THE NIV APPLICATION COMMENTARY

ON THE BIBLE

ONE-VOLUME EDITION

THE NIV APPLICATION COMMENTARY SERIES

Old Testament Volumes

Genesis, John H. Walton
Exodus, Peter Enns
Leviticus, Numbers, Roy Gane
Deuteronomy, Daniel I. Block
Joshua, Robert L. Hubbard Jr.
Judges, Ruth, K. Lawson Younger Jr.
1 and 2 Samuel, Bill T. Arnold
1 and 2 Kings, August H. Konkel
1 and 2 Chronicles, Andrew E. Hill
Ezra-Nehemiah, Donna and Thomas Petter
Esther, Karen H. Jobes
Job, John H. Walton
Psalms Volume 1, Gerald H. Wilson
Psalms Volume 2, W. Dennis Tucker Jr. and Jamie A. Grant
Proverbs, Paul E. Koptak
Ecclesiastes, Song of Songs, Iain Provan
Isaiah, John N. Oswalt
Jeremiah, Lamentations, J. Andrew Dearman
Ezekiel, Iain M. Duguid
Daniel, Tremper Longman III
Hosea, Amos, Micah, Gary V. Smith
Jonah, Nahum, Habakkuk, Zephaniah, James Bruckner
Joel, Obadiah, Malachi, David W. Baker
Haggai, Zechariah, Mark J. Boda

New Testament Volumes

Matthew, Michael J. Wilkins
Mark, David E. Garland
Luke, Darrell L. Bock
John, Gary M. Burge
Acts, Ajith Fernando
Romans, Douglas J. Moo
1 Corinthians, Craig L. Blomberg
2 Corinthians, Scott J. Hafemann
Galatians, Scot McKnight
Ephesians, Klyne Snodgrass
Philippians, Frank Thielman
Colossians, Philemon, David E. Garland
1 and 2 Thessalonians, Michael W. Holmes
1 and 2 Timothy, Titus, Walter L. Liefeld
Hebrews, George H. Guthrie
James, David P. Nystrom
1 Peter, Scot McKnight
2 Peter, Jude, Douglas J. Moo
Letters of John, Gary M. Burge
Revelation, Craig S. Keener

THE NIV APPLICATION COMMENTARY

ON THE BIBLE

ONE-VOLUME EDITION

Old Testament Editor: Nancy L. Erickson

New Testament Editor: Christopher A. Beetham

Consulting Editors: Karen H. Jobes, Tremper Longman III, Scot McKnight, Douglas J. Moo, and John H. Walton

Abridging Editor: Adam T. Barr

ZONDERVAN ACADEMIC

ZONDERVAN ACADEMIC

The NIV Application Commentary on the Bible

Requests for information should be addressed to:

Zondervan, *3900 Sparks Dr. SE, Grand Rapids, Michigan 49546*

Zondervan titles may be purchased in bulk for educational, business, fundraising, or sales promotional use. For information, please email SpecialMarkets@Zondervan.com.

ISBN 978-0-310-53080-0 (hardcover)
ISBN 978-0-310-53081-7 (ebook)

Cover design by Faceout Studio, Molly von Borstel
Cover photo: © muratart / Shutterstock
Cover pattern: © BitterHeart / Shutterstock
Interior design: Kait Lamphere

Printed in the United States of America

25 26 27 28 29 30 31 32 33 34 35 36 /TRM/ 18 17 16 15 14 13 12 11 10 9 8 7 6 5 4

CONTENTS

INTRODUCTION

This one-volume abridgment has been years in the making and is built on decades of scholarship. The pages here represent hundreds of thousands of hours of research, writing, and editing, from the first volumes published in 1995 (*1 Corinthians, Galatians, Philippians*) to the final volume released in 2021 (*Ezra/Nehemiah*). The labor of love can be seen on the card page (p. iv), where each author is attributed to their work. The names represent some of the best scholarship over the past three decades. Review the list and be amazed! Some scholars wrote their volumes early in their career, and we now reap the benefit of a plethora of their works in the field. Others wrote near the end of their career, their contribution in the NIV Application Commentary series representing a lifetime of study.

The initial vision for the NIVAC series was aimed at the church. The volumes were to demonstrate excellent scholarship and at the same time provide tools and resourcing for pastors and interested laity. For this reason, the NIVAC volumes are touted as the best go-to complete commentary series for the church, and herein lies the heartbeat behind the one-volume here. The idea to abridge the entire series into one volume came from Nancy's husband Dan Erickson (one of many ideas that have since inspired forthcoming projects). The sentiment was captured by Nancy and brought to a conversation with Stan Gundry, then senior vice president and group publisher of Zondervan Academic, Zondervan Reflective, and Study Resources and editor-in-chief of Zondervan. In many ways, the pages here sing a tribute to Stan's lifelong dedication to providing exceptional scholarly work for the church.

By our estimate, the complete NIVAC series boasted over ninety million words and forty-four volumes. The abridgment here, into a single volume, now includes just over one million words. The goal was to retain the most useful and relevant content for each volume in proportion to the biblical canon. This means that a larger percentage of content was retained for the abridgment of the book of Isaiah as compared, for example, to the book of Esther. The exception here is to a preference for slightly higher percentages of content for the New Testament volumes.

The abridgment process was no small feat and was tasked to Nancy and Chris, Old and New Testament editorial counterparts for Zondervan Academic. We set out with specific guidelines when it came to the abridgment, namely, significantly reducing book introductions and outlines; removing the Bridging Contexts sections; avoiding footnotes and internal notes unless otherwise necessary; updating NIV quotations and references to the NIV 2011; and revising, when necessary, content in the Contemporary Application section (funny how reference to floppy disks and dial-up internet were not all that long ago!). The format of each book with its commentary includes the following: Introduction, Book Outline, Original Meaning, and Application.

Abridgment did not fall on our plates exclusively. When it became clear that our editorial plates were too full to make significant progress on the project, we chose the abridging assistance of our esteemed friend and co-laborer, Adam Barr (thanks for the introduction, Ryan Pazdur). Adam's work in this abridgment process is nothing short of excellent. As a pastor, he knew the volumes well, and it quickly became clear that he was in his element when it came to the work of abridging the content. Well done, Adam! It is because of your fine work that this one-volume is now available. After Adam finished his work, Nancy and Chris reviewed every line, making changes and updates as we deemed necessary and regularly referring to the original published volumes.

We'd like to thank Amie Vaughan, proofreader extraordinaire. This may be the longest proofreading project that Amie has worked on for the Zondervan team, and for that, thank you, not just for your steady commitment but to your sharp eye for readability and accuracy. Our colleague Lee Fields also had his hand in the project at a later stage, helping incorporate necessary corrections. In many ways this was a full team effort, from the marketing team to editorial; Kari Moore and Kelsey Kaemingk, we see you!

Like the initial purpose of the multivolume set, we hope that this one-volume commentary finds its way into the hands of the church. May it be an ever-rich resource pointing to the reading and study of Scripture.

Nancy L. Erickson, Old Testament editor
Christopher A. Beetham, New Testament editor

GENESIS

INTRODUCTION TO GENESIS

Biblical traditions connect the Pentateuch (the first five books of the Bible) in general with Moses, and the biblical profile given of the man Moses makes him perfectly suited, indeed, a most logical candidate, to compile the book of Genesis. Acceptance, therefore, of the biblical traditions concerning the canon and the man leave little foothold for doubt about the significant role played by Moses. It is easy to imagine the Israelites at Mount Sinai or in the desert as the audience for the material addressed in Genesis.

Nevertheless, equal confidence is not provided by specific claims of the book of Genesis or for sweeping absolute statements. Willingness to accept a significant role for Moses still leaves many issues undecided. How much of his role was authorial as opposed to editorial? This is not a theological question because inspiration can take place through editors just as easily as it can take place through authors. If the purpose of the book is accomplished through activities such as selection, arrangement, and emphasis, then the editorial role is crucial.

It is entirely plausible to expect that Moses had many sources of information available to him, both in written and oral form. In this scenario, inspiration enabled him to select sources that were accurate and to weave that material together into a purposeful composition that is essentially the book of Genesis as we have it today. Whatever limited additions or revisions may have been made after the time of Moses must likewise be considered inspired. We contend, however, that the principal inspired, purposeful, and creative mind behind Genesis was Moses.

BOOK OUTLINE

I. Creation: Cosmic World (1:1–2:3)
II. Before the Patriarchs: The Need for a Covenant People—*Toledot* of Heavens and Earth; *Toledot* of Adam; *Toledot* of Noah; *Toledot* of Shem, Ham, and Japheth; *Toledot* of Shem (2:4–11:26)
III. The Patriarchs in Palestine: The Establishment of a Covenant People—*Toledot* of Terah; *Toledot* of Ishmael; *Toledot* of Isaac; *Toledot* of Esau (11:27–36:43)
IV. The Patriarchs in Egypt: Incubation for the Covenant People—*Toledot* of Jacob (37:1–50:26)

GENESIS 1:1–5

Original Meaning

Literary Introduction (1:1). *In the beginning.* It sounds so simple, yet the moment we begin to ponder the phrase, its cloudlike simplicity dissipates to reveal rugged mountain peaks. Does it refer to some creative activity that preceded the seven days (in which something that can be designated heaven and earth were created), or does it introduce and summarize the activity of the seven days (during which heaven and earth were created)? There are two evidence that offer support for the second option.

1. The book of Genesis operates literarily by introducing sections with a summary statement. For example, beginning in 2:4 and ten additional times throughout the book, a *toledot* ("accounts") statement introduces a section.
2. Even more persuasive is that the account of the six days closes with the comment that "the heavens and the earth" were completed (2:1).

God created. The author's concerns were much like others in the ancient Near East, where the greatest exercise of the power of the gods was demonstrated in the fixing of destinies. Each year at Babylon's New Year's enthronement festival, the gods fixed the destinies for the coming year, thus reasserting their power. Here in Genesis, Israel's God also demonstrates his power by the assigning of roles and functions. This is an affirmation of his exclusive sovereignty.

God and the Forces of Chaos (1:2). *Formless and empty.* There is a clear establishment of order from disorder. That disorder is described in 1:2, starting with the Hebrew terms *tohu* and *bohu* (NIV, "formless and empty"). Analysis of the Hebrew confirms the conclusion that these terms indicate that the cosmos was empty of purpose, meaning, and function—a place that had no order or intelligibility, a desertlike wasteland.

Darkness over the deep. While both darkness and the watery deep (Heb. *tehom*) are elements of chaos, neither is personified here. There is nothing sinister or menacing about this chaos in Genesis; it is simply the indication that God has not yet done his work.

Spirit of God. Hebrew uses the same word (*ruah*) for wind or spirit. Exegetical analysis suggests that the *ruah* here represents an extension of God's power, like his hand or his breath.

Our conclusion can be conveniently summarized in the following paraphrase: "The earth was nonfunctional; primordial, watery darkness prevailed, and a supernatural wind that was permeated with the power of God circulated over the surface of the waters."

Day One (1:3–5). *Light.* In Genesis 1:5a the NIV translates, "God called the light [Heb. *or*] 'day' [*yom*], and the darkness he called 'night.'" When God said, "Let there be *or*," we understand it as "Let there be a period of light." Day one does not concern itself with the creation of "light" as a physical entity with physical properties. On day one, God created *time*. This is the first of the functions God will use to bring order to the chaos of the cosmos: the orderly and regular sequence of time.

Evening and morning. Why is evening listed first? The coming of evening and then of morning marked the first series of transitions and completed the cycle, showing that what God had set up had now taken effect. In other words, on day one there was no morning as a transition, simply God's creative act of daylight. The first transition after the creation of daylight/time was evening. In the rest of the narrative, God's activity will take place during the daylight hours, after which the established transitions, represented by evening and morning, will again take place.

The first day. This at last brings us to the discussion of "day" (*yom*). In the semantic range of *yom* we must include (1) the daylight hours, (2) a twenty-four-hour day, (3) special days (e.g., day of his death), and (4) a plural use that can refer to a few days or even a year. Furthermore, (5) the definite article can be added to *yom* to make it mean "today," or (6) a preposition can be tacked on the front and a demonstrative pronoun associated with it to say "in that day" or simply "when." The important point to be made here is that these categories cannot be merged carelessly. Though it is true that *yom* sometimes refers to an extended period of time, that usage is limited to certain expressions and collocations, and its meaning cannot be so glibly transferred to Genesis 1.

It is extremely difficult to conclude that anything other than a twenty-four-hour day was intended. It is not the text that causes people to think otherwise, only the demands of trying to harmonize with modern science. Perhaps, however, after the functions approach to the text has been understood, the twenty-four-hour day will not be seen as posing the problem it has in the past—but that discussion will have to wait until the end of chapter 1. For now, on day one God created time.

Application. When the ancients wanted to describe or discuss creation, they had little interest in the material structure or the formational history of the cosmos. Rather, their concerns focused on the functional cosmos. The text communicates a universal reality—how all peoples throughout time have *experienced* the cosmos. It affirms that though people have often perceived the cosmos as a threat to their survival, God set up the cosmos to operate this way, and it was just right.

Young earth creationists, old earth creationists, and theistic evolutionists have been locked in an argument concerning who offers the best picture of creation's formational history. Each want to claim that it has a *biblical* view of creation's formational history. The problem exists because from a biblical point of view, it is an oxymoron to speak of "creation's formational history," in that *the Bible's view of creation is not concerned with formational history*. If we come to the Bible expecting it to discuss creation in terms of material structure, we will be sadly disappointed.

By distinguishing the text from science in this way, I am not endorsing the argument that science and religion have nothing to do with one another. It is not science that is the enemy, it is naturalism. The scientific endeavor by its very nature operates by means of what I would call an "atheistic premise"—that is, it tries to figure out the natural world without resorting to supernatural explanations. If we were to assume that something happened without God's intervention, how would it have happened?

We need to defend the teaching of the text, not a scientific reconstruction of the text or statements that are read between the lines of the text. Our best theological, hermeneutical, and scientific minds need to work to forge a new consensus for the relationship between science and Scripture, as was done in the wake of the Copernican revolution, rather than sacrificing more Galileo-type martyrs on the altar of stone-rigid, quasi-scientific presuppositions dressed up as if they were the word of God.

GENESIS 1:6–13

Original Meaning

Day Two (1:6–8). Day two describes the setting up of the next function, focusing on the *raqia* ("vault"), perceived by the Israelite audience as a solid dome. The function of the *raqia* was to regulate the weather, as is evident from the description of the waters above it. In a functional approach, the author has apparently used the cosmological language available to him to describe weather. Given the need to affirm that God created the cosmos with an operational weather system, the setting up of a *raqia* would be the logical choice. The intention of the text is not to convey structure but function.

Day Three (1:9–13). Day three has two elements attached to it: the separation of water and dry land, and the production of vegetation. From a literary standpoint this helps to establish parallelism between days 1–3 and days 4–6. While these literary observations accurately assess the narrator's art, they do not fully disclose the nature of the relationship between the two sets. This relationship will be explored in detail in the discussion of days 4–6. For now, however, it is important to understand that the two elements are intrinsically related in a functional approach. The two elements brought together on the third day focus on a cosmos designed to provide for vegetation and agriculture.

Application. Along with time, weather/climate and agriculture are the three functions of the cosmos of most significance to us. They are beyond our control, yet they define our existence. We can only rediscover who we are as we come to understand who God is. He is utterly and eternally coherent. When he drew order out of chaos and made the world functional, he created coherence and established meaning for the cosmos and for each life.

GENESIS 1:14–2:3

Original Meaning. Thus far we have argued that Genesis 1 is not the record of the creation of physical matter but a divine organization and assignment of functions to the cosmos. Days four, five, and six fall in line with this same overall theme but turn attention to the functionaries.

Day Four (1:14–19). Signs function theologically in the Old Testament as indicators through which God conveys knowledge and reveals himself. The second function indicates that the celestial bodies serve for identifying *moadim* ("sacred times"), the related festivals and religious feast days of the liturgical calendar. The third and last function in the list indicates that the calendar was established through celestial observations. This functional approach is mirrored both in biblical and in Mesopotamian literature regarding the celestial bodies.

In 1:16 the NIV translates, "God made two great lights." The Hebrew verb for "made" here (*asah*) has a wide range of meanings. Is this saying that the Lord *manufactured* all of these things in these six days and that he *manufactured* the heavenly bodies on Day Four? The text does not address how or when the bodies originated; rather, the assignment of function is described in the text by the verb *asah*. The report of the fourth day concludes with the presentation of other functions of the heavenly bodies: giving light and dividing and ruling over the day and night.

Day Five (1:20–23). While we may be inclined to identify these creatures as whales, sharks, and the like, that is not what the Hebrew word (*tannin*) would have communicated to its audience. Other uses of this word associate it with the chaos monsters that were believed to inhabit the cosmic waters. So, for instance, Psalm 74:13–14 puts Leviathan, a multiheaded beast, in the category of *tannin*. Polemic comes to the surface, as these creatures are not antagonists that have to be defeated, but creatures that have been given functions just like any other.

In 1:20 is the first occurrence of the designation *nepesh hayya* ("living creatures"). The same designation is used for land animals in 1:24 and includes some sea creatures and birds in 1:28; in 2:7 it indicates what Adam became when God breathed into him. Though people will be differentiated from the animal world by the image of God, they hold in common with all creatures the quality of life.

Day Six (1:24–31). *Animals.* The categories are divided into domesticated animals (Heb. *behema*), wild herd animals that often serve as prey (*remes*), and wild, predatory animals (*hayya*). In keeping with the functional emphasis, this does not describe a biological process but a functional relationship.

Use of plurals. The use of the plural pronouns ("us" and "our") in 1:26 has occasioned constant discussion among the commentators. In the Old Testament, the heavenly court is made up of angels, or more specifically, the "sons of God." If we are going to link our interpretation to the sense that the Israelite audience would have understood (and methodologically I believe that is essential for maintaining the authority of the text), the heavenly court is the most defensible interpretation and poses no insuperable theological obstacles.

Image of God. The governing work of God is seen in Genesis to be accomplished by people (1:28). But that is not all there is to the image of God. Information from other contexts that can be gleaned about the image includes that (1) the image of God is not lost at the fall (9:6); and (2) it does differentiate people from animals (9:6), though that does not mean that anything that differentiates is part of the image.

Perhaps most significant, 5:1–3 likens the image of God in Adam to the image of Adam in Seth. This goes beyond the comment about plants and animals reproducing after their kind. The image of God in people provides them the capacity not only to serve as God's vice-regents (his representatives containing his essence), but also the capacity to be and act like him. Thus, 5:1–3 is perhaps the most significant for determining how we ought to interpret the image of God.

The blessing. While the image of God defines a role for humanity (vice-regents for God), the blessing indicates the functions that people will have as a result of the role to which they were created. The first function is to "subdue" the earth, the second to "rule" it (1:28). "Subduing" is associated (grammatically, not semantically) with the prior verb, "filling" (1:28), and has the earth as its focus. "Ruling" is directed toward the animals and implies domestication or some other level of use or control. Of course, this does not legitimize slaughter, abuse, or neglect.

Day Seven (2:1–3). The seventh day is marked by God's ceasing the work of the previous six days and by his settling into the stability of the cosmos he created, perhaps experiencing refreshment as he did so. By blessing it, he extends his favor to it.

Application. Being made in the image of God confers on us *dignity*, entrusts us with *responsibility*, and implants in us a certain potential, namely, the *capacity* to mirror our Creator. As Christians, our redemption has greatly enhanced this capacity and, in the process, has made us more sensitive to the responsibility we have and the dignity shared by all humankind.

GENESIS 2:4–25

Original Meaning. From this point on the text proceeds from section to section by tracing the *toledot* ("accounts") that provide linkage and continuity from that initial period through the eras that lead eventually to Abraham.

The Formation of Adam (2:4–7). *Toledot.* The *toledot* formulas in Genesis are introductions that can be paraphrased "developments that arise out of. . . ."

Shrub . . . plant. The point made by 2:5 is that there is no food growing in uncultivated areas, and there is no cultivation for the arable land.

Streams. Verses 5–6 in an interpretive paraphrase is: "No shrubs or plants were yet growing wild (for food) because God had not yet sent rain; and people were not yet around to work the ground (for irrigation), so the regular inundations saturated the ground indiscriminately (thus no food was being grown)."

Dust. The Hebrew word *apar* ("dust") represents what people return to when they die.

Breath of life. God breathes it into every person who is born. It was not just a first-time thing with Adam.

The Garden of Eden (2:8–17). *Garden . . . Eden.* Gardens of this variety were a common feature in palace complexes in the ancient world (e.g., Nebuchadnezzar's famous hanging gardens). The produce of these temple gardens was used in offerings to the deity. The picture presented is of a mighty spring that gushes out from Eden and is channeled through the garden for irrigation purposes.

Location of the garden. The geography used here is not a topographical geography but a cosmic geography. Its location is given so that its strategic role can be appreciated. All fertility emanates from the presence of God.

Specific trees. Two specific trees are mentioned as holding a prominent place in the garden. The tree of life is well known in the Bible and the ancient Near East, while the tree of the knowledge of good and evil is known only from this text.

We should view the *tree of life* as having fruit that extends life rather than instantly grants immortality. Understanding the second tree depends heavily on our ability to identify the meaning of the phrase "knowledge of good and evil" (2:17). Knowing good and evil is characteristic of God (3:22) but not of children (Deut 1:39; Isa 7:15–16), the elderly (2 Sam 19:35), or the inexperienced (1 Kgs 3:9); when people gain the knowledge by eating the fruit, they can legitimately be described as being like God.

Work and care. The tasks given to Adam are of a priestly nature—that is, caring for sacred space. In ancient thinking, caring for sacred space made one a participant with God in the ongoing task of sustaining the equilibrium God had established in the cosmos.

Command and threat. A paraphrase of Genesis 2:17 is: "When you eat of it, you will be sentenced to death and therefore doomed to die." Consequently, death will be a certainty.

Adam and Eve (2:18–25). *Suitable helper.* What is the implication of identifying the woman as a "helper suitable" for man? The word "helper" is a description of someone who comes to the aid of or provides a service for someone. Nothing suggests a subservient status of the one helping; in fact, the opposite is more likely. The second word, *kenegdo* ("suitable"), is a combination of two prepositions with the appendage of the third masculine singular pronominal suffix that suggest "complementary." I would choose a translation such as "partner" or "counterpart."

Rib. The text portrays God as taking a handful(?) of bone and flesh out of Adam's side to use in the construction of Eve. In this case, the preposition connected to the word "woman" may simply introduce the purpose of the action: "Then the LORD God built up the side he had taken from the man for (the purpose of making) a woman" (author's translation, 2:22).

Responses to Eve. Adam's response to Eve recognizes her similarity to him and her derivative nature. We would be mistaken to think that Adam names Eve here. He rather indicates what category she belongs in. The narrator's response in 2:24 does not speak exclusively of sexual desire, though sexual desire may be the mechanism that drives it. Conceiving children (being fruitful) is the idea.

Naked without shame. Their nakedness (Heb. *arummim*) is contrasted to the serpent's craftiness (*arum*) by means of wordplay. In this sense their nakedness is an indication of a level of naiveté. It serves as the "before" picture that will be contrasted to the "after" picture in 3:7.

Application. My opinion of Genesis 2 is that it offers no establishment or articulation of gender roles. Regardless of what conclusions can be drawn about the issue as a whole once New Testament texts are considered, this text is concerned with human roles, not gender roles. Man and woman serve together.

GENESIS 3:1–7

Original Meaning

The Serpent (3:1a). It is important to recognize that the serpent is simply classified as one of the wild animals. There is no god or demon or genie lurking beneath the guise of the serpent.

The Temptation (3:1b–5). The serpent's statement can be paraphrased something like, "Don't think that death is such an immediate threat." According to the serpent, it was never really God's intention to put them to death. In effect, then, the serpent does not actually contradict God; he only suggests that there is nothing to worry about.

Adam's Role (3:6). It should be noted that all the verbs in this section are plural. Why does the man not correct the woman's statement? The text offers no explanation.

The Results (3:7). They were not ashamed because they were unaware of their nakedness, and conversely, when they become aware, they feel shame. Fig leaves are the largest leaves found in Canaan and provide limited covering for the shamed couple. It is intriguing that the fig tree becomes a symbol of fertility.

Application. God offered nothing less to Adam and Eve than the privilege of freedom and the joy of dependence. Our society treats this as an oxymoron and labels God a tyrant. In rejecting dependence on God (though in no way escaping from it) people choose a far more costly dependency—on themselves and their own resources. In seeking autonomy, freedom, and power, they only forge new chains.

GENESIS 3:8–24

Original Meaning

God in Garden (3:8–13). What else could "wind of the day" (author's translation, 3:8; NIV "cool of the day") mean? Akkadian terminology has demonstrated that the word translated "day" also has the meaning "storm." If this is the correct rendering of the word here in Genesis 3, we can translate 3:8 in this way: "They heard the roar of the LORD moving about in the garden in the wind of the storm." The context makes this new rendering a possibility, but one that can only be held tentatively.

Serpent Curse (3:14). We should not think of the curse of eating dust as a description of the diet of snakes. The curse on the serpent can be understood as wishing upon it a status associated with docility (crawling on belly) and death (eating dust).

Seed and Enmity (3:15). The most important interpretive question here concerns the nature of the conflict being described. Throughout the history of the church, this has been read as the first foreshadowing of Christ's defeat of Satan. The verbs NIV translates "crush" and "strike" are now properly identified as belonging to the same Hebrew root, *shwp*. Given the repetition of the verb and the potentially mortal nature of both attacks, it becomes difficult to understand the verse as suggesting an eventual outcome to the struggle. The verse is depicting a continual, unresolved conflict between humans and the representatives of evil.

Woman (3:16). Two important exegetical issues center around the words "pain" and "desire," both of which must be explored and clarified.

Pain. The first half of 3:16 is an extended merism (two endpoints used to refer to everything in between) referring to the anxiety that a woman will experience through the whole process from conception to birth. A resulting paraphrase of 3:16a is: "I will greatly increase the anguish you will experience in the birth process, from the anxiety surrounding conception to the strenuous work of giving birth."

Desire. One possibility, and the one I favor, is that the word simply refers to one's basic or inherent instincts. In 3:16, then, since the context has already addressed the issue of reproduction, the term "desire" can easily be identified as a basic instinct of woman. If reproduction is going to be so fraught with anguish, why do it? The answer is found in the woman's instinct, her desire to have children.

Man/Ground (3:17–19). What does it mean for the ground to be cursed? The verbal root used here (*'rr*) is recognized as the opposite of bless (*brk*). In English, the best equivalent for *'rr* is the word "damn." The ground is being removed from God's favor, protection, and blessing. The impact of this curse is that, though food is still made available to people, it will be much harder to produce.

Skin Garments (3:20–21). It is a serious error to read sacrifice between the lines of 3:21. The institution of sacrifice is far too significant an occurrence to leave it entirely to inference. This provision should probably be seen as an act of grace by God, preparing them for the more difficult environment he is sending them into and providing a remedy for their newly developed shame.

Sentence Passed (3:22–24). Banishment from the garden and cutting off access to the tree of life are the means by which the death penalty is carried out. The cherubim guard the way to the tree of life, now forbidden property of God.

Application. As always, the serpent is most successful in contexts in which what is true or right can be twisted around to create an obstacle. The fact is that we can defend certain beliefs without defaming or castigating those who have come to different conclusions with integrity. Failing to exercise the grace that we should naturally extend to fellow Christians, we have adopted a Reformation zeal concerning issues that come nowhere near the significance of the battles fought by Calvin and Luther, while we comfortably make our beds amidst the cultural landmines that are exploding all around us.

GENESIS 4:1–16

Original Meaning

Birth of Cain and Abel (4:1–2). There is nothing in the syntax or grammar that locates intercourse relative to the fall. The first intercourse would logically follow the fall and pronouncement as we have interpreted them and would certainly be a suitable moment to address the naming of Eve.

The Sacrifice (4:3–5). The problem with Cain's sacrifice does not have anything to do with the absence of blood. We must look elsewhere to identify the fault in Cain's offering. In the end, the only thing the text makes clear is that Cain, in some way, does not "do what [was] right" (4:7). Whatever the cause of Cain's rejection, the text is more interested in his response to it than it is in delineating the details.

Confrontation (4:6–7). The threshold at which Cain is poised is indicated in 4:7b by a line that comes from 3:16. The vocabulary is the same ("desire" and "rule") though the pronouns are reversed. "Desire" is best understood as a basic instinct (here the instinct would be to deprave). "Sin" is personified as a crouching demon waiting to strike.

Murder and Its Aftermath (4:8–16). In 4:9 God's question is parried by deflecting blame to others. Cain's response is simply a lie ("I don't know," 4:9), followed by an evasive denial of responsibility.

As 3:13 introduced the pronouncement with a statement that assigned guilt, so 4:10 introduces Yahweh's pronouncement with essentially the same statement. As in 3:17 the ground was put under a curse, so now Cain himself is put under the same sort of curse. Based on what appears to be a clarifying statement in 4:12, I am inclined to translate, "cursed are you relative to the ground." Becoming a "restless wanderer" (4:12) is a consequence of the land not providing for his food; rather, he will be forced to wander to get food.

Who does Cain think is out there to kill him, and what is the mark affixed by Yahweh? The presence of other people can either be attributed to the idea that Adam and Eve are only one of many couples that were created or that the other people represent a rapidly expanding family from the offspring of Adam and Eve. The text of Genesis is silent in this regard, but Pauline theology leads us to favor the second option. It is difficult to determine how sin came to all humanity unless all humans are descendants of Adam and Eve. This theological inference cannot be elaborated since the text offers no further information.

The "mark" (4:15) placed on Cain plays a parallel role in this narrative to the garments provided for Adam and Eve in 3:21. Just as it did not matter where God got the animal skin or what it looked like, it is of little importance what the sign is like and how it functions. In both cases the importance of the gift is in the One who gave it.

Application. When we refuse to take responsibility for our sin, to accept blame for the consequences of our actions, and to be held accountable for what we do and say, we burn down the bridges of reconciliation. The only way back to reconciliation, forgiveness, and God has as its first step a recognition of the problem and repentant desire to do something about it.

GENESIS 4:17–5:32

Original Meaning

Arts of Civilization (4:17–22). In Cain's line we find record of the first building of a city as well as the earliest development of the arts of civilization. Because Cain and his family were forced to their extremities, they could only survive by means of human advancement. There is nothing to reflect rebellion here, only an indication that even Cain's line continues to enjoy the blessing by subduing and ruling.

Lamech's Boast (4:23–24). The most notable member of Cain's descendants is boastful Lamech. The twenty-one words of his speech constitute what is often considered an example of earliest poetry. The parallelism makes it clear that a single incident of combat is the subject of the triumphant declaration, so that the "man" and the "young man" (4:23) are one and the same. The text has moved from unrepentant Cain to defiant Lamech. Violence is glorified, and the mark of Cain no longer stands as a stigma of exile but as a badge of honor that brings protection equivalent to invulnerability. The human situation is degenerating.

Calling on the Name of the Lord (4:25–26). The line of Seth is associated with religious practice. When God calls on the name of someone, he appoints or designates that person for a particular role (Bezalel in Exod 31:2; Cyrus in Isa 45:3–4; stars in Isa 40:26). When people "call on the name of the LORD" (Gen 4:26), this similarly constitutes a designation and recognition of Yahweh as God. This is the beginning of worship and shows that the development of civilization did not bring a total abandonment of the Lord.

Genealogy (5:1–32). *Enoch.* The text does not say where Enoch was taken, a possible indication that the author did not profess to know. We can properly assume that he was believed to have been taken to a better place, for this fate was seen as a reward for his close relationship to God, but the text stops short of saying he went to heaven or to be with God.

Names in the genealogies. Anyone even casually familiar with the Bible has noticed how many Israelite names end in *-iah* or *-el* or start with *Jeho-* or *El-*. All of these represent Israel's God. This type of name is called a *theophoric* name and affirms the nature of the deity, proclaims the attributes of the deity, or requests the blessing of the deity.

The only theophoric names in the genealogies of Genesis 4 and 5 (Mehujael, Methushael, and Mahalalel) feature the divine name El, which indicates a Semitic language setting. Current scholarly consensus accepts that Hebrew did not develop as a language until the first half of the second millennium BC, in which case it is logical to conclude that these are translations from a language used in earlier sources.

The most significant name in the list is Noah because of the reason given for the name (5:29). This hope has been thought to find its complement in 8:21. It may have been Lamech's hope that Noah would somehow bring about the reversal of the curse (*'rr*), but the flood's destruction does not accomplish this end in that every intention of humanity was evil.

Long lifespans. The long lifespans have been a continual curiosity among Bible readers. None of the proposals has been able to provide a solution that encompasses all of the data. If we accept the biblical account at face value, there are reasons one might expect long lives in the shadow of Eden. Whether one would speculate that the long lives testify to the gradual penetration of sin (and death) or to the enduring effect of Adam and Eve's temporary (pre-fall) diet from the tree of life, the accuracy of these numbers can be defended.

Application. These chapters illustrate how, from nearly the beginning, the conditions existed for good and evil to flourish in one another's company. The influences of good (represented by the blessing) and of evil (represented by the curse) are so intertwined as at times to become inseparable.

This is how God works in a fallen world. Since he has chosen not to eradicate a fallen race but to redeem it, he does his work in an imperfect context. Until the final blow is struck, evil will always find ways to pervert that which has the potential to do good and will prosper under the umbrella of protection created by the aura of that which is good.

GENESIS 6:1–4

Original Meaning. The "Nephilim" (6:4) are referred to only in this passage and in Numbers 13:33, where they are listed among the inhabitants of the land of Canaan at the time of the conquest. Three approaches have been used to try to identify them.

1. *Etymology.* Since the Hebrew root *npl* means "to fall," meanings such as "fallen ones" or "those who fall [i.e., prey] on others" have been common suggestions. Etymology, however, is an unreliable guide to meaning, and so this option should be held at arm's length.
2. *Association.* In Numbers 13:33 the spies speak of the descendants of Anak, who were of considerable size. The descendants are associated with the Nephilim in that passage, so some consider the Nephilim giants.
3. *General context.* In both passages the Nephilim appear as renowned warrior heroes. They are identified with the "heroes of old" at the end of Genesis 6:4, but their relationship to the children born to the sons of God is a bit more tenuous. I am inclined to take 6:4 as indicating that the actions of the sons of God took place during the heroic age, though perhaps they were also seen as the offspring of these unions.

Application. What happens when oppression becomes institutionalized? In Genesis 1–11 the institutionalization of oppression is the last step that eventuates in the condition described in 6:5. If rulers and leaders are oppressive or corrupt, there is either a *double standard* (by which the population is held accountable to a level of behavior from which the rulers are exempt) or the *moral fiber* of the population erodes away following the example of its leaders. This phenomenon is observable at every level of behavior, whether violence breeds violence, corruption (e.g., bribes or extortion) breeds corruption, racism breeds racism, sexual misconduct breeds sexual misconduct, or lies breed lies.

GENESIS 6:5–8:22

Original Meaning

Reason for the Flood (6:5, 11–13). The text makes it clear that the problem leading to the flood was simply the wickedness of the human heart and the behavior that resulted.

Some elaboration of this occurs in 6:11–13, which specifically cites violence and corruption. The Hebrew word translated "violence" (6:11) is a general term that ranges from international contexts to social injustice. The word for "corrupt" (6:12) is taken up in a number of ways in this chapter. Violence and corruption are the types of offenses that have been illustrated in the text up to this point, so the conclusion is that sin has reached critical mass and divine response is now inevitable.

God's Grief (6:7). Passages using terminology such as God's being sorry, repenting, or changing his mind have been the source of theological confusion, consternation, and debate. There are three ways to seek resolution.

1. We can simply rethink our view of God. This is exactly what is happening in the new theology called the "openness of God."
2. We can justify the terminology by seeking to understand ways in which anthropomorphic language is used in describing God's actions without imputing human limitations to him. This is the path followed in most commentaries.
3. We can reassess the lexical data to see if we are on the right track when we translate terms in particular ways. The need for this is especially evident when there is a lack of cohesion in how a term is translated or when the theological implications of a translation indicate that something may be amiss. Both of these situations exist in the word used here ("regret"), so a reexamination is in order.

I propose that "regret" can be best understood in accounting terms. In bookkeeping, the ledgers must always be kept in balance; debits equal credits. If the books get out of balance, something must be adjusted. Whenever transactions are made, entries must be made accordingly. The verbal form of *nhm* ("regret") in 6:7 can be viewed in terms of acting to keep personal, national, or cosmic "ledgers" in balance.

When God has set a course for punishment, it can at times be counterbalanced by an act of grace that revokes that punishment and brings the "ledger" back into balance (Jer 26:13; Jonah 3:9–10). God is disturbed when people have sinned and been warned of the coming consequences of the imbalance represented by their wickedness, but they refuse to balance their ledgers with repentance (Jer 8:6). God is known as a God who does not allow evil to stand on the books but balances it with either grace and mercy (Joel 2:13; Jonah 4:2) or with punishment (Jer 18:10). In Genesis 6:6–7, Yahweh is seeking to redress the situation.

Noah's Righteousness (6:9). Noah's righteousness and blamelessness is *in comparison to the people of his time*. We should note that no statement is made concerning the spiritual condition of the rest of Noah's extended family. This probably means that the eight of them enjoy God's protection as a corporate group either because Noah's righteousness has been duplicated and imitated by the members of his family, or because the reward of his righteousness includes the deliverance of his loved ones.

The Ark (6:14–16). The dimensions of the ark are easy enough to determine, and the general shape of it is therefore discernible. Based on 1 cubit equaling 18 inches, Noah's ark is 450 feet long, 75 feet wide, and 45 feet deep. It is evident that Noah's ark was not designed to be navigated. Consequently, the fate of the company aboard was left in the hands of God.

Flood (6:17). The Hebrew word for Noah's flood, used twelve times in Genesis 6–11, is *mabbul*. Outside of this section it occurs only once (Ps 29:10). Broader cultural usage suggests that the word may have had broader currency as a cosmic water-weapon wielded by a deity.

Animals (6:19–20; 7:2–3). While the initial instructions indicate that pairs of all living creatures are to be taken into the ark, when more specific instructions are given, one pair of unclean animals and seven pairs of clean animals are to be taken. The distinction between clean and unclean animals was not an innovation established at Sinai, but here is seen as early as Noah.

Length of Flood (7:4) and Length of Stay in Ark. The biblical text sets the period of rain at forty days and nights. The one hundred and fifty days that the water prevails (7:24) and the additional one hundred and fifty that it recedes (8:5), added to several periods of waiting (7:10; 8:6, 10, 12), amount to just over a year spent on the ark.

Mountains of Ararat (8:4). The mountains of Ararat are located in the Lake Van region of eastern Turkey in the area of Armenia.

Birds (8:6–12). One of the enduring pictures of the biblical account is that of Noah sending out the birds to gain information about the conditions outside the ark. Ancient navigators used birds to find land, but Noah is not navigating, and he is on land. His use of the birds is not in order to find direction but to determine the readiness of the land for habitation.

Sacrifice (8:20–21). The purpose of Noah's sacrifice is not stated. The burnt offerings that Moses's audience were familiar with are usually associated with petitions or entreaties set before God. Noah's purpose is likely to request God's favor and blessing.

Application. We can see from the flood narrative that God is able to bring restoration where he has brought destruction. The re-creation theme in the flood narrative shows God's starting again with humanity. This theme is developed later in Scripture in relation to Israel's great political and theological crisis, the exile. In that context, the prophet Jeremiah is initially given a message that focuses on plucking up, breaking down, destroying, and overthrowing (Jer 1:10). Yet in the introduction to the new covenant (Jer 31:27–28), God shows the flip side of these actions in another re-creation context.

It is more than just salvation here; God is committed to salvage operations. Noah and his family are saved; the world and human civilization are salvaged. Salvaging involves retrieving that which is valuable from the wreckage. This concept is at the heart of Israel's remnant theology, but we can also find God's salvage work in individual lives. It is this quality of God that finds, amidst Saul's destructive, skeptic zeal, Paul's apostolic vision for the church. The same God finds and nurtures in each one of us that which transforms our lives from sinful rubble to useful ministry. God is in the business of re-creating, and our lives testify to that grace. We are saved from our sin and its condemnation; we are salvaged for ministry and its service to God.

GENESIS 9:1–29

Original Meaning

Blessing (9:1–7). After the fall, the ground would not be cooperative, so that food was not as easily obtainable. Likewise, here we find that animals will not be cooperative, with the result that obtaining food will continue to be a challenge. It is likely that permission to use animals for food should be seen as a concession of grace.

In giving permission to eat this meat, the text introduces two caveats.

1. That the animal is living. This presumably rules out feeding from dead carcasses found in the wild.
2. That the meat cannot be eaten with the lifeblood in it. Ritually speaking, the draining of the blood before eating the meat was a way of returning the life force of the animal to God who gave it life.

Human life, because of the image of God, remains under the protection of God. Accountability to God for preserving human life is put into humanity's hands. In Israelite society, capital punishment was the recognized right of the family and was considered an act of justice.

Covenant (9:8–17). Perhaps the closest concept to a covenant in our society is a legal contract. Here the covenant is used as a means for God to formalize a pledge that he will not undo the blessing again. He again gives human beings reproduction and food procurement, and he will not negate them again by returning the earth to watery chaos. In this way, the covenant is tightly connected to the blessing theme.

The designation of the rainbow as a sign of the covenant does not suggest this was the first rainbow ever seen. The function of a sign is connected to the significance attached to it. Since the word for rainbow is the same Hebrew word as that used for the bow weapon, this offers an interesting image. It is a pregnant image to have God hanging up his bow. This should not change our interpretation of the rainbow, but it does hint at other subtle images and nuances floating in the background.

Noah's Vineyard (9:18–23). The phrase "man of the soil" (9:20) probably connotes more than simply "farmer." The NIV's "soil" translates the Hebrew *damah*, which has been a significant term in these early chapters. As a man of the *damah*, Noah is mortal and must continue to struggle with the curse. At the same time, the *damah* has survived, and Noah finds himself again on *terra firma*, with a second chance for humanity.

After Noah plants the vineyard, he becomes inebriated from its produce. The text does not explain, excuse, or condemn Noah's drunkenness. This does not mean that there is no explanation, no excuse, or no condemnation; it simply indicates that the text is not willing to be deterred from its purpose. The parallel to the fall is in Ham's action, not in Noah's condition.

If Ham's offense is parallel to the fall (as other literary indicators throughout this section suggest), then we should look for the common denominator of the parallels for clues. This does not mean that Ham's offense is the same as Eve's, but we can look for some point of comparison. We begin with observations. Both Eve and Ham are betrayed by their eyes. Eve *saw* that the fruit was desirable, and Ham *saw* his father's nakedness (was there something desirable about it?). Moreover, both Eve and Ham seek to entice others to join them in the offensive act.

Pronouncement (9:24–29). *Nature of the pronouncement.* Many have wondered why Canaan is cursed when apparently Ham committed the offense. This question can be resolved when we recognize the nature of Noah's statements. Verses 25–27 fit into the category of "patriarchal pronouncement." These pronouncements concern fertility of the family and ground and the question of who will dominate whom. Such pronouncements often include both negative and positive statements and are often given by a father on his deathbed, but they need not be limited to that situation. They can be influenced by various factors, including mood.

Details of the pronouncement. The Hebrew reads literally: "May God extend Japheth and may *he* dwell in the tents of Shem" (9:27, author's translation). We need not be overly concerned with identifying a fulfillment of this situation in history. Since there is no question concerning the slave status assigned to Canaan, any situation in which Canaan is under someone else's power qualifies.

Function of the pronouncement. Both times Ham is mentioned by name, the text informs us that he is the father of Canaan. The author is more interested in Canaan than he is in Ham. He implies that the Canaanites got off on the wrong foot from the beginning; thus, it is no surprise that by the time of Moses and his audience, they have earned the wrath and punishment of God.

Application. God has pledged that *he* will not bring the return of chaos through his actions. But that does not mean he will prevent us from bringing ecological doom on ourselves. The security we may derive from God's commitment should not make us so comfortable that we consider ourselves invulnerable to ecological catastrophe, with license to be as reckless as our indulgences demand.

GENESIS 10:1–11:26

Original Meaning

Table of Nations (10:1–32). The organization of the list of nations in chapter 10 is quasi-genealogical, but genealogy is not its purpose. Japheth is first. Ham's line is addressed in 10:6–20. Shem's descendants are delineated in 10:21–31. Two expansionary statements occur: the earth's being divided in the time of Peleg (10:25) and the region occupied by the line of Joktan (10:30).

Tower of Babel (11:1–9). *The project.* The alluvial plains of southern Mesopotamia had no stone available. As a result, as early as the Late Uruk period at the end of the fourth millennium BC, we see the development of kiln-fired brick (11:3).

The text refers to a "city" and a "tower" (11:4). In the early stages of urbanization, the city was comprised of public buildings such as administrative buildings and granaries, which were mostly connected with the temple. This brings us to the tower. Most interpreters have identified the Tower of Babel as a ziggurat, and I concur. Not only is it sociologically right for the context, even the terminology supports it.

The ziggurat did not play a part in any of the rituals that are known to us from Mesopotamia. The ziggurat was a structure that was built to support a stairway. This stairway was a visual representation of that which was believed to be used by the gods to travel from one realm to another. At the top of the ziggurat was the gate of the gods, the entrance into their heavenly abode. At the bottom was the temple, where hopefully the god would descend to receive the gifts and worship of his people.

The offense. With the development of urbanization people began to envision their gods in human terms. The needs and nature of the deities who would make use of a ziggurat stairway reflect the weakness and distortion of deity brought about by the Babylonian anthropomorphization of the gods. The offense in this passage, then, is to be found in the beliefs that resulted in the project and what it stood for in the minds of the builders. It went beyond mere idolatry; it degraded the nature of God by portraying him as having needs.

The response. The builders construct the ziggurat so that the deity can come down into their midst—and indeed Yahweh does come down (11:5), but he is displeased. He views this as a first step with inevitable results—human beings have crossed a significant threshold from which there will be no turning back. This is expressed in his observation that now "nothing they plan to do will be impossible" (11:6). The inhibitions that may prevent them from further corruption have been overcome. The confusion of the language makes cooperative living impossible and therefore scattering unavoidable.

Shem's Descendants (11:10–26). This is the line that finally takes us to Abram. Here in 11:10–26 the intention is to trace the genealogical line from Noah to Abram as a means of establishing continuity from the blessed line of Shem to the forefather of the Hebrews.

Application. God's power is an awesome thing. We dilute God when we try to tap into that power in order to redirect it for our own purpose or benefit. We are called to be the channel of that power. This becomes a problem when, instead of letting his power work through us or in us to carry out his plans, we want him to do our bidding. We are often delighted for God's power to work wonders in our lives but reluctant to allow his power to purify us.

GENESIS 11:27–12:20

Original Meaning

Chronology of Abraham (11:27–30, 32). Abram's entry into Canaan can be plausibly placed somewhere between 2100 and 1875 BC. Since the narrator elsewhere ties up loose ends further in time before moving along his chosen course, it is not unusual for him to report Terah's death before turning all his attention to Abram, even though Terah died long after Abram left his hometown.

Abram's Homeland (11:31). A quick check of the maps at the back of most Bibles confirms a consensus in popular circles concerning the identification of Abram's hometown, Ur of the Chaldeans. This consensus is the result of the spectacular archaeological excavations done at the Sumerian site of Ur in southern Mesopotamia by Sir Leonard Woolley from 1922 to 1934. Though it makes for a convenient identification and there is no other archaeological site that carries the ancient name of Ur, there are reasons to remain skeptical about this identification. The question ought to be considered an open one, unresolved until further information comes to light.

Covenant Offer (12:1–3). Though Terah leads a portion of his clan to Haran, Yahweh makes the covenant initiative offer to Abram (12:1–3). He must decide whether to abandon his land in favor of the land Yahweh offers. He must decide whether to abandon what family he still has in favor of the family Yahweh promises. Abram must trust Yahweh to deliver what he has offered in order to give up so much that Abram already has to gain.

Abram's Itinerary and Offerings (12:4–9). The trip from Haran to Canaan is about five hundred miles and takes the better part of a month, even if Abram travels at normal caravan pace (about twenty miles per day). The stops indicated by the text, Shechem and Bethel, both become major sacred sites in later Israelite history. At each one Abram builds an altar. What function do these altars serve? It is of interest that the text makes no specific reference to offering a sacrifice at either site (though that may be implied in his calling on the name of Yahweh in 12:8).

It is not possible that the altar is simply built so that the clan can conduct their worship during the time they remain there. When he builds the altar at Hebron in 13:18, its purpose seems simply to service his worship needs while he is there.

Shechem and Bethel are both located in the central hill country, thirty-five miles north of Jerusalem. Perhaps because of its proximity to Mount Gerizim and Mount Ebal, it has had a long history as a sacred site. The strategic position of Shechem, at the east entrance to the pass between these mountains, also made it an important trading center. Bethel is usually identified with Beitin just over ten miles north of Jerusalem. There was a major fortified city on the site during the Middle Bronze Age.

Abram in Egypt (12:10–18). *Move to Egypt.* Modern archaeologists and geologists have found evidence of a massive three-hundred-year drought cycle that occurred during the end of the third millennium and the beginning of the second millennium—one of the time periods to which Abram is dated. There is a built-in theological question here when Abram goes to Egypt. The famine represents a crisis in food provision. This, in turn, raises questions about the ability of God to take care of his followers. The temporary solution to the food problem creates a family problem, as Sarai is taken into the harem of Pharaoh.

Strategic ruse. This is the first of three narratives in which a patriarch attempts to identify his wife as his sister to avoid problems with the power establishment of the region (chs. 12, 20, 26). Interpreters have proposed many ingenious explanations for this behavior. At the present time we remain ignorant of what sociological realities commended this course of action to Abram. The original Israelite audience undoubtedly knew what advantage was to be gained from the ruse, so there was no need for the author to explain it. For our part, we accomplish nothing by welcoming or devising solutions designed to either vindicate or vitiate Abram.

Sarai's beauty. Our culture has persuaded us that beauty is closely connected with sensuality, youth, and certain facial and bodily features. We need not think that every culture is so superficial in their assessments of beauty as ours is. We need not therefore assume that Sarai has miraculously retained the stunning beauty of youth. Her dignity, her bearing, her countenance, her outfitting may all contribute to the impression that she is a striking woman. There is no reason to dismiss Sarai's beauty as existing only in the eyes of a doting husband.

Diseases. There is no indication of what diseases afflicted the household of Pharaoh. A sudden onslaught of disease would naturally lead to an investigation of activities that may have upset the gods. Pharaoh's reprimand of Abram is not a judgment of Abram's ethics, but a chastening for putting him in jeopardy.

Application. When we think of ourselves as recipients of grace, we inevitably think of salvation. The grace of God's sending his Son who died for us so that we can experience forgiveness of sins and spend eternity with him shines so brightly in our spiritual experience that everything else pales—stars washed out by the rising sun. Genesis gives us a chance to explore the brightly shining stars in the dawn of the theology of grace. What shines brighter than anything else is the grace shown by God as he reveals himself to and through his people. And though we are not wrong to be in constant awe of the grace of our salvation, we cannot afford to lose our awe of the grace of revelation.

In grace, he condescended to communicate concerning what pleases him and what angers him. We don't have to guess. He has opened to us his character, his attributes, his heart. How sad it is that the reality of revelation has become so commonplace to us. What a tragedy that we take it for granted. Though we have every reason to revel in the thrill of our eternal destiny, we would be terribly remiss if we failed to realize that greater than the privilege of living forever is that of knowing God.

GENESIS 13:1–15:21

Original Meaning

Separation from Lot (13:1–18). The land of Canaan had a limited number of water sources as well as limited grazing areas. It is not surprising, then, that the needs of Abram and Lot soon outgrew the available resources. As always, competing needs lead to conflict, and Abram and Lot finally decide they must go their separate ways.

Lot's attention is drawn to the "plain of the Jordan" (13:10). By moving to the vicinity of the cities of the plain, Lot has gone outside the land of Canaan, leaving it entirely to Abram. It is also important to notice the occurrence of "toward the east" in 13:11. Every movement away from God thus far in Genesis has been designated as toward the east (3:24; 4:16; 11:2).

Once Lot moves out of the land, the Lord gives Abram the land of Canaan (13:14–17). His itinerant wandering now takes on new purpose, almost equivalent to conquest, since everywhere he walks will be given to him and his family. Lot takes the road toward Jericho and the Jordan Valley, moving south to the vicinity of Sodom and Gomorrah. Abram takes the road south through Jerusalem and Bethlehem and into the Negev to arrive at Hebron.

The city of Hebron (13:18) is located in the Judean hill country. The construction of an altar here, as at Bethel, transforms it eventually into an important religious site, and its subsequent use as a burial place for the ancestors established its political importance.

The Rescue of Lot (14:1–16). *The kings.* The kings of the east remain obscure despite numerous attempts to link them to historically known figures, though the geographical areas they represent can be identified with some confidence. The names of the kings of the East are authentic enough, but none of them have been identified or linked to the kings of these respective regions at this time period. We certainly have no information of Elamite control of sections of Palestine as suggested in 14:4, but it must be admitted that there are many gaps in our knowledge of the history of this period. None of the five kings of Canaan are known outside the Bible.

Defeated territories. The itinerary of conquest is given as is common in chronographic texts. The route goes from north to south along what is known as the King's Highway, the major north-south artery in Transjordan, just east of the Jordan Valley. The towns of Sodom and Gomorrah have not been located with any certainty, though some think that their remains are beneath part of the Dead Sea. After the battle in the Valley of Siddim (location unknown), the four kings travel along the west side of the Jordan and go as far as Dan, in the north of the land of Canaan, before being overtaken by Abram and his men.

Returning to the narrative, when the battle turns against the Canaanite cities, the tar pits come into the narrative (14:10). Tar pits are common in this area of the Dead Sea, which is so rich in bitumen that large amounts bubble to the surface and even float on the Dead Sea. The word translated "pits" (14:10) generally refers to a spot that has been dug out. These pits provide refuge for the kings. The verb form used may mean that they fall into them, but the context may also be read to suggest that the pits are used for hiding places (they throw themselves into the pits).

In 14:13 Abram is referred to as "Abram the Hebrew." The use of the designation "Hebrew" in early texts only occurs when Abram's family or the Israelites are being identified with respect to foreigners.

Upon receiving word of the attack, Abram responds with his 318 retainers. Though the number seems small, this army is a match for any other armed force in the region. Besides the 318 who are "born in [Abram's] household" (14:14), Abram has three allies (14:24) who likely supply men to the effort as well.

Victory Reception (14:17–24). Melchizedek is introduced as the "king of Salem" (14:18) and is portrayed as the principal king of the region in that he receives a portion of the booty. Salem is generally considered to be Jerusalem (based on Ps 76:2). Whether Melchizedek is Canaanite, Amorite, or Jebusite cannot be easily determined. The name of God that he uses to bless Abram, *el elyon* ("God Most High," 14:19, 20), associates the common title Elyon with the name of El. In the Old Testament, Yahweh is referred to as El or, more frequently, as Elohim. El is also the chief Canaanite god. Since El Elyon could represent the designation of a Canaanite god, we have no reason to think of Melchizedek as a worshiper of Yahweh or even as monotheistic. His joint role as king and priest is common in the ancient Near East.

The communal meal Abram and Melchizedek share indicates a peaceful agreement. Melchizedek is anxious to make peace with such a proven military force, and Abram submits to the chief king of the region by paying a tithe, thereby acknowledging Melchizedek's status by giving him a portion of the spoils.

The other king involved is the "king of Sodom" (14:21, 22). He acknowledges that Abram has a right to the booty but asks that the people be returned to him. Abram refuses any share due him with the explanation that he is under oath to El Elyon (whom he identifies as Yahweh) not to profit from his military action.

Ratification of the Covenant (15:1–21). *Theophany.* This is the only chapter where God's communication with Abram takes place through the medium of a vision (15:1). The first topic for discussion concerns an heir. It does not take a lot of thought to realize that all of God's promises are dependent on

Abram's having a son. It was common practice in the ancient world for childless couples to adopt a son to care for them in their old age and receive the inheritance when they died. It appears that Eliezer currently has that role.

Yahweh's response is to assure Abram that the heir will be his biological son. God shows Abram the stars and indicates that his offspring will be equally innumerable. Abram accepts this confirmation regarding family, but he still has questions regarding possession of the land. This becomes the topic of the second half of the chapter.

Abram's belief. In the English combination of "believe" and "in," the total is equal to more than the sum of the parts. To "believe" someone simply means to accept what he or she says as valid, accurate, or credible. To "believe in" someone is to adopt a much more comprehensive faith and trust. When we say someone "believes in" God, we are using the combination idiomatically to represent a belief system. The Hebrew does not express a comprehensive belief system with these words.

Does the combination used in Genesis 15:6 refer to trusting God for salvation from one's sins? A survey of the passages indicates that salvation from sins is never under discussion when this phrase is used. The phrase in question ("Abram believed the LORD") concerns taking God at his word—believing that what he says will become reality and then acting on that belief. As a result, we conclude that Genesis 15:6 is saying the same thing. Abram's belief has nothing to do with salvation and nothing to do with a faith system. He simply believed that, though he had no children and no hope of having any, God could make his offspring as numerous as the stars of the sky.

What then of the second half of the statement? How does taking God at his word become "credited to him as righteousness" (15:6b)? If Abram's belief is not in the realm of soteriology, it would follow that neither is his righteousness. The verse can therefore not refer to the technical, imputed righteousness that modern theologians associate with justification (a meaning that the word never has in the Old Testament). The righteousness that is credited to him creates a legacy (in this case, a covenant; see Num 25:13).

In summary, Genesis 15:6 should be seen as the premise on which the covenant is ratified. Because Abram takes God at his word, God credits him with a legacy on the basis of the "rightness" of his faith. God accomplishes this by formally establishing the covenant with Abram. Recognized righteousness becomes the basis for blessing.

The ritual. When God speaks of giving him the land, Abram seems skeptical: "How can I know?" (15:8). Why the difference between the two responses? The difference is that the first will come about in his lifetime (he will have a son), while the second will not. God shows no frustration or disappointment at Abram's request for surety.

The ritual of dividing a series of animals in half and in some way passing between the halves is not widely attested. Texts from Mari and Alalakh feature the killing of animals as part of the ceremony of making a treaty. In these texts, walking through this sacrificial pathway can be seen as a symbolic action enacting the treaty as well as a curse on the one who violates the promise. This sort of explanation is less satisfactory in Genesis 15 because it is unclear what significance a self-curse can possibly have for God. Abram's driving away the birds of prey is identified as symbolic of future protection from Israel's enemies provided by Abram's faith.

In 15:17 a "smoking firepot" and a "blazing torch" make their appearance. The firepot functions as an oven principally for baking, including the baking of grain offerings (Lev 2:4). The torch can be used to provide light, but it is also used in military contexts or to speak of God's judgment (Zech 12:6). While in Mesopotamia the torch and oven represented particular deities, here they represent Yahweh, perhaps as the purifier. This is one of many instances where the Lord uses familiar concepts and motifs to reveal himself.

Application. Not only do God's plans often involve difficulties that we do not expect, but they also often take a long time to unfold. If someone is in a hurry, it is easy for that person to grow impatient with God. Genesis shows us a God who is not in a hurry. We cannot hurry him along, and we dare not grow impatient with him. When everything we do can be done faster and faster, thus accommodating our impatience, we are encouraged to be in a hurry ourselves and expect everyone else to match our pace.

We are an increasingly impatient people. When God doesn't perform his operations in nanoseconds, our impatience begins to show as our expectations go unfulfilled. How can we begin to resolve this problem? The key is to recognize that there is a certain tension between expectations and relationship.

Relationships operate in the here and now, while expectations are always looking to the future. Parents who manage to cherish each stage of development and focus on the present tolerate whatever drawbacks accompany each stage in deference to the sheer enjoyment of their child. This is the focus on *present relationship* rather than *future expectation*. If we are to achieve the goal of putting relationships ahead of expectations, we must learn to see relationships as a matter of greater consequence than expectations.

GENESIS 16:1–18:15

Original Meaning

Abram's and Sarai's Decision and Its Outcome (16:1–16). *Hagar's role.* Sarai has not borne any children for Abram.

Consequently, Sarai makes the suggestion of a way that Abram can have a son as the Lord has promised. It seems an unusual course of action, but in the context of the ancient world, this was not only appropriate but at times contractually dictated. Bearing children is a sign of God's blessing, both culturally and in the context of the blessing of Genesis 1.

Hagar's spite and feeling of superiority came from her confidence that a deity had blessed her and that Abram was now dependent on her since she carried the heir to the family in her womb. Sarai's accusation against Abram is that he has neglected the necessary steps that would keep Hagar remembering her appropriate place within the household. When Abram puts the matter in Sarai's hands to show Hagar her place, Sarai's mistreatment of the girl drives her to desertion.

This situation now represents triple jeopardy.

1. The covenant promises are in jeopardy because of the absence of the true heir.
2. An attempt at resolution of the initial jeopardy creates the second jeopardy of a son who will be a competing heir.
3. The makeshift heir is now in jeopardy of being lost to Abram and Sarai before he is even born.

Hagar's flight. The "angel of the LORD" makes his first appearance in Genesis in 16:7. The message of the angel shows distinct covenantal overtones in making reference to a numerous seed. She is going to be fruitful and multiply.

The pronouncement in 16:11–12 starts with a birth pronouncement, similar to that found in Isaiah 7:14. The name is given as a reminder of God's response to her suffering at the hands of Sarai. Verse 12 does not sound at all positive. Moses undoubtedly found in it an accurate description of the Bedouin lifestyle of Ishmael's descendants (see 25:18).

Hagar affirms a supernatural identity for the messenger and may well believe that the messenger was indeed a deity, but we would expect little in terms of spiritual insight or discerning subtleties from an Egyptian slave girl. Most likely Hagar is expressing surprise that she has encountered in such an unlikely place a deity inclined to show favor to her. In 16:13 the narrator identifies the deity as "the LORD" (i.e., Yahweh) but gives no indication that Hagar knows the deity is Yahweh.

Theophany and Circumcision (17:1–27). *Name change.* In chapter 15 God had only given legal ratification of his promises. This remained one step away from relationship since it was still one-sided. By analogy, the situation is progressing from providing a notarized document to entering a business partnership.

One of the first elements in this partnership is God's assignment of new names to Abram and Sarai. The names themselves indicate an expansion of the covenant. In chapter 12 it was promised that God would make Abram a great nation. The new name "Abraham" indicates that he will be "a father of many nations" (17:5).

It is true that naming is an act of authority, but we must also recognize it, as Abram undoubtedly did, as constituting a great privilege. When parents gave a name, it often expressed their hopes and dreams. Considering God's sovereignty, his giving of a name is much more determinative. Up until now, God has been interacting with Abram and directing him, but this is more like taking him into the household. He promises "to be your God and the God of your descendants after you" (17:7).

Everlasting covenant and everlasting possession. In 9:16 the covenant with Noah was identified as an "everlasting" covenant; that same terminology is used here (17:7, 13, 19). Additionally, the land is identified as an "everlasting" possession (17:8), correlating to 13:15, where God promised to give it to Abram's offspring "forever." The Hebrew word for "forever" is *olam*.

There are many contexts where *olam* clearly has more to do with an open-ended perpetuity than an absolute eternity. What, then, should be understood when the text speaks of a covenant that is *olam*? The implication of the terminology is that these agreements are permanent in the sense that no other alternative arrangement to serve that purpose is envisioned. This does not mean that the purpose it serves will never be obsolete. Circumcision, for example, became obsolete even though it is designated here as a covenant *olam*.

The history of circumcision. Circumcision was practiced widely in the ancient Near East as a rite of puberty or marriage. The Israelite reader was well aware of this fact. It was obvious enough to them that God was adopting a well-known sociological practice and adapting it for a unique theological function.

Although the Israelites are not the only people in the ancient Near East to circumcise their sons, what is unique in their practice is that the ritual is used as a theological rite of passage into the covenantal community rather than a passage into adulthood or a new family group through marriage.

Abraham's response. It has taken twenty-five years for Abraham to receive complete information. First God was going to make a great nation of him (12:2), then it was clarified that his heir would be his biological son (15:4), and now it is stated that the heir will also be Sarah's biological son (17:16). Abraham's bemused incredulity about Sarah's bearing a son is practically cut off in midstream as the wider implications sink in: Where does this leave Ishmael?

The poignancy of this question is lost if we fail to realize that for the last thirteen years, Abraham has lived in the belief that Ishmael, the son of his old age, is the promised son and that God's covenant will be carried out through him. All of his love, all of his hopes, and all of his dreams have been poured into this boy, and it is not unlikely that they have already discussed

Ishmael's covenant destiny. Abraham has not been anxiously awaiting the arrival of another son. In response to Abraham's expression of concern, God extends certain of the covenant benefits to Ishmael, but he also makes it clear that the covenant program is going to proceed through Isaac.

Three Guests (18:1–15). The text treats the visit of the three men as a theophany. Abraham's treatment of the men includes nothing to indicate whether he recognizes their supernatural nature. The bowing, foot-washing, and offer of refreshment in the shade and a meal are all standard aspects of meticulous hospitality.

The question in 18:9, "Where is your wife Sarah?", is designed to evoke an admission. If the question is to be explained in this way in this passage, Abraham's response that Sarah is in the tent constitutes some sort of admission. Perhaps the question is prompted by the fact that Abraham is waiting on them rather than Sarah. One of the most common reasons for a woman to be confined in her house or tent is when she was menstruating.

The timing must be precise here. In 18:6 Abraham asked Sarah to bake some bread, an activity often forbidden to menstruating women in Abraham's time, so at that point her period has not begun. Yet she would not be confined to her tent unless she actually had her period. If this is the issue, then, she presumably experienced the onset of her period as dinner is being served. It would have constituted a remarkable sign of the resumption of her fertility.

I want to make it clear how tenuous I regard this suggestion. The author has no need to clarify the linkage for his reader, though the customary confinement of menstruating women in the culture may have made the situation as clear to the native Israelite as our cryptic comment, "It's that time of the month." I only offer it as an option that makes sense of all the elements in the text.

Sarah's laughter is often a topic of conversation when this text is studied. Both Abraham's and Sarah's laughter expresses an incredulity that we can easily understand, given the circumstances. But Abraham's incredulous laughter is immediately followed by a statement that shows he accepts the pronouncement regardless of how unbelievable it is. In contrast, Sarah's question is left hanging in the air and begging for a response.

The question about why Sarah laughs is simply the lead into the more important statement of 18:14. The word translated "hard" here refers to that which goes beyond what human workmanship can attain. The sense of the word goes beyond "wonderful" or "astonishing" to something more like "mystical" or "supernatural." Here we see a clear statement of what the text is teaching about God.

Application. In chapter 16 Abraham makes decisions, but we are not told whether they are good ones or bad ones. More important, Abraham does not even know whether they are good or bad. In the thirteen-year gap between 16:16 and 17:1 we should be startled to discover that Abram has not been informed that Ishmael is not going to be the ultimate heir that the covenant had promised. For all these years he thinks that he is on the right track. His heart is devoted to Ishmael.

We need not think of digressions as failures or as unproductive. God in his sovereignty and providence does not waste our experiences. As long as we are not ignoring his signals or indulging our self-will, we can be sure he is shaping us for his service. Perhaps we too often think of God's plan for our lives as a perfectly straight track leading to his perfect will, with sidetracks deviating left and right as pitfalls and senseless distractions that seek to waylay us. It is more helpful to think of our lives in terms of a complicated model train set in the basement, with inside tracks, outside tracks, and many crisscrossing tracks. It doesn't matter whether we are on the inside or the outside track or cutting across. Sometimes we may feel as if we are going in circles, which is OK as long as we don't derail. Our goal is not to "get somewhere" but to serve. We must remember that we are on the rails and God is at the switch. What is most important about our faith is not where we are going but what we are becoming.

GENESIS 18:16–19:38

Original Meaning

Sodom and Gomorrah (18:16–33). Genesis 18:20–21 portrays the Lord again on a fact-finding mission. Statements as these should not be viewed as compromising attributes of God such as his omnipresence or omniscience but as reinforcing attributes such as justice. In 19:13 it is specified that the mission of the messengers is to destroy the city. Nevertheless, a fair judge sees the evidence firsthand.

It is the "outcry" (18:20) that has motivated God's response (18:20–21; 19:13). Innocent bloodshed cries out to the Lord for vengeance (cf. 4:10).

Location. Sodom and Gomorrah have stood throughout history as an example of wickedness and divine judgment. How strange it is, then, that there is little recollection of the location of these "cities of the plain." Their association with Zoar and the bitumen pits in "the Valley of Siddim" (14:10) both point to the southern end of the Dead Sea.

There are five sites of Early Bronze cities on the southeast plain of the Dead Sea, demonstrating that fairly large populations once existed here. Only Bab edh-Dhra and Numeira have been excavated extensively, and the destruction of these cities by fire has been set by archaeologists at about 2350 BC, seemingly too early for Abraham, though chronological reckoning of this period is difficult.

Wickedness (19:1–14). The sin of the Sodomites is self-evident and multileveled, blatant and unambiguous. No inhibitions interfere with their threats of violence or demands to indulge their lust. The text also makes it clear that the wicked behavior is not isolated (19:4). Though we have seen that "all" can be hyperbolic, the addition of the merism "both young and old" (19:4) indicates widespread participation.

Lot's response to the demand of the men in 19:8 is startling. Is Lot truly offering his daughters to be gang-raped and probably murdered? An alternative is that his suggestion implies a more subtle, "I would as soon have you violate my family members as violate those whom I have taken in and offered hospitality!" It would be like sarcastically saying to your mortgage company, "Why don't you just take the clothes off my children's backs and the food off their plates?" Such a comment is not suggesting that they will really do that. If this is the correct way to read 19:8, Lot's offer of his daughters is intended to prick the conscience of the mob.

The mob refuses to be placated or dissuaded from its intentions and indicates that it is even willing to treat Lot with the same violence that it threatens his guests with. Lot is beyond any power to enforce the law or punish violators. It is the divine messengers who come to his rescue as they strike the mob with blindness.

The word for "blindness" (19:11) here is used elsewhere only for the Aramean army at Dothan (2 Kgs 6:18). It is a term related to an Akkadian word for day-blindness (pertinent to 2 Kgs 6) and, evidently from this passage, also serves in Hebrew (as in Aramaic) to refer to night-blindness.

Lot now seeks to influence those who have other reasons to respect him. In 19:14 he lobbies his sons-in-law. Since his daughters appear to live in his house while his sons-in-law live elsewhere, it is logically assumed that the marriage agreement is somewhere in process. One would expect men in such a situation to do most anything to ingratiate or patronize their father-in-law. Yet their assessment of Lot's warning leads them not to take him seriously.

Escape, Destruction, and Lot's Wife (19:15–26). The space and time logistics become important here for understanding the details of the text. First, we must make two observations.

1. Lot's family and the angels leave the city at dawn (19:15), and the destruction begins when the sun is high in the sky (19:23). This means that they cannot have traveled more than ten miles.
2. The angel states that he cannot do anything until they reach Zoar (19:22), and the destruction indeed does not begin until they get there (19:23–24). This means that when Lot's wife looks back, the destruction has not yet begun.

If the five sites that have been identified archaeologically are the five cities of this passage, Zoar is in the middle of the group. That means that one would not have to look back to see the destruction. We therefore conclude that the angel's prohibition does not concern looking at the destruction. After all, people standing on the city walls of Zoar would have been able to watch the carnage take place. I conclude that the three commands form a sequence: (1) Get out of here; (2) don't turn back; and (3) don't stop before reaching your destination. This means that the verb used in 19:17 and 26 (*nbt*, "looked") must have idiomatic value that goes beyond looking.

There is a passage that suggests the city has so captured her attention that she actually returns to it. In Luke 17:28–32 Christ is comparing the day of Sodom's destruction to the coming of the kingdom of God. Here Jesus clearly implies that Lot's wife returned to Sodom. In this interpretation the command of the angel is broken not by glancing over one's shoulder and seeing what should not be seen but in directing attention back and returning to the city.

The result that Lot's wife becomes a pillar of salt need not be seen as an arbitrary and instantaneous transformation. The destruction is described in terms of sulfur (brimstone) and fire "raining down" (19:24) on the cities. The scene is one of divine retribution, and the use of brimstone appears here and elsewhere as an agent of purification and divine wrath on the wicked.

Lot and His Daughters (19:27–38). The five cities of the plain are the only cities in the region. With the destruction of those cities, it most likely seems to them that they are the last people on earth. This may be the reason behind the plot of Lot's daughters to become pregnant by their father. The text does not pause to condemn their action, though the audience would not have needed prompting to recognize it as reprehensible.

Lot is exonerated in that the daughters realize they have to get him drunk in order to carry out their intentions. This implies that he would not have agreed to the course of action they propose. Despite the vileness of the strategy, it is not impossible that Lot's daughters may be viewed in some quarters as tragic-heroic figures who are willing to do what is unimaginable and distasteful in order to achieve what is necessary. But while the text does not explicitly denounce their conduct, neither does it lionize them as tragic heroines. Their judgment concerning how to resolve a difficult situation is as unacceptable as their father's is.

Application. Righteous people have always been and will always be a minority. Still, individually and as the corporate church, God expects us to have an impact for righteousness in the world. Examples of such individuals abound. From the apostle Paul to Martin Luther to Mother Teresa, there are those who have refused to think they were too insignificant for God to use. Their impact came not because they were full of self-importance and thought themselves capable of big things, but because they humbly did what needed to be done. Understanding the task at hand, they boldly went about doing what God led them to do. In most cases, an impact is not accomplished amidst great fanfare and does not necessarily enjoy popular support. Mother Teresa worked in virtual anonymity in the squalid conditions of the diseased and the destitute for decades before gaining the popular recognition and acclaim that she received in her last years. Martin Luther and other Reformers were met with official resistance that threatened their lives, health, and welfare.

More often than not, making an impact for righteousness in a fallen world entails a good deal of "plodding." It may take time for the church to have an impact on the world. We can only be faithful to the call of Christ and do what needs to be done. The harvest is his and will come as his will determines.

GENESIS 20:1–21:34

Original Meaning

Abraham and Abimelek (20:1–18). Abraham's itinerant lifestyle, not a famine, drives him to Gerar. Verse 1 distinguishes between where Abraham settles (between Kadesh and Shur) and where he wanders (NIV "stayed" [20:1]—in Gerar). The former is his base of operations; the latter is one of the stations for his flocks and herds. Gerar is about thirty-five miles from Hebron (where Abraham was in the previous chapters). This is the second time that the text records Abraham's identifying Sarah as his sister, but it is not unlikely that this is their regular custom when they are in unfamiliar places (20:13).

God informs Abimelek of his offense in a dream. In ancient Near Eastern literature there is a category called auditory message dreams. In auditory message dreams, God appears and sometimes startles the person awake. Here the accusation concerns the potential of adultery. Hittite laws, Middle Assyrian Laws, and the Laws of Hammurabi all contain legislation against adultery.

Verse 7 contains the first occurrence of the term "prophet" in the Old Testament. God identifies Abraham as one who is capable of intercession on Abimelech's behalf. Generally, the prophet offered a message from the deity, but here Abraham is praying for healing (cf. 20:17). This reflects the broader view of a prophet as one who has powerful connections to the deity, such that he can initiate or remove curses. In the ancient Near East, this role is typically played by an incantation priest, who would recite incantations and perform appropriate rituals. He also received omens to enable him to proclaim that the danger had passed.

It is clear that the plague on Abimelech's house has something to do with barrenness or, more likely, with sexual dysfunction since Abimelek also requires healing. It appears that Sarah has not spent much time under Abimelech's control, so the plague most likely manifests itself rather quickly. Anything that prevented childbirth could be described as "closing the womb" (20:18), in that the diagnosis of medical conditions in the ancient Near East tended to be symptomatic (identifying consequences) rather than ontological (identifying causes).

Abimelek responds generously, probably as an act of appeasement to Abraham's God. Unspecified amounts of cattle and slaves are given in addition to freedom to move about the land and 1,000 shekels of silver. In weight it equals about 25 pounds of silver, but in value it is more than a common worker could expect to make in a lifetime.

Isaac and Ishmael (21:1–21). The long-awaited birth of Isaac is reported in 21:1–7. In the plot of Genesis, this should be a significant climax, yet it is reported briefly and without fanfare. The scene has been well set for the name Isaac ("laughter," see 17:17; 18:12–15), but there is an ill turn on the name in 21:9 ("mocking"). In 21:10 the text is not clear whether Ishmael has done something that warrants the drastic response of Sarah. God's directions to Abraham neither vindicate Sarah nor confirm an offense on the part of Ishmael.

The text's statement in 21:11 appears cryptic. Which son? We might expect Abraham to share Sarah's concern about Isaac's inheritance, but the following verses make it clear that his distress is over the welfare of Ishmael.

For a second time (see 16:10–13) Hagar receives a visitation from God. He not only comforts her with a promise (21:18) but provides for her immediate needs (21:19). Few individuals in the Bible are favored with two theophanies and can claim to have been rescued by receiving divine instruction. This is another indication of the blessings that surround Abraham and those associated with him.

The Treaty (21:22–34). In a land of seasonally-confined rainfall, wells are extremely important to the welfare of the human population and their herds and flocks. The area of Beersheba where Abraham had dug a well is apparently under the political jurisdiction of Abimelek but is unowned land (as much of the land in this region is). Abraham is claiming no ownership of the land, only the rights to the water in the well that he has dug.

As in chapter 20, Abimelech's servants take something

that belongs to Abraham, and Abimelek excuses himself as not knowing about the offense. In chapter 20 Abimelek gives sheep and cattle to Abraham (20:14), while in chapter 21 Abraham gives sheep and cattle to Abimelek (21:27). Abimelek gives Abraham 1,000 shekels in 20:16 to signify that Sarah still belongs to Abraham, and Abraham gives Abimelek seven ewe lambs in 21:28 as a testimony that the well belongs to Abraham.

The designation of significance to a name (21:31) is not necessarily a suggestion that the name originated at that time. The ancients were less concerned with the origin of a name than they were with the significance the name acquired.

Abraham's worship is expressed in 21:33 in a couple of different ways.

1. He plants a tamarisk tree. The tamarisk grows in sandy soil. Bedouin commonly plant this hearty tree for its shade and the branches. Images were made from its wood, and it was at times connected with cosmic stability. In this sense, planting a tree can have as much significance as building an altar.
2. Abraham "calls on the name of the LORD" (21:33). That seems to be the case here in that the epithet "Eternal God" (Heb. *el olam*) is attached to explain how Abraham designates God. In Isaiah the epithet is part of the prophet's presentation of Yahweh as the God who holds history, the nations, and Israel's destiny in his hands (e.g. Isa 40:28).
3. Finally, Abraham's dwelling is identified as "the land of the Philistines" (21:34). The first-known mention of the Philistines outside the Bible is in the records of Pharaoh Ramesses III (1182–1151 BC). As part of the invading Sea Peoples, they settled in five city-states along the southern coast of Canaan and were employed by the Egyptians as mercenaries and trading partners. This story may thus represent contact with an earlier group of Philistines who settled the area prior to the Sea Peoples' invasion, or perhaps it is an anachronistic use of the name *Philistines* for the area rather than the people Abraham encountered.

Application. Does the fact that God can open the womb mean that women who cannot bear children ought to pray for God to give them the ability to bear children, as Hannah did (1 Sam 1:5–6, 10–11)? Such petitions are on the same level as prayers for healing from those who are sick. We pray because we know that God is able, but we must also be ready to hear a "no" answer. If God chooses not to grant fertility, we can only accept his wisdom and seek to honor him as we are. God's decisions will be designed to serve his purposes.

It is counterproductive to our service of God to allow bitterness to infect our spirits, whatever our complaints against him may be. When Christ was questioned about the offense that caused a man to be born blind (John 9:1–5), his answer is instructive. He did not answer the question in terms of cause but in terms of purpose. It is immaterial what caused the man's condition, he said; what is important is that God be honored through it. We cannot determine cause; we cannot assume disfavor. We can only turn our attention away from the past and look toward the future, seeking to honor God in whatever situation he places us in.

GENESIS 22:1–24

Original Meaning

God Tests Abraham (22:1). When God tests, he tests some value, quality, or attribute by stretching it to its limits. In most cases he is testing the faith and faithfulness of individuals or of Israel by expecting them to obey in difficult circumstances.

Human Sacrifice (22:3–12). The command to sacrifice his son would not have been as shocking to Abraham as it is to us. In the Canaanite worldview, the god who provided fertility (El) was also entitled to demand a portion of what had been produced. This was expressed in sacrifice of animals and grain and in the sacrifice of children. Abraham's compliant acquiescence, as much as it reflects the power of his faith, also suggests that human sacrifice is familiar to his conceptual worldview.

God's Provision (22:13–14). The verb translated "provide" by the NIV in 22:8, 14 is the verb "to see." This usage approximates one of the idiomatic uses of the verb "to see" that we also have in English to convey that the details will be taken care of. But the idiom also suggests Abraham is convinced that the Lord will work out all of the details (22:8).

It is also significant coming from the mouth of Moses, the narrator, that "to this day it is said 'On the mountain of the LORD it will be provided'" (22:14). The only two other mountains that are ever referred to as "the mountain of the LORD" are Jerusalem and Sinai. Both places are easily recognized as locations where God took care of details—the details of the law at Mount Sinai and the details of sacrifice at the temple in Jerusalem.

Renewed Covenant (22:15–24). The reiteration of the covenant contains several elements worthy of note.

1. Yahweh swears an oath in his own name (22:16). This element was not included in any of the previous statements of covenant promises. Consequently, when the rest of the Old Testament mentions "the land I swore to Abraham," it is referring specifically back to this passage. This oath represents an advance in the

covenant in that it strengthens even further Yahweh's obligation.

2. This reiteration is also an advance because it explicitly promises that Abraham's descendants "will take possession of the cities of their enemies" (22:17). This is the first indication of a conquest (repeated in Genesis only in 24:60) and would be particularly meaningful to the Israelites in the desert. As a result of conquest, the nations will want to bring themselves under Israel's blessing. This can be understood as the nations ingratiating themselves to the Israelites, who are clearly favored by God.
3. Finally, note that the oath and the accompanying advancements in the covenant agreement are here cited as a consequence of Abraham's obedience (22:18). In all prior statements, the covenant promises were motivated purely by God's grace with no indication of conditions or suggestions that God's favor was earned. The statement made here does not suggest that the promises are conditional on the future obedience of Abraham and his descendants, but it does identify his obedience as having served as a stimulus for this advance.

Application. When we are not in control, it is easy to become anxious and fearful. The distance between a response of fear and one of exhilaration is the belief we have that the situation truly is under control, even if it is not our control. We may feel that we are free-falling through life, but we are held by God, who is in absolute control. It may not quite be exhilaration that we feel when life takes a dive, but having faith that the situation is never out of God's control can calm our fears.

GENESIS 23:1–25:18

Original Meaning

Hittite Land (23:1–3). It is difficult to determine whether the Hittites mentioned here are related to those of the Hittite Empire known from Anatolia a few centuries later. Abraham's era is far too early to coincide with the dissemination of the Hittites into Syro-Palestine that took place in the aftermath of the turmoil associated with the Sea Peoples around 1200 BC.

Arable land was so precious in the ancient world that owners usually refrained from selling it to anyone outside the kinship group. But Abraham is not trying to buy farmland, only property for a burial site. Most often a family tomb was used by several generations. A body was laid in a prepared shelf. Later the skeletal remains were removed and placed in another chamber or an ossuary box or simply swept to the rear of the tomb to accommodate another burial.

Negotiations (23:4–16). Four hundred shekels of silver is a substantial price—equivalent to about 7.25 pounds of silver. Abraham is likely anxious to pay full price because a discounted price could be later connected to family debt problems and also allow the heirs of Ephron to reclaim the land.

Mamre, Hebron, and Machpelah (23:17–20). The city of Hebron is in the Judean hill country about halfway between Jerusalem and Beersheba. Mamre is identified as Ramet el-Khalil, about two miles north of Hebron. Excavations indicate a wall around an ancient terebinth there already in the Second Temple period.

The Servant's Oath (24:1–9). Abraham's insistence that Isaac's wife be chosen from among family rather than from the people of the land (24:3) is a covenant matter, but we must keep in mind that Abraham's relatives are no more monotheistic than the Canaanites. At this early stage, intermarriage with the people of the land would risk assimilation and thus jeopardize the covenant promises of the land to Abraham's descendants. This also allows the Israel of Moses's audience to understand that the people they are to drive out of the land are not related to them in any way.

The servant takes the oath with the symbolic gesture of placing his hand under Abraham's thigh. This is in the vicinity of the genitals, and some even maintain that this procedure involves placing one's hand on the genitals. This would make sense to the extent that the oath concerned not just Isaac but ultimately all of Abraham's offspring.

The Prayer and the Oracle (24:10–21). Aram Naharaim ("Aram of the Two Rivers"), containing Haran on the Balikh River, includes the general area between the Euphrates River and the Habur River triangle in northern Mesopotamia. Trips to a well were generally made during the cooler hours of the day, and most of the women of the town appeared there. It was normal protocol for a stranger to ask permission to use a town's well, and it was customary for the people of the town to provide the hospitality of offering a drink.

The prayer of Abraham's servant uses an oracular approach for identifying Isaac's bride-to-be. In an oracle a yes/no question is posed to a deity and a mechanism of some binary nature is given so that the deity can provide an answer (the oracle). In post-Sinai Israel the priest carried the Urim and Thummim to use in oracular situations.

Abraham's servant must be creative as he devises a mechanism for procuring the oracle. The yes/no question he poses is whether the girl he approaches is the right wife for Isaac. His oracular mechanism is based on a question he will ask the girl: Will she give him a drink? The expected answer to that oracular question would be yes, so that the only logical unique answer would be no. Thus, for the alternative the servant must choose something far out of the range of expectation—such as the girl's volunteering to water all his camels.

A camel that has gone a few days without water can drink as much as twenty-five gallons. Ancient jars used for drawing water usually held no more than three gallons. In other words, this offer involves perhaps from eighty to a hundred drawings from the well. Such an unbelievable proposal would indicate that God is working to override human nature in specified ways. Rebekah passes the test of Abraham's servant.

Negotiations (24:22–54). The giving of gifts—the nose ring and bracelets—serves several functions. On the most basic level it can be thought of as an exorbitant payment for exorbitant service. But no one would have taken this as a pay-for-hire situation. The gifts give evidence of his master's wealth and serve as motivation for the eventual proposal to be taken seriously. Finally, they serve as a down payment on a bride price.

Bracelets were bands worn around the wrist as bangles. They were popular items and are often found on the arms and wrists of females in tombs. By placing them on Rebekah's arms, the servant may be symbolizing the marriage contract. A 10-shekel bracelet weighs about four ounces. Legal materials from this time period suggest a worker might expect to make at most 10 shekels of silver per year and less. Gold shekels were even more valuable. In other words, these extremely costly gifts from Abraham would have undoubtedly caused a stir of great excitement.

Laban eagerly takes the servant in, and the bulk of the chapter contains the repetition of the story. The retelling of the story is significant because of the evidence that it offers that this marriage is divinely sanctioned (esp. 24:40, 48, 50).

Blessing and Marriage (24:55–67). For a marriage to be arranged, the groom's family must provide a bride price while the bride's family provides a dowry. The silver and gold objects and the garments presented to Rebekah are part of her transformation into a member of Abraham's household. The presents given to her brother Laban and her mother demonstrate Abraham's wealth and the desirability of the marriage.

It was unusual in the ancient world for the woman to have any part in major decisions. Rebekah is not consulted with regard to the marriage (24:50–51), but when the servant asks to leave right away, the men look to Rebekah for consent. She is probably consulted because of the substantial risk involved in leaving family protection under such unusual circumstances.

With Rebekah leaving home, the family recites a blessing that reiterates some of the elements that have by now been identified firmly within the covenant benefits (24:60). The increase of descendants goes back to Genesis 1, but the possession of enemy cities was not included until Genesis 22. These themes have become programmatic in the family blessings of Genesis (22:17; 27:27–29).

When the group arrives in Beer Lahai Roi, Abraham's servant identifies Isaac in the fields, and Rebekah dons her veil. Since she has gone unveiled during the journey, she is probably now indicating that she is Isaac's bride. Brides were veiled during the wedding but went unveiled as married women. By taking Rebekah into his mother's tent, Isaac demonstrates that she is now the mistress of the household.

Abraham's Second Family and Death (25:1–11). The use of the plural "concubines" in 25:6 and the lack of any temporal clause stating clearly that Keturah came on the scene after Sarah's death suggest that Keturah may have entered the family at an earlier period (between Ishmael and Isaac). The narrator only picks it up here as an appendix of sorts to close out the issue of inheritance and other miscellaneous items connected to Abraham. The author does not always relate everything in chronological order.

Of the children of Keturah, Midian is the most familiar to the modern Bible reading audience. In the Pentateuch the Midianites initially have neutral standing as the traders who transport Joseph to Egypt, then a favorable standing because Moses marries into the family of the priest of Midian, Jethro. By the end of the period, however, they are in collusion with the Moabites.

Ishmael's Family (25:12–18). This section constitutes a separate *toledot* ("accounts"), the seventh and the shortest of the eleven *toledot* sections. This is another case of the narrator pursuing the unimportant line and drawing it to conclusion before coming back and discussing the line he is interested in following. Thus, Ishmael's descendants are enumerated before Isaac's descendants. In 16:12 the angel told Hagar that Ishmael would live in hostility to his brothers. It is a fitting conclusion, then, for 25:18 to note that that is exactly how it turned out. In 21:18 the angel told Hagar that Ishmael would become a great nation. In 25:13–16 the text indicates the fulfillment of that statement as well. Eight of these twelve sons of Ishmael appear again in Scripture, but only a few times each.

Application. In the process of discerning God's will in our lives, there are aspects that are our responsibility and others that are God's responsibility. It is our responsibility to be committed to doing his will. Our prayers should focus on ferreting out self-will and selfish motivations. Instead of asking for miraculous signs, we should ask God to help us to be motivated only by what pleases and honors him. We should ask him to help us think clearly about the decision and to direct our thinking. If we faithfully do our part, it is then his job to guide us to the right decision. He can do this through abnormal circumstances that carry his unmistakable mark, but more frequently he will do it through closed and open doors, through our own thinking process, and through his Spirit working within us. Asking for signs may indicate that we do not trust God enough to allow him to work in our minds and hearts to give us godly discernment.

GENESIS 25:19–27:46

Original Meaning

Oracle and Birth (25:19–28). This section begins the *toledot* of Isaac. Though the barrenness obstacle that we saw in the Abraham story recurs in this generation, the text does not dwell on it. Instead, the obstacle in immediate focus is that once Rebekah conceives, she is troubled by a problem pregnancy. The terminology "to inquire of the LORD" (25:22) usually indicates the asking of an oracle.

Genesis 25:23 records the content of the oracle, which by its very nature suggests it was provided by a human expert or by a theophany since mechanistic oracles do not give verbal messages. The focus of the text is on the content of the oracle, not its source. The jostling Rebekah feels signifies that she is carrying twins and that there will be conflict between them, with the younger prevailing. It is this conflict and reversal (the younger prevailing) that define the dominant obstacles for the new generation. The oracle concerns the destiny of the descendants but gives no instruction for parenting the individuals.

Names in the ancient world most often made statements about a deity, but they also sometimes offered commentary on circumstances surrounding one's birth. A creative name might do both—one directly and the other through wordplay. This is apparently the case in Jacob's name. The name *Yaqub-el* is common in West Semitic and means "May the God El protect." At the same time the noun using the same three root letters (*ʿqb*) means "heel." Thus, the name combines the standard sentence name with a comment on the circumstances of Jacob's birth.

The contrast between the two continues in their preferred lifestyles, and the conflict between them is energized by the favoritism shown by the parents. The verb translated "love" (25:28) is indicative of favor, choice, and preference. Rebekah undoubtedly loves both her children, but Jacob is her favorite and receives preferential treatment from her.

The qualities that endear Jacob to Rebekah are summarized in 25:27. The description of Jacob likely has to do with being an organized, administrative type of person who is conscientious, detail-oriented, well-rounded, and efficient. Such can only be speculation from what we observe about Jacob, for there are no occurrences of the adjective sufficiently nuanced in context to clarify these alternatives. The second description of him, staying "among the tents" (25:27), identifies him as engaged in seminomadic pastoralism rather than being a hunter like Esau.

Birthright (25:29–34). *The prize.* We must first be clear about what is at stake. The birthright was the oldest son's share of the material estate of the family. In the ancient world the firstborn typically received a double share of the inheritance. The fewer the number of sons, the greater the discrepancy. In the case of Esau and Jacob, Esau would receive two-thirds—twice what Jacob would receive. The sense of injustice would be substantially increased when the second born is a twin. Thus, it is easy to understand the sort of bitterness and jealousy that could result from such inequity.

The setting. Jacob is cooking stew. In a large household such as Isaac's, one would expect servants to do this sort of work. We may also ask why Esau does not appeal to Isaac to get the food that is being withheld. The most logical solution is that the setting is not at their home base but at a shepherd camp. Most realistic is a setting in which Jacob is in charge of one of the groups of herders at a grazing site.

Esau's condition and capitulation. Is it possible that this skilled hunter is truly on the brink of starvation, or is he simply using careless hyperbole? Giving Esau the benefit of the doubt, we may accept that he believes that hunger threatens his life. The original audience would react to Esau's blunt statement ("What good is the birthright to me?" 25:32) with horror, regardless of his extremity. There was intrinsic value connected to a birthright, not just utilitarian value. The only evaluation the text offers comes in the last verb of 25:34: "Esau despised his birthright." This verb does not reflect Esau's feelings about the birthright but comments on his valuation of it.

Isaac and Abimelek (26:1–35). *Covenant.* Verse 1 is clear that this is a different, though admittedly similar, episode. As Abraham insisted that Isaac stay in the land in 24:6, the Lord also instructs him to stay in the land. That leads to a reiteration of the covenant promises

What are the obligations, decrees, and instructions that the patriarchs live by? An example of "command/obligation" is when Lot was told to flee Sodom or when Abraham was told to sacrifice Isaac. An example of "decree/regulation" is the ordinance of circumcision. An example of "law/ instruction" is that circumcision should be done on the eighth day.

Wife-sister. Isaac's rationale for the ruse is the same as Abraham's (26:7), but Rebekah is not actually taken by the ruler as Sarah had been on both occasions. Discovery of the ruse does not come through divine revelation (20:3) or because of plagues (12:17), but through a chance glimpse of Isaac's intimate interaction with Rebekah. We can note, therefore, a decreasing danger in the accounts.

Wells. After the protagonists are sufficiently spread out across the land, the conflict is resolved, and they eventually ally themselves together by oath. Perhaps most important to the author, the men of Gerar recognize God's blessing on Isaac and, as the covenant has suggested, they seek to join themselves to him.

Isaac's Blessing (27:1–46). This narrative begins with Isaac's health in sufficiently fragile condition that he decides that the time has come to give his blessing. In reality, Isaac lives for many more years. Nevertheless, Isaac desires to put his house in order by giving a blessing to Esau. The occasion of the giving of the blessing is obviously celebratory.

Isaac is planning to give the patriarchal blessing, which must be distinguished from the material inheritance (birthright) discussed at the end of Genesis 25. The blessing has nothing to do with material goods or birth order. It is also important to distinguish the patriarchal blessing from the covenant blessing, though there may be areas of overlap. The covenant blessing is passed on to Jacob by Isaac in 28:3–4 but, more important, is confirmed by God in subsequent settings (e.g., 28:13–15).

These pronouncements can be viewed from three different perspectives: social, theological, and canonical. From the *social* perspective, there is no question that these pronouncements are taken with the utmost gravity by both father and son. They expect the pronouncements to impact the destiny of the son. The significance attached to the pronouncement is evident in what Rebekah and Jacob are willing to do to procure it as well as in Esau's distress when he loses it. The power of the pronouncement is vested in its being spoken. That is why Isaac cannot take it back after he learns he has been tricked.

Theologically these pronouncements are not presented as prophetic messages from the Lord. They simply represent the hopes and wishes of a father for his son(s). Consequently, Isaac uses first-person grammatical forms to indicate his ownership of the statements (27:37). There is no intrinsic authority vested in the blessing.

When we look at the situation from a *canonical* perspective, however, we must admit that their inclusion by the narrator indicates a sense that the pronouncement also enjoys God's seal of approval and that it turns out accurately to reflect the son's destiny. Whether we would say that the patriarch is blessed with divine insight in the making of the pronouncement or that God sees fit to honor the pronouncement is just semantics.

As we are reminded of Abraham's practice of giving gifts to his children and sending them away (21:11–14; 25:6), singling out Esau opens up the possibility that Isaac is intending to send Esau away. While admittedly no such exigency is referred to either by Isaac or the narrator, it makes some sense in the context of the grief Esau is causing his parents because of his marriages (26:35) and explains his being summoned individually. How ironic it would be if Rebekah and Jacob unwittingly interfere with the sequence that would have resulted in Esau's being sent away. Instead, it is Jacob who ends up being sent away.

The story is well known, and there is little in the detail that cries out for clarification. We will focus our comments, then, on a few of the unusual twists. What first strikes one as Rebekah's scheme unfolds is the sheer improbability that this can possibly work. Can goat meat be made to taste like venison? Can goatskin feel like human hair? How can Jacob possibly pass as Esau when his voice can so easily give him away? We must conclude that beyond being blind, all of Isaac's senses are dulled—not only his five senses but his common sense and his sense of reason as well. Jacob is thus again exploiting the vulnerability of his relatives.

A second unusual twist is Rebekah's offer to take the curse on herself if Jacob is discovered (27:13). We might recall the curse that Canaan/Ham drew from Noah when they provoked his ire. Rebekah seeks to allay Jacob's qualms by suggesting that she will take any resulting curse on herself. How can she do that? As we will see, a blessing is not transferable, so why should a curse be? Rebekah is likely referring to the consequences of the curse rather than the curse itself.

Isaac conducts five tests concerning the identity of his son: logic (27:20), touch (27:21–22), sound (27:22), his word (27:24), and scent (27:27). Jacob dissembles through the first and the fourth, and his disguise gets him through the second and fifth. Only the middle one, the sound of his voice, fails. Having been adequately satisfied that this is Esau, Isaac proceeds with the blessing. In this blessing we can recognize the standard elements of patriarchal pronouncements: fertility of the land and authority over others.

The suspense continues as Esau arrives right on the heels of Jacob. As the deception is revealed, Jacob's name is seen to reflect the reality of his character. At birth Esau was "heeled" by Jacob's grasp, and now in adulthood he is "heeled" by the ambition of Rebekah and Jacob's grasp for the blessing (27:36).

Esau's desperation creates a dilemma for Isaac, who would like to accommodate his son's request but has little to offer. The resulting blessing is far from ideal. The first part uses the same words as he has just spoken to Jacob but to the opposite effect. Jacob was to receive abundance *from* heaven's dew and *from* earth's richness (27:28). In contrast, Esau's dwelling will be *away from* heaven's dew and *away from* earth's richness (27:39). In the second part of the blessing, all Isaac can do is to indicate that Esau's descendants will eventually be able to break free from Jacob's.

The narrative now moves rapidly to the unsurprising results: escalated tensions and greater conflict. Rebekah shares in this consequence as she is forced to send her favorite away. In this sense, the resulting curse is on her. Despite her hopes that the separation will be brief, "a while" (27:44) turns into twenty years. The jeopardy to the covenant is encapsulated in Rebekah's expression of her worst fear: "Why should I lose both of you in one day?" (27:45). The covenant again hangs by a thread with the frighteningly realistic prospect that both Isaac and Jacob could be lost in a twinkling.

Application. It is particularly painful when a son or daughter shows no concern for the rich heritage and solid upbringing they have received. In the famous parable, though the prodigal son did not fail to appreciate his inheritance, he did reject the value system of his father. Just as Esau is painted as one who did not adopt the value system of his family, many today turn aside from their family's values and in the process forfeit God's blessing in missed opportunities.

What can we expect from God when we show ourselves unworthy of his blessing by despising the values that comprise our spiritual heritage? Christians who have grown up in difficult family situations may often fantasize about growing up in a loving, nurturing Christian environment. But the Bible and history are replete with examples of those who have grown up in the homes of great spiritual leaders but have found the pathway less than smooth. Enough stories are available about prodigal preacher's kids and missionary's kids for all to be aware of the problems.

GENESIS 28:1–22

Original Meaning

Jacob's Departure (28:1–9). Jacob is already seventy-seven years old. The marriage instructions are similar to those given by Abraham to his servant almost one hundred years earlier when Isaac was ready to marry. In addition to the instructions, Jacob is sent away with the covenant blessing (28:3–4). Jacob is going away, and this is part of the process of parting. This is the only place in Genesis where a patriarch confers the covenant blessing on his son. We note, however, that only blessings are spoken, not promises. These are Isaac's wishes for his son; it is left to God to make promises to Jacob (28:13–15).

Jacob's Dream and Vow (28:10–22). The 550-mile trip from Beersheba to Haran would have taken Jacob over a month. It probably takes several days to get as far as Bethel, sixty miles from Beersheba. What Jacob is dreaming comes from the cultural world of the ancient Near East. In Mesopotamia the comparable word to the one used here describes the stairway used by a messenger of the gods moving from one realm to another. It is this same stairway that is architecturally depicted in the famous ziggurats in Mesopotamian cities.

In Genesis 28 the messengers of God are using this stairway to travel between realms. Angels (messengers) descended to embark on their errands throughout the earth and ascended when returning with reports. Note carefully that Yahweh is not seen descending by the stairway; he is standing beside it. Thus, the dream is thoroughly embedded in the imagery of the worldview that it features but is distinct in how God relates to it.

The important part of all of this is the content of the message conveyed by it. This is Jacob's first theophany, and it parallels the "Yahweh theophany" that Abraham received in Genesis 15. As indicated there, Yahweh theophanies tend to be land oriented. Obviously, the descendants element is not ignored (28:14), but the main thrust of the message is that Yahweh will bring Jacob back to the land. Note too that Jacob is virtually the same age as Abraham was when God asked him to leave his home and travel to a new land (12:1–4).

When Jacob awakes, he has two responses.

1. He recognizes the nature of the place. Since Jacob has seen a portal here, he identifies the space as sacred space, a house of God. Jacob sets up the stone as a pillar. Sacred pillars and standing stones are familiar in the religious environment of the ancient world. Anointing the pillar constitutes its dedication. Jacob names the place Bethel, meaning "house of God" (28:19), which formalizes his new information about the place.
2. The second response is a personal one from Jacob that comes in terms of a vow. Vows are promises made (almost always to God) with conditions attached. Here the conditions include provision and protection from God that will result in Jacob's return as Yahweh promised in the dream theophany. The tangible element of Jacob's gift is a tithe of all he receives from the hand of God.

Jacob most likely anticipates that any wealth coming to him will be in the form of flocks and herds. In such a case the tithe will be represented in sacrifices at Bethel. Genesis 35 does not mention sacrifices being made, but Jacob does build an altar, thereby making it all the more likely that he fulfills this part of his vow by sacrifice.

But there was also a more intangible element to Jacob's promises. In 28:21 he specifically names Yahweh as his God. In other words, if Providence smiles on him and returns Jacob to this land, Jacob will recognize that Yahweh is behind that Providence and is guiding his destiny. Since Genesis 35 records Jacob's fulfillment of his vow, he carries out this part by setting aside other gods (35:2).

Application. God is a good teacher, full of patience and grace despite our arrogance and conceit. Dare we dictate to God the terms of our commitment or suggest that our service will only be rendered when he proves himself worthy? That is what Jacob is doing when he makes his vow.

In our lives, we may imagine we have done God a favor and deserve his attention and blessing, but no one can make that a premise for requests for blessing. The reason is that God has done far more for us in sending his Son to die for us. Whatever we do for God is small repayment compared to that. God has unlimited grace; yet, in our attitudes we can presume upon his grace and tire him with our self-serving requests.

Perhaps God would be pleased if more of our requests focused on spiritual gain: stronger faith, purification of thoughts, straightening out of attitudes, patience in hardship, love for those we find difficult to love, sensitivity to his leading, and increased commitment to his service. These are the sort of requests that never presume upon his grace. They will achieve his purpose of helping us come to an understanding of our true nature and our dependence on him.

GENESIS 29:1–31:55

Original Meaning

Family Reunion (29:1–14). The early verses describe a typical pastoral scene of shepherds and sheep gathered near a well. The conversation is likewise typical as is the shepherding contract referred to (29:3, 8). Contracts are necessary where water is scarce, and distrust is often warranted.

Jacob's warm welcome of Rachel and her resulting excitement is understandable given that there may have been no news of Rebekah since she had left with Abraham's servant nearly a century earlier. Laban's enthusiasm need not be attributed to his anticipation of profit because the prospect of family news from Jacob is cause enough for the joy and celebration. Nevertheless, we have a hint of what is to come when Laban comments that Jacob is his own flesh and blood (29:14). This is, of course, an innocent statement on Laban's part, but the reader has already gotten a taste of Jacob's nature, and in Laban we will encounter one "cut from the same cloth."

Wedding-Night Surprise (29:15–30). Jacob is impressed by Rachel's appearance. In contrast to Rachel, the text suggests that while Leah is not without striking features, she pales in comparison to Rachel's overall beauty. The agreement reached between Laban and Jacob is intended to provide for the bride price that was an essential part of marriage contracts. This was a payment made from the groom or his family to the family of the bride. Its function was to serve as a trust fund of sorts to provide for the support of the wife should the husband divorce her or die. Laban will garner Jacob's would-be wages and secure them into a bride-price account of some sort.

Marriage customs in the ancient Near East combined legal and festive elements in different ways from current Western practice. The legal aspect was reflected in a private marriage contract drawn up by the families involved. When the agreed-upon time arrived, a marriage feast was held to honor the couple. It included a ritual, celebratory meal and concluded with the couple retiring to consummate the marriage. Even after the feast the bride continued to live in the house of her father for several months and receive conjugal visits. Often the conception of a child signaled the time for the couple to begin their own household.

The traditional feast is held in 29:22–24. A bride was veiled during these public festivities, and it was not uncommon for the celebratory mood to lead to drunkenness. Though we have no indication that Jacob is drunk, that is one way to account for his inability to recognize the substitution of Leah for Rachel. In 29:25, the text offers only a summary statement of what must have been a very distressed response from Jacob in the morning.

The details are worked out, and Jacob ends up obliging himself to seven more years of work, though he is allowed to marry Rachel in short order. Now Jacob's bevy of spouses is set with wives Leah and Rachel and eventual concubines Zilpah and Bilhah. The scene is also set for the favoritism that will be a significant factor in the next generation: Jacob loves Rachel more than Leah (29:30).

Children (29:31–30:24). As God begins to provide a family for Jacob, we see a new twist on an old theme of the unloved and the firstborn. With Abraham, Hagar was likely unloved, and though Ishmael was loved by Abraham, he was rejected and sent away. Isaac's firstborn, Esau, though preferred by his father, was, like Ishmael, not the chosen son and was rejected by God. Now it is the unloved wife, Leah, who produces the firstborn child. He will eventually be rejected as a result of his behavior. It is clear from the names given to her sons that Leah is haunted by her inability to elicit favor and affection from Jacob, though providing four sons would be expected to gain her some standing in his eyes.

The old, familiar obstacle of barrenness continues to be endemic in the line of Terah. Given the context of tension, conflict, and jealousy, it is perhaps no surprise that Rachel's condition occasions angry frustration (30:2). Consequently, Rachel, as Sarah had before her, encourages Jacob to resort to her handmaid to provide a child to their marriage through a surrogate. Rachel's naming of the son Dan ("vindication") indicates that she feels vindicated; her infertility would bring at least the tacit accusation that she is suffering punishment for (undoubtedly) secret sins.

The family continues to grow. Leah goes through her own period of infertility, likely curbing her scorn of Rachel, and the handmaids continue to have their role in producing children. The names by and large reflect the tension in the family. Yet Rachel is still without children. When Leah's son Reuben finds some mandrakes, Rachel thinks they may help her. The mandrake (*Mandragora officinarum*) is a stemless, perennial root in the potato family that grows in stony ground. It has narcotic and purgative properties, which explain its medicinal use. Its shape and pungent fragrance may be the origin of its use in fertility rites and as an aphrodisiac.

The exchange between the women concerning the mandrakes again illustrates the bitter conflict and rivalry between Leah and Rachel. Ironically, the night with Jacob that Rachel trades for the mandrakes brings renewed fertility to Leah rather than a child to Rachel.

In 30:22 Rachel's barrenness is resolved as God opens her womb. Finally getting pregnant herself completes the process of erasing her public disgrace (30:23). The end to this portion of the family history does not come when all the children have been born, but when Rachel is no longer barren. This suggests that Rachel's barrenness is at issue rather than the general concept of extending the family to the next generation. Since Jacob has no shortage of children, why is Rachel's barrenness an issue? What is it an obstacle to? We must conclude that it is not an obstacle to the covenant from a family standpoint but only to the audience, who is well aware of the importance of Joseph.

Prosperity (30:25–43). It is not coincidental that Jacob requests permission to take his leave of Laban only after Joseph is born (30:25). If a woman has not borne children, she can easily be discarded or demoted. The only protection she had came from her father's family, who then took responsibility for her. Prior to Joseph's birth, a request to leave would have been inappropriate from Jacob's standpoint and risky from Rachel's, for it would rob Rachel of her protection.

Though Laban is relieved of his concern for Rachel's well-being, economic issues lead him to negotiate for Jacob to stay. There are few indications of Laban's religious practices, but here we see him engaged in divination. An Israelite audience may be shocked at the thought that Yahweh would communicate by means of divination, but the text stops short of suggesting that. Rather, Laban claims that his divination has led him to conclude that Yahweh has blessed him because of Jacob. God occasionally chooses to use methods that are generally prohibited, as the Bethlehem star attests.

Laban's offer results in an agreement to give Jacob part ownership of the herd and the potential to increase his interest as time goes on. Jacob gets all the goats that are not totally black and all the sheep that are not totally white. Dark and spotted animals usually represented a smaller proportion. The passage thereby suggests that Laban has the better end of the deal.

Is Laban doing anything different from what Jacob has anticipated in his proposal? A simple reading of the NIV translation suggests that in 30:32 Jacob proposes to remove the designated sheep from Laban's flock for his wages. If so, then Laban's actions in 30:35 appear to be a violation of this agreement. Alternatively, since Jacob has insisted in 30:31 that Laban give him nothing, we must conclude that Jacob's intention in the proposed deal is to separate out the type of animals he has spoken about and perhaps mark them in some way as Laban's. Then any spotted or speckled that are born *from that point on* will be his wages. If this is correct, Laban's unanticipated action in 30:35 is the total removal of these spotted animals from the breeding pool—a move that, under normal circumstances, will greatly reduce the number of spotted and speckled goats and dark-colored lambs being born.

Not to be deterred, Jacob applies the science of his day to compensate for Laban's shrewd strategy. Any shepherd knows that strong parents breed strong lambs and kids. Jacob therefore engages in common sense selective breeding as a means to produce strong, healthy offspring (30:41). This strategy is combined with folk traditions that conditions during breeding, such as what is in the animals' visual field, may have an impact on the offspring. Whatever level of success Jacob enjoys while using this procedure is attributable only to God, regardless of the conclusions Jacob may have drawn.

Flight (31:1–21). Jacob's decision to return to Canaan is a combination of his awareness of the hostility of Laban's sons toward him and direction from God. The willingness of Leah and Rachel to leave is premised on an accusation against their father concerning his handling of their inheritance. Jacob, of course, gave no bride price but his labor, so the equivalent of his wages should have been set aside for the women. Apparently, that was never done. Jacob's labor has benefited Laban, not the women; thus, it is as if he has "sold" them to Jacob. If their father's house holds no economic security for them, they have no reason to stay.

They choose sheep-shearing time to make their escape because they know that Laban will be away and preoccupied. The text also includes Rachel's theft of the household gods (*terapim*). These were images of either the ancestors or the patron gods of the ancestors. They were believed to bring prosperity and protection. Given how Rachel is able to conceal them, these must be very small.

Confrontation and Parting Agreement (31:22–55). The site of Mizpah (where Laban catches up to Jacob) is not known, but from Haran to the northern end of the hill country of

Gilead is approximately three hundred miles. To reach that spot in ten days, Jacob would have traveled thirty miles per day, an incredible rate. Caravans usually managed twenty-three at most. Sheep and goats cannot achieve or maintain that pace (see 33:13), and women and children likewise slow down the speed of travel. Given the circumstances, Jacob cannot expect to make more than about ten miles per day.

Whenever the text refers to a journey (Heb. *derek*) of a particular number of days, the number is one, three, or seven, suggesting the possibility that the expression is idiomatic rather than precise. Yet that does not solve all the problems, because if Jacob travels at a rate of only ten miles per day, one would expect Laban to catch him long before he arrives at "the hill country of Gilead" (31:21).

If Jacob is traveling twelve or thirteen miles per day and Laban seventeen, Laban would catch Jacob after about seven days (as the text seems to suggest). But they would only be about 110 miles from Haran, putting them somewhere near Ebla, only one third of the way to the hill country of Gilead. The only conceivable solution that explains Laban's not catching up to Jacob before the area of Gilead is to assume that it takes Laban a week or ten days to prepare for the trip before he can set out and that he cannot travel very fast (after all, he is over one hundred and fifty years old now).

When Laban and Jacob finally meet face to face, there is a major confrontation between them. Laban's complaints focus first on Jacob's furtive flight, turn to the stolen gods, and climax in the claim that all of Jacob's prosperity has been at his expense. Jacob's grievances begin with Laban's general untrustworthiness. He then reminds Laban of the hardships he has suffered in his employ while maintaining an unblemished record. The only thing both agree on is that Jacob's God has protected him and prospered him. Rachel's deception is added to her theft as she lies about her condition as an excuse to prevent Laban from finding the stolen images.

The covenant Laban and Jacob make is designed to protect each one against hostility or ill-treatment at the hands of the other. The use of a heap of stones as a boundary marker, a memorial to an event, or a witness to a covenant appears several places in the biblical text. The fact that both Jacob and Laban erect a "pillar" (31:45) here and give each a name suggests an invoking ritual in which the god(s) of each party are called to witness the treaty-making ceremony and to enforce its stipulations.

The stipulations placed on Jacob concern the proper treatment of Laban's daughters and a prohibition against taking other wives. These stipulations protect the rights and status of Laban's daughters in Jacob's household, since Laban will not be there to vouchsafe them. In addition to serving as a witness, 31:52 suggests that the stones serve as a boundary marker between Jacob and Laban. The covenant is sealed with a ritual meal, as is customary.

Finally, a word must be said about the "Mizpah benediction" in 31:49. It is not unusual today to hear this intoned by a minister as the benediction to the congregation at the end of a service or even to find it inscribed on wedding rings. In using it this way, we show our misunderstanding of the words. Here in Genesis, the words express suspicion. A paraphrase is, "I don't trust you out of my sight, but since I can no longer personally hold you accountable, may God do so." It is hardly the sentiment that one would want on a wedding ring, and although a minister may feel that way about a congregation, it is not in good taste to express it so unequivocally.

Application. We live in a society that has taught us to "look out for Number One." This means taking whatever steps are necessary to assure ourselves of success and achieve our goals or ambitions. Many Christians can compete with Jacob as master manipulators, making their own way through life and taking their destiny into their own hands. But that is not God's way. God wants to be recognized as the source of our success. Shrewd or cunning strategies, especially when they involve a level of dishonesty, are counterproductive to God's work in our lives. Just as God negated Jacob's attempts to succeed in order to replace them with his own blessings, God sometimes uses failure in our lives to draw us to depend on him.

This is not to say we should never plan or strategize. But it does point out the need to acknowledge God as the source of our prosperity and to give him credit for all that works out well in our lives.

GENESIS 32:1–33:20

Original Meaning

Placating Esau (32:1–21). The chapter opens with another indication that God is directing the events of Jacob's return. Just as his dream twenty years earlier had led him to name a place Bethel, so this second encounter with God's messengers produces the name Mahanaim ("Two Camps"). Literarily, these two occurrences form what is called an *inclusio*. Here the *inclusio* of these angelic appearances sets apart Jacob's time outside the land.

Jacob decides that it is best to inform Esau of his return. He probably assumes that his father has died by now. If his father has died, Esau may have come into the entire inheritance, Jacob's status or whereabouts being undetermined. We find, then, that in Jacob's initial communication (32:4–5) he makes three basic points.

- "I have been staying with Laban and have remained there till now" (32:4). Implication, "I have not been hiding, avoiding you, or sneaking around behind your back."

- "I have cattle and donkeys, sheep and goats, male and female servants" (32:5a). Implication, "I have plenty. I am not going to try to trick you out of anything or lay claim to anything that you have acquired."
- "I am sending this message . . . that I may find favor in your eyes" (32:5b). Implication, "Why don't we let bygones be bygones?"

The answer he receives makes him ill at ease in its ambiguity (32:6–7).

In these difficult straits we finally find Jacob resorting to prayer. He begins by referring to his roots. Yahweh is the God who had directed and provided for Abraham and Isaac. He does not yet call him "Yahweh, my God." The prayer is further compromised as he sounds as if he is collecting on a debt and that God needs to be held to his word.

Jacob is at his best in 32:10 as he acknowledges his unworthiness and God's faithfulness. That leads into his actual petition in 32:11: He wants deliverance for himself and his family. Unfortunately, 32:12 finds him again sounding as if he has to hold something over God's head to persuade him to act on his behalf. At least he realizes something that will eventually put him where God can do something with him: He cannot rely on his own skills to assure the safety of his family.

This realization, however, does not prevent him from doing all of the strategic planning we have come to expect from Jacob. In 32:13–21 he selects the gifts he sends to Esau. This gift is larger than towns were likely to pay in tribute to foreign kings. In addition to seeking Esau's favor as a response to his generosity, Jacob plans three strategic advantages.

1. If they were planning an ambush, Esau's band would have to set it up each time a group arrives. After five times it is unlikely that they are as alert for combat as they may have been at first. By that time Esau and his men will probably have given up the idea of an ambush altogether.
2. As the gifts arrive, Esau becomes more and more encumbered in his travel. The animals will force him to move more slowly and will make his band much noisier.
3. As Jacob's servants bring the gifts, they join the march of Esau's band. How effective can any of Esau's intended military strategies be if he has to cope with members of Jacob's household mixed in among his own retinue of soldiers?

These tactics along with the divisions of his camp using the river as strategically as possible exhaust all of Jacob's reserve, yet he still feels vulnerable to Esau's attack. This is precisely where God wants him—feeling in need with no recourse left but to rely on God. Now the real struggle begins.

The Wrestling Match (32:22–32). Note that Jacob is ninety-seven years old at this point in the narrative. When the text tells us that Jacob's opponent cannot overcome him, it is not suggesting that Jacob is physically besting the man. The ease with which he inflicts physical damage on Jacob (32:25) indicates that any inability must be in the spiritual arena, not the physical one. If the wrestler is unable to overcome Jacob spiritually, it is because Jacob is not willing to yield. Only when the man threatens to go without offering assurances of God's help does Jacob show his willingness to negotiate in the critical issues.

The turning point comes when Jacob informs the stranger that he will not release him unless he receives such assurances (i.e., a blessing). I believe this indicates Jacob's willingness to submit himself to God's demands on him. Jacob's persistence is now going to work to his benefit. He is ready to do whatever it takes. The blessing comes in the form of a name change. This is significant for Jacob since his name has embodied his character throughout the narrative. A name change therefore signifies a character change.

Jacob accepts the name change, which in this case is equivalent to accepting a change in character. As always, with God one has to lose in order to win. It is possible that Jacob's request for the wrestler's name is a last attempt to retain some control, but the wrestler evades the request.

Who is this stranger? The narrator refers to him throughout the episode as "a man" (Heb. *ish*), which is as noncommittal as our referring to "an individual" who wrestles with Jacob. At the end of the episode, Jacob designates the individual as *elohim* (32:30). This word usually is a designation for deity but can be used for any supernatural being. The clearest statement comes in Hosea 12:4, where the prophet indicates that Jacob struggled with an angel.

What implications attach to this pericope in the context of the ancient Near East? Fords were understood as a gateway guarded by the gods or their servants. Just as the stairway of Jacob's dream would have been at home in the general culture of the ancient Near East, so the appearance of struggling with a deity upon entrance to his territory would have been familiar.

Another common motif is prevailing upon a detained deity to procure a blessing. While there are important similarities, there are of course also significant differences. But we need not go into them at this juncture. The point is that to the Israelite audience this episode may not have seemed as unusual as it does to us.

The name "Israel" is now introduced (32:38). It is theophoric, making a statement about God, El. Comparative Semitics offers little help. Consequently, exegetes can offer little lexical illumination beyond the explanation cited in the text.

The last element in the narrative to deal with is Jacob's *yarek* ("hip," 32:25). The "socket" of his *yarek* is "touched" and as a result is "wrenched" (32:25). Consequently, Jacob limps (32:31). *Yarek* usually refers to flesh or muscle rather than the pelvic bone. The word translated "socket" (Heb. *kap*) when associated with the hand or foot is usually translated palm or sole. Usage suggests that it is not the appendage of a bone but one of flesh.

Whatever this part is, it is most logical that this is the part that is injured. The text says that in the morning he is limping—it does not say that he has a limp the rest of his life. It is therefore not a requirement that the terms we have been looking at be understood in a way that produces a debilitating injury that will not have healed over time.

Meeting with Esau (33:1–11). When the dreaded meeting finally takes place, Jacob is as humble and submissive as possible. For his part, Esau is sentimental and interested in catching up on family news. Esau is flattered by Jacob's generous gifts and tries to return them, but Jacob will not hear of it. This is a family reunion of the sort where dysfunctions have, for the moment, faded into the background.

Parting and Settling (33:12–20). Esau offers several options to accompany Jacob or to provide protection for him, but Jacob declines them, and the two part company. Sometime later Jacob and his family moved to Shechem, about thirty-five miles north of Jerusalem. Its strategic location at the crossroads of major transportation arteries attracted frequent settlers. The area also provides both farming and grazing land. It is here that Jacob purchases land to live on. As with previous narratives, the author draws attention to any occasion on which land is purchased with an eye toward the covenant promises.

In addition to the land purchase, Jacob builds his first altar here and so identifies with the religious practices of his forefathers. This is the first instance, however, in which an altar was named. The name shows at last a personal appropriation of the God of Jacob's fathers. In his conversation with Esau earlier in the chapter, the transition can be detected as in process. Here he acknowledges God as *the* God, his own God, with the name change no less—"El Elohe Israel," meaning "God, the God of Israel" (33:20). The transformation of Jacob's character is largely complete; it only has to be formalized in Genesis 35.

Application. Most marriage counselors consider it important to communicate to the happy couple that if the marriage is to succeed, both must be willing to accept the other as he or she is. God's relationship with us is not like this. While it is true that God loves us as we are, it is his desire and his right to transform us. Additionally, unlike a spouse, God has the power to transform us. The problem is that most of us are not motivated to change. We must see there is a problem and be given a reason to change before we submit, just as we must be persuaded that something is drastically wrong with our bodies before we willingly put ourselves under the surgeon's knife.

The first step is trust in the surgeon. God can transform us. God can resolve the conflict that is the result of character flaws. Sometimes our response to conflict is a prayer that God will work on the other person to produce harmony. Perhaps we need to be more willing to pray that God will change us—take away our bitterness, overcome our habits, help us step back from our expectations, and weaken our pride.

GENESIS 34:1–36:43

Original Meaning

Dinah and Shechem (34:1–24). Dinah's role in the act is not clarified by the terms used in the text. The word the NIV translates as "raped" (34:2) is not used only for rape situations where the girl is simply a victim, though it does imply that the man takes the initiative. In the end, however, the text does not need to clarify the role of Dinah, because the focus of the account is not the relationship between Dinah and Shechem. That is just a set-up for the violence of Simeon and Levi, which is the author's real focus.

It is intriguing that Dinah's brothers are outraged because such "an outrageous thing [is not done] in Israel" (34:7). There was no territory named Israel. This stands as a good example of the author's use of anachronism. A number of law collections from the ancient Near East that predate Sinai contain prescriptions against illicit or violent sexual relationships. This is therefore not a case of Jacob's sons holding their neighbors responsible for a higher standard of conduct than they would have maintained in their own community.

Though neither Dinah's nor Jacob's motivations are explained in the text, the motivations of the other parties are evident. Jacob's sons are motivated by the prospect for revenge in the name of the family honor. In addition to the personal impact on Dinah, Shechem's act is disrespectful to the family and has taken something of value from them. Shechem himself is motivated by infatuation (34:11–12, 19), while his father and the rest of the town are motivated by economic prospects (34:21–23). The situation is ripe for deceit, and it is attributed to Jacob's sons rather than to Jacob. It comes in the form of a prerequisite of circumcision. The procedure was painful and would virtually debilitate the adult male population for several days.

The decision by the men of Shechem takes place at the city gate. This was the common place of assembly for legal and business transactions or public meetings to occur. That the men of the town agree to the proposal set before them demonstrates how eager they are to reap the economic benefit of intermarriage even though that which is required of them involves a degree of pain.

Simeon and Levi (34:25–31). Archaeological excavations have identified Shechem as having been resettled in about 1900 BC. The presence of a gate suggests sufficient size that it seems incredulous that two men could wipe out all of the male population by themselves. Alternatively, we may assume that Simeon and Levi recruited a band of servants to go with them.

Beyond the slaughter of the entire male population, the brothers take all the women and children as well as all the goods in the city as plunder. Presumably the brothers rationalize their conduct by insisting that such is the mandated bride price for the violation of their sister. Nevertheless, the level of brutality is incomprehensible and far exceeds any justifiable retribution for the crime of the city's prince.

Jacob at Bethel (35:1–15). When Jacob originally made his vow (28:20–22), he included three promises: acknowledgement of Yahweh as his God, setting up a shrine, and paying a tithe. The instruction of 35:1 addresses the latter two most directly. Presumably Jacob's altar would be used for sacrifices that constitute the tithe of his possessions that he is giving to Yahweh. Before Jacob proceeds to Bethel, however, he engages his entire household in a purification ritual.

Perhaps the idols and earrings are from the plunder taken at Shechem. The fact that the purification takes place at Shechem rather than Bethel suggests that it may have had as much to do with the slaughter of the Shechemites as it did with the fulfillment of the vow. These alternatives are not mutually exclusive and may both be involved.

Burying idols (35:4) is not the same as destroying them. When the family of Jacob arrives at Bethel, Rebekah's nurse, Deborah, is also buried under a tree (35:8). Perhaps more important in the author's communication to his audience is this first instance of disposing of other gods. There has been little discussion thus far in Genesis about the issue of other gods and no clear call to monotheistic belief or practice. But here a statement is made in the actions of Jacob.

Genesis 35 has another theophany for Jacob. It is the El Shaddai theophany, meaning "God Almighty" (35:11). These theophanies are important in the author's tracing of the advancement of the covenant. They are watersheds in the developing relationship between God and his people and in his ongoing revelation of himself to them.

As in Abraham's El Shaddai theophany, a name change is involved, here reiterated and formalized from the initial context in Genesis 32. The mention of "nations" and "kings" (35:11) is prominent, but the land is also mentioned. Jacob responds to the theophany by setting up another pillar and again anointing it (35:14; cf. 28:18). In addition, he pours out a "drink offering" (35:14).

Family Matters (35:16–29). The chapter closes with a short narrative and a summary that completes the family history for Jacob. Rachel's death in childbirth was not an uncommon occurrence in the ancient world. On her deathbed Rachel names her son in accordance with the misery she faces. Jacob is unwilling to let that name stand as a sad reminder of the circumstances of his son's birth, so he changes it. Rachel's burial place remains somewhat controversial. There is a memorial known today as Rachel's tomb about a mile north of Bethlehem, but this identification goes back only to the fourth century AD, and the structure built there is of Crusader design.

Esau's Family (36:1–43). With the summary of Jacob's family (35:23–26) and the death of Isaac (35:27–29), the Jacob story comes to an end. Before proceeding to the account of what comes from Jacob (the Jacob *toledot*, 37:2), the text first disposes of Esau, following the procedure that the line that is of less interest is addressed first. This identifies the origins of some of Israel's neighbors to the desert audience. Most notable of these from the biblical record is Amalek, the son of Esau's son and a concubine (36:12). Also of interest is that just as there were twelve tribes from Jacob, there are twelve from Esau (36:9–14). This may suggest that in some senses Esau has enjoyed a blessing on an equal footing with Jacob.

As in the table of nations in Genesis 10, many of these names are presented as clan names connected to chieftains rather than individual names. Moreover, the text includes a section that appears to have been added later, listing the kings of Edom "before any Israelite king reigned" (36:31). Another notable name is Uz (36:28), which is the home of Job.

Application. God's patient work in Jacob's life offers a lesson as we assess how God can bring us each along step by step in the process of spiritual maturity. Sometimes we may look back with shame or embarrassment at things we did in the past that at the time we considered spiritual. At these times hindsight may allow us to recognize those actions in reality as naive, shallow, or self-serving. Other times we may look back and think of all the wasted time and opportunities. But we do not please God by wallowing in regret. Instead, we should thank God for his patience in bringing us along and move forward in faith, commitment, and service.

Finally, we may at times look at where we are in our spiritual walk and feel as if we haven't gotten anywhere. We can feel overwhelmed by our failures and our inability to master the Christian life. Those are the times when we need to pause and look back so that we can gain an appreciation of how far God has brought us. When my Hebrew students experience frustration near the end of the first semester over their struggles with the language, I have only to remind them that three months earlier even the alphabet looked like chicken-scratch. It helps for them to see how far they have come. As is evident in his dealings with Jacob, God does not demand instant perfection, but he leads us little by little, making inroads into our self-centeredness and doing his work in our lives one step at a time.

GENESIS 37:1–47:26

Original Meaning

Joseph's Status (37:1–4). When this account begins, Jacob and his family have been back in the land of Canaan for about a decade. They have resumed their vocations as itinerant herders. The favoritism that Jacob felt for Rachel has apparently transferred to her older son, Joseph, for Jacob bestows special status on Joseph. Most scholars acknowledge that status, not just favor, is what the special coat represents. Most commentators favor something along the line of a full-length coat or a long-sleeved coat, either of which would indicate that Joseph is management, not labor.

Joseph's Dreams (37:5–11). Dreams in the ancient world were considered derived from the divine realm and were thus taken seriously. Dreams by prophets and kings often contained theophanies offering divine revelation. The ordinary dreams of common people were believed to contain omens that communicated information about what the gods were doing, though they usually made no reference to deity. Dreams were often filled with symbolism, necessitating an interpreter, though at times the symbols were reasonably self-evident. The information that came through dreams was not believed to be irreversible. Dreams of a rise to power like the ones Joseph had are known in the ancient Near East. There is nothing in Joseph's dream that leads them to consider that Joseph's eventual prominence will extend beyond the confines of the family. It is only his family members who bow down to him. It would not have occurred to any of them that Joseph would rise to the position of second-in-command of a dominant world power.

A curious feature of the second dream (37:9–10) is the symbolic presence of his mother and all eleven brothers. After all, his mother died giving birth to the last brother. The inclusion of his parents is of significance here, because the dream does not just suggest that Joseph will be first among his brothers. It suggests Joseph's eventual prominence in the ancestral line, superseding even his parents in significance. This justifies the inclusion of family members living or dead.

Brothers' Revenge (37:12–36). From the home base in the Valley of Hebron (37:14) Shechem is just over fifty miles, and Dothan is about fourteen more. The journey would have taken Joseph four or five days. Joseph fails to find his brothers at Shechem and receives direction from a stranger (37:15–17).

Joseph's brothers see him coming and begin to formulate a plan. We can imagine that at first the plan is just an idle suggestion, expressing their hatred of their brother. Even so, it quickly takes a serious turn. The text refrains from indicating which brother or brothers make the initial suggestion and, in so doing, implies that it represents something of a consensus. Reuben is the only objector as he adopts part of their suggestion (the cistern) but seeks to avoid violence. The text reports his intent to get Joseph back to the safety of his father. We do not know whether this reflects Reuben's sense of responsibility as the oldest and wisest or if he is seeking ways to regain his father's favor after the debacle of 35:22.

Cisterns were either hollowed out of limestone bedrock or dug in the ground and lined with plaster. Since most of Israel's rainfall is confined to three or four months of the year, these cisterns collected the rainwater and made it available during the dry period. It was not unusual that during part of the year they were dry. After Joseph is stripped of his status and manhandled, the brothers sit down comfortably to eat. Dothan is on the normal caravan route from Gilead to Egypt. It is no surprise that a caravan should pass that way, but the timing is providential.

This caravan is made up of Midianites and Ishmaelites (37:25, 28). Midianites are descendants of Abraham through Keturah (25:2), while the Ishmaelites descended from Abraham through Hagar, so these are kinfolk. The forebears of these two peoples were half-brothers to one another (and to Isaac), and so uncles to Jacob; therefore, these traders are second or third cousins to Joseph and his brothers.

Most commentators consider "Midianite" and "Ishmaelite" as variant terms for the same group. Some suggest that perhaps "Ishmaelite" had already become less an ethnic designation and more a term like gypsy or Bedouin, which describes a way of life. This is not impossible, but certainly another alternative is to see the caravan made up of Midianite merchants who serve as middlemen for Ishmaelite businessmen. The Midianites do the business (37:28, 36), while the goods belong to the Ishmaelites, who finance the caravan (37:25–28; 39:1).

Judah is the one who offers the idea of selling Joseph rather than killing him. This is the first appearance of a number of significant actions by Judah in the narrative as he begins his own personal journey. It is probably significant that in all three of the narrative contexts of the Joseph story where Judah plays a role, he successfully persuades others to do as he suggests. Each speech is longer than the previous one, and each one is more commendable than the previous one.

As modern readers we must be aware of the role Judah is already playing to most of the ancient audience. While Reuben's motives are clarified by the text (37:22), Judah's are left unelaborated. Is he trying to save Joseph or just get rid of him conveniently? From his statement it appears as if he has inhibitions against killing relatives but has no concern for Joseph's welfare (37:26–27). The twenty-shekel sale price is typical for slaves in this period and represents about two years' wages for a common shepherd.

When Reuben returns (from wherever he has been), his dismay reflects his sense that, as the oldest, he is the one ultimately held responsible for Joseph's safety—so much for regaining Jacob's favor! We are not told which brother comes up with this plot to deceive Jacob about Joseph's fate. Jacob is allowed to draw his own conclusions and is literally inconsolable. The text leaves the reader to decide whether or not Jacob's deep grief causes the brothers any remorse for their actions. Indication of a residue of guilt only surfaces in 42:21–22.

The chapter concludes with a note concerning to whom Joseph is sold in Egypt. This is just enough to indicate that he has not been written out of the narrative never to be heard from again. His whereabouts are known, but his fate hangs in the balance. The narrator will now leave the reader in suspense for a while as he formulates an important concept for consideration.

Judah's Problem (38:1–11). Judah's problem begins when his oldest son dies by the hand of the Lord for his wickedness (38:7). Levirate marriage laws required that if a woman's husband died without offspring having been produced, it was the duty of his brother to bear a child by her in order to continue his dead brother's line. This custom is established as legislation in the Mosaic law (Deut 25:5–10). When Onan refuses to do his duty by Tamar, he is punished by God and likewise expires.

Onan's refusal is explained by his knowledge that the son will not be his (38:9). Onan is punished by death for preserving his inheritance rights by disposing of the competition.

Judah, like his father before him, is being treated in the same way that he has treated others, especially Joseph. Though Judah is the fourth son of Jacob, it can be argued that his three older brothers have already disqualified themselves for birthright status. As things stand in Jacob's family, however, these disqualifications may have simply made it more likely for Jacob to exercise his choice rather than simply follow birth order. If so, Joseph could easily be seen as a threat to Judah's inheritance (see 1 Chr 5:1–2). It is to Judah's advantage, therefore, to dispose of Joseph. If this is so, the indictment pronounced against Onan (38:8–10) hangs over Judah's head as well. Recognition that the deaths of his sons may well be punishment for his treatment of Joseph give plausibility to his fear that his last son, Shelah, will meet the same fate as his brothers (38:11).

Tamar's Solution (38:12–23). The formulation of the Hittite law regarding levirate marriage stipulates that when a widow marries her late husband's brother, if he dies, she is then to marry his father (i.e., her father-in-law). This is not how the later Israelite legislation reads, but it appears to be the procedure that Tamar is following. She carries out her scheme by means of yet another masquerade as Jacob's resort to deception continues to echo through the family history.

Judah's encounter with Tamar takes place around sheepshearing time (38:12–13). Judah's guarantee of payment for his act of prostitution is his seal, cord, and staff. The seal is most likely a stamp seal engraved with a design that would uniquely identify Judah. It would be used by him for any transaction or correspondence, much as we use a signature today. Taking this as a pledge for payment ensures a quick response on Judah's part because seals were used with some frequency. Seals were often worn around the neck on a cord, so that is probably the cord referred to here. His staff is a walking stick but may have been a symbol of authority in his clan. If so, Tamar holds in her possession symbols of his individual and corporate identity—in modern terms, items akin to someone's driver's license.

Denouement (38:24–30). When Tamar's pregnancy gives evidence of her behavior, Judah is at first harsh in his criticism. If he considered it possible that the death of his first two sons was the result of some sort of hex put on them by Tamar, her prostitution is just another sign of her utter wickedness. He would be happy for the excuse to get rid of her and bring this long, unfortunate chapter of his life to a close. But he is made aware of his own complicity and culpability when he is shown the things he left as a pledge and is forced to identify them. In this he is put in a position similar to that of Jacob at the end of the previous chapter, where Judah, along with his brothers, confronted their father with a sign of Joseph's identity (his coat that was torn and bloodied). Though many of the details are different, there is a degree of reversal as the narrative turns on the presentation of a sign of identity.

In a brief two verses Judah moves from demands that Tamar be burned (38:24) to the declaration that she is more righteous than he (v. 26)—that is to say, that her actions are more justifiable than his. This is the first hint of a change taking place in Judah as he admits to moral failure. This stands in stark contrast to Joseph's moral resilience in the next chapter and is the first step that leads eventually to the transformed Judah in 44:18–34.

The conclusion of the story is the report of the unusual circumstances surrounding the birth of the sons of Judah and Tamar. It seems an odd way to end an odd story, but it is the oddity of this birth that brings forth the point of the narrator.

From Slave to Prisoner (39:1–23). Potiphar was an important official in Pharaoh's court. His name, meaning "he whom

Re gives," occurs occasionally in Egyptian inscriptions, generally between the seventh and third century BC, but as early as the eleventh century BC. The two titles given to him, "one of Pharaoh's officials" and "captain of the guard" (39:1), are both fairly general in nature. The former uses a Hebrew word that is sometimes translated "eunuch" but can be used broadly for a courtier.

In the second title, the first word ("captain") is clear and undisputed. The second, which the NIV translates "guard," is more controversial. Elsewhere the Hebrew word refers to slaughter, mostly of sacrificial animals. The LXX therefore chose a term that is translated "butcher," apparently making him one of the kitchen staff. The Targums agree, but the Vulgate and Syriac go more in the direction of the NIV. Either of these directions can be supported by Hebrew usage. A military identification is favored by the reference to the prison being in the house of the captain of the guard (40:3).

In contrast to the detail in the last chapter that God put Judah's sons to death, here the Lord is with Joseph, and he prospers (39:2). As in the relationship between Jacob and Laban where Laban recognized that the Lord's favor was with Jacob (30:27), Potiphar sees the same in Joseph and trusts him with responsibility. As a result, the blessing side of the covenant continues to be realized on a small scale as Potiphar and his house are blessed through Joseph (39:5–6). But his success is short-lived.

The account of the seduction of Joseph shows him in a positive light. The details are given in such a way as to confirm Joseph's unquestionable innocence. He does not lead Potiphar's wife on or allow himself to enjoy her company at any level. He is compromised only by a desperate and spiteful act, supported by bold-faced lies that none can contest but the accused. Her summary accusation identifies him as a Hebrew slave brought to "make sport" of her (39:17).

1. This statement represents an accusation against her husband, which puts him on the defensive by attributing to him devious motives.
2. The Hebrew word translated "make sport" is the same one that provides the root for Isaac's name and that has been repeatedly used as a motif in the text.
3. Note that once again Joseph is being identified by his cloak that has been taken from him. Here it is supposed to incriminate Joseph, just as the sign of Judah's identity incriminated him of sexual malfeasance in the last chapter. The difference is, of course, that Joseph is being falsely accused.

Potiphar responds by "burn[ing] with anger" (39:19). Given his wife's slander of his own motives, the proven trustworthiness of Joseph, the fact that he is going to lose the services of a competent slave, and his knowledge of his wife's character or lack of it, Potiphar's anger arguably burns at his wife, not at Joseph. This is further suggested by the fact that Joseph is only put in the king's prison. If Potiphar believed his wife and was truly angry with Joseph, Joseph would probably have been executed on the spot, no questions asked. In contrast, the king's prison was a place for political prisoners and would hardly have been expected to accommodate foreign slaves guilty of crimes against their masters. Potiphar is in a difficult position here—he cannot discount his wife's accusation without publicly humiliating her, even if he were certain she is lying. The action he takes against Joseph is as minimal as it can be while still retaining his family's honor.

It also appears that the prison is on Potiphar's premises, for 40:3 identifies it as "in the house of the captain of the guard," using the same title previously given to Potiphar (39:1). The end result of this incarceration is that it puts Joseph in a place where he will become acquainted with members of Pharaoh's court. It also offers another opportunity for the text to draw attention to the favor that Joseph enjoys with everyone he encounters, despite his hardships.

Dreams in Prison (40:1–23). Since two years separate the dreams of this chapter from Joseph's elevation to high position (41:1) and he is thirty years old when elevated (41:46), Joseph spends eleven years in Potiphar's house and in prison, though there is no indication how that time period divides. The officers whom Joseph encounters in prison are high-ranking members of the court. They are responsible for safe-guarding two of the ways that a potential assassin could strike the king. They not only had to be extremely trustworthy individuals of unquestioned loyalty to the king, they also had to be fine judges of character lest an enemy with intent to poison the pharaoh infiltrate their staffs.

Genesis 40 gives no hint what sequence of events has landed these officials under Joseph's care. Offenses against Pharaoh certainly could take many forms. Whether these officials are suspected of involvement in a conspiracy or just guilty of displeasing the king in the disposition of their duties is impossible to tell. Perhaps Pharaoh got sick from a meal, and they have come under suspicion. Perhaps they are under house arrest, awaiting the investigation of charges against them.

In the ancient Near East, dream interpretations were sought from experts who had been trained in techniques and methods of the day. Both the Egyptians and Babylonians compiled what are called "dream books," which contain sample dreams along with a key to their interpretation. Though some of the interpretations in the biblical accounts may seem transparent or self-evident, dreams often depended on symbolism, and the symbols might not stand for what was most logical. The dream books preserved the empirical data concerning past dreams and interpretations and therefore offered the security of scientific documentation. It was believed that the gods communicated generally through dreams but that they revealed the meanings of dreams by giving wisdom in the expert's research.

Joseph was not familiar with any of the "scientific" literature, so he consulted God. Regardless, his interpretation follows the way the dream literature interpreted comparable symbols. A full goblet, for instance, was indicative of having a name and offspring. Carrying fruit on one's head was indicative of sorrow. As is common in Mesopotamian literature, Joseph draws a time indication from a number featured in the dream.

The operative difference between the interpretations given for the two men turns on the phrase, "Pharaoh will lift up/off your head" (40:13, 19). In Hebrew the phrase is exactly the same, but the surrounding context gives each a different meaning. For the cupbearer, the king will lift up his head (i.e., give favor and forgiveness) and restore him. For the baker, the king will lift up his head also, but the added prepositional phrase "off" changes the idiom from one of favor to one of execution. In this case the baker would have been beheaded and then hung in public view for birds and insects to devour.

The third day, Pharaoh's birthday, brings about exactly the result that Joseph's interpretation has indicated. Literature from Egypt only evidences the granting of amnesty on Pharaoh's birthday in the Greek period, though there is more ample evidence of amnesties being extended on the anniversary of his accession to the throne, which can also be described as his birth as a god. The cupbearer's good fortune, however, goes for naught as in his joy at being restored, he forgets (for the time being) his debt to Joseph.

Pharaoh's Dreams (41:1–38). The author of Genesis does not mention any pharaoh by name, so it is not unusual that the name of the pharaoh of the Joseph story is unknown. The chronological information within the biblical record calculates to an earlier time in the Middle Kingdom's twelfth dynasty (1963–1786 BC). Nevertheless, insufficient evidence exists to identify a particular king with confidence.

In the ancient Near East, dreams sometimes received special emphasis when they were repeated or came in a set of two (cf. 41:32). Here the pharaoh has two visions that warn of the coming famine in Egypt.

Since the pharaoh was considered divine, it would be unusual for him to seek out an interpreter for his dreams. The Hebrew word used to describe the specialists whom the pharaoh sends for (NIV "magicians," v. 8) is from a technical Egyptian term often translated "lector-priest," thought by some to describe dream interpreters. It is used to describe the famous official Imhotep in a late inscription (second century BC), where he is portrayed giving advice to Pharaoh concerning a seven-year famine.

Like Solomon and Daniel, Joseph is presented as a wise man whose skills exceed those of his contemporaries. His wisdom is demonstrated in his interpretation of dreams, his eloquent speech, and his insightful plan to deal with crisis. These were all valued skills in Egypt. When he is finally brought before Pharaoh, he is careful to deny that he is a trained expert in dream interpretation. Whatever success he has, he insists, comes from God (41:16). He assures Pharaoh that God will give him the "answer he desires" (v. 16).

The text says literally that God will answer the "*shalom* of Pharaoh." This expression is not used anywhere else in the Old Testament, so we can only judge its meaning by context. It may simply mean that "God will provide an answer just as you have asked," but then what is the role for the Hebrew word *shalom*? Alternatively, Joseph may be saying that God will address (= answer) Pharaoh's "welfare" (an alternative translation for *shalom*) by solving the mystery—giving him the meaning of a troubling dream, even if the interpretation turns out to be negative. At least he will know what is going on, thus offering "peace of mind." This is similar to how someone with chest pains might go to the doctor to get the peace of mind from a sure diagnosis, even if that diagnosis is not good news.

As Joseph presents the interpretation, he also treats the dream as a message from God (41:25). He does not specifically identify the God Yahweh as the deity who has sent the message. He uses generic terminology, and Pharaoh is left to draw his own conclusion about which deity is responsible. Certainly, any deity who could foist such a severe famine on Egypt must be a powerful one. Egypt does not depend on rainfall for its food production but on the flooding of the Nile, which is much more dependable. Rarely, then, did the country suffer extended famine. The gods connected to the Nile and its annual flooding were considered to be powerful gods who would have to be restrained in some way (or angered by some offense) for the inundation to fail for seven years.

Often dreams or oracles that were interpreted negatively were associated with some sort of offense. Here there is no suggestion that the deity sending this dream is angry or seeking appeasement. No cause is offered for the coming famine. Indeed, the whole sequence would not have worked that way because the first seven years are years of plenty and therefore typically indicate the pleasure of the gods. It would appear odd for a dream to carry prospects of both tremendous prosperity and devastating tragedy. What could possibly be motivating any deity to offer such mutually exclusive determinations? At any rate, Joseph is clearly no malcontent conspiratorially speaking ill of the throne, nor is he a flatterer trying to get on Pharaoh's good side by offering joyous news of divine favor. It is not surprising, then, that Pharaoh deems him intrinsically credible and decisively trustworthy.

In addition to speaking eloquently and offering an indisputable interpretation of the dreams, Joseph shows himself quick on his feet as he promotes a plan for action that already has specific suggestions in mind. This includes a team of administrators exacting a 20 percent tax in kind (41:34) to be stored in escrow and doled out later. What he proposes is also attractive from the government's standpoint. Not only does the plan provide a strategy by which the country and its people will be able to survive, it does so in a way that is economically advantageous. It procures the excess food through taxation, and then sells food back to the very people who have contributed it. When finally the people have no money left to buy food, the government can take their land.

It is no surprise that Pharaoh is amenable to such a profitable course of action. His assessment of Joseph is that he is one who possesses the "spirit of God" (41:38). What would this comment mean coming from the mouth of a pharaoh? Pharaoh is acknowledging that in his estimation the deity is indeed the source of Joseph's wisdom.

Elevation of Joseph (41:39–57). The text goes into significant detail concerning the elevation of Joseph to high office. This section contains the most information that can be checked against Egyptian practice and history. The first step for Pharaoh is to give Joseph his signet ring. This ring was necessary for Joseph to do business in Pharaoh's name since it was used to seal official documents. The linen robes and the gold chain are part of the investiture that signifies his rank, status, and office. Chariots were the limousines of the day, so it is arranged that Joseph will ride in style. The men going before him clearing the way are the equivalent of the Secret Service protection that is offered to important dignitaries and officers in the United States.

Placing Joseph second-in-command may mean several different things. The second-in-command in all administrative matters in ancient Egypt was the Grand Vizier. It is not impossible that Joseph is given that position, but there are other posts that could make the claim of being second-in-command in the area of their responsibility. This is similar to a company today that has a President/CEO and a staff of vice presidents: Vice President of Production, Vice President of Marketing, Vice President of Legal Affairs, and so on. Each of these individuals can legitimately claim to be second-in-command in his or her particular area.

Even if we possessed a complete list of Grand Viziers for this period (we do not) and Joseph was not found on the list, there would be no cause for concern. Certainly, one of the most appropriate known titles to describe Joseph's duties is "Overseer of the Granaries of Upper and Lower Egypt." It is not unusual to find accounts of officials elevated from lowly status to high positions of authority. Such a display for a non-Egyptian was uncommon prior to the Hyksos period (1750–1550 BC), when a greater number of Semites served in Egypt.

The meaning of Joseph's Egyptian name is uncertain but may be "the God has spoken and he will live" or "the one who knows." An example of renaming a Semite official elevated to high office with an Egyptian name is also found in the reign of Pharaoh Merneptah (1224–1208 BC). The marriage arranged for Joseph places him within the circle of one of the most powerful priestly families in Egypt.

The last section of Genesis 41 confirms that everything works out exactly as Joseph has said and that his policies are successful in dealing with the crisis. In 41:56–57 we discover that the famine not only affects Egypt but all the countries around as well. Thus, the covenant blessing echoes through the passage with all the nations of the earth being blessed by Abraham's family, now represented in Joseph, ruler in Egypt.

The Brothers' First Visit (42:1–38). The brothers of Joseph are providentially driven by God toward Egypt and the inevitable encounter with Joseph. We find out incidentally that the impact of Joseph's disappearance remains evident in Jacob's protectiveness of Benjamin (42:4). One can only wonder what Benjamin, now in his twenties, thinks of his father's zealous attention. The text moves in a surprisingly rapid manner to the initial meeting between Joseph and his brothers (41:6) because, after all, there is no suspense about whether they will meet, only about what will happen when they do.

Again, a masquerade figures in the plot as Joseph "pretended to be a stranger" (42:7). There is also reversal as Joseph treats his brothers harshly, though different from their harsh treatment of him. As Joseph accuses them of being spies, the situation is heavy with irony and becomes almost laughable as the brothers protest their honesty (42:11), though it takes on a sad tone as they remark about their brother who "is no more" (42:13). As Joseph's plan unfolds, he indeed is testing his brothers as he says (42:15), but not concerning whether they are spies. The purpose of Joseph's test is to determine whether his brothers have reformed.

Putting his brothers in prison continues the line of reversal, but the test has two important elements in it that go well beyond revenge.

1. By keeping Simeon (42:24) he gives them the chance to abandon one of their brothers to prison and slavery as they previously did to him. The text does not indicate why Simeon is chosen. Given the nature of the test, it may be that, for whatever reasons, Simeon is the one who will be most readily abandoned by the others (since that had been Joseph's situation). The test will be most effective if there is no strong motivation to bring the

brothers back except their own sense of mercy (if they have found any).

2. Joseph also requests that they bring Benjamin back with them. He needs to have Benjamin there for the test he has in mind to discover whether his full brother is being treated in the same way he was.

In 42:21–23 we discover that in the thirteen intervening years, the guilt and recriminations experienced by Joseph's brothers have enslaved and imprisoned them no less than Joseph's chains had done to him. They clearly recognize their culpability and acknowledge that punishment is therefore due. They confess to hard-heartedness (42:21) and bloodguilt (42:22). Though their confessions bring an emotional response from Joseph, he is determined to see the test through to the end to test the mettle of his brothers' remorse.

When, back home, the brothers discover that they still have their silver, they continue to attribute their misfortune to punishment from the hand of God (42:28). Jacob is less specific as he laments, "Everything is against me!" (42:36). Being unaware of the sins of his sons, he has no point of connection to make between crime and punishment. He is not inclined to see his bereavement as ongoing punishment for the faults of his earlier years, and the narrator suggests nothing of the sort.

The chapter ends with Jacob's resolve not to part with Benjamin, despite the excessive surety offered by Reuben. Reuben and Judah continue to be the only active brothers in the drama. In each case Reuben's efforts are ineffective while Judah's, for good or ill, accomplish their goal. The audience of Genesis in this way sees Judah's tribal leadership begin to emerge.

The Brothers' Second Visit (43:1–34). When Judah finally persuades Jacob to allow them to go and take Benjamin, his statement is reminiscent of the persuasion used by Jacob's mother many years earlier when he was reluctant to act. Just as Rebekah told Jacob that she would bear the brunt of Isaac's curse (27:13), now Judah asserts that he will bear the blame if Benjamin does not return. With no alternatives, Jacob sends Benjamin with them again, having taken every precaution (43:11–12; cf. 32:13–21), praying for God's mercy (43:14; cf. 32:9–12), and then fatalistically settling down to await the outcome (43:14; cf. 32:7–8, 22). In the products that the brothers carry, they have become the caravan merchants going to Egypt with one of Rachel's sons in tow.

If the first visit brought their guilt and remorse to the surface, the second visit keeps them entirely off balance with events that are incongruous and bewildering. The first shock comes when they are invited guests at a feast at the home of this important man. They can only imagine the worst of intentions (43:18). The reply to their hurried explanations about the silver is met with a second shocking occurrence as the steward interprets their good fortune theologically: "Your God, the God of your father, has given you treasure in your sacks" (43:23). This cryptic statement is exactly the opposite of their own interpretation—that God was punishing them (42:28).

There are several interesting elements here.

1. We must note the use of the Hebrew word *shalom*. In chapter 37 the brothers could not speak *shalom* to Joseph (37:4). Now in 43:23 the steward's remarks are prefaced by speaking *shalom* (lit., "*shalom* to you—don't be afraid"; NIV "It's all right... Don't be afraid"), and in 43:27 Joseph checks on their welfare (*shalom*).
2. We may wonder what the word "treasure" (43:23) hints at in this statement. This word typically refers to something of great value that is hidden. Is there some level of metaphor attached to the word in the steward's use of it? What is the metaphorical treasure that God has put in their sacks? Grace? Blessing? Mercy? They have little time to ponder this before the flurry of activity continues.

In Joseph's home the care for their needs is meticulous. Joseph provides the picture of hospitality at its finest. The bounty they are served is generous, but it pales in comparison to what is set before Benjamin. The special treatment of Benjamin is important, for it repeats the special treatment he himself had received in the special coat that had stimulated the jealousy of his brothers. As in his own case, the brothers' needs are well cared for, but one is singled out for preferential treatment. Will they respond with jealousy toward Benjamin just as they had toward him? The silver cup used in the next chapter provides an opportunity for them to act on any jealousy.

The Silver Cup (44:1–34). The test of the silver cup is designed to see if the brothers are still inclined to abandon one of Rachel's sons who receives preferential treatment. When Joseph's servant catches up to the brothers and sets forth the accusation, they are so sure of their innocence that they invoke the death penalty on anyone who is found with the treasured cup. This echoes the offer made by Jacob when Laban accuses him of stealing the household idols (31:32). The finding of the silver cup offers yet another example of the steward's comment of the day before that God put treasure in their sacks.

Though the brothers propose that the one found with the cup will be killed while the rest of them will be enslaved, that scenario would not accomplish Joseph's intent. The counterproposal of the servant is that the one with the cup will be enslaved while the others go free. In this way the situation of Joseph's sale into slavery is most comparably reconstructed. The grief of the brothers upon the discovery of the cup in Benjamin's sack gives an early indication that they are indeed changed men.

But the charade must be played out to the very last scene, and they all shuffle back to Egypt.

Joseph's statement when they are again before him is another of the cryptic statements woven through the narrative: "Don't you know that a man like me can find things out by divination?" (44:15). Divination in Egypt was generally only accessible to people of high status. Not much is known concerning the most popular techniques. The brothers would not be surprised that a high official uses such methods.

But it is possible that Joseph insinuates more than this. In the immediate context, Joseph is reading the omens of their behavior to determine whether they are changed men. Indeed, he is using the cup for this divination. Joseph has begun to see God's plan. In the larger scheme of things, his early dreams had indicated the destiny that he has now fulfilled, and he is beginning to understand what God is doing through him.

The scene rushes to its conclusion. In 44:16 the brothers admit their corporate guilt and desire to establish their innocence. Their goal is now the same as Joseph's—he also wants to see whether they have become innocent rather than treacherous men. So, he gives them one last chance to repeat their crime as he sets the opportunity for them to escape at Benjamin's expense (44:17). This is the pivot point of this section of the Joseph narrative.

As in Genesis 37, Judah's speech sets the course of the narrative. Just as he had made the suggestion to sell Joseph, thus bringing about the whole sequence of events that the narrative has recounted, so he is the one who steps forward, now refusing to "sell" Benjamin. Judah's speech reveals important information that is critical to Joseph's test. It becomes clear that the brothers have a new sensitivity to their father's feelings. Judah even tries, subtly, to make Joseph feel guilty about the complicity he will have in Jacob's death from grief (44:31).

Moreover, Joseph discovers what Jacob has believed about his fate all these years (44:28). He thus is made aware that his father actually believes him to be dead. Most important, it becomes clear that Judah has become altruistic. He would rather bear slavery than blame. He is selflessly willing to accept his own misery rather than put others in misery. This transformation of the brothers represented in Judah is every bit as miraculous as the transformation in the status of Joseph.

Joseph Revealed (45:1–28). When Joseph finally is convinced of the transformation that has taken place in his brothers, he reveals himself to them. The first statement he makes, "I am Joseph," is logical enough, but the next one seems odd: "Is my father still living?" (45:3). The brothers have been speaking all along of the actions and statements of Jacob. They have reported on Jacob's involvement up to the very moment of their departure. Why ask such a question?

A couple of observations can address the issue.

1. Joseph is hereby ending his masquerade. The question he asks is less important than the choice that he now makes to call Jacob "my father" instead of "your father."
2. It is likely that the Hebrew word *hay* ("living") asks not so much whether he is above ground or below ground, heart beating or not. It is the equivalent of our question, "Is my father well?" He wants to know on a personal level how his father is doing. Up until now the communications have been given to him as an outsider. He wants more intimate and detailed news of his father.

Meanwhile, the brothers are understandably stunned into speechlessness. As they cower in fear and shock, Joseph has to draw them back to him. He then seeks to calm their fears by voicing the theology that is the centerpiece of the Joseph story: God has sovereignly directed the sequence of events in order to accomplish his purposes. It serves as a transition to the third segment of the story, which involves the resettlement of the covenant family in the land of Egypt.

The first suggestion of this plan comes from Joseph in 45:9–11. The argument to support this major departure from patriarchal policy is, first of all, that God has clearly sanctioned Joseph's leadership and judgment. Next is the fact that their very existence requires this move to be made. Joseph's suggestion is reiterated in a generous offering from Pharaoh to provide the best for them while they are in Egypt—another sign of God's blessing. This will incidentally give the Israelites of the exodus generation a far more complimentary picture of Pharaoh than they have seen in their lifetimes.

A few interesting details close the chapter.

1. The Joseph story began with favoritism expressed through the gift of a special coat. As it is drawing to a close, Joseph communicates his favoritism by giving extravagant amounts of silver and five sets of clothes (45:22).
2. Joseph admonishes his brothers not to "quarrel" on the way back (45:24). What does he expect them to quarrel about? "Quarrel" is the translation most commonly chosen, but the Hebrew term (*rgz*) does not mean that anywhere else. Joseph anticipates that his brothers may be fearful that he will have second thoughts and send an army after them—perhaps accusing them of plundering and thievery—and slaughter them all.
3. Finally, news is brought to Jacob and, with some effort, he is at last persuaded that Joseph is alive and determines to go see him.

Jacob's Move to Egypt (46:1–27). Jacob's movements in and out of the land have been marked by angels and theophanies. Thus, it is no surprise that his preparation to leave the land and settle in Egypt is marked by a vision. This theophany is briefer and makes only passing reference to the two covenant benefits. There are three significant differences to note.

1. God identified himself; here he is "God, the God of your father" (46:3). By now this is recognizable as a reference to the God of the covenant. Consequently, the instructions to leave the land should be seen as part of the big covenant plan, not a change.
2. The next significant difference concerns a detail left dangling for twenty chapters. In 15:13 when God ratified the covenant with Abraham, he told him that his people would be in a land not their own for four hundred years and that there they would be enslaved and mistreated. The small word "there" is finally revealed as Egypt, where the family will grow into a nation. Moreover, regardless of how it may look from the vantage point of those who were slaves in Egypt, God is the one who brought them there as part of his covenant plan.
3. God will go down to Egypt with Jacob (46:4). In Genesis 28 it can be said that God was extending his arm of protection from Canaan to cover Jacob in his journeys. Here in Genesis 46, God is packing up and going with Jacob to Egypt. All of this takes place at Beersheba, the southern boundary to the land.

Jacob and his family ignore Pharaoh's advice to leave their belongings behind (45:20) as they pack everything up for the journey (46:6). The text makes a point of saying that all Jacob's offspring go to Egypt (46:6–7) to make it clear that no part of the family is left behind to hold the fort and preserve the family holdings while the main part leaves. In that sense this is a complete act of faith.

The list of those who go to Egypt has some similarities to the table of nations in Genesis 10. There most of the lines extended only to the second generation, with selected expansions to the third. The degree to which each line extended was carefully chosen to arrive at the total of seventy. In this list there are twelve sons to trace instead of three. That means that for the total seventy to be reached, a lesser degree of extension is necessary.

We need not expect genealogies to operate in the Israelite culture the same way they operate in ours. If they have a different function in the culture, different methods can be used to construct them, and different criteria must be used to evaluate their accuracy.

It may be best to consider the list in Genesis 46 as a document listing those who are considered charter members of the Goshen settlement rather than something like an airplane's manifest or a census document. That this is the case is indicated somewhat in the text itself as it notes that the number does not include the sons' wives (46:26). They would have physically participated in the journey and resettlement, but their charter status is represented in their husbands.

Settlement in Egypt (46:28–47:12). In 46:28 the emergence of Judah takes its next step forward as he is given a role of responsibility by being sent ahead to Joseph for the family. This role is going to be finalized in the blessings of Genesis 49 and, of course, is represented in the reality of the exodus generation and eventually in the kingship of the Davidic dynasty.

Goshen is a Semitic term most likely referring to the delta region of Lower (= northern) Egypt in the area of the Wadi Tumilat. Egyptian texts from the Hyksos period (ca. 1750–1550 BC) refer to Semites in this region, and it is an area that provides excellent pasturage for herds, which is what Jacob and his sons need. In 47:11 it is referred to anachronistically as the "district of Rameses." Joseph meets Jacob there for their emotional reunion.

Joseph's instructions to his brothers concerning their occupation (46:31–34) and their subsequent conversation with Pharaoh (47:1–4) highlight the low opinion of shepherds in Egypt (46:34). "Shepherds" may be ambiguous, referring not only to a vocation that was legitimate and acceptable (since there is no indication of dishonor attached to the profession in Egypt), but also to a group of people who were already infiltrating the land and, as a group, were despised. Joseph would want to ensure that his family was classified in the former category rather than the latter. Immigrants can easily be stereotyped by their vocation, with that vocation then being adopted as a derogatory designation for the group.

The meeting with Pharaoh is successful in procuring permission for Jacob's family to settle In Goshen. But it reaches its climax in the conversation between Pharaoh and Jacob. Both at the beginning of the conversation (47:7) and at the end (47:10) Jacob blesses Pharaoh, adding another illustration of the covenant promise that "all peoples on earth will be blessed through you" (12:3).

Joseph's Policies (47:13–26). Though it may appear as if Joseph's policies are economically repressive, hard times require hard solutions. The text documents the sequence of how the people were impoverished by the famine. First, they spent all their money buying food (47:14–15), then they traded away their livestock (47:16–17), and finally, they gave up their land and worked as tenant farmers (47:18–20). Their rent for the land was 20 percent of the produce—a lower than normal percent in the ancient world. This was a progressive tax in that it was proportioned according to income. Theoretically, then, a prosperous farmer could have rebuilt his wealth when the famine ended, though It is not clear whether he would have been allowed to buy back the land. This turned Egypt into a state in which all the wealth was centralized in the government. The priests shared in the centralization of wealth since they were subsidized by the government. This was the common practice in Egypt and led to significant wealth (and therefore political power) being attached to long-standing priestly families.

Despite the personal hardship and servitude that resulted, the people are grateful for their lives (47:25). Once more, then, the point is made that through Joseph, the representative of Abraham's family, people are experiencing deliverance and blessing.

Application. When I play the computer in chess, it is an exercise in futility and inevitability. Since I am not very good at chess, I usually find that the computer continually puts me into positions where I have to respond with certain moves, yet those very moves lead inevitably to further the computer's strategy and ultimate victory. In the rare cases that I feel free to choose a move that furthers my game strategy, I usually discover that my choice is not a particularly good one. If I inadvertently try to make an illegal move, the computer does not allow it. If I make a stupid move, the computer makes me pay for it as it weaves my stupidity into its strategy. If I make a move with evil intent, the computer parries it (handily) and usually uses it to its own advantage.

Compared to God, we are all like bad chess players competing against a computer. There are differences, of course. God is not just in it to win, and God's moves are not mechanically programmed. In one sense it can be said that when he wins, we win. He is driven by love and compassion. Yet, just as in the illustration, we can at times feel caught in the current of the events that surround us, not understanding how we can be winning when it feels so much like losing.

The computer does not make me move one way or the other, but it limits my choices and sometimes forces my hand. It is in absolute control of the game, even though I am making independent choices. Whatever choices I make are powerless to hamper its strategies. Neither the word "cause" nor the word "allow" describes the computer's role in my moves. Since I cannot find a word that describes the computer's role in my moves, it is only possible to describe the computer's role in the game (of which I am involved). It accepts me as an opponent, but its mastery is complete. It controls the game, and I cannot even minutely divert its strategies, let alone defeat it.

I cannot pretend to offer any language that resolves all the problems of reconciling God's sovereignty with the presence of evil in the world. It should be noted, however, that the Bible's own attempt to reconcile these issues is not represented by detailed and technical philosophical treatises. Instead, the important theology is clarified by illustration because, as we all know, where language may fail, illustration can succeed. The story of Joseph, therefore, can stand as a living treatise on the theology of God's sovereignty.

GENESIS 47:27–50:26

Original Meaning

Jacob's Request (47:27–31). We must not miss the strong covenant language in the opening verses of this section.

1. The Israelites have acquired property, albeit in Egypt (47:27). The promise for the land of Canaan (17:8) had become a reality but only on a small scale (23:4), though it had also been part of a tantalizing temptation (34:10).
2. Moreover, 47:27 indicates that the Israelites have become fruitful and multiplied. This again draws together the blessing to all humankind from 1:28 and the covenant blessing in 17:20 that Abraham's family would become a great nation with many descendants. In other words, God has granted them covenant-type blessings in Egypt in a mini-fulfillment of the promises that will eventually come to full fruition only in the return to Canaan. The time in Egypt is not an interruption of the covenant but an incubation of the covenant people.

Jacob's use of deferential language when addressing Joseph (47:29) may simply be a reflection of Joseph's office, but as the narrative develops it seems rather to indicate a new status for Joseph as the head of the clan—a fulfillment of the dreams in Genesis 37. Typically, the head of a clan was responsible for the funeral and for the continued care of the deceased. In some cultures, this included funerary offerings and veneration of the ancestor, though no such practices have been observable in Abraham's family. Minimally, it required attentive care to the gravesite and the bones of the ancestor.

The idea that there is a transfer of status here also helps explain what has historically been a difficult phrase in the second half of 47:31, which the NIV translates, "Israel worshiped as he leaned on the top of his staff." Jacob's bowing at the head of his bed is an acknowledgement of divine care that has allowed him to pass clan leadership successfully to his son Joseph.

Blessing of Ephraim and Manasseh (48:1–22). In this second transition segment, Jacob adopts Ephraim and Manasseh as replacements for Reuben and Simeon. The translation by the NIV blurs this by rendering 48:5 "just as Reuben and Simeon are mine." A literal translation of the Hebrew reads: "Like Reuben and Simeon they will be to me." That is, they become the firstborn sons of Jacob. This, in effect, provides the double portion of the firstborn's inheritance to Joseph, though in a roundabout way. Theoretically, Joseph receives his portion, while Ephraim and Manasseh receive the portions of Reuben and Simeon, giving Joseph three shares. At the same time, it is still possible that Judah receives the double portion, though 48:22 suggests that Joseph has that role (cf. 1 Chr 5:1–2).

Jacob begins his speech by recapitulating the covenant promises (48:3–4). The connection of this to the adoption proceedings is unclear until the discussion turns to the inheritance of property at the end of 48:6. The land was given to him, and this adoption dictates how he will allocate it. Likewise, 48:7 may seem like pointless rambling until we make the connection that Jacob legitimates the adoption of Ephraim and Manasseh on the basis of the premature demise of Rachel. Just as a man who dies without children can have his line perpetuated by his surviving widow's production of descendants that become legally his, so Jacob sees Rachel's line, prematurely cut short, as perpetuated by her survivor, Joseph. Jacob thus considers Joseph's two sons as legally his. He lost Rachel during his wandering years (48:7), and Ephraim and Manasseh were born before his wandering came to a conclusion in Egypt (48:5).

The ceremony begins in 48:8 with the question, "Who are these?" This question is not indication of Jacob's blindness but the initiation of the ceremony, just as in modern-day weddings when, near the beginning, the minister may ask, "Who gives this woman to be married to this man?" The ceremonial response, "Her mother and I do" is also paralleled in Joseph's ceremonial response. The sons were given by God, and they are the very ones born in Egypt (48:9), thus meeting Jacob's criteria for the adoption. The ceremony continues without delay or surprise until, despite Joseph's careful arrangement, and then his verbal protest, Jacob insists on favoring the younger Ephraim over his older brother.

The actual blessing occurs in 48:15–16, 20. Since Ephraim and Manasseh have no natural brothers, there is no reference to domination over brothers. Likewise, the common element of fertility of the land is absent. Only the blessing for large families is here. In this way it can be seen as differing from the normal patriarchal pronouncements. Of course, being primarily an adoption pronouncement (48:16b), this is to be expected. The only real oddity in the blessing is the reference to the angel (48:16a). The grammatical parallel indicates that the angel need not be a title for deity but may simply be positioned parallel to God. In other words, Jacob is blessing Ephraim and Manasseh by putting them under the care of God, who shepherds, under his angel, who delivers.

That a blessing on Joseph is also specifically included can be seen in 48:22, which has, like 47:31, been consistently elusive to translators. Historically, this must refer to the conquest of Shechem (or should we call it the slaughter of the Shechemites?) by Simeon and Levi. Jacob did not approve of this act and was not proud of it, but it was irreversible and undeniable. The land is therefore his to give since it was taken in his name and by his clan. This justifies his use of the first person ("I took," 48:22). In this blessing, Joseph is given immediate clan leadership (as one over his brothers), though, as the next chapter's blessing will indicate, Judah is destined for eventual tribal rule.

Blessing of the Sons of Jacob (49:1–28). In this last and most extensive example of patriarchal pronouncement, we must again observe that the patriarch's words are *not* fashioned as a prophetic message from God. This does not mean that the pronouncement does not carry authority or that it has no impact on the future. It would not have been viewed as prediction as much as a determination of individual and tribal destiny. Just as the giving of a name was believed to have some role in determining the destiny of an individual, so these pronouncements were taken seriously.

Reuben, Simeon, and Levi (49:3–7). These sections focus on the past and function as indictments. The only reference to their resulting destiny is that at least Simeon and Levi will be "dispersed" (49:7) in Israel. As tribal history goes, Simeon's claim is to villages scattered in Judah's territory, and Levi has no claim as the Levites are distributed among the tribes to serve their priestly functions.

In the saying connected to Simeon and Levi, the word that the NIV translates "swords" (49:5) occurs only here in the Old Testament and is highly disputed. I favor reading it as a noun form from the verb *krt*, "to cut," a verb occasionally used for circumcision (e.g., Exod 4:25). In this reading their "cutters/knives" (used for the circumcision of the men of Shechem) became weapons of violence.

"Hamstrung oxen" (49:6) may also mean "they castrated an ox." This in turn may be understood metaphorically, as demonstrated in Ugaritic where the equivalent word for "bull" is sometimes used metaphorically to refer to "princes." Thus, we understand the statement to mean "they mutilated the genitals of a prince," alluding to the Shechem incident.

Judah (49:8–12). Here the focus turns away from the past to the future. At the same time, the blessing now adopts the use of animal metaphors, which become characteristic of many of the remaining sayings. This is the only saying that appears to carry relevance that extends beyond the land divisions that occur in the period of Joshua and Judges.

In 49:8–10 Judah assumes the role of the younger son, who is emerging to a place of leadership. The indication that his father's sons will bow down to him (49:8) puts him on a par with Joseph. Joseph's dream and its eventual fulfillment in 42:6 had a more immediate focus, while Judah's role is for future days. Genesis 49:8 also shows some similarity to previous patriarchal pronouncements by addressing the relationship among the brothers. But certainly, the largest problem of the chapter concerns the reference to 49:10.

The most important item for the understanding of this verse is related to the conjunction universally translated "until" (49:10). Even those who interpret the verse either in a Davidic or messianic way are troubled by this because in neither case did the scepter depart from Judah. David/Messiah is a representative of Judah, not a replacement for him.

This saying, in effect, points to Judah as the primary channel of blessing to all the nations of the earth in the future, even though Joseph filled that role in the context of Jacob's immediate family. Again, we can see the emphasis on the blessing clause of the covenant in this section of Genesis and Judah's emergence as the tribe destined for leadership.

Zebulun, Issachar, Dan, Gad, Asher, Naphtali (49:13–21). The territory allotted to Zebulun after the conquest was the area of Western Lower Galilee. At no point does this territory reach the sea. The area along the sea north of the Carmel promontory was assigned to Asher. The coastal territory south of the Carmel promontory was assigned to Manasseh. Certainly, then, we can conclude that this blessing does not simply reflect a description of the territories as they existed after the conquest. In addition, there is no known period when Zebulun controlled the coastal regions. This is problematic and makes interpretation of this saying difficult.

Issachar was allotted most of the Jezreel Valley when Israel came into the land. In fact, the idea of lying down between sheep pens can describe the way in which Issachar's territory jutted south between the Carmel range and the Gilboa range. The description of the land as pleasant (49:15) describes the Jezreel Valley as appropriately as any other region in the country. Besides being fertile, the main highway from Egypt to Babylon passed through the Jezreel Valley so that any country trying to control the trade routes would seek to take control of that region. It is therefore understandable that the one inhabiting that region would be subject to forced labor.

The saying associated to Dan has nothing to do with territory. Dan's assigned territory had been west of Ephraim and Benjamin, including the coastal area around modern Tel-Aviv. The saying focuses on the characteristics and function of the tribe, not its location.

There are three problems in 49:16–18.

1. What is the role and identity of "his people" in 49:16? If Dan refers to the patriarch, it goes without saying that he will provide justice for his people (i.e., his descendants). If, as is more likely, the saying refers to the tribe, then "his people" must logically refer to some group outside the tribe. An intriguing alternative is to understand "his people" as the subject of the verb rather than the object. The fact that the verb "to provide justice" is a play on the name Dan justifies this kind of statement being made. An alternative that suits the context a little better is to take the verb here as deriving from the Hebrew root *dnn*, "to be strong," rather than from the Hebrew root *dyn*, "to judge." This also resolves the obscurity of the second line comparing Dan to one of the tribes of Israel. The resulting translation is: "Dan—his people will be strong like one of the tribes of Israel." It suggests that Dan will eventually take its proper place among the tribes.
2. The use of the serpent metaphor is transparent enough, though it remains unclear why the metaphor is suitable to Dan (49:17).
3. The final problem is the concluding prayer in 49:18. Does the "I" mark the line as something Dan says or something Jacob says? The latter is more likely, but why is such a statement inserted here in the middle of the blessing? It should also be noted that this three-word (in Hebrew) statement contains the only reference to Yahweh in the blessing. In fact, that name for God has not been used since 39:23 and, aside from chapter 39, is not used at all in the Joseph story (though it does appear in 38:7–10). Jacob has not been shown using the name Yahweh since his prayer in 32:9.

   Perhaps it is no coincidence that on either side of 49:18 there are references to attack and that in both cases the attack targets the heels. It will be recalled from the naming of Jacob in 25:26 that the word "heel" is similar to Jacob's name. Yet these tribes are not being attacked at the heels; they are portrayed as the one attacking the heels. This is not out of line in that Jacob was the one who grabbed onto the heel of his brother. Just as Jacob had been at a disadvantage when he took hold of his brother's heel, so both Dan and Gad are in tenuous positions, perhaps leading Jacob to express the hope of deliverance. The verse remains entirely obscure.

There is little light that can be shed on Gad and Asher. The statements about them are rich in wordplay with little to offer about the patriarch or tribe's situations.

Finally, the main controversy surrounding the Naphtali statement concerns what animal metaphor is being used. The alternative to the traditional doe with fawns is a reference to a lambing ewe with lambs. The issue is difficult and technical with no resolution resulting.

Joseph and Benjamin (49:22–27). All major translations present the initial metaphor as a plant metaphor ("fruitful vine," 49:22), but the technicalities of this translation are too complex to discuss here since it would take us far beyond the scope of this commentary. Regardless of the extent that kingship implications may or may not be involved for Joseph, there is a clear distinction articulated between Joseph and his brothers in the last line of the saying. Joseph's ruling position has also been established in the surrounding narrative context. But Joseph's ruling role is in the present; there is nothing to compare or compete with the role given to the tribe of Judah for the long term.

The saying concerning Benjamin is straightforward enough as far as translation goes, but as with the sayings associated with the other minor tribes, it has little obvious connection to what we know of Benjamin as a person or of the tribal history.

In case there were any remaining doubt, 49:28 shows that the emphasis is on tribes, not just sons.

Jacob's Death and Burial (49:29–50:14). The phrase "gathered to my people" (49:29) may reflect not only burial in the family tomb, as evident in the next sentence, but also the contemporary perspective on the afterlife. The Israelites had as yet no revelation that offered them a hope of heaven, but perhaps we can speak of an ancestral village in the netherworld where the spirit of the individual who has died rejoins the spirits of the ancestors. Caution is necessary here, however, and we should be reluctant to draw firm philosophical conclusions from stock phrases.

The burial instructions remind us of information brought out in previous narratives. This recollection of the ancestral burial grounds would certainly preserve a strong tie between the Israelites and Canaan during their centuries of sojourn in Egypt. After the death of Jacob, he is embalmed in accordance with Egyptian practice.

Although it was a common practice in Egypt (for any who could afford it), embalming of Israelites is found only in this chapter. The fact that the bodies of Jacob and Joseph are embalmed may suggest the desire of the Israelites to soothe the feelings of the Egyptians, but it also serves the purpose of preserving their bodies for later burial in Canaan. The seventy-day period of mourning for Jacob (50:3) may include the forty days required to embalm the body plus the traditional thirty-day mourning period (see Deut 34:8).

The accompaniment by Egyptian dignitaries and a military escort reflects the importance of Joseph and the dignity that is thereby accorded to Jacob. It also serves a theological purpose, showing how far this little family of Abraham's has progressed. God promised to make Abraham's name great and to bless him. Now all of Egypt stops and pays attention with great pomp and circumstance at the passing of his grandson.

Joseph's Legacy and Death (50:15–26). Verses 15–21 show that Joseph's brothers have not fully assimilated his forgiveness. In their possibly manufactured message from their now-deceased father, we find the first acknowledgement of guilt by the brothers, yet even now they offer it in the context of a message from their father rather than owning up to it themselves.

The indirect repentance of the brothers, the forgiveness extended by Joseph, and the theological statement concerning God's purposes contain the climax to the Joseph story and, in some ways, the message of both this story and the entire book.

In 50:25 Joseph refers to the transportation of his bones. This language probably reflects his upbringing in Canaan more than his adopted Egyptian culture. Nomadic groups often practiced secondary burial, in which survivors transported the skeletal remains of relatives to a traditional site long after death. If Joseph were anticipating mummification, he would not have referred to transportation of his bones.

Joseph died at age one hundred and ten, which was considered the ideal age for an Egyptian, despite the fact that examination of mummies has demonstrated that the average life expectancy in Egypt was between forty and fifty.

Application. What kind of teacher is God? God's solution to the plight of humankind is not to provide for systematic breaking, though the results of the fall make us vulnerable to brokenness and in need of something to distract us from our self-will. Instead, God's solution is self-revelation. By showing us what he is like, he gives us something to aspire to.

Life can break us because we live in a fallen world. God can use such circumstances, for he intends them for good. Moreover, God can break us if that is the kind of student we turn out to be. But he has given us the revelation of himself in the Bible so that we may not drown in self but learn to swim toward him stroke by stroke and finally, diving in, be totally submerged in him as we submit to his will and yield our lives to his mastery.

But as committed as we may be to attain this end result, we must acknowledge that whatever path we take, the separation from self and sin cannot be painless—the surgeon must cut to heal and the builder must demolish to rebuild.

EXODUS

INTRODUCTION TO EXODUS

The authorship of Exodus (and the Pentateuch) has been a disputed point, not only over the past three hundred years of Old Testament scholarship but earlier as well. Several theories that account for the present state of the Pentateuch have without doubt overreached the biblical evidence. It is equally clear, however, that data in the Pentateuch and the book of Exodus complicate the matter of identifying an author with any certainty. In a manner of speaking, it is the Pentateuch itself that raises the question of authorship. For instance, nowhere in the Pentateuch is Moses described as the writer of the whole work. To be sure, he *is* said to write—the first instance being the episode with the Amalekites (see Exod 17:14). Elsewhere in the Pentateuch where Moses is said to write, the reference is to the law (24:4; 34:27, 28; Deut 31:9, 24), the only exception being Deuteronomy 31:19, 22, which tells us that Moses wrote down the words of a song (Deut 32:1–43). The Pentateuch has no more to say on the subject. With this in mind, an attitude of reverential open-mindedness seems most consistent with the evidence.

BOOK OUTLINE

- I. Departure From Egypt (1:1–15:21)
  - A. Prelude (1:1–7:7)
  - B. Plagues 1–9: Prelude to Israel's Release and Egypt's Destruction (7:8–10:29)
  - C. Departure (11:1–15:21)
- II. Mount Sinai: Law (15:22–24:18)
  - A. Journey to Sinai (15:22–18:27)
  - B. Arrival at Sinai and Moses's First Trip up the Mountain (19:1–25)
  - C. Ten Commandments (20:1–21)
  - D. The Book of the Covenant (20:22–23:19)
  - E. A Final Warning Against the Worship of Other Gods (23:20–33)
  - F. The Covenant Is Signed and Sealed (24:1–18)
- III. Mount Sinai: Tabernacle (25:1–40:38)
  - A. Instructions for the Tabernacle (25:1–31:18; 35:1–40:33)
  - B. Rebellion and Forgiveness (32:1–34:35)
  - C. Building the Tabernacle (40:34–38)

EXODUS 1:1–22

Original Meaning. One can begin to understand Exodus by thinking of it more as a chapter of a book (the Pentateuch) than a book in its own right. Although not reflected in the NIV, the Hebrew text shows that 1:1 does not begin simply with the words "These are the names. . . ." Rather, it begins with the harmless word "and" (the Hebrew letter *waw*). Although the presence of "and" at the beginning of the book may seem odd, it functions to join the book of Exodus to what has come before.

Furthermore, the language of 1:7 is creation language, calling to mind the language found in Genesis 1:28 and 9:1: The Israelites "were exceedingly fruitful; they multiplied greatly, increased in numbers." The Hebrew of Exodus 1:7 is even more explicit than the NIV: "The Israelites became fruitful and swarmed; they increased in number and became exceedingly strong" (author's translation). "Swarm," also used in Genesis 1:21 and 8:17, is another description of what God's *created* beings do. The presence of such creation language in Exodus 1 is indication that this book is to be read in the context of Genesis.

Two immediate questions come to mind with respect to 1:8.

1. Who is this pharaoh?
2. How much time has passed since the demise of Joseph's generation?

The biblical writer, however, is not interested in giving these details. Why not? This is anyone's guess. It may be that in providing too many concrete historical details he runs the danger of limiting the timelessness of the message of Exodus. Another reason may be that some of these details are simply not worth mentioning since they do not add to his purpose, a purpose that is evidently more theological than journalistic. Exodus is the story of *God's* deliverance of his people.

Although some of the details of the story are lacking, what is clear is that this new pharaoh is not at all happy with what he sees. What troubles him is the increasing number of Israelites (1:9). To put it another way, Pharaoh is opposed to their fulfillment of the creation mandate to be fruitful and increase (cf. Pharaoh's words in 1:9 with 1:6–7). In this respect, Pharaoh represents not only a force hostile to God's people by enslaving them (1:11–14) but a force hostile to God himself, who wills that his people multiply.

The final solution is the murder of all male infants (1:22) by throwing them into the Nile. In keeping with his taciturn prose, the writer does not tell us anything that transpires after the giving of this insidious decree. It is evident, however, that either many other male infants escaped as well or (more likely) that the decree was eventually rescinded, since Moses was not the only male of his generation to survive! Nevertheless, the text does not give us information regarding the sweeping ramifications of this decree. All we are told is that one special child escaped Pharaoh's evil intention.

Application. Why does God let this happen? Doesn't he see what's happening? I thought being a Christian meant always feeling God's presence. God's people through all time have struggled with his apparent disinterest in their personal affairs. All believers go through periods of spiritual dryness where they struggle with feelings of God's absence. These things do not happen because of lack of faith. The lesson, rather, is that neither our present circumstances nor our perceptions of God's absence determine reality. We cry out to the Lord honestly, and he hears us.

EXODUS 2:1–10

Original Meaning. When Moses's mother looked at the child after his birth, she saw that he was "fine" or "good" (*tob*, 2:2). Why did the writer feel it necessary to include such an apparently incidental comment in this otherwise terse narrative? Are we really to conclude that Moses's mother simply saw how good-looking he was? A more fruitful line of inquiry is to understand the birth of Moses—in keeping with the re-creation theme in chapter 1—as not merely about the birth of one man but representative of the birth of a people.

The boy is set in an "ark" (*tebah*) and set afloat on the Nile (2:3). *Tebah* provides a clear connection to Genesis. In all of the Old Testament, this Hebrew word is found only here and in the flood story (Gen 6:14–9:18). Moses's safe passage through the waters of the Nile not only looks backward to the flood story but also looks forward to the passage through the sea in Exodus 14 for all of God's people.

Big sister (presumably Miriam, not mentioned by name until 15:20) watches her little brother float along and sees the vessel retrieved by the handmaidens of Pharaoh's daughter. The sister seizes the moment and offers, somewhat matter-of-factly, that it might be of benefit to all concerned if the child were nursed—at least for the time being—by someone else, say, a Hebrew woman she just happens to know (2:7–8). Pharaoh's daughter agrees to this arrangement and even pays the nurse for her efforts (2:9).

Application. Did Moses grow up hating his new mother because she was not an Israelite? Or is it more likely that he came to rely on her, look up to her, depend on her—love her? What is our proper posture toward an unbeliever? The model of "opposition" is certainly well known and has ample biblical precedent. This model, however, is not deserving of universal application. We share with others the love of Christ, who was a friend to sinners. In doing so, we bring the good news to them in many different ways, which is something that God's people are called to do. But do not be surprised if in the process the Lord uses these same people to change you.

EXODUS 2:11–25

Original Meaning. By the time we reach 2:11, Moses has apparently grown to be a man, as the following narrative makes clear. Moses goes out to be with his people. It is not clear whether he at this point has already consciously identified himself with his true countrymen. Nowhere in this passage do we see Moses consider himself an Israelite. The fact that he goes out to observe the suffering of his countrymen certainly suggests a strong degree of compassion but not necessarily blood-kinship.

The Egyptian's "beating" the Hebrew slave (2:11) evokes a strong action on Moses's part. However conscious Moses is of his own background, it is clear that Moses is incensed enough at what he sees to kill the Egyptian, thus severing his ties with the Egyptian aristocracy.

In 2:13 Moses intercedes in another conflict, but now between two Israelites. This incident serves to introduce two interconnected themes that recur throughout the Pentateuch: Israel's rebellion and the rejection of Moses. Moses's role as redeemer at its very beginning is already met with his own people questioning his authority.

Pharaoh's determination to kill Moses drives Moses away to Midian. His choice of haven is significant. Midian serves to tie Moses to the patriarchs. Perhaps most significant, Moses's departure from Egypt into the Sinai desert foreshadows the exodus itself.

Regarding Moses's marriage, anyone familiar with the patriarchal narratives will be reminded of Genesis 24 and 29, where Isaac and Jacob, respectively, meet their wives. The clear difference between these narratives is that Isaac and Jacob marry descendants of Abraham, while Moses marries a foreign woman. Moses finds acceptance apart from his own people, first by being raised in an Egyptian household and now by starting his own household on foreign soil with a foreign wife. Once again, Moses's circumstances anticipate Israel's forty-year "exile" in the desert.

In 2:23–25 the Israelites "groan" and "cry out." God responds because he remembers "his covenant with Abraham, with Isaac and with Jacob" (2:24). With these concluding verses, the stage is set. The next scene of the drama of Israel's redemption is about to unfold. How, then, will God aid his covenant people?

Application. Humility is a central quality that defines the Christian. There are times, however, when humility is not something we choose but is thrust upon us. Moses chose to help his Hebrew brother; he never intended to flee his home as a result. Christians often find themselves in a state of enforced humility simply by virtue of their Christian witness. We who are Christ's ambassadors can expect nothing less than that which our Lord himself endured.

EXODUS 3:1–4:17

Original Meaning

The Burning Bush (3:1–10). The precise identity of the angel of the Lord has always been a matter of debate. Throughout the Old Testament this mysterious figure is closely identified, if not equated, with Yahweh himself. Nevertheless, it is best not to think of the two figures as simply equated. We should see this in the context of the ancient Near East, where messengers normally spoke for the sender. In the final analysis, the angel of the Lord remains a mysterious but prominent figure in the context of God's self-revelation to his people, and his role is ultimately fulfilled in Christ.

Another common element that regularly accompanies God's self-revelation is fire, a frequent sign of God's presence in Exodus. The fact that the bush is not consumed demonstrates that the fire's natural property is temporarily suspended. This episode presages the upheaval of the natural phenomena in the plagues and the crossing of the Red Sea.

Yahweh sets the tone immediately: Moses must know first and foremost that he is in the presence of a holy God. Why must he remove his sandals? This is a sign of reverence common in the ancient Near East. Yahweh announces himself to Moses (3:6). Whereas God's first words to Moses are an announcement of his holiness, his second words are a reminder of the past.

Yahweh continues speaking in 3:7; he knows what his people have been enduring under Egyptian oppression. Israel is "my people." He will "bring them up" from one land and into another, from the land of Egypt, which meant captivity and slavery, and into "a land flowing with milk and honey" (3:8).

The announcement has been made. As soon as the chosen messenger relays God's word to the Israelites, they will begin to feel the sought-after relief from their misery. But how will this messenger react? Will he be a willing participant in God's mighty act?

Moses Doubts Himself: "Who Am I?" (3:11–12). Who is the "I" that is going to be doing the saving, Moses or Yahweh? God's response to Moses's question in 3:12 settles the matter: "I will be with you." Moses's assertion that *he* cannot do this task is correct but entirely beside the point. He is not doing the saving. Moses says, "I cannot do this." Yahweh responds, "You're not, I am."

Moses Doubts His Reception: "What Is Your Name?" (3:13–22). "I AM WHO I AM" is not God's name but a preparatory comment that introduces the following announcement. The divine name, instead, seems to be "I AM" (3:14). It seems the purpose of 3:14–15 is not to introduce a new name but to underscore the precise identity of the God who is now addressing Moses. God is saying to him: "I am Yahweh, the 'I AM,' the God of the patriarchs. The one you have heard about is the one speaking with you now." Moses is to bring his message to the elders of Israel (3:16) and must tell them that God will bring them up out of Egypt and into the promised land.

What is of more immediate concern is the nature of the request that Moses and the elders are to make (3:18). Most commentators suggest that "three-day journey" simply indicates the amount of time needed to get to where they need to go for their celebration without necessarily implying a return trip. Moses's words are not a display of cunning but a bold command to let the people go.

Yahweh continues his speech to Moses by predicting that Pharaoh will not listen to reasoned persuasion (3:19). Only a "mighty hand" will compel him. Not only will Pharaoh send them away, but the Egyptians will have such pity for the slaves that they will not allow the Israelites to go away empty-handed (3:21–22).

Moses Doubts His Reception: Three Signs Are Given (4:1–9). Moses is concerned not with whether *Pharaoh* will recognize his authority but whether *Israel* will. God answers Moses's objection by providing him with three signs.

1. The first sign is turning Moses's staff into a snake (4:2–5). Why a snake? Likely because the snake represents a sign of Egyptian royal authority.
2. The second sign is the skin disease (4:6–7). The significance of this second sign seems to be authority over disease and sickness and may anticipate some of the plagues (e.g., boils).
3. The third sign, turning water into blood, symbolizes God's power over the elements, similar to the burning

bush. It also symbolizes the power of Israel's God over the power of the Egyptian gods and the Egyptian nation, whose life force was the Nile.

Moses Doubts His Reception: "I Have Never Been Eloquent" (4:10–12). Moses's fourth objection focuses on another reason why he might not be received by his countrymen. The precise nature of Moses's problem is difficult to identify. Whatever the problem, legitimate or illegitimate, it is not enough to deflect God from his path of action. The significance of God's answer in 4:11–12 is that God is in control not only of the elements and of the Egyptian government, but he is also in control over the messenger.

Moses Refuses God's Call (4:13–17). Moses's last objection is not based on some legitimate circumstance; Moses just doesn't want to do it. He is simply putting his foot down and saying "no." Hence, the Lord becomes angry with him for the first time (4:14).

Verses 15–16 suggest that Moses's final refusal is closely related to his previous objection. Apparently, what concerns Moses is his speech difficulty. Moses and Aaron will now become a team, but not a team of equal partners. Aaron will be Moses's mouth, but Moses will be Aaron's God (4:16).

The dialogue between Moses and God ends somewhat abruptly: "Don't forget your staff, Moses." The staff is to become a conspicuous player in the plague narratives. God will use this symbol of lowliness and unimportance to bring about the central salvific act of the Old Testament. "Don't forget your staff, Moses."

Application. Although doubts and struggles will certainly arise in conjunction with God's call, it is the very spirit of Christ that the Father imparts to us in that call. God's promise to be with Moses is fulfilled in us to a degree that neither Moses nor any of the Old Testament saints ever envisioned. God is not *with* us but *in* us—and we are *in* Christ. This intimacy is greater than what Moses experienced. This powerful presence of God in our lives does not preclude doubt and struggle. Rather, it serves as the proper theological setting in which to view our struggle. Brothers and sisters of the risen Christ are in a privileged situation.

EXODUS 4:18–31

Original Meaning

Moses's Departure (4:18–23). Note how 4:19 echoes the deliverance from Egypt of the following chapters. When Moses left Egypt, he was a wanted man. But now those who intended him harm are themselves dead. Later in the book, the Egyptians who seek to harm the Israelites meet their own demise in the Red Sea. In this sense, 4:19 is an announcement to Moses that the first installment of the exodus has commenced. Those who enslaved the Israelites are dead—the process has begun.

Moses's family is nowhere mentioned explicitly as arriving in Egypt with Moses. Exodus 18:2 is explicit in telling us that Moses had previously sent his family away to live with Jethro, presumably to keep his loved ones out of harm's way. Where Moses's family went in 4:20 or how they might have gotten to Midian is not something the narrative is pleased to disclose.

Verse 21 introduces an inherent theme in Exodus that raises serious questions about God's justice and the freedom of the human will. In 3:19, Pharaoh's resistance seems to be his own doing; in 4:21, it is the will of God. This is the real tension of the narrative. The point of all this should not be lost: The deliverance of Israel from Egypt is entirely God's doing and under his complete control. The impending Exodus is a play in which God is author, producer, director, and principal actor. The purpose of 4:21, then, is not to introduce some abstract philosophical notion of God's sovereignty. Rather, it is further confirmation of what we have seen earlier in chapter 4—that God is with Moses and with Israel.

Verses 22–23 conclude the Lord's final talk to Moses before beginning his mission. God's demand for Israel's release is not simply for Israel to be free *from* service to Egypt but for Israel *to* serve the Lord. The reason for Israel's release goes beyond vague notions of "freedom from oppression." Rather, God's son, Israel, is now to enter into a close father-son relationship with God.

The Circumcision of Moses's Son (4:24–26). Of all the things that the Israelites need to hear before their departure, why is so much time spent pointing out the necessity of circumcision, a rite that won't even become relevant until well after their departure? What we see in 4:24–26 is the zeal with which the Lord guards this most important rite. We must remember that circumcision as a sign of God's covenant was commanded of the patriarch Abraham (Gen 17:1–27). This connection to the patriarchs also imposes a covenant obligation on Moses and the Israelites. They have been delivered by the God of Abraham, Isaac, and Jacob. They are, therefore, to observe the command given to them: Circumcise your male children.

Moses, Aaron, and the Israelites (4:27–31). In 4:27–31, God's words to Moses on Mount Horeb are realized: Moses meets with Aaron as promised (4:14). The fact that Aaron and Moses meet on the "mountain of God" (4:27) is significant. As God had earlier commissioned Moses on Mount Horeb, Moses is now inaugurating Aaron. After Aaron's initial debriefing, they both go to meet with the elders of Israel. In this meeting

Aaron, not Moses, is the one who relays the message to the people, thus fulfilling God's earlier promise that Aaron will speak for Moses (4:16). The good news for Moses is that the people seem to accept him enthusiastically, thus allaying his fear of rejection (4:31).

Application. For Christians, our guilt for not doing what we ought needs to be tempered by a knowledge that we are God's children and he is our Father. If my children do something wrong, I want them to feel guilty, but I do not want them to be paralyzed with guilt. Nor do I want them to be guilty about silly things. They need to learn which things are worthy of guilt and which are not. However gracious we are to our children, we know that the God of the exodus is, in Christ, more gracious still with us.

EXODUS 5:1–21

Original Meaning. Perhaps nowhere is Pharaoh's hardness of heart demonstrated more clearly than in the first words he utters in the Exodus narrative: "Who is the LORD?" (5:2). As we saw in chapter 1, the true battle in Exodus is not between the Israelites and Pharaoh, nor even between Moses and Pharaoh. Rather, it is between the God of Israel and Pharaoh. The Israelites have been fulfilling God's creation mandate, and the biblical writer's aim is to present Pharaoh as one whose ultimate purpose is to oppose God.

As mentioned earlier, "three-day" (5:3) indicates not the time away from Egypt but the approximate time it would take to get to the proper site for the celebration without in any way implying that a return to Egypt is in view. Verse 3, then, is not a cowering response on Moses's part, who, after Pharaoh's rebuff, is willing to settle for the next best thing. Moses says: "Read my lips; perhaps I didn't make myself clear. It is *God* who met with us. *He* came to us with this message. *God* is speaking to you now, not two old men."

Pharaoh's eagerness to further his godless claim on the lives of this growing population is made more explicit beginning in 5:6. From now on, the Israelite slaves will have to gather their own straw to make their quota of bricks. This is no random decree but one calculated to drive a wedge between Moses and the people.

Pharaoh's decree pits him squarely against God. Pharaoh does not simply reject and disobey God's command ("keep working"), he counters it with yet an even more severe measure ("work *more*"). Specifically, Pharaoh says he wants to make their "work harder" (5:9). The irony, of course, is that as Pharaoh punishes Israel by making the people work "hard," his own heart is "hardened," which results in *his* punishment—the plagues and the Red Sea incident.

In 5:10 the slave drivers and foremen preface their message by saying, "This is what Pharaoh says." The wording is surely not accidental but a deliberate echo of 5:1 and 4:22: "This is what the LORD says." Yahweh gives the command to release the Israelites, but Pharaoh, the "false god," commands that they stay—and he even increases their labor to boot.

Verses 13–14 then tell us that the Israelite foremen are beaten by their Egyptian slave drivers. The foremen are understandably taken aback by this and say, in effect, "Why are you beating *us*? *Your* people are the ones who have stopped supplying us with straw. It's their fault. If anything, beat them."

Pharaoh not only refuses to heed their cry, but he mocks them as well. He repeats his accusation of 5:8: "Lazy, that's what you are—lazy" (5:17). Moses's command at the beginning of this chapter has so incensed the king of Egypt that he turns a deaf ear and now borders on the irrational. He simply tells them to get back to work (5:18).

For now, Pharaoh's strategy of disparaging Moses's reputation among the people has worked. The foremen leave Pharaoh's presence, perhaps dumbfounded, and see Moses and Aaron waiting to meet them. Immediately, the foremen turn on them and pronounce a curse on them (5:21). How ironic it is to call God's judgment down on the very one whom he has chosen to deliver his people! The foremen have it backward: This Moses, whom they treat so disrespectfully now, is not the reason for their oppression but God's instrument to end that oppression.

Application. Evangelism, properly executed, is not accompanied by timidity, but not so much because the evangelist has confidence in herself or himself but because the evangelist's focus shifts from the messenger to the originator of the message. This is what enables Moses to march into Pharaoh's court—not a conviction about his own preaching skills but a boldness that comes from knowing and being known by God. The message we preach, then, is not our own. Nor are we somehow indispensable in bringing this message to others. We are, rather, the most privileged of God's creation to be given this most honorable task of being coworkers with God himself to reconcile the world.

EXODUS 5:22–7:7

Original Meaning

God (Again) Promises Deliverance (5:22–6:12). The section begins with Moses seemingly at the end of his rope, exasperated. In effect, Moses is calling into question God's character. God said he was planning to bring the Israelites out of Egypt with Moses as his chosen vessel to bring it about. For now, however, things seem to be skidding out of control, and Moses concludes that God is actually bringing trouble on them.

God's response to Moses recalls three prominent elements of their previous conversation:

- 6:2: I am Yahweh (see 3:14)
- 6:3–4: I am the God of the patriarchs (see 3:6, 15–17)
- 6:5: I have heard your complaint (see 3:7 [and 2:24–25])

By repeating these vital elements, God is saying to Moses, "Let's try it again, but this time listen closely. This is who I am; I am Yahweh [6:2]. I made a promise to the patriarchs that I have every intention of keeping [6:3–4]. I know what is happening, and I am now poised to do something about it [6:5]. So, stand back and watch."

No discussion of this passage can pass by 6:3, one of the more difficult, controversial, and widely discussed verses in the entire book. According to the mainstream of critical scholarship, 6:3 is all but impossible to reconcile with 3:14, since both seem to *reveal* God's name. How can God reveal his name to Moses twice? Exodus 6:3 does not say that God is now giving a *new* name but that God's name is now going to be *fully* known; that is, the *significance* of the name is going to be understood at this most pivotal time in Israel's history. Verse 3, then, may be paraphrased as follows:

> I appeared to Abraham, Isaac, and Jacob, but only partially —in the capacity of El Shaddai. But who I am fully, which is what my name Yahweh captures, I did not make known to them. This is made known first only now, to you, the exodus generation, who will witness my mighty saving power.

Armed, then, with this reaffirmation of God's character and his presence with Moses and the Israelites, Moses is again sent back. The focus of God's message to the Israelites is on who *he* is, and their assessment of the situation must be based squarely on that immovable fact. The reaction of the Israelites, however, is not unlike that of Moses at the beginning of the passage: They will not be fooled again. (6:9).

But inasmuch as the Israelites have not yet learned their lesson, apparently neither has Moses. The Lord tells him to go once more to Pharaoh (6:11), but Moses responds (can we really blame him?), as it were: "It's no use, LORD. If my own people won't listen, what makes you think Pharaoh will? Besides, I speak with faltering lips."

The Genealogy (6:13–27). Verses 10–12 and 28–30 surround the genealogy. Moreover, 6:28–30 essentially repeats 6:10–12. In both passages God gives Moses the order to go to Pharaoh and both times Moses reminds God, somewhat feebly, that he has a problem speaking. These two passages are not separate events but one and the same. That is, 6:28–30 repeats 6:10–12 in an effort to "frame" the genealogy. Hence, this repetition shows that the insertion of the genealogy here is purposeful. What is that purpose? Verses 26–27 provide the answer: It establishes the pedigree of Moses and Aaron—or perhaps more accurately, of Aaron. Both are of the tribe of Levi.

Aaron Speaks for Moses (6:28–7:7). There is one significant difference between God's response to Moses here and that given in 4:15–16. In their first conversation on Mount Horeb, God tells Moses that he will be God to *Aaron*. Here the roles played by Moses and Aaron are presented differently: Moses is to be God directly to *Pharaoh* (7:1). That is, Moses will be an authority figure to Pharaoh rather than just to Aaron. We may think of this as an extra dose of power that God bestows on Moses for the purpose of confronting the king of Egypt. The halting dismissal that Pharaoh gave the first time will not be repeated. From now on, albeit not all at once, Pharaoh, too, will know that Moses is God's representative and is therefore someone to be reckoned with.

Application. As Christians, we have been re-created in God's image. In our union with the Son, we, like him, are true image-bearers. Although not yet fully, we *truly* reflect the image-bearing status that was lost in the garden but that will once again be fully realized in eternity. Such knowledge ought to have an effect on how we live from day to day. It seems an almost natural tendency among the Christians I know (including myself!) to follow the pattern of Moses rather than that of Christ. We have doubts regarding our status as being re-created by the Father, in Christ, for a glorious purpose. We are known by God. He gives us a new start, a fresh beginning, but that high reality does not always translate well in our contact with the world in which we live.

EXODUS 7:8–10:29

Original Meaning

Preview of the Plagues: The Snake (7:8–13). In 7:8–13 Aaron and Moses confront Pharaoh with God's power. The initial audience with Pharaoh (5:1–21) did not go as well as they had hoped, but things will be different now. Aaron casts his staff before Pharaoh and it turns into a snake. Pharaoh's magicians duplicate the feat, but Aaron's snake swallows those of the magicians.

The overarching point is clear: This encounter is an initial sparring between rival gods. This one brief incident embodies the main elements of the ten plagues that follow: God shows his power and Pharaoh resists the obvious conclusion that he is no match for the God of Israel. He should concede victory to Yahweh, but he does not, which will yield disastrous circumstances.

It seems odd that a different Hebrew word is used for "snake" (*tannin*) in this passage from what was used before (*nahash* in 4:3). Might there be some theological significance to these terms? I think so. One way of looking at this is to connect this passage with creation, which we have seen throughout the opening chapters of Exodus and will continue to see in the Exodus narratives. *Tannin* in the Old Testament as well as in the ancient Near East represents the chaotic forces of nature that God conquers at creation. The staff of Aaron, then, as it swallows the *tannin* of Pharaoh, is another example of this theme. The king represents an anti-God, anti-creation force, which the true God conquers.

Snakes represent Egyptian power. The pharaonic headdress, so famous from such popular images as King Tut's coffin, looks like a cobra. In this sense, the swallowing of the snakes is a striking illustration to all present of what Israel's God thinks of Pharaoh's might.

First Plague: Water to Blood (7:14–25). Egypt's greatness as a civilization was wholly dependent on the life-giving waters of the Nile. An attack on the Nile was nothing less than an attack on Egypt itself. The Nile was personified and worshiped as a god in Egypt. An attack on the Nile is in effect an attack on Egypt's gods and, hence, reflects the conflict that drives the Exodus narrative as a whole. The fight is not between Israel and Pharaoh, nor even between Moses and Pharaoh; it is between God and Pharaoh. If the previous sign (staff to a snake) served as a preview of the ensuing plagues, the plague on the Nile was the first toll of the bell that signaled Egypt's demise. Judgment has come.

Although some biblical scholars dismiss outright an event such as water turning to blood as mere fantasy, others admit to its historicity but attribute to it a naturalistic explanation. A common approach is to see the blood of the Nile as an interpretation of the sediment of red earth that occasionally discolors the water. Were this merely a natural phenomenon, Pharaoh could simply have countered, "But this happens all the time, Moses! Can't your God do any better than this?" But the fact that the magicians had to appeal to their "secret arts" (7:22) suggests that there was more here than red sediment pouring into the Nile. Even if the blood can be explained as a natural phenomenon (itself a debatable point), the fact that this phenomenon happened *at God's command* is the central concern of the biblical writer.

The plagues and the Red Sea incident are nothing less than a series of creation reversals: God is unleashing his creative forces on Egypt for punishment but employing those same forces for Israel's benefit. This culminates in the parting of the Red Sea where God, in a new act of creation, once again divides the water from the land (cf. Gen 1:9–10), only to bring those waters crashing down on the Egyptians while the Israelites march safely across.

Second Plague: Frogs (8:1–15). This is the first plague that involves the animal kingdom. As with the previous plague, the relevance of frogs is usually thought to reflect a polemic against Egyptian religion. Heqet, a goddess of childbirth, is depicted in Egyptian art with the head of a frog. A plague of frogs can be understood as an attack on the Egyptian fertility goddess for the Egyptians' previous attempt at eradicating the Israelites' male infant population (Exod 1). In light of this, it is, like the first plague, a pointed theological statement: Yahweh is bigger than the gods of Egypt and will unleash the forces of creation to drive this point home.

With the second plague we see the first sign of Pharaoh's weakness. He sees that Israel's God, despite his magicians' ability to mimic the plague, is a power to be reckoned with. But if Pharaoh is now convinced by the plague of *Yahweh's* might, why does he capitulate only after his magicians produce frogs on their own? It may be that Pharaoh has recognized not only that God has the power to produce frogs but that *only* God has the power to get rid of them. To show the king the extent of Yahweh's might, Moses gives him the choice of when the plague will stop. This timing demonstrates to Pharaoh that this is no trick manipulated by Moses.

As soon as the plague is out of sight, it is also out of mind. Yahweh's second display of his control over creation is not enough to convince the king of Egypt that he is no match. But in the end, we will see that Pharaoh's reluctance to capitulate is less a result of his own stubbornness and more a result of God's desire to keep him pinned against the ropes, long after the bell should have rung. God will not allow Pharaoh to quit so easily.

Third Plague: Gnats (8:16–19). This plague differs from the previous two in that it comes upon us abruptly. The plague of gnats receives the shortest account. This is also the first plague that Pharaoh's magicians are unable to reproduce, which raises the obvious question: Why? The proper answer is to be found perhaps not in the types of creatures but from where they originate. The first two plagues concern the water, which is the life and power of Egypt, politically, economically, and religiously. The gnats, however, come from the dust of the earth, which is not the Egyptian "power source." Their magic and secret arts are empowered by the Nile, but with the third plague the magicians are out of their element. The God of Israel is the God of all nature.

The magicians recognize that they are in over their heads by confessing, "This is the finger of God" (8:19). The Hebrew is somewhat ambiguous, however. It may simply mean, "This is the finger of *a god*." In other words, this is not necessarily a confession on their part that Yahweh has done this. Rather, they may simply be saying, "This is too big for us," or, "This is no trick." In any event, this plague does represent a movement *toward* recognition of Yahweh as the mighty God, which is, in the words of the Exodus narrative itself, one of the central purposes for the plagues.

Fourth Plague: Flies (8:20–32). The identity of the creatures employed by God in this plague is not entirely clear, but a fly of some sort is nearly universally accepted. It is unlikely that this represents a polemic against Egyptian religion since no god was thus depicted. Of more significance is that this plague is from the air, whereas the previous two are of the water (where the Egyptian magicians exercised power) and earth (cf. comments above). God shows the extent of his power by releasing on Egypt creatures from the dust and air as well.

This is the first plague to make a distinction between God's people and the people of Pharaoh. This distinction is maintained throughout the remainder of the plagues (except for the locust plague), either explicitly or implicitly, and culminates in the tenth plague, where the "destroyer" sees the blood of the Passover lamb on the doorframes of the Israelites and passes them by. God unleashes his creation power for the benefit of Israel but for Egypt's destruction. It is not just God's power in the plagues that displays his glory, but his election of Israel as a special people.

Pharaoh does capitulate, but his motive appears to be half-hearted: He will allow the Israelites to sacrifice, but they must remain in Egypt to do so (8:25). Moses's response in 8:26 seems to be, "Oh, no. We don't want to offend the Egyptians' religious sensibilities. They might stone us as a result." Rather than doing a polite political dance with Pharaoh, Moses is really saying: "Don't even try it, Pharaoh. You know as well as I that if we even tried to sacrifice to our God on Egyptian soil, which you believe is home to your gods, the Egyptians will stone us to death. We're a little more clever than that! You think you can give the appearance of letting us have our way, but the end result plays right into your hands! Forget it! No deal! We're leaving just as we said we were. It's all or nothing."

Pharaoh sees that his subtle maneuver has not worked. The hardness of Pharaoh's heart can be seen: "*I* will let you go to offer sacrifices" (8:28, emphasis added). But Pharaoh's repentance is only on the surface. Nevertheless, Moses prays a second time for the cessation of the plague. As we see throughout the narrative, the cessation of the plague is as much a display of Yahweh's might (and correspondingly of Pharaoh's impotence) as the plague itself.

Fifth Plague: On Livestock (9:1–7). Whereas God's "finger" (8:19) brought about the plague of gnats, the force of his "hand" (9:3) is now about to come on the Egyptians. The "hand" of God to deliver the Israelites is a common term in Exodus (e.g., 3:19; 6:1; 13:3) and is normally associated with some mighty act of judgment. The precise nature of the fifth plague itself is not specified, but that is not important. The narrative's focus is clearly on what was afflicted: Egypt's livestock. Perhaps this is a polemic against Egyptian religion, since Hathor, the mother and sky goddess, was depicted as a cow, in which case we see another psychological blow to Pharaoh's perceived source of strength. Some also see a continuation of the creation reversal theme: Animals that were once given to humans for the purpose of being ruled by them (Gen 1:26) are now taken from them.

A problem routinely discussed concerns the reference to *all* the livestock of Egypt having died (9:6). If all the animals died, how can animals be mentioned later (e.g., 9:9, 19)? Probably the writer does not expect the reader to take this "all" literally. The use of "all" in 9:6 simply means "a lot."

Sixth Plague: Boils (9:8–12). This is the first real demonstration to the Egyptians that their lives are in danger. Heretofore it has been pesky frogs and insects or plagues on livestock. Now humans bear the brunt of God's judgment. This plague represents a concrete step toward the ultimate, irrevocable outcome, the death of the firstborn and of the Egyptian army in the sea. Taking soot from the kiln is poetic justice for the kiln-baked bricks the Israelites had to make as Pharaoh's slaves.

The nature of the plague is said to be "festering boils" (9:9). The magicians have lost their power, but Moses and Aaron are far from done. The magicians have been unmasked and exposed, and their magic cannot even save *them*. The effects of the plagues are moving closer to the power center. This plague marks another turning point, for here is the first time that Pharaoh's refusal to heed the sign is attributed to *Yahweh's* hardening of Pharaoh's heart.

Seventh Plague: Hail (9:13–35). The nature of the seventh plague itself is significant. Hail is often associated with an act of judgment on God's part (Josh 10:11; Ps 18:12; Isa 28:2, 17; 30:30; Ezek 13:11–13; 38:22). In fact, weather disturbances of a variety of sorts often represent theophanic language—that is, not just that God is judging, but that God is present.

For the first time in our narrative, Pharaoh is offered some chance of protection. He is advised to "give an order" (9:19) that the livestock be brought inside for safety. This is a test for Pharaoh to see if he will take steps to comply with Yahweh's warning and thus tacitly acknowledge Yahweh's authority. No mention is made whether Pharaoh heeds Moses's advice; only those who fear "the word of the LORD" respond to Moses's warning (9:20). Such laconic prose serves to highlight Pharaoh's stubbornness.

When the plague finally arrives, the hail hurts not only human beings and animals but "everything growing in the fields of Egypt" (9:22). According to 9:25, the hail "beat down everything growing in the fields and stripped every tree." Verse 27 brings us to the point we have been expecting—what appears as a truly heartfelt capitulation by Pharaoh.

However authentic this repentance seems to be at first blush, it is certainly short-lived. No sooner does the plague cease than Pharaoh "sins again" (9:34). Note once again that neither Moses nor his God are taken by surprise by Pharaoh's tactic. As we have seen (9:12, 16), Pharaoh's stubbornness is by God's design.

Eighth Plague: Locusts (10:1–20). After Moses announces the plague, he and Aaron simply leave Pharaoh's presence without giving him any chance to respond. The time for discussion is over. God has hardened Pharaoh's heart. His sorry state stands in sharp contrast to the desire on the part of his court officials to let the Israelites go (10:7). Pharaoh is the last to catch on. His magicians abandoned him long ago (8:19); now his court officials ask, "how long," a clear echo of the words Moses and Aaron are told to bring to Pharaoh in 10:3. This turn of events also serves to move the focal point of God's judgment to where the readers have anticipated since the beginning of the book—to Pharaoh, the anti-God figure of the book. The confrontation between the true God and the false one is now beginning to draw to a climax.

In a certain sense, however, Pharaoh is making measured progress. Here, for the first time, he says he will actually allow the Israelites to leave Egypt—at least, the men (10:11), presumably because only men were needed to fulfill religious obligations. When Moses responds that everybody is to leave, Pharaoh is upset (10:10–11). It has taken now eight plagues for Pharaoh to acquiesce to Moses's request to allow the Israelites to go sacrifice to their God. But at precisely this moment, when, according to Pharaoh's perspective, the judgments should have ceased, God's full intention is made known to Pharaoh, and this contributes to the hardening of his heart—which is exactly what God wants to do with him in the first place.

This unprecedented event of a locust plague brings Pharaoh to his knees. He quickly calls for Moses and Aaron and confesses, once again, that he has sinned (10:16–17). Whether such a confession is truly heartfelt is hardly a debatable point. Moses prays for the plague to be removed, and it is—not for Pharaoh to repent but in order to give him another chance to see God's might. When the locusts are gone, God again hardens Pharaoh's heart.

Ninth Plague: Darkness (10:21–29). A plague of darkness is almost certainly intended to be understood as a polemic against an Egyptian solar deity, possibly Re, a common sun god throughout Egypt's history. For the God of Israelite slaves to have his way with such a powerful Egyptian god would send a clear message. This would speak to Pharaoh even more directly, since Egyptian kings were sometimes referred to as the son of Re. Once again, creation does not work against the Israelites but for them. The phrase "had light" at the end of 10:23 is an almost unmistakable echo of Genesis 1:3, "Let there be light."

Pharaoh once again seems to capitulate, but this time with one seemingly inconsequential stipulation: They are to leave the animals behind. This is likely a ploy by Pharaoh to get the people to return. It is not the case that he needs these animals but that he knows the Israelites do. How long would they survive without them? Pharaoh wants some security that the people will have to rush back.

Furthermore, as Moses points out correctly, if also diplomatically, such a request cannot be reconciled with Pharaoh's concession to allow the Israelites to leave and worship their God (10:24), for without livestock, there is no worship of Yahweh. In other words, without the animals, their release is no release at all. The very purpose for leaving Egypt, we have been told repeatedly throughout the narrative, is so the Israelites can worship the Lord. Thus, Pharaoh's compliance with Moses's request fails to appreciate the reason for the request at its very heart.

Pharaoh receives no chance for rebuttal: God hardens his heart (10:27). How he may have responded if left on his own is not the point, nor should we become preoccupied with reconciling such decisive action on God's part to our own images of how a fair God should behave. God is bringing this contest between himself and Egypt's king to a speedy resolution. At this point, Pharaoh, ironically, cuts off the only means of salvation he has by banishing Moses from his presence forever.

Application. The point of the plagues for today is not so much in what *we* do with it but in having our hearts and minds opened to what *God* has done and thereby understanding *him* better. In the final analysis, the story of the plagues is not about what God does to save *you*, or perhaps even so much a story of how he saved Israel. It is about God, period; for when all is said and done, we all need to be reminded of *him* now and then. The question, then, to ask of our passage is not, "What does this have to do with me?" We must at least first ask, "What does this tell me about who God is?"

Perhaps the application is, in a word, doxological. We praise, that is, worship God for his fearful might and great love, both of which he has employed for the sake of his beloved children. Praising God is not a lesser form of application. Rather, it is what so much of the Bible is driving us toward. It is the goal of redemption itself—not to feel self-important by being part of God's club but to turn ourselves away from our sinful inclination toward self-centeredness and toward God. This, I suggest, is how the ancient Israelites properly "applied" the plagues.

They saw what God had done for them, and they fell back in awe—and they remembered.

EXODUS 11:1–13:16

Original Meaning

The Announcement of the Tenth Plague (11:1–10). The conversation between Moses and Pharaoh that follows is a continuation of the conversation of 10:24–29. It is as if, while leaving, Moses turns to Pharaoh and says, "Oh yes, one more thing before I go." With the announcement of the tenth plague, the confrontation between the two is ended. They will meet once again but only for Pharaoh to capitulate fully to Moses's demand to release the Israelites (12:31–32).

The significance of this plague may be seen partly in that Pharaoh is considered a son of the sun god Re in Egyptian religion—a fact that lends some continuity between the ninth and tenth plagues. This plague can be construed as an attack on Pharaoh's power. In addition to the connection with the ninth plague, the death of the Egyptian firstborn takes us back to the first chapter of Exodus. In 11:4 Moses warns Pharaoh that God is coming at midnight to kill the firstborn of Egypt. This is clearly retribution for Pharaoh's attempt to kill the male children of Israel in chapter 1. The tenth plague is certainly a "measure-for-measure" punishment.

Verses 9–10 summarize both what has gone before and what will soon come about. Pharaoh's heart has been hardened by God (11:9). Pharaoh is being used by God. His actions have been scripted so that God can execute his plan.

Regulations for the Passover and Feast of Unleavened Bread (12:1–28). The drama of the departure from Egypt gives way to what seems like a liturgical interlude. But, as noted above, this is much more than an aside or an intrusion of legal, ritualistic mumbo jumbo. The purpose of these celebrations is clearly for the benefit of those generations who did not participate in the exodus itself. There is more to the exodus than simply delivering slaves from Egypt. God's field of vision is far and broad. The deliverance from Egypt is a new beginning for Israel; from now on, every glance at the calendar will remind them of this fact. It also provides a connection to Genesis and creation. At the exodus, God's people are being "re-created"; they are starting over with a fresh slate.

At this prescribed time, each household is to take a one-year-old male lamb without defect. The blood of the young lamb is to be drained into a basin, a hyssop branch is to be dipped into it, and the tops and sides of the doorframes are to be painted with the blood. This will be a sign that the occupants of that house are placing themselves under God's protection and so will be spared.

Furthermore, they are to "roast" the meat and eat it with "bitter herbs" (12:8) and "bread made without yeast" (12:15). The significance of bitter herbs is not made explicit, although it is tempting to see in them a reminder of the "bitter" service of the Israelites. The journey is to be made in haste, so there is no time to let the dough rise. This meal is to be called "Passover" (*pesah*), and while it is being celebrated, God will bring judgment on Egypt and their gods.

The focus of this section of Exodus is not simply on the regulations. This celebration is to be a lasting, eternal ordinance. Passover is not just an event, and it is not just for one night. The Israelites from now on are to remember this night, impress it on their collective consciousness, and pass it on to their children (12:26–27). By celebrating the Passover and the Feast, God's people in some mysterious sense participate in the exodus themselves.

The Departure from Egypt (12:29–42). God's threat is made good (12:29–30). Loud wailing is heard throughout Egypt. This prompts Pharaoh, once again, to call for Israel's release (12:31–32). He has done so before (9:27–28; 10:16), but here there is a new sense of urgency, for he calls to them at night, right then and there, without a moment to lose, saying as it were: "Just get out! Take what you want, but just get out!"

This is total capitulation on Pharaoh's part. Even the people "urge" the Israelites to leave at once (12:33), which they do, but not before they plunder the Egyptians. The Israelites march out of Egypt through the front door with dignity—not like dogs crawling through the back fence but like God's people. This exaltation of Israel is another humiliation for Egypt.

It is important to note that bread made without yeast is mentioned again in 12:34, 39. The repetition of the regulations for both the Passover and the Feast throughout 12:1–28, in addition to Israel's obedience in following the commands regarding the unleavened bread, underscore how inextricably bound the rituals are to the departure itself. The theology of this narrative will not allow us to separate the departure from Egypt from the rituals that remind the people of the lasting significance of that event.

Two numbers are mentioned in this summary statement, both of which have engendered discussion.

1. We are told that "six hundred thousand men" leave, not including women and children (12:37). Most commentators mention that such a large number would require a total population of roughly two million, a number that the archaeological data do not support. That a large number of Israelites departs is expected, since it was their rapid growth that caused Pharaoh to panic in the first place (ch. 1). But what are we to make of this number? It seems best for us to remain agnostic on this matter.

2. The second number is the 430-year stay in Egypt. Is this an exact number? It seems so, since the four hundred years spoken of in Genesis 15:13 (cf. Acts 7:6) is most likely a round number. Note, too, the emphatic point made that the Israelites left Egypt 430 years "to the very day" after they entered (Exod 12:41). But if this is an exact number, it raises the question why a round number, six hundred thousand, has just been used above. We have come to expect our author to use nonliteral numbers. Recall, too, the genealogy of chapter 6, which refers to four generations from Levi to Aaron—clearly an example of a telescoped genealogy. When all is said and done, how these numbers are to be understood is not clear.

Additional Regulations (12:43–13:16). In 12:43–49 we are given additional Passover regulations. Here again the narrative of the departure is interwoven with liturgical stipulations. The regulations concerning foreigners seem to reflect the fact that non-Israelites left Egypt along with the Israelites (see 12:38). Non-Israelites are not excluded from the meal simply on the basis of their ethnicity. They must, however, put themselves under the sign of the covenant (i.e., circumcision) in order to participate.

We have here an attractive mixture of exclusivism and, ultimately, universalism. This is another hint that God's purpose for bringing the Israelites out of Egypt is for a broader purpose. Although God has throughout made a distinction between the Israelites and the Egyptians, those who are willing may nevertheless partake of this holy celebration. The appeal to circumcision also emphasizes that, although the meal is to be celebrated inside the home, it is more properly considered a community affair. This is not private worship. It is a community of believers bound by circumcision to their covenant God.

The regulations concerning foreigners clearly pertain to the Israelites only after they have left Egypt. Like so much of this chapter, these regulations are future oriented. For example, mention of foreign slaves, temporary residents, and hired workers is not applicable to the Israelites while they are slaves themselves. In light of this, 12:50–51 does not seem to refer to Israel's obedience regarding the regulations that are given immediately before. Rather, this statement seems intended as an object lesson for *future* generations, for whom the foregoing regulations are actually relevant.

Exodus 13:1–16 reiterates and expands on the regulations concerning the Feast of Unleavened Bread (13:3–10) and the future consecration of the firstborn (13:11–16). However redundant such repetition may seem to us, these regulations form the heart of the exodus story. This section specifies that the new first month is the month of Abib (12:2), corresponding to our late March and early April. Exodus 13:5 articulates what has been hinted at earlier, that these more detailed regulations are for future generations.

The Feast of Unleavened Bread is to be scrupulously observed, and its meaning is to be impressed on the children from generation to generation. The ceremony will be "like a sign on your hand and a reminder on your forehead" (13:9). This statement gave rise to the use of phylacteries (see Matt 23:5), which are still used by observant Jews today. They are always to remember who they are—or better, *whose* they are. Israel's identity is a function of what God has done for them.

Likewise, after they enter the land they must be careful to consecrate to God the firstborn of every womb in Israel, whether human or animal, a point made plain later in Exodus 22:29–30. We should understand this ritual in light of the tenth plague itself: Israel as God's son (see 4:22) was redeemed (delivered from Egypt) by the death of Egypt's firstborn sons. The point is that the firstborn of every womb belongs to God, but in the case of the Israelites he will not claim his right fully; a substitute will take their place.

We see, then, a hint of what becomes clearer almost fifteen hundred years later on a cross near Jerusalem: Life comes from death, or better, life can *only* come from death. The tenth plague was not a divine temper tantrum where God flexes his muscles before the Egyptians and really lets them have it. It is the necessary implementation of a redemptive pattern, one that requires death as a means to fuller life. The consecration of the firstborn, therefore, is a reminder of the once-for-all substitutionary death of the beloved firstborn son who is to come.

Application. The most obvious point of application of the Passover is instituted by Christ himself and concerns the church as a whole—the regular celebration of the Lord's Supper by Christians around the world and through all time. As we celebrate the Lord's Supper, we are celebrating our redemption through Christ and the glory that awaits us. But we should also remember that the Lord's Supper is itself a fulfillment of that Israelite meal at an earlier stage of God's redemptive work. By partaking in communion, we are participating in the effects of God's redemptive work that he began to execute in Israel's day and that came to completion on Easter Sunday. It seems, then, that we, like the Israelites, in celebrating the Lord's Supper, are not merely *remembering* what God has done. By partaking of the body and blood of Christ, we are, in some mysterious sense, participating in his death and resurrection.

Perhaps the greatest source of commonality between Passover and the Lord's Supper lies in their future orientation: Neither meal is merely for the historical moment in which it was first instituted. These rituals are to be observed for successive generations. Although this is not a constant refrain in the Lord's Supper (the narrative is much briefer than with Passover), Jesus's command that the meal be done in remembrance of him (Luke 22:19) suggests as much. Moreover, the eschatological references in Luke 22:16 and 18 (which refer to the coming of the kingdom of God) imply a continued observance until such time (see also 1 Cor 11:17–34).

EXODUS 13:17–14:31

Original Meaning. Finally, the Israelites leave Egypt! The story takes an unexpected twist, however. God leads the Israelites on the longer route rather than the shorter. The reason stated is that the shorter route will bring them into military conflict with the Philistines. Yahweh does not want the Israelites to become discouraged and change their minds, so he has them avoid this region entirely. But why, after such an irresistible display of power in Egypt, does the possibility of armed conflict give God such pause for thought (if we can even speak this way)? Can he not continue fighting for Israel and use such military engagement as another source of *encouragement* for the Israelites?

Another strange phrase is that the Israelites march out "ready for battle" (13:18). What sense does this phrase make in the context, since verse 17 tells us that God wants to *avoid* war? The fact of the matter is that the Hebrew word translated in the NIV as "ready for battle" has posed problems for interpreters and translators throughout history, and its meaning is still uncertain. I suggest with other commentators that the military overtones should not be stressed.

It is significant that the move forward out of Egypt does not commence without a look backward: Moses remembers to take the bones of Joseph with them, thus fulfilling the patriarch's wish that his bones be taken to Canaan when the Israelites leave Egypt (Gen 50:24–25). Inasmuch as the reference to Joseph's bones is a reminder of the past, so too is the mention of the pillar of cloud and of fire in 13:21–22. Although this is the first time we encounter these phenomena, which will become prominent throughout the desert period, we have had a hint of them in 3:2 with the burning bush. Hence, we arrive at a partial understanding of the significance of the burning bush: It is another element in the early chapters of Exodus that presages the subsequent events of the exodus.

With 14:1 the narrative shifts back to the action at hand. The departure from Egypt takes another unexpected turn. One would think after all the Israelites have gone through that a speedy, painless, undelayed departure would be in order (especially since God himself ordered the departure to be hasty [12:11]). But God is not finished with the Egyptians yet. He devises what by common military standards is a foolish strategy: March the Israelites toward the sea, leaving them no escape route. Then entice Pharaoh to follow the Israelites so he and Pharaoh can engage in one final battle, one that will show Pharaoh who is truly God.

The paradox of God's plan to harden Pharaoh's heart and of the latter's decision to pursue begins in 14:5. Pharaoh apparently expects the Israelites to go only on a three-day journey, which is what Moses asked for from the beginning and which Pharaoh probably means in 12:31 when he finally gives the command to go. Although the text does not spell this out, it is reasonable to conclude that after three days have elapsed, Pharaoh is told that "the people . . . *fled*" (14:5), meaning that they have kept right on going.

The thought that the Israelites will not come back is too much for Pharaoh, so he chases them. He musters all his power. He calls the best and brightest of Egypt's troops (14:7). The irony, of course, is that Pharaoh has gone to fight Israel's God, the God of the plagues, with mere chariots, horsemen, and troops (14:9). These may be the best of the best, but they will prove of no avail. Things are proceeding according to God's design.

But this turn of events comes as a great shock to the Israelites. In one sense one can hardly blame the Israelites for reacting the way they do (14:10). Still, their moment of panic is not painted by the author in a sympathetic light. Their cry, so soon after they have witnessed God's mighty acts in the plagues, is nothing less than capitulation to the appearance of their immediate circumstances of which the events of the previous thirteen chapters should have cured them. They have still not learned that *their* circumstances are not the final standard on which to view the work of God.

It is in this context of the Israelites'denicrssness in light of what God has done that we should understand 14:14. In Hebrew the last part of the verse is a mere two Hebrew words, which are best translated as "Shut up!" This is no word of comfort but an angry denouncement of Israel's paper-thin faith. This lack of trust in light of the plague narrative is startling, and perhaps it is meant to be. It is a harbinger of things to come.

Why is it, after the *Israelites* cry out in 14:12 and Moses rebukes *them* for their lack of faith in vv. 13–14, that *Moses* is reprimanded by God for crying out (v. 15)? We have seen earlier in Exodus that Moses is a representative of his people. Moses embodies what all Israel will soon come to experience. There is a close identification between Moses and the people he is leading. He is "one" with them, and as such he can represent the people to God. He is the mediator who connects the people to God (e.g., 32:9–14). What we see in 14:15, then, is one reflex of this close identification between Moses and the Israelites: Their guilt becomes his.

What makes the rebuke of 14:15 unusual as well is the

fact that it is over so quickly. It is a curt rebuff and the action resumes. God tells Moses to raise his staff so that the water will be divided and the Israelites can walk through on dry ground (14:16). Once again, as in the plagues, the elements obey Moses's command to bring deliverance for the Israelites but punishment for the Egyptians.

In 14:19 we meet, somewhat unexpectedly, "the angel of God." Who is this figure? We get a hint from 13:21 where we read that the LORD went ahead of the Israelites in the pillars of cloud and fire. The fact that the angel of 14:19 is said to perform the same function leads to the conclusion that he is a concrete manifestation of God's presence with his people.

Verse 21 brings together a number of other statements in Exodus. In 14:16 Moses is told to raise his staff to divide the water. Verse 21 begins in the same way, "Moses stretched out his hand"; but then we read that the LORD is the one who does the parting. Who, then, is responsible for the parting of the sea? As the mediator between the people and God, Moses takes on characteristics of both. The ambiguity is a window into the manner in which God has brought Israel back to himself. Indeed, it is a hint of how God will once again, more than a millennium later, save "Israel" through one who identifies both with the people and with God.

The sea is parted and the Egyptians follow in pursuit, hardened against the horrible end that surely awaits them. But they finally grasp that all hope is lost, for in their pursuit God throws the Egyptians "into confusion" (14:24). This is not mere intellectual confusion, as if they are confused about what course of action to take. This is a *terrifying* confusion, and it takes the form of wheel trouble (14:25)—most likely either that their wheels come off or that they get stuck in the muddy road that once was the bottom of the Red Sea. This tactic hits the Egyptians at their symbol of power—their mighty chariots—which earlier struck fear into the Israelites. It is precisely that element that God mockingly derails.

Verses 29–31 end the narrative of the departure from Egypt. The redemption of the Israelites has been accomplished. The promise to the patriarchs—at least the first installment of that promise—has been kept. Egypt is in their rearview mirror, and the people are about to embark on the second stage of their journey.

Application. As Christians we have crossed over from our slavery to sin and death to a new beginning as God's people, in subjection to him. We who are in Christ have moved out of one country and into another (or more accurately, we are moving toward another country), which itself is a preview of our entrance to the heavenly country that awaits us. The application of the exodus theme to our lives could not be more central.

EXODUS 15:1–21

Original Meaning. This song is a poetic rendering of the narrative of the death of Egypt's army described toward the end of chapter 14. Perhaps more importantly, it is also the gateway to what will be the focus of attention for the remainder of the book. It reminds the reader not only of what has just transpired but gives a glimpse of what will soon take place. It is the bridge that closes the first half of the book and begins the second half. After we leave this passage, Egypt will remain in Israel's rearview mirror and her desert wandering will have begun.

Verses 1–12 recount the destruction of the Egyptians. Verse 13 introduces the purpose for which the Israelites have been permitted to escape the doomed Egyptian army: God "redeemed" his people in order to lead them to his "holy dwelling." What is the identity of this dwelling? We can say that God is bringing his people out of Egypt in order that he might be present with them, and that presence will be manifest in "sacred space" that takes three forms. God's self-revelation at Sinai, although itself a frighteningly powerful reality, is a prelude to the permanence of his presence in the land and the temple.

The building of the temple under Solomon is the culminating stage in which God's presence will abide with his people. For the ancient Israelites, the building of the temple was not an afterthought, nor was it, like church buildings today, "a nice thing to have but you don't really need it." Jerusalem and the temple are where God chooses to make his dwelling. It is his house. As we will see with respect to the tabernacle (the forerunner to the temple), it is more than simply a place where God chooses to dwell. It is constructed in such a way that brings to mind God's first earthly dwelling with his people, Eden—the first "temple." And Eden itself represents God's heavenly throne room, where God's presence is most full.

The allusion to the temple raises another issue. Is this reference not anachronistic, since the temple will not be built until several hundred years after the crossing of the sea? This has led some scholars to conclude that the Song at the Sea was written either in whole or in part well after the events themselves. Such a theory also seems to be supported by 15:14–16. One should not glance over the fact that 15:14–15 mention the Philistines, Edomites, Moabites, and Canaanites. These are peoples with which Israel will not come into contact until well after they leave Sinai. In fact, the Philistines and Canaanites will not be encountered for at least another forty years.

To make such an assertion is not to deny the reality of prophecy in the Old Testament. What I am suggesting is that the *written version of the poem as we have it* is the product of the mature reflection on the crossing of the sea from the point of view of those who have not only the exodus but also the conquest behind them. Moses and the Israelites *did* sing the

Song at the Sea, but the inspired version of that song, the one that achieved canonical status, gives us, the readers of today, the added benefit of seeing how the significance of the exodus was understood and celebrated by Israelites who lived some time after the initial event itself. Most important perhaps, placing such a song with its allusions to subsequent events in the context of the crossing of the sea apparently does not present a problem for the biblical author. However odd this may seem to us, we see once again that our expectations should not exert undue influence in how we approach and what we see in the biblical data.

The song concludes in a most fitting way (15:18). The rule of God is eternal, and if the Israelites are to learn anything from the death of the Egyptians, it is that the exodus story is about more than the exodus. The exodus is about God and who he is. The focus of the song is not on what happens to the Israelites or the Egyptians, but on God, who "reigns for ever and ever." The deliverance of the Israelites is an act in this cosmic drama, a drama that transcends the particulars of the world while at the same time being directly involved in that world.

Application. Although neither I nor anyone else can prove the point, I do not think that the songs of the Old Testament were spontaneous outpourings of worship quickly jotted down and then preserved in a glass jar for future generations to gawk at. They are, rather, models for worship. They were written down precisely so that they could be pondered, studied, and reflected on—and not just for ancient Israelites, but for those who live in the light of the resurrection of God's Son. They are not trophies on a mantel but inspired examples, not so much because they have to be followed word for word but because they give us a glimpse of who God is and, therefore, what our proper stance toward him should be.

EXODUS 15:22–17:7

Original Meaning

Water at Marah (15:22–27). Exodus 15:22–17:7 are three stories that should be taken together. These three rapid-fire stories of rebellion in the desert stagger the imagination. This first story concerns the provision of water at Marah. Three days have passed since the Israelites have crossed the sea. The harsh realities of a desert march set in, and they begin to fear that they may die of thirst.

Moses responds in a manner familiar to us; he "cries out" (15:25)—the same way the Israelites earlier responded to their oppression in Egypt. God, in turn, responds in a manner reminiscent of the plagues and the exodus: He performs another water miracle. The wood thrown into the water reminds us of the wood of the staff that Moses used to perform the two great water miracles of the departure narrative: the first plague and the parting of the sea.

What do the "commands" and "decrees" mentioned in 15:26 refer to? What God is telling his people at this crucial juncture in their young life as a people is: "Stick to me and you will never relive the horrors of Egypt again. If you ignore my law, although you will not return to Egypt physically, you will be treated as they were."

As the reference to commands foreshadows Sinai, the reference to "Elim" (15:27) foreshadows another climactic event in Israel's existence: entrance into the promised land. The numbers twelve and seventy should probably be seen as numbers of completion: The Israelites have plenty of springs for water (perhaps one for each tribe) and palm trees for shade. Elim is a reversal of the desert environment and a foretaste of things to come.

Manna and Quail (16:1–36). Surely, having just seen again God's care for them, rebellion is now out of the question, right? Wrong! A mere month has passed since the departure from Egypt. Is their memory so short?

The Israelites bring what is an absurd charge against their leaders, well in keeping with the absurdity of this passage as a whole (16:3). Only the most callused heart or the most stupid mind could conceive of such a ridiculous charge.

Without any hint of anger or malice, God provides for his people again but with one minor provision. They are only to gather as much bread as they need for each day. This is a test, a point explicitly made in 16:4, to see if they will follow God's instructions. In view of Israel's behavior thus far, a test is certainly in order.

The main purpose of sending manna and quail is certainly not just to test the Israelites or simply to fill their stomachs. It is rather to teach them something about God, or as 16:6 puts it, so that the Israelites will "know that it was the LORD who brought you out of Egypt" (see also 16:12). That the Israelites will "know" is another echo of the departure narrative. God is not yet finished teaching his people who he is. In fact, he has hardly begun.

God provides bread in the morning and quail at night. All he asks is that they gather only as much as they need for one day and not keep any until the next morning (16:16). This gracious provision of food is not to be hoarded, but God is to be trusted anew every day, a lesson they will have to learn for their long trek in the desert and their life as a nation thereafter.

As might be expected, not everyone obeys God's simple instructions to gather only what they need (16:20). Some of the Israelites do not see the necessity of obeying the God who has saved them, and they go out on the Sabbath anyway. A second act of disobedience is met with a stunning rebuke by

God: "How long will you refuse to keep my commands and my instructions?" (16:28). This pattern becomes commonplace throughout the trek in the desert: rebellion in the face of God's clear commands. Lack of obedience will have dire consequences.

Although talk of the quail recedes to the background, the manna takes on added significance (16:33–36). The manna seems to be a foretaste (literally) of the blessings of Canaan. Some of the manna is to be kept in a jar as a perpetual reminder to future generations that God brought the Israelites out of Egypt. The point here is not simply to fill their stomachs but to teach his people something that will be passed on for generations.

Verses 34–35 are significant because of a sudden and anachronistic reference to the "covenant law" (i.e., the ark of the covenant, which is not built until 37:1–9). This is no veiled prophecy but a backward look to the desert era from the perspective of someone who lived at the very least sometime after Moses died. Are these two verses merely editorial additions updating a Mosaic work, or are statements such as this clues as to the authorship of the whole? As interesting as this question is, it need not detain us here, for that would divert attention from the theological focus of the narrative.

Water From the Rock at Rephidim (17:1–7). The third rebellion episode is the famous incident at Rephidim of getting water from the rock (17:1–7). Rephidim is the Israelites' last stop on their way to Sinai, and here they again complain to God about the lack of water. To have two similar episodes so close to each other in the narrative points out the absurdity of Israel's lack of trust in God. Like Pharaoh before them, how many times do they need to see God work before they understand?

As before, Moses responds by reminding the people that a complaint against him is really a complaint against God. Yet when he turns to God, his focus is directed toward himself. Is Moses still harboring doubts about his mission?

Moses is instructed to walk ahead to Horeb with some of the elders and strike a rock with the staff with which he struck the Nile (17:5–6). The imagery is obvious. The water from the rock is another exodus-like event: A staff touches water and the people are saved. The power that has brought the Israelites out of Egypt is the same power that is sustaining them in the desert and that will bring them, eventually, safely into the land God promised to Abraham. It shows that Yahweh is Lord of the desert as he has also shown himself to be Lord of Egypt. The desert is a hostile place, as was Egypt, but both are at God's command.

We have in this passage three stories of grumbling and complaining, which are lovingly and patiently answered by God. Despite all they have seen, perhaps they still need a clearer picture of the holy God who has called them into being. That clearer picture is soon to come on Mount Sinai in chapter 20, but two other episodes must first be addressed.

Application. We are in a privileged position of living in the age in which the kingdom of God has indeed already come in Christ, although we still await its final implementation at his second coming. Still, grumbling and complaining as our Israelite ancestors did remains a live option for us. And thus we must make every effort to guard against this in view of the clearer vision we have of God's goodness that is ours by virtue of the Spirit who dwells in us. Indeed, it is precisely because of the Spirit's indwelling that we are able to resist.

EXODUS 17:8–16

Original Meaning. The Amalekites are a mysterious people. We meet them first somewhat abruptly in Genesis 14:7. When we meet them in Exodus 17, we only learn of their apparently unprovoked attack on the Israelites. The struggles of the Israelites with the Amalekites do not end, however, after crossing the Jordan. They actively stand in their way (Judg 3:13; 6:3, 33; 7:12; 10:12). They are not defeated until Saul's campaign recorded in 1 Samuel 15, although David has to finish the job later (1 Sam 30).

A number of elements of the exodus story are mentioned here for the first time. In 17:9 Joshua is referred to. His name appears four times in this brief passage. Joshua's appearance here foreshadows the many military encounters the Israelites will have later on, especially during the conquest. Since Joshua will be leading the Israelites at that time, it is only fitting that he be prominently displayed here.

In 17:10 we read that Joshua obeys Moses's command to fight the Amalekites. This is another hint of what is to come. It is precisely Joshua's obedience that makes him a fitting successor to Moses. As the Pentateuch progresses, Joshua's obedience is often contrasted to the disobedience of the Israelites.

Verses 11–13 recount one of the more unusual events in this book. Moses goes up to the top of the hill and raises his hands. As long as his hands are up, the Israelites prevail in the battle. Whenever they drop from fatigue, the Amalekites gain the upper hand (no pun intended). Finally, to ensure that his hands remain in the correct position, Aaron and Hur hold Moses's hands up until sunset. It is plausible to understand Hur's and Aaron's helping of Moses as another foreshadowing of things to come: the division of labor in chapter 18.

There is another important first in 17:14. It is one of only a few places in the Pentateuch where Moses is said to "write." Here is another foreshadow of Sinai, where Moses will again be instructed to write at God's command.

It seems best to understand the reference to blotting out the Amalekites in Exodus 17:14 as God's promise of what he will eventually do through Saul and David. Perhaps the events of 17:8–16 do not actually bring an end to these peoples, only their sound defeat and the promise of their inevitable demise.

Reference to an altar in 17:15 is another foreshadow of later events. Moses is commanded to build another altar in 20:24–26, and he builds one at the foot of Mount Sinai in 24:4. This altar connects Moses to the past. The purpose of the altar here is not for sacrifice but, in keeping with the meaning of 17:14, a means by which Israel will remember what God has done for them in the desert. Hence, like the writing in the scroll in 17:14 and several other acts in the previous chapters, the view here is once again toward the future.

Application. The defeat of the Amalekites is an early manifestation of a grander and more basic battle, one that comes to a head on the cross and in the empty tomb. It is one battle that is part of a bigger picture. This is the proper perspective from which to apply the defeat of the Amalekites to our lives. The true identity of the enemies of God's people has finally been unmasked. They are not tribes or nations, kings or princes. They are a spiritual entity, and they have been defeated already.

EXODUS 18:1–27

Original Meaning

Jethro's Acknowledgment of the God of Moses (18:1–12). The word of Yahweh's victory over Egypt has spread so as to reach Jethro's ears. Unlike the nations of 15:14–16 who tremble at such news, Jethro is attracted to it, and so he comes to Moses. These verses form a concrete reminder to the readers of where Moses *and the Israelites* have been. This is why the names of the sons are mentioned. We meet again Gershom, who is a reminder not only that Moses was a foreigner in Midian (see 2:22) but that the Israelites experienced a similar alienation in Egypt. And here we meet Eliezer (18:4), meaning "my God is helper." He is a reminder of deliverance not only for Moses but for Israel.

The meeting between Moses and Jethro in 18:7–8 should jar our memory a bit. Moses here experiences a second reunion with a family member in the desert (cf. the reunion with Aaron in 4:27–28). Moses kisses his father-in-law, just as earlier he kissed Aaron. Exodus 4:28 parallels somewhat 18:8–9: In both places, Moses recounts "everything" God has done or said.

Jethro's confession "now I know" (18:11) is standard Exodus language (see 6:7; 7:5; 8:10; 9:29). Although neither the Egyptians nor the Amalekites get it, Jethro, the Midianite, has learned the lesson of the exodus: "The LORD is greater than all other gods" (18:11). This is, I suggest, the central theological point of this chapter, and it gives us a good hint of why this story should be included in Israel's saga at all. Midian is the one nation that gives a proper response to God's deliverance of his own people.

The reference to "a burnt offering and other sacrifices" (18:12) should not be passed over too quickly. This sacrifice presumably takes place in "the tent" (18:7; likely Moses's tent). Note also the meal that Jethro, Moses, Aaron, and the elders have "in the presence of God" (18:12). The meal provides a hint of what is to come in 24:11.

Jethro's Advice to Moses (18:13–27). Verses 13–27 record the second topic of this chapter: Jethro's advice to Moses to divide the labor of judging the people's disputes. Moses is said to "judge" (18:13), which in context means arbitrating legal issues between parties based on the standard of "God's decrees and instructions" (18:16). This adjudication between parties proves too much for Moses. He is dead tired after keeping up the pace all day. Jethro sees what is happening to his son-in-law and offers sound advice: Get some help.

Jethro's advice (18:17–23) is detailed and may indicate that he had experience in these matters, being a priest.

1. Moses is to have superiority over his chosen helpers in that he is the "people's representative before God" and is to "teach" the people God's laws (18:19–20).
2. Moses is to "select capable men," each of whom is to act as judge over an assigned group of people for the "simple" cases (18:21–22); Moses will get only the "difficult" ones (18:22). Note also the qualifications of these judges. They are to be "men who fear God, trustworthy men who hate dishonest gain" (18:21).

Moses listens to his father-in-law and puts the plan into operation (18:24–26). It seems that the reason why Moses obeys Jethro is not to be polite or to try it to see if it works. Jethro's advice is also God's command. Verse 23 of the NIV has, "If you do this *and God so commands*, you will be able to stand the strain" (emphasis added), which assumes that the second clause (in italics) is part of the protasis (the "if" clause). This may be the case, but it makes more sense to read this clause as Jethro adding "punch" to his advice: "If you do this—God commands you—you will be able to stand the strain." By dividing the labor, Moses was following God's order given through Jethro.

Jethro and Moses part company in 18:27. Presumably Moses's family remains behind since Gershom's descendants serve as priests (Judg 18:30), although Zipporah is not mentioned again. Interestingly, according to Numbers 12:1 Moses had a Cushite wife. This may be a second wife in addition to Zipporah or a wife after the death of Zipporah (not recorded); any suggestion is conjecture.

Application. As Exodus 18 shows us, the nations are part of God's plan. This is no less true today. No, this is not going to be a pep talk for overseas missions. Rather, I wish to stress that the response of the nations to God's acts, as seen adumbrated in Jethro's response, has *already* happened. The church is universal. The call to preach the gospel (Acts 1:8) has come to pass. Belief in the God of Israel is no longer located in the tiny strip of land in the Middle East. Nothing more needs to be done for God's general purpose to bring the gospel to all the world to be "accomplished." This is *not* to say that missionary activity can cease! It means that the dividing wall of hostility between the Jews and gentiles has been broken down because of the resurrection of Christ (Eph 2:14–18). The gospel now goes freely to the whole world.

EXODUS 19:1–25

Original Meaning. God's first speech to Israel is a simple message: remember. This is the basic content of 19:4. At the beginning of God's self-disclosure to them, the Israelites are to think back to what he has done in destroying Egypt and bringing them to himself.

Not only are the Israelites to remember what God has done but that memory is to motivate them to *obey* (19:5). The Israelites are not to keep the law in order for God to save them. The law he now gives is what is expected of a people *already* redeemed. The people do not earn their salvation, but once saved, they are obligated to act in a manner worthy of their high calling. This is true in the New Testament as well. The clause "keep my covenant" (19:5) is a call to Israel to remain faithful to the covenant initiated with Abraham—the covenant that will be given greater substance in the following chapters.

Note especially the three consequences of Israel's obedience (19:5–6): Israel will be a treasured possession, a kingdom of priests, and a holy nation. Israel is royal property, purely by virtue of God's own will and desire. As holy and priestly, Israel is the means by which God will *bring the nations to have knowledge of him*. God is not just making a statement about Israel's new inner character as a special and separate people. He is also making a statement about the *international implications* of Israel's favored status. Israel is a holy and priestly nation that God has chosen to work through to bring about his broad, far-reaching plan.

Moses descends the mountain for the first time (cf. 19:3) and tells the elders what is required of them (19:7–8). They respond with an unqualified "yes." We will see, however, that much of Israel's subsequent history falls far short of this enthusiastic and perhaps well-intentioned assent.

Moses goes back up the mountain and brings Israel's answer to the Lord (19:8b); their second conversation is recorded in 19:9–13. In order to obviate any subsequent opposition to Moses, God will speak to Moses directly out of the cloud in the hearing of the people.

Verses 10–13 relate another set of instructions: The Israelites are to prepare themselves to approach the mountain and meet their God. They are about to do something that no other nation has ever done—to meet their heavenly King and listen to his voice. They are given two days to prepare themselves, and part of that preparation involved the outward act of washing their clothes. Perhaps this is a sign of respect.

The fact that limits are placed around the mountain accents the holiness of God's dwelling. You do not simply walk up to it in street clothes and chat with the occupant. The way is barred. You must prepare yourself first, and then you must wait until the occupant is willing to receive you.

Having been consecrated, the people are now ready to meet God. But it is certainly not anything they may have expected. Not only are they surrounded by thunder, lightning, and thick clouds (standard theophany language) but by a loud trumpet blast, too. This trumpet blast signals to the people to approach God (cf. 19:13), which they do, coming to the foot of the mountain (19:16–17). The climax of the scene comes when Moses and God converse, thus fulfilling what was promised in 19:9. Unfortunately, we are not told what they speak about. It is clear that 19:20–25 does not represent the content of this discussion, since it is further information Moses is to bring to the people. Apparently, all thedenicle need to hear is that Moses and God do speak to each other.

God's command to Moses in 19:21–22 is difficult to understand fully in the context. Although there is confusion for us in some areas, many elements come through loud and clear. If we look past the confusion, we will see that God repeats essentially the same warning three times (19:12–13, 21–22, 24).

Verse 25 reports Moses's third descent down the mountain (cf. vv. 18, 20). He again reports to the people what God has said. The Israelites have been reminded of what God has done for them, encouraged by their privileged status as his special people, exhorted to keep the covenant, and given a lesson in what it means to be in God's holy presence. These things have prepared them to listen to the words of God and to hear the laws their holy God requires of them, which will further define them as servants of God, both now and for generations to come.

Application. First Peter 2:4–12 is not interested in making an abstract connection between Israel and the church. The purpose of making the equation is for practical reasons. The church as the new Israel is to exhibit impeccable behavior, which is what Old Testament Israel essentially failed to do. The intention of God to reconcile the world to himself through a select and holy people—a plan first announced in Genesis 12:1–3 and more clearly in Exodus 19:5–6 and that has come to a climax in the death and resurrection of Christ—is something God is still working out. As instruments of God's plan, we are to live holy lives before God *and humanity*. This is a just summary of the path that all Christians are to walk. Both elements are crucial.

EXODUS 20:1–21

Original Meaning

The Setting and Prologue (20:1–2). Verse 2 reminds Israel *who God is and what he has done*. God has brought the Israelites out of Egypt. The relationship between them has already been established. The law, in other words, is connected to grace. It is based on God's gracious act of saving his people; it is not a condition of becoming God's people.

The Ten Commandments (20:3–17). (1) *First commandment (20:3).* This first commandment is the basis from which the other nine derive their meaning. If the prologue provides the motivation for obeying the commandments, the first commandment provides the conceptual framework from which the others are to be understood. Yahweh alone is God, and he is speaking to the people who belong to him.

(2) *Second commandment (20:4–6).* Idols that the Israelites had seen were idols of other gods, a ubiquitous ancient custom. This command is longer than the first, for it includes a threat to those who disobey and a promise to those who obey. God is jealous for his people to remain truly faithful to him.

(3) *Third commandment (20:7).* Even today, many Jews make no attempt to use or even pronounce the name, referring to God simply as *Hashem* (Heb. for "the name"). This is the name by which Israel, the saved people of God, his treasured possession, his holy people, know him. This is why his name is to be treated with utmost respect.

(4) *Fourth commandment (20:8–11).* The Israelites are told to "remember" (20:8) the Sabbath day. This is not merely a cognitive exercise any more than remembering your wedding anniversary means simply recalling it. As any forgetful husband can well attest, some concrete demonstration of remembrance is expected. Biblical remembrance requires action. "Keeping it holy" (20:8) should be understood as the resulting effect of remembering. "By remembering the Sabbath, Israel, you are treating the day as separate from the other six days. You are treating it as holy."

(5) *Fifth commandment (20:12).* Honoring one's parents means long life in the land. But this should not be understood in an individual sense. The reference to length of stay in the land is a warning to the Israelites as a whole (cf. Deut 4:40; 5:32–33), a fact that underscores just how important this command is.

(6) *Sixth commandment (20:13).* The command clearly does not mean that *any* taking of a human life is wrong. Killing is something both God and the Israelites, by God's approval, do throughout the Old Testament. The Hebrew word translated "murder" is a common one in the Old Testament. It is a restricted term, generally referring to the killing of someone who is not an "enemy" of the people. In other words, it is not used in contexts of war or just punishment for a crime.

(7) *Seventh commandment (20:14).* Maintaining the physical sanctity of marriage is a central element in the maintenance of social cohesion, which is not a small consideration in light of Israel's impending entrance into the land, but it is also an earthly symbol of the intimacy between God and his people.

(8) *Eighth commandment (20:15).* Clearly the Israelites have some notion of ownership and rightful property for such a command to make sense. Stealing from one's "neighbor," as with the seventh commandment, is a threat to society. It breeds distrust and strife.

(9) *Ninth commandment (20:16).* Giving "false testimony" refers not to lying in general but to bearing false testimony in court. Israelite justice depended on witnesses to a much larger extent than in modern times.

(10) *Tenth commandment (20:17).* Coveting refers to an inward desire that, if fanned, will lead to action. In driving home the importance of this command, the Israelite is taken on a tour of his surroundings. Look around you: your neighbor's wife, his servants, his animals—in fact, anything that belongs to him. Coveting his wife will lead to adultery and the breaking of the seventh commandment. Coveting his servants, animals, or other property will lead to breaking the eighth commandment.

The Epilogue (20:18–21). The people beg Moses not to have God speak to them again. Verse 20 can be paraphrased: "Do not be afraid. God is giving you a taste of himself so that this memory will stick with you to keep you from sinning." The people's fear is to be tempered by the fact that God is giving them this experience for a reason. A debilitating fear will give way to a healthy fear, one that will result in faithfulness on their part.

Application. As we apply the Ten Commandments to our lives as Christians in today's world, it is important that we keep in mind what they are. They are a charter of conduct for a people already redeemed, who already participate in God's redemptive plan by being walking and talking examples of what it means to be created in God's image. They are, in other words, commands of God to be understood in a redemptive context, a context that defines their promulgation in the Old Testament and reiteration in the New.

EXODUS 20:22–23:19

Original Meaning. We come now to a complex body of laws known as the book of the covenant. It covers a wide variety of legal issues, including worship, protection of property, and personal injury. It is no accident that the book of the covenant begins and ends with matters of worship. The structure of the book of the covenant reminds us that secular and sacred intertwine. More precisely, there is no "secular" realm in ancient Israel. God's law to Israel pertains to *all* matters of conduct.

Worship: Idols and Altars (20:22–26). Both the Ten Commandments and the book of the covenant begin the same way, with a declaration that Yahweh and Yahweh alone is worthy of Israel's worship and is therefore to be obeyed. Why are instructions on altars needed? The central point of this section is that the attention the writer pays to worship at the outset of the book of the covenant indicates the proper context within which to view the laws that follow. There is, in other words, a triad of (1) *redemption* from Egypt that prepared Israel for meeting God, (2) proper *worship* of God, and (3) *law*. These three elements are not to be dissociated from each other if any one of these elements is to be understood properly.

Social Responsibility (21:1–22:17). *Freedom and servitude for Hebrew slaves (21:1–11).* Why does this main body of regulations begin with a lengthy discussion of Hebrew slavery? In the context of the book, the reason seems obvious: The Israelites were slaves themselves in Egypt.

Having said this, however, one curious element strikes us immediately. If Israel ought to be so concerned not to abuse others as they had been in Egypt, why not abolish slavery altogether? It seems that people, even "free" Israelites, could be owned by other Israelites. Whatever ethical misgivings modern readers may have regarding 21:1–6 are augmented in 21:7–11. Male slaves may go free in the seventh year, but female slaves may not. Moreover, it seems that Hebrew fathers could sell their own daughters into slavery!

The point of the law is not to question the existence of this social condition but to give clear guidelines for how people in such a condition must be treated. The writer's focus is on the proper, godly treatment of those Israelites on the lowest rung of the social ladder. They are fellow countrymen, the people of God, a part of the kingdom of priests and the holy nation (see 19:6).

Humans injuring other humans (21:12–27). Like the previous section, this one also deals with proper treatment of fellow Israelites—this time personal injury in general. The first point made here is a distinction between an intentional, premeditated killing and unintentional, accidental killing.

One's conduct toward one's parents is also prominent here. Verses 15 and 17 mandate death to anyone who attacks or curses his or her parents. The NIV text note suggests "kills" as an alternate translation to "attacks," and this is likely correct. What it means to curse one's parents is ambiguous. It seems best to think of this as some egregious act of disrespect or repudiation, for example, neglecting their duty to care for their parents in old age.

The laws mentioned in 21:12–17 are grievous enough to result in certain death to the perpetrator. The remaining laws in this section (21:18–27) deal with more ambiguous matters. Again, they do not cover any and every circumstance but merely a sampling.

Verses 22–25 are among the best known in the book of the covenant for two reasons: Many find a biblical argument against abortion in 21:22, and 21:23–25 contain the famous phrase "eye for eye, tooth for tooth." Verse 22 suffers from some of the same ambiguities as does the rest of the book of the covenant and should therefore be used with great caution in any modern debate. Even if it were relevant for the debate, a convincing argument would have to be mounted for why the principles behind this law should be adhered to but not many of the others in the book of the covenant (e.g., 22:16–17).

The remaining law in this section (21:26–27) concerns personal injury to a servant. The slave's injury is not on the same level as a free man's, otherwise the restitution would be the same. The freedom granted the servant simply means that the master who did the injuring suffers merely financial loss; he can always get another servant. The servant, however, is without an eye or tooth. Moreover, he or she must now find some other manner of support.

Various injuries involving animals (21:28–36). We move from injuries inflicted between human beings (slave and free) to injuries involving animals, either inflicted by them or to them. These laws clear up a matter left ambiguous in the preceding laws concerning the value of a slave's life. In 21:28–32, the clear implication is that the life of a free person is worth more than that of the servant. Whereas injury by animals as a result of human negligence deserves some recompense, so too injury done to animals by negligent humans (21:33–34). The final scenario is loss of one animal by another (21:35–36). Having begun with human against human, the laws then treat in turn animal against human, human against animal, and now animal against animal.

Concerning matters of property (22:1–17). This section extends not simply to 22:15, as is indicated by the NIV headings, but through 22:17. The NIV is somewhat generous in its estimation of the status of certain classes of women in Israelite society. The only reason for separating the case of a virgin from the cases of property in 22:1–15 is the assumption that virgin daughters are more than simply property. This may be the case, but the specific law in 22:16–17 has more in common structurally with what precedes than with what follows.

A virgin who is not pledged to be married and who is seduced by a man shall become that man's wife (this is not rape, hence some consent on the part of the woman is implied). It is important to understand this law from the point of view of the wronged party: It is not the virgin who suffers a loss in such a situation but her father. As I suggested above, this law falls under the category of "property damage," not "social responsibility." If a virgin has sexual relations with a man outside of marriage, she is "damaged goods," which means the father will not be able to exact the bride-price for her. That is why the man who seduced her will have to make restitution *to him*, not to her (22:17). Marriage, which would help the daughter save face, is something the father can refuse, but the bride-price must be paid to him nonetheless.

Worship and Social Responsibility (22:18–23:19). *Worship: sorceresses, bestiality, and false sacrifices (22:18–20).* These three laws are brief. Sorcery probably involves calling on forces other than Yahweh, which thus constitutes an act of false worship. Bestiality (22:19) is a religious practice of Israel's neighbors. There is more to the prohibition than simply the fact that bestiality is a sick, demented, gross act. This law should be understood within a cultic context.

The third law Is the most explicitly cultic of the three: Sacrificing to other gods is punishable by death. Note that the Hebrew used here indicates the surrendering of something to God for the purpose of utter and complete destruction. Throughout Joshua, for example, this word is used with respect to the destruction of Canaanite cities.

Social responsibility: oppression and loans (22:21–28). These three laws highlight what we have seen throughout the book of Exodus: God loves his people dearly. He is protective of them against any abuse, including abuse at the hands of fellow Israelites. God's people must not show any sign that they are becoming like the Egyptians who oppressed them. This includes both in how they worship and in how they treat others, whether fellow Israelites or aliens living among them.

Verse 28 forms the conclusion to this section. The warning not to blaspheme God or curse the rulers pertains to the previously stated laws. Blasphemy should not be understood as simply some abstract verbal assault on God but a failure to follow God's law. So, too, cursing the rulers shows contempt for civil authorities whose job it is to uphold God's law.

Worship: offerings, firstborn, holiness (22:29–31). The Israelites are reminded here that their best belongs to God. Of course, a human firstborn was to be redeemed with (i.e., substituted by) a lamb, as could a firstborn donkey (13:12–13). Firstborn cattle and sheep also belong to God, but they must stay with their mothers for seven days and given over on the eighth day. There is a clear parallel here with circumcision on the eighth day (Gen 17:12), another type of dedication to God. This period of time likely represents a period of completeness after which the subject is adequately "prepared" to be given to God.

Verse 31 contains another reminder—that Israel is to be God's "holy people" (an echo of 19:6). What are we to make of the specific law mentioned in 22:31b? Why should the meat of torn animals be such an issue? This law must be read in light of what we see in Leviticus 17:15 and 22:8. Eating meat torn by wild animals (carrion) makes one unclean.

Social responsibility: testimony in court, an enemy's animal, oppression (23:1–9). The final cycle of laws pertaining to social responsibility focuses mainly on matters of legal justice. The godly Israelite is to make no attempt at perverting justice by making the guilty look innocent. This law, and the others that follow, are explications of the ninth commandment. God's people are called upon to do what *is* right, not what *feels* right.

Verse 3 is a bit surprising in the context of other laws we have seen in the book of the covenant. The rights of the poor are emphasized, but here the Israelites are warned not to take this to the extreme. No one should assume that the rights of the poor are emphasized to the point that favoritism can be shown them! This is no more justice than is abuse of the poor. Verse 3 must, however, be read in conjunction with 23:6. Although the poor are not to be shown favoritism, they are not to be denied justice either.

Verses 4–5 are case laws. They envision situations in which one Israelite should go out of his way to help another. In fact, you are even to help your enemy. These verses are aimed not at the welfare of animals but that of the enemy. "Love your enemies" is not a sentiment found only in the New Testament.

The final verse of this section repeats the essence of 22:21. Israelites are to deal fairly (lovingly) with everyone in their midst: fellow countrymen, whether poor or rich (23:1–3, 6–8); enemies (23:4–5); and even non-Israelites, the "foreigners." As a kingdom of priests, they are not to oppress those to whom they are to reflect the glory of God.

Worship: Sabbaths and festivals (23:10–19). The book of the covenant ends with a number of regulations concerning worship, namely, laws regarding the Sabbath, the three annual festivals, and stipulations regarding sacrifice, presumably relating to these festivals.

The Sabbath year is an extension of the fourth commandment (see Lev 25:1–7). Note that the means by which the Israelites are to "keep it holy" (see Exod 20:8) is not by offering the produce of the seventh year to God in the form of a cultic offering but by leaving it for the poor (23:11). We should be careful not to pit the humanitarian concerns of 23:12 against the more "theological" motive of 20:11. They most certainly complement each other.

Verse 13 serves as a sort of transition to the cultic matters of 23:14–19. I suggest it serves to introduce the following topic: faithfulness to God. Specifically, Israel is not to invoke the names of other gods—a reiteration of the first two commandments. It is fitting to end the book of the covenant with a reminder to the Israelites that they are a worshiping community, a reality that extends to every area of life but that is most clearly seen in the ceremonies by which they worship God.

This leads us to a number of cultic regulations that the Israelites are commanded to keep (23:14–17). The three annual festivals correspond to three different stages in Israel's agricultural year. The command to keep these festivals is given in 23:14 and 23:17, thus framing the description of the festivals themselves.

The first feast is the Festival of Unleavened Bread. This ceremony is to be understood in conjunction with the Passover night described in Exodus 12. This ceremony is a yearly commemoration of that deliverance. The allusion to offerings at the end of 23:15 indicates that the Festival of Unleavened Bread is more than a private celebration of Passover but a community festival complete with offerings of some sort. The offerings of 23:15 are most likely agricultural in nature.

The second feast is the Festival of Harvest, also referred to as the Festival of Weeks (34:22). This feast entails offering to God the firstfruits of one's produce; it symbolizes the harvest that is to come. The third feast is the Festival of Ingathering, celebrated at the end of the agricultural year. The land's ability to produce is a gift from God. It is at these agriculturally significant times that Israel is to be reminded that all these gifts come from God. Every element of life, whether social or agricultural, is to be lived out in God's presence. He is the source and the goal of everything they do. The law comes *from* God, and through obedience Israel will move closer *to* him.

The injunction against yeast (23:18) certainly reflects the Feast of Unleavened Bread. Nor may the fat remain until morning (see 12:9–10). The reference to firstfruits (23:19) likewise suggests a connection to the Feast of Harvest. The final law in the book of the covenant is one that for some captures the obscurity (and contemporary irrelevance) of the Israelite legal system: "Do not cook a young goat in its mother's milk" (23:19). What does this mean? A number of explanations have been suggested but they are all speculative. It seems to have been a practice of Israel's neighbors, as is suggested in a Ugaritic text, so it may be that this injunction is a polemic against pagan practices.

Application. It is important to communicate that the book of the covenant is not meant to be mined today for those laws that seem applicable. The law reflects the nature of God, but it does so in a historical context. The book of the covenant is *God's* law, but it reveals God to a people living at a particular point in time and for whom he has a particular purpose. I remain convinced that what we as Christians are supposed to glean from the book of the covenant is an understanding of the nature of God and what he requires of his people, what Jesus summarized as loving God and treating your neighbor as yourself. The Christian's view of the law must first be rooted in the knowledge of what God has already done apart from the law. He has called us from darkness into light.

EXODUS 23:20–33

Original Meaning. Worship and land have formed the backdrop for much of the book of the covenant and even Exodus as a whole. Regarding worship, the Israelites were redeemed from Egypt so that they might "serve" Yahweh rather than Pharaoh. The promise of the land is implicit throughout the book of the covenant since its laws form a manifesto for how the Israelites are to conduct themselves in the land they are about to receive. By focusing on these two central themes of worship and land, the writer not only reiterates what he has said before but prepares his readers for what is to come.

Verses 20–26 fall into two parts, each with a command followed by consequences of either obeying or disobeying the command. Listening to the angel will result in the nations being driven out of Canaan (23:20–23). By worshiping Yahweh alone, Israel is promised well-being, long life, and offspring (23:24–26).

What is somewhat striking here is the warning that the angel will not forgive Israel if they rebel. What are we to make of this, especially in light of the fact that forgiveness is precisely what we find throughout Israel's desert experience? Hyperbole is not unknown in the Old Testament, and this is what we may be dealing with here. It simply will not do to give a warning in any other way! Imagine God saying, "Listen to the angel, but if you do not, don't worry, I'll forgive you anyway." This could hardly be! A warning *must* be made in no uncertain terms. It is by obeying the angel that Israel will possess the land (23:22–23).

Verses 27–30 continue the theme of Israel's entrance into the land but adds a somewhat expected detail: The conquest will take place little by little. As the angel will go ahead of the Israelites in their journey, God says that he will send his "terror" (Heb. *emah*) ahead of the Israelites to throw the nations into confusion (23:27). This "terror" is the report that Canaan will hear of Yahweh's dealings with the Egyptians.

Verses 29–30 anticipate a problem that this fledgling community will encounter. Their numbers are not yet large enough to take complete and sudden possession of the land. Canaan certainly supports a much larger population than the Israelites who will be displacing them. Simply annihilating or chasing off the inhabitants will leave the land to be overrun by wild animals. Its arable land cannot be cultivated in the absence of a sufficient number of workers and will therefore become desolate. Hence, the conquest will take place little by little, in stages—just how many years we are not told—until the population can sustain the land God will give them.

Verses 31–33 reinforce the notion of Israel's complete possession of the land. The general borders God intends for Israel's possession are given. Verses 32–33 remind the Israelites once again about worshiping other gods. What anchors the message of this entire section is Yahweh's insistent teaching to his people that they belong to him and him alone. If they do not remember this foundational fact, if they do not let this truth seep into their hearts, the laws are nothing but hollow precepts and the promised land nothing but another plot of earth.

Application. The "angel" is still with God's people. We do not look back at the abiding presence of the angel with the Israelites and heave a sigh of resignation for bygone days. The angel is more deeply felt now than ever before. The spirit of the risen Christ, the Holy Spirit, is always with us. This is Jesus's final statement to his disciples (Matt 28:20). Christ does now what the angel did for the Israelites. He is truly with us at every step in our journey. He was there at our redemption, not with arms folded waiting to see if we would make the right choice but calling us into his presence. And having called us, he now walks ahead of us to guard us and guide us home.

EXODUS 24:1–18

Original Meaning. Moses, after receiving the instructions of 24:1–2, makes his way down the mountain to tell the people what God has told him. Likely "words" and "laws" (v. 3) are a shorthand reference to the Ten Commandments and the book of the covenant. The people respond in almost the exact same words of utter enthusiasm as before. This enthusiasm is short-lived.

After recording God's words to him, Moses builds an altar (24:4). Burnt offerings are typically made for atonement for sin and consecration, that is, devotion and commitment to God. Fellowship offerings celebrate fellowship with God. The nature of these two offerings parallels how the blood of the sacrifices was used. One half was sprinkled on the altar while the other half was put in bowls (24:6) and was sprinkled on the people (24:8). The former represents sin atonement (burnt offerings), the latter fellowship.

After this confirmation of the covenant, we proceed to the next scene, a return to what was introduced in 24:1–2: Moses, Aaron and his sons, and the elders "went up and saw the God of Israel" (24:9–10). The Israelites are at a crucial point in their redemptive journey. The covenant stipulations have just been given and the covenant confirmed by the sprinkling of blood. By showing himself to the leaders, God is giving them an added dose of his presence to solemnize what has just happened and to prepare them for what is to come.

When meeting the heavenly King, their gaze does not rise higher than his feet. But even this low view of God is startling. Even this vision of God's feet and the ground under his feet is too much for words. The best the writer can do is to say it is "*something like* a pavement" (24:10, emphasis added). This pavement is lapis lazuli. This is a striking gem of opaque blue. Its beauty and blue color is used to describe not only the clear-as-sky pavement in 24:10 but also the throne of God in Ezekiel 1:26 and 10:1. The company on the mountain eat and drink a "covenant" meal (Exod 24:11; cf. 18:12).

After the meal it is time for Moses to leave the others behind and proceed up the mountain (24:12–18). Joshua is allowed to come part of the way, although just how far is not mentioned. While Moses is meeting with God on Sinai, Aaron and Hur are in charge of settling disputes. As Moses ascends the mountain, he has left things in what he no doubt thinks are trustworthy hands: his older brother Aaron, whom God appointed as his partner, and Hur, a respected member of the community. The anger he shows later is an appropriate response (32:19–20).

There is a clear connection between Mount Sinai and the tabernacle. Both are where God's glory resides in the form of a cloud. Sinai is not a reflection of the tabernacle but the other way around. God meets with his people at Mount Sinai, and the tabernacle is a way of making that presence "portable." God's glory rests on the tabernacle as it does on Mount Sinai. This is why the tabernacle is to be built according to the divine *pattern*, according to what is given Moses *on the mountain* (25:9, 40).

Application. The application of this aspect of Exodus 24 should not be sought so much on the private level but on the communal and theological level. We do not continually confirm our covenant with God; this was done once for all in Christ. What the church does do, however, is celebrate the

Lord's Supper as a continual reminder both of what God has done in Christ and of the final eschatological meal to be shared by the universal church in the presence of God at the end of the present world order.

EXODUS 25:1–31:18; 35:1–40:33

The Tabernacle. The matter of the tabernacle spans thirteen of the remaining sixteen chapters of Exodus. The ultimate goal toward which God is leading his redeemed people is possession of the land. On the way toward that end we have the more immediate goal of the giving of the law and the building of the tabernacle and religious system it represents, both of which will be of central importance once the land is conquered. As I hope to make clear, the building of the tabernacle is more than simply a matter of building a worship site in the desert. It is a piece of heaven on earth. Even though the list of building materials, lampstands, and incense altars may seem repetitive and tedious to modern readers, it is precisely the mass of this material that alerts us that we have arrived at the heart of the matter from the ancient point of view.

This being said, however, the length and repetitive nature of this material pose a problem for organizing this section of the commentary. For one thing, chapters 35–40 essentially repeat the content of chapters 25–31 with only insignificant and minor additions and/or deletions. I have thus decided to group together the parallel sections under one heading. For example, immediately below we begin with the writer's treatment of the offerings for the tabernacle, which is his topic not only in 25:1–9 but also 35:4–9. To treat each passage in a separate Original Meaning section is both tedious and pointless.

To say this, however, is not to minimize the organization that the biblical writer himself deemed necessary. In fact, I must confess it goes against my grain to treat this material in the way I have planned. It is far too common for commentaries and other monographs to deal with the entire tabernacle section first and then treat as almost an appendix the "intervening" chapters 32–34, without trying to account for why the biblical writer set things up the way he did. My point in organizing the material in this way is not to lend credence to such a misapprehension of the biblical text but todenicrtate the goals of this commentary as a whole.

Original Meaning

Offerings for the Tabernacle (25:1–9; 35:4–9). This is the beginning of what God speaks to Moses upon entering the cloud (24:18). The reader is provided with a list of the materials that are to be brought before God for the purpose of building the tabernacle and related items. It is a fitting introduction to the tabernacle section in that the list of materials amounts to an overview of what is to come. And this is no list of simple, everyday items one might expect of desert dwellers. We have precious metals, expensive yarns and linen, acacia wood, olive oil, spices, precious stones, and gems. The only possible source of these items that can be inferred from the text is the Egyptians themselves, whom the Israelites plundered (12:36), although it bears mentioning that nowhere is this connection made explicit.

God commands Moses to build the tabernacle precisely according to the pattern he will give (25:9). The reason for such precision seems to be implied in 25:8: "And I will dwell among them." God intends to be present with his people in a way he has not been before. The suitable abode for God is one that reflects the "pattern" given to Moses. This is an early indication that the tabernacle is an earthly symbol of a greater, heavenly reality; we will return to this idea at various points.

One important point should be mentioned here, mainly because this will be developed more clearly later on and seems to form a central concern of the biblical writer. Commentators for centuries have noticed that the phrase "the LORD said to Moses" occurs seven times in chapters 25–31. The first six concern the building of the tabernacle and its furnishings (25:1; 30:11, 17, 22, 34; 31:1), while the final introduces the Sabbath command (31:12). It seems clear that the purpose of this arrangement is to aid the reader in making the connection between the building of the tabernacle and the seven days of creation, both of which involve six creative acts culminating in a seventh-day rest.

It should also be mentioned that the theme of sanctuary building by divine pattern and over a seven-day span is not unique to Israel. As early as approximately 2200 BC the Sumerian King Gudea of Lagash undertook a similar project. As we have seen elsewhere in Exodus, the manner in which God reveals himself to his people, at least in terms of its basic structures and patterns, would not seem odd to the ancient Israelites.

The Ark (25:10–22; 37:1–9). We now begin with specifics. The first thing to be mentioned is the ark. This may strike us as a bit unexpected. We would expect first to have the instructions for the tabernacle, since this structure will house the articles like the ark. The "displacement" of the ark here is further suggested by the fact that the actual building of the ark in 37:1–9 *follows* the building of the tabernacle in 36:8–38. So the sequence here is reversed. Why?

Apparently the writer wants to stress the importance of the ark. By placing the ark first, the reader's attention is drawn to the central concern of the tabernacle narrative. The ark is the focus of God's presence with his people, the central point of contact between heaven and the tabernacle, the earthly symbol of heaven.

The holiness of the ark is no doubt why it is not to be touched. You cannot simply walk up to it, pick it up, and move it as you might a basket of laundry. Rather, a system of rings and poles is necessary to transport it. As we read in the well-known story of Uzzah, to touch the ark means death (2 Sam 6:3–7; 1 Chr 13:9–10).

As with the tabernacle in general, the ark also has ancient Near Eastern parallels. In King Tut's tomb, for example, was found a cedar chest complete with rings and poles. Depositing the law inside a sacred place (Exod 25:16, 21) is also known from other ancient sources. The same is true of the cherubim that sit atop the cover of the ark. These were common symbols in the ancient world, and the Israelites were no doubt familiar with them. Moreover, the sudden reference to these creatures implies that they need no explanation for the Israelite readers. Cherubim appear not only over the cover but throughout the design of the tabernacle, a sign that the tabernacle is a symbolic representation of God's heavenly dwelling.

The presence of the cherubim also emphasizes the holiness of the ark. Over the ark, which measures approximately 3 feet and 9 inches long by 2 feet and 4 inches wide and high, is the "atonement cover" (v. 17), so called because the Hebrew word *kapporet* derives from the root *kpr*, which often refers to atonement in the Old Testament. From above this cover, between the cherubim, God will meet with his people and speak with them (25:22). It is God's location above the cover and between the cherubim that has led some scholars to regard the cover as God's throne and the ark itself his footstool. This is not just a scholarly conjecture. A number of passages speak of God being *enthroned* between the cherubim (1 Sam 4:4; 2 Sam 6:2; Pss 80:1; 99:1).

We know little else about these cherubim and why God chooses this image in particular for such an important and holy purpose. Perhaps the most we can say is that they are angelic, heavenly beings who live in God's presence (much like the seraphs of Isa 6:1–7). Since any image of God was strictly forbidden, the best Israel can do is make an image of those beings closest to him. Thus, his holiness is emphasized. Moreover, the fact that the law, God's supreme self-revelation to his people, is kept inside the ark also indicates that the ark is the "center of gravity" of God's presence with his people.

The Table (25:23–30; 37:10–16). The table is constructed apparently for the singular purpose of holding the bread of the Presence (25:30). Its dimensions are 3 feet long by 1 foot and 6 inches wide and 2 feet and 3 inches high; it is made of acacia wood overlaid with pure gold. Like the ark, it has a system of rings and poles for carrying. It will be placed in the Holy Place along with the lampstand and the incense altar.

This passage is cryptic in a number of places. For example, what are the plates and dishes mentioned in 25:29 used for? According to Leviticus 24:9, priests are to eat of the bread, but this information is not given here. Also, the pitchers and bowls mentioned in the same verse are for "the pouring out of offerings," but just what type of offerings is not mentioned (37:16 gives a little more information by speaking of "drink offerings").

Likewise, no explanation is given here for "the bread of the Presence" (25:30). According to Leviticus 24:6, twelve loaves of bread (two rows of six) are to be placed on the table, the number no doubt representing the tribes of Israel. According to 24:8–9, this bread is to be set out afresh weekly, on the Sabbath, and the priests are to dispose of it properly, that is, by eating it within the confines of the tabernacle. The term *bread of the Presence* is an ambiguous term, which may simply mean "bread that is in the presence [of God]." We should not look at this in mystical terms, as if God is present "in" the bread. It is the bread that is placed before God, who is in the Most Holy Place, over the ark.

As to any further significance of the bread, we are given little information. Clearly, the placement of the bread on the table at the entrance of the Most Holy Place indicates its status relative to the other furnishings of the tabernacle. This is the second time within the span of two chapters (cf. 24:11) that we have seen Israel's leaders partaking in a meal in God's presence. Perhaps the bread of the Presence along with the drink offering implied in 25:29 are elements in another covenant meal between God and Israel's leaders. The bread and the wine, situated as they are just outside the Most Holy Place, are a continual reminder of the covenant that the holy God, who is located behind a curtain just several feet away, has made with his people.

The Lampstand (25:31–40; 37:17–24). The lampstand and its lamps are made of pure gold with no wood. This is because these items are small enough, although a talent of gold (about 75 pounds) is needed. There is no clear indication of their symbolic meaning, but the matter of tending the lamps is serious business. As we read in Leviticus 24:1–4, it is the high priest's responsibility to do so "from evening till morning, continually" (24:3). Their function is likely ritualistic and symbolic, though precisely what we do not know.

What the lampstand represents is something God may or may not be pleased to reveal. And even if such significance is hidden from Israel, it has no bearing on how they are to behave. The lampstand is to be made as he said, and the light is to be kept burning. Perhaps the mystery will be further revealed as Israel continues to obey God's command. But for now, "See that you make them according to the pattern shown you on the mountain" (Exod 25:40).

The Tabernacle (26:1–37; 36:8–38). It is only after the instructions for the ark, table, and lampstand are given that we finally come to the tabernacle itself. The amount of space devoted to its description only begins to tell the story of its vital significance for Israel's religious practices.

The tabernacle is basically a series of curtains and frames. The curtains covering the entire structure are to be made of fine linen and colored yarn. Cherubim are to be worked into them, an ever-present reminder that the tabernacle is an earthly representation of the heavenly tabernacle. This first layer of curtains must be covered on the outside by a second layer made of goat hair, most likely to protect the inner curtains from the elements. There are apparently two further layers of ram skins and hides of sea cows covering the layer of goat hair (26:14). These curtains are to be keptdenicrer by a system of bronze clasps and loops.

The frames anddenicrars that support the curtains are to be made of acacia wood, doubled in the corners for strength. The crossbars are overlaid with gold and kept together with gold rings. Despite the information given, just how the structure holds together is not clear.

After giving the instructions for the frame and the large curtains that form the roof and walls, the Lord reminds Moses once again to adhere strictly to this plan (26:30). This is a fitting reminder here, since 26:31 commences with instructions concerning the curtain to separate the Holy Place from the Most Holy Place. This curtain seems to be made in the same manner as the first layer of curtains described in 26:1. Another similarly constructed curtain is to be placed at the entrance of the tent (i.e., between the Holy Place and the outer court). Note that this curtain has no cherubim worked into it since this is one step removed from the Most Holy Place.

Much has been made of the dimensions of the tabernacle, and rightly so. The entire structure measured 150 feet on the north and south sides and 75 feet on the east and west, thus forming a rectangle made up of two squares 75 feet by 75 feet. The one square constituted the outer court, in which was placed the altar of burnt offering, roughly 7 feet by 6-inch square structure, and the wash basin at the entrance of the Holy Place. Inside the other square was the Holy Place, a rectangle measuring 30 feet by 15 feet, the same proportions as the tabernacle as a whole. The adjoining Most Holy Place measured a perfect 15-foot square.

The three-part structure of the tabernacle, moving from lesser to greater degrees of holiness, reflects the gradations of holiness on Mount Sinai. The tabernacle is modeled after a higher, cosmic reality: the dwelling place of God.

This brings us to a matter of great importance for understanding the meaning of the tabernacle in its original setting. The precise measurements of the structure combined with the symbolism of the curtains and the furnishings are not without deep significance. The tabernacle seems to represent a microcosm of creation itself. The splendor and beauty of the materials used—fine fabrics, precious metals, and stones—affirm the goodness of the created world. The precise and perfect dimensions of the tabernacle indicate a sense of order amid chaos.

In pointing this out I am not offering suggestions as to how we might approach the theological significance of the tabernacle today. Rather, I am suggesting, as others have done, that to think of the tabernacle as an act of cosmic re-creation is precisely what the building of the tabernacle originally intended to convey. We have already seen a couple of examples of the creation theme in the tabernacle ("created" in seven segments; the cherubim). The ornate and orderly structure of the tabernacle itself is another.

In the midst of a fallen world, in exile from the garden of Eden—the original "heaven on earth"—God undertakes another act of creation, a building project that is nothing less than a return to pre-fall splendor. The tabernacle, therefore, is laden with redemptive significance, not just because of the sacrifices and offerings within its walls but simply because of what it is: a piece of holy ground amid a world that has lost its way. If this is a correct understanding of the tabernacle, we begin to see why the writer of Exodus devotes so much space to its description.

Altar of Burnt Offering (27:1–8; 38:1–7). The altar measures 7 feet by 6 inches square and is 4 feet by 6 inches tall; it is to be located in the outer court. This altar is for offering burnt offerings, an appropriate act of sin atonement considering the fact that God "resides" only several yards away in the Most Holy Place. Details of this sacrifice are presented in Leviticus 1:1–17.

One of its curious characteristics is a horn at each of its four corners. Why are they there? Do they perform a function? Are they merely ornamental, or are they in some way symbolic? We read in 29:12 and Leviticus 4:7, for example, that blood is to be put on the horns, thus suggesting some type of redemptive symbolism, but just what is not clear. We do know that clinging to the horns of the altar was a way of seeking refuge in God's presence from some harm (1 Kgs 1:50–51; 2:28). We are not told, however, what about the symbolism of the horns inspires such action.

One area where the worlds of biblical studies and archaeology come together is with respect to altars. Although the Israelite altar of burnt offering from the tabernacle has not been found, others like it have been discovered. The presence of horned altars in antiquity is well established, which lends credence to the historicity of the altar described here.

The Courtyard (27:9–19; 38:9–20). As mentioned above, the courtyard is a rectangle of 150 feet on the north and south ends, and 75 feet on the east and west. The courtyard, therefore, is the entire enclosure, not to be confused with the outer court. The entrance to the courtyard is to be centered on the east side, 30 feet long. Most of this description concerns the making of curtains and the system of posts, bases, and hooks for keeping the structure together.

Oil for the Lampstand (27:20–21). It is not clear why the instructions for the oil are not given immediately following the instructions for the lampstand. Clear olive oil is to be used, as it produces little smoke and gives off better light. Such a stipulation is not given for the anointing oil or the oil added to the grain offerings, likely because the lampstand is located in the Holy Place whereas the other oils are used mainly in the court. As mentioned above, the lamps are to be kept burning by Aaron, although here Aaron's sons are included (cf. Lev 24:1–4).

Here for the first time the tabernacle is referred to as "the tent of meeting" (Exod 27:21), although the term will be used another thirty-two times before the end of the book. Once again, a new piece of information is placed before the reader somewhat suddenly. The choice of this term does not seem particularly significant here. To call the tabernacle the tent of meeting is not an indication of what the Israelites did but what God did.

Priestly Garments (28:1–43; 39:1–31). This lengthy section treats the garments that Aaron (28:1–39) and his sons (28:40–43) are to wear when ministering in the tabernacle. As we have seen with the tabernacle itself, precisely what these garments look like cannot be said with any precision. Although the description of the garments may not be entirely clear, their purpose is spelled out nicely in 28:2: The garments are to give Aaron "dignity and honor," and they are to be prepared in advance of his consecration (28:3). No doubt the manner in which this dignity and honor are conferred is by the use of expensive materials. Moreover, these materials are not just costly, but they also parallel the materials used to make the tabernacle: gold, blue, purple, and scarlet yarn, fine linen, onyx, and other precious stones.

This similarity between the priestly garments and the tabernacle is hardly accidental, and thus we catch a glimpse of the meaning of these garments. By being decked out as the tabernacle itself, the high priest in his service becomes the focus of God's presence for the people of God—a mini-tabernacle, as it were. I am not suggesting that we extend the analogy to say that the spirit of God resides "in" the priest as he does in the Most Holy Place. Their garments, rather, reflect the holiness of the place in which they are called to minister. One might well ask, "How *else* should we expect them to dress? Everyday clothes?" Out of the question!

Several particulars are worth noting. The ephod is likely an apron-like garment. As with a number of other elements throughout chapters 25–40, similar garments are known from Ugaritic and Assyrian texts. We are not told here what its purpose is, but other biblical texts indicate that it is a means of finding out God's will (1 Sam 23:9–11; 30:7–8). The high priest functions not only in a sacrificial role but also as a conduit for God's revelation to the people.

Over the ephod is a "breastpiece for making decisions" (28:15). This garment sports four rows of three stones, each of which is engraved with the name of one of the tribes of Israel. Also placed in the breastpiece are the Urim and Thummim (28:30). This verse gives a tantalizing piece of information: "Thus Aaron will always bear the means of making decisions for the Israelites over his heart before the LORD." The Urim and Thummim have been a point of scholarly debate for some time.

Of course, this matter must be left open in view of the paucity of information we have. What can be said, however, apart from their role in decision making, is that the Urim and Thummim must certainly have predated Moses. The people must have known what they were and how they were to be used since they simply appear here in Exodus 28 without any explanation (see also Lev 8:8; Num 27:21; Deut 33:8).

Another cryptic piece of information occurs in Exodus 28:35: Aaron is to wear a robe beneath the ephod, whose decorations include gold bells. Their purpose, apparently, is to ring when he enters or leaves the Most Holy Place "so that he will not die."

Next we read of the plate of pure gold on the front of the turban, on which is engraved: "HOLY TO THE LORD" (28:36). What precisely is so designated? This should probably be connected to the notion of bearing guilt mentioned in 28:38, but this does not make things clear either. What guilt needs to be borne? Perhaps it is to make these sacred gifts acceptable to God. This seems to be the intention of the final part of 28:38. The words on Aaron's forehead are a reminder to God that the offerings Aaron is bringing are "acceptable to the LORD."

The final garments mentioned are tunics, sashes, headbands, and the undergarments. What is conspicuously absent from the list is shoes, perhaps because of what has already been suggested in 3:5: "Take off your sandals, for the place where you are standing is holy ground." These words were spoken to Moses as he approached God on Mount Horeb. As we have seen, the tabernacle is an earthly representation of a heavenly reality—a portable Mount Horeb/Sinai. Although 3:5 is not explicitly reiterated in chapter 28, this connection seems a fruitful avenue of approach. The priests stand in God's presence and must conduct themselves appropriately.

Consecration of the Priests (29:1–46). Chapter 29 is devoted to the sacrifices involved in the consecration of the priests; their actual consecration is mentioned only in passing in 40:12–16. This is a deviation from the pattern we have seen: instructions in chapters 25–31, execution in chapters 35–40. This can be easily explained, however. The focus of chapters 35–40 is on the building of the tabernacle and its furnishings. The matter of the consecration of the priests occurs several chapters later in Leviticus. Note, too, that much of Leviticus is an extended conversation between God and Moses at the tent of meeting, the tabernacle. Leviticus picks up where Exodus leaves off.

Aaron and his sons are to be consecrated by a series of sacrifices and offerings, an anointing with oil, and the donning of the tunics, headbands, and sashes. The entire ceremony is neatly summarized in 29:1–9. The end of 29:9 already begins to focus the reader's attention on Aaron's descendants, not just his own sons but in perpetuity: "The priesthood is theirs by a lasting ordinance" (cf. also 29:29–30, 42).

The sacrifices Are of three types: a bull for a sin offering, a ram for a burnt offering, and another ram for a wave offering. This sequence is significant. The sin offering cleanses the priests from sin; it is understandable why the ordination process begins this way. Next, the burnt offering is an expression of devotion and commitment on the part of the worshiper. The second ram, along with a loaf of bread, a cake made with oil, and a wafer, are to be a wave offering.

It Is not clear what a wave offering is. The phrase occurs about twenty times in the Pentateuch, but no description is given. Obviously, an act of waving is involved, but what purpose does the offering itself have? According to Leviticus 7:28–36, a wave offering is a type of fellowship offering, the purpose of which concerns the establishing of communion between God and his people. This is the expected finale to the consecration ceremony. The element of communion is further indicated in Exodus 29:31–34 where Aaron and his sons eat a meal made up of the fellowship offering. As we have seen in 24:11, Israel's leaders eat in God's presence.

The fact that the ordination process takes seven days (29:35–37) is worth noting. It is not the case that every mention of the number seven in the Old Testament or even in Exodus is automatically an allusion to creation (cf. Jethro's seven daughters in 2:16). Perhaps in this context the number seven simply expresses "completeness." But why does the number seven embody such meaning? The reason is that the world was created in a seven-day pattern. Seven is the number of completeness because it is the number of creation. Furthermore, when we keep in mind that Exodus as a whole and the tabernacle in particular abound in creation imagery, it is appropriate to suggest such a connection here. The ordination ceremony of the priest lasts seven days since he is to be a priest in the tabernacle, the microcosm of the universe.

Verses 38–43 describe the institution of the regular morning and evening sacrifices "for the generations to come" (29:42). Here we have apparently left the topic of the consecration of the priests. What justifies the shift in topic is the reference to sacrifices on the altar throughout this section. It also helps draw together the twin topics of the consecration of the priests and of the tabernacle, a point made explicit in 29:44. The daily sacrifices are the focus of the priests' duties; it therefore stands to reason to bring these two strands together.

Verses 42–46 reiterate a number of themes treated elsewhere. The tabernacle is the place where God's glory dwells and where he has chosen to meet with his people. It is God's presence, his glory, that actually consecrates the tabernacle (29:43; cf. 29:44: "*I* will consecrate," emphasis added). It is not the ceremonies that consecrate the tabernacle or the priests but God himself, no doubt through the ceremonies. In other words, there is nothing magical or manipulative on the part of the people to make it happen. It is God's tabernacle, his priesthood, his people. He will prepare his people to be a suitable dwelling for himself.

The final three verses of chapter 29 are a fitting end to the topic at hand. The writer ties together the tabernacle and priesthood with the exodus itself. The tabernacle and the priests have been consecrated and God now dwells with his people. Now the people are to think back at what God has done in bringing them out of Egypt. In this way the people will *know* that Yahweh is their God (29:46). As we have noted many times, the purpose of the exodus was not simply to free slaves. It was to bring God's people into a covenant relationship with him through the law, tabernacle, and priesthood.

Altar of Incense (30:1–10; 37:25–28). This altar measures about 1 foot 6 inches square and 3 feet tall. It is to be placed in the Holy Place (30:6) and therefore must be constructed of gold. Like the altar of burnt offering, it has horns.

One might have expected *all* the items in the tabernacle to be described before the instruction on consecrating the priests in chapter 29. Perhaps these items are mentioned after chapter 29 because none of them are needed in consecrating the priests. If so, its effect is to place emphasis on the importance of the consecration of the priests. The reason for organizing the various descriptions of the tabernacle and its furnishings is to bring the instructions regarding priestly consecration into the picture as quickly as possible. This, if anything, reminds us that the tabernacle and the priesthood are twin concepts in the book of Exodus. Chapters 25–40 are not just about the building of the tabernacle but the institution of an entire cultic system.

The incense itself (30:8) is not treated fully until 30:34–38.

A question left unanswered is the symbolism of the incense: What is its purpose? Is it to counter the smell of dead animals that permeates the tabernacle? Its use was certainly common in the ancient Near East. It has been suggested that the placement of the altar immediately between the priest and the Most Holy Place indicates that the incense performs a protective function: Its smoke conceals the atonement cover from the priest so he will not die (cf. Lev 16:12–13). It is a barrier that the high priest crosses only once a year on the Day of Atonement. Little else can be said about the subject.

Atonement Money (30:11–16). This brief reference to atonement money (which does not occur in chs. 35–40) seems somewhat out of place. The passage begins with the second "creative word" given to Moses from God (see 25:1 for the first). As we noted earlier, there are seven occurrences of the phrase, "Then the LORD said to Moses," which correspond to the seven days of creation.

The passage begins, "When you take a census" (30:12). Why would they do this? A census might be taken as preparation for war (Num 1:2–3, 44–47), but is that relevant here? Whatever the reason, the context clearly implies that it is a dangerous undertaking since a census is to be accompanied by a ransom payment. In this way a plague on the people will be avoided.

The description of this procedure calls to mind 2 Samuel 24:1–17 where David is punished with three days of plague for taking a census of his fighting men. But if this episode is relevant for understanding Exodus 30:11–16, it would seem more reasonable to read simply, "Do not take a census, for it is wrong to do so." Rather, we find here the assumption that a census will be taken from time to time, and some provision is necessary in order to avoid calamity. It may be that the ransom is a reminder to Israel not to rely on her own strength.

The more pertinent question is what all of this has to do with the tabernacle. Verse 16 justifies the logic of including a description of atonement money: The money is to be used for "the service of the tent of meeting." We are not told precisely what the money will be used for (purchase of oil? gold? yarns and linens?) but that it involves the tabernacle is clear. But the money is to be used for more than purchasing power. It is also a "memorial for the Israelites before the LORD" (30:16). At the risk of sounding redundant, just what this means is not certain.

If I may put the pieces together, the money is a reminder to the Israelites that atonement has been made for their lives. This is circular, however, since the very reason atonement is needed is because a census has been taken. Of course, this scenario assumes that the content of verse 16 is directly related to what comes before. If I may put a slightly different spin on it, it seems that the human penchant for assessing self-worth is something God will "tax" for the good of the tabernacle and as a prodding reminder to the people of who really has worth.

The Basin for Washing (30:17–21; 38:8). The basin for washing is to be placed in the courtyard between the curtain to the Holy Place and the altar of burnt offering. The priests are to use it to wash themselves before entering the Holy Place. As with other elements of the tabernacle ceremony, there is no room for negotiation: If they do not wash, they will die.

This washing likely has a practical as well as a ceremonial function. The slaughter that takes place at the altar will certainly leave the priests bloody. Washing the blood off will make them more presentable. But again, this explanation is a conjecture and finds no explicit basis in the text. The washing may also symbolize the cleansing from sin (cf. 29:4).

No dimensions for the basin are given. Since it is not in the inner courts of the tabernacle, it is not made of gold but of bronze. Throughout these chapters, the material used to make the tabernacle and the furnishings reflect the gradations of holiness of the structure itself.

The parallel description of the wash basin in 38:8 offers a surprising piece of information not found in its counterpart in 30:17–21: The bronze basin and stand are to be made from "the mirrors of the women who served at the entrance to the tent of meeting." Once again, we are given a tantalizing tidbit only to have any hope of further explanation dashed. Mirrors in the ancient world were not made of glass but of polished bronze. Hence, this verse explains the source of the bronze. But who were these women and what does it mean that they "served"?

First Samuel 2:22 is routinely brought into the discussion, since it also mentions women serving at the entrance to the tent of meeting (this verse and Exod 38:8 are similar in Hebrew). The problem with this connection, however, is that 1 Samuel 2:22 speaks of the sin of Eli's sons in engaging in sexual activity with these women. The reference, in other words, is to the ubiquitous ancient Near Eastern practice of cult prostitution. We can safely rule out this option, since otherwise the biblical record of what constitutes proper worship of God would be completely overturned. But this verse may simply refer to a *perversion* of an otherwise commonly accepted (although to us unknown) practice involving some sort of service of women at the tabernacle.

The Anointing Oil and Incense (30:22–38; 37:29). The basin for washing began with the third repetition of the creation-phrase, "Then the LORD said to Moses" (30:17). Instructions concerning the anointing oil (30:22) and the incense (30:34) are the fourth and fifth instances. I have grouped these two together for the sake of convenience, since the two are mentioned together in one sentence in 37:29.

The recipe for the oil is about 16 pounds of cinnamon and spices and 1 gallon of olive oil—an expensive and even extravagant recipe. The purpose of the oil is to anoint the tabernacle and the furnishings, thereby consecrating them (as was the high priest, 29:7). Both are to be set apart for a holy purpose.

The anointing oil and the incense are to be kept only for cultic functions. It is not to be used for self-adornment of any sort, the penalty being to be "cut off from their people" (30:33; cf. this same phrase in 12:15, 19, regarding the keeping of the Passover). If we may bring 31:14 into the discussion here, being cut off apparently means more than banishment; it denotes being put to death.

This is not totally surprising since we have seen similar harsh penalties throughout this section. Death is the expected penalty for not following God's directions fully. One may be tempted to ask, "What is the big deal about anointing oil and incense?" This is not a biblical question to ask. The fact of the matter is that the oil and incense *are* worthy of such respect on Israel's part. I would add that the fact that both the oil and incense begin with the creation-phrase is itself an indication of their relative importance.

I must confess, however, that I do not see the logic of why the seven creative words are dispersed as they are. The following elements in chapters 25–31 are introduced by the creation formula: offerings for the tabernacle (25:1), atonement money (30:11), wash basin (30:17), anointing oil (30:22), incense (30:34), appointment of Bezalel and Oholiab (31:1), and Sabbath (31:12). Although the overall theological significance of this pattern of seven seems clear, why certain elements and not others are introduced in this manner is difficult to determine.

Bezalel and Oholiab (31:1–11; 35:30–36:7). Two men, Bezalel and Oholiab, are singled out for the task of putting all the information together and building the tabernacle and all its furnishings and other elements (the list in 31:7–11 is quite complete). To do so they are filled with the spirit of God (31:3, perhaps the same spirit of God that was present at creation in Gen 1:2). Perhaps such divine skill is needed in view of the paucity of information given. More likely is the fact that what needs to be built is of great importance and seriousness. Not just anyone can rush into this occupation foolishly. On the other hand, the seriousness of the matter may have discouraged most from even attempting such a task were it not for special divine empowerment.

We know precious little of Bezalel and less of Oholiab. The latter is mentioned only in Exodus and the former is mentioned outside of Exodus only incidentally (1 Chr 2:20; 2 Chr 1:5). If it is even valid to seek significance in the etymology of names (a last resort when other information is lacking), Bezalel probably means "in the shadow/protection of El [*el*, a name for God]." Oholiab can mean either "father is my tent" or perhaps "father is a tent." Thus, the names themselves may be an allusion to the tabernacle.

The Sabbath (31:12–18; 35:1–3). As mentioned previously, the instructions concerning the building of the tabernacle end with the command to keep the Sabbath. The is the seventh passage of the tabernacle section to begin with the creation-formula, "Then the Lord said to Moses" (31:12).

The plural "Sabbaths" refers to the regular keeping of the Sabbath day week in and week out, not to a multiplicity of differing Sabbath days. The observance of the Sabbath will be a lasting "sign" between God and Israel (31:13). Verses 16–17 spell this out: The Sabbath is a sign of the covenant God has made with Israel. God's conduct toward Israel in bringing them out of Egypt and establishing them as his people, an event that culminates here in the construction of the tabernacle and the institution of Israel's religious system, is tied to creation in 31:17.

It is most fitting that the Sabbath be the sign of this covenant. Israel, as we have noted, is a new creation. This is a new people of God, whom he intends to use to undo the work of the first man. Also, the tabernacle is a microcosm of the created order, a parcel ofdenicc splendor established amid the chaos of the world. The Sabbath is not just a reminder of the original creation in Genesis 1 and 2 but a reminder of God's re-creation of the cosmos in the tabernacle.

The purpose of the Sabbath is "so you may know that I am the Lord, who makes you holy" (31:13). It is, in other words, a reminder of who God is and what his intentions are for his people. We also see here what Jesus meant when he said, "The Sabbath was made for man, not man for the Sabbath" (Mark 2:27). The regular keeping of the Sabbath serves a purpose for our benefit, to help us along in a deeper understanding of who God is.

Failure to keep the Sabbath ("desecrates," 31:14), therefore, is to be met with severe punishment, death—or, as we have seen also with the oil and incense, being "cut off from their people." This penalty seems harsh, but not when we realize what the Sabbath was intended to do. By not keeping the Sabbath, the Israelite was showing that he or she was not interested in "know[ing] that I am the Lord" (31:13). Desecration means to do work, though as we saw under the fourth commandment, the Bible does not provide us a list of what constitutes work. In this respect, attempts in the history of Judaism to define what precisely is work are understandable.

The instructions concerning the building of the tabernacle and its furnishings end in 31:18. The two tablets of the covenant law are to be placed in the ark. It is worth mentioning again that 35:1 picks up right where 31:18 leaves off without missing a beat—as if to say that the intervening episode of rebellion (chs. 32–34) and the near dissolving of the covenant relationship on God's part (see 32:9–14) are forgotten. The framing of the rebellion narrative with the Sabbath law indicates that God's plan is now going forth unabated.

Finally, the reference to the Sabbath at the end of the first part of the tabernacle section has further significance beyond that of continuing the connection of exodus to creation. The building of the tabernacle, as we have seen, is a microcosm of the created world—heavenly order amid earthly chaos. It is a true sanctuary where Israel continually experiences connection to their God who brought them out of Israel. The tabernacle is like no other place on earth. It is built according to a divine plan to reflect a heavenly reality. It is a piece of holy ground.

To put it another way, the tabernacle is holy space. The Sabbath, by contrast, is holy time. By building the tabernacle and setting apart one day in seven, God is truly recreating heaven in *space* and *time*. Weekly Sabbath worship is on holy ground in holy time. There is no more holy spot on the face of the earth than the tabernacle on the Sabbath. We can see how important the tabernacle, and later the temple, was to Israel's identity as God's people. We can also see how utterly devastating the destruction of the temple by the Babylonians was. By entering the tabernacle, Israel entered God's house; by keeping the Sabbath, Israel entered God's rest.

Collecting of Materials (35:10–29). This is the first passage in the second part of the tabernacle section that is not treated in the first part, although 35:11–19 is similar to 31:6–10. The narrative of the collection of the building materials logically precedes the presentation of Bezalel and Oholiab in 35:30–36:7, but the latter was treated above in conjunction with its parallel in 31:1–11.

Verses 10–19 review what the Israelites are to build: the tabernacle, its furnishings, and the priestly garments. Verses 20–29 recount the actual collecting of the materials necessary to do the work. The emphasis here seems to be on the willingness of the Israelites to give and the participation of both men and women. Women are particularly singled out by the writer as spinners of yarn and goat hair (35:25–26).

The reference to acacia wood is interesting (35:24). How is this to be understood? Are we to think of Israelites carrying planks of wood out of Egypt? The tree was common in the Sinai Peninsula, so it is conceivable that the Israelites felled the trees and shaped the planks, even though this is not described in the Exodus narrative. Verse 24 refers merely to "everyone who had acacia wood," a statement that does not imply the cutting of planks.

Also, 35:28 seems to suggest that the oil for the light and anointing are not pounded by the Israelites but are simply in their possession. This implies that these materials were part of the plunder brought from Egypt.

List of Materials Used (38:21–31). We have here a list not only of the materials used but of their weights. This list is recorded by the priests under the direction of Ithamar, one of Aaron's four sons. It takes 300 shekels to make one talent. The approximate weights of the material listed, in today's measures, are as follows: 2,193.25 pounds of gold; 7,544.38 pounds of silver; 5,310 pounds of bronze. To put it in perspective, the total weight in precious metals the Israelites carried out of Egypt was about 15,000 pounds. This may seem like an excessively heavy amount in the abstract, but it comes to only approximately .025 pounds for every adult male Israelite—pocket change. There is no need to suggest, as some have done, that these weights are exaggerated numbers.

The Work Is Completed (39:32–43). This reference to the completed work (esp. 39:33–41) includes a list more complete than the ones found in 31:7–11 and 35:11–19. This passage recounts Israel's obedience, provides a summary of what is made, and relays Moses's inspection. Verse 32 explicitly equates the tabernacle and the tent of meeting.

We have seen a number of creation connections. Several more are found here.

1. In 39:32, the work is "completed." The Hebrew root (*klh*) is also used in Genesis 2:2 for the completion of God's creative work.
2. Moses inspects the work and sees (*r'h*) that the Israelites have completed the work well, according to plan (Exod 39:43). This is an allusion to God's inspecting his creative work and "seeing" (*r'h*) that it was good (e.g., Gen 1:31).
3. Moses "blesses" (*brk*) the people after completing the work (Exod 39:43) as God "blessed" (*brk*) his creation (Gen 1:22, 28; 2:3).

These allusions to creation are not accidental. They confirm that the biblical writer wishes the reader to view the construction of the tabernacle as an act of creation.

The Tabernacle Is Set Up (40:1–33). The narrative of the tabernacle concludes, appropriately, by recounting how it is set up. Verses 1–11 are the detailed commands given by God to Moses concerning what needs to be done: The tabernacle is to be set up, the furnishings put in their places, and both the tabernacle and the furnishings are to be anointed. Verses 12–15 follow with the commands concerning the anointing of the priests. After the summary acknowledgment that Moses obeys God fully (40:16), the details of the set-up are recounted (40:17–33).

There is also creation language here. In fact, this section ends (40:33) by repeating almost verbatim the language of Genesis 2:2. Only Genesis 2:2 has the clause "by the seventh day," but both say that God/Moses *finished* (Heb. root *klh*) *work* (Heb. *ml'kh*). Moses's overseeing the construction of the tabernacle is like God building the universe.

We also see that the tabernacle is set up "on the first day of the first month in the second year" (40:17). As we saw in 12:2, the exodus inaugurated a new calendar in Israelite life: The month in which the exodus took place would be the first month of the year. The deliverance of Israel from Egypt marked a new beginning for God's people, a "new creation." It is no surprise, therefore, that the tabernacle, itself a microcosm of creation, is also set up one year later on the first day of the first month. It, too, is a new creation.

A final creation connection here is perhaps more subtle but worth pointing out. We see not only in this passage but throughout the tabernacle section that marked attention is given to the precision by which the tabernacle and its furnishings are to be made and where precisely the furnishings are to be placed in the tabernacle. This uncompromising attention to details is another indication that the tabernacle is an act of creation: It reflects the order that God originally created in the universe. There is no room for human disorder or for chaos to invade this holy space. Everything must be exactly as God has commanded. The order of the tabernacle reflects God's very nature, a nature that creation itself reflects.

Application. How does one "apply" the tabernacle? As we have just seen, the New Testament points us in the direction we should go. Christ fulfills the symbolism of the tabernacle/temple, and Christians, because they are in Christ, have also become the dwelling place of God, the "temple" (to use Paul's word). What does it mean for God to take up residence in us? How does this work out concretely in our lives?

A proper understanding of the theology of the tabernacle does not provide us with specific guidelines for what we ought to do. Applying the tabernacle must be approached from a different angle. Rather than tell us *what* we ought to do, it tells us *why* we ought to do it. It is the tabernacle as a whole that we should seek to apply. It is the big picture that gives us a proper theological framework within which to view our daily activities. A proper understanding of tabernacle theology motivates us to live so as to please God. It does this simply by *reminding us* of who God is and who we are in relation to him. An understanding of the tabernacle helps shape our minds to reflect more the way God wants us to think.

Thus, the tabernacle—what it looked like, how it functioned, what it represented—is one reminder of who God is. There is perhaps no thought more important than to be clear on the question of what God is like. What is the picture of God that we see in the tabernacle?

For one thing, we have noted repeatedly that the tabernacle is a microcosm of creation. In it we see the God of all creation dwelling on earth in a structure intended to reflect the perfect created order—a piece of heaven on earth. Then, at the climactic stage in redemptive history, God took up residence in Christ, the temple who "tabernacled" among his people. He is not a building constructed to reflect heavenly glory. He himself is from heaven and is therefore the concrete manifestation of what the tabernacle symbolized. And finally, inexplicably, the God of creation has built us up to be his house so he can take up residence in us. He has fashioned us with material far more precious than gold or silver, dyed yarn, or fine linen. We are created in the very image of the risen Christ so that even we reflect a piece of heaven. We are worthy of the Spirit's indwelling because we have been re-created by the power of God into heavenly beings.

What does this mean? The paths to understanding and applying this profound mystery are endless. But I want to point out two implications for how we, as tabernacles, should reflect the order of God amid the chaos around us: how we worship and how we live.

1. The tabernacle was a place of worship, a place of giving God praise and acknowledging that he alone is worthy. It was a place of "connecting" with God. Worship may be described as the place where heaven and earth meet. This is why we "go to church" on Sunday. When the saints of God meet on Sunday mornings, they, like the Israelites before them, are worshiping in holy time and space.

   Going to church is also a testimony to the chaotic world around us. As redeemed people we participate in heavenly reality. Worshiping God collectively one day in seven is a sign to the world that there is something other, something higher, than the private universes people create for themselves. Whether in the end the world is attracted to this alternative is the Lord's doing, not ours. But we bear visible, tangible witness that God's order is not the order of the world. We demonstrate that we follow different rules, God's rules, and in doing so God is glorified.
2. We also reflect divine order by how we live day to day in a fallen world. When we think of our bodies as the temple of God, it puts sinning in a different perspective. This is really Paul's point in 1 Corinthians 6:18–20 where he equates individual Christians at Corinth with the temple. Some in Corinth were engaging in sexual immorality. Paul's rebuke essentially amounts to this: "What, are you crazy?! How can you *possibly* think of doing anything like this?! Don't you know God himself resides in you?!"

Some things are unthinkable in God's house. No one, for example, would put a pornographic magazine stand alongside the pulpit of a church (although in our day and age, I am not so sure). Well, we are God's house, and some things should be unthinkable for us. In fact, if we wish to expand the analogy with the Old Testament tabernacle, *any* sin is repulsive. Just like the construction of the tabernacle and its furnishings, not even the slightest deviation from the divine norm can be tolerated. To introduce sin to the holy dwellings God has made us is unthinkable.

EXODUS 32:1–34:35

Original Meaning. The rapid pace with which we move from the final instructions for the tabernacle (31:18) to the rebellion at the foot of the mountain (ch. 32) is almost numbing. Suddenly we find ourselves caught up in an event that could threaten to unravel God's entire plan. There is no indication as to what actually motivates the Israelites to do what they did. All we read is that they see that Moses has been delayed and so they gather around Aaron to make their request.

We must remember that Moses is the only means of contact that the Israelites have with God. It is possible to read the story not as an act of godless rebellion but as an act of panic on the part of a people who fear they have lost their contact with God. There is more to Israel's act, however. They approach Aaron and refer to Moses as "this fellow Moses" (v. 1), a phrase that communicates a sense of derision and contempt. We have already seen such contempt in Exodus and will see it again later in the Pentateuch. Perhaps the contempt here is a result of the delay. However we explain their motives, the Israelites will later be punished by God for what they are about to do.

Aaron responds to this threatening situation in a way that, perhaps, we can hardly blame him for. He tells the people to take off their gold earrings, which he will then use to form an idol in the shape of a calf. In light of the repeated references to gold in the tabernacle section, it is hard not to see the connection. By building the calf out of gold the people want what the tabernacle was intended to do—provide a concrete point of contact between the people and God.

The choice of a calf is not arbitrary. It was a common idol image in the ancient Near East. It is commonly accepted by Old Testament scholars today that the ancients did not *equate* an idol with the god, but it was some sort of earthly *representation* of that god. Specifically, it was thought that calves or bulls functioned as pedestals for the gods seated or standing over them. In this sense, the calf is analogous to the ark (the fact that both are made of gold strengthens this connection).

This is important to remember because it is unlikely that the calf *itself* is being declared "god" by the Israelites, as if they actually think that *it* has brought them out of Egypt. Rather, like the ark, it is the place above which God is enthroned, thus ensuring his presence with them. The calf is thus a pagan *representation* of the true God. Put otherwise, the Israelites are not saying that this calf and *not* Yahweh brought them out of Egypt, but that Yahweh's *presence* is now associated with this piece of gold. By making the golden calf, Israel has broken not the first commandment but the second.

Aaron asks for gold and the people respond willingly, an act that parallels nicely the freewill offering the people will make for the tabernacle. It is becoming more clear that the calf represents an alternate point of contact between God and his people.

The Israelites claim that "these gods" are the ones who have "brought [them] up out of Egypt" (32:4), I do not think this means that they are claiming that this calf and not Yahweh has been responsible for their deliverance, only that this calf is the earthly representation of Yahweh. But this does not make the offense any less severe! We must remember how the Ten Commandments begins (20:2). Israel's act here is more than simply idolatry. Israel is fashioning a new, false religion according to the pattern of what God revealed to them earlier.

In 32:5 Aaron builds an altar, a parallel to the altar that will be built for the tabernacle. He proclaims that there will be a "festival to the LORD" the next day (cf. 10:9; 12:14; 13:6). Throughout Exodus we read the refrain that Israel is to leave Egypt to hold a festival to the Lord. That festival is the Passover and the Feast of Unleavened Bread. But the Israelites at the foot of Mount Sinai turn it into something else.

At least two of the phrases in 32:6 are reminiscent of what we have seen in chapter 24, which is a celebration of the confirmation of the covenant God made with the Israelites. In 24:4–5 Moses rises *early* and sacrifices *burnt and fellowship offerings*. The similar wording in 32:6 suggests that the festival here is a reversal—indeed, a perversion—of the true celebration of chapter 24. Israel's actions are systematically, step by step, undoing what has been done.

The same goes for the eating and drinking mentioned at the end of 32:6. Remember that this is what the leaders of Israel did in 24:11 after they were given a brief glimpse of God himself. Now the Israelites, who were not given that earlier glimpse, fashion themselves as being "in God's presence" and partake of a covenant meal of their own. An added twist is that they also engage in what the NIV translates as "revelry" (32:6). The Hebrew word has connotations of sexual activity (see Gen 26:8; 39:14, 17). To say the least, this is not the festival Israel was intended to celebrate at the foot of God's holy mountain.

God reports the activities of the Israelites to Moses (32:7–10). By referring to the Israelites as "your people" (i.e., Moses's people), we see already an ominous hint of what is to come. Israel is no longer "*my* [God's] people." Up to this point in Exodus God has been zealous to refer to Israel as "my firstborn son" (4:22), but here he has had enough. They have "become corrupt" (32:7). They have been "quick to turn away" (32:8). The drama of Israel's sudden turnabout after all that has happened to them, after all they have seen, should leave our heads shaking. In 32:9 God continues to use derisive language to speak of Israel, referring to them as "*these* people," a phrase that brings to mind the Israelites' reference to Moses as "*this* fellow" (32:1, emphasis added).

God's solution is to have his "anger . . . burn against them" (32:10) and start over with Moses: "Then I will make *you* [Moses] into a great nation" (emphasis added). By saying what he does to Moses, God is in effect going back to Genesis 12 and posing Moses as a new Abraham. God is threatening to wipe out the Israelites and to start over again.

But this is not where the story ends. Moses comes through. Rebellion is followed by mediation. He reminds God of the very things that God himself regularly enjoins the Israelites to remember, that God delivered Israel with "great power and a mighty hand" (32:11). He also reminds the Lord that his own honor is at stake. Had he not just finished dismantling the Egyptian army and their gods? Will he now turn around and give these very same enemies a reason to rejoice in Yahweh's defeat? Never! Moses bases his argument ultimately on the very element that God seems to have discounted in the previous verses: the promise to the patriarchs (32:13).

Moses's argument has the desired outcome. God turns from his anger and does not bring about the threatened disaster (32:14). What can we say about this change of heart? It certainly seems that Moses, through argument and pleading, has been able to get God to alter his plans. To put it in plain English, Moses gets God to change his mind. There is really no other way to read this, and we should not try to avoid it.

How can God's sovereignty be reconciled to the fact that he here changes his mind? I suggest that we should look at this in the broadest context possible. The Bible gives us a varied portrait of the nature of God. At times we seem to be peering into heaven itself. At other times, the Bible presents God in human pictures. The dialogue of 32:11–14 is more in keeping with the latter category than the former. The reason for this here seems to be that the writer is focusing his attention on Moses's role as intercessor, not on the inner workings of God's psyche (as if that is *ever* the topic in the Bible!). Moses has finally begun to grow into the role he so adamantly rejected when he first met God on Mount Horeb.

However we seek to understand this interchange, Moses's pleading works. He then turns to go down the mountain with the two tablets in his hands, which have God's writing on both the front and back. The author mentions this in order to prepare the reader for the devastation of the breaking of these tablets (32:19). Moses will smash something very sacred.

On his way down the mountain, Moses meets up with Joshua (32:17). Joshua is unaware of what is happening in the camp below. He surmises on the basis of the sounds that he hears that there must be war in the camp. Moses informs Joshua of what is actually happening (32:18).

Moses reacts to what he sees in the camp by throwing the tablets to the ground, breaking them to pieces. Moreover, his "anger burns" against the people (32:19; cf. the similar reference to God's anger in 32:10). But whereas Moses successfully appeased God's wrath, Moses, upon actually seeing the depth to which his people have sunk, does not follow his own advice.

The breaking of the tablets is more than just a graphic, even impulsive, depiction of intense anger. Like so much of this narrative, it is symbolic. By smashing the tablets on which is written the law—by God's finger, no less—the law is symbolically undone. Moses's act says to the Israelites that if they are not prepared to obey the law, they do not deserve to have it.

This would not bring a sense of relief to them, as if now they are finally rid of the burden of God's law. Rather, this shocks them into a clearer understanding of just what it is they have done. The smashing of the tablets, with one resounding crash, tells the Israelites below that the party is over. Their attempt to create a religion of their own design has failed.

One curious element concerns the grinding of the golden calf into powder, mixing it with water, and making the Israelites drink it. This is obviously some sort of ritual that the text itself does not explain but that to the original audience was clear enough. Why are the Israelites made to drink the concoction, and what does that mean? It may be helpful to bring Numbers 5:12–31 into the discussion. This section describes an elaborate ceremony whereby a woman suspected of adultery is made to drink a mixture of water and dust from the tabernacle in order to determine her guilt or innocence. Even though Exodus 32 does not draw on this ceremony, it may well be the significance of the act described here.

Verses 21–24 record a confrontation between Moses and Aaron that appears somewhat pathetic and almost comical on the surface: "What did these people do to you, that you led them into such great sin?" Perhaps the question is sarcastic: "Aaron, you know better! You are the high priest! The only way I can see you doing something so stupid, to commit such a 'great sin,' is that 'these people' did something to you first!"

There are two ways of looking at Aaron's response. Either this answer is so lame that it serves no other purpose than to portray Aaron as a weasel and to expose the utter madness of the act, or it has a more serious meaning. I am strongly inclined toward the former, not only because Aaron's answer does indeed appear ridiculous (a circular argument, I know), but also because Moses himself gives no response, as if to say that he will not even dignify it with an answer.

In the wake of this disaster, it is the Levites who rally to Moses's side. The fact that all the Levites come forward indicates that God's house is still in order. The rebellion is grievous and serious, but it is not the final word. The guilty parties will be put to death—and by those responsible for maintaining order in the community, the Levites.

The next day Moses announces his intention to go up the mountain to make atonement for the people (32:30). The text implies two levels of guilt in the making of the golden calf. The "more guilty" party, perhaps those directly or extensively involved, have been put to death by the Levites. The rest of the Israelites are apparently also guilty in some sense, otherwise atonement would not have to be made; but they are not so guilty as to deserve death along with the three thousand.

In his attempt to make atonement by pleading for the life of his people, Moses's argument essentially amounts to "take me instead." He has certainly changed from his first encounter with God on Mount Horeb. He is neither timid nor reluctant to be the mediator between God and his people, and he is showing his commitment to the task by his willingness to pay the ultimate price. The Lord responds by rejecting Moses's offer (32:33). Sinners, not the guiltless, will be blotted out—for now at least. The mediator has negotiated a solution that will guarantee Israel's existence and keep God close by them, but God still reserves his right to punish later on. The timing and form of this punishment is indicated in v. 35.

The story continues with tension and suspense (33:1–6). It seems as though things have been patched up between God and his people. He tells them to "leave this place" (i.e., "Mount Horeb," 33:6). God announces that he himself will not be going with them (33:3).

The significance of this turn of events cannot be stressed too highly. The whole purpose of the exodus was for God and his people to be together. God's presence with them will be firmly established in the proposed tabernacle. By saying "go ahead, but you're going without me," the events of the previous thirty-one chapters are being undone. This is not merely a setback; it means the end of the road.

The reason God gives for not going with them is twofold: They are a stiff-necked, stubborn people, and God is afraid he "might destroy [them] on the way." Again, we see a very "human" portrait of God. As we have seen above, the writer is not concerned to reveal to us the absolute, abstract essence of God but God in the context of his dealings with his people.

The relevance of 33:7–11, which refer to the tent that Moses pitches outside the camp, is a source of bafflement. What, if anything, does it contribute to the flow of the story? This passage does indeed follow logically from the golden calf narrative. It is the events of chapter 32 that prompt the action of 33:7–11. The fact that a temporary tent of meeting is set up and that God does meet with Moses as a representative of the people signals to the reader that God has not entirely abandoned Israel. This so-called "tent of meeting" (33:7) will soon give way to the splendor of the tabernacle, the true tent of meeting. The cloud will soon descend to guide the entire camp.

I am not convinced that 33:7–11 describe a recurring event, which is how the NIV interprets it. I do admit, though, that the NIV's translation is possible. Verses 10–11 can also indicate a single action and can be translated:

> *So* the people saw the pillar of cloud standing at the entrance to the tent; they all stood and worshiped, each at the entrance to his tent. *Then* the LORD *spoke* to Moses face to face, as a man speaks with his friend. Then Moses *returned* to the camp, but his young aide Joshua son of Nun did not leave the tent. (emphasis added)

If this translation is accepted, 33:12–23 recount the conversation between Moses and God implied in 33:11. If the translation in the NIV is accepted, a stronger case is made for 33:7–11 being essentially a lull in the action and no more.

The conversation between God and Moses begins with the latter issuing a challenge. What is Moses asking for here? Does he want to know who will go before them and lead, such as the angel? Perhaps. But Moses may also be asking, "I know you want me to lead, but which people are going out with me?" In other words, Moses wants to know who will be left after the purge of 33:5?

Such an understanding of 33:12 provides a different perspective from which to read the conversation to follow. When Moses continues, he seems to be saying, "I know how special *I* am to you, but what about everybody else?" Moses does not want to make the journey alone. He sees no honor in being the only one to reach Canaan. So, he reminds God in 33:13, "Remember that this nation is your people."

In this respect, God's response in 33:14 can be seen as somewhat of a veiled denial to Moses's pleading: "My Presence will go with *you*, and I will give *you* rest" (emphasis added). Rest should not be understood psychologically, as if God is promising that Moses's mind will be put to ease. It is an expression used for entering the land and receiving rest from engaging enemies in war. Hence, what God seems to be saying to Moses, albeit subtly, is, "Don't worry, Moses. I'll be with *you*."

This perspective also helps makes sense of 33:15–17. Moses responds by asking that God's presence go up "with *us*," meaning all the people, not just Moses. He is not giving in. If in 33:14 God was promising that his presence would be with *all* the people (taking the singular "you" as a plural, which is certainly possible in Hebrew), why does Moses keep pressing the point in 33:15? Why would he ask for the very thing that God has just conceded? It makes more sense to read 33:14 as referring to Moses alone and 33:15 to be Moses's gentle retort.

In other words, the argument of 33:12–16 serves the singular purpose of ensuring that the people will not be left behind. The clincher for Moses is 33:16, which, like 32:11–14, is an appeal to God's reputation among the people of the world: If God's presence is not with *us*, the people, then no one will know that Moses and the people are special.

The argument concludes by God's promising to do as Moses asked (33:17). Why? Because he is "pleased" with Moses and knows him "by name." God will be present with the people for Moses's sake. Once again, Moses has succeeded in moving God to compassion.

The following verses (33:18–23), where Moses asks to see God's glory, must be understood within this context. This is not simply to satisfy his curiosity or some deep spiritual longing. He is in effect asking God for some demonstration of the promise he has just made. He is asking God to "put it in writing."

God says that he will cause all his "goodness" to pass in front of Moses. Moreover, God again proclaims his name, "the LORD," to Moses. This is an allusion to the initial encounter in 3:14–15, where God first proclaimed his name to Moses. God is willing to start over, and Moses is once again called upon to lead his people.

The meaning of God's words in 33:19b are not clear in the context. What does it mean that his "mercy" and "compassion" are at his will? I suggest it is a summary of what God has done for Israel in bringing them out of Egypt, an act of pure mercy.

Verse 23 is a captivating image. God is "there" in some tangible form, passing by in front of Moses. The anthropomorphism is apparent, but we should not conclude, on the basis that God does not have a body, that Moses does not see anything. He most certainly does see something, something that God himself refers to as his back. This is not to imply that God appears to Moses in bodily form, only that he sees something. If we dwell on what precisely Moses sees, we lose sight of the point of the story as a whole. No one knows what it means to speak of God's hand, back, and face, but perhaps this is precisely what is intended. God's appearance is a mystery, a mystery that even Moses himself is able to see only partially.

As with the theophanies in Exodus 3 and 24, this one serves a similar function. It is a boost of God's presence for the task that lies ahead. After the disaster of chapter 32, when all seems lost, Moses is recommissioned with a seriousness not seen in the previous theophanies. His authority as God's chosen leader is thus emphasized amid the near disqualification of the people.

The beginning of chapter 34 reinforces that the covenant between God and Israel is reestablished after the golden calf incident. Once again, Moses will have tablets of stone with the words of God's law written on them. The fact that Moses has to chisel them may indicate God's displeasure with him at having smashed them (32:19).

In 34:6–7 God proclaims his name—the double repetition of the divine name lending emphasis to what is about to take place. As we noted in chapter 3, "the LORD" (Yahweh) is God's "salvation name." This is precisely what he is once again committing himself to do for Israel, even after the events of chapter 32. This list of attributes is true not only of God's behavior in chapter 34 but throughout Exodus.

Moses's response in 34:8–9 appears to be petitioning God for what he has just granted. Despite God's words of forgiveness, Moses wants some added evidence or proof that God will go with his people. He wants God to "document" in some way his intentions.

God responds to Moses's doubt not by reprimanding him but by giving him what he wants, some sign of his continued presence with his people. He will make "a covenant" with the people (34:10). To put it more accurately, he will *renew* the covenant. What follows in 34:11–28 is essentially a repetition of a number of things we have seen in previous sections of Exodus. Such repetition forces the reader to understand what is happening as a *renewal* of the covenant.

As before (24:18), Moses stays on the mountain for forty days and nights, although this time we read that he neither eats bread nor drinks water (34:27–28). After receiving the synopsis of the law, Moses writes it on the tablets he chiseled and makes his way back down the mountain. This time, however, he is not greeted with the sound of "singing." Instead, the people are afraid. Why? Because Moses's face has become radiant (34:30). Although the reason why Moses's face shines is not made explicit in the text, it is probably to impress on the people that God's authority and presence rest unequivocally with Moses. A little fear is good for them. They must relearn what they first experienced in chapter 19: Being at the foot of the mountain is serious business. They are receiving God's law.

What, then, are we to make of the veil? Its purpose is to cover Moses's face in the presence of the people after he enters "the LORD's presence" (34:34). Within the broader context of Exodus, we may think of Moses's veil functioning in a similar way to the veil or curtain in the tabernacle. Just as the people could not enter the Most Holy Place to behold God's glory, now they cannot behold the glory of God reflected in Moses. He has, therefore, become the embodiment of the tabernacle.

It is only after the covenant has been renewed and the relationship between God and his people has been repaired that the plans for building the tabernacle can be carried through to completion. The fact that the action picks up *after* the rebellion in the same place as *before* the rebellion means that Moses's intercession has been *completely* successful. The people are *totally* restored. The subsequent silence concerning this event adds to this notion. Forgiveness is complete. The main thrust of chapters 32–34 now becomes clear. It is not so much a story of rebellion as it is a story of God's forgiveness and Moses's role in making this happen.

Application. Applying the Bible does not mean that we simply transport the action of this story into our contemporary setting. Exodus 32 is relevant today because in it we see how God does *not* act now. This is not to drive a wedge between the Testaments and to proclaim the story passé. It is rather to understand this one story in the context of the whole. In other words, Exodus 32–34 is not to be *applied* in any conventional sense of the word. We do not read the story, make a mental image of God being angry, and then imagine him acting similarly in contemporary settings of our choosing. Rather, it is to help us to see what God is like, what he expects, and how Christ completes the picture. In doing so the significance of the story is not rejected but properly understood.

Israel's sin at the foot of Mount Sinai occurs before there is any official means of sin atonement. The tabernacle has not yet been built, and the priestly system has not yet been inaugurated. At this point these things have only been planned for. This is why Moses himself needs to step in and say, "I will go up to the Lord; perhaps I can make atonement for your sin" (32:30). For Israel, the official means of atoning for sin is still in the future. For the church, the final, complete, once-for-all atonement for sin *has* happened. The means of atonement Moses offered, substituting himself for his people, which God did not accept, is what Christ was able to do!

EXODUS 40:34–38

Original Meaning. As we come to the conclusion of the exodus story, we find God present with his people in a powerful way. The reappearance of the cloud in particular attracts our attention. God was with his people in the form of a cloud at a number of important places in Exodus. The recurring appearance of this symbol ties various parts of the book together and communicates loud and clear that the God of the exodus is still with his people. The same can be said for the use of "travel" and "set out" on a journey. As with the cloud, this word has occurred a number of times previously in Exodus. It, too, indicates that God is moving ahead with the plan he announced earlier.

Exodus 40:36–38, in other words, prepare us for what will become a dominant element in Numbers and Deuteronomy: the relentless push toward the land of Canaan. The purpose of these closing verses of Exodus is to explain how this will happen. When God moves, the people move. Israel's eventual arrival in the promised land will be solely by God's guidance and direction, by his will and in his time.

God's presence is so "thick," as it were, that even Moses cannot enter. Moses is unable to enter *because of* the cloud and the glory. Something powerful is happening in the midst of the community, and it is fitting that it should be so. In light of what we have seen in chapters 32–34, it is important to remind the people of God's holiness, that there are times when even Moses may not come near. This is a lesson the Israelites, unfortunately, will be slow to learn.

Nevertheless, the fact that God is still present with his people, and in such an intense way, reminds the people of something else: All is forgiven. The exodus-God, the God who has led his people out of Egypt with fire and cloud (14:19, 24) is still at work (40:38). The mission, at least the first stage, has been completed and the plan is proceeding full steam ahead.

Thus, the first phase of Israel's story comes to an end. One chapter of this grand story is closing and another is beginning, so our gaze is directed forward to the next phase in Israel's journey. Along that journey, Israel's prophets and psalmists will from time to time call Israel back to remember what God did in bringing them out of Egypt. They will be challenged to remember that neither Egypt's might nor Israel's stubbornness—nor even God's own anger—have been able to thwart his plan. After all, he made a promise to Abraham. Nothing will get in the way. This is the story of the exodus.

Application. The end of Exodus is among the more applicable parts of the book. Verses 34–38 have something to say to us since we, too, have been delivered and are waiting to arrive at the final destination. We, like the Israelites, are poised to reach our rest.

On this journey, we follow our holy Redeemer as he guides us to the promised land. Admittedly, there is no cloud overhead, but we have the spirit of Christ dwelling in us. He brings us to the goal of our salvation just as surely as the cloud guided the Israelites to their ultimate destination. The people of God should take great comfort in this. The God of Exodus is still guiding. God is present with his people wherever they go, for he still leads and guides them, not to Canaan but to a "better country—a heavenly one" (Heb 11:16).

LEVITICUS

INTRODUCTION TO LEVITICUS

Leviticus consistently maintains that the chief recipient and transmitter of its divine speeches was Moses. The New Testament, including direct speech of Jesus, refers to legislation in Leviticus as authoritative and from Moses. The book is, however, strictly speaking anonymous. While we can acknowledge what Leviticus says about itself in terms of basic divine-Mosaic origin, we do not know how it reached its final form, who was involved in the writing-editing process, or how long this took because no hard evidence regarding these questions has come to light.

BOOK OUTLINE

I. Sacrificial Worship (1:1–7:38)
   A. Prescriptions for All Israelites (1:1–6:7)
   B. Additional Sacrificial Instructions for Priests (6:8–7:38)
II. Description of Ceremonies That Founded the Ritual System (8:1–10:20)
   A. Consecration of Priests and Sanctuary (8:1–36)
   B. Inaugural Service (9:1–24)
   C. Tragic Disruption (10:1–20)
III. Purity Versus Impurity (11:1–15:33)
   A. Distinctions Between Pure (Permitted for Eating) and Impure Animals (11:1–47)
   B. Physical Ritual Impurities from Human Sources (12:1–15:33)
IV. Purgation of Sanctuary and Camp on Day of Atonement (16:1–34)
V. Holy (Sacrificial) Slaughter (17:1–16)
VI. Community Holiness (18:1–20:27)
   A. Sexuality (18:1–30)
   B. Comprehensive Life of Holiness (19:1–37)
   C. Terminal Penalties for Inexpiable Offenses (20:1–27)
VII. Special Holy Entities (21:1–27:34)
   A. Holy Priests (21:1–24)
   B. Holy Offerings (22:1–33)
   C. Holy Times (23:1–44)
   D. Holy Light and Bread; Holy Divine Name (24:1–23)
   E. Holy Land (25:1–55)
   F. Holy Covenant (26:1–46)
   G. Holy Consecrations, and Redemption of Them (27:1–34)

LEVITICUS 1:1–17

Original Meaning. While most of Leviticus consists of laws, this legislation is placed within a narrative framework that picks up where the story of Exodus ends. The rituals prescribed in Leviticus require the sanctuary that is described and set up in Exodus. While the physical structure of the sanctuary was crucial, it was the resident presence of God that made the place powerful. This is where Leviticus comes in. Here at the heart of the Torah, the focus is on the way God's people are to interact with divine holiness.

When the Lord calls to Moses from the "tent of meeting" (1:1), he wastes no time launching into a series of commands regarding the heart of worship: sacrifice. Given that animal sacrifices are foreign and even repulsive to us, how do we begin to understand the divine message and get something out of it? Where is the meaning in a ritual?

Systems of activity. A ritual is a system of activities. Do you get ready for work on Mondays? What activities are necessary for this? At the very least, you need to get dressed. Before you get dressed, you must get out of bed and locate the clothes you will put on. We could call these *prerequisite* activities. Then you start the actual process of dressing. Although some things must be done before others, your routine is capable of some flexibility. Because your *goal* is the reason for the activity system, it determines the activities you must include and shapes their order.

Dressing may belong to a larger activity system, such as getting your family ready for the day. This illustrates the fact that activity systems, like all other systems, are *hierarchical*, with systems consisting of smaller systems and making up larger systems. When you finish dressing, you may need to tidy your room by putting away the items you decided not to wear. This would be *post-requisite* activity.

Burnt offerings involve some of the same kinds of factors that can be found in connection with your dressing for work. While your dressing may have become fairly regularized as a routine, any relevant external authority (e.g., your company or society) is concerned only with the result and does not dictate the steps of your procedure. There are some routines, however, that are *fixed/formulaic*. For example, to withdraw money from an ATM or to go online, you must follow the protocol set by the bank or your internet provider. If you fail to go through the series of specified steps in just the right order, your process will be invalidated. Similarly, rituals are fixed/formulaic activity systems. The Lord is concerned with the burnt offering *procedure* as well as its *result*.

The meaning of a ritual is found in its unusual goal. Leviticus 1:9 tells us that the *overall goal* of the burnt offering is to provide a gift of pleasing aroma to the Lord. The word for "food offering" here is usually understood to mean something like "a burnt offering" (NIV). The Lord receives his "food offering" in the form of smoke by "smelling" ("pleasing aroma"). The Lord receives his meat in an extraordinary way, through smoke. What appears to be impractical wastefulness is due to the fact that the receiving party in the *transaction* (transfer of something of value) is superhuman. He does not belong to our ordinarily accessible material world.

Through rituals the Israelites could enjoy limited *interaction* with God. They could come to the sanctuary, the "tent of meeting" (1:1, 3, 5, etc.), and give something tangible to him to express their devotion, thanks, or desire to receive forgiveness. In the case of the burnt offering, they could give him a token food gift (1:9) and receive his gracious response of expiation, that is, removal of evil ("make atonement"; 1:4).

Application. Rituals, including Christian rituals of baptism and the Lord's Supper/communion, transcend the boundary between the seen and unseen realms. So does prayer. We are not completely cut off from God. Through prayer and ritual, it is as though we can reach out and touch him. When Jesus came, people could touch him because he came without a "bubble" to isolate him from the moral and physical disease of the fallen human race. His death and resurrection make it possible for us to be restored to face-to-face communion with God so that rituals will no longer be needed (cf. Rev 21:22).

LEVITICUS 2:1–16

Original Meaning. In 2:1–3 the grain offering handed over to the priest was to be semolina/grits of wheat. Although this was not the "finest flour" (2:1) in terms of texture, it was fine in the sense that it was choice food rather than ordinary flour. The oil helped the offering burn on the altar and the incense enhanced the pleasing aroma (2:2). Both oil and incense are associated with joy (Prov 27:9).

A grain offering involved no butchering, blood, or hide to serve as a priest's commission, so the priest kept the remainder of the grain offering after he scooped a handful from it and burned that part as a token portion for the Lord on the altar (2:2). This was the procedure for grain offerings on behalf of non-priests. The grain offering for a priest, by contrast, was completely burned on the altar (6:23) with no commission, because the priest was both the offeror and the one performing the offering.

Leviticus 2:11–13 present two general rules. The first is a prohibition against yeast because of the even broader rule that no yeast/leaven or honey may be turned into smoke as a food gift to the Lord. This does not apply to offerings that are not burned on the altar, including firstfruits of processed foods (2:12) and leavened loaves made of wheat (23:17).

The second general rule is a positive one: The "salt of the covenant of your God" must be included with all grain offerings, again as an application of a more general rule: All offerings, implicitly including animal sacrifices, must be salted (2:13).

Whereas the earlier instructions in Leviticus 2:1–10 concern grain offerings from semolina of wheat, 2:14–16 tell what to do if you bring a "firstfruits" grain offering. This section resumes the series of subcases within the overall category of cooked grain offerings. This makes sense because its preparation includes a kind of cooking (2:14). The ritual process at the sanctuary is the same as in the other cases (2:16), but Leviticus 2 separates this parched variety from the earlier cooked offerings because it includes incense like uncooked offerings (2:15), it consists of "heads of new grain" (2:14) rather than a ground wheat product, and it is mandatory rather than voluntary.

Application. Bloodless Israelite sacrifices of grain have helped us to understand that we can truly offer ourselves to God as a "living sacrifice" and "be transformed by the renewing" of our minds rather than conforming "to the pattern of this world" (Rom 12:1–2). By meeting the needs of other people, we can give gifts that are "a fragrant offering, an acceptable sacrifice, pleasing to God" (Phil 4:18). "Through Jesus, therefore, let us continually offer to God a sacrifice of praise—the fruit of lips that openly profess his name. And do not forget to do good and to share with others, for with such sacrifices God is pleased" (Heb 13:15–16).

LEVITICUS 3:1–17

Original Meaning. Leviticus 3 outlines the procedure for the *shelamim* sacrifice, which can be translated "well-being offering" (so-called "peace" or "fellowship" offering). The translation "well-being" comes from the idea of *shalem* ("whole/sound"), reflecting the fact that this sacrifice is offered for happy circumstances. The well-being offering is called *zebah shelamim* (Lev 3:1) because it belongs to the *zebah* category of sacrifices. This category differs from burnt and purification offerings in that those who offer *zebah* sacrifices eat the meat, thereby materially benefiting from their own sacrifices.

While well-being offering animals, like burnt offerings, must be without physical defect, there are two differences.

1. While a bird can be a burnt offering (1:14–17), birds are not used for well-being offerings.
2. Whereas burnt offerings from the herd or flock must be male (1:3, 10), a well-being offering can be either male or female (3:1, 6). In Leviticus 3 a physiological difference between sheep and goats requires that these flock animals be treated separately: The suet/fat of the sheep that is turned into smoke on the altar includes its fat tail (3:9), which a goat does not have (cf. 3:14).

Application of blood to the sides of the outer altar is the same as in the burnt offering. However, the suet (hard fat) portions are removed and only those parts are turned into smoke. While the offering as a whole is brought to the Lord (3:1, 6, 12) and the fat is burned for him (3:16), the breast and thigh are allotted by God to the priests as their commission and the offeror eats the rest. So, there is a three-way distribution of the body of the animal among the Lord, the priests, and the offeror.

The offeror's portion is sacrificial meat from an animal that has been dedicated to God. It is a sacred meal. So, the Lord's ritual rules follow the food out of the sacred precincts to govern some aspects of its consumption (7:15–16). Because the meat is holy and therefore must not be brought into contact with ritual impurity, the offeror must be ritually pure in order to eat it (7:19–21).

At the end of Leviticus 3, verses 16b–17 state general sacrificial rules regarding suet/fat and blood that are especially relevant to the well-being offering because its fat is removed for the Lord and the flesh is consumed by the offeror.

Application. Like ancient Israelites who brought well-being offerings to the sanctuary, we can joyfully express thanks to God in all kinds of ways, including prayer, praise through music, and tangible gifts to him and his work of service for others. We can also fulfill vows of commitment, resources, or service, and we can simply express love and devotion to him anytime we wish. In these ways we can learn to live in God's presence.

LEVITICUS 4:1–35

Original Meaning. Leviticus 4 introduces the *hattat* sacrifice, which is commonly translated "sin offering." It is clear that *hattat* as a kind of sacrifice should be understood as "purification offering" (as in NIV84), a rendering that covers both purification from sins and purification from physical ritual impurities. The usual translation "sin offering" is misleading because it implies that the *hattat* sacrifice deals only with sin as moral fault and that it is the only sacrifice to do so. The interpretation "sin offering" generates problems that do not really exist, such as the question: How has a woman sinned in giving birth, so that she must sacrifice a "sin offering" (12:6–8)? She has not sinned at all. Rather, she has enjoyed the divine blessing to "be fruitful and multiply" (Gen 1:28). Her sacrifice is for physical ritual impurity, which is not "sin" in the sense of moral fault. The category *hattat* ("purification offering") includes a much wider variety of rituals than any of the other types of Israelite sacrifices.

The purification offerings prescribed in Leviticus 4 are required to remedy inadvertent violations of any of the Lord's commands (4:2), once the sinner realizes what they have done. Leviticus teaches us about the nature of sin and about what God thinks of it. While an inadvertent fault is not as serious as a wrong that is motivated by an attitude of rebellion, it is still a sin that must be taken seriously and properly remedied.

The most important procedural difference between purification offerings in Leviticus 4 has to do with locations of blood applications. On this basis we can distinguish between what can be called "outer sanctum" (4:3–21) and "outer altar" (4:22–35) purification offerings.

"Outer sanctum" purification offering. In Leviticus 4 either the high priest (4:3–12) or the entire community (4:13–21) sacrifices a bull. The procedures for the high priest and community are the same, with the qualification that in the latter case, the representative elders rather than the high priest lean their hands (one hand each) on the head of the victim (4:15). The high priest officiates both rituals.

Notice that the high priest performs two applications of blood in the outer sanctum. First, he sprinkles it seven times in front of the inner veil (4:6, 17). Then he daubs some blood on the horns of the altar of incense (4:7a, 18a). Following these applications, he goes out to the courtyard and disposes of the remaining blood by pouring it at the base of the outer altar (4:7b; 18b).

"Outer altar" purification offering. The outline of activities belonging to the "outer altar" purification offering appear three times in 4:22–35 to allow for variations concerning the offeror and the animal victim. A chieftain is required to bring a male goat (4:22–26), but a commoner offers a female flock animal, whether a goat (4:27–31) or a sheep (4:32–35).

The "outer altar" ritual differs from the more elaborate "outer sanctum" type in several respects.

1. The "outer altar" sacrifice uses flock animals rather than bulls.
2. An ordinary priest can officiate it.
3. There is only one application of blood to the horns of the altar *outside* the sacred tent.
4. The officiating priest eats the meat.

Application. Forgiveness is not to be taken for granted as if it is easy, to be dispensed the way we hand out compliments.

To for*give* means to *give* up something. True forgiveness is tough. It is not automatic and it has a cost, even for God—especially for God, who absorbs the prerequisite cost in the sacrifice of his Son. We should have a forgiving attitude as Jesus did when he was being crucified (Luke 23:34).

LEVITICUS 5:1–13

Original Meaning. *"Graded" purification offering.* Leviticus 5:1–13 continues a major organizing principle of the book: Gradations of sacrificial victims/materials are presented in order of descending value, beginning with, and therefore honoring, the more valuable offerings even if the lesser ones may have been sacrificed more frequently in actual practice.

By comparison with chapter 4, we see that the rituals in 5:1–13 comprise a related but distinct subcategory of purification offerings. While it does make allowances for the poor, the fact that its function is distinguished from the chapter 4 rituals in other ways as well—noninadvertence and prior confession—indicates that it is not simply a poor person's purification offering.

A bird cannot be offered by itself as a purification offering, presumably because it is too small a victim, so it is accompanied by another bird for a burnt offering (5:7–10). Whereas the priest simply drains out the blood of the burnt offering bird against the side of the altar (1:15), he sprinkles some blood of the purification offering bird there (not on the horns as in other purification offerings) and then drains out the remainder at the base of the altar (5:9; cf. 4:7, 18, 25, 30, 34).

That the bird rituals are a unit is shown by the fact that the expiation formula is stated only once, covering both rituals as a single complex (5:10). The combination of a purification offering with a burnt offering serves as the functional equivalent of a single purification offering of a flock animal (cf. 5:6). So, the burnt offering supplements the *quantity* of the purification offering. It is true that a burnt offering expiates (1:4; 16:24; cf. 14:19–20; Job 1:5; 42:8), but in combination with a purification offering its function is subsumed to provide what amounts to a greater purification offering.

In Leviticus 5:11–13 the purification offering of grain is like the uncooked semolina offering in 2:1–3 except that its quantity of flour is specified as one tenth of an *ephah* and no oil or incense are added because it is for an unjoyful occasion of sin. After the priest turns the token portion to smoke on the altar, the remainder belongs to him (5:13). Although it consists of grain, it is not a *minhah* ("grain offering"); the text insists that this is a purification offering (5:11–12). Like other purification offerings, it provides expiation prerequisite to forgiveness (5:13). However, it is unique as the only mandatory expiatory sacrifice that lacks blood (cf. Heb 9:22).

Application. If mercy and justice are crucial components of God's love, which he offers to us (Rom 5:5), it stands to reason that we should think about how to implement them *together in a balanced way*. Mercy and justice are principles to be implemented as decisions; they are not simply emotions. Justice is the standard/rule governing a given situation, which serves as an anchor to keep you from falling over as you extend mercy.

LEVITICUS 5:14–6:7

Original Meaning. *Making reparation to heal a wrong.* Under certain circumstances, an Israelite was to offer a kind of sacrifice labeled as an *asham* ("reparation offering" [author's translation], 5:15, 18; 6:6). The customary rendering "guilt offering" (NIV) is inadequate because it fails to capture the sense that an *asham* redresses a liability that has been incurred. Furthermore, "guilt offering," like the translation "sin offering" for the purification offering, is too general.

Misusing the Lord's property. In 5:14–19 there are two subcases. In the first subcase an Israelite violates the boundary of holiness by inadvertently misappropriating something that belongs to the Lord for his or her own purpose. An example could be eating produce that has been dedicated as tithe or firstfruits. Such misuse must be committed inadvertently (5:15) in order to be expiable by sacrifice. Before the reparation offering is performed, the sinner must repay the misappropriated amount plus a 20 percent penalty to the Lord via the priest. Because of the seriousness of sacrilege, a reparation offering victim is always a ram, the most valuable animal ever required of a commoner.

The second subcase (5:17–19) is baffling if it is read in isolation, but it makes sense in context. The sin is inadvertent violation of any of the Lord's prohibitive commandments ("Thou shalt not") without knowing it *and continuing to not know about it*. The unknowing individual has pangs of conscience associated with consequences of sin, suggesting that all is not well with the divine-human relationship. Beyond this vague prompting, the sinner is clueless. To cover any contingency, he offers the sacrifice that would cover the worst possibility: the reparation offering. However, without even knowing for sure that sacrilege is involved, it is impossible to make prior reparation, so this requirement is waived.

Misusing human property along with misusing the Lord's name. In 6:1–7 misappropriation of another human being's property is not said to be inadvertent. A sinner who has wronged both a human being and God in this way must remedy the offense by making reparation to the wronged human party (including a 20 percent penalty) and by offering a ram as a reparation offering to the Lord (6:5–6). As with the graduated purification offering, while sacrifice expiates for sin, it does not replace fulfillment of duty.

Application. We can give up our guilt feelings to God. Unidentified guilt hang-ups drive people to distraction, despair, drinking, drugs, and divorce. Unresolved guilt is one among many causes of anxiety disorder, and unidentified guilt erodes assurance and gives birth to depression. But thousands of years ago Leviticus 5:17–19 supplied God's people with a solution: They could be freed from worry by giving the burden of *suspected* guilt over to God at his sanctuary through a reparation offering.

LEVITICUS 6:8–7:10

Original Meaning. *Burnt offerings.* No portions of burnt offerings are eaten by human beings. So, 6:8–12 concerns maintenance of the altar fire (cf. 1:7). A threefold repetition emphasizes that keeping the fire going is of paramount importance (6:9, 12, 13). Leviticus 9:24 will later tell us why: The Lord himself lit it! So, when the altar fire consumes a sacrifice, it is the Lord consuming it by fire.

The directions in 6:10–11 for removing and disposing of ashes from the outer altar to keep the fire going are the only biblical information we have about physically cleaning the sanctuary. In this procedure, we see clear demarcations between boundaries of categories relevant to the sanctuary: holy, profane (nonholy), and pure. The ashes must be transferred from the holy domain to the profane realm outside. Because they come from holy sacrifices, the part of the profane realm to which they go must be pure rather than impure. Holiness is compatible with purity but not with impurity (cf. 7:20–21).

Grain offerings. Verses 14–23 are subdivided into two parts. The first specifies the way priests must eat their portions of grain offerings brought by laypersons (6:14–18). The second, introduced with a new divine speech, gives directions for grain offerings brought by priests (6:19–23). Here is recorded a kind of cooked grain offering not included in chapter 2 because it is mandatory. It is offered by Aaron and the succession of those among his descendants who fill the high priestly office, starting at the time when he is anointed and continuing regularly after that (6:20, 22). Paralleling the daily burnt offering complex, the high priest offers half of his grain offering in the morning and the other half in the evening (6:20).

Because the high priest sacrifices his special grain offering on his own behalf, it must be wholly burned up (6:22), with no portion serving as an agent's commission. Verse 23 places this instruction within a general rule that also applies to grain offerings of ordinary priests.

Purification offerings. Chapter 4 did not say what happens to the remaining meat of an "outer altar" purification offering, which is sacrificed on behalf of a chieftain or commoner (4:22–35). Leviticus 6:24–30 now fills in the blank: It belongs to the officiating priest. Because the meat is "most holy" (6:29), it carries restrictions: The priest must eat it in the courtyard of the tabernacle, and it can only be shared with males among priestly family members.

Verse 30 reminds us of a limitation that we already know from 4:11–12, 21 regarding the "outer sanctum" sacrifices of the high priest and the entire community. This also applies to the special purification offerings that purge the entire sanctuary with blood on the Day of Atonement (16:27).

Reparation offerings and priestly portions. As with the purification offering, the meat of a most sacred reparation offering must be eaten by a male of the priests in the sacred precincts (7:6–7). Since the text has just referred to priestly ownership of purification and reparation offerings (7:7), the following verses (7:8–10) take the opportunity to continue conveniently summarizing priestly perquisites for most holy sacrifices.

Application. At the center of ancient Israelite worship was holy fire. At its core, the religion of God's people was not a social club, political bloc, or system of dogma. It was an ongoing encounter with the divine. For this experience to continue, the "pilot light" had to remain lit. Sparks of any other kindling were ruled out.

As in Old Testament times, God's ministers of the twenty-first century AD are to be keepers of the flame and teachers of instruction (torah) from the Lord, not lighters of the fire and inventors of their own doctrines. Rather than presuming to preach and teach our own thoughts in order to polish our popular image, we are obliged to allow God's word, illuminated by his Spirit, to kindle inspiration. Like the Olympic torch, God's gospel fire is to be relayed around the world in all kinds of ways, but it must come from the source—the sacred, eternal flame.

LEVITICUS 7:11–38

Original Meaning. *Lay consumption of well-being offerings.* Although 7:11–21 falls within the major block of supplementary instructions addressed to the priests, we can assume that the priests were responsible for sharing such knowledge with the people. In later books, priests were to be custodians and teachers of torah, divine instruction (2 Chr 15:3).

The motivation of thanksgiving affects a well-being offering in a way that is not specified in chapter 3. Along with a "fellowship offering of thanksgiving" a person must offer special grain items (7:12–13). After giving one of each kind of cake or wafer, to be utilized by the officiating priest rather than burned on the altar, the offeror can eat the rest.

While thank offerings must be eaten on the day they are offered, the rule for votive and freewill offerings is more flexible in that they can be consumed the next day as well (7:15–16). However, anything left over on the third day must be incinerated (7:17). The offeror is responsible for making sure that neither he nor she nor anyone else (e.g., a guest) desecrates the meat, which is still holy even though it has reached the limit of its ritual function, by transgressing the time limit by eating it on the third day. Such a violation retroactively invalidates the benefit of the entire sacrifice because it is "impure" meat (Heb. *piggul*; 7:18). Verses 19–21 state additional restrictions on consumption of well-being offering meat for the sake of preserving its sanctity.

General prohibition against consuming fat or blood. With the earlier directions for well-being offerings came the general rule (3:16b–17). Leviticus 7:22–27 reiterates and expands this. The prohibition of consuming suet/fat applies to sacrificeable species even if such an animal dies from something other than slaughter by a human being (7:23–25). Because all suet of such animals belongs to God, for a human being to consume it constitutes sacrilege, which is punishable by being cut off (7:25).

The prohibition of eating blood, that is, meat from which the blood is not drained out at the time of slaughter, is not restricted to sacrificeable species. This command has its roots much earlier than the Israelite sacrificial system in the instructions that God gave to Noah after the flood, when God permitted him and his family to eat meat but not blood (Gen 9:3–4). The blood prohibition applies to any bird or land animal (Lev 7:26–27) but not fish. Notice that neither Leviticus 3 nor 7 says that all blood is the LORD's. While sacrificial suet is consumed by the Lord's fire, there is no indication that all blood must be consumed this way.

Priestly portions. The priestly portions of a well-being offering consists of (1) the breast (7:30)—and (2) the right thigh, which is dedicated without a ritual gesture (7:32, 34).

Verses 37–38 conclude the first major portion of the book of Leviticus—chapters 1–7, which provide prescriptive rules governing performance of sacrifices. This summary lists types of sacrifices in the order of their treatment in 6:8–7:36 but inserts "the ordination offering" (*milluim*) before the well-being offering (7:37). The ordination offering is part of the complex of rituals through which the priests are consecrated for their function as the Lord's special agents (Exod 29; Lev 8).

Application. Our ability to effectively express joy in worship is dependent on Christ and his sacrifice. We need Christ for joyful worship because all of our communication with heaven is dependent on him. As the divine "Word" who "became flesh" (John 1:1–5, 14), he serves as Jacob's ladder, a highway of interaction between heaven and earth (John 1:51; cf. Gen 28:12). Without him and the priestly mediation bought by his sacrifice, we would have no access to God. Even the prayers of the saints (i.e., "God's people," NIV) need the mediation of holy incense to accompany them as they come up before God in his heavenly temple (Rev 8:3).

LEVITICUS 8:1–36

Original Meaning. *Beginning of the sanctuary's ritual function.* Chapter 8 describes the ceremonies by which the sanctuary and its priesthood were consecrated and the priests ordained.

Consecration ceremony. The description of consecration in chapter 8 fulfills the detailed prescription in Exodus 29, thereby contributing to the linkage between the two books. We can outline Leviticus 8, which describes the consecration service, as follows:

Preliminary
- God commands Moses to assemble materials, participants, and congregation (8:1–3)
- Moses carries out the command to get ready for the service (8:4–5)

Anointing
- Moses washes Aaron and his sons (8:6)
- Moses dresses Aaron in his high priestly regalia (8:7–9)
- Moses anoints the tabernacle (8:10)
- Moses anoints the altar (8:11)
- Moses anoints Aaron's head (8:12)
- Moses dresses Aaron's sons in their priestly vestments (8:13)

Sacrifices
- Moses officiates a purification offering on behalf of the priests (8:14–17)
- Moses officiates a burnt offering on behalf of the priests (8:18–21)
- Moses officiates an ordination sacrifice on behalf of the priests (8:22–29)

Anointing
- Moses sprinkles anointing oil and blood from the altar on the priests (8:30)

Concluding
- Moses instructs the priests to eat ordination meat and to remain seven days (8:31–35).
- Aaron and his sons fulfill Moses's concluding instructions (8:36).

Before dressing Aaron's sons, Moses consecrated three things by anointing them with the sacred anointing oil: the tabernacle, the altar, and Aaron's head. These represented the three major parts of the sanctuary infrastructure, with Aaron standing for the priesthood. While the other priests also received anointing oil later on (8:30), Aaron's anointing on his head was special, so that he and each high priest who succeeded him could be called the "anointed priest."

At the heart of the ritual complex were three sacrifices on behalf of the priests. The first sacrifice had the primary goal of purifying and consecrating the outer altar (8:15). The priests benefited from the purification offering in the sense that the altar's qualification made possible their subsequent officiating on it.

The remainder of the "outer altar" purification offering was incinerated outside the camp rather than eaten by Moses as an agent's commission (8:17). Although he officiated on this occasion, he was not an Aaronic priest qualified to partake of the most holy sacrifices.

Ordination sacrifice to authorize priests for their job. While the first two kinds of sacrifices—purification offering and burnt offering—were to be performed on other occasions as well, the third was unique to the ordination event. The label for the ordination sacrifice is *milluim* (8:22, 28, 29, 31, 33), an abstract plural meaning "filling." This expression refers to having one's hand filled with the tool(s) or insignia of one's job. By extension it signifies authorization to fulfill an official function. Ordination was not simply a badge of honorable status; it was a commission to do a job for the Lord.

The ordination sacrifice had strong affinities Iith the holy (not most holy) well-being offering. Aside from the fact that it was a "pleasing aroma," a food gift to the Lord (8:28), Moses elevated the breast and kept it as his portion for officiating (8:29). Furthermore, the offerors ate the remaining meat (8:31–32), and the sacrifice involved special grain items like the thank offering (8:26).

Two major aspects of the ordination offering made it unique.

1. Before dashing the blood of the ordination ram on the sides of the outer altar, Moses put some of the blood on the lobe of Aaron's right ear, on his right thumb, and on his right big toe. Then he did the same to his sons (8:23–24). In this way he connected Aaron and his sons to the Lord and his altar by a bond in blood, as he had linked the Israelites to the Lord through covenant sacrifices by tossing half of the blood on the people after dashing the other half on an altar (Exod 24:5–8).
2. Before turning the suet portions, right thigh, and grain items into smoke on the altar, Moses linked them together with each other and with the priests by laying the grain items on the suet portions and right thigh, placing these in the hands of Aaron and his sons, and elevating them to the Lord (8:26–28).

Oil and blood had been separately applied to the priests (8:12, 23–24), but then these elements came together when Moses sprinkled anointing oil and some blood from the altar on Aaron and his sons and their garments (8:30). The anointing oil consecrated them by virtue of its holy nature. The blood from the altar consecrated them because it was taken from the altar that was earlier consecrated.

Completion of the priests' "rite of passage" required completion of a seven-day period (8:33–35). This element of time—seven days, as in the initial process of creation by God (Gen 1) and as in other ritual transitions, including purification from severe ritual impurities—was essential to elevation of status. During the week, a purification offering was to be performed each day to purify the outer altar. Because the priests were in a transitional/liminal and therefore vulnerable state, they were not to leave the sacred precincts (Lev 8:33–35).

Application. It is the Spirit who empowers Christians for leadership and the authority that goes with it, just as he distributes all other spiritual gifts (1 Cor 12). If Christians had solved their questions of leadership by following God's leading and guidelines (including Paul's letters to Timothy and Titus) during the past couple of millennia, imagine how much trouble and bloodshed would have been avoided. By turning sacred offices into positions of political domination rather than humble spiritual leadership, Christianity has suffered disunity, loss of real spiritual power and divine protection, and disenfranchisement of many believers as God's "royal priesthood" (1 Pet 2:9). Christians are called and consecrated to go out into the world to praise God for transformation from darkness to light that has been wrought by Christ.

LEVITICUS 9:1–24

Original Meaning. Following the seven days of consecration, the complex of sacrifices that Aaron and his sons performed on their first officiation on the eighth day (9:1) consisted of the following:

Sacrifices on behalf of the priests
- Purification offering for the priests: bull calf (9:8–11)
- Burnt offering for the priests: ram (9:12–14)

Sacrifices on behalf of the nonpriestly community
- Purification offering for the nonpriestly community: male goat (9:15)
- Burnt offering for the nonpriestly community: calf and lamb (9:16)
- Grain offering mixed with oil for the nonpriestly community (9:17)
- Well-being offering for the community: ox and ram (9:18–21)

There were seven animals plus a grain offering, making a total of eight sacrifices. Every major kind of sacrifice prescribed in Leviticus 1–7 is represented except for the reparation offering, which never appears as a public sacrifice, presumably because its role is specialized to cases involving certain or suspected sacrilege.

After Moses issued preliminary instructions for assembling materials and people (9:1–7), Aaron approached the altar to make his debut as Israel's high priest, assisted by his newly ordained sons. We are not told what Aaron and Moses said when they blessed the people, from where Aaron had to step down (from the altar?), or why Moses and Aaron entered the sacred tent. Comparison with the dedication of Solomon's temple, at which the king prayed (1 Kgs 8:22–53) between blessing the people twice (8:14–21, 54–61), suggests that Moses and Aaron entered the tabernacle to pray that God would accept the sanctuary, its priesthood, and their sacrifices. The fire that consumed the inaugural sacrifices and thereby legitimized the Aaronic priesthood was henceforth to be kept continually burning on the altar to preserve the miracle of divine acceptance.

Application. Christ appears "for us in God's presence" (Heb 9:24) as our advocate/mediator (1 John 2:1). He pleads our case/cause by presenting evidence, as in a court of law. The evidence is not a CV (Curriculum Vitae) that we have produced, but the fact that we have acknowledged him (Matt 10:32), thereby accepting his CV (Christus Victor), which he has accomplished by his sacrifice and which proves God's right to justly forgive us (Rom 3:24–26).

Christ's CV is not printed on paper or uploaded to the internet but engraved in his flesh (John 20:24–28). John, the beloved disciple, saw him in heaven symbolically depicted as a Lamb that had just been slaughtered but had not yet crumpled to the ground from loss of blood (Rev 5:6). The point is that Christ continually carries the altar/cross event with him *as if it were happening right now* in order to drive home the evidence that gives us peace with God (Rom 5:1) and secures what we need. Even if we have no earthly mediator to speak up for us and nobody here below is praying for our need, we can be certain that Jesus is interceding for us.

LEVITICUS 10:1–20

Original Meaning. Leviticus 10:1–2 cryptically records the ritual mistake of Nadab and Abihu and their destruction by divine fire. Just enough is said to make clear that their offense was to burn incense to the Lord with unauthorized fire, the use of which he had not commanded for this purpose. This fire must have consisted of live coals from a source other than the authorized sacred fire on the outer altar that God himself had lit.

Nadab and Abihu may have had what seemed to them to be a good rationale for doing what they did under the circumstances, just as Uzzah later had a good reason to grasp the ark of the covenant in order to steady it when its cart jolted (2 Sam 6:6–7). In any case, the reasons of these three individuals were not good enough to prevent their sudden death by divine agency. For those who came this close to the "nuclear reactor" of divine presence, there was no leeway for deviations from protocol.

In response to the death of his nephews, Moses conveyed the Lord's interpretation of the event to Aaron, their father. This potent divine speech with double-edged meaning is cast in poetic parallelism (10:3). By stark contrast with the people's joyful shouting only a short time before (9:24), Aaron's response was dead silence (10:3).

The remains of Nadab and Abihu could not be left where they had fallen. So Moses summoned two nonpriestly Levites to approach and carry them to a location "outside the camp" (10:4). Outside the camp is where sacred ashes from the altar and incinerated remains of sacrifices were disposed of. Aaronic priests were supposed to approach the Lord to officiate sacrifices that were burned on his altar, so it is ironic that here Mishael and Elzaphan had to approach priests who had offered unauthorized fire (10:1) and whom the Lord had burned (10:2) in order to grimly carry them out of the holy area.

To prevent further misrepresentation of God and loss of life, the Lord commanded Aaron and his surviving sons, Eleazar and Ithamar, to abstain from mourning in the usual ways of disheveling hair and tearing garments (10:6). By virtue of their consecration, the priests and their vestments belonged to the sacred sphere that was to be dissociated from death and corpse contamination.

Despite the tragedy, Moses sought to ensure that the surviving priests completed the inaugural sacrifices on behalf of the people by eating their meat portions, which functioned as agents' commissions (10:12–18). Life must go on. Even deep personal grief compounded by horror must be held in check so that the community can be served. After the traumatizing deaths of Nadab and Abihu it is hard to imagine a time when Aaron and his surviving sons would be less interested in eating, but eat they must.

When Moses discovered that instead of properly eating the remainder of the purification offering on behalf of the people (cf. 9:15) the priests had incinerated it like the earlier purification offering on behalf of themselves (9:11), he "hit the roof" ("was angry," 10:16). Undoubtedly, he suspected that Eleazar and Ithamar were reckless like their dead brothers. What's the matter with this generation? Can't they get anything right?

In the process of upbraiding Aaron's surviving sons, Moses uttered words with profound implications for the meaning of the purification offering. Verse 18 simply refers to the rules in 6:24–30, but 10:17 adds a vital element to our understanding of purification offerings: Through eating the meat of such a sacrifice, an officiating priest bears the culpability (NIV "guilt") of the offeror and thereby makes an integral contribution to the process of expiation. No wonder Moses was upset!

Now it was Aaron's turn to speak (10:19–20). Aaron's abstaining from the meat was not a careless ritual mistake but a choice based on priestly reflection regarding implications of the sin of Nadab and Abihu. The priests were unworthy to bear the culpability of others on the very day that their family had fallen under divine condemnation. Moses's approval implies that the sacrifice remained valid despite this departure from the norm.

Application. We do not literally bear the names of tribes over our hearts as Aaron did when he ministered before the Lord (Exod 28:15–21, 29), but we can metaphorically bear on our hearts the names of our family members, work associates, fellow church members, neighborhoods, acquaintances in need, and so on. By serving others and by interceding for them in prayer, we have the privilege of assisting Christ in his priestly ministry. Like Aaron, Eleazar, and Ithamar, we must sometimes carry on for the sake of others in spite of private pain. It is when other people become our own that we most truly "carry each other's burdens" (Gal 6:2)

LEVITICUS 11:1–47

Original Meaning. *Pure and impure animals.* Leviticus 11 continues two themes from chapter 10: eating meat and making distinctions. Not surprisingly, the reason for observing the Lord's dietary distinctions is to emulate the Lord's holiness, which is opposed to impurity (11:44–45).

The last verse of chapter 11 summarizes distinctions that apply to the animal kingdom (11:47). These distinctions have to do with two issues.

1. The first is whether an animal defiles a person who eats/ingests it.
2. The other is whether the carcass of an animal can also defile a person who merely touches it. The carcass of a *tame* ("unclean") animal or of a permitted/pure animal that dies by itself contaminates by touch. The defiled individual incurs a light ritual impurity remaining until evening (11:24–40), which has the consequence that contact with holy things is forbidden during this time. This state of impurity implies that the person must ritually bathe. Carrying any part of an "unclean" carcass or eating from the carcass of a permitted animal that has died of itself requires laundering of clothes as well (11:25, 28, 40). Within the unclean category, eight exceptional species that move along the ground also contaminate nonhuman objects (11:29–38).

When the Lord created the animals, he pronounced them all "good" (Gen 1:21, 25), but Leviticus 11 has to do with the unnatural matter of eating animals that were not created to be eaten. A camel, donkey, or horse may be excellent for something else, such as a means of transportation, so God says that they are not good for eating.

Once the categories are in place, the next question is how to tell which creature belongs to which category. Some are specified by criteria, others by lists of specific species, and still others by both. Leviticus 11 uses criteria if possible, both for the sake of convenience and economy. However, where adequate criteria are not available, as in the case of birds, a list appears instead.

Criteria are of several kinds, including especially a creature's physiology of locomotion (divided hoofs, cleft-footed, paws, jointed legs, fins) as well as outer covering (scales) and manner of digestion (chewing cud). All of the criteria in Leviticus 11, including behavioral characteristics of locomotion and digestion, are apparent to someone who observes a live creature itself without the need to study external factors such as diet, society, mating behavior, and so on.

The conclusion 11:43–45 emphasizes the most important point of the chapter: Observing the Lord's dietary regulations has the purpose of emulating the Lord's holiness, which is antithetical to impurity. If God's people make themselves odious by what they eat, they misrepresent him. So, living according to the dietary distinctions outlined in chapter 11 is vital for maintaining the health of the divine-human relationship.

Application. If we really want to help ourselves, the best way to do it is to follow the comprehensive "manufacturer's handbook," that is, the Bible. It is true that the Bible cannot deal with every detail of our lives, some of which were not known when it was written (e.g., smoking), yet it covers all the major bases to the extent that we can apply those principles to particulars that crop up. The Bible rightly places our well-being within the context of our covenant connection with God, whose grace alone can give us ultimate health as a gift, not because we earn it.

LEVITICUS 12:1–8

Original Meaning. Leviticus 12 is the shortest chapter in Leviticus. The first week or two of a child's life, depending on the sex of the child, is treated like the regular ritual impurity of a menstrual period (12:2, 5). This impurity is communicable to persons by touch (15:19), and whatever the woman lies or sits on conveys impurity to those who contact them (15:20–23).

When the period of impurity is over, the mother must bring a pair of sacrifices to the sanctuary: a young (year-old) sheep for a burnt offering and a dove or pigeon for a purification offering

(12:6). If the mother cannot afford a sheep for a burnt offering, she can offer a bird instead. While the officiating priest would slaughter a bird at the altar because of its small size (Lev 1:15; 5:8), there is no indication in 12:6 that the offeror is not permitted to slaughter a sheep, as usual (cf. 1:4–5, 11). In this case the offeror happens to be a woman, which shows that women could participate in sacrifices as offerors.

By translating *hattat* as "sin offering" in 12:6, 8, English versions of the Bible raise the question: How has the mother sinned? Closer examination shows that the goal/meaning of the ritual procedure is to remove physical ritual impurity from the woman so that she is ritually pure, not to remove moral fault from her in preparation for divine forgiveness. So, her *hattat* is a "purification offering."

Now we run into a longstanding crux of interpretation. Postnatal purification of a mother is affected by the sex of her child. Why does a mother's ritual impurity last twice as long if she has a girl? Interpreters have suggested a variety of answers. Since some vaginal bleeding can occur on the part of a newborn girl, the doubled time of the mother's purification could be based on the actual and potential genital discharge of both females.

Application. The fact that the effects of sin are already present at birth shows that they pervade our being (Pss 51:5; 58:3). It is no accident that Christ gave forgiveness with healing during his earthly ministry. This is a foretaste of the gift provided by his sacrifice, the ultimate purification offering. We think of this as a sacrifice for sin, and so it was (John 1:29). However, by overlooking the fact that purification offerings addressed not only *acts* of sin but also the state of *mortality* that results from sin, Christians have missed a magnificent fact.

LEVITICUS 13:1–59

Original Meaning. Since the symptoms of skin disease in chapter 13 are rather complicated and potentially ambiguous, it is no wonder their interpretation was left for priestly experts. This chapter contains a number of obscure Hebrew medical terms, the most important of which is the overall designation for ritually impure skin conditions: *tsaraat*.

The common translation "leprosy" has arisen from the LXX (Septuagint) translation of *tsaraat* as *lepra*, the word that also appears in the New Testament (Matt 8:3; Mark 1:42; Luke 5:12–13). Just as Hippocrates appears to have used Greek *lepra* with reference to several skin diseases, Hebrew *tsaraat* applies to a complex of conditions, including some that resemble psoriasis and vitiligo. Some scholars have contended that Hebrew *tsaraat* and Greek *lepra* do not refer to modern "leprosy," now known as Hansen's disease, for which Greek could use another term: *elephantiasis*. Although diseases can change over time and *tsaraat* in Leviticus 13–14 applies to a variety of conditions that can even affect fabrics and houses, some key symptoms of the chronic form of human *tsaraat* in Leviticus 13 correspond to those of Hansen's disease. Therefore, it appears that biblical *tsaraat* could have at least included an ancient form of the loathsome disease we now label "leprosy."

These considerations point to the key for understanding Leviticus 13–14. The concerns here for diagnosis and quarantine are not with one or more medical conditions per se but with recognizing outward appearances that place persons or things in the ritually impure category, which must be kept separate from the sacred sphere. Because we are dealing here with the world of religious ritual rather than medicine, scientific identification of skin disease is not crucial for understanding the biblical message.

Here is a reader's digested outline of the diagnoses and other instructions in Leviticus 13, following the introduction to divine speech in 13:1:

Impure skin disease on persons (13:2–44)
Prescribed behavior of skin diseased persons (13:45–46)
Impure spoiling = mold in fabrics (13:47–59)

In Leviticus 13:2–44 the diagnostic procedure is logical. A person suspected of having skin disease is brought to a priest, who inspects the affected area. If he observes a clear manifestation of the disease according to the criteria listed above, he pronounces the person ritually impure. If there is a question, however, the priest quarantines the person for a week, after which he examines the affected area again. If it betrays signs of skin disease, it is pronounced as such, but if the case is still ambiguous, there is another week of quarantine. If no changes for the worse identify the condition as skin disease, the priest declares the individual "clean," that is, free from that serious impurity. However, apparently as a result of a two-week quarantine for suspected skin disease, the person has incurred minor impurity that requires laundering his or her clothes (13:6, 34).

In 13:47–59 a parallel procedure of priestly examination at one-week intervals is applied to fabrics affected by mold or mildew, with the following differences:

1. The priest does not pronounce a fabric impure without quarantining it for at least a week.
2. The affected material is washed before a second week of quarantine if it is necessary.
3. If the abnormal condition fades after the fabric has been washed and quarantined for a second week, the priest tears/cuts out the affected area.
4. An impure fabric is destroyed by fire.

Application. Like the other biblical laws regulating ritual impurities, the instructions in Leviticus 13–14 are obsolete in terms of our obligation to observe them. However, from "skin disease" we learn about the human condition in relation to God. This impure affliction is a powerful metaphor for the human state induced by sin. Since the fall (Gen 3), our state of mortality progressively and inexorably moves us in the direction of decay and death (Rom 5:12; 6:23).

Although our healthy mortality is not as ugly and its trajectory is not as precipitous as the heightened state of mortality represented by skin disease or leprosy, it is all a matter of degree. Even if a priest should declare us "clean," this is only relative. Still mortal, we remain unable to bask in the full glory of God's presence. Still longing for immortality like the legendary Gilgamesh or a fountain of youth like Ponce de León, the Spanish explorer, we must await the divinely appointed day when "the perishable must clothe itself with the imperishable, and the mortal with immortality." (1 Cor 15:53).

LEVITICUS 14:1–57

Original Meaning

Purification after Healing from Skin Disease (14:1–32). A person healed from skin disease undergoes an elaborate purification process in phases that occur on the first, seventh, and eighth days. Each of these phases progressively moves the individual toward full purity status so that he or she can be reinstated into the society of the Lord's people, who dwell within the bounds of the camp where God's sanctuary is located.

- First-day procedures (14:4–8)
  - Bird ritual (14:4–7)
  - Shaving and ablutions (14:8)
- Seventh-day shaving and ablutions (14:9)
- Eighth-day sacrifices (14:10–20)

When a person banished outside the camp because of skin disease believes that the condition has gone away, he or she calls for a priest to come out and make an inspection. The priest must come out because the person is not permitted to come inside the camp to him. If the priest confirms that the skin disease is gone, he presides over a nonsacrificial elimination ritual employing two birds (14:4–7).

One bird is slaughtered over water from a flowing source, such as a spring. The priest takes the other bird, still alive, along with cedar wood, crimson yarn, and hyssop, and dips them all in the blood of the slain bird that has mixed with the water. Then the priest sprinkles the blood-water mixture seven times on the person undergoing purification and sets the living bird free into open country. In this way the ritual impurity is transferred from the person to the living bird via the blood of the slain bird, and the living bird carries the impurity away into oblivion.

Both here and in the parallel ritual for purifying a house (14:49–53), sending a living bird away shows some similarity to the way Azazel's goat (the so-called "scapegoat") is sent off into the desert on the Day of Atonement after the completion of the purgation of the Lord's earthly dwelling (16:10, 20–22). Unlike Azazel's goat, the live bird receives blood from a slain creature within the same individual ritual as an integral part of the same purification, not as a subsequent phase.

Following the bird ritual, the candidate for cleansing must launder his/her clothes, shave off all hair, and bathe in water. At that point the individual becomes ritually "pure." In this context "pure" means "pure enough for this stage," which allows for entry into the camp. However, because some impurity remains, the person must stay outside his or her tent. On the seventh day there is another shaving, laundering, and bath, after which the person is "clean" again (14:9).

Once the first- and seventh-day procedures have restored the healed person's level of purity to the point that coming to the sanctuary is permissible, the final stage on the eighth day requires the Israelite to offer a group of sacrifices at the sanctuary (14:10–20). Because the reparation offering is unusual, it is outlined in considerable detail (14:12–18). Rather than simply taking the blood and dashing it on the sides of the altar, the priest takes some of the blood and puts it on the right extremities of the offeror who is undergoing purification.

Next, the priest sprinkles some of the oil with his finger seven times before the Lord, apparently to enhance the dedication already accomplished by the elevation. Then he applies some of the oil to the same right extremities of the Israelite, on top of the blood. Lastly, the priest puts the remaining oil on the head of the Israelite and completes the rest of the sacrifice, thereby finishing the reparation offering phase for the offeror (14:18).

The next sacrifice is the purification offering (14:19). Performance of the burnt and grain offerings bring the expiatory complex to successful conclusion and finally, for the last time, the Israelite is "clean" (14:20)! Restoration is done.

Since the eighth-day sacrificial process involves three animals—two male lambs and a yearling ewe—it is expensive. Thus, for those who cannot afford it, 14:21–32 outline a parallel procedure with two birds substituted for the purification and burnt offering animals. There is no substitute for the male lamb of the reparation offering, which is the first and most important sacrifice on this occasion.

Fungus in Houses (14:33–53). The diagnostic procedure for a house (14:35–45) largely resembles that of chapter 13 with regard to persons and garments. If the priest finds "depressions" (14:37), he places it under quarantine and examines it again after seven days to see whether it has spread. If it has, the material of the affected area is replaced (cf. 13:56).

A quarantined house makes any person who even enters it unclean until evening, and the residential activities of lying down or eating there require laundering of clothes as well (14:46–7). The house conveys its severe impurity by "overhang," contaminating everything within its enclosed space, even without direct contact. Because the priest is the one who places the house under quarantine, he is also the one who determines when its impurity begins. This explains why the priest orders that the house be emptied before he inspects it so that movable belongings do not become impure when he commences the quarantine (14:36). Clearing out the house also facilitates total inspection of its walls.

Here is additional evidence that Leviticus 14 is concerned with legal-religious categories. Just as a city ordinance condemning a house and forbidding anyone to enter takes effect when it is announced and posted, so the Israelite priest's declaration of quarantine carries legal force that determines when the house begins to defile by overhang. Obviously, this is not the way medical science works. If you come in contact with an individual carrying a contagious disease before examination by a physician, you are no less at risk than if your contact was after the exam.

If after its repair the house suffers a relapse of fungous infection, it is "unclean" and must be demolished (cf. 13:52, 55, 57). By contrast, if priestly inspection reveals that replacement of the infected material has solved the problem, he pronounces the house "clean" because the infection is gone (14:48). To decontaminate (14:49) the house pronounced "clean," the priest performs an elimination ritual with two birds, just like the first-day procedure for a person, but in this case he sprinkles on the house. By doing this the priest purges the house from ritual impurity so that it is "clean" (14:53).

Application. In our age of instant gratification, we want leaps rather than steps. But most human progress happens in steps. A reason for steps is to understand and/or teach how a process is accomplished. Seeing a polished PowerPoint presentation can be enlightening and enjoyable, but witnessing a demonstration of the steps that have gone into the final product raises the level of appreciation and the possibility that others can learn to make contributions by using the tool.

In addition to providing comprehension, steps are encouraging because they show measurable progress that would not register if shown in leaps. This is part of the phenomenal success of the twelve-step program of Alcoholics Anonymous for overcoming alcohol addiction. Another part is the fact that the program treats afflicted individuals as whole persons, including the physical, emotional, spiritual, and social dimensions.

LEVITICUS 15:1–33

Original Meaning. Discharges from genital organs are private matters. Thus, in Leviticus 15, determination of ritual impurities from these sources requires no examination by priests (contrast chs. 13–14). Another difference is the fact that some impure genital fluxes (i.e., nocturnal emission, ejaculation during intercourse, and menstruation) are healthy rather than abnormal.

Two patterns characterize the order in which chapter 15 treats genital discharges: male precedes female and the abnormal and normal categories create a chiasm.

a abnormal male (15:2–15)
  b normal male (15:16–18)
  b′ normal female (15:18–24)
a′ abnormal female (15:25–30)

Since 15:18 deals with the ritual impurity of sexual intercourse, which involves both genders, it provides a smooth transition from male to female discharges.

Because seminal emissions are of short duration, they give rise to light impurities that only require a man to bathe, launder any fabric or leather with semen on it, and wait until evening (15:16–18) for restoration to purity, which allows contact with holy things. In the case of intercourse, these rules also apply to the woman (15:18).

The slower *zwb* flows are more serious. For normal menstruation, impurity lasts seven days. If a flux is abnormal, a period of impurity persists as long as the symptoms continue, plus seven days beyond their cessation. As sources of impurity, the nonseminal fluxes communicate impurity to other objects and persons in a variety of ways. Objects are secondarily affected when the impure Israelite lies or sits on them. Persons are contaminated by contacting the impure individual or anything that has been under him or her.

A man with an abnormal discharge defiles anyone on whom he spits (15:8) or anyone he touches (unless the man with the discharge has recently rinsed his hands, 15:11). He also contaminates some objects by touch, including an earthen vessel or wooden implement (15:12).

Except when contact is by sexual intercourse, secondarily affected persons incur light impurities that require laundering clothes and bathing and waiting until evening. Sexual intercourse is a more intimate form of contact. So just as a woman shares equally in the light impurity of a man with whom she has intercourse (15:18), a man who has intercourse with a menstruating woman shares her seven-day impurity.

Menstruation is a fairly severe impurity, lasting seven days. But because it is normal and regular, purification calls for no sacrifices. The text does not mention bathing either, but it can be assumed from the fact that purification with water is necessary even for the more minor impurities. Since the regulations for a woman who has given birth and one who has a chronic discharge follow those of menstruation (12:2; 15:25), we can assume that these women must also bathe.

While monthly menstruation was undoubtedly inconvenient, an ancient Israelite woman was not ritually impure and therefore barred from participation in worship at the sanctuary as often as we might suppose. Women married young and generally had as many children as they could. There would not have been a market for contraceptives even if they had been invented. In other words, during much of her childbearing phase of life, a woman was in a state of pregnancy, which interrupts menstruation, or breast-feeding, which can suppress it. Furthermore, it appears that the onset of menstruation at puberty was later and its termination at menopause earlier than in modern times.

When an Israelite with an abnormal discharge is "clean" (15:13, 28) in the sense of physically healed, he or she must wait seven days. At the end of this week the person must launder, bathe in "fresh water" (i.e., flowing water/spring water, 15:13), and at that point becomes ritually "clean" (15:13, 28). In context, the meaning is "pure enough for this stage" (cf. 14:8–9), since there is more to the process.

On the eighth day the individual undergoing ritual cleansing must offer two birds as a purification offering supplemented by a burnt offering (15:14–15, 29–30). This pair is the same as the poor mother's postpartum offering (12:8). The goal is to expiate for (i.e., purge) the person from his or her discharge (15:15, 30). This means that the sacrifice removes the remaining ritual impurity from the offeror.

Leviticus 15:32–33 summarizes by listing the various kinds of cases covered in chapter 15, but 15:31 puts serious teeth into the legislation. Here at the end of the section of the book regulating physical ritual impurities, the Lord warns Moses and Aaron.

In 15:31 the words "defiling my dwelling place" do not limit the possibility of the sanctuary's defilement to an impure person physically entering the sacred precincts. The implication is that anyone in the camp could defile the sanctuary simply by being illegitimately impure, that is, without undergoing proper purification. If it seems strange that impurity could travel through space in this way, keep in mind that we are dealing with dynamic conceptual categories rather than contagious transmission of physical entities (e.g., microorganisms). Remember that a person could become impure simply by entering an "unclean" house (Lev 14:36, 46–47). More to the point, a corpse in a tent contaminated persons and objects within that defined space (Num 19:14–15). The Israelite camp was simply a larger unit of defined space, within which severe enough impurity defiled that which was most sensitive to it: the sacred domain of the sanctuary (cf. Num 5:1–4).

Application. In ancient Israel the concept of mortality could spread like a virus through the influence of physical contact or location within a defined space. It was crucial that this contagious influence not reach and infect sacred things. The sphere of holiness/life was so opposed to that of impurity/mortality that the Lord could not even allow indirect contact between the two. It was not that death itself could actually make God mortal in the same way that it spread to all humankind. Rather, such contact would misrepresent the nature of God to the Israelites.

Erosion of respect for God's immortal nature, which contrasts with human mortality, inevitably leads human beings to underestimate their accountability to him. They lose the healthy fear of God that Christ encapsulated (Matt 10:28). As the immortal Source and Sustainer of life, God holds absolute power over human beings who can and do die. He allows sinners to die so that they will not immortalize sin and all the infectious misery that goes with it (Gen 3:22–24).

While we are no longer required to literally observe the rules of Leviticus governing ritual impurities, reverence for God's holiness is as important as ever. How do we portray God's nature and character? This question applies on a number of levels, including our individual and family lives, our church communities, and our nation. One attitude or act of reverence or irreverence leads to another.

LEVITICUS 16:1–34

Original Meaning. Leviticus 16 can be described as the "inner sanctum" of the Torah. Throughout the year, sacrifices at the Israelite sanctuary removed sins and severe physical ritual impurities from those who offered them there. Once a year, the high priest performed a special complex of rituals to purify the entire sanctuary (Lev 16). Its biblical name is *yom hakkippurim* (23:27–28), "the Day of Purgation," known today as Yom Kippur or the Day of Atonement.

Preparatory Activities (16:1–10). To prepare for special interaction with God in the inner sanctum, the high priest bathed his entire body. Then he donned sacred linen garments reserved for this occasion (16:4). Once the high priest was ready and the required animals were assembled in the courtyard of the sanctuary, he performed a unique preparatory casting of lots to determine the respective ritual roles of two goats provided by the people.

Purification Offerings (16:11–19). The core of the ritual procedure begins in 16:11. After slaughtering the purification offering bull, the high priest was to deposit a censer in the inner sanctum ("the Most Holy Place") to provide a cloud of incense smoke (16:12–13) to shield him from God's lethally glorious presence by covering the *kapporet* (the so-called "atonement cover," NIV, or "mercy seat," ESV, NKJV, etc.). Then he was to bring the bull's blood into the inner sanctum where he would sprinkle some of it once on the *kapporet* and seven times in front of it (16:14). Notice that by sprinkling he would avoid touching it.

Before applying the bull's blood to other parts of the sanctuary, the high priest was to slaughter the Lord's goat (16:6–9) on behalf of the lay community and similarly sprinkle once on and seven times before the *kapporet* (16:15). In this way he would begin the purification offering of the goat before completing that of the bull.

The first part of 16:16 states what the high priest would accomplish by sprinkling the blood of the bull and of the goat in the inner sanctum. By sprinkling on and in front of the ark, the high priest was to remove ritual impurities and two kinds of moral faults—transgressions and sins—that had belonged to the priestly and lay communities from the area of the inner sanctum, including the ark located there.

Having cleansed the inner sanctum, the high priest was to purify the outer sanctum (16:16b), that is, the rest of the tabernacle. The priest was to purge the area and its contents by applying the blood of the bull and of the goat once to a central object and seven times in front of that object.

Exiting to the courtyard, the high priest was to daub the mixed bloods of the bull and goat on the horns of the outer altar in order to purge it (16:18). He was to sprinkle seven times on the altar itself to reconsecrate it (16:19b). The altar needed an extra dose of restoration because the Israelites had brought their sins and impurities to it throughout the year.

Live Goat (16:20–22). Next on the agenda was removal of the moral faults away from the community and its camp by means of the live goat. The high priest, representing his nation, was to lean both his hands on the head of the live goat (16:21). Why would the high priest use two hands rather than one? Perhaps to signify that the goat bears numerous sins of all Israelites and/or to identify a different kind of relationship between the goat and the Israelites. In any case, double hand-leaning plus confession cannot carry the same meaning as leaning one hand on the head of a sacrificial animal to identify its owner as the offeror. For one thing, the high priest has already identified its new owner as "scapegoat" by casting lots (16:8). For another, because he does not offer the live goat to the Lord for his utilization, this is not a sacrifice.

The nonsacrificial procedure with the live goat is an elimination ritual that transfers evils away from people and disposes of them by abandonment. From the sanctuary he removed *physical ritual impurities*, inexpiable rebellious sins, and expiable sins (16:16), but on the live goat he placed *culpabilities*, inexpiable rebellious sins, and expiable sins (16:21).

A (presumably lay) man was to lead what we can call the "tote goat," bearing the moral evils of the Israelites, away into the desert (16:21). Once in a "remote place," an inaccessible place from which the goat could not return to the camp, the assistant leading the goat would turn it loose (16:22).

Concluding Activities of the High Priest (16:23–25). Having completed the dangerous process of expelling moral evil from the sanctuary and camp, the high priest was to bathe again before arraying himself in his ornate vestments and performing the supplementary burnt offerings for the priests and laity at the outer altar (16:23–24).

The core of the "Day of Purgation" (or Day of Atonement) ritual procedure began with the purification offerings (16:11–19) and ended with them (16:25). In between were the live goat ritual (16:20–22), the high priest's transition (16:23–24a), and the burnt offerings (16:24b). So, the purification offerings form a structural "frame" around the other rituals to hold them together as a unified group that coordinates to remove from the sanctuary and camp all Israelite ritual impurities and moral faults accumulated at the sanctuary throughout the year.

Post-Requisite Tasks of Assistants (16:26–28). Leviticus 16:26–28 prescribes some required cleanup activities that are ritual in nature but follow the procedural core and are performed by assistants who are not required to be priests. Contact with these victims defiles each person involved in carrying them outside the camp and incinerating them. Purification of an assistant is like that of the live goat's handler: laundering and bathing (16:28).

Concluding Wrap-Up (16:29–34). Having outlined the ritual procedures to be performed at the sanctuary (16:1–28), this chapter wraps up instructions for the "Day of Purgation" in two ways: (1) by commanding the Israelites to practice self-denial and refrain from work on the tenth day of the seventh month (16:29–31); and (2) by summarizing the main performer (high priest) and beneficiaries of the yearly purgation (16:32–34).

Application. We have found that purging the ancient Israelite sanctuary once a year signified the clearing of God's reputation with regard to his treatment of people who had made different kinds of choices regarding him. Since Christ's ministry in God's heavenly temple has superseded the Aaronic services (Heb 7–10) at the earthly "copy and shadow" (Heb 8:5), the possibility arises that Christ as victim-priest may address a burden of God's reputation that is borne at his headquarters in the temple.

This possibility is strengthened by the fact that "heavenly things" had to be purified by Christ's sacrifice at the beginning of his priestly ministry in God's temple (Heb 9:23), just as part of the earthly sanctuary received purging blood when Aaron and his sons were consecrated. If Christ's better sacrifice has this function at the beginning of his priestly ministry, perhaps it also cleanses the heavenly sanctuary later on in some way that is analogous to the purgation accomplished by the Israelite high priest on the "Day of Purgation."

LEVITICUS 17:1–16

Original Meaning

Bringing All Sacrifices to the Lord (17:1–9). This first warning puts teeth into the rule that the Israelites must bring all sacrifices to the sanctuary for officiation there by the Aaronic priests. A violator is guilty of bloodshed and condemned to suffer the divine penalty of being "cut off," that is, probably extirpation of his or her line of descendants (17:4, 9). The reason for the warning is to stop the Israelites from offering sacrifices out in the open country

The fact that in chapter 17 some Israelites were sacrificing in the open country, away from the sanctuary and its altar (17:5, 7), indicates that they regarded these "goat idols" as supernatural beings. The idea that male goats in uninhabited regions could represent the supernatural is reinforced by a parallel with Isaiah 13:21. That the Lord did not immediately strike dead the Israelites sacrificing to "goat idols" implies that he mercifully recognized that they did not understand the full implications of what they were doing. However, his warning in Leviticus 17 puts an end to any such ignorance.

Warning against Eating Fat or Blood (17:10–14). This second warning puts teeth into the Lord's prohibition against eating any fat or blood. Here he provides the reason: The life is in the blood, which is why he has assigned it the function of ransoming the lives of offerors on the altar (17:11).

Warning against Neglect to Purify Oneself (17:15–16). Verses 15–16 issue the third warning, this time against neglect to make oneself clean. This case has to do with a "pure"/permitted animal dying of a cause other than slaughter by a human being. In 17:15 we read of the two main ways that such an animal could die: naturally by itself or violently by the agency of one or more wild animals. Unlike the earlier warnings, this one (17:15–16) provides no rationale and the penalty for violation is stated differently: "He shall bear his culpability" (author's translation; 17:16). The law applies only to nonpriests. A later law holds priests to a higher standard of purity, as befits their holiness, by prohibiting them from eating such animals altogether (22:8).

Application. How do biblical laws, including those of Leviticus 17, speak to us today? They do not comprehensively specify every detail of the ways we should act and think. Rather, they provide illustrations that reveal the character and values of the divine Lawgiver, thereby establishing the constitution/charter of covenant life with him.

Are Christians expected to keep any of the biblical laws, or are there any from which we would gain benefit by voluntarily observing them? We are not talking about a legalistic, works-oriented approach to salvation, but about people who are already saved enjoying fuller "new covenant" life and service by following divine guidance and thereby revealing God's character to others.

For the purpose of determining whether or how various kinds of Old Testament laws apply today, Christians have traditionally divided them into categories, such as the following:

1. *moral laws*, consisting of the Ten Commandments, which express timeless and universal principles governing relationships with God and other human beings
2. *ritual laws*, which served as "types" or "shadows" until they met their fulfillment at the cross
3. *civil laws*, which were applicable only under Israel's theocratic government
4. *health laws*, which have ongoing value because human bodies function the same today as they did in ancient times

While such categories have some validity and usefulness, we should recognize that the Bible does *not* delineate categories such as those stated above. They are more recent analytical constructs. Biblical law does not even make the sharp distinction between religious and secular categories to which we are so accustomed. Since every aspect of life as the people of God came under his jurisdiction, laws belonging to what we would classify as the religious and secular domains often appear together.

Can we reduce the above into a single, simple rule of thumb to determine whether the Bible intends for Christians to keep a given Old Testament law? Here is an attempt: *A law should be kept to the extent that its principle can be applied, unless the New Testament removes the reason for its application.*

LEVITICUS 18:1–30

Original Meaning. *Incest.* The main area of legislation in chapter 18 is incest. Verse 6 reads: "No one is to approach any close relative to have sexual relations [lit., to uncover nakedness].

I am the LORD." Elsewhere the verb "approach" by itself can be a euphemism for "made love" (Isa 8:3). In Leviticus 18 the combination of "approach" with "to uncover nakedness" unambiguously refers to sexual activity.

In Leviticus 18, incest is defined more broadly than our modern understanding in that relatives by marriage, to whom a man would have easy access within the household, are off limits in addition to blood relatives. Forbidden relatives who marry into one's family include a wife of one's father (18:8), aunt by marriage (18:14), daughter-in-law (18:15), and sister-in-law (18:16). Each of these laws prohibit marriages of widowed or divorced women to men who are related to them by marriage. However, Deuteronomy 25:5–6 recognizes the notable exception of "levirate" marriage.

Leviticus 18:17–18 prohibits a man from sexual unions with two women who are blood relatives of each other: a woman and her daughter or granddaughter (18:17) or a woman and her sister while the first is alive (18:18). Only in this last case is the prohibition limited to bigamy. Whereas it is forbidden to marry a woman and her daughter or granddaughter at all, whether sequentially or simultaneously, it is only forbidden to take (i.e., marry) a sister-in-law while one's wife is still alive, thereby producing rivalry between the two sisters (cf. Leah and Rachel in Gen 29–30).

Misuse of "seed." Leviticus 18:19–23 describes five laws that come under the topic of the Lord's statutes, by contrast to those of Egypt and Canaan (18:2–5), but not under the heading of incest laws (18:6). Nevertheless, four out of five of them also have to do with sexuality.

Intercourse with a menstruating woman is absolutely forbidden in 18:19, and in 18:29 the consequence of this and other offenses is the divine penalty of being "cut off." So how do we explain the fact that in 15:24 a man having sexual relations with a menstruant only incurs a seven-day impurity? Since 15:24 deals with ritual consequences irrespective of intention, it covers situations of accidental violation in which a couple has intercourse without knowing that the woman is menstruating, but they learn this after the fact. In chapters 18 and 20, by contrast, the divine penalty is for deliberate violation; it would be pointless to forbid an accident.

The prohibition of adultery, involving the consent of both parties, is already part of the Ten Commandments (Exod 20:14), but the broader scope of Leviticus 18:20 also includes rape. While becoming impure through intercourse with another man's wife is generated by the physical act, this is not merely the ritual pollution. Rather, it involves permanent moral defilement, for which no ritual remedy is provided.

At the center of the final group of five laws is a prohibition against sacrificing children to the god Molek (18:21), who was worshiped especially by the Ammonites. This law has to do with idolatrous worship of another deity rather than sexual relations, but the close parallel between the wording of 18:21 and the previous verse forges a link for us. Just as you shall not give your penis for seed (i.e., sperm) to the wife of another (18:20), you shall not give any of your seed (posterity/children) to pass through for Molek (18:21). "Sacrifice" in this context means pass through fire (cf. 2 Kgs 16:3; 23:10). Molek worship parallels adultery: Both violate covenant relationships by disloyally giving precious "seed" to parties forbidden to receive it.

Verse 22 reads: "Do not have sexual relations with a man as one does with a woman; that is detestable." The language is devastatingly untechnical, leaving no room for ambiguity. Leviticus 20:13 reiterates, but with a penalty directly attached. This condemnation of homosexual practice as offensive to God is not "politically correct" today, but our task here is to understand what the Bible says, not to rewrite it. Notice, however, that Leviticus does not condemn persons who have homosexual tendencies, as long as they do not act on them.

The last law in chapter 18 prohibits bestiality, whether by a man or a woman. For a man the terminology is almost the same as in 18:20 but slightly more specific and therefore graphic: (lit.) "You shall not put your penis in any animal to become impure by means of it." The language is different for a woman, who is forbidden to initiate mating with an animal by presenting her body to it for this purpose. Again, Leviticus 20 mandates capital punishment for both the human and animal parties (20:15–16).

The conclusion of Leviticus 18 provides powerful incentives to follow the Lord's directives (18:24–30). If the Israelites defile the Lord's land by morally polluting themselves, they will be expelled like the Canaanites, as vividly described by the metaphor of vomiting (18:24–28). The second incentive is to avoid the divine penalty of being "cut off" (18:29–30).

Application. Some regard the biblical approach to homosexuality as "gay bashing." However, according to the Bible, God loves sinners and wants to save individuals who are now gay by transforming them. If God loves them, should we be afraid to love them too? Ultimately it is far more compassionate for God and for us to warn them of danger and to hold out hope for the divine gift of conversion than to say "Peace, peace," when there is no peace (cf. Jer 6:14; 8:11), by condoning gay marriage.

While the church has no biblical license to sanction the practice of homosexuality in any form, Christ's approach demands that it be a haven of support to help precious people—including gays, lesbians, and bisexuals—in their often painful and traumatic journeys of recovery from all kinds of lifestyles. To restore the church as the trusted friend rather than the enemy of sinners requires a major shift of attitude on our part.

LEVITICUS 19:1–37

Original Meaning. It is easy for us to look back with 20/20 hindsight and underestimate the magnitude of the contribution made by Leviticus 19, in which relationships among human beings are to be based on love (19:18)—not power, greed, a self-serving desire to have a good image, or even self-preservation, but love. Yet love is ultimately the best path to self-preservation because without it, mutual assured destruction (MAD) comes sooner or later.

Bases of holiness in the Decalogue. Following the overall command to be holy because the Lord is holy (19:2), 19:3–4 reiterate several of the Ten Commandments.

Ritual holiness. Verses 5–8 repeat the ritual instructions governing acceptable consumption of the offeror's portion of the well-being offering (7:16–18), with the clarification that eating it on the third day profanes the Lord's holy things and the culpability incurred leads to being "cut off."

Social and ethical holiness. Verses 9–10 move to a social matter: Do not be too thorough when you harvest but leave some agricultural produce for the poor and resident aliens to glean. Leviticus 19:11 prohibits stealing, as well as deceiving and lying. Continuing the theme of honesty, 19:12 forbids falsely swearing by and thereby profaning the Lord's name (cf. Exod 20:7). Alongside fraud and robbery, 19:13b prohibits withholding the wages of a hired man, who depends on them, as if they were a deposit or pledge (cf. 6:2). Continuing the idea of protection for disadvantaged members of society, 19:14 prohibits treating a physically-challenged individual disrespectfully or harmfully by taking advantage of that person's weakness. Further upholding social justice, 19:15 addresses the judicial system.

Holiness in the heart. Leviticus 19:16–18 addresses damaging behaviors and the underlying attitudes toward other people that cause or prevent them. Verse 16 speaks against spreading slander and profiting by (lit., "standing upon") the blood of a fellow person. By starting malicious rumors, it is possible to hurt or even destroy a person and, in the process, gain advantage.

Verse 17 strikes at the root of antagonistic behavior. By rebuking rather than hating, a person avoids bearing blame/culpability with regard to someone else in two ways: (1) by preempting one's own sinful action that could result from hatred; and (2) by fulfilling the responsibility to warn the other person. Remarkably, this law controls an *internal attitude.* No human legislative body would dream of formulating such a decree because not even the FBI, with the latest surveillance technology, can enforce it. The Lord can hold people responsible to love (19:18) rather than hate (19:17) or covet (Exod 20:17) because his perception penetrates human thought.

Holiness of mixtures. Leviticus 19:19 prohibits mixtures in breeding cattle, sowing seed in the same field, and manufacturing garments. These laws do not state their rationale and appear strange to modern readers who wear clothes made of all kinds of mixtures of cotton, wool, dacron, rayon, polyester, and so on. The key is in Deuteronomy 22:9, where produce from a mixed vineyard is "forfeit(ed)" (NRSV; NJB). Forfeited to whom? The Hebrew behind these translations literally means "will become holy." In other words, a mixture was holy, and any mixtures were to be forfeited to the holy realm of the sanctuary, where mixtures were appropriately found in some of its fabrics and priestly garments, as well as in the cherubim guarding the ark. The cherubim remind us that in ancient Near Eastern art and literature, mixed beings, including composite guardian creatures, belong to the supernatural realm of the gods. In other words, the laws regarding mixtures seem intended to protect the distinction between the ordinary domain of laypersons and the sacred sphere of the sanctuary.

Sexual holiness. Leviticus 19:20–22 deals with an unusual case of sexual misconduct. The young woman is a slave assigned for another man in advance of her redemption or manumission, that is, while she is still a slave. Because of her nonfree status, she is not betrothed and therefore another man who has sexual relations with her does not commit the equivalent of the capital crime of adultery. Consequently, there is an inquest. If her slave status is confirmed, the sexual partners are not put to death.

Although violation of a designated slave woman is not a capital offense, it is immoral activity offensive to God, violating the spirit of the seventh commandment of the Decalogue, which prohibits adultery. Thus, a man who commits this wrong must sacrifice a reparation offering to the Lord.

Why a reparation offering? Specification of this sacrifice implies that before offering it, the offending man must pay reparation to the wronged party, who has lost property through a deliberate ethical offense (6:4–5). The fact that the biblical text does not specify the one entitled to receive compensation seems to imply that the legal inquiry was to sort out such details. As a result of his required reparation offering, the offending man is forgiven from his sin (19:22).

Holiness of horticulture in the holy land. In 19:23–25 the Lord commands the Israelites to regard the fruit of trees that they plant for food as "uncircumcised" (see NIV text note; i.e., "forbidden" to eat) for the first three years. The metaphor of uncircumcision may have been chosen for at least three reasons.

1. The immature fruit still enclosed in its bud is analogous to a foreskin in that it is removed and discarded.
2. By referring to immature fruit in this way, God encourages compliance by memorably stigmatizing its unfitness to eat. Who would want to eat something referred to as a "foreskin"?

3. The basic rationale for the law seems to be that the Lord claims the promised land and the trees on it just as he claims sons, whose connection to him is shown by their circumcision.

In the fourth year the first fruit considered edible is holy, which means that it, like other required firstfruits, belongs to the sacred domain and presumably must be given to the priests to eat. Encouraging obedience is the promise that the yield of the tree would be increased (19:25).

Holiness versus divination and death. Verse 26 seems to reiterate the command to abstain from eating blood (17:10–14). However, here "blood" is not the direct object. Rather, Israelites are prohibited from eating *on/over* the blood. In this context, and because we know that in some parts of the ancient world blood was poured into the ground to netherworld deities, it has been suggested that eating over the blood may involve occult consultation of ancestral spirits.

Holiness in various areas of ethical and religious conduct. Leviticus 19:29–36 wraps up the chapter by revisiting various areas of ethical or religious life touched on by the earlier laws: sexuality and protection of subordinate females (19:29), respect for divinely appointed authority and Sabbaths (19:30), avoiding consultation of pagan/occult sources of information regarding the future (19:31), treatment of the physically and socially weak (19:32–34), and honesty (19:35–36).

Application. The nature of the love in view in Leviticus 19:18 is clarified by its antithesis: taking revenge or bearing a grudge. This is not romantic or easy love, but tough love that faces a challenge and is linked to action. In an imperfect world and society, people inevitably have differences among themselves, but they must get along in spite of those differences. Everyone is tempted to unlove, but what God forbids is to cherish and nurse a grievance, which can become a seething volcano that erupts into a Vesuvian explosion of violence.

LEVITICUS 20:1–27

Original Meaning. Human sacrifice by passing one's child through/in fire was part of Syro-Palestinian worship of the underworld god Molek. This was a particularly heinous form of idolatry because it showed cruel disrespect for precious life entrusted to parents. Whereas 18:21 simply outlaws giving any of your children to Molek and thus profaning God's name, 20:2–5 adds several elements.

1. The law also applies to resident aliens (20:2).
2. The people living in the land are to stone a violator to death (20:2), implicitly purging the holy land.
3. A Molek worshiper nominally connected with God, whether an Israelite or a resident alien in God's holy land, not only profanes his holy name (20:3), he also defiles his sanctuary (20:3).

   Divinely administered "cutting off" goes beyond capital punishment. When someone deserves more than one death penalty, human justice is stymied; the malefactor has but one life to give for his crime(s). But God can do plenty more: He can make the punishment fit the crime by seeing to it that the sinner's line of descendants becomes extinct so that he is not even history. God can also deny the offender a positive afterlife.
4. Anyone who ignores the abhorrent practice of Molek worship and fails to act decisively by carrying out the death penalty is condemned to the same divine punishment (20:4–5).
5. In 18:21, giving "seed" to Molek parallels the sexual offense of giving "seed" to another man's wife (18:20), but in 20:5 the sexual analogy is explicit: Molek worship is spiritual prostitution/promiscuity.

In 20:25–26 the closing exhortation recapitulates 11:43–47, where the Israelites are commanded to be holy as God is holy by abstaining from defilement through impure animals.

Because 20:27, condemning occult practitioners, comes after the concluding exhortation in 20:22–26 rather than with 20:6, which also deals with the occult, some scholars regard 20:27 as an appendix to the chapter. They explain it variously as creating a framing structure for chapter 20 (cf. 20:7, 26), serving as a transition to chapter 21 or tacked on after the rest of the legislation in chapter 20 had been completed. In support of the framing structure idea, we can expand the frame as follows:

Penalty of stoning (for Molek worship; 20:2)
  Prohibition of occult (20:6)
    Be holy because God is holy (20:7)
      "Keep my decrees" (20:8)
      "Keep all my decrees" (20:22)
    Be holy because God is holy (20:26)
  Prohibition of occult (20:27)
Penalty of stoning (for mediums; 20:27)

The choice of laws against occult activities to occupy strategic positions in this frame could be due to a correspondence between the penalty of stoning in 20:27 and the same punishment at the beginning of the chapter in 20:2, a need for transition to chapter 21, and/or an emphasis that occult practice is the antithesis of holiness.

Application. We shudder at those horrible ancient days when children were sacrificed at temples of doom. But is the situation really much better for kids these days, when pictures of thousands of missing children are posted on public flyers, the internet, and television? Many are found, dead or alive, molested or not, but hundreds each year are never recovered. It appears that some are exploited for pornography, pedophilia, and/or prostitution, then disposed of. Unlike Molek worship, these are crimes against families, with parents as secondary victims rather than perpetrators. Another global issue that strikes at the heart of the legislation in Leviticus 20 is selling children into sex slavery, thereby condemning them to moral degradation and, in many cases, death. This is not far from Molek worship: sacrifice of a child for personal gain.

LEVITICUS 21:1–24

Original Meaning. Priests in general must guard their holiness in several ways.

1. They must not incur corpse contamination, except to bury close relatives (21:1–4).
2. Priests may not practice the pagan mourning customs of making themselves bald or shaving the edges of their beards (21:5–6).
3. A priest's holiness prevents him from marrying two kinds of women: a woman defiled by prostitution or a divorced woman (21:7).

Leviticus 21:8 touches on the responsibility of all Israelites toward a priest: They must treat him as holy because he offers "the food" (i.e., sacrifices) of their holy God (cf. 21:6), who makes them holy. For the people to maintain the benefit of their relationship with God, they must have priests who live holy lives.

A priest's family members participate in his holiness. This is true both because they are related to him and because he shares with them the holy (but not most holy) portions of sacrificial food (cf. 22:12–13). For a priest's daughter the good news is that she enjoys an elevated status of holiness, but this privilege carries moral responsibility. The bad news is that if she profanes/desecrates herself by promiscuity, she not only shames her father, but she also profanes his priestly holiness. Since this is a particularly grave evil, which affects all Israelites by morally sullying the priesthood, the penalty is harsh even if she is not betrothed or married (21:9).

The high priest is especially consecrated for uniquely intimate access to God on behalf of all Israelites. Correspondingly, he must live by the strictest rules of all (21:10–15). In addition to the regulations for all priests, he may not dishevel his hair or tear his garments (21:10), including his nonpriestly clothes. The high priest is forbidden to incur corpse contamination at all (21:11). The high priest may not leave the sacred precincts for the purpose of participating in a funeral and/or mourning. A high priest's marriage options are limited to a virgin of his own people/kin (21:13). This rules out a widow, in addition to the three classes of women forbidden to ordinary priests (21:14; cf. 21:7).

Although priests who are seriously defective in that they are blind, lame, disfigured, and so on may eat most holy and holy sacrificial food, they are forbidden to desecrate the sanctuary by engaging in priestly officiation (21:16–23). The priesthood constitutes the Lord's corps of special servants who must be in harmony with his holy, immortal, perfect sphere to the greatest extent possible. Only in this way can they properly represent the nature and character of God to the people.

Application. Although the New Testament has no earthly mediatorial priesthood, as spiritual leaders in the community of faith, Christian ministers and their families carry some of the same burdens that were laid on the ancient priests and their close relatives. The reason is essentially the same—to rightly present the Lord's character to the people. We know that ministers and their families are human and therefore imperfect, but it is devastating to congregations (including radio or TV audiences) when they fall in a serious way. The press, lawyers, anti-religionists, and the devil have a field day, but the people who matter suffer damage to their faith in God.

Ministers must take responsibility for their actions like everyone else, but trying to trip them up is unconscionable and self-defeating. A ministry is a terrible thing to waste, but it is also a wonderful thing to nurture. Rather than exhausting valuable creative energies in contention and criticism, congregations benefit themselves, their communities, and the cause of God by focusing their energies on upholding dedicated leaders and walking with them on the path of holiness.

LEVITICUS 22:1–33

Original Meaning. Leviticus 22 continues the topic introduced in the last part of chapter 21: disqualifications with regard to sacred things. In 22:1–7 Moses deals with *temporary* disqualification of nondefective priests from officiation as a result of contracting physical ritual impurity. A priest must be careful not to illegitimately use sacred things that the Israelites dedicate to the Lord (22:3). Impurity that represents human mortality may not be brought into contact with holiness that characterizes the pure, immortal sphere of God.

In the context of restrictions on what priests may eat, 22:8 prohibits priests from eating animals not slaughtered by humans, i.e., whether they die of themselves or are killed by animals. While *most holy* sacrificial portions must be eaten in the sacred precincts by the officiating priest himself or a male member of a priestly family, *holy* portions may be shared with other family members as part of their livelihood. The boundaries of a priestly family authorized to partake of sacred offerings are specified in 22:10–13. In accordance with the procedure already established in 5:16, if an unauthorized person inadvertently eats a holy thing, he or she must make reparation (22:14).

Verses 15–16 exhort the priests to prevent desecration of the people's offerings. Verse 16 adds that if the priests do desecrate the sacred things that laypersons dedicate to the Lord by permitting them to eat the priestly portions of what they give, they will cause the Israelites to bear culpability of liability that requires reparation (22:16).

Leviticus 22:17–25 continues the overall topic of qualifications in regard to sacred gifts. From earlier sacrificial regulations we know that in order to be acceptable, a sacrifice had to be unblemished (21:18–21), that is, free from serious defect. Leviticus 22:22–24 specify the kinds of defects that render animals unfit.

The rules in chapter 22 only apply to cattle, sheep, or goats (22:19), and the defects listed in 22:22–24 are limited to those that are outwardly visible. Verses 26–30 wrap up the topic of ritual qualifications. Apparently out of respect for life, a baby animal may not be taken from its mother as a sacrifice during the first seven days of its life (22:27), and an animal and its young are not to be sacrificed the same day (22:28).

Leviticus 22:29–30, reiterating the rule that a thanksgiving offering must be eaten the same day (7:15), complements 19:5–7, which repeats the requirement that other kinds of well-being offerings must be consumed by the second day (7:16–18). Thus 19:5–7 and 22:29–30 form an *inclusio* that binds together chapters 19–22, which emphasize spatial and personal holiness.

A concluding exhortation (22:31–33) contains elements that parallel ingredients of exhortations in chapters 18–21:

- summary command to keep the Lord's regulations
- reminder that "I am the LORD" (in each verse)
- warning against profaning God's holy name
- warning that the Lord must be treated as holy among the Israelites
- reminder that it is the Lord who makes Israel holy
- reminder that the Lord brought the Israelites out of Egypt to be their God

Application. Do we devote our best to God in terms of time, energy, and other resources? Or do we condescendingly give him leftover bits of the day, such as spare time (what's that?) and spare change, as if he is a beggar? Obviously, our resources are finite and we have families to support. But do we ever "sacrifice" anything from our abundance for anyone else? Or do we only give to others what we would otherwise haul to the dump or use to clothe a scarecrow in the garden?

Another way to dump problems on God is to expect him to do for us things we can and ought to do for ourselves. When we ask him to bless us in spite of the fact that we violate the cause-and-effect principles through which his blessing comes, we are being unreasonable. Why should he give us success when we are sloppy, provide us with health when we abuse it, make our families happy when we are selfish, or take us to the mountaintop of spiritual fulfillment when we choose forms of entertainment that pull us down in the opposite direction?

When God appears harsh, unfeeling, or unresponsive, sometimes it is because he is unwilling to support our addiction to sin by entering into a codependent relationship with us. Just as family members of those addicted to destructive drugs, alcohol, illicit sex, or gambling need to learn redemptive "tough love" by refusing to bear responsibility that is not theirs, God reinforces our willpower by teaching us the nature, consequences, and power of our own choices.

LEVITICUS 23:1–22

Original Meaning. Leviticus 23 attaches the expression "proclamation of holiness" (NIV "sacred assemblies") to the weekly Sabbath (23:3) plus seven yearly festival days. Why should holy days be occasions of rest? Although the Creator rested only on the weekly Sabbath (Gen 2:2–3), at that time he established cessation from work as the way to enact holiness in the dimension of time (23:3).

Verses 5–8 remind the Israelites to celebrate Passover on the fourteenth day of the first month and the seven-day Festival of Unleavened Bread immediately thereafter. Exodus 12:16 establishes a paradigm for Leviticus 23 by labeling the first and seventh days of the festival proclamations of holiness, when work is forbidden except for food preparation.

Verses 9–21 concern two observances, fifty days apart, that celebrate and implicitly thank God for the beginnings of the barley and wheat harvests, respectively, after they are settled in the promised land. First, the Israelites are to bring to the sanctuary the first sheaf of grain that they harvest in the spring, which is undoubtedly barley. A priest dedicates the sheaf to the Lord (23:11–12). On the same day, the people are required to sacrifice a burnt offering with its grain and drink accompaniments (23:12–13). By giving the Lord a token portion before eating any of the new harvest, they act out "saying the blessing," acknowledging that the harvest is from him.

Up to this point everything is clear, but on what day is the sheaf to be elevated/waved? Verse 11 specifies: "on the day after the Sabbath" (see also 23:15). But to which Sabbath does this refer—a weekly Sabbath (23:3) or a ceremonial Sabbath belonging to the Festival of Unleavened Bread (23:7–8)? By the Second Temple period a fierce interpretive controversy raged over whether "the day after the Sabbath" meant the first weekly Sabbath after Passover (Nisan 14) or the ceremonial Sabbath on the first day of Unleavened Bread, which always came on Nisan 15.

It is difficult for us to appreciate why a ritual detail should generate such a heated fuss. When so many people have a stake in the same ritual—the correct performance of which is deemed crucial for divine favor on the entire nation—the particulars matter. To complicate matters, the timing of the sheaf ritual was the base point for calculating when the subsequent Festival of Weeks was to be observed (23:15).

Counting the day when the barley sheaf is elevated as day 1, the Festival of Weeks comes after seven complete Sabbaths (23:15). Confirmation that "Sabbaths" in this context mean "weeks" comes from Numbers 28:26, where the usual word for weeks refers to the same period of time. The fact that in Leviticus 23:15 "Sabbaths" are weeks buttresses the argument that "the day after the Sabbath" earlier in the same verse refers to the weekly Sabbath rather than a yearly ceremonial rest day.

For the Festival of Weeks the Israelites were to bring a corporate firstfruits offering of new grain, in this case, from the wheat harvest. The wheat was to be baked in two loaves of *leavened* bread (23:16–17) and presented along with a group of animal sacrifices (23:18–20). Like the earlier barley sheaf, the two loaves constituted an elevation offering (23:17), acknowledging that the Lord provided the harvest.

It may appear strange to present firstfruits for thanksgiving at the beginning rather than the end of the harvest. Yet there is a sense in which a crop ready for harvest represented successful completion of an agricultural growth process, for which the people were grateful to God, on whom they could depend for the rest of the harvest (cf. Phil 1:6).

Through acknowledging God as the one who sustains the lives of his creatures by giving them food, the Israelites honored him as their Creator. Since the weekly Sabbath celebrates creation, it makes sense that timing the relationship between the sheaf ritual and the Festival of Weeks (23:15–16) is saturated with Sabbath connections. Because the Festival of Weeks has to do with harvest, 23:22 appends a reminder to leave something for the poor and alien to glean (cf. 19:9–10).

Application. Ironically, one of the greatest blessings of the commandment to abstain from work on the Sabbath is the very fact that the Bible presents it as an absolute requirement. A goal-oriented, driven, "type A" workaholic needs it to be a command from the Lord himself or he or she will rest-lessly continue to work and thereby incur damage from burnout. It is an immense relief to halt work for twenty-four peaceful hours in order to enjoy God through church, family, and walks in the woods or by a lake without feeling the slightest twinge of guilt for doing so! Obeying God's command in order to receive his blessing of genuine Sabbath refreshment is not legalism.

LEVITICUS 23:23–44

Original Meaning. Directions for the first day of the seventh month are brief (23:23–25). The only unique element is a reminder accomplished by "trumpet blasts" (23:24). The short blasts at commencement of the seventh month convey special urgency. On the first day of the seventh month (23:24), Israelites will hear the trumpet signal, reminding them that their Commander-in-Chief, King, and Deliverer is with them. This is ten days before the Day of Purgation (Atonement), when the Lord affirms his relationship with those who show loyalty but rejects those who neglect to do this. Only the loyal will benefit from divine deliverance. So, the short blasts on the first day of the month also imply the solemn responsibility of repentance and reformation.

Following reinforced reiteration of the commands to practice self-denial and abstain from work on the Day of Purgation (23:26–32), vv. 33–36 concern the Festival of Tabernacles (NIV; Booths, ESV, NASB, etc.). This major pilgrim festival celebrates God's goodness at the end of the harvest, which is why Exodus 34:22 calls it the Festival of Ingathering. Its purpose is similar to that of the American Thanksgiving holiday.

The Festival of Booths runs for seven days, from the fifteenth to twenty-first days of the seventh month (23:34), plus a connected but distinct solemn assembly on the eighth day (23:36). This seven-plus-one day sequence of contiguous festival days balances the one-plus-seven day sequence of Passover plus Unleavened Bread in the spring, creating a symmetrical pattern.

Following a conclusion in 23:37–38, verses 39–43 append important supplementary instructions regarding the Festival of Booths. During the seven days of the festival, the Israelites are to rejoice before the Lord with various kinds of foliage and live in booths as a reminder of life in the desert when the Lord brought them out of Egypt. Thus, not only do they rejoice in his creative power over agriculture; they also relive his historical redemption, accomplished by his creative power as demonstrated by the signs/miracles he performed for them in Egypt, his parting of the Red Sea to save them from Pharaoh, and his provision for their physical needs in the desert. The tight link between the Lord's creative and redemptive roles also appears in the fact that both of them are motives for keeping the Sabbath. For the Israelites, religious rejoicing climaxed with the pilgrim Festival of Booths.

The sequence of autumn festivals is logical. On the first day of the seventh month, there is a reminder that the Lord is Israel's sovereign deliverer. On the tenth day (Day of Purgation), God judges between his loyal and disloyal subjects. From the fifteenth to twenty-first days of the same month (Festival of Booths), the Lord celebrates his kingship with his loyal subjects.

For all blessings, the Israelites were dependent on their divine King to whom they were accountable for loyalty.

Application. Christians who accept salvation and receive forgiveness must continue in their faith (Col 1:23), just as the ancient Israelites were to maintain their loyalty. It is not enough to have done God's will in the past, even if that included prophesying and performing miracles. God "has set a day when he will judge the world with justice" (Acts 17:31). Believing in Christ does not exempt us from judgment. Speaking to Christians, Paul wrote: "For we will all stand before God's judgment seat" (Rom 14:10). However, there are two pieces of good news. For those who are forgiven and remain reconciled to God, judgment reaffirms assurance; it does not take it away. When Christ comes in glory, he will know who are really his. The deciding factor will not be words of commitment but whether people have followed through by honoring him in the way they have treated others.

LEVITICUS 24:1–23

Original Meaning. *Regular maintenance rituals in the outer sanctum.* Verses 2–4 remind the Israelites of their ongoing duty to supply olive oil as fuel for the lamps on the golden lampstand. Every morning Aaron is to trim the lamps and fill them with fresh oil, and every evening he is to kindle them. By burning through the night, the lamps parallel the evening regular burnt offering on the outer altar (6:12).

Within the Israelite ritual system, the lampstand, table, and incense burner served as the Lord's furniture in his dwelling place. The complex of rituals performed regularly by the priest in the outer sanctum, such as tending the lamps and burning incense, constituted the work of a servant for his Lord, who was enthroned behind the curtain in the Most Holy Place.

Another regular (24:8) priestly ritual duty in the outer sanctum was to renew the "bread" of the presence each Sabbath on the golden table (24:5–9). This special presentation offering of grain, consisting of twelve loaves plus incense, was placed on the table in two "arrangements" (24:6; NIV "stacks"). A "memorial" (token) portion of incense was "by" each pile (24:7), most likely in containers.

Brawling and blasphemy. Leviticus 24:10–23 is a narrative reporting a person's sin against the sphere of holiness, which results in his death. The circumstances involved in the narrative of 24:10–14 directly generate the ensuing legislation regarding blasphemy and physical assault (24:15–22). In fact, the laws are framed by the divine sentence of death on the blasphemer (24:14) and the report of his execution (24:23).

The problem starts when a man whose mother is Israelite but whose father is Egyptian, and who therefore is camped with the mixed multitude of non-Israelites, goes out of his area into the Israelite encampment. A fight ensues between the half-Israelite and a full Israelite (24:10), which likely has something to do with the fact that the former is in the wrong neighborhood. Because the full Israelite is not later indicted and punished, the intruder must be at fault.

Apparently frustrated and angry that he is not achieving his objective, whatever it is, the half-Israelite pronounces "the name," that is, "YHWH," the sacred personal name of Israel's deity, and curses. The shocked Israelites apprehend him and bring him to Moses for determination of his fate (24:11).

Saying God's name could also be proper, positive, and permissible in Old Testament times (e.g., Ruth 2:4). However, the half-Israelite does not simply take God's name in vain as a construction worker might when he accidentally whacks his thumbnail; he curses (Lev 24:11).

He assaults the Lord by cursing *him* personally, as shown by the way the following legislation begins (24:15–16). This reiterates the command of Exodus 22:28. Because a curse was regarded as a real and potent weapon in ancient times, such an attack was not merely figurative. Using the power of speech against God, who created the world for the human species by speaking, is the height of ingratitude and rebellion.

Once the Israelites bring the blasphemer to Moses (Lev 24:11), Moses does not know whether God himself will directly administer capital punishment or whether he will delegate this to the community. Pending a divine oracle to clarify the question, the blasphemer is put under guard (24:12). When the Lord speaks, he specifies the execution procedure (24:14). "Outside the camp" is to avoid polluting the camp with a corpse.

It appears that hand-leaning by witnesses must do more than designating the culprit and acknowledging responsibility for his death. This is probably related to the high priest's leaning both hands on the nonsacrificial live goat and loading the moral faults of the Israelites on it before sending it away (16:21–22). By leaning their hands on the blasphemer, they briefly make a connection for the sake of rejection: Yes, they have heard the curse, but no, they were not party to it; therefore, its consequences belong to the blasphemer alone.

After telling Moses what to do with the blasphemer in particular (24:14), the Lord formulates his ruling into an ongoing law against cursing God and blaspheming his name (24:15–16). There is another objectionable aspect of the blasphemer's behavior: physical violence. The following legislation lays down a series of penalties for various kinds of violence related to the case at hand by logical extension (*lex talionis*), including murder, assault, and killing animals belonging to others (24:17–22).

Application. While the *lex talionis* made good sense for ancient Israel from the viewpoints of justice, theology, and practicality, it would be viewed as "cruel and unusual punishment" today, even for those who perpetrate cruel and unusually painful and damaging crimes. Nevertheless, Leviticus teaches us the importance of respecting the sanctity of another person's body, facing the full consequences of one's physical violence, treating everyone equally before the law, and protecting the rights of victims.

LEVITICUS 25:1–55

Original Meaning. *Chronology.* The counting of sabbatical years was to begin when the Israelites conquered Canaan and owned their own fields (25:2–3). After seven sabbatical years totaling forty-nine years, the Jubilee year is the fiftieth year, beginning on the tenth day of the seventh month, which is the Day of Purgation (Atonement; 25:8–11).

Because the fiftieth (= first) year was fallow, this would leave only five regular years of agricultural work (years 2–6) between the forty-ninth-year sabbatical and the seventh-year sabbatical of the following cycle. At first glance this would seem to conflict with Leviticus 25:3. However, six years was simply the norm. Compare the fact that the weekly Sabbath commandment reads, "Six days you shall labor and do all your work" (Exod 20:9), but extra ceremonial Sabbaths (Lev 23) could reduce the number of workdays to five in a particular week.

The relationship between sabbatical and Jubilee years in Leviticus 25 parallels the relationship between seven weekly Sabbaths and the Feast of Weeks on the fiftieth day (23:15–16). Here the integration is simpler because the 7 x 7 = 49 + 1 = 50 cycle of days is not immediately followed by an identical cycle.

Fallow years. The Sabbath of the land in the seventh year was "to the LORD" (25:4), so letting the land revert to its natural state carried religious significance. Because there would be no sowing, whatever grew by itself from kernels spilled during the previous harvest would belong to anyone, human or animal, who needed it. Since there was no reaping, even of that which sprang up by itself (25:5), the whole population would live off the land from day to day.

Even with eating what the land would produce by itself, the question arises: "What will we eat in the seventh year if we do not plant or harvest our crops?" (25:20). God answers in the context of the last sabbatical period in the Jubilee cycle (25:21–22). Here is the same principle as God's promise to provide a double portion of manna on the sixth day of the week so that the Israelites would not need to collect any on the Sabbath. But the triple harvest in the sixth year had to provide for that year and last over a fallow sabbatical year, immediately followed by a fallow Jubilee year.

Real estate release. The heart of the Jubilee law is in 25:10. Here is the ultimate New Year, a time of beginning again for disenfranchised Israelites. If they had been separated from their land (by sale) or from their clan (by entering servitude), they would be reunited with them. The Israelites as privileged servants of the Lord were to recover their landed property and independence after a succession of seven sabbatical years, during which there were no crops.

The starting point for consideration of Israelite ownership of the land is the premise that it was all "crown property" in the sense that it belonged to the divine King (25:23). He gave it to the Israelites (25:38) to be subdivided equitably among their clans. To protect this distribution from permanent alienation of ancestral land by sale, the Lord decreed that *nobody* outside the clan to which a given property was attached could hold more than a temporary interest in it (25:23–24). In the event that a piece of such land was sold, its value was to be prorated according to the number of years remaining until the next Jubilee (25:13–18). So, it was use of the land, not the land itself, that was sold.

The Jubilee law is concerned with ancestral real estate necessary to maintain an agricultural livelihood. This includes houses in unwalled villages, which are zoned with open country, but not urban dwellings in walled cities (25:29–31). For ensuring that the land of a clan would be kept for the support of its members, the Jubilee release was the remedy of last resort. If a person became poor and sold part of his land, his kinsman should redeem it (25:25), that is, buy it back. If he had no redeemer but his situation later improved, he could redeem the property himself at a price that was prorated until the next Jubilee year (25:26–27). Failing the above options, the land would revert to the original owner at the Jubilee (25:28).

Real estate belonging to Levites was unique. Because this tribe was to have cities surrounded by pastures (Num 35:1–8) rather than large territories, their urban dwellings were to be released in the Jubilee as if they were in unwalled villages (Lev 25:32–33). Their pastures could not be sold at all.

Application. Why manage our resources well? So we can be secure and have more to spend on ourselves, like a rich man with an edifice complex, of whom Jesus spoke (Luke 12:15–21)? No. Our good management is the first phase of a ministry of sharing. By taking good care of the blessings God gives us and passing them on, we acknowledge that they are not simply our own. Even with all our efforts, we would have nothing without the ability that he has given us (Deut 8:17–18). We can't take it all with us anyway.

While it is important that the church not try to take over functions of the state, the church is not exempt from addressing social problems, such as poverty and equality or ecological concerns, just because the state is working on the same problems.

Leviticus 25 teaches us that for those who believe in God, faith and ethics impact the larger context of our lives.

LEVITICUS 26:1–46

Original Meaning. The brief unit of 26:1–2 forms a structural tie with the same commands in 19:4, 30, where the theme is holy living because the Lord is holy. Staying away from idolatry, keeping Sabbath, and reverencing the Lord's sanctuary are basic ways that the Israelites can show loyalty to him.

Leviticus 26:3 begins a series of blessings with "if" (Heb. *im*). The much longer section of curses similarly begins with "but if" (26:14). Repetitions of "if" in 26:18, 21, 23, 27 threaten progressively more dire consequences if fulfillments of earlier curses do not stop the Israelites in their tracks. A final "but if" in 26:40 brings the juggernaut of catastrophe to a screeching halt and turns the seemingly inexorable situation around.

The blessings in 26:3–13 touch the major aspects of life that are dear to an ancient Israelite. The Israelites can trust the Lord's goodwill toward them because he has already definitively proven it by delivering them from the heavy burden of Egyptian oppression (26:13).

If the contrast between blessings and curses seem shocking, it is meant to be. The curses in 26:14–39 invoke a comprehensive catalogue of calamities. They are much more extensive than the blessings, partly because the blessings are simpler and more obvious and partly because negative motivations need to be more substantial in order to serve as an effective deterrent.

In 26:14–17 there is fear, sickness, plunder of agricultural produce by enemies, military defeat, and subjection to enemy rulers. In 26:18–20, introduced by another "if," the Lord threatens to multiply the punishments for their sins by seven. Although this is a figure of speech for many times over, seven is also the sabbatical number of completeness and holiness. Thus, it is both appropriate and ironic that divine retribution is sevenfold. In response to the hardness of their hearts, the Lord will make the sky like iron and the ground like copper so that agricultural effort will be spent in vain (26:19–20).

Following yet another "if," 26:21 threatens further increase of affliction by seven times. Thus, the downside of covenant cause and effect is proportional to exacerbation of the sin problem. Moreover, rejecting the repeated warnings of the divine Judge, whether through his messengers, conscience, Scripture, or providential punishments, constitutes "contempt of court."

If the Israelites throw away the blessing of having predatory animals removed from their land (cf. 26:6), the Lord will commission such beasts to thin the population of humans and domestic animals (26:22). As in some large cities today, even muggers will be afraid to go out.

Surely by now the people will call a moratorium on their self-destructive rebellion! In case they don't, the fires of affliction are just getting warmed up. If they decide not to walk with God by keeping his covenant (cf. 26:3), he will walk on a collision course with them (26:24) and bring them all the miseries of military attack. They can run, but they cannot hide (26:25–26).

The next unit that begins with "if" is much longer (26:27–39) and constitutes one of the most frightful warnings in the entire Bible. The dam restraining retributive justice bursts open with a vengeance, disclosing the ultimate horrors of starvation during siege (26:29), appalling devastation of the land (26:30–32), and scattering of the people into exile (26:33–35).

In the rubble we see one of the main causes for divine judgment (26:30). It is fitting that the presumed holiness of these idols be defiled by corpse contamination because they are like lifeless, impure corpses anyway. In 26:31, God will destroy "*your* [plural] sanctuaries" (emphasis added; contrast 26:2: "have reverence for *my* sanctuary").

When the people are in exile and the land has been so devastated that even the enemies of Israel who move in are devastated/appalled by the sight (26:32), the following ironic link to chapter 25 occurs (26:34–35). If the people deplete the land by failing to grant its sabbatical respites, they will be deleted from it. It is as if the exhausted land heaves a mighty sigh of relief and settles down to a long nap to recover from its sleep deficit.

The survivors in exile will be a miserable lot (26:36). Unable to stand (26:37), they revert to their pre-exodus state, before the Lord set them free to walk upright (26:13). In exile they will rot away in their culpability and the culpabilities of their ancestors (26:38–39).

After all that has happened, it is a wonder that anyone has survived at all! But 26:40–45 pries open a door of hope at what looked like a dead end. We would expect a requirement of extreme expiation for prodigal Israel to be reaccepted by the divine Father, but there are no animal sacrifices here. Indeed, how could there be with the people in exile and the temple destroyed? Moreover, what sacrifice could they bring for deliberate, high-handed rebellion that called for nothing but their extirpation?

Here at the climax of Leviticus there appears at first glance to be a massive letdown, like a dramatic pause in a Beethoven symphony: "if [the Israelites] will confess their sins. . ." (26:40). That's all—only confess. No elaborate ceremonies. Only humbling themselves before the Lord, admitting they have made bad choices, and putting themselves at his mercy, where they really have been all along but wouldn't admit it.

It sounds too simple, but what the Lord has wanted all along is for his people simply to return to loyalty and dependence on him. Verses 43–45 repeat the promise to make sure it sinks in. Although the Israelites will in some sense pay for the debt of their culpability through suffering, God will remember his covenant with their ancestors whom he brought out of Egypt (cf. 26:42). By referring to the exodus generation, the breathtaking finale to Leviticus comes back to the original audience of the book according to the narrative framework of the Pentateuch (26:46).

In 26:45 is the forty-ninth and last instance of "I am the LORD" in the book of Leviticus. Is it coincidence that this key expression is used the same super-sabbatical (7 x 7) number of times as the seven weeks of days between the elevated sheaf and the Feast of Weeks (23:15) and the seven weeks of years between Jubilees (25:8), as well as the number of separate applications of purification offering blood by which the sanctuary is restored on the Day of Purgation (16:14–19) when the Jubilee year begins (25:9)? Associated as this multiple of the sacred number seven is with the Lord's identity and sacred occasions, the number forty-nine carries a connotation of high holiness. Thus, we find that Leviticus, like other great artistic works such as Bach's *St. Matthew Passion*, makes connections by patterns under as well as on the surface.

Verse 46 concludes the Sinai revelation of chapters 25–26 by stating that the Lord gave these "decrees," "laws," and "regulations" between himself and the Israelites on Mount Sinai through Moses. The expression "between himself and the Israelites" (26:46) means that the legislation was placed within the framework of the covenant relationship.

Application. Our pursuit of happiness will be successful only if we allow happiness to pursue us! Our approach must be indirect. As the ancient Israelites found out through long and bitter experience, directly chasing happiness will only chase it away, as if it were a wild antelope. We get happiness to pursue us by pursuing a positive relationship with God, the source of all blessings (Matt 6:33). It is a matter of priorities. If we want God first, we will have happiness, especially in the age to come (Rev 21–22).

The happiness that God gives is not exactly the same as our human definition of "happiness." It is *far better* (1 Cor 2:9; cf. Isa 64:4). If we are hell-bent on happiness as we define it, with God left out of the picture, relegated to the sidelines, or used as a mere tool, we are doomed to failure. The ancient Israelites had to learn this the hard way even though God had told them the final score in advance (Lev 26). According to the Bible, there is simply no such thing as full, genuine happiness without God and the guidance he offers.

LEVITICUS 27:1–34

Original Meaning. Leviticus 27 regulates gifts to the sanctuary. The focus of this chapter on holy things links it with earlier portions of Leviticus. Verse 2 introduces the topic of votive gifts in typical case law style. Apparently, what is extraordinary about such a vow is that the gift is a human being. Rather than human sacrifice or lifelong service at the sanctuary, the Lord will receive what amounts to a redemption price. The variables are gender and age. In this list, ages begin with the prime of adulthood and decrease to infancy, after which valuations of elderly persons are specified. Verse 8 makes a concession for a poor person who wants to make such a vow but cannot afford the usual amount. The priest lowers the valuation of the vowed person in proportion to the vower's ability to pay.

Verses 9–10 constitute a subcase. If that which is vowed is a sacrificeable animal, it becomes holy so that no other animal can take its place, even a better animal. Attempted substitution will result in both animals becoming holy to the Lord, meaning that they will belong to the sanctuary (27:10).

An Israelite can also vow an unclean and therefore unsacrificeable animal that can be used by the priests for work or sold (27:11). In this case a priest will assign the value of this gift to the Lord (27:12). The value will be relevant for sale of the animal to someone else or for redemption if the owner wants to keep the animal, in which case he or she will pay the value plus one fifth (27:13). This 20 percent charge is the same amount as the penalty for sacrilege in 5:16. Although redemption is not a sin and requires no reparation offering, it is related to sacrilege in that it withdraws something from the holy domain.

Verse 14 opens up a new main case of nonvotive dedications/consecrations. Unlike vows, which are conditional promises to be fulfilled in the future, such dedications go into effect immediately. Consecration of a house works like a vow of an unclean animal: The priest sets the value, and any redemption requires that amount plus a fifth (27:14–15).

Unlike a house, ancestral land cannot be permanently sold, but it reverts to its original owner in the Jubilee year. Therefore, the value of a piece of land is based on its potential agricultural yield—as indicated by the amount of seed required to sow it—until the next Jubilee. Verses 16–25 deal with two possibilities: Either the dedicator is the original owner (27:16–21) or he has bought (really leased) someone else's land (27:22–25). Redemption by the original owner requires an extra fifth, as expected (27:19).

The meaning of 27:20–21 is not transparent. By dedicating it to the sanctuary after already selling its use to someone else until the Jubilee, the original owner indicates his intention to dedicate something over and above that which he has already sold, namely, permanent ownership. Therefore, at the next Jubilee, when the property would normally revert to him, it instead becomes the permanent property of the priesthood.

It is like *herem* property—something irrevocably banished to the sphere of holiness.

Verses 28–29 concern the intense *herem* category of proscribed things or persons that have been irredeemably consecrated to the divine sphere and therefore are "most holy to the LORD" (27:28). We are most familiar with this category in terms of sacral devotion to destruction within the context of warfare against other nations. Leviticus 27:28–29, however, refers to a peacetime *herem*.

Tithes are like a firstborn animal in that they are already holy to the Lord and can be redeemed (27:30–32). When a tithe consists of every tenth animal, no substitution can be made without forfeiting both animals (27:32–33).

The book of Leviticus ends: "These are the commands the LORD gave Moses at Mount Sinai for the Israelites" (27:34). This echoes the earlier conclusion in 26:46.

Application. What is a person worth? A person made in the image of God (Gen 1:26; 9:6) is of inestimable value. How can anyone put a price on the image of God? Because we do not fully comprehend the Original, we cannot appraise our own worth. Life that comes from the holy Creator is sacred. Therefore, treating others as if their lives are cheap is profanity and sacrilege.

Any notion that we may have figured out our intrinsic worth is swept aside by a mystery: "For God so loved the world that he gave his one and only Son, that whoever believes in him shall not perish but have eternal life" (John 3:16). God's gift was not a conditional vow, neither was it a money substitute, nor was his beloved Son only made in his image as a human being, nor was he given merely to provide live service (cf. Col 1:19–20). His love puts the value of every human being *way* beyond price.

NUMBERS

INTRODUCTION TO NUMBERS

As with Leviticus and the other Pentateuchal books, Numbers is an anonymous work but is ascribed by tradition to Moses, who served as the intermediary between God and Israel within its narrative framework. The New Testament (including Jesus) accepts the idea that the entire Pentateuch is basically Mosaic (e.g., Luke 16:29; 24:27; John 1:17; 5:46; 2 Cor 3:15). This does not rule out participation of others in the writing/editing process. For example, it has long been recognized that the affirmation of Moses's unparalleled humility in Numbers 12:3 was likely penned by someone else.

In its final form, the book of Numbers shows evidence that it draws on a variety of materials, such as administrative lists, legal records, the story of Balaam (chs. 22–24), and written historical accounts, including the explicitly cited "Book of the Wars of the Lord" (21:14). Critical scholars have spent a great deal of energy attempting to isolate and date individual strands of authorship with varying perspectives, reconstructing the composition process by disassembling the "sources" of Numbers and then reassembling them in chronological sequence. Even though they have often drawn conclusions that go beyond the surviving evidence, they have contributed to our understanding of the book by highlighting interdependence between Pentateuchal books and the remarkable diversity of literary genres and styles that have been combined to provide a rich portrayal of Israel's life with God.

BOOK OUTLINE

I. Preparations for Journey from Sinai Desert (1:1–10:10)
   A. Military Census and Introduction to Duties of Levites (1:1–54)
   B. Arrangement of Military Camp and Marching Order of Tribes (2:1–34)
   C. Census and Duties of Levites (3:1–4:49)
   D. Laws of Community Purity and Holiness (5:1–6:27)
   E. Final Preparations of the Sanctuary Infrastructure (7:1–8:26)
   F. Exodus from Sinai (9:1–23)

II. Journeying in the Desert (10:11–19:22)
   A. Departure from Sinai (10:11–36)
   B. Rebellions in the Desert (11:1–14:45)
   C. Laws and Narrative Regarding Loyalty Versus Disloyalty (15:1–41)
   D. Rebellion of Korah & Co. and Its Aftermath (16:1–18:32)
   E. Law of Purification from Corpse Impurity (19:1–22)

III. Up and Down Road to the Borders of the Promised Land (20:1–25:18)
   A. Kadesh Again and More Bad News (20:1–29)
   B. Initial Victories (21:1–35)
   C. Attempt of King Balak to Destroy Israel Through Balaam (22:1–24:25)
   D. Apostasy by the Jordan at Shittim with the Baal of Peor (25:1–18)

IV. Preparation for Occupation of the Promised Land (26:1–36:13)
   A. Déjà vu: Second Census of Surviving Younger Generation (26:1–65)
   B. Transfers to Persons of Younger Generations (27:1–23)
   C. Calendar of Cyclical Sacrifices (28:1–29:40)
   D. Law of Vows (30:1–16)
   E. War of Vengeance Against Midianites (31:1–54)
   F. Allocation of Transjordanian Land to Reuben, Gad, and Half of Manasseh (32:1–42)
   G. Summary and Instructions for Conquest and Settlement in Canaan (33:1–35:34)
   H. Keeping Land in the Family When Inherited by Daughters (36:1–13)

NUMBERS 1:1–54

Original Meaning. Just as Leviticus begins with a speech by the Lord to Moses "from the tent of meeting" (1:1), Numbers commences with a divine speech "in the tent of meeting" (1:1). This verse provides additional information regarding the geographical and chronological setting.

Before the Israelites resume their journey, the Lord commands that they take a military census of men twenty years old or more who are to serve as soldiers (1:2–3). This is preliminary to the organization of an army with no upper age limit for retirement, which can exert maximum force to conquer Canaan. Although the census report, with its names, numbers, and repetitions, may not excite the modern reader, the event surely would quicken the pulse of the Israelites because it heralds dramatic events leading to the fulfillment of the Lord's promise to give them the promised land, where at last they will have a permanent home.

The count is accomplished fairly quickly (cf. 1:1; 10:11) because it is organized like a modern election in that groups simultaneously collect their own tallies of names and then hand them over to a higher level of supervisors (tribal chiefs and Moses). Later, during the Israelite monarchy, several censuses served basically the same purpose—to assess and organize military human resources.

As we would expect for a tribal nation, the Numbers 1 census is structured according to hierarchical social groups determined by the patriarchal family tree (1:2). A chieftain representing each tribe (1:3–16) assists Moses and Aaron, the high priest. Each tribe constitutes a major army division, within which members of the same "house" belonging to each clan will fight alongside each other.

The high priest's involvement is appropriate because the Israelites are preparing for *holy* war, in which they will fight under the Lord's direction. Priests are to be involved with warfare in several ways. Before each battle the high priest is to encourage the troops that God is with them to give them victory (Deut 20:2–4). Also through him, undoubtedly by means of the Urim and Thummim in his breastplate, the army can inquire of the Lord for guidance in making military decisions (Judg 20:27–28).

The fact that Moses promptly implements the census on the same day the Lord gives him the command (1:17–19) conveys the impression that he is eager to get rolling. Verses 20–43 list the total number of potential fighting men from each of the twelve tribes. These numbers range from a high of 74,600 for Judah (1:27) to a low of 32,200 for Manasseh (1:35). The grand total is 603,550 (1:46).

The military census does not include a thirteenth tribe—Levi—because the Levites are not to be part of the regular army. Rather, their job is to guard and take care of the tabernacle. Thus, they are counted separately later on (chs. 3–4). There are thirteen tribes because faithful Joseph, the oldest son of Jacob's first love, Rachel, received a double inheritance when Jacob gave Joseph's two sons, Ephraim and Manasseh, equal status with his own sons (Gen 48). Because of the uniquely loyal role of the Levites at the time of the golden calf episode, God gave them privileged status as his servants at the sanctuary (Exod 32:26–29).

Numbers 1 concludes with a simple notice of compliance (1:54). This obedience is the initial benchmark for the book of Numbers, but as the book progresses we will find that on more than one occasion the people do *everything but* what the Lord commands through Moses.

Application. Do Christian family members need to fight alongside one another today? In Ephesians 6:10–12 Paul describes a battle "against the spiritual forces of evil" in which each Christian is involved. We need each other's support as a "family" of believers (Gal 6:10; cf. 1 Pet 4:17). This "family" encompasses all spiritual "brothers and sisters" (cf. Gal 3:26–29; 1 Pet 3:8), including physical family members (e.g., Eph 5:21–6:4; 1 Pet 3:1–7). Like the ancient Israelites, we are stronger together as bonded units than if we try to fight alone. If anyone thinks that he or she is as strong spiritually as Samson was physically, remember that as a one-man army, solitary Samson made no lasting impact (Judg 14–16).

NUMBERS 2:1–34

Original Meaning. If the Israelite men were to be organized into an army, their camp had to be a military camp. So Numbers 2 outlines the arrangement of tribal groups within the war camp. Numbers 1:52–53 has already briefly summarized the overall plan, and to resume this topic, 2:2 reiterates: "The Israelites are to camp around the tent of meeting some distance from it, each of them under their standard and holding the banners of their family."

The rest of chapter 2 specifies the locations of the various tribes around the sanctuary. The twelve tribes, not including Levi, are to be divided into four groups of three tribes each. With reference to the sanctuary and Levite camp in the middle, each group of three tribes occupies a position to one of the four directions of the compass. The text lists these directions in clockwise rotation beginning with east, the direction of sunrise and the standard starting point for Israelite directions: east, south, west, and north. Each of the four groups is led by one of the three tribes of which it is composed, so that the groups are called "the camp of Judah" (2:9), "the camp of Reuben" (2:16), "the camp of Ephraim" (2:24), and "the camp of Dan" (2:31).

The Israelite encampment is arranged as a square. The center of the Israelite war camp is occupied by the Lord's sanctuary. As Balaam later observes, the Israelites enjoy the power and protection of a Leader in their midst who is not only royal; he is truly divine (Num 23:21)!

Just as the Lord's sanctuary occupies the protected middle of the camp, which protects it in the event of an attack (cf. Exod 17:8), so it travels with the Levites in the middle of the marching column in case the Israelites are attacked in front or behind (cf. Num 21:1). Because the order of encampment corresponds to the marching order (2:17), the Israelites can hit the road or set up camp with optimum efficiency. Aside from cutting stress and fatigue, this prevents "road rage" disputes that could easily develop by people and animals getting in each other's way. It also enables the Israelites to react quickly in case of emergency.

Application. Our modern culture revels in personal independence. Living in private dwellings, perhaps in restricted access communities, we can live our own lives the way we want and control much of our contact with other people. We have voice mail and e-mail to facilitate limited communication according to our schedules. Now we can do much of our business from home over the internet. Everything is designed around us for our security, convenience, and comfort. In our private cars we have wraparound sound. Commercials bombard us from all directions to reinforce what we already know: We are the center of the universe, and our desires govern it. We cannot be the center of our own religion if we want to claim the religion of the Bible. Placing ourselves, anything, or anyone in place of God makes us his enemy.

NUMBERS 3:1–4:49

Original Meaning. *Ministerial exemption from military duty.* Because the Levites were the Lord's ministers, performing vital service that was continually necessary for the well-being of the nation, they were not drafted into the army. As a result, they were not included in the general military census (1:49). Numbers 3 fills in details regarding the tribe of Levi, within which the family of Aaron is singled out for the priesthood. Verse 4 adds a detail not found in Leviticus 10: When Nadab and Abihu died, they left no sons to carry on lines of descendants. So in effect, they were "cut off" from Israel. Consequently, the priesthood is limited to the two branches from Aaron's surviving sons: Eleazar and Ithamar.

Non-priestly Levites are to assist the priests by performing duties pertaining to the sanctuary infrastructure (3:6–9). However, Aaron and his sons are to guard their priestly prerogatives. Any unauthorized person (i.e., nonpriest, including Levites) will be put to death if he attempts to "approach" the sanctuary (in the restricted, technical sense of usurping or encroaching on an exclusive priestly function; see 3:10).

Although Levites are not soldiers, it is necessary to count them and organize their workforce. Rather than counting males twenty years of age or more who can serve in the army, the register of Levites (3:14–37) begins with babies one month old (3:15) because the members of this tribe substitute for firstborn male Israelites (3:40–41), who are to be redeemed with five shekels when they are one month old (18:15–16). One month conveniently allows some time for the payment following the birth and means that parents do not have to pay the redemption price in the tragic event that a baby dies soon after birth. Even though Levite males are counted down to the age of one month, there are still far fewer Levites than members of any other tribe: only 22,000 (3:39; cf. 1:35; 2:21).

The census report of Levites covers their clans in the order of Gershon, Kohath, and Merari. Numbers 3:21–26 provide several kinds of information regarding the Gershonites. Verses 27–32 supply the same categories of data regarding the Kohathites (3:31). Since the Kohathite clan is that of the priests, the administrative chief of all the Levites is a Kohathite: Eleazar, son of Aaron, the high priest (3:32). Finally, the Merarites are to camp on the north side of the tabernacle and take care of the entire framework of the sanctuary (3:33–37).

The encampment of Moses and the priests is to guard the sanctuary on the east, where it is most vulnerable because that is where its entrance is located. Again the text warns that an unauthorized person who encroaches on priestly prerogatives is to be put to death (3:38). This is no empty threat. The unsqueamish zeal of Phinehas exemplifies the readiness of priests to use weapons in order to defend holiness (25:6–8).

We may have thought that substitution of the Levites for the male firstborn (3:12–13) involves an inexact kind of abstract equivalence. Now we learn that there is to be one-to-one numerical correspondence between the Levites and the firstborn whose place they take. A census of firstborn males in the other twelve tribes yields a total of 22,273 (3:40–43). So, 22,000 Levites replace 22,273 firstborn. Surely that is close enough! But no. While 22,000 firstborn are redeemed by the substitution of the Levites, the remaining 273 must be redeemed another way: with five shekels apiece, totaling 1,365 shekels (3:44–51). Such monetary redemption is required for all subsequent firstborn (18:15–16).

The five-shekel redemption price for each Israelite firstborn male and the lifelong dedication of Levites to God's work at the sanctuary in place of the firstborn serve as tokens of redemption, ongoing reminders of the roots of Israelite freedom. When Egypt refused to free Israel, whom God called "my firstborn son" (Exod 4:22), the Lord struck down the firstborn of Egypt (Exod 12:29) but spared the firstborn Israelites.

Levite labor. In Numbers 4 another census is needed to determine the number of Levites available for the actual work of the sanctuary by men thirty to fifty years of age, that is, mature and in their physical prime. As we would expect in any normal population group, these numbers are significantly less: 8,580 (4:48).

The job description of the Kohathites (4:4–20) is by far the longest and most complicated because it involves careful coordination with the priests, who are to cover the sacred objects of furniture before the other, nonpriestly Kohathites can carry them. Packing up for a journey begins with the most sacred item of furniture (the ark of the covenant), which is appropriately covered with the most sacred fabric (the inner veil). Over the veil goes a leather protective covering and over that a violet cloth. In addition, the long carrying poles are to be put in place (4:5–6), implying that they are detached when not needed for transport.

Coverings on the pieces of sanctuary furniture in transit are color-coded according to whether these items belong in the Most Holy Place, the Holy Place, or the court. The ark of the covenant from the inner sanctum has violet cloth over its leather covering (4:6). Leather is on the outside of the other pieces (with their auxiliary utensils), but whereas the furniture of the Holy Place has violet cloth under the leather, the cloth under the leather covering the outer bronze altar is red-purple.

When the Kohathites have emptied the sanctuary of its furniture and utensils, the Gershonites are to pack up and carry away all the fabric and skin coverings of the sanctuary and its court, including the ropes that go with them (4:24–28). After they have stripped the portable sanctuary down to its skeleton, the Merarites are to carry the disassembled pieces of this framework and everything pertaining to it (4:31–33).

Application. *No service for the Sovereign is small.* Nehemiah was a waiter, the personal cupbearer of Artaxerxes, king of the Persian Empire (Neh 1:11; 2:1). The monarch implicitly trusted Nehemiah to make sure there was no poison in his wine. With frequent, intimate access to the king, Nehemiah was a high-ranking member of the royal court who ended up rebuilding the walls of Jerusalem and serving as governor of Judah. His cup-bearing role was by no means menial because the one he was serving was important.

At the ancient Israelite sanctuary, the Levites do what appears to be menial labor: maintenance, guarding, packing, and hauling. But all of it is honorable and vitally important because it is for the divine King. Similarly, the smallest and most insignificant task that contributes to God's work today is important: cleaning the church, changing its light bulbs, preparing food for a social event, visiting a sick person, teaching a scriptural song to a child, encouraging a neighbor, and so on.

As in Bible times, service for God is anywhere he leads, not just at church. Some find his work in the classroom, others in the boardroom. Some help the least of Christ's brothers and sisters on the streets of San Francisco or Calcutta, others the more outwardly fortunate in posh apartments and country clubs. Everyone has a place and a role to play. For the person who seeks to do everything to God's glory (cf. 1 Cor 10:31), life is holy. It is as though every meal is a sacrament, every word a prayer, and every deed an act of worship.

NUMBERS 5:1–31

Original Meaning. *Physical ritual impurity.* As in Leviticus 12–15, Numbers 5:1–4 has to do with physical ritual purity from human sources. The more stringent rules in Numbers 5:1–4 regarding genital discharge and corpse contamination appear to reflect an elevation in the sacral status of the Israelite war camp. Under normal conditions only skin-diseased persons are to be banished, but the war camp is a special situation. The reason for sending impure persons away is not to avoid the spread of ordinary sickness but to avoid defiling the holy camp in which the Lord dwells among his people (5:3). Around the sanctuary, with its three gradations of holiness—the Most Holy Place, the Holy Place, and the court—there is a fourth gradation: the camp.

Ethical wrongs. Numbers 5:5–10 supplements the law of reparation for an ethical wrong involving sacrilege (Lev 6:1–7). The main innovation of the Numbers 5 unit is in verse 8, which deals with the contingency that the wronged person dies and leaves no kinsman to whom reparation can be paid. The solution is that the person who committed the wrong pays the reparation to the priest, as the Lord's representative, along with the required reparation offering of a ram of "atonement" (5:8).

Suspected adulteress. The first two sections of Numbers 5 regarding ritual impurity (5:2–3) and ethical sin by a man or woman involving sacrilege (i.e., unfaithfulness, 5:6), brief as they are, pave the way for 5:11–31. Here a remarkable law concerning a woman suspected of adultery intertwines matters of impurity (5:13–14, 20, 27–29) and unfaithfulness to a husband (5:12, 27) within the social context of the Israelite community.

The case is particularly problematic because (1) it deals with suspicion rather than clear-cut guilt, (2) guilt or innocence can be impossible for a human tribunal to establish as a result of the secret nature of the offense, (3) the stakes are high—adultery is a capital offense (Lev 20:10), (4) unresolved suspicion can wreck a marriage, and (5) suspicion could be lethal to a woman, since men controlled legal matters.

The protasis consists of two possible scenarios.

1. The first concerns a wife who actually goes astray and is unfaithful to her husband by having sexual relations with another man; this defilement of herself goes undetected, but her husband is overcome with an anxious spirit/feeling of jealousy.
2. The other one concerns a husband who is jealous even though his wife has not defiled herself.

With regard to the first possibility, 5:13 tells us in four ways the crucial factor that the woman who has defiled herself by adultery cannot be brought to justice by human agency: "hidden," "undetected," "no witness," "not caught." The suspected adulteress passage never uses a word which specifies adultery that is punishable by human agency when humans apprehend the guilty parties (Lev 20:10). Only God can adjudicate.

From 5:15 on, the remainder of the chapter constitutes the apodosis, which states the results of the conditions set up in the protasis. In this instance, the apodosis consists of a ritual prescription. To invoke the Lord's jurisdiction, the jealous husband must bring a grain offering on behalf of his wife. This grain offering of jealousy, which serves as a reminder of culpability, lacks oil and incense (5:15), two elements associated with happier occasions (Lev 2:1, 15).

The priest has the woman stand before the Lord (Num 5:16), that is, in the courtyard. The Supreme Court of Israel is in session, with God himself as Judge! Next the priest takes some holy water, probably from the sacred laver/basin. He adds to it some dust from the dirt floor of the holy tabernacle (5:17), presumably enhancing the potency of the water. The point is not the water's dirtiness but its holiness.

The priest prepares the woman for her ritual role by removing her headdress to loosen her hair, which is elsewhere associated with mourning, and by placing the grain offering of jealousy in her hands while he holds the vessel containing the holy water (5:18). He then places her under oath before the Lord (5:19–22).

The oath consists of two parts, corresponding to the contrasting possibilities stated earlier—guilty or innocent (5:12b–14)—but in reverse/chiastic order—innocent or guilty. If she is innocent, she will be immune to the effects of the water (5:19). But if she is guilty of having defiled herself by committing adultery (5:20), she will be punished.

Adultery involves physical ritual impurity that is forbidden and is therefore morally wrong because it is incurred with the wrong party. The presence or absence of such illegal defilement is the deciding factor in the dynamics of the suspected adulteress ritual.

If a suspected adulteress is guilty, the punishment will fit the crime. The Lord will put/set her as an imprecation among her people by putting physical maladies in the relevant area of her body (5:21–22, 27). While scholars have not agreed on the gynecological implications of the Hebrew terminology, they sound painful and clearly cause sterility (contrast 5:28). So the conditional imprecation, to which a suspected woman must assent by saying *amen, so be it* (5:22, italics added), specifies outcomes that any Israelite woman dreads: social stigma, physical suffering, and inability to bear children. Although the oath provides a powerful incentive for a guilty woman to volunteer a confession before saying *amen*, the text does not say whether her punishment is mitigated if she does confess.

The ritual continues. The priest writes the curses and then physically rubs off the words into the holy water so that it symbolically contains the curses (5:23; cf. Jer 51:59–64). Then he takes the grain offering of jealousy from her, dedicates it to the Lord by elevating/waving it before him, and burns a handful of it on the altar as the Lord's token portion (Num 5:25–26).

The next move is startling and brings the entire procedure to a climax: The priest has the woman drink the holy water that is now bitter with conditional curses (5:26b; anticipated in 5:24). If she is guilty of defiling herself and committing unfaithfulness against her husband, the water causes the bitter suffering specified in the oath (5:24, 27). But if she is pure/innocent, she is vindicated and "will be able to have children" (5:28).

Verses 29–31 conclude the chapter by labeling and summarizing "the law of jealousy." Verse 31 adds an important concept: A husband who takes his wife to the sanctuary for the suspected adulteress ritual remains clean/free from culpability, that is, even if she is innocent, but his wife bears her culpability if she is guilty. His suspicion is not an accusation for which he would be culpable if she were innocent (cf. Deut 19:16–19; 22:13–19).

Application. Grass is greener on the other side of the fence (Prov 9:17)—maybe for an initial rush of exciting chemistry. But when lustful curiosity is sated and glamour fades like yet another episode of a soap opera, adultery is shallow and boring, and it leaves an aftertaste of guilt. There is no comparison to the sustainable emotional and spiritual depth of "your own cistern" (Prov 5:15). Decades ago, a married man who enjoyed dating around justified himself by saying to me, "Variety is the spice of life." Although not yet married, I replied: "The spouse is the spice."

As marriage partners are to each other, God is the exclusive covenant partner of his people. Covenant intimacy demands this exclusiveness. He forbids his people to engage in idolatry or worship of other deities because he is "a jealous God" (Exod 20:5; 34:14; Deut 4:24; 5:9; 6:15).

NUMBERS 6:1–21

Original Meaning. Why would someone choose to become a Nazirite? By not specifying a motivation, the biblical text leaves open a range of possibilities that could suit a variety of individuals and circumstances. Commitment to Naziriteship could simply be an expression of devotion and gratitude to the Lord, or it could be tied to a request for some kind of tangible or spiritual benefit from God.

In Numbers 6 there are three lifestyle restrictions that a temporary Nazirite must scrupulously observe throughout the entire period of dedication.

1. A Nazirite must remain separate from all alcoholic beverages, vinegar, and any other grape product even if it is not fermented (6:3–4).
2. The Nazirite must not have his or her hair cut (6:5).
3. The Nazirite must not go near a dead person, even of a close relative (6:6–7).

The reasons for the first and third of these requirements are readily apparent. All priests, including the high priest, are forbidden to drink wine or other fermented drink when they enter the tent of meeting (Lev 10:9). Ordinary priests are allowed to incur corpse contamination for certain close blood relatives (21:1–4), but the high priest is totally barred from corpse contamination (21:11).

The Nazirite's uncut hair is the outward symbol of separation to special holiness to the Lord (Num 6:5, 8). The high priest is consecrated to special holiness by a symbol of separation on his head, in this case anointing with oil (Lev 21:10, 12). Another symbol on his head is a golden "emblem" (Exod 39:30; cf. 29:6; Lev 8:9). The holiness of the Nazirite is analogous in some ways to that of the high priest.

Accidental annulment. In addition to the usual purification for corpse contamination on the third and seventh days by sprinkling water containing ashes of the red cow (19:11–12, 17–19), the Nazirite must shave his or her head (6:9). This removes the sign of Naziriteship.

On the eighth day a sacrifice of two birds, serving as a purification offering supplemented by a burnt offering, provides expiation for the unintentional sin of breaking the vow (6:10–11). Impurity has simply occurred through adverse circumstances, without any failure of intention, carefulness, vigilance, or memory on the part of the Nazirite.

The same day as the purification and burnt offerings, the Israelite must begin the period of Naziriteship all over again, (re-)consecrate his or her head, and bring a lamb for a reparation offering (6:11–12). The reason for this type of sacrifice, which remedies sacrilege, is implied (6:12).

Completion of the Nazirite period. Numbers 6:13–21 outlines a ceremony for termination of a successfully completed Nazirite period, after which the Nazirite restrictions are lifted. The ritual procedure includes several sacrifices, among which is a purification offering ("fellowship offering" [6:14, 16]).

It appears that the purification offering of the Nazirite has basically the same function as that of the priestly consecration service—carrying out purification before offering consecration gifts to the Lord. The difference is that whereas the priests offered their consecration gifts at the *beginning* of lifelong service at the sanctuary, Nazirites offer theirs at the *end* of temporary, voluntary periods of holiness. As part of the completion ceremony, the Nazirite must shave his or her head and put the hair on the altar fire under the fellowship offering (6:18; cf. Acts 21:23–24).

Application. Numbers 6 made provision for any of God's people to be special as a Nazirite. With this privilege and honor came restrictions. Life is often like that. With a promotion and pay raise come increased responsibilities and less free time. But paradoxically, some restrictions bring freedom. A person who abstains from alcoholic beverages (including a Nazirite) is free from fear that he or she might get into trouble as a result of being intoxicated. Faithful marriage partners spare themselves many health and emotional risks. Restrictions on leaders and their families protect them from physical or character assassination.

NUMBERS 6:22–27

Original Meaning. God himself gives his priests the words to "bless" his people, that is, to put his name on them by invoking him as their deity so that he will bless them (6:27). We have already encountered an occasion when words like these would have been appropriate—at the conclusion of the inauguration service (Lev 9:22; cf. 9:23).

The blessing here is brief (Num 6:24–26) but poetic, with three pairs of parallels. Each pair begins with Yahweh as subject and wishes for him to have a favorable attitude: blessing, making his face shine, and lifting up his face. These ancient expressions of favor appear in other texts (Ruth 2:4). The second member of each pair wishes for Yahweh to do something positive for his people: guard, be gracious, and give well-being.

The language of Numbers 6:27 is related to that of 6:26. Notice how 6:27 encapsulates the blessing by referring to the beginning and ending ideas but in reverse (chiastic) order. In this structural pattern, the Lord's putting his name on the Israelites (6:27a) is the functional equivalent of giving them well-being (6:26b). Implied is reinforcement of the idea that through their connection with God, whose name represents his presence and character, his people receive well-being.

Application. Hebrews 4:14–16 invites Christians to ask as they approach God's throne through their sympathetic High Priest in heaven to receive mercy and grace in time of need. So why don't we ask more? If our prayers are real to God, are they real to us? Do we have confidence that our praises and petitions to God, feeble and unfocused as they are, have been successfully transmitted to him with the aid of his Spirit (Rom 8:26)?

NUMBERS 7:1–89

Original Meaning. The chieftains, representing their tribes (not including Levi), brought their gifts to the sanctuary when Moses anointed and thereby consecrated it (7:1–2). The chiefs give six wagons and twelve oxen, two for each wagon, which logically go to the Gershonite and Merarite Levites for transporting the sanctuary (7:3–8). This helps to explain why the present archival account is placed here in the book of Numbers. The gifts meet needs created by the Levite job descriptions (ch. 4).

The Kohathites do not need wagons because they transport the sacred furniture on their shoulders by poles (7:9).

This requires manpower, but it protects the precious items from the kind of jolting that later cost Uzzah his life when he reached out to steady the ark of the covenant on its cart (2 Sam 6:3–7).

Having introduced the twelve tribal chieftains in Numbers 7, the rest of the chapter (except for 7:89) continues with an inventory of the chieftains' other offerings, even though they brought them earlier for the service of the outer altar when it was initiated/inaugurated shortly after it was anointed (7:10–88; cf. 7:1). Although this inventory belongs between Leviticus 8 and 9 from a chronological perspective, its present location maintains thematic cohesion by avoiding interruption of the grand consecration-inauguration process in Leviticus and by keeping the chiefs' presents to the sanctuary together.

The word for "initiation" (NIV "dedication") of the altar is *hanukkah* (7:10, 11, 84, 88). This noun denotes the first use of a structure for the purpose for which it was intended. Thus, a house (Deut 20:5), city wall (Neh 12:27), or image (Dan 3:2–3) could be initiated, as was Solomon's temple (1 Kgs 8:63; 2 Chr 7:5) and its altar (2 Chr 7:9). The Jewish holiday of Hanukkah in December celebrates the initiation of a new altar when the Maccabees purified and reconsecrated the Second Temple (1 Macc 4:52–59).

At first glance, the last verse of Numbers 7 (7:89) looks isolated, but it harks back to the beginning of the chapter, which refers to Moses's setting up and consecrating the sanctuary. As the Lord promised when he provided directions for constructing the ark of the covenant (Exod 25:22), Moses heard the Lord's voice "speaking to him from between the two cherubim above the atonement cover on the ark of the covenant law" (Num 7:89).

The initial occasion when Moses could enter the tabernacle after its consecration and encounter the divine glory like this was at the conclusion of the public inauguration service (Lev 9:23; cf. 9:6), for which sacrificial victims and other materials (9:1–5) undoubtedly had been provided by the chieftains. At that time Moses and Aaron blessed the people (9:22–23; cf. Num 6:22–27). So, Numbers 6:22–7:89 contains a cluster of connections to the founding events of Israelite worship on which any progress would be based.

Application. Like the Israelite chieftains who brought gifts to the Lord at the sanctuary (Num 7) and the Magi who paid rich homage to the newborn King (Matt 2:11), we have the privilege of joyfully acknowledging him with tangible gifts as well as prayers, songs, and testimonies. When modern people initiate the use of a church and provide it with a van, kitchen utensils, and food for God's work in their community, they are following in the worthy footsteps of Nahshon, Nethanel, Eliab, and their fellow leaders.

NUMBERS 8:1–26

Original Meaning. *Forward lighting.* This brief passage repeats the divine instruction in Exodus 25:37 where the lamps appear for the first time. Numbers 8:3 provides the only new information: Aaron complies with the instruction after the inauguration of the sanctuary. Numbers 7–8 refers to initiation of all three major portions of the sanctuary: the outer altar (7:10–88), the inner sanctum (7:89), and the outer sanctum (8:1–4).

Separating the Levite workforce. Before the Levites can begin their sacred duties of transporting the sanctuary and its sancta (8:5–19), they must be ritually purified and set apart from the other Israelites (8:7). Sprinkling remedies any corpse contamination that the Levites may have incurred. Diametrically opposed to holiness/life, this kind of severe impurity defiles the sanctuary even from a distance if it is not removed (19:13, 20).

Unlike the ordination of the priests (cf. Lev 8), the authorization service for the Levites does not include consecration with anointing oil. Members of the Israelite community are to lay their hands on the Levites, presumably to designate them as the ones who will perform the work of the sanctuary as representatives of the community (Num 8:9–11). Then Aaron is to dedicate the Levites as a "wave offering" before the Lord from the Israelites (8:11). As part of the service, the Levites are also to receive expiation through the sacrifice of two bulls as a sin offering pair (8:12).

Verses 14–19 explain the work of the Levites at the sanctuary. The Levites are to do the work of the sanctuary on behalf of the rest of the Israelites and are to ransom them so that no plague will strike the community if some Israelites approach the sanctuary, that is, cross boundaries of authorized access.

We think of this kind of ransom for life as accomplished through animal sacrifice or the half shekel ransom at the time of a census. In fact, by leaning their hands on the Levites and elevating/waving them, the Israelites and Aaron, respectively, treat the Levites as if they are a corporate sacrificial victim. Although they are not offered on the Lord's altar, they are responsible for guarding the sanctuary against encroachment, literally with their lives. If they fail to stop this evil by putting the offender(s) to death (1:51), they will bear the culpability, but the other Israelites will be spared.

The end of Numbers 8 specifies the ages of men included in the Levite workforce: twenty-five to fifty (8:23–26). After the age of fifty a Levite is to retire from the strenuous work of moving the sanctuary, but he can still assist with guard duty (8:26). This passage is at variance with chapter 4 (4:3, 23, 30, 35, 39, 43, 47—seven times), where the census of the Levite workforce ranges from thirty to fifty years of age. When the sanctuary later found a permanent resting place at Jerusalem and the

Levites' job description changed from carrying it to less rigorous duties at the temple, David instructed that they be counted from age twenty with no upper age limit (1 Chr 23:24–27).

Application. Just as Levites were specially set apart to do tasks for the benefit of the priests and the Israelite community (Num 3:6–7; 8:5–22), deacons were set apart to serve the Christian community by doing administrative tasks so that the apostles could be free for spiritual leadership (Acts 6:1–6). Of course, there are important differences between Levites and deacons. The deacons were dedicated to assist apostles by dealing with matters such as daily distribution of food (Acts 6:1), not to help priests by taking care of the infrastructure for ritual worship at a sanctuary/temple. The dedications of Levites and deacons reinforce the concept that seemingly mundane tasks for the Lord and his community are sacred.

NUMBERS 9:1–23

Original Meaning. The drama of deliverance is continuing. The Israelites are about to exit the Mount Sinai region and resume their journey toward the promised land (Num 10). Numbers 9 tells how God reminds the Israelites to celebrate Passover (9:1–5) and makes provision for those who are ritually unclean to observe it later (9:9–14), and then describes how the Lord's cloud guides the people in their journeys (9:15–23). At first glance, the topics of Passover and the divine cloud seem unrelated to each other, but we must remember their connection in the book of Exodus: The Lord commanded Passover, the Israelites left Egypt, and God in his cloud guided and protected them (Exod 12–14).

Numbers 9:6 introduces a problem: Some Israelites are not able to celebrate Passover at the proper time because they have become ritually impure from a corpse. Celebrating the Passover involves eating a holy sacrifice, but the Israelites are strictly forbidden to eat sacrificial food while in a state of ritual impurity (Lev 7:20–21).

It is clear that the impure Israelites have not arranged to be disqualified from Passover so that they can skip it. Rather, they approach Moses and Aaron right away to express frustration that extenuating circumstances beyond their control, which we would call "a death in the family," are preventing them from joining the rest of the people in the privilege of presenting the Lord's offering (9:6–7). Theirs is a refreshing kind of complaint!

The Lord's solution is to establish an ongoing second date for Passover observance, a month later on the fourteenth day of the second month, for those prevented by corpse contamination from celebrating it at the normal time (9:8–12). To this concession, he graciously adds its application to individuals who might be away on long journeys at the usual time of the festival in the first month (9:10). Presumably this will go into effect when the Israelites are settled in Canaan.

Numbers 9:15–23 continues the transition to resumption of the desert journey by reiterating the behavior of the divine cloud (cf. Exod 40:34–38). Its movements prompt the Israelites to set out or to camp.

Numbers 9 appears to be out of chronological sequence. Verse 1 puts God's reminder regarding Passover "in the *first month* of the second year after they came out of Egypt" (emphasis added). This must be early in the first month before the Israelites are to celebrate the festival on the fourteenth day of the month (9:3). So, the Lord gives this reminder before his command in chapter 1 to carry out a military census, which he issues "on the *first day of the second month* of the second year" (1:1; emphasis added). Why this reversal?

The problem vanishes when we take into account the content of the new legislation in chapter 9: The second Passover on the *fourteenth day of the second month* is to be observed after the census has begun and just before the Israelites leave Mount Sinai on the twentieth day of the second month (10:11).

Application. For the Israelites to be with God's resident presence they must move with him. It is no use lingering to venerate the spot where he has been, nor is it worthwhile trying to guess where he may go next and running ahead to get there first. The important thing is to know where his cloud is and to follow it.

God's leadership calls for readiness to move at any time and also patience to stay put until he directs otherwise. For an individual who wants to set his or her own agenda, this arrangement can be intensely irritating and unsettling, but it is fine for someone who wants to be with God more than anything else. Such a person can feel content, like a baby carried by a parent, unworried about the specifics of the route as long as Mama or Papa is there.

NUMBERS 10:1–36

Original Meaning. *Trumpet signals.* Two signal trumpets of silver are to be blown by the priests at the sanctuary in order to assemble the people or to announce the break of camp (10:1–8). "Headquarters" are always guarded by priests, who notice movements of the cloud, and from this central location the trumpet blasts can be heard throughout the camp.

Different types of trumpet blasts signal a variety of activities, to which a wide range of emotions are associated. Variables in trumpet calls include (1) one or two trumpets, (2) the kind of blast: long or short, and (3) the number of blasts. Unlike assembly and celebration (both long), breaking camp and going to war (both short) involve moving out.

On the march! Only twenty days after announcement of the military census (1:1), "the cloud lifted from above the tabernacle of the covenant law" (10:11). The departure from Mount Sinai toward the desert of Paran (10:12) is a major transition in the Israelites' experience. The Lord has kept them at Mount Sinai long enough to make them into a functioning nation so that they can be unified under his benevolent rule and stay that way once they spread out in the promised land. Now they are ready to fulfill his dream and theirs!

As the Israelites are about to leave Mount Sinai, Moses urges "Hobab son of Reuel the Midianite, Moses's father-in-law [*hoten*]" to come with them (10:29). It is not clear whether the description "Moses's father-in-law" applies to Hobab or to Reuel. Exodus 2:18 refers to Moses's father-in-law as Reuel, who was the "priest of Midian" (2:16). In 3:1 and 18:1 Moses's father-in-law and "priest of Midian" is called Jethro. Thus, "Reuel" and "Jethro" are alternative names for the same man.

At least for the first three days of travel from Mount Sinai, the ark of the covenant goes before the Israelites (10:33). This indicates that unlike the rest of the tabernacle furniture, the ark precedes the entire column of Israelites. Perhaps the divine cloud that hovers over them (10:34), apparently for shade and protection, moves over the ark when it is time to halt.

Attached to the end of this chapter are two prayers that Moses pronounces, the first whenever the ark sets out and the second whenever it comes to rest (10:35–36). The second prayer can be taken in any or all of three ways, depending on whether the Lord returns *to* the Israelite hosts, is Lord *of* the Israelite hosts, or *is* the hosts of Israel, that is, Israel's strength, as in the traditional expression "Lord of hosts [NIV: "Almighty"]" (e.g., 1 Sam 1:3, 11; 4:4; 15:2): "Return O Lord the myriads of thousands of Israel" (10:36, author's translation). In translating this verse, the NIV, NASB, and NKJV insert "to" (preposition understood); the NRSV has "of" (Heb. construct); and the NJPS has "you who are" (apposition).

Application. The concept that God's people benefit from cooperation with him runs through the Old Testament. Divine-human coordination also appears in the New Testament. Why does the Lord have human beings do something, no matter how small, when he wants to do something amazing for them? Obviously, it is not because he cannot do those things, and far more efficiently too. Rather, it is because human activity is an expression of faith.

Cooperation with God requires first learning what he wants and then doing it, so that our work cooperates with his. If our prayers are simply one-way monologues in which we speak to him without listening for his voice or his "trumpet" or looking for his "cloud," we miss opportunities for his direction to guide our work.

NUMBERS 11:1–35

Original Meaning. *Grousing.* We have made it through ten chapters of the book of Numbers without hearing of anyone having a bad attitude. In 11:1, however, we hit a sour note that sounds like déjà vu all over again. Experiencing the discomforts of travel, the people ungratefully complain. Whereas the divine cloud has been appearing like fire at night to protect the Israelites (9:15–16), now the Lord answers grumbling with destructive fire at the outskirts of the camp, reminiscent of the fire that consumed Nadab and Abihu.

The next episode is about the Lord's cafeteria menu, the staple of which is manna (Num 11:4–6). The disgruntled riffraff are the catalyst for complaining. Because the non-Israelites would have lived at the outskirts of the camp, outside the areas designated for the twelve tribes, the fact that the Lord struck that portion at "Taberah" (11:3) implies that the riffraff instigated the grumbling there as well.

As expected, the divine King does not take kindly to insulting rejection of the heavenly bounty that he has daily provided. Ominously, he becomes "exceedingly angry" (11:10). Exacerbating the gravity of the situation is Moses's burnout. Whereas he interceded at Taberah with a prayer to God (11:2), he now offers a complaint of his own (11:11–15). Just as the people are sick and tired of manna, Moses is sick and tired of them! This is the same Moses who earlier pleaded for Israel's life, even if it meant blotting his own name out of God's book (Exod 32:32). Now the Lord has two problems on his hands: Moses as well as Israel.

The Lord first addresses Moses's need, telling him to gather seventy elders (Num 11:16) so that they can be empowered to help him carry the burden of managing the people (11:17). Whereas Jethro earlier advised Moses to delegate judges for handling disputes between the people (Exod 18:13–26), here it is the Lord who takes initiative to make tribal elders an extension of Moses and a buffer between him and their people.

Turning to the people's craving for meat, God commands that the people sanctify themselves (11:18). Such "consecration" includes washing their clothes and abstaining from sexual relations along with bathing in preparation for a special encounter with God the next day. It sounds as though the Israelites are to enjoy sacrificial meat, but their wish-come-true will turn to punishment that fits their crime when they will have it coming out their noses (11:19–20).

Sharing the Spirit. When the Lord puts the Spirit on seventy elders, they temporarily prophesy (11:24–25). The text does not say what this prophesying entails. Their prophesying alarms Joshua, who is apparently concerned that leadership extending to the elders should be associated with Moses at headquarters (11:27–28). Rather than being jealous of the spiritual gifts granted to others, Moses rejoices and desires the best for all of God's people.

Quail. Having answered Moses's need by putting his Spirit (Heb. *ruah*) on the elders, the Lord delivers fresh meat to the people by airmail, sending a literal wind (also *ruah*) that blows quail in from the sea (11:31). He has sent them quail before (Exod 16:13), but this time the birds come in prodigious quantities. The biblical text says that the wind left the quail around the camp about 2 cubits "above/on" (Heb. preposition *al*) the surface of the land. This can as easily mean that the wind impels the quail to within reach of the Israelites and leaves them there just above and on the ground where they can readily be caught and slaughtered.

The people greedily gather quail around the clock all day, all night, and all the next day and spread them out around the camp, presumably to cure by drying, so that their excess of "ten homers" of quail each (11:32) can last for the next month, as the Lord promised (11:18–20). Six hundred thousand men (11:21) collect more than thirty-five bushels each, for a total of more than twenty-one million bushels. Undoubtedly women and children help with the gathering process, but they may have shared in the "ten homers" minimum that belonged to their men. Even if there were only five birds per bushel (a low estimate given their relatively small size), there would be a total of more than 105 million birds, still a flock of staggering proportions that would have occupied a vast area while in full flight before becoming bogged down and concentrated around the Israelite camp.

The influx of quail in the biblical story is related to a natural phenomenon. Large numbers of quail migrate across the Sinai Peninsula from Africa on their way to Europe and Asia. Since these birds have relatively heavy bodies and do not fly well, they partly depend on prevailing winds to assist their flight, and they become exhausted by long journeys. In Numbers 11 the quail come from the sea, as we would expect, but three unusual elements signal divine intervention: The arrival of quail is timed to serve as the Lord's answer to the Israelites' demand for meat, the wind that carries the flock is from the Lord, and the number of birds is miraculous.

The people's indulgence for a month until quail comes out their noses (cf. 11:20) is interrupted. God's anger burns against them and he strikes them a great blow (11:33). This may involve sickness, such as a form of bacterial food poisoning that induces vomiting (possibly including out the nose). Whatever the precise nature of the "severe plague" (11:33) resulting from quail, its acute onset is deadly, as implied by the name given to the place: Kibroth Hattaavah, meaning "the graves of craving" (11:34).

Application. Freedom allows for the possibility of complaining. God knows that faith has a "learning curve." After giving the Israelites evidence on which to base their trust, he then expected them to trust him more and held them accountable for the quality of their faith in his beneficence. After a year of living in total dependence on him, they knew where to get help when they needed it. When grumbling about food arose again, it was not simply complaining—it was rebellious refusal to trust the Lord. He had to cure them of this attitude in a desert "boot camp" because they could not survive a military assault on fortified Canaan without implicit trust in miracles that only he could provide.

Complaining is alive and well today, especially with regard to little aggravations, inconveniences, aches, and pains. Obviously, there is a place for directing legitimate grievances to those who have caused our problems or can do something about them, whether they are other people or God (cf. Job, many psalms, and Habakkuk), but grumbling behind someone's back is destructive. This includes unfocused complaining, which implicitly implicates God as the ultimate cause and denies that he cares about every aspect of our well-being (Luke 12:6–7).

Instead of simply complaining, which tends to depress ourselves and others, we can accomplish something positive if we take our complaints directly to God in prayer, believing that he will hear us (cf. Ps 142:1–3). A complaint to God that is a petition of faith can end up strengthening the faith of others when the Lord answers the prayer (cf. 142:7).

NUMBERS 12:1–16

Original Meaning. Unless Moses married a second woman, for which there is no clear evidence, why would Zipporah be labelled a "Cushite" here (12:1)? We don't know for sure. In any case, Miriam and Aaron are irritated at Moses's non-Israelite wife, but this is only the outer symptom of a deeper grievance: They feel that Moses is unduly dominating their prophetic triumvirate (12:2). Why now? Moses has just appointed seventy elders to receive the prophetic gift and share responsibility with him (11:24–26), thereby decentralizing power away from Miriam and Aaron. Although the arrangement is the Lord's idea (11:16–17, 24), Miriam and Aaron can easily associate it with an earlier initiative to relieve Moses by decentralizing judicial responsibility, which was sponsored by Jethro, Zipporah's father (Exod 18:13–26). Who would have a greater interest in reducing Moses's burden now more than the "first lady" of Israel (whether Zipporah or another wife)?

"First lady"? That may explain why Miriam is mentioned before Aaron as the instigator of criticism (12:1). With her brothers, she was a leader of the exodus (Mic 6:4). It was "Miriam the prophet, Aaron's sister," who took a tambourine and led all the Israelite women in a song of triumph at the Red Sea (Exod 15:20–21). Now she likely feels displaced, perhaps by one who has never experienced the horrors of slavery and the trauma of leaving Egypt.

While Moses does not defend himself, the Lord takes decisive action (12:4). He does not deny the claim of Aaron and Miriam to prophetic inspiration (12:6). But Moses has experienced more intimate access to God than any other human being (12:7–8) and is an active participant in dialogue with him. Miriam and Aaron should be afraid to speak against Moses (12:8), which is tantamount to speaking against God.

When the divine warning is punctuated by Miriam's case of skin disease, Aaron undoubtedly remembers the way Moses produced and reversed such disease on himself as a sign of divine power (Exod 4:6–7). Assuming that Moses is angry, Aaron implores him for forgiveness and for healing for Miriam (12:11–12). However, all Moses can do is to cry out for the Lord to heal her (12:13). It is ironic that Aaron and Miriam, who are supposed to be prophets, are utterly dependent on the intercession of Moses.

Because the Lord has disgraced Miriam, who apparently was more at fault than Aaron, it takes some time to restore her. A quick fix would trivialize the gravity of the situation. During the week of delay, all Israelites have plenty of opportunity to reflect on the deadly "disease" of rebellion against God's leadership through Moses (12:15). Many years before, big sister Miriam had waited for baby Moses (Exod 2:4); now he waits for her.

The humblest? Numbers 12:3 parenthetically informs us that Moses was the most *anaw* man on earth. English versions generally render this word as "humble." For those who believe the traditional view that Moses was the author of the Pentateuch, 12:3 raises a question: If Moses wrote that he was the humblest man on the face of the earth, wouldn't this constitute a boast that would invalidate his humility? It can be argued that the explanation in 12:3 was written by an editor of the Pentateuch, not by Moses himself (cf. Gen 12:6; Deut 34).

Elsewhere the Hebrew word *anaw* refers to those who are poor, needy, socially weak, afflicted, and/or humiliated (e.g., Isa 61:1; Amos 2:7). While Moses was a powerful leader and in this sense was not socially weak, he was afflicted by his people and, at Hazeroth, was ill-treated and humiliated by his own sister and brother (12:1–2). Thus, in addition to the idea that Moses lacks arrogance, it appears that at least part of the point in 12:3 may be that he is so bowed down and burdened that he is unable to stick up for himself, which explains why the Lord has to step in to defend him.

Application. The fact that Moses's wife is described as "Cushite" only in the context of derogatory talk regarding her by Miriam and Aaron (12:1) suggests that they look down on her for having darker skin (cf. Song 1:6). While a racial slur is only on the "skin" of an underlying issue of status and control, the Lord's punishment of Miriam indicates that he takes her xenophobia seriously by making her skin "as white as now" (12:10). It is as though he were saying to her: "Miriam, if you can't get used to the idea that dark is beautiful, see if you like your own skin, which pales by comparison!" What is so bad about racism? As in the story of Miriam and Aaron, it is always about status and control, and it is always an insult to God.

NUMBERS 13:1–33

Original Meaning. Numbers 13 and 14 recount a major turning point in the desert journey of the Israelites—the expedition of scouts and the impact of their reports on the willingness of the people to trust the Lord's promise that he will give them the promised land. When the chieftains return to the community, they stage a much anticipated "show and tell." "Pomegranates and figs" provide material confirmation of the land's superlative agricultural quality, as encapsulated in the expression "flow with milk and honey" (13:23, 26–27). Most impressive is a gargantuan "cluster" (*eshkol*) of grapes that two scouts carry between them on a pole (13:23) the way Kohathite Levites carry sacred objects belonging to the sanctuary (4:6, 8, 11, 14; 7:9).

The scouts quickly move over agriculture to dwell on the human demographics of Canaan. Matching the abundant and sizeable fruits are numerous and powerful peoples with large, fortified cities (13:28). As the people's euphoria vaporizes, there is an uproar. Observe how Caleb, the scout from Judah, needs to silence the people before telling them that they can and should go up and take the land (13:30).

At this point the biased attitude of the other scouts bursts into the open as they categorically contradict Caleb and defame the land they have earlier praised, claiming that it "devours those living in it" (13:31–32). If they are saying that Canaan is an unhealthy place, they are contradicting themselves. How can its inhabitants be so big and strong if the land devours them? Perhaps they mean that the land metaphorically devours its people through war. But if the people of Canaan are decimated and weakened by war, how can they be so numerous, prosperous, and secure as to pose an insurmountable obstacle to the Israelites?

To drive a final nail in the coffin of hope, the ten scouts volunteer a category of information regarding which Moses has not asked: the physical size of the inhabitants of Canaan. The most intimidating aspect of Canaan is the (undoubtedly exaggerated) generalization that "all the people we saw there are of great size" (13:32). To traumatize overwrought imaginations, the chieftains describe some of the giants as Nephilim (13:33), descended from the mighty men of renown who lived before the flood (Gen 6:4). It is not clear how the Israelites suppose that the line of antediluvian Nephilim has survived the flood (cf. 7:21–23). Details aside, they readily buy the idea that the Canaanite giants are a vastly more powerful class of human beings than they are and succumb to catatonic terror.

Application. For the person of faith, obstacles are temporary because God is real. For the disbeliever, obstacles are permanent because God is not real enough. Thus, the key to exegesis of exigencies is an existential question: Is God real to me? Do I believe, act, and live as if he is alive?

Do we have evidence that God is real? In Scripture we have an accumulated record of divine activity, including descriptions by human beings who experienced it. Most impressive is the testimony of eyewitnesses regarding the incarnate Christ (1 John 1:1).

What about something that we can personally experience? Paul cites the evidence of creation as basic for all inhabitants of earth (Rom 1:20). We may never experience a dry path through a body of water, food from the sky, or an awesome voice from the top of a mountain, but if we pray to treat someone with more unselfish love than yesterday and if that prayer is answered, we have the most important miracle of all.

NUMBERS 14:1–45

Original Meaning. Persuaded by the negative scouts (13:31–33) that it is hopeless to attempt to conquer Canaan, the Israelites conclude that the Lord is their enemy and their best option is to mutiny against Moses and return to Egypt (14:3–4). With Moses and Aaron prostrate (14:5), apparently in a position of silent petition to God, Joshua and Caleb take over the defense (14:6–9). Their argument that the "protection" (6:9) of the people of Canaan is gone may allude to God's promise to Abraham (Gen 15:16). If so, Joshua and Caleb are saying that God's protective mercy on the inhabitants of the land is finished and the time for Israel to receive Canaan has arrived.

Joshua and Caleb employ wise strategy. Nevertheless, the two faithful scouts get nothing for their trouble except talk of stoning them, which likely threatens Moses and Aaron too (14:10). The murderous threats transgress the bounds of tolerable free speech. Preempting their fulfillment, "the glory of the Lord appeared at the tent of meeting" (14:10b), undoubtedly turning rampaging rage into trembling terror. Although the mob constitutes the collective "defendant," God says nothing to them. Rather, he addresses Moses to announce their sentence: death and replacement with a better nation descended from Moses (14:11–12).

Moses finds his voice to plead for the lives of those who have heaped abominable abuse on him (14:13–19). The Lord does indeed forgive the Israelites as Moses asks (14:20), namely, in the sense of preserving the corporate covenant relationship by not destroying all of them at once (14:15). However, merciful amnesty for the nation by no means rules out capital condemnation of a significant number of rebels, as God states in a formidable exception clause that he sets in concrete by swearing an oath (14:21). The Lord swears by his *life* that the people (i.e., the adult generation) who have *seen* his glory, which fills the whole earth, will *die* in the desert without *seeing* the promised land (14:21–23).

"Ten times" (14:22) appears to be idiomatic for "[too] many times." Ironically, the Lord has graciously given the Israelites his glorious Ten Commandments, but they have repaid him with ten tests of patience.

There is an exception to the exception: Although Caleb belongs to the condemned generation, he will permanently enter Canaan because he has completely followed the Lord (14:24). Later God also includes Joshua with Caleb (14:30).

Accepting the Israelites' own decision to return toward Egypt rather than appropriate their own territory (14:3–4), the Lord orders them back into the desert along the way leading to the Red Sea (14:25). They refuse to live in the promised land, so they will suffer by dying in the unpromising and uncompromising desert.

In his next divine speech, the Lord specifies how the adult generation will meet its demise (14:26–35). To make the punishment fit the crime, the Lord will bring on the Israelites the very thing they wished for when they grumbled against him. Their corpses will fall in the desert (14:29; cf. 14:2) but not all at once, so that the Lord will accomplish his goal of purifying Israel without damaging his own.

Those who will die without seeing Canaan are the grumblers who were earlier included in the military census (men twenty years of age and older), not including the Levites (14:29). To be counted is to be accountable. The text does not specify the fate of adult women, but it appears that they are to die in the desert along with their husbands. Ironically, the children whom the men regarded as helpless (14:3) will be the only ones to survive (14:31). Nevertheless, for forty years they will bear the result of their parents' "unfaithfulness" to God by being shepherds in the desert rather than enjoying the promised land (14:33).

Like the Israelites' punishment of exclusion from the land they have spurned, the duration will exquisitely fit their crime: forty years, one year for each of the days that the scouts explored hostile territory (14: 34; cf. 13:25). Thus, the Lord answers his own question (14:27).

Through a divine plague, the ten spies who were the catalyst for rebellious grumbling have the distinction of being the "firstfruits" of extinction (14:36–37). After mourning their fate (14:39), which kills any doubt as to the seriousness of the

Lord's intentions, the Israelites arise the next morning, confess their sin, and insist they are ready to go into Canaan (14:40).

The Israelites were afraid to enter Canaan with God on their side, but now they boldly go without him, as if they can do it by themselves. Here is a classic case of salvation by human works arrogantly attempting to take the place of salvation by grace through faith, as if human beings are greater than God. This isn't courage; it is stupidity.

The Israelite soldiers already doomed to die in the desert only succeed in hastening their demise. They get themselves bashed in pieces by the Amalekites and Canaanites all the way down to a place subsequently called Hormah (14:45). The place receives this name decades later when the Israelites devote Arad to the Lord for total destruction (21:1–3). Thus, for an audience of a torah reading, the ignominious Israelite retreat "to Hormah" likely evokes the idea that they are battered to destruction.

Application. Just as modern fads sweep through society because people exert strong influence on each other, the negativity of naysaying Israelite scouts is wildly contagious to people who share a lack of adequate trust in God. How do we protect ourselves and others from negative tipping points, such as giving in to temptation and strife, and promote positive ones, such as decisions to wholeheartedly follow the Lord? Here are a few tips:

- Foster a healthy influence on others, especially with regard to attitudes or attitude-shaping pieces of information that can be passed on without control from one person to another (e.g., avoiding gossip, slander, paranoia, or sensationalism).
- Critique influences on you, no matter how compelling they look. Don't allow them to lead you to make damaging choices.
- Keep things in perspective and don't run or jump just because all the other lemmings do.
- Be aware of spiritual, social, intellectual, and emotional environments that provide fertile ground for sudden change, whether for better or for worse.
- Maintain personal anchor points of faith and ethics to hang on to when everything else seems to be shifting fast.

NUMBERS 15:1–41

Original Meaning. *"Eye" of the "hurricane."* After the breathtaking narrative of the previous chapter, we are in the tranquil "eye" of a narrative "hurricane" that will strike again with full fury in chapter 16. The very fact that the Lord is willing to continue as Israel's Lawgiver and accept sacrificial gifts from the people is a good sign, and so is explicit application of these laws to future life in the promised land (15:2, 18), where they can offer him its products such as grain and wine (15:2–21). This legislation affirms his promise to bring the younger generation into Canaan.

It also highlights the need for loyalty to him by making a drastic contrast between inadvertent sin, for which he offers a sacrificial remedy leading to forgiveness, and defiant sin, for which there is only terminal condemnation (15:22–31). This chapter, with its thematic balance between God's justice and mercy and its strong warning against disloyalty, simultaneously makes Korah's revolt (ch. 16) appear more shocking and unreasonable to the listener/reader.

Sacrificial accompaniments and first dough. Numbers 15:1–16 formulates a general rule: Grain and wine offerings must accompany every sacrificial gift. The word "sacrifice" (*zebah*) here does not refer to sacrifices in general but to the class of sacrifices that includes fellowship offerings, from which offerors are permitted to eat. The fact that grain and wine accompaniments are included implies that they are burned on the outer altar.

Numbers 15:4–12 specifies in ascending order the amounts of the grain offerings and drink offerings of wine that must accompany each flock animal (sheep or goat), ram, or bull in accordance with its size/value. The same rules for sacrificial accompaniments apply to resident aliens (15:13–16). Verses 15–16 emphasize remarkable equality: Resident aliens share the same legal status before the Lord as other Israelites.

Verses 17–21 present another law that applies when the Israelites enter the promised land (cf. 15:2). When they eat the bread of the land, they must set aside a dedication/gift and present it to the Lord via his priest: a loaf from the first bread-making vessel(?) or dough(?) of each new harvest. Because it is processed dough from ground grain rather than standing grain, this firstfruits offering applies to both nonfarmers and farmers.

Forgivable versus unforgivable sin. The text goes on to contrast expiable inadvertence with defiant sin, for which there is no sacrificial remedy, but only the divinely administered terminal punishment of being "cut off" (15:30–31). Numbers 15:22–31 presents two notable differences to Leviticus 4.

1. Instead of a purification ("sin") offering bull (Lev 4:14), the community must now sacrifice a burnt offering bull, with its grain and wine accompaniments, in addition to a male goat for a purification offering (Num 15:24). What difference does the modification make? The most obvious one is that Numbers 15 distances the purification offering of the community from that of the high priest, both of which call for bulls in Leviticus 4. Why change the ritual in this way? The text does not say. Perhaps the answer lies in the relationship between

Numbers 15 and its narrative context, where sins of the community that include conflict with the high priesthood feature so prominently (chs. 14; 16–17).

2. The other notable difference to Leviticus 4 is the fact that Numbers 15:30–31 explicitly condemns defiant sinners without any opportunity for the sacrificial expiation. This contrast warns those tempted to rebellion against God that there is a point of no return. By their own choice, human beings can permanently and irrevocably destroy their relationship with him. Defiant sin is the spiritual equivalent of jumping off the Golden Gate Bridge. If biblical warnings sound harsh, they are to prevent that from happening.

Apparently to illustrate inexpiable sin, 15:32–36 places the brief narrative of a man scrounging for firewood on Sabbath within the legal setting of Numbers 15. This happened sometime during the period when the Israelites were in the desert (15:32), where the climate was warm and the people had manna to eat. So, a fire for warmth or cooking would not have been urgent even if it were not Sabbath. It looks as though this man was going out of his way to violate the Sabbath command, of which the people were reminded every weekend when they received a double portion of manna on Friday and none on the Sabbath (Exod 16:22–30).

The Ten Commandments do not specify punishments. Thus, as in the case of the blasphemer, the penalty for breaking the Sabbath was not clear, so the offender was kept under guard pending a divine oracle (Num 15:34). Again, the divine verdict communicated to Moses was death outside the camp through stoning by the community (15:35–36).

Tassels. Numbers 15:37–41 prescribes an ongoing strategy to jog the memory of the Israelites regarding all of the Lord's commandments—tassels on their garments to help them obey and be consecrated to the Lord rather than by going wherever their hearts or eyes should lead them (15:39).

A violet (Heb. *tekelet*) cord (Heb. *petil*) attached to the tassels (15:38) is to symbolize consecration of the Israelites to the Lord (15:40) as a "kingdom of priests" (Exod 19:6). Violet was a color of royalty because only royalty could afford this kind of dye. Violet was also connected with the priesthood because it was used in the priestly garments. In fact, aside from the violet cord on the tassels in Numbers 15:38, violet cords only appear in the context of the high priest's ornate vestments, connecting the breastpiece to the ephod (Exod 28:28; 39:21) and the gold plate to the turban (28:36–37; 39:30–31).

Application. The fact that God is incredibly merciful should bring hope to *any* sinner who desires salvation. However, it should not lead any to suppose that it is safe to presume upon his grace by stubbornly sliding down the slippery slope of apostasy with assurance that the gravity of depravity can be reversed at any time with a simple hop onto the "chair lift" to heaven. Going down does not make it easier to get back up. The problem is not for God to be willing to forgive but for a sinner to want to be forgiven.

NUMBERS 16:1–35

Original Meaning. *Fighting words.* The Israelites have previously talked about choosing someone to replace Moses and Aaron (14:4). Now Korah announces his candidacy—a Kohathite Levite, closely related to Moses, Aaron, and Miriam. With Korah are Dathan, Abiram, and On from the tribe of Reuben (16:1). Since the Reubenites and Kohathites both camp on the south side of the tabernacle (2:10; 3:29), the tents of the rebel leaders are close to each other.

Backed up by a formidable group of 250 reputable chieftains, Korah and his associates confront Moses and Aaron (16:1–3a) with fighting words (16:3b). Korah & Co. have armed themselves with a kind of covenant theology. As the Lord himself said, the whole nation is holy (Exod 19:6), so how can Moses and Aaron claim higher status and presume to condemn others? The rebels are not a disorganized mob venting riotous indignation. They are well-organized leaders who are, humanly speaking, qualified to run the nation.

Deadly challenge. Moses responds by challenging the rebels to burn incense in order to test their claim to holiness on a par with that of the Aaronic priests (16:5–7). It is supposed to work like a ritual litmus test for a suspected adulteress (5:11–31) in the sense that variable results will depend on variable states of persons who come in contact with certain kinds/degrees of holiness.

The test proposed by Moses is deadly dangerous, and his warning (16:7) is no empty threat. Even though Aaron's sons Nadab and Abihu were authorized priests, they perished for offering incense with unauthorized fire (Lev 10:1–2). What will happen to someone who offers incense if the Lord has not chosen him?

Rebuking the rebel Levites with laser-like focus, Moses inversely mirrors the introduction of Korah & Co.: "Is it (too) small for you . . . ?" (16:9, author's translation). Is their special work for the Lord so insignificant that they should also seek the priesthood (16:9–10)? Moses's punch line hits the proverbial nail on the head (16:11). At issue is theocratic leadership of the community.

Refusing Moses's summons, Dathan and Abiram send an insulting message that begins with language like that which Moses used on Korah (16:13). As far as they are concerned, Moses is the problem blocking the way to real progress.

Moses has put up with a lot in the past, but the outrageous

defamations hurled at him by Dathan and Abiram turn him into an anti-intercessor (16:15). This is the only place where the Pentateuch says that Moses was "very angry."

Swallowing those who fail to swallow their pride. It is surprising that Korah & Co. show up at the court of the sanctuary the next day for an incense duel with Aaron (16:18). Apparently ambition blinds them to their peril. Predictably, their invocation is provocation. Incensed, the Lord serves notice that he is about to finish off "this assembly," that is, the entire Israelite community (16:20–21).

Rather than getting out of the Lord's way, Moses and Aaron desperately attempt to intercede. Their question of theodicy (16:22) is reminiscent of Abraham's plea for Sodom (Gen 18:25). In response, the Lord commands Moses to save the majority of the people by isolating the rebel leaders (Num 23–24). To do this, Moses goes to the Reubenite encampment of Dathan and Abiram, who have not been willing to come to him (16:25–27).

Whereas the incense test is between Aaron and the Levites who challenge him over the priesthood, now Moses proposes a test of his own divinely mandated leadership. This challenge consists of a conditional funeral oration: If the rebel leaders die natural deaths, Moses's commission from the Lord will be invalidated. If, however, God will "create a creation" (16:30, author's translation) by having the earth swallow them alive, the Israelites will know that these rebels have "treated the Lord with contempt" (16:30). In the Bible only God can create. Ironically, this present unprecedented miracle of creation will be for destruction.

The rebels have opened their mouths against the Lord and sought a higher place, but now the earth opens its mouth to gulp them down to a lower place. Loss of any innocent family members who belong to them, such as young children, is punishment on the rebels themselves, not on the innocents. Korah's men likewise descend (16:31–33). The seismic swallowing is all over in seconds. The Israelites run for their lives lest pits of perdition await them too (16:34).

Now that Moses and Aaron are separated from the 250 wannabe priests who have flunked their test, these men receive their "F" = Fire (16:35), as would be expected from the demise of Nadab and Abihu (Lev 10:2). Since the Israelite adults are already condemned to die in the desert, some of them have presumably thought they had nothing more to lose by further provoking the Lord. Think again!

Application. It is easy to point at Korah & Co. with horror and disgust, affirming that we would never have a falling away as they did. Indeed, the drama of their last moments would be a tough act to follow, but the subsurface cause of their failure gives us pause because we too can neglect the private inner world where our spiritual connection to God resides. Rather than wait for that sinking feeling when we do something irreparably stupid, it is better to replenish our subterranean aquifers from the Source that supports the ground of our being.

NUMBERS 16:36–17:11

Original Meaning. *Mess and "martyrs."* While the men were perishable, their censers were not. These objects were consecrated by the same divine fire that consumed those who wielded them. Therefore, they had to stay at the sanctuary, but what could be done with them?

God's solution is to have Eleazar, son of Aaron, retrieve the censers from the charred human remains and have them hammered out as a supplementary plating to overlay the outer altar. This plating will serve as a warning to any inclined to freelance priestly activities (16:36–40).

When the Israelites deliberately attribute the work of God to the powers of darkness, as if Moses and Aaron have killed the rebels (16:41) by some sort of black magic, there is nothing more he can do to shape their attitudes through further works of mercy or discipline. Moses and Aaron fall on their faces (16:45b). But now there is no time even for a short prayer of intercession. Only Aaron's rapidly mobile mediation with incense saves the community from extermination (16:46–48). The precise nature of the divine "plague" is not stated, but the aftermath shows a high body count (16:49).

Chief of staffs. To put the final nail in the coffin of opposition to his divine election, the Lord sets up one final test, this time a peaceful one. The staff of the man whom the Lord has chosen as priest will miraculously sprout (17:1–5).

As can be expected, it is Aaron's staff that sprouts. There is no doubt that it is Aaron's because his name is written on it (17:3). The extent to which the Lord abundantly emphasizes his choice is startling: Aaron's staff has also blossomed and produced "almonds," all overnight (17:8)! Aaron's staff has produced a *tsits* ("blossom"; 17:8). This happens to be the same word that describes the golden emblem worn by Aaron on the front of his high priestly turban (Exod 28:36–37).

Why almonds? The cups of the golden lampstand in the tabernacle were "shaped like almond flowers with buds and blossoms" (Exod 25:33–34; 37:19–20). The Hebrew word for "almond" is derived from the verb *shqd*, which means "watch/be awake." The connection is that the almond tree blossoms in the spring before other trees. Watchfulness is the point of the sanctuary lamps burning all night (Exod 27:21; Lev 24:3).

Application. Like modern "baby boomers," whose worldview has been shaped by events such as the Vietnam War and Watergate, the Israelites of the exodus generation had difficulty trusting authority. The Lord gave them magnificent options so that they could break out into the open air of mental and spiritual freedom, but ultimately, they clung to their melancholic, twisted perspective and treated his gifts as punishments.

With all his omnipotence and omniscience, God failed to satisfy the adult Israelites whom he so gloriously redeemed from bondage. His example teaches: Love people consistently and persistently with everything you have, but if they ultimately choose to reject you, let them go because you can't force them to be grateful or to love you in return. Like Moses, Aaron, and the later Hebrew prophets, we are accountable for the quality of the service we give, not the responses we get.

NUMBERS 17:12–18:32

Original Meaning. After the Lord has unleashed his terrible swift sword against the Israelites (16:46–50), they are thoroughly traumatized and fear that they will perish, especially if they come near the tabernacle of his presence (17:12–13). God allays their fears by altering the rules of engagement: The Levite tribe, including the priests, will henceforth bear the culpability of the sanctuary, and the priests alone will bear the culpability of their priesthood (18:1; cf. 18:23). This means that if one or more non-Levites violate the sanctity of the sanctuary, divine wrath will break out only against the Levites, in addition to the unauthorized persons themselves. The Levites were earlier designated to prevent such outbreaks from falling on the entire community (1:53), but now their incentive to stop a violator literally dead in his tracks (cf. 1:51) is to protect themselves.

Similarly, if a nonpriest (including a Levite) encroaches on a priestly prerogative, God will also hold the priests responsible (18:3) because it is up to them to ensure that this does not happen (18:7; cf. 3:10, 38). However, the Lord will no longer unleash his destruction against the whole community, as he threatened to do when the 250 unauthorized chieftains burned incense (16:21) and as he started to do when the Israelites sided with the rebels (16:41–50).

In 18:7 Aaron and his sons "must guard their priesthood with regard to everything connected with the (outer) altar and with respect to that which is within the (inner) veil" (author's translation). Two loci of priestly officiation are mentioned here—outer altar and inner sanctum—but not the outer sanctum.

In 18:7 the altar and inner sanctum represent the outermost and innermost areas of priestly officiation. So, this combination can easily be understood as a merism, which refers to the entire priestly domain, including the outer sanctum, by specifying its extremes.

The remainder of Numbers 18 reiterates and further details the portions of sacred gifts that belong to the priests and Levites. Placement of this legislation here accomplishes two things.

1. The Lord further affirms his choice of the Aaronic priests and the Levites who assist them.
2. The Lord rewards them for their potentially hazardous work at the sanctuary.

In lieu of a separate tribal territory in the promised land, the priests and other Levites will receive wages from the Lord consisting of agricultural tithes given to him (18:20–24) so that they can devote themselves to his service rather than spending all their time supporting themselves by farming. In this sense he will be their share and inheritance (18:20). Jacob had said that Levi would be dispersed in Israel (Gen 49:7), but the Lord turns this into a blessing. The priests will receive seven items as their perpetual entitlement:

1. Portions of most holy sacrifices (18:9–10; cf. Lev 6–7).
2. Dedicated portions of sacred gifts (Num 18:11), such as the breast and right thigh of holy (not most holy) well-being offerings (Lev 7:30–36).
3. Firstfruits offerings of olive oil, new wine, and grain (Num 18:12–13).
4. Every irrevocably devoted thing (Heb. *herem*; 18:14).
5. The meat of sacrificeable (clean domestic) firstborn animals (18:15–18).
6. Every portion set aside from holy offerings given by the Israelites (18:19). Here this perpetual entitlement is also called a perpetual "covenant of salt."
7. A tithe (tenth) of the tithes received by the Levites (18:25–32).

Application. The New Testament does not specify a tithe as a means of support for the Christian ministry. However, it is easy to see how the tithe principle could be applied for maintaining a stable source of support for the Lord's work. Since most of us are not farmers, our income consists of money rather than net agricultural produce (not including seed for replanting). So, we can give a tenth of our net money income and take God up on his offer to bless us (Mal 3:10).

Some Christian denominations encourage payment of tithe or even require it, just as it was required for ancient Israelites. Some Christians who feel that God has especially blessed them voluntarily add a second tithe, which they also give to their churches. Some set aside a portion of their incomes for helping disadvantaged people, as the Israelites were to do every third year (Deut 14:28–29; 26:12).

I have never heard of Christians consciously setting aside a percentage of their incomes for generous religious-social rejoicing as the Israelites were to do with their second tithe (Deut 12:17–19; 14:22–27). It would be fascinating to experiment with application of this concept, not forgetting to invite our ministers as the Israelites were to include their Levites (12:18–19; 14:27), and see what happens to attitudes toward God.

NUMBERS 19:1–22

Original Meaning. *Cleansing from the impurity of death.* Even though ritual impurity contracted from a corpse by a live person was secondary, it was serious. This makes sense in light of the rationale underlying the ancient Israelite system of physical ritual impurities: Mortality involved in the birth-death cycle of human beings is opposed to divine holiness, which is characterized by life. What could represent mortality more than a corpse?

At first glance it is peculiar that the full prescription for remedying the prominent impurity of corpse contamination does not appear until Numbers 19, after several passages have referred or alluded to the problem of this kind of impurity (Lev 10:4–5; 21:1–4, 11; Num 6:6–7, 9–12; 8:5–21), and Numbers 8:7 has even mentioned the "water of purification." However, placement of the remedy for corpse contamination in chapter 19 is appropriate in view of the expanding prominence of death in the narrative. By now thousands of Israelites have perished by divine judgments, and the entire adult generation of non-Levites is doomed to die in the desert, except for Caleb and Joshua.

The fact that corpse contamination was considered such a powerful impurity posed a problem for remedying it: The impure person could not come to the sanctuary in order to sacrifice a purification offering, so ritual decontamination had to take place outside the sacred precincts. Also, because priests were to avoid corpse contamination (Lev 21:1–4, 11), the purification rite needed to be administered by a layperson.

To remedy corpse contamination subject to these constraints, Numbers 19 prescribes a unique procedure consisting of two parts.

1. An unusual ritual outside the camp, officiated by a priest, involved burning a reddish cow, thereby producing a supply of ashes to be stored for future use (19:1–10a).
2. When an Israelite needed cleansing, a few of the ashes were mixed with water as a "ready-made, instant" purification offering, and a layperson sprinkled them on the affected individual (19:10b–22). This economical approach had the additional advantage that it spared grieving Israelites the burden of expensive sacrifices after they had just buried their dead.

Red cow purification offering. Verses 1–10a provide instructions for acquiring sacrificial ashes. The victim supplied by the community is to be female, like other purification offerings for the benefit of individual commoners. It must be a cow, the largest female sacrificeable animal, so that it will supply a maximum quantity of ashes. It must be reddish to evoke the color of blood. Like other sacrificial victims, it must be unblemished. Additionally, even though the ritual is outside the camp, the cow must not have been used as a work animal.

The son of the high priest is to supervise the sacrificial slaughter of the cow (19:3) and then "take some of its blood on his finger and sprinkle it seven times toward the front of the tent of meeting" (19:4). Since the ritual is performed outside the sacred precincts, this gesture establishes symbolic interaction with the sanctuary in order to make the procedure a sacrificial one.

Next the priest must supervise incineration of the entire cow (19:5), which is burned more completely than any other Israelite sacrifice, including the burnt offering of which the hide was saved for the priest. The verb for "incinerate" (NIV "burned," 19:5) here appears elsewhere in purification offering contexts as the method by which to dispose of unused animal parts outside the camp (Lev 4:12, 21; 6:30; 8:17; 9:11; 10:16; 16:27).

Into the midst of the fire where the cow is burning, the priest must toss cedar wood, hyssop, and crimson yarn (Num 19:6). The reddish hide of the cow, cedar wood, and crimson yarn emphasizes the color red. This is in keeping with the fact that the ashes contain blood, and when they are later mixed with water, the liquid will function like blood.

Not only is hyssop an ingredient of the ashes (19:6), but laypersons are to mix the ashes with fresh water and use hyssop to sprinkle it (19:18). Similarities are striking between cleansing from corpse contamination and the first-day ritual to treat a person or house for the ritual impurity of skin disease, in which hyssop, along with cedar wood and crimson yarn, was dipped into a mixture of blood and fresh water, which was then sprinkled on the person/house undergoing purification (Lev 14:4–7, 49–52). Skin disease, like corpse contamination, was closely connected with death.

After incinerating the cow, a ritually pure lay assistant must gather the sacrificial ashes and deposit them in a pure place outside the camp, to be kept for use in the "water of cleansing" (Num 19:9). The word here is *niddah*, which elsewhere usually refers to menstrual impurity but can also be used as a metaphor for moral impurity (Lev 20:21). Apparently, the connection between menstruation and sprinkling for corpse contamination is the idea of spattering blood or its equivalent.

Applying ash water. Numbers 19:10b–22 outlines the procedure and rules for applying the water and explains how this form of impurity is contracted. After the sprinkling on the seventh day, cleansing also requires laundering clothes, bathing, and waiting until evening (19:19). Remaining in a state of impurity by neglecting the ritual will have the grave consequence of defiling the Lord's tabernacle, for which the culprit will suffer the divine penalty of being "cut off" (19:13). The ashes are available at no charge and the procedure is quick and easy, so there is no excuse for noncompliance.

Corpse contamination is so virulent that if a dead body

is located in a tent, that is, in an enclosed dwelling space, any person or lidless vessel is defiled simply by being in the same space (19:14–15). Out in the open the effect is less intense: Pollution requires actually touching a corpse, human bone, or grave (19:16).

Application. Death of a red cow in the past gave Israelites ongoing assurance that they could be freed from their corpse contamination. The cow provided an *ongoing* supply of ashes to be mixed with fresh/living water and sprinkled on many impure persons whenever burial or other contact with the dead occurred. There was no need to bring an animal to the sanctuary and sacrifice it as a purification offering. The sacrifice had already taken place; all that was needed was to apply its benefit.

Hebrews 9:13–14 speaks of another death that provides assurance. Here "the ashes" refers to application of ash water, functioning like blood, from the red cow/heifer. If this procedure could affect cleansing from ritual impurity, which was associated with mortality, how much more does the once-for-all death of the Son of God make abundant *ongoing* provision for cleansing us morally, spiritually, and ultimately from mortality itself (cf. 1 Cor 15:51–54) by his blood?

When the Israelites sinned or incurred impurity, God gave them adequate opportunity to avail themselves of his remedies. In the meantime, they were covered by corporate sacrifices on their behalf, including daily burnt offerings and additional burnt and purification offerings performed on Sabbaths, new moons, and annual festivals (Num 28–29). Having this opportunity available was no substitute for personally taking it. Similarly, Christ's sacrifice has provided the only way out of our dilemma (Acts 4:12), with daily opportunities for restoration. His sacrifice is our only assurance.

NUMBERS 20:1–29

Original Meaning. *This is a sad chapter.* The deaths of Miriam at the beginning (20:1) and Aaron at the end (20:22–29) frame a dispute of the Israelites over water at Kadesh (20:2–13) and Edomite refusal to let the Israelites pass from Kadesh through their territory (20:14–21). The chapter is united by the location at Kadesh and the fact that Aaron dies at Mount Hor on the way around Edom for his failure with Moses regarding the water (20:24). The gloom of this chapter is only implicitly relieved by the fact that Israel and its high priestly office survive to trudge on toward better days.

Good-bye to Miriam. Miriam's obituary is a simple one (20:1). The year is lacking, so we do not know how long she lives after recovering from skin disease (ch. 12). Mention of Kadesh in 20:14 appears to seamlessly connect the events concerning Edom and Aaron's death, which occur near the end of the forty years in the desert (cf. 33:38–39), to Miriam's death and the contention over water at the same location (20:1–13). This suggests that Miriam dies near the end of the desert sojourn.

Striking failure. At Kadesh the Israelites dispute (Heb. *ryb*) with Moses because there is no water (20:2–3). This verb can denote verbal or physical contention/quarreling (e.g., Gen 26:20), lodging a complaint (Judg 21:22), or pursuing a lawsuit (Prov 25:8–9). At Kadesh the grievance is *grievous* (20:3). The Israelites regret that God did not slay them along with those who perished in the wake of Korah's revolt (chs. 16–17). The Lord was provoked enough on that occasion, but he spared them on account of the intercession of Moses and Aaron (16:20–24, 44–50), whom the people now accuse of abusing their God-given (and therefore legal) responsibility to take care of his community (20:4–5). Notice that although the Israelites primarily dispute with Moses (20:3), they also oppose Aaron (20:2) and frame their demand in plural address (20:4).

As at Rephidim (Exod 17:5–6), the Lord instructs Moses to take the staff to a rock so that water will come out of it (Num 20:7–8). At Rephidim Moses struck the rock (Exod 17:6), but this time, even though he will have his staff in hand as a reminder of the earlier miracle, he and Aaron are to merely speak (plural) to the rock (Num 20:8). This will be an even greater miracle, as there is no possibility that a physical blow will simply dislodge the natural plug to an aquifer.

Moses follows the divine directions up to a point (20:9–10a). However, apparently the sight of all those recalcitrant people gathered in front of the rock is too much for Moses. Uncharacteristically "losing it," he angrily lashes out verbally and then physically, whacking the rock with his staff—not just once, but twice (20:10b–11a).

While a lot of water gushes out for the people and their livestock, it is not the miracle God intended. Aaron did not participate in the miracle and thereby affirm his co-leadership, and Moses spoke to the people instead of the rock, which he struck. Although Moses sinned in the heat of the moment, apparently without premeditation, it is a grave offense committed in full view of the community to which he is supposed to be an example. For this failure, God denies Moses and Aaron the privilege of leading the Israelites into the promised land (20:12).

No way! Although Moses diplomatically appeals to the sympathies of the Edomites as relatives of the Israelites descended from Isaac through Esau (cf. Gen 25, 36) and pledges to respect their resources, their king resoundingly refuses to grant them right of way (Num 20:14–21). Moses's message to Edom in Numbers 20:14–17 comes at the beginning of a continuous stream of events leading to the Israelite conquest. Deuteronomy 2:14 puts the encounter with Edom in relative chronological perspective. Numbers 20 skips almost everything that happens during the thirty-eight years as unworthy of mention. These are just dull decades of death in the desert.

Aaron too. Aaron dies at Mount Hor according to divine plan (20:22–29), almost "with his boots on." Aaron's son Eleazar accompanies Aaron and Moses up the mountain so that Moses can transfer Aaron's high priestly garments to Eleazar after the people see Aaron for the last time but before he actually breathes his last (20:27–28). Presumably this procedure avoids corpse contamination of the sacred vestments, and Moses, not the new high priest, buries his brother. This transfer of garments is all it takes to invest Eleazar with his status (cf. Lev 8).

When only Moses and Eleazar descend the mountain from their grim errand, the Israelites know that Aaron has expired, and they mourn him for thirty days (20:29). Numbers 33:38–39 provides additional chronological information: Aaron dies at the age of 123 "on the first day of the fifth month of the fortieth year after the Israelites came out of Egypt." So, this is at the end of the desert wandering period.

Application. As God's servants our job is to do what he says and let God be God. This is easier said than done. It can be excruciating to exercise such restraint. By punishing Moses and Aaron, the Lord shows that no amount of human merit amassed through past obedience can atone for even one sin. Jesus said to his disciples, "So you also, when you have done everything you were told to do, should say, 'We are unworthy servants; we have only done our duty'" (Luke 17:10). To be responsible for living and responding to God at a high level as an example to other people is simply one of the duties and occupational hazards of being his servant.

NUMBERS 21:1–35

Original Meaning. *Victory and venom.* The Israelites backed down in the face of an armed threat from the Edomites (20:20–21). By contrast, they devote the Canaanites of Arad to the Lord for utter destruction, thereby fulfilling a vow that invokes divine aid by faith (21:1–3). Why do they treat the people of Arad so differently? Unlike the Edomites, these Canaanites are not their relatives, inhabit part of the land promised to Israel, and actually attack first.

Rather than occupying Arad/Hormah and penetrating Canaan from the south, as the earlier plan went before the ten scouts discouraged them at Kadesh (chs. 13–14), the Israelites now prolong their journey in order to enter the promised land from the east. Apparently, this alteration of direction responds to a shift in the military landscape of Canaan that make its eastern defenses relatively more vulnerable at this time.

With all the extra travel, the Israelites become impatient (21:4). Complaining that their appetite loathes manna (21:5), they insult God as at Kibroth Hattaavah (11:6). This time, instead of quail, he sends snakes that are fiery, apparently in the sense that their venom feels like fire, by which he has punished people on several occasions. The invasion of reprehensible reptiles is like the plagues on Egypt by which the Lord demonstrated his sovereignty over nature (Exod 7–10). If the Israelites prefer to live in Egypt, they will die like Egyptians.

When the Israelites confess their sin and call for help, God does not simply call off the serpents. Rather, he commands Moses to employ a visual antivenom (21:8), which Moses does by sculpting and displaying a snake out of bronze (21:9). In light of other ancient cultures, some have suggested that this effects a kind of magic.

The bronze snake, however, is appointed by God, who alone is capable of healing his people. So although it is symbolic, it is not magical. Nor is it an offering to the Lord. To confront the serpent sculpture is to confront one's own sin and its result. It is the spiritual equivalent of looking in the mirror. That unspoken confession is all it takes to live.

Obtaining water and land. Journeying northward, the Israelites pass Moab and then camp along the Arnon river in a desert area belonging to the Amorites, just to the north of Moabite territory (21:10–13). A quotation from the "Book of the Wars of the LORD" emphasizes that the Arnon formed the border of Moab, so the Israelites are outside Moab (21:14–15; cf. Judg 11:18). This lost historical source (cf. the "Book of Jashar" in Josh 10:13; 2 Sam 1:18) is not mentioned anywhere else in the Bible.

Moving on, another potential crisis over water turns into a refreshing example of divine-human cooperation when the Israelites dig a well at the Lord's direction (Num 21:16–18a). Stated in the imperative, the words "Spring up, O well!" (21:17) celebrate claiming the divine promise, as if to say: "We know you're down there, water, so just go ahead and get on up here as God said you would!" This is only the second recorded occasion on which the Israelites sing for joy when they receive divine assistance. The previous time also had to do with water, but it was at the Red Sea where the Lord drowned Pharaoh's army (Exod 14–15).

To proceed further north in order to reach the Jordan River and enter Canaan from the east, the Israelites ask to pass through the territory of Sihon, king of the Amorites. Not only does Sihon punctuate his refusal to their diplomatic request with a military response as the king of Edom had (cf. 20:20); he comes out to attack Israel (21:23) as the Canaanite king of Arad had (21:1). Like the Canaanites, the Amorites are not related to the Israelites, who have no qualms about crushing them and seizing their domain. Although this is not part of Canaan, it is the first land that the Israelites occupy (21:25, 31).

In fact, it eventually becomes a permanent part of their holdings (see ch. 32).

As supported by reference to some early poetry about Heshbon, Sihon's capital city, the king had earlier extended his border to the Arnon at Moab's expense (21:26–30). The fact that he ruled from the Arnon in the south to the Jabbok in the north when Israel defeats him and that Israel does not enter Ammonite territory (21:24; cf. Deut 2:24–37) later becomes Jephthah's key argument in his dispute with the king of Ammon, who claims that the Israelites have taken the area between the two rivers from his people (Judg 11:13, 15, 19–23).

Like Sihon, King Og of the fertile region of Bashan in the northern Transjordan greets Israel with his army and suffers a similar fate (21:33–35). According to other passages, he is a giant (Deut 3:11; Josh 12:4) and his people are Amorites (Deut 4:47).

Application. When we truly sense that because Christ has already won, we who believe in him are all winners together, we too become energized, follow the game plan, and sacrifice rather than make up excuses. We too give generously, encourage rather than criticize, and assist others rather than vying with them to see who can become the greatest. Like the victorious Israelites, we can come together to a refreshing "well," a source of life that God has given to sustain us through the "desert."

NUMBERS 22:1–41

Original Meaning. *The maledictorian.* With so many Israelites so close, King Balak of Moab and his people are seized by sickening dread because they see what Israel has done to the Amorites (22:2–3), who earlier defeated Moab (21:26–30). Slim indeed are your chances of winning against a team that has handily defeated another team that earlier defeated you!

According to Deuteronomy 2:9, the Lord has already commanded Moses not to disturb the Moabites or take any of their land, but poor Balak does not know this. So, ruling out a preemptive military strike, even with the help of his Midianite allies (Num 22:4), he comes up with an alternative proactive strategy to utilize a secret weapon: a curse by Balaam. Balak does not expect Balaam to destroy the Israelites but only to soften them up and thereby even the odds to manageable proportions so that his ground troops will have a fighting chance (22:5–6). Balaam, a diviner who originated from the northeast by the Euphrates River, has an international reputation for pronouncing effective blessings, and when it comes to curses, you could say that he is the maledictorian in his class (22:6b).

For persuading Balaam to come on his errant errand, King Balak uses verbal flattery, an impressive delegation of Moabite and Midianite leaders to convey the gravity of the request, and divination fees (22:6b–7). Balak's message does not identify the Israelites as such (22:5, 11), perhaps so that Balaam will not recognize a conflict of interest that pits the Lord against his own people.

Balaam keeps the messengers overnight so that he can receive an answer from the Lord (22:8). This non-Israelite diviner is a kind of prophet and expects a revelation in the night. An eighth-century BC group of inscriptions from Deir ʿAlla, Jordan correlates with the biblical story in important ways. These inscriptions, which present literary similarities to the biblical Balaam oracles, are written in a Northwest Semitic dialect (with some affinities to Aramaic), which may be a form of Hebrew spoken by Israelites who lived in that Transjordanian region. In terms of content, the most striking feature is that Balaam son of Beor is remembered as a seer of the gods, who conveys a disturbing message to him in an oracular vision at night.

The Deir ʿAlla writings are saturated with polytheism, express belief in divination, and portray Balaam as interacting with a number of gods in various ways—by receiving visions and through involvement with divination and possibly exorcism. If he was a polytheist, as depicted here, it appears that he would have dealt with whatever supernatural beings were relevant to the needs of his clients. Perhaps the Deir ʿAlla account reflects a stage in Balaam's life that came after an apostasy from monotheistic devotion to Israel's deity (Yahweh), but there is insufficient evidence to establish this.

Not taking Balaam's divinely directed "no" for an answer, desperate Balak offers Balaam a tempting "blank check" to fill in any amount he wishes for his "honorarium" (22:15–17). The first part of Balaam's answer (22:18) is a model of piety that would make him a biblical paradigm of loyalty to the Lord, whom he claims as his God, if it were not for the rest of the story.

Balaam's next words, however, betray a certain ambivalence. He invites the messengers to stay so that he can find out what else the Lord may have to say (22:19). This is odd. Why would Balaam think the Lord might change his mind? Or perhaps we should ask: Why would Balaam *hope* the Lord might change his mind? The answer to this question is rather obvious: King Balak has upped the ante to the point that Balaam cannot resist!

Surprisingly, the Lord's answer is indeed different: Balaam can go to Moab on condition that he do only what God tells him. Undoubtedly delighted at the prospect of satisfying his greed with his professional integrity intact, thereby having his cake and eating it too, Balaam wastes no time lest the Lord should withdraw permission. In the morning he rises, saddles his female donkey, and sets out with two servants (22:20–22).

Journey on a jenny. Although God allows Balaam to go, he is angry when the diviner leaves. To forcefully convey divine displeasure, "the angel of the LORD" takes his stand in the road as a *satan* (i.e., adversary) to Balaam (22:22; see also 22:32). Elsewhere in the Hebrew Bible, *satan* can designate the adversary of God and his people (Job 1–2; Zech 3:1–2), namely, Satan. But here the term refers to a role played by an angel or messenger of God. Balaam is trotting into heavy opposition!

Balaam values his own insight and wisdom, but his life is saved by the lowly beast of burden that he mistreats for irritating him (Num 22:33). She is his greatest asset. When the Lord uncovers Balaam's eyes and he sees what she did, he reacts similarly (cf. 22:27) by prostrating himself before the awesome angel blocking the way with sword drawn (22:31).

The angel issues Balaam a ticket for reckless driving (22:32). The Hebrew verb that the NIV renders "is a reckless one" is *yrt*, which shows up only here in the Hebrew Bible. It is clear from the context that the Lord, represented by his angel, disapproves of what Balaam is doing and is determined to alter his course of action.

Although Balaam confesses and offers to return home, as well he might (22:34), the angel tells him to continue with the condition that he "speak only what I tell you" (22:35). When King Balak meets Balaam at the Moabite border, Balaam cites this condition of complete divine control (22:38) as an escape clause in case Balak should be dissatisfied with his utterances.

Balak extends hospitality to Balaam by sacrificing animals at Kiriath Huzoth and sending them to Balaam and the princes with him, apparently primarily for them to enjoy a feast (22:39–40). The text does not identify the deity to which these non-Israelite sacrifices are offered, but it appears that they are related to the Israelite *zebah* (so-called "sacrifice") class of sacrifices, from which the offeror(s) could eat (Lev 7:15–21).

The following morning, Balak takes Balaam up to a place with a view—Bamoth Baal, "high places of Baal"—where he can visually connect with Israel from a safe distance (22:41) in order to aim his imprecatory smart bombs.

Application. Needless to say, this should have been a humbling experience for Balaam. He thought he was special because God spoke through him, but now God spoke through his donkey, to whom he considered himself so superior. Hearing God speak to us is no indication that we are unusually spiritual or mature or important. God is able to communicate with whomever he chooses.

Whether we are human or donkey, male or female, young or old, rich or poor, educated or uneducated, asking who is superior to whom is to miss the point: God can use whomever or whatever he chooses, including even stones (Luke 19:40; cf. Matt 3:9; Luke 3:8). It is God who is superior, and none of us are excluded from service to him. Here is a call for humility and for treating each other with respect (cf. Rom 12:10; 1 Cor 12:21–25).

NUMBERS 23:1–30

Original Meaning. *Not even a sorcerer's apprentice.* At Bamoth Baal (22:41), Balaam instructs Balak to put his best foot forward by providing the Lord a rich complex of burnt offerings on seven altars (23:1–2). It is by no means clear that the burnt offerings, which basically serve as instruments of divination to evoke communication from the deity, provide the Lord with a reason for giving Balaam a revelation. Israelite prophets were never required to offer sacrifices before they received divine messages. It appears that God meets with Balaam (23:4–5) *in spite of* the sacrifices.

Then Balaam utters his oracle (23:7). The Hebrew word for "oracle" is *mashal,* which refers to a discourse constructed with parallelism, often employing figurative language. In Numbers 23–24 the same phraseology introduces seven oracular speeches of Balaam (23:7, 18; 24:3, 15, 20, 21, 23), affirming that the number seven is indeed significant for the God of Israel.

Balaam's first oracle (23:7–10) employs seven (this number again!) couplets. He is now fully aware of the identity of the people whom Balak wants him to curse: Jacob/Israel (23:7; cf. 22:5, 11). Balaam quickly moves to the basic problem—his conflict of interest. Since he is God's spokesman, how can he "curse . . . denounce" (*qbb . . . z'm*) those whom the Lord has not cursed/denounced (23:8)?

From his vantage point, Balaam views Israel as separate rather than just another nation, and metaphorically he refers to their innumerable multitude in terms of "dust" (23:9–10a). This is what God promised Abraham and Jacob that their chosen offspring would be like (Gen 13:16; 28:14).

At the end of Balaam's speech, he wishes for himself to die like straight/upright (i.e., righteous ones), referring to the Israelites, and (in poetic parallelism) he wants his afterlife to be like theirs (23:10b). In light of the first part of the same verse, the desirability of a righteous person's fate lies largely in the assurance of having abundant posterity to live on and multiply after one dies. Ironically, the Lord makes Balaam express admiration for and identification with those whom he has set out to curse!

King Balak has hired Balaam as a master sorcerer, a powerful practitioner of black magic, but he isn't even a sorcerer's apprentice. He is just a diviner who is mastered by divinity to heap divine blessings on the enemy (23:11). Balaam is playing a dicey game between the Lord's vested interest in Israel and Balak's antagonism toward the same nation. But Balaam has his escape clause ready for Balak: He can only speak God's words (23:12).

Not giving up, Balak hopes that moving the curser to a different location will help him delete his blessings. So, he takes Balaam to where a narrower field of vision will help him retain his focus (23:13–14a). Curses and narrow outlooks go together!

After sacrificial preparations (23:14b), Balaam receives his second oracle (23:15–17), which consists of ten parallel units (23:18–24), expanding on the theme of his earlier speech. There is no trouble or sorrow among the Israelites. Rather, they have the battle cry of the divine King in their midst (23:21). The couplet "God brought them out of Egypt; they have the strength of a wild ox" (23:22) alludes to the initial expressions of Moabite fear in 22:4–5 but reversing the order of the "ox" and "out of Egypt" ideas.

Balaam continues by affirming that no divination is effective against Israel. The point is not what Israel can do but "what God has done!" (23:23). The last simile of Balaam's speech sounds even more terrifying than a wild ox: Israel is like a devouring lion (23:24). If Balak is disappointed by Balaam's first oracle, this devastating blessing of Israel is a catastrophe. It would be better if Balaam said nothing (23:25).

Desperate and still vainly imagining that the divine attitude can be altered by the venue, Balak relocates Balaam (23:28). It is unlikely that even a human being would be so fickle as to change from pro- to anti-Israelite in this way.

It is remarkable that Balaam plays along with the futile charade, directing Balak to waste fourteen more valuable animals (23:29–30). Having no vested interest in either Israel or Moab, Balaam is clinging to hope for reward no matter what the outcome.

Application. The Lord's firm resolve to bless the children of Abraham is also for Christians who are truly God's people through faith in Christ (Gal 3:26, 29). The promise includes salvation, a future home, and adoption into a multitude of literal and spiritual descendants of Abraham—the patriarch who set the paradigm for faith (cf. Heb 11:10, 12). With the divine King in our "camp" (cf. Num 23:21), we have ultimate "social security."

NUMBERS 24:1–25

Original Meaning. *Three strikes and you're out!* At the top of Peor (23:28), Balaam gives up seeking to meet omens/divinations (24:1), apparently referring to the divine Source with which he connected on previous occasions. To short-circuit the Lord's control, he skips going off by himself and simply sets his face in the direction of the desert where Israel is encamped (24:1). He is bent on sorcery without interference by the Source in order to satisfy Balak and claim his reward.

Since Balaam has not come to the Lord, the Lord comes to him with some short-circuiting of his own. He possesses Balaam as a prophet (24:2), thereby bypassing his volition and overpowering his ability to say anything contrary to the divine will. So, Balaam introduces his third oracle (24:3). The Hebrew word for "prophecy" here (see also 24:4, 15–16) is *neum*, which refers to a prophet's inspired utterance or a declaration of the Lord.

The third oracle contains twelve parallel units (24:3–9). That there are twelve is appropriate because Balaam is looking at "Israel encamped tribe by tribe" (24:2). The second member of each of the first three couplets refers to Balaam's visionary gift (24:3–4). He also "hears the words of God" (24:4a). The third couplet (24:4b) alludes in reverse (chiastic) order to 22:31, where the Lord uncovered his eyes so that he could see the "angel of the LORD," and then he bowed and prostrated himself.

In the fourth to seventh couplets, Balaam extols Israel's war camp, of which the beauty is in tents (24:5–7a). Among other similes, likening the tents of the Israelites to aloe trees provides a satisfying Hebrew wordplay. After figuratively referring to water (24:6), 24:7a affirms the Israelites' literal abundance of that crucial resource.

The eighth couplet (24:7b) speaks of Israel in royal terms. In his second oracle, Balaam described Israel as already having a king, that is, the Lord (23:21). However, in 24:7 the verbs are in the imperfect tense/aspect and may refer to a future human king of Israel.

The ninth couplet (24:8a), recalling the exodus and likening Israel to a wild ox, reiterates part of Balaam's second oracle (23:22). The tenth parallel unit (24:8b) would be particularly disquieting to Balak because it describes Israel as devouring nations that are its enemies, breaking their bones, and striking them with arrows. Here the only figurative expression is "devour." The rest of the language is devastatingly literal, calculated to intimidate Balak into peaceful relations with Israel.

In his eleventh parallel unit, Balaam continues to intimidate by likening Israel to a lion (Num 24:9a), affirming the ongoing validity of Jacob's prophetic blessing on Judah (Gen 49:9). Let sleeping lions lie! In his previous oracle, Balaam has already warned of what the Israelite lion will do if aroused (Num 23:24).

As Balaam's punch line, the twelfth and final parallel hammers home God's unequivocal bottom line toward Israel: "May those who bless you be blessed and those who curse you be cursed!" (24:9b). In his first oracle, Balaam said he could not curse those whom the Lord had not cursed (23:8). In his second oracle he admitted that he could not change God's command to bless (23:20). Now he speaks of blessing and cursing together (cf. 22:12), adding the motivational concept that the way people treat Israel determines whether they are blessed or cursed (24:9). By building to this climax, Balaam has arrived at the full formulation of God's promise to Abraham (Gen 12:3).

Infuriated that his persistence has backfired, King Balak fires Balaam and orders him to flee home without giving him any honorarium, severance package, or even a token consolation prize (24:10–11). Nevertheless, by blaming the Lord for keeping Balaam from his reward, Balak acknowledges divine control (24:11b).

For the last time, Balaam cites his escape clause (24:12–13). However, this time he repeats the fuller version that he stated to Balak's second group of messengers (24:13; cf. 22:18).

Parting shots. Before leaving, Balaam delivers unsolicited divine counsel regarding what the Israelites will do to the Moabites in the latter days, that is, in the distant future (24:14). Balaam begins his "latter days" oracle as a prophetic speech, using the same words with which he commenced his third oracle (24:15–16; cf. 24:3–4). But this time he adds a line at the center of his introductory section of three parallels (24:15–16), describing himself as one "who has knowledge from [lit., "knows knowledge of"] the Most High" (24:16a). He has access to information that is otherwise inaccessible to humans, in this case because it concerns future events.

The following couplets (24:17–19) are startling. Balaam sees a future ruler whom he metaphorically depicts as a "star" or "scepter" who will originate from Israel and strike the heads of the Moabites (24:17). Unlike Balaam's third oracle, this is not a conditional threat that the Moabites will be defeated if they disturb Israel (cf. 24:8–9); rather, it is a prediction.

Israel will also take possession of Edom/Seir, which treated Israel as an enemy (24:18). The Lord protected the Moabites and Edomites from the Israelites because they were related to them (Deut 2:4–5, 9), but this protection will end because both nations have treated the chosen people with hostility rather than brotherhood and thereby incurred the curse of Abraham (Gen 12:3; Num 24:9).

Balaam concludes his salvo with three brief discourses against other nations—(1) Amalek, (2) Kenites, and (3) Assyria and Eber (24:20–24)—each of which is introduced as a *mashal* (see comments on 23:7). Numbers 24 ends anticlimactically by simply reporting that Balaam goes home and Balak goes on his way (24:25). With this "gruesome twosome" splitting up, we could assume that their threat to Israel is over. However, we will discover that such a conclusion is premature (cf. chs. 25; 31).

Application. While Balaam's words describe a prophet who receives special revelation from the Lord, there is also a sense in which the same principles can apply to those who preach and teach God's word. Today, no less than in ancient times, spokespersons for God need clear vision to see what he wants to show them, whether in his written word, in his creation, or in providential circumstances. They need to be ready at all times to hear communication from God, even when it comes in a "gentle whisper" (cf. 1 Kgs 19:12), rather than drowning it out with all kinds of other noise, including their own exuberant verbosity. They need knowledge of the Most High, including both knowledge from him and about him. They need to gain their vision from El Shaddai (see Gen 17:1; 35:11; Exod 6:3; Job 37:23), be awestruck by his power and glory as Isaiah, Ezekiel, Daniel, and John were (Isa 6; Ezek 1; Dan 7:9–14), fall prostrate before him in humility, and allow him to uncover their eyes to see the "angel of the LORD" (Num 22:31).

NUMBERS 25:1–18

Original Meaning. Camping at Shittim east of the Jordan River (25:1a), the Israelites are just across from the promised land. At Shittim the Israelite men are distracted by Moabite women, who effectively use sex appeal to lure them to sacrifices honoring Moabite gods (25:1b–3). A significant number of Israelites prostrate themselves to worship the Moabite gods, presumably in the form of idols (25:2).

To turn away divine wrath from corporate Israel and thereby save the nation from destruction, the Lord orders Moses to take all the chiefs of the people, who are apparently the leading culprits, and expose them (i.e., their dead bodies) before the Lord in full public view (25:4).

Apparently not long after Moses conveys the divine verdict to the Israelite judges, who are to execute it (25:5), lo and behold (Heb. *hinneh*), an Israelite man "brought (Heb. *qrb*) . . ." (25:6). Since this word is the usual term for bringing a sacrifice to the sanctuary (e.g., Lev 1:2–3, 10; 4:3, 14), it would be logical for the reader to expect that the Israelite devoutly sets out to make amends with the Lord. Alas, what he has in tow is not an animal victim but a lass—and a Midianite one at that (Num 25:6a)! His mission is not expiation but fornication.

Rather than sneaking his foreign pleasure into the camp, the Israelite blatantly parades with her (25:6b). Phinehas sets out to meet the crisis (25:7). Since his grandfather, Aaron, has died and his father, Eleazar, has become high priest (20:23–29), Phinehas has inherited Eleazar's former position as head of the Levites in charge of guarding and caring for the sanctuary (cf. 3:32). In the tent where the Israelite and Midianitess have gone, Phinehas summarily kebobs both of them together (25:7b–8).

Phinehas' "officiation" accomplishes expiation (Heb. *kipper*) for the Israelites (25:13) in the sense of destroying offending persons to remove disruption of the covenant relationship between the Lord and his corporate people. Consequently, a plague of divine retribution against them is stopped (25:8b). By the time Phinehas grabs his spear and uses it, a divine plague has already killed thousands of Israelites (25:9).

The body count of 24,000, an average of 2,000 from each of the twelve tribes, is the highest ever suffered by the Israelites during their long and painful passage from Egypt to Canaan. It is even higher than at Kadesh, where 14,700 died in addition to Korah & Co. before Aaron's propitiatory intercession (16:46–49). The only divine punishment on Israel during biblical times that slew more was the plague that took the lives of 70,000 as a result of David's census (2 Sam 24:15).

The Lord highly commends Phinehas for his decisive action and grants him a covenant of peace/well-being (Heb. *shalom*; 25:12) and of eternal priesthood (25:13). This implies that religious leadership through the high priesthood will flow through his line of descendants.

God's covenant of eternal priesthood for Phinehas is similar to the later divine covenant of dynastic monarchy for David (2 Sam 7). Both covenants promise loyal individuals that they and their descendants will fill existing institutional positions of national leadership within the framework of the covenant established with Israel at Sinai.

Who thought up the brilliant and devastatingly effective strategy of using sex and food as lethal weapons to kill Israelites by luring them to commit capital offenses punishable by their own deity? When the Israelites later attacked the Midianites to avenge the deaths of those whom the Lord slew, "they also killed Balaam son of Beor with the sword" (31:8). What was he doing with the Midianites? Hadn't he gone home (24:25)? If we connect the dots, Balaam came up with a scheme and returned to counsel the Midianites and Moabites to use their women to incite Israelites to rebellion against the Lord (31:16).

Application. When it comes to the deceptive inroads of apostasy into the church, Christians may need to face corporate conflicts head-on. Like the proactive priest of Numbers 25, Jesus demonstrated this when he drove out those engaged in business at the courts of the temple (John 2:17). Like zealous Phinehas, Christ identified with God to the extent that there was no difference between defending the honor of God and that of himself.

NUMBERS 26:1–65

Original Meaning. The second census of Numbers 26 shows that the torch has passed to the new generation. Chapter 26 lists clans within each tribe that receive their names from the earliest descendants of the twelve patriarchs. Thus the chapter reads like a combination of genealogy and census.

With the genealogical component are some notices of special circumstances that affected certain lines of descendants: the rebellion and deaths of Reubenites Dathan and Abiram along with Korah & Co. (26:9–11; cf. ch. 16); the deaths, also divinely administered, of Judah's oldest sons, Er and Onan, in Canaan (26:19; cf. Gen 38:7–10); and the fact that Zelophehad of Manasseh has only daughters (26:33). The significance of these daughters will come to light in chapters 27 and 36.

The order of tribes in this second census report is the same as in the first report of 1:20–43, except that Manasseh is placed before Ephraim (26:29–37; cf. 1:32–35). Numbers 26:51 adds up the total number of Israelite fighting men twenty years of age and older as 601,730. This is slightly less than the total of the first census: 603,550 (1:46).

The numbers tell how the various tribes fared during the decades of desert wandering. Some flourished, such as Manasseh. Others declined, most notably Simeon, the tribe of Zimri (slain by Phinehas; 25:6–8, 14), which lost more than half its number. A serious factor was retributive justice meted out by the Lord on rebellious Israelites, which took out 14,700 at Kadesh (16:49) and 24,000 at Shittim alone (25:9). Since the last of the condemned older generation already died within thirty-eight years after the people left Kadesh and before the Baal of Peor incident (Num 25), the 24,000 slain in the plague at Shittim (25:9) belonged to the younger generation.

In addition to its military function, the second census is to determine the size of the territories that will be allotted to the tribes when they conquer the land (26:52–56). Distribution of inheritances by casting lots will be fair in that the Israelites will be distributed evenly throughout the promised land. By making sizes of territories proportional to tribal populations, which were affected by loyalty/disloyalty to the Lord during the desert period, he rewards the tribes according to their levels of faithfulness during that time.

As earlier in Numbers, Levites are counted separately because they do not serve in the regular army, and their males are counted from the age of one month instead of twenty years (cf. ch. 3). Furthermore, they will not inherit land along with the other tribes (26:62). Numbers 26:57–62 reports the second census of the Levites who total 23,000 (26:62), as compared with 22,000 earlier (3:39).

The second census gives the Israelites a new beginning. About to conquer Canaan, they are back to the same situation as at the time of the first census, after losing nearly four decades. The second census has another important purpose—to make sure that the entire generation excluded from Canaan because of the rebellion at Kadesh (ch. 14) is dead. So, the end of chapter 26 delivers this crucial piece of information: Except for Caleb and Joshua, the second military census includes none counted in the first census (26:63–65). At last, the Israelites will be permitted to enter the promised land.

Application. If the Lord can't accomplish his purposes through the strong, he turns to the weak. When the Israelites lamented that any attempted invasion of Canaan would result in their children being taken captive by the enemy (14:3), God responded by saying that he would give the promised land to those same defenseless children (14:31–32). If he cannot use some people to carry out his goals, he turns to others, even if they seem inadequate and even if he must wait for another generation. While the Lord inexorably moves his plans for human beings through to fulfillment, none of us is indispensable for carrying out his will.

While we are privileged to participate in God's plan, our realization that its success does not depend on us provides rest and security. We are to bear each other's burdens (Gal 6:2), but no matter how important our positions of leadership may be, the Herculean weight of responsibility for the world does not rest on our shoulders, as if anything that puts us out of action will bring everything crashing down. There is another who carries the weight, and he is indispensable because he is not an ordinary human being (Isa 9:6).

NUMBERS 27:1–23

Original Meaning. *Transfer of inheritance from Zelophehad to his daughters.* In biblical days, justice was for the dead as well as the living. Thus, Zelophehad's daughters seek to redress inequity by asking to inherit their father's possession of landed property (27:1–4). Having no legal precedent on which to base an answer to the young women, Moses turns to the Lord, who confirms that Zelophehad's daughters are right (27:5–7). As on other occasions when Moses sought divine legal counsel, God gives him permanent legislation surrounding the case in question (27:8–11).

Transfer of leadership from Moses to Joshua. Aaron has already died. Now Moses's turn is approaching. Unlike the Israelites who died in the desert, including Zelophehad, Moses will at least be permitted to see the promised land from the top of a mountain before he dies (27:12–14). Deuteronomy 3:27 and 34:1 identifies the place as Pisgah, the same as the name of the mountain where Balaam uttered his second oracle.

With utmost gravity, Moses appeals to "the LORD, the God who gives breath to all living things," to appoint a good "shepherd" in his place (Num 27:15–17). The Lord responds by identifying Joshua and instructing Moses to commission this worthy successor (27:18–21).

Joshua cannot talk with the Lord face-to-face as Moses has. However, he is to ascertain God's will through the Urim (and Thummim, understood) worn by the high priest. In accordance with this guidance, he will command the Israelites what to do (27:21).

Transfer of power requires only a simple, straightforward, but elegant ceremony in which Moses leans his hand on Joshua and then commissions him while he stands before Eleazar the high priest and the whole assembly (27:18–23). By commissioning Joshua to take some of his majesty/authority (27:20), Moses shares leadership while he is still alive in order to ensure a smooth transition when he dies.

Application. Like sheep, people need someone they trust to lead them rather than to drive them. In short, they need a "shepherd." If they are "like sheep without a shepherd" (27:17), they scatter and are defenseless. When Jesus saw crowds, "he had compassion on them, because they were harassed and helpless, like sheep without a shepherd" (Matt 9:36).

Not any shepherd will do. Sheep need a *good* shepherd who protects his sheep with his life, not a cowardly "hireling," a "sheep in sheep's clothing," who cares primarily about protecting himself (John 10:11–13). Nor do they need a shepherd who exploits and scatters them (Jer 23:1; Ezek 34:1–8).

Being a good shepherd or herdsman can demand toughness and courage, involving exposure to all kinds of discomforts, irritations, and perils (Gen 31:40; 1 Sam 17:34–35). Being a good shepherd of human beings is no less challenging. It requires toughness and humility, courage and ability to lead rather than drive.

NUMBERS 28:1–29:40

Original Meaning. In the ritual calendar of Leviticus 23, the emphasis was on outlining overall observance of sacred times. The parallel calendar in Numbers 28–29 fills in important details by providing a comprehensive inventory of public sacrifices that must be performed at the sanctuary on regular and festival occasions.

Daily worship. Numbers 28 begins by reiterating the prescription given earlier at Sinai (Exod 29:38–42) for regular burnt offerings, which must be performed every day as the foundation of the sacrificial system (Num 28:1–8). "Food" is the operative metaphor. The two burnt offerings with their accompanying grain and drink offerings (28:5, 7a; cf. 15:4–5) constitute the daily symbolic "meals" of the Lord that are essential for maintaining his presence among the Israelites.

In addition to the usual offering of wine/fermented drink at the outer altar to accompany the regular burnt offering, 28:7b prescribes a unique libation. This beverage is to be offered in the *qodesh* ("Holy [Place]," i.e., inside the tabernacle). Usually *shekar* is interpreted as strong/fermented drink, an interpretation for which there is considerable support. That alcoholic beverages would be offered at the holy sanctuary for symbolic utilization by the Lord as part of his daily "meal" seems inconsistent with the rule in Leviticus 2:11, presumably because these materials included or were susceptible to fermentation associated with death, which was antagonistic to holiness. The concept that something holy should be kept free from contact with fermentation/intoxication also appears to be behind the divine commands that priests must not drink wine when they enter the sacred tent (Lev 10:9), and Nazirites must abstain from these beverages during their periods of consecration (Num 6:3; cf. Judg 13:4, 7, 14).

Even if it is to be argued that sacrificial wine should be poured out beside the altar at its base rather than on its hearth, the offering raises a special problem because it is to be poured out to the Lord inside the sacred tent (28:7). Perhaps one or both types of drink offerings are unfermented, with *yayin* and/or *shekar* referring to the same kinds of juices that become alcoholic *if* fermented. But there is no clear evidence to settle this issue.

Whereas the ritual of renewing the bread of the presence takes place once per week on the Sabbath (Lev 24:8), the context in which the *shekar* libation is prescribed (Num 28:7b) indicates that it is performed twice daily, like the drink offerings of wine accompanying the regular morning and evening burnt offerings.

Liturgical year. After prescribing the regular daily sacrifices, the ritual calendar of Numbers 28–29 moves to additional sacrifices performed weekly on the Sabbath (28:9–10), monthly at new moons (28:11–15), and yearly at the annual festivals of Passover and Unleavened Bread (28:16–25), Weeks (28:26–31), Trumpets (29:1–6), the Day of Atonement (29:7–11), and Booths (29:12–38). The order is the same as in Leviticus 23, going from smaller to larger cycles and moving through the yearly festivals in chronological order from spring to autumn.

The calendar richly illustrates ritual hierarchy. We find in ascending order of complexity: (a) individual rituals; (b) small complexes consisting of combinations of individual rituals, such as a burnt offering with its accompanying grain and drink offerings; (c) larger complexes in which several smaller complexes are embedded, such as groups of burnt offerings with their accompaniments; (d) individual festival days on which several large ritual complexes are performed; and (e) multiday festivals.

The number seven, which is associated with the weekly Sabbath and conveys the idea of holiness, is prominent in the Israelite system of new moons and festivals. At new moons and on each festival day, seven or fourteen (= 2 × 7) lambs are offered as burnt offerings. The ritual year culminates in the seventh month. Since Unleavened Bread and Booths last for seven days each, the total number of each kind of animal offered during these festivals is a multiple of seven. During the seven-day Feast of Booths, a total of seventy (= 7 x 10) bulls are offered as burnt offerings, including seven on the seventh day (7/21). These instances of the number seven suggest that the cyclical holy times of special worship (cf. Lev 23:2–4, 7–8, 21, 24, 27, etc.) are, in a sense, extensions of the weekly Sabbath. The large numbers of sacrifices during the Feast of Booths acknowledge God's blessings at the thanksgiving season of harvest.

Application. The earthly sanctuary and its sacrifices are gone, but there remains the need for everyone who enjoys a new covenant relationship with God to maintain it on a daily basis. The point is not that the Lord is dependent on our service and will immediately reject us if we miss a day, but that *we need* frequent and regular reaffirmation of our connection to him.

Daily and festival sacrifices at the Israelite sanctuary, with their smoke ascending heavenward, showed that a healthy relationship with God was available to anyone, anywhere, anytime. Now our prayers ascend to where our sacrificial Lamb is depicted as if he has just been slaughtered (Rev 5:6), that is, carrying the cross event with him to continually offer its healing to all who will avail themselves of it. Those who have him have assurance of life.

NUMBERS 30:1–16

Original Meaning. A vow to God is supposed to be an absolute promise. But what happens if you take on such a binding commitment and then discover that another obligation to the Lord, such as honoring your parents (Exod 20:12), conflicts with your vow?

To provide a baseline for the exceptional situations treated later, chapter 30 begins by affirming a man's obligation to not violate a vow he has made or a pledge that he has bound on himself by swearing an oath (30:2). A vow is a solemn promise to the Lord, and an oath taken by his name should not be taken in vain and profaned by swearing falsely (Exod 20:7; Lev 19:12).

The main concern of Numbers 30 is not with the binding nature of vows and oaths taken by men but with the tension that can arise when dependent women bind themselves by obligations to God that may conflict with the will of their fathers or husbands, to whom they are legally subordinate in ancient Israelite society (30:16). The vows/obligations of widowed or divorced women, who are independent, are binding like those of men (30:9).

The thrust of this legislation is to benefit dependent women by absolving them of guilt before God when their fathers or husbands do not allow them to fulfill their vows or oaths. Three cases are cited here, following the progression of a woman's life from single to married status:

- unmarried women subject to their fathers (30:3–5)
- women who marry while they are under vows or pledges previously taken (30:6–8)

- married women who make vows/pledges while subject to their husbands (30:10–15)

The Lord does not allow males to exercise their authority in an arbitrary manner. If a father or husband does not approve of the vow or pledge made by his daughter or wife, he can forbid it only when he first hears of it, in which case God will automatically forgive her for not fulfilling her obligation (30:5, 8, 12). These are the only instances in the Bible of forgiveness automatically guaranteed by statute. If the man does not express disapproval the first time the woman's obligation comes to his attention, his silence constitutes binding consent (30:3–4, 6–7, 10–11, 14). Therefore, if he later breaks her obligation, he is responsible and will bear her culpability (30:15).

Verses 6 and 8 refer to a woman becoming married while still under obligation from a *mibta* of her lips. This noun appears only here in the Hebrew Bible. It is generally interpreted as a rash/thoughtless utterance in accordance with the fact that in Psalm 106:33 the verb from the root *bt'* describes the rash utterance from Moses's mouth when he was angry at the waters of Meribah (cf. Num 20:10). However, because *mibta* appears only in a case that involves a change of a woman's status from single to married, it seems clear that her "rashness" is not necessarily a character flaw. Rather, it seems to reflect her inability to foresee the potential effects of a change in circumstances, coming under the jurisdiction of a husband who may feel adversely affected by an obligation she incurred while single.

Singled out for special mention is a husband's right to confirm or annul any obligation that his wife takes to practice self-denial. Presumably it will be of no consequence to him if she chooses to fast for a limited time. However, he will be affected if her self-denial includes other aspects of this kind of mourning observance, especially if she committed herself to abstain from sexual relations.

Application. Modern Western society is not patriarchal, at least not to the degree that men have almost exclusive control over the legal structure. Nevertheless, Numbers 30 contains some important principles that transcend the differences between cultures.

1. Promises made to God are serious.
2. We should consider the effects that our vows/pledges may have on other people. Binding obligations, including the marriage vow, should be taken carefully, prayerfully, sparingly, and in counsel with others.
3. Family harmony within the context of a given culture should not be disturbed unless absolutely necessary.
4. By being willing to waive his own rights, the Lord teaches us that we do not always need to insist on our rights.
5. People who control other individuals should not be arbitrary or fickle. Sometimes it is necessary to annul someone's decision, but there should be a good and consistent reason for doing so.

NUMBERS 31:1–54

Original Meaning. *Battle against the Midianites.* Moses has a few more miles to go and promises to keep before it is time for him to sleep. One major piece of unfinished business is to fulfill the divine command issued after the Baal of Peor scandal (25:16–18). Because Midian is a tribal confederation constituting a kind of nation, corporate retributive justice requires a major military operation.

Along with the Israelite army of one thousand from each tribe (31:3–5), Moses sends Phinehas, the priest (31:6). This is a holy war commanded by God. Phinehas and the unspecified holy objects that he takes with him represent the Lord's presence with the troops. When he blows on a silver trumpet (cf. 10:9), they will know that the divine King in their midst (cf. 23:21) will give them victory. Another reason to send Phinehas, specifically, is the fact that this unsqueamish priest has energetically begun the process of vengeance by slaying Kosbi (25:8, 15). So, his presence will inspire the Israelite soldiers to finish the job.

Rather than relishing the gory details, Numbers 31 describes the actual battle with brevity (31:7). Among the slain are the kings of five major subdivisions of the Midianite tribal nation (31:8a). In addition, the Israelites "also killed Balaam son of Beor with the sword" (31:8b). The unprofitable prophet must have returned from home to incite the Midianites and Moabites to deception against the Israelites at Shittim (31:16). The success of this tempter and his female agents was their own undoing because they succeeded in arousing the Lord and his people to deadly resolve.

When the triumphant Israelite warriors return with captives and spoils of war (31:12–13), having destroyed all Midianite men (31:7), we expect Moses to be overjoyed. Instead, he is angry with the army officers for keeping alive the Midianite women, who have been the most dangerous enemies as instruments of apostasy to penetrate the Israelite camp (31:14–16). Moses thinks they should have known what to do.

Having attempted to destroy the Israelites, the Midianites have forfeited mercy. So, Moses orders summary execution of all captives except for 32,000 young virgin girls (31:17–18, 35). These can be assimilated into the Israelite community by marrying Israelite men, who will provide them with new family identities. Absorption of the girls will help to restore the Israelite population depleted by loss of the 24,000 who died at Shittim (25:9).

Purification and distribution. All soldiers who have come in contact with corpses are required to remain outside the main encampment, where the holy sanctuary is, and to undergo ritual purification (31:19) to avoid bringing the conceptual sphere of impurity/death into association with divine holiness/life.

Operating under the assumption that the surviving girls have contacted dead bodies, the Israelites also purify them for a week (31:19b), during which time they have to babysit these unhappy campers before they can be placed in new homes. In addition to persons, a wide variety of objects taken into battle or captured from the Midianites require purification from corpse contamination. Regarding these, Eleazar the high priest picks up where Moses left off (31:20), conveying supplementary instructions that Moses received from the Lord (31:21–24). It is appropriate that the high priest should serve as God's spokesman concerning such matters, especially because Moses will soon be departing from the scene and the people need to get used to listening to someone else.

Metal objects are to be purified by fire and the "water of cleansing" (31:22–23a), which contains the ashes of the red cow (cf. ch. 19). Other things that cannot withstand fire are to be passed through water instead (31:23b).

The rest of Numbers 31 describes distribution of the spoils of war (31:25–54). The captured girls and animals are to be equally divided between the warriors and the rest of the community. Part of each of these half portions is to be set apart for the Lord and his sanctuary, one five-hundredth from the soldiers and one fiftieth from the community.

Both of the mandatory contributions to God are much lower percentages than the voluntary tithe Abraham gave the priest Melchizedek after his victory over four kings (Gen 14:20). Perhaps the numbers of captured girls and animals are simply too great for the sanctuary, priests, and Levites to absorb at the 10 percent rate. For one thing, there are more sheep than the total number of Israelite men counted in the military census (Num 31:32; cf. 26:51)!

Gold purified through fire. The distribution just described deals only with captured persons and animals. All other plunder belongs to the soldiers who have taken it, every man for himself (31:53). However, the army officers are grateful to God that their casualties amount to a miraculous zero. So, as a valuable offering before the Lord (31:50b), they present the crafted items of gold—primarily jewelry—that they have seized (31:48–54). This ransom is like the half shekel census tax (Exod 30:12–16) in the sense that the lives of those who were counted (cf. Num 31:4–6) have been spared. Notice that rather than holding a grudge against Moses for upbraiding them for failing to slay the Midianite women (31:14–16), the army officers treat Moses with great respect (31:49).

Moses and Eleazar bring the commander's contribution into the sacred tent as a memorial/reminder for the Israelites before the Lord (31:54), testifying to the fact that their lives have been ransomed. The rich endowment shows the fine attitude of Israel's military leaders who care about the men under their command, are unselfish, respectfully acknowledge the human authority over them, and are grateful to the Lord. This is a breath of fresh air for Moses, who can end his career on an upbeat. His ransomed people are becoming like that memorial—gold purified through fire (cf. 31:22–23; Rev 3:18).

Application. We confront the hard reality that our approach to the ethics of "holy war" genocide depends on our answer to a religious question: Which deity is true and therefore has ultimate authority over human life? Problems such as the political and ideological environment of the Middle East will never be satisfactorily and permanently solved at any conference table as long as moral attitudes and ethical judgments are founded on different religions. If we could agree that because theocracy no longer exists on Planet Earth, there is no such thing as "holy war" in the twenty-first century and therefore indiscriminate slaughter is unconscionable, inhumane, and universally condemnable, we would have a solid basis for resolution of conflict.

As Christians, what we need is not less of religion, but more of *truer* religion (cf. Matt 5:20) that is permeated by Christ's self-sacrificing love. Leaving vengeance up to God to administer according to his wisdom (Deut 32:35; Rom 12:19; Heb 10:30), we must love others as ourselves (Lev 19:18; Matt 22:36–40; John 13:34–35; Rom 13:8). The holy war that we are to wage is love.

NUMBERS 32–34

Original Meaning. *Home on the range.* When the Reubenites and Gadites approach Moses and other leaders to request the Transjordanian territories as their possession (32:1–5), they cause a major misunderstanding by concluding their petition with the words: "Do not make us cross the Jordan" (32:5). Moses hits the roof and delivers one of the most sizzling speeches of his oratorically distinguished career (32:6–15).

Moses thinks he has just aborted a rebellion by a "brood of sinners" (32:14) and no doubt expects the representatives of Reuben and Gad to slink away with their tails between their legs. He must be surprised when they courageously come closer to him instead (32:16). They clarify their intentions and outline a plan for their men to go not just *with* the rest of the Israelites but to be deployed in advance of them to help them fight for their inheritance on the other side of the Jordan (32:16–18). Moses approves, provided that they will follow through (32:20–24). So, the Gadites and Reubenites reinforce their promise by repeating it, referring to their idea as their lord's (Moses's) command (32:25–27). They are rapidly learning the art of diplomacy!

When Moses grants Transjordanian land to Gad and Reuben, he also allots a portion east of the Jordan to half of the tribe of Manasseh (32:33). The biblical text does not explain why Manasseh enters the picture at this point. Perhaps after Reuben and Gad pave the way with Moses, some Manassites decide they want to live in the Transjordan too. In any case, it serves Moses's interests to have the tribe of Manasseh straddling the Jordan. At least members of the half-tribe of Manasseh on the east will have a strong vested interest in assisting their fellow tribesmen on the west and making sure that the Reubenites and Gadites join them in this. Later the two and a half tribes east of the Jordan do make good on their pledge to send their army across the Jordan in front of the other Israelites (Josh 4:12), after which they return home (22:9).

Incredible journey, homeward bound. God's people maintain a balanced perspective by reviewing their journey and remembering how he has led. In this way they simultaneously reinforce their sense of dependence on him and confidence that he will take care of them each step of the way.

The summary in Numbers 33 is more complete than the accounts in Exodus and earlier in Numbers, which concentrate on places where memorable events have occurred. While we know the overall contours of Israel's movement from Egypt to Canaan, modern scholars have not succeeded in definitively working out all the details because there is inadequate evidence to pinpoint all the locations named in the Bible. Remember that the Israelites were camping in an uninhabited area without building anything that would remain.

Verses 3–15 cover journeys from Egypt to the Desert of Sinai (cf. Exod 12–19). Numbers 33:4 adds that the Lord has accomplished judgment on the gods of the Egyptians. In other words, the plagues were not simply to discomfort the Egyptians; they were strategically calculated to attack their religious system by displaying God's power over things they worshiped.

Numbers 33:15–16 includes the Desert of Sinai, where the tabernacle was constructed and the laws of Leviticus were given, as just another stop along the way. Verses 16–49 cover the decades of travel from the Desert of Sinai to the plains of Moab by the Jordan River (cf. chs. 10–25), listing many place names that we have not encountered earlier in Numbers because no noteworthy events occurred there during the years of wandering.

According to Numbers 33, after leaving the Desert of Sinai (33:16a), the Israelites camped at Kibroth Hattaavah (33:16b), at Hazeroth (33:18a), and then at a series of places not mentioned earlier in Numbers (33:18b–36a), before arriving at Kadesh in the Desert of Zin (33:36b). This is the Kadesh where the "waters of Meribah" were located (20:1–13) and from which Moses petitioned the king of Edom for passage (20:14). The question is: Why doesn't Numbers 33 mention the long stay at Kadesh? Was it perhaps a different Kadesh from the one where the Israelites stayed thirty-eight years later?

The summary of past journeys in Numbers 33 returns to the present at the plains of Moab by the Jordan, where the Israelites are encamped (33:49). Here, across from Jericho, the Lord instructs them how to treat the Canaanites when they cross the Jordan: Drive them out, destroy all their objects of worship, and settle in their land, dividing it up by casting lots (33:50–56).

Numbers 34 addresses the settlement and division of the land. First, the boundaries of the promised land are specified in the order: southern (34:3–5), western (34:6), northern (34:7–9), and eastern (34:10–12), aside from the Transjordanian territory of the Gadites, Reubenites, and half-tribe of Manasseh (34:13–15). Next, chapter 34 lists the leaders who will be responsible for dividing up the land (34:16–29). Reuben and Gad are not represented among these leaders because their inheritance is on the other side of the Jordan (see ch. 32).

Application. Because Moses was running a nation, he had to delegate in all kinds of ways, but this was not always easy for him. Jethro found him trying to do the job of ten men and urged him to appoint judges, which he did (Exod 18:13–26). The Lord found him crushed by the burden of leading the people and instructed him to choose seventy elders, which he also did (Num 11).

Moses was not jealous for his own authority or afraid that others could do things better than he could (see 11:29). Nor would this former prince of Egypt have lacked training. However, Moses was concerned for God to maintain authority (e.g., 16:5–11) and he was conscientious, knowing that the stakes involved in cooperation with the divine will were high. So, when it came to matters of crucial importance, it is not surprising that he would have some reservations about depending on others, especially when even his own brother let him and the Lord down by making a golden calf at Sinai (Exod 32).

If we don't feel comfortable with the strong way God and Moses ordered the Israelites to do things *or else*, we should keep in mind that these people had just come out of slavery. In many areas of life, a lot of them had low interest, motivation, and skill, so they needed the "telling" approach. Even if we are well motivated, highly skilled, and therefore ready for someone to lead us by "delegating," we can still learn a lot from prescriptive passages of the Pentateuch. Formulation of messages as law in this part of the Bible is part of the leadership style and does not invalidate the messages themselves as "legalistic."

NUMBERS 35–36

Original Meaning. *Towns for Levites and for refuge.* Because the Levites are to receive tithes instead of territory, they will not have a part in the division of the promised land (ch. 34). Nevertheless, they do need to live somewhere. So, chapter 35 instructs the Israelite tribes to give the Levites forty-eight towns distributed throughout their territories, surrounded by pasture lands for their animals (35:1–8). Spreading out the Levite ministers of the Lord in this way will help to maintain the religious unity of the nation.

Six of the Levite towns, three on each side of the Jordan River, are to have special legal status as places of asylum/refuge to which any person (Israelite or alien) who has inadvertently killed someone can flee (35:6, 9–15). This plan will make it possible for a manslayer to receive a fair trial without being lynched by an avenger from the family of the one whom he has killed (35:12).

Either of two criteria for what we call "first-degree murder," however, disqualifies a killer from asylum so that capital punishment is to be administered by the avenger (35:16–21):

1. if death occurs by striking with a hard object of metal (iron), hand-held stone, or a hand-held object of wood that is capable of functioning as a deadly weapon (35:16–18);
2. if death is caused by shoving someone, throwing something at him/her, or punching that is motivated by hostile intention (35:20–21a). Unintentional manslaughter, for which the killer is eligible for protection at a city of refuge, lacks both of the factors just described (35:22–25).

Once an Israelite killer runs to a town of refuge, the community will take him and judge between him and the "avenger of blood" (representing the deceased) according to the criteria in this legislation (35:24). Undoubtedly the bulk of the debate centers on questions of intent that require witnesses to testify regarding the history of the relationship between the killer and the one slain. If the community judges the accused guilty of capital murder, he is to be put to death (Deut 19:12—by the avenger). But if he is acquitted, the community is to return him to the city of refuge. Only by staying there will he enjoy legal immunity to the avenger until the high priest dies, after which he is free to return home (35:25–28).

Numbers 35 concludes with injunctions for safeguarding justice and preventing corruption (35:29–34).

1. Establishing capital murder requires more than one witness. So, a single grudge-bearer cannot abuse the judicial system to destroy another person.
2. No ransom can save any condemned murderer from the death penalty. Thus, wealth or power cannot subvert equal opportunity punishment.
3. Temporary exile to a city of refuge is mandatory for accidentally taking a human life, and no ransom can enable a manslayer to return home before the death of the high priest.

In support of the law that a murderer must die (35:31), 35:33–34 explains that blood(shed)/murder pollutes and defiles the land where the Lord dwells among his people. This is a serious problem because his holiness is incompatible with impurity. Unremedied, defilement of the land may ultimately lead to exile. It can only be expiated/purged through the blood of the person who shed the blood (35:33).

Female inheritance and marriage. Numbers 36 consists of a postscript to 27:1–8, where the Lord allowed the daughters of Zelophehad, a Manassite descended from Gilead, to inherit his property. The heads of the clan of Gilead, to which Zelophehad belonged, detected a potential problem: If Zelophehad's daughters marry men from another tribe, they will thereby join that tribe and take Zelophehad's property with them, thereby diminishing the allotted territory of Gilead (36:1–3). The Jubilee release, which applies to real estate transferred by sale (cf. Lev 25) but not by inheritance or marriage, will change nothing. They and their property will have been permanently alienated from Gilead (Num 36:4).

The Lord has a simple solution. An heiress will be required to marry within her father's clan so that her property will stay in the family (36:6–9). The daughters of Zelophehad comply (36:10–12), and that is the end of the story. We can hope that they lived happily ever after. In keeping with this gentle resolution, which reminds us of the compliance report setting the standard for faithfulness at the beginning of the book (1:54), Numbers concludes quietly with a simple summary (36:13).

Application. It is true that Christ commanded love for enemies, forgiveness, and reconciliation rather than retaliation. These principles are already in the Old Testament. For example, Leviticus 19:18 says: "Do not seek revenge or bear a grudge against one of your people, but love your neighbor as yourself." However, a few chapters later, the same book stipulates: "Anyone takes the life of a human being is to be put to death" (24:17). Is this a contradiction? Not if we realize that chapter 19 is addressed to individuals, but chapter 24 is for the community. God's people were not to seek revenge, but a murderer was condemned to execution by the civil community. The latter was not revenge; it was divinely mandated retributive justice.

In Matthew 5:38–42, Christ was speaking to individuals, some of whom were undoubtedly inclined to seize on the *lex talionis* (law of retaliation: eye for an eye, etc.) as justification for vengeance, especially against the Romans. Although they may have thought they should control society, they did not possess civil judicial power. Neither did the New Testament church have civil power to inflict physical punishment. The only executions in the context of the church were of Ananias and Sapphira, slain by God himself (Acts 5). However, Romans 13 makes clear that even outside theocracy, God mandates state civil power to maintain order in society by restraining and punishing wrongdoers.

The bottom line is that the Bible gives society the authority to administer capital punishment for some kinds of clearly established crimes, such as murder. If some people oppose any form of capital punishment, that is their right, but their position does not harmonize with that of the Bible.

It is important to keep in mind that although a person who justly suffers capital punishment has forfeited the present life, it is possible for him or her to enjoy the promised paradise to come. When a dying criminal on the cross next to Jesus expressed his belief and repentance, Jesus promised that the man would be with him in paradise (Luke 23:42–43).

DEUTERONOMY

INTRODUCTION TO DEUTERONOMY

Prior to the rise of the source-critical method, both Jewish and Christian readers assumed Mosaic authorship of the book of Deuteronomy, a fact reflected in the common designation of the Pentateuchal books outside the English world as the Five Books of Moses. By the second half of the nineteenth century the documentary approach to Pentateuchal studies was firmly entrenched, and Deuteronomy had been isolated as a source separate from J (Yahwist), E (Elohist), and P (Priestly). Critical scholars generally agree that on the one hand Deuteronomy either provides the occasion or is the result of the Josianic reform, and on the other hand that the speeches in Deuteronomy are pseudepigraphic, being fictionally attributed to Moses to lend weight to the voice of the parties whose interests are represented in the book. But this reconstruction of the origins and provenance of Deuteronomy is diametrically opposed to the internal evidence of the book.

In accordance with ancient Near Eastern literary conventions, strictly speaking the book as we have it is anonymous. We may speculate when the individual speeches of Moses were combined, arranged, and linked with their present narrative stitching. Although the speeches of Deuteronomy derive from Moses himself, the book as we have it was produced later. A reasonable *terminus a quo* (earliest possible date) would be during the tenure of Joshua after the Israelites had crossed the Jordan; a *terminus ad quem* (latest possible date) would be the ninth century, prior to the ministries of Elijah and Elisha, after which the style of prophetic preaching seems to have changed dramatically.

BOOK OUTLINE

- I. Moses's First Address: Remembering the Grace of Yahweh (1:1–4:43)
  - A. Moses's First Address (1:1–4:40)
  - B. The Epilogue to Moses's First Address (4:41–43)
- II. Moses's Second Address: Explaining the Grace of Yahweh (4:44–29:1[28:69])
  - A. Moses's Second Address (4:44–26:19)
  - B. Interlude: A Call for Covenantal Renewal in the Promised Land (27:1–26)
  - C. Moses's Second Address Continued (28:1–29:1)
- III. Moses's Third Address: Trusting in the Grace of Yahweh (29:2–30:20)
- IV. The Death of Moses (31:1–34:12)
  - A. Preparing for the Death of Moses (31:1–32:47)
  - B. Announcing the Death of Moses (32:48–52)
  - C. The Benediction of Moses (33:1–29)
  - D. Recounting the Death of Moses (34:1–12)

DEUTERONOMY 1:1–5

Original Meaning. Although Deuteronomy consists largely of proclaimed divine truth, the voice of God is heard directly only five times: 31:14b, 16b–21, 23b, 32:49–52, and 34:4b. This introduction alerts the reader to the voice of Moses, which we will hear throughout. But his voice is not an independent voice; he speaks only what Yahweh "had commanded him" (1:3). The addressees are identified as "all Israel" in 1:1 and "Israelites" in 1:3, two expressions that are scattered throughout the book. The former suggests that Moses speaks to the community of faith; the latter highlights the nation's ethnic cohesion (they are the descendants of Jacob/Israel).

The syntax of 1:1b creates the impression that Moses delivered these addresses in the desert, somewhere in the Arabah. The following list of place names seems to refer to a series of way stations along the route the Israelites took from Sinai/Horeb to Kadesh Barnea. Moses delivers these addresses after the defeat of the two Amorite kings east of the Jordan. The victories over Sihon and Og provide concrete proof that when Israel is faithful to Yahweh, he will fight for them.

The book opens with "These are the words Moses spoke." Verse 3 reiterates that Moses "proclaimed" (*dibber*) to the Israelites all that Yahweh commanded him. This suggests that in this book Moses does not function primarily as a lawgiver but as a prophet and as the people's pastor, delivering his final sermons before he passes from the scene.

Deuteronomy involves two kinds of torah: oral and written. Deuteronomy 1:5 and 4:8 classify Moses's first address as the former. However, within the reports of Moses's second and third addresses, we find numerous references to a written torah, which refers to the transcribed version of his oral speeches. As if to dispel any doubt about the genre of the book, the introduction concludes with a verb of speech rather than legislation. Moses stands before the people as pastor, delivering his final sermons at the command of Yahweh and pleading with the Israelites to remain faithful to their God once they cross the Jordan and settle down in the land promised to the ancestors.

Application. For many Christians the Old Testament in general and Deuteronomy in particular is a dead book. Consequently, the favorite book of Jesus is ignored, the source of much Johannine and Pauline theology is discarded, and the life-giving power of the word of God is cut off. Unless we rediscover this book, we will not treasure the Old Testament as a whole. As we will see in the commentary, this book presents the gospel according to Moses. This is a gospel of divine grace lavished on undeserving human beings. Moses's vision for his own people serves as a microcosm for the divine vision of humanity as a whole. The book points the reader to the Lord God, who has redeemed his people and assigned them the mission of radiating his grace to the world.

DEUTERONOMY 1:6–18

Original Meaning

The Command to Leave Horeb (1:6–8). Moses begins with a verbatim quotation of Yahweh's speech to the Israelites thirty-eight years ago, instructing the Israelites to leave Horeb and head for Canaan (1:6–8; cf. Num 10:11–13). The order consists of three parts.

1. Moses recalls Yahweh's telling the people that they had camped at the mountain long enough; his goals at Horeb had been achieved.
2. Moses describes the destination.
3. Moses reiterates Yahweh's promise to the ancestors (1:8). With deliberately legal language Yahweh announces he has given the land into the hands of his vassal Israel.

Administrative Details (1:9–18). Verses 9–18 divide into three sections: (1) Moses's explanation of the need to reorganize Israel's administrative structures (1:9–12); (2) his explanation of how the assistants were appointed (1:13–15); and (3) his report of the charge given to those who had been appointed (1:16–18).

1. In the first part (1:9–12), Moses acknowledges that the burden of the Israelites had become heavier than he could bear (1:9). Remarkably, the underlying cause was Yahweh's faithfulness: He had fulfilled his promise to the ancestors and transformed Israel from a small clan into this innumerable host (1:10). Moses's plea to God to multiply them a thousandfold suggests that the number of people was not the real problem (1:11). The problem lay with the character and conduct of the people (1:12).
2. To take the pressure off himself, Moses proposed that the people pick men of wisdom, understanding, and experience from each of the tribes as leaders over them (1:13–15). Moses emphasizes the leaders' maturity and intellectual qualifications. Moses identifies the officials who were chosen with three expressions: "leading men," "commanders," and "tribal officials" (1:15).
3. Moses reports his charge to the officials whom he had installed as leaders of the Israelites (1:16–18). In the charge Moses makes four basic points.
   a. These men were instructed to hear the people's disputes and judge "fairly" (1:16b).
   b. The men were not to "show partiality" in their judging (1:17a); they were expected to hear the cases of the small and the great alike (cf. Lev 19:15).
   c. The officials were to judge boldly ("do not be afraid"); they must not fear the accused, a member of the accused's family, or a superior, because the "judgment belongs to God" (Deut 1:17b).
   d. The officials had to recognize their limitations (1:17b). Moses invited the officials to bring cases they found too difficult to handle to him.

Application. The law was not the end goal nor did it represent the essence of God's call. While the covenant and the revelation of God's will were to be received as incredible graces, the promise looked beyond Sinai, and the mission lay far beyond. This is not to minimize the significance of the law, it is simply to emphasize that possession of it is not the end goal. The Lord calls us that we might delight in the fulfillment of his promise and that in that fulfillment the world may see what he can do for them.

DEUTERONOMY 1:19–2:1

Original Meaning

Moses's Charge to Take the Land (1:20–21). The opening to Moses's reminiscences of Kadesh Barnea contains three promising observations: the Israelites had arrived at their destination (1:7, 19); Yahweh had placed his grant of land before them (cf. 1:8); and Yahweh, the God of their ancestors, had kept his word.

The People's Faithless Act of Rebellion (1:22–33). The Israelites responded to Moses's charge by proposing to send a party of men to scout out the territory. This account differs dramatically from Numbers 13:1–2, but neither report claims to tell the whole story. In this rendition Moses agreed to the people's request, selected a man from each tribe, and sent them out (1:23; cf. Num 13:4–16.). The detail with which he now recounts the people's infidelity in 1:26–45 suggests Moses may have acted on his own, and after thirty-eight years of reflection he seems to have recognized this was a wrong move.

Verses 24–25 describe the scouts' mission and report. His recollection illuminates the ironies of the situation. They went out to gain information to be used to determine military strategy, but their report focused on fruit, concrete evidence of the fertility of the land. They reported that the land was good, but promptly demonstrated they did not think it worth the risk of an invasion. They referred to the land as "a good land that the LORD our God is giving us" (1:25), but they refused to accept it from his hand.

In 1:26–33 Moses recalls the people's reaction to the scouting report. Omitting many details found in Numbers 13–14, he concentrates on their shameful attitude (1:26–27a) and reprehensible actions (1:27b–28). He describes the former with three expressions: they were unwilling to go up; they rebelled against the command of Yahweh; and they muttered/grumbled in their tents.

Trying to correct the people's flawed perspective, Moses's response focused entirely on Yahweh. After an opening call for calm and confidence (1:29), he tried to encourage them with three arguments (1:30–31):

1. Yahweh was present with them and going before them;
2. Yahweh, the Divine Warrior and captain of his hosts, would fight for them;
3. Yahweh had taken care of them in the past by defeating the Egyptians and sustaining them through the great and terrifying desert (1:19).

With sensitive pastoral touch, Moses compared Yahweh's care to that of a father who carries his son through danger to safety.

It is obvious from 1:32–33 that Moses's exhortation had no effect. Reiterating how foolish and faithless the people had been, he reminded the present generation that their security and success rested neither with human generals nor in human wisdom; Yahweh always marched ahead of them. The real challenge was neither physical nor military, but spiritual. Would they trust God? Verse 32 declares that they would not!

Yahweh's Reaction to the People's Faithlessness (1:34–40). Moses's recollection of Yahweh's response abbreviates Numbers 14 drastically. He simply announces Yahweh's anger at the sound of the people's words and moves immediately to his final decision, expressed with an oath. Yahweh swore that he would give the land to the little children of that faithless generation. Innocent children who could not distinguish good from bad would replace "this evil generation" (1:35).

Within the context of Yahweh's oath, Moses's personal gripe in 1:37 is intrusive. He blames the Israelites that he is unable to enter the promised land with Caleb and Joshua. The reasons given for God's refusing Moses entrance into the promised land in the earlier narratives relate to an entirely different incident—his failure to treat Yahweh as holy by striking the rock rather than speaking to it at Meribah (Num 20:2–13). How then could he blame the Israelites for his failure to enter the land? The answer is actually simple. If the Israelites had trusted Yahweh at Kadesh Barnea and entered the land at his command, the event recorded in Numbers 20 would never have occurred.

The People's Presumptuous Act of Rebellion (1:41–2:1). The key expressions in this paragraph are "rebelled against the LORD's command" and "arrogance" (1:43). Defying their divine commander and without any assurance of divine protection, they attacked those whom they had feared only a short time ago. Adding the sin of presumption to rebellion, they forgot that God is not obligated to those who do not take him seriously.

Moses's observation that they milled around in circles for many days in the vicinity of Seir represents a classic understatement. During these thirty-eight years (cf. 2:14) the Israelites made no progress whatsoever toward the fulfillment of the mission on which they had embarked when they came out of Egypt. For almost four decades Israel was a death camp, a walking mortuary, in which the dominant sound was the death wail. The irony is inescapable. So long as they were slaves in Egypt, Israel's population mushroomed; as soon as they were free, it shrank.

Application. Sadly, like Israel the church as a collective and Christians as individuals have often proved faithless, being more impressed by the power of the enemy than the power of God and the resources he makes available to his people. But the example of Caleb inspires us in our pursuit of God and provides the key to passing the tests we face: possession of a different spirit, that is, the Holy Spirit of God, and unqualified commitment to God and his mission. To those who persevere the Lord promises not a plot of land but the eternal reward of an inheritance with him (Eph 1:3–14).

DEUTERONOMY 2:2–23

Original Meaning

Moses's Recollections of Seir/Edom (2:2–8a). In this opening episode, Moses remembers Israel's encounter with the Edomites. After circling Mount Seir for many days, Yahweh broke his silence, telling Moses that they had milled around long enough and that the time had come to head north. Moses does not recount how the Israelites conducted their negotiations with the Edomites. In 2:2–7 he simply recalls verbatim the divinely prescribed policy for dealing with Edom: The Israelites were simply to pass through, treating the Edomites with respect and not provoking them in any way.

This policy appears to have been based on five considerations.

1. The Edomites were the Israelites' relatives (2:4a).
2. The Edomites were fearful of the Israelites (2:4); apparently the story of their escape from Egypt and defeat of the Amalekites forty years ago had reached them.
3. Just as Yahweh had allocated the land of Canaan to Israel, so he allocated Seir as the rightful possession of Esau and his descendants. Whereas ancient Near Easterners tended to perceive patron deities as having jurisdiction only over their own territories, Yahweh, the God of Israel, exercises supranational authority and providential care over other nations. As Yahweh's vassal, Israel was not to claim territory given by him to another (2:5).
4. Yahweh prohibited the Israelites from looting or stealing from the Edomites; instead, they were to pay for any food or water that they would need with silver (2:6).
5. Israel was to continue relying entirely on the direct provision of Yahweh (2:7). Yahweh's speech represented a test of faith for the new generation. From what follows, they obviously passed this test.

Moses's Recollections of Moab (2:8b–15). When the Israelites arrived at the edge of Moab (2:8b), Yahweh commanded that the policy that governed their treatment of Edom was also to apply to Moab. They were not to harass them or pick a fight with them (cf. 2:5). Just as Yahweh had given Seir to Edom, so he gave Ar to the Moabites as their possession. Remarkably, Yahweh posed as Moab's patron deity, claiming a role normally ascribed to Chemosh, the god of Moab.

Verses 10–12 function as a footnote, clarifying ethnographic and geographic issues raised in Moses's speech. Syntactically 2:14–15 also function as a parenthetical footnote. The recollection of Yahweh's charge to cross the Zered (2:13) triggered a reflective glance backward. The generation that had been lost in the desert perished not for lack of water or food but because Yahweh had become their enemy and had taken action against them, just as he had sworn.

Moses's Recollection of Bene Ammon (2:16–23). Once the last warriors of the faithless generation had died, Yahweh ordered the Israelites to move into the homestretch of their long journey, past the territory of the Ammonites. Yahweh prohibited the Israelites from harassing the Ammonites or from trying to take any of their territory, for he had given their land as their own possession. Here he claims authority normally attributed to Milkom, the acknowledged patron deity of Bene Ammon.

The remainder of the report concerning Bene Ammon is taken up with a parenthetical note concerning the persons they displaced as occupants of the land (2:20–23). Just as Yahweh had enabled the descendants of Esau to dispossess and destroy the Horites in Seir and to occupy their land (2:22), so he had destroyed the Zamzummites and allowed the Ammonites to dispossess them and occupy their land (2:21).

Verse 23 adds a puzzling reference to historical events far away in the region of Philistia on the southwest coast of Palestine, where the Avvites were destroyed and dispossessed by the Caphtorites or Philistines (cf. Josh 13:3–4). In the providence of God, the Philistines arrived in Palestine (which is named after them) from the west at the same time as the Israelites were moving in from the east and trying to establish their authority over the land. Conflict was inevitable.

Application. This text teaches Israel and all who read it that land is a gift delivered by Yahweh himself. The references to these fearful peoples highlight the truth that when God begins to do his work of grace, no one can stand in his way. The enemies may appear huge, numerous, and strong, but the church must remember that Yahweh, the God of Israel, is mightier than all. Greater is he who is in you than he who is in the world (1 John 4:4).

DEUTERONOMY 2:24–3:29

Original Meaning

The Conquest of Sihon of Heshbon (2:24–37). Yahweh's command to the Israelites consists of six imperatives (the first is not represented in the NIV): Arise! Set out! Cross the Wadi Arnon! Begin! Take possession! Engage him in battle! (2:24). This charge is accompanied by two significant promises: Yahweh had already given Sihon into the Israelites' hands, and from this day on, he would send shockwaves throughout the earth, causing people to tremble in fright when they heard of Israel's triumphs. Remarkably the statement highlights Israel's actions and places Yahweh in the background. The peoples throughout the world (lit., "the peoples under the whole heaven") would tremble and writhe (in anguish) *before them* when they heard reports *of them* because they were in dread *of them* and in awe *of them*. Rahab's testimony in Joshua 2:9–11 and the narrator's comment in Numbers 22:3 indicate that this actually happened among the Canaanites and Moabites.

Although, like Pharaoh, Sihon was inexcusable for his disposition, Moses attributes his response directly to Yahweh, who "made his spirit stubborn" and "his heart obstinate" (2:30). He also declares explicitly the divine purpose in hardening Sihon: "in order to give him into your hands" (2:30). With the concluding phrase in 2:30, lit., "as [it is] this day," Moses draws attention to a present reality whose roots lay in past actions. In 2:31–37 Moses describes the battle against Sihon.

The Conquest of Og of Bashan (3:1–11). Omitting a command from Yahweh to continue the campaign northward (cf. 2:24), Moses recalls rather matter-of-factly that the Israelites "turned and went up along the road toward Bashan" (3:1), as if this were merely one more stage in Israel's itinerary. Og interpreted the Israelites' movements as a hostile military maneuver. The voice of Yahweh broke through to Moses with a word of encouragement and a challenge (3:2). Yahweh encouraged him and challenged Moses to deal with Og exactly as he had with Sihon in Heshbon.

In 3:3–7 Moses describes the course of the battle. Moses concludes his recollections of the battles against Sihon and Og with a summary statement of the Israelites' conquests (3:8). Verse 9 interrupts the review with another parenthetical comment, this time clarifying the reference to Mount Hermon. Apparently Mount Hermon was the Israelite name for a mountain that the Sidonians (representing the Phoenicians) called Hermon Sirion and one that the Amorites (who previously controlled it) called Senir. In 3:10 Moses reiterates the scope of the Israelites' conquests, focusing on the highlands. Moving from south to north, he lists the conquered regions.

A final footnote at the end of Moses's recollection of the defeat of Sihon and Og notes that as a Rephaite, Og was one of the last survivors of the gigantic pre-Amorite aboriginal peoples in this region. As concrete evidence of his size Moses refers to Og's bed, which apparently was on display in Rabbah of Bene Ammon (the Ammonite capital) at the time this note was written. Og's bed was impressive. It was huge: 9 cubits long by 4 cubits wide (13.5 feet by 6 feet). And it was made of iron. Since iron was a precious metal in the Late Bronze Age, this was probably a bed made of wood and adorned with iron. This note invites the ancient reader to check the narrator's veracity and to confirm the magnitude of Israel's victory.

Moses's Assignment of the Transjordanian Lands (3:12–17). Moses's recollection of the distribution of the Amorites' lands to the tribes of Reuben, Gad, and the half-tribe of Manasseh differs from the procedure Yahweh prescribed for the apportionment of the land west of the Jordan (Num 26:52–56) and from the process actually followed in the event (Josh 14–19). Numbers 32 tells the full story. Observing that the hills of Gilead and Bashan were ideal for raising livestock, the tribes of Reuben and Gad approached Moses for permission to claim this land as their possession (32:5). At first Moses interpreted the request as an act of rebellion against Yahweh (32:14–15), but when they assured him they would cross the Jordan with the rest of the tribes and assist them in the conquest of Canaan, he granted their request.

Moses's Charge to the Transjordanian Tribes (3:18–20). Having authorized the two and one-half tribes to settle east of the Jordan, Moses charged them to aid the rest of Israel in the conquest of the actual promised land (cf. Josh 1:12–15). The charge consists of four parts.

1. Moses credits Yahweh with granting the land to the two and one-half tribes.
2. Moses issues the specific command: The two and one-half tribes must commit all their "able-bodied men" to the campaign so that the "Israelites" can wage war on the other side of the Jordan.
3. Moses authorizes the women, children, and livestock belonging to the two and one-half tribes to remain east of the Jordan in the towns he granted them.
4. Moses defines the time the two and one-half tribes are to commit themselves to the greater national interest—until "the LORD gives rest to your fellow Israelites" (3:20), just as he had given rest to those across the Jordan.

Moses's Public Charge to Joshua (3:21–22). Having reminded the two and one-half tribes of their obligations to their kinsmen, Moses recalls his earlier charge to Joshua as well. Moses's charge to Joshua consisted of three elements.

1. He reminded Joshua of his own past experience of Yahweh's intervention on Israel's behalf, which Joshua had seen with his own eyes.
2. Moses declared that Yahweh's triumph over Sihon and Og was paradigmatic for what he would do against the kingdoms on the other side of the Jordan.
3. Moses promised the continued presence of Yahweh, for Yahweh is the divine Warrior fighting for them.

Moses's Private Prayer (3:23–29). This prayer takes up only verses 24 and 25, but it contains several typical features of biblical prose prayers.

1. **The invocative address: "Sovereign LORD."** The double invocation establishes contact with God (3:24; cf. 9:26).
2. **The description.** "You have begun to show to your servant your greatness and your strong hand. For what god is there in heaven or on earth who can do the deeds and mighty works you do?" (3:24). The question obviously anticipates an emphatic negative response: "There is no god like Yahweh!"
3. **The petition.** Next comes Moses's petition: "Let me go over and see the good land beyond the Jordan—that fine hill country and Lebanon" (3:25). Moses expresses his desire forthrightly and passionately. The intensity of his pain at the prospect of missing this opportunity is reflected by his heaping of adjectives to describe the goal: "the good [i.e., fertile] land," "that fine [i.e., fertile] hill country," "and Lebanon," which serves as a metaphor for any lush landscape.

Moses concludes his recollections of this painful episode abruptly by noting simply that he and the people remained in the valley opposite Beth Peor on the plains of Moab (34:1), the place where he delivered this address.

Application. The apportionment of the land east of the Jordan to the two and one-half tribes (3:12–17) illustrates the ambiguities that often characterize the life of faith. Although their request seemed reasonable, in the long term it proved a disaster. The episode reminds readers today to set their affections on things above, not on things below (Col 3:2). It is not that what seems attractive to us is fundamentally wrong; it may even be logically defensible and economically wise. But when earthly considerations eclipse the divine agenda, we are in danger of losing our place in both.

DEUTERONOMY 4:1–8

Original Meaning

Here Now, Israel, hear (4:1). In a sense, 4:1–8 summarizes the entire chapter, highlighting the importance of obedience as the proper response to Yahweh's grace expressed by the revelation of his will. Moses was the communicator and interpreter of divine revelation, not its source. Moses declares his pedagogical goals in 4:1b (cf. 30:11–14). His immediate objective is to inspire Israel to "follow" the decrees and laws. What he offers is not theoretical speculation but practical instruction for life demonstrated through obedient action.

Why Obedience to the Torah Is Crucial (4:2–8). In 4:2–8 Moses declares that *only* that which he (on Yahweh's behalf) prescribes is normative, and by warning them not to delete anything from his word, he declares that *all* that he (on Yahweh's behalf) prescribes is normative. Obedience to the torah is the key to life (4:3–4); in fact, as Moses will reiterate at the end of his final address (30:15–20), obedience to Yahweh is a matter of life and death. This was demonstrated recently in the treacherous worship of Baal at Peor, which Moses takes to be paradigmatic. As at Kadesh Barnea thirty-eight years earlier and more recently at Baal of Peor, the people's fidelity will be tested every day once they have entered the promised land.

Obedience to the torah is the highest privilege imaginable (4:6–8). Compliance with the law is not a burden imposed on the people; it is a special privilege that will make them the envy of the nations. Observing Israel's "wisdom" and "understanding," they will ascribe "great nation" status to them, thereby fulfilling God's promise to Abraham (4:6). In 4:7–8 Moses declares that the nation's greatness does not derive from her own qualities but from Yahweh their God. God is near to them and he answers their prayers.

The Israelites are uniquely privileged because they know what their God expects of them, and what he expects is absolutely righteous. For Moses, righteousness is not an abstraction but adherence to an objective norm, demonstrated in concrete ethical acts that seek the interests of others and result in perfect harmony between them and their ruler. Israel's laws are righteous because they derive from God—who is absolutely righteous and upright (32:4)—and because adherence to them always achieves righteous results. His intent is that they might be a blessing (Gen 12:2–3; 18:18; 22:18; 26:4; 28:14) and light (Isa 42:6; 49:6; 51:4) to the nations.

Application. The torah and the rest of the Scriptures have not been given to us to display in beautifully decorated family Bibles on the coffee table or to be the subjects of high-sounding creedal statements on the inerrancy and infallibility of the Scriptures. A high view of God's revealed will is demonstrated in lives that conform to God's will as revealed. Moses spends much more time calling his people to orthopraxy than to orthodoxy. The missional goal of God's people is not fulfilled with precise theological formulas but through the life-giving and transforming power of the divine word.

DEUTERONOMY 4:9–31

Original Meaning

The Grace of Covenant Past: The Origins of Yahweh's Covenant with Israel (4:9–14). Verses 9–14 involve one long sentence governed by the twofold appeal to absolute vigilance. The verb "forget" does not mean simply a loss of memory but failure to take into account what the memory recalls—the special relationship Yahweh had established with his people. The Israelites' greatest enemy will not be the Canaanites out there but their own mind and heart within them.

Moses's recollections of Horeb focus on actions, first by the Israelites (4:10–11) and then by Yahweh (4:12–14). On that day the people stood before Yahweh their God. The combination of fire and light on one hand with cloud and darkness on the other introduced the Israelites both to the radiance of divine glory and to its lethal force. The Hebrew word for "to revere" (4:10) could denote either fright or reverence and awe in the presence of a superior. The latter is obviously the case here. For Israel this sort of "fear" will be a precondition to unqualified obedience, which in turn will be a precondition to life and prosperity in the land.

Like all covenants involving Yahweh in the Old Testament, this covenant is monergistic, that is, Yahweh initiates it, identifies the covenant partner, defines the terms, and determines the consequences for compliance or noncompliance. Moses associates the covenant with "the Ten Words" (4:13, lit.). Here the early Greek translation of Decalogue should be followed, that is, "the ten words/declarations" or even "the ten principles of covenant relationship."

Having declared the foundational principles of the covenant, Yahweh produced two written copies of the document on tablets of stone. The provision of two identical copies follows the ancient Near Eastern custom of giving each party to a covenant a copy of the agreement. Deuteronomy 10:5 notes that both Yahweh's and Israel's copies of the Decalogue were stored in the ark of the covenant.

The Grace of Covenant Present: The Essence of Yahweh's Covenant with Israel (4:15–24). Verse 20 represents the focal point of this passage, highlighting the utter treachery and perversion of idolatry. Moses highlights Israel's special relationship with Yahweh with three statements.

1. They are the product of Yahweh's gracious saving actions.
2. They were rescued from the furnace specifically to be Yahweh's covenant partner.
3. They have been claimed by Yahweh as his own "special possession" (Exod 19:5; Deut 7:6; 14:2), highlighting Yahweh's loving and caring relationship with this nation.

Verses 23–24 represent the climax. Once more Moses charges his people to guard against forgetting "the covenant" (4:23) and against manufacturing any images that would supplant Yahweh in this relationship. He grounds this warning with, "Yahweh is Consuming Fire; he is Impassioned El" (4:24; author's translation). Here the fire represents not merely the personal presence of Yahweh but his burning fury in the face of covenantal infidelity. Moses's characterization of Yahweh as "Impassioned El" is equally dramatic. The translation of "jealous"in 4:24 is misleading because jealousy is commonly understood as an illegitimate disposition akin to envy or covetousness. However, in the Old Testament, this term usually speaks of the legitimate passion that is aroused when interference from a third party threatens a proper relationship, particularly a marriage relationship when another lover enters the picture.

The Grace of Covenant Future: The Permanence of the Covenant (4:25–31). Now Moses shifts his gaze to the role of the covenant in the distant future. Moses envisions Israel's descent into idolatry when they are well-established in the land. Then he lists consequences of infidelity that await the Israelites. Exposing the folly of idolatry, Moses observes sarcastically how roles have reversed. Instead of the creature worshiping the creator, the creator worships the creature: Idols are the work of human hands.

But suddenly the tone changes (4:29). Beyond the judgment Moses sees a change in the people's disposition. From the land of the Israelites' exile and from the land where they worship their worthless idols, they will again seek Yahweh, and amazingly he will let himself be found by them. In the end, Yahweh's disposition and character guarantee their hope: "the Lord your God is a merciful God" (4:31). Israel may forget the covenant of Yahweh (4:23), but Yahweh will never forget the covenant of the "ancestors" (4:31). Israel's future is as secure as the eternal covenant and the unchangeably gracious character of God.

Application. In our text, idolatry involves reverential acts of homage and submission to objects other than God—objects made either by human hands or by God's own hands. While modern Westerners tend not to create concrete objects to be worshiped, we are constantly crafting new substitutes for God. Indeed an idol may be defined as anything (whether concrete or abstract) that rivals God—anything to which we submit and which we serve in place of God himself. The stuff of idols is not necessarily bad. The sun, moon, and stars are good; they govern the universe. Wood and stones are good and useful for limitless projects and tasks. But when we pervert their function and treat them as ultimate things on which our well-being and destiny depend, they rival God—and that makes them an idol.

DEUTERONOMY 4:32–40

Original Meaning

The History Lesson, Part I (4:32–34). Moses invites his audience to engage in exhaustive historical research in pursuit of the answers to four questions. The first two questions are general; the third and fourth are more specific.

1. Has any great event like this ever happened before?
2. Has anybody ever heard about anything like this?
3. Has any people ever heard the voice of God? And having heard it, have they lived to tell about it?
4. Has any god dared to do what Israel's God has done in taking for himself one nation from the midst of another nation?

Moses declares that Yahweh's rescue of Israel from Egypt is unparalleled either in historical records or in fictional portrayals; the notion is unheard of, the experience is intolerable, and the divine power displayed is awesome.

The Theology Lesson, Part I (4:35). The purpose of Yahweh's awesome acts was revelatory: These events demonstrated that he alone deserves the title God and that there is no other in his class.

The History Lesson, Part II (4:36–38). Moses begins to address the second pair of rhetorical questions from 4:33 and 4:34 by affirming that Yahweh is *both* in heaven—his true residence—*and* on earth in the very midst of the fire (cf. 4:11–15). In 4:37b–38 Moses addresses the fourth question, summarizing again Yahweh's great past and anticipated future acts on Israel's behalf.

Moses's declaration that Yahweh has chosen Israel and is acting on the nation's behalf "because he loved your ancestors" (4:37) introduces us for the first time to a key theological motif in Deuteronomy. This statement is revolutionary, since the notion of love is virtually absent from the vocabulary of divine-human relationships in the ancient Near East.

The Theology Lesson, Part II (4:39). Reiterating the statement of 4:35, Moses heightens the urgency and relevance of acknowledging Yahweh for the Israelites poised to cross the Jordan by adding "this day." What the people had witnessed at Sinai has enduring significance. The people may cross the Jordan confidently, knowing that though Yahweh is supreme in heaven, he is present with them on earth.

The Practical Lesson (4:40). Moses appeals to his people to obey the will of Yahweh for their own good and for the good of their descendants. If they will keep alive the memory of Yahweh's gracious actions, if their theology remains pure, and if their response is right, God's mission for them will be fulfilled.

Application. For Israel, God's saving actions involved the plagues of Egypt, through which he not only declared Israel to be his chosen people but also revealed to the watching world his glory and grace. But what he did for this nation of slaves is paradigmatic for what God has done for sinners, enslaved not to an evil earthly empire but to sin. In fact, in the death and resurrection of Christ, we witness a surpassing demonstration of power and glory by which he proves that he is indeed supreme over all. In 2 Peter 1:16–17, Peter gathers the motifs of story and power, divine majesty, honor, glory, and the voice of revelation from heaven on the sacred mountain. But in Christ, God's glory and grace are revealed even more dramatically.

DEUTERONOMY 4:41–43

Original Meaning. From a literary perspective, this short paragraph is a narrative epilogue to Moses's first address. By setting aside three towns of refuge east of the Jordan, Moses fulfilled part of Yahweh's instruction in Numbers 35:9–34 (cf. Josh 20). The narrator is content to record his actions and to offer a summary statement of the function of these towns. The principles underlying the towns of refuge accord with the humanitarian interests of the book of Deuteronomy as a whole.

Application. Whereas this provision presupposes that the Israelites will execute murderers, it recognizes the danger of potentially escalating cycles of revenge. It also recognizes that whenever one person accidentally or inadvertently causes another's death, there are actually two victims: the one whose physical life was taken and the one deprived of social life. This policy illustrates the need for all judicial systems to take into account the lives of potential secondary victims. Even as it grieves over accidental loss of life, a just society will guard against unwarranted violent responses to innocent acts.

DEUTERONOMY 4:44–5:5

Original Meaning

The Prologue to the Second Address (4:44–5:1a). Like the introduction to the first address, the prologue to the second describes the historical context of the speech. By itself, 4:45 seems to suggest that Moses delivered this address when the Israelites left Egypt. However, in 4:46 he clarifies the situation, linking the speech to the defeat of the Amorite kings and describing the geographical scope of those campaigns. In so doing he collapses the first forty years of Israel's history as a nation into one short statement.

The Context of the Revelation of Covenant Relationship (5:1b–5). The second address divides into two parts. The first (5:1b–11:32) is largely sermonic, while parts of the second (12:1–29:1[28:69]) are more formal, making more direct use of previously revealed prescriptions and concluding with covenant blessings and curses. However, throughout we hear the voice of Moses the pastor. In the first section we hear a pastoral exhortation to covenant faith, and in the second, more detailed pastoral application of covenant faith to life.

Chapters 5–11 subdivide into three parts, each of which begins with "Hear, [O] Israel" (5:1b; 6:4; 9:1). Homiletically, these three parts represent three constituents of authoritative preaching:

1. the Scripture lesson (5:1b–6:3), highlighting the foundations of covenant relationship;
2. the theology arising from the Scripture (6:4–8:20), focusing on the essence of covenant relationship;
3. the appropriate response arising from that theology (9:1–11:32), demonstrating love for Yahweh as evidence of covenant relationship.

Moses's purpose in 5:1b–5 is twofold: to challenge the present generation to seize hold of what their parents had rejected at Sinai and to highlight the importance of his teaching.

His message is the same as that revealed at Sinai, and he delivers it as the very message of God.

Verses 4–5 summarize the roles played by the respective parties when Yahweh made his covenant with Israel at Horeb. On the one hand, Yahweh spoke directly with the people from the midst of the fire (5:4). But on the other hand, Moses stood between Yahweh and the people to declare the divine word to them (5:5).

Application. It is possible for us today to hear the voice of God and still not hear the voice of God. The exodus generation heard Yahweh's voice clearly, but because of the hardness of their hearts, they rejected what they heard. Consequently, like the branches of a vine that refuses to bear fruit (John 15:6), they were cut off by the vinedresser and thrown into the fire. Those who abide in the vine bear the fruit of belief and covenant commitment (love) shown in obedience to the revealed will of God. This passage declares that if we reject the revelation of God, we reject God himself.

DEUTERONOMY 5:6–22

Original Meaning

The Historical Prologue (5:6). Behind this document lie the gracious actions of the divine superior, where obedience to God's will as outlined in the commands that follow represents a supreme act of worship, involving reverential human acts of submission and homage before the divine sovereign in response to his gracious revelation of himself.

The Covenant Stipulations (5:7–21). The terms of the covenant create a worldview intended to govern the relationship between the redeemed and their redeemer on the one hand, and among members of the community on the other. This document functions as an Israelite version of a bill of rights. However, unlike modern bills of rights, the document does not protect one's own rights but the rights of the next person.

The first principle of covenant relationship: Yahweh's right to exclusive allegiance (5:7–10). Israel is to have no other gods besides Yahweh. Verses 8–10 serve as commentary on 5:7. This first principle of covenant relationship (5:7–10) represents "the Supreme Command," which Moses has in mind whenever he uses the singular expression "the command" in connection with the plural forms "the decrees and laws" (5:31; 6:1; 7:11).

The second principle of covenant relationship: Yahweh's right to proper representation (5:11). A literal rendering of "You shall not misuse the name of the LORD your God" is "You shall not bear/carry the name of Yahweh your God emptily." The idiom derives from the ancient practice of branding slaves with the name of their owner. To bear the name of Yahweh means to claim him as one's owner and to accept the role of representing him (cf. Isa 44:5).

The third principle of covenant commitment: the right of all members of the household to humane treatment (5:12–15). Although the weekly Sabbath rest was designed to serve several functions, the Old Testament offers remarkably little information on how the Israelites were to keep and sanctify it. The pattern was in place before the Israelites got to Sinai: It was not part of the ritual system associated with tabernacle or temple worship but a fundamentally ethical ordinance.

The fourth principle of covenant relationship: parental right to respect (5:16). The motive clause links people's well-being with their disposition toward their parents. Well-being is a blessing granted by Yahweh in response to proper respect for one's parents.

The fifth principle of covenant relationship: the right to life (5:17). The command is rooted in the unique sanctity of human life that derives from our status as the image of God (Gen 9:6). To take the life of another person is to rob God of a representative and deputy, which is the highest form of treason. Unlike Babylonian laws, this command draws no distinctions in value of life based on status, race, or gender.

The sixth principle of covenant relationship: the right to fidelity in marriage (5:18). Like murder, adultery pollutes the land and ultimately causes it to spew out its inhabitants (Lev 18:20, 24–25). And like murder, adultery is not only a crime against one's spouse or children or parents; it is a crime against God (cf. Gen 39:9).

The seventh principle of covenant relationship: the right to own property (5:19). This is a categorical prohibition of all theft, particularly of items one is tempted to covet, as listed in the last principle (5:21b).

The eighth principle of covenant relationship: the right to an honest and fair hearing in court (5:20). The concern is testimony that does not move the case forward, that hedges the truth or that detracts from the pursuit of justice with misleading and trivial responses. The seriousness of false testimony is reflected by the call for the death penalty in 19:15–21.

The ninth principle of covenant relationship: the right to marital security (5:21a). Here Moses elevates the marital relationship above all other domestic relationships. Whereas the sixth command sought to ensure the purity of marriage, this ordinance seeks to ensure the security of the relationship.

The tenth principle of covenant relationship: the right to secure ownership of household property (5:21b). Having separated the wife from the rest of the household, Moses forbids Israelites from lusting after their neighbor's economic assets. The aim of these last two commands is to create a climate of trust and security within the covenant community.

The Transcriptional Epilogue (5:22). By reciting the Decalogue, Moses has laid the foundations for the rest of the second address. The transcription of the Decalogue on a pair of durable tablets of stone rather than perishable materials like parchment or papyrus reflects both its official nature and its permanent validity. Exodus 32:15 observed that the words of the Decalogue covered the stone slabs front and back, reinforcing the conclusion that Yahweh gave Moses two identical copies: one for the people and one for himself.

Application. The Decalogue is addressed to those who have been redeemed. The ten principles of covenant relationship were not revealed to the Egyptians or Canaanites but to the people of God chosen to represent him and proclaim his grace and glory among the nations. Impulses to post the Decalogue in public schools and courthouses are fundamentally misplaced. The problem with American society is not that people do not keep the Ten Commandments; it is that most have never left Egypt. It is unrealistic and unbiblical to expect those who have not been redeemed to live according to the principles and commitments of the redeemed. They have neither the motivation nor the indwelling Spirit to empower them do so.

DEUTERONOMY 5:23–6:3

Original Meaning

The People's Response to the Theophany at Horeb (5:23–27). Upon hearing the thunder of Yahweh's voice, a delegation consisting of all the leaders of the tribes and elders approached Moses. Yahweh's fiery presence has convinced them that he is indeed the living God, but they fear that the One who lives will take their life. To ward off the danger, the people request that Moses serve as mediator (5:27), and they promise from now on to listen to him and to treat the voice of Moses as if it were the voice of God.

Yahweh's Response to the People's Proposal (5:28–31). Yahweh acknowledged that he overheard the people's request to Moses (cf. 4:28) and affirmed their response. He also expressed his wish that the Israelites would never lose their present reverential disposition toward him. If they would demonstrate it by obedience to all his commands forever, then their well-being would be assured forever.

The Mediator's Exhortation (5:32–6:3). Moses speaks of Yahweh's commands as a road down which he has commanded his people to travel, and he warns them not to get sidetracked by turning off "to the right or to the left" (5:32). If they stay on course, they will reach the threefold goal of life, well-being, and length of days in the land they are to possess (cf. 28:1–14).

Moses's second charge (6:1–2) focuses on what Yahweh has commanded him to teach the people. As pastor-teacher, he opens his third charge (6:3) with an appeal to listen, followed by a call to "be careful to obey" by doing. Oozing with milk and honey, the promised land represented the antithesis to the desert, where for nearly forty years these people had had nothing to eat but manna.

Application. The proper human disposition before the glorious and gracious God remains fear, the deep sense of awe in his presence, which alone will produce acceptable liturgical response and the worship of daily obedience. Where there is no fear, there is no sense of obligation and no sense of gratitude that we have stood in the presence of God and lived to tell about it. Without fear, the privileged life of obedience is reduced to a burdensome duty.

DEUTERONOMY 6:4–9

Original Meaning

The Focus of Covenant Commitment (6:4). The Shema is one of the most important symbols of Judaism. To this day, orthodox Jews recite 6:4–5 twice daily as part of their prayers (cf. 6:7). Moses's concern is whether God's people would remain devoted exclusively to Yahweh or be seduced by the gods of Canaan. By uttering the Shema the Israelites were declaring their complete, undivided, and unqualified devotion to Yahweh. This is a cry of allegiance, an affirmation of covenant commitment that defines the boundaries of the covenant community.

The Locus of Covenant Commitment (6:5). Moses calls on the people to back up the verbal commitment expressed in 6:4 with wholehearted and full-bodied love. Calling all Israelites to love God without reservation or qualification, Moses begins with the inner being, then moves to the whole person, and ends with all that one claims as one's own. This is the yoke of the kingdom—covenant commitment rooted in the heart but extending to every level of one's being.

The Dimensions of Covenant Commitment (6:6–9). Moses emphasizes that this unreserved commitment is to permeate all of life. The commitment expressed in the Shema must be indelibly written on one's own inner being (6:6). This covenant commitment is to be a family matter, demonstrated by the indoctrination of children and the spontaneous discussion of the issue with the members of one's household (6:7). This commitment is to be a public matter. Moses continues his pattern of triadic expression by charging his people to bind these words on their hands, apply them as phylacteries on their foreheads (lit., "between their eyes"), and inscribe them on the doorposts of their buildings. The binding concretizes the declaration of allegiance and ownership by Yahweh as declared orally in the Shema.

Application. Moses taught his people and he teaches us and Christians everywhere that true spirituality arises from the heart and extends to all of life. Those who claim to be religious tend to be subject to two temptations: either to treat spirituality as primarily interior and private or to treat it as a matter of external performance. True love for God is rooted in the heart, but it is demonstrated in life, specifically a passion to speak of one's faith in the context of the family and to declare one's allegiance publicly to the world. This passage suggests that the very decoration of our homes should bear testimony to our faith, declaring to all guests and passers-by the fundamentally theological outlook of those who live within and serving as reminders to residents to live in dependence on God and to realize that blessing is contingent on obedience.

DEUTERONOMY 6:10–25

Original Meaning

The Nature of the Test (6:10–19). Moses sets the stage for the warning in 6:12 by describing the context in which the temptation to forget Yahweh will arise: when Yahweh has brought them to the land that he swore to their ancestors (6:10a), when they have eaten, and when they are full (end of 6:11). In 6:13–19 Moses describes how the Israelites should respond to prosperity. Whereas in the past Israel's loyalty to Yahweh had been tested by deprivation, in the future they will be tested by being "satisifed" (6:11). Crises of need tempt people to demand a response from Yahweh, but crises of prosperity tempt them to forget him and to become self-sufficient. In 6:18–19 Moses pleads for loyalty to Yahweh one more time.

The Response to the Test (6:20–25). Here we witness Moses at his pastoral best, instructing his congregation on the importance of passing the faith on to succeeding generations. This short paragraph consists of a child's question (6:20) and the adult's prescribed response (6:21–25). Moses assumes that when faced with the challenge of competing cultures, children will ask their parents for an explanation of their way of life. The question the child asks concerns the stipulations, decrees, and laws that Yahweh commanded Israel (cf. 4:45). Whether the question arises out of ignorance, curiosity, or cynicism, the child is in effect asking, "Why are we governed by this set of regulations?" In 6:24–25 Moses addresses the question raised in 6:20.

Application. With the wealth and excess we in the Western world enjoy, it is easy to forget that everything we have is a gracious gift of God. Sadly, too many of us fail the test of fidelity and faith that prosperity represents. We become like the rich farmer of Jesus's parable (Luke 12:14–21)—smug and self-sufficient in our excess but paupers toward God. Difficult days for a congregation test the faith of God's people, but so do times of growth and apparent effectiveness. When our buildings are large and our congregations huge, then more than ever we must guard ourselves so that our commitment extends beyond glib confessions of love for God, regurgitation of creedal affirmations, or emotional passion in cultic worship to the daily obedience of faith.

DEUTERONOMY 7:1–26

Original Meaning

The Nature of the Test (7:1–16). *The context of the test (7:1–2a).* Deuteronomy 7 opens with a series of temporal clauses that set the stage for the presentation of the test of Israel's love for Yahweh (7:2b). The policy is to be implemented when (1) Yahweh has brought the Israelites into the promised land, (2) he has cleared away the opposition, (3) he has delivered the Canaanites into the hands of the Israelites, and (4) the Israelites have defeated them. As in 6:10, the test of Israel's love for Yahweh will come when God's promises have been fulfilled.

The elements of the test (7:2b–5). The emphatic construction rendered "you must destroy them totally" (7:2b) signals the principal element of the test and reinforces the sacred nature of the agenda. The noun *herem* and its cognate verb *hrm* ("to commit to *herem*") combine military (3:6) and sacred nuances (13:15–17[16–18]). The root itself means "to consecrate" for divine service. In the remainder of 7:2b–5 Moses explains how this policy should work. The consequences of compromise on the issue described in the last clause of 6:4 reflects the seriousness of this policy: To adopt the lifestyle and the religious commitments of a Canaanite is to render oneself a Canaanite and thus provoke the ire of Yahweh.

Having specified prohibited actions and dispositions within Israel's *herem* policy, in 7:5 Moses outlines the actions the policy demands. At one level the demolition of sacred objects was intended to eradicate evidence of the pagan practices of the Canaanites within the land. However, at a deeper level, it represented a polemic against idolatry. The lesson for Israel should have been obvious: If idols cannot defend themselves, of what use are they to their worshipers?

The basis of the test (7:6–8). Moses's discussion of Israel's version of the *herem* policy reaches a climax in 7:6–8, where he specifies its grounds. Moses reflects on Israel's awesome privilege as Yahweh's covenant partner. Moses contemplates the question, "Why does God love Israel?" He does not actually answer the question, except to suggest that God loves Israel because God loves Israel. Driven by fidelity to his promise to the forefathers and his covenant commitment to their descendants, through a miraculous act of grace, Yahweh secured Israel's freedom and called this nation from the kingdom of darkness into the kingdom of his marvelous light (cf. 1 Pet 2:9).

The importance of the test (7:9–15). Thematically, 7:11–12 function as the fulcrum of this passage: Moses renews his charge to the people to keep the Supreme Command (cf. 5:31; 6:1) and the detailed stipulations of the covenant that he is issuing. According to the logic of this paragraph, knowledge of the character of Yahweh and his fidelity to the covenant, whose terms include both blessings and curses (7:9–10), is the precondition to scrupulous conformity to his will (7:11). At the same time, scrupulous conformity to Yahweh's will (7:12a) is the precondition to experiencing the blessings rather than the curses (7:12b–13a).

In 7:12b–16 Moses elaborates on the blessings promised to those who respond to grace with obedience. Moses tries to motivate fidelity with three promises, each expressed with a single word. If the Israelites will be faithful, Yahweh will demonstrate his covenant commitment (NIV "love," 7:12b, 13) to them, bless them, and multiply them. Whereas the size of Israel's population had nothing to do with their election (7:7), in the future an increase in their numbers will be their reward for obedience.

The concluding call for obedience (7:16). Verse 16 is transitional, bringing the preceding conversation to a conclusion with a plea for decisive action against the Canaanites and setting the stage for the response expressed in 7:17.

The Response to the External Test of Covenant Commitment (7:17–26). *The question (7:17).* We may readily imagine that as Moses lays the challenge of 7:1–16 before the people, he picks up nonverbal signals of incredulity or despair from some in the crowd. His hypothetical interlocutor raises a problem: the obvious numerical superiority of the nations the Israelites are about to face. Speaking for all Israel in first person, he asks, "How can I dispossess them?" (author's translation).

Moses's answer (7:18–26). Moses's response divides into a promise (7:18–24) and a warning (7:25–26). In 7:18b–20 Moses encourages his audience with two principal points: Remember what Yahweh has done for you in the past (7:18b–19) and recognize that Yahweh is with you in the present (7:20). His point is that if Yahweh was able to rescue them from the Egyptians, then these petty kingdoms, which have for some time been subject states to the pharaohs, are nothing at all to him.

In 7:22–24 Moses explains how this awesome God will pursue his campaign of conquest. As the supreme commander of Israel's forces and the Divine Warrior who fights for them, his strategy is clear: He will clear away the nations of Canaan before the Israelites (7:22); he will hand them over to the Israelites (7:23); he will throw them into great confusion until they are destroyed (7:23; cf. 7:2); and he will deliver the kings of Canaan into the Israelites' hands (7:24). With these promises, Moses challenges his people to trust in Yahweh. This is his war, not theirs. His awesome presence will create pandemonium among the enemies' forces, and he will deliver their leaders into Israel's hands.

Shifting from promise to warning in 7:25–26, Moses's mood changes significantly. Borrowing a verb from the ninth command, he warns against "coveting" the silver and gold used in the manufacture of images. He hereby forecloses the temptation to rationalize salvaging and recycling the precious metals when carrying out the policy of *herem* against enemy establishments.

The Hebrew word *toebah* ("abomination"; NIV "detestable") in 7:25 and 7:26 serves as Moses's favorite expression for the abhorrent nature of idolatry. In 7:26 he identifies the root of the problem. Idolatry is not only seductive ("a snare") and an abomination to Yahweh; the "abomination" is contagious.

Application. For the everyday struggles with sin and the pressures posed by the kingdom of darkness, Deuteronomy 7:17–24 is particularly relevant. This paragraph presents three indispensable keys to a victorious Christian life.

1. Recognize God's past grace in salvation.
2. Recognize his power in the present.
3. Recognize our own responsibility to engage the enemy by keeping ourselves unspotted from the world.

DEUTERONOMY 8:1–20

Original Meaning

The Nature of the Internal Test (8:1–10). *The context of the test (8:1).* Moses begins by reminding his audience of Yahweh's ancient goal for Israel: life and prosperity in the land that he had sworn to give to their descendants.

The desert experience as a paradigm for the future test (8:2–5). This paragraph forms a self-contained unit framed by the appeal to remember in 8:2 and the appeal to draw the right theological conclusions in 8:5. Moses declares that Yahweh's relationship to Israel is like that of a father to a son. Yahweh's fatherly disciplinary action is always administered in love for the good of his people. This is the lesson the present generation must take with them as they cross the Jordan into the promised land.

The nature of the future test (8:6–9). How will the Israelites respond to prosperity and excess? Moses's literary style rises to a new semi-poetic register as he describes the Edenic world that awaits his people beyond the Jordan. This "Ode to the Promised Land" breaks down into five stanzas, each introduced by the word "land" and each lauding the land for a particular contribution it will make to Israel's well-being.

The correct response to the future test (8:10). It was one thing for the previous generation to lean on Yahweh in the desert when they were directly dependent on God for food, but for this and future generations the test will be the opposite. In response to the gift of the land and the food it produces, the people were to acknowledge Yahweh.

The Response to the Internal Test (8:11–20). *The wrong response to the test (8:11–17).* Having described the nature of the internal test and the correct response, Moses goes on to describe the wrong response (8:11–17). The threat envisioned is not the Canaanite nations but the Israelites themselves. The potential problem emerges in 8:14: Instead of blessing Yahweh, the Israelites' hearts will be tempted with pride. Moses clarifies what he means in 8:17: This is a disposition that causes people to take credit for all their successes and to think that their wealth is the result of their own efforts. Verses 14b–16 highlight the tragedy of this response to the test by reviewing the kindnesses Yahweh has lavished on Israel.

The correct response to the future test (8:18). In contrast to the wrong response to the test (8:11–17), Moses now provides three elements of the correct response.

1. When the Israelites prosper in the land, they must "remember the Lord."
2. Even if the Israelites prosper through hard work, they must recognize that the skill and energy needed to do that work is a gift from Yahweh.
3. They must remember that Yahweh gives strength not primarily for their prosperity but to confirm his covenant with the ancestors.

The final warning (8:19–20). Moses ends this topic with a final frightful warning. If the Israelites go after other gods, they will surely perish like the nations whom Yahweh destroyed before them. The final clause reminds Moses's hearers of the reason for their horrible fate: They refused to listen to the voice of God.

Application. The first stage on the road to idolatry is ingratitude. Moses reminds his audience and us that the only appropriate response to eating of the bounty that God provides is to bless Yahweh. But this chapter exhibits a downward spiral, in which forgetting Yahweh (8:2, 11) leads to ingratitude (8:12–16), which leads to self-sufficiency (8:17), which leads to idolatry (8:19). Paul plots a similar course in Romans 1:21–23.

DEUTERONOMY 9:1–24

Original Meaning

The Nature of the False Claim (9:1–6). *Introduction (9:1–3).* The challenge facing this generation is no different than it had been thirty-eight years earlier. The quotation in 9:3 has a proverbial ring. This reminder of the enemies' apparent invincibility sets the stage for Moses's confident declaration in 9:3. Whereas in 4:24 the reference to the fiery passion of Yahweh was intended to motivate Israelite fidelity and warn against worshiping other gods, here Moses promises that the same fury will be turned against the enemy.

The hypothesis (9:4a). In 9:4a Moses introduces a hypothetical speaker who imagines himself to be virtuous, but the word speaks of smug self-righteousness and inflated self-esteem.

Moses's counter-thesis (9:4b–6). Moses weaves his counter-thesis. Far from claiming "righteousness" (9:4b) as their characteristic attribute, the Israelites are fundamentally "a stiff-necked people" (9:6). This idiom is based on the image of draft animals, especially yoked oxen, whose locus of power is perceived to be in the neck but who often refuse to work as their master directs.

The Refutation of the Claim (9:7–24). Moses identifies Horeb as a symbol of Israel's true character (9:8–11). This was the mountain where the Israelites were formally received as Yahweh's covenant partners. This was also the place where they had demonstrated their true colors. While Moses was on the mountain on official business on behalf of the people, they searched for a replacement for him (Exod 32:1). In his recollection Moses highlights the transformation in the symbolism of Horeb from a place of grace and glory, of revelation and response, of covenant and promise, to a place of human rebellion and divine fury.

After announcing Israel's rebellion and providing background information, Moses shifts attention to Yahweh's response (9:12–14). Yahweh's determination to "blot out their name from under heaven" (9:14) is shocking. If Moses's presentation of Yahweh's fury is stronger than in the earlier narrative, the same is true of the honor Yahweh promised him (9:14b). Whereas Exodus 32:10 had simply echoed God's general promise to make Abraham a great nation, Moses remembers it as a promise to make of him into a nation stronger and more numerous than the Canaanites.

Moses's reaction to Israel's rebellion (9:15–21). Moses's report of his own actions consists of four summary parts.

1. He smashed the tablets (9:15–17).
2. He interceded before Yahweh (9:18–19).
3. He interceded for his brother Aaron (9:20).
4. He disposed of the calf (9:21).

Moses's smashing of the tablets (9:15–17). These actions were both legal and symbolic, analogous to the Mesopotamian custom of breaking tablets on which contracts were written when the agreement had been violated. By smashing the tablets Moses declared the covenant null and void even before the people had a chance to see the divinely produced written documentation.

Moses's intercession for the people (9:18–19). Moses the statesman becomes Moses the prophetic intercessor par excellence. The definite article on the word for "sin" (9:18) suggests a specific crime, in this case and generally elsewhere, the violation of the first commandment. Moses feared that Yahweh would destroy his people. The relief in his voice is still evident thirty-eight years later when he adds, "But again the LORD listened to me" (9:19).

Moses's intercession for Aaron (9:20). Through Moses's intercession, Yahweh's threat on Aaron's life was also lifted. Nonetheless, for his involvement in this event, Aaron was barred from entrance into the promised land.

Moses's disposal of the golden calf (9:21). Moses concludes this phase of his report of the rebellion at Horeb by describing how he disposed of the calf itself.

The postscript (9:22–24). Moses summarizes in a sentence what he had described in great detail in 1:26–43. Here the Israelites' refusal to enter the land from Kadesh Barnea was paradigmatic of their rebellion, unbelief, and disobedience (cf. 1:26, 32). Moses concludes with one final sweeping generalization: They have been in revolt against Yahweh from the day he was first introduced to them. Although this is obviously rhetorical hyperbole, the history of sour relations between the people, on the one hand, and Yahweh and Moses, on the other, can be traced as far back as Exodus 5:20–23.

Application. The call to relationship with God is never based on merit. Moses demonstrates that the Israelites had been undeserving of the mission to which God had called them; if they had been rescued from Egypt and would be handed the promised land as their grant, these were privileges granted by grace alone. With respect to the call to salvation, human righteousness counts for nothing with God. Indeed, apart from God's grace we are all Canaanites.

DEUTERONOMY 9:25–10:11

Original Meaning

The Nature of Moses's Plea (9:25–29). With the vocative opening to the prayer, Moses uses the personal name of God and acknowledges his own vassal status. Moses immediately launches into his demands.

1. "Do not destroy your people" (9:26).
2. "Remember your servants Abraham, Isaac and Jacob" (9:27a).
3. "Overlook the stubbornness of this people, their wickedness and their sin" (9:27b).

Moses's third demand was the most dramatic (9:27). Neither excusing his people nor minimizing their crime, Moses daringly warned Yahweh that if he destroyed the Israelites, the nations would conclude that either he was unable to carry through on his mission of bringing them to the land or that he had intentionally brought them in the desert to slaughter them. Moses therefore argued that Yahweh's own reputation was at stake; he could not afford to destroy his people. Moses concluded his prayer with a positive foundation for this appeal. Repeating his opening statements, he declared that Israel was Yahweh's people; they were his personal possession and saving them was to his advantage.

The Lord's Response to the Plea for Renewal of Favor (10:1–11). *Yahweh's reaffirmation of the Israelite covenant (10:1–5).* Yahweh's commands were simple.

1. Moses was to cut out two tablets of stone to function like the original tablets.
2. Moses was to make an ark and put these new tablets into it. This was not the permanent ark of the covenant later placed in the Most Holy Place of the tabernacle. That ark had not yet been made, and in any case, it was crafted by the divinely endowed craftsman Bezalel (Exod 35:30–36:1).

Moses reports the outcome of Yahweh's instructions in 10:3–5. In keeping with ancient Near Eastern custom, by placing the tablets of the covenant in the ark and later depositing it before Yahweh in the Most Holy Place, Yahweh was invoked as a witness to and guarantor of the covenant.

Introduction of the custodians of the covenant (10:6–9). Moses's report is interrupted briefly by a geographical comment (10:6–7) and an explanation for the Levites' current role. The Levitical priests were responsible for maintaining the relationship between the two parties to the covenant. Whereas the rest of the tribes of Israel would receive real estate, Yahweh promised himself as their grant.

Moses's narrative epilogue (10:10–11). When Moses's own voice returns in 10:10–11, he resumes the main subject at hand: Yahweh's reaffirmation of his covenant with Israel. Yahweh responded as he had done previously (cf. 9:19) and withdrew his threat to destroy his people. The reminder of the promise of land to the ancestors provides concrete proof that the covenant relationship was fully restored.

Application. Lest we be seduced into thinking that prayer is simply a formula by which we manipulate God to get anything we want, it is important to emphasize that in this case, Moses actually sacrificed his own self-interest in the interests of his people. Furthermore, in his forty-day wrestling bout with God, his single interest was the will and reputation of God, which he was convinced would be best served by sparing the people who had rebelled against him rather than starting over with Moses. When wicked people turn from their sin in full repentance (Jonah 3) or when a righteous intercessor pleads with God on behalf of sinners, God's fury is turned back and his grace is extended to undeserving people. This is one more exhilarating dimension of the gospel according to Moses.

DEUTERONOMY 10:12–11:1

Original Meaning. *The issue raised (10:12a).* Moses begins his reflection on the practical implications of the covenant with a question. The result is a glorious theology of covenant relationship built on three pillars of cosmic theology and grounded on three marvelous acts of grace.

Moses's first answer (10:12b–15). Moses's first response consists of five infinitive phrases, all of which have been heard before and will be heard repeatedly hereafter. This combination captures in a nutshell the message of this book, especially as it relates to the human response to divine grace. Fear is primary and love (covenant commitment) is at the core. Without these, the actions are legalistic efforts to gain the favor of God. Without the actions, fear and love are useless and dead.

Moses signals the shift to the grounds for these demands in 10:14. Whatever cosmic entity one may imagine to exist, it all belongs to Yahweh, the God of Israel. But Yahweh is also sovereign over the earth and all it contains, human beings as well as animals large and small. Although Yahweh owns everything in the universe, he chose Israel's ancestors to be the object of his affection and love and to be his covenant people.

Moses's second answer to the question (10:16–19). Moses's charge in 10:16 consists of two commands: Circumcise the foreskin of your hearts and stop stiffening your necks. He does not explain at this point what he means by "circumcise your hearts" (10:16), except to contrast it with "stiff-necked" in the second command. Moses suggests that a circumcised heart/mind represents a disposition that is soft and sensitive toward Yahweh and has ceased resisting his will. In 10:17–18 Moses grounds the demand for spiritual circumcision on Yahweh's supremacy over all powers. Moses combines these transcendent attributes of Yahweh with four verbal declarations of his immanence.

Moses's third answer to the question (10:20–22). Moses begins his presentation of the grounds for this demand with a third doxology (10:21). In 10:21b Moses explains how Yahweh has manifested himself in Israel through "great and awesome" demonstrations of power. What has happened to Jacob's descendants can only be attributed to a marvelous work of Yahweh.

The issue concluded (11:1). Moses reduces the divine requirement to two simple statements, the first of which abbreviates the Supreme Command (6:5), and the second reiterates the call for obedience to the revealed will of God in its entirety.

Application. The principal question God's people should always be asking is: "What does the Lord ask of us?" Like Israel, we often forget that unless we are walking in the ways of the Lord during the rest of the week, nothing we do in corporate liturgical worship on Sunday or any other day will impress God. This text reminds us again that walking in the ways of the Lord, accepting our vassal status before him, and obeying his commands are the fruit he seeks as evidence of reverent awe and covenant commitment (love) to him. Mouthing words of devotion ring hollow without the life of devotion.

DEUTERONOMY 11:2–28

Original Meaning

A Lesson from History: Reviewing the Mighty Acts of God (11: 2–7). Moses opens with a thesis statement: "Know today the lesson of Yahweh your God" (author's paraphrase). The subject of study is Yahweh's actions, but through those mighty acts the Israelites learn about him. The actual lesson divides into two parts: three simple pointers to Yahweh's person (11:2b) and a series of manifestations of Yahweh's power (11:3–6). With the final note, "how the LORD brought lasting ruin on them" (11:4), Moses acknowledges the results of a momentous event: Israel is standing on the threshold of the promised land.

Moses's ends his recitation of Yahweh's powerful acts with a reminder that the people in his audience were eyewitnesses to the events he has just described (11:7). Awareness of how fearful it is to fall into the hands of the living God (Heb 10:31) should provide lasting motivation for uncompromising covenant fidelity and a constant reminder that the benefits of covenant relationship with Yahweh should never be taken for granted (11:8–25).

A Lesson from Economic Geography: Recognizing the Gracious Provision of God (11:8–28). *Part I: The land as gift (11:8–12).* Moses opens his discussion of the place of the land in Israel's relationship with Yahweh with a charge to keep the Supreme Command in all its dimensions. By following this command with two purpose clauses, he presents it as a virtual condition for the fulfillment of the promise that follows (11:8b–9). Each purpose statement ends with a comment on the land.

Moses's excitement at Israel's prospect of entering the land (11:9b–12) is evident in his excursus extolling its virtues. With this speech Moses tries to excite his people about the prospects awaiting them on the other side of the Jordan. Moses envisions the promised land through the eyes of faith. In 11:12 Moses adds a fourth reason why the land is special: It is the object of Yahweh's special attention and care.

Part II: The land as test (11:13–21). Moses presents life in the land as a test with significant consequences. The land symbolizes a choice between two ways: the way of blessing, prosperity, and life or the way of the curse, adversity, and death. Moses begins by defining the passing grade, the correct response to the test (11:13–15). His injunctions are not for the distant future but are to be applied immediately. By speaking with Yahweh's voice in 11:14–15, Moses draws attention to the following statements as both *divine* promise and *divine* evaluation of their response to the test.

In 11:16–17 Moses declares that open-mindedness toward the worship of gods other than Yahweh is fatal. If the people fix their devotion elsewhere instead of being the objects of Yahweh's favor, he will unleash his fury against them. Consequently, the Israelites will perish quickly from the good land that they had received as a gift.

Verses 18–21 hold the key to the future relationship of deity, people, and land. In order to ensure that God's design for Israel will be realized, the people must commit themselves wholeheartedly to him and his covenant. Yahweh's desire is to see their population explode as the lifespan of each generation increases on the land that he had promised the ancestors.

Part III: The land as promise (11:22–25). Having offered the land as a test in 11:18–21 and concluded with a glorious word of promise, in 11:22 Moses yanks his audience back to reality with a third expression of conditionality. Using strong military language, 11:23–25 spells out the rewards for having met these conditions: Yahweh will dispossess all the Canaanite nations in advance of the Israelites (11:23a), and Israel will "possess" nations stronger and mightier than they are.

Part IV: The land as opportunity (11:26–28). As pastor, Moses concludes this part of the sermon with a climactic appeal for decision; he is handing them the options of "blessing" and "curse." Moses summarizes the conditions determining which of these the Israelites will experience in 11:27 and 11:28. With his call to decision in 11:26–32, Moses challenges the new generation to respond with greater fidelity than their parents had done. Their future in the land depends on it.

Application. For those who claim to be God's people, every day is a day of decision. Our commitment to Yahweh must not only be renewed at significant junctures in our lives, but daily. The blessings associated with the covenant are not to be taken for granted or viewed as automatic rights. The covenant established by Christ involves a special relationship, which demands constant investment of energy and devotion. The options open to the Israelites—blessing and curse—are open to us, but how we experience them depends on our covenant commitment to Christ, demonstrated by active obedience.

DEUTERONOMY 11:29–32

Original Meaning. Moses's attention shifts from the present covenant renewal ceremony to an anticipated event on the other side of the Jordan. Moses's description of the ceremony is sketchy, consisting of only nine words in the Hebrew (11:29b). Having identified Mounts Gerizim and Ebal as the place for the ceremony, by means of a complex rhetorical question Moses offers a convoluted description of the location.

In 11:31 Moses confidently announces the end of the journey for his people. They are about to cross the Jordan to receive their gift of land from Yahweh. Moses concludes the first section of his second address (5:1b–11:32) with another appeal for the Israelites "today." There is no point in dreaming about the future if they do not commit themselves *now* to full obedience to the decrees and laws that he is giving them.

Application. This passage reminds us that God is faithful; he always keeps his promises. Just as he had held the land of the Canaanites in reserve for his people as their special grant and inheritance, so he holds in reserve for those who believe in Jesus the Christ an eternal heavenly grant (Eph 1:3–14). Our possession is not an earthly allotment but a spiritual reality; we have been redeemed and have been given the Holy Spirit as a pledge of our inheritance to the praise of his glory. Like every other benefit, this is an unmerited and undeserved gift from God.

DEUTERONOMY 12:1–14

Original Meaning

The First Invitation to Celebrate in the Presence of Yahweh (12:2–7). Moses's discourse on the decrees and laws begins with instructions on Israel's vertical relationship with Yahweh. This first version of the invitation anticipates two phases of application: purging the land of any vestiges of Canaanite idolatry (12:2–3) and replacing these pagan practices with those approved by Yahweh (12:5–7).

Moses's charge to clear the land of Canaanite worship consists of three parts: an emphatic general command to destroy all pagan cult centers (12:2), a specific command to destroy all cult paraphernalia (12:3a–d), and a sweeping command to eliminate all the claims that Canaanite deities might have to the land (12:3e). Moses concludes with a simple but direct command not to behave like the people whom the Israelites will displace (12:4). Moses follows this general proscription with a positive alternative in 12:5–7, a remarkably gracious invitation to a more personal relationship with Yahweh their God.

Verse 5 contains the first of twenty-one occurrences of "the place formula" in Deuteronomy. The formula occurs in a variety of forms. It is a place that Yahweh will *choose*. The place will be chosen "from among all your [pl.] tribes," referring to the territorial tribal allotments predicted in Numbers 34 and fulfilled by Joshua in Joshua 14–19. The place will have Yahweh's name on it. The phrase indicates divine ownership. The place will be the goal of Israel's pilgrimages.

Verses 6–7 declare the purpose of Yahweh's invitation by explaining what is to happen at the place Yahweh establishes. Moses invites the Israelites to bring all their sacrificial gifts to the place. He invites the Israelites to eat in the presence of Yahweh their God. In the ancient world, eating together was an act of fellowship and communion, often the culmination of a covenant-making ritual. Moses views worship as the joyful and celebrative response of everyone in the community to Yahweh's invitation to his presence.

The Second Invitation to Celebrate in the Presence of Yahweh (12:8–12). This paragraph clarifies the key issue raised in 12:2–7: the centralizing of national worship, beginning with an appeal to stop current problematic practices (12:8–9). The motive clause in 12:9 recognizes that Israel is still in a transitional historical stage. Only when they have come to their "resting place" and the "inheritance" of land Yahweh has reserved for them will the ideal of exclusive devotion to Yahweh be matched by exclusive worship at a central shrine (12:9). In 12:10 he establishes the context for Yahweh's revelation of the place he has chosen for his name.

A Concluding Exhortation (12:13–14). Moses concludes the present instructions on worship with a warning not to make decisions regarding worship practices on the basis of personal preferences and a specific charge to offer their sacrifices only at the place that Yahweh chooses. He reiterates that Israelites are to worship Yahweh only at the place he will choose within one of the tribal allotments.

Application. Deuteronomy 12:1–14 offers a profound theology of worship. Worship must be designed to please the object of worship, not the worshipers. If Moses had to call a stop to the Israelites of his day worshiping in any way they pleased (12:8), the same is true today. In the end, the divine verdict on our worship is the only verdict that matters. Contrary to some, ultimately acceptable forms and styles of worship are not determined by worshipers, let alone the unregenerate or marginally spiritual.

DEUTERONOMY 12:15–28

Original Meaning

Moses's Instructions on Profane Slaughter (12:15–16, 20–25). In these passages Moses expresses his positive disposition toward profane slaughter. Verse 15 specifies the context as "in your gates" (lit.), a figure of speech for "your towns" (NIV), within the allotted tribal territories where the Israelites reside (cf. 12:12). Moses's own clarification in 12:20–21 confirms this interpretation: eating profaned slaughter will be approved when Yahweh has fulfilled his promise and enlarged the individual's territory, and the person lives far from the place "where the LORD your God chooses to put his Name."

Moses highlights the craving for meat with the threefold repetition of "in all the desire of your soul/person" (author's translation of 12:15, 20b, 21b) and casting it in direct speech, "I would like some meat" (12:20a). Moses responds to this craving by opening wide the door to "profane" consumption. Having opened the door to the consumption of meat of domestic animals away from the central sanctuary does not mean that Israelites can treat these animals callously or that this slaughter could be considered amoral or secular. Verses 16 and 23 specify that when they kill an animal, the blood must not be consumed but poured out on the ground like water. Because life is sacred and the blood is identified with the life, consuming blood is viewed as an attack on life itself. Although the blood of an animal slaughtered for its meat did not require satisfaction, in a sense all slaughter is sacrificial and substitutionary: a life for a life.

Moses's Instructions on Sacred Offerings (12:17–19, 26–27). In 12:17–19 Moses reminds his people of the other side of this coin. Permission to slaughter domestic animals in all their towns whenever they crave meat does not mean that all livestock are candidates for profane consumption. Animals and produce of the field that have been set apart as sacred offerings may be consumed only in the presence of Yahweh at the place he chooses.

Moses follows up the command to eat these products as sacrificial meals at the central sanctuary by specifying who may participate in these events (12:18a). Verse 18 concludes with another invitation to celebrate before Yahweh with all the products of the Israelites' labor. Almost as an afterthought, Moses ends with a stern warning not to neglect the Levite as long as the Israelites live on the earth (12:19).

Verses 26–27 follow Moses's more detailed instructions on profane slaughter (12:20–25). Once again he restricts the meals authorized for consumption in the towns by excluding sacred offerings. For these offerings the Israelites should go to the place Yahweh chooses. With burnt offerings the flesh and blood are consumed entirely by fire on the altar; with the rest, the meat is consumed by worshipers and the blood is poured out on the altar.

Conclusion (12:28). Forever the pastor, Moses concludes his instructions regarding the central sanctuary and profane slaughter with a final exhortation to pay careful attention to all that he has said. Heeding his instructions is the precondition for the well-being of the present generation and their descendants in perpetuity.

Application. Even as this passage encourages us to enjoy the provision of God, it does so with a profound ethical sensitivity. The slaughter of animals for meat could easily degenerate into savagery and a ruthless disregard for the life of the animal. However, the ritual of draining the blood reminds the persons who slaughtered the animal and those who eat its meat that even the life of the creature is sacred. While the flesh is sanctioned for human consumption, life itself is inviolable, and God remains the guarantor of the sanctity of the life of the animal.

DEUTERONOMY 12:29–13:18

Original Meaning

The General Warning against Spiritual Defection (12:29–32). Once again, the test of Israel's faith will come when they are enjoying the fulfillment of the promise to Abraham. Moses cautions the people against fascination with the gods of the nations in Canaan. He identifies the most despicable offense; they even offer their children as burnt offerings to their gods.

The Specific Warnings against Spiritual Defection (13:1–18). *Apostasy instigated by a prophet or an oneiromantic (13:1–5).* False prophets represent the first potential source of spiritual sedition. The second, oneiromancy (divination through dreams), was widespread in the ancient world. Moses anticipates that prophets and dreamers who call for defection to other gods will try to prove their authenticity with an attesting "sign or wonder" (13:2a). Moses recognizes that false prophets are sometimes able to work wonders (Exod 7:11, 22; 8:7[3]).

In 13:3–5 Moses explicitly charges the Israelites to refuse to give prophets or dreamers who incite spiritual sedition an ear (13:3–4). Whatever the origin or source of a temptation to abandon Yahweh, such occasions always constitute a test of love for him. Moses instructs the people on how to treat a prophet or dreamer who incites sedition (13:5a). The sin of sedition is like a virus whose influence can only be stopped by exterminating those infected with it.

Apostasy instigated by a member of the family (13:6–11). The second seditious scenario involves treachery at home. To highlight the potential problem Moses lists five close acquaintances who might incite defection away from Yahweh. Viewed as a whole, this list imagines those who are closest as potential conspirators intent on leading the family and the community away from the worship of Yahweh.

To modern readers the demand to execute the conspirator in 13:9–10a seems ruthless and heartless. But allegiance to Yahweh must take precedence over family ties. Because Israel's identity was bound up with her covenant relationship with him, defection was a capital offense. By stoning the criminal, the executioners avoided direct contact with objects contaminated by holiness/unholiness.

As Israel's pastor, in 13:10b Moses returns to his principle concern: guarding the relationship between Yahweh and his people. The close relative or neighbor is to be executed because he tried to lure a person away from Yahweh his God. All Israelites have a vested interest in taking drastic measures, even against close relatives or neighbors. Fear of a similar fate should deter anyone else who might be tempted to promote spiritual sedition.

Apostasy instigated by anyone else in Israel (13:12–18). The third scenario is the most serious—defection of an entire town. Because this scenario envisages rumors of spiritual sedition rather than direct contact with those who lead in the defection from Yahweh, instead of immediately calling for the death penalty, Moses demands careful investigation (13:14a). Once it is established that the rumors are true, Moses calls for the indiscriminate slaughter of all living things in the town (13:15). The inanimate material found in the renegade town is to be totally burned up as a sacrifice (13:16). The tone reflects the seriousness with which Yahweh looks on spiritual defection. The only way to placate his burning wrath and to renew his compassion is to offer up an entire town to Yahweh as a whole burnt offering.

Application. Yahweh had called Israel to a position of praise and fame and honor above all the nations, but if they follow the gods of the nations, they will lose their identity in the mass of humankind and attract the fury of their own God. This chapter reminds Christians today that commitment to Yahweh is not only a national affair; it must also be rigorously pursued at the personal, family, and community level.

DEUTERONOMY 14:1–21

Original Meaning

The Guests at Yahweh's Table (14:1–3). Without 14:1–3 the dietary regulations in 14:4–20 are external laws imposed by a suzerain upon a vassal (cf. 5:6). The introduction changes everything. By opening this unit with "Sons you are to Yahweh your God" (14:1, author's translation), Moses announces that whatever follows reflects Israel's acceptance of this privileged status.

The Fare at Yahweh's Table (14:4–20). Because Israelites are the holy people of Yahweh, the meat in their diet must be like the food that God "eats" in the sacrifices offered to him. Through everyday observance of the dietary boundaries, Israelites declared to one another and to outsiders their unique proximity to Yahweh. In the end we admit that the Old Testament never spells out the reasons for the boundaries. They may seem arbitrary to modern readers, but they are simply to be accepted because they represent the will of the divine Lord.

We might have expected the opening statement in 14:4 to be followed by principles by which kosher animals could be identified. Instead, Moses lists ten animals permitted as food (14:4b–5). Having listed clean animals, Moses explains that permissible meat may come only from animals with split hooves that chew the cud (14:6). The most detailed listing of animals involves aerial creatures. Moses concludes with a brief reference to "insects" (14:19).

A Final Reminder for Those Who Eat at Yahweh's Table (14:21). In the epilogue (19:21) Moses returns to the fundamental issue that has occupied his mind since the beginning of this chapter: Israel's status as Yahweh's holy people. Yahweh's covenant people must avoid meat from animals that have died a natural death. The prohibition is probably connected with the need to drain the blood of animals before eating it.

The proscription on boiling a kid in its mother's milk remains a riddle. Its association with the annual pilgrimage festivals suggests it may allude to fertility rites performed in honor of a Canaanite deity.

Application. The significance of the dietary regulations for Christians is probably best understood as a corollary of Israel's sacrificial system. If indeed Deuteronomy 14 involves Yahweh's invitation to eat of the food in which he himself takes delight in the form of sacrifices (12:5–14), then with the termination of all sacrifices in Christ, these food regulations also become passé. Since we no longer present these offerings to God but celebrate the sacrificial work of Jesus Christ, whenever we partake of the bread and the wine of communion, we participate in the feast to which the Lord has graciously invited us.

DEUTERONOMY 14:22–29

Original Meaning

The Annual Tithe Festival (14:22–26). Although this paragraph begins with an emphatic command to set aside annually one tenth of all that the fields produce (14:22), the remainder reads more like an invitation to a celebration than a cultic ordinance. Moses declares the purpose of the banquet: that the Israelites may learn to revere Yahweh. It is not the eating that teaches people to fear Yahweh, but eating in the presence of Yahweh. Thus, the presentation of the tithe provided a means by which the settled people could participate annually in the kind of event that the elders of Israel had experienced on Horeb (4:10; Exod 24:9–11). Reverent awe and gratitude were to characterize the people of Yahweh.

To Moses the tithal meal was obviously not intended as a burdensome legal or ceremonial requirement. It was to be welcomed as an occasion for eating and celebrating in the presence of Yahweh their God. For this reason, he makes it easy for all citizens to participate and redundantly invites not only the heads of families but entire households to eat anything that their hearts desire at the festival. Remarkably, the text omits any reference to the most common foods (cf. 14:23). Apparently, meat was always desirable fare for a banquet.

The Triennial Tithe Festival (14:27–29). Concerned about the Levites' general economic well-being throughout the year, in 14:28–29 Moses calls for a third-year tithe. In the third and sixth years the farmers must deposit their tithes in their towns. Here they can be stored and distributed to the Levites. Moses expands the economic safety net to the alien, the fatherless, and the widow. These should all be invited to the gates to receive food they can take home and eat until they are satisfied.

Application. It seems that when we ask, "Do Christians need to tithe?" we have asked the wrong question. At issue is not the institution but the heart and mind of God, which are to be reflected in the hearts and minds of his people. This passage is about providing another occasion to celebrate in the presence of God and to encourage generosity. Consequently, we should rephrase the question this way: How might Christians demonstrate the compassion that the institution of the tithe tries to foster? This gets us off the externals and focuses on the primary issue: soft hearts and open hands.

DEUTERONOMY 15:1–18

Original Meaning

Showing Kindness to the Poor (15:1–11). *The year for canceling debts (15:1–5).* In general terms Moses calls on creditors to release their claims on debtors. The Hebrew expression reflects the ancient custom of leaving property with a creditor as collateral and a guarantee that one intends to repay the loan. By this understanding the present statement does not mean the absolute cancellation of all debts, nor even the suspension of payments during the sabbatical year, but the return of all properties that a creditor is holding against loans by those indebted to him.

Instructions on how to treat the poor (15:7–8). In 15:7–11 Moses appeals to Israel's sense of family. He is not interested in the personal sin that might underlie the poor person's indebtedness but the propensity of the rich to sin against their poor brothers (15:9). Israelites are to be softhearted and openhanded.

Warnings against hardheartedness and tightfistedness (15:9). The text identifies pathological dispositions that plague those who are economically well-off.

Further instructions on how to treat the poor (15:10–11). Verses 10 and 11 go on the offensive, describing the disposition and actions that should characterize the rich and adding the consequences of such conduct. In 15:10b Moses declares that Yahweh will bless the creditor "in all your work." In 15:11 Moses ends this paragraph with another realistic reminder that the poor will always be around.

Showing Kindness to Debt-Slaves (15:12–18). *Principles governing the treatment of indentured Israelites (15:12–15).* Moses here instructs the Israelites on how those with means were to treat indentured countrymen. He permits them to use the services of indentured Israelites for six years. Verses 13–14 charge those whom the impoverished person has served to help "jumpstart" their economic independence.

Principles governing an exceptional case (15:16–17a). In 15:16–17 Moses contemplates the possibility of an Israelite preferring permanent servitude to economic independence.

The concluding appeal (15:18). Moses ends with a motive clause: The reward for this gracious disposition toward persons who are granted their freedom will be the blessing of Yahweh on all that the creditor sets his hands to do.

Application. Although Christians for the most part do not live in the land of Israel and are not brothers and sisters in an ethnic sense, the relevance of the principles arising from Deuteronomy 15:1–11 and 12–18 are obvious to all who have eyes that see. We the redeemed remember that God in his grace has rescued us from the bondage of sin and adopted us as his children, lavishing on us his provision in accordance with our needs. Knowing not only the pain of deprivation and slavery but also the grace of redemption, we look at the world through the eyes of our heavenly Father and are inspired to treat others as he has treated us.

DEUTERONOMY 15:19–23

Original Meaning. The paragraph opens with a forthright command, calling Israelites to consecrate the firstborn in their herds and flocks to Yahweh their God. Although the text does not specify the time of year to consecrate the firstborn, the expression "each year" (15:20; "year by year," [lit.]) suggests they were to be presented at the central sanctuary at one of the annual festivals.

Verse 20 invites the head and the entire household to a banquet in the presence of Yahweh when the firstborn are consecrated. Although Yahweh himself does not eat the meat, as divine host he invites his family to partake of food that has been dedicated to him. Lest they become careless about their offerings, Moses reminds the Israelites that the only meat worthy of Yahweh's table is that which comes from flawless animals (15:21).

Application. This is a problem in our own day. We often view the Lord's blessing as a right rather than a privilege. But God's people cannot afford to lose sight of the grace of covenant relationship with him, concretized in his blessing on our work and his invitation to worship in his presence. Success in every venture, whether agricultural, industrial, academic, or domestic, depends on God's favor. And every meal is still a sacrifice, but it is also a gracious provision of God.

DEUTERONOMY 16:1–17

Original Meaning

The Festival of Passover (16:1–8). *The charge to keep the Passover (16:1).* Abib was the first month of the year, which may suggest that this celebration also functioned as a New Year Festival.

Instructions for keeping the Passover (16:2–7). Like the other Pentateuchal accounts of the Passover, Deuteronomy 16:1–8 offers only a bare outline of the rituals involved in the festival. We may rearrange the four significant stages as follows.

1. The Passover animal is slaughtered in the evening as the sun sets (16:6), to coincide with the timing of Israel's exodus from Egypt.
2. The meat of the animal is cooked (16:7). This probably involved roasting it directly over a fire or indirectly in a pan.
3. The people eat the Passover. The reference to the Passover as "the first day" (16:4) assumes the conjunction of Passover with the Festival of Unleavened Bread.
4. Having eaten, in the morning the worshipers return to their tents (16:7b)—temporary dwellings that the people have pitched in the vicinity of the central sanctuary.

The charge to keep the Festival of Unleavened Bread (16:8). The instructions on Passover conclude with a final summary, highlighting features of the Festival of Unleavened Bread.

The Festival of Weeks (16:9–12). *The timing of the Festival of Weeks (16:9).* Instead of specifying a date for its celebration, twice in Hebrew the opening statement calls on the people to "count off seven weeks" (cf. NASB). The festival would have fallen in the month of Sivan (May-June) so that the Festivals of Unleavened Bread and Weeks respectively served as bookends on either side of the grain harvest.

The essence of the Festival of Weeks (16:10–12a). The Festival of Weeks is to be a joyful celebration (16:11), an opportunity to celebrate before Yahweh. The catalogue of participants includes every imaginable member of the community. By associating what was otherwise an agricultural festival with Egypt, he highlights the conviction that everything Israel has is to be received as a gift. Like his provision of salvation, Yahweh's provision of harvest calls for free and spontaneous expressions of gratitude.

The concluding charge to observe the Festival of Weeks (16:12b–c). The instructions on the Festival of Weeks conclude more formally than any witnessed previously with a double call ("follow carefully," lit., "and you shall keep and you shall observe") to observe these ordinances.

The Festival of Booths (16:13–15). *The timing of the Festival of Booths (16:13).* Leviticus 23:34 and Numbers 29:12 fix the date on the fifteenth day of the seventh month (Tishri 15 = September-October). This results in a remarkably symmetrical calendar with important observances in the first and seventh months at opposite ends of the cycle anchoring life.

The essence of the Festival of Booths (16:14–15). These verses suggest the Festival of Booths serves two purposes.

1. It affords Israelites an occasion to celebrate their sense of community in a weeklong festival of joy.
2. Coming at the end of the agricultural cycle, the Festival of Booths affords the Israelites an opportunity for corporate thanksgiving in the presence of Yahweh at the place he would choose as his residence. When the Israelites come to worship Yahweh at the Festival of Booths, they are to be overflowing with joy and prepared to express that joy for an entire week.

The Summary Statement (16:16–17). The summary statement in 16:16–17 recalls Yahweh's words in Exodus 23:14–17. Yahweh graciously allows himself to be sought and encountered at the place he chooses. While noting with Exodus 23:15 that worshipers are not to appear before Yahweh empty-handed, here too Moses notes this and (cf. Deut 16:10) adds that these gifts are to be proportional to the blessing that Yahweh has lavished on the worshiper. The divine host delights in the generosity of his people.

Application. Apart from the Lord's Supper, the New Testament never prescribes specific festivals and celebrations for God's new covenant people. However, this should not be interpreted to suggest we need not bother with commemorative rituals and events. On the contrary, the church as a whole and individual congregations would do well to establish memorial festivals that bind us to believers everywhere (Easter, Pentecost, Christmas, etc.) and to keep alive in our minds the reality of God's work on our behalf. But even as we celebrate the ecumenical festivals of the church year and the commemorative festivals of our local congregations, like the ancient Israelites we must beware of the danger of mere externalism.

DEUTERONOMY 16:18–17:13

Original Meaning

A Call for Communal Commitment to Righteousness (16:18–20). Whereas in the earlier text Moses had installed leaders whom the people presented to him, here he assigns responsibility to the people. Moses's call for judges to "judge the people fairly" (16:18) is the only comment in this entire unit concerned with the conduct of judges, calling them to render righteous judgments. In 16:19 Moses calls on the people to imitate Yahweh in not perverting justice through partiality or bribery.

Three Examples of Righteousness Violated (16:21–17:1). The first command warns against spiritual syncretism (16:21). In Canaanite religion Asherah was a female goddess, the consort of El, who represented the female principle in the fertility religion. The meaning of the second prohibition is less certain (16:22). The association of pillars with Asherim in 7:5 and 12:3 suggests this is a stone erected to symbolize Baal, who represents the male principle in the fertility religion. However, the singular form may suggest a symbol of Yahweh himself, who claimed responsibility for the productivity of the soil and the livestock (7:12–14). The third prohibition shifts from overtly apostate actions that Yahweh hates to apostate dispositions that he finds detestable (17:1).

The Prescription for Righteousness Violated (17:2–13). **Panel A: How to deal with idolaters (17:2–7).** *The problem (17:2–4a).* A report of the crime to the community is to trigger the response that follows.

The prescription (17:4b–7b). The prescription for confirmed spiritual defection is execution by stoning (17:5). Executing criminals in the gate would make a spectacle of them and demonstrate the heinousness of their "evil deed" (17:5b).

The goal (17:7c). Yahweh's agenda requires a people united in its devotion to him and rigorous in its preservation of its own character as a holy people.

Panel B: How to deal with difficult cases (17:8–12). *The problem (17:8a).* Moses announces the issue: cases for judgment that are too difficult for the local court to settle in the gates.

The prescription (17:8b–12b). Although Moses introduces Levitical priests and a judge as final adjudicators (17:9), his primary addressee continues to be ordinary citizens. While the actions of the priest/judge are presented in one short statement (17:9c), those required of the people are presented in two stages: their duty to present the case to the central tribunal (17:8b–9), and their responsibility to execute its decision (17:10–12b).

When confronted with an insoluble case, the people are to "arise and go up" (17:8b, author's translation) to the place that Yahweh will choose. Moses suggests that the central sanctuary will not only be a place of worship but also a court of last resort; he thus implies the role of God in the pursuit of righteousness.

How would this tribunal operate? As priestly "judge," the designated official is heir to Moses, who at first heard all the disputes of the people and then inquired of God (Exod 18:15–16). However, unlike Moses, the priestly judge could probably use the Urim and Thummim to determine the mind of God.

Moses's charge to execute the verdict of the tribunal is the center of gravity (Deut 17:10–12b). When the Israelites execute the divine tribunal's decision, they pursue righteousness. Failure to execute the judgment as prescribed is the height of presumption and defiance against God (17:12a–b). Refusal to listen to the priest who stands in the service of Yahweh or to the judge who declares Yahweh's verdict, is as reprehensible as idolatry itself and deserves the death penalty.

Conclusion (17:13). Moses concludes the unit that began in 16:18 by repeating a point made in 13:11. Here that goal is served through the severity of the punishment of those who defy God by not executing his judgments.

Application. Righteousness is not served by a system that expects defense attorneys to convince a jury to acquit the guilty or prosecuting attorneys to condemn the innocent by smooth arguments, evasion of evidence to the contrary, and looking for loopholes in the law. Nor is righteousness served when those with means are able to hire the most skillful legal defense team while the economically or ethnically marginalized are at the mercy of assigned lawyers who would rather be on the other side of the case.

DEUTERONOMY 17:14–20

Original Meaning. The regulation regarding horses is intended to stifle militaristic impulses. The prohibition against multiplying women views the harem as a threat to spiritual fidelity to Yahweh: The women will turn the king's heart away. The warning concerns defection into idolatry. The proscription on excessive accumulation of silver and gold is shorthand for wealth and opulence, generally amassed at the expense of the people by taxing the citizens and demanding tribute from subject states.

Moses's positive instructions for the king are even more remarkable than the preceding prohibitions. The king must copy the torah for himself. By the act of copying the torah, the king declared his spiritual subordination to the priests and to the torah, the symbol of the covenant that bound Yahweh and Israel.

Application. Godly leaders embody the ideals of covenant relationship to which God's people are committed. Leaders in the church *must* be walking according to the revealed will of God. In so doing, they model the link between knowing the word and fearing and obeying the Lord.

DEUTERONOMY 18:1–8

Original Meaning

The Basis of the Levites' Entitlements (18:1–2). To compensate for their landless status, Yahweh offers himself as the Levitical priests' grant (18:2b). In effect, Yahweh invites them to eat from his own table; that which the people present to him, he passes on to them.

The Nature of the Levites' Entitlements (18:3–5). Yahweh may be the Levitical priests' possession, but he takes care of them by means of the sacrifices that the people bring to him. Verse 5 is official court language, authorizing them to enter the Sovereign's presence to minister to him or to receive a commission from him.

The Range of the Levites' Entitlements (18:6–8). In 18:6–7 Moses invites all Levites to participate in the prerequisites described in 18:3–5. Moses affirms the impulse of a Levite driven by a personal desire to worship at the place that Yahweh has chosen, granting full permission not only to worship at the central sanctuary but also to join fellow Levites in ministering in Yahweh's name. In 18:8 Moses finally gets to the point of this paragraph: equal prerequisites for equal service.

Application. Divine service is a vocation, not a profession. "To stand before God" means that we listen carefully to his voice and commit ourselves to doing his will, and "to serve in his name" means that we receive our authority from him and that everything we do is driven by the passion to glorify him. Whereas the Scriptures concerning Israel speak of these as privileges reserved for angels, prophets, and priests, the New Testament teaching on the priesthood of all believers (1 Pet 2:9) means that because of the work of Jesus Christ, believers collectively have direct access to God and responsibility to represent him to the unbelieving world.

DEUTERONOMY 18:9–22

Original Meaning

The Foil for the Promise of a Prophet Like Moses (18:9–14). The last clause of 18:9 functions as a theme statement for 18:9–14. Verses 10–11 are not exhaustive, but they provide the fullest catalogue of divinatory expressions in the Old Testament. The practices in this list are all intended to manipulate deities, supernatural forces, and the spirits of the deceased to act in the worshiper's favor. Moses's restates his hostility toward these practices in 18:12–13.

Verse 14 concludes with an awkward but emphatic note, "But you not thus [i.e., listening to fortunetellers and diviners] did Yahweh your God grant [permission]" (author's translation). Moses rejects any appeal to divine revelation to justify pagan forms of communication with Yahweh.

The Nature of the Promise of a Prophet Like Moses (18:15–20). Because Yahweh promises to provide Israel with prophets, there is no need to resort to divination, magic, and necromancy to determine his will. Impulses that drive others to abhorrent magical practices will be satisfied in Yahweh's provision of the prophetic institution.

In 18:16–20 Moses assures his people that Yahweh will not leave them without authorized teachers when he is gone and they have crossed into the land. Moses concludes with Yahweh's appeal to take his prophets' messages seriously. For the prophet to "speak in my name" (18:19) is to speak with Yahweh's authority and on his behalf. Yahweh reinforces the *gravitas* of the prophetic ministry with an impassioned word to those who will abuse the office by prophesying falsely.

The Challenge to the Promise of a Prophet Like Moses (18:21–22). Verses 21–22 focuses on the marks of false prophecy. If one can identify a false prophecy, one may identify a false prophet, who should be executed. On the surface, Moses's answer is not helpful. If utterances that a prophet claims to speak in the name of Yahweh are not fulfilled, the prophecy is false, and the prophet is a charlatan. However, if a prophecy concerns the distant future, the veracity of a statement and the proof of a genuine prophet will be delayed, and the prophet may not live to witness his vindication. Moses does not answer this dilemma but concludes this discussion with counsel regarding the proper disposition toward prophets whose words do not come true.

Application. This passage reminds readers in all ages and contexts to be vigilant in testing the validity of all who preach and teach in God's name. Sounding more like Moses than many realize, 1 John 4:1 warns Christians not to believe every spirit. Similarly, Paul encourages the believers at Thessalonica that even as they welcome prophetic utterances, they must be vigilant in testing all messages, holding fast to what is good and rejecting all that is evil (1 Thess 5:20–22).

DEUTERONOMY 19:1–14

Original Meaning

The Provision of Asylum for Innocent Manslaughter (19:1–3). Verses 2–3 prescribe three actions.

1. They must designate three towns in the heartland to complement the three already set apart east of the Jordan.
2. They must establish the routes to the towns of asylum.
3. Having identified these three focal points, the Israelites were to divide the entire territory into three regions, for which the towns would function as umbrellas of protection for those fleeing from avengers of blood. The last sentence of 19:3 declares the purpose of these towns: to serve as refuges for those who inadvertently cause another person's death.

The Need for the Provision of Asylum for Innocent Manslaughter (19:4–7, 10). Whereas Numbers 35:16–23 focused on the legal rules of evidence, the present text pursues righteousness by providing an illustration of its necessity. In keeping with the sermonic nature of this address, Deuteronomy 19:4 is best read something like, "Here is an illustration of the killer who flees there [to the town of asylum] that he might live, that is, a person who unintentionally strikes down his neighbor, without having exhibited any prior hostility toward him" (author's translation). Verse 10 offers a rationale for the policy: Towns of asylum are needed to prevent innocent blood from being shed in the midst of the land.

The Expansion of the Provision of Asylum for Innocent Manslaughter (19:8–9). Should Israel's territory expand beyond the original tribal allotments, three towns of asylum on each side of the Jordan would be inadequate. Therefore, Moses calls for the addition of three more towns of asylum to serve the people living beyond the narrowly defined promised land (19:9b).

The Exception to the Provision of Asylum for Manslaughter (19:11–13). In proposing a hypothetical scenario that is the opposite of 19:4–10, Moses recognizes the potential for criminals to abuse the institution and reaffirms the demand in Numbers 35 for discrimination between intentional murder and accidental death. Moses concludes these instructions with a reminder that Israel's well-being depends on rigorous defense of innocent blood (19:13b).

Righteousness and Greed (19:14). The inviolability of boundary markers is fundamental to a settled agricultural economy, where ownership of land is critical for well-being. Israelite law viewed Yahweh as the true owner of the land, and the allotments to tribes and families were inviolable.

Application. No crime against another human is as heinous as willful homicide, for it involves the intentional elimination of an image of God. Because the demand to execute the perpetrator is rooted in a divine charge to the ancestor of all (Noah), this principle may not be dismissed as an Israelite civil law abrogated in Christ. As Moses declared in Deuteronomy 19:13, personal dispositions, the intimacy of relationships, and sentimentality may not interfere with this righteous demand.

DEUTERONOMY 19:15–21

Original Meaning. The guidelines regarding witnesses in judicial proceedings flesh out the eighth command of the Decalogue. The text divides into two uneven parts: (1) a call for more than one witness in all cases (19:15), and (2) instructions on how to deal with malicious witnesses (19:16–21). Both are driven by a concern for righteousness in judicial procedures.

Verses 17–18 describe the appropriate response to miscarriage of justice.

1. Accuser and accused must appear before the priests who are serving as judges, where participants would be conscious of Yahweh's supervision of the legal process, heightening the implications of malicious testimony.
2. The adjudicators are to investigate the case thoroughly (19:18a). Moses draws attention to the announcement of the verdict with "and behold" (Heb. *hinneh*, not translated in the NIV). The malicious witness has indeed testified falsely against his brother. Repeating the purgation formula, in 19:19b–20 Moses presents the rationale for this response. Verse 21 fleshes out verse 19.

Since false accusations damage personal relations and the very fabric of the community, this principle provides a means of nipping such social cancers in the bud.

Application. When Jesus calls New Testament believers to turn the other cheek toward those who abuse them rather than to retaliate with "eye for eye and tooth for tooth" vengeance (Matt 5:38–42), he does not establish a new ethic. Rather, he reminds his followers that those who bear the name of God live by a distinctive ethic. We do indeed insist that society and the courts uphold the rights of all citizens and protect all from social predators. However, with respect to our own personal relationships, instead of retaliating when our own rights are violated (which may be our legal right), righteous Christians will turn the other cheek and forgive their enemies.

DEUTERONOMY 20:1–20

Original Meaning

Encouraging the Troops for War (20:1–9). *The priest's exhortation (20:1–4).* Moses begins by describing the context that calls for courage. For Moses the primary issue in 20:1–9 is fear. He reassures Israel that if Yahweh could liberate them by defeating the superior Egyptians, his presence will surely guarantee victory against the Canaanites.

The officials' speeches (20:5–9). Verse 5 introduces a new group of interlocutors, literate nonmilitary officials, perhaps Levites charged with mustering the troops and keeping records of their names and numbers. This text suggests they were also responsible for screening recruits.

The officials' second speech (20:8–9). The second speech exempts a would-be warrior from military service out of respect for the psychological effect of his presence on his comrades. After the "officers" (20:8) have delivered their speeches and after those with legitimate reasons for exemption and those who are fearful have returned home, the officials are to appoint "commanders" (20:9) to lead the army into battle.

Instructions for the Troops in Battle (20:10–20). *Instructions for distant campaigns (20:10–15).* Upon approaching a targeted town, the Israelites are to offer it a chance to surrender peacefully. To accept the offer means to accept subject status, though without the horrendous consequences of defeat in battle. Alternatively, if they reject peace and "engage you in battle," then the armies of Israel may go on the offensive in subduing the town (20:12). The ultimate fall of the city will be credited to Yahweh, who delivers it into their hands (20:13a).

They are to slaughter all the male inhabitants (20:13b), who represent the key to resistance and the backbone of the town's economy and administration. They may plunder the town (20:14a) and they can make use of the booty (20:14b), receiving it as a gift from Yahweh. In 20:15 we learn these instructions apply to campaigns against "all the cities that are at a distance from you," in contrast to these towns that "belong to the nations nearby."

Instructions for campaigns nearby (20:16–18). Building on the law of *herem* as prescribed in chapter 7, Moses calls for the total destruction of Canaanite cities as their dedication to Yahweh. The policy demands the slaughter of the entire human population of the Canaanite towns. Whereas the women and children of distant towns that reject Israel's peaceful overtures are to be spared, in the cities of the land Yahweh is giving to Israel, as their grant, nothing "that breathes" is to survive (20:16). The exception created for distant towns demonstrates that this was never intended to be a fundamental part of Israel's military policy (20:1–15).

This policy did not originate with politicians or military leaders but derives from Yahweh himself. The addition of "as the LORD your God has commanded you" in 20:17 drives both hearer and reader to search for antecedent texts. Here Moses seems to have in mind the treatment of Canaanites prescribed by Yahweh at Sinai (Exod 23:23–33, 34:11–16) and reiterated on the plains of Moab (Num 33:51–55). The *herem* policy was driven by religious rather than genocidal or military considerations. For Israel, implementing *herem* on a town not only secured its absolute transfer to the divine sphere, it was also intended to secure Israel's survival.

Instructions for troops in siege warfare (20:19–20). Moses speaks about preserving the natural environment around the town, charging the people not to destroy the fruit trees by wielding their axes against them. Since the Israelites will have conquered the fields around the besieged city and eventually will occupy the city, it is contrary to self-interest to ruthlessly cut down the orchards around the city.

Application. Since the people of God are no longer defined nationally or ethnically, none of the wars in which contemporary nations engage can be equated with Israel's wars against the Canaanites, and efforts to claim "God is on our side" generally sound presumptuous and arrogant. The church is indeed engaged in warfare; but this conflict is not against flesh and blood but against principalities and powers arrayed against God and his church.

DEUTERONOMY 21:1-9

Original Meaning

The Problem (21:1). The purpose of this unit is not to show how to solve the murder, but how to resolve the spiritual crisis that an unsolved murder creates for the community.

The Prescription (21:2–8b). Moses's instructions seem simple: Measure the distance from the location of the corpse to the towns in the region to determine which is nearest. The purpose is to identify the community that should take responsibility for purging Israel of its bloodguilt.

The ritual action of the elders (21:2–8b). The elders represent the town and nation in the expiatory ceremony. We may recognize four discrete stages in the ritual to be performed.

1. The elders must select a young heifer (21:3b). Since the ritual involves breaking the animal's neck, an uncontaminated specimen was needed.
2. The elders remove the heifer to a flowing wadi (21:4a). The instructions envisage a virgin river valley where plants grow naturally, rather than a place watered by a stream only in the rainy season.
3. The elders break the heifer's neck at the wadi (21:4). It seems best to view the ritual as a reenactment of the murder, with the goal of banishing the defilement of the land. An innocent life has been taken in an innocent locale, with rituals performed in such a way that the land does not lose its innocence by absorbing additional blood.
4. The elders wash their hands over the heifer (21:6). While it is unclear why the elders should wash their hands over the heifer, it provided residents of the town a means whereby they (through their representatives) could declare their innocence before God.
5. The elders declare their innocence and plead for mercy (21:7–8b). As in Moses's intercessory prayers, the elders of the town are to cast themselves and their people on the mercy of Yahweh.

Application. This short unit not only reinforces the conviction of the sanctity of human life, but it also goes beyond that text in recognizing the corporate responsibility of the entire community for the crimes of the individuals. Criminals are indeed responsible for the crimes they commit, but they are not *solely* responsible. Unless the community responds to the crime, the guilt of the individual rests on the heads of all.

DEUTERONOMY 21:10-23

Original Meaning

Righteousness in the Treatment of War Brides (21:10–14). *The nature of the degradation (21:10–12a).* The description of the warrior's treatment of the war bride sounds calloused, but Moses's disposition is hinted at by the final clause (21:14).

Protecting the dignity of the captive woman in marriage (21:12b–13). Moses instructs the Israelites how to respect the rights and dignity of wives whom they have captured. The monthlong quarantine expresses respect for the woman's ties to her family of origin and her own psychological and emotional health.

Protecting the rights of the captive woman in divorce (21:14). Whatever the cause, Moses issues two prohibitions for the Israelite husband who would divorce his war bride: By no means may he sell her for silver, nor may he treat her as chattel property. He concludes with a rationale for the compassionate treatment of war brides even in divorce.

Righteousness in the Treatment of the Firstborn (21:15–17). Moses does not explicitly outlaw the father's prerogative to choose the primary heir, but he cautions against making this common practice once the Israelites have settled in the land. Responding to this potential situation, 21:16–17a declare that once the father divides the assets, he may not rob the eldest of his rights and status (21:16). Moses hereby seeks to protect the rights and dignity of the less-favored wife by prohibiting husbands from making children pay for strained relationships between or among parents.

Righteousness in the Treatment of a Rebellious Son (21:18–21). The description suggests the parents have done all they could to raise their son properly, but he is incorrigible and will not listen to either father or mother. The prescription for this son seems simple. The parents are to seize him, take him to the assembly of the elders in the town where they reside, present their case orally, and leave him with the men of the town, who will stone him to death (21:19–21a).

Righteousness in the Treatment of a Criminal's Remains (21:22–23). Moses prescribes the treatment of the criminal's body that has been hung from a tree (21:23a–b). The rationale for burying the body is couched in ambiguous terms: "A person who is hanged is a curse of God" (author's translation). How should we interpret the phrase "a curse of God"? The NIV's "[he] is under God's curse" has dominated Christian interpretation from the beginning.

Application. In Galatians 3:13 Paul states the truth concerning ourselves—that we all are sinners deserving the death of the criminal in view in Deuteronomy 21:22–23. This applies also to Jews who try to find salvation by keeping the law rather than by faith, casting themselves on God incarnate in Jesus Christ. Paul also declares the glorious gospel that Christ himself became the curse that we all deserve by virtue of our sinful state.

DEUTERONOMY 22:1–12

Original Meaning

Righteousness Demonstrated in Care for Domestic Animals (22:1–4). Both scenarios in 22:1–4 involve a fellow Israelite's animal in a threatening situation. This paragraph assumes that the covenant love Israelites have for their neighbors extends to livestock.

Righteousness Demonstrated in Respect for Sexual Distinctions (22:5). Similar to 22:9–11, this injunction seeks to preserve the order built into creation, specifically the fundamental distinction between male and female. For a person to wear anything associated with the opposite gender confuses one's sexual identity and blurs established boundaries.

Righteousness Demonstrated in Care for Wild Animals (22:6–8). This appeal for a tender and sympathetic disposition toward wild birds is unparalleled in the Old Testament. The wisdom of this counsel is obvious: Taking the mother but sparing the young would have meant the death of all, for unhatched eggs and fledgling birds depend on the mother. Israelites are not to kill for killing's sake. The scope of righteous living extends to respect for the life of helpless creatures.

Righteousness Demonstrated in Care for One's Household (22:8). Without a barrier around the perimeter, people could step off the roof and fall to their deaths. The final clause of 22:8 holds the head of the household responsible for the life of anyone whose death is the result of negligence.

Righteousness Demonstrated in Farming the Land (22:9–11). *The prohibition on seeding a vineyard with other seeds (22:9).* The proscription addresses a common practice in ancient and modern times ("intercropping"), making use of every inch of arable land. The clause implies consecration of the produce, which means treating it like produce presented at the sanctuary.

The prohibition on plowing with two species of animals (22:10). The animals' unequal strength and stamina could cause the more vigorous to exhaust the weaker. However, these factors were probably less significant than forcing a bond between clean and unclean, which happens when ox and donkey are yoked together.

The prohibition on wearing divergent kinds of fabric (22:11). This taboo fits logically with the taboo on mixing crops and mixing draft animals. It seems that all these prohibitions were intended to guard against boundary violations that defy the order of the universe (Gen 1). However, the concern goes beyond order in everyday life. These instructions draw clear boundaries between that which is appropriate for deity (mixtures of all sorts) and that which is appropriate for mortals (no mixtures at all).

Righteousness Demonstrated in Dress (22:12). Like words of covenant commitment written on hands and foreheads and on the doorposts of houses and gates (Deut 6:4–9), the tassels reminded the one who wore both them and outsiders of Israel's special status as the covenant people of Yahweh.

Application. Few Christians today heed Moses's prohibitions on mixing different varieties of plants in a single plot of land or wearing two different fabrics. However, underlying these commands is a profoundly theological concern for order. The blurring of boundaries symbolizes chaos. The lives of the redeemed should be characterized by order and resistance to everything that causes disintegration of that order in one's life.

DEUTERONOMY 22:13–30

Original Meaning

Righteousness in the Face of Marital Infidelity (22:13–21). *The primary case (22:13–19).* Since the elders find the woman innocent, the punishment appropriate to the crime for which the woman is charged (in this case, death by stoning) should be execution of the man (cf. 19:15–21). However, since he is merely chastised and forced to pay compensation to the woman's father suggests that the primary issue here is not the veracity of the husband's charges, but the innocence of his wife. The striking ending of the motive clause in 22:19 assumes that sexual sins are also crimes against the entire community.

The counter case (22:20–21). Moses completes the discussion by instructing the court how to proceed if the husband's accusations are confirmed. Moses's demand that "the men of her town" (22:21) rather than the men of the town where she and her husband lived is remarkable. This forces the community that hosted the sinful acts to come to terms with the crime. Radical surgery is required to remove those who flaunt contempt for the covenant by promiscuous behavior.

Righteousness in the Face of Sexual Promiscuity (22:22–30). *Adultery involving a married woman (22:22).* The opening formula indicates this case is not about rumors but about adulterers discovered in the very act: A man lies with another man's wife. The text seems to assume that the person(s) who discovered them in the act would notify the elders of the town and testify against them in a public hearing, whereupon they would be publicly executed by stoning.

Adultery involving a virgin engaged to be married (22:23–27). These instructions subdivide into two panels representing a primary case (22:23–24) and a counter case (22:25–27). The primary case (22:23–24) concerns an adulterous act committed within the walls of the town, where residents live in close proximity to one another. Since no one heard the woman's cry for help, it is assumed she did not cry out, which suggests the sexual act was consensual. Therefore, both the man and the woman are to be brought to the gate of the town and executed by stoning.

The counter case (22:25–27) highlights the role of the woman as victim. This hypothetical encounter transpires in the open field, where, even if she had cried for help, no one within earshot would have heard her cry. Consequently, she is given the benefit of the doubt, while the man is considered guilty.

Adultery involving a virgin not engaged to be married (22:28–29). The prescribed response focuses entirely on the man. Because he has deflowered and degraded the woman, he must pay the father of the woman 50 shekels. Unlike 22:19, this payment is not considered a fine but the bride price, since upon its payment she becomes his wife in a marriage from which there is to be no divorce as long as they live (cf. 22:19).

Respecting one's father's sexuality (22:30). Since girls married at a very young age in ancient times, Moses may also be contemplating a scenario in which a man is attracted to his father's former wife, who is free either because of divorce or the husband's death.

Application. The narratives of the Old Testament expose the problems with patriarchy. The solution offered by the Old Testament (and New Testament) is not to replace these structures with some sort of egalitarianism that neutralizes gender distinctions and homogenizes roles, but to plead for transformed leadership.

DEUTERONOMY 23:1–14

Original Meaning

Righteousness in the Assembly of Yahweh (23:1–8). *Defending the sanctity of the assembly of Yahweh (23:1–6).* The first category is emasculated men. While the etymology of the word is uncertain, this seems to refer to offspring of prostitutes who lived at pagan cult sites. The permanent exclusion of Ammonites and Moabites seems odd (23:3–6) in light of the disposition toward Edom in 23:7. Moses cites their refusal to greet the Israelites with bread and water when they came up from Egypt and their engagement of Balaam to curse them.

Opening the doors to the assembly of Yahweh (23:7–8). The conciliatory tone toward Edom may reflect Yahweh's special interest in the direct descendants of Abraham (cf. Gen 27:39–40; 36). Because the Egyptians hosted them during a precarious phase of their history, they are rewarded. Verse 8 qualifies the openness.

Maintaining Righteousness in the Camp of Israel (23:9–14). *Theme: a call for purity in the camp (23:9).* When the Israelites go out on campaigns, they are to guard against anything "unclean."

In this context the danger is internal and theological; the Israelites are to guard themselves against every spiritual danger.

Exposition: the procedure for maintaining purity in the camp (23:10–13). Moses begins with instructions regarding seminal emissions (23:10–11). In 23:12–13 attention shifts to defecation. The association suggests its impurity derives from its source inside the human body rather than the repulsive nature of feces.

Rationale: the importance of purity in the camp (23:14). In 23:14 the tone and style change from clinical and hygienic objectivity to theological principle. These clauses portray him as a divine commander inspecting his troops; if he finds any cause of defilement as he walks about the camp, he will abandon them.

Application. As a spiritual body, the true Israel recognizes the boundaries that separate this community from the world at large. The assembly of Yahweh welcomes those of genuine faith, but it maintains the highest standards of holiness. Those who stand in opposition to covenantal standards by personal conduct, religious compromise, or indifference and opposition to the work of God are not at home in the church.

DEUTERONOMY 23:15–25

Original Meaning

Safeguarding the Rights of a Slave (23:15–16). The prohibited action "to shut someone in" (lit.) means to apprehend and imprison the fugitive until the owner arrives, when he would be delivered into the master's hands. By calling the Israelites to provide safe haven for fugitives, Moses treats the entire land as *terra sancta*.

Safeguarding the Sanctity of the Cult (23:17–18). The involvement of such persons in prostitution here reflects an imitation of foreign cults. The expression that "the LORD your God detests them both" (23:18) places their actions in a category with carved images of pagan deities and pagan service to gods, including child sacrifice, sacrificing blemished animals, divination, sorcery, magic, transvestism, and dishonesty in business. These gifts are rejected as "dirty money."

Safeguarding the Economic Health of the People of Yahweh (23:19–20). By addressing would-be lenders rather than borrowers, Moses makes interest-free loans a responsibility for those with means rather than a right of the poor. The ban on interest for loans does not extend to foreigners. The persons envisioned here might have been merchants who bought and sold goods for profit rather than the sheer need for survival. If their business ventures did not succeed, they could always go home.

Safeguarding Promises (23:21–23). The statement in 23:21–23 highlights three fundamental principles underlying vows.

1. Vows are entirely optional.
2. Once vows are made, they must be kept.
3. Yahweh holds persons accountable for the vows they make.

Safeguarding the Trust of Neighbors (23:24–25). Within an agrarian economy, the right of passers-by to pick grain or fruit from the trees for the journey from the fields they were crossing could create several problems. On the one hand, landowners could be greedy and unreasonable. On the other hand, especially in harvest time, people passing through would be tempted to carry containers and fill them with grapes or to bring a sickle, cut standing grain, and stuff it in their bags. Moses's instructions are simultaneously realistic, generous, and responsible.

Application. It is unrealistic to expect secular governments to operate by biblical norms, but the harsh disposition of many evangelicals toward unregistered aliens in this land violates both the spirit and the law of Moses. We must address the illegality of unregistered aliens, not only by insisting on obedience to the laws of the land but especially by genuine friendship and efforts to help them legalize their presence among us.

DEUTERONOMY 24:1–5

Original Meaning

Righteousness in the Face of Divorce (24:1–4). *The problem (24:1a–c).* The man is disappointed because of "something indecent." The expression is best interpreted as some menstrual irregularity. The result is a constant state of impurity, curtailing many normal marital activities and rendering her incapable of bearing children. But instead of responding with compassion, he divorced her.

The complication (24:2–3). Moses imagines two developments that could complicate the woman's life.

1. A second husband's disposition toward her may change to rejection.
2. Her second husband dies.

The proscription (24:4). Moses declares the original husband may not change his mind and remarry his wife. As in Deuteronomy 21:14, the issue is the degradation of the woman. The man has already degraded her, first by refusing to be gracious to a needy spouse ritually defiled through no fault of her own, and second, by publicizing her personal issue through the divorce proceedings. The shift to second person reminds the people that if they allow a man to remarry his former wife after she has been married to another, they would bring guilt not only on themselves but also on the land they have received from Yahweh.

Righteousness in the Face of a Call to Arms (24:5). Husbands of new brides are exempt from all communal obligations so they may devote themselves to the happiness of their wives. With keen pastoral insight Moses has painted a picture of marriage that contrasts sharply with that portrayed in 24:1–4.

Application. The culture of divorce in the West offers Christians an extraordinary opportunity to be countercultural. To the extent that in these matters we have behaved like the world, we must repent. To the extent that we model biblical ideals of marriage, we declare to the world the kind of relationship they may enjoy with God through Jesus Christ, the self-sacrificing head and husband of the church.

DEUTERONOMY 24:6–22

Original Meaning

Depriving a Person of Access to Food (24:6). To demand a millstone as a pledge meant depriving a household of the basic instrument for making essential food (bread), which was tantamount to claiming the debtor's life as a pledge.

Depriving a Poor Person of Life Itself (24:7). Moses identifies the kidnapper as a "fellow Israelite" in relation to his victim. By calling for the death penalty to purge the evil from Israel's midst, Moses places this offense in a class with other capital crimes.

Righteousness in Heeding Authority (24:8–9). Moses reinforces his appeal for compliance by linking the voices of Levitical priests with his own and ultimately with God's voice. Moses calls for careful attention to the voice of experience, charging the people to remember what happened to Miriam (Num 12:10–15). This reminder suggests that the real concern here is not the skin disease but the importance of heeding the instruction of the priests.

Depriving a Person of Clothing (24:10–13). The illustration in 24:10–13 changes from 24:6, but here we find additional instructions on how creditors may lend to the poor. As elsewhere, the goal is a community built on ethical values of trust and compassion. This response to the poor promotes a healthy relationship between creditor and debtor and pleases Yahweh.

Depriving a Person of Rightful Due (24:14–15). Moses addresses the temptation of employers to exploit their workers. In 24:15 Moses explains what he means: day laborers must be paid at the end of the day in which they perform their services. He concludes with four reasons why they should do so.

Righteousness in Accountability for Crimes: Protecting the Innocent (24:16). Knowledge that they will be held responsible for the effects their sins have on their families should deter them from actions that violate Yahweh's covenant. Significantly, Old Testament examples of children being punished for crimes committed by parents all involve fundamental violations of the covenant.

Depriving the Poor of Justice (24:17–18). Now Moses returns to the primary issue of this chapter: demonstrating righteousness toward socially and economically vulnerable persons, specifically promoting the well-being of aliens, the fatherless, and widows. In 24:18 Moses seeks to motivate compassion by reminding all Israelites of their own experience in Egypt.

Depriving the Poor of Food (24:19–22). These instructions build on earlier legislation (Lev 19:9–10; 23:22), where Yahweh had called on landowners to leave the corners of their fields uncut and leave for the poor and the alien whatever they dropped while harvesting the crop. These instructions are even more pastoral, seeking to instill in the covenant community a spirit of generosity that goes far beyond the original legislation.

Application. This chapter of Deuteronomy highlights the responsibility of the community to care for individuals, especially those with limited means for taking care of themselves. At the same time, it refuses to allow the members of the community to be dragged into the net of other individuals' misdeeds, especially when this involves actions subject to human judicial decision. The principle of righteousness precludes human courts from imposing the sentence for one person's crimes on another person.

DEUTERONOMY 25:1–16

Original Meaning

Safeguarding Righteousness in the Administration of Justice (25:1–3). The specific instructions on the execution of the punishment in 25:2–3 reflect keen concern for justice for both parties. To ensure the executioner does not overstep the bounds of the sentence, the punishment must be administered in the presence of the judge, and the number of lashings must be correlated with the severity of the crime. To protect the dignity of the accused and to prevent excessive public humiliation, Moses sets forty lashes as the absolute maximum sentence.

***Safeguarding Righteousness in the Treatment of Animals* (25:4).** The concern for animals in 25:4 accords with the trajectory we have observed repeatedly in Deuteronomy. The pursuit of righteousness on the farm will involve care for the creatures in one's charge, just as God himself does.

***Safeguarding Righteousness in Relation to Male Sexuality* (25:5–12).** *Maintaining righteousness in the face of shameful male behavior (25:5–10).* A levirate marriage is a legally sanctioned union between a widow whose husband has died without having fathered offspring and the brother of the deceased. By marrying the deceased's widow, the brother-in-law offered her economic security and physical protection. However, the primary concern here is securing progeny for her deceased husband. The levirate addressed the worst curse imaginable—to have one's "seed" cut off and one's name forgotten.

Verses 5b–6 describe the righteous response to this situation. Verse 6 assumes that the marriage and sexual intercourse achieve their intended goal; the woman conceives and gives birth to a son. This son represents the deceased's line; through him both the deceased's name and the integrity of the family patrimony are preserved.

The instructions for the corollary case (25:7–10) assume the possibility of exemption for men who prefer not to perform the duties of a levir, though this refusal was not to be taken lightly and involved the stigma of shame. The man who refused to guarantee the memory of his brother may indeed build a house of his own. However, in perpetuity his progeny will bear the stigma of his shameful conduct.

Maintaining righteousness in the face of shameful female behavior (25:11–12). The primary issue is not the fact that she would defend her husband, but her tactics: She reaches out and grabs his genitals. From the grammar and syntax of the passage as well as the severity of the punishment, this is no innocent gesture; her action is deliberate.

***Safeguarding Righteousness in Business Transactions* (25:13–16).** This text warns against having two different sets of weights, the lighter one to be used when calculating payment one owes and the heavier to calculate commodities or money one was owed.

Application. A more relevant issue in the entire book than the call for integrity in all economic transactions can scarcely be imagined. Honest and fair calculation of transactions and scrupulous payment of debts should be the hallmark of those who claim to be God's people. In a society that seems to become more unethical by the day, Christians should stand out for the fidelity and integrity with which they conduct their business.

DEUTERONOMY 25:17–19

Original Meaning. Moses's rhetorical style cites three actions by the Amalekites against Israel that demand response. They (1) opportunistically "attacked" the Israelites along the way when they came out of Egypt; (2) committed barbaric and cowardly atrocities; (3) did not fear God. The paragraph ends with a final appeal to the Israelites: "Do not forget!" (25:19). Forget what? It seems best, therefore, to see this as the preceding command to blot out the Amalekites.

Application. While this text speaks eloquently to the issue of the just pursuit of war, it has little to contribute to contemporary debates about theories of just war. Like his instructions regarding the Canaanite nations listed in 7:1, Moses's charge regarding the Amalekites is exceptional. Under no circumstances are these policies to be generalized into national policies of genocide or justification for violent expressions of revenge.

DEUTERONOMY 26:1–15

Original Meaning

***Celebrating the Faithfulness of God* (26:1–11).** Verse 1 sets the stage for a series of ritual actions that extends through 26:11.

Phase 1: The worshiper's first set of actions (26:2–3a). The worshiper is to take some of the first harvestings brought in from his land and go to the place that Yahweh has chosen to establish his name. The high priest receives the gifts on behalf of his colleagues and on God's behalf.

Phase 2: The worshiper's first declaration (26:3b). With this declaration, the worshiper recognizes the priest as both a symbol of divine presence and the official witness to his declaration. Whereas outside Israel harvest festivals celebrated the fertility of the land, here the occasion is transformed into a commemoration of Yahweh's fidelity to a greater agenda—the gift of the land itself.

Phase 3: The high priest's actions (26:4). The priest's actions declare symbolically that Yahweh has accepted the worshiper's expression of devotion.

Phase 4: The worshiper's second declaration (26:5–10a). Having observed the priest's actions, the worshiper is to recite a summary history of his people's experience with Yahweh. Many have recognized that what follows is an early creedal statement (cf. 6:20–25; 11:2–7) cast in celebrative prose, summarizing the Israelites' basic beliefs concerning their origins.

The particle "and now," followed by "look/behold" (not translated in the NIV), signals a shift from the past to the worshiper's present ritual performance (26:10a). With the shift he declares his personal participation in the nation's history, and by giving thanks for the land from which the firstfruits have come, he transforms an annual fertility celebration into a celebration of a historical event: Yahweh's gift of the land to Israel.

Phase 5: The worshiper's actions (26:10b–11). He is to set the basket with the firstfruits before Yahweh, and then in a gesture of homage and submission prostrate himself before him. Having done so, he is to invite his entire household, as well as Levites and aliens from his town, to join him in celebrating.

Affirming Fidelity to the Covenant (26:12–15). (1) *The prerequisite to acceptable confessional worship (26:12).* After Israelite farmers have demonstrated covenantal loyalty to Yahweh by taking care of the poor, they are to make a pilgrimage to the central sanctuary and perform the verbal ritual that follows.

(2) *The nature of acceptable confessional worship (26:13–15).* The farmer has scrupulously set aside one tenth of all his produce. Here charity toward the poor is seen as representative of compliance with the covenantal stipulations as a whole. The worshiper's focus shifts from the function and the beneficiaries of the tithe to their proper handling. Once a gift had been designated as an offering for the deity, its sanctity must be scrupulously guarded. The worshiper acknowledges he is a vassal of Yahweh and declares that he has obeyed Yahweh fully. Locating these instructions at the end of the second address invites readers to interpret this ritual as a token confession of fidelity to the covenant as a whole. The ritual concludes with a prayer (26:15).

Application. God's people are a thankful people. This text reminds readers of every era of the importance of specific celebrations devoted to thanksgiving. But true thanksgiving recognizes that God is much more than a fertility deity who provides for his people in the annual cycle of seedtime and harvest. Yahweh's rescue of Israel from the bondage of Egypt was paradigmatic of our redemption from the slavery of sin and our rescue from the kingdom of darkness through the death and resurrection of Jesus Christ.

DEUTERONOMY 26:16–19

Original Meaning. Verses 16–19 summarize key theological issues of the book and provide a hinge between Moses's lengthy exposition of the specific stipulations and his recitation of the consequences upon the nation for their response in chapter 28. Whereas 26:1–15 looked forward to the time when Israel would be well-established in the land, with the opening phrase "this day" in 26:16, Moses refocuses his hearers' attention on the present moment of decision.

By declaring that Yahweh will set Israel high above the nations that he has made, Moses casts his gaze far beyond the Cis- and Transjordanian regions to the world as a whole. The NIV rendering suggests that the goal is Israel's praise, fame, and glory. However, given the flow of the book as a whole and later echoes of this text, it is best to ascribe the glory to God. Neither in Deuteronomy nor anywhere else is Israel's standing among the nations ever to be a source of national pride.

Application. If Yahweh was glorified through the righteous and faithful conduct of his people Israel, the same is true of the new Israel of God. Indeed, Jesus reminds his disciples that his Father is glorified in this—that the disciples prove to be his disciples by bearing much fruit (John 15:5).

DEUTERONOMY 27:1–26

Original Meaning

Completing the Covenantal Triangle: Yahweh–Israel–Land (27:1–8). *Panel A (27:2–3).* Moses announces that the rituals to follow are to be performed "on the day" (author's translation; NIV "when") the Israelites cross the Jordan into the land that Yahweh has promised them.

Erecting stone monuments. This part of the ritual would echo the original covenant ratification ceremony celebrated at Sinai (Exod 24:4).

Plastering the stones. The plaster probably involved a white alkaline compound. These instructions call for a one-time ritual use involving the text of the torah Moses has been promulgating.

Writing the torah on the stones. The scribes were to include all of Moses's present addresses on the pillars.

Panel B (27:4–8). Verses 5–7 instruct the people on the rituals to be performed on Mount Ebal. Whereas the Sinai event had sealed the bipartite relationship between people and deity, the third party (the land) was missing. The purpose of this ritual was to celebrate the completion of the triangle.

The Charge of Moses and the Levites (27:9–10). Covenantal fidelity is demonstrated through listening to Yahweh's voice (27:10a) and scrupulously observing the commands expounded upon by Moses. His instructions are not to be treated merely as museum pieces or literary artifacts, but as guides to life.

Appealing for Covenantal Fidelity in the Promised Land (27:11–26). *The prescribed arrangements for the blessings and the curses (27:11–13).* Mounts Ebal and Gerizim are present not only as witnesses to the blessings and curses, but as the repository to the torah itself (the inscribed pillars), and the land of Canaan (now Israel) is also engaged as a vital partner in the covenantal relationship.

The imprecatory ritual (27:14–26). Verses 15–26 consist of twelve imprecations, which has led scholars to refer to this text as the *Dodecalogue* ("the twelve words").

1. *Private household idolatry (27:15).* Moses characterizes such a practice as "detestable" to Yahweh.
2. *Disrespectful treatment of parents (27:16).* This is referring to any verbal or physical action by which children demean parents.
3. *Moving a landmark (27:17).* Moving a boundary stone was viewed not only as a violation of others' right to their own property, but also as a crime against Yahweh, the ultimate owner of the land.
4. *Misleading the blind (27:18).* This is the first of two curses addressed to those who take advantage of others' misfortune.
5. *Subverting the rights of the marginalized (27:19).* Like the curse on those who move boundaries (27:17), the wording derives from earlier instruction in 24:17.
6. *Incest with one's father's wife (27:20).* "For he would uncover the skirt of his father" (author's translation) is a euphemism for violating the sanctity of the marriage.
7. *Intercourse with an animal (27:21).* Apparently, bestiality was deemed such a heinous offense because it blurs the boundaries between the creaturely world and humankind created as image-bearers of God (Gen 1:26–28).
8. *Incest with one's sister (27:22).* This practice was common in royal circles of ancient Egypt, and apparently in Phoenicia.
9. *Sexual intercourse with one's mother-in-law (27:23).* Leviticus 20:14 condemns this act and calls for capital punishment in the form of burning.
10. *Striking one's neighbor in secret (27:24).* It is unclear whether this curse involves simply striking one's neighbor or intentionally killing a person. The formulation may be intentionally vague to cover any physical violence.
11. *Accepting a bribe to condemn an innocent person (27:25).* Here the case involves either paying a bribe to a witness or paying a bribe to a judge so he condemns an innocent person to death.
12. *Failure to uphold the terms of this torah (27:26).* The imprecations conclude with a general curse on all who will not uphold "the words of this law." This imprecation calls for Israelite fidelity to him and invests Moses's words with permanent canonical authority.

Application. These rituals signify Israel's security and hope in Yahweh. Of course, the peace they celebrate is made possible only through the work of Jesus Christ, whose sacrificial work underlies all these rituals. And the peace they will celebrate at Gerizim and Ebal expresses in microcosm the peace we enjoy and the heavenly inheritance we will one day claim in the very presence of God.

DEUTERONOMY 28:1–29:1

Original Meaning

The Way of Blessing and Summary of the Way of the Curse (28:1–19). *The preconditions to blessing and curse (28:1–2; 28:15).* While the words for "blessings" and "curses" are the same as those encountered in 11:26–29 and 27:12–13, here and throughout the chapter the concepts are portrayed as animate beings that come upon their targets.

The formulaic declarations of blessing and curse (28:3–6; 28:16–19). These formulaic blessings and curses define Israel's well-being in agricultural terms and are grounded on the underlying premise that the land belongs to Yahweh; he determines whether it fulfills its role within the covenantal triangle involving deity, people, and land. While Israel's neighbors looked to fertility gods for their economic security, these opening statements declare that Israel's well-being depends on their fidelity to Yahweh.

The way of blessing (28:7–14). Although 28:7–13 expounds on 28:3–6, this paragraph exhibits independent stylistic and structural integrity. As a whole the unit summarizes the rewards for covenant obedience, though 28:9 and 28:13b–14 remind the hearers that these benefactions are not unconditional entitlements (cf. 28:1–2). Within this relationship, Israel will never be able to claim credit for the blessings they enjoy, but they will be held fully liable if the blessings do not materialize. Appearing in the center of chiastically arranged benefactions (28:9–10), Moses highlights Israel's special relationship with Yahweh, envisioning a glorious future in which the covenantal triangle is fully operative and *shalom* pervades.

Since this prosperity will happen on the land that Yahweh had sworn to the patriarchs, the blessing is linked to the ancient promises. Moses concretizes the image of prosperity in 28:12a by portraying Yahweh as the owner of a heavenly "storehouse," who opens the chute and lets the rains gush out on the land. Moses hereby declares polemically that the productivity of the land is determined by Yahweh, not Baal. Speaking metaphorically, he declares that Yahweh will make them "the head" of all and "the tail" of none (28:13a). This hegemony will involve total military (28:7) and economic (28:12b–13a; cf. 15:6) superiority over the nations.

When Yahweh establishes Israel as his holy people, then all the nations of the earth will see that Israel is branded with his name. This expression derives from the practice of inscribing or branding one's name on property. When the nations read Yahweh's name on Israel, they will recognize both that he owns them and that their well-being is a reflection of their divine suzerain. As his "holy people," Israel was chosen to bear the name of their divine redeemer and of the creator of all nations (26:19). They represent humanity in microcosm, exercising authority on Yahweh's behalf and evoking the response of awe from those over whom they exercise dominion.

The Way of the Curse (28:20–68). **1. The way of doom: the first volley (28:20–46).** Verses 20 and 45–46 frame the first volley of woes, announcing the issues involved. While linked in substance, the styles of these bookends differ. The reference to the long-range effects of Yahweh's actions against Israel in 28:46 represents the most striking difference: They will be a "sign" and "wonder" forever. Between these borders Moses threatens a litany of disasters, illustrating the curse, panic, and frustration referred to in 28:20.

The first alarm (28:21–26). The first alarm involves three agents of disaster: the plague (28:21–22a), crop failure (28:22b–24), and military defeat (28:25–26). In 28:22 Moses becomes more specific, listing seven afflictions with which Yahweh will strike his people.

The next two verses (28:23–24) spell out the crop afflictions. Like the four expressions for human illnesses, the meanings of the terms for crop diseases are uncertain. These verses echo Leviticus 26:19, which also portrays the heavens as a sheet of metal preventing moisture above the firmament from watering the earth and the ground as hardened and resisting cultivation.

Verse 26 concretizes the horror of defeat in battle. The corpses of the slain are left out in the open field as carrion for scavenging birds and mammals—perhaps the greatest indignity of all.

The second alarm (28:27–34). The curses in 28:27–29a, 34 threaten the personal health of the Israelites. A pair of identical clauses highlights Yahweh's role in Israel's future disaster (28:27a, 28a, cf. 28:35a) to be followed by a list of agents he will engage. Verse 28 may refer to the bewilderment that attends the kinds of disasters described in this chapter.

Verse 29 illustrates how these mental disorders manifest themselves. This declaration, coupled with the expressions of hopelessness in 28:29, 31, and 32, suggests the effects of an overwhelming military defeat. Compounding the crisis, 28:29b announces the theme of utter futility, which is then developed by means of a series of futility curses involving grievous domestic and economic abuses.

1. *The futility of betrothal* (28:30a).
2. *The futility of home construction* (28:30b).
3. *The futility of agricultural efforts* (28:30c).
4. *The futility of owning livestock* (28:31).
5. *The futility of having children* (28:32).
6. *The futility of all human effort* (28:33). Verse 33 summarizes the tragedy of the preceding. The Israelites will not eat the fruit of their own ground or consume any products of their toil.

The third alarm (28:35–44). Like the first alarm, this paragraph subdivides into three parts, dealing successively with illnesses (28:35), military defeat (28:36–37), and famine (28:38–42). It ends with a warning of the internal social effects of Israel's calamities (28:43–44).

Picking up the motif mentioned in 28:27, verse 35 returns to "the boils of Egypt," though now Moses adds that they will affect the knees and legs particularly, rendering movement difficult. Not only will this plague be incurable; the boils will cover the entire body from the soles of their feet to the crowns of their heads.

Whereas the first alarm spoke explicitly of Yahweh causing Israel's defeat at the hands of enemy armies (28:24–25) and the second dealt with oppression of Israel's citizens that will attend such a defeat (28:29b–34), the third predicts Israel's exile from the land (28:36–37). Moses declares that there, among the nations, the Israelites "will worship other gods, gods of wood and stone" (28:36). Their privileged status as vassals of Yahweh will be exchanged for vassaldom to lifeless idols. Verse 37 summarizes the effects of these calamities on Israel's standing among the nations.

In 28:38–42 Moses resumes his threat of famine as judgment, but his tactics change. Now the lack of food will not be caused by drought and plant diseases but insects. "Locusts" (28:38) are grass-eating insects that fly in vast swarms and devour everything in sight. "Worms" (28:39) refers to fruit grubs that attack the grapes. The meaning of "swarms of locusts" (28:42) is uncertain, but it probably refers to a species of beetle that kills vegetation by attacking leaves or stems.

Verses 43–44 reverse the blessing in 28:12–13 (cf. 23:20). "The foreigners" (28:43) could refer to foreign nations, but this is better interpreted as a divinely imposed reversal whereby Israelites in the land are targeted for judgment while sojourners and guest workers are spared.

In 28:45–46 Moses provides a summary conclusion to the litany of disasters (identified as "all these curses") described in 28:20–44. These threats describe Israel's certain future if they abandon Yahweh and serve other gods (28:29).

2. The way of doom: the second volley (28:47–57). *The underlying causes of Israel's demise (28:47–48).* Moses begins by declaring that ultimately Israel herself will be responsible for the threatened disasters (28:47). Because the Israelites refuse to serve their benefactor, Yahweh will provide alternative masters (28:49).

The character and tactics of Yahweh's agent (28:49–52). Moses frames this paragraph with declarations of Yahweh's involvement in Israel's demise (28:49, 52). However, between these frames his focus shifts from Yahweh, who will be immediately responsible for Israel's demise, to the terrifying nature and tactics of his agent. Verses 49–50 characterize Yahweh's agent of doom. The ruthless disposition of Yahweh's agent is matched by his ruthless actions (28:51–52). In 28:52 Moses predicts that all the fortifications in the land that Yahweh had granted to Israel will come crashing down before the invader. The deity–nation–land covenantal triangle will collapse like the walls of Israel's cities.

The horrific consequences of Yahweh's actions against Israel (28:53–57). Borrowing images from Leviticus 26:27–29, this paragraph opens with a general thesis statement, which is followed by two frightful scenes of cannibalism. Moses develops this theme in two parallel panels, illustrating how men and women respectively respond to the crisis precipitated by the siege (Deut 28:54–55, 56–57). Both panels begin by highlighting the cultural refinement of the people who are reduced to eating their own children. While fathers are described as "most gentle and sensitive" (28:54), Moses concretizes mothers' delicacy by describing those who consume their children as being unable to bear the thought of letting the soles of their feet touch the ground (28:56). These characterizations reflect the dehumanization that results from the actions of Yahweh's agent.

3. The way of doom: the third volley (28:58–68). Moses opens this section with a reminder to his immediate audience that the horrific fate described in this chapter is inevitable if they do not live scrupulously according to "all the words of this Torah that are written in this document" (28:58, author's translation), and if they "do not revere this glorious and awesome name—the LORD your God." The literary construction in 28:58 ("keep by doing . . . and by fearing," [lit.]) reminds the Israelites that covenantal fidelity involves both obedience to the will of the covenant Lord and due concern for his honor. Moses threatens the Israelites with a complete reversal of their salvation history by means of plagues and diseases (28:59–63b), dispersion (28:63c–67), and enslavement (28:68).

The literary construction of 28:63 signals a new and shocking dimension in this litany of horror: the termination of the nation–land association by dispersing the population among the nations (28:63–67). Where previously Yahweh had delighted in causing Israel to flourish, now he will delight in their destruction. These statements reflect the other side of Yahweh's passion: When his people trample underfoot his grace, his passions will be ignited against them.

Verses 65–66 describe the Israelites' physical and emotional state in exile: Yahweh himself will rob them of all joy and meaning in life, and the distress over their demise will haunt them wherever they go. In 28:66–67 he concretizes their despair by introducing hypothetical interlocutors, whose lips express their emotional state.

Moses's warning of Israel's doom concludes in 28:68 with an unequivocal image of the reversal of Israel's history. Back in Egypt they will try to sell themselves to their enemies to serve as male and female slaves, but even as slaves they will be deemed worthless.

Colophonic Conclusion (29:1). The characterization of the covenant as "that which Yahweh commanded Moses to make ["cut," literal] with the descendants of Israel" (author's translation) highlights Moses's role as authorized interpreter of its stipulations and the one who presides over the covenant renewal ceremonies reflected in Deuteronomy. When Moses "cuts this covenant," he supervises new ceremonies whereby the new generation commits itself to the old covenant. This means that as a result of his exposition, the people have a fuller understanding of the original event and the stipulations revealed at Horeb, but also that they commit themselves to Moses's interpretation in this address of the words associated with that covenant (the Decalogue, book of the covenant, instructions on holiness, etc.). In short, the covenant referred to in 29:1 should not be viewed as a new covenant but as a supplement to the one made at Sinai, which itself represented the fulfillment and elaboration of Yahweh's covenant with Abraham (Gen 17:7–8).

Application. The warnings in such texts are intended to guard against presumption. Like the Israelites of the Old Testament, Christians may be tempted to presume upon the grace of God and take their standing with him for granted. However, these warnings aim to elicit both hope and fear; in so doing they provide an antidote to apostasy and rebellion.

As a corollary, this passage reminds readers in every generation that prosperity and freedom may never be regarded as fundamental and unconditional rights. The call to relationship with God in Christ to bear his name is a glorious privilege (Deut 28:8–10; cf. 1 Pet 4:12–19), to which we must respond with faith demonstrated through obedience to the revealed will of God. Fidelity to him may provoke the ire of others, but it will win the Lord's praise. However, failure to live according to the will of the suzerain may win the praise of others, but it will provoke the ire of God.

DEUTERONOMY 29:2–28

Original Meaning

Act I: Celebrating the Grace of Covenant Today (29:2–13). *Remembering Yahweh's past grace today (29:2–9).* Since most in the assembly were born during the forty years in the desert and did not witness the nation's rescue from Egypt, Moses draws all of them into Yahweh's past actions by speaking as if they were eyewitnesses to those events. Through their renewal of the covenant, the present generation may identify with their predecessors, who saw the amazing signs and wonders that Yahweh performed in Egypt.

Verse 4 is difficult, but retaining the word order of the Hebrew may help: "But the LORD has not given you a mind that understands or eyes that see or ears that hear, until this day" (author's translation). Following the reference to the understanding "mind," "eyes" and "ears" denote mental capacities of perception and understanding. Whereas the exodus generation as a whole did not grasp the revelatory, redemptive, and covenantal significance of Yahweh's actions (9:1–24; cf. 1:19–46), this generation knows; through Moses's final pastoral addresses Yahweh has given Israel a heart to know, eyes to see, and ears to hear.

Within the chapter as a whole, 29:9 is a hinge. Here Moses challenges his audience to continue to prove their faith in Yahweh, keeping the words of this covenant by doing them. The clause "so that you may prosper in everything you do" highlights the future importance of maintaining the commitment the Israelites had shown in their victory over the Amorite kings. The dimensions of this prosperity are summarized in the blessings of 28:1–14.

Claiming Yahweh's grace today (29:10–13). Moses lists the participants in the covenantal proceedings. Beginning with a comprehensive expression "all of you" (29:10), he provides the longest catalogue of participants in a formal religious event in the entire Old Testament. This assembly had two purposes.

1. Through these rituals the people "enter into the covenant of Yahweh your God and his oath" (29:12, author's translation). Moses refers to this covenant as Yahweh's covenant, not Israel's, and the oath as "his oath." The oath involved a conditional imprecation, calling for the curses if the party taking the oath fails to keep the terms of the treaty.
2. Through these rituals Yahweh confirms Israel as his people and himself as their God. The covenant with Abraham and his descendants is the covenant he established with Abraham's descendants at Sinai (Exod 19–24), and he now confirms it on the plains of Moab with the generation about to move in and take the promised land.

Act II: Despising the Grace of Covenant Tomorrow (29:14–28). **Setting the stage (29:14–17).** The construction of 29:14–15 is emphatic, both by a second reference to "this covenant, with its oath" (referring to the privileges and warnings built into the covenant) and by its word order (29:14). The commitments made here by Israel and Yahweh were binding for future generations.

In 29:16–17 Moses digresses with reflections on the Israelites' life in Egypt and their crossing through the territory of other nations on their journey to the present location. However, the journey itself is not his concern. Rather, it is the shocking sight of the idolatry of the nations through whose lands they passed. Moses's epithets for idols reflect his disposition toward idolatry. These designations for idols emphasize their worthlessness and repugnancy.

The personal consequences of infidelity (29:18–21). Moses warns the present and future generations that, unlike the gods of the nations, Yahweh will brook no rivals (29:18). He warns against tolerating an individual in their midst who should turn away from Yahweh to serve other gods. Poison and wormwood function metaphorically for the unsavory and lethal effects of idolatry.

In 29:20–21 Moses predicts Yahweh's reaction. Though Moses might have declared Yahweh as unwilling to spare that man, he speaks of refusing forgiveness. Nothing will change Yahweh's disposition. By his idolatry and highhanded response to the warnings, the idolater has sealed his own fate.

The geographic consequences of collective infidelity (29:22–28). *The first speech (29:22–23).* Moses begins with a general designation, "later generations." According to 29:23 the speech is precipitated by the sight that greets these observers. These expressions are shorthand for all the curses in 28:20–68, though they bear closest links with 28:59. The sight reminds observers of the utter devastation of Sodom, Gomorrah, Admah, and Zeboiim.

The second speech (29:24). The introduction of new speakers highlights the irony of the situation. Whereas Yahweh's design was that the nations should witness Israel's privileged status (26:19; cf. 28:1), here "all the nations" witness her demise.

The third speech (29:25–28). Moses does not identify the speakers behind the third speech, though they seem well aware of Israel's special relationship with Yahweh and the covenant he had made with them. The speech itself divides into two virtually equal parts, the first (29:25–26) dealing with human causation behind Israel's fate and the second (29:26–27) with Yahweh's response.

1. Israel's treachery is the ultimate cause of their fate (29:25–26). Here the speakers realize that Israel's destruction is the result of rebellion against their divine Lord. They prostrated themselves before strange gods, in contrast to Yahweh, who had called Israel to an intimate covenant relationship with himself and had claimed Israel as his special allotment (32:9).
2. Yahweh's fury is the immediate cause of Israel's fate (29:27–28). This speech is filled with irony. Like those

who had come out of Egypt (cf. 29:4), the future generation of Israelites envisioned here seems clueless about spiritual realities, apparently having forgotten Yahweh their God, his covenant, and the event at which they formally became the people of Yahweh. The concluding note, "as it is now" (29:28), does not refer to the immediate rhetorical situation but reflects the context and perspective of the interlocutor. "Now" is the day of Israel's judgment.

Application. This chapter highlights the tragic missiological consequences of infidelity. Yahweh did not establish his covenant with Israel in a corner, nor did he intend for her to be insular in her enjoyment of his blessing. He chose Israel in the first place that she might be a kingdom of priests, a holy people among the nations, intervening on their behalf before him and serving as his agents of revelation and blessing. If the prosperity of Israel redounds to the glory of God among the nations, the opposite is also true when they observe the horrendous consequences of infidelity.

DEUTERONOMY 29:29–30:10

Original Meaning

Today: Wondering about Covenant Grace (29:29). Moses's insertion of this statement provides a psychological buffer between the darkness of chapter 29 and the brilliance of chapter 30. Like the intermission between acts in a theatrical performance, this esoteric reflection on wisdom prepares for the change in tone and direction.

The Restoration of the Bilateral Relationship between Yahweh and Israel (30:1–3). Moses has been trying to inspire fidelity with promises and with warnings. When his predictions have been fulfilled, the events foreseen in 30:1b–3 will occur (cf. 4:30). They will "return to the Lord" (30:2). Yahweh's disposition toward Israel will change; he will show compassion to them. Instead of turning from Israel and operating as their enemy, he will turn toward them and act on their behalf. Whereas previously he had scattered them among the nations, now he will gather them.

The Restoration of the Trilateral Relationships Involving Yahweh, Israel, and the Land (30:4–7). Moses begins this subunit by addressing the nation–land relationship of the triangle (30:4–5). The picture will be complete when Yahweh fulfills his ancient promise to Abraham to multiply his descendants once more. In fact, Yahweh will cause the population to exceed that of their ancestors before the exile.

Verse 6 brings us close to unraveling the mysteries of divine providence and grace. Moses declares that Yahweh will secure permanent and total devotion through circumcising the hearts of those whom he brings back from the exile and of their descendants. With this heart surgery the covenantal triangle will be totally restored. Yahweh will repair their standing among the nations, imposing the sanctions that his own people had experienced.

The Human Proof of Restoration (30:8). Moses's optimism regarding Israel as a nation presupposes a divine act of heart circumcision. He expresses no confidence in the human will to maintain the course.

The Environmental Proof of the Restoration (30:9–10). Moses draws his hearers' attention back to Yahweh, who causes the land to fulfill its role in the tripartite covenant relationship. In describing the environmental evidences of this new order, he highlights Israel's special relationship with Yahweh by what these two will do for each other. Moses brings this section to a close with one more reminder that although the triangular covenantal relationships will be fully restored, the Israelites must pay full attention to the voice of Yahweh, which means ordering their conduct according to his commands and decrees. Israel must return to Yahweh her God with all her heart/mind and her entire being.

Application. The work of Christ, whose mission was established before the foundation of the world (1 Pet 1:18–21), provides the basis for all God's covenants. Through Christ's work the holiness of God is satisfied and his wrath toward us is lifted and replaced with mercy.

DEUTERONOMY 30:11–20

Original Meaning

The Accessibility of the Revelation of God (30:11–14). In 30:11–14 Moses reiterates that the demands of covenant relationship are not unknowable, unreasonable, incomprehensible, or impossible. On the contrary, they are accessible and doable. Seldom in the book has the argumentation been so tight. If we read the main body of this covenant renewal oration as a continuous narrative, 30:11–14 expand on "all the words of this law [torah]" (29:29) that have been revealed to the Israelites.

Verse 14 indicates the revelation is extremely near, in their mouths and in their minds/hearts; by recitation they commit it to memory. While every generation will produce individuals who are righteous and loyal to Yahweh (i.e., true Israelites), here the concern is spiritual recidivism of the nation as a whole. Their success depends on the fidelity of the group.

The Two Ways (30:15–20). Moses the teacher/preacher presents two options and outlines the consequences of each. Israel obeys the commands of Yahweh that Moses is commanding them "to love" Yahweh their God, "to walk" in his ways, and "to keep" his commands. The kinds of behavior that bring on death and disaster involve a change in disposition away from Yahweh, demonstrated in disobedience and worship of other gods (30:17–18).

"Life" (30:19) means a long life in which the effects of sin and premature death are staved off. But it also means dwelling in the land that Yahweh had promised on oath to give to their ancestors. With this last reference to the ancestors, Moses has come full circle, ending where he began—with the people on the verge of the promised land and with Yahweh's sworn promises ringing in his ears. Yahweh always keeps his word; the question here is, will the people keep theirs?

Application. People's standing before God and their ultimate destiny is in their own hands. Such is the gospel according to Moses, and such is the gospel according to Jesus (Matt 7:13). This is not only a warning against choosing the wrong path that leads to death and destruction, but also an invitation to choose the path of life. Thanks be to God!

DEUTERONOMY 31:1–30

Original Meaning

The Installation of Joshua as Moses's Successor: Part I (31:1–8). *Moses's challenge for the people (31:1–6).* Verse 1 shifts attention from the nature of covenantal relationship to steps taken to "put the house in order." Whereas other death stories tend to begin with the narrator's announcement of the character's old age and impending death, here Moses announces his old age and his inability to lead the people any longer.

Moses directs their attention to Yahweh's continued presence (31:3–5). The people will be led by Yahweh and his designated agent (31:3a, d). Yahweh will deal with the Canaanite nations himself. Moses promises that Yahweh will destroy them (31:3b), and then he reminds Israel of recent victories (31:4–5a). Moses concludes this brief speech with an impassioned appeal to his people to take courage and put full confidence in Yahweh (31:6).

Moses's challenge for Joshua (31:7–8). Moses publicly passes the mantle to his trusted lieutenant so that Joshua will be seen as the divinely chosen successor. The hortatory framework, "Be strong and courageous" (31:7) and "Do not be afraid; do not be discouraged" (31:8), sets the tone of this speech. Verse 8 offers Joshua the grounds for courage: Yahweh goes before him and guarantees his presence.

The Deposition of the Torah (31:9–13). The narrative preamble (31:9) highlights three specific actions by Moses in relation to the torah.

1. Moses wrote down this torah. For the first time he appears as a scribe.
2. Moses hands the torah to the Levitical priests and to all the elders of Israel. The narrator also notes the involvement of all the elders of Israel. The involvement of priestly and civil authorities anticipates the bifurcation of roles after Moses's death.
3. Moses charges the Levitical priests and elders to read the torah regularly before the people. This charge, which takes up the bulk of this paragraph, consists of three principal declarations: read this torah (31:11); assemble the people (31:12); let their children hear and learn to fear Yahweh (31:13). Future readings of the torah will provide succeeding generations with regular opportunities for renewal and actualization of their covenant relationship with him.

The Installation of Joshua as Moses's Successor: Part II (31:14–15, 23). Now we hear the voice of Yahweh speaking directly to Moses, inviting him and Joshua for a private audience with him in the tent of meeting. When Moses and Joshua present themselves, Yahweh appears in a pillar of cloud, which stands at the doorway of the tent.

Joshua is not a part of the picture until 31:23, which contains Yahweh's commissioning speech for him as Moses's successor. In 31:23 Yahweh summarizes Moses's installation speech in 31:7–8. It seems that Yahweh's private commissioning may have been for Joshua's personal benefit, reassuring him that he is the divinely appointed successor to Moses.

The Preamble to Israel's National Anthem (31:16–22). *The problem: Israel's apparently inevitable apostasy (31:16–18).* Beginning abruptly by announcing Moses's imminent death, Yahweh describes the consequences of this event as a chain of actions and responses. Moses's death has great significance not only for himself but especially for the people. Yahweh describes the Israelites' anticipated response to Moses's departure with four verbs.

1. They will "rise" (untranslated in the NIV) in rebellion against Yahweh.
2. They will "prostitute themselves" to foreign gods of the land they are entering.
3. They will "forsake" Yahweh.
4. They will "break the covenant."

The three expressions Yahweh uses to describe his response to Israel's apostasy reflect the intensity of his rage (31:17a). The idiom "to hide the face" signifies the withdrawal of favor.

In ancient courtly contexts, for a king to turn his face from a subject signaled disaster, though the idiom was often applied to gods as well. As in extrabiblical texts, when a deity hid his face, the effects were devastating (31:17b). The people's demise is indeed the result of divine wrath, but the ultimate cause is their abandoning of the covenant that Yahweh made with them.

The Solution: A Song (31:19–21). Instead of appointing a pastoral successor to hold the nation together spiritually and to keep it on its covenantal course, he commissions a song. Indeed 31:19–21 suggests that Yahweh's primary reason for calling Moses and Joshua to the tent of meeting was to communicate to them this song, which would serve as a sort of national anthem for the people.

Verse 20 summarizes *vaticinium ante eventum* (prediction before the event), future historical developments that necessitate the song. Yahweh will deliver into their hands the land, which will yield its produce and enable them to eat, be satisfied, and grow fat. They will turn to other gods, serve them as vassals, spurn Yahweh, and break his covenant.

"Many disasters and calamities" (31:21) represent new participants in Israel's future and serve as a shorthand expression for all the covenant curses outlined in 28:15–68. In this desperate context the words of the song will testify to the fidelity and grace of Yahweh and the ingratitude and rebellion of his people. But it also offers hope. Like the ending to Moses's third address, it declares that after judgment Yahweh will vindicate his reputation and his people. After recounting Yahweh's speech, the narrator reports that Moses did as Yahweh had instructed him (31:22).

Moses's Concluding Speech (31:24–29). Based on the subject matter, this short paragraph divides into three parts:

1. a preamble to Moses's speech (31:24–25);
2. final instructions regarding the torah (31:26–27); and
3. instructions regarding Israel's national anthem (31:28–30).

Although the latter two may represent separate utterances associated with earlier elements of this chapter, by combining them the narrator suggests the depositions of the torah and the song reflect a common concern.

1. By noting that Moses's charge to the Levites is issued after he has finished writing the words of the torah, the narrator links what follows to 31:9–13.
2. By handing the written copy of the torah to the Levites, Moses designates them as custodians of the document, and by having them place it beside the ark, he acknowledges Yahweh as its source and divine guarantor.
3. Moses's instructions concerning the song in 31:28–29 consist of a command to the Levites to act (31:28a), the purpose of that action (31:28b–c), and a rationale for it (31:29).

Verse 29 reinforces v. 27, showing that Moses shares Yahweh's pessimistic view of the spiritual state of the people. The narrator has the last word in this chapter, reporting that Moses recited all the words of this song in the hearing of the whole assembly.

Application. Yahweh always provides the leadership needed to fulfill his calling. While every generation of leaders must hand the baton to successors, thankfully, neither new leaders nor the people in their charge are left to their own resources. The keys to the fulfillment of God's mission remain acceptance of the commission received from him and trust in his promised presence.

DEUTERONOMY 32:1–47

Original Meaning

The Exordium: A Call to Acknowledge the Perfections of Yahweh (32:1–4). Verse 1 suggests this is a song of praise to Yahweh from the lips of a human that the world needs to hear. Verse 2 focuses on the refreshing effect of his words. Verse 3 signals a shift in attention from the words of the song to the singer's intent—to glorify Yahweh. Verse 4 is a confessional statement, announcing the theme of Israel's national anthem.

The Recollection: A Call to Acknowledge the Imperfections of Yahweh's People (32:5–18). *Stanza I: The thesis statement (32:5–6).* The first stanza indicates that corruption involves violation of the Supreme Command through idolatry. The rhetorical questions of 32:6 confirm that 32:5 has contrasted the perfections of Yahweh (32:4) with Israel's deep-seated imperfections. The rhetorical question in the first line calls for a negative answer, but the characterization of the Israelites suggests they have answered it positively. The second half of 32:6 uses another rhetorical question to hint at the nature of their corruption: Yahweh is their father, but they have treated him shamefully.

Stanza II: A call to remember Yahweh's grace (32:7–14).

1. *Yahweh's election of Israel and her special relationship with him (32:8–9).* With elegant parallelism the elders recall the establishment of Israel's special relationship to Yahweh. This text emphasizes the relationship between Yahweh and his people.
2. *Yahweh's rescue of Israel from a threatening situation and his care for her in the desert (32:10–12).* This verse suggests a slow death of thirst or the sudden attack of hungry desert creatures. However, apparently just in time Yahweh came by and "found" Israel (32:10). Verse 11

introduces another image of divine care, referring to actions an eagle might take to secure the well-being of its young. If the Israelites ever made it through the desert, it was entirely to Yahweh's credit (32:12).

3. *Yahweh's endowment of Israel with all good things (32:13–14).* The last strophe envisions Yahweh's leading Israel through the promised land in triumphant procession. The first line portrays Israel's arrival as an army of chariots riding over the "heights of the land" (32:13a). The rest of 32:13–14, then, highlights the agricultural benefits that the land yields for Israel.

Stanza III: Trampling underfoot the grace of Yahweh (32:15–18). The concern of this stanza is Israel's violation of the Supreme Command. The subject is presented from two sides: Israel's abandonment of Yahweh (32:15, 18) and their pursuit of other gods (32:16–17). The reference to Israel as "Jeshurun" (32:15), Yahweh's affectionate epithet for his people, heightens the tragedy. The description of Jeshurun that follows suggests the name is used ironically. The "straight one" (author's translation of "Jeshurun") on whom Yahweh had lavished his affection has acted perversely through abominable acts of devotion to other gods.

Verses 16–17 shift the focus from Israel's foolish response to Yahweh to their ridiculous response to other gods. The Israelite objects of devotion are nongods. They are novelties ("gods that recently appeared" [32:17]) in contrast to Yahweh, who has been operating in Israel's interest since the day the nations were distributed among the sons of God (32:8).

Verse 18 returns to the notions with which the strophe had opened (32:15): Israel has forgotten Yahweh. By portraying Israel as the child of Yahweh, who exhibits both fatherly (32:6) and motherly (32:18) qualities, the song highlights Israel's dependence on Yahweh for her very existence. In forgetting Yahweh, they have truly trampled underfoot his grace.

The Confession: A Call to Recognize the Justice of Yahweh (32:19–35). **Stanza I: Yahweh's justice in dealing with his own people (32:19–25).** *Yahweh's disposition toward his people (32:20–21).* The first statement recalls Yahweh's prediction in the narrative preamble to the song (31:16b–18). The second line is not an expression of openness, as if Yahweh has no awareness or control over Israel's destiny. Verses 20c–21b summarize the basis for Yahweh's rejection of his people, presenting first the external (32:20c–d) and then the internal grounds (32:21a–b). In 32:21c–d Yahweh declares his intention in rejecting Israel.

Yahweh's actions against his people (32:22–25). The expression of divine fury begins cosmically (32:22) and then zeroes in on the Israelites themselves (32:23–25). Yahweh's fury against the cosmos gives way to a particular target, specified in 32:25 as young men and young women, nursing children, and "those with grey hair." None will survive the attack of Yahweh's agents of wrath.

Stanza II: Yahweh's justice in dealing with Israel's enemies (32:26–35). In the end we learn why he did not utterly reject his people, despite their ingratitude and rebellion. Verse 27 explains Yahweh was troubled by the possibility that the enemies would draw false conclusions regarding their role in Israel's demise. They may have been chosen as instruments of divine judgment, but this decision was not based on their inherent qualifications or moral superiority. To the contrary, 32:28–29 highlight the enemy's stupidity. Verse 29 presents evidence of the enemy's ignorance by posing a hypothetical and unreal condition. Were the nations wise, they would get it, that is, grasp their end (cf. 32:20).

In 32:30 the speaker asserts that the Israelites' survival is due entirely to the work of God. The shift to first person plural in 32:31 signals a new speaker who recognizes the uniqueness of Yahweh among the gods of the nations. Verse 32 signals another shift in perspective, returning to the voice of Yahweh, which will carry through to the end of 32:35.

The rest of 32:32 and 32:33 suggests the grapes are poisonous and their clusters deadly—as deadly as the venom of serpents and as cruel as the poison of cobras. With the references to Sodom and Gomorrah, Yahweh subtly hinted at the enemies' destiny (v. 32; cf. v. 29). Yahweh has kept under lock and key the poisonous wine from Sodom and Gomorrah, reserved for the day when he will serve it to Israel's enemies. According to 32:35, because Yahweh controls the nations' fate, their judgment is certain. Poisonous wine now stored in Yahweh's storehouse is about to be served.

The Gospel: A Call to Treasure the Compassion of Yahweh (32:36–42). In 32:37 Yahweh quickly resumes his speech. While Yahweh and Moses deem Israel's future infidelity and judgment to be inevitable, already in 4:31 Moses had declared the present assertion of divine empathy to be rooted in Yahweh's character as a compassionate God. The second half of 32:36 sets the context of his change in disposition. Yahweh notices that the Israelites are at the end of their resources.

In 32:37–38 Yahweh's voice returns and carries on through 32:42. He begins by taunting the Israelites for having put their confidence in other gods. In 32:38 the mockery turns to idols themselves. The triad of action verbs reinforces the sarcasm: "Let them rise, assist you, and be your hiding place" (32:38, author's translation). These expressions all play on the reference to the gods as "rock" in 32:37.

The remainder of 32:39 and indeed 32:40–42 elaborate on Yahweh's exclusive control over the fates and fortunes of human beings. If Israel has suffered, this has indeed been the work of Yahweh, but the switch to an imperfect verb turns this statement into a promise: Yahweh will certainly heal his people.

The final strophe (32:40–42) seals Israel's future. Yahweh assures Israel that he will deal with their enemies once and for all. Verses 41 and 42 reinforce the substance of the divinely sworn affidavit, beginning with a reference to the context—when Yahweh, the Divine Warrior, prepares his weapons for battle. In 32:42 Yahweh portrays his sword and arrows as carnivorous beasts that cannot get enough of human blood and human flesh. Yahweh will rise on behalf of his people and punish their enemies for their arrogance and brutality to Israel.

The Coda: A Call to Celebrate Yahweh's Deliverance (32:43). Israel's national anthem ends on a festive note, appealing to the nations to join in the celebration of Yahweh's gracious acts on behalf of Israel. Verse 43 presents the hosts of heaven and the nations with three reasons to celebrate and pay homage to Yahweh.

1. Yahweh has restored his relationship with Israel.
2. Yahweh has taken vengeance on Israel's (and his own) enemies.
3. Yahweh has made atonement for the land. In so doing he has reversed the earlier dissolution of the tripartite relationship involving deity–nation–people precipitated by Israel's idolatry.

The Epilogue to Israel's National Anthem (32:44–47). Having quoted Israel's anthem, the narrator draws the reader back to the context in which the song was delivered. But Moses is not content with merely reciting the poem. As Israel's pastor he adds an exhortation in 32:46 for all the assembled people. In 32:47 Moses reiterates the importance for Israel's future of heeding his instruction.

Application. The song presents a frank assessment of the human condition, especially our propensity to bow down to idols that are pathetic figments of the human imagination. An idol is anything that robs God of our devotion and in which we trust, to which we look for significance, meaning, and security. The idols of our day include money, pleasure, beauty, science, human reason, and power.

DEUTERONOMY 32:48–52

Original Meaning. Following a narrative introduction, this paragraph is cast entirely as divine speech. The skeleton of the speech is represented by the quartette of commands: "go up," "view," "die," "be gathered" (32:49–51). It concludes with a climactic indicative statement (32:52), which must have been the most painful of all. Yahweh's tone is stern. Moses may indeed "see" the land visually, but he may not "experience" it.

Application. The privilege of leadership over God's people comes with a heavy burden. From those who have been given much, much is required (Luke 12:48). Those who are called to lead must lead according to the will of the one who has called them.

DEUTERONOMY 33:1–29

Original Meaning

Introduction and Exordium (33:1–5). The narrative preamble (33:1) reminds readers that what follows is part of Moses's preparations for his death. The exordium proper takes up 33:2–5, portraying Yahweh in glorious theophanic form, coming from the mountains in the desert, presumably to deliver his people and to be acknowledged as king over all the tribes of Israel. Taken together, vv. 2–3 paint a picture of Yahweh's universal authority.

The third person reference to Moses and the reference to the giving of the torah in 33:4 catch the reader by surprise. However, linked to the previous verse, this torah may be identified with his commands that have now become the special "possession" of the Israelites (cf. 4:8).

Verse 5 suggests the gathering of the tribes on the plains of Moab was a royal event. In the face of his own imminent death, Moses hereby declares publicly that although he will be departing, their divine king will lead the way into the enemy territory.

The Blessings of Reuben and Judah (33:6–7). The collection of benedictions opens unannounced with the blessing of Reuben. Moses's blessing is extremely modest. It consists of four lines, beginning with a plea to Yahweh to hear the Judahites' prayers—apparently when they head into battle—and to provide protection so they may return safely from their campaigns.

The Blessing of Levi (33:8–11). The length of the Levites' blessing reflects Moses's relationship to this tribe (Exod 6:16–27) and their spiritual role among the people. While 33:11 hints at a military role for this tribe, the emphasis is on their spiritual ministry among the people. This blessing envisions four responsibilities for the Levites, all of them custodial: of the Thummim and Urim (33:8), the covenant (33:9), divine revelation (33:10a–b), and the sacrificial liturgy (33:10c–d).

The Blessings of Benjamin and Joseph (33:12–17). After blessing three Leah tribes, the benediction turns to the tribes descended from Rachel: Benjamin and Joseph. Here Benjamin is not merely the beloved son of his father (cf. Gen 44:20), but the "beloved" of Yahweh (cf. 2 Sam 12:25). The blessing proper focuses on Benjamin's security under Yahweh's protective care.

The blessing of Joseph opens with an effusive prayer for blessing of the land. The blessing marshals the entire cosmos in Joseph's interest. The list concludes with a declaration that prosperity is dependent on the good will of Yahweh, identified here by the unusual epithet, "the one who inhabits the bush" (33:16, lit.). Verse 17 elaborates on Joseph's status as firstborn with impressive bovine imagery.

The Blessings of Zebulun, Issachar, and Gad (33:18–21). In 33:18–25 Moses addresses the six northern tribes in five short fragments. He honors Zebulun by departing from the birth order and naming the younger tribe first. Zebulun and Issachar are to rejoice wherever they are. Moses speaks of these tribes harvesting the products of the sea and the seashore. This blessing envisions Zebulun and Issachar along the coast in Phoenician territory rather than inland as described in Joshua 19:10–23.

The blessing involving Gad (Deut 33:20–21) actually pronounces the benediction on the one who enlarges Gad, that is, Yahweh himself. The enlargement of Gad represents a fulfillment of the name, which means "good fortune." The last three lines praise the Gadites for their spiritual commitments.

The Blessings of Dan, Naphtali, and Asher (33:22–25). Moses's blessing of Dan is the shortest of all (33:22). Dan is compared to a lion cub leaping from Bashan (cf. Gen 49:9). The blessing of Naphtali (Deut 33:23) sounds like a collage of expressions that have been heard earlier, but they are now combined in the first two lines to present an image of superlative well-being and satisfaction with the favor and the blessing of Yahweh. The last line charges Naphtali to take possession of the west and the southland.

In the blessing of Asher, Moses prays for both fertility and security. The material dimension of that favor is expressed by a curious idiom, "let him bathe his feet in oil" (33:24). The expression imagines the olive trees of Galilee so productive that streams of oil run down the hills.

The Coda (33:26–29). The opening line of 33:26 declares the incomparability of God. This imagery recalls Canaanite myths of the storm god Baal, one of whose stock epithets was "rider of the clouds." By claiming these epithets for Yahweh, Moses declares his jurisdiction over all the spheres that Canaanites had distributed among the gods.

The first two lines of 33:27 declare in a nutshell the Israelites' basis of security. They know their God is eternal. The Israelites are secure because Yahweh is their defender. Moses created the image of a strong father who provides a safe and secure home for his family and who holds them in a protective embrace. But Yahweh's actions on Israel's behalf are also offensive; he goes before Israel, defeating the enemy and sending out his agents with the charge "Destroy him!"

Verse 28 functions as a fulcrum between two hymnic celebrations of privilege, describing a domestic scene of perfect bliss. The last two lines of 33:28 highlight Israel's prosperity. As staple agricultural products, grain and wine function as a merism referring to full prosperity.

Whereas the coda had begun by declaring the incomparability of Israel's God, it ends by declaring the incomparability of God's people. They are the beneficiaries of his rescue and protection. With the last line, Moses presents the image of subjugated persons cringing prostrate before their victor and the victor placing his foot on their backs.

Application. As in the Lord's Prayer, issues relating to physical well-being are framed by and subordinated to the sheer privilege of calling God our father, king, savior, and defender. To bear the name of Christ and to hear him address us as his beloved are reasons enough to celebrate and keep our focus on him.

DEUTERONOMY 34:1–12

Original Meaning

The Report of Moses's Death (34:1–6). As the final death report, Deuteronomy 34 recounts Moses's ascent up Mount Nebo, his observation of the land (34:1–4), and his death and burial (34:5–6). Although chapter 34 opens with a report of Moses's ascent, the bulk of the paragraph focuses on Yahweh's actions (34:1b, 4, 6).

In 34:4, Yahweh addresses Moses, declaring to him that this is indeed the land he had promised on oath to the ancestors. For Israel this declaration brings the book to an end on a hopeful note, but for Moses it was extremely painful. Yahweh reminds him once more that he will not cross over there. Moses may only gaze at the prize with his eyes.

The announcement of Moses's death in 34:5 is brief and to the point. But even his death confirms Yahweh's fidelity, for his demise transpires "as the Lord had said." Although the word "servant" may denote menial status, phrases like "servant of the king" for court officials demonstrate that in contexts like this, it bears honorific significance.

From a hagiographic perspective, the notice of Moses's burial in 34:6 is striking. Moses was buried by Yahweh himself. Moses had reached his heavenly destination without having reached his earthly home. God had been with Moses throughout his life, but Moses was alone with God in his death.

The Response to Moses's Death (34:7–8). As the Israelites had done for Aaron, they mourned Moses's passing for thirty days (34:8).

Epitaph: The Narrator's Commentary on Moses (34:9–12). The grammatical construction of the first sentence of 34:9 shifts the attention from Moses to Joshua son of Nun, but in so doing it still honors Moses. The expression "spirit of wisdom" represents a special divine endowment for the fulfillment of a divinely ordained role. Joshua was divinely endowed with the spirit of wisdom *because* Moses ordained him. The narrator concludes his biography of Moses with an unrestrained eulogy.

Application. Moses was a shepherd after the order of Christ as described in 1 Peter 5:1–6 and after the order of Yahweh as celebrated in Psalm 23—perhaps the finest pastoral text in Scripture. Like Yahweh—incarnate in the Good Shepherd, Jesus Christ—Moses provided his people what they really needed: nourishment and rest. He guided them in paths of righteousness; he walked with them through valleys of deepest darkness; and he invited them to come and celebrate in the presence of the Lord. May the Lord raise up for his work in our day pastors in the order of Christ our Shepherd.

JOSHUA

INTRODUCTION TO JOSHUA

Jewish tradition claims that Joshua wrote the book named after him, but few affirm that today. More likely, the book of Joshua is named for its main character whose exploits as Israel's leader after Moses dominate its contents. The Old Testament nowhere explains how the book of Joshua came to be, so internal clues offer the only illumination on the matter. Joshua comprises an edited compilation of source materials.

Key terms in Joshua echo the language of Moses in Deuteronomy. The same Deuteronomic influence is evident in Judges, 1–2 Samuel, and 1–2 Kings. Many scholars now believe that this Deuteronomistic History (DH) appeared in two successive editions, the first during the reign of Josiah (seventh century BC) and the second during the exile (ca. 550 BC). Acceptance of a Deuteronomistic historian does not deny the antiquity of the contents of much of Deuteronomy, nor does it preclude the possibility that the DH, or at least parts of it, may have found written form as early as the early monarchy.

Despite the shadow of ethnic cleansing that haunts Joshua, it also reflects a surprisingly inclusive stance toward non-Israelites. Joshua's main plea is that Israel must vigilantly guard against corrupting Canaanite influences rather than totally get rid of them. To be sure, the Canaanites pose a deadly danger to Israel's loyalty to Yahweh, and Yahweh holds Israel accountable to its covenant commitment. But the book of Joshua seems to leave the final solution to Yahweh—and perhaps also to leave the door open to other Rahabs and Gibeonites from among the Canaanite enclaves who might choose submission over resistance.

BOOK OUTLINE

I. Report: The Conquest of the Land (1:1–12:24)
   - A. Preparations for Entrance (1:1–2:24)
   - B. Jordan Crossing and Two Battle Reports (3:1–8:35)
   - C. Conquest of Canaan Proper (9:1–12:24)

II. Report: The Settlement of the Land (13:1–24:33)
   - A. The Distribution of Inheritances (13:1–19:51)
   - B. Two Special Land Provisions (20:1–21:45)
   - C. Three Concluding Reports (22:1–24:33)

JOSHUA 1:1–18

Original Meaning

Joshua's Marching Orders (1:1–9). *The introduction (1:1a).* The brief opening report formula, "after the death of Moses," signals that Joshua 1 picks up where Deuteronomy 34 left off and pushes the story forward. The death of Moses leaves a leadership vacuum in Israel, so it is no surprise that the book immediately turns to a speech by Yahweh (1:1b).

Joshua's commissioning (1:2–9). Yahweh's commissioning speech sounds like a king issuing battle plans to his field general. Joshua and Israel are to "cross the Jordan" (1:2b). "I am about to give" stresses the land as the generous gift of Yahweh, Israel's mighty Savior from slavery and gracious covenant partner.

The gift includes the *whole* promised land. Yahweh quotes Moses's own words in a slightly expanded form (Deut 11:24) to reiterate the promise spoken through him (Josh 1:3–4). "Every place where you set your foot" (1:3) stresses that Israel's new territory is so vast that wherever he walks, Joshua will never leave it. The traditional boundary markers (1:4) trace Israel's borders in a crisscross pattern: south ("the desert) to north ("Lebanon"), then east ("the Euphrates") to west ("the Mediterranean Sea"). Slight embellishments of Moses's original words paint Israel's new land as huge and fabled.

But for Joshua the crucial question is not the extent of the terrain but its conquerability. A divine promise, applying to Joshua words that Moses spoke to Israel, accompanies the divine command to cross. It reassures the new leader that no human enemy can "stand against you [Joshua]" no matter how long he lived (1:5). This astonishing invincibility comes from the presence of Almighty God with Joshua—the very presence that won Moses's stunning victories.

For his part, Joshua receives Yahweh's command to "be strong and very courageous," reiterated three times (1:6, 7, 9). The present context directly parallels the wording of Deuteronomy 31, where both Moses (31:7) and Yahweh (31:23) invoke it in appointing Joshua as Moses's successor. For Israel this installation marks Joshua as the chosen leader whom Yahweh expects them to follow. His specific task is to lead them to inherit the promised land (Josh 1:6b).

Undergirding Joshua's confidence is the simple fact that he is not alone. Yahweh, all-powerful, leads the way and surrounds him with his presence. That is why 1:7–8 detail the single proviso that Joshua must observe. Joshua's actions must carefully conform to what Moses taught. Indeed, the very success of his future endeavors hangs upon his never wavering from Moses's teachings (1:7b).

How can Joshua align his conduct with Moses's teaching and thereby assure its successful outcome? The key is "this Book of the Law" (1:8), an allusion to a document that, according to Deuteronomy, Moses wrote shortly before his death. Joshua should treat the book's contents as something to read in the hearing of others—to be shared with the community rather than hoarded to oneself.

Joshua Passes the Word (1:10–18). *To the officers (1:10–11).* Joshua puts in motion the divine commander's marching orders. First, he orders his officers to prepare the people for crossing the Jordan (1:10–11), then he addresses the Transjordanian tribes (1:12–18). The "officers" in 1:10 probably are civilian administrators supporting Joshua rather than military officers. In lists of Israelite leaders, the term is often paired with "elders" or "judges" rather than with "(military) officers" or "soldiers." They are to fan out through the Israelite camp and command the people to prepare provisions for a departure in three days (1:11).

To the eastern tribes (1:12–18). Second, Joshua deals specially with the Transjordanian tribes—Reuben, Gad, and half of Manasseh (1:12–18). They have already received their inheritance from Moses. Numbers 32 even implies that they have already conquered it, rebuilt its cities, and lived in houses. "Remember the command that Moses the servant of the LORD gave you" (1:13) recalls Moses's decrees in Numbers 32.

Nearly quoting Moses verbatim (cf. Deut 3:20), Joshua reiterates the two conditions that must prevail before they can go home: when Yahweh finally has given their fellow Israelites the same "rest" they themselves have already sampled and when their west-bank kin also possess their inheritance (Josh 1:15). All Israel will bear its burdens, suffer its losses, pay its prices, and share in it victories.

The chapter concludes with the reply of the two-and-a-half tribes (1:16–18). A subtle argument undergirds their words: If the Transjordanian tribes with no personal interest in west-bank land affirm what follows, how much more so the others. The east-bank tribes promise Joshua the same obedience they gave Moses (1:17). Given the context, this last affirmation is especially significant. It signals the successful transfer of tribal allegiance from Moses to Joshua (1:16–17a).

Finally, after affirming Joshua's authority the Israelites address Joshua personally. They themselves reiterate Yahweh's command that Joshua "be strong and courageous" (1:18b). Paraphrased, their point is this: "We're with you—and anyone who rebels will be executed. Your job, Joshua, is to be brave and firmly resolved."

Application. Fear lurks in the background of Joshua 1. Fear is an experience that all humans share. Joshua 1, however, points to four truths as the antidote to such fears: our unique identity as God's people, our dependence on God's word, our bond of unity with other believers, and God's powerful presence with us.

JOSHUA 2:1–24

Original Meaning

The Spy Mission (2:1–21). *Joshua's commission (2:1).* Joshua secretly commissions two unnamed men as spies to "go, see the land, Jericho" (2:1, lit.). Yahweh has assured Joshua of certain victory (1:2–5), so why send the spies at all? Despite receiving God's emphatic reassurance, he opts for a cautious rather than a bold first step forward.

Inside Jericho (2:2–8). The young pair's first move is to lodge in the house of a prostitute named Rahab. Someone notices their arrival and informs the king (2:2), who sends word demanding that Rahab hand them over (2:3). Observation of Israel's comings and goings by Canaanite scouts may partly explain how the king knows the two spies' whereabouts. Suddenly, the mission has turned sour. But, for reasons yet to be explained, Rahab risks her life and cunningly protects her two guests.

She concedes that the men "came to me" but denies knowing from where (2:4). Next, Rahab lies about their present whereabouts (2:5). She explains that the men left before the city closed its gate for the night. Swallowing Rahab's lie, the king's men hotly pursue the allegedly fleeing Israelites down the road to the river.

For the spies, these mark ominous developments. Like it or not, their fate rests in the wily prostitute's hands. Clearly, she is no "dumb broad" or garden-variety madam. On the contrary, she seems the most competent character in the story, with quick wits and decisive action. Indeed, her intervention surprisingly transforms the calamity into deliverance.

Rahab strikes a deal (2:9–21). Rahab finally explains herself (2:9–11). She knows that Yahweh has given Canaan into Israel's hands (2:9). The perfect verbal expression "has given" states the truth as a done deal—an already established fact soon to become reality. She reveals the popular mood in Canaan, that a terrible dread of Israel now grips the land. If Yahweh has given the land to Israel, then Israel must be unstoppable—and a Canaanite massacre inescapable. The Canaanites also had warrior gods, but according to Rahab those gods are no match for Yahweh. Plainly, whatever firm determination the inhabitants once had has become terrified panic.

To conclude her explanation, Rahab returns to Yahweh, the cause of the current disarray in Canaan (2:11b). By honoring Yahweh's victories at the Red Sea and over Sihon and Og (2:10), Rahab tacitly affirms the superiority of his power. But she stops short of saying that Yahweh is the *sole* sovereign of the universe. She refers to Yahweh as "your [the spies'] God" (2:11). Yahweh is not yet her God; she has not yet made him her most important, much less her only, God as an Israelite would. Rahab's words mark a step in the direction of a more complete, if not exclusive, commitment to Yahweh.

Now Rahab makes the request for which her statement paves the way (2:12–13). She asks them to swear an oath in the name of Yahweh, the God whose greatness she has just affirmed. The oath obligates Israel to spare the lives of her whole family when they take Jericho (2:13). Notice the nature of the agreement in play here. Israel is not offering the Canaanite Rahab a covenant and thereby violating its obligation to impose *herem*. Rather, it is Rahab who affirms the sovereignty of Yahweh and accepts his purposes—a basic confession of her faith—and who, on that basis, asks Israel (and, implicitly, Yahweh) to promise to spare her life. The spies readily grant her request (2:14).

Rahab lowers the pair by a rope dropped from her window (2:15). To avoid meeting the pursuit team, she instructs them to go west into the hills (the latter word is emphatic) and hide there three days. Once free of Rahab's trap, the young spies regain the initiative and prolong the conversation rather than silently vanish into the hills (2:17–20). They attach two new stipulations to the oath they have just taken. Rahab accepts the new conditions and sends them on their way (2:21a). In tying the crimson cord in the window (2:21b), she fulfills the first of the spies' two stipulations.

The Spies Debrief Joshua (2:22–24). Having paused for a long conversation, the story now hurries to its conclusion. While Rahab obeys the two spies, the two spies obey her. Their escape route now free of scrutiny, the two fugitives descend the eastern slope, cross the Jordan, and reach Joshua (2:23a). To conclude the story, the author has the spies basically borrow two of Rahab's lines (2:24). This positive report sharply contrasts that of Moses's infamous twelve spies (Num 13).

Application. We must confess our reluctance to welcome outsiders, especially those with problematic pasts or presents. Normally, we Christians settle into comfortably snug small groups of friends who are like us. Even if we avoid forming actual cliques, we tend to associate with people with whom we have a lot in common. Jesus models a lifestyle of hanging in with people in trouble, people in need, people on the margins, people others avoid. We, his followers, can do no less, but *how* can we do this? We need to overcome our natural skittishness. As Rahab welcomed the Israelite spies, outsiders in her world, so we are to welcome outsiders into ours.

JOSHUA 3:1–5:1

Original Meaning

The Report of the Jordan Crossing (3:1–17). *Preparations for crossing (3:1–8).* The morning after the spies' return, Joshua and Israel shift their camp to the Jordan (3:1). Three days later, the officers pass through the camp to instruct Israel about the crossing (3:2–3). They order the people to watch for the ark with its priestly bearers and follow it (3:3b). This comment marks the book's first mention of the ark of the covenant. Israel understood the space between the winged cherubim to be the royal throne over which Yahweh invisibly reigns. Here it symbolizes Yahweh's royal presence with Israel and his sovereign leadership of the coming invasion.

Specific instructions follow in three brief narrative snapshots (3:5–8).

1. Joshua commands the people (3:5) to prepare themselves personally ("make yourselves holy," lit.). The requirement for ritual purity signals that this river crossing is a solemn religious ritual, not an ordinary military invasion.
2. Joshua's next command, this one to the priests (3:6), confirms this.
3. In the final snapshot, Yahweh addresses Joshua with a personal promise (3:7). With their own eyes Israel will recognize Joshua as their new Moses, the divinely appointed leader to trust and to obey.

Yahweh concludes the final snapshot with a terse instruction through Joshua for the priests carrying the ark. At first glance, it makes little sense (3:8). How can they possibly do that, given the river's current flow at flood stage (3:15)? The vague, curious instruction anticipates what follows, especially the stunning event soon to ensue.

The crossing (3:9–17). After Israel has assembled, Joshua addresses them (3:9–13), immediately driving home the key point: "The living God . . . among you" is, indeed, about to drive out the seven peoples inhabiting Canaan (3:10).

Wordplays in 3:13 underscore the significance of the amazing event. The event's trigger is the entry of the "soles of the feet" (lit.) of the priests into the river, a key phrase in both 3:8 and 3:13. The Old Testament often associates the expression (NIV "set foot") with the conquest of enemies. Also, Yahweh asserts his authority over the Jordan River and all land westward. The waters are to stand in a "heap (of water)" (*ned*, 3:13), a term that elsewhere only describes what Yahweh did at the Red Sea (Exod 15:8; Ps 78:13). The pun hints that Yahweh is about to perform at the Jordan as stunning a miracle as he did at the exodus.

Suddenly, the speech ends and the narrator steps forward to report that the crossing proper takes place exactly as expected (Josh 3:14–17). The Jordan is at its mightiest—at flood stage, angrily swollen by melting snow and spring rains. It is almost as if the river defiantly dares Israel to attempt a crossing! But the trigger that ignites the miracle is the moment that the priests' "soles" wade into the water's edge. That instant marks the clash for sovereignty between ark and river, a conflict that the ark easily wins.

The "dry ground" motif in 3:17 also echoes another mighty, salvific act of Yahweh, his stunning parting of the Rea Sea at the exodus (Exod 14:21). Further, the crossing apparently transforms "the whole nation" of Israel itself. Verse 17 marks the first time that the book calls Israel a "nation" (*goy*) rather than "people" (*am*).

Yahweh's Two Commissions of Joshua (4:1–24). *Yahweh's first commission (4:1–14).* Yahweh commissions Joshua to select twelve men, one from each tribe (4:2) and commands them to carry twelve stones from the spot where the priests' feet rested in the dry Jordan and deliver them to Israel's next campsite (as yet, unnamed). Clearly, the importance of the stones is their connection with that historic spot.

Joshua hastens to explain the purpose of this unusual mission. The stones serve as both "sign" and "memorial" (4:6–7). They authenticate that the past event actually happened and remind Israel of its continuing significance for later generations. But the stones bear no self-explanatory inscription. Instead, their mute testimony will cause curious Israelite children to ask in the future, "What do these stones mean?" This is significant: The text assumes visits to the site by future generations, probably for some ritual remembrance, if not reenactment, of the river crossing.

The twelve men carry out Joshua's orders (4:8). Each carries a stone from the middle of the Jordan and deposits it at Israel's campsite. Parenthetically, twelve other stones unexpectedly merit mention. These are ones that Joshua himself unilaterally erects in the middle of the Jordan, right where the priests' feet stood (4:9; see NIV footnote). With those symbolic memorials in place, the narrative resumes the main plot—the dramatic crossing.

In the Old Testament, "forty thousand" (4:13) is a round number meaning "huge army." This throng passes in review before Yahweh, their commander, armed and ready for war. These comments cast Israel's crossing not as a migration but as an invasion by a numerically formidable force.

Most importantly, that day Yahweh keeps his promise to exalt Joshua before Israel (4:14a). Indeed, henceforth, Israel accords Joshua the same consummate respect given Moses during his lifetime. Of course, theologically Joshua merely represents in human form the loving sovereignty of Israel's covenant lord, Yahweh.

Yahweh's second commission (4:15–24). As soon as the priests set foot on dry land (4:18a), the Jordan's waters return to their former place, again swelling its banks (cf. 3:15). "Waters . . . returned" probably marks another allusion to the exodus, the return of waters over the dry path through the Red Sea. The timing of the momentous event—the tenth day of the first month (4:19a)—recalls dates associated with Passover, thus forging a further link between the Red Sea and Jordan crossings. The crossing date also anticipates and explains the Passover celebration four days later (5:10–12).

Joshua's statement to the people (4:20–21) reprises the question-and-answer ritual from 4:6–7, but the language and length of the adult's answer here differs significantly. The answerer is to "inform" (NIV, "tell")—to improve their knowledge (4:22a)—not just "say." The answerer is also to reply with a specific formula. Further, unlike 4:7, in 4:23 Joshua explicitly credits Yahweh with drying up the Jordan's waters and compares the act to his drying up of the Red Sea at the exodus. Whenever Israel sees the stones—whenever the child asks and the adult answers—Israel remembers the might of Yahweh and rekindles their awe of that great God.

Epilogue: International Reaction (5:1). Israel's presence in Canaan—and especially the miracle that opened the entry gates—is no secret to their prospective adversaries. With the crossing, the die is cast: Conflict with the land's inhabitants is inevitable.

Application. We all face the problem of remembering—or, put differently, our tendency to forget. Part of the problem is that we have so much to remember these days. The cluttered mind poses a unique danger to our lives. It makes us forget things which matter most, including our walk with Christ. Joshua erected twelve stones at Gilgal so that future Israelite generations would remember what had happened there. It would drive them back to a firm, steady, convinced, life-altering fear of him. Like Joshua, Jesus took pains to ensure that his followers remember his death. At the Last Supper, he declared, "Do this in remembrance of me" (Luke 22:19).

JOSHUA 5:2–6:27

Original Meaning

Preparations at Gilgal (5:2–12). *The circumcision ceremony (5:2–9).* In his first speech since 4:15–16, Yahweh decrees that Joshua must lead Israel in a circumcision ceremony using flint knives (5:2–9). Unlike their ancestors who died in the wilderness, the generation born in the wilderness had not been circumcised (5:4–7). At issue is a question that echoes throughout the book: Will *this* generation—the one Yahweh graciously preserved in the wilderness (5:7)—obey him and keep (not lose) the land? Joshua himself obeys by circumcising the "nation," ensuring that the earlier sad history not repeat itself (5:8), at least not for now. The ritual marks this younger Israel as Yahweh's covenant people and ritually fit to occupy the land.

The Passover observance (5:10–12). The observance of Passover marks the second important prebattle activity (5:10–12). This takes place four days after Israel's arrival, with the people encamped at Gilgal in the plains of Jericho. The last recorded observance of Passover took place at the beginning of Israel's second year out of Egypt (Num 9). Thus, as Israel's first Passover in the new land, this celebration signals a new beginning for their national life. Indeed, the narrator highlights two notable events in successive days to confirm the dawning of a new day for Israel.

The day after Passover the people feed themselves for the first time with food grown in their new land (Josh 5:11). The point is that the food is "homegrown" in Canaan, not provisions brought with them. The second notable event occurs the next day. Since Israel now eats off the land, their daily supply of manna stops (5:12). The note that "there was no longer any manna for the Israelites" interprets this event as the end of an era—the exodus-wilderness period. Ahead lies the new era ("that year") of living off the land of Canaan (see Exod 16:35).

The Ritual Siege of Jericho (5:13–6:27). *The mysterious stranger (5:13–6:1).* A brief scene involving a mysterious stranger shifts attention from preparation to conquest. Interestingly, the phrase "drawn sword" (5:13) elsewhere occurs only with "the angel of the LORD" (Num 22:23; 1 Chr 21:16) and, thus, creates the expectation in readers (but not in Joshua) that the "man" is in fact a divine messenger in human form. It is almost comic to watch Joshua, oblivious to the other party's true identity, commandingly confront and interrogate him.

Joshua's question in 5:13 ("Are you for us or for our enemies?") seeks the man's military affiliation. The visitor's answer underscores what is important, his identity as God's on-site commander, not his loyalties to either Israel or Canaan. Once the stranger's words hit home, Joshua falls face down on the ground and worships him (5:14b), a gesture of high respect that an inferior pays a superior. Joshua acts out his recognition that the "army" is God's almighty, invisible host and the stranger is an angelic figure in human form (see also Gen 18; Judg 13). Joshua no longer needs to ascertain the man's loyalty—the man is clearly a "friend" come to support Israel.

Surprisingly, the commander orders, "Take off your sandals, for the place where you are standing is holy" (5:15a). The command virtually quotes Yahweh's familiar orders to Moses at the burning bush (Exod 3:5). Literarily, the echoed wording links the two scenes, reconfirming Joshua as Moses's successor and—more importantly—forever marking this episode as Joshua's "burning bush experience."

The ritual siege of Jericho (6:2–25). The supreme commander speaks (6:2–5). He reassures Joshua with the assurance-of-victory formula (6:2). God's instructions (6:3–5) sketch a general overview with few details. Israelite soldiers are specifically to "encircle" (not merely "march around," NIV) the city once each day for six days (6:3)—a six-day, symbolic siege of Jericho. In effect, the circuits of the ark enclose Jericho in a deadly ring of Yahweh's power and doom it to fall before that power. The seventh day marks the ceremony's climax. On that day, with the troops in place, the trumpet-bearing priests are to march around the city seven times, blowing steadily on their instruments (6:4b–5). After the last circuit, they are to sound a long blast, the signal for the people to raise a mighty shout (6:5a).

Immediately, Joshua issues an order to execute Yahweh's battle plan (6:6–7). Seven priests, each with a ram's horn, are to lead the priests carrying the ark of the covenant (6:6; cf. 6:4). Joshua also commands the people, "Move out! Surround the city" (6:7, author's translation). "Surround the city" repeats the instruction given the soldiers (6:3); the people, too, are symbolically to besiege the city.

Joshua adds a further detail: An armed vanguard and "rear guard" are, respectively, to precede and follow the ark in its daily circuits of the city (6:7b, 9b). Since the ark needs no human defense, this gesture must be symbolic. In my view, the vanguard, rear guard, and ark together personify that Israel as a whole is engaging in Yahweh's war.

Jericho: Day One (6:8–11). Now the action starts, with Israel dramatically obeying the commands of Yahweh and Joshua. But, on Joshua's orders, the people keep silent as stones; no traditional war whoops for them today (6:10). The combination of blowing ram's horns and dead silence may strike terror in the hearts of the Canaanites watching the scene. The human actors play important roles. But ultimately, that wooden box, the symbol of Yahweh's powerful presence, commands center stage and identifies him as Jericho's true attacker.

Jericho: Days Two to Seven (6:12–25). Israel continues to obey Yahweh and Joshua. Interestingly, here the focus falls on the seven priestly trumpeters, their ongoing sounds, and the ark's front and rear guard details (6:14a). The prominence accorded the priests fits the chapter's pattern and sounds an important theme: Israel participates ceremonially in this episode of Yahweh's war, but it is Yahweh's presence that is decisive in toppling Jericho.

Day Seven begins not just "early" (NIV) but at "daybreak," and today the whole camp ("they"), not just Joshua, rises to greet it (cf. 6:12). Today, however, all Israel ("they") takes center stage rather than the ark. The procedure is the same as days one to six, but today—and only today—they circle Jericho a climactic seven times as Yahweh has commanded (6:15b; cf. 6:4).

More important, a second formal formula ("[it happened] the seventh time around") dramatically sets off the decisive, electric, long-awaited moment—the seventh and final walk round the city (6:16). Joshua commands them, "Shout!"—but then issues his final instructions concerning the city's fall (6:16–19). The surprising digression abruptly postpones the climactic war cry and the falling of the wall (6:20). The literary effect is to heighten the scene's suspense and to underscore the importance of his instructions.

In fact, this marks the first instruction in the book concerning the treatment of conquered Canaanites and the debut of the important concept of *herem* (NIV "devoted things"; 6:18). In a context of Yahweh's war, *herem* takes on a specific religious meaning. It requires the devotion to Yahweh of anything classed as *herem* either through special custody provisions or through its total destruction. Destruction constitutes the way Yahweh requires Israel to implement his exclusive ownership. Thus, Joshua's declaration of Jericho as *herem* affirms that Yahweh owns it exclusively and seals the fate of everything in it—everyone, of course, except "Rahab the prostitute," as Joshua quickly clarifies (6:17b).

At last, the people answer the trumpet's call with their long-awaited victory shout (6:20). And, as 6:5 promised, the wall collapses where it stands. Inside, Israel obeys Joshua's instructions, and the slaughter is total. Indirect-object-first syntax singles out the lone exception (6:22), Rahab and "her entire family" (lit.), whom the spies lead safely from Jericho (6:23). They locate them somewhere "outside the camp of Israel" (6:23b), presumably to maintain its ritual cleanness.

Postscript: Joshua's curse and reputation (6:26–27). To conclude, the narrator returns Joshua to center stage to pronounce a curse on Jericho (6:26). Why single out Jericho for cursing? To foreign passersby, the charred ruins were evidence of judgment by some deity; to passing Israelites, mute testimony to Yahweh's first great victory in Canaan. Deuteronomy 13:17 might lead some Israelites to read Jericho as a city destroyed and abandoned for heresy. From this angle, ruined Jericho would silently warn Israel of the terrible fate awaiting those who abandon Yahweh for other gods.

Finally, Yahweh's stunning victory further enhances Joshua's public stature. It confirms convincingly that "the LORD was with Joshua" just as he promised (Josh 6:27a). An Israelite leader can have no better reputation.

Application. We are not at peace but at war, the Jesus War. History illustrates one important thing about the Jesus War: Jesus Christ has already won its decisive battles. To us, the tide of war often seems turned against us, but his victories have in reality decisively turned it in our favor. To paraphrase Joshua, Jesus has already "given the enemy into our hands." The cross and the resurrection mark Jesus's most decisive victory. At Calvary and the empty tomb, God through Christ decisively defeated humanity's bitterest enemies, sin and death.

JOSHUA 7:1–8:35

Original Meaning

Ai Attack I (7:1–26). *A deadly secret (7:1–15).* Without preface or fanfare, the narrator describes a highly serious, treacherous breach of trust between Yahweh and Israel. The culprit, the one who took items from Jericho, is a man named Achan with an impressive, prestigious pedigree (7:18). His tribe will soon produce Israel's royal dynasty. Readers know about the crime, the criminal, and God's fury (7:1), but Joshua and Israel remain in the dark, oblivious to the readers' sense of foreboding.

As with Jericho, Joshua acts on his own, dispatching another reconnaissance team to spy out the region around Ai (7:2). As at Jericho, the spies' report on Ai is positive (7:3): no need to march the whole army up there. Joshua sends "about three thousand" soldiers to Ai but with shocking results: Ai's "few" defenders send the group of soldiers packing (7:4).

The greatly outnumbered few kill about thirty-six Israelites then go on the offensive, chasing the invaders from their front gate. They overtake the Israelites at the nearby town quarries and clobber them as they retreat (7:5a). Grave doubts suddenly plague Israel: Will God enable them to take even one more city, much less the whole land?

Joshua tears his clothes and joins the tribal leadership in tossing dust on their heads and in laying face down before the ark until the evening (7:6). About nightfall, Joshua finally speaks (7:7), addressing God with a typical formula of deference. He then asks an accusatory question: Why did Yahweh bring "this people" across the Jordan only to hand "us" over to the Amorites for destruction? Given Joshua's ignorance of Achan's perfidy, one may forgive him the frustration and indignation with which his words ring. He still addresses Yahweh with a formula of respect, bowing to Yahweh's authority as a preface to his next cry of frustration (7:8). Worse, the retreat has damaged Israel's psychological advantage over the peoples of Canaan (7:9). Joshua ends his soliloquy the way he began it—with a question to drive home what he sees as ultimately at stake here for Yahweh.

Yahweh barks with obvious irritation (7:10). In God's eyes, Joshua's posture and procedure are totally out of line—in modern terms, he just doesn't get it. This is not about divine inattention but about Israel's sin (7:11). In highly provocative words, Yahweh rapidly ticks off what has him so ticked off. This outrage explains the disaster at Ai (7:12). In short, Israel itself has now become what it stole—*herem* ("destined for destruction")—and unless they do what they should have in the first place Yahweh refuses to be with them.

Yahweh spells out the conditions (7:13–15). Joshua must "consecrate the people," ordering them to "consecrate yourselves" for a ceremony the next day (7:13a). There is *herem* somewhere in the camp right now, and they will not win another victory until they completely "remove" it (7:13b). The oracle also details the removal procedure (7:14–15). Tomorrow morning, Israel is to present themselves before God by tribes so that Yahweh may sift out the mystery man's tribe, clan, and family step by step.

The penalty is severe. The individual and everything he has will be burned—and for two reasons: He has violated the covenant and "did an outrageous thing in Israel" (7:15b). In short, this is not a petty crime but deadly serious business, and the direst of consequences follow. Singlehandedly, the man has returned Israel to their precrossing state of uncleanness and driven Yahweh from their midst.

Joshua's discovery (7:16–26). The scene is high drama, the atmosphere tense. Quickly, the process identifies the tribe (Judah; 7:16), the clan (the Zerahites), and the family (Zimri; 7:17). Finally, the lot nabs the traitor from among Zabdi's males, Achan, and the narrator ticks off his illustrious lineage (7:18). Subdued comments probably ripple through the crowd at the shocking revelation, and a mini trial ensues. Joshua addresses Achan as "my son" (7:19), the way superiors speak to subordinates (1 Sam 3:16; 4:16; 2 Sam 18:22). He commands him to "give glory to the LORD . . . and . . . honor" (Josh 7:19). The command assumes that Achan's crime somehow violates Yahweh's honor and praiseworthiness, so now Achan must offset that offense.

Achan does so (7:20), invoking a typical confession declaration formula and then fully confessing his crime (7:21). For the first time and from the now-unmasked traitor's own lips, all Israel and Bible readers hear a full accounting of his secret crime. Roaming Jericho's ruins, he spotted three things: "a beautiful robe from Babylonia, two hundred shekels of silver and a bar of gold weighing fifty shekels" (7:21). He "coveted them" and took them to his tent and hid them underground. Achan's greed simply got the better of him.

Joshua dispatches messengers who run to Achan's tent and—yes, indeed!—they find the stuff hidden there just as he had said (7:22). They bring them and "spread [literally, poured] them out before the LORD" (7:23). "Before the LORD" is appropriate in two respects. First, the goods really belong to him. Second, Yahweh is the judicial authority sponsoring the trial.

All Israel joins Joshua as he leads Achan, the stolen goods, his children, animals, tent, and everything he owns from Jericho to the Valley of Achor (7:24). At Achor, Joshua pronounces the death sentence. Achan's innocent victim, the entire community, stones him to death, burns him with fire, and then stones everything else (7:25b). Thus, Israel meets Yahweh's demands: They remove the *herem*, the source of their current troubles, and in so doing, restore the community to its pre-Achan ritual cleanness. Finally, they "heaped up" over Achan's charred remains a great pile of stones, "which remains to this day" (7:26a). Fittingly, Yahweh turns "from his fierce anger," the driving force behind the catastrophe (cf. 7:1b), a divine signal of Israel's safe return to his good graces.

Ai Attack II (8:1–29). *Yahweh's commands (8:1–2).* Yahweh immediately takes charge, addressing Joshua with language typical of Yahweh war. To encourage him, he invokes the twofold formula of reassurance ("Do not be afraid/discouraged"). Yahweh also orders Joshua to lead "the whole army" up to attack Ai—ironically, the exact opposite advice given Joshua the last time by the returning spies (7:3). This time, Israelites may help themselves to plunder and livestock (8:2).

Joshua's compliance (8:3–9). Joshua promptly prepares the whole army for Ai II (8:3). He selects thirty elite units as an ambush team and sends them to Ai at night. Before the elite force embarks, Joshua issues crucial orders that flesh out Yahweh's general concept into a detailed, coordinated battle plan (8:4–9).

The trap: set and sprung (8:10–23). Carefully crafted narration unfolds the dramatic scene. An opening wide shot shows Joshua mustering the army, then a close-up follows him and Israel's elders leading the troops uphill toward Ai (8:10). The view then quickly widens to show the ascent and dramatic arrival of the entire force with Joshua at the very front of the city (8:11).

The narrative now builds tension in anticipation of the coming battle. It briefly backtracks, reviewing the prior, secret placement of the ambush team of "about five thousand men" (8:12). It then reports the final double checks by Joshua's officers. That night Joshua himself spends the night in the valley, perhaps positioning himself to lead his troops into battle (8:13). Everyone quietly awaits the dawn.

The next morning, the king of Ai sees something threatening. The king and his army immediately "hurry" out to battle Israel somewhere east of the city (8:14). Joshua and all Israel feign being routed and flee eastward down the wilderness road. Meanwhile, "lured away" from Ai (cf. 8:6) just as Joshua planned, Ai's entire military force hotly pursues him (8:16). The fact that every male from Ai and nearby Bethel have abandoned the city to pursue Israel leaves its gates open and its inhabitants defenseless (8:17). Unexpectedly, Yahweh himself speaks, ordering Joshua to stretch out the "javelin" (Heb. *kidon*, "scimitar") in his hand toward Ai because "I will deliver the city" (8:18).

As if on cue (i.e., just as Joshua's arm extends), the hidden ambush team suddenly appears, runs into the city, captures it, and sets it on fire (8:19). The visible conflagration confirms the successful ambush, so the fleeing Israelites turn around. They deny Ai's stunned forces any hope of escape and spring the fatal trap (8:20–21). The arrival of the ambush team from the city swamps Ai's helpless troops in a sea of Israelites (8:22). The resulting slaughter is total—no survivors or escapees—with one exception. The Israelites single out the king of Ai and bring him alive to Joshua, an action that signals absolute victory (8:23).

The king's fate (8:24–29). Joshua does not lower the symbolic scimitar until "he" has utterly "destroyed all" Ai's inhabitants (8:26). Yahweh permits Israel to keep plunder and livestock from Ai, a policy Israel gladly carries out (8:27). Joshua accomplishes two key things.

1. He reduces Ai to a permanent pile of burnt rubble—a state still evident in the writer's day (8:28).
2. Joshua executes the king of Ai, impaling him on a post until evening (8:29). At sunset, Joshua has his corpse taken down and thrown down at the entrance of Ai's city gate, exactly obeying Moses (Deut 21:22–23). The royal rock-pile tomb at Ai testifies to a great victory by Yahweh the warrior.

The Altar-Building and Sacrifices (8:30–31). The altar building carries out Moses's commands, especially the stipulation that only large, uncut fieldstones be used. The people immediately offer on it the "burnt offerings" and "fellowship offerings" that Moses commanded (8:31). It is a simple, happy scene, with God and his people sharing a joyful, friendly fellowship meal.

It is striking that the wording in 8:31 echoes language in the covenant-making ceremony at Mount Sinai (Exod 24:5). Since the offerings mark the people's only direct action here, their actions probably signal their recommitment to the covenant. But consider also that the elevation of Mount Ebal (2,867 feet) offers a commanding view of virtually all of Canaan except the Negev. More important, Shechem also has ties to Israel's patriarchs. Both Abraham and Jacob built altars there when they, too, entered Canaan (Gen 12:7; 33:20).

The altar raised by Joshua on Mount Ebal probably stakes a similar claim for the present generation. This may explain why Joshua 8 gives primacy to the altar construction (8:30) rather than to the writing of the law on plastered stones (8:32). The reordering makes the altar a powerful symbol of Israel's land claim on Canaan, signals the end of Israel's old nomadic society, and inaugurates a new one in Israel's new land.

The Writing of the Law (8:32–33). Once the sacrifices conclude, the people apparently descend the mountain since they next appear in the valley below (8:33). Joshua then writes on the stones a copy of the "instruction of Moses" (author's translation) that the latter had himself written (8:32). The reference may be to Moses's writing of "the book of the covenant" (Exod 24:4, 7), apparently at the Israelite camp though not specifically "in the presence of the Israelites," as Joshua 8:32 says. The term "instruction of Moses" more likely recalls his writing of "this law" at the plains of Moab since the context has the Israelites present (Deut 31:7, 9).

The participants include everybody: leaders, priests, Israelite citizens, resident aliens (Josh 8:33, 35), as well as "women and children" (8:35). Everyone is present for this public, corporate event. Moses's teaching authorizes the participation of aliens in Israel's worship life—Sabbaths (Exod 20:10), Passover (Exod 12:19, 48, 49), and other major festivals (Deut 16:10–14; 26:10–11). Meanwhile, whether native-born citizen or immigrant, all stand side by side in two large groups, half at the foot of Mount Gerizim and half at the foot of Mount Ebal. They wait patiently below as Joshua writes. This ceremony serves a single purpose, to bestow on the people Yahweh's blessings.

The Reading of the Law (8:34–35). Joshua turns from writing to reading. He reads aloud, specifically the blessings and curses (8:34; cf. Deut 28). The act is momentous—the first recorded public reading of the instruction since the death of Moses. Finally, the author underscores that Joshua reads the entire instruction—every single word (8:35). The comment both enhances the portrait of Joshua as a worthy successor to Moses and pictures the instruction of Moses as consummately authoritative.

Application. What sins today might compare to Achan's? As we saw, Achan sinned by keeping to himself things that Yahweh had declared to be his own exclusive property (*herem*). The answer to our question, thus, lies in identifying things that God today claims to be his own. Certainly, the church and other Christians ultimately belong to only God and not to us. The church is the bride of Christ himself (Rev 19:7), a spiritual union based on Jesus's loving sacrificial death on the cross on behalf of the church (Eph 5:25, 29). Jesus deeply cares for his bride, so it would be Achanesque to do anything to harm the church, as Achan's sin did grave harm to Israel. Therefore, the example of Achan warns against doing anything that sullies the public reputation of the church, puts a strain on its relationship with God himself, or brings disunity to the body. What applies to the church as a whole likewise applies to our treatment of fellow believers. Woe to us if we lead them astray, confuse their minds, harm their walk with Christ, or disillusion them about the gospel.

JOSHUA 9:1–10:43

Original Meaning

The Gibeonites: Trick and Treaty (9:1–27). *The Gibeonite trick (9:1–15).* News of Israel's capture and destruction of Ai (and perhaps Jericho) galvanizes Canaan's kings into action (9:1). The threat Israel poses is a real one. At stake is the Canaanites' ancient way of life, precisely what Yahweh intends to replace with a whole new society. In self-defense, the kings join forces to battle Joshua, their leadership counterpart, and Israel (9:2).

Verse 3 quickly shifts from the massing armies to report the reaction of a single group, "the people of Gibeon," who have also heard the same news. The narrative contrasts the "kings" of the cities with the people of Gibeon, a city that apparently has no king (9:3–4). Like Rahab, the Gibeonites thrust the reader eyeball-to-eyeball with real live Canaanites and their real live fears.

The news of Joshua's threat galvanizes the Gibeonites into action, but they eschew the violence of the warrior kings in favor of a simple "ruse" (9:4a). What the Gibeonites considered cleverness Israel will call treachery here. The Gibeonites present quite a bedraggled, woeful picture as they enter the Israelite camp at Gilgal to meet Joshua and Israel (9:6a). They apparently expect their looks to do the talking, for they open with an abrupt, vague introduction: "We have come from a distant country," they lie. Then they boldly ask that Israel make a treaty with them (9:6b).

The subsequent conversation pits wary Israelites against cagey Gibeonites. "Perhaps you live near us" puts the Israelites' wariness into words and explains their reluctance to enter a treaty (9:7). To dispel Israelite misgivings, the Hivites reply by, in essence, surrendering themselves fully into Israel's hands (9:8a). But Joshua still presses them for details about their identity (9:8b).

Their answer is at the same time expansive and evasive. They completely breeze past the request for an ethnic name, and "very distant country" (9:9) names no specific homeland. They emphasize the reason for their trip: The magnet of Yahweh's "fame" has drawn them to visit the Israelites (9:9a). They cite reports of his victories over Egypt (9:9b) and Sihon and Og east of the Jordan (9:10). What they heard drove the elders and people back home to authorize the long trip and to supply them with provisions. They are empowered to surrender their people into Israel's hands and make a treaty (9:11). How could Israel ever deny a people who honor Yahweh and want peace?

But Israelite suspicions remain. To allay such suspicions once and for all, the visitors point out hard evidence that verifies their "very long journey": dry, moldy (not warm) bread, patched (not new) wineskins, and tattered clothes and worn shoes (9:12–13). Some Israelite men (but not Joshua) take the bait. They sample the alleged provisions but (alas) do not seek Yahweh's advice ("mouth," lit.) on the matter (9:14). Their actions naively trust the matter to their human senses rather than to divine guidance. Whatever his misgivings, Joshua makes a treaty to spare the lives of these pathetic strangers, and Israel's leaders ratify it with an oath (9:15).

The Gibeonites' indenture (9:16–27). The treaty is only three days old, and Israel learns that their new "foreign" partners are in fact Gibeonites, a people on the *herem* hit-list (9:16). The oath prohibits Israel from attacking their treaty partner but does not prevent the Israelite community at large from grumbling against the leaders who took it (9:18).

Israel's only alternative is to let them live (9:20). The leaders apparently assume that Israel may not simply declare the treaty null and void because it was concluded under false pretenses. Again, no one consults with Yahweh, who could have either voided the treaty or voiced approval of it. Instead, leaders publicly pronounce their formal decision ("Let them live," 9:21), but they also limit the Gibeonites to a specific social role—to serve the community as "woodcutters and water carriers" (9:21, 27).

Joshua summons the Hivite leaders and addresses them (9:22). Joshua indicts the Gibeonites for cunningly covering up crucial facts to gain personal advantage. Not surprisingly, Joshua next does what victims of deceit typically do: He curses the whole Hivite people (9:23a). Joshua's curse adds an important detail—the Gibeonites' wood-cutting and water-carrying will always serve "the house of my God" (9:23). In assigning the Gibeonites to the sanctuary, the sacred realm over which only priests preside, Joshua exercises an authority akin to that of Moses.

The Hivites defend their actions (9:24): They have simply responded to what someone had told them. They concede that Joshua's "hands" hold their fate and submit (9:25). Joshua "did for them accordingly" (9:26, lit.)—in other words, what he deemed "good and right" under the circumstances. Specifically, he "saved them from the hands of the Israelites" (9:26, lit.) in whose grip revenge, if not death, might be likely.

A change to more formal literary style ("That day he made . . .") brings the scene to a close (9:27). From distant hindsight, the narrator reiterates Joshua's twofold assignment of the Gibeonites: to provide wood and water "for the assembly" at large and "for the altar of the LORD" (i.e., for sacrifices). In a sense, this honors them: Their tasks may be lowly, but their workplace enjoys the highest rank and serves Yahweh Most High himself.

Duped but Not Defeated (10:1–39). *Israel to the rescue (10:1–14).* News of the treaty and of Ai's capture and destruction has reached King Adoni-Zedek (10:1). This is terrifyingly bad news to Adoni-Zedek, who fears a domino effect of falling cities—a seismic shift in the balance of power—that threatens his own kingdom. So Adoni-Zedek rallies the kings of four other powerful city-states—Hebron, Jarmuth, Lachish, and Eglon (all south and southwest of Jerusalem)—to rendezvous at Jerusalem and join him in attacking Gibeon (10:3–4).

The five Amorite kings muster their armies at Jerusalem, proceed to Gibeon, set up camp, and lay siege to it (10:5). In response, Joshua leads the entire army, including all its "best fighting men" (10:7), on an all-night march to defend Israel's beleaguered ally, Gibeon. God invokes the common biblical formula of reassurance (10:8a), the soothing words directly addressing Joshua's anxiety about the battle ahead.

Joshua's unexpected, early-morning arrival takes the encamped besiegers by complete surprise (10:9). No sooner has Israel arrived than Yahweh unleashes a terrifying vanguard to lead Israel's advance (10:10). As the enemy flees from Israel, Yahweh showers them with huge hailstones (10:11). Since Israel could not have won it on their own, the victory is ultimately Yahweh's.

Verses 12–13 mark one of the book's best-known and most-discussed parts. This intriguing and important text has stirred much discussion. In my reading, five lines of a poem that Joshua quotes (10:12b+13a) comprise the centerpiece of 10:12–14. The author reminds the reader (10:13b) that the lines are preserved in the Book of Jashar, apparently a collection of early Israelite epic or lyric poetry.

Strikingly, while the cosmic scale of the text's claims are what amaze modern readers, what stuns the narrator is the terrestrial scene—that Joshua prays and (unbelievable!) Yahweh obeys by fighting for Israel (10:14). He views it as an event without past precedent or likelihood of future recurrence. As I see it, what astonishes the author is that God heeds a request of such cosmic magnitude. He readily deploys cosmic forces, his two primary celestial lights, to help fight his great battle on Israel's behalf. In effect, he fully honors Israel's covenant renewal at Mount Ebal (8:30–35) and leaves the treaty with Gibeon out of consideration.

Scholars, however, have interpreted 10:12–13 variously. The traditional view, one still held by many today, assumes that the earth literally stops rotating, thereby lengthening the day to give time to attain victory. Others find that view implausible because the universe apparently shows no traces of such a cosmic event and, besides, such a cosmic stoppage of nature seems out of keeping with God's character. Instead, they propose solutions involving natural phenomena.

The interpretation of 10:12–14 is difficult, but an important starting point is to take seriously its poetic nature—that its thought world is phenomenological and metaphorical rather than historical or scientific. The best option is to read 10:12–13 figuratively as a poetic depiction of the military conflict on a cosmic scale. It compares to the claim of another poem, the song of Deborah (Judg 5:20). The poetic excerpt invokes cosmic terms rhetorically to magnify the majestic power of God that won this great victory.

The fate of the royal ringleaders (10:15–27). The five kings flee for their lives and hide in the cave at Makkedah (10:16). They hope to hide themselves out of sight until the crisis passes and Israel leaves the area. Alas, information as to their whereabouts reaches Joshua at the Israelite camp (10:17a).

The author quotes Joshua at length (10:18–19): They are to roll large stones over the cave opening—an instant prisoner-of-war cell!—and to post men to guard the captured kings. This will prevent any rescue by loyal troops or an escape by the monarchs themselves (10:18). The rest are to chase after "your enemies," attack them from the rear, and cut off their escape to safety in fortified cities. Rather than describe the ensuing battle, however, the narrator skips ahead to underscore its results (10:20).

That is what happens when God fights for Israel (10:14b and 10:42b). Israel can now peacefully camp in the Amorite heartland, surely a harbinger of their later, larger settlement there. But the five kings must be dealt with, so Joshua orders the caves opened and kings brought outside to him (10:22).

Joshua seizes the moment for a symbolic action to benefit his troops. Surrounded by the entire force, he commands the troop commanders to step forward and place their feet on the necks of the presumably prostrate kings (10:24). Joshua then addresses his men, urging them to be neither "afraid" nor "discouraged" (10:25). They can be strong and courageous because Yahweh will similarly defeat all the enemies they are now battling (10:25b).

Joshua next strikes and kills the five kings, then hangs (probably impales) their corpses on wooden stakes until evening (10:26). At sunset, he has the corpses taken down per the instruction (Deut 21:22–23) and thrown back into the cave (Josh 10:27). Though inhumane to modern readers, the gesture was typical of ancient warfare.

The southern blitzkrieg (10:28–39). Despite an astounding day of victory, other battles remain for Joshua and Israel, but to treat them the narrator adopts a style with repeated formulae (but not slavishly or in lock-step order) and occasional hyperbole (e.g., "everyone in it," 10:28). The following comprise its core items (in general order of occurrence):

1. The city's capture (10:28, 32, 35, 37, 39)
2. The siege and attack (10:29, 31, 34, 36, 38)
3. The city, everyone put to the sword (10:28, 30, 32, 35, 37, 39)
4. No survivors remain (10:28, 30, 33, 35, 37, 39)

5. Israel implements the "ban," (i.e., "totally destroyed," 10:28, 35, 37, 39)
6. The king suffers the same fate as the king of city-X (10:28, 30, 32, 35, 37, 39)

Summary of the Conquest (10:40–43). Borrowing terms from 10:28–39, the author credits Joshua with leaving "no survivors" (10:40)—in obedience to Yahweh's command. The author stakes out the boundaries of Joshua's swath of victory with the typical Old Testament way of describing large territory. Verses 41–42 celebrate Israel's conquest (but not necessarily control) of the land. After a remarkable blitzkrieg that, in essence, won them the southern half of Canaan, Joshua and Israel return to base camp at Gilgal (10:43).

Application. Joshua 9–10 in no way justifies the use of violence to achieve Christian goals. The gospel does not advance by military coercion. To eschew violence is not to deny that there is a spiritual war going on as I write this. There is, in fact, a war out there (and "in here," too). Indeed, the first aspect of contemporary meaning is to recognize how Joshua 9–10 offers a microcosm of the big picture, the gospel enterprise in history. Whatever one's moral compunctions about the conquest, theologically it marks a step forward in God's plan to establish his kingdom on earth. It confronts the ruling powers of the day (the Amorite kings) with the demand that they submit to Yahweh's sovereign rule. It puts his representatives—his chosen people, warts and all—smack dab in the middle of the nations of the world.

For Christians the war is a spiritual one. Rather than confront enemies of "flesh and blood," they face "the rulers . . . the authorities . . . the powers of this dark world and . . . the spiritual forces of evil in the heavenly realms" (Eph 6:12). Like Israel, God has also dispersed his representatives—his own redeemed people—right in the middle of the world's many nations. The arrival of gospel messengers anywhere provokes modern Amorites to hostile opposition and people like the Gibeonites to peaceful inquiry.

JOSHUA 11:1–23

Original Meaning

The Northern Campaign (11:1–15). *The battle of Merom (11:1–9).* In the Late Bronze Age, Hazor undoubtedly was the largest, most influential city in all of Canaan. Its size was huge—200 acres, an estimated population of 30,000—and ideally situated for economic and political dominance. The reader rightly imagines a dramatic scene around the Merom spring: a huge military force determined to stop Israel's advance into Galilee—and with frightening firepower.

The narrative assumes that Joshua knows the enemy's moves, because Yahweh opens the battle report with a word of assurance, a promise, and an instruction for Joshua (11:6). True to his word, Yahweh gives the coalition troops into Israel's hands (11:8). Joshua does to them precisely what Yahweh commanded (11:9). The reader imagines a scene of fire, rising smoke, hobbled warhorses, and no enemy in sight.

Special notice: Hazor (11:10–11). Sometime later, Joshua "turns back" from wherever he is and captures the city of Hazor (11:10). The writer quickly explains that Hazor fell not because of an Israelite preemptive strike but because of its longstanding, regional dominance ("head of all these kingdoms," 11:10). Hazor finally receives its just desserts for the bloodshed. Its demise ends the last bastion of Canaanite rule and inaugurates the Israelite period.

Conclusion (11:12–15). The other cities and kings suffered the same fate as Hazor (11:12). Israel does not burn any northern cities built atop mounds except for Hazor. Presumably, this proviso leaves the Israelites ready-made cities in Galilee in which to settle after the land distribution.

In Praise of Joshua: Conquest Summary (11:16–23). *Geographical summary (11:16–17a).* A survey of Canaan's major geographical regions asserts the extent of Joshua's conquests.

An interpretive surprise (11:17b–20). The writer adds that the ultimate reason for the long conquest is the Canaanite kings' refusal to seek peace with the Israelites: In short, God himself stiffened their resolve ("hardened their hearts," 11:20) to meet Israel in battle. The Canaanites could have escaped disaster by making peace with Israel, but they refused because Yahweh steeled their resolve to attack instead. By the same token, the comment also implies that God did *not* harden the heart of the Hivites of Gibeon, leaving them free to seek peace rather than rally for war. Theologically, the comment suggests divine awareness of the Hivites' inclination in that direction, an inclination that God permits to run its course. Indeed, it seems tantamount to an act of divine grace toward an otherwise condemned people. In short, amid the dark horrors of war and *herem* a small candle of mercy shines on a group of humans whose attitude pleases God.

Special notice: the Anakites (11:21–22). The Anakites were descendants of Anak son of Arba and, ultimately, of the fabled Nephilim (Num 13:33). Their stunning height and gigantic size had especially terrified the Israelite spies (13:28). No Anakites survive except in Gaza, Gath, and Ashdod, three Philistine cities along the Mediterranean where they either lived or fled for refuge. The mention of Gath is significant: It anticipates the later debut of Goliath.

"The end" (11:23). The present campaign had been long and grueling, but in Yahweh's mighty power Joshua has won the

victory at last. The "quiet" gives Israel a chance to beat their swords into plowshares and their spears into pruning hooks. They can stop being soldiers and start being farmers, vineyard owners, and cultivators of fruit trees.

Application. The encouraging words "Don't be afraid" echo across the biblical landscape. Fears plague us all, especially when we are keenly aware that a spiritual battle swirls around us. Some Christians may fear actual physical harm for their faith in Christ. Certainly, believers who suffer under oppressive regimes know that fear intimately. Still yet another fear of Christians is the fear of failing and disappointing God. Behind this lies a deep sense of inadequacy in light of the imagined enormity of what God expects. It is true that the Christian life is no lazy stroll through the park. But the reassuring "Don't be afraid" spoken by Jesus (e.g., Matt 10:26, 28; 28:10) applies to fears of persecution, ostracism, and personal inadequacy. It offers us a powerful antidote to the stresses they inflict on us, his daily presence with us.

JOSHUA 12:1–24

Original Meaning

Two Fallen Eastern Kings (12:1–6). The recapitulation of Israelite royal conquests begins at the beginning, with their victories over two kings and land acquisitions "east of the Jordan" (12:1). Biblical tradition remembers Sihon and Og as a paradigmatic victory of Yahweh on behalf of Israel. Literarily, they comprise a "down payment" on the eventual realization of Israel's full inheritance.

The Fallen Western Kings (12:7–24). *Narrative preface (12:7–8).* Now comes the list of the thirty-one kings whom Joshua and the Israelites struck down west of the Jordan. The report is anachronistic, affirming in advance what is to come later, namely, that Joshua did in Cisjordan what Moses did in Transjordan. Joshua gave it to Israel tribe-by-tribe as their "possession" (12:6).

The list proper (12:9–24). To reinforce this point, a stylized list of kings now follows (12:9–24). Except for 12:24 (one king plus the total), each line lists two kings in stereotyped form. The literary effect is to highlight their social position and the fact they are all gone.

The total triumph comes from one God, Yahweh, and one united people, Israel. Besides drawing the conquest to a close, the list also literarily anticipates what follows. With Tirzah, the list returns the reader to the Israelite heartland, the place where the long process of allocation will soon begin. Further, the roster omits significant ancient cities—notably, Shechem—thus foreshadowing the theme of *un*conquered land with which the following chapter opens.

Application. Politicians, religious leaders, famous athletes, film idols, rock stars, and founders of movements all proclaim, "Follow me!" They eagerly beckon for enthronement as king—or, at least, as "kingpins." Given the felt need for either, many garner sizeable followings.

What rightful claim does Jesus have to being king? Why choose him over modern Canaanite ones? One thing, first of all, sets the reign of Jesus apart: He is a *good king.* My mind imagines him mobbed by crowds as he enters and makes his way through each town or village. The people are thinking, "Wow, the famous rabbi has come to *our* backwater!" It is a Jesus who mills among the locals shaking hands, giving occasional hugs, joking with the crowd, and asking about what has been going on. It is a Jesus who loves ordinary people and loves to be with them.

Jesus is also a *king who saves.* As savior, Jesus rescues us from all kinds of things. I know this from long years of personal experience, as do (I presume) many readers. His forgiveness unshackles the chains of sin that bind me, freeing me from my slavery to it. His power bails me out of the messes that I sometimes create for myself. His grace gently lifts me up when I fall, so he and I can go on together. His patience also warmly embraces me when I fail him, and his smile dispels the dark clouds of discouragement and shame that often envelop me. His soothing presence shepherds me through the dark valleys of despair through which I sometimes must pass.

JOSHUA 13:1–19:51

Original Meaning

Yahweh's Commission to Joshua (13:1–33). *The commission proper (13:1–7).* Joshua's advanced age leads Yahweh to raise an important matter. What is to be done about the "very large areas of land [still] to be taken over" (13:1). After twice celebrating that "Joshua took the entire land" (11:16, 23), the book's mention of unconquered areas may strike some readers as a contradiction. The comment should not surprise us, however, since (as noted above) the existence of areas of Canaan still awaiting conquest is implicit both in the conquest narrative (chs. 6–11) and in the celebratory list of kings (ch. 12). In 13:7, Yahweh formally ("And now . . .," lit.) commissions Joshua to "divide" the entire land.

Retrospective review (13:8–33). This section reviews Moses's prior land allocations east of the Jordan to two-and-a-half tribes (cf. Num 32:33–42). He did so on one condition—that they fight to win inheritances for the other tribes on the west side of the Jordan. Thematically, this retrospective adds details to the description in Joshua 12:1–6 and anticipates Joshua's later dismissal of the east-bank tribes to their lands (ch. 22).

Joshua 13:32 sums up the entire retrospective ("this is the

inheritance Moses had given . . ."). It anchors the historic moment at its historic site (Num 22:1; 26:3). For the second time the writer mentions that Moses gave no inheritance to the tribe of Levi (Josh 13:33). The rationale this time, however, is that Yahweh himself is Levi's inheritance, just as Yahweh promised them. Set aside for Yahweh's service (Exod 32:26–29), the tribe of Levi enjoyed the special blessing of ongoing contact with him and his personal provision of their financial needs (i.e., Israel's tithes and offerings). In sum, Joshua 13 affirms that Moses gave Israel's Transjordanian tribes their inheritances—and, thereby, the basis for their land claims—and reasserts that, despite the barrier of the Jordan, they help comprise larger Israel.

Joshua's Obedience: The First Allotment (14:1–17:18). *Introduction (14:1–5).* Opening and closing formulae ("Now these are the areas/territories . . . ," 14:1; 19:51) bracket the lengthy summary (chs. 14–19) of what lands the Israelites received as their inheritances. Indeed, the formulae stamp the summary as primarily retrospective—a backward look at the results of the process, not necessarily a report of how it was done.

At the same time, the writer's summary report (14:2–5) does explain the distribution as the work of the high priest, Eleazar, Joshua, and the tribal leaders. The presence of the high priest and the use of lots per Yahweh's explicit command also mark the land distribution as specifically a *sacred* act (14:2). The main point of chapters 14–19, however, is to confirm that Joshua faithfully executes his commission to apportion Canaan among the nine-and-a-half tribes.

A special allotment: Caleb (14:6–15). The first allotment opens with a narrative concerning a special allotment for Caleb (14:6–15), then details the allotments to Judah (15:1–63) and the Josephites, Ephraim and Manasseh (16:1–17:13). It concludes with a supplementary allotment for the latter pair (17:14–18).

A Judahite visit with Joshua at Gilgal (14:6a) sets the context for a speech by Caleb, who presumably accompanies them there (14:6b–12). Caleb, of course, is the wilderness hero who represented Judah among the twelve spies and favored a bold Israelite attack into Canaan rather than a frightened retreat back to Egypt (Num 13–14). The sensitive reader imagines the poignant moment when Joshua and Caleb, two aging veterans of so much history, meet at Gilgal—itself a site where powerful memories echo—surrounded by Judah's representatives. Caleb reminds Joshua, his only ally among the spies, of "what the LORD said to Moses . . . about you and me" long ago at Kadesh Barnea (Josh 14:6b).

The promise rewards Caleb's one sterling trait: He "followed the LORD . . . God wholeheartedly," a trait the context recalls verbatim three times (14:9; cf. vv. 8, 14). In other words, what Caleb did was wholeheartedly—that is, resolutely, unswervingly, unhesitatingly—to obey God's will rather than his own or that of someone else. Therein lies what set him apart from his unfaithful comrades (14:24).

Caleb remarks (with apparent hyperbole) that God, as he promised, has kept him alive to age eighty-five—and just as vigorous and battle-ready as ever! (14:10–11). The motif implicitly points the reader to the steps he followed in order to enjoy the divine blessings of long life and the retention of ancestral land.

Judah's allotment (15:1–63). The larger process begins with a long report of Judah's inheritance (15:1–63). The boundary description (15:1–12) traces in considerable detail its southern (15:2–4), eastern (15:5a), northern (15:5b–11), and western borders (15:12).

Caleb returns on stage in a brief interlude (15:13–19) that also features his daughter Acsah. The narrator recalls that Hebron (or Kiriath Arba) is Caleb's inheritance and lies within Judah's inheritance (15:13). He also reports officially that Caleb destroyed three descendants of Anak at Hebron (15:14). Nor is old Caleb finished. He marches to Debir, fifteen miles southwest of Hebron, and offers his daughter Acsah in marriage to anyone who captures it. Caleb's nephew, Othniel, does so and claims the prize (15:15–17). At his new wife's urging, Othniel gets Caleb to grant them a field, and Acsah herself wins "a special favor" from her father—the area's upper and lower springs (15:18–19)—because the property lies in the "land in the Negev" (i.e., the desert). The wedding present permits them to irrigate land in the Negev's semiarid climate. This vignette implies that, besides Hebron, Caleb also held territory southwest of the city in the southern hill country of Judah and the Negev.

The inheritance of Judah concludes with a lengthy list of Judah's towns (15:20–63) neatly organized by four geographical regions. Many readers will find the Judah section—hands down, the largest in chapters 14–19—tediously detailed. But that is the point: Its sheer quantity underscores Judah's importance within Israel. Later history will confirm the importance of Judah's foothold in the land for it constituted the remnant of the twelve tribes that enabled Israel to continue its mission to the world.

For the first time, however, the book reports that a tribe did not destroy (15:63) indigenous people occupying its inheritance. In this case, it is the Jebusites who live in Jerusalem, and the author adds that in his day they still "live with the Judahites in Jerusalem" (lit.). This comment is surprising because it assumes that Jerusalem belongs to Judah, whereas the border of Judah excludes it (15:8) and 18:28 assigns Jerusalem to the inheritance of Benjamin. The best explanation for 15:63 is to read it as reflecting the writer's Judahite perspective and probably a Davidic or post-Davidic time of writing.

The allotments of the Joseph tribes (16:1–17:18). The two tribes of Joseph now receive their inheritance (16:1–17:13). The author again sounds the did-not-destroy theme. The Ephraimites forced them to work for the Israelites (16:10). This seems to imply criticism of Ephraimite efforts in the matter, unless the force required to compel labor is less than that necessary to destroy the Canaanites. The text clarifies that the inheritance of West Manasseh (17:1–13) concerns six clans of Manasseh other than those of Makir or East Manasseh (16:1–2, 6b), already an inheritance recipient (13:28–31). West Manasseh receives ten sections of land in Cisjordan in order to accommodate them (17:5–6).

Finally, an unexpected dialogue between the Josephites and Joshua closes both the Josephite allotment report and the larger first allotment section (17:14–18). Strikingly, the narrator phrases it in first person singular, as if the two tribes were speaking as a single individual (17:14). Joshua's reply turns the petitioner's premise around. If the hill country of Ephraim lacks room, he challenges Joseph to wield his large population as a powerful saw against the forest where the Perizzites and Rephaites live (17:15). In short, behind the difficulty lurks an opportunity.

Contextually, of course, the Josephites apparently have a short memory and feeble faith. The contrast with the bold and fearless eighty-year-old Caleb (chs. 14–15) is also stark and disappointing. That Caleb (14:6–12) and Zelophehad's daughters (17:4) appeal to God's prior promises of land likewise casts Joseph's approach in an arrogant, self-serving light.

Joshua's final ruling (17:17–18) parries both prongs of the Josephite argument.

1. He encourages them not to sell themselves short.
2. He turns their "one lousy portion" against them and reiterates his earlier challenge concerning the opportunities that the forest offers.

The Second Allotment: the Shiloh Assembly (18:1–19:51). *Instructions and compliance (18:1–10).* At first hearing, Joshua's opening statement ("How long will you wait . . . ?") sounds like an accusation that faults the seven tribes for laziness (18:3). In reality, the seven have received no prior mandate to occupy land, so his seemingly blunt statement is merely motivational rhetoric to get them moving on his plan. The plan (18:4–5, 8) calls for three men from each tribe—probably twenty-one in all—to survey the land still available outside the territory already occupied by Judah and Joseph. Then the surveyors are to return to Joshua, who will cast lots before God and Israel to decide who gets what (18:6–7).

Tribal allotments (18:11–19:48). The text itself offers no explanation of the lot-casting procedure.

Benjamin (18:11–28). The first lot identifies Benjamin (18:11a) and his land (18:11b). The list of Benjamite towns—the third longest after those of Judah (ch. 15) and Levi (ch. 21)—now follows (18:21–28), subdivided into eastern (twelve towns) and western (fourteen towns) districts.

Simeon (19:1–9). The second lot identifies the inheritance of Simeon. It consists exclusively of towns within Judah's territory. The writer explains that Simeon benefited from the fact that Judah's portion exceeded Judah's needs (19:9). Structurally, the list subdivides the towns into districts of thirteen (19:2–6) and four (19:7–8) along with their surrounding villages. The thirteen lie in southern Judah, while the four include two in the Negev and two in the western lowlands. Baalath Beer marks either the southernmost village or the southern boundary within which they fall (19:8a).

Zebulun (19:10–16). The third lot falls to Zebulun. Structurally, opening and closing formulae (19:10a, 16) bracket an extensive boundary description (19:10b–14) and a short town list (19:15). Zebulun is a small tribe set snugly between Asher (west), Naphtali (north and northeast), Issachar (southeast), and West Manasseh (southwest). The writer says that Zebulun's towns number twelve, plus their villages, but lists only five relatively obscure places (19:15).

Issachar (19:17–23). Issachar receives its inheritance with the fall of the fourth lot. As with Zebulun, opening and closing formulae (19:17, 23) set off the list of sixteen towns with villages (19:18–21), with possibly a terse description of its northern boundary ending at the Jordan (19:22). Place names and the descriptions suggest that the allotments of Zebulun, Issachar, and Napthali all meet near Mount Tabor.

Asher (19:24–31). The fifth lot identifies Asher. Opening and closing formulae set off the report (19:24, 31). In sum, Asher occupies a narrow swath of land east-to-west between the Mediterranean and Zebulun and south-to-north between the Kishon River and somewhere north of the Litani River. The text's unique combination of borders and town lists serves to support Israel's ancient territorial claim, based on God's will spoken through lots, and to keep hope alive for reclaiming it during periods when it falls into alien hands.

Naphtali (19:32–39). The sixth lot concerns Naphtali, and again opening and closing formulae (19:32, 39) set the section apart. Structurally, the author offers a boundary description (19:33–34) and a list of nineteen towns (19:35–38). In short, the territory of Naphtali occupies the eastern part of Lower Galilee and most of Upper Galilee west of Asher and east of the Sea of Galilee and the Jordan above it.

Dan (19:40–49). Finally, the seventh lot falls on Dan. Again, opening and closing formulae (19:40, 48) enclose this report, the final section of the second allotment. That several of the towns also appear in Solomon's second administrative district (1 Kgs 4:9) has fueled scholarly speculation that the latter may be the source of the Danite list. The narrative omits a final tally of Dan's towns (Simeon is the only other tribe of the seven without one), a concession perhaps to the historical reality known to the original audience. A parenthetical comment explains how Dan, unable to possess its allotment, militarily succeeds in settling way up north (Josh 19:47). The comment ("Dan's territory left them," lit.) seems to blame the land for skedaddling rather than Dan for failing. The text implies sympathy—in modern terms, "it was just one of those things."

Joshua's Allotment (19:49–50). The allotment narrative opened with Joshua (13:1) and now fittingly returns to him (19:49). The tribes have received their allotments from Joshua, and now the collective body ("the Israelites") returns the favor, gifting him with his own inheritance. They give him what he asks for, the town of Timnath Serah in the middle of Ephraim, his own tribe (Num 13:8). Joshua makes the town liveable and settles in (Josh 19:50b). The absence of Timnath Serah from the list of Ephraimite towns suggests that it may have been Joshua's own personal possession—a special land grant to him from a grateful nation.

Summary (19:51). This concluding formula looks back over the proceedings of chapters 18–19 and draws them to a close. The literary effect is to bring solemn closure to the giving (and receiving) of inheritances and to introduce a narrative pause in the book. As we will see in chapters 20–21, however, two more distributions await their moment before one may finally consider the settlement an actual reality.

Application. Joshua 13–19 begins with Yahweh's conversation with aging Joshua concerning "the land that remains" (13:2). He surveys the terrain not yet in Israelite hands, leaving Israel to do its part and promising to drive out the Sidonians himself. An important contemporary theme emerges from this conversation: Given our human weakness, we always carry out God's tasks imperfectly, but God is strong and caring; he stands ready to aid our efforts rather than tolerate our compromise.

The more I read Scripture and listen to the Holy Spirit, the more aware I become of areas of my person and my way of life not yet surrendered to the lordship of Christ. In my soul still lurk dark corners that I keep Jesus out of lest he discover the sin, self-centeredness, and rebellion hiding undisturbed there. The air in this closet reeks of fear and panic—and plain faithlessness. I suspect that my readers have dark, secret closets of their own where they shut out the searching light of Jesus, lest it expose the inner corruption and spiritual detritus stockpiled there.

As an eight-year-old I was "converted to Christ" in a genuine moment of personal commitment that launched my long life of discipleship. In reality, however, the more I learn about myself, the more I reckon myself among the partly converted. There is much about me that remains *un*converted. For my conversion to become more complete, I need to dismantle those hidden and forbidden closets deep down in my soul, thoroughly clean up the space, and toss their contents into the trash.

This is where the second part of this theme comes into play. God promised to give Israel the land, and Joshua 13–19 demonstrates that he did so. Similarly, God promises us his power to compensate for our imperfections and failures as Christians. As God's power compensated for Israel's military weakness against Sidon, so also his power offsets our spiritual weaknesses. God supplies this deficit in order to encourage us as we contend on his behalf against our spiritual Sidonians.

When we feel the weakest, that is when we are the strongest! At that moment, the powerful grace of God comes into play. The trick, of course, is to relax and let that power take over. Here is what I suggest to surrender to God's power: Memorize Philippians 4:13, and when you feel yourself in need of God's power, simply say, "I can all this through him who gives me strength." When you dread going to work: "I can do all this through him. . . ." When you fail and need to repair a relationship: "I can do all this through him. . . ." When you have no idea how to solve a problem, "I can do all this through him. . . ." When you feel like you cannot live another day: "I can do all this through him. . . ." You will experience the paradox of the gospel: It demonstrates its incredible power at the moment we feel at rock bottom.

JOSHUA 20:1–21:45

Original Meaning

The Cities of Refuge (20:1–9). The Israelites are to implement what Yahweh told Moses by setting aside cities of refuge (20:1–2). The term "cities of refuge" links Joshua 20 with the provision of Numbers 35:6. The ancient custom of blood revenge—retaliation in kind against a killer by the victim's kin—stands in the background of Joshua 20. In Israel one duty of close male relatives was to avenge such deaths by killing the person thought responsible. But a pattern of unrestrained retaliation poses a threat to the continuation of stable social order. The provision of cities of refuge seeks to break that cycle of blood revenge. But 20:3 clarifies that it only applies to accidental and unintentional killings (Num 35:11–15).

The act of killing nevertheless incurs blood guilt and legitimates retaliation by the aggrieved family. Thus, Yahweh outlines the procedure to be followed to obviate the latter (Josh 20:4–6). If the killer desires refuge, he is to flee to the closest city of refuge and must argue his case at the city gate before the elders (20:4). Since a full trial follows (20:6), this process amounts to a preliminary hearing to determine whether his case qualifies for asylum. Once satisfied, the elders may admit him to the city and provide him a place to live during his long stay. If a blood restorer tracks him there, the city's leaders may not hand the killer over since his actions seem to have been unintentional and not driven by anger (20:5). Curiously, when the current high priest dies, the refugee receives an amnesty that permits his return home. Verse 9 reiterates the purpose of the institution.

The Cities for the Levites (Joshua 21:1–42). *The summary report (21:1–8).* Once again, an interested party proffers a petition before Eleazer, Joshua, and the tribal leaders at Shiloh. This time the petitioners are the heads of the three Levite families, and they ask for what Yahweh had promised them through Moses (21:2b). Again, echoing the theme of Israel's obedience, the people do so (21:3). Verse 8 again states that the Israelites obeyed Yahweh's command delivered by Moses; they allotted towns and pasturelands to the Levites. Literarily, the summary report prepares the reader to understand the distribution that follows.

The allotment details (21:9–42). A simple, somewhat formulaic structure forms the skeleton of this long section. The underlying structure of 21:9–42 includes the following elements:

1. Introductory formula: "to family X [they gave] . . ." (21:9, 11, 13, 20, 27, 34)
2. Tribal source formula: "from tribe X + town list + total number of towns" (21:9, 11, 13–16, 17–18, 28–29, 30–31, 32, 36–37)
3. Summary formula ("All the towns . . .") with tally (21:19, 26, 33, 40)
4. Grand total tally for all Levites (21:41)
5. Conclusion (21:42)

The Aaronides (21:9–19). The paragraph on the Aaronides —Aaron's descendants who are priests—is the most detailed and complex one. It especially underscores the priority of the Aaronides "because the first lot fell to them" (21:10).

The Kohathites (21:20–26). Israel gives the nonpriestly Kohathites ten towns and their land belts, four each from Ephraim, including Shechem and Dan, as well as two from West Manasseh.

The Gershonites (21:27–33). The Gershonites also receive thirteen cities, two from East Manasseh, including Golan (a city of refuge [21:27]), four from Issachar and Asher, and three from Naphtali, including Kedesh (a city of refuge [v. 32]). Geographically, two of their towns lie way east of the Sea of Galilee, the rest spread north, south, and northwest of it.

The Merarites (21:34–40). Finally, the Merarites receive four towns from Zebulun, Reuben, and Gad (v. 39).

Retrospective summary (21:43–45). The Joshua editor now steps forward personally to deliver a powerful closing comment. It marks one of the most important moments in the entire book. His simple words dramatically bring down the curtain on both the conquest of Canaan (chs. 1–12) and its settlement (chs. 13–21). He writes retrospectively, looking back on past events to underscore their significance. Quietly, he weaves together four unmistakable linguistic echoes from chapter 1 to form a thematic *inclusio* around chapters 1–21.

1. He affirms that "the LORD gave Israel all the land"; that is, he kept his oath to their ancestors (21:43a; cf. 1:6).
2. The author affirms that Israel "took possession of it and settled there" (21:43b). Again, he writes retrospectively; to "take possession" was what, on Joshua's orders, the officers told the people in order to motivate them in their preparations for the Jordan crossing (1:11; cf. 1:15).
3. The narrator recalls another fulfilled patriarchal promise —Yahweh's gift of "rest on every side" (21:44a). Clearly, this "rest" that Yahweh accomplished concerns his defeat of enemies opposing their settlement in Canaan.
4. The writer affirms that nothing Yahweh promised was left undone; it all came true (21:45; cf. 23:14). All credit goes to Yahweh.

Application. The Old Testament cities of refuge offered mercy for unfortunate Israelites. In my view, one aspect of their contemporary meaning is to challenge churches today to be "churches of refuge." What traits typify a "church of refuge"?

1. Its primary concern is with today and tomorrow, not yesterday. When people approach its front door, they sense they are entering a nonthreatening, safe place. They sense a place where their past will never get in the way of relationships or come back to haunt them.
2. Yes, churches have rules—biblical standards of conduct and expectations—but refuge churches apply them only when necessary, and then gently and sorrowfully. They let people be who they are—warts and all!—and leave the transformation business to God. He is a lot better at it than they are, anyway.
3. A safe church grows members well aware of their own warts. Its rank structure is—well, it has none. People may serve different organizational functions within it, but they enjoy the same status: They are all forgiven sinners, nothing more, nothing less.
4. Finally, a safe church gives people the God-treatment. It treats people the same way God has treated them—with mercy and compassion. It works hard to live out Jesus's teaching that among his people the "greatest" is the "slave" who serves everyone else first (Matt 20:26; Mark 9:35; Luke 22:26).

JOSHUA 22:1–34

Original Meaning

Scene 1 (Shiloh): "Troops, Dismissed!" (22:1–8). *Joshua's remarks (22:1–6).* With the fighting done and west-bank land secure, Joshua summons the Transjordanian tribes (Reuben, Gad, East Manasseh) to a private meeting (22:1). He recalls that long ago Moses had granted their requested inheritances in Transjordan on one condition—that they not occupy them until they and the other tribes had together conquered Cisjordan (Num 35). Joshua affirms that they have fully met both obligations, obeying both Moses and himself (Josh 22:2). Specifically, they did not abandon their brothers, although the hardships implicit in the conquest narrative (chs. 1–12) gave them many reasons to bail out (22:3).

Most importantly, Joshua affirms that, ultimately, their service was not to fellow Israelites but to Yahweh himself. Now that the job is done Joshua orders them (22:4) to turn and head home. In brief detail Joshua makes sure the returnees remember what is ultimately most important (22:5). They must stay on their guard to scrupulously observe everything Moses taught them.

Finally, Joshua pronounces a blessing over them (22:6). The implication of Joshua's Mosaic-like vocabulary and blessing is that Joshua regards the east-bank tribes as an integral part of Israel despite their distant settlement location. Cleverly, the narrator wields these words to set the scene for those subsequent events.

Scene 2 (Transjordan): What's Going On? (22:9–31). *Report: the altar building (22:9–10).* The two-and-a-half tribes leave Shiloh in Canaan and proceed to the land of Gilead, where they own land by God's command through Moses (22:9). The narrator invokes terminology that noticeably contrasts the east and west-bank areas. It seems to represent a Cisjordanian perspective: "Shiloh in the land of Canaan" versus "the land of Gilead"; "children of Reuben, Gad, and half-Manasseh" (lit. for all three) versus "the children of Israel."

This contrast raises a question: If Canaan is the true land of promise and the Israelites its recipients, what is the status of these two-and-a-half tribes outside it? The reader may rightly wonder how soon such sensitivity concerning their status might surface among those tribes. In any case, the travelers reach the area along the Jordan's west bank, presumably at a major crossing point, where they build an altar (22:10).

A delegation to Transjordan (22:11–14). A report (or rumor?) concerning this striking structure beside the Jordan soon reaches the Israelites (22:11). The report about the unsettling discovery conveys shocked urgency, as if the altar were scandalous and posed a serious threat to west-bank well-being. The news sparks a rush of the "whole assembly of Israel" to an emergency pow-wow at Shiloh (22:12). Israel meets to prepare for war against the two-and-a-half tribes.

First, however, the Israelites dispatch a delegation to the Transjordanian tribes (again, names spelled out) in Gilead with a priest, Phinehas son of Eleazar, as its head (22:13–14)—the only member explicitly named. To put a priest in charge assumes the issue to be a religious one, and this particular priest has an interesting past history. He is best known for his decisive, violent action at Baal Peor that ended a devastating plague in Israel's camp and won him special praise from Yahweh (Num 25). If the situation demands a ruling on altars or bold, daring initiative, Phinehas is certainly the right man for the job.

The west-bank view (22:15–20). Phinehas and the ten VIPs reach Gilead and, at an unnamed site, at length address the gathered Transjordanian tribes (22:15–20). The opening messenger formula presents the speech as spoken, not by a single individual like Phinehas but by the community of Yahweh as a whole (22:16). Subtly, it also implies some serious problem with the standing of the east-bank tribes in the eyes of Yahweh and Israel.

The dignitaries' first question levels a blunt, strongly worded accusation—the severest of crimes against God, one that imperiled all Israel. The delegation assumes that, since Yahweh has authorized only one altar—the one in Canaan (cf. 22:19)—the new altar must honor another god. Therein lies the Transjordanian revolt, the visitors argue; it is apostasy, plain and simple.

With a second question ("Was not the sin of Peor enough for us?" 22:17), the speech moves from blunt accusation to an appeal to spare everyone terrible consequences (22:17–20). Peor recalls the place just east of the Jordan where Yahweh sent a terrible plague to punish Israel for worshiping an idol, the Baal of Peor, in Numbers 25. The plague took 24,000 lives.

To avert this disaster, the visitors propose that the two-and-a-half tribes leave "defiled" Transjordan and settle among the other tribes in Canaan, "in the LORD's land," near the tabernacle (Josh 22:19). This comment shares the same Israel/non-Israel distinction seen earlier. It assumes—perhaps hyperbolically for sake of argument—that Transjordan is not "the LORD's land" but land belonging to some other deity. It voices the Cisjordanian perspective that east-bank land is not holy as Canaan is.

The second shameful episode (22:20) is the more recent one, the horrid treachery of Achan. If the scandal at Peor marks the classic case of apostasy, Achan denotes the classic case of treachery. The Israelites climactic (perhaps even melodramatic!) cry that "[Achan] was not the only one who died for his sin" (22:20) powerfully drives home their message.

The east-bank view (22:21–29). The opening rhetorical flourish, a string of orthodox names for Israel's God, aims immediately to dispel the visitors' doubts about their orthodoxy (22:22). There is, they claim, another side to this story. They strongly affirm that Israel's God understands the real situation. If their altar announces rejection of Yahweh (and, by implication, his altar in Canaan) and pledges loyalty to another god through sacrifices, they ask Yahweh himself to "call us to account" (22:23). Thus, they deny the accusations; they claim to have nothing to hide. They share the visitors' conviction that Israel performs sacrifices to Yahweh only at Shiloh.

But now the Transjordanians reveal something new—they fear that future descendants of the present accusers will deny their own descendants to have access to Yahweh (22:24a). They also quote a possible objection that future Cisjordanians might raise to exclude their descendants (22:24b–25a). But what really makes them shudder—their worst fear—is the frightening result of their exclusion: The Transjordanians' descendants will "stop fearing the LORD" (22:25b). The altar offers tangible testimony of the Transjordanian commitment to sacrifice only at Yahweh's west-bank sanctuary, not to fall into rebellion and apostasy.

This perspective rules out of bounds any west-bank attempt to deny them access to their "share in the LORD" in Canaan (22:26–27). Coming generations of Transjordanian pilgrims can point to it, "a replica of the LORD's altar," as silent evidence of their connection to Yahweh at his official site, not at the riverside one (22:28). As a final, dramatic gesture, the Transjordanians voice a negative oath: "Far be it from us" to "rebel" (Heb. *marad*, 22:29) against Yahweh by sacrificing at any spot other than at the altar in front of the tabernacle.

Resolution (22:30–31). Suddenly, the Cisjordanians find the tables turned on them; the would-be accusers now find themselves the accused! The fact that the Transjordanians mount a defense longer than the original accusation implies that the sympathies of the biblical author also lie with them. The lengthy explanation by the Transjordanians pleases the entire delegation (22:30).

It falls to Phinehas the priest, the delegation's leader, to respond officially on their behalf (22:31). The easterners have given Yahweh no reason to abandon Israel. Phinehas accepts the heart of the Transjordanian concern—they are full members of Israel. Phinehas acknowledges emphatically that "now"—because of your persuasive explanation—the east-bank tribes "have rescued the Israelites from the LORD's hand." The claim of rescue probably describes the result of their persuasive answer.

Scene 3 (Shiloh): No Problem! (22:32–34). *The good report (22:32–33).* The report concerning the return trip of Phinehas and the other leaders from Transjordan marks the transition to the brief third scene (22:32a). The centrality of the hero, Phinehas the priest, in the narrative fully legitimates the altar. At least, nothing is said about tearing it down. And no doubt the crowd also feels a welcome sense of relief, since they immediately "praise ("bless," lit.) God" and say nothing more about going to war (22:33b).

The altar's name (22:34). No one tears the altar down. Instead, Reuben and Gad give it an appropriate sentence name: "A Witness Between Us—that the LORD [and absolutely no one else] is God" (22:34). Implicit also is the unspoken tagline, "and on both sides of the river, too!"

Application. The Jordan River was the symbol of theological tensions that could have divided Israel. In my view, little Jordans, capable of eroding Christian unity, flow quietly through every congregation. A variety of religious experiences may populate a congregation. Such differing experiences raise divisive questions about what the church should be doing. They also often cause divisions about how the church should worship—formal, informal, or blended worship style? Rather than confront each other over every little thing, there are times simply to let things pass because we trust each other—and we trust the unseen work of the Holy Spirit. As the Transjordanians shout, "The LORD! He knows! (22:22).

JOSHUA 23:1–16

Original Meaning

Remembrance and Exhortation, Part 1 (23:1–8). Driven by the urgency of age, Joshua summons all Israel, including its major officials, to hear his farewell address (23:2a). Joshua quickly turns to remembrance (23:2–5), shifting the focus from himself to the audience and what "you yourselves [emphatic pronoun] have seen" (23:3).

Joshua redirects to the people commands that Yahweh originally addressed only to himself in (23:6). Joshua commands them, "Be very strong!" Like Joshua, on their own they must also "be careful to obey" what Yahweh commands (1:6). Specifically, Joshua cites things to avoid: to associate or intermingle with the remaining nations and to take an oath on the name of their gods or swear by them (23:7). Instead, they are "to hold fast" to Yahweh alone (23:8). To cling firmly to Yahweh is to embrace him so tightly—to observe such exclusive loyalty to him—as to leave not even the smallest crack for other gods between the two of you.

Remembrance and Exhortation, Part 2 (23:9–13). From exhortation Joshua returns again to the past deeds of Yahweh that they themselves have seen (23:9–10). Joshua repeats a phrase heard earlier in the book to highlight what Israel saw. Just as he promised, they were so unstoppable that one solitary Israelite could rout a thousand Canaanites (23:9b–10)! For that invincibility under Yahweh to continue, Israel must "be very careful to love the LORD your God" (23:11).

But why should Israelites protect themselves? The threatening influence in 23:6–8 will derive from Israel's simply hanging around and doing business with Canaanites. But in the long conditional warning (23:12–13), the threatening influence is actual intermarriage with them. Israel should fully grasp the disastrous consequences they are risking (23:13).

Final Warning (23:14–16). In short, Joshua's concluding warning brings his farewell speech to a rhetorical climax. He dispels any illusions Israel might have about getting along with both Canaanites and Yahweh. Such attempts at accommodation are foolhardy and futile, the risks grave. Joshua has lived long enough to know that such well-intended experiments are doomed to failure; he knows where in the wilderness the bodies of Israel's ancestors are buried. For a people to perish is to vanish from history—and, in Israel's case, to trash centuries of postponed hope endured by their patient, longsuffering ancestors. Joshua's point is that, for Israel, idolatry is nothing but stupid. Alas, notwithstanding Joshua's warnings, a disastrous period of Canaanization—Israel's defection from Yahweh and adoption of Canaanite culture—will characterize the early post-Joshua period (see Judg 2:11–13).

Application. Every Christian has his or her own story to tell of something amazing God did for them. Sometimes Jesus just lifts our spirits, gives us new insight into ourselves or others, or heals simple sicknesses. Other times his loving rebuke steers us around pitfalls, or his gentle nudge gets us past our reluctance to do the right thing. These, too, are amazing feats, albeit on a smaller scale, and rightly lead us to celebrate with gratitude and joy over what God has done.

JOSHUA 24:1–33

Original Meaning

A Look Backward and Call for Decision (24:1–15).

The setting (24:1). The text opens with a report that Joshua assembled all the tribes of Israel and their leaders for a meeting at Shechem. Besides its patriarchal associations, the city's location offered an ideal place for Israel to convene. It sits in central Canaan with excellent accessibility by road, and its surrounding valley could easily accommodate such a large gathering.

Yahweh's speech (24:2–13). Joshua launches the proceedings by addressing the assembled crowd. The address reviews Israel's ancestral history beginning with Abraham (24:2–4). The people know the story well: It marks the beginning of Yahweh's connection with them as a people. The driving theme of the speech concerns Israel's exclusive devotion to Yahweh alone. The change of subject from plural ("[they] lived," 24:2) to "I" (24:3) colors what follows as Yahweh's personal testimony, a highly selective thumbnail sketch of Genesis 12 to Joshua 22.

Yahweh appeals to their own experience ("you saw with your own eyes what I did . . . ," 24:7), an echo of a common phrase of Moses in Deuteronomy. There it recalls Israel's witness of Yahweh's victories over the Amorite kings Sihon and Og, the god Baal of Peor, the rebels Dathan and Abiram, Pharaoh in Egypt, and the Egyptian army at the Red Sea. In Israelite memory, these kinds of events epitomized Yahweh's awesome and overwhelming miraculous power. Here they rhetorically display Yahweh's unquestioned superiority over both mighty earthly kings and would-be rival deities, all in support of the central appeal to Israel that soon follows.

Joshua 24 highlights details of the Red Sea crossing. Their special inclusion may sound a thematic echo of the continuity emphasized earlier between the Red Sea and Jordan River crossings (cf. 4:21–24). Further, the broad statement "you lived in the wilderness for a long time" quickly summarizes that forty-year period (24:7b). His focus remains on the good he has done for Israel—grammatically, the indicative mood—to tap into their reservoir of gratitude and win a favorable response (the imperative mood).

One memorable event in Transjordan—how Moab's king Balak tried to get the seer Balaam to curse Israel—receives full treatment (24:9–10). Again, many in the listening audience would remember this famous episode from personal experience. The theme of divine rescue marks one of the speech's key themes, another of a string of divine deliverances from hostile enemies over the centuries. The implication is that had Yahweh not intervened, there would be no Israel for him to address on this or any other occasion. Enemies would have overwhelmed them long ago.

But the story then moves closer to home, to the events of Joshua 3–12: the Jordan crossing, Jericho, and the defeat of Canaan's seven peoples (24:11). Yahweh highlights how widespread was enemy resistance to Israel—and how sweeping the victory. Like the two Amorite kings, all seven fell to "the hornet" (24:12), a kind of advanced guard that "I" sent to drive them out before Israel arrived.

That means that Israel's possession of the land is God's gift, pure and simple ("I gave you [pl.]," 24:13)—the fifth and final such gift in Yahweh's testimony. Israel had a hand neither in the land's conquest nor in its construction. Yahweh generously handed over to Israel ready-made fields, vineyards, and olive groves to feed themselves, and ready-made cities in which to live. In short, the defeat of Canaan and the land gift are all Yahweh's doing. They mark the capstone of the stunning saga of salvation that he has singlehandedly orchestrated for Israel's benefit since the call of Abram.

Joshua's closing exhortation (24:14–15). A subtle, seamless shift from the divine "I" to the third person signals that Joshua speaks from here on. Verse 14 mentions two places where Israel or their ancestors had lived long enough to put down roots, Mesopotamia and Egypt. Israel may serve Yahweh or their ancestors' gods, but not both; polytheism is no longer an option.

So Joshua urges his hearers "this day" to make a choice one way or the other (24:15). Joshua's transition ("but as for me") draws a firm line between his household and the alternatives: "We will serve the LORD" (24:15). In one sense, this announcement is no surprise; Joshua has a sterling track record behind him. The issue is whether other Israelite households will join his or whether his alone will serve Yahweh.

The Ritual Dialogue: Loyalty Reaffirmed (24:16–24). The decision phase of the process (24:16–21) opens in 24:16 with the people's opening line, "Far be it from us . . ." (in modern terms, "No way!"). They state their rationale just as Yahweh did, in their own historical review, their own testimony of what—and this is the main point—Yahweh "our God" (not other gods) has done for "us" (24:17–18a). The people's response to Yahweh's mighty deeds is that "we too will serve the LORD" (24:18b).

At first glance, Joshua's reply sounds like an irritated rebuttal (24:19; in modern terms, "In your dreams!"). But his seeming rejoinder in fact dispenses to theologically naive Israel a strong dose of divine reality in order to dispel a dangerous delusion. Probably Joshua senses in Israel's response (24:16–18) a mistakenly narrow preoccupation with Yahweh's ability to protect. The danger is that they fail to reckon fully with Yahweh's unique character compared to the gods they have known.

This leads Joshua to issue a stern conditional warning (24:20). If Israel does, indeed, break its solemn word, "disaster" will surely follow. Joshua disabuses Israel of the misperception that Yahweh's goodness toward them will continue no matter what. On the contrary, Joshua says, make no mistake: The "[very] bad" (NIV "disaster") will replace the "good" should Israel drop Yahweh and take up with foreign gods.

But Joshua's stern warning does not deter the people, who again commit themselves to serve Yahweh (cf. 24:18b). Joshua's tone now softens, and the confirmation phase of covenant-making follows (24:22–24).

The Ceremony: The Book and the Stone (24:25–28). The people take on themselves the covenant here enacted as a permanent, official, self-imposed public policy that Israel will serve Yahweh alone.

1. Joshua writes down "these things" in "a book of God's instruction" (24:26, lit.)
2. Joshua erects a large stone under the oak tree at Shechem. The custom of raising a stone (or stone pile) to memorialize memorable events or people is well attested in the Old Testament, especially in Joshua. Finally, the narrator reports that Joshua dismisses the assembly, each participant returning "to their own inheritance" (24:28).

Joshua's death and burial (24:29–31). This small section reports the simple fact that "Joshua son of Nun . . . died" (24:29) and that "they buried him" (24:30a). The Bible says nothing about Joshua having a wife or children, so the indefinite "they" probably refers to more distant relatives.

A deft, subtle narrative touch also bestows on Joshua a telling posthumous award. His previous title had simply been "Moses's aide" (1:1), but here the writer honors him with the title "the servant of the LORD" (24:29). This is the same posthumous title awarded Moses at his death (Deut 34:5).

A brief narrative eulogy lauds Joshua for the fact that "Israel served the LORD" during his entire lifetime (Josh 24:31). Through it the writer reasserts the connection made earlier in the chapter between Yahweh's acts and the demand to "serve" him (see comments on 24:1–28). The comment further redounds to the glory of Joshua as a great leader.

The burial of Joseph (24:32). The box of long-carried and now-buried bones tucked into the earth symbolizes the long epic journey from Genesis to Joshua. Implicitly, those bones echo the last sound of one of the book's central themes, God's fulfillment of his promise to the patriarchs.

The burial of Eleazar (24:33). With Eleazar's burial, a generation of Israelite leadership—the two successors of Moses and Aaron, respectively—passes from the scene and the momentous book of Joshua ends. For the narrator, the ending is not sad but satisfying. It provides an appropriate moment to draw one of the book's key themes to a close—the exemplary, successful leadership of Joshua. More important, the burials mark the closing bookend of the long epic from a promise received in Genesis to a promise realized in Joshua.

Application. What makes something usually thought normal or healthy a god? It might be a god if we willingly yield it excessive authority to direct our lives. For example, we may follow its advice or demands without even considering whether God has anything to say about the matter. It might be a god if it in any way plays a more significant role in our lives than God does. That was what Israel did that so seriously offended Yahweh. They trusted other gods *instead of* Yahweh; they granted those deities a large role in their lives and ceded them authority over them rather than Yahweh. In short, the danger of polytheism is that we may be completely committed to the lordship of Jesus Christ, yet still rely on and trust in other things with such a commitment and passion that makes them gods. We may worship (i.e., highly value) them, give them offerings (i.e., spend money on them), and serve them (i.e., devote time and energy). Joshua 24 calls us to renounce all other gods and to serve only Yahweh.

The three burial reports that conclude Joshua demarcate the end of one era and the dawn of another. Similarly, the resurrection of Jesus marks the crucial turning point in human history. Besides defeating death, our bitterest enemy, Jesus injects a new power—resurrection power—into our lives to strengthen us to finish the race.

JUDGES

INTRODUCTION TO JUDGES

The book of Judges is anonymous. It is apparent that the book is a collection of various blocks of material concerning the different judges. Some of the stories may have existed very early in oral or written form, but none of these blocks is attributed to any particular source in the text. Modern scholars have expended great amounts of time and energy in an attempt to identify these sources, but with limited success. Since the book demonstrates very clear and deep interconnections, and hence a compositional unity, whatever the precise sources, this book is the work of a real author, not simply an editor.

The reference in 18:30 to "the time of the captivity of the land" seems to refer to the exile (either 722 or 586 BC) and suggests that the final edition of the book came from the exile or afterwards. Thus, the precise author and date are uncertain, but this should hardly deter the reader from understanding the book's message.

BOOK OUTLINE

I. Double Introduction (1:1–3:6)

II. Judges (3:7–16:31)
- Major judge cycle: Othniel (3:7–11)
- Major judge cycle: Ehud (3:12–30)
  - Minor judge: Shamgar (3:31)
- Major judge cycle: Deborah and Barak (4:1–5:31)
- Major judge cycle: Gideon and Abimelek (6:1–9:57)
  - Minor judge: Tola (10:1–2)
  - Minor judge: Jair (10:3–5)
- Major judge cycle: Jephthah (10:6–12:7)
  - Minor judge: Ibzan (12:8–10)
  - Minor judge: Elon (12:11–12)
  - Minor judge: Abdon (12:13–15)
- Major judge cycle: Samson (13:1–16:31)

III. Specific Conditions During These Times (17:1–21:25)
- Difficulties with domestic religious idols—the origin of the premonarchic sanctuary of Dan (17:1–18:31)
- Domestic wars with the herem being applied —the Benjaminite atrocity and civil war (19:1–21:25)

JUDGES 1:1–2:5

Original Meaning

"Who Will . . . Go Up?" (1:1–2a). Chapter 1 opens with an important phrase, "after the death of Joshua" (1:1a). Judges recapitulates the position of Joshua (how much of the land Israel would occupy) before going on to the central question of Judges: Why could they not completely occupy the land?

The phrase "the Israelites asked the Lord" (1:1b) expresses the idea of obtaining a declaration of the divine will. Thus, at the beginning of the narrative, the Israelites seek guidance in the proper manner as to "Who of us is to go up first to fight against the Canaanites?" (1:1c). The question is who will be the first chronologically? While a series of campaigns by individual tribes is envisioned, the concept of a united Israel remains.

Judah Goes Up (1:2b–21). "I have given the land into their hands" (1:2b). This is the same phrase that Yahweh used when he promised Joshua victory in the land. So far, so good. The Judahites, however, immediately make a deal with the Simeonites (1:3). It was God's intention that each tribe trust him in the process of conquering its allotment. Thus, by making this treaty, the two tribes undercut this process. Even so, the Judahites and Simeonites will see general success in their campaigns since they are willing to go up and fight the Canaanites.

In fulfillment of Yahweh's oracle above, the Canaanites and Perizzites are given into the hands of the Judahites (1:4). The next three verses are devoted to a description of the lord of Bezeq's capture, mutilation, and death. The lord of Bezeq admits that he has suffered only what he deserved. The brutality is justified (from the victim's own mouth!) as divine retribution. Amazingly, this is an enemy king, the embodiment of evil, and a Canaanite who has a limited comprehension of God. Ironically, if the same measure of justice were placed on Israel, Israel would face a similar fate as the lord of Bezeq.

The Judahites have great success in conquering Jerusalem, too. Using the stereotypical statements characteristic of conquest accounts, they capture and destroy it like Jericho, Ai, and Hazor in the book of Joshua.

Othniel, a younger relative of Caleb, is the champion of Judah capturing Debir. He is rewarded with marriage to Aksah. Aksah has already received from her father "land in the Negev" as a dowry (1:15). Now she strengthens its value by obtaining adequate water rights. It is likely that a wife in ancient Israel retained some potential rights over her dowry, even though the dowry became part of the husband's property. Her initiative is still extraordinary.

It is important to remember that the land in the Old Testament carried spiritual overtones. This is true here as well as in the story of the daughters of Zelophehad. The actions of all these women are strongly commended. The story demonstrates that the claim of the descendants of Othniel and Aksah to this land is based on a legal bequest by the original recipient of the territory. Aksah's request is not transitory but generational in its impact.

In the more extended context of the book of Judges, Aksah serves as a contrast in two important ways.

1. As a positive paradigm of a daughter being given to an ideal hero, she is juxtaposed to the notice of Israel's apostasy of intermarriage with the inhabitants of the land.
2. The contrast between Aksah and Delilah could not be more stark! Aksah was the wife of Othniel (who will be described later in the book as the ideal judge). She took the initiative to procure greater blessing for her husband and progeny. In contrast, Delilah was the consort of Samson (the worst of the judges). She used her initiative to bring down her man, all for filthily gained money.

The Simeonites obtain their allotment (1:17). They attack the city of Zephath and "totally destroy" it. The city is renamed Hormah (derived from Heb. *herem*). It is ironic that the Simeonites, a numerically insignificant tribe, are the only tribe in the narration of the occupation of the land who obey Yahweh and implement the *herem* thoroughly. Yet they will not be mentioned in the book of Judges again.

Verse 19 states that "the LORD was with the men of Judah." (a direct reference back to 1:2b). While the victory seems complete with even Gaza, Ashkelon, and Ekron falling to the Judahites, the unit emends this with the last statements "but they were unable to drive people from the plains, because they had chariots fitted with iron" (1:19). In light of this general success of the Judahites, the Benjamite failure in 1:21 contrasts starkly.

The House of Joseph (1:22–36). The process of subjugation is observable in a four-stage decline in Israelite spirituality. The four stages are:

Stage 1 (1:1–20): The general success of Judah is recounted through a number of very short stories. The Judahites, having enlisted the Simeonites as their allies, are able to "drive out" the Canaanites everywhere except in the plain. No Canaanites "live among" the Judahites (1:19).

Stage 2 (1:21–30): Benjamin, Manesseh, Ephraim, and Zebulun do "not drive out" the Canaanites, and the Canaanites "live/lived" among them (1:27, 29, 30), though some Canaanites are forced laborers (cf. Josh 16:10; 18:11–28).

Stage 3 (1:31–33): Asher and Naphtali do "not drive out" the Canaanites, the inhabitants of the land, but instead these tribes "live among" the Canaanites. A few Canaanites become forced laborers.

Stage 4 (1:34): There is no statement about "driving out" or "living among." Instead, the Amorites oppress or confine Dan, not allowing them into the plain. This utter failure of the Danites anticipates their move in chapter 18. The word "driving out," translated "oppressing" in Exodus 3:9, where the Egyptians "oppress" the Israelites, anticipates Judges 2:18; 4:3; 6:9; 10:12.

The account in Judges 1 corresponds in significant ways to the narration in Joshua 13–19, in both perspective (the moral degeneration of Israel) and content (the geographic tribal descriptions).

The Messenger of Yahweh (2:1–5). The indictment brought against the Israelites is that they have broken Yahweh's covenant (Heb. *berit*, "treaty"). Interestingly, the Israelites are not indicted in 2:2 with failing to expel all the Canaanites but with entering into covenant (treaty) with them. In other words, the process of dispossession and occupation would have been completed in due course if the Israelites had fulfilled their obligations to Yahweh, but now their disobedience has put the completion of the conquest in jeopardy (2:3).

Application. Like ancient Israel, Christians also are in covenant relationship to God, albeit through a better covenant. Nevertheless, the stipulations of that covenant—the law "to love one another," as Paul puts it—require obedience (Rom 13:8–10; see also Jas 1:25). While the warfare in which Christians are engaged is not physical but spiritual, the necessity of walking by faith in loyalty to Christ's covenant is the only hope of victory.

JUDGES 2:6–3:6

Original Meaning

Preface: From Joshua to "Another Generation" (2:6–10). In 2:6–10 there is a specific contrast between two different generations: the faithfulness of Joshua's day and the infidelity of the subsequent generation. Joshua sent the people away to their inheritances in order to possess the land (what should have transpired, instead of what is narrated in 1:1–2:5). The people serve Yahweh in the generation of Joshua and the elders (who saw the great deeds that Yahweh had done). When that generation died, another generation arose.

The description of this second generation is stark. In contrast to the previous generation, they "knew neither the LORD nor what he had done for Israel" (2:10). They did not have a relationship with him, nor did they even know about the mighty acts he had done on their behalf. The result is anticipated: They "did evil in the eyes of the LORD and served the Baals" (2:11). This was an active choice on their part, as Joshua 24 reinforces.

Cyclical Pattern of History (2:11–19). *Apostasy in Israel (2:11–13).* The initial statement that "the Israelites did evil in the eyes of the LORD" will be the opening declaration for every major judge story in the book. The following statements elaborate on this initial declaration and further define this apostasy from Yahweh.

The chiastic pattern A-B-C-B′-A′ unifies the paragraph. The idea conveyed in the A, B and B′, A′ elements—that is, "forsaking/abandoning" (*azab*) Yahweh and "serving" (*abad*) Baal—are really two sides of the same coin. They define more precisely "the evil" that the Israelites do in the eyes of Yahweh. These elements encircle C, with its emphasis on false worship, with the resultant anger of the Lord. The idea of "going or walking after (*halak ahare*) other gods" (lit.) clearly contrasts with the biblical idea of "walking with [*halak et*] the LORD." And the idea of "worshiping" (*shahah*) these other gods is a blatant violation of Exod 20:5, "You shall not bow down to [*shahah*] them."

Yahweh's anger—oppression as punishment (2:14–15). In this second part, Yahweh's anger at the Israelites results in the oppressions that he brings on them as punishment. The clauses that Yahweh "gave them" (2:14, i.e., "sold") the Israelites into the hands of oppressors or raiders are framework statements.

In Judges 2:15, the NIV's "to defeat them" misses the mark. The term is *raah* (misfortune, calamity) and is an obvious play on the term *ra* (evil) in 2:11a. Because the Israelites did "evil" (*ra*) Yahweh ensured that when they went out to battle, the outcome was a calamitous disaster. This is declared to be the promised result according to earlier solemn declarations of Yahweh.

Yahweh's compassion—deliverance by judges in spite of Israel's continued apostasies (2:16–19). Yahweh has compassion on his people and raises up judges (i.e., tribal rulers) to deliver them. Although the judges deliver the Israelites, their response is to return quickly to doing evil. The text clearly implies that each successive generation experiences a greater degeneration in sin and corruption than with the previous one (2:19). Thus, the picture is not just cyclical but downward. Israel is spiraling down into a spiritual abyss.

Yahweh's Punishment: The Nations Left as Punishment (2:20–3:4). Yahweh's punishment is a fulfillment and expansion of his promise in 2:3. Both that passage and this one record the people's transgression of the covenant, their disobedience to Yahweh, and his vow to halt the progress of the subjugation of the land.

Summary Conclusion to the Whole Introduction (3:5–6). The last section here, 3:5–6, is the final summary conclusion to the whole introduction. It stresses three things: (1) The Israelites "live among" (*yashab*) the peoples of the land; (2) they intermarry with the peoples there; and (3) they "serve" their gods.

Application. The myth of secularism is that there are no idols because there is no God. But if idolatry is worshiping the creation, or some part of it, instead of the creator (cf. Rom 1:18–23), then the process of sacralization (the process by which created things become central to life, invoking religious-like awe and submission) provides numerous examples of idolatry in modern contexts. One object of sacralization is money and material possessions. This is the idol of Mammon (Matt 6:24), which leads on to sins such as covetousness. Underlying this idol is the fundamental belief that utopia exists and that its essence is material well-being.

JUDGES 3:7–11

Original Meaning. As is the case with all six cyclical judge narratives, the initial framework statement is: "The Israelites did evil in the eyes of the LORD" (3:7). Yahweh subjects those who have served (*abad*) foreign Baals and Asherahs to serve (*abad*) a foreign king for eight years.

On account of this oppression, the Israelites cry out to Yahweh. This is not a penitential plea, as though the Israelites have repented. Rather, it is a simple anguishing cry of pain. Yahweh intervenes on Israel's behalf solely on the basis of his compassion for the Israelites in the midst of their distress, not on the basis of their repentance.

The enemy that Othniel defeats is Cushan-Rishathaim, king of Aram Naharaim. The name means "dark, doubly wicked!" and is clearly a pejorative. The obvious implication is that he is the worst of the oppressors.

But Othniel "overpowered him" (3:10). Only here in this cycle does this phrase describe Yahweh's delivering of the oppressor into the hand of the judge. Othniel appears as the paragon by which the other major judges are assessed.

Application. In an age when many choose a different path, not uncommonly bringing on themselves oppression that is the result of sin (i.e., like a Cushan-Rishathaim), it is wonderful to see a model like Othniel who simply walks in tandem with God and overcomes evil. The simplicity and faithfulness of Othniel is in radical contrast to the complexity and self-gratification of the final judge of the book of Judges, Samson.

JUDGES 3:12–30

Original Meaning

Introduction (3:12–15a). Only here does the writer say that Yahweh actively "gave . . . power" (3:12) to or strengthened/empowered the oppressor against Israel. The cyclic description continues with Israel's crying out to Yahweh in stress and pain (not repentance). Yahweh raises up a savior/deliverer: Ehud. This savior is "left-handed" (3:15). But this left-handed savior is ironically a Benjamite (meaning "son of the right hand"). From a literary standpoint, Ehud's left-handedness is explicitly noted because it explains how he smuggles his dagger in. The palace guards, assuming he is right-handed, would not have checked for a left-handed weapon-carrier.

Presentation of Tribute (3:15b–18). The Israelites send their savior/deliverer Ehud with tribute to Eglon. This provides the opportunity for Ehud to take a daring personal initiative. Ehud crafts a double-edged dagger, likely about a foot or less in length. His improvisation is undoubtedly a prefiguring of the improvising of other weapons: Shamgar's oxgoad (3:31), Jael's tent peg (4:21–22), Gideon's jars and torches (7:20), the certain woman's millstone (9:53), and Samson's donkey jawbone (15:15). But here, as opposed to the other instances, Ehud's action is deliberate and calculated.

The Assassination of Eglon (3:19–26a). The focus on the execution of the plot (3:19b–26a) is heightened by satire and irony, the principal target of which is Eglon. The satire centers mainly on Eglon's famed fatness. Eglon has fattened himself on the tribute he has extorted from Israel. While his fatness symbolizes his greed, it also hints at his vulnerability to Ehud's swift left-handed thrust of the blade. Eglon has become plump, defenseless, stupid game. Like a dumb animal, he is completely unaware of the danger.

He dismisses his bodyguard (3:19) then rises from his throne to receive this secret "message from God" (*debar elohim*, 3:20). The Hebrew word *dabar* is ambiguous and can mean "word, message, thing, or matter." Ehud's words, like his double-edged dagger, have a double meaning: the one that Eglon naively accepts ("the word/message of God") and the one that the reader already knows, namely, that "the secret [thing] from God" is the dagger!

The actual description of the killing (i.e., sacrifice) is given in grotesque detail. The term translated "fat" (*heleb*) is the sacrificial term used for the choicest parts of the sacrifice, the entrails (see Lev 3–6). At this climatic moment without the dagger being removed, Eglon's anal sphincter explodes. Eglon got the point of the message! The scatological satire continues with the comic scene of 3:24–25, in which Eglon's servants belatedly discover their master's corpse.

Liberation from Moabite Oppression (3:26b–29). Ehud's rallying words, "Follow me . . . for the LORD has given Moab, your enemy, into your hands" (3:28) is not just battlefield rhetoric. Based on the narrative, it is a reference to the tangible grounds for such assurance: The Moabite despot has already been given into the hand of Ehud and is dead. Thus, Ehud now stands revealed as Yahweh's chosen savior/deliverer. Moreover, the words demonstrate that for Ehud the entire process has been a matter of trust in Yahweh and assurance of Yahweh's deliverance.

Application. How are we to wage spiritual warfare against those who abuse, exploit, and persecute the church? While the warfare in which Christians are engaged is spiritual, not physical, the necessity of walking by faith in loyalty to Christ's covenant is the only hope of victory. We are certainly not to fashion our own daggers as Ehud did, but rather to engage the world with a better weapon already supplied—the sword of the Spirit, the word of God.

JUDGES 3:31

Original Meaning. This brief account (made up of one verse consisting of three Hebrew sentences) follows the story of Ehud and continues that story's satirical tone. Shamgar, the next judge, delivers Israel through a single-handed act with an agricultural implement. Again, the enemy is not only defeated but made to look utterly ridiculous, as the reader's attention is drawn to the improvised weapon.

Application. See the comments at the end of the last three minor judges (12:8–15) (pp. 211–12).

JUDGES 4:1–5:31

Original Meaning

The Narrative of Deborah and Barak (4:1–24). The Israelites return to their apostasy. As expected, Yahweh sells them into the hand of an oppressor, "Jabin king of Canaan" (4:2). He only plays a role in the story's prologue and epilogue, but immediately the prologue introduces Jabin's commander, Sisera, who will be the up-front antagonist in the story.

Deborah (meaning "honeybee") is a prophetess; she is leading/judging Israel at that time (4:4b). It is her role as prophetess that is catalytic in this narrative. As a prophetess, Deborah stands in a long tradition, starting with Miriam (Exod 15:20) and continuing throughout the Old Testament.

In 4:6 Barak (meaning "lightning") is introduced (note that Deborah "sends" for him and then "commands" him). Clearly Deborah is the one who is taking the initiative, not Barak. She stands as God's envoy, the means by which God issues his call to Barak.

Since Barak is at first reluctant to respond positively to the prophetic word, Deborah is used as a foil to promote Barak's negative characterization. The first rhetorical question (4:6) literally reads: "Has not Yahweh, the God of Israel, commanded, go?" Thus, this is not her opinion about his calling and how things ought to work out but the sure word of Yahweh. Deborah's commissioning of Barak (4:6–7) suggests that he ought to fulfill a role comparable to Othniel. His response, however, is hardly the stuff of an Othniel or even an Ehud.

Deborah's response that she will go seems to allay the problem of Barak's hesitation. But then she issues another prophecy (4:9). The reader has only one woman to suspect as the possible fulfillment—Deborah. But the ironic twist is just over the horizon.

For the second time, Deborah anticipates Barak's reluctance to follow her instructions from Yahweh by using the rhetorical construction: "Has not the LORD gone ahead of you?" (4:14). This underscores the certainty of the victory but serves to heighten Barak's reluctance without great assurance.

Perhaps stimulated by the assurance, this time Barak's response is appropriate. Barak goes down to fight with the ten thousand men following and wins the battle, but he loses Sisera (in accordance with Deborah's prophecy). Yahweh routs Sisera and his army with its iron chariots. The Hebrew of 4:15 literally states: "Yahweh threw Sisera . . . into a panic [*wayyaham yhwh*]. . . ."

Like Shamgar, Jael is a non-Israelite, specifically a Kenite. Jael intentionally goes out to meet Sisera and entreats him to come into her tent as a place of safety. Her words (4:18) and her hospitality disarm the Canaanite warlord. Having entered her tent, he makes his own entreaty: "I'm thirsty. . . . Please give me some water" (4:19). Jael demonstrates ancient Near Eastern hospitality in giving him milk and covering him up.

Sisera falls asleep as a result of the exhaustion of the battle and escape. Then Jael, having set her victim at ease, picks up a tent peg and hammer and drives the peg through Sisera's temple into the ground. The narration of the killing of Sisera by Jael is in the same vivid style as Eglon's killing by Ehud (3:21–22).

To the attentive reader, the similarities between Jael's murder of Sisera and Ehud's assassination of Eglon are transparent. As Ehud's manipulation of Eglon and his courtiers serves to satirize Eglon and his men for their gullibility, so Jael's manipulation of Sisera by means of verbal ambiguity satirizes him for his gullibility. Eglon's courtiers discover their lord fallen (*nopel*) on the ground dead (*met*); Barak discovers Sisera fallen (*nopel*) dead (*met*). The result of all this is to ironically picture Barak playing a role analogous to that of Eglon's courtiers. Without his general Sisera, Jabin was no threat and was quickly subdued.

The Song of Deborah (5:1–31). After the prose setting of the song (5:1), an initial call to praise contains a report of Israel's need (5:2–8). It opens with an invocation to praise (*barak*, not to be confused with the name Barak [*baraq*]) Yahweh (5:2). The first line of 5:2 that the NIV translates "When the princes in Israel take the lead" is perhaps better translated "because hair was unbound in Israel." It suggests dedication to the purposes of Yahweh, either a vow similar to that of a Nazarite or to intense military dedication that results in unkept, shaggy hair.

The act continues with an exhortation especially addressed to royalty, that is, to kings and rulers (5:3), to pay attention. The singers draw attention to Yahweh's epiphany, which is described in terms of storm and quake upon the earth. Yahweh comes forth from the barren regions of the southeast with an awesome, overwhelming storm with the earth and mountains shaking from the lightning and thunder.

The picture is clearly one of oppression. People abandoned the use of the normal roads and resorted to windy back pathways (likely due to safety and security issues on the main roads). This was the situation "until I, Deborah, arose . . . a mother in Israel" (5:7). The phrase, "mother in Israel" is a significant metaphor. In the context of the song, there is obviously the later contrast with the mother of Sisera (5:28).

Israel's choices concerning new gods was the thing that brought military humiliation and servitude, including the very weapons of war (shield and spear) necessary to overcome the oppression. When God's people chose to worship other gods (new gods), the Lord brought severe oppression on them; but it also stresses Yahweh's victorious intervention all the more.

There are two causes for praise and response of the people (5:11 and 5:12–13).

1. The voice of the singers at the watering places concerning Yahweh's victories and those of his warriors stimulates a response.
2. The leadership of Deborah and then Barak.

In the ancient Near East, victory songs usually extol the might and power of the king in his victory over his enemies. Only a victory song for "the people of the LORD" would choose to extol the inferiority of its own army in the face of oppression in order to praise the people's king, Yahweh (5:11b–c).

The third and central act of the song gives a full picture of the tribal mobilization. It is a recognition and assessment of the tribes who participated and who did not (5:14–18). Although they are theoretically united by their worship of Yahweh and the covenant with him, the Israelites manifest a serious deficiency of political and military solidarity.

The fourth act expounds the battle and presents a transition: the curse of Meroz. As with so many battles in the ancient Near East, an army was often composed of troops from numerous small vassal states with their kinglets or chiefs leading them. While the Canaanite kings joined to Sisera fought, they had no success, no plunder.

At this point, the poetry paints a magnificent portrait of divine intervention. The Kishon River "swept them away" (5:21). The previous verse states: "From the heavens the stars fought, from their courses they fought against Sisera" (5:20). This may seem to moderns a strange confusion of meteorological and astronomical phenomena, but it was perfectly understandable in ancient Near Eastern thought, where weather phenomena were part of the same celestial phenomena as lunar, solar, stellar, and planetary phenomena.

It is interesting that not one single line of the poem shows the Israelites directly involved in the hard and dangerous work of warfare. The poet seems to purposely choose not to give such a depiction in order to allow all the honor to go to Yahweh.

The transition of the curse of Meroz is pronounced by the angel (or messenger, *malak*) of Yahweh (5:23). From the placement of the curse it is plausible to interpret the failure of Meroz as one of denying immediate aid to the pursuing Israelite warriors rather than as a failure for mustering troops at the beginning of the campaign.

The fifth and final act is a double portrait of Jael's deed and Sisera's mother, which lead to the climactic conclusion of this song. Jael would not typically be expected to get involved. But she has risked everything to execute the enemy of God and to aid God's people. By contrast, the Israelite tribes and city of Meroz, who could be expected to participate and render aid, did not.

The second portrait is a taunt of Sisera's mother (5:28–30). The picture shifts to Sisera's mother looking out of the window, anxiously awaiting the return of her son. The lady and her attendants fantasize about a huge amount of booty (ironically including women) as the cause for his delay; they never (openly) suspect the possibility of his demise.

The climactic conclusion is a double invocation for God to bring such a judgment to pass on all who defy him and for God to bring blessing on those who love him. This double invocation, therefore, is a fitting conclusion to the extraordinary poem known as the song of Deborah.

Application. Both the narrative and the song celebrate the saving work of Yahweh. The double accounting in prose and poetry stresses God's sovereignty over human events. This passage thus encourages us to perceive God's sovereignty over history and our own lives. Whether it is in his chastening, in his compassionate deliverance, in his financial provision, or in his leading and guiding decisions, God is sovereign over life, and he is at work bringing his plan to fruition.

JUDGES 6:1–10

Original Meaning. The familiar cycle opening component, "the Israelites did evil in the eyes of the Lord" (6:1), stands in abrupt contrast to the praise of Yahweh that has just been sung in the previous chapter. This component stresses the fickleness of the Israelites, who lack resistance to the lures of the other gods.

The description of the oppression pictures a reversal of lifestyles. The settled Israelites revert to living in caves, as nomadic groups often do in the southern Levant. By contrast, the nomadic Midianites come and plop all over the land.

Accordingly, the Israelites cry to Yahweh (with, of course, no hint at true repentance). This is as they have done in the past, but things are different this time; Yahweh sends a prophet (6:8a). The prophet is formally indicting the Israelites for a breach of the covenant.

Application. In a practical sense, this passage addresses a common problem in the area of prayer. We turn to God in a moment of need, even when we have not been walking in his ways. Yet we expect God to answer our prayers because (and often for no other reason than) we are in need! Over and over the Bible (including the book of Judges) addresses this issue of manipulation in prayer (e.g., Jas 4:1–6). Relationship with God is never a mechanical process.

JUDGES 6:11–32

Original Meaning. In order to explain his plan for the deliverance of Israel, Yahweh resorts to a theophany (a manifestation or appearance of God) to communicate his choice to Gideon. Gideon is the only judge in the book of Judges who is called by God personally through a theophany.

There is great irony in this statement by the angel of Yahweh. Gideon is hiding from the Midianites, threshing wheat in a winepress. Gideon's name (*gidon*) means "hacker" ("to hack, break to pieces"). Not only is this an indication of his warring ability, but it also has a connection to the covenant stipulations (Deut 7:5; 12:3; cf. Judg 6:25–32). This man is the Lord's choice to save Israel. But Gideon is characterized by fearfulness and reluctance, although Yahweh's words are correct (i.e., he will be a great warrior at the end; see Judg 8:4–21).

In the dialogue with the angel of the Lord, Gideon will mount a three-point opposition, which, in each case, anticipates later plot complications.

1. His response to the angel of the Lord's initial call is a dull, cynical question and diatribe about God's treatment of the nation (6:13). He manifests a dispassionate disregard for Yahweh's primary concern about Israel's covenantal disloyalty (anticipating 6:25–32; 8:24–27).
2. Although Yahweh encourages Gideon, Gideon's objection in 6:15 is an attempt to evade personal responsibility for the conquest because of his clan's smallness (anticipating 7:2–8).
3. After Yahweh's assurance (6:16), Gideon's request for a sign in 6:17 discloses his preoccupation with tangible manifestations of the divine (anticipating 6:36–37, 39; 7:10–15; and especially 8:24–27).

While the theophany is especially reminiscent of the call of Moses (Exod 3:7–10), Gideon is no Moses. Like Moses, there is a problem with the will. But in the case of Gideon, there are additional problems of perception (of the presence of the Lord and the reason for Israel's distress) and faith (Gideon will have a much harder time with trust in Yahweh than Moses, as the narrative will show).

In 6:17 Gideon begins his requests for signs. The NIV's "give me a sign" is more accurately translated "perform a sign for me." Gideon's offering is not in accordance with any Levitical sacrifice. Nevertheless, in spite of Gideon's motives, the Lord accepts the sacrifices with miraculous fire coming from the rock to consume the meat and bread—an outcome totally unexpected by Gideon. God's actions are not just concerned with Gideon but are centered on delivering Israel. Hence, Gideon builds an altar (the first in the narration) and names it: "Yahweh-Shalom" (NIV "The Lord is Peace," 6:24).

God's command to Gideon (6:25) contains two demands —a negative one followed by a positive one.

1. He must tear down his father's altar to Baal and cut down the Asherah pole that is beside it (note the pair of idolatrous items).
2. Gideon must build an altar to Yahweh and sacrifice a burnt offering. By his command to Gideon to destroy the pagan altar and rebuild a proper altar to Yahweh on this pagan site, Yahweh seems to be ordering him to reclaim this apostate shrine locale.

Fearing the repercussions of the destruction of the Baal altar and Asherah pole, Gideon takes ten of his servants and carries out Yahweh's orders under cover of night. He demolishes the Baal altar, cuts down the Asherah pole, builds a proper altar to Yahweh, and sacrifices the second bull on the new altar.

The utter outrage and hostility of the town reflects the true spiritual condition of the nation. Gideon recognizes that his own family and the people of his village will choose to defend the Baal altar and Asherah pole before choosing to defend him. The Israelites were so disloyal to God's covenant that they are willing to kill a fellow Israelite for the cause of Baal, which is directly counter to what they should be doing according to Deuteronomy 13:6–10, where Israelites unfaithful to Yahweh were to be put to death.

Joash's decision is a ploy to save face, and to save Gideon at the same time, by referring the case to higher authority (6:31). The townspeople back down, and Gideon receives a new name: Jerub-Baal (6:32, meaning "Let/May Baal contend/indict"). In one sense, it designates him as living proof of Baal's impotence. Thus, Gideon begins his career by driving the deity Baal from the field of battle (Baal cannot contend with him). But he now must face the challenge of driving the human foe, the Midianites, from the field of battle.

Application. *Divine level.* On the divine level, this section of the Gideon/Abimelek cycle emphasizes the grace of Yahweh. God's compassion for his people, with all of their grave transgressions and weaknesses, provides once again the impetus to deliver Israel. Moreover, God surprises us by remaining faithful in the midst of persistent cynicism and doubt.

Human level. The story of Gideon's call serves as a notable illustration of the dangers of not remembering God's mighty acts. The product can be cynicism and an inability to perceive God. It can lead to an ignorance and misunderstanding of God's Word and why things happen in the world.

JUDGES 6:33–7:18

Original Meaning. With the narration of Gideon's call and name change complete, 6:33–35 resumes the description of the oppression of the Midianites and their alliances. Like the Moabites (and their allies) in 3:13 and the massively armed Canaanites in 4:13, this horde presents an almost insurmountable challenge to the undermanned Israelites.

The reader's expectations for the same type of deliverance as in the earlier cycles are quickly dashed in 6:36–40. Gideon suddenly confronts God with the need for a sign, proof that God will really save Israel through him. Note that God has already said that he would, and Gideon knows it (6:36). Thus, while the phrase "the spirit of the LORD came on [lit. "clothed," (Heb. *labash*) Gideon" (6:34) sounds spiritually positive, it is important to recognize the irony built into the context. The spirit of Yahweh "comes/clothes/is strong" upon the out-group judges more frequently than upon the in-group judges (five times vs. one time). It is especially clear from the usages in the Jephthah narrative and the Samson episodes that the phrase does not necessarily carry a positive comment on the individual's spirituality.

In the case of Gideon, the Spirit's work reflects God's sovereign will to set things in motion for the deliverance he has planned, not Gideon's condition of faith or spirituality. Although Gideon has much popular support and has a considerable fighting force at his disposal, he hesitates. His almost immediate "fleecing" of God speaks to his unbelief, his lack of spirituality. In fact, the fleece incidents are Gideon's second request for a "sign" from God (cf. the earlier request in 6:17), and this second sign request needs to be doubly confirmed! Sadly, unlike Yahweh, Gideon will not be true to his word after the first fleece incident. Therefore, in spite of the polite entreaty, we should not be blind to the manner in which Gideon is trying to manipulate God.

Contrary to popular interpretation, these fleecings have nothing to do with discovering or determining God's will. The divine will is perfectly and absolutely clear in Gideon's own mind (note the wording in 6:36). These "signs" reveal his lack of faith.

It is not insignificant that throughout the pericope concerning the fleecings the divine personal, covenantal name of Yahweh is missing. Instead, the rather generic designation Elohim ("God") is used. This fleecing process is nothing short of a pagan divinatory test of the deity. Apparently, being clothed with the Spirit is not sufficient. Gideon needs tangible signs obtained through divinatory processes in order to believe God.

Perhaps one may inquire of Baal this way, but this is not the way to treat the God of Israel. Remarkably, Yahweh responds to Gideon's tests. One may argue that the narrator includes this pericope to construct a sharper picture of Gideon's unbelief and questionable religious practices. Finally, on the basis of the structure of this section, it should be observed that just as Yahweh uses the pair of fleecings with their pagan divinatory overtones to encourage Gideon to deliver Israel, he will also use two Midianites—one relating his dream, the other interpreting it (also with pagan divinatory overtones)—to encourage and motivate Gideon to action. What great lengths God is going to in order to save Israel from the hand of Midian! In short, God performed the signs with the fleece because he intended to save Israel; he will not let Gideon's unbelief derail his plan.

The two central episodes deal with the issue of fear. The double reduction (7:1–8) of Gideon's fighting force begins with the removal of all the fearful Israelites (7:1–3). The result is a twenty-two-thousand-man reduction.

Then God directs Gideon to go down to the water for the further reduction of his remaining ten-thousand-man force (7:4–8). Commentators are divided in their understanding of the process of reduction. It seems best to understand the process as based on purely arbitrary criteria. Whether the process of selection is based on positive or negative evaluative criteria is not as important as the reduction in number to an extremely small force—three hundred men. Along with this drastic reduction in his forces comes a further word of reassurance (7:7). The reason for the reductions is stated explicitly in 7:2. This motive will, unfortunately, be undercut, as we will see.

In the second central episode (7:9–11), Yahweh, knowing that Gideon himself is still fearful, directs him to go down to the enemy camp to overhear the enemy. Gideon and his servant arrive at the Midianite camp at the precise moment that a Midianite is relating his dream to his comrade. God has clearly devised his own sign for Gideon. Gideon hears the exact same words that Yahweh had already spoken to him (7:14; cf. 6:16, 36). The irony is rich. Hearing the promise directly from Yahweh did not convince Gideon but hearing it from the lips of a Midianite soldier does convince him.

In 7:15–18 it is evident that this reported dream has its intended effect on Gideon: He worships God (7:15). Gideon now musters his small band of men with the confidence that Yahweh will truly give them the victory. At this moment, he believes God. After worshiping God as the result of this final sign, Gideon will not worship God again. Rather than having a wonderful song of Yahweh's glorification after the battle (cf. ch. 5), there will only be Gideon's increasing usurpation of God's glory for the victory in the battle and its outcomes.

Application. It is impossible to engender faith without the word of God. General revelation demonstrates that there is a God (Rom 1:18–23), but only the word of God reveals his attributes, his character, and his person. It is difficult, if not impossible, to have faith in someone that you don't know or barely know. It is extremely hard to trust someone that you misunderstand or are misinformed about. Gideon's ignorance about the word of God was a strong factor in his inability to trust Yahweh, for he had misconceptions about Yahweh and misunderstood the very nature and character of God. If we do not inculcate the word of God in our lives (Rom 10:17), we will manifest the same unbelief—even stubbornness to believe—that Gideon did.

JUDGES 7:19–8:21

Original Meaning

The First Battle: Cisjordan (7:19–8:3). Gideon and his men reach the Midianite camp at just the right time: the changing of the guard. Once again, the narrator shows that Yahweh's sovereign hand is at work in the victory. The blowing of the trumpets, the breaking of the jars, the flashing of the torches, and the shouting of the men (7:20) all proliferate utter chaos and horror in the Midianite camp.

The pursuit of the defeated Midianites is narrated in two

stages. In the initial stage (7:22b–23), the troops from Naphtali, Asher, and all Manasseh are called out to pursue the Midianites along a route described in 7:22b. In the second stage (7:24–25), Gideon calls out the troops of Ephraim.

The brief epilogue that follows this battle (8:1–3) demonstrates Gideon's diplomatic skills. Gideon's reply to the Ephraimites implies that they have accomplished much more than he and the other Israelites in the initial attack (8:2). Accordingly, now with the external threat removed and internal peace restored, the reader naturally anticipates the narrative frame component: "and the land had peace for X years."

The Second Battle: Transjordan (8:4–21). However, quite unexpectedly, the story is resumed in 8:4. If the narrative ended roughly with 8:3, Gideon would be considered one of the heroic judges of ancient Israel, notwithstanding his problem with fear and lack of faith. However, the narration continues, and the portrayal of Gideon becomes bleaker and bleaker. The moment that he and his men cross the Jordan, a whole new Gideon emerges.

In contrast to the first Gideon, who was a timid "hacker" and who succeeded by the grace of God, this second Gideon is a forceful, resourceful, avenging "hacker," whose very success breeds even worse failure. Like an animal on the prowl, his pronounced purpose is to capture "Zebah and Zalmunna, the kings of Midian" (8:5). Gideon's threats of revenge are totally uncalled for. There are no indications of Yahweh's involvement in this second battle. In fact, the statements of God's involvement, so prominent in the buildup to and description of the first battle, are entirely lacking here.

Using a route that the Midianite remnant does not anticipate, Gideon brings down on them a furious attack at Karkor. This oasis is located about 170 miles (273.6 km) southeast of Mount Moreh in the Wadi Sirhân. To pursue these Midianite leaders this distance is an indication of Gideon's determination. Yahweh's silence and noninvolvement in this second battle and subsequent events is a foreshadowing of the Jephthah narrative, in which Yahweh's silence and noninvolvement is paramount.

Gideon's motive in pursuing the two Midianite kings is revealed in 8:18–19: revenge. Zebah and Zalmunna had killed his brothers. Zebah and Zalmunna are executed, not because they are the enemies of Yahweh but because of Gideon's personal vengeance.

Application. We can be thankful that we have the example of Gideon's obedience and victory over the Midianites. The story of God's working through his call of Gideon to accomplish the victory in the Cisjordanian battle is an encouragement to Christians that God can use us to accomplish beneficial results for the kingdom of Christ. Positive examples of faith can enhance the application of faith in our lives. Marvelous is the victory when it is solely of God. Gideon and his puny three hundred were not the reason for the victory in this battle; rather, they were simply used by God to achieve his victory. When we trust God and see his great victory, so often in spite of us, we need to give him the glory.

JUDGES 8:22–32

Original Meaning. Immediately after the slaughter of the last pair of kings, Gideon's countrymen offer him dynastic rule. But 8:22 is more than just a dynastic offer to Gideon; it also states the reason (in the Israelites' thinking): "because you have saved [*yasha*] us out of the hand of Midian."

The Israelites make three errors in their proposition.

1. As Gideon correctly notes, he cannot be king over them since Yahweh is already supposed to be king over them.
2. Though Gideon does not mention this, Yahweh is the one who has saved Israel, not him. Yet Gideon does not correct their mistake regarding who has saved them. By allowing that statement to stand, he endorses it de facto.
3. According to the Israelites' logic, the one who has saved them should be their king. The text shows that the Israelites do exactly the opposite of what their own thesis requires, for their deliverer has been Yahweh. This is summed up in the next section, in 8:34: The Israelites "did not remember the LORD their God, who had rescued them."

Gideon's concocting of an ephod from the Midianite (Ishmaelite) golden earrings is analogous to Aaron's casting the golden calf from the Egyptians' golden earrings (Exod 32:1–8). Both Gideon's and Aaron's idols served as illegitimate cult objects for Israel to worship after a miraculous deliverance that Yahweh worked on Israel's behalf. If Gideon is somewhat like Moses in his calling, he is definitely like Aaron in this act.

Since in biblical texts there is a connection between the ephod and the Urim and Thummim used by the high priest for obtaining divine guidance, it is possible that Gideon's ephod had divinatory intentions. Although the narrator does not reveal the nature of the image, some interpreters argue that it seems most likely that Gideon reconstructed the shrine to Baal that he had torn down earlier at Yahweh's command (6:25–32).

Instead of glorifying Yahweh, who has clothed him with his Spirit, and properly worshiping him in a victory song, Gideon creates his own idol and clothes it with pagan materials. If Yahweh's altar effectively replaced Baal's altar at Ophrah, then Gideon's cult image, the ephod, effectively replaces the Asherah cult image.

At the beginning of the Gideon story, Ophrah is the hub of a clan cult, a family affair. At the end, it is a center for national religious prostitution (under Gideon's oversight). Thus, things have come full circle.

Hard on the heels of the description of Gideon's idol comes, ironically, the stereotyped frame components (8:28). While the cycle seems to be ending, in reality the seeds for its continuation are sown on either side of these statements. The introduction of the ephod worship above and now the narration in an epilogue (8:29–32), which relate the birth and naming of Abimelek, set the stage for the complementary sequel that follows.

Application. When God works through us, whether in a formal or informal ministry situation, we must give him the honor and glory. The deep-rooted pride of achievement can blur our vision as to how we got to where we are. God has gifted men and women, and therefore whatever they accomplish ultimately redounds to his credit. The athlete, the intellectual, the businessman, the preacher—all owe their achievements and accomplishments to God's endowment.

JUDGES 8:33–9:57

Original Meaning

The Prologue (8:33–35). The Israelites set Baal-Berith (literally, "lord or master of the covenant," 8:33) as their god and do not remember Yahweh (even though Yahweh is the actual Lord of the actual covenant, not Baal). There can be no doubt that Gideon's ephod has contributed greatly to this rapid return to Baalism and the resultant unfaithfulness to his family.

The Rise of Abimelek (9:1–24). Abimelek addresses two groups in order to enlist them in his plot: his mother's brothers in Shechem and all his mother's clan. Thus, he appeals to the immediate family as well as the complete extended family or clan. Abimelek is not happy with his position as an outsider, and he is dominated by a ruthless craving to change his marginal existence.

The citizens/lords of Shechem trust the conspirator and give him seventy shekels of silver to hire reckless scoundrels. With their aid, Abimelek murders his (paternal) brothers, the seventy sons of Jerub-Baal, on a single stone (ironically a single stone will kill Abimelek, 9:53). But one of these sons, Jotham (the youngest son), escapes by hiding. With seemingly all opposition removed, Abimelek is made king (*melek*) in Shechem (9:6).

Jotham, the lone survivor of the Ophrah massacre, appears on the scene in 9:7 to confront the men of Shechem with the evil they have done. Invoking the men of Shechem to listen, he appeals to a higher moral plane—the issues of honor, integrity, honesty, and a divine standard of justice—and calls on God to witness their response. He adapts a four-part plant fable to his purpose (9:7–15), but the main point of the speech is not in the fable itself but in its application to the present situation in the form of a curse (9:16–20).

In the context of the passage, not only is Jotham's speech crucial, so is his very name. Jotham is a combination of the short form of the divine name Yahweh and the short form of the term *tamim*, with the resultant meaning of "Yahweh is perfect, blameless, honest, has integrity." One of the key words in Jotham's speech is also this *tamim*.

The fable itself (9:7–15) is relatively straightforward. In the fable, the trees go out to anoint a king over them. They approach four different plants (the first three of which have significant value in the Israelite agricultural context, producing valuable products for human beings). Each is offered the kingship, but the first three have a declining response. Finally, the trees make an offer to the thornbush (9:14), whose response is parabolic (9:15). Only the thornbush, a useless plant (Abimelek), accepts the trees' (Shechemites') offer with an absurd condition.

Jotham's implied thrust is this: Since the trees (i.e., the citizens/lords of Shechem) have done the absurdity of trying to make the thornbush (i.e., Abimelek) their king, then perhaps fire will come out of the thornbush and consume the trees and forest!

Jotham's application of the fable is contained in a curse (9:16–20). The curse is conditional (though rhetorical). The conditional clause is stated twice in 9:16. The clause contains two possible situations that the NIV translates as three questions: (1) "Have you acted honorably and in good faith by making Abimelek king?" and (2) "Have you been fair to Jerub-Baal and his family? Have you treated him as he deserves?" The parenthetical aside demonstrates that the implied answer to the conditional clause is that the Shechemites have not acted with integrity in a blameless and honest manner.

Jotham reminds them that Gideon took great personal risk—indeed, needing the prompting of God at every moment—yet the citizens/lords of Shechem "have revolted" (9:18) against Gideon's family, murdering his sons and installing Abimelek, an illegitimate son (hence a "thorn"), to the throne. Verse 19 resumes the question or condition and concludes with a sarcastic statement. Verse 20, however, gives the second situation and the real, intended curse. Because the crime has already been committed and the outcomes are irrevocable, the curse is really a pronouncement of sure judgment.

The laconic statement that "Abimelek . . . governed Israel three years" (9:22) is especially significant in that the time period is by far the shortest of any oppression or judgeship in the book. God does not put up with Abimelek and the Shechemites very long; his retribution is the swiftest in the book. He intervenes by stirring up "animosity between

Abimelek and the citizens of Shechem" (9:23). Yahweh is the architect of the estrangement between Abimelek and Shechem's folk. Former allies become mortal enemies. It is important to recognize that it is God who begins the process of avenging the wrongs done by both Abimelek and the Shechemites. In this instance, he will use each to judge the other.

The Fall of Abimelek (9:25–57). The Shechemites initiate hostilities against Abimelek—and this happens immediately after God sends the evil spirit (i.e., creating the animosity/bad attitude) between Abimelek and the citizens/lords of Shechem. Shechem's second act of treachery, given in full, is narrated in 9:26–41. The entrance of the character Gaal is deliberately patterned after that of Abimelek. This is a comment not only on the character traits of Abimelek (i.e., both Abimelek and Gaal are raw opportunists who resort to dirty politics in their quest for power) but also on the character qualities of the citizens/lords of Shechem (disgruntled and fickle). In the midst of a reveling festival in the temple of El-Berith, they curse Abimelek. Seizing the moment, Gaal (like Abimelek earlier) uses rhetorical questions to heighten his popularity and undermine that of the current government.

Abimelek's response is quick. He deploys his troops to ambush the city (9:34). Gaal leads the citizens/lords of Shechem out to fight Abimelek, but Abimelek's ambush succeeds, and Abimelek slays many while chasing Gaal to the entrance of Shechem (9:39–40). Abimelek stays in Arumah while Zebul expels Gaal and his brothers from Shechem (9:41). At this, one might expect the conflict between Abimelek and Shechem to be resolved, since the antagonist Gaal is out of the picture. But Abimelek is the son of Jerub-Baal—as much as he despised his father—and his personal revenge is only now beginning.

The next day the common people of Shechem resume their daily routine and go out into the fields. Abimelek divides his troops into three companies and sets another ambush in the fields. The use of the term "people" (Heb. *am*, 9:42) indicates that this group includes women. Moreover, it is a group hardly expecting battle; hence they are no doubt unarmed. Abimelek's company seizes the city gate, and the other two companies press the attack. The helpless victims are slaughtered in the fields, putting up whatever feeble resistance that they can.

The massacre is great, and the city is captured and destroyed. The scattering of salt over the ground of the city is an attempt to condemn it to perpetual barrenness and desolation. Hence, just as Abimelek has made Jerub-Baal's family barren, so now he makes Shechem barren. Again, one might expect the conflict between Abimelek and Shechem to be resolved since the city is out of the picture, but his personal revenge is still far from over.

On hearing of the demise of the people, the citizens/lords in the tower of Shechem (Beth Millo) enter the stronghold of the temple of El-Berith (9:46). Abimelek perceives their vulnerability (9:47). He and his people ascend Mount Zalmon. He cuts off branches and sets them on his shoulders (9:48a). Now, for the first time since 9:2, Abimelek speaks (cf. Gideon's instructions in 7:17). His troops imitate him as though in a trance (9:48b–49a). They pile these branches up against the stronghold and set them on fire (9:49a). All of the people, men and women—one thousand in number—die in the conflagration (9:49b). Once again, one might expect the conflict between Abimelek and Shechem to be resolved since the stronghold of Beth Millo has been removed from the picture, but Abimelek is the son of Jerub-Baal—as much as he despised his father—and his personal revenge is still far from over. In fact, one is beginning to wonder if anything can stop it!

In blitzkrieg fashion, the narrative states that Abimelek goes, besieges, and captures Thebez (9:50). All the people (men and women) flee to the tower and ascend to the roof. Abimelek attacks the tower and approaches the entrance to the tower in order to burn it (9:52). Based on the repetition of the previous reprisals, the reader's expectations are set for another of Abimelek's massacres. However, unexpectedly the narrative introduces "a woman" who drops an upper millstone on Abimelek's head and cracks his skull (9:53). Stunned, Abimelek orders his servant to kill him lest a woman be credited with his death. He is stabbed and dies (9:54). Then, when the troops see that Abimelek is dead, they return home without completing the attack on Thebez (9:55).

The upper millstone, usually made of basalt, though sometimes sandstone, was the smaller upper stone of a hand mill or saddle-quern. For most women, grinding was a daily domestic task. It was humiliating for a man to do such work. Therefore, it was also humiliating to be struck by such a stone hurled by a woman. As in the case of Jael in 4:21, this woman uses what is normally a domestic, everyday object and turns it into weapon.

The fire with which Abimelek destroys the tower of Shechem in 9:47–49 is obviously the fulfillment of Jotham's curse about fire consuming the citizens/lords in 9:20. But what about the fulfillment of Jotham's curse about Abimelek being consumed by fire? The answer appears to be in a pun on the word "woman" (*ishshah*). The word for fire is *esh*. Thus, the words for woman (*ishshah*) and fire (*esh*) form a wordplay. Abimelek's attempt to burn the tower of Thebez with fire (*esh*) "backfires" when a woman (*ishshah*) drops a stone on his head.

God has repaid the evil committed by Abimelek and the evil committed by the men of Shechem. The curse of Jotham, son of Jerub-Baal, comes on them. Thus, Yahweh works vindication and justice.

The primary theme of the Abimelek account is the notion of revenge: getting even (when in the human context) or retribution (when in the divine context). The pattern of divine retribution in the cycles section so far has been one of sin → punishment → compassion → deliverance. In the Abimelek narrative, however, the pattern appears to be sin → exact retribution.

Yahweh himself has had to resolve two complications that result from Gideon's covenantal failings—his ephod production with its consequent return to Baalism and his conjugal relations with a Canaanite woman. The moral degeneration within this major judge cycle underscores how great the unmerited favor of the Lord is toward Israel.

Application. This text certainly underscores the results of sin. Our sins cannot be measured in a lifetime. They have an impact on the next generation and beyond. Whether it is our families, our communities, or our nation, the impact will be felt. The harvest of the seeds of sin may not necessarily come in our generation but in innumerable ones beyond us.

JUDGES 10:1–5

Original Meaning

Tola (10:1–2). Tola's socioeconomic status may be reflected in the fact that he is the only judge for which a genealogical connection is given back to a third generation. Often in the Old Testament, such a genealogical statement is evidence of high social standing. But from whom did Tola save Israel? The text is deliberately ambiguous. Surely the narrator could have been more direct, but then such might have obscured the cycles message of moral degeneration.

Jair (10:3–5). Jair is Transjordanian, and he "led [literally, judged] Israel twenty-two years" (10:3). One thing is certain: Jair is a powerful man. In order to have thirty sons, one has to have a harem. Following as it does so soon after the Gideon/Abimelek cycle, the issue of kingship seems to be clearly in view.

Application. See the comments at the end of the last three minor judges (12:8–15) (pp. 211–12).

JUDGES 10:6–16

Original Meaning. Seven groups of foreign deities are listed in 10:6. By identifying seven sets of deities, the text meant to be symbolic, conveying that the Israelites went completely after other deities. What follows in 10:15–16 (Israel's confession of sin and removal of the foreign gods) seems on the surface to reflect a genuine repentance. But Israel is attempting again to manipulate God to meet their immediate specific need of deliverance. Their hearts are not really devoted to God except for convenience.

Jephthah will not be a fitting judge for the nation, and yet that seems to be just the point. With each round of apostasy, the nation seems to plunge deeper, God's response is more serious, and the judge for the nation is less qualified for the role. There is a correspondence between the nation's unfaithfulness to Yahweh and his torah and the quality of the judge raised up to deliver them.

Application. Believers are entirely capable of going through the motions, of offering God insincere and superficial repentance. They can do the right rituals, play their parts, and certainly put on a convincing performance; at least as far as other human beings are concerned. But the Lord sees through the charade; he knows our hearts. He will not be manipulated by us.

JUDGES 10:17–11:11

Original Meaning. The leaders or elders of Gilead are pictured as taking the initiative to maintain their social and political status. Like the Shechemites in the story of Abimelek, the leaders of Gilead do not depend on the Lord to raise up a deliverer. Instead, they choose their own.

Presumably this is why it is not said of Jephthah that Yahweh raises him up to deliver Israel. The absence of such a statement only reinforces how ill-advised the elders' oath is to choose "whoever" (10:18) to be head of their clan.

Jephthah is introduced in a parenthetical flashback (11:1–3). The first thing emphasized in the narrative introduction is that "Jephthah . . . was a mighty warrior" (cf. Gideon in 6:12). But the second part of the verse adds a problem: His father was a man named Gilead, but his mother was a prostitute. In addition, Gilead's wife had sons, and when his father died, his brothers went to court to sue on the grounds that Jephthah's adoption was not valid because, in their opinion, the son of a prostitute could not be adopted. The elders ruled in favor of the brothers and legally disinherited Jephthah.

Verse 3 explains how Jephthah became known as a mighty warrior. He had fled from his brothers, settled in the land of Tob, and became the leader of a gang. He is the leader of a group of vagrants, morally empty men, and is thus pictured in the same terms as Abimelek.

The elders' initial offer of 10:18 was that "whoever" saved them would become their tribal chief. But in their first approach to Jephthah (11:4–5), they make the lesser offer of "commander" (Heb. *qatsin*, 11:6). It may be that the elders first offer Jephthah the title *qatsin* instead of the title *rosh* ("head") because he had been disinherited.

The essence of Jephthah's response in 11:7 is a rejection of their offer. Jephthah rejects the elders because they have previously rejected his case in court and have annulled an adoption agreement that his father made in his favor. Moreover, their offer of making Jephthah commander is rightly perceived for what it is.

Only after Jephthah's objection (11:7) do they raise the offer to its initial level. Their haggling shows how unprincipled these opportunists are. They seek to hire Jephthah "cheap" by offering him less than what they offered a full citizen of Gilead (10:18). They would gladly abuse him to accomplish their ambitious ends.

Jephthah lays down the condition for which he was willing to go fight the Ammonites (11:9). If they could have obtained Jephthah without reinstating him to his inheritance, they would have. But they also have no hesitation to reverse their earlier decision and disinherit Jephthah's brothers in order to get their man.

Jephthah, seeing his chance for promotion in Gilead, is equally as ready to perform an illegitimate cultic vow to guarantee the military victory he needs to retain the status that he acquires through his negotiations with the elders. The error in both cases is the same: placing ambition above covenantal loyalty, familial loyalty, and proper cultic performance.

The ratification ceremony takes place at Mizpah. Their ritual ceremony uses the Lord's name, but the Lord is absent from the process of raising up Jephthah. Just using the divine name does not mean that God is in it.

Application. What is especially disturbing in this passage is that the raw opportunists are the political and spiritual leaders of Israel! Could such raw opportunists be found in the church today? It is a chilling thought, but the better part of wisdom recognizes that such situations can and do exist.

JUDGES 11:12–28

Original Meaning. Immediately after Jephthah's installation at Mizpah, he sends messengers to the Ammonite king asking why the Ammonites are attacking. The Ammonite king's response is hardly satisfying: Israel has stolen Ammon's land; surrender it, and there will be peace (11:13). In the lengthy speech that follows, Jephthah uses a common ancient Near Eastern form known as the royal covenant/treaty disputation.

Jephthah starts the speech with the assertion that Israel did not take the land of Moab or the land of the Ammonites (11:15). This assertion (if true, and it is) undercuts the Ammonite claim right from the beginning. Israel cannot give back to Ammon that which was never Ammon's.

Not only does Jephthah's rehearsal of the area's history function to undercut the Ammonite claim—he will further the argument shortly—it also functions as a mocking warning to the Ammonite monarch. Just as Israel sent messengers to the Transjordanian kings, so Jephthah has sent messengers. Just as the Transjordanian kings chose a negative response (especially Sihon), so the Ammonite king may choose a negative response. But just as Yahweh gave Sihon into the Israelites' hands, so will he give the king of Ammon into their hands. Just as Israel utterly defeated Sihon and his army, so the Israelites will defeat the Ammonite king and his army (if he chooses the same response as Sihon).

Jephthah uses what appears to be a logical argument—an argument commonly asserted in the ancient Near East: A people must accept the will of its god. Therefore, the Ammonites will possess the lands that Chemosh, their god, gives them, and the Israelites will possess the lands that Yahweh, the God of Israel, gives them (in this case, the disputed area!).

For all his apparent piety, Jephthah identifies faith in Yahweh with the practices of the surrounding national cults rather than the ideals of biblical faith. He localizes Yahweh as though he is just like Chemosh, Milcom, Baal, and so on.

Now Jephthah follows up with a series of questions related to Balak (11:25). These, on the surface, seem strong arguments. Jephthah's last rhetorical question is preceded by an assertion. The essence of the argument is this: Since no Ammonite king (or Moabite, either, for that matter) has ever attempted to claim the land area in dispute for over three hundred years, nobody in his right mind would claim it now. Thus, the claim is rejected.

Jephthah's conclusion is found in 11:27. This brings the disputation to its climax. Often such disputations were but a preamble to the violence of the battlefield.

Jephthah mocks the Ammonite king for pondering war with the Israelites, since war with them is war with Yahweh. His mockery only compels the Ammonite king onto the battlefield, where he will be, like Sihon, greatly humbled. As in his dealings with the elders (11:9), Jephthah voices a recognition that the victory belongs to Yahweh (11:21, 27). But like his negotiations with the elders, this is only a tacit recognition, for Jephthah is a pragmatic Yahwist.

Application. Theological ignorance and error lead to devastating results. In addition, we live in a world that has, over the course of a century, continually depreciated the worth of theological matters. A knowledge of the Bible is not considered important today. In our drive for technology, knowing God's word is seen as having little or no value. Knowing the Bible does not put bread on the table, so the argument goes.

JUDGES 11:29–40

Original Meaning. As pointed out in the discussion of the spirit of Yahweh clothing Gideon (6:34–35), this does not presuppose any particular level of spirituality on the part of the recipient. It affirms Yahweh's involvement in empowerment but does not guarantee the recipient's spirituality.

Following this statement is a fourfold repetition of the same verb (*abar*, variously translated in the NIV "crossed . . . passed through . . . advanced against . . . went over") in 11:29b–32a, which serves to link Jephthah's endowment with Yahweh's Spirit with his Yahweh-given victory. His crossing, passing, advancing, and going over functions to intensify Jephthah's actions, building up to the climax of Yahweh's giving the Ammonites into his hands (11:32b).

It is very tragic that almost immediately after the spirit of Yahweh comes on Jephthah, he disrupts the flow toward the climax in Yahweh's victory by vowing to perform a sacrifice if Yahweh should give the Ammonites into his hand (11:30–31). Jephthah's vow is nothing short of making a deal with the deity, an attempt to exert control over God. The irony is stark. Jephthah delivers the Israelites from the Ammonites, who along with their neighbors sacrifice their children to their gods; then he sacrifices his daughter to Yahweh, who does not accept human sacrifice!

Does Jephthah intend to imply a human sacrifice in his vow? It may seem odd to Western readers for sheep or cattle to come out of one's house. But the typical four-room house of this period contained a room that housed animals. Hence, in his vow, Jephthah most likely had this in mind.

The focus is on the daughter's innocence and Jephthah's ignorance. While it was sin to break a vow (Num 30:2), God did provide for the redemption of vows made without full reflection of their ramifications. Tragically, had he known about this, Jephthah could have redeemed his daughter (Lev 27:1–8)!

Application. The tragedy of this passage is repeated again and again in our modern society. Jephthah was an illegitimate son, born of a prostitute, rejected and disinherited by his family, leader of a gang. He became a man who was hurt, angry, bitter, ambition driven, abusive of his daughter, and doing what is right in his own eyes for his own gain. He made his daughter responsible, blaming her for the disaster that he would inflict on her and making himself the victim of his rash vow. In many ways this nameless daughter represents all the courageous daughters of abusive fathers.

JUDGES 12:1–7

Original Meaning. The Ephraimite accusation and threat come from the ancient Near Eastern context of the covenant disputation. They have the same rhetorical effect as the earlier threat of the king of Ammon (11:13). It is as though, having delivered Gilead from the external threat of the Ammonite king, Jephthah must now face this internal threat from one of the tribes of Israel.

Jephthah's reaction, however, lacks the same high quality of divine righteousness as that which characterized Jephthah's diplomacy with the king of the Ammonites. Without waiting for a response to his rhetorical question at the end of 12:3, Jephthah calls out the Gileadites and fights against the Ephraimites.

Interestingly, Yahweh is not involved in this battle in any way. Yahweh is not mentioned anywhere. This is an intertribal feud that God has hardly sanctioned. This episode is a foretaste of the intertribal war that erupts in Judges 19–21. Just as Jephthah through his word (11:30–31) murders a daughter within his tribe—in fact, within his own family—so Gilead through a word (*shibbolet*/*sibbolet*, 12:6) murders a confederated tribe.

Application. Contentious people produce contention. Jealousy, envy, and every sort of evil (Jas 3:14–18) can consume God's people. So it is with the petty, unimportant, and unnecessary fights that consume many a church. While forty-some thousand may not die, the emotional and physical damage can be astronomical—especially in its long-term effects. There is a need for humility and repentance.

JUDGES 12:8–15

Original Meaning

Ibzan (12:8–10). After the Gideon account and its complementary sequel about Abimelek, the references to the number of sons of the judges seems to indicate that, from Gideon on, judgeship is always on the verge of turning into kingship, with sons succeeding fathers to office. Thus, the self-interest motif continues in both the cyclical/major and noncyclical/minor judges.

Elon (12:11–12). Nothing is really reported about Elon the Zebulunite except the length of his judgeship and the place of his burial. His name is usually interpreted to mean "oak" or "terebinth."

Abdon (12:13–15). Oddly, Abdon has fewer grandsons than sons. The opposite is what would be expected. In light of the Deuteronomic covenantal blessings and cursings (namely, Deut 28:4, 18), is this a subtle allusion to unfaithfulness?

Application. The noncyclical/minor judges give evidence (like their major judge counterparts) of a spiritual and moral degeneration. Rather than living up to their responsibilities in saving

Israel and stimulating Israel to godly living, aside from Shamgar and Tola, they are, in the main, characterized as self-interested materialists hungry for power. Such a negative characterization serves as a warning to us today. In a culture that promotes self-interest and materialism and that worships power, such activity does not work the works of God.

JUDGES 13:1–25

Original Meaning

Opening Narrative Frame (13:1–2). The well-familiar opening narrative frame components begin the narration of the cycle in 13:1. Yahweh's utilization of the Philistines has already been anticipated in the introduction to the Jephthah story (10:7). The length of the oppression is forty years, double the next longest oppression. This may speak to its severity.

Instead of the usual third component, "and the Israelites cried out to the LORD," there is only silence. In the last two cycles (Gideon/Abimelek and Jephthah), this issue of crying out to Yahweh has come under close scrutiny. Israel does not deserve to be delivered and cannot manipulate Yahweh to intervene through false repentance (as Yahweh himself emphasizes in 10:10–16). In the Samson episode, Israel is utterly passive.

In light of Israel's stubborn rebellion at this time, it is much more remarkable that Yahweh will not only intervene but will do so in the context of a miraculous birth reminiscent of Abraham and Sarah. This intervention in the days of Samson demonstrates the tremendous long-suffering grace of God so that, in spite of Israel's lack of response, he will act purely out of faithfulness to his covenant with them.

First Theophany to Manoah's Wife (13:3–7). In the first theophany to Manoah's wife, the angel of Yahweh makes an unsolicited appearance to offer two predictions. The first prediction is fulfilled in 13:24. The second prediction is fulfilled progressively over chapters 14–16: Samson only begins the process of deliverance; he will not accomplish it. God knows that Samson will not actually finish the job; he will only arouse Israel from its oppressive slumber.

The Nazirite vow in given in Numbers included three basic prohibitions:

- to refrain from consuming wine (*yayin*) or other intoxicating drink (*shekar*), in fact, anything from the vine (6:1–4);
- to refrain from cutting one's hair for the duration of the vow (6:5); and
- to avoid coming into contact with a dead body (6:6–12).

Interestingly, Samson is twice sacred to Yahweh: first in being the firstborn and second in being consecrated to Yahweh as a Nazirite at conception.

Second Theophany to Manoah's Wife (13:8–23). Manoah is incredulous, even cynical, about his wife's report of this first angelic visit. Obviously, he is unwilling to trust the Lord's word already revealed through his wife's testimony, and, as a result, he unnecessarily delays the fulfillment of God's plan.

Remarkably but graciously, God responds to Manoah's request and sends the angel back. No additional revelation concerning Samson is communicated through the angel's second visit. In the end, it only reveals Manoah's unwillingness to believe what was announced in the first visit to his wife.

In contrast to the theophany to Gideon, where Yahweh himself gives the reassurance (cf. 6:23), here the reassurance that they will not die comes from Manoah's wife (13:23), who thus chides Manoah for not comprehending the purpose of the divine visits. She says this not because of brilliant theological insight on her part but from basic common sense: Why would the angel of the Lord appear twice, repeating his prediction and the requirements concerning the son to be born, if he was planning to kill them? That would be truly stupid. Poor Manoah still does not truly believe!

This incident reveals Manaoh's spiritual dullness and his attempt at manipulating Yahweh. Manoah's attempt at hospitality receives a rebuff (13:16). Apparently, Manoah's intention is to detain and obligate his divine visitor through feeding, a concept well-attested in ancient Near Eastern religions, where feeding a deity or his envoy provided the basis for the supplicant's expectation of divine action on his behalf.

But Manoah is not done with his attempted manipulation. He now asks the question, "What is your name, so that we may honor [*kabad*] you when your word comes true?" (13:17). In the ancient Near Eastern context, knowing the name of a heavenly being provided power over that being. So, Manoah is still seeking manipulative power through special knowledge. Manoah asks his name in order to honor him—not immediately but after "[his] word comes true" (13:17). In other words, Manoah still is doubtful about Yahweh's words.

Closing Narrative Frame (13:24–25). Ironically, it is his mother who gives the baby the name Samson (*shimshon*) (13:24a), a name related to the Hebrew noun *shemesh* ("sun"), which is also the name of the Canaanite sun-god (as well as in other Semitic) languages. This is hardly a name that would be expected after such a double theophany of Yahweh to his mother! Even so, by God's grace, the boy grows up, and Yahweh blesses him.

Application. This passage calls us to an attitude check. Have we grown apathetic in our Christianity? Are we sensitive to God's calling in our lives? Has compromise with the world caused us to be unresponsive to God's word, to his standards of morality, to his promises and expectations for our lives? Have we become dull, not being able to discern his voice? Do we demand personal verification, unwilling to trust his self-revelation in his word?

JUDGES 14:1–15:20

Original Meaning

First Account Linked to Samson's Timnite Wife (14:1–20). All of the problems narrated in this entire second section stem from the first episode (14:1–4). This verse clearly reveals the character of Samson. The text's emphasis on "seeing" stresses that Samson is a man dominated by his senses, not logic. He follows his sensual instincts, instincts that find foreign women more intriguing than those of Israel. These carnal proclivities overwhelm his perception of matters that any thinking man would know better. Samson's personality seems to be a degeneration of the other out-group judges.

Moreover, Samson's demand to his parents reveals a total disregard for authority in his life, whether parental or divine. The emphasis in 14:2 is on "now." This reveals his unwillingness to delay his gratifications, to let reason, and more importantly God's word, have a chance.

Manoah emphasizes the woman's unacceptability. None of this persuades Samson. His mind is made up. Samson is insensitive and disrespectful toward his parents and their grief over the matter. In short, he dishonors his father and mother.

However, in the parenthetical statement of 14:4, the narrator assures the reader. Yahweh's seeking does not imply that he is inciting Samson's lustful desire for the Timnite woman. Rather, it suggests that Samson's sinful actions are turned by Yahweh to accomplish his will. Samson's marriage to a Philistine causes all of the events of 14:5–15:19.

In the second episode of chapter 14 (14:5–7), Samson's parents capitulate and go down to Timnah with Samson to arrange the marriage. At the vineyards of Timnah, suddenly (Heb. *hinneh*) a young lion roars. Empowered by the spirit of Yahweh, Samson easily tears the lion in two. While this is a truly marvelous feat, Samson deliberately withholds any mention of this incident to his parents. Why?

Samson has, in dealing with the lion, produced a corpse. There is nothing wrong in protecting himself, but according to the Nazirite vow, one had to go immediately to the tabernacle and undergo a lengthy restoration ritual. To do all this would really cramp Samson's style! It is inconvenient to travel to the tabernacle, and it would waste time, money, and resources. Besides, he has a woman on his mind. Quite simply, God and his law are not important to Samson, only what is right in his eyes.

This is even clearer in the next episode (14:8–9). Some time later Samson returns to marry the Timnite. On the way, he deliberately turns aside to see the lion's carcass, in flagrant violation of his Nazirite status. As an ordinary Israelite, Samson should have left the honey in the corpse alone (Lev 11:24–40, especially 27); as a Nazirite, even more so. Instead, he scoops out some honey that the bees have made, eating it and giving some to his parents to eat. Of course, he does not tell them about the corpse for the same reason as before. Not only does he not care about his own ritually unclean status, but he cares little for that of others, including his parents, who are now ritually unclean because of his action. The only thing that matters to Samson is the satisfaction of his own appetites and cravings. Furthermore, his action shows that he knows what he is doing is in contrast to his Nazirite status.

Samson receives thirty Philistine "companions" (14:11), whom he challenges with a riddle and a bet. Of course, after three days of frustration the companions turn to Samson's wife. Through threat and intimidation, they cajole and coerce the woman to find out the answer. Ironically, Samson, who refused to tell his own mother and father about the lion, gives in to his bride's hounding on the final day. She promptly tells the companions (4:17). Thus, the companions are able to give the answer in their own poetic form (14:18).

Empowered by the spirit of Yahweh, Samson goes to Ashkelon (20 miles/32.2 km away), murders thirty Philistine men, and robs them of their clothes—just so he can pay his debt to his companions for losing the bet over his sure winner of a riddle. His unbridled anger sets the stage for his bride being given to another.

While Samson is at home sulking, his wife is given to his companion who attended him at his wedding (14:20). In other words, his father-in-law sees an opportunity to marry his daughter to one of his own people—no doubt a better social move on his part. Such a move is stimulated by Samson's return to his father's house, which leads his father-in-law to assume that Samson is displeased with his daughter and has divorced.

Second Account Linked to Samson's Timnite Wife (15:1–20). With Samson's belated return (15:1), the plot thickens. He suddenly shows up in Timnah with a young goat, assuming that nothing has changed. His father-in-law stops him at the door (literally) and proposes a new arrangement, his younger daughter, who is more attractive than her older sister (15:2). Samson swears revenge.

Samson then captures three hundred foxes, ties them tail to tail in pairs, and fastens a torch to every pair of tails—an act of prowess on his part! Lighting the torches, he lets them loose in the standing grain of the Philistines, burning the shocks, standing grain, vineyards, and olive groves—a thoroughgoing destruction! While truly an amazing feat, it is motivated purely on Samson's desire for retaliation and is wrong.

Not that the Philistines are so good. They, in turn, now inquire as to the arson and, having determined that it is Samson, burn his wife and father-in-law. So, the conflict escalates even more (15:7). He attacks them viciously and slaughters many of them. All of this is the result of a personal vendetta for revenge. While revenge was a common modus operandi in the ancient Near East, Yahweh had declared that vengeance belongs to him.

Perhaps tired, the lone-ranger-judge escapes to a cave in the rock of Etam. The Philistines, intent on finding Samson, come and camp near Lehi (meaning "jawbone," an anticipatory mentioning since the name was received after the incident that now unfolds).

The series of dialogues between the Judahites and Philistines and between the Judahites and Samson is revealing (15:10–11). All three parties are concerned about what is being or has been done to them. For the Philistines, Judahites, and Samson, the only thing that matters is reprisal and counter reprisal.

Having obtained an oath from the Judahites that they will not kill him, Samson allows them to tie him up with two new ropes. The Judahites lead him from the rock to the Philistines near Lehi ("jawbone," a second anticipatory mentioning). Empowered by the spirit of Yahweh, the binding of the ropes is easily broken. His loosing is entirely the work of Yahweh. Yet, he immediately finds an unclean object, a "fresh" jawbone of a donkey (15:15), and slaughters a thousand Philistines. Practically speaking, Samson uses what is available, but it was ritually unclean. So, in picking up this item, he again shows his disregard for his Nazirite vow.

The epilogue to this climactic slaughter of the Philistines records Samson's first prayer, the first time that he calls on Yahweh. But it is immediately plain that this is only due to the exhaustion from the massacre, a desperation of thirst. From the tone of Samson's prayer, it seems clear that this is little more than a demand for water (cf. Israel's demands in the wilderness).

Application. The passage is a warning to us concerning what characteristics we should not want in our lives. In Samson, Israel has a judge who determines what is right and wrong purely based on his senses. Today we are encouraged to live life in this way. We are persuaded by commercials to "just do it," that if we like something to go for it. Ads are directed to our senses—appearance is everything. If you don't have the right stuff, you're nothing. Sex is used to sell everything from cars to ice cream, even rice! Samson lived in a fashion that our culture would endorse—at least in his willingness to gratify every inclination of his heart.

JUDGES 16:1–31

Original Meaning

Downfall of Samson (16:1–22). Just as all of the problems of the second section (14:1–15:20) stemmed from Samson's "going" to Timnah and "seeing" a Philistine woman, so the problems in this final section stem from Samson's "going" to Gaza and "seeing" a prostitute. Samson's going to a prostitute is once again indicative of his lack of regard for God's law.

His insolent act endangers him (16:2). The people of the city discover his presence, even though going to a prostitute usually involves stealth. The feat in 16:3 is impressive, a truly miraculous exploit. City gates were not light objects. For cities like Gaza, they were typically two stories high, and their heavy posts were set in firm sockets. To haul this gate for some considerable distance to the hill opposite Hebron multiplies the magnitude of the act. The distance between Gaza and Hebron is about 40 miles (64.4 km) and involves an ascent of more than 2,000 feet. While Samson does not carry the gate structure all the way to Hebron (only to a hill opposite Hebron), he must have carried it some considerable distance.

But the feat is completely self-serving. Samson only acts to save himself. He has not delivered one Israelite from the hands of the oppressors, the Philistines. The feat is unnecessary—at least carrying the gate any distance. Simply breaking down the gate would have been sufficient.

After Samson humiliates the Gazites by this feat, they become preoccupied with discovering the secret of his strength so that they, in turn, might humiliate him. Once again, it is Samson himself who supplies the Philistines with the opportunity through his sensual weakness (16:4). While Samson may be able to uproot the gates of the city of Gaza and carry them almost forty miles uphill, he cannot withstand the wiles of a woman.

Significantly, Delilah is the only woman in the Samson cycle whose name is supplied. By only supplying Delilah's name and using it seven times, the narrator singles her out as the most portentous of the four females in the story.

The "rulers" (literally, "tyrants," 16:5) of the Philistines make the most of this opportunity. This time there is no threat or coercion (as there was in the case of Samson's wife); rather, they offer Delilah an extraordinary bounty for information concerning the secret of Samson's strength. They each offer her 1,100 shekels of silver, giving her a total of 5,500 shekels (an absurdly fantastic amount for this time period). This demonstrates how much they wanted Samson out of the way.

Samson is most commonly pictured as a hulk, a mammoth of incredible size and strength. But Samson must have been a relatively ordinary-looking man in size and weight. His strength is not even in his long, seven-braided hair. Therefore, his strength is not in the obvious; it is in Yahweh, who is working through his special, Yahweh-called, Nazirite status. Moreover, it is clear in what transpires that the Philistines are convinced that Samson's strength lies in supernatural or magical contexts.

Four attempts to subdue Samson follow in which Delilah unleashes a verbal attack on Samson in order to subdue him and receive her payment. In her third attempt, Delilah repeats the same line as the second (16:13). Samson's answer is perilously near the truth since it concerns his hair. This may indicate that his will is breaking.

In her final attempt, Delilah crowns her attack: "How can you say, 'I love [*aheb*] you,' when you won't confide in me?" (16:15). Samson's answer to this fourth attempt is exasperated and true (16:17). Ironically, he bears his soul on this most intimate of matters to a pagan woman, one who is not even his legal wife! Sadly, Samson's confession demonstrates that he has known all along that he is a Nazirite. This is a powerful comment on all of Samson's previous acts in which he has demonstrated total disregard for his Nazirite status.

Samson's confession is foolish. Yes, Delilah has worn him down. But Samson is so absorbed with her that he, like Eglon, makes himself an easy, dumb, animal sacrifice for the wily Delilah. The reversal of judgeship is preeminent here. Instead of the judge overthrowing the oppressor (Ehud vs. Eglon, 3:12–30), the judge is undone by the oppressors' hired gun.

Perhaps one of the most tragic verses in the Hebrew Bible follows: "He awoke from his sleep and thought, 'I'll go out as before and shake myself free.' But he did not know that the LORD had left him" (16:20). The spirit of Yahweh is no longer empowering him. As each of the seven braids is cut, so is the Nazirite status finally severed. The gap between the breaking of the first two Nazirite prescriptions and the breaking of the third has provided the narrator with time to underline God's long-suffering.

As a result, Samson is blinded and bound, and, after being taken to Gaza, he is set to work grinding. Grinding grain was considered a slave or female occupation, and so the Philistines greatly humble their nemesis. From their perspective there is ironic justice in Samson's grinding the grain since he burned up their grain earlier.

Death of Samson/Death of Dagon (16:23–31). Dagon is the Hebrew form of the important Upper Mesopotamian and West Semitic deity Dagan, an important grain deity. The Philistines apparently adopted the deity from the local Semitic population, no doubt in some syncretistic form with an original Aegean grain deity. In the biblical texts, he appears as a grain deity. In this connection, Samson's burning of the grain stocks is seen to be more serious. Likewise, in their excitement over the capture of Samson, it is understandable why the Philistines in their victory give the credit for this to Dagon.

To complete the humiliation, the Philistines bring Samson out of prison to the temple to perform. Samson requests to be placed near to the pillars that support the temple, a request that is anticipatory of what is to come. The temple is fully crowded with men and women, plus all the tyrants of the Philistines. Some three thousand are on the roof (to get a better view of Samson?). In this context, Samson utters his second prayer to Yahweh (16:28, author's translation), which states:

> O Lord Yahweh, please remember me.
>   Please strengthen me! Just this once! O God!
> And let me revenge [*naqam*] myself with one revenge
>   [*naqam*] on the Philistines for my two eyes.

The first line of this prayer raises expectations that perhaps finally Samson is genuinely turning to Yahweh in humility and proper faith. But the next two lines dash this. This is truly an egocentric prayer. Although ostensibly addressed to Yahweh, it is dominated by first-person pronouns, which occur five times in this short prayer. Samson is not concerned about Yahweh's reputation, only his personal revenge on the Philistines for his eyes.

Gropingly finding the two support pillars, Samson bellows his last words (16:30). Pushing the columns out of their sockets, he brings down the temple structure on the Philistines and himself. It is perhaps ironic that unwittingly Samson keeps the law about tearing down cultic installations (Deut 12:2–3) when Yahweh empowers him to destroy the temple of Dagon. Samson serves as a microcosm of Israel for its respective failures to fulfill their obligations to Yahweh.

Application. Samson's spiritual apathy is truly stupefying. Spiritual apathy concerning one's calling can lead to open rebellion, as Samson's union with the prostitute of Gaza illustrates. Throughout the Samson cycle, self-interest serves as the motivation, not only for his exploits but also for Delilah, the one who brings him down. When self-interest serves as the motivational factor in one's life, eventual devastation will come—in some cases not surprisingly from another person whose motivation is also driven by self-interest.

JUDGES 17:1–18:31

Original Meaning

The Idolatry of Micah the Ephraimite (17:1–6). Whereas at the beginning of the period of the judges the Israelites had difficulties with the foreign gods of the peoples in the land (2:6–3:6), the Israelites are presented now, in the first conclusion, as perfectly capable of manufacturing their own idols.

The narrative introduces a man named Micah from the hill country of Ephraim, who confesses that he has stolen 1,100 shekels of silver from his unnamed mother (obviously a woman of substantial wealth). The name Micah is a short form of *Mikayahu*, meaning "Who is like Yahweh?" This is ironic since Yahweh is so absent from this story.

This sum (1,100 shekels of silver) provides a tangible link to the foregoing narrative, where Delilah takes precisely this amount from each of the five Philistine lords (16:5). Micah's theft is not a business transaction for services rendered (as in the case of Delilah); it is nothing but the product of raw covetousness.

Micah's mother utters a curse, and this seems to motivate Micah to return the stolen silver, principally because he is afraid of the fulfillment of this curse. The reaction of his mother is to counteract the curse with a blessing (17:2). What seems to underline Micah's mother's curse and blessing is the ancient Near Eastern concept of magic.

After the promised return of the silver, Micah's mother solemnly consecrates the silver to Yahweh in order for her son to make an idolatrous object (or objects). She contributes, however, only two hundred shekels of the silver toward this project (evidently pocketing the rest?).

In addition, 17:5 notes that Micah made an ephod and teraphim (Heb. *epod uterapim*, NIV "ephod and some household gods"). The mother contributes the silver for production of the "idol" (*pesel umassekah*, 17:4), emphasizing the fabricated aspect of the image. Micah contributes the material for the production of the *epod uterapim*, emphasizing the oracular aspect of the cult shrine.

In any case, the production of the first is in obvious violation of the second commandment, not to mention the specific Deuteronomic curse (Deut 27:15). The making of an ephod was wrong for the same reasons that it was wrong in the case of Gideon. The use of *terapim* (household gods) for divinatory purposes is attested elsewhere. Thus, there is also a violation of the first commandment.

Micah places all the cult paraphernalia in his own house, where he makes a shrine. He installs one of his sons as the shrine's priest. The installation of someone other than a Levite as a priest was obviously in violation of the law. This action undercut the divinely ordained priestly authority at Shiloh.

Disregard for parental well-being, theft, homemade idolatrous objects of pilfered silver, private shrines, personal priests, self-made religious paraphernalia—these are hardly the proper trappings of one whose name means "Who is like Yahweh?" Ironically, while thinking that they are doing right, both Micah and his mother perform actions contrary to Yahweh's cultic requirements as prescribed in Deuteronomy 12. Small wonder this initial story ends with the first occurrence of the refrain, "In those days Israel had no king; everyone did as they saw fit" (Judg 17:6). This refrain, of course, serves as a transition to the next section.

The Installation of the Levite at Micah's Shrine (17:7–13). In the next episode, a young Levite traveling from Bethlehem in Judah finds his way northward to Micah's house. He has been "living" (literally, "sojourning," 17:7) in Bethlehem. Why is a young Levite living in Bethlehem in Judah? Bethlehem is not a Levitical town in Judah. Thus, this Levite should not have been living in Bethlehem in Judah.

The Levite comes to Micah's house (17:8). In light of the offer that Micah makes to him in 17:10, it is clear that the Levite is motivated primarily by material concerns. The fact that later he accepts an even more attractive offer confirms his materialistic motivation.

This seems right in the eyes of the Levite. Micah treats him like one of his sons (i.e., quite well, 17:11). Installing the Levite as his priest probably means the demotion of his own son, but having a genuine Levite as his priest gives Micah's shrine an air of legitimacy and prestige. This conclusion is supported by the statement of Micah in 17:13. Micah evinces an ignorance of the law in its most basic teachings.

What makes the passage even more ironic is the setting. All the action (the making of the carved image and a cast idol, the making of Micah's son a priest, the hiring of a wandering Levite) takes place in the hill country of Ephraim, the very tribe where the tabernacle of Yahweh is located (i.e., Shiloh).

The Migration of the Danites (18:1–31). Just as the wayward Levite sought a place to settle, so now the text describes a wayward tribe seeking a place to settle. This is the initial link between the two stories. Just as the Levite happened to come to Micah's house, so the Danite spies happen to come to Micah's house and spend the night. And just as the Danites' quest for new territory is illegitimate, so is their quest for a cult other than that of Yahweh.

The narration backs up slightly to the time of their approach to Micah's house when they recognize "the voice" (18:3) of the young Levite. The word "voice" (Heb. *qol*) probably refers to the Levite's accent. Consequently, they bombard the Levite with questions about how he got there, what he is doing there, and why he is there.

The Levite replies that Micah "has hired me and I am his priest" (18:4). The answer does not disturb the Danites in the least. Instead, they solicit an oracle: "Please inquire of God to learn whether our journey will be successful" (18:5). Notice that they use the term "God," not Yahweh.

The Levite gives them exactly what they want to hear: "Go in peace, your journey has the Lord's approval" (18:6).

Ironically, the Levite, who has barely found his own way, now confidently and authoritatively pronounces Yahweh's approval of theirs.

Presumably, the next day the spies leave and go to Laish. Without proper defenses or effective alliances, Laish was easy prey. The spies return to Zorah and Eshtaol (18:8) and give their report, which stresses the prosperity of the land and the vulnerability of its inhabitants (18:9–10).

The writer portrays the Danites and their spies not only as too fearful to conquer their own territory (cf. 1:34–36) but also as willing to cruelly conquer a defenseless territory and to victimize the weaker Micah. They are characterized as eager perpetrators of injustice.

Six hundred men of the Danites set out to attack the unsuspecting town. Arriving at Micah's house, the five scouts inform their tribesmen that the house contains a shrine with all the trappings. The Levite priest questions them, but they make him an offer (18:19). The Levite's reaction is immediate and positive: "The priest was very pleased" (18:20). The appeal to his vanity and materialism are sufficient to obtain his commitment.

The men who live near Micah are called out to help recover the pilfered gods. Ironically, Micah is concerned about the loss of gods who could not even protect themselves or their maker. His anguish is that of one whose life is centered on powerless gods (18:24). Micah, who at the beginning of the story was portrayed as a thief, is himself the victim of theft.

Coercingly, they reply, "Don't argue with us, or some of the men may get angry and attack you" (18:25).Their intimidation works; Micah departs without his gods, and the Danites continue on their quest. With the cultic materials and priest securely in their possession, the Danites confidently attack the unsuspecting town of Laish. In the same ruthless manner that they had stolen the powerless gods from the helpless Micah, who had manufactured them, the Danites exterminate the powerless, helpless inhabitants of Laish.

The Danites rebuild the city and rename it Dan, after their forefather. They also set up the image that Micah made and install "Jonathan son of Gershom, the son of Moses" as priest (18:30). The Levite's Yahwistic name, Jonathan (meaning "Yahweh has given"), and his genealogical connections to Moses heighten the irony of the entire story. Thus, the problems of religious syncretism and spiritual decay have infected the very institution designed to combat these problems, not to mention one of the most revered households in ancient Israel.

It is interesting that Judges 17–18 concludes with a reference to the legitimate "house of God" (*bet haelohim*) at Shiloh (18:31). This is a clear condemnation of Micah's illegitimate shrine and the cult objects he made, which have now become the Danites' cult materials (18:30a, 31a). Just as Judges 13:1–16:31 culminates in a portrayal of Samson's personal failings, so Judges 18 (as well as 1:34–36) depicts Dan's tribal failings. As Samson moves from physical strength to weakness because of ritual impurity, so Dan moves from a position of military weakness to one of strength, albeit by thuggery and at the expense of cultic and covenantal loyalty.

Application. When God's word is unknown or ignored, the results are human manufactured, culturally conditioned innovations. Self-consumed individuals (and a group) dominate this passage, which itself, at its very root, is immersed in the misconception of human manipulation of deity (i.e., idolatry). The participants in both parts of the story here appear quite silly in all their efforts and activities. Don't they realize what they are doing?

JUDGES 19:1–30

Original Meaning. By focusing on Levites in the concluding episodes, the narrator communicates the extent of Israel's moral decline. The corruption that has infected the people and their deliverers has even spread to those entrusted with the Yahwistic instruction and with upholding Yahweh's holiness in their lives.

In this case, the Levite lives in a remote area of the hill country of Ephraim. This Levite "took a concubine [Heb. *pilegesh*] from Bethlehem in Judah" (19:1). A concubine was a second-class wife—a woman who performed marriage duties without the same legal rights as a full wife. This may imply that the Levite has another wife, but the text contains no record of that. His concubine "was unfaithful to him" (19:2). The young woman initiates a separation and goes straight for her father's house in Bethlehem.

After a four-month delay (which the text does not explain), the Levite goes to Bethlehem to win her back. He speaks kindly to her. This may suggest that she has not left without some provocation on his part (his later callousness toward her seems to be a strong indication of this).

His father-in-law gladly welcomes him, probably because the separation of his daughter and her husband is a matter of disgrace for the family, and he gladly welcomes the prospect of the reunion of the two. The father-in-law shows normal hospitality over a three-day period.

The father-in-law's hospitality borders on the excessive: Six times he offers hospitality, persuading the Levite to spend five days with him. In fact, the father-in-law's delays explain why the Levite and his party end up in Gibeah, only halfway home by nightfall at the end of the fifth day.

The model of hospitality enjoyed by the Levite while in Bethlehem heightens the contrast with the treatment received in Gibeah. Thus, while bordering on the excessive, its redundancy conveys the potentially endless hospitality that the Levite may have enjoyed had he chosen to remain in Bethlehem of Judah as over against that which he gets in Gibeah.

The delayed departure from Bethlehem forces the fateful decision of 19:12: "No. We won't go into any city whose people are not Israelites. We will go on to Gibeah." Ironically, by seeking to avoid the potential inhospitality of a foreign city, the Levite and his party suffer that very fate, or even worse, in Gibeah, an Israelite city.

At sunset, the little group reaches Gibeah. The narrator goes to great lengths to demarcate the atrocity itself by the signposts of sunset and daybreak: Night falls upon arrival at Gibeah, and the ordeal begins (19:14); daybreak marks the end of both the outrage and the victim (19:26). Entering the city, the group sits in the city square waiting for someone to show hospitality and take them home with them for the night. No one offers. The people of Gibeah abuse (in general) the Levite and his party passively (by refusing basic hospitality) before the rapists abuse them actively (19:15, 22).

Finally, an old man from Ephraim, a temporary resident in Gibeah and not a Benjamite, comes by and questions the party. In his response, the Levite presents himself as a weary traveler returning home after a visit to Bethlehem.

The old man welcomes them to spend the night at his house, "only don't spend the night in the square" (19:20). The latter clause—and for that matter the entire scene at Gibeah—is reminiscent of the story of Lot in Sodom in Genesis 19:1–11. At his house, the old man at first appears to be the model host. He fodders the Levite's donkeys, provides the people with water to wash their feet, and gives them food and drink (Judg 19:21).

Then, suddenly (*hinneh*), everything is overturned. While they are enjoying themselves, some wicked men of the city surround the house and demand the host to bring out the Levite so that they can rape him. The old man's response in 19:23–24 is appallingly Lot-like.

Thus, the old man, who appears initially to be the model host, ends up being the one who comes up with the idea of throwing the concubine (and his own virgin daughter) to the horde at the door. That he should volunteer his own daughter is one thing; that he should volunteer the Levite's concubine is another; but that he volunteers either is unimaginable. The man condemns the horde for thinking of doing this outrageous act upon the Levite and yet, ironically, ends up doing a foolish thing in making such an offer.

Amazingly, there is no protest from the Levite! When they refuse to listen to the old man, it is the Levite who seizes his concubine and hands her over to the horde. Obviously this selfish act in the extreme saves him from the horde but reveals the depths of depravity in his heart.

Having tossed his concubine to the pack of men, the Levite went to bed! If the people of Gibeah were callous to the sons of Belial, then this Levite shows a deeper level of callousness, because this is a woman that he is in relationship with.

This statement, in turn, heightens the next one. Her master, the Levite, commands her with almost unbelievable callousness to "get up" (*qum*, 19:28) because he is ready to go. How can he be so cold-hearted? There is no answer.

Immediately after his return home, the Levite takes a knife and cuts her up, limb by limb, into twelve parts and sends these into every tribe in Israel. In the beginning of the story, there was a "small separation," in that the Levite was separated from his concubine by her going to her father's house. But at the end of the story, there is a "big separation," for the Levite is separated from his concubine by cutting her up and sending her parts to the tribes of Israel.

The intention of the dismemberment, on the surface, seems to have been to awaken Israel from its moral lethargy and stimulate justice. But what are the real motives of this nameless Levite? The act of dismemberment is a graphic means of calling everyone to arms. It is highly ironic that the one who issues such a call for justice is himself so selfishly insensitive and self-involved in the crime itself. But the outrageous dismemberment achieves its intended outrageous response.

Application. There are many victims like the concubine in our world today. They are the hapless, ill-fated casualties of a world that either ignores God or outright rejects him. These victims most often are the less important people in our society; or better, what our society, in one way or another, deems the less important people: women, children, minorities—that is, people with no power to defend themselves. They deserve our compassion. They need Jesus Christ's love.

JUDGES 20:1–48

Original Meaning

Incitement to Battle (20:1–17). The reader knows the Levite's systematic dismemberment of the concubine is nothing but an expression of the self-centered callousness he displayed toward her at Gibeah; however, to those at the assembly who have received the ghastly pieces it is interpreted as a zealous act of covenant fidelity and a call to religious war.

Not only is the turnout massive, but also impressive (20:2). Benjamin is aware of the assembly but is not apparently called out as a participant. The Levite is called upon as the sole witness. The leaders of the assembly hear and accept his testimony alone, which will have a devastating impact on all Israel.

Very simply, the Levite bears false witness. It is not a grossly distorted account. The general story line is correct, but the intended impression is different from the picture conveyed in chapter 19. Any possible culpability of the Levite in the incident at Gibeah is eliminated by his testimony.

"Some wicked men" (literally, "sons of Belial") in 19:22 become in his testimony "men of Gibeah" in 20:5. Thus the members of the assembly apparently understand that the crime has been committed by the leading men of the city, not some lower-class men of the baser sort. In the previous account, the wicked men demanded the old man to bring the Levite out so that they could have sex with him (19:22). The Levite now testifies: "Me they intended to kill" (20:5, author's translation).

In other words, the Levite's report glosses the sexual danger to him, and yet at the same time heightens his status as an innocent intended victim of murder. He later recovered her body and, in outrage for the crime, he sent the dismembered pieces to the tribes. The Levite's testimony to the assembly is deceptively simple in assigning guilt for her death to the men of Gibeah (20:5).

Without any additional testimony (contrary to the law that required two or more witnesses, Deut 19:15), the tribal assembly condemns the crime against the Levite's concubine and takes steps to punish the guilty. All actions are based on tribally determined loyalties. This led to the support of a fellow-tribe member in this dispute, regardless of moral questions.

While the term *herem* does not occur in the description of the action against Benjamin, the concept is clearly present. It seems that the procedure for placing Gibeah under the ban (*herem*) derives from a law recorded in Deuteronomy 13:12–18. While the law there specifically applies to idolatry, the abomination committed by the wicked men of Gibeah may have been understood as contrary to proper covenantal behavior.

Unfortunately, while this may be the case, the Israelites do not adhere to the stipulations of this law in their implementation. The leadership of the assembly does not follow the clear stipulation that "you must inquire, probe and investigate it thoroughly" (Deut 13:14a). They simply accept the Levite's version of what has happened. Moreover, they determine a military course of action before they attempt diplomatic overtures. In fact, rather than dealing directly with the city of Gibeah, they raise the issue to a higher intensity level by sending men throughout the entire tribe of Benjamin, demanding that they hand over the wicked men so that the evil may be purged from Israel. The very fabric of Israel is being threatened.

Three Battles (20:18–48). The Israelites' first inquiry is, "Who of us is to go up first to fight against the Benjamites?" (20:18a). Yahweh's response is that Judah is to go first, but there is no promise of victory (20:18b). Though the Israelites attack Gibeah en masse, they are severely defeated (20:19–21).

In the preinquiry actions, the Israelites encourage one another and again take up their positions (20:22). They also weep before Yahweh (20:23a). Yahweh again replies, "Go up against them" (20:23b). The Israelites once again attack en masse, and once again they are defeated severely by the Benjamites, though not quite as badly (20:24–25).

Before the second battle, the Israelites wept before Yahweh; now in their preinquiry actions, they weep, fast, and offer sacrifices (20:26). Yahweh responds "Go, for tomorrow I *will give* them into your hands" (20:28b; emphasis added). The Israelites set an ambush and destroy all the towns, including the animals.

Application. It is not uncommon today that the religious charlatan, the spiritual quack (like the Levite in this narrative), gets the biggest response from gullible Christians who do not inquire about the real credentials of the imposter. Some of these frauds tell convincing stories to invoke action on the part of their listeners. They can inspire many almost to a frenzy, to the point that they are willing to sacrifice their hard-earned money to support a man whose testimony is false and motivated by self-interest. Yet the truly biblical preacher will find the assembly perhaps emotionally moved, but with no real resolve to follow God.

JUDGES 21:1–25

Original Meaning

Oaths at Mizpah (21:1–5). The Israelites have sworn two oaths at Mizpah before the battles, and these create dilemmas. The first, given in parenthetical flashback in 21:1, is that the Israelites had promised not to give their daughters in marriage to the Benjamites. The excessive slaughter of the Benjamites and the endangerment of tribal extinction expose the rashness of the oath. Obviously this is like Jephthah's vow (also taken before the battle). With the passion of battle spent and with all the Benjamite women, children, and animals having been slaughtered, the Israelites suddenly realize that there is no way of providing wives for the six hundred male survivors, due to their oath. Hence a tribe of Israel will go extinct.

The people assemble at Bethel, raising their voices and weeping bitterly. But Yahweh does not answer. Early the next day the Israelites resume the inquiry by building an altar and presenting burnt offerings and fellowship offerings (21:4).

Wives for the Benjamites: Part 1 (21:6–14). Verses 6–7 record the Israelites emotional dilemma created by their first oath: "How can we provide wives for those who are left?" (21:7). Ironically (and certainly unfortunately for those in Jabesh Gilead), it is discovered that Jabesh Gilead did not send any contingent to the war. So, the second oath sworn at Mizpah (21:5) is now conveniently implemented. Since the city of Jabesh

Gilead did not send warriors for the war against Benjamin, they are not bound by the oath not to give their daughters to the Benjamites.

Thus, a force of twelve thousand is dispatched at once with instructions to put the defaulters under the ban (*herem*), all the inhabitants of the town except the virgins. Just as the Danites had attacked the unsuspecting town of Laish, putting it under the *herem* (Judg 18:27–28), so the Israelites attack the unsuspecting town of Jabesh Gilead, putting it under the *herem*. The difference, however, is that in the latter case the unsuspecting town is inhabited by fellow Israelites. So, the *herem* is abusively applied both to Benjamin (ch. 20) and to Jabesh Gilead (ch. 21).

The operation yields only four hundred young women, who are brought back to Shiloh "in Canaan" (21:12) and are "given" to the Benjamites as an offer of peace (21:13–14). But they are two hundred short of the required total. This shortfall will lead the Israelites to their final solution.

Wives for the Benjamites: Part 2 (21:15–25). The only other time that the elders of the entire nation of Israel are mentioned in this book is 2:7, where it describes the elders under whom the Israelites served Yahweh. In contrast, the elders in 21:15–25 are the devisers of a shameful plan to supply the Benjamites with the necessary women to make up the shortage from Jabesh Gilead.

Verses 15–18 are repetitious of 21:6–7. The repetition links the two erroneous solutions. This time, rather than exercising a *herem* ban against an Israelite city, the elders devise a plan that is nothing short of another rape!

The annual festival of the Lord provides the context. This festival may have been a local one, or in light of the reference to vineyards (21:20), it may refer to the Feast of Tabernacles. The elders instruct the Benjamites to hide in the vineyards, and when the girls of Shiloh come out to dance, seize a wife from these girls of Shiloh.

With the Benjamites "seizing" wives, the fathers are not technically "giving" them to the Benjamites. The legal intimidation of the threat of the oath's curse eliminates the fathers from making any objection.

The Benjamites return and rebuild their cities (21:23) so that the entire implementation of the *herem* has been undercut. In the end, what has been accomplished? Not only has justice not been served, but many injustices have happened in the feeble attempt to implement justice for the atrocity. No positive thing has really occurred in all the outcomes of the narrative. Not only have many wrongs occurred, but no rights have ultimately been championed.

The book ends with the powerful refrain, "In those days Israel had no king; every man did what was right in his own eyes" (21:25, author's translation). Sadly, the accuracy of the second line of the refrain is forcefully made in this final story.

Application. Whenever religious reasons are used to justify actions, there is room for a closer look. If in the process God's moral laws are broken, the actions are invariably wrong. We should be careful never to use one law or oath to circumvent another, for destructive tragedy will surely follow.

When God's kingship is unacknowledged, when his law is ignored, when the morality that he advocates is circumvented, incredible, appalling disasters are the outcome. When rash oaths in his name are used to manipulate and abuse people, when leaders use the ends to justify the means, when God does not exist in the lives of his people, the consequences are outrageously appalling.

RUTH

INTRODUCTION TO RUTH

The book of Ruth contains a wonderful love story, which, while set in the period of the judges, contrasts greatly with the general chaos and disobedience of that period. In a refreshing way the book provides an antithesis to the incessantly negative message about the conditions in Israel during that time by underscoring God's tremendous blessing in the midst of great familial distress.

Quite simply, the author of the book of Ruth is unknown. The date of the book's composition is, in many ways, a more difficult matter. The evidence seems to suggest a late preexilic to early postexilic date.

BOOK OUTLINE

I. Prologue and Act 1: Naomi's Return (1:1–22)
II. Act 2: Ruth and Boaz in the Fields (2:1–23)
III. Act 3: Ruth and Boaz at the Threshing Floor (3:1–18)
IV. Act 4: Boaz Arranges to Marry Ruth and Epilogue (4:1–22)

RUTH 1:1–22

Original Meaning

The Prologue (1:1–6). *The setting (1:1–2).* The story is set in the period of the judges (1:1a). Such an allusion must have conjured up for the original audience visions of the moral and spiritual declivity with the consequent oppressions and chaos that prevailed in that time

Verse 1 quickly adds that "there was a famine in the land. So a man from Bethlehem in Judah . . . went to live for a while in the country of Moab." Ironically, the man comes from Bethlehem, which means "house of bread," but there is no bread/food in that city.

Double bereavement (1:3–5). Although tragic is the loss of her husband, Naomi's aloneness is mitigated by the fact that her two sons are alive. The sons die after a ten-year period; the story compresses this time interval, creating the impression that Naomi is left battered by the relentless onslaught of one tragic event after another.

Hint of change (1:6). This is the first time Yahweh is mentioned in the story, and it is in the context of his compassionate provision for his people. As Yahweh has provided food for his people, will he yet provide fertility to Ruth and an offspring for Naomi?

Act 1: Naomi's Return (1:7–22). *On the road to Judah (1:7–19a).* Naomi, Ruth, and Orpah set out on the road to Judah (1:7). They probably have not gone very far—perhaps they have not even left Moabite territory—when Naomi speaks up. Naomi urges her daughters-in-law to return "each of you, to your mother's home" (1:8). Naomi's urging must have been with some mixed feelings. To urge Orpah and Ruth to return to Moab necessitates that she will travel home completely alone.

Naomi pronounces a blessing of *hesed* (NIV "kindness") on the women because of their *hesed* to the deceased. The young women refuse to leave Naomi alone, insisting that they will go with her. Naomi makes it abundantly clear that, at least in her understanding, she is the target of God's overwhelming power and wrath.

Orpah kisses Naomi good-bye (1:14). Naomi's powerful argument has convinced her that a normal life back in Moab is preferable to life with Naomi in Israel. Ruth swears her commitment to Naomi in the name of Israel's God, thus acknowledging him as her God. The essence of the oath is that only death will separate Ruth from Naomi.

Naomi and Ruth arrive at Bethlehem (1:19b–22). Naomi has returned home empty, unfulfilled, and bitter. In Naomi's anguished response to the delighted cries of the women of Bethlehem—all absorbed in her own world of pain and bitter affliction—she fails even to acknowledge Ruth's presence with her. In a subtle touch of the narrator, Naomi utters her complaint as though Ruth, whose words of loving commitment still ring in the readers' ears, has never pronounced these words at all! Yahweh has indeed not brought Naomi back empty.

Application. What the world attributes to large impersonal forces of nature and chance, the Scriptures attribute to the sovereignty of God. This is a fundamental teaching of the Bible, and the book of Ruth stresses it throughout its pages. How we respond to the circumstances that God may bring into our lives often determines further outcomes.

RUTH 2:1–23

Original Meaning

Scene 1. Ruth Gleans in a Field Belonging to Boaz, Naomi's Relative (2:1–3). Verse 1 serves as a parenthetical digression in which one of the major characters is introduced. He is described first in relationship to Naomi, "a relative on her husband's side"

(2:1a). This relative is further described as "a man of standing" from the family/clan of Elimelek (2:1b).

Verse 2 picks up the story where 1:22 left off. God established at least two ways through which widows could have their needs met. However, the law also gave the following provision for the poor and the foreigner. This was what Ruth intended to do according to her statement in 2:2. The storyteller then adds an important clause: "As it turned out, she was working in a field belonging to Boaz . . ." (2:3). God, who is constantly working behind the scenes, is pictured as directing and controlling this situation through his gracious providence.

Scene 2. Ruth and Boaz Meet on the Harvest Field (2:4–17a). The initial greetings between Boaz and his workers in 2:4 build suspense by focusing on Boaz, a man whose first words are a blessing on his workers in the name of Yahweh. Such a greeting speaks to his character and foreshadows his generosity.

Boaz immediately inquires from his overseer about the identity of the unknown young woman gleaning in his field by probing her origins (2:5). The overseer's perspective serves as a foil to heighten the magnanimity of Boaz in the passage. He insinuates to Boaz that this Moabitess is not like the other poor gleaners because she is gathering too much grain.

Boaz addresses Ruth, not the overseer. In a series of six short statements with a final seventh conditional statement (2:8–9), Boaz outlines a beneficent program for Ruth in his field despite the fact that she is a Moabite woman (and in spite of the report given to him by the overseer).

In his seven statements Boaz is granting her more than the ordinary rights of gleaning. She is to glean in that portion of the field normally off limits to poor gleaners. Boaz instructs her to stick close to his young women workers, and he instructs his workers not to interfere with her. Finally, if she is thirsty, she can drink from the more immediately available water jars rather than seek refreshment elsewhere and lose time in gleaning. Boaz's provision is extraordinary.

Verse 10 records Ruth's reaction and reply. Overwhelmed by Boaz's unexpected protection and generosity, she falls to the ground. This gesture consists of dropping to the knees and touching the forehead to the ground. Both Ruth's action and her accompanying words exhibit that she is completely surprised at what Boaz has said to her. This confirms that he has granted her far more than she has requested. Boaz's action is once again evidence of God's providence.

Boaz's reply is the high point of the scene in 2:11–12. In a concise and straightforward manner, permeated with praise and admiration, he affirms what Ruth has solemnly vowed to Naomi in her stirring words of commitment in Moab. Boaz then wishes that Yahweh will "repay" Ruth for her actions and prays that she may "be richly rewarded by the Lord" (2:12). Like a defenseless starling, Ruth sits securely under Yahweh's mighty wings.

Ruth expresses her gratitude in 2:13. Boaz's kindness has greatly assured her that her mission will succeed. Ruth refers to herself here as "servant," although she does not really even have this status. The term is an expression of Ruth's humility.

In 2:14–16 Boaz welcomes her to the intimacy of the noon meal, invites her to glean, and bestows so much roasted grain on her that she eats all she wants and has some left over. Thus, Boaz transformed a rather ordinary occasion—the noontime meal—into another demonstration of his compassion and generosity (i.e., his *hesed*).

Scene 3. Naomi Evaluates the Meeting (2:17b–23). Ruth has threshed roughly enough for the two women to eat for a little more than a week. The large quantity and leftovers from the noon meal clearly lead into Naomi's surprised reaction and excited questions in 2:19a. It is clear from Naomi's two questions that she is not concerned about finding out a particular geographic location where Ruth has gleaned but is concerned about who the owner of the field is.

Naomi pronounces a specific blessing on Boaz: "The Lord bless him! . . . He has not stopped showing his kindness [*hesed*] to the living and the dead" (2:20a). Naomi also now adds some crucial information: "That man is our close relative; he is one of our guardian-redeemers [*goel*]" (2:20b). Naomi's revelation of Boaz's relationship to them is important to the plot because it creates anticipation of events to come.

In 2:21 Ruth is, through her excitement, expressing understanding of Boaz's actions, now that she knows of his relationship to them, including the fact that he has accorded her the same extraordinary gleaning privilege throughout the rest of the harvest.

At the end of this two-month period, 2:23b stresses that Ruth is still living with her mother-in-law. This is significant to the plot of the story. Ruth has gleaned for both the barley and wheat harvests in the fields of Boaz, but there has been no development in their relationship. What looked like a clear solution to their widowed situation seems to have died out.

Application. It is certainly the case that Boaz and Ruth represent ideal models of extraordinary character. It is not in some religious setting that Ruth or Boaz manifest their hesed. Rather, it is in the daily workplace, the place where too often *hesed* is lacking. Such manifestations of *hesed* are the result of commitment to the Lord, and both Ruth and Boaz exhibit *hesed* qualities to those around them. Certainly, the writer intends that his readers (both ancient and modern) look to these two individuals as didactic models for life.

RUTH 3:1–18

Original Meaning

Scene 1. Naomi Discloses Her Plan for Ruth and Boaz (3:1–5). Naomi instructs Ruth to do three things: bathe, put on perfumed oil, and put on her "dress" (Heb. *simlah*; NIV "best clothes," 3:3). The most likely explanation of Naomi's instructions is that they mean that Ruth should end her period of mourning and so signal her return to the normal activities and desires of life, which, of course, would include marriage. This change in her appearance, with its symbolic meaning, will indicate to Boaz both her availability and the seriousness of her intentions.

Ruth's response demonstrates her willingness to engage in this risky endeavor: "I will do whatever you say" (3:5). It should be remembered that things could go wrong in the plan. For example, Boaz could mock her request for marriage to him. Or even worse, Boaz could use the night's opportunity for his sexual pleasure, bringing on her great humiliation. Yet Ruth demonstrates her radical commitment to and trust in Naomi.

Scene 2. Ruth Executes Naomi's Plan and Boaz Offers to Be Kinsman-Redeemer (3:6–15). Verse 7 narrates that Boaz is in good spirits. Thus, he will be receptive to the request communicated by Ruth's symbolic actions. Ruth approaches, uncovers his legs, and lies down. The narrator has built the suspense to a peak.

The utter surprise of Boaz is captured in the narration (3:9). Ruth's words are carefully chosen. She uses *amah*. When used this way, *amah* suggests a female petitioner's weakness and need for help or protection when presenting a request before a more powerful male.

Next, Ruth invokes Boaz to "spread the corner of your garment [*kanap*] over me" (3:9). The choice of the term *kanap* can be construed as a general plea for protection. The term *kanap* may also refer to the symbolic investment connected with marriage. Ruth's actions and words seem to achieve the desired effect. Boaz takes them to be an invitation to marriage.

There is no doubt that this scene on the threshing floor is sexually provocative. But the narrator constantly and consistently depicts both Ruth and Boaz as individuals of unmatched character, whose lives exhibit that faithful loyalty to relationships described by the Hebrew word *hesed*. It is evident that Boaz's silence means to imply here that they meet this moment of choice with the same integrity. The sexual connotations of the scene are used by the narrator to convey the sexual and emotional tension felt by the characters.

Boaz's first words are a blessing (3:10). Boaz goes on to assure Ruth (3:11). While the last clause may be formulaic, it nevertheless stresses Boaz's commitment to Ruth. Boaz acknowledges his responsibility, but he also recognizes the fact of hierarchy within the clan structure. Boaz's symbolic action of promise in 3:15 is parallel to his first act of generosity in 2:14–17. It is clear from the gift that this is meant as a symbol of his commitment to the relationship.

Scene 3. Naomi Evaluates the Encounter (3:16–18). Naomi's response to Ruth reveals that she fully understands the meaning of Boaz's symbolic gift. She counsels Ruth to sit tight. Her confidence in Boaz's integrity is undiminished, even greater than when she sent Ruth to the threshing floor. This dialogue between Ruth and Naomi comprises the last words that either of them utter in the story. Poised on the threshold of fulfillment, they both step aside, with Boaz taking center stage. His action will now dominate the story's resolution.

Application. Ruth and Boaz demonstrate their pure motives in chapter 3. It is the issue of purity in motives that is the very heart of the issue of integrity. As Christians, ultimately we are called to serve the Lord and therefore ought to speak and act out of pure motives that will bring honor and glory to his name. Honesty with God and honesty with ourselves as we reflect on what we are doing and why we are doing it goes a long way in helping us to evaluate our motives and to act with integrity with others.

RUTH 4:1–22

Original Meaning

Act 4: Boaz Arranges to Marry Ruth (4:1–12). *Boaz confronts the unnamed kinsman (4:1–8).* Boaz, true to his words, "went up to the town gate and sat down there just as the guardian-redeemer he had mentioned came along" (4:1). The Hebrew construction here translated "just as" is meant to convey surprise. Thus, this is not simply coincidence but the hidden hand of Yahweh at work.

Having called the man over, Boaz now procures ten elders of the city. The text strongly suggests that Boaz does not simply wait in the gate with the other redeemer until ten elders of the city chance to pass through on their way to the fields. Instead, he actively seeks these individuals out so that the legal proceedings can start.

Having assembled the elders, he confronts the nearer *goel* ("guardian-redeemer," 4:3). This verse introduces a totally new item to the story. Without a single prior word on the subject, the narrator has Boaz inform the nearer redeemer that "Naomi, who has come back from Moab, is selling the piece of land that belonged to our relative Elimelek" (4:3).

It is clear that the text is not describing an outright sale of land by Naomi. Instead, this refers to a transaction in which only the right of use of the land is being transferred for a stipulated value. Naomi must have inherited rights to the field of Elimelek. Boaz appeals to the nearer redeemer to buy back the rights from the unnamed third party.

This nearer redeemer has not taken any initiative to help Naomi and/or Ruth. In other words, in contrast to Boaz, who had already functioned as a *goel* of sorts for Naomi and Ruth, this man has done nothing. It seems likely that this nearer redeemer has been thinking along different lines. In all probability he knows about the field of Elimelek. Since there is no descendant of Elimelek, the field will, at a certain point, merge into his possession. Whatever the price paid for the redemption will be offset by the annual crop yields. With such self-interest in mind, the nearer redeemer quickly consents to redeem the field when Boaz brings the issue forward.

However, Boaz is a crafty fellow. He now drives home the second responsibility of the *goel*: "On the day you buy (acquire the usufructuary rights of) the land from Naomi, you also acquire Ruth the Moabite, the dead man's widow, in order to maintain the name of the dead with his property" (4:5).

The nearer redeemer is not up to fulfilling the social and moral responsibilities. He states: "Then I cannot redeem it because I might endanger my own estate [*nahalah*]. You redeem it yourself. I cannot do it" (4:6). Nonverbal action closes the scene. The nearer redeemer (*goel*) removes his sandal and hands it to Boaz as a symbolic act declaring his abdication of his own right of redemption.

Boaz acquires the right to redeem Naomi and Ruth (4:9–12). Calling the entire assembly to be his witnesses, Boaz formally declares in a full and detailed form the two obligations that the nearer redeemer has ceded to him. Through this solemn and emphatic declaration, Boaz reinforces the issue of restoration of the clan—the memory of the deceased may not perish.

The elders and all those at the gate declared their witness of the legal proceedings. They then pronounce a threefold blessing on Boaz (4:11–12). Boaz is certainly a praiseworthy man. While the offspring of Boaz and Ruth will count in the family line of Elimelek, he will also count as a genuine scion of Boaz.

Epilogue (4:13–17). The resolution to the death and emptiness that have afflicted Naomi are truly resolved in these few verses. The women of Bethlehem joyously celebrate the son born to Ruth and Boaz as the one who restores life and fullness to Naomi. She who was left alone without her two sons (Heb. *yeladim*, 1:5) now takes the boy (*yeled*), holds him, and becomes the one who cares for him (4:16).

Finally, a surprise identification is given. The child is "the father of Jesse, the father of David" (4:17). It is at this point that the reader can perceive how precarious the situation was: Without Ruth, the line of Elimelek would be extinguished, as, too, the line of Boaz, and hence no David.

Coda (4:18–22). The theme of family continuity becomes the theme of national continuity. The book of Ruth is the bridge between the era of Israel as family or tribe and Israel as nation. Far from being peripheral to the main narrative sequence of the Bible, Ruth dramatizes its principal theme: the continuity of the people Israel in their land. Moreover, in Yahweh's providence, the *hesed* of Boaz, Ruth, and Naomi lays the foundation for a salvation that extends to the ends of the earth for a lost world.

Application. Christians can learn much from Boaz. Because we live in a world that demands to get its own way and is often more than willing to bypass or short-circuit any ethical issue that stands in the way, the church finds itself infected with this way of living. Clear scriptural directives for reconciliation are ignored in order to achieve one's goals. Unsupported testimony (i.e., gossip) filters its way throughout congregations in order to gain its intended aims. The very idea of "doing *hesed*" does not cross the minds of many a church attendee, who are more interested in having his or her needs met.

1 SAMUEL

INTRODUCTION TO 1 SAMUEL

The books of Samuel are anonymous, like many other Old Testament books. Over the past six decades, biblical scholars have devised a theory to explain the origins and composition of 1–2 Samuel, and it is fair to say we have reached something of a consensus. The books of Samuel appear to have been a portion of a longer work tracing Israel's history from Moses to the destruction of Jerusalem by the Babylonians in 586 BC. This longer history was comprised of Deuteronomy (at least in part) plus Joshua, Judges, 1–2 Samuel, and 1–2 Kings. These books present a theological history of Israel, evaluating Israel's past in light of the covenant relationship established in Deuteronomy and relying on the so-called retribution theology established there. Based on the curses and blessings of Deuteronomy 28, the doctrine of retribution assumes the idea of reward for obedience to the covenant and punishment for disobedience. Such a guiding principle evaluated national and individual successes and failures in terms of the consequence of faithfulness or disobedience to Mosaic, or Deuteronomic, law. As a result, this extended history, which includes the books of Samuel, is commonly referred to as the Deuteronomistic History.

First Samuel details the transition from theocracy to monarchy, an agonizing process in the life of ancient Israel. First Samuel 1–7 describes the prelude to the monarchy, chapters 8–15 its advent, and chapters 16–31 its establishment.

BOOK OUTLINE

- I. Israel's Need for a King (1:1–7:17)
  - A. Shiloh Narratives (1:1–4:1a)
  - B. Ark Narratives (4:1b–7:17)
- II. The Rise and Fall of Saul, Israel's First King (8:1–15:35)
  - A. Saul Becomes King (8:1–12:25)
  - B. God Rejects Saul (13:1–15:35)
- III. The Rise of David Begins, Israel's Promised King (16:1–31:13)
  - A. David in Saul's Court (16:1–20:42)
  - B. David and Saul Estranged (21:1–31:13)

1 SAMUEL 1:1–28

Original Meaning

Background of Hannah and Her Problems (1:1–8). This opening paragraph contains several features that illustrate the righteousness of Samuel's parents. Elkanah is depicted as an upstanding Israelite who cares deeply for his family and carefully attends to his religious commitments. The law of Moses mandated regular trips to the tabernacle to worship (Deut 16:16), and Elkanah is a faithful Israelite, concerned to fulfill his vows to Yahweh. Elkanah carefully and generously distributes meat to his family, likely a common practice during the festivals in which certain sacrifices were offered (1:4). Finally, Elkanah loves Hannah deeply, despite her unenviable position as a barren wife (1:5, 8). Hannah's intense pain is exacerbated by the insufferable cruelty inflicted on her by her counterpart, Peninnah.

Hannah's Prayer (1:9–18). While at the Lord's temple for the festival at Shiloh, Hannah weeps and prays earnestly, making a vow to Yahweh (1:11), which implies the so-called Nazirite vow. The term *nazir* ("Nazirite") is defined in Numbers 6, where a man or woman can make a special vow of separation to Yahweh. After the period of separation was over, Numbers 6 prescribed a ritual for terminating the vow. Hannah is offering her unborn child as a permanent Nazirite, whose life will be wholly and exclusively God's.

The encounter between the priest Eli and Hannah contains an ironic twist. The spiritual leader of the nation is unable to discern the spiritual significance of this woman's struggle. In the end, he recognizes in her the faith he was supposed to represent (1:17).

The Birth of Samuel (1:19–20). These verses reveal a quick answer to Hannah's prayer. After their return trip home, Elkanah "made love to Hannah his wife," which in Hebrew is simply he "knew" her (1:19). The original language is graphic at this point. Elkanah knows her and Yahweh remembers her, as he remembered Rachel when he opened her womb (Gen 30:22). God's remembering someone in the Old Testament does not mean that he has forgotten them, only that his memory is consistent with his promises and that he will take action (Exod 2:23–25).

Birth narratives play an important role in biblical literature. Clearly the birth of Samuel into such circumstances marked for the narrator the dawning of a new day in Israel. Birth narratives in the Old Testament commonly use paronomasia or wordplays in announcing the name of a child. The Hebrew words for "ask" (*shaal*) and "request" (*sheelah*) are enough like the name

"Samuel" (*shemuel*) to make Hannah's name-giving typical of other Old Testament examples. Her play on Samuel's name is not attempting a precise etymological connection. It is a rather typical naming wordplay, and it emphasizes her confidence in God's faithfulness to answer prayer.

Hannah Fulfills Her Vow (1:21–28). Hannah decides not to accompany Elkanah and the rest of the family during the annual festival. But when the boy is old enough to live in Shiloh permanently (two or three years old), Hannah feels able to fulfill her vow (1:21–23). She takes him to Shiloh and worships Yahweh in gratitude for his gracious gift (1:24).

In a striking wordplay that continues the play on Samuel's name, Hannah states that Yahweh has granted her petition (*sheelati*), which she had requested (*shaalti*, 1:27). In language that illustrates how appropriate her response is, she dedicates him (*hishiltihu*, from the same verbal root) to Yahweh; all his life Samuel will be dedicated (*shaul*) to Yahweh (1:28). Having come to God with nothing, she now returns to Shiloh to give back that which means everything.

Application. When a nation is in such despair, the only hope is the appearance of righteous individuals, both in national leadership and in the common citizenry. First Samuel 1 announces both. Samuel is the coming new leadership, and he is given to the nation through a righteous family. As illustrated by chapter 1, God desires to use godly leaders to reform nations. Through her suffering and trials, Hannah was used as an instrument of God to initiate spiritual rebirth in Israel. Like Elizabeth and Mary after her, she was honored by God with miraculous conception in order to show God's mercy and grace and to continue his salvation story. But without a host of other, nameless Israelites who also prayed and lived their lives in quiet devotion, such reform would not be possible.

1 SAMUEL 2:1–36

Original Meaning

Hannah's Song (2:1–11). Old Testament historical narratives occasionally insert poetry to supplement a particular episode. This little poem plays an important structuring role in 1–2 Samuel generally. It corresponds in a kind of point-counterpoint fashion with two poems near the conclusion of the two-volume book (2 Sam 22:1–51, 23:1–7). Hannah begins 1–2 Samuel by celebrating what Yahweh has done and will do in the future, while David concludes the book by celebrating Yahweh's faithfulness.

Hannah's prayer spans the height and depth of Israelite theology and relates it to her circumstances. She begins with an introduction (2:1) that announces the personal joy she has in her relationship with Yahweh. The concept of the exalted horn appears to be a metaphor in which the horns and head of an animal are held high as a symbol of triumph and power.

Hannah's joy and triumph are firmly rooted in the singular holiness of Yahweh (2:2). Only he is transcendent in power and moral character. From this certitude flows her confidence, and she bursts forth in a stream of assertions that result from it.

In the closing phrases of the poem, we return to the idea of the exalted horn, which forms an *inclusio*, or literary envelope, for the whole (2:10b). This is the first time the king of Israel is referred to as "anointed." These concluding phrases of Hannah's song emphasize the Lord's anointed as especially chosen by God and empowered for the task of leading Israel. This description of Yahweh's anointed becomes programmatic for the narratives that follow.

Contrast between Eli's Sons and Samuel (2:12–26). The general statement of 2:12 sets the tone for 2:12–17. The designation "scoundrels" (literally, "sons of Belial") in these opening chapters of 1 Samuel refers to cultic abuses, that is, a lack of regard for the proper worship of Yahweh. It is ironic that Eli earlier mistakenly assumed Hannah was a "wicked woman" (1:16; literally, "daughter of Belial"). Hannah was a righteous woman, but Eli does not know righteousness when he sees it.

The specific nature of the sins of Hophni and Phinehas has to do with their rights as priests. The Old Testament law provided proper and just ways for priests to share in certain meat portions of animals offered at the tabernacle (Lev 7:28–36; Deut 18:3). But Eli's sons at Shiloh have devised their own system. The narrator summarizes their great sin as "treating the LORD's offering with contempt" (1 Sam 2:17).

The positive evaluation of Samuel and his family likewise begins with a general statement, setting the tone for 2:18–21. The linen ephod was a garment worn by priests, and the "little robe" supplied by his mother each year may have been an outer cloak worn over the ephod. This ideal scene, so lovingly describing the adorned little priest, is surely a dramatic contrast to the grasping and avaricious sons of Eli.

Meanwhile, Eli is either unwilling or unable to control his wayward sons. When he learns of their sexual exploits and their public reputation (2:22–23), he rebukes them and warns them of the inevitable consequences of their actions. But they reject his words (2:25). Samuel, by contrast, continues to mature physically as well as spiritually (2:26).

Prophecy Against Eli's Priesthood (2:27–36). The sudden and unexpected appearance of "a man of God" (2:27) in Old Testament narrative is seldom good news. Such anonymous prophetic figures often bring messages of impending judgment. This pericope contains the features of prophetic speech often used by such prophets. Such prophetic speech has a discernible form: introduction, followed by accusation, and then by the announcement of judgment. As is typical, the prophetic "Thus says Yahweh" introduces the whole speech (NIV "This is what the LORD says," 2:27). It is followed by the accusation, which here takes the form of a question. This particular accusation in fact contains three questions (2:27–29).

The final stage of the prophetic speech is the announcement of judgment, which begins with the "therefore" in 2:30. Yahweh reminds Eli that he had committed himself by divine oracle to the Elide house as priests, that they would minister before the Lord "forever." But as elsewhere in the Bible, such divine eternal promises are conditioned on continued faithfulness.

The specifics of God's judgment against Eli are both corporate and personal. The entire house of Eli will suffer the consequences of the present wickedness. Every one of its members will die early, making Eli the last old man in his priestly line (2:22). But the immediate and personal application for Eli relates to his sons, Hophni and Phinehas (2:34–36): They will both die on the same day! Yahweh will raise up in their place a faithful priest (2:35). The fulfillment of this prophecy comes in stages.

Application. The contrast between Samuel and Eli's sons in this chapter is a lesson for all religious professionals, as well as for individuals deeply involved in the life of their local congregation. There is something about throwing oneself into the everyday affairs of the church, into the routine business of doing church work, that is deceptive. It soothes our conscience and makes us feel we are in the right state of mind spiritually. But proximity to God's work is no substitute for submission to the grace of God.

1 SAMUEL 3:1–4:1A

Original Meaning

The Word of the Lord Was Rare (3:1). Easily lost in our familiarity with this narrative is the way the historian has framed the account with an emphasis on "the word" of Yahweh. Our author has a special appreciation for the importance of living under the authority of Yahweh's word. Without such direction, the nation (or any individual) will wander aimlessly and eventually fall into self-destructive behavior.

The Word of the Lord Came to Samuel (3:2–14). Yahweh's call of Samuel is narrated in 3:4–10 and the divine message conveyed to the prophet-in-the-making in 3:11–14. Samuel's recurring self-announcement ("Here I am; you called me") is the expression of those who volunteer themselves for service. It is especially significant when someone hears and obeys the divine call (Gen 22:1, 11; Exod 3:4; Isa 6:8).

Samuel is still inexperienced in the way of Yahweh (3:7). That is about to change. His willingness to serve, together with his holy parentage and his childlike acceptance of religious instruction, prepares Samuel to experience Yahweh in a new way. His lack of knowledge of Yahweh leads to confusion in this moment of call, but eventually Eli discerns that it is God who is calling the youth (3:8).

After calling Samuel three times, Yahweh now "came and stood there" (3:10). Apparently, Samuel is now receiving not only a word but also a vision, significant because we have been told that both word and vision were rare in those days (3:1). The call of Samuel thus far has been an idyllic, childlike exchange. But when Yahweh reveals the message to Samuel (3:11–14), it is anything but idyllic or childlike. Yahweh informs Samuel that he is about to fulfill his word spoken through the anonymous "man of God" regarding the end of Eli's priesthood (2:27–36). There is no turning back now (3:14).

Samuel the Prophet (3:15–4:1a). Samuel is afraid to tell Eli the dreadful message. But when Eli presses him, Samuel tells the elderly priest the truth, to which Eli responds with gloomy resignation. Surely he understands that the sovereign Yahweh is free to punish sin and is just in doing so. The emphasis of 3:19–21 is the validity of Samuel's prophetic ministry. The narrator itemizes four facts that confirm Samuel's important role as Israel's new hope for revival and deliverance from her spiritual lethargy.

1. Yahweh continues to grant his supernatural presence to Samuel as he matures. The abiding presence of Yahweh demonstrates that the circumstances of his life (and career) are not left to human influence alone.
2. The historian informs us that Yahweh "let none of [Samuel's] words fall to the ground" (3:19). This particular expression denotes the success of Samuel's prophetic words.
3. The validity of Samuel's ministry is demonstrated in his public acclaim (3:20). The expression "from Dan to Beersheba" designates the northern and southern most extremities of united Israel.
4. The final legitimizing feature of Samuel's new role is the continued manifestations of Yahweh to Samuel at Shiloh, where God reveals himself "through his word" (3:21). The night call is not an exceptional appearance of Yahweh to Samuel, but rather the first of a series.

Application. In God's appearance to Samuel, his word functions both to inform and to invite. God's word in the Bible refers to things around us, but it also relates to us directly. He speaks both to *inform* us and to *form* us, both for *information* and for *formation*. The word that God addresses to contemporary believers is both an instrument of government, whereby he informs us how we ought to live, and also a means of fellowship, whereby he invites us into personal relationship with him.

1 SAMUEL 4:1B–11

Original Meaning

War with the Philistines (4:1b–4). During the judges period, Philistine encroachment resulted in the relocation of the tribe of Dan (Judg 18). Now continued aggression threatened to result in more losses in Israel's heartland. In 1 Samuel 4:2, the Philistines rout the Israelites. The question asked by the elders of Israel in 4:3 about this defeat reflects the Israelite concept of the sovereignty of Yahweh. They assume that Yahweh has brought this defeat on them. In a sense, they are right. The sins of Eli and his sons Hophni and Phinehas have national and military consequences.

Yet the course of action chosen by the elders is misguided. They presume they can reverse the horrible events of that day by treating the ark of the covenant as though it were a magical wand. But God cannot be manipulated. The subtle reference in 4:4b reminds the reader that along with the ark come the wicked sons of Eli. As long as this situation persists, Yahweh will not bless Israel's wars, and the ark will not serve a military role.

The Ark of the Covenant Arrives (4:5–9). Ironically, the Philistines prove to be more adept at interpreting Israelite history than the Israelites themselves. The Philistines understand that Israel's God is more powerful than anything they have ever experienced. Note 4:7: "Oh no! Nothing like this has happened before." Unfortunately, Israel has become negligent in its worship of this miracle-working God. Strangely, the fear and alarm caused by the Israelite war cry arouses the Philistines to fight even harder (4:9).

The Capture of the Ark (4:10–11). The loss of thirty thousand ground infantry is indeed a "very great" slaughter (4:10). However, we should be sensitive to the hyperbolic way in which ancient Israelite authors used numbers. The loss may well be a metaphoric statement for an excessively large number of military casualties.

The losses of 4:1b–11 are due to a theological crisis in Israelite society that goes far beyond a failed military strategy. The causes of the defeat are to be found in the failure of the Elide priesthood, even if not stated unequivocally. The culmination of Samuel's prophecy in chapter 3 and its acceptance by Eli, along with 4:12–22, remove all doubt: Israel lost this war with the Philistines because of the wickedness of Eli and his sons.

Application. Living for Jesus does not mean we are always right or that we will always "win." Sometimes we will need correction and the discipline provided by others. Unlike the Israelites in this passage, we must never assume that God owes us something or that we can control the outcome of personal conflict by appealing to our relationship with God. After all, our life with God is all of grace and depends not one bit on our own merit.

1 SAMUEL 4:12–22

Original Meaning

The Death of Eli (4:12–18). The messenger's pitiable report contains four parts building in climactic fashion (4:17). First, the Israelite army has been put to flight before the Philistines. Second, he reports the news of heavy casualties. Third, Eli's own sons are both dead. Fourth, the ark of God has been captured. We are not told of Eli's reaction to the first three pieces of news. But at the mention of the ark's capture, he falls, and because of his advanced age and great girth, he does not survive the fall. The narrator intends us to understand that Eli is practically unaffected by the news of his sons' deaths, supposing that he has given up on them as hopeless.

The Birth of Ichabod (4:19–22). The birth and naming of Ichabod appears to be patterned by the narrator after the birth of Benjamin to Rachel (Gen 35:16–19). When read in this way, this pericope is significant not only for Ichabod's name (see just below) but also because of the contrast between his birth and Benjamin's. As here, Rachel's midwife tried to comfort the mother by assuring her that she is giving birth to a son. Also like this passage, Rachel names her son with her dying breath. But in this case, the wife of Phinehas seems to draw no comfort from the fact that she is delivering a son (4:20). The name "Ichabod" presumably means "no glory." Another possibility is that the name means, "Where is the glory?"

The use of repetition in 4:21–22 reveals the narrator's concern. He is afraid we may misunderstand Ichabod's mother and the true source of her distress in this, her moment of death. She sees no glory left to Israel because of the capture of "the ark of God" in addition to the deaths of her father-in-law and husband (4:21b). The focusing restatement of 4:22 removes all doubt.

Application. The deaths of Eli and his sons had been announced by the anonymous "man of God" and by the young Samuel. Chapter 4 then describes the nation's defeat at the hands of the Philistines, which leads us to this section on the death of Eli and his sons. The point of this prophecy-fulfillment pattern is that these events are divinely driven, that God's word through his prophets is true, and that God's will is being accomplished in and through these events. Prophetic history marches with certainty from word to fulfillment. God's word is to be trusted and his prophets believed.

1 SAMUEL 5:1–7:1

Original Meaning

The Ark of the Covenant in Philistia (5:1–12). Ashdod was apparently the chief city of the Philistine pentapolis. Scholars believe the Philistines arrived in Israel around 1200 BC. They appear to have adapted to Canaanite culture nicely, and the acquisition of Yahweh's ark would have been typical of ancient Near Eastern religious syncretism. Placing the ark "beside Dagon" (5:2) would confirm that Israel's deity was now supporting their efforts to establish hegemony. The Philistines could only have been encouraged by this development.

But on the first morning after placing the ark next to Dagon, the Philistines find Dagon in a position of subservience and worship, prostrate before Yahweh's ark (5:3). On the following morning, Dagon has lost his head and hands (5:4). Decapitation and cutting off hands was not infrequent in ancient warfare. Thus, the condition of Dagon's torso on the second morning is a sign of military defeat. The added detail that the executed Dagon's extremities are found "lying on the threshold" explain why "to this day" priests of Dagon step over the threshold of the temple of Dagon in Ashdod (5:5). The superstitious custom of jumping over the threshold of a sacred place was known in ancient Israel, even practiced by idolatrous priests in Jerusalem (Zeph 1:4, 9).

In the Philistine mind, there is no doubt that the plague of tumors is due to the hand of Yahweh. The Philistines have now learned the hard lesson, which the Israelites themselves learned in 1 Samuel 4. No one can manipulate or control Yahweh simply by obtaining possession of the ark of the covenant. They have both grossly underestimated his power and holiness.

The Philistines Send the Ark of the Covenant Back (6:1–12). The Philistines decide they have seen enough; it is time to return the ark to Israel. The recommended offering for Yahweh (6:4) apparently uses sympathetic magic. The departure of the golden statues is probably intended to affect the removal of the rodents and disease from the region of the Philistine pentapolis. Ironically, the Philistine priests and diviners are now urging their people to give glory and honor to Yahweh, the God of Israel. What a fascinating turn of events!

The proof that Yahweh was the genuine source of the Philistine's afflictions comes in the nature of the ark's return to Israel (6:7–12). The cows act against nature (because their new calves are not with them) but under divine compulsion (without turning to the right or to the left), taking the cart straight to Beth Shemesh.

The Ark of the Covenant at Beth Shemesh and Kiriath Jearim (6:13–7:1). The people of Beth Shemesh join in worshipful thanksgiving by sacrificing the cows to Yahweh before the ark. But it is short-lived. The loss of seventy citizens of that city may have been the result of disease passed from Philistine contacts. But in the minds of the Israelites, it is because they have not properly cared for the sacred symbol of Yahweh's covenant (6:19).

The pitiable question of the citizens of Beth Shemesh acknowledges the loss of Shiloh as the proper cult center for the fledgling nation (6:20). The driving question is: Where should the ark be housed now that we have lost Shiloh and now that Eli's family is dead? The people of Kiriath Jearim accept the task, consecrating Eleazar the son of Abinadab to "guard" (literally, "keep," 7:1) the ark. These events form the inspiration for the psalmist's mediations in Psalm 78:60–62, 65–69.

Application. At the very time when many postmoderns are seeking God in illegitimate ways, God seems evermore distant. Deism still clings, for God seems for many to be as far away as ever. But biblical revelation breaks into this worldview and shatters it. Biblical truth offers an alternate view of reality that makes the others impossible. God, the transcendent Creator of the universe, is also immanent and thus immanently involved in the world.

In this text he crashed into the Philistine world in order to teach them that their various ways of explaining and understanding divine presence are all wrong. The message of this text is greatly needed in today's world. It illustrates that the Philistine worldview—which is so similar in many ways to today's postmodern New Age perspective—is inadequate. God is not coterminous with the forces of nature, nor is he created in our image. He is not susceptible to the forces of magic or idolatry. He cannot be manipulated or pressed into service whenever we feel threatened or at risk. The God of Israel is in fact immanent and in control; he is victorious over all the forces of our world, just as he was victorious over the Philistine god Dagon.

1 SAMUEL 7:2–4

Original Meaning. Israel is still living in relationship with Yahweh. She has been plagued with sin and failure. But through it all, he graciously continues to find a way to save her and draw her closer to himself. Whereas their mourning in 6:19 was the result of the tragedy at Beth Shemesh, their remorse in 7:2b is accompanied by seeking after Yahweh.

Verse 3 contains the most important Old Testament expression for repentance. To "return" to the Lord implies acknowledging, confessing, and forsaking sinful behavior, making it possible to be reinstated in a right relationship with him. The combination of "returning" with "all your hearts" refer to the seat of one's intellectual commitments rather than singularly to human emotions, as we tend to use it in modern English.

The paragraph ends with the terse but encouraging statement, "So the Israelites put away their Baals and Ashtoreths, and served the LORD only" (7:4). Samuel's preaching is effective, and the Israelites are now prepared to be led into their future.

Application. First Samuel 7:2–4 teaches there is a natural connection between committing ourselves to the Lord exclusively and ridding ourselves of the foreign gods, whatever they may be in our contemporary context. For today's believers, any object of our affection may potentially become a "foreign god," interfering with our relationship with God. Whenever and wherever this happens, the message of the prophet needs to be heard again: Return to the Lord wholeheartedly by ridding yourselves of foreign gods, committing yourselves to the Lord, and serving him only!

1 SAMUEL 7:5–17

Original Meaning

Repentance at Mizpah (7:5–6). Mizpah was located in the tribe of Benjamin, just eight miles north of Jerusalem. As an important city in early Israel, it was an appropriate location for national confession. It is possible that the water ceremony (7:6) symbolized the washing away of corporate guilt.

Israel's confession in 7:6 makes a significant contribution to the overall message of 1–2 Samuel: "We have sinned against the LORD." The historian responsible for the books of Samuel seems especially interested in defining and illustrating the nature of genuine confession and repentance.

Decisive Victory (7:7–11). In 1 Samuel 4 the Israelites lost to the Philistines because they attempted to manipulate God by bringing the ark of the covenant into the battle. They had no leadership to warn them against such action, and the military defeat was at the same time a spiritual failure. Now, the people implore Samuel to continue interceding on their behalf (7:8). Nothing has really changed—and yet everything has changed.

"Ebenezer": The Lord Has Helped Us (7:12–14). This stone monument is more than a reminder for future generations that Yahweh helped in this battle against the Philistines. It is that, but it is more. It also serves the present generation by driving a benchmark in the ground and acknowledging that this victory is not a result of their own strength or brilliant military strategy. Yahweh had spoken with a loud thunder (7:10), and this stone acknowledges his help.

Summary of Samuel's Ministry (7:15–17). The spectacular victory over the Philistines and the concluding reference to "peace" in 7:14 draw deliberate comparisons between Samuel and the charismatic leaders in the book of Judges. But there are differences as well. Samuel is established on a more permanent basis, partly because of the loss of the priesthood and the cult shrine at Shiloh. His jurisdiction is broader than previous judges. He is truly a pivotal figure in the transition from tribal confederation under the temporary leadership of various judges to a centralized monarchic government.

Application. We have many monuments in America. As important and meaningful as these national monuments are, none of them speaks to the needs addressed by Israel's Ebenezer monument. The Ebenezer stood in Samuel's day as a reminder of what *God* had done for the nation of Israel. God had been faithful to his word; God had *acted* on their behalf. America could use such a monument.

1 SAMUEL 8:1–22

Original Meaning

Israel Asks for a King (8:1–9). The Israelites are justified in planning for the future, and we certainly cannot fault them for approaching Samuel about what they should do after his death. The problem arises in the nature of their suggestion. When the elders ask Samuel to appoint a king to "lead" them (8:5, 6), they clearly have in mind more than a simple change of leaders. This is a request for a paradigm shift of political structures, rejecting the older form of charismatically chosen judges. Requesting a "king" to "lead" is tantamount to a rejection of Samuel's godly judgeship and ministry of prophecy.

Motivation for such a request is stated succinctly: "such as all the other nations have" (8:5). This alarming statement reveals a profound dissatisfaction with who they are as a people. They are grasping for something they fail to understand and will lose the very things they hope to ensure by having a king.

At first sight, Yahweh's response to Samuel may seem harsh (8:7). Yahweh cites the long-standing pattern of sin and rebellion since the exodus as evidence that the people of Israel will persist in their demand for a king (8:8). In fact, this speech of Yahweh uses characteristic vocabulary to illustrate that their request is tantamount to other episodes of rebellion from Israel's history: "forsaking me and serving other gods" (8:8). He is painfully aware that even given the warnings against kingship, Israel will not relent.

Samuel Warns Against Kingship (8:10–18). Yahweh was not opposed to an Israelite monarchy. Rather, he was opposed to the *kind* of monarchy Israel is now demanding! She wants a king *like the nations around her*, a kingship that will bring her power and political influence. The portrait of kingship that Samuel paints appears to be an authentic description of the semifeudal Canaanite political structure as it existed prior to and during the time of Samuel. He objects that having a king like "all the other nations" is not what Yahweh has in mind. Such an unchecked human institution will become militaristic, conscript Israelite men (even women!) into military service, confiscate property, and lead ultimately to enslavement (8:11–17).

Israel's Informed Decision (8:19–22). The desire to be "like all the other nations" is repeated (8:5, 20). To this is added, "with a king to lead us and to go out before us and fight our battles" (8:20). The lust for territorial security is stated in general terms here. Apparently, the people of Israel have not learned sufficiently enough from the genuine repentance and glorious victory over the Philistines recorded in chapter 7. After Yahweh confirms that he will indeed grant a king, Samuel dismisses the assembly and instructs the people to leave Ramah and return to their homes (8:21–22).

Application. All too often, Christians become more like Israel than we care to admit, forsaking the security of the lordship of God and grasping after a compromised authority in order to become something we were never meant to be. In our clearest and most honest moments, we all too often seek security by conforming to the zeitgeist, the spirit of the times, rather than serving in the world as God's counterculture, as we were created to do. Like Israel, we tend to forfeit the lordship of God in order to become "like all the nations."

1 SAMUEL 9:1–10:27

Original Meaning

Saul Looks for Donkeys and Finds a Kingdom (9:1–10:8). Saul is an impressive young man. His father's lengthy genealogy implies the family has great wealth. Saul himself strikes an imposing figure, literally standing out in the crowd (9:2; 10:23–24). Saul and a servant set out to find a group of lost donkeys belonging to his father (9:3–4). They traverse the tribal territories of Benjamin and Ephraim but cannot find the lost animals. At the servant's suggestion, the two of them decide to inquire of a "man of God" (9:6) at a certain town in the district of Zuph. The text does not mention the name of the town or the name of the man of God. Having thus built a satisfying amount of suspense, in 9:14 we learn, finally, that this is Samuel himself.

In a parenthetical paragraph, the author informs us that Yahweh has prepared Samuel the day before Saul's arrival (9:15–16). Thus, the prophet is prepared to anoint him as "leader" ("prince, ruler," Heb. *nagid*) over the nation Israel. This term is used in Samuel and Kings for the king-designate, as the one officially chosen and appointed by Yahweh to rule his people Israel.

However, the term *nagid* likely connotes even more than the primacy of Yahweh's choosing. It seems probable that this word was initially a military term and may have referred to the "commander" of the national militia under the old tribal confederation. The choice of *nagid* rather that the common Hebrew word for "king" (*melek*) emphasizes the limited nature of Saul's kingship. Perhaps *melek* is avoided here because *Yahweh* is Israel's king.

In 9:17–27 Saul and Samuel meet for the first time. Yahweh informs Samuel that this young visitor is the one who will "govern" Israel (9:17). There were much more common Hebrew verbs available, but here we have a verb that usually means "restrain." The other terms for "rule" may have been avoided to indicate that this will be a governance under the strict lordship of Yahweh, thus again stressing the distinctiveness of Israelite kingship. Saul is to be a ruler-deliverer, who operates under the direct authority of Yahweh and his prophet.

Samuel immediately sets Saul's mind at ease about the missing donkeys. Samuel then unexpectedly includes his guests in a banquet for that evening at the high place outside the town. Without warning, Saul becomes the center of attention, being given a place of honor and a specially designated portion of food.

In the morning, Samuel prepares Saul to receive a private word from God by asking that he send his servant on ahead of them (9:27). Once alone, Samuel anoints Saul. The use of oil is a symbol of the spirit of Yahweh in several Old Testament passages and represents the empowerment of Yahweh.

The transformation of Saul from an unassuming youth to the king-designate is certainly a drastic change for him personally, but it is also revolutionary for the nation. Samuel prophesies three events that will happen to Saul on his return home, which will confirm his selection, at least privately (10:2–7).

1. At Zelzah near Rachel's tomb, two strangers will report to Saul that the lost donkeys have been located and that his father is worried about his safety (10:2).
2. Three men near Tabor will greet him and offer him bread (10:3–4).
3. At Gibeah he will be met by a group of prophets playing musical instruments. The spirit of Yahweh will come upon him, he will join them in their prophesying, and he will be "changed into a different person" (10:6).

Samuel concludes these signs of confirmation with a command to wait for seven days at Gilgal to receive further instructions.

At that time, Samuel will sacrifice burnt offerings and fellowship offerings (10:8).

"Is Saul Also among the Prophets?" (10:9–16). All three of the signs meant to confirm his anointing are fulfilled that very day. Only the third sign, however, is detailed in the text. When Saul reaches Gibeah, he meets the band of ecstatic prophets, as Samuel has prophesied. The spirit of God comes on him and empowers him to join the prophets, arousing the derision of the local inhabitants, who apparently know him and his family well.

The question "Is Saul also among the prophets" (10:11) has several possible connotations. It serves as a rhetorical question expecting a negative answer. In this light, the question affirms Saul's new spiritual gifts, not because he belongs naturally to the band of prophets but because he is the legitimate new ruler of Israel. It affirms his anointing by Samuel, and he accepts his new role. This naturally provokes questions from his uncle (10:14–16). Saul's reticence to answer them is in keeping with the private nature of his encounter with Samuel and ensures that his selection by lot will be unsoiled.

Coronation at Mizpah (10:17–27). Samuel calls another national convocation at Mizpah, the site of Israel's humble repentance and victory (7:5–17). In stereotypical prophetic language, he reminds the people that Yahweh brought them out of Egypt and delivered them from its power. Interestingly, the prophetic speech pattern used here is one well known throughout the Old Testament for announcing judgment. In fact, the selection of Saul is inserted at the very point where we would expect an announcement of judgment. This being the case, Yahweh's act of providing a king for Israel is itself an act of divine wrath (see Hos 13:11).

When Saul is selected by a process of elimination, he is nowhere to be found. Is Saul hiding because of his humility or his cowardliness? Because this king-designate has been prophetically anointed, has received three signs confirming his divine appointment (1 Sam 10:1–7), and has been empowered by the spirit of God, this hesitancy to take up the task reflects badly on Saul.

Once located, Saul is presented to the people, who enthusiastically approve. The exultant "Long live the king!" (10:24) has survived into modern times and universally implores health and success for a new monarch in the hopes that he might lead the people to better times. But this great "leader" has to be dragged before his subjects from behind the baggage, which does not bode well for the future.

Application. An awareness that God is at work in the world today should make believers more sensitive to his unexpected and unseen influence in our everyday lives. Not that we should look for the spectacular and miraculous around every bend, but we should recognize and acknowledge his work in our own lives and in those around us. Saul and his servant were casually looking for his father's lost donkeys when God unexpectedly visited him through the prophet. Abraham was resting by the entrance to his tent when God paid him a visit (Gen 18). Moses was pasturing sheep when God came and called him to service (Exod 3). God does not miraculously send us a prophetic word every day or meet us in a burning bush. Nevertheless, we should learn to be faithful while attending to the routine, the ordinary, and the familiar. For in these, God often leads and directs his people.

1 SAMUEL 11:1–15

Original Meaning

The Ammonite Threat (11:1–3). During the judges period, the Ammonites had threatened Israelite territory more than once (Judg 3:13; 10:6–9; 11:4). Claiming Jabesh Gilead, a city strategic in the defense of the east bank of the Jordan, would solidify Nabash's stranglehold on Gad and Reuben and constitute a further threat to all Israel in general. This comes at a time when Philistia was already a concern on Israel's western flank.

The question that plagues the minds of the elders of Jabesh Gilead is whether there is anyone to "deliver" (NIV "rescue," 1 Sam 11:3) them. Thus, the text establishes the suspense. Will Israel's new king be up to the task, or will he fail to deliver, as the troublemakers of 10:27 suspect?

Saul Defeats the Ammonites (11:4–11). This passage is especially reminiscent of Judges 19–21. In the earlier tragic episode, the Levite's concubine had been killed while he was spending the night in Gibeah of Benjamin. Out of desperation, he brought the crime to the attention of the Israelite tribes by dismembering her body and sending the pieces to the tribes for judicial decision. Saul appears to have intentionally mimicked this method when he kills the team of oxen and sends the pieces throughout Israel as a call to arms. When the tribes joined to take action against Benjamin for the crimes against the Levite's concubine, the inhabitants of Jabesh Gilead had not participated in the battles (Judg 21:8). Reprisals were swift and severe (21:10–14). As a result, the inhabitants of the city probably have little reason now to hope that the tribes on the western side of the Jordan River will join together in order to defend them from the Ammonites. Their plea for seven days to find out if they have the support of their kindred tribes is not a ruse but a genuine question of concern (1 Sam 11:3). Saul's ability to unite the tribes and lead them against the Ammonites in defense of a cause that is in doubt is an impressive beginning.

As in the previous passage, the "spirit of God" comes on Saul to empower him (11:6). The text uses nearly identical phraseology as in Judges. The Spirit fills the judge with divine indignation and empowers him for military service. The earlier Spirit-empowerment of Saul was temporary, but this one is apparently more permanent, continuing until Samuel anoints David as Saul's replacement.

The Ammonite victory in chapter 11 functions as the testing stage for Saul's kingship. In the overarching narrative of his rise to power, this victory is not the one pictured in his anointing and commissioning, which speaks instead of the Philistine threat (9:16; 10:5). Rather, this victory was Saul's first test and prepares for his final coronation at Gilgal.

Saul's Kingship Renewed (11:12–15). After this spectacular victory over the Ammonites, it seems only logical to the people that they execute those who first opposed the Lord's anointed. The people of Israel ask for the death penalty because of their understanding of sacred justice. But Yahweh has achieved a great deliverance on this day, which certifies his anointed king, Saul. This little paragraph illustrates the role of the king as anointed or as messiah. The anointed one, whom Yahweh has publicly confirmed through victory, is the only one who has the ability to forgive crimes and abolish the demands of divine justice.

Application. It is not always easy to know whether we are definitely moved by God's spirit or by our natural instincts. It is easy to be confused about what we are supposed to do and when we are supposed to do it. In this text, we are presented with an Old Testament example of a chosen servant of God, prepared in many ways to fulfill God's mission for his life and also open and responsive to God's prodding, direction, and timing. We can learn much from such examples.

1 SAMUEL 12:1–25

Original Meaning

Samuel's Faithful Ministry (12:1–5). It is time for Samuel to clear the air. Under his tenure, things were fair and equitable. The claim that Samuel has not *taken* anything unlawfully or unjustly relates this speech with the one in 8:11–18. There Samuel detailed "the way of the king," who would "take" everything they hold dear, including their freedom.

Samuel has vindicated himself and has also emphasized the responsibility of the new king to maintain the same high standard of just and righteous leadership. The Israelites are to consider his faithfulness "in the presence of the LORD and his anointed" (12:3). In Samuel's reference to the Lord's "anointed," he stresses the role of the new king to uphold Yahweh's rule among his people. Now the burden rests on Saul.

Samuel's Farewell Charge to the Israelites (12:6–15). The expression "present yourselves" in 12:7 and 12:16 mark these units as distinct (NIV "stand here" and "stand still"). Both usages prepare the audience to consider the mighty deeds of Yahweh. In the first (12:6–15), Samuel locates the people's recent demand for a king in the context of their national history and confronts them with a choice for the future. In the second (12:16–25), the venerable prophet performs a new "great thing" (12:16) of Yahweh in order to demonstrate the prophetic ministry they have forfeited and urges them to be faithful in the future.

Samuel emphasizes in particular the judges period in order to show that regardless of how far short their ancestors fell, Yahweh never abandoned them. The cycle of sin, oppression, repentance, and judge-provided deliverance was oft repeated and had, in fact, preserved the nation. Now this current generation of Israelites has grown dissatisfied with the theocratic system, just as their ancestors had grown tired of the manna in the desert.

So, Samuel drives home their choice. He forces them to face the reality of a human king as opposed to the divinely provided judge-deliverers. Verse 13 is the hinge or central theme of the chapter. It is as if Samuel were saying, "Here! Here you are! This is the king you have chosen. You asked for him; you got him! Yahweh has given him to you." They have indeed received a king, but he comes with divine restrictions. Then, to prove that this is no omnipotent monarchy, Samuel outlines the conditions for its success (12:14–15).

Samuel Redefines His Role as Prophet (12:16–25). For the sake of future generations, it is critically important for the Israelites to properly define and understand the role of the new king. But just as important is the role of prophets in the new government. In order to make a lasting impression on this point, Samuel calls for a thunderstorm at wheat harvest (12:16–18). Israel may have a new king and a new political structure, but they must never neglect the word of the servants of Yahweh, the prophets.

Samuel's words and the miraculous storm drive the people to repentance and to a plea for Samuel to intercede on their behalf (12:19). Samuel begins his answer by reminding the people that they themselves have demanded a king (12:20–22). They have acted wickedly, but they are not without hope. If they remain true to Yahweh, avoiding all idolatry, he will not reject them. Despite the new political system, Yahweh still wants the intimate relationship with Israel, but only under the old-covenant terms.

Having duly charged the people to remain faithful, the rest of Samuel's answer addresses his own responsibilities (12:23–25): Samuel's new role arises from his prophetic relationship with Yahweh. His service will now consist in two things.

1. He will intercede with Yahweh for the people.
2. He will instruct them in "the way that is good and right" (12:23).

Application. God was constantly giving Israel second chances. At some point, one would wonder if God's grace might give out. When does one exhaust the mercy of God and begin to worry that God might withhold his forgiveness? Once again, we see that the Old Testament narratives illustrate a truth taught explicitly in the New Testament. The scandal of God's grace is evident here not only in his forgiveness but also in his willingness to send Samuel to Israel in the first place. God's grace to forgive takes shape first of all as grace to convict and uncover the hidden sinfulness of the human heart. Most Christians today stress only forgiveness as the ministry of God's grace. But here the hard words of the prophet, bringing awareness that one is in need of forgiveness, are also a gift of God's grace.

1 SAMUEL 13:1–22

Original Meaning

Philistine Wars Renewed (13:1–4). The opening verse has suffered textually, and it leaves us without the chronological details of Saul's reign. The Hebrew says only "two years," which is doubtlessly incomplete. Regardless of the reason for the incomplete reference to Saul's reign in 13:1, it seems ironic that it heralds Saul's flawed reign. The regnal formula introducing Saul is as defective as the king himself!

Jonathan appears for the first time with little fanfare. He is not identified specifically as Saul's son until 13:16. His skirmish with a Philistine outpost escalates into the full-fledged war that everyone is expecting and for which Saul has been anointed king.

Saul Offers Up the Burnt Offering at Gilgal (13:5–15). When the Philistines muster what seems like insurmountable odds, many of Saul's troops begin to scatter (13:5–7). Saul has been directed by Samuel to wait seven days, after which the prophet will arrive, offer the appropriate sacrifices, and commission Saul and the troops to enter the battle. The text demonstrates the unique nature of the Israelite version of ancient Near Eastern monarchy as well as the unique nature of prophecy in Israel. Standing beside every Israelite king was to be a prophet speaking God's word for the situation.

Unable to hold his army together and desperate to get things underway, Saul offers the sacrifice himself (13:9). Saul's offense is not the mere fact that he offers a sacrifice but that he disobeys God's word through the prophet Samuel. No sooner has Saul finished than Samuel appears to announce his folly (13:13).

Saul has lost the opportunity to establish an eternal dynasty. He himself will keep the throne, but it will not pass to his descendants and endure forever, as eventually will be promised to David. Instead, Yahweh will give the kingdom to "a man after his own heart" (13:14). The new king will exhibit a certain "like-mindedness" with Yahweh. The circumstances of Saul's selection were marred by the insolent demand of the people. The implication is that David is chosen on the basis of different criteria, that is, divine criteria unencumbered by the exigencies of human demands.

Philistine Strategic and Tactical Advantages (13:16–22). The Philistines hold a decisive military superiority over the Israelites during this period. They substantially outnumber the troops of Saul and Jonathan. This personnel superiority is accompanied by a superiority in military equipment. By controlling a monopoly in metallurgical technology and technicians, the Philistines are able to limit Israel's arsenal. The result is that on the day of battle, only Saul and Jonathan among the Israelites are armed with sword and spear (13:22). Presumably the Philistines know how inadequately Israel is prepared for war. It seems clear: Saul and his forces are in danger of annihilation.

Application. Consider the features of Saul's actions that contribute to the anatomy of sin.

1. Saul allows the circumstances of his current crisis to overtake him.
2. Saul commits himself to partial obedience.
3. When Samuel confronts Saul with this infraction, he fails to accept responsibility. He continues the kind of recrimination we have come to expect (and use ourselves!) since the garden of Eden.

1 SAMUEL 13:23–14:52

Original Meaning

Jonathan Attacks the Outpost at Mikmash (13:23–14:15). The unit opens with the account of Jonathan's daring raid on the Philistine detachment at Mikmash. Against all odds, he and his armor-bearer attack an outpost of Philistines. Jonathan is unimpressed by the enemy's greater numbers and undeterred in his belief that Yahweh will deliver Israel from this dreaded enemy. His words to the armor-bearer reveal his character and commitment (14:6).

In fact, the Lord honors Jonathan's brave leadership. In this opening sortie, these two men alone kill around twenty Philistines in a small area (14:14). By implication the paragraph is showing what kind of king Jonathan would have been as his father's successor. But alas, the text has already informed us that Jonathan will not be king because of Saul's unfaithfulness (13:13–14).

While Jonathan and his armor-bearer are on their secret mission, Saul is in Gibeah administering his kingdom. The passing reference to Ahijah in 14:3 is important for our reading of this unit. What is remarkable here is Ahijah's carefully phrased genealogy. The narrator has detoured from direct descent in the line of Aaron in order to highlight meticulously an uncle, Ichabod, thus recalling the checkered history of Eli, Phinehas, and Shiloh. The reference in 14:3 to the rejected priestly house thus stresses the rejection of Saul's royal house. Moreover, it reveals something of the inner life of Saul, who has apparently lost the prophet Samuel as his spiritual advisor.

Saul and the Israelites Rout the Philistines (14:16–23). This paragraph continues the contrast between Saul and Jonathan by illustrating how Jonathan is a leader who takes action, while Saul simply responds. When Saul sees what is happening, he calls for Ahijah to bring the ephod, apparently in order to ask Yahweh whether he should join the battle with the Philistines or not. But inexplicably, Saul suddenly stops the inquiry and rushes to the battlefield (14:19–20). Such sudden reversals expose Saul's uncertainty and remind the reader of his previous failure to wait for Samuel's arrival in order to offer sacrifice. The battle appears to have been nearly won before Saul even arrives on the scene (14:20).

Saul's Foolish Ban against Eating (14:24–46). Saul's impetuous, even careless, actions continue. Saul places an unnecessary and unreasonable burden on his troops by disallowing them to eat food during the day of battle. He may have been motivated by a desire to create a "holy war" setting, which is reasonable in this context. But however commendable his reasons for such a ban, the result is that his men are famished and exhausted.

This paragraph's unusual events illustrate again the contrast between Jonathan and Saul. Jonathan, unaware of his father's foolish ban, does not hesitate to refresh himself with honey. His "brightened" condition (14:27, 29) proves that he has better understood God's will for the troops than his father. He quickly condemns Saul's ban and accuses him of making trouble for Israel (14:29). Later, when Saul seeks divine guidance concerning a surprise night attack, there is no response from Yahweh. This divine silence is tantamount to divine displeasure, and Saul begins an investigation to find the guilty party. When Jonathan proves to be the guilty party, Saul is faced with revolt in his own army.

Saul has gradually alienated himself first from Samuel, then from his army with the foolish ban against eating, and now finally from his own son (14:39). The result is a lost opportunity. The day that began with prospects of a final and decisive victory over the Philistines ends in a draw (14:46).

Summary of Saul's Reign (14:47–52). These brief notices about Saul's reign are typical of the Deuteronomistic Historian, who also provides royal summaries for David and commonly in the books of 1–2 Kings. It has been suggested that Saul's summary is more notable for what it does *not* say than for what it does say. Unlike David's summary, for example, there is no mention of Yahweh. Especially important is the concluding verse (14:52). The Philistine threat was Saul's reason for serving Israel as king (9:16). But the final subjugation of Philistia will have to await a greater king.

Application. Once he stops listening to Samuel and the prophetic voice withdraws from Saul, the "destructive darkness" of his life begins to become more apparent, and his course is set. Christians are not supposed to navigate their own course. We must recognize that we are incapable of finding within our own beings the measure by which we must rule our lives. Just as Saul needed Samuel to direct and guide him, so we need God to shine his light on our paths (Ps 119:105). As Saul was condemned once he turned from Samuel to find guidance in other sources, so modern believers must be warned against neglecting or abandoning God as the source of truth and light.

1 SAMUEL 15:1–35

Original Meaning

Saul's Victory over the Amalekites (15:1–9). The Amalekites were the first people to oppose the Israelites after the exodus (Exod 17:8–16) and are portrayed as terrorists who preyed on weaker opponents, showing no regard for God (Deut 25:17–18). Because of their cowardly tactics on an unsuspecting nation, Yahweh promised to extract vengeance against them in some future day when Israel was established in the promised land (Exod 17:14; cf. Deut 25:19).

Samuel returns to announce that now is the time to accomplish Yahweh's vengeance against Amalek (15:2–3), and Saul is the king to do this. The ambiguity of the text toward Saul is still apparent. He has lost all hope for an enduring dynasty—but he is still God's anointed one. Yahweh still has an important mission for him, and even now his destiny is uncertain. Who knows, good conduct might yield a divine change of mind.

Samuel's instructions for warfare are clear (15:3). The description given is familiar to us as what has become known as "holy war," though this terminology is not used in the Old Testament itself. In such wars, Yahweh himself initiates the conflict and ensures its success. Samuel's words in 15:3 are an important part of this "holy war" tradition. The term "totally destroy" occurs eight times in this chapter and is an important concept in understanding why Saul is rejected. The word denotes a special act of consecration to God. This paragraph ends on a note that Saul and his army are *selectively* obedient to Yahweh's instructions.

Samuel Confronts and Condemns Saul (15:10–31). Yahweh informs Samuel that he regrets making Saul king (15:11). This precipitates an encounter between Samuel and Saul, in which Saul first tries to deflect the blame, then tries to justify it, and finally tries to minimize its seriousness. All in all, we would say Saul fails to take responsibility for his actions.

When they first meet, Saul greets Samuel (15:13). Apparently, he is oblivious to the extent of his crimes. He has replaced Samuel as his spiritual adviser (ch. 14), and now he has failed to fulfill the mission as defined by Yahweh. Samuel's blunt questions shatter the delusional world in which Saul is living (15:14). Saul has rationalized his sparing of Agag and the best of the cattle as a delay. In Saul's mind, this is only a temporary postponement in fulfilling Yahweh's command. But Samuel's booming "What then is this bleating of sheep?" (15:14) breaks into Saul's world and reveals his deception for what it truly is—a selfish rejection of God's message.

Samuel has arrived on the scene merely to point out the obvious. The series of statements made by the king in his defense before Samuel in this passage reveals a pitiable soul who is sorry only that he has been caught. His instincts are to defend himself against his prophet accuser.

First, Saul tries deflection, hoping to divert the blame onto the soldiers (15:15). It is, after all, really the troops who have spared the best of the cattle, not strictly speaking Saul himself. Such recrimination is as old as the garden of Eden. But Saul is no more successful at averting guilt than Adam and Eve. Samuel reminds the king that it is Yahweh's command that made him king and that it is also Yahweh's command that he has now rejected (15:17–19).

Once deflection of blame fails, Saul's second strategy is argumentation (15:20–21). In his defense, the central issue in his argumentation is a redefinition of Yahweh's command. In one breath, Saul argues that he did in fact execute the terms of holy war (i.e., complete annihilation of the enemy) *and* brought back Agag the king! But this is a self-condemning contradiction. This too is a common strategy for escaping condemnation. In the face of exposed disobedience, many have attempted to redefine what it actually means to obey.

Samuel's response is unequivocal (15:22–23). Yahweh desires obedience over everything else. Even sacrifice is unacceptable if it becomes only a ruse for real submission to God's will. Samuel announces the judgment of Yahweh, which is strictly commensurate with the nature of Saul's sin (15:23). Now Saul has lost not only his dynasty (as in ch. 13) but his right to serve as king.

After hearing the irrefutable statement of rejection, Saul changes his strategy again and for the first time we hear something like a confession. This strategy might be called self-serving confession (15:24–25). Technically, he uses the right words. But this is followed by many more words revealing the compulsory and obligatory nature of that confession, contrived and motivated by self-interest. It is disingenuous, and Samuel responds by reaffirming Yahweh's rejection of Saul as king (15:26–29).

The unit concludes with a climactic "I have sinned," in which Saul acknowledges his guilt a second time (15:30). The repetition of Saul's confession (15:24–25, 30) is common in Old Testament narrative as a technique for emphasis. The differences in the second occurrence often reveal the main theme of the narrative.

In this text, the second confession serves a climactic role near the end of a unit and reveals the spirit of Saul's ploy. He has replaced "forgive my sin" with "honor me before the elders" (cf. 15:25 and 15:30). Saul seems more concerned with *his* people than with *Samuel's* God.

Samuel and Saul Part Company (15:32–35). In the closing scene, Samuel executes the Amalekite king. The job unfinished by the king is now left for the prophet himself, who gave the original order (see 15:3). The public execution of Agag is itself an implicit rebuke of Saul, who allowed him to live in the first place.

Finally, there are words of sorrow. Samuel mourns for Saul, and Yahweh is grieved that he made Saul king. Everyone seems full of sorrow and regret—except Saul. The text ends by implicitly emphasizing that Saul is unrepentant, showing no true remorse or contrition.

Application. This text illustrates how we only make our situation worse by failing to learn the true nature of worship and confession. Church attendance and tithing are worthless unless they come from the heart, just as the Old Testament sacrifices made Yahweh nauseous unless they were genuine. It is possible simply to go through the motions while neglecting the internal realities of our tortured souls. Samuel reminds us with his word to Saul that obedience is better than sacrifice. If we miss the reality of internal worship and confession, no amount of attention to externals, such as church attendance or involvement in Christian causes, will atone for disobeying God's Word.

1 SAMUEL 16:1–13

Original Meaning

Samuel Goes to Bethlehem to Anoint a New King (16:1–5). Yahweh commands his prophet to move forward regardless of his sense of personal loss (16:1). Jesse is the grandson of Ruth and Boaz (Ruth 4:17–22) and comes from the tribe of Judah (Ruth 4:12). From this time forward, the name of Jesse, the city of Bethlehem, and the tribe of Judah will always be linked to Israel's messiah. The last phrase of 1 Samuel 16:1 contains a subtle but powerful statement about David, though the NIV's rendering obscures its significance. A better translation is: "I have provided *for myself* a king from among his sons" (author's translation). This suggests a contrast with the circumstances surrounding Saul's selection, when Yahweh made a concession for the sake of the people (8:22).

Samuel is evidently aware of Saul's hostile intent toward him because he fears for his life if it were known that he has anointed David (16:2). But Yahweh assures Samuel that he will make known to the prophet what he should do. He consecrates Jesse and his sons and invites them (and presumably the elders of Bethlehem) to the sacrifice.

Samuel Anoints David (16:6–13). When Samuel meets Jesse's sons, he assumes the firstborn, so striking in appearance, is Yahweh's choice as king (16:6). Yahweh immediately tells Samuel that this young man is not to become king and that Samuel should not be unduly influenced by external features, such as Eliab's handsome appearance. This is followed in 16:7 by a particularly memorable saying contrasting human abilities with God's ability. People and God do not perceive reality in the same way. In order to anoint the right son of Jesse, Samuel will have to overcome his human reliance on his own ability to see.

The other sons of Jesse parade before the great prophet, but none is the "chosen" one (16:8–10). No one feels it necessary to include the youngest son of Jesse. He is apparently so unlikely a candidate it hardly seems necessary to summon him from his work following the sheep (16:11). Once he is summoned, however, Yahweh quickly confirms his choice (16:12). Samuel immediately obeys and anoints David in this private setting. As in the case of Saul, anointing for kingship is accompanied by the arrival of the spirit of Yahweh, empowering the king-designate for service.

Application. This text is especially concerned with the kind of person God seeks. When you and I consider the qualities of the people around us, we are inevitably influenced by what we see with our eyes. But God has used the uneducated, the poor, the disenfranchised. The fact is that you and I simply cannot see the human heart the way God does; thus, we may often be surprised by what God sees in others.

1 SAMUEL 16:14–23

Original Meaning

Saul Needs a Harpist (16:14–18). Just as the arrival of the spirit of Yahweh marked David as someone destined and supremely fitted to *become* king of Israel (16:13), so the departure of the Spirit from Saul marks him as destined not to *remain* king. The narrative explains further that the departure of God's spirit is followed by the presence of "an evil spirit from the LORD" (16:14), which overwhelms and terrifies Saul. The spirit of Yahweh comes to bestow strength and power for service, while the evil spirit *from* Yahweh torments. The ruinous spirit comes from Yahweh because of Saul's persistent and unrepentant stance, and it is the source of his problems, plaguing him throughout the rest of the narrative.

Saul's courtiers believe music is the answer. They offer to find an appropriate harpist to soothe the ailing Saul whenever his fits occur. David has now become well known, at least to this unnamed courtier. He uses several important descriptors for David. The most ironic and telling, however, is the last: "The LORD is with him" (16:18). A contrast is established between Saul and David: Yahweh is with David and has departed from Saul.

David Enters Saul's Service (16:19–23). This little paragraph introduces three themes that will recur in chapters 17–31: Saul is in decline, David prospers because "the LORD is with him," and Saul is deeply attached to David.

Application. As Christians, we are committed to the *idea* that God is at work in our lives—directing, guiding, and in some instances, cajoling. But we are not often *consciously aware* of the specifics of his involvement. First Samuel 16:14–23 does not provide any of this detail about the inner thought processes of David. It is not written to expose his emotions and doubts concerning his arrival at the royal court. Little does David realize it is through his musical talents that he will eventually gain access to the court and that Samuel's anointing oil designates something quite specific in God's will for David. All this will happen sooner rather than later in David's life. But he has to walk through circumstances somewhat in the dark. He is left simply to do his best without having the big picture. So it often is with modern believers.

1 SAMUEL 17:1–58

Original Meaning

Battle Lines at the Valley of Elah (17:1–3). The battleground between Socoh and Azekah places this event in the western foothills of Judah. The Valley of Elah (Valley of the Terebinth) separates the opposing armies, presumably with the Philistine troops on the southern slopes of the valley and the Israelite forces on the northern slopes.

Description of Goliath and His Challenge (17:4–11). Peculiar to this Israelite-Philistine battle is the appearance of a single infantryman who challenges Israel to match him in representative combat. In this way the issue of the war between the two nations might be settled in single combat (17:8). Man-to-man combat as a substitute for full-fledged battle between opposing armies was possible in the ancient world as a means of settling disputes without recourse to extensive bloodshed. But in most of these examples, representative individual combat seldom succeeded as a means of limiting warfare. As in our text, the warring parties often continued with the battle after the contest between the designated representatives was over (17:52–54).

Goliath is not designated a "giant," as we might imagine from children's stories like "Jack and the Beanstalk." Rather, he is portrayed as an exceedingly tall warrior whose very height strikes terror in the hearts of his potential foes. The NIV's note "about 9 feet 9 inches or about 3 meters" (17:4) represents the Hebrew text. The narrative's description of Goliath's impressive stature reminds the reader of another impressive leader (10:23). In other words, Saul is the best match for Goliath. Indeed, there is an implicit condemnation of Saul in Goliath's description, since King Saul would be expected not only to motivate his troops but to lead them forth against the Philistines. But on hearing Goliath's words, "Saul and all the Israelites" are paralyzed with fear (17:11).

Description of David (17:12–16). Goliath is enormous, protected by impressive armor, armed with potent weapons, and accompanied by his own shield bearer for added protection. He must have looked overpowering, even invincible. By contrast, David can hardly look more vulnerable and insignificant.

The text further characterizes David by contrasting him with everyone else in the story. His oldest brothers are in Saul's military, stationed at the camp of the Israelites. Goliath is in the habit of taking his defiant stand morning and evening for forty days. The descriptions of David and Goliath in 17:4–16 subtly differentiate the powerful and defiant enemies of God in the world against the unassuming innocence of God's faithful shepherd boy from Bethlehem.

David Arrives at the Valley of Elah (17:17–30). David has been given the menial task of carrying provisions to the commander of his brothers' unit. But one day, when David delivers the rations, he arrives just as the army is going forth to battle, and he personally witnesses Goliath's defiant challenge. In his subsequent conversations with the troops, David learns that there will be a substantial reward for the Israelite soldier powerful and brave enough to defeat the terrifying Philistine champion. His oldest brother, Eliab, rebukes David because he believes his kid brother is conceited and has come to the front lines only to criticize their lack of initiative in answering Goliath's challenge. But David has matured enough to speak for himself, and he ignores his brother's disapproval.

The central question of the paragraph is David's in 17:26. The Israelite troops see a terrifying and seemingly invincible warrior who brings reproach on all Israel. But David sees only an uncircumcised Philistine who worships deities that are not even alive. This worshiper of dead idols has the audacity to reproach the armies of the living God. Thus, the soldiers' words of resignation are contrasted with David's words of indignation. David has learned to see things others cannot see.

David Volunteers and Prepares to Meet Goliath (17:31–40). David's conversations with the troops contain an implicit offer to fight Goliath. Saul is at least willing to entertain the possibility. But when they meet and David volunteers to fight Goliath, Saul cannot accept the idea that this inexperienced youth could go up against Goliath.

David's explanation of how he might be able to prevail against the Philistine also reveals his profound faith in Yahweh. Since the Hebrew word translated "paw" in 17:37 is the same for "hand," David is relating the hand/power of the Philistine with that of the lion or bear. Just as Yahweh delivered from the hand of the lion and bear, so he will deliver from the hand of Goliath. In young David's mind, all the enemies of God are reduced to the same level; they are nothing but dumb beasts. David has moved from reciting his own bravery and skill (17:34–36) to acknowledging that Yahweh is the source of deliverance (17:37).

It is possible that Saul's offer for David to use his royal armor is a calculated effort to bind the two together in a way that will make it possible for Saul to take credit for David's victory, should he actually succeed in defeating the Philistine champion. In any event, Saul appears all too willing to loan his fighting gear to someone else, since he is not prepared to use it himself, especially against Goliath.

David Kills Goliath (17:41–51). After getting a good look at this young Israelite challenger, Goliath is incredulous. Despising David's shepherd staff as a "stick" (17:43), he curses David in the name of the Philistine gods and threatens to expose his corpse to the wild animals.

In a beautiful speech that dramatizes the conflict between Israel and the enemy nations around her, David emphasizes that Goliath is trusting in his own superior military resources. In contrast, David repeats his theme by promising that everyone present, both Israelite and Philistine, will learn that Yahweh's salvation is not by means of sword or spear, because the battle already belongs to the Lord (17:47). The narrator returns to this theme to stress its centrality (17:50).

No doubt, this young shepherd boy is unlike any other

warrior Goliath has ever seen. But superior strength and military resources are useless against the representative of Yahweh. The contest is over before it begins. David kills Goliath with one of his choice stones. Since he does the job without a sword in his hand, Yahweh has been true to his word: He saved "not by sword or spear" (17:47).

Israel Routs the Philistines (17:52–54). The location of the account is a deliberate narrative technique in the book's structure. After Saul's anointing, the narrator recorded the new king's military victory over the Ammonites (10:1–2; 11:1–11). So here, the text moves from David's anointing to this victory over Goliath and the Philistine nation generally (16:13 and ch. 17). It seems important to illustrate in each case that Yahweh's chosen is qualified to lead Israel victoriously into battle.

Saul Determines David's Identity (17:55–58). In perplexing fashion, the narrative presents a Saul who does not seem to be aware of David's identity, which is difficult to square with his great love and appreciation for David in 16:21–22. Some have speculated that Saul's unstable mental condition has resulted in a loss of memory (see 16:14), or perhaps Saul wants to know more about David's parentage because he had promised to give his daughter in marriage to the one who killed Goliath (17:25). However, it is possible to interpret chapter 16 as Saul's initial pleasure with David as a court musician, while here he is interested in David as a warrior.

Application. Christians should not be surprised when they encounter opposition to what God has called them to do. The Bible teaches in a variety of ways that there will often be challenges to God's sovereign rule in the world. Church history presents many examples of Christians who failed to interact redemptively with hostile surrounding cultures. For example, the Christian community in Germany failed to reject radical nationalism and to oppose vigorously the growth of Nazism in the early twentieth century. The church essentially failed to function as a transforming element of the culture. The way in which today's Christians in North America respond to postmodernism and the growing possibility of anti-Christian sentiment may pose a discomfiting parallel.

1 SAMUEL 18:1–30

Original Meaning

Jonathan's Covenant with David (18:1–4). The specific Hebrew verb for "love" used here has important political overtones (18:1). So, for example, Saul loved David in 16:21, and Hiram king of Tyre loved David in 1 Kings 5:1. Indeed, the relationship between David and Jonathan is a classic example of a covenant between individuals, and the language used to characterize that relationship is typical of ancient kinship and mutual kinship obligation. The political overtones of Jonathan's love for David are marked by their "covenant" (18:3) and by Jonathan's extravagant gifts (18:4).

It is also possible that the specific idiom for "became one in spirit" (18:1) has a similar kind of double meaning, referring again to the political nature of their relationship. David's and Jonathan's immediate bonding and personal friendship apparently leads the crown prince to renounce his throne, and the gifts of 18:4 are symbolic of his commitment to defer to David's right to be king.

Saul First Becomes Jealous of David (18:5–9). This section emphasizes Saul's anger and jealousy of David. The historian carefully sets up a screen around David's intimate responses to other characters and to events as they unfold by withholding from the reader David's thoughts or feelings. We learn what kind of person he is by his speeches, by his impressive military exploits, and by what other characters feel about him. But the narrator never makes statements about *David's* feelings or reveals his inner thoughts.

By contrast, the narrator exposes in this chapter the feelings and emotions of everyone around David. Jonathan is entirely motivated by love and devotion for David. The general populace are motivated by admiration for David (the military officers are pleased when he is promoted, and the women celebrate his victories). Saul is motivated by fear, anger, and jealousy. Michal, like Jonathan, is motivated by her love for David (18:20). All of these emotions are stated flatly by the narrator. But David's inner life is revealed more opaquely and is held in suspense throughout most of the narratives. This technique focuses our attention squarely on David as the central figure, as everyone around him seems likewise focused.

Saul Attempts to Kill David (18:10–16). Saul obviously has deep psychological problems. This chapter contains the first of several references to his fits of jealousy over David's popularity, and Saul is afraid. But as always in biblical narrative, the historian is more interested in the theological causes than historical details.

The omniscient narrator knows who loves whom (Jonathan and Michal love David) and who is jealous of whom (Saul is jealous of David). More impressively, the writer knows that an injurious spirit from God comes upon Saul, that Yahweh is with David, and that Yahweh has abandoned Saul. The theme of the paragraph is repeated twice: Yahweh is with David, and Saul is afraid of David (18:12, 14–15; cf. 18:28–29). These statements form the theological centerpiece of the chapter and give the narrator's underlying foundations for what is happening historically in the family of Saul and in Saul himself. In this paragraph, what begins as anger and jealousy (18:8–9) moves to murderous and irrational fear.

The text is also clear about the causal connection between Saul's fear and David's successes. Yahweh is with David in order to make successful everything he attempts, and therefore Saul is afraid (18:12, 14–15). The irony that plays out in the subsequent narrative is that David will not himself raise a hand against Yahweh's anointed, Saul.

Saul's Daughters, Merab and Michal (18:17–30). The rest of the chapter relates Saul's attempts to rid himself of David. First, he offers in marriage his oldest daughter to David, which is the expected reward for the warrior who defeated Goliath. But this offer is a ruse, because in exchange for Merab, Saul also seeks David's commitment to continue the military struggle against the Philistines. Saul's motive is revealed in 18:17, but Saul changes his mind and gives Merab to another man.

When Saul learns of Michal's love for David, he sees it as another opportunity to ensnare the young rival (18:21). This time using more diplomacy, he persuades David to earn the right to Michal's hand by acquiring "a hundred Philistine foreskins" as a bride-price (18:25). Saul hopes such a requirement will actually cost David his life. The irony of the text is clear in the repetition of the expression "he was pleased" in 18:20 and 18:26. Saul is pleased because he sees Michal's love for David as another opportunity for entrapment of David, but David is pleased because he sees it as an opportunity to become the king's son-in-law. This ironic twist illustrates the nature of Saul's relationship with David.

Application. Even when an enemy of God, motivated by anger, jealousy, or hatred, attempts to intervene forcibly against the progress of what God is accomplishing, that very intervention itself can be used by God to further his purposes. This principle has been illustrated in American history in the second half of the twentieth century in the civil rights movement, thanks largely to the use of Christian principles in the civil disobedience of the movement's leadership.

Christians are called to refuse retaliation and to live in such a way as not only to *overcome* but *transform* the oppressors. Though Saul had set his course and would not allow himself to be deterred, David was faithful to what God placed before him, and God was "with" David. As Christians, we must bear testimony to God's grace in our lives in good times and in bad, and we must remember that a loving response to opposition can transform our enemies and transform ourselves as well.

1 SAMUEL 19:1–17

Original Meaning

Jonathan Attempts Reconciliation (19:1–7). The opening verse of the text states laconically that Saul now resolves to draw others into his conspiracy against David. Because of his friendship and commitment to David, Jonathan arranges to serve as an intermediary in order to accomplish a reconciliation with his father.

Jonathan has carefully planned what he will say. In persuasive fashion, he makes his case before Saul, with David waiting in the wings. He argues that David is in fact innocent of any wrongdoing. Jonathan's logic and eloquence win the day, and his father and friend are reconciled. But the peaceable relations are short-lived.

Saul's Second Attempt on David's Life (19:8–10). More military glory for David results again in more problems with Saul. As before, his victories ignite jealousy in Saul, which leads to yet another spontaneous and unexpected attempt on David's life.

Michal Helps David Escape (19:11–17). Michal's ruse shows just how morbid and insane Saul's preoccupation with David is. She anticipates the soldiers may search the house and so places an "idol" (19:13) in David's bed with appropriate disguise. The precise nature of such an idol in the Old Testament is much disputed, and it is apparently only here that one appears large enough to pass for a human under bed coverings.

The ruse works, giving David time to escape. But when Saul realizes what Michal has done, he becomes angry with her. In order to calm the unpredictable Saul, she deceives him, now for a second time. Michal appears to have no hesitation about the deceptions, and the narrator relates the events in an apparently approving tone.

Application. Saul was obsessed with killing David, so that Jonathan and Michal were justified in their actions. We should be careful here and not assume that in our context we have frequent situations in which it would be desirable to mislead or deceive another person. Such extreme steps are required only when we are confronted with life-threatening choices.

1 SAMUEL 19:18–24

Original Meaning

Saul Sends Men to Capture David at Ramah (19:18–21). Having fled from Saul's wrath and having no place else to go, David returns to Samuel, whose center for operations is at Ramah. Though we have not heard anything from Samuel since David's anointing, he is evidently active as the leader of a band of prophets at Ramah. The irony of David's presence in Ramah with Samuel should not escape us. Though the text of chapter 10 does not say so explicitly, it appears that this is also where Saul first received the promise of the spirit of God and where his heart was transformed (10:6, 9). Now, however, the tide has turned, and it is David who meets Samuel at Ramah.

Samuel takes David to "Naioth at Ramah" (19:18–19). The Hebrew word translated "Naioth" is probably not a proper noun (as in NIV) but rather a reference to "camps" or remote country dwelling places, which could become the residences of shepherds and could be associated with the dwelling place of God. When Saul's espionage sources tell him where David is, he sends three detachments to these camps at Ramah to capture David. But in all three instances, his envoys become enamored with the feverish worship, and they also prophesy in the spirit of God and are thereby distracted from their unworthy errand.

Saul Prophesies at Ramah (19:22–24). Finally, out of frustration and desperation, Saul goes himself to the camps at Ramah. But before he even reaches the group, the "spirit of God" comes, and he begins prophesying as the others before him. It is possible to interpret this "spirit of God" (19:23) as the same evil spirit *from* God that had plagued Saul (16:14; 18:10; 19:9). Others have suggested that only Saul lies before Samuel "all that day and night" (19:24) in this ecstatic state of external unconsciousness. In this reading, the text is condemning Saul irrevocably as someone who has resisted God's grace and opposed God's purposes with regard to David. The soldiers who prophesy under the Spirit's influence are not detained so long because they are mere emissaries on Saul's behalf. In any case, Saul's prophetic ecstasy before Samuel lasts an entire day, giving David plenty of time to escape.

The question closes the chapter, "Is Saul also among the prophets?" (19:24). Its earlier use in 10:11 implied a positive evaluation of Saul. But here, the question, which must have been used in earliest times to characterize Saul, can only imply a negative evaluation. The irony of the question challenges the genuineness of Saul's prophetic behavior and thus also his legitimacy as king of Israel.

Application. The presence of God's empowering Spirit is no *guarantee* of future blessing. Gifted persons and inspired leaders often begin to feel invincible. The evangelical church in the last quarter of the twentieth century saw several of its most visible leaders stumble or even completely lose their ministries. There is innate danger in the heresy that Spirit-led ministry is invincible, irrespective of continued faithfulness.

This, of course, has implications for all of us as individuals since we cannot live today on the spiritual blessings of our childhood or early adulthood. But the wider implications for the church are also obvious. No generation can afford to enjoy the spiritual benefits of their ancestors without giving any thought to their own responsibility in service and ministry. The church is always only one generation from extinction.

1 SAMUEL 20:1–42

Original Meaning

Jonathan and David Devise a Plan (20:1–23). Jonathan had earlier established a covenant with David and had essentially abdicated his right to succeed Saul as king of Israel (18:1–4). David therefore feels he can trust Jonathan to act surreptitiously in order to learn the true disposition of the king and to help determine what he should do next. They agree on the ruse at the next day's New Moon festival as a test case for Saul's true intentions.

The elaborate speeches of Jonathan contain more than a simple plan to determine Saul's intentions toward David. Acknowledging that David will certainly one day be king, Jonathan confirms his covenant commitment to David and desires to protect his own children when David in fact becomes king. He also speaks frankly and prophetically about David's future international rule, which is a new theme in the books of Samuel. These speeches legitimize David's rule as the rightful successor to the throne of Israel and underscore the future relationship between the house of Saul and the house of David.

Saul's New Moon Festival (20:24–34). At first glance, David's absence at Saul's table seems like no more than a simple gaffe in social etiquette, though it could also represent a preference for David's ancestral line over the rightful place of Saul's royal lineage. Such an explanation may indicate that David's absence betrays his own royal aspirations, or so Saul may have assumed.

Whatever the implications, the reader is hardly prepared for the violent reaction of Saul in 20:30. After hearing the full explanation for David's absence (20:28–29), Saul erupts into a full-fledged tirade in which he insults Jonathan personally. Some of the modern translations concur with the NIV's "You son of a perverse and rebellious woman!" as an English euphemism for a more graphic insult intended by the original (as in NLT's "You stupid son of a whore!" and NJB's "Son of a rebellious slut!").

Saul's shocking outburst reveals a new element in his obsession with David and helps explain why Jonathan and David finally realize they must abandon all hopes of reconciliation with Saul. In 20:31, Saul's suspicion of David becomes a conviction that David's rapid rise not only threatens Saul personally but also Jonathan and the hopes of a Saulide dynasty in Israel.

When Jonathan tries yet again to defend David's motives, Saul reaches for his spear to kill even Jonathan! Jonathan is sure of Saul's resolve to kill his friend. Sadly, the time has come for Jonathan and David to part company. Jonathan must remain with Saul; David cannot.

Jonathan and David Say Farewell (20:35–42). Jonathan meets his friend at the predetermined location and communicates the bad news by the agreed-upon ruse. After the youngster is sent away, the two bid farewell in an emotional scene. One might ask if it is safe to meet in such a fashion, why was it necessary to use the elaborate ruse in the first place? But David and Jonathan have no way of knowing in advance if they will be able to speak face to face, and the secretive way of communicating seems wise.

Once alone and aware that circumstances have worked against them, they are overcome with emotion. Characterized as it is by physical signs of respect, mutual devotion, and sorrow (bowing, embracing, and weeping), this text powerfully illustrates the depth and profundity of the relationship between Jonathan and David. In this tearful good-bye, it is Jonathan who recognizes their only recourse: "Go in peace" (20:42). This he follows with one last reminder that their oath of loyalty is witnessed by Yahweh himself, which Jonathan hopes will assure peaceable relations between his descendants and David's. This text, of course, creates a tension throughout the rest of 1 and 2 Samuel, resolved finally in David's relationship with Jonathan's son, Mephibosheth (2 Sam 9; 21:1–14). After this scene, David and Jonathan will only see each other on one other occasion (1 Sam 23:16–18).

Application. The message of fidelity in covenanted relationships speaks as powerfully today as it did in the biblical context. Especially compelling is the *permanency* of the commitment between David and Jonathan, which grew out of their covenant relationship rooted in love (20:17). The relevance of this discussion on faithfulness for contemporary culture in North America should be readily apparent and applicable on several levels. Our society today longs for models of such permanency or lasting commitment in relationships.

Generally, Christians today bemoan what is happening in our culture concerning the abandonment of children by parents, the crumbling of traditional marriages, and the broken and dishonorable way in which business is conducted in today's marketplace. Thus, the Bible opens up a whole different perspective into the potential of human relationships. Against much of modern pop culture, this text teaches that it is possible for humans to build relationships that are durable and employable in God's plan for the future.

1 SAMUEL 21:1–22:23

Original Meaning

David Flees to Ahimelech the Priest (21:1–9). You can learn a lot about a person by seeing where they turn in times of trouble. When David first found it necessary to run from Saul, he went to Samuel at Ramah. Now officially on the run, David is in immediate need of food, arms, and shelter. In desperation he goes to Ahimelech, the priest at Nob, where he receives "the bread of the Presence" (21:6) of Yahweh and the sword of Goliath, reminding him of his reliance on Yahweh at other times of conflict and crisis. He enthusiastically accepts Goliath's sword, which is unique in its ability to prompt images of strength and victory in Yahweh's cause.

Earlier he received the aid of the old prophet Samuel; now he gets the assistance of a priest of Yahweh in the old traditions of the tabernacle at Shiloh. The reminder of the military victories of his youth in the name of Yahweh (referred to twice here, 21:9, 11), together with his contacts with prophet and priest, helps David turn to the faith of his childhood. In his greatest hour of need, David is reminded that Yahweh has been his help in time of trouble.

David Flees to King Achish of Gath (21:10–15). Having benefited all he could and not wishing to endanger further the gracious priests at Nob, David needs to continue to distance himself from Saul. This paragraph narrates his failed attempt to join himself to the Philistines. Interestingly, the servants of Achish identify David as "king of the land" (20:11), which probably means they think of him as a local chieftain or ruler. At any rate, they must not have realized his real status as a refugee on the run from Saul.

David at Adullam and Mizpah (22:1–5). Being driven off by the Philistines, David now withdraws to Adullam, where he is met by family members and four hundred malcontents, who join forces with him in a loosely organized army. Those men who are drawn to David are unhappy with the way things are going for one reason or another. They are oppressed, in debt, or otherwise embittered by their circumstances. It is from this motley band of men that David begins to form a fiercely loyal inner circle of followers, which is to become a personal army. This group will grow into at least six hundred and become an important ingredient of the rest of his rule over Israel.

The Slaughter of the Priests of Nob (22:6–23). As the scene opens, Saul is surrounded with all the trappings of power: seated on a hill in the royal city, spear in hand, powerful officials all around (22:6). Yet the point of the narrative is that he is in fact powerless to do anything about David, no matter how outrageous and abhorrent his attempts. When Saul accuses his court officials of conspiring against him to conceal Jonathan's support of David, only Doeg the Edomite responds. This character was introduced in passing as "one of Saul's servants" in 21:7, where he happened to observe David's activities in Nob. Doeg, being an Edomite and having no compulsion about sparing David or the priests at Nob, sees this as an opportunity to turn his good fortune into political advantage. He informs Saul about Ahimelech's aid for David, and Saul promptly condemns the priests to death, despite Ahimelech's denial of participation in a conspiracy. When the Israelite officials uniformly refuse to carry out Saul's death sentence, Doeg is conscripted to perform the ghastly service for Saul.

Only one member of the priestly family escapes, Abiathar. When he runs to David with the news, David takes full responsibility for the terrible consequences of his relationship with Ahimelech. However, the reader knows that which David can only surmise. The real causes for the disaster are Saul's irrational pursuit of David and the treachery of Doeg the Edomite.

Interpreters usually comment on Saul's slaughter of the priests of Nob as legally unjustified and morally outrageous, explicable only as the desperate actions of a madman. But recent investigations of legal and cultural conventions from the ancient Near East challenge this interpretation, making it possible to see Saul's actions as based on conventional ancient practice, though still an act of desperation. Specifically, oracular priests and diviners were sometimes required to take oaths of loyalty to the king, committing themselves to serve in essence as informants if they learned of any rebellion in the land. By Ahimelech's own admission, he made oracular inquiry on David's behalf rather than Saul's and failed to inform Saul of David's activities, implicating himself and his fellow priests as coconspirators in rebellion. The result of such sedition was usually the death penalty. Thus, Saul's actions can be understood as a rational act, though still a desperate and evil attempt to maintain power by relying on human power structures.

David implores Abiathar to remain with him where he will be safe, so that David becomes the protector of the last surviving priest. As a result, king-elect and priest-elect join forces as fellow fugitives, and they forge a relationship that will last throughout David's reign.

Application. The overarching theme of the text is that God's word is certain and true. Certainly, our world needs to hear precisely this message. In previous decades many attacked the validity of the Bible and challenged the trustworthiness of God's word. In today's emerging postmodernism, we are faced with a different challenge. The postrationalistic nature of our emerging generation rejects the idea that truth is absolute and purely rational. Many today dethrone human intellect altogether and turn instead to other paths of truth besides reason, such as emotions and intuition. Though there are positive aspects of such a shift, it is still necessary to communicate this simple truth of the gospel: God will be faithful to his word. This message comes as comfort to the believer and cause for alarm for the unbeliever.

1 SAMUEL 23:1–29

Original Meaning

David Saves Keilah (23:1–6). The Philistine threat, which played a role in the rise of the monarchy itself, has receded into the background of the narrative tracing David's rise to power. Now these people are once again threatening the borders of central Judah. David's reliance on the Lord is accented here. He uses Abiathar the priest to discern Yahweh's will concerning whether he should go to Keilah or not. When his men balk because of Philistine superior strength in the area, David checks again in order to confirm the message from God.

The reference to Abiathar and the priestly ephod ties these events together with the previous episode and presumably means David's inquiries are answered by means of the sacred lots, the Urim and Thummim stored in the ephod. The specifics of how these worked is not clear, but they served as a form of divinely sanctioned lot-casting, which may have functioned something like our "heads or tails."

This important feature of David's relationship with God is central in the contrast between Saul and him. Yahweh has long since stopped answering Saul's inquiries, presumably because Saul has made up his mind before asking. By contrast, Ahimelech earlier inquired of Yahweh on David's behalf, which may be when David learned the value of such inquiries.

David Escapes Keilah (23:7–14). Saul should have rejoiced in the deliverance of Keilah from the Philistines. But his only thoughts are of how much easier it will be to trap David. David is still painfully aware of his role in the tragic deaths of the citizens of Nob, and he fears the same will happen now at Keilah, as his prayer reveals (23:10). It is a shocking fact that Saul is mustering his troops to capture *David* rather than to take advantage of the victory to pursue the Philistines further. The citizens of Keilah would be anxious to avoid the same fate as Nob, regardless of how grateful they may be to David. They would be compelled to surrender David to Saul. In order to avoid more innocent bloodshed, David and his men escape into the desert of Ziph.

As Saul's hostility against David intensifies, the narrator informs us that "God did not give David into his hands" (23:14). This reminder keeps before us the question of royal authority in Israel. Yahweh, the true king of Israel, is in charge, and ultimately his plan will be accomplished.

Jonathan Reassures David (23:15–18). As in other texts where Jonathan and David appear together, the crown prince acknowledges the future greatness of David, though this statement is the most explicit of all. Jonathan's intent is encouragement. David is no doubt encouraged by their long-standing friendship, but perhaps more by Jonathan's certainty and optimism about the future (23:17).

Saul Pursues David Farther South (23:19–29). Saul continues his pursuit of David with the help of the Ziphites. The same Yahweh who delivered the Philistines into David's hands now protects David from the hand of Saul. The irony here is again the role of the Philistines. Just as Saul is closing in on David and feels he has him trapped at long last, word comes of another Philistine raid, forcing Saul to abandon his pursuit of David. The hand of Yahweh is clearly behind these events, since he is free to use any means necessary to protect David, even the perennial threat of the Philistines.

The text also contributes to the extended narrative's emphasis on the contrast between Saul and David. Saul's pathetic reliance on rumors and reconnaissance missions is a reminder that Yahweh has ceased answering his pleas for help. Saul has long since stopped seeking messages from Yahweh, depending instead on his own political and strategic decision-making abilities. In his desperate obsession with killing David, he is completely dependent on his own wisdom and whatever information he can gather from informants—all of this while the king should have been concerned instead about the Philistines.

By contrast, David is himself inflicting losses on the Philistines and doing so with the help of Abiathar. This text presents us with two occasions when David consults the priestly ephod for guidance. This practice of consulting Yahweh becomes David's standard modus operandi throughout much of his reign. By contrast, Saul has executed the priests who could have helped him, and he seems incapable of hearing God's word.

Application. What are the primary methods by which God communicates today? Without denying a role for modern prophets or the *possibility* of audible voices or some other dramatic means of communication, we must begin by stating that God's *primary* means of communication today is through Scripture. Our identity as Christians means we are a people of the book—more specifically, sixty-six books divided into Old and New Testaments. In seeking the guidance of God, we should never separate the work of the Holy Spirit from the role of Scripture (Eph 6:17).

1 SAMUEL 24:1–22

Original Meaning

Chance Encounter in a Cave near En Gedi (24:1–7). Saul's desperate state of mind is illustrated by his willingness to deploy a significant military contingent to pursue David, even while the Philistine threat still looms in the shadows. Saul's purpose for entering the cave is clear (NIV "to relieve himself," 24:3). Seeking privacy and thinking he is alone, he has no idea David and his men are in the same cave. The assumption on the part of David's men that Yahweh has miraculously provided this opportunity to kill Saul is only natural; God has delivered Saul into David's "hands" (24:4).

David's cutting a corner of Saul's robe is probably more than a means of proving his goodwill toward Saul. It seems likely here that David's cutting of the hem of Saul's garment has enormous symbolic significance, denoting perhaps not only that Saul's hold on the kingdom is over but that David's has now begun. So, David takes a portion of Saul's garment rather than his life. Though it looks merciful at first sight, we learn immediately that David is conscience-stricken by his deed.

As we have seen in 1 Samuel, the anointed of Yahweh is endowed with Yahweh's Spirit, and the idea of striking such a one is repulsive to David. Even in the case of Saul, from whom the spirit of Yahweh has departed, David's act symbolizing the transfer of power is in a sense lifting the hand against Yahweh's anointed.

Saul Acknowledges David's Right to Rule (24:8–22). Saul has become an Ichabod figure, meaning the spirit of Yahweh has been withdrawn from him, while David grows in the strength and spirit of Yahweh in each narrative. David's long eloquent speech in 24:9–15 is juxtaposed with Saul's choked cry in 24:16–21. Saul's speech culminates in an admission that David is in the right and will in fact be king. Nothing legitimizes David's reign more than a confession on the lips of Saul himself that David is the legitimate anointed one (24:20).

David is respectful of Saul's position, both in terminology (24:8) and body language. He persuasively details his case. He is innocent regardless of the false rumors Saul has been receiving (24:9). He is loyal to King Saul, which is proven by the piece of robe in his hand. He pleads for divine intervention, asking that God may vindicate him before Saul (24:14–15).

In response, Saul can only evoke the awkward question reminiscent of their earlier close relationship (24:16). After acknowledging that David is in the right, Saul makes a profound confession (24:20). Here there is no recrimination as we have come to expect from Saul (cf. 15:10–31). He seems genuinely to understand that he will be placed aside in favor of David, but his admission is too late.

Having nothing else to say, Saul seeks to ensure that David will not exterminate his family once he replaces Saul as king of Israel (24:21). As the narrative progresses, there is a growing consensus that David will be king. First, Samuel (ch. 16), then Jonathan, and now Saul come to realize that David will become king and that a Saulide dynasty is impossible. The reader, too, gradually comes to accept the inevitability of David's reign and becomes convinced of his innocence and legitimacy.

Most of Saul's sons are eventually killed by the Philistines (31:2) and the Gibeonites (2 Sam 21:1–14). The historians responsible for the final books of Samuel want the reader to understand that David does keep his promises to Jonathan and Saul. Unlike most ancient monarchs, David shows a God-pleasing, compassionate magnanimity toward his enemies; in this sense, he is truly a man after God's own heart.

Application. The text's message of reverence and trust speaks volumes. Reverence for God is more than respect for the pastor and the church. If we want to mimic the attitude of David in this passage, it has to be more than focusing on the way we speak about God or avoiding certain explicatives with "God" in them. David in this text exemplifies a radical reverence for God that controlled his thoughts and actions. He refused to succumb to a bloody resolution to his problems, even while his trusted allies around him assured him it was "God's will" that he kill Saul. This is vital reverence resulting in obedience, even when it is unclear which action is the obedient action to take.

1 SAMUEL 25:1–44

Original Meaning

The Death of Samuel (25:1). It is not insignificant that the reference to Samuel's death follows immediately on the heels of Saul's confession in 24:20–21, which was a public announcement accepting Samuel's judgment on him. Saul has now come to see the truth of what Samuel predicted concerning him and his reign, though it is too late for Saul (chs. 13–15).

Nabal Rejects David's Request (25:2–13). Here we encounter for the first time Nabal, who is wealthy but boorish. His name in Hebrew means "foolish," which becomes an ironic part of the narrative (25:25). However, as rude and unsavory as Nabal is, his wife Abigail is "intelligent and beautiful" (25:3). Her name means "my father is joy(ous)," and her beauty is more than skin deep.

David's delegation asks for no more than payment for protection they have voluntarily rendered earlier. Indeed, ancient Near Eastern customs of hospitality and Old Testament laws suggest that Nabal, who is more than able to provide such modest provisions, is under obligation to aid David.

Nabal's response brings a swift reaction. David's command to each one to "strap on your sword!" (25:13) leaves no doubt about his intentions. Verse 13 contains the word "sword" three times in the Hebrew, revealing a dependence on armed force we have not seen in David before. David acts impetuously and violently, which does not bode well for his future as ruler over Israel.

Abigail Intercedes (25:14–35). Nabal's servants feel it useless to try to reason with him directly. Instead, one of them goes immediately to his remarkable wife, Abigail. She recognizes the seriousness of the situation at once and takes decisive action. Just as she and David approach each other, David is premeditating the vengeful action he is about to take (25:21–22). His intentions are clear and his mind is set.

Abigail's speech shows remarkable wisdom and skill (25:24–31). Abigail softens David first with her "gift" (25:27) and then addresses him as a superior (25:24). In a speech full of subtleties and polite innuendo, she flatters and cajoles in order to prevent David from bringing bloodguilt on himself. She recognizes that David will one day be king and seems more conscious than he that such bloodguilt would be unworthy of the anointed one of Yahweh. She fully expects the Lord to work out a better way, and she urges David to return good for evil, as he has consistently done to Saul. In 25:29, she makes passing reference to Saul, who still torments him even now in the different form of Nabal, and to Goliath, over whom David won a great victory with the Lord's help.

Abigail has made it nearly impossible for David to extract his revenge on this beautiful and gifted woman, who so humbly and persuasively intervenes on behalf of her master's servants and herself. More importantly, she has reminded David of who he is. David recognizes that Abigail has saved him from wrongdoing and that Yahweh himself is at work in these events to prevent the guilt of bloodshed (25:32–34).

Nabal Dies and Abigail Becomes David's Wife (25:36–44). As usual, God turns a negative into a positive. Not only does Nabal's death suddenly confirm David's actions, but it makes the way clear for this remarkable woman, Abigail, to become David's wife. Her wisdom and strong character make her a suitable partner for David, and she is in many respects his equal.

The political significance of his marriage should not be missed. David's exile from Saul's court means he has lost his power base in Gibeah, where he was hailed as a military hero. His marriages to Abigail and Ahinoam give him ties to the Hebron and Jezreel areas, perhaps giving him a new power base among the inhabitants of Judah. David's compliance and teachability are turned to good use in the movement toward a new kingdom, so that once again the Lord hammers out his will on the anvil of human circumstances.

Application. The issues we have discussed in the previous section have to do with discipleship. The nature of Christian discipleship involves "learning," since a disciple is, after all, a "learner" and the rabbi is a "teacher." This text serves as a reminder that disciples must be teachable; they receive the word of God and must act on it, adjusting their lives accordingly. David learns that patience and personal restraint are a better way, a God-pleasing way of acting as king. Thus, he quickly changes his mind.

All of us are on a journey to somewhere; all of us are in the process of becoming someone. Christian discipleship adopts a certain understanding of the nature of growth in grace. In one sense, growth does not really change the nature of the thing itself or, in this case, the essential nature of the person. An oak seedling simply cannot grow into a mature pine or maple tree, no matter how much growth occurs. So, a new believer, immature in faith at first, should grow naturally into a mature believer.

1 SAMUEL 26:1–25

Original Meaning

David in Saul's Camp (26:1–12). The Ziphites were Saul's informants once before concerning David's location. They were apparently spying out David's movements throughout their areas of southern Judah in order to gain the favor of King Saul.

Saul once again expends a significant corps of troops to chase David. But David learns that Saul has camped in a vulnerable location; he daringly enters the camp with Abishai. With the aid of a "deep sleep" from Yahweh, the two are able to slip into the midst of the camp and take Saul's spear and water jug (26:12). Saul was once before supernaturally hindered from finding David, when the spirit of God seized him and prevented him from apprehending David (19:23–24). Now Saul and his entire regiment are unaware of David's presence because of God-induced sleep. In both episodes, the text emphasizes Yahweh's personal and active involvement in David's rise to power.

When Abishai wants to take advantage of Saul's vulnerability, David's reaction is similar to that in the cave of En Gedi. There is significance in the variety of ways in which David suggests Saul might meet his end (26:10). The idea that Saul might die in battle anticipates chapter 31. But David has also learned his lesson from the Nabal episode (ch. 25), that the Lord might directly strike his adversary with untimely death.

David and Saul's Last Meeting (26:13–25). Having absconded with Saul's spear and water jug, David now confronts Saul with the irrationality and injustice of his vile pursuit. He begins by chastising Abner, the general of the army, for failing to protect adequately Yahweh's anointed (26:15–16). In the ensuing dialogue, David pleads his innocence and implores the king to consider how irrational is his obsession with capturing David. He argues that whether the source of his delusional actions is divine or human, there are other more reasonable means of handling them (26:19–20).

David again implies that the king's reckless pursuit is useless because he, David, is harmless (26:20; cf. 24:14). The reference to himself as "a partridge in the mountains" (26:20) seems obscure, but David uses an interesting wordplay on Abner's desperate question in 26:14. The Hebrew for partridge is literally "he who calls on the mountains," which is ironically appropriate for David who calls to Saul and Abner on a mountain (26:13–14).

Saul admits his guilt and makes more concessions than he has before (26:21). David ignores Saul's invitation to return to the royal court and his promises not to attack David again. It is simply too late. David merely returns Saul's spear and expresses his faith that God will honor his actions and deliver him from trouble (26:24). David concludes it is safer to rely on Yahweh for protection, even in exile in the desert, than to trust Saul and his unpredictable temperament.

Saul's parting words, "You will do great things and surely triumph" (26:25), are more prophetic than Saul could have known and certainly more than he intends. This is to be the last meeting between the two anointed ones. David "went on his way" with the blessing and protection of Yahweh. Saul "returned home," a king in name only (26:25).

Application. David will not always be exemplary as a paragon of faith, but at least in this text, he is convinced of God's guidance, even if he does not have immediate confirmation. This is also a natural part of Christian discipleship. As we grow and mature in our faith, we also become more confident about God's guidance, and we spend less time seeking constantly for evidence of his moving.

Unfortunately, in our modern context, the opposite development is taking place. As Christians become more comfortable in the conviction that God is at work in the details of life, the world around us has made less and less room for God. The premise that God exists and that he defines human moral responsibilities has been an underlying principle for two millennia of Western civilization. But in the closing decades of the twentieth century, Western cultures have been experimenting with the prospects of defining our responsibilities without the benefit of God. Modern humankind has learned to live without God.

1 SAMUEL 27:1–12

Original Meaning

David Flees to Gath and Receives Ziklag (27:1–7). This is David's most desperate hour. He realizes his only lasting means of escaping Saul's evil intentions is to go into exile in Philistia (27:1). He is being driven from Yahweh's presence and forced to live where pagan gods are served. As David once fled from Gibeah and the royal court (19:18–24), now he is forced to flee from the desert recesses of southern Judah.

We have encountered Achish before (21:10–15). His city, Gath, is one of the five principal cities of the Philistines, governed in a so-called pentapolis. It is not to David's advantage to settle actually *in* the city of Gath. As we will learn, David must operate somewhat independently of Achish's close observation. It is also possible that Achish is more than happy to consign David and his six hundred men and their families to a less conspicuous location, thereby free from the burden of feeding and caring for them. Ziklag appears to be ideal for David's purposes. In 27:6 the narrator gives a hint at the success with which David occupies Ziklag: "So on that day Achish gave him Ziklag, and it has belonged to the kings of Judah ever since."

David's Campaigns and His Deception of Achish (27:8–12). David's custom during the sixteen months he lives in Philistia (27:7) is to conduct raids against Judah's desert neighbors. While living in Philistia on the run from King Saul, he has actually become a defender of Judahite causes. At the same time, he is also able to endear himself to the Philistine king, leading him to think David is fighting Philistia's enemies. David has it both ways: the inhabitants of Judah and the Philistine king love him.

Achish believes David is raiding areas of southern Judah itself, when in reality he is assaulting enemies who are troublesome to Judah. The Philistine ruler naively believes David has burned his bridges, irreparably alienating himself from his own people. He accepts David's word and assumes the citizens of Israel must hate him so much by now that David will have no choice but to remain loyal to his new Philistine colleague (27:12).

Application. This text presents us with examples of David's taking decisive action that affect the role he will play in God's plans for the future. He bases his decisions on the logical and rational circumstances around him and appears to have simply trusted God to guide the process. Because we often lust for the tangible and the safety of the discernible, this type of trust is usually difficult for us.

1 SAMUEL 28:1–25

Original Meaning

Renewed War with the Philistines (28:1–2). David is now in an impossible situation. Achish joins his fellow Philistine overlords in mustering their forces against Israel's heartland, and it is time for David to "fish or cut bait." David's response seems carefully crafted to be noncommittal, though it satisfies Achish.

Circumstances of Saul's Final Humiliation (28:3–6). Saul had banished all "mediums and spiritists" from Israel (28:3). The narrator anticipates the witch's initial objections (28:9). Even Saul himself, at some point earlier in his reign—perhaps under the direction of Samuel—had forbidden the use of necromancy. But as we will soon see, driving the specific sin of necromancy from Saul's land did not drive the roots of that sin from his heart.

The battle lines are being drawn in the fateful Jezreel Valley, where armies often gathered for battle. The two armies are facing off for battle. Saul's position on Mount Gilboa places him strategically on a type of observation deck so he can observe the outcome.

The narrator prepares us further for what follows by exposing Saul's inner life. The statement that he "inquired of the Lord" (28:6) is significant in light of this phrase's other occurrences in 1 Samuel. The extended narrative has contrasted Saul and David by showing that David often "inquired of Yahweh." Saul *finally* "inquires" but receives no answer.

For Saul, it is too late. Yahweh has long since stopped answering Saul since the king is more inclined to make up his mind before asking. When his "foxhole" prayer brings no satisfaction, he becomes desperate to discern the plan of God. His next action represents the lowest point of his troubled reign as king over Israel.

Saul Consults the Medium at Endor (28:7–14). In a desperate move, Saul asks his attendants to help him locate a medium who can communicate with the dead. Against the wishes of the prophets and the leaders of normative religion in ancient Israel, some Israelites apparently persisted in the Canaanite custom of necromancy and other death rituals. In such rituals, actions were directed to the deceased in an attempt to appease the dead or to secure favors from them. This text, then, represents a vestige of the customs and religious practices of Canaanites and of some Israelites, despite the disapproval of normative Old Testament religion.

Saul's visit at night may have been a simple military necessity. But nighttime may also have been the approved time for such séances, the darkness of night being the appropriate time to communicate with those who live in darkness. The idea that Saul needs the medium to "bring up" (28:8) someone reflects the concept of Sheol as a place for the dead beneath the earth's surface, to which people descend at death.

Ironically, the medium is hesitant. He who wanted to eliminate necromancy from the land (28:3) has come to her with just such a request, and she who communicates with the dead is worried about joining them prematurely. Once Saul guarantees her safety, the medium is ready to hear the name of the departed individual whom Saul wishes to contact. Now we learn for the first time that it is Samuel.

At his appearance, the woman shrieks and immediately recognizes her client (28:12). At this point in the narrative, we are left with unanswered questions. Why precisely should the woman be shocked at the apparition if she were accustomed to such séances? Does Samuel's appearance differ significantly from other specters? Why does she suddenly discern Saul's identity?

Without becoming sidetracked with questions that are finally unanswerable, we can state that the essentials are clear. Samuel appears to Saul one last time and communicates with him through this medium. Saul himself is not able to see Samuel, at least not initially, since he has to ask the medium about Samuel's appearance (28:14).

Samuel's Answer and Its Result (28:15–25). Given an audience with his former mentor, Saul summarizes his situation succinctly and factually (28:15). Samuel's reply has no advice concerning the impending battle with the Philistines (28:16–19). The message of the deceased Samuel was the same as the living Samuel. He simply reiterates the divine judgment against the king announced when he was alive. Though there is no advice concerning the Philistines, there is this: "tomorrow you and your sons will be with me" (28:19). The time of Saul's judgment has arrived. The theme of Yahweh's rejection of the first anointed one, Saul, arrives at a climax in 28:20.

Application. It would be simplistic for us to limit the application of this text to blatant heretical practices such as the occult and magical incantations. Rather, we should also consider how easy it is to use good things in a magical way in an attempt to manipulate God. For example, consider the magical use of prayer, church attendance, and tithing among modern believers. Saul's reliance on a nonbiblical worldview needs to be applied to such cases in which perfunctory observance of the standard means of grace can come to represent the means by which we exact God's good favor. In other words, some believers come to expect good things from God, even believe that God *owes* them something, because they (we!) have fulfilled certain obligations. One's relationship with God can be quickly reduced to a sort of previously arranged agreement, a sort of quid pro quo, in which all we have to do is keep our end of the bargain and God will be forced to keep his.

1 SAMUEL 29:1–30:31

Original Meaning

David Is Rejected by the Philistine Rulers (29:1–11). As the Philistines muster for war, David and his men are organized as the rearguard. But the Philistine commanders object, quoting the famous Israelite ditty that memorialized David's great military victories. The generals are aware of the danger of mixed loyalties during the strain of combat, and they apparently have experience with Hebrew soldiers who easily switched from one army to another. They insist that Achish send David away.

David's questions in 29:8 feign shock and disappointment. Particularly his third question seems to contain an ironic ambiguity: "Why can't I go and fight against the enemies of my lord the king?" Achish would naturally assume that he himself is the king David refers to, but the reader must assume, in light of the context, that David is loyal only to Saul and the Israelite troops. For David, the real "enemies" *are* the Philistines, and "my lord the king" must refer to Saul. This question implies that if David were forced to join the battle, he would indeed turn on the Philistines.

Achish is truly enamored with David. He appears to be concerned that David might try to force himself on the generals and demand that he fight in the battle. So, he urges him to "get up early" (which always indicates determination to take action) and go back as soon as possible (29:10).

The irony of Achish's speech is impressive. David's worst-case scenario has developed, and he appears to have no means of avoiding the battle. Now ironically one of the Philistine rulers praises David's character and reluctantly *prohibits* him from staying. Achish thinks he is disappointing David by driving him away. The manner in which David is disencumbered from this trap leaves us breathless.

The Amalekite Raid of Ziklag (30:1–6). The importance of David and his rule over Israel is demonstrated in this fact: David is the instrument of Yahweh's vengeance against Amalek. In this episode David exacts vengeance because of the Amalekite raid of Ziklag. The Amalekites have once again acted ruthlessly, plundering David's adopted city and taking alive all the women and children of his men, including David's own two wives, Ahinoam and Abigail.

As if this were not enough, David's own men for the first time question his leadership (30:6). Their bitterness over losing their families is so severe that they now talk of stoning David.

This brings us to another crisis in David's life, which is narrated in such a way as to heighten the contrast between him and Saul. Like Saul in chapter 28, David is now surrounded with trouble. Saul was pressed all around by the Philistines with little hope of victory, while David is surrounded by his own grieving men and likewise appears to have no hope of retrieving their families. Both men are at their lowest ebb.

The contrast between Saul and David becomes most apparent in the closing phrase of 30:6: "But David found strength in the LORD his God." In Saul's greatest moment of crisis, he had tried to inquire of Yahweh but found that the Lord had abandoned him (28:6). By contrast, David strengthens himself in Yahweh at the moment of his greatest crisis. Even though God graciously makes faith possible, it is up to us to respond to his grace. Here David musters up his strength in his greatest moment of crisis.

David Avenges the Amalekite Raid (30:7–25). David calls for Abiathar to bring the priestly ephod containing the Urim and Thummim, the divinely sanctioned and approved means of seeking divine guidance. The particular terminology used in 30:7–8 refers to the practice of "inquiring" (literally, "asking") of Yahweh, that is, seeking his will in specific situations. The good priest Ahimelech had earlier inquired of Yahweh on David's behalf. David's rise to kingship is characterized by the importance he attached to seeking guidance from God.

The victory over the Amalekite marauders is narrated in such a way as to highlight an important feature of David's character. He identifies with people and understands their needs. First Samuel 30 highlights two such episodes.

1. David is generous and gracious in his treatment of an Egyptian who had been an Amalekite slave (30:11–15).
2. David intervenes in a dispute among his followers concerning the distribution of their plunder. He magnanimously decides to include those too exhausted to make the journey to the Amalekite encampment and opted to stay with the supplies. David thus establishes the principle of equality that lasts throughout his reign (30:24).

The reversal of David's losses at the hands of the Amalekites is a stunning victory. Through his faith in Yahweh and his resolve to avenge his losses and those of his men, he turns an impossible and hopeless situation into a great victory. While Saul is preparing for his final battle, which is doomed to failure, David is leading his meager forces in victory against one of Israel's greatest enemies. While Saul has proven himself ill-equipped and inadequate for leading God's people, David seems perfectly suited for the task.

David Supports the Cities of Judah (30:26–31). With this victory, David now takes the daring step of sharing the spoils with his "friends" in Judah. By giving them portions of "the plunder of the LORD's enemies" (30:26), David continued to endear himself to the citizens of Judah, whom he will soon rule as king. Presumably many of these "friends" are the same who will shortly anoint him king "over the house of Judah" at Hebron (2 Sam 2:4).

Application. Where do we turn for help in our time of need? As modern believers, we seek the face of God through the portals of his written word. Being convinced by the truth in his word, we must seek to act boldly on it, with confidence and hope.

We present-day believers must choose between paths that lead either to the medium of Endor or to Abiathar, son of Ahimelech! By the living of our everyday lives, we establish patterns of seeking advice and help, either from Endor or from Abiathar—that is, finding answers in naturalism (or postmodernism, or New Age gurus, etc.) or from the God of heaven and earth, who has revealed his truth in Scripture. These are really the only two options. In time, we will become like Saul, incapable of making right decisions, or we will become like David, who makes right decisions almost instinctively.

1 SAMUEL 31:1–13

Original Meaning

The Deaths of Saul and Jonathan (31:1–6). The description of Saul's death brings the contrast between David and Saul to a climax. Chapter 30 has just related David's great success against the Amalekites; he rescued Ziklag and saved the lives of everyone associated with him. By contrast, Saul and everyone associated with him die in this losing battle with the Philistines. Saul had been commissioned as king specifically to provide victory against the Philistines (9:16), which makes his death at their hands especially ironic.

The Philistines Desecrate Saul's Body (31:7–10). The result of the debacle at Mount Gilboa is devastating for Israel. The subsequent evacuation of the towns in the area leaves the Philistine military in control of Israelite territory. Saul's decapitated body is fastened "to the wall of Beth Shan" (31:10), a city that stands impressively over the junction of the Jezreel and Jordan valleys, guarding access to both. Saul's armor is placed in "the temple of the Ashtoreths" (31:10), which may refer to the goddess Astarte worshiped principally at Sidon but is more likely a derogatory reference to the unnamed principal goddess of Beth Shan.

Saul's worst fears of bodily desecration at the hands of the Philistines become a reality. Moreover, his defeat and death become occasions for proclamation of glad tidings in the temples of foreign idol gods, implying the victory of those gods over Yahweh in the minds of the Philistines. The national tragedy, painful though it is, serves merely as the backdrop for Saul's failure to vigorously defend and honor the name of Yahweh.

Citizens of Jabesh Gilead Bury Saul's Remains (31:11–13). Even in this dreary moment, the anointed of Yahweh cannot be left in such degrading circumstances. The residents of Jabesh Gilead never forgot how Saul rescued them from the Ammonites (ch. 11). Now they will repay his kindness with their loyalty. Their actions paid homage not to the king of Israel as fallen hero but to the king of Israel as the anointed one of Yahweh. This is no rejection of God's judgment on Saul but of the atrocities of the victorious Philistines in their jubilant celebration. Their kindness in return for Saul's kindness provides the king some dignity in his otherwise ignoble death.

Application. Death is not the end of our story. Contemporary believers should read 1 Samuel 31 in a way that leads to hope for the future. Just as ancient Israelite readers would have read this text in anticipation of the coronation of David and the rule of the ideal anointed one, so we know there is more to the story. The coming of David's greater Son has given us reason to hope that a new day will dawn in which death will no more claim its wretched price (1 Cor 15:54–57).

2 SAMUEL

INTRODUCTION TO 2 SAMUEL

While 1 Samuel details the transition from theocracy to monarchy, 2 Samuel narrates its growth. Second Samuel 1–20 describes the consolidation of the monarchy under David, while chapters 21–24 function as an epilogue to the books generally. See also the Introduction to 1 Samuel above (p. 225) for commentary on the authorship of 1–2 Samuel and Deuteronomistic History.

BOOK OUTLINE

I. The Continued Rise of David (Continued from 1 Samuel), Israel's Promised King (1:1–4:12)
II. The Reign of David, Israel's Greatest King (5:1–20:26)
  A. The Consolidation of His Rule (5:1–8:18)
  B. The Question of David's Heir (9:1–20:26)
III. Epilogue (21:1–24:25)
  A. Famine Due to Gibeonite Massacre (21:1–14)
  B. Notes on Wars Against Philistine Giants (21:15–22)
  C. David's Song of Thanksgiving (22:1–51)
  D. David's Last Words (23:1–7)
  E. Soldiers' Hall of Fame (23:8–39)
  F. David Conducts a Census (24:1–25)

2 SAMUEL 1:1–27

Original Meaning

The Report of Saul's Death (1:1–10). The account of the Amalekite messenger appears incongruous with the narrative given in 1 Samuel 31, as any cursory reading of the two chapters together will show. It seems logical that the historian has placed these two chapters together intentionally to portray the Amalekite as a liar. The reference to David's recent military campaign against and defeat of the Amalekites not only places this text in historical perspective but prepares us for the irony of what follows (1:1). David's return and the conclusion of the battle on Mount Gilboa are roughly contemporaneous.

The messenger is not identified as an Amalekite until his speech to David (1:8). His identity as an Amalekite would automatically raise suspicion among David's men and call into question his role in the events on Mount Gilboa. This messenger is not likely to arouse sympathy among those who have just rescued their families from the Amalekites.

How the royal insignia of crown and armlet come to be in David's possession is an important issue to clarify (1:10). Perhaps many in Israel suspect David has in fact killed Saul and Jonathan. By explaining the chronology, the narrator has made it clear that David is probably just returning from the Amalekite campaign while the debacle at Mount Gilboa is taking place. He simply could not have killed Saul and Jonathan because he could not have been in two places at once. More importantly, as the text will soon show, David could never have taken such actions against Saul because his loyalties have always been with Yahweh's anointed one and his son Jonathan.

David Mourns Saul and Kills the Amalekite Messenger (1:11–16). Some may have expected David and his men to rejoice at the death of Saul. But instead of rejoicing, David and his men show signs of catastrophic grief, and they are unanimous in their mourning and sorrow (1:11–12). Furthermore, his execution of the Amalekite messenger manifests the theological point, namely, David has the highest reverence for the sanctity of the Israelite king, the anointed one of Yahweh. David does not know the Amalekite is lying. It makes no difference; he has confessed to a terrible crime (1:16).

David's Lament for Saul and Jonathan (1:17–27). In one of the most emotional and moving scenes of the Bible, David's genuine pain comes through with singular clarity. In a series of vocatives, David addresses first the nation Israel, then the specific geographical location of the fateful battle (Mount Gilboa), and finally the "daughters of Israel" (1:19, 21, and 24). The theme of the dirge is clear from the phrase repeated three times (1:19, 25, and 27): "How the mighty have fallen!" This simple phrase (only three words in Hebrew) powerfully captures the depth of David's emotions and serves as a literary marker for the structure of the poem.

Application. Power itself is not inherently evil, but the way people use it often is. The Bible has much to teach us on this point. At this transitional chapter in the books of Samuel, it is appropriate to consider Saul's abuse of power as narrated in 1 Samuel, and this chapter serves to demonstrate the results. Conversely, David has served in 1 Samuel as an example of the right use of power, and he will continue to serve this way in the next few chapters. Unfortunately, however, David will not be so exemplary throughout all of 2 Samuel.

2 SAMUEL 2:1–7

Original Meaning

David Becomes King at Hebron (2:1–4a). Earlier, Samuel had anointed David (1 Sam 16:13). Now that David's predecessor Saul proved himself unworthy and is dead and properly buried, it is time for this private and prophetic anointing of David to be repeated in public. Now is the time for David to move into action and claim the promises of God.

But as so often happens, it is difficult to know when one should take action and when one should wait upon God's guidance. Fortunately for David, he does not have to rely on his own instincts and intuition, as valuable as they are. The expression "David inquired of the LORD" (2:1) tells it all. This dependence on Yahweh for guidance characterizes David and is partly what the text refers to when it describes him as the ideal king of Israel.

David's move to Judah is permanent; he has no intentions of returning to Philistia, as is evident by the reference to his entire company of people: the men with him, their families, and David's own two wives (2:2–3). With God's guidance revealed clearly through the Urim and Thummim, surrounded by his retinue of family and personal troops, David is finally ready to be anointed king by the inhabitants of Judah. Gathering at Hebron, they use the traditional Israelite custom of anointing as a means of formalizing the royal status of David (2:4). Prophetic anointing indicates divine approval. Here, however, anointing is by the people, which represents the public acceptance of David as king.

David's Proposal to Jabesh Gilead (2:4b–7). This paragraph is all about loyalty. There had been a special relationship between Saul and the citizens of Jabesh Gilead. David, realizing the need to have supporters in the north, offers himself as the logical and convenient successor to Saul. The loyalty of the people of Jabesh Gilead is a significant confirmation of David's right to rule the whole of Israel rather than Judah only.

When Saul needed their help, the citizens of Jabesh Gilead responded by jeopardizing their own lives to provide him a proper burial (2:5). Now both Yahweh and David will come to the city's aid (2:6), since presumably the rise of the Philistines and Saul's death will once again threaten Jabesh Gilead. David's proposal is that the good people of Jabesh Gilead should strengthen themselves for the decision to be loyal to David in the full knowledge that Saul is dead and buried and that he, David, has been made king in Judah. Their loyalty to Saul must now be transformed to David (2:7).

Application. Perhaps you have heard it said (or have said yourself): If only I could have the same kind of experience with God as Moses (or David, or X-biblical saint), then surely, I would be as faithful as they were. In reality, we have the advantage over these biblical saints because of where we stand in relation to God's redemptive acts in history and because we have in our possession the entire Bible.

2 SAMUEL 2:8–4:12

Original Meaning

Rival Monarchies (2:8–11). Events in the north quickly move against David, and his hopes for a peaceful transition of power over a unified Israel are not to be realized. For the first time, our historian tells us of "Ish-Bosheth son of Saul" (2:8). His name means "man of shame" and is probably a euphemistic substitution for Ish-Baal, "man of Baal" (referring to the Canaanite fertility god Baal). Abner we have met before as the commander of Saul's army. He was one of the most powerful men in Saul's kingdom, and this text is clear that Abner was the real power behind Ish-Bosheth's kingship. All hopes for a lasting Saulide dynasty in the north rested with this rugged military man. This is strikingly clear in the Hebrew causative verb of 2:9 ("he made him king"), which is the same terminology used when Samuel the prophet made Saul king over Israel (1 Sam 8:22; 12:1).

Mahanaim seems to have functioned as the administrative seat for Gilead in Saul's day and throughout most of the early monarchy. If Abner wants Ish-Bosheth to claim the throne of Israel, his power play may have a better chance if based in this municipal center far away from political and social forces in the south. Our text portrays this move as a calculated power play. It is a daring maneuver, but one that Abner and Ish-Bosheth take boldly when they assert control over "all Israel" (2:9). Unfortunately for these conspirators, the house of Judah follows David (2:10).

The specific phraseology used in this paragraph seems intentional in order to underscore the contrast between David and Ish-Bosheth. Unlike David's rise to power, there is no mention here of divine direction or approval, nor is there mention of public anointing or popular support. Ish-Bosheth is part of a political power move. By contrast, David rises to power through sensitivity to Yahweh's guidance and timing. David's is no power play; rather, his is a "faith play."

War between the Rival Monarchies (2:12–32). The account of the civil war between the house of David in the south and the house of Ish-Bosheth in the north is held together literarily by the march of the generals with their armies from their respective capitals to Gibeon (2:12–13) and by their return after the conflict (2:29–32).

The first section records an example of the ancient custom of representative combat, in which man-to-man fighting substituted for full-fledged battle between opposing armies in an effort to settle disputes without recourse to extensive bloodshed. But the twenty-four champions are all killed, and no side can claim an undisputed victory (2:14–16).

As a result, the hostilities continue, and the bloodletting becomes severe. Our historian summarizes the events of that day (2:17). Joab's presence at Gibeon in Benjamin, the home tribe of Saul, may indicate Joab's army had made successful advances north into Ish-Bosheth's territory. Abner's proposal to use representative combat may have been an attempt to impede Joab's advance.

The episode between Abner and Joab's brother Asahel serves two purposes in the narrative (2:18–28).

1. In the immediate context it explains how the death of Asahel sickens both sides (2:23). As a result, both sides lose the heart and will for warfare and declare a truce (2:28).
2. In the larger narrative, the episode explains why hostility between Joab and Abner continues.

Summary of the War Years (3:1–5). Rather than recount further gruesome details of the civil war, the text merely states that it goes on "a long time" (3:1) and that David gradually gains strength while Ish-Bosheth grows weaker. The inclusion of a list of David's sons seems curious here. In light of the emphasis on the growing strength of David contrasted with the waning strength of Ish-Bosheth, most likely this list of David's sons born while he rules from Hebron is intended to intensify the contrast.

Death of Abner (3:6–39). Abner, the general of Ish-Bosheth's army, has grown in political influence and strength in the house of Saul (3:6). Sexual relations with a king's wife or concubine in the ancient world was tantamount to a claim to that king's throne. Ish-Bosheth suspects Abner will use his strength to take the throne of the Northern Kingdom. But Abner defiantly proclaims that he has been stubbornly "loyal" (3:8) to the house of Saul but has decided to turn all of Israel over to David (3:10). He then defects to David.

Abner is insulted by Ish-Bosheth's accusation against him (3:8). Abner expresses twice his decision to do for David what Yahweh has sworn (NIV "promised") to do, that is, to transfer the house of Saul into David's hands (3:9, 18). Abner does not offer ulterior motives. He appears to be doing the best he can in a nearly impossible situation.

In narrating Joab's murder of Abner, the narrator goes to great lengths to emphasize David's innocence. David sent him away "in peace" (three times in 3:21–23). When Joab summons Abner with the clearly premeditated intent to kill him, we are told explicitly, "David did not know it" (3:26). Finally, David personally leads the throng at the funeral for Abner (3:31–35). All the people of Israel accept David's innocence and are greatly pleased by everything he has done (3:36–37).

Death of Ish-Bosheth (4:1–12). Our passage's final summary statement emphasizes the reactions of Ish-Bosheth and his people to the loss of Abner (4:1). It remains only for Baanah and Recab to strike the *coup de grâce*. As in the narration of Abner's death, the biblical historian is concerned to document David's innocence. Any hint that Ish-Bosheth's murder was engineered by David could hinder the king's attempt to win the loyalty of the northern tribes. So, David's quote reminds us there is a right way and a wrong way to become king, and the cruel murder of "an innocent man" is not the right way (4:9–11).

Note the reference to Mephibosheth in 4:4. This is the first time we meet Jonathan's son, and the intrusion here prepares the reader for his role later in the court history of David. Although this verse disrupts the flow of the present narrative, its inclusion highlights the pitiable end of Saul's progeny. This mention of crippled Mephibosheth reminds us that David's coming rule over all Israel has a corresponding truth: Saul's descendants will *not* rule Israel.

Application. In the case of the early church, Christian believers waited patiently in prayer as instructed by Jesus for the promised Holy Spirit of God to become a reality (Luke 24:49; Acts 1:4, 14). This devotion was not unlike David patiently waiting for God's time and place to fulfill his promises. Sadly, the church has not always been so patient or, for that matter, so obedient to God's call. At times the body of Christ on earth has been more like Ish-Bosheth than David.

David is celebrated in these texts as the ideal king who willingly submits to God's timing and direction and consistently repudiates the way of power politics and force. Jesus fulfills all that was right about David. Like David, he could have chosen the wrong way to accomplish his divine mission. In fact, Satan even tempted him with that (Matt 4:1–11). But Jesus is the ideal king of Israel because he became king in the right way, through submission to his divine vocation as the Son of David and through patient waiting and service.

2 SAMUEL 5:1–6:23

Original Meaning

David Becomes King over All Israel (5:1–5). The importance of this part in our story is highlighted by the presence of "all the tribes of Israel" with David at Hebron (5:1). Also here are the "elders of Israel," who deal directly with "King David," an appellative that takes on new meaning from this point forward (5:3). The elders assert something equally significant: "We are your own flesh and blood" (5:1). The tribes of Israel, through their representative elders, present themselves to David at Hebron and are ready to commit to his rule over a united monarchy, if he is willing to include the northern tribes.

This is a high-water mark to which the narrative has been building since 1 Samuel 16. David now reigns as king over all Israel. The books of Samuel argue for the legitimacy of David because of *theological* causation: Yahweh has chosen him. In the biblical worldview, this is most important, and there is nothing incompatible about these perspectives.

David Captures Jerusalem (5:6–10). Without doubt, Jerusalem is the most important city of the Bible. It is mentioned over eight hundred times in the Bible. The name "Zion" occurs over 150 times in the Old Testament and refers originally to the southeast hill of the city, which is equated in our text with the "City of David" (5:7). Like Jerusalem, the etymological meaning of Zion is unclear, but it comes to be used as a synonym of Jerusalem and takes on enormous theological significance in Psalms, Isaiah, and elsewhere.

A Palace for David in Jerusalem (5:11–12). With the aid of the powerful king of Tyre, who later helps Solomon in the construction of the temple (1 Kgs 5:7), David now receives a palace in Jerusalem. This is vivid confirmation that Yahweh himself has established David as king for the sake of the people of Israel. As a result of these blessings, David now grasps fully his indebtedness to Yahweh.

The events narrated in this section are not given in chronological sequence. The biblical historian has collected events topically in this unit in order to produce the full impact of David under the blessing of Yahweh (5:10). Just as these historical developments serve to confirm in David's mind that God has blessed him and established his kingdom (5:12), so they serve the same role for the readers.

David's Children Born in Jerusalem (5:13–16). Though the extended narrative portrays David under the blessing of Yahweh, there may be hints of future trouble here. The new king has taken more wives and concubines in direct violation of the royal law of Deuteronomy 17:17.

Two Victories over the Philistines (5:17–25). Philistines could tolerate an anointed King David in the south, but the idea of a united Israel with David as king is a threat they attempt to prevent (5:17). These paragraphs narrate two battles against the Philistines, who attack Judah's heartland in an apparent attempt to drive a wedge between David's two constituencies. As we have seen throughout this unit, the events are reported thematically, not in chronological sequence.

The Valley of Rephaim was a plain just southwest of Jerusalem, a portion of which lay on the border between Benjamin and Judah. By attempting to cut David off from his new northern supporters, the Philistines present a critical moment early in David's rule. It is difficult to overstress the joy and celebration in the narrator's voice in reporting these Israelite triumphs over the Philistines.

The significance of these victories is highlighted by subtle references in the text.

1. The idea that the Philistines abandon their idols is a powerful image. This reference conjures up the horrifying shadows of the first battle of Ebenezer, when the Philistines captured the ark of the covenant (1 Sam 4:1b–11). David's glorious victory is an apt reversal of those misfortunes.
2. The Israelites in that earlier battle with the Philistines had recklessly attempted to create the circumstances of holy war. Here, however, the terminology and imagery of divine armies marching in the balsam trees and Yahweh's "going" in front of Israel's army (2 Sam 5:24) is reminiscent of ancient theophanic poetry, in which Yahweh and his celestial armies come to help in holy war. Where earlier attempts failed, David succeeds.
3. Finally, the repeated information that "David inquired of the Lord" (5:19) is a familiar theme. David's rise to kingship is characterized by the importance he attaches to seeking guidance from God—in contrast to Saul, who sometimes made up his mind in advance or failed to ask altogether. Now that David is king, he defeats the hated foe of God. But he continues to take steps that are directed and guided by Yahweh's loving response. Here again, David becomes the portrait of the ideal king of Israel.

David Brings the Ark to Jerusalem (6:1–23). This chapter's location is significant in light of the immediately preceding paragraphs. David has captured Jerusalem and transformed the city into a political force by driving the Philistines back to their traditional borders and unifying the tribes of Israel at their new capital city. The new political role for Jerusalem is now supplemented by a new religious significance. The entrance of the ark of the covenant into the city is the culmination of a long and painful sojourn since the fall of Shiloh and the loss of a central cult center (1 Sam 4:12–22). Thus, the chapter's location builds on the political and military accomplishments of David in 5:6–25 by narrating an event of substantial religious significance in 2 Samuel 5.

The unusual designation for the ark in 6:2 calls for comment in the text. Such a long and cumbersome designation probably indicates the use of a formal cult-related title for the ark and indirectly for the God of Israel. The ark was the divine throne itself. The expression "who is enthroned between the cherubim" (6:2) is a sacred epithet used of God by the early Israelites in worship.

While the theological import of this move of the ark to Jerusalem seems central, it clearly has political significance as well. Shiloh was an important Israelite religious center prior to the rise of the monarchy (cf. 1 Sam 1–3). David is most likely attempting to transfer the former authority and power of Shiloh, now sadly lost for decades, to the newly designated capital city.

David must have meant well, but the process of bringing the ark into the city is disastrous. In a way that seems especially foreign to present-day readers, the unfortunate Uzzah illustrates the holiness of God present in the ark. The Israelites have not taken his power and holiness seriously enough, and now David is left with the question (6:9): "How can the ark of the Lord ever come to me?" The text implies that the ark (and hence God's presence) can and will come into David's life, but his power and holiness come with it.

Finally, we must make a comment about the difficult references to Michal. Note that Michal is identified in her first appearance in this unit as the "daughter of Saul" rather than the "wife of David." In her objections and demeanor, she manifests her father's disposition rather than her husband's. While nation and king celebrate the joyous occasion, Michal sulks as though *Saul* would have done better. She has forgotten that Saul had neglected the ark (and God!) and refused to heed the warnings of the prophet Samuel.

Whatever the details of Michal's objections may have been, she functions in this text as a remnant of the old Saulide line. The closing phrase of the unit implies her childlessness is her punishment. Saul, Jonathan, and Ish-Bosheth are dead; Mephibosheth is crippled; Michal is barren.

Application. When this text portrays David as kingdom builder, the informed reader realizes he is not building simply another earthly nation but Yahweh's kingdom. The Christian reader recognizes at once that David's accomplishments are truly cosmic, nothing less than laying the foundation for the Lord's Zion, the city of all future salvation.

The eschatological dimension of the text calls for faith on the part of the reader. By affirming Christian faith and becoming a member of the community, one joins in the journey to Zion. Like Abraham we march to a celestial city (Heb 11:10). Having the rest of the story gives today's Christian readers an appreciation for David's anointing and his building of Jerusalem. We know the consummation of these events in their glorious finality. With Christ before us as the Son of David and his eternal city as our destination, we march onward in faith. These two—king and city—symbolize our "hope of glory" in that we expect to participate in King Jesus's resurrection glory, a hope kept alive in us by his presence within (Col 1:27).

2 SAMUEL 7:1–29

Original Meaning

David's Intentions to Build a Temple (7:1–3). The mention of David's "palace" in 7:1 assumes knowledge of the capture of Jerusalem (5:6–9) and the building of a royal palace with Phoenician help (5:11). The statement that Yahweh had given David rest from all the enemies around him assumes David's success at driving the Philistines out of Israelite territory (5:17–25). Beyond the immediate context, these verses are also reminiscent of Deuteronomy 12:10–11. Surely this is a propitious time for the new energetic king to build a permanent structure for God's dwelling.

With the reference to David's "palace" in 7:1, the narrator introduces a theme word for 2 Samuel 7—*bayit* ("house"), which occurs fifteen times in the chapter. It will recur several times in the next few verses, all referring to a physical structure, either a royal palace (as here in 7:1) or a temple.

The Lord's Alternate Plan (7:4–17). During the night, Yahweh reverses the plan. Will David hear Nathan's prophetic voice any differently from how Saul heard Samuel's voice? Will David refuse to hear the divine oracle as Saul did, or will he submit to Yahweh's will? This chapter, more than any other, answers these questions irrevocably: David is not like Saul. He is as much an ideal ruler of God's people as Saul was an inadequate one.

Yahweh's objection to David's plan (7:5) has historical reasons (7:6–7). He has not needed a physical home since the time of the exodus until the day of David. Furthermore, Yahweh has not requested such a house. Temples were for deities who were tied down. Israel's God cannot be manipulated or contained in a temple, a point made carefully when the temple *was* eventually built (see 1 Kgs 8:27).

Instead, Yahweh has an alternate plan (2 Sam 7:8–17). The plan is stated first generally (7:8–11a) and then specifically (7:11b–17). The general statement emphasizes the special relationship Yahweh has with David, signaled at the outset by the epithet "my servant David" (7:5, 8). One of the driving theological convictions of the history of David's rise has been that David succeeds where Saul fails because Yahweh has blessed David with his divine presence. David is the legitimate anointed one who suitably rules God's people because he is the Immanuel figure; God is with him.

Yahweh promises, furthermore, to continue these blessings in the future. Through David, Yahweh will provide security for all Israel and will "give [them] rest" (7:11) from their enemies. The promise of rest in the land is an important unifying theme throughout the Deuteronomistic History. Now that Jerusalem has been established, this chapter introduces the theme of a temple for Yahweh, which means the long-awaited "rest" is possible. This rest has now been secured in David and will be ensured by his perpetuating dynasty.

Next, Yahweh details his plan more specifically for David (7:11b–17). Rather than David's building a "house" for Yahweh, God declares he instead will build a "house" for David (7:11b). David will be succeeded by a son, thus establishing the first royal dynasty in Israel. That son will build the temple (7:13). More sons will follow. Yahweh will be a father to them, and they will be his sons (7:14). When they sin, Yahweh will graciously restrict his punishment to that appropriate for humans, but he will never withdraw his steadfast covenant love as he withdrew it from Saul (7:14b–15). Saul's progeny will not last; David's is forever (7:16)!

David's Prayer (7:18–29). Perhaps here more than anywhere else we see the contrast between David and Saul. Put simply, David acquiesces to "the word of the LORD" (7:4). In response to Nathan's oracle, David enters in and sits before the Lord, presumably inside the temporary tent before the ark of the covenant. David's opening question admits that his tribal family has no legitimate dynastic expectations (7:18). Yahweh will make David's house stand forever, and David is greatly humbled by the promise.

David's opening question is also reminiscent of Saul's (1 Sam 9:21). But the similarity ceases there. Saul's humility soon turns to defensive self-preservation, while David's drives him to further dependence on Yahweh. David is driven from humility to adoration of God's greatness (2 Sam 7:22–24). He rightly understands that this promise to establish a permanent Davidic dynasty is related to God's great saving acts of old, his deliverance of Israel from Egypt and the conquest of the promised land (7:23). Israel has become Yahweh's people, and he is her God (7:24), which is covenant language again emphasizing the continuity of this promise to David with God's mighty acts of the past.

David closes with supplication. As elsewhere in the Old Testament, Israel's prayers, when at their best, call on God to be fully God in their lives and base the request on God's own reputation and character (7:26). By making this promise to David a reality, Yahweh will demonstrate his great faithfulness to Israel and show himself different from the whimsical gods of the ancient Near East.

Application. David's prayer is a model of yielding to God while at the same time boldly imploring that God truly be God, keeping faithfully his promises. Likewise, present-day believers must avail themselves of every opportunity to receive the grace of God: church attendance, Bible study, prayer, involvement in missions and outreach, commitment to serve the poor, and so on. Just as David lived close to the established means of God's grace, so must today's believers learn to revel in the different ways in which God speaks today. The historian of the books of Samuel has offered David as an example for future kings through the narrative thus far. As such he functions as a model for all of us who worship the Son of David today.

2 SAMUEL 8:1–18

Original Meaning

Catalogue of Defeated Nations (8:1–6). The Philistines are unable to continue encroaching on Israelite territory once David is anointed king over a unified Israel. As we have seen, shortly after his coronation, David drove the Philistines from Judah's heartland and confined them to the coastal plains (5:17–25). The victory mentioned here probably indicates that he reclaims disputed territory and almost completely subjugates them (8:1).

The rest of the paragraph lists David's victories over enemies in the Transjordan (Moab) and the north (the Arameans of Zobah and Damascus). His cruel treatment of Moabite prisoners of war is surprising in light of his Moabite ancestry and the fact that the Moabites had helped his parents during their enforced exile (Ruth 4:21–22; 1 Sam 22:3–4).

David Collects the Spoils of War (8:7–14). The recurring phrase that gives structure to chapter 8 ("the LORD gave victory," 8:6 and 8:14) referred to military victory in 8:1–6. Here it relates to collections of the spoils of war. The narrative brings into focus what David does with the booty in Jerusalem. David consistently "dedicated" (8:11) the captured articles to Yahweh. Once again in contrast to Saul, we learn who may suitably serve as Israel's king. When God blesses, the true anointed one gives thanks and obeys.

Thus far in 2 Samuel, the historian has described the transformation of Jerusalem into a new capital city, the construction of a royal palace, the expulsion of the Philistines from Judah's heartland, and union between Judah in the south and Israel in the north. David has reached a point where he can turn his attention to Israel's perennial foes to the east and south (Edom, Moab, and Ammon).

David's Officials (8:15–18). With this list of royal officials, the historian has taken us a step further in understanding the new Israelite institution of monarchy. The organization of the state under the new institution is considerably different from the tribal organization operative at the beginning of 1 Samuel under the able leadership of the prophet Samuel. The previous social stratification based on kinship has given way to a structure based more on skill and ability. So, in this list of royal officers, a series of functional roles (generals, recorders, priests, secretaries, and advisers) has replaced the elders of Israel and Judah as the power structure.

In a summarizing sentence, the narrator assesses David's monarchy (8:15). David is the embodiment of Yahweh's rule on earth. He is Yahweh's chosen, anointed one, who rules as Yahweh himself wants his people to be governed. David becomes the example for all future kings—the standard by which they will be judged. But as we will see in the rest of 2 Samuel, this is not the whole story.

Application. This chapter illustrates that God is faithful to his word and strengthens his servants for the task to which he has called them. So, what can it mean for today's believers to have victory wherever we go? It means that God has already won the victory and has promised to strengthen us for the tasks we are called to perform in the church and in the world. As David defeated Israel's enemies, so today's believers can expect to accomplish successfully our God-given and God-ordained tasks, with the help of his Holy Spirit. This catalogue of military victories should inspire confidence in all believers that God is at work fulfilling his word through his people.

2 SAMUEL 9:1–13

Original Meaning

David Searches for a Descendant of Saul (9:1–5). The military summary provided in chapter 8 fulfills the words of Jonathan in 1 Samuel 20:15. Second Samuel 8 makes it clear that Yahweh has indeed cut David's enemies off, giving him victory wherever he went and providing the promised "rest" for the land. So now is the time for David to keep the covenant he and Jonathan established.

We may question David's sincerity and his motives for showing kindness to Mephibosheth. Perhaps David is attempting to solidify the otherwise tenuous unity between northern Israel and southern Judah by incorporating into his royal household the vestiges of the Saulide dynasty, so popular among the northern tribes. Or perhaps this act of kindness is simply a desperate attempt to ease David's guilt-ridden conscience, assuming he somehow has felt responsible for the end of Saul's line.

But all such hypothetical and psychological speculation takes us beyond the message of 1–2 Samuel, which are clear in explaining David's motives at critical junctures. As far as the text is concerned, David's motives are singularly focused on Jonathan; his reasons for showing kindness now are simply "for Jonathan's sake" (9:1, 7).

David Shows Kindness to Mephibosheth (9:6–13). Regardless of what Mephibosheth may have hoped, it can hardly be good news for him to be summoned to the royal palace. David brings him from obscurity in Lo Debar and identifies him as the son of Jonathan and grandson of Saul (9:6). In the central and pivotal section of our text (9:7), David begins by alleviating his visitor's fears. The king will not only permit Mephibosheth to live, but he will show kindness to him for Jonathan's sake.

That kindness takes the form of two blessings.

1. David will give him the property of Saul's estate, making Mephibosheth a wealthy man instantly.
2. David grants the privilege that was lost to Mephibosheth when Saul and Jonathan were killed, that is, the right to eat at the king's table.

Application. You and I are tempted to show kindness and to keep our covenant commitments only when it is convenient to do so or when it shows particular promise of return. In the workplace, in schools, dare I say even in the church, we tend to keep covenant with those who will repay us in some way. In this text, David serves as an example because he keeps covenant and shows mercy to someone who cannot advance his own causes. Unlike Saul, who abused (or attempted to abuse) his royal power, David uses power *in this passage* in a way consistent with his calling as shepherd of God's flock. As such, he also anticipates his greater Son, who will never use power for self-aggrandizement but only for the advancement of his Father's kingdom. Unfortunately, David will not always represent such an example of the use of power, as we will soon see.

2 SAMUEL 10:1–12:31

Original Meaning

Diplomacy with the Ammonites Breaks Down (10:1–5). David apparently does not expect war with the Ammonites. Most likely Nahash, the Ammonite king who has died here (10:1) and an old adversary of Saul (1 Sam 11), was David's ally during the difficult days of Saul's reign. David logically seeks to maintain friendly relations with the Ammonites after Nahash's death. The specific terminology used to reveal David's intentions ("I will show kindness," 10:2) is reminiscent of David's kindness to Mephibosheth in the immediately preceding chapter (9:1, 3, 7) and may mean David has an actual covenant or treaty with Nahash.

Details on why the shaved beard and cut garments represented the ultimate insult are not entirely clear (10:4). The beard was apparently the pride and joy of an Israelite male, which was cut only for periods of mourning or as an act of humiliation. Since garments in the biblical world often reflected status, power, or identity, the added insult of cutting their garments at their hips exposes David's men to further humiliation.

These two kings are busy "sending" to and against each other in the strategic play for power. Their "sending" is all about human power structures and about who has access to the most strength in order to dominate the other. David's decisive victory over the Arameans brings the power motif into focus and characterizes him as the legitimate king of Israel, who has the God-given power and authority to "send." David does indeed have royal power, and as we will see, this motif returns in frightening ways in chapters 11 and 12.

Ammonite Wars (10:6–19). The first battle described here takes place near the city of Rabbah itself (10:6–14; cf. 12:26). Once the Arameans arrived in the Transjordan, they successfully out-maneuver Joab so that he is forced to fight on two separate fronts (10:9–12). Joab divides his troops and encourages them to be strong and fight bravely, adding that Yahweh will do whatever seems best in his sight (10:12). The irascible general is seldom a paragon of virtue, but here Joab's quote illustrates the healthy balance between effort and faith. As someone has said, saints pray as though the outcome depends solely on God and work as though it depends on them.

To the disappointment of the Ammonites, their Aramean allies flee before Joab. The Israelite victory is probably tempered by losses, so that Joab is unable to continue his siege on the city itself and has no alternative but to return to Jerusalem (10:14).

The next battle is between Israel and the Arameans themselves and will determine the fate of all of Syria-Palestine (10:15–19). David leads the troops himself this time in what becomes a decisive victory. With the Aramean allies effectively neutralized, all that remains for David to control the Transjordan area is conquest of Ammon itself (12:26–31).

David Remains in Jerusalem (11:1). The first is a temporal clause, translated literally "And at the return of the year, at the time of the marching forth of the kings." That the events recorded in this chapter take place in the spring is probable, and therefore the NIV ("In the spring") and most other translations are not entirely wrong, though somewhat misleading. Instead, the "return of the year" refers most likely to the coming around of the one-year anniversary of the time when the Aramean kings marched against Israel (10:6–19). The text is less concerned with this detail than it is to show that David's adultery with Bathsheba occurs approximately one year after the Ammonite-Aramean wars began, so the military action of 11:1 is intended to finish what was begun by Hanun and his Aramean allies. In striking irony, David is thus described as performing his rightful role as king of Israel; that is, he is defending the nation. The irony, of course, is that David stays home, and rather than defend his subjects, he abuses them (i.e., Bathsheba and her family).

The second portion of the verse seems emphatic that all able-bodied men are in the field: Joab, the king's servants, and *all* Israel. The last clause directs our attention to David *sitting* alone at home, in contrast to all the others who are *destroying* and *besieging*. This verse contrasts David not only with the Israelites on the battlefield but also with other kings who have gone forth for battle. By placing in the foreground the picture of Israel's adversary kings marching off to war, the narrator has put the spotlight on David sitting at home.

David, Bathsheba, and Uriah (11:2–27). After the carefully crafted introduction in 11:1, 11:2 portrays the king loitering about on the roof of the palace after first lounging on his couch. While so occupied (or unoccupied!), David sees a beautiful woman bathing on a nearby rooftop. The narrator emphasizes Bathsheba's beauty and immediately alarms the reader that danger lurks around the corner.

The narration is further characterized by three occurrences of our theme word, "send" (11:3, 4, 5). David *sends* someone to find out more about Bathsheba. The reported facts apparently do not deter David: The woman is the daughter of a prominent individual (Eliam) and the wife of Uriah the Hittite, whom we learn later is one of David's faithful fighting heroes (23:39). Such details might arouse relief in the reader at first, but they eventually serve only to highlight the premeditated intent of David's next action.

David then *sends* again, this time with the intention of fetching Bathsheba to the palace. The specific verbs used in 11:4 to describe David's actions are painfully clear: He sends, he takes her ("take" is slightly obscured by the NIV's "David sent messengers *to get* her"), and he lies with her. Mercifully brief, with no account of conversation or mitigating circumstances, the verse coldly recounts David's crime.

The little phrase near the end of 11:4 sounds an ominous note. The point of the clause is that Bathsheba is cleansing herself ritually because of menstruation. Such a detail clarifies a few further facts about the episode. (1) She is not currently pregnant prior to intercourse with David. (2) Intercourse with David takes place precisely at the most opportune time for conception. (3) Since Uriah is off in the battlefield, he cannot possibly be the father. A small phrase with big implications!

David is not the only character who "sends" in this episode, for Bathsheba *sends* a succinct message that changes everything. David exercised power in chapter 10 and thus far in chapter 11 by "sending." But when Bathsheba "sends," David must deal with a different kind of power. The power of wronged Bathsheba, the power of David's own sin—these are powers that David will now attempt to answer with more "sending" (11:6). But ultimately, Yahweh will "send," and David will relent (12:1).

The second episode of chapter 11 narrates David's first attempts to cover up the unfortunate consequences of his affair with Bathsheba (11:6–13). His machinations reveal a pitiful dependence on human power structures reminiscent of King Saul. Our unit's theme word ("send") occurs three times in 11:6. David has the royal authority and power to *send* a decree to Joab, who has the military power to *send* Uriah back to Jerusalem from the battlefield. In order to cover his guilt, David tries subterfuge and deceit. He has faith in his plan, and he believes his royal power is sufficient for the task. So, as elsewhere, David *sends* in order to control and dominate, and also this time to conceal.

When Uriah arrives in Jerusalem, David's hypocritical questions in 11:7 are likely intended to give Uriah the impression that David has summoned him from the battlefield in order to get an accurate military report. But the reader knows better! In light of what David has just done, his feigned concern leaves the reader unsettled. How can our hero, the anointed of Yahweh, be so hypocritical?

David's pathetic attempts to manipulate and control Uriah bring the king's hypocrisy to the foreground (11:8–13). His suggestion that Uriah go home and "wash his feet" (11:8) may be a euphemism for sexual intercourse, which is evidently how Uriah understands these words. Obviously, David wants Uriah to spend a night at home with his wife, creating the possibility later that Uriah is the father of Bathsheba's child. David was desperate. All would be well if Uriah would only spend a night relaxing at home with Bathsheba.

David has grossly underestimated Uriah's character. He disregards the king's invitations for two reasons: religious convictions and loyalty to his fellow soldiers (11:11). The great irony of our text is that this convert of foreign ancestry is more righteous than the Israelite king. Yet King David, the anointed one of Yahweh, has abused his God-given power and attempts to manipulate a faithful and righteous servant in a desperate scam to save himself.

The third episode is the shocking account of murder (11:14–25). David is not finished *sending* yet. His next step is to write Uriah's own death warrant and "send" it to Joab by Uriah's own hand (11:14). As David had sent and taken Bathsheba (11:4), as he had sent and retrieved Uriah from the battlefield (11:6), now he sends and kills Uriah. His powerful royal prerogative has been turned to evil purposes. He becomes so intent on destroying Uriah in order to save himself that he jeopardizes his army's actions against Rabbah and trivializes the deaths of Israelite soldiers that he himself has caused.

David had shown the capacity to grieve deeply over the deaths of men who were his adversaries (Saul and Abner in 1:11–27 and 3:31–39 respectively). In this case, Uriah is no adversary but a faithful warrior who has apparently been with David many years. Yet David does not mourn. His flippant response to the news of Uriah's death (11:25) is shocking illustration of how far David has gone.

The fourth part of our chapter is the (apparent!) conclusion of the story (11:26–27): David takes Bathsheba as his wife, and she bears him a son. After the official time of mourning is over, David "sent and brought her" (literally, 11:27; NIV "had her brought") to the royal palace. This is the last time in our text David is the subject of *sending*. From now on, God or Joab will do the *sending* (12:1, 25, 27). From David's perspective, that is the end of the matter.

In reality, what ends the story in human eyes is really only the beginning of the struggle from God's perspective. Sin has been concealed from human view, but there is much more to reality than only the human view. The little clause that ends the chapter injects a different element, a divine element, that reverberates throughout chapter 12.

Nathan the Prophet: You Are the Man! (12:1–12). The return of our theme word "send" in 12:1 is ironic: "The LORD *sent* Nathan to David." David had sent, first in order to commit adultery, and then in order to cover up his crime. Now just when it appears David has gotten away with it and the story is over, Yahweh does some sending of his own.

The best way to expose David's hypocrisy is to have him condemn himself. Nathan's parable about the rich man and the poor man arouses David's indignation, and he quickly condemns himself by condemning the rich man (12:1–6). With decisiveness and passion, the king quickly declares that the rich man is guilty and deserving of death, though as king he will allow severe reparations as punishment (12:5–6).

David has announced his official royal judgment on any man who would behave in such a way. Nathan comes immediately to the point of his parable (12:7): "You are the man!" David's sin is that he has "despise[ed] the word of the LORD" (12:9) by committing evil in God's sight (cf. 1 Sam 15:23, 26). The Lord has given him everything, but he wants more. As David chose the way of violence to cover his sin, using "the sword of the Ammonites" (12:9), so the sword will never depart from his royal dynasty. God's punishment matches the crime. Furthermore, calamity (literally, "evil") will arise against David from within his own household (12:11–12).

Death of Newborn; Birth of Solomon (12:13–25). Here we learn David's real character. Certainly, he is remembered for the heinous sins of chapter 11. But his response to the prophetic word in 12:13 is why David became known as Israel's ideal king. Unlike Saul's repentance in 1 Samuel 15, David's words,

"I have sinned" (12:13), are full of genuine remorse and sorrow. There is no attempt to blame or dodge. In fact, it is possible that David has been miserable with guilt and actually welcomes Nathan's reproach.

A king in David's position could easily have simply killed Nathan and asked for another prophet, one who would say only nice things. But the books of Samuel are teaching us that Israel's kings are different—indeed, they have to be different, because in reality it is Yahweh who rules. On a more personal level, this passage also shows that David is someone who wants to be what he is called to be. Ultimately, this is the difference between believers and unbelievers, the difference between Saul and David, between David and lesser kings.

The biblical understanding of sin is defined elsewhere but is illustrated in chapter 11. Likewise, biblical understandings of repentance and forgiveness are defined elsewhere but are illustrated here. True repentance (12:13a) is met instantly with genuine forgiveness (12:13b). God is merciful. Nathan's reassuring words contain one of several metaphors for forgiveness in the Old Testament: "The LORD has taken away your sin" (12:13b). Its implication is essentially spatial: Sin is removed, carried off to a great distance.

David's repentance is genuine, especially when compared to Saul's in 1 Samuel 15. More importantly, the text illustrates the truth expressed in one of Israel's ancient creeds: Yahweh is a "compassionate and gracious God . . . , forgiving wickedness, rebellion and sin" (Exod 34:6–7).

At the same time as 2 Samuel 12:13 illustrates God's merciful forgiveness, 12:14 illustrates the unmitigated consequences of sin, even though forgiven by God. The punishment of death has been turned aside from David because of his repentance, but the aftermath of sin remains; the child will die. Sin that has been forgiven and forgotten by God may still leave human scars.

The death of Bathsheba's new son leaves today's readers with one of the most difficult aspects of Old Testament faith. Why is David forgiven while the innocent newborn has to die? The answer lies in the Bible's distinction between punishment and consequence. The child's death is a result of David's sin, but this is not the same as punishment. It is a fundamental principle of life that God may forgive and cleanse us of all wrongdoing, but the consequences of our sin may, and in fact often, remain.

A second part of the ancient creed just quoted from Exodus 34:7 acknowledges the fact that Yahweh "punishes the children and their children for the sin of the parents to the third and the fourth generation." A variant of this creed in the Ten Commandments (Exod 20:5–6) emphasizes that God may allow sin's consequences to endure for three, perhaps four generations, but his love extends for "a thousand generations of those who love me." In other words, Yahweh graciously limits the duration of sin's consequences that would otherwise continue on their own indefinitely, but his love is extended to a thousand generations of one's descendants. Because of Yahweh's nature, sin has a limited life span, but love lasts forever.

The episode of the child's death and David's reversal of conventional mourning customs leaves many interpreters perplexed (2 Sam 12:15–23). The normal period of mourning lasted seven days, and the child died on the seventh day (12:18). Since David assumes an attitude of mourning while he prays for the sick boy, he has already fulfilled the customary period of mourning proleptically, and there was no need to continue his futile prayers for the boy's life (12:21–23). Though modern scholars (like his ancient courtiers) are confused by David's disregard for social customs, there may be nothing more intended here than the depth of David's passion and hope in God.

The birth of another son between David and Bathsheba holds great symbolic significance (12:24–25). Bathsheba is called David's "wife" rather than the "wife of Uriah the Hittite" (cf. 11:3; 12:10). More importantly, Yahweh loves the new son, who bears two names, Solomon and Jedidiah. Though other children are born to this union, he will have special significance in fulfilling the covenant promises of 2 Samuel 7.

David Captures Rabbah (12:26–31). The historian now returns to an annalistic-style military report of David's Ammonite wars, narrating the capture of the royal city. This paragraph is a historical flashback used as a literary frame. It serves together with 10:1–11:1 to create a literary envelope for the whole.

Joab and the army (formerly including Uriah the Hittite) capture Rabbah's water supply, and it will only be a matter of time before the city falls into Israelite hands. In the last occurrence of our passage's theme word, Joab uses his power to "send" (12:27) a message to David. Just as the war was precipitated by the sending of messengers (10:2, 4), so now it is concluded.

Application. American culture has fallen prey to the lie that our highest human fulfillment is partially attainable through self-indulgent, unrestrained erotic expression rather than through faithful, enduring, monogamous love. But this falsehood is as old as human civilization itself, and this text reveals the ancient lie for what it is. David surrenders impulsively to his most basic instincts, which lead him down a path that grows darker with each step. Rather than reaching his highest level of personal fulfillment, David discovers the darkness of his own soul. Likewise, instead of enabling us to reach our highest human fulfillment, reckless and illicit eroticism ensnares us in animalistic self-destruction. It is a hopeless cycle that ends only and always in death (Prov 7:21–23, 27).

2 SAMUEL 13:1–14:33

Original Meaning

Amnon's Love for His Half-Sister, Tamar (13:1–2). Verse 1 sets the stage for a new episode by introducing the principal actors, Amnon and Tamar. However, the Hebrew syntax (obscured by NIV) highlights Absalom's role. Thus the narrator lifts Absalom into the foreground and makes us aware that this is not simply a story about Amnon and Tamar, for it participates in the larger narrative of Absalom. Since chapter 14 ends with the word "Absalom," these two chapters begin and end with Absalom. Amnon's crude but honest explanation for his love-sickness (13:2) shows that his "love" for Tamar is not love in any meaningful sense, but only lust.

Amnon Rapes Tamar (13:3–22). The previous two verses presented Amnon's problem: he cannot have the woman he desires. Here we meet his solution: the nefarious advice of a friend. More than a friend, Jonadab is the "son of Shimeah, David's brother." Now we get a picture of the strife pervading David's extended family, which seems divided into opposing camps. Tamar and Absalom are allies on the one hand, while Amnon and his cousin Jonadab are on the other. Amnon's speech proclaims love for Tamar, but his actions are about to unveil a more sinister passion.

Amnon follows Jonadab's advice by feigning illness in order to draw Tamar into the trap (13:6–14). The Hebrew of this text uses a wide array of literary devices to emphasize the irony and injustice of the shameful act. The interchanging use of "sister" and "brother" in the dialogue focuses on the familial relationship between Amnon and Tamar and heightens the tragedy about to occur. After driving everyone out of the room so they can be alone, Amnon reveals his true intent to Tamar (13:11).

Tamar's impressive speech desperately raises numerous objections and shows her to be a woman of integrity. She begins with a firm and resolute refusal, with another subtle use of "my brother." Amnon may have hoped for consensual relations with Tamar in the privacy of his bed chamber. But her prohibition, "Don't force me!," uses a specific verb decrying the act for what it would be: rape. His proposal is a "wicked thing" and will only make a fool of him. In a more practical vein, Tamar uses great foresight in warning that if he rapes her, he will ruin both their lives. Finally, Tamar asserts that marriage is not out of the question and that following the proper procedures may work in Amnon's favor.

This narrator is fond of thematic analogies between episodes. So here it seems likely that Amnon's lying on his feigned sickbed is similar to David's rising from his siesta bed. One summons his forbidden sister in order to abuse her; the other summons another man's wife to abuse her. Thus, Amnon's actions are subtly drawn together with David's in a cause-and-effect relationship: David's sin has come to rest now in his immediate family.

Amnon is not to be deterred. With staccato-like precision and brevity, details of the deplorable act are recorded (13:14–15). Having earlier seized Tamar (13:11), Amnon has not released her to this point. He now overpowers her, which emphasizes the raw physical violence with which he forces himself on her, removing any trace of doubt about Tamar's innocence.

The next sequence of events is clarified when we keep the Pentateuchal law in view, regardless of how much or little it was enforced in the royal court of David. In his hatred, Amnon wants to drive Tamar away (13:15). But Israelite law (and presumably earlier Hebrew mores) required that a man who had sexual intercourse with a virgin must marry her. Tamar objects that "sending" her away now will be worse than Amnon's first offense—a reference to the Old Testament provision for divorcing a wife (Deut 24:1). Amnon and Tamar are not married, of course, but Tamar's use of the technical term for divorce is a plea, a reminder that two wrongs do not make a right.

The mention of Tamar's "ornate robe" (2 Sam 13:18) is interesting because this is the only other example of the expression used to describe Joseph's famous coat (Gen 37:3). We have no clear indication of the precise nature of the robe that makes it so distinctive. Whatever the term's etymological significance, the narrator has thankfully left us a note explaining the symbolism of Tamar's robe: It signified her status as an unmarried princess. Once she tears it, the robe symbolizes the ruin of her life.

The laconic 2 Samuel 13:21 states that when David learns what has happened, he is furious. The abrupt ending of the verse is an indictment of his inactivity. It seems likely that David's consciousness of his own guilt paralyzes him. How can he chastise Amnon in light of his own sin? Perhaps David could have prevented what will soon take place. Instead, he appears the overindulgent father, who becomes a passive, silent sufferer throughout the rest of the extended narrative (i.e., through ch. 20). Absalom refuses to speak to Amnon, but he treasures the hatred in his heart (13:22). The narrative that began with love (13:1–2) now ends with hatred (13:21–22). At its center stands the act of violence that has turned love into hatred (13:14–15).

Absalom Kills Amnon (13:23–39). Absalom's two-year wait, during which he likely nurtures his hatred and plots his revenge, comes to fruition in the murder of Amnon. Though rape is roundly condemned in the Old Testament, the punishment was not murder, and Absalom's actions are totally unjustified. Not unlike David's murder of Uriah, Absalom's execution of Amnon involves cold-blooded intrigue and secrecy.

The expression "all the king's sons" (13:23, 29, 30, 33; without "all" in 13:35, 36) is probably a technical term designating those sons of David besides the crown prince, who is himself in line to inherit the throne. Thus, Amnon is the crown prince and the object of Absalom's plot, while the other princes are only a decoy (13:27). The question of succession to David's kingdom is a theme just below the surface of this text. Amnon's murder serves both to avenge his shameful rape of Tamar and to clear the way for Absalom to claim the royal throne.

In 13:37–39, the narrator gives a brief report of the ensuing three years. Absalom is forced into exile in Geshur, where he receives the hospitality and protection of his grandfather on his mother's side. The narrative seems to have reached an impasse: David is incapable of administering justice in his own family, and Absalom is unable to return home. The narrator tells us Absalom stayed in Geshur for only "three years," which promises a resolution to the impasse and also creates a transition to the next chapter. In addition, David is now able to deal with the loss of Amnon and is ready for reconciliation with Absalom (13:39).

The Wise Woman of Tekoa (14:1–20). Joab takes action presumably because Absalom remains the crown prince, and his absence from Jerusalem could complicate a smooth transition of royal power to a new leader when the time is right. Being fully aware of David's desire (14:1), Joab makes arrangements to persuade David it is acceptable to bring Absalom home.

Joab is in need of a gifted and eloquent actress in order to persuade David to take action. In Tekoa, he finds a remarkable woman, noted for her articulate, persuasive speech. Joab supplies the words, the Tekoite woman the rhetorical and thespian skills.

As supreme judge of the nation, David must have felt an obligation to avenge Amnon's death as required by law. Keeping Absalom safely tucked away in Geshur saves David from any unpleasantness and makes it possible for him to avoid taking action. David needs to think in wholly different categories. Once he declares that the Tekoite woman's son will be spared, it suddenly becomes admissible to consider an exception in the case of Absalom.

David and Absalom Reconciled (14:21–33). The result of the impressive Tekoite woman's audience with David is a changed situation. Once David places the woman's only remaining son under royal protection, David is forced to reconsider his own position on Absalom. His situation is considerably different. But the wise woman is able to press on David the parallels between her case and his. David relents, and Absalom is allowed to return to Jerusalem.

The rest of this chapter characterizes Absalom further and prepares us as readers for the tragic events to follow. Absalom's impressive appearance is prelude to his claim to be king. Just as Saul's height and David's manly appearance served them well, so Absalom's striking good looks will serve him well. The physical characteristic of full, thick hair is an important detail that the narrator hopes we will remember (14:26; see 18:9). His manipulative and violent treatment of Joab further warns us of an avaricious side to Absalom that does not bode well for the future. The reconciliation between father and son is described (14:33).

Application. The vicious cycle of apparently unending hatred and violence is characteristic of human nature. Our world is filled with examples, each with its own lengthy string of unforgiving acts of violence. The teenage bomb-thrower in Northern Ireland, the rock-throwing youth in Palestine, or the gun-toting Israeli soldier often has no knowledge, or at least no recollection, of the long history of violent hatred behind his actions. Ireland is still burdened with atrocities committed by Oliver Cromwell in the seventeenth century, Palestinians are avenging memories from five decades of injustices, and the Jews of modern Israel live with the haunting memories of centuries of anti-Semitism and pogroms in Europe.

The sad fact is that each of us repeats the failures of Adam and Eve in the primeval garden, eating the goodly fruit of the tree of the knowledge of good and evil to learn for ourselves. Thus, each of us contributes to the communal hatred that plagues humankind and constantly threatens to erupt at any moment in self-destructive violence. For this is the additional lesson of the story of David's family: All hate-driven violence inflicts as much harm on the avenger as the victim. Amnon and Absalom both come to an ignoble and violent death, which contributes further to our full-orbed understanding of the nature of sin.

2 SAMUEL 15:1–20:26

Original Meaning

Absalom Steals the Hearts of the People of Israel (15:1–12). The theme of this paragraph is the summarizing statement that Absalom "stole the hearts" of the Israelites (15:6). The "heart" in Old Testament Hebrew is often the seat of one's intellect as well as one's emotions. Thus, rather than win the affections of the Israelites, Absalom stole their minds—that is, he deceived or duped them. This paragraph, then, is the account of the precise strategies Absalom uses in his seditious efforts to deceive and distort in order to overthrow David.

Absalom begins building support for his rebellion against David by means of three strategies.

1. He acquires a chariot and horses, with a personal escort of fifty men (15:1). This constitutes no less than a claim

to royal status since such accessories were normally the privilege of the king.

2. Absalom assumes the position and role of judge for the people, which ordinarily was the function of the king (15:2–4). His accusatory tones assume that David, in Absalom's opinion, no longer fulfills his responsibility to provide justice for the people.
3. Absalom begins to receive anyone coming to him—not as a crown prince but as the king himself (15:5).

After four years of building his base, Absalom is now ready to instigate open rebellion against his father (15:7). He appears as patient and calculated in rebellion as he was in revenge. His request to go to Hebron to fulfill a vow to the Lord sounds suspiciously like his earlier request to allow Amnon his brother to join his sheepshearers at Baal Hazor (13:23–27).

The narrator is clear that the two hundred men accompanying Absalom are duped into being present; they do not know about "the matter" (15:11). Once there, they will automatically be associated with the sedition, and any attempts to extract themselves will be nearly impossible. The important figure, Ahithophel, is introduced into the narrative here for the first time (15:12). He is a powerful ally because his counsel is valued so highly by both Absalom and David (16:23).

David's Retreat (15:13–16:14). The opening paragraphs begin David's flight and exile from Jerusalem (15:13–23). He wisely discerns that he will need time to organize his forces and prepare for a defense against Absalom (15:14). Otherwise, all will be lost, and lost quickly. Though fleeing for his life, David's popularity among the country citizens is apparent by the loud weeping as he and his entire entourage cross the valley.

The text emphasizes especially the foreign troops who have remained loyal to David over the years. The phrase "Kerethites and Pelethites" connotes a royal bodyguard he assembled while living in exile at Ziklag (15:18). These crack troops were attached directly to the king and were loyal only to him.

David's magnanimous spirit and the fierce loyalty of his men are illustrated in the exchange with Ittai the Gittite (15:19–22). Having only just joined David's royal bodyguard, it seems unfair for Ittai to risk his life and family by getting involved in this dispute. David grants him a full pardon and releases him from his commitments. Ittai's moving statement of devotion to David, whether in life or death, is reminiscent of Ruth's classic expression of loyalty to Naomi (Ruth 1:16–17).

The next portion of the narrative (2 Sam 15:24–16:14) continues David's flight from the city. Now begins the series of so-called "meeting scenes." David first encounters Zadok the priest, then Hushai, Ziba, and Shimei. The action is delayed while important speeches carry forward the salient ideas in this unit.

These scenes portray David's reactions under fire. David calmly works through his grief with resolve and wisdom, always with a righteous deference to Yahweh's will. He is a man of great faith but also of great planning and strategy. He is being humbled by the course of political events, but he need not be naïve.

As to the meeting with Zadok, David's resignation expressed in 15:25–26 is not simple fatalism. Rather, he seems to acknowledge the events as the just punishment for his sins, and he submits to the will of God, whatever the outcome. At this sad moment in his life, David is not the least bit grasping or manipulative. He appears utterly submissive to Yahweh's will.

We should not move too quickly past David's decision to send the ark of the covenant back into Jerusalem. David illustrates here that he has learned to see beyond personal ambition and accomplishment. He would rather be right in his relationship with Yahweh than be the winner of this conflict. He refuses to turn possession of the ark to political advantage, but he humbly trusts God to do what is best in his life.

When he turns Zadok and Abiathar back into Jerusalem, David sees the opportunity to establish a system of priestly spies to inform him of Absalom's activities (15:27–28). The venerated priests will themselves learn the most up-to-date information available, and they will use their sons, Ahimaaz and Jonathan, as runners to carry the news to David.

As if David needs more bad news, he learns that his trusted counselor, Ahithophel, is among the conspirators (15:31). In a text revolving around the question of loyalty, this news of a disloyal adviser is devastating. But again, we see a combination of faith and strategy. David's prayer is that Yahweh will turn Ahithophel's counsel—otherwise always dependable—into foolishness. But this is followed immediately by David's arrangement with Hushai the Arkite (15:32–37). Hushai returns to Jerusalem prepared to serve as a double agent. He will offer his services to Absalom, but his mission will be to counter the advice of Ahithophel. David also informs Hushai of the ring of priestly spies prepared to carry the information to the king in the desert. The suspense and intrigue begin to build.

The remainder of this section narrates two episodes linked to David's relationship to the house of Saul: the encounters with Ziba and Shimei. Just beyond the summit of the Mount of Olives, David meets Ziba (16:1–4). The picture of a representative of Saul's house meeting and supporting David at this moment is somehow ironic. David is, after all, running from his own son, just as he once ran from Saul. This image contributes to the theme of loyalty in this extended narrative. Who is loyal to whom?

The last episode, also related to the house of Saul, is the cursing by Shimei (16:5–14). As the king and his retinue pass his town, Shimei takes the opportunity to pour down on them insults and stones. It seems likely that Shimei is expressing the resentment of others who felt David's rise to power was illegitimate and not condoned by Yahweh.

When Abishai offers to bring an end to such blasphemy, David demurs. Now is not the time for further violence, especially against the family of Saul, the former anointed of Yahweh. Moreover, David wants to be submissive to the Lord's will in every respect. Perhaps this curse is itself from God (16:10–11). Even these many years after Saul's death and in such extreme circumstances in which his own son and close advisers have proven disloyal, David by contrast remains loyal to Saul, the anointed of the Lord, and to Yahweh's will, whatever his own fate.

Ahithophel's Advice Defeated (16:15–17:23). The opening paragraph (16:15–19) reminds us of the narrative's central theme, that is, loyalty. Upon learning that his trusted counselor failed to remain loyal, David prayed that the Lord would turn Ahithophel's counsel into foolishness, and he enlisted Hushai to make it possible (15:31–37). Now the question becomes: Will Hushai be loyal, or will he too join the conspiracy?

When Hushai meets Absalom, he repeats the standard loyalty oath (16:16): "Long live the king!" This phrase may actually serve as a sort of pledge of allegiance. In this context, the expression raises further the question: Does Hushai intend to support Absalom or David? By pledging loyalty to "the king," does he mean the young usurper king or the banished King David?

Absalom may have become suspicious, so he pushes Hushai further about his loyalty to David (16:17). The implication is that Absalom can do without Hushai's support if, in fact, he is so fickle. Absalom's question puts Hushai in a tight spot. His response is the picture of diplomacy, and it admirably convinces Absalom that Hushai is great in wisdom and can be trusted (16:18–19).

Nonetheless, Hushai's task is a difficult one. Ahithophel's counsel is nearly always right, as though God himself has spoken from Mount Sinai (16:23). His first piece of advice is rather strange: Absalom should appear publicly sleeping with David's royal harem (16:21). Sexual relations with a king's wife or concubine was tantamount to a claim to that king's throne. Absalom quickly obeys Ahithophel's advice, which must have given the impression to the inhabitants of Jerusalem that the insurrection is in fact successful, and Absalom is king (16:22). It also constitutes a definite and irreversible break between Absalom and David.

Of course, Absalom's appearance with David's concubines is also the fulfillment of Nathan's pronouncement to David in 12:11–12. This explicit intertextuality ties together the events of chapters 13–20 with the king's own violent and sexual sins in chapter 11. David continues to reap what he has sown.

The conflict between Ahithophel's counsel (16:20–17:4) and Hushai's (17:5–14) is not unlike our own English wisdom proverbs: "Strike while the iron is hot" and "Look before you leap." Ahithophel advocates striking while David's position is weakened, while Hushai argues that only a carefully planned and well-staffed attack will be successful against so experienced an opponent as David. Hushai's speech is once again impressive, especially the subtle reminders of David's abilities in guerrilla warfare and his use of propaganda (17:8–10). Absalom and all the men of Israel are persuaded, and Ahithophel's advice is disregarded (17:14a).

However, lest the reader place too much credit on Hushai's rhetorical flare, the narrator intrudes with a rare, explicitly stated theological assessment (17:14b). This pronouncement is the turning point—the moment at which the reader learns how the story will end. God has acted, and we have only to follow the course of events as Absalom's otherwise successful rebellion comes to ruin and David is restored to the throne.

The next portion of this unit shows David's espionage ring in action (17:15–22). The sons of Zadok and Abiathar are well positioned to take reports of Ahithophel's advice to David (see 15:27–29, 35–36). The two younger priests narrowly escape capture.

The informants manage to avert attention thanks to the benevolent aid of an unnamed couple in Bahurim, and they successfully reach David with the vital information. David and everyone with him cross the river and head to Mahanaim in order to prepare for the coming battle (17:22).

The brief note on Ahithophel's ignoble death is surprising (17:23). We can only assume this seasoned politician realizes his cause is irreversibly lost once Absalom rejects his advice. David's prayer has been answered (15:31).

Absalom's Forces Defeated (17:24–19:8a). Absalom and "all the men of Israel" enter the Transjordan and set up camp in Gilead (17:24–26). Interestingly, Mahanaim was the center of Ish-Bosheth's power (2:8–9), and the northern Transjordan area was important for Saul's reign. The irony of David escaping from Absalom and finding shelter here is heightened when he is met by friendly local authorities who support him and his troops with much needed provisions (17:27–29).

Apparently Hushai's delay tactics have given David enough time to reach Mahanaim, which is presumably well fortified, and has provided time to organize his supporters into three companies (18:1–2). He originally planned to join the troops in the field but is dissuaded by their pleas that he will be worth more in the city than in the field of battle (18:3).

The account of the actual battle is brief (18:6–8). The rebellion has a superior force, and it appears to command an impressive advantage. Implicit in the words of David's men (18:3) is the realization that they are grossly outnumbered. The location of the "forest of Ephraim" (18:6) is uncertain. The significance of the forest, however, is clear: It is difficult terrain for fighting and gives the advantage to David's men (18:8).

The historian tells us that Absalom's head is caught in a tree and the mule rides on, leaving him dangling (18:9). The symbolism of Absalom's predicament is related to the use of the mule during the early monarchy as the usual mount for princes and kings. As Absalom has lost his mule from under him, so he has also lost his royal seat. There may be further symbolism intended in Absalom's suspension "between heaven and earth" (18:9, author's translation of NIV "in midair"). His rebellion has left him without the ground beneath his feet, unable to fulfill his life as prince or king and incapable of serving in the kingdom of God.

The description of Absalom's death occupies the center of this section. David's prebattle instructions are preoccupied with Absalom's safekeeping (18:5). Once Absalom is captured, one of Joab's men reminds him of David's concerns (18:12).

We have seen foreigners deliver to David what they thought would be received as good news before. When Joab sends a Cushite to David with the news of Absalom's death, one recalls the Amalekite who reported Saul's death (1:1–16). Joab takes no chances here. This will not be unmitigated good news for David, and he refuses to send Ahimaaz son of Zadok.

The account of the two messengers running to David slowly builds suspense as we are forced to wait for David's reactions (18:19–19:7). Ahimaaz appears to have been genuinely ignorant about the specifics of Absalom's death (18:29). When he is forced to "stand aside" (18:30) and wait for the Cushite to deliver the vital piece of missing information, we as readers are also left waiting for the moment when David learns of Absalom's death. We may have anticipated at least an ambivalent response: David rejoicing because of the military victory but melancholy because of the death of the prince. But there is no joy here—only grief.

David's powerful sense of loss (18:33) towers over the landscape of this narrative, turning the army's spectacular military achievement into defeat (19:2). His anguished "my son" is repeated five times in 18:33 (and another three times in 19:4) and reflects David's inconsolable attempt to fathom the loss.

Life must go on, even if David cannot bear to imagine it without Absalom. Joab takes the role of the realist, who forces David to continue with life without trying to talk him out of his grief (19:5–7).

David's Return (19:8b–43). Now that Absalom is dead, the pro-David voices return. He is, after all, the one who defeated the Philistines, and it is not likely that the nation will find a better ruler. These pro-David voices among the northern tribes argue that they should move quickly to bring David back into power in Jerusalem (19:9–10).

However, Judah is apparently slower to act, and David realizes he can never rule effectively in Jerusalem without Judah's support. He sends messengers to the "elders of Judah," stressing his kinship with them and offering to make Amasa the general of the Israelite army (19:11–13). All Judah acts to bring David back across the Jordan River. They meet him at Gilgal to escort him back into the city.

At this point in the narrative, we read of three encounters corresponding to the meetings David had on his way out of Jerusalem across the river into the Transjordan. First comes Shimei, who, of course, is anxious to make amends. David's magnanimity is a picture of a true anointed one, who is confident enough of his reign to forgive a man like Shimei.

David meets Mephibosheth, who argues fervently for his innocence against the slander of Ziba. This is a case of conflicting testimonies and counterclaims, and David sees immediately that he will never be able to sort it all out. David's compromise leaves Mephibosheth with something and still rewards Ziba for his support during the crisis.

David meets the aged Barzillai the Gileadite (19:31–39). Barzillai had been part of the delegation from the Transjordan that supported David during the crisis. David always appears ready to reward loyalty, and he wants particularly to reward the powerful Barzillai. But Barzillai is beyond caring for palace attractions (19:35) and prefers instead to live out the rest of his life at home. In his place he offers Kimham, assumed by most interpreters to be one of his younger sons.

Unfortunately, the end of Absalom's conspiracy is not the end of difficulties for David (as Nathan predicted, 12:10). The final paragraph of this unit illustrates the divide between Judah and the northern tribes (19:40–43). The tenuous union in national Israel is achieved only through the strong personal leadership of David. But even during his reign the union threatens to dissolve into intertribal conflict at the slightest provocation. Such acrimony sets the stage for the open conflict described in chapter 20.

Rebellion Finally Crushed (20:1–22). An unscrupulous individual named Sheba capitalizes on the instability in the north and takes the opportunity to incite a rebellion (20:1–2). The description of him as "a troublemaker" (20:1) uses the expression "man of Belial," which is the Old Testament way of describing someone who is at least a worthless scoundrel. His cry of revolution in 20:1 is similar to that of secessionists after Solomon's death and may be a conventional rallying cry for traditionalists in the north. The phrase "all the men of Israel" (20:2) denotes the geography of the secessionists, not the extent of their rebellion.

The information about the ten concubines seems bizarre for contemporary readers (20:3). David's action in confining them to house arrest for the remainder of their lifetimes may be an act of repentance. On the other hand, royal women have played an important political role in Israel's early monarchy.

When David returned to the throne after Absalom's conspiracy, he promised to replace Joab with Amasa as the commander of the army (19:13). Since Amasa himself commanded Absalom's army during the revolt, this is a certain compromise meant to appease those who objected to Joab's leadership (17:25). However, in Amasa's first assignment as the commander of the army for David, he fails (20:5).

David understands that Absalom's rebellion posed a threat to the king, whereas Sheba's revolt threatens the kingdom itself. He can ill afford to delay in responding to the threat, and perhaps he is having doubts about Amasa's loyalty. His solution is to send out his crack troops as an advance party under the leadership of Joab's brother, Abishai. When Amasa greets Joab as an ally, Joab strikes him down in a single blow. As Amasa draws his last breath, no one cares beyond removing him as a mere inconvenience from the path so the troops can get on with their business (20:12–13).

As it turns out, Sheba's revolt is not serious. Joab is able to corner easily this rebel. But ironically, in the midst of all this military power and strategy, it is a "wise woman" (20:16) who intervenes and delivers the town from destruction. Her persuasive use of words and skillful rhetoric save the town and the kingdom.

David's Officials (20:23–26). The literary unit beginning in chapter 15 is now concluded with a little paragraph corresponding to a similar list at 8:15–18. These were probably lists of officials from, respectively, early and late in David's reign. They serve literarily to conclude extended narratives in 2 Samuel and to summarize the organization of David's government. Thus, the entire narrative in chapters 9–20 finds conclusion in these words, which signal the end of the action of Absalom's rebellion and Sheba's revolt. Things are getting back to normal in Jerusalem.

Ironically, Joab is back in power (20:23). David attempted to replace him, but Joab is not a man easily persuaded to give up power. The lessons of the wise woman of Abel seem to have been lost on Joab.

Application. Rebellion can often look like vocation. In other words, we easily justify our rebellion because it appears to be a way to accomplish something we are genuinely called to accomplish. Taking Absalom as our departure point, it is clear that he, as crown prince, had at his disposal large amounts of legitimate power. He could probably assume that he would one day become David's successor and rule all Israel. Over time, he began to believe he had no reason to wait for David's (and God's!) timing. As David sent and took Bathsheba simply because he *could*, so Absalom took the kingdom because he believed it was eventually to be his anyway, and *he had the ability* to take it. It was one way of fulfilling his calling.

This is often the nature of temptation. In fact, temptations are hard to recognize because they regularly offer us ways to take control and use our own power (God-given power!) to falsely realize a true vocation. The abuse of God-given power to accomplish a God-given mission is a great temptation for contemporary believers today. Absalom serves precisely in this way as a warning for all of us who fail to resist this temptation.

2 SAMUEL 21:1–24:25

Original Meaning

Famine as a Result of the Gibeonite massacre (21:1–14). After three years of famine, David fervently prays in order to discern the cause of the plague. The Lord reveals to David that the famine is the result of Saul's treason against the Gibeonites. The text assumes knowledge of Joshua 9:3–27, in which the Gibeonites, non-Israelite residents of cities north of Jerusalem, tricked Joshua into a peace treaty.

Rizpah loses two sons in the carnage (2 Sam 21:8). Her extreme actions are perhaps motivated by a desire to prevent the most shameful burial possible for an ancient Israelite, that of exposure to the birds and wild animals (21:10). However, it is also possible she is protecting her sons and the others from the curse reserved for covenant violators. Her loyalty to these descendants of Saul reminds David of Saul's and Jonathan's own ignominious deaths and moves him into action. He does what Rizpah cannot do; he gives the fallen from the house of Saul a proper burial in their own family tomb. All these many years later, and near the conclusion of 1–2 Samuel, the house of Saul is finally laid to rest.

Apparently, these actions meet the needs of justice and honor, and God answers prayer "in behalf of the land" (21:14). Israel is delivered from the famine. This formula for answered prayer is repeated in the last verse of the book (24:25) and emphasizes the effectiveness of King David's prayer. The portrait of Israel's king, established by these parallel accounts, fixes the ideal anointed one for Israel's future: David's repentant leadership provides a context in which Yahweh can answer prayer.

Notes on Wars against Philistine Giants (21:15–22). These four episodes presumably occur at various times in David's early wars with the Philistines and are held together literarily by two common threads (summarized in the concluding 21:22).

1. Each relates the victory of one of David's warriors in crucial battles against the Philistines.
2. In each episode, one of David's impressive soldiers is credited with the execution of one of the "descendants of Rapha" (21:22).

The descendants of Rapha are a frightening lot. They were probably a distinct group of the Rephaim in the Old Testament and may have been the Transjordanian equivalent of the Anakites west of the Jordan. In light of references to the weight and size of their spears (21:16, 19), we can probably assume they are giants like Goliath in 1 Samuel 17, making this a list of David's "giant-killers." The unnamed "huge man" with six digits on each hand and foot (2 Sam 21:20) is especially compelling. More importantly, this list illustrates that giants in the Bible generally portray a negative image, usually representing pagans who deserve God's displeasure and are worthy of his wrath. When he taunts Israel, David's nephew Jonathan justifiably cut him down (21:21).

The verse about Elhanan of Bethlehem is difficult for a number of reasons (21:19). The larger problem is the statement that this Elhanan kills "Goliath the Gittite." In light of the importance of the David and Goliath account of 1 Samuel 17, one must ask: Who then killed Goliath, Elhanan or David?

The most preferred attempts at harmonization originated in early Jewish interpretation and removes the difficulty by claiming "Elhanan" is an alternative name for "David." Thus 1 Samuel 17 and 2 Samuel 21:19 are referring to the same event. But this suggestion requires the further step of asserting that "son of Jair" is a textual error for "son of Jesse," while at the same time requiring this exceptional use of "Elhanan" in a passage where "David" is common (2 Sam 21:15, 17, 21, 22). More compellingly, the inclusion of Elhanan/David in a list of his own mighty men is problematic. Is it really possible that his own victory over Goliath was nonchalantly included as third in a list of four such battles attributed to his mighty warriors? Ultimately, this explanation is wholly unsatisfying.

It must be admitted that we currently have no easy answer to this question. Most scholars dismiss the parallel in 1 Chronicles 20:5 as an obvious harmonization. In light of the textual corruption of 2 Samuel 21:19, it is best to leave open the possibility that this verse originally referred to a brother of Goliath, who was the more famous of the two, as in the Chronicles parallel. Another way around the impasse is to admit that contradictions of this sort were not necessarily as disconcerting to ancient Israelite authors and editors as they are to modern readers.

David's Song of Thanksgiving (22:1–51). The poems at the beginning and end of the books of Samuel serve an important function as literary frames for the whole (Hannah's prayer in 1 Sam 2:1–11 and David's psalm and last words in 2 Sam 22:1–23:7). The poetic frame articulates more directly and explicitly the books' core theological assertions. Fittingly, then, in these concluding sections of 1–2 Samuel, the historian has included this praise song, which should be taken as a theological commentary on the entire history of David.

The scholarly literature on David's song is enormous for a number of reasons, not the least of which is its repetition in Psalm 18. The differences that are present are mostly minor textual or scribal variations, making the parallel editions a textbook example of the way ancient writings were preserved and transmitted. It seems likely that other minor changes were intended to make one rendition suitable for use in a liturgical collection (Ps 18) and the other for a theological summation of narrative related to David (2 Sam 22).

This particular psalm is of a type most often called a "song of thanksgiving," though it is also a "royal psalm." At the heart of thanksgiving psalms is typically a story of deliverance or salvation, which may be summarized succinctly at the beginning, as it is in the introduction to our psalm (22:4).

In general, the psalm in chapter 22 can be summarized by the keywords that recur in its stanzas and give the overall hymn a unified theme: "rock" and "save, deliver."

1. "Rock" is a common epithet for God in the Old Testament (e.g., 2 Sam 22:32, 47; Isa 26:4; Ps 18:31), as it was among other nations of the ancient world to describe their own deities. Referring to God in this way is similar to our "solid as a rock" or to the metaphorical ways we use "mountain" to connote stability and strength.
2. The other key word is the verb "save, deliver" and its related noun "salvation" (22:3, 36, 47; also 23:5). David celebrates the assurance that Yahweh is a God who can be trusted, who rescues him and delivers him from certain death.

The brief historical introduction in 22:1 is almost identical to the superscription of Psalm 18. Its formulaic nature is similar to other songs inserted into narrative contexts. This is followed by the introduction to the poetry proper, which launches us immediately into a celebration of Yahweh's deliverance (2 Sam 22:2–4).

As is typical for Hebrew thanksgiving psalms, the general statement of deliverance in 22:4 is expanded significantly in 22:5–20. David defines his situation as that of certain and imminent death (note the theme "death," "destruction," and "grave/Sheol," 22:5–6). This is followed again by the assertion that he called out to God in the midst of his distress, and God heard his cry from his heavenly abode. David claims that earnest and righteous prayer is effective.

There follows in 22:8–20 a theophany (or divine appearance) phrased in language similar to other such appearances in the Old Testament. The general theme is that Yahweh delivers the king in his time of trouble and equips him for warfare. The primary image associated with Yahweh throughout the theophany is that of the Divine Warrior. As in other such appearances of God, his arrival is accompanied by the quaking of the earth and mountains (22:8). He comes as the warrior storm god, breathing smoke and consuming fire (22:9). His thunderous arrival is meant to strike terror in the hearts of his enemies, a terror justified because of the arrows and bolts of lightning he uses against them (22:13–15).

The conclusion of the spectacular theophany is that Yahweh has brought David out "into a spacious place" (22:20). He has reached into David's tight spot, depicted as hemmed in by the cords of the grave, covered with the waves of death, and plunged into deep waters (22:5, 6, and 17), and God has set him down safely in the open.

David's hymn of praise now takes a turn that seems unusual for modern readers. In the next section, the king maintains his innocence and righteousness and asserts that Yahweh was only being faithful in saving David (22:21–30). Yahweh has dealt with David in wonderful ways in accordance with the king's righteousness and clean hands (22:21). In general, David claims to have maintained his relationship with God by keeping the law and spurning evil (22:22–25).

David is not claiming here to have never sinned, a claim that can hardly be read seriously in light of the previous narration about Bathsheba and Uriah. Rather, he is taking the standard Old Testament view that deliverance is also vindication of one's relationship with God.

The next section of the poem celebrates David's military victories, all of which have been won in the strength of Yahweh (22:31–46). David begins with a sort of confession of faith, declaring God's way is perfect and his word flawless (22:31). This leads him to extol the incomparability of Yahweh in the form of two rhetorical questions (22:32). These questions call for an emphatic negative answer ("No one!"), and they contain an implicit monotheism. It is Yahweh who made David swift in flight (which he often needed against Saul) and strong in battle (22:33–35). David's indebtedness to God is clear from the fact that God is the subject of all the verbs in 22:32–36. David then lists his great military victories, in which he has subdued all his enemies (22:38–46). As a hymn of praise, the poem offers these victories as evidence of God's strength and power, not of David's own military prowess. It celebrates the king as a great warrior—but only penultimately, because it knows that Yahweh, not David, is the one who wins the battles.

At the close of the hymn, the psalmist bursts forth in exultant praise (22:47–51). In this closing stanza, we encounter again themes used elsewhere in the psalm: God as rock and salvation (our two key words discussed above) and victory over enemies.

There is, however, something new here. For the first time in the poem, the term "anointed" (22:51) is used specifically to refer to David. This is yet another way in which our psalm is similar to Hannah's prayer, because it likewise concludes with a reference to the anointed one of God (1 Sam 2:10).

But the way in which blessing and favor are specifically tied to David in 2 Samuel 22:51 is noteworthy. As we near the conclusion of this book, in which we learned about the Lord's promise of an eternal dynasty for David (ch. 7), the final phrase of the poem becomes even more significant, especially for Christian readers. God's blessing and favor will be poured out on his anointed one, David, and on his "descendants forever" (22:51b). This king whom God has blessed with such favor is no singular individual but David *and* his offspring forever, which refers then to the royal family of David and ultimately to Christ (Matt 1:6–16).

David's Last Words (23:1–7). In the thanksgiving psalm of the previous section, David has looked back at the mercy and faithfulness of Yahweh during his life and reign. Here in his last words, he looks forward, trusting in the promises he has received from God. David extols the benefits and virtues of a righteous kingship. His must be just such a kingship because God has made "an everlasting covenant" with him (23:5).

The designation of David as "the man anointed" (23:1) or "messiah" links this poem with the preceding one because of its use of the same term in its concluding verse (22:51). Together they form a poetic core at the center of the passage's chiastic structure.

The prophet-like speech of David commends the beautiful benefits of righteous rulership for all who are so ruled (23:2–4). Such a righteous ruler may be compared to the grandeur of the early morning sunrise, to warm sunshine on a cloudless morning, and to fresh life-giving rain.

But David then turns to an even more meaningful concept. His own kingship is regarded by Yahweh as acceptable because his dynasty has been granted an "everlasting covenant" (23:5). This is a technical term in the Old Testament that has semantic parallels in the ancient Near East related to legal contracts with no anticipated terminus point; that is, they exist in perpetuity. The expression is used in the Old Testament for all of the covenants (Noah, Abraham, Moses, and David). Thus, David's kingship is both a blessing for all humankind and an enduring promise more specifically to Israel. David's rule is just and right and is a lasting blessing for all his subjects. Such concepts became foundational for Israel's messianic hopes, and it is just such a king that Israel longs for.

More specifically, the three poetic sections that provide literary shape for 1–2 Samuel also give theological shape to the books' portrayal of David (1 Sam 2:1–10; 2 Sam 22:1–51;

23:1–7). In fact, the messianic themes of the narratives are clarified, perhaps even intensified, by the poetic frame. Certain claims central to the messianic expectations expressed in these books are reiterated in the three poems and may be summarized as follows:

1. The messiah or anointed one is God's appointed ruler (1 Sam 2:10; 2 Sam 22:51; 23:1).
2. David trusts in God and is upheld and rescued by him (2 Sam 22:2, 38–43, 49).
3. David leads God's people in battle, and God gives him power over the surrounding nations (2 Sam 22:28, 45–46, 48).
4. The king is to rule God's people justly (2 Sam 23:3–4).

Thus, Hannah's prayer, David's thanksgiving psalm, and his last words bring into sharp focus the most important themes in the narratives, especially those with messianic implications.

Soldiers' Hall of Fame (23:8–39). We come now to a military honor roll, which matches the list at 21:15–22 and like it may have come from an official military archive. In succinct fashion, this passage lists the heroes who supported David, along with a few of their more spectacular exploits. From a human perspective, these are the valiant and loyal soldiers who made David's kingdom possible, and our historian honors them enthusiastically with this Soldiers' Hall of Fame. At the same time, the narrator reminds us that the human perspective is inadequate to explain their successes. After relating two of their amazing feats, the text adds "the Lord brought about a great victory" (23:10, 12). Even when celebrating the decorated war heroes, one must remember the source of their strength.

The "Three" and the "Thirty" referred to in this text (23:23) were presumably ranks of honor, whose precise relationship to the other, larger groups is unclear. Their members changed over time as some died and others were replaced, so at the time of this list there are actually thirty-seven in the "Thirty" (23:39). These two groups were special corps of David's elite troops.

Our passage has a simple two-part structure.

1. The narrator has included stories about "the Three" who are honored above the rest (23:8–12).
2. The text describes "the Thirty," first by relating particularly striking examples of their heroism and loyalty and then simply listing their names (23:13–39). The notes on Abishai and Benaiah (23:18–23) are included to explain that both were honored above the Thirty but did not belong to the rank of the Three.

The water retrieved by the three unnamed soldiers illustrates not only their love and loyalty to David but his own devout instincts, which, of course, made his men love him all the more (23:13–17). After his men risked their lives to bring him the very water to satisfy his nostalgia, his reaction may seem ungrateful to modern readers. But the particular verb for "poured it out" (23:16) refers to the pouring out of libations, and when poured out "before the Lord," this is terminology specifically reminiscent of offerings to Yahweh as an act of devotion. David honors his men even more by offering it to Yahweh as a sacrifice. As Israelites were not allowed to drink the blood of a sacrificial animal, so David refuses to drink this water, turning it into sacred blood worthy of sacrifice to Yahweh.

The names of the soldiers appear to have no particular order in the list of 23:24–39. Surprisingly Joab is not mentioned, though his armor bearer is powerful enough to make the list (23:37). Perhaps Joab is so powerful it is not necessary to include him. His influence and power stand at the top of this list, just as his presence is felt throughout the narratives related to David.

If so much subtlety is involved in the list, then certainly the last item is intended to convey irony: "and Uriah the Hittite" (23:39). As impressive as these war heroes were, it was enough to recall that even the greatest warrior of them all, David, was flawed.

David Conducts a Census (24:1–25). At first glance, our historian appears to have chosen a peculiar way in which to conclude 1–2 Samuel. Upon further reflection, this narrative plays a role in the overall contribution of chapters 21–24 generally to the message of 1–2 Samuel. Chapter 24 returns to one of the central characterizing features of David as the ideal king of Israel. In short, this narrative reinforces the ideal portrait of David as someone willing to place aside his royal power in deference to Yahweh's will and authority.

The opening verse of this text presents modern readers with a number of perplexing questions. Why is the Lord angry? Here we are simply not told why Yahweh is angry with David, and to read emotions or motivations into the text is to be guilty of "psychologizing" the character of God.

The text assumes through the words of Joab that the census reflects a shift in David's object of faith—a shift from reliance on Yahweh to win battles to a reliance on access to military might (24:3). It is sinful because David is acting like a typical ancient Near Eastern king instead of an Israelite king.

The question on why the Lord would incite David to sin in the first place is more complicated. In the closely related parallel passage in 1 Chronicles 21:1, the source of the problem has been redefined. Traditionally, Jewish and Christian interpreters have harmonized these two statements by asserting that God's permissive action is expressed in 2 Samuel 24:1 and Satan's instrumentality is the emphasis of the Chronicles parallel. This sometimes gives the impression of exegetical sleight of hand and is often less than satisfying.

Without attempting to address this question thoroughly here, I suggest simply that we need to give more credence to ancient Israelite formulations of theology and the way that theology evolved over time during the Old Testament period. As we have seen elsewhere in this commentary, ancient Israelites were not initially concerned with secondary causes. Their emphasis on Yahweh as the creator and supreme God of the universe often found expression in the Bible in their crediting him with disaster or calamity. We modern readers are usually more interested in defending God's goodness than ancient Israelite authors, who were first and foremost interested in his power. Subsequently and late in their history, they saw a role for "Satan" in the power structures of world administration. Ultimately, however, it must be admitted once again that we may need to learn to live without neat and tidy answers to questions raised by this text.

After nearly ten months of arduous work, Joab is able to give David a report of the census (24:8–9). But then David has a change of heart. Interestingly, 24:10 gives no hint of prophetic intervention or condemnatory oracle. The real point of the narrative seems to be David's important words, "I have sinned" (24:17). The confession is strategically placed to remind us of another time David used almost the identical words to admit his guilt before Nathan and Yahweh (12:13), only this time there is no prophetic "You are the man" to expose David's hypocrisy and call for repentance.

Gad the prophet comes to David the next day, *after* David has confessed and pleaded for forgiveness (24:11–13). This final narrative of 1–2 Samuel portrays David as a king who has learned how to confess and seek forgiveness and restoration. This time he does not need a prophetic intermediary to threaten him or parabolic sermons to persuade him of his guilt. David sees his own guilt, and he quickly and genuinely repents and seeks to reverse what he has done.

Yahweh makes David "pick his poison." Required to choose between famine, military defeat, or plague (24:13), David surprises us again. He concludes that the judgment of mortals is unpredictable, whereas God's judgment is consistently moderated by his mercy (24:14). He trusts God enough to fling himself on God's mercy rather than calculate the costs of suffering at the hands of mortals. In this again, David has become this narrative's portrait of the ideal king of Israel.

In the closing paragraphs of 2 Samuel, we encounter another rather bizarre episode. The tender-hearted King David is tortured by the realization that his people (24:17) suffer because of his actions. He intervenes on their behalf, pleading that the Lord lay his vengeful wrath on him and his own family rather than on the people of Jerusalem, which the angel of death is about to strike with the plague (24:16). At Gad's instruction, David acquires "the threshing floor of Araunah the Jebusite" (24:18), builds an altar to Yahweh on it, and offers burnt offerings and fellowship offerings. The Lord responds, and the plague ends (24:18–25). At the end of the day, it is David's relationship with Yahweh that saves Jerusalem. All is well.

Threshing floors were normally on a hill where the grain was collected for threshing and winnowing. They were also traditional sites for theophanies and receiving divine messages. The context of this final paragraph implies that the threshing floor in question is north of David's city. The Chronicler provides the missing detail that, in fact, this threshing floor becomes the site chosen for Solomon's temple, having been duly purchased with David's money and made sacred by his offerings (1 Chr 22:1; 2 Chr 3:1). The final paragraph, therefore, establishes the sanctity of the future site of the temple.

Moreover, the cost of Araunah's threshing floor is significant. David insists on paying a fair price, and his assertion about the nature of sacrifice in 24:24 has profound significance. David understands the need to sacrifice a portion of his personal wealth to honor Yahweh. Otherwise, his worship will be cheap and his service meaningless.

The final verse of the books of Samuel therefore produces an interesting reminder (24:25): "David built an *altar* to the Lord there" instead of "David built the *temple* of the Lord there." David is the ideal anointed one—but not because he is invincible and accomplishes everything he wants. He is ideal because he is repentant and forgiven. He is ideal because while David is king, he is only viceroy of Israel; Yahweh is the true king. He is ideal because he banks on the mercy of God rather than trusting the fickle judgement of mortals (24:14) and because he pays the cost of true worship (24:24). David is someone well suited for kingship in Israel.

All others in Israel's future will be measured by David as the standard of Israelite kingship. But few measure up. Each royal failure only serves to drive the hope, the longing, for an ideal Son of David further into the future. So, Jesus becomes the fulfillment of this longing for another David—not because David is perfect, but because he is submissive to God's rulership and is used by God to establish the kingdom. Jesus fulfills David's promise in an unexpected way and in a way no one else could (Matt 4:17).

Application. The New Testament found this portrait of the ideal king of Israel useful for its christological affirmations. In the first Gospel, the prophecy-fulfillment motif leans heavily on the Davidic ancestry of the Messiah. This is especially apparent in Matthew's carefully constructed genealogy of Jesus, where Abraham and David are benchmarks (Matt 1:1, 17). The title "Son of David" is common on the lips of those who need help from Jesus (9:27; 15:22; 20:30; see also 12:23; 21:9, 15). This title in Matthew is equivalent to "Messiah" and provides an explicit link to the Davidic roots of Israel's messianic expectation.

In Luke-Acts, the promise-fulfillment pattern gives way to an emphasis on the flow of salvation history, which nonetheless continues to give a central role to Davidic messianism. In a paradigmatic text for Luke's Gospel, several features of the Nathan oracle appear together (Luke 1:32–33): Jesus will be made great, he will be considered Son of God, he will inherit the throne of his ancestor David, and he will rule over God's people forever. Jesus is the Lord's Anointed One, born in Bethlehem of David (Luke 1:27; 2:4, 11, 26). Jesus's resurrection is the fulfillment of the Davidic promise in Psalm 16 (Acts 2:24–32), and Jesus's ascension into heaven is the fulfillment of the Davidic promise in Psalm 110 (Acts 2:33–36). Paul assumes Jesus's Davidic descent, but in general these messianic themes are not as central in Pauline formulations of Christology. However, the expression "descendant of David" (literally, "seed of David") appears to be a proof of Jesus's messiahship based on the Davidic covenant (Rom 1:3–5; 2 Tim 2:8; cf. 2 Sam 7:12, 14).

Thus, Jesus comes to establish the kingdom of God as David established and built the kingdom of God in old Israel. Jesus is upheld and vindicated by God's power and is victorious over God's enemies. Jesus is God's Anointed One, the Messiah, who rules his people in justice and truth. As the one sent from God, Jesus prods us, as he did his first disciples, with the question (Mark 8:29): "But what about you? . . . Who do you say I am?" With Peter and Christians everywhere, we assert, "You are the Messiah." At least a portion of what we mean in our confession of Jesus as the Christ is to affirm the messianic expectations of 1–2 Samuel, their interpretation in Israel's Scriptures, and the christological development of these expectations in the pages of the New Testament.

1 KINGS

INTRODUCTION TO 1 KINGS

Joshua through Kings does not make a claim to being the work of one individual and has not been preserved in a form in which it is the work of one individual. In the Hebrew canon the entire narrative from Genesis to Kings is presented as a continuous history—a Deuteronomistic History seeking to develop a national identity on the basis of covenant loyalty.

The treatment of themes in the books of Kings is convincing evidence for dating a version of the Deuteronomistic History to the time of Josiah. Two themes—covenant obedience and the promise to David—reach their climax in the reign of Josiah. The optimistic outlook for the kingdom during the reign of Josiah is unmistakable. The catastrophe of the exile, then, requires a revision of the history. The severity of covenant disobedience takes on tragic reality for the nation, but the exile does not remove the hope of the promise. Whatever the future of the kingdom of Israel, the kingdom of God as promised to David will prevail.

The content of 1 Kings continues the narrative of the books of Samuel. It is a direct extension of the account of the kingdom of David told in Samuel. In 1 Kings we learn of the reign of David's son Solomon, the building and dedication of the temple in Jerusalem, and the subsequent demise of the united monarchy—the divided kingdom.

BOOK OUTLINE

I. Succession to David (1:1–2:46)
II. God Confirms Solomon's Rule (3:1–28)
III. Administration of Solomon (4:1–34)
IV. Royal Building Projects (5:1–7:51a)
V. Dedication of the Temple (7:51b–9:9)
VI. Solomon's Wealth and Wisdom (9:10–10:29)
VII. Demise of the Kingdom (11:1–43)
VIII. Division of the Kingdom (12:1–14:31)
IX. Conflict and Civil War (15:1–16:34)
X. Battle with the Baal Cult (17:1–19:21)
XI. Battles with the Arameans (20:1–43)
XII. Murder for a Vineyard (21:1–29)
XIII. Troubled Alliances (22:1–53)

1 KINGS 1:1–2:46

Original Meaning

Advancing Debilitation of David (1:1–4). The inability of David to function as king creates a crisis in the young kingdom. His inability to stay warm when provided an abundance of coverings is a sign of impending death. David's political advisers and protectors attempt to assist him by seeking out a beautiful young woman to provide him with personal care. None of this would be unusual in a society that expected kings to have the services of a large harem. The narrative provides no indication that Abishag is sought for the purpose of restoring virility.

Enthronement of Solomon (1:5–53). The attempted coup by Adonijah and the counter coup of Solomon are the outcome of moral compromises of David's reign. Adonijah is David's fourth son (2 Sam 3:4) and apparently the oldest surviving son. Amnon, the oldest son of David, was killed by Absalom because of the rape of his sister Tamar (2 Sam 13:28–29). Absalom, the third oldest son, died in his revolt against David (2 Sam 18:14–15).

Adonijah believes he is entitled to be heir and attempts to take over the throne; David is either negligent in the matter of not fulfilling his earlier oath to Bathsheba (1 Kgs 1:13, 17, 30), or he secretly sympathizes with the ambitions of Adonijah. Nathan the prophet intervenes. David has not been in control of his own household (1:6), a pattern seen during his reign. After Solomon is installed as king by the authority of David, the group supporting Adonijah disbands, and Adonijah is offered conciliation.

Adonijah is aggressive in seizing the throne (1:5, 7, 9). He employs a personal chariot force and guard of honor to give him the status of king and to prepare for his coup. Joab, the powerful military leader of David's army, joins in the revolt, along with Abiathar, a leading priest.

Joab is a relative of David and the ruthless leader of David's army (2 Sam 3:27; 18:14; 20:10). With Joab at the head of the conspirators, Adonijah has access to the entire army, a far greater force than the palace guard of Benaiah. Abiathar the priest has served David from the beginning of his struggles (1 Sam 22:20–23); he escaped from the slaughter of the priests at Nob, took refuge with David, and became a priest in the kingdom along with Zadok. Adonijah calls together the royal family and all the men of Judah, his own clansmen, who under Joab constitute the striking force of the national army.

The counter forces consist of Zadok the priest, Benaiah the general of the standing army, Nathan the prophet, and Shimei, who had the status of friend of the king (1 Kgs 1:8). Zadok appeared after David's occupation of Jerusalem (2 Sam 8:17) and functioned as a leading priest along with the representative of the line of Eli. Benaiah also took office after David's conquest of Jerusalem (2 Sam 8:18); he was the commander of the royal army. Nathan the prophet emerged after David took office in Jerusalem as well (2 Sam 7:2). He was always associated with the king and had sufficient influence such that he could confront and correct the king, as in the Bathsheba affair (2 Sam 12:1–15). Adonijah underestimated the resistance of those loyal to Solomon, and he overestimated the power of his forces to overcome them (1 Kgs 1:12).

Nathan the prophet previously served as the conscience to the king. Knowing the oath of succession, Nathan is committed to ensuring the promise is fulfilled. This time Nathan brings his rebuke through the influence of Bathsheba. David would feel a sense of obligation to her, especially since the oath was initially made to her (1:17). Nathan arrives as a messenger to report to David that the investiture of Adonijah is in progress. As on previous occasions, Nathan directly addresses the failure of the king without violating royal prerogative or rousing the anger of the king.

When confronted with his failures, David accepts responsibility for his wrong. His oath assures Nathan and Bathsheba that he will keep the vow made earlier (1:29–30). Prophet, priest, and general (Nathan, Zadok, and Benaiah) are to commence the coronation of Solomon immediately. Solomon mounts David's private mule, dramatic and visual evidence that royal authority has been turned over to the rightful heir.

Zadok the priest anoints Solomon as king with the authority of Nathan the prophet. The trumpet blast announces the installation of the new king. With this, prophet, priest, and general set out with the royal guard (1:38). A joyful procession follows (1:40), marking this as a most significant occasion.

The tumult of the coronation attracts the attention of Adonijah's party just down the valley. Jonathan, the son of Abiathar the priest and a man of status, is apparently present at the proceedings of the anointing of Solomon and reports everything that has transpired. The last word, spoken by David himself, is a thanksgiving prayer that the dynasty will continue (1:48). The party of Adonijah quickly disperses, unwilling to challenge the will of David and the forces who are with Solomon. Adonijah himself seeks refuge in the sanctuary. The sanctuary protects the innocent, but it is of no help to the guilty. Adonijah seems to think he is able to bargain for mercy. Solomon grants him security on the condition that he conduct himself with loyalty and honor.

Solomon Consolidates His Rule (2:1–46). *David's charge to Solomon and his death (2:1–11).* This chapter is a sequel to the enthronement of Solomon. The charge of David to deal with Joab and Shimei serve as a prolepsis for the task Solomon will have in securing his throne. The problem of Abiathar and Adonijah has already been established in the anointing of Solomon. Joab had a role in those events (2:28), though he was not mentioned, and Shimei humiliated David when he fled from Absalom (2 Sam 16:5–14). The previous episode of Solomon gaining the throne is continued by introducing the role David had in securing the throne in the midst of various rivalries that carried over from his time.

The charge of David to Solomon (1 Kgs 2:2–4) is typical Deuteronomistic theology, expressing the ideology of the kingdom. The fundamental obligation of the king is to rigorously observe the divine mandate (2:3a), which is "written in the Law of Moses"—that is, Deuteronomy. Faithfulness to the covenant is the single discriminating factor in determining whether kings are good or bad. These final words of David are the fundamental first words for every succeeding king. They express the need for uncompromising faithfulness if the dynastic succession is to continue as God has promised (2:4).

As is the case in any transition of power, some matters need immediate attention to prevent continuation of the kind of conflict experienced with Adonijah. During David's reign there had been rivalry for power within the military. Joab and his brothers Abishai and Asahel were a central force in David's wars against the house of Saul (2 Sam 2:17–18). Abner was the chief of the military for the Benjamites, but he eventually defected to David in an agreement to unite the two political powers (3:12–21). Abner in self-defense had earlier killed the fleet-footed Asahel (2:18–23). When Abner made peace with David, Joab lured him back into the gate of Hebron, where he killed him (3:24–27). This was a serious setback for David since the people of Israel held him responsible for the death of their military leader.

Worse still was the murder of Amasa, a kinsman of David who replaced Joab at the head of the military (2 Sam 19:13–14). Joab, under the command of Abishai, pursued the rebels, but in a fit of jealousy treacherously killed Amasa when he came to meet them at Gibeon (20:7–10). Joab regained his status as head of the army (20:23) through the death of those better than himself (see 1 Kgs 2:32). Solomon must now use his political savvy to accomplish what David failed to do in bringing stability to the military.

David owes a favor to Barzillai, a Gileadite of Rogelim, who brought food and supplies to him and his followers at Mahanaim during Absalom's rebellion (2 Sam 17:27–29). David insists that Barzillai's son, Chimham be rewarded for this deed of loyalty (19:37–38).

David was never able to overcome the hostility between Benjamin and Judah. The rift of north and south was evident during the rebellion of Absalom when Shimei, a Benjamite relative of Saul, publicly cursed David and accused him of bloodguilt in supplanting the house of Saul (2 Sam 16:5–13). When the rebellion was quelled, Shimei petitioned David for his life, and David granted him an oath of clemency (2 Sam 19:16–23). Solomon cannot allow such resistance to go unchecked, and David instructs him to find occasion to deal with it coercively.

David then dies and is buried in the city of David, the walled fortress of the Jebusites that was first conquered by David and his personal striking force (2 Sam 5:6–9). Though Peter makes reference to the tomb of David as known in his time (Acts 2:29), it is no longer possible to authenticate the place. The summary of David's reign repeats the information given earlier (cf. 2 Sam 5:4). The regnal résumé in customary fashion summarizes several key events in the life of David.

The consolidation of Solomon's reign (2:12–46). The investiture of Solomon does not settle the question of succession. Adonijah uses the influence of Bathsheba to rally support for his right to rule as the older brother. Solomon recognizes the popular support that Adonijah would have as the older brother (2:22), and that he also has the support of a leading priest (Abiathar) and military leader (Joab). Adonijah's request for Abishag becomes the occasion for Solomon to rid himself of the adversary he has reluctantly spared (cf. 1:52). Solomon takes a double oath (2:23–24) to express the certainty that Adonijah must die. He ordered his death through the agency of Benaiah (2:25), who is responsible for the royal guard.

The role of Bathsheba in the proceedings is left somewhat enigmatic in the narrative. She has complied with Adonijah's request, though he is a rival and feels that his right of kingdom has been taken away (2:15). Bathsheba is well aware of Solomon's claim to the throne because of the promise to David (2:24). It is possible that in delivering the request she knows Solomon will have sufficient reason to bring closure to the question of succession through eliminating his rival.

Solomon bans Abiathar to Anathoth, where he is to make a living from his own estate and never again receive support from the sanctuary (2:26–27). The sentence given to Abiathar as a man marked for death (2:26) is commuted; this may be the regular form for an accession amnesty. Abiathar can no longer function as a priest; according to the judgment of Deuteronomistic theology, this is a consequence of the sins of the house of Eli in Shiloh (1 Sam 3:12–14). The genealogy from Eli to Ahimelech, priest of Nob, Abiathar's father, is never given explicitly (22:20), but there may have been independent tradition to confirm it.

The banishment of Abiathar signals to Joab that his time is up (2:28–35). Even the most fierce and fearless warrior will die by the sword as he lived by the sword. Joab seeks refuge at the altar and determines to die there if necessary. He may have hoped that Solomon will not resort to execution, at least not in the temple, but Solomon's resolve is undeterred.

Solomon gives amnesty to Shimei (2:36–38) but at a considerable cost. He is confined to Jerusalem, which prevents him from again rallying support against the Davidic dynasty in the Benjamite countryside. It also prevents him from managing his own lands. In the forced absence of their master, the servants are free to act on their own initiative and in their own interests. Two of them run away (2:39).

Shimei obviously knows the risks of pursuing his servants in seeking to protect his economic interests. Solomon has forbidden him to cross the Kidron (2:37), a valley just to the east of ancient Jerusalem that separated it from Shimei's territory in Bahurim. Shimei goes south and west to Gath, perhaps taking literally the prohibition of not crossing the Kidron, in the hope that this will not violate his oath. He returns with his servants before Solomon finds out about his departure, but this does not spare him. Solomon executes the oath according to its intent, if not the exact letter of the law.

Application. The enthusiastic statements about the celebration of Solomon's rule leave no doubt about the conviction of the Deuteronomistic Historian (1 Kgs 1:47–48). For the sake of the kingdom of God, it is important that the throne be made secure under Solomon's dominion, and to that end it is necessary and good that all opposition to his rule be quelled. The skeptical reader will find this to be an indictment of the low spiritual ideals of the time, demonstrating an attitude that the end justified the means. A desire to find God's will in these events inevitably lends legitimacy to the charge that implicit approval is given to the methods of Solomon. The contemporary Christian faces a similar cynicism when attempting to discern God's will in current events.

A high theology in this narrative may be discerned in the blunt presentations of the flawed actions of each of the characters. There is no flattering portrayal of a champion; the deeds of each individual are frankly described, even though this may diminish the reader's estimation of all of the characters. The prophetic authors present a realistic and believable portrait of the succession to David's throne. They hold God in highest esteem; God alone is allowed to be the hero in an otherwise sordid tale. Understanding the dynamic between human volition and divine purpose becomes particularly difficult in dealing with the depraved behavior of human conflict.

In a democratic society, Christians are asked to be a part of the process by which leaders come into power. Admittedly the procedures are often not fair and equitable, and sometimes the leaders are flawed. Nevertheless, these procedures are regarded as a means ordained by God to accomplish his purpose in the world in which his people live. As with Solomon, God carries out his purposes through imperfect people using imperfect methods of achieving their goals.

1 KINGS 3:1–28

Original Meaning

The Divine Gift of Wisdom (3:1–15). Solomon is an eminently successful king renowned for his wisdom and wealth. His success is the result of a superior administration, enabling him to raise revenues far beyond anything previous to that time. The introductory note about Solomon's marriage to the daughter of Pharaoh (3:1) is significant in relation to his worship at Gibeon and the building of the temple. Solomon has become allied to Pharaoh, likely in connection with Egyptian campaigns into Philistine country (9:16). The mention of Pharaoh's daughter calls attention to Solomon's prominent international position early in his reign. The first part of Solomon's reign is most magnificent.

Solomon's choice to worship outside of Jerusalem (3:4) is normal before the completion of the temple (3:2), but the choice of Gibeon is politically expedient. Gibeonite territory was one of the first areas to become a part of Saul's kingdom, and a new king would need to renew the connection with the Gibeonites, possibly through a treaty, in order to become recognized as their ruler.

Gibeon is also home to the largest "high place" (*bamah*, 3:4) in the country, a prominent location for the worship of Yahweh before worship at the temple in Jerusalem is established. But once worship at the temple in Jerusalem is established, these other centers are not regarded as legitimate places for worship of Yahweh.

Solomon is seeking guidance and blessing from Yahweh. When Yahweh appears in the dream, Solomon makes his request in terms of the covenant relationship established with David his father (3:6). "Great kindness" is an expression of covenant loyalty, describing integrity in a relationship. As a new king Solomon is inexperienced; he is not really a "little child" (3:7) since he already has a son when he begins his reign. Solomon rules forty years (11:42), and his son Rehoboam is forty-one when he begins to reign (14:21).

As king, Solomon has the well-being of the people at heart; his request is to be able to rule with justice, having the wisdom to hear both sides of every story with a discerning mind (3:9). As a king whose first concern is the welfare of the people, Solomon is also granted that which he does not request: wealth, honor, and a long life.

Justice of a Wise King (3:16–28). The exceptional wisdom granted to Solomon is next demonstrated in a difficult judicial case. The evidence of both parties is presented as given orally before the king (3:16–22), and the king sums up the argument (3:23). It is his responsibility to render a decision when there are no independent witnesses and where there is a great deal of bitterness between the two litigants.

Several features in the story about Solomon settling the dispute between the two women call attention to his insightful and sympathetic rule. Ancient prostitutes were generally slaves, often daughters who had been sold by their own parents. Or they were poor women who had never had an opportunity to marry or who had lost their husbands and were not supported by their own families. Kings were the highest recourse for justice, expected to take up the case of the widow, the orphan, and the oppressed. Note how Solomon has time for the most vulnerable of his subjects, not only in terms of their poverty but also in terms of their vices.

The judgment of Solomon shows both mercy and justice. The Hebrew text makes the circumstances of the death explicit. The two women are together with "no one" present (3:18); the women have no family. Since none was present, the death of the infant can only be the responsibility of its mother. The mother of the dead child is charged with being careless, suffocating her child during the night by lying on it (3:19); this fact can hardly have been known, since the death occurred while the other was asleep. This is a case of the word of one against the word of the other, and there are no witnesses.

Solomon's judgment does not deal with the circumstances of the death of the child or with the various accusations being made. His concern is with the bonding relationship of a mother and her child, which he presumes to be present by virtue of the fact that the case has come before him. The living child has no father, but the true mother is determined to care for her child and to give it hope in this world.

Faced with the horror of watching her child die, the emotions of the true mother compel her to acquiesce to the demands of her wicked partner (3:26). Once Solomon knows the identity of the true mother, he does not engage in further punishments, either to deal with the cause of the first death or the subsequent criminal actions in switching the children. The circumstances of prostitution and the death of the child are regarded as punishment. Justice is best served when tempered with mercy; the life of a child is preserved and the bond of motherhood restored, and there is renewed opportunity to make the best of a bad situation.

The judgment of the new king causes the people to be filled with awe. The response is that of respect due to a king, but there is recognition that this king possesses wisdom beyond that of other mortals. Solomon has received a divine gift that is at work in enabling him to resolve an otherwise impossible case.

Application. Under the new covenant no one government represents the kingdom of God, but government makes possible the advancement of the kingdom. This is true even when a government is hostile to Christians and restricts or persecutes expression of faith in Christ. The apostle Paul was able to spread the gospel across Asia Minor and as far as Rome because of the security and order provided by *pax Romana*. Prayer for government is important not only to provide for good order, but because it is God's will that all should be saved and come to knowledge of the truth (1 Tim 2:3–4).

1 KINGS 4:1–34

Original Meaning

The Chief Officials (4:1–6). The roster of chief officials mentions eight distinct offices as compared with five in 2 Samuel 8:16–18 and six in 20:23–25. The priest heads the list (1 Kgs 4:2) as the most influential of the officials. The secretaries (4:3a) keep records and prepare correspondence. The recorder (4:3b) regulates the ceremonies of the palace, introduces people to royal audiences, and serves as master of ceremonies on an official tour.

The commander of the army (4:4a) may have also served in administrative responsibility as a kind of secretary of war. The officer over the district governors (4:5a) is responsible for the provisioning system for the palace. The personal advisor to the king (4:5b) is the king's most intimate confidant and perhaps a chief officer of government administration. The officer in charge of the palace (4:6a) is responsible for all the royal property, including lands and buildings. The officer in charge of conscripted service for the king (4:6b) is responsible to provide the necessary labor for the king's projects. The list has been transmitted with variations, the result of historical and textual developments.

The District Governors (4:7–20). The districts of Solomon's administration are defined according to tribal territory and groups of cities. This is the only administrative document pertaining to the official organization of the kingdom. There are other comparable documents from this time that can serve as a basis for comparison with this list of Solomon's reign. Several features of these lists parallel the list of Solomon's governors. An introduction defines the contents of the list and designates the individuals listed; it is followed by a series of entries with a personal name and a place name, and finally there is a concluding entry distinctive from all its predecessors. The administrative list in Kings has been incorporated into the narrative to show how the practical prudence of Solomon brings satisfaction to his citizens (4:20).

Provisions for the Kingdom (4:21–28). The extent of Solomon's kingdom and the prosperity of the people are fulfillments of the covenant with Abraham (Gen 15:18). Solomon reigns from the Euphrates River to the border of Egypt (1 Kgs 4:21). The subservience of all these kings bringing tribute to Solomon shows the farthest extent of the kingdom of Israel. It comprises a territory more vast than the land God had promised Abraham.

The list of provisions for a single day (4:22) are for the entire palatial establishment, including servants and guests (4:27). A comparison of the texts for Solomon's stalls suggests that 4,000 is the original number. The records indicated that Solomon has 12,000 horses in 4,000 stalls and probably about 3,000 chariots, a formidable force comparable to others of the time.

The Wisdom of Solomon (4:29–34). In addition to the wisdom required for the governance of a vast kingdom, Solomon has a breadth of knowledge (4:29) that rivals that of all ancient time. Mesopotamia and Egypt were famous for wisdom, some aspects of which are preserved to the present time. Ethan and Heman are noted in their contribution to the Psalter (Ps 88–89). "Sons of Mahol" (1 Kgs 4:31) does not refer to physical ancestry but to their skill as musicians or dancers. Wisdom, poetry, and music are closely connected. "Ezrahite" (4:31) means native and may indicate that this knowledge of musical instruments and poetry goes back to the pre-Israelite occupants of Canaan. Wisdom is expressed with skill and impact by means of poetry and song.

Solomon is not only known for his songs (4:32) but also for his proverbs. There are collections of Solomon's proverbs, as indicated by the divisions in Proverbs. The "proverbs of Solomon" (Prov 10:1–22:16) contain 475 proverbs, the numerical value of the name *Solomon*. The proverbs of Solomon inspire other collections of proverbs (e.g., Prov 25:1) long after Solomon's death.

Ancient wisdom encompassed not only music and poetry, along with proverbial sayings for prudent conduct, but also much of what is now called science. The reference to Solomon's wisdom concerning nature (4:33) is not just that nature served as a basis for proverbial sayings. Solomon's classification of creatures into beasts, birds, reptiles, and fish may have been another aspect of his comprehensive knowledge.

Application. Wisdom is knowledge of how to live with other people and how to live in harmony with the world of nature. These two kinds of knowledge are the basis of getting on well in this world. Living in harmony with the world of nature is a continuing challenge. The "green revolution" has enabled the production of food many times beyond what previous generations could have imagined. It has also endangered plant species and polluted or dried up water supplies. The development of energy has been a vast resource, but there is the constant threat that demand will outstrip supply or that the consumption of energy will alter the earth so it becomes a much less hospitable place for human existence.

Wisdom of how to live with people is an even greater challenge. Conflict and violence are part of social relations from the smallest units of society to the largest: homes, communities, nations, and between nations. The ideals of Solomon's wisdom and administration are rightly remembered as the goal to which every society must strive.

1 KINGS 5:1–7:51A

Original Meaning

Preparations for Building the Temple (5:1–18). Solomon's preparations for building are described in two sections. The first section (5:1–12) explains the alliance between Hiram and Solomon through which Solomon acquires the necessary materials and craftsmen. The second section (5:13–18) describes the workforce that Solomon marshals to accomplish his building projects.

Alliance between Hiram and Solomon (5:1–12). The alliance of Hiram with David and Solomon serves as the grounds for Solomon to make his appeal, either through letter or as an oral communication (5:1–2). The actual request is made at the conclusion of the appeal (5:6). The delay in building the temple must first be explained (5:3–5); David has been involved in warfare to gain control over his empire. The request of Solomon to Hiram makes the declaration that Yahweh gave David rest from his enemies. The rest given to David was a divine gift.

Chronicles develops theologically the reason why David could not build the temple; it was because of his shedding blood in warfare (1 Chr 22:7–8; 28:2–3). Solomon gives a historical reason: David was too occupied by warfare. Chronicles gives the theological reason: The peace of God's kingdom is incongruous with a person constantly involved in warfare.

Hiram's response is to praise Solomon's God for the succession of a wise king like Solomon (1 Kgs 5:7). Hiram is noted for his own temple buildings to the god Melqart (Heracles), but it is appropriate for him to give praise to Solomon's God in observing the success of Solomon. Hiram's reply is constructed around his obligation and Solomon's obligation; Hiram will give Solomon trees, and Solomon will give Hiram food (5:8–9).

Lebanon refers to the double range of mountains parallel to the Mediterranean coast. Solomon provides Hiram annually with over fifty thousand bushels of grain and over one hundred thousand gallons of purified olive oil. The treaty (5:12) is a mutual benefit, since the cliffs of Tyre are not conducive to producing food and Solomon requires the skills and materials of the Phoenicians.

The cedar tree (5:8, 10) is renowned for its beauty and impressive height, reaching as high as thirty meters. The kings of Egypt, Mesopotamia, Phoenicia, Assyria, Babylon, Persia, and Greece all used cedar timber for building temples and palaces. Cedar wood was also desired for its fragrance. The pine tree (often translated juniper or cypress) may be a collective name for several species of fir. The trees are bound together in rafts so they could be driven by water as far as Jaffo (Joppa), where they can be disassembled and taken overland to Jerusalem. Solomon in turn gives to Hiram food supplies that include the finest oil (5:11). The oil was of exceptional quality for the lamps in the tabernacle (Exod 27:20) and the preparation of flour offerings (29:40).

Administration of building projects (5:13–18). The second section of building preparations (5:13–18) gives some detail of the work of Adoniram (cf. 4:6), the chief officer in charge of the conscripted labor force. Hiram has determined that his workers will bring the wood down from Lebanon (5:9), but according to this description they are assisted by Solomon's workforce as well. The amount of labor required to quarry and shape the stones to lay the foundation of the temple makes them costly (5:17).

The Construction of the Temple (6:1–7:1). The building of the temple begins and ends with a chronological notice (6:1, 37–38). The introduction sets the month in which the foundation is laid in reference to the exodus. This is significant for two reasons.

1. The temple represents the worldview of the Israelites that Yahweh rules in all the earth, so they calculate their chronology from the founding of the temple.
2. The exodus is the redemptive event through which the Israelites experience the rule of God in the world (Exod 15:13, 18).

The description of the building itself lacks details, except for a brief notice concerning the windows (6:4), but there is a detailed description of the doors to the inner sanctuary (6:31–32). The intention is to report selected details and ornamentations to illustrate the intricate designs and splendor of the temple as the edifice that represents the divine presence in Israel. The account of the temple construction consists of three sections. The first describes the exterior of the temple (6:2–14), the second its interior (6:15–28), and the third some particular features of the furnishings of the temple and court (6:29–36).

1. The exterior of the temple. The description of the exterior concludes with a statement that the building has been completed (6:9a); this is followed by a parenthetical note on the construction of the roof, the room extensions around the sides of the building, and the exterior paneling (6:9b–10). This section ends with an exhortation to obey the covenant (6:11–13); the covenant, not the temple, is the means to divine presence. The building account resumes with a repetition of the statement that Solomon built and completed the temple (6:14; cf. 6:9); this repetition marks the transition to the second section.

The temple is a small structure adjacent to the much larger palace in the royal compound. The dimensions (6:2) indicate the interior size of the building, not taking into account the thickness of the exterior walls or those that separated the three rooms. The length of sixty cubits includes the main hall and shrine; the porch is measured separately (6:3). The cubit varied in length in different periods (cf. 2 Chr 3:3), but reasonable estimates can be established. The temple of Solomon is about 27 meters long (87.5 feet), 9 meters wide (29 feet), and 13.5 meters high (44.8 feet). The length and breadth of the temple are double the dimensions of the tabernacle constructed at Mount Sinai.

The porch runs the full width of the building and extends ten cubits in the front of the long room (6:3). Windows are recessed in the walls (6:4). For comparison, the portico of the ʿAin Daraʿ temple was open on one side, but the walls of the temple extended to form two walls, and two massive pillars (like Boaz and Jakin) supported a roof. This appears to be the model of the portico on Solomon's temple.

The windows in the walls are apparently ornamental; the wall panels in the first room of the ʿAin Daraʿ temple included at least two window frames carefully cut into the stone. The stone windows had reliefs in the upper half. The walls of Solomon's temple have similar decorative stone reliefs. Light and ventilation is apparently provided through openings on the upper part of the building.

A platform built of large blocks extends along the wall all around the building (6:5) and serves as a foundation for three-storied auxiliary wings. These stones are placed as lifted from the quarry, without the use of iron tools in construction (6:7). The outside walls of the temple are recessed at the level of each story, so the adjoining wings are not bound into the temple walls (6:6). Each successive story is, therefore, one cubit wider.

In Solomon's temple a door on the south side at the front of the temple serves as an entrance to the lower story (6:8). The second and third stories are reached by means of stairs, probably winding or reversing. The roof (6:9) is constructed with rows of reticular beams (forming squares) and recessed panels. Each level of the side rooms has a ceiling (called a platform) adjoined to the temple walls by cedar beams (6:10). The temple building is relatively simple and modest in size, especially in comparison to the assembly hall.

The use of undressed stones taken directly from the quarry conforms to the requirement that no iron tools were to be used on stones for altars used in worship (Exod 20:25; Deut 27:5–6). The prohibition of dressed stones is another way of distinguishing an Israelite place of worship from the Canaanite shrines. Israelite altars are to be unadorned, made of earth or unhewn stones and without steps (Exod 20:24–26). The temple symbolizes the divine rule but in no sense the actual image of a king, not even in the construction of the building itself.

2. The interior of the temple. The temple's interior is finished with costly materials: cedar for the wall panels and juniper for the floor panels (1 Kgs 6:15–16). The interior walls of the temple have carvings of gourds and open flowers, cherubs and palmettes (6:18, 29). At the extreme interior of the hall a special area is constructed as the Most Holy Place (6:16b). It is constructed equal in all directions, extending twenty cubits into the hall and twenty cubits toward the ceiling (cf. 2 Chr 3:8).

The building is thirty cubits high. The Most Holy Place is prepared as a repository for the ark, which contains the terms of the covenant. The interior of the Most Holy Place is covered with pure gold (1 Kgs 6:20). Nothing is said about the veil in front of the Most Holy Place (cf. 2 Chr 3:14), but reference is made to gold chains pulled across its front (1 Kgs 6:21). Perhaps the curtain is pulled with these chains.

An altar built of cedar (6:20) stands in front of the Most Holy Place. Though not stated, the altar inside the temple is for the offering of incense, as in the tabernacle (Exod 30:1–10; 1 Chr 28:18).

Cherubs were a distinguishing feature of thrones in ancient Mesopotamia, Syria, and Canaan. They were composite creatures, signifying union of the highest powers of strength, speed, and sagacity. The cherubs of Solomon's temple (1 Kgs 6:23–28) are distinct because they are not designed to serve as a human throne. They are attached to the ark, which serves as a footstool to the throne (cf. 1 Chr 28: 2).

3. Particular features of temple furnishings. The third section of the temple description (1 Kgs 6:29–36) notes particular features about the larger temple complex. Cherubs, palm trees, and open flowers are engraved on all the walls, inside and outside. Special attention is given to the wood doors leading to the Most Holy Place.

The design of the doors is unclear. The two doors of juniper wood providing entrance into the main hall each have two panels (6:34). For the first time it is explained that the gold is inlaid over the engraved figures (6:35). A wall consisting of three layers of shaped stones with an ornate cedar beam on the top encloses the temple in an inner court (6:36). The temple is a separate section within the great court, which includes the temple and the entire palace compound (6:36). The concluding chronological reference to the seven years of temple building (6:37–38) includes notice of the thirteen years it took to build the palace (7:1).

The Construction of the Palace Complex (7:2–12). The first building described (7:2–5) is the great assembly hall, which also serves as an armory. Based on the medium size cubit, the structure is 44.5 meters (146 feet) long, 22.25 meters (73 feet) wide, and 13.35 meters (43.8 feet) high. The structure is supported by four rows of cedar pillars and cedar cross beams above them. It is known as the "Palace of the Forest of Lebanon" (7:2) because its many pillars give it the appearance of a great forest. The structure of the building, however, is not clear; salient features are given to indicate its grandeur.

The description of the assembly hall is particularly ambiguous in 7:3, as a comparison of translations makes evident. The cedar roof is built over three "beams" (*tselaʿ*), which are above the pillars. In the temple description, "beam" describes stories of storage rooms (6:5, 8), rows of cedar boards (6:15), and panels of a door (6:34). The referent of the term in 7:3, then, may be either beams or storage rooms. It is likely that the hall has storage rooms since it also serves as an armory.

Analogies to similar structures suggest that four rows of pillars form three long open naves, allowing a large assembly hall on the ground floor. Three stories of rooms, fifteen at each level, are constructed on top of each of the two outside naves. Each of the three stories has rows of windows at the ends of the great halls, each corresponding to or opposite the other at the three levels (7:4).

The three sets of doorways serve as entrances to the great halls and are perhaps placed at the ends, opposite each other (7:5). The doorways and doorposts are square. Whatever the arrangement of the rooms, doors, and windows, the "Forest of Lebanon" is a hall fit for a great assembly with plenty of rooms for an armory.

The hall of pillars (7:6) does not seem to be an independent building but a colonnade that serves as an entrance to the great assembly hall. The length of 50 cubits (44.5 meters; 146 feet) is equal to the width of the assembly hall. It is unclear as to what structure is described in front of the colonnade. A hall along the front of the porch has a protective barrier guarding entrance into the building. It is likely that this porch is built to serve as the judgment hall (7:7).

The palace of Solomon (7:8) and the quarters for all his servants are set in another court back (west) of the hall. The public buildings are situated in a separate court; the palace is not accessible to the public but has an entrance to the public court as well as the inner court of the temple. The palace of Solomon and that of Pharaoh's daughter are similar in construction to the other buildings, since all of them are royal edifices.

Special notice is made of the costly stonework (7:9–12) that is part of the buildings and the courts. It is costly because the stones are all hewn to measure inside and outside. Dressed stone is used from the foundation to the framework—or to the roof overhang, if stonework is mixed with the woodwork, as is often done. This seems to have been the case in the royal buildings, as the stonework and woodwork are made to measure on the upper levels (7:11). The stonework extends as far as the large public court. The foundation stones are large (3.5 to 4.5 meters; 11.5 to 14.6 feet) but not excessive by building standards. The larger outer court is built with three levels of stone and a row of cedar timbers (7:12), like the inner temple court (cf. 6:36).

Artifacts for the Temple (7:13–51a). The first of the artifacts described are the two pillars set in the porch of the temple (7:15–22). They are made of bronze and are 8 meters (27 feet) in height. Their circumference was over 5 meters (17.5 feet), making them almost 2 meters (6 feet) in diameter.

The height of each pillar is extended by a capital at the top formed of bronze, just over two meters (over seven feet) in height (7:16). These are ornately decorated (7:17–18). The two capitals have the shape of a lily; there is a bowl-shape in the capital just below the lily, where two hundred pomegranates hang in rows (7:19–20). The pillar to the south is named Jakin and the pillar to the north Boaz (7:21). The significance of the names can only be guessed; Jakin ("it is firm") may refer to the promise of the kingdom, and Boaz ("in strength") may have been a prayer for the king. The pillars perhaps have a structural as well as symbolic function.

The second item described is a giant water container (7:23–26), over four meters (fifteen feet) in diameter and over 2 meters (7.5 feet) in height, cast with two rows of gourds beneath its rim, which have the shape of a lily. Twelve bulls face outward beneath it, three in each direction. It holds about 11,000 gallons of water. Its significance is to be found in the name "Sea" (7:23). Water has a practical use in ritual cleansings in Solomon's temple (2 Chr 4:6), but the size of the great water basin is not practical for that purpose. Its primary purpose in the temple court is to represent the rule of God over the cosmos.

In addition to the great Sea, the temple has ten water tanks in the shape of a bowl to distribute water for cleansing purposes (1 Kgs 7:27–39). Each of these tanks is six feet in diameter and holds about 220 gallons of water (7:38). It is estimated that the weight of each stand with its water reservoir full would be 3.5 tons. They are equipped with wheels, but they are not readily mobile.

The bases of the lavers are six feet square and three feet high, made of bronze, with frames and supports (7:27–28). These are elaborately decorated with cherub figures and borders, above and below, with delicately worked spiral designs (7:29). Each base is equipped with wheels, legs, and supports beneath the laver (7:30), each of the supports adjacent to the spiral designs. The opening of the box-shaped frame has within it a circular rim to support the laver (7:31), with engravings on the square frame that hold the laver support. The wheels are over two feet in diameter (7:32), similar to a chariot wheel with rims, spokes, and a hub cast together (7:33) and attached to the legs with axles in sockets. The circular rim of the laver protrudes at the top of the base frame, which has handles and supports (7:35), possibly to assist in moving the laver. All the space on the panels, frames, and handles is appropriately filled with cherub figures and palm trees (7:36). All ten lavers are identical (7:37), disposed in two groups at the south and north corners at the temple (7:39), with the great Sea being further to the east on the south side.

Huram is responsible for a variety of artifacts used for the altars (7:40), including ash containers and shovels, and containers for sprinkling (cf. Exod 27:3). The bowl shape of the capitals has not been mentioned previously (1 Kgs 7:41); it is not certain if this is the same aspect as the "bowl-shape" mentioned earlier (7:20). The items are made with polished bronze (7:45) and smelted in earthen molds in the Jordan Valley north of Jerusalem (7:46), just north of the Jabbok River east of the Jordan.

The gold items are located inside the building next to the specially constructed throne room at the back (7:48–50). The incense altar (cf. 6:20, 22), the table with bread, and the ten lampstands (each with seven arms) are elements in the temple to represent access to the presence of the divine. Other floral decorations are part of the lampstands and lamps to provide decoration and light. The highest quality of metal distinguishes the sacredness of the area.

Application. For the leaders of Judah, the temple was reduced to a place of ritual; their sacrifices, festivals, and even their prayers in the temple were an abomination to God (Isa 1:11–15). Though they had fervent dedication to the temple, their city and land were equivalent to Sodom and Gomorrah (1:10). The grandeur of the temple was not sufficient to assure that God would be God in the land of Israel.

One of the most decisive influences in the lives of the faithful is their understanding of God. A subtle deception for Christians is the assumption that belief in the Bible alone will lead to a true understanding of the God of the Bible. Though mortals can never understand God fully, it is possible and necessary to understand God truly. It is also possible to come to a seriously distorted understanding of God through improper, though sincere, reading of the Scriptures. Misunderstanding God may be no less disastrous for a church than it was for those who celebrated the construction of Solomon's temple.

1 KINGS 7:51B–9:9

Original Meaning

Installation of the Ark (7:51b–8:13). After the building's completion, its function as a temple must be established. The articles dedicated to God by a vow are brought to its treasuries (7:51b), and the ark is placed in the Most Holy Place. When the priests bring the ark into Solomon's sanctuary, the glory of the divine presence takes possession of it (8:11), just as the glory accompanied it in the desert.

Solomon assembles the elders of Israel, the heads of the tribes, and the ancestral chieftains to bring the ark up to the temple (8:1). Several groups of people are distinguished: the ordinary people are brought together with their leaders, while the priests actually carry the ark (8:2–3).

The ark processional takes place in the seventh month. Since the temple was completed in the eighth month (6:38), the inauguration of the temple seems to be almost a year later. The ark and the "tent of meeting" (8:4) are brought up to the temple—the former to be put in the sacred throne room, the latter to be stored with the other sacred items. With the building of the temple that tabernacle has no further function but is kept as a sacred treasure.

When the ark is placed beneath the cherubs, the poles are still visible (8:8). The poles, as a permanent fixture, indicate the presence of the ark. The ark contains only the tablets of the covenant (cf. Exod 25:21; Deut 10:5). The pot of manna (Exod 16:33) and the branch of Aaron that budded (Num 17:10) are also sacred objects associated with the temple or Holy Place but are never said to be actually inside the ark in the Old Testament.

The ark is set in the Most Holy Place in thick darkness. A poem recited by Solomon celebrates the significance of this "magnificent temple" (1 Kgs 8:12–13). God's temple is the heavens (8:39, 43, 49), but the Most Holy Place with the ark and the cherubs now represent his heavenly temple.

Patronage of David (8:14–21). The blessing of the assembly begins with a declaration of the blessedness of God (8:14–15). Blessedness is an epithet of God, an acknowledgment that he is the source and dispenser of blessing. The blessedness of God is his fulfillment of the promise that the son of David was destined to build a temple as a focus for Israel's prayers and worship.

Solomon's words express the importance of the temple in the history of the nation and the role it will have in future relationships between God and his people. The presence of the temple assures the people that God has secured a royal dynasty for his people (cf. 2 Sam 7:12–17). The temple is the place where the ark of God's covenant finds its rest (1 Kgs 8:21). The ark represents the special legal bond uniting God and Israel. The presence of the ark of the covenant makes the temple the focal point for prayer, no matter where the prayer is uttered.

Dedication Prayer (8:22–53). Solomon takes a position at the altar in front of all the people and begins his prayer of dedication. Standing with one's hands spread toward heaven is a customary posture of prayer (8:22), though Solomon is later said to have been kneeling (8:54). Standing before a seated deity signifies an attitude of readiness for service; kneeling or sitting depicts humility in the presence of the deity.

Solomon prays before the assembled crowd in the presence of the altar (8:22, 54). Presumably this is the bronze altar in the court (8:64), though it has not been previously mentioned in the furnishings of the temple made by Hiram. The prayer emphasizes the loyal faithfulness of God in his covenant with those who are faithful (8:23). "Covenant of love" in 8:23 is a paraphrase for loyalty; the Hebrew word *hesed* is used primarily to describe loyalty to a commitment made by oath. Divine loyalty is evident in the promise to David already fulfilled (8:24); Solomon's prayer is that the divine promise might now be fulfilled in the continuity of David's descendants on the throne (8:25–26). The covenant blessing is conditional on the faithfulness of the covenant partners (8:46). Solomon pleads for the temple to receive the divine mercy when the people pray.

The presence of God is not to be conceived as limited to the temple, since even the heavens cannot contain the Creator (8:27); this is the place God has chosen for his "Name" (8:29). Solomon's purpose is to build a central temple for "the Name" of God (8:17, 19). Solomon prays that "the eyes" of the LORD will always be open to the place where petitions are made (8:29, 52).

In the prayer, seven petitions are intended to be representative of any future situation that the people of the covenant might encounter. The first circumstance describes a dispute that cannot be resolved, leading the parties to give testimony by oath to determine guilt and innocence (8:31–32). Solomon's first request is that justice might function as it should in the determination of guilt and innocence.

The petitions of Solomon make specific reference to the curses of Deuteronomy. One of the curses of covenant disobedience is that Israel will be struck by her enemies (8:33). There may also come a time when no rain falls, when the sky turns to bronze and the earth to iron (8:35–36). Enemies will attack their fortified cities (8:37). War and illness are both matters of individual as well as national concern (8:38). God is the one who knows the inner attitude (8:39), the one who can forgive the truly penitent.

Knowledge of the covenant is the wisdom of Israel in the presence of all the nations (Deut 4:6–8). There will be those from other nations who voluntarily join the society of the covenant. They no less than any others are the object of Solomon's concern; his prayer is that they, in the same way as other Israelites, might find mercy before God (1 Kgs 8:41–43).

Solomon's petition returns to the themes of war (8:44–45) and exile (8:46–53). In war the people experience God's judgment. Solomon prays that God may "uphold their cause" (8:45). This is an appropriate rendering of God's acting on their case to give them justice. However, it may be impossible for God to defend his people in war because of their covenant violation.

Exile is the consequence of a ruptured relationship with God. Captors may take them into an enemy land (8:46); if in the land where they were taken captive they turn in their minds and make confession to God (8:47–48), if they turn wholeheartedly to the city God has chosen, God may hear and forgive (8:49–50). Defeat by enemies is evidence of sin and failure (8:46); the only recourse in captivity is to turn back to God in repentance, remembering his covenant and his promise. God redeemed his people and made them his special possession at Mount Sinai (8:53; cf. Exod 19:5–6). Solomon's prayer is that God's work may be completed.

The prophetic concerns of a total exile are evident in the final two petitions of this prayer. The situation of defeat in war has already been contemplated (1 Kgs 8:33–34); it is now repeated (8:44) with allusion to the curse of Deuteronomy that God may send them and their king into foreign territory. A petition for time of exile (8:46–53) follows that of being sent away in war (8:44–45).

There were many exiles in the history of Israel, but complete destruction of Jerusalem and its temple will be the greatest challenge to faith. The mention of land, city, and temple suggests a total destruction, not a partial exile (8:48). The promise of the exodus (8:53) has to be reaffirmed. The petitions (8:45, 50) and the covenant promise (8:51–53) are particularly important in a time when the temple might no longer be present. Even then, prayer could be directed to God in heaven, who would hear and forgive.

Dedication Exhortation (8:54–61). Following the long dedicatory prayer Solomon stands to bless the people by giving praise to God for fulfilling his word (8:56–58). The prayer switches to the first person with two concluding petitions (8:59–61). Solomon asks for justice as each day requires, so that all nations may know the truth declared at Mount Sinai: There is but one Lord (8:60; cf. Deut 4:35, 39). Solomon in turn petitions for undivided loyalty from the people (1 Kgs 8:61). Ironically, this prayer fails to be realized in Solomon's lifetime (11:4).

Dedication Sacrifices (8:62–66). The closing summary of the temple dedication at the Festival of Booths brings the account back to the events of the introduction (cf. 8:1–2). Further details are added. The sacrifices previously described as being without number (8:5) are here enumerated in terms of oxen and sheep (8:63). Communal peace offerings introduce the sacrifices and appear to be the central aspect of the dedication. The main function of these offerings is to provide food for the table; these sacrifices are for joyous occasions of celebration. The quantity of these offerings is so great that the great bronze altar does not have sufficient capacity (8:64). The entire court was consecrated for the occasion.

Covenant Confirmation (9:1–9). The vision is less an affirmation of the initiatives of Solomon in temple building than a warning of the dangers of covenant failure. God has been faithful in fulfilling the promise that he has given (9:5). The promise of an eternal house of David is always contingent on absolute faithfulness of the Davidic kings (9:6–7). This is not to dismiss the possibility of grace and forgiveness. The problem is to expect grace while persisting in compromise of the covenant. This is the warning of the vision, with specific attention to the fact that no splendor of building or eloquence of prayer can serve as a substitute for obedience (9:8). The vision is also an exhortation, which becomes personal in its use of the second person plural (9:6–9). The demand for obedience not only pertains to the king, it pertains to the entire people.

Application. The Christian calling has a fundamental continuity with the function of the temple as expressed in Solomon's dedication prayer. Solomon's mission in building the temple was to memorialize and perpetuate the great works of Yahweh, the kingdom anticipated in the promise to David. The calling of the Christian church is to show the purpose of God for creation as it is accomplished in his world. Those called to Christ are destined according to the purpose of the one who does all things according to the intent of his will, to be to the praise of his glory (Eph 1:11–12).

Belonging to the church demands that Christians learn to live in accordance with that calling, learning harmony and unity with each other (Eph 4:1–3). Fundamentally, living as a Christian requires a new way of thinking (4:17–24). Outside of Christ human values are governed by self-interest, the deceit of greed. All divisions of humanity are bridged in Christ; all races and classes are brought into harmony, as they are transformed in knowledge according to God's image (Col 3:10–11).

1 KINGS 9:10–10:29

Original Meaning

Labor Provisions for Building Projects (9:10–25). It is not clear why Solomon gives territory to Hiram. Solomon's payment of twenty settlements is not expressed as a sequel to the material contributions of Hiram (9:11). The main clause explains Hiram's displeasure when the transactions are completed at the end of twenty years (9:12). Hiram apparently thinks twenty settlements in northern Galilee are a miserly remuneration for the amount of gold given. At minimum Hiram has given Solomon several tons of gold.

The account of conscripted labor (9:15–23) has a long introduction (9:15–19), which enumerates the various projects that form a part of Solomon's building activities. These include the fortifications of Jerusalem and strategic points in the provinces.

Six cities are named as part of the fortifications. These form a line of defense from north to south. The list concludes with an inclusive reference to all centers developed for administrative and defensive purposes (9:19). Excavations at cities like Lachish have revealed large buildings with long, narrow rooms that served for storage.

Conscripted labor that Solomon uses to maintain his building projects consists of native Canaanite peoples who lived as subordinates after the conquest (9:20–21). These are to be distinguished from the temporary conscriptions that Solomon laid on the Israelites to construct the buildings (5:13). The Israelites were never subject to continuous servitude.

A concluding summary on the temple (9:23–25) notes three disparate items: the number of the chief supervisors, the move of Pharaoh's daughter, and the three annual festivals. The offerings Solomon makes are not to suggest he is acting as a priest but rather to show he makes provision for daily and yearly rituals of the temple (9:25b).

International Fame and Fortune (9:26–10:25). In addition to internal administration of his kingdom, Solomon has extensive involvement in foreign affairs. These include trade with distant lands, which he carries out in cooperation with Hiram (9:26–28; 10:22). The shipbuilders of Tyre had access to many types of wood and imported materials for sails and ornamentation. Solomon used magnificent ships for voyages to fetch the treasures of Ophir.

The account of the queen of Sheba further illustrates the fame, wisdom, and wealth of Solomon (10:1–13). A distinguished monarch as far away as southern Arabia is impressed by reports of his accomplishments. Southwestern Arabia was an important territory, controlling trade routes between India, east Africa, and the Mediterranean. The queen of Sheba controlled an enormous amount of wealth, as indicated in the size of the caravan that attended her (10:2). She comes to test the wisdom of Solomon with riddles (10:1), to obscure metaphorical references like the kind Samson used to test the Philistines (cf. Judg 14:14). His answers and accomplishments are enough to take away her breath (1 Kgs 10:5).

Solomon's wealth is indicated by the enormous gifts the queen needs to give in order to be significant (10:10); the gold alone is equivalent to what Solomon has received from Hiram (cf. 9:14). With the mention of Hiram, wealth is stressed as much as wisdom in the visit of the queen of Sheba. The gold Solomon receives in one year may have been the income in one particular year rather than an annual income (10:14). Solomon also collects taxes from foreign traders and local merchants (10:15).

Solomon makes two hundred large shields covered with gold and three hundred small shields (10:16–17). Large shields were body length, possibly three sided; small shields were a light protection worn on the arm. The weight of gold in each small shield is just over 3.5 pounds, just under 2 kilos. The weight measure of the large shields is not given, but shekel is likely to be inferred, a weight four times that of the small shields. Guards display the shields as the king goes up to the temple (cf. 14:27–28).

The throne of Solomon is a work of grandeur. The six steps may indicate that the throne is situated on a platform, which constitutes the seventh step (10:19). Lion figures stand at the sides of each step and beside each armrest (10:19–20). The throne has ivory inlays and is covered with gold.

Prosperity and Security in Jerusalem (10:26–29). The wealth of Solomon provides for strong military, security, and spectacular luxury in the capital city. The enumeration of horses, chariots, and military cities summarizes information given earlier (4:26; 9:19). Solomon obtains his horses from Egypt and Kue, located on the Cappadocian seacoast in Asia Minor near the Taurus Mountains (10:28).

Solomon's merchants buy horses and chariots and trade them along the way with the Hittite and Aramean kings (10:29). Egypt may have been a recipient in the trade of horses and chariots. Commentator G. H. Jones (*1 & 2 Kings*, NCBC) suggests that Solomon may have controlled trade between Egypt and Syria.

Application. Wealth is never an individual matter; no one can achieve wealth in isolation from a community or a broad work environment; people with wealth should always honor God as the giver. We must live our Christian lives with these principles in mind. The use of money is fundamental to living out Christian values. The story of Solomon has important lessons on God's view of wealth, its significance, and its use.

The wealth of Israel was not the personal possession of individual Israelites, as though they earned it themselves, nor was it the possession of the king who made their national economy possible. God granted wealth in Israel the same way as he provided manna in the desert. The Israelites were to remember that they were unable to become independently wealthy. Theologically, resources are a gift from God; sociologically, they are received as a community and are a product of the collective work of individuals.

Christians need to think carefully about their view of the world in relation to wealth. Industrialized societies tend to view the world as a resource of unlimited good. If this is so, wealth can be generated by hard work; hard work done honorably brings about God's blessing, and the wealth earned is the sole responsibility of the individual. Christians need to remember that resources are limited for particular people in particular places. Not everyone is able to generate a living through relentless hard work, let alone wealth. Those in the kingdom of God must look beyond their own interests both in how they acquire wealth and how they share it with those who do not have the same opportunities.

Solomon is an important example to all Christians who have considerable material well-being in comparison to other people of the world. God must be honored through the riches he has given us through the collective support of a whole economic system. We are privileged to have the blessing; we need not apologize for it. Our challenge is to use this blessing to bring about peace and good, the kind of kingdom envisaged for Solomon (Ps 72).

1 KINGS 11:1–43

Original Meaning

Prophetic Judgment of Solomon (11:1–13). This section has been characterized as a theological review. It contains offenses and judgment statements that evaluate the king according to prophetic orthodoxy. The prophetic indictment is given as a word from Yahweh without any specification as to the occasion or manner in which that word is delivered (11:11–13). Judgment against Solomon is mitigated by the promise to David (11:12–13).

Solomon attaches himself to foreign women (11:2), accommodating their practices. He builds altars for them in the presence of the temple (11:7–8), though it is not said that he actually worships with them. The covenant contained specific warnings about intermarriage with the nations (Deut 7:1–5). This review of Solomon's reign has a particular focus on that failure.

The numbers of wives and concubines with their children are deemed beyond enumeration. The wives are princesses, women of high political rank (1 Kgs 11:3). Though these relationships may have begun as a matter of political expediency, the end result is the catastrophe Deuteronomy warned would happen.

"Ashtoreth" is a form of the name of the Canaanite goddess Ashtart (11:5). The pronunciation is sometimes deemed to be a deliberate parody. She was the Canaanite counterpart to the Akkadian Ishtar and Sumerian Inanna, a goddess of war and sexuality. Milcom is the national god of the Ammonites, also pronounced Molek (11:5, 7), a name that meant kingship. This god is associated with child sacrifice (2 Kgs 23:10; Jer 32:35). Chemosh, the national god of the Moabites, is also worshiped in Syria. A Moabite king offered his son in sacrifice to his god in desperation in his war with the Israelites (2 Kgs 3:27).

Enemies of Solomon (11:14–25). The adversaries of Solomon are human political opponents designated by God to punish Solomon (11:14, 23, 25). In later Hebrew this word (*satan*) for "adversary" meant "prosecutor," in some instances a member of God's court (Job 1:9; 2:2; Zech 3:1–2); eventually the term became a name for the devil.

Two kings named Hadad are known from the genealogies of Edom (Gen 36:31–39). David conquered Edom as one of the expansions of his empire (2 Sam 8:13–14) and a certain Hadad king of Edom was an adversary of Solomon (1 Kgs 11:14–22, 25).

Nothing is said of the fate of Hadad, but his servants take the young prince to Midian, east of the Gulf of Aqaba, then to Paran in the western Sinai. There they solicit the help of guides familiar with the territory and finally find refuge in Egypt. The reigning pharaoh not only gives the young prince a home, provisions, and land; he makes him a member of the royal family. David and Joab are his dreaded enemies (11:21); when they die, Hadad renounces the security and luxury of Egypt and enters into some type of guerilla warfare against Solomon (11:25).

David's defeat of Hadadezer king of Zobah is described in some detail (2 Sam 8:3–8). Rezon, a rebel against Hadadezer, organized a guerilla movement and eventually gained control of Damascus (1 Kgs 11:23–24). Rezon founded a dynasty that became the kingdom of Aram-Damascus, the most powerful Syrian state in the days following Solomon. As an independent power he resisted Solomon during the whole time of his rule (11:25).

Revolt of Jeroboam (11:26–43). Jeroboam is the servant of Solomon who becomes his successor (11:11, 27–28). Solomon recognizes the capability of Jeroboam and makes him supervisor over the compulsory state service required from the house of Joseph. The location of the two construction sites mentioned is not specified. Solomon may have needed to expand his fortifications to the south and east, which require building up the wall bases and closing the breaches.

"About that time" does not indicate chronological sequence (11:29) but indicates a general temporal relationship with previous events. The prophetic endorsement comes sometime during Solomon's reign, because Jeroboam flees to Egypt and seeks refuge there until Solomon dies (11:40). Where the prophet meets Jeroboam is not specified, but it is not a coincidental encounter.

Prophets often communicate in dramatic fashion (e.g., Isa 20:1–6). The action of Ahijah is particularly dramatic as he tears up the new garment of Jeroboam. The seizing of the garment indicates it belongs to Jeroboam (1 Kgs 11:30), because such an action would not be pertinent to his own coat. The newness of the garment is stressed twice (11:29–30), making it a fit item for the prophetic sign.

The action of Ahijah persuades Jeroboam to initiate an insurrection against Solomon's autocracy, but it gains him nothing more than exile in Egypt (11:40). God will grant Jeroboam his desire to rule (11:37), but it will not happen because of his own initiative. It is the work of a prophet to stir people to action in order that God's purposes may be accomplished through them in his time.

The words of Ahijah amplify the judgment given earlier in the narrative. Judgment is the result of Solomon's promoting worship of foreign gods (11:33); judgment is mitigated because of God's promise to David (11:34–36). The leadership of David is described as a lamp at the time he was rescued from mortal danger by his soldiers. A son of Solomon will continue to rule one tribe to preserve this light (11:36), an acknowledgment of the political reality that territorially the tribes of Benjamin and Simeon are absorbed and Judah exists as a single territory.

Ahijah declares Jeroboam to be a true successor of David (11:38); the promise of dynasty applies to Jeroboam as it had to David. The phraseology of Nathan's prophecy to David is strikingly adapted to Jeroboam, legitimizing the Northern Kingdom (2 Sam 7:9a, 16a). But unlike David, where the kingdom is promised in perpetuity, the house of Jeroboam is made contingent on his uncompromised obedience. The house of David will be humbled, but a ruler will remain in Jerusalem for the sake of David (1 Kgs 11:34).

Solomon becomes aware of Jeroboam's plot, which apparently is not limited to Jeroboam himself (cf. 11:26b, 30). Jeroboam finds refuge in the court of Shishak, the first king of the Twenty-Second Dynasty in Egypt (ca. 945–924 BC). His treatment of Jeroboam is an indication of a change in Egyptian policy to Solomon. The length of his stay is not specified.

Application. The glory of a king blessed by wisdom is a critical aspect of the story of Solomon, but the lessons of Solomon taught in the narrative of Kings are much more sobering. A great and wise king may at the same time be a foolish and weak king. This is the irony of Solomon's life; wisdom has the power to produce wealth, but the seductive power of wealth can erode the wisdom of following God. The narrative of Kings calls everyone to be a person greater than Solomon. None might compare to Solomon in the glory of his reign or the wisdom discovered by the queen of Sheba, but all need the wisdom of faithfulness to God.

The persistent lesson of Solomon for those who live under a new covenant is the importance of faithfulness. Success at any one point in the life of an individual—spiritually, materially, or both—is no assurance of continued loyalty to God. This message is skillfully articulated in the prophetic portrayal of Solomon's reign.

1 KINGS 12:1–14:31

Original Meaning

Jeroboam Made King over Israel (12:1–24). Dynastic succession did not have an established procedure in the early days of the kingdom. Solomon had to overcome the forces of Adonijah in succeeding David to the throne. In the same way, Rehoboam, son of Solomon, has to travel to Shechem to develop a consensus on his claim to the throne. Deuteronomy was structured around the requirement of a tribal commitment at Mounts Ebal and Gerizim, where Shechem was located (Deut 11:29–32; 27:1–14). The fulfillment of this requirement was made a central point in the arrangement of the book of Joshua. If Rehoboam is to secure the loyalty of the northern tribes, he must do so at Shechem.

When Rehoboam arrives in Shechem, the representatives of the northern tribes begin negotiations to gain concessions from the heavy load of taxation and conscripted service. The king is not at liberty to make an independent decision on this vital matter. He sets a time of three days to take counsel with the "elders" and the "young men," two groups who have a critical role in the political process (1 Kgs 12:6, 8, 10).

Elders traditionally exercised considerable influence in royal decisions. When Absalom revolted against David, the elders of Israel were an influential force in critical decisions (2 Sam 17:4, 15; 19:11). These elders were distinguished from officials, nobles, and guardians (Judg 8:14; 1 Kgs 21:8; 2 Kgs 10:5) who had official roles in governance.

The "young men" are described as those who have grown up with Rehoboam (1 Kgs 12:8). Since Rehoboam is forty-one years old when he becomes king (14:21), it seems that the reference to "young men" does not necessarily imply youth. Rather, they belong to another generation and have different values from the more experienced elders.

As might be expected, the opinions of the two groups of advisors are diametrically opposed. The elders, well-tempered by years of political experience, urge moderation (12:7). The younger princes, having enjoyed a sense of power and status all of their lives, urge the new king to proceed in an autocratic manner (12:10). The sting of the "scorpion" is apparently a weighted or spiked lash that can be wielded by a taskmaster (12:11).

Rehoboam chooses not to follow the counsel of the elders. Though this is a foolish political choice, it is not just politics that influences his choice. The values of the covenant and the role of the king as a brother have already been lost by Solomon. The judgment of the prophets has already been declared; this turn of events is from Yahweh's fulfilling the declarations of the prophet Ahijah (12:15). Yet it is wrong to interpret this statement as divine control over Rehoboam's mind. Rehoboam has no inner desire to follow Yahweh or the way of the covenant. He makes choices in accordance with his own values, which he has learned through his father.

Rehoboam proceeds to follow the path of political coercion and sends Adoram, the commissioner over those conscripted into royal service, to deal with the unrest. Adoram may be an abbreviation of Adoniram, the commissioner who regulated the conscripted workers during the time of Solomon (4:6b). Whether or not he is known from an earlier regime, the people are in no mood to listen to new policies for regular terms of state service. They kill him, and Rehoboam flees to Jerusalem.

Rehoboam has not lost all capacity to respect the prophetic word. In accordance with the advice of the "young men," Rehoboam prepares a considerable army to enforce his will over the rebellious tribes (12:21). A godly man named Shemaiah reminds him that though these tribes have rejected his rule, their rejection of his rule is not a judgment against them but the evidence of a divine judgment against Rehoboam himself. Rehoboam respects this judgment sufficiently to refrain from further political conflict and self-destruction.

The death of Solomon and the revolt of the northern tribes provides the occasion for Jeroboam to return from his exile in Egypt and assume leadership over the new political entity of Israel (12:20). It seems that Jeroboam is not summoned to the assembly until after the murder of Adoram, when it becomes known he has returned from Egypt (12:20). Earlier references to Jeroboam indicate he is present during the negotiations at Shechem (12:1–3, 12). Presumably, Jeroboam has had a role in inspiring the verdict that Israel has no inheritance in the dynasty of David (12:16).

Innovations in the Northern Kingdom (12:25–32). Jeroboam creates a distinct kingdom in the north through various changes.

He fortifies Shechem to make it a royal residence, then Penuel across the Jordan (12:25), and finally Tirzah (cf. 14:17). He establishes places of worship in Bethel and Dan so the people will not go to Jerusalem for the pilgrimage festivals; he makes the Canaanite bull the symbol of divine presence and providence (12:27–31). Archaeological evidence indicates that in the days of Jeroboam the sanctuary at Dan extended over a relatively large area. This area, with its various structures, storerooms, and open spaces paved with stone, may be the various "shrines on high places" (12:31).

Jeroboam alters the priesthood, ordaining those not from the tribe of Levi; he establishes the eighth month as the time of the great fall pilgrimage (12:32). The ordination of non-Levitical priests may have been part of the policy to forge a separation between the kingdoms of David and Jeroboam. Levitical priests would naturally have had a loyalty to the temple as well as David, and most may have been unwilling to serve at a separate shrine.

Prophetic Condemnation of Jeroboam (12:33–13:34). Jeroboam's ascent to the altar on the first day of the festival is the initiation of the high place he has built. A man of God from Judah calls Jeroboam to account for his worship at Bethel (13:1–10). There is an old prophet from Bethel who tests this word from Yahweh (13:11–32).

The disobedience of Jeroboam to the word of Yahweh leads him to the same fate as the disobedience of the man of God who came from Judah. The faithful man of God becomes unfaithful, just as Jeroboam, the anointed king of Israel, goes his own way and becomes the object of the word of judgment. The man of God from Judah proclaims God's word in declaring the folly of Jeroboam but then chooses the way of folly himself in disobeying what he knows to be God's word given to him.

A second revelation given to the man of God from Judah is pivotal in understanding the message of this story about two prophets. Three times we are told the man of God from Judah is not to eat bread, drink water, or return by the way he came. The first occurs in his encounter with Jeroboam. The king suffers paralysis of his arm in demanding that the prophet be seized (13:4). The prophet prays for the king and his arm is restored (13:6), and the king in turn offers the man of God hospitality (13:7), possibly as a sign of solidarity and affirmation of his new position. The prophet refuses, citing the prohibition of Yahweh given to him (13:8–10).

When the old prophet from Bethel invites the man from Judah to return for food and drink, the latter repeats the prohibition, which he knows to be Yahweh's word (13:16–17). The prophet from Bethel lies (13:18), averring that a messenger from Yahweh has told him the man from Judah should return and eat bread with him. Following the lie does not excuse the man from Judah, who has demonstrated with a sign that he knows the word of Yahweh (13:5). When the word of judgment comes to the prophet from Bethel, the prohibition of eating and drinking is repeated (13:22). The disobedience of the prophet from Judah with its attendant judgment becomes a demonstration of the judgment that rests on the house of Jeroboam.

The context and sequences of the story depict the judgment that awaits Israel. Jeroboam has built altars, which become a sin for the people (12:25–33). The obedient man of God proclaims judgment against the altar at Bethel as Jeroboam stands by (13:1–10). But the prophet himself compromises his mission by returning to eat and drink, contrary to God's word (13:11–19). The prophet of Judah is condemned by a word of Yahweh given by the prophet from Bethel and falls prey to a lion (13:20–25a). The donkey stands helplessly beside his body, just as Jeroboam stood beside the shattered altar. In subtle terms this scene shows Jeroboam to be a dumb animal.

In the final scene the prophet from Bethel retrieves the body from the presence of the lion, which has not molested the body or mauled the donkey (13:25b–32). The lion's abstention from eating serves to emphasize retrospectively the transgression of the man of God in eating prohibited food. The warning at the altar does nothing to change the ways of Jeroboam (13:33–34). He proceeds to ordain priests to serve at the high places. This is the sin of Jeroboam that leads to the dissolution of the nation and its ultimate destruction.

Prophetic Judgment against Jeroboam (14:1–20). Judgment against the house of Jeroboam begins with the illness and death of his son Abijah. The name of his son meant "my father is Yah(weh)," suggesting a pretentious claim on the part of the king. The illness of the son is so severe the king seeks the help of the prophet Ahijah, who brought him the original oracle of his appointment as king. He sends his wife to Shiloh in Ephraim, where the prophet resides. She is to be disguised so Ahijah will not know who is coming with the request, possibly because Jeroboam hopes to receive a more favorable response. She carries a modest gift as a tribute to the prophet. The physical sight of Ahijah has failed, but he has inspired vision, which not only enables him to identify his visitor but declare the harsh message he has for her.

The condemnation of Jeroboam is in terms of his call (14:7–11; cf. 11:33–35). Jeroboam has received the kingdom at the expense of the Davidic dynasty because Solomon failed to be loyal to God. That Jeroboam is "more evil than all who lived before [him]" (14:9) is stereotyped language found repeatedly in Kings; David was not evil as Jeroboam, but Jeroboam has committed the same sins as Solomon and leaders before David. The judgment that came on Solomon will also come on

Jeroboam. His whole royal house will die without receiving a proper burial (14:10–11).

The judgment against Jeroboam begins the moment his wife enters the city (14:12–13). His son will die and will be mourned by all Israel. Only this child of the house of Jeroboam will be buried with dignity. Yahweh will raise up another king in place of the descendants of Jeroboam (14:14), but ultimately the whole nation will go into exile beyond the Euphrates because of his sins (14:15–16). The metaphor of a reed shaken in the water may refer to the many dynastic changes that will shortly take place or to the uncertainty that comes with the instability of leadership. The Asherah poles, which are so offensive to Yahweh (14:15), are associated with the worship of Baal, representing the goddess of fertility.

The concluding notice of the reign of Jeroboam makes special note of his great feats in warfare and rule (14:19–20). Information from the royal annals of the kings must have been incorporated into the sources the prophetic authors used to compile their history. Reference to these records becomes a fixed and formalized framework for the reign of each king.

The Reign of Rehoboam (14:21–31). The introductory regnal résumé introduces Rehoboam at the death of Solomon (14:21–24); he reigns from 930–913 BC. Most notable about Rehoboam is the way he leads Judah in the sins of Canaanite worship, no less than what Jeroboam does in the north. This includes the erection of sacred stones along with the sacred poles representing Asherah, the goddess of fertility. Worst of all are the "shrine prostitutes" (14:24). Sexual relations were part of sacrificial rites as a means of achieving fertility and prosperity (Hos 4:14). Cult practices and prostitution were explicitly forbidden by the covenant (Deut 23:18).

One of the main events of the reign of Rehoboam is the invasion of Shoshenq I of Egypt, known to the Hebrews as Shishak (1 Kgs 14:25–28). The division of Israel, along with internal union and peace in Egypt, provide opportunity for political and commercial exploitation. A fragmentary victory stela from Thebes (Karnak) provides a description of a border skirmish that may have been the immediate occasion for the invasion.

The general course of Shishak's campaign can be inferred from a topical list inscribed on the pylon of a temple in Karnak. Shoshenq with the main army goes up a well-traveled route by Ajalon and Gibeon to secure the submission and tribute of Rehoboam in Jerusalem. From there he travels north to Megiddo, possibly through Tirzah, the capital of Jeroboam. Of greatest significance is the cost of the campaign to the wealth and splendor that Solomon accumulated. The temple and palace are stripped; mere bronze shields replace the gold ones Solomon made. The ceremonial marches to the temple lose much of their former splendor.

Application. Jesus, in his high priestly prayer for his disciples, did not ask that God take them out of the world, but that God would keep them from the evil one; they were not of this world, just as Jesus himself was not of this world (John 17:15–16). Christians have struggled with this concept and debated it in many ways. Christians understand that they live by the values and conduct of the kingdom of God, but it is not easy to know how these are to be exercised in particular circumstances. To some extent believers must conform to the culture around them as part of the world they live in, but in certain ways their lives need to manifest a different value system.

It is easy for Christians to become consumed with the pursuit of wealth and a better standard of living. Such a standard is a good goal but not if it becomes the purpose for work and use of one's time. Christians understand that good relationships within family and community must be a high priority, but it is difficult to maintain good relations in the stress of daily life and encounters with difficult individuals.

As in the days of Jeroboam and Rehoboam, there is an expression of faith that has compromised biblical life and values so it is indistinguishable from the surrounding culture. Jesus did not ask that his followers be taken from the world, but that they would be sanctified in the truth of God's word and sent into the world (John 17:17–18). Purity from this world must begin with clear Christian thinking. Failure to clearly distinguish Christian faith from postmodern relativism will lead Christians to conform to the ways of the world.

1 KINGS 15:1–16:34

Original Meaning

Conflict between Judah and Israel (15:1–24). Abijah (Abijam in Hebrew) succeeds Rehoboam. Abijah's mother is Maakah daughter of Abishalom, understood to be a variation of Absalom. Maakah may have been a foreigner, possibly of Aramean descent, which may account for her idolatry (15:13). It is not possible to identify the mother of Abijah as daughter to Absalom the son of David. It is best to accept the information given rather than to harmonize or assume contradictions. It is unlikely that Rehoboam would have married a daughter of Absalom, a cousin through his father's older brother.

Kings condemns Abijah; he follows in the idolatry of Rehoboam. His territory is preserved only because Yahweh desires to keep the lamp of David preserved in Jerusalem (15:3–5). Abijah continues his father's policy of war with Israel (15:6–7), but there is no acknowledgment of divine blessing on his reign.

The forty-one years of Asa are from 910–869 BC (15:9–10). He takes initiative against the male and female cult prostitutes serving at the country shrines and removes Maakah as the leading lady (15:12–13). Maakah holds the office of "queen mother" (15:13). The queen mother is the first lady of the realm, taking precedence over all the women of the harem. Normally she holds the office as long as she lives, and on her decease the title passes on to the mother of the heir apparent.

Official functions of the office of queen mother in Israelite monarchy are nowhere more specific than in 15:13. The patronage of Maakah to the Asherah cult may have been one aspect of fulfilling her court responsibilities to legitimizing the rule of the king, but this is speculative. Maacah may have been a woman with particular personality force and influence.

Asherah in the Bible is usually a pole, possibly a phallic symbol. She is well known from the Canaanite Ugaritic literature, where she is the wife of the supreme god El and the mother of seventy children, including Baal. The queen mother has a shrine dedicated to this goddess. Asa has the object cut down and burned. Though Asa is unable to remove the shrines, he is committed to the restoration of the temple treasuries (15:14–15). He was able to restore some of the artifacts of the temple through booty, which he and his father dedicate for temple use.

The war with Baasha brings the Arameans into conflict with Israel (15:16). Baasha apparently attempts to prevent Israelites from having contact with Asa by fortifying Ramah (15:17). Asa takes whatever treasures Shishak has left and whatever he has managed to restore and sends them as a bribe to the Aramean king Ben-Hadad to attack Baasha. The mention of Asa's father may indicate that Abijah has already made an agreement with Ben-Hadad (15:19).

Ben-Hadad is more than willing to accept money from both Baasha and Asa in their war against each other (15:19–20). The Aramean breaks his treaty and attacks northern Israel, capturing all the land of Naphtali. The absence of Hazor from the list of cities taken by Ben-Hadad is remarkable since it was the major fortified city of the area. Baasha may have been able to resist the Aramean army and retain the territory around Hazor. The northern attack forces Baasha to abandon his southern fortification.

After the withdrawal of Baasha, Asa conscripts workers to use the materials at Ramah to rebuild Geba and Mizpah. According to the concluding formula, Asa fortifies other cities in Judah as well (15:23–24). His death from disease was regarded as evidence of divine disfavor.

Civil War and Idolatry in Israel (15:25–16:34). The only son of Jeroboam to succeed him is Nadab, whose two-year reign, according to nonaccession year reckoning of Israel, is chronologically a bit more than a year (909–908 BC). Baasha assassinates him while he is occupied with a siege at Gibbethon (15:25–31). Baasha not only assassinates Nadab but also carries out a blood purge against the entire royal lineage of Jeroboam, fulfilling the judgment that Ahijah the prophet proclaimed against him.

The war between Baasha and Asa is discussed as part of the reign of Asa (15:17–21), so Baasha's reign can be summarized with the synchronism and length of his reign (15:32–33) and a theological assessment (15:34). His guilt lies in following the sins of Jeroboam; Jehu son of Hanani delivers the sentence.

The speech against Baasha (16:1–4) is given in the rhetoric found in the judgment against Jeroboam. Baasha is appointed as a leader over Israel but causes Israel to sin and offends Yahweh (16:2; cf. 14:9). The threat to "wipe out Baasha" is an abbreviation of the threat to "burn up the house of Jeroboam as one burns dung" (16:3; cf. 14:10). Exposure of the corpses is described in the same manner (16:4; cf. 14:11). Content of the prophetic speeches provides a conscious continuity between the house of Jeroboam and the house of Baasha. The regnal summary provided for the reign of Baasha includes the activity of Jehu the prophet (16:5–7), which makes explicit the parallel to Jeroboam.

The house of Baasha ends with the type of violence Baasha inflicted on the house of Jeroboam (16:8–14). Zimri, an army commander responsible for half of the chariot force, murders Elah in a conspiracy. The judgment announced by the prophet Jehu is fulfilled, just as that announced by Abijah against Jeroboam (16:12–13; cf. 15:29–30). Elah dies because of false worship of "worthless idols" (16:13), meaning gods of no real existence.

Zimri is reckoned as one of the kings of Israel even though his reign only lasts seven days (16:15). When Omri, the field commander in Gibbethon, hears the king has been killed, he has himself proclaimed king by the army. He marches to Tirzah and lays siege to the capital. When Zimri sees his cause is lost, he chooses death in the flames of the palace rather than execution by Omri.

Omri is unable to claim the kingship of Israel with the death of Zimri. Tibni the son of Ginath makes a bid for the throne (16:21), so the country is divided for a period of about four years (cf. 16:21–22). At the death of Tibni, Omri becomes the undisputed king.

The twelve-year reign of Omri is shared with Tibni for the first five years (885–874 BC). Omri receives the briefest attention; his great deeds are mentioned in a general summarizing fashion (16:27). The one achievement mentioned is the establishment of a new state capital, Samaria (16:24). Its summit reaches over 1,400 feet overlooking the main coastal road connecting Egypt and Judah with the Jezreel Valley and northern routes to Phoenicia and Damascus. Though the hill was occupied before Omri, the earlier buildings at the site indicate the presence of a family estate producing oil and wine.

The twenty-two-year reign of Ahab ends with the battle at Qarqar (874–853 BC). His regnal summary occurs several chapters later (22:39–40) since the account of his reign is intertwined with the Elijah stories. Ahab extends the idolatry of Israel, making worship for the Baal cult exclusive. He builds a temple for Baal in Samaria and promotes the cult of Asherah (16:32–33). Alliance with the Phoenicians, with the marriage of Ahab to Jezebel, daughter of the Sidonian king (16:31), facilitates the state promotion of the Baal cult.

Rebuilding Jericho, one of many cities Ahab restores, brings about the curse of Joshua (16:34). Specification of the eldest and youngest sons is a merism ("from oldest to youngest"), indicating the death of all the children of Ahiel. Laying the foundations is the first stage of building and hanging the doors its completion.

Application. Most of the Christian past involves conflict, like the history of Israel and Judah. This conflict goes back to the earliest times of the New Testament itself. The apostle Paul encounters intense conflict with the church at Corinth and avoids a further personal confrontation by writing a painful letter (2 Cor 1:23–2:4). There are those who took satisfaction in the suffering and imprisonment of the apostle Paul and preached Christ with the goal of adding affliction to his imprisonment (Phil 1:15–18).

As Christians look back on their past, it is important to understand clearly their perspectives. Only then is it possible to understand the way in which the church struggles and fails in dealing with the forces of this age. It is then more possible to respect considerable divergences within the Christian faith. Above all, it is important to see how God continues to be at work accomplishing his purposes, sometimes through the deeds of wicked individuals who seek only to promote their own interests and sometimes through individuals willing to sacrifice their lives in doing the will of God on earth.

1 KINGS 17:1–19:21

Original Meaning

Drought in Israel (17:1–24). Elijah is introduced as a prophet from Gilead, though the precise place of his origin remains in doubt. He is introduced as a "Tishbite, from Tishbe" (17:1a). The NIV note suggests "Tishbite, of the settlers," perhaps indicating nothing more than that Elijah is a settler in the wild, forested, and largely unsettled territory east of Jordan in Gilead.

The message to King Ahab is given with divine sanction: "by the life of Yahweh" (17:1b, author's translation), which invokes an oath asserting the truth of the words spoken. The threat of drought by the oath of Yahweh is a direct challenge to the powers of Baal. Baal was the rider of the clouds, the god of rain and fertility, and therefore of riches. The protagonists in the present story are Yahweh and Baal, represented by Elijah and Ahab respectively.

Immediately after delivering the message, presumably in Samaria, Elijah is directed to go outside Ahab's territory. He hides by a little brook overlooking the Jordan called Kerith. Elijah needs sustenance and protection from Ahab. Provision for Elijah becomes even more dramatic after the brook dries up. Elijah is directed into the heart of Baal territory in Phoenicia. Not only is Baal incapable of overcoming the drought, but the provision of Yahweh for the faithful prophet takes place right in the heart of Baal territory.

A widow in this foreign territory provides for Elijah. Usually widows were the poorest of all the citizens, though the reference to her household may suggest she is a woman of some means (17:15, 17). She is herself preparing to die with her son because the drought has exhausted their entire food supply (17:12). Her favorable response to the prophet's request for water prompts him to ask her for bread as well. The woman, though a Sidonian, answers in the name of the God of Elijah. Elijah tests her faith and self-renunciation by asking that she first provide a small loaf for him, then another for herself and her son. Yahweh will ensure that the flour in the jar and the oil in the jug will be sufficient until the rains again restore the fertility of the ground. The woman trusts the God of the prophet and does as he instructs. Her faith is rewarded, the prophetic word is confirmed, and the God of Israel is shown to be the giver of life.

The illness and death of the woman's son (17:18, 20, 21–22) is taken as evidence that Elijah is not a benevolent prophet to a foreign woman; instead, she is being punished for her sins. The woman addresses Elijah in great distress (17:18).

Elijah takes the lad upstairs to his own private room, where he stretches himself over the lifeless body three times (17:21). The action may be an acted-out prayer typical of the prophets, but it could be a self-sacrificial intercession in which he takes the role of the sacrificial victim, identifying himself with the ultimate uncleanness of death. It should not be thought that Elijah prays for the restoration of the "soul" (Heb. *nephesh*) of the child to the body (17:21, KJV). The Hebrew word *nepesh* is better understood as "breath" or "life," such as animals possess as well. Life is restored to the child, demonstrating that God, not Baal, is the giver of life.

Confrontation on Mount Carmel (18:1–46). *Elijah and Obadiah (18:1–15).* "The third year" (18:1) describes a severe drought that did not end the year after it began but continues on into a third year. Elijah arrives back in Israel when Ahab and Obadiah, his administrator of palace property (cf. 4:6), are scouting the land in the hope of finding sufficient provision so the animals will not need to be destroyed. Obadiah is a God-fearing man (identified by later Jewish rabbis as the writing prophet Obadiah, though this is not certain) who has risked his own life when he hid and fed a hundred prophets in caves to preserve them from the sentence of death by Jezebel (18:3–4). Ahab has completely misplaced priorities. He is busy trying to preserve the animals (18:5), but apparently has no concern for the prophets whom Jezebel has cut off (18:4). There are two droughts in the land; while hunger from drought is severe (18:2), hunger for the prophets is caused by the wiles of a wicked woman. Ahab and Obadiah are not only going in different directions geographically in their search for water (18:6), they are in pursuit of opposing values.

The encounter between Elijah and Obadiah (18:7–15) reveals how Elijah is in control of life in Samaria. Obadiah the prophet has the opposite response of the widow in Zarephath when Elijah asks him to report to Ahab (18:8–9). While the pagan widow immediately complied with a demanding request (17:13–15), the man who fears Yahweh responds with fear. As the widow makes Elijah responsible for the death of her son by bringing her sin to light (17:18), so Obadiah feels that Elijah will be the cause of his death if he should report to Ahab (18:9, 12, 14).

Elijah and the prophets of Baal at Mount Carmel (18:16–40). The meeting between Elijah and Ahab contrasts his apostasy with the faithfulness of Obadiah (18:16–20). While the latter has respectfully greeted Elijah by falling to the ground (18:7), Ahab accuses Elijah as being the one who had put a hex on Israel (18:17). This accusation of Ahab is itself a contradiction. If Baal is truly god, Elijah could have no power over Israel at all. If Elijah does have power to bring drought, then Baal is not really god.

Ahab accepts the order to gather the prophets of Baal and Asherah to Mount Carmel (18:19–20). His acquiescence may have been because of his fear of Elijah since Elijah does have control over the kingdom, in spite of Jezebel's zeal. The choice of Mount Carmel is significant as the center for the worship of a local deity that functioned as Canaanite Baal. Its proximity to the Phoenician border places the challenge to Jezebel right at her doorstep. Carmel is also the natural place to worship the storm god who can calm the winter gales and turn the storms into rain.

The contest at Mount Carmel shows that the Lord of Israel will tolerate no compromise; Elijah challenges the people to "stop hopping between two boughs" (18:21, author's translation). The word for "bough" (Heb. *seippim*) is also used to refer to thoughts (e.g., Job 4:13). Just as boughs branch off from trees, so thoughts and opinions can branch off in more than one direction. This wordplay describes the prevarication of the people in their professed worship.

The contest Elijah proposes shows the folly of attempting to serve two masters (18:22–24). The prophets of Baal hop about, seeking a response from their god (18:26); this ritual dance, which may have included music and song, is meant to attract the attention of Baal. Elijah may have alluded to this ritual in describing the people as hopping between two opinions.

Baal ritual seems to be alluded to in Elijah's taunting questions (18:27). The question about sleep probably refers to the death of Baal. In the assumption that Baal rituals follow a seasonal pattern, the death of Baal in the ritual would signify the hot dry period of summer. The customary gashing with knives and blades may be part of a blood ritual seeking the first rainfall. Bloodletting was a rite of imitative magic to prompt a release of vital rain. These rituals would take place at a fall festival for the Baal cult in anticipation of the early rains.

Once the time for the Baal offering has passed, Elijah makes preparations for the evening burnt offering (18:29). This takes place on an altar restored for the purpose (18:30), indicating that the worship of God is not fully centralized with the building of the temple. Disrepair of the altar is presumably a result of the oppression Jezebel has inflicted on the prophets. The animal is prepared on the wood, and everything is soaked with water three times. Elijah then prays that the hearts of the people will be turned back to Yahweh (18:36–37), bringing fire to consume the offering.

The "fire of the LORD" (18:38) anticipates the advance of the rain. The fiery apparition indicates the divine presence. Fire also attests the divine acceptance and approval of the sacrifice. Fire may indicate both approval of the sacrifice and the divine presence, as with Gideon (Judg 6:20–22) and Moses (Lev 9:22–24).

The actions of Elijah signal the restoration of Israel. An altar of twelve stones (18:31) and twelve dousings with water (four jars emptied three times) both recall the twelve tribes and the crossing of the Jordan. Building an altar, forsaking false gods, and restoring the name Israel (18:30–31) follow the pattern of Jacob when he built the altar at Bethel (Gen 35:1–9). The Carmel event is no less significant than the exodus; the renewal of Israel does not allow for the continuance of Baalism (18:40).

Elijah and the resumption of rain (18:41–46). With Israel reborn, Elijah turns his attention to Ahab. Ahab must prepare for a feast to celebrate the coming of rain. A sevenfold repetition indicates the fullness of prayer (18:43–44); each time the servant ascends one of the peaks of Carmel for the best view. At the first sign of a small cloud the company begins its descent from the mountain lest the rain bog them in the valley below. As Ahab rides furiously toward Jezreel, Elijah runs on ahead. Running before the king indicates service to that king, now with the intent that the king will fulfill his proper mission in service to God.

Confirmation at Mount Horeb (19:1–21). With the slaughter of the prophets of Baal, Jezebel asserts her authority as the patron of the Baal cult (19:1–2). Her reputation is well established; now she appears in person with an oath against the life of Elijah. The names of the protagonists reveal the combatants: Jezebel (meaning "Where is the prince [Baal]?") is pitted against Elijah (meaning "Yah[weh] is my God"). Jezebel sends her messenger with a verbal threat. She prefers to avoid personal confrontation, perhaps because of the following Elijah has achieved at Carmel. If she can persuade Elijah to leave the country, she can pursue her ends without interference from the prophet and without exacerbating the situation by violent conflict.

The prophet Elijah appears to be a contradiction of himself in his fearful withdrawal from Jezebel (18:3–8) and his accusations against the faithlessness of the people (18:9–11). He seems to have felt confident in confronting Ahab, but he is not prepared to face the real proponent of the Baal cult, in spite of the dramatic victory that has just taken place on the mountain. He ignores the dramatic conversion of the people (18:39), forgets the courageous faithfulness of the Obadiah (18:3–4), blames the people for the vengeful attack of Jezebel (19:10, 14), and regards himself as utterly isolated in his struggle against the Baal cult.

Jezebel achieves her desired ends. Elijah flees south out of Israel to Beersheba, the southern limit of Judah. There he dismisses his servant (19:3), signifying that he intends to leave the land of Israel's heritage altogether. After another day's journey south Elijah finds shelter under a broom tree (19:4), a desert shrub that grows four to twelve feet high with straight long branches and small leaves.

Alone in the desert, Elijah desires nothing other than death. "No better than my ancestors" (19:4) may recall Moses, who asks for death when the people grumble about their conditions in the desert (Num 11:15). Elijah is twice strengthened by divine provision of food and refreshed by sleep (1 Kgs 19:5–7) before he continues his journey toward Horeb for forty days and forty nights (19:8).

Driven from the promised land by fear, Elijah arrives at the mountain of God where he takes up residence in a cave (19:9a). At Mount Horeb, just as Moses before him, Elijah hears the word of Yahweh (19:9b), addressing him twice with the same question: "What are you doing here, Elijah?" (19:9c, 13c).

Elijah's answer to the question shows that he is a prophet worthy of encountering Yahweh at his mountain (19:11a); his function as a prophet is restored. The narrative intentionally makes Elijah a prophet like Moses. Storm, earthquake, and fire recall the original appearance of God to the people at Mount Sinai. Elijah wraps his face in his garment, the equivalent of Moses being protected by the rock as the glory of Yahweh passed by (19:13; cf. Exod 33:21–22).

Elijah has restored the people to a relationship with God after failure. Like Moses, Elijah has brought God's word to the people (cf. Deut 18:16–18); he occupies a position above that of the other prophets. Elijah experiences the divine presence, though it is not possible for him to encounter directly the divine majesty. After the storm, earthquake, and fire, God speaks in the silence. The divine word comes to Elijah, renewing his commission to judge the compromise of the covenant and bring about a renewal.

The commission of Elijah is the pledge that conflict with Baal will end in victory over the house of Ahab (19:15–18). Anointing the kings of Aram and Israel is the harbinger of judgment on the nation for its political compromise and a purge of the Baal cult within Israel. Jehu, the successor to the Omride dynasty, carries out a total purge of the Baal cult and is rewarded with a dynasty of four generations, even though he does not institute pure Yahweh worship (2 Kgs 10:30–31). The anointing of Elisha assures Elijah that the prophetic challenge will not end with him.

From Horeb, Elijah proceeds to commission Elisha (19:19) as he makes the journey northward to Abel Meholah. Elisha (meaning "God is my salvation") is in charge of twelve pairs of oxen. Elisha evidently comes from a relatively prosperous family. The hairy mantel that Elijah throws over Elisha is a garment distinctive to some type of prophet, especially significant to Elisha but known in other circles (cf. Zech 13:4). Transfer of the garment signifies a transmission of the mission and the ability to accomplish it.

Elisha recognizes God's call and prepares to separate from his family (19:20). Elijah grants permission with an enigmatic question: "What have I done to you?" There is no indication the question is a rebuke. It may indicate that the calling of Elisha does not need to sever natural family affection, but without clarification it leaves the future mission of Elisha a mystery. Elisha's sacrifice is a thank offering for his call, in which neighbors are naturally invited to join. The burning of the yoke of the oxen signifies a complete break with the past. From that time on Elisha becomes the protégé of Elijah.

Application. In ancient times, material well-being required that the gods be satisfied in order for them to bestow their bounty. In part, religion served materialist desires; to a measure, materialism was the basis for religion. In modern times, materialism has itself become a religion.

Philosophical materialism is the theory that physical matter is the only reality and that everything, including thought, feeling, mind, and will, can be explained in terms of matter and physical phenomena. Modern society continues to operate largely on the materialistic premises of such thinkers as Charles Darwin, Karl Marx, and Sigmund Freud. Convinced that the only reality is material, true explanations become reductive. Thought is treated as the irrational product of environment or brain chemistry; reductionism permeates society from politics and social sciences to literature and the performing arts.

One of the legacies of materialism is coercive utopianism; this is the belief that the perfect society may be engineered through social science and planning. One version of this is the modern welfare state, in which government becomes ever more intrusive as planners ally themselves with the tools of materialist social science. In the name of social science and humanity, social scientists claim the right to remake society without having to obtain its consent. They believe in their own power to bring about complete material well-being and implicitly believe that this is the highest good, since it is the basis of fulfilling all other desires.

Such materialist objectives, even if achievable, cannot bring about the utopian promise. Materialist doctrines of moral relativism and denial of personal responsibility undermine the ideal society of materialist dreams. Materialist religion is as deceptive, destructive, and pervasive as Baalism in Ahab's Israel.

1 KINGS 20:1–43

Original Meaning

The Battle for Samaria (20:1–21). The battle for Samaria results when negotiations break down between the Aramean king and his Israelite vassal (20:1–11). The demands begin when the Aramean forces are able to break down Israelite control of its provinces and besiege Samaria (20:1). The thirty-two kings were not heads of state but tribal chieftains who roamed with semi-independence in the area of Damascus. The title "king of Aram" (20:1) refers to the control Ben-Hadad has in mustering these chieftains against Ahab. Aram is an ethnic rather than a geographic term, and the "kings" are rulers of various tribes or confederacies.

The negotiations are arranged in three sets of dialogue between Ben-Hadad and Ahab: 20:2–4, 5–9, and 10–11. In the middle set Ben-Hadad addresses Ahab (20:5–6), Ahab has exchanges with his elders (20:7–8), and he finally responds to Ben-Hadad (20:9). The subordinate situation of Ahab is indicated by his acceptance of the Aramean king (20:4) and a willingness to be subservient to his demands of taxation.

Ben-Hadad demands that his officers conduct the taxation as they see fit, including possession of members of the royal family, leaving Ahab to rule as a vassal (20:5–6). Ahab follows the advice of his elders in resisting this demand. Ahab still defers to the Aramean king as his "lord" (20:9) and concedes to his original demands, but Ahab will not be reduced to Aramean occupation of his territory. Ben-Hadad responds to this with an oath that he will turn Samaria into dust scooped up by his soldiers (20:10), but Ahab replies with a proverb of his own (20:11): Boasting only comes after the battle.

On hearing this response, Ben-Hadad orders his troops to attack Samaria (20:12). By midday Ben-Hadad has become scandalously drunk. Ahab in turn is given assurance by an unnamed prophet that God will win the battle as in the time of the exodus, so the Israelites may know the meaning of the name Yahweh (20:13). The word of proof offered by the prophet (20:14–15) is that Ahab will appoint 232 elite troops engaged in the protection of the provinces, who will be joined by seven thousand of the regular troops marshaled for the occasion.

The report goes out to Ben-Hadad that the troops have left the capital of Samaria. In his drunken and arrogant state, Ben-Hadad demands they be seized alive, whether their intentions are for peaceful negotiations or war. The Israelites meet the Aramean army man for man, pursue them, and inflict heavy casualties. Ben-Hadad manages to escape with his horsemen, but the Israelites decimate their cavalry as well (20:21).

The Battle for Aphek (20:22–34). Though Ben-Hadad should have been forced into a conciliatory position, it is Ahab who continues to be reticent. Ahab is given a prophetic warning (20:22). Ben-Hadad revises his battle strategy to make better use of his superior cavalry (20:23–25). The Aramean king is advised to abandon the ineffective alliances with area chieftains and bring his military forces directly under his control, with officials he appoints himself. He further needs to tally a force equal to the troops and cavalry that desert him.

When the entire Israelite army is mustered, it has the appearance of two exposed flocks of goats (20:27). The prophet responds with a message identical to the one given before the first battle (20:28), with the same assurance the God of the exodus will be with them in defeat of his enemies.

The battle at Aphek is described briefly (20:29–30), depicting the victory in terms of holy war. The armies face each other seven days and the walls of Aphek fall. The Israelites shatter the Arameans. Ben-Hadad himself manages to seek security within a secret room.

Ben-Hadad is left with no alternative but to appeal to treaty loyalty, which he expects from Ahab (20:31). "Merciful" (Heb. *hesed*) in 20:31 is a covenant term denoting loyalty to a relationship. Course black cloth attached to the waist is a sign of penitence. A rope on the head indicates servitude.

Ahab responds to this with a willingness to continue a treaty relationship: "He is my brother" (20:32). The envoys are looking for an omen, some sign that their mission will succeed; they test Ahab by suggesting a renewed loyalty (20:33). Ahab sends for Ben-Hadad and invites him into his chariot. Ben-Hadad agrees to restore territory he has taken and to set up preferential commercial relations in Damascus; in return Ahab agrees to release Ben-Hadad.

Prophetic Confrontation with the King of Israel (20:35–43). A message for Ahab comes from one of the "company of the prophets," a group associated with Elisha, mentioned only here in connection with Elijah (20:35). The message of the prophet is delivered through an enacted parable. The prophet demands that someone from his company strike and injure him. The refusal of his request is a disobedience that results in death by a lion (20:36), a fate consistent with that of the disobedient prophet from Judah (cf. 13:24). A second companion does strike and injure him, allowing him to disguise himself for the king.

The story of the prophet to the king assumes that a prisoner of war was the property of his captor and that his escape is a breach of pledge demanding restitution. The exorbitant price for the loss of a slave may have been a way of impressing the king with the severity of breaching the divine covenant and causing the death of the entire nation. The king in rendering his judgment assumes he is indicting a wounded soldier with a punishment determined by the soldier himself. He does not realize that "your life for his life" (20:39) is a verdict he is bringing on himself and his people.

The king recognizes the prophet the instant he removes his disguise. The doctrine of holy war requires that the spoils belong entirely to God (cf. Josh 6:18). A prisoner in such a case cannot be treated as common property; anything so devoted cannot be sold or redeemed by substituting something else. According to prophetic theology, the Aramean king is under such a ban (Heb. *herem*, 1 Kgs 20:42), and it is not Ahab's prerogative to make a treaty with him. The king, learning of the judgment pronounced on him and his country, returns to his capital resentful and angry.

Application. Judgment is conspicuously absent in contemporary concepts of God. Judging is a bad odor, always equivalent to judgmentalism. Knowing God in acts of divine judgment is regarded as primitive, even primordial in the development of moral understanding. Unconditional love is regarded as equivalent to unconditional forgiveness. The God of popular imagining is less father than uncle. Judgment, especially in relation to God, is regarded as arbitrary and capricious.

The church may shoulder its share of blame for this perception; divine punishment has often been attached to rules that have little to do with morality or requirements of faith that have little to do with biblical theology. It may also be the consequence of a permissive culture in pursuit of personal freedom without responsibility for the consequences of such choices. A therapeutic culture has replaced judgment with validation of feelings.

1 KINGS 21:1–29

Original Meaning

Judicial Murder of Naboth (21:1–16). The double mention of Jezreel in 21:1 is not superfluous because a significant point in the story is that the property is located in Ahab's hometown. Jezreel is a royal center of the Omride dynasty, though Omri established a capital in Samaria (16:24).

The royal center was built concurrently with Samaria; the planners and architects of both sites followed the same architectural layout. The various buildings included a central building that served as a royal residence. The size and imposing nature of the fortifications express the need to show the strength and position of the royal dynasty. These grandiose public works are a means of social control over the local population. This function of Jezreel in the royal possessions conforms well to the desire of Ahab to enhance his presence by taking possession of Naboth's vineyard.

Naboth refuses Ahab's offer of purchase from the viewpoint of ancestral inheritance: All the land belongs to God; the Israelites are sojourners. It is not their prerogative to sell land in perpetuity or to alienate it from the family.

Ahab responds in the manner of an embittered king but apparently does not intend to overcome Naboth's opposition (21:4). Jezebel perceives Ahab's response as weakness (21:7). She writes letters and signs them in the name of the king. In Israel the corruption of authority extended to supervising elders and freemen with the power to exercise judicial authority.

Naboth himself appears to have been the head of an influential local family, as he is given a place of honor at the sacred occasion (21:9). However, his refusal to cooperate with the royal request makes him a rival to the supporters of the king. It is an offense to curse a ruler of the people (Exod 22:28), so it is not difficult for unscrupulous witnesses to bring a sentence of death against Naboth. The ease with which such a plot is accomplished demonstrates the pervasive corruption of Ahab's reign. Once Jezebel receives word of the execution, she informs her husband that the vineyard is now his for the taking. This criminal act has been achieved with full judicial authority.

Judgment of Ahab (21:17–29). Yahweh commissions Elijah to confront Ahab in Naboth's vineyard. Ahab has gone from Samaria to Jezreel to inspect his property (21:16, 18b); Ahab "who rules in Samaria" (21:18) is a reference to his normal habitat at his royal residence rather than his personal presence there. Elijah is to confront Ahab at the scene of the crime.

The judgment against Ahab is that the dogs will lick up his blood just as they did that of Naboth (21:19). The dogs do literally lick up the blood of Ahab in Samaria when the chariot in which he dies is washed (22:38), but they also lick up his blood in the vineyard of Naboth when the body of his son Joram is thrown there (2 Kgs 9:25–26). Human injustice is succeeded by divine judgment in a double sense; Ahab will die in battle, and his dynasty will end with the death of his son. The judgment against Ahab is not that every male will be cut off (1 Kgs 21:21), but that all the royal descendants will be exterminated. His death, and that of Jezebel, are described in the terms of Jeroboam and Baasha (21:23–24; cf. 14:10–11; 16:4).

Ahab's response to Elijah betrays knowledge of his own guilt: "So you have found me, my enemy!" (21:20). Elijah is Ahab's enemy because the latter has violated his responsibility as a king under the covenant. Elijah describes Ahab's guilt for what it is (21:20). Greed has led Ahab into the sin of murder and theft, so there is none who can be compared to him (21:25). Though Jezebel is an accomplice in his crime, Ahab is still culpable as the instigator of her actions. Murder and theft are the results of desecrating the covenant (21:26), a manifestation of his disrespect for God and the relationships that are divinely ordained.

The ending of the narrative offers a surprising turn on the character of Ahab (21:27–29). One would not expect a king described as more abominable in his deeds than the Amorites (21:25–26) to have a change of heart at the proclamation of judgment. Ahab shows his repentance by wearing sackcloth, fasting, sleeping in sackcloth, and conducting his affairs with gentleness. Though Elijah is not commissioned with any message for Ahab, God does inform the prophet that his punishment will be mitigated and will come to fruition in the days of his son. Though Ahab does die violently in battle, he is buried in the royal sepulcher (22:39–40), and his dynasty continues for another fourteen years under the rule of his sons.

Application. The story of Naboth is a biblical paragon for injustice, as it exemplifies how the powerful take advantage of the weak to add to their wealth. It has all the features that are typical of such instances. The actions are done "legally" because they are in the power of the state; they are justified by the people in power, so the victims may not even be able to make a case for their deprivation being unjust. As a society becomes corrupt because of oppressive leaders, there is increased opportunity for such individuals to ply their trade.

1 KINGS 22:1–50

Original Meaning

The Battle for Ramoth Gilead (22:1–40). Three years is a typological number rather than an exact chronological statement. Plans for the attack are laid during a state visit by Jehoshaphat. Ahab's question concerning Ramoth Gilead is intended to arouse shame and resentment (22:3), since the Arameans are violating the agreement made earlier at Aphek.

Ahab does not have sufficient resources to attack the Arameans on his own (22:4), so he solicits help from his ally in enforcing the treaty. Jehoshaphat affirms his support, but he refuses to proceed unless there is divine confirmation that the venture is within the divine will.

The inquiry unfolds in two scenes. In the first, four hundred prophets of the king affirm Ahab's intention to go to war (22:5–6). The message of Ahab's prophets is affirmed and reiterated in a circumstantial amplification (22:10–12). Their leader, Zedekiah, makes himself iron horns to act out the message of how the Arameans will be utterly defeated.

In the second, Micaiah is first persuaded to verbally confirm the message of Ahab's prophets (22:7–23): Yahweh will give Ramoth Gilead over to the king's control (22:6b, 15b). But the king knows Micaiah is only giving him the answer that will confirm the loyalty of his prophets rather than the divine word. At the request of Ahab, Micaiah elaborates that the armies of Israel will be scattered like sheep without a shepherd and will return home without leaders (22:17). In other words, Ahab will die. The contradiction with Micaiah's first response is clarified with a vision (22:19–23), which explains the behavior of Ahab's prophets and how it is possible for the initial words of Micaiah to conform to them.

Micaiah does not claim, as charged by Zedekiah (22:24), that the spirit of Yahweh has left Zedekiah and gone over to him. Micaiah can only speak the truth he has seen in the vision (22:14). In Micaiah's vision, the heavenly court is the counterpart of a royal council; the king is surrounded by his attendants, each assigned to fulfill specific roles (22:19). In that vision these are divine beings in service to God. The question to the heavenly court is how to entice Ahab to go into battle at Ramoth Gilead. The persuasion of Ahab is to accomplish the invincible will of God. This persuasion is to guarantee that Ahab will fall in battle; his judgment is decreed.

The effective accomplishment of the divine will can take place without the conscious participation of his prophets—either positively, as in the case of Jeremiah (Jer 20:7, 10), or negatively, as in the case of Ahab's prophets (1 Kgs 22:21–22). The punishment on Ahab and his prophets is determined by their own hardness of heart, just as Pharaoh hardened his heart and then came under divine judgment of an unchanging will that led to his destruction (Exod 4–14).

A crux in this passage is the intent of the enticement as a "deceiving spirit" (1 Kgs 22:23). The LXX renders this as a "false spirit" (*pneuma pseudes*), taking the Hebrew *ruah sheqer* as deception by the divine messenger. However, the question as to how the spirit will try to persuade Ahab suggests that the *ruah sheqer* is not a deception on the part of the messenger but a description of the effect his message will have on the king. Ahab is deluded; this delusion begins with his adoption of the message of his own prophets and his implicit recognition that Micaiah speaks the truth, contrary to Ahab's own prophets.

The confrontation with Micaiah reaches its climax in the assault of Zedekiah (22:24) and the confinement imposed by the king until the truth of his words can be verified (22:26–27). Restraint imposed on the prophet will prevent him from disseminating his pernicious views among the people. Micaiah for his part simply responds according to the prophetic test of truth as found in Deuteronomy 18:21–22. If Zedekiah and Ahab are vindicated, death is his well-deserved fate.

With the consultation at an impasse, the scene moves to the battlefront. Ahab's plan is to go into the battle disguised as a soldier, with Jehoshaphat filling the role of military leader. The king's disguise is his response to the prophecy that the army will return without its king (22:17). Though he has chosen to disregard the oracle, he is not able to ignore it.

The strategy of the Aramean chariot commanders is to single out the king of Israel (22:31). Since Jehoshaphat alone is distinguished by the insignia of the military leader, the warriors focus their attention on him (22:32). The outcry of Jehoshaphat informs them he is not the king of Israel. Ahab is hit by an inadvertent shot that pierces the scales of his armor at a vulnerable point. The shot is not an accident, however; it confirms the judgment that has been pronounced by Micaiah.

The wounded king demands to be taken from the troops; this is the first step in separating his fate from that of the army (22:34). The end of the day seals the separate destinies of king and army. At evening the king dies (22:35b), the blood from his mortal wound draining and collecting at the bottom of the chariot. At sunset, the army disperses; each of the soldiers returns to his own place of residence (22:36). By the end of the day the king's effort to subvert the word of doom spoken against him fails (22:35). The central occurrence of the battle is the death of the king at Ramoth Gilead and the return of the armies in peace without their shepherd.

The death of the king is the first oracle to receive fulfillment on that fateful day. The body of the king is returned to Samaria, where the chariot is washed (22:37–38). Dogs lick up the blood of the slain king, fulfilling the judgment pronounced by Elijah for slaying Naboth (cf. 21:19). The defiance of Ahab in his death stands as a stark contrast to his humility when Elijah denounced him for the murder of Naboth.

The epilogue on Ahab's reign notes his significant achievements and his royal burial as a great king (22:39–40). He fortified and developed various cities, including Samaria the capital. The reign of Ahab is among the most influential and, by temporal standards, an almost incomparable success.

The Reign of Jehoshaphat (22:41–50). According to the Hebrew text, Jehoshaphat begins his reign in the fourth year of Ahab (22:41), so that his twenty-five-year reign extends into the fifth year of Joram son of Ahab (2 Kgs 8:16).

In Kings, events of the reign of Jehoshaphat are related in accounts of his wars with Israelite kings. His own reign is recounted in a regnal résumé. He is given credit for purging the "male shrine prostitutes" (1 Kgs 22:46). Apparently, the king attempts to renovate the ships used by Solomon, but they prove to be unseaworthy and never leave port. The Judean mariners are not prepared for such voyages, but Jehoshaphat refuses the assistance of Ahaziah, whose alliance with Phoenician expertise may have been of great assistance (22:49).

The two kingdoms ally themselves against the Arameans, but Jehoshaphat determines to maintain his economic and territorial independence. His control of Edom supports Israel because it cuts off Aramean access to the Red Sea. For this reason, Israel, Judah, and Edom unite to resist Moabite aspirations for independence (2 Kgs 3:4–27).

Reign of Ahaziah (22:51–53). The introductory summary of the reign of Ahaziah is regular in providing a synchronism with Jehoshaphat and giving the length of his reign. The last year of the reign of Ahab was the battle of Qarqar in 853 BC, a firm date in ancient Syrian chronology.

Application. Though the secular role of the state is necessary, it is absurd to think that faith is a purely private matter. If religion has no role in public society, then secularism becomes a state religion of its own, imposing its own values on people of all faiths and religion. This is really no different than Ahab choosing his own prophets who always say what he wants them to say. Values for ethics and law cannot be established apart from convictions that have a personal faith base, and in that sense are always religious. Freedom of religion in the secular state must not only allow for the public expression of various faiths, it must also allow for rational expression of faith convictions. To the extent that a state fails to do this, it will succumb to its own vices, just like Ahab and the state of Israel in listening only to their own prophets.

Christians in this manifestation of a postmodern society often find themselves in the unhappy lot of Jehoshaphat. Having a desire to seek an independent course of action, they are pressured in various ways to conform, even at risk to their own well-being. While they seek to do what is right, the high places remain and compromise the way of life they value most.

2 KINGS

INTRODUCTION TO 2 KINGS

Second Kings continues the narrative in 1 Kings. Its separation into two books is otherwise artificial. The book witnesses the ups and downs of the divided kingdom and concludes with the fall of both. The story continues to describe the prophetic ministries of Elijah and Elisha and introduces the ministry of the prophet Isaiah during the Assyrian crisis. See also the Introduction to 1 Kings above (p. 272) for commentary on the authorship of 1–2 Kings, Deuteronomistic History, and the two primary themes in the books of Kings.

BOOK OUTLINE

I. Judgment on Ahaziah (Continued from 1 Kings) (1:1–18)
II. Ascension of Elijah (2:1–25)
III. Battle against Moab (3:1–27)
IV. Mission of Elisha (4:1–44)
V. Healing of Naaman (5:1–27)
VI. Deliverance in Times of War (6:1–8:15)
VII. Revolution in Israel (8:16–10:36)
VIII. Revolt against Athaliah (11:1–20)
IX. Reign of Joash (11:21–12:21)
X. Survival of Aramean Decimation (13:1–14:29)
XI. Demise of Israel (15:1–38)
XII. Apostasy of Ahaz (16:1–20)
XIII. End of Israel (17:1–41)
XIV. Faithfulness and Failure (18:1–20:21)
XV. Idolatry in Judah (21:1–26)
XVI. Reform of Josiah (22:1–23:30)
XVII. Last Days of Judah (23:31–24:17)
XVIII. Fall of Jerusalem (24:18–25:30)

2 KINGS 1:1–18

Original Meaning

The Death of Ahab and Confrontation with Elijah (1:1–18). The death of Ahab brings about a new era in the Omride dynasty. Moab rebels almost immediately, with both Edom and Libnah gaining independence during the reign of Joram. The days of the Israelite Empire are over. The alliance of Ahab with the Arameans at the battle of Qarqar is the end of a period of international influence for Israel.

Ahaziah is an apostate like his parents, but his particular sin is the act of seeking an oracle from Baal-Zebub, a god of the Philistines (2:2). Baal-Zebub (meaning, "lord of the flies") may have been a god to control disease. It is likely that the name was originally Baal-Zebul ("lord of a lofty or exalted place"), an epithet used for Baal in Ugaritic literature.

The desire to receive an oracle from Baal-Zebub, as if there were no God in Israel (1:3), becomes the occasion for Elijah to confront once again the apostate house of Omri. The messenger of Yahweh commissions Elijah to intercept the messengers of the king with an oracle of doom, telling the king that he will not recover from his injuries (1:3–4).

The impact of the struggle in the narrative is achieved through the double meaning of the word "messenger" (*malak*). This Hebrew word refers to both the "angel [of the LORD]" and to the "messengers [of the king]" (1:3). God exercises his authority through the first messenger, while King Ahaziah can do nothing more than extend his power through military messengers. The king's messengers in effect return with an oracle from Yahweh rather than Baal-Zebub (1:5–6).

The king recognizes Elijah by his description as a hairy man (1:8) and takes up the challenge by immediately sending a military unit to arrest him (1:9–14). The military officers are no match for the power of Yahweh through Elijah and are repeatedly consumed by fire. In the end the king's messengers finally get their way (1:15–16), but it has nothing to do with their power. The messenger (angel) of Yahweh comes to Elijah again, instructing him to go down to the king so that Elijah may personally deliver the same oracle to the king.

When the king gets his request to meet his nemesis Elijah face to face, the result is nothing more than a repetition of the inevitable oracle of doom. The repeated exchange of the messengers dramatizes the superior and dangerous power of God connected with the prophetic oracle. Each of Ahaziah's actions moves him inexorably toward the judgment reserved for him because of his rejection of the God of the covenant.

With the appearance of Elijah before the king, Ahaziah's death according to the divine oracle is simply reported. The narrative concludes with the summary of his reign and the introduction of the next king. The usual formula appears somewhat disjointed in the Hebrew text. The accession of his successor is given before the typical concluding summary (1:17b–18). The sole rule of Jehoram began in the fifth year of Joram son of Ahab (8:16), at the end of the twenty-five-year reign of Jehoshaphat.

Application. The authority of Elijah was grounded in his uncompromising allegiance to God in the teaching of the covenant. The authority of Jesus was established with the people through his use of the Scriptures. He promised that this power would be with his followers always, even to the end of the world. This power continues to be the authority of the church. The church has often claimed and used temporal powers, but often not to the advancement of its mission in the world. Temporal power does not assist the church in the accomplishment of its mission, but neither can temporal power prevent the growth of the church.

It is vital that church leaders always adhere to the genuine source of their authority, which is found in faithfulness to the revelation of God for his world. Their power lies in teaching this truth to the people. Government powers of this world cannot control this power.

2 KINGS 2:1–25

Original Meaning

Departure of Elijah (2:1–18). The topic of the chapter is introduced by saying that Elijah is taken up to heaven in a storm. The force and power of the wind are symbolic of the majestic and holy presence of the divine. During the time of Samuel, Gilgal became an important religious center and may have been the site of an ancient temple.

The whole narrative is designed to build suspense. Elijah suddenly receives the revelation that he is to go as far as Bethel and urges Elisha to stay behind. When they arrive at Bethel, they are met with news of a prophetic revelation. Elijah then receives a message that he is to go to Jericho. A second band of prophets from Jericho comes with news of the same revelation. Mixed emotions of impatience, sorrow, and anger may be intended in the words, "I know. Be quiet!" (2:3, 5, author's translation). Yahweh then calls Elijah to the Jordan; Elisha is determined to follow his master, refusing to compromise his vow, though repeatedly challenged.

Elisha asks for a double portion of Elijah's spirit, an expression used elsewhere to refer to the right of inheritance of the firstborn as double that of the others (Deut 21:17). Elisha is not requesting twice the prophetic spirit of Elijah, but rather the right to the office of Elijah. "My father" is repeated (2 Kgs 2:12), an expression of the honor attributed to the leader.

"The chariots and horseman of Israel" (2:12) must refer to the vision of Elijah departing into glory. Elijah introduced the cloak as a symbol of succession (2:13) when he first anointed Elisha as his successor (1 Kgs 19:19). In the return crossing of the Jordan, Elisha calls for the same demonstration of divine provision as was given Elijah (2 Kgs 2:14). The same miraculous crossing assures Elisha that he is indeed the true successor to Elijah. The prophetic band in Jericho confirms that Elisha will continue the work of Elijah (2:15–18).

Confirmation of Elisha (2:19–25). The first event to confirm that Elisha has succeeded Elijah as the prophet like Moses is the curing of the waters at Jericho. The effect of the sterility caused by the water is not clear; it could be that it caused the land to be unproductive, or it caused the people to be childless.

Elisha asks for a "new bowl" (2:20). The point of the salt in the new jar is to distinguish this prophetic action from all other common techniques that might be used in "healing" the water. The waters remain pure until the time the accounts of Elisha are recorded (2:22). The power of Elisha is reminiscent of that of Moses in "healing" the waters at Marah (cf. Exod 15:22–26).

The taunting of the young men should not be viewed as immature juvenile activity (2 Kgs 2:23). If a prophet were known because he was a hairy man (1:8), taunting Elisha as a bald man is to deny that he is a prophet, or at least to deny that he is a prophet like Elijah. The mauling of the youthful mob is not vindictive anger on behalf of Elisha but divine judgment for culpable denial of the divine purpose. The bears are no less divinely appointed than the whale that swallowed Jonah. With the return to Mount Carmel, Elisha completes the transition to being successor to Elijah (2:25).

Application. God has always chosen and empowered his leaders for times of political threat against his people. Jesus gave his followers the same assurance that the kingdom of God would prevail. At Caesarea Philippi, Peter recognized Jesus as the Anointed One ("the Christ") who fulfilled the promises of the prophets for the kingdom of God (Matt 16:16). This confession was not by means of some special discernment but was itself a revelation granted by God (16:17). As the one who had received this revelation, Peter became that rock on which the church would be built (16:18), with the assurance that "the gates of hell shall not prevail against it" (KJV). The "keys of the kingdom" were entrusted to Peter (16:19), with the assurance that no earthly power would ever be able to stop the will of God on earth.

Though Jesus directed the beatitude specifically at Peter (16:17), it must be remembered that the blessing belonged to all the disciples (cf. 13:16–17; 18:18). The heavenly Father had revealed his Son to his disciples (11:25–30). The church was built on the foundation of the apostles and prophets (Eph 2:20) as a sacred temple to the Lord. Peter is singled out as a representative apostle, the first person to be called a disciple, the son of John called Cephas (John 1:42), who loved Jesus and was called to feed his sheep (21:15–17).

2 KINGS 3:1–27

Original Meaning

Political and Military Crisis (3:1–12). The regnal summary of Joram (3:1–3) is given with a synchronism to the eighteenth year of Jehoshaphat. Joram is credited with removing the memorial pillar that Ahab had set up in honor of Baal (3:2). Standing stones were objects of veneration and worship, conventionalized aniconic representations of a deity. Such stones were not symbols of the transcendent being but evoked an actual presence.

Moab had been subservient to Israel from the time of David (2 Sam 8:2). As a vassal of Israel, Mesha was required to pay a levy. His refusal to bring tribute is the result of the weakening military control of Israel.

Joram attempts to regain dominance over Moab by mustering his forces and reinforcing them with assistance from Judah. Edom is still subservient to Judah at this time, so Edom's army is part of the alliance.

The route of attack takes the armies through Edom around the southern end of the Dead Sea. The journey around the Dead Sea would have taken considerable time. In typical prophetic style it is described as "a march of seven days" (3:9), the emphasis being on the time-consuming effort of a difficult journey rather than a precise calculation of time. The whole expedition is jeopardized by a lack of water as the armies march through desert land.

Joram realizes that the eminent failure of his armies is a sign of divine judgment on him (3:10). Jehoshaphat comes to the rescue in a nonmilitary fashion by proposing they seek direction from a true prophet (3:11). Elisha is known through Elijah; "pouring water over the hands" (3:11) was apparently a gesture of respect shown by a servant to his master or a host to his guest. Jehoshaphat recognizes Elisha as a true prophet who can bring them a word from Yahweh (3:12). Joram has been alienated from Elisha (3:13) and could not have sought his assistance without the mediation of Jehoshaphat.

The Prophetic Assurance (3:13–20). When the king of Israel appears before Elisha, the prophet confronts him in uncompromising and forceful terms. The king ought to be consistent with his own policy of following in the ways of Jeroboam the son of Nebat (3:13). Though Joram follows the prophets of his parents in official policy, he also knows that his dire situation is a result of the judgment of the God of Elisha (cf. 3:14). Joram knows that only the God of Elisha can be of assistance. Elisha grants Joram a concession (3:14); though he regards Joram, the leader of the group, with disdain, Jehoshaphat is worthy of receiving a word from Yahweh.

The procedures for entering the mystic state of prophecy are veiled in tantalizing incidental comments. Elisha calls for music in order that he might experience the power of the Lord. The use of music is only one means of entering the mystical experience.

The word of Yahweh through Elisha declares that every depression in the dry valley bed will become a receptacle for water. The prophet is not commanding them to make ditches (3:16); the valley itself will become pools. Though such occurrences are not infrequent, there is nothing natural about the deliverance experienced by the three armies. The water comes according to the word of the prophet.

The prophetic word assures Joram and his allies that they will be successful in the battle against Moab (3:19). The ruin described in the victory over Moab is a contradiction to the rules for war provided in the covenant (Deut 20:19). Elisha does not order the destruction of trees and arable land but describes the totality of the ruin that will come to Moab in the conflict.

The Military Outcome (3:21–27). When the Moabites realize the coalition is at their boundary, they muster what army they can to stop them at the border (3:21). Their soldiers are described as bearing arms, meaning lightly armed skirmishers or those carrying a sword. In the light of the early morning sun the water gathered in the hollows appears to the Moabites to be red like blood (3:22).

There is a notable wordplay here; while waiting in the red sandstone ground of Edom (*edom*), the Moabites mistake water that appears blood red (*adummim*) for actual blood (3:22). They come to the conclusion that the coalition has turned on itself and the spoil is theirs for the taking (3:23). This is a fatal error (3:24); as the Moabite army moves into the Israelite camp, the Israelites continue on the attack against the Moabites. The resulting destruction is exactly as the prophet said (3:25); the cities are overthrown, every field ruined with stones, the water sources filled, and the trees felled.

The Israelites advance as far as the city of Kir Haresheth. Warriors with slings lay siege to the fortification and attack it in an effort to capture the Moabite warriors. The Moabites attempt to break out of the siege by breaking through the Edomite line, the weak link in the circle of forces that surround the city (3:26). When this fails, the king of Moab sacrifices a young man on the walls of the city in full view of the attacking armies (3:27).

The final outcome of the campaign fails to regain control

over the territory and restore the tribute of Moab. Neither the presence of Jehoshaphat nor the word of Elisha can turn the tide of judgment against Israel. In spite of the rout of the Moabites through divine intervention, Joram cannot achieve his goal to subjugate Mesha; rather, he is forced to retreat precipitately.

Application. Christians must reconcile the doctrine of the Divine Warrior with the particular historical wars that are a part of the present order. Just as God was active in human affairs in times past, exercising his rule among human kingdoms and giving them to whomever he willed (Dan 5:21), so God continues to be at work in human affairs.

A particularly difficult question for the faithful is how to relate to the government in its legitimate role of the control of violence and the exercise of judgment. Though this is a God-ordained function, it is scarcely possible to point to a government at any time that consistently carried out this function as a legitimate representative of divine authority. War is always a matter of fallible human governments making judgments in matters of life and death. At their best they have their share of evil, and at their worst they are the greatest enemy to their own people.

2 KINGS 4:1–44

Original Meaning

Oil for a Widow (4:1–7). The story of God's provision is told without embellishment. Elisha asks two questions about the widow's need and resources, to which she responds. He then tells her what to do, and she dutifully obeys. The provision of oil takes place behind closed doors, with only the woman and her sons present. The oil is a divine gift that is not dependent on the presence of the man of God and cannot be viewed as some kind of trick. The form of the verb "pour" seems to indicate that the oil is made to pour continuously until all the jars are filled (4:5). No details are given following Elisha's final instruction (4:7), but it may be assumed that the woman obeys without question. Her debts are paid, and her family remains together.

A Son for the Childless (4:8–37). In the previous story, a widow of one of the prophets supporting Elisha seeks out his assistance in her dire need. In this second story a woman of means urges the prophet to accept her hospitality whenever he passes by on his journeys through the Jezreel Valley (4:8).

Elisha has occasion to pass the location regularly on his journeys from Carmel (4:9); like Samuel (1 Sam 7:15–17), he probably follows a circuit in the administration of his duties. Elisha is regarded as a holy man, distinguished from the other prophets who continue to have regular vocations. The room is furnished simply but adequately for a regular guest. This woman is not independently wealthy but secures permission from her husband to build a special hospitality suite for this notable guest.

The second part of the story introduces Gehazi, the assistant to Elisha, as intermediary between Elisha and the woman (2 Kgs 4:12–17). The scene depicts a deference and appropriate protocol between Elisha and his patron, who holds him to be a holy man of God. Through Gehazi, she first makes herself available to Elisha (4:12), then she comes to be present in the doorway (4:15).

Elisha poses the same question for his benefactor as he did for the widow who came to plead her case (4:13; cf. 14:2). His suggestions of intervening with the king or military commander show that Elisha has come into a position of political influence. As wealthy people, the woman and her husband carry a heavy liability for maintaining the state and its military. The woman declines political intervention, saying she is secure within her clan. She has no need of social and material assistance, unlike the first woman who is about to lose her sons.

Discussion with Gehazi reveals her real need: Unlike the widow, she cannot lose her children, because she has none. Elisha asks her to be present in person for his announcement that in a year she will embrace a son. Like Sarah at the announcement of Isaac (Gen 18:12), the woman finds the promise incredible (2 Kgs 4:16); she does not dare to hope lest she be disappointed. In spite of her doubts, her desire for a child is fulfilled.

The narrative immediately advances to another day, some years later, when the child has grown (4:18). The third division of the story deals with the disappointment the woman fears (4:18–28); in spite of the miraculous birth, she does not now have a son. The woman is depicted as resolute in her plight. When the child dies in her arms, she immediately lays the body on the bed of the man of God and prepares to confront him. Her husband is presented as uncompassionate and skeptical (4:22–23). The woman silences her husband with a single word for well-being (Heb. *shalom*, "That's all right," NIV); an amorphous term, it can be interpreted as a dismissal or a confidence.

The woman goes with all the speed she can manage (4:24), resolved to express her distress to the man of God himself. Elisha sees her coming and sends Gehazi to meet her (4:26); she dismisses his inquiry with the same uncertain response she had for her husband (*shalom*). Like the woman at Zarephath (1 Kgs 17:18), the woman from Shunem feels that there is something sinister about this man of God; he has deceived her (2 Kgs 4:28). From the start she has been loath to believe it was possible she should have a son. Surprisingly, Elisha confesses to being mystified by this turn of events (4:27).

He admits to Gehazi that he has received no word from Yahweh on this matter.

The final division of the story shows that the woman has not lost her faith in God or his servant (4:29–37). She is hurt, confused, and anxious. Elisha treats the situation with urgency, sending Gehazi with his staff (4:29). The mission to place the staff of Elisha on the lad is an assurance that the prophet himself is on his way to Shunem. The woman refuses to go with Gehazi; her vow to stay with Elisha is identical to that of Elisha in his refusal to leave Elijah (4:30; cf. 2:2, 4, 6).

When Elisha arrives he shuts the door so the miracle will be private (4:33), just like the multiplication of the oil (4:4–5). The actions of Elisha are similar to those of Elijah in reviving the child of the woman at Zarephath but are described in significantly more detail (4:33–35). The actions of the woman are similar to her reporting the death of the child (4:27); she falls prostrate at the feet of Elisha, this time in gratitude rather than grief.

Food in Time of Famine (4:38–44). Both stories involve the prophetic bands that support Elisha in his efforts to teach the ways of the covenant in a state devoted to the Baal cult. In the first story (4:38–41), a famine leaves the band short of food, with the necessity of foraging for what they can find. Ignorance results in a "death pot" that threatens the health of the men. Elisha responds immediately to the crisis with the authority that is his alone as the man of God; the food is made wholesome and the welfare of the band preserved.

In the second story a stranger offers food to the band, but it is insufficient for the entire group. Elisha twice gives exactly the same command: "Give it to the people to eat" (4:42, 43). The protest that it will be insufficient is met with a word from Yahweh indicating that it will be more than sufficient. This word is fulfilled (4:44); Elisha provides for his prophets, just as he had for the widow. Each of these events establishes the authority of Elisha with the prophets as well as his ability to care for them.

Application. Life in this world is characterized by need and struggle as typified in these stories about Elisha. The pain of various situations and individuals is not really comparable; who is to say that losing a child to a creditor is more painful than never to have had a child at all or that the pain of food deprivation is more injurious than the loss of children (4:1, 14, 38, 43)? Empathy is a somewhat risky business, since one can never know the feelings or pain of another. Perhaps this unknown is part of the divine mystery of grace. God sovereignly dispenses his mercy to particular situations in his care for all his children. Mercy by its very nature is not justice, so the children are not able to demand whatever they consider to be their right, nor can they expect that their experience with God will be like that of someone else. Every age has a need for a mission like that of Elisha: to care for the needy, intervene for justice, and provide for the well-being of the marginalized.

2 KINGS 5:1–27

Original Meaning

The Cure of a Mighty Leper (5:1–14). Naaman is the field marshal of the king of Aram. The fame and valor of Naaman is expanded three times to emphasize his distinction (v. 1). He also has one other distinction; he is a leper. This one single word at the end of a string of accolades compromises all the others.

Naaman's disease has caused whiteness (v. 27), something like vitiligo in which pigment is lost from areas of the skin. Naaman continued to have access to the court of the king of Aram in Damascus (v. 4), an indication that his distress is more aesthetic than contagion.

Naaman has been conducting raids in the territory of Israel, and in the course of war has taken citizens captive, including a young girl who serves in his household. She suggests to her mistress that if her master were to go to the prophet in Samaria he might be cured. Her remark begins a series of transmissions that travel like lightning.

The Aramean king prepares a letter for the Israelite king. Naaman prepares a large gift to establish diplomatic relations with the king of Israel (v. 5). Naaman then sets out for Israel with the letter and with the enormous royal gift.

The content of the letter shifts the focus to the dramatic response of the king, who takes the letter as an incitation to war. The king of Israel, knowing his precarious situation with the Aramean armies and the prophets of Elisha, reads the letter as a demand that he demonstrate his authority over matters of life and death (5:7). The story mocks the impotence of kings and royal protocol, especially when the God of the covenant is being actively rejected.

The account now brings Elisha directly onto the scene as the main character of the first division (5:8). Elisha interrupts the royal exchange, telling the unbelieving king of Israel that an Aramean general will come to know the power of a true prophet.

Naaman proves to have a pride of his own (5:9–12). He interprets the prophet's indifference to royal protocol as an affront to his own status as someone esteemed by the mighty king of Aram. The prophet refuses to grant even a personal audience and does not come out to pray and offer a gesture of healing. Instead, he suggests the cure can be found in waters vastly inferior to those of his own country.

The Conversion of a Conqueror (5:15–19). Naaman's arrogance has become humility, and he now qualifies for his wish to have a direct audience with the prophet. He makes his confession to the God of Israel (5:15), proving the earlier words of Elisha to be true (5:8). The master of the servant girl now becomes the servant of the Israelite prophet.

Elisha refuses his proffered reward with a vow (5:16); Elisha can accept no responsibility for the mercy received. Grace granted by God cannot be rewarded with material benefits. As a confirmation of his confession, Naaman then makes two further requests of his own. He now wants two mule loads of earth to take back to the land of Aram. The earth is to build an altar to worship in Aram because he acknowledges no God in all the earth except the God of Israel. The second request is related to the first. As a servant of his lord he will be required to worship the God of thunder. Naaman will be required to participate with the king as his right-hand man. Elisha dismisses him with a simple blessing: "Go in peace" (5:19). Elisha does not question Naaman's loyalty. His humble petition serves as its own affirmation of his genuine faith.

The Curse of Envy (5:20–27). Naaman shows the true character of faith while Gehazi, the servant of the prophet, betrays his master and his trust in God. Gehazi vows in the name of God to obtain at least a portion of the gift (5:20), though his master has vowed that he cannot accept material gifts for a gift of grace (5:16).

Gehazi sets off in hot pursuit to rectify what he thinks to be an injustice, but Naaman expresses concern only for the well-being of the prophet (5:21). Though Gehazi professes that all is at peace (5:22), he is in the very process of violating that peace. He not only prepares to lie but puts the lie in the mouth of his master. Somehow Gehazi knew about the size of gift that Naaman planned (5:5) and contrives his request accordingly (5:22).

When Naaman urges him to take more, he packs the loot and readily accepts the help of two servants to take it back (5:23). While Naaman's reputation precedes him (5:1), the servants precede Gehazi with the booty of his treachery (5:24). As soon as they are back at the safety of the acropolis in Samaria, Gehazi deposits the goods in the house and dispatches the servants (5:25). Naaman is again on his way, and Gehazi resumes his position in the presence of his master as though nothing has happened.

The closing episode shows Elisha to be a true prophet who is fully aware of the implications of what has transpired. The duplicitous response of Gehazi to the question of where he has been does not deceive Elisha (5:25–26a). The sharp rebuke of Elisha comes in the form of an enigmatic question (5:26b).

Strangely, Elisha goes on to name items Gehazi has not actually taken: fields of olives and vineyards, sheep, cattle, and servants. At most it may be thought that Gehazi intends to purchase these with the money he has acquired. The sin of Gehazi is deception, unbelief, and the disparagement of "this Aramean" (5:20). The question indicates that the sin of Gehazi is not merely greed and theft. The envy of Gehazi is immoral, as is his indifference to the profound conversion of Naaman to trust in the God of Israel.

Application. As a pastor I have too often observed those who would reprimand others for failure of faith, with little understanding of their own compromises in their accusations. Not long ago I was ordering a meal on Sunday in a town well known for its abundance of churches. When the pleasant and cheerful table waiter came to take the order, I thanked her for such delightful attention to her customers, even when she had to work on a Sunday. She responded by saying my appreciation was a rather different attitude than the one she had just received. A couple had ordered their meal and discovered that the person serving them was a church member. They gave her a long lecture on the sin of working on Sunday, seemingly quite oblivious to the fact that if they thought such work on Sunday was a sin, they would do well to do their eating where someone else did not need to work for them.

2 KINGS 6:1–8:15

Original Meaning

Mercy at the Jordan (6:1–7). The "iron axhead" in 6:5 was undoubtedly a valuable instrument and was "borrowed" ("begged or prayed for," literally), making the loss so much more distressing. The story's focus is entirely on the miracle of recovering the axhead from the Jordan; the only connection for its being placed here in the Elisha collection of stories is that it relates another miracle of Elisha at the Jordan (cf. the Naaman story).

Military Secrets at Dothan (6:8–23). The first episode of this story presents Elisha as a spy in the Aramean camp, warning the Israelites where the enemy is planning to attack (6:8–10). The Aramean king plans an attack against Israel, but Elisha sends a warning to the king of Israel about the place of attack (6:9). The king then sends a warning to his commander (6:10), so the Arameans are stymied repeatedly, and no attack actually takes place.

In the second episode (6:11–14), a frustrated Aramean king rages against his own advisors, accusing one of them of being a spy for Israel. Apparently, the king has his own spies in the Israelite camp because one of his assistants is able to inform him that the prophet Elisha can hear what is said in the walls of his bedroom. The king further learns that the prophet is residing at Dothan, a city north of Samaria on the road leading into the Jezreel Valley. The king is determined to capture Elisha, either to avenge the sabotage of his army or to enlist him as an intelligence informant in his own forces. In order to ensure the success of his efforts, he dispatches a heavy force deep into the Israelite territory. The force enters under the cover of darkness and surrounds the city.

The third episode contrasts the army of the Arameans with the army of God (6:15–17). The Arameans have surrounded the city. The mighty army of the Arameans surrounding the city (6:15) is no match for one man of God surrounded by the chariots of Yahweh's army (6:17).

The Aramean army is not struck down by the swords of soldiers but by a blinding light. This is not ordinary blindness but a bright light that causes a temporary distortion of vision. In this fourth episode the Aramean army is taken captive by Elisha and led to the capital (6:18–20). Elisha then prays a prayer virtually identical to the one that enabled his servant to see the heavenly armies (6:20; cf. 6:17). The eyes of the soldiers are opened and they see their man, but they also see that they are now surrounded by the enemy army.

In the final episode the king of Israel believes he has an opportunity to inflict a debilitating defeat on the Aramean army (6:21–23). Matters, however, are not in his control; he has not been responsible for taking the soldiers captive and requires permission from the prophet, respectfully and unusually addressed as "father" (6:21). These soldiers are not to be slain or taken captive as the spoils of war and made slaves; instead, they are treated lavishly with food and drink and sent on their way. The result is a halt of the border wars.

Famine in Samaria (6:24–7:20). Ben-Hadad was probably a dynastic name for Aramean kings. The usual assumption of historians is that the Ben-Hadad in this Elisha story is Ben-Hadad son of Hazael (cf. 13:3). One of the tactics of siege warfare was to create famine so the citizens within a fortified city would be forced to surrender. Siege warfare reduces populations to extremes, which can include cannibalism.

The pathos of the story surfaces in the appeal of the woman who cries out to the king for help (6:26–31). Her complaint is not that she had been reduced to eating the corpse of her own child for food, but the injustice she feels when her neighbor refuses to honor the agreement they have to equally share their grisly fare. The revulsion of the story is her apparent lack of feeling for the death of her own child and that of her neighbor; the normal compassion of motherhood is subordinated to the desperation to survive.

The king assumes she is asking for food, and his helplessness is seen in the retort that only God can provide help in such circumstances (6:27), for the royal storehouses have been exhausted. When he learns of the real concern of the woman, he can only tear his clothes in grief. The rip reveals his own despair, as it exposes the coarse cloth of lament he is wearing underneath his regular tunic.

Contrary to the previous story, where Elisha is in total control, the prophet is now threatened with death by his own king. Elisha preached divine judgment against the descendants of Ahab (e.g., 2 Kgs 3:15–19), and the encounter with Naaman and his treatment of the Aramean army in Samaria demonstrate his good standing with the Arameans. Elisha is a logical target for the frustrations of an impotent king.

The threat the king makes against Elisha is irrational, but it is not idle. He dispatches a messenger to ambush the prophet while he is conferring with the leaders of the city (6:32–33); it is not only the members of the prophetic band who listen to Elisha. Elisha is fully aware of the king's intentions and instructs the elders to block the door and hold the executioner until the king arrives. He knows the king is right behind and that he has relented from his rash order.

The narrative moves quickly, showing the control of the prophet and the despair of the king. This disaster is part of God's sovereign purpose; the king can do nothing, not even pray. Elisha responds to the king with a word from Yahweh pertaining to the next day (7:1). The officer who is the immediate assistant to the king finds this announcement unbelievable (7:2). The prophet assures the officer that he will see this reversal of fortune but not enjoy the benefits.

The fulfillment of Yahweh's word begins with four lepers outside the gate of the city. Caught in a death trap, the four decide to go to desert to the enemy camp (7:3–4). When they arrive there, they find the enemy has fled in terror, having heard the noise of a mighty army. The Aramean soldiers have fled for their lives (7:7).

The divine message comes full circle as the lepers report back. The king, acting with prudent skepticism, suspects an enemy ploy to dupe his soldiers, draw them out of the city, capture them alive, and take the city. Subordinates point out the only real danger—missing an opportunity for relief from the famine. His army has been defeated (7:13); nothing is lost in taking a few of the remaining horses and confirming the report.

Food prices become exactly as the prophet earlier announced (7:16). The death of the officer takes place when he is appointed to be in charge of the gate and is trampled by the stampeding people. The final verses bring closure to the story by repeating the prophetic word (7:18–20), which determines the course of events.

Land Claims at Shunem (8:1–6). Elisha continues to assist his patroness from Shumen, this time warning her to leave because of a famine that is about to devastate the land of Israel (8:1). The woman takes refuge in the land of the Philistines (8:2).

When the woman returns, she finds her properties have been taken over. Though Elisha is no longer present, his influence comes to her assistance in getting a hearing with the king.

The legal details for loss of land tenure are not given. The text indicates that the problem is one of confiscation; in her absence the properties have been taken over, possibly by another family member or neighbor. The property is legally hers, possibly through inheritance, but she has no access to it.

The activities of Elisha are of interest to many during his lifetime, including the king. The arrival of the woman of Shunem to lodge her complaint, accompanied by her son, provides an immediate opportunity to verify the event of his being raised back to life. The king is moved by her story and appoints an officer to be in charge of restoring her property. This king acts much more nobly than his predecessor Ahab, who had no hesitation in confiscating the property of Naboth.

Regime Change at Damascus (8:7–15). Elisha is in Damascus on the occasion of King Ben-Hadad's being ill. The fame of the prophet is well known in Damascus, so it is only natural that the king should inquire about the outcome of his illness. The king sends Hazael, one of his trusted deputies, with a substantial remuneration to receive a word from the prophet. Though this is the gift of a king, forty camel loads must be read as hyperbole (8:9).

The encounter is not what Hazael expects; Elisha commissions him with the message that the king will live, though in fact the king will die (8:10). The message is mixed; the king will not die of his illness, but he will die at the hands of an assassin. The news so shocks Hazael that his gaze remains transfixed until he feels embarrassed (8:11); it is broken only by the weeping of the man of God.

God has already declared that Hazael will be the instrument of punishment to Israel (1 Kgs 19:15–17); here stands the man who will crush innocent citizens of Israel. The prophet knows that Hazael will become king of Aram (2 Kgs 8:13) and that war against Israel will be the inevitable outcome.

Events transpired as the prophet says (8:14–15); Hazael is well known in history as the usurper who took over the Aramean throne in Damascus. The "feat" that Hazael will accomplish (8:13) is described from an Aramean point of view. The crushing of children and slashing of pregnant women might be victory to a conquering king, but they are not great feats to the most vulnerable victims of war.

Application. The Israelites experience the activity of the Divine Warrior in many different ways, depending on their situation, but the presence and activity of God is at work through his prophets. The rule of God is demonstrated through Elisha the man of God rather than the king. Protecting the poor, bringing life and justice, leading armies, and acting as a covenant champion are all part of the ideal royal profile.

The apostle Paul reminds the Ephesians that the situation is no different for them (Eph 6:10–13). They need to be strong in the Lord and in the power of his might; they must put on the whole armor of God so that they can take their stand against the wiles of the devil. They are not struggling with an enemy of flesh and blood, but against rulers, authorities, and mighty forces of this dark world, against spiritual wickedness in the heavenly places. Behind the evil forces at work in the world are transworldly forces that put Paul into prison. Equipped with the spiritual armor of God it is possible for Christians in this world to stand against such forces. This spiritual armor is nothing other than faith in the truth of the gospel (Eph 6:14–17); above all it is prayer to the Divine Warrior (6:18), and steadfast prayer at all times for all the saints.

In the essentials of spiritual warfare, the present world is no different from the tortured topsy-turvy world of Elisha. Christians in many different places are ravaged by the turbulence of war, just as the faithful in the days of Elisha. Where actual physical warfare is not present, Christians struggle against ideologies and social forces designed to undermine the rule of God in this world, the way of life God has ordained through his word for those created to represent him as his image. Everywhere the faithful are called to be like Elisha and his followers; they must resist evil and show mercy, as they are able. As with Elisha, their weapon is prayer and their assurance is that the Divine Warrior will act on their behalf, even as he did in the distressing days of Omride apostasy.

2 KINGS 8:16–10:36

Original Meaning

Apostasy of the Kings of Judah (8:16–29). The synchronism of Jehoram with the fifth year of Joram son of Ahab (8:16) marks the end of the twenty-five-year reign of Jehoshaphat. The summary of Jehoram's reign states that the mercy of God preserves the dynasty of David in spite of the fact that Jehoram follows in the ways of the house of Ahab (8:18–19). The promise to David is a light that continues to shine. Though the dynasty is preserved, Judah suffers the loss of territory and influence.

Jehoram tries to bring Edom into submission but without success (8:20–22). Jehoram and all his chariot forces conduct a night raid on Edom, but the Edomites surround him and the chariot officers, and the army flees back to its tents. The note that the revolt of Edom continues "to this day" (8:22) shows a special interest in territorial claims when Judah regains its military strength.

Ahaziah, son of Jehoram, begins to rule Israel in the twelfth year of Joram (8:25) and rules briefly until his death in

Megiddo at the hands of Jehu (9:27). The mother of Ahaziah is Athaliah, here said to be a "granddaughter [descendant] of Omri" (8:26). The queen mother could exercise considerable influence in affairs of the court, as we saw in the case of Maacah (cf. 1 Kgs 15:13). The influence of Jezebel in fostering foreign cults in Jerusalem continues through her daughter Athaliah. These are best described in terms of "the house of Ahab" (2 Kgs 8:27), who was renowned for his support of the prophets of Baal against Elijah. The end of Ahaziah's reign does not have the usual burial formula. His death is recorded in the following narrative (9:27–28).

The Revolt of Jehu (9:1–37). The anointing takes place clandestinely and hastily, as is necessary if the revolt were to take place with the army leaders while they are on active duty. Ahab had failed in his attempt to capture the city (1 Kgs 22:29–36). Elisha plays a relatively minor role in the anointing of Jehu, especially given the prominence of the commission of Elijah (1 Kgs 19:16). Jehu evidently is known to the prophetic envoy; he identifies him among the officers gathered at Ramoth Gilead (2 Kgs 9:5). The prophetic oracle (9:7–10) against the house of Ahab is certainly exploited by Jehu and his party.

The oracle has the two standard elements: There is a judgment relevant to the immediate situation (9:7), followed by the stereotyped curse (9:8–9). The oracle against Jezebel (9:10) is specifically a fulfillment of the prophetic word (1 Kgs 21:23). The judgment speech brings to a climax the accumulated sins of Israel from Jeroboam to Joram.

Calling the prophet a "maniac" (9:11) is a derogatory reference to the eclectic nature of prophets. But prophets did have influence, even when their ability to declare the divine will was disregarded. The officers know the prophetic emissary with Jehu, and his announcement is regarded as the occasion to act. The followers of Jehu immediately turn the bare steps into an ascent to a royal dais and declare Jehu as king. Blowing a trumpet served as a public announcement to formally submit to the new monarch. Following the accession ceremony, a proclamation to announce the anointed as king was normal procedure. Though the prophetic herald is spoken of disparagingly, his word is effective.

The narrative moves to the scene at Jezreel where the coup actually transpires (9:14–15). Jehu relies on the element of surprise in returning to Jezreel, demanding that no one betray a coronation that has just taken place. Joram will naturally expect that his chief officer is bringing him news from the battlefront when the watchmen see him approach.

The threefold repetition of the question asking whether all is well shifts attention to the actual disruption of peace (9:18, 19, 22). In the first instance, Joram still functions in the role of king, as the messenger is sent with an order: The king is asking, "Do you come in peace?" (9:18). Jehu knows Joram is no longer king, and his reply directs attention to the problem: What does the house of Ahab have to do with peace?

Jehu's response brings his mission into focus. The rider is in the service of a king who represents the crime of Ahab against Naboth in spilling innocent blood; he has nothing whatever to do with peace. If the rider is asking about whether Jehu's advance is war, the answer is the same: Jehu is bringing revolution to Jezreel. When the rider joins Jehu's troop, a second messenger is sent with the same question.

The narrative further joins Jehu with the prophetic message by describing his driving as "like a maniac" (9:11, 20). Joram acts in naivety, denial, or desperation; the narrative is ambiguous regarding his state of mind. Joram finds Jehu at Naboth's plot and asks whether the mission is one of peace (9:22). Perhaps he thinks his presence can change the course of Jehu's action.

Joram is powerless before Jehu (9:18–23). Jehu has come unannounced, with a formidable force, and has not allowed the messengers to return. Joram is not himself responsible for the sins of his mother that robbed the land of justice (9:22). There can be no peace for Joram.

Joram wheels about in a desperate attempt to escape his fate (9:23). His cry of "treachery" (*mirmah*) functions as the opposite of peace (*shalom*). The reign of Ahab was characterized by lies and deceit. His dynasty ends by means of the same treachery that characterized it.

The callous violence of Jehu is carried out in the sense of fulfilling divine judgment. As Joram slumps in the chariot, Jehu recalls how he and his commander Bidkar were riding side by side when the divine utterance was made against the house of Ahab (9:25–26). Jehu is determined to remove not only the ruling descendant of Ahab but also members of the royal family. Thus, Jehu pursues Ahaziah, giving orders to shoot him as well (9:27).

Ahaziah flees south. He is shot and wounded. Knowing that he cannot count on the speed of his chariot in the hills of Samaria, Ahaziah turns west toward Megiddo, perhaps in the hope that it is still loyal to Joram. He finds refuge but dies there from his wounds and is brought back to Jerusalem, where he receives a proper burial. The summary of the reign of Ahaziah is inserted as the conclusion to his burial (9:29).

Jehu then returns to Jezreel to deal with Jezebel; her attendants join the revolt and throw her down to be trampled on the ground (9:33). Jehu goes on to celebrate (9:34).

The abandonment of the cadaver of Jezebel to the scavenger animals (9:35–37) is a particularly disparaging insult against the woman who was queen. The fate of Jezebel emphasizes the fulfillment of the prophetic word (cf. 1 Kgs 21:23). The proverb about her body being as dung is possibly a further insult to her name, calling attention to a second meaning for *zebel* as "manure."

The Reign of Jehu (10:1–36). The destruction of Ahab's house is described in two episodes. The first episode begins with letters calculated to inspire terror in any of the leaders that may still be loyal to Joram. Jehu's objective is to eliminate all the claimants to the throne, described as seventy sons of Ahab. It is not clear whether the letters go to the leaders of Jezreel (10:1); if the officials of Jezreel are meant, they must have fled to Samaria where the letters are sent.

The letters challenge the members of the former regime to contest the regency of Jehu if they are so inclined (10: 2–3). The chief steward of the palace, the governor of the city, the officials, and the guardians of the royal sons concede immediately, refusing to install a rival king (10:5). Jehu then asks that the heads of the royal descendants be brought to Jezreel. There appears to be a deliberate ambiguity in the request since it is not clear if the chief leaders ("heads," 10:6) are to be brought or the decapitated skulls. This may have been the ruse Jehu uses to claim innocence in the whole affair (10:9) and imply the massacre is the result of a popular rebellion against Joram. The officials take the corporeal meaning, dutifully bring the decapitated heads of all the members of Joram's family and, on the orders of Jehu, heap them in two piles at the gates of Jezreel (10:8). The bloody spectacle is an effective tactic of intimidation.

Once Jehu has the situation in Jezreel fully in his control, he proceeds to the capital Samaria (10:12). The narrative does not explain the circumstances of this encounter with the brothers of Ahaziah. Jehu discovers them while doing reconnaissance. The text may be read to say their intent is to "avenge" (Heb. *shallem*, NIV "greet") the deaths of the family members of Joram and Jezebel, the queen mother (10:13), rather than to seek their peace. If this is the correct link to the narrative, it explains the presence of the force that Jehu has with him that enables him to kill forty-two of them. It is imperative for Jehu to control resistance movements in Judah, as there are undoubtedly loyalties to the house of Ahab there as well.

Jehonadab the Rekabite seeks out Jehu on the way in order to join his campaign against the Baal cult. Jeremiah describes the Rekabites (Jer 35:5–11) as examples of fidelity to their word, in contrast to the infidelity of Judah in its covenant with Yahweh. Rekabite austerity and rejection of sedentary life in Canaan are in themselves insufficient to explain Jehonadab's resolution to join Jehu in the extermination of the Baal cult. Jehonadab joins Jehu in his chariot to Samaria, where Jehu immediately eliminates all the remnants of the house of Ahab.

The second objective of Jehu in Samaria is to purge the ministers of the Baal cult and raze its temple to the ground (10:18–28). Jehu's demand that all the prophets, ministers, and priests of Baal be present is carried out under threat of death (10:19). The call extends to the whole territory of Israel, so the entire temple is filled (10:20–21). Care is taken to be sure all the proper vestments are provided and that none but the Baal ministers are present (10:23). Once the sacrifices are underway, Jehu assembles a force of eighty military officers, guards, and lieutenants outside the temple. Under pain of death, they are to make sure no individual escapes (10:24); their mission extends to the inmost shrine of the temple to ensure their purge is thorough (10:25).

The sacred pillar is then burned and crushed (10:26–27). The whole temple complex is torn to the ground; it is unlikely the whole complex is a "latrine" (10:27) but more likely a dung heap, a permanent public dump.

The summary of Jehu's reign (10:29–36) gives Jehu credit for the change of religion he has brought about in Samaria. The dynasty of Jehu continues for four generations (10:30), enduring for almost a hundred years—by far the longest in Israel. This achievement is not without compromise or cost. It is twice noted that Jehu fails to rectify the fundamental problem of cultic worship at Dan and Bethel (10:29, 31). The military is so severely weakened that Israel is subjected to Hazael in the Transjordan (10:32–33).

Application. The contemporary world has many examples of a *cause célèbre* equivalent to that of Naboth's vineyard. These can range from local issues, such as the plight of the homeless in any major city, to national issues, such as the loss of land by aboriginals, or to international issues, such as disruptions caused by the phenomena known as "globalization"—labor issues, free trade, debt, and emerging markets. Governments at various levels share culpability and responsibility in these matters and must be accountable. Injustice must be addressed but not in a manner that creates an equal evil in turn.

Although the necessary changes instituted by Jehu are commended for the necessary change they effect, Hosea condemns Jehu's methods as bringing inevitable judgment. His brutal actions are designed to achieve his personal ambitions as a military leader, under the guise of terminating the injustices of the Omride dynasty. Often attempts to deal with evident injustice are so governed by passion, haste, and personal ambition that other victimization occurs in the process.

As Aquinas observed, the passion most immediately associated with injustice is anger. Anger is often justified, inspired by love and respect for those persons whose rights are perceived as being violated. Anger recoils at injustice; it strikes out at what is wrong. It strains to change unjust structures that deprive the vulnerable of political, social, economic, or personal rights that human dignity demands. A good dose of anger can be helpful; anger is creative energy that can be used for positive action. It is like a fire; in a controlled environment, it is a powerful force for good, but out of control it can do irreparable damage. Anger can lash out in harsh words, biting insults, violence, riots, and even war.

2 KINGS 11:1–20

Original Meaning

The Conspiracy of Jehoiada (11:1–16). When Ahaziah dies at the hands of Jehu's forces (9:27), Athaliah attempts to kill all the heirs and assume the throne herself (11:1, 3). Her conduct is consistent with that of Jehoram, who killed all the other sons of Jehoshaphat when he came to the throne (2 Chr 21:4). The elimination of all rival claimants furthers the goal of retaining Omride power in Judah. Athaliah may have prevented Jehu from entering Judah and reuniting Judah and Israel. She is able to retain control of the army and retain the independence of Judah for six years.

The despotism of Athaliah is unsuccessful. Jehosheba, sister of Ahaziah, is able to hide Joash, son of the king and heir to the throne, in the temple. The temple must have remained relatively undisturbed by the Baal cult during Athaliah's reign, as the heir to the throne is not discovered.

Jehoiada is in complete charge of the temple and its guards. He swears the guards to secrecy and shows them the surviving heir to the throne. Jehoiada summons all the temple guards, who apparently serve on a rotation of one week out of three (11:5–7). Those on duty he assigns to positions at three locations (11:6–8). Highest care is taken to protect the king.

All the guards assigned to the palace and the temple take their stations with their weapons as instructed (11:9). The focus of activity shifts to the anointing of the king at the temple on this extraordinary Sabbath day. The officers are all given spears and shields, apparently ceremonial armor appropriate for the anointing of the king (11:10). The guards take up their stations around the temple, from south to north around the altar, in order to protect the king (11:11). The guards seem to have formed a semicircle around the front of the temple.

Once the officers and guards are stationed, the king is brought out for the ceremony. The anointing with oil, the blowing of the horns, and the shouts of the people are reminiscent of the coronation of Solomon (1 Kgs 1:39–40) or Jehu (2 Kgs 9:13). Joash receives a crown and a copy of the covenant. A diadem served as a sign of royalty in ancient Israel. The king was required to keep with him a testimony of the covenant as a constant reminder that he must rule according to divine order (Deut 17:18–19).

The tumult of the coronation rouses the attention of Athaliah, who makes her way to the temple to investigate (11:13). Gathered there are the civic leaders who are part of the coronation ceremony (11:14, 18, 20). Their presence is required to confirm the accession of the new king; they represent the residents of the land. When Athaliah sees the king, she recognizes immediately that her time as queen is over; she is seized by force and taken to the entrance of the Horse Gate. She is summarily executed, allowing no time for her supporters to raise resistance to the new king.

The Renewal of the Covenant (11:17–20). The anointing of a new king requires renewal of the covenant. The covenant with Yahweh (11:17) is different from the covenant Jehoiada made with the officers and the guards (11:4). This is the first occasion that the making of the covenant is mentioned during the time of the monarchy.

Both the Chronicler (2 Chr 23:16, 18) and Josephus (*Antiquities* 9.141) emphasize the restoration of the Davidic line. This is primary, since the "lamp" of David has come near to extinction. The coronation includes the covenant obligation of the young king in the presentation of the crown jewels (2 Kgs 11:12); these affirm the renewal of the Davidic dynasty and the commitment of the king to lead the people according to the book of the covenant kept at his side.

The leaders then follow the pattern of Jehu in the north by purging the land of Baal influence (11:18). This is not the end of the Baal cult in Jerusalem, however; Hezekiah again removes altars and shrines of Canaanite religion (18:4), as does Josiah following the days of Manasseh (23:4). But a new beginning is established with Joash. Special custodians are appointed for the security of the temple (11:18b–19).

The report of the restoration of the temple and the destruction of the Baal temple is concluded by summarizing statements of the coronation of the king and the death of Athaliah (11:19–20). The restoration of a true Davidic king and the death of Athaliah bring an end to the domination of the Baal cult in Judah.

Application. The church in this world may feel threatened, even as the temple seemed to be threatened in the time of Athaliah. At the confession at Caesarea Philippi, Jesus assures Peter that he is the rock on which the church will be built and the gates of death will not prevail against it (Matt 16:13–18). The light of the church is as secure as the lamp of David (2 Kgs 8:19); indeed, it is a lamp shining in its own right. Matthew's Gospel is the account of Jesus Christ, Son of David, Son of Abraham (Matt 1:1). Both the blessing of Abraham and the promise to David find their fulfillment in the person of Christ.

The specter of an Athaliah determined to eliminate the worship of God will continue to arise in different places and different times. The church must not fear, not even at the prospect of great suffering, as has happened so frequently. The "lamp" of David will not be snuffed out. One of the important lessons of the Deuteronomistic History is the preservation of the promise; that promise will prevail in spite of the eventual failure of the kingdom and the exile of the dynasty. As the history concludes, hope is still to be found in Babylon.

2 KINGS 11:21–12:21

Original Meaning

The Repair of the Temple (11:21–12:16). The reign of Joash is linked with the preceding narrative by giving his age at the time he begins to reign followed by the synchronism with Jehu (11:21–12:1). Jehoiada has taught the king well and apparently has considerable influence early in his reign, even choosing his wives (2 Chr 24:3). The priestly training of Joash influences him to take the initiative in temple restoration, with Jehoiada playing a minor role.

In repairing the temple (2 Kgs 12:4–16), Joash is compelled to introduce a new method of financing temple maintenance. The temple restoration under Joash refers to two sources of income for repair: the funds brought to the temple (12:4) and the money in the possession of the priests (12:5), which never comes to the temple (12:16).

In time, enthusiasm for the maintenance of the temple wanes, and the priests no longer contribute personal money. Joash reaches a new agreement with the priests (12:7); they will be absolved of responsibility to repair the temple, but they will no longer be in charge of the offerings brought to the temple. A cash box is installed south of the altar to provide for voluntary donations; when an Israelite enters the temple, the Levitical guards at the entrance will receive offerings and deposit them in the box.

This system of collecting voluntary contributions is effective. Periodically the king's recorder and the high priest collect the money and count it. Once the silver is valued, it is used to pay the workers for repairs (12:11) and the craftsmen needed to prepare the wood and the stone (12:12). The refurbishing of the temple artifacts used in worship is temporarily suspended to concentrate on the building itself.

The Invasion of Hazael (12:17–21). The reforms of Joash in his twenty-third year (813 BC) take place just after the end of the twenty-eight-year reign of Jehu (814 BC). His death ends the treaty he had with the Assyrians, and Hazael may have taken that opportunity to extend his control in his war with Assyria.

Joash successfully buys him off with the sacred vessels and temple treasures. Hazael does not seriously consider a conquest of Judah; his goal is to subjugate and control Joash, providing himself taxation revenues in the process. His main goal is to control trade routes along the coast, as he had in the Transjordan.

The summary of the reign of Joash tells of his assassination by his own court officials. No explanation is given, but his capitulation to Hazael and stripping the temple to meet the demands of the Arameans bring about political discontent. Chronicles further tells of dissention with the priesthood that results in Joash's killing Zachariah, son of Jehoiada (2 Chr 24:20–21). The assassins are probably professional soldiers hired to do the job, but no details are given as to who is behind the conspiracy.

Application. The situation is different for the church today; the church is best served when it is not supported by the state. It has the right to be protected by the state, as do all other citizens. Often the church faces the hostility of the state; this should not be surprising. The state represents the world, the powers of this age. Jesus warns his followers to expect the hostility of the world (John 15:18–20). The church cannot expect understanding from the world; it can only hope for tolerance and equal treatment with all other groups in society.

The necessity of secular government is readily accepted in a pluralistic society. The tension between the secular and the sacred remains as difficult as the cooperation of royalty and priesthood under the covenant in Old Testament times. The story of Joash is a warning of the dangers that can lead to self-destructive conflict. Avenues of compromise will be found on many issues if the church is to live in harmony with the state and if Christians are to participate in secular power with ethical integrity.

2 KINGS 13:1–14:29

Original Meaning

Reprieve from Aramean Oppression (13:1–25). The severely decimated power of Israel after the purge of Jehu allows for Aramean expansion in the Transjordan (10:32–33). Hazael and his successor, Ben-Hadad III, are able to oppress Jehoahaz king of Israel during most of his seventeen-year reign (13:1–3, 7). Even so, a prophetic word declares that Yahweh will send deliverance to Israel (13:3–5), which enables the dynasty to survive.

The prophetic note explains that Jehoahaz prays for deliverance and that Yahweh sends a savior to help them (13:5). This deliverer may have been a political figure, but historically there is no outstanding king who may be regarded as bringing relief to Israel. In the context of the Elisha passage (13:14–21), it is more likely that the savior intended by the Deuteronomistic Historians is a prophetic figure. If Elisha were this figure, it would be about forty years after his activity in the anointing of Jehu to succeed the Omride dynasty.

Ten-thousand foot soldiers of Jehoahaz (13:7) are a marked contrast to the ten chariots left to his forces. This statement still serves as an explanation for his subjugation to the Arameans, because a large number of infantry does not provide resistance to the speed of chariots. Israel is crushed like dust before the Arameans

Jehoahaz is succeeded by his son Jehoash (13:10–13), the same name as his counterpart in Judah. The significant events of the reign of Jehoash are only mentioned within the regnal summary of his reign (13:10–13), indicating that these events have been excerpted from the historical records of Jehoash. His victory over Ben-Hadad III is given with a summary of the domination of the Arameans (13:22–25), and his war with Amaziah is given as part of the history of the Judean king (14:8–14). The fortunes of Israel begin to rise significantly during the reign of Jehoash until it becomes a formidable and wealthy country under his son, Jeroboam II.

The reign of Jehoash is followed by a report of his visit to Elisha. The visit of Jehoash is to bring his last respects as Elisha is dying. The location of this visit is not given; if Elisha dies in the vicinity of his burial near Moab (13:20), it may be near his home in Abel Meholah (cf. 1 Kgs 19:16). The encomium of Jehoash is the same as that spoken by Elisha to his master, Elijah (2 Kgs 13:14; cf. 2:12). Elisha, unlike Elijah, has had active military leadership in the conflicts of Israel against the Arameans (cf. 3:11–19; 6:13–17); the words of Jehoash acknowledge that role and attribute to Elisha the same distinction that belonged to Elijah.

The last action of Elisha is to give a message of promise to the dynasty of Jehu, not unlike the final blessing of other leaders. The king of Israel is instructed to shoot an arrow east toward Aphek, east of the sea of Tiberias. Ahab successfully defended Aphek from an attack of the Arameans (1 Kgs 20:22–30), but it had since come under Aramean control. The arrow represents complete victory in regaining Aphek.

The king is then instructed to strike the ground with his arrows. His three strikes signify only a partial recovery from the dominion of the Arameans. The significance of this action is like that of the prophet Ahijah in the call of Jeroboam (1 Kgs 11:29–32). They are communicative and interactive, a message with a persuasive dimension. The anger of the prophet is instigated by the king's limited faith and resolve.

The legacy of Elisha is last of all remembered in a story about his burial. His prophetic anointing is again attested after his death, as contact with his bones leads to life-giving power. Like the episode with the arrows, it signifies the life-giving power of the prophet for the nation through the declaration of the divine will.

A summary of events in the Aramean conflict brings the focus of the narrative to the political fortunes of the dynasty of Jehu. The aggression of Hazael constituted the greater part of the reign of Jehoahaz, whose seventeen-year sovereignty extended into the eighth century. The delay of the judgment of Israel under Jehu's dynasty is in keeping with the covenant promise according to Deuteronomistic theology (2 Kgs 13:23; cf. Deut 6:10–12).

Rise of Israelite Power (14:1–29). After the summary of Jehoash's reign in Israel and a notation of his successes against the Arameans (13:12–13; 22–25), the narrative turns to Amaziah. The topic does not substantially change, because Amaziah becomes subject to Jehoash. Jehoash does not attempt to bring Judah under his rule, since the time for such a union is past, but Judah may have been a vassal to Israel. The disastrous reign of Amaziah ends with his exile and execution in Lachish (14:18–22). His unsuccessful war against Jehoash demonstrates the dominance of Israel (14:8–12). The long twenty-nine-year reign of Amaziah (14:2) and the fifty-two-year reign of Azariah (14:29; 15:2) undoubtedly involve a significant period of coregency.

Though Amaziah is said to do what is right, the ominous note of his rule is sounded in the observation that his reign is not like that of David but rather like that of his father Joash (14:3–4). The high places, not necessarily those of foreign gods, remain in place until the time of Josiah. These were not to be tolerated once the temple was built and designated as the place Yahweh chose for his name to dwell.

Succession to the throne is not without conflict (14:5–6). Joash, father of Amaziah, was assassinated in a political plot (12:21); Amaziah does not deal with the assassins until he has secured his place on the throne (14:5). Those who assassinated Joash are individuals with status and influence, who now threaten the rule of the new king. Special care is taken to point out that Amaziah follows the covenant regulation in the extent of the executions (14:6; cf. Deut 24:16).

The circumstances of the battle with Edom (2 Kgs 14:7) are not specified, though Chronicles indicates that Amaziah initiates the attack (2 Chr 25:11). The initial conquests in the north are probably achieved with the assistance of the king of Israel, with the aim of dominating the southern portion.

If Amaziah has allied with Jehoash of Israel in his efforts to gain control of lucrative trade routes, the cooperation ends in sharp disagreement. Border warfare may be the occasion for Amaziah seeking some type of negotiation with Jehoash (2 Kgs 14:8). Jehoash's response indicates that the negotiation initially carries with it a threat of military force (14:9–11). Amaziah seriously overestimates his military capability after his defeat of Edom. Jehoash is not intimidated; his reply is laced with scorn.

In a decisive victory, Jehoash takes Amaziah prisoner, then marches unhindered to Jerusalem, breaks down part of its wall, and plunders it (14:12–14). The hostages are likely nobility or members of the royal family, kept under guard or held for ransom. The plundering of the temple is reminiscent of the attack of Hazael against Joash.

Amaziah's death and the succession of Azariah (14:19–22) are unexpected after the closing notice of his reign (14:18). The narrative sequence may be explained by the unusual circumstances of his succession. After his death and burial it is stated that the people of Judah install Azariah as king in his place (14:21). A crown prince normally succeeds at the death of his father. The statement indicates that Azariah begins to rule while his father is still alive; Amaziah continues to be a titular king. The instability of his position is indicated by the measures he takes to secure his rule (14:5) and by the fact that he is driven into exile and executed (14:19). Discontent mounts following this humiliation inflicted by Jehoash. The conspirators include highly positioned political and military people, since even fortified Lachish proves to be unsafe.

The political power of Judah is totally eclipsed by Israel under the reign of Jeroboam, the successor to Jehoash (14:23–29). The synchronisms for the reign of Jeroboam indicate that political stability and military strength are achieved through Jeroboam's coming to power while his father is still king. The fortunes of the Jehu dynasty rise to impressive heights during the forty-one-year reign of Jeroboam (14:23–29). His victories reestablish the territorial limits of the reign of Solomon (14:25; cf. 1 Kgs 5:1; 8:65).

With the death of Jehoash and the rule of Azariah in Judah, it seems the royal houses of Samaria and Israel come to a new level of cooperation. Vast areas of productive agricultural land, from the prairies of Bashan (Amos 4:1) to the plantations of Carmel, produce abundant harvests of grain, wine, and oil (Hos 7:14). The Transjordan caravan routes are under Israelite control, as well as the Jezreel Valley and the Sharon Plain.

The closing summary of Jeroboam's reign is difficult both textually and historically (14:28–29). The least change of the text is to read "Judah and Israel," with the interpretation that the two countries are allies in receiving tribute from Hamath and Damascus. Ahab had established preferential commercial relations with Damascus (1 Kgs 20:34); Jeroboam is able to restore that measure of economic control, and it must be assumed that Judah shares in the prosperity of Israel until Assyria begins to exert pressure on Israel in the middle of the eighth century.

Application. The religious leaders of Israel appear to be scarcely aware of their grievous sin in making God's mercy an occasion for the imposition of injustice to the poor. Long term is what the prophets are thinking; immediate and lavish material gains achieved with disregard to the injury done to the powerless will bring death to the nation in just one generation.

The prophetic warnings of judgment against the oppressive rich are continued for the church. In the visions of the last plagues, the apostle John sees the judgment of Babylon, the great representative of wealth and oppression in the world (Rev 18:2–3). The safety of the church depends on her having no association with this Babylon and its sins (Rev 18:4–8). Babylon the Great will receive double for all the evil she has afflicted on others. Those who enjoy the wealth of this great harlot will lament when they see her smoke ascending, destroying the vast wealth accumulated.

Individual Christians and congregations by necessity are a part of this great and greedy commercial venture. They must be vigilant in using such wealth to seek first the kingdom of God. This is the only way to dissociate from Babylon, to avoid participating in her sins (Rev 18:4). Seeking first God's kingdom in the wealth of this world is a daily discipline, a continuous and conscious choice to use money and resources to further the values of the kingdom of God and to bring others into that kingdom. The choices are not easy, and they are not without compromise. The mercy of God is to be found for the motives of those who participate in the economy of the great harlot, as they are in this world, but at the same time we must seek always to bring justice and good news to the weak and the needy.

2 KINGS 15:1–38

Original Meaning

The Reign of Azariah (15:1–7). Azariah is also known as Uzziah; outside of Kings he is known by the latter name (2 Chr 26–27; Isa 1:1; 6:1). Though Azariah has a long and prosperous reign, his achievements are left unrecorded in the Deuteronomistic History. The single detail of his life for which he is remembered was that he has leprosy (2 Kgs 15:5). He is unable to perform his administrative and official duties to "the people of the land" (15:5). This privileged group receives particular services from the king in judicial matters and ritual duties (with leprosy Azariah is not permitted to enter sacred space). Jotham is appointed to carry out the responsibilities of the king in place of his father.

Uzziah's burial is variously said to be with his ancestors (15:7) or in the burial field that belongs to the kings (2 Chr 26:23). Inscriptional evidence indicates that the grave of Uzziah was moved. An inscribed plaque in Aramaic and dated to the first century BC was discovered in Jerusalem. The inscription indicates that the bones of Uzziah are located in a solitary tomb. "The garden of Uzza" (2 Kgs 21:18, 26) may have been the burial place of Uzziah.

Disintegration of the Israelite Monarchy (15:8–31). The death of Jeroboam brings an end to the dynasty of Jehu, which was prophesied to continue for four generations (10:30). Social and moral decay, vividly chronicled in Amos, has its effect in the political upheavals that come with the death of Jeroboam. Zechariah rules six months (15:8) and Shallum his successor for one month (15:13). Indications are that the political rivalries that follow the death of Jeroboam are territorial.

The assassination of Zechariah takes place at Ibleam, according to the Old Greek (15:10), which is often taken to be the correct text (cf. RSV, NEB). This is a change of only one letter from the Masoretic Text (the Hebrew Bible); the translation "in front of the people" (NIV) is problematic.

Menahem launches an attack from Tirzah against Shallum in Samaria (15:14). Menahem is also said to have attacked Tiphsah (15:16). The notation is connected with the assassination of Shallum (15:13–16) rather than the summary of Menahem's reign (15:17–22), indicating that this takes place at the time Menahem seizes the throne.

Menahem can only achieve and maintain his power through alliance with Pul, king of Assyria (15:19–20). Pul is the hypocoristicon by which Tiglath-Pileser is known in later historical writings (cf. 15:29). Menahem submits to the Assyrians in payment of tribute and in return gains their support so he can secure his kingdom (15:19). Fifty shekels was the price of a slave in Assyria at that time. At 3,000 shekels to a talent (cf. Exod 38:25–26), the tribute would pay sixty thousand soldiers.

The ten-year reign of Menahem is followed by a two-year reign of his son Pekahiah (742–740 BC). He is assassinated by Pekah, his chief officer, in the citadel of the palace in Samaria (2 Kgs 15:25). Pekah is assisted by a military unit from Gilead. His reign of twenty years must overlap with that of Menahem; he apparently has a rival rule in Gilead after the death of Jeroboam II.

The year of Pekah's ascension to the throne in Samaria is the same year that King Azariah (Uzziah) dies (15:27; cf. Isa 6:1). From that point on, the politics of both Damascus and Samaria are dominated entirely by the activities of Tiglath-Pileser (2 Kgs 15:29). During the last days of Pekah (734–732 BC), Tiglath-Pileser directs a number of campaigns against Israel in the coastal plain, Galilee, and Transjordan, reducing Israel to the rump state of Samaria ruled by Hoshea as a vassal king. The conspiracy of Hoshea against Pekah is through the military force of Tiglath-Pileser (15:30).

The Reign of Jotham (15:32–38). The reigns of Azariah and Jotham overlap with those of the last kings of Israel; the fate of Judah is determined by the vicissitudes of Israel. Jotham becomes king when Azariah is smitten with leprosy (15:5), in the second year of Pekah (15:32). He lives beyond his sixteen-year reign into his twentieth year, when Pekah is assassinated (15:30). The complexity of the synchronistic data betrays the political turbulence of this period; political struggles lead to various alliances vying for power.

Jotham begins to reign in 750 BC, ten years before the death of Azariah, and lives beyond the time that he actually retains control over the kingdom. Apparently, a pro-Assyrian faction raises Ahaz to the throne in the seventeenth year of Pekah in 735 BC (16:1). The sentiments in Judah have shifted; powerful officials have come to regard Israel as a threat and Assyria as a potential ally. Rezin of Aramea and Pekah of Israel attempt to coerce Jotham into an alliance against Assyria (15:37), but Ahaz attempts to gain independence from them through the assistance of the Assyrians (16:5–9). The pro-Assyrian policy effectively ends the reign of Jotham, but it does not deliver Judah; within a generation the armies of Assyria surround Jerusalem, and citizens from Judah are exiled as well.

The reign of Jotham is scarcely independent of either his father Azariah or the domination of the pro-Assyrian forces that put Ahaz into power. Aside from the notation that he exercises royal authority in the place of his father (15:5), the only achievement of his reign given in Kings is that he renovates one of the gateways of the temple (15:35). Temple repair is of special interest to the worship concerns of the historian; nothing is known of the circumstances requiring repair at this gate.

Application. The religion of modern secular societies does not concern itself with service, with forgiveness and reconciliation. Goals for justice have little to do with victims; crimes are deemed to be against society and against its order of rule, not against individuals who suffer. These kingdoms all perish, like those of Jeroboam and Uzziah, because they exist through power rather than the provision of justice and mercy to their people.

From a political perspective, the kingdoms of Jeroboam and Uzziah can be regarded as a remarkable success. From the perspective of observing the values of God's kingdom, they are failures, a dark period that comes under divine judgment. Though human kingdoms fail, God's kingdom does not fail. It finds fulfillment in the remnant that turns to God; it finds fulfillment in the proclamation of the Savior who came as the child promised by Isaiah in those dark days. The kingdom of God continues to find expression within the great kingdoms of this world. These kingdoms will crumble, just as surely as all the others before them, but Christ will build his church, and the gates of death will not prevail against it (Matt 16:18).

2 KINGS 16:1–20

Original Meaning

Political Compromise (16:1–9). Ahaz becomes king twelve years before Hoshea begins to reign (17:1). Tiglath-Pileser may have accorded him some recognition of authority, which north Israelite records count as his formal accession. His independent rule begins in the sixteenth year of the reign of Jotham, though Jotham lives another four years.

The attack of Rezin and Pekah (16:5) is partly an attempt to force Judah to join an alliance in resisting the Assyrian advance.

The result noted here is the same as that indicated in Isaiah 7:1: The aggressors fail to engage the Judean army, or at least fail in their attempt to lay siege to Jerusalem.

Ahaz's appeal to Tiglath-Pileser for help (2 Kgs 16:7–8) is a critique of Ahaz based on sources from the court and temple. The wealth sent to the Assyrians is not a "gift" (NIV) but a "bribe" (Heb. *shohad*). This exchange should not be compared with submitting tribute as a vassal. The historian portrays Ahaz as voluntarily submitting to the Assyrian yoke, a grievous misdeed in addition to his promoting idolatry in the high places.

Temple Innovations (16:10–20). The political compliance to Tiglath-Pileser requires Ahaz to meet him in Damascus to bring tribute. While there, he sees an altar that apparently meets the deficiencies of the altar of Solomon, which is described as too small (1 Kgs 8:64). The altar is built by Uriah the faithful high priest (Isa 8:2), according to the model and design Ahaz has prescribed. When Ahaz returns from Damascus he conducts the inaugural ceremony, just as Solomon did at the dedication of the temple. The new altar is elevated, so the king must mount it in order to make the offerings (2 Kgs 16:12).

The offerings include those totally burned, the dry offerings of grains, the libations of liquid produce such as oil and wine, and the peace or fellowship offerings, which are consumed by the worshipers (16:13). The old bronze altar is moved from its place in front of the sanctuary entrance to the north side. All the regular offerings for the king and his officials (16:15) are to be brought to the new altar. The old altar is for the exclusive use of the king, where he will worship and pray. The sense of how Ahaz will seek (*baqqer*, 16:15) Yahweh is not specified, but no cultic practice is implied. The involvement of Uriah the priest suggests that Ahaz does not intend worship contrary to what has been prescribed.

Ahaz removes the frames from the wheeled stands (cf. 1 Kgs 7:27–30) with their elaborate metal work, probably as part of the payments made to Assyria (2 Kgs 16:17). He also takes down the large basin from the bronze oxen that support it and places it on a stone bed. The "Sabbath canopy" may have been a metal awning (16:18). All these changes are regarded negatively as an accommodation to Assyrian influence.

Application. Biblical prophecy has left Ahaz as a paradigm for the choice to trust in God for one's well-being. In seeking to protect his earthly inheritance, he loses it all. Had he been willing to trust God with his kingdom, he and his people could have been secure. Jesus in the same way promises his followers that all the needs of this earthly life will be provided to those who make the kingdom of God their concern (Matt 6:25–33). By contrast, those who seek treasure on this earth will find it will rust and decay (6:19–21), if it is not taken away, as Tiglath-Pileser strips the treasures of the temple.

The choices of Ahaz are typical of the values of the wealthy seeking security for their possessions. He chooses to trust political and economic forces rather than God. In so doing he is willing not only to desecrate the temple by robbing it of its valuable metals but to set up in its precincts foreign altars. In all of this, God is still with Ahaz. During his reign the kingdom of Israel disappears entirely, the nation that he so fears, but his own people come under the domination of the same Assyrians. Wealth is important to life in this world but not as an end in itself. Pursued as a goal, it brings judgment and is lost. Wealth used in dependence on God and in furthering the kingdom of God enables his presence and blessing. But Ahaz chooses to make his god to be the security of his wealth through temporal forces, and in so doing he loses the blessing of the sign of Immanuel. Christians, who have experienced the blessing of the fulfillment of Immanuel, must beware of falling into the same condemnation.

2 KINGS 17:1–41

Original Meaning

Fall of Samaria (17:1–6). The end of Hoshea's reign is described in two-verse pairs (17:3–4 and 5–6), each of which notes an invasion by Shalmaneser. The report begins with an emphatic irony: Hoshea, who did not sin as did the kings of Israel before him (17:2), is the king whom Shalmaneser attacks (17:3). In 17:3–4 the author recalls the vivid memory of the attack that ended the nation of Israel and the reason for it. Hoshea rebelled from his servant status and with Egyptian assistance attempted to gain independence; as a result, the Assyrians invaded and imprisoned the king. The author then describes the effect of the invasion for the city of Samaria and the population of the country (17:5–6); after a three-year struggle, the city fell and large numbers of people were deported.

Israel's deportation takes place in the years following the fall of Samaria after the death of Shalmaneser V. That death delays the consequences for Israel; Sargon II recaptures the city, and the deportations follow. Others of the Israelites are deported (17:6). These become skilled workers in building projects or are assigned as farmers to lands owned by state officials in the main part of Assyria. Several years later (after 716 BC), other deportees are less fortunate; they suffer the hardships of living in a frontier region described as "towns of the Medes" (i.e., in the Zagros Mountains, 17:6).

Punishment of Idolatry (17:7–23). A prophetic sermon details the sins that are responsible for the fall of Israel (and

Judah; cf. 17:19). The sermon falls into two main sections (17:7–13 and 14–19), with a conclusion that recapitulates the sins of Jeroboam that started Israel on the path into idolatry (17:20–23). These two main sections are well balanced: Each begins with a general statement of the sins of Israel (17:7–9a and 14), followed by a detailed list of the misdeeds of the people (17:9b–12 and 17:15–18). The first section concludes with the warning that God gave Israel through the prophets (17:13), the second with the warning that Judah received through the fall of Israel (17:19).

The only mention of Israel's kings here is in the general introduction of the sins of Israel (17:8b). The translation in 17:9 that the Israelites "secretly did things against the LORD" is doubtful (cf. RSV, NIV); the Hebrew word translated "secretly" occurs only in this verse, and its meaning must be inferred from context. It more likely means that the Israelites attributed to God things that are not true (cf. NEB), such as worshiping Yahweh under the image of a molten calf. This was the adoption of foreign practices introduced into the worship of Yahweh. The erection of stone pillars and Asherah are also examples of this (17:10).

Religions of Samaria (17:24–33). The exiled Israelites are replaced with people from other lands. Sargon II's deportations differed from those of Tiglath-Pileser III, which were unidirectional. Sargon II continued the policy of securing the Damascus-Megiddo-Egypt route and quick access to the Philistine states, but the rump state of Samaria was not particularly integral to that objective. Samaria was important as a trading center, and thus Sargon populated it with Arabians as well as those from the diverse areas of Assyria. Not only did this divert some of the Arabian trade to that area, in which nomads played an important role, it also repopulated desolate and impoverished areas to reinforce the western border of the Assyrian Empire.

The five nationalities noted in 17:24 correspond with Mesopotamian locations conquered by Sargon II in the latter part of the eighth century. The repatriation of a priest to Bethel to teach the newcomers how to fear Yahweh (17:27–28) also accords well with known Sargonic policy. The peoples brought to repopulate Israel add Yahweh to the gods from their homelands as another god to worship (17:33). The Bethel sanctuary continues to function as the place to worship Yahweh, but other temples at high places are built in various cities for the worship of other gods, led by their priests (17:28–29).

Persistent Covenant Disobedience (17:34–41). In the worship fostered at Bethel and the other high places before the deportation, the people did not "fear the LORD" (17:34, NASB). They included unacceptable elements of other religions and, of course, did not accept or use the temple at Jerusalem. The end of Israel becomes the occasion for a concluding exhortation on the failure of the covenant from the time of the exodus "to this day" (17:34). The final summary repeats the phrase: "To this day" the people fail to observe the loyalty of the covenant oath they have taken (17:40–41). Repetitive phrases are typical in Hebrew narrative to mark the beginning and end of a distinct literary unit within a larger composition.

Application. The failures of the old covenant lamented by the Deuteronomists could not be corrected by greater resolution to obey precepts as a means to a relationship with God. This fundamental misunderstanding of the covenant relationship continued to distort a true understanding of a genuine relationship with God. The possibility of a relationship with God from the start was a divine initiative that made those of his covenant "his treasured possession" (Deut 7:6).

God created Israel to be his bride; he voluntarily entered into an oath with them. The fundamental requirement of that relationship is stated in the primary confession of the covenant book (Deut 6:5). God never demands perfection in keeping the pledge; his love is perfect and abundant to pardon. Our God is one who will always forgive our sins and heal our diseases (Ps 103:3). God requires a loyalty to that promise; as with the oath of marriage, the covenant partner must always receive uncompromised fidelity.

The failure of the covenant relationship that resulted in the exile did not bring an end to the promise of God or his love for his people. The church continues the work of God, for which the prophets longed. In this new covenant there is forgiveness of sins; each one teaches the other to know the Lord, as Jeremiah promised. Jesus turns the Passover into a confession of this new covenant. The wine is his blood of the covenant, shed for many for the forgiveness of sins (Matt 26:28). Paul declares the cup of the Passover is the new covenant in the blood of Christ; eating the bread and drinking the wine must be done in remembrance of Christ until he comes (1 Cor 11:25–26). The Eucharist is the confession of the new redemption that follows the failures of the old covenant.

2 KINGS 18:1–20:21

Original Meaning

The Faithful King (18:1–12). In contrast to all the previous kings of Israel and Judah, Hezekiah is introduced as the faithful king, one who reformed Judean worship and moved Judah toward the ideal of the covenant. Hezekiah is the very model of the Davidic ideal (18:3, 5). His faithfulness results in the preservation of Jerusalem, a stark contrast to the captivity of Israel.

This point is made explicit by recounting again the fall

of Israel, which takes place early in Hezekiah's life, while he is coregent with his father, Ahaz. Hezekiah's independent rule begins in 715 BC, fourteen years before the siege against Jerusalem. He is rewarded for his faithfulness, not only in successfully resisting the Assyrian advances but also in securing his boundaries toward the Philistine territories (18:7–8). Hezekiah's trust is particularly evident when he refuses to yield to the Assyrians, even when the fortified cities of Judah are destroyed and the Assyrian armies have encircled Jerusalem.

Devastation of Judah (18:13–16). The success and prosperity of Hezekiah come to an abrupt end with Assyria's invasion of Judah. A monumental wall relief from the palace of Sennacherib in Nineveh commemorates the battle over Lachish and the deportation of its inhabitants. This commemoration of that siege demonstrates its strategic importance in Assyria's military advance.

Deliverance of Jerusalem (18:17–19:37). The biblical events are part of a larger Assyrian campaign into Philistia and Judah. Jerusalem attracts a heavy military force under the direction of the top generals (18:17). The Tartan (NIV "supreme commander") is the highest official after the king (cf. Isa 20:1); the Rabsaris (NIV "chief officer") is often dispatched on duties at the head of Assyrian forces; the Rabshakeh (NIV "field commander") is the personal attendant of the king. Eliakim, the royal steward in charge of the palace (cf. 1 Kgs 4:6), is at the head of Hezekiah's delegation (2 Kgs 18:18); the "secretary" and the "recorder" are the other chief-ranking officers. In the ensuing speech, Hezekiah is always referred to by his personal name, while the Assyrian king is designated "the great king."

The field commander is the spokesman for the Assyrians, quite possibly because of his fluency in languages (18:26–27). His attack centers on the question of trust (18:21–25). Reliance on Egypt is compared to a splintered reed (Egypt had many marshy waters) that will pierce the hand rather than serve as support. Trust in God is undermined because presumably Hezekiah has insulted Yahweh by removing the high places. Thus, the only reasonable alternative is to enter an agreement with the Assyrians. The Assyrian even claims that his presence at Jerusalem indicates the Judahite God has abandoned his people and joined the Assyrian side.

The shouting to the people on the wall is designed to intimidate. Though the envoys of Sennacherib and the Jerusalem delegates know Aramaic well, the international language of the day, the field commander insists on speaking Judahite (18:28), the Hebrew dialect of the south. He threatens the people with the dire consequences of starvation, which is the typical result of siege warfare (18:27; cf. 6:24–31).

As is typical of brutal conquerors, his promise is one of prosperity and independence (18:31–32). Sennacherib boasts of conquests of Aramean cities that have been captured much earlier (18:34); Hamath and Samaria were captured by Sargon, Arpad by Tiglath-Pileser III (cf. 17:24). Hezekiah is duly humbled by this intimidation (19:3); it is a day of distress, rebuke, and contempt. Yet in spite of such threats, the prophet Isaiah assures Hezekiah that Sennacherib will soon hear news that will drive him back to his own land.

The message of Isaiah leads to a transition in the narrative. The report of the arrival of the Egyptians causes an Assyrian withdrawal (19:8–9a). "So he again sent" (19:9b) can also mean "so he returned," since the Hebrew verb *shub* can be adverbial ("again") or can mean "return." The narrative reads sensibly as a sequel; the Egyptians do not affect a withdrawal of the Assyrians, so Hezekiah must go to Isaiah a second time to receive words of assurance.

The repeated boasts of Assyrian conquests are impressive (19:12). In response to such taunts, Hezekiah prays; he is granted access to the temple where he prays before the cherubim (19:15), who represent the throne of the Creator of the universe.

Isaiah delivers an answer to Hezekiah's prayer as a mocking song (19:21–28). The sentiment of the song is typical of Isaiah; the divine plan has been determined from the beginning of the world (19:25; Isa 40:21; 46:10). The Assyrian boasts of his conquests; the people are rendered powerless, dismayed, and confounded, and fortifications have been shattered. However, the Assyrians will not escape the destruction of war, which they have executed as part of God's judgment (cf. Isa 10:5–7). God knows their every action, their every pursuit (2 Kgs 19:27). Assyrians led their prisoners by placing rings in their lips and attaching ropes to them; they themselves will be taken captive as wild animals with hooks.

The assurance that Sennacherib will be turned back to the way he came is given twice (19:28c, 33–34). Judah will feel the effects of the foreign presence; it will be two years before a normal agricultural cycle of sowing and harvest can resume (19:29–30). Though there will be a great deportation of peoples, those who survive will take root as a healthy plant, once again making the country prosperous (19:30). The second oracle makes it clear that there was no actual siege against Jerusalem as at Lachish and the other fortified cities of Judah (19:32–34). God protects Jerusalem for the sake of his own name and because of his promise to David.

The Bible ignores the twenty years that elapse before the assassination of Sennacherib. The point is that divine judgment is meted out on the cruel Assyrian invader. The Babylonian Chronicle confirms the assassination of Sennacherib.

Deliverance from Illness (20:1–11). Hezekiah's illness receives a loose chronological link with the time of the Assyrian invasion.

The message of Isaiah for Jerusalem is affirmative but initially not so for its king. On receiving the news of his impending death, King Hezekiah turns to God. Isaiah returns with the message that Hezekiah will be delivered, as will Jerusalem, because of God's reputation and the promise made to David (20:6).

The healing of Hezekiah from some type of skin disease is facilitated with a fig cake plaster. The healing is followed by a request for a sign. The prophetic sign is given as evidence of the significance of the healing.

Failure of Faith (20:12–21). The visit of the Babylonian envoys has the same general chronological link to the time of the Assyrian siege. The sequence is arranged to show the threat to Jerusalem and the Davidic dynasty, the basic purpose of the Deuteronomistic History. No purpose for the visit is stated; it is probably an effort to maintain goodwill between common enemies of the Assyrians.

For this perfidy with the Babylonians, Hezekiah receives the ultimate judgment; his dynasty will end with his descendants going into exile. However, during Hezekiah's time, the city of Jerusalem is spared judgment. Hezekiah is famous for his defenses of the city, particularly in securing a water supply (20:20). This involved cutting a tunnel under the walls of the city to carry the waters of the Gihon spring to the Siloam Pool. An inscription at the entrance to the tunnel commemorates this feat of ancient engineering. The tunnel is over 500 meters (over 1,600 feet) long.

Hezekiah resigns himself to the declaration of judgment he receives (20:19); the word of Yahweh is appropriate. The statement of self-interest, that there will be peace during his days, is drawn into Kings from Isaiah's account. The failure of peace is a motif in Isaiah (Isa 48:22; 57:21). Hezekiah does not fall into the category of the wicked, but his faithlessness in the matter of the Babylonian embassy is one more example of why Judah goes into exile.

Application. Faithfulness is primary in any relationship and is the most fundamental requirement in a relationship with God. A covenant is the highest commitment of faithfulness; for Hezekiah, the covenant is both collective and personal. He represents the people who have entered into a divine covenant and leads them to faithfully observe it. This is possible only because of his own faithfulness, seen in both his response to the Assyrian threat and his illness.

Christians in the same way are called to faithfulness, both collectively and individually. In writing to the Corinthians, Paul exhorts the believers to be faithful to Christ, because all things are theirs in Christ (1 Cor 3:21–23). He uses the metaphor of a steward to describe the calling of Christians to represent God in his world. All things belong to Christ and, by extension, to his followers. When Paul refers to "stewards of the mysteries of God" (4:1, NASB), he means that Christians fulfill the work of God's kingdom in this world until such time as it is consummated in the second coming of Christ. As stewards responsible for the work of the kingdom in this world, faithfulness is the one fundamental requirement (4:2).

Such stewardship is much more than just giving money or being prudent with material possessions. It means to use every moment of time as a gift from God in a way that honors God. In this respect Christians must not become unduly introspective; Paul himself notes that he does not spend time on self-examination (1 Cor 4:3–5). He knows of nothing that will compromise his faithfulness, but that judgment belongs to the Lord. When the Lord comes, he will make manifest our intentions more clearly than we can know them now.

Hezekiah is a model of the exhortation the apostle Paul leaves Christians. The motives of Hezekiah can be questioned in the way he dealt with the Assyrians, in his prayer during the time of his illness, and particularly in his culpability in exposing his wealth and military capabilities to the Babylonian emissaries. In all of these matters, Hezekiah is simply presented as a king in pursuit of faithfulness, doing the best he can within his own circumstances.

Sometimes faithfulness requires the ultimate commitment of dying for the truth. Since the time of the martyrs, who were the seed of the church, many have suffered and given their lives in faithfulness to the gospel. The writer to the Hebrews exhorts Christians to be faithful in time of suffering (Heb 10:32–39). They suffered public humiliation and identified with those who so suffered; they suffered the plundering of their possessions. Endurance of suffering for the sake of the kingdom is the mark of faithfulness, which will bring a great reward.

2 KINGS 21:1–26

Original Meaning

Abominations of Manasseh (21:1–18). The dates of Manasseh's reign must be calculated from the time of the captivity. The Babylonian Chronicle gives the exact date when Nebuchadnezzar captures Jerusalem and takes Johoiachin prisoner to Babylon. The reign of Manasseh must have begun in 696 BC, giving him a ten-year coregency with Hezekiah. Manasseh reigns the longest of all the Judean kings.

Manasseh must have had the support of the leaders of Judah in his practice of foreign worship. Assyria has not yet met the disaster declared by Isaiah (Isa 10:12–19). There may have been a reaction to the reforms of Hezekiah, especially by those who worshiped at the various shrines in the countryside before Hezekiah dismantled them. Manasseh reverses the policies of his father, both in the practice of faith and in the submission to Assyria.

Manasseh advances foreign worship in a number of ways. The host of heaven is worshiped in the two temple courts (2 Kgs 21:3, 5) and on the roof of his palace (23:12). Jeremiah witnesses family worship of the Queen of Heaven in Jerusalem (Jer 7:18). Worship of astral deities also occurs—a Canaanite practice that Israel was warned about before their entry into the land (Deut 4:19; cf. 17:3).

Passing the sons through the fire is named along with sorcery and consultation of mediums. This again is a specific violation of the covenant (Deut 18:10–11). Passing one's sons through the fire probably concerns funeral rites, as may be suggested by its association with consultation of ghosts and spirits of the dead. Rituals that involved children do not indicate that the children were slaughtered for these rites (cf. Jer 7:32; 19:5; 32:35). Incineration of bodies took place at a dedicated location called a *tophet* by archaeologists (based on the Hebrew references). Such a place had a low enclosure wall and was used for generations. Those buried were primarily premature, stillborn, and young infants, buried with a special ceremony.

The carved image of the Asherah implies something even worse than the standard Asherah pole (2 Kgs 21:7). Setting the image in the temple is a desecration of the one place that represented divine ownership and fulfillment of the promise to David.

The narrative leads into divine speech with the citation of the promise to David and the condition to rest in the land (21:7b–10). The "plumb line" of Samaria (21:13) is a graphic image used by the earlier prophets (cf. Amos 7:7–8). Ordinary tools of construction become God's standard of destruction. Jerusalem's being wiped clean as a washed pan turned upside down is an equally graphic proverb. God has had his fill of Judah's sinning; the city will be emptied out, its social order turned completely upside down.

The good remnant found in the reforms of Hezekiah will be uprooted and cast out. The nation is no longer God's inheritance, unique among the other nations (2 Kgs 21:14). The shedding of innocent blood is also a metaphor for injustice against the poor, one of the greatest offenses committed by those who had themselves once been slaves (Isa 1:15–17). Manasseh is the only king to have misdeeds noted in the concluding formula (2 Kgs 21:17).

The Assassination of Amon (21:19–26). Amon is born when his father is forty-five, making it unlikely that he is the oldest son. The reign of Amon is brought to an abrupt end by conspirators from his own court. No details are given concerning the uprising. Perhaps this is an anti-Assyrian uprising, possibly in connection with disturbances during the reign of Ashurbanipal (640 BC). Whatever the case, the plot fails. Representative civic leaders dispatch the conspirators and make Amon's son Josiah king.

Application. The effects of the sins of one person can extend to many others. Other individuals are drawn into errant ways, and many victims suffer the results of evil. This is particularly true when transgressions are committed by persons in political power. Most often oppressive actions are exercised under the rubric of peace and liberty. Commonly, the results are irreversible for generations, and many pay a terrible price, as is the case with Manasseh. Religion and race are often a part of malevolence exercised against others.

2 KINGS 22:1–23:30

Original Meaning

Discovery of the Book of the Covenant (22:1–20). The thirty-one-year reign of Josiah ends in 609 BC when he dies fighting the Egyptians in their campaign to the Euphrates against Haran (23:29–30). Josiah's reign begins in 640 BC, and he reigns during the declining years of the Assyrian Empire. The reign of Josiah takes place during massive transitions of power in international affairs.

The conspirators of Amon are themselves killed by certain civic leaders (21:24), who then place Josiah on the throne at age eight. Regents from this group must have been responsible for the king during the years of his minority. The account of Josiah's reign is introduced (22:2) and concluded (23:25) with the standard formulas for keeping the covenant: He does not turn to the right or to the left (Deut 5:32; 17:20) but loves God with all his heart, soul, and strength (6:4).

The disastrous state of the temple must have taken place during the apostate reign of Manasseh. In that time the book of the covenant seems to have been entirely forgotten. Josiah begins to seek the God of David in the eighth year of his reign and to remove the idolatrous high places from Judah and Jerusalem in the twelfth (2 Chr 34:3). The temple purification begins in his eighteenth year, at which time the book of the covenant is discovered (2 Chr 34:8, 14). Reforms thus begin before the discovery of that book when Josiah turns twenty, the age of majority (2 Chr 34:3).

The Deuteronomistic History has a particular focus on the book of the covenant; thus, the events are associated with it during the reign of Josiah. It is not difficult to understand why the book may have been moved from its proper place beside the ark of the covenant (Deut 31:26); Manasseh would not have wanted it there, nor would the priests have wanted to provoke him by leaving it there.

Hilkiah, the priest responsible to refurbish the temple,

was not likely present during the reigns of either Manasseh or Amon. Hilkiah probably receives his position early in the reign of Josiah and initiates a change in the state-sponsored religion present in the temple.

The book found in the temple is readily identified as "the Law" (2 Kgs 22:8). Josiah becomes profoundly repentant when he learns about the neglect of the covenant and takes immediate action. He dispatches a delegation to the court prophetess. Huldah is the only woman prophet during the kingdom period; she belongs to priestly circles, and her husband is likely the uncle of Jeremiah, instrumental in the reforms of Josiah (Jer 32:7). The message of the prophetess is an unequivocal application of the book's message to the inhabitants of Judah and Jerusalem. The curse of the covenant rests on them (e.g., Deut 28:58–68).

The only mitigation to be found in the words of Huldah is a personal application to the king. His penitence will prevent the disaster of the exile from taking place during his lifetime. The "curse" on the inhabitants of the kingdom cannot be averted (2 Kgs 22:19), but Josiah will die in peace. In all other circumstances this would signify a natural death, not a death in war as befalls Josiah (23:29–30). Peace for Josiah means he will be buried in his own grave with other distinguished kings of Judah.

Renewal of the Covenant (23:1–20). The inclusion of both civil and religious leaders as representatives makes the covenant effective in both civil and religious jurisdictions. This is a high point in the history of the nation; the people not only enter into a covenant with God, but the covenant becomes the legal foundation of the political order. Renewal of the covenant is enacted with the purification of worship at the orders of King Josiah.

Purification begins in Jerusalem and focuses on the temple (23:4–14). The cult practices are those of Canaanite religion, which apparently flourished under Assyrian domination during the days of Manasseh. Cult objects of Baal and Asherah, male and female fertility deities, and the "starry host" (23:4) are burned in the terraces of the Kidron Valley.

Purification extends to idolatrous objects and to those who led in such practices. A wooden cult statue of Asherah is removed from the temple and burned; the image installed there by Manasseh (cf. 21:7). The "quarters of the male shrine prostitutes" (23:7) are probably rooms connected to the cult of Asherah.

Nothing is known of cultic installations at the city gates. "The gateway" (*hashearim*, 23:8) has been read as "goat demon" (*hasheirim*), a cult mentioned elsewhere (cf. Lev 17:7). A gate named Joshua Gate in Jerusalem is not known. The rural priests who come into Jerusalem do not have the same status in Jerusalem, but they do have provision of food (2 Kgs 23:9). Their restrictions are similar to physically blemished priests (Lev 21:22–23); their limited rank is likely dictated by the nature of the reform in the allocation of priests.

Manasseh and Amon, the "kings of Judah" (2 Kgs 23:12), were responsible for altars and images of other cults in different parts of the outer temple courts, the upper levels, and the roof over the stairway or ascending ramp of Ahaz. Ahaz renovated an exterior entranceway, and some feature of the structure served as a sundial, erected by Ahaz for the worship of astral deities. Manasseh also built fire pits for various rituals in the burial of children (23:10). It is likely there were legitimate uses for such fire pits, but they came to be identified with other gods. Idolatrous gods functioned as a king, and children are burned to various gods such as Adrammelek and Anammelek (17:31). Horses were used in the worship of the sun god (Shamash); in Mesopotamia the emblem of the sun god rode a horse-drawn chariot on festal days.

Josiah's purifications involve the removal of shrines that go back to the time of Solomon (1 Kings 11:5–7). The "Hill of Corruption" (2 Kings 23:13) is a wordplay on the Mount of Olives; instead of the "mount of anointing" (*har hammishkhah*) it is the "mount of destruction" (*har hammaskhit*). Filling the idolatrous places with human bones renders them untouchable (cf. Num 19:16).

Josiah has a special interest in Bethel as a territory that once belonged to Judah. Jeroboam set up a border shrine there in establishing his kingdom. Josiah's desecration of the altar by burning the bones of the graves on it fulfills the words of the prophet from Judah in the time of Jeroboam (1 Kgs 13:1–2). The bones of the prophet are spared, along with those of the old prophet from Bethel. The purging of the shrines in the cities of Samaria also fulfills prophecy (1 Kgs 13:32). Josiah shows no tolerance for the priests of those high places but punishes them according to the instructions found for the treatment of idolatrous cities (Deut 13:12–18).

Celebration of the Passover (23:21–25). Celebration of the Passover is an essential aspect of covenant renewal. Its introduction resumes the account of the renewal ceremony (23:1–3), which is interrupted by the lengthy description of Josiah's reforms and concludes the account of Josiah's bringing Judah into conformity with the covenant requirements. The last reported covenant renewal was in the days of Joshua (Josh 8:30–35); the covenant of Josiah is the first occasion since that time when the Passover was celebrated as a national festival with official leaders.

The renewal also involves purging all false prophecy in Israel. Consultation with the dead was a usual method for receiving a divine oracle. "Mediums and spiritists" refer to some type of necromancy (2 Kgs 23:24). The use of "household gods"

(23:24) also goes back to ancient practice (Gen 31:19). These images are of various sizes, always associated with communication with a deity.

Death of Josiah (23:26–30). Egypt becomes an ally of Assyria in the crucial days of its collapsing power. When Ashuruballit II, the last Assyrian king, forms a rump state around Haran after the fall of Nineveh (612 BC), Egypt supports him with troops. The march of Necho's army toward the Euphrates three years later is directly related to this support of Assur.

Necho's ambition is to assume control in the former Assyrian provinces. Egyptian forces previously supported weak Assyrian armies in their battles against the Babylonians. Josiah's encounter with the Egyptians at Megiddo meets with disaster. His tragic death is a calamity. According to the Chronicler, Jeremiah composes a long lament song for his funeral, which remains to his time (2 Chr 35:25). As at other times, certain civic officials assume leadership and appoint one of Josiah's younger sons to the throne.

Application. In the Dallas Museum of Fine Arts hangs a painting by Thomas Hart Benton, a twentieth-century Missouri artist. The late afternoon sun casts harsh shadows across a twisted landscape. A man stands at the side of an empty road with a suitcase tied together with pieces of rope. He stares across the road to an abandoned farmhouse, wooden walls weathered gray, roof falling in. In one corner of the painting is a bleached skeleton of a steer. As the man looks across the rutted road, he scratches his greying beard as if pondering something. The painting seems poised to tell a story; the tile on the wall reads: "The Prodigal Son."

As Benton illustrates that parable, the prodigal has waited too long. The home that would have welcomed him has become a ramshackle ruin; the fatted calf that once would have fed a homecoming feast is now only bones drying under a tortured, unforgiving sky. The viewer may protest; this is not the way to tell the story. That is the story of Josiah measured by the fate of the nation.

Josiah reads like a story of too little, too late. This would not have been his own assessment of his life's work. The oracle of Huldah leaves some ambiguity as to the extent of the exile that threatens, but the book of the Law that was found is clear enough about its possibility. The king knows that it is possible in his lifetime. Even if he knew exile would happen in his lifetime, he would likely have done exactly as he did; the book of the Law instructed him as to his course of action. His reforms are right, irrespective of the eventual outcome for Judah. His action is to the glory of God—which is always the ultimate goal and a goal that is achievable. If Josiah had as his only goal the preservation of Judah, it is too little, too late.

Success in leadership must be measured by the impact it has on people. It has been said that leadership is getting people to go where they want to go by getting them to do what they do not want to do. The success of such a task is a matter of perspective. Within his time, Josiah is immensely successful in the matter of reform, more than any other king who preceded him. He leads the nation in an unprecedented revival, going back to times before the monarchy even began (23:22). Though the fate of the nation is sealed, Josiah is instrumental in preserving the covenant. This is especially evident in the life of Jeremiah.

2 KINGS 23:31–24:17

Original Meaning

Egyptian Intervention (23:31–35). The civic leaders of Judah appoint Shallum to succeed Josiah (23:30). Shallum is the fourth son of Josiah according to the Davidide genealogy (1 Chr 3:15); he receives the throne name Jehoahaz when he is anointed king. His mother comes from the countryside of the Shephelah. Jehoahaz is appointed by the same leaders who made Josiah king (2 Kgs 21:24), in the hopes that he will continue the policies of his father. Necho imprisons him in Riblah, an Assyrian administrative center on the Orontos River in the north Lebanon Valley. Necho levies an indemnity against Judah, making it a vassal of Egypt. There is no concluding regnal summary for Jehoahaz, since he dies in Egypt; the place of his tomb is not known. Necho makes Eliakim the king of Judah on his successful return from Haran (23:34).

Babylonian Control (23:36–24:17). Political forces change during Jehoiakim's reign. Pharoah Necho fails to restrict the power of the Babylonians at Haran. Egypt controls the Levant for about four years, until the Babylonians conquer Carchemish in 605 BC. Jehoiakim, enthroned by the Egyptians, soon comes under the domination of the Babylonians, the successors of the Neo-Assyrian Empire.

Nebuchadnezzar marches to Egypt in his fourth year but fails to gain a victory. Necho followed up his victory by invading the southern coast and taking Gaza (cf. Jer 47:1). This is the time of Jehoiakim's rebellion against Babylon (2 Kgs 24:1). Jehoiakim is caught in the power struggle; Nebuchanezzar stays in Babylon rebuilding his army in his fifth year, which gives Necho the opportunity to rebuild his position in encouraging a coalition against Babylonia.

In his sixth year Nebuchadnezzar again goes west (599 BC). The main entry for his seventh year is the capture of Jerusalem (24:2). Jehoiakim dies before the city surrenders and is followed by his eighteen-year-old son, Jehoiachin. He reigns only three months (24:8). Nebuchadnezzar himself arrives to join the army besieging Jerusalem, and Jehoiachin surrenders, sparing the city from destruction (24:11–12). Jehoiachin pays for the policy of his father with exile. The temple and the palace are emptied of their treasures, as was common practice (24:13–16).

Before leaving Jerusalem, Nebuchadnezzar installs Mattaniah as his vassal king, the youngest son of Josiah; he has the same mother as Jehoahaz (24:17–18). His throne name is Zedekiah; he rules until the fate of the kingdom of Judah is sealed.

Application. The traumatic upheaval of the Russian Revolution and Civil War was particularly devasting in Ukraine. Living in the rich heartland of Ukraine, devout, hardworking, and self-sufficient German colonists could not anticipate the violence and chaos that would come with revolution and counterrevolution. I grew up hearing of these stories from my grandparents, who also survived that era.

As a young teenager I remember visits with my maternal grandparents. I remember the poverty and the struggles of those bereft of everything coming to a foreign land and struggling with language as they tried to find a way to earn a living on the farm. What I have come to appreciate more than ever is their unwavering faith. It is said that God is all you need, but you do not know that until God is all you have. That was the faith story of my mother and her parents.

The same story is true for the Israelites in exile. They suffered the same alienation and ignominy. The story preserved in Kings is testimony to the strength and resolution of their faith.

2 KINGS 24:18–25:30

Original Meaning

Breach and Plunder of Jerusalem (24:18–25:21). Zedekiah begins his eleven-year reign when Nebuchadnezzar takes Jehoiachin captive to Babylon. Zedekiah takes the throne as a sworn vassal of Nebuchadnezzar. The Babylonians expect little resistance from Judah; the deportation of military personnel and high officials requires that a new administration must be restructured. Zedekiah has a difficult time maneuvering among the various factions.

It is not clear what inspires Zedekiah's rebellion (24:20). Zedekiah breaks his treaty with Babylon by sending messengers to Egypt to ask for horses and troops (Ezek 17:15). The Babylonians encounter no resistance to their advance through Palestine. Nebuchadnezzar chooses to attack Jerusalem first, besieging it in 588 BC. Earthen ramps are thrown around the city to prevent anyone from escaping.

The siege of Jerusalem lasts for about a year and a half. The royal party is captured in the level area at Jericho. The group is taken to the military headquarters in Riblah, where the king witnesses the death of his sons before being blinded and led to Babylon.

The destruction of Jerusalem is thorough. Temple, palaces, and houses are burned, the temple vessels including the enormous bronze Sea and the wheeled bronze stands are broken and taken as booty—all those items described in the account of Solomon's construction of the temple. With the capture and destruction of Jerusalem, the kingdom of Judah ceases to exist.

Reign of Gedaliah (25:22–26). The Babylonian policy for conquered territory did not involve rebuilding destroyed cities. Under a Babylonian official, the rural population was expected to carry on with their lives; de-centralization made a national uprising hard to organize. Gedaliah belongs to a prominent noble family; his grandfather was a scribe during the days of Josiah (22:3); his father was a member of the mission sent to Huldah (22:12), and he also intervened to save Jeremiah from the mob (Jer 26:24). Jeremiah supports Gedaliah, appointed by the Babylonians as governor at Mizpah (Jer 39:14). The army officers enter into oath with Gedaliah (2 Kgs 25:24); they need assurance there will be no reprisals for their having fought against the Babylonians. They are granted amnesty to now serve the Babylonians.

After a short time, Gedaliah and the Babylonians at Mizpah are murdered by a band led by Ishmael son of Nethaniah, a member of the royal family. It is not certain if Ishmael is contesting Gedaliah's position as a leader of Judah. The murder is hardly an act of rebellion against the Babylonians; it is a vendetta against those who are viewed as collaborating with the Babylonians.

The people of Judah, fearful of Babylonian revenge, flee to Egypt, forcing Jeremiah and Baruch to go with them (Jer 43:4–7). The report of their flight indicates that the judgment of exile is carried out in totality. Gedaliah's death is the extinction of all national existence.

Release of Jehoiachin (25:27–30). Awel-Marduk, son and successor of Nebuchadnezzar, reigns for two years (561–560 BC). His accession year becomes the occasion to grant amnesty to prisoners. Jehoiachin was apparently charged with some act of treason and was thrown into prison until the death of Nebuchadnezzar. Jehoiachin is then granted a favored status in relation to other captive kings; it is not specified what these privileges actually mean. He is confined to the court of the Babylonian king, with his family. Seven sons are born to him in exile (1 Chr 3:17–18).

Application. Death is a process. The process itself can be long and agonizing, or it can be swift and unexpected, whether it be the death of an individual, a marriage, or any other relationship. Depending on the process and the circumstances, the pain is experienced in different ways and at different levels. In many respects, the death of a marriage in divorce or the death of a community is more painful than physical death. In physical death there is an absolute termination; the death of a marriage or community is like a death that does not die. If children are involved in the death of a marriage, something of continuity with the former relationship is unavoidable. In the death of a community, like that of Judah, there is much continuity with the past but also much alienation, in which highly valued relationships and customs end.

It is said that those who lose all their possessions lose a lot, those who lose their friends lose a lot more, and those who lose hope have lost everything. The exiles have lost their possessions and were separated from many of their friends, but they never lose hope. Their memory of the exile is one expression of the faithfulness of God—and implicitly therefore hope in the faithfulness of God for the future.

1 CHRONICLES

INTRODUCTION TO 1 CHRONICLES

The books of 1–2 Chronicles are an anonymous composition. The stylistic and linguistic similarities with Ezra–Nehemiah have led many biblical scholars to conclude a single "Chronicler" was responsible for all four books. At one time there was an overwhelming consensus that Ezra and Chronicles were the product of a single author, but the identification of the Chronicler with Ezra the scribe has not been universally accepted.

More recent biblical research has questioned the literary ties between Chronicles and Ezra–Nehemiah. The comprehensive analysis of the Chronicler's language has led most Old Testament scholars today to acknowledge the unity of the two books of Chronicles but reject the idea of common authorship of Ezra–Nehemiah. The exact relationship of the Chronicler's writings to the books of Ezra–Nehemiah remains an open question.

The Chronicles, along with Ezra-Nehemiah, are probably the latest books of the Old Testament in respect to the date of composition. The time of writing for the Chronicles is usually assigned to the postexilic period of Hebrew history. Dates range anywhere from the reforms of the prophets Haggai and Zechariah (ca. 515 BC) to well into the Greek period (sometime between 300 and 160 BC).

First Chronicles includes a long genealogical list, beginning from the patriarchs through the time of Saul (chs. 1–9). Chapter 10 briefly describes the reign of Saul but otherwise turns the narrative to focus on David and his reign. The story of David's reign continues through the rest of the book. In its last pages, First Chronicles describes David's farewell and death (29:10–30).

BOOK OUTLINE

- I. Genealogical Prologue (1:1–9:44)
  - A. Patriarchs (1:1–2:2)
  - B. Israel's Sons (2:3–3:24)
  - C. Families of Judah (4:1–23)
  - D. Simeon (4:24–43)
  - E. Reuben, Gad, Manasseh (5:1–26)
  - F. Levi (6:1–81)
  - G. Issachar, Benjamin, Naphtali, Ephraim, Asher (7:1–40)
  - H. Saul (8:1–9:1a)
  - I. Returning Exiles and Saul's Genealogy (9:1b–44)
- II. United Monarchy (10:1–29:30)
  - A. King Saul and King David Contrasted (10:1–12:40)
  - B. David Returns the Ark of the Covenant (13:1–17:27)
  - C. David's Conquests (18:1–20:8)
  - D. David's Preparations for the Temple (21:1–29:9)
  - E. David's Farewell and Death (29:10–30)

1 CHRONICLES 1:1–2:2

Original Meaning. The genealogical prologue found in chapters 1–9 contains the most extensive and complex genealogies of the Bible. The basic purpose of the genealogy is to identify kinship relationships between individuals, families, and people groups. It is evident the genealogies of chapters 1–9 serve multiple purposes, especially in legitimizing the authority of Levitical priesthood as the rightful successors to the royal authority of Davidic kingship and in asserting the continuity of the Hebrew people through the national distress of the Babylonian exile. There is even a sense in which the juxtaposition of certain genealogies (e.g., that of Esau and Israel or Saul and David) works to express movement in history according to God's redemptive plan.

The Chronicler's panoramic sweep of ancient history from Adam to Noah to Abraham and Israel transports the audience into the accounts of the book of Genesis. There the emphasis was on God's dealings with humanity both in terms of creation and redemption. Equally important are the great theological themes the story of Noah establishes, themes that course through the rest of the Bible—especially the covenant relationship with God (Gen 9:11) and the twin truths of God's judgment of human sin and rebellion and his sustaining grace in preserving the righteous (Gen 6:7–8).

The family of Abraham is located strategically in the middle of the listing of names from Adam (1 Chr 1:1) to Israel (2:1) and is appropriately paired with the family of Esau as a foil, illustrating contrasting responses to covenant relationship with Yahweh. Not coincidentally, the listing of the twelve sons of Israel follows the genealogy of Esau, a reminder that the Hebrews persist as the people of God.

The final passage of the section simply lists the twelve sons of Jacob, later named Israel. The catalog of the twelve sons of

Israel sets the stage for the remainder of the genealogies comprising the prologue of Chronicles. Both Zebulun and Dan are slighted by the Chronicler, and Naphtali's descendants are mentioned in a single verse (7:13). This selectivity in the presentation of the genealogical records further underscores the Chronicler's pointed interests in the lineage of Judah and the institution of kingship as well as the lineage of Levi and the office of the priesthood.

Application. The identity crisis in postexilic Judah was only secondarily a matter of historical circumstance. The real crisis in postexilic Judah was one of theological understanding. The Chronicler's generation had misinterpreted the message of the earlier prophets concerning the nature and the timing of the restoration of Israel. By the time of Ezra and Nehemiah, the postexilic community had resigned itself to hierocratic or priestly rule as well as economic and political subordination in the vast Persian Empire. Whether verbalized or not, the Chronicler's audience suspects that God's word has failed.

The Chronicler uses the literary form of the genealogy to locate postexilic Judah in a larger historical framework—a metanarrative. For the Chronicler, the theological locus of the biblical metanarrative is the God of Israel. Especially important to the formation of the theological baseline for his metanarrative are the words of God emphasizing divine promise and fulfillment. The Chronicler's theology of hope is credible for the Jewish restoration community because the God of Israel has proven faithful to his word across the generations from Adam to all those listed in his genealogy—the prominent and the obscure.

By appealing to those books and records already a part of the Hebrew Bible as resources for his preaching and teaching, the Chronicler offers his audience the flawless, true, and eternal word of God himself. Such is the pattern for apostolic preaching in the New Testament, and so it remains for preaching and teaching in the church today. The unfolding drama of God's redemption of humanity as recorded in Scripture continues to provide the legitimate metanarrative for the Christian faith.

1 CHRONICLES 2:3–3:24

Original Meaning. Broadly outlined, the genealogical prologue showcases Judah. The emphasis on the tribe of Judah demonstrates that the purposes of God's election to provide righteous leadership through Judah were still at work despite Judah's unfaithfulness that led to the catastrophe of the Babylonian exile. The genealogy of Judah highlights the family of David and implicitly evokes thoughts of the Davidic covenant. For it was through this covenant of kingship that God would be glorified as the ruler of Israel and the nations and Israel would enjoy rest in the land granted to the descendants of Abraham. The royal family of David (3:1–24) is sandwiched between records of the other sons of Judah (2:1–55 and 4:1–23) in a highly stylized literary structure.

Judah to Hezron (2:3–8). This brief portion of Judah's family tree (2:3–4) contains a number of subtle theological ideas that become themes or motifs for the Chronicler's genealogical prologue. For instance, the birth reports calling attention to the mothers of Judah's sons (daughter of Shua, 2:3, and Tamar, 2:4) are a recurring feature of the genealogical prologue. The Chronicler effectively uses the birth report to promote his agenda of inclusivism in the face of the growing separatist nationalism of the later postexilic period. This literary vehicle enables the Chronicler to give prominence not only to women in the genealogical prologue but also to non-Hebrew women like the Canaanite Shua, the Geshurite Maacah (3:2), or the Egyptian Bithiah (4:18).

Other theological themes embedded in this list of Judah's sons include the demotion of the firstborn son (2:3; cf. 5:1), God's just punishment of wickedness among the Hebrew people as his elect (2:3; cf. 5:26), and God's faithfulness in sustaining the line of Judah (2:4; cf. 4:10).

Descendants of Ram (2:9–17). The family tree of Ram is listed first even though he was not the firstborn son of Hezron (2:10; cf. 2:9). The Chronicler showcases Ram because his interest in Judah centers on the clan of Hezron and the family of David through Ram (2:13–17). The roster of names from Ram to Jesse (2:10–12) repeats the genealogy of Ruth (Ruth 4:19–22).

Descendants of Caleb (2:18–24). Analysis of Caleb's genealogy is complicated by two factors: The genealogy is divided into several sections (2:18–24, 42–55; 4:1–8), and there is some question as to whether or not Caleb son of Hezron (2:18) and Caleb son of Jephunneh are distinct individuals (cf. Num 13:6).

Descendants of Jerahmeel (2:25–41). The genealogy of Jerahmeel shares the emphasis on women with the preceding family tree of Caleb (cf. 2:26, 29, 34, 35). The Chronicler's strong interest in the role of non-Hebrews in the genealogical prologue surfaces as well in the reference to the Egyptian Jarha (2:34).

Descendants of Caleb (2:42–55). This extension of Calebite genealogy consists of two distinct sections, each one probably representing a separate literary source. The first section is framed by opening and closing formulas. Caleb's descendants are ordered in a three-part arrangement according to their different mothers, including an unnamed wife (2:42–45), a concubine named Ephah (2:46–47), and a concubine named Maacah (2:48–50a).

The second section (2:50b–55) continues the family tree of Hur, born to Caleb and Ephrathah (2:19; cf. 4:4b). Each of the three sons of Hur is identified as the founding father or important chieftain of a well-known Judahite city (2:50–51). The reference to Bethlehem is a natural prelude to the family tree of David beginning in the next section of the Judahite genealogy (ch. 3).

Royal Family of David (3:1–24). The family of David is the feature attraction of Judah's genealogy. The Chronicler's emphasis on David stems from his knowledge of prophetic statements about the unbreakable covenant God made with David and the reestablishment of Davidic kingship in Israel (cf. Jer 33:19–22). He then offers this hope to his audience through the repetition of the word of the Lord to Nathan announcing the Davidic covenant (1 Chr 17:4–14, esp. vv. 10–14; cf. 2 Sam 7:4–16). The record of the royal line continues the genealogy tracing David's ancestry from Ram to Jesse (1 Chr 2:10–17). The chapter divides naturally into three distinct sections: David's children (3:1–9), the kings of Judah (3:10–16), and the postexilic descendants of David (3:17–24).

David's sons are registered in two lists according to the capital city in which they were born: Hebron (3:1–4) or Jerusalem (3:5–9). The genealogy highlights birth reports citing the name of the mother (e.g., 3:1), concluding tallies (e.g., 3:4), and name lists (e.g., 3:5).

The birth reports citing the name of the individual mothers of David's sons recall the annals of the kings of Judah, where similar information is preserved (e.g., 1 Kgs 15:2). Theologically, the practice reflects the association of the "offspring of the woman" promise (Gen 3:15) with the line of David (cf. 2 Sam 7:16). Tamar (1 Chr 3:9) is mentioned because she is the only daughter of David; her story is known from 2 Samuel 13.

The Chronicler reports the complete list of Davidic kings reigning in the Southern Kingdom of Judah during the period of the divided Hebrew monarchies (3:10–16). Jehoiachin (1 Chr 3:16), the next to last king of Judah, was taken captive by King Nebuchadnezzar and exiled as a prisoner of war in Babylonia (2 Kgs 24:15). His release from prison upon the ascension of Awel-Marduk (2 Kgs 25:27–30) serves as the postscript for the book of Jeremiah (Jer 52:31–34) and rekindled hope for the restoration of the Davidic monarchy after the Babylonian exile. It is for this reason that the Chronicler introduces the last section of the Davidic genealogy with King Jehoiachin "the captive" (1 Chr 3:17).

The final section of the royal genealogy contains the register of the postexilic descendants of David (3:17–24). The key figures of the list include Shenazzar, probably the same "prince of Judah" named Sheshbazzar, who led the initial wave of Jewish emigrants back to Jerusalem with the help of King Cyrus of Persia (cf. Ezra 1:8–11), and Zerubbabel, who headed up a second Hebrew migration from Persia sometime later (Ezra 2:2). Zerubbabel, son of Shealtiel (through Pedaiah, 1 Chr 3:17–19), served as governor of postexilic Judah for a time (cf. Zech 4:6–10). It was Haggai's blessing of Zerubbabel as God's "signet ring" that overturned Jeremiah's curse on the line of King Jehoiachin and restored royal authority to the descendants of David (Hag 2:23; cf. Jer 22:28–30).

Application. The Chronicler's genealogical prologue works for his audience because they have been initiated into the shared secret of the community of faith—covenant relationship with Yahweh, the covenant maker. They have also experienced the disruption of the Babylonian exile, as threatened by the prophets. For these reasons, they are in a position to embrace the "wisdom" of the Chronicler's theology of hope rooted in God's faithfulness over the course of their history as illustrated in the genealogical record. Appropriately, the Chronicler calls his contemporaries to respond to his "historical sermon" with praise and worship of the God of their Hebrew ancestors.

1 CHRONICLES 4:1–23

Original Meaning

Clans of Hur and Shobal (4:1–8). The initial portion of the genealogical appendix to the tribe of Judah contains supplementary materials tracing the clans of Hur and Shobal to Perez. The village of Zorah is important to the Chronicler because it was resettled by Judeans after the Babylonian captivity (Neh 11:29). This emphasis is in keeping with the Chronicler's theme of establishing the continuity of the restoration community with past Israelite history.

The genealogy of Etam (1 Chr 4:3–4) appears to be an unrelated intrusion in the registers of Hur and Shobal. The name Hazzelelponi (4:3) is a curiosity but should be retained as original to the text. Women (wives as well as sisters) are featured in the Chronicler's genealogies, and the formula introducing the name of this "sister" has a parallel in 7:15.

The expression "father of" common to the genealogies in this section may be understood in the sense of ancestor and/or as "settler" or even "founding father" of a town or village. Thus it is possible that Penuel (4:4) and Jered (4:18) were cofounders of the city of Gedor (or Jedur?). The name Hushah is attached to the village of Hushan (some five miles west of Bethlehem), and two of the members of David's elite guard are identified as "Hushathites" (2 Sam 21:18; 23:27; cf. 1 Chr 11:29; 20:4; 27:11). Again, the Chronicler's selection of genealogical materials here seems to be motivated by his concern to establish continuity between the restoration community and earlier Israelite history.

Jabez (4:10–11). This note on Jabez is an independent literary unit and is theological in character. There is a play on words with the name Jabez (*yʿbts*) as a result of the "pain" (*ʿtsb*) his mother endured during his birth. Jabez is remembered as an honorable man, more so than his brothers. The efficacy of prayer to the God of Israel is an important theme in Chronicles. The Chronicler seeks to remind his audience that God's responsiveness to prayer in the past is an invitation to offer prayers addressing present needs and concerns.

Kelub (4:11–12). The name Kelub is sometimes rendered Chelub (so NRSV). None of the persons included in this genealogy are mentioned elsewhere in the Old Testament, and Chelub's parents are unidentified. The importance of this independent genealogical unit seems to be the connection of Chelub to the "men of Recah."

Clans of Othniel and Caleb (4:13–16). Kenaz was the younger brother of Caleb and the father of Othniel (cf. Josh 15:17; Judg 1:13; 3:9, 11). Caleb was one of the twelve spies sent into Canaan to reconnoiter the land before the Israelite conquest (Num 13:6, 30; 14:6). Along with Joshua, Caleb returned with a favorable report and was commended by God for his faith and duly rewarded with an inheritance in the land of Canaan (Num 14:24; Deut 1:36).

Othniel, Caleb's nephew (or younger brother, as in the NIV), was known for his conquest of Debir at the behest of Caleb (for which he received Caleb's daughter Acsah in marriage, Josh 15:16–17). Othniel was also known for his leadership as a judge in delivering the Israelites from the king of Aram (Judg 3:9–11). The Chronicler includes the genealogies of Othniel and Caleb because both were responsible for expanding the boundaries of Israel during the days of the judges. Their example was meant to encourage postexilic Judah by reminding the people that God was still capable of enlarging the borders of diminished Judah through the efforts of faithful individuals.

Clan of Ezrah (4:17–20). Apart from the (disputed) locations of Gedor, Soco, and Zanoah, nothing is known of people or places mentioned in 4:17–18. This section of the extended Judahite genealogy is interesting because of the prominent place it gives to women, especially Miriam (a Calebite relative of Ezrah, 4:17) and Bithiah (daughter of Pharaoh, 4:18). There is some question as to whether or not "Pharaoh" is a royal title in this context. At the very least it suggests the inclusion of Egyptian elements within the tribe of Judah.

Clan of Shelah (4:21–23). The reference to Shelah, the oldest surviving son of Judah, echoes 2:3 and forms an inclusio or envelope construction marking 2:3–4:23 as a larger literary unit. The parenthetical statement attesting the antiquity of the genealogy (4:22) and the reference to the king (4:23) indicate these records date from the preexilic period of Israelite history.

Application. The Chronicler's subtle exhortation to his postexilic audience for an "evangelistic openness" to relationships with non-Jews calls to mind the parable Jesus told about the good Samaritan (Luke 10:25–37). The story is well known and often told. The question raised in applying the parable to the contemporary setting still haunts the Christian and the Christian church: "Who is my neighbor?"

1 CHRONICLES 4:24–43

Original Meaning. The destiny of Simeon and Judah was entwined socially and politically. By the time of David, the towns and villages within the territory of Simeon were recognized as Judean holdings (4:31). The genealogy of Simeon offers a partial explanation for the subordinate position of the tribe of Simeon in relation to the tribe of Judah. One wonders if this fact is incidental to the Chronicler's purposes or if it conveys a theological message. Given the highly selective nature of the genealogies in Chronicles, the latter seems more likely.

Perhaps the Chronicler is making a pejorative statement about intermarriage among God's people, resulting in the lack of offspring among the Simeonites. Or maybe the postexilic historian emphasizes the lineage of Shaul as an example of Yahweh's universal love for the nations, similar to the story of Ruth. No doubt the faithful among the Chronicler's audience discern both messages in this notation.

Theologically, the focus is faithfulness—the faithfulness of God's word concerning the destiny of Simeon as uttered by Jacob (Gen 49:5–7), the faithfulness of the Simeonites in possessing the land allotted to them by Joshua (note the correspondence of the place names between Josh 19:2–9 and 1 Chr 4:28–33), the faithfulness of God in helping the Simeonites overcome their enemies (cf. Deut 1:30; 3:22), and the faithfulness of Shimei's family in trusting God for the expansion of the Simeonite tribal holdings (1 Chr 4:38–43). These are all important examples of a faithful God blessing his faithful people—a necessary history lesson for the Chronicler's audience.

Application. The Chronicler is attempting to reconcile the historical distance and theological disparity between the Davidic ideal and the reality of Persian occupation of Judah for a discouraged audience in postexilic Jerusalem. The New Testament mentions other kinds of tensions between the biblical ideal and actual human experience that have the potential to produce similar feelings of anxiety and despair in individual believers and in the Christian community at large. Note, for example, the ongoing conflict between the kingdom of light and the kingdom of darkness, sound doctrine compromised by false teaching, and an ethic of social justice eroded by oppression and prejudice. Some mediation of the biblical ideal and present reality is essential because the unresolved tension poses a threat to personal faith and spiritual growth. The greater the discontinuity between the ideal and the actual, the more room for seeds of doubt to germinate, undermining one's hope in God and robbing one of the joy of the Lord.

1 CHRONICLES 5:1–26

Original Meaning. The chapter may be divided into five distinct sections: the genealogy of Reuben (5:1–10), the genealogy of Gad (5:11–17), a historical note on the war against the Hagrites (5:18–22), the genealogy of the half-tribe of Manasseh (5:23–24), and the summary statement of sin and exile (5:25–26). The purpose of the passage is twofold.

1. The account explains the prominence of the tribe of Judah even though Reuben was the firstborn son of Jacob (renamed Israel).
2. The record contributes to the Chronicler's goal of including all the tribes of Israel in the ideal "all Israel" identity he seeks to establish for the postexilic community.

Reuben (5:1–10). Reuben was the firstborn son of Jacob by Leah (Gen 29:32). The name Reuben means "he [the LORD] has seen my misery," so pronounced by Leah with the hope of gaining Jacob's love and respect. The Chronicler recites Reuben's crime of engaging in sexual intercourse with his father's concubine (Bilhah) in order to explain the prominence of Judah and the Joseph tribes in later Israelite history. From Judah came the "ruler" (1 Chr 5:2), no doubt a reference to King David. And to Joseph's sons, Ephraim and Manasseh, was transferred the firstborn rights of Reuben (Gen 48:5–20). Implied in this forfeiture of the birthright is the double share due the firstborn son on the basis of Mosaic law (Deut 21:15–17).

Gad (5:11–22). The unit of Gad contains two distinct parts. The first pertains to the tribe of Gad (5:11–17), while the second refers collectively to the two and one-half tribes located in the Transjordan (5:18–22). The genealogy of Gad is unusual in that it begins with a geographical note (5:11) and omits materials from the other Gadite genealogies (e.g., Gen 46:16; Num 26:15–18; 1 Chr 12:9–13). This emphasis on the territorial holdings of Gad forms an envelope for the genealogical record.

There is some question concerning the reference to "Jotham king of Judah" in the chronological footnote (5:17) since the Transjordan tribes were part of the Northern Kingdom. The reference may suggest separate genealogical registers compiled by each of the divided monarchies or even a synchronistic chronicle composed in two columns. It seems more likely that events in Israel were simply synchronized historically by reference to the occupant of the Judahite throne. In any case, the census mentioned dates to around 750 BC.

The battle report of the coalition of Transjordan tribes against the Hagrites (5:18–22) probably represents a summary of expansion during the period of the united monarchy by the coalition of Transjordan Israelite tribes against the Hagrites, not an account of a single battle or event. The Hagrites, along with the Moabites, Edomites, and Ishmaelites, were among the traditional enemies of Israel located in the Transjordan.

More than the size of the muster tallies, the Chronicler's focus is on the theology of warfare. The war with the Hagrites and their allies was God's battle (5:22). The men of Reuben, Gad, and East Manasseh trusted in God and prayed to him, and he answered their prayers by helping them in battle (5:20–21).

East Manasseh (5:23–26). Like the genealogy of Gad, this section contains two distinct units. The first pertains to the tribe of East Manasseh (5:23–24), while the second refers collectively to the two and one-half tribes located in the Transjordan (5:25–26). The concluding passage (5:25–26) agrees with the books of Kings on the Northern Kingdom's sin of idolatry (2 Kgs 17:7). The writer also correctly understood the "vomit theology" laid out by Moses in the book of Leviticus (Lev 18:24–30). Once the Israelites became guilty of the sins for which God punished the Canaanites, the Israelite occupation of the land of covenant promise was in jeopardy.

The Chronicler's consistent understanding of God's sovereignty is worth noting. It is God who stirred the spirit of the king of Assyria to judge the sin of Israel (1 Chr 5:26). Likewise, it is God who stirred the spirit of the king of Persia to permit the Jews to return to their covenant homeland (cf. 2 Chr 36:22–23).

Application. In a way, the Chronicler plays the role of a press-box commentator watching a long-distance race, since his attention is fixed on the "starts" and "finishes" of the tribes across the history of Israelite and Judean monarchies. One way in which the New Testament enhances the message of Chronicles is that of example through character study. For instance, we have the account of the life of the apostle Paul, introduced to us as the chief of sinners (cf. 1 Tim 1:16) but transformed into the apostle of the gentiles (Acts 9:15). The name Demas is associated with the more tragic story of one who apparently started well (cf. Col 4:14) but who quit the race and deserted Paul because "he loved this world" (2 Tim 4:10).

1 CHRONICLES 6:1–81

Original Meaning. Along with Judah and Benjamin, Levi was one of the three prominent tribes in the Chronicler's retelling of Israelite history. The importance of Levi is attested both by its central position in the tribal genealogies and its length, second only to the register of Judah (2:3–4:23). The genealogy may be divided into two sections: Levitical genealogies (6:1–53) and the settlement of the priests and Levites (6:54–81).

The Priestly Line of Levi (5:1–15). The sons of Levi (Gershon, Kohath, and Merari) are always ordered according to age (cf. Gen 46:11; Exod 6:16; Num 3:17). The focus of the initial genealogy of Levi, however, is Kohath (1 Chr 6:2) since he was the ancestor of the Aaronite high priests (6:3). The listing of the Aaronite high priests preserves twenty-one generations from Eleazar to Jehozadak, but it is not a complete genealogical record. The first six generations of the register (Levi to Phineas) have been extracted from the family record of Moses and Aaron (Exod 6:16–25).

The genealogy highlights two priests with anecdotes: Azariah, who served as priest in Solomon's temple (1 Chr 6:10), and Jehozadak, who was deported to Babylonia at the time of Jerusalem's exile (6:15). Both events were watersheds in Israelite history. The erection of a permanent sanctuary for the worship of Yahweh in Jerusalem redefined the Levitical priesthood, while the Babylonian exile indelibly marked Israelite history and theology.

The Sons of Levi (6:16–30). This section of the genealogy introduces the three sons of Levi, each one as a founding ancestor of a major division of the Levitical corps: Gershon, Kohath, and Merari. The Chronicler's source for the listing is the record of the Levitical clans found in Numbers 3:17–20 (cf. Exod 6:16–19). The genealogies of Levi's descendants demonstrate breadth (or horizontal relationship of offspring from a common ancestor) for two successive generations for each of Levi's three sons (1 Chr 6:16–19). Furthermore, they demonstrate depth (or the listing of successive generations) in recording seven generations of Gershonites (6:20) and Merarites (6:29). The clan genealogies appear to descend (i.e., arranged from father to son) to the time of Saul and David (given the reference to Samuel's sons in 6:28 [cf. 1 Sam 8:2–3] and the reference to Asaiah in 1 Chr 6:30 [cf. 15:6]).

The family tree of Samuel (6:26–28) has been added to the clan of Kohath's genealogy in basic agreement with 1 Samuel 1:1 and 8:2. The tragic record of the unfaithfulness of Samuel's sons to the commands of the Mosaic covenant and their heritage as priests is found in 1 Samuel 8:2–3. As a result of their corrupt leadership, the Israelites requested a king to rule the tribes (8:4–5).

The Temple Musicians (6:31–47). King David's preparations for a permanent sanctuary for the worship of Yahweh necessitated a reorganization of the nonpriestly Levites, whose services were no longer required as porters, assemblers, and custodians of the portable sanctuary. The Chronicler summarizes the reassignment of Levitical duties under the dual headings of music for the house of God (6:31–32) and duties related to the tabernacle (6:48). The families of Heman, Asaph, and Ethan, each representing one of the three sons of Levi, were appointed as music directors for temple worship. Apparently, the Levitical musicians split the duties of the music ministry between the "house of the LORD" in Jerusalem where "the ark came to rest" (6:31; cf. 15:1–3) and the tabernacle in Gibeon (cf. 16:39–42) until the completion of Solomon's temple (6:32).

Heman (6:33) oversaw the ministry of music in the house of the Lord (6:31; cf. 15:16–17). He was among those charged to sound the bronze cymbals when the ark of the Lord entered Jerusalem (15:19). The genealogy of Heman is traced through twenty-two generations of the clan of Kohath of the tribe of Levi (6:33–38).

Asaph was appointed the first associate of Heman ("served at his right hand," 6:39); his genealogy is traced through fifteen generations of the clan of Gershon of the tribe of Levi (6:39–43).

Ethan headed a third musical guild as a result of the reorganization of the Levites by King David (6:44–47; cf. 15:16–17). Ethan's genealogy is traced through Mushi, son of Merari, son of Levi (6:47). Ethan's family tree is the briefest among the directors of the three temple musical guilds, counting only twelve generations.

Priestly Duties (6:48–49). The blessing of the tribes of Israel highlights a twofold function for the descendants of Levi: "watching over" God's word through the teaching of the Mosaic law to the Israelites and guarding Yahweh's covenant with Israel by attending to the sacrificial rituals of Hebrew worship (Deut 33:8–11). Here the Chronicler distinguishes between the "fellow Levites" (1 Chr 6:48) and the priesthood descended from Aaron with respect to liturgical duties. The context indicates the Chronicler differentiates between the Levitical musicians (6:31–47) and the priests assigned to perform the sacrificial liturgy of the sanctuary (6:48–49). While the Levites were called to assist the priests in numerous ways (cf. 1 Chr 23:28–31; 2 Chr 30:16; 35:11), the sacrificial altar was the exclusive domain of the Aaronic priesthood (cf. Num 18:1–7).

The Chronicler summarizes the work of the Levites broadly as "all the other duties of the . . . house of God" (1 Chr 6:48; cf. Num 3:6–9). The priests were responsible for the altar of burnt offering, the altar of incense, and the work of the Most Holy Place in general, under the threat of divine wrath against all Israel should they shirk their responsibilities (1 Chr 6:49; cf. Num 18:5).

The goal of the priestly sacrificial ministry was "making atonement for Israel" (1 Chr 6:49). The word "atonement" (Heb. *kpr*) essentially means "to cover." God ordained that sin be "covered" by means of animal sacrifice, whether offered for individuals (e.g., Lev 4:29, 31) or the entire nation of Israel on the Day of Atonement (cf. Lev 16). Prayer and forgiveness are vitally linked in the Chronicler's theology of atonement (cf. 2 Chr 7:14; 33:18–19). The section closes with special emphasis on the fact that the priesthood served in compliance with the demands of the Mosaic law (1 Chr 6:49).

The High Priests (6:50–53). The list of high priests is an abbreviated version of the descendants of Aaron found previously (6:3–8). The register of names completes the thought of 6:49, given the reference to Aaron and the duties associated with the high priests. Zadok was a contemporary of David (2 Sam 15:27; 19:11), while Ahimaaz was the high priest during a portion of Solomon's reign (1 Chr 6:8–9). Breaking the list of high priests off at this juncture is logical because David reorganized the priesthood (6:31–32) and Solomon built the temple where divinely ordained priestly tasks were performed (6:49).

The Levitical Cities (6:54–81). The Chronicler's list of Levitical cities is parallel to Joshua's allotment of towns to the Levites (Josh 21:5–39). The list in Chronicles tends to abridge the version found in Joshua. The omission of the references to Dan (1 Chr 6:61, 69; cf. Josh 21:5, 23) may represent the modernizing of the register by the Chronicler in an attempt to reflect the tribal realities of his own day rather than bias on his part.

The Chronicler also reorders the Levitical settlement list from Joshua, placing the allotment of towns for the descendants of Aaron first (6:54–60; cf. Josh 21:9–19). The emphatic position of the Aaronides no doubt calls attention to the centrality of the priestly line in postexilic Judah, given the collapse of Davidic kingship. The list of Levitical cities stood as a permanent testimony to the reality that the Lord was the share and inheritance of Aaron and his descendants (Num 18:20).

The Chronicler has retained only two of the explanatory notes from the parallel list of Levitical cities in Joshua. Both are references to "a city of refuge" (6:57, 67), and both occur in a shortened form (cf. "a city of refuge for one accused of murder," Josh 21:13, 21, 27, 32, 38). The city of refuge was a safe haven from the avenger of blood for a person who committed accidental manslaughter (20:2–6).

Application. The priests and Levites rightfully play a key leadership role in postexilic Judah, given the demise of the kingship. The role of the priests and Levites as worship leaders goes beyond the sheer maintenance of the form and order of the sacrificial liturgy. Israel's right relationship with God was to be accomplished primarily through the teaching ministry of the Levitical corps (Deut 33:10). The curriculum for this educational initiative in "spiritual literacy" is the law of God.

Historically, the church of Jesus Christ has promulgated his gospel in a similar manner, that of instruction by clergy invested with the office gift of pastor-teacher and by laypeople endowed with the spiritual gift of teaching. The goal, or "preferred outcome" educationally speaking, of this instruction is consistent with that of the priestly ministry: freeing people from bondage to sin through a knowledge of God's truth about the human condition and his redemptive plan to remedy our plight (cf. John 8:32; 2 Tim 3:14–16).

1 CHRONICLES 7:1–40

Original Meaning. This section of the Chronicler's genealogical prologue contains the final installment of Hebrew tribal lists, broadly classified as northern and, in certain cases, Transjordan tribes. The listing is in keeping with the Chronicler's overall purpose in the retelling of Israelite history. The inclusion of both the prominent and obscure northern Hebrew tribes is necessary for presenting a complete historical overview of Israel to the restoration community.

Issachar (7:1–5). Issachar was the ninth son of Jacob, the fifth son born to him by Leah (Gen 30:17). His name means "hired workman," and Jacob's deathbed blessing of Issachar plays on that meaning in predicting that Issachar's descendants will toil in forced labor gangs (Gen 49:15).

The names of Issachar's four sons match those lists found in Genesis 46:13 and Numbers 26:23–24. The reference to David (1 Chr 7:2) indicates that the purpose of the tribal lists is to accent the role of King David in uniting the tribes of Israel. That the tribal lists of Issachar are incomplete is attested simply by checking the math of the muster tallies, since the total cited (87,000 in 7:5) is greater than the sum of the tallies of 7:2, 4 (58,600).

Benjamin (7:6–12). Benjamin was the youngest son of Jacob and the second son born to Rachel, who died giving birth to him (Gen 35:19, 24). The name Benjamin was given to the boy by his father and means literally "son of the right hand." The insertion of the Benjamite genealogy at this juncture serves to introduce the more extensive family tree of Benjamin that follows in chapter 8. The highlighting of Benjamin calls to mind the fact that this tribe was also the transitional tribe of Hebrew kingship. King Saul hailed from Benjamin, and the Chronicler uses his genealogy and royal history as a preface to the history of the Davidic dynasty.

Naphtali (7:13). Bilhah was one of Jacob's concubines and the mother of Naphtali (Gen 46:24–25).

Manasseh (7:14–19). Manasseh and Ephraim were the sons of Joseph by his Egyptian wife, Asenath (Gen 41:50–51). Manasseh and Ephraim are the so-called half-tribes or Joseph tribes of Israel. First Chronicles preserves separate genealogies for the Transjordan clans of Manasseh (5:23–26) and the western clans of Manasseh (7:14–19). The genealogy of Manasseh may have been separated from its original location for theological purposes. It is helpful to remember that the Chronicler has selected and arranged genealogical materials from a number of ancient sources for theological purposes related to the postexilic restoration of Judah. The Chronicler has included genealogical records of the Joseph tribes primarily in order to round out the ideal number of the twelve tribes.

One of the historical sidebars of this section is the reference to Asriel's Aramean mother (Manasseh's unnamed concubine, 7:14). This seems to be yet another example of the Chronicler's openness to the nations in affirming God's sovereignty in fulfilling the "blessings" clause of the Abrahamic covenant (Gen 12:3).

Ephraim (7:20–29). The sequential treatment of the two Joseph tribes is logical, fitting the biblical pattern of treating Ephraim and Manasseh as a related sociopolitical entity (cf. Deut 34:2). Often Ephraim is placed first when paired with Manasseh because of Jacob's blessing of Ephraim prior to Manasseh, though Manasseh was the older of the brothers (Gen 48:20). The Chronicler's order of Manasseh followed by Ephraim is explained on the basis of geographical location of the northern tribes.

The genealogy concludes with Joshua son of Nun, descendant of Ephraim and successor of Moses (1 Chr 7:27; cf. Deut 34:9). The reference to Joshua is in keeping with the Chronicler's emphasis on the Israelite conquest and occupation of the land of covenant promise. The historical anecdote sandwiched between the two halves of the genealogy seems to serve the same purpose.

The story of Ezer and Elead is unique to Chronicles. The Chronicler inserts the account as an example of temporary loss and setback overcome providentially by human initiative. What better way to remind his audience that the setback of the exile was only temporary? The addendum to the historical footnote celebrating Sheerah as the builder of Beth Horon is remarkable for the prominence accorded a woman, but not out of character for the Chronicler. This story too, emphasizing the accomplishments of an individual, serves to encourage each member of the postexilic community to become involved in restoring Israel to its former glory.

Asher (7:30–40). Asher was the son of Zilpah, the handmaid of Leah (Gen 46:18). Asher concludes the tribal list. The attrition in the muster roll to 26,000 (7:40) from 41,500 (Num 1:40–41) and 53,400 (26:47) testifies to the misfortunes experienced by this tribe.

Application. The inclusive nature of the covenants, old and new, permits the application of an unchanging biblical principle to changing historical and cultural circumstances—the principle of inclusion itself! The theme of including the gentiles in the covenant promises to Israel encases the message of the entire Bible, much like an envelope or even bookends. The opening chapters of Genesis introduces the table of nations (Gen 10) and God's promise to bless all nations (12:1–3), and the concluding book of the Bible depicts the nations surrounding the throne of God in worship (Rev 5:9–10; 7:9–10; etc.).

1 CHRONICLES 8:1–9:1A

Original Meaning. The genealogy of the tribe of Benjamin serves as an introduction to the genealogy of Saul in 9:35–44. The tribal territory of Benjamin is important since it represents a portion of the covenant promise made to Abraham about a specific geographical region (Gen 12:1–3). Beyond that, however, the tribes of Benjamin and Judah essentially formed the Southern Kingdom of Judah and, later, the postexilic province of Judah.

The Families of Bela and Ehud (8:1–7). The focal point of the genealogy is the clan of Ehud more than the family tree of the tribal patriarch Benjamin. The Ehud clan of Benjamites is associated with Geba (8:6), one of the cities allotted to Benjamin as part of the tribal inheritance of Canaan supervised by Joshua (Josh 18:24). The deportation (or migration?) of Ehud's sons to Manahath (1 Chr 8:7) cannot be placed historically, given the limited data available.

The Family of Shaharaim (8:8–13). The setting for the episodes concerning the family of Shaharaim is Moab (8:8). Nothing else is known of Shaharaim apart from the Chronicler's genealogy. Moab was a satellite state under Israelite control during the reigns of David and Solomon (cf. 2 Sam 8:2).

The Benjamite genealogy includes the curious report that sons were born to Shaharaim by a third wife, Hodesh, after he had divorced two others of his wives (1 Chr 8:8). This anecdote is in keeping with the Chronicler's style of personalizing the genealogies with sidebars that highlight unusual events or call attention to marginalized people (like women and non-Hebrews).

The Descendants of Elpaal (8:14–28). Little is known about those individuals included in the genealogy since most of the names occur only here in the Bible. Perhaps geography is an organizing principle in the splicing together of the Benjamite materials since there is a general movement from the periphery of the territory of Benjamin to the city of Jerusalem. The dual themes of tribal expansion and tribal unity are important to the Chronicler's theology of hope for postexilic Judah. In fact, he illustrates that the city of Jerusalem belongs to all Israel by naming citizens from several tribes resettling there after the exile (9:3).

The Family of Saul (8:29–40). The central character of the last section of Benjamin's genealogy is Saul—the most famous of all the Benjamites. The naming of Kish (8:33) prompts the recitation of the genealogy of King Saul (8:33–38). The list is the most extensive record of Saul's family in the Bible and is repeated (with minor variations) in 9:39–44 as an introduction to the death of King Saul (ch. 10). The Chronicler's genealogy of Benjamin is both a reminder to the postexilic Benjamites of their noble heritage and a call to emulate their example of faith and intertribal cooperation.

Application. Part of the story of the Bible is the conflict between faith in God (and the truth he has disclosed through general and special revelation) and false gods and false teaching espoused by humanistic philosophies and superstitious religions. In recent decades the church has had to combat an equally insidious false teaching that promotes health, wealth, and happiness—all the while eschewing pain, suffering, and adversity as symptoms of a stunted spiritual development. This gospel of "gain with no pain" must ignore the biblical stories featuring the adversity and suffering of God's people.

1 CHRONICLES 9:1B–44

Original Meaning. The purpose of the genealogical introduction was twofold:

1. to legitimize the restoration community as the rightful heirs of the promises made to the patriarchs and kings of Israel; and
2. to bolster the morale of those Hebrews returning to Judah from Babylonia and inspire full participation in the restoration initiative.

Families Resettling Jerusalem (9:1b–34). The repetition of "Israel" in 2:1 and 9:1a suggests an envelope construction encasing the genealogies of 2:1–9:1a as a complete literary unit. The genealogy as a whole calls attention to the priests, Levites, and temple personnel resettling Jerusalem. The citations to the tribe of Benjamin at the beginning of the list serve as a bridge between the genealogy of Benjamin (ch. 8) and the account of Saul's kingship (9:35–10:14).

The introduction (9:2–3) to the list of people resettling Judah after the Babylonian exile subtly confirms the linkage of the postexilic Jewish community with earlier national Israel. The Chronicler's report of the reoccupation of Jerusalem (9:3) is another important tie between the present and the past for the postexilic community. The resettling of Jerusalem is a sure sign of God's blessing and a hopeful omen since the prophetic promises for the rebuilding of the nation of Israel are centered in the city of David (Isa 44:26, 28; Jer 33:16).

The Chronicler abbreviates the list of descendants of Judah (9:4–6) found in the parallel of Nehemiah 11:4–6. The difference in tabulations (468 in Neh 11:6 and 690 in 1 Chr 9:6) may be due to the breadth of the census takings ("men" specified in Neh 11:6, "people" in 1 Chr 9:6). The Chronicler's total may also reflect the growth in the families of Judah from the earlier census of Nehemiah.

The Chronicler's list of the descendants of Benjamin (9:7–9) contains even more variation from the parallel account in Nehemiah 11:7–9 than the Judahite genealogy. Numerous solutions have been proposed for reconciling the differences, but suffice to say that each writer makes selective use of a common and more complete genealogical record.

The list of priestly descendants resettling Jerusalem (9:10–13) is also abbreviated when compared to the parallel account in Nehemiah 11:10–14. Both census takings number less than half of the priests who initially returned from exile. This may indicate that even priests were reluctant to live in the ruined shell of Jerusalem upon return from Babylonia. As one might expect, the Chronicler (9:14–16) slightly expands the genealogy of the Levites when compared to the parallel in Nehemiah 11:15–18.

The Chronicler's section on the gatekeepers is an extensive expansion of a single verse in Nehemiah (Neh 11:19). In addition to their Levitical descent, this listing emphasizes their exemplary behavior in heeding the call to live in Jerusalem (1 Chr 9:22, 25) and in their self-sacrificing spirit as they willingly accept additional tasks (9:26–32).

Four chief gatekeepers are identified, as there were four entrances to the temple precincts. A gate was located on each of the cardinal compass points, with the east gate being the most important. According to 26:13, the gate assignments of the chief gatekeepers were originally determined by the casting of lots. The gatekeepers worked their shifts in pairs for seven-day periods (9:25), and in all they manned twenty-two stations around the clock (26:17–18).

The gatekeepers provided leadership in the day-to-day operations of the temple by continually guarding the premises and its contents and opening the gates for temple services every morning (9:27). In addition, the gatekeepers supported the temple ministries by maintaining the furniture and the implements used in the worship rituals and by preparing the ingredients required for the priestly sacrifices and offerings (9:29–30).

The word translated "musicians" (9:33; so NIV, NLT) literally signifies "singers" (so NKJV, NRSV). It is unclear if the singers are the Levites mentioned in 9:14–16 or gatekeepers (9:17–32) who double as temple musicians. The Chronicler's stylized genealogical record of all Israel, past and present, represents the religious ideal for God's people. The focal point of the genealogies is Jerusalem and the services of temple worship orchestrated by the priests and Levites.

The conclusion to the list of people resettling Jerusalem (9:34) essentially repeats 8:28 (with the addition of the word "Levite"). The verse serves as a transition between the Levitical musicians (9:33) and the genealogy of Saul (9:35–44). Most commentators note the echo of "Jerusalem" marks an inclusion with 9:3 and forms an envelope construction for the section.

Genealogy of Saul (9:35–44). This genealogy repeats the register of Saul's family tree (with minor variations) found in 8:29–38 as one segment of the genealogy of Benjamin. These minor variations may be explained as either textual corruption or to an ongoing process of transformation of names because of language changes over time.

Application. The story of Israel is a story of fresh starts by God's grace. In fact, the story of the Bible is the story of God making and remaking, "doing new things" (Isa 43:19; cf. Jer 31:22). The New Testament, especially the Gospels and Acts, tells a similar story. There one reads of dramatic examples of fresh starts, people whose lives are changed because of an encounter with Jesus of Nazareth. The story of fresh starts initiated by the grace of God is not confined to biblical history. As one reads church history, there is a delightful repetition in the annals of Christian faith. These new beginnings, flashing like meteor showers across the timeline of church history, testify to the faithfulness of God through the ages.

1 CHRONICLES 10:1–12:40

Original Meaning

Saul's Death (10:1–7). Saul was anointed king over Israel in order to deliver God's people "from the hand of the Philistines" (1 Sam 9:16). Ironically, Saul and his sons were killed by these very same Philistines. In the end, Israel actually lost more territory than it gained in these wars. The national hopes that fueled the fervent clamor for a king were dashed.

The dramatic narration of the inexorable "press" of the battle against King Saul and his sons (1 Chr 10:2) helps illumine the Chronicler's assessment of the conflict: "so the LORD put him [Saul] to death" (10:14). In like manner, the naming of Saul's slain sons foreshadows the Chronicler's commentary on the cessation of his royal dynasty. The reference to Jonathan (10:2) no doubt stirs memories in the Chronicler's audience of Jonathan's covenant of friendship with David and King David's eulogy of King Saul and Jonathan.

Both Samuel and Chronicles agree as to the wounding of King Saul by Philistine archers (10:3; cf. 1 Sam 31:3). The refusal of his armor-bearer to honor Saul's request to kill him with the sword prompts the first king of Israel to fall on his own sword. The Chronicler offers no theological commentary on the propriety of Saul's suicide, a rare occurrence in the Bible. The report of the desecration of Saul's body indicates his fear of abuse by the enemy is justified (1 Chr 10:9–10). The deaths of Saul and his sons at Mount Gilboa have the practical outcome of demoralizing the Israelite militia who flee the battleground.

Saul's Burial (10:8–12). The rescue of the exposed corpses of Saul and his sons by the valiant men of Jabesh Gilead (10:11–12) may have been prompted by King Saul's deliverance of Jabesh Gilead from the aggression of Nahash the Ammonite (1 Sam 11:1–11). The burial site under "the great tree in Jabesh" (1 Chr 10:12) was an important local landmark and probably a sacred site. The seven-day duration of the fast by the inhabitants of Jabesh Gilead attest their fierce loyalty and high regard for King Saul.

Demise of Saul's Dynasty (10:13–14). The Chronicler concludes the story of Saul's death with a unique theological commentary on Saul's reign. Saul fails miserably on three crucial counts: he was unfaithful, he did not keep the word of the Lord, and he neglected to seek guidance from the Lord. Unfaithfulness and failure to seek the Lord are prominent themes in Chronicles and inevitably result in divine judgment. The Chronicler's narrative of Saul's death has a twofold purpose.

1. The Israelite kingdom and kingship belong to God.
2. God had good reason for transferring the kingdom from the family of Saul to the family of David.

All Israel Supports David's Kingship (11:1–12:40). *David enthroned at Hebron (11:1–3).* The report of "all Israel" gathering to lend support to David's kingship (11:1) is echoed throughout the narrative (11:4, 10; 12:38). The passage references several key concepts connected with kingship after the

Davidic ideal: the pastoral image of king as shepherd of the people, the "king" (*melek*) as "ruler" (*nagid*; the term has military connotations and calls to mind the language of the Davidic covenant, 2 Sam 7:7–8), and the act of anointing (the public recognition of a divine commission for an office of leadership, cf. 1 Sam 16:3, 12). Moreover, the ancient city of Hebron was home and burial ground for the patriarchs and matriarchs of Israel. No doubt implicit in the Chronicler's association of David with the patriarchal site of Hebron geographically is the splicing together of the Abrahamic and Davidic covenants theologically.

David conquers Jerusalem (11:4–9). According to the Chronicler, the conquest of Jerusalem is the first major act of David's kingship (11:4). This narrative is important to the purpose of portraying the development of a united Israel under King David's leadership.

The prominence given to Joab in the Chronicler's version of the conquest of Jerusalem may be due to his fierce loyalty to King David, part of that strong support David enjoys from his cadre of military leaders. In contrast to Saul's unfaithfulness (10:13), David expands his base of power in Israel because "the LORD Almighty was with him" (11:9). The Chronicler rightly acknowledges David's faithfulness to God and his obedience to God's law as the standard by which his successors will be measured.

David's mighty men (11:10–47). The roster of David's mighty men and the reports of their heroic exploits has its precursor in 2 Samuel 23:8–39. The lists of soldiers in both Samuel and the Chronicles parallel makes reference to the "Three" and the "Thirty" (2 Sam 23:8, 13, 17, 23; 1 Chr 11:15, 20, 25). These elite troops are the ancient equivalent of both the modern-day special forces military units and the secret service, charged with the protection of our highest elected officials. The Chronicler's interest in these heroes is found in the "strong support" they give to David as king (11:10). The Chronicler recognizes that the survival of the postexilic community to which he writes depends on this kind of unanimity of support for the leadership God might restore in Jerusalem.

The roster of David's mighty men begins with the names and exploits of those known as "the Three": Jashobeam, Eleazar, and Abishai (11:11–14, 20). Perhaps the most striking feature of 11:11–14 is the theological assessment of the heroism of the Three, that "the LORD brought about a great victory" (11:14). The Chronicler's theology of hope for postexilic Judah rests not on the exploits of mighty warriors but on the LORD.

It is unclear whether the account of the three anonymous mighty men securing water for King David from the heavily guarded well at Bethlehem (11:15–19) should be connected with the names of David's heroes preceding or following the story. What is unmistakably clear is the Chronicler's emphasis on David's ability as a leader to inspire remarkable bravery and unshakable loyalty among his followers.

Next the Chronicler showcases two additional heroes of special status, ranking somewhere between the "Three" and the "Thirty" (11:20–25). Benaiah is accorded special honor because of his role as the chief of King David's bodyguards (11:25).

The list of David's "mighty men" in 11:26–47 is longer than the parallel found in 2 Samuel 23:24–39. The differences in the two lists enumerating David's mighty men suggests not only the Chronicler's access to additional historical sources but also the natural fluidity in the composition of a group of military heroes during David's long reign.

Early tribal support for David: Benjamin (12:1–7). This section of the larger literary unit (chs. 10–12) furthers the Chronicler's theme of the wide support King David enjoys from all Israel. The purpose of chapter 12 seems to be that of telling the story of the building of David's "great army" (12:22). Chapter 12 divides neatly into two parts: the defectors from Saul's army who join David while he is a fugitive as the rival king (12:1–22) and the assembly of the Israelite militia at Hebron for David's coronation (12:23–40). This material has no parallel in the Samuel narrative, suggesting the Chronicler preserves an untitled military document from the period of the united monarchy.

The account of the defection of certain warriors from the tribe of Benjamin to David's guerilla band dates to the time when David was seeking asylum among the Philistines (12:1–7). The ambidextrous skill of these Benjamite warriors as both slingers and bowmen is noteworthy. The addition of a contingent of twenty-three experienced soldiers to David's army does not seem too impressive to the modern reader. Yet we learn from the Amarna correspondence from an earlier historical period that a small cohort of experienced archers could turn the tide of a battle.

Early tribal support for David: Gad (12:8–15). The list of eleven Gadite defectors (12:9–13) is framed by exploit reports emphasizing the caliber of the warriors joining David's ranks (12:8, 14–15). Unlike the archers and slingers from the tribe of Benjamin who are effective in battle from a distance (12:1–7), the Gadite soldiers excel in hand-to-hand combat because of their speed and strength.

Early tribal support for David: Benjamin and Judah (12:16–18). The text recounts the story of a special group of soldiers from Benjamin and Judah who seek asylum with David. The motive for their shift in allegiance from Saul to David is unclear. David himself is suspicious of their intentions and challenges their loyalty under oath (12:17).

The reference to the "Spirit" coming on Amasai (12:18; literally, "the Spirit clothed Amasai") signifies the anointing of God's spirit and marks his speech as a type of prophetic utterance. Amasai's speech makes oblique reference to the Davidic covenant in the clause "your God will help you" (12:18; cf. 17:7–14). In response to David's question of allegiance, Amasai replies, "We are yours" (12:18a). The second half of Amasai's speech plays on the key words prompting David's skepticism, "peace" (*shalom*, translated "success" 3x in 12:18) and "help" (*ʿzr*, 3x in 12:17–18). The Chronicler essentially tells his audience that "God helps those who help David and his descendants."

Early tribal support for David: Manasseh (12:19–22). The theme of "help" joins this passage with the preceding unit (12:16–18). Amasai's generalized prophecy of God's "help" in bringing about success for David's kingship (12:18) is fulfilled specifically through the loyal "help" of others against the Amalekite bandits (12:21–22).

The tribes anoint David at Hebron (12:23–40). The purpose of this report of the tribal gathering at Hebron is the transfer of Saul's kingdom to David (12:23). The Chronicler also notes that all this is done according to the word of the Lord (12:23). The muster roll names eleven tribes and two half-tribes, the most complete tribal register in the Old Testament. All this is further evidence in support of the Chronicler's basic premise that "all Israel" supports David's kingship (12:38).

The section concludes with representatives from the Hebrew tribes gathered at Hebron for the crowning of David as king over all Israel (12:38–40). The emphasis of the Chronicler on Israel as the people of God is seen in the various segments of Hebrew society joining in the coronation, including the professional military (12:1–22), the volunteer militia (12:23–37), and the rest of the Israelites (12:38). Chronologically, this closing paragraph completes the narrative begun in 11:1–3, the account of "all Israel" assembling at Hebron to anoint David as king. David's coronation sets the stage for the rest of the Chronicler's history.

The Chronicler is careful to report that the outcome of tribal unity is "joy in Israel" (12:40; cf. 29:22; 2 Chr 7:8–10; 30:21–26). He is hopeful, no doubt, that this recipe for joy will be the experience of postexilic Judah as well.

Application. The writer of Chronicles appeals to David's example of fierce loyalty to God because of the spirit of unity it inspired among the tribes of Israel. After all, support of the Israelite monarchy was essential to the success of the postexilic community. The Chronicler seems to be simply calling his audience to do the right thing—quite apart from the hope of any tangible reward for the individual or the larger community.

The crisis of loyalty addressed by the Chronicler is not as far removed from the Christian church as we might think. Popular culture naturally infiltrates and influences the Christian subculture over the course of time. One example illustrates the point. The contemporary social doctrine of "political correctness" has created a "PC" mindset that now permeates popular culture. To be politically correct means to conform to a belief that language and practices that might offend another sociopolitical or religious group are to be eliminated.

This relativizing of God's truth as revealed in Scripture mutes convictions and thus fosters a pseudo-neutrality that grants the "truth of Islam" or the "truth of Hinduism" as on equal footing with the "truth of Christianity." Hence, the Christian church is now embroiled in an intramural controversy involving the exclusive claims of the gospel of Jesus Christ and its implications for the doctrine of salvation in an age of religious pluralism.

1 CHRONICLES 13:1–17:27

Original Meaning

First Stage of the Ark's Return (13:1–14). The book of 2 Samuel treats the transfer of the ark of God as a military event initially (2 Sam 6:1). The Chronicler adds the details that David consults not only with his military leaders but also the religious leadership of Israel (priests and Levites) and the general populace (1 Chr 13:2). David's call to "bring the ark of our God back to us" connotes a spiritual journey as much as it denotes a geographical one (13:3a). Implicit in David's summons to restore the ark to its proper place in Israelite worship is the cause-and-effect link between Saul's demise and Israel's defeat by the Philistines and the neglect of the ark of God (13:3c).

Affirming the prominent theme of Israelite unity under King David, the Chronicler indicates in threefold repetition that "all the Israelites" participate with King David in the processional to return the ark of God (13:5, 6, 8). The Chronicler's elaboration on the extent to which this multitude represents the breadth of the territory of Israel is noteworthy (13:5). The Chronicler's definition of the borders of Israel occurs elsewhere in the Old Testament only in Joshua 13:2–5. The Chronicler may be making two statements in his appeal to the precursor text in Joshua.

1. The rarely used geographical description maximizes the sweeping extent of David's support.
2. It may offer commentary on Joshua 13:2–5 in the sense that under King David, the conquest of Canaan is finally completed.

The portrayal of Yahweh as "the LORD, who is enthroned between the cherubim" (1 Chr 13:6) is an infrequent but powerful image of the God of the Hebrews (cf. 1 Sam 4:4; 2 Kgs 19:15). The idea of the mysterious and majestic presence of God enthroned between the cherubim of the ark of the covenant is based on the understanding that this is where God meets his people (Exod 25:22).

The deadly mishap involving Uzzah (1 Chr 13:9) dramatically and immediately changes the mood surrounding the transfer of the ark of the covenant. King David's response of both anger and fear to the tragedy is also readily reported (13:11–12). David's visceral reaction seems to be based on the assumption that Uzzah is an innocent victim and that God has capriciously shown his disapproval for the enterprise of transferring the ark. The death of Uzzah resulting in the bungled transfer of the ark of the covenant is one of two failures of King David reported by the Chronicler (the other is the census-taking, ch. 21). God is a consuming fire, and he will show himself holy before all people. The Chronicler's repetition of the word "break out" (Heb. *prts*) in this section of the narrative seems to draw attention to this terrifying dimension of God's character (cf. 13:11; 14:11; 15:13).

David's refusal to press on with his quest to transfer the ark to Jerusalem marks two important character traits of this beloved shepherd-king (13:13–14).

1. His disposition to deposit the ark at the nearest convenient location indicates his submission to God's will.
2. Whether out of abject fear or outright reverence, David refuses to manipulate God for personal advantage through control of the sacred symbol of divine presence.

There is some question as to the identity of Obed-Edom. There is no doubt, however, about the purpose of the Chronicler's report of God's blessing on the house of Obed-Edom for those three months the ark resides in his keeping. David and all Israel (as well as the Chronicler's audience) need to know that the transgression against God was not the transfer of the ark itself but the faulty way in which it was carried out. God demands proper means to achieve good and right ends.

King David's Fame Spreads (14:1–17). King Hiram of Tyre was an ally of both David and Solomon (14:1–2). Most likely Hiram ruled from about 980–950 BC, but scholarly estimates vary widely. Hiram's gift of construction materials and craftsmen for the building of David's palace may have been part of a trade agreement, much like that arranged later with Solomon.

The Jerusalem birth report and name list assume the audience's knowledge of the Hebron birth report and name list (2 Sam 3:2–5). Unlike King Saul's dynasty, which died out (1 Chr 10:6), David's house is a "fruitful vine" (Ps 128:3).

The news of David being anointed as king of Israel prompts a Philistine invasion of Judah, presumably an attempt to dethrone him before their former vassal has sufficient time to solidify his power among God's people (1 Chr 14:8–12). Unlike King Saul, who "inquired" of the medium of Endor (1 Sam 28:7), David "inquired" of the Lord and was assured victory (1 Chr 14:10). The Philistines abandon their gods on the battlefield, symbolic of their impotence before Yahweh, the true God (14:12). David burns the relics of false worship in accordance with the law of Moses (Deut 7:5; 12:3).

The Philistines launch a second offensive at the same location (1 Chr 14:13–16). As before, the narrative reports that David appropriately "inquires" of God as to his response to the Philistine aggression (14:14). Once again, David is assured of God's help in battle, but this time the tactics are changed. The rustling of the leaves in the trees is most likely the spirit of God, since David is told God will go before him in battle.

The spread of David's fame and the fear of Yahweh among the nations are interrelated (14:17). As God blesses David's faithfulness, so David's success brings glory and honor to God. Presumably the Chronicler intends this account of the reversal of fortune for Israel under King David as a message of hope and encouragement for his audience.

Jerusalem Made Ready for the Entrance of the Ark (15:1–24). The report of the "tent" David pitches for temporarily housing the ark (15:1) emphasizes the thoroughness of his preparations for transferring the ark (cf. 15:12). More important to the venture of relocating the ark of God in Jerusalem is the role of the Levites as porters (15:2). This time the ark is to be carried by the Levites, not driven on a cart. God himself may have revealed this to David through the king's study of the Mosaic law (Deut 10:8: 18:5).

The Chronicler is careful to include the priests ("descendants of Aaron") and the "Levites" (1 Chr 15:4) in the assembly of "all Israel" (15:3). The Chronicler also lists three additional families in 15:8–10, all descendants of Kohath. The Kohathites were the clan charged by Moses to attend and transport the ark. In his appointment of the proper Levitical clan to transport the ark, King David again demonstrates his faithfulness to God's commands.

David's preparations for the transfer of the ark extend beyond the readying of a site for housing it to the personnel responsible for transporting and attending the sacred chest (15:11–15). The word "consecrate" (15:12, 14) means to set things or persons apart from impurity and profane use and dedicate them to the service of God in holiness. The Chronicler makes it clear that faulty procedure that fails to recognize the holiness of God is responsible for the aborted attempt to transfer the ark (15:13). This time David and the religious leaders of Israel follow the prescriptions of the Mosaic code. The concluding section of the report summarizing David's extensive preparations for the transfer of the ark to Jerusalem (15:16–24) showcases the priests and Levites as musicians, another theme in Chronicles.

Second Stage of the Ark's Transfer: The Processional into Jerusalem (15:25–16:3). David's priestly role in the processional is tacitly approved by the detailed reference to the king's garb: a linen robe and linen ephod (15:27; like that of the Levites, cf. Exod 39:27–29). By contrast, David earns the disapproval of his wife Michal (1 Chr 15:29), Saul's daughter. In one sense she represents the last vestige of King Saul's unfaithfulness, and her story provides yet further justification for God's rejection of Saul's dynasty.

This portion of the account concludes with the successful installation of the ark of God in a tent, a temporary structure erected by David for housing the ark until a permanent shrine can be built. The Jerusalem tent is not to be confused with the Mosaic tabernacle, apparently located at Gibeon during David's reign (cf. 16:39; 21:29).

The "burnt offerings" (16:2) are sacrifices for sin and demonstrate dedication to God. The "fellowship offerings" (16:2) signify the completion of a vow (13:3) and thankfulness on the part of all Israel for the blessings of God in sustaining the nation and establishing David as king (cf. Lev 3). The communal blessing and ritual meal are part of a covenant-renewal ceremony (cf. Exod 24:11). By installing the ark in Jerusalem, David is reestablishing God's rule over Israel and Israel's loyalty to Yahweh's covenant with his chosen people.

Yahweh Enthroned on Israel's Praise (16:4–43). The psalm of thanksgiving commemorating the installation of the ark in Jerusalem, in one sense, is the theological center of the Chronicler's retelling of Israel's history. The installation of the ark marks Israel's return to God under David's leadership and a renewal of the nation's covenant loyalty to the God of their ancestors. The ark itself symbolizes the covenant agreement established by Yahweh with Israel at Mount Sinai. The Chronicler's song of praise celebrates God as both covenant maker and covenant keeper, the lynchpin in his theology of hope for postexilic Judah.

King David's appointment of certain members of the Levites to attend the ark indicates a division of labor among the Levitical corps. One group of Levites and the priests are stationed at the shrine in Gibeon housing the Mosaic tabernacle (16:39; 21:29). The other group of Levites are stationed in Jerusalem to minister before the ark of the Lord (16:4). The priestly and Levitical ministry centered in Gibeon remains one of maintaining the sacrificial worship of Israel. The Levitical ministry before the ark in Jerusalem is primarily musical in nature.

The psalm of thanksgiving (16:8–36) is a composite of selections from three psalms (Pss 105:1–15, 96:1–13, 106:1, 47–48). The psalmic composition, however, is not a random rearrangement of earlier poetic materials. The Chronicler has been influenced in his selection of poems from the Psalter by the vocabulary found in the immediate context of the narrative.

The theological themes of the three divisions of the composite psalm rehearse the key emphases of 1–2 Chronicles as a "biography" of God.

1. The first unit (1 Chr 16:7–22) from Psalm 105 highlights God as a covenant maker and keeper and Israel's unique place among the nations as his elect (16:15–17).
2. The second unit (16:23–33) from Psalm 96 extols God as creator and sovereign over all the nations and over all their gods.
3. The third unit (16:34–36) from Psalm 106 praises the goodness and mercy of the God of salvation.

Last, and not to be overlooked, the entire composite psalm repeats the covenant name Yahweh some sixteen times.

Obed-Edom apparently serves in the dual role of musician and gatekeeper (16:38; cf. 15:18, 21, 24). The relationship of this Obed-Edom to the Obed-Edom who housed the ark for three months after David's first attempt to transfer the ark failed is unclear (cf. 13:13).

The reference to the Gibeon sanctuary is important to the purpose of Chronicles because it demonstrates that King David has not neglected the Mosaic tabernacle. Likewise, the perpetuation of the morning and evening sacrifices commanded by the torah is a further witness to David's adherence to the law of Moses. Perhaps more crucial from the Chronicler's perspective is establishing the historical and theological continuity between David's tent-shrine in Jerusalem and the Mosaic tent-shrine in Gibeon. It seems likely that implicit in Zadok's assignment to Gibeon as chief priest (16:39) is the appointment of Abiathar as chief priest in Jerusalem (cf. 15:11).

Clearly the ministry of music on the part of the Levites is central to worship at both tent-sanctuaries. Both Heman and Jeduthun are known elsewhere as directors of Levitical musical guilds (cf. 25:1, 6). The musical refrain describing the thanksgiving of the Levites ("his love endures forever," 16:41) emphasizes the covenant loyalty, faithfulness, and steadfast love of God for Israel.

The Davidic Covenant (17:1–27). David's desire to build a temple for Yahweh is typical of royal behavior in the biblical world (17:1). It is only natural that David seeks to honor his God in like manner. Beyond this, David is shamed that Yahweh, as the true king of Israel is confined to a tent-sanctuary while he himself enjoys the luxury of a palace of cedar.

Nathan enters the scene rather abruptly in the narrative (17:1–2). The idea behind the word "prophet" (17:1) in the Old Testament world is that of a servant who stands in the council of the gods and then reports exactly what he heard as a divine messenger or herald. Nathan is a strategic religious-political adviser in the early Hebrew monarchy, as evidenced by his role in securing Solomon's succession to David's throne (cf. 1 Kgs 1).

Elsewhere we learn that Nathan the prophet is also a court historian since the Chronicler references his "records" (cf. 29:29; 2 Chr 9:29). The combined good intentions of King David and the blessing of the prophet Nathan, however, are rebuffed by God.

Previously God's presence had not been localized permanently at one specific geographical site. The idea of a permanent and centralized structure for the worship of Yahweh is not the issue in God's veto of David's plan to build a temple. The problem is not the erection of a temple for Yahweh, but David. David's legacy as a warrior means he will serve only as Solomon's contractor for the building of the temple (cf. 22:8; 28:3).

The promise of an offspring to succeed David on the throne of Israel echoes God's similar promise to Abraham and Sarah (cf. Gen 12:1–3). King David has the assurance of God that despite his own death, his dynasty will be firmly established (1 Chr 11:11). The temple as "God's house" can have significance for God's people only after God has built "David's house."

Biblical commentators have noted a high degree of correspondence between David's prayer in 17:16–27 and its precursor in 2 Samuel 7:18–29. This is the first of several prayers offered to God by Israelite kings inserted in the Chronicler's retelling of Israelite history. In fact, this is a subtle agenda item of the Chronicler—to draw the people of postexilic Judah back into conversation with God through prayer. The emphasis on prayer fits naturally into his concern for worship renewal because prayer ultimately issues in the glory of God (17:24).

The *introduction* to the prayer precedes its text and calls attention to the content of the prayer. The *invocation* or address to God (17:16b–19) sets the tone of the prayer. The *declaration* serves either to praise God or justify the suppliant's petition. Here in David's prayer the declaration (17:20–22) praises the uniqueness of God and his power as revealed in Hebrew history. The thumbnail sketch of Israelite history highlights the exodus, when God "redeemed" a people for himself, and makes an allusion to the conquest and settlement period of the judges in the phrase "driving out nations" (17:21). David's *petition* is brief (17:23–24). He simply asks God to follow through and bring to completion what he has already promised—to raise up a descendant who will complete the task of building the temple and to establish firmly an everlasting Davidic dynasty.

The final structural element of the formal prayer is the *recognition* of God's response to the prayer (17:25–27). David acknowledges that he has already received a partial answer to his prayer. God has blessed David's house in that his divine promise will not fail (17:19, 23). The conclusion of David's prayer is a doxology of sorts, as the word "bless" (*brk*) occurs three times in the final verse (17:27). David understands all this is the gracious work of God, not the genius of human scheming or the chance of fate.

Doubtless, the Chronicler expects his audience to learn (or be reminded of) basic theological truths embedded in David's prayer. The first is a repeated message in Chronicles: God both hears and answers the prayers of the righteous by doing great things that ultimately bring glory to his name (17:19, 24, 26). The second is implicit in God's promise to build a lasting Davidic dynasty. The covenant granted to the house of David establishes the rule of God on earth. The present reality of the kingdom of God embodied in the nation of Israel is the cornerstone of the Chronicler's theology of hope.

Application. The community of faith in ancient Israel and the early Christian church used signs and symbols in much the same way. By "sign" we mean a practical and visible representation of reality, whether a spiritual quality or characteristic, a biblical doctrine or truth, or even a key biblical figure. A sign conveys information that leads to personal action. For example, the sign of Christian baptism points to the theological idea of the "virtual" death, burial, and resurrection of the believer in Jesus Christ (cf. Rom 6:3–4).

A "symbol" may be understood as a visual representation of an idea or a reality beyond or more than itself. The religious symbol points to a spiritual reality outside of itself, participates in its power, and makes intelligible its meaning. Genuine religious symbols are divinely created in the sense that they find their origin in Scripture. For example, the dove is a symbol of the reality of the empowering Holy Spirit (Matt 3:16), and the sacrificial lamb is a symbol of the reality of the redemptive nature of Jesus Christ's life and ministry (John 1:29; Rev 5:6). For the sake of imparting the legacy of Christian worship, instruction, and evangelism to the generations now being raised in this age of technology and visual media culture, the church must rediscover the value of symbolic communication.

1 CHRONICLES 18:1–20:8

Original Meaning. The recounting of David's campaigns are included primarily for the purpose of explaining why David is prohibited from building Yahweh's temple: David is a warrior who has "shed much blood" (22:8; 28:3). According to Deuteronomy, God would choose a dwelling place for his name once the Israelites had "rest" from their enemies (Deut 12:10; 25:19). That rest has not yet occurred. The repetition of the victory formula suggests divine approval of David's expansionist policy, almost as a type of second Joshua engaging in the conquest of the promised land (cf. 1 Chr 18:6, 13). Although a secondary emphasis, the booty David and his armies plunder from their enemies and subsequently dedicate to the Lord provides the funds for the eventual construction of the temple (18:8, 11; cf. 22:3, 14; 29:3).

David's Campaigns (18:1–13). Strategically, subduing the Philistines secures the western flank of David's empire. The Chronicler preserves a more lengthy account of the campaign against a coalition of Aramean states to the northeast (18:3–10). David opposes Hadadezer's declaration of sovereignty, perhaps because he has designs on controlling the trade route known as the King's Highway.

Among the spoils David takes from Hadadezer and the cities of Zobah are large quantities of bronze. The Chronicler adds the fact that the booty is later used by Solomon in casting the bronze vessels for the temple (18:7–8). This not only provides further detail as to what became of the plunder, but also it is another way in which the Chronicler connects David to the preparations made for building Yahweh's temple.

The news of Israel's success against the kingdom of Zobah and the Arameans of Damascus prompts Tou, king of Hamath, to befriend King David with gifts of gold, silver, and bronze (18:9–10). This is likely intended to forge some kind of political alliance between King Tou and King David.

The survey of David's campaigns concludes with a brief report of the Edomite war (18:12–13). Edom becomes a satellite state of Israel like Aramean Damascus and Moab. Edom is among the nations paying tribute to Israel during the reign of Solomon (cf. 1 Kgs 4:21).

Important to the Chronicler's message is the theological commentary found at the midpoint and end of the chapter (1 Chr 18:6, 13). The God who "gave David victory" is the God of the Chronicler and postexilic Judah. That same blessing of divine approval awaits those who dedicate themselves in expectant faith to the spiritual and physical restoration of Jerusalem, even as King David dedicates the silver and gold plundered in war to the work of the Lord (18:11).

David's Royal Cabinet (18:14–17). Three distinct departments comprise David's royal cabinet: a war office, a priestly office, and an administrative office. Joab becomes David's general. Abiathar and Zadok (18:16) appear to function as joint high priests. The cabinet post of "recorder" (18:15) may have been a position similar to that of the royal herald in the Egyptian court. The herald was a personal secretary to the pharaoh in charge of royal protocol and served as the public spokesman for the monarchy.

War Against the Ammonites (19:1–20:3). David intends his commissioning of a delegation representing his administration at the "state funeral" in Ammon as a gesture of goodwill (19:2). The men are seized, however, and accused of spying (19:3). The beard was the symbol of manhood in the ancient world, so to shave off half the beard was both an insult to the Israelite emissaries and an affront to the virility of King David (19:4–5). The further humiliation of the Israelite dignitaries in the cutting of their robes is an act of open contempt for King David, publicly shaming him since ambassadors acted on behalf of the king.

The Ammonite preparations for war consist largely of hiring Aramean mercenaries (19:6–7). The thousand talents of silver (19:6) translates into more than thirty-seven tons of the precious metal. This incredible sum speaks to the desperation of the Ammonites.

David's response is swift and thorough: the mobilization of the entire Israelite army against the Ammonites under the command of Joab (19:8). The Arameans and the Ammonites are deployed on two fronts. Shrewdly, Joab positions his elite forces against the Aramean mercenaries, with the remaining forces pitted against the Ammonites (19:10–11). He also devises a plan B calling for the consolidation of the Israelite troops in case the battle should go against his army (19:12).

Finally, Joab encourages his troops by reminding them they are fighting for all the Israelite people and "the cities of our God" (19:13a). This phrase, coupled with the command to "be strong and . . . fight bravely," alludes to Yahweh's covenant with Israel and to the conquest of Canaan by Joshua (cf. Josh 1:6–7). Joab concludes his precombat exhortation with a prayer, committing the outcome of the battle to the sovereignty and goodness of God (19:13b). Expressions of such trust in the providence of Yahweh are an important feature of the Chronicler's theology of hope for postexilic Judah.

The answer to Joab's prayer comes almost immediately. The Aramean mercenaries flee. The Ammonites retreat into the walled city. Joab chooses not to lay siege to the city of Rabbah but returns to Jerusalem (19:15b). It may have already been late in the year, and the winter rains would stymie any protracted siege of the city. Joab's defeat of the coalition of Ammonite and Aramean armies is not decisive. The Aramean troops (19:16) are summoned to wage war with Israel in an attempt to check David's growing military strength.

The result of the battle is similar to the previous engagement led by Joab (19:14–15). David is victorious as the Arameans again are routed and flee the battlefield (19:17–18). Hadadezer's general is killed in battle (19:18).

The Ammonite campaign resumes in the spring of the following year, tactically a more opportune time to lay siege to a walled city (20:1). The Chronicler omits the lengthy (and lurid) story of David's tryst with Bathsheba (2 Sam 11:2–12:25), although a hint of that royal scandal is retained in the cryptic reference to the king's decision to remain behind after sending Joab and the Israelite army off to war (1 Chr 20:1b). The transition from Joab's sacking of Rabbah (20:1c) to King David claiming the crown of the Ammonite king (20:2) is awkward.

Critics have questioned the accuracy of the biblical figures for the weight of the Ammonite crown in 20:2 (a talent of gold would weigh more than sevety-five pounds!). The piece in question is probably an ornamental tiara symbolizing Ammonite kingship and may have been displayed at certain royal occasions. Most likely this royal headdress is lifted to David's head briefly by his personal attendants as a public declaration of Israel's sovereignty over Ammon.

War against the Philistines (20:4–8). The Chronicler returns to the Philistine problem to conclude his summary of David's wars. The Philistines were the nemesis of the Israelites. The ongoing conflict stemmed primarily from the fact that the Israelites needed a seaport, as the kingdoms of Saul and David were landlocked. The narrative relates border skirmishes settled by duels between champion warriors more than full-scale war.

Our passage consists of three exploit reports, each of which records a contest between an Israelite warrior and a Philistine warrior descended from the Rephaites. The Rephaim were people of enormous size and strength (e.g., Goliath was more than nine feet tall, 1 Sam 17:4; Og king of Bashan required a bed thirteen feet in length, Deut 3:11). The relationship of the Philistine Rephaites to the giants of the Transjordan, also called Rephaim or Anakim, is unclear (cf. Deut 2:10–11).

One can only muse over the factors influencing the Chronicler's selective appeal to the summary accounts of the wars of King David. No doubt, the stories of the success of David and his army in the face of seemingly insurmountable odds are a source of inspiration for postexilic Judah. They are also a stirring reminder of the power of God to deliver his faithful servants from dark circumstances. The Chronicler's audience needs to hear that!

Application. The warfare motif is not restricted to the Old Testament. The church at Ephesus learned about spiritual warfare from the apostle Paul, an ongoing cosmic battle between God and the unseen powers of evil (Eph 6:11–12; cf. 2 Cor 10:3–4). The eschatological kingdom of God ushered in at the second coming of Jesus Christ will result in a new heaven and earth and rid evil from God's creation once and for all. In fact, according to Paul, Jesus Christ will yield his kingdom to the Father only after he has defeated all dominions and powers, subdued all his enemies, and destroyed the last enemy—death (1 Cor 15:21–26).

As was the case in the Old Testament with David's wars, so too the battle belongs to God in the New Testament era. King David sang with joyful confidence that "with God we will gain the victory" (Ps 60:12). In like manner, the apostle Paul rejoiced with the Corinthian church that God "gives us the victory through our Lord Jesus Christ" over sin and death (1 Cor 15:57).

1 CHRONICLES 21:1–29:9

Original Meaning

David's Census (21:1–22:1). The Chronicler brings his own unique perspective to bear on the census. His primary concern is the relationship of the census-taking story to the centerpiece of his retelling of Israelite history—the Jerusalem temple. The purchase of the threshing floor becomes the foundational event for a series of actions by David to make ready for the building of Yahweh's temple. In the Chronicler's mind, what better place for God's permanent sanctuary than the site identified as the prime location for repentant prayer and divine absolution? The story of David's census-taking consists of three main episodes.

Episode 1 (21:1–7). Most likely the tally of the census (1,570,000 fighting men) should be understood as 1,100 units or cohorts (of an unspecified number of soldiers) of militia or even 1,100 "chiefs" or "outstanding warriors." More significant theologically is the Chronicler's understanding of the role of "Satan" in inciting David in 21:1. The word "Satan" is the transliteration of the Hebrew word *satan*, meaning "adversary;" in the Old Testament it is not so much a personal name as it is a role or function. As a result of God's progressive revelation during intervening centuries, the Hebrews came to understand the agency of Satan in relationship to God and the problem of evil. That is, as sovereign Lord, it is God's prerogative to use Satan as his agent of testing and/or judgment to accomplish his redemptive purposes in the created order. This fact, however, does not absolve David of his personal guilt in the matter.

Episode 2 (21:8–17). This episode opens with David's confession that he has "sinned greatly" (21:8). It seems that the offense is not so much a breach of ritual protocol as it is David's motive. Joab's strenuous objection to the king's request suggests that David orders the census as a tribute to his own strength and power rather than a testimony to God as the true warrior of Israel and the builder of Israel's army (21:3).

This episode also introduces Gad the prophet as David's "seer" (21:9). God sends him to David in response to the king's initial prayer of repentance for his action (21:8), and he offers the king three possible punishments as divine judgment for the folly of numbering of Israel (21:10–12).

The reaction of David and the elders of Israel to the sight of the destroying angel suggest they expected greater leniency in submitting to three days of the sword of Yahweh (21:16). Only then is David fully aware of the depth of his sin and the horrific consequences of his choice of punishment. All this brings David full circle to reiterate his admission that the census was his doing and that the people of Israel are "sheep," that is, innocent (21:17).

Episode 3 (21:18–27). The Chronicler interprets the divine command through Gad to build an altar at the site of Araunah's threshing floor as legitimizing a new altar for the sacrificial worship of the central shrine (cf. 21:28–29). The dire urgency of the situation is seen in the fact that the destroying angel is already at the threshing floor, presumably ready to kill Araunah and his sons (21:20).

The fire sent from heaven on the altar in answer to David's prayer of mercy is reminiscent of Elijah's contest with the prophets of Baal at Mount Carmel (1 Kgs 18:38). The sign of this fire confirms God's approval of David's atoning prayer and sacrificial offerings, as evidenced by the staying of the plague (1 Chr 21:26–27).

The difference in the price paid for Araunah's threshing floor as recorded in the parallel accounts of the transaction is usually attributed to the cost differential between the threshing floor proper (fifty shekels of silver, 2 Sam 24:24) and the tract of adjacent land required beyond the site for the altar in order to accommodate the entire temple complex (six hundred shekels of gold, 1 Chr 21:25).

Conclusion (21:28–22:1). The Chronicler adds a conclusion to this story to demonstrate the God-ordained continuity between worship centered in the Mosaic tabernacle (located in Gibeon) and the future temple of Yahweh in Jerusalem. The answer to David's prayer for God's mercy by the sign of fire sent from heaven upon the altar is presented as divine confirmation of this shift in the location for Israel's worship center (21:26). The theological addendum also explains why the Israelite sanctuary is transferred from Gibeon to Jerusalem, since David is unable to go to Gibeon to inquire of the Lord because of the "destroying angel" (cf. 21:16).

Preparations for the Temple (22:2–19). *David conscripts workers and gathers materials (22:2–5).* The emphasis in this paragraph is on the comprehensive nature of David's preparations for the building of the temple. The proximity of his own death and Solomon's youth and inexperience combine to motivate David's remarkable effort to organize the labor and secure the raw materials for the monumental project. In one sense, David is the prefabricator of Solomon's temple.

Four types of craftsmen are drafted into service as laborers for the temple project: stonecutters, masons, carpenters, and metal workers (22:2, 15; cf. 2 Chr 2:17–18). The "foreigners" (1 Chr 22:2) are non-Israelite inhabitants of territories occupied and controlled by Israel. The temple craftsmen work with four types of raw materials: stone, iron, bronze, and wood (22:2–4). The temple is a theological statement to the nations (22:5) about God's faithfulness to his covenant with David and the embodiment of his kingdom in the Israelite monarchy.

David's charge to Solomon (22:6–16). David's counsel recorded here is a private charge to his son Solomon to build Yahweh's temple, in anticipation of the later public commissioning of the crown prince (cf. 28:9–10). The section contrasts David as a "man of wars" with Solomon as a "man of peace and rest" (22:9) and is laden with allusions to Joshua's succession of Moses as Israel's leader.

The introduction to David's charge to Solomon (22:7–10) is generally understood to be a commentary of sorts on the Davidic covenant. The prophet Nathan's announcing the Davidic dynasty has been amplified in three ways: David may not build Yahweh's temple, Solomon may build the temple because the land now has "rest," and Solomon is recognized as the heir of the promise for the continuation of Davidic kingship (cf. 17:11).

The repetition of theme and the transfer of royal authority from David to Solomon reflect the commissioning of Joshua by Moses as his successor (22:11–13; cf. Deut 31; Josh 1). For example, both Moses and David are disqualified from achieving their ultimate goals, while both Joshua and Solomon lead God's people into an era of "rest" and "blessing."

The phrase "discretion and understanding" (22:12) occurs elsewhere only in King Hiram's letter to King Solomon, affirming these qualities in David's successor ("intelligence and discernment," 2 Chr 2:12). This expression combines the ideas of intelligence and insight. As in the case of Joshua's commission, however, true wisdom is connected to obedience to God's law (Josh 1:7–8).

David's actual charge to Solomon to build the temple is an invocation or prayer that offers encouragement, delineates the task at hand, and gives assurance of divine help. This threefold structure has been identified as the pattern in what is called the "induction into office" formula in Old Testament literature. Typically, the induction formula begins with a word of encouragement to the one about to enter the office. It then includes a description of the task to which the individual is called and concludes with the promise of divine accompaniment as enablement for the successful completion of the commission.

Many scholars consider the astronomical amounts of gold and silver that David provides for the temple project a form of hyperbole that means David gathers materials in quantities beyond measure or that he spares no expense in making extravagant provisions for Yahweh's temple. Whether or not the Chronicler's figures are a literary device or reflect reality, most biblical commentators miss the main focus, which is not on the opulence of the temple but on David's understanding of the inestimable worth of God.

David's charge to Israel's leaders (22:17–19). Following the private charge to Solomon, David issues a royal edict to all the leaders of Israel, who are expected to "help" (22:17) Solomon—a tacit admission that undertaking a building project of this magnitude demands the full support of the nation.

The same contingency for success given to Solomon applies

to the leaders of Israel (cf. 22:12). They too must "seek" the Lord (22:19), recognizing that this is the act of obedience to God's law, not a search for divine guidance. David envisions two distinct purposes for the temple as the sanctuary of God: housing the sacred vessels and furniture essential to Israel's worship, especially the ark of the covenant, and exalting the name of the Lord before his people and the nations (22:19).

Duties for the Levites (23:1–32). *Introduction (23:1).* The expression "old and full of years" is an epithet connoting great honor and places David among the Old Testament heroes of the faith (e.g., Abraham, Gen 25:8; Isaac, 35:29; Moses, Deut 34:7; Job, Job 42:17).

The census of the Levites (23:2–6a). The report of the census of the Levites provides the background for the subsequent registers of the three sons of Levi. David organized the Levites according to four distinct categories of labor: the work of the temple, officials and judges, gatekeepers, and musicians (23:3–5). This census should not be seen as a contradiction to the ill-advised military census previously ordered by David and implemented by Joab (ch. 21). The purpose of this census of the Levites is to establish a rotation of Levitical service for temple worship.

The three sons of Levi (23:6b–24). The genealogical table of Levi highlights his three sons in keeping with the order found elsewhere: Gershon, Kohath, and Merari. Apart from Moses (23:15–17), each family in the register is represented by three generations of descendants. The expression "heads of families" (23:24) in Chronicles denotes clan leaders or family elders (cf. 27:1). The census counts twenty-two families, nine each from Gershon and Kohath and four from Merari. The lack of harmonization with the twenty-four divisions of Levites enumerated later (chs. 24–25) and the twenty-two families of Levites outlined in the genealogical table suggest that this list dates to a different time period. We have already seen that the practice of annotating genealogies is common in Chronicles, so these expansions need not be regarded as secondary additions to the record.

Both the priests and the Levites are called "to minister" before the Lord and "pronounce blessings" in his name (23:13; cf. Deut 10:8). The distinctive service of the priests consists of consecrating holy things and of offering sacrifices (1 Chr 23:13). The priests are responsible to sanctify the vessels and furniture of the Lord's sanctuary and to maintain the holy status of these objects as they are utilized in worship. The expression "offer sacrifices" (literally, "burn incense" or "go up in smoke," 23:13) refers in general to the various types of ritual sacrifices superintended by the priests.

The duties of the Levites (23:25–32). Originally the Levites were porters for the tent-shrine and its furnishings. The shift from a portable to a permanent sanctuary for Israel's worship of Yahweh means that the duties for the Levites must be reassigned. David anticipates this need to restructure the duty roster of the Levites, perhaps on the basis of Moses's prediction that one day Israel will worship at a central sanctuary (cf. Deut 12:10).

In general, the Levites assist the priests in the service of the temple (1 Chr 23:28a). They are charged to help the priests minister before the Lord in three distinct realms: guarding the temple precincts (23:28b), cleaning and maintaining the precincts (23:28c), and aiding the priests in the daily sacrificial rituals (23:29). This duty roster for the Levites is less detailed than the catalog of Levitical services found earlier in the Chronicler's narrative (cf. 9:28–32).

In addition to their role as a supporting cast to the priesthood, the Levites are also in charge of the music that accompanies the rituals of temple worship (23:30–31). The key idea of the passage is the contribution of the Levites to the continuity of Israelite worship through the faithful discharging of their responsibilities, first in the tent of meeting and then in the temple of David and Solomon (23:32).

The Divisions of the Priests (24:1–31). *The descendants of Aaron (24:1–19).* The emphasis here is not one of liturgical function but rather one of organization for service (24:1–5). This is another case where the Chronicler has assumed the audience's knowledge of the priestly duties associated with the sacrificial worship of the temple. The writer's concern is twofold: the formal sanctioning of that duty roster by King David (24:3) and the propriety of carefully ordering priestly service by means of lot-casting (24:5).

The reference to "drawing lots" underscores the impartiality of the method in the assignment of priestly duties (24:5). The exact meaning of the titles "officials of the sanctuary" and "officials of God" is unclear (24:5). The phrases may be understood in apposition so as to clarify the nature of their position or the character of their service.

Shemaiah the scribe is mentioned only here (24:6) in the biblical records. The scribal tradition's association with the priestly class has a long history in the Old Testament, however (cf. Josh 18–21). By analogy to the institution of the Israelite monarchy with its royal "recorder" and royal "secretary" (2 Sam 8:16–17), it seems logical that the institution of the Israelite priesthood also had its official record keepers.

It is not clear if the names listed in the priestly register represent individuals or families or both. Many of the names found in the roster occur only here, so it is possible that the contents of the priestly rota (a fixed order of persons or duties) represent the divisional structure of the priesthood at the time of the writer.

The rest of the Levites (24:20–31). The roster of additional Levitical families updates the register found in 23:6–23 and assumes the reader's knowledge of that list. This section reporting the divisions of the priests is understood as a supplement to the report of David's organization of the Levites (ch. 23). The concluding report of the enrollment of the Levites by lot serves to link this unit (24:20–31) with the rota of priests (24:1–19).

The Temple Musicians (25:1–31). *The three musical guilds (25:1–7).* The Chronicler traces the origin of the temple music ministry in three Levitical families: Asaph, Heman, and Jeduthun (25:1). There is a sense in which these families represent musical guilds, as witnessed in their contribution to the Psalms (cf. Ps 73–89). Perhaps each family or guild has its own distinctive musical style or repertoire, or some other distinctive feature (note, e.g., the musical notations introducing the psalms of the Asaph and Korah collections, Ps 73–89).

David's organization of a corps of Levitical temple musicians is important to the legitimacy of music in worship as temple liturgy developed. This is another way for the Chronicler to connect his present with Israel's past, especially since the postexilic community is still bereft of Davidic kingship. For the Chronicler, the community is still linked to Davidic kingship, at least indirectly, through the temple worship he organized.

King David appoints the temple musicians in consultation with "commanders of the army" (25:1a). Although strong associations between musicians and the military are known in the ancient world, it is unclear whether these consultants are military personnel or Levitical officers since the meaning of the word "army" is flexible.

Music and singing are connected with Hebrew liturgy from its inception in the covenant code ratified at Mount Sinai. Singing to instrumental accompaniment seems to be the norm in the Old Testament. It is not surprising that David organizes the Levitical musical guilds responsible for the music of the temple liturgy since he himself accounts for nearly half of the songs in the Psalter. No doubt, his example of exuberant and skillful musicianship serves the Levitical corps well as they direct the worship of Israel.

The three families of musicians trace their lineage to Levi. Asaph is a descendant of Gershom, a son of Levi (6:39). Jeduthun is identified as a Levite; his ancestry is not traced, although the name appears in the titles of three psalms (Ps 39; 62; 77). Heman is a descendant of Kohath, another son of Levi (1 Chr 6:33; cf. Ps 88). The four sons of Asaph, the six sons of Jeduthun, and the fourteen sons of Heman account for the twenty-four divisions of temple musicians. Each is under the supervision of their father.

The twenty-four divisions of Levitical musicians (25:8–31). The opening verse bridges the two sections of the chapter in the collective reference to the preceding roster of Levitical musicians ("young and old alike, teacher as well as student," 1 Chr 25:8) and in the introduction of the lot-casting for assigned duties. The casting of lots is also the method used to determine the order of ministry for the priestly divisions (24:31) of the Levites and the gate assignments for the gatekeepers (26:13). The Israelites considered the drawing of lots (24:5) as an impartial selection process as well as a divinely superintended one, since they understood that the decision of the lot is from the Lord (Prov 16:33). It is unclear whether the lot-casting determines the composition and ministry routine of the Levitical singers or their rotation of liturgical service.

The reference to "young and old alike, teacher as well as student" (25:8) suggests a conservatory-like environment with emphasis on technique and skill level through training and rehearsal in addition to scheduled appearances for music ministry in the temple liturgy.

The Temple Gatekeepers (26:1–32). *The divisions of gatekeepers (26:1–19).* The first section of this chapter identifies two families of Levitical gatekeepers: Meshelemiah (26:1–3, 9) and Hosah (26:10–11). The family of Meshelemiah traces their heritage to the line of Korah through the family of Izhar and ultimately Kohath, one of the three sons of Levi (6:1–2, 22; 26:1).

The family of Hosah are descendants of Merari, another son of Levi (cf. Exod 6:16–19). During the days of the tabernacle, the Gershonites and the Merarites were the porters of the structural materials of the tabernacle (Num 4). Hosah is mentioned elsewhere as a gatekeeper in connection with the return of the ark of the covenant to Jerusalem by David (1 Chr 16:38). Shimri has the distinction of preeminence among Hosah's sons, despite the fact he is not the firstborn son (26:10, a practice known elsewhere in the Old Testament; cf. Ephraim in Gen 48:14).

The next unit (1 Chr 26:12–18) is a table of organization outlining the service assignments of the temple gatekeepers. Earlier in Chronicles we learned that during the days of the portable shrine, or Mosaic tabernacle, Phinehas was in charge of the gatekeepers (9:20). Beyond that, the status and authority vested in the temple gatekeepers come about as a result of the roles of King David and Samuel the seer in appointing the Levites (9:22). Clearly, the Chronicler does not want this fact lost upon his audience. The essential purpose of the expansion to his record of temple gatekeepers is the recounting of the ceremony for the specific gatekeeper assignments.

The final unit of this section enumerates a duty roster of sorts, indicating the number of Levites stationed at the various posts during the daily watches (26:16b–18). The temple gatekeepers serve two by two, and there are apparently twenty-four daily assignments.

The summary statement tracing the divisions of the temple gatekeepers to two of the sons of Levi, Kohath indirectly (from Izhar to Korah) and Merari (directly), legitimizes or sanctions these Levitical servants by means of their genealogy (26:19). The conclusion also attaches the family of Obed-Edom to the Kohathites through Korah (cf. 26:15, 19).

Treasurers and administrative officials (26:20–32). The second section of this chapter may be divided into two distinct units: the list of Levites who serve as treasurers (26:20–28) and those who hold administrative posts outside the temple precinct of Jerusalem (26:29–32). The two rosters complete the catalog of the various registers of Levites and their assigned duties (chs. 23–26). The unity of the two paragraphs is supplied by the genealogical framework of the four Kohathite families mentioned by the Chronicler (or his source, 26:23).

Other Levites have supervision of the two temple treasuries: one identified as storage for the treasures of "the house of God" and the other for the storage of "dedicated things" (26:20). Such duties are logical assignments for the Levites since the storehouses are located near the temple gates.

Two special groups of Levites are placed in charge of public administration in regions west of the Jordan River (26:29–32). The two Levitical families singled out for civil service outside the environs of Jerusalem and among the Israelite tribes in the Transjordan are the Izharites (26:29) and the Hebronites (26:30–32). Thus, three of the four Levitical families mentioned earlier (26:23) are accounted for, namely, the Amramites, who serve as temple treasurers (26:24–28); the Izharites, who serve as "officials and judges" (26:29); and the Hebronites, who discharge duties related to the "work of the Lord" and the "king's service" (26:30–32). Though cited as one of the four Levitical families contributing to the civil-service workforce (26:23), the Uzzielites are not mentioned.

The date formula (26:31) suggests these Levitical assignments are made in the last year of David's reign. The Chronicler's purpose in reporting the Levitical presence in the public administration of the united monarchy is unclear. He may be attempting to legitimize the role of the Levites in offices of civil service at his own time or calling for their involvement in that role based on the earlier precedent.

Military and Political Officials (27:1–34). *David's military commanders (27:1–15).* The first verse should be understood as the heading to the section treating the divisions of David's army (27:2–15), not the entire chapter. Rather than a standing army, the military divisions described in 27:2–15 represent a militia or citizen army, perhaps akin to our National Guard. David carefully organizes his army in twelve divisions.

Tribal officers (27:16–24). The brief but important paragraph explaining why no census statistics are recorded for the tribes of Israel in the book of the annals of King David (27:23–24) is significant. The report of Joab's failure to complete the census is not an effort by the Chronicler to transfer blame from David to Joab. Rather, the writer assumes the audience's knowledge of the parallel account in Samuel. The record notes Joab's aversion to the task and God's judgment against David and Israel for the king's presumption in equating political strength with the size of his military forces (2 Sam 24:3, 10; cf. 1 Chr 21:3, 7–8).

Implicit in the reference to the Abrahamic covenant to make Israel as numerous as the stars in the sky is the sovereignty of God in "growing" Israel as a nation (27:23; cf. Gen 12:2). David has compromised God's rule over Israel.

The king's overseers (27:25–31). A portion of the revenue necessary to meet the expenses of the bureaucracy established by King David is generated by income from crown properties. Material wealth is not only necessary to offset expenditures of the centralized government, but it enhances the king's prestige. Generally, the Old Testament sees such wealth as a sign of God's blessing on the king's reign, although the Mosaic provision for kingship prohibited the amassing of large treasuries by the king (Deut 17:17). Naturally these crown properties need responsible supervision, and the twelve officials named as overseers are in keeping with the pattern used by David in the administration of both the religious and the political sectors.

David's advisers (27:32–34). This list of David's personal advisers is usually contrasted with the registers delineating the king's public counselors and the official members of his royal cabinet (cf. 18:14–17; also 2 Sam 8:15–18; 20:23–26). It seems clear that the contents of the roster span the long reign of King David. The chapter concludes the description of the structure and key personnel of David's administration. Beyond the inauguration of governmental organization by David, the real purpose of chapters 23–27 for the Chronicler is the important message that "all Israel" is behind the king in his plans to build the temple.

Architectural Plans for the Temple (28:1–21). *David's charge to the leaders of Israel (28:1–8).* It is unclear exactly how this assembly of Israelite officials (28:1) compares with other reports of administrative personnel summoned to Jerusalem in this larger unit of the Chronicler's history (chs. 22–29). This congress of leaders is probably distinct from the "whole assembly" in 29:1 since the "people" were a part of that larger gathering (see 29:9).

The opening lines of David's speech are a historical summary of sorts, outlining his aspirations for building Yahweh's temple (28:2–3). The expressions "house . . . of rest" for the temple and "footstool" (28:2) for the ark of the covenant are found only in Psalm 132 and Chronicles. Clearly, Psalm 132 is important to the Chronicler because it contains reflections about David's restless ambition to build a sanctuary for God.

The royal footstool (1 Chr 28:2) is a symbol of a king's authority, a symbol of the peaceful rest enjoyed by his kingdom. By means of this symbol the Chronicler recognizes that Israel's "rest," whether in David's time or his own, is entwined with God's restful presence among his people.

It is widely agreed that the next segment of David's speech to the officials of Israel serves to legitimize his dynasty both retrospectively and prospectively. By way of the past, David traces his lineage to the tribe of Judah, the tribe given the "scepter" in Jacob's blessing of his sons (cf. Gen 49:8–12). By way of the future, David points to the selection of Solomon as his successor. Indeed, God's choice of Solomon from among David's many sons makes his divine election all the more remarkable (1 Chr 28:5; David had nineteen sons, see 3:1–9).

The emphasis on Solomon as the "chosen . . . son" (28:6) among David's children leads naturally to the understanding that God's kingdom and David's kingdom are inseparably linked. In one sense, God adopts Solomon as his own son (28:6), and the Davidic throne is also the "throne of the kingdom of the LORD over Israel" (28:5). Perhaps most importantly, as David passes the baton to his son Solomon, he exhorts Israel to look to God for their hope and help—not to himself or even his dynasty (28:8).

David commissions Solomon (28:9–10). The public transfer of power accomplished "in the sight of all Israel" (28:8) completes the succession ritual begun with David's private charge to his son (22:11–13). Both admonitions link Solomon's success to his obedience to God's law, and both urge the new king to "be strong" (22:13; 28:10). The king's general exhortation to obedience continues that thematic emphasis in 28:9 and is followed by the specific command to build the Lord's temple (28:10).

The Chronicler's understanding of Solomon's divine election to the Davidic throne is unusual in that he is the only Old Testament writer to apply the word "chosen" to Solomon (28:10). All those individuals "chosen" by God to fill leadership positions in the earlier Old Testament era did so by means other than those established by socially accepted convention—except Solomon. There is a sense, however, in which Solomon's accession is also out of the ordinary in that he is not David's oldest living son and hence is not the logical heir to the throne.

Transfer of the temple plans (28:11–21). The detailed instructions handed over to Solomon deal with temple architecture (28:11–12), temple personnel (28:13), temple furnishings (28:14–19), and the final commissioning of Solomon as the crown prince (28:20–21). The influence of the tabernacle narrative is clearly evident in the vocabulary and theology of the passage. For the Chronicler, the temple is the continuation of all that the tabernacle represented in Israelite religion, and David plays a role similar to that of Moses as God's agent in establishing the institution.

The exact nature of the plans and instructions David gives to Solomon for the execution of the temple building project is unknown. It seems clear they are written plans, probably sketches or blueprints of sorts containing specific directions (28:19). Since the actual floor plan of the temple sanctuary proper is similar to the dimensions of the tabernacle, the plans most likely deal with issues related to the permanence of this structure in contrast to the portable tabernacle. In addition, the portico, the anterooms, and the courts are new elements in the construction plans, and they receive primary attention (28:11). The two treasuries are prominently featured in the plans (28:12), most likely because they were cited previously in connection with the duties of the Levites (26:22–28).

The accessories important to the temple rituals include gold and silver vessels and implements (28:14–17). The gold and silver vessels are especially important to the Chronicler because they are among the goods the Persians restored to the Jews when they returned to the land after the Babylonian exile (cf. Ezra 1:7–11). Thus, they are tangible representations of the continuity of postexilic temple worship with preexilic temple worship. But more important, they are tokens of God's faithfulness in preserving and restoring his covenant people.

The table displaying the consecrated bread (1 Chr 28:16) is a notable feature of both the tabernacle and temple furnishings because it symbolizes God's constant presence and provision for his people. The "chariot" (28:18) is unmentioned elsewhere in the listings of tabernacle and temple furnishings. The ark is given special emphasis in the inventory of temple furnishings by virtue of its placement at the end of the list (28:18).

David's final speech concludes with a third charge to Solomon as his successor to the throne of Israel (28:20–21). It is significant that the third and final charge to Solomon as he is inducted into office mentions a supporting cast that includes the religious leaders, the various guilds of craftsmen, the political leaders, and all the people (28:21). The temple is to be a national response to the God of Israel by his covenant people—not a monument to King David!

Gifts for Temple Construction (29:1–9). *David's speech (29:1–5).* David's exhortation to the people to fully support Solomon, given his youth and inexperience, echoes concern in the king's first speech (cf. 22:5). The first speech contained a general call to the leaders and the people to support Solomon by devoting themselves to God (22:19). This third speech provides the tangible means to demonstrate their devotion to God and support for the crown prince, Solomon—sacrificially giving of their material resources to the temple building fund.

The parallels between the giving of the Israelites for the

building of the Mosaic tabernacle and the Solomonic temple are widely recognized. The identification of the gold given by David as "gold of Ophir" (29:4) probably refers as much to the quality of the gold as to its source of origin. As with the tabernacle, only the best of natural and human resources is to be given for the construction of Yahweh's earthly sanctuary.

David's speech includes several unusual terms, each one highlighting a theological truth important to the transition of power from father to son. The word translated "palatial structure" (29:1) is used to describe a citadel or a fortress elsewhere in the Old Testament. Only the Chronicler uses the expression as a synonym for the temple. The word is an apt reminder to Solomon and the people that the kingdom belongs to God and that he is the one enthroned over Israel.

A second word, "personal treasures" (29:3), is typically used to describe Israel as God's "special possession." This "treasure" is highly valued personal property of the king; this cache was extremely important to rulers in the biblical world because it was kept in reserve as insurance against unforeseen political misfortunes or natural calamities. David's example of selfless giving in the yielding of goods stored for his own personal security becomes the catalyst for the generous outpouring of gifts for the temple project from the leaders and the people.

Last, the repetition of the verbal root meaning "gave willingly" (Heb. *ndb*) introduces a key theme in the entire chapter (cf. 29:5, 6, 9, 14, 17). The word often denotes freewill gifts and offerings, giving that is not required but prompted by a willing heart or spirit. The issue is not the amassing of glittering jewels and precious metals but the pouring of themselves as God's people into building the temple as a symbol of the wholehearted worship that will soon take place in that sanctuary.

The people's response (29:6–9). Several themes important to the Chronicler are knit together in the response of the Israelites to David's speech. The first is that of unity among the leadership. A second emphasis is that of a charitable attitude—they "gave willingly" (29:6b). It is a proven leadership principle that generosity needs an example. The open-handed giving of Israelite leaders serves as an inducement for a similar response on the part of the people.

The quantities of precious metals given by the leaders of Israel are enormous (about 190 tons plus another 185 pounds of gold and about 375 tons of silver). These contributions nearly double the gifts of gold and silver made by David (29:4). The Israelites honor God with their wealth since it all belongs to him anyway.

Application. Leadership is a matter of universal importance, and effective supervision is essential to the survival of any social group, political organization, or religious institution. The impact of good or bad leadership has been felt by every generation of human history. The same is no less true today—and perhaps more so, given the "global village" that the new communications technologies have created. The challenges confronting effective leadership, however, are timeless because basic human needs remain essentially the same regardless of the historical period. Naturally, successful management principles discovered by leaders in bygone eras are often understood to be transferable, as the plethora of self-help books appealing to historical figures as models for today's executives attest.

No biblical character is more prominent as an example of leadership than King David:

- David had charisma. More important than his abilities, however, was the empowerment of the Holy Spirit in his life (1 Sam 16:13).
- David well understood the importance of vision, as demonstrated in his conquest of Jerusalem (2 Sam 5:6–10). That victory legitimized King David and propelled Israel into nationhood. It also became the impetus for David's lifelong quest to build a sanctuary for Yahweh in the very city that God helped him capture (cf. 1 Chr 22:1).
- This section of 1 Chronicles (21:1–29:9) offers an excellent illustration of David's ability to define the vision (i.e., build a house for Yahweh), structure the plan to accomplish the vision, and motivate others to implement and fulfill the vision.
- David clearly understood the benefits of delegating authority to others as evidenced by his roster of cabinet appointees.
- David shows us that a servant-leader can survive a grave mistake, an error of judgment, or a near fatal flaw because of God's mercy.
- The final acts of David's kingship included naming his successor and providing that individual with all the resources needed to carry on David's vision for Israel (cf. 21:1–29:9). David built a bridge to the future through Solomon for all Israel for several centuries beyond his own death.

1 CHRONICLES 29:10–30

Original Meaning

David's Prayer (29:10–20). *Doxology (29:10–12).* A hymn or doxology tends to offer praise to God in general terms for his greatness and faithfulness as creator. The repeated word "praise" (Heb. *baruk*, 29:10, 20) may be rendered alternately in English as "praise" (so NIV) or "bless" (so NRSV). Here David "blesses" God as an act of homage or reverence because God is the source of all blessing.

The key theme of the doxology is the eternal kingdom of God (29:11d). David equates God's kingdom with the entirety of the created order (29:11c, 12a) and acknowledges that temporal human kingdoms (including his own) can only survive and thrive as they concede all power and strength and honor and wealth belong to God alone.

Thanksgiving (29:13–16). Typically, a song of thanksgiving opens with a statement of the worshiper's gratitude (29:13), moves to a narration of some past experience of God's gracious help in a time of need (29:14–15), and concludes by confessing Yahweh's graciousness and goodness (29:16). David continues his priestly role here, expressing the gratitude of the people in the collective "we" (29:13). David appeals to the imagery of the resident alien to remind his audience that they are utterly dependent on God for their security and physical well-being. No doubt the Chronicler inveighs David's blessing for the purpose of inspiring this same attitude of humble faith in his own audience.

To reinforce the idea that God's people are resident aliens in this life, David offers the evidence of the brevity and frailty of human life ("our days . . . are like a shadow," 29:15). The concluding confession in 29:16 reiterates 29:12 in extolling God as the source of all gifts.

Supplication (29:17–19). David's blessing closes with a petition for the people of his realm: "Keep their hearts loyal to you" (29:18). The Chronicler can seek nothing more significant for his own audience. The heart is crucial to physical and spiritual life. David knows that divine tests are essential to a healthy spiritual life (29:17), and prominent on the answer key are two words, "integrity" and "honest intent" (29:17).

Finally, David is sensitive to the need of a role model for the people, an individual who can foster honesty and integrity within the Israelite community by virtue of personal example. Hence, David petitions for his son Solomon, that he might exhibit "wholehearted devotion" through obedience to the law of God (29:19).

Response (29:20). The worship response of the people includes the recitation of a doxology and bodily prostration, a common worship posture in the Old Testament. David mentions the "God of our fathers" in his prayer (29:18), and this phrase is repeated in the report of the people's worship response (29:20). Spiritual linkage to the past is a crucial element in the Chronicler's theology of hope for the postexilic nation, demonstrated in the more than twenty-five occurrences of this phrase in Chronicles.

The report that the people do obeisance in reverence to "the Lord and the king" is both striking and theologically significant. The king of Israel is the anointed of God, and the occupant of the royal office is God's servant. The throne of Israel, however, belongs to Yahweh, and to bow to the king is ultimately to bow to God, who has installed the king as his agent of justice and righteousness.

Solomon Anointed a Second Time (29:21–25). The second day of the festival (29:21) is a celebration of God's provision of an heir to David's legacy. The Chronicler indicates Solomon is anointed a "second time" (29:22). It seems likely this installation ceremony for King Solomon is the formal and public sequel to the hurried and private appointment of Solomon as David's successor. The anointing of Zadok probably refers to his promotion (or reappointment under a new king) to the office of high priest.

The record of the pledge of loyalty by David's mercenary guard and the other princes (29:24) is a significant political datum. The stability of the Davidic throne was twice challenged by rivals within the royal family: by Absalom (2 Sam 15–18) and by Adonijah (1 Kings 1). Solomon knows that such an oath of allegiance is crucial to the smooth transfer of power in the aftermath of Adonijah's attempted coup. It is significant that the prince (i.e., Solomon), with the support of David's mercenary guard, is eventually installed as David's successor.

The summary statement touting the glory of Solomon's reign prior to the account of David's death is unusual. The alteration in the format calls attention to the place of "all Israel" (29:25) in this new regime, a key theme in Chronicles. In fact, the word of measure, "all," occurs frequently in this literary unit. It expresses both the totality of God's rule and the unity of the Israelites as God's people. No doubt the Chronicler envisions a similar scenario: all Israel once again unified under a divinely ordained Davidic ruler.

David's Death (29:26–30). Unlike Kings, the Chronicler inserts the phrase "son of Jesse" (29:26). The point is to remind his audience of the selection process by which David came to the throne of Israel (cf. 1 Sam 16). I suspect the key episode in the whole narrative for the Chronicler is the criterion by which the prophet Samuel was instructed to make his choice among the sons of Jesse (1 Sam 16:7).

The role of David and Solomon in solidifying the tribes into a nation cannot be overlooked, given the repetition of the phrase "all Israel" for the fourth time (1 Chr 29:21, 23, 25, 26). Implicit in all this is God's faithfulness in making good on his promise to make Israel into a great nation (Gen 12:2; 22:16–18). The reference to Solomon as David's successor (1 Chr 29:28b) is both a statement of simple fact and a subtle reminder that in Solomon God has fulfilled his promise to the house of David through Nathan the prophet.

The bibliographic citation to the records of the prophets Samuel, Nathan, and Gad (29:29) probably refers to the books of Samuel and Kings and perhaps an additional source available to the Chronicler. The writer is careful to inform his audience that his record of David's reign is based reliably on the authoritative word of God's prophets.

The interplay of the nation of Israel with the kingdoms of the other people groups surrounding the Hebrews is an important dimension of the Chronicler's history because God's sovereign hand is seen in that arena as well. Thus, the reference to foreign policy in this passage serves as a retrospective summary of the record of David's imperialistic expansion found in chapters 18–20. This phrase is prospective in that it anticipates Israel's interaction with the nations in 2 Chronicles, especially the ancient superpowers of Assyria and Babylonia.

Application. Social critics have observed that the American right to pursue happiness in the form of instant emotional "fixes" has created a society addicted to fun but bereft of joy. Interestingly, the thematic structure of the psalm of lament speaks to this dichotomy in that the lament typically concludes with a "vow of praise." The vow of praise is testimony both to the sovereignty of God in human circumstance (i.e., affirmation of Yahweh's ability to change the situation if he wills to intervene) and to the goodness of God's character (i.e., the recognition that God is good whether or not he chooses to intervene and remedy a situation). This helps explain the Chronicler's report that the people of Israel "ate and drank with great joy in the presence of the LORD" at the coronation of King Solomon (29:22). He apprehends the theological truth that joy is connected to the person and presence of God (cf. 16:27).

2 CHRONICLES

INTRODUCTION TO 2 CHRONICLES

Second Chronicles begins with Solomon's reign of the united kingdom. His rule includes the construction and dedication of the temple (chs. 2–7). Upon Solomon's death (ch. 9), the narrative turns to describe the long history of the divided kingdom and the eventual demise of both kingdoms. The last chapter in the book details the fall of Jerusalem (36:15–21). See also the Introduction to 1 Chronicles above (p. 320) for commentary on the authorship, composition, and dating of 1–2 Chronicles.

BOOK OUTLINE

I. United Monarchy (Continued from 1 Chronicles): Solomon's Reign (1:1–9:31)
II. Early History of Judah (10:1–32:33)
- A. Four Kings and the Prophetic Voice (10:1–21:3)
- B. Judah and the Dynasty of Ahab (21:4–23:21)
- C. Three Kings and the Decline of Judah (24:1–26:23)
- D. Three Kings and the Assyrian Threat (27:1–32:33)

III. Later History of Judah (33:1–36:21)
- A. Three Kings and Repentance (33:1–36:1)
- B. Four Kings and the Exile of Judah (36:2–21)

IV. Epilogue: The Decree of Cyrus (36:22–23)

2 CHRONICLES 1:1–9:31

Original Meaning

Solomon's Kingship (1:1–17). *Solomon's worship (1:1–6).* The Chronicler provides narrative connectors as the story shifts from the rule of King David to King Solomon by means of intertextuality (i.e., the demonstration of a literary interdependence between texts or documents through the repetition of words, phrases, and ideas). For instance, the reference to "all Israel" (1:2) hearkens back to the unity of God's people under King David as Israel's divinely appointed leader. Solomon's assembly at Gibeon (1:3) is clearly patterned after the account of David's plans to relocate the ark of the covenant in Jerusalem (including references to the same Hebrew officials, worship by means of the bronze altar and the tent of meeting, and the repetition of the verb "to inquire of" the Lord, cf. 1 Chr 13:1–6).

Solomon begins his rule over Israel with an act of public worship (1 Chr 1:1–6). In terms of biblical chronology, Solomon's accession to David's throne occurs around 970 BC. The prayer and ritual sacrifice offered at Gibeon is symbolic of the new king's primary task, as the acts of piety show Solomon to be a fitting candidate for building Yahweh's temple.

The pilgrimage to Gibeon is a reconnection with the ancient Hebrew religious traditions. Solomon's petition for wisdom and knowledge (1:10) is rooted in his worship experience before Bezalel's altar (cf. Exod 38:1–2). It is clear that in identifying Solomon as a "second Bezalel," the Chronicler understands the greatest demonstration of his wisdom to be the construction of the temple itself. The king's presentation of burnt offerings on the altar in Gibeon stands as a witness to his intentions to keep his father's charge to obey the laws of the Lord and thereby preserve the worship of his ancestors (cf. 1 Chr 28:7–8). The propensity "to inquire" (2 Chr 1:5) of God is one measure of the faithfulness of the leaders of Israel (e.g., 1 Chr 10:14; 2 Chr 22:9).

Solomon's wisdom (1:7–13). Solomon seeks God by means of ritual sacrifice (1:6) and prayer (1:8–10). Interestingly, in response to Solomon's worship at Gibeon, God inquires of Solomon by asking him to request anything he wants—a blank check of sorts signed by God himself (1:7). This divine invitation prompts Solomon's petition for wisdom (1:10).

Here Solomon is a model of how the righteous should pray, because he first inquires or seeks God. He then couches his prayer in the history of God's "great kindness" to David (1:8), acknowledging that the Lord has indeed proven himself as a good God. Next, Solomon voices his humility and dependence on God in his rhetorical question, "Who is able to govern this great people of yours?" (1:10). Beyond this, Solomon seeks spiritual blessing over material blessing in asking God for wisdom and knowledge to rule instead of personal wealth and riches (1:10–11).

In his petition to "confirm" the promises made to his father (1:9), Solomon is not placing demands on God in his arrogance as David's successor. Rather, he is simply asking God to be consistent with his character. With his request for "wisdom and knowledge" (1:10), Solomon looks forward to the fulfillment of God's promise to David, since it is tied to the completion of the temple (6:17).

Both Kings and Chronicles agree on the purpose of Solomon's request: able leadership "to govern" the people of Israel (1:10; cf. 1 Kgs 3:9). Solomon asks for wisdom and knowledge and receives wealth, riches, and honor as a bonus (2 Chr 1:11–12).

After worshiping in Gibeon, Solomon returns to Jerusalem (1:13). The summary statement "and he reigned over Israel" (1:13b) reconnects the Gibeon experience with Solomon's efforts to establish himself as king in Israel. Clearly the Chronicler wants his audience to understand a cause-and-effect relationship between Solomon's worship of God and his firm rule of Israel.

Solomon's wealth (1:14–17). The third defining characteristic of King Solomon's reign is his accumulation of unprecedented riches. The Chronicler's rationale for framing the story of Solomon with the description of the staggering wealth possessed by the king is to demonstrate God's faithfulness in fulfilling his promise cited in 1:12. Implicit in the reference to the size of Solomon's bank account is the idea of God's favor resting on a faithful king. In this way the Chronicler affirms God's adoption of the Davidic dynasty as "his son" (cf. 1 Chr 17:13). The threefold measure of Solomon's wealth includes military hardware (2 Chr 1:14), precious metals (1:15), and profits from international trade (1:16).

Construction of the Temple (2:1–5:1). *Solomon's preparations for building the temple (2:1–18).* The Chronicler understands Solomon's building campaign as a two-phased undertaking—the "temple for the Name of the LORD" and his own royal palace (2:1). This datum helps explain the timing of the Lord's appearance to Solomon, after both the temple and the palace complex have been completed (7:11). The actual construction of the temple begins in the fourth year of Solomon's reign (ca. 966 BC; cf. 1 Kgs 6:1) and is completed six years later (960 BC).

Solomon makes requests of Hiram in 2 Chronicles 2:3–9. In return for raw building materials, Solomon will provide Hiram with supplies of wheat, barley, honey, and olive oil (2:10). The foodstuffs bartered for the lumber are sent overland to Tyre, while the timbers are floated down to Joppa from Tyre in rafts (2:16). The more interesting features of the correspondence are the synopsis of temple worship (2:4) and theological treatise (2:5–6) Solomon offers the Phoenician king.

The ritual observances cited by Solomon show a full knowledge of the Mosaic law: the daily altar of incense and bread of presence offerings (cf. Exod 25:30; 30:7), the morning and evening burnt offerings (cf. 29:38–39), and the offerings pertaining to the ritual calendar (i.e., Sabbath, New Moon, and the pilgrimage festivals; cf. 23:14–19; 31:13; Num 10:10). As to theology, Solomon underscores God's omnipotence and transcendence to his royal counterpart in Phoenicia—quite an apologetic to the Tyrian worshiper of Baal!

The census of Solomon's labor force (2 Chr 2:17–18) clarifies the earlier report of the numbers of workers conscripted for the temple and palace building projects (2:2). This census clearly followed the ill-fated numbering of Israel by David (2:17b).

Solomon builds the temple (3:1–17). The Chronicler compresses the temple construction into fourteen verses (3:1–14). The building of Yahweh's temple at Mount Moriah fulfills the plans made by David for the structure in the purchase of Araunah's threshing floor (3:1; cf. 1 Chr 21:25–26). The reference to Mount Moriah awakens memories of the Lord's appearance to Abraham at the near sacrifice of Isaac his son (cf. Gen 22).

The Chronicler has placed the focus on the floor plan of the structure. Ancient Israel used two different standards for measuring the cubit (2 Chr 3:3). The short cubit (17.4 inches) and the long cubit (20.4 inches) were based on an Egyptian standard of six and seven palm lengths. The dimensions of Solomon's temple rendered in contemporary equivalents (using the short cubit) compute as follows: The sanctuary proper is ninety feet long, thirty feet wide, and forty-five feet high (with the Holy Place measuring 60′ × 30′ by 45′ and the Most Holy Place measuring 30′ × 30′ × 45′); the porch or portico extends the temple by another fifteen feet in length (i.e., 30′ wide × 30′ high). The walls of the portico are overlaid with gold (3:4b), not only enhancing the beauty of the entrance but having the practical effect of reflecting light into the building.

The Chronicler next describes the sanctuary of the temple (3:5–7; cf. 1 Kgs 6:20–22). The pinewood walls of the main hall are overlaid with gold and decorated with palm tree and chain motifs (2 Chr 3:5). The precious stones collected by David also adorn the main hall in some unspecified way. The rest of the interior is also overlaid with gold from Parvaim (an unknown site, 3:6–7a).

Winged cherubim are also engraved on the gold overlay of the temple walls (3:7b). The cherubim of the Bible are angelic creatures combining numerous human and animal features (e.g., Exod 37:7–9; Ezek 41:18–19). The combination of extensive gold overlay and the presence of the cherubim represent the beauty and majesty of a royal throne room, a fitting dwelling place for the Lord. Two cherubim are fixed atop the cover of the ark of the covenant as well (Exod 25:18–20). The repeated artistic motifs of the palm tree and the chain design may represent the ideas of life and eternality—the domains of God as creator.

The extravagant use of gold overlay extends into the Most Holy Place (2 Chr 3:8–9). Much of the description of the Most Holy Place is devoted to the two massive sculptures of cherubim figures with outstretched wings that fill the room (3:10–13). Like the cherubim that guarded the entrance to the garden after the fall (Gen 3:24), these creatures guard the ark of the covenant eventually installed in the Most Holy Place (2 Chr 5:7–8). Except for that one day in the year when the high priest entered the Most Holy Place to sprinkle the blood of the Day of Atonement sacrifice, this sacred space was pitch black. Yet, in terms of the symbolic divine presence resting there, the Hebrews know that "darkness is as light" to God (Ps 139:12).

A veil woven of blue, purple, and scarlet yarn separated the Holy Place from the Most Holy Place in the Mosaic tabernacle or tent of meeting (Exod 26:31–36). The veil of Solomon's temple replicates that tapestry, including the decorative embroidery of cherubim worked into the fabric (2 Chr 3:14). The temple also has wooden doors overlaid with gold, including the inner doors to the Most Holy Place (4:22).

As with the veil, the bronze pillars in the front of the temple are given separate attention (3:15–17). Beyond the uncertainty of the origin and the function of pillars, they achieve additional notoriety because of the enigmatic names ascribed to each (Jakin and Boaz, 3:17). Jakin means "he establishes," and Boaz may mean "strength is in him."

The temple furnishings (4:1–5:1). The Sea of cast metal (4:2–5) replaces the laver of the Mosaic tabernacle (cf. Exod 30:17–21). It holds 3,000 baths (about 17,500 gallons). The ten golden lampstands replace the one lampstand featured in the Mosaic tabernacle (2 Chr 4:7; cf. Exod 25:31–36). The ten tables are mentioned only here in the Old Testament descriptions of the Solomon's temple (2 Chr 4:8). The Chronicler seems to assume that the ten lampstands rest on the ten tables. The insertion of the description of the courtyard of the priests completes the report of the Sea by noting its location in the southeast corner of the courtyard (4:9–10). The summary of Huram-Abi's achievements (4:11–16) completes the record of the skilled smiths sent by King Hiram of Tyre (2:13–14).

The reference to the deposit of David's war booty in the temple treasuries (5:1) serves as a transition to the account of the installation of the ark of the covenant. This verse also recalls the plunder taken from the Egyptians used in the construction of the Mosaic tabernacle (Exod 12:36). In both cases, the wealth of the nations contributes to the building of God's sanctuaries.

Dedication of the Temple (5:2–7:22). *The installation of the ark of the covenant (5:2–6:2).* The transfer of the ark of the covenant comes almost verbatim from 1 Kings 8:1–13. The ark was the single most sacred object associated with the Mosaic tabernacle. The Chronicler is careful to note that the Levites serve as porters for the ark while in transit, while the priests are required to station the ark in the Most Holy Place (2 Chr 5:4, 7–8). The installation of the ark and the dedication of the temple are held in conjunction with the Feast of Tabernacles (5:3). The rest of the sacred furniture from the tent of meeting, as well as the tent itself, is also transported to the temple precinct (5:4–5).

Simultaneously with the installation of the ark, Solomon and the assembly of Israel offer sacrifices in the temple court (5:6). The reference to the tablets of Moses as the only contents of the ark of the covenant (5:10) indicates that the Chronicler is familiar with the tradition that the ark held additional contents at one time.

The reference to the Levitical musicians (5:11–13) in the final paragraph (5:11–6:2) reflects the Chronicler's special interests in the musical tradition of the temple. The hymnic refrain "he is good; his love endures forever" (5:13) is a liturgical response associated with other festal gatherings in Chronicles. The word "good" calls to mind God as creator and the goodness of his creation, while "love" evokes the Mount Sinai experience and God's covenant relationship with Israel.

Following the pattern of the dedication of the tabernacle, the cloud of God's glory fills the temple after the priests install the ark in the Most Holy Place (5:14; cf. Exod 40:34–35). This account of the event is told from a priestly perspective in terms of their service rendered in the temple. Later the event is retold from the perspective of Solomon and the assembly of Israel as the ceremonies for the temple dedication come to an end (2 Chr 7:1–2).

Solomon addresses the assembly of Israel (6:3–11). After Solomon has turned from the dazzling spectacle of the cloud of Yahweh's glory filling the temple (5:14), he addresses the "whole assembly of Israel" (6:3). Like his father, David, Solomon assumes a priestly or pastoral role when addressing the nation of Israel (cf. 1 Chr 16:43). The Chronicler, however, portrays Solomon as one who represents the interests of the people more than the office of the Levitical priesthood. He blessed the populace as one of them.

The contents of Solomon's blessing show him to be not only a pastor, but also a theologian. Appropriately, the king begins his address with praise to God—a blessing learned from his father. The reference to the "God of Israel" (6:4) and the repetition of the word "chosen" (6:5–6) allude to the Abrahamic covenant (Gen 12:1–3). The allusion to the exodus (2 Chr 6:5) reveals that Solomon understands the historical and theological continuity between the Mosaic covenant and the Davidic covenant. Finally, the acknowledgment that Jerusalem is now the place identified with God's "Name" (6:6) demonstrates Solomon's awareness of the teaching of Deuteronomy concerning an eventual permanent worship site in Israel (cf. Deut 12:11, 21).

The second half of Solomon's address to the people of Israel is basically a prayer of thanksgiving, acknowledging God as a promise keeper (2 Chr 6:7–11). The king specifically cites his succession to David's throne (6:10a), the completion of the temple (6:10b), and the installation of the ark of the covenant (6:11) as proof positive that Yahweh is faithful to his word.

Solomon's prayer of dedication (6:12–42). The fact that Solomon's prayer occupies more text than the actual construction of the temple further substantiates the argument that the Chronicler is making a theological statement to his own audience about the centrality of prayer in the life of the postexilic community.

The opening paragraph lists the preparations undertaken by Solomon for his dedicatory prayer for the Jerusalem temple (6:12–13). Chronicles expands the Kings' version by including details related to the bronze platform on which the king offers his prayer to the Lord God of Israel (6:13; cf. 1 Kgs 8:22).

The bronze platform is most likely a temporary structure erected in the outer court of the temple precinct. Solomon's posture of standing before the altar and the assembly of Israel prior to praying suggests he has taken on a priestly role as a representative of the people (2 Chr 6:12). The backdrop of the bronze altar of burnt offering for the prayer of dedication points to the idea that prayer is also a form of sacrifice. Standing, kneeling, and spreading the hands are common prayer postures in biblical times.

Solomon first petitions God to bless him with a posterity so that the Davidic throne may be established forever (6:14–17; cf. 2 Sam 7:13, 15). The threefold repetition of God's covenant name, "Lord, God of Israel" (2 Chr 6:14, 16, 17) addresses his majesty as Lord of creation (cf. 6:18), while the emphasis on his covenant love speaks to his uniqueness and incomparability as the one true God (6:14). Solomon's prayer for the continuation of the Davidic dynasty is ultimately the Chronicler's prayer as well.

This section of Solomon's entreaty includes two distinct segments: the fundamental theological principles of intercessory prayer (2 Chr 6:18–21) and the circumstances prompting intercession (6:22–39).

1. To understand prayer is to acknowledge the paradoxical truth of God's simultaneous transcendence and immanence. Solomon recognizes that the vast expanse of the heavens cannot contain the unique otherness of the creator; how much less can a building like the temple (6:18). Yet somehow the Jerusalem shrine is the earthly interface of the Lord's divine presence and absolute holiness because it is at this place that God has chosen to set his name (6:20). Solomon's temple becomes the symbolic focal point of God's interest in and care for humanity, for it is here that his eyes and ears are continually open to the supplications of both Israelite and foreigner alike (6:21; cf. 6:32–33).
2. The list of circumstances prompting intercessory prayer should be regarded as representative and not comprehensive (6:22–39). The examples of personal injustices (6:22–23), warfare (6:24–25, 34–39), and natural calamities and disasters affecting the land (6:26–31) are universal experiences in the agrarian society of biblical times.

The most extensive alterations of the earlier version of Solomon's prayer of dedication for the temple occur in the final section (6:40–42), suggesting that this portion of the prayer is especially important to the Chronicler. The parallel in 1 Kings 8:50b–53 grounds the expectation for God's favorable response to the prayer in the special relationship between Yahweh and Israel established by the Mosaic covenant. By contrast, the Chronicler omits the reference to Moses and the exodus and grounds this expectation in God's promises to David (6:41–42).

The repetition of God's "great love" and the phrase "David your servant" in the final verse (6:42) has the effect of forming an *inclusio* or envelope construction with the opening petition of Solomon's prayer (6:14–17). The invitation to Yahweh to arise and enter his "resting place" (6:41) anticipates the Lord's return to his temple as prophesied by Zechariah (Zech 1:16). The Chronicler's reordering and change of wording in his appropriation of Psalm 132:10 in 2 Chronicles 6:42 is an allusion to the "everlasting covenant . . . promised to David" (cf. Isa 55:3). Both Psalm 132:10–11 and Isaiah 55:3 stress the Lord's promise to continue David's dynasty—a message the Chronicler's audience needs to hear!

Dedication of the temple (7:1–10). The Chronicler omits Solomon's blessing of the assembly (1 Kgs 8:55–61) and instead inserts the report of fire raining down from heaven and consuming the burnt offerings and sacrifices (2 Chr 7:1b–3). The simultaneous events of fire from heaven falling on the bronze altar and the cloud of Yahweh's glory filling the temple prompt a predictable reaction from the people—prostration in worship (7:3).

The dramatic depiction of God's issuing fire from heaven on an altar is a familiar motif in the Old Testament. In a similar manner, each aspect of the divine response to the temple dedication ceremonies orchestrated by Solomon is crucial to the inauguration of the new sanctuary as the central Israelite worship center.

1. The fire from heaven that engulfs the sacrifices on the bronze altar affirms that the Lord God has accepted the work of Solomon in building the temple and the worship of the priests and people in dedicating the edifice to the service of Yahweh.
2. The cloud of glory that fills the temple and prevents the priests from entering the structure signals God's approval of this new "house of prayer" as his abode among his people.

National unity is a recurring theme for the Chronicler, and it resurfaces in the report that the king, the people, and the priests and Levites all join in the ceremony of dedication for the new temple (7:4–6). Regardless of whether one understands the tally of animals sacrificed in a symbolic or a literal fashion, the point is that the magnitude of this worship response to

God makes Solomon's new bronze altar inadequate for the task (cf. 7:7).

The week-long dedication of the temple precedes the week-long Feast of Tabernacles celebration. Solomon holds a sacred assembly on the eighth day (7:9). The Feast of Tabernacles (or Ingathering) was a pilgrimage festival, thus explaining the large assembly in Jerusalem (Exod 23:16).

The reference to "Lebo Hamath to the Wadi of Egypt" (2 Chr 7:8) constitutes the ideal boundaries of ancient Israel, the possession promised to the patriarchs (cf. Gen 15:18; Num 34:5, 8). The Chronicler adds the clause "for they had celebrated the dedication of the altar" (2 Chr 7:9), since the temple was both a house of prayer and a house of sacrifice (7:12). The act of dedication was a formal initiation of something or someone for a divinely ordained role—in this case, the bronze altar for burnt offerings (cf. Num 7:10–11).

The Chronicler is careful to note that the people are blessed through David and Solomon as divine agents—it is the Lord himself who has done the "good things" for Israel (2 Chr 7:10). The report of the temple dedication is a formulaic summary of joyful worship that includes a chronological statement, a list of the participants, and the ceremonial rituals observed (cf. 15:9–15; 30:13–27; 35:1–19).

The Lord appears to Solomon (7:11–22). The second half of chapter 7 describes the Lord's appearance to Solomon "at night" (7:12). The dream report may be divided into two uneven segments: an introduction (7:11–12a) and the divine address (7:12b–22).

The Lord's speech to Solomon on the occasion of his second dream theophany may be outlined in three distinct parts: the Lord's acceptance of Solomon's prayer of dedication and his approval of the Jerusalem temple as the place for his name to dwell (7:12b); the Lord's promise to Solomon and the people he shepherds (7:13–18); and the Lord's threat of punishment for disobedience (7:19–22).

The Lord's promise to Solomon confers the right to rule to the household or dynasty of King David (7:13–18). This theological truth is reinforced by the Chronicler's insertion of the word "covenanted" for the word promised in the divine charge to Solomon (7:18; cf. 1 Kgs 9:5). The fulfillment of the promise, however, is conditioned by two separate but related factors. The first is the obedience of the people to the laws of God (1 Chr 7:13–16); the second is the obedience of the king to those same divine decrees and laws (7:17–18). Little has changed in the theological progression from the Mosaic covenant to the Davidic covenant—the blessing of God still requires the response of faith acted out in loving obedience to God's revelation.

The paragraph of the Lord's speech to Solomon addressing the call to repentance and the promise of forgiveness is unique to Chronicles (7:13–16). The word "humble" (7:14) means to subdue one's pride and submit in self-denying loyalty to God and his will. "Pray" is a shameless acknowledgment of personal sin and a plea for God's mercy. "Seek" is often used in desperate situations in which God is the only possible hope for deliverance. "Turn" is the Old Testament term for repentance and signifies a complete change of direction away from sin and toward God.

The call to repentance and the promise of forgiveness in 7:14 is also the Chronicler's sermon to his own audience. The postexilic Jewish community needs the reminder that God's choice of Jerusalem as the place to set his name is still valid. The second temple, like Solomon's sanctuary, embodies the truth that God will forgive the repentant sinner.

Although contextually the Lord's threat (7:19–22) is addressed to Solomon and the people of Israel, the Chronicler clearly understands that the threat of divine punishment is still in force for his own audience. The question-and-answer schema couched in the conversation of the casual stranger passing by the rejected temple (7:21–22) emphasizes the sin and guilt of the people precipitating such calamity. The words are no doubt a grim reminder to the Chronicler's audience of what once did happen, and could happen again, to the temple.

Solomon's Other Activities (8:1–9:31). *Additional building projects (8:1–6).* The twin priorities of erecting a temple for the worship of Yahweh and Solomon's establishing his own administrative center require twenty years of building activity (8:1). The report of the cities given by Hiram of Tyre to Solomon seems to reverse the report found in the Kings' parallel, in which Solomon gives the Phoenician city-state king twenty towns (towns restored to Solomon because Hiram is "unhappy" with them, 1 Kgs 9:10–12).

It may be possible to harmonize the reports in one of two ways.

1. Perhaps Kings and Chronicles refer to two different occasions in which cities are exchanged as a part of agreements arranged between Hiram and Solomon.
2. Chronicles may be the sequel to the Kings' account in that Hiram held the twenty cities temporarily as collateral for the timber supplied to Solomon until such time as a cash payment (of gold) could be made.

The capture of Hamath is the only reference to a military campaign by King Solomon in all of Chronicles. The oasis and caravan stop of Tadmor (Palmyra of Greek sources) affords a shortcut along the desert trade route into Mesopotamia some 120 miles northeast of Damascus. The writer seems to be calling attention to the extent of the ideal borders of Israel achieved under David and Solomon.

The twin towns of Upper and Lower Beth Horon were

strategically located on a ridge guarding the approach to Jerusalem from the coastal plain along the road linking the interior with the coastal highway. The emphasis on store cites and chariot cities (8:6) highlights the priority Solomon gives to the related activities of trade and military defense. The summary statement (8:6c) lauding Solomon's achievements indicates he has both the political power and the economic resources to build at will throughout his empire.

Slave labor force (8:7–10). This passage distinguishes clearly between Solomon's treatment of his own countrymen and the subjugated non-Israelite people groups (8:8). The writer emphasizes how Solomon puts fellow countrymen in positions of leadership (8:9–10).

The removal of Pharaoh's daughter (8:11). The parallel passage in 1 Kings 9:24 concurs with the report in Chronicles that Solomon relocates this unnamed Egyptian princess in her own special quarters once that structure is completed. Only Chronicles records the rationale for the displacement of Solomon's Egyptian wife, ostensibly because of issues of ritual purity.

The altar of the Lord (8:12–15). Not only does King Solomon obey the law of Moses, but he is also careful to implement his father's instructions concerning the reorganization of the priests and Levites (8:14–15; cf. 1 Chr 23–26). As the juxtaposition of the preceding report of Solomon's success in a range of activities verifies (2 Chr 8:1–11), obedience to God's word as well as his instructions to the previous generation is the key to success.

Summary statements (8:16–18). The review of Solomon's other significant royal activities concludes with a summary statement concerning the completion of the Jerusalem temple (8:16) and a synopsis of the cooperative maritime operations Solomon negotiated with Hiram, the Phoenician king of Tyre (8:18). The summary statement that Solomon perseveres in the task of building the temple from the foundation to its completion conveys the idea that Solomon cuts no corners and spares no expense in getting the job done. For the Chronicler, Solomon's role as king is summed up in his work of completing the temple.

The Phoenicians were well known in the ancient world for their shipbuilding technology and seamanship, so Solomon's alliance with Hiram of Tyre for the purpose of maritime trade is a natural one (cf. Isa 23:1–4; Ezek 27:4, 8–9). These joint Israelite-Phoenician maritime expeditions are three-year trading junkets. Gold, algumwood (ebony?), gemstones, silver, ivory, and exotic animals are among the other goods returned to port at Ezion Geber (cf. 2 Chr 9:10, 21).

Queen of Sheba visits Solomon (9:1–12). The story of the Queen of Sheba's visit balances the opening chapter (ch. 1) in that God has honored Solomon's obedience in giving the wealth accumulated by David to the building of the temple by restoring wealth to the monarchy through trade and gifts from other nations.

The story also illustrates the key themes of the larger literary unit (chs. 1–9), namely, Solomon's wisdom, wealth, and fame—all gifts from God. For example, Solomon petitioned God for wisdom and was blessed with promises of wealth and fame as well (1:11–12). As a result of her visit with King Solomon, the Queen of Sheba testifies of Solomon's unsurpassed wisdom (9:5) and contributes to Solomon's wealth with lavish gifts of gold, spices, and gemstones (9:9). Beyond this, the queen bears witness to the fact that Solomon's wisdom and wealth are the result of God's blessing on the king and his love for the nation of Israel (9:8).

God's covenant with Abraham and Sarah included a clause that their descendants, the nation of Israel, would be a blessing to the nations (Gen 12:3). Declaring the glory of God among the nations is a minor theme in Chronicles, and the report of the Queen of Sheba's visit to Jerusalem contributes to Asaph's exhortation to make God known among the nations (1 Chr 16:8, 24).

Solomon's splendor (9:13–21). The Chronicler includes a collection of related materials reporting Solomon's great wealth as a summary statement asserting the incomparability of his riches and wisdom (cf. 9:22). The review of the opulence of Solomon's kingdom further enhanced the king's (and Israel's) reputation among all the other kingdoms (9:19). The objects of his splendor are organized in three categories: gold and its abundant use (9:13–16), the ivory throne (9:17–19), and the king's "household articles" (9:20–21). The account stands as a testimony to God's faithfulness in keeping his promise to give Solomon unsurpassed wealth and honor (cf. 2 Chr 1:11–12).

Encomium on Solomon's glory (9:22–28). The encomium is an extended (in this case, prose) lyric praising an abstract quality or general character type. This encomium combines both features as it is the abstract quality of wisdom that defines the character type of King Solomon. By way of literary structure, 9:22–28 completes the envelope construction introduced in 1:14–17. The two texts recite the symbols of Solomon's great wealth and in so doing frame the entire literary unit (chs. 1–9).

Theologically, chapters 1–9 complete the idealized biographies of King David and his son and successor, King Solomon. These biographies represent the fulfillment of the Davidic covenant in that God has built David's "house" (i.e., dynasty) in establishing Solomon as king, and Solomon has fulfilled the commission of his father to build Yahweh's "house" (i.e., the temple). Of special import is the declaration that Solomon's wisdom and wealth are the result of God's favor, since foreign potentates come to Jerusalem from all over the world to hear "the wisdom God had put in his heart" (9:23).

Concluding regnal résumé (9:29–31). The regnal résumé of Solomon's reign essentially repeats the summary found in 1 Kings 11:41–43. There are two notable variations.

1. The phrase "from beginning to end" (2 Chr 9:29) is a characteristic of the Chronicler's style in the regnal résumés (cf. 1 Chr 29:29; 2 Chr 12:15).
2. The Chronicler cites three prophetic records as the historical sources for Solomon's kingship (9:29). These prophetic sources are probably sections contained within other documents (e.g., the Elijah and Elishah stories of Kings) or an even larger compendium of monarchic records.

The phrase "rested with his ancestors" (9:31) signifies both a peaceful death and a long and prosperous life. The Chronicler omits altogether the unfavorable theological review of Solomon's idolatry-tainted reign found in 1 Kings 11:1–13, as well as the opposition recorded in 11:14–40.

Application. The establishment of Solomon's temple in Jerusalem brings a renewed emphasis on prayer to Israelite religious thought and life. Solomon's prayer of dedication for the temple places great importance on prayer in maintaining Israel's covenant relationship with God (cf. 1 Kgs 8; 2 Chr 6). Specific circumstances mentioned by Solomon that provide the impetus for prayer either to maintain or to repair relationship with Yahweh include: prayers of personal supplication (6:21); prayers of confession and repentance for sin (6:24, 26); petitions and intercessions concerning natural disasters and health afflictions (6:29); prayers of homage offered by the foreigner (6:32); petitions and intercessions offered during times of national emergency (e.g., war; 6:34); and prayers seeking restoration should sin cause Israel to be exiled from the land of covenant promise (6:39). Practically speaking, this made the temple a house of prayer for King Solomon (cf. 6:40).

Following the example of the prayer-book tradition, some kind of personal or familial adaptation of morning and evening prayers can easily be developed as one type of spiritual discipline. The special seasons of the church year also lend themselves readily to the hours of the daily office with certain modifications.

The call for a return to some form of the daily prayer office is not necessarily a call to monasticism, although monastic retreats are gaining in popularity in Christian circles. Neither is the corporate or personal observance of the daily office of prayer encouraged simply because "more is better" or because formality is more effective. Christian prayer is first and foremost a matter of heart and attitude, not vain repetitions. Exploring the Christian tradition of the daily office permits the Christian and the local Christian church to learn the ancient rhythm of prayer. Participation in the daily cycle of prayer hearkens back to the temple as the house of prayer and the idea that prayer is one means for recovering order out of chaos.

2 CHRONICLES 10:1–21:3

Original Meaning

King Rehoboam (10:1–12:16). *Israel rejects the Davidic dynasty (10:1–11:4). The Israelite tribes assemble at Shechem (10:1–4).* Rehoboam travels for his public coronation to Shechem (10:1)—a strategic military, political, and religious center for Israel from ancient times. Rehoboam may be hoping the long Israelite tradition associated with this site will contribute to easing political tensions. No doubt Jeroboam was monitoring the situation from afar and so makes his way to Shechem during the interim period between the national mourning over Solomon's death and the installation of Rehoboam as his successor.

Because of his earlier commissioning by the prophet Ahijah, Jeroboam is dubbed as spokesman for "all Israel" (10:3, here the phrase refers to the northern tribes that will soon constitute the Northern Kingdom). Two issues of primary concern must be settled in order for the northern tribes to guarantee loyalty to the new king: "harsh labor" (i.e., forced labor gangs) and a "heavy yoke" (i.e., taxation, 10:4).

Rehoboam consults with his advisers (10:5–11). Rehoboam consults two groups of royal advisers. The first is a cohort of elders left over from Solomon's reign (10:6). The "young men who had grown up" with Rehoboam comprise the second advisory council (10:8).

The advice of Solomon's elders is conciliatory—win their approval and earn their support by "being kind" (10:7). A "favorable answer" to the assembly at Shechem would be a wise move, a gracious gesture, and a culturally appropriate response for the new king. The advice of Rehoboam's cronies (10:8–9), by contrast, threatens the implementation of an even more severe policy.

Rehoboam is not so young as inexperienced (he is forty-one years old at his accession; 12:13). Nothing in chapter 10 suggests that he is especially malicious or cruel—only foolish. Whether out of fear that he may appear weak or for the sake of pragmatism, he rejects the good advice of the elders and follows the bad advice (10:14).

The division of Israel and Judah (10:12–19). After the three days specified for reaching a decision have elapsed, Jeroboam and his retinue and Rehoboam and his entourage reconvene the assembly at Shechem (10:12). It is interesting to note that David's coronation lasts three days and the celebration includes feasting as part of a covenant meal, sealing a pact or treaty between the tribes (cf. 1 Chr 12:39).

Biblical historians note that this "turn of events was from

God" (2 Chr 10:15a; cf. 1 Kgs 12:15). The Chronicler connects his commentary to Ahijah's prophecy predicting the split of Solomon's kingdom as punishment for his sin of idolatry—thus assuming his audience's knowledge of the story (2 Chr 10:15b; cf. 1 Kgs 11:29–40). The northern tribes are not reprehensible in their role in splitting the united monarchy. Rather, they become odious to God and the biblical historians because of their subsequent sin—idol worship.

The repetition of Rehoboam's refusal to "listen" to the people further underscores the intransigence of the king (2 Chr 10:15–16). The poetic fragment that commemorates the split of the united monarchy is the traditional rallying cry of the northern tribes. What a stark contrast between the taunt tossed at Rehoboam and the vote of confidence King David received. The clause "so all the Israelites went home" signifies both the rejection of Rehoboam in the act of dismissal and also the finality of the decision—the negotiations are over (10:16d).

Adoniram (10:18) is one of Jeroboam's successors as an overseer of the forced labor gangs established by Solomon (cf. 1 Kgs 11:28). The secretary of labor is promptly stoned to death by the civil servants under his charge (2 Chr 10:18b). Apparently, Rehoboam has accompanied Adoniram on the peace initiative because he barely escapes with his life from the unspecified location of the meeting (10:18c).

Shemaiah brokers peace between Israel and Judah (11:1–4). The civil war that later characterizes the first fifty years of coexistence of the divided kingdoms of Israel and Judah is averted early on by prophetic intervention (11:2–4). Shemaiah is one of several preclassical prophets mentioned briefly in the Old Testament historical books. No collections of their oracles have been preserved, only extracts of sermons and prophecies—as in the case of Shemaiah's message to Rehoboam (11:3–4). This time Rehoboam heeds the advice offered, without asking for a second opinion.

Judah supports Rehoboam (11:5–17). The passage divides neatly into two sections, a summary of Rehoboam's defensive measures against foreign invasion (11:5–12) and the support Rehoboam received from the northern tribes after the split of the united monarchy (11:13–17). The unit continues the emphasis on God's reward for faithfulness and introduces for the first time the religious apostasy of Jeroboam (perpetuated by all the rulers of the Northern Kingdom).

The report of priests and Levites migrating from Israel to Judah after the split of the united monarchy offers a Southern Kingdom perspective on the false worship centers established in the Northern Kingdom by Jeroboam (11:13–17; cf. 1 Kgs 12:26–33). The Levites are probably rejected as candidates for religious service in Jeroboam's "calf cult" because they remain loyal to the Jerusalem temple as the legitimate worship center for all Israelites. Interestingly, these Israelites have "set their hearts on seeking the LORD" (2 Chr 11:16), something King Rehoboam ultimately refuses to do (12:14).

The influx of loyal priests and Levites and faithful Israelites from the northern tribal districts strengthens Rehoboam's rule and bolsters morale in Judah (11:17a). For a brief time, unfortunately only three years, the kingdom of Judah demonstrates faith in God and obedience to his commandments after the manner modeled by David and Solomon (11:17b).

Rehoboam's family (11:18–23). The report concerning the family of Rehoboam is unique to Chronicles. The insertion of the genealogical material may explain the cryptic reference to the records of Iddo the seer "that deal with genealogies" in the regnal résumé (12:15).

It should be noted, in addition to his own eighteen wives and sixty concubines (11:21), Rehoboam is responsible for supporting his father Solomon's harem (since royal women were property of the state in perpetuity). This obligation may have had something to do with his decision to levy a tax hike on his subjects. The appointment of Abijah as "crown prince among his brothers" (11:22) is tantamount to implementing a coregency for the purpose of guaranteeing an orderly transition of power when Rehoboam dies.

The concluding verse of the regnal résumé lauds Rehoboam's wisdom in "dispersing some of his sons throughout the districts of Judah" (11:23). Rehoboam apparently imitates his father's practice of delegation of royal authority, but he makes those appointments from princes within the royal household rather than from tribal leaders.

Pharaoh Shishak raids Judah (12:1–12). The Chronicler understands Shishak's invasion of Judah as punishment for sin, in that Rehoboam and all Israel have "abandoned the law of the LORD" (12:1). The reason for the lapse in Judah's loyalty to Yahweh after three years of walking faithfully in the ways of David and Solomon is unclear (cf. 11:17). The phrase "he had become strong" (12:1) suggests that pride and self-reliance have replaced Rehoboam's dependence on God.

Shemaiah the prophet (12:5) is known as a "man of God" (11:2) and earlier warned Rehoboam not to wage war against the northern tribes of Israel after the split of Solomon's kingdom (11:4). He now brings a message of both judgment (12:5) and mercy to Rehoboam and the leaders of Judah (12:7–8). The response by Rehoboam and the leaders of Judah that "the LORD is just" (12:6) is essentially a confession of sin. God accepts this confession as an act of "humbling oneself" (12:6–7), a form of repentance that brings the sinner back to God.

God mercifully decrees that Judah will experience a "qualified" deliverance from Shishak (12:7b), but they will not escape the consequences of their disobedience—they will "become subject to him [i.e., Shishak]" for a time (12:8). The report of the "treasures" of the Jerusalem temple and royal palace "carried off" by Shishak suggests the loot is given as tribute to buy off Shishak rather than taken as booty through war (12:9–11).

The word "humbled himself" (12:12) means to forsake one's pride and yield in self-denying loyalty to God. This action appeases God's wrath and spares Rehoboam and Judah from total destruction. God delivers on his promise to respond with forgiveness and healing to those who humble themselves before him in prayer (7:14).

Concluding regnal résumé (12:13–16). The theological review in 1 Kings 14:22 indicts the people of Judah for the blatant religious apostasy during Rehoboam's reign. By contrast, the Chronicler places blame for idolatry directly on Rehoboam, even adding the commentary that the king "had not set his heart on seeking the Lord" (2 Chr 12:14).

The Chronicler's citation of additional historical sources may help explain why his account of Rehoboam's reign is three times longer than the parallel in 1 Kings. Moreover, these references indicate the breadth of historical sources available to the Chronicler as well as a concern for accuracy in his reporting.

King Abijah (13:1–14:1). *Opening regnal résumé (13:1–2a).* The opening regnal résumé is based on 1 Kings 15:1–2. The citation to the eighteenth year of Jeroboam (2 Chr 13:1) is the only synchronism with the Northern Kingdom in all of Chronicles. Jeroboam ruled as king of Israel for twenty-two years (930–909 BC). Abijah's three-year reign over Judah is thus fixed from 913–910 BC. The name Abijah is consistently rendered Abijam in the Kings' narrative (whether this is an issue of orthography or perhaps the difference between his given name and throne name is unclear).

War with Israel (13:2b–21). Setting the stage (13:2b–3). The story begins with a blunt announcement that civil war has erupted between the kingdom of Israel (led by Jeroboam) and the kingdom of Judah (led by Abijah). The Chronicler's report of the size of the two opposing armies proves troublesome for some commentators. However one chooses to understand the numbers, the basic meaning of the tallies is clear—the troops of Israel outnumber the troops of Judah two to one.

Abijah's speech (13:4–12). King Abijah of Judah addresses his rival Jeroboam and the vast Israelite army from Mount Zemaraim (13:4). Abijah's speech is propagandistic, given the military context of the address; psychological warfare is not a modern development.

The speech contrasts the faithfulness and loyalty of Abijah with the rebellion and disloyalty of Jeroboam in two issues: the Davidic covenant (13:4–8a) and God's temple in Jerusalem (13:8b–12). In order to create dissension and separate Jeroboam from his troops, Abijah refers to his northern counterpart in the third person and characterizes his leadership as "rebellion" against Solomon (13:6), since he was formerly a court official under David's successor (1 Kgs 11:26). Implicitly, Jeroboam has rebelled against God since God has given the kingdom to David and his descendants (2 Chr 13:5).

The second half of Abijah's speech contrasts Jeroboam's forsaking of the Lord's temple and his banishment of the Levitical priesthood with Abijah's compliance with the Mosaic law related to the proper worship of God (13:8b–12). Like the first half of the address, this segment includes a rhetorical question based on the conviction that Israel ought to know they are the party in the wrong (13:9). The installment of a pseudo-priesthood aside (13:9b), the most damning indictment against the northern tribes are "the golden calves that Jeroboam made to be your gods" (13:8b). The punch line of Abijah's oration is eminently theological and decidedly practical: "God is with us" (13:12a). What kind of folly is it to "fight against the Lord" (13:12b)?

The battle at Mount Zemaraim (13:13–19). God responds by allying himself to the army of Judah and routing the forces of the Northern Kingdom (13:15). The divine-warrior motif is revisited in that overwhelming odds present no problem when his people rely on him (13:18). Though Judah is outnumbered two to one and outflanked on the battlefield, Israel loses more than half its military force, and the remainder flee in panic (13:16).

The entire battle report turns on a key verb—the men of Judah are victorious "because they *relied on* the Lord" (13:18, emphasis added). The significance of the attached phrase "God of their ancestors" should not be lost—God has done this kind of thing before! The capture of Bethel is significant because it means the cessation of the calf-cult worship there for a time (13:19).

The aftermath (13:20–21). The heavy losses sustained by Jeroboam at the battle of Mount Zemaraim cripple his capacities for further aggression against the Southern Kingdom. The verb "strike down" (13:20) often denotes a divine plague or blow executed by God as a Divine Warrior who brings judgment on rebellious and sinful people. The Chronicler's insertion that Abijah "grew in strength" and married fourteen wives and fathered thirty-eight children is usually taken as a statement of God's blessing on the king (13:21).

King Asa (14:2–16:14). *Early years (14:2–15).* King Asa was a religious reformer (14:3–5) and a builder of fortifications for the defense of Judah's perimeter (14:7). The repetition of "seeking the Lord" in 14:4 and 14:7 sets the theme for the entire section. The "peace" and "rest" (14:5, 6, 7) that Judah enjoys under Asa is due in part to Abijah's victory over Jeroboam (13:19–20) but is also a reward for Asa's faithfulness to God (14:7). This accords well with the Chronicler's emphasis on the retribution principle in Israelite history; that is, obedience to

God's commands results in reward whereas disobedience brings punishment.

The story of Zerah the Cushite's march against Judah (14:8–15) has no parallel in the Kings' version of Asa's reign. Asa has a large and well-equipped army (14:8). But Zerah's army is vast (literally, "a thousand thousands" 14:9). The story turns on Asa's prayer for "help" from the Lord (14:11). His prayer seems to be modeled on Solomon's exhortation for the Israelites to pray toward the temple and God will hear from heaven and "uphold their cause" (6:34–35). The Chronicler includes this story of Judah's victory over Zerah and the Cushites as evidence of the king's faithfulness and reliance on God.

Reforms (15:1–19). The prophet's sermon (15:1–7) explains the occasion of King Asa's reforms. Azariah is charged to go and find King Asa (15:2a). God's prophet serves as the conscience of the divided monarchies, so it is appropriate that Azariah's message is delivered to the king and the people of Judah and Benjamin (15:2b).

These are the themes highlighted in the prophet's message: God is with those who side with him, and he rewards obedience (15:2, 7); and God will be found by those who seek him but forsakes those who abandon him (15:2). In good homiletical style, the sermon ends with an exhortation to continue the good work already begun because God will honor it (15:7).

The king's obedience to God's word through the prophet Azariah launches sweeping religious reforms in Judah. The report of Asa's reform and covenant renewal ceremony (15:8–15) expands the earlier summary statement of the king's eradication of false worship in Judah (cf. 14:3) and should be understood as parallel accounts. The covenant ceremony may have been associated with the Feast of Weeks or Pentecost, as the spring pilgrimage festival would have naturally necessitated the gathering of all Israel in Jerusalem at that time of year (15:10).

For the Chronicler, acts of obedience to God (like swearing the covenant oath) are also acts of worship, and worship erupts in "rejoicing" (15:15; cf. 23:13, 21; 30:21, 25). The shouts of the people and the blasts of trumpets and horns (15:14) are external expression of an internal reality, echoing Asaph's psalm of thanksgiving in celebration of the transfer of the ark of the covenant to Jerusalem (cf. 1 Chr 16:10).

The covenant ceremony marks the beginning of a twenty-year period of peace under King Asa. The word "rest" occurs three times in the review of Asa's reign (2 Chr 14:6, 7; 15:15) and signifies the blessing of God for a peaceful and prosperous life as a reward for covenant obedience.

Maakah, Asa's grandmother, is removed from her position of authority as queen mother because of her idolatry (15:16). The Asherah pole was a cultic symbol of the Canaanite fertility goddess Asherah in the form of a tree or tree trunk. The pole represented the tree of life in Canaanite religion. Asa smashes this pole and burns it in the Kidron Valley southeast of Jerusalem, a garbage pit and refuse dump sometimes used for the disposal of such religious objects.

Nevertheless, Asa fails to remove the high places from Israel. Rather than see this as a contradiction to the record of the king's reforms (15:17; cf. 14:3), it is probably better to assume that the writer distinguishes between the high places of Judah and Israel. The theological review that Asa's "heart was fully committed to the Lord all his life" (15:17) is difficult to harmonize with the details of chapter 16.

Later years (16:1–10). After two decades of peace, conflict once again breaks out between the kingdoms of Israel and Judah (16:1). King Baasha of Israel is the aggressor in that the defensive measures he takes to fortify Ramah also threaten the territory of Judah economically and militarily. Asa resorts to paying tribute to a third party for the purpose of engaging an aggressor nation on a second front (16:3–4).

God responds to Asa through Hanani the seer (16:7–9). Nothing is known of this prophet apart from the sermon recorded here. The key word in the prophet's speech is "rely" (16:7). Earlier in his reign, Asa "relied" on God, and Judah prevailed over the Cushites who mustered a vast army against them (14:11). History should have been Asa's teacher (16:8). Here in this crisis, Asa shuns divine aid and trusts in his own power—his political savvy and human instincts to deliver Judah.

Surprisingly, God intended to grant Judah victory over both Aram and Israel, had Asa trusted God for deliverance (note 16:7). Somehow Asa has foolishly lost sight of God's sovereignty—hence the reminder that "the eyes of the Lord range throughout the earth" (16:9). The heart fully committed to God demonstrates such allegiance by relying on the Lord in all things—and God himself works in the faithful to strengthen that resolve. Asa's response to Hanani constitutes the first incident of royal persecution of a prophet of God recorded in the Old Testament (16:10).

Concluding regnal résumé (16:11–14). The Chronicles version of the regnal résumé expands the report of King Asa's foot disease with theological commentary (16:12; cf. 1 Kgs 15:23b). The Chronicler's point is that at times divine judgment takes the form of illness (e.g., 2 Chr 21:16–20; 26:16–23). The writer implies that the sickness is an unheeded warning from God, expressing his displeasure over Asa's response to recent events. The statement that Asa seeks human help in the form of physicians rather than divine help for healing (16:12b) impugns his faith in God, not ancient medical practitioners.

King Jehoshaphat (17:1–21:3). *Character of his reign (17:1–19). Theological review (17:1–6).* The kings of the divided monarchy (ch. 10–36) are evaluated against the gold standard of kingship,

King David himself. Jehoshaphat is compared favorably to David because he is single-minded in his obedience to God (17:3).

The demonstration of wholehearted devotion to God is the removal of the symbols and practices of false worship (17:6). Echoes of the Davidic prayer of dedication of the gifts for the temple may be seen in the statement "the LORD established the kingdom under his control" and in the "wealth and honor" that come to Jehoshaphat (17:5). There are also overtones of the Davidic covenant in the theological review of King Jehoshaphat. God's faithfulness to his word is seen in the succession of Jehoshaphat and the continuation of the Davidic dynasty (17:1) in that God has cut off the enemies of Judah (17:2), and in Jehoshaphat's leadership in shepherding the people into the way of God through his religious reforms (17:6).

Religious instruction for Judah (17:7–9). If the historical reconstruction understanding a three-year coregency between Asa and his son Jehoshaphat is correct, Jehoshaphat marks the beginning of his own independent rule over Judah with an initiative aimed at spiritual reform. The king's religious instruction program is supervised by five civil officials (17:7) and ten Levitical officials (eight Levites and two priests, 17:8). This "theological faculty" engages in "distance learning" of sorts, in that they launch an itinerant teaching ministry throughout the towns of Judah (17:9).

Military organization (17:10–19). God's blessing rests on Jehoshaphat's reign; as a result, "the fear of the LORD" falls on Judah's neighbors (17:10). The writer's ordering of the material is significant insofar as the details concerning the organization and size of Jehoshaphat's army follows the report about the dread Judah inspires among the surrounding nations (17:14–19). Clearly this is a deliberate ploy, lest anyone mistakenly equate the king's military might with the Lord's work in establishing Jehoshaphat's kingdom (cf. 17:5). Respect for Judah's political clout results in the payment of tribute from peoples to the west and south (17:11).

The flow of wealth into Judah permits the building of fortifications and store cities (17:12–13). Jehoshaphat's army totals 1,160,000 soldiers (17:14–18). Our understanding of numerical data must take into consideration the range of possible meanings for the word "thousand" in context, whether a "chieftain," a "military cohort" of some size, or a literal "thousand."

Alliance with Ahab (18:1–19:3). Proposal for war (18:1–4). The gist of the opening report is King Jehoshaphat's consent to partner with King Ahab in a war against Ramoth Gilead (18:3). Ahab's design in waging war with Aram is to recapture former Israelite territory. Perhaps his motivation for war is triggered by Ben-Hadad's treachery in breaking an earlier treaty (cf. 1 Kgs 20:34). Jehoshaphat consents, but he then requests Ahab to "seek the counsel of the LORD" (2 Chr 18:4). The king is looking for some kind of divine assurance that the military campaign will be successful.

Prophetic counsel (18:5–27). Ahab obliges his counterpart from Judah by assembling four hundred prophets, all of whom predict victory for Ahab and Israel (18:5). Jehoshaphat remains unpersuaded, perhaps even suspicious, since he knows that the true prophets are often dissenters in the face of popular opinion, and he requests yet another prophetic judgment (18:6). Micaiah son of Imlah is summoned, but Ahab remonstrates that this prophet only speaks "bad" about him (18:7).

Apart from his confrontation with Ahab and Jehoshaphat (18:12–24), nothing else is known of Micaiah. The king's envoy attempts to coach Micaiah as he enters the situation (18:12). But Micaiah staunchly refuses to compromise any message from the Lord (18:13). His response to Ahab's initial inquiry must have been sarcastic, a parody of the king's four hundred yes men (18:14). Exasperated, Ahab ironically demands the truth from the Lord's prophet (18:15).

Micaiah's prophecy takes the form of two visions. The first depicts a scene of sheep without a shepherd on the hills (18:16–17). Ahab presumes the prophet portends his death in battle, which he does (18:17). But Micaiah's message has a double meaning, in that the people of Israel currently "have no master" (18:16b). Ahab's corrupt rule has led the people far from God—how sardonic that the sheep will have "peace" (18:16c) when the shepherd is gone!

Micaiah's second vision offers a window into the throne room of God, where the divine council discusses the battle of Ramoth Gilead and the fate of King Ahab (18:18–22). Typically, the role of divine council in Israel's warfare is mustering the heavenly army to fight on behalf of Israel, but here the council plots the death of Ahab and the defeat of the combined armies of Israel and Judah.

Micaiah's message about the "deceiving spirit" sent from God unmasks the fraudulent prophets of Ahab (18:20–22). Ahab accents his rejection of Micaiah's message by having the prophet thrown in prison in Samaria (18:25–26; cf. v. 9). Amon must have held a position in the city of Samaria similar to that of mayor.

Micaiah responds to Ahab's declaration that he will return safely (18:26b) with a death threat (18:27). The king's death in battle will vindicate Micaiah and verify the truth of his message.

Battle of Ramoth Gilead (18:28–34). By engaging in the battle against the Arameans at Ramoth Gilead (18:28), Ahab fulfills Micaiah's prophecy about the king being lured to his own destruction (cf. 18:20–22). Ahab's ploy to disguise himself is perhaps an attempt to thwart the word of the prophet that the king fears may be true (18:29).

Who, then, becomes the target of the Aramean charioteers?

King Jehoshaphat of Judah, dressed in his royal robes (18:31). The Chronicler interprets Jehoshaphat's cry as a prayer and adds the clause "and the LORD helped him" (18:31). The "random" arrow that pierces a chink in Ahab's armor is certainly God's arrow (18:33), verifying that God has indeed spoken through Micaiah the prophet.

Jehu's prophecy (19:1–3). Jehu the seer (19:2) is the son of Hanani the seer, who rebuked King Asa of Judah for entering into a foreign alliance with Ben-Hadad of Aram (16:1–9). By allying himself with King Ahab of Israel, Jehoshaphat is a partner to "the wicked" and an accomplice of "those who hate the LORD"—offenses deserving of the "wrath of the LORD" (19:2). The evil of *alliances* with foreign nations in lieu of *reliance* on God is a repeated theme in Chronicles. The moral still has currency for the Chronicler's audience, for the full restoration of Judah will be accomplished by trust in God, not by brokering alliances with foreign nations.

Judicial reform (19:4–11). Jehoshaphat's revival (19:4). The section opens with a brief account of Jehoshaphat's activity as an evangelist throughout Judah after the debacle at Ramoth Gilead (19:4). The phrase "he went out again" probably implies the king's earlier teaching mission through his emissaries (17:7–9). The king's spiritual fervor seems to be motivated by the curse of God's wrath placed on him by Jehu the seer (19:1–3).

Jehoshaphat's appointment of judges (19:5–11c). Jehoshaphat's decision to place judges and establish forums for legal proceedings in the "fortified cities" is a logical one (19:5). The strategic location of these fortified cities makes them accessible for the general population. The role of the judge is that of an agent for God, not the king (19:6). The injunction against showing favoritism or bribery (19:7) was a foundational judicial principle in the Mosaic legal tradition.

In addition to hearing cases and rendering fair verdicts, the judge must also warn (or instruct) the citizenry who come before the bench not to commit further sin against the Lord, lest the "wrath" of God come against them and their family (19:9–10). This "fear of the LORD" is understood as a deterrent to further criminal activity (19:9); it permits all the citizens of Judah to enjoy the protection afforded by the law. In addition, the just application of the law to everyday life will lead to an equitable society—the ideal social dynamic of the covenant community.

The clause "in every case that comes before you from your people who live in the cities" suggests that the judges in Jerusalem act as a court of appeals for the provincial courts in the outlying districts of Judah (19:10). The main purpose of setting up an appeals court system is to prevent "sin against the LORD" so as to avoid "his wrath" (19:10).

To ensure some separation of power and introduce a check-and-balance mechanism into the judicial organization, the king gives the chief priest Amariah jurisdiction over religious matters (19:11a). He then grants jurisdiction in all crown or civil matters to Zebadiah, the leader of the tribe of Judah (19:11b). The Levites serve as "officials" and assist the courts as clerks and bailiffs (19:11c).

Jehoshaphat's final admonition (19:11d). Jehoshaphat's final admonition is more positive. Instead of warning the judicial appointees not to sin (19:7, 10), the king exhorts them to "act with courage" and invokes the Lord's presence with them as they discharge their duties (19:11d).

War with Moab and Ammon (20:1–30). Judah prepares for war (20:1–4). The phrase "after this" (20:1) refers to the revival among the people of Judah after the debacle at Ramoth Gilead (19:4) and presumes a chronological ordering of the Jehoshaphat narrative. A coalition of three nations invades Judah (20:1). The expression "vast army" is the Chronicler's way of describing the overwhelming numerical superiority of the invaders (20:2).

After Jehoshaphat's initial panic has subsided, he inquires of the Lord with deep resolve and proclaims a national fast (20:3). The fact that people from "every town" (20:4) in Judah rally together to seek the Lord indicates the lasting spiritual impact Jehoshaphat's revival has upon the nation.

Jehoshaphat's prayer (20:5–12). The emphasis on the "assembly" (20:5, 14, 26) stresses the unity of the people as they face this dire circumstance. Jehoshaphat's prayer takes the form of a community or national lament.

Jehoshaphat's prayer-speech appeals widely to other Old Testament texts. For example, his address to God, "LORD, the God of our ancestors" (20:6), echoes David's prayer before the assembly of Israel after the gifts for the temple were collected. The expression "Abraham your friend" (20:7) hearkens back to Genesis 18:17–19. Finally, the king repeats the idea from Solomon's temple dedication prayer that God will hear his people when they pray before they go to war—and he will uphold their cause (2 Chr 20:9; cf. 6:34–35). Jehoshaphat's prayer makes allusions to three important Old Testament covenants in a few short sentences: the Abrahamic covenant, the Mosaic covenant, and the Davidic covenant.

Jahaziel's salvation oracle (20:13–17). God's answer to Jehoshaphat's prayer comes immediately, perhaps from an unexpected source. Jahaziel the Levite is empowered by God's spirit to deliver a word of knowledge to the king and the people of Judah (20:14). The Chronicler's special interest in the Levites is shown in the recital of Jahaziel's impressive pedigree, tracing his lineage back to Asaph of King David's era (20:14).

A number of the Yahweh-war motifs are continued in the prophetic speech of Jahaziel: the exhortation to take courage and stand firm (20:15, 17); the numerical superiority of the enemy armies ("vast army," 20:15); the Israelites not having to fight because Yahweh will wage war for them (20:15, 17); and the promise of certain victory because God will sustain his people with his presence (20:16–17). The prediction that the people of Judah will see God's victory "tomorrow" (20:17) is a reminder of the urgency of the situation, as the coalition armies are only a day's march from Jerusalem!

Liturgical response (20:18–19). The response of Jehoshaphat and all the people of Judah and Jerusalem to the prophetic oracle of Jahaziel has affinities to both covenant-renewal liturgy and the temple liturgy in Old Testament corporate worship: worship proper (demonstrated by prostration before God) followed by enthusiastic praise (20:18–19; cf. Neh 9–10; Ps 95).

Yahweh's victory (20:20–26). The army of Judah sets out "early in the morning" for the Desert of Tekoa (20:20), suggesting a sense of expectation and confidence in what God is about to do in achieving deliverance for his people. Jehoshaphat paraphrases the priestly exhortation and adds the words "have faith in his prophets and you will be successful" (20:20). This statement affirms the efficacy of the prophetic word prompted by the spirit of God and may even signify canonical prophetic literature by this time.

The report of an army going into battle singing the praises of God is unique in the Bible, although music accompanies the appearance of the Divine Warrior when he executes judgment on the earth (Ps 47; 96; 98). The text the Levites sing in praise of Yahweh was Psalm 136:1, an often-repeated refrain in Chronicles (2 Chr 20:21; cf. 5:13; 7:3; 1 Chr 16:34). Interestingly, the Levitical chorus initiates God's battle strategy against the enemy coalition (2 Chr 20:22). Whether God terrifies the coalition armies with the appearance of his heavenly army (as in 2 Sam 5:24; 2 Kgs 7:5–7) or sends a spirit of confusion and mistrust among the allies (as in Judg 7:22; 2 Kgs 3:23) is unclear. What is clear is that God stirs the Transjordan armies into a spirit of frenzied self-destruction (2 Chr 20:22–23).

It takes the army of Judah three days to plunder the spoils from the battlefield, one day for each army of the coalition (20:25). The fourth day is devoted to worship in praise of God's victory; the name given to the valley where the Lord upheld his people is the Valley of Berakah, meaning "praise" (20:26; cf. 20:20).

March of triumph to Jerusalem (20:27–28). Fittingly, the story of the Yahweh war against the Transjordan coalition ends where it began—at the temple of the Lord God of Israel. The march of triumph is depicted almost as a festival worship processional; the musical instruments that accompanied the singing of the Levites in battle (20:21) are now employed in the joyful celebration of the victory God has given them over their enemies (20:27–28).

The aftermath (20:29–30). Characteristically, Yahweh war leaves in its wake "the fear of God" among the nations (20:29) and the "peace" and "rest" of God for his faithful community (20:30).

Concluding regnal résumé (20:31–21:3). King Jehoshaphat's twenty-five-year reign may be dated between 872 and 848 BC (20:31). Jehoshaphat is likened to his father, Asa, as a king who did "what was right in the eyes of the LORD" (20:32). He receives a favorable but not unqualified theological review from the biblical historians. Much like his father, Jehoshaphat was rebuked by God's prophet for entering into foreign political alliances (19:1–3; cf. 16:7–9), and he failed to remove completely the high places—vestiges of Canaanite worship still infecting Hebrew religion (20:33; cf. 15:17). Although Jehoshaphat "followed the ways of his father Asa" (20:32), neither Asa nor Jehoshaphat is given the epitaph of Hezekiah and Josiah (29:2; 34:2).

The writer calls attention to the fickleness of the people, whose hearts are not fully set on God (20:33). The Chronicler's commentary here seems to be directed at his own audience as much as it reports Judah's history. Whether for Jehoshaphat's generation or his own, the need for unswerving faithfulness to God and constant vigilance to his commandments must be set before God's people on a continual basis.

Jehu's father, Hanani the seer, rebuked King Asa for his alliance with Ben-Hadad, king of Aram (16:7–9). The "annals of Jehu" are part of larger historical materials documenting the Israelite monarchies (20:34).

Like the commentary that calls attention to the incomplete religious reforms of Jehoshaphat (20:33), the insertion of the failed maritime venture in partnership with Ahaziah, king of Israel, appears to be yet another qualification of the "good" king's reign (20:35–37). The prophecy from Eliezer predicting catastrophe for Jehoshaphat's fleet (20:37) fits a pattern of prophetic rebuke and divine judgment of the king of Judah for entering into political and commercial alliances with the Northern Kingdom of Israel or other foreign nations. Biblical historians are careful to portray the full humanity of the characters on stage in the Old Testament so that God is praised as the key actor in the drama of history, not "super saints."

Application. The idea of relevance is not a recent cultural invention. People, whether living in an ancient, modern, or postmodern society, seek relevance because at some level "theory" and "practice" must overlap for life to have meaning and purpose. In fact, if Chronicles is indeed a "theology of hope" for postexilic Judah, then in one sense the two books are all about the relevance of earlier Hebrew history for the contemporary generation. For the Chronicler, that relevance or applicability is found in things like the example of humble obedience to the commandments found in God's word, the efficacy of heartfelt prayer to the Lord God of heaven when trouble looms large on the horizon, or the experience of joy associated with the proper worship of Yahweh at his temple.

Why are the Old Testament prophets relevant, and what makes their message spoken to ancient Israel more than twenty-five centuries ago applicable to contemporary culture? They do not speak *of* our age but *to* it because the word of Yahweh is in their mouths as his messengers. But here is the rub: I fear we do not know the message of the prophets.

I am inclined to surmise that many of our Protestant traditions perpetuate a "practical Marcionism" because they send students to college who have little or no acquaintance with the Old Testament story. Naturally, the home and the church must work together in the biblical education of Christian young people, and the impact of Christian home schooling and Christian elementary and high school education is encouraging. But the general lack of Old Testament knowledge among students entering Christian colleges is a disturbing trend.

The significance of the prophetic voices in this section of Chronicles is not the application of their message to our times but an exhortation to find out what that message was so we can then make contemporary application. King Jehoshaphat's charge to "have faith in his prophets" (20:20) is still our directive in the sense that we, too, accept the Old Testament prophets as Yahweh's clarions, trumpeting his word to God's faithful across the generations. The Chronicler would call us to "have faith" in God's prophets to the point where we indeed believe that they were divinely commissioned messengers who spoke the very words of God.

One way for the Christian church to "gather around" the Hebrew prophets is to utilize the prophetic books of the Old Testament on a regular basis—thus giving credence to Paul's instruction (1 Tim 4:13). In addition to the public reading of the Old Testament as a part of the Scripture lessons in the service of the word in corporate worship, the corpus of the Old Testament prophets must also be a resource for Christian preaching. Christians can experience the immediacy of God's word from the preaching of the Old Testament as well as the New. The practical benefits of exploring the relevance of the Old Testament prophets for the Christian church are timely, even crucial as modernity gives way to postmodernity. This is true primarily because the ideology of religious pluralism is the shared common denominator between the cultural contexts of the biblical prophets and contemporary North American society.

2 CHRONICLES 21:4–23:21

Original Meaning

Jehoram (21:4–20). Jehoram's crime of fratricide is the first of four acts of violence against the house of David in this narrative unit (21:4, 17; 22:8–9, 10–11). The Chronicler traces the wickedness of Jehoram directly to his marriage to "a daughter of Ahab" (21:6). Tragically, the corruption of godly kingship through intermarriage is a repeated theme in the history of the Israelite monarchy. In the present case, the affiliation of the house of Judah with the house of Ahab through the marriage of Jehoram and Athaliah is a recipe for self-destruction.

The report of rebellions against Jehoram and Judah by Edom and Libnah (21:8–10a) closely follows 2 Kings 8:20–22. According to the Chronicler's theology of immediate retribution, there is direct correspondence between a king's political power and his faithfulness to the tenets of Yahweh's covenant. Jehoram's political weakness is attested by his failure to control former Judean satellite states and cities. The author's theological commentary on the two revolts against Jehoram places blame directly on the king's sin of idolatry, implied in the references to the "high places" and the activity of the people in "prostituting themselves" (21:10b–11).

Along with royal speeches and prayers, the report of Elijah's letter to King Jehoram is typical of the kinds of material peculiar to the Chronicler in the nonsynoptic portions of his history. Elijah was alive during part of Jehoram's reign since he was apparently a coregent with Jehoshaphat as early as 853 BC. Prophetic documents like letters and written oracles are known at the same time period (cf. 1 Chr 29:29; 2 Chr 20:34).

The letter's contents reflect Elijah's confrontation with the house of Ahab in both subject matter and tone. The body of Elijah's letter is characteristic of Old Testament prophetic speech. The messenger formula (21:12) identifies the source and authority of the message. The pattern of indictment followed by the pronouncement of judgment is typical of the structure of preexilic prophetic oracles. Jehoram's crimes are twofold: adhering to the ways of the kings of the rival Northern Kingdom and murdering his own brothers (21:13). The phrase "the ways of the kings of Israel" (21:13) refers to Jeroboam's sin of idolatry, perpetuated by all his successors in Israel (1 Kgs 14:9; cf. 15:34).

The king's punishment, a hideous and lingering disease (2 Chr 21:15), strikes at the heart of Jehoram's sin—his failure to recognize that kingship belongs to God and not to any human being. The humiliating malady exposes his mortality and mocks his dignity as royalty.

The report of the revolt on the part of the Philistines and Arabs (21:16b) validates the prophecy of Elijah against the royal household (21:14) and underscores the theme of immediate divine retribution in Chronicles. The capture (and eventual execution) of the royal family and the plundering of royal spoils (21:17) strikes a telling blow at the core values of kingship, humanly speaking.

The focus of the report of divine judgment against the house of Jehoram shifts to the king himself (21:18–19). Again,

God is identified as the agent of justice in the punishment of Jehoram's sin (21:18; cf. 21:10). Jehoram is afflicted with a humiliating and an incurable illness, described only as an excruciatingly painful disease of the bowels (21:15, 18). Tragically, this descendant of David dies ignominiously, and even his own people refuse to honor him in death with the customary royal funeral fire (21:19; cf. 16:14).

The last words concerning Jehoram are both a parting insult of his person and a final assessment of his reign—he is denied burial in the royal tomb complex of the Davidic family (21:20d). This is a fitting end for Jehoram, since he has walked in the ways of the house of Ahab, not David.

King Ahaziah (22:1–9). The Chronicler hurries to tell the story of Jehoram's son Ahaziah. His reign is treated almost like an extension of Jehoram's rule. The insertion that Ahaziah takes counsel from the "house of Ahab" (22:4) again signals the Chronicler's concern over the impact political alliances have on the history of the two monarchies.

The account of King Ahaziah's reign consists of three brief reports: the regnal résumé and theological review (22:1–4), the alliance with Joram of Israel (22:5–6a), and the death report (22:6b–9). The one-year reign of Ahaziah is dated anywhere from 845–841 BC, depending on the source. His brief tenure in the royal office is best placed in 842 or 841 BC.

The raiders in league with the Arabs who are responsible for slaying the older princes of Judah are probably Philistines (22:1; cf. 21:16–17). Ahaziah is thus the sole surviving heir of Jehoram and the Davidic line (21:17). The name of Ahaziah's mother, Athaliah, is included in the regnal résumé for two reasons (22:2).

1. Her relationship to the dynasty of Omri as daughter of Ahab and Jezebel explains the influence of the "house of Ahab" (22:3) on the kingdom of Judah.
2. As a member of Ahab's family, Athaliah takes it upon herself to destroy the royal family of Judah (22:10). By virtue of her role as queen mother, she holds the important position of royal adviser, thus poisoning the counsel received by both her husband Jehoram and her son Ahaziah. The status and authority she enjoys as queen mother also enables her to fill the power vacuum left by the death of her son and to usurp the throne of David.

The Chronicler offers one example of such lethal counsel in the decision of Ahaziah to join forces with King Joram of the rival Israelite kingdom against a common enemy, Hazael king of Aram (22:5–6a). Such an alliance with the apostate state of Israel is doomed to failure, as the unfolding story demonstrates.

We learn from the narrative that King Joram is wounded in battle at Ramoth Gilead by the Arameans (22:6a). Hoping to speed the healing of his injuries, Joram retreats to the safety of Jezreel. It is there that Ahaziah visits his recuperating ally, only to meet his end (22:6b).

The Chroniclers' theological commentary bluntly states that God "brought about Ahaziah's downfall" (22:7). The message of the passage is alarmingly clear: God repays evil for evil almost immediately on those who fail to emulate David's example of righteous rule. Although the sins of the house of Ahab perpetuated by King Ahaziah are unnamed in Chronicles, it seems they include idolatry, witchcraft, and a failure to trust in God as the sovereign of Judah, as evidenced by "unholy" political alliances.

The death of Ahaziah returns us to the theme of this section of the narrative: the conflict between God's promise to David of a dynasty forever and the apparent lack of an heir to the throne. The house of David has been purged of sin, but the end result seems worse than the combined reigns of Jehoram and Ahaziah. The "lamp" of David (21:7) is in jeopardy of being extinguished by powerful Athaliah (22:9c).

The Interregnum of Athaliah (22:10–23:21). *The asylum of Joash with Jehosheba's help (22:10–12).* Athaliah seizes the Davidic throne. It seems likely that Athaliah is the daughter of the Phoenician princess Jezebel and King Ahab of Israel. Like her mother she worships the Canaanite fertility god Baal and foists Baal worship on the citizenry of the kingdom through manipulation of the king. She attempts to do what God himself will not do—completely destroy the house of David (22:10). Whatever her motivation, Athaliah seeks to eliminate all rivals to the throne of David.

One woman, Athaliah, seeks to destroy the family of David and rules the land for six years. The other, Jehosheba, works courageously and covertly to preserve the family of David during those same six years (22:11). Jehosheba is the daughter of Jehoram and probably the stepsister of Ahaziah. The name Jehosheba means "Yahweh vows." Fittingly, God uses this faithful woman to keep his oath to maintain the lamp of David (cf. 21:7).

The accession of Joash with Jehoaida's help (23:1–11). The coup led by Jehoiada the priest occurs during the seventh year of Athaliah's rule (or about 837 BC). The revolt against Athaliah is carried out by a coalition of military and religious leaders in Judah. Jehoiada is not driven by selfish motives; rather, he appeals to the promise of God anchored in the Davidic covenant (23:3b).

Jehoiada the priest is a clever strategist, planning his coup in three stages: first assembling a coalition of conspirators (23:1–3a), then strategically deploying armed guards to ensure the safety of the king (23:3b–7), and finally presenting Joash for public installation as king of Judah (23:8–11).

Jehoiada's coup is a well-planned and carefully orchestrated event. There is no dissension in the ranks, as everyone does as he is ordered (23:8). The conspiracy is shrewdly coordinated with the Sabbath observance (23:8b). The Chronicler takes pains to note that the priests and Levites rotating off-duty for the Sabbath remain in the temple area as a show of solidarity for the new king.

The distribution of weapons is a precautionary measure (23:9). The spears and shields are probably ceremonial weapons (cf. 1 Chr 18:7). The strategic deployment of armed guards completely encircles the child-king as he is presented to the public for installation (2 Chr 23:10). The installation of a king includes a coronation, anointing with oil, and the presentation of a "copy of the covenant" (23:11).

The execution of Athaliah (23:12–15). Athaliah goes to investigate for herself rather than send a royal servant (23:12). She is abruptly greeted by the sight of a coronation, that of a child-king wearing a crown and standing by his pillar at the entrance to the temple (23:13). In characteristic fashion, the Chronicler singles out the singers and the musicians for the role they play in the coronation of Joash.

The cooperation of the priests with army commanders suggests that a coalition of religious and military leaders is responsible for the coup that elevates Joash to the throne. Jehoiada the priest also decrees that Athaliah be executed outside temple precincts so not to defile the sacred site (23:14).

Covenant renewal in Judah (23:16–19). The coronation of Joash climaxes with a covenant-renewal ceremony led by Jehoiada the priest (23:16). Two distinct but related covenants are enacted in the aftermath of the coup against Athaliah. The first covenant is ratified by the king and the people of Jerusalem, reestablishing the authority of Davidic kingship in Judah. The second pact is a covenant-renewal ceremony binding king and people in obedience to the law of Moses.

The first covenant rids the land of Athaliah, the illegitimate usurper of the Davidic throne, and reinstates Davidic kingship in Judah. The second covenant renews Yahweh's relationship with Judah as God's people and reorganizes temple worship according to the law of Moses. The destruction of the Baal temple in Jerusalem and the purification of temple worship mirrors similar reforms taking place in the Northern Kingdom at the same time under the leadership of Jehu. For the Chronicler, the restoration of proper temple worship is no less important than the reestablishment of Davidic kingship in Judah.

The installation of King Joash (23:20–21). The installation of Joash on the royal throne (23:20) marks the end of the interregnum under Athaliah. Thanks to Jehosheba and Jehoiada, there has been, in one sense, no interruption of Davidic kingship in Judah—Joash has been there all along.

Application. As modernism gives way to postmodernism and both secular society and the Christian church recover a new sense of collective identity in their denial of individualism and rediscovery of community, let us not forget the Chronicler's affirmation of human individuality. His emphasis on named individuals in the genealogical prologue and the narrative history of the Israelite monarchies reminds each of us of our uniqueness and importance. In the stories of a man like Jehoiada and a woman like Jehosheba, the Chronicler proclaims that each person is indeed fearfully and wonderfully made in the image of our God (Ps 139). More than this, the Chronicler reminds us that each person of faith in the God of the Bible becomes an integral player on the stage of redemptive history as he or she steps out and "shows strength" with the help of the Holy Spirit (2 Chr 23:1). His record of Hebrew history becomes an invitation and exhortation to renew our partnership with Yahweh in the making of "His-story" as Jesus Christ continues to build his church in the world!

2 CHRONICLES 24:1–26:23

Original Meaning

Joash (24:1–27). *Opening regnal résumé (24:1–3).* The forty-year reign of Joash is dated variously between 840 and 796 BC. The Old Testament chronology informing this study dates his rule from about 835 to 796 BC. The Chronicler divides the reign of Joash into two distinct and contrasting periods: the good years of his early rule under the tutelage of Jehoiada and the later years of apostasy. The Chronicler refers to the progeny of Joash (24:3), and one assumes it is registered as part of the king's favorable theological review since children are a sign of divine blessing (cf. 11:18–21; 13:21). The arrangement of two marriages for Joash by the priest Jehoida (24:3) is in keeping with the Mosaic law. It is probably an attempt to ensure the viability of the Davidic line, given the recent episodes of fratricide and infanticide against the royal family.

Jehoiada and Joash (24:4–16). The favorable report concerning Joash's reign centers on the dual themes of the renovation of Yahweh's temple and the figure of Jehoiada as the ideal high priest. Athaliah not only usurped the Davidic throne but also seized the temple and implemented Baal worship there. The desecration of the sanctuary included structural damage as well (24:7).

Jehoiada is the model high priest for the Chronicler because of his role as royal guardian and adviser. The ideal of shared power between the civil and religious sectors in the oversight of Israel can be traced back to the leadership of Moses and Aaron after the exodus. In one sense Jehoiada is a prototype for the high priests of the later postexilic period since he wields considerable civil authority. Unlike those priests of the later period, however, Jehoiada shows great concern for the preservation of legitimate kingship in Israel.

The expression "old and full of years" is an idiom signifying honor and respect, and Jehoiada's longevity is a sign of divine favor (24:15). Jehoiada is remembered especially for two things: leading Israel in covenant faithfulness and leading in the initiative to refurbish the temple (24:16). Ironically, Jehoiada is accorded a better burial than Joash eventually receives ("buried with the kings," 24:16; cf. 24:25).

Joash's apostasy (24:17–26). The expression "paid homage" (24:17) may suggest that the leaders exploit a character weakness in Joash through flattery. The elders prefer to return to the policies of Joash's father. Perhaps such religious policy is advantageous socially and economically. For the Chronicler, however, to abandon the temple is to abandon God (24:18).

God voices his displeasure with Judah through the message of an unspecified number of prophets—but to no avail, as the people will "not listen" (24:19). One of those divine messengers is the priest Zechariah, son of Jehoiada (24:20). Zechariah's message is delivered in two parts typical of prophetic speech: an indictment followed by a pronouncement of judgment. The indictment is posed in the form of a rhetorical question, rebuking the king's disobedience to divine commands (24:20b). The pronouncement of judgment is built on the wordplay of "abandon" (NIV "forsake"): Even as God returns to those who return to him, he also abandons those who abandon him (24:20c).

Ironically, Joash has Zechariah murdered in the courtyard of the temple, the very site where "Jehoiada and his sons" (23:11) anointed Joash as king of Judah (24:21). Zechariah's dying words (24:22b) should not be regarded as a plea for vengeance. Rather, it is a petition for God to mete out divine justice according to his righteousness. Zechariah's words soon come to pass with the assassination of Joash (24: 25).

The "turn of the year" (24:23a) probably indicates the spring season. This is the time for military campaigns in the ancient world since the dry season is beginning and agricultural activity slackens. The kingdom of King Hazael of Aram (and his son Ben-hadad) sporadically oppressed both the kingdoms of Israel and Judah. God often accomplishes the judgment of sin among his people by means of foreign invasion. Such is the case here, including the slaying of Judean officials and the plundering of Jerusalem (24:23b-c).

The Chronicler reports that the small contingent of Aramean soldiers is victorious because "the LORD delivered" the larger army of Judah into the hands of the Arameans (24:24a). The sovereignty of God as just judge and lord of history is further highlighted in the extensive wordplay in the Chronicler's account. For example, even as Joash has abandoned God (24:20), so the Arameans "leave" or abandon the king for dead (24:25). All of this comes about because Judah has "forsaken" or abandoned the Lord (24:24). In each case, the same Hebrew word (from the root *'zb*) is employed.

The writer is careful to note that prominent among the conspirators are Zabad and Jehozabad—both sons of non-Hebrew women (24:26). It is as if the Chronicler seeks to emphasize the irony of the situation since these "mixed-blood" Israelites have a greater sense of justice than the king and citizens of Judah.

Concluding regnal résumé (24:27). The word "annotations" (*midrash*) occurs elsewhere only in 13:22, where the historical source is associated with Iddo the prophet. Presumably the idea of *midrash* here is theological commentary on the annals of the monarchy. If the prophetic oracles or burdens (Heb. *massa*; NIV "prophecies") mentioned in this concluding résumé refer to the prophetic ministry of 24:19, then the translation "oracles *against* him" (NRSV, emphasis added; NIV "about") may be closer to the Chronicler's intended meaning.

Amaziah (25:1–28). *Opening regnal résumé (25:1–4).* Amaziah seems to share a lengthy coregency with his son Uzziah (cf. 2 Kgs 14:23; 15:1). The capture of Amaziah by Jehoash of Israel may have necessitated the extended period of coregency (cf. 2 Chr 25:23). Amaziah rules the kingdom of Judah from approximately 796 to 767 BC. Second Kings 14:3 qualifies Amaziah's righteousness as a ruler by reporting that he follows his father Joash's example rather than David as the ideal king. The Chronicler offers the same assessment but inserts the report about Amaziah's execution of the assassins responsible for murdering his father (2 Chr 25:3–4).

Chronicles take pains to demonstrate Amaziah's strict adherence to the prescriptions of Mosaic law in not executing the sons of the conspirators. Amaziah obeys the law of Moses selectively, bringing just punishment against the conspirators responsible for his father's murder but ignoring the injunctions against false worship in the Canaanite high places.

The campaign against Edom (25:5–13). The mustering of militia along tribal subdivisions follows the pattern of previous kings. Conscripting males aged twenty and older for military service goes back to the census of the Israelites taken by Moses after the exodus (cf. Num 1:18–19). The fact that the tribe of Benjamin is explicitly mentioned in the muster roll suggests that Judah still controls that region, which buffered the kingdoms of Judah and Israel.

The expression "man of God" (2 Chr 25:7) is often a title for a prophetic figure. This unnamed individual is one of two anonymous prophets who approach King Amaziah with a message from God. At times God's prophets remain unnamed so as to highlight the message rather than the messenger. The first prophet advises the king to reject the help of mercenaries from the kingdom of Israel because "the LORD is not with Israel" (25:7). Amaziah needs to be reminded that Judah's power and might reside in God as her ally, not in the sheer number of soldiers marshaled for battle.

Amaziah's decision to dismiss the Israelite mercenaries (25:10) is not risk free. The man of God makes no promises that the campaign against Edom will be completely void of trouble. Each soldier goes back to Israel with three shekels (or about three months of wages) for sidestepping the battlefield. Perhaps not bad pay for no work but what an insult to the professional soldier! Their "great rage" (25:10) portends evil for Judah, as the Chronicler reports (25:13). Judah's defeat of Edom is both decisive and bloodthirsty (25:12).

Amaziah responds favorably to the word of the man of God in the matter of the Israelite mercenaries (25:10). But the same cannot be said for the enraged soldiers who are dismissed and sent back to Samaria. Their fury against Amaziah and the kingdom of Judah is vented in a raid. The attack leaves three thousand citizens of Judah dead. This event prompts Amaziah to "challenge" King Jehoash of Israel (25:17).

Amaziah's apostasy (25:14–16). Perhaps Amaziah assumes that Judah's defeat of Edom is due in part to a shift in loyalty of the Edomite deities to the cause of Judah. This would explain his need to placate these gods in some way. The words "bow down" and "burn sacrifices" (25:14) are terms signifying acts of worship reserved solely for Yahweh according to the Mosaic law.

A second nameless prophet is commissioned by God to rebuke Amaziah (25:15). According to the sanctions of the Davidic covenant, idolatry by the royal family puts the whole nation at risk of being exiled from the land (cf. 7:19–22). The petulant Amaziah interrupts the prophet mid-sentence and commands him to desist in his indictment, upon threat of death (25:16). Although the prophet stops his oracle, God's message cannot be stopped—to reject the counsel of God's prophet is to reject God himself. The course of events will soon demonstrate that Amaziah can ignore the prophet's counsel—but not God's!

The campaign against Israel (25:17–24). It is unclear whether Amaziah's invitation to meet Jehoash (25:17) is an act of diplomacy for the purpose of arranging a political marriage between the Northern and Southern Kingdoms (25:18) or a veiled challenge to cross swords in a military engagement in order to seek revenge (cf. 25:13). King Jehoash of Israel clearly interprets the initiative as the latter.

Jehoash responds to Amaziah's challenge with a fable about a thistle trampled by a wild beast (25:18). Jehoash identifies the motivation behind Amaziah's challenge, pride, and arrogance as a result of his success against the Edomites (25:19a). His warning threatens doom not only on Amaziah but also Judah (25:19b).

The Chronicler again emphasizes that Yahweh is sovereign (25:16, 20). God utilizes Amaziah's pride and obstinacy to accomplish his purposes of judging the king's sin and punishing the nation of Judah for their breach of covenant loyalty. According to the battle report (25:21–24), King Jehoash goes on the offensive in response to Amaziah's challenge and routs Judah at Beth Shemesh (25:21–22). In a further show of force, Jehoash batters down a lengthy section of the wall of Jerusalem and plunders the temple of its gold and silver (25:24).

Concluding regnal résumé (25:25–28). It is likely that Amaziah's false worship is the catalyst that bonds a group of conspirators from Judah to plot Amaziah's assassination for some fifteen years. Most likely it is a coalition of priests along with civil and military leaders similar to the one that elevated Joash to the throne of Judah. The report of Amaziah's assassination includes his flight to Lachish. Assassins from Jerusalem hunt him down there, execute him, and convey his corpse back to Jerusalem for burial in the royal tomb complex (25:27–28).

Uzziah (26:1–23). *Opening regnal résumé (26:1–5).* The writer of Kings prefers the name Azariah, apparently a variant of Uzziah. Perhaps the Chronicler's preference for Uzziah is a deliberate attempt to avoid confusion with Azariah the priest (26:17–20). The Chronicler's assessment of Uzziah as one who does "right . . . just as his father Amaziah had done" (26:4) is hardly a ringing endorsement, since in the end Amaziah was an apostate king (25:27). Uzziah rules the kingdom of Judah for fifty-five years, from approximately 792 to 740 BC (ruling as coregent with his father from 792–767).

Uzziah's fame (26:6–15). The report of Uzziah's prosperity (26:6–15) has no parallel in 2 Kings. The litany of achievements attesting divine favor include military victory over Judah's archenemies (26:6–8), extensive building activity and agricultural bounty (26:9–10), and the marshalling of a large, well-trained, and well-equipped army (26:11–15). The unit is framed by a formula of prosperity that highlights Uzziah's "fame" and "power" (26:8, 15). In combination these two epithets are a recipe for pride and eventual self-destruction since a proud heart tends to "forget the LORD" (Deut 8:14).

The Chronicler summarizes Uzziah's foreign policy by reporting his military campaigns against the Philistines, Arabs, and Ammonites (26:6–8). King Uzziah's domestic policy is characterized by building achievements and agricultural prosperity (26:9–10). Both are typically understood as signs of divine favor in the Old Testament world. No doubt, some of the construction is to repair the damage done by King Jehoash of Israel in his assault on Jerusalem (25:23). A considerable amount of archaeological data supports the biblical account of Uzziah's building activity, especially the reference to towers and cisterns (26:10). Not since Solomon has there been a king with such agrarian interests (cf. 1 Kgs 4:33).

Uzziah's pride and God's judgment (26:16–21). The report of Uzziah's pride is the focal point of the Chronicler's review of his reign. The ominous words, when the king "became powerful" (26:16a), link the commentary on the two phases of Uzziah's rule: the early years of God's blessing (26:5–15) and the later years of divine judgment (26:16–21). The expression "was unfaithful" (26:16) becomes a regular theme in the Chronicler's retelling of the history of Davidic kingship (cf. 28:19, 22; 29:6, 19; 30:7; 33:19).

Uzziah's haughtiness so impairs his judgment that he attempts to enter the temple and burn incense to the Lord, thus usurping the role of the priests (26:16). Only the Aaronic priesthood was allowed to attend to the altar and burn incense there. Like Kings Saul and Jeroboam I, who also sought to assume the priestly role, Uzziah is rebuked by a priest (26:17–18). This challenge to royal authority is done at great risk, given the recent horror of Joash's murder of the priest Zechariah (cf. 24:22).

Azariah identifies the key issue in the conflict with Uzziah. Even as the Davidic king is anointed to shepherd the Israelite nation, so the Aaronic priest is anointed to serve God and the people through the ministry of ritual sacrifice. Azariah's threat to Uzziah is cast generally as a censure of divine honor for the king (26:18).

Enraged at the priests for intercepting him in the temple and thwarting his attempt to burn incense on the altar, Uzziah is afflicted by God (26:20). It is important to notice that God's anger breaks out against Uzziah only after he has vented his anger against the priests (26:19). His disregard for the Lord's priests and the Lord's sanctuary implicitly signals a disregard for God himself. Uzziah thus joins the ignominious list of other kings afflicted by God with a disease as punishment for unfaithfulness, which results in becoming ritually impure and socially unclean. More significant is the dishonor of being excluded from worship in the temple of the Lord (26:21).

Concluding regnal résumé (26:22–23). The record of Isaiah son of Amoz is one of several prophetic resources in the Chronicler's bibliography. The details concerning Uzziah's skin disease and his place of burial are important to the Chronicler for two reasons.

1. The Chronicler is a priest, and ritual purity is paramount for his fellow members of the Levitical orders.
2. Preservation of Uzziah's banishment from the royal tomb complex serves to further the legitimation of the priestly hierocracy in Judah during the postexilic period.

Application. We have already learned from the lives of kings Joash, Amaziah, and Uzziah that receiving instruction and accepting counsel demand listening skills and that such skills are directly related to the fear of the LORD. It is the biblical notion of the fear of the Lord that fosters reliance on God and receptivity to divine wisdom, in contrast to self-reliance and dependence on one's own understanding.

2 CHRONICLES 27:1–32:33

Original Meaning

Jotham (27:1–9). The brief report of King Jotham's reign is little more than a postscript to King Uzziah's tenure on the throne of Judah. Harmonizing the chronological data for Jotham's reign proves challenging. Typically, his sixteen-year rule is dated from 750–735 BC. It appears that Jotham serves as a coregent with his father, Uzziah, for the first ten years of his kingship (750–740 BC). The reference to the twentieth year of King Jotham (2 Kgs 15:30) is usually understood to mean that Jotham's reign also overlaps with that of his son Ahaz. If so, then Ahaz is coregent and junior partner with his father Jotham commencing in 735 BC. Jotham probably dies in 732 BC.

Jotham is the first king of Judah since Abijah to receive an unqualified theological review from the Chronicler (27:2; cf. 13:1–22). Jotham's righteousness is illustrated by both a positive and negative analogy to his father Uzziah. The theme of individual responsibility reappears in the Chronicler's report in that Jotham's reign has little impact on the corrupt practices of the citizenry of Judah (27:2c).

The Chronicler's review of Jotham's reign applauds achievements on three fronts: his building program, his military success, and his consolidation of political power (27:3–6). Jotham's war with the Ammonites (27:5) is not mentioned elsewhere in the Old Testament, but the campaign extends his father's military expansion from areas southwest of Judah to the east. But unlike his father, Jotham does not fall prey to the temptation of pride and turn away from God. His success is attributed directly to the fact that he "walked steadfastly before the LORD" (27:6).

The repetition of age of accession and length of reign from the opening résumé is unusual. The resulting *inclusio* or envelope construction serves to emphasize the significant accomplishments of a youthful king in a comparatively brief period of time. In contrast to his father, Uzziah, Jotham is buried in the city of David in the royal tomb complex (27:9).

Ahaz (28:1–27). *Opening regnal résumé (28:1–4).* The Chronicler's negative theological review of Ahaz is uniquely phrased in that he is measured against King David and then indicted (28:1–2). The negative theological review is supported by a shocking list of covenant violations, such as idolatry (28:2), child sacrifice (28:3), and participation in the false worship associated with the Canaanite high places (28:4). The Valley of Ben Hinnom (28:3) was located immediately south of the Temple Mount and was the site of the city dump, where fires continually burned dead animals and garbage. The ritual of human sacrifice is associated with this valley elsewhere in the Old Testament. Perhaps the most striking comment in this résumé is the observation that King Ahaz is guilty of perpetuating the very sins for which God previously judged the indigenous Canaanites (28:3).

Defeat by Syria (Aram) and Israel (28:5–15). The account of the Syro-Ephraimite war in Chronicles differs from that in 2 Kings 16 by downplaying the coalition of Syria (or Aram) and Israel and stressing instead the extent of Judah's defeat. The large numbers of casualties and captives reported by the Chronicler (28:6, 8) have troubled biblical commentators. Beyond the sheer totals, the devastating losses to Judah are compounded by the deaths of key officials (28:7). The deaths of three members of Ahaz's cabinet would have had a crippling effect in the administration of political and military affairs in Judah.

The Chronicler often uses prophetic intervention and oracular speech as a vehicle for his theology of immediate retribution. Interestingly, Oded is a prophet of Yahweh from Israel, whose ministry is centered in Samaria; clearly God still has a voice in the Northern Kingdom (28:9). His indictment of Israel serves as the source for the Chronicler's interpretation of the events of Ahaz's reign, as it is God who hands over Judah to Aram and Israel (28:9; cf. 28:5). The Chronicler's positive portrayal of the Northern Kingdom should not go unnoticed, as he links both Israel and Judah to the same God (28:10) and identifies the citizenry of each as "fellow Israelites" (28:11). Unlike King Ahaz and their Judean counterparts, the leadership of Israel responds to the word of God through the prophet Oded and repents of their actions (28:12–13).

Further defeats of Judah (28:16–21). King Ahaz faces enemy aggression on two fronts, the Syro-Ephraimite coalition in the north and the alliance of the Philistines and Edomites in the south. The heavy losses suffered at the hands of the invading Israelites and Arameans (28:5–15) forces Ahaz to seek the "help" (28:16) of Tiglath-Pileser III, king of Assyria (745–727 BC). This dangerous diplomacy of playing one ancient superpower (i.e., Assyria) against another (i.e., Egypt) as an ally in petty border wars with neighboring nations was a ploy of the Northern Kingdom of Israel during the reign of Jeroboam II—a tactic soundly condemned by Hosea the prophet (Hos 7:11).

In one sense, Ahaz is paying for the success of his predecessors since the Edomites seek retaliation against King Amaziah (cf. 2 Chr 25:14) and the Philistines seek to recoup earlier losses to King Uzziah (cf. 26:6). Given his predicament, Ahaz seeks help from the Assyrians despite the fact that God helped faithful kings of Judah in times past. According to the Chronicler, all this comes about to "humble Judah" because of the wickedness of Ahaz (28:19). The reference to Ahaz as the "king of Israel" (28:19) serves as a stern reminder that the responsibility for Judah's plight lies with Ahaz as the Davidic shepherd of the people.

Rather than "help," Ahaz receives "trouble" from the Assyrians (28:20). Judah not only suffers depleted economic resources because of the imposition of annual Assyrian tribute (28:21) but also loses its political autonomy—as Judah, Ammon, Moab, Ashkelon, Edom, and Gaza are all subordinated to Assyria as vassal states.

Ahaz's apostasy (28:22–25). Ahaz's "time of trouble" (28:22) affords the king the opportunity to seek the Lord in penitent prayer. But instead of turning to God, he strays even further by worshiping the gods of the victorious Syrians or Arameans (28:23). By failing to acknowledge the God of Israel as sovereign Lord, Ahaz rejects the one source from which he may have received the help he so desperately pursues.

The proliferation of false worship under King Ahaz (28:24–25) echoes the apostasy of Jeroboam I at the time of the schism (cf. 13:8–9). The idolatry of Ahaz has even greater affinities to the reign of King Ahab of Israel, however, in that both Ahaz and Ahab institutionalize the worship of false gods as the state religion of their respective kingdoms.

Concluding regnal résumé (28:26–27). Like King Uzziah before him (26:23), Ahaz is denied the honor of proper burial "in the tombs of the kings of Israel" (28:27)—the ultimate negative theological review for the Chronicler.

Hezekiah (29:1–32:33). *Invitation to purify the temple (29:1–11).* The genre of report comprises all of chapters 29–31, which document Hezekiah's temple reforms and festival keeping. Unlike Jehoshaphat, who was likened to King David during the early years of his reign (17:3), King Hezekiah is fully compared to David (29:2). In fact, the reference to David foreshadows several direct analogies between that ideal king and Hezekiah later in the narrative.

Hezekiah's invitation to purify the temple (29:3–11) is dominated by a royal speech (29:5–11) directed to the priests and Levites (29:4). The king's speech to the priests and Levites contains two injunctions: a call to the religious leadership to "consecrate" themselves and an instruction to them to "remove all defilement from the sanctuary" (29:5).

The rest of the royal address rehearses the neglect of the temple by Hezekiah's predecessors (29:6–8). The depth of Judah's apostasy under Ahaz is underscored in the fivefold emphasis on their wicked deeds (29:6). It is for this reason that Yahweh's wrath fell on Judah, resulting in costly losses in battle and the exile of many citizens of Judah (29:9).

In advocating covenant renewal, Hezekiah is almost a Moses-type figure, acting as intercessor for the nation (29:10). Hezekiah adjures the priests and Levites against continued apathy and dereliction of duty (29:11). By appealing to them as "sons" (29:11), the king acknowledges their key role and encourages their renewed participation in the religious life of the Hebrew community.

Renewing temple worship (29:12–36). The purification of the temple (29:12–19). The name list serves both to memorialize the contributions of key leaders in Israelite history and to remind the present audience that God's work is accomplished through the cooperative efforts of faithful individuals. The Chronicler records the names of fourteen individuals (29:12–14) who serve as the leaders of the purification ritual of the temple (29:15–19).

The actual cleansing of the temple takes two weeks, one week for the outer courts and another week to purge the sanctuary itself (29:15–17). The Chronicler is careful to indicate the work is done in accordance with the "the word of the LORD" (29:15). The work of cleansing the temple involved a two-stage process:

1. the purification of the temple and its courts by the removal of everything "unclean" (29:16), and
2. the consecration of the temple structure and its furnishings and implements by ritual sacrifice (29:20–36).

King Hezekiah includes the fact that all the temple utensils have been recovered and cleansed (29:18–19). Presumably they were stored or simply discarded in one of the anterooms of the temple during the reign of "unfaithful" Ahaz (29:19). The purified temple implements are arrayed before the altar of burnt offering, thus setting the stage for the report of the ritual sacrifices necessary for consecration and the resumption of the temple liturgy (29:20–36).

The consecration of the temple (29:20–36). The ceremony for the consecration of the temple is a multifaceted event.

1. The initial phase addresses the issues of sin and purification in the community (29:20–24).
2. The next phase features burnt offerings signifying the dedication of the religious and civic leaders and the sanctuary to the service of God (29:25–30). The burnt-offering ritual is accompanied by instrumental and choral music from the Levitical musicians and concludes with prostration in reverent worship (29:29–30). There is some question as to whether the sin offering and burnt offering are sequential or simultaneous events.
3. The final stage includes participation by the assembly of people from Jerusalem and Judah (representing "all Israel") through additional burnt offerings and thank offerings (29:31–36).

The Chronicler's emphasis on Hezekiah's orchestration of the consecration ceremony is unmistakable as the king "gathers" the civic leaders (29:20a), "commands" the priests to perform the ritual sacrifice (29:21b), and "gives orders" for the proceedings to begin (29:24). The multiples of seven in the list of sacrificial animals suggest the completeness of both the extent and the degree to which the sin offering is to be applied to the nation of Judah (29:21).

The consecration ceremony emphasizes the dedication of the purified religious and civic leaders and the temple structure to the service of Yahweh (29:25–30). The Chronicler takes great pains to demonstrate the legitimacy of the rituals associated with the consecration ceremony by establishing direct connections to earlier traditions originating with David and sanctioned by God's word through the prophets (29:25–26).

It is clear to all that Yahweh is King in Israel, not Hezekiah, for he, too, bows before the Lord with the assembly (29:29). The blending of joy in the singing of praises and reverence in bowing down are significant. The atonement ritual is not perceived as an end in itself but rather as a necessary preparation for the responses of praise and thanksgiving to God. The reference to Asaph the seer (29:30) recalls the commissioning of certain members of the Levitical musical guilds for the ministry of prophesying.

During the final phase of the consecration ceremony (29:31–36) the rites of purification and dedication are extended to the "assembly" (29:31) and "all the people" of Judah (29:36). Unlike the public sacrifices atoning for the sin of the civic and religious leaders, the sacrifices of this final stage are freewill offerings presented by individuals "whose hearts were willing" (29:31).

The Chronicler commends the spirit of the Levites in assisting the priests in flaying the animals for sacrifice (29:34a). Apparently, a spirit of apathy still plagues the priesthood since some are slow to respond to Hezekiah's reforms (29:34b). Obviously, the reign of Ahaz has cast a long shadow over temple worship and the priestly corps who serve there.

The rejoicing reported by the Chronicler celebrates the rescue of the people of Judah by God, since they now realize they had come perilously close to sharing the fate of the Northern Kingdom. That the restoration of temple worship is truly an act of God is seen in the fact that it is accomplished so quickly (29:36).

Invitation to celebrate the Passover (30:1–12). The introductory section of the chapter recounts the decision to celebrate the Passover in Jerusalem at the reopened temple (30:1–5). King Hezekiah and the "assembly" make this decision (30:2); the latter is apparently an advisory council comprised of ordinary citizens, tribal leaders, and royal officials. The "assembly" figures prominently in the Chronicler's narrative of Hezekiah's Passover and provides yet another link between this king and the populist reigns of David and Solomon.

The actual text of Hezekiah's letter is summarized in the second section of the unit (30:6–9). Curiously, the letter itself does not mention the Passover celebration—although this is the theme of the entire pericope. The so-called Passover letter is sent "throughout Israel and Judah" (30:6) as Hezekiah seeks to reunite the tribes in the aftermath of the Assyrian conquest and annexation of the Northern Kingdom. The reference to "Ephraim and Manasseh" (a word pair often used for the Northern Kingdom of Israel, 30:10; cf. 34:9) is inserted almost as a point of clarification or special emphasis. Israelites who live anywhere from Beersheba to Dan are invited to the Passover.

The Chronicler's report (30:6–12) continues to emphasize King Hezekiah's role in the initiative to reunite Israel and Judah through worship at the site chosen and consecrated by God (30:8). The text of the letter has affinities to the Levitical sermons and prophetic speeches of Chronicles. In addition to calling the people to repentance, Hezekiah's letter admonishes the Israelites to cease being "unfaithful" (30:7) and "stiff-necked" (30:8) like their ancestors. The time to break with the past is long overdue. Hezekiah's letter holds out hope to those who have escaped the wrath of God meted out through Assyrian kings. The appeal to the Lord, who "is gracious and compassionate" (30:9), seems to allude once again to Solomon's dedicatory prayer, beseeching God to induce Israel's conquerors to show mercy on his people should they sin and be overtaken by their enemies (cf. 1 Kgs 8:50).

Predictably, Hezekiah's invitation to renew festival worship in the reopened Jerusalem temple receives a mixed response (2 Chr 30:10–12). The majority of Israelites in the regions of Ephraim, Manasseh, and Zebulun spurn the invitation, while others make the pilgrimage to Jerusalem (30:10–11). The overwhelming response of those in the kingdom of Judah to obey the king is a remarkable demonstration of solidarity and is attributed to the "hand of God" on the people (30:12).

Celebrating the Passover and the Feast of Unleavened Bread (30:13–31:1). The Chronicler's report alternates between the description of the Feast of Unleavened Bread (2 Chr 30:13–14, 21–27) and the Passover (30:15–20). Hezekiah's festival may be outlined in three broad movements: the assembling of large numbers of Israelites making the pilgrimage to Jerusalem (30:13, 17–18), the cleansing and consecration rituals (30:14–16, 19), and the sacrifice of joyful praise extended over a two-week period (30:21–27). The reference to the size of the crowd gathered in Jerusalem for the festival is significant not so much for the sake of the sheer numbers as its composition of people from all over Judah and Israel (30:10–13). The inclusion of worshipers from the northern tribes speaks to the theme of reunification under King Hezekiah (cf. 30:18).

The rituals associated with the Passover are the focus of the Chronicler's report in 30:15–20. The religious leaders in charge of instructing the people in the law of Moses and in mediating the sacrificial worship of Israel are outdone by a righteous laity. Shortly thereafter the priests and the Levites are consecrated, so they, too, are careful to follow the prescriptions of the Mosaic law in discharging their duties as mediators of the Passover (30:16).

The Chronicler makes an important theological observation that intent of heart and acts of repentance, when combined with intercessory prayer, override the letter of the law when it comes to the worship of God (30:18–19). The result is answered prayer in the form of God's "healing" of the people (30:20).

The Levites return to center stage through their ministry of praise music during the week-long festival (30:21–22). Hezekiah's affirmation of the Levites is a poignant personal touch preserved by the Chronicler (30:22).

The seven-day extension of Hezekiah's Passover and Unleavened Bread festivals (30:23–27) has its precedent in the protraction of the ceremonies accompanying Solomon's dedication of the temple (cf. 7:8–10). The joy experienced by those participating in the festival affords the Chronicler a further opportunity to compare King Hezekiah with the Davidic and Solomonic ideal (30:26). No doubt, there is a less-than-subtle message about the relationship between right worship and answered prayer for the Chronicler's audience (30:27).

Hezekiah's further reforms (31:2–21). The cleansing and reopening of the temple brings about the restoration of the temple liturgy. Hezekiah reinstates the system of tithes and offerings designed to both worship God and financially underwrite the ministry of the priests and Levites (30:2–3). These reforms are necessary because presumably the priestly orders devoted to the sacrificial liturgy and the Levitical divisions assigned to various ministries were abolished when Ahaz closed Yahweh's temple (28:24).

Hezekiah restores the divisions of the priests and Levites implemented by Solomon (8:14). The Old Testament is unapologetic about the daily provisions secured for the priests and Levites by means of the tithes and offerings brought to the temple by the citizenry. This enabled the temple personnel to devote themselves to the study and teaching of "the Law of the Lord" (2 Chr 31:4).

The response to the king's command to bring the firstfruits of the produce of the field and tithe of the herds and flocks is overwhelming (31:5–8). No doubt, the Chronicler understands these actions as signifying the genuineness of the people's repentance. The contributions come from all Israel, including the citizens of Jerusalem as well as the residents of Judah and the Israelites from the northern tribes who have emigrated to Judah (31:4, 6).

The Chronicler associates the king's blessing with those of Kings David and Solomon (31:8; cf. 1 Chr 16:2; 2 Chr 6:3). He equates the people's abundant giving with the overflow of contributions collected for the building of the tabernacle and the temple (cf. Exod 36:2–7; 1 Chr 29:6–9). Finally, the Chronicler carefully reports that the bounty of goods received is inventoried, properly stored and maintained, and distributed with equity among the families of the priests and Levites (2 Chr 31:11–19).

The concluding theological review (31:20–21) of Hezekiah is an extension of the favorable assessment found in the opening regnal résumé (29:1–2). The review also links Hezekiah with David in his wholehearted devotion to God and with Solomon in his concern for the Lord's temple, ranking him among the great kings of Israel (cf. 7:11). Hezekiah's sterling record of obedience and faithfulness to Yahweh elevates him as a premier example of the Chronicler's retribution theology and foreshadows the providential turn of events reported next.

Sennacherib besieges Jerusalem (32:1–23). Along with the building of Solomon's temple and the fall of Samaria, Sennacherib's invasion of Judah is one of the most important events in the history of the Southern Kingdom. The Assyrian campaign is dated to 701 BC, during the fourteenth year of Hezekiah. The Chronicler assumes a thorough knowledge on the part of his audience of the earlier parallel accounts (2 Kgs 18–19; Isa 36–37). The Chronicler's summary of the event largely consists of two speech acts: one by Hezekiah (32:6–8) and one by an officer of Sennacherib's army (32:10–15). This is followed by the report of a prayer by Hezekiah and Isaiah the prophet (32:20).

Hezekiah's defensive preparations (32:1–8). The Chronicler's report of Hezekiah's efforts to make ready for an Assyrian siege against Jerusalem has no parallel (32:2–5). Hezekiah's defensive precautions should not be interpreted as a lack of faith in God but rather as an example of prudence on the part of a wise king.

The defensive measures Hezekiah uses to thwart the Assyrian army include the stoppage of springs supplying fresh water around the environs of Jerusalem (32:3–4), repairing the walls and towers of Jerusalem and fortifying this reconstruction with a second "wall outside" (32:5a), and stockpiling an arsenal by making weapons and shields (32:5b).

Finally, Hezekiah organizes the citizens of Jerusalem into a militia of sorts with oversight by select military personnel (32:6). As commander-in-chief he encourages the people with a motivational speech (32:6b–8a). The king's appeal to the people is a theological treatise, not a nationalistic or patriotic rally cry.

The people take heart from the king's words and gain confidence to face the crisis because Hezekiah is able to articulate that his confidence is deeply rooted in the Lord their God. For the Hebrews, that epithet "the Lord our God" (32:8) is a reminder of God's election of the nation of Israel and his mighty deliverance of his people from Egyptian oppression at the exodus.

Sennacherib's invasion of Judah (32:9–19). It is likely that Sennacherib's Judean campaign unfolds in two stages. The first phase includes the capture of the environs of Jerusalem, and the second phase includes the siege of the city itself. The reason for Sennacherib's failure to withdraw from Judah after receiving Hezekiah's tribute is unclear, although the Assyrian king is no doubt motivated by greed to possess all the wealth of the Jerusalem temple—not just a portion of it.

The message delivered to King Hezekiah by the officers of Sennacherib (32:10–15) is a call to surrender the city of Jerusalem or die in the siege. King Sennacherib's emissaries offer two logical reasons for Judah's capitulation to the invading army.

1. The success of the Assyrian campaign in the outlying regions of Judah is interpreted as necessary retribution against Hezekiah because he has offended the gods in his purge of the "high places" (32:11–12).
2. Recent history has shown that none of the gods of the other nations was able to deliver their people from the Assyrian juggernaut (32:13–15).

The final section of the Assyrian message to Hezekiah and the citizens of Jerusalem is a taunt against the God of Israel, mocking his impotence in the current crisis (32:16–19). The gibes are delivered in the form of insulting letters written by Sennacherib himself (32:17). Sennacherib and the Assyrians will soon experience the dire consequences of putting God to the test by profaning his name in this manner.

God defends Judah (32:20–23). God's deliverance of Hezekiah and the people of Judah is achieved through prayer. The Chronicler heightens the direct intervention of God against the Assyrians by reporting that "the Lord sent an angel" into the enemy camp (32:21). The "death angel" annihilates the Assyrian army, including officers and troops. Sennacherib withdraws from Jerusalem in disgrace and returns to Assyria with the remnants of his decimated army.

No doubt the Chronicler has certain psalms in mind in which the enemies of the righteous are turned back in shame and disgrace (cf. Ps 6:10; 40:14; 70:2). His account compresses time in such a way to suggest that Sennacherib is assassinated immediately upon his return to Nineveh, perhaps to accent the retribution principle for his audience. In actuality, Sennacherib is murdered by his son Adrammelech while worshiping in the temple of Nisroch some twenty years later (ca. 681 BC).

Far more important to the Chronicler is God's deliverance of Hezekiah and Judah from the superior forces of the Assyrians (32:22). The key question of the story line has been answered: God has "saved" the king and the nation (32:22). The words of Hezekiah's speech have proven true: God's power is greater than that of the Assyrians, and he indeed fought the battle for Judah (32:8). The "offerings" brought to the Lord (32:23) are probably thank offerings or vow offerings (presented for deliverance when a vow is made on that condition).

Hezekiah's pride and death (32:24–33). The expression "in those days" (32:24) is intended to closely link Hezekiah's illness with the Assyrian invasion in a chronological sense. The actual healing of Hezekiah's life-threatening ailment is reported briefly, as the Chronicler apparently assumes his audience's knowledge of 2 Kings 20:1–11.

The direct relationship between divine blessing and God's forgiveness recorded in 2 Chronicles 32:27–31 repeats a motif associated with righteous kings (e.g., David, Solomon, Jehoshaphat, Uzziah). The reference to Hezekiah's "great wealth and honor" is another parallel the Chronicler draws between this king and Solomon (cf. 1:12; 9:22).

The concluding regnal résumé (32:32–33) references the "vision of the prophet Isaiah" as the source of the Chronicler's information. The burial formula is expanded to include a more detailed description of Hezekiah's tomb and the honor accorded him by the general populace at his death (cf. 16:14; 21:19).

Application. Three times the Chronicler conspicuously reports how Hezekiah speaks words of encouragement to the people, affirming their service to God and instilling confidence in them despite the dire circumstances portended by Sennacherib's invasion of the Southern Kingdom (cf. 30:22; 32:6–7, 8). The repetition of this character trait in the king of Judah seemingly makes the topic an obvious one for a contemporary application of this passage.

Naturally this raises the question of exactly what a virtue is. In its simplest form, a virtue is defined as "a commendable quality or trait." Given this understanding of virtue, Hezekiah's ability to encourage others is indeed a "commendable trait"—and one worth emulating! In fact, there is a biblical mandate to be a "Hezekiah" of sorts, as the New Testament itself *encourages* Christians, whether pastors or not, to be *encouragers*.

To encourage is to embolden another to overcome a paralyzing fear or deep-seated reluctance. To encourage is to inspire, to hearten, and to offer hope to another through word or deed. The New Testament values encouragement as a Christian virtue because it serves to embolden the timid in the service of Christ (1 Thess 5:14). The encourager also contributes to the righteous endurance of the Christian in that daily mutual encouragement prevents the heart from being hardened by sin's deceitfulness (Heb 3:13; cf. 10:25). The encourager thus helps build the kingdom of God because those who endure "will . . . reign with him [i.e., Christ]" (2 Tim 2:12).

2 CHRONICLES 33:1–36:1

Original Meaning

King Manasseh (33:1–20). *Judah's relapse into false worship (33:1–10).* Manasseh rules longer than any other Israelite king. His fifty-five-year reign probably includes a coregency of several years with his father, Hezekiah. The dates of his reign extend from about 696 to 642 BC. As an aside, it bears mention that Manasseh was probably born into the royal family during the fifteen-year extension of Hezekiah's life granted by God in response to his prayer for healing from a fatal disease (cf. 2 Kgs 20:1–6).

This entire section turns on the juxtaposition of the evil deeds of Manasseh and the identification of God's "Name" with the Jerusalem temple (33:4–5, 7). The litany of the king's detestable practices possibly represents the conflation of two independent sources (i.e., 33:3–6 and 33:7–9), given the repetition of the desecration of the temple precincts. The specific catalog of abominations promoted by Manasseh as "alternative religion" for the kingdom of Judah invites comparison with the Mosaic prohibitions against false worship. Among the taboos borrowed wholesale from Canaanite culture are idolatry associated with the fertility cult deities Asherah and Baal, astral worship, infanticide, and the occult (33:3–6).

The Chronicler hints at Manasseh's role in Judah's exile by referring to the "nations" driven out by the Lord when Israel entered the land of Canaan (33:2). Manasseh's responsibility for the welfare of Judah is made more clear in the Chronicler's allusion to the Davidic covenant and Israel's security in the land of covenant promise (33:7; cf. 2 Sam 7:10). The king leads the people astray by breaking the first commandment (2 Chr 33:7). The carved image he erects in God's temple symbolizes his rejection of God's rule at both the personal and the national level.

Once the Israelites renounce their covenant loyalty to Yahweh and become more evil than the nations he destroyed in the land of Canaan, God has no choice but to invoke the covenant curses on his people (cf. Deut 28:36–37). The conclusion of the first report (2 Chr 33:10), however, shifts some of the responsibility for the Babylonian exile to the people of Judah as well. They shoulder blame for the catastrophe because they refuse to heed the word of the Lord through his prophets.

Manasseh's exile and repentance (33:11–13). While Manasseh's exile has no parallel in 2 Kings and is uncorroborated by extant Assyrian sources, it seems likely that he is a coconspirator with the Babylonians in the revolt against Shamash-shum-ukin in Babylon. The nose "hook" and "bronze shackles" (33:11) are typical of the humiliation inflicted on captives in the biblical world.

God often brings trouble against his people in the Old Testament to punish and to purify them. Unlike King Ahaz, Manasseh turns to God in his distress and finds favor with the Almighty (33:12). Manasseh's plea issues from a contrite heart (33:12). This signifies true repentance, demonstrated by a broken spirit coupled with acts of penance for personal sin and disobedience to God. For this reason, the report of Manasseh's repentance and prayer of forgiveness is reminiscent of the language of God's promise to King Solomon to restore those who "humble themselves and pray" (7:14).

The expression "the LORD was moved" (33:13) is unusual and marks a theological distinctive of the God of the Bible. The stark contrast between God who listens to the plea of Manasseh and the people who pay no attention to God (33:10) would not be lost on the Chronicler's audience.

Manasseh's infrastructural repairs and spiritual reforms (33:14–17). Manasseh's reforms are both political and religious in nature, suggesting God's acceptance of the king's prayer of repentance. The rebuilding of the city wall of Jerusalem (33:14) may refer to repairs made necessary when Manasseh was taken captive by the Assyrians.

The depth, extent, and duration of Manasseh's religious reforms remain an open question. Clearly, the temple is purified and proper worship is restored at least for a short time. We are told, however, that false worship is pervasive during the reigns of the next two kings of Judah (33:22; 34:3–7). The impact of Manasseh's religious reforms seems restricted to Jerusalem and its immediate environs, given the Chronicler's reference to ongoing worship in the high places (33:17).

Concluding regnal résumé (33:18–20). Manasseh's concluding résumé is significant theologically because of the emphasis on the king's prayer of entreaty and God's response to his repentance (33:18–19).

King Amon (33:21–25). Amon's rule lasts only two years (642–640 BC, 33:21). He is judged an evil king because he perpetuates the false worship established in Judah by his father (33:22). The reason behind his assassination is unspecified (33:24). Clearly the general populace is not in sympathy with the coup since they execute those palace officials party to the conspiracy (33:25a). The expression "people of the land" (33:25a) may be an idiom for a coalition of religious and political leadership centered in Jerusalem since they also function as kingmakers in other succession crises (cf. 22:1; 26:1; 36:1).

Josiah (34:1–36:1). *Josiah's religious reform (34:1–7).* Josiah's reign can be dated with confidence to 640–609 BC. According to 34:3, Josiah begins his reform initiatives at age twenty. The age of twenty was the age of majority in Hebrew culture and, more than coincidentally for the Chronicler, the age when the Levite began his service to Yahweh (cf. Num 1:3; 1 Chr 23:24). There is a growing consensus among scholars that Josiah's reform movement predates the discovery of the law scroll in 622 BC and his later reforms associated with the temple renovation and eradication of false worship centers.

Temple repair and finding of the law scroll (34:8–33). Josiah's temple renovation (34:8–13). Josiah's plans to repair the temple serve as the setting in the Kings narrative for the discovery of the law scroll and the subsequent sweeping religious reforms in Judah. The report of Josiah's renovation of the temple in Chronicles is linked to the early reforms of the king by the insertion of the clause "to purify the land and the temple" (2 Chr 34:8; cf. 34:3). Thus, the Chronicler understands the report of the temple repair as one episode in a series of related events in Josiah's comprehensive reform movement.

The need for skilled craftsmen such as carpenters and masons indicates the temple is in a serious state of disrepair (34:10–11). Chronicles places blame for the ruin of the temple on the kings of Judah. No doubt the negligent kings the writer has in mind included Manasseh and Amon, perhaps going as far back as Ahaz. The Chronicler connects the success of the temple repairs to the faithfulness of the workers and effective supervision by the Levites (34:12–13).

Discovery of the law scroll (34:14–18). The reference to the money collected by the Levites for renovating the temple links the previous section with this segment of the story (cf. 34:9, 14). Surprisingly, while the discovery of the law scroll is the key event of the chapter and the turning point of Josiah's reign, its actual uncovering is mentioned only briefly (34:14b–15a). Its discovery becomes a reward of sorts for Josiah's faithfulness in attending to God's sanctuary.

The scroll is given two titles in the narrative: "the Book of the Law" (34:15) and "the Book of the Covenant" (34:30). The puzzling question for biblical scholars has been the identity of this book. The general consensus favors the book of Deuteronomy or an earlier version of that book. We can only speculate as to why the law scroll disappeared from the collection of Hebrew religious documents. Was it suppressed, or lost, or hidden? Presumably the scroll fell out of circulation because of the need to hide it for the sake of preservation at the threat of military invasion, or else it was censored by rulers and/or concealed by the priests during one of the lapses of Israel into religious apostasy.

Interpretation of the scroll (34:19–28). Josiah's twofold response to Shaphan's reading of the scroll is immediate and decisive. Recognizing the message of the scroll as the very word of God, Josiah tears his clothes (34:19)—a tangible expression of grief in response to personal or national crises.

The king perceives that the message of the law scroll has profound implications for both him and his subjects. This explains Josiah's decision to appoint envoys to seek an interpretation of the scroll and to ask for counsel in addressing the disturbing news about God's anger revealed in the law scroll.

Hilkiah's visit to Huldah seems to be based on his relationship with Shallum, her husband. Shallum is "keeper of the wardrobe" (34:22) for the priests and the Levites, which means he has oversight of the production and maintenance of the vestments and robes of Levites. Thus, Hilkiah is in regular contact with Shallum. Huldah is not mentioned elsewhere in the Old Testament, although she is among a handful of Hebrew women titled as a prophetess. She is respected as a servant of Yahweh because she is consulted, and her interpretation of the law scroll is received as a word from God.

That interpretation is delivered to Hilkiah, Shaphan, and the others in a two-part message.

1. An oracle of punishment (34:24–25) assumes the curses of Deuteronomy 28. They will be inflicted on Jerusalem and the people of Judah as divine judgment for sins associated with idolatry.
2. An oracle of salvation (34:26–28a) is prompted by Josiah's repentance as demonstrated in his acts of humility and contrition.

Covenant-renewal ceremony (34:29–33). The expression "the Book of the Covenant" is a rarely used technical term for the entire Pentateuch in later Judaism (34:30). Thus, this book title likely refers to the core of the Sinai covenant code, Exodus 19–24, or perhaps the book of Deuteronomy. More important is the theological significance of the term "covenant," which denotes an agreement that creates new relationships in accordance with stipulations outlined in advance.

The key issue for our study is the creation of relationships by means of a covenant ritual, and this through the voluntary act of the individual (or community). Covenant renewal for ancient Israel was repairing or restoring a relationship with God, a relationship broken because of their willful violation of the stipulations regulating the relationship. Repentance or humbling oneself is the first step in renewing a covenant relationship with God.

Josiah's covenant-renewal ceremony combines elements of the Mosaic covenant and of the Davidic covenant. Beyond treaty definition and form, the idea of covenant combines both judgment and hope for Israel: judgment in the form of divine curse for disloyalty to the treaty demands and hope in the form of divine blessing for loyalty to the treaty demands. By God's design, almost frighteningly so, Israel's destiny lies in the decision of the people to choose "life and prosperity" or "death and destruction" (Deut 30:15). Thankfully in this instance, because of the strong leadership of Josiah, the people chose life—for a time.

In keeping with the prescription of the Mosaic law, all the people gather for the reading of the law scroll and the covenant-ratification ceremony (2 Chr 34:29–30). Theologically, the idea of God's grace extended to the disobedient people of God is not lost on the Chronicler. What God did in Israel by way of religious reform and spiritual renewal through the covenant-renewal ceremonies of Asa, Hezekiah, and Josiah is repeatable history for the Jews living in postexilic Judah—if they too humble themselves and pray and pledge covenant loyalty to Yahweh.

The final verse of this section (34:33) summarizes the impact of the discovery of the law scroll and the covenant-renewal ceremony on Josiah's reign by means of allusion to the extensive religious reforms carried out in Judah. The Chronicler emphasizes how Josiah purges false religion "from all the territory belonging to the Israelites."

Josiah's Passover (35:1–19). The Passover is the preeminent religious festival for postexilic Judah and the apex of temple worship for the Chronicler. The reason for the prominence of this feast in the Jewish restoration community stems from the Passover observed after the completion of the second temple in 516 BC and the understanding that the return from Babylonian captivity is a second exodus for God's people (cf. Ezra 6:19–22). The Passover, more than any other Hebrew religious festival, drew the nation of Israel back to her roots, since it was at Mount Sinai that the former Hebrew slaves were constituted as the people of God.

The preparations for the festival (35:1–6). The Chronicler specifies the precise date for the observance of the Passover (35:1) in order to demonstrate that Josiah is in compliance with Mosaic law. Like Hezekiah, Josiah is also an "encourager" (35:2; cf. 30:22; 32:6).

The reference to transferring the ark of the covenant back to the temple is obscure (35:3), since there is no record that it was moved from the sanctuary. The authority behind the specific instructions for the change in the ritual duties of the Levites is based on the decrees of Kings David and Solomon in recognition of the shift from portable sanctuary to permanent temple (35:4).

Quite apart from the technicalities of sacrificial worship, we cannot overlook the essential calling of the Levitical priesthood as mediators (35:3, 5–6). The Levitical priests are to mediate the holy presence of God in Israel by making atonement first for their own sins and then for the sins of the people (Lev 9:7). Hence the Levites must first prepare themselves (2 Chr 35:4) before they can serve the people in the ministry of sacrificial worship (35:5–6).

The provision of sacrificial animals (35:7–10). The key piece of information in this section is the report of the generosity of the king in providing the sacrificial animals for the Passover. In addition to the sheep and goats from Josiah's personal flocks (35:7), his royal officials and the administrators of the temple also contribute animals for the Passover offerings (35:8–9).

The Chronicler notes that the civil and religious leaders of Judah are not only generous but also willing (35:8). No doubt the Chronicler seeks to impress the importance of the virtue of generosity on his audience as well. In terms of the sheer numbers of animals to be sacrificed, Josiah's celebration doubles the size of Hezekiah's Passover (35:7–9).

The ritual service of the offerings (35:11–15). This third unit describes the actual Passover ceremony. The ritual consists of two segments: offering the animal sacrifices (35:11–12) and eating the Passover meal (35:13–15). The shift in the locus of the Passover from the home to the temple as the central shrine radically alters the ritual character of the Passover. The priests are now responsible for slaughtering the Passover lambs (35:6, 11), sprinkling the blood of the slain animal on the altar of burnt offering (35:11; cf. 29:22; 30:16), and then skinning the animal for cooking (35:11; cf. 29:34). Moreover, the priests and attending Levites supervise the roasting of the sacrificial animals and serve the Passover meal to the assembly (35:13).

The Chronicler emphasizes how the priests and Levites fulfill all the requirements of the ceremony demanded by the king and the law of Moses (35:10, 16). In fact, the eager ministry of the Levites supersedes the requirements of the ceremony. They not only serve the people "quickly" as a reminder of the hasty meal eaten at the first Passover (35:13), but they also are a model of servanthood at the communal meal by making additional preparations for their fellow priests, musicians, and gatekeepers, who remain on duty at their posts for the entire day (35:14–15).

The epilogue (35:16–19). The Chronicler reiterates the detailed diligence of the priests and Levites in carrying out the instructions of the king and the law of Moses. The declaration that Josiah's Passover is unrivaled as a religious festival in Israel anticipates a comparison with Hezekiah's Passover celebration (cf. 30:26). The Chronicler's statement may be one of kind more than totality, since he is probably referring to the centralized celebration of the Passover linked to the Jerusalem temple.

In keeping with his thematic emphasis on "all Israel," the Chronicler uses the name "Israel" (35:18) to refer to the divided kingdoms of Israel and Judah as recorded in 2 Kings 23:22. For him, the Passover is a unifying festival in the life of Israel since it brings the king, the priests, the Levites, and all the people together in fellowship over a ritual meal.

Battle report of Josiah's death (35:20–25). The expression "after all this" (35:20) cues the reader that some time has elapsed since Josiah's celebration of the Passover. Specifically, the narrative leaps chronologically from the Passover festival in Jerusalem in 622 BC to Josiah's death in battle at Megiddo in 609 BC. Given the dominant theme of the retribution principle in Chronicles, Josiah's death poses a narrative problem for the writer, namely, how to explain the untimely end of a righteous king.

By way of historical background, we must remember that the military might of the ancient superpower of Assyria is now on the wane, while the greatness of the Babylonian Empire is swiftly and brutally on the rise. Only a year prior to Josiah's ill-advised campaign against Pharaoh Necho (610 BC), the Babylonians forced the last Assyrian king, Ashur-uballit, to flee the capital city of Haran and set up a provisional government in Carchemish. Pharaoh Necho apparently seeks passage through Israel to bring his large army to reinforce the beleaguered Assyrian army for a final stand against the Babylonians at Carchemish (35:20).

Pharaoh Necho indicates he has no quarrel with Josiah or Judah; he simply wants a right of way through Judah so he can show loyalty to his Assyrian ally (35:21). The Megiddo pass lies on the international coastal highway, an ancient trade route connecting Egypt with Syria, northern Mesopotamia, and Anatolia. The site of Megiddo guards this bottleneck on the route through the Mount Carmel foothills. To meet up with the Assyrians at Carchemish, Necho must move his army through the Megiddo pass. It is at this strategic location that Josiah (foolishly) chooses to intercept Pharaoh Necho and the Egyptian army.

The key statement in the Chronicler's rendition of Josiah's death is the clause "he would not listen to what Necho had said" (35:22). Previously, Josiah was commended by Huldah the prophetess for his responsiveness to God (34:27). Now he actually stands in opposition to God's word spoken through Pharaoh Necho—to his own destruction (35:21b).

The Chronicler is careful to note that Josiah receives a proper burial in the "tombs of his ancestors" (35:24). In this regard, the words of Huldah's prophecy over Josiah are fulfilled: He is buried in the tombs of his fathers in peace (34:28).

Josiah has been a popular king, for "all Judah and Jerusalem" mourn his death (35:24). The shock wave of Josiah's death sends tremors through Judah from which the nation never recovers. Not only do his religious reforms die with him in battle, but also the kingdom of Judah itself will soon "die" in the Babylonian onslaught.

Concluding regnal résumé (35:26–36:1). The expression "acts of devotion" (35:26) is better rendered "covenant loyalty," commemorating the covenant-renewal ceremony convened by Josiah and ratified by all Judah (34:29–31). The Chronicler also adds the phrase "in Jerusalem" to the succession formula (36:1), presumably to remind his audience that God made good on his promise to restore his people and his name in that city.

Application. The preacher both comforts and disturbs the audience through the act of preaching, the proclamation of the word of God. The messenger must deliver the message of the One who sends the servant—not an invented message (cf. Amos 3:8; 2 Pet 1:21). The preacher "earths" the word in the world by communicating God's truth with relevance and pertinence to our ever-changing society. The "preaching" of Chronicles informs contemporary preaching at two levels.

1. In terms of content, the disturbing message of preaching is the call to repentance.

2. In terms of style, the narrative approach permits the preacher to locate the disturbing message in a larger story that also includes the message of comfort.

2 CHRONICLES 36:2–21

Original Meaning. The four brief accounts of the reigns of Jehoahaz (36:2–4), Jehoiakim (36:5–8), Jehoiachin (36:9–10), and Zedekiah (36:11–14) summarize the deadly game of "musical thrones" that sees the end of the kingdom of Judah. This final section of the Chronicler's history is driven by both a documentary impulse (i.e., telling *what* happened) and the literary impulse (i.e., telling *how* it happened). The repetition of the twin themes of the exile of the last Judahite kings and the repeated plundering of the Lord's temple explains *what* happens to the kingdom of Judah (36:4, 6–7, 10, 18, 20). The descriptions of King Zedekiah (who does not humble himself and will not turn to the Lord, 36:12–13; cf. 7:14) and the priests and all the people (who are unfaithful, 36:14; cf. 30:8) illustrate *how* all this happens to Judah.

The historian of 2 Kings identified Manasseh as the culprit responsible for the Babylonian exile (2 Kgs 24:3–4). The Chronicler, however, extends blame to the entire nation, not to any one individual. King Zedekiah, the priests, and the people are all unfaithful to God and equally accountable for the fall of Judah (2 Chr 36:14). The corporate interpretation of the exile is a key component in the "all Israel" theology of the Chronicler.

Likewise, all Israelites are heirs of God's promises for the restoration of Israel announced by the prophets. The Chronicler knows that his generation will be successful in obeying the word of the Lord only by recognizing their vicarious relationship to the tragic events of the past and the anticipated blessings of the future. The general categories of sins attributed to the people ("detestable practices" and "defiling the temple," 36:14) serve as warnings to the Chronicler's contemporaries.

The Chronicler implicitly addresses the retribution principle conditioning the Mosaic covenant by noting the cause-and-effect relationship between Judah's desecration of the temple (36:14) and the despoiling of the temple by the Babylonians (36:18). The response of divine blessing for obedience to the stipulations of God's covenant and the response of divine judgment for violation of the same frame Israel's relationship to Yahweh. The references to God's messengers and prophets further underscore the emphasis on the retribution principle in the Chronicler's assessment of the fall of Jerusalem. The blessings and curses theology of the Mosaic covenant is foundational to prophetic ministry because it is on this basis that these divine messengers forecast either blessing or judgment for God's people.

The Chronicler hurries past the last four kings of Judah to report the fall of Jerusalem for good reason (36:15–21). The Chronicler needs to guard against wrong thinking and bad theology, lest God be blamed for Judah's calamity. Essentially, the Chronicler offers his generation a twofold rationale for Judah's expulsion from the land of the promise.

1. Both king and people have rejected God's word spoken by his prophetic messengers (36:16).
2. The people of Judah have failed to keep the covenant stipulation of giving the land "its sabbath rests" (36:21).

Here again the compiler assumes his audience has a working knowledge of the Torah and the Prophets in the intertwining of the covenant curse (Lev 26:34) and the word of Jeremiah (Jer 29:10).

More important theologically, the Chronicler understands the exile as God's work. The Lord himself brought the Babylonians against Judah and handed his people over to Nebuchadnezzar in fulfillment of the words of Jeremiah the prophet (36:17, 21; cf. Jer 25:8–11; 29:10). It is of vital importance that the Chronicler affirm God's faithfulness to his word. The postexilic generation needs assurance that God keeps his word, whether it be a word of blessing or judgment (Ps 33:4–5).

Application. Reflective writings on the topic of theodicy are not limited to the Hebrew Bible or the ancient world. Thankfully, the Christian has an advantage over the Old Testament faithful in the discussion of theodicy because we have the rest of the story. The disciples of Jesus testified that they believe that Jesus came from God (John 16:30). Interestingly, however, this Advocate from heaven does not decree the end of human suffering. Rather, he bluntly informs his followers that "in this world you will have trouble. But take heart! I have overcome the world" (John 16:33). This means the righteous should not necessarily expect to escape the problem of evil in this fallen world. Instead, they are assured God will uphold them in their suffering by the help of his Holy Spirit (1 Cor 10:13; Rom 8:9–11). Only a sovereign God of infinite power and eternal goodness is able to use human sufferings to cultivate godly virtues in the righteous that lead to the crown of life (Rom 5:3–4; Jas 1:12).

2 CHRONICLES 36:22–23

Original Meaning. The quotation of Cyrus's decree functions as a coda, offering a hopeful summary statement to the Chronicler's history and directing the audience (or reader) to the continuation of the story of the repatriation of Jerusalem found in the books of Ezra-Nehemiah. It seems only logical to regard the epilogue as the work of the Chronicler since he retells the history of Israel as a theology of hope for his postexilic audience.

The epilogue includes a date formula, "the first year of Cyrus king of Persia" (36:22; the year is 538 BC). The famous clay barrel or inscribed cylinder of Cyrus records his conquest of Babylon without a battle and his overturning of the foreign policy of previous regimes. Although the Hebrews are not specifically mentioned in the text of the Cyrus Cylinder, the decree includes those Israelites previously exiled by the Assyrians and Babylonians. The document cited by the Chronicler is most likely a formal extension of the original decree for this specific people group.

According to Ezra 1, King Cyrus restores numerous articles taken by the Babylonians as booty from the temple of Yahweh to the first band of returnees under the leadership of Sheshbazzar. This is yet another way in which God "moves the heart of Cyrus" for the benefit of his chosen people (36:22). Well in advance of the fact, God through the prophet Isaiah named Cyrus as the subduer of nations and deliverer of the exiles from the land of Judah (Isa 45:1–4, 13).

This echo of the oracles of Isaiah is yet another reminder from the Chronicler that God's word is sure. Even more, the restoration community in Jerusalem can be assured of God's ongoing sovereignty over the nations. Although still under Persian control, postexilic Judah has the guarantee of God's word for complete restoration and the historical evidence that Israel's God controls the destinies of the nations. The excerpt from Cyrus's edict calling for the rebuilding of Yahweh's temple in Jerusalem is probably a veiled reference to the fulfillment of Isaiah's prediction that Cyrus will be God's agent for restoring Jerusalem after the exile (Isa 44:28).

In one sense, not only is King Cyrus Yahweh's shepherd, but he is also Yahweh's prophet in his proclamation permitting the restoration of Jerusalem and the rebuilding of the temple. The aftermath of Cyrus's decree—the waves of Jews emigrating from Mesopotamia to Palestine as a type of second exodus and the rebuilding of the Jerusalem temple—is recorded in the books of Ezra-Nehemiah.

Application. On the one hand, the Bible declares with certainty that God is the sovereign Lord of the nations. Yet on the other hand, the Assyrias, Babylonias and Persias of contemporary history still rage against God and persecute the church of Jesus Christ. This side of the second advent of our Lord, the Chronicler's solution for reconciling the biblical doctrine of God's sovereignty with the political reality of the nations roaring like the waves of the sea as they churn up the mud and mire of wickedness and rebellion against God is still worthy of careful consideration (cf. Isa 17:12–13; 57:20–21).

There is something significant in the incomplete citation of Ezra 1:3 in the Chronicler's epilogue. The expression "may go up" (2 Chr 36:23) is both an invitation and a directive to worship. The psalmist uses the verb "go up" to depict ascending the Temple Mount and worshiping in God's holy place (Ps 24:3; 122:4). Like the psalmist, the Chronicler recognizes that the formal worship of Yahweh is the integrating component of life lived in a fallen world. It is only as the psalmist (here Asaph) experiences God in temple worship that he can gain perspective on the seeming incongruities between the experiences of the wicked and the righteous (cf. 73:13–17). Only as the finite contemplates the Infinite One, only as the creature ponders the Creator, only as the filthy consider the Holy One, can the temporal take on meaning in the light of the eternal. The Chronicler's call for postexilic Judah to "go up" to the temple and worship makes the apostle Peter's words all the more penetrating when he says:

> But you are a chosen people, a royal priesthood, a holy nation, God's special possession, that you may declare the praises of him who called you out of darkness into his wonderful light. (1 Pet 2:9)

EZRA

INTRODUCTION TO EZRA

Ezra-Nehemiah (traditionally considered to be one book originally) should be viewed in four distinct parts: the first return (Ezra 1:1–6:22), the second return (Ezra 7:1–10:44), the third return (Neh 1:1–13:3), and an epilogue (Neh 13:4–31). The books cover a period of about one hundred years (539 BC–433 BC). In light of this long span of history, it is no surprise that modern scholars have debated the context(s) of the composition and redaction(s) of the volume. It is the conviction of the authors that the final edition of Ezra-Nehemiah reflects a higher degree of compositional and editorial clarity than is sometimes discussed by some scholars. It seems reasonable to assign a place of preeminence for both Ezra and Nehemiah in the compositional and editorial process that resulted in the final form of the books (around 430 BC) not long after the events.

The book of Ezra details the first and second returns. Chapters 1–6 narrate the first return under the leadership of Zerubbabel and Joshua and describe the events leading to the completion of the temple. Chapters 7–10 describe the second return under Ezra, the priest and scribe. His return entailed a reinstatement of the law of God.

BOOK OUTLINE

- I. The First Return: Zerubbabel/Sheshbazzar Restore the Temple (1:1–6:22)
  - A. Fulfillment of Prophecy (1:1–11)
  - B. The People Returning to Jerusalem (2:1–70)
  - C. The Rebuilding Begins (3:1–13)
  - D. Opposition to the Rebuilding (4:1–24)
  - E. Rebuilding Resumes and Temple Completed (5:1–6:22)
- II. The Second Return: Ezra Restores the Law (7:1–10:44)
  - A. Ezra Comes to Jerusalem (7:1–28)
  - B. The People Returning with Ezra and the Journey (8:1–36)
  - C. Marriage Problems and Ezra's Response (9:1–15)
  - D. The People's Response to Ezra's Prayer of Confession (10:1–44)

EZRA 1:1–11

Original Meaning

Cyrus's Proclamation: The Hope and Help (1:1–4). *Fulfilled prophecy (1:1).* In 539 BC the Persians, together with the Medes, diverted the waters of the Euphrates and marched into well-fortified Babylon (Dan 5). With a bloodless transition the Babylonian Empire fell to the Persians. The author of Ezra, however, wants the reader to see that Cyrus's first year was not to be interpreted merely from the vantage of international politics. Instead, it was much more. God takes action and intervenes.

The acquisition (1:2a). Cyrus acknowledges his successful military acquisition derives from "The LORD (1:2a)." This precise designation appears only one other time in Ezra-Nehemiah and it comes from the praying lips of Nehemiah (Neh 1:5).

The appointment (1:2b–3). Cyrus acknowledges the task of [re]building Yahweh's earthly dwelling in Jerusalem (1:2b). This would include financial backing and any other resources to make it happen.

Cyrus's surprising use of the covenantal name Yahweh (NIV "LORD") is not an acknowledgement that Cyrus had experienced Yahweh in the same way as an Israelite. Rather it is an acknowledgement that Yahweh is Israel's God who resides in Jerusalem.

In Ezra 1:3 Cyrus commissions the Jews for a special building project. Embedded in the edict are two important factors for the successful execution of the project. On the one hand, it depends upon the willingness of some people to leave Babylon. On the other hand, it depends entirely on divine presence/favor, as Cyrus states, "May their God be with them" (1:3).

Cyrus solicits community-wide support (1:4a). The king enables those who wish to go up by rallying support, first from those Jews who wish to stay but also from the non-Judean community.

Cyrus solicits needed resources (1:4b). The building project required not only willing souls but also money and materials.

The Response to Cyrus's Proclamation (1:5–11). *Leaders respond (1:5).* The first responders were leaders from the tribes of Judah and Benjamin. Yet as the numbers in chapter 2 make clear, not many chose to return. The author deliberately mentions that priests and Levites were among a second group who also responded. Without these spiritual leaders in particular, the renewal process would not have been possible.

Neighbors respond (1:6). The Hebrew literally says, "they strengthened their hands." The way the neighbors enabled those going to Jerusalem was through giving.

Cyrus responds (1:7–8). God moved the Persian king to further action. Roughly two hundred years earlier, Isaiah prophesied that God's people would return to Jerusalem and that "the articles of the LORD's house" would be involved (Isa 52:11–12).

Cultic provisions (1:9–11). The chapter closes with a tally based on the numbering in verse 11. All of this empirical evidence affirms Cyrus's best wishes (1:3). It is the author's implicit way of showing that the Lord is with his people, thus practically fulfilling his word spoken by Jeremiah.

Application. God is going to keep his word no matter what obstacles are stacked against him! The significance of knowing that God keeps his word to restore all things unto himself, especially in times of separation from him due to sin's consequences or on account of living in this world, is critical. Without such a worldview, we lose our view and perspective on life.

EZRA 2:1–70

Original Meaning

Those with Documentary Proof of Descending from Israel (2:1–58). *The people and the leadership (2:1–2).* The captive people return to their homeland of Jerusalem and Judah. Another exodus is taking place, one promised by the prophet Isaiah (48:20–22).

As the narrative in Ezra-Nehemiah makes clear, both Zerubbabel and Joshua, the first two names on the list (Ezra 2:2), emerge as key players in the restoration and rebuilding process. Zerubbabel has a position in the Davidic line—a hope of reestablishing kingship. Joshua, as Judah's high priest, gives solid spiritual leadership and is associated with rebuilding the altar (3:2).

Lay People: Connections with the past by family of origin (2:2b–20). The list commences with a broad umbrella category of lay people designated as "the men of the people of Israel" (2:2b–35). The use of "the people of Israel" (2:2b) is a reminder of the ties and connections these people have to a past that defined them. The expectation, based on a typical genealogy, is to have the present heads of the families mentioned. Instead, the family name of an important ancestor in preexilic Israel is cited. Using the ancestral name rather than the current family head is the author's implicit way of stating that these people have a legal connection to the land.

Lay People: Connections with the past by city of origin (2:21–35). In Ezra 2:21–35 twenty-one geographical names emerge on the list. The list associates the people who are going up to Jerusalem and Judah with towns in the region, not an ancestor.

Ministers: Connections with previous personnel (2:36–58). After enumerating lay people (2:3–35), the author lists five distinct categories of ministers who return (priests, Levites, musicians, gatekeepers, and temple servants). Four families of priests are noted first (2:36–39). Along with the priests, two families of Levites are named (2:40).

The list also includes musicians associated with the "descendants of Asaph" (2:41). There is mention also of six families of gatekeepers (2:42). As with the musicians, David organized the gatekeepers. The list concludes with thirty-five families of temple servants and an additional ten families associated with the servants of Solomon (2:43–58).

Those Without Documentary Proof of Descending from Israel (2:59–70). Although family records were apparently lost for both lay people and priests (2:59, 62), the wording of the latter verse draws attention to the specific search pertaining to the priests since "exclusion" from the priesthood is mentioned as a result of the unsuccessful search. The Urim and Thummim would ultimately determine God's intentions for them once a priest was again officiating with these sacred instruments. The larger point of the account here is that it remains unclear whether the priests under scrutiny could be consecrated for the Lord's work. Reestablishing true worship in Israel cannot effectively be done if lay people and ministers of the Lord have questionable identity as the people of God.

Summary and conclusion (2:64–70). Verse 64 functions as a numerical summary. The chapter concludes with what appears to be a total head count of people and their possessions, including servants and animals, that set out and eventually settled in Jerusalem. However, the total of the "whole company" listed in 2:64 does not mathematically equate when adding the numbers together, but that is not surprising as often lists are incomplete without intending to be exhaustive.

Application. As we journey in becoming the people of God, we need to be reassured that when we lose our spiritual markers of identity because of our own wrongdoing or life's circumstances, we are still God's! The fact of the matter is this: we make our own markers of identity as a result of trying to figure out who we are. The problem with the markers of identity that we establish is that they do not stand the test of time because they are of human origin. We need, therefore, to have a purpose that is not grounded in ourselves. It might be summed up this way: we don't know who we are until we know whose we are.

EZRA 3:1–13

Original Meaning

The Altar Rebuilt (3:1–6). *Rebuilding the altar (3:1–2).* The seventh month represents more than a chronological peg. From a literary perspective, it structures the unit of thought in 3:1–6. It also signals movement forward from both a practical point of view (to rebuild the temple) and a theological perspective (to rebuild worship).

Joshua and Zerubbabel (3:2). As high priest, Joshua was the nation's spiritual leader, providing access to God. As Joshua and Zerubbabel provide spiritual and administrative leadership, 3:2 orients the reader to the specific goals of the covenantal community. Ezra 3:2 announces the stated project, "to build the altar of the God of Israel," but the verse also reflects the stated purpose for building the altar, "to sacrifice burnt offerings on it." Furthermore, Joshua and company have the stated authority backing their efforts, "in accordance with what is written in the Law of Moses the man of God." Their worship to the Lord is rooted and grounded in the word of God.

Context of rebuilding: Fear and outcome (3:3). With the altar rebuilt according to Mosaic specifications, the people were ready to reengage worship of Yahweh on a daily basis. Although the returnees labored under adverse conditions, they were not paralyzed so as to stop the work altogether on the altar.

Outcome of rebuilding: yearly and monthly worship (3:4–5). The Feast of Tabernacles was a celebration deriving from the fact that God graciously protected and provided for their ancestors when they lived in tents during their forty-year desert discipline. With the altar rebuilt, the people were ready to engage the Lord with all the required sacrifices built into their calendar year.

Summary of activities in the seventh month (3:6). In the seventh month the altar was rebuilt, most of their sacrificial system was in place, and all this happened prior to the building of the temple. This information explains that true worship is possible even without the temple.

Supplies and Personnel (3:7–9). After completing the altar, the returnees immediately turn their attention to preparations for rebuilding the temple, starting with the foundation. The preparation includes securing building supplies as authorized by Cyrus.

The administrative and spiritual leaders (Zerubbabel and Joshua, respectively), as well as the priests, Levites, and "all who had returned from the captivity" (3:8), worked. The Levites who were age twenty and older were appointed to supervise all the work. This appointment parallels that of King David to some degree (1 Chr 23:4–32). The intentionality here of the author to make connections with the past seems evident.

The Hebrew in 3:9 reads that the families are "as one" (*keehad*), or joined together, to supervise the work. The language expresses unity of purpose.

Temple Foundation Completed: Responses (3:10–13). *The scene: first worship service after exile (3:10–11).* The praise of the returnees was rooted in a keen awareness of Yahweh's strong and unshakable character, without which the return from exile and the completion of the temple foundation would not have been possible.

Contrasting Experience (3:12). Although the environment is joyful, the eyewitnesses of Solomon's temple were underwhelmed at what they saw and wept loudly.

Praise to the Lord (3:13). The author wants the reader to know that not only was the sound of Israel's praises to the Lord loud (indicative of a renewed heart), but also the sound reverberated outside the community. In fact, their renewed witness in the land sets the stage for the trouble described in the chapter that follows.

Application. God's character enables us to look at life's difficulties (self-imposed or otherwise) and see God presently is good. But it also enables us to look forward with great assurance when we face life's difficulties (self-imposed or otherwise) and see that God will still be good.

EZRA 4:1–5

Original Meaning

Opposition under Cyrus's Reign (4:1–5, 24). The biblical writer intentionally gives a lot of literary space (roughly three consecutive chapters, 4:1–6:12) to the topic of opposition and only ten verses to narrate the completion and celebration of the rebuilt temple (6:13–22). The point is that one must understand the completed task in light of its opposition.

For the first time, the Jews faced serious, external opposition from the locals or "peoples around them" (4:4) in regard to rebuilding. The narrator further identifies these locals as "the enemies of Judah and Benjamin" (4:1). But in the recorded speech, they self-identify as exiles, people also carried away from Assyria to Samaria by King Esarhaddon (4:2). The boast "like you, we seek your God" becomes their rationale for offering assistance. Perhaps a sense of entitlement based on the long residence in the land prompted the offer of help.

Regardless, Israel's leaders respond with a united voice demonstrating discernment and uncompromising theological conviction. Purity, for the sake of preserving the identity of the people of God, was the premise of rebuilding the new community. A lack of purity could not be tolerated given their sordid past but especially in light of this second chance.

The wise decision to exclude these folks because of legal and theological convictions was not without a cost for the reestablished community. Those excluded most likely felt angry and rejected, which led to retaliation. The goal of their tactic was to "discourage," literally, "weakening the hands of (*merappim yedey*)" the people of Judah (4:4). When this phrase appears elsewhere in the Bible, it describes a crippling effect caused by deep despair and dismay (e.g., 2 Sam 4:1 Isa 13:7; Jer 38:4). Indeed, the enemies' tactic, whatever it was, produced fruit. Eventually the Jews, worn out by the opposition, voluntarily stopped their work on the house of God for sixteen years.

Application. This short narrative invites the reader, but especially a leader, to lead with conviction and to count the cost of conviction. It shows that such a thing exists as a theology of saying no! There is a time for religious intolerance.

EZRA 4:6–24

Original Meaning

Later Opposition under Xerxes and Artaxerxes: Work Ceases (4:6–24). The first of the two instances of opposition concern an accusation leveled at the people early in the reign of Xerxes. The author offers no information about the nature of this complaint but merely lists it first. The second instance concerns a piece of correspondence. The recipient is King Artaxerxes of Persia. The complaint has the backing of people of rank, and it is geographically widespread (Tripolis, Persia, Erech, Babylon, and Susa; 4:9–10). Put another way, the complaint verbalized in the letter carries some weight.

After the letter's salutation in 4:11, the formal complaint begins. The heart of the complaint pertains to loyalty (4:14–16). Those crafting the letter prop themselves up and appear to have a staunch loyalty. Since rebuilding a city wall is akin to gaining strength and independence, it was viewed as a compromise of loyalties, posing a serious threat to the empire.

The informants describe Jerusalem's interactions with past political administrations as rebellious. Rebellion here means a political revolt against international powers whereby the vassal breaks allegiance with the suzerain. According to the king's informants, the city was destroyed on account of such rebellion (4:15), and they are justified in their complaint. Their human perspective, however, contrasts with the divine perspective about the city's fall (2 Chr 36:15–19).

The section closes with a record of the king's response and action to the supposed threat (Ezra 4:17–23). It speaks of three orders: one to look into the matter, another to stop the work, and a hypothetical order that might grant rebuilding at a future time. This literary interlude (4:6–23) fills out the bigger picture of opposition that the Jews faced. The author then returns to the subject at hand, the temple building project, and will complete his thoughts on that topic in what follows (5:1–6:22).

Application. The staunch opposition and nasty accusations faced by the Jews in their effort to rebuild reflect what we know, this side of the cross, to be spiritual warfare. What looks like a fight against flesh and blood is really a fight against the principalities and powers in the heavenly places (Eph 6:10–12). We often forget, and perhaps even deny, that theologically speaking we are in a time of war, not peace. With Jesus's resurrection, the age to come has broken into this present age. But the present age is not benign. It is the present evil age (Eph 6:12). This is why some receive salvation and others do not. This is why we see some healings, but not all the time. This is why we ultimately experience opposition, individually and corporately as the church. This is the reason why the nations are not yet reached for the gospel. This is why some nations remain closed to Christianity. This is why evil prevails. This is why the church looks defeated, thwarted, and even stopped! We are living in the age of tension.

EZRA 5:1–17

Original Meaning

Haggai and Zechariah Motivate People: Work Resumes but Is Challenged (5:1–5). *Prophetic players (5:1).* The author wants to communicate that God intervened after the long, sixteen-year hiatus to fulfill the intended goal of rebuilding the temple (1:1–11).

Prophetic response (5:2). This verse in Ezra demonstrates how true prophecy was meant to motivate, bring change, and work in the lives of God's covenantal people.

Persian officials (5:3–5). Once again Persian officials challenge the Jews about the rebuilding process but with an entirely different spirit. Their challenge is not necessarily to deter but to do things according to government regulations. Verse 5 reveals the heart of the matter—God's seeing eye leads to protection from harm.

Investigation Pursued (5:6–17). *Speculations (5:6–10).* The second section of chapter 5 concerns the first of two pieces of royal correspondence in Ezra 5:1–6:12, Tattenai's letter of inquiry to Darius. The officials are loyal informants of the king but of a different stripe from those mentioned in 4:12–16. They simply wish to obtain government clearance on the building project.

The Persians do not acknowledge Israel's God as the only God, but as one among many (see Ezra 1:1–3). He was, however, chief God for the Israelites. No malice seems intended in the investigation. In fact, the Persian officials affirmed both the workers and the work (5:8). These officials also wanted to know names of those from the Jewish community; the more information, the better in bringing the matter to a conclusion.

Jews' response (5:11–17). Ezra 5:11–17 gives a confident response by the Jews to the inquiry of the Persian officials. The Jews confidently provide Darius with a historical sketch about the temple. Notice that Solomon's name was omitted above in reference to the first temple (5:12). Perhaps this reveals a deliberate strategy of the Jews for Darius's investigation? The Jews may have put forward only the names of those who could be traced in the official documents. The focus on chapter 3 pertains to the building, but here in chapter 5 the focus is on the evidence allowing the Jews to build.

Application. Not unlike the Israelites under Persian rule, US residents have legal recourse to protect their First Amendment rights (freedom of speech). Free debate is encouraged, and there is an ability to seek help and reform through democratic means. Historically and legally, freedom of speech allows one to defend the Christian worldview. On this basis, it would appear a Christian in the USA (and other parts of the Western world) may be able to stand somewhat secure in her or his rights and freedom to worship (unlike the suffering and persecuted underground church elsewhere in the world). Nevertheless, this sense of security is false in many aspects since our confidence and freedom must stem from something surer than political constitutional rights.

EZRA 6:1–12

Original Meaning

Evidence Found and Response to Investigation by Darius (6:1–12). *Scroll of Ecbatana (6:1–5).* In 6:1–5 the needed documentary evidence was found in Ecbatana, the summer residence of Persian kings. Both the measurements and the materials give governmental specs. In this way, the Jews were in the clear.

Darius's response (6:6–10). Ezra 6:6–10 contains Darius's letter of response to Tattenai. He prohibits interference physically (6:6b). In addition, 6:8 suggests that the king prohibited any financial interference. It was not uncommon for Persian kings to look after the religious interests of their subjects. By so doing, they were attempting to secure both public and divine favor from the gods their subjects served.

Penalties (6:11–12). Finally, Darius closes his response with the enforcement of a penalty to those who would disobey the decree or attempt to destroy the Jerusalem temple (6:11–12). Such threats of punishment and curses for disobedient subjects were typical parts of covenantal agreements in the ancient Near East.

In short, opposition will be met with opposition. Thus, Darius not only sanctioned that the work continue, but he also guaranteed protection of God's people in the process of its completion. Opposition does not last forever because God eventually (on his timetable) intervenes in governments of the world. But divine intervention here is twofold. Not only does God intervene by raising up the prophets Haggai and Zechariah from within the covenantal community (5:1–5), but God also intervenes by raising up individuals, outside the covenantal community and from the government, to support and encourage his people and to achieve his broader purposes. It is fitting, therefore, that Ezra 6:1–12 concludes the narrator's discussion on temple building opposition with such a definitive statement.

Application. If the restoration of Zion is nonnegotiable because it is tied to the very promises of God that "whoever curses you I will curse" (Gen 12:3), then God's people can have a staunch assurance that opposition toward kingdom work will end. We can be assured that in the end, God will do something radical to oppose those who are opposed to him.

EZRA 6:13–22

Original Meaning

The Temple Rebuilt and Celebration (6:13–22). *Temple completion (6:13–15).* Ezra 6:13–15 not only tells of the finished work (1:1–6:22), but it also shows in a succinct summary statement how, why, and when the rebuilding was completed, as well as the results. First, from a practical point of view, the lack of governmental interference enabled the Jews to continue to build (6:14). Second, from a spiritual point of view, the "preaching" of the prophets motivated the Jews, enabling them "to build and prosper" (6:14).

Verses 13–14 communicate how and why the temple ultimately was rebuilt. The human side of the equation (work decreed by Persian kings) operated in tandem with the divine side (work commanded by God). The "command of the God of Israel" (6:14) likely refers to the prophetic words of Haggai and Zechariah that enabled the finished project.

Verse 15 also gives the answer to the when question. The date corresponds to March 12, 515 BC, some years after Haggai and Zechariah started preaching in Aug–Dec of 520 BC (Hag 1:1; Zech 1:1, second year of Darius).

Dedication, installation, and celebration of the building (6:16–18). As was done in earlier building phases, with the altar and foundation respectively (3:3–5, 10–13), the returnees celebrated and worshiped. The previous celebrations, however, were a mixed bag of fear (3:3), joy, and sadness (3:12–13). Joy alone characterizes this present celebration (6:16, 22 [2x]).

This moment recalls, too, the dedication of Solomon's temple, when the king, along with all Israel, offered sacrifices before the

Lord (1 Kgs 8:62–63). Although only Judah, Benjamin, and Levi remained of the twelve tribes at this point in the nation's history, the narrator attempts to represent the past with the realities of the present. This building dedication, installation, and celebration was just as valid as previous building dedications.

Ultimate result: Passover worship (6:19–22). With all the cultic installations in place (a new temple and cultic personnel), the community resumes and conducts worship in the traditional way with the celebration of Passover. The day of Passover was followed by the week-long Feast of Unleavened Bread. These combined feasts were intended to bring the worshiper back to God, to remind the worshiper who was responsible for the joyous occasion. This celebration of Passover in Ezra not only connects them with their past, but it celebrates another rescue mission—Israel's deliverance from exile—and the motif of the second exodus resurfaces.

Accordingly, measures were taken to ensure a proper celebration. The Levites slaughter the Passover lamb (6:20). Likewise, those partaking in the meal had to demonstrate purity. Such devotion to the God of Israel required cutting all other religious ties, allegiances, and ways of worship. Again, the exclusive rather than inclusive nature of those participating in worship is important because the identity and purity of God's people is at stake.

Thus, in Ezra 6:13–22 the narrator summarizes how, why, and when the second temple was completed but zooms in on the ultimate result—the worship of Yahweh and the people's devotion to him, a reestablished relationship with their God who is mighty to protect and save. The real victor over all obstacles and opposition is not Cyrus, not Darius, but Yahweh.

Application. Dedication and celebration! As temples of the living God, our lives should be marked by full service and dedication to God. Celebration leading to worship should naturally flow from our lives/temples as a result of what God has done; it should be our goal to "keep the Festival" as Paul exhorts (1 Cor 5:8). Peter exhorts that the Old Testament Passover lamb, although a reality for the Israelites, merely foreshadowed the ultimate and final Passover Lamb, Jesus. Through his perfect life and sacrificial death, Jesus was our only option to rescue us from death to life (1 Pet 1:19–21).

EZRA 7:1–10

Original Meaning. Ezra's lineage in 7:1–6 ties him to a great line-up of staunchly loyal and prestigious priests who served in powerful regimes. The author name-drops in order to underline Ezra's pedigree. "This Ezra" is not just any Ezra, but one with distinction (7:6).

Next, the author reveals Ezra's social and religious standing within the priesthood (7:6b). The NIV's "well versed in the Law of Moses" may also be translated as "experienced" or "skilled" with respect to the law. The designations show that Ezra fulfilled an important role in the postexile phase, a role further unpacked by the statement in 7:10.

Ezra had a strong resolve—he "devoted himself" to a task (7:10). A more helpful reading would be "he made firm his heart" or "had set his heart" (author's translation) to a task. This preferred reading gives proper attention to the Hebrew verbal form used, which indicates an internally causative action.

What Ezra did in Babylon, he would continue to do in Israel. His entire life was given over to that purpose. His IOS (internal operating system) was oriented toward the word of God. The fruit of his study was personal piety and application of the truths of God's law. Thus Ezra 7:10 highlights Ezra's critical role and his depth of character.

The author reveals that Ezra had favor with the Persian king (7:6, 11–26). However, the favor Ezra experienced was not because of his impressive credentials as priest and teacher but for one main reason: "the hand of the Lord his God was on him" (7:6). Here the author shows how and why Ezra ended up in Jerusalem—on account of divine favor for the divine purpose of reviving the law in the covenantal community after years of neglect and deficit.

Application. Placing a premium on God's word has the power to bring revival to individuals and churches. Church history testifies to this fact. What place does the word hold in our churches and lives? While it is true that not everyone is called to be a reformer of the caliber of Luther or a scribe of the caliber of Ezra, the latter's specialized role does reveal the continued need to have experts in the church to help restore God's people. Institutions like Bible colleges and seminaries have a critical role to play as a result. In this regard professors with a heart for the word, teaching at a seminary, are critical to the church's mission.

EZRA 7:11–28

Original Meaning

A Letter Legitimizing Ezra's Return (7:11–28). *Orders to Ezra and the Israelites (7:12–20).* In the first set of orders, Artaxerxes entrusts Ezra with two main things: amassing a volunteer team of people (7:13–14) and the acquisition of financial aid (7:15–20).

The statement in 7:14 is revealing: "You are sent by the king . . . to inquire about Judah and Jerusalem with regard to the Law of your God, which is in your hand." Artaxerxes, without knowing it, portrays Ezra as a lawgiver and keeper akin to

Moses (Exod 31:18) or one of the nation's great kings, such as Josiah (2 Kgs 22:1–23:32) and Hezekiah (2 Chr 31:21). Ezra, like Moses, was a lawgiver, another important tie to preexilic Israel.

The second item the king entrusts Ezra with concerns money. Artaxerxes entrusts Ezra with no small amount of finances deriving from three different sources to aid sacrifices for temple worship (7:15–17). In this context Artaxerxes also trusts that any financial surplus not used for temple services would be used by Ezra "in accordance with the will of your God" (7:18). The will of God is knowable because Ezra possesses God's will in his hand (7:14). The law of God and God's will are one and the same. For this reason, the king has tremendous confidence in Ezra.

Orders to the treasurers of Trans-Euphrates (7:21–24). Another set of orders is directed toward the king's officials living in Judah and Jerusalem (7:21). The king requires that government workers in his territories abroad trust Ezra, relative to matters of worship, upon his arrival. Likewise, the treasurers may not collect any revenues (taxes) from the temple clergy (7:24).

Orders personally to Ezra (7:25–26). The last part of the letter is orders directed toward Ezra: "And you, Ezra" (7:25). Artaxerxes entrusts Ezra with governmental affairs! He asks him to dispense justice in the land by delegating people like himself to the task, people "who know the laws of your God" (7:25a). Finally, this section closes with a strong word reminding Ezra of the consequences for those who break either God's or the king's laws (7:26). Disobedience to the law would not be tolerated, and Ezra, along with those appointed by Ezra, were to hold lawbreakers accountable.

Ezra's own understanding of how and why he got to Jerusalem (7:27–28). The final section of this chapter brings Ezra's personal point of view back to the reader. It is Ezra's first-person interpretation of how and why he ended up taking the trek to Jerusalem and a preface to the list of people who volunteered to follow him in this new exodus (8:1–14).

Application. The hope of a national transformation by applying the truths and principles of God's word was the goal of Ezra and the Persian king. This teaches us how the Bible becomes critical as a source of wisdom, not just at the personal level but in the public sphere as well. The presence or absence of godly principles directly affects the well-being of a nation. To remain Christian and have an influence means we need to retain the Bible. America and other Western nations threaten to spiral into decline by turning away from the Bible. A nation that has the word or is attempting to apply its principles (however those principles have come to that nation, such as a pagan king, a missionary, a pastor/teacher) will be better off than without it.

EZRA 8:1–36

Original Meaning

List of the Returning Families (8:1–14). The list in Ezra 8:1–14 numbers about one thousand five hundred Jews who returned with Ezra from fifteen different families, relatives of those who went to Jerusalem previously (ch. 2; Neh 7). The list commences with the needed workers for temple services in Jerusalem, family heads associated with the priestly lines of Phinehas and Ithamar and descendants of David (Ezra 8:2–3). With regard to the former, the lineage of Aaron is followed. By this the author draws attention to the prestige of the preexilic priestly line. With the mention of David's descendants, it lauds the preexilic royal line.

The Journey: Problems and Preparations (8:15–20). The men Ezra chooses to send are described in an intentional way by the use of relative clauses in 8:16. They are "leaders" and "men of learning" who "go to Iddo, the leader in Kasiphia" to recruit attendants for the house of God (8:16–17). Among the recruits were also 220 temple servants to aid the Levites, an arrangement made previously by David and his court officials (8:20). The mention of David here recalls 3:10, connecting postexilic worship to preexilic. Once again, the author wishes to reestablish that what was normative for preexilic Israel remains so for the postexilic people of God.

Ezra attributes the success in recruiting Levites to God's good hand on them corporately (8:18). Ezra's own interpretive grid for daily life was God. He understood that the practical things that fall into place, such as obtaining Levites and traveling mercies, all stem from God.

The Solution about Safety and Finances and their Safe Arrival (8:21–36). Once the Levite problem was solved but before the journey could begin, Ezra put into place two more preparatory elements. The first concerned a fast for their physical safety; the second was a delegation of the finances to the priests and Levites for safekeeping (8:28–29).

Seekers of God (in this context Ezra and company, but ultimately anyone) experience God's favor. Ezra knows both cognitively and experientially God's favor and disfavor. Help in the face of potential enemies, therefore, is Ezra's hope. The outcome of fasting and praying was not just a safe journey to Jerusalem but a to the king testimony of God's character. Accordingly, in Ezra's mind there was more on the line than just a safe journey physically to Jerusalem. Yahweh was clearly different than the gods of the Persian pantheon.

Ezra's concern in 8:24–30 is for the safekeeping of the finances that poured in from donors back in Babylon (8:25). These donations were to be handled by twelve priests (8:24).

Both the donations and those bearing them were deemed "consecrated to the LORD" (8:28). All of this (the holiness and purpose of finances) was an indirect charge to be faithful to the task. It reflects the importance Ezra placed on godly stewardship leading to worship of Yahweh.

Verses 31–32 show how God answered the pleas for help through fasting and praying. On the journey, the returnees were indeed "rescued" (Heb. *natsal*; author's translation; NIV "delivered") from opposition. Likewise, all was carried out as planned with the finances (8:33–34). Verses 35–36 return to third-person narrative, and the chapter closes with a note of celebration. Now with the lawgiver and his entourage back in Jerusalem, yet another celebration ensues, and Ezra has made it abundantly clear that divine assistance was given to the people of God every step of the way.

Application. This Ezra passage invites us to contemplate our own perspectives about the journey we are on in life. Navigation in this world to do kingdom work is not easy nor without hassle, but God has graciously given us a system to navigate it with success. The text invites us to recall that we are on a journey with a clear destination—to arrive home safely at the house of our God, to be in relationship with him. It also reminds us that the journey is not hassle free. Needed help may not necessarily be available and at times it may be unsafe. Moreover, the journey requires a God-dependent mindset. That is, we must be aware and assured of divine assistance when problems arise.

EZRA 9:1–15

Original Meaning

Ezra Mourns and Confesses Corporate Sin (9:1–5). *Ezra approached (9:1–2).* What the leaders, priests, and Levites have done is no less than defiled themselves like Israel of old. The mission to restore the sanctity of Zion has come to a screeching halt and faces an existential threat.

Ezra mourns (9:3–5). Ezra's use of first person makes it especially dramatic and gives the reader a window into how he was personally affected by the circumstances. Ezra draws a crowd of like-minded, courageous people around him, those that feared God and revered God's word. In this entire act of mourning, subduing his bodily desires and dying to self, Ezra revealed a visceral reaction to sin. All he had to fall back on was his deep awareness of God's merciful and gracious character.

Ezra's Prayer (9:6–15). *Awareness and confession of guilt (9:6–7).* The grief and guilt associated with lifestyle choices not aligned with God's word weighed Ezra down physically and spiritually. Just as preexilic Israel was guilty, so is postexilic Israel (9:7). Even after suffering the exile, the consequence of breaking God's law, and even after returning to the land, the consequence of God's grace and mercy, God's people were still guilty and not able to keep God's law.

Awareness and confession of God's mercy and grace (9:8–9). As Ezra's prayer continues, the awareness of God's grace takes center stage. The Hebrew of 9:8 says that the two purposes of God's grace manifested itself in "leaving an escaped remnant" and "giving us a peg" (author's translation). The term for "peg" (*yated*) is rendered as "secure hold" or "firm place" in English translations (ESV, NIV). It is a term associated with the instrument that holds up the tabernacle (Exod 27:19; 35:18). The metaphor affirms that God has given them something firm in the renewed sanctuary: a secure place where, indeed, one can tangibly see a manifestation of God's grace.

Ezra admits in 9:9 that God has, as the NIV puts it, "shown us kindness." This translation of "kindness" for the Hebrew term *hesed* misses some of the nuance of the rich term. Its use redirects God, Ezra, and the gathered crowd to reflect on previous moments where God displayed such loyalties, moments where God demonstrated his *hesed*. Ezra's present interpretive lens for dealing with sin, therefore, is God's relentless, gracious, and merciful character.

Awareness of accountability (9:10–12). "But now, our God, what can we say after this?" (9:10). This rhetorical question captures the intensity of the moment. The answer, of course, is nothing! Their neglectful behavior relative to the application of God's word is yet another connection to preexilic Israel. Their character flaw is great (lack of loyalty in the relationship), and they deserve his wrath, not mercy.

Awareness of what is deserved (9:13–15). As Ezra's prayer draws to a close, he asks in 9:14, "Would you not be angry enough with us to destroy us?" He concedes that their ongoing guilt deserves God's full wrath, particularly in light of his grace. The existence of God's people hangs in the balance, not unlike the threat that existed with the golden calf prior to Moses's intercession (Exod 32–34).

The theology that surfaces from this part of Ezra's prayer reveals how the sin-guilt cycle endemic to God's people exposes a bigger problem. Guilty people cannot legally stand before a holy God. Ezra knows that the future existence of the exiles is based solely on the fact that God is and always will be the God of Israel.

Application. God's people blow it by engaging in a particular unfaithfulness resulting in sin's consequences, the equivalent of the exile. Because of God's merciful restoration, the equivalent of the return from exile, they experience his grace and joy. For a time, and out of deep, genuine gratitude, they do everything according to the word of God as it relates to regulating their worship of him (chs. 1–6). With the passing of time, gratitude for his mercy and favor fade, and people can easily slip back into their old patterns of unfaithfulness. When it comes to the attention of our spiritual leaders that we have fallen back or backslidden, the hope is that they are grieved and cry out to God on our behalf. In this way, the application of this text is perhaps closer to the surface for us than some other Old Testament texts.

EZRA 10:1–44

Original Meaning

Confessions of Unfaithfulness in Community and Action Taken (10:1–17). *Community conviction (10:1).* The shift to third-person narrative (rather than Ezra's first-person perspective) gives specific attention to those in the community and their critical viewpoint on the event. The emotional effects of sin in the camp were deep and not confined just to Ezra.

Unfaithfulness and hope (10:2–4). The reported speech of Shekaniah confesses two things: their unfaithfulness and yet their hope, two seemingly contradictory points. Remarkable ownership of their sin is witnessed by this confession.

The second thing that Shekaniah confesses in 10:2 is hope for the nation. Hope is obviously needed because the threat of destruction or another exile looms large yet again (9:14–15). Shekaniah seems to be contextualizing concerns of the law as Ezra has done.

The "covenant" in 10:3 was to be agreed upon by Ezra and other leaders who feared God's commands, a gesture showing compliance "according to the Law." How could the specific arrangement of this covenant—sending away the women and their children—be done according to the law? In the statement in 10:3, "Let it be done according to the Law," the "it" refers to the terms of the covenant and the legal requirement of the oath associated with covenant making. In this regard the people of God are covenanting afresh to keep all of God's law in general, but more specifically and in this context, not to have any other gods besides Yahweh, since marrying foreigners equates to idolatry.

A pledge and prayer (10:5–6). Ezra acts in two specific ways. First, he secures the group's consensus by calling for an oath or pledge of allegiance to follow through with the arrangements of the covenant. The second way Ezra acts concerns a return to prayer.

Ezra returns to prayer and fasting, but this time in private. Ezra returns to praying and fasting in hopes to avert God's wrath (10:6). Accordingly, he continues to mourn. Likewise, the group assembled recognizes the urgent need to avert God's fierce anger.

A proclamation (10:7–8). A communication was then put out for "all the exiles" (10:7). The stern nature of the communication was expressed in the need for timeliness in getting to Jerusalem. They were to assemble within a three-day period, a time that would allow those farther away to participate. The stern nature of the communication, however, was expressed by two parts. The first part of the ultimatum was to assemble or forfeit property. The second part of the ultimatum was to assemble or be an exile among the exiles. They would become like the ones they have married: non-Yahwist foreigners!

Call to confession and reform (10:9–11). Ezra cuts to the chase and does what a faithful priest in the covenant community ought to have done. As their spiritual leader, he holds them accountable for their actions and calls them to reform their ways. The NIV translation of 10:10, "you have been unfaithful," does not fully do justice to the emphasis of the original. The Hebrew reads, "You, you have been unfaithful" or "You yourselves have been unfaithful." The statement by Ezra reinforces the accountability of God's people for their actions, expressed in Shekaniah's confession (10:2). Not only was preexilic Israel guilty, but now postexilic Israel is guilty.

Ezra commands them accordingly to "honor the LORD, the God of your ancestors" (10:11a). Ezra also commands "and do his will" (10:11b). Doing God's will entails both praise and reform. This leads to the third command, "separate yourselves" (10:11c). He reminds them of the previous agreed upon action of sending away what appears to be the defilement in the land, their foreign wives and children (10:3).

Ironically, the returnees are re-defiling the land by their affiliation to women who worship other gods, a defilement that God warned about previously (9:11–12, cf. Deut 13). Thus, the forced departure is not unlike the forced removal that God imposed on the inhabitants of Canaan through Joshua's conquests. The expulsion of the women and children represents a re-conquering of the promised land. It was a cleansing of the land that would enable them to remain and for the promises of God to be furthered in the life of the community.

Assembly's response (10:12–17). The people's swift response shows awareness, not denial, of their transgression and guilt, and a healthy fear of God's just anger with respect to it (10:13–14). They actually believe their reforms will avert God's wrath and more consequences for sin, which is not an unhealthy motivation for change. With the exception of four people who stood against the idea for unknown reasons (10:15), Ezra gets the surprising but hoped for cooperation evidenced in the unified and loud voice of the assembly (10:12). This loud, unified voice should not be glossed over. Rarely does one see such quick admission of wrongdoing in the biblical text. The people of God express admission and confession of guilt and their intention to reform.

The Guilty Parties (10:18–44). *Guilty priests (10:18–22).* Sixteen offending priests are noted. At the top of the list was Joshua, the son of Jozadak, the high priest at the time. Those following Joshua in the priestly lineup derive from the family of the high priest. Their poor example is now made right. Thus, the offending priests confessed their own sins, and, by offering a guilt offering, they were ministering as appropriate in the community for unfaithfulness (Lev 5:14–19).

Guilty laity (10:25–43). The list of offending laity comes next. From the general population of Israelites, mentioned as noteworthy for their guilt are the descendants of Elam who include Mattaniah, Zechariah, Jehiel, Abdi, Jeremoth, and Elijah (10:26).

Summary of the event (10:44). This verse represents a final summary statement by the author with respect to the events that unfolded beginning in chapter 9.

Application. There is still hope for God's guilty people. The wrongdoing in our lives clearly makes us guilty, but how do we handle both the ongoing wrongdoings and the feelings of deep guilt associated with it? Perhaps we handle it by harsh judgment and condemnation of ourselves and of others? Some of us prefer our own rigid works righteousness to appease a guilty conscious. If you find yourself working, it might suggest a self-reliance and not a God-reliance. Ultimately, we must look to the cross where our true hope is found.

NEHEMIAH

INTRODUCTION TO NEHEMIAH

The book of Nehemiah details the third return from Babylon (continued from the book of Ezra) under the leadership of the governor Nehemiah. Chapters 1–13 narrate the restoration of the walls and sanctity of Zion. The book concludes in 13:4–31 with an epilogue, noting Nehemiah's final attempts at reform. See also the Introduction to Ezra above (p. 374) for commentary on the composition and dating of Ezra-Nehemiah.

BOOK OUTLINE

- I. The Third Return (Continued from Ezra): Nehemiah Restores the Walls and Sanctity of Zion (1:1–13:3)
  - A. Nehemiah's Prayer (1:1–11)
  - B. Nehemiah's Commission (2:1–8)
  - C. Initial Impressions in Jerusalem (2:9–20)
  - D. The Rebuilding of the Gates and Repairing the Walls (3:1–32)
  - E. Physical Threat (4:1–23)
  - F. Internal Threat (5:1–19)
  - G. Personal Threat (6:1–19)
  - H. Genealogical Record (7:1–73a)
  - I. Covenant Renewal (7:73b–8:18)
  - J. Historical Retrospective (9:1–37)
  - K. Covenant Ratification (9:38–10:39)
  - L. Resettling the Land (11:1–36)
  - M. Lineage of Priests and Levites (12:1–26)
  - N. Dedication of the Wall and Restoration of Worship (12:27–13:3)
- II. Epilogue: Nehemiah's Final Attempts at Reform (13:4–31)

NEHEMIAH 1:1–11

Original Meaning

Nehemiah's Prayer (1:1–11). *The setting (1:1–4).* The plot of the book is wrapped in the report provided by Hanani (1:2). Nehemiah asks a pointed two-part question: first, regarding the "Jewish remnant that had survived the exile" (1:2a); and second, the query focuses on the actual city of "Jerusalem" (1:2b). The devastating news of Jerusalem (1:3) fits squarely within the Sinaitic covenant equation of judgment-destruction (Deut 28:52). Disloyalty to Yahweh results in foreign invasion and exile.

Nehemiah 1:4 breaks down Nehemiah's reaction to the report into three parts. As soon as he heard the news, he "sat down." This immediate reaction is then followed by weeping and mourning. The context suggests the idea of many days, since the next chronological marker is found in 2:1: "in the month of Nisan," some four months later.

The prayer (1:5–11). By attaching the familiar "God of Heaven" to Yahweh (NIV "Lord"; 1:5), Nehemiah's invocation anchors the prayer to the Sinaitic revelation of God to Moses (Exod 6:2–3) and thereby sets the theological context for the rest of the prayer. "Covenant of love" (Neh 1:5) should be read as "Yahweh who keeps the covenant and *hesed*" (author's translation). This appeal to *hesed* gives Nehemiah the boldness to petition Yahweh. Nehemiah's prayer reflects a conviction that without a confession of sin, no promises of God can be fulfilled for the exiles.

Verse 7 continues the confession of sin: "we have not obeyed the stipulations, decrees and laws," which is the typical preexilic tripartite designation for Deuteronomic law (Deut 4:44–45). Nehemiah appeals to truths that Yahweh originated and gave to his servant Moses.

Nehemiah 1:8–10 marks the shift in the prayer from confession to petition by appealing directly to the Deuteronomic promise of return from exile following the repentance of the people (Deut 30:1–5) to "the place the Lord your God will choose from among all your tribes to put his Name there for his dwelling" (Deut 12:5). This rich and textured theological phrase emphasizes the significance of Jerusalem in the Deuteronomic theology of the divine presence.

While it would be appropriate to include Nehemiah 1:11b as part of the whole prayer (following the NIV and most other translations), it perhaps fits the context better to single out the last part of the prayer as a hinge that introduces the next chapter of Nehemiah's memoir. Now the prayer has a focus: the encounter with the king in chapter 2 and the reality that this meeting was, to use a popular phrase, "bathed in prayer."

Application. Nehemiah's opening prayer underscores the significance of confession of sin for our own lives, for those of our family, and for the sins of others. We as Christians have a responsibility in our own particular cultural contexts to identify with and weep for the aftermaths of the sins of our ancestors. A posture of humility will prevent us, in turn, from smugness, arrogance, and defensiveness when confronted with our own corporate past.

NEHEMIAH 2:1–8

Original Meaning

Nehemiah's Commission (2:1–8). "I had not been sad . . . before" in 2:1 provides a unique background that sets the context for the ensuing conversation and will change Nehemiah's destiny forever. As a result of a brief exchange, he will pack up his bags and find himself in Yehud, placed in charge of the restoration of Zion!

As soon as the king notices Nehemiah's incongruous mood, Nehemiah becomes convinced he has reached the point of no return. Now is the time for action and for the request to be presented. Will he find favor with the king as he has been praying for several weeks now?

Nehemiah's rhetorical response in 2:3, "Why should my face not look sad," deftly omits the political designation of the "city" as Jerusalem and places the emphasis on Nehemiah's ancestral roots.

Nehemiah himself might have been taken aback at how effective his own scheme panned out since the text interjects a new line in the narrative sequence. We expect the framing formula of "and I answered the king" (2:5), but instead we hear that Nehemiah prayed (2:4). In this heightened tension, he draws closer to the God of heaven.

In presenting his formal request for a commission, the goal is plainly stated: "so that I can rebuild it" (2:5). Nehemiah could have asked for a detachment to shore up Ezra's efforts or requested an emissary to the local satrap to intervene for the rebuilding of the city. But that is not what he asked. Instead, he enters the arena and hopes to become the lead character in this process of rebuilding Zion. Verse 6 leaves no suspense in narrative time as to what the king's answer will be.

The next and final section of the formal exchange at the court (2:7–8) represents a unit that we might call the "let's put this in writing part" and reveals just how well-prepared Nehemiah was for the meeting, as there is no indicator that the events described at the court happened over an extended period of time (as in the case of Esther; see, e.g., Esth 1:1–12). Once Nehemiah receives the go-ahead from the king, he also secures crucial documents that will give him the legal and material means to finish the task of restoring Zion.

Application. There are numerous examples in church history for when the people of God pray to see the will of the Lord accomplished. The work of God in building the spiritual building of the church continues to this day. This is the ministry to which you and I have been called as intercessors. We should not think that this kind of success is restricted to the covenant people in the history of redemption. As God's people we, too, are writing the history of redemption of the people the Lord has placed on our path, and we, too, are called to see the rebuilding of the church take place.

NEHEMIAH 2:9–20

Original Meaning

Initial Impressions in Jerusalem (2:9–20). *The new conquest (2:9–10).* Verse 9 functions as a concluding summary to Nehemiah's audience with the king. In addition, the mention of an imperial escort further stresses Nehemiah's role as a new political force to be reckoned with in the eyes of the regional establishment. Verse 10 launches a major theme of Nehemiah's memoirs and provides a neat literary connection with the documenting of oppositions chronicled in Ezra 4.

Surveying the extent of the damage (2:11–15). Literarily, the description of the night survey introduces us to the actual building project described in both chapters 3 and 4 of Nehemiah. The background details of the account reveal Nehemiah's characteristic deftness and discretion in negotiating the restoration of Zion with authorities, whether through the stealth of a concerted time of prayer before meeting the king of Persia in chapter 1 or the stealth of a pedestrian night survey before addressing the people of Yehud.

Addressing the local Jewish leadership (2:16–18). The "officials" (mentioned twice in 2:16) refer to the local Jewish officials that would answer to Nehemiah as the newly minted governor of Yehud. Nehemiah's succinct address (2:17) intentionally repeats the familiar vocabulary of both chapter 1 and his address to the king in chapter 2. The removal of "disgrace" (2:17) recalls the cause-and-effect Deuteronomic relationship between the restoration of Zion and the absence of disgrace. Verse 18 describes another foundational theme of answered prayer.

Responding to his enemies (2:19–20). His counterparts' strong reaction in 2:10 is developed in 2:19–20 and underscores the epic political struggle Nehemiah faces with the local governors of the Trans-Euphrates. However, Nehemiah is equally forceful in his reply. These three antagonists have no claim to Zion, in the past, present, and its future.

Application. Just as the early church faced the reality of opposition, we will face opposition in the building of Zion, the people of God in the new covenant. Nehemiah's approach may sound intolerant in an age of pluralism, tolerance, and inclusivity. However, in the eyes of the majority church elsewhere in the world, especially in areas facing persecutions, this no-compromise approach makes sense since it is matter of physical survival of the community of believers.

NEHEMIAH 3:1–32

Original Meaning

The Rebuilding of the Gates and Repairing the Walls (3:1–32). Nehemiah 3 functions as an introductory summary of the building narrative (Neh 4–6) and offers parallels to the list of those who resettled Jerusalem in Nehemiah 11 and especially to the dedication of the sacred enclosure in chapter 12. Literarily, connections between these sections of the book are rich: those who are involved in the restoration of Zion are specifically singled out by name along with topographical and architectural landmarks (both monumental and domestic) that relate to the restoration project. Each of these sections follows a highly formulaic genre which, in the case of chapter 3, is reminiscent of ancient Near Eastern building inscriptions, with the marked difference that rather than having a first-person account that lauds the achievements of the king (e.g., "I built this"), we now have an official record of the participation of the people by name. The shift to the third-person narrative voice and Nehemiah's noticeable absence from this list underscores the involvement of the community as a whole. The amazing degree of consensus reflected in chapter 3 also anticipates a similar unity when the covenant is renewed in chapter 8, in contrast to other moments of disunity in the book (chs. 5, 13). Chapter 3 builds upon the string of Nehemiah's successes following his extended time of prayer and mourning: both the king and the people wholeheartedly embrace Nehemiah's project of restoration, and now the diverse community of Yehud gets involved.

Formulaic emphasis. Nehemiah skillfully structures his name list with formulaic language. Beyond the identification of the participants, the chapter recounts the restoration of the enclosure wall, with a particular emphasis on the rebuilding and restoration of some gates in the first half of the account (3:1–15) and the wall in relationship to individuals' houses and other landmarks in the second half (3:16–32). From a historical standpoint, chapter 3 is a treasure trove of historical-geographical information, and we ought to capitalize on this ancient "Bible atlas" of fifth century BC Yehud.

Building and repairing. As a building project, the language of "repaired" and "rebuilt" dominates the account. In the formulaic language pertaining to the building of the gates, attention is drawn to the work on the "doors" (3:3). The gates needed to be rebuilt from scratch since the Babylonian and subsequent attacks on Jerusalem destroyed them (see 1:3). Thus, when it says gates were rebuilt, we should probably understand this to mean new doors were installed. This new construction would provide explanation as to why the high priest felt the need to "dedicate" the Sheep Gate (in the sense of making it holy, 3:1).

For building activities pertaining to walls, the verb "to repair" dominates the account. This emphasis on strengthening or shoring up an existing feature bears significance. First, it might explain why no building supplies from quarries are mentioned in the account. The needed stonework would be recycled from the existing building materials found in the debris caused by the damage of the 586 BC destruction. This would also explain the rapidity with which the community restored the sanctity and (relative) safety of Zion.

Identification and individuals. Next to the actual parts of the walls that were affected, the identification of individuals dominates the chapter, and significant elements for interpretation are embedded into the names, occupation, and tasks.

Patrimonial heads of the community carried out the majority of the work. In tribal societies then and now, nothing gets done without the consent and participation of the tribal leaders.

Several tribal heads also function as "ruler" (3:9, 12, 14, 15, 16, 17, 18, 19) of a "half-district" (3:9, 12, 16, 17,18) or "district" (3:14, 15). As Persian officials in Yehud and according to Artaxerxes's commission to Nehemiah, they lead no less than six building projects (3:9, 12, 14, 15, 16, 19), thereby validating the legitimacy and legality of the enterprise and, conversely, underscoring the illegal nature of the opposition by Nehemiah's opponents.

Including members of outlying communities (e.g., "men of Jericho"; 3:2) points to a geographical distribution of the effort that encompassed the Jordan Valley ("Jericho") and the highlands surrounding Jerusalem. The effort was not a phenomenon limited to the community in Jerusalem but reflects a widespread geographical participation throughout the province of Yehud.

"Priests" (3:1, 22) feature prominently at the beginning of the list and also toward the end. Other members of the religious class also include "Levites" (3:17) and "temple servants (3:26)." These three groups play a central role later in the account (see chs. 8–12).

Specialized craftsmen, "goldsmiths" (3:8, 31; literally, "refiners"), "perfumers" (3:8), and "merchants" (3:32), are involved as well. Further pointing to socio-organizational diversity, the "daughters" of "Shallum," "ruler of a half-district of Jerusalem" also participated in repairing a section of the wall (3:12).

Gates and walls. Details on the gates' construction (3:1–15) are covered by the recurring phrase "[they] put its doors and bolts and bars in place" (3:3, 6, 13, 14, 15). The phrase emphasizes the sanctity of the site has been restored (see 13:19) and also confirms the gates as the focal point of the Babylonian and subsequent destructions (e.g., 1:3).

Details pertaining to wall restoration abutting the gates are signaled by the formula that includes the following elements: participant(s) + "repaired" + "next to him/them" (e.g., 3:10, "Hattush son of Hashabneiah made repairs next to him").

Supplementary details occur for every gate except for the Sheep Gate and the Dung Gate. These details offer us a window into the extent of the damage and where most of the work needed to take place. We may assume other gates mentioned in the second part of the report required no work (e.g., "Water Gate," 3:26; see also Neh 8:1) since they are not mentioned as a repair project.

Application. What is clearly intentional in this account is the remarkable diversity of representation for the building project. People of all walks of life participated. Qualification for participation does not relate to one's particular skillsets but is based on the desire to rebuild Zion, which for us means the edification and sanctification of the body of Christ. This image painted by Nehemiah 3 prepares us for the unity of the body of Christ reflected in the list of Romans 12:1–8, which allows a diversity of roles and functions so that the whole body/temple (1 Cor 3:16; Eph 2:22) is built together.

NEHEMIAH 4:1–23

Original Meaning

Physical Threat (4:1–23). *Sanballat's Brinkmanship (4:1–3).* Evidently, Sanballat was predisposed to undermine the galvanizing effect of the newly appointed governor of Yehud, but what took him by surprise was the scope of involvement. The taunting is accentuated by a reported speech framed as a series of rhetorical questions (4:2). Sanballat gives a counterpart speech to motivate his troops as Nehemiah did to the leaders of Yehud in 2:17–18, with equal success. "Tobiah the Ammonite" (4:3) is re-introduced without his title of "servant," but the echo-chamber effect of his rhetorical question supports the idea of his role as Sanballat's junior partner.

Nehemiah's corporate prayer (4:4–6). Nehemiah himself led this prayer, rather than the religious authorities. The prayer fits the genre of imprecation, common in the psalms, where the Yahwist prays down Deuteronomic curses upon his enemies' head.

Verse 6 summarizes the situation at the halfway point and functions as a bridge statement, serving both as an explanation for the strongly worded opposition and looming threat of the "army of Samaria" of the preceding paragraph (4:1–5). It also prepares us for the impending struggle of the rest of the chapter.

Escalation of the crisis (4:7–9). This summary paragraph is structurally a mirror image of the sequence of 4:1–5. As in 4:4–5, the escalating threat is met by the prayers of the community (4:9), which points to the determination of the community to face the threat with keen spiritual awareness. To counter the physical threat will require spiritual means.

The spiritual reaction to the physical threat continues to mirror the structure of the previous paragraph (4:9, 4:4) but is now conveyed in the narrative voice. This statement sets the tone for the rest of the chapter: the community answers Sanballat's brinkmanship via both spiritual and physical means.

Nehemiah's address to the community: remember and fight! (4:10–15). In quick succession, three reported speeches expose the depth of the threat at the half-way mark and set the stage for the events narrated in the rest of the chapter. The first reflects the sentiment of the community at large: the extent of the devastation seriously hampers the debris clearing process. The second speech (4:11) shifts the focus to an impending threat from the "enemies." The third speech (4:12) continues the movement toward an escalation of the conflict, now outside the bounds of Jerusalem proper. Jews in outlying communities are feeling the imposition from Sanballat's tribal alliance. It appears the enemy has seized the opportunity created by the fluid situation in Jerusalem to assert a more robust regional stance over Jewish settlements outside the city. This in turn places intense pressure on Nehemiah at the outset of his governorship to provide protection for the Jewish communities living outside Jerusalem. He is potentially facing a regional conflict between the varying populations in Yehud.

The rest of the section chronicles the success of Nehemiah's approach and speaks to his deftness as a motivator in the community. By calling them to remember and fight, Nehemiah accomplished the dual purpose of not only averting a serious physical threat to the work but also motivating the community to return to their work in spite the logistical difficulties. Verse 15 represents a significant marker in Nehemiah's narrative and provides the theological summary of why the community went from a high state of military readiness to the resumption of the work. To the end of the chapter, and in the rest of the account, the community will not face a similar sense of physical danger.

Total commitment (4:16–23). From 4:16 to the end of the chapter, the tide has turned. The builders have regained the initiative. Preparedness, solidarity, and unity of purpose, along with the inevitable sacrifices, dominate the account. To rebuild the wall demands total commitment. Nehemiah makes a significant shift to the strategy of rebuilding. He himself moved frequently on the site and functioned as the overall supervisor of both the work and the defense of the city.

Verse 19 introduces us to Nehemiah's next major speech in his memoirs. Nehemiah again looks beyond the adverse circumstances, as he did during his time of prayer and fasting, and looks up to "our God" who "will fight for us" (4:20), but not without addressing the question of preparedness in the case of an attack: "whenever you hear the sound of the trumpet, join us there" (4:20). Verse 21 provides another summary.

The final detail in 4:23 speaks to Nehemiah's own determination to guard the community: "neither I nor my brothers nor my men nor the guards with me" let down their guard since no one removed his garments at night for personal hygiene. Instead, he kept his weapon, "even when he went for water" (4:23).

Application. While Satan is not mentioned in the account, his tactics of intimidation remain the same today. The principal lie is that we cannot change the consequence of the past, that what we have done is irreversible. The role of the enemy is to remind us of our past and the failures of the past, but the restoring power of the Holy Spirit breaks through this lie and changes the circumstances accordingly.

NEHEMIAH 5:1–19

Original Meaning

Internal Threat (5:1–19). *Three famine-related problems (5:1–5).* Specific immediate complaints also uncover deeper-seated problems within the community. The brief introductory statement exposes the seriousness of the matter since it is a widespread sentiment. The cause of this second existential threat no longer comes from a common external enemy. Instead, the opponent is now identified as "their fellow Jews" (5:1).

The first concern (5:2) focuses on the immediate and urgent need for food. Thus, the newly appointed governor is confronted with an unforeseen effect of his call for an all-out effort on the building of Zion. How to feed all these people?

The second complaint and the reference to a "famine" (5:3) provides crucial background and underscores how this food shortage quickly escalates into a full-blown crisis that threatens to tear apart the community. The final round of complaints (5:4–5) reflects a situation that has gone from bad to worse: the selling of human property (slavery) for cash in order to pay property taxes to Persian authorities ("the king," 5:4). The threat that tribal identity could be erased is real and needs to be addressed before the work on the wall can be completed.

Nehemiah resolves the dispute with the tribal leadership (5:6–13). Nehemiah's reaction matches his opponents' strong emotional reactions in previous encounters (4:1, 7). Rather than reacting on the spot, he "pondered" in his "mind" what the proper course of action should be (5:7). The verb "accused" (5:7) reflects the lawsuits Yahweh brought against his people in Deuteronomy 32 and carried out by his prophets in preexilic history (e.g., Isa 1), when the people stand liable before God's law. Nehemiah here acts as formal arbitrator and governor with considerable authority over the rulers.

Underlining the grave situation the community is facing, Nehemiah calls for a "large meeting to deal with them" (5:7b). Nehemiah's address to the group (5:8) convincingly argues that at stake is not simply an economic issue, but one of solidarity and identity. For Nehemiah, the problem boils down to a fundamental value that family members do not sell one another into slavery.

In light of the people's silence, Nehemiah is emboldened to continue (5:9) and state in plain terms: "What you are doing is not right." This rebuke not only rests on the spiritual need for covenantal loyalty to Yahweh ("fear of our God") but also on the practical reality of the existential threat posed by Sanballat et al. (5:9). The imperative that includes himself ("let us" in 5:10) now shifts to a command directed at the community leaders in 5:11: "Give back to them immediately" all land and property.

The people's silence of the first part of the address is now broken with a stunningly unequivocal response (5:12a). Nehemiah immediately seeks to ratify the promise by a formal oath ceremony (5:12b) with "priests" officiating. Nehemiah himself enacts an imprecatory curse formula by shaking the fold of his garment (5:13a).

Two examples from Nehemiah's integrity as governor (5:14–19). Nehemiah sets himself in sharp contrast to his predecessors (5:15). The theme of the fear of God literarily links this part of the chapter to the preceding one. For Nehemiah, the focal point of his governorship was the task for which he was commissioned in the first place. The single-minded focus on the task at hand kept Nehemiah from falling into the greedy practices of his predecessors.

As a closing statement, Nehemiah appeals not to human rewards but to God's "favor" (5:19) with respect to his single-minded dedication to the task, and, more importantly, to the people.

Application. Churches should always be on the lookout for those in need within their midst, and leaders should keep a particularly keen eye on these matters instead of growing complacent and ensconced in the material blessings they enjoy. Inequity among the people of God tears a community apart and represents a bad witness to the Lord. We are supposed to be known for our acts of compassion toward one another and to take care of our own within the community. Economic slavery of the day is debt and economic oppression.

NEHEMIAH 6:1–19

Original Meaning

Personal Threat (6:1–19). *Intimidation and distraction tactics from Sanballat and Geshem (6:1–4).* Without the wooden doors, the city remains vulnerable to unwanted intrusion. The moment seems opportune for the opponents to neutralize Nehemiah's direct influence in this reconstruction project. The location of the rendezvous places the meeting at the border between the provinces of Samaria and Judah, away from any protection for Nehemiah. In keeping with the official nature of the relationship between two Persian officials, Nehemiah is obligated to respond via courier.

Accusation of sedition (6:5–9). The conflict escalates to the accusation of sedition. It proved effective prior to Nehemiah's arrival in the province (Ezra 4:23), and now, since the work has progressed significantly, the scenario provided by Sanballat and Geshem would no longer ring hollow in the ears of Artaxerxes as it did when Nehemiah first arrived in Jerusalem (Neh 2:19). Nehemiah chooses the approach of full disclosure in the ensuing diplomatic exchange, which in turn allows him to mount a forceful denial of the allegations.

Tobiah the Godfather (6:10–15). The identity of Shemaiah remains a mystery beyond this incident. From the context of 6:12 ("he had prophesied"), we can safely surmise he belonged to the guild, along with a female prophet Noadiah. Nehemiah feels no obligation to fill in details, since his main point is to project the image that Shemaiah is an insider whom Nehemiah would consider friend rather than foe.

Nehemiah is not one to be duped. The specificity of the designation "temple" and the call to "close the temple doors" (6:10) raises red flags in Nehemiah's mind. Nehemiah would know that no one is allowed in this sacred space, let alone be confined inside the temple with its doors closed. His greatest concern is not his own personal safety but the sanctity of Yahweh's sacred space. By entering the temple's sacred space, Nehemiah would have been discredited in the eyes of the faithful community of Yahwists and would have seriously compromised his larger plan to restore the sanctity of Zion.

This episode marks the conclusion of the attempts on Nehemiah's life. The text quickly pivots to a summary that the task of building the wall was completed in "fifty-two days" (6:15). The rapidity with which the task was completed underscores the reality that the true purpose was to restore the sanctity of the site rather than to rebuild Zion as a military fortress worthy of a king.

Victory (6:16). Verse 16 is a hinge verse and functions in the manner of an official bulletin announcing the cessation of hostilities.

Post scriptum: letters of intimidation by the nobles of Judah (6:17–19). The text does not elaborate on the content of the letters; unlike the correspondence between Sanballat and Nehemiah, their mail remains unopened to us. However, 6:18 explicitly states why open channels of communication existed between Tobiah and the nobles: "many in Judah were under oath to him" because of marriage alliances that span two generations. This long list of patronymics speaks to the extent of the alliance and circles back to the reasons why Ezra and Nehemiah both speak so strongly against intermarriage within the context of the sanctity of Zion.

Verse 19 adds an additional layer of correspondence. Clearly these nobles were not on the side of Zion. Tobiah in turn tried also to "intimidate" (see 6:14) Nehemiah in his work. Verse 19, therefore, holds interpretive significance for the whole of Nehemiah's opposition and qualifies the sense of unity that existed at the outset of his mission in chapters 1–3. His situation remained precarious throughout, since some remained very much in the camp of the local authorities.

Application. *Dealing with bullies.* Nehemiah's experience of betrayal by those he thought he could trust is not an unfamiliar one in ministry. It would be naïve to think that everyone has our best interests at heart as we focus on the building up and edification of God's people in our respective callings. We should not be surprised how entangled the ministry of the gospel can be with folks with ulterior motives such as greed and power. Opposition to the building up of Zion comes in all sorts of ways, and Nehemiah offers some solid advice on how to conduct ourselves, especially among those friends-turned-foes, whether through bullying, intimidation, or the uncovering of hidden ungodly alliances.

NEHEMIAH 7:1–73A

Original Meaning

Genealogical Record (7:1–73a). Chapter 7 consists mostly of genealogies extracted from existing archives and plays an important role in the enterprise to which Nehemiah has been commissioned by both Yahweh and the king of Persia—to restore and protect the sanctity of Zion.

Completing the task of securing Zion (7:1–3). Nehemiah 7:1 captures the chronological emphasis of the text: "After the wall had been rebuilt and I had set the doors in place." In 7:2 Nehemiah will only entrust the guarding of the "citadel" (Heb. *birah*) to his own trusted blood brother. Hananiah's credentials are then listed. Nehemiah knows to focus first on the character of a person in relationship to God. Verse 3 speaks of three sets of specific instructions given to both Hanani and Hananiah ("I said to them").

Divine initiative to register people (7:4–5). Nehemiah is now setting his sight on the next task: rebuilding the city itself and setting up a relocation program so that people of the province of Yehud actually move back in permanently. Nehemiah plainly and clearly explains why he is summoning the people (7:5): he needs legal evidence that the people he is gathering actually belong to Israel, a noted designation that symbolizes the beginning of the restoration promised by the prophets.

List of returnees (7:6–73a). The role of the list of returnees for Nehemiah is to repopulate Zion after the rebuilding of the wall and gates.

Application. Nehemiah's divine prompting to find lists of names is equally valid to the divine promptings to go preach the gospel to a land/place/city/people the Lord puts on the hearts of his people. Divine guidance is not only for tasks pertaining to spiritual activities alone. In the comprehensive call to restore the sanctity of Zion and to prepare the city of God for the return of the King, we should take the so-called menial tasks of data entry, compiling directories, or schedules seriously. Legitimate membership in the community of faith is especially important, since we, too, face strong opponents in the proclamation of the gospel. We need to know who is who—or perhaps, who is whose!

NEHEMIAH 7:73B–8:18

Original Meaning

Covenant Renewal (7:73b–8:18). *Reading of the Law (7:73b–8:8).* The seventh month represents, along with the first month and the Passover in the spring (Lev 23:6), the high point in the calendar year (Lev 23:24, 27, 34) with the Feast of Trumpets on the first day (today's Rosh Hashanah), the Day of Atonement (today's Yom Kippur) on the tenth, and the Feast of Booths on the fifteenth (kept for one week). As the narrative unfolds, however, it is the third feast that receives special attention.

Ezra dons two hats. He is curator of the law when asked to bring out the book of the law in 8:1, but as he is about to read from it, he is designated "priest," (Heb. *kohen*) as he "brought the Law before the assembly" (8:2).

Ezra "read . . . aloud" (8:3) to a captive audience from dawn to noon, which at this time of year represents about six hours. In short order, the text pivots back to the audience itself, defined a second time as "men, women and others who could understand" (8:3; cf. 8:2). The imagery is that everyone was leaning forward to pay attention. Their ears are opened, and they have become active listeners.

Verses 4–5 provide further background to the morning scene of the reading of the law by Ezra that was described in 8:2–3. Prior to the assembling, a "high wooden platform" (literally, a "tower of wood") had been "built for the occasion. (8:4). Whether the men stand with Ezra on the elevated platform or are on the ground on both sides is not clear, but the overall picture is akin to Israel's great addresses in the past (Deut 29; Josh 8:30–35) and the covenant renewals during the late Judean period.

The peoples' response comes in quick succession (author's translation):

- *all the people* answered: "Amen! Amen!" (Neh 8:6), with their hands above
- they bowed
- they worshiped the LORD, faces to the ground (literally, "earthward")

That "all the people" (8:5) lifted their hands was a clear sign of worship, adoration, and honor to God. We will never know what specific words Ezra used to bless the Lord, but we do know what all the people said in response: "Amen! Amen!," which is a transliteration for the interjection *amen* in Hebrew and is connected to the meaning "believe, trust."

Thirteen Levites were dispatched into the crowds and "instructed the people in the Law" (8:7) as the law was being read by Ezra. The Levites functioned as simultaneous interpreters, probably providing quick words of clarification, all without disrupting the actual reading of the Law by Ezra.

Holy day of celebration (8:9–12). The content of the reported speech focuses on the people's reaction to the morning address. The imperative to the assembly, "do not mourn or weep" (8:9), goes at the heart of the mood of the day. There will be time for repentance and confession (see ch. 9)—but not today. In verse 10 Nehemiah commissions a celebration banquet (8:10, literally, "eat the fat and drink the best wine"). The third speech in 8:11 is there for continued emphasis and allows the Levites to weigh in.

The Feast of Booths is observed (8:13–18). Under Ezra's leadership, the tribal leaders reconvened by themselves the following day. They "found written in the Law" (8:14) that the whole assembly should immediately regather to Jerusalem and celebrate the Festival of Booths (NIV "temporary shelters").

As on the first day, the people respond right away and return (8:16) and build booths within the city of Jerusalem at specific locations. The exceptional nature of this particular addition cannot be overstated, since now Zion stands again as a protected sacred site. Indeed, "their joy was very great" (8:17), which is pursuant to the injunction by Nehemiah for the people to rejoice.

In conclusion (8:18), the account fittingly summarizes the role of Ezra in the daily attending to the reading of the "Book of the Law of God" and the atmosphere of celebration for the duration of the feast.

Application. The obvious application of this text across cultural and ethnic fault-lines centers around the centrality of God's word in Christian ministry, regardless of our diversity. The history of Christian mission attests to the amazing adaptability of the word of God to different cultures. The common denominator will be a high view of Scripture and its authority.

NEHEMIAH 9:1–37

Original Meaning

Historical Retrospective (9:1–37). *Call to worship (9:1–6).* The time of confession is set in the broader context of a public reading of the "Book of the Law of the LORD their God" (9:3) that alternated between times of confession and repentance, and the reading of the word. The time of confession remains anchored in the context of celebration of the past week (Feast of Booths).

"You alone are the LORD" (9:6) captures only a fraction of the redundant and emphatic nature of the syntax in the original pertaining to the uniqueness of Yahweh. It makes for an awkward sequence in English, but it certainly gets the point across:

> You are he Yahweh, you alone, you, you made the heavens . . . [and] the earth. (9:6, author's translation)

The covenant with Abraham (9:7–8). The recalling of the promise of the land made to Abraham puts the emphasis on the name change and his response of faith to Yahweh. His faithfulness to the promise to Abraham reveals that Yahweh is righteous. However, it would be too reductive to limit Yahweh's righteous acts to his faithfulness to Abram, as the prayer will demonstrate.

Exodus (9:9–11). The next installment of Israelite recapitulative history is anchored on the exodus event. This decisive victory was the crowning moment of Yahweh's revelation as the uncontested one God over all the gods of Egypt (Exod 15:11): "You made a name for yourself" (Neh 9:10).

Sinai (9:12–15). The guidance of cloud and fire serves as prolepsis (9:12) and as a connecting verse to the next main event. The Sinai account circles back to the wilderness journey by highlighting God's provision.

The people's arrogance and Yahweh's hesed *(9:16–18).* One cannot help but think the history so far serves as an introduction to the main point of the prayer, which is to highlight the people's disobedience in the midst of Yahweh's mighty acts of salvation, protection, and provision. In response to this perfect record of faithfulness, "they, our ancestors, became arrogant" (9:16). The text adds the one word coined in the crucible of the Israelites' disobedience: "stiff-necked" (9:16; see Exod 32:9), an animal husbandry term that characterizes a stubborn beast of burden. However, in response to this paradigm of inflexibility and rebellion, the prayer pivots to Yahweh's revelation of his character, which serves as a point-by-point response to the Israelites rebellion (Neh 9:17b).

Wilderness (9:19–21). The recalling of wilderness years (see Deut 8:1–4) concludes the whole first part of the history of Israel. The appeal is to the character of Yahweh as revealed in the declaration of the divine name at Sinai.

Conquest and settlement (9:22–25). Verse 22 returns to a well-rehearsed dimension to the conquest of Canaan in Israelite lore (Num 21:23–35; Deut 2:24–27; 3:1–11). The prayer pointedly recalls that the land promise is not complete without the presence of "children as numerous as the stars in the sky" (Neh 9:23), along with the accompanying subduing of the Canaanites and numerous material blessings as fruit of conquest.

The time of the judges as paradigm of Israelite history (9:26–31). The people's response to Yahweh's *hesed* at the time of the exodus (9:17a) is matched at the time of the settlement in Canaan and throughout the time of the monarchy. But there were many times (NIV "time after time") that Yahweh continued to display his "compassion" by delivering them (9:28).

The dramatic conclusion of this summary of Israelite history is marked by a relentless lexical repetition of themes parallel to Israel's response with the golden calf incident (see 9:16–17a). In addition, the list returns to the theme of the warning of the prophets, now clearly associated with the activity of the Spirit (9:30, cf. 9:20), along with a modified version of the vivid imagery of 9:26. Yet, in spite of this tremendous list of catastrophic failure on the part of Israel, Yahweh's "great mercy" (9:31) prevails in the end.

Confession: We have acted unfaithfully while you have been righteous (9:32–35). Yahweh has been fully justified in his actions to judge Israel and the verdict is in: Yahweh is righteous, while the people "acted wickedly" (9:33). The postexilic community recognizes the universal and pervasive guilt shared by every sphere of society.

By invoking the divine name (9:32), the appeal is to both Yahweh's covenant-keeping actions and his *hesed*. As elsewhere, Yahweh's character of faithfulness to the covenant and of *hesed* is not only the centerpiece of their appeal, it is the only one.

Petition: We are slaves! (9:36–37). If there is a formal petition, it is intentionally oblique ("we are slaves today," 9:36) and remains permeated with a deep sense that their lot is fully deserved ("because of our sins," 9:37) and of the undeserved favor of God toward them (the squandered gift of the land). We are essentially taken back to square one in this magisterial and sweeping overview of the history of Israel, which parallels Ezra's own prayer in Ezra 9:9.

Application. The biblical narrative is our narrative. It is our story. One of the great themes of the story of God's people is that once they lost the narrative of Scripture, they lost the narrative of their lives. Without spending time in the Scripture, we are flying blind and remain woefully unaware of our sinful condition. The Scripture provides a diagnostic, a sort of health report of where we stand and what adjustment we need to make to stay close to God. Without these regular checkups, we do not know how healthy or unhealthy we are. Just as with our own health, to avoid doctor checkups and regular diagnostics (what to eat or not eat, etc.) is akin to flying blind. We do not have a sense of what is ahead on the journey. We should not wait until we crash and burn spiritually to get our lives with God back on track. The Scripture is our guide. Nehemiah 9 is a bitter realization that without his word, the Israelites grew cold and stiff-necked with God—with the consequences that they had essentially returned to Egypt in the province of Yehud. We need to heed the wise words of the psalmist: "I have hidden your word in my heart that I might not sin against you" (Ps 119:11). By embracing the narrative of Scripture and the big picture of the cycles of creation-sin-judgment-deliverance-redemption in our lives, we grow in our dependence upon God's *hesed* as revealed in the person of Jesus Christ. We are rooted in him, the one who has fulfilled all righteousness.

NEHEMIAH 9:38–10:39

Original Meaning

Covenant Ratification (9:38–10:39). *The binding agreement (9:38).* The prayer of chapter 9 seamlessly morphs into the basis of a "binding agreement" the community makes (9:38). While the word "covenant"' is not actually present in 9:38, the verb used (NIV "we are making") is the idiomatic "cutting" (Heb. *karat*), which is always used in the context of covenant making (Gen 15:18). Thus, it says, "we are cutting a binding agreement" (author's translation).

The list of signatories (10:1–27). The organization of the names follows the pattern anticipated from 9:38. To weave in names that hark back to the past, along with names from the context of the present, thus reflects the expected sensitivity of the tribal characteristics of belonging in a past, present, and future sense.

The rest of the people join in (10:28–29). Verse 28 adds "the rest of the people" (10:28) to the list of those who are also committing themselves to what is now unmistakably couched in preexilic Sinaitic covenantal terms: they "are entering" (author's translation; NIV "join") into a "curse and an oath" (10:29) in a ceremony strongly reminiscent of the one in the plains of Moab (Deut 30:11–19) and at Mount Ebal (Josh 8:30–35; cf. Deut 27). No one is coercing them to join in this covenant. The people are willingly signing up, in large part because the God of the spiritual leadership is also their God.

Promise to maintain their own sanctity (10:30–31). The first set of three promises (10:30–31) are carefully delineated by the use of three modal (i.e., imperative force) verbs, strongly reminiscent of a form found in Old Testament laws such as the Ten Commandments (e.g., "you shall not . . ." Deut 5:8).

The first "we shall not" (Neh 10:30, NIV "we promise") fittingly relates to the practice of intermarriage (cf. 10:28). In effect, the people are making a promise not to repeat the mistakes of the past: we will not get entangled with the "peoples of the land" (10:30, author's translation, NIV, "peoples around us") and will maintain our own sanctity. The second "we shall not" (10:31a, NIV "we will not buy") keeps the focus on the peoples of the land but now extends to economic partnerships, particularly in the context of buying and selling "merchandise or grain" on the "Sabbath . . . or on any holy day" (10:31a). The third is a positive one, "we will cancel" (10:31b). In this context, the specific reference to "debts" (Heb. *masha*) directly connects to the commitment not to repeat the problems of injustice described in chapter 5.

Promises to maintain the sanctity of Zion (10:32–39). The rest of the promises (10:32–39) are specifically tied to the worship of Yahweh and "the service of the house of our God" (10:32). Heading off the list of promises (10:32–33) is the collection of a temple tax for the maintenance of the raison d'être of the temple: "offerings," including "grain," "burnt," and "sin offerings to make atonement for Israel" (10:33). Following the temple tax, the entire community is involved through the very practical task of collecting firewood. The text is almost disarming in its practicality: without wood supplies, there can be no sacrifice.

Another essential dimension to worship was the bringing of "firstfruits" (10:35) to Yahweh and the "storerooms" of the temple (10:37). Here, the list is also itemized and includes typical commodities associated with agriculture and horticulture. The "tithe" (10:37), another well-known revenue stream in the law, must be collected through the Levites. In turn, from this tithe a tenth must go to the "house of our God" to be stored in the "storerooms of the treasury" (10:38).

As a final note, all "the people of Israel" (10:39) are responsible to bring in "contributions of grain, new wine and olive oil" to the storerooms "for the ministering priests, the gatekeepers and the musicians." This last point underscores that, without the people's active involvement in supplying foods to the temple personnel, worship will not be sustainable.

Application. Making a commitment to support the work and worship of God is not optional if we desire a continuous worship among God's people. It is hard to imagine proper worship without sacrifices and consistent contributions to the house of the Lord and the work of God. In other words, supporting the material needs of worship on a permanent basis is an essential part of worship! It is not enough to build programs, read the Bible, and confess sins; worship always involves giving. The imagery of supplying firewood evokes the mundane and unappealing. However, appeals for these supplies in a modern context are equally important (building maintenance and payroll come to mind in today's context).

NEHEMIAH 11:1–36

Original Meaning

Resettling the Land (11:1–26). Chapter 11 represents the fourth list of names (one remains in Neh 12) in the book of Nehemiah, in line with the official nature of the record from the governor of the province of Yehud in the empire of Persia.

Summary of the resettlement of the holy city and the land (11:1–3). In this introductory and formal record of who repopulated the "holy city" (11:1), the theme of contribution to the work of the house of the Lord continues in earnest from the preceding chapter. The summary provides equal legitimacy to those who lived in the city and those who lived in the province.

Judah and Benjamin (11:4–9). The list begins appropriately with the one surviving eponymous tribe, "Judah" (11:4), with a list of "men of standing" (11:6) that further underscores the courage and the honor given to them for living in Jerusalem. Of note, the list of "descendants of Benjamin" outnumbers the list of Judah (11:8).

The priests (11:10–14). As with the list in the previous chapter, the names could refer to individuals or families. In addition to rooting the priests in genealogies that hark back to preexilic times, the list also focuses on the particular tasks of those who relocated in the temple area. The term "Haggedolim" (11:14) probably was an epithet meaning "the great one" (Heb. *gdl*) rather than a proper name per se, and reflects the warriors of ages past in Israel.

The Levites and the gatekeepers (11:15–19). The mixing of religious duties and protective duties continues with the list of Levites.

Other temple attendants (11:20–24). In addition to "the rest of the Israelites" (11:20), the list now extends to others who are also closely related to the temple and worship. The musicians come under Persian supervisory rule (11:23). The crown will allow the worship of Yahweh to proceed but not entirely without supervision.

Allotments in the province (11:25–36). In the form of an onomasticon (i.e, a list of place names), the historical geography reveals a map that is a mere fraction of the original Israel-Judah territory. The settlement patterns in fifth century Yehud strongly suggest that designations such as "Judah" and "Benjamin" should not be taken at face value and in a literal territorial sense. Instead, Israel consisted of individual settlements in a region occupied by many ethnic groups in the provinces comprising the province of Yehud. In other words, "x marks the spot" only indicates that Israelite presence was in a particular settlement, which may or may not have overlapped sites historically connected to preexilic territories. This composite map serves as further indication of the level of opposition the community faced in claiming Jerusalem as their own territory, in claiming to rebuild the walls, and now in claiming that the worship of Yahweh can resume there. In addition, it also gives a stark visual as to the challenge not to intermarry and interact with the peoples of the land who were all around them. The protection of Yahweh's sacred space continues to take precedence over the reality that the people of Yahweh continue to be very much a minority in the land.

Application. Through the ages of Christian history, believers have not always applied the principles outlined above. Temporal aspirations and ambitions for territorial expansion have to give way to the focal point of maintaining the sanctity of Zion, which now is defined as the people of God. Paul compares the church to a foundation of truth in 1 Timothy 3:15, and thus Scripture continues to challenge us by giving us marching orders away from unhealthy attachments to temporal categories (buildings, rituals, and theocratic aspirations) and toward spiritual ones. We need to realize we will never be a majority voice in the present evil age, from which Jesus came to save us (Gal 1:3–5). Even in the age of megachurches in the West and parts of Asia and Africa, from a standpoint of demographics, what is, for example, a 20,000-member church in a city of five million people? The Christian patterns of settlement in the present evil age will never be swayed in our favor. This radical redistribution will only occur when Christ establishes his kingdom on earth, in the new heaven and new earth (Isa 65:17; 66:22; 2 Pet 3:13; Rev 21). Our global map will always resemble the postexilic patterns of settlement in Yehud rather than the settlement patterns of the time of Joshua and Judges. Thus, our task remains the same as those of the temple attendants in Yehud. We, as Levites (a royal priesthood, 1 Pet 2:9), are called to populate the holy city with God's people from the Jerusalem "above" (Gal 4:26), making sure that we remain holy as he is holy (1 Pet 1:16).

NEHEMIAH 12:1–13:3

Original Meaning

Lineage of Priests and Levites (12:1–26). *Unbroken lineage of priests and Levites to the present (12:1–26).* While a return to priestly genealogical records in Nehemiah may appear unnecessary, the genealogy in this context targets the priests and Levites ("gatekeepers" are added at the end, 12:25–26) in a more comprehensive way than the list of Nehemiah 7, along with a practical rationale—the resumption of worship can begin in earnest since everything and everyone is in place.

Dedication of the Wall and Restoration of Worship (12:27–13:3). *Celebration and dedication of the walls (12:27–43).* No temporal framework is provided to situate the "dedication"

(12:27, Heb. *hanukkah*). Before the celebration can begin, in keeping with the larger theological purpose of the entire project, the priests and Levites "purified themselves" and "purified the people, the gates and the wall" (12:30). The restoration project thus has come full circle from chapter 3.

In a way recalling Nehemiah's own journey on the wall a few months prior (2:13–14), one of the processions went up on the wall going to the "right" (or south) toward the Dung Gate (12:31). "The second choir" (12:38) went "the opposite direction." The last stop was right at the entrance of the temple: "the Gate of the Guard" (12:39). The two choirs "took their places" (12:40) in the temple area proper, including Nehemiah himself with half of the officials, who remain anonymous.

The second action verb after "took their places" in 12:40 is the first of several verbs that creates a dynamic picture ("on that day," 12:43) and serve as the fitting and dramatic conclusion to an extraordinary past few months for Nehemiah and the rest of the people:

- The "choirs sang" (12:42; "caused to hear," author's translation)
- "under the direction of Jezrahiah" (12:42)
- They offered "great sacrifices" (12:43, which then explained why so many of them are mentioned by name)
- They rejoiced (Heb. *smh*, 12:43)

This act of rejoicing echoes the "joy of the Lord" of 8:10 and is directly attributed to "God" himself who has "caused them to rejoice [Heb. *smh*] with great joy [*smh*]" (author's translation; NIV "God had given them great joy," 12:43). To add to the picture and further recall the events of chapter 8, "the women and the children also rejoiced [*smh*]" (12:43). As in a crescendo, the atmosphere of rejoicing receives one last main verb describing a mood of extraordinary joy:

- "rejoicing [*smh*] in Jerusalem could be heard far away" (12:43)

Thus, in quick succession, the root for "joy" occurs five times in the original Hebrew text. The projected and public nature of the joy serves as a fitting conclusion that the enemies of Zion could not prevail and take away the joy of a community who put their faith in Yahweh.

Securing the ongoing support for the house of the Lord (12:44–47). Nehemiah wants to make sure the worship and service to the temple take on a permanent format beyond the events of the day and the past few months. He knows that unless people willingly contribute to the service of the house of the Lord, as promised in chapter 10, his efforts and success in restoring Zion could be reversed, especially since Jerusalem remains surrounded by hostile neighbors. As the current governor of Judah and successor of Zerubbabel (12:47), he is also accountable to the crown to make sure that everyone involved in the service of the temple ("musicians and gatekeepers" along with Levites and the "descendants of Aaron," 12:47) are supported to fulfill their respective duties, including temple security and the protection of the sanctity of the site.

As a concluding thought (12:47), "all Israel" was true to the promise to provide for the affairs of the temple attendants (musicians, gatekeepers, Levites, and descendants of Aaron). The obvious parallel between the "days of Zerubabbel" in the first return and those "of Nehemiah" (12:47) underscores a return to normalcy and strongly hints at the success of Nehemiah's mission.

One final warning about their hostile neighbors (13:1–3). The final act of "that day" (13:1) is the public reading of "the Book of Moses," which underscores its newly gained importance and forms a literary *inclusio* to the sequence of events launched only a few weeks ago. The community has gathered around the hearing of the law ("in the hearing of the people," 13:1) one more time. On this occasion, however, the reading appears brief and targeted to an essentially direct quotation from Deuteronomy 23:3–5. The added interpretation, "Our God, however, turned the curse into a blessing" (13:2), recalls the work of the Levites among the people in chapter 8 to clarify the law. Upon hearing this injunction ("law"), "they excluded from Israel all who were of foreign descent" (13:3), which is a further connection with Israel's distant past.

Application. In the West, Christian short-term outreach teams do prayer walks routinely (on one occasion we walked around the main plaza in Mexico City several times), as do church staff in their neighborhoods. What is the significance of all these processions? The proclamation of God's faithfulness in a very public way is an act of worship to him. We are declaring to the world around us that God is at work and that he is faithful to carry out his purposes. It took courage for the fledgling minority in Yehud to have such a public display on the walls of the city, but they (men, women, and children) did it with their whole heart, so much so that their joy was heard from afar (12:43).

NEHEMIAH 13:4–31

Original Meaning

Nehemiah's Final Attemps at Reform (13:4–31). Nehemiah's final chapter of his scrambling amongst Yehud documents the methodical and point-by-point unravelling of his work of restoration of "the house of my God and its services" (13:14):

- A compromised priesthood (13:4–9/10:30)
- Disrupted worship in the temple since the Levites and the singers are no longer supported in their work (13:10–13/10:37–39)
- Sabbath-day transactions with the "peoples of the land" (13:15–22/10:39)

- Compromised sanctity of the temple (13:22/12:30)
- Intermarriage (13:23–29/10:30; 13:3)
- Defiled priesthood and dereliction of duties (13:30/12:30, 44–47)
- Shortage of firewood and contributions (13:30–31/10:30–39; 12:44–47)

Dealing with Eliashib (13:4–9). At the heart of what Eliashib had done was an illicit partnership with Tobiah (e.g., Lev 21:1 as an example of associations that make unclean). Tobiah needs no introduction in his twin role as joint-chief protagonist and double agent by marriage alliance (Neh 6:18). A catastrophe does not even begin to describe what is going on, and it thrusts us back to the dark ages of the preexilic systemic neglect of the worship in Judah. The syntactical structure of mainline verbs formats Nehemiah's response in expectedly swift and decisive terms (13:7–9).

Restoring the support of the house (13:10–14). The next round of reforms is given no chronological marker and must be assumed to have occurred within the same context, in light of Eliashib's failure and Tobiah's disruptive presence within the sacred space of Zion. Nehemiah's response mirrors his decisiveness in dealing with Tobiah.

Upon summoning the community, "all Judah" returned their contributions to the storerooms (13:12). Nehemiah promptly transitions Eliashib out of his position and replaces him with three individuals all mentioned by name. In this intercessory prayer, Nehemiah realizes all too well that the work accomplished to restore Zion could quickly be wiped out as a result of Eliashib's grievous failure. The uncompromising standards of holiness in the worship of Yahweh continue to loom large in this narrative.

Restoring the sanctity of Zion and of the Sabbath (13:15–22). The reforms continue at a rapid pace ("in those days," 13:15), organized by three pointed addresses. Nehemiah "warned" those who are violating the Sabbath (13:15). The people had stopped caring for the house of Yahweh and conducted business as if the worship of Yahweh was unimportant.

The second address elicits a second question: "What is this wicked thing you are doing?" (13:17). The focus of Nehemiah's ire, the fish trade from Tyre (13:16), combines the violation of the Sabbath law along with trading with the peoples of the land—non-Israelites. Nehemiah turns his attention to re-securing the sanctity of Zion by guarding who is allowed to come in on the Sabbath (13:19). In a similar protocol to the measures related to the storerooms (13:13), Nehemiah focuses on the prevention of violations. For this task, specific steps are taken, all marked by action verbs in the first person. In conclusion, the purpose of the Sabbath reform is made explicitly clear: "in order to keep the Sabbath day holy" (13:22).

Restoring the sanctity of marriage (13:23–27). The temporal tempo, marked by another "in those days" (13:23), continues unabated and returns to a well-worn theme. The structural format as a sequence of main verbs characterizing the report of reforms, continues as well (13:25). The oath itself focuses on the exchange of "daughters" and "sons" (13:25) and essentially repeats the one that had already been taken in Nehemiah 10:30. Nehemiah's final question to them underscores the "terrible wickedness" and the unfaithfulness "to our God by marrying foreign women" (13:27).

Restoring the sanctity of the priesthood (13:28–31). The final round of reform focuses on the priestly leadership, starting at the highest echelon. The action taken by Nehemiah is as terse as it is effective: "I drove him away from me" (13:28). Nehemiah holds both the high priest and the culprit in equal contempt of God's law. The reference to the "covenant of the priesthood" (13:29) is unique but may very well deal with the covenantal obligations pertaining to them within the broader covenant of Sinai.

Nehemiah concludes his account with the focus on what ultimately mattered most to him: the preservation of the sanctity of Zion, including its leadership. All these tasks were, of course, supposed to be overseen by the priests and Levites themselves. However, in light of the catastrophic failure witnessed upon his return, he, as a governor and non-Levite, took it upon himself to carry out the maintenance of the worship in Jerusalem, the holy city.

In the context of this tremendous (and lonely) responsibility comes the final "remember" prayer (12:31). Nehemiah thus ends his account on a wonderfully hopeful note. Nehemiah's prayer has been answered in ways far greater than he could have ever imagined.

Application. The call to remember the zeal of Nehemiah is also our call. We want to be remembered for what we have accomplished for the Lord, just as Phinehas was (though now we look to Christ for substitutionary salvation with his death and resurrection). We, too, uphold the sanctity of Zion as the will of God for our lives (1 Thess 4:3). Now, however, Christ is the one who makes us holy by faith in him (Acts 26:18).

The zeal of Nehemiah ultimately falls short, as did Saul of Tarsus (Gal 1:14) and everyone else who thinks building the kingdom of God is accomplished through our own will power, aptitudes, or an unhealthy focus on ritual (see Matt 23). The sanctifying process of Zion finds its fulfillment, as does our zeal for God's people and the establishment of his kingdom, in Christ alone. He alone is our sanctification (1 Cor 1:30), and he is the one at work in us to do and will according to his good and perfect will. We offer ourselves as "living sacrifices," which is our "proper worship" (Rom 12:1–2). At the cross, Jesus reveals for us the weightier matters of the law: self-sacrifice, love of our enemies, and self-emptying (Phil 2), rather than the pursuit of vainglorious ambition.

Christ's work on the cross was not a senseless act of violence but was a self-sacrifice by God the Son who chose to offer himself up as an atoning sacrifice for the despondency of the people of Zion in Yehud, in our days, and in the future—until he returns to establish his kingdom. Thus, apart from Christ's work on the cross, we will not understand the implacability of God's holiness and his complete intolerance for the presence of sin in his presence (including Ezra's actions to break up marriages and Nehemiah's advocacy to separate). However complex these ethical questions get, we do know that at the cross, Christ experienced the injustice of a violent death as an innocent party. Christ tasted injustice. We put our trust in him and in the vindication against all injustice. The resurrection is the beginning of the restoration of justice that will be fulfilled when he returns. He will judge everyone according to what he or she has done (Rom 14:10). Those who have placed their faith in him will be found justified (whose justified state will be justified by their just actions), and those who continued to reject his gracious offer of salvation will find themselves permanently outside the gates of the holy city (Rev 22:15). Thus, as we, too, are the guardians of Zion, we continue to make the gates of the city open at daytime, as it were, so that whosoever believes in him would not perish but have eternal life (John 3:16).

ESTHER

INTRODUCTION TO ESTHER

The author of Esther opens the book with the same Hebrew formula (*wayehi*) that opens the historical books of Joshua, Judges, and Samuel, as well as the book of Ezekiel. The author apparently intends his readers to think of the story he is about to tell as events that really happened. Nothing in this book has been shown to be historically untrue, though a number of questions have been raised concerning its historical accuracy. None of these problems is beyond explanation, and some may result from the legitimate use of poetic license. Even when taken together they do not compel the conclusion that the story is entirely fiction.

The use of poetic license in biblical narrative to interpret the significance of the events told does not compromise the integrity of Scripture. Thus, some of the questions we have and "problems" we see with the book of Esther arise because we value historical accuracy and precision where the author valued poetic license for the purpose of interpretation. We who rightly insist on the historicity of biblical events must also fully appreciate the literary genre and the author's use of poetic license, and not press the story historically where the author did not intend his readers to do so.

BOOK OUTLINE

- I. The Jews of Persia Are Threatened (1:1–5:14)
  - A. Life in Persia Is Dangerous (1:1–22)
  - B. Esther, Mordecai, and Haman (2:1–3:15)
  - C. Esther's Defining Moment (4:1–17)
  - D. Esther's Intervention (5:1–14)
- II. The Reversal of Destiny (6:1–9:19)
  - A. The Reversal Begins (6:1–14)
  - B. Haman Is Executed (7:1–10)
  - C. The Counter-Edict Is Issued (8:1–17)
  - D. The Day of Conflict Arrives (9:1–19)
- III. Purim Is Established (9:20–28)
- IV. Epilogue: Mordecai Is Esteemed as National Hero (9:29–10:3)

ESTHER 1:1–8

Original Meaning. These events occurred during the time of Xerxes, the Persian king who reigned from 486–465 BC. Xerxes was known for his consolidation of the Persian Empire from "India to Cush" (1:1), corresponding to the regions of modern Pakistan and northern Sudan, respectively. The reference to 127 provinces has been taken by some scholars as a historical inaccuracy. In 1:1, however, the Hebrew word used does not mean "satrapy" but "province" and probably refers to a smaller metropolitan region that encompassed a city.

The description of the banquet focuses on the opulence of its setting in the king's garden and the abundance of wine, "in keeping with the king's liberality," served in goblets of gold (1:7). The might and glory of the Persian Empire were at Xerxes' disposal in order to reward those who would remain loyal to his cause and obedient to his command.

Application. Through the centuries and around the world, political and military might have been glorified as the epitome of a nation's strength. America, too, must take heed that, though perhaps founded for Christian liberty, its might and power are nonetheless worldly might and power. For the Christian, the sovereign power of the Lord is of greatest comfort. To be in Christ is to be on the winning side of history, to be victors even in the face of life's greatest threats.

ESTHER 1:9–12

Original Meaning. After seven days of drinking, when Xerxes was "in high spirits from wine" (1:10), he sent for his queen to display her royal beauty before the men of Susa. The beautiful Vashti, wearing her royal diadem, was a living trophy of his power and glory. Because Xerxes was displaying his power and might in order to solidify his nobles as he went to war against Greece, the refusal of his own queen to obey his command must have been extremely embarrassing. No wonder Xerxes became furious and burned with anger! He needed his men to obey his commands as they went to war, but in his own palace he could not even get his own wife to obey!

Application. Like Xerxes of long ago, modern kings, presidents, and rulers make decisions from purely political motives. Like Vashti, people today unwittingly make decisions that have long-reaching consequences far beyond what they could have foreseen. These events may be completely secular and perhaps made by people who give Christ no thought. Nonetheless, through them God is moving all of history forward to accomplish all that must happen before the return of his Son, Jesus Christ, the true King of kings.

ESTHER 1:13–22

Original Meaning. Xerxes' reaction highlights the political ramifications of Vashti's defiance. Irrevocable royal decree rather than personal reconciliation will determine Vashti's fate. The decree will formalize permanently what Vashti had chosen in one moment. Because she refused to come to the king, she will be demoted to the status of those who may not enter the king's presence.

Although Xerxes invites the counsel of his seven advisors concerning what is to be done to Vashti in this one instance, the advice he gets goes beyond this instance. What began as an issue between two people suddenly is escalated into a crisis of empire-wide proportions. By universalizing the incident, Memukan can express his personal anxiety and fears in terms of the good of the empire and thereby manipulate the king to his own ends. Haman later uses the same tactic against the Jews in 3:8.

Vashti is assumed to have such influence on the women of the empire that when they hear of her disobedience, they will similarly respond to their husbands, starting with the wives of the king's seven advisors. Therefore, the king must make sure that these women also hear that Vashti has been deposed as a result of her insolence. When the women see what harsh consequences follow disobedience, they will be intimidated into "respect[ing] their husbands, from the least to the greatest" (1:20). Xerxes and the seven nobles find this reasoning to be sound, and so the king issues a decree throughout his empire "to each province in its own script and to each people in its own language" (1:22).

Application. The scene in 1:13–22 is an inside look at just what makes the world go round. Law and justice may be the public ideal of every great government, but people in power, compelled by their own fears and anxieties, all too often abuse the power with which they have been entrusted. Absolute power held by flawed leaders is a terrifying scenario.

ESTHER 2:1–11

Original Meaning. Vashti refused to come to King Xerxes in the third year of his reign, 483 BC. Esther was made queen in the seventh year of his reign, 479 BC (2:16–17). During the intervening years Xerxes was off fighting a disastrous war with Greece. His humiliating defeat depleted the treasuries of the Persian Empire and discredited him in the eyes of his subjects. Shortly after his return from Greece, Esther was chosen as his new consort.

In addition to one or more wives, Persian kings typically had many concubines, women who came as virgins to the king's bed and then lived in luxurious desolation in his harem. Artaxerxes II is said to have had 360 concubines of surpassing beauty in his harem.

Mordecai is introduced as "a Jew of the tribe of Benjamin," a descendant of a man named Kish (2:5). These verses suggest that Mordecai was taken into exile with Jehoiachin, king of Judah, in 597 BC. The author's point in mentioning the exile of the king of Judah is to associate Mordecai with the exile out of the promised land and all that it connotes, thereby providing a historical context within which to understand the events that are about to transpire

Esther is introduced as Mordecai's "cousin . . . whom he had brought up because she" (2:7) was an orphan. By describing Esther's beauty, the author is aligning her with the women already mentioned in the story, beautiful queen Vashti and the beautiful young virgins, thus creating a certain expectation of how Esther will fare in the Persian court.

Esther is also known by her Hebrew name, Hadassah. The name Esther may be the Persian word for star, or it may be a Hebrew transliteration of Ishtar, the name of the Babylonian goddess of love and war. Esther is the only person in the story with two names. It was not uncommon for Hebrew peoples to have both a Hebrew name and a second name taken from the culture in which they lived.

Esther "was taken" (2:8) into the harem where the virgins were gathered. Regardless of how she felt about it or whether she cooperated, Esther was at the mercy of a ruthless pagan king, just as her people were. The use of the passive voice is appropriate in this story, for it expresses life from the perspective of being caught up in and swept along by circumstances beyond one's control.

Mordecai commands Esther to conceal her "nationality and family background" (2:10), even though it would certainly mean compromising whatever fidelity to the torah she had. The ambiguity of Esther's thoughts about her situation raises questions about her observance of God's law and her practices as a Jew. Unlike Daniel and his friends, Esther does not protest. Because she could so successfully hide her identity as a Jew, she apparently had adopted Persian dress and customs at least to the extent that she was indistinguishable as a Jewish woman.

Application. The story is not about conflict between any two hostile peoples, it is about the hostility of the world against God's people. Against all odds, in some inscrutable and mysterious way, the events of human history work to fulfill the promises of the covenant the Lord made with his people at Sinai. While God may be good to all his creatures in general, he is in a special relationship of protection and preservation with his covenant people.

ESTHER 2:12–18

Original Meaning. Xerxes spared no expense to prepare his women for one night in his bed. For twelve months they were lotioned and perfumed. After twelve months of preparation, the woman was given "anything she wanted" (2:13) to take with her to the king. The phrase may refer to jewelry and clothing, but also to aphrodisiac potions or other such items to enhance pleasure. After spending one night in the king's bed, the woman was returned to the harem of concubines, where she would spend the rest of her life in luxurious but desolate seclusion. She could not leave the harem to marry or return to her family. The woman would not even see the king again, unless he asked for her by name. Children conceived by the king in these unions were raised to serve their father in high positions, but they were not legitimate heirs to the throne.

After her twelve months of beauty treatments, Esther's turn with the king came. She asked for nothing except what Hegai, the keeper of the harem, suggested she take with her. Esther's deference contrasts with Vashti's defiance and implies a different outcome.

Given the sensual atmosphere created by the author's description of the period of preparation and the competition Esther faced, the reader can hardly avoid wondering just how she won Xerxes in just one night with him. Did God give her favor with Xerxes? The text does not explain it that way. However, it is certain that because this young Jewish virgin apparently did whatever it took to please a lascivious pagan king, she won the position of queen, through which she later saved the whole of her nation, the nation from which the Messiah later came.

Application. This episode from Esther's life offers great encouragement and comfort when we find ourselves in situations where every choice is an odd mix of right and wrong. Only God knows the end of our story from its beginning. We are responsible to him for living faithfully in obedience to his word in every situation as we best know how. Esther's story shows that we can entrust our situations to the Lord and move on.

ESTHER 2:19–3:15

Original Meaning. Mordecai happened to overhear a plot to assassinate Xerxes while he was "sitting at the king's gate" (2:19). This phrase refers to holding an official position in the court. Mordecai foiled the assassination plot by reporting it to Queen Esther, who in turn reported it to Xerxes, giving due credit to Mordecai. All of this was recorded in the annals of the king.

At this point, a new character is introduced into the story: Haman the Agagite. Xerxes had promoted Haman to a high position, though no explanation of why he deserved this honor is given. Given Mordecai's demonstrated loyalty to the king, promotion would have been an appropriate reward. The author places the promotion of Haman just where the original readers would have expected a report of Mordecai's reward as a benefactor of the king. Haman's introduction forms an unexpected twist when juxtaposed with Mordecai's unrewarded loyalty.

A subtheme in this conflict between Mordecai and Haman is again that of respect commanded and respect refused. Interpreters throughout the ages have offered explanations for Mordecai's refusal. It is known from other sources that in general, Jews did bow to pagan officials of the Persian court. Some interpreters have suggested that Haman, being a pagan, wore an emblem of an idol on his garment to which Mordecai refused to pay homage.

In Hebrew narrative the characteristic described when a character is introduced is key to understanding his or her role in the story. When Mordecai is introduced in 2:5, he is identified not as a wise man or as an official in the court, but as a Jew of the tribe of Benjamin. When Haman is introduced, he is identified as an Agagite. The author implies that the perennial relationship of enmity between the Jews and the Agagites is mirrored in the personal relationship between Mordecai and Haman. The original readers would expect the relationship to be characterized by conflict and aggression. Agag was the king of the Amalekites at the time Saul (also of the tribe of Benjamin) was the first king of Israel (1 Sam 15).

Haman need not have been genetically descended from the Amalekites to have earned the name Agagite. By using this term, the author is characterizing him as anti-Semitic, an enemy of the Jews. The original readers would have understood this one clue as introducing yet another episode of the age-old conflict between Israel and the powers that sought to destroy her.

Esther had been queen for five years when Haman skillfully manipulates the king to gain support for his evil plan. He begins by bringing an accusation certain to arouse the king's attention—that there is "a certain people" (3:8). Haman then appeals to the king's need to replenish the treasury depleted by Xerxes' disastrous war with Greece. Haman's offer to provide ten thousand talents of silver (about 300 tons) represents a substantial contribution to the royal coffers.

To determine the propitious time for an attack on the Jews, Haman consults the *pur* (plural, *purim*) or "lot" (3:7). The *pur* (or *goral*) was used also by ancient Israel to query Yahweh.

For instance, Joshua cast lots before the Lord to learn how to assign the land to the various tribes (Josh 18:6). Haman casts the lot in the first month, Nisan, the month the Jews celebrate Passover. It falls on the twelfth month, Adar.

Application. Most of us like to think that through thoughtful planning and wise living we can successfully direct the course of our lives. Our sense of ultimately being in control is at times revealed by life's circumstances to be an illusion. Only God knows the end of a matter before it has even begun. God works mysteriously, patiently, and inexorably through a series of events and human decisions, even those based on questionable motives and evil intents. All of the "chance" events in life are really working toward the end that God has ordained.

ESTHER 4:1–17

Original Meaning. Upon hearing of the king's decree, Mordecai tears his clothes and puts on sackcloth and ashes in an act of deep mourning and distress. This gesture was common throughout the biblical period. The Persians in Susa would have recognized the significance of Mordecai's behavior, for they, too, tore their clothes in grief when they were defeated by the Greeks in battle at Salamis.

Although apparently separated from direct contact with Mordecai during the first five years of her marriage to Xerxes, Esther remains concerned for him. She sends clothing to him to replace his sackcloth. However, it is only when he refuses to accept her gift that she attempts to find out what is actually troubling her cousin.

When Esther's attending eunuch, Hathach, however, brings Mordecai's entreaty that she go to the king to plead for "her" (4:8) people, she begs off, explaining that she no longer routinely sees the king. Moreover, as Mordecai well knows, she cannot go to the king uninvited without risking her life, for unless Xerxes extends his golden scepter, her life will be taken on the spot. Surely Mordecai does not mean to suggest she jeopardize herself like that!

Mordecai pointedly remarks that even if the queen should decide to continue to hide her Jewish identity, as he himself had previously advised, she will face certain death, but the Jews will be helped "from another place" (4:14). If "from another place" is a euphemism for God, Mordecai's statement means that if Esther fails to act, God himself will intervene. This understanding is problematic, for it is not a choice between Esther's delivering the Jews or God's delivering them. Rather, it is a question of what human agency God will use to deliver the Jews since they have no king. Mordecai's point is that the Jews will be delivered somehow, but that Esther's doom is certain if she fails to act.

In Mordecai's thinking, Esther's life *may be* in jeopardy if she goes to the king uninvited, but her doom *is certain* if she does not. Mordecai's remark is unsettling. If Esther fails to act as he is suggesting, is he threatening to reveal her identity as a Jew, thus bringing her under Haman's decree? Or is he invoking divine judgment on her for her apparent apathy toward her people? Esther probably wondered the same thing.

Mordecai's words also suggest that there is a purpose in all that has happened that exceeds Esther's own interests. He asks, ". . . and who knows but that you have come to royal position for such a time as this?" (4:14). Mordecai points out that all of the previous circumstances of Esther's life that led her to the Persian throne may have been just for this moment when she can intercede for her people.

It is only after hearing this remark containing both a veiled threat and a suggestion of a greater purpose that Esther decides to act as Mordecai wishes. After deciding to go to the king, she gives Mordecai a command, which he "went away and carried out" (4:17). Esther commands Mordecai to call the Jews of Susa to a fast.

Application. It is unlikely that any of us will ever be in Esther's dire predicament, but every one of us faces defining moments in our own lives. Certainly, the most fundamental of them comes when we hear the gospel of Jesus Christ and decide how to respond to it. However, the new birth is only the beginning of decisions. It is followed by a continuous sequence of defining moments throughout life as we daily face decisions that demand we choose either to identify ourselves with Christ by obedience to his word or to live as pagans in that moment. Only if we live as Christ commands, in every moment and every decision, will we be the agents through whom the promises of the new covenant are fulfilled.

ESTHER 5:1–14

Original Meaning. After three days of fasting, Esther does not just try to make herself beautiful for her uninvited audience with the king, she appears before him in her "royal robes" (5:1). At the same time as she decides to identify with her people, she also claims her authority and power as the Queen of Persia in going before the king. The threat of death passes when Xerxes extends the golden scepter to her.

For the first time in the story, Esther is directly addressed as "Queen Esther" when Xerxes offers her up to half of the kingdom (5:3). This expression was an idiom commonly used by ancient royalty and was not intended to be taken literally. It simply meant that the king was disposed to be generous in meeting a request.

In answer to the king's direct question, Esther invites the

king to a festive meal and asks him to summon Haman as well. This pleases the king, and both he and Haman go to the banquet Esther has prepared. Esther now has Xerxes and Haman, the two most powerful men of the Persian Empire, responding to her initiative.

At the banquet while the king is drinking wine, he again asks Esther why she appeared uninvited in her royal robes in the throne room. Previously in the story when Xerxes was drinking wine, Vashti ended up losing her royal position and power. Using a delay tactic, Esther again asks only that Haman and the king come to a second banquet on the next day. At that time Esther assures the king she will present her request. The suspense is heightened, not only for the king but also for the reader.

Haman's prideful excitement at being invited to a private dinner of the king and queen is marred when Mordecai shows no gesture of deference as Haman leaves the palace. Emboldened by the presumption that he stands solidly in the favor of both King Xerxes and Queen Esther, Haman takes the advice of his wife. Haman builds a gallows of extraordinary size, seventy-five feet high, not realizing that its size is the measure of his own pride.

Application. We have the benefit of knowing the end of the story and how Esther's decision led her to power and fame. But at the time Esther made that decision, she did not know how her story would end. At that point her decision could have just as well ended her life, either in the king's throne room or during the execution of Haman's decree. Esther could not have known at the time she decided to risk her life that it was that very decision that would fulfill her personal destiny as well as the destiny of her people.

In the original decision of conversion to Jesus Christ and in all subsequent decisions, we become the women or men God has created us to be by aligning ourselves with his covenant in Christ. As Paul wrote in Galatians, that covenant issues in the life-changing work of the Holy Spirit within us. Like Esther, we too need a transformation of our character so that we may no longer live as pagans. Without this transformation of character by the Holy Spirit, none of us can attain the full potential of our humanity. Without the work of God's spirit, we cannot be the persons God created us to be, nor can we attain fully to the purpose of our lives as agents of God's redemptive work in history.

ESTHER 6:1–14

Original Meaning. This is arguably the most ironically comic scene in the entire Bible. While Haman plots Mordecai's outrageous death, the king plans to honor Mordecai's faithful service. Haman's splendid humiliation results from a series of coincidences, each believable in itself, and yet a series that is completely out of Haman's control.

After the king's intriguing banquet with Esther, he is unable to sleep. Xerxes decides to review court business. "The book of the chronicles" (6:1) was the official record of the Persian kings, in which every official transaction of the court was recorded. From this official transcript the king would draw up a list of those who were to be rewarded for faithful service to the throne. The king was mortified to find that nothing had been done to honor Mordecai publicly, who some five years before had foiled an assassination plot against him.

Haman's proposal for what "should be done to the man the king delights to honor" (6:6) may seem unusual by modern standards. Believing the honors would go to himself, Haman could not ask for a promotion because he was already second only to the king in his authority over the empire. He apparently had all the wealth and luxury such a high-ranking position could afford in opulent Persia. His request to wear the king's robe and ride the king's horse was intended both to honor the king and to reinforce Haman's relationship with him.

For Haman no other honor was left to him but to partake of the king's own power, prestige, and stature. To have such an intimate gesture bestowed instead on Mordecai, the Jew, is a crushing humiliation. More importantly, it foreshadows the reversal of fortune that is about to inexorably unfold before Haman's horrified eyes. When he plotted the destruction of "a certain people" (3:8), he failed to mention their identity to the king or to his wife and friends. When Haman's wife, Zeresh, and his friends later learn that Mordecai is Jewish, they reverse their earlier advice. Not only will Haman's plan against Mordecai be frustrated, but Haman himself will come to ruin for the attempt. The full extent of Haman's tragic miscalculation begins to emerge.

Application. The author of Esther implies a consistency in God's rule of human history that is based on his word, not on circumstances. Regardless of how circumstances appear, God is ruling history according to the ancient covenant he made with Israel at Sinai. God's promise to Israel made at the beginning of their nation still stood. God was not capricious like the gods of the pagans. He was not locked in some struggle with other deities that gave him control only on certain days or in certain situations.

What a great God we serve! Any deity worth his salt can do a miracle now and then. Our God is so great, so powerful, that he can work without miracles through the ordinary events of billions of human lives through millennia of time to accomplish his eternal purposes and ancient promises.

ESTHER 7:1–10

Original Meaning. While drinking wine, Xerxes asks Queen Esther for the third time to reveal her request and again assures her of his positive and generous response. Her reply is rhetorically structured exactly as was his question. By framing her response using the king's rhetoric, Esther is saying that her destiny is one with her people.

Esther quotes the exact words of Haman's edict (cf. 3:13) but by using the passive voice, she delays mentioning Haman's name or the fact that it was the king himself who sold the Jewish people for ten thousand talents of silver (cf. 3:9, 11). Xerxes' indignation and anger erupt with the demand that she tell him, "Who is he?" and "Where is he—the man . . . ?" (7:5). Apparently, the death edict has made so little an impression on the king that Esther's quotation of it does not even ring a bell.

Esther's words send Xerxes into an enraged quandary that drives him out of the banquet room and into the garden. Clearly Haman realizes that the king's fury is upon him. He also knows Xerxes well enough to realize that the king never made his own decision. It was the manipulative agenda of others that drove his actions, a ploy Haman himself had used so successfully in the past. Thus, his only chance of survival lies in the hands of Esther, whom he begs to intercede with the king for his life.

Harem protocol dictated that no one but the king could be left alone with a woman of the harem. That Haman should actually fall on the couch where Esther is reclining is unthinkable. Precisely at this moment of impropriety Xerxes returns and finds his quandary about what to do with Haman resolved.

When Harbona suggests that Haman be hanged on the gallows he had built for Mordecai, Xerxes concludes that Haman perhaps had secret sympathies with his attempted assassins (7:9). The English word "gallows" connotes death by asphyxiation. Persians built "gallows" that were wooden stakes on which they impaled their victims.

Application. Human evil, wherever it occurs and for whatever motivation, always sets itself against God, because God is the definition of goodness and righteousness. Divine justice inevitably and inextricably means the destruction of evil. In order to deliver the Jewish people from annihilation, as God promised in his covenant with them, God necessarily had to destroy the evil that threatened their existence. In this case that evil came in the person of Haman. Mercy on Haman would have been inconsistent with God's covenant.

ESTHER 8:1–17

Original Meaning. Because Haman was executed as a traitor to the throne, his property was confiscated. Because Esther was the person wronged by Haman, the king bestows Haman's estate on her. Immediately, Esther summons Mordecai into Xerxes' presence, who gives to Mordecai, the man who had years before saved the king's life, the signet ring previously worn by Haman. In a great reversal Mordecai is vested with all the power and authority previously wielded by Haman (cf. 3:10).

Esther pleads with Xerxes to "put an end to" Haman's evil death decree that still stands against her people (8:3); but the king is unable to do so, for the decree of death is irrevocable. The only solution to their dilemma is to write another decree to counteract the first with equal force.

As Haman had done, Mordecai writes in the name of King Xerxes. His message is that the Jews may take whatever measures are necessary to defend themselves. He seals the edict with the king's signet ring—the same one used by Haman to seal the decree of death against them—and sends out the edict by mounted couriers to every part of the empire.

The author of Esther has constructed a contrast of reversals in chiastic order. Haman's original edict had caused "great mourning among the Jews, with fasting, weeping and wailing. Many lay in sackcloth and ashes" (4:3). Mordecai had clothed himself in sackcloth and ashes. Now, as the counter-decree goes out, Mordecai comes from the very presence of the king "wearing royal garments of blue and white, a large crown of gold and a purple robe of fine linen," and he goes throughout the city in joyous procession (8:15; cf. 4:1–2).

Haman's sudden death and Mordecai's rise to power brought such fear to "many people of other nationalities" that they "became Jews" (8:17). The Hebrew word translated "became Jews" occurs only here in the Old Testament, and its meaning is debated. How are we to understand this "conversion"? Some have argued that the Persians recognized the improbable series of events as the hand of God and thus responded in true, heartfelt conversion to the God of the Jews.

Application. From the beginning of time God's war has been against sin and evil. It is easy to think wrongly of sin and evil as being abstractions apart from people. We seem to want God to destroy sin and evil but leave people alone. However, sin and evil do not exist apart from beings who sin and beings who do evil, whether angelic or human. Because we are all sinners and evildoers, we all have God's irrevocable decree of death against us. God could have justly destroyed the earth and everyone on it, for none of us is good by God's high standards. Instead, he chose to issue a counter-decree to redeem a people out of sin and evil and into righteousness, removing them from the realm of his destruction to the realm of deliverance.

ESTHER 9:1–19

Original Meaning. In the armed conflict on Adar 13, the Jews struck down, killed, and destroyed those "who hated them" (9:1). Five hundred men fell in Susa on the thirteenth and another three hundred the next day; seventy-five thousand died throughout the empire. The author is careful to say three times that the Jews "did not lay their hands on the plunder" (9:10, 15, 16) even though Mordecai's decree allowed it. Mordecai's decree included the permission to plunder because he was reversing the exact terms that Haman's decree had previously established. However, unlike the Agagite's intent, the Jews understood the execution of Mordecai's decree as governed by the ancient command of holy war against the Amalekites.

In actual fact, Israel's execution of holy war was often less than holy and tainted with their own sin. Throughout its history, Israel took illicit plunder, trusted in the strength of its own army instead of waiting on the Lord, and generally lived no better than the wicked people they were to war against in God's holy name. Israel's first king, Saul, violated the trust of holy war when he failed to destroy completely the Amalekites.

In Esther, the author's emphatic statement three times over that the Jews did not lay a hand on the plunder suggests that this episode against Haman and those who hated the Jews was understood as holy war, not as an opportunity for looting and personal gain. The Jews of Persia succeeded where Saul failed.

Esther requests that the bodies of Haman's sons be hung, that is, impaled, on gallows for public humiliation, just as their father had been. Though perhaps barbaric by modern standards, this also was a custom in ancient warfare. The author makes no attempt to exonerate the queen or to justify her request. The Bible is remarkable in revealing the darker side of God's chosen leaders, often just at their shining moment.

On the other hand, Esther's reasons for the second day of killing in Susa may have been legitimate, even though they are unknown to us and were also possibly unknown to the author. Haman was, after all, second only to the king, and he likely had many in Susa who were loyal to him and his decree. Esther's request is another instance of the disquieting moral ambiguity that characterizes this story. Rather than attempting to resolve it, we should reflect on it.

Application. The Bible assures us that the full expanse of human history, including the days in which we now live, is encompassed by God's redemptive plan. Even those whose sinful pride, like Haman's, pit them against God and the gospel are, in the final analysis, players in the universal plan of redemption. One would hope that before their end they will turn to Christ and be counted among the people whom God has called out from both the Jews and gentiles to be saved from his destruction of evil. For all who have come to know Christ have been saved from God's wrath, whether Jew or gentile.

ESTHER 9:20–28

Original Meaning. It is fitting that the fulfillment of God's promise to the Jews in Persia should also be written down and commemorated. This gave the promise both divine authority and perpetuity. The events of the Esther story show a fulfillment of this promise many centuries later and far away from the place it was made, illustrating the efficacy of God's word.

The authority on which Purim is based is unlike that of the feasts commanded by Moses in the Pentateuch. The celebration of Purim is therefore different from the feasts prescribed by the Torah. Rather than being imposed on the people from above as God's commandment, Purim began as the spontaneous response of God's people to his omnipotent faithfulness to the promises of the covenant.

In explaining the origin of the holiday, the author of Esther also explains the origin of its name, Purim (9:26). It is derived from the word *pur*, which was not originally a Hebrew word. *Pur* refers to the "lot" or "die" (singular of "dice") that Haman cast in divination to determine the day of death for the Jewish race.

Therefore, the name of the feast, Purim, is a double entendre, signifying that the lot, or destiny, of God's people would not be determined by Haman's casting of lots before his gods. Only Yahweh determines the roll of the lot, and only Yahweh determines the lot of his people.

Application. The book of Esther is part of the spiritual heritage of Christians bequeathed to us by Jesus Christ. Its significance has been transformed by his resurrection. The deliverance of the Jews in Persia foreshadows the redemption of those from all nations who enter into God's covenant through Jesus the Messiah. Christ reveals a new destiny, a destiny beyond death.

ESTHER 9:29–10:3

Original Meaning. Now Esther reappears. At the beginning of her story, she is referred to as "Esther (the young woman Mordecai had adopted, the daughter of his uncle Abihail)" (2:15). At the end of her story her Jewish identity and Persian position are integrated in the reference to her as "Queen Esther, daughter of Abihail," who writes "with full authority to confirm this second letter concerning Purim" (9:29). Esther is remarkable in biblical history not only for her role in the deliverance of God's people, but for the authority she achieved to write—though she most likely used the scribes to record her words, just as Haman and Mordecai had done.

Nevertheless, in chapter 10 it is Mordecai who gets the last word. When life returned to normal after the crisis, Mordecai continued to use his rank as second only to the king for the benefit of his people. When Haman had worn Xerxes' signet ring, he was effectively, though not formally, the king of the enemies of the Jews. Now Mordecai wears that same ring and is effectively, though not formally, king of the Jews.

Application. Christian men are not only husbands and fathers, nor are Christian women only wives and mothers. Both have a wider range of interests, talents, gifts, and calling from the Lord. Unfortunately, the question of women's roles in the church has been too narrowly focused on the question of ordination.

In fact, relatively few Christians—either men or women—are heading for ordination, and so the discussion completely overlooks the reality of life for most members of the church. Judging from the state of the discussion, one would think that the church has no vision for the significance of a woman's life in Christ other than motherhood or ordination. Women need a positive statement from the church validating their roles as other than wives and mothers and affirming their calling as responsible adults living and working for the glory of God.

JOB

INTRODUCTION TO JOB

The Hebrew of the book of Job is the most difficult in the Old Testament, and while we do not know the author or the date of the book of Job, this lack of information does not affect our interpretation of its contents. How much of the book is literary artifice and how much is a journalistic reporting of real events? Either option could be legitimate genres for canonical texts and could provide the authority for sacred writ. We must keep foremost in our mind that this book is manifestly and unarguably in the genre category of wisdom literature, not historical literature. As wisdom literature it makes no claims about the nature of the events. In that sense the discussion about whether the events are real events is misplaced.

A second understanding that is important is that as wisdom literature, this book would fit easily into the classification "thought experiment." In such a case the author is using the various parts of the book to pose a philosophical scenario that will be used to address wisdom themes. If the book of Job is a thought experiment, the reader is supposed to draw conclusions about God from the final point, not from every detail along the way. Consequently, for example, the opening scene in heaven is not intended to be used as a source of information about God's activities and nature. We would not rule out the possibility that such a scenario could happen, but we would be mistaken to think that author seeks to unfold a series of historical events. It is wisdom literature.

BOOK OUTLINE

- I. Prologue (1:1–2:13)
- II. Dialogues (3:1–27:23)
    - A. Job's Opening Lament (3:1–26)
    - B. Cycle 1: Consolation (4:1–14:22)
    - C. Cycle 2: The Fate of the Wicked (15:1–21:34)
    - D. Cycle 3: Specific Accusations (22:1–27:23)
- III. Interlude: Wisdom Hymn (28:1–28)
- IV. Discourses (29:1–42:6)
    - A. Discourse 1: Job (29:1–31:40)
    - B. Discourse 2: Elihu (32:1–37:24)
    - C. Discourse 3: God (38:1–41:34)
- V. Job's Closing Statements and Epilogue (42:1–17)

JOB 1:1–22

Original Meaning

Job's Profile (1:1–5). *Uz.* Job's homeland has yet to be positively identified. Regardless of its location, this detail is significant because it indicates that Job is not an Israelite. Intriguingly, however, the book frequently evidences an Israelite perspective, which suggests that the story of the non-Israelite Job gives the book a voice in the context of Israelite ideas about God and his expectations.

Job's qualities. The terms "blameless" (*tam*) and "upright" (*yashar*) in 1:1 do not describe people who live lives of sinless perfection; rather, they describe those who have found favor in the eyes of God and other humans. Job is also described as one who "fears God" (*elohim*, 1:1). As we would expect in Job, the author does not identify him as one who "fears Yahweh" specifically. In a non-Israelite context, fearing God could refer to being ritually or ethically conscientious, and the context of Job requires nothing more than this definition. In sum, Job is a paragon of devotion and integrity.

Job's possessions and status. In 1:2 and 1:3 Job's prosperity is described in terms of his family and his possessions. Everything about Job is ideal, portraying him as the ultimate example of a person who is beyond reproach and who has achieved success by the highest standards.

Job's piety. Why are these feasts the setting for the potential offense of cursing God? Why does Job even imagine that his family might curse God in their private conversations at these feasts? The description of Job leaves no doubt that he is righteous. But the chosen example does not clarify his motives for being righteous and his picture of God. Once we see the issue in this light, we can see how these two verses lead directly to the challenge posed in 6:1–12. If Job is engaged in appeasement mentality, no motivation remains for righteousness except to reap benefits from a patronized god. The stage is set for the challenger to raise the issue of Job's motives and through them to raise questions about God's policies.

First Conversation (1:6–12). *Angels.* The phrase "angels" (*beney ha'elohim*, 1:6) relates to the idea of a divine council, where "the sons of God" (author's translation) are the functionaries who make up the council. This divine council meets to give reports and make decisions; it is where the business of heaven is done. In the ancient Near Eastern polytheistic cultures, this council was populated by the chief gods. Divine authority was distributed among these gods, and each had their area of jurisdiction. In Old Testament monotheism this concept is revised but not eliminated. These administrative functionaries possess no independent divine authority, but they have delegated roles in the administration of Yahweh's authority.

The Challenger (*hasatan*; "Satan" NIV). The Hebrew word *satan* has traditionally been transliterated with capitalization as the proper name "Satan"; most translations follow the tradition. This decision, in turn, leads casual readers to associate this challenger with the devil, named as Satan in the New Testament. This conclusion is not necessarily valid.

I conclude that *satan* refers to one who challenges. Such a challenge could be made with positive or negative intent, and it could be designed to preserve a system through accountability or to destabilize a kingdom. Consequently, not only must we identify *satan* here as a functional designation, but we also must consider the possibility that, as a function, it is not intrinsically evil.

The text does not attribute to God or to the challenger any personal emotional response to Job's tragedy; God carries more responsibility for striking Job than the challenger (implied in 1:12 and 2:3), and both lack any sympathetic response. There is no expression of glee; there is no diabolical chuckle. Nothing personal, Job . . . there is a major philosophical issue on the line that supersedes individual circumstances. The result of this profile is that we are not in a position to claim that the challenger in Job should be identified with Satan as we know him in the New Testament.

Accolade. Yahweh praises Job (1:8), using the same language that the narrator has used in 1:1.

Challenge. The challenger is questioning God's blueprint for divine-human relations—the validity of a moral order in which the righteous unfailingly prosper, or what we can call the retribution principle. By pointing out all that Yahweh has done to bless and prosper Job, he raises the point that Job's motives are open to question: Is he truly righteous or just acting in ways that will gain him benefits?

Curse/Bless. The challenger's claim stems not from some identified flaw in Job but from his experience with human nature. He has no specific evidence that would impugn Job's character, though perhaps Job's ritual customs betray some crack in the façade. If he really had any evidence, the whole challenge would be invalid and fruitless. The challenger's confidence is that God's policy is misguided and ill-advised.

Devastation of Job (1:13–22). *Sabeans and Chaldeans, fire of God and mighty wind.* We can see that the challenger uses all the resources at God's disposal—human foes, divine judgment from heaven, and natural disaster. Even though all of these disasters come from the hand of God (2:3), they fit into different categories—another way of showing the totality of the devastation.

An Israelite audience would readily recognize all the disasters because they are among those delineated in the covenant curses for disobedience (Deut 28:31–35). This recognition would heighten the poignancy for the Israelite reader and would also evoke further connections with retribution theology—here on the corporate level.

Job's response. Job's initial response reflects the normal customs of mourning (1:20). Job acknowledges by his prostration that God has performed a remarkable act, and Job accepts it as such; he abases himself in response to the great power that God has demonstrated. The challenger said he would "bless" (= euphemism for "curse," so NIV; 1:11) God to his face. Job does "bless" God to his face, but here, we must conclude, with no euphemistic connotation. The narrator concludes that Job does not attribute wrongdoing to God. Job is not calling God to accountability; this accords with Job's words in 1:21. This is not Job's final posture, but his reflection at this stage; we will later see that Job does call God to account.

Application. We should not conclude that the text is providing us with a biblically authorized response to suffering in the character of Job; we must maintain the distinction between description and prescription. Undoubtedly, God was pleased with Job's response (indicated by his repeated praise of Job in 2:3; see also Ezek 14:14), but a variety of other responses may have been just as acceptable. This part of the book is not designed to detail "the" right response to suffering.

JOB 2:1–13

Original Meaning

Second Conversation (2:1–6). *Job maintains his integrity.* The text indicates that Job continues to cling to his integrity. We can easily conclude that Job maintains not only his blamelessness but also his other commendable qualities. In short, Job's actions have revealed no flawed motive such as the challenger earlier suggested.

Ruin without reason. Who is responsible for Job's predicament: the challenger or Yahweh? Yahweh is accountable and responsible despite the role that the challenger plays. Nothing that happens to Job can be construed as punishment for some offense; Job's righteousness continues to be confirmed from all sources. If the retribution principle represents justice, it must be carried out in proportion: the punishment must suit the crime. In Job's case, no such proportionality can be sustained.

Affliction of Job and the Arrival of Counselors (2:7–13). *Advanced trial.* The first round of trials took away that which was positive in Job's life—that is, his prosperity; this second round adds the negative by causing physical suffering. The first round brought mental anguish associated with loss, while the second brings physical problems associated with pain.

Job allows no possibility that his affliction is caused by another party: the bad comes from God (2:10). In the first trial God took away the good (1:21); in the second, God brings the bad (2:10). Job accepts God's right to do both without cursing him.

Role of Job's wife. Job's wife has advised Job to capitulate to his tragic fate by cursing God (2:9) and accepting the inevitable punishment of death. Contrary to "cursing God to his face," Job has not sinned with his lips.

The arrival of the friends. Eliphaz, Bildad, and Zophar now enter the picture. The friends come together by arrangement and with a specific purpose: to commiserate or sympathize and to offer condolences and assuage his grief.

Application. Job assumed that his suffering came from the hand of God. God did indeed play an active role, but we must remember that the book is not trying to give us a model for how God is regularly involved in what people suffer. What vocabulary should we use to describe God's involvement? I would suggest that one of the major lessons of the book of Job is that no such language suffices. Whenever we choose a verb to communicate God's relationship to suffering, we are proposing what can only be a simplistic understanding of what God does. In the scenario laid out in Job, he happened to be right—his circumstances were from the hand of God. But it would be reductionistic and inaccurate for us to characterize all suffering as coming directly from the hand of God.

JOB 3:1–26

Original Meaning

Cursing the Day of Birth (3:1–10). In this chapter we find the only curse Job utters, a curse that focuses on the day of his birth rather than on God.

Chaos incantation. If God were not to call forth the light, the sun, or the day, the day would not exist. The sequence of images expresses a variety of ways that the day could be negated.

Rousing Leviathan. Who are "those who curse days" (3:8)? Akkadian literature speaks of a class of scholars known as the *ummani le'uti* ("able scholars"). Deities, especially Enki/Ea, the god of divination, or his son, Marduk, are capable of powerful incantations. Demons known as the *utukke lemnuti* in ancient Near Eastern literature were considered responsible for disruption of order. In the end I would view Job's statement as having an intentionally indefinite referent (lit., "whoever curses days and rouses Leviathan, may they do so," author's translation).

The Netherworld (3:11–19). Job expresses his belief that the netherworld would be a better place to be than his life on earth; he depicts the netherworld as a place of comfort, rest, ease, and tranquility. In modern-day terms, someone who was starving might look forward to prison, where they could get three meals a day.

The Misery of Life (3:20–26). *What I feared has come upon me (3:25).* In 31:23 Job clarifies that he specifically dreaded destruction from God. Job 1:4–5 shows that Job was fearful of actions that would cause him or his loved ones to lose the favor of God. His fears have been realized, though he can imagine no actions of his that could have been the cause of his circumstances. Job's words do not betray the reasons for his foreboding apprehension, and so the book remains ambiguous concerning Job's motives (and now his fears).

Application. God can use hedges that we perceive as negative, but which are ultimately for our good—that is, disciplinary hedges. In Hosea 2:6 God builds a hedge around Israel to prevent her from finding her way. The hedge is intended to drive her back to her Lord, to prevent her from wandering. It manifests itself not in misfortunes but in lack of success in worldly endeavors. When we experience these, we should reconsider our motives and our goals to pursue greater dependence on God.

JOB 4:1–14:22

Original Meaning

Eliphaz (Job 4:1–5:27). Eliphaz's first exhortation for Job occurs in the problematic verse 4:6, which the NIV renders, "Should not your piety be your confidence and your blameless ways your hope?" Eliphaz identifies Job's fear of God as an irrational confidence. Given Eliphaz's observations in 4:7–11, he seems to be accusing Job of denial in 4:6. In this interpretation, the translation should not be "Should not . . . ," but something more like, "Is not your [self-proclaimed] piety the basis for this irrational confidence? Is your only hope really in the [presumed] blamelessness of your ways?" In Eliphaz's view, the incontestable retribution principle (4:7–11) gives the lie to Job's delusion of righteousness and exposes his hope as vain.

Eliphaz's mystical experience (4:12–21) occurs in a vision (NIV "dreams," 12:13). Eliphaz is claiming revelation; in effect he says, "God gave me a message for you, Job." The NIV renders 4:17 in the traditional way: "Can a mortal be more righteous than God? Can . . . man be more pure than his Maker?" We propose the reading of Job 4:17 as: "Can a mortal be righteous in God's perspective? Can a man be clean in the perspective of his Maker?" The rhetorical thrust is not much different from those who have translated, "Can a mortal be righteous before God," but the nuance is subtly different: meeting God's minimal standards for ritual acceptability ("before" God) versus meeting God's maximum standards in the broader moral/ethical realm ("in God's perspective"). The latter relegates Job's confidence to vanity.

Eliphaz's main point in 4:12–21 reflects ancient Near Eastern beliefs—namely, that the gods have far more regulations than humans know or recognize; there are so many ways one might offend the gods in one's ritual performance, one can never claim not to deserve what the deity has sent. Such confidence would truly be irrational.

In 5:1 Eliphaz speaks of "the holy ones," another way of referring to members of the divine council (i.e., the "sons of God"). This is highly ironic since Eliphaz is more correct than he knows. No appeal to the divine council will resolve this before its time. This is also the first suggestion of Job initiating legal action. Eliphaz, however, implies that summoning one of the council would be fruitless.

Instead, Eliphaz counsels Job to appeal directly to God (5:8). Job has an entirely different idea in mind, for rather than seeking an oracle from God to identify his offense, he plans to appeal to God for vindication.

Eliphaz also points out that Job should look on his situation as the disciplinary correction of God (5:17). Having received God's attention in a negative way, Job can now have some confidence that God will also respond to Job's repentance and bring restoration. The rest of Eliphaz's speech anticipates this restoration (5:18–27).

Job (Job 6:1–7:21). After Job again calls for his own death (6:8–9), he evaluates his stance in which he takes consolation (6:10). This verse is pivotal but also difficult to understand. The phrase the NIV renders "words of the Holy One" (*imrey qadosh*) occurs nowhere else in the Old Testament. The LXX and several translations preferred to treat the word as an adjective and render the phrase "holy words," which I believe is preferable here, since no holy one has spoken. The holy words would refer to the traditional teachings of the fathers, frequently referred to in this book by other descriptions (e.g., 8:8; 15:18).

I offer the following interpretation of 6:10: Job consoles himself that he has not softened the blow of holy words (= traditional teaching) as Eliphaz did when he suggested that "everything's going to be OK" (5:18–27). Job is at least prepared to face the facts and wishes for death. As he expresses the misery of his condition, Job finds consolation only in his refusal to accept a sugar-coated view of reality (6:10).

From this point, Job launches into his first full-scale verbal assault on his friends (6:14–30). He challenges them to cease their platitudes and reveal his specific offense (6:24). Job considers this important because his integrity is at stake (6:29). Job's demand of his friends is a bit stronger than the "relent/reconsider" of the NIV in 6:29; he wants them to "take back" their malicious words because his "integrity is at stake."

After another lament concerning his condition, Job finally—and for the first time—turns his attention and remarks directly to God (7:7–21). Job primarily accuses God of being overattentive and unrealistic in his expectations. Job claims that, unlike the chaos creatures, he is no threat to order and therefore doesn't warrant constant attention.

Job continues in this vein as he asks, "What is mankind that you make so much of them?" (7:17). Job conveys the terrifying and negative prospect of God's singling out humanity as a whole—or worse still, a single person. Job labels God a "watcher of men" (7:20, author's translation). Job uses a term that often bears a positive connotation, indicating care and protection, but, as so often in this speech, he ironically turns this positive language upside down.

Before we move from Job's first speech, we must consider whether Job continues to consider himself innocent of wrongdoing. We can explain the language in both clauses of 7:21 as a request for God to cease and desist his actions, which have presumed a trial and a guilty verdict. Job does not own up to such offenses, but he wants God to give up the prosecution of this court action.

Bildad (Job 8:1–22). Bildad sees clearly the implication of Job's words and therefore launches into a speech of his own, a speech filled with rhetorical questions designed to affirm that God upholds justice. In these statements he denies that God would "pervert" justice and righteousness (8:3). Is Bildad justified in his tacit accusation of Job, or is he caricaturing Job through hyperbole? Job has not charged God with perverting justice (yet), but in Bildad's view of the world, that would be the only logical conclusion if Job can sustain his claim of innocence. Bildad is therefore confronting Job with the ultimate destination of the dangerous path he has taken.

Bildad clearly doubts Job's claims of innocence, reflected here in his words, "If you are pure and upright..." (8:6). Here we find Bildad holding forth the possibility that God will restore Job should Job show himself to be untainted; a few speeches later, however, Bildad reveals that no one can claim to be untainted. This shows that Bildad is simply patronizing Job in 8:6.

Bildad also has his own implied accusations as he unwraps the implications of the retribution principle: "Surely God does not reject one who is blameless or strengthen the hands of evildoers" (8:20). These convictions lead him to characterize Job implicitly as "godless" and one who forgets God (8:13).

Job (Job 9:1–10:22). Job immediately latches on to the idea of entering into legal action with God. Given God's power, he is now understandably worried about facing God in a courtroom setting. Job's hymn (9:5–13) is an aside to explain why Job trembles at the thought of opposing God in court.

Verses 5–9 address cosmic geography. We would not translate Job 9:5 as "God causes mountains to move" (implied in the NIV translation of "He moves mountains"), but "God traverses the mountains." This would parallel his treading on the seas in 9:8. The first clause of 9:6 contains terminology commonly used for earthquakes. It is difficult to understand what the pillars are doing, but the context gives us some confidence based on the parallel between the two lines. The earthquake continues the theme of punishment against those who resist.

The punishment theme moves heavenward in 9:7. Job recognizes God as the one who seals off the stars in the second phrase of 9:7. Sealing the stars would refer to shutting them out so they could not enter the paths to shine in the heavens. We can read 9:7 as a continuation of God's cosmic judgment against those who resist him (9:4).

As translated by the NIV, 9:8 appears to concern God's creation, but close attention to the words shows otherwise. The first act refers not so much to stretching out the heavens, but to lifting them up. We can see the idea of "lifting up" as God raises up the corner to step in under it.

To interpret 9:9 we need a better understanding of constellations in the ancient world. Regardless of which constellations chapter 9 refers to, the more important question is why the constellations are brought into the discussion. Constellations often are the subject of omens (for good or ill) in Akkadian literature. These are also used for judgment.

The point of the section is that God uses all of the cosmos as a weapon against those who would oppose him. Though Job anticipates facing God in court rather than in combat, Job is justified in feeling apprehensive. In Job's perception, God's ways are imperceptible (10:11); he is accountable to none (10:12). The latter is again ironic in that God is allowing the challenger to hold his policies accountable.

Rahab (9:13) is another of the enemies of order generally connected to the sea. In the Babylonian Creation Epic, Tiamat, the chaos creature associated with the sea, rebels against the gods with the aid of her consorts. This section shows God handily defeating even the most fearsome chaos creatures; if that is so, what chance does a human have in confronting God at any level?

This mode of thinking continues Job's characteristically deficient view of God, evident almost since the beginning of the book. He has viewed God as petty and overattentive, and now as one likely to abuse his power. Job's rhetoric escalates as he throws caution to the winds (9:21) and makes his boldest statement yet: "He destroys both the blameless and the wicked" (9:22).

Though Job identifies God as the source of destruction for all, he still believes there is a justice system. The fact that he can consider himself to be tried and found guilty (9:29) and that a courtroom scenario is possible (9:32) shows that there is still a justice system; Job has not claimed there is no justice—only that God is the sole target of his complaint. Job requests a courtroom scenario in which an arbitrator will serve on his behalf (9:33).

Chapter 10 shows us that Job continues to think the world ought to operate according to the retribution principle (cf. 10:3). God as judge does not need to gather information like a human judge. Job questions God's omniscience as part of his defense.

In 10:8–12 Job wonders why God bothered making him at all if he only intends to destroy him. He uses language typical of the ancient world to describe his making: molded like clay (10:9a). The biblical and ancient Near Eastern accounts demonstrate the view that it was not just the first human who was made of dust/clay; every human is so made. Every human is molded by deity and every human returns to dust. We find this archetypal view throughout the ancient world.

Just when it seemed that Job could not get any bolder, he stunningly claims to know the mind of God (10:13). This brash and arrogant declaration shows once again Job's deficient view of God. God's statement about Job in 42:7–8 has inclined us to exonerate Job totally and consider his view of God to be accurate and appropriate, but how can we reconcile this inclination with the near blasphemous accusations he hurls against God in this chapter? Job finishes his speech of despair (over getting a fair trial) by wishing again for death (10:18–22), a reprise of his lament in chapter 3.

Zophar (Job 11:1–20). Zophar accuses Job of "idle talk" (11:3). Zophar is characterizing Job's stance about his innocence as a farcical travesty. Zophar characterizes Job: "We all know you are guilty Job. It's obvious! Why keep the charade going?"

As he wishes for God to address this subject, Zophar observes that "true wisdom has two sides" (11:6). I would suggest an interpretation something like: "Competent, responsible thinking has to consider the other side of the equation; think of how much worse it could be if God decided to punish *all* your sins."

Zophar argues for God's inscrutability in 11:7–12. He thinks that Job takes too much on himself in supposing that he can match God in court. In one sense this anticipates part of what God will say when he appears in chapter 38. This illustrates that the words of the friends are not utter foolishness. Their arguments derive power from the accepted, sound thinking on which they are based. The problem is often not a theology that is entirely wrong but in drawing wrongheaded conclusions in a flawed assemblage of ideas or the intermixture of presuppositions that are not essential.

Zophar lays out his recommended course of action in 11:13–20. His advice in 11:13 is difficult to argue against—all followers of God should do such things. His assumption in 11:14, however, begins to show the deviation, and 11:15–20 reveal Zophar's perception of the goal. He assumes that Job has indeed sinned and so brought this punishment down on himself—a flawed conclusion. The goal he holds out for Job is restoration of prosperity.

Job (Job 12:1–14:22). Job is not willing to look at his case in isolation; God should be concerned about those who are wicked and hold them in contempt (12:5–6). This observation rests on the premise that justice should be proportional and relative.

We may note in passing that 12:9 makes the only reference to Yahweh outside of the narrative frame and the Yahweh speeches in chapters 38–41. The hymnic section (12:10–24) expresses God's authority to revoke the power of corrupt or repressive leaders.

In chapter 13, Job turns his attention back to his desired court case, beginning with a rebuke to the friends (13:4). The more stinging complaint against them, however, comes as he accuses them of speaking "wickedly on God's behalf" (13:7). The friends are not giving testimony *to* God because they are not on trial; they are not giving false testimony *about* God, because they are not giving bad theology; they *are*, however, giving false testimony *on behalf of* God when they presume to represent God's testimony about Job and his supposed sin. The second clause of 13:8 confirms this interpretation.

The next textual puzzle to solve is in the famous statement of Job in 13:15, "Though he slay me, yet will I hope in him." Unfortunately, the most familiar and popular sections in Job are often among the most difficult. Does the last word (Heb. *yhl*) describe "hoping" or "waiting"? The impetus for interpreting the verb as "waiting in silence" concerns Elihu (32:11, 16), who waited while the others spoke; the usage of the verb throughout Job confirms such an interpretation. The meaning of hope only comes in secondarily as those who are suffering often wait with hope for God to bring relief. I would therefore translate, "Even though he may slay me, I will not wait [in silence]"—that is, Job is going to continue pressing for the court appearance.

After concluding his plea for a legitimate hearing, he shifts to a discussion of human mortality and frailty (13:28–14:14). In 14:7–14 we find the strongest statements in the book about Job's beliefs concerning the afterlife, beliefs that prove bleak. Like everyone in the ancient world, Job believes that life continues after death, but such a belief offers little hope if life in the netherworld is dreary drudgery. Trees can resprout (14:7–9) but humans have no such prospects (14:10, 12)—they are more like the riverbed that simply dries up (14:11). Job wishes it were otherwise, that he could take refuge in the grave and then be brought back to life (14:13), but he realizes that such an option does not exist.

In 14:14 Job is hoping that his turn will come. This leads seamlessly into 14:15, where God will summon Job and Job will have the chance he has been looking for to have his case heard. As Job dreams of this new day, we should observe that his objective is restored relationship (14:15–17), not restored benefits. This continues to be the most important aspect of Job's posture. When Job thinks of restored relationship with God, he envisions a coming day after his reconciliation with God when he will be given the benefit of the doubt and will receive mercy based on a track record of good behavior, even if God is dogging his steps.

Application. We must ask whether our faith can be sustained when our desires are not granted, when healing does not come, when broken homes are not restored, when the goals we pursue remain beyond our reach.

As Christians we must first conclude that being motivated by righteousness and faith rather than by benefits should be our goal. For some they never get there. They only think of Christianity as a benefits system, and if there is nothing in it for them, they lose all motivation. Yet Christ has told us that the cost of discipleship is high. We lose our lives, not gain them. Once this course is set, we must determine that righteous behavior earns us nothing and that even if it gains us nothing, God is worthy of this life response. He is a righteous God and has created us with the capacity to imitate him. It is in the imitation of him that we find relationship with him—our highest joy. Our faith and its accompanying righteousness ought not to be self-serving. Righteousness should have its desired end in relationship with God, not in gaining reward from God. This is the teaching of the book of Job, and it is a lesson we still desperately need to learn.

JOB 15:1–21:34

Original Meaning

Eliphaz (Job 15:1–35). Though Eliphaz evaluates Job's arguments as nonsense, he more importantly accuses Job of sinful words. He makes six accusations in three parallel pairs (15:4–6). Eliphaz first says that Job "undermines piety" (15:4a). Eliphaz does not accuse Job of nullifying piety itself but of negating his own claims to piety by contradicting himself.

The second phrase indicates that Job has "hindered devotion to God" (15:4b). Eliphaz is saying that Job's words have not only nullified his claims to piety, but they have effectively reduced the persuasiveness of the claim that he would make against the deity. In this phrase, "undermine" works better than in the first phrase. Eliphaz claims that Job's response has weakened his case considerably and undermined the respect of his peers.

The second pair of accusations (15:5) concern Job's motives and methods. Eliphaz first claims that "your sin prompts your mouth." Eliphaz is suggesting that Job has rationalized his sins so much so that he is not aware of them. That is, the sinful deeds he has committed have taught his mouth how to rationalize so that the sins are not recognized for what they are. The second line in 15:5 follows up on this course of thinking by suggesting that Job has adopted "crafty" language to accomplish his rationalization. Eliphaz is accusing Job of what we today call "spin."

In the third parallel set (15:6) Eliphaz expresses his assessment of Job's current position—he stands condemned by his own words. Eliphaz uses legal language to identify Job's mouth as both the source of his verdict and the witness that has provided testimony to arrive at that verdict.

Eliphaz then attacks what he assesses as Job's arrogance. He clearly identifies "the first man ever born" as a person of great wisdom (15:7). As readers, we detect the irony of Eliphaz's rhetorical question concerning Job's involvement in God's heavenly council (15:8) since it was the meeting of the council that precipitated Job's situation. Had Job been privy to the discussions in the divine council, he would have understood his predicament more fully.

One wonders what Eliphaz has in mind when he speaks of God's "consolations" (*tanhumot*) in 15:11. Eliphaz may refer to the revelation that he divulged in 4:12–21. This speech would be considered a consoling word because it suggested that Job was not alone—all humanity shares his deficiency of righteousness (4:17).

Just before Eliphaz explicates the fate of the wicked, he returns to a theme addressed in previous speeches. His opening line in 15:14 alludes to Job's question in 7:17. This statement in 15:14 returns to the key point in Eliphaz's first speech (4:17). Here, as in 4:18, he follows his initial statement with an assertion concerning God's lack of trust in his holy ones (15:15). Even God's heavenly servants are accountable. Eliphaz is suggesting that even those things that seem to be unblemished from our perspective are not so to God.

We cannot pause to consider each detail of 15:17–35, but a few matters stand out. The speech primarily focuses on the destiny of the wicked man rather than on his acts (15:20). In 15:25, however, Eliphaz unequivocally places Job in the category of the wicked. Finally, we also should note that Eliphaz sees prosperity and other benefits as the ultimate payoff and greatest potential loss. He still does not seem to comprehend that Job is not concerned with these things.

Job (Job 16:1–17:16). Job continues to delineate new charges against God. Though he voices accusations in 16:11–14, his main charge is summarized in 16:9. Three verbs portray God as a savage, predatory beast: "assails," "tears," and "gnashes his teeth." Again, Job accuses God of making him a target.

Job turns again to his long-desired court case. In 9:33 he anticipates some help in his litigation. In 16:18–21 we see a variety of terms. If we combine information from the context of Job, the Old Testament, and court documents from the ancient Near Eastern cultural background, we can infer that Job hopes for a member of the divine council to call God to account on his behalf.

In chapter 17 Job returns to the topic of death. Again, it is clear that he sees no vindication after the grave; he cannot return from the grave (16:22) and death offers no relief (17:1, 13). In 17:15–16 he again makes it clear that he has no hope in the afterlife.

Chapter 17 also affirms Job's tenaciously held and accurate view of righteousness. In light of all of the abuse that he has suffered at the hands of friends and strangers, his declaration in 17:9 makes his position clear. Not one whisper comes from Job about the righteous getting all their prosperity back. Truly righteous people are concerned about their integrity, not the rewards they receive.

Bildad (Job 18:1–21). When Bildad speaks of the earth's abandonment and the rocks' removal, he is speaking metaphorically to convey how radically Job is challenging traditional wisdom. Bildad, the traditionalist in the group, reasserts traditional wisdom concerning the plight of the wicked. In so doing he illustrates what the friends have done all along in their interpretation of the retribution principle. It is one thing to say that the wicked will suffer, but it is quite another to conclude that anyone who is suffering must be wicked; this, however, is the inference drawn by the friends.

Bildad's litany concerning the doom of the wicked contains a particularly obscure statement: "death's firstborn devours his limbs" (18:13b). The description speaks not of a slowly progressing disease but of the total destruction of the body in the grave.

Bildad ends on a stinging insinuation. He has described the plight of the wicked using a number of statements that coincide with Job's experiences, and in 18:21 he concludes that such things happen to those who do not know God. Has it come to this? Not only is Job considered guilty of wicked deeds, but now Bildad tacitly suggests that he has no knowledge of God. It matters little whether Bildad means that Job lacks a relationship with God or accurate information about God (or both)—this is a devastating judgment.

Job (Job 19:1–29). It is no surprise that Job feels crushed by the words of Bildad. His sense of abandonment leads him to reiterate that his friends have deserted him and to claim blatantly that God has wronged him (19:6). This begins a series of accusations specifying how God has brought disaster, which parallels Bildad's litany of the plight of the wicked. Job, however, still refuses to admit that this treatment might be God's response to his behavior.

This leads us into one of the most familiar yet controversial sections of the book. In 19:25 we find the much beloved declaration, "I know that my redeemer (*goel*) lives," immortalized in Handel's "Messiah." Even more than 13:15, this verse stands in many people's minds as representing the posture and hope of Job. A christological interpretation is clearly indicated by those translations that capitalize "Redeemer," despite the fact that the New Testament never integrates this verse into its own Christology or suggests this was a prophecy fulfilled in Christ.

Unfortunately, in the analysis that follows, we will see little that is certain in 19:23–27. As we sort through the problems in translation, we must also seriously consider how these verses fit with what Job and his friends are saying throughout the rest of the book. These verses ought not be interpreted as an inexplicable departure from the context.

The issues with the Hebrew text are myriad and complex; we will address the problems as they arise in the following analysis.

Job 19:23–24. Because Job does not expect to be around much longer to present his case personally, he wishes for a permanent record of his sufferings and claims for posterity.

Job 19:25. A *goel* is also one who enters a legal situation on behalf of another. The job of the *goel* is to recover losses and to salvage the dignity of one who has suffered loss. It is not surprising, then, to hear Job speak of a *goel* who might act on his behalf. Job is persuaded that his *goel* is alive and that this one will arise to take a stand. The place is stipulated as *al-apar* (NIV: "on the earth"). Evidence suggests that Job expects his *goel* to arrive and testify at the place where he is mourning and where he has expected to lie down and turn to dust (2:8).

Job 19:27. Job's statement in 19:27, "I myself will see him with my own eyes" (NIV), further substantiates the idea that Job will enjoy restored favor with God in his own flesh. Does Job mean that he will see the God he has long been familiar with rather than the God of his recent experience, who seems to be a stranger? This understanding is unlikely, for God would not be appropriately classified as an outsider. Does Job mean that he himself will see God, rather than a stranger standing in for him? This is also improbable, because a person standing in for him would be authorized to do so. Does Job mean that he will not be a stranger to God or perhaps that God will no longer treat him as a stranger? I consider this last idea the most likely, as it parallels nicely the idea of being received back favorably into God's presence; no longer an outsider, Job is welcomed back into fellowship.

In summary, I would offer the following expanded paraphrase:

"I firmly believe that there is someone, somewhere, who will come and testify on my behalf right here on my dung heap at the end of all this. Despite my peeling skin, I expect to have enough left to come before God in my own flesh. I will be restored to his favor and no longer be treated as a stranger. This is my deepest desire!" (Prosperity has nothing to do with it).

Zophar (Job 20:1–29). Finally, the theologian speaks—but his words can only echo what the mystic and the traditionalist have already asserted: It is the wicked who suffer. Eliphaz made his case based on his observation and experience (15:17). Bildad, as the traditionalist, couched his observations in aphorisms; now Zophar grounds his argument in God's actions against the wicked: He takes away their riches (20:15), rains down blows on them (20:23), and carries away all that they have (20:28–29). The reader knows that even though Job has experienced these things, they do not result from the wrath of God, as Zophar suggests (20:28). Zophar indirectly accuses Job of pride (20:6) and of concealing evil (20:12). As always, the friends observe Job's circumstances but draw illegitimate conclusions about God's motives and Job's conduct.

Job (Job 21:1–34). In response to these three speeches about the plight and destiny of the wicked, Job offers his own observations about the wicked—diametrically opposed to the neat and tidy perspective of the friends. Job confronts them with evidence that contradicts the traditions they have been spouting—the wicked often prosper (21:7–33). This is information that they all know but prefer to ignore. Job is preparing his case that the system is broken, for whether people have a secure and prosperous life or a miserable life of destitution, they all die (21:26). This sentiment picks up a theme well-known from Ecclesiastes.

Application. The force of the argument in this second series of dialogues concerns the suffering of the wicked. Job's friends insist that the wicked do suffer, and Job's concluding speech questions whether experience affirms such consistency. What should we think about this, and how does it factor into our own worldview?

Certainly, both Old and New Testaments encourage us to think that God delights in good behavior and that he will judge the wicked. We reap what we sow (Gal 6:7), yet our own experiences and observations lead us to share in Job's skepticism. I propose that we should adopt a modified view of the retribution principle, understood in proverbial and theological terms. In other words, the retribution principle is useful to describe God's nature, and it therefore helps us to identify general trends in human experience, but it offers no guarantees and cannot be applied consistently or universally in this fallen world.

This interpretation suggests several important conclusions:

- We cannot draw conclusions about people's behavior from their circumstances.
- We should not expect wicked people to get their just punishment in this life.
- We should never rejoice in the misfortune of an enemy, though we may take consolation that justice is sometimes served in this world.

On the last point we would distinguish between judicial actions and personal circumstances. In the former case, justice is vindicated when a corrupt politician is caught, indicted, tried, and punished for his or her crimes. Without indulging vindictive feelings, we can rejoice that justice was served and that the system worked. However, we should not respond gleefully when someone we consider an enemy or a wicked person suffers personal tragedies (i.e., they lose a loved one or contract a serious disease). We should rather defer to Christ's teaching that we love even our enemies, and we cannot legitimately assess their circumstances as God's judgment of wickedness.

JOB 22:1–27:23

Original Meaning

Eliphaz (Job 22:1–30). Eliphaz's opening line sets the tone for the remainder of his speech as he targets the issue that Job has been holding as his defense. In 22:2–3 Eliphaz is in effect saying, "A mediator will do you no good; your proposed lawsuit would have no chance of success." In 22:4 this rhetoric is continued with: "Is it for your piety that he rebukes you?" Of course not! Eliphaz concludes his point in 22:5 with the rhetorical question that offers the alternative. This then leads to the enumeration of Job's many sins (all presumed, not observed).

In 22:6–9 we find the friends' only attempt to accuse Job of specific sins. The list alleges injustice toward three vulnerable classes: the debtor (22:6), the hungry/thirsty (22:7–8), and the widow/orphan (22:9). Knowing that the accusations of injustice are speculative and unfounded, we must also question the validity of Eliphaz's claims concerning Job's speech. In 22:13 he alleges that Job has said, "What does God know? Does he judge through such darkness?" These questions do not match up with any words that Job has actually spoken, so we must take them as Eliphaz's synthesis of what Job has "in effect" said.

As Eliphaz continues his discourse, we see further connections to Job's last speech. In 22:15 he is urging Job not to think that he can follow the path of the wicked that Job has just described. His comments in 22:17–18 contain the same wording that Job attributes to the wicked in 21:14–16.

In 22:21 Eliphaz begins his exhortation to Job and picks up the verb *skn* ("submit") that he used in 22:2. Eliphaz advises Job to pay attention to God—to reengage with him and stop arguing. Eliphaz's understanding of reengaging with God is, however, far different from Job's understanding.

Concluding his final speech, Eliphaz turns from his exhortation to the anticipated results. Here he emphasizes restored favor with God (22:25–27) but with the twist that renewed favor will put Job in a position to influence God. This is a more subtle temptation for Job to respond in anticipation of benefits rather than retain righteousness for righteousness' sake.

The last verse (22:30) is unfortunately problematic. We might surmise that Eliphaz refers to a category of individuals who are caught in the legal system. Accused of guilt and unable to establish innocence (not unlike Job), this person's reputation and integrity have come under suspicion. Perhaps Eliphaz is suggesting, then, that when Job is restored, he could help people who are suffering the same thing he has endured. Presumably he could urge them to return to God, just as Eliphaz has urged him.

Job (Job 23:1–24:25). In chapter 23 Job ponders his status before God. He is torn between optimistic confidence (23:6b–7, 10) and frustrated attempts at justification (23:8–9). He is filled with continuing plans for his legal defense (23:4–5) and affirmations of his righteousness (23:11–12). Both his suffering (23:2) and his terror of God (23:13–17) remain.

In chapter 24 Job turns his attention to the injustice in the world as he wonders why God does not respond. Job here complains, "God charges no one with wrongdoing" (24:12). Job 24:13–17 identifies the characteristics of those who love the dark ("rebel against the light," 24:13). Murderers, adulterers, and thieves comprise the three categories of offenders.

We have mentioned already that the Hebrew of the book of Job is the most difficult in the Old Testament; worse still, this section of Job 24 is often considered the most obscure in the book. Job would not hesitate to suggest that the wicked die like everyone else. A problem would occur only if Job specifically refers to God's judgment of the wicked, because he has been denying this all along (24:12, "God charges no one with wrongdoing"). Job 24:22 ("God drags away the mighty") poses just such a potential contradiction. It is therefore important to note that the subject of 24:22 is not specified in the Hebrew text; "God" has been supplied by the translators. We must reconsider whether this is the best choice.

The addition of "God" as the subject in 24:22 is followed in most all translations and commentaries. This single factor causes these statements to sound foreign to the mouth of Job. I propose it is unnecessary either to supply "God" as the subject or to significantly emend the text to arrive at a suitable translation. I suggest the following paraphrase for 24:22–23:

> He (a wicked person) uses his power to draw along the mighty; he rises (to positions of influence), but his life is in constant jeopardy. Though he has provided for his own security, he has to keep his eyes on them (the mighty) all the time.

In this analysis, Job observes that wickedness offers no advantage, but he does not suggest that the wicked are called to account by God. They fall prey to their own schemes and to their own mortality. This sort of statement would not be out of place in the mouth of Job.

Bildad (Job 25:1–6). Bildad's last speech is only six verses long. The brevity is defensible in light of his entrenched traditionalism, which, at this point in the dialogue, has reduced him to platitudinous reiteration of his major salient points.

Job (Job 26:1–27:23). Job 26:5–6 describe the dead and the netherworld. The Akkadian myth "The Descent of Ishtar to the Underworld" recounts Ishtar's passage through the seven gates of the netherworld. It is intriguing to see all of these elements (the opening of the netherworld, nakedness, and trembling) grouped together in both Job and the "The Descent," but the contexts are very different.

If we follow the traditional understanding of 26:5–6, the hymn moves from God's control of the realm of the dead and powerful spiritual or cosmic creatures to his control of the upper cosmos. The cosmic geography expressed in 26:7 has attracted considerable attention, since some have asserted that it reflects some modern, scientific models that conceive of the earth suspended in space. Careful attention, however, shows this not to be the case. Job 26:7 indicates what the "earth" is suspended on. In the ancient functional ontology, people saw the earth/netherworld as suspended on the functionless cosmic waters below, parallel to the heaven stretched out over the upper cosmic waters.

The imagery of cloud-enveloped waters in 26:8 likewise fits the ideas current in the ancient world. An Assyrian artifact in the British Museum provides our only graphic representation of this phenomenon. It depicts the winged deity with drawn bow in the skies, flanked by bags containing hail or rain. The point of their inclusion in chapter 26 is largely self-evident as it speaks of God's control: He does not allow the bags to burst under the weight of the water.

Just as the earth is supported by pillars, so too are the heavens in 26:11—or, more specifically, the dome of heaven. The pillars may refer to mountains since some mountains were believed to intersect the sky and perhaps hold it up.

In 26:12–13 Job continues his hymnic description of God's primordial ordering of the cosmos. The churning of the sea has been generally considered an element of the typical mythical scene in which the restless cosmic ocean disturbs the creatures (monsters, beasts) that represent chaos and disorder. The cosmic creature Rahab is roused by the agitation of the sea. God's power enables him to stir up the sea, but it is his understanding that gives him victory. It takes specialized skill to dispatch a great cosmic creature like Rahab.

Job 27:1–6 is extremely significant, for it contains Job's final response to the case of his friends. The oath formula that begins Job's speech shows that Job is not simply making a serious statement but is delivering an ultimatum to his friends—further debate will be useless.

Job's two statements in 27:2 concern what God has done to him: "denied me justice" and "made my life bitter." Though at one level they can be affirmed, these two statements summarize Job's flawed view of God. The flaw is not in the blunt facts (Job's suffering at God's hand) but in what he implies about God's character as he reiterates those facts.

The first phrase uses the same root that described Job's devotion in the early chapters of the book (1:1). Here, however, God has caused justice to turn aside. In particular, Job probably means that God has denied him the right to defend himself in court. Job nonetheless expresses his lifelong commitment in six phrases in 27:4–6.

Job begins 27:7–10 by cursing his enemies. By this point in the book we might well imagine that Job counts his three "advisors" as enemies, in that they have opposed and condemned him. This understanding follows naturally from 27:1–6. Just as they have implicitly condemned him, he now does the same to them.

In 27:11–12 Job again addresses the friends directly. Job initially asked for their instruction (6:24), which they offered in the form of teaching (8:10). Now Job again turns the tables, assessing their instruction as nothing but "meaningless talk" (27:12). I interpret the word as referring to that which is incapable of bringing ultimate satisfaction or contentment.

Job now returns to a discussion of God's interaction with the wicked (27:13–23). Unlike his previous treatment of this topic (24:18–24), Job here specifically mentions God's retributive action (though God is only named in 27:13). Still, in this context, Job only speaks of a general fate allotted by God, not a specific act of judgment; thus, he does not contradict his statement in 24:12.

Application. Humans (especially Americans) tend to be motivated by self-interest: "What is in it for me?" we ask. We have not only adopted our own self-fulfillment and happiness as a goal, but nearly consider it a right (subconsciously emending the Declaration of Independence to indicate what to us is indeed self-evident, that we have inalienable rights to life, liberty, and the pursuit of happiness). Not only has happiness become our ambition, it has often become a spiritual expectation. Our relationship to God looks much like the Great Symbiosis, in that our commitment is premised on anticipated benefits. Often in the process we expect much of God and little of ourselves.

If the book of Job promotes disinterested righteousness as a moral principle, we should explore what this value looks like for our faith to get beyond self-interests. If our righteousness is for righteousness' sake, what will it look like? Taking the lead from the book of Job, we would have to conclude that such a faith would not abandon belief even if life gets difficult. But it is important that we also consider the proper motives for our behavior and our choices. How should we discern what God expects of us and what we should expect of ourselves? How should we live if we want to pursue a faith not premised on self-interests?

Ideally, we should aspire to holiness, not because of benefits we can gain as a result but because God is God, and our righteous behavior is one of the ways we honor him. Regardless of whether we experience any advantages in life because of these decisions, we choose this path because of who God is.

JOB 28:1–28

Original Meaning

Mining (28:1–11). Mining was an important industry in the ancient world. Mined materials were used in a wide variety of practical and aesthetic undertakings. These materials served as the foundation for technological advancement, production of art, and accumulation of wealth. The discovery of mineral deposits, the technology for extracting them from the earth, and the techniques for refining them were all considered somewhat esoteric, evoking awe and wonder. As the passage outlines, mining requires deep delving in dark, obscure places and produces stunning products (sapphire/lapis lazuli, gold) from what looks common (dust, rock). These aspects will be applied to the search for wisdom; the last line, brings "hidden things to light" (28:11), provides a summary and transition to the topic of wisdom.

Elusive Wisdom (28:12–19). One can search for precious metals and find them, given sufficient technology and knowledge. Likewise, though it is difficult, it is possible to explore and discover the sources of rivers. In contrast, wisdom cannot be found and cannot be purchased. It is inaccessible from a human vantage point and beyond value.

Source of Wisdom (28:20–28). Job 28:20 reiterates 28:12 with a change in the verb: "Where can wisdom be found" in 28:12 and "Where then does wisdom come from" in 28:20. This crucial adjustment distinguishes the message of 28:12–19, in which wisdom cannot be "found," from 28:20–28, which suggests that wisdom "comes from" God. The first concerns a search—ultimately unsuccessful; the second concerns a source. In 28:14 it was the deep and the sea who answered; in 28:22 it is Destruction and Death who answer. The distinction is again an important one. In 28:12–19 the quest focused on the land of the living, where deep and sea are located. In 28:20–28, the quest is extended. Since wisdom is hidden from every living thing, Destruction and Death are consulted. They have word of it, but they confess that wisdom is not to be found in their realm either. One does not achieve wisdom by moving into the next realm. Sheol offers no heightened levels of awareness.

The word translated "Destruction" in 28:22 is *abaddon* and "Death" is the familiar *mawet*. As with deep and sea in the last section, these are personified but not deified (though in Ugaritic mythology Mot/Death [cf. *mawet*] is a deity who contends with Baal). Abaddon occurs only five times in the Old Testament. In intertestamental literature (1 Enoch 20:2) it takes on the persona of an angel, also evidenced in the New Testament (Rev 9:11) where its Greek name is Apollyon. Despite those later developments, in the Old Testament Abaddon is a place name, sometimes personified as here, and not a demonic creature. Demonology is largely absent in the Old Testament; it developed in Hellenistic Judaism under the influence of the ancient Near Eastern and Persian worldviews.

Finally, the poem begins moving to its conclusion with the first reference to God in 28:23, who then becomes the subject of the remainder of the sentences. Previously the path to wisdom and its place of dwelling were unknown; now the poem affirms that God knows both path and place. God's relationship to wisdom is elaborated in 28:24–27.

"And he said to the human race, 'The fear of the Lord—that is wisdom, and to shun evil is understanding'" (28:28). Fear of the Lord is expressed in righteous behavior—turning away from evil, but not in appeasement of a deity presumed to respond to people based on the ways they meet his needs. In this way of thinking, fear of the Lord does not look for patronizing a needy god so that he will leave you alone; fear of the Lord looks for upright behavior—true ethical righteousness as Job has insisted.

Application. We express our fear of the Lord when we trust him with our circumstances—as uncomfortable or confusing as they may be. We trust him enough to accept that there need not be an explanation. We trust that his just nature is unassailable even though there is no identifiable justice in the circumstances in which we find ourselves. We trust that he has set up the system in the very best (= wisest) way possible even when we are suffering the consequences of a system broken by the fall. We trust his love for us, and we trust that even in our difficulties, he can show his love and strengthen us through the trials.

JOB 29:1–31:40

Original Meaning

Job 29:1–25. Never in Job's description of God's blessing in his life does he suggest that he deserved or had earned such treatment. In evaluating the nature of Job's special blessing, the reference to God's "intimate friendship" (Heb. *sod*) in 29:4 is of particular interest. Previously, Job used *sod* in relation to his friends who betrayed him (19:19), with whom he once shared confidences, counsel, and trust. Here in 29:4, this word is grammatically linked to the word for God.

In Job 29:7–10 and 21–23, Job describes the universal respect he received from leaders and the general populace. Job may well have been wise, kind, and upright, and his attractive qualities certainly may have contributed to the respect he enjoyed. Ultimately, however, his success and prosperity were the primary factors behind his social position. Presumably his wisdom and kindness did not change, but when he lost his prosperity, he lost respect from those around him.

Job's musings conclude by equating his high social standing to the role of a chief or king. The passage's imagery nuances the specific form of control he exercised: he "chose" their way, and he was like a king "among his troops" (29:25). These phrases suggest unquestioned loyalty from his followers and portray Job as a compassionate leader, not an oppressive tyrant over unwilling subjects.

Job 30:1–31. The scene shifts as Job's thoughts turn to his current state. His recent disasters have obliterated past glories, and Job details the shame that he now endures. He identifies his mockers in 30:1 and comments on their shiftless fathers in 30:1–8. It would be bad enough to be passively neglected by upstanding citizens, but it is far worse to be subject to abuse by the dregs of society.

Verse 15 concludes the exposition of Job's sad state. The word "terrors" (Heb. *ballahot*) was used in 18:14 when Bildad spoke of a "king of terrors" parallel to the "firstborn" of death (18:13) in a string of personifications (Terrors and Mot). If Terrors is indeed a personal entity, "night" in 30:17 may also be a personification parallel to Terrors, and either or both could serve as the subject of the masculine singular verbs in 30:18–19.

By 30:20–23 Job has indeed returned his attention to God. Once again, the text does not explicitly mention God, but it employs second person forms, and it is unlikely that Job here is beseeching personified Terrors and Night. Rather, in Job's perception, God has joined Terrors and Night in behaving toward Job as a chaos creature, as author of disorder and death.

The chapter ends with Job's summary reflections on his plight (30:27–31). Not only has God brought disaster, but he also refuses to act on Job's behalf or respond to his pleas. As a result, Job himself has become an outcast (30:29), like the worthless men described earlier in the chapter. He is now the mourner (30:31) with no one to comfort him.

Job 31:1–40. Job 31:1 opens with reference to a covenant. Job has made a covenant regarding his eyes—that much is clear. Job's covenant regarding his eyes cannot be interpreted as a commitment to asceticism because he already has a wife. The logical alternative is that the statement concerns the acquisition of a harem. A large harem was an indicator of power and status in the ancient world. Job eschews amassing multiple wives and concubines, and he characterizes this decision as a covenant regarding his eyes in order to underscore the point that he is not even "on the prowl." This avowal mirrors his statement in 31:24–25 that he is not absorbed in the pursuit of wealth. Job has undertaken neither a vow of poverty nor a vow of chastity, but rather avoids the obsessive pursuit of prestige.

Verse 2 leads into the chapter's effectual introduction. Job demonstrates his ongoing commitment to the retribution principle in his assertion that the wicked will suffer. Verse 4 combines the philosophical premise of 31:3 with the theological affirmation that God scrutinizes Job's actions. These two principles give Job's oath of innocence its bite: swearing a false oath, especially one so replete with claims, would be an evil worthy of punishment, and God is paying attention. Therefore, if God does not act against Job, Job may claim vindication.

The potential offense described in 31:9–12 concerns sexual purity. These two examples demonstrate the oath's application to a wide range of sexual misconduct and indicate that illicit sexual relationships, rather than merely any illicit sexual acts, are its target. The projected punishment is loss of legitimate sexual relationship. Another man would take Job's wife, and Job would become the injured party instead of the neighbor. The image of Job's wife "grinding another man's grain" (31:10) is a sexual euphemism: She will process what another man produces (i.e., children).

The wisdom saying that closes the section (31:12) bears resemblance to the one that encapsulates the message of Song of Songs: "Love is as strong as death, its jealousy unyielding as the grave. It burns like a blazing fire, like a mighty flame" (Song 8:6). Passion cannot easily be extinguished and, as the text indicates, will burn to Destruction. When Job states that such passion would have uprooted his harvest, he acknowledges that sexual misconduct would have undermined all his positive effort and blessing.

The broad range of activities described in 31:13–23 finds order within a rubric of justice. Per Job, the person who does justice shows compassion and performs acts of charity. His list of just behavior includes hearing grievances (31:13); meeting the needs of the poor (31:16a); comforting the bereaved (31:16b); and providing bed and board for the orphan (31:17–18), clothing for the needy (31:19–20), and legal defense for the powerless (31:21). Job took every available opportunity to enact compassion and justice, as anyone who is able should, and therefore he considered himself above reproach.

Attention now turns in 31:24–28 to sources of trust and security. Job raises two possibilities. The first is the familiar faith in material wealth. The second potential locus of trust is the gods, particularly the astral deities (sun and moon). The offense to which Job refers involves perception followed by a response of worship (31:27b). Job reminds God that he is obliged to take action if Job has committed any of these errors, including in this case "unfaithfulness" (31:28) to God. The word rendered "unfaithful" comes from the Hebrew root *khsh*, which in the Piel stem often connotes dissociating or disowning. Job identifies such behavior as sufficiently serious to necessitate retribution from God.

The overarching theme of 31:29–32, 38–40 may be termed "grace to outsiders"—outsiders being identified as those who are not members in good standing in the community. The text references various categories of people: enemies (31:29–30), strangers (31:31–32), and landowners (31:38–39).

Job 31:33–37 serves as a transition to the key verses of the chapter: Job's signature to his oath (31:35–37). In 31:33, Job comments that he has not hidden offense in the "fold of his garment" (author's translation); the word appears only here, so there is some uncertainty as to its exact meaning, but it is generally agreed that it refers to his clothing rather than physiology (e.g., NIV, "heart").

Job's oath reaches its grand finale in 31:35–37. In the absence of an advocate or judge, he sets his signature to the dossier of oaths. Job calls not only on El Shaddai (NIV "Almighty") to answer him (although he may not expect an answer), but also on anyone who wishes to contest his claims of innocence.

Job's imagery (bearing the indictment on his shoulder, donning it as a crown) also suggests that he will publicize any claims against him. The implication is Job's eagerness for the opportunity to respond to formal legal charges.

Job's final formal speech thus concludes on one of the book's high points. He has adamantly denied any wrongdoing and has taken a decisive (and risky) step to try to force a response from God. If God remains silent, Job, though undoubtedly still dissatisfied, could at least theoretically claim vindication (i.e., God did not strike him dead for a false oath) in order to facilitate social reintegration and restoration of his status and identity. Such an accomplishment would enable Job to restore his sense of coherence.

Application. What theological price are we willing to pay in order to achieve coherence in our lives? Do we prioritize our coherence above God's reputation? Do we give more concern to our reputation than God's reputation? If we truly believe what we say we believe about the Bible—that it is God's revelation of himself in which he offers an understanding of his character that is both right and true—then that biblical revelation takes precedence over our feeble attempts to discern coherence in our world and over any defense we may wish to make of our reputation.

JOB 32:1–37:24

Original Meaning

Elihu's Identity and Status (32:1–5). Who is Elihu? He does not come among the three friends introduced in 2:11. He is identified as a Buzite. Buz was a brother of Uz in Genesis 22:20–21, and thus Elihu is related to the Israelites as part of the international family of Abram. Such identification still distances Elihu from national Israelites. I might suggest that just as the friends represented the common logic of the ancient Near East, Elihu represents a more theologically sophisticated and nuanced opinion that might have predominated among the Israelites. Those Israelites who would have scoffed at the blatant attempts of the friends to prompt Job to action in order to restore his prosperity and favor with God would likely find Elihu's thinking more persuasive.

Elihu is seen as a raging, angry young man. The narrator indicates this four times in the text itself. The text is clear that this anger is not just because Job considers himself righteous. More specifically, Elihu is angry because Job regards his own righteousness more highly than he regards God's. Elihu directs his anger against the incompetence of the friends on two counts.

1. They have condemned Job without having found fault.
2. They had run out of arguments without having succeeded.

Elihu's Premise (32:6–22). In Job 32:8 Elihu asserts "But it is the spirit in a person, the breath of the Almighty, that gives them understanding." We might justifiably connect the breath of life/the Almighty with the image of God in Genesis 1, which could easily be associated with the human attribute of wisdom. In this sense, Elihu's statement can be viewed as merging anthropological concepts found in Genesis 1 and 2.

Elihu goes further, however, to suggest that this "breath of the Almighty" (Job 32:8) serves as a person's spirit (Heb. *ruah*). Elihu identifies the spirit particularly as the source of the wisdom that he declares he possesses. It is the spirit within him (not the Holy Spirit) that compels him in 32:18; he is energized and impatient to speak.

In 32:12–14 Elihu reiterates the failure of the friends to answer Job satisfactorily and proceeds to differentiate himself from the three friends.

In 32:15–22 Elihu's description of himself resembles Jeremiah's description of how he is compelled to deliver his prophetic message. We should not, however, conclude that Elihu is claiming a prophetic office or role.

Elihu concludes this part of his speech by insisting that he will not engage in flattery or show partiality. Readers will recall that when the friends began their speeches, they acknowledged the wisdom and righteousness of Job. Only as the dialogues continued did they begin accusing. Elihu is not inclined to such diplomacy; he jumps directly to confrontation. Just as Job continually insists on keeping his integrity intact, Elihu identifies his own guiding mantra as boldly proclaiming hard truths.

Elihu's Theory Statement (Job 33:1–33). "The Spirit of God has made me; the breath of the Almighty gives me life" (33:4). Even though the NIV capitalizes "Spirit," the parallel with "breath" suggests otherwise. The statement that the spirit "has made me" is parallel to the statement that God's breath "gives me life." God "made" him by giving him life and wisdom.

Even though Elihu does not directly quote any of Job's lines, Elihu fairly summarizes Job's overall position in 33:8–11. In 33:12 Elihu begins by warning Job that no one can "out-God" God (33:12). Elihu avers on principle that this can never be the case. This theological commitment is Elihu's strength, and it is what makes his position more acceptable than Job's.

Specifically, Elihu contends that God has not been silent; rather, Job has not been listening on the right frequency. He presents dreams and visions as the first examples of the media God uses for communication (33:15–18). Elihu adds physical pain to the list of divine communications in 33:19 along with distress. He identifies all of these communication strategies as having corrective intentions (33:17–18). In other words, Elihu considers these communications to be instructive and constructive rather than punitive. In this he offers a perspective not represented in the thinking of Job or his friends. Rather than restoring the sufferer to the path of life, however, such experiences often lead instead to depression and a decline toward death.

How can this discrepancy (decline toward death rather than restoration to life) be addressed and the cycle broken? Elihu offers his theory in 33:23–28, but it is not an easy one to sort out. Questions arise as to whether the messenger (NIV "angel") is an angelic mediator or a human one. I believe that Elihu is referring to his own role. He views himself as the messenger/mediator who is going to interpret Job's situation and advise him what he needs to.

If this is the case, rather than Job being provided the equivalent of a public defender (as he has requested numerous times), Elihu is serving in the role we might recognize as federal mediator to bring the sides to a mutual understanding. Nevertheless, Elihu is hardly the sort of mediator whom Job has been seeking.

Verdict: The Justice of God (Job 34:1–37). Elihu's articulation of Job's position in 34:5–9 is confusing. It is certainly true that Job considers himself innocent and maintains that God has denied him justice (34:5). He also considers his position to be truthful and the scourge of God to be disproportionate to his guilt (34:6). But what is Elihu referring to in 34:7–9? In 34:7 Job is said to "drink scorn." Job indulges in mockery as easily and frequently as he drinks water. In this view, rather than being mocked by others, Job is being accused of engaging in mockery of God. The content of this mockery would be the accusations that Elihu has already identified in 34:5. The shape of the metaphor would thus favor seeing Job as the object of scorn, whereas the context would favor seeing Job as the one who is scorning.

The issue has to be resolved by sorting out 34:8–9. It has certainly not been proven that Job "keeps company with evildoers" (34:8). Is 34:9 a claim that represents Job's thinking accurately? Verse 9 needs to be read as the complement of 34:8. Job has tacitly taken up company among the wicked when he concludes that associating with God does not produce personal benefit. Thus 34:8 is a logical deduction rather than an empirical observation; that is, Job is accused of aligning himself philosophically with evildoers by default when he sets himself against God.

In this deduction, Elihu is wrong. We should recall that the whole question of the book is whether Job's chosen behavior is based on potential gain. Job has "maintained his innocence" (27:1–6) by not pursuing regaining his prosperity. Elihu's statement assumes that if Job finds no benefit in throwing in his lot with God, he is therefore going to throw in his lot with the wicked. This would be a logical deduction only if Job's alignment with God were based on the expectation of benefit. Job in fact believes that it *should* work that way (i.e., the retribution principle should work), but the whole book is designed to demonstrate that Job is not *motivated* by that expectation. After all, that had been the challenger's claim from the beginning. This is important because in this sense, though Elihu is more justified in the sort of offense that he identifies in Job (self-righteousness), the accuracy of that assessment still does not compromise or undermine the central question of the book. Though Job *is* guilty of self-righteousness and disparaging God's justice (as Elihu contends), he is *not* guilty of pandering—following God only because of the benefit such a relationship brings. In this misrepresentation of Job, Elihu is no better than the friends. The difference is that he does not misrepresent God as the friends do. He is right about Job's offense; he is wrong in his inference about Job's motivation.

In 34:10–20 Elihu offers his basic presuppositions. In 34:10 he indicates that the justice of God is his bedrock. Elihu's insistence that God would not pervert justice echoes the words of Bildad's first speech (8:2). It is strong language, and in using it Elihu may be guilty of maintaining a simplistic tautology.

Elihu continues to wax eloquent on the loftiness of God in 34:13–15. He affirms that God is not a contingent being (not accountable or dependent on another). In theological terms, he is asserting God's aseity (his existence has its source only in himself). Conversely, human beings are absolutely and totally contingent (34:14–15). Consequently, we do not surpass God in his attributes, including that of his justice.

Elihu continues by posing a rhetorical question in 34:17, but it again reflects reductionism. No one has suggested that God hates justice. Job, for his part, has wondered how important justice is to God and whether he carries it out consistently. So again, hyperbole, though perhaps rhetorically acceptable, here weakens Elihu's case. Yet as he returns to expressing the attributes of God, his affirmations are legitimate. In 34:17b–20 Elihu again addresses human contingency in reference to the most powerful humans. People cannot hold God accountable (34:17b), but it is God who condemns wicked rulers, shows no partiality to the wealthy, and exacts punishment. It is true that God acts in this way. The question that Elihu fails to consider is whether his policies are defined by and grounded in such involvement. Does God have options?

What we are seeing is that just as Job has drawn false inferences about governance from his understanding of God (inferences about the centrality and execution of the retribution principle), Elihu is drawing other inferences (based on his reinterpretation of the retribution principle). Though both have a basically sound comprehension of the attributes of God, both are wrong (in different ways) about what inferences can therefore be drawn.

In 34:21–30 we find the next stage of Elihu's case for God. He begins by affirming God's omniscience, particularly as it relates to his omnipresence. God has access to every place, and thus, in his role as judge, he has immediate access to all pieces of evidence.

In 34:29–30 Elihu turns his attention to an issue that is closer to home. Up to this point he has been talking about God taking responsibility to maintain justice, but what if God remains silent? Elihu maintains that God has a right to such a silence and thus implies that Job is presumptuous to be critical of God on this count.

Having offered a defense of God's apparent indifference (which addresses indirectly one of Job's major complaints), Elihu now proposes a hypothetical course of action (34:31–33). In this sequence Elihu has characterized Job accurately in terms that are consistent with the dialogue section of the book. As Job has refused to repent, Elihu makes his case as he asks Job what he expects God to do (34:33). Elihu implies that he has expressed Job's expectations in this confrontation and thus insinuates that Job's request is impious. Though Elihu has characterized Job's posture correctly, has he rightly identified Job's expectation? What *does* Job expect to result from the legal confrontation that he requests?

Elihu's assessment is that Job wants God to "reward" him on Job's terms. This posture of Job's is what Elihu then identifies in 34:36–37 as he summarizes what he perceives to be Job's offense. That offense is not something that occurred prior to his downfall, but it has become evident in his response to his downfall. Elihu's call, then, is: "Stand down, Job!"

Transcendence of God (Job 35:1–16). Elihu's summary of Job's putative position presents Job as expecting to benefit from his righteous behavior (35:3). As I indicated earlier, that may indeed be Job's expectation, but that does not mean it is his motivation. If, however, we could imagine Job's response to Elihu (which he never gives), he might object that he is *not* looking for profit or gain from not sinning; he *is* expecting that he would be protected from major devastations. The semantic distinction might be that any profit Job might expect would be in protection, not in material prosperity. Argue as we may, however, it is Elihu's rhetorical style to be reductionist and to engage in hyperbole.

Elihu's first point of reply is that any human being's righteousness or wickedness has no effect on God whatsoever. In these affirmations Elihu offers a concise refutation of the Great Symbiosis. This symbiosis is benefit-focused: The gods reap benefits from the labor of humans, and the humans reap benefits from the favor of the gods.

In 35:8–13 Elihu contrasts two different ways of approaching God. The first involves prayers for relief from oppression (35:9); the second involves a search for God and recognition of his grace as he teaches wisdom (35:10–11). Elihu suggests that God is not responsive to the former (35:12–13). In this he suggests that people should be more interested in coming to know God better rather than on trying to get God to solve their problems. He should be the object of our inquiry rather than the object of our complaints. He is not at our beck and call and cannot be called to heel like a dog—he is our *Maker*!

As Elihu thus emphasizes God's transcendence over his immanence (introduced in 35:5), he suggests that we need to show a little more recognition of our place. We should think in terms of responding to God rather than God responding to us. God responds according to his own purposes and timing. People cannot call him to account for the way he interacts with them nor to criticize him in accordance with their own expectations. In Elihu's view Job has diminished God by the way he thinks about him.

Summary and Closing Remarks—The Acts of God (Job 36:1–37:24). As Elihu introduces his last speech, he again indicates that he views himself as speaking on behalf of God. Elihu appears to have an elevated view of himself (36:3a; 36:4b). When he describes himself as "perfect [in] knowledge" (36:4b), he is only saying that his opinions are consistent and coherent.

The view of God that Elihu offers balances the ideas that though God is inexorable, he does not therefore simply run roughshod over humans indiscriminately. He has a determined posture and steadfast policy regarding his treatment of humanity, though that does not mean he is predictable. Again, Elihu identifies this divine policy as the retribution principle—the wicked are punished while the righteous are rewarded (36:6–7). He elaborates by asserting that not only does God act according to this principle, but he also communicates (36:9–10), thus giving people opportunity to change their ways and their circumstances (36:11–12). As before, God's character is accurately perceived, but his policies are misrepresented.

After characterizing the wicked as unresponsive to God's promptings (36:13–14), Elihu makes a bold transition from third-person plural forms to second-person singular in 36:16–21 to draw out the implications for Job personally. Elihu portrays Job as disinclined to accept the generous offer of God to resolve his situation. In Elihu's mind, Job has demonstrated this disinclination by refusing to back down and adopt a submissive posture before God.

In summary, Elihu suggests that if Job seeks to regain wealth and power through evil, he will simply be exchanging his current affliction for another one. It could not be fairly said that Job *chose* his current affliction, but if turning to evil is the choice he makes, he *will* be choosing the affliction that will inevitably result.

The description of God's cosmic power in 36:22–37:13 is one of the most eloquent in the Hebrew Bible. When Elihu declares that God's years are unsearchable, we may prefer to translate the Hebrew *mispar* (NIV "number") as "account" because the *count* of the years is ultimately insignificant. That is, can God's biography be written? Elihu's few meager observations scarcely begin this report.

Now we come to Elihu's recitation of some of the mighty acts of God, mostly related to precipitation, thunder, and lightning. His description of precipitation in 36:27–28 has drawn some interesting comments over the years. In Elihu's comments he is describing divine action not material mechanisms.

Elihu's discourse on the weather continues in 36:29–37:5 with discussion of thunder and lightning. The focus is still on God's control of these phenomena and the evidence they provide of his rule (36:31). His rule is expressed in providing the food supply necessary for survival. It is by means of providing or withholding food that God brings justice on the people.

This reminds us that the focus of Elihu's discussion is on God's justice. Elihu illustrates the way this unfathomable instrument of judgment works in 37:6–13. Elihu concludes this section by returning to his main point: Through this activity God punishes or shows his favor—weather is an instrument of his justice (37:13).

Elihu's speech concludes as he addresses Job directly again in 37:14–24 and urges him to consider the "wonders" (37:14) of God. Elihu's posing of rhetorical questions to prompt Job's recognition of God's great works in nature (37:15–16) foreshadows the approach of God in the next chapter.

As Elihu concludes his speech, he confronts Job with a question that Job himself has considered (to paraphrase): "What in the world do you think you would say to him if you got your request of a day in court?" (cf. 37:19). Elihu wonders why anyone would ask for the inevitable trouble that would result (37:20). When God approaches, his majesty is overwhelming. Elihu's description of this in 37:22 anticipates Yahweh's entrance a few verses later. Elihu, however, is mistaken in his assertion that God is beyond human reach, though he is right that God is exalted in power (37:23). God is going to demonstrate that he is both beyond human reach (transcendent) yet accessible in his immanence.

As interpreted in the NIV, Elihu ends with a rhetorical question (37:24). His words are, however, more of a statement—a final conclusion that God cannot be swayed by those who would qualify as the wisest among humanity (whether in the estimation of others or in their self-assessment). People fear (= respect) him because they are no match for him.

Application. Elihu's opinion was that when anyone thinks of God as paying close attention to the details of our lives and micromanaging our circumstances, we are giving ourselves too much importance and trivializing God's role in the cosmos. Yet what is the alternative? Do we believe that God is not really involved in the details and is only engaged in the larger issues? Here lies mystery. While we can err on the deism extreme or on the micromanagement extreme, we can also err by thinking we can sort it all out and figure out how God works or does not work. The error of "God too small" is committed when we misrepresent at one extreme or the other, but it is also committed when we think we can fully describe the nature of his involvement. To believe that his work could so easily be defined is to reduce him to something manageable. We must be content with mystery.

JOB 38:1–41:34

Original Meaning

Introduction (38:1–3). We must first notice that it is *Yahweh* who speaks in 38:1. This marks a shift in terms because throughout the dialogues and discourses of the book, the deity has most often been identified as El Shaddai ("Almighty") or Elohim ("God"). The use of Yahweh in the prologue and now in the divine speeches may well have significance, but it is not transparent what it might be.

A second observation is that Yahweh comes in the storm. The storm sets the tone for the nature of the theophanic speeches of Yahweh. Yahweh is not simply taking up the role of wisdom instructor; the tone of his words should be understood as a rebuke. The storm does not simply convey his power; it conveys his wrath.

Consequently, as Yahweh characterizes Job, we see a clear distinction from the open admiration expressed in the prologue. The contrast is not contradictory but suggests that although Job's conduct is above reproach, his understanding is flawed. Yahweh is about to offer a corrective. The reprimand takes the form of an examination as Yahweh turns the tables. Instead of Job playing inquisitor, a role he has taken throughout the book, Yahweh will ask the questions.

Macrocosmic Operation (Job 38:4–38). In these verses Yahweh expresses his control, which comprises his power and wisdom. He communicates about macrocosmic operations using the terminology and understanding of the ancient world—Job's world. As is true throughout the Bible, God communicates to his people on the basis of their understanding when it comes to scientific matters. It is primarily in theological matters that he pushes them beyond their cultural understandings.

We should pause for further comment on a few of the details of this section. In 38:7 we encounter one of the few references in the Old Testament to the *beney elohim* (literally, "sons of God; NIV "angels"). In our brief discussion of the term in Job 1:6, the sons of God were seen as members of the divine council. Here we have additional information that presents them as parallel to "the morning stars" (38:7). This association between the members of the divine council and the stars also occurs in ancient Near Eastern literature. In this way, Yahweh's speech reflects common thinking in the ancient world. The difference is that in Israelite theology, the divine council is not composed of gods with whom Yahweh shares divine authority, though he may at times delegate tasks to them.

A second issue of particular note arises in 38:25–27. Throughout the book, Job has assumed the retribution principle and therefore has embraced the belief that the world operates according to justice. The flaw in this logic is that one cannot move automatically from the justice of God to the necessity of the world's operations being just. Yahweh makes this point in 38:25–27, where he notes that rain falls in places where no one lives. If justice reigned in the cosmos, rain, the provider of blessing and fertility, would target the deserving. Although we affirm God's control of the forces of nature, we don't believe that he micromanages the system with justice in mind for each moment's activity. Thus, Job's perception of the cosmos is undermined, and his reliance on the retribution principle crumbles under scrutiny.

Finally, a word should be said about the constellations. We have already discussed in some measure the constellations in relation to Job 9. Mesopotamian cosmology held that the constellations and their movements were used as a source of omens and could thereby bring favor or disaster. These verses accordingly ask whether Job is able to bring about justice through the manipulation of constellations that theoretically determine fortunes on earth.

In conclusion, this section about macrocosmic operations intends to show that Job is incapable of taking control of the cosmos to bring about justice. He has overestimated his ability to devise a cogent philosophy of the operation of the world and has underestimated the complexity of the system. Job has questioned God's design and execution, so in this section God focuses on Job's faulty understanding of design and his inability to execute.

Microcosmic Operations (Job 38:39–39:30). In the ancient world, it was a common academic exercise to make lists of plants, animals, stars, and many other things. Such lists were a type of wisdom, so it is no surprise to find a list such as this in a biblical wisdom book.

Though each of these animals could be discussed in turn, space demands that we narrow our focus. The most problematic section is the one addressing the ostrich (39:13–18). Some have objected that Yahweh's description does not accurately portray ostrich behavior, but it should be noted that the comments in the text deal with perception. Yahweh does not say that the ostrich was given wisdom that humans cannot understand—a different kind of wisdom, as it were—but that he did not endow the ostrich with wisdom at all. Yahweh is adopting the perspective common to humans at the time rather than making universally verifiable statements about the ontological nature of ostriches.

Job's First Response (Job 40:1–14). In 40:1–2 Yahweh concludes his first discourse by again demanding an answer from Job. Job's reply (40:4–5) is appropriately one of submission and humility, but he stops short of recanting. He is speechless and has adopted a stance of neutrality: "I will say no more" (40:5). Job has been cowed and intimidated—an outcome he had anticipated as early as 9:3 and which was not without a level of validity—but he has not yet understood the extent of his folly.

As in 38:3, Yahweh opens in 40:7 by challenging Job to prepare to answer as one who has wisdom. In this second challenge, however, Job is identified as one who has discredited Yahweh's justice (40:8) in contrast to one who has questioned the wisdom of his design (38:2). Furthermore, Yahweh accuses Job of having defamed Yahweh in order to justify himself. We have noted from the beginning that Job considered his own righteousness the only factor of which he could be certain. Yahweh is taking Job to task for not valuing God's justice more than his own righteousness.

Yahweh offers a challenge: Let Job take up control of the cosmos using the retribution principle that he has adopted and imposed on Yahweh. If Job were "God for a day," could he execute the retribution principle consistently in bringing justice?

In God's challenge, if Job could don the mantle of divine power and demonstrate that his concept of just cosmic operation could actually be sustained, his righteousness would be vindicated and he would be "saved." He must demonstrate that the system he envisions (and to which he wants God held accountable) can actually work. Only in such a system would suffering be taken as evidence of unrighteousness.

Cosmic Fringe Operations: Yahweh's Second Speech (40:15–41:34). In this section the discussion is no longer about Job being God for a day or Job's limitations. Instead, the focus moves to how God's system should properly be seen. The discussion shifts from reprimand to instruction, from what Job cannot do to what God has done. In the dialogues, Job wonders why God is treating him like a chaos creature (7:12); in the discourses, Job suggests that God is acting like a chaos creature (ch. 30). Here in God's second set of speeches, Yahweh picks up both of Job's charges and alters Job's fundamental assumption: Chaos creatures are, in fact, part of God's ordered world.

The passages about Behemoth and Leviathan appropriately follow Yahweh's challenge to Job to bring low all the proud (40:11), for Leviathan is identified as the king over all who are proud (41:34). It is no surprise that Behemoth and Leviathan evince connections to both the world of nature and the world of myth. These associations make them recognizable to the audience and inform their use. In the end, however, it is not the roots of the ideas or the associations they may evoke that are most important; it is their literary use in Job.

Job is compared to Behemoth (40:15). Job, like Behemoth, is the first of God's works (cf. 15:7) and withstands all turbulence. God brings his sword against Job (40:19) and by a snare he penetrates Job's anger (40:24). Yahweh does not speak of Job doing anything *to* Behemoth, but when the discussion switches to Leviathan, the first eight verses use the second person. I therefore suggest that Leviathan is to be compared to Yahweh (41:3, 10–11, 34)—he won't beg you for mercy and won't speak with gentle words; you can't put him on a leash, subdue him, or rouse him. These all discuss what *Job* can't do to Leviathan, and they are also things that Job must learn he cannot do to Yahweh.

If this is what the text is doing, it does not matter what relationship these creatures have to zoology or mythology; rather, the point of the text lies elsewhere. Yahweh's message would be clear: "Job, be strong and content like Behemoth, and don't think that you can domesticate or subdue me any more than you can Leviathan." Job needs to have more respect for Yahweh. Yahweh now *is* addressing Job as if he (Job) were a chaos creature (cf. 7:12), and he *is* likening himself to a chaos creature (cf. ch. 30)—but all within the confines of his ordered world.

The point is not that God can subdue Leviathan and therefore he can subdue Job—that was never in question. Rather, the passage indicates that since Job cannot bring Leviathan to heel, he cannot expect to domesticate Yahweh.

Application. The book of Job is not intended to bring comfort to the suffering, but to bring understanding that might prevent us from simply blaming God. The alternative is to trust God, and the book gives us a focus for our faith. Too often we focus our faith on believing that God will heal, relieve our suffering, or protect us from pain. Sometimes our faith lies in the belief that God will somehow come to us and give us explanations. Other times we place our faith in our ability to force our experiences into a coherent, meaningful narrative. All these approaches are unrealistic. Our faith should be directed toward embracing an all-wise God and asking him for help to live well before him regardless of our plight in this world that continues to display both order and disorder.

We should recognize, then, that the book of Job does not seek to explain God to us—such an endeavor would be impossible, as the book demonstrates. The book instead exposes our false and misguided ideas about God, the world, and suffering. It does not replace the rejected concepts with a comprehensive list of particulars but simply gives direction for thinking. If we can avoid the standard list of misperceptions and begin moving in the right direction, the book will have achieved its purpose.

That does not mean that there are never reasons for suffering that might need to be recognized. Sometimes we suffer the consequences of bad choices, and we need to acknowledge that and make changes. Overall, however, we are not encouraged to immerse ourselves in anguish over what may have caused our suffering. We definitely should not assume that if we are suffering, we must have done something to deserve it. People are often prone to respond to suffering with the question, "Why me?" I would propose that it is when we have *not* suffered or when we are unexpectedly granted *relief* from suffering that we should pose the puzzled question, "Why me?"

If we shouldn't expect explanations or relief, what should we expect? We should expect that God is able to sustain us through suffering and even strengthen us through it. We please and honor God by trusting him in faith. We find purpose in suffering if we allow it to draw us closer to him in dependence instead of driving us further from him (though this should not be confused with ultimate cause or treated as a reason). We serve and honor God by being people of faith and helping others who might also be suffering to find the same solutions.

JOB 42:1–17

Original Meaning

Job's Second Response (42:1–6). Job acknowledges God's wisdom and power (42:2) then admits the validity of God's accusation that he (Job) has obscured knowledge and spoken ignorantly (42:3). He concedes that he spoke of things too "wonderful" to know (42:3).

In 42:5 Job distinguishes between secondhand experience ("my ears had heard") and firsthand experience ("now my eyes have seen"); in light of the comparison, he "despises" and "repents" (42:6). The first verb ("despises") connotes considering something or someone as nothing or as having no value. The second verb ("repents") should be distinguished from others that can be translated "repent." It would not be misguided to see in Job's statements that he regrets his previous statements, his characterization of God, his presumptuous belief in his own understanding, and his arrogant challenges. Nevertheless, his statement here focuses elsewhere. "Repent" in 42:6 means to reconsider something or to put something out of mind—to forget all about it. In this verse, that "something" is Job's dust and ashes. The preposition cannot be read as Job repenting "in" dust and ashes; rather, he "reconsiders dust and ashes," or "puts dust and ashes out of his mind." He has thereby announced the end to his mourning as he has accepted his reality.

Narrative Epilogue (42:7–17). The epilogue comprises two parts: the reprimand and reconciliation of Job's friends (42:7–9) and the restoration of Job's prosperity (42:10–16). After God expresses his anger at the three friends, he twice identifies the reason for his displeasure: "You have not spoken the truth about me, as my servant Job has" (42:7, 8).

It is difficult to understand why Job seems to receive exoneration for his statements about God, particularly in light of the harsh indictment that immediately preceded this section. In contrast to his friends, Job did speak what is right (or valid) in certain ways, even though in other ways he misspoke. I believe this offers the most profitable direction for interpretation. Although Job spoke more truly than his friends, God does not exonerate his behavior as a whole.

In 42:8 God states that if Job offers a sacrifice and prays for the friends, "I will accept his prayer and not deal with you according to your folly." This translation avoids a problem evident in the Hebrew text, which has no second person pronoun attached to the noun folly (*nebalah*). The Hebrew thus appears to require the translation "lest I commit folly in my treatment of you."

Can God act this way? In light of preceding chapters, we must answer in the affirmative, for a reversal of norms is precisely the manner in which God has acted toward Job: God brought suffering on that righteous man even though convention dictated that he should prosper. Here, then, God threatens that Job's friends are not immune to similar treatment. They too are vulnerable to loss and misery, contrary to their confidence in the retribution principle.

Finally, Job offers a prayer for his friends after they have offered the requisite sacrifices. This action serves as an *inclusio* with chapter 1, where Job offered sacrifices for his children. When Job acted as priest for his children, his behavior revealed flaws in his theology and exposed him to questions regarding his motivations, which led to his suffering. In contrast, when Job acts as intercessor for his friends at the end of the book, he does so in reflection of God's compassion not in suspicion of God's unreasonable character; as a result, this behavior leads to Job's restoration (42:10). Job conducted his former rituals in order to hedge against the possibility that his children had cursed God; now their rituals and his prayer are required because his friends did not speak what was right about Yahweh—a fact, not a vague suspicion.

Application. I am not convinced that we should view suffering as "God's will," by which I mean that it is not his desire for us to suffer. God desires that we learn perseverance and wisdom and that we mature. Suffering is part of the disorder in the world and God can bring good from it. Disorder has remained part of the cosmos as part of God's plan. But instead of responding to this disorder righteously, we have responded to this disorder with sin, which sometimes results in suffering. We should not rejoice over our sin and over the chaos and suffering that ensue as a result. Positive results can follow sin when we recognize it, suffer the consequences, repent, and thereby grow strong against it—but that does not make sin God's will.

We should not think of suffering as God's way to teach us a lesson and that our continued suffering means we have not yet learned the intended lesson. God can teach lessons through our suffering, but we should not think of it as his will to do so. Likewise, we should not think in terms of "blaming the world." We must resist finding a focus for blame, for that is not the point.

God's plan for history and the cosmos entails a gradual process of expanding order. While that process remains incomplete, we cope with the disorder that remains. God could have chosen to act differently, but it is not our role to second-guess God or to suggest better options, as the book of Job has taught us. When we distinguish between God's permissive will and his perfect sovereign will, we reflect our desire to craft theology to justify our experience. Such systematizations run the risk of committing the same fault as Job and his friends: reducing God's policies to a simple formula.

PSALMS

INTRODUCTION TO PSALMS

The composition of the individual psalms covers a period of more than eight hundred years. Add to this the time involved in gathering and shaping the Psalter collection and you have almost a millennium. The book of Psalms then represents the end result of a long history of composition, transmission, collection, and arrangement. It contains some of the earliest and some of the latest texts in the Old Testament and is in a sense a microcosm of the whole Old Testament corpus.

Scholars generally agree today that most of the psalms (some even say all) were composed, not for private prayer, but for public performance in the temple worship of ancient Israel. If this is so, then even the individual psalms were not composed simply for private use but were intended to be presented—performed if you will—within community worship. Some of the psalm headings even include mention of specific worship settings.

It appears that the psalm headings developed over a considerable period of time. Certain elements—probably the liturgical instructions—were appended quite early, while others (designation of authors and historical notices) continued to be added over time. If the evidence of the Qumran scrolls suggests continued fluidity in psalm collection and the addition of psalm headings, then this process does not seem to have been completed before the mid-first century AD.

Although the Psalter is often considered a collection of 150 separate psalms, closer inspection, especially of the headings or superscriptions, suggests otherwise. At some point, perhaps late in its compositional history, the Hebrew Psalter was divided into five "books": Psalms 1–41; 42–72; 73–89; 90–106; and 107–50. The recognition of a five-book arrangement to the Psalter is not a recent development in scholarship but extends far back in history.

BOOK OUTLINE

I. Book 1: Establishment of Davidic Covenant (1:1–41:13)
II. Book 2 (42:1–72:20)
  A. Davidic Covenant Continues (42:1–71:24)
  B. The Hope of the Davidic Kings (72:1–20)
III. Book 3 (73:1–89:52)
  A. Crisis for the Community (Asaph Psalms (73:1–83:18))
  B. A Focus on Zion (84:1–89:52)
IV. Book 4 (90:1–106:48)
  A. Introduction to Book 4 (90:1–92:15)
  B. The Enthronement Psalms (93:1–99:9)
  C. Responses to the Kingship of God (100:1–106:48)
V. Book 5 (107:1–150:6)
  A. The Return from Exile (107:1–43)
  B. A Davidic Collection (108:1–110:7)
  C. Calls to Praise God (111:1–112:10)
  D. The Egyptian Hallel (113:1–118:29)
  E. A Meditation on the Torah's Centrality for All of Life (119:1–176)
  F. The Songs of Ascent (120:1–134:3)
  G. An Appendix to the Songs of Ascent (135:1–136:26)
  H. An Imprecation against the Enemies of Israel (137:1–9)
  I. A Final Davidic Collection (138:1–145:21)
  J. The Final Hallel (146:1–150:6)

PSALM 1:1–6

Original Meaning

Guilt by Association (1:1–2). The blessed man is one *who does not walk . . . stand . . . sit (1:1)*, which describes a negative example of a lifestyle to be avoided, not emulated.

Delight . . . in the law of the LORD (1:2). Most likely torah ("law") here implies the traditional commandments of God in *the* Torah as well as the life-giving guidance God gives elsewhere in Scripture. Psalm 1 stresses careful, diligent attention to Scripture, seeking God's guidance for life.

Fruitful Living (1:3–4). The image of the tree is known from the similar passage in Jeremiah 17:7–8.

Ultimate Consequences (1:5–6). The reader is presented with a choice: the way of righteousness that God oversees or the way of wickedness that will ultimately perish.

Application. When we meditate on and memorize the psalms, we are planting our roots deeply into the life-giving water of God's word. This is the same "living water" that Jesus offers to the Samaritan woman at the well (John 4).

The power of the psalms is not that they present us with a neat, theologically consistent package we can assent to (or reject!) intellectually. Instead, they confront us with the messiness and conflict of the life of faith lived out in the real word of body, mind, and spirit. In so doing they allow God's word to penetrate deeply to "dividing soul and spirit, joints and marrow," laying bare our inward contradictions, yet at the same time encouraging us to "approach God's throne of grace with confidence, so that we may receive mercy and find grace to help us in our time of need" (Heb 4:12–16).

PSALM 2:1–12

Original Meaning. Psalm 2 is the first example in the Psalter of the category of psalms known as "royal psalms"—compositions primarily concerned with the human kings of Judah who understood themselves to be uniquely authorized and empowered as Yahweh's adopted sons.

International Conspiracy (2:1–3). The opening section of Psalm 2 describes an international conspiracy against the authority of Yahweh and his "anointed" representative (2:2c). They have no allegiance to him and are depicted here as fomenting rebellion to cast off his overlordship.

Divine Response (2:4–6). Yahweh sees these human beings, knows their plots and pretensions, and is unconcerned. Divine laughter turns to "anger" and scoffing to "rebuke" (2:5) as Yahweh himself pronounces judgment on the assembled conspirators.

Covenant of Kingship (2:7–9). The king takes center stage to testify in his own voice to the authorizing covenant established between Yahweh and the king. The background of this relationship is clearly the Davidic covenant described in 2 Samuel 7:4–16. The nations are to become the king's "inheritance" (2:8). The image is one of divine judgment but also emphasizes the fragility of the seemingly great and powerful nations of the world.

Warning to the Nations (2:10–12). The narrator returns in the final section of the psalm to issue a stern warning to the rebellious kings—a warning founded on the preceding description of the covenant that exists between Yahweh and his anointed king.

Application. Whenever we buy into the world's way of placing self before all else, we become "the nations," negating the work of Christ to bring us into the family of God.

PSALM 3:1–8

Original Meaning

Surrounded by the Enemy (3:1–2). One can almost sense the panic as the psalmist sees only the multitude of enemies about to overwhelm.

A Shield Around Me (3:3–4). The psalmist responds with a cry of his own directed to God. The cry of confidence has the appearance of hindsight gained after the fact of actual deliverance.

The Realization of Deliverance (3:5–8). The final segment of the psalm exudes an almost eerie sense of confidence and security. Yahweh is the unshakable source of human dignity and honor.

Application. Sometimes when we are under attack, we can begin to question our own worth to others, to ourselves, even to God. At moments like these we need to tap into the vision that proceeds from God and can only be made real in the heart of each individual by God himself lifting up the head of the person under attack.

PSALM 4:1–8

Original Meaning

Invocation and Critique (4:1–2). The opening section of Psalm 4 is divided into a plea directed to Yahweh (4:1) and a rebuke directed to the psalmist's own people (4:2). It assumes a legal setting where God renders a verdict regarding the actions of the parties in relation to what is expected.

Wise Counsel (4:3–5). Having condemned the opponents for seeking a solution to their difficulties by worshiping false gods, the psalmist now offers sage counsel for appropriate response in the circumstances. It seems clear that the psalmist assumes the opponents are within the covenant community of Israel when he advises them to "offer the sacrifices of the righteous" (4:5).

Expression of Confidence (4:6–8). The final segment of the psalm turns from critique and counsel of the opponents to the psalmist's own affirmation of confident joy in the provision of Yahweh. The "who" (4:6) of this sentence clearly refers to the multiple gods and goddesses of the pagan pantheon. In contrast, the psalmist trusts in the steadfast love of Yahweh—a love that never ceases.

Application. This psalm is a call to practicing the presence of God.

PSALM 5:1–12

Original Meaning

Opening Plea (5:1–3). The psalmist begins with a trio of imperatives in synonymously parallel phrases directing God's attention to the psalmist's "words" (5:1). The psalmist's speech is a loud "cry for help" (5:2) rather than any other form of quiet meditation or reflection.

The Character of God (5:4–6). The psalmist finds the grounds of confidence to approach Yahweh in the very character of God himself. These two verses emphasize God's absolute rejection of evil and those who commit evil acts.

Hope for Deliverance (5:7–8). Yahweh's holiness has two sides. Not only is it incompatible with evil; it is also characterized by relentless goodness. From the beginning, God's only intent was and still is to bless his creation. Judgment and mercy, therefore, are not two competing characteristics of Yahweh but are two inseparable consequences of his holiness. Relentless goodness is the flip side of incompatibility with evil.

The Benefit of the Righteous (5:11–12). While the enemies will fall under the weight of their own rebellious plotting, those who revere Yahweh (5:7) and make him their refuge will "be glad" and "ever sing for joy" (5:11). Trust is more than a temporary desire for protection or security. It evidences a willingness to commit one's whole destiny to God. If there is any primary message here, it is that who God essentially is and how humans respond to that essence determines what humans ultimately receive from his hand.

Application. Those who take refuge in God find hope in God's holiness both because he is incompatible with evil *and* because he is relentlessly good.

PSALM 6:1–10

Original Meaning

Invocation of God (6:1–5). The first subsection (6:1) pleads that Yahweh will not prove himself right at the psalmist's expense. The second subsection of the first unit (6:2–3) changes from the request that Yahweh refrain to entreaties for divine action. The third subsection (6:4–5) contains the word "turn" (6:4), regularly used to describe a change of action or direction. The mercy of Yahweh could lead him to respond with a revocation of decreed judgment. If Yahweh continues to "forget" the faithful in this life, there will be no one left above ground to praise him!

The Torment of Suffering (6:6–7). The extended suffering occasioned by Yahweh's delay of action has reduced the psalmist to nocturnal episodes of uncontrollable weeping and anguish.

Confrontation of Foes (6:8–10). Confrontation and rejection of the psalmist's enemies (6:8a, 10) bracket a confidence in Yahweh (6:8b–9). Yahweh will deliver the psalmist, and the opponents will receive a public comeuppance.

Application. We must realize with the psalmists that the experiences of personal pain are all evidences that we live in a disordered world that is at present far less than the world God created. It is a world that in many ways defies the good intention of the creator.

PSALM 7:1–17

Original Meaning

Appeal to Yahweh (7:1–2). The psalmist is in desperate straits and feels pursued by ravenous beasts who threaten to tear him apart. He takes refuge in Yahweh. Placing oneself in the protective care of Yahweh is foundation enough for confident hope for deliverance from the savage attacks of the psalmist's enemies.

Protestation of Innocence (7:3–5). The passage is divided into an "if" section (7:3–4), describing possible wrongs of which the psalmist claims innocence, and a "then" section (7:5), where consequences of proven guilt are laid out. The kind of guilt envisioned stains the hands and may suggest some ritual hand-washing ceremony to demonstrate purity.

Yahweh Called to Judgment (7:6–9). Having established innocence through this protestation, the psalmist now turns to Yahweh in his role of righteous judge. With an initial string of imperatives, he calls on Yahweh to arise in righteous indignation and to assume his seat as judge. Surrounded by the assembly of all peoples, Yahweh, exalted overall, is ready to hear the case and render righteous judgment.

Yahweh Prepares for Judgment (7:10–13). The God who judges righteously also metes out the consequences of that judgment. The psalmist describes how Yahweh now responds as a "shield" and defender for those proven to be righteous (the "upright in heart," 7:10). He also prepares to mete out judgment on the wicked. The psalmist clearly has personal enemies in view here.

The Fate of the Wicked (7:14–16). The psalmist moves on to describe the fate of the wicked themselves. Heaping up words relating to conception and birth, the psalmist scorns the one who is "pregnant with evil" (6:14a) and trouble. Such a one, saturated with evil, gives birth to a "lie" or "falsehood" (6:14b, NIV "disillusionment"). The enemy ultimately falls into the trapping pit prepared for the psalmist.

Concluding Praise (7:17). Yahweh is to be praised because he is a righteous judge who can as a result be trusted to exonerate and uphold the righteous while punishing the wicked.

Application. How comforting it is to think of God as our refuge. Yet often, precisely when we need that refuge most, we feel unable or unworthy to enter in. As a result, we do not take the steps to healing and wholeness that God provides.

PSALM 8:1–9

Original Meaning

The Thematic Framework (8:1a). The "name" of God lays claim to divine authority. Earth and heaven mark the two extremes of all that God has created and declare all to be permeated with the majestic name of Yahweh.

The Creative Power of Yahweh (8:1b–2). Toddlers and nursing children are particularly dependent on others. The psalmist uses this image to create a dramatic contrast with the presumed power of those who oppose God and his faithful ones.

Human Frailty (8:3–4). The psalmist begins with awed wonder at the creative power of Yahweh displayed in "the heavens" (8:3) and is then drawn to reflect on the significance of earthbound humans (8:4).

Empowerment and Responsibility (8:5–8). Humans, who can seem so powerless and small in the scheme of things, are invested with stupendous worth and responsibility by the creator.

The Thematic Framework Revisited (8:9). At the beginning our praise began by affirming the magnificence of the creator. At the end, we stand in awe at the unexpected grace that has elevated his human works to unimaginable heights.

Application. This psalm opens a new window on who we really are. Although we see ourselves as weak and insignificant, God sees us as only a little lower than he himself.

PSALM 9:1–20 AND 10:1–18

Original Meaning. Psalms 9 and 10 introduce us to a phenomenon encountered several times: Two adjacent psalms seem to have been read together as a single composition. Most often this special relationship is marked out by the second psalm lacking a heading while the heading of the first psalm does double duty for both.

Anticipation of Thanksgiving (9:1–3). It is clear from the body of the psalm that the psalmist is still suffering; yet the psalm begins with this expression of confident thanksgiving. We get to see the whole process of suffering, plea, deliverance, and thanksgiving telescoped in a single composition.

Judge of the Nations (9:4–8). Verse 4 acts as a hinge, with 9:4a offering a concluding reason for the psalmist's opening praise ("you have upheld my right"), while at the same time 9:4b introduces the theme of Yahweh as "righteous judge" (9:4) that dominates the following section. The psalmist uses perfect verb forms to describe Yahweh's activity of judgment as already decided but awaiting enforcement in the future. The dominant emphasis in these verses is on Yahweh's character as a *righteous judge*. In a series of parallel phrases, the psalmist describes the divine judgment on the opposing nations.

A Refuge for the Oppressed (9:9–14). Confident that Yahweh is a righteous judge who eternally sits ready to pass judgment for the righteous and against the wicked, the psalmist is ready to proclaim him as trustworthy refuge and stronghold for those who are "oppressed" and "in times of trouble" (9:9). The same Hebrew word appears behind the NIV translation for both "refuge" and "stronghold" in this verse. This word describes a high, rocky spot that is inaccessible and thus provides protection from encroaching enemies. The psalmist sees God as a remote and protected spot to which the psalmist can flee out of the press of trouble.

Judgment on the Nations (9:15–20). Psalm 9 concludes with a description of the divine retribution visited on the wicked as the just due for their violent oppression of the weak and needy. Once again, the interplay in these verses between the "nations" and the "wicked" allows flexibility in understanding the enemy as the wicked individuals opposing the psalmist or as the evil nations oppressing Israel. One gathers the impression that an originally personal psalm has been adapted to speak to the situation of the exilic community by identifying the wicked with the nations.

The Arrogant Wicked (10:1–11). Psalm 10 opens with agonized questions directed to God, revealing a sense of isolation and divine absence that contrasts with the confident affirmation of Yahweh as "refuge" in Psalm 9. Deliverance is not yet at hand in Psalm 10, and for the psalmist God seems hidden and removed (10:1). The questions and the attendant sense of abandonment set the stage for the long acrimonious description of the arrogant wicked that dominates 10:2–11.

The wicked oppressors of Psalm 10 are primarily the more localized enemies of the community, identified with the "nations" only by a single subtle statement near the end of the psalm (10:16). The description of the wicked is divided into two sections of five verses, each concluded by a quotation of the wicked who arrogantly assumes independence from divine scrutiny (10:6, 11).

Plea for Deliverance (10:12–15). The psalmist's response to this finely drawn portrait of arrogant human self-determination is to suggest that it is divine absence or delay that has allowed opportunity for the wicked to work. The portrait was prefaced (10:1) with the psalmist's pointed questions regarding the reasons for God's delayed response to the pleas of the needy and the injustice of the wicked. Now he follows his critique with a call for divine action coupled with a second set of questions regarding the wicked's almost casual assumption of divine ignorance or unconcern (10:12–13).

Yahweh as Eternal King (10:16–18). The combined psalm concludes by acknowledging Yahweh as the eternal king, protector of the afflicted and defender of "the fatherless and the oppressed" (10:18). An unusual number of terms for these defenseless classes of persons who require the protection of the monarch are used in this psalm. Thus, one major concern of the psalmist appears to be revealed: the oppression of the defenseless people by the wicked. Since Yahweh is the eternal righteous king, he will take the side of the weak (10:18).

Application. The arrogant pride that marks the wicked in Psalm 10 in particular (10:2–11) has none of the sense of wonder and awe that marks the psalmist's encounter with the creator in Psalm 8. Set immediately following the wondrous pronouncements of Psalm 8, this prideful dismissal of God is stated in its most shocking and extreme fashion. The result is as much a warning for the faithful not to allow the seeming absence of God (10:1) to erode confidence in his active concern and presence as it is a rebuke of the faithless for their ignorance and pride.

PSALM 11:1–7

Original Meaning

Refuge or Flight (11:1). The psalmist establishes the confident tone of the psalm by creating a studied contrast between the consuming fear generated by those who counsel flight and the psalmist, who takes refuge in Yahweh.

What Can the Righteous Do? (11:2–3). "Upright" (11:2b) occurs eighteen times in the psalms. The term can be applied to straight, smooth roads or straight, direct persons. These people are attacked by the wicked but will ultimately be justified by Yahweh.

Yahweh the Examiner (11:4–6). Yahweh is "in his holy temple" seated "on his heavenly throne" (11:4). This picture shows Yahweh in control. From his vantage point in the heavens, he is able to examine the chaotic human events on the earth and render righteous judgments.

Affirmation of Yahweh's Righteousness (11:7). Our psalm concludes by affirming Yahweh's righteousness and his love of justice. These twin attributes provide the basis of the psalmist's confident hope.

Application. According to this psalm, in foundation-shaking circumstances we have two basic choices: Either we can flee to the hills or take refuge in God.

PSALM 12:1–8

Original Meaning

Grounds of Complaint (12:1–2). The psalmist drives home the complaint in the language of hyperbole. Lying and deception are universal. This heightens the sense of oppression and leaves God little choice but to act.

Plea for Deliverance (12:3–4). Still operating in hyperbole, he demands that Yahweh remove the offending elements of speech (12:3). The self-absorption of the wicked is reflected in their own arrogant words (12:4).

Divine Response and Promise (12:5). Yahweh takes his kingly role as protector of the defenseless seriously.

Confident Expectation (12:6–7). Using the analogy of the smelting and purification of precious metal, the psalmist describes the "words of the LORD" (12:6). This purity of the divine utterance shows up the self-focused and grasping nature of the liars' words.

Reprise of Complaint (12:8). The wicked still strut about unhindered. But the faithful see through the eyes of the psalmist that Yahweh is the God of the pure, effective word, who takes the side of the needy when all others malign them.

Application. Most could provide a long list of ways that words are used deceptively. It is usually easier to point to others in this regard.

PSALM 13:1–6

Original Meaning

Questioning God (13:1–2). This questioning is a response to the experience of the hiddenness of God. Such questions reveal a faith seeking to understand in the midst of painful experiences.

Plea for Deliverance from Approaching Death (13:3–4). The psalmist's sense of desperation is voiced in a series of pleas to God that expand in almost inexorable fashion. Without the hoped-for divine intervention, the psalmist can only anticipate rapid decline, defeat, and death.

Trust and Confidence (13:5–6). This psalm concludes with an expression of trust and confidence based on an understanding of the character of God as well as previous experience of goodness from Yahweh's hand.

Application. Many today struggle with feelings of unworthiness, believing in the result of some wrong within themselves. Such inner turmoil often grows out of self-condemnation and can lead to anger, paralysis, and despair.

PSALM 14:1–7

Original Meaning

The Folly of the Evildoers (14:1–3). The foolish wicked are led astray by their arrogant assumption that there is no limit to their personal power and control. This is expressed in 14:1 by the quotation: "There is no God." By taking this counsel "in his heart," the fool is deliberating in the center of moral and ethical decision-making. Folly is not simply uninformed stupidity but a moral decision for evil.

Judgment on the Wicked (14:4–6). The foolish wicked are identified as "evildoers" (14:4).

Hope for Restoration from Exile (14:7). The psalm concludes with a previously unanticipated expansion of the perspective of the narrator to include the experience of the exilic community. From preoccupation with the nature and deeds of the wicked, the psalm turns decisively at the end to a communal expression of the desire for restoration.

Application. What immediately comes to your mind as you read Psalm 14:1–6? When we hurry to class ourselves with the righteous poor, we often fail to acknowledge the many ways our abundant lifestyle is founded on the exploitation of the "two-thirds" world who have so little.

PSALM 15:1–5

Original Meaning

The Thematic Question (15:1). The opening question initiates the theme that provides the backdrop for the whole psalm.

Eleven Answers (15:2–5b). Having set the scene and theme of the psalm, the psalmist now supplies eleven answers to the foundational questions of 15:1. Together these answers offer a comprehensive, if not exhaustive, response to the central concern of the psalm: What style of living prepares one for living in the presence of Yahweh?

Confident Summation (15:5c). Whoever emulates the lifestyle need never fear being "shaken," a verb that describes the kind of insecurity experienced when one's feet are on rough, untrustworthy ground.

Application. The one who is ready to enter God's presence is *not* the one who knows how to adopt the requisite outer attitudes of worship. Instead, the one who lives a life of transparency is ready to meet God.

PSALM 16:1–11

Original Meaning

The Initial Plea (16:1). The plea is more a desire for continued protection than for deliverance from specific trouble.

Profession of Faith (16:2). Competing translations of 16:2 concern who is speaking in the confessional words of 16:2a. The choice is between the first-person voice of the psalmist or the second-person voice of another. The choice made affects and is affected by the translation of 16:2–4, especially the understanding of who the "holy people" and "noble ones" are in 16:3.

Refusal to Worship Other Gods (16:3–4). The NIV takes *qedoshim* in 16:3a to mean "holy people," a positive commendation of the faithful in the land of Israel, and connects the verse with the preceding statements in 16:1–2. Other commentators, however, drawing on evidence that *qedoshim* is a reference to Canaanite deities, link 16:3 with the negative comments in 16:4. In this case, the expression of delight in the "noble ones" (16:3) becomes a negative example of false allegiance to pagan gods.

Commitment to Yahweh (16:5–8). The psalmist knows that it is Yahweh who apportions the land to whom he will and who provides for its security and prosperity. The pleasant circumstances that surround the psalmist are the result of the blessing of Yahweh.

Confidence and Joy in Yahweh (16:9–11). The reasons for the psalmist's feeling of security fall into three categories:

1. deliverance from death (16:10);
2. continued guidance (16:11a); and
3. the gift of divine presence (16:11b-c).

Application. Where do we find security? In a society obsessed by the possession of things, concern for security against robbery has grown to epidemic proportions. Even at the most unstable moments, Yahweh is *still* our "portion and . . . cup" (16:5).

PSALM 17:1–15

Original Meaning

Plea and Claim of Innocence (17:1–5). From the beginning, Psalm 17 is couched in the voice of the innocent sufferer. Verse 1a ought to be interpreted in light of the parallel phrase in 17:1b to be the psalmist's plea that Yahweh pay attention to his cause or just plea. Yahweh is called to "hear" and "listen" since the psalmist's declaration is without deceit.

The psalmist invites divine scrutiny and examination, confident there is no fault to be uncovered. The examination moves from the "heart" (17:3a) to the "mouth" (17:3c) to the outward actions (17:4). The final statement of 17:5 ("my feet have not stumbled") may function either as further evidence of the psalmist's loyal adherence to the teaching of Yahweh or as a grateful acknowledgment of the security provided by divine guidance.

The Enemy Attack (17:6–12). The psalmist introduces two images of the protective care and concern of Yahweh. The first relates the psalmist to the pupil of the eye, which is to be carefully guarded from injury. The second image is the desire to be hidden "in the shadow of [God's] wings" (17:8). This image refers in the most general sense to the protection of small birds under the wings of their hovering parent.

Enemies assail the psalmist on every side (17:9). The surrounding enemies are like hungry lions moving in for the kill.

Final Plea (17:13–15). From his seat on his throne of judgment, Yahweh is to stand in order to render judgment and enforce it. The resolution of his hope is in coming near to Yahweh and experiencing the secure blessing of the divine presence. The psalmist recognizes that it is only the righteous who can stand in Yahweh's presence (17:15) and who can hope to "be satisfied with seeing" the likeness of God. The theme of coming into the divine presence was introduced in Psalm 11:7. In 14:5 the theme is renewed when we learn that "God is present in the company of the righteous." Psalm 15 then describes the character of the one who would enter the divine presence, and Psalm 16 lays claim to the "joy in [Yahweh's] presence" (16:11).

Application. The "face of God" has fearsome potential for judgment (1 Pet 3:12). By contrast, the faithful "will *see the face of the Lord*" (Rev 22:3–4, emphasis added). In other words, the New Testament preserves the same tension as the Old between those who will experience the face of God as judgment and the faithful who discover both blessing and satisfaction when God's face shines on them.

PSALM 18:1–50

Original Meaning

Introductory Praise (18:1–3). The psalmist begins with a first-person address of his love to Yahweh (18:1) and then continues in the third person to heap up epithets of Yahweh that call forth the psalmist's praise. All these epithets respond to Yahweh as source of refuge, protection, and deliverance. The theme of "refuge" in Yahweh is a prominent one in the Psalter.

Narrative of Deliverance (18:4–19). The narrative begins with a generalized description of distress (18:4–6), continues with a theophany (18:7–15), and concludes with a description of divine deliverance (18:16–19).

The attack experienced by the psalmist is life-threatening. It is clear that he understands the circumstance as being bound over to the power of death (18:4–5). Life is going under and only Yahweh can save. When the psalmist calls, Yahweh hears and responds (18:6).

The narrative of deliverance now moves to an extended theophany, in which the approach of God into the profane world of human existence is described with all its fearsome effects. The awesome power and majesty of the divine glory entering the human world is not business as usual. God's holy otherness places sinful humanity under threat, and even the created order suffers by direct exposure to his presence. The created world cannot contain the creator, and its usual laws and order are stretched to the breaking point by this divine intrusion.

The final segment of the narrative shifts the focus from the power of Yahweh displayed in the storm and in his successful conflict with the chaotic waters to the psalmist's personal experience of deliverance. This connection is made by viewing the distress as being overwhelmed by "deep waters," from which Yahweh extracts the psalmist (18:16). These threatening "waters" are identified with his real enemies 18:17—those "who were too strong for me." Yahweh, however, is the psalmist's "support" (18:18b), and he swoops down to pull the despairing psalmist to safety. Divine aid is the consequence of divine "delight" (18:19) in the psalmist.

Instruction in Righteousness (18:20–29). Three subsections alternate between the personal experience of the psalmist (18:20–24, 27–29) and more general instruction to the faithful (18:25–26).

The first subsection is clearly marked off by an *inclusio* of almost identical verses at beginning and end (18:20, 24), which set out the primary theme of the whole larger section: Divine deliverance is a consequence of personal righteousness, loyalty, and cleanness of hands.

The second subsection (18:25–26) uses the device of repeated reciprocity to encourage the faithful to adopt a fruitful relation to Yahweh.

The third subsection (18:27–29) offers a series of summary statements that move the discussion from the more general acknowledgment of the previous section that Yahweh is the hope of the faithful (18:25–26) to the more specific and personal recognition that Yahweh is indeed the psalmist's own source of strength against the enemy.

The Way of Victory (18:30–45). A change from first-person direct address to third-person description of God signals the shift to the fourth major section of the psalm—a description of the victory that the faithful experience when they trust in the "perfect" way of Yahweh (18:30).

Yahweh perfectly fulfills what is expected of the divine covenant partner. His "way" (18:30) of dealing with humans and the world cannot be faulted: Yahweh is *tamim*, meaning "whole, complete, intact, integrated," just as the psalmist has claimed to be *tamim* (18:23). This means Yahweh can be trusted to do what he says, to act according to his promises and commitments.

Along with giving strength, Yahweh also provides sure footing in the conflicts of life (18:32b–33). God himself supports the weary warrior in the midst of the fight (18:35b-c). The "enemies" (18:40) are left vulnerable to the attack of the psalmist (18:42).

In a series of "you" statements the psalmist describes Yahweh's saving and equipping acts (cf. 18:35–36, 39–40, 43). Then in each case he moves to describe a personal experience of the consequences of this divine empowerment (18:37–38, 41–42, 44–45), the first two of which are marked by repeated "I" language.

Conclusion of Praise (18:46–50). The psalm concludes with a song of praise to Yahweh for deliverance and victory. This section begins by referring to Yahweh as the psalmist's "Rock" (18:46), linking back to the opening lines of the psalm (18:2) as well as to the opening of the previous section (18:31) and bringing this important theme of the psalm to an appropriate end.

The psalmist's promise to "sing praises to" the name of Yahweh among the nations (18:49) clearly took on heightened significance for the exilic community, who were "scattered among the nations" (cf. Ps 44:11).

Application. Many of us today have real difficulty imagining the presence of God in earthshaking and awe-inspiring terms. In many contemporary congregations, God through Jesus has become a familiar friend rather than a holy God. While I do think it is important to understand that God is our helper and friend, I also think something essential is lost when we *never* experience the shock of God's holy presence as did Moses (Exod 3:1–6), Jacob (Gen 28:10–22), Isaiah (Isa 6:1–9), and Paul (Acts 9:1–19). God is, of course, a friend who loves and comforts us, but he is also the holy God who knocks our socks off and shakes us to our very foundations. We need to experience God as both if we are to keep our faith in the right perspective.

PSALM 19:1–14

Original Meaning

Revelation of God in the Heavens (19:1–4b). What we usually recognize as inanimate creation is here given life and voice as the heavens and skies "declare," "proclaim," and "pour forth speech" in praise of the creator (19:1–2). This is, then, a continual outcry of nature to God from the moment of creation until now and on into the future.

The All-Seeing Sun (19:4c–6). In the middle of 19:4, the psalm takes a new turn by introducing an extended metaphorical description of the sun. In the present context, this description represents a move from the more general works of God—heavens, firmament—to a specific example of those works. The shift is akin to a metonymy, a literary device in which a part is introduced as representative of the whole. The sun is a part of the heavenly features through which the glory of God has been displayed and communicated since the beginning.

Revelation Through Torah (19:7–11). For those called to know God through his creative works, the divine scrutiny illustrated by the constant arcing of the sun overhead implies the need for a guide in order to satisfy God's will and expectation. The psalm now moves to consider how the torah (the law) fulfills the role of admonition and guide to reward (19:11), through which Yahweh's will is revealed to those who fear him. The section consists, for the most part, of a series of adjectives describing the character of torah, each accompanied by a verbal phrase revealing how torah impacts the life of the faithful.

Human Response (19:12–14). Having wondered at the revelation of God declared through heavens and sun and having rejoiced in the admonition and guidance offered through God's torah, the psalmist turns at last to the appropriate human response of those who adopt the proper attitude of "fear of the Lord" (19:9). The final statement is a model of the kind of submission to the will of God admonished in the whole psalm.

Application. Humans are not left alone and forlorn with no purpose or meaning in life. God's word is a delight because through it we discover who God is and how to assume our place within his creation.

PSALM 20:1–9

Original Meaning

Hope for Divine Intervention and Victory (20:1–5). A string of eight imperfect verb forms linked in pairs dominates the first section of the poem. The linked pairs ask for divine hearing and protection (20:1), divine help and support from the temple (20:2), God's favorable response to the king's offerings and sacrifices (20:3), and successful fulfillment of the king's military plans for victory (20:4).

Assurance of Divine Support (20:6). A distinctive and singular voice breaks into the communal recitation of hope that has characterized the psalm thus far. The identity of the speaker is not clear from the context. Drawing on the similar context of 2 Chronicles 20, many commentators assume the speaker to be one of the Levites serving in the temple, who here speaks prophetically to assure king and people of a positive divine response and certain victory.

Confession of Trust in Yahweh (20:7–8). By trusting in "chariots" and "horses" the misguided opponents are doomed to fall (20:7a). In contrast, those who trust in Yahweh "rise up and stand firm" (20:8b).

Final Plea (20:9). The psalm concludes with a final plea that draws together the intercessory and personal prayers of the assembly.

Application. We are called to trust in the God who has delivered us and has called us into a relationship of commitment and trust.

PSALM 21:1–13

Original Meaning

In Praise of Yahweh's Strength (21:1). As Psalm 20 ends with direct mention of the king (20:9), so Psalm 21 begins with a similar reference to the king (21:1) rejoicing in the strength of Yahweh, which provides the king with victories.

Blessing on the King (21:2–6). The king is a model of integrity; what he desires in his heart he requests with his lips. Yahweh's response to the king's integrity pours out in blessing. The king has asked for life, and God has given him abundant, long-lasting life. The "rich blessings" bestowed on the king beginning in 21:3 are summed up as this section comes to a close.

Confession of Trust (21:7). The distinctive nature of the verse is revealed by the appearance only here of third-person reference about Yahweh rather than the second-person address to him that dominates the rest of the psalm. In this central verse, the king responds to the description of divine blessing and presence with a confession of trust in Yahweh.

Divine Judgment on the Enemy (21:8–12). The presence of God is a two-edged sword. For the faithful who trust in him, God brings blessing and salvation, while for the rebellious who resist his rule, God's coming means judgment. In 21:8–12 the psalmist describes the hoped-for consequences of Yahweh's "appearing" (21:9a) on the enemy. God—through a consuming fire—is depicted as "swallowing up" and "consuming" his opponents (21:9b).

Concluding Praise of Yahweh's Strength (21:13). The final call is for Yahweh to be "exalted" because of his many acts of "strength."

Application. We want to be in control of our lives, and we want to take the credit for the victories we achieve. Yet we are too often forced to admit just how little control we really have. Do we understand our victories—however great or small—as God's deliverance?

PSALM 22:1–31

Original Meaning

Thematic Introduction (22:1). "My God, my God, why have you forsaken me?" The opening words of this psalm have become so familiar to us from Jesus's use of them from the cross that it is difficult for us to separate them from that much later context. If we read these words *only* as words about Jesus, we ignore the original and continuing word of God to *us*.

The Silence and Absence of God (22:2–11). The first major section of the psalm emphasizes the theme of abandonment through two sets of contrasts between the psalmist's current sense of God's complete absence and past reports of God's very present help in time of trouble. The first contrast focuses on God's *silence* (22:2–5), while the second is concerned with his *failure to act* (22:6–11).

Vicious Attacks by the Enemies (22:12–21). The psalmist's enemies are depicted as fearsome beasts that surround him and cut off all escape. The animals are introduced in a particular order—bulls (22:12), lions (22:13), and dogs (22:16)—that is reversed in the plea for deliverance: dogs (22:20), lions (22:21a), and wild oxen (22:21b).

The fierce attack reduces the psalmist to fear and weakness. The signs of physical weakness are common ones. His strength departs like water "poured out" on the ground (22:14a), so that his body feels awkward and out of control ("all my bones are out of joint," 22:14b). Similarly, the psalmist's "heart" (or courage) melts away like wax before a fierce flame (22:14c-d). He feels weakened by fear (22:15a) and has a bad case of cotton mouth (22:15b), fearing the approach of death (22:15c).

Promise to Praise (22:22–31). The final stanza of ten verses turns decisively toward praise. The stanza is subdivided into two segments, each introduced by a second-person address to Yahweh promising to proclaim praise to the psalmist's fellow worshipers in the temple (cf. 22:22, 25). Both promises are followed by a passage in which Yahweh is mentioned in the third person, and others are encouraged to praise him by a rehearsal of reasons he is praiseworthy (cf. 22:23–24, 26–31).

The first subsection of this final stanza begins with a vow to declare Yahweh's name in worship. That temple worship is intended is clearly indicated by the phrases "in the assembly" (22:22b) and "in the great assembly" (22:25b).

The concluding praise section of the psalm (22:26–31) moves out in almost apocalyptic fashion to describe the global effects of Yahweh's righteous rule. The themes addressed include:

- the welfare of the poor who are satisfied (22:26a);
- the submission of the nations to the rule of Yahweh (22:27–28);
- the leveling of society in acknowledged dependence on Yahweh (22:29); and
- the continued praise and proclamation of the righteousness of God (22:26b, 30–31).

The psalmist envisions a future in which the current state of affairs is turned on end and the true purposes of Yahweh are realized in the world of human events. God comes near, and humans—rich or poor, Israelite or non-Israelite—will acknowledge his lordship and bow before him.

Application. The faith modeled by Jesus on the cross was no fair-weather religion that trusted in God when the going was good. Neither was it a faith that fled like the disciples when confronted by the harsh realities of rejection, persecution, and, indeed, execution. His was a faith that experienced the worst the world had to offer—knewing what it was to feel abandoned by God—and yet just when it was darkest, as life was slipping away, he was able to proclaim with a final certainty: "It is finished!" (John 19:30). Having won his way through to the end, Jesus surrendered his spirit into the hand of God the Father (Luke 23:46). Psalm 22, with its hopeful vision of a future restored to its original purposes, encourages us to do the same.

PSALM 23:1–6

Original Meaning

Introduction (23:1). That David should speak of Yahweh as "*my* shepherd" (emphasis added) is a way of acknowledging that Yahweh is indeed the power behind the throne of David.

Abundant Life (23:2–3). The shepherd leads his sheep in pleasant places full of all the necessities of life.

Secure Life (23:4). From a life of abundant ease, the psalmist moves to a description of fearful threat.

Blessed Life (23:5). To sit at Yahweh's table is to enjoy fellowship and communion with him. To do so "in the presence of my enemies" is to have one's special relationship to God declared publicly in a context of divine blessing and security.

Dwelling in Yahweh's House (23:6). Not only does the psalmist sit as an honored guest at the table with God, but he looks forward in confidence to dwelling in Yahweh's house forever. To dwell with God is a potent image of eternal security and ongoing relationship.

Application. Being in Christ does not mean that the troubles of this world are simply removed from us. We remain "in the presence" of our enemies. We need also, however, to ask and constantly remind ourselves in what ways, day by day, God is setting a table for *us* in the presence of our enemies.

PSALM 24:1–10

Original Meaning

Yahweh's Creative Authority (24:1–2). The introductory verses affirm the authority of Yahweh over the whole earth, its contents and inhabitants. Because he created it, the earth belongs to Yahweh. In certain passages "earth" and "world" emphasize the stable character of the cosmos Yahweh creates and sustains (1 Sam 2:8; 1 Chr 16:30). In other contexts, the emphasis is on the authority that attaches to Yahweh as the creator of the cosmos (Pss 33:8–9; 89:11).

Preparation to Enter the Presence of God (24:3–6). Having affirmed the creative power and continuing authority of Yahweh over the whole world, the psalm now turns its gaze on the creature who would enter the presence of this creator God. The liturgical nature of the psalm becomes clearer in a series of antiphonal questions and answers. Many commentators have pictured a throng of pilgrim worshipers approaching the Temple Mount in Jerusalem, preparing to go up to participate in worship.

The King of Glory Comes (24:7–10). Having gained admission to the temple precincts, the gathered pilgrim worshipers anticipate the arrival of Yahweh himself. The temple can never fully contain the glory that is Yahweh; rather, it serves only as the meeting place of God and humans.

Application. When we realize that our life is in God's hands, we are emboldened to make decisions that are based on the well-being of the cosmos, not just personal benefit or concern.

PSALM 25:1–22

Original Meaning

Statement of Trust (25:1–3). The psalm begins with a confident declaration of trust in Yahweh (25:1), followed immediately by a plea that the speaker not be "put to shame" or defeated by the enemy (25:2). This plea does not undermine the statement of trust because it is grounded in the theological observation that follows in 25:3; because Yahweh will never allow those who trust in him to be put to shame, the psalmist is free to claim personal application of that truth. Unlike the treacherous idol worshiper of 24:4, he declares, "I lift up my *nepesh*" (author's translation; NIV idiomatically, "I put my trust") to Yahweh, who alone is trustworthy (25:1).

In Praise of God's Faithfulness (25:8–10). A shift to third-person reference about God signals the beginning of a new section. The content shifts as well from plea to descriptive praise of Yahweh for his enduring love and faithfulness (25:10a). This section responds point for point to the pleas in 25:4–7 (instructive guidance, enduring mercy, and love), grounding confidence in the characteristic nature of God.

Those Who Fear Yahweh (25:12–15). Following the pivotal confession of sin, the psalm shifts once again to the third person, indicating a new section. These verses describe the blessings that accrue to those who "fear the LORD" (25:12a, 14). Moving from the singular reference in 25:12 to the plural reference in 25:14 has the effect of linking the experience of the psalmist to the more general experience of the community to which he speaks. The section moves in two directions: It admonishes the larger community to adopt the stance of fearing Yahweh, and it provides a foundation for the psalmist's confidence of deliverance, since he claims the kind of total reliance on Yahweh that fearing him entails (cf. 25: 15).

The Final Plea (25:16–21). The final section of the psalm is marked out by another shift to second-person direct address of Yahweh, accompanied by a new string of seven imperative verb forms that signal the psalmist's final plea for deliverance.

Communal Plea for Redemption (25:22). This final verse broadens the narrow focus of the psalm by identifying the pleas of the individual psalmist with the communal concern for the redemption of Israel "from all their troubles."

Application. The message of both Old and New Testaments is clear: Those who enter the eternal kingdom of God's grace are those who acknowledge their sin and trust in the gracious mercy of God while surrendering self-power and pride. May our eyes ever be on Yahweh, for only he will release our feet from the snares of life (cf. 25:15).

PSALM 26:1–12

Original Meaning

Plea for Vindication (26:1). While the ultimate result of the examination is the declaration of the psalmist's "blameless life," the invitation to judge prepares the way for the following verbs of examination and scrutiny in 26:2.

Submission to Divine Examination (26:2–7). The repeated synonyms for testing drive home the psalmist's willing submission to God's examination. Yahweh looks on the interior motivation of humans insofar as he examines the psalmist's "heart" (literally, "my kidneys") and "mind" (literally, "my heart," which in Hebrew is the center of reflection and decision making). By offering these parts of life to the divine gaze the psalmist is demonstrating complete openness.

Standing in the Presence of Yahweh (26:8–11). The psalmist is filled by a sense of love for the temple as the place where God and humans come together. That the temple is the "house" where Yahweh's glory "dwells" (26:8) is clearly established by a variety of passages (especially 2 Chr 7:1–3; Ezek 43:4–5; 44:4).

Confident Expectation (26:12). The psalm ends with a statement of the psalmist's firm conviction that God will act in his behalf. All fear of slipping is gone. As a result, the psalmist's praise of Yahweh wells forth in the "great congregation."

Application. As Romans 5:1–5 makes abundantly clear, righteousness gives us confidence to stand in the presence of a holy God without fear and to anticipate with great joy "the hope of the glory of God" (5:2).

PSALM 27:1–14

Original Meaning

Confidence in Yahweh (27:1–3). In the affirming parallelism of 27:1, the first two phrases ("my light and my salvation") are paralleled by the expanded phrase "stronghold of my life," suggesting that these three terms provide nuances to the psalmist's understanding of Yahweh's protective role. Yahweh is the light that vanquishes the "darkest valley" (23:4). That light marks out the "right paths" (cf. 23:3; 25:4, 9). Yahweh is also the life-saving stronghold that delivers the psalmist. Because of that guidance and protection, he is unafraid (27:1:b, d; cf. 23:4).

The protective presence and care of Yahweh encourages the psalmist in the face of enemy attack (27:2–3). In spite of the severity of the attack, the psalmist remains confident and unafraid (27:2d).

Desire to Dwell in the House of Yahweh (27:4–6). To seek God in this way is a sign of commitment to the way of life he demands and provides. Dwelling in the house of Yahweh is not just an experience of aesthetic delight in the gracious hospitality of God. There is a protective benefit to the nearness of God. Freed from fear of the enemy by the presence of Yahweh, the psalmist is free to sing praises and to offer sacrifices of thanksgiving to God.

Plea for Deliverance from Enemies (27:7–12). This cry underscores the reality of his suffering in spite of a strong confidence in Yahweh's saving nature. The rest of the plea is divided into a desire for divine presence in the face of God's seeming absence (27:8–10), a desire for divine instruction in the right way (27:11), and a desire for divine vindication in the face of "false witnesses" (27:12).

Confidence and Encouragement (27:13–14). In this final section the psalmist returns to the confident stance of 27:1–3. He "remains confident" that he will see the "goodness of the LORD in the land of the living" (27:13)—a clear reference to an expectation to be delivered in this life. The two verbs "be strong" (*hzq*) and "take heart" (*'mts*) are the same used in Joshua to encourage the Israelites as they cross the Jordan River to take the promised land (Josh 1:6, 7, 9, 18; 10:25).

Application. Where or to whom do you go when life seems too much to handle? Perhaps to your spouse or a close friend, a trusted minister, your parents? For the psalmist, God is the stronghold of his life—the secure place when all else fails.

PSALM 28:1–9

Original Meaning

Opening Plea for Deliverance (28:1–2). Drawing on the lack of aural acuity associated with deafness, the psalmist entreats Yahweh not to "turn a deaf ear" (28:1b) to the psalmist's cries. If God does "remain silent," the psalmist will "be like" those who descend to death in Sheol (28:1c). He entreats Yahweh as "my Rock" (28:1a), a characterization that links back to 27:5. God is the psalmist's secure high place.

Call for Retribution (28:3–5). The psalmist seeks to distinguish himself from the wicked and to avoid the punishment he thinks they so richly deserve. The enemy uses a facade of cordiality to mask an inner attitude of malice. God looks on the heart and expects one's attitudes, desires, and commitment to reflect consistency with one's outwardly observable actions.

Praise for Deliverance (28:6–7). The psalmist experiences the certainty that Yahweh has indeed heard his plea for divine favor. This certainty is expressed in words that almost parallel the plea itself in 28:2. Because of this assurance he praises Yahweh (28:6–7).

Call for Communal Deliverance (28:8–9). Psalm 28, like many individual psalms in the Psalter, exhibits at its end a shift from purely individual to more communal concerns. The individual image of Yahweh as the psalmist's "shield" (28:7) has been expanded to include the whole community in 28:8.

Application. God's purpose in calling his church out of the world is not to escape. He has called us out in order to experience a new wholeness and to experience the world's brokenness for what it really is—a direct contradiction of God's intention for humanity and his whole creation. We have been sent back to the world to make its suffering our own and so to redeem it.

PSALM 29:1–11

Original Meaning

Call to Worship and Testimony (29:1–2). The NIV's choice of the translation "heavenly beings" in 29:1 for *beney elim* (literally, "sons of gods") obscures the fact that *elim* is the plural of the common ancient Near Eastern word for "god" (*el*). Its underlying purpose is to enhance the majesty of Yahweh at the expense of foreign deities, bowing down in worship of his holiness (29:2).

Theophany of Yahweh in the Storm (29:3–9). Psalm 29 stands as a response to the plea in Psalm 28 that Yahweh not remain silent (28:1). Notice how the phrase "the voice of the LORD" appears seven times in 29:3–9. The descriptive phrases picture a massive storm originating over the Mediterranean Sea (29:3), moving ashore at the heavily forested Lebanon range to the far north of Israel (29:5–6), and then across the Desert of Kadesh (29:8). The pinnacle and climax of the theophany comes at the height of the storm's power, as all those gathered in the temple worship Yahweh.

Yahweh's Enthronement as King (29:10–11). In the temple, the ark of the covenant in the Most Holy Place served as the place where the invisible God of Israel sat with his people—enthroned between the wings of the cherubim as Israel's king.

Application. How long has it been since you were overwhelmed in this way by a sense of God's powerful presence?

PSALM 30:1–12

Original Meaning

Declaration of Praise (30:1–3). Just as Yahweh "exalted" the psalmist above his surrounding enemies (27:6), so now the psalmist seeks to "exalt" Yahweh by making known his saving acts (30:1). The psalmist's suffering may have been occasioned by a desperate illness. The psalmist appears almost to have been plucked out of the line of those currently waiting to enter Sheol.

Call to Join in Praise (30:4–5). The psalmist now calls on the listening/reading "faithful people" (30:4) to join in the praise of Yahweh—another indication that the setting of the psalmist's recitation is likely temple worship.

The Psalmist's Narrative (30:6–12). In the rest of the psalm, the psalmist gives an account of the changing mental and emotional processes that accompanied his downfall and deliverance. The psalmist begins with an almost naive sense of safety and security (30:6). The tension between real and false security is played out in 30:7.

To "hide the face" in 30:7 is an expression indicating the withdrawal of divine presence and appears frequently both inside and outside the Psalter. Awareness of vulnerability leads the psalmist to seek deliverance and divine favor. The rhetorical questions at the end of 30:9—each assuming the answer "No!"—realize that the only thing "gained" that humans represent to God lies in their praise and acknowledgment of his faithfulness.

Psalm 30 concludes with the psalmist's joyful memory of deliverance realized. His rites of mourning have become instead a dance.

Application. When we acknowledge that without God life is formless and void, when we admit our own powerlessness, when we acknowledge that he alone has the power to save, then regardless of its circumstances, life with God at the center can be marked with enduring contentment.

PSALM 31:1–24

Original Meaning

Plea for Deliverance (31:1–5). The related terms pile up in these verses ("refuge" in 31:1, 2, 4; "rock" in 31:2, 3; "fortress" in 31:2, 3), emphasizing the theme of reliance and trust that underlies the whole psalm. To take refuge in Yahweh is to trust that Yahweh affirms the righteousness of the faithful and to hope confidently that he will indeed act to establish that essential righteousness publicly.

To commit one's "spirit" to God (31:5) is not simply to trust for physical deliverance of the physical being, but it is to make the ultimate surrender of the very animating force of life into the care of the God from whom it comes and who may sustain or remove it as he pleases. The psalmist's act of commitment, coming as it does at the end of the opening plea, reflects complete surrender of self-control and submission to God's will.

Commitment and Confidence (31:6–8). Verse 6 contrasts the futility of trusting in gods other than Yahweh ("cling to worthless idols") with the psalmist's own confident reliance on Yahweh ("I trust in the LORD"). The phrase "worthless idols" (*hable shaw*) is instructive. The Hebrew combines two words—"Nothingness, void" and "worthless, in vain, false"—to refer rather obliquely but pointedly to the ineffective emptiness of idols on which the wicked rely. The remaining verses celebrate the psalmist's assurance of Yahweh's love (31:7) and deliverance (31:8).

Plea for Mercy (31:9–13). The psalmist returns briefly in 31:9 to the plea for deliverance with which the psalm began (cf. 31:1–4). But here the plea introduces an extended narrative of suffering that serves as the motivation for divine deliverance. The description uses images of drastic physical deterioration, which might be associated with symptoms of extreme illness as analogies to the painful waning of life force as the result of constant attack from without. The disgraceful public shame the psalmist experiences is falsely induced, but it produces a context of contempt in which the psalmist feels terrified, under attack, and threatened.

Trust and Anticipation of Deliverance (31:14–18). Following the intense description of the demoralizing situation the psalmist faces, it is as if he says: "Contrary to what one might expect under the circumstances, I do not despair, *but I* surrender in trust to the hand of God" (31:14–15), naming Yahweh as the only source of hope. This is no simplistic fatalism in which the psalmist, confronted by life-threatening circumstances, simply shrugs and says, "Whatever!" Rather, it is a call to be perceptive observers of life and sensitive to the character and purpose of God, and to respond appropriately in each time.

Proclamation of God's Goodness (31:19–20). The poem shifts at this point into the mode of praise. These two verses have the effect of generalizing the circumstances of the psalmist to incorporate the whole community of the faithful. His experiences are seen not as isolated personal events but as part of the great tapestry of dealing between God and his faithful people. As God has stored up goodness for those who fear him, so goodness is in store for the suffering psalmist.

Call to Praise (31:21–24). In this section praise of Yahweh remains the psalmist's aim (as in the preceding verses). Here, however, the focus returns to his more specific context, as evidenced by the use of first-person singular pronouns "I" and "me" throughout. If in the former passage the psalmist was generalizing to include a larger group of believers in praise, now the object is to give testimony to this larger group from his own experience.

Application. What do you do? How much do you make? Whom do you count among your friends? Often these criteria drive our perception of our value. And if our context should change—a job lost, a spouse dead or divorced, a moral failure tarnishing a reputation—then our value is tarnished as well. In what appear to be hopeless circumstances, God arrives to provide refuge and hope.

PSALM 32:1–11

Original Meaning

Proclamation of Blessing (32:1–2). The psalm begins with a twofold repetition in 32:1–2 of the Hebrew term *'ashrey* ("blessed")—the same word that begins the whole Psalter (1:1). Forgiveness comes to the one who confesses sin completely and openly without deceit or reservation.

A Personal Example (32:3–5). In these three verses, the psalmist describes a personal experience that moves from initial resistance to confession (32:3–4) to reluctant but complete admission of sin (32:5). It was commonly understood that sin could bring divine retribution in the form of physical illness. In Psalm 32, the psalmist has sinned, with illness as the consequence. The destructive effects of repressed and unexpressed emotions and anxieties can be powerfully experienced in physical pain and psychological disintegration.

Exhortation and Personal Testimony (32:6–7). The exhortation in these two verses is styled as direct address to God, but the purpose is clearly to encourage humans to seize on the hope engendered by the psalmist's experience of divine grace extended in response to honest confession.

Admonition and Instruction (32:8–10). The readers are warned not to deaden their perceptive senses so that they end up resisting the divine will and must be disciplined by the "many . . . woes" (32:10a) that come on the wicked. By contrast, those wise ones who trust in Yahweh find themselves surrounded by his "unfailing love" (32:10b).

Final Call to Praise (32:11). This final verse, with its invocation to praise Yahweh, provides the occasion for the voicing of praise in the following Psalm 33.

Application. Our obvious (at least to ourselves) failure to live up to the "shoulds" and "oughts" of our lives causes many of us to hide our failings behind a façade of apparent success. Having a community of faith willing to hear your wrongs as fellow sinners rather than perfectionist judges has broken through years of helplessness and denial to offer freedom.

PSALM 33:1–22

Original Meaning

Invocation to Praise (33:1–3). A "new song" (33:3) is a logical response to a "new act" of deliverance. For such new joy, the old expressions of joy just will not do! New praise must find its way to the singing lips and playing fingers. It also seems understandable that by association, the ultimate eschatological act of deliverance requires the ultimate "new song" (33:3), as Revelation recounts.

Motivation for Praise (33:4–11). In the second major section of the psalm, the psalmist lays out in sixteen lines the motivating reasoning behind the call to praise. The motivation falls into three categories: the right and faithful *character* of God (33:4–5), the powerful and creative *word* of God

(33:6–9), and the enduring and unshakable *purpose* of God (33:10–11).

Exhortation to Trust Yahweh (33:12–19). Verse 12 links back to the preceding discussion by using singular forms of the same nouns used to describe the "nations" (*goyim*) and "peoples" (*ammim*) in verse 10. Israel's plans and purposes are subjected to the same sovereign will of Yahweh as the rest of the nations. Israel, however, is "blessed" (33:12a) above all other nations because the righteous God has chosen Israel for special relationship—to be their God. Israel, by divine election, has become God's "inheritance (33:12b)"

The remainder of the section builds on this beginning in three movements that balance those of the preceding section: divine scrutiny holds humans to the standard of Yahweh's righteousness (33:13–15); reliance on human power is doomed to failure in comparison to the power of Yahweh (33:16–17); and Yahweh's purpose for those who hope in him is deliverance (33:18–19).

Concluding Affirmation of Trust (33:20–22). The psalm concludes with a communal affirmation of trust in Yahweh, using vocabulary that links back to the immediately preceding section. The affirmation of hopeful "waiting" on Yahweh in 33:20 links to the mention in 33:18 of "those who wait hopefully for his unfailing love" (author's translation; NIV "those whose hope is in his unfailing love"). The speakers trust Yahweh because he provides the kind of protective covering in the midst of the fray that a shield provides the soldier in combat.

Application. I am convinced that autos are produced with planned obsolescence. Designs change and equipment fails, necessitating replacement parts or replacement vehicles. I have grown to understand that one does not place trust in a car, no matter how new or well-maintained it may seem to be.

Psalm 33 celebrates the enduring quality of God's creation. But it is not the enduring creation—as lasting and stable as it appears to be—that fills the psalmist with trust. It is, instead, the creator God himself who inspires hope and confidence.

PSALM 34:1–22

Original Meaning

Invocation to Praise Yahweh (34:1–3). Psalm 34 begins with an invocation to praise Yahweh, in which the psalmist first proclaims personal determination (34:1–2) and then invites the listener/reader to join with him. The first three lines (34:1–2a) follow the theme of the psalmist's personal praise of Yahweh, while the fourth line (34:2b) shifts to the invitation of a larger audience.

Personal Testimony of Deliverance (34:4–7). The psalmist here presents a personal testimony of deliverance by Yahweh, interwoven with encouragement to others to entrust themselves to his care. The movement from specific personal testimony to general exhortation occurs twice in these four verses: specific testimony (34:4), general exhortation (34:5), specific testimony (34:6), general exhortation (34:7).

The angel of Yahweh encamps around God's people, surrounding them with divine protection from their enemies.

Proverbial Instruction (34:8–22). Verse 8 sets the tone for the following collection of proverbial aphorisms that make up the remainder of the psalm. This verse is an exhortation to discover the goodness that Yahweh represents and to "take refuge in him." That 34:8–22 form a collection is indicated by the parallel phrase "take refuge in him" in 34:8 and 34:22. The expression signals bookends (*inclusio*) for the section. The former (34:8) is an exhortation to trust Yahweh while the latter (34:22) is a promise of divine protection.

Those who "fear the LORD" (34:9) receive what they need from him. Young lions may be unable to meet their own food needs, but those who "seek [*drsh*]" Yahweh (34:10) as the psalmist "sought [*drsh*]" him (34:4) will lack nothing.

Having established "fear of the LORD" as the foundation of security, the psalmist lays out for the reader/listener the nature of this most important relationship (34:11–14). The next two verses (34:15–16) provide contrasting examples of Yahweh's response to the righteous and those "who do evil" (34:16). Verses 17–20 are intended to be an encouragement that Yahweh hears and acts on their behalf (34:17).

The psalm concludes with a final contrast between the wicked and the righteous in the classic tradition of wisdom literature. While it is not unambiguously stated *how* evil slays the wicked, the parallel line suggests that it is their evil acts (their failure to fear Yahweh and turn from evil) that leads to divine condemnation. By contrast, those who "take refuge in" Yahweh (34:22) need not fear condemnation.

Application. We too often identify divine blessing with "getting the goods" in one way or another. The trouble is that we may come to associate divine blessing *exclusively* with such external evidence. The people of Jesus's day struggled with this sort of thinking (John 9:1–12).

PSALM 35:1–28

Original Meaning

Plea for Divine Action and Deliverance (35:1–3). The psalmist begins by requesting that Yahweh respond to the psalmist's enemies in a style of confrontation related to their attack (legal and military): Yahweh should "contend" with those who "contend" and should "fight" with those who "fight" (35:1). The remainder of the introductory plea describes the anticipated action of Yahweh in more militaristic terms. Yahweh's ringing voice is heard above the din of battle, shouting "I am your salvation!" (35:3). This encourages the beleaguered psalmist to hang on until deliverance arrives.

Military Attack (35:4–8). With the assurance of Yahweh's approach ringing in the ears, the psalmist turns to a plea for retribution (35:4). Like chaff blown by the wind, they will be driven away.

Verses 6–7 illustrate the retributive expectations of the psalmist. Punishment received is equivalent to the offense committed. Those who hid a net to entrap him (35:7) will be entangled themselves (35:8). Those who dug a pit for him (35:7) will fall into it instead (35:8).

Response and Promise of Praise (35:9–10). The first major section of the psalm concludes with the psalmist's personal response to the anticipated salvation of Yahweh (cf. 35:3, 9) by promising to rejoice and praise God. The various verbs used to express the psalmist's testimony of rejoicing and delight emphasize a visible and audible expression of joy in a public setting. That testimony is encapsulated in the exclamation preserved in 35:10: "Who is like you, LORD?"—a rhetorical question with only a single obvious answer, "No one!"

Legal Conflict (35:11–16). The psalmist now describes a situation of confrontation in a legal setting. He is opposed by "ruthless witnesses" (35:11). What is depicted is damaging false testimony in a case involving the death penalty.

The psalmist's distress at this legal attack is increased by the opponents' callous disregard for his favorable treatment of them in the past. They repay his goodness with evil. To return evil for good, then, is one of the greatest insults imaginable and is a sign of great disrespect, insolence, and rejection of one's authority.

Personal Plea and Promise of Praise (35:17–18). The description of the legal attack against the psalmist concludes with a plea for divine rescue that develops the picture of the attackers as beasts of prey introduced in 35:16. He wishes to be saved from the "ravages" of the attackers, characterized as acting like "lions" (35:17b). The psalmist questions "how long" (35:17a) God can view the enemies' depredations and sit still without acting. Plea leads to thanksgiving as the psalmist promises to offer the testimony of thanksgiving in the corporate setting of temple worship.

Let Them Not Gloat Over Me (35:19–27). The psalmist now enters into a series of pleas for deliverance (35:19–21), vindication (35:22–25), and retribution (35:26–27) directed toward those who rejoice (in 35:19, 24, 26) over the psalmist's distress. Once again, he characterizes these attacks as baseless (35:19; cf. 35:7). The psalmist's enemies are hostile and present false testimony, claiming to be eyewitnesses (35:20–21).

The caustic exclamation "Aha! Aha!" (35:21) attributed to the false opponents flows from a sense of having the upper hand and is, therefore, a public form of finger-pointing that intends to cause public shame and disgrace of the individual.

The psalm concludes with the hopeful psalmist promising to testify regarding Yahweh's righteousness that has vindicated him against the false witnesses.

Application. The psalmist's desire for vindication ultimately turns away from self-seeking altogether. More than his personal vindication, condemnation of the enemy leads to public acclamation of the righteousness of *God*. The point of the public discrediting of the wicked is that others will see God at work (35:27).

The psalm cautions us to be clear about our motives when we seek public vindication for ourselves and even wish for the downfall of our detractors. God is not in the vengeance business. There is innocent suffering that needs to be confronted and judged, but the psalmist reminds us that what is finally at stake is not *our* reputations or even our well-being, but *God's* glory and righteousness.

PSALM 36:1–12

Original Meaning

The Arrogant Wicked (36:1–4). The psalm opens with prophetic utterance (*neum*). This Hebrew word implies that the psalmist is acting as a prophet to communicate insights provided by divine inspiration. Rather than a typical oracle of judgment as encountered in the Prophets, Psalm 36 might better be called an insight into the fate of the arrogant who exhibit no "fear of God" (36:1) and yet often seem to prosper.

The Boundless Love of Yahweh (36:5–9). The psalmist now turns to a portrait of Yahweh's boundless love that provides a sure foundation. Employing an intricate merism, he praises Yahweh's love that fills the whole of creation—reaching from heaven (36:5) to earth (36:6), from the mighty mountains to the great deep (36:6). Not only does Yahweh's love provide abundant pleasures, but it also offers access to the life-sustaining refreshment of the "river of delights" (36:8) and the "fountain of life" (36:9).

Plea for Yahweh's Continued Love (36:10–11). Trusting in the abundant goodness of Yahweh as the source of life, the psalmist can also trust that the present preeminence of the arrogant wicked is not God's plan and will. Thus, in calling for divine action to set things right, he is at once expressing his personal desire and aligning that personal desire with the will and purpose of Yahweh.

Final Call to Confidence (36:12). In the eye of the psalmist, God has implanted a vision of the fall of the wicked that gives the lie to their apparent present dominance and power.

Application. The poet finds the strength to live today, not in some hoped-for future but in the ongoing provision of God for the faithful; his unfailing love provides refuge as well as the abundant delights of God's house.

PSALM 37:1–40

Original Meaning

Call to Trust Yahweh (37:1–11). Verses 1–2 admonish the reader/listener not to be concerned because of the apparent success and invulnerability of the wicked, because their ultimate destiny is defeat and destruction. Following the negatively stated admonition of 37:1, the psalmist shifts (37:3–6) to a series of positively stated imperative directives to the hearers. A pair of balanced statements, each involving two positive imperatives and the call not to fret (37:7–8), leads to a clear statement of the future destiny of the wicked (37:9).

The unit concludes with the basis of a positive response to the psalmist's demands. In two balanced verses, he repeats the opening theme with a negative and positive inducement to the reader. The evil have only "a little while" before they are "no more," but the "meek" who "hope in the LORD" will "inherit the land" (37:9–11).

The Ultimate Fate of the Wicked (37:12–22). Four illustrations of the futility of the wicked's attempts at self-power (37:12–13, 14–15, 20, 21–21) bracket a contrasting exhortation to righteousness and blamelessness (37:16–19). The purpose is to contrast the secure future of the righteous with the certain disappearance of the wicked.

While the wicked may plot against the righteous (37:12) and even cause them trouble and pain, Yahweh remains unimpressed and unconcerned, even laughing at their pretense to power. God knows, as the psalmist understands and declares to the hearer, that the days of the wicked are already numbered (37:13). The wicked may draw their sword and bow to oppress the poor and needy (37:14), but the evil they intend will return on them decisively (37:15).

The Blessings of the Faithful (37:23–29). The psalm now moves from a description of the ultimate fate of the wicked to a consideration of the blessings that accrue to the faithful. Again, a series of extended proverb-like compositions, each consisting of four poetic lines, explore the subject.

The first aphorism introduces the theme with the image of the protective care of Yahweh along the path of the righteous, making each step sure and firm and offering a steadying hand should the righteous stumble (37:23–24). As the righteous "delight" in Yahweh and commit their "way" to him (37:4–5), so Yahweh "delights" in the way of the righteous and makes their "steps firm" (37:23).

This second collection of aphorisms ends much as does the first collection—and the introductory admonition as well. As in those earlier cases, we read a contrasting description of the fate of the wicked, who are "completely destroyed," and the righteous, who will "inherit the land" (37:28–29).

Contrasting Presents (37:30–34). An extended wisdom saying about the present reality of the righteous (37:30–31) is immediately followed by a contrasting picture of the devious plots of the wicked (37:32–33). The psalmist exhorts the faithful to wait patiently for Yahweh while keeping "his way" (37:34). Despite what seem to be contrary indications in the present circumstance, Yahweh will ultimately act.

Contrasting Futures (37:35–38). Just as the righteous and wicked occupy conflicting positions in the present, so the future holds much the same in store. The psalmist offers a personal observation that confirms the promise. He has "seen" the prosperity of the wicked that seemed rooted and grounded like a flourishing tree established in its native soil suddenly, unexpectedly, disappear (37:35–36).

The psalmist then calls the reader/listener to share in the observation. If they will but "consider the blameless" and "observe the upright" (37:37), they will reach the same conclusion (37:38).

Confidence in Yahweh (37:39–40). Once again, the theme of Yahweh as "refuge" and "stronghold" of the righteous takes the stage. Because the body of the psalm is preoccupied with the eventual defeat and demise of the wicked, the conclusion offers a hopeful way forward.

Application. The realization of this darkness without and within can tempt us to view God as the "big fix," which can take us out of our suffering and pain. During one particularly difficult period I was earnestly seeking God's presence in my life through prayer, meditation, Scripture—certainly not bad things in themselves. Yet God continued to seem distant and absent. One day, however, I realized what I was doing. I was making God into a "big fix" to take me out of my misery.

I wanted an ecstatic experience with God that would so fill me with his spiritual presence that I would no longer be aware of the suffering that surrounded me and filled me. I was shocked by the realization of how similar my desire for God was to the need of the addict for a narcotic high or an alcoholic haze that obliterated—even for a moment—the pain of the real world. When I set aside this unrealistic view of relationship with God, I began, little by little, to experience the presence of God *within* the distorted world in which we live.

PSALM 38:1–22

Original Meaning

The Invocation of Yahweh (38:1–4). Verses 1–4 establish the perspective and tone for the remainder of the composition. The psalmist experiences physical suffering as the rebuke of Yahweh for personal sin. He does not deny the assumed accusation but freely admits his guilt (38:3–4).

From the psalmist's view Yahweh is acting out of "anger" and "wrath" (38:1, 3), regular terms used to describe the experience of God's displeasure with human sin. However, the atmosphere of instruction fostered here provides a context that somewhat mitigates the harshness of divine anger/wrath by understanding it as a part of divine instruction.

The consequence of this divine attack is a rapid decline of the psalmist's physical health. The effects of the disease are all-consuming (38:3), inner as well as outer physical pain and deterioration. Add to this the psychological torment of "guilt" (38:4), and the psalmist's absorption by disease is complete.

Narrative of Suffering (38:5–20). This account can be divided into two parts: 38:5–10, where the focus is on the physical consequences of suffering, and 38:11–20, where relational effects between the psalmist and friends or enemies are explored.

The description uses language of extreme gangrenous infection. The afflicted psalmist's diseased body exhibits "wounds" or sores that emit a foul odor (38:5). The psalmist is "bowed down" by this malady (38:6); he experiences searing back pain as well (38:7). He acknowledges the suffering as a consequence of personal sin and "folly" (38:5) to which he now responds with mourning and repentance. The psalmist feels "feeble and utterly crushed," and he is able to respond only with inarticulate groans and sighs (38:8–9).

The psalmist's condition has disruptive effects on relationships with others. Those whom he might count as positive relationships—friends, companions, neighbors—distance themselves (38:11). At the same time, his opponents consider the sickness an opportunity to gain advantage.

Unable to answer his accusers, the psalmist waits for Yahweh to act as defender and vindicator (38:15). The narrator feels at a crisis point and is wracked with pain (38:17). This sense of vulnerability and lack of control leads him at last to the full confession of sin and an expression of remorse.

Final Plea for Deliverance (38:21–22). The psalmist returns at the end to directly address Yahweh, pleading for God's immediacy of presence in deliverance. At the bottom of personal resources and hope, he recognizes that Yahweh is synonymous with salvation.

Application. Often Christian leaders enmeshed in moral failures feel unable to confess their sin or to seek help. Some even choose suicide rather than confession. Our psalm helps us to see that acknowledging sin is the only way out of this trap of fear and destruction.

PSALM 39:1–13

Original Meaning

The Agony of Silent Waiting (39:1–3). It is difficult to know just what words the psalmist kept from speech that might be considered "sin" (39:1). The key may be found in 39:2, where the psalmist says that silence—"not even saying anything good"—only increased his anguish. In this event the speech he "muzzles" (i.e., keeps in check) would be a caustic diatribe against the "wicked" who are "present" (38:1). The struggle is, then, between striking out verbally at the wicked or alternatively speaking something "good" (39:2). The inner turmoil ultimately forces him to break his self-imposed silence (39:3c) with the good word of the body of the psalm.

The Frailty of Human Life (39:4–6). Rather than a diatribe against evil or even an anguished complaint to God, the psalmist offers an informed meditation on the fragility of human life. The psalmist wishes to know the "end" of his life and the "number" of his days (39:4), not in order to have mastery over life but to gain an appropriate appreciation for the tenuous and fragile nature of human existence. Yahweh does supply the hope of the psalmist.

This new perspective leads to a pessimistic evaluation of human life and its lasting accomplishments that is reminiscent of Ecclesiastes. The continued thought in 39:6 focuses—as does Ecclesiastes—on the empty accomplishment of human endeavor.

Acknowledgment of Sin (39:7–11). Having established the frailty of human life and the futility of human endeavor, where can the psalmist turn for effective help? He finds hope for deliverance from sin and the "scorn of fools" in Yahweh (39:7–8).

Deliverance comes at the price of confession of sin (39:8, 11), and the psalmist acknowledges that the suffering endured is from God (39:9–11) and is intended as "rebuke and discipline" (39:11).

Final Plea for Deliverance (39:12–13). The psalmist concludes with a final plea to Yahweh for deliverance. Unless Yahweh relents and ends the punishment, he has no hope but to depart and be no more.

Application. Meditative silence can allow us time to reflect on the real reasons behind our anger and pain before our lashing out jeopardizes relationships by distorting and confusing the real issues involved.

PSALM 40:1–17

Original Meaning

Description of Past Deliverance (40:1–4). The theme of "waiting" for Yahweh in the midst of trouble that began in Psalm 37 and continued through Psalms 38 and 39 is sounded once again in 40:1. It seems significant that the enduring expectancy commanded in 37:34, affirmed by the psalmist's commitment in 38:15, and reflected in the narrative of Psalm 39, should reach such a definite conclusion in the emphatic construction of 40:1. Whereas in the former psalms Yahweh's response was anticipated and hoped for, here it is an experienced reality.

The purpose of the "new song" (40:3) is testimony. It will draw others to "fear" Yahweh. In our passage, the positive content of fearing Yahweh is put forward as "trust" in him (40:3) and is clarified further by the blessing in 40:4.

Avowal of Personal Faithfulness and Witness (40:5–10). In this new section the psalmist testifies to the "wonders" Yahweh has done (40:5–6) and declares personal loyalty to him (40:7–10). The "wonders" of Yahweh are too numerous to detail (40:5) as his plans for us are too vast to enumerate.

Verses 6–8 are often taken as a general condemnation of the sacrificial system of Israelite temple worship. Perhaps another way to understand these seemingly harsh words about sacrifice is to take them as referring only to the specific experience of the psalmist. In this case the psalmist is testifying that rather than demanding gifts and sacrifices as payment for the psalmist's sin, what Yahweh really wanted was "opened" ears of the psalmist (40:6), attentive to God's instruction, and a heart willing to allow the torah ("law") to guide it (40:8).

The Need for Divine Aid (40:11–12). After establishing a foundation of personal faithfulness, the psalmist appeals to Yahweh for mercy. This appeal also includes the psalmist's desperate circumstances as justification for divine deliverance, using imagery normally reserved for descriptions of pounding surf. Isolated and desperate, the psalmist is on the brink of losing all hope ("my heart fails," 40:12).

Speedy Delivery (40:13–17; 70:1–5). As a concluding plea for deliverance, the psalmist uses five verses that are—except for a few significant variations—identical with the freestanding Psalm 70. There has been considerable debate concerning which version of these verses (40:13–17 or 70:1–5) is earlier, with most concluding that Psalm 70 is an original, independent poem adapted for use at the end of Psalm 40.

Verses 13–17 bring Psalm 40 to a conclusion in an unexpected fashion. The earlier part of the psalm was directed to the psalmist's testimony to the faithfulness of God before the congregation and desire for deliverance from the unspecified troubles that have resulted from sin. Now, without previous mention, these final verses focus on his enemies, whom the psalmist wants Yahweh to recompense for their attacks. The one link with the earlier portion of Psalm 40 is the continuing theme of trusting Yahweh.

Application. Our communities of worship and faith must take care that the important role of confession as a means of proclaiming God's righteousness, truth, and salvation does not become the exclusive domain of twelve-step groups and other psychological support groups.

PSALM 41:1–13

Original Meaning

The Foundation of Confidence (41:1–3). The first stanza begins with the important Hebrew word *ashrey* ("blessed, happy"). This term here seems intentionally positioned to cause the reader to reflect back to the opening blessings in Psalms 1 and 2 and to read the present psalm—with its rather tenuous portrait of a king at risk—against that more powerful earlier picture of the king as established and empowered by God. The one who knows how to deal appropriately with the weak can anticipate appropriate treatment from Yahweh when weakness overtakes him.

The Complaint (41:4–9). Two stanzas of three verses each expound the malice and calumny of the psalmist's enemies (41:5–6) and friends (41:9), who speak false cheer to the patient (41:6), spread groundless rumors, and plot together to take advantage of the situation (41:7–8). The section is introduced (41:4) by the psalmist's confession of sin and a plea to Yahweh for mercy.

Final Plea and Confidence (41:10–12). The psalmist now seeks mercy from God and restoration to health. The psalmist's hope is not only for forgiveness and restored health but also for being requited against the enemies—balancing the account sheet between them.

The Doxology (41:13). Verse 13 presents the first of four similar doxologies that function editorially to mark the conclusion of the first four books of the Psalter. This verse marks the end of the first Davidic collection of psalms (Pss 3–41).

Application. Psalm 41 offers insight into the kind of integrity that leads to being upheld by God. This kind of integrity is a consistent way of acting that has its beginning and end in God. There may be individual stumbles along the way, but the integrated person is the one whose eyes remain firmly fixed on the goal.

PSALMS 42:1–43:5

Original Meaning. Psalms 42 and 43 should be read as a unified composition. This idea is confirmed by a number of ancient manuscripts of Psalms that do treat these two psalms as one. The two psalms share a repeated refrain that appears regularly in a combined composition (42:5, 11; 43:5), dividing the whole into three segments of relatively equal size.

Longing to Meet God (42:1–5). Few images in the Psalter exceed the beauty of the opening lines of this psalm. The emphasis is not just on the psalmist's utter dependence on God for life; it is rather the joy and pleasure of being in God's presence that the psalmist misses and longs to restore.

This psalm does not provide us with a clear reason for the psalmist's inability to participate in temple worship. The taunts of the enemy and the implication of 42:6 that he is located outside the land of Israel lends itself to an exilic interpretation.

Overwhelmed and Forgotten (42:6–11). Picking up on the terminology of the refrain, the psalmist acknowledges his "soul is downcast" (42:6a). But immediately the refrain follows into a new terrain of hope: "Therefore I will remember you . . ." (42:6b). Rather than remembering the "things" of worship, he now remembers God himself—the living God, the source of life and hope. He discovers an island in the midst of the sea. God is the "Rock" (42:9) who provides firm footing and protection.

Still, no matter how powerful, the song does not remove the darkness. Psalm 42 draws to an end with the repetition of the earlier refrain. Left as it is the psalm offers but a somber hope.

Plea for Vindication and Joyous Return (43:1–5). The first two imperatives suggest a legal context but note that the opponents described are "an unfaithful nation" (43:1). Thus, it is perhaps better to understand the pleas as expressing the desire that the psalmist's hope and faith in God will be rewarded and publicly acknowledged.

In 43:2, following the imperative plea for vindication and before the following imperatives seeking divine light and guidance (43:3), the psalmist's sense of rejection and suffering become an integral part of motivating God to action.

The poet pictures with relish the consequence of a return to the temple and praising God to the tune of the harp. In this joyous concluding context, the final repeated refrain seems much less somber and clearly more hopeful.

Application. The psalmist suggests another way to remember God's faithfulness: to long for and avail ourselves whenever possible of opportunities to stand together with those who are worshiping God. Even if we feel distant or abandoned, the celebration will have the effect of renewing our certainty and hope. One of the roles of the worshiping congregation is to worship when I cannot, to celebrate the resurrection of Christ when I am mourning the death of a loved one or struggling with my own sin. The congregation is to declare the wonderful works of God even when I can no longer see him or sense his presence.

PSALM 44:1–26

Original Meaning

The Testimony of the Ancestors (44:1–3). The psalm begins by referring to the constant repetition of the patriarchal history and the mighty acts of God enjoined on Israel in the Deuteronomic literature (Deut 4:9). The psalmist describes how the recorded and transmitted history of God's activity with the ancestors of the faith provides the foundation of confidence to present believers (Ps 44:2).

Contemporary Appropriation of Tradition (44:4–8). Faced with a contemporary context of suffering, the people *remember* past evidence of Yahweh's good intent and powerful action on behalf of their ancestors, and in these verses, they seek to follow the advice of the repeated refrain of Psalms 42–43.

Contemporary Israel reaffirms in the present the ancient commitment of the ancestors to Yahweh alone. The single voice that speaks at this point may well be the king who acknowledges that any human efforts at rulership and control must submit to the ultimate sovereignty of God. The singular voice reappears again and again in what follows (cf. 44:6, 15–16) so that the king is pictured as leading the people in recognizing the absolute dependence of human kingship on the gracious mercy of God.

Description of Present Suffering (44:9–16). The Hebrew word *'ap* (meaning "also, yet"), with which 44:9 begins, introduces a radical shift in the tone and content of the psalm. It must in the context be translated as a strong "but now," marking extreme contrast with what has preceded. In 44:1–8 all had been confidence and assurance.

Israel's experience did not live up to her expectation. Victory eluded them, and the reality of defeat took its place. The description suggests severe destruction, societal dislocation, and even deportation (44:11). Regardless of its origin, the psalm would have resonated with the ongoing circumstance of the Diaspora community.

With harsh and pointed language, the psalmist leaves no doubt that the cause of Israel's suffering and disgrace is God himself. The emphatic litany of "You!" with which each verse begins in 44:9–14 is directed to God. The embarrassing words of shame and disgrace pile up in the last verses of this segment like a cairn of stones intended to mark the scene of some scandalous infamy.

Protestation of Innocence (44:17–22). The new departure in this segment is not that Israel suffers defeat and exile. It is not even that the exile is attributed to God. The Deuteronomistic History and viewpoint had already driven both those points home forcefully. Where Psalm 44 departs is in the community's earnest protestation of innocence of any guilt that might justify the punishment meted out in the exile.

Plea for Deliverance (44:23–26). With typical language intended to rouse the hearer to action, the beleaguered community makes its desire for deliverance known. They want God to bring this period of extended rejection to an end (44:23; cf. 44:9). They want his forgetfulness, which led to their current misery, replaced by active memory (44:24). The psalm concludes with a final entreaty for God to "rise up" and redeem his suffering people (44:26).

Application. The community's protest is no claim of complete sinlessness but a claim to have fulfilled their essential obligations to the covenant. Most of us would have to admit that accepting the sacrificial death of Christ as Savior has not yet perfectly removed all our tendencies toward selfishness, anger, lust, greed, and other more subtle forms of sin. I am grateful to know that my moments of weakness and failure, while serious in their own right and in need of repentance and confession, do not drive an irreparable wedge between myself and God.

PSALM 45:1–17

Original Meaning

The Introduction (45:1). The psalm opens with the psalmist's declared purpose to write verses "for" the king. Perhaps the king is the poet's patron, who has commissioned this poem for his wedding day.

In Praise of the King (45:2–9). The psalmist's inspired "good word" begins with an extended section both praising the king and encouraging him to exercise his majestic power and splendor in the service of "truth, humility and justice" (45:4). The anticipated result of this display of kingly power is the defeat of his enemies (45:5) and the establishment of an eternal kingdom of justice and peace (45:6). The major portion of the description is bound at beginning and end by verses that proclaim the king's excellence over other humans (45:2, 7).

In Praise of the Bride (45:10–15). The direct address of the psalm now shifts to the bride, who is depicted as a "daughter" (45:10) forsaking her people and the house of her father to assume her role as wife to the king. The impending marital relationship depicted in a few words is instructive. The king craves the bride's "beauty" (45:11a), while the bride is counseled to "honor" the king because he is her "lord" (45:11b). This rather one-sided relationship is consistent with what is known of the ancient Near East during this period.

The rich and glorious attire of the bride is recounted. Clothed in rich brocades interwoven with gold and in embroidered cloth, the bride "is led [*ybl*] to the king" (45:14), a verb that most often describes bringing something as a gift, sacrifice, tribute, or even booty. This heightens the sense of a political arrangement rather than a marriage of equals or even a love match.

The King's Future (45:16–17). The poem concludes as the bride and her entourage enter the king's palace. Besides the possibility of political alliance with another nation, the marriage also represents the potential for dynastic succession through the production of sons, who will "take the place" (45:16) of the king's fathers. This description of dynastic succession seems to presume a long line of royal antecedents preceding the present king.

Application. The ambiguous statement in 45:6, "Your throne, O God, will last for ever and ever," seems to equate the bridegroom king with God himself. This ambiguous statement allows the possibility that the king, who appears here to be called "God," is in fact being understood as the Messiah, who will usher in God's kingdom. If so, then the marriage ceremony may well already be understood as between Messiah and the people of God, as in the later understanding of this psalm.

PSALM 46:1–11

Original Meaning

Radical Trust in Yahweh (46:1–3). The radical confidence of the psalmist is exhibited in an ability to stand without fear in the face of what constitutes a threat of uncreation. The flood (Gen 6–9) threatened to dissolve creation order into precreation chaos by allowing these restricted waters to exceed and ultimately erase their established boundaries.

God's Protective Presence (46:4–7). From the roar of the rushing waters, we come to the more peaceful description of the well-watered "city of God" (46:4). The river is almost placid by contrast to the raging waters of the previous verses. Rather than destruction, this river offers rejoicing.

The psalmist affirms that unlike the mountains in 46:2 that topple into the sea, the city of God bolstered by his saving presence "will not fall" (46:5). This second section of the psalm concludes with the first statement of a refrain repeated at the end of the psalm: "The LORD Almighty is with us" (46:7, 11).

Trusting Yahweh (46:8–11). The invitation to "come and see what the LORD has done" (46:8) introduces a series of affirmingly parallel lines describing militant actions with an edge of violence. These works of God are reasons for horror to those who want to rule the earth with military might.

Application. When we participate in war, we are not participating in God's creation intention but something that grew out of human sin and disobedience. We are not even participating in something that will last—wars will cease to the ends of the earth!

PSALM 47:1–9

Original Meaning

Yahweh Subdues the Nations (47:1–5). I suggest that the Hebrew expression *taqaʿ kap* in our passage does not mean "clap the hands . . . *of joy*" (emphasis added); rather, in keeping with its regular usage to "strike hands" as confirmation of a bargain or contract, the "nations" are being called to come to agreement regarding their relationship to Yahweh, God of Israel (47:1). It is fitting in this context of universal sovereignty where all humankind is called to acknowledge the kingship of Yahweh, God of Abraham, that the title "Most High" (47:2), with its implication of superiority over the lesser gods of the pagan world, should be applied to Yahweh.

Yahweh Rules as King (47:6–9). The second stanza focuses on the kingship of Yahweh. This is reiterated three times (47:6b, 7a, 8a) and mentions his enthronement as well (47:8b). The kings of the earth in their submission to Yahweh have become his possession (47:9), and there are no longer any who compete with the divine authority of Yahweh as king.

Application. God's purposes move unhindered to their completion despite the chaotic brokenness of our world. God subdues the nations and provides Israel with her true inheritance.

PSALM 48:1–14

Original Meaning

The Presence of Yahweh in Zion (48:1–3). The psalm begins typically for a song in praise of Yahweh. It is only in 48:2 that the focus on the city/mountain where Yahweh makes himself present becomes clear.

The Flight of the Foes (48:4–7). Because of the presence of Yahweh, Zion stands firm in the face of the enemy. The opposing kings are depicted as joining forces for a combined attack (48:4), reminiscent of the conspiracy of the "kings of the earth" against Yahweh and his anointed described in 2:2.

The approaching enemy is astonished and rendered numb by what they see. Whether it is the lofty, fortified city itself (as the NIV implies) or the presence of Yahweh within her that stuns the enemy host is uncertain. The response of the enemy to what they see is described in a series of verbs and expressions indicating astonishment and terror (48:5–6). The end result is total destruction of the enemy army (48:7).

Thematic Center (48:8). The enemy hosts look on Mount Zion, tremble, and flee to their destruction. By contrast, the psalmist and his readers look at the "city of our God" (48:8) and find enduring security.

The Worship of Praise (48:9–11). The setting of the psalm within temple worship becomes explicit by the mention of the "temple" in 48:9. The emphasis here is on the temple as the abode of God—the place where he is present among his people as king. Because of Yahweh's righteous judgments the whole of the Israelite nation rejoices.

Future Hope (48:12–14). The psalm concludes with a mental tour of the defense works of Zion. Yahweh is the eternal God who guides his people like a shepherd.

Application. No matter how impressive our battle works, they are an empty hope unless God is there.

PSALM 49:1–20

Original Meaning

The Sage's Introduction (49:1–4). The psalmist begins with a pluralized form of the classic opening to the Shema—Israel's call to faith—"Hear!" Those called to hear are also described as those "who live in this world" (49:1b). The "world" intended here is the world of *time*—akin to the Greek concept of *aion* ("the world at this time)" rather than *kosmos* ("the world in space"). That is, the emphasis is on those who live in this transitory age.

Like the sages of Proverbs, Ecclesiastes, and Job, the psalmist desires to "give . . . understanding" (49:3), drawing insight from deep within ("my heart"). Since the heart is the seat of moral reasoning and decision-making, such "heart talk" is neither emotional nor intellectual claptrap but represents the deep and enduring outflow of the moral character of the speaker.

The Futility of Human Wealth (49:5–12). The apparent collapse of righteous order that the prosperity of the wicked seems to herald does not undermine the psalmist's confidence in the ultimate good intent of God for the righteous. He acknowledges the reality of "evil days" (49:5a) and the corrupting influence of the crowd of "wicked deceivers" (49:5b), who press their view of the efficacy of wealth (49:6) and use it to intimidate and oppress the poor.

The naming of lands after oneself (49:11b) was a prerogative normally reserved for conquering kings. Here the rich practice the naming of lands in a vain attempt to ensure some immortality for themselves. The psalmist ironically observes that the only land they will continue to possess after death is the tombs in which they are buried.

The Fate of Those Who Trust Themselves (49:13–20). The second stanza begins with a descriptive heading that sets the scene for what follows: "This is the fate of those who trust in themselves" (49:13). Until now it has been the power of wealth that was trusted, but the subtle shift indicates the real issue, namely, the attitude of self-reliance that refuses to acknowledge dependence on Yahweh alone. It is this latter acceptance of one's absolute dependence on the undeserved mercy of Yahweh that is at the core of Israel's understanding of "the fear of the LORD." Such fear is not terror but submission of one's whole being to the vulnerable state of Yahweh's control. This is what the arrogant rich lack in our psalm—which in turn leads the psalmist to describe them as "like the [unthinking] beasts that perish" (49:20b).

Application. Those who trust in themselves and wealth or power are doomed to the decay of death. Those who, however, trust in God will find their significance there.

PSALM 50:1–23

Original Meaning

God the Judge (50:1–6). The introductory passage sets the scene for the two divine speeches that occupy the body of the psalm. God (identified as Yahweh only in the opening verse) comes in theophanic glory (50:3) to sit as judge (50:4, 6) over his covenant people (50:5, 16). At the same time his appearance is linked with sun imagery (50:1–2), a not completely unexpected phenomenon since the sun is often linked with judgment in the ancient Near East. God's subpoena is for both witnesses (heavens and earth) and defendants ("this consecrated people," 50:5) to gather for the hearing of the case.

The First Accusation (50:7–15). The first accusation is a parody of the Shema, the essential call to acknowledge Yahweh as the one and only God to whom Israel gives allegiance and obedience (Deut 6:4). By bringing together both Shema and the giving of the law, the psalmist emphasizes the core of the covenant tradition as allegiance to Yahweh alone and obedience to his covenant demands.

It is the intersection of faithfulness to the covenant demands and sacrifice that are at issue in the remainder of the psalm. It is clear that sacrifices are being made in abundance (50:8). God does not rebuke Israel for failing to sacrifice at all. It is, however, Israel's *understanding* of sacrifice that appears to be defective.

In this first section, the problem seems to be that those who sacrifice believe their sacrifices are *essential* to God—that in some sense their sacrifices meet a need that God has. This was common in the Mesopotamian context. Israel must have agreed with the general Mesopotamian view that sacrifice met the needs of God and offered an opportunity for humans to manipulate him.

The section concludes with an exhortation to right sacrifice. The point of offering "thank offerings" (50:14) is that such sacrifices acknowledge the offeror's absolute dependence on Yahweh's grace and mercy. Such people will "fulfill [their] vows" (50:14) to God and will experience the deliverance they seek (50:15).

The Second Accusation (50:16–23). Israel's wickedness is that they lack the inner commitment to Yahweh that would give their ritual sacrifice meaning (50:17). The psalm offers six examples of covenant-breaking wickedness, presented in synonymous pairs. In a general sense, the psalmist envisions failure to maintain relationships of honesty and respect.

The psalmist exhorts the people to adopt a renewed understanding of sacrifice and to offer evidence of one's inner reliance on Yahweh alone. Forgetting God has severe consequences. The image used for divine judgment is that of a ravening beast tearing its helpless prey. Sacrifice is not a form of self-expression or self-power but a way of acknowledging thanks to God.

Application. Let's not mistake praise and thanks for worship. They are vital parts of worship, but *only part*! True worship requires the fear of Yahweh, acknowledgment of sin, and petition of forgiveness. Then our thanksgiving and praise will be sincere. True worship involves opening our eyes to see the hurts of the world outside our gathering place. It means acting on what we see. Then our praise will have meaning beyond our own well-being and will sound with new sweetness in God's ears.

PSALM 51:1–19

Original Meaning

Plea for Forgiveness (51:1–2). The psalmist appeals to the "unfailing love" (*hesed*) of God as the basis of hope for forgiveness (51:1). Although the psalmist has failed through sin, Yahweh does not fail but continues in his commitment to sinful humans who acknowledge their sin and rely on God's merciful forgiveness and love. The forgiveness sought is described in a series of imperative verbs for cleansing. Some ritual of confession, repentance, and cleansing may be in mind here.

Along with the three verbs for cleansing, the psalmist uses three nouns for sin. Rather than focus on specific types of sin, the use of all three terms seems intended to be comprehensive, so that the psalmist's confession is far-reaching and complete.

Confession of Sin (51:3–6). That the sin is against Yahweh "only" (51:4) may seem to belittle the offense against Bathsheba, against her husband, Uriah, or against society as a whole. But the intent is perhaps to heighten the sense of offense by acknowledging that ultimately violations of the covenant are offenses against God himself. The psalmist concedes that his sin proceeds from a longstanding sinful nature. In his expressions of self-awareness, the psalmist exhibits the kind of transparency God desires (51:6).

Plea for Cleansing (51:7–9). The psalmist pleads with Yahweh in 51:9 to "hide [his] face"—not from the psalmist but from his *sins*. Such an act implies that God chooses not to take one's failings into account but to "blot out" (51:1, 9). Such restoration is predicated on the "unfailing love" and "compassion" of Yahweh (51:1).

Plea for Spiritual Restoration (51:10–12). In these verses, the psalmist emphasizes the need for a transformed inner attitude characterized by a "pure heart," a "steadfast spirit," and a "willing spirit."

Vow of Praise and Public Contrition (51:13–17). The psalmist's anticipation of deliverance leads to vows of public acts of praise and contrition that provide instructive exhortation to right actions for other sinners (51:13). Deliverance loosens his tongue to joyous proclamations of public praise (51:14–15).

Plea for Restoration of Zion (51:18–19). The concern expressed for the rebuilding of Jerusalem has the effect of adapting this individual plea for deliverance to the circumstance of the exilic Jewish community.

Application. Admitting sin and working on it is painful, and I don't like to face pain. Usually, however, once I have chewed on it for a while, I am finally able to get around to doing something about it. I get so sick of seeing it out there in front of me that I at last consent to let it be gone.

PSALM 52:1–9

Original Meaning

The Arrogance of the Wicked (52:1–5). The psalmist must have felt under attack by those who knew well how to control and manipulate language with destructive effectiveness (52:4b). The arrogance and evil intent of these enemies come together when they feel free to "boast" of their evil "all day long" (52:1b). Here the tongue of the wicked takes on almost a life of its own as it plots out its destructive course. Its deceptive power to lie and mislead is put in the foreground in chapter 52, as "deceit" and "falsehood" are the operative terms (52:2a, 3b, 4b). The final result of the enemy's arrogant falsehood and deceit is judgment.

The Response of the Righteous (52:6–7). The fall of the deceitful wicked provides an object lesson the righteous can take to heart. Behind the laughter stands a clear admonition not to follow this path to destruction.

Trust and Praise of the Psalmist (52:8–9). Unlike the wicked who will be pulled out of the nourishing soil of the land of the living (52:5), the psalmist will be like a tree planted deep in the life-giving earth of Yahweh's own dwelling, flourishing with abundant foliage (52:8a). This blessing of Yahweh's continued presence is linked to the psalmist's trust in God's "unfailing love [*hesed*]" (52:8b). Trust and blessing shift over to praise and hope in the final verse.

Application. One need not experience the rooting out reserved for the wicked. Trust in God rather than in self.

PSALM 53:1–6

Original Meaning

The Folly of the Evildoers (53:1–3). See the commentary on 14:1–3 for discussion on these verses.

Judgment on the Wicked (53:4–5). Having described the corruption of human beings (53:1–3) in terms that seem absolute, the psalmist now indicates there are those oppressed by the powerful fools and who receive divine care and protection. As a result, the wicked are condemned for treating the poor as consumable objects. In Psalm 14, the emphasis is placed on the protective power of God on behalf of the poor, while in Psalm 53, God's power is unleashed in judgment on the wicked.

Communal Hope for Restoration (53:6). As in Psalm 14, our present version concludes with an expression of the hope of the community for restoration.

Application. There are those in my society who *are* being consumed in a radical way, such as throw-away children and young men and women forced into the sex trade. Such individuals have become equivalent to consumable products like bread and potatoes to satisfy an appetite.

PSALM 54:1–7

Original Meaning

Call for Hearing and Deliverance (54:1–2). The psalm begins with a plea for God to "save" the psalmist (54:1a). Along with deliverance, the psalmist also desires vindication (54:1b).

The Psalmist's Plight (54:3). The attackers are called *zarim*, a Hebrew term that normally refers to a non-Israelite. Perhaps the intent is to use a particularly harsh term to describe fellow Israelites in order to emphasize just how far they had removed themselves from true covenant relationship.

Statement of Confidence (54:4). The central message of the psalm is confidence in God.

Plea for Retribution (54:5). In 54:5 the psalmist asks that God the judge render justice on his enemies.

Vow of Sacrifice and Praise (54:6–7). As in many laments, this psalm concludes with a vow to offer sacrifice and praise.

Application. When we keep our eyes on God and allow him to be the helper, we can know fulfillment even when our most intimate human connections fail to provide.

PSALM 55:1–23

Original Meaning

Invocation of God (55:1–2a). A typical plea for God to hear the psalmist's complaint opens the psalm. The speaker of 55:1–2 desires God to "answer."

The Psalmist's Distress (55:2b–8). The psalmist's circumstance is dominated by mental and emotional turmoil. The Hebrew root of the verb *yamitu* (NIV "bring down") in 55:3 is well known with the meaning "shake, quake, move" and is commonly used in the psalms to speak about either shaken or unshakable foundations. The enemy's angry attack against the psalmist (55:3) is described with the verbal root *stm*, normally rendered "bear a grudge against, harbor animosity toward." Other commentators translate this verb as "hunt," "persecute," or even "revile."

The distress is so great and so all-consuming that the psalmist wishes only to flee. Wild "doves" (55:6) often nested in remote and inaccessible cliffs in more deserted regions—thus the psalmist's image of fleeing to the security and rest of the desert. The poet is tempted not to wait for divine deliverance but to exercise *self*-deliverance by fleeing to a "place of shelter" (55:8).

Plea for Judgment on the Enemy (55:9–11). Indicating that the problem faced is hostile speech, the psalmist appeals to God to "confuse" and "confound" (literally, "split") the enemy's tongue (55:9). Our passage recalls the Tower of Babel story in Genesis 11, where Yahweh "confuses" the "language" of the unified people building the city in the plain of Shinar. The psalmist may be drawing on the Tower of Babel narrative to speak a word of divine condemnation to the contemporary context. Confusion of speech is needed in his view because the city has become a place of violence and strife.

The Faithless Friend (55:12–14). The attacker is an intimate associate, whom the psalmist knows well from long experience and as a "close" confidant (55:13). The "sweet fellowship" (55:14) shared is confidential conversation between friends who trust each another. The location of the "sweet fellowship" is the temple precincts, so that the two have been spiritually connected and compatible. This last comment heightens the travesty represented by the betrayal.

Renewed Call for Judgment (55:15). The calumny of betrayal by an intimate associate brings the psalmist to harsh words. Tricked by death, they should be brought down to Sheol (55:15; NIV "realm of the dead") while still alive—an indication of the abrupt and unexpected nature of their departure.

Statement of Confidence (55:16–19). In contrast to the quick and certain destruction of the wicked, the psalmist is confident of divine deliverance. His confidence is founded on the eternal enthronement of Yahweh as king (55:19).

Reprise: The Faithless Friend (55:20–21). The psalmist returns to the subject of treacherous attack by a close friend. Slippery language cloaks the real sentiment and motivation of the opponent behind false words. The enemy's words appear "more soothing than oil" used to anoint and soften, while in reality their intent is to cut and maim like "swords" (55:21).

Confident Trust in God (55:22–23). This last section contains the psalmist's call to others to trust God by casting their cares on him (55:22), a statement directed to God expressing confidence of judgment on the wicked (55:23) and a brief profession of faith and confidence in God (55:23c).

Application. Just to be associated with certain words is destructive, even if the words are untrue. Our words can affect the way someone is viewed by others. They can even undermine the way one feels about oneself.

PSALM 56:1–13

Original Meaning

Opening Plea for Mercy (56:1–4). The enemy is depicted like a hound in full pursuit, snapping at the fleeing psalmist's heels. The attack is continual, as indicated by the repetition of the phrase "all day long" no less than three times in the first five verses (56:1b, 2a, 5a). The opponents attack the psalmist from a position of advantage (56:2; Heb. *marom* ["elevation of ground; high social position"] rather than the NIV's "in their pride").

Desired Defeat of the Enemy (56:5–11). They "twist [his] words," plot harm, and wait for the opportunity to snuff out his life (56:6). The psalmist appeals to God for redress (56:7), pleading that his enemies not escape their just punishment. But he makes an unexpected turn here by requesting that God bring down not such social detractors and opponents, but "the peoples" (*ammim*, NIV "nations, 56:7), a reference to the many ethnic and tribal communities that make up the nations and the world population. This broadened reference probably reflects a postexilic viewpoint of the Jewish Diaspora.

The psalmist wants God to record his lament so that it will not be forgotten and will lead ultimately to action. The psalmist seems to imply that if God remembers the plea, he will act so that his enemies will be defeated and "turn back" (56:9). The call for redress against the enemy concludes with the second appearance of the refrain.

Vow of Thanksgiving (56:12–13). Vows are promises to give something to God. Fulfillment of a vow normally took place in the context of public worship.

Application. God's word is a source of confidence to those who are beset by enemies. Only God sees the true state of our affairs. Only he is able to pronounce a true judgment of righteousness and failure.

PSALM 57:1–11

Original Meaning

Plea for Deliverance (57:1–5). Rather than focusing on the treacherous attack of the wicked as does Psalm 56, the psalmist here brings to the foreground a confident sense of God as the place of "refuge" (57:1). The psalmist's desire to seek refuge is based on an understanding of God that inspires confidence. God "sends forth his love and his faithfulness" (57:3). In expressing the desire that God be exalted "above the heavens" (57:5) and that his "glory [*kabod*] be over all the earth," the poet is using a merism to inculcate God's rule over everything that is.

Promise of Praise (57:6–11). Following the hopeful refrain, the psalmist returns again to the enemy's attack, but this time with a decided difference. Here the evil of the opponents is seen to return upon themselves (57:6c-d). The placement of the refrain (57:5) in the middle of the discussion of the enemy attack (57:4, 6) demonstrates literarily what the psalmist hopes to experience in reality: God's protective presence in the midst of trouble.

Like Psalm 56, this psalm shifts somewhat to include a more international perspective as the psalmist promises to sing God's praises "among the nations . . . among the peoples" (57:9). Again, this may represent an adaptation of an originally more individually focused psalm to continue to speak to the circumstances of the postexilic Jewish community.

It is an overwhelming sense of God's loyalty and faithfulness that motivates the psalmist's outbreak of praise. As God comes in his glory, evil and its effects are vanquished and the faithful affirmed in their enduring loyalty to God.

Application. Yahweh is *above* the heavens, outside what he made. Yet God's glory can fill creation. This God loves, and he can be known and loved in return.

PSALM 58:1–11

Original Meaning

The Evil Influence of the Wicked (58:1–5). Corrupt judges are likened to dangerous, venomous cobras, so intent on their evil from birth that they have become completely inured to any persuasion or control, wanting only to lash out and harm.

Plea for Divine Judgment (58:6–8). The psalmist switches imagery to call for divine judgment on the corrupt judges. He calls on God to render them impotent and toothless. A string of changing images follows, expressing the psalmist's desire that the oppressive wicked may cease to enjoy effective existence. In the harshest rebuke, the psalmist wishes that the wicked had never been born, nipping the long process of their wayward wickedness (cf. 58:3) in the bud.

Expression of Confidence (58:9–11). Psalm 58 now turns to expressions of confidence in deliverance. Bathing the feet in the blood of the enemy is a traditional ancient Near Eastern way of expressing the utter defeat of the enemy. The image is wading through blood left as the result of the carnage of battle.

Vindication comes with the public recognition and acknowledgment that the righteous are "rewarded" (58:11) by God. The final line drives home the reality that the justice humans mete out ought to be reflective of the kind of justice God himself would (and eventually will) render as judge of the earth.

Application. I long for restoration when evil will be destroyed and creation harmony reigns at last between human beings, humans and animals, and all of us with the physical world itself.

PSALM 59:1–17

Original Meaning

Introductory Plea (59:1–2). The psalmist pleads for deliverance and protection from enemies. In 59:2 these opponents are further described as "evildoers."

The Enemy Attack (59:3–9). It is not immediately clear that the enemy attack is a matter of "slander" (59:10). The enemy lie in wait/ambush and attack (cf. 56:6) the psalmist for no cause (59:3c, 4a). His protestation of innocence is no protection from their rushing attack.

In 59:6 and again later (59:14), the enemy is characterized as a roving pack of dogs that roam the city looking for vulnerable prey. The enemy's verbal attacks are likened to vicious thrusts with a sword (59:7b), thinking they can speak and act with impunity: "Who can hear us?" But the psalmist is confident that God does hear.

Like the watchman of a besieged city straining to see the expected arrival of the relieving troops, the psalmist "watches" (59:9) for the appearance of "my God on whom I can rely" (59:10a). This refrain ends the first major section of the psalm.

Punishment and Confidence (59:10–17). Following the first refrain, the psalmist shifts to a description of the hoped-for response by God to the empty pride of the enemy. He desires both public vindication and the destruction of the enemy. He does not ask for a complete decimation of the opponents ("do not kill them," 59:11), but the ultimate consequence is, of course, the final destruction and disappearance of the enemy (59:13). This object lesson has two purposes:

1. to punish the enemy for their arrogant slander (59:12a, b); and
2. to make it clear that God is the effective ruler of Israel (59:13b).

The concluding refrain takes on a subtly different meaning. In its first occurrence (59:9), the psalmist responded to the enemy's attack by watching diligently for the coming of God's strength as deliverance. Here God's "strength" (59:16) has already become a cause for praise, and the psalmist moves to acknowledge that God is the source of his own strength.

Application. Not only is God creator and sustainer, sovereign and all-powerful, but he is a loving God as well. Without the last, God would be a powerful deity with whom we had to deal, but we would not likely *trust* him. It would be a little like living under a totalitarian dictatorship. The government would exercise the power of life and death over all aspects of our world, and we would have to deal with it and consider it in all our decisions and actions; but we would not have to trust it.

PSALM 60:1–12

Original Meaning

The Lament (60:1–4). The psalm laments a particularly significant defeat that is interpreted as divine judgment on Israel. God is described as the source of Israel's suffering in a series of verbal expressions that extends through 60:3. The "banner" (60:4) is a type of standard or flag used in battle to provide visibility during hand-to-hand combat and to offer a rallying point.

Oracle of Deliverance (60:5–8). The psalm moves into a confident promise of divine power and victory. This section begins with a renewed plea for deliverance (60:5) and continues with a word from God himself. This divine word expresses

God's power and authority over all those national enemies who confront his people.

Plea for Divine Leadership and Deliverance (60:9–12). Psalm 60 concludes with a plea for God to act as he is capable and to enable his people to defeat their enemies. The plea stands in tension between the confidence that God is *able* to defeat all enemies (as the preceding verses have demonstrated) and the continuing awareness that Israel is experiencing divine abandonment and rejection (60:1–3, 10). The psalmist calls on God directly to aid his people against their enemies (60:11a) and acknowledges that human power is ultimately of no avail (60:11b). The confident assurance of 60:12 must be read as a hopeful profession of faith, standing as it does in such close proximity with the preceding pictures of divine abandonment and human powerlessness.

Application. Our failures do not mean that God has failed. Destruction, no matter how desperate, can be mended (60:2). God offers deliverance from sin.

PSALM 61:1–8

Original Meaning

Opening Plea for Hearing (61:1–5). The cry is urgent because he is speaking "from the ends of the earth" (61:2a). Isolated and distant, the psalmist's heart "grows faint" (61:2b). One can almost see the psalmist frantically reaching upward along the rock and seeking the down stretched hand of God to pull him to safety.

The psalmist switches metaphors to envision an even more secure life dwelling in the "tent" of God "forever" (61:4). The psalmist's vow to praise God's name in the face of such threatening isolation is a measure of his faith (61:5).

Long Life for the King (61:6–7). In an unexpected shift, the psalmist moves from an individual plea for protection to a prayer for a long life and enduring reign for the king.

Concluding Vow of Praise (61:8). The psalm ends with a promise to praise God's name daily as a fulfillment of the vow mentioned earlier in 61:5.

Application. The psalmist cries out even with a weak heart because God has been a refuge and a strong tower against the foe in the past.

PSALM 62:1–12

Original Meaning

The Assault of the Wicked (62:1–6). The first section of the psalm describes an assault on the psalmist by the wicked. This description itself takes up two central verses (62:3–4) bracketed before and behind by a near *inclusio* (62:1–2, 5–6) which includes the psalmist's expression of unshakable trust in God as "my rock," "my salvation," and "my fortress." The effect of the *inclusio* is to surround the attacking enemy with the power and protection of God, so that any strength or effectiveness attributed to the enemy is nullified from the start.

God as Rock and Refuge (62:7–8). These central verses provide the transition from the more individual reflections in 62:1–6 and the community-oriented aphorisms in 62:9–12. The "glue" that holds the two together is the brief reflection in these verses on God who is the "fortress" and "refuge" of both psalmist and community (62:2b, 7b).

Exhortations to the Community (62:9–12). The final section of Psalm 62 is a collection of three aphorisms that drive home the preceding exhortation for the community to place their trust in God as refuge. These sayings are similar in structure, content, and vocabulary with comparable aphorisms known from the biblical wisdom literature.

The section concludes with a numerical saying similar to those found in Proverbs 30:7–31. The twofold description of the character of God provided in this saying offers the necessary basis of confidence and trust that was missing in human status and corrupt power. God can be trusted.

Application. With eyes on the storm, there seems no hope to overcome it. With eyes turned toward self, there is no personal power equal to the task. Only when one is able to focus on God alone does the power of the storm recede in response to his command: "Quiet! Be still!" (Mark 4:39).

PSALM 63:1–11

Original Meaning

Thirst for God (63:1). The psalmist begins with imagery of a parched traveler searching for life like looking for water. For the psalmist, God is just such a rare and life-giving commodity for which he longs. The verb "seek" (63:1) has the edge of an "earnest, intent, focused" search.

Satisfying Vision of God (63:2–8). In the midst of the psalmist's isolation and an earnest search for God, he experiences a vision of God that sustains him. The psalmist's vision is of God "in the sanctuary," reminiscent of Isaiah's vision (Isa 6:1–9) and reminding the psalmist in an almost overwhelming way of God's "power and . . . glory" (Ps 63:2). The remainder of this section of the psalm follows this division as the psalmist first praises God for his power (63:3b–5) and then commits faithfully to cling to God's sustaining love (63:6–8).

Remembering God while "on my bed" or "through the watches of the night" (63:6) means the psalmist is not calmly sleeping but wakefully worrying! In the midst of this nocturnal tension, however, he recalls the vision of God's enduring, committed love (*hesed*) and is sustained by that memory.

Confidence of Deliverance (63:9–11). The life of the enemy "pours out" upon the "handles" of a (violently thrusted) "sword" (author's translation, 63:10a; NIV "given over to the sword"). In 63:10b the body of the slain enemy becomes "food for jackals." King and people *will* find cause for rejoicing and praise.

Application. The teaching of both Old and New Testaments agrees that knowing God and his love is more satisfying than life itself.

PSALM 64:1–10

Original Meaning

Plea for Deliverance (64:1–2). The problem is a terrifying and life-threatening attack by his enemies. The attack is characterized as a "conspiracy" (64:2).

The Arrogance of the Wicked (64:3–6). The deadly words of the enemies cut and pierce (64:3–4). He is "innocent" and completely unprepared for the "ambush" that comes without warning (64:4). The utter arrogance of the wicked is displayed in their sense of impunity.

The enemy find courage in numbers and plot their attacks in advance. They convince themselves their plan has no possible flaw. The section concludes with the ironic comment of the narrator (64:6c). Perhaps a more apt translation of would be: "The inward deliberations of a man and his heart are impenetrable!" You can almost see the psalmist's head shaking with ironic confusion over how the enemy could come to such a misguided and totally erroneous conclusion.

Judgment Is Coming (64:7–8). Far from carrying out their plot in secret, they will be exposed to public ridicule as "all who see them" unite in shaking "their heads in scorn" (64:8c).

Concluding Praise and Trust (64:9–10). The righteous, the psalmist affirms, need have no fear of such attackers but should take refuge in Yahweh, assured of his protective care.

Application. Hope for justice has a double edge. We sinners have no complaint when we receive from God the justice we wished on others.

PSALM 65:1–13

Original Meaning

Forgiveness of Sin (65:1–4). Here, distress is the result of sin (65:3a), and praise is a response to God's forgiveness (65:3b). Acknowledging an overwhelming sense of guilt for sin (65:3a), the psalmist nevertheless affirms past experience of God's forgiveness and restoration (65:3b–4).

God's Stabilizing Power (65:5–8). Not only does God forgive sin, but he also provides a stabilizing influence on a world beset with turmoil. God hears the prayer of the sinner and responds "with awesome and righteous deeds" (65:5a). The Savior God is acknowledged as the powerful creator of the mountains, who was able to provide effective boundaries to the chaotic waters at creation and will similarly provide limits to the power of the "nations" and "the turmoil" that results from their striving (65:7).

The result of God's continuing control of the universe and the human powers within it is that those who dwell at its furthest limits are amazed by God's wondrous power and righteousness (cf. 65:5, 8) and are inspired to shouts of joy.

The Blessings of the Land (65:9–13). The final segment of the psalm centers around the abundant blessings of the land enriched by God's care (65:9). God so "cares for" or loves the land that he pours out his blessing on it. Everything is described in terms of excess. All this excess is clearly attributed to the gracious care and effective power of God, who rules the earth from "where morning dawns, where evening fades" (65:8). As a result, the land throws a party! (65:13).

Application. God's redemption is *inclusive* and not *exclusive.* God wants peoples near and far to fear his wondrous works, not by standing on the outside and looking in longingly but by standing shoulder to shoulder and joining in the chorus of praise.

PSALM 66:1–20

Original Meaning

Call to Universal Praise of God (66:1–15). This first major section of chapter 66 is further subdivided into three segments, each marked by an imperative call to participation. The first subdivision (66:1–4) opens with a call to the universal praise of God by "all the earth" (66:1a). The basis for this universal recognition of God's glory is his mighty deeds, which leave no doubt about his authority and power. Overwhelmed by the glory of God, the world falls to its collective knees in wonder and praise to his name (66:4a-c).

The second subsection (66:5–7) describes the works of God. What God has done has both a specific Israelite component and a more universal edge. National celebration is coupled with a more universal recognition of the ruling power and authority of God (66:7).

The third subsection (66:8–12) begins, as did the first, with a universal call to praise God. What follows constitutes Israel's personal testimony before the nations. Despite fierce suffering, God's intentions for his people were good from the beginning (cf. 66:9) and proved to be blessing at the end when the community of faith admitted that God "brought us to a place of abundance" (66:12c).

Personal Testimony (66:16–20). The final section of the psalm begins again with an invitation to a larger community of participants—presumably those gathered to worship in the temple. In this case it is "all you who fear God" who are invited to witness the psalmist's testimony to God's gracious deliverance (66:16).

In the context of the extended group of Psalms 56–68, Psalm 66 becomes the testimony of Israel among the nations that God is in decisive control over the world (66:2–7) and delivers those who adopt the proper attitude of repentance of sin (66:17–20). Israel's loss of national identity and independence in the exile is to be understood as divine testing of the faithful, which will ultimately lead to abundant life (66:8–12). The goal of this testimony is to call "all the earth" (66:1) and the "peoples" (66:8) to experience the blessing and to join in the praise of God.

Application. We sometimes think that God's power can only be displayed when we live charmed, painless lives of abundant goodness. Such a perspective inhibits us from talking honestly and openly about the failures, struggles, hurts, and attacks that characterize our lives. But it is in our weakness that the power of God is made known.

PSALM 67:1–7

Original Meaning

Communal Benediction (67:1–3). Verses 1–3 describe the salvation of God as extending to other nations, who learn to "fear him" (67:7).

The Just Rule and Guidance of God (67:4–5). Verses 4–5 continue the note of universal thanksgiving. God's salvation is known through his extending his authority to the whole earth.

The Universal Blessing of God (67:6–7). The psalm concludes with abundant crops, a sign of God's blessing (67:6b). The final verse reintroduces the theme and universal language that stitches together the group of Psalms 56–68. The growing theme has reached its climax, and all is ready for the celebration to begin.

Application. God has promised to guide us himself, to go before us and to make his way known. Our attention to the details of God's rule among us will sharpen our vision along with our faith to follow him.

PSALM 68:1–35

Original Meaning

Desire for God to Scatter His Enemies (68:1–3). The psalmist uses the imagery of the dissipation of smoke before a wind and the melting away of wax before a flame to describe the utter defeat of God's enemies, who scatter and flee in total disarray before him (68:2–3). While the wicked will perish when God comes (a natural result of the conflict between their sin and his holiness), the righteous have nothing to fear.

Praise for Protection of the Defenseless (68:4–6). The coming of God is an occasion for great joy, and the gathered worshipers are called to join in singing his praise (68:4). God appears in association with the power of the storm (cf. 68:33–34) and is proclaimed the one "who rides on the clouds" (68:4)—an epithet also known to be applied to the Canaanite deity Baal. This may be the reason the divine name Yahweh is introduced at this point, so that no mistake can be made. Elsewhere in the psalms God is also associated with powerful storm phenomena (cf. especially Ps 29).

God Appears as Abundant Rain (68:7–10). In contrast to the environs experienced by the "rebellious" (68:6), the faithful experience Yahweh as refreshing showers that provide bounty even in the wasteland. In what appears to be an allusion to the exodus and subsequent conquest of Canaan, God is described as going before his people and marching with them "through the wilderness" (68:7). This allusion is heightened in the following verses by the phrases "God, the One of Sinai" (68:8c), "inheritance" (68:9), and "settled in it" (68:10). The exodus-conquest motifs of desert wandering and entry into the land are artfully expanded in these verses by the inclusion of storm imagery, which both displays God's power and affirms his concern to provide for his people.

The Divine Word Scatters the Enemy (68:11–14). Not only does Yahweh provide bountiful crops for his people, but he also removes the enemies that threaten them. The primary message is clear: Yahweh comes, and "kings and armies flee" (68:12a) and are scattered like snow on the mountaintops (68:14). The "word" that God pronounces at the beginning of this passage (68:11a) is possibly the announcement of his impending visit (cf. 68:17). Even the prospect of God's coming is enough to send the mighty kings of the earth into a panic.

Yahweh Comes to His Sanctuary (68:15–27). The craggy mountains of Bashan gaze down with envy, not because of Zion's great heights or rugged beauty but simply because it is the place "where God chooses to reign" (68:16). The very presence of God gives this simple location stature.

As a victorious king entered a city and sanctuary, God ascends the throne, from which he rules his kingdom. The victory procession of a returning king was common in the ancient Near East. Captives were paraded as a visible representation of the king's far-flung conquests. Even the "rebellious" (68:18) will hurry with gifts to prove their loyalty to God.

God's presence in his sanctuary is a source of hope for his people. Yahweh "daily bears [their] burdens" (68:19b) and provides "escape from death" (68:20b). Therefore, God is acknowledged as "Savior" (68:19a).

Yahweh, the king, intends to bring his conquered enemies to Jerusalem so that the people there can see and even share in the defeat of their opponents. The conquered come from Bashan. The "sea" mentioned as the source of additional defeated enemies (68:22b) is the Mediterranean, which borders Israel on the west. The psalmist mixes the image of the victorious king entering his capital city—defeated enemies following in his train—with the cultic procession of celebrants to the Jerusalem temple.

The Nations Submit to God's Power (68:28–31). The victory of Yahweh brings submission by the nations of the earth to his rule. Because of his "power" and "strength" (68:28), they hasten to bring gifts and tribute, acknowledging their allegiance to him (68:29–30). "Egypt" (along with "Cush," i.e., Upper Egypt) is explicitly mentioned in 68:31 as sending envoys in order to submit to the authority of God and to entreat peace with him.

The Kingdoms of the Earth Praise God (68:32–35). In a reprise of earlier praises, the psalmist reissues the call to "sing to God" (68:32), first heard in 68:4. As there, God is associated with storm phenomena (particularly thunder, 68:33). Having been brought captive to Jerusalem, the nations witness the awesome power of Yahweh as he enters his sanctuary. Once having seen his glory, these rebellious nations are unable to resist the praise of God, who is king both in the heavens and on the earth (68:34). Yahweh's power is manifest in his temple, and his presence in Israel imparts "power and strength to his people" (68:35).

Application. To experience God in this way is to experience him with all the guards let down and the boundaries removed. It is to know the terrible, awesome, fearsome, threatening being of the one who created us and yet is now unleashed among us to challenge our sinful beings to provide any justification for our continued existence. Isaiah's response to such a theophany (Isa 6:1–9) shows us just how scary that kind of experience can be!

PSALM 69:1–36

Original Meaning

Plea for Deliverance from Enemies (69:1–4). The imagery the psalmist chooses to dramatize the situation is the desperate struggle of a shipwreck survivor trying to stay afloat in a pounding sea. The real threat is not the pounding waves of the sea but the pounding attack of enemies who seek to destroy. Like the ceaseless waves, the psalmist's enemies are everywhere and seem without number. The enemy attack is more than a misguided vendetta; it is a purposefully deceitful attempt to "get" the psalmist by distorting the truth—submerging any protestations under the flood of their false accusations.

Folly and Scorn (69:5–12). Although the psalmist characterizes the enemy's attacks as groundless and false, the second section begins with an admission—directly to God—of his "folly" and "guilt" (69:5). The psalmist acknowledges that individual failing has corporate consequences. Whatever the nature of the guilt the psalmist admits to God in 69:5, the scorn he experiences results from his commitment to God rather than personal failing.

He endures both scorn and shame because of his "zeal" for God's house (69:9). The following verses (69:10–11) suggest a public display of weeping, fasting, and wearing of sackcloth. The public response to the psalmist's fervent and visible grief is ridicule and mocking (69:11–12).

Renewed Plea for Deliverance (69:13–18). Having described the experience of communal shame and ridicule, the psalmist returns again to entreat God for deliverance. The resulting prayer entreats Yahweh for a time of divine favor in which the proper human response is trust and God's appropriate action is enduring salvation.

The psalmist's desperation is illumined by the repeated appearance of the imperative call "answer me" in 69:13, 16, 17. The grounds for his assumption that *now* is the appropriate time for divine favor is the perception of God's "great love" (69:13) and "mercy" (69:16).

This section concludes with the plea that God end his inactive and hidden state and come quickly to the psalmist's rescue. For God to "hide [his] face" (69:17) from his covenant people was considered a sign of divine rejection and punishment for sin.

Continued Description of Scorn (69:19–21). This painful lack of concern—even sadistic toying with the urgent needs of the suffering—is used in the New Testament to describe the scornful treatment of the suffering Christ on the cross.

Desire for Divine Judgment on the Enemy (69:22–29). The psalmist's experience of such unjust suffering wrenches out a rather angry desire for divine retribution on the heartless enemies. The "snare" and "trap" (69:22) are frequently used metaphorically for sudden entrapment of humans by their own deeds. Here, for the deeds and accusations of the enemy to return on them would be fitting "retribution" (69:22b).

These honest expressions of anger are placed within the context of anticipated *divine* retribution (69:24). The blindness, constant burdens, decimation of descendants, and striking of the enemy's name from the "book of life" (69:28) are God's actions against those who injure people under his protection.

Interestingly, however, in calling for divine action against the enemy, the psalmist acknowledges that God is already in the process of disciplining him as well (69:26). It seems that the opponents are not so much accusing the psalmist falsely as they are ridiculing his acts of grief and contrition in response to the chastisement of God. These, says the psalmist, deserve to be excluded from the saving grace of God's "salvation" (69:27).

The psalmist concludes this section with a plea for God's salvation and protection (69:29).

Vow to Praise God's Name (69:30–33). The shift mentioned above is further indicated by a change of mood and content from distressed plea for deliverance to a vow to "praise God's name in song" (69:30). In addition, it is in these last verses that allusions to the circumstances of the exilic community are more readily apparent. They are Yahweh's "captive people" (69:33) who look forward to the day when God will "rebuild the cities of Judah" so that people "will settle there and possess it . . . inherit it, and . . . dwell there" (69:35–36).

Concluding Call to Praise (69:34–36). In the final segment of the psalm, the psalmist calls "heaven and earth," the "seas," and their inhabitants (69:34) to join in the praise of God. The shift begun at the end of 69:33 continues as he envisions God's salvation of Zion (69:35a) and the reconstruction (69:35b) and repopulation (69:35c) of the devastated cities of Judah. This future event is cast in terms reminiscent of the original conquest of Canaan (69:36).

Application. Like sacrifice, undeniably good actions can be set in motion by undeniably bad motivation. It is like salt, Jesus says (Matt 5:13). What identifies salt, Jesus says, is *invisible* to the eye. But just put a bit on the tip of your tongue and you will know: It *tastes* like salt. Similarly, if we are connected to God through his Son, that relationship will work itself out in visible ways; we will be distinctively different from those who have not entered God's kingdom.

PSALMS 70:1–71:24

Original Meaning. Psalm 70 serves to introduce the more extensive plea of Psalm 71, and several connecting links bind these two psalms together both thematically and verbally.

Invocation (70:1–5). Psalm 70 is framed at the beginning and end by the psalmist's pleas for speedy assistance. Without the addition of Psalm 71, the reason for this sense of urgency remains unclear, since the distress described in 70:2–3 centers around those seeking to disgrace and ruin the psalmist. Psalm 71 makes clear that it is the psalmist's advancing years (71:9, 18) that heighten the need for immediate action lest his tenuous hold on life slip away altogether.

Psalm 70:2 introduces the theme of shame, confusion, and disgrace, which returns as a major motif in the combined chapters of 70–71. In the independent Psalm 70, the psalmist offers contrasting hopes for the enemies (70:2–3) and the faithful sufferer (70:4). The term translated "confusion" (70:2) in the NIV is more usually rendered "be ashamed, abashed, dismayed."

The "poor" and "needy" (70:5) throughout the psalms are those who are vulnerable to the manipulation and control of others. Consequently, their only recourse in the face of oppression is to trust in God for deliverance and redress. The psalmist acknowledges his weakness and reliance on God and couples this desperate vulnerability with an expression of confidence (70:5).

Renewed Petitions (71:1–4). The opening section of Psalm 71 introduces the new theme of "refuge" that dominates verses 1–8. The theme of shame and disgrace reappears as well. A concern with shame resurfaces twice more in 71:13, 24.

The refuge God provides is always available to those in need to enter (71:3). It is unclear in the NIV translation just who is to be commanded and how delivery is anticipated. It is better, in my opinion, to take this phrase as referring back to the earlier "rock of refuge" and to render the construction as "[which] you have decreed for my deliverance."

The Foundation of Hope (71:5–9). The psalmist turns to the foundation of hope on which the preceding plea for deliverance is grounded. For the first time it becomes clear that he is speaking from the experience and vulnerability of old age. He realizes that dependence on Yahweh predates even birth, to the time when he was being formed in his mother's womb. Verse 9 does double duty, providing transition to the following complaint section while concluding the preceding segment.

The Complaint (71:10–13). The enemies' speech concerning the psalmist (71:10) may refer (as in the NIV) to their general attacks, or it may look ahead to the quotation attributed to them in 71:11. The opponents are pictured watching closely for an opportunity to press their attack home. The psalmist, knowing that their perceptions and accusations are false, turns desperately to God for immediate deliverance (71:12) and desires shame and disgrace to pour out on them (71:13).

Praise and Confidence (71:14–24). Direct from the enemies' attack, the psalmist returns to the theme of "hope" (71:14), introduced earlier in 71:5. Two elements dominate this expression of praise and confidence: the righteousness of Yahweh and his saving deeds. The former is mentioned three times (71:15, 16, 19) while the latter appears four times (71:15, 16, 17, 19).

This section emphasizes the psalmist's vow to testify to the mighty acts of God. Beginning in 71:14, a series of verbs and expressions for speaking/proclaiming pile up, illustrating his determination to make God's deeds known.

In 71:18 the psalmist pleads to God not to be forsaken in old age so that this lifelong testimony to the praiseworthy acts of Yahweh can be transmitted to a new generation, thereby extending the efficacy of praise and testimony beyond his own lifetime.

"Who is like you, God?" (71:19). This expression of God's incomparability is on the one hand the pinnacle of the psalmist's praise of Yahweh, while on the other hand it provides the foundation for his confidence expressed in 71:20–21.

"From the depths of the earth . . ." in 71:20 might suggest resurrection from the grave, but it probably indicates the psalmist's confidence of being delivered from a life-threatening circumstance.

Verse 24 returns to the concerns expressed at the beginning of chapters 70–71. There the psalmist called on Yahweh for speedy deliverance (70:1). In 71:24 he concludes with the answering assurance.

Application. While aging is becoming an increasing concern of society, our concern is not so much to enhance spiritual, emotional, and physical health and satisfaction among the aging population but to delay or eliminate the effects of aging—at all costs.

PSALM 72:1–20

Original Meaning

Opening Entreaty (72:1). The psalm opens with a direct entreaty for God to empower "the king" with the necessary resources for just and righteous rule.

Just Rule (72:2–4). If the king takes God's righteous judgments to heart, the result will be continued evidence of just rule over his people by their human monarchs. God is the source of right rule, and those monarchs who allow themselves to be so empowered will rule so that the defenseless are protected, the oppressor crushed.

Enduring Reign (72:5–7). The "sun" and "moon" (72:5), established by God at creation, antedate humankind and often serve as symbols of longevity and endurance. Longevity of just reign is the foundation of prosperity and blessing. Because the monarch pours righteous judgment on the land, the "righteous" will "burst forth" (NIV "flourish," 72:7).

Worldwide Dominion (72:8–11). The psalmist envisions the right rule of the monarch as having effects far beyond the borders of Israel. The monarch is here envisioned as establishing the intended creation order—God's kingdom—throughout the whole earth.

Ultimately "all kings . . . and all nations" (72:11) will submit to his authority. While these hopes were clearly never completely fulfilled in any one of the historical kings, the language continued to express the hopes of the exilic community for a future "son of David"—the Messiah—who will usher in the kingdom of God.

Compassionate Justice (72:12–14). The king has the task of defending those who are unable to defend themselves in society (72:13–14). The king will use his world power to "save" and "rescue" those who are oppressed by violence and on the verge of losing their lives.

Prosperous Kingdom (72:15–17). The psalm draws to a conclusion with a renewed expression of the desire for the enduring and prosperous reign of the king. Such a king will be loved by his people, who will pray daily for his well-being (72:15c) and bless him (72:15d).

The psalm concludes on a note of universal benediction *for* and *from* the golden king of Israel. In a subtle interweaving of the covenantal promises to David (2 Sam 7:8–16) and Abraham (Gen 12:2–3), the nations are said to "be blessed through him" at the same time they "call him blessed" (72:17).

Doxology (72:18–19). As the final psalm in Book 2 of the Psalter, Psalm 72 concludes with a doxology, blessing Yahweh.

The final word of the doxology is an entreaty that "the whole earth be filled with his glory" (72:19b). This sentiment is another one particularly well suited to bring to a close the developing theme of the preceding group of Psalms 56–72.

Concluding Postscript (72:20). The very end of Psalm 72:20 is marked by the only appearance in the Psalter of an instructional postscript. The term for "prayers" used here is the Hebrew *tefillah/tefillot*, which most commonly reflects petition or entreaty on behalf of the sufferer.

Application. Psalms 72 calls us not only to pray for the well-being of our leaders but for their wisdom to see that all justice is ultimately God's justice and that righteousness is not measured by what works but by the character of God, who empowers leaders and who will ultimately set all things right "from sea to sea and from the River to the ends of the earth" (72:8).

PSALM 73:1–28

Original Meaning

Orientation (73:1). Asaph reminds the reader that "surely God is good," and in 73:28 he states that "it is good to be near God." This common Hebrew poetic technique is known as an *inclusio*—a bracketing function that draws the reader's attention to the key theme of the poem or text.

Disorientation (73:2–17). Asaph's is a very personal crisis, but it is one to which many believers throughout the centuries can relate. Why do the wicked prosper when God's people seem to struggle so much?

A major part of the problem was the way he *perceived* things. These people are not just the ordinary wicked, they are the oppressive (73:8) wicked who exploit the weak and mock the Creator in doing so. As we shall see in a moment, Asaph's envy was based on an illusion.

Asaph *believes* that God is good (73:1), but he *knows* that he is suffering (73:13–14). Herein lies the crisis of faith and experience —Asaph believes one thing, but his experience tells another.

Stanza 73:15–17 marks a turning point in the psalm, pivoting from lament to praise and declaration of faith. The importance of community is accentuated by the confession that individual contemplation has failed to provide resolution for Asaph (73:16). Clearly, it is in meeting with God in his sanctuary that Asaph's internal torment finds release. The psalmist came to see things from God's perspective (73:21–22).

Reorientation (73:18–28). In 73:18–20 we witness Asaph's dawning realization that those who reject the ways of Yahweh are as insubstantial as the dust of the street.

It was ignorance of God's mystery and his inability to bring to mind the fact that God is simply bigger than our human understanding that led to Asaph's overemphasis on temporal, as opposed to eternal, reality (73:21–22).

The psalmist's meeting with God awakens the poet to a profound awareness of the immense gift of divine presence. This God protects, just as a parent holds the hand of his child while crossing the street. Asaph's realization that he is the one who is truly rich continues in the following verses (73:25–27).

Final Summary (73:27–28). God's justice will not be denied. Sometimes it is realized by his intervention into current events of humankind; always it will become clear at the final judgment.

Application. The sovereign God sees our hearts and knows our moods and precisely how we see things. If we are disappointed or angry with God, he is fully aware of that fact, and there is no point in offering a politely dishonest prayer.

PSALM 74:1–23

Original Meaning

The "Why" Question (74:1–3). To ask, "why have you rejected us *forever*" (emphasis added, 74:1), could indicate the doubts that arose with the lengthy passage of time in exile. The pain of God's rejection is accentuated by the recollection of their own identity as a flock under the care of Yahweh.

As is so often the way in the Psalms, despair leads to prayer. The combination of "purchased" and "redeemed" in 74:2 resonates with the language of the Song of Moses (Exod 15:13, 16, 17).

Of course, the irony of Psalm 74:1–3 is that the *enemies* of Judah have become the *instruments* of Yahweh.

Destruction and Doubt (74:4–9). From the psalmist's perspective he cannot comprehend why God allowed these things to happen. The stanza of 74:4–9 points to the great offence perpetrated by Judah's enemies in their assault on the temple.

The lack of "signs" (74:9) may refer to the silence of God in response to the fall of Jerusalem. What is more, there are no prophets left declaring the will of God, and the people have no idea for how long this state of affairs will continue.

How Long? (74:10–11). Yahweh's inactivity is a complete mystery to the poet. Knowing that Yahweh is capable of acting makes his inactivity all the more inexplicable from the psalmist's perspective.

The Power of the Creator God (74:12–21). The psalmist speaks of Yahweh's intrinsic character (74:12), which cannot change even if the community's present circumstances are difficult to understand.

The graphic presentation of Yahweh in 74:13–16 is designed to illustrate his power over chaos. This prayer to God is a proclamation of the ultimate nature of his power, probably as a reminder both to the psalmist himself and to the exiled people of God.

Remember and Rise Up! (74:18–23). Yahweh is encouraged to remember the mocking of his name by Judah's enemies (74:18, 22), to remember his covenant (74:20), and not to forget his afflicted people forever (74:19). The command to "rise up" (74:22) is an exhortation to action directed toward Yahweh as Judge. The loss of the temple in Jerusalem was not just a sociopolitical phenomenon resulting from the vagaries of ancient Near Eastern politics at that time. It was a challenge to the very nature of Yahweh and, therefore, to the faith of his people.

Application. It may be hard for us to discern just how God's hand is at work in the (often traumatic) events of our own experience, so—as with Psalm 74—this practice is one best worked out communally in our congregations of faith. Challenging as it may be, however, we should practice such discernment. We should ask God to reveal to us how and where he is at work in our own situations and, also, ask what role he would have us play as his people in this generation.

PSALM 75:1–10

Original Meaning

Giving Thanks for a God Who Is Near (75:1). It is particularly poignant that the psalmist chooses to celebrate the nearness of God's "Name" following a lament in Psalm 74 over the loss of the temple.

Divine Proclamation (75:2–5). The writer of the preceding psalm challenges God to, "Rise up . . ." (74:22), and here, in the very next psalm, God responds. Not only will God judge (75:2), but God holds the earth and keeps it secure (75:3)—he will deal with the arrogant and the mocker (74:4–5).

The Exalting and Humbling God (75:6–8). In the preceding verses God speaks of himself as Judge and as the one who brings down the boastful. In these verses the psalmist himself, in turn, portrays God first as the exalting and humbling God (75:6–7) and then as Judge (75:8).

Praise and Justice (75:9–10). The psalm closes with a double declaration in which both statements are made in the first-person singular. The first statement (75:9) is the psalmist's determined declaration that he will both declare God's authority and judgment forever and, as a result, "sing praise to the God of Jacob," while the final declaration of judgment is another divine oracle (75:10).

Application. Often the way in which we see our reality is very different from God's perspective of intending to bless us for our *eternal good*, though not necessarily for our *present ease.*

PSALM 76:1–12

Original Meaning

God Who Is Known in Zion (76:1–3). God is not distant (76:1). God still dwells in Zion (76:2)! Israel's God ends wars (76:3).

The Warrior God (76:4–6). The imagery in 76:4–6 speaks of God's great and unquestionable majesty. Israel's God is by nature more glorious than the hills and stronger than the lion. The God who ends wars leaves rebellious armies devastated and powerless (76:5).

Awesome God (76:7–10). The idea of a sovereign's "being feared" (76:7) in the ancient world was used in much the same way we would use the word "awesome." Whenever God speaks his decree from heaven, the earth is hushed to silence.

The working of God's justice is never capricious or nasty. The aim is always to bring peace and restore righteousness on the earth. Not only does God save his own people by bringing human rebellion to an end, but in doing so he also brings about the transformation of those very people who rebel against him.

Responding to the Awesome God (76:11–12). The closing two verses of Psalm 76 address the question of response to such a God. The first three stanzas speak about God as Warrior and Judge. This final stanza sets out to answer the question of how we respond to such a God.

Application. Jesus made a public spectacle of all the powers of evil that would keep us from coming to God—he triumphed over them by the cross.

PSALM 77:1–20

Original Meaning

The Call of Lament (77:1–2). The intensity of these prayers is seen in the language used—the language of crying out, being in distress, seeking the Lord, stretching out untiring hands, and refusal to be comforted. The psalmist is relating an account of a protracted time when he grappled with God in prayer.

Painful Reflection (77:3–6). The poet's memory of past grace made his present suffering all the more difficult to bear. Verse 4a paints a picture of a God who refused the psalmist sleep, thus forcing him to maintain his vigil of reflection. Despite his wakefulness, the psalmist finds himself unable to speak (77:4b). It is possible that the songs which the speaker remembered in the night were songs of praise to Yahweh.

Powerful Rhetorical Questions (77:7–9). The rhetorical questions speak for themselves and lead the psalmist to a conclusion grounded in faith that belies the difficulties of his present circumstances. This self-interrogation reminds the speaker of what he knows about his God and, once again, this reminder brings remarkable transformation.

Appeal to the Past (77:10–15). Psalm 77:10 serves as the pivot around which this poem revolves. Equally, the verses that follow speak of the poet's remembrance of the saving works of Yahweh in the past and his goodness toward his own people (77:11–15). The psalmist has found a new focus for his prayer that had somehow fallen by the wayside in his previous intercession. What is more, the speaker acknowledges that the experience of deliverance has been their norm for many years, and, despite the present difficulty, Israel's God has not changed.

Remembering Past Victory (77:16–20). The poet commemorates what is arguably the most miraculous of all the miracles worked by Yahweh to secure the release of his people from slavery, namely, the parting of the Red Sea (Exod 14). The imagery of Psalm 77:17–18 is typical of psalmic accounts of theophany (cf. 18:7–15). Clouds, thunder, lightning, and the quaking of the earth typically mark the physical manifestation of God on earth in the Old Testament.

The Good Shepherd (77:20). The image of God as Shepherd in the ancient Near East speaks of both divine kingship and of divine care. Just as the flock is obliged to follow the shepherd, so also the shepherd is expected to look after the sheep.

Application. Our spirituality must be marked by remembrance of the past as much as it is marked by vision for the future.

PSALM 78:1–72

Original Meaning

Learning from History (78:1–8). The opening words of Psalm 78 are replete with the language of Old Testament wisdom literature. Psalm 78:1–2 presents the reader with a context for understanding what is to follow.

The psalmist continues his instructional theme by discussing the transmission of teaching from one generation to the next (78:3–4). This emphasis on the importance of transmission is reminiscent of the instruction of Deuteronomy (Deut 6:4–5). As each generation learns what it means to have the commandments of the Lord on their own hearts in their own context (Ps 78:6), so they bear the obligation to teach these commandments to the succeeding generation (78:7).

The purpose of the present generation's teaching task is expressed both positively (78:7) and negatively (78:8). As well as cultivating trust and torah-obedience, the aim of this act of education is also that those who follow should avoid the failings of those who have gone before.

Failures of Faith and Miracles Galore (78:9–16). Verses 10–11 give clear reasons for Ephraim's failure. The poet describes their downfall as having a threefold root: failure to keep God's covenant with them, refusal to walk in the ways of God's law, and forgetfulness regarding God's miraculous works in the past.

In Psalm 78:12–16 the psalmist is outlining the miraculous past deeds that Yahweh worked on behalf of his people. Yahweh performed miracles in securing their release and nationhood (Exod 13–17). Such a God should never be forgotten!

Miracles, Rebellion, and Retribution (78:17–31). Verses 17–31 show that the psalmist has in mind the forgetful "ancestors" mentioned in 78:12. The exodus generation set the tone for the generations to follow. Testing (78:18) is the theme of the book of Numbers—it is the primary characteristic of the wilderness generation (Num 14:20–25). The Israelites constantly tested Yahweh, and by doing so they cast doubt on both *his love* for them (Exod 14:11) and, as in this case, *his ability* to help them (Ps 78:19–20).

The harm of forgetfulness is illustrated by God's response in Psalm 78:21–22. The people's grumbling attitude damaged the covenantal relationship and had to be addressed.

Despite the rebellion of the people, Yahweh continued to prove his good character and unquestionable competence by providing the very things they had so skeptically demanded. Verses 23–25 first draw attention to the provision of manna from heaven. Verses 26–29 then retell the miraculous provision of meat in the flocks of quail that landed in the Israelite camp (Exod 16). The imagery is of provision that is gracious and generous rather than reluctant and miserly.

Yahweh had provided for the Israelites the very things they craved, but his provision should not be seen as a tacit acceptance of the people's rebellious behavior and distrust (Ps 78:17–21). Verses 30–31 make it quite clear that Israel's God is not to be toyed with!

The Stubbornness of Rebellion (78:32–39). Throughout the Bible, God's punishment is presented as a means of securing repentance (e.g., see Deut 29:22–29; cf. 30:1–10). Despite divine judgment, however, this generation *continued* in rebellion against Yahweh (Ps 78:32). The people's failure to relate rightly to Yahweh inevitably led to wrong behavior and empty lives (78:33). The irony, of course, is that this generation is the one freed from Egyptian slavery. What an amazing opportunity to enjoy and delight in their release, yet their faithless rebellion led them to futility, not freedom.

Verses 34–35 present a picture similar to the one we find in the book of Judges. God's repeated rebuke would bring a repentance that was far from genuine (78:36). The people would, in a sense, say the right things (78:35) and, in a sense, do the right things (78:34). But their words and deeds were only superficial and did not reflect a true change of heart (78:37).

They received God's rebuke—designed to bring real transformation—yet they would not change (78:34, 37). Still, it appears that the people thought of God as a plaything in their own hands—one to be manipulated at their own will. Genuine devotion to Yahweh was far from them. Their response to God was more functional than it was real, and this kind of response is always a danger in the practice of religion.

Remarkably, Yahweh did not respond to his people in kind. His character remains unchanged despite his people's failings (78:38). Verse 38 is an unusual verse in the Old Testament because it speaks of God's atoning for his people's sin (translated "forgave" in the NIV). Normally in the Old Testament this work is that of the priest. Here, however, Yahweh himself takes on the role of the one who does what is necessary to deal with his people's sinfulness.

Whereas Israel's remembering God in Psalm 78:35 lacked sincerity, we see here that God *remembers* his people's human frailty, and this remembrance leads him to compassion.

Rebellion Despite Release (78:40–55). Verses 40–41 draw attention to the repeated failures of the exodus generation while they were in the desert. Their rebellion was not just a one-off or even an occasional matter. Time and again, this newborn nation rebelled against their Redeemer.

Israel's rebellion is made all the more difficult to comprehend because they were forgetful not only of God's miraculous salvific power but also of his shepherding care for them (78:52–55). God's manifest power should have made Israel fearful of forgetting. His loving care should have inspired an affection that kept Israel from forgetting.

The underlying image is of the God of promise who is at work in the temporal realm to do whatever is necessary to benefit his people. Sometimes this work is a display of power *against* those who oppose his children (78:42–51, 55). Sometimes his power miraculously *opens pathways* for his people (78:52–54). Sometimes his power *provides* for the needs of his flock (78:25–29). Whatever the specific expression of God's power may be, the psalmist reminds his readers that his multivalent activity serves the purpose of blessing his people.

Failure and Withdrawal (78:56–64). The focus switches from the exodus generation to Israel throughout the period of the judges until the reign of David. The settled people repeated the mistakes of their ancestors in *testing* God and *rebelling* against him (78:56), as is made explicit in 78:57.

While *forgetting* was the order of the day for the exodus generation (78:11, 42), the people in the land resorted to idolatry (78:58). Psalm 78:59–64 highlights the full extent of Israel's unfaithfulness by recounting the severity of Yahweh's response to it. The people repeatedly turned to useless idols rather than to God. So, when God hears their prayers to lifeless statues—with the ironic implication that *Yahweh alone* hears these prayers—he becomes very angry. While God's withdrawal from his people was not permanent, the consequences were stark (78:61–64).

Forgiveness and Renewal (78:65–72). The image of the drunken warrior awaking from his stupor is not entirely accidental. Once Yahweh's attention is refocused on Israel's plight, the people witness again the raw power of the warrior God who freed his people from Egypt with a mighty hand (78:42–51).

The remarkable surprise of these verses is compounded by the very fact that no reason is given for the sudden change of heart. The psalmist does not draw attention to any act of national repentance. Quite simply, the poet makes it plain that divine intervention is based on divine choice. Yahweh chose Judah and Zion and David.

This lengthy psalm ends with the poignant image of David as the shepherd-king. He is chosen by God, and the pastoral imagery of caring for sheep is transposed to caring for God's people on a national scale. The presentation of David is idealized. We see here the author's hope in a coming king from the line of David who would truly represent the best of everything the historical David offered. The concluding voice of Psalm 78 speaks clearly of a future hope. The psalmist's hope is founded on the remembrance of a God who keeps his promises.

Application. Christians living in the twenty-first century should not be too quick to shake our heads at the fickleness of the exodus generation, for we often fall prey to exactly the same tendencies. For a generation in which Christianity is becoming increasingly marginalized in the Western world, it is easy to look at the license and permissiveness of the world in which we live and to say, "It's too hard to be a Christian! I want to go back to the life I had before!"

We can all face this tendency on the journey that is the Christian life of faith. Sometimes the cost of being different just seems too high. As we meditate on the true character of God, as we consider the self-sacrifice of Christ, as we recall the indwelling presence of the Holy Spirit in our hearts, our perspectives on life now and life before are transformed.

PSALM 79:1–13

Original Meaning

Reminding God of the Cost (79:1–4). Psalm 79 begins by *reminding God* of the events that his people have faced in the fall of Jerusalem and the exile. Moses's prayer in Deuteronomy that Yahweh would spare the people likewise describes Israel as God's "inheritance" (79:1; Deut 9:26–29). Yahweh's people and place have been violated by pagan nations who worship false gods.

Lament: The Cry of Despair and Hope (79:5–8). It is clear in the poet's mind that the people of Judah deserved their punishment, but this reversal in 79:6–7 urges Yahweh to respond to the gross criminality of the nations during the fall of Jerusalem. The psalmist asks for forgiveness of sins (79:8a) and the swift expression of God's mercy (79:8b), and he puts these requests in context by stressing the great need in which the people find themselves (79:8c).

A Prayer for Mercy, a Prayer for Justice (79:9–13). The Old Testament community viewed the saving nature of God in terms of divine activity on their behalf. Salvation is a much more physical and practical concept in the Psalter. Verse 10 implies that the best way to restore Yahweh's standing among the nations is through the restoration of Israel and the bringing of God's just punishment on those nations who have mocked his character.

The psalmist's prayer in 79:11 picks up on exodus imagery by calling on God to intervene on behalf of his people. The book of Exodus reminds the exilic generation that Yahweh heard the groaning of his people once before and remembered his covenant (Exod 2:23–25).

The people have sinned and received God's rebuke for it. Their lament is grounded in their view of their own circumstances, and they believe they have suffered enough and have learned their lesson—hence their reminder to God that they are his people. Their prayer is for permanent restoration and that renewed community will be marked by continual, grateful praise.

Application. Why pray if God already knows? Prayer is about more than "getting things done"—it is about relationship with a God who loves us and whom we love.

PSALM 80:1–19

Original Meaning

Calling on the Shepherd God (80:1–2). Psalm 80 renews the call for restoration by the Shepherd-King. The psalmist's plea seeks a fresh expression of Yahweh's mighty works in the exodus.

The Refrain (80:3, 7, 19). The three parts of Psalm 80 are divided by a repeated chorus in verses 3, 7, and 19. The essential content of these verses is the same: a call for restoration followed by an appeal for blessing toward the specific end of deliverance for the people.

Calling on the Warrior God (80:4–6). After praying for restoration in the refrain, the psalmist's prayer is directed toward the Almighty, all-powerful God *who is the cause* of their present suffering! *His* anger smolders (80:4). *He* fed his people with the bread of tears (80:5). *He* caused enemies to mock them (80:6).

The Parable of the Vine (80:8–18). Psalm 80:8–18 recounts the exodus story using the vine metaphor for God's people. Yahweh's hand was behind Israel's preexilic success, as we see in the psalmist's use of "you" throughout this section. These verses show the great care taken by Yahweh to ensure that this vine takes root and bears fruit. Verses 12–13 return to the removal of divine protection. This poetic imagery points to the spoiling of Israel by foreign nations. Psalm 80:14b is a prayer for a renewed exodus (Exod 2:25).

The psalmist's implied willingness to endure God's scrutiny (Ps 80:14c), however uncomfortable doing so might be, is explained in 80:16—they would rather endure fire that purifies than fire that simply destroys.

Only by way of Yahweh's merciful help will they be able to live in the manner that pleases him. Only with divine mercy and help can the people remain true. The psalm closes with the final rendering of the refrain, which seeks the blessing and practical help of Yahweh.

Application. The psalmist knows that only when God's hand of blessing is upon his people will they be able to remain true to him. Equally, Jesus's description of himself as the "true vine" in John 15 encourages a healthy attitude of dependence. It is by remaining in him and relying on him that we are enabled to be fruitful. An attitude of dependence is realistic and drives us to prayer—dependence *has* to be a good thing.

PSALM 81:1–16

Original Meaning

The Call to Worship (81:1–5b). Note the compelling nature of the commands that we read in these opening verses. As we see in many of the Psalter's calls to praise God, there is something almost vociferous about the psalmic expectation regarding our worship of God. Psalmic worship is not a tepid affair—rather, it is whole-hearted and full of gusto. At least part of the rationale for this praise is found in 81:1a—sing for joy to "God our strength." The praise command is a reminder that God remains unchanged even in the people's experience of distress.

The Prophetic Oracle: Part 1 (81:5c–10). Verses 6–7 once again recall God's liberating work in the exodus from Egypt. As well as reminding Israel of his powerful work in securing their release, God also reminds them of the fact that he did hear and answer the prayers of his enslaved people. Inattentiveness is Israel's problem, not Yahweh's.

Verses 9–10 make explicit what is implied in the preceding verse. The reminder of the Shema draws the reader to thoughts of devotion to Yahweh alone, and that singular devotion becomes the express focus of 81:9–10.

Yahweh is more than able (and willing) to provide abundantly for his people, if only they will put their trust solely in him. He provided generously in the exodus and will provide generously again for his people . . . if only they will listen and trust.

The Prophetic Oracle: Part 2 (81:11–16). In Psalm 80 the psalmist asks God "Why?" and "How long?" with regard to the exile. The second part of Yahweh's soliloquy in 81:11–16 answers both questions. First, the answer to the "Why?" question of 80:12 comes in 81:11–12. The exile occurred because Israel would not listen! Nor would they submit to God.

The prophet-poet's answer to the "How long?" question follows in 81:13. How long will the exile last? Well, if the people would finally *listen*, they would then see just how quickly Yahweh responds to their change of heart!

Application. In praise we are reminded of who God is and how God works, so our praises can be important in shaping our perspective on our life and present experience.

PSALM 82:1–8

Original Meaning

Assembly of "the Gods" (82:1). Yahweh has called a meeting, and all the heavenly beings are obliged to attend.

Gods of Injustice (82:2–4). Yahweh has delegated power to rule but expects them to do so in accordance with his own standards. Since the gods have failed, he calls them to task.

Judgment (82:5). These so-called deities did not even realize that social justice is the hallmark of a good society.

Mortality of the "Gods" (82:6–7). Yahweh reminds the "gods" (82:6) that they owe their status to the Most High God in the first place. He conferred status on them and can remove that status just as quickly. Rejection of Yahweh's standards leads to death.

The Appeal (82:8). The prayer is the logical conclusion that follows from the neutralizing of the gods by Yahweh's judgment on them (82:6–7). The psalmist cries out in prayer to Yahweh, that he reassume control over "all the nations" (82:8) as his inheritance, not just Israel.

Application. Social justice is basic to the nature of the God of the Bible.

PSALM 83:1–18

Original Meaning

The Nations Conspire (83:1–8). Psalm 82:8 ends with the call for Yahweh to rise up and judge the earth. Psalm 83:1 picks up on this theme with a threefold prayer that God will not be silent!

The psalmist moves to lament in 83:2–8. The nations are in rebellion against God and his design for the world. In the mind of the poet, standing against God's people is standing against God's will and purpose and, therefore, against God himself (83:3–5).

Covenant is a solemn and serious agreement of association. The nations listed in 83:6–8 are intent on conscious rebellion against Yahweh through the annihilation of his people. Ten neighboring nations are listed in 83:6–8 as those who have entered into covenant against Israel.

Intercession Seeking Intervention (83:9–18). It seems that in 83:9–12 the psalmist is focusing particularly on the victories of God during the time of the judges (Judg 4:17–24). Oreb, Zeeb, Zebah, and Zalmunna, Midianite noblemen, died in Gideon's campaign against this people's oppression of Israel (Judg 6–8).

Psalm 83:13–15 expand this prayer for divine deliverance from military persecution. The victory requested in 83:9–12 is spelled out in these subsequent verses. The poet demands that these forces, which seem so substantial, become inconsequential before the power of Yahweh.

In some ways we naturally balk at the violent overtones of the prayer in 83:9–15, yet the end purpose of the prayer is quite remarkable. The psalmist effectively prays that Yahweh would make the enemies who had conspired to eradicate the covenant community part of that selfsame family of God's people!

Application. Injustice and evil should be named for what they are, and our prayers should reflect the revulsion the Creator feels when his laws and his people are violated. That repentance and justice should be the focus of our prayers is part of the message of Psalm 83.

PSALM 84:1–12

Original Meaning

Dwelling with the Lord (84:1–4). Psalm 84 begins with describing the beauty and benefits of dwelling in the presence of God. The language of the "soul" and "heart" and "flesh" is used to express the completeness of desire (84:2). If the birds of the air can make their homes at the temple, how much more should God's people?

The Blessings of the Way (84:5–7). Although the poet speaks longingly of his desire to enjoy God's *special presence* in Jerusalem, he is fully aware that God's blessing and protection are with his people wherever they may be. The very presence of the pilgrims en route to Jerusalem transforms challenging landscape into a place of streams and pools. The pilgrims who have set their heart on the worship of Yahweh are equipped with divine strength.

The Psalmist's Prayer (84:8–9). The next section of the psalm moves from celebration of the delights of God's presence to a prayer for protection on behalf of the king.

The Locus of Hope (84:10–12). One day in the "real" presence of God in the Jerusalem temple is better than a thousand days spent anywhere else. Verse 11 crystallizes the hope that is evident throughout the psalm. The two images, of course, speak of light and protection.

Psalm 84 closes with another beatitude (cf. 84:4–5). In 84:12 we are reminded that because he is the God who reigns, not only is he inclined to do good toward people, but he is also capable of ordering all circumstances for their benefit! Surely trust in him brings great blessing.

Application. There is great happiness to be found in coming together with other believers to worship God. Such fellowship is a source of great joy and a reservoir of strength to keep going in the Christian faith (Heb 10:25).

PSALM 85:1–13

Original Meaning

Rich Forgiveness (85:1–3). The language in 85:1–3 understands sin to be a burden. Through forgiveness, God lifts that weight from the Israelite's shoulders. In forgiving the sins of his people God also sets aside his righteous anger.

The Conundrum (85:4–7). The psalmist is confident to pray because he knows that salvation is something properly basic to the character of God. The questions of 85:5–6 are rhetorical, for the psalmist has *witnessed* the fact that Yahweh does not prolong his anger through all generations. God will also bring life to the people again. Such spiritual renewal results in a people who are grateful in heart and rejoice in their relationship with God.

God Speaks Peace (85:8–9). We can choose to focus on the inadequacies we experience—or we can actually listen to God himself. God himself—by his spoken word—recreates that peace and wholeness of relationship. It is because of sin that God's people find it difficult to accept his acceptance. So, the psalmist urges his readers to turn away from all behaviors that lead them to doubt God's love and acceptance.

Covenantal Tensions Resolved (85:10–13). With a beautiful sense of the poetic, the psalmist points the readers again to a God of grace and unmerited love, a God who does for them what they could not do for themselves. The psalm ends with a reminder of the righteousness of God.

Application. Like the psalmist expresses, we too can struggle to accept that God still loves us and that his grace is sufficient to forgive all our sins.

PSALM 86:1–17

Original Meaning

The Poet's Intercession (86:1–7). The poet is under severe pressure, and he desperately needs God's help. The complete dependence that lies at the heart of 86:2 is echoed in the prayer of the following verse. In the face of great trouble, the psalmist calls out to God for mercy because prayer is his only source of hope. Verse 5 is reminding God of God's very nature! God will hear because of who *he* is rather than because of who the supplicant is or what the supplicant does. The declaration of 86:7 becomes a statement of faithful determination.

The Incomparability of God and the Inclusion of the Nations (86:8–10). The psalmist turns to praise of God based on the incomparable greatness that sets him apart from all the gods of the nations. The nations themselves will come to realize that Yahweh is far greater than the gods they worship. Yahweh is so great in his character and deeds that everyone who stops to consider the reality of his being will surely come to realize that he alone is the true God (86:8, 10).

A Prayer of Devotion in Times of Trouble (86:11–17). The poet now prays for God's help that he might continue to live a life of commitment to Yahweh. The first aspect of this prayer for devotion is cognitive (86:11a). The second element of this prayer of devotion to Yahweh centers more on the idea of holistic, heartfelt devotion to God (86:11b).

This singularity of devotion is repeated in the poet's commitment to holistic praise of Yahweh and the desire to bring glory to him (86:12). Verse 13 gives a clear reason for the exemplary devotion witnessed in the preceding verses.

Verses 14 and 17 give some insight into the poet's current difficulties. He faces persecution from those who oppose him and reject God (86:14). The poet is aware that he need not fear the character of his enemies because he knows the character of God (86:15).

Application. Missional activity that is biblically based speaks about the reality of a God of love and forgiveness who has done wonderful things for humanity.

PSALM 87:1–7

Original Meaning

The Centrality of Zion (87:1–3). Zion is founded by God as a place of special holiness, as becomes explicit in the following verses. Zion bears unique significance even within Israel as a whole.

The Rebirth of the Nations in Zion (87:4–7). God's proclamation of Zion's greatness begins with the inclusion of Israel's archenemies among those who "acknowledge" (87:4; lit., "know") him. Rahab is frequently used as a metaphor for Egypt (see Ps 89:10; Isa 30:7). The concluding statement of Psalm 87:4 clearly implies that a sense of belonging is extended to nations outside Israel. God himself enters these nations in his list of citizens! The psalmist points to a future reality—ordained and brought into being by Yahweh himself—in which these countries will ultimately become part of God's people.

Application. The onus is on those of us in the church to make newcomers and seekers feel welcomed and loved despite the differences that may exist between us.

PSALM 88:1–18

Original Meaning

The Prayer of Desperation (88:1–5). The poet lambastes God for failing to hear and respond to his prayers . . . yet he continues to pray to God. Verses 3–5 give us insight into the depths of the psalmist's despair. Verse 5 summarizes the full extent of the psalmist's pain and suffering. He is so close to death as to be indistinguishable from the dead. So deep is his pain and so lengthy its extent that the poet believes God has forgotten him—a spiritual dynamic that adds to the torment of his present physical suffering.

The Source of Suffering (Psalm 88:6–9). Take note of the pronouns used throughout this section of the psalm: "*you* have put me in the lowest pit"; "*your* wrath lies heavily on me"; "*you* have overwhelmed me"; "*you* have taken from me my closest friends" (88:6a, 7a, 7b, 8a; emphasis added). The issue is not simply a matter of the mystery of divine inactivity, for from the psalmist's perspective God is actually *proactive* in causing his suffering. Naturally, we balk against such readings. Our response as readers should be to associate with the speaker, to empathize with him rather than to deny the legitimacy of his conclusions.

Unanswered Prayer and Rhetorical Questions (88:9b–12). The psalmist believes that the God to whom he prays is in some way responsible for the suffering, yet he continues to pray to this selfsame God. This seemingly paradoxical activity emblematizes the natural tension of lament. The poet lays out his complaint because he believes that God has not been faithful. But his only source of hope is the faithfulness of God. The psalmist desires to maintain relationship with his God despite experiencing what that might mean.

Darkness is my Closest Friend (88:13–18). The poet's prayer is constant (88:13), yet it remains unheard (88:14). His suffering is made all the more difficult as he considers the root of his affliction (88:15b–16). Quite simply, his circumstances have taken him to a point that is beyond his ability to bear. The psalmist feels like he is drowning (88:17), and despair has taken over. Psalm 88 closes with the cry of dereliction—*utter darkness!*

Application. Job grappled with God himself while interacting also with his friends. It appears that one implication of Yahweh's commendation of Job may be found in the *relational* aspect of his lament.

PSALM 89:1–52

Original Meaning

The God of Covenant (89:1–4). The psalmist begins with a confident outpouring of praise to God because of his devoted love and faithfulness to the community of faith. The root of this great and confident celebration is to be found in the promise of God to David (89:3–4). Yahweh himself had spoken his decree that a king in the line of David would rule throughout all the ages, and this promise filled the poet with a great sense of assurance. Yahweh's invisible rule over the whole of the earth and humankind was, in a sense, "incarnated" through the line of the sons of David. Their political rule was the visible symbol of Yahweh's absolute governance over the whole earth.

The Created Order Declares Yahweh's Praise (89:5–18). Verses 5–8 take the reader into the realm of the metaphorical "heavenly council." The implication of 89:8 is that Yahweh can be trusted implicitly, whereas the other gods of the ancient world are capricious and changeable. Verses 9–10 speak to God's control over all the powers of chaos in the created order.

The imagery of God's "strong arm" in 89:10 is completed in the following verses, where his "arm" and "hand" (89:13) extend over the whole earth, as well as the heavens and the sea. God's sovereign rule is asserted through the language of possession. These metaphors commonly refer to God's ability to work out his purposes in the historical reality of his people.

Verse 14 uses the language of covenant, a concept that is so central to this poem. "Righteousness" (*tsedeq*), "justice" (*mishpat*), "love" (*hesed*), and "faithfulness" (*'emet*) are all key components of the covenantal relationship between Yahweh and his people and key components of the relationship between Yahweh and David.

The truth of God's covenantal faithfulness (89:1–4, 14) and sovereign rule over all creation (89:5–13) can lead to only one proper response: worship (89:15–16). As we respond by worshiping him, human beings find the essence of happiness in their lives.

The idea of vicegerency is seen in 89:18's description of the king. Just as Yahweh is a shield and refuge for the people, so should the king be.

Calling to Mind the Covenant with David (89:19–37). Psalm 89:19–37 recalls in poetic form the covenant made between God and David as king of Israel (see 2 Sam 7; 1 Chr 17). The first stanza of this account of the Davidic covenant focuses on David as a warrior. The psalmic representation of the covenantal promise focuses on the fact that David, as king of Israel, would neither be defeated by those who would attack the nation (Ps 89:22–23) or thwarted by those nations that he would attack (89:25). In Psalm 89:24b Yahweh provides strength for the people beyond their status, and he does just the same for their king.

The second aspect of the promise to David is that of a continuous line of successors to perpetuate the monarchic dynasty (89:27–29). Following this discussion of security for the nation and a line for David is a caveat (89:30–37): What happens if David's heirs do not love Yahweh in the manner that he did? Clearly, covenantal election can never be an excuse for license. This truth applied to Israel (Deut 28) and also to the Davidic dynasty (Ps 89:32).

The rest of this strophe focuses on the promise of God's continuing love for David, expressed by way of God's continuing grace toward his ancestral line (89:33–37). God's covenant is based on his sovereign choice. God's faithfulness to the promise he made to David could not be thwarted even by the unfaithfulness of David's heirs. If God is absolutely faithful to his promise, then why has the Davidic line ceased to exist, as the psalmist acknowledges it has?

The Faithfulness of God Questioned (89:38–51). The psalmist believed the promises described above, but he now faces a historical reality that contradicts his beliefs. In that confusion he cries out in 89:38–39. The promise of security (89:22) has been dashed by the humiliation of military defeat (89:40–41). The promise of divine strength (89:21) seems to have been transferred to his enemies (89:42). The promise of an eternal line of descendants (89:27–29) has been brought to a crushing end in real time (89:44–45). The once exalted status of the anointed one of Yahweh (89:20) has been rejected and cast down to the very dust of the earth (89:39, 44–45).

The exclamation "How long?" seeks an end to the conflict of faith and experience. It all boils down to the essential question in 89:49. There is no way for the psalmist to reconcile his understanding of God's nature with his historical experience. With that lack of understanding comes prayer, for he believes that it is only in relationship with Yahweh that he can make sense of all the theological incongruities of life.

The Final Doxology (89:52). Most scholars accept that the doxologies found at the end of each of the books of the Psalter (Pss 41:13; 72:19–20; 89:52; 106:48; 146–50) function as editorial signs that indicate the conclusion of each of the books of the book of Psalms. So, there is a sense in which Psalm 89:52 applies to the whole of Book 3 of the Psalms, thus concluding the collection that is Psalms 73–89. But it is equally inescapable that this verse is added to the end of Psalm 89 as a part of the poem itself, so 89:52 has an influence on this psalm as well as concluding the book as a whole. There is no resolution implied in 89:52. It does not change or deny the paradox voiced in the lament; rather, as with every lament, this verse simply acknowledges the dichotomy. The doxology reminds the reader that God is worthy even when his people are conflicted in their experience of him.

Application. It is as we learn the worship of God that we are equipped to deal with the complexities and incongruities of life. In worship we are shaped and equipped to find our strength in God, even when we do not really understand what God is doing.

PSALM 90:1–17

Original Meaning

Sovereign throughout History (90:1–6). Yahweh is still—and is always—the "dwelling place" of his people (90:1). The essence of the people's security is found in the eternal and unchangeable nature of God (90:2). This focus contrasts strongly with the discussion of the brevity of *human* life in 93:3–6. The reminder is that the events of human history, although significant for each generation in turn, are but a moment from God's perspective and are all under his control as Creator and the one who ordains life and death. God is in control because he is the eternal Creator God.

Divine Rebuke and the Human Experience (90:7–11). Psalm 90:8 gives the clear reason for the divine anger mentioned in the previous verse—human sin has provoked a response from God. Experiencing God's anger simply adds to the frustration of living a brief and troubled life (90:9–11). The psalmist cuts to the quick at the culmination of his reflection on the frustrations of life in the light of divine wrath (90:11). God's righteous anger should always provoke a response of faithfulness in his people.

The Prayer of the Finite (90:12–17). "Teach us to number our days, that we may gain a heart of wisdom" (90:12) reflects the central theme of this psalm, namely, awareness of our human finitude and weakness and the importance of responding properly to that realization. In Psalm 90:12–17, the poet's prayer seeks the *mercy* of God. Whereas the laments of Book 3 were focused on the injustice and divine abandonment felt by the people, the lament of Psalm 90 centers on the mercy of God in response to sin. The supplication is not grounded in demands based on the covenantal promises; it seeks a gracious response from God *despite* the people's sin. The concluding prayer of 90:17 presents the inescapable resolution to this tension: it is only by the undeserving grace of God that any relationship with the holy God can be maintained.

Application. Our lives are brief and frail, and without that realization we will never adopt the right attitude of dependence on God that should characterize our every day!

PSALM 91:1–16

Original Meaning

A Determined Declaration of Faith (91:1–2). The basic point being made in Psalm 90 is that God's people should look away from the apparent crisis of their present political situation and see the *ultimate* security that is theirs because of their covenantal relationship with the Creator God. Psalm 91 continues that line of thought by painting a very vivid and graphic picture of the individual who chooses to trust in Yahweh above all else. It is not enough that the people have trust, for faith is not an abstract entity. It is the object of their trust that is important: God himself, and nothing less.

Divine Protection in the Face of Trial (91:3–13). The poet is being explicit about the correct *object* of one's trust. He then goes on in 91:3–8 to paint a picture of a world full of a wide variety of dangers. Each of the two stanzas in this section of Psalm 91 ends with a description of the believer's status in the thick of surrounding turmoil. God must be a dwelling place for his people, a refuge and place of security even in dark and troubled times. Throughout 91:3–13 there is a transformation of the believer from one who is constantly buffeted by the dangers and misfortunes of life to one who triumphs over these selfsame challenges, thus bringing order out of chaos.

Yahweh's Assurance of Protection (91:13–16). It becomes immediately apparent who the speaker is, given the language of these verses. The "rhetorical" transformation is remarkable because it moves the poem from making statements of faith *about* God to statements *from* God. This shift brings a whole new level of certainty to the reader's experience of Psalm 91. It is one thing to be encouraged by the poet to believe these things; it is quite another experience to hear this promised protection in the form of a prophetic word "directly" from God. The assurance that rings out speaks of a covenantal God who is *never* absent from those who take refuge in him, and especially not in their times of greatest distress.

Application. Psalm 91's promise ultimately is that God will be present, not that life will be easy. Yet the promise of deliverance and salvation is still there.

PSALM 92:1–15

Original Meaning

The Joy of Praise (92:1–3). It is a good thing to praise the living God! Verse 2 provides the rationale for the poet's assessment of praise as good. In the ancient Near East it was common to praise gods for fear they might turn nasty. But it is good to praise God because he himself is good.

Works, Thoughts and Judgment (92:4–8). The works of the Lord give the psalmist reason to delight in worship. Not only are the Lord's works a great encouragement, so are his thoughts, and anyone who fails to realize this truth is nothing other than a fool (92:5–6). Whatever exaltation oppressors may enjoy in this world, it is brief. The eternal Creator, on the other hand, is praised forever.

The Fall of the Lord's Enemies (92:9–11). The blessing and stability of the righteous comes to the fore as the concomitant effect of divine intervention in the events of this world. The imagery combines to describe the strength and restoration of the believer at the hand of Yahweh. He intervenes in a hostile world to provide strength and to refresh his once-wearied people.

The Righteous Flourish (92:12–15). Those rejecting Yahweh are like grass (92:7). The righteous, however, are like the palm tree and the cedar (92:12). These arboreal similes communicate images of perpetual growth and fruitfulness. In remaining close to Yahweh, the believer lives life under his blessing, protection, and providential care, thus allowing her to experience the fullness of human existence that springs only from communion with God. The concluding voice of Psalm 92 is a voice of praise and assurance.

Application. We pray "your kingdom come; your will be done" (Matt 6:10), and we rejoice when that kingdom does come little by little, more and more fully in our day.

PSALM 93:1–5

Original Meaning

Yahweh Reigns (93:1). Yahweh is characterized by such evident glory and power that there is no mistaking his high office within the created order.

Establishment and Security (93:1d–2). God has always been King. But that kingship becomes a visible reality in the creation of the universe.

Yahweh: Mightier than the Seas (93:3–4). The seas of 93:3–4 could refer to the power of the sea or, more metaphorically, either to the surrounding nations that oppose Israel or to the mythical forces of chaos.

Stability and Decoration (93:5). In the psalmist's mind, there is no doubt as to God's power. Equally, *his character* is beyond question.

Application. Many things in life *are* entirely beyond our control. That is why the psalmist reminds us not only of the power of God but also of his character.

PSALM 94:1–23

Original Meaning

How Long Will the Wicked Be Jubilant (94:1–3). This opening plea is clearly a call for God's justice to be worked out in the face of present oppression. The psalmist's plea is not based on some sort of understanding of God as a wrathful vigilante; rather, his appeal is to the ultimate Judge of humanity to work out justice within his present historical setting.

"They crush your people, Lord" (94:4–7). The poet voices his indignation at the open arrogance of those who do evil in society. They trumpet those activities of which they should be ashamed. Their pride is vocal as well as behavioral. Such flagrant self-glorification of their own power and ability to oppress rubs salt into the wounds of the community.

The Folly of Disdain (94:8–11). We can almost hear the tone of mocking laughter on the psalmist's lips. The foolish wicked of 94:4–7 shows their great disdain for God in the words of 94:7, but the true reality is that God has nothing but disdain for them! Verse 11 is an affirmation that the intentions of the wicked will come to nothing.

The Blessing of Discipline (94:12–15). Verse 12 makes the link between discipline and teaching. The implication is probably that there is a lesson that can still be learned *before* God brings his punishment. True happiness is to be found in *walking in God's paths*, not rejecting them! God's people never experience "days of trouble" apart from the presence of God (94:13).

God's Comfort in Difficult Days (94:16–19). Yahweh will respond by arising and standing up against the evildoers, but the question also makes a rhetorical challenge that the readers claim the courage of their convictions by taking a stand against social wrongs. The voice of testimony remembers so as to shape the reader's perception.

An End to Oppression (94:20–23). The office of these oppressors, in a formal sense, associates them with Yahweh, but it is one's behavior that draws a person near to or distances from the Creator God—offices and titles are meaningless. The psalmist acknowledges a security that goes far beyond the reach of those who hold temporal office. Yahweh himself is the psalmist's fortress and refuge. The poet is absolutely certain of the ultimacy of divine judgment. Effectively, the speaker is making his stand alongside the poor and voiceless of society—he is absolutely with them in their struggle and certain of their vindication.

Application. Our task is to associate actively with the voiceless and to declare his justice in our societies before he comes to avenge and judge the earth.

PSALM 95:1–11

Original Meaning

Come and Worship the Creator God (95:1–5). The exhortation to draw near is plural, thus addressing the whole community of God's people, and the verbs call for noisy worship. Why should the people worship Yahweh as opposed to any other god? Because he is the "great God" and "great King" (95:3).

Come and Worship the God of the Covenant (95:6–7c). As a community, the worshipers celebrate their God loudly because he is Creator, but they also bow before him because he is King. This God is Israel's God, but this identification works two ways, for Israel is also Yahweh's possession, his flock.

Learning from Past Mistakes (95:7d–11). The issue is not about whether God's voice is audible to his people—it is rather that the worshiping community should be careful to *listen* to his voice when they "hear" it (95:7d). The verb (Heb. *shm*ʿ) takes on an implication of *obedience* rather than the simple physicality of hearing or listening. The exodus generation's enjoyment of the covenantal relationship with their Creator and Redeemer was spoiled by their consistent refusal to listen and trust. According to the psalmist this is the very reason that the people failed to enter the promised land. It was because the desert generation explicitly and continually denied God's good character that they were excluded from entry into the land as a place of rest.

Application. The need for identity is basic to human existence, so Israel responds in joyous worship *because* they know to whom they belong. There is a sense of inevitability about this joyful response.

PSALM 96:1–13

Original Meaning

The First Call to Worship (96:1–3). Typically, the call to worship is characterized by plural commands of vocal praise and the language of approach. The call to worship in Psalm 96 incorporates these elements (96:1–2a) but goes beyond by including commands of proclamation and declaration (96:2b–3). The real surprise is the full extent of the address: *the whole earth* is called to praise.

The First Rationale (96:4–6). The psalmist's strategy of poetic proclamation is to encourage the nations to compare the insignificance of their gods with the significance of Yahweh. "The heavens" (96:5) represented the sphere of existence in which the people of the nations believed their gods lived. The implied polemic then becomes clear: the worthless gods may (or may not) live there, but in either case it was Yahweh who created that dwelling space.

The Second Call to Worship (96:7–10). In 96:9 the call to "worship" is literally an invitation to "bow down." Such a clear act of commitment draws the nations into the flock as they offer their allegiance to Yahweh. Yahweh reigns, and if this statement is true, then it requires a response.

The Second Rationale (96:11–13). The environmental response in 96:11–13 shows the significance of the natural world in God's grand design for humankind. God is absolutely worthy of praise—and as such it plays a sanctified role in the call to worship that goes out to all the nations of the earth.

Application. Any song of praise and worship to God that truly reflects his identity will speak of the way he has and does reach out to restore and renew sinful humanity and of how he draws us into a new relationship with him. Our songs should be acts of worship to God that declare his character as a missionary God.

PSALM 97:1–12

Original Meaning

Responding to Yahweh's Rule (97:1). The poet again extends the benefits of Yahweh's rule far beyond the bounds of Israel—the whole created order, including the foreign and distant nations, rejoices in his kingship.

Revelation by Theophany (97:2–6). We see similar language used to describe God's appearance before Israel at Mount Sinai in Exodus 19–20. There is, of course, irony in the fact that clouds and thick darkness actually bring the light of revelation (Ps 97:11). The very basis of Yahweh's rule is righteousness and justice. Psalm 97 (like the other psalms in this collection) foresees a day when all peoples will see and acknowledge his true character (97:6b).

Worship the God of Gods (97:7–10). Israel's monotheism was probably more functional than ontological. In the Hebrew mindset the main question was one of worth and value rather than an abstract concept of existence. The question is: Whose God/god is actually worth worshiping? The answer is clear. Whether or not the gods of the nations exist, they are false and are subject to Yahweh's lordship. So, they too are called to worship him.

The Call to Rejoice (97:11–12). It is not the inhabitants of Zion or Judah mentioned in 97:8 who receive light and joy; rather, it is whoever responds to God in righteousness and uprightness of heart.

Application. God is King and Judge. His kingdom rule should be our habitual practice. The standards and priorities that he sets should govern our daily living.

PSALM 98:1–9

Original Meaning

The Call to Worship (98:1–3). All the nations should worship Yahweh because he has done marvelous things. In remembering his covenantal promises to Israel, God's activity in human history acts as a testimony to the nations.

Participating in Noisy Worship (98:4–6). The song of the goodness of Yahweh's character and the power of his hand may be new on the lips of the nations, but it gives good *reason* to praise: reason to bring praise that is vocal, praise that is musical, praise that is full of joy. The establishment of God's authority, given his nature, gives the whole earth good cause to rejoice.

The Choir of Creation (98:7–9). The imagery in this final stanza is the recognition of Yahweh's inherent worth by the whole created order because he is the universal Judge. The fact that the created realm acknowledges Yahweh's right to judge further emphasizes the inherent and unquestionable nature of that right.

Application. As God's steadfast love and faithfulness are worked out in the church, others are drawn to join that community of faith. As the church experiences the blessings of God openly and without embarrassment, others are drawn to know and love this God who does great things.

PSALM 99:1–9

Original Meaning

The Rule of the King (99:1–3). Israel's God reigns absolutely, and the whole world should respond accordingly. These images remind the original Israelite hearers that God is near but also that his presence in Jerusalem has a significance that goes far beyond Zion, Judah, and Israel.

The Character of the King (99:4–5). Verse 4a literally reads: "And the might of a king, he loves justice." Probably the best option, without emending the Hebrew text, is to translate this line thus: "And a King's might is his love of justice." In the remaining lines of this verse the psalmist goes on to verify that Yahweh, as High King, has established equity, justice, and righteousness.

Pleading with the Holy God (99:6–9). The psalmist highlights the intercessory ministry of these three Old Testament figures of faith. They prayed to Yahweh and he responded to their petitions. They were also associated with the teaching of the torah and obedience to God's revealed word. Following the reminder of God's gracious response to the prayers of his leaders, the poet draws attention to God's grace, but his mercy should never be abused.

Application. Our God is a holy God, and therefore he is absolutely consistent in his response to his people. When God's people cry to him for mercy, he hears and answers their prayer, regardless of the circumstances.

PSALM 100:1–5

Original Meaning

Delight in the King! (100:1–3). The invitation to draw near with confidence *is premised on the realization that he is the one, true God, Creator, and King over the universe.*

Enter with Praise! (100:4–5). Normally, non-Israelites would have been excluded from the inner court of the temple, but in 100:4 they are encouraged not only to "enter his gates with thanksgiving" but also to enter "his courts" (i.e., go beyond the outer court and enter the inner court). For the nations, this call invites a privileged and unprecedented level of participation.

Application. As a church, we need to consider more carefully our public praise of God as outreach.

PSALM 101:1–8

Original Meaning

A Determined Song (101:1–2). The first two verses set the tone for the rest of the psalm in expressing the poet-king's determination to live in accordance with God's standards—his "justice" (101:1)—and the psalmist expresses this determination in an attitude of praise. The theological point of these opening verses seems to be that the poet-king will reflect the ways of Yahweh's rule in his own human and political kingship.

Turning Toward by Turning Away (101:3–8). Although this form of negative expression is perhaps uncommon in the modern world, the significance of the characteristics rejected by the poet-king is quite powerful in the context of the Psalms and the Old Testament more broadly. The poet-king pronounces rejection of the behavioral consequences of a wicked worldview. Surely the wrong attitude of heart will ultimately lead to wrong moral actions. The faithful dwell with the king, but those who practice deceit will not be allowed to do so.

Application. It strikes me that part of the "well-regulated slumber" of the contemporary Western church is an unnatural focus on "being nice." We see being noncontroversial as an essential part of our witness. Yet our emphasis on niceness can lead to the absolute denial of the church's awkward, angular, prophetic office that is so clearly outlined both in the prophets and the teaching of Jesus in the Gospels.

PSALM 102:1–28

Original Meaning

The Personal Lament (102:1–11). The graphic images in 102:3–11 imply suffering to the extent that the poet believes his life is about to be painfully extinguished. There is little left for him, and all seems hopeless. The reader is drawn to feel the anguished despair of the poet, whose body is failing him (102:5). The second aspect of lament is focused on the opposition of enemies and expressed in terms of loneliness and social isolation (102:6–8). The sickness and physical decay of the lament is exacerbated by the mocking of enemies (102:8). The third element of this introductory lament section focuses on God as the prime mover and ultimate cause of the psalmist's torment (the God lament). Even when enemies are the proximate cause of an individual's suffering, Yahweh is always viewed as being ultimately responsible either for causing or failing to prevent the pain that causes lament.

National Crisis and Future Hope (102:12–22). The second section of the poem transitions from personal complaint to an expression of sadness at the demise of Jerusalem, but also of hope in the city's future restoration. The movement from the individual to Zion is a surprising one, but such a transition is not altogether uncommon. Nevertheless, there is hope! Israel's God still reigns, despite all appearances to the contrary. Yahweh is the *eternal* King (102:12), and the psalmist hopes that God will evidence his kingship through the restoration of the city. He not only sees, but he also pays attention to the realities of his people and acts in an efficacious manner. The aim of his observation is to hear the needs of his people *and* to set free those imprisoned *so that* his name will be declared in the midst of his people.

Passing Life, Eternal God (102:23–28). The fleeting brevity of human life, particularly a life apparently being cut short by illness, is contrasted with the eternal reign of God (102:24b–27). In some ways the contrast is stark. The poet decries the abbreviation of his life in juxtaposition with the timelessness of God, yet ultimately there is comfort to be found in the eternal reign of the Creator because he is "my God" (102:24). The psalm ends with a voice of hope for restoration in the future. The psalmist's days may be shortened, but God has made covenantal promises to his people, so there is hope for the longer term. God is a God of restoration (102:16).

Application. The poet is not so focused on himself that he fails to see the world around him. Nor is he so focused on his own pain that he forgets the character of God. Remembering God's faithful work in the world brings hope to even the darkest of personal circumstances. Prayer is a deeply personal matter, but Psalm 102 models an attitude to prayer that goes beyond the solely personal. We should follow its example.

PSALM 103:1–22

Original Meaning

Blessing Yahweh (103:1–2). The reminder to his own "soul" (103:1) to praise the Lord is a personalized call to worship. Just as the psalmists will frequently call Israel, the priesthood, or Yahweh's followers to give thanks (118:2–3) or call the nations and peoples to praise him (117:1), so here the poet addresses his very inner being with the call to praise the Lord. The explicit, negative command not to forget affirms the implication in the opening verse: It is easy to forget in our inner being the many reasons we have to praise God.

The Benefits Listed (103:3–6). The second section of the psalm (103:3–6) gives a powerful rationale for praise. It outlines the character of God by listing his actions through a series of personal participles. The Lord is the one who forgives, heals, redeems, and so on. The catalogue lists five actions that typify the character of God, the first of which focuses on the forgiveness of sins. Often in the Hebrew Bible, first place in a list indicates the priority of the author's emphasis, as is certainly the case in Psalm 103, where the remainder of the poem is so strongly focused on the forgiving love of God toward his people.

The Loving Forgiveness of God (103:7–19). The psalmist's reflection on the divine self-revelation in Exodus 34:6 is made explicit with reference to Moses (Ps 103:7). This direct quotation from Exodus 34:6 continues the poet's focus on God's grace, compassion, and forgiveness. The compassionate love of a father for his children is the only human experience that can approximate God's love for his children. God's people respond to his grace by a commitment to love him through mindfulness of his teaching. The King speaks into every area of life, and the proper covenantal response is to apply his standards to every aspect of our lives and the world around us.

Blessing Yahweh in the Cosmic Realm (103:20–22). This call to worship addressed to the angelic armies of the Lord is the logical consequence of his cosmic reign focused on in the previous verse. As throughout the psalm, in these concluding verses the emphasis remains on *doing* the word of God. The angels do his word in order to heed the sound of his word, thus providing an example for all humans whose desire is to worship God with their lives (103:18). Psalm 103 moves from the poet's self-exhortation to praise to a cosmic call to worship.

Application. Together with the psalmist, we must remind ourselves of God's eternal love for us (103:17)—a love that will not be tempered by our human weakness (103:13–16).

PSALM 104:1–35

Original Meaning

Praise God Who Made the Heavens (104:1–4). The voice of praise here sets an important tone of worship and joy that permeates the poem (104:1, 15, 24, 26, 33–35). Why praise? Because God is *very* great! God's greatness is often implied in statements of his character or works. Here the poet provides himself with an immediate justification for praise based on God's ontological nature. He is, quite simply, very great—and therefore worthy of praise. Continuing the image of Yahweh's cosmic kingship using the terminology of God's miraculously powerful appearance in theophany, the psalmist presents him as riding the clouds, commanding the winds, and sending out lightning bolts.

The Creation of the Earth (104:5–23). *The Waters (104:5–18).* The earth is not established because it is the earth. The earth is established because it was created and set in place by Yahweh, who is "very great" (104:1). In most cosmogonies (stories regarding the origins of cosmos), the waters represented threat and chaos. Far from being a chaotic threat that is barely held in check, the waters are part of Yahweh's sovereign purpose for the earth. They have a vital role to play in God's provision for all the living creatures that populate his earth (104:10–18).

The Times (104:19–23). From right places, he moves on to consider appropriate times and seasons. Just as the cedars of Lebanon provide an appropriate home for the birds of the air, so also the moon marks off appropriate seasons and the sun knows when to rise and set (104:19). This sense of right and appropriate order continues throughout the ensuing verses of this section (104:19–23). As God has worked in the creation of the universe, work and rest are both ingrained within that natural rhythm of the day. The implication of 104:23 is that there should be a time for rest once the evening comes.

A Declaration of Praise (104:24). The association between God's wisdom and his works of creation is a common one in the poetic texts of the Old Testament (see Job 28, 38–41; Prov 8). The creation-wisdom link implies that God's ways are somehow deeply ingrained in the natural order. The rhythms of day and night, passing seasons, sun and moon and constellations all taking their rightful places in the skies—all these phenomena point to a divine decree etched into the cosmos so that everything works as it should (Job 28:23–28).

The Creation of the Sea (104:25–26). Most frequently the seas are a symbol of threat and chaos (e.g., Ps 93). Psalm 104, however, presents the oceans as a playground for ships and sea monsters (104:26)! It really is a delightful image that continues the sense of purposefulness from the previous stanza (104:10–23). The high mountains are *for* the mountain goats. The crags are *for* the hyraxes. Here, quite amazingly, the implication is that the sea is *for* the ships to sail in and *for* Leviathan, the mythic sea monster, to play in. Once again, there is a glorious sense of artifice and delight in the way in which God made the seas.

The Sustainer of Life (104:27–30). The image in 104:27–28 demonstrates creaturely dependence on the Creator. Alternatively, when the Creator hides his face and takes away their breath, creatures die (104:29). The message is simple: all living beings, be they animals or people, are completely and utterly dependent on their Creator in each and every moment of life. We often celebrate human "autonomy" and "endeavor"—the things we ourselves achieve. But the truth of the matter is that we cannot demand our next breath. It is a gift from the Sustainer of life. This dependence is cause for praise (104:31–35)!

Concluding Praises (104:31–35). The earth continues as long as it gives glory to God. The implication of the juxtaposed phrases is that "his works" (104:31) continue as long as they give glory to God. Note the psalmist's determination for praise that results from his reflection on creation. The two acts inevitably go hand in hand. When people of faith reflect on the reality of the created order, it inclines the heart and mind to praise God. The poet expresses his desire that anything which taints or tarnishes God's glory should be removed from the created order.

Application. There is a delightful physicality in the images in Psalm 104. These products were staples in the ancient world—staples to be enjoyed. God gives human beings a beautiful world and good gifts. It is a human, spiritual, and eschatological tragedy if we do not enjoy these gifts, this world, this life.

PSALM 105:1–45

Original Meaning

The Call to Praise (105:1–7). The opening call to praise consists in eleven commands (105:1–5) followed by an address (105:6) and a rationale (105:7). The eleventh command, in 105:5 ("remember"), introduces the key idea for what follows in Psalms 105 and 106—divine remembrance and human forgetfulness. This theme of remembering God and his faithfulness dominates, and Psalm 105:5 sets the tone for what follows. The call to mindfulness is bifocal: remembering his *works* encourages remembrance of his *word*. The idea is Deuteronomic in nature. If God's people remember the goodness of his character and the gracious power of his actions on their behalf, then surely they will want to call to mind his instructions and live in accordance with them.

The Covenant with Abraham (105:8–15). God has always been faithful to his people because of the promise he made to Abraham. God *always* remembers that covenant, and he is *always* working the circumstances around his people in accordance with that promise of blessing, even when it does not appear to be so. That promise of blessing included the promise of a land (105:11), which would, again, have been a comforting assurance for those living in the fragile setting of the return from exile. Verses 12–15 reference that period of the promise when the patriarchs were in the land but not owners of it.

Providence through Trial in the Joseph Story (105:16–22). Verses 16–22 continue this poetic take on the early stages of the covenantal history by giving a brief rendering of the Joseph narrative. Tellingly, the psalmist's emphasis in recounting this part of the story is that God's plan is still at work even during periods of great hardship. Famine destroys the food supply for the patriarchal family (105:16), *but* Yahweh sent a man before them (105:17). The efficacy of the divine plan comes to the fore with the declaration that the "slave" of 105:17 has become "master" and "ruler" by 105:21. The massive irony shows that Yahweh's plan ("the word of the LORD" [105:19]) is always effective, even when that plan is shrouded in mystery and hardship for those who participate in it.

Moses and the Miracle of the Exodus (105:23–38). This section of Psalm 105 begins and ends with the language of entrance and exit. Israel came to Egypt (105:23), but it was the Egyptians who rejoiced when they departed (105:38). The Egyptians were sons of Noah just as much as the Israelites were (Gen 5:32, 1 Chr 1:8). Shared origins remind Israel that their election is from among their brothers. They are no better or stronger or more righteous than any other nation (Deut 7). They were chosen by God not because of any sense of inherent value in and of themselves; rather, they were chosen for a particular task (Ps 105:43–45).

Desert Provision and the Opportunities of the Land (105:39–41). Interestingly the cloud, which is normally presented as going before the people in leadership (Exod 13:21–22), is here presented as covering the people in protection (Ps 105:39a). The psalmist continues with reference to the miraculous provision of food and water in the desert before drawing his didactic conclusions in the final stanza.

Theological Commentary and Conclusions (105:42–45). The psalmist ends the main section of the psalm (following the introductory call to worship) by recounting Yahweh's mindfulness of his covenantal promise once again (105:8; cf. 105:42). Yahweh remembers his holy promise in a relational sense. Covenantal faithfulness is not just a point of principle—it is also an indication of God's great love for his chosen people. The land becomes an open forum in which God's chosen people are to live in accordance with his instruction. In so doing, they live lives so different, so godly, that the surrounding nations look on and are attracted to the ways of Yahweh. This missional tone resonates throughout Psalm 105.

Application. It is often noted that there is no mission in the Old Testament, but Psalm 105 strikes the tenor of Old Testament mission: Yahweh's great worth is declared by lives lived out openly in community, according to the standards of his torah, for everyone else to see. Living in this way will lead to such an attractive way of being that others will see Jesus in us and be drawn to his message. *Lifestyles* of self-denying love lived out in local communities in which all are welcomed and people seem somehow different from the rest of the world—*that* is a truly powerful message in this cynical world in which we live.

PSALM 106:1–48

Original Meaning

Introductory call to praise and intercession (106:1–5). The poet's intercessions at the beginning and end of the psalm (106:4–5, 47) and his account of Israel's continuing history are completely predicated on the awareness of Yahweh's fundamental goodness and his loving commitment to his people. The history of the nation would never have continued for as long as it did apart from God's steadfast love even for a rebellious people. Just as it is impossible to express fully or even adequately God's worth in praise, so also it is impossible to give an account of all God's activity in human history for the benefit of the covenant community. Divine remembrance of the individual implies that Yahweh will be faithful to his covenantal promises.

Forgetfulness from the Beginning (106:6–12). The writer of Psalm 106 confesses the sinfulness of his own generation alongside the sins of his fathers. Clearly, reflection on the events of the exile led the people to a sober understanding of their own failings. Failure to reflect on God's miraculous works on behalf of his people combined with their failure to remember the *many* kindnesses he had shown to them led to their rebellion in a time of stress. Yahweh saved Israel because he was true to himself, not because the people responded well to the threat they faced. Being true to his own character means that God will be true to his nature as a missionary God.

Hurrying to Forget in the Desert (106:13–18). All too soon after God's mighty deliverance, the people's selective amnesia returns, and they rebel. Verses 14–15 probably refer to the almost absurd rebellion in Numbers 11:4–35, where the people complain about the miraculous provision of food in the desert and start whining about the lack of meat. The second desert rebellion reprised by the psalmist (Ps 106:16–18) is found in Numbers 16. Once again, the essence of the issue is right relationship with Yahweh. The rebellions called into question the goodness of God's character and his design for the people.

Forgetting God at Sinai (106:19–23). There is an implied sense of absolute incredulity in 106:19–20. The actions are unbelievable and the location even worse. Making an idol from metal and declaring that inanimate thing to be the living God is farcical enough, but doing so at Sinai, the place of ultimate revelation prior to the incarnation, exacerbates the crime. To have seen the miracles worked in their own historical reality and then to make an idol from metal that they themselves knew full well had *nothing* to do with their release from Egypt combined, as far as the psalmist is concerned, to make the ultimate absurdity.

Failing to Believe the Promise of a Land (106:24–27). The next failing highlighted by the psalmist is the people's response to the report of the ten spies (Num 13–14). The verb used in Psalm 106:24a implies the rejection of the divine plan. The root cause of this rejection is failure to believe (106:24b). Similarly, 106:25 begins with an action resulting from a failure to do what was expected of them. Verse 27 telescopes the effects of the fathers' failings and focuses on the impact in the psalmist's generation. Faithlessness has a cross-generational impact that resonates through the ages from exodus to exile.

Provoking Yahweh through Idolatry (106:28–33). Their being "yoked" (106:28) leads to a string of events that shows the ups and downs of a community's unraveling and veering away from its true identity. The events of Numbers 25 describe an idolatrous orgy of cultic prostitution quelled only by the radical intervention of Phinehas. Just as Moses's prayer saved them from Phinehas's destruction (Ps 106:23), so Phineas' intervention saved them from the plague, but neither of these representative actions was enough to bring a change of heart and behavior on the part of the people. They troubled Moses by rebelling. The action for which Moses is punished is rooted in the constant, vexing rebellion of the people.

Polluting the land with blood (106:34–39). The conquest command was not rooted in any sense of ethnic cleansing. It was, rather, a moral imperative to prevent the pagan worship practices that resulted in the slaughter of innocents through the habitual sacrifice of children. As with the previous generation, the issue boils down to one of simple obedience. They knew that mingling with the Canaanites meant running the risk of adopting their abhorrent religious practices. The people were meant to be distinctive from all the other tribes and nations. God's people proved themselves unworthy of their calling, so the punishments of Deuteronomy 28 were bound to unfold as promised by God.

Punishment and Grace in Exile (106:40–46). Given the truncated history recounted to this point, the conclusion of 106:40 is absolutely inevitable. By summarizing the history of Israel in this manner—focusing on the many and repeated failures of the nation—the psalmist makes it plain that Yahweh could respond in no other way. The exile was the inevitable consequence of the nation's action. Despite this image of decay and decline, once again grace triumphs over rebellion (106:44–46). Even having disobeyed for so long and with such determination that they incurred the ultimate covenantal curse of exile (cf. Deut 28:64–68), yet God's people experience his mercy.

Intercession, Praise, and Conclusion to Book 4 (106:47–48). The prayer for salvation places the psalmist with the people in the exile. Whether exile is his literal or metaphorical location is difficult to say. But the prayer resonates through all generations and communities of faith. The concluding call to praise serves as a doxology that indicates the close of Book 4 of the Psalter as well as the logical conclusion of the psalm.

Application. Most Christians, at some point, feel condemned and dismayed by the repeating pattern of seeking forgiveness followed by sudden relapse. The poet was able to believe that God's grace was bigger and more determined than the often-repeated sins of the people. How much more should we, having seen what he has done for us in Jesus, be able to trust in God's great love?

PSALM 107:1–43

Original Meaning

The Steadfast Love of God (107:1–3). The commitment of Yahweh to his people may not be fully captured with the word "love" (107:1). The *hesed* of the Lord shapes the community's understanding of their own history and God's faithful, covenantal commitment throughout it, but the term also reminds the community of the foundational hope for deliverance, past and future.

To limit the interpretation of 107:3c to a geographic understanding alone fails to capture the full range of possible meanings. The people are to give thanks to the Lord because he has gathered them from the lands, but also because he has delivered them from the "north" and the "south" (lit., "sea," so NIV footnote) from places that threatened to unleash chaos into the lives of God's people.

Deliverance from the Desert Wasteland (107:4–9). The first scene depicts a group lost in the wilderness with no hope of delivering themselves. So far off the beaten path are they, the psalmist says, that they cannot even find a city in which to dwell. In each scene of deliverance, the psalmist recounts how the people cried out to God and how they were delivered (107:6, 13, 19, 28). Because of the Lord's steadfast love and his capacity to perform "wonderful deeds" (107:8), the people are delivered from "their trouble" and "their distress" (107:6). They are given a city to live in, and their appetites are satiated (107:7b, 9).

Deliverance from Prison (107:10–16). The second scene depicts individuals suffering in captivity. Unlike the first scene, however, those in prison make a correlation between their dire circumstances and their lack of faithfulness to God (107:11). Similar to the hopelessness in 107:4–9, the psalmist now notes "there was no one to help" those "subjected . . . to bitter labor" (107:12). Consequently, the people cried out to Yahweh (107:13), and he delivered them (107:14). Because of this act of covenantal faithfulness, the people are invited to give thanks for the steadfast love (*hesed*) of Yahweh.

Deliverance from Sheol (107:17–22). From the perspective of the psalmist, those who were foolish and turned aside or rebelled (107:17a) from the ways of God followed a pathway that appeared to lead to the gates of death (107:18b). Later in this section, these gates of death are referred to as "the grave" (107:20). Strikingly, however, the psalmist personalizes the term by adding a third-person masculine plural suffix to the end of the word—an ending that would result in a literal rendering of the word as "their pit." In other words, their iniquities have led to their pit. Nonetheless, those sick under the weight of sin cry to Yahweh for deliverance (107:19), and he delivers them from their oppression or distress.

Deliverance from the Sea (107:23–32). Three times the psalmist refers to the sea in terms that are metaphorically rich in meaning (107:23b, 24b, 26a). Frequently these terms connote chaos and the threat of death (cf. 69:1, 2, 15). Similar imagery is employed in the book of Jonah as well (Jonah 2:3, 5). So great was the storm that the sailors were "at their wits' end" (Ps 107:27). Literally the Hebrew reads, "all their wisdom was swallowed up"—perhaps another allusion to Jonah.

A Hymn on the Power of God (107:33–41). Following the four narrative portions of the psalm, the psalmist offers a poem that celebrates the awesome power of God over all aspects of creation. Verses 33–34 open the final hymn with a stark reminder of Yahweh's power. This particular exercise of Yahweh's power is a response to the wickedness (Heb. *ra'*) of those who dwell in the land. The theology of the poor plays a significant role in the theology of the Psalter as a whole, and elements of such a theology are reflected in 107:39–41. Yahweh lifted them out of their affliction and blessed them by increasing their families.

Wisdom Conclusion (107:42–43). The final two verses make clear the paraenetic-didactic purpose of the psalm. The upright are instructed to "see" (107:42) and learn from the stories of deliverance and the testimonies of Yahweh's transforming work in the world. Should they do so, they will be led to rejoicing, while those engaged in wickedness will have their mouths shut in the light of Yahweh's power. The psalm concludes by returning to the same idea (107:43b). Those who consider or understand the *hesed* of Yahweh will not only have reason to give thanks (107:1a); they will also be well on their way to becoming wise (107:43b).

Application. In our technological age, people are falling into exile in new and more sophisticated ways. When circumstances become challenging or conversations become difficult, people resort to social media as a means of escape. Rather than engaging others, people withdraw into a sophisticated form of isolationism. Ironically, for many people deliverance is associated with being exiled from others—a concept foreign to the psalmist and to the church.

PSALM 108:1–13

Original Meaning

A Song of Praise to God (108:1–4). The psalmist is announcing that he will make a confession concerning all that God has done on behalf of his people—and that he will make that confession among the peoples and the nations. The psalmist provides an explicit rationale to this claim in 108:4.

The Divine King Is Mighty to Save (108:5–6). The psalmist's request for God to rise up and be exalted over the heavens in 108:5 establishes the ground for the petition that follows in 108:6. Because Yahweh has assumed his rightful place over the heavens as Sovereign over the created world, the psalmist has confidence that God, and God alone, will deliver his people.

The Response of God (108:7–9). The anticipated response to the psalmist's request follows in the next section of the psalm, 108:7–9. While this divine oracle does provide a verbal answer, it indicates much more; the response suggests God's intent to act on behalf of his people by bringing deliverance.

Prayer for Help against the Enemies (108:10–13). The confident claim made in the divine oracle stands in grave tension with the realities articulated in 108:10–13. The threat of enemies poses serious issues related to protection and deliverance. The psalmist concludes with a plea that God will come to the aid of his people followed by a confession (108:13b) that God and God alone can tread down Israel's foes.

Application. The psalmist refuses to believe in a second-hand god because he refuses to allow the circumstances that surround him to define God.

PSALM 109:1–31

Original Meaning

The Complaint (109:1–5). The first five verses refer repeatedly to acts of speaking. In 109:1 the psalmist announces that he praises God, while a few verses later he explains that those around him continue to assault him with lying words. In 109:2–5 the psalmist rehearses the situation that has prompted this prayer. The social relationships of the psalmist have been skewed as loyalty and friendship (109:4a, 5b) have given way to accusation and hatred.

Request for an Accuser (109:6–7). In 109:6 the psalmist makes a request. As he has been charged by a wicked person (109:2), the psalmist requests that a wicked person be appointed over those who have made false claims. In the second half of 109:6 the psalmist requests that an accuser, or *satan*, stand against the enemy. Although the word *satan* accrues additional meaning in later biblical texts, the meaning here suggests a prosecutor. Even if the enemy offers up a plea to Yahweh, the psalmist requests that such a prayer would "condem him" (109:7), or, better yet, that such a prayer would simply "miss the mark."

Request for a Just Sentence (109:8–19). The psalmist then provides a lengthy list of presumed punishments that should be exacted upon the enemy. Such an unadulterated list of curses challenges the modern reader. The apparent vitriol in 109:8–15, however, may best be understood if the reader considers the psalmist's claim in 109:16–19. Not only did the enemy fail to show compassion to the most vulnerable, he actually thrived on the cursing of others (109:17). To be more precise, the Hebrew in 109:17 actually says, "He loved cursing and it entered him."

Request for Deliverance (109:20–25). The psalmist pleads with Yahweh for the sake of Yahweh's name or, better yet, for the sake of his reputation. The psalmist then requests that Yahweh deliver him "out of the goodness of your love" (109:21). The word *hesed* ("love") appears again in this psalm, and once again it suggests covenantal faithfulness and loyal love. Whereas Yahweh is depicted as the master, capable of delivering the psalmist (109:21b), the psalmist describes himself as the servant, one of the "poor and needy" (109:22). Without the aid of Yahweh, life is quickly coming to a disastrous end. The psalmist has grown thin and emaciated; his very appearance invokes the scorn of others.

Request for Deliverance (109:26–29). The third petition of the psalmist appears in 109:26–29, where attention turns to the enemy. In 109:26 the psalmist pleads for Yahweh to save him "according to your unfailing love" (*hesed*). The psalmist, therefore, requests that Yahweh bless him (109:28b) while clothing the accusers in shame (109:29). At first glance such a request may appear retaliatory, but in a culture dominated by honor and shame, if Yahweh shows his "hand" (109:27), delivers the psalmist, and clears the psalmist of any wrong, then the enemies have lost face. They are "wrapped in shame as in a cloak" (109:29).

Promise of Praise (109:30–31). The poem concludes in a manner typical of a lament psalm by promising worship of Yahweh and declaration of his name in the presence of others. In the opening of the psalm, the poet suggests that God's perceived inactivity and silence suggest something of God's apparent absence in the midst of the situation of great suffering and unjust accusation. By declaring in the final verse that Yahweh stands at the right hand of the needy, the psalmist asserts his belief that God must be standing alongside him as well.

Application. To speak of injustice in docile and hushed terms, as perhaps we may prefer, only masks the devastating work of injustice in the world. The language of this psalm strips away such a veneer, thus exposing the inhumanity experienced by one trapped by injustice. This psalm asks us to acknowledge injustice but then to declare that injustice does not have the final word. Our prayers are meant to be joined with all those seeking justice so together we might proclaim that the God we serve is indeed a God of justice.

PSALM 110:1–7

Original Meaning

The Announcement of Victory over Enemies (110:1–3). The term "my lord" in 110:1a suggests a hierarchical relationship between the person speaking and the one being addressed. The king being addressed is invited to sit at the right hand of Yahweh, and as such implies a position of honor. The image and implications of Yahweh and the king as his co-ruler are spelled out in 110:2.

A Priest Like Melchizedek (110:4–7). In 2 Samuel 7 the Lord swore to David that he will establish a kingdom for David, and Yahweh affirms that he will not change his mind. Similar to Melchizedek (110:4; cf. Gen 12:18–20), the king will serve as mediator between Yahweh and his people. Yahweh's appearance at the right hand of the king implies protection and support. In this role, however, Yahweh is not passive. In 110:7 the king signals that he is the beneficiary of Yahweh's judgment against the nations.

Application. Those who stand in opposition to the work of God and who appear to have power are not our source of hope.

PSALM 111:1–10

Original Meaning

Introduction (111:1–2). The verb "extol" (111:1) can mean to praise, but it can also mean "confess" or "proclaim." This poem is not spoken *to* God by the psalmist; instead, it is a psalm spoken *about* God *to* the congregation (111:1). In 111:2 the psalmist introduces the theme: the "works of the LORD" (111:3, 4, 6, and 7).

The Works of God in History (111:3–6). Verse 3 functions as an introduction to the first major section in the psalm. Through its language the verse invokes the image of Yahweh as Divine King, while 111:4–6 describe the works as constitutive of a life-sustaining world established by God. The works or deeds of Yahweh are evidence that Yahweh is the God he claims to be.

The Torah as the Work of God (111:7–10). The second line in 111:7 redirects the reader's attention to God's covenant law. The precepts of God are reliable because they introduce a world filled with faithfulness and justice. For this psalmist, the fear of the Lord is connected to living out the torah of God. If one carries out the precepts of God, then there will be a reward.

Application. The works of God call us, even now, to root our lives in the story of God *and* in the values and commitments expressed in his word.

PSALM 112:1–10

Original Meaning

Introductory Beatitude (112:1). The psalmist rightly knows that the blessed life is the one that is oriented toward God and God's purposes in the world. In Psalm 111 the psalmist calls people to delight in the *works* of God, while here in Psalm 112 the emphasis shifts to the *words* of God.

Markers of a Blessed Life (112:2–5). "Mighty" offspring (112:2) are not a *reward* for faithful living; rather, they are the *result* of faithful living. Those who have wealth and riches have received them *from God*, but they are to be used *for the community.* Beginning in 112:4, there are social implications for how one conducts his or her life.

The Fear of God and the Absence of Fear (112:6–9). Those who fear Yahweh have no reason to fear anything in life. Psalm 112:7–8 addresses two issues that likely would have produced anxiety and fear: bad news and the presence of enemies. Those who fear and trust in God possess hearts that are firmly established.

The Fate of the Wicked (112:10). According to Psalm 112, while the wicked may gnash their teeth, ultimately they will melt away in the light of the one with greater strength. The final line of the psalm sums up the fate of the wicked. It mirrors the fate of the wicked in Psalm 1:6—both will come to an end.

Application. According to the psalmist, this blessed life is one that lives in relationship with God and one that finds "great delight" in the purposes of God in the world (112:1).

PSALM 113:1–9

Original Meaning

Praise the Name of the Lord (113:1–3). The psalmist opens with an extended call for the servants of the Lord to praise him. The final line clarifies the expansive rule of the Mighty One. The praise of the Lord's name should fill the entire earth, from horizon to horizon.

The Lord is Exalted (113:4–6). All three verses point to Yahweh as the exalted Lord who reigns on high. Yet Yahweh's exaltation above the heavens does not suggest abandonment by God. To the contrary, his location above the heavens ensures the faithfulness of God and his capacity to deliver.

The Lord Delivers the Weak (113:7–9). The claims of radical transcendence in 113:4–6 are met with claims of radical immanence in 113:7–9. Yahweh is worthy of Israel's praise because he is in fact the Divine King enthroned on high, but also because he is the Divine King who acts as a king by delivering the most vulnerable.

Application. Although he reigns on high, he has come among us. Praise the Lord—hallelujah!

PSALM 114:1–8

Original Meaning

Deliverance and Election (114:1–2). In the opening strophe the psalmist recounts the decisive moment in Israel's history in 114:1 and then draws theological conclusions from that event in 114:2.

Nature's Response to God's Work (114:3–4). These verses build on the images associated with the exodus and the entry into the promised land.

The Questioning of Nature's Response (114:5–6). The psalmist has modified the narrative in 114:3–4 so that the same information now reads as rhetorical questions.

The Presence of the Lord (114:7–8). The final strophe calls all creation to acknowledge God as the Divine King. Even as he can turn rocks into pools of water, so also can God turn a people into his sanctuary.

Application. In unison with the psalmist, we echo "tremble, earth"—tremble indeed (114:7).

PSALM 115:1–18

Original Meaning

Petition to the God of Heaven (115:1–3). The opening strophe of Psalm 115 presents the theological crisis that confronted the people of God (115:2). In response, the psalmist offers a short confession in 115:3. This confession functions like a thesis statement by presenting the community's primary response to the crisis articulated in 115:2.

The Impotence of Other Gods (115:4–8). In the second strophe the psalmist invites a comparison between "our God" (115:3) and "their idols" (115:4). The juxtaposition of the living God, who acts on behalf of his people, with the other nations' impotent idols/gods, which are incapable of action, reinforces Israel's monotheistic claim.

Call to Trust in Israel's God (115:9–11). The third strophe appears as a litany with a threefold call for each group to trust in the Lord and to acknowledge that he is their help and shield. Those who trust in lifeless idols have no hope, but those who trust in Yahweh have a deliverer and a protector.

Communal Assurance of Blessing (115:12–13). Those praying this psalm find themselves in a situation in which the honor of God's name needs to be restored. The circumstances are such that the nations are questioning the presence of Israel's God. The assertion that God has remembered his people signals that deliverance is on the way.

The Power of Israel's God (115:14–15). In 115:14–15 the speaker (priest) replies to the communal confession by issuing a prayer for the people. The prayer focuses on a simple request, namely, that God would increase his people and that the present generation and those to follow would be the beneficiaries.

Vow of Praise to the God of Heaven (115:16–18). Having acknowledged the futility of the foreign gods and the power of Israel's God, in the final strophe the community makes a vow to praise God. The twofold confession returns to the theme of God as the creator to whom belongs all creation while also introducing a new theme, that of the vocation of praise.

Application. Our way forward is through God and with God.

PSALM 116:1–19

Original Meaning

Declaration of Trust (116:1–2). The opening lines of Psalm 116 provide the fundamental reason for the psalmist's song of thanksgiving: God has heard his prayer. Yahweh's faithful action in the past (116:1b, 2a) prompts the psalmist to respond in the future.

Recollection of Deliverance (116:3–6). Following the declaration of trust, the psalmist recounts the scene of deliverance that prompted the song of thanksgiving. He recounts the depths of his plight in verses 3 and 6b, thereby creating an *inclusio* around the verses that deal with Yahweh's capacity to deliver.

Self-Exhortation in the Light of Deliverance (116:7–9). The psalmist turns to reflect on his own condition in the present. The earlier verses mentioned the sense of confinement experienced by the psalmist. In this section such oppressive, life-threatening conditions have been abated and replaced by conditions of hope.

Confession of Trust (116:10–11). The confession of trust in 116:10–11 links back to the declaration of trust in 116:1–2. In essence, these two sections create an *inclusio* around 116:3–9 by opening and closing the thanksgiving song with affirmations of the psalmist's trust in God's capacity to deliver. Verses 10–11 serve as a recapitulation of thanksgiving.

Act of Thanksgiving (116:12–14). The poet considers his response to God: "What shall I return to the Lord for all his goodness to me?" (116:12). In the context of the subsequent verses, 116:17–19, verses 13–14 refer to the psalmist's participation in a sacrificial thanksgiving meal. His expression of praise is manifested in action before the people of God.

Confession of Trust (116:15–16). As part of the act of thanksgiving, the psalmist offers up the third confession of trust in 116:15–16. In both verses he explains why God has sought to deliver him.

Thanksgiving Sacrifice (116:17–19). The poem concludes with the psalmist's promise to give a thanksgiving offering while once again calling on the name of the Lord (116:17). Then his deliverance will be full and complete. Such deliverance is worthy of the psalm's final admonition: *hallu-yah*, "Praise the Lord" (116:19).

Application. Perhaps there are others who need to know the same truth about *our God*. And while ministers can climb into the pulpit weekly to make that proclamation, what most people really want to hear is a testimony grounded in unadulterated thanksgiving.

PSALM 117:1–2

Original Meaning. The hymn opens with a call to the "nations" (*goyim*), typically non-Israelite nations (117:1). The psalmist contends that the very fact of Yahweh's love and faithfulness will elicit praise from the nations.

Application. This God is the hope of us all (Rom 15:12).

PSALM 118:1–29

Original Meaning

Call to Thank God (118:1–4). The psalmist calls the people to do more than simply have a thankful attitude; their giving thanks carries with it the sense of giving testimony about Yahweh's goodness and steadfast love. Verses 2–4 contain a short litany in which the psalmist invites Israel, the house of Aaron, and those who fear God to make a confession: "his love endures forever."

Deliverance from Peril (118:5–18). In the second major section of the psalm, the poet shifts to recounting his past deliverance. This section provides the rationale for the call to give thanks found in the opening and closing sections of the psalm. The psalmist recounts how "all the nations" had surrounded him (118:10), but Yahweh had brought him into a "spacious place"(118:5) and delivered him. Within this section there are two interludes (118:8–9, 15–16); both play a critical role in the theology of the section. The first interlude makes use of language from the wisdom tradition, while the second one invokes imagery associated with the exodus.

Thanksgiving Celebration (118:19–28). The final section of the psalm rehearses a thanksgiving or *todah* ceremony that would have probably taken place near or within the temple precinct. The participants in this liturgy likely included the individual psalmist (118:19, 21, 28), the temple priests or ministers (118:20, 26–27), and the worshiping community (118:22–25). Following the declaration by the priests in 118:27 that Yahweh is God, the psalmist speaks again in affirming not only that Yahweh is God but also that Yahweh is *his* God, that there is a relationship between Yahweh and the psalmist (118:28). The language in 118:28 follows closely the language in Exodus 15:2b by declaring the psalmist's intent to praise or confess God and magnify him.

Concluding Verse (118:29). The psalm concludes by repeating the opening verse of the psalm. The psalm opens with this affirmation, but the deliverance recounted in 118:5–18 and the events of the thanksgiving celebration in 118:19–28 give reason anew for the call to give thanks.

Application. At times thanksgiving has been reduced simply to the act of saying "thank you." As such, the expression is merely the final statement made in a series of exchanges between two or more parties. The lengthy recitation in 118:5–18, however, poses a different model for thanksgiving. The psalmist opted to recount at length the depths of his trouble and the reality of his helplessness. In this section of the psalm such images are juxtaposed with God's intervention in the psalmist's life. Rather than simply offering a perfunctory "thank you" to God, we also might do well to describe the depths of our own trouble and the reality of our own helplessness. Perhaps we are too self-reliant and too ashamed of our inability to save ourselves, but when we confess the depths of our need, we are confronted above all with our need for God. As we make this recitation-turned-confession, we are also reminded of the greatness of God's deliverance. It is in those moments that we may find ourselves overwhelmed with a sense of true thanksgiving.

PSALM 119:1–176

Original Meaning

Aleph (119:1–8). Psalm 119 begins with the same word that begins Psalm 1: *'ashrey*, "blessed." In Psalm 119 the poet acknowledges that the ways of the "blessed" are blameless because they walk in the ways of the torah of Yahweh and seek instruction with their heart. In the first half of the strophe (119:1–4) the psalmist describes the blessed life as one rooted in the torah of Yahweh. In the second half of the strophe, he refers to the tumultuous circumstances that appear to threaten him. The psalmist worries about being put to shame (119:6) and left forsaken (119:8). Thus, the opening strophe holds in tandem the desire to live a blessed life that is rooted in the torah of Yahweh and the reality of a threatened existence. Psalm 119 reminds the reader of the need to root one's life in the instruction of God amid such challenging circumstances in life.

Beth (119:9–16). The second strophe begins with the question, "How can a young person stay on the path of purity?" (119:9a). In 119:9b the psalmist explains that a person must live according to God's "word" (Heb. *dabar*). The term itself can refer either to the written revelation of God, or it can refer to God's direct communication to his people (cf. Jer 1:4; Ezek 1:3). The entire strophe is bracketed by the term "word." In the strophe's opening verse, the psalmist announces that the pure path is reached by choosing to live according to God's word, and in the final verse the psalmist pledges not to forget God's "word." In 119:11 the poet declares that he has "hidden your word" in his heart so that he might not sin against God. The heart of the blessed person becomes a storehouse of God's words.

Gimel (119:17–24). In the opening strophe (Aleph) of Psalm 119 the psalmist alluded to the difficult circumstances he faces (119:6). The Gimel strophe makes clear the impact this threat has had upon him. In the second half of the strophe the psalmist refers to those who are plaguing him. Together they slander the psalmist and rain down on him scorn and contempt. He explicitly defines them in 119:21 as "those who stray from your commands." Over against the threatening group, the psalmist self-identifies as "your servant" in verses 17 and 23. Although the psalmist feels pressure from his enemies, he longs for God's laws (119:20), for they are his counselors (119:24); they provide the needed and necessary guidance amid the challenges he confronts.

Daleth (119:25–32). The lament uttered in the Gimel strophe continues in this strophe. The psalmist describes his plight by saying, "my life clings to the dust" (author's translation, 119:25). This plight is juxtaposed with his confession in 119:31. Although his life is *clings* to the dust (119:25), he confesses that he *clings* (NIV "hold fast") to the statutes of God (119:31). As a result of Yahweh's instructing the psalmist, he can exclaim, "you have broadened my understanding" (119:32). Just as trouble is imagined as being in a tight spot, so deliverance is imagined as being in an open space. On the one hand, by following the paths of Yahweh's instruction, his understanding will be enlarged. On the other hand, the reference to paths and open spaces in this verse suggests deliverance.

He (119:33–40). The He strophe shifts the focus to petition. Every line in this strophe begins with an imperative addressed to Yahweh. The symmetry is further extended in the first seven lines with each verb appearing in the *hiphil* form (based upon the guiding letter for the strophe, *he*). Even more deliberately than in previous strophes, Yahweh is depicted as the teacher for his pupil, the psalmist. In the two middle verses, the psalmist asks God to remove those things that can prove distracting: "selfish gain" (119:36) and "worthless things" (119:37). Both terms are meant to suggest that the value of Yahweh's torah surpasses all things. In 119:38 the psalmist refers to the covenantal relationship that defines his life with Yahweh.

Waw (119:41–48). The Waw strophe opens with another petition directed at Yahweh. In this initial petition the psalmist requests that Yahweh's "unfailing love" (*hesed*) and "salvation" (*teshuah*) come to him (119:41). The taunting of the enemies has prompted this plea (119:42). The coming of Yahweh's *hesed* would signal God's covenantal loyalty and rebut the claim of the enemy. Because the psalmist trusts in God's "word" (*dabar*, 119:42), he declares that he can "walk about in freedom" (119:45), in a wide, open space. So certain is the psalmist of God's promises (119:41) that he pledges to speak of Yahweh's "statutes" (119:46) in the presence of kings. The strophe draws to a close with the psalmist's confessing his loyal love to the ways of Yahweh.

Zayin (119:49–56). The focus of the Zayin strophe is the thrice repeated word *zakar*, "to remember." In 119:49 the psalmist implores Yahweh to remember his "word" (*dabar*) to his servant (cf. 119:17, 23) in the midst of the arrogant and mocking throng. In this context the psalmist declares that he "remembers" Yahweh's ancient laws (119:52). Despite the sense of being without a land (119:54, "wherever I lodge"), the psalmist confesses that the decrees of Yahweh have been a comfort and a source of joy. In the midst of his sense of dislocation, the psalmist confesses that at night he "remembers" the name of Yahweh (119:55). As with previous strophes, the psalmist holds in tension the reality of his world with his tenacious commitment to the torah of Yahweh.

Heth (119:57–64). In the previous strophe (119:54) and the Gimel strophe (119:19), the psalmist declares that he is a sojourner, a person without a land. In response to that assessment of his condition, the psalmist opens the Heth strophe by describing Yahweh as his "portion" (119:57). While he feels like an alien, he is not without a home. Yahweh will be his portion. The psalmist confesses that he has not only a home but also a community (119:63). Until this point in the psalm the image has been that of the lone, faithful psalmist against his godless enemies; but in the Heth strophe the image shifts. The wicked remain a present danger (119:61), but that threat is not faced in isolation.

Teth (119:65–72). In the Teth strophe the operative word is "good" (*tov*). The word begins the first two verses of the strophe and, likewise, is the first word in the last two verses, thus serving as a framing device. Beyond these four uses the word *tov* begins 119:68, and the verbal form of the term appears later in the verse. In the book of Deuteronomy *tov* represents the life-sustaining gifts or blessings of Yahweh, particularly as related to Israel's faithfulness to the covenant (cf. Deut 10:13). In Psalm 119 the poet explains in verses 67 and 71 that, like the enemies, he too had gone astray. Whatever gain he may have achieved by following the ways of the arrogant, the psalmist now concludes that the only source of value is the law (torah) that proceeds from God's mouth (119:72).

Yodh (119:73–80). The opening line of the Yodh strophe refers to human creation. Whether the psalmist is alluding specifically to Genesis 1–3 or to the creation motif more generally is difficult to determine. What is not difficult to discern is the rationale for invoking creation language. The psalmist declares that he was fashioned by God and, consequently, designed to live out God's commandments. Human life and faithful obedience are intertwined in this strophe with the larger truth that true life, as fashioned by God, includes faithfulness to God's instruction. The psalmist indicates that it is God's *hesed* and mercy that provide comfort to him so that he may live (Ps 119:77). Yahweh is not only the creator but also the sustainer of those who delight in his law (119:77a).

Kaph (119:81–88). The Kaph strophe and the strophe to follow (Lamed) function as the center of Psalm 119, both literally and figuratively. The Kaph strophe provides the most explicit account of the psalmist's plight and serves to anchor the lament element of the psalm. In the Teth strophe the psalmist indicated that he had been afflicted in the past because he had gone astray (119:67). In this strophe, however, he confesses that everything happening now is "without cause" (119:86). Consequently, the psalmist can do nothing other than to petition Yahweh for help (119:86b). The strophe concludes with the psalmist invoking Yahweh's *hesed*, "unfailing love" (119:88).

Lamed (119:89–96). The Lamed strophe emphasizes the psalmist's cause for hope, namely, the faithfulness of Yahweh and the enduring strength of his torah. Yahweh's enthronement in the heavens secures his rightful place as the cosmic king over all creation. Similarly, the psalmist contends that Yahweh's word stands firm in the heavens. Whatever political and social machinations may occur on earth, they do not undermine the authoritative power of Yahweh's word or his faithfulness; it "endure[s] to this day" (119:91). It is because of that enduring power that in 119:94 the psalmist confesses, "I am yours." With this declaration the psalmist recognizes God as his patron and seeks the deliverance that only he can bring.

Mem (119:97–104). The Mem strophe continues the praise of Yahweh's torah. As with the author of Psalm 1:2, the writer of Psalm 119 confesses that he meditates on Yahweh's laws all day long. In Psalm 1:2, the verb "to meditate" is *hagah*, but in Psalm 119:97 it is *siah*. Although the terms differ, they are synonymous in meaning. In Psalm 1:2 the psalmist employs a merismus ("day and night") to capture the sense of continual meditation. In Psalm 119:97a the poet confesses that he meditates "all day long," thus conveying a similar meaning. He has received instruction from Yahweh himself (119:102). Like honey, Yahweh's instruction has been life giving and life sustaining (119:103). It is because of all these things that the psalmist begins the strophe with his declaration, "Oh how I love your law!" (119:97).

Nun (119:105–12). The Nun strophe opens with what may arguably be the most well-known verse in Psalm 119. More popularly, this verse is applied to a broader understanding of Scripture, but it actually serves to bind the Mem and Nun strophes together around the idea of "path." The psalmist needs a lamp to light his way because of the darkness that threatens the path. This darkness is the result of the affliction he is enduring (119:107) and the traps being set by the wicked to snare him (119:110). The light of God's word (119:105) will enable the psalmist to see such snares and avoid them altogether. The psalmist does not allow those elements to take him off the path determined by God. Instead, he confesses that his life is focused on keeping the decrees of Yahweh.

Samekh (119:113–20). The strophe opens with the psalmist's announcement of his antipathy for "double-minded" people (119:113a), people with divided commitments. Throughout the Samekh strophe the psalmist signals that he remains single-minded in his commitment to Yahweh: "I love your law" (119:113b); "I may keep the commands of my God" (119:115b); and "I love your statutes" (119:119b). Those who remain double-minded will be rejected by Yahweh (119:118a) and ultimately cast aside like dross. The final verse in the strophe reiterates his posture of piety before Yahweh. In 119:120a the Hebrew reads literally, "My flesh trembles because I fear you," and the verse concludes with his confession that he stands "in awe of your laws."

Ayin (119:121–28). In the Ayin strophe the psalmist stresses the urgency of his situation. The first two verses (119:121–22) refer to the oppression he is experiencing at the hands of the arrogant—an oppression so great that his eyes have started to fail and grow weary in watching for deliverance (119:123). The entire situation leads the psalmist to register his formal complaint in 119:126a: "your law is being broken [*hepar*]." The word *hepar* occurs regularly in texts that report the breaking of the covenant, but in this instance, it is the torah of Yahweh that has been abrogated. As a result, the poet announces, "It is time for you to act, LORD" (119:126). The psalmist appeals to his patron to act on behalf of his servant. The psalmist affirms that he has honored his commitments to Yahweh. In return, the psalmist requests that God respond.

Pe (119:129–36). This strophe highlights the "wonder-working" power of the torah. Yahweh's instruction provides light in the darkness (119:130), satisfies the thirsty (119:131), and directs the paths of God's people (119:133). While the allusions are indirect, they arguably point to events associated with the wilderness wandering, as does the request that Yahweh make his face shine upon his servant (cf. Num 6:25). The psalmist also pleads with Yahweh to turn to him (Ps 119:132) and, even more, to redeem (*padah*, 119:134) him from human oppression. The verb *padah*, "to redeem," appears in the book of Deuteronomy in reference to Israel's deliverance from oppression in Egypt (e.g., Deut 7:8). In the concluding verse of the Pe strophe the psalmist weeps because of the rampant disobedience that characterizes his society.

Tsadhe (119:137–44). The recurring root in the Tsadhe strophe is *tsdq*, "righteous(ness)," which appears five times in these verses (119:137, 138, 142 [2x; lit., "your righteousness is an everlasting righteousness," NASB], 144). Broadly speaking the root *tsdq* refers to "the policy that God wills and enacts as ruler of the universe." The psalm opens with the declaration that God is "righteous" (*tsaddiq*) and then repeatedly contends that Yahweh's instruction is righteous (119:138, 142, 144). Although the enemies ignore God's words (119:139), the psalmist confesses his love for those words (119:140). He also acknowledges the reality of his plight: he is lowly and despised, and his life is marked by trouble and distress (119:143). The strophe concludes by declaring God's statutes as "righteous" (119:144) They are the psalmist's source of life.

Qoph (119:145–52). The psalmist longs for the coming deliverance of Yahweh. In 119:148 he declares that through the watches of night he meditates on God's promises, perhaps in anticipation of the morning. The psalmist declares that, although the godless who devise evil schemes remain near, "you are near, LORD" (119:151). While in the present moment the psalmist is harangued by the enemy, he takes heart that the justice of God has been from "long ago" and is meant to "last forever" (119:152). The nearness of the enemy is momentary, but the enduring justice of God, as evident in his torah, remains the psalmist's hope.

Resh (119:153–60). The language of complaint in the previous strophe continues in the first two lines of the Resh strophe. Three times the psalmist recounts his faithfulness to God's law (119:153a, 157b, 159a), and twice the psalmist observes the insolence of the enemies against it (119:155b, 158b). Matching the three times the psalmist confesses his commitment to God's instruction, three times (119:154, 156, 159) he asks for Yahweh to "preserve his life." The psalmist's faithfulness and his claim to deliverance are linked. His desire for deliverance is not wishful thinking; rather, it is rooted in God's "promise" (119:154), God's "compassion" (119:156), and God's "love" (119:159).

Sin and Shin (119:161–68). The strophe opens with a reference to the "rulers" (119:161) who persecute the psalmist. And while one should shudder or be in fear of such worldly powers, the psalmist confesses that his heart trembles before the word of Yahweh. While military victors may collect the spoils of war following a successful battle, the psalmist declares that he has found a "great spoil" in the instruction of God (119:162). Those who are victorious in battle may find "great peace" (119:165), but the psalmist announces that "great peace" awaits those who love the law of God. The poet refers to "loving" (*'ahab*) two additional times, thus making the threefold repetition of this claim a central motif in the strophe (119:163, 165, 167). His love of the law is so great, in fact, that he praises God seven times a day (119:164).

Taw (119:169–76). The final strophe in the psalm opens with a series of four petitions, including language associated with lament (119:169, 170) and concluding with language of praise and thanksgiving (119:171, 172). In the second half of the strophe the psalmist turns to the actions requested of God (119:173–75). What binds both sections of this strophe together, however, is the relationship between faithfulness to the torah of Yahweh and the sheer gift of life that it brings. He concludes the psalm by confessing that, while he has not forgotten the commandments of God, he is a frail creature of dust, a "lost sheep" (119:176) who stands in need of the mercy of God. The psalmist remains committed to God until the end in the certainty that the same can be said of God's commitment to him, and even more.

Application. Both the Matthean beatitudes and Psalm 119 reflect the perilous circumstances faced by followers of God. In both texts the faithful encounter persecution (Ps 119:86, 157, 161; Matt 5:10, 11), and in both texts they experience the derisive insults of the ungodly (Ps 119:23; Matt 5:11). Yet each of the Matthean beatitudes begins with "Blessed," even as Psalm 119:1–2 opens with "Blessed." Both texts describe the life of the faithful as they await the fullness of God's work in the world. Waiting and hoping involves living in and living into the ways of God in the here and now. But even more, these texts remind us that *our work* is that of faithfulness; *his work* is that of deliverance (119:173–76). And so we wait—in abiding faithfulness and with much hope, we wait.

PSALM 120:1–7

Original Meaning

Recollection of the Past (120:1). God's capacity to deliver the psalmist from a previous threat provides the assurance that God can redeem him from another context.

Plea for Deliverance (120:2). The nature of the distress currently experienced by the psalmist appears initially in 120:2.

Rhetorical Challenge of the Foe (120:3–4). Beginning in 120:3 the discourse shifts and the psalmist turns to address the enemy rhetorically. Their lives will be laid waste even as cities were laid waste by arrows and flames of fire.

Lament Regarding Crisis (120:5–7). In the final strophe of the poem the psalmist provides further explication concerning the situation. Verses 5–7 suggest that the one with a deceitful tongue has a proclivity toward violence, presumably against the psalmist.

Application. Psalm 120 invites us to give words to the human hunger for place, both physical and social stability (120:5b).

PSALM 121:1–8

Original Meaning

Confidence in the Lord (121:1–2). "Mountains" in 121:1 likely refers to the mountains of Zion, the mountain of God.

The Watchful Care of Yahweh (121:3–4). The psalmist may have sought to label Yahweh as the Guardian of Israel. Yahweh remains on watch to protect his people because God will not "slumber nor sleep" (121:4).

The Lord Is your Shade (121:5–6). Because the soldier carried his shield in his left hand, the right side of his body remained vulnerable. A friend at his "right hand" provided protection (121:5).

The Lord Will Protect Your Life (121:7–8). The phrase "coming and going" (121:8) functions as a merismus referring simply to the general activity of life. The poem may have been included in the Songs of Ascent because of the image evoked by the phrase.

Application. Those who pray this psalm do not walk alone.

PSALM 122:1–9

Original Meaning

Joy in the Pilgrimage (122:1–2). The psalmist may be pleased to receive this invitation to journey to the house of Yahweh, but the real source of joy remains being in the presence of God himself. Verse 1 recounted the moment when the psalmist was invited to make the pilgrimage to Jerusalem; verse 2 records his arrival at the gates of the city.

Descriptions of Jerusalem (122:3–5). The psalmist offers a description of Jerusalem more generally, followed by two recollections associated with the importance of the city. Jerusalem is a refuge. From the thrones in Jerusalem go forth the decisions that can lead to peace, *shalom*, for the land.

Pray for Peace (122:6–9). The theme of *shalom* dominates the final strophe. In 122:6–8 the word "peace," or *shalom*, appears once in each verse. The name "Jerusalem" itself (122:6a) reinforces the theme of peace, given that the Hebrew root for "peace," *shlm*, comprises part of the city's name, "Jeru*salem*."

Application. Like the pilgrims in Psalm 122, we, too, may continue to celebrate a way of life rooted deeply in the presence of God.

PSALM 123:1–4

Original Meaning

Expression of Trust (123:1–2). Even as the slave would wait for any signal from the hand of the master, those who were enduring hardship were looking to the hand of Yahweh in the face of their current plight.

Petition for Mercy (123:3–4). The language employed in these two verses remains general, precluding identification of the social context. The references could signify a small group of the faithful who have been shamed or Israel humiliated by its conquerors.

Application. We wait with anticipation and certainty that the King over all will stoop down and pick us up from the ash heap (113:7).

PSALM 124:1–8

Original Meaning

The God Who Is for His People (124:1–5). The idea in this section might be better construed in English as "it was Yahweh (who acted), but if he had not," then this is what would have happened (the "unreal situation"). Had not Yahweh been on the side of Israel, they would have met with death.

Thanksgiving for God's Deliverance (124:6–7). The psalm shifts to what *did* happen. Verse 7 presumably refers to the lifting of a siege or some other kind of deliverance from a foreign occupier. In Psalm 124 the community celebrates their deliverance from such a dire fate.

Declaration of Trust (124:8). The concluding verse in Psalm 124 stands in stark relief to 124:2b. Where in 124:2 the community remembers "when people attacked us," the threat is little match for the "Maker of heaven and earth" in 124:8.

Application. Amid a world of swirling waters and fowler's snares, the Maker of heaven and earth is our help. He is for us.

PSALM 125:1–5

Original Meaning

A Declaration of Trust (125:1–3). This psalm of trust opens with two comparisons meant to encourage confidence on the part of those who pray the psalms—Mount Zion and the mountains that encircle Jerusalem. In 125:3, however, the psalmist explains what Yahweh will do to eradicate the threat that is before the people.

The Petition (125:4–5). Members of the community must choose one of two paths. Either they can align themselves with those who choose to do good, or they can align themselves with those who "turn to crooked ways" (125:5). The word for "crooked ways" (*ʿaqalqal*) suggests a twisting or winding path. Toward each kind of person, Yahweh acts with justice.

Application. God's presence and God's protection prove sufficient in a world that appears unruly and unstable.

PSALM 126:1–6

Original Meaning

Remembering Yahweh's Return to Zion (126:1–3). A dream in the ancient Near East was understood as a medium for divine revelation. Thus, when the community declared that they were dreamers, they were announcing that Yahweh's work of restoration was at hand. The confession made by the nations in 126:2b appears on the lips of the community in 126:3.

Petition for God's Work of Restoration (126:4–6). Simple agricultural images prove powerfully rich metaphors of hope. God will come and restore the fortunes of his people; barrenness will be transformed into a future filled with shouts of joy and arms full of the harvest.

Application. The harvest will bring shouts of joy, but the harvest will come only if the seed has been planted—weeping and all. To plant anything is an act of faith. The end cannot be known, only trusted.

PSALM 127:1–5

Original Meaning

The Involvement of the Lord in Life (127:1–2). The first strophe of the psalm explains the necessity of God's involvement in human life by alluding to two spheres of it: the home and the city. To live one's life apart from the involvement of God proves unsuccessful and meaningless.

Children Are a Heritage from the Lord (127:3–5). In the second half of Psalm 127 the poet turns to familial matters and considers the blessings associated with a larger family. Similar to the claims made in 127:1–2, the latter strophe in the psalm focuses on the activity of God in human life.

Application. Those of us who live in the United States are well acquainted with the rhetoric of the "American dream." Because we believe success is contingent upon effort, we are compelled to work harder, we are resigned to "toiling for food" (127:2).

PSALM 128:1–6

Original Meaning

A Blessed Life (128:1–4). The psalmist rightly knows that the blessed life is the life that is oriented toward God and God's purposes in the world. One does not "fear the LORD" (128:1) because of what he can do in the sense of judgment but of what he can bring—life in all its fullness.

Blessings from Zion (128:5–6). Psalm 128 closes with blessings upon the pilgrims making their journey from their homes to Mount Zion. The last line in the psalm reiterates the desire for peace upon Israel, a desire expressed elsewhere in the collection of the Songs of Ascent.

Application. Those who seek to order their lives rightly will soon realize that the goal of life is not to *earn* divine blessing but to *receive* the simple elements of life *as* divine blessing.

PSALM 129:1–8

Original Meaning

Recalling Israel's History of Oppression (129:1–4). Despite repeated episodes of oppression, the community gives thanks because God has consistently delivered his people. Although the use of first-person language might warrant interpreting the verb as referring to personal or individual attacks, the context of the psalm suggests that Israel's larger history of oppression is in view.

Imprecations against the Enemy (129:5–8). In the second strophe of the psalm the poet turns to a series of curses or imprecations. The curses in 129:5–8 suggest that a persistent threat remains—a threat that must be redressed by Yahweh. The psalmist shifts metaphors and language in 129:5, before returning to agricultural imagery in 129:6–7.

Application. We should acknowledge the true injustice in the world and long for God's redeeming and redemptive work that will overturn this injustice. Such an approach can be heard in the teaching of Jesus (Matt 5:6).

PSALM 130:1–8

Original Meaning

Cry to God (130:1–2). Although the spatial distance between the poet and God is highlighted, the potential for such distance to be overcome is also signaled in the reference to Yahweh's capacity to hear.

A Statement of Confidence (130:3–4). To remedy his plight, the psalmist confidently asserts that there is forgiveness with Israel's God. The relationship once broken by sin is restored, not by us but by God. Forgiveness results in faithful service.

Waiting for the Lord (130:5–6). In ancient cities, guards were stationed on the city walls to keep watch over the city during the night. Just as the guards await the morning, so too does the psalmist wait on God.

The Redemption of Israel (130:7–8). The "I" in 130:1–6 turns and exhorts the community to adopt the same posture of waiting that he himself has adopted. Just as the psalmist waits and hopes, so too should the community.

Application. As we reflect on our own sinfulness we might be inclined to turn away from God. The psalmist turns to God and cries out. And we are invited to do the same.

PSALM 131:1–3

Original Meaning

Declaration of Humility (131:1–3). Psalm 131 begins with "LORD," followed by three statements meant to indicate the piety of the psalmist. The first two refer to relationship with others, while the last statement refers to God. Psalm 131 refers to a posture of trust. Like the infant child resting upon its mother, all Israel is called to trust in God, with the assurance that its collective life will be cared for "both now and forever more" (131:3b).

Application. We need the posture of a child, the very model of the one invited into the kingdom of God (Matt 18:1–4).

PSALM 132:1–18

Original Meaning

David Vows to God (132:1–5). The strophe opens with a petition for Yahweh to remember David. The oath that David made to Yahweh (132:3–5) anchors the first strophe by providing a rationale for God's remembrance. David spared no effort in ensuring that there were proper resources available for the construction of Yahweh's temple. Second Samuel 6 recalls David's bringing the ark to Jerusalem, the site of his newly conquered capital, with the primary intent of finding a resting place for the ark.

Allusion to the Ark Story (132:6–10). The second strophe of Psalm 132 recounts the movement of the ark from Kiriath-Jearim to Jerusalem, as well as the words uttered by those who accompanied the ark into Jerusalem. Rather than using the third person to speak of those involved, as though merely recounting history objectively, the community uses the first-person plural, "we," and in doing so they place themselves within the story.

God's Vow to David (132:11–12). Just as the name "David" provided an *inclusio* in the first half of the psalm (132:1, 10), so too does it in the poem's second half. References to David appear in the first strophe and final strophe (132:11, 17). David's name functions as a bookend of sorts. The second half of the psalm places the focus on Yahweh's fidelity both to the Davidic dynasty and to Zion, the place of Yahweh's dwelling (132:13).

Yahweh's Blessing upon David (132:17–18). The final petition in the first half of the psalm urged Yahweh not to turn from or reject the anointed one (132:10). The final strophe in the psalm answers this petition by confirming Yahweh's faithfulness to the line of David. Despite the failure of previous kings, the dynasty has not reached its full and final end. Just as Yahweh will bless the priests, the laity, and the poor, Yahweh will bless David and his progeny; he will make a "horn" (132:17) grow for David. The horn symbolizes royal power and suggests that it will "grow," or "sprout up" (Heb. *tsamah*) yet again (132:17).

Application. Psalm 132 invites us to think more deliberately about how we cultivate memory, how we nurture hope. Pilgrimages do not happen by accident, nor do cultivated memory and nurtured hope, but they are necessary. They are necessary for those who seek to walk in the way of the Lord.

PSALM 133:1–3

Original Meaning

Wisdom Saying (133:1). Psalm 133 begins with a wisdom saying that clearly could stand alone and perhaps did at some point in its history. The saying commends a particular way of life, namely, that of familial unity.

Explanatory Similes (133:2–3b). The poet employs two similes to illustrate the claim articulated in 133:1: oil and dew. The first simile suggests a festal setting, while the second suggests a reference to the mountains of Zion.

The Centrality of Zion (133:3c–d). The blessings of God pour forth from Zion. But these blessings are best received when God's people gather in unity.

Application. Amid real threats and anticipated hopes, the pilgrims leaned into their identity as the people of God.

PSALM 134:1–3

Original Meaning

Call to Praise the Lord (134:1–3). Within the framework of a covenant, or even a patron-client relationship, the master or lord would bestow favor on the servant, and in return the servant would speak well of, or bless, the master. In the Old Testament, God bestows blessings upon his people, and in return his people speak well of God.

Application. We lift our hands to God, the Maker of heaven and earth, assured that from him all blessings flow.

PSALM 135:1–21

Original Meaning

The Call to Praise God (135:1–4). The call for the people to praise God dominates the initial strophe, with the verb *hallu* ("praise") appearing four times, and a related term, *zamar*, which means to make celebratory music, appearing once. Following the repeated call to praise, the psalmist puts forth two reasons justifying this call (135:3). The reference to the kingship of Yahweh in 135:4 presages the more explicit references to Yahweh's kingship in the following verses.

God's Kingship over All Creation (135:5–7). Although perhaps strange to our modern ears, the mention of storm clouds, wind, and rain in 135:7 likely evoked the images of the Canaanite god of storms and weather—Baal. The point, however, was not to compare Yahweh to Baal but to declare that Yahweh alone reigns in, through, and over creation.

The Power of God against the Nations (135:8–14). In the third strophe of this poem, the psalmist turns to consider the display of God's power among the nations. The use of names and actions recorded in Psalm 135 presupposes that the readers had a general familiarity with Israel's canonical history as expressed in the Pentateuch. As a result, the psalmist has no need to rehearse the entirety of this history, nor does he provide considerable detail.

The Powerlessness of Idols (135:15–18). In this strophe the psalmist adopts an abbreviated form of Psalm 115:4–6, 8. In Psalm 115, as in Psalm 135, the psalmists lampoon the idols for their inability to speak, see, and hear. Psalm 135:17b inserts a text from Jeremiah's critique of idols (see Jer 10:14). The lack of breath in their mouths suggests that there is no life in them (Gen 2:7). So too are those who make them and rely on them (Ps 135:18).

Invitation to Praise God (135:19–21). In the final strophe of the psalm the poet returns once more to Psalm 115 and models the final section of Psalm 135 after the language found in Psalm 115:9–11. Although Psalm 135 traces the early history of Israel up to the point of their entry into the land, the emphasis on Zion in the concluding verse serves to create an arc back to the Songs of Ascent (Ps 132:13; 133:3; 134:3).

Application. The point of the hymn is to confess what we know about God, and what we know about God begins with election (135:4). It is only because God has made us his treasured possession that we come to understand that "our Lord is greater than all gods" (135:5). And it is because God has chosen us as his covenantal partners that he has acted on our behalf to secure our future.

PSALM 136:1–26

Original Meaning

Call to Confess Yahweh (136:1–3). Psalm 136 opens with a call for Israel to confess that Yahweh is good—a claim appearing in Psalm 135:3 as well. The reference to the divine name in 136:1 is the only appearance of the term in the psalm. Other appellations are used in referring to Yahweh, most notably in the first strophe (136:2–3) and in the last verse.

Yahweh's Mighty Works in Creation (136:4–9). Following the opening call for the people to confess their faith in Yahweh, in the second strophe the psalmist turns to consider Yahweh's work as Creator. The focus of the strophe is not cosmological in nature (i.e., how the universe came to be) but decidedly theological.

Yahweh's Victory of the Powers of Egypt (136:10–15). In the third strophe the psalmist turns to God's demonstration of power against the Egyptians. In Psalm 136 the poet refers to the smiting of the firstborn in Egypt (136:10), the coming out of Egypt (136:11), and the crossing of the Red Sea (136:13–14)—all constituent elements within the exodus tradition.

Yahweh's Defeat of the Kings (136:16–22). The fourth strophe begins with Israel's departure from Egypt and culminates in their arrival in the land. The principle focus, however, is not on the journey itself but on the demonstration of Yahweh's power in defeating the kings who threatened Israel's entrance into the land.

God's Deliverance of the Present Generation (136:23–25). In the final strophe the psalmist breaks with the previous strophes by introducing first-person plural language (i.e., "our low estate," "our enemies," 136:23a, 24a). The subtle shift in person and number suggests the hermeneutical move being made by the psalmist. The story is not merely of a generation dead and gone, but of *us*.

A Concluding Call to Confess Yahweh (136:26). The psalm concludes by repeating the opening exhortation to give thanks to Yahweh. Having rehearsed Israel's history and recounted Yahweh's decisive acts in Israel's behalf, the community can do nothing less than confess or praise this God. The idea of Yahweh as the God of the heavens emphasizes Yahweh's role as Divine King and disqualifies any human king's claim to supremacy.

Application. We do more than simply recall a story—we confess a truth and lean into a vision. God's faithfulness to us in the past compels us to hope in a future in which God's vision of reality continues to unfold.

PSALM 137:1–9

Original Meaning

Recalling the Experience in Exile (137:1–4). From start to finish 137:1–4 recalls the events associated with Babylon. The image in Psalm 137:1 is not that of a group who decided to sit down by a river one day to weep but rather of a community whose home in exile was there by the rivers.

An Oath to Jerusalem (137:5–6). In the second strophe the psalmist continues the theme of remembering. The very structure of the second strophe itself reinforces this theme and its significance. The intent of the confession is to state one's own commitment or belief, but even more, to invite the community to believe similarly.

Imprecatory Plea against Edom and Babylon (137:7–9). The final strophe turns attention away from the psalmist and his community and instead calls on Yahweh to remember. In particular, the psalmist implores Yahweh to remember, or call to mind, the actions of the Edomites and the Babylonians. The admittedly disturbing language and imagery in 137:9 is rooted in the tactics of warfare as practiced in that cultural setting.

Application. This psalm reminds us that we should be less concerned about how this psalm fits neatly into "our world" and more concerned about those for whom this psalm describes their world.

PSALM 138:1–8

Original Meaning

Pledge to Confess God (138:1–3). The first strophe in the psalm includes the psalmist's pledge to confess God (138:1) and spells out the content of that confession (138:2–3). The act of confessing Yahweh "before the 'gods'" (138:1b) asserts Yahweh's supremacy over all other presumed deities.

Kings Will Confess God (138:4–6). In the second strophe the psalmist declares that the world powers, the "kings of the earth" (138:4), will join with the psalmist in making a confession about Israel's God. The kings of the earth hear the words of Yahweh's mouth, thus leading them to confess him and sing his praises while acknowledging that he reigns as the King on high.

God Preserves the Lowly (138:7–8). In 138:6 the psalmist recounts Yahweh's commitment as Divine King to lift up the lowly. That declaration serves not only as evidence for the anticipated confession of the kings in 138:4–5 (as suggested above), but also as the ground of hope for the psalmist in 138:7–8. In this final strophe the psalmist moves from a general claim about Yahweh to its significance for his predicament.

Application. To see the world differently necessitates a proper view of divine transcendence, a divine transcendence that is capable of reaching into the present moment while also pointing to the divine future.

PSALM 139:1–24

Original Meaning

God's Examination of the Psalmist (139:1–6). The opening strophe of the psalm considers Yahweh's comprehensive knowledge of the psalmist. The poet captures the fullness of God's knowledge through several examples of merism. A merism is a poetic technique that expresses a totality by mentioning two parts, typically polar opposites. For example, Psalm 139 includes "when I sit" and "when I rise" (139:2a), "my going out and my lying down" (139:3a), and "behind and before" (139:5a). Poetically speaking, a merism provides vivid images that are meant to replace more abstract concepts such as "all," "every," or "always." Yahweh completely surrounds the psalmist.

The Psalmist's Thoughts on Fleeing from God (139:7–12). The second strophe continues the theme of God's pervasive presence. Verse 7 contains two rhetorical questions placed in parallel. Both questions concern the scope of God's spirit or presence. In 139:8–9 the psalmist returns to the use of merisms to convey the spatial sense, both vertical and horizontal, of God's presence. The final two verses in this strophe appear to contain another merism. If he were in the darkness, then perhaps finally he would find a place apart from God. The psalmist quickly recognizes the fault in his own logic, however, because darkness quickly ceases to be darkness because of the radiant light of God.

God's Presence from the Beginning of Life (139:13–18). In the third strophe of Psalm 139 the poet continues his reflection on God's presence by highlighting God's involvement in the life of the psalmist from its very beginning. The focus on his birth, however, is not an afterthought but actually serves to buttress the claims made in the first two strophes. The first strophe concentrates on the comprehensive nature of God's knowing presence, and the second highlights the psalmist's inability to escape the pervasive presence of God. These claims make sense "because" (139:14) God has been with the psalmist from the beginning of his life.

The Threat of Enemies (139:19–24). The final strophe abruptly shifts from the hymnic language of the first three strophes to more petitionary language in the final strophe. In these six verses the psalmist utters a petition (139:19–20), a declaration of commitment (139:21–22), and a concluding plea (139:23–24). Verse 18 ended the third strophe with the psalmist's affirmation that he remained in the presence of God. In 139:19–24 he introduces the presence of yet another party, the enemies. Through his petitions the psalmist aligns himself with God and asks for God to redress his present circumstances.

Application. Many of the great hymns of the Christian faith give considerable attention to the personal relationship between God and the individual. The chorus of one hymn ("In the Garden") reads, "And he walks with me and he talks with me, and he tells me that I am his own." Hymns such as these tend to highlight the "fascination," or the comfort, gained from God's presence. Rarely do hymns remind us of the kind of pervasive presence of God in our lives that might prompt a sense of holy fear. We are content with having God near us, but preferably not *too* near.

PSALM 140:1–13

Original Meaning

Lament over the Enemies (140:1–5). In Psalm 140 the psalmist stands in need of deliverance because of the life-threatening actions of the enemy that have closed in on him. From planning to execution, from heart to hand, the enemies are working toward the downfall of the petitioner. The psalmist implores God to keep watch over him.

Confession of Trust (140:6–8). In the third strophe the psalmist utters a confession of trust predicated on his relationship with God (140:6). His hope for deliverance is grounded in his affirmation of God's protective care in the midst of battle, whether literal or figurative (140:7). The enemies have been plotting to crush the psalmist, and in 140:8b the psalmist pleads with Yahweh to frustrate their plans.

Curse on the Enemies (140:9–11). The fourth strophe contains a series of three curses levied against the wicked. The psalmist prays that the scheming plans of the enemies mentioned in strophes 1 and 2 be turned back upon them. The fourth strophe is not an unfiltered rant against the enemy but a request for justice to be enacted.

Declaration of Faith (140:12–13). In the final strophe the psalmist expresses his confidence in Yahweh's capacity to deliver. Although deliverance has yet to occur, its delay is only temporary. Because of Yahweh's action on behalf of the poor, the righteous will confess Yahweh's name, and the upright will enjoy his presence (cf. Ps 107:41–42). The world will be rightly ordered once more.

Application. We are reminded of the reality of evildoers and the presence of violent people in the world. We are reminded of the pervasive nature of sin and injustice. But even more, we are reminded that these evils do not have the last word.

PSALM 141:1–10

Original Meaning

Petition to Be Heard (141:1–2). Psalm 140 concluded with the confession that the upright will (eventually) live in God's presence (140:14). In Psalm 141 the psalmist acknowledges the challenges that remain, including the sense that he remains apart from the presence of God. The request that God give ear, coupled with his plea for Yahweh to "come quickly" *to him* (141:1), suggests that the psalmist perceives a chasm between himself and God.

Request for Aid in Resisting Temptation (141:3–6). In this strophe the psalmist requests three things—two provided by God and a third by a fellow community member. The poet's request consists in the divine guarding of his mouth and keeping of his heart from following evil so that he will not act accordingly. Then in 141:5a–b he asks that someone correct his paths.

Plea for Deliverance (141:7–10). In the final strophe the psalmist acknowledges the desperate plight of the faithful while confessing that their hope rests solely with God. The psalm opened with his request for God to "come quickly" (141:1), and it concludes with the poet's affirmation that his eyes are fixed on the God who has come near. Because the God of the covenant has come near, the psalmist can take "refuge" in him (141:8).

Application. Like the psalmist, we may perceive there is a chasm that exists between God and us; the vagaries of life have overwhelmed us, and we feel as though God stands at a distance. In those moments we would do well to reflect on Psalm 141. He fixes his eyes upon God and musters the courage to declare, "in you I take refuge" (141:8).

PSALM 142:1–7

Original Meaning

Declaration of Lament (142:1–2). The psalmist employs four verbs declaring his intent to utter a lament. This strophe remains in the third person. Perhaps the psalmist is making his declaration in the presence of the congregation or a smaller group within the community.

The Complaint of the Psalmist (142:3–4). The poet expands the description of his current situation. The circumstances that surround the psalmist have caused his spirit to "grow faint" (142:3) and become exceedingly weak. Despite his circumstances, he has confidence in God.

Confession of Trust (142:5). Having recounted his desperate plight in the second strophe (142:3–4), the psalmist cries to Yahweh in 142:5 with his confession of trust. Once more the psalmist shifts the metaphorical field to communicate claims about Yahweh.

Petition for Yahweh to Act (142:6–7). In the final strophe the psalmist petitions Yahweh for deliverance. In 142:6 a complaint follows each petition. Verse 7a contains a petition but breaks the pattern by issuing a promise to praise God instead of a complaint (142:7b).

Application. Scripture reminds us that our troubled existence is always intermingled with our assurance in a God who has worked, and is working still, for the redemption of his people.

PSALM 143:1–12

Original Meaning

Opening Petitions (143:1–2). The psalm opens in 143:1 with three petitions meant to move Yahweh to action in the poet's behalf. By contrast, 143:2 calls Yahweh to *inaction*. The petitions both for action and inaction reflect the psalmist's longing for the mercy of God. The psalmist understands that he, like all humans, has done nothing to garner God's aid, only God's judgment. Nonetheless, he implores Yahweh to withhold his judgment and instead deliver him from his enemies (143:3–4).

Formal Complaint (143:3–6). Following the petitions in 143:1–2, the psalmist outlines the threats that currently plague him. The language of threat involves metaphors and imagery associated with death (143:3–4), thus indicating the perceived gravity of the situation. The rehearsal of the threats is followed by a recollection of the past (143:5) and then a brief description of the psalmist's posture of prayer in the present (143:6).

Petitions (143:7–12). Verses 7–10 contain a series of seven imperatives and jussives, with each calling on Yahweh to act in particular ways on behalf of the psalmist. With the request to "answer me" (143:7), the psalmist implores Yahweh to act with haste. The motif of God's attentive care in the morning serves as a cause for both hope and celebration. In the final line (143:12c) the poet declares himself the servant of God and so reinforces the rationale for divine action—covenantal faithfulness.

Application. The very environment that we think frees us actually confines us, while our only hope for true freedom is found in our willingness to enter into a relationship with God—a relationship initiated and sustained by God. It is in this relationship that we discover a hopeful word for our lamenting cries.

PSALM 144:1–15

Original Meaning

The Psalmist Praises God (144:1–2). The psalm opens with a series of descriptive statements meant to highlight the relationship between the psalmist and his God. The relational nature of the comments is emphasized by the repeated use of first-person singular language. The psalmist draws much of his imagery from Psalm 18.

Reflection on the Human Condition (144:3–4). In the second strophe the psalmist turns to consider the nature of the human condition. He confesses that human life is like a "breath" (Heb. *hebel*), the same word that appears throughout the book of Ecclesiastes (cf. Eccl 1:2, "meaningless," NIV) and a word that stresses the ephemerality of life.

Petitions to Yahweh (144:5–8). In these verses the language and imagery draws considerably from Psalm 18, but they have been adapted to address the current plight. The psalmist envisions Yahweh as the God of the heavens, but he seeks to close that spatial distance (144:5). The cosmological language employed reinforces the significance of the threat.

Praise and Petition (144:9–11). The fourth strophe contains a vow of praise followed by a petition. The reason Yahweh deserves praise (144:10a–b) provides the warrant for the petition. Yahweh's faithfulness in the past provides the rationale for the petitions that follow in 144:10c–11.

Communal Statement of Confidence (144:12–14). The psalm shifts from first-person singular language ("I," "me") to first-person plural language ("we," "us"). In these verses the community describes their life once Yahweh has rid the land of the oppressive enemies. The scarcity of resources and the threat of survival stand behind the imagery present in 144:12–14.

Closing Beatitude (144:15). The psalmist announces that "blessed" (*'ashrey*) are the people whose lives reflect that which is described in 144:12–14. The second beatitude (144:15b) suggests that such a "blessed" existence is only possible because Yahweh is Israel's God.

Application. We are asked to renounce our sense of self-sufficiency and the hubris associated with claims of self-deliverance. We are asked to acknowledge what we know to be true—we are mere fleeting shadows. Because we know what *we are*, we must lean fully into who *he is*—the Divine King (Ps 145), the heavenly Divine Warrior, our Rock and Shield.

PSALM 145:1–21

Original Meaning

Vow to Praise God (145:1–2). In the opening line the psalmist confesses Yahweh as "My God the King." In the light of his confession the psalmist commits to three actions: "exalt," "praise," and "extol" (145:1, 2). All three verbs are part of the vocabulary of praise that dominates the first half of the psalm. In the first two verses the psalmist refers to the "name" (Heb. *shem*) of God twice.

Praise of God (145:3–7). The second strophe begins with a succinct statement about the character of God in 145:3, followed by the praise of God uttered by all generations. The declaration that Yahweh is great in 145:3 complements the earlier confession that he is *the* King (145:1a). Yahweh's "awesome" (145:6) works should inspire fear and awe in both the recipients and the beneficiaries.

Confession of Yahweh's Character (145:8–9). Following the rehearsal of God's faithful action on behalf of Israel in 145:4–6, the psalmist returns to explicit statements concerning the character of God. In celebrating God's character, the poet references the "graciousness formula" of Exodus 34:6–7 in which Yahweh self-describes. Psalm 145:8 quotes the Exodus text nearly verbatim.

Interlude (145:10). The psalmist pauses to claim that all God's works "praise" who he is; they bear witness to his identity as the great King. In 145:10b the psalmist shifts to declare that the faithful people of Yahweh will "extol" him. God bestows blessings upon his people, and his people in return speak well of God; they bless or praise God for the good he has brought to them.

In Praise of Yahweh's Kingdom (145:11–13). Within this short section of the psalm, the word *malkut* ("kingdom") appears four times, each time referencing Yahweh, the Divine King.

Characteristics of Yahweh's Just Rule (145:14–20). In the final strophe the psalmist builds on the fourfold reference to Yahweh's kingdom in 145:11–13. In this lengthy strophe the psalmist confesses Yahweh's sovereign care over all creation (145:14–16) and in particular over those who call on him (145:18–20). In accord with the confessions made in Psalm 121, Yahweh watches over his people, but the way of the wicked he will destroy (cf. Ps 1:6).

Postlude (145:21). The psalm concludes by repeating three words from 145:1: "praise" in 145:21a, and "name" and "praise" (*barak*, "to bless") in 145:21b. In 145:21 the psalmist expresses his desire for "every creature" (literally, "all flesh") to praise or bless God, thus bringing the psalm to a fitting conclusion. Even as his kingdom is everlasting (145:13), so too must our praise be "forever and ever" (145:21c).

Application. The psalmist explains that a people of praise are those who remember and tell, recall and proclaim.

PSALM 146:1–10

Original Meaning

Introductory Call to Praise the Lord (146:1–2). The psalm opens with an exhortation to "Praise the LORD" (*hallu-yah*) in 146:1a, an exhortation that repeats at the close of the psalm in 146:10c. The two together create an *inclusio* around the entire psalm, as is characteristic of all the psalms in the Final Hallel (Pss 146–150).

Wisdom Reflection on the Human Condition (146:3–4). Indirectly, 146:3–4 provides a rationale for the call to praise God in the first strophe. The psalmist emphasizes the ephemerality of humans and human power.

The Divine King as Creator and Redeemer (146:5–9). After acknowledging that all human power is frail and ephemeral, the psalmist places the focus on Yahweh, the Divine King. Beginning with a beatitude (146:5) followed by nine participial phrases and two additional statements (146:9b–c), the psalmist recounts the activity of this God who merits our praise.

Conclusion (146:10). The hope for all generations in Zion rests fully with the Divine King, the one who demonstrated his dominion over human power in the exodus and stands poised to do so once more (146:10b).

Application. We can spend our life singing praises because "he remains faithful forever" (146:6c). God indeed is our maker and defender, redeemer and friend, because he is the God who reigns forever.

PSALM 147:1–20

Original Meaning

Praise the God Who Cares for His People (147:1–6). Following the initial call to praise God (147:1a), in 147:1b the psalmist provides an initial justification for doing so prior to offering a more comprehensive rationale in 147:2–6. Verses 2–3 introduce two images, those of builder and shepherd. The Great Shepherd heals the brokenhearted and the wounded. Rather than being "sustain[ed]" (147:6), those who have been scattered need to be lifted up. This image stands in contrast to the fate of the wicked in 147:6b, whom Yahweh "casts . . . to the ground."

Praise the God Who Sustains the World (147:7–11). The community is invited to sing in a spirit of thanksgiving.

The remaining verses in the strophe identify the things for which they have reason to give thanks. Verses 8–9 allude to Yahweh's providing food for his creation. With the language in 147:10 the psalmist conjures up impressive images of imperial war machines. Despite the impressive power associated with such military might, the psalmist confesses that Israel's God delights in those who "fear him" and hope in his "unfailing love" (*hesed*, 147:11).

Praise the God Who Gives His Word (147:12–20). In similar fashion to the two previous strophes, the final strophe opens with a call for the community to praise Yahweh, followed by a lengthy justification for this call. In 147:13–14 the psalmist identifies four ways in which Yahweh demonstrates his concern for Jerusalem. The final two lines shift the focus from the role of God's word in ordering the world (147:15–18) to the role of God's word in governing his people (147:19–20). God's "word" (*dabar*) reminds them of the one with whom they are in covenant, namely, the Divine King.

Application. The God who sends his word to order and sustain creation is the God who continues to come to us in his word, and in the Word, so that we too might be ordered and sustained by the very power of God that is at work in the world. Because he continues to come to us, because he continues to sustain us, and because he continues to shape us, we are invited to praise the Lord.

PSALM 148:1–14

Original Meaning

Exhortation for the Heavens to Praise Yahweh (148:1–6). The psalm opens with an exhortation to "Praise the LORD" (*hallu-yah*) in 148:1a, an exhortation that repeats at the close of the psalm in 148:14. The two together create an *inclusio* around the entire psalm. Verses 1b–5a call on the heavens and all that inhabit them to praise Yahweh. The strophe concludes with a threefold acknowledgment of the creative power of Yahweh's spoken word (148:5b–6). No power on earth or in the heavens can thwart what Yahweh has created and established.

Exhortation for the Earth to Praise Yahweh (148:7–14). In the first half of Psalm 148 the poet called upon the heavens and its inhabitants to praise Yahweh. In the second half he turns his attention to the inhabitants of the earth and calls on them to do the same. Verses 7b–8a include three pairs of objects: sea creatures and ocean depths; lightning and hail; and snow and clouds. Verses 9–12a continue the pairing of terms, beginning with nature. Humans are not mentioned until 148:11–12. Yahweh himself is lifted high.

Application. Psalm 148 invites us to reorient our worship and our words, and yes, even our very lives. We are asked to dispense with our own idolatrous constructs about the nature of God and even ourselves, and instead we are called to find our rightful place in a chorus comprised of all creation as we lift our voices to the one true God who indeed stands over the entirety of earth and heaven.

PSALM 149:1–9

Original Meaning

The Divine King and His Care for His People (149:1–4). The first strophe invites the congregation to sing praises to God based on the community's relationship with God in the present (149:4a) and their belief in the work that is yet to come (149:4b). The psalmist's "new song" (149:1) has little to do with his song's being a "new" composition. These songs announce the coming of a new and just world.

God's Royal Rule (149:5–9). The second strophe resumes the call to praise in 149:5–6. A series of statements concerning the demonstration of Yahweh's rule over the world follows in 149:7–9.

Application. In Psalm 149 God invites his people to join him in establishing his kingdom. Much prayer and much formation have come prior to arriving at this psalm and at this understanding. As we pray the Psalter, we learn of God and his ways in the world. *His* vision of the kingdom slowly becomes *our* vision of the kingdom.

PSALM 150:1–6

Original Meaning

Praise the Great King (150:1–2). The first two verses focus on the God who is to be praised, and in particular on his role as the Sovereign over all creation.

Offer Praise to the Divine King (150:3–5). In 150:3–5 the psalmist declares that the praise of God as the great King begins in the context of celebratory worship.

Exhortation to Universal Praise of God (150:6). With this final exhortation the psalmist extends the summons beyond the temple to all creation, thus inviting all creation to praise God.

Application. When we praise God, we are doing far more than simply listing all the good qualities God possesses—we are uttering a confession about the reality of our God. We are declaring that the Divine King is coming still.

PROVERBS

INTRODUCTION TO PROVERBS

The attribution to Solomon at the head of the book sets the book of Proverbs in that historical context. Yet the contemporary reader may be surprised that foreign names are credited with some sections of the book. Of the seven superscriptions that organize the book of Proverbs, three name Solomon (1:1; 10:1; with "the men of Hezekiah," 25:1), two name "the wise" (22:17; 24:23), and the last two name Agur (30:1) and Lemuel (along with his mother, 31:1), persons about whom we know hardly anything. There is no compelling reason to doubt that Solomon is to be associated with much of the book as author and patron, even as we recognize that it is not possible to discern by any scholarly criteria what is directly attributable to Solomon and what is the work of later hands who carried on his tradition of wisdom. So it is that his name appears first, perhaps as tribute and dedication.

BOOK OUTLINE

- I. The Proverbs of Solomon Son of David, King of Israel (1:1–9:18)
  - A. Prologue (1:1–7)
  - B. Instructions (1:8–9:18)
- II. The Proverbs of Solomon (10:1–22:16)
  - A. Mostly Antithetical Proverbs (10:1–15:33)
  - B. Mostly Synonymous Proverbs (16:1–22:16)
- III. The Sayings of the Wise (22:17–24:34)
- IV. More Proverbs of Solomon, Copied by the Men of Hezekiah King of Judah (25:1–29:27)
  - A. Mostly Synonymous Proverbs (25:1–27:27)
  - B. Mostly Antithetical Righteous/Wicked Proverbs (28:1–29:27)
- V. The Sayings of Agur Son of Jakeh (30:1–33)
- VI. The Sayings of Lemuel King of Massa (31:1–31)

PROVERBS 1:1–7

Original Meaning. At the beginning of the book of Proverbs, we have an introduction that declares "the fear of the Lord is the beginning of knowledge" (1:7). We should always pay attention to beginnings and endings of literary works because writers tend to put their most important thoughts and images there. In this case, "fear of the Lord" not only concludes this prologue and the first part of the book of Proverbs (i.e., chs. 1–9; cf. 9:10), it also appears at the end of the entire book (31:30).

Application. Wisdom is not so much a goal to be attained as a posture of humility, a willingness to receive instruction. A wise person is a learning person, a person in process, not a finished product. The book of Proverbs assumes that its readers are daily learning new ways to put into practice the teachings of wisdom.

PROVERBS 1:8–19

Original Meaning. The literary setting for the instruction in chapters 1–9 is the home schooling of a young man coming of age. Three invitations appear in Proverbs 1. The young listener is told to pay attention to the teaching of his parents (1:8) and the correction of Woman Wisdom (1:33) but to ignore the offer to join violent men (1:10, 15). In essence, each invitation is a call to join or identify with a way of life.

If the prologue of 1:1–7 presents the purposes of the book and the benefits that can be gained from its study, the sections that immediately follow offer two vivid examples of wisdom instruction. The invitation to join violent men (1:8–19) and the first speech of personified Wisdom (1:20–33) are lessons in learning how to discern true speech from false.

Application. The parent's first lesson in wisdom asks its readers to practice discernment in listening, to pay attention to outcomes, and especially to do these while watching out for temptations to greed. This first lesson in wisdom, then, asks each of us to think about the messages we hear. Wisdom offers to guide us, as we will see in the following section.

PROVERBS 1:20–33

Original Meaning

Wisdom's Call to All (1:20–23). The first of Wisdom's addresses calls out to anyone who will hear. The "simple" (1:4) can learn if they leave their simple ways behind, but if they love those ways and hate knowledge, they become fools who hate wisdom and discipline (1:7). Mockers do not merely choose to ignore; their rejection is active; they scoff and ridicule. Wisdom's rebuke is correction, an offer of instruction that is personal and direct.

Wisdom's Call Rejected (1:24–27). Just as the gang's evil was repaid with evil in the parent's earlier instruction, so it will be for those who ignored Wisdom's rebuke. As they mocked, so will she.

Wisdom's Refusal to Answer a Call (1:28–33). Wisdom's third address begins in 1:28 with an echo of her own calls. Rejection of Wisdom is now revealed for what it really is: a rejection of the Lord. Wisdom stresses that this rejection has not been done out of ignorance but out of choice. The final call also promises safety to those who will listen; it offers a confirmation to those who have already chosen to walk along Wisdom's path. Like the prologue, it encourages the reader to continue reading the book and to walk in the ways of wisdom.

Application. Wisdom's warning and correction tell us the truth about human nature. In a word, we can easily be led astray. We also learn that we are at a new crossroads every day, and every day must choose to follow Jesus again. And every day, the other path that leads away from him beckons. We may not abandon his way completely like those addressed by Wisdom, but if we are honest, we recognize that we also wander.

PROVERBS 2:1–22

Original Meaning

"If You" (2:1–4). The three "if you" phrases work together to portray this search for wisdom as strenuous, requiring all the strength one has. The rewards make the work worthwhile.

"Then You Will Understand" (2:5–8). The first reward of diligence is not wisdom, as we might expect, but God. The quest for wisdom, understanding, and insight (2:3) brings one to "the fear of the LORD" (2:5), the beginning of knowledge (cf. 1:7)—here set in parallel with "the knowledge of God." Wisdom, in the final accounting, is a gift of God (2:6), but what a contrast that gift makes with the sweaty, fervent, and even desperate work of study just described!

Four descriptions of the traveler in 2:7–8 put responsibility on right living—that traveler is upright, blameless, just, and faithful. In sum, the search for wisdom brings the wonderful gifts of knowledge, especially knowledge of God, and as a result, the protection one needs to walk on the way.

"Then You Will Understand" (2:9–11). "Wisdom" and "knowledge" (paired again) are internalized in 2:10, entering the diligent heart and forming a character that seeks to do right by others. Discretion and understanding, thus internalized, offer protection.

"Will Save You" from Wicked Men (2:12–15). The danger lies not in what the men will do to the young man but in their invitation to join them on their evil. The six descriptions of their way not only repeat the idea of leaving the straight path, but they also stress the fact that they love doing it.

"Will Save You" from the Adulteress (2:16–19). The strange or adulterous woman appears four times in Proverbs 1–9. Each description highlights the false and seductive nature of her words and the deadly end of her way. Just as the violent men will meet a violent end, so the path of adultery is a path of folly that leads to death.

"In Order to Walk" Safe in the Land (2:20–22). For ancient Israel, land was not considered a possession as much as a privilege. Its inhabitants lived on the land not as overlords but as stewards, enjoying the fruits of obedient relationship with God. The wicked and the faithless enjoyed no such benefit.

Application. The teaching of this chapter urges parents to take seriously the task of wisdom education. Families must give it attention since parents are the primary teachers. Education is taking place all the time in the home, and so it seems reasonable to ensure that teaching in biblical wisdom be included in the process.

PROVERBS 3:1–35

Original Meaning

Five Admonitions (3:1–10). The three benefits of long life, prosperity, and good reputation appear at the very start of the first instruction (3:1–4). However, these objects of desire do not come as ends in themselves but as the result of effort in learning wisdom and living wisely.

Descriptions of a good name (3:4), straight paths (3:6), bodily health (3:8), and overflowing barns and wine vats (3:10) are all variations on the theme of the good life. It is better to think of these benefits as results rather than rewards. Wisdom writers understood the life of *shalom* as a gift that Yahweh intends for the enjoyment of all.

In sum, the first instruction of chapter 3 sets its sights on the heart and its relation to God. It is the heart that gives direction to a life by making the primary choice between arrogant self-reliance and trust. The heart that trusts Yahweh, fears Yahweh, and honors Yahweh understands and knows that life can only be found in paths that lead straight toward him, not away.

Blessings of Wisdom (3:11–20). The "discipline" (3:11; Heb. *musar*) spoken of here is primarily that of teaching and correction. It is not equivalent to punishment, although Proverbs uses the word in a few contexts where the translation "punishment" is warranted, usually in association with folly. Verbal discipline both teaches and corrects.

The admonition is followed by a hymn-like poem in 3:13–18. Personified Wisdom makes her second appearance in Proverbs, although she does not speak as she did in chapter 1. Two sets of images follow the blessing of the one who finds wisdom and gains understanding; in the first, images of silver, gold, and rubies compare her worth and profit to the world's greatest wealth (3:14–15) A second series of images complements the offer of long life and prosperity from 3:2. The "tree of life" (3:18) in Proverbs appears as a source of good life and health rather than of eternal life.

In 3:19–20 a depiction similar to the creation account from Genesis 1 makes a surprising appearance, almost as if the tree of life triggers other thoughts about creation. Here "wisdom," "understanding," and "knowledge" are the guiding principles. The same wisdom that made a place for life by dividing the waters above from the waters below also lets down from above only enough water at a time to allow life to flourish.

Five Prohibitions (3:21–35). The goal of wisdom teaching is the formation of a person of discernment. As in chapter 2, "sound judgment and discretion" (3:21) are associated with images of safety and security. Yahweh will keep the wise son safe; he will also keep his foot from being snared. Safe passage by day is paired with peaceful rest at night, confident that someone is standing guard (cf. Ps 91:5; 127:2). Yahweh protects all the time. The assurance that he will be the son's confidence comes again in Proverbs 3:31–32, restating the disaster of the wicked in 3:25.

The list of five prohibitions against bad treatment of neighbors in 3:27–32 stands in structural symmetry with the five admonitions to honor Yahweh in 3:1–10. The structure seems to say that right relationship with God moves one to right dealings with one's neighbors.

The final three verses continue the series of contrasts that began in Proverbs 3:32, each comparing Yahweh's dealings with the righteous and the wicked. God's opposition to the wicked takes on a social dimension, mockers being mocked in return and fools held up to shame in the community. Verse 35 reverses the order of the previous contrasts so that the wise come first and fools come in dead last.

Application. There are really only two commands in this chapter. The first, said in many ways, is "find wisdom," with its implications of learning the teachings so we can learn to love. The second is "keep a close watch on your hand," making sure it does not hold back or grasp what is not ours in the first place. Notice these are not far from Jesus's command to love God and one's neighbor.

PROVERBS 4:1–27

Original Meaning

Grandfather's Teaching (4:1–9). Here we find the most detailed depiction of wisdom instruction in the book of Proverbs. The father, representing both father and mother, describes his own training. It is striking that the plural is used to introduce the remembered example of one-to-one instruction. One can imagine the instruction taking place in any Israelite home, especially since the issues it touches are universal.

The connection between "a father's instruction" (4:1) and the teaching of past generations comes through the father's quotation of words he first heard long ago. The remembered teachings of the father's father are short and direct: "Get wisdom! Get understanding!" (4:5).

A double meaning may stress that wisdom is of supreme worth; therefore, she comes first in value and first in time. The point is that many generations have proved the worth of wisdom, and this also puts the father to the test. The sons can ask if experience has proven his claims, and what is more, sons can observe their fathers to see whether what they say is true. One wonders whether the son might ask if his father has received the garland of grace and crown of splendor (4:9).

Paths of Righteousness and Wickedness (4:10–19). The repeated words "path" and "way" contrast the clear and well-lit path of the righteous with the dark and treacherous way of the wicked. The verse that does not use the metaphor of the path is 4:13, where the imagery shifts to guarding a treasure. Set in the context of the journey on the path, the image portrays a traveler who watches his coin purse, keeping it closely hidden. In summary, this section of instruction contrasts the benefits that come to the righteous and the woes of the wicked.

Anatomy of Righteousness (4:20–27). An anatomy of righteousness follows, urging the son to keep the father's words before his eyes and in his heart so they can direct the action of his mouth, lips, and feet. The heart that holds onto teaching is a source of life. This source of life was maintained not by keeping bad things out of it but by putting good teachings in and keeping them there (4:20–21). The heart, the seat of intentions, thoughts, and emotions, served as the control center for the rest of human anatomy, especially the organs of speech. A guarded heart and straight speech go together (4:23–24).

The next set of body images shows the outflow of a heart that is guarded; perversity and corrupt talk are placed far from the mouth and lips, eyes look straight ahead, and the feet do not turn right or left from level and sure paths (4:24–26). The Hebrew terms contrast what is straight and crooked in all three.

The ethical life is not only an inheritance, but also a life work. For this reason, the father appeals to the son to take his teaching with him on the journey, here symbolized as choosing a good mate, a good path, and a good heart.

Application. The images of wisdom as a life partner, a path for life, and a guard are symbols of lifelong commitments that direct everyday choices. A person heading out on a long journey on foot, as people did in Bible times, would always choose a good traveling companion. You would choose a well-traveled and safe path, and you would take care to watch how you use your body members, keeping eyes on the goal and feet on that path.

PROVERBS 5:1–23

Original Meaning

Avoid the Adulteress (5:1–6). The teacher warns that single-minded faithfulness can be compromised by the temptations of adultery (5:3–6). The principal contrast here is drawn between the deceptively sweet and smooth lips of the other woman and the lips of the young man that are to preserve knowledge and wisdom. She represents both the folly of adultery and all that is foreign to the way of wisdom.

Do Not Give What Is Yours to Others (5:7–14). The son is told to make his path *far* from the woman. The motivations or reasons for the charge in 5:9–14 are all negative. Death (5:5–6) is here defined as loss of strength, years, substance, and reputation, the reverse of wisdom's benefits of long life, riches, and honor. In going after a strange woman, one that is not his own, the son could lose all that is his own to strangers.

The teacher then fast-forwards this fictional narrative to the end of the son's life. He tells the young man he "will groan" (5:11) the way a heart groans in anguish from a sick and wasted body. Perhaps the most potent source of regret is the shame that comes to light in the last few words of 5:14.

Drink from Your Own Well (5:15–23). Just as the speech of the adulteress tasted like honey and oil that turned to bitter gall, so here drinking water becomes a metaphor for faithful sexual expression with one's spouse. What do these various symbols of water and drinking stand for? The suggestions made by interpreters include: the pleasures of physical love, the production of offspring, the squandered seed that does not produce offspring, or the wife herself. We may take a clue from Song of Songs 4:12–15. It is even more important to take the verses as a whole. They direct the son to have physical relations with his wife alone. To take one's intimacy to strangers is to risk losing all to strangers; to drink from one's own well is to keep all that is one's own, including one's life.

Application. The portrayal of adultery in this chapter highlights not only the losses that follow this reaching out of bounds, but the lies that come before. It is no accident that the description of the other woman centers on her words, not her beauty, because she represents the lie that sexual pleasure can be enjoyed in ways it was never designed for.

PROVERBS 6:1–35

Original Meaning

Avoid the Way of Pledges, Sluggards, and Scoundrels (6:1–19). *Get free from pledges (6:1–5).* In 6:1–5 a warning against a potential danger of pledging security presents another instance in which the young man is in danger of losing his livelihood to strangers. Most likely the teacher speaks against the guarantee of security for someone else's loan. The teachers of Proverbs took a dim view of such pledging; each mention of the practice in the book warns against getting involved.

Go learn from the ant (6:6–11). Having just used the analogy of the survival instinct of a bird from a trap (6:5), this second warning concentrates on the ant's foresight and hard work (6:6). Such analogies taken from the animal kingdom were common in the ancient Near East; Solomon taught about plants and animals as a sign of his wisdom and learning (1 Kgs 4:33).

The term translated "sluggard" (Prov 6:6) occurs fourteen times in Proverbs. The sluggard exemplifies folly (19:15; 21:24–26; 26:12–16), particularly in matters of food production. Therefore, the sluggard must look to a lowly creature to learn wisdom, one of the topsy-turvy motifs of wisdom literature.

The example of the ant's diligence and planning challenges avoidance of one's duties and responsibilities. It urges the young man to prevent being caught in the position of needing a loan and a guarantor.

Watch out for the scoundrel (6:12–15). Second-person address suddenly shifts to third-person description in 6:12. Mouth, eye, feet, and fingers are all used to communicate false and damaging messages. They are outward expressions of internal plotting and deceit (6:14). The disaster that pursues the scoundrel will come suddenly, making its appearance all the more frightening (6:15).

Hate the seven things Yahweh hates (6:16–19). The numerical pattern not only has the feel of a riddle, but it also places emphasis on the final statement as a kind of climax. In this case, the last two items in the list are not body parts at all but persons recognized by their actions: the "false witness" and the "person who stirs up conflict" (6:19). Thus, the climax to this section brings together the parts into one hideous whole, rephrasing and intensifying the description of the scoundrel in 6:12–15.

Avoid the Way of Adultery (6:20–35). Threats and warnings continue as the teacher reminds the son that no one who touches another man's wife will go unpunished. The commands and corrections are likened to a lamp that keeps feet from stumbling in the dark and onto a path to life (6:23). The need for reminders and protecting guides becomes clear in 6:24, namely, to keep the son from the immoral woman and her smooth tongue.

Again, the negative consequences of reaching out of bounds come more from the way life works than from God's direct intervention. Three comparisons, all painful, once again direct the young man to consider the costs before turning away from his parents' teaching.

Application. The teachers of Proverbs see that both pledges and laziness are forms of shirking responsibility for one's self and livelihood. Their message is deceptively simple: Take responsibility for what is yours, and do not take responsibility for what is not. Both use animal images to urge the use of our survival skills; trapped animals struggle to get free and ants model foresight, self-initiative, and industry. In fact, both recommend learning wisdom to be able to see negative outcomes before they arrive. The warning against pledges tells us to avoid bad commitments or to get out of them as soon as possible, while the picture of the sluggard tells us to keep commitments that are good. The knack for learning how to decide which is which is the mark of godly wisdom, for the problem facing many if not most Christians today is not idleness but overcommitment.

PROVERBS 7:1–27

Original Meaning

Call to Attention—Protected from the Woman (7:1–5). The first call to listen (7:1) once again urges the young man to keep and store the words and commands of his parents. The whole person—eye, hand, and heart—is to be dedicated to the task. Keeping the teachings, symbolized as a relationship with Wisdom, will keep the young man from the other woman and her seductive words (7:2, 5).

A Simple Young Man Wanders (7:6–9). We cannot say for certain who the speaker of chapter 7 is, for the text does not tell us. It may be the father, but it could be the mother. What is clear is that trouble is on its way.

Watching those who are passing by, the speaker notes that among the "simple" and "young men is one who "had no sense" (7:7), most likely the teacher's preview of the way the story will unfold. He is walking in the direction of the woman's house. It is twilight, just as the dark of night is falling. The repetition signals the wrong choice.

The Woman Described and Quoted (7:10–20). The Hebrew text uses *hinneh* (7:10; literally, "look now!") to create a "you are there" experience and signal the sudden appearance of a woman, heading in his direction to meet him. Before we hear her, we see her. She is "dressed like a prostitute" (7:10). Her attire signals her intent. Like a hunting animal, she grabs the unsuspecting youth and kisses him. Her brazen face is literally made strong and hard.

Three enticements follow: the sacrifices at home offer the delicacy of meat to eat (7:14), the bed at home offers the pleasures of love (7:16–17), and the husband *not* at home promises a sense of security (7:19–20). Having touched his lips with a kiss, all her other seductions come from her words. She is able to appeal to all his senses and make it sound as if her home is a place of paradise. What the young man does not know is that these words are the bait of a trap. The contrast between her many words and his silence is telling.

A Simple Young Man Is Slain (7:21–23). "With persuasive words she led him astray" (7:21). The persuasive words are literally "much teaching," making a play on the Hebrew root *lqh*, which can mean "take" or "receive teaching." The persuasive words lead the young man astray to his death, which the narrator likens to animal slaughter.

Second Call to Attention—An Image of the Woman's Slain Victims (7:24–27). The final image the parental teachers wish to leave in their son's mind is that of the highway to *sheol* ("grave," 7:27), mixing metaphors to liken her house to that way. It was the house and its awaiting pleasures that seemed so alluring, yet it became a home of the dead.

Application. I don't think I've ever heard a sermon on this chapter of the book of Proverbs. Certainly, it is appropriate to use discretion in speaking about matters of sexual behavior, but our embarrassment over the issue should never promote silence. Instead, we must help young adults understand their sexual desires and their needs to enter into a whole relationship with a life partner.

PROVERBS 8:1–36

Original Meaning. Here for the second time in the book, personified Wisdom calls out like a street preacher, seeking hearers and followers. She describes herself, her qualities, and her gifts and speaks of her existence at the dawn of creation. Her words not only contribute to our understanding of that creation but also to our understanding of the Word, who was with God in the beginning (John 1:1).

The speech of Wisdom in chapter 8 stands alone as a work

of art but also as a strategic answer to all that has come to the reader's attention since her last appearance. In chapters 7–9, the juxtaposed speeches of Folly and Wisdom follow a chiastic pattern.

A 7:14–20	Speech of the other/strange woman
B 8:4–36	Speech of Wisdom
B′ 9:5–6	Speech of Wisdom
A′ 9:16–17	Speech of the foolish woman

Unlike the strange woman, Woman Wisdom offers good teaching in 8:1–21.

8:1–5	Wisdom speaks to all humankind
8:6–11	Wisdom speaks what is noble and precious
8:12–16	Wisdom gives righteous counsel to rulers
8:17–21	Wisdom gives love, honor, and wealth to those who love her

Even the most casual reader will notice a shift in topic that marks the second half of Wisdom's speech in Proverbs 8:22.

1. It is the only verse in the whole speech to begin with the Hebrew *yhwh*, placing special emphasis on "the LORD," who is the main actor in all that follows. Wisdom is happy to say that only *she was there* when Yahweh made the heavens and the earth.
2. The scene changes from a description of the present to a recollection of the primeval past. Wisdom takes her listeners back to the dawn of creation to claim that she was a witness to God's great work of setting out the boundaries of the world. In asserting that she was there first, Wisdom continues to establish her credibility; that is, she enhances her authority to speak on behalf of God.

It is important to keep in mind that the speech moves toward the call to listen in 8:32. More than a recap of 8:6, that final call defines the purpose of the entire speech. Wisdom speaks about her role in the founding and administration of the world *so that* she can make a claim that sounds like Jesus's words, "No one comes to the Father except through me" (John 14:6).

The second half of Wisdom's speech in 8:22–36 is organized chronologically:

Wisdom was there *before* anything else (8:22–26)
Wisdom was present *when* the orders of creation were set in place (8:27–31)
Wisdom is *now* the one to whom we must listen (8:32–36)

This structure highlights the authority of her ways and words (8:32–33). To ignore them is to hate them, and to hate her is to love death (8:36). Thus, both chapters 7 and 8 end with the word "death" (Heb. *mawet*), a bitter frame surrounding the images of creation and life.

Application. Wisdom's call to all who will listen extends to readers in the twenty-first century, directing us to consider the nature of her words and the decisions it requires of us. We have seen that the rhetorical strategy of the first half of Wisdom's speech emphasizes reference to her own righteousness in speech and action, to establish her credibility and to serve as a model for rulers and citizens alike. Americans who have become cynical after learning that their presidents have lied about war, wiretapping, and womanizing now listen with a critical ear. They will not tolerate speech that distorts or traffics in half-truths, presenting only what serves the speaker's purposes. Therefore, righteous speech is ethical; it speaks the truth out of concern for another and rejects self-serving distortions.

The New Testament portraits of Jesus who was present and instrumental in creation did not claim one-to-one identification with these portraits of Wisdom but rather used the principle of analogy to say that Jesus, the wisdom of God, is *like* these various earlier portraits. In other words, the writer of Proverbs did not intend to describe a messiah or the person of Jesus; rather, later inspired writers (such as Paul) saw a correspondence and used a form of typology to make it clear to their readers.

PROVERBS 9:1–18

Original Meaning

Wisdom's Invitation (9:1–6). The speaker again introduces Wisdom's speech, setting it at the highest place in the city. From this visible and central location, she invites her hearers. Wisdom builds a house in which she dwells and offers her teaching, symbolized in the lavish banquet. The seven pillars are "hewn" (see NIV note on 9:1), possibly the way a stone cutter shapes rough stone. The number seven is often associated with seven days of creation and completion. If Wisdom has built her house, it is finished and it is good—nothing else is needed.

Wisdom's speech is less a public address than a public invitation to her table. In contrast to the other woman, her meat and drink will bring life, not death. But to come to her is to leave those simple ways behind and to walk in a new way, the way of understanding.

Learning Wisdom (9:7–12). The section that follows Wisdom's invitation appears to intrude, interrupting the contrast with the invitation of Folly. The structure of the section begins with the responses of the mocker and the wise person (9:7–9) and ends with their rewards (9:11–12). In the central position of this frame, "the fear of the LORD" links response and outcome, explaining the difference as fear of Yahweh (9:10). Therefore, juxtaposition of elements that appear dissimilar on the surface need not be taken as a sign of patchwork; the chapter is more like a skillfully sewn quilt, beautiful in its assembly of varied pieces.

Folly's Invitation (9:13–18). Wisdom's banquet invitation is followed by a nearly identical call from Folly. The differences are significant. Whereas Wisdom was portrayed as hardworking and generous, Folly is loud and boisterous, simple, and without knowledge. Just as Wisdom calls from the highest places, Folly takes a seat at the high places and calls to those who pass by, going straight on their way. Folly's identical call to the simple to "turn in here" (author's translation, 9:16a; cf. 9:4) takes on a new meaning in this context. She calls away those who want to walk a straight path.

Application. Knowing the fear of the Lord helps us with our fears about bad influences. Wisdom recognizes that positive and negative influences are out there, but instead of attempting to shut negative messages out, she tries to help the reader learn to discern and decide.

PROVERBS 10:1–32

Original Meaning

Prologue: Wise and Foolish Sons and the Watching Yahweh (10:1–5). *10:1.* The intended contrast is between the honor or shame that comes to both parents based on their son's choices.

10:2. For anyone who takes moral shortcuts in acquiring wealth, those riches will not offer security.

10:3. Desire brings life or death, depending on the intention that guides it.

10:4. This general truth should not be taken as a promise that God is constrained to fulfill but as a description of what generally happens.

10:5. The one who gathers is wise, but the one who sleeps is a shameful son.

Blessing and the Life of the Community (10:6–21). *10:6.* In contrast to blessings that come on the head is violence that overwhelms the mouth of the wicked.

10:7. Like the body, reputations can putrefy and disappear.

10:8. The wise are silent and learn, while the fool's lips are too busy prattling to learn what would prevent ruin.

10:9. The contrast warns against loss of reputation, not the physical danger that a reader might expect.

10:10. This saying presents not a contrast but a twofold picture of wickedness. Both come to a grievous end.

10:11. "Fountain of life" is used for righteous speech that refreshes and maintains life.

10:12. Hatred stirs up, love smooths over.

10:13. There are two contrasts, the first between the wisdom that is found on the lips and the punishment that falls on the back, the second between the person who has discernment and the one who lacks judgment.

10:14. The wise in their knowledge know when to share it and when it is best to keep it in reserve; fools, lacking such discretion and self-control, speak in ways that eventually will come back to harm them.

10:15. The point centers in the metaphor that one stores knowledge for protection.

10:16. Only the wages of righteousness can give final security.

10:17. Walking and wandering recount the major themes of chapters 1–9. The contrast with "life" in 10:17 is similar to that in 10:16; one expects to read "death" but instead finds wandering or erring, a kind of "lead[ing] others astray."

10:18. The difference between hiding hatred and spreading it through slander is one of action, not intent; both forms of deceit have the potential to be equally destructive.

10:19. Words are like sheep; the more there are, the better the chances that some will go astray.

10:20. The contrast of worth ("choice silver" versus "little value") traces the outflow of the tongue to its source, the heart. To be lacking in heart is to lack judgment and character (10:13; cf. 4:23).

10:21. The wise speak in a way that benefits others; the fool speaks in a way that leads to his own ruin.

Blessing of Yahweh and the Ends of the Righteous and Wicked (10:22–32). *10:22.* The blessing of Yahweh brings wealth that does not come with trouble.

10:23. The contrast between the fool's evil and the love of wisdom highlights different tastes in what brings pleasure and delight.

10:24. The unwanted dread of the wicked will still come, while that which the righteous desires will be given.

10:25. Read together, 10:24 and 25 suggest that the righteous desire and are given long life.

10:26. The proverb may recommend getting rid of the sluggard like one who spits out vinegar or moves out of a smoky place.

10:27. The theme returns to the respective futures of the righteous and wicked, reminding the reader of 10:16.

10:28. The wicked not only fail to get what they desire (10:28), they do receive what they fear (10:24).

10:29. Having considered the blessing and fear of Yahweh, the proverb now recommends the "way" of Yahweh.

10:30. The image is of a plant pulled up by its roots.

10:31–32. This final proverb pair should be read together, since the second lines of both describe the tongue.

Application. The proverbs encourage the value of diligence. However, we make a mistake if we take these texts as proof that our kids need a kick in the pants and in so doing, only give them a message of rejection.

PROVERBS 11:1–31

Original Meaning

Yahweh Detests Dishonest Scales (11:1–19). *11:1.* Ancient dealers sometimes kept two sets of weighing stones, one for buying and one for selling.

11:2. Pride points to the arrogance of those who believe they can abuse others and not be brought to account.

11:3. This contrast imagines roads filled with dangers. One would be glad to have a guide in such situations.

11:4. The next seven verses present variations on the word for righteousness and its use in 11:4. The vocabulary of the proverb reminds the reader of 10:2.

11:5. Verses 5–6 form a pair contrasting the fates of the righteous and the wicked.

11:6. Righteousness keeps its bearer safe and free while wickedness ensnares and destroys.

11:7. Because the wicked have no desire for the enduring treasures of wisdom, their hopes and dreams die with them.

11:8. The irony of the sages shows that the wicked bring their own trouble on themselves.

11:9. These next six proverbs are clustered around the theme of speech. We may not be protected from the verbal assaults of others, but we will be rescued from the backlash that uncontrolled speech brings on itself.

11:10. The sounds of rejoicing may come when outcomes are fitting because too often they are not.

11:11. The life of the city is affected for better or worse by the character of its citizens.

11:12. The words of the wicked destroy by deriding others or by breaking confidence. The discerning and trustworthy person keeps silent on both counts.

11:13. This proverb applies to personal relationships, but business practices are included as well.

11:14. Just as negative words can tear persons and cities down, good counsel builds up and brings victory.

11:15. Admonition to neighbor love is qualified by this warning against surety.

11:16. As the NIV translates, the kindheartedness of the woman wins her the favor of others while the ruthlessness or aggression of men wins wealth.

11:17. Kindness and cruelty done to others turn back on the doer.

11:18. There is a wordplay on the Hebrew terms for "deceptive" (*shaqer*) in 11:18a and "reward" (*saeker*) in 11:18b.

11:19. "Life" and "death" complete each line of 11:19, which contrasts a person of true righteousness and one who pursues evil.

Yahweh Detests Perverse Hearts (11:20–31). *11:20.* Like the dishonest scales of 11:1, perverse hearts are "an abomination to the LORD" (author's translation).

11:21. The contrast is between sure punishment of the guilty and sure grace to the righteous.

11:22. The saying is less a putdown of beautiful and foolish women than of men who might prefer them.

11:23. This verse makes the connection of the verses in 11:20–23 clear, pitting good desires against wicked hope.

11:24. The theme of generosity versus withholding runs throughout this section.

11:25. The one who nurtures others will be nurtured in turn.

11:26. While the honor that comes from others is not the primary motivation for doing good, it is not discounted.

11:27. Continuing the themes of public favor and rewards, 11:27 compares two seekers: one who seeks good and finds goodwill, the other who pursues evil for others only to have it "come to" him.

11:28. A false sense of security in what one owns motivates the evil behaviors. Sadly, the one who turns that belief into action falls dead like a dried-up leaf.

11:29. The negative recompense for evil even extends to one's family. Proverbs about the fool who serves the wise will appear.

11:30. The wise promote life, they do not take it away.

11:31. A straightforward statement of just rewards both summarizes the theme of the chapter and lends its assurance that Yahweh hates perversity and loves righteousness; therefore, rewards will be forthcoming.

Application. Daily we are given countless opportunities to seek good instead of evil. In "seeking good" we are also seeking the kingdom of God and his righteousness.

PROVERBS 12:1–28

Original Meaning

Learn and Stand (12:1–7). *12:1.* This proverb contrasts love of discipline, a sign that one loves knowledge, with hating correction, a sign that one is "stupid."

12:2. The one who is good shapes life according to values outside of the self while the one who schemes only looks within to one's own intentions.

12:3. Yahweh told the prophet Jeremiah he would pull up the roots of those who establish themselves through wickedness (Jer 1:9–10).

12:4. The instruction of this proverb is to value character above beauty.

12:5. The contrast focuses attention on the intentions of persons, their deliberations on what they will and will not do.

12:6. The proverb has the upright delivered by the very means the wicked meant for harm.

12:7. The theme of permanence first stated in 12:3 is echoed here.

Praise and Blame (12:8–12). *12:8.* The proverb reminds us of the importance of shame and honor as motivators for many cultures.

12:9. The "better . . . than" saying is a typical form of proverb.

12:10. Better to be the righteous person's horse than the wicked person's neighbor!

12:11. A proverb about the rewards of labor moves the imagery from the stable to the field.

12:12. This verse restates and summarizes the theme of the section.

Speech and Silence (12:13–23). *12:13.* "Oh, what a tangled web we weave, when we first practice to deceive." (Sir Walter Scott)

12:14. Just as speaking is a form of doing, so both hands and mouth can be put to purposes good or evil.

12:15. The first of two proverbs about fools contrasts two counselors.

12:16. The contrast in both 12:15 and 12:16 is between the loud fool and the silent sage.

12:17. There are times in which an honest witness must make a report to counteract the lies of the false witness.

12:18. Words are rarely neutral, and they usually leave their mark for good or bad.

12:19. Lies may look as though they can bring security, but in fact, they build on a precarious branch. It sometimes takes time for truth to show itself strong.

12:20. The wise one absorbs what is heard so it can be offered to others and the joy shared.

12:21. The joy of *shalom* described in 12:20 also brings with it freedom from fear.

12:22. That which Yahweh "detests" is an abomination.

12:23. This proverb provides a humorous explanation for why knowledge so often seems in short supply!

Diligence and Laziness (12:24–28). *12:24.* The contrast between hands that work like a servant yet rule like a king shows the same kind of reversal of expectations as the hands that seek rest but wind up working in forced or conscripted labor.

12:25. Speech to oneself from the anxious heart is contrasted with the external word that brings joy.

12:26. The way of the wicked is no way at all, for it leads nowhere, and those who take it become lost.

12:27. Like the wicked, lazy people have nothing to give others, for they cannot even take care of themselves!

12:28. This last saying connects the themes of this chapter with the recurring motif of the two ways, life and death.

Application. The proverbs of this chapter continue to encourage openness to instruction by reminding its readers that wisdom and folly will make themselves known. Neither remains hidden for long.

PROVERBS 13:1–25

Original Meaning

Discipline and Eating (13:1–6). *13:1.* While responsibility is set squarely on the learner, the parent's responsibility to teach is upheld.

13:2. A similar contrast is intensified in 13:3, where the contrast is between "life" and "ruin" or destruction.

13:3. These sayings caution us to watch what our mouths put out as well as what they take in to satisfy their desires.

13:4. A proverb about the sluggard completes this cluster of sayings about appetite and desire.

13:5. The contrast in 13:5 pits falsehood against its result of shame and disgrace.

13:6. This saying personifies righteousness and wickedness as protector and destroyer.

Riches and Virtues (13:7–11). *13:7.* Riches are not as clear an indication of status and worth as we often believe.

13:8. This verse allows that riches can get one out of trouble, but only as it reminds us that it is better to hear no threat of trouble at all.

13:9. The image of the lamp signifies a long and happy life.

13:10. The source of contention ("pride") is defined as an unwillingness to listen and learn.

13:11. The first line can read "meaningless wealth" (author's translation). The contrast with the second line suggests that it is wealth gained from no labor—perhaps theft or speculation.

Desire Fulfilled (13:12–19). *13:12.* Although this proverb contrasts hope deferred and longing fulfilled, it simply makes the contrasts and observes its effects.

13:13. The contrast between one who pays and one who is paid is in view here.

13:14. The fountain of life is associated with righteous speech, the fear of Yahweh, and understanding.

13:15. This saying compares "good judgment" that can be acquired with the "way" or actions of those who reject it.

13:16. Demonstration of learning, or lack of it, is at the heart of this proverb.

13:17. If you sent someone into a conflict situation, you would want one who would make it better, not worse.

13:18. The key word "discipline" (Heb. *musar*) appears, marking the beginning, middle, and end of this chapter.

13:19. Fools who refuse to turn from evil will certainly not enjoy the sweetness of fulfilled desire; their actions will bear their fruits.

Prosperity and Inheritance (13:20–23). *13:20.* Fools not only refuse to turn from evil, but they also fail to choose good company.

13:21. Fools and sinners not only find trouble; here trouble is personified as seeking them.

13:22. The reward of 13:21 can be passed on to one's children and grandchildren.

13:23. The blessings of God and nature may favor the poor, but an astute observer will also note that their gain can be taken by injustice.

Discipline and Eating (13:24–25). *13:24.* This verse can never be taken as support for corporal punishment. The issue is one of instruction, not the means used to bring it about.

13:25. The contrast of this proverb suggests this hunger is a reward, but given what we have seen of the wicked and their undisciplined desires, it is a just one.

Application. The discipline of loving instruction makes the difference between "longing fulfilled" and "craving" that is not. We receive this discipline, shaping our lives around it so that we offer it to those who come after us.

PROVERBS 14:1–35

Original Meaning

The Wise and Foolish Compared (14:1–7). *14:1.* The sages speak here of our main direction in life.

14:2. The walk of the wise in 13:20 is here shown to contrast with the fool who rejects Yahweh.

14:3. The contrast between a fool's "mouth" and a wise person's "lips" is linked to their rewards, punishment, or protection.

14:4. It costs grain to keep an ox, but with the ox there is a greater return on the investment.

14:5. The false witness is a "lie breather" (author's translation).

14:6. Knowledge comes quickly and easily to the one who has cultivated discernment, for it is this quality that the mocker lacks.

14:7. If mockers have not found wisdom, neither will knowledge be found with the fool.

The Prudent and Foolish Compared (14:8–15). *14:8.* The contrast in this saying is completed with an unexpected contrast between thoughtful consideration of the way one walks and deception.

14:9. The contrast stands between a scornful attitude toward reconciliation and a way of life that rarely needs it.

14:10. Even while our lives are shared with others, our deepest thoughts and feelings remain hidden.

14:11. The Hebrew word for "flourish" (*prḥ*) typically refers to plants that sprout or bud.

14:12. "Way" points to the choices that require foresight, while the "end" describes outcomes, rewards, and reality.

14:13. When read alongside 14:10, the first and second lines correspond—the first on the theme of inner hurt, the second on the word "joy."

14:14. The "faithless" are "those whose hearts have turned" (author's translation).

14:15. These are the naive people that Wisdom tried so desperately to reach, but Folly was never far away.

Fear of Yahweh, Life, and Refuge (14:16–27). *14:16.* Verses 16–17 are linked by images of hair-trigger temper and folly, and they are framed by the simple/prudent distinction in 14:15 and 18.

14:17. The comparison here is between one who does foolish things on impulse and one who does evil that has been carefully planned and premeditated, a product of scheming.

14:18. In both lines of the saying, the rewards not only correspond to the qualities of "folly" and "prudence," they foster and nurture them.

14:19. The proverb and its imagery offer hope to those who too often see the good bowing down before the power of an evil person.

14:20. When read together, the main contrast is between the self-interested love shown to the rich and the selfless kindness shown to the poor.

14:21. The saying turns the focus away from the experience of the poor in 14:20 to the responsibility of those who help or fail them.

14:22. Those who plan evil are rewarded with going astray, so it is better to plan for good and enjoy its return in love and faithfulness.

14:23. The contrast of mere talk and effort is that of intention and follow through, emptiness and payoff.

14:24. Fools who cannot see the difference between talk and effort are left with the foolishness they began with.

14:25. In a court of law we depend on the truthful witness to free innocent people.

14:26. The "fortress" is a confidence or reliance in which one trusts.

14:27. To animals, the difference between a spring of water and a net is life and death, but the human capacity to worship actually turns us from one to the other.

Kings, Subjects, and Servants (14:28–35). *14:28.* The larger the kingdom, the larger the status, but the second line shows that even a ruler's power is dependent on the quality of relationships in the kingdom.

14:29. If it is hard to believe that one displays wisdom by holding one's temper, the reverse picture of uncontrolled anger is certainly convincing.

14:30. The ancients knew that jealousy, passion, and envy eat one from the inside out, thus rotting the bones.

14:31. The absence of the fear of Yahweh gives a person the temerity to oppress the poor whom God loves.

14:32. Verse 32 repeats the image of "refuge" from 14:26; here also the righteous are protected from the "calamity" that brings down the wicked.

14:33. Wisdom is with both the discerning and fools, yet she only stays with the former.

14:34. To be righteous lifts a nation's reputation high, but sin brings it disgrace.

14:35. A good kingdom requires good citizens, righteous people, and prudent servants.

Application. The pervasive presence of evil described in the proverbs can sensitize us to harsh treatment of others. How can one person do anything about individual and corporate greed? While the answers are not simple, a commitment toward exploring them makes a good start.

PROVERBS 15:1–33

Original Meaning

Words and Speech (15:1–8). *15:1.* The first saying of this chapter picks up the topic of anger from 14:35 and turns the focus toward speech that turns away wrath.

15:2. Another saying on speaking distinguishes the wise and foolish by what their mouths produce.

15:3. Human tongues speak and heavenly eyes watch.

15:4. Speech that does damage is deceitful; by implication, then, speech that heals is truthful.

15:5. Wisdom to speak and teach others is learned in listening.

15:6. Only the righteous receive rewards that one would like to keep and share.

15:7. The desire to spread knowledge as an antidote to folly is the mark of a wise person and a caring teacher.

Yahweh Sayings (15:8–11). *15:8.* Worship may never be divorced from our day-to-day actions.

15:9. The proverb contrasts two paths, indicated by use of the words "way" and "pursue."

15:10. The warning is not just for the wicked; whoever wishes to stay on the path had better prepare for correction or reproof.

15:11. "How much more" sayings take an accepted truth and apply it to a new situation.

Death and Hatred/Life and Love (15:11–18). *15:12.* The "mocker" appears in wisdom's speeches and a number of individual sayings.

15:13. This proverb does not contrast external joy with internal sorrow but rather the wide range of our emotional states and their effects.

15:14. A heart that seeks knowledge will find it; folly, by contrast, is hardly gourmet fare.

15:15. This last of the heart sayings sets the stage for another pair of sayings on contentment in 15:16–17.

15:16. Mitigating factors may make having little preferable to having much; by implication, "fear of the Lord," like wisdom, is worth more than gold or jewels.

15:17. Taken together, 15:15–17 redefine what is to be considered a good feast, namely, the cheerful heart.

15:18. One's response to a situation influences it for good or bad.

Sluggards and Fools (15:19–24). *15:19.* Thorns and briers in the path certainly slow the way and make traveling miserable; they may be a sign of folly, for who would choose such a route?

15:20. The second line implies the link between wisdom and love.

15:21. Folly has its delights, but the person of understanding is not misled.

15:22. A wise person listens to advice.

15:23. The proverb celebrates the wisdom that knows how to speak the right word at the right time.

15:24. At root, everyone wants "life," but too many pursue it in ways that lead to death.

Yahweh Sayings (15:25–33). *15:25.* Yahweh brings down the high and mighty and lifts up the lowly.

15:26. The saying highlights Yahweh's look at intentions that motivate right and wrong behaviors.

15:27. The greedy person thinks only of gains, not consequences.

15:28. When that inner work is ignored, the mouth pours out folly and its close cousin, evil.

15:29. If we read 15:28 and 29 together, the evil speech of the wicked is the counterpart to the prayers of the righteous.

15:30. The proverb is about messages that come from the good heart and bring health and life to those who receive them.

15:31. Rebuke brings life because it brings wisdom.

15:32. Those who ignore discipline not only disrespect others, such as the wise, they hate themselves.

15:33. Fear of Yahweh, a stepping down from self-rule (becoming small), is instruction in wisdom.

Application. The principles we have discerned in this chapter about wise speaking, the heart's desires, and the goodness of life lived in the fear of Yahweh translate easily into the concerns of our own day, and preachers and teachers may be surprised to find examples in every walk of life. These sayings on speech commend gentleness and truthfulness. Such speech turns away wrath, brings healing, and calms quarrels.

PROVERBS 16:1–33

Original Meaning

Yahweh Sayings (16:1–9). *16:1.* Humans act according to their intentions, but God is somehow at work in those acts of word and deed.

16:2. Yahweh is better able to discern our motivations than we are.

16:3. We might paraphrase: "Plan, pray, then act."

16:4. Yahweh does what he purposes, even while there are those who seek to work out purposes that are contrary to Yahweh's.

16:5. The wicked do not undo God's intentions for the world by opposing his intentions.

16:6. The contrast of punished pride is sin atoned. "Fear of the LORD" takes on new significance here as both motivation and means for avoiding moral evil.

16:7. "Peace with God, peace with others" might paraphrase the proverb.

16:8. Because interests sometimes conflict, one should learn to choose righteousness and justice over profit.

16:9. Human plans and God's oversight are in cooperation, not conflict.

King Sayings (16:10–15). *16:10.* Lips and mouth are frequently paired; here they point to the king's responsibility to enact "justice."

16:11. Even when there is human intent to deceive, God's justice will eventually win out.

16:12. As the king shares Yahweh's abhorrence to the deeds of the wicked, the throne is established.

16:13. Just as kings detest the wrong, they love those who do right.

16:14. Wise persons know how to assuage anger, and they know how to speak the truth so that it need not be aroused.

16:15. The juxtaposition of opposites—the sun that shines brightly and a dark rain cloud—surprise the reader with their similarity; both are welcome and necessary for a good crop.

Wisdom Better Than Gold (16:16–19). *16:16.* Gain without the integrity of wisdom loses its value.

16:17. The straight way also turns away from evil, and in so doing watches over life as well.

16:18. The Hebrew could read, "Before destruction, pride, and before stumbling, a haughty spirit" (author's translation).

16:19. Communities are contrasted here: one in which goods are divided, but with gloating and perhaps resentment at having to share; the other where there is no wealth to divide, only joyful sharing and company.

Wisdom Sweet on the Lips (16:20–24). *16:20.* Trust believes that God's way is the best way and so gladly follows it.

16:21. The charge to gain wisdom carries with it a second charge to pass it on to others by means of persuasive teaching.

16:22. The contrast is between "understanding" (author's translation, NIV "prudence") and "folly" along with each one's results, "life" and "punishment."

16:23. The second line could be translated "adds learning to the lips" (author's translation), perhaps a reference to the ongoing learning of the wise.

16:24. Honey is the symbol for the teaching that brings life, a sign that all is well.

Evil Fire on the Lips (16:25–30). *16:25.* This saying states our need for an external reference point by which we set our course.

16:26. The repetition of the word "appetite" (Heb. *nephesh*) from 16:24 (where it is translated "soul") suggests that we compare the overflowing sweetness of the honeycomb with the intense hunger that motivates a worker.

16:27. A "scorching fire" quickly spreads, destroying everything in its path as it burns out of control.

16:28. The similarity between the two lines is the absence of goodwill and unity. The difference is that one can create it loudly or quietly.

16:29. A strong contrast stands here between the teacher who spreads health and peace and the "teacher" who spreads division and finally violence.

16:30. The image of pressing both the eyes and lips seems to be a common act of "perversity," linking this verse with the dissension and gossip of 16:28.

Patience, Reverence, and Endurance (16:31–33). *16:31.* Long life is a reward for walking the righteous way even when one wants to quit.

16:32. Better to exhibit self-control than to control others.

16:33. Both lots cast and stones drawn out point to Yahweh's desire for decisions that reflect his will.

Application. If the first fifteen proverbs of the chapter present a picture of leadership exercised in full recognition of God's authority, the second half of the chapter offers implications. Servant leadership rejects pride in favor of humble identification with the lowly and oppressed, foregoes personal gains, and holds wisdom as more valuable than gold.

PROVERBS 17:1–28

Original Meaning

Households, Sons, and Brothers (17:1–6). *17:1.* The irony is plain: If the goal of harmony is not met, what good is a sumptuous table?

17:2. Status, like material prosperity, means little if it is not matched by wise character.

17:3. "Tests" here is set in parallel to the crucible and furnace that removes impurities and tempers the metal, naming "the LORD" as tester and the heart as tested.

17:4. It is ironic that one who lies can be taken in by the same sort of deception in others.

17:5. Attitude is an action waiting to happen, and so the way we view others determines the way we will treat them.

17:6. Perhaps an encouragement to set a wise example is implied in this statement of the ideal.

Eloquent Fools and Lying Rulers (17:7–11). *17:7.* The climax in the saying comes with the "how much more"; it is even worse to find lying lips with a leader or noble.

17:8. The saying is descriptive and does not commend the practice of paying bribes.

17:9. The observation leads to the general truth that it is better to forgive and forget.

17:10. Blows *won't* work if words won't.

17:11. One can seek reconciliation, or one can seek rebellion; the choice is clear.

Dangers of Fools and Folly 17:12–15. *17:12.* The salt of the proverb compares the danger of a bear *without* her cubs to fools whose folly goes *with* them wherever they go.

17:13. Evil in its shortsightedness is just plain dumb.

17:14. As water cannot be brought back under control once released, a quarrel can escalate beyond expectation.

17:15. False judgments are detestable in Yahweh's eyes.

Fools and Money, Brothers and Friends (17:16–20). *17:16.* Wisdom is a gift of God and must be acquired through study, and even if wisdom could be bought, the fool lacks the sense to know what to do with it.

17:17. The saying implicitly rebukes those who claim friendship but are nowhere to be found when they are needed.

17:18. This proverb pair advises readers to avoid trouble, not a neighbor in need.

17:19. If loving or holding onto an offense leads one to build a "high gate" (presumably to keep away neighbors), one trusts in a false hope.

17:20. This proverb is one of the many sayings that link "heart" and "tongue" to represent the whole person's thoughts and actions.

Suffering Fools in Secret (17:21–24). *17:21.* If 17:20 depicts the effects of folly on the person who practices it, this proverb reminds us that the effects spread throughout the family and to others as well.

17:22. In Proverbs, the "crushed spirit" is brought on by heartache and is hard to bear.

17:23. Like the hidden heart that reveals its conditions in word, deed, and even the condition of the body, so a bribe given in secret does its damaging work.

17:24. This saying contrasts the person who keeps wisdom nearby and the fool who looks everywhere else for answers.

Fools Thought Wise When Silent (17:25–28). *17:25.* The second of the sayings about bearing a foolish son, this variation on the theme adds the "bitterness" of the mother to the father's "grief."

17:26. The proverb recommends fair judgment for all members of society.

17:27. This saying presents two signs of a person who has gathered "knowledge"—that one moderates both words and temper.

17:28. Reserve and restraint are so powerfully communicative that even fools can appear wise.

Application. The evangelical church is just as prone to bitter conflict as the rest of the world, perhaps even more so. No wonder Jesus prayed for the unity of the church—he knew what was coming! Conflict and its roots in inordinate desire have always been with us.

PROVERBS 18:1–24

Original Meaning

Sayings on Speech and Fools (18:1–8). *18:1.* The picture of isolation and quarreling here continues the theme of behaviors that bring strife.

18:2. Interested only in showing what he knows, the person in this verse accomplishes just the opposite.

18:3. "Contempt" goes with the wicked everywhere they go.

18:4. Words, like deep waters, can mislead. The "fountain of wisdom" reminds readers of the fountain of life.

18:5. One should not clear the guilty and condemn the innocent.

18:6. It is not certain whether the blows are the result of a fight or punishment.

18:7. If 18:6 notes the reaction of others, this verse makes it clear the fool has no one to blame but himself.

18:8. Tidbits of gossip may be stored for evil purposes.

Sayings on Strength, Safety, and Pride (18:9–12). *18:9.* "One who is slack" lets drop what is in the hands, but the destruction that results from such negligence is no accident.

18:10. The phrase "name of the Lord" occurs only here in Proverbs, but frequently in the Psalms it is a sign of refuge.

18:11. Wealth is only a strong city and high wall as "they imagine it."

18:12. It seems that either attitude leads inexorably to its opposite.

Sayings on Speech and Disputes (18:13–19). *18:13.* Fools only like to hear themselves talk.

18:14. The connection between spirit and body links the proverbs that mention the crushed spirit.

18:15. The ear of the wise not only searches for knowledge but does so by sorting knowledge from folly.

18:16. If the ear of 18:15 seeks to acquire knowledge, the gift only seeks to buy access to power.

18:17. There are always two sides; it is better to wait until both are heard before passing judgment.

18:18. One is also reminded that Yahweh's decisions are compared with the lot, and perhaps there is some sense that the lot gives the decision over to God.

18:19. One expects the brother to stand with, not against, so sibling conflict is the worst example of good relations perverted.

Sayings on Speech and Its Rewards (18:20–24). *18:20.* This saying might be paraphrased, "we'd better be able to stomach what we say" (author's translation).

18:21. The one who loves the tongue understands its power and uses it for good.

18:22. Wisdom's words about herself in 8:35 remind us that wisdom is a gracious gift of God, yet available to all who ask for it (Prov 2). As Wisdom calls out and offers herself, so does Yahweh; yet humans must seek her and Yahweh diligently.

18:23. More often than not, the poor must plead with someone who holds power over them, while the rich can answer harshly to those of lower status.

18:24. In contrast to the previous verse, where there is no friendship, this saying compares many friends to one who loves and sticks close like a brother.

Application. All of our speaking and listening end up in the "inmost parts," so make a conscious effort to reject gossip and other forms of put down.

PROVERBS 19:1–29

Original Meaning

Fools, Friends, and False Witnesses (19:1–9). *19:1.* A blameless walk and a crooked tongue mix metaphors in typical proverbial style, the path of the feet and words of the mouth serving as expressions of either wisdom or folly.

19:2. This proverb holds out patience and caution as knowledgeable companions of desire.

19:3. The fool, having ruined his life all by himself, now wants to blame God for his misfortune!

19:4. The proverb points out the painful truth that most would rather be a friend to the rich.

19:5. If one gains wealth or courts friendship through falsehood, that perverse use of speech will eventually be repaid.

19:6. The friendship is hollow for both parties, being based only on self-interest and personal gain.

19:7. The poor person is deserted even by relatives, so it is not unexpected that friends also keep their distance.

19:8. An upbeat saying intrudes on this unhappy series of proverbs, assuring the reader that those who acquire "heart" (author's translation, NIV "wisdom") care for themselves.

19:9. The crime of perjury is more than a preference for the rich over the poor; it is outright attack.

Fools, Rulers, and Families (19:10–14). *19:10.* Fools usually do not live in luxury, but sometimes exceptions prove the rule.

19:11. It is when we seek to protect our honor or status by quarreling that we stand to lose it the most.

19:12. If it is wise to practice patience and restrain one's anger, it is also wise to do everything possible to keep from provoking anger in one more powerful.

19:13. The continual dripping of the quarrelsome wife is not like the annoyance of a leaky faucet; the dripping roof is destructive and dangerous, a fitting parallel for the ruin of the foolish son.

19:14. Again the mysterious correspondence between decision and blessing is held up but not explained.

Sluggards and Discipline (19:15–24). *19:15.* As laziness *only* brings on sleep, the appetite of the indolent goes hungry.

19:16. To refuse guidance is to despise one's way, to be careless about where one walks.

19:17. While the poor often cannot repay, Yahweh always can.

19:18. The proverb urges parents to exercise such discipline "for in that there is hope," the possibility for a good outcome.

19:19. The saying not only recommends the value of a cool temper, but it also offers advice on handling the one who has not cultivated it.

19:20. Wisdom is a lifelong project, not a job order that one fulfills and moves on.

19:21. Once again, the proverb urges its readers to consider final outcomes and ends.

19:22. It is better to be poor and honest than to have great gain through lies.

19:23. To fear Yahweh is to fear nothing else.

19:24. Although no one is really that lazy, the exaggeration shows that sloth will leave one hungry.

Mockers and Knowledge (19:25–29). *19:25.* The contrast is plain; beat a mocker as an example to the simple, because the mocker is beyond learning.

19:26. The danger of failing to honor and care for parents is real, especially when the son's foolishness has left the parents destitute.

19:27. In Proverbs, a young learner can be led astray by another woman, a sign of one's own folly (5:20, 23), wine and beer (20:1), and evil men (28:10).

19:28. Desire without knowledge is not good, for you may swallow poison!

19:29. The beatings of 19:25 will take place, and while they may not instruct the mockers or fools, they will teach one willing to watch and learn that God's justice is not mocked.

Application. In our haste to fulfill our wants we can easily misstep. Proverbs would have us learn another way. Instead of worrying about how well we are doing, we can worry about how well those with less are doing. Seeing that what we have is a gift, we are free to give it again.

PROVERBS 20:1–30

Original Meaning

Foolish Behaviors of Brawling and Loafing (20:1–4). *20:1.* This proverb recognizes that alcohol can impair one's judgment and therefore compares it to two figures known to be a negative influence.

20:2. The wise take warning, but fools provoke it and pay with their lives.

20:3. Those who quarrel will not gain the respect they fight for but will actually lose standing.

20:4. The comic example of the sluggard who makes no preparation but still looks for a result recommends both foresight and industry.

Discerning Hidden Intentions through Behavior (20:5–9). *20:5.* Like water from the bottom of the well, human "purposes" can be drawn out if one has "insight."

20:6. This proverb on faithfulness recalls the friendship themes of the previous chapter.

20:7. Children can also be the beneficiaries of a parent's faith (14:26).

20:8. The king's work of discernment is akin to that of Yahweh, who judges in righteousness.

20:9. The point is not so much that there are people who claim to be without sin, but that there are more people who claim to have dealt with it than really have.

Seeing as Yahweh Sees (20:10–12). *20:10.* False measures are rejected as an abomination to Yahweh.

20:11. Whether old or young, actions reveal character to those who have learned the wise art of discernment.

20:12. God made eyes and ears to perceive and understand, and he is pleased when they do.

Business Practices, Foolish and Wise (20:13–17). *20:13.* The one who sleeps could become dispossessed or lose the inheritance.

20:14. Here there are two kinds of speaking, one for negotiating and one for boasting.

20:15. The proverb asks, what do we value the most?

20:16. Ironically, one who makes an unwise pledge may well have given his shirt, for he will surely lose it.

20:17. False speech fills the mouth that produces it with dirt and stone.

Counsel, Not Cursing (20:18–21). *20:18.* One should seek out advice, practical and ethical, from one who speaks words of knowledge.

20:19. The practical wisdom of this observation teaches that if you hear a confidence, someone else will probably hear yours.

20:20. The extinguished "lamp" can refer to the light that goes out when it is most needed, but it may be a metaphor for losing one's life.

20:21. Inappropriate behavior at the start cannot lead to blessing, divine or human, at the end.

Judgment, Divine and Human (20:22–30). *20:22.* Just as wisdom teaches us to hold back our words in general, here words of vengeance are warned against specifically.

20:23. This proverb is a variation on 20:10.

20:24. This juxtaposition of human plans and intentions with God's sovereign action in human affairs is not meant to discourage planning but rather to guide it.

20:25. The metaphor of the trap should register with anyone who has made a promise, only later to wish he or she had been more careful.

20:26. To "winnow" is also to scatter the chaff to the winds, so wisdom is also power.

20:27. The image of God's light searching human interior spaces fits in well with neighboring proverbs on the interior life.

20:28. The same throne that winnows out evil is protected by love.

20:29. Time offers every young person an exchange; if strength is spent wisely, the return is a long life, symbolized by the gray head.

20:30. One can either acquire the capacity for discernment to discipline self or fail to learn discernment and suffer the discipline of another who has.

Application. The idolatry of sin is imagining we have ultimate authority to make our own way and therefore to exercise ultimate authority over our behavior, becoming a law unto ourselves. It begins in boasting, when our talk is bigger than the strength we actually have.

PROVERBS 21:1–31

Original Meaning

Yahweh Looks at the Heart (21:1–3). *21:1.* Just as water is directed by digging irrigation ditches and building dams, so the king's heart will follow Yahweh to establish justice.

21:2. Yahweh alone can determine what is known and what is hidden from a person's own self-perceptions.

21:3. The comparison does not demean devotional practices but does observe that it is easier to have sacrifice without right living than it is to have right living without religious practice.

Sins of a Proud Heart, Lies, and Violence (21:4–8). *21:4.* Haughty eyes and arrogant kings will be brought low, but kings who reject arrogance are promised a long dynasty.

21:5. Here "haste" is another form of laziness.

21:6. The "fleeting vapor" and "deadly snare" negate security, often expressed in Proverbs as a long life.

21:7. Those that refuse to do justice for others will have it done to them.

21:8. Character and deeds match more often than they do not.

Final Outcomes and Judgments (21:9–19). *21:9.* The humor in this proverb breaks up the seriousness of the sayings on pride and injustice.

21:10. How can a person centered only on self show mercy to a neighbor?

21:11. Even a naive person can learn from example.

21:12. Throughout the wisdom writings it is God who overthrows the wicked and frustrates the words of the unfaithful.

21:13. The "cry of the poor" may be their ever-present need or their response to a specific injustice.

21:14. Both lines of this saying emphasize the hiddenness of the bribe-gift, a sign it is given to pervert justice.

21:15. The picture of justice victorious in broad daylight is in view here as both the righteous and evil see the outcome.

21:16. The traveler who strays from the good path will not end up in a good place.

21:17. To love wine and oil and not the work that produces them is shortsighted.

21:18. The righteous are rescued from the trouble that rightly comes on the wicked instead of them.

21:19. Better to live without a house in the desert than in a miserable domestic situation.

Examples of Wise Moderation and Strength (21:20–23). *21:20.* This saying contrasts one who practices moderation and foresight and the fool who swallows everything in gluttony and shortsightedness.

21:21. In seeking these virtues, one also finds the three primary desires of the proverbs: life, prosperity, and honor.

21:22. The last Hebrew word translated as "they trust" is key, pointing out the confidence placed in strength and numbers and contrasting it with the wise person's trust in God.

21:23. It is harder to guard one's speech than a city.

Sins of Pride and Power (21:24–29). *21:24.* "Insolent fury" describes the rages that come on one who exercises no control over mouth and tongue.

21:25. How often laziness and gluttony go together!

21:26. If the righteous give without sparing, the giving goes beyond what one has to spare.

21:27. Evil deeds have been named "detestable" throughout Proverbs, so certainly the hypocritical sacrifices of a wicked person will draw the same response from Yahweh.

21:28. The discerning person will endure.

21:29. One attends only to the self and its preservation, the other attends to the larger picture of life lived uprightly and in harmony with Yahweh's creation and community.

Yahweh's Victory (21:30–31). *21:30.* The terms "wisdom," "insight," and "plan" may have military connotations that are made more explicit in the next verse.

21:31. The two proverbs name different but related errors. The first and most obvious is to go against God; the second is more subtle is to forget to thank God for victory and trust in one's own foresight and strength.

Application. Most of us are vulnerable to sins of omission. Even if we do not actively take advantage of the poor, we do often fail to hear their cries and act on their behalf (21:13). However, common to both is the principle of reversal, that what we do to or for our neighbors will eventually come back to us.

PROVERBS 22:1–16

Original Meaning

Proverbs about Riches and Consequences (22:1–7). *22:1.* The "good name" implies that good character will make itself known around town.

22:2. To make such distinctions is to dishonor Yahweh, the "Maker of them all."

22:3. The prudent, knowing the effects of evil, see it coming and hide, while the simple, not even knowing the danger, walk straight toward it.

22:4. "Riches and honor and life" comes to those who seek higher ideals and lower status.

22:5. One who is vigilant guards "life" (Heb. *nepesh*).

22:6. A proverb is not a promise; therefore, this one is no guarantee for any method of parenting.

22:7. Many commentators take this saying as a warning to the poor against borrowing, but perhaps a more general observation about the responsibilities of power is intended.

Proverbs about Speaking and Judgments (22:8–16). *22:8.* This version of "you reap what you sow" extends the idea of responsibility from Proverbs 22:7.

22:9. The attitude behind sharing with the poor has more in common with 22:2 than 22:7 and 16.

22:10. The proverb does not advocate the suppression of conflict, only unnecessary arguing.

22:11. The person who practices wise and good speech is welcomed by the king.

22:12. Yahweh not only judges how "knowledge" leads one to live, but he also "frustrates" wicked persons.

22:13. Although few real excuses are as wild or transparent as this one, the scene reminds readers that Yahweh can tell whether one's words come from knowledge or deception.

22:14. We would expect the one who falls into the pit of her words will incur wrath, but we get the reverse!

22:15. Better the rod used for discipline than a trap of sin and death—though this rod can also be symbolic of parents' teaching.

22:16. Oppressors wake up to find they have become one of the group they oppressed!

Application. Certainly, one of the most vexing problems awaiting address by the evangelical church is a moral climate that is at best only mildly disturbed by the growing gap between rich and poor. Yet this concern was first and foremost in the minds of those who produced the words of the wise and Proverbs. Yahweh takes up the case of those who have been crushed and plundered. Therefore, to respond as God does is to become an advocate for the poor, using whatever resources and authority are available to offer mercy and work for justice.

PROVERBS 22:17–23:35

Original Meaning

Pay Attention, Give Sound Answers to One Who Sends (22:17–21). *22:17.* A prologue of sorts includes a call to attention and motivations for learning, much like the prologue of 1:1–7.

22:18. The motivation in 22:18 envisions a synthesis, wisdom that is perhaps greater than the sum of the parts.

22:19. Knowledge and wisdom are not the source of one's confidence; teaching is to inspire trust in Yahweh, integrating intellectual study and faith.

22:20. For the first time in Proverbs, oral teaching has given way to teaching by means of text.

22:21. Verse 21 sets out a secondary goal, that is, to show how one might return reliable words in answer to one who sends.

Sayings of Counsel and Knowledge (22:22–29). *22:22–23.* "Exploit" in 22:22 is translated "rob" in other contexts, suggesting exploitation is one way to take what belongs to another. "Take up their case" (22:23) echoes the voice of the prophets, who portray Yahweh as judge, prosecutor, and executor.

22:24–27. The matched sections of 22:24–25 and 22:26–27 present familiar warnings about avoiding certain persons and practices, juxtaposing new motivations. A number of the proverbs warned against a "hot-tempered" person but describing this person's influence as a snare is new. The "pledge" was compared with a trap in 6:1–5, but here the teacher warns against repossession.

22:28. To move the marker for financial gain is to defraud those most vulnerable.

22:29. If earlier proverbs about the king stressed his responsibilities for executing justice and his capacities for discerning evil intention, these instructions give advice about working for such a person.

Deceptive Delicacies and Fleeting Riches (23:1–8). *23:1–3.* Putting a knife to the throat is not a threat of death but rather holding a knife to one's desire. We can allow "delicacies" (23:3) and the status they bring to cloud our judgment, tempting us to make them the goal of life instead of faithfulness and love.

23:4–5. Riches are also deceptive; therefore, one should not become weary in their pursuit but have the wisdom to know when to stop or show restraint (cf. 23:2).

23:6–8. Usually, a meal is a sign of hospitality and friendship to all who come by; yet there are other meals where either guest or host is tested, where motives other than friendship are present. Just as Wisdom offered a banquet of life and Folly a meal of death (9:1–18), so here food and appetite are used as metaphors for the attitude one brings to riches and the kind of teaching one desires.

Teaching and Traditions (23:9–14). *23:9–11.* Just as one should take care in speaking at the table, so one should take care when speaking to a fool who will not listen to instruction. The fatherless do have kin, after all, just as the poor have a defender in Yahweh.

23:12–14. A renewed call to attention repeats the words "heart" and "ears" from 22:17, this time with a call to "apply" oneself (23:12). The teaching of 23:13–14 is not an endorsement of corporal punishment as much as a call to the responsibility of teaching and correcting.

Signs of Wisdom That Bring Parents Joy (23:15–21). *23:15–18.* Two conditional sayings work individually and as a pair in 23:15 and 16. The teacher's whole "inmost being" rejoices at this meeting of wise heart and upright speech.

Wisdom first looks to Yahweh, then toward the prosperity of others with improved vision. "Envy" and "zeal" are both derived from the same Hebrew word (*qanah*) for an intense feeling of love and desire.

23:19–21. The warning combines fears of gluttony and laziness; the "drowsiness" (23:21) may come from the wine or simply from love of sleep. This teaching calls for restraint when encountering food and drink that fail to nourish or satisfy, as well as independent thinking in the face of peer pressure.

The Seductions of Sex and Wine (23:22–35). *23:22–25.* Having warned the young learner about negative influences, the parental teachers again speak of gladness at their son's wise choices. This young man honors his parents by honoring their teaching. Parents' rejoicing is in each of the four lines.

23:26–28. To give the heart is to entrust it to the one who will direct it through *teaching*, although some affection is certainly involved. The motivation for this charge is the danger of the prostitute or harlot, whose promiscuous ways are a deep pit. Just as those who are not careful to watch their ways can fall into a pit, so they can be easy picking for predators who wait along the back roads.

23:29–35. A series of rhetorical questions begins with general descriptions of woe and sorrow and ends with the hangover problem of eyes that are bloodshot. If we have a riddle in (23:29), the answer is provided: The person who has these problems is the one who lingers over wine (23:20). The braggart claims he is not hurt, but in reality he is addicted to this form of self-abuse.

Application. We can practice regular reflection about our activities and pursuits as well as the effect they have on our inner lives. A first step in the right direction is taking an inner inventory of our pursuits and the satisfaction they bring. This is not to say that only what satisfies is good; rather, it is an attempt to turn things around, to seek what is good because it satisfies. In our age of plenty, when many middle- and upper-class people do not struggle for basic needs and economic survival, if a pursuit is not satisfying, this can be a sign that we are into something bad.

PROVERBS 24:1–34

Original Meaning

Advocacy, Not Envy (24:1–12). *24:1–2.* The choice of companions often begins in the desire to emulate. But what kind of company can one have with people who think and speak about trouble?

24:3–4. While warnings against greed and threats of danger have been associated with wealth in other parts of the book, here the motivations are like those of Woman Wisdom, who holds life in one hand and wealth and honor in the other.

24:5–6. The might of the wise is gained through the teaching of others. The theme of strength in 24:5 does not become victory until the last line.

24:7–10. If guidance and counsel help one win a battle, the fool has none to give at the gate, where public decisions and judgments are made.

Verses 8–9 are linked by the catchword "scheme." Strong language links this figure with the detested mocker, one who makes plans as though there were no one to call those plans to account. The one who falters in 24:10 is one who has little strength.

24:11–12. There are no valid excuses for standing idle when it is possible to help. The fourth line restates a common theme, that Yahweh will pay back according to deeds. What is new here is that the threat is directed at the reader, not some wicked third party.

Trust and Hope, Not Violence or Gloating (24:13–22). *24:13–14.* A pair of sayings compare the sweet taste of honey and its nourishment to the goodness of wisdom that builds, fills, and fortifies a house.

24:15–16. "Lurk like a thief" reminds readers of the violent men of 1:11. The righteous may fall, but they rise again—not like the wicked, who are brought down for good.

24:17–18. In each case, one seeks or is made glad by the misfortune of another. Yahweh would rather have us rejoice over rescues and leave matters of judgment to him.

24:19–20. Being righteous is one thing, but the next step is trusting in that ultimate judgment when life does not move in predictable ways.

24:21–22. The dangers of bad association have been highlighted throughout the words of the wise; this final word assures us that there is no alliance that can withstand the wrath of God and king.

Diligence and Honesty, Not Partiality (24:23–34). *24:23–26.* The image of blindfolded justice continues this ancient tradition that a case is not judged on the basis of who is involved (or what they can do for the judge). Verse 24 expands this idea. Verses 25–26 present a picture of those who judge rightly. The kiss in the ancient world communicated loyalty as well as affection.

24:27–34. An extended teaching on fields and their upkeep frames a pair of prohibitions against false witness and vengeance. The proverb about work in 24:27 recommends putting first things first. It is folly to have a house to live in but no provisions to live on.

This direct imperative to work is framed with two sayings about lips, honest and deceitful (24:26, 28). The first speaks to the aggressor who hopes to take advantage of the legal system, and the second speaks to the victim. Yahweh oversees the matters of justice and reward, forbidding any attempt to take vengeance into one's hands. Diligence demonstrates wisdom and is essential for successful living. Negligence exacts a high price.

Application. These teachings remind us that in choosing wisdom we acquire a home and stores aplenty, that we have food that is delicious and nourishing, and that these come with responsibility to watch over our fields and work them. If we teach against envy, then we must also teach about the house and its treasures; if we speak against vengeance, we must also speak about the rich taste of honey and its future hope; and if we speak against laziness and irresponsibility, we must speak about the blessings that come on those who are diligent to speak and judge rightly. In other words, we who preach and teach are charged to point toward the fullness and richness that so many pass by in their pursuit of vanities.

PROVERBS 25:1–28

Original Meaning

Kings and Honors (25:1–7). *25:1.* Hezekiah and Solomon are remembered for their wonderful exploits of leadership but also for leaving kingdoms that did not survive them.

25:2. The wise hide truth to invite seekers to investigate. It is a king's duty to search out matters of truth in human affairs.

25:3. Just as no one can fathom all there is to know of Yahweh, so the heart of the king is never fully known, perhaps even to himself.

25:4–5. No one prefers a corrupt government any more than anyone wants impure silver; it is in this sense that the throne is "established through righteousness" (25:5).

25:6–7. Let the king bestow honor. If you claim it for yourself, you will be put in your place.

Neighbors and Testimony (25:8–10). *25:8.* Just as one should not move too quickly to a high position, so one should not be too quick to contend that one is right before a judge.

25:9–10. If it is foolish to go before legal authorities too quickly, it is also possible to speak rashly when the time comes to argue a case. The result is shame plus a bad reputation that never goes away.

Rulers and Words (25:11–15). *25:11–12.* A word of reproof or correction must find a receptive listener. The sender must be careful not only to craft persuasive words but also to exercise discernment in determining when it is best to speak.

25:13–15. A proverb about the power of persuasive speaking is preceded by a pair of sayings about personal reliability, all three together showing the difference between speaking faithfully and falsely. The soft tongue that breaks a bone speaks of quiet determination that persuades, not a sign of weakness but power.

Neighbors Good and Bad (25:16–20). *25:16–17.* Just as too much of a good thing becomes the opposite, so friends and neighbors are good, even sweet, as long as visits are not too frequent or too long.

25:18–20. This trio of sayings uses experiences of pain to describe people who cannot be trusted or counted on. In each case, what is needed is lost or missing. Each action is inappropriate and therefore hurtful.

Waters and Words (25:21–26). *25:21–22.* But what does it mean to heap burning coals on the enemies' head? Three of the four lines are clear, so we should keep Yahweh's reward for kindness to enemies at the forefront as we try to make sense of a puzzling image. The search for a similar practice in ancient Near Eastern culture has discovered a variety of practices:

Coals placed in a tray were carried on the head as a gift to the poor or as a sign of repentance; burning coals were also placed directly on the head to punish, to heal wounds, or to relieve suffering for a person dying of rabies!

25:23–24. Secret words about others will be heard and produce results. Anger and quarreling may drive an embattled spouse out of the house.

25:25–26. A pair of similes compare good and bad sources of drinking water to the positive and negative experiences of life. To people who relied on messengers, good news from far-away was like cold water on a parched throat. One expects a spring to provide drinkable water and the righteous to remain true. Whether the "righteous who give way to the wicked" is a victim or someone who fails to stand, the outcome for those who need clear water is the same.

Honey and Honor (25:27–28). A person who does not know when to stop eating honey or to refrain from seeking accolades is a person who lacks self-control. Self-discipline is self-defense.

Application. Restraint and reflection are the sages' remedies for self-centered and unwise living. On a personal level I know I need to cultivate the habit of pausing to ask whose interests are being served in a particular decision or action. Too often I have found that actions I thought were loving were not seen the same way through another person's eyes.

PROVERBS 26:1–28

Original Meaning

Fools and Sluggards Wise in Their Own Eyes (26:1–16). *26:1.* Snow does not come in summer, rain is not welcome during harvest, and so glory should not come to a fool.

26:2. The metaphors of fluttering sparrows and swallows depict birds one never sees at rest (23:5); so also an "undeserved curse" never lands.

26:3. If a rod is recommended, it is assumed that the fool is no smarter than beasts of burden.

26:4–5. This famous pair of contrasting sayings show that it is not always easy to know how to make a fitting response to a fool. Some argue the point of the teacher's dilemma: Although one should not have to dialogue with the fool, it is the sage's job.

26:6. It is not clear whether the harm described is done to the sender or to others, but the former is more likely.

26:7. Anyone can memorize a collection of sayings and apply them inappropriately.

26:8. Giving honor is not only inappropriate but also dangerous.

26:9. When spoken by a fool, a proverb has little effect.

26:10. Sending a fool creates danger for all.

26:11–12. The dog's actions make holding on to folly seem particularly distasteful. As dangerous as the fool might be, there is more chance that the fool will learn than someone "wise in [his] own" eyes.

26:13–16. These verses present a series of vignettes on the sluggard, three that demonstrate his laziness, and the fourth to show that like the fool, he is "wiser in his own eyes" (23:16). Verse 13 reports what the sluggard *says*; verse 14 indicates that he *does* even less. The picture of a hand that is buried or hid in the dish suggests a deep scoop, but even this effort is left off since now he is too tired to bring it back to his mouth (26:15). Although the proverbs have associated the sluggard's behavior with folly, he does not see it that way, and perhaps this is his greatest folly of all.

Quarrelers and Deceivers (26:17–28). *26:17–19.* Continuing the theme of 26:17, the extended saying of 26:18–19 depicts one who does not take seriously the ruinous effects of his actions.

26:20–22. Three proverbs about gossip, quarrels, and damage extend the theme of 26:17–19. Taken together, one can see the need to excise both the behavior and the person who stirs up quarrels, just as one takes away wood to put out a fire. Morsels of "gossip" (26:20) have a negative influence on one's mind and heart.

26:23–25. Three proverbs develop the theme of deception from 26:18–19, describing it as an attractive surface that hides the ugliness lying beneath. Speech can be charming, even beautiful, but it conceals seven abominations.

26:26–28. Three examples of evil deeds that backfire begin with the ultimate end of deception. When malice is exposed, everyone will know. Getting caught in a trap set for others is a common motif of Psalms as well as Proverbs. So also, the false tongue not only hurts others, but it also hurts itself because it leads to its own ruin.

Application. If we are to apply the principles of these proverbs to our own day, we may as well admit that at times we have all played the fool or the troublemaker to some degree. Who has not sought honors by dropping a name? Who has not said an unkind word, hoping to prove that we are right or better than the one singed by the fire? The problem is that we are messing with the basic chemistry of communication and are in danger of blowing up the lab, hurting others as well as ourselves.

PROVERBS 27:1–27

Original Meaning

Praise and Rebuke (27:1–6). *27:1–2.* Lips were made for building up one another with teaching and correction, not for building up ourselves.

27:3–4. We may think ourselves burdened by the folly of others, but who among us has not been knocked down by our own jealousy?

27:5–6. Reproof is painful but profitable. Friendship sometimes brings praise and sometimes wounds, but those wounds are also faithful.

Family and Safety (27:7–12). *27:7–8.* The theme of reversed expectations continues into this pair of proverbs about rejection. One whose hunger is satisfied literally walks past or tramples honey, while someone who strays from home is like the bird that leaves the safety of the nest.

27:9–10. The sweet smells of incense cause the heart to rejoice, just as the sweetness of a friend and neighbor is better than one's own counsel. Neighbors, like family, are precious and should not be rejected or abandoned.

27:11–12. If this son learns wisdom, his father will rejoice. A father is also glad to see his son exercise prudence.

Bad Neighbors and Quarrelsome Wives (27:13–16). *27:13–14.* A proverb pair about treating strangers like neighbors and neighbors like enemies shows that friendly actions are inappropriate when they do too much.

27:15–16. Little can be done with a contentious person.

Iron to Iron, Face to Face (27:17–22). *27:17–18.* Two proverbs speak about good relations with neighbors and employers. The comparison with striking iron points out the need for two to hone the edge. Those who tend a garden enjoy its produce. It is by serving well *and* keeping the employer sharp that servants receive the "honor" (27:18).

27:19–20. The parallel use of body parts draws a contrast; if kind hearts can reflect one another in friendship, it is also true that greedy eyes can devour another's life.

27:21–22. The NIV translation suggests that the way we react to the praise of others reveals our motives, honorable and dishonorable. Verse 22 presents the point that folly cannot be separated from the fool, for it is too deeply ingrained.

Care for One's Animals (27:23–27). *27:23–27.* Unlike the collection of proverb pairs that precedes, these last five verses make up an extended poem, notable for the pastoral imagery. The person is to know the "condition" (literally, "face," 27:23) of the flocks, just as the wise study and know the human heart. One never arrives at the place where work is not necessary.

Verses 26–27 describe the payoff for diligence. While some interpreters think the message of the poem was directed to landed young men called into service at the court, the metaphor for attentiveness and diligence applies to many areas of life.

Application. Stories in broadcast and print media make it seem as though one either lives for self, like a robber baron, or for others, like Mother Theresa. We do not want excess; we want to have "enough." Still, in the backs of our minds, we wish there could be a little more, just a little more to take the edge off our financial worries and make things a little easier.

It is therefore hard to see when that legitimate concern for well-being turns the corner into avarice, the immoderate desire for possessions that makes them into gods. The proverbs and poem of this chapter help us to see that there is an approach to life and possessions that sets them in proper perspective so that we realize that we need one another, not things we can own. It is possible, then, to have "enough" for ourselves and also to have plenty to share.

PROVERBS 28:1–28

Original Meaning. *28:1.* Righteous confidence is contrasted with the fear that plagues the wicked, always looking over their shoulders as they flee.

28:2. People will rebel unless led by a person of wisdom.

28:3. The natural image of torrential rain that flattens grain is clear.

28:4. The righteous not only keep their ways straight but make sure others do the same.

28:5. This saying contrasts those who "do not understand" with those who "understand all things" (author's translation) because they seek Yahweh.

28:6. In both cases the only essential possession is integrity.

28:7. A person can be discerning or disgraceful.

28:8. Ill-gotten wealth goes to one who will give it back to the poor.

28:9. If you won't listen to God, God will not listen to you.

28:10. This proverb presents a vivid picture of an evil person leading another along a path strewn with his own traps, reminding readers of 1:17–18.

28:11. We would expect the contrasting poor person to be humble, with downcast eyes. Instead, this person has eyes to see through the bravado.

28:12. People know that the character of a leader will have consequences for them.

Fates of the Wicked and the Righteous (28:13–28). *28:13.* People may forgive a person who truly changes.

28:14. A hard heart knows no correction and therefore no change; it will hide, not confess.

28:15. In Proverbs, the king's wrath is like the lion's roar (19:12, 20:2); here the roar is like a wicked person ruling over the helpless poor.

28:16. This saying presents a contrast between the tyrant

who rules with "great oppression" (author's translation) and the good ruler who "makes long the days" (author's translation), that is, has a long life.

28:17. Sins of blood start a justice in motion that cannot be derailed.

28:18. The blameless are "kept safe" (or "saved"), although the protector is not named.

28:19. This saying is nearly identical to 12:11.

28:20. If one seeks the goal of possessions alone, even more will be lost.

28:21. People will risk great penalties for small amounts of gain, even a piece of bread.

28:22. Acquiring wealth just to hold onto it makes a poor goal for a life.

28:23. The honest tongue earns favor, not a "flattering" one.

28:24. Parents who have given of their means and very selves to their children deserve care when it is their turn in their later years.

28:25. Greed brings "conflict"; trust brings prosperity.

28:26. Although it seems logical that we know our needs and can look out for our own best interests, nothing is further from the truth.

28:27. The key is to be able to see need, but many prove unwilling to try, shutting their eyes.

28:28. The wicked will perish and not from natural causes; after that, the righteous will thrive.

Application. However true it is that Christians are first called to live as an alternate community to the ways of the world, balancing radical identification and distinction, Christians are also called upon to vote and serve as community leaders. They will be (or should be) asked to lend voice and muscle to the business of living in neighborhoods, towns or cities, and nations. While the church exists as a model of what might be, challenging and inspiring the rest of the community, its members are also faced with the daunting prospect of stating their views on matters social and political and of lending support to local civic bodies and service organizations.

PROVERBS 29:1–27

Original Meaning

Cycles of Thriving Righteousness and Wickedness (29:1–16). *29:1.* The ox that would not bend its neck for a yoke became a symbol for recalcitrant Israel.

29:2. Wisdom and folly are never experienced in isolation, but their effects are especially pronounced when practiced by someone in authority.

29:3. This saying pits love of wisdom against prostitutes, similar to personifications of wisdom and folly throughout the book.

29:4. "Justice" is the highest responsibility of the king.

29:5. It is not clear whether "their feet" goes with the neighbor or the flatterer. If the first, the contrast is between the smooth words of flattery and the harsh capture of the net. If the latter, the proverb is like the saying "what goes around comes around."

29:6. The net spread out for others (29:5) is also the sin that traps the trapper.

29:7. "A righteous one knows the rights of the poor, a wicked one does not understand such knowledge" (author's translation).

29:8. This saying is the first of a series on the theme of speaking and listening (29:8–12).

29:9. The wise may calm anger but not the rage of a recalcitrant fool.

29:10. The evil intent of the "bloodthirsty" who hate integrity and the contrast with those who love it are clear.

29:11. The wise give their words beauty and persuasiveness.

29:12. The implied admonition urges persons in authority to weed out the word of falsehood before it takes root.

29:13. The imbalance of power is restored with one look at the One who gives them the ability to see each other.

29:14. Association with Yahweh who judges the poor faithfully is strong, as is the theme of stability.

29:15. The parent who does not give needed correction risks receiving unwanted shame.

29:16. In its literary context, this proverb on corporate character is equally applicable to courts and households.

Discipline of Sons and Servants, Justice for Nations (29:17–27). *29:17.* This proverb stresses the positive aspect of discipline; the son who receives "discipline" gives peace and delight.

29:18. This proverb is too limited in its teaching if it is only taken as support for church programs and goal setting.

29:19. Servants were expected to follow orders, and at times more than a verbal prodding was necessary.

29:20. The observation on the dangers of rash speech is simple enough, but to say that there is more hope for the fool is to use the hyperbole to show how serious the matter is.

29:21. Discipline provided early on will lead to a happier ending.

29:22. As wrath goes uncontrolled, so does its damage.

29:23. Better to be called up higher than put lower.

29:24. To hold back testimony when it is called for is a crime of complicity.

29:25. One can show kindness without fear since Yahweh rewards.

29:26. The proverb lends assurance for those times when no justice from a ruler can be obtained.

29:27. "Detest" communicates more than a feeling of mutual distaste; instead, the two ways of life are totally incompatible.

Application. Many believe that most decisions about behavior are a matter of personal choice. The faulty logic of this thinking was exposed by a series of antidrug ads. Young people looked into the camera and said, "I killed a drug runner"; "I bribed police"; "I helped so and so die of an overdose." By participating in the drug trade, all sorts of unspeakable crimes take place.

PROVERBS 30:1–33

Original Meaning

The Oracle of Agur (30:1–14). *30:1–5.* Agur's message begins with confession of ignorance: "For more beast than man am I" (30:2, author's translation). The beast was a symbol that acknowledged the unique capacity of human nature to perceive spiritual matters and to be in relationship with its Creator. To lack such perception is to be like an animal that is only concerned for its food and safety.

Four questions in 30:4 initiate a series of "fours" that runs throughout the chapter. Many commentators find here a motif of ancient Near Eastern literature; common to many human attempts to ascend to heaven is the great gulf that separates the human and divine realms. The questions imply that God acts to create and maintain a world, but God also speaks (30:5). That pure word shows that God is a "shield" to those who take refuge (30:5).

30:6–10. The series of "fours" continues with four appearances of the phrase "do not" ("do not add"; "do not refuse"; "do not give" [NIV "but give me only"]; and "do not slander"). Verses 5–6 are linked around the theme of God's words. Any additions to those true and faultless words will prove false. To talk when we should be listening is never wise.

The theme of falsehood continues into 30:10, for slander of a servant is probably to bring a false report. Such bad talk brings a curse. In sum, then, four prohibitions against false speaking follow the proclamation that God's word is fire-tested, true, and flawless.

30:11–14. Each of the next four verses begins with the Hebrew word *dor* ("generation"; NIV "those who"). Each describes "one of a generation" who rejects the way of wisdom, the opposite of God's intention for humankind. God's intention is shown by the sons of the wise woman of worth, who praise her (31:28).

Numerical Sayings (30:15–31). *30:15–17.* The leech's twin daughters are repulsive and sobering metaphors for a greedy generation. The first of the following "three–four" (30:15b) sayings brings together four more leech-like consumers that will take all they can.

30:18–20. The second of the "three–four" sayings brings together four phenomena about which the speaker says, "I do not understand" (30:18), echoing the words of Agur's lament. All four creatures move in ways both wonderful and mysterious through God's created order. Each knows how to make its way in its part of the created order: Eagles don't try to swim, snakes don't try to fly, and ships that go on rocks are destroyed. Therefore, men or women who despise the mystery of love and sex and move outside of its boundaries are like those who step out of their place in created order. The contrast between the wonder of 30:18–19 and the contempt of 30:20 is striking.

30:21–23. Just as the "way of an adulteress" (30:20) is out of step with the created order of wisdom, so the four items listed threaten to overturn that order. In ancient Near Eastern thinking, the earth shakes when the natural order is disturbed. In the view of the sages, there is an order to life, and as long as it is just and fair, it should not be disturbed.

30:24–28. As in the other "three–four" sayings, the statement of the number also offers the key to the puzzle that follows. Readers are to ask: How are these things small and yet "wiser than the wisest?" (author's translation). These small creatures teach great lessons about being a people, asking ancient readers: "What kind of people do you want to be—strong, led by a king? You don't need that as much as you need wisdom."

30:29–31. The final "three–four" saying names things "stately in their stride"; in slang, they are "walking good." The use of "king" in 30:31 brings together its occurrences in 30:24–28, suggesting that we understand these brave and stately four in light of the small and wise four. Again, power comes not from strength or numbers alone but from wisdom.

Epilogue on Pride and Strife (30:32–33). Fools either exalt themselves or plan evil, and the two are not that far apart. The remedy in Hebrew is short and direct: "Hand over your mouth!" (30:32). Speech is for defending others, not for plotting and speaking evil. The three lines of 30:33 are linked by the repetition of the translation "produces." There are three churnings, but perhaps the lack of a fourth signals that the advice can be heeded, and that folly can be averted in favor of wisdom.

Application. Courage like this comes from having a healthy assessment of who we are—limitations, sins, and all—but also in being able to see who God is as well. Pride subverts both, driving us to gobble all we can in insatiable hunger and to speak in ways that churn up anger and violence. Agur's oracle looks in another direction, at first in despair of having looked for wisdom without finding it, but then turning to the One who inspires wisdom by revealing a vision of himself.

PROVERBS 31:1–31

Original Meaning

Kings Speak Out for the Poor (31:1–9). *31:1–2.* These sayings are not really Lemuel's but his mother's, a reminder that women serve as teachers throughout the book.

31:3–5. The concern over the distractions of harems and drinking and the resulting impaired judgment were common throughout the literature of the ancient Near East. The ideal king protects the poor and defenseless, caring for them instead of amassing wealth and building great palaces.

31:6–9. The poor can drink and forget their poverty, for they are the ones who suffer. Behind this recommendation to give drink is a concern for responsible execution of judgment and care. In my view, the "wine" (31:6) is both a real comfort and a symbol of the fair judgment and rule that a king gives to his people. Moreover, the offer of drink is not the only solution; we would be more concerned about this counsel were it not followed by the call to speak out for the poor.

The Woman of Worth Brings Her Husband Good (31:10–31). *31:10–18.* The "wife of noble character" in 31:10 has been mentioned before. We can also translate "a *woman* of noble character," observing that she enacts more roles than wife. "Who can find?" (31:10) communicates that faithful character is valuable because it is rare.

From the start we are given a clue that somehow this poem is a summary of all that has been said about wisdom in Proverbs. The first of the praises describes this woman's character as a treasure. Her husband recognizes her worth, for he "lacks nothing" (31:11). What some would take by force comes to those who seek what is most important. In sum, this woman works and trades night and day to provide for herself and her household; she is as wise as the evil characters of chapter 30 are foolish and self-centered.

31:19–20. Her palms take hold of the spindle and open themselves to the needy. The wordplay creates a contrast between the hands that close on her tools of production but open to share of her rewards with the poor.

31:21–29. The husband and household appear twice, first as beneficiaries, then as those who praise her. The benefits are presented in chiastic fashion, drawing attention to the honor that comes to the husband.

A No fear of snow—household *clothed* in scarlet (31:21)
  B She is clothed in *linen* and purple (31:22)
    C Husband respected at the gate (31:23)
  B′ She makes and sells *linen* and sashes (31:24)
A′ Laughs at future—she is *clothed* in strength and dignity (31:25)

The wordplay in 31:25 clothes her in "strength and dignity." The husband is not the only one who speaks wisely, for she "opens her mouth in wisdom" (author's translation, 31:26a), just as Lemuel was instructed in 31:8–9. The "faithful instruction" (31:26b) is both true to the tradition and to the marginalized people it serves. If the husband speaks for justice at the gates, she does the same in the home. If the start of the poem lauds the good she brings to her husband, the end rewards it with praise, from her children and her man.

31:30–31. More important than any beauty, charm, or even work is the fear of Yahweh, which shapes all that this woman is. What else can we readers do but join in giving her "praise" (31:30)?

Application. Perhaps the most important aspect of the conclusion to the book of Proverbs is that both Lemuel's mother and the woman of noble character teach and model the orderly life of wisdom. Let us be taught not only to live sober and responsible lives but also to "speak up for those who cannot speak for themselves" (31:8). Let us manage our affairs so as to provide well for family and stranger. In this way the public concerns of the queen mother and the private concerns of the wife of character come together.

ECCLESIASTES

INTRODUCTION TO ECCLESIASTES

Christians are called to live in this world that God has created and loves, even while anticipating a world to come. We are no less in need, therefore, of advice about living (as well as about waiting), about the pitfalls of wealth and wisdom, about the folly of attempting to control our destinies, about the importance of living life fully and daily in the certain knowledge of death, about the centrality of God to the good life, and about our response to puzzlement and pain. Ecclesiastes, as part of the Scripture that is given us for shaping faith and life, offers us such advice, correlating as it does with extensive sections of the New Testament that also touch on such themes.

Ancient tradition held that Solomon, "son of David, king in Jerusalem" (1:1b), was the author of the book. There are good reasons, however, to believe that Solomon was not himself the author. Even in the "Solomonic" sections of the book, it seems evident from verses like 1:16 and 2:7, 9 that the "real" historical location of the speaker in the book is at some distance from the era of Solomon. Instead, modern scholarship attributes the work to a speaker that identifies as "Teacher" or "Qohelet" (based on the Hebrew word *qohelet*) in 1:1a.

BOOK OUTLINE

I. Introduction (1:1–11)
II. Wisdom, Pleasure, and Joy (1:12–2:26)
III. A Time for Everything (3:1–22)
IV. Achievement and Oppression (4:1–16)
V. True Worship (5:1–7)
VI. The Pursuit of Wealth (5:8–6:12)
VII. Wisdom Is a Shelter (7:1–12)
VIII. The Universe Beyond Our Grasp (7:13–29)
IX. Dealing with an Unjust World (8:1–17)
X. Living in the Face of Death (9:1–12)
XI. The Way of Wisdom (9:13–10:20)
XII. The Mysterious God (11:1–8)
XIII. In the Days of Youth; Qoheleth Was a Wise Man (11:9–12:14)

ECCLESIASTES 1:1–11

Original Meaning. The Hebrew word translated "Teacher" in 1:1a is *qohelet*. Qoheleth addresses his gathered listeners, the Israelites. He is "son of David, king in Jerusalem" (1:1b). Qoheleth himself is presented to the reader by still another person—the one who transmits his words to us and who makes himself known to us explicitly in 12:9–14. There is no conflict between Qoheleth and his editor. Both wish us to understand, as the foundational truth on which Qoheleth premises all his words, that life is "like a breath" (NIV "meaningless," five times in 1:2 and thirty-eight times in the book).

The point is not that human activity intrinsically, whether in the realm of thought or action, is "meaningless" (1:2)—Qoheleth clearly does not believe this. The emphasis lies not on whether certain ways of being or doing possess *meaning in themselves*, but on whether these ways of being or doing succeed in *achieving the goals* that humans often set before themselves. Qoheleth thinks not. The human attempt to impose self on reality in this way is a foolish undertaking, which can only end in pain and frustration.

The world is an essentially unchanging place, unaffected by the "generations" that come and go (1:4). The wind blows (1:6). The water cycle remains the water cycle (1:7). All these various natural phenomena toil steadily away, around and around, going about their appointed tasks without variation (1:8); there is "nothing new under the sun" (1:9), no "thing" (1:10) that breaks the rule of regularity and predictability seen in "all things" (1:8). The human participants in the drama of creation are relatively insignificant when considered in this context.

Application. To all those who try to gain from life, whatever it is they claim to be doing, Qoheleth presents stark reality—reality that does not change simply because we wish it to but remains fundamentally as it is in spite of all that comes under the heading "progress." The more things change, the more they stay the same. This life on earth is intended to have as its center the God who created everything and who holds everything in his hand. He calls us to love him and our neighbor and to care for the garden he has entrusted to us.

ECCLESIASTES 1:12–2:26

Original Meaning

Wisdom as an Instrument for Understanding the World (1:12–18). The first-person testimony of the-speaker-as-Solomon tells us a different story from the one we might have expected on the basis of the narrative account of his life. The passage comes to us in two sections (1:12–15 and 1:16–18), each with its own statement of what Qoheleth set out to do and what he discovered, and each with its own concluding proverb. The first section essentially tells us of the role that wisdom played in leading Qoheleth to the point of view expressed in 1:1–11, while the second offers some comments on wisdom itself.

If the first part of 1:12–18 has viewed wisdom as an instrument through which to view reality and has found it useful in coming to a clear perception of the world in all its futility, the second part (1:16–18) now turns to consider wisdom in itself. Although wisdom and knowledge are good and useful, they paradoxically bring with them "sorrow" and "grief" (1:18)—not least, one suspects, because they enable people like Qoheleth to gain particular clarity as to just how evil the business of living can be.

Joy, Work, and Profit (2:1–11). Gladness of heart, joy, pleasure—it is not that these things are not good in themselves in Ecclesiastes. Yet Qoheleth has discovered that the *pursuit* of them with the hope of gain is just as pointless as the pursuit of wisdom and knowledge for that purpose. He treads one path with his body while taking another with his mind, hoping in his intoxicated state to experience the full depths of "folly" (2:3) and to arrive at discernment.

The overall intention of the experiment and the means by which it was conducted having been described, its detail is now laid bare. The king set out to transform his environment and thereby to facilitate his enjoyment of life. He put superhuman effort into what he did. Houses, vineyards, gardens, and parks are all mentioned. The enormous wealth of the king is portrayed (2:7–8) in terms of unparalleled numbers of herds and flocks, hoards of treasure that have been gathered in part from "kings and provinces" (2:8) who have either been plundered or have brought tribute, and unspecified numbers of human beings devoted to the task of pleasing him.

While engaged on the experiment on its inside, as it were (and even though mentally detached from it to some extent), he found joy as his reward; but considering it coolly from the outside after its completion and bringing to it the mentality of the balance sheet, he pronounced it all a "chasing after the wind" (2:11). The reward was not an adequate one when measured by the aspirations that drove the experiment.

Further Reflections on Wisdom (2:12–16). The question arises in Qohelet's mind: What does he "gain by being wise" (2:15)? This question once again concerns ultimate, extrinsic gain, rather than the kind of intrinsic profit that is plainly acknowledged as a reality in 2:13. Not only can wisdom not offer mortal beings release from the evil business of living (1:12–18); it also cannot solve the problem of death.

From Despair to Satisfaction (2:17–26). The reality of death overshadows Qohelet's life to the extent that he now confesses his hatred for life (2:17). Life lived from such a perspective is full of pointlessness (2:17, 19, 21, 23), despair or hopelessness (2:20), misfortune (2:21), pain, grief, and restlessness (2:23). Those who seek control of life only and always "chase after the wind" (2:17), that is, grasp after what cannot be grasped. Death is the ultimate statement of mortal lack of control, which must always pass to another who will benefit from his predecessor's input (2:19). Only God has ultimate control, even though mortals may briefly possess some degree of it.

It is madness and folly, indeed sin, to seek for profit from life; and the consequence is misery for those sufficiently perceptive to see the pointlessness of it. Wisdom, by contrast, acknowledges God and not the self as the center of existence and gladly embraces the limitations of the creature set within the larger, massive reality of creation. Reality having been embraced, it is possible to know joy.

Application. It is not difficult to understand the application of Ecclesiastes 1:12–2:26 when it is remembered what the reality of our modern culture is that underlies its confident, abrasive tone, and its pretensions to divinity. The reality is the widespread sense of futility and weariness that Qoheleth himself describes in this passage—the first-person testimony that contradicts the story that is usually told in public, and which provides a very different perspective on the culture. Empiricism has undeniably brought great gains to humanity, but it can only partially grasp what is true, and it cannot tell us the meaning of things.

ECCLESIASTES 3:1–22

Original Meaning

Human Experiences as a Tapestry of Times (3:1–8). The opening verses picture human experience as a tapestry woven of "times." The totality of life is captured here, utilizing the literary figure of merismus, in a series of opposites. It is not always clear whether the pairs are to be understood literally or metaphorically. If there are some difficulties in 3:1–8 in understanding precisely what is being said in the detail, it is important to remember that it is not the individual elements of themselves that are important but the elements taken together as an overall description of life.

Life in the Context of the Creator (3:9–15). "What do workers [or better, simply "the human actor/doer"] gain from their toil?" (3:9). We have returned to the perspective of the person interested in profit or gain from life, for whom the whole business of life is evil. What is evil about life from this point of view, of course, is that it cannot be controlled and manipulated so as to render the rewards sought after.

The problem facing the human actor is that there is another Actor whose actions are decisive ones: "He has made everything beautiful . . . no one fathom what God has done" (3:11). This Creator has made everything "beautiful" in its time—probably in the sense of "beautifully fitting," given the emphasis of 3:1–8, rather than in the sense of "intrinsically beautiful." There is an elegance about how life works, as time succeeds time.

Yet Qohelet's point is this: Mortal beings cannot "fathom [literally, "find"] what God has done from beginning to end" (3:11). If it is true that only God truly understands and controls the times and that the human sense of time is insufficient for the task of truly understanding or controlling them, then it is unsurprising that those who continue in the quest for gain from toil will only know frustration. As in chapter 2, however, there is an alternative course of action open to mortal beings. It is to give up on the quest for profit and to reorientate life toward the Creator.

Only when what is done under the sun takes account of and responds to what is done *by God* can it be other than pointless. To struggle for anything other than harmony with this reality is to act insanely and with the utmost futility. Instead, the only rational response to reality is to "fear him [God]" (3:14), issuing in a life centered on God.

Divine Control and the Reality of Death (3:16–22). In the closing verses of chapter 3 we discover some new lines of thought that are nevertheless clearly related to what has gone before. Verses 16–17 pick up and develop the theme of divine control of "the times," using it to address the question of injustice in the world; and 3:18–22 returns to the theme of death as an ultimate reality, which renders the striving life futile, now developing this theme in relation not just to wise and foolish human beings (as in 2:12–26) but to human and animal life.

We are to live life not in the hope of gaining some advantage over the rest of creation with which we share dust and breath but simply for its own sake, finding joy in it and receiving that joy as itself the reward that living brings us. When the dust settles and we arrive out of breath at the end of the journey, that will be all that remains. This was the insight that "Solomon" first gained in 2:10, even while journeying at that time on a different path.

Application. We cannot truly understand or control "the times," and so we are cast back on God who holds our times in his hands and alone knows the span of our individual days. Yet the God on whom we are cast is good, and he is *for us* (Rom 8:31). Our response to his grace and blessing should be to seize the time that we have and live it well and joyfully to his glory and praise.

ECCLESIASTES 4:1–16

Original Meaning. In the Bible, oppression involves cheating one's neighbor of something. It involves making an unjust gain, including the profit made from interest on loans. It is the abuse of power, financial and otherwise, perpetrated on those who are not so powerful and are indeed vulnerable—the poor, widows, orphans, and strangers. Thus, it is often associated with violence and bloodshed in the Old Testament and with the denial of rights and justice.

Power, economic or otherwise, is not to be abused; people, whether less powerful than we or not, are not to be treated as objects out of which profit can be squeezed, but as human beings made by the same God who created us all. Human beings as we find them "under the sun" (4:1) are, however, in rebellion against God and thus generally careless of their neighbor. The world is, therefore, a miserable place for many people, who live without anyone to comfort them with the real prospect of change in their circumstances. More fortunate than both the living and the dead are those who have not yet been born. They are blessed who have not yet looked on it.

The fuel that feeds the fires of this human striving after gain is envy that drives us on in the mad rush after gain. In pursuing out of envy the neighbor above us on the ladder, we inevitably step on the head of the neighbor below us. As disastrous as this is for the people who are trampled on, it is also futile for the person who is upwardly mobile at their expense.

The life of striving is fundamentally anti-neighbor. The point of life, when viewed from this perspective, is to get ahead of one's neighbors rather than to participate in community with them. Verses 7–8 paint the picture of a person "all alone" (literally, "having no second person," 4:8), without "son or brother" to inherit his wealth. An alternative vision of the world involves at its heart the notion of community (4:9–12).

The closing verses of 4:13–16 show that poverty with wisdom is better than advancement with folly. Advancement all too often brings with it the loss of the self, as people lose touch with where they have come from. It brings with it even greater toil than before, but no greater thanks.

Application. The religious individualism that lays great emphasis on a person's relationship with God but little emphasis on a person's social, economic, political, and religious relationships with other people has little in the end to do with the Bible. The Bible is about *persons-in-community*, whether in the Godhead of Father, Son, and Spirit, or in the church, or in the world at large. The proper goal of the Christian is to be found in right relationship with God, neighbor, and God's world *now* and in the future, which will include by God's grace a future beyond death.

ECCLESIASTES 5:1–7

Original Meaning. In worship, the first task of the worshiper is to "go near to listen" (5:1), with a view to obeying the divine voice (cf. the same language in Deut 5:27). The wise person comes before God carefully and with due attention, for such a person, unlike the fool, knows that God is really God. The wise person listens, therefore, rather than speaks (Eccl 5:2).

The making of a vow is a particular form of speech and is the focal point of 5:4–6. Temple vows were a common feature of Old Testament worship and involved promises to consecrate such things as sacrifices or money to God in return for granting a request in prayer. The temptation presented to the worshiper was to avoid fulfilling the vow once the prayer had been answered.

Application. Silence is undervalued in the noisy, intrusive world that most of us inhabit. Noise deafens us to reality. Silent reflection—deliberate inactivity—is necessary if we are to regain perspective and remember who God really is, what that really means, and what, therefore, the church is *for*.

ECCLESIASTES 5:8–6:12

Original Meaning. As in Ecclesiastes 4:1–16, we turn from oppression to consider its root causes. Envy was the focus of 4:4–6; in 5:10 Qoheleth fixes attention on the love of money itself. Like all false gods, money never fulfills those who pursue it but only feeds the insatiable desire for more.

The world of the rich is indeed a world of "abundance" (5:12), which does not in fact satisfy (5:10) and permits no sleep. The world of the worker, by contrast, is one in which there may be less consumption, but at least he has peace of mind that permits restful slumber. The pursuit of profit brings not only oppression to others but also damage to the self.

This is not the only grievous evil that exists, however. Qoheleth has seen wealth both hoarded and lost in the course of the wealthy person's involvement in the "evil/miserable business" (4:8) of life. Unlike the driven man of 4:7–8 who has no family to leave an inheritance, the consequence is that this man who has a son but loses his wealth from misfortune is unable to pass on any inheritance; he has literally "nothing in his hand" to give him (5:14). For those who pursue gain, then, and who oppress the poor in doing so, there is no contented consumption but only dissatisfaction, restlessness, frustration, affliction, and anger.

With this reality in mind, Qoheleth returns to his earlier advice about how to gain or find contentment. It is good for a person to eat and drink and to "see the good" (author's translation, NIV "find satisfaction," 5:18) in all toil. Wisdom lies in accepting these things from the hand of the good God as they come to us as an aspect of the times he gives us. As we adjust ourselves to the reality of the universe and to the reality of God who made it, it is possible to find peace of mind and joy in the midst of our lives.

It is not that it is impossible to know God and to know joy even in the midst of wealth and possessions (5:19–20). Yet what Qoheleth himself seemingly gives with one hand he immediately takes away with the other, as he returns to reinforce what he has said in 5:8–17. The fact of the matter is that all too often God gives someone wealth, possessions, and indeed honor and yet does not grant him the ability to "enjoy them" (literally, "eat them," 6:2). A stranger "eats" them instead. This verse echoes the preceding passage (cf. 5:11, 14), even though we are not told here precisely why someone else, not the wealthy person himself, consumes what he has. We are not dealing here with another "evil" (6:2) but are merely exploring further the reality already presented—an evil or bad situation that multiplies. It is possible to have all that the heart desires (6:2) and yet to find no joy in it.

The paradigm case is the man who (presumably theoretically and for emphasis) has a hundred children and lives many years. Long life and abundance of offspring are characteristic indicators of God's blessing in the Bible. Yet of what use is the mere possession of multitudes of days and offspring if a person cannot be satisfied with these good things, if "he cannot enjoy his prosperity" (6:3)?

Verse 7 sums up the madness of it all: toil undertaken in pursuit of things to consume, yet powerless to fill the gaping void that is human appetite. Although the Hebrew of its second part might better be translated as "what advantage does a poor man have who knows how to meet life's challenges" (author's translation), verse 8 is best taken as the question to which 6:9 is the answer. What is the profit that wisdom has over folly? It lies in understanding that we should rest content with what lies before us and resist the temptation to wander off in search of more (6:9).

Reality has once again been brutally exposed by Qohelet. As he brings this section of his reflections to a close (6:10–12), he underlines that it is something that must be accepted rather than debated. There is simply no point in multiplying words, therefore, in a vain attempt to change the nature of reality. Acceptance of reality is a necessity. "For who knows what is good for a person in life" (6:12) other than God, who creates the good and blesses mortals with it? It is certainly therefore not a rational course of action to seek anything other from life than harmony with creation as it really is and with God who made it thus. Life lived in any other manner can only end in tears.

Application. The words that often drown out the word of God are those of the advertisers—those great prophets and evangelists of mammon. Perhaps the first step toward defiance of the idols of mammon among Christians is conscious resistance to their rhetoric and myth-making; yet we will not even realize that the advertisers are telling us lies about reality if we do not take steps first to deal with the hold that the idols they worship also have on our hearts.

ECCLESIASTES 7:1–12

Original Meaning. The reality of death lies at the heart of the opening verses (7:1–6). Recognizing the brevity and preciousness of life, we should live life *seriously*. In this spirit Qoheleth commends to us in 7:2 mourning rather than feasting. There is a way of living that is *centered* on feasting, on the pursuit of joy, on empty laughter and singing. This is life lived in denial of the true nature of things, hoping to push reality to the margins by flooding the senses with sensation and drowning out quiet contemplation with noise.

By contrast, there is a way of living that is centered on reality. From the point of view of focusing the mind on the business of living, the day of death is the "better" (7:2) of the two. Depth is, in fact, a characteristic of the person who lives in the light of reality, just as superficiality is the mark of the life in denial. The wise person knows the value of things. Verses 11–12 sum up the value of wisdom for "those who see the sun," that is, for all human beings. To embrace wisdom is to embrace life itself, along with all the gifts that may be bestowed with life—length of days and riches and honor. But to embrace and pursue riches and honor of themselves is to head for disaster.

Application. We live in an escapist culture. The materialist mansion that we as modern people have constructed for ourselves has become for many an unbearably oppressive prison whose spiritual emptiness is all too apparent. The sensible course of action is to visit the archives, find the building plans, and begin a discussion of what has gone wrong. The alternative choice is escapism, that is, the modern attempt to have our materialist cake and to eat it just to drown its taste with strong wine. The healing of our pain of which the Bible speaks requires us to confront reality rather than to seek to escape from it.

ECCLESIASTES 7:13–29

Original Meaning. Possessing wisdom is far from enabling complete mastery over existence, and it certainly does not solve the problem of death. The wise person accepts the limitations that God has set on mortal life. Thus does Qoheleth continue to balance appreciation for wisdom with critique of its potential and, no doubt, of the way that it was sometimes used within his own culture and time.

Wisdom is not a key that can be used in independence of the Creator to unlock the secrets of the universe, to shape existence after mortal desires, and to control life. Thus, the wise person accepts the world as he or she finds it, receiving both good and bad from God and acknowledging that either might lie in the future (7:14).

The surprising advice of 7:16–18 should be understood in this context. Wisdom is clearly attractive to many people, as the book has shown, precisely because it appears to offer the possibility of control over life. Yet this represents, for Qohelet, a profound misunderstanding of the nature of things.

Verses 19–22 further explain the message of 7:15–18. Although wisdom may be pursued from bad motives and its pursuit may result in bad consequences, it is in itself a good thing. It is vastly superior, in fact, to political or military power, which is dependent on wisdom for its success. Yet the wise person will still be a flawed person because he or she is a human being.

With 7:23–25 we move toward the conclusion of the whole chapter. Although wisdom in itself may not be found and a comprehensive grasp of reality cannot be attained, some individual findings are possible. Verses 26–29 recount some such findings.

The precise way in which we are to understand the second part of 7:28 in this context is a matter of debate. The overriding perspective of the whole book of Qoheleth is, of course, resolutely male, as has been most recently demonstrated by 7:26 (it does not speak of the man who is a snare to women). Qoheleth's findings thus represent a drop in the ocean of experience, and they are a male drop at that.

Application. We should remember fundamentally that God is God and we are not. When we forget this, we make the basic human mistake. The consequences of this mistake, when human power is wielded in defiance of divine power, is disaster for other people, for creation more generally, and eventually for ourselves. The only safe kind of human wisdom is wisdom rooted in God and centered in Jesus Christ, which thus knows its limitations and boundaries.

ECCLESIASTES 8:1–17

Original Meaning. As the focus of the passage now shifts more explicitly to the wise man at court, the emphasis falls in the first instance on obedience (8:2). This much is clear, even though the best way precisely to understand 8:2b–3 is not. Taken together the verses should be read as advocating withdrawal from the royal court rather than opposing the king, which may involve the uttering of an oath by way of indicating the seriousness of the opposition. The wise man will think more than twice before opposing the king in this way. He will not rush to speech and action.

The wise person is advised to disguise his true feelings while in the king's presence, for "a king's word is supreme" (8:4). The theme of power is prominent throughout the passage. It may be true that wisdom makes one wise man more powerful than ten rulers, but the truly wise person knows not to flaunt his wisdom when confronted by a foolish ruler, for there is a serious risk if he does so (8:5).

Verse 7 reaffirms the lack of control that human beings have. Various images of mortal lack of control are then given in 8:8 to underline the point. These truths are general ones that might apply to anyone and in particular to the wise person, who may be tempted to think that he can change things by his words and actions that cannot in fact be changed for the moment.

Verses 9–10 then bring the whole section to an intermediate conclusion. The present "time" that is under consideration is characterized (8:9) as that in which a man exercises power that results in "hurt." The statement in 8:9 is ambiguous (literally, "there is a time when a man exercises power over a man for hurt to him"), and perhaps deliberately so in the light of the preceding verses. Does the "hurt" fall only on the king's victims, or ultimately on the king himself?

The final sentence of 8:10, referring to futility, is better taken with what follows it than what precedes it. It is one of the unfortunate results of divine patience with human beings in their sinfulness, which may mean that "the sentence for a crime is not quickly carried out" (8:11a) that foolish hearts are "filled with schemes to do wrong" (8:11b).

The wicked may sin massively and yet live a long life. This is admittedly puzzling if God is good and just and truly governs the universe. The clear implication of his thinking must be that there is some "time" beyond the "times" of life in which wrongs can be righted and imbalances corrected; yet as we have seen, Qoheleth is agnostic about life after death (3:18–21). Unable finally to resolve the puzzle himself, he then characteristically advocates that the reader get on with life and not worry too much about the details, which lie with God. That is precisely the direction in which he moves in 8:15–17.

Application. One of the most serious idolatries is "God and country." It has milder and stronger forms. In its milder form, there is only a subtle, but certainly dangerous, elevation of the nation-state to a position in one's life in which it is spoken of in the same breath as God. It is only a short step to the stronger and more deadly form, however, in which God is enlisted in support of one's country, one's culture, and one's way of life.

ECCLESIASTES 9:1–12

Original Meaning. The point of 9:1 is to emphasize that the righteous and the wise, perhaps against their expectation, will experience in life both "love" and "hate," which may simply be another way of saying "good and evil." Their experience is in this respect no different from that of the wicked and the foolish—*everyone* has a mixed experience of life. The point is then developed in the remainder of 9:2, as those who share both the common life and the common fate are enumerated—the "destiny" in question (as in 2:14) being death, as will become clear.

We should understand 9:3 as somewhat reiterating, in reverse order and with emphasis on the negative, the contentions of 9:1–2. There is a common human destiny (death), and during life both the righteous and the wise are by no means untouched by misery and folly. In the terms used in 9:1, they know hate as well as love.

The unsatisfactory life, at least in degree, comes to an unfortunate and absolute end. Anyone who is currently among the living may be certain that he or she will know some misery and then death. It is the fact that the living thus knows *something*, however, whereas the dead know nothing (9:5), that brings to Qohelet's mind what looks like another traditional proverb: "A live dog is better off than a dead lion" (9:4). His interest here, so far as we can tell, is only in the contrast between life and death in the single regard that the living are conscious while the dead are not.

With this stark description of reality articulated, Qoheleth now turns once again to advice for the living (9:7–10), picking up the thread from 8:15. Life is indeed a mixed bag; death awaits us all. What is the wise response? It is to seek joy where it may be found.

Verses 11–12 provide a tailpiece that underlines the message of 9:1–10. Life's outcomes (other than death) are not predictable in their specifics; good and bad come to all. The human situation is somewhat akin to that of fish or birds. A fish does not anticipate the moment of capture in a "cruel" net (9:12), nor does a bird have any idea that in a moment it will find itself entrapped in a snare. Thus, do evil or bad times come on us "unexpectedly" or suddenly (9:12).

Application. We are people much given to prediction, and prediction implies control. We imagine we understand the world; we can see how it is going. Yet we are constantly surprised. We live in a world in which cause and effect are often visibly in connection with each other. I press a light switch, and the light comes on. This promise of control is a seductive one and lies at the heart of much of the advertising with which we are every day deluged. To control our lives—so it is suggested—we need only buy this product, eat this kind of food, and avoid that sort of drink. No longer need we be the victims of our frailty and mortality. The idea that we have any such control, Qoheleth and other biblical writers remind us, is a myth. It is true that the universe is an ordered place and that cause and effect are features of its reality. Yet the universe is not a machine. It is a personally created and governed space, whose Originator and Sustainer is the living God.

ECCLESIASTES 9:13–10:20

Original Meaning. The implication of 9:15–17 is that wealth and social class are far more impressive to people than wisdom, and that people will listen more readily to people of great wealth and high social class than to a poor but wise man. This reaffirmation of wisdom's value leads to a number of sayings concerning wisdom's value, many of them dealing with leaders and with foolish or wise speech.

In chapter 10, verses 2–3 develop the general point about the bizarre and different choices that people make in life. The inner lives of the wise and foolish persons are set in completely different directions. The fool has no idea, in fact, of his destination and how to get there. The launching pad for this whole section was the contrast between the wise poor man and the rich and foolish "ruler"—the focus in 10:4–7.

Verses 8–9 have in common that they concern unforeseen happenings in which a person suffers hurt. The completion of everyday tasks results not in satisfaction and well-being but in injury. The context suggests that the figure of the angry and foolish king with his unpredictable policies is still at the forefront of Qohelet's mind.

Verses 12–14 speak further about the wise man's speech in contrast to the self-destructive words of the fool, which begin in folly and end in wicked and verbose madness. The fool's words devour him.

The closing verses of chapter 10 envisage two contrasting scenarios (10:16–17): a land whose king was previously a "servant" and, being ill-equipped for government, presides over a ruling class that is dissolute and neglectful of responsibility; and a land whose king himself originates from the ruling classes and who keeps a firm hand on the reins of government.

It is not surprising that 10:20 goes on to speak of reviling the king and cursing the rich, for in a country governed in such a way, the temptation to indulge in such bad-mouthing would be great. Yet it is unwise to think such thoughts, for thoughts can easily spill out into words, and even words spoken in private may find their way back to the rich and powerful, who can do the subject damage.

Application. We live in a world where information is widely privileged over wisdom. We are bombarded with "facts" and expected somehow to accommodate all of them and to integrate them into our lives. But we are like the readers of a complicated novel who read all the sentences yet cannot grasp the plot. The truth is that we have never known so much and understood so little. We live in a world, in fact, in which wisdom is routinely suspected, mocked, and despised.

ECCLESIASTES 11:1–8

Original Meaning. The opening verses (11:1–6) remind the reader of our human inability to control the times, emphasizing the lack of knowledge that mortals possess. In the light of all that we do not know, Qoheleth offers his advice. In the midst of uncertainty, but in the expectation sooner or later of trouble, various kinds of actions are to be considered wise. Verse 1 counsels long-term investments. Verse 2 advises distribution of risk.

What these same readers should *not* do is described in 11:4. They should not try to beat the system, attempting to find some patterns in the complex combination of predictable and unpredictable events that will enable them to manipulate reality to their own ends and profit.

In 11:6 Qoheleth advocates a course of action opposite to that described in 11:4. Given that reality is the way it is, the wise course of action is not to refrain from sowing and reaping but to engage vigorously and continuously in these activities, knowing that some projects will succeed and some will fail.

It is the theme of living life to the full while not being unaware of the darker side of things that is taken up in 11:7–8. There is no reason to think that one cannot "enjoy" (11:8) life under the sun. Yet all will not always be sweetness and light. It should never be forgotten that there will be dark days as well.

Application. Modern people tend to view the movement of history, as far as human beings are concerned, as being from primeval swamp to divinity. The beginning was unpromising, but quite against expectation the forces of evolution have propelled us along to a point where we stand on the verge of greatness. The Bible presents us with a rather different view of history. It replaces the myth of endless rising up toward divinity with the harsh fact of fallenness, as the mortal seeking immortality brings with it alienation and wickedness. It knows of technological progress but also knows that it can coexist with barbarism. Whereas those who tell the first story look ahead to boundless possibilities stretching into the future, the Bible knows of a sudden ending to everything, as God's sovereignty over his universe is displayed in an ultimate way. Here is the reality that must be juxtaposed with our modern myths.

ECCLESIASTES 11:9–12:14

Original Meaning. Qoheleth now turns to the young man who, because the time of youth is also brief (11:10), has a still shorter period in which to make the most of his opportunities.

In view not only of death (12:6–7) but also of the slow and steady intrusion of death into life as people age (12:1–5), the young man is urged to live life to the full (11:9–10). This is not an invitation to hedonism. Yet joy *is* indeed to be pursued. A life marked by brevity need not be a life of futility, if life is embraced for what it is and joy is pursued therein.

The Creator encompasses this whole section, just as he encompasses the whole of life. That the bowl is golden and the cord from which it hangs is silver speaks of the preciousness of the life that is thus given by God and then in due course taken away (12:6–7). Verse 8, which brings our section to a conclusion, is virtually identical to 1:2, thus bringing all the words of Qoheleth to a conclusion as well.

With the closing verses of Ecclesiastes 12 we once again hear the voice of the person who has been reporting the words of Qoheleth to his "son" (12:12) and to us. Qohelet's consistent advice throughout the book has been to live joyfully and reverently before God in the midst of what is often a complex world, believing that God himself will judge every human work. The words of Qoheleth are designed so that we may live well before God, reverencing him and bearing always in mind that the universe is a moral place in which there is accountability for the way in which we spend our days.

Application. The biblical narrative—and all the texts that are bound up with it, reflect on it, and comment on it—provides us with the map we need both for our own journey through life and for helping others find the best path. Qoheleth paints a corner of the map. He suggests to us that the young person needs to be told about the reality of decay and death and what this signifies about God and ourselves. This is important because young people often think themselves indestructible. The young person also needs to be told, however, about the goodness of God and to be encouraged to live responsively to that goodness. This involves virtue, of course, but it also involves joy. It is important to speak about both.

SONG OF SONGS

INTRODUCTION TO SONG OF SONGS

It has been the common Jewish and Christian view up until modern times that Solomon wrote this song. Yet Solomon only appears in this book in third-person references. Moreover, when the essentially negative character of most of the material mentioning "the king" is recognized, the case for Solomonic authorship is further weakened.

The heading itself can signify that the song *concerns* Solomon. In Song of Songs, the focus of attention is on his famed possession of women. This feature allows the biblical author to explore love and sexual intimacy and to present to us a particular vision of the world for consideration.

BOOK OUTLINE

I. The Lovers Presented (1:1–17)
II. Springtime in Palestine (2:1–17)
III. The Terrors of the Night (3:1–11)
IV. A Man Enraptured (4:1–5:1)
V. The Lovers Entranced (5:2–6:10)
VI. The Dance of Delights (6:11–7:13)
VII. Love Strong as Death (8:1–14)

SONG OF SONGS 1:1–17

Original Meaning. The best of biblical songs opens with the words of the female protagonist, expressing a passionate desire for her lover. In 1:4 the woman seems in part to identify herself with this wider group of female admirers, while in part distinguishing herself from them.

The second line of 1:4 is better understood not as expressing a desire but as referring to a past action: "The king brought me into his chambers" (author's translation; NIV "Let the king bring"). Evidence will accumulate as we move through this song that the king and the lover are certainly *not* to be identified.

Our speaker's attention has moved from her beloved man to a wider circle of women and then back once again at the end of 1:6 to her beloved. In 1:7 she wishes to know where she can find him, so that she can go directly to the spot, for she fears otherwise that she will be mistaken for a prostitute.

The vulnerability of the woman is also implied in the man's response to the woman in 1:9. Pharaoh's chariots were typically drawn by stallions hitched in pairs; a mare placed among them would have caused great disruption and distraction, as her scent or mere presence was detected. Both the woman and the man are aware of the likely consequences in terms of unwanted male attention, should this "most beautiful of women" (1:8) wander aimlessly through the countryside.

It seems that we have three main characters rather than simply two.

1. There is the woman, who has come to the royal court yet longs to return to the outside, where her special friend is to be found.
2. There is the king, who inhabits the inside world of the court and knows the woman (perhaps sexually, although this is not explicit) as a member of his royal harem.
3. There is, finally, the man who is to be found in the outside world, represented by grazing lands, vineyards, and forests. He is certainly romantically and sexually (although this is still only implicit) involved with the woman.

Application. The Song of Songs does not speak in favor of sexual repression. But neither does it speak in favor of sexual license and the kind of pursuit of "rights" (by men or women) that in the end destroys all humanity. The sexual intimacy of this song is intimacy in the context of commitment—the kind of commitment that in actuality and in mutuality gives up "rights" in pursuit of relationship.

SONG OF SONGS 2:1–17

Original Meaning. The woman compares herself in 2:1 to two flowers, and her lover responds in 2:2 by agreeing with her self-description, and possibly even praising her more highly than she herself does. This affirmation from her beloved now leads the woman into an extended reflection on her love for this man who chases after her, woos her, and delights—but exhausts—her (2:3–13). The sign (2:4; NIV "banner") that the man hangs is "love," indicating that love is the defining activity in which the man and the woman engage.

As the lovers embrace, the woman (or possibly the man) addresses the puzzling aside in 2:7 to the "daughters of Jerusalem." Because of the devastating and overpowering results of love, they should ensure that it is awakened only when the timing and circumstances are right.

The scene now changes as the imagery of the gazelle is

developed in 2:8–17. The gazelle is swift and athletic as well as beautiful, and he speeds across the mountains and hills toward the woman who waits for him (2:8–9). He desires her to come out and be seen.

To this plea that the woman should emerge from the shadows and the safety of her home and fly away with her lover, the words in 2:15 are best understood as a female response. The "vineyards" in 2:15 are the very women whom men would like to persuade to come outside, and the "foxes" are presumably those men intent on sexual conquest. If the woman's lover and his friends really do wish women to come out into the countryside, then, they are invited first to ensure their safety.

In 2:16–17 the lover's hopes have been realized, and he is invited in all his athletic beauty to bestride "the rugged hills" (2:17)—hills cut by a deep valley. These are most naturally understood in the context as referring to the beloved's breasts. The lovers are together for an extended period and revel in each other's company.

Application. Christians are the heirs of a long-standing tradition that has characterized a spiritual person as someone who disguises and or trivializes his or her own beauty, and perhaps even comes to deny it or hate it. The Song of Songs, especially chapter 2, offers the church both challenge and healing. It challenges false dichotomies between the earthly and the heavenly, demanding that we give up all notions that beauty is somehow incompatible with godliness and even with God. It legitimates the enjoyment of and the mutual embrace of beauty as an aspect of the enjoyment and the embrace of God, and it encourages the affirmation of each other in our beauty.

SONG OF SONGS 3:1–11

Original Meaning. The major interpretative question concerns the precise relationship between the two parts of the chapter. The dream of 3:1–4 bespeaks her fear of loss, and even a longing to return to the safety and security of her youth. The vision of 3:6–10 bespeaks her resentment of royal possession and her longing for release from royal coercion.

A good case can be made for taking Song of Songs 3:6–11 as a dark and bitter satire concerning Solomon and his string of sacrificial female victims. Verse 6 is an allusion to a victim who lies on the "altar," which is Solomon's bed. She is not moving across a (real) desert in the direction of Jerusalem. She is arising from the royal bed. To name the royal bed a desert is to contrast most forcibly the lovemaking that happens there with the lovemaking that happens elsewhere in this song, which is so routinely associated with fertility and abundant vegetation.

The first part of our chapter concerns an individual woman who is in love with an individual man and initiates an anxious search for him. There is, by contrast, no true intimacy experienced in the desert, which is the extraordinary royal bedchamber. Her purpose is to offer a stark contrast between her relationships with the two men already introduced in chapters 1–2. She is an eager participant in one of these relationships and a reluctant victim in the other.

Application. Sex is often bound up in this troubled world with power and its abuse. That which was gifted to us so that we could witness through it to the Love that governs the universe has come to symbolize everything that has gone wrong with human relationships in the world. The need that many men appear to have to dominate and to conquer women sexually is still a marked feature of our world. The Song of Songs lauds romance while reminding us not to be romantic about a world in which coercion and violence all too often mark human affairs.

SONG OF SONGS 4:1–5:1

Original Meaning. The return after the terrors of the night to the quiet normality of the relationship described in chapters 1–2 is signaled immediately by the return to familiar language in 4:1, whose opening words are exactly those of 1:15. It is perhaps significant, after the impersonal sexual activity implied in 3:6–11, that the lover should begin with his beloved's eyes, even though he cannot see them clearly; for to look into the eyes is to encounter a person, not simply a body.

It is the beloved's unique, individual beauty that transfixes him in its totality (note "altogether" in 4:7), as he considers first her head and neck. Only after he has surveyed this scene does he move on to still-familiar territory (4:5–6), mentioning those breasts that have been alluded to already in 2:17, in the context of a browsing in the lilies and an intimacy that lasts "until the day breaks and the shadows flee" (4:6). She is not to him merely one woman among many, coveted for sexual charms. She is the one and only woman for him, a person to be looked in the eyes.

The woman who is to Solomon only one among many daughters of Jerusalem—readily available and coerced to join him in his desert-prison—is to her lover an expansive and fertile landscape, magnificent, flawless (4:7), and, as we will see, self-possessed. She is to be affirmed and enjoyed rather than controlled.

The woman's full participation in this relationship and her personal control over this participation is underlined in 4:8–15, as her inaccessibility to the man is also again emphasized. As a garden she is unparalleled. At the same time, she is also a spring that waters the garden. Both the garden itself and its water supply are described in 4:12, significantly, as "locked up." Entry can only be attained by those who possess permission or a key.

The hope is expressed that the wind will blow on the garden, sending its fragrance out into the countryside and guiding the lover to find it as he searches for his beloved. Verse 1 of chapter 5 reports the resolution of the whole situation. The man finds the garden and consumes what is within.

Application. We live in a world saturated by sex while desperate for love. True erotic love is in short supply in it. Eros focuses on the particular woman, the particular man—the beloved himself or herself. In the midst of the reality of the sexualized and depersonalized world (represented in Song 3:6–11) in which men and women question their unique worth and beauty, experience assaults on their sense of self, and know deep alienation, eros calls us to affirmation, respect, and intimacy—the antidote prescribed in 4:1–5:1.

SONG OF SONGS 5:2–6:10

Original Meaning. As the passage opens (5:2), the woman is asleep, even though her heart is "awake." She hears her lover knocking at her door. She seems at first resistant to his pleas. The woman's resistance does not last long. She goes to the door in response to his words, and, finding him already gone, she goes out immediately in search of him.

She does not find *him*, but the city watchmen do find *her*. They inflict violence on her and take away her cloak (5:7). The beating is followed only by a plea that others should help in bringing the lovers back together again.

Here the dream and the reality merge into each other. She has only dreamt of the loss, yet now, in an anxious state, she seeks her absent lover in reality and urges the daughters of Jerusalem to tell the man, should they see him, that his beloved is lovesick. It is their response to this request in 5:9 that leads to the woman's description of her beloved in 5:10–16.

He is a particularly striking man, one who stands out from the crowd. As chapter 5 closes, then, the man is still separated from the woman. But the daughters of Jerusalem at least have a description of him and an answer to their question about why the search is so important. As chapter 6 opens, we find the theme of separation briefly continued.

Yet now it transpires that the search is unnecessary and the fears that have come to expression in the dream are groundless. The woman knows where her lover is. He was never really lost to her. He is to be found in his own garden (6:2)—that female "place" where he is accustomed to spend his time and whose fragrances are complementary to his own.

The union of the two now permits yet another direct address by the man to the woman in 6:4–10. There is wondrous beauty, but it is beauty with an edge—an awesome loveliness that induces trembling as well as devotion. This aspect of the woman's beauty is picked up at the beginning of 6:5, where her eyes are said to "overwhelm" the man. He can hardly bear to look into them. The poem here is intended to remind the woman of her identity as far as those who truly love her are concerned; even the royal harem agrees with this description.

Application. We recognize in the ideal relationship that the Song of Songs presents to us the intimacy that we ourselves crave. But we are perhaps glad for the recognition in this song itself that real relationships only approximate at certain times and in some ways to the ideal. It is no different in our relationship with God. The Christian life is not a life of uninterrupted intimacy with God. We know of divine absence as well as divine presence. The truth about God, of course, is that he is not only transcendent but also very near; and not only near, but absolutely committed to his creatures; and not only committed, but proactive in wooing them.

SONG OF SONGS 6:11–7:13

Original Meaning. The garden the man visits in 6:11 is a fertile area bursting with the new growth of springtime. The woman herself is again clearly in mind, and the imagery may be deliberately chosen to evoke the intimate parts of her body. Certainly, the experience of going down to the garden (6:11) has a profound effect on the man, even if it is a little difficult to be certain as to what exactly that effect is.

Song of Songs 6:12 is widely considered to be the most difficult verse in the book, yet it is not impossible to make sense of it. Our best lead as we make the attempt lies in the mention of "chariots." Chariots in the Song of Songs speak of male desire for a woman. The man is pictured as out of control, either caught by surprise by the speed with which he joins the herd of "stallions" straining after the beloved or disconcerted by it and not quite recognizing himself in his own behavior. He begins his journey to the nut grove in possession of himself; he ends it possessed by the object of his desire.

With this interpretation of 6:11–12 in mind, it is now perhaps easier to understand 6:13, which begins with words spoken by a group and ends with a response to this group by the lover. The main point is that these men are looking for the woman to present herself before them for their pleasure and entertainment. The lover objects to this. He does not accept their right to view his beloved in the same way he has viewed her hitherto in this song.

He marvels at this woman. The man's eyes moved up from his beloved's feet to her head (7:1–6); now his body wishes to follow. He hopes that his arrival at his destination will lead him to the enjoyment of the aforementioned fruit. He also looks forward to tasting the "apples" (7:8), which are to be found still higher up this amazing, multifaceted tree, at the site of the beloved's mouth and nose. The man eagerly anticipates drinking the wine that flows there.

The woman is no longer a dancer observed but a lover aroused. No sooner has the man expressed his own wish to taste her wine than she responds with the fervent hope that he will indeed enjoy it (7:9b). She invites him (7:11–13) to go with her to those fertile regions of the countryside where his own desire for her was first kindled.

The "mandrakes" of 7:13 are plants with aphrodisiac qualities which are pictured as growing in this locale where lovemaking will take place. The "locale" is, of course, as much the woman herself as a "place" to which both lovers go, as it was in 6:11. This is particularly clear in the remainder of 7:13, which speaks of a "door" giving access to "every delicacy" that has been stored up for the man—an opening already hinted at in the opening of the blossoms in 7:12.

Application. Marriage has become the target of bitter humor and the focus of widespread suspicion. It is a dark pit into which we will certainly fall unless we, like the prodigal son, "come to our senses" in sufficient time (Luke 15:17). Perhaps the real problem with marriage, however, is not that we come to our senses too late but that we come to our senses at all. Love has drawn us out of ourselves and enabled us for a while and to an extent to behave unselfishly. It has even led us to a place in which we find ourselves making promises to another person about commitment.

God never "comes to his senses" in his love affair with us, withdrawing from us out of a desire for self-protection. The wounds that still mark Jesus's hands and side witness to his ongoing vulnerability and indeed to the true nature of reality, in spite of mortal claims to the contrary. "Reality" is self-giving Love. It is those who insist otherwise who dwell in unreality.

SONG OF SONGS 8:1–14

Original Meaning. The opening scenes of the Song of Songs concern a woman whose brothers have previously been angry with her and have made her take care of the vineyards (1:6). The only possible reason for the anger that could be found in 1:6 lies in her claim that she has not taken care of her own "vineyard." She is in love with a man, who is associated (like the vineyards) with the countryside. She now finds herself at the royal court and at the beck and call of the king—another male figure who interposes himself between the woman and her lover (as in 3:6–11). There are thus significant obstacles to be overcome if the lovers are to continue their relationship.

Chapter 8 draws many of these threads together as the Song of Songs comes to its conclusion. The obstacles to the coveted relationship are implied already in 8:1–5 in the references to those who would "despise" the woman for her kisses (8:1) and in the allusion to the king's bed (8:5a). The woman's brothers themselves apparently speak in 8:8–9, drawing a sharp retort from the woman in 8:10–12, which establishes her independence from both the brothers and Solomon. The passion of the lover's relationship, finally, is powerfully communicated in 8:5b–7, and the song ends with their words to each other as they transcend all obstacles and reaffirm their love (8:13–14).

In response to Solomon's claim to ownership of her as "vineyard," she responds most forcibly: "My own vineyard is mine to give" (8:12). Money has nothing to do with true love. She will not be possessed by any man other than the one she has chosen. She invites him to run like a gazelle or a stag over the spice-laden mountains, her breasts—an immediate invitation to sexual consummation.

Application. The myth that "death cannot stop true love" is a powerful one, which continues to captivate our souls. We have an insatiable desire to have it told to us again and again. Hollywood regularly obliges, knowing that the myth will always sell. Against all sense, human beings will not accept that fairy stories are only fairy stories. They have a deep need to believe them to be true, even as they have ceased to believe in any God who might reveal to them what truth is.

Our culture insists, against all the evidence, that good, in the end, defeats evil. Since it is at least a faith of some kind, romanticism is in the end much closer to the truth than nihilism, for it recognizes, however imperfectly, that Love lies at the heart of things. Only the gospel supplies the larger framework, however, in which its lacks can be made up and its errors corrected. For it tells us of a wooing God whose love makes sense of ours.

ISAIAH

INTRODUCTION TO ISAIAH

The book of Isaiah cites no other author than "Isaiah son of Amoz" (1:1) of Jerusalem, stating that he received his vision during the reigns of Uzziah, Jotham, Ahaz, and Hezekiah, that is, during the last half of the eighth century BC. This was the view of the church up until the eighteenth-century AD, when the scholars of the Enlightenment began to insist that all truth claims had to bow at the bar of human reason. The idea of multiple authorship of the book gained widespread scholarly acceptance as a result.

There is no a priori reason why God could not have used multiple authors to create a unified work of theology like the book of Isaiah. He is God, and he can do what he likes. But the question is, what does the book itself claim? Here there seems to me to be no question. The book claims to have come through one human mind, that of Isaiah ben Amoz, who lived in the eighth and seventh centuries BC and was gifted by God to see the future in such a way that it would forever demonstrate that Yahweh of Israel was not one of the gods. Yahweh's ability to tell the future in detail was the ultimate evidence that he was not a personification of the forces of creation but was the Creator of creation, the One who made it, continued to direct it, and would eventually redeem it.

BOOK OUTLINE

I. Introduction: God's Servants, Now and Then (1:1–5:30)
   A. God's Denunciation, Appeal, and Promise (1:1–31)
   B. The Problem: What Israel Is Versus What She Will Be (2:1–4:6)
   C. A Harvest of Wild Grapes (5:1–30)
II. A Call to Servanthood (6:1–13)
III. Lessons in Trust—the Basis of Servanthood (7:1–39:8)
   A. God or Assyria? No Trust (7:1–12:6)
   B. God: Master of the Nations (13:1–35:10)
   C. God or Assyria? Trust (36:1–39:8)
IV. The Vocation of Servanthood (40:1–55:13)
   A. Introduction: The Servant's Lord (40:1–31)
   B. Motive for Servanthood: Grace (41:1–48:22)
   C. Means of Servanthood: Atonement (49:1–55:13)
V. The Marks of Servanthood: Divine Character (56:1–66:24)
   A. Human Inability (56:1–59:21)
   B. The Lord Has Glorified You (60:1–62:12)
   C. Divine Ability (63:1–66:24)

ISAIAH 1:1-9

Original Meaning. The opening nine verses of Isaiah introduce the author and time of composition and summarize the charge against the people of Judah. We know nothing more of Isaiah than what is mentioned in the book. Chapter 6 makes it plain that Isaiah's ministry began in the last year of King Uzziah, about 740 BC.

The charges are those of rebellion (1:2) and corruption (1:4), which have resulted in desolation. Isaiah concludes (1:9) that only because of the mercy of God does the land continue to exist at all. In 1:5–8 Isaiah uses two graphic figures to depict the nation's spiritual condition. It is a sign of the depth of their rebellion that even with the evidence of judgment all around them, they will not turn back.

Application. Given the character of God as defined in the Bible and particularly in Isaiah, the alternative to rebellion is not mechanical obedience. For God has not prescribed every action for us. He has merely defined the outer limits beyond which we may not go without hurting ourselves. Just as the law of gravity does not render us mindless robots, neither does the law forbidding stealing.

ISAIAH 1:10-20

Original Meaning. In 1:9 the author says that it is only because of the mercy of God that Israel and Judah have not already been destroyed like Sodom and Gomorrah. In 1:10 he reinforces the comparison. If the Israelites will just do all the rituals more carefully, God will have to avert the coming judgment and give them his blessings. God responds to such an idea with dripping scorn in 1:11–15.

If God's people intend to take the way of increased religiosity as the way of solving their problems, they are taking a dead-end street. Why? A clue appears in 1:15. There is perhaps a bit of double entendre here. Yes, their hands are full of the blood of sacrifice, but they are also full of the blood of the innocent. They want God to bless them while they are the source of destruction and curse for those around them.

This becomes explicit in 1:16–17. What God wants is right

and just behavior, especially toward those who are helpless. Anyone can perform rituals, but the person who acts like God is the person who has entered into a life-changing relationship with him, and that is clearly what God wants.

In 1:18 God is challenging us to do our best thinking. If one way of acting brings destruction (1:20) and another brings not only forgiveness and restoration (1:18) but all the blessings of life (1:19), which choice makes the best sense?

Application. How easy it is to think that when we go to church regularly, read the Bible, pray, tithe, and don't engage in substance abuse, God somehow owes us something. Moreover, how easy it is to think that when we have done all these things, God should be grateful to have such faithful servants as us. Then, when difficulties come to us, we are angry at God, accusing him of being unfair after all we have done for him. It is easy for these behaviors to become substitutes for real biblical faith.

ISAIAH 1:21–31

Original Meaning. The prophet describes the present situation in a series of contrasts between what the Lord intended and what he actually got. He intended faithfulness and got harlotry; he intended righteousness and got murder. Instead of silver he got dross; instead of pure wine, tasteless dilution. Instead of rulers he got rebels; instead of defenders of the helpless, takers of bribes. True religion is not to be a dilution of godly and self-serving principles but a pure distillation of the former.

It is apparent that God's people considered themselves in a position of privilege. How it must have stung when Isaiah said that they were *not* God's favorites but his enemies, on whom he would be avenged (1:24)! But God's judgment is never intended to be his last word. The fires of the exile will be terrible and painful, but he will use those fires to fulfill God's intention for it (1:26).

Verse 27 shows an interesting double usage of "justice" and "righteousness." On the one hand, it is the justice and righteousness of God that will accomplish the ultimate redemption of Zion. But on the other hand, that justice and righteousness is available because people have repented of their own unjust and unrighteous behavior and have reaffirmed their willingness to emulate God's behavior.

This segment introduces a prominent theme of the book, that of "Lady Zion." In many ways Zion is seen to be the wife of Yahweh. The same imagery is to be found in Hosea and Ezekiel. Yahweh has betrothed himself to this lady, and he expects faithfulness and loyalty in return. Sadly, that is not the case. Yet in spite of that, God intends to find a way to woo her back to himself (Isa 49:15–21; 66:7–11).

One of the characteristics of Isaiah is that no matter how promising his oracles of salvation may be, he never lets them give his audience a false comfort. The good news is only available to those who make a radical turnaround. Those who persist in their rebellion *will* be destroyed (1:28–31).

Application. For almost two hundred years Christendom has been a dominant force in the West, especially in America. Now we see the church increasingly marginalized as a force to change society, even losing its ability to maintain its own identity. What should be our attitude? Surely Isaiah would say that we ought not to be trying to increase our power and influence. Nor should we be wringing our hands and crying, "All is lost." Rather, we should each be looking inward at our own lives and outward at a lost and broken world, confident God does not intend to harm us but aware he demands purity, selflessness, and love in all our relationships.

ISAIAH 2:1–5

Original Meaning. While Zion may not be the highest of the mountains, it is still *the* mountain where the one true God is to be found. This is the mountain where humanity should seek God. The reason they should do so at this place is because this is where God has instructions (torah) on how to walk in his ways. Thus, the nations do not come to Jerusalem for power or mystical union with the divine but in order to learn how the Creator intends his creations to live.

When the nations walk in God's ways, they will be submitting to his lordship. The concept of "judgment" in Hebrew (*shapat*, 2:4) involves the administration of the world, the establishment of governmental order. Thus, the expected outcome of God's word among the nations is harmony.

It is not just any god who is doing this, but the "God of Jacob" (2:3). He has condescended to become involved in the specifics of their lives in order that the world may know him and be redeemed. If that is true, then there is all the more reason why the family of Jacob (2:5) should walk in the light of the Lord. If it is true that even the gentiles will one day seek out God's ways so that they can walk in them, surely God's chosen people ought to be walking in those ways now.

Application. There are two dangers with a passage like this. One danger is to take it too seriously, and the other is not to take it seriously enough. The danger of taking the passage too seriously is that we try to create utopian societies where conflicts cannot occur. These inevitably fail. And the danger of not taking the passage seriously enough is that we simply relegate God's promises to an unknown future, thereby dismissing ourselves from any responsibility to see them fulfilled in any real way now.

So, what must we do? We must reaffirm the truth of these promises: God is the God of the whole world. We must not allow the world to define our faith for us. We must put God's ways into practice in our own lives. We must start living lives of grace and nonviolence. We must start reaching out to the poor and the helpless. We must give up our lust for riches and power.

ISAIAH 2:6–4:1

Original Meaning

General Statement of the Principle (2:6–22). Because Israel and Judah have abandoned the Creator, they are doomed to be terribly humiliated. The theme is addressed in three sections: 2:6–22, 3:1–15, and 3:16–4:1. The section here is marked by the repetition of a refrain in 2:11 and 2:17. God alone is "high and exalted" (cf. 6:1), and any attempt on our part to claim some of that glory for ourselves is doomed to fail.

Verses 6–10 begin with a sharp contrast to 2:5. Here Isaiah says God has abandoned the "descendants of Jacob" because instead of being filled with the ways of the true God, they are full of human wisdom (2:6). The East was understood as the origin of wisdom and learning. Undoubtedly the complex religious thought of Mesopotamia had a terrific appeal over against the simple and austere religion of Yahweh.

Not only have the Israelites filled themselves with the world's learning; they have filled themselves with the world's values: wealth and power. In Isaiah's time "horses" and "chariots" (2:7) represented the most powerful weapons of war available.

Placing a premium on human wisdom and human values issues in human self-worship, and the outcome is idolatry—conceiving of the divine in human terms. Again and again throughout the book, Isaiah mocks the practice of idolatry and questions how something made by us can possibly take care of us (17:8; 30:22; 40:18–20; 44:9–10; 46:5–7).

The cryptic injunction "Do not forgive them" at the end of 2:9 may be the prophet's cry to God not to be too gracious to these people who have filled themselves with all the wrong things. But it may also be his injunction to other humans not to let fellow humans too easily out of the consequences of their self-exaltation.

Verses 12–18 amplify this theme of the Lord's sole glory by contrasting him with every "high" thing in creation. That includes trees (2:13), mountains (2:14), fortifications (2:15), and beautiful, tall-masted ships (2:16). Nothing in all creation can compare to the Lord. He is another order of being altogether. So how can mere humans and the gods they have created hope to stand up to him (2:17–18)?

All this is brought to a blistering conclusion in 2:19–22. The prophet declares that those things that human hands created and human minds pronounced holy will be hastily cast away to "the moles and bats" (2:20), the most unclean of animals. The study of opposites in the section is thus brought to its climax. Our attempt to make humanity holy actually ends up making us unclean, and our attempt to give ourselves significance renders us worthless. Why would the Israelites put their trust in something worthless and unclean when they can put their trust in the living God?

Illustration of Human Arrogance (3:1–15). This section illustrates the theme of arrogance producing humiliation by looking at the leadership of Judah. The Judeans have idolized the great men, somehow believing that such people will deliver them from their difficulties. But God is going to deprive the people of their false security (3:1–3). Instead of great men, mere "youths" will be their leaders (3:4), people lacking either the maturity or the moral authority to administer the nation in a just way. The result will be anarchy, with violence undermining the last vestiges of order (3:5).

It is probable that Isaiah has in mind here typical conditions following the defeat of a nation and the exile of its leaders and craftsmen (cf. Jer 40–42). The connection with exile is further reinforced by the vignette in Isaiah 3:6–7. Since no one with natural leadership skills is left to govern "this heap of ruins" (3:6), even the possession of a cloak (as a badge of office?) will be considered all that is necessary to assume a leadership position—but such a person will not take the job. This is how far, the prophet says, we are going to go in humiliation after having exalted our great men so high.

The connection with 2:6–22 is underscored by 3:8–9. Judah's sin is arrogance. Ultimately, it is to commit the sin of Sodom and Gomorrah, which was not first of all sexual sin but the insistence of the residents that they had the right to determine right and wrong for themselves. The only result of such pride is "disaster" (3:9).

Verses 10–11 underline the cause-and-effect nature of relations with God. He is not arbitrary in his judgments. We have been made to operate within certain parameters. If we do so, we may expect positive results. If we choose to live outside those parameters, we should not be surprised if negative results follow.

Verses 12–15 detail God's judgment on the leaders whom Judah has idolized. Why will they be removed? Why will they be taken into captivity? Why will their nation be humiliated? The simple answer is that they are not great men at all. Their behavior makes it plain that they are not qualified to lead. They are "youths" and "women" (3:12), two categories of persons who in that society had neither the training nor the status to give leadership. These elders of the people oppress the poor, "grinding" their "faces" (3:15) in the dirt. Instead of denying themselves to tend the Lord's "vineyard," the nation of Judah, they have "ruined" it with their greed for gain and their lust for power (3:14).

Another Illustration of Human Arrogance (3:16–4:1). This third section on human arrogance is the most graphic of all. Most commentators believe it is addressed to the wealthy women of Judah and Jerusalem. And it may have been, originally. However, in the context in which it now occurs, I believe it is being used to symbolize the nation as a whole. This conclusion is reinforced both by the use of "women [literally, daughters] of Zion" in 4:4 and by the way in which Zion is personified in 3:25–26.

Once again, the prophet presents the contrast in the strongest terms. The arrogant heads will be bowed in shame, the beautiful hair shaved off to reveal sores seeping pus (3:17). All the beautiful clothing will be stripped off and replaced with a strip of burlap and a piece of rope (3:24). The city will be reduced to utter destitution.

In 4:1 the prophet gives the final graphic illustration of humiliation. In that society it was a great shame for a woman to have no family connections. Yet Isaiah foresees a day when so many of the men have died in plague or been killed in war that there are not enough fathers and husbands to go around. In utter humiliation, seven women will beg one man to give them his name with no obligation on his part at all. Here is the final degradation of human pride.

Application. The terrible irony of life is that we humans must have something beyond ourselves to live for! So, the existentialist philosophers argued that we must each create our own pattern of meaning, all the time knowing that there is no meaning. This, of course, means that no one can claim that his or her system of meaning is *the* meaning of life; there is no such thing. Thus today, although the person on the street cannot explain the philosophical basis for his or her ideas, it is still obvious that existentialism has come to rule the day.

ISAIAH 4:2–6

Original Meaning. Commentators are divided as to the intent of the phrase "the Branch of the LORD" (4:2). There is a clear eschatological tone that calls for an understanding of the phrase in light of the fulfillment of the messianic promises.

The promises here are not in place of judgment but through it. The "survivors" (4:2) are the remnant left after the "fire" of judgment (4:4) has done its work. There are three results of that raging firestorm.

1. The people will be "holy" (4:3); that is, they will belong to God alone and will reflect the character of their owner.
2. They will be cleansed of their "filth" and "bloodstains," that is, the accumulated guilt of all their sins (4:4).
3. They will experience the presence of God not as a threat but as a blessing (4:5). By his presence ("the glory"), he will provide the very security for which they had turned to idols. The imagery of the "cloud . . . by day" (4:5) and "fire by night" is reminiscent of that used in Exodus (Exod 40:38). In short, Isaiah sees the messianic kingdom as a return to what the exodus was meant to produce.

Application. In many cases, the adversity is the judgment of God. We have sinned, and we are now experiencing those results. But it is not a cruel God who brings those things upon us, and it is not a rejecting God who abandons us to the fire. Rather, it is a loving God who sees no other way to bring us to the place where he can live in us.

ISAIAH 5:1–30

Original Meaning

The Vineyard (5:1–6). Throughout the book, Isaiah makes use of illustrations to bring his point home. Here, in one sense, the author sums up everything he has said thus far in one powerful image. This image of the vineyard would have special poignancy for the Judean audience that Isaiah is addressing, because grapes is the crop that grows best in Judah.

But, as the illustration makes plain, a grape crop demands a great deal of preparation and care (5:2). This is the work of an entire year. Then the finest vines that one can afford must be purchased and carefully set out. During that second year the cleared rocks must be built into fences and watchtowers in order to keep out marauders, both four-footed and two-footed. Finally, in the third year, the fruit of all the previous labor is ready.

It is easy to imagine the Judean farmers being right with the speaker as they anticipate the sweet harvest. And it is also possible to imagine their outrage when they are told that for all that effort, the outcome is only bitter grapes (5:2). So, when Isaiah announces that he is going to tear down the wall and let the wild animals in and even pray the heavens to stop raining on that vineyard (5:5–6), we can imagine the hearers shouting, "Yes, do it!"

Explanation of the Vineyard (5:7–24). But the hearers suddenly realize Isaiah is talking about them. In the succeeding verses Isaiah tells his hearers what those bitter grapes are. He begins with a general statement in 5:7 and then gives the specifics in a series of "woes" in 5:8–24. This is a word associated with funerals. A death lies ahead, all the more tragic because it is so unnecessary. The woes describe the sins of the people in relation to the kinds of lives God had called for them to live in the Sinai covenant. Just as the vineyard of bitter grapes will be destroyed because of what it produced, so will Israel.

Greed. The particular expression of greed addressed in 5:8 is greed for bigger houses and more land. The rich man buys more and more land, dispossessing the former owners one by one until at last he lives alone on a vast estate, with the former owners as his serfs. This kind of sin was particularly offensive to God because in the covenant God retained ownership of the land, giving it in the form of grants to his servants to be maintained in the respective families for all time. In 5:9 and 10 God announces a punishment that fits the crime.

Self-indulgence. The "bitter grape" given most attention is the one of self-indulgence (5:11–17), and much of the passage is the announcement of judgment on this behavior. This is not an attack on all physical enjoyment. Rather, it is attacking the paying of attention to these things as if they are the only things that matter. Once again, the punishment fits the crime. As these wealthy and noble people have focused on what goes down their throats, the day will come when nothing goes down (5:13). And just as they have opened their mouths wider and wider to take in more, so death will open its mouth. Verse 17 depicts the sheep that once provided the expansive meals for "the rich," now feeding quietly among the "ruins" of the banqueting halls of the rich.

Cynicism. From the more fleshly sins of greed and indulgence, the prophet proceeds to the underlying attitudes that both precede and follow the sins of the flesh. The first of these attitudes is cynicism that dares God to take action (5:18–19). These are people who delight in sinning, who seek out ways to do it more aggressively, all the while insisting that if such a course of action was so bad, the great God, this "Holy One of Israel" (5:19) Isaiah keeps going on about, will certainly take some action against it. In the meantime, they intend to keep right on pleasing themselves at all costs.

Moral perversion. The fourth woe (5:20–21) takes the situation one step further. Now it is not merely daring God to condemn sin. Rather, it is declaring that there is no such thing as sin, that in fact what was previously declared to be wrong is actually right and that what has been considered right is actually wrong. Such persons have dismissed God from the picture entirely. What is going on is not merely asserting one's right to choose one's own moral conventions but is rather a revolt against any moral authority at all.

Social injustice. The final woe (5:22–24) speaks ironically of those who are great at what does not matter (mixing drinks) and therefore neglect what does matter—justice. The nobility of Judah, instead of standing up for truly noble causes, has turned to ignoble pursuits.

This is not accidental. The people have rejected the instruction (NIV "law," Heb. *torah*) of the One being who stands outside of time and space, the One being in the universe who has the right to be called "Holy," the One who has yet condescended to give himself in covenant to Israel (5:24b). That is, the people have rejected the instruction of the One being in the universe who is in a position to give such instructions.

The Calling of the Enemy Nations (5:25–30). In these closing verses of chapter 5, the intimations of exile in the preceding verses are brought together and made explicit. Isaiah uses a refrain he will repeat again several times in 9:8–10:4: "For all this, his anger is not turned away, his hand is still upraised" (5:25b). These great powers are instruments in the hands of God. They come in response to his signal (5:26). In 5:27–29 Isaiah uses short, terse couplets to create a sense of urgency and impulsion.

Application. The Christian church today faces a crisis of worldview. Our culture has lost the idea that there is a God outside of myself to whom I owe obedience. As a result, we are becoming lawless, because there is not enough force in the world to make a nation of people obey if they do not want to obey.

The challenge to the church is that this kind of thinking is creeping in among us as well. We are slowly losing our grip on the idea that there is a Creator whose character is absolutely consistent and who has created humans in his image. We are losing the idea that this Creator has built into his universe certain spiritual principles that are as unchangeable as any of the natural principles.

ISAIAH 6:1–13

Original Meaning. With Uzziah's death, Judah's truly hopeless situation emerges. The Assyrian emperor Tiglath-Pileser III has clearly established himself as a military conqueror to be feared. But as long as the powerful Uzziah was on the throne, the immediacy of the threat was blurred. But when Uzziah was removed from the scene, the danger could no longer be ignored.

The images and language used to describe God emphasize majesty and holiness. In the ancient Near East, "holy" was not used especially widely, and when it was used, it was not given special prominence. But for the Hebrews, the idea of the holy was decidedly different. Beginning with Exodus 6:3 and continuing on through 19:6 and throughout the entire Old Testament, the people of Israel had learned that there is only one being who is truly other than this world, and they had learned that it was his character, even more than his essence, that set him apart from us humans.

This is why Isaiah knew there was no hope for him once he had heard the seraphs describe the Lord. He knew that his character was utterly unlike that of the Holy One. But why does Isaiah say that his lips are unclean? Why not his heart? Two suggestions may be offered.

1. It may be that the lips are being referred to as the evidence of what is really in the heart.
2. A related possibility is that having just heard the golden tones of the seraphs, Isaiah knows that his lips, having been used to praise himself, put others down, and generally serve his own ends, could never be used in such holy service.

Isaiah sees his situation as being so hopeless that he does not even bother to ask for cleansing or deliverance. But here he underestimates the grace of God. God has not given him this vision in order to annihilate him. Rather, he brings these terrifying things into the prophet's life in order that he might be delivered into his true vocation.

Isaiah is called upon to preach a message that, given the already-hardened hearts of his generation and several of the following, will only push them farther away from God. But some will turn, among them faithful followers of Isaiah, who will preserve his words until the day when the cauterizing fires of the exile fall and there will finally be a generation willing to listen. When the forest has been felled and even the remaining stumps have been burned, one of those stumps will still have life in it.

Application. We have all heard many people tell how they were dragged kicking and screaming into the Lord's service. Why is that? I suspect it is because we have grown up never really feeling the wonder of having been forgiven of our sins and given new life.

ISAIAH 7:1–25

Original Meaning

The Call to Trust (7:1–9). While we do not know the precise date of the events described in these verses, it seems probable that they occur about 735 BC. We do not know the specific reason why Syria and Israel are attacking Judah. However, it seems probable that they are attempting to force Judah to join a coalition with them against the Assyrians. At any rate, the two neighboring kingdoms are attacking Judah with the express purpose of deposing Ahaz and putting someone named Tabeel on the throne in his place (7:6).

Most likely Ahaz is looking over the city's water supply in preparation for the coming siege. While there were no foolproof procedures for breaking into a well-defended, walled city, it was possible to force such a city to surrender if its water supply could be cut off. Ahaz wants to be sure that such a thing does not happen.

Throughout chapters 7–11 children are important figures. The first is presented here, accompanying his father to confront the king (7:3). This child's name means "only a remnant will return." If Isaiah introduces his son to the king, the conversation may have started off on a rather grim note!

The prophet addresses the king's fearfulness, telling him that it is not necessary (7:4–9). In the end it does not matter what Rezin and Pekah say (7:5–6). It only matters what the "Sovereign LORD" (7:7; lit., "the Lord Yahweh") says, and he says that their threats will amount to nothing. In fact, in "sixty-five years" (7:8), probably a way of saying within one person's lifetime, they would not even be a people. Isaiah concludes his appeal to trust God. If he will firmly believe in God, then he can stand in quiet confidence no matter how desperate the immediate circumstances may appear.

The Sign of Immanuel (7:10–25). God takes Ahaz a step further by offering him a sign to prompt faith. But Ahaz refuses the challenge (7:12). Maddeningly, he does so with an appeal to piety. He says that to ask God for a sign would be to test God, something forbidden in the Torah (Num 14:22; Deut 6:16). But the testing referred to in the Torah is not believing God's promises! To step out in faith is nothing like the rebellions in the desert. Ahaz's supposed piety is only a mask for the same kind of unbelief.

Isaiah clearly recognizes this as he responds with frustration (7:13). God begins to wonder how much longer he must put up with that king. So, God says he will give Ahaz a sign anyway (7:14). On the surface the sign seems to be that before a child conceived at the time of the saying is twelve years of age, the two nations that so frighten the house of David will be destroyed (7:16).

However, there are three factors in the sign itself that raise some question about this apparently straightforward interpretation.

1. God himself urges Ahaz to ask for a remarkable sign (7:11). On the surface there seems nothing remarkable about the sign that God actually gives.
2. The second unusual feature is that the Hebrew word *almah* in 7:14 is not the normal term for "woman" but a relatively unusual one meaning "young woman of marriageable age" (NIV "virgin"). The LXX translates the word with "virgin."
3. Finally, the choice of a name for the child ("Immanuel," 7:14) is a bit strange since its immediate relevance to the historic situation is not clear.

Taken together, all of these suggest that there is more going on in this sign than meets the eye and that Matthew (1:23) has not merely (mis-)appropriated some ancient text for his own purposes, as some modern commentators suggest he did. I believe that the sign as originally given had a single meaning but a double significance. Its meaning is that God is with us. The first significance is for Ahaz's own day.

But is God *really* with us? The answer to the question is "yes." God has come to take up residence with us as one of us. How has that fact been accomplished? By giving him a human mother but no human father.

At any rate, before this child who is shortly to be conceived is able "to reject the wrong and choose the right" (7:15–16), Syria and Israel will be destroyed. This phrase most likely refers to the age of accountability.

The child is a sign that God is with Judah in two ways, one positive and the other negative. Since God is with them, they need not fear their two small neighbors. But since Ahaz has acted as though God is not and Assyria is, he will discover God who *is* with us, bringing against him the very thing he has trusted (7:18–19).

Application. We need to seek God's word—something Ahaz did not do. We need to seek it in the Scriptures, in the counsel of godly elders, in the nature of the circumstances, and in our own hearts. What we must avoid at all costs is what Ahaz did, deciding what we want and then asking God if he could please bless what we want.

ISAIAH 8:1–22

Original Meaning

Birth of Child and Significance of Name (8:1–10). Isaiah is to write down the child's name even before he is conceived as evidence of predictive prophecy. Heathen gods cannot tell the future since they are as much imprisoned in time as humans are. But God stands outside of time and can declare what is to happen before it happens.

The language of 8:3 is similar to that of 7:14. This suggests that the two verses may be referring to the same event. There is a strong case for identifying Maher-Shalal-Hash-Baz with the first fulfillment of the Immanuel sign. If this is so, the child will not be able to speak clearly before Damascus and Samaria have been plundered.

Verses 6–10 encapsulate Isaiah's (and God's) perspective on history. The nations come and go at God's command and serve his plan being worked out through his people. God is with Israel; thus, if Israel tries to live as if that were not so, there will be tragic consequences (8:6–8). At the same time, the nations must never forget that they are but instruments in the hand of the Holy One of Israel. If they think they can wipe out his people in order to achieve their own geopolitical goals, they are mistaken, because God *is* with his people and will achieve his goals through them, regardless of what any other nation on the face of the earth does (8:9–10).

The People's Blindness and Its Consequences (8:11–22). Jerusalem in 735 BC was like a pot on the boil. Not only was there a resurgent Assyria to worry about, there was the nearer problem of Syria and Israel. In the middle of this whirlpool, God comes to Isaiah with specific instructions. In the first place, he is not to lose his focus on God. He should not be swept off his feet with the latest conspiracy theory, and he should not fall into the trap of fear. Instead, he should focus his attention on serving and pleasing the God in whose hands our destinies reside. The attention to "fear" in 8:12–13 is important. The fear of the unknown is a defiling kind of fear, but the "fear of the LORD" is clean (see Ps 19:9). This phrase describes a way of life that pays primary attention to learning and obeying the ways of the only one who can truly be called "holy" (Isa 8:13).

God tells Isaiah that if he gets his attention focused properly, God will be a sanctuary (8:14) for him. The one who has focused on God will be at peace. But those who refuse to give God that central place in their lives will find a "stone" in the road to "stumble" over (8:14).

Here we come again to the dual significance of "God is with us." God's presence is the one inescapable fact of human life. We *will* encounter him in one way or another. Those who make a place for him find him to be the glue that holds everything together. Those who ignore him find their lives to be askew and cannot understand why.

So, what should Isaiah do in such a climate? Shall he simply give up in frustration? Or shall he keep hammering away at a people who cannot even understand what he is talking about? The answer is the middle way (8:16–17). He should not give up declaring God's word, but he should do it particularly to disciples who will "bind up" (i.e., treasure, 8:16) those words for another day when God's face will no longer be hidden from his people.

In 8:19–22 we read what happens when people refuse to trust and obey God. They have God's word given to them in the Torah and the Prophets, yet they refuse to consult it. They prefer instead to consult the dead! They have been trusting all these other things instead of the revealed God, and all of them have failed.

Application. It is interesting to watch the fascination of modern people with so-called "conspiracy theories." But Isaiah calls us to give up the fascination with "what really happened." He calls us to believe that God is at work in history and that we can trust him to work all things together for the good of those who are called according to his purpose (Rom 8:28).

ISAIAH 9:1–7

Original Meaning. Choosing their own way rather than God's way, the nation has plunged itself into darkness. But that is not where God intends to leave them. God promises that the light will dawn. The people of Israel have done nothing to deserve this; it is nothing but God's grace.

The Assyrian conquests began in the tribal territory of Zebulun and Naphtali (9:1a). Not only was this a lush agricultural area, but it was also the place through which the main trade route from Mesopotamia to Egypt ran ("the Way of the Sea," (9:1b). Thus, it is easy to see why it was high on the priority list for conquest. But God is greater than Assyria, and he promises that just as these people have experienced the grief and despair of conquest, they will also experience the joy and triumph of victory (9:3–5). As Gideon defeated Midian in the Valley of Jezreel (Judg 7), so God will defeat Israel's enemies in that same place.

But how will God accomplish this great feat? Through the birth of a child (Isa 9:6)! For the third time in as many chapters, the birth of a child is filled with great portent. The repetition of birth and the close connection in the meaning of the three signs argues that all three are expressions of Immanuel. Clearly the person being referred to here is the promised Messiah, who will reign with a kind of justice and righteousness that no mere human descendant of David ever achieved. The government and the social and personal integration he will produce will be eternal (9:7).

Application. The good news is that the God who is with us is a God who wants to turn our darkness into light, our conflict into *shalom*, our loss into abundance, our despair into joy. Have we allowed the Child-King to take over the government of our lives? Only then can we know the benefits of God with us. We cannot have the light, the honor, the joy, the abundance, or the integration that he offers in any other way.

ISAIAH 9:8–10:4

Original Meaning

Arrogance (9:8–12). The charges God lodges against Israel all have to do with ethical behavior, with the covenant providing the background. The first is specifically focused on the Northern Kingdom of Israel, in the final decade of its existence. "Rezin's foes" (the Assyrians) as well as Israel's former allies, the "Arameans" (the Syrians), and their perpetual enemies, the Philistines, will all be brought against them (9:11–12).

Adulation of Great Men (9:13–17). When God is forsaken, the natural substitute is human leaders. God will deprive Israel and Judah of all such false leaders. It does not matter who these leaders are (9:15); they will all be swept away.

Lack of Brotherly Love (9:18–21). The breakdown of social structure as a result of sin is burning up the land (9:18), and God's righteous judgment adds tinder to the flame (9:19). As the terrific pressure of Assyria's demand for tribute mounts higher and higher, everyone scrambles to save his or her own neck. Ultimately, as the final siege begins, the devouring of one's "own offspring" ceases to be metaphorical and becomes a horrible, literal fact (9:20). In a world where self reigns supreme, they turn on their brother tribe to the south: Judah (9:21).

Social Injustice (10:1–4). In a world characterized by human arrogance, justice becomes a rarer and rarer commodity, with the poor and the helpless being least able to secure it. God's particular anger is reserved for those who consciously use the legal system to oppress the poor and make themselves rich (10:1–2). There will not be enough "riches" (10:3) to deliver them from captivity.

Application. When we think of God's anger, we must avoid thinking: "Oh, that's just an Old Testament misunderstanding of things. We know better now. Since Jesus, we know that God is really a God of love." God's anger and love are found in both Old and New Testaments. Jesus himself became terribly angry on several occasions. If we allow God to be passionately involved with his creation in a positive way and call that "love," we must also allow that the same passionate involvement might express itself in the negative way known as "anger." The two terminologies express two sides of the same phenomenon.

Does God get angry? Yes, but it is not the selfish anger of a fallen human. It is the heartbroken response of an Artist who watches his artistic creations doing things that are not only a violation of his original dream but are a violation of their very natures.

ISAIAH 10:5–34

Original Meaning

A Message against Assyria (10:5–19). Assyria is the "rod" (10:5) that is held in God's upraised hand (9:12, 17, 21; 10:4), and it is raised up to punish "a godless nation" (10:6). This expression must have seemed unjust to many. Surely the Assyrians are the ones who are "godless" and perverse. But the fact is, the Israelites know better, yet they pervert their way by turning their backs on the truth revealed to them.

The Assyrians' "purpose" (10:7) is to conquer and "destroy" as many nations as possible. This idea is expressed in the quotation put in the mouth of the Assyrian king in 10:8–11.

The king has no qualms about saying that he is superior to everything on earth, including all its gods. He is so great that even his "commanders" (10:8) are the equivalent of the kings of other lands. He is truly the king of kings. He is superior to God and will do to Jerusalem whatever he wants.

But as Isaiah points out, when Jerusalem's punishment is complete, at least for the moment, Assyria's punishment will begin (10:12). That punishment will be because of Assyrian "pride" (10:12), which is expressed in another quotation from their king (10:13–14). That king does not recognize that he is a tool in the hand of God. Rather, he boasts that it is his "hand" (10:13) that has captured the nations.

But they are tools in the hand of Yahweh (10:15). God said he would cut down the forest of Judah's pride (6:13), and Assyria is the "axe" in God's hand to accomplish that task. God also said that he would punish his people for their sin (5:25), and Assyria is the instrument of that punishment.

Because Assyria refuses to recognize the truth, God will turn the tool over to destruction. The "flame" (10:16) of God's holiness will be turned on those who refuse to admit that there might be One superior to them. The metaphors of field and forest are used again to convey the idea of glory destroyed (10:17–19). Not only the least in Assyria ("thorns" and "briers"; 10:17) but also the greatest ("forests and fertile fields"; 10:18) will be consumed—and all "in a single day" (10:17). This most likely refers to the destruction of the Assyrian army in 701 BC (see 37:36–37).

A Remnant Will Survive (10:20–23). "In that day" is an expansive term referring to any future time of God's judgment and/or restoration. Thus, it is not necessary to refer it directly to the events of 701 BC nor even to the events of 620–609 BC, when Assyria was finally destroyed. Rather, here it speaks of that future time when all the punishment at the hands of the nations will be over and the purified "remnant" (10:21) of God's people (see 4:2–6) will be brought home.

As is typical of this part of the book, Isaiah is trying hard to guard against false expectations. No one should get so focused on the future survival as to forget the terrible judgment that precedes that survival. Thus, he insists to his hearers that even though the destruction will not be complete, it will be thorough. It has been so "decreed" (10:22). But the remnant will be different from their predecessors in at least one respect. They will no longer "rely on" (10:20), or trust, their worst enemy before they will trust "the Holy One of Israel."

The Lord's Protection of His People (10:24–34). In view of the fact that Assyria will be judged and that a remnant of the nation will survive, "therefore" (10:24) the people of Judah should not live in fear of Assyria. Their foreign policy and their spiritual outlook should not be shaped by either the offers or the threats of that great power. As Isaiah earlier said to Ahaz, no emergency action is necessary (10:25).

In 10:26 the prophet turns to two experiences from the past as confirmation of the Lord's power to protect his people from massive threats. Neither was any match for the power of the "LORD Almighty" (literally, "Yahweh of armies"). The heavy "yoke" of oppression that the Assyrian kings used to boast about putting on the necks of conquered peoples will be "broken" off (10:27).

Verses 28–34 have occasioned a great deal of scholarly discussion, primarily over whether they describe a literal historical event. The route described diverges from the normal one that begins to the north of Jerusalem and travels instead down the east side of the ridge line. Probably the reason for this is to express the almost unstoppable approach of the enemy army. It does not matter that the route is rugged and filled with obstacles—on they come! This is a metaphor for Assyria. On they have come year after year. Nothing can stop them. Judah must come to terms with them or be destroyed.

But Isaiah tells his hearers they should look at another reality. For at the moment when the Assyrian ax believes it will topple the Judean tree, Judah's God turns the ax upon the ax! In a moment a forest as mighty as that covering the Lebanon mountains falls to the ground. Human pride cannot stand before the true "Mighty One" (Heb. *'addir*, 10:34; note the similar Hebrew term *'abbir*, "a mighty one," in 10:13, which is what the Assyrian king called himself). The true Mighty One is the one whom Judah should be relying on, not on the ax in the Mighty One's hand.

Application. Any nation that attempts to put itself in the place of God cannot survive. Will the United States learn this lesson? What is it that God wants to do through us in the world today? Will we make any serious attempt to discover that? And if we do, will we carry out our tasks in humility, recognizing the terrible risks of pride? The history of nations in the Christian West is not encouraging in this respect. One after another has come to power proclaiming its dependence on God, and one after another has exited the scene in disgrace, having come to believe that they were ultimate in themselves.

ISAIAH 11:1–16

Original Meaning

The Coming Descendant of Jesse (11:1–9). Why is the Messiah here attributed to the family line of Jesse and not more directly to that of Jesse's son David? The One who is coming will not be merely one more descendant of the royal line that is now so thoroughly besmirched; rather, he will spring from the very roots of that dynasty. Israel's pride has been thoroughly cut down and burned. In this field of stumps, there is still life in the original root, a life that resides finally in the faithfulness of God.

This descendant of Jesse will rule with the spirit of the Lord. Thus, the Messiah will not rule in the power and the motivation of the fallen human spirit but by the life and breath of God himself. How different he will be becomes clear in 11:3–5. He will not be biased in favor of the rich and powerful. Nor will the powerful escape if they are among the "wicked." His words will be more powerful than the mightiest "rod," and the "breath" (Heb. *ruah*, "spirit") of his lips will not only pronounce the sentence of the "wicked" but will actually kill them (11:4).

"Righteousness" and "faithfulness" (11:5) will be at the very heart of this person's existence. The result of this kind of leadership will be peace—not merely the cessation of hostilities but the unification of that which was formerly divided. The imagery used to convey this point in 11:6–9 has captured thinkers and artists across the centuries.

The means by which this will be accomplished is cited in the final colon of 11:9: "The earth will be filled with the knowledge of the LORD as the waters cover the sea." The Hebrew language does not recognize any distinction between knowledge that is an accumulation of information and knowledge that is personal acquaintance. For the Hebrews, all true knowledge is based on experience. The prophet speaks of insight into reality born of a close and intimate relationship with the LORD. The Messiah will make it possible for all people to know God intimately.

The Messiah as the Banner (11:10–16). As God previously ran up a "banner" (5:26) to call the enemy nations, now the Messiah is a "banner" (11:10, 12) calling the nations to himself. The places cited in 11:11 emphasize the worldwide nature of this return. There is no part of the earth too far away for God's hand to reach.

The precise intent of "a second time" in 11:11 is not clear. The worldwide extent of the dispersion was greater than anything that happened between 722 and 586 BC, and the return in 538 BC was only from Babylon. This invites us to consider that the "second time" may point to a second return from exile.

The prophet envisions a day when hostility, stretching back to the division after Solomon's death and even further, will be permanently healed. The division between Samaria and Judea at the time of Christ was one continuation of that hostility. When Christ drew some of the Samaritans to himself (John 4), he was beginning to bridge the gulf.

Again in 11:15 it is unclear how literal the prophet intends these figures to be taken, but the point is clear. There will be no effective barrier to the return of his people either from the south ("the gulf of the Egyptian Sea") or from the north ("the Euphrates River"). Isaiah 11:16 continues the imagery of ease of travel.

Application. Just as there will be a literal return of Christ, there will also be a literal new heaven and new earth over which Christ will reign; it is to that kingdom that this chapter is looking forward. The logic of creation calls for a time when God's creatures will experience creation as it was meant to be.

ISAIAH 12:1–6

Original Meaning. God should be trusted simply because he is God, but how much more he should be trusted when we realize that he himself has turned his righteous anger to "comfort" or encouragement (12:1). As on the shores of the Red Sea, the people can say what they have learned about God: He is "strength," he is "defense" (NIV footnote, "song"), he is "salvation." Who would not trust such a God as this?

Verse 4 gives a short course in the behavior of the believer: thanks, prayer, and witness. Works like those the Holy One has performed cannot be proclaimed with a long face. They must be sung "to all the world" (12:5).

Application. God reconciled us to himself through his own work on the cross. There was nothing we could offer to God in the way of negotiation. We were condemned sinners, estranged from God and alienated from life. But God found a way to satisfy his own justice in that Christ has died in our place. In place of judgment, he has come to offer us encouragement.

ISAIAH 13:1–22

Original Meaning

Address against Babylon (13:1). The fact that the first oracle (chs. 13–14) begins with Babylon, which was not a world power in Isaiah's lifetime, is often taken to be proof of the late date of the book. We are told, however, that "Isaiah son of Amoz," not some later editor, saw this oracle against Babylon.

The Terror of Coming Judgment (13:2–8). In this stanza the terror of the coming judgment is emphasized. Once again, a signal "banner" is run up to call the various nations to come against God's enemy in judgment (13:2). But these armies come from the very "ends of the heavens" (13:5). This is not a merely historical judgment but an eschatological one. Even the mightiest and most glorious of earth's nations is no match for God (13:7–8).

The Sin of Pride (13:9–13). As seen in the earliest chapters of Isaiah, the greatest of all the sins of creation is the sin of pride.

Oftentimes, the pagan deification of humanity expresses itself in the fiction that the gods, made in human form, are the stars. In fact, says Isaiah, the opposite is true. They are the dutiful servants of the Almighty. He will darken them and shake them (13:10, 13).

The Collapse of Power (13:14–22). Isaiah now takes up a somewhat more historical note, although the language still retains a distinctly universalistic tone. Verses 14–15 describe the break-up of the collection of city-states out of which every ancient empire was crafted. There would be no protection (13:16).

The "Medes" (13:17) were a warlike people from the Zagros Mountains east of the Tigris River (in what is today Iran). With prophetic inspiration, Isaiah recognizes that the Medes are the ones who will undo Babylon, so that Babylon's destruction will be complete (13:19–22).

Although the Medo-Persian conquest of Babylon did not signal the city's immediate demise, it did signal the beginning of the end. The greatest city in the ancient world went into a slow decline so that in the eighteenth-century AD, even its location was unknown. Isaiah's prophecy about its becoming a haunt of "hyenas" and "jackals" (13:22) came true with a vengeance.

Application. We give our allegiance to flesh and blood, to physical things, as though they can give us significance and worth. In fact, they are all passing faster than we can imagine. So, wisdom asks: What will survive the wreck of all human accomplishments? Rather, we should be looking to the eternal, which will not pass away. Why trust the veil when we may trust him who is behind the veil and will assuredly one day pull that veil to the ground?

ISAIAH 14:1–27

Original Meaning

Words of Promise to Israel (14:1–4a). Between the announcement of the destruction of Babylon in chapter 13 and that of Babylon's king in chapter 14 are words of promise to Israel. Once more the prophet affirms that the coming destruction is not because the Mesopotamian powers are so great that God cannot stop them. No, those powers are mere tools in his hand, and once their work is finished, they too will come in for judgment while Israel will be restored to all the promises.

Rest for People on Earth (14:4b–8). A typical lament might begin by saying how earth's inhabitants are struck over the news of the departed's death. But here the poet tells in anticipation how grateful the people on earth are to have "rest" (14:7) from the repeated blows of the oppressor's rod (14:5–6). Nor is it just human beings who are glad to know that the reign of terror is over. The whole creation, including the trees, are glad (14:8). Human pride sees both humans and nature as fodder, so even nature breathes a sigh of relief when the news of that pride's death is announced.

The Underworld (14:9–11). The picture changes from the earth to the underworld. In place of the peace and quiet that the tyrant's death has brought to the earth, the underworld is in an uproar. Verse 11 is a masterpiece of sarcasm and irony. We see that the beautiful bier and its coverings are nothing but a writhing mass of "maggots" (14:11). Human pretension is no match for the grim reality of death and decay.

A Message from Heaven (14:12–15). The language here has intriguing overtones of several ancient stories about both human and divine hubris. Isaiah has taken a number of themes familiar to his hearers and woven them together into a new creation to make his unique theological point. In verses 13–14, the egotist has made four boasts about what he will do. But this man, who thought to make himself equal to God, is mocked by death, which has taken him from the "heights" (14:13) of his own pretensions to the "depths of the pit" (14:15) in one terrible moment.

The Tragedy of the Fallen King (14:16–21). No single individual is being addressed here. This "king of Babylon" is a composite of all the proud, despotic kings who have ruled on the earth. Verses 16–20 show people staring at the mangled corpse of the tyrant lying in a heap of other corpses in a pit (see especially 14:19). This agrees with the idea of a battlefield death. Instead of a dignified death and an honorable burial, the corpse is abandoned in the field, perhaps in a hasty retreat. The point is one of final and complete humiliation for the most vaunting arrogance.

But not only does the proud king have no decent burial, neither does he have any continuing dynasty. Verses 20b–21 express the hope that the oppressor will have no offspring to carry on his name. Thus, his destruction is complete.

Conclusion (14:22–27). In 14:22–23 the thought of the immediately preceding verses is continued and expanded. Not only will the king of Babylon have no offspring and thus no living memorial, neither will Babylon itself. In 14:24–27, the prophet gives a specific example of this destruction of Babylon, namely, the coming downfall of Assyria. Any person or nation that lifts itself up against the "plan" and "purpose" of God (14:24, 26–27) marks itself for destruction. Verse 25 seems to refer to the destruction of Sennacherib's army in Judah in 701 BC (as described in 37:36).

Application. Any attempt to make ourselves ultimate has results that are just as predictable as are the results of jumping off a tall building. We have been made to reflect the glory of the only God. If a mirror says, "No, I will reflect only myself" and pulls down all the shades and turns the lights off, it should not be surprised to discover there is nothing to reflect. The mirror has violated the terms of its creation. So it is that when we humans say, "I will live only for myself," we should not be surprised to discover that there is no life to be lived.

ISAIAH 14:28–32

Original Meaning. It seems probable that Ahaz died in 716 BC and that Hezekiah either began to reign then or assumed full regency after having been coregent for some time. But it is not clear what the significance of Ahaz's death is for the meaning of this oracle.

If Ahaz had been a threat to the Philistines, it would be natural to say he was the broken rod who had struck the Philistines. But 2 Chronicles 28:18 indicates that Ahaz lost several cities to the Philistines. Perhaps the date is significant because the Philistines had revolted against Assyria at this time and were urging the new king, Hezekiah, to join them because Assyria, "the rod that struck [us] is broken" (Isa 14:29a). If that is correct, Isaiah quickly disabuses them of such a false notion (14:29b).

Verses 30 and 32 strengthen the suggestion that the Philistines are inviting the Judeans to join them in revolt. To this proposal, Isaiah answers that the Lord will take care of Judah without any help from the Philistines.

Application. The church today is often in the position of Judah. We feel beleaguered on every hand, and we look for allies. The history of the church's attempts to do this is a pretty sorry one. All too often we discover that the world's "best products" carry with them understandings of reality that are alien to everything the church stands for. The Bible says, "Trust in the LORD with all your heart and lean not on your own understanding" (Prov 3:5). That is what Isaiah is saying.

ISAIAH 15:1–16:14

Original Meaning. The oracle against Moab takes a very different tone, at least on the surface, from the ones against Babylon and her king. There, even though the oracle against the king took the form of a lament, there was no question that the prophet, speaking for Judah and Israel, took delight in the destruction of the proud oppressor. Here there seems to be genuine sorrow over the coming destruction of Moab.

With the exception of Kir (15:1), the towns and villages mentioned in 15:1–4 all are found in the northern part of Moab. Although several of the sites mentioned in 15:5–8 are unknown, those that are known are in the southern part of Moab, south of the Arnon River. This north-to-south movement would have been characteristic of the flight of the Moabites southward before a marauding army heading south along the King's Highway from Damascus.

If the southward flight suggested in chapter 15 is correct, it would be natural for the fugitives to have sought refuge in Edom. But in fact, that is not the case. The prophet knows that Moab's only hope is in the Lord and in the Messiah he has promised.

Isaiah 16:1–4a are the cries of the refugees for help. In 16:4b–5 Isaiah takes an opportunity to speak about the ultimate trust not only for the Moabites but for the whole world. This short statement is reminiscent not only of 11:1–16 but also of 9:1–7.

As he has already done several times in the book, Isaiah once again follows a familiar pattern: After a glimpse of that future hope, which should give people the basis for living lives of trust in dark hours, the prophet swings back to the grim present realities (16:6–13). Those who attempt to exalt themselves only ensure their eventual downfall, and those who labor to manipulate the forces of this earth for their own sakes only exhaust themselves in futility.

Isaiah 16:14 commits the prophet to a test. He asserts that within three years of these words having been uttered, calculated as carefully as an indentured servant would calculate the days remaining on his servitude, the predictions will be fulfilled. There was a major destruction of Moab by the Assyrians in 715 BC, so these words may have been first spoken in 718 BC. The prophet is not merely speaking in generalities; he is speaking for the God of truth, who is the Lord of history, and he dares to stake both his reputation and God's on the fulfillment of what he says will happen.

Application. There is no hope in our achievements, whether they be the refined culture of Europe or the rough accoutrements of a village on the steppes. None of our accomplishments can save us from the brutality of humans run amok. Even if our lives are lived out in peace, cruel death will make us all refugees in the end, leaving all we have on the road to be pillaged by those who come after us.

We may be justly proud of the things we have done, but if that is the source of our eternal hope, our hope is small indeed. Perhaps the pyramids of Egypt will endure to the end of time, but what do they tell us about their builders? Next to nothing.

It is the same for us, whose accomplishments are a lot less stupendous than those ancient Egyptians. What will we leave behind when we take the road? Everything! And it will soon be scattered to the four winds. All our efforts to gain control of our environment, whether it be home or office or love of life, will only end in a final exhaustion. In the end, the only final hope is to be found in the "man" of Isaiah 16:5—the man, Jesus Christ. Only in his eternal kingdom is there true freedom and justice.

ISAIAH 17:1–11

Original Meaning. Isaiah 17:1–3 speaks of the fall of Aram (Syria). Cities will be reduced to "ruins," where "flocks" will feed (17:1, 2). The fading glory of Jacob then becomes the main topic in the rest of the segment (17:4–11). It begins with an extended comparison of Israel's fate to that of a harvested field or orchard (17:4–6). Hardly anything of the nation will remain, though there *will* be something left.

Thus, 17:7–8 speak of that future day when the Israelites will be purified by judgment and will turn their backs on their idols. The key emphasis is on worshiping "their Maker" (17:7) instead of what "their fingers have made" (17:8). A day will come when the remnant will finally abandon idolatry.

In 17:9–11 Isaiah once more demonstrates his familiar pattern. Yes, there is the hope that in the future the trust in the human creatures of idolatry will be abandoned. But between then and the present, there is the awful reality of judgment. Why? Because they have "forgotten God" (17:10).

Isaiah 17:10b–11 express this again in imagery that is familiar to these largely agricultural people. They have done everything that their human strength can do. They have purchased the finest "imported" vines (17:10b), perhaps an allusion to alliances with foreign nations. But even if they are such skillful agrarians that they could cause the plants to bud and bear fruit in a single day (something they obviously cannot do), the harvest would be worthless. Judgment is coming and cannot be averted by human skill. The best of human effort is not enough to solve the human problem. Someday the remnant of Israel will learn that fact.

Application. The epidemic of pornography today is a contemporary manifestation of an age-old problem. It is tragic that millions of dollars can be raised to combat pollution of the physical environment while the much more serious pollution of the spiritual environment proceeds apace with influential voices raised to defend it.

To paraphrase the prophet, we may be able to import the finest digital technology and use the most professional skills in photography, we may have a website up in a day and have ten thousand "hits," we may make millions of dollars, but "the harvest will be as nothing in the day of disease and incurable pain" (17:11). Instead of a society that is genuinely fruitful, because people are turned outward and are able to sublimate their desires to accomplish worthwhile goals, we will have a society that is wholly given over to pleasing itself and is ultimately barren.

ISAIAH 17:12–18:7

Original Meaning

The Raging of the Nations (17:12–14). The prophet compares the nations to the raging sea. It seems as though they are the ultimate reality with which we must come to terms. But in fact, the One who sits in the heavens is the ultimate reality. Before his breath, the nations are no more substantial than bits of "chaff" or a rolling "tumbleweed" (17:13). They have their day but suddenly night falls, and in the morning nothing is left of what seemed so enduring (17:14). In other words, Isaiah is attempting to get his people to focus beyond apparent realities and onto the One who is reality in himself.

Messengers for Cush (18:1–3). In about 740 BC the Ethiopian Piankhy (also known as Piye) took over Egypt. He along with his successor, Shabako (715–702 BC), brought a new energy to Egyptian affairs. Most likely both of them attempted to cement alliances with various surrounding countries in order to counter the Assyrian threat. We can imagine the stir made in Jerusalem by the tall, regal-looking Ethiopian envoys, who came up the Mediterranean coast in their strange "papyrus" craft (18:2). But Isaiah says that envoys should instead go to Ethiopia to tell them to beware of the true Ruler of the world. It is his battle flag and his war trumpet for which they should be on the alert (18:3).

A Message from God (18:4–7). God's activity often seems unnoticeable. But in a masterful way the prophet reminds his hearers that just because something does not draw much attention to itself does not mean it is powerless. He uses two comparisons to make his point (18:4). Neither comes with fanfare or pageantry; they are simply present and inescapable. So is God. And in his harvest he will cut down the enemy nations like unproductive branches on a vine (18:5–6). Judeans should remember that the day will come when the Ethiopians will be giving gifts to the God of Jerusalem (18:7).

Application. When we think of the prediction that the Ethiopians will come to Jerusalem bearing gifts to the Lord (18:7), we remember the Ethiopian eunuch who became a believer (Acts 8:26–39). He represents all those other nations who have brought their gifts to God in Jerusalem, both before the birth of Christ and even more since.

ISAIAH 19:1–20:6

Original Meaning

Prediction of Egypt's Fall (19:1–15). *Isaiah 19:1–4.* In several places Israelite writers appropriate the imagery of the Canaanite storm god Baal to say that the Lord rides upon the clouds (e.g., Deut 33:26; Pss 68:4; 104:3). So here it is not the Assyrian armies from the north whom the Egyptians should fear but the God from the north, whose chariots are the clouds (Isa 19:1). The "idols" of Egypt (19:1, 3) are utterly helpless.

The Egyptians were an orderly people. As a result, when rapid change came, they tended to "lose heart" (19:3), and order quickly gave way to disorder. Many possibilities exist for the identity of the "cruel master" of 19:4, but the point is that this person will only rule at the sufferance of Yahweh, the God of Israel.

Isaiah 19:5–10. The Egyptians referred to their land as "the gift of the Nile." That is literally true. If not for the Nile River, Egypt would be an extension of the Sahara Desert. Egypt and the Nile are inseparable. But Isaiah envisions a day when the mighty river will run dry, along with all the activities dependent on it: agriculture (19:7), fisheries (19:8), and flax-making (19:9–10).

Isaiah 19:11–15. Egypt was known in the ancient world for its wisdom and culture. It is tempting to think that there is an allusion to the Joseph narrative in the inability of all the Egyptian wise men to tell the pharaoh what the Lord has "planned" for Egypt (19:12).

The language of 19:14 is like that found in chapter 28, where the prophet condemns the leaders of Judah for giving foolish counsel (cf. 28:7–8). "Head or tail, palm branch or reed" (19:15) are figures of totality, like the English "top to bottom." Egypt's entire collection of counselors is helpless to discern what Israel's God is going to do with them and their land.

Egypt's Coming Worship of God (19:16–25). There are not only negative reasons why Egypt should not be trusted, but there is also a positive reason why trusting in Egypt is foolish: The Egyptians will one day turn to Judah's God! Four different prose statements are made here, each headed by the phrase "in that day" (19:16, 18, 19, 23). This phrase does not refer to some specific twenty-four-hour period but to a more general time in the future. A good English equivalent is "at that time."

Verses 16–17 form a transition in that they are in the prose form of what follows, while their message is more like that of 19:1–15. The Egyptians will be plunged into terror when the God of Judah acts. Because it is Judah's God who is at work, the very name of Judah will frighten the people of Egypt.

But God's ultimate goal is not to destroy the people of Egypt. Isaiah 19:18–25 shows that his ultimate purpose is to bring them to worship him together with Israel and Assyria. This is an amazing thought, showing the truly universal character of Old Testament religion. The ultimate vision of the Hebrew prophets is that Israel will be a blessing to the nations as it leads them to the one true God. All the peoples will worship him together.

The hope of Egypt is expressed in three movements.

1. Several cities will speak Hebrew and swear allegiance to the Lord (19:18).
2. The Lord will be worshiped in Egypt, with an "altar" in the center of the land and a "monument" on the border (19:19). The building of an altar or the setting up of memorial pillars was a way of acknowledging God's presence and of thanking him for his care.

The language of Isaiah 19:20–22 appears to have been consciously chosen to demonstrate that Egypt will share the same kind of relationship with the Lord as Israel did. They will be subject to the same kinds of divine discipline ("oppressors," 19:20; "plague," 19:22), and they will have available to them the same kinds of divine deliverance ("savior," 19:20; "heal," 19:22). He will reveal himself to them, and they will "acknowledge" (19:21; lit., "know") him.

1. The final expression of God's positive plans for Egypt is, if anything, even more shocking than the previous two. He is not merely going to deliver Egypt and Israel from the Assyrian oppressors; he is going to join the three countries together in the common worship of the Lord! Israel will fulfill the function that God promised to Abraham for his descendants (Gen 12:3). They will be a blessing to the world, a means whereby the blessings of God can come to all peoples (Isa 19:25).

Certainty of Egypt's Judgment (20:1–6). There is uncertainty whether Isaiah is fully nude during this three-year period. The Hebrew word *'arom* (20:2; NIV, "stripped") can connote either full or partial nudity, such as only wearing a loincloth, which would leave the "buttocks bared" (20:4). In any case, Isaiah is acting out what is going to happen when the Assyrians strip the captive Egyptians and march them off into captivity.

This is the only recorded example of Isaiah's performing symbolic actions. In the pagan view, what was done to the symbol was necessarily done to reality. To act something out was to bring it to pass. By contrast, in Greek philosophical understanding, which has shaped modern thinking, there is no necessary relation between the symbol and the reality.

The biblical understanding stands somewhere between these extremes. While the symbol is not identical with reality, it does "partake" of the reality. Thus, certain symbols have a uniquely powerful ability to depict and evoke a given reality. As such, they cannot be freely alternated with other symbols. But at the same time, there is never the sense that because the prophet has performed some symbolic action, the corresponding reality *must* occur. The symbol has evocative power, not causal power. The law of transcendence has forever broken that understanding of causation.

Application. Will the promises recorded here be fulfilled? Yes, they will. In fact, from one point of view they already have been fulfilled. For the first half of the first millennium, Egypt was one of the major centers of Christian, that is, biblical, faith. But we should be careful to avoid two extremes. On the one hand we should not say that the only possible fulfillment is a literal one according to my, or my group's, definition of "literal." On the other hand, we should not say that the spiritual teaching of these predictions is all that is important. If God is God, then history is still his arena to act in as he chooses.

ISAIAH 21:1–17

Original Meaning

The Desert by the Sea (21:1–10). The first verse states, literally, "the burden of the desert of the sea" (author's translation, 21:1a). Clearly, that is a contradiction in terms. The desert is not wet, and the sea is not dry. So, what is the writer intending to convey? Verse 9 suggests that the subject is Babylon, so why use this obscure expression? The most likely possibility is that it is a play on the name of Marduk-Baladan's (39:1) homeland in extreme southern Mesopotamia, "the Sealand." Is the great Babylonian rebel in a position to offer Judah any help? Yes, just about as much as a desert might offer!

Verses 1–2 depict the suddenness of destruction. Like a whirlwind in the "southland" of Judah, the destruction will sweep in. Babylon's power, like Assyria's before it, will be built on betrayal and plunder. But the day will come when the tables will be turned. Both "Elam" and "Media" (21:2) were occasionally allies of Babylon, and both turn against her at various points.

Probably the best explanation for the grief that racks Isaiah in 21:3–4 is that he is lamenting for those who put their trust in Babylon and will be destroyed when that trust fails (see 22:4). But he may also be experiencing vicariously the grief of those who are tortured and taken into exile.

Verse 5 reminds the reader of the scene in Daniel 5, where Belshazzar is feasting in Babylon while the enemy is at the gates. The scene of feasting is quickly changed to one of frantic preparation for war ("oil the shields," Isa 21:5), but the preparation is far too late.

While the overall sense of 21:6–9 is clear enough—that is, look for the message to come that "Babylon has fallen" (21:9)—the specific significance of the repeated references to chariots and teams of horses is not. Perhaps they are suggestive of the fleeing, defeated remnants of an army. Verse 10 continues that thought. The people of Judah had been crushed under the sled of Assyria, so it looks as if Babylon offers a ray of hope. But Isaiah, the watchman, sees a false hope. Babylon is no more able to help than any other nation on earth.

The Dumah Oracle (21:11–12). This two-verse oracle is a puzzle. Perhaps the thought is that even the Edomites turn to Isaiah, the Judean "watchman," to see what is happening in the east. Because of his God he is able to see the future in ways the ordinary seer cannot.

An Oracle on Arabia (21:13–17). The oasis of "Tema" (21:14) was located in an area of northwest Arabia known as Kedar (21:16). Tema is significant because this is where the last king of Babylon made his headquarters for most of his reign. It is not clear who the "fugitives" mentioned in 21:14 are. Perhaps they are Babylonians fleeing the destruction of their city. But 21:16–17 make it clear that Kedar itself will not escape the disaster.

Application. These three oracles speak of the fickleness of human promises. Are people depending on us? Are we only interested in using them for our own advantage? These are serious questions. One of the reasons they are so serious is because of the immense capacity for self-deception that human self-interest provokes.

ISAIAH 22:1–25

Original Meaning

The Valley of Vision (22:1–14). A valley is not where one goes to get a long view of things. Perhaps the prophet is condemning the Judeans. They are in the bottom of a valley, having lost all perspective on reality and what it means.

All the inhabitants of "the Valley of Vision" can see is short-term relief (22:1–2). They cannot see the longer view that the prophet has, namely, the events just before the fall of Jerusalem. The people are rejoicing over a short-term lifting of the Assyrian threat, while the prophet sees how this whole episode will end 125 years later and weeps "bitterly" (22:4). Verses 5–7 probably continue Isaiah's view of the distant future, when the besieging armies will be camped around the city.

In 22:8–14 the prophet makes his pronouncement against the Valley of Vision. Note the recurrence of verbs for seeing in 22:8, 9, and 11. Temporal realities have been looked at instead of eternal ones. It is not clear who the repeated "you" is in 22:8–12. It is probably Hezekiah, because we know he strengthened the walls of Jerusalem and had the famous tunnel dug to bring water from the spring of Gihon to the pool at the foot of the old city (2 Chr 32:1–5); if so, he is not named. Although the first verb of the succession of second-person verbs is singular (Isa 22:8), the rest are plural (22:9–11). Perhaps the point is that Hezekiah is not himself responsible for the misplaced priorities (22:15–19).

Jerusalem exists as the capital city of Judah only because of the grace and power of God (22:11). The land is a covenant gift from their covenant Lord. Thus, the most important thing to do in a moment of danger and threat is to be sure that they are acting within the covenant Lord's will and that their relationship with him is intact so that they can continue to receive the promised blessings of the covenant.

But they are acting as if the most important things they can do are the human things they do for themselves, such as tearing down the houses to "strengthen the wall" (22:10) and also so that troops can easily be rushed to any point where an attack is being made.

It is for this reason that God is calling for weeping and wailing (22:12). This is no time for self-congratulation and partying. But all the indications are that they have neither the interest nor the attention to learn those lessons. Thus, since the people will not weep and wail over their sins, it falls to the prophet to do it (22:4). He sees that apart from confession, repentance, and the attendant mercy of God, there is no possibility for the sins of the nation to be "atoned for" (22:14), and that is a source of terrible grief for him.

A Picture of Two Men (22:15–25). After a discourse, the prophet's point is reinforced with a concrete picture of what has just been said. Here the picture takes two parts, revolving around two different men. The first illustration (22:15–19) is negative, while the second (22:20–25) is more positive.

Shebna carries great responsibility for the well-being of the country, both spiritually and materially, but he is building himself a fine rock tomb. Instead of losing himself in order to bring life to his country, he is trying to make sure he will be remembered in death!

It is easy to think of the prime minister driving one of his splendid chariots (22:18), one of the perks of his office, out to see how the work was coming. But when he arrives at the site, he finds an unwelcome visitor, the prophet Isaiah. Isaiah tells Shebna that far from being important and significant, he is a "disgrace to [his] master's house" (22:18). Instead of being memorialized before all the people, he will be wadded up and thrown away like an old rag (22:17–18).

For a person like Shebna, the tokens of importance were significant to him. Thus, to have his official uniform ("robe" and "sash," 22:21) taken from him and given to another will be terribly humiliating. The "key" referred to in 22:22 represents absolute authority to determine who will have an audience with the king and who will not. Unlike Shebna, who is only concerned for himself, Eliakim will be concerned for the people under his charge and will act as a "father" (22:21) to them.

But there is a danger that can befall anyone who is truly responsible and reliable. That danger is spelled out in 22:23–25. There seems to be a suggestion that Eliakim's family will become a special burden to him (22:23–24). Eventually, he will crack under the strain, and all that has been dependent on him will come crashing down (22:25).

Application. We may choose to be Eliakim or Shebna. We may focus on the temporal or the eternal. If we focus on the temporal, we and all our works will perish with the temporal. If we choose the eternal, then none of our temporal works will ever be lost (Rom 8:13). Like Eliakim, we will be given authority (Matt 16:19).

ISAIAH 23:1–18

Original Meaning

Tyre's Destruction (23:1–14). Isaiah begins his discussion of Tyre's destruction with the word reaching the merchant ships homeward bound from the West. The reference to "the island" in 23:2 is a recognition that Tyre consisted of both a mainland city and an offshore island, with the harbor between the two. Verse 3 notes that Tyre was a shipper for Egyptian "grain." The Nile Valley produced much grain that was of no use to the Egyptians unless they sold it. For shipping it elsewhere they were dependent on the Phoenicians.

In 23:4 the Canaanite sea god Yam cries out like a parent bereft of children. Tyre, his foremost child, is gone, and it is as though he has never had any children. When the word reaches Egypt, the Egyptians "will be in anguish" (23:5).

Verses 6–12 are addressed to the Phoenician colony of Tarshish as the Lord calls on them to think about the implications of what has happened. Tyre was a "city of revelry" (23:7), a place of wealth and pleasure. It was also an "old" city, a mother city that had given birth to Tarshish and probably more colonies that we do not know of now (23:7). These colonies were so powerful and wealthy that each had its own king. Tyre's merchants had become so wealthy that they were no longer considered businessmen but rather were a part of the nobility (23:8).

Yet Isaiah sees the day when all of that will come to a screeching halt. The revelry will cease (23:12), and Tarshish will have to become self-subsistent, since the Egyptian grain will no longer be available (23:10). Tyre will not fall by accident or because of the superior might of the Assyrians, the Babylonians, or the Greeks. It will fall according to the eternal purposes of the Holy One of Israel.

There seems little evidence to support such an outlandish claim. Yet God said it, and that was enough for Isaiah. Nor were the plan and purpose of God's merely arbitrary. Rather, like all the other pagan nations, Tyre exalted itself against the Creator (23:9). God's hand is extended against pride in all its forms.

The reader is invited to compare the fate of Babylon with that which is coming to Tyre (23:13). Sargon brought heavy destruction on the city of Babylon in 710 BC and Sennacherib brought even greater destruction in 689 BC. Thus, the two cities that begin and end the sequence of oracles are brought together here. Neither will escape the judgment planned by God.

Tyre's Turning to the Lord (23:15–18). Isaiah foresees a day when Tyre will turn to the Lord. It is not clear what the seventy-year period in 23:15 refers to. Perhaps it is simply an indefinite time of punishment, with seventy referring to completeness. In any case, after this time the Lord will permit Tyre to regain some of its former eminence (23:17).

Application. Tyre's love was for money and the luxury and influence it could buy. It is difficult to separate money from what we think it can buy. How big a house is big enough? How many cars are enough? And how much do we need for a "comfortable" retirement? What are we looking for? Comfort, pleasure, and security—the things humans have been looking for since the beginning of time. And what will give these to us? Money, the more the better! In other words, we are little different from Tyre. We have forgotten or ignored Jesus's words in Mark 10:25: "It is easier for a camel to go through the eye of a needle than for someone who is rich to enter the kingdom of God."

ISAIAH 24:1–23

Original Meaning

The Destruction of the Earth (24:1–13). There can be no question of the focus of chapter 24: the destruction of the earth. But why is this destruction coming? It is the result of the choices that earth's inhabitants have made. Verses 4–13 use one of the common images of this early part of the book to make this statement—the vine. The earth "dries up" and "withers" (24:4) like a vine (24:7). Earth's inhabitants have "disobeyed the laws" of life (24:5a). They have "broken the everlasting covenant" (24:5b). Like Paul in Romans 1, Isaiah insists that there are laws that God the Creator has written on the human conscience. Thus, he will not admit any argument of ignorance as justification for sin.

The "covenant" in 24:5c may refer to the Noachic covenant of Genesis 9:1–17 with its prohibition of bloodshed. Here again is an understanding between the creature and the Creator that is not dependent on special revelation. Rather, it has been passed down through the ages as common human heritage.

One of the features of covenants was the custom of the parties calling down curses on themselves for failure to keep the covenant. That is what has happened to earth's inhabitants. They are under a "curse" and bear "guilt" for what they have done (24:6).

The "city" of earth (24:10, 12) lies silent and desolate. The forced and artificial gaiety induced by alcohol (24:7, 9, 11) vanishes like a vapor before the awful realities of judgment and destruction. The city offers wealth, glamour, excitement, pleasure, intrigue, and power—all the things humans are prone to sell their souls for. But as mighty and alluring as the city of earth is, a day of harvest is coming when all the fruit will be stripped off and nothing will be left (24:13).

A Dramatic Contrast (24:14–18a). These verses are something of a riddle because of the dramatic contrast between 24:14–16a and 24:16b–18a. The first segment speaks of overflowing shouts of "joy" coming from the ends of the earth because of the "glory" and "majesty" of the Lord (24:14–15). This is immediately followed with an unidentified "I" (24:16; the prophet?) protesting that he is wasting away because of the "treachery" and "terror" (24:17) that characterize the earth.

It seems most likely to me that the first segment is the cry of joy from those who have been oppressed by the evil earth-city. They are looking joyously at the end of the story. But the prophet cannot move so quickly beyond the present dark realities. He sees all the horrors that must take place before that final resolution, and he is stricken by them.

The Entire Creation Subject to God (24:18b–23). The imagery of 24:18b–20 is reminiscent of the description of the flood in Genesis 6. But the water is only an image. The real weight that crushes the earth is the "guilt of its rebellion" (Isa 24:20). Again, the issue is clear, as it has been from the earliest verses of the book: the human problem of rebellion against God.

Isaiah 24:21–23 expand the theme from the earth to the entire creation. People in the ancient world considered the "powers in the heavens" (24:21)—that is, the stars, the sun, and the moon—to be deities. But the God of Israel insists they are not. If God chooses, he can turn off their light and shut them up in a dark "prison" (24:22). Compared to the light of "the Lord Almighty," their light is something to be ashamed of (24:23).

There is only One who has the right to be called King of the universe. Where will be the seat of his rule? He will rule on "Mount Zion," and the "elders" will be his courtiers (24:23). Thus, we are prepared for the shift to hope that occurs in the following chapter.

Application. Only God is eternal, and he will one day bring down the curtain on earth's stage. It will be too late to get ready for that day when it arrives. Either we are ready every day, or we are not ready at all.

ISAIAH 25:1–12

Original Meaning. As I have said previously, the book of Isaiah makes it clear that judgment and destruction are never God's intended last words. Rather, he intends that those harsh words will pave the way for the happier words of hope and redemption. This is the case in Isaiah 24 and 25. From the silence of the shattered city, we move to the joy of a feast where the host is the Lord.

Israel's Lord has been faithful to his promises and has "done wonderful things" (25:1). In 25:3 is the hint of a significant addition to this picture. Redemption and deliverance are not for Israel alone but for all peoples who turn to God in faith and humility. This theme is developed in 25:6–9. There is no sense in which God glories in the destruction of the wicked. He wants to invite "all peoples" (25:6–8) to his feast.

Verse 9 emphasizes once again the overarching theme of chapters 7–39: the trustworthiness of God. God can be trusted when nothing and no one else on earth can. If we trust the nations of humanity instead of God, they will turn on us and destroy us.

But the thought of this unit does not end on this glorious note. Yes, God is merciful and compassionate, slow to get angry, and quick to forgive. But no one dare presume on that grace. Sin *will* be punished, and its deadly consequences will not be immediately curtailed.

Application. This passage has one of the clearest teachings on resurrection in the Old Testament. As such it speaks to the greatest issue in the modern world—the issue of death. Death takes away the possibility of individual human significance. The only alternative is to say that humanity will go on after I die and that therefore I have some significance as a part of the race. But that is my only significance, and a very small one.

But we have not been created for death but for life. Death has lost its sting, and the grave has been robbed of its victory (1 Cor 15:55). God the Father has defeated death forever in the death and resurrection of his Son, Jesus Christ. To be sure, we await the final day when the King will make his promised pronouncement and death will cease to be. But until then we can live in the assurance that we do have individual significance and that death cannot destroy that. Furthermore, we can know that trust in God and renunciation of our pride are ultimate values that will make all the difference in whether we conquer death or death conquers us.

ISAIAH 26:1–27:1

Original Meaning

Thanks for God's Deliverance (26:1–6). The opening song of thanks picks up themes from chapters 24–25. Instead of the silent and ruined city of the earth (26:5), there is now the city of God, peopled with the faithful singing his praises (26:1–2). It has the open gates of confidence, open to those who choose to live in the ethical righteousness of the covenant. One is able to behave in this way because of a complete inner integrity that stems from complete dependence on God: "trust" (26:3). This trust is eminently justified because the Lord is as secure as a "Rock" that is "eternal" (26:4) and because he will bring the "lofty city" of earth down into the dust (26:5–6).

Dependence on God (26:7–19). In 26:7–11 the prophet asks God to speed that day of retribution. He begins by talking about the "path" or way of life on which God calls the "righteous" to walk, "level" and "smooth" (26:7). God only asks them to live in the way they were made for.

The righteous do not say they trust God and then rush ahead to take care of themselves in ways that violate God's regulations for fruitful living. God's honor and reputation have become the believers' deepest desire (26:8). They want to live in a way that will bring honor to him and not disgrace. This thought is deepened in 26:9. Isaiah is longing for the ethical evidence of God's presence to be unmistakably seen, because this is the only way "the people of the world" (26:9) will learn what is right.

Verses 10–11 express a profound truth. In the absence of repentance, "grace" may actually be counterproductive. Unless the "wicked" experience the results of their having broken God's just regulations for life, his "judgments" (26:9), they will see no reason to change. The nations believe they have conquered through their own power and glory, in spite of the Lord. God must demonstrate to the world that this is not the case. He must rise up against the wicked on behalf of his people and make the consequences of sin clear.

Verses 12–18 reflect further on this thought. The people have been unable to accomplish God's work in the world, and they call on him to demonstrate his delivering power there. This reflection begins with a testimony of his grace on their behalf in the past (26:12–15). Verses 16–18 continue the previous theme, but the focus changes from the might of God to the helplessness of the people.

This last thought in 26:18 appears to be reflecting on Israel's larger mission to be a blessing on the nations. Not only does Isaiah long to see God's justice applied to the world in regard to Israel (26:9–11), but he also wants to see God's salvation made available to the world through Israel.

In 26:19 the prophet, speaking for God, tells them not to despair. Though years have passed and many of the faithful have died, with no effect either on the nation or the world, death does not have the last word; God does.

Promises to the Faithful (26:20–27:1). The illustration that is used in 27:1 is almost certainly taken from Canaanite mythology, in which the chaos monster is a sea serpent named Leviathan. Isaiah is simply making use of emotive images familiar to many in his audience to make his point. No enemy can defeat God's plan and purposes.

Application. These verses in Isaiah are written for just such an ambiguous time as ours—when the lines are not clear. In many cases we have allowed the culture around us, through media domination, to saturate our vision. The result is that many of us know nothing of inner serenity. The scriptural admonition, "Do not be anxious about anything" (Phil 4:6), becomes almost laughable. We are anxious about everything.

What must we do? We must first of all guard much more closely what we let into our minds. This begins at home. Are our homes places of quiet, beauty, and serenity? Hardly! Many of our homes are places where cluttered minds reveal themselves in cluttered living spaces. When will Christians admit that we are countercultural and begin to embrace that reality?

ISAIAH 27:2–13

Original Meaning. Here we have the opposite picture from the one we saw in chapter 5. There God called in the wild animals to destroy the vineyard of bitter grapes, his nation. Now we see the vineyard from the other side. The vineyard of "Jacob" is going to be so fruitful that it will fill "the world with fruit" (27:6).

What accounts for this radical shift? Surely God *was* angry with his people, angry enough to destroy them. Yet here he talks as if those words had never been said. Verses 6–11 explain the matter. Yes, God had indeed driven Israel out (27:8), but his purpose was not annihilation but cleansing (27:9).

Isaiah 27:12–13 cap the Lord's promises to his people. The writer begins with the metaphor of harvest. The same point is made with a different metaphor, the trumpet call of muster for battle (27:13). The exiles from north and south are called to "worship the LORD on the holy mountain" (27:13).

Application. God's actions in our lives today continue to be not for the purpose of destruction but for refinement. If trouble and adversity have come our way, our attitude about God will make all the difference in how we receive them. If we think of God as passionately loving "the old house" that we are, then the ripping of the saw and the crashing of the hammer will still be painful but much easier to bear.

ISAIAH 28:1–29

Original Meaning

Pronouncement against Ephraim (28:1–6). Throughout this stanza, there is a play on "wreath." The drunken partygoers in Samaria wear these wreaths on their heads as they try to forget the terror facing them. The battlements of the city sitting on its hilltop at the "head" of the "valley" (28:1, 4) give it the appearance of one of these wreaths. But Isaiah sees a day when all these wreaths will be thrown to the ground and trampled. The pride of the Northern Kingdom is going to be snatched up like a ripe "fig" (28:4).

In contrast, there is another "wreath," the Lord himself (28:5). He will be the source of beauty and glory for those who have abandoned their own pride in glad submission to him. He will give "justice" to the judges and "strength" to the soldiers (28:6).

Continuing Pronouncement against Ephraim (28:7–13). Verses 1–4 spoke of the political leaders and the nobility, whereas 28:7–8 show that the priests and prophets are no better off. Alcohol abuse is a problem for them, but it is only a symptom of their deeper problem, an unwillingness to surrender their needs and desires to the Lord. The result is that those who should be giving clear guidance and teaching in that desperate hour are "befuddled" (29:7) and staggering around in a stupor. The "tables" (28:8) "are covered with vomit," expressing the depths of his disgust with what is taking place. Verses 9–10 express the mockery of these religious leaders for the true prophet. Of course, childishness is just what alcohol does to a person, but it makes them unable to recognize the fact.

The prophet responds in 28:11–13 by saying that since this is what they think they are getting, it is exactly what they *will* get, only from other lips than his. Since they refuse God's invitation to rest in him, they will learn his truth through "foreign lips and strange tongues" (28:11). If the people will not learn the easy way of faith, then they must learn the hard way of experience (28:13).

A Message to the Leaders in Jerusalem (28:14–22). The focus now shifts to the leaders in Jerusalem. A "scoffer" (28:14) is someone who not only rejects the truth but also makes light of it. Like the leaders in the north, these Judean scoffers have laughed at the foolishness of trusting God and have made their cynical covenants "with death" (28:15a). Probably this is a reference to an alliance with Egypt. They have allied themselves with a "lie" (28:15b), namely, the idea that human power is a better means of protecting oneself than God's power.

God's response to the "covenant of death" appears in 28:16–19b. He begins by asserting once again that he alone is trustworthy. The "stone" (28:16) is probably to be understood as an agglomeration of all the elements of God's trustworthiness. When any other trust is measured against him, its faultiness becomes apparent at once, as is the case with the "covenant with death" (28:18).

In 28:17c–19b God declares that the "hiding place" the leaders have so craftily built is going to be swept away like a hut in a windstorm. The flood will not come just once but again and again ("morning after morning," 28:19). This is an accurate reflection of the Assyrian tactics, as they came back to an area again and again until it was completely destroyed.

Isaiah 28:19c–22 give us the prophet's reflection on the Lord's words. Just as the Lord struck down the Philistines with a flood at "Mount Perazim" (28:21) and scattered the Canaanites with hail in the "Valley of Gibeon" (28:21), so now he will treat his own people like those enemies (cf. 1:24). The scoffers had better "stop [their] mocking" of the word of God and had better start listening to what "the Lord, the LORD Almighty" is actually saying (28:22).

Illustration from the World of Agriculture (28:23–29). "Listen and hear my voice" (28:23) has overtones of wisdom literature, with which the royal counselors would be familiar. Also, the comparison of one activity, royal counsel, with another, farming, is characteristic of wisdom literature. A farmer knows that there are certain appropriate ways to do things. He does not keep on plowing forever, as though that were an end in itself. When he plants, he does not mix up all the different seeds together. Each has to be grown separately. When he threshes, he uses appropriate tools to the size of the grain involved. To use a heavy threshing sledge or a stone roller on the tiny "caraway" and "cummin" seeds (28:25, 27) would crush them to dust. Instead, he uses a jointed "stick" (28:27), called a "flail" in English. Neither does one use a threshing sledge to grind up the grain for flour. There are other tools for that.

In each of these cases, Isaiah says these peasants have learned these principles from God, the Creator. His natural revelation has taught them how life works. Why cannot these wise counselors, who have the benefit of both natural and special revelation, be as intelligent as an uneducated peasant when it comes to understanding that God can be trusted and humans cannot?

Application. There are spiritual principles that are as simple and ironclad as physical ones. The pagans of Isaiah's day had observed these and had written them into their civil law codes. They knew that no human society could survive where lying, stealing, murder, and adultery occurred with any regularity. The pagan cultures, with no real concept of transcendence and thus no true doctrine of creation, could not explain it, but they recognized it to be so. Thus, such behaviors were forbidden in all the legal codes of the ancient Near East. It waited until biblical revelation for the explanation to be made clear.

The Creator is a God of truth, integrity, love, and faithfulness, and thus his creation reflects that character. Obedience to the covenant did not require some strange, occult activities outside of human experience. It involved nothing other than living out the lifestyle that others had discovered before them but doing it for the sake of the love of God.

Modern legal theory is deeply opposed to the idea of "natural law." Isaiah would merely shake his head and point to the farmer. Are there "natural laws" in nature? he would ask. If so, why would we think there are none in the rest of the natural world, that is, the world of the spirit?

ISAIAH 29:1–14

Original Meaning. This second "woe" is addressed to Jerusalem (29:1), also called "Ariel." One possible meaning of the word is "altar hearth," which is the most probable explanation (so NIV, 29:2). This would fit in with the general emphasis of the passage on the cultic activity that took place at Jerusalem (29:1, 13).

As in Isaiah 1, Jerusalem's problem is that they believe they have immunity from judgment because they have the true cult of Yahweh (29:1, 13). But as there, Isaiah says this worship is worthless because it is not from the heart (29:13).

Verse 2 suggests that all of Jerusalem will become an altar hearth on which the people themselves will become the sacrifice. Note that there is no mention of Assyria here; God is the enemy who besieges the city (29:3).

Verse 4 is perhaps an allusion to the worship of the dead and to spiritism. While priding themselves on their pure worship, the people of Jerusalem and Judah are secretly engaging in many pagan practices.

But because it is God, not Assyria, who puts his people into the dust, it is also God who can make Jerusalem's enemies as insubstantial as "fine dust" (29:5). They appear so weighty and terrifying, but before God they are as thin and as vaporous as a "dream" (29:7, 8). Jerusalem will be drawing pilgrims from all over the earth thousands of years after the capitals of those nations have ceased to exist.

But the Judeans are equally "blind" (29:9) to the reality of the Lord's work. In 29:9–10 the interplay of causation is significant. The people have blinded themselves, yet at the same time God has made the prophets unable to see the truth. We may endlessly debate which of these comes first, but the fact is that nothing happens apart from both those causes. As a result, the word of God ("this whole vision") is a closed book to God's people (29:11–12). From God's side it is sealed up and cannot be opened; from the human side, it cannot be read when it is opened.

Consequently, Jerusalem's religion has become only a performance with themselves as the audience. There is no real connection between the worshipers and the One being worshiped. They go through the motions with no expectation of any real encounter with the living God, no sense of wonder. So, the LORD promises to do wonders (29:14), but the clear implication is that the coming wonders of the God they thought they had under their control will become their enemy (cf. 28:21).

Application. Since Hebrew worship was similar in form to that of the pagans, it was easy for the Hebrews to fall into a pagan understanding, namely, that because certain human activities have been performed, the gods must do certain things. The result is that the activity has much more to do with manipulation than with worship. Because I have given God a very expensive gift, he is obligated to bless me. Again and again the Old Testament speaks out against such an idea. God is transcendent; that is, he is radically discontinuous from this world. Thus, he cannot be manipulated through anything done in this world. He forgives through his grace alone.

ISAIAH 29:15–24

Original Meaning. This third "woe" is composed of both judgment (29:15–16) and hope (29:17–24). The prophet accuses the counselors of trying to hide their counsel. They have made their "plans" (29:15) secretly, without consulting the Lord's prophet, foolishly hoping he will not find out. False hope! Isaiah says this is like the pot telling the potter how to do his work (29:16).

The promises made in 29:17–24 are more far-reaching than for mere physical restoration. They deal primarily with the spiritual needs of the nation. They promise a day when the kinds of attitudes and behaviors that have brought the nation to this dark day will be radically changed.

The reference to the "scroll" (29:18) connects the thought back to 29:11–12. No longer will the word of God be closed to God's people. Verses 19–21 deal with the social results of this restored sensitivity to God's leading and will.

Isaiah 29:22–24 gives the results of all of this, as signaled by the opening "therefore." Gracious redemption will result in holy living and a transformed attitude toward God's truth. Redemption is expressed in a figure that appears frequently in the last section of the book—many children (cf. 54:2–3; 66:7–11). God will not allow his promises to Abraham to fail.

This is, of course, covenant language. Those who are in covenant with God are committed to replicating God's holy character, his "name" (29:23), in their own behavior. No longer will the descendants of Jacob take "the Holy One" (29:23) for granted. Instead of the stubbornness, willfulness, and general hardheadedness that tend to characterize all humans, not just Israel, there will be a grasp of "understanding" (29:24) and a genuine teachability.

Application. To a large extent, the Old Testament is the story of Israel's failure to be a holy people. Here in Isaiah God promises that the day will come when they can actually fulfill the demands of the covenant. We now live in that day. Now, through what Christ has done for us in forgiving the sin of the broken covenant and in giving us his Spirit, it is possible for us to fulfill all the "righteous requirements of the law" in real life (Rom 8:3–4).

ISAIAH 30:1–33

Original Meaning

Foolishness of Looking to Egypt (30:1–7). This section is composed of two parts: The first (30:1–5) states the foolishness of trusting Egypt; the second (30:6–7) illustrates this message. God has carefully reared them, but they do not consult their Father for his counsel and advice but hastily make their own "plans" (30:1). Because they are "wayward in spirit" (29:24), they refuse to be led by God's spirit.

On the surface, Egypt is large enough and powerful enough to be like a large palm tree, whose fronds offer "shade" (30:2) from Assyria's blazing sun. But God sees things differently. There may be impressive "officials in Zoan" (30:4), the town where the Hebrews were once enslaved (Ps 78:12, 43), but there is nothing substantial behind the facade. Everyone who puts their trust in Egypt will be disgraced (Isa 30:5).

This idea of Egypt's helplessness is illustrated in a two-verse "prophecy" (30:6–7). The mention of "envoys" (30:6) suggests that this is a diplomatic mission and that the caravan is carrying a large payment for the Egyptian "help" (30:7). In a touch of sarcasm, Isaiah creates an oxymoron to describe Egypt. *This* Rahab is a toothless old monster, too lazy to move.

Judah's Coming Devastation (30:8–18). In 30:8 Isaiah offers the purpose of writing down prophetic words, so that when the predictions came true, people will know it (cf. 8:1, 16; 29:11, 18). He defines the rebellion of the people more clearly.

They do not want to hear "the LORD's instruction" (30:9) or "what is right" (30:10). Instead, they ask the prophets to say pleasant things to them. They do not want Isaiah to confront them. Undoubtedly, they do not actually ask for "illusions" (30:10), but Isaiah says that is what they are actually asking for when they demand that he stop telling them about "the Holy One of Israel" (30:11).

Ironically, Isaiah's response to that demand is to tell them "what the Holy One of Israel says" (30:12). They have rejected the truth that God alone can be trusted and instead have trusted in "oppression" (30:12) and lies, grinding the poor to get money to pay Egypt for its worthless help. As a result, their destruction will come as suddenly as a collapsing wall.

God has told them again and again the prescription for their condition. They must turn back to him in "repentance" and "rest" in him (30:15). In quietly trusting him instead of frantically rushing around trying to solve their problems for themselves, they will find both "salvation" and "strength" (30:15). But the patient has refused the physician's prescription.

Isaiah 30:16 offers a strong contrast with 30:15. Instead of quietness and trust, there will be rapid flight. There is only one problem with that course of action: The "pursuers" will be swifter yet. As a result, they will be as forlorn as a tattered flag whipping in the wind, with nothing but corpses surrounding it (30:17).

So, what is God's course of action in the face of this reality? Will he wash his hands of them? No, in one of the greatest statements in all of Scripture, he says that since Israel will not wait for (trust in) him, he will have to wait (NIV "longs") to be gracious to them (30:18). Isaiah presents the picture of the Creator of the universe patiently standing, waiting for us to discover what fools we have been and to turn back to him to receive the grace and compassion that are in his fatherly heart.

Promises of Redemption of God's People (30:19–33). This last section details what will happen when the Israelites finally come to their senses and turn back to God. Three kinds of promises are made: The first one (30:19–22) involves spiritual regeneration; the second one (30:23–26) speaks of the physical blessings God intends to pour out on his people; and the final one (30:27–33) prophesies defeat for all of Israel's enemies, particularly Assyria.

Isaiah sees a day coming when the people will "cry" out to God, and he will "answer" them with grace (30:19). Their spiritual eyes will be open to see all that he is teaching them through these experiences (30:20). No longer will they be like a stubborn mule. Now their spiritual ears will be so sensitive they will only need the merest whisper in their ear to turn them to the right or the left (30:21). This will result in a despising of all the expensive idols on which they have lavished such attention (30:22).

Verses 23–26 are closely related to the first promise. When his people are responsive to him and have stopped their attempts to manipulate the physical, social, and spiritual world to their own advantage, God will give all those blessings freely. Verses 23–24 express the blessings in agricultural terms.

Verses 25–26 contrast "slaughter" with "healing." This may refer to earth's final battle (cf. Zech 14:1–4; Mal 4:1–2). It may also refer to the destruction of pride, because height, barrenness, and darkness are associated with pride elsewhere in the book (Isa 2:12–17; 8:21–22; 47:5). Barrenness will be replaced with abundant water, and darkness will be replaced with incredible light.

In the final promise (30:27–33), the language has a certain "end of history" flavor. It is highly emotive and loaded with vivid imagery. Yet 30:31 makes it clear that the ultimate subject of God's wrath here is Assyria. This should make us cautious about what passages we assign as end-time promises.

Perhaps the reason for the unusually vivid language here is to convince the hearers of the certainty of the promises. In all of this, one recurring feature is a reference to the Lord's mouth, breath, and voice (30:27, 28, 30, 31, 33). Just as his word is life and health to those who respond to it, it is sudden, terrible death to those who reject it. In Malachi, the same sun that heals the wounded is the one that draws the last moisture from the chaff (4:1–2).

Application. The fundamental idea behind repentance in the Old Testament is to turn around or to turn back. It is to stop going in the direction you were, namely, one of self-dependence and self-pleasing, and to turn away from that life to one of depending on God and pleasing him. To talk about resting in the Lord while still keeping hold of one's life and its direction is a contradiction in terms. By the same token, to stop committing certain sins and to clean up one's act merely for the sake of avoiding punishment is not to turn back to God. It is only to turn away from sin and may be just as selfish as any other act.

Just as the Old Testament put the correct relationship with God within the context of absolute loyalty to a covenant king, the New Testament calls us to turn from loyalty to ourselves and become the glad subjects of heaven's King. If we find real trust difficult, perhaps it is because there has never been a real change of king in our lives. The idea that we can have the benefits of the kingdom without turning away from our own kingship is a fallacy.

ISAIAH 31:1–9

Original Meaning. The woe in 28:1 was against the drunken leaders in Ephraim; in 29:1 it was against those in Jerusalem who depended on cultic righteousness; in 29:15 it was against those who tried to hide their counsel from the Lord; in 30:1 it was against "obstinate children" who would not bring to the Lord their plans to make an alliance with Egypt. The present "woe" is specifically against "those who go down to Egypt for help" (31:1). Thus, the climax (or the nadir) has been reached. Drunken leaders who focus on the wrong things have given ungodly advice that rebellious people have adopted without consulting God.

The result is now baldly stated: They have chosen to trust men and horses instead of "the Holy One of Israel" (31:1). They have chosen to trust the creation rather than the Creator. This is foolish, as 31:2–3 explains.

Up to here, Isaiah has been counseling the Israelites not to trust Egypt because Egypt cannot help. In 31:4–9 he develops the other side of the argument: Trust the Lord because he is the only One who can deliver you. He makes three points: God will defend Jerusalem (31:4–5); turn back to him and away from idols (31:6–7); Assyria is no match for the Lord (31:8–9).

Just as 31:1–3 is the most specific in denouncing the counsel to trust Egypt, so 31:8–9 is the most specific in promising deliverance from the Assyrian threat. The promise that they "will fall by no human sword" (31:8) surely sounds like what is described in 37:36. Again, Isaiah's main point is that it is much wiser to trust God than Egypt in the face of the Assyrians.

Application. The statements here about God's shielding Jerusalem (31:5) and about his furnace being Jerusalem (31:9) raise questions for us about the appropriate attitude Christians should take toward Jerusalem and Israel today. While I believe that God's promises for physical Israel will be fulfilled, I suspect they may be fulfilled in very different ways than a simplistic, literal reading of the Bible would suggest. The Jews in Jesus's day read the prophecies of the Messiah in that way and were almost completely unprepared for the way in which they were actually fulfilled. We need to be reading the text with faith and yet openness; God loves to do things in new ways.

ISAIAH 32:1–8

Original Meaning. Chapters 32–33 speak of the true leader and the characteristics of his reign. What is described here is more than the best of human kingdoms. Thus, there seems good reason to see this material as God's promise of his Messiah in view of the failure of all the human messiahs.

Instead of devouring their people for their own sakes (chs. 28–29), these leaders will be a blessing to their people. Their blessing is described in four vivid similes in 32:2: a "shelter," a "refuge," "streams of water," and shade (NIV "shadow") in the desert. In this new kingdom, "eyes" will see, and "ears" will hear (32:3). Instead of dullness and insensitivity, hearts will have knowledge and understanding.

In 32:5–8 is a lengthy contrast between the "fool" and the "noble." Many times in life a "fool" is treated as a "noble" simply because he has gained power and wealth. Those are called "noble" (32:8) have learned that the gracious God can be trusted to supply their needs, and thus they no longer need to be grasping but can become giving.

Application. We in the church today run the same danger just described. We give honors to people who do not deserve them. Money has no morality, but the people who make it and give it do. The "fool" believes that he or she owns you now and has the right to tell you how to conduct your business in a more up-to-date (read "less Christian") way. And because we feel beholden to our benefactor, we are cautious about offending him or her.

ISAIAH 32:9–20

Original Meaning. The unit shows a consistent train of thought as it continues to address the issue that everything in chapters 7–39 ultimately goes back to trust and security. Verses 9–14 condemn "women" who are "complacent" and "secure" (32:9), for in only one year, all that will be changed. They should start mourning now (32:11–12) because of the agricultural disaster about to come on them.

Verse 13, with its use of "thorns and briers," suggests that the prophet has more in mind than a mere physical disaster (5:6; 27:4). Not only will the land itself become barren and deserted, but this is the condition of the nation as well. "Merriment" and "revelry" will cease (32:13), and all the places where strength and rule could be expected will be abandoned (32:14). All the false trusts will have failed.

But that will not mean God has failed. As so many times previously, the prediction of tragedy and defeat is immediately followed with God's promise of hope (32:15–20). If the nation has trusted in all the wrong things and become barren and unproductive, God has something in mind that will make possible true productivity and security, namely, his own "Spirit" (32:15).

In the messianic kingdom, God will pour out his Spirit from "on high" (32:15). The Spirit will fall on barren hearts, and the things that the covenant required but could not produce—"justice" and "righteousness"—will spring up (32:16).

Application. Just as Isaiah had promised, the Messiah, through the Holy Spirit he has given, makes it possible for Christians to live a life of true nobility. There are inner resources with which to meet everything that comes to us and to triumph over them.

ISAIAH 33:1–16

Original Meaning

The Woe and an Appeal to God (33:1–6). The emphasis on betrayal in 33:1 has suggested to many that the specific occasion for this woe was when Sennacherib accepted Hezekiah's payment to break off his attack on Judah and then did not break off the attack. However, if that were the case, the material has been placed here in a much larger theological context. The fact that Assyria is not named is indicative of this. All the destructive and deceptive character of earth's nations is used as a foil to depict the radically different character of the biblical God and of the kingdom he will build.

The Lord is the only One who is truly "exalted" (33:5). His character will provide a "foundation" (33:6) on which people can live with confidence (cf. 28:16–17). That foundation is "justice" and "righteousness" (33:5), and on it can be erected "salvation," "wisdom and knowledge" (33:6). All of this is available to the person who acknowledges that God is the Lord and gives him reverent obedience (33:6).

Deliverance to Come from God (33:7–16). Verses 7–9 paint a picture of hopelessness. But there *is* hope. Assyria started a fire sweeping across the ancient world with its imperial aggression and oppression, and one day God will bring that fire back on Assyria's own "peoples" (33:12). He is the "everlasting burning" (33:14) with whom people must somehow come to terms. But how can mere humans "dwell" with him (33:14)! In fact, it is not God's mystical essence that separates us from himself; rather, it is his character. Thus, all that is required is a change of character on our part.

The opening words of 33:15 give a general description of this character: Do and say "what is right." In 33:15c–16, the specifics of "right" behavior are spelled out. As is usually the case in such lists, the behaviors are primarily relational. Persons who will survive the fire value others just as God values others. Such a person can "dwell" with God on the "heights" (33:16). In that setting they will be secure (NIV "refuge") and will have all their needs supplied. God can do what human leaders cannot and what Egypt cannot. Should he not be trusted?

Application. No one can earn a place with God by righteous behavior. Rather, we are *given* that place, just as the Israelites were given freedom from Egypt. God gives us that place because Jesus Christ has died in our place. But God has not only given us eternal life, he has also given us his Spirit so that we can do what the Israelites could not.

ISAIAH 33:17–24

Original Meaning. In the context of chapter 33, there can be little question that the "king" referred to in 33:17 is the Lord. Not only is it clear in 33:1–16 that he is the monarch of the earth, but 33:22 specifically identifies "the LORD" as "our king." The "king" here is the One to whom Hezekiah goes in humble subjection (37:16–20) and who thereby removes the Assyrian siege "towers" and tribute (NIV "revenue") from Jerusalem (33:18). This divine king makes it so that the alien Assyrian speech is not heard in Judah for a long time (33:19).

The city will have peaceful "rivers and streams" (33:21) flowing through it, a symbol of peace and abundance. Isaiah underscores the peaceful nature of God's supply when he says no vessel of war ("galley," 33:21) will sail on the rivers of Zion. Why? Because of the righteous character of the Lord, who is Israel's "king" (33:22).

It is not clear who is being addressed in the first half of 33:23. However, in the overall context, it is most likely the destroying, betraying nation with which the chapter began. This warship tried to sail against Zion, but it came up against a greater enemy in the Lord than it had planned for.

The final promise for the Zion ruled by the Messiah is that it will be a place of health, both physical and spiritual. All the effects of "sin" (33:24) will be done away with, and creation will be seen again in the manner in which it was first intended.

Application. In Christ there are *endless opportunities.* He does not press us into a mold in order to produce robots who will serve him. Rather, he calls us friends, allowing each of us to achieve the maximum of what we were designed for. He allows each of us to develop in our own way because he, our King, delights to serve us. In such a relationship and with all the power of heaven at our disposal, even the most restrictive of earth's situations offers endless openings.

ISAIAH 34:1–17

Original Meaning

General Announcement of Judgment (34:1–4). The language in 34:1–4 is that of the court. God calls the defendants to hear the decree pronounced against them. But the judgment does not merely involve the "earth" (34:1); it affects the entire cosmos (34:4). God's anger is particularly directed against the "armies," which aptly symbolize the arrogance and pride of "nations" (34:2). This is a conflict between the Creator and those who have rebelled against him, a conflict with cosmic consequences.

Edom as an Example (34:5–17). When it is asked why Edom should be singled out to represent the nations of the earth in their hostility to God and their eventual destruction, the answer seems clear. As early as the entry of Israel into the land of Canaan, Edom opposed God's plan (Num 20:14–21).

The section on Edom can be divided in two parts. The first (Isa 34:5–8) speaks of the bloody destruction that is going to fall on Edom for Zion's sake. The second part (34:9–17) speaks of the desert that Edom will become.

Verse 5 emphasizes the representative role of Edom among the nations. The repetition of "blood" and "fat" (34:6–7), terms commonly used in instructions for sacrifices, makes the sacrificial setting that much clearer. The destruction of the nations is intended "to uphold Zion's cause" (34:8).

The description in 34:9–17 goes into considerable detail to make its point. The language of 34:9–10 is reminiscent of the destruction of Sodom and Gomorrah in Genesis 19. This may be another reason why Edom is chosen to represent the destruction of the nations: Its territory is largely desert, which is nearly uninhabitable. Thus, it fits what Isaiah wants to say about the results of trusting human glory.

Verses 16–17 assert that the prediction about the birds and animals nesting in Edom is a certainty. To establish this certainty, the prophet appeals to "the scroll of the LORD" (34:16a), where the hearer can supposedly read that each of the animals mentioned will be there. In the book of nature as established by the "mouth" of God (34:16b), there are certain fixed realities, like the mating of animals. Just as God has assigned the places and conditions of the animals, so he has also assigned the places and conditions of humans. He is like a landowner who can divide up the plots of land as he wishes. Thus, there is a fixed rule in the moral universe that is no more changeable than the laws of nature. The nations of the earth have chosen to flaunt their rebellion and must pay the price for doing so.

Application. What are our churches trusting in? Large budgets, impressive facilities, powerful preaching? If so, we have put our trust in the creature. The place given to prayer in a local congregation is a good measure of where a church's trust really is. If its only focused praying is the Sunday morning pastoral prayer, that congregation is headed into the desert. Whatever they may say, they as a church are trusting the creature. By contrast, when a congregation like the Brooklyn Tabernacle makes real, earnest prayer a top priority, it is actually making a practice of trusting God and is headed into a garden. The pastor who teaches the congregation to pray and the congregation who teaches their pastor to pray has gone far toward a change of allegiance from the world to God.

ISAIAH 35:1–10

Original Meaning. This chapter is the mirror image of Isaiah 34. That passage spoke of the fate of the arrogant nations and all who trusted in them. This one speaks of the destiny of those who turn from that path to a resolute trust in God. In a powerful contrast, God will turn the "desert" into a garden (35:1). The "burning sand will become a pool," and the places "where jackals once lay" will become grassy meadows (35:7).

Verses 3–6a and 8 make it plain that this restoration is a spiritual one. Those who are discouraged and fearful will be given courage and strength. In an apparent allusion to Isaiah 6, the promise is made that those who did not remain faithful—the "blind" and the "deaf" (35:5), the spiritually "lame" and "mute" (35:6)—will be delivered from their afflictions and become full participants in the community of faith.

This idea is furthered with an additional image in 35:8–10, namely, that of a "highway." In the rugged highlands of Judah and Ephraim as well as in the desert east and south of Judah's central ridge, a straight and level highway would be a wonderful thing. There is ready access to him and to all the blessings of his creation.

This highway is the way to God, as seen in its title, "the Way of Holiness" (35:8). It is the way of holiness on which the "redeemed" walk (35:9). Verse 10 describes the end result of this journey through the desert. It is to come to the city of God, Zion, where "gladness" and "joy" will forever displace "sorrow and sighing" (cf. 25:7–8).

Application. God has delivered us from our sins so that we can participate in his life and character. This is what Paul has in mind when he says that believers are to "work out your salvation with fear and trembling, for it is God who works in you to will and to act in order to fulfill his good purpose" (Phil 2:12–13). God has come to us and day by day makes it possible for us to walk with him in greater and greater likeness to him.

ISAIAH 36:1–37:7

Original Meaning

The Speech of the Field Commander (36:1–22). The "field commander" (36:2) is the third highest-ranking officer in the Assyrian army, so this move against Jerusalem is a serious one. The main army is engaged in the siege of Lachish, the last remaining Judean walled city except Jerusalem; all the rest have fallen to the Assyrians (36:1). As long as Jerusalem holds out, she poses a danger to the troops surrounding Lachish. So, it is to Sennacherib's advantage to persuade the leadership in Jerusalem that their situation is hopeless and that their only option is to surrender.

It is significant that the field commander stands in exactly the same spot where Isaiah stood some thirty-four or thirty-five years earlier when he had confronted Ahaz (36:2; cf. 7:3). The warnings Isaiah gave over the folly of trusting Assyria instead of God are all coming true with a vengeance.

The field commander's speech hammers the fearful Judeans

with every possible argument that might undermine their trust—and trust is clearly what this conflict is about. His opening words make that clear (36:4). Then he proceeds to demolish, from his point of view, each possible basis. He starts with military power and says they are trusting a "splintered reed" (36:6), Egypt, for their strength. That reed will break if they put any weight at all on it (36:5–6).

The commander then turns to another possible source of help, the Lord (36:7). Here he betrays a deficiency in his background briefing, believing that God is unhappy at the destruction of the high places outside of Jerusalem where local people were worshiping him. The pagan Assyrian cannot understand that the unity of God is undermined by worship of him in places other than Jerusalem.

Assyria could afford to give two thousand horses to Judah and still be confident of defeating them. Little Judah cannot muster two thousand trained horsemen to ride the horses even if they were given. In that light, the help from Egypt is useless (36:9), because Judah cannot make good use of whatever military assistance they might receive.

Then the Assyrian field commander switches gears again, asserting that "the LORD," the God of Israel, has directed him to "destroy" the "land" (36:10). It may well be that the Assyrian foreign office has discovered these were the kinds of things the prophets of Israel were saying. Yet the field commander's assertion that his king can defeat Judah's God just as he has every other god (36:18–20) makes it clear that all he really believes in is power. It is clear from the interchange in 36:11–12 that a part of the purpose of the field commander's expedition is to erode the morale of the city.

It is interesting that the Assyrian refers to his master as "the king" on several occasions (36:8, 13, 14, 16, 18) but refers to the king of Judah only by his name. Here is one more part of the power play: The ruler of this petty nation does not even have the right to be called a king in any comparison with the true king of the universe, Sennacherib. How does he dare to oppose his will to that of the only true king?

The real issue comes out in 36:14–20. It is a contest between the Lord and the king of Assyria. Note that it is not a contest between the Lord and the gods of Assyria, but between the mightiest and most glorious man of the age and the Lord God. Here is the height of the human arrogance that has been attacked throughout the book thus far, and here all the teaching of the book thus far comes to its climax. Will we trust human glory, a humanity that dares to call itself "king"? Or will we trust the One who *is* Glory, the One who *is* King, and be given a message of hope for the nations? The Assyrian officer says in the bluntest of terms that Hezekiah "cannot deliver you" (36:14), because "the LORD will [not] deliver" them (36:18–20).

Hezekiah's Response (37:1–7). Hezekiah's response to his advisors' report is instructive (37:1). He does not closet himself with his advisors and consider what spin to put on the events. Not only does Hezekiah himself turn to God, but he also sends an impressive delegation to consult with Isaiah (37:2). Hezekiah is particularly concerned about the disgrace that this situation brings on God. Hezekiah wonders if God will let that go by (37:4).

The response God gives to Isaiah makes it clear he does not intend to let the challenge pass unaddressed. The king may be terrified, but the God who speaks through Isaiah is not. He has been blasphemed. As a result, he will not allow the Assyrian to succeed in his plans but will send him home. There, Sennacherib will die by the "sword" (37:7).

Application. If there are any practices or relationships in our lives that will give others a chance to say that we talk a good show but are really no different from the world in the way we live, we must get rid of them now. These kinds of decisions are personal, between us and the Lord, but the real issue for all of us is: Do I really trust the Lord for the supply of my needs, or does my behavior say that I lie?

ISAIAH 37:8–38

Original Meaning

Hezekiah's Prayer (37:8–20). Sennacherib does not want to relax any of the pressure on Hezekiah. Unable to spare the highest officers this time, he sends messengers with a letter directly from himself. No longer is it a question of Hezekiah's deceiving the people about God's deliverance (36:14). Now the challenge is directly to God: "Do not let the god you depend on deceive you" (37:10). Sennacherib's fatal mistake is that he does not realize that Judah's God is not man-made, like all the rest.

This time Hezekiah does not ask Isaiah to pray; rather, he goes directly to God himself. His ascription of praise in 37:16 is a marvelous compendium of the attributes and character of God. Hezekiah's petition (37:17) particularly stresses the fact that God is not an idol but is the "living God." Hezekiah prays as Elijah did on Mount Carmel (1 Kgs 18:36–37), with the confidence that his God not only can hear but wants to hear. Perhaps the most striking thing about this prayer is its focus on God's vindication rather than on the deliverance of the people.

Hezekiah admits that what the Assyrian has said about the other kingdoms and cities and their gods is right (Isa 37:18–19), but he insists that they are not gods at all. Isaiah 37:20 brings the prayer to a fitting climax. Why does Hezekiah pray for the deliverance of his city? One reason alone is given: "so that all kingdoms on earth may know that you, LORD, are the only God." In many ways this is the climax of all the teaching found in chapters 7–35.

God's Response to Hezekiah's Prayer (37:21–38). God's response to this prayer comes through Isaiah and is recorded in 37:21–35. It appears in three parts, the first of which is addressed directly to Sennacherib (37:22–29). The second is addressed to Hezekiah (37:30–32), and the third is spoken of Sennacherib (37:33–35). If the message of the field commander betrayed a certain familiarity with Judean life and thought, this oracle shows remarkable familiarity with the Assyrian royal annals, especially 37:24–25, which quote the boasts of Sennacherib, much like what appears in those annals. Possibly there were publicists with the Assyrian armies who circulated these kinds of poetic celebrations of Assyrian might. If so, Isaiah has picked up on them and uses them to show how foolish they are in the light of the reality of the living God.

The opening phrase "Virgin Daughter Zion" (37:22) suggests that the Assyrian attack on Jerusalem is comparable to a dominant male seeking to rape a beautiful young girl. But Assyria, the would-be rapist, has not taken into account "the Holy One of Israel" (37:23). He has put himself on the level of God, lifting his "eyes in pride" (37:23) and in the process blaspheming God by bringing him down to Sennacherib's own level.

Verses 24–25 seem to extol Sennacherib by reference to extremes. But what he does not know is that all of this has been "long ago ... planned" by the God of one of the little countries the Assyrian has so contemptuously trampled on (37:26). Assyria is a puppet being moved by Israel's God! God has "brought it to pass" that Assyria has conquered the "fortified cities" and reduced their inhabitants to wilted, "scorched" "plants" (37:27). As a result, Sennacherib cannot hide from God. Just as God has brought him on the stage, he can take him off again (37:28–29).

Verses 30–32 constitute a sign to Hezekiah that this is indeed a word from God. Like several of the other signs in the book (7:14; 8:3; 16:14), God has gone on record that he will do what he says and has given a means for checking the veracity of what he has said. Probably the three years in 37:30 entails parts of three different calendar years.

In God's mind, the more important point is that he will preserve a harvest for himself from among his people (37:32). All God's promises are summed up in 37:33–35, where Isaiah makes two assertions about what will happen—one negative (37:33) and one positive (37:34)—and then gives a supporting reason for these assertions (37:35). The negative assertion is that the Assyrian will not mount any kind of an attack against the city. Not only will they not conquer God's city, but they will also not even "shoot an arrow" there (37:33). On the surface of it, this is amazing. Not only will the Assyrians not mount a siege against the city, but they will leave the area completely (37:34). The reason given for this amazing turn of events is that God "will defend" the city "and save it" (37:35). Sennacherib has said he will destroy the city, whereas God has said he will save it. Now we will see who is right.

Verses 36–38 are stunning in their terse, matter-of-fact reporting. They are so plain and unadorned as to be almost anticlimactic. Perhaps the point is to show that there is simply no contest here. This is not some earth-shaking conflict between evenly matched contestants. This is definitely a "no contest" match. God simply sends the angel of death. And the angel is not finished on the Philistine plains. Just because Sennacherib is at home in what should have been the safest place on earth for him ("the temple of his god," 37:38), God's word is still true (37:7), and his rule is still effective. His own sons "killed him with the sword" (37:38) and flee. Despite all his boasts, Sennacherib cannot stand against the living God. Hezekiah has proved that it is foolish to trust the nations in place of the living God, "the Holy One of Israel" (37:23).

Application. This is maturity: having a correct estimate of your abilities and your liabilities, one that is not dependent on the opinions of others and being secure in who you are and who you are becoming. But this is not really possible without the perspective of heaven. When we get ourselves "off our hands" and into God's hands, we no longer need to worry about how we are looking. Now it is God's reputation that matters to us, and we are freed from that debilitating self-concern that will otherwise eat us up. That is the picture we see in Hezekiah's prayer. Here is a man whose personal success and survival are no longer paramount. This is a free man.

ISAIAH 38:1–22

Original Meaning

Hezekiah's Prayer (38:1–8). Although Hezekiah's prayer in 38:3 is not as lofty and unselfish as that in chapter 37, it is still a model of the direction the trusting heart takes in the time of crisis. It is interesting that Hezekiah does not actually ask for lengthened life. What he does is simply remind God that he has conducted his life with faithfulness and "wholehearted devotion" (literally, "a perfect heart," 38:3). This is reminiscent of God's command to Abraham in Genesis 17:1. In short, Hezekiah, who was only thirty-nine years old at the time, is saying to God that he has met God's requirements for long life (cf. Ps 34:11–14) and is asking by implication if it is fair to cut his life short as though he were a wicked man (cf. Ps 37:35–36).

God responds to this argument and sends Isaiah back with a different word, one of fifteen additional years. Like his father before him, Hezekiah is offered a sign to confirm God's gracious promise of deliverance. Ahaz refused the sign because he had already made arrangements to take care of himself. Hezekiah has no such encumbrance, so he is happy to receive whatever evidence God cares to give.

Hezekiah's Lament (38:9–20). These verses are often referred to as Hezekiah's psalm of thanksgiving for his deliverance from death. However, the meter of the Hebrew lines is that of a lament. In fact, the psalm seems to be largely a meditation on mortality.

In 38:10–14 Hezekiah speaks of the untimeliness of the announced death. The tent is never very long in one place as the shepherd keeps moving to follow the flock. And although a cloth seems permanently attached to the loom, there must inevitably come a day when it is "cut" loose (38:12). Life is just as impermanent. But just as death is from the Lord, so is life. If there is to be any hope, it is from "the heavens"; if any "aid," it is from the Lord (38:14).

It is unclear whether 38:15 is to be taken negatively or positively. The point seems to be that all of "this," both the disease and its subsequent removal, is the work of God. What lesson should Hezekiah draw? He should certainly not stride through life in arrogance as though his life were his own. He believes that the "anguish" he went through has been beneficial (38:17). Perhaps one benefit is a new realization of God's "love" and mercy (38:17).

Verses 18–19 express the idea that it is to God's benefit to keep the faithful alive since those in the "grave cannot praise" God for his "faithfulness" (38:18). Rather, it is "the living" who praise God and who pass along their testimony of his faithfulness to their children (38:19). Verse 20 moves to an unambiguous note of praise. Hezekiah promises that as long as he is alive, there will be joyful music to the saving God in his "temple."

Additional Notes (38:21–22). In my judgment these last two verses were not part of the original in Isaiah. They do not fit with each other, and they appear to be out of context. This is especially clear when we look at the parallel account in 2 Kings 20, where they are integrated into the flow of the narrative. I propose that the Isaiah account and the Kings account were both dependent on a common source and that the original Isaiah did not include these details, perhaps in order to highlight the psalm. But a later editor, comparing the two accounts, thought that the details had been unintentionally left out and added them on at the end, not wanting to disturb the flow of the original.

Verse 20 shows us that healing is from the Lord even if some intervening means is used to promote the healing. Verse 21 may explain why the sign involved the "stairway of Ahaz" in 38:8. As the sun moved up and down that stairway, so Hezekiah would once again move up and down the stairs of the "temple."

Application. God does not change his mind concerning the basic nature of things. But God will gladly change what he has said about us if it can become a greater means to our blessing. God sees that his intervention will be a means of greater blessing for both Hezekiah and his people. Did God know that before? Of course he did. But the issue is whether Hezekiah will turn to God in faith at such a moment. If he will not, then there is little God can do for him and through him.

ISAIAH 39:1–8

Original Meaning. "Marduk-Baladan"(39:1) was a Babylonian leader who was twice able to make himself king of Babylon in defiance of the Assyrians. Obviously, he was interested in encouraging any others in the Assyrian Empire who were potential allies or who would draw Assyrian attention away from him and onto themselves. It is easy to understand why Hezekiah would be glad to receive the "envoys" (39:2). After all, there is something immensely flattering when someone whom we consider more important than ourselves pays attention to us. But there is also something dangerous as well, namely, that we will succumb to the temptation to convince the important person that the attention being given is justified. Sadly, that is the temptation into which Hezekiah falls.

This is not how we would like to remember such a good man. Yet this is how Isaiah has chosen for us to remember him. And when we recall that this event probably occurred before those of chapters 36–37, we are forced to ask why the material has been ordered in this way. In actual fact, Hezekiah rose above this point in his trust in God when faced with Sennacherib. So why are we not allowed to remember him in that way instead of this?

By showing that Hezekiah is both mortal and fallible, Isaiah shows that trust is intended to be a way of life, not a onetime experience. Something more was necessary to enable such trust in an unreserved way. What that something was must yet be revealed, but it would be in the chapters to come. There is no final salvation in a human being, no matter how good he might be. Our hope is not in the perfectibility of humanity. The Messiah we look for is better than that.

Application. The person who has cultivated a life of trust, who knows that everything he or she has is a gift from God, will be constantly deflecting the praise and honor from himself or herself to God. Who is getting the glory?

ISAIAH 40:1–31

Original Meaning

God's Promised Deliverance (40:1–11). No longer is the prophetic message to be primarily one of judgment. That point has been made and will be confirmed in the fires of the exile. Now, however, the message is to be one of hope. Verses 1 and 2 provide an introduction and set the tone for the following three three-verse stanzas. Isaiah sees a day when God's servants will feel sure that all is lost. But the message to be proclaimed to them is that this is not so.

In the first stanza (40:3–5), some of the language of chapter 35 is resumed. God comes to helpless Zion to set her free. Nothing can prevent his swift coming to his people's aid, neither mountains nor valleys. If there is to be deliverance for God's people, it must come from God's direct intervention. There is no other hope.

That fact is underlined in the second stanza (40:6–8). On the one hand, Judean flesh is like grass. They have been consumed by their sins, and there is no permanence in them at all, nor is there anything they can do to help themselves. But it is also true that Babylonian flesh is as grass. If the Judeans are to be delivered, God will have to do it. But if he *does* decide to do it, there is nothing the Babylonians can do to prevent it. If God speaks a promise, that "word" (40:8) will stand.

Because that is so, "Zion" (40:9) has a word to declare to the surrounding villages. The most natural way to read the Hebrew is that Zion is this messenger of good tidings. The good news is about the intervention of God in the world: He "comes" (40:10). The Creator breaks into his world, both to break the power of evil with his strong "arm" (40:10) and, "like a shepherd" (40:11a), to gather up the broken in his gentle "arms" (40:11b).

God's Ability to Deliver His People (40:12–26). The first section (40:1–11) has verified God's desire and intention to deliver his people, but can he do it? Isaiah's approach to answering the question is to assert that God is unique. He is able to deliver not because he is greater than the Babylonian gods; he is able to deliver because *he is the only God!*

Isaiah 40:12–26 can be divided into two sections that parallel each other in general ways (40:12–20 and 40:21–26). Each unit begins with an assertion, in the form of rhetorical questions, that the Lord is the sole Creator (40:12–14, 21). This is followed by an affirmation that the Lord is the Ruler of all nations and rulers (40:15–17, 22–24). Next is a rhetorical invitation to compare God with anything else (40:18a, 25). Finally, there is the claim of absolute superiority over the gods, whether conceived of as idols (40:18b–20) or as the heavenly host (40:26).

In 40:12–14 the prophet employs a series of rhetorical questions intended to bring the reader to the point of saying that Yahweh is the sole Creator. The doctrine of creation is important to the argument of this part of the book. The prophet has received it and accepts it gladly, insisting that God is other than creation.

Verses 13–14 seem particularly aimed at the polytheistic religions, where a counselor/magician among the gods assists the other gods in realizing their purposes. Isaiah insists that there are no such beings, that "understanding" (40:14) originated with the Originator of all things. To think otherwise is to give up transcendence, and to give that up is to be dropped into the morass where life is only the outworking of a deterministic cycle coming from nowhere and going nowhere.

Compared to the One who holds the oceans in his hand, the nations of the earth are "nothing" (40:17). Verse 16 illustrates this point by saying that no earthly sacrifice is sufficient to manipulate him in favor of earthly concerns. If all the forests of Lebanon were set on fire and all its animals burned on the fire, it would not affect him at all.

Thus, if the Lord is the sole Creator and the Lord of the nations, will we say that an idol is comparable to him? Certainly not! The diatribe against the idols in 40:18b–20 is the first of several in this part of the book. It is the complement to the prophet's insistence on the transcendence of God. The emphasis on the making of the idol is surely intentional. How can something made by humans possibly be the maker of the humans who made it?

The cycle begins again with 40:21, where the prophet asserts that God is not only other than the world but also other than the heavens, having stretched them out "like a tent" (40:22). As a result, he is not overawed by the "rulers" (40:23) of this earth. In fact, their destiny is in his hands. The tender plants of humanity are no match for the eternal judgments of God (40:24).

Thus, once again we, the readers, are asked—this time by God himself—if we know of anything to compare with him. Is the product on the same plane as the maker or the sheep on the same plane as the shepherd? No, the stars only exist because of the "mighty strength" of Judah's God (40:26).

Waiting in Hope (40:27–31). In 40:27 the prophet anticipates the attitude of the exiles. So, he speaks of both the being and the person of God. Thus, his question in 40:28 is rather incredulous. How could you say such things about God when you know perfectly well who he is and what he is like? Here we come back to the theme of trust. To "wait" on God is not simply to mark time; rather, it is to live in confident expectation of his action on our behalf. The God of all strength can give them exactly what they need at the right time, whether to "soar," "run," or "walk" (40:31).

Application. The Bible is increasingly lost in Western society, and with it we have lost its central idea, the idea of transformation. So, we fight for individual rights, and yet we increasingly deny any responsibility for our choices, arguing that we really do not have any choices since we are conditioned by society, our family, some tragedy, or even our genes. What has happened? We have kept the Bible's conclusion but denied its premises. We have accepted human worth while buying into deterministic evolution.

ISAIAH 41:1–20

Original Meaning

God's Challenge to the Nations (41:1). This first verse introduces an imaginary court case between God and the idols. By this means God will demonstrate to his fearful people that their captivity in Babylon in no way calls his power or lordship into question.

God's Activities as Evidence (41:2–7). As his first evidence (41:2–4), God begins with a rhetorical question in 41:2 and then repeats and answers it in 41:4. Not only does Isaiah say that God has called Cyrus forth, he also says that it is God who has given the "nations" into his hand (41:2). Cyrus is able to subdue every nation he encounters with ease, treating them like grain to be threshed because this is in the God of Israel's plan.

When the nations of earth hear of Cyrus's earth-shaking conquests, they will be terrified (41:5–7). But what can they do? They know of no gods who rule history on the basis of a righteous plan. So, they do the only thing they can do: make better idols. It is hard work to make your maker.

No Need for God's People to Fear (41:8–20). In this section God asserts that unlike the powerful nations around them, the Judean captives have nothing to fear. God is "with" them, to "strengthen," "help," and "uphold" them (41:10b). God is not at some far-off point, shouting instructions. He is personally present with his people, so they have nothing to "fear" (41:10a).

They are also afraid that their many enemies will overpower them. That is the issue addressed in 41:11–16. God will protect them, and their enemies will simply evaporate before the Lord (41:11–12). God will demonstrate his lordship by helping his people (41:13–14). He will take an active hand in their defense.

In 41:15–16 God continues to offer his people protection from their enemies. A "threshing sledge" (41:15) was constructed from pieces of wood with sharp stones ("teeth") driven into them. This device was pulled around over a pile of cut grain so that the kernels of grain were separated from the husks both by the weight and by the cutting effect of the stones. God will use Israel in his plan of world history. Verses 17–20 are a graphic summary of what has been said to this point. God can do what is new and unheard of. He can make "rivers" flow on mountaintops and cause "pools" to spring up in the "desert" (41:19).

Application. With the help of the entire universe at our backs, why should we be afraid? It is the almighty, independent Creator, who freely comes to stand at our sides and do through us what we cannot. Why does he not just tell us to stay out of the way and watch him do his work? He has given us the dignity of sharing his own image, and he will not demean us by making us merely robots to speed his cause. What an unimaginable task, and yet what an incredible honor!

ISAIAH 41:21–42:9

Original Meaning

The Case against the Idols (41:21–29). Once more God calls on the idol worshipers to present their case. Here Isaiah strikes directly at the heart of the pagan worldview. The prophet calls on the idolaters to give evidence that their idols have ever specifically predicted the future.

In fact, the gods are incapable of doing anything of a free or unconditioned nature (41:23). They are a part of the cyclic functioning of the cosmic system and must do what the cycle requires. So, God pronounces judgment (41:24). In attempting to deify creation, the pagans have actually committed an offense against it. In 41:25–27 God responds to the challenge. He does have a plan for history, and what will be unfolding before the exiles' eyes will be the evidence of it.

It is one thing to assert that Cyrus's coming is at the direction of "Jacob's King" (41:21), but it is quite another to prove that the assertion is so. Anyone can make the claim to have done so after the fact. But Isaiah is ready for that approach, and he has both negative and positive evidence. First of all, none of the idols predicted Cyrus's coming at all (41:26). The God of Israel did make such a prediction in advance (41:27). In fact, that is exactly what he is doing through Isaiah, his "messenger of good news" in this very writing.

Isaiah 41:28–29 is the pronouncement of judgment on the idol worshipers. All who worship something other than the true God are doomed to become like their gods: nothing, worthless, wind, and chaos. Their lives are doomed to become as meaningless as their gods are.

An Address to the Servant (42:1–9). As in 41:1–21, the court case against the gods is followed by an address to the Lord's servant. Just as he was able to bring down the Babylonian Empire through Cyrus, so he will bring "justice" (42:1, 3, 4) to the earth through his "servant" (42:1). Verse 9 makes the connection clear by stating explicitly that the prediction concerning the servant is one of the "new things" that the gods could not declare in advance but that the Lord can do so with impunity.

The reiterated statement that this person is going to bring justice on the earth, that God's spirit will be on him (42:1), and that his accomplishment of this end will not be through oppression (42:3) reminds us of the prophecies of the Messiah in Isaiah 9, 11, and 32. Thus, we have a complementary picture to the one there. There we had the servant as King. Here we have the king as Servant.

Application. The Servant brings God's right order into the world not from a position of strength but of weakness. He does not break an already-bent reed, nor does he quench a candle flame that is already flickering. Christ disarmed his enemies with love and grace and gentleness. We must minister in the same way.

ISAIAH 42:10–43:7

Original Meaning

A Hymn of Praise (42:10–17). Isaiah calls on the whole world to give praise to God (42:10–12). The extremities of earth are particularly emphasized, probably as a way of expressing totality. Likewise, the "sea" (42:10), the "wilderness" (42:11a), and "the mountaintops" (42:11b) all convey the idea of the extremes of earth. Isaiah is emphasizing that the Lord is the God of the whole world, and what he is going to do for Judah has joyous implications for the whole world.

Verses 14–17 expand on the promise of 42:13, where God is depicted as "warrior" coming to the defense of people. If it seems to them that he has "kept silent" (42:14) for a long time as they have endured the exile, that time is coming to a rapid close. God is going to birth a new thing on behalf of his people. Whatever obstacles may stand in the way, whether forested mountains or rapid rivers, they will present no obstacle to God (42:15). Even though they are "blind," he will lead them, giving them "light" for their darkness (42:16). This means that their worst fears—that God has either abandoned them or is helpless to come to their aid—are groundless. By contrast, the Babylonian gods will be helpless to assist their people (42:17).

The Issue of God's Deliverance (42:18–43:7). Verses 18–20 remind us that servant Israel is not in a position to do anything for herself or for the world. But now the prophet commands the "deaf" to "hear" (42:18). Perhaps the tragedy of the exile will unstop their ears a little. He calls on them to ask why they are in exile (42:22–24). God brought them down to destruction in punishment for their sin, but no one seemed to get the point.

So, what is God to do after the looting and plundering have become fact? The shift in tone from 42:25 to 43:1 is breathtaking. What God will now do is grace. God simply declares, as in 40:1–2, that he has "redeemed" (43:1) them. It is a completed fact.

The key to all of this is the personal relationship of God to his people. The recurrence of the pronouns "I" and "you" throughout 43:1–7 is striking. In 43:5–7 the promise first made in 11:11 is reiterated: God will recover his people from all the lands where they have been taken. Even if the exiles themselves do not go home, their children, who are God's own "sons" and "daughters" (43:6), will. God's promises will not fail.

Application. One of the fundamental principles of the kingdom of God is that his grace precedes everything else. To be sure, God calls his people to listen to and believe the promises he makes to deliver them. But his grace is declared to them even before they are necessarily prepared to listen and believe. The most concise statement of this truth in the New Testament is found in Romans 5:8. God did everything necessary to deliver us from the consequences of our sin before there was any indication that we would respond to that free act.

ISAIAH 43:8–44:5

Original Meaning

God's Courtroom Scene (43:8–13). Isaiah 43:8, which almost certainly refers to the servant Israel, leaves no doubt that their hope is not in themselves. The One who is both judge and defendant turns to his blind and deaf servant and says, "You are my witnesses" (43:10). God is going to have to do an amazing work on their behalf so that they can be the evidence he deserves.

Verses 10–13 relate in general terms what Israel's relationship is to God and what they know to be true if only they will open their eyes and ears. They have been called into a relationship with God whereby they will "know" (affective) and "believe" (volitional) and "understand" (cognitive) that "I am he" (43:10). This is God's ultimate statement of identity. A more colloquial translation might say, "I'm the one."

God has not merely "revealed" truth about himself to them, nor has he merely "saved" them, nor has he merely "proclaimed" the meaning of what he has done (43:12). He has done all three together and simultaneously so that his revelation is a wholistic one, touching the whole of human personality. God is saying that he is the totality of deity, as revealed by what he has done on the earth for and through the Israelites.

Promises of Deliverance (43:14–21). In 43:14–21 God tells his people once again that he is going to deliver them from

Babylon. But how is he going to deliver them? Verses 16–17 invite the people to remember what he did in the exodus. There God demonstrated his lordship over both nature and human nations. He also showed both his desire and his ability to save.

But after reminding them of those facts, he suddenly says in 43:18 that they are to "forget" all that. What is going on? God is not predictable like the gods. He is the Creator, who loves doing things in "new" ways (43:19). God promises to transform the desert created by arrogance and false trust into a place of "streams" where his "chosen" may have all their needs supplied (43:20). As a result, his people will "proclaim my praise" (43:21).

The Present Reality (43:22–28). Then, in ways we saw several times in chapters 1–39, the prophet steps back from that glorious future to talk about present reality. Not only does Isaiah point to the unbelief during the exile but to the unbelief rampant in Isaiah's own day, for which judgment is still to come (43:28). There is an implied charge that it seems unfair of God to have sent his people into exile in the first place.

God's answer to this charge reflects the kind of hyperbolic, ironic language that the prophets often resort to when discussing ritual and cultic activity. God says that, in fact, they have not been calling on him at all; rather, they have wearied themselves with their sacrifice (43:22). They have not really brought sacrifices to God when they did these things, and in fact God never said that he wanted such things (43:23). What have they done? They have just piled up more and more sin until God could not bear it any longer.

The Hebrews were continually falling back into the worldview of their neighbors, in which, since the gods are a part of the cosmic system, doing something to the system does something to the gods. But God is not part of the system, and instead of the ritual having automatic effects, it was intended to symbolize a change in personal relations.

God does not have to be manipulated into forgiving us. In fact, he cannot be so manipulated. He has already done that (43:25), and he has done it for his own sake. We have only to receive what he has done. The sacrifices were to be symbols of changed hearts and changed lives. Thus, God suggests in 43:26 that his people might want to review the "case" they are making against him. Far from being unfair because of their careful ritual, the exile became the more necessary because of them.

God's New Work (44:1–5). But, as always in this book, destruction is not the last word God intends to speak. Once again, he implores his people to "listen" (44:1). Israel must not rely on mechanical rituals but enter into a relationship by listening to the One who speaks, who has been speaking since the dawn of time.

Again, the appeal is to creation. If the exiled Israelites are tempted to think that God has given up on them, that their sin has become too much for him to do anything about, they should remember that God has a special interest in them. If a mother cannot forget her child, God cannot forget those he created.

Just as God is strong enough to do something about their physical captivity, so he is great enough to do something about their persistent sinning. Not only has he found a way to forgive their sin without destroying the justice on which the world rests; he has also found a way to transform a proud, self-centered people, who seem incapable of giving themselves away, into those who will gladly find their central identity in their surrender to their Father. The means of that transformation is his Spirit (44:3). No longer will they try to retain ownership to themselves while trying to manipulate God with sacrifices.

Application. Notice that there is no command to be witnesses here. Rather, God simply declares a fact: "You *are* my witnesses" (43:10; emphasis added). Jesus says the same thing (Acts 1:8). Like it or not, we have been changed. We *are* evidence of his divine, delivering, transforming power. One's witness is the expression of one's experience. The exiles were not expected to make speeches but to report what they knew to be so out of their own lives.

ISAIAH 44:6–22

Original Meaning

God's Absolute Uniqueness (44:6–8). In words and phrases that are now familiar to anyone working straight through the book, Yahweh declares his absolute uniqueness. But he first identifies himself inextricably with Israel. Although he is the only God, he is also the one who has made himself known in the context of a relationship with a small, insignificant people. The people of Israel are "witnesses" to that fact (44:8).

Charges against the Idols (44:9–20). In contrast to the Rock (44:8), what do the other peoples of earth have to cling to? Nothing. They "treasure" worthless things, trash, and as a result have become "nothing" themselves (44:9). This thought is developed further in a general way in 44:10–11.

In 44:12–17 the prophet describes the process of making idols in great detail, showing how difficult it is to make one's own gods when the true God can be so easily found. Isaiah takes us backward through the complex process, beginning with the last step of plating the wooden form with precious metal (44:12). Then he describes how the carpenter made the wooden form (44:13). Next, he describes the process of choosing the wood for the form (44:14). In all of this he describes the difficulty and the complexity of the process.

In 44:15–17 Isaiah comes to the heart of his argument. How in the world, the prophet asks, can a piece of wood, another part of which has been used to cook food and supply warmth, ever be expected to save a person, especially when so much human effort has had to be lavished on it to make it what it is? The answer is, of course, that it cannot do so, and anyone who thinks it can has been mentally and spiritually blinded (44:18).

The ultimate seriousness of paganism and its consequences is seen in 44:19–20. It is not mere hyperbole when he calls the idols an "abomination" (NIV "detestable thing," 44:19). In the Old Testament an "abomination" is to use a created thing in a way that violates its character. That is surely the case with idolatry. For us to elevate nature to the place of God and bow down to that which was made for us is just such a violation.

A Call to Take Heart (44:21–22). These two verses give us God's appeal to his people on the basis of what he has just said. They have not made their God; rather he has "made" them (44:21). If they will "remember," they need not fear that he will "forget" them (44:21). If he determines to forgive their "offenses" and to redeem them from their captivity, he will find a way to do those things (44:22).

Application. The meaninglessness and pointlessness of life in a world where the transcendent God has been shut out is vividly portrayed in all the media today. We are already reaping the bitter fruits of the view that this world is all there is. Can things made with human hands save us from ourselves today any more than they could then? Not in the least. So, the god and goddess of unlimited sex, the god of power through wealth, the god of alcoholic gaiety, and the goddess of beauty must all be rejected by Christians today as we seek the face of the one God more than anything else.

ISAIAH 44:23–45:13

Original Meaning

A Call to Praise (44:23). This verse functions as a transition between the former unit and the following one, just as 42:10–17 did. It is a call to praise. Nature, in whom God's creative "glory" is seen, is called upon to praise God for his greater redemptive "glory" that will be displayed "in Israel."

God's Redemptive Plans (44:24–28). The "Redeemer" (44:24) now spells out in the greatest detail yet what his redemptive plans are. Verses 24–28 comprise a single sentence consisting of a succession of participles that define "I am the LORD" in 44:24. Here God identifies himself and demonstrates his lordship by what he does. He is the Creator. He is the Lord of history (44:25–26a). He is the Redeemer (44:26b–28). Because he is the Creator and the Lord of history and the Redeemer, he is even able to use a pagan emperor to accomplish his purposes.

The Commission of Cyrus (45:1–8). Cyrus is specifically said to be God's "anointed" or messiah (45:1). The victories that will come to him will be gifts from God's hand (45:1–3). They will not be his own accomplishments but will come from God for two purposes: that Cyrus himself might know that Yahweh, "the God of Israel," is "the LORD" (45:3), and that his work in history might be done "for the sake of Jacob my servant" (45:4).

Twice is it said that God has called Cyrus "by name" (45:3, 4). This underlines the importance of the naming of Cyrus as an act of predictive prophecy. Isaiah has repeatedly insisted that God alone can tell the future and that the attempts to do so by the devotees of the gods only make them look like "fools" (44:25).

One of the pieces of evidence of God's lordship is that he knows the name of one who does not know God's name (45:4–5). Even if Cyrus has never heard of Yahweh of Israel, Yahweh knows about Cyrus even before he is born. The statement that Cyrus will recognize this eventually is an interesting one and depending on how the identity of Darius in the book of Daniel is resolved, that book may give evidence of the realization of the promise (cf. Dan 6:26–27). At the same time, Cyrus's acknowledgment that he was called by the Lord to release his people (cf. Ezra 1:2) may be as much as this statement intends for him to do.

This segment ends much as the previous one (Isa 44:23–28) began: with a declaration of the absolute uniqueness of God (45:5–8). There is none like him, and his goal is that people all over the world will recognize his uniqueness. Three different times the Lord makes the statement that there is no other god than he (45:5–6).

God as Sole Creator and Redeemer (45:9–13). But does God have the right to use someone who does not even know him to save his believing people? Surely if God were going to raise up a deliverer for them, it would be someone like Moses. God responds to this idea with strong words. He pronounces doom ("woe," 45:9–10) on those who challenge the rightness of his activity.

If the exiles will not let God deliver them in his own way, they have not learned the lesson of his lordship. He is still their "God in a box," to do with as they choose. So, in 45:11–12 God once more asserts that he is not only Israel's "Holy One" and "Maker," but also the Maker of the whole cosmos and the Creator. If he does not have a right to set his "exiles free" (45:13) as he chooses, who does?

Application. We as evangelical Christians need to be careful that we do not fall into the trap the Pharisees did. It was people who zealously studied the Scriptures who could not believe that Jesus could be the promised Messiah. It was people who wanted to please God who could not accept his friendship with notorious sinners. It was people who had almost made a life's work of studying God's ways who could not allow Jesus to deliver people in ways that seemed to violate how God was supposed to act. We may say that they had not studied the Scriptures well enough or that they were more concerned about justifying God's ways to themselves than they were about applying them to human hearts. But the question here is whether that behavior is descriptive of me and whether the strong words of Isaiah and Jesus might be directed at me.

ISAIAH 45:14–46:13

Original Meaning

God's Ability to Save (45:14–25). This segment opens with a picture of people from the ends of the earth coming humbly to Israel, admitting that Israel's God is the only God (45:14). The next three verses offer some reflection on this picture. The gods of the idol makers will fail them and leave them in "disgrace" as they "go off" into captivity (45:16). But God's people will not be "disgraced," for the opposite thing will happen to them: They will be "saved" from captivity (45:17).

Verses 18–19 give the reason why this affirmation can be made: God is the sole Creator of the universe, and he created it for a purpose. Though he may be hidden in his transcendent essence, he is anything but hidden in his desire for relationship with his human creatures. He has revealed this desire as he has "spoken" to them again and again, inviting them to "seek" him (45:19).

After this introduction, the idol makers are once more called to present themselves before God (45:20). But their description here is unusual. They are the "fugitives from the nations" (cf. 45:14). In other words, the discussion has proceeded to the point where the idols are now seen as having failed, and their worshipers know this. So, they come into the assembly carrying their useless images. In 45:21 the Lord once again asks who predicted this situation, and the answer is that he alone has done so. Thus, he is the only God.

What follows next is surprising. We might expect words of judgment, but instead we have an invitation to these people from the "ends of the earth" to "turn" to the Lord "and be saved" (45:22). This expresses God's ultimate purpose in the conflict with the idols. He does not want to destroy the idol makers but to save them.

Illustration of God as the Only Savior (46:1–7). The theme of God as the only Savior is now graphically illustrated. Those who have depended on the Babylonian gods "Bel" and "Nebo" load their idol gods onto oxcarts to be "carried" off "into captivity" (46:1–2). The worshipers, instead of being saved by their gods, have to save the gods! In an especially poignant rejoinder, God reminds his people that he is the one who has "carried" (46:3) them ever since their conception in the womb, and he promises to continue to carry them through their "old age" (46:4).

The alternative is spelled out in 46:5–7. If people choose to make their own gods, they will have to carry what they have made. When they put the god down, it will not move an inch from where it is put. Would we compare the Maker and only Savior of the world to that? Surely not!

Final Appeal to Idol Worshipers (46:8–13). These verses constitute the final summation and appeal in the disputation with the idols. The case has been presented several times, moving from the inability of the idols to explain the past or tell the future to their inability to save those who worship them. Now God calls on his people to make their decision.

Cyrus, "the bird of prey" coming "from the east" (46:11), will arrive in direct fulfillment of the prediction and purpose of God. These things show that Yahweh is God alone and that "there is none like" him (46:9). The issue now is whether the exiles will believe it and keep their faith through forty-five dark, uncertain years so that when Cyrus is revealed, there will still be a remnant who can reach out and take hold of God's hand.

Application. Meaning, purpose, identity, and fulfillment are ultimately only things God can provide. We truly begin to experience God's carrying of us when we take our hands off these things and relinquish them into God's hands. And why should we not? Until we are willing to do what the remnant did during the exile and release our survival into God's hands, we are allowing our fears to keep us from knowing God's care and deliverance.

ISAIAH 47:1–15

Original Meaning

Babylon's Humiliation (47:1–4). Babylon was the queen of the world, the mightiest of the mighty, but she will soon meet one mightier than she, who says that she must leave her "throne" (47:1). Although she is beautiful, she will be forced to do menial labor (47:2). More than that, she will be sexually humiliated. This language is used elsewhere in the Old Testament to describe being taken into exile (cf. 20:4). This introductory stanza is brought to a conclusion with an ejaculation of praise to the One who is bringing all this to pass.

Babylon's False Pride (47:5–11). The Babylonians thought that they could do whatever they wanted to captive nations

(47:6) because there was no one greater than they. They made the fatal error of thinking that they were self-existent and self-perpetuating (47:8, 10). It never occurred to them that they might be the agents of One infinitely greater than they who will hold them to account for their actions (47:7), a deadly mistake.

Part of the deadliness of that mistake is complacency. Queen Babylon is so convinced of her ascendancy that she cannot imagine herself as a widow bereft of children (47:8–9). Her complacency robs her of beneficial self-criticism, so "wickedness" runs rampant (47:10). Part of that wickedness is the attempt to control the spirit world through magic "spells" and "sorceries" (47:9). The Babylonians were devoted to mastering magical arts, sure they can ward off any "calamity" (47:11). They do not reckon with a God who is beyond all magical manipulation, who is complete in himself, and who knows nothing of fate or destiny (cf. 65:11).

Babylon's Helplessness (47:12–15). On a sarcastic note, the prophet tells Babylon to go ahead with her magic (47:12). But of course, it is futile. All the energy expended to divine the future and control its events has been wasted (47:13). What the sorcerers have set in motion is like a fire that does no one any good; it will only burn up those who started it (47:14).

Application. Intelligence not surrendered to God can be a terrible curse for the human race. Our tremendous intelligence is, as it was for the Babylonians, aimed at making ourselves self-existent and self-perpetuating. How long will it be before the Redeemer, whose name is Yahweh of Heaven's Armies, the Holy One of Israel, tells us to get off our throne and to take our place in the dust?

ISAIAH 48:1–22

Original Meaning

Opening Words (48:1–2). The people consider themselves to be God's people. But Isaiah says they have been stubborn and rebellious (48:4, 8). They have a name, but their behavior has shown that they do not have a relationship.

The Nature of Israel's God (48:3–11). The people have heard all the predictions God has made, and they know all his predictions have come true (48:3). He made the predictions precisely so that when the events occurred, it would be impossible to say that some idol god performed the actions (48:4–5). In 48:6a Isaiah calls the people to "admit" the truth of their experience and to draw the appropriate conclusions from that experience.

Then in 48:6b, the prophet turns to the future. He will predict new things that have not been heard before. What these things are is not specified, and indeed that is not the point of the statement. The point is that God can do new things, something the idols cannot do. He is the Creator and can therefore say and do things that have never happened before. He is doing this precisely so that no one can "defame" him by comparing him to an idol and so that no idol may share his "glory" (48:11).

God's Appeal to His People (48:12–22). These verses sharpen God's appeal to his people. Three times they are commanded to listen (48:12, 14, 16). As with a number of Hebrew words, the word *shama'* ("listen") does not permit a separation between perception and action. Thus, if you truly *hear* an admonition, you will obey it. If you do not obey it, then you evidently did not *hear* it. Here, then, if God's people *listen* to what God says, they will believe his words and act accordingly. They will retain their faith in him in spite of adverse circumstances.

Verses 12–16 recap the reasons why the people should listen to (and put their faith in) God. He is the sole Creator (48:12–13). He is the Lord of history (48:14–15). Just as he summons the stars of the heavens and they obey (48:13), so he can also summon a Persian emperor who will do what God has purposed all along (48:14). No idol can predict such a thing in advance as God has because they are captive to the cycles of time and fate. The challenge to hear is summed up in 48:16 with a reiteration of the claim that God is the speaking God.

Verses 17–22 sum up everything that has been said in the chapter and, in some ways, in the entire subdivision (chs. 40–48). In keeping with this idea of summation, 48:17 identifies God by a group of his names and titles: "the LORD . . . your Redeemer, the Holy One of Israel," and "your God." The last three of these denote the special relationship of God to Israel. If they had "paid attention" (48:18) in the past, none of the tragedies that are to befall them in the exile would have occurred. Instead, all the promises that God had made to them would have been fulfilled (48:18–19).

But even though they did not listen in the past, that does not mean God has been defeated by their sin and has given up on them. If they will believe God now, they can be delivered from Babylon, into which their deaf ears and hardened hearts have delivered them. Just because no one had ever gone home from exile before does not mean it cannot happen. The Creator can break in and make "water flow" (48:21) from rocks if he chooses.

The allusion to the exodus is clear here. What he has done in the past shows that he can be equally creative to redeem his people again. "Announce this with shouts of joy!" (48:20). But joy is not the final note here. As always in this book, the prophet is careful not to let the wonderful promises of the future delude his hearers into believing that they can leave their present condition unaddressed (48:22). If they persist in wickedness, none of these promises are for them. They must change their way of responding if they are to have a part in the coming joy.

Application. We can leave the "Babylons" that have enslaved us. We can be delivered from the guilt and shame of all our past sins. In Jesus Christ, God has made a way for us. If ever there was a new thing, the coming of Christ was it. God can do the impossible and bring about genuine change. He can do for us what we cannot do for ourselves.

ISAIAH 49:1–13

Original Meaning

The Salvation Task of the Servant (49:1–6). We can imagine Isaiah's readers saying, as they come to the end of what is now chapter 48, "Alright, we're listening, and we can believe that God can and will restore us from Babylon by means of Cyrus. But who can restore us to God? That's the real problem." Isaiah's answer is given in these verses. The prophet is continuing to unfold God's plan, which calls for yet a further obedient, believing response. But now it is the servant himself who calls for the entire world to listen to what he is going to reveal.

The first revelation is one of call and confidence. The servant has no doubt of his call (49:1), his divine enablement (49:2–3), or his ultimate vindication (49:4). He has been called from the womb, so his vocation is no secondary thing. Furthermore, like a "sharpened sword" or a "polished arrow" (49:2), he will accomplish exactly what God wants at the appointed time. The Messiah will be "Israel" as Israel was meant to be. He will display the Lord's "splendor" (49:3) as an obedient Israel might have done, and in so doing, he will be the One "to restore the tribes of Jacob" to the Lord (49:6).

How that will be done is left unanswered here, but it will be answered a few chapters later. Whatever it is will be so far-reaching that it will reach to the ends of the earth, including even "Gentiles" in its scope (49:6).

The Servant's Task as Representative of God's Covenant (49:7–12). Although the servant is "despised," a day will come when kings and princes will honor him because of God's faithfulness in his life (49:7). In particular, the servant's task is to be a representative of God's "covenant" to his people (49:8). Like a new Joshua he will settle the people in a land of freedom and abundance, where the God of "compassion" will tend them as a shepherd tends his flock (49:10). While 49:12 may be intended to speak of the remnant returning from all directions, it may also be another indication of the worldwide scope of the servant's ministry.

Outburst of Praise (49:13). As in 42:10–17, the announcement of the work of the servant results in an outburst of praise. As there, nature is called on to sing the praise of its Creator and Redeemer.

Application. As those who participate in the life of the Servant, we too can have that sense of enablement by God. We too can become aware of being a "sharpened sword" or a "polished arrow" in his hand (49:2). As we perform what may seem to be simple tasks, they may have more significance than we will ever know on this side of the grave. We can have that sense of having been divinely fitted for just what it is we are doing.

ISAIAH 49:14–50:3

Original Meaning. This passage consists of the people's negative response to the proclamation of the servant's redemptive work (49:14) and God's extended rejoinder (49:15–50:3). In words reminiscent of 40:27, the people declare that the great promises about the servant's ministry are in vain because it is plain that "the Lord has forgotten" them (49:14). To this God replies that he can no more forget them than a nursing mother can forget her baby (49:15–16). He goes on to declare that the proof of his love for them will be seen in the abundance of descendants that will be born to Zion when she thought herself forever barren (49:17–21). God will cause the nations to bring the lost children home (49:22–23).

But these promises elicit another pessimistic answer: Who can break the grip of the captors (49:24)? Again, God responds that he can do that very thing (49:25–26). The next response is only implicit, but on the basis of God's response in 50:1–3, it seems to be something like: "But you are the one who (arbitrarily) sold us to those captors in the first place." To that God responds again that he has not cast them off and has the power to restore them at will.

But the astonishing thing is that he cannot do these things for his people if they will not give him an opportunity by putting their trust in him. Chapters 40–55 focus on the motivation to trust God. Chapters 7–39 have amply demonstrated that God can and should be trusted. But ultimately it is only the grace of God that can actually motivate persons to believe what he says and to exercise that trust (cf. 12:1–2). This passage in chapter 49 is an expression of that grace, reaching its climax in the passionate words of 50:1–3, where God insists that he has both the will and the power to redeem his people.

To be sure, it is no accident of history that the Judeans experienced the exile; it was because of their sin (50:1). But just as no nation on earth can stand up to God, neither can sin. Do they think he has divorced them? Where is the certificate? There is none. Do they think he was somehow forced to "sell" (50:1) them against his will? Of course not. But just as he alone could deliver them from the power of the nations, he alone has the power to deliver from sin. His "arm" is not "short" and weak (50:2a); rather, it is full-sized and powerful. He can "dry up the sea" and turn off the sun (50:2b); what is so difficult about defeating sin?

Application. When we rush ahead to solve our problems in our own way without waiting on God to show us how he wants to deal with those problems, we have effectively said to him that we know better than he does and we are better able to solve the problem than he is. This is why Jesus required his disciples to wait in Jerusalem for him to fill them with his Holy Spirit. They and their devices were not the way to carry out Jesus's command to make disciples of all nations. God was going to use them in dramatic ways to fulfill that purpose, but it was going to be in his way and through his power, not theirs.

ISAIAH 50:4–51:8

Original Meaning

The Obedience of the Servant (50:4–9). The song in 50:4–9 reveals yet more clearly that the servant's obedience to the Lord will result in suffering for him. If the message is declared, there is going to be abuse (50:6) The servant is willing to bear that abuse because he knows that God will vindicate him in the end (50:7–9).

Words of Transition (50:10–11). This brief introduction to the commentary on the servant's words highlights the emphasis on obedience to his message that will be prominent in the commentary proper (51:1–9). It also contains a significant synonymous parallel between the Lord and the servant. To "fear the Lord" is synonymous with obeying "the word of his servant," and vice versa (50:10). More and more clearly, this servant is in a unique position.

Clearly, one's response to the servant is in the nature of a watershed. Those who have "no light" (50:10) can walk safely if they will entrust themselves to God in the way that he has revealed. But those who reject God's revealed way and try to manufacture their own light will find that the way they have chosen leads to "torment" (50:11).

A Commentary on the Servant's Words (51:1–8). The commentary may be divided into three stanzas: 51:1–3, 4–6, and 7–8.

1. In 51:1–3 God and the servant call on the righteous ("Listen to me") to remember God's dealings with Abraham and to recognize the creative power that brought the world into existence in the first place.
2. The emphasis in 51:4–6 is the universal and eternal work of the servant. This deliverance that will be accomplished is not merely for the children of Abraham but for the children of Adam, the light that the servant brings to the "nations." What God will do for his people truly has universal impact.
3. The third stanza of the commentary also begins with a call to listen (51:7). Israel needs to be encouraged (comforted) by the assurance that God has not abandoned them and that their commitments to know God and to do his will have not been in vain.

Application. Those who seek God today and attempt to live in the light of his covenant commands can draw even further strength from the lessons taught here. We too can look back on the goodness of the Creator's intent and on the election love of Abraham's friend. But we can also look back on the coming of the promised Servant, the Son of the Father. With those things to look back on, we can look ahead with confidence.

ISAIAH 51:9–16

Original Meaning. Assuming 50:10–51:8 is a commentary on 50:4–9, Isaiah 51:9–16 opens the unit (51:9–52:12) that stands between two songs of the servant. This larger unit of 51:9–52:12 progresses through three stages from question to affirmation: 51:9–16 deals with the uncertainty over why God has not yet acted; 51:17–23 affirms that it is now Zion's oppressors who will suffer; and 52:1–12 announces the imminent deliverance from captivity.

Isaiah 51:9–11 presents the question and 51:12–16 gives the Lord's answer. The opening verses have some of the characteristics of a community lament in that they express both doubt and hope. "Why hasn't the Lord acted on our behalf long before now?" After all, he was the One who redeemed Israel from Egypt, so there is no question of his ability. None of the powers of evil in the world can stop him, so it is time for that mighty arm (51:9; cf. 51:5) to swing into action.

At the same time, there is the confidence that God will indeed act. Isaiah 51:11 looks forward to the day when the ransomed will return to "Zion with singing." So, the captives no longer doubt that God *will* act, but they wonder why he is waiting so long.

God does not directly answer the question, but he does respond by calling on the captives to be sure that their focus is on him and not on their oppressors. The double "I" in 51:12 highlights this emphasis. There is no point in focusing on the "oppressor" (51:13), because he will soon be gone. The One who does rule asserts that the "prisoners . . . will not die in their dungeon" (51:14). Far better to focus on the Comforter, to whom both the seen and the unseen worlds bow in obedience (51:15). The servant's ministry is to reveal God. He will declare God's words, and nothing will be able to thwart those plans for him.

Application. The biblical lament is a wonderful piece of literature insofar as it bridges two attitudes in life that are often treated as excluding each other: doubt and hope. The result of this exclusion is that people are often deprived of the encouragement and assurance that can be theirs. We are often told that if you entertain doubts, you do not have faith and hope is impossible for you. As a result, there are people who never face their doubts and are forced to live lives of denial and superficiality. By contrast, there are those whose doubts are undeniable and who therefore conclude that faith is impossible for them. Both kinds of persons need to look carefully at passages such as this and at the longer laments in the Psalms (e.g., Pss 6; 22).

ISAIAH 51:17–52:12

Original Meaning. One of the recurring images of Scripture is the "cup of wrath," found from Psalms through Revelation. The cup symbolized the sum total of a person's allotted experience (Ps 16:5). So, those who have sinned against God must drink the cup that their sins have filled up. In Israel's case, that cup was the apparent destruction of her heritage. With the destruction of the Northern Kingdom and then the Southern Kingdom, it looked as if the mother would die alone, her children dead and destroyed (Isa 51:18–20). But now, God says, the day of destruction is past, and the cup of God's wrath is placed in the hands of the "tormentors" for them to drink (51:23).

Isaiah 52:1–12 represents the climax of God's promises not to allow his people to remain alienated from himself. This segment falls naturally into two parts. In 52:1–6, just as God demonstrated his unique deity in delivering his people from Egypt, so he will do again in delivering them from this new bondage (52:4–6). Once again, an important piece of evidence for that uniqueness is his ability to predict the whole thing in advance (52:6).

The second part of this climactic unit (52:7–12) brings to a conclusion all that has been said about redemption, not only since 49:1 but indeed since 40:1. Both the ability and the desire of God to restore his people to himself have been amply demonstrated; all that remains is for the paeans of song (52:9) to begin. As is so typical of this book, Isaiah utilizes a graphic illustration to conclude the point.

Suddenly, the watchmen on the walls of the city begin to "shout for joy" (52:8). They have seen a messenger far away on the mountain, and he is signaling the "good news" (52:7) of victory. God has laid bare "his holy arm" (52:10), defeated the enemy, and "redeemed Jerusalem" (52:9). Nothing remains but for Israel to lay hold of this promise in faith and to leave behind the old way with its sin and uncleanness. They are free, free indeed, through the power of God.

Application. Why does God wait until we are helpless, or at least aware of our helplessness, before he acts? One of the main reasons is that we are usually unwilling to give up our control of the situation until we come to that extremity. As long as we think the solution to our problems is somehow in ourselves, we are liable to think of God as an assistant or as a fallback device. But to think of the almighty Creator in such a way is to deprive ourselves of his aid. He is not our servant. This is especially true in regard to our relation to him. As long as we think that we can do something to earn his favor, we are unlikely to cast ourselves on the Savior whom God has provided. It is only when we admit that there is nothing we can do for ourselves to remove our sins and our sinning that we will turn to the Savior and receive the forgiveness, cleansing, and empowerment he has been wanting to give us all the time.

ISAIAH 52:13–53:12

Original Meaning

Introduction (52:13–15). The poem begins with a note of triumph. There is no question about the outcome of the servant's work. A day will come when the very same words will be used of him ("high and lifted up," 52:13) as are used only of God elsewhere in the book (6:1; 57:15). It is important to note that the poem closes on the same note of triumph (53:12). The spoils belong to the victor. There is a reason why that point is made both at the beginning and the end of the poem. It is because nothing in between looks in the least like victory.

This anomalous view is presented immediately after the opening words. The disfigurement of the servant is utterly shocking. He hardly appears to be human. He is not the attractive figure that so many of the world's conquerors have been or pretended to be.

If we retain the meaning "sprinkle" (NIV and NASB) and assume that the object being sprinkled is not stated, then the sense of 52:15 is that the kings are struck dumb by the thought that the supposed conqueror has actually come to purify the nations by sprinkling something (blood? sacred water?) on them.

Rejection of the Servant (53:1–3). Isaiah makes it explicit that this servant is "the arm of the LORD" that had been promised (53:1). But that report is clearly disbelieved. Why? Three reasons are given.

1. He comes onto the scene in a quiet and unassuming way (53:2).

2. He has no extraordinary beauty or attractiveness to draw people to him; his "appearance" (53:2) was quite ordinary.
3. Finally, he is rejected because he takes on himself the pain and "suffering" of the world (53:3).

We find pain and suffering disturbing, both because we do not know what to say in sympathy and because it reminds us of our own vulnerability. So, we try to ignore it ("hide [our] faces," 53:3) and not to think about it. The servant has come to take away the sins of the world, but no one pays any attention to him.

The Servant's Carrying of Sin (53:4–6). If there were any question about why the servant suffers, these verses answer the question once and for all. Despite what "we" thought, he is not suffering because God has inflicted deserved punishment on him (53:4). It is our suffering that he bore, and it is for "our transgressions" and "our iniquities" that he suffered (53:5). The repetition of first-person plural pronouns hammers home that the servant has suffered in "our" place. Verse 6 drives this point home with imagery. "We" (53:6), the blind, rebellious people of God (cf. 42:18–25), are the sheep who have gone astray, but he is the one who gets beaten for our willfulness!

The Results of Carrying Our Sin (53:7–9). This stanza details the servant's innocence and submission and the injustice of the treatment he receives. The servant is now compared to a sheep, and with very different results. In him it is the mild, defenseless nature of the sheep that is the basis of comparison. Although his suffering is manifestly unjust, he accepts it without protest (53:7). It is significant that the only extended metaphor in the poem deals with sheep, the animals of sacrifice.

The injustice of what the servant suffered is further underlined in 53:8–9. He is deprived of justice, but he is also "cut off" (53:8) in the prime of life. As a final insult, he is buried with the rich. But is this an insult? Isaiah's statement in 5:8 reflects the view of such prophets as Hosea and Amos (and Jesus). In their view, riches have all too often been amassed through violence and deceit. The contrastive "though" in 53:9b seems to make clear that that is the sense here. The servant is buried with the rich even "though" he did not do what they did.

The Atoning Nature of the Carrying (53:10–12). Why have these things happened to the servant? The answer is given in this final stanza. They were not accidental; they were intended. Moreover, it was God's intention. The opening lines of 53:10 are terrible. What good father could *wish* for his son to be crushed? It is only possible if there was some unquestionably greater good to be obtained. And what greater good could possibly justify the crushing of the servant? The answer is given in the second half of the verse. It is when the "life" (53:10a) of the servant is offered as a sin offering that God's purpose in bringing him to this place is realized ("prosper," 53:10b). Then will the injustice of being deprived of children and a long life be rectified. The servant did not come to tell people what God wants; rather, he came to *be* what God wants *for* us. But how can someone who has been cut off from the land of the living without descendants ever have these things? It certainly looks as though resurrection is the only answer.

Verse 11 gives a more theological statement of what was accomplished in the servant's death. When his life has been offered up for others, he will "see" it and be "satisfied." The hard struggle will have been worth it.

But what does that struggle accomplish for people who accept it on their own behalf? The second half of 53:11 answers that question in a tightly connected statement. Because the servant knows God in intimate relationship and indeed shares God's own righteousness (lit, "the righteous one, my servant," 53:11b), he will in turn be able to make many people righteous. How? By bearing "their iniquities" (53:11b).

Why does God give his servant the victor's wreath? "Because" he was treated like one of the rebels when he was not and thus could bear their punishment and make "intercession" for them (53:12). If there are any remaining question about how the servant brings God's justice to the world, this verse should clear it up.

Application. Can humans thwart the will of God? Not in any ultimate sense. There *will* be a new heaven and a new earth, and all the redeemed *will* inhabit them. There *will* be a great crowd of the redeemed. But those who are invited first may choose not to come in (Luke 14:16–24). From God's side he has done everything necessary, and whoever will may come. But we must accept the offering made on our behalf.

ISAIAH 54:1–17

Original Meaning

Restoration and Hope for a Disgraced Woman (54:1–10). In these ten verses God speaks to Israel in the image of a disgraced woman. She is the barren one (54:1–3), the widow (54:4–5), and the divorced one (54:6–8). To each of these, God promises restoration and hope, and the promises are brought to a climax in 54:9–10.

This does not mean that Israel will no longer be subject to condemnation and punishment, as later history shows. It means rather that somehow God is now reconciled in himself to his people. Whatever was necessary to satisfy the righteous anger of God at human sin has been done, and God can proclaim that there is no longer any barrier to persons experiencing that reconciliation.

In the ancient Near East almost the worst fate that could befall a woman was to have no children. Here (54:1–3) God says that those who have experienced his grace will no longer be fruitless but will live lives of unexpected abundance, with more descendants than they can account for.

Widowhood was also considered a disgrace in many parts of the ancient world (54:4). God says that Israel should no longer consider herself to be a widow. Her "Maker" is her "husband" (54:5). Who is this one who has married her, delivering her from the disgrace? Verse 5 rings with his titles.

But there was an even worse disgrace than childlessness or widowhood: divorce. At least in widowhood your husband had left you alone involuntarily. The divorced woman was one who had been found wanting in some way and was willfully "rejected" (54:6). This was Israel: She had failed God and was cast out of her home. But God has found a way and brought her back to himself. His "anger" was for a "moment," but his "compassion" is "everlasting" (54:7–8).

Restoration and Hope for a Ruined City (54:11–17). The image now changes from disgraced woman to a ruined city. The people are like a city that has been "lashed by storms" (54:11), subjected to "tyranny" and "terror" (54:14) and experienced "havoc" (54:16) within it. But since God is the one who brought all that to pass (54:16), he is the one who can change it all (54:15, 17).

Again, the promises are lyrical in tone. In place of weathered, broken walls stained with smoke, there are "battlements of rubies" (54:12) glittering in the sun. In place of tyranny and terror, there is true learning, "peace" (*shalom*), "righteousness," and security (54:13–14). These blessings are for those who gladly accept the role of "servants of the LORD" (54:17). How can sinful, rebellious Israel enter into such a role? Through the ministry of the servant of the Lord.

Application. This passage shows us the heart of the gospel of Christ. God has reconciled his lost world to himself. He has not waited for us to find a way to bridge the gap between him and us, as he certainly could have in his own righteousness. After all, we are the ones who created the breach between him and ourselves, so let us find a way across it. Yet the amazing thing about God is that he gets no satisfaction from the richly deserved death of the sinner. Not even the death of the most heinous criminal brings a grim smile of satisfaction to the face of God. Rather, there is grief in his heart.

ISAIAH 55:1–13

Original Meaning. We turn now from the announcement in chapter 54 that all is forgiven to the invitation to experience that forgiveness. In 55:1–5 the invitation is expressed in the strongest terms to those who have no resources in themselves. It begins in physical imagery (55:1–2) and moves onto a more spiritual plane (55:3). God's invitation is not merely to find a supply of bodily needs but to satisfy a person's whole being with true life. The old covenant was broken and thus legally annulled. But God promises another covenant, this one on the pattern of the unconditional one given to "David" (55:3).

But more is going on than simply a similarity between the covenants. It is plain that in some sense this "everlasting covenant" (55:3) *is* the covenant with David. For what David was in part, "a witness to the peoples" (55:4), the nation now will be able to bring to fulfillment. The nations of the world will flock to restored Israel because of their God (55:5). This is, of course, exactly what was predicted in Isaiah 2.

Verses 6–11 address the universal problem of people who hear the invitation of God with clarity. They cannot deny the reality of the choice before them: to stay where they are in unbelief or to go forward in immense uncertainty. Surely for people in Isaiah's own day, but no less so for those who read these words in the exile, the message of what is now 52:13–53:12 was largely a mystery. What in the world was God talking about? Who is this person, and how in the world can what he did make it possible for God to be *eternally* reconciled to his people?

God's challenge to these people is to exercise faith first and let understanding come afterward. God promises that what he says (his "word," 55:11) is indeed reliable and that forgiveness and abundance are theirs now and in the future, if they will only seek him sincerely and unreservedly.

All of this is brought to a close in 55:12–13. While much more than deliverance from physical captivity is being talked about, that imagery would communicate most immediately in the circumstances of the exile. All nature will rejoice in the redemption of humanity, and in place of sorrow and sighing there will be "joy" and "peace" (55:12) as the captives return to their God.

Application. Nothing has changed since the garden of Eden. We do not wish to be told by our Creator that something is wrong for us when everything appears so delightful. Neither do we wish to be told that something is good for us when it looks as though it is going to take a lot of effort and may actually bring us some pain. We want to hold the place of God in our lives and have God serve us, supplying our needs as we dictate. So, faith always involves letting go of secure footholds and (apparent) certainties to do things God's way.

ISAIAH 56:1–8

Original Meaning. A careful reader will note an apparent contradiction between the teachings of chapters 1–39 and those of chapters 40–55. This seeming contradiction may be illustrated by the differing uses of the word "righteousness." In chapters 1–39 it is used exclusively for behavior that is in keeping with the statutes of God. But in chapters 40–55, the term refers to God's "righteousness" in faithfully delivering his people in spite of their previous sin. In a remarkable way, chapters 56–66 synthesize the teaching of the two earlier sections, showing that actual righteous living is a requirement for the servants of God (i.e., chs. 1–39) but that such righteousness is only possible through the grace of God (i.e., chs. 40–55).

Verse 1 provides an immediate illustration. It calls on the reader to "maintain justice and do what is right" in language similar to that found repeatedly in chapters 1–39. But in the same breath it says we should do this because God's "righteousness"—that is, his "salvation"—is at hand (56:1). We can only do righteousness because of God's righteousness made available to us.

It may have been easy for persons reading chapters 40–55 to conclude that it was really one's birthright that secured salvation. But 56:3–8 radically refute such an idea. The person who is pleasing to God is not the purebred Israelite who is doing his part to continue the physical line of Abraham. If the "eunuch," who cannot pass that line on, chooses to live in obedience to God's "covenant" (56:4, 6), God will give the eunuch a better heritage than children, "an everlasting name" (56:5).

But this righteousness is more than legalistic law-keeping. Verse 6 speaks in relational terms of binding oneself to God as an act of love, service, and worship. Those who do this will be brought into God's "house of prayer," there to participate in the worship of that place, because God's purpose is to gather "all nations" to himself (56:7–8).

Application. Unless our adoption into a new family changes our behavior into the likeness of the head of that family, there is reason to doubt the reality of the adoption. Christians today must recover the understanding that while it is indeed by grace through faith, not our works, that we are saved (Eph 2:8–9), it is *for* good works that we have been saved (Eph 2:10).

ISAIAH 56:9–57:13

Original Meaning

Words of Judgment to the Leaders (56:9–57:2). This section begins with an attack on "Israel's watchmen" (56:10), who are compared to "dogs" who do not bark because they are asleep with full stomachs (56:10–11). They are stupid "shepherds" (56:11) who are only interested in taking care of themselves and have no concern for the flock. Clearly this is the leadership of the nation, and with what follows, they are evidently the religious leaders. The nation is in a desperate spiritual condition, and the leaders do not care.

Isaiah is implying that simply a return from captivity will not guarantee a new set of behaviors for the people. If the leaders continue to be self-centered and power hungry, the flock entrusted to them will continue to be overtaken by their spiritual enemies (56:9). Moreover, there will be so little spiritual perception that the disappearance of the "righteous" (57:1) from among them will go unnoticed.

Words of Judgment to the People (57:3–13). Now Isaiah turns directly to the people, addressing them as "you" (57:3). In strong language he speaks to those who believe that they are the elect and that cultic righteousness is all that is required of them. Like those who worship rocks and trees (57:5–7), who engage in ritual prostitution (57:8), and who sacrifice their children (57:5, 9), their only real desire is to manipulate divine power to their own advantage. Of course, the attempt to manipulate divine power to one's own advantage is hard work (57:10).

Following the description of the people's behavior, God pronounces his judgment. He begins with a question. This is the God who graciously delivered them. How could they have not "remembered" (57:11) all this and instead turned to the religions of their own making?

In an ironic aside, he asks whether it is because he has not spoken to them that they do not fear him. Of course, he has spoken to them again and again. No, the answer to these two questions lies in the depravity of the human heart. It is simply that God asks them to give up control of their lives and to abandon themselves into his hands in glad obedience (57:13b). That is too much. So, they would rather construct a religion that seems to give them control. But such a religion cannot stand up when the winds of adversity blow upon a life. It will collapse and blow away (57:13a).

Application. In so many ways the satisfaction of supposed needs is all-important to us: We drink to excess, we eat to excess, we cannot get enough sex of all sorts, and we sacrifice our children, both the unborn and the living, to the satisfaction of these needs. What is the answer? The key is in self-surrender. Paul calls it dying to oneself (cf. Rom 6:11; Gal 2:20; Col 3:3–5). We surrender our needs to him, determined to be faithful to him and his ways above all else, leaving the fulfillment of our needs in his hand. Here there is freedom without excess, satisfaction without satiation, because we know that in the end it is God we want and that another half-gallon of ice cream will never satisfy that longing.

ISAIAH 57:14–21

Original Meaning. These verses stand in sharp contrast to 56:9–57:13. There the stress was on the inability of humans to live the righteous lives that their redemption called them to live; here the focus is on the activity of God. There the focus was on the failings of "you" (e.g., 57:12); here the focus is on what God will do for his people.

Once more the highway imagery comes to the fore. But this is a highway on which the "contrite" (57:15) can return to God. In one of the most beautiful statements in Scripture, the One who is utterly separated from the inhabitants of earth in his "holy" place says that his dwelling is also with the lowly and the contrite (57:15). His intention is not merely to punish (57:17) but to go beyond that to giving his people a changed nature, where rebellion and pride will be replaced by "praise" and "peace" (57:19).

Because the wicked refuse to recognize their sinfulness and turn from it, they cannot experience the peace (*shalom*) that God promises. These final verses emphasize once again that God's promises are not for the nation as a whole merely because they are the descendants of Jacob but specifically for those inside the nation—and outside—who recognize their need and turn to God in contrition.

Application. We evangelicals need to come to God in contrition—contrition that our "standing" before God has been more important to us than our relationship with him. The good news is that God is merciful. He wants to live with us and in us. He wants to heal us. The worst thing we can do is to return to the kind of legalistic righteousness of earlier generations. No, the message of these verses, and indeed of this entire last part of the book, is that while God expects real righteousness and justice in our lives, he also expects to do that in us and for us as a by-product of our loving relation with him.

ISAIAH 58:1–14

Original Meaning. Verses 1–3 introduce the subject. The people give every appearance of piety and genuine concern to know God's will. But in fact, says Isaiah, they are in a state of "rebellion" (58:1). The evidence of this fact is in their approach to their cultic behavior. They are engaging in the behavior for the very same reasons the pagans do, to manipulate God to act in their favor.

Verses 4–12 expand on this theme. Instead of abandoning themselves and their needs into the hands of God and instead of giving themselves away to others, their religious activities have become self-serving. Verse 5 suggests this self-serving aspect with the phrase "people to humble themselves" (literally, "to afflict oneself"). The worshiper is merely doing something to himself to show how devoted he is.

God calls for behavior that is self-forgetful and outward-looking. Let acts of self-denial be for the sake of others and not for one's own sake (58:6). Eat less in order to have food to give to the "hungry" (58:7). Wear less-expensive clothes in order to clothe the "naked" (58:7, 10). This is the kind of cessation and self-affliction God has "chosen" (58:6).

The reference to "light" in 58:8 and 10 looks both backward and forward. It looks back to the promises to the servant in 42:6 and 49:6. By means of the servant, God's light of justice will shine through his people to be a light for the nations. The theme reaches its climax in 60:1–3. Through God's people the blessings of his covenant will be extended to the whole earth.

Verses 13 and 14, speaking about the Sabbath, are connected to the preceding as a way of further saying what kind of cessation God *would* like. He would like his people to stop doing as they "please" (58:13) on the Sabbath day (cf. 58:3). The Sabbath is enjoined as one of the feast days and is to be considered as a time of delighting in the Lord and in all his blessings to us. It does not manipulate God but is a means of developing the all-important relationship with him.

Application. We are still just as tempted to use religious behavior as a way of manipulating God for our selfish ends as our Israelite forbears were. It is interesting that Isaiah uses fasting, because that continues to be a practice of Christians today who seek a more disciplined life. Other activities, however, have replaced Israelite cultic activities, such as church attendance, daily devotions, prayer, tithing, and so on, and these are all liable to the same dangers. The danger is that we engage in them in order to wring blessings from a God who, we feel, is disinclined to give blessings unless we manipulate him in some way.

ISAIAH 59:1–15A

Original Meaning. Verses 1 and 2 seem to hark back to the opening of Isaiah 58. From their point of view, the people have done everything necessary to procure God's blessings for themselves. Yet it does not seem to be happening. Their lack of blessing is not God's fault but theirs. Their "iniquities" and "sins" have come between them and God (59:2). And as chapters 57–58 have shown, some of those sins are their very religiosity. Coupled with that are the twofold evidences of a broken social system: violence and injustice (59:3–4).

The closing of 59:4 seems to provide the basis for yet one more of Isaiah's graphic illustrations. The things they give birth to, or produce, are like the "eggs of vipers" and the webs of spiders (59:5–6a). They are not only "useless" (59:6a) but worse, deadly.

This thought is further expanded upon in 59:6b–7. All the faculties of these persons are given over to evil. In contrast to the highway of holiness that God will prepare for his people (35:8), these "roads" are "crooked," and those who embark on them will find destruction and disintegration, not "peace" (59:8; cf. 52:7; 57:19).

In 59:9–15a the prophet moves from condemnation to shared confession, using first-person plurals. Here he is speaking for all the faithful of the land. It would have been easy, becoming so intimately allied with the holy God and being aware of just how terrible the sin of the people was, to consider oneself above such things. But if the prophet was closely allied with God, he was also still inextricably part of his human community. The mark of the truly great prophets was that they did not forget the latter in their absorption in the former.

This confession is one of a person who has reflected deeply on the human condition. In 59:12, in words reminiscent of Psalm 51:4, the prophet makes it plain that the reason injustice and unrighteousness are first of all acts of "rebellion" (59:13) against the Lord of the universe. Having revolted against God and thereby denying the "truth" of our existence, there is no truth in any of our relationships to the extent that those who take a stand against "evil" become the target to be attacked (59:14–15).

Are humans doomed to continue in sin, recognizing that they ought to do differently but are constitutionally unable to do so? Isaiah is definitely not saying that. Rather, he is showing the need for something other than merely stern discipline and good intentions if God's commands are to be fulfilled. What that something is will be uncovered in the next segment.

Application. Why do we do things that are so obviously destructive of even our own best interests in the long run? Why do we choose to do things to one another that are not merely self-serving but egregiously vicious and cruel? God created the universe as an expression of his own goodness. But he has permitted his creatures the possibility of choosing not to live within his purposes, and that choice on the part of our first parents was like introducing a virus into the body. It has infected the entire system, most especially the human system. Thus, just as cancer cells are able to capture the cells around them and turn them to their own destructive purposes, the Bible insists that there is a moral cancer let loose in the human system.

ISAIAH 59:15B–21

Original Meaning. God's people seem unable to keep his commandments. So, what is to be done? The answer is found in 59:15b–21. God will come and do for his people what neither they nor anyone else can do for them. The servant will now defeat the sin that reigns in them and will make it possible for them to be, in truth, the servants of the Lord. Whereas in 52:13–53:12 the servant was submissive, undergoing the punishment the erring sheep had brought on themselves, now the arm of the Lord is revealed as a conquering warrior (59:17).

He is not coming here to vindicate the righteous (59:1–15a made it abundantly clear there are no such persons). No, he has come to do what the people, sinners and righteous alike, cannot do, namely, defeat the power of evil in their lives. People all over the world will be affected by the witness of a righteous Israel. They will give God "glory" and turn to him in obedience (59:19).

Verse 21 concludes all that has been said in chapters 56–59. God's goal for his people is for them to be witnesses to the world of his nature and character, that he, the only God, is indeed the only Savior. The "Spirit" of God (59:21) can fill the lives and mouths of his people, making the witness promised in 2:1–5 not just a possibility but a reality. This is the fulfillment of the "covenant of peace" (54:10; 55:3–5).

Application. Through the gift of the Holy Spirit, we can keep covenant with God, with no credit for the feat accruing to us but with all glory to the conquering Christ. He enables us to live "blameless" lives (1 Thess 5:23), to walk in a "blameless" manner (Gen 17:1), and to keep us in that walk until the coming of Christ.

ISAIAH 60:1–22

Original Meaning

Poetic Introduction (60:1–3). The emphasis on "light" in 60:1–3 is all the more striking because of the contrast with 59:9. Where there was complete "darkness," there will now be "light" like that of the rising sun. Something has occurred that makes it possible for the glory of the Lord to be seen in his people. Zion will be the lamp out of which that light shines on the nations (60:3).

The purpose of God's sharing his glory with his people becomes explicit in 60:2–3. Israel has a mission: The nations are in darkness because they do not know the one Creator, who is thereby the one Savior. When the light of God dawns in Israel, the nations will recognize it for what it is and "come" (60:1, 3) flowing to it. Zion's light is not for itself but for others.

Return of Zion's Dispersed Sons and Daughters (60:4–9). In 60:4–9 Isaiah emphasizes the worldwide nature of the pilgrimage of the nations. They will come with every kind of conveyance, from camels to ships. The wealth will be of every sort as well. But there is no question what this wealth is intended to honor (60:6, 9). Zion is only the lamp from which the light shines. The "splendor" (60:9) with which God endows his people is an expression of his own generous abundance, but even more it is so that the world may know him.

Along with their wealth, the nations will also bring back Zion's "sons" and "daughters" (60:4, 9). If the promises to Abraham are to have any meaning, the forced dispersion of Abraham's descendants cannot be permitted. In a coming day, all those who wished to return will be able to do so; moreover, the nations that carried them off will be the ones to bring them home (60:4, 9).

Submission to Zion (60:10–14). The nations will not only bring their wealth to Zion, but they will also come to serve her (60:10), and if not, their "kingdom . . . will be utterly ruined" (60:12). Two points are being made.

1. Those who oppress God's people, even as an instrument in his hand, are accountable for their behavior.
2. A choice is implied in the two kinds of passages. If one does not choose to become a participant in worship with God's redeemed people, the only other option is to become their servants.

Restoration of Israel to God (60:15–22). Isaiah closes by asserting that all of the benefits that will accrue to God's people result from one thing alone: the gracious power of the Lord. Twice he asserts that "the LORD will be your everlasting light" (60:19, 20). It is he who will transform Zion from being "forsaken" and abandoned (60:15) to being suckled at the "breasts" of royalty (60:16). It is he who will replace silver, iron, and stones with gold, silver, and bronze (60:17). It is he who will take away violence, ruin, and destruction (60:18) and give peace and righteousness (60:17), salvation and praise (60:18) in their place.

Isaiah does not foresee a day when Israel will finally "get it all together" and bring in the kingdom of God. Rather, he sees a day when Israel will finally allow God to do his work in them and through them. The ultimate transformation that the Savior produces is not changing bronze into gold or iron into silver. Rather, it is changing people who are helpless in sin, incapable of acting in righteous ways, into "righteous" people (60:21).

Application. Glory is never for oneself. It is always to be shared, given away, reflected. In Hebrew the word "glory" (*kabod*) does not have the ephemeral connotations that "glory" has in English. In fact, it is just the opposite. *Kabod* connotes what is weighty, significant, even real. This is what Christ has come to give us—the very reality of God. But just as he has given it to us from God, we are to give it back to him. As the light of his reality shines in us, it is not to draw people to us but to God. No accolades should come to us but to the God who shines through us.

ISAIAH 61:1–11

Original Meaning. In this chapter we are introduced once again to the means whereby God's people will be enabled to live righteous lives, which will in turn draw the nations to God. That means is the anointed one, the messiah (61:1–3a). Then follows a list of the benefits that the messiah's people will receive (61:3b–7). In 61:8–9 God speaks, making it explicit that covenant righteousness is what he desires and that he is the one who makes that righteousness possible. Finally, the servant people break forth into a psalm of praise to God, who makes them a righteous people in the sight of the nations (61:10–11).

The results of the messiah's work are detailed in 61:3b–7, beginning with God's people becoming "oaks of righteousness" (61:3). This is the opposite of what was said of them in 1:27–31, where they were an "oak with fading leaves" (1:30) because of the unrighteousness and injustice practiced among them (1:21). The servant/messiah's work will not only deliver but also transform.

As has happened before when the work of the servant/messiah is presented, the response is a paean of praise. Israel sees herself as a bride whom the groom has dressed in beautiful wedding garments. What are the garments? They are "salvation" and "righteousness" (61:10). The figure changes in 61:11. Now Israel sees herself as a fruitful field in which God has planted the seeds of flowers, namely, "righteousness" and "praise." In the overall context of Isaiah 56–66, there can be no doubt of the import of these words. God will give his people the righteous behavior they have been unable to produce in themselves. He will do this for his own praise and glory before the nations as a witness to his almighty power.

Application. Too often we allow the accuser to defeat us. We do not see instant, painless change in our behavior and so we allow doubt to replace faith. But the point of failure is the point at which we must ask God to show us what in us is preventing his power from being released in us. As we give God the freedom to probe around in our persons and to excise what is killing us, we may enter into a painful process. But it is also a process that leads to wonderful freedom and joyous growth.

In the end, the only question is one of belief. Do we believe that Christ wants to deliver us from habitual sinning? Do we believe he can do that? Will *we*, personally and intentionally, believe him to do that in our lives? Will we keep on believing him to remake us into his image, despite setbacks and difficulties, right to the end of the road?

ISAIAH 62:1–12

Original Meaning. The theme introduced in 61:4–11 (and paralleling that of 60:1–22) continues here. It is introduced in

62:1 with a declaration of God's intent for Zion. This statement is followed by eight verses (62:2–9) of direct address to Israel. The theme of these verses is an insistence that God has not cast off Zion (62:4) but that he "rejoices" (62:5) over her as a groom does a bride (cf. 61:10).

In this statement of God's joy in his people, the idea of the display of his handiwork before the nations is never far from the surface. "The nations will see" the "glory" that is their "vindication" (62:2). The nation will be a beautiful "crown" in God's "hand" (62:3).

The concluding segment (62:10–12) actually concludes the unit that began at 60:1. As already mentioned, these verses show some interesting parallels with chapter 40, with its call to build up the "highway." This is the same language used in the discussion of the messianic kingdom in chapter 11. Here Isaiah is drawing together strands from throughout his book in an effort to call the people to take action to receive the promises God is making to them. They *can* be the righteous people of God, his "Holy People" (62:12), who will draw all nations to him.

Application. We live in a time of strange paradoxes. One of those is that we have never had such emphasis on self-esteem coupled with such a high suicide rate. What explains this? I am not suggesting that our emphasis on self-esteem is causing the suicides, of course. But I would suggest that increasing our (artificial) attempts to induce self-esteem does not address the problem. What causes feelings of self-worth? What enables people to go on living when problems seem to mount above eye level?

Oddly enough, self-esteem outside of a positive complex of relationships is not a good thing but a bad one. The serial killer often feels good about himself and has nothing but contempt for his victims. In other words, we are focusing on the wrong thing. We should be helping people to find complex, stable webs of relationship in which they play a vital and necessary part. In such a setting they will know themselves to be of worth, but that worth will not be the most important thing to them. What will matter is that we find our "self" by giving it away to others.

ISAIAH 63:1–6

Original Meaning. How can an unrighteous people manifest the light of God that will bring the nations to his feet? The answer is the Divine Warrior. God will defeat every enemy of his people, including the most dangerous of all, sin.

Israel's problem is that they are weak because they are sinful. In response, God does not say in 63:1–66:24 that he will destroy their physical enemies in spite of their sinfulness. Rather, he will destroy the sinners *among his people* and will vindicate those among his people who allow him to make them righteous, using these latter people to call the nations to worship the righteous God. They are his true servants (65:13–16; cf. 54:17).

Thus, the blood that stains the garments of the victor (63:1, 3) is the blood of sinners from all nations, including his own nation, who have defied him. This is not destruction for its own sake. Rather, it is for the purpose of making redemption and "salvation" (63:4–5) available. Until sin and those who propagate it are defeated, there is no genuine salvation available. The idea that redemption and continued sin can coexist is not biblical; it is certainly not Isaianic.

Application. If Christ is the Divine Warrior who will eventually triumph over sin in the world at large, the time is now to let him defeat sin in our own lives and to give us a thoroughgoing hatred of it in all its forms.

ISAIAH 63:7–14

Original Meaning. After introducing God's ability to defeat sin in all of its forms, Isaiah returns to a discussion of the human inability to do what is right (from 63:7 to 65:16). There is not only a lament over the failure but also the question why God allows this condition to persist.

The groundwork for this question is laid in 63:7–14, and then the question itself is brought out in 63:15–64:12. The forceful answer from God appears in 65:1–5. In 63:7–14 the prophet begins the discussion by rehearsing the theological significance of the exodus.

The exodus events reveal the rebellious character of God's people. After all God had done for them, the Israelites turned against him. Interestingly, Isaiah does not say that they broke their covenant or they disobeyed their king. Rather, they "grieved [God's] Holy Spirit" (63:10). That is the language of personal relationship.

This atmosphere is reinforced by such language as "lifted them up and carried them" (63:9; cf. 46:3–4). A Father's love, care, and concern has been treated as worthless. The result is that their lover became their "enemy" (63:10). Love and personal relationship do not invalidate the law of cause and effect.

But if the exodus events illustrate both the undeserved grace of God and the shocking rebellion of the people, they also illustrate what older theologians called the "biddability" of God. For in spite of the rebellion of the first generation in the desert, God did not abandon his people. Can he not deliver them from their persistent rebellion and grieving of the Holy Spirit?

Application. Isaiah calls us to return to our first love. It is not the stern Judge or the distant King who calls us but the One who has carried us through all the years (cf. 46:3–4).

ISAIAH 63:15–64:12

Original Meaning

The Complaint (63:15–19). These verses, spoken by the prophet as a representative of the people, express the complaint element of the lament. In brief, God has "withheld" his "might" and "compassion" from them (63:15). This is not right because God is the true "Father" (63:16) of Israel, much more so than "Abraham" and Jacob ("Israel"). Isaiah understands that Israel is not merely an ethnic, linguistic, or national group. They are first and foremost a spiritual group. They are who they are because of the covenant love of God. If that love should ever be withdrawn, their reason for existence would be called into question.

Unless God softens the depraved and hardened human heart, there is no way we can ever turn to him (cf. 1:9). But the fact is, he has already done all that is necessary for that softening to occur. God has not changed. If his people will return to him, he will return to them.

Isaiah 63:18–19 continues the complaint. As those in despair often do, the speaker has magnified the tragic and minimized the positive. God's people carried his name and possessed his sanctuary for a long time. But looking back, it seems like such a short time.

The Petition (64:1–5). Isaiah moves from complaint to petition, calling on God in the name of the people to leave his isolation in the "heavens" and to come to their aid (64:1). God's actions in the past demonstrate that this petition is not based in fantasy (64:3–4). Whenever God had manifested himself in the past, dramatic things occurred. In sum, God can act and he has acted, so it is not foolish to ask him to act again.

But if Isaiah knows that God can act, he also knows that there are conditions for that to occur (64:4–5). God acts on behalf of those who "wait for him" (64:4), that is, those who put their trust in him. One evidence of such a trust is a life of godliness.

The Contradiction (64:6–7). Relationship with a holy God while doing what is contrary to his character is a contradiction of terms. The recognition of the contradiction at the end of 64:5 is now expanded. If the people tended to blame God for their hard-heartedness, at least they did not minimize the reality of their condition (64:6).

Further reflection occurs in 64:7. Here we are at the conundrum again: We are wasting away in our sins because we won't turn to God, and we won't turn to him because he has hidden his face from us. What is to be done?

The Petition Repeated (64:8–12). Once again Isaiah asserts that the nation only exists because of God, the "Father," who brought them into existence, the "potter" who formed their "clay" on his wheel (64:8). He should not allow the people's "sins" to make him forget that they are his creation (64:9), nor should he overlook the fact that all the sacred spaces that he presumably treasures are in ruins (64:10–11). The closing verse picks up the original plea of 63:15.

Application. Paganism saw all of life as directed by the fates, where the position of the stars on the day of your birth determined the possibilities for the rest of your life. In a stunning contrast, the Bible declares that every person has real choices to make regarding the meaning and purpose of life and that every person will be held accountable for those choices.

ISAIAH 65:1–16

Original Meaning

God's Continuing Revelation (65:1). In the previous section, 64:7 stated that "no one calls on [God's] name," because "you have hidden your face from us." Isaiah 65:1 directly refutes that statement by saying that in fact God had "revealed" himself to people who did not call on his name.

Israel's Problem (65:2–7). So, what was their problem? Three ideas—obstinacy, devising one's own ways, and ways that are not good—describe in a brief compass precisely what the human problem is. Rather than obediently submitting to the ways of living that the Creator has designed for us, we have rebelled and tried to devise other ways of living for ourselves.

So, what is it we humans have devised? We have devised worship practices that we believe will make it possible to manipulate God to act in our favor while we retain the option to live our lives for ourselves. The worship practices described in 65:3–5, 7 look markedly like the preexilic Canaanite practices that were so attractive to the Israelites.

In these circumstances, the people's pretensions to holiness procured by ritual magic are ludicrous (65:5). That being the case, they might rather prefer for God to remain silent instead of responding to their lament and rending the heavens to speak to them! But the prophet says God "will not keep silent" (65:6). They want God to act? Well, act he will—and he will fully repay them for all they have done (65:7).

A Remnant of the Faithful (65:8–11). But if God castigates the spurious holiness of those who think that they can manipulate him through their rituals, it does not mean that there is no remnant of the faithful among the people. These are the ones God calls his "servants" (65:8). These are the people who "seek" the Lord (65:10).

To seek the Lord is to seek his ways, to seek to please him, to seek his presence. These are the primary goals of a believer, not his blessings. The servants of God stand in stark contrast with those who try to bypass a submissive relationship with God and seek to gain control of "Destiny" through religious behavior (65:11).

God's Promises Remain (65:12–16). "Jacob" will have "descendants," and "Judah" will possess the land of promise (65:9), but that does not mean everyone called by the names of Jacob or Judah will share in the promise. It is not birthright but behavior that marks the servants of God. Thus, 65:13–16 details the differences between "you" (i.e., those who have been trying to manipulate God for blessings) and "my servants" (i.e., those who seek God for himself with changed lives).

Application. If we gauge our Christian faith by external behaviors alone—any external behaviors—it is all dust and ashes. Unless we have come to the place where our service to God is growing out of a glad servant heart, it is all in vain. Can you imagine a bridegroom asking a minister how many hours a month he has to spend with his bride to keep the marriage in force? If he does ask this question, we know something is severely lacking in his devotion to his bride, and we also know the relationship is doomed.

ISAIAH 65:17–25

Original Meaning. The fact is that all the effects of human choice are not experienced in this life. Justice is not entirely served here, as any of us can relate. All the good that is done here is not rewarded here, and all the evil that is done here is not punished here. So, if God says that his servants will be blessed, as he did in 65:13–16, either he is a liar, or this world is not all there is to reality. These verses tell us that the latter is the case.

God will "create" (65:17–18) something that, while being in continuity with what had been, will yet be a completely new expression of that reality. The earthly realities give shape to the new realities instead of the earthly expression being merely a duplication of what already exists in heaven. But because they are new, the tragic realities of this world need not be repeated. Thus, we may experience the reality of joy without the reality of weeping (65:18–19). Likewise, we may experience the delight of birth without the despair of death (65:20). The satisfaction of building will not be accompanied by the fear of destruction and conquest (65:21–23).

So, God says that what he has said is true: Those who believe his word, who obey him, and who live his life *will* be "blessed" (65:23). There are consequences to our choices; they begin now and will come to their ultimate fruition when the Creator concludes his creative activity in the coming days. What we have here is not merely a poetic expression of the certainty of justice in some general sense but a prediction of real events in the age to come.

Application. If it is true that the reality we experience in the days to come will be shaped by our choices now, then those choices are of critical importance. Far from saying with the television comic, "the devil made me do it," we need to be thinking about the cosmic effects of our choices on the world to come. Our actions are not predetermined. Instead, our actions will bear fruit from now on and forever. This ought to make us think a good deal more soberly about what we do. Far from being merely a duplicate of something that has always existed, we have the possibility of shaping the reality that is to come.

ISAIAH 66:1–24

Original Meaning

A Final Diatribe against Ritualism (66:1–6). Empty ritualism that does not symbolize a genuinely repentant and obedient heart is worse than useless. From the outset of the book and up to its very end, the central problem it has identified in the human race is that of self-exaltation. We try to solve the basic problem of our extreme fragility, both physically and psychologically, by lifting ourselves up in order to gain power. For it is by means of power that we can protect ourselves and ensure the satisfaction of whatever we consider our needs to be. When all is said and done, that is what ritualistic religion is about.

God says here that it is the "humble and contrite in spirit," who tremble at his word, whom he esteems (66:2). To try to use ritual to enhance one's own power or to satisfy one's own needs is to do nothing other than to choose one's "own ways" (66:3), even if the rituals are those promulgated by God himself. Once again, God insists that it is not he who has been silent when they called, as they had charged in 64:12. Instead, the very opposite is true. He has "called," and they have been silent (66:4). They have devised their own ways of relating to God, and when he calls them to a different kind of response, they are deaf.

In 66:5–6 God turns to speak once again to the remnant, those whom he designated as his "servants" in chapter 65. These are the people of whom he spoke in 66:2, those "who tremble at his word" (66:5). God says that the lowly have one powerful thing going for them—God! He will vindicate those who care more about what God says than whether their needs have been met.

Hope and Abundance (66:7–14). This next unit describes Zion. Here the promise made in chapter 1 comes to its fruition. The dross has been purged away, and instead of being a harlot, Zion has become the faithful city, the mother of nations (cf. 1:25–27). The pagan fertility rituals were focused on the critical need to maintain the fertility of field and womb if life was to defeat death in the world. But Isaiah says that the only real life is that which is given as a free gift by God in response to surrender and obedience.

God's gifts are out of all proportion to whatever we have done. His gifts are childbirth without labor (66:7–9). Our needs are not met by our work but by our being in a position to receive the results of God's work. This is the significance of nursing at the "breasts" of Zion (66:11). A baby does nothing to satisfy its own needs; it must simply own its absolute dependence and receive what has been provided.

In such a position there is rest, rejoicing, and wholeness, or "peace" (66:12). As in 12:1 and elsewhere, the idea behind the word "comfort" (66:13) is to encourage. Those who have felt the weight of their sin, have known their own powerlessness to deal with that sin, but have still come to God in penitent faith, believing that he can do something about it, will find themselves encouraged just as a child does on its mother's lap.

But if judgment is never God's intended last word, neither is hope without conditions. Isaiah never wants his readers to be left in a position where they are so secure in God's election love that they forget the real possibility of judgment. The Lord's "hand" (66:14) of deliverance, redemption, and power will be revealed to "his servants," but it is "his fury" that "will be shown to his foes." Once again, the question emerges: Am I among his servants or his foes?

Judgment and Hope (66:15–24). This section concludes the book in a characteristic fashion, with an interplay of the twin themes of judgment and hope. Just as the two have been intertwined throughout the book, they are intertwined here. The beginning (66:15–17) and the end (66:24) speak of the judgment that lies ahead for those who rebel against God and attempt to gain control of his power for themselves. For the present, God has taken the fire of his judgment into himself in the person of his servant. But that will not always be so. A day will come when that "fire" (66:15–16, 24) will be unleashed against an unrepentant world.

But judgment is not what God wants, and that is equally clear in this final section. Isaiah 66:18–23 speak of the universal redemption that is God's desired way of bringing this sinful world to its close. God will use the very sins and schemes of the rebellious to reveal the glory of his salvation. The people of Zion who "survive" all the attempts of an evil world to destroy them will be sent to all the "nations" with a "sign" of God's "glory" (66:19). Israel has a mission to declare God's glory to the nations in such a way that they will be drawn to him.

The response of the nations to Israel's mission will be to restore the last remnants of the Israelites (66:20) to Israel in a last great ingathering. Then comes the most stunning statement of all: "I will select some of them also to be priests and Levites" (66:21). While we cannot be absolutely certain of the antecedent of "them" in this statement, the most obvious one is "the nations." This is the strongest statement in the book that the election of Israel is not for Israel but for the world. That understanding is furthered by 66:22–23, which speaks of the entire human race coming to worship God. This is the goal of all that God has done on earth—that we, his creatures, may have fellowship with him.

But what about 66:24? Why end the book on this grisly note? The answer goes as far back as chapter 1. There Isaiah could speak of the day when the unfaithful city, whose sins he has carefully delineated, will be transformed by righteousness and justice into "the Faithful City" (1:21–27). But just as he would not leave his hearers there in chapter 1, ending that chapter instead with an announcement of the destruction awaiting those who did not repent, neither will he leave them with unmitigated hope here. For the wonderful promises of God have nothing to do with any who persist in rebellion. If the rebels are lulled into complacency by these good promises, they will be lost.

On the one hand, the promises of God are yea and amen (2 Cor 1:20): There *will* be a new heaven and a new earth (Isa 66:22), and those who rejoice to worship the one true God *will* participate in it. On the other hand, whether any of us participate in those promises is strictly up to us, and Isaiah never wants that to be forgotten.

Application. God has delivered us from each of our Egypts by the blood of Jesus Christ. He has done this in order to write his covenant on our hearts through the power of the Holy Spirit and thus to take up residence in the tabernacle he desires most of all—the tabernacle of our hearts. He longs to fill that tabernacle with the glory that fills the earth. He wants to move each of us from that place where we cry out in horror, "Woe to me . . ." (6:5), to the place where we can "come and see [his] glory" (66:18)—and not merely to survive the experience but actually to have that glory reside in us. That is the goal of life.

JEREMIAH

INTRODUCTION TO JEREMIAH

Already in the fifth year of Jehoiakim Jeremiah had instructed Baruch, his scribal companion, to produce a written scroll of his oracles (604 BC; Jer 36:2, 9). During the reign of Zedekiah Jeremiah corresponded with Judeans in Babylon (ch. 29). After Gedaliah's murder he and Baruch were still engaged in prophetic activity in Egypt, where there was a substantial Judean community (chs. 43–44). Thus, there were likely written copies of some of Jeremiah's oracles in Palestine, Egypt, and Babylonia even before the prophet's death.

The circle(s) responsible for the final form of Jeremiah are not well known, even though some who helped Jeremiah preserve and disseminate his oracles are named in the book. Baruch certainly had a major role in preserving the Jeremiah traditions (i.e., oracles, sermons, and narratives about Jeremiah); perhaps it was even a family affair, since Baruch's brother Seraiah (a Judean official) also assisted Jeremiah with the deliverance of a prophetic message to Babylon (51:59–64). In addition to these scribal companions, there must have been disciples who learned the gist of his message and who passed along his words in the aftermath of Jerusalem's fall.

The vantage point of the final compilers of the book was similar to that of the historical Jeremiah and Baruch in one very important respect: They too lived after the tragic fall of Judah. Virtually every line in the book is preserved to help explain the recent past to readers. Finally, the book points to a future that lies open to the action of God in history, even though some of the hopes for that future are as yet unrealized.

Within the final composition of the book there are two distinct subsections: (a) Jeremiah 30–33 and (b) Jeremiah 37–45. (a) The four chapters of 30–33 do not, however, form a simple unity in themselves. Chapters 30–31 are largely poetry, while 32–33 are prose. Chapters 30–31 are often called by interpreters the Book of Consolation or the Book of Hope because they contain proclamations of Israel and Judah's restoration to the promised land. No concrete setting in Jeremiah's ministry is given for the proclamation of chapters 30–31 as there is with chapters 32–33. The latter are set in the last days of the Judean state (587 BC), the tenth year of Zedekiah and the eighteenth of Nebuchadnezzar (32:1; 33:1).

(b) Chapters 37–45 form a subsection dealing primarily with the reign of Zedekiah and the fall of Jerusalem. Most of the material concerns the details of the Babylonian siege during the last two years of Zedekiah's reign (588–586 BC), his capture and ignominious transport to Babylon (39:4–7), and the tragic aftermath of the city's capture when Gedaliah, the Babylonian-appointed governor, is assassinated and Jeremiah is dragged to Egypt with a pitiful Judean contingent (chs. 40–44). A word of hope granted to Baruch concludes the section (ch. 45), dated to the fourth year of Jehoiakim (45:1; i.e., 605/604 BC). These narratives are a collection of accounts that have a thematic coherence to them.

BOOK OUTLINE

- I. Judgment and Hope (1:1–25:38)
  - A. Call of the Prophet (1:1–19)
  - B. Corporate Failures Identified (2:1–6:30)
  - C. Sermon at the Temple (7:1–8:3)
  - D. Additional Corporate Failures Identified (8:4–10:25)
  - E. Sermon on Covenant Breaking (11:1–17)
  - F. Threats to the Prophet and His Laments (11:18–12:17)
  - G. Signs of Judgment and More Corporate Failures Identified (13:1–15:9)
  - H. Additional Threats to the Prophet and His Laments (15:10–21)
  - I. Additional Signs of Judgment and More Threats to the Prophet and His Laments (16:1–20:18)
  - J. Judgment on Leaders (21:1–23:40)
  - K. More Signs of Judgment (24:1–10)
  - L. Nebuchadnezzar and Exile (25:1–38)
- II. Judgment and Hope (26:1–52:34)
  - A. Narratives about Judean Failures (26:1–28:17)
  - B. Letter to First Wave of Exiles (29:1–32)
  - C. Hope and Consolation (30:1–33:26)
  - D. Oppression of Slaves (34:1–22)
  - E. Sign of the Rechabites (35:1–19)
  - F. Writing and Burning of the First Scroll, Part 1 (36:1–32)
  - G. Narratives During and After the Final Siege of Jerusalem (37:1–44:30)
  - H. Additional Writing and Burning of the First Scroll, Part 2 (45:1–5)
  - I. Oracles About and Against Other Nations, Including Babylon (46:1–51:64)
  - J. Rehearsal of Jerusalem's Fall and Note of Jehoiachin's Release (52:1–34)

JEREMIAH 1:1–3

Original Meaning. Like most prophetic books, Jeremiah begins with a superscription indicating the time of the prophet's ministry. The forty-plus years given for Jeremiah's ministry (ca. 627–584 BC) cover some of the most tumultuous and tragic events of the nation's history. Jeremiah was from a priestly family of Anathoth, a village about three miles north of Jerusalem, the capital city of Judah.

King Josiah attempted to free Judah from the control of Assyria and to set Judah on the road to spiritual reform. His thirteenth year coincides with the demise of Assyria's last strong king, Assurbanipal, and probably also includes his initial steps to alter Judah's politically subservient and religiously degenerate path. The eleventh year of Zedekiah is among the most somber in all biblical history. Jerusalem was captured and destroyed by the Babylonians, Zedekiah himself was seized and blinded, and many Judeans were taken into exile by their captors.

Application. The prophetic superscription reflects a form of incarnational theology. Just as God's supreme revelation was his word become flesh in Jesus Christ, so God's word took historical form in the life of Jeremiah and acquired written form in a book. Jeremiah's words provide testimony that God uses both people and events to further his purposes and to instruct the faithful.

JEREMIAH 1:4–19

Original Meaning. The rest of chapter 1 contains an account of Jeremiah's call and appointment to prophesy (1:4–10), followed by two divine oracles (1:11–12 and 1:13–19) assuring the prophet that God is with him as he delivers a judgmental word to Judah.

Verse 5 has paired phrases indicating that God's decision to use Jeremiah came prior to his birth. "Set apart" is a rendering of the Hebrew verbal root *qdsh* whose basic meaning is to be holy. The term assumes that what God designates as holy is reserved for a particular task. God has appointed Jeremiah a "prophet to the nations" (1:5). Jeremiah's protest that he is too young and inexperienced is countered by God's assurances. Each of these assurances is a way to define a prophet. He or she is designated by God for a task and is granted his presence and guidance, and what is spoken by the prophet is God's word for the occasion in which it is given.

In the call's conclusion, 1:10 offers an elaboration on the phrase prophet to the "nations," with the comment that Jeremiah's appointed activities are to tear down and to overthrow as well as to build and to plant. The verbs of 1:10 describe succinctly what Jeremiah's words will do. They will tear down much that his audience believes, and only after the terrible toll of Judah's failures has been reckoned will his positive words begin to build up and plant.

The first oracle of assurance (1:11–12) is a pun in Hebrew. The Hebrew word for "almond tree" (*shaqed*) sounds like the Hebrew verb to "watch" (*shoqed*). The almond tree becomes a sign to Jeremiah that God is watching over his word to bring it to fulfillment.

The second oracle (1:13–19) concerns the effects of an overturned pot of boiling liquid. The pot is a metaphor for the threat to come on Jerusalem and Judah because of the people's disobedience. There is also an initial reference to those who will oppose Jeremiah (1:19); there will be much more in the book about them. Finally, the repetition of the assurance from 1:8 reminds the reader that God will be with Jeremiah to deliver him from his opponents.

Application. God does not call all believers to be prophets; some, however, are called to engage in prophetic activity, and all are called to trust the efficacy of the prophetic word in Scripture. Two related elements in Jeremiah 1 have continuing significance for understanding prophetic activity: dependence on God for vindication rather than popularity among one's contemporaries and the likelihood that such activity will result in opposition.

JEREMIAH 2:1–37

Original Meaning. It is clear from the Hebrew text that chapter 2 alternates the manner in which the audience is addressed. Unfortunately, English words do not offer a similar kind of specificity in translation because the English pronoun "you" can refer to masculine singular, feminine singular, and corporate entities, whereas these are all differentiated in Hebrew.

A. 2:1–2 address Jerusalem (cities are personified as female in Hebrew) as the bride of the Lord.
B. 2:3 refers to Israel.
C. 2:4–13 is for the people who are addressed with a plural "you."
D. 2:14–16 continues the address to Israel.
E. 2:17–25 shifts the address back to Jerusalem.
F. 2:26–32 addresses Israel and Judah, both of which are corporate designations of the people.
G. 2:33–37 addresses Jerusalem again.

2:2–3. The combined imagery of 2:2–3 is that of Israel's devotion to and dependence on the Lord for both identity and sustenance. It recalls by inference the exodus from Egypt into the desert, the covenant ceremony at Mount Sinai, and God's sustaining of his people in the arid desert. This period of intimacy is contrasted with the estrangement from God depicted for Jeremiah's contemporaries in the rest of the chapter.

2:4–13. Israel is defined here in covenantal terms as "my people" (2:13; i.e., the people of God). Corporately Israel is accused of having defected from its first love to pursue "worthless idols" (2:5). Baal, a popular Canaanite deity, is named specifically in 2:8.

Also in 2:8, Jeremiah singles out Judah's leadership for particular criticism (cf. 2:26). Priests had the sacred task of interpreting God's presence and will among the people and having facility with torah. The word translated as "leaders" (2:8) is more literally rendered as "shepherds." God, who is the great shepherd of his people, demands that the leadership of the people share in this shepherding role. Finally, the "prophets" (2:8) are singled out for their perfidy in seeking inspiration from Baal rather than the Lord.

The Lord's historic faithfulness (2:6–7) is contrasted with the emptiness of Baal and other idolatries. Succinctly stated: "My people have exchanged their glorious God for worthless idols" (2:11) and have committed two evils: They have rejected the Lord and attempted vainly to support themselves (2:13). Jeremiah compares the labor-intensive work of repairing cisterns with the idolatry of following other gods, whereas the Lord is a fountain of living water.

2:14–19. The tragic example of Israel (here, the Northern Kingdom) serves to highlight the precarious position of Jeremiah's contemporaries in Judah. This indictment presupposes a close relationship between an idolatrous and false worship on the one hand and a disastrous political agenda on the other. Just as Judah seems willing to trust any deity in the Canaanite pantheon, so the state seems willing to grasp at straws in an attempt to save itself by making deals with Egypt and Assyria. Verse 19 predicts that Judah's wicked acts will also be the measure of its judgment.

2:20–25. Because of their defection, the people are depicted through a personification of Jerusalem as a prostitute. By analogy she/they are also like animals in heat who are unrestrained in seeking a mate. The valley mentioned in 2:23—where the people seek the Baals—is likely the Valley of Hinnom, the probable site of child sacrifice to Molek or Baal (see also 7:30–34).

2:26–32. In matters of religious devotion, Jeremiah describes the people as calling on other gods through the symbols of trees and stones, with Judah having as many gods as towns (2:26–28). In fertility cults, a tree is often the symbol of female fertility and a stone (in the form of a pillar) the symbol of male fertility. The consequences are severe: The Lord has rejected those forces in which Judah has put its trust.

In 2:29–32 the prophet carries on a dialogue or dispute with the people. Apparently, some among them have accused God of negligence, while God, through the agency of prophets, has accused the people of defection—which earlier in the chapter was described as prostitution. Forgetting is associated with not honoring God or with being disobedient, just as remembering is associated with doing what is expected.

2:33–37. Jerusalem is again addressed, now personified as a prostitute or an adulteress. Verse 34 understands the prostitution as more than a defection from the worship of the Lord. The image is that of blood spattered on a garment, blood from innocent people whose lives have been consumed by the adulterous activities of Jerusalem. This adds the element of what can be called social criticism. Injustice and unrighteousness also flow from a defective understanding of who the Lord is and what he desires from his covenant partner.

The final image is that of personified Jerusalem walking away with her hands on her head. This is the posture of mourning and resignation, and it probably refers to the posture used by captives who are being led away. Those entities (e.g., Assyria, Egypt) in whom she has trusted will be unable to help her in time of need.

Application. In the United States, churches are often invited (tempted?) to make alliances for gain or influence. Conservative churches may unite with a Republican or a politically conservative figure and more liberal churches with a Democrat or a more politically liberal figure. Thus, in political campaigns collections are taken up in congregations. The question here is: Who is using whom? Are not both parties using the other? Is it possible that there will be long-term pain for short-term gain in these alliances? The answer may not be simple or obvious, but it is important to ask the questions of primary identity and covenant loyalty.

JEREMIAH 3:1–4:2

Original Meaning. The manner in which the audience is addressed varies in this collection, as it did in chapter 2. An underlying metaphor is the identity of the people as members of the Lord's household or family. Thus, they can be depicted as Jerusalem, as the spouse or covenant partner of the Lord, as unfaithful sisters who are married to the Lord, and as children who have rebelled against the dictates of the Lord, the head of the household.

A. 3:1–5. Following the last section of chapter 2, the opening figure in chapter 3 is Jerusalem.
B. 3:6–10. This prose section represents "faithless Israel" and "unfaithful . . . Judah" as adulterous sisters.
C. 3:11–13. Israel (i.e., the adulterous Northern Kingdom) is addressed in a poetic oracle in 3:12b–13.
D. 3:14–18. The people, scattered because of their sinfulness, are addressed as God's children and called to resettle the area of Judah and Jerusalem.

E. 3:19–20. Jerusalem is addressed.

F. 3:21–22a. The people are addressed as wayward children from the house/family of the Lord.

G. 3:22b–25. The people, personified as prodigal children, offer a liturgy of repentance.

H. 4:1–2. The voice of the Lord concludes this section with a statement about repentance.

3:1–5. Jeremiah uses the relationship of a husband and his divorced wife as an analogy of the relationship between the Lord and his disobedient covenant people. This passage also presupposes the instruction of Deuteronomy 24:1–4 concerning divorce and remarriage. That text from the Torah raises the question whether a woman, once married but then divorced and married to another man, can then remarry her first husband (Deut 24:4). The answer is *no*.

Jerusalem, representing the people of Judah, is the spouse who has married many lovers in her defection from the Lord. As a result, she is in a defiled state, estranged from her first husband and incapable of mending the relationship. The language of 3:2 contains a Hebrew term so uncompromising and harsh in its depiction of adultery that the scribes who compiled the Masoretic Text (the Hebrew Bible) provided a substitute word to be used in public reading. The NIV choice of "ravish" catches something of the physical and offensive nature of the term.

3:6–10. In this prose section, perhaps compiled as an interpretive comment for readers of the poetic oracle in 3:1–5, the fate and infidelity of Israel are compared to the (worse) circumstances of Judah. Israel and Judah are described as sisters who have both committed adultery against their spouse. The adjective "faithless" (3:6) used for Israel is part of the wordplay on the concept of turning/repenting. Literally, one could translate the phrase as "turning Israel," as if she is constantly turning this way and that in seeking lovers. Surprisingly, Judah has learned nothing from the fall of Israel.

3:11–13. The Lord calls faithless Israel to return (Heb. *shub*) to the Lord. This oracle is preserved as part of an autobiographical section (3:11). The oracle is intended for remnants of the former Northern Kingdom. God promises to be gracious and receptive, foregoing the anger proper to a spurned spouse. Although no date is given for this oracle, it probably fits early in Jeremiah's prophetic ministry, during the time when King Josiah made overtures to remnants of the covenant people in the territory of the former Northern Kingdom.

3:14–18. The NIV attempts to keep the metaphor of marriage by translating the Hebrew term for master/owner as "husband." The passage begins with an address to children, however, and not to a personified entity who plays the role of spouse. The Lord will bring back the prodigal children and establish them in their homeland.

One way to grasp the significance of the ark of the covenant in 3:16 is its portrayal as the throne (or royal footstool) of the cosmic Lord. Yet in the future, in a renewed Jerusalem, no one will long for the lost ark because the whole city will be "The Throne of the Lord" (3:17). Remnants from both Israel and Judah will inhabit the city and surrounding land. Even other nations will come to the city. This restoration will come about even though the initial passage of the section (3:1) assumed that according to the torah, "remarriage" was impossible.

3:19–20. Both the marriage (unfaithful wife) and familial metaphors (children able to inherit) are again used to indicate Judah's sin.

3:21–25. The language of "returning" (*shub*, 3:22) and of healing the people's "faithless[ness]" and "backsliding" (3:22) are used in the promises of these verses. They offer confession of sin and repentance in 3:22b–25. Apparently, the passage depicts a state of affairs to come after the judgment of the exile.

4:1–2. When that time comes, God calls for a sincere "return" (*shub*, 4:1) to him. The future restoration of God's people will lead other nations into finding a blessing in the Lord. This last element plays on the foundational promise of Genesis 12:3—that all the nations of the earth will find a blessing in Abraham's descendants.

Application. Christians are the bride of Jesus Christ, God's Son. Christ's disciples are bound to him through his resurrection, and the working of the Holy Spirit is present within them and the church, the corporate body of Christ. Disobedience ("sin") is not just failure to observe a norm of behavior but the breaking of a bond and an affront to one's Lord. Adultery in theological terms is a crime against grace; it is infidelity against God who in Christ has called us into an intimate fellowship and who has formed a church as the holy bride of Christ.

JEREMIAH 4:3–6:30

Original Meaning. This section of Jeremiah is essentially a collection of prophecies concerning judgments to befall Judah. It is interspersed, however, with quotations attributed to Jeremiah, God, Jerusalem, and the people, all of which give this section a dialogical character (e.g., 4:10; 5:1–6).

As with the previous section, the individual prophecies in this collection likely date from various times in Jeremiah's public ministry. The primary theme is judgment on Judah and Jerusalem through the historical process, as God sends disasters and enemies against his people.

4:3–4. Repentance toward God is symbolized by a circumcision of the heart. Removal of the foreskin from the male genitalia is a sign (Gen 17:11) of the covenant, a mark in the flesh that represents the bond established by God with Abraham and his descendants. Circumcision of the heart, the organ of understanding and will, is obviously a metaphor for preparing a wholehearted commitment to the Lord and proper obedience to the revelation of his will. This metaphor in Jeremiah presupposes that the fleshly mark is inadequate apart from personal commitment.

There are similar references elsewhere in Jeremiah and in Deuteronomy to the significance of both the terms *circumcision* and *heart*. In Jeremiah 17:1–10 the sin of Judah is described as engraved on the tablets of their hearts. According to 17:9–10, the heart of the people is desperately sick. In 24:7 God promises to give a new heart to his people. Similarly, Deuteronomy 10:16 preserves the imperative to Israel to circumcise their hearts, and Deuteronomy 30:1–10 preserves the prophecy that after the coming judgment, the Lord will circumcise the hearts of his people so that they will love him with all their heart and soul. These various references presuppose that Israel must make a radical commitment to God but also that God's people will be unable to fulfill that commitment unless he acts decisively to renew and transform them.

4:5–13. Judah and Jerusalem are called to assemble, to put on sackcloth, and to lament the approach of a foe from the north. The approach of this enemy is in reality the approach of the Lord, who comes against the people like a lion or whose blast of anger is like a searing wind.

Verse 10 is an autobiographical comment that accuses God of deceiving the people by giving a word of "peace" (Heb. *shalom*) when in actuality a mortal threat is at hand. Perhaps the prophet's charge assumes the words of the prophets and priests mentioned in the previous verse, who may have assured the people that deliverance will come (cf. 6:13–14; 8:11–12). A related possibility is that Jeremiah's own words about judgment to come have been proclaimed for several years, but, as yet no catastrophic blow has fallen. Those prophets and priests who have proclaimed peace have been right (so far), and in both frustration and alarm, Jeremiah wonders how God can allow these circumstances to exist.

4:14–22. The prophet beseeches Jerusalem to cleanse her heart and remove her wicked thoughts. God reminds Jerusalem of the dire consequences of her activity. Her own "conduct and actions" (4:18) have brought these appalling circumstances to light.

In his own *heart* (note again the catchword) Jeremiah expresses horror at the realization of Jerusalem's impending doom (4:19–22). In striking fashion his emotional reaction to this doom is translated into physical reaction, with writhing "in pain" (4:19). The prophet lays the responsibility for failure with the people, who are described as "fools" and "senseless children" (4:22).

A close reading of this section brings together the voices of Jeremiah, God, and the people in an amazing way. It begins with Jeremiah addressing Jerusalem in almost frantic fashion. The emotion fits that of the prophet, but the refrain of 4:17 ("declares the Lord") indicates that this concern for the city is also that of God. The writhing pain of 4:19–20 may be that of Jerusalem as she watches her land and inhabitants being consumed, or perhaps it is that of the prophet, who has begun to grasp the enormity of the tragedy to come. The third party to this emotion-laden conversation is God himself. The sad comment in 4:22 that the people "do not know *me*" (emphasis added) can be no other than the voice of God himself, as represented through the prophet. The conversation and mixing of voices are such that they blend together. In the final analysis, no one—people, prophet, or God—remains aloof from the horror of it all.

4:23–26. In the visionary perspective of the prophet, the Judean landscape is transformed into something "formless and empty" (4:23), the same two terms used in Genesis 1:2 to describe the chaos of creation before the creative spirit of God began its work and God spoke order into existence. Judah's sinfulness takes on a type of cosmic context in this visionary account, as if the people's folly makes them complicit in a consuming cosmic chaos.

4:27–31. The prophet returns to the horror that will befall Jerusalem. God will speak and judgment will come, just as surely as in the creation account God spoke and order was brought out of chaos. Verse 28 states that the earth will "mourn" or languish. This sad comment reflects a synthetic understanding of existence, whereby the personified land is affected by the folly of the people's sinfulness.

In 4:31 the prophet depicts Jerusalem's cries like those of birth pains. It is not, however, the joy of giving birth but the fear of death that is on her lips. She is in collapse before murderers!

5:1–9. This section contains an interchange between God and the audience in Jerusalem, mediated by the prophet, who offers commentary in 5:3–6. The passage begins with a challenge for people to search Jerusalem for anyone who "deals honestly and seeks the truth" (5:1). One can also translate "deals honestly" as "does justice" (Heb. *mishpat*). Apparently, no one fits these requirements.

In 5:3–6 Jeremiah himself attempts a search, but "their rebellion is great" (5:6). God's reply is that forgiveness is not presently an option (cf. 5:9 with 5:29).

5:10–17. Jerusalem is now personified as the possessor of vines and branches, which symbolize people. Not only have both Israel and Judah refused to accept that their misfortune is the Lord's judgment on them, but there is even a sense among some that the Lord is not active and will not judge in the future either. Verse 12 places a quotation in their mouth to the effect that neither sword nor famine will strike them. Apparently, these sentiments are provoked by "prophets" since Jeremiah replies that these prophets "are but wind" (5:13). Underlying a text like this is heated debate among prophets, all of whom claim to represent the will of God.

The Lord makes Jeremiah's prophetic word of judgment like a fire consuming wood (5:14). More specifically, the Lord declares that a foreign nation is coming to devastate the people (5:15–17). This depiction is one of the catchword topics used repeatedly in chapters 4–6. One result of their onslaught is that the people will be carried away and serve foreigners in a strange land (i.e., the exile).

5:18–19. In this short prose section, the Lord offers commentary on the previous verse and its reference to exile. Two sentiments are expressed succinctly.

1. Exile from the promised land does not bring an end to the existence of the people.
2. The Lord also reinforces the exile as a just reward for the polytheistic deviations of the people in forsaking him. In the exile they will serve foreigners.

5:20–31. Jeremiah describes the people as "senseless" (5:21) and employs the rhetorical device of describing them as possessing eyes that do not see and ears that do not hear. Jeremiah's invective continues by noting that they refuse to "fear" the Lord (5:22); that is, they do not hold the Lord in awe and serve him with reverence. Verse 25 then underscores the correspondence between act and consequence. The Lord indicts both priest and prophet for misleading God's people in the concluding verses of the chapter.

A general breakdown of common decency, not to mention the covenant responsibilities of an elect nation, is described in 5:26–28. Greed and violence go hand in hand.

6:1–9. Chapter 6 functions like a summary of chapters 4–5. It contains calls to flee from the enemy (6:1) and to mourn the fall of the city (6:26). Disaster is imminent for Judah and Jerusalem. The city is the "Daughter Zion" (6:2), so beautiful and yet so tragic. Verse 6 depicts a siege along with a succinct statement of the reason. In 6:9 the prophet returns to a theme articulated in 5:10: The enemy will glean the vineyard of the Lord, making sure that even a surviving remnant feels the brunt of judgment.

6:10–15. Announcements about the coming judgment have fallen on deaf ears. Jeremiah, speaking for himself and for God, wonders to whom else can he speak? He confesses that he is wearied at holding in God's wrath, and he hears the command to pour it out on the city that has known no shame. The priests and prophets have led the people astray with their proclamations (6:14). The people are so shameless that they do not know how to blush (6:15)!

6:16–26. Through his prophet, the Lord asks the people to (re-)consider the "good way," the "ancient paths" (6:16), that lead to security. The prophet, as vocal mediator, represents God and the people in conversation, while the people rudely contravene or reject divine guidance. They are reminded that God raised up "watchmen" (6:17) who warned the people—but to no avail. The people continue to reject God's "law" (6:19). The fate to befall them is actually the "fruit of their [own] schemes" (6:19). Correspondingly, God rejects the sacrifices of the people as inadequate in light of their moral and spiritual disobedience. As part of their judgment God will put "obstacles" (6:21) in their way. This may be another way to refer to the foe that is coming from the north to attack the land. Jeremiah utters a severe warning about this foe.

6:27–30. Jeremiah's prophetic role is that of a "tester of metals" (6:27). The refining process of calling for repentance and announcing judgment has not separated the wicked from the righteous but simply confirmed that the people as a whole are corrupt. These verses provide something of a commentary or definition of the prophetic office. Prophets are raised up by God as refiners.

Application. A legitimate interpretation of Jeremiah's words for the contemporary church is not required to announce judgment on the audience (as Jeremiah did to his contemporaries), but his words should drive the interpreter to note the failings of Judah and Jerusalem and then to ask if corresponding failures inhibit the life of God's people today. Even if contemporary sins differ somewhat in kind from those enunciated by Jeremiah, his words should also drive the reader to repent for failures and to seek moral and spiritual renewal.

In the modern West, there is great concern in some quarters about the decline in order and civility. Among many Western churches there is corresponding concern over the diminished morality of members and declining spiritual vitality. Are these factors related, and is a visionary depiction of coming chaos an accurate assessment of trends? Jeremiah's vision of chaos emerges spiritually from his deep involvement with a people who are heedless of divine standards and skeptical that God will actually judge them. Does this not sound familiar to Western ears? Is it not the case that Western society has essentially capitulated to the demands of secular pluralism that moral and values-based judgments be restricted to the private realm, where they will not intrude on public policy decisions? And does the rising perception that society is spinning out of moral control because of its spiritual bankruptcy not point to a future chaos?

JEREMIAH 7:1–8:3

Original Meaning. *7:1–15.* Jeremiah warns worshipers not to trust in deceptive words that give them false hopes concerning the security of the temple or the efficacy of their religious activities. Three times the phrase "[this is] the temple of the LORD" is repeated in 7:4. It seems to function like a mantra, as if simply repeating it or even asserting it makes it true. Just because the temple sits in Jerusalem, worshipers should not assume that they can fail in their covenantal responsibilities to God and neighbor and then come to the temple and cry, "We are safe!" (7:10).

Jeremiah has no intention of denying that the majestic temple on Mount Zion belongs to the Lord. Speaking for God, however, he asserts that the Lord is not bound to preserve the temple at all costs in the face of the people's flagrant disobedience. The prophet points to the shrine at Shiloh during the time of Samuel and Eli (1 Sam 1–4) to say that God may send judgment even on a place of worship that bears his "Name" (Jer 7:10, 11).

In Deuteronomy 12:5, 11 God promised to choose a place from among the Israelite tribes designated for animal sacrifice and certain other ritual acts of worship. It would be a place for pilgrimage—the only appropriate site for these endeavors, in contrast to the Canaanite inhabitants, who had many "high places" for sacrificial worship. Deuteronomy does not give the name of the place God would choose; that Jerusalem became the location, however, is clear from the dedicatory prayer of Solomon in 1 Kings 8:23–53.

There was nothing magical about the temple in Jerusalem with respect to divine presence. The claim that God's name dwelt there was a metaphorical way of saying that God could be personally encountered at that site. It was a place of his choosing. At the same time, God recognizes that he is not tied to the structure or somehow bound irrevocably to its fate.

The prophet refers to the basic covenant stipulations in Jer 7:9 as they are known in the Decalogue (Deut 4:13). Moreover, in Jeremiah 7:6 the prophet charges that Judah has oppressed the alien, the widow, and the orphan. Specifically cited in 7:9 are stealing, murder, adultery, and false witness. Each of these comes from the so-called second table of the law, where communal relations are regulated. Burning incense to Baal and following other gods, however, reflects the first commandment. Taken as a whole, the prophet charges that those attending temple service love neither God nor neighbor according to the standards of the torah. Instead, they grasp at the magical properties of the temple in hopes that God will protect the city against the enemy.

7:16–34. Jeremiah reveals that God has commanded him not to intercede for the people. Why should Jeremiah intercede for the people when some of them have turned to the worship of the Queen of Heaven and other deities? Their trust is misplaced. Jeremiah is but one in a line of prophets whom God sent to his people, each of whom was rejected. The hardhearted people have refused to heed their warnings and announcements of judgment. Sacrifices are not acceptable when flagrant breaches of covenantal ethics are rampant. They are no more efficacious for a sinful, obdurate people than the temple will be in the day of assault by the enemy.

In a nearby valley nicknamed "Slaughter" (7:32), the Judeans participated in the horrifying rites of child sacrifice (cf. 19:1–15). Which valley near Jerusalem is an interesting question; probably it is the valley along the western and southern boundaries of the current old city known as the Wadi er Rababi. "Topheth" (7:31) is a term of uncertain derivation, but it refers to a place where human sacrificial and cremation rituals took place. Some Judeans must have believed that they appeased the Lord by partaking in these rituals, since God protests through the prophet that he has not commanded such activities. Elsewhere these activities are associated with Baal and Molek (2 Kgs 23:10; Jer 19:5). Jerusalem itself will become a place of slaughter (like the nearby Topheth) because of her rejection of the Lord.

8:1–3. These words may have been appended to the sermon because they reflect the horror of manipulating and exposing human corpses. The Topheth rites in 7:30–34 apparently included sacrificial rites with corpses (of children). Without repentance, death will be the only future for Judah.

Application. Jeremiah's address assumes a doctrine of Israel as God's people who assemble for worship and depart for service. Similarly, worship of God is the reason for Christian assembling, and service to him in word and deed is its goal. The temple was an institution by which God made himself present and known among the people. The church is an institution by which God makes himself present in the world and known among the nations.

One hears today the phrase that "theology matters." Its proponents believe that the visible church suffers from a lack of clarity about the uniqueness of the gospel, a diminished sense of authority for the classical tenets of the faith, and an overreliance on individualism and human experience as keys to Christian identity.

Theology does matter, not because God insists on a rigid intellectual system, but because unless we understand who God is, we will be in basic error about everything else that is ultimately important. The church will not save anyone (nor did the temple or animal sacrifice); it is a means to a goal, not the end itself. Understood correctly it is a means to know God and be rightly related to him.

Jeremiah's address means not only that "theology matters," but that it matters in the practical applications of the Christian life. His indictment of the immorality of the people illustrates the old adage that "I may not believe everything you say, but I believe everything you do." Behavior matters for it is a key to a person's or an institution's allegiance. Christian ethics, like the social institutions and actions of Jeremiah's day, are a means to an end—to worship and serve the living God.

JEREMIAH 8:4–10:25

Original Meaning. *8:4–12.* The prophet engages his hearers with rhetorical questions and accuses them of moral stupidity and a culpable spiritual dullness. Speaking for God, the prophet states: "I have listened attentively, but they do not say what is right" (8:6). It is also assumed that the people of Jerusalem do not do what is right. God is almost incredulous at the stupidity of the people. Verse 7 continues a theme seen elsewhere in Jeremiah: God's people are woefully and willfully ignorant of God's "requirements" of behavior, which are designed to regulate life. Even a stork knows that there are appointed seasons, yet God's own people seem clueless.

To the reply from the people in 8:8 that they are indeed "wise" and "have the law of the LORD," Jeremiah charges that scribal interpretation has made God's truth into a lie. The deceitful interpretation of God's instruction is explained as blunting its judgmental force against iniquity. God's torah *is* wisdom (see Deut 4:5–8). Priest and prophet alike are proclaiming "peace" (Jer 8:11) when all is not well. This too is a theme Jeremiah stresses elsewhere (cf. 6:14). The charge that the people are shameless and don't even know how to blush is likewise found in 6:15.

Possibly we have here Jeremiah's accusations about the eventual collapse of Josiah's covenant reforms. Religious leaders might have blunted the sharp edge of those reforms sparked by a (re)discovery of a book of the Torah of the Lord during temple repairs (2 Kgs 22–23). Presumably the interpretive skills of the priests have kept God's word from performing its basic tasks of challenging and instructing the people, as if they have explained away the force of divine imperatives. Jeremiah himself was from a priestly family and thus familiar with the tasks of interpreting and applying divine instruction.

8:13–17. The people belatedly realize that God's judgment is upon them. Jeremiah depicts them as coming to the sudden and terrifying realization that the enemy is approaching, and that God is in the process of judging them for their transgressions. The reference to the enemy horses at Dan indicates that the enemy is approaching from the north. Dan was at the northern border of the Northern Kingdom of Israel.

The unrealistic hope of the people for peace is now seen for what the previous passage indicated it always was: self-delusion and a rejection of God's law. "Poisoned water" in 8:14 likely refers to the problems with water stored in cisterns rather than to some form of divine action in actually poisoning wells. Sieges typically result in heavy reliance on poor resources stored in cisterns. Perhaps we should read 8:17 similarly: The "venomous snakes" (8:17) that the Lord will send denote the deadly work of the invaders.

8:18–22. Interpreters are divided over the implied speakers throughout this unit since it is difficult to tell at some points whether the voice is Jeremiah's or the Lord's. A suggested outline for 8:18–22 is as follows:

> [**prophet**] You who are my Comforter in sorrow,
> my heart is faint within me.
> Listen to the cry of my people
> from a land far away:
> "Is the LORD not in Zion?
> Is her King no longer there?"
> [**Lord**] "Why have they aroused my anger with their images,
> with their worthless foreign idols?"
> [**prophet**, quoting the people] "The harvest is past,
> the summer has ended,
> and we are not saved."
> [**prophet**] Since my people are crushed, I am crushed;
> I mourn, and horror grips me.
> Is there no balm in Gilead?
> Is there no physician there?
> Why then is there no healing
> for the wound of my people?

Jeremiah's prophetic poignancy demonstrates that he is not aloof or indifferent to the suffering of the people. Indeed, three times (8:19, 21–22) the people are called "my people," a phrase appropriate also in the mouth of God. This point should not be lost on the reader. The sorrow Jeremiah feels at the fate of his people is that felt by God as well. Prophetic person and prophetic message converge to reveal not only the God of righteous judgment but the God of sorrows at the plaintive cry.

9:1–11. As with the previous section, readers encounter a merging of Jeremiah and God's voices. A suggestion of "voices" for 9:1–11 is as follows:

> [**prophet**] 9:1–2: "Oh, that my head were a spring of water...."
> [**God**] 9:3: "They make ready their tongue like a bow, to shoot lies...."
> [**God** to Jeremiah] 9:4–6: "Beware of your friends...."
> [**prophet**, speaking for God] 9:7–11: "See, I will refine and test them... I will weep and wail...."

If this sequence of voices is correct, we have a conversation between God and prophet in 9:1–6, followed by an announcement of judgment on the people in 9:7–11. Note that in 9:10 God weeps and wails (like Jeremiah) for the destruction to come.

9:12–22. Picking up the theme of wisdom and judgment from chapter 8, the rhetorical question of spiritual discernment is again raised in a series of divine oracles. Note the introductory formula for divine communication (e.g., "The LORD said") in 9:13, 17, 22. Judgment has fallen on Judah for her sins. Following the Baals is a blatant example of the people's folly.

Mourning cries mark the demise of shameful Judah. Exile is upon them. Death too has arrived and is personified as climbing into homes and roaming the doomed cities of Judah. Verses 17 and 20 refer to wailing women; they presuppose that women played a leading role in funeral lamentation.

A precise context for these prophecies is not given. Perhaps they reflect the initial Babylonian constriction of Jerusalem under Nebuchadnezzar in 598/597 BC or the devastating drought mentioned elsewhere in Jeremiah (14:1–6).

9:23–26. These verses are further prophetic responses to the previous announcement of judgment. Verses 23–24 return again to the theme of wisdom in such a time as this. With 9:25 comes the typical introduction to a prophetic depiction of the future. Note that markers for divine saying are found in each of the verses in 9:23–25.

Verses 23–24 are almost proverbial in form. There is a valid form of boasting, which comes with the realization of correct priorities. True wisdom is not only the recognition that God has sent judgment on Judah; it is, above all, knowledge of the Lord and his character. God reveals himself as One who practices and takes delight in kindness (Heb. *hesed*), justice (*mishpat*), and righteousness (*tsedaqa*). As 9:25–26 make clear, those nations who spurn the moral integrity of God—whether Egypt or Israel, circumcised or not—will see his judgment. The criticism of Israel as uncircumcised of heart picks up a theme from 4:4.

10:1–16. These verses contain an extended critique of idolatry and affirmations of the Lord as Ruler over all. Idolatry is described and defined variously. Verse 2 refers to astrological divination. Verses 3–5 criticize the making and veneration of a wooden image. Verse 9 notes that a wooden piece can be decorated with silver and gold and clothed in royal colors—but this does not make it divine. Verse 11 is a proverb written in Aramaic, which has been incorporated into the critique of idolatry. Perhaps it is a traditional saying that the prophet adopts here for emphasis. Divine images are succinctly judged in 10:15 with the claim that they are "worthless, the objects of mockery."

The lifeless images of other deities are contrasted with the uniqueness of the "living God," who is the Creator of heaven and earth (10:10–12). His cosmic kingship is twice affirmed (10:7, 10). This God, the "Maker of all things," is also the "Portion of Jacob" (10:16). Even the wisdom from other nations is folly compared to God's truth.

Much of this section is intended to instruct Israel and Judah in the time of the exile. Not that it is irrelevant to the circumstances of Judah before the Babylonian onslaught, but the text is cast in a teaching mode rather than as a list of reasons why Israel is being judged. Assimilation, if not downright capitulation, to a dominant culture was a real issue for Israelites and Judeans among other nations

10:17–22. One may see the voices in 10:17–22 as follows:

[**prophet** to Jerusalem] 10:17–18: "Gather up your belongings. . . ."

[**Jerusalem** to herself] 10:19–20: "Woe to me because of my injury! . . ."

[**prophet** to Jerusalem] 10:21–22: "The shepherds are senseless and do not inquire of the LORD. . . ."

10:23–25. The poetic collection of 8:4–10:25 concludes with the prayer of a chastened individual. The speaker is almost certainly Jeremiah; the question is whether he speaks personally or as a member of a wounded and judged people. The prayer contains a frank admission that human resources themselves are not enough to keep a person on the pathway marked out by God. God is humbly implored to correct the errant ways of the one who prays—but in a manner that reveals God's justice and that does not continue in judgment (as is appropriate for those who do not know the Lord).

There is more wisdom than resignation in the way the prayer begins. A person does not ultimately direct his or her own pathways; rather, they are in the hands of God. Recognition of this fact is a first step toward wisdom. Much of the prayer is about justice: God is implored to judge the enemy who has devoured Jacob.

Application. The role of Christians and the church in engaging the world requires a passionate identification with the folly of the world. Those who would offer a grave spiritual diagnosis must love the patients and not stand aloof from them. This is a model of the church, which is not only the recipient of a judgmental word from Jeremiah, but also which, by God's grace, seeks a prophetic ministry among society's ills. Jeremiah may be a prophetic reminder of the deep sorrow that should meet all Christians when they reflect on the circumstances of those who do not know God. The lost are, after all, estranged siblings of the Lord, who wept and died for them.

God's anguish and anger are, in reality, the only basis for hope in this world. His passions grow from love; the opposite of love is not anger but indifference. Were God indifferent to the predicament of a fallen creation, there would have been no prophetic ministry in Israel and no Son to engage evil and to die to expend its curse.

Among these prophecies of judgment, readers will also find indications of what God intends for his people in their corporate life. These are the marks of the wisdom Jeremiah finds lacking among his generation. Among such marks are the recognition of repentance as a conscious rejection of evil, an embracing of God's standards for moral integrity, a willingness to hear God's word as judgment on human pretensions and sinfulness, a passion for those whose folly has trapped them in evil consequences, a humble boasting in the sufficiency of God whose own ways are just and right, and an aversion to idolatry whereby someone or something becomes the supreme value for people's affections rather than the one God of heaven and earth.

JEREMIAH 11:1–17

Original Meaning. This passage is composed essentially in prose and is concerned with the covenant-breaking activities of Judah and Jerusalem. A closer examination of this section indicates that there are subunits within it. Verses 1–5 comprise the initial unit, an address from God to Jeremiah that instructs the prophet about the people's failures to maintain fidelity to "this covenant" (11:2–3; cf. 11:6, 8, 10).

Verses 6–14 offer a second communication from God given to the prophet, though the content is clearly intended for the people. Jeremiah is the human vessel to deliver the words.

The Lord recognizes that much, if not all, of Jeremiah's report to the people will fall on deaf ears and hard hearts. As a result, the prophet is commanded not to pray for the people. Verse 14 assumes that intercession will do no good because the people will remain incorrigible. Verses 1–17 appear to be a summary of reflections on the failure of Judah and Jerusalem to keep God's covenant rather than a report of the prophet's actual presentation to the people.

Two conclusions may be stated from this succinct analysis.

1. God's people have broken the covenant, and the prophet's task is to communicate that message to them.
2. There are consequences for disobedience, in that judgment will fall on the people.

Details in 11:1–17 offer further perspective on the term *covenant*, but they also leave a number of things assumed on the part of hearers/readers. "This covenant" is something God "commanded" the ancestors of Judah and Jerusalem (11:3–4, 10), who were slaves in Egypt. Their redemption from such slavery is the presupposition of the covenant. Obedience to what God commanded Israel to do is expected, since he redeemed Israel and they belong to him. "This covenant" (11:2) also includes as part of its content an "oath" (11:5) God swore to the ancestors, a promise that the land of Canaan would belong to their descendants. According to 11:4b God asked for obedience to his word and promised, "You will be my people, and I will be your God." This last phrase states succinctly the essence of the covenant, from which blessings like children and land would emerge.

One may compare the basic marriage formulation ("I will be your husband, and you will be my wife") with that of the covenant between God and Israel. They are linguistically similar formulations, and both presuppose an exclusive, intimate relationship as the basis on which a broader community is built. Thus, the covenant was predicated on God's gifts of deliverance and instruction, it is extended by him to the people, and it also contained curses for the people's disobedience to the covenant stipulations (11:3, 8, 11). Accusations in 11:9–13 that Judah venerates other gods is a violation of the covenant God established with the people (Deut 5:7–10) and the reason for reminding them of the curses for disobedience.

As the previous comments indicate, the particulars of Jer 11:1–17 assume a historical and theological context for the first hearers and readers that spans the biblical storyline from the promises to Abraham and descendants, the deliverance of the ancestors from Egypt, covenant-making at Mount Sinai, and guidance to the promised land. But there is more to be considered with respect to Jeremiah's own lifetime. King Josiah had undertaken a movement for covenant renewal (2 Kgs 22–23) by calling Judah back to the fundamental principles of the Sinai/Horeb covenant. He read to the assembled people from the newly discovered book of the covenant (probably Deuteronomy), he officiated at a ceremony of covenant-making, and the people responded affirmatively from their side (23:1–3). His reforming efforts coincided with the call of the young Jeremiah.

Two elements about the role of Josiah's reforming activity may help in interpreting Jer 11:1–17.

1. The book of Deuteronomy is essentially a covenant-renewal document, for it reports the last addresses of Moses to the Israelites prior to his death. Moses emphasized that it was time for the younger generation who came out of Egypt to respond affirmatively to the covenant claim that God had on them. He mediated with them a covenant-renewal ceremony on the plains of Moab. This set a pattern that Josiah would follow. Jeremiah, a prophet like Moses for his generation (cf. Deut 18:18), takes up a similar role of calling the people back to their first love and reminding them of the consequences.
2. Moses commanded that the words of God's torah be read every seven years at the Festival of Booths (Deut 31:9–13). It is possible that Jeremiah's sermon as summarized in chapter 11 is influenced by the prophet's support for the covenant reform measures instituted earlier by

Josiah (although they seem to have been short-lived) as well as by the opportunity to reflect on God's covenantal instructions as they were read periodically in Judah.

Application. It is a mistake simply to assume that people who try harder will succeed in their commitments. There will be no lasting success apart from a lasting transformation. Such transformation as God in Christ supplies is a process that begins with a gracious acceptance of the claims of the gospel and continues unto and beyond death. The prophet addresses God's people, and his message is profoundly theological. "Trying harder" in secular terms is a bandage on a mortal wound.

JEREMIAH 11:18–12:17

Original Meaning. *11:18–23.* In a moment of consternation Jeremiah is shown the true intentions of neighbors. God reveals to him that they intend to humiliate him and to bring his prophetic work to an end. Indeed, the phrase "cut him off from the land of the living" (11:19) indicates murder, as does the threat of 11:21.

Jeremiah describes himself, therefore, as a lamb led to slaughter. A lamb led to slaughter carries with it the imagery of nonaggression and nonculpability on the part of the lamb. Jeremiah's predicament is not God's judgment on him but the plot of others who oppose his message and seek to harm him.

The short prayer of the prophet in 11:20 is based on the conviction that God is a righteous judge. Jeremiah asks not only for deliverance—which is one task a judge can perform—but also for God to judge those who persecute him unjustly.

Verses 21–23 reveal a judgment on those who seek Jeremiah's life. Both 11:21 and 22 contain the formula "This is what the LORD says," giving a double emphasis to the judgment to come on the persecutors of the prophet.

12:1–6. The case or issue that Jeremiah brings is not just that of threat to his life; it is also the question of why a righteous God allows the way of the wicked to prosper. If God is so clearly opposed to the activity of the wicked, then why not judge them and be done with it? Readers can see why this passage follows that of the description of Jeremiah's persecution in 11:18–23.

God's reply (12:5–6) does not deal with the larger question of evil's prosperity or even the more restricted question of immediate judgment on those who oppose Jeremiah and ruin the land. Instead, God speaks to Jeremiah as the one called to be a prophet to the nations. God does not take the bait and offer a defense of his providence. He simply calls the prophet to keep on the task at hand.

12:7–13. God sets forth his own complaint and announcement of judgment over the loss of his people. Verse 7 describes Judah as God's house, as his inheritance, and as the one whom God loves. As the head of his household, God experiences pain at its ruination and at the perversion of his inheritance. Verse 8 describes the city as transformed into an animal against God, and God's comment is that he "hates" (12:8) her. In this case the hatred is not the opposite of love, which is indifference, but the sad effects of betrayed and wounded love.

12:14–17. This word about the neighboring states around Judah anticipates elements in the oracles concerning foreign nations in chapters 25, 46–51. It sits somewhat surprisingly in this context, but it offers important perspective on the function of judgmental prophecies. The announcement of judgment may be in service to a larger design for blessing and reconciliation.

Application. Family and friends alike apparently opposed Jeremiah's prophetic activity. His opposition, his despair, and even the threats to his life came not from his sinfulness but from the exercise of his faith in responding to God's call. This is a perennial issue for Christians, more likely in some cultures and settings than in others, but a perennial issue nevertheless.

JEREMIAH 13:1–27

Original Meaning. *13:1–11.* This is the first of several acts Jeremiah performs to portray his message. God commands Jeremiah to take a linen waistcloth, clothe himself with it, then remove it and take it to the bank of the Perath and leave it. Scholars have debated whether the river or stream named Perath is the well-known Euphrates (ca. 300 miles from Jerusalem) or the seasonal stream near Anathoth with a similar name (cf. Parah in Josh 18:23). If there is significance attached to the river in this symbolic act, it is implicit and not explicit in the text. The textual emphasis falls on the linen waistcloth, not on the river.

Just as the waistcloth was to be bound to its wearer, so Israel and Judah have been formed by God to be bound to him. The verb "be bound" in 13:11 is the same word used in Genesis 2:24 to describe the man who leaves his parents to "be united" to his wife and to become "one flesh." The soiling of the waistcloth came because Jeremiah removed it and buried it near the bank of the water. So, Israel and Judah—whose separation from the Lord was caused by their faithlessness—were like the ruined waistcloth. Israel and Judah were formed for God's "renown and praise and honor" (Jer 13:11), but they are no better than dirty underwear.

13:12–14. Wineskins are created to hold wine. In this scenario the intended function of the wineskins is ruined in similar fashion to the waistcloth. Neither waistcloth nor wine jars fulfill their intended functions and thus are failures.

13:15–19. Jeremiah utters judgments against the pride that leads to a fall. Verse 16 employs the unusual command to "give glory to the LORD your God" before the darkness of judgment falls on the people. Perhaps this command functions as a call for them to admit the justice of the judgment about to befall them. It is possible, however, that the call to "give glory to the LORD" is a way to avert the disaster to come. If so, then Jeremiah's message functions as a call for repentance and change on the part of the people.

Verses 18–19 point to a particular source of pride, the king and queen mother. This short section is the only one in Jeremiah in which the role of the queen mother is taken up.

13:20–27. Jerusalem is called to see the foe from the north who comes in judgment. Should she wonder why destruction has come to her, Jeremiah quotes a proverbial saying (13:23). Just as neither Ethiopians (Africans) nor leopards can change the distinctive color of their skin, so the evil propensity of God's people cannot be removed by their own hand. The evil of Jerusalem is also personified as a prostitute, whose private parts are shamefully exposed.

The concluding question, "How long will you be unclean?" (13:27), assumes that even though Jerusalem is incapable of righting herself, she could at least recognize her plight and seek the Lord, who alone can heal her failures.

Application. Perhaps modern Christians should give more consideration to the impact of symbolic acts as part of their discipleship. Communication is not just words but deeds. Is not this true on both an individual and a corporate scale? A church that refuses to move from a changing neighborhood is making a statement as surely as is the church that moves. A Christian who volunteers in the nursery program "speaks" as surely as the teacher of a class. The church that refuses to play the insidious games of nationalism or racism speaks, no matter what it prints on paper.

JEREMIAH 14:1–15:9

Original Meaning. The different speaking voices in 14:1–15:9 comprise a pattern of oracle from the prophet, followed by words from the people. The prophet, speaking for God, has the first and last word:

A. 14:2–6: The prophet speaks of Judah's mourning.
B. 14:7–9: The people as a whole confess sin and offer a petition.
C. 14:10–16: The Lord speaks to Jeremiah about judgment on the people and other prophets.
D. 14:17–18: At God's command, Jeremiah delivers a lament over the fate of the people.
E. 14:19–22: The people as a whole confess sin and offer a petition again.
F. 15:1–9: The Lord speaks to Jeremiah about judgment on the people.

It is difficult to know how one should read the two corporate confessions/petitions of the people (14:7–9, 19–22). After both comes language of divine judgment. We have at least two options in seeking to make sense of this section in the context of Jeremiah's ministry.

1. The corporate confessions/petitions of the people are actually insincere.
2. These confessions/petitions are confessions that Jeremiah is offering to the people, if only they would take the confessional content to heart.

14:2–6. Judah and Jerusalem mourn over the devastating effects of a drought.

14:7–9. The people confess their sin against God. In confessional terms God is described as Israel's hope (Heb. *miqveh*) and Savior (*moshia*) in troubled times (14:8). Verse 9 reflects the tradition of God as a valiant warrior who defends and delivers his people.

14:10–16. This mostly prose section records the give-and-take between God and the prophet. Verse 10 contains a poetic oracle that God does not accept the people. In 14:11 and 14 come autobiographical introductions: "Then the LORD said to me." Jeremiah is bidden not to pray for the people. Prophets who have led the people astray receive sustained attention. They are obviously making Jeremiah's life more difficult by speaking in the Lord's name and contradicting his own prophecies of judgment.

14:17–18. These two verses offer an example of lament in which it is difficult to know who is speaking, Jeremiah or God. "My Virgin Daughter, my people" reflects more naturally on God as speaker than the prophet.

14:19–22. The second corporate confession/petition of the people asks plaintively if God has completely rejected Judah and Zion. With the confession of sin also comes the refrain "for the sake of your name do not despise us" (14:21; cf. 14:7, 9) and a plea for God to remember his covenant with them and not to annul it.

15:1–9. The reference to Moses and Samuel as mediators and intercessors (15:1) evokes memory of past events in Israel's history (Exod 32:30–35; 34:1–27). In the period before the monarchy, the people entreated Samuel to cry out to the Lord on their behalf, and eventually the Philistine threat was subdued (1 Sam 7:8–17). In the work of Moses and Samuel, one finds models of intercessory prayers and accounts of the preservation of the people in spite of the divine judgment that had fallen on them.

For God to dismiss the work of Moses and Samuel as efficacious in the present moment of Judah's sin is, in effect, to say that no prophetic mediator will be accepted and that judgment cannot be averted. Total destruction had been averted through their mediation. Now, however, it will be different. Judgment to come is announced and described graphically in 15:2. Jeremiah cites the lingering effects of Manasseh as reasons for the inevitability of judgment. This accusation has parallels in 2 Kings 21:1–18; 23:26; 24:3–4, where the judgment to come on Judah and Jerusalem in Jeremiah's day derives from the overflowing wickedness of Manasseh's reign.

Application. Many prayers for rain are heard frequently during months of drought. Arid conditions are an effective reminder of how easily life can get out of balance and how circumstances of drought can only be ameliorated from above. Nevertheless, when rain finally comes, drought conditions are quickly forgotten. Jeremiah 14 is a salutary reminder of the true source of life and of the One who calls a people into existence for his glory and praise.

JEREMIAH 15:10–21

Original Meaning. This section is structured around a give-and-take conversation between the prophet and God, which unfolds as follows:

A. 15:10: Jeremiah laments the day of his birth and the curses of people that are now directed at him.
B. 15:11: God replies that he will deliver Jeremiah for a good purpose.
C. 15:12–14: God pronounces judgment on the people.
D. 15:15–18: Jeremiah expresses his frustrations to God.
E. 15:19–21: God replies to Jeremiah.

There are difficult textual and syntactical issues involved in the translation of this section, particularly with 15:12, a verse that has a significant role in the way the lament/complaint is interpreted. Perhaps the best option is to interpret 15:12–14 as a word from the Lord pronouncing judgment on Judah.

15:10. In this verse Jeremiah laments his birth. This provides another, somewhat broader context in which to hear the language of personal woe. Jeremiah is similar to Job. His contemporaries curse him, and the pain of his ostracism has made even God seem deceitful and unreliable to him.

In lamenting the day of his birth, Jeremiah offers an evaluation of his life and prophetic ministry. He feels as if there is no purpose for him to continue to live. Such language should be taken seriously as an indication of despair, though not literally as the announcement of suicide. Jeremiah describes the "curses" that have come to him.

15:11. God replies that he will deliver Jeremiah for a "good purpose" and will bring his enemies to a place where they will need to plead with him. This last comment perhaps leads to the further pronouncement of judgment on Judah in 15:12–14.

15:12–14. As noted above, the text of 15:12 and the interpretation of these three verses is difficult. The best overall option is to see all three verses as a judgment speech on Judah. They repeat material found in 17:3–4, where the context is clearly judgment on the people.

15:15–18. Jeremiah turns once again to the Lord. As part of his lament/complaint he notes that his enemies are also God's enemies. Jeremiah suffers his reproach because he represents God's word to the people. In 15:16 he describes his encountering of God's word with the surprising claim that he "ate" them, and they became his joy. Whether this means that Jeremiah was instructed by a document like the book of the covenant discovered during Josiah's reign or another preserved text cannot be known. The emphasis falls on the prophet's joy at that time as opposed to the despair and rejection he now encounters.

Jeremiah confesses that it is God's hand that he feels on him, that God is the source of the indignation he experiences. As his emotions boil over, the prophet asks God why his (Jeremiah's) pain is unending and why he (God) has become like failing water.

15:19–21. God's reply is not to deal with the particulars of Jeremiah's anger but to remind him that the path of the faithful and obedient prophet is still open to him. One should not conclude that Jeremiah has failed or that God has failed the prophet, but rather that God has called him to prophesy in this historical hour of judgment.

Verse 19 has two plays on the verb "turn/return" (Heb. *shub*). If Jeremiah will "repent" (i.e., change his tune and direction), then God will "restore" him (15:19a). These are the NIV renderings of *shub* in both cases. Moreover, using the same verb, God states that the people should "turn" to Jeremiah, but that Jeremiah should not "turn" to them (15:19b). Verses 20–21 are reminiscent of Jeremiah's initial call in 1:18–19. He still has the same task ahead of him and the same assurance that God is with him.

Application. Ministry can be painful and costly. Jeremiah's lament shows one of God's chosen vessels suffering because of his service to God. His life is an Old Testament form of Jesus's call to discipleship: Take up your cross and follow me. Even when stretched seemingly to the breaking point, God reminds Jeremiah of his call to prophetic ministry. For the prophet there is no alternative but to turn (return) once again to the Lord, who called him and promised him protection.

JEREMIAH 16:1–21

Original Meaning. *16:1–9.* God commands Jeremiah not to marry or have children (16:2), since judgment is coming soon and many parents and children in Judah will die. There are, perhaps, at least two reasons for including this command as part of the book.

1. In a society where marriages were arranged between families, celibacy was comparatively rare. Thus, Jeremiah's celibacy might surface as a hot-button issue for his detractors to seize upon. They can portray him as crazed and out of touch with reality. But Jeremiah's celibacy is not a denial of the goodness of marriage or even the voicing of his own preferences in the matter. For all we know, he may well have desired a wife and children. Yet his desires, like much about his personal circumstances, recede behind the presentation of his prophetic work.
2. Since destruction is imminent, this is no time for marriage (16:3–5). His celibacy is part of his embodiment of the message he proclaims; it is a symbolic act as surely as was Hosea's marriage of a prostitute (Hos 1–3) or Ezekiel's refusal to mourn publicly the death of his wife (Ezek 24:15–27).

Jeremiah is not to enter a house for feasting or celebration either (Jer 16:8–9), for the joy of a bride and groom will also be silenced in the coming devastation. Here again he bears the mark of his ministry.

16:10–13. This text presupposes that Jeremiah passes on the substance of the Lord's messages to him about constricting his social activities. Judgment is at hand. "Why such judgment?" the people ask (cf. 16:10). The answer is the familiar (to readers of the book) and crushing reply that both ancestors and the current generation have forsaken the Lord, been disobedient to his instruction, and served other deities. The current generation is particularly recalcitrant and motivated by an evil heart. The punishment for "defiling" (16:18) God's land is to be cast from the land and humiliated in exile by worshiping other deities.

16:14–15. These verses announce an abrupt change through the rhetorical formula, "the days are coming." God announces that the judgment of the exile will be matched by the saving exodus from foreign territory and back to the promised land.

16:16–18. Verse 18 makes it clear that God is speaking about bringing judgment upon the failures of Judah, so that we see a return to the language of historical judgment. The announcement of fishing and hunting for offenders in foreign lands (16:16), however, is obscure. Perhaps they are a reply to the sarcasm of people who say that in exile God will not see and judge them for their sins. Certainly, Jeremiah affirms that God is not limited by geography or spatial distance in bringing to pass what he desires.

16:19–21. The chapter concludes with the voice of one who prays on behalf of himself and his sinful people. Contextually this must be Jeremiah, for the concluding verse makes it clear that God is behind the sentiments expressed and that he intends to teach his people a lesson about his power. Along with the confession of the people's sinfulness is an affirmation that "the nations will come" to God (16:19). God is the prophet's refuge and strength—characteristics that separate him from the folly of idols. This in turn leads to the declaration that God has acted in history in order that people may know that his name is Yahweh (cf. Exod 6:3).

Application. As noted elsewhere, knowledge of God is not mere intellectual comprehension or cognition—the devil and his minions believe that God exists (Jas 2:19). True knowledge of God is formed in relationship with him and in obedience to his claims of exclusive worship. God serves as a fortress and refuge to those who trust him and who humbly seek to follow his revealed will. God is also a righteous judge, whose timing in judging iniquity should not be confused with either indifference or caprice.

JEREMIAH 17:1–27

Original Meaning. *17:1–4.* This brief passage—that Judah has rejected God's instruction and will be judged accordingly—is similar to many preceding parts. Judah's sinfulness is described as "engraved with an iron tool . . . on the tablets of their hearts" (17:1). This metaphor underscores the indelible nature of sin and its corrosive effects on the people.

Verse 2 mentions the "Asherah poles" as evidence for Judah's defection from the Lord, along with the people's embracing of false worship. In recent years several inscriptions have been discovered in and around the ancient territory of Judah. On more than one occasion there is the reference to "YHWH and his Asherah." These texts demonstrate a kind of unhealthy syncretism, if not outright polytheism, from the time of Jeremiah and other prophets.

Canaan is actually the Lord's inheritance, but the people were granted a life in it as part of God's covenant promises to them. Punishment means they will lose their place in his inheritance. This is tantamount to saying they have lost their place in the household (i.e., family) of the Lord.

17:5–8. This passage reads like a "play" (i.e., a serious pun) on Psalm 1. The contrast is between trust in human effort and design, and reliance on God.

17:9–13. Verse 9 represents the heart as the seat of human deceitfulness. The depths of its possible depravity are difficult to measure. Indeed, only God can accurately measure it. According to 17:10, this knowledge, which belongs to God, enables him to "reward each person according to their conduct." The connection between act and consequence is further elaboration of the blessing-and-curse contrast presented in the previous unit. Part of what God does in overseeing blessings and curses is to connect the disposition of the human heart and the deeds that flow from it. This is not a law of physics but the operation of a sovereign God, who cannot be bound rigidly by a formula.

Verse 11 is another proverbial statement: Riches gained unjustly are like a bird hatching eggs it did not lay. Here again the connection between act and consequence is set out. Jeremiah's use of this proverb suggests a connection between Judah's "gains" from idolatry and the sad loss of its land and freedom. Only a fool would want such gains.

17:12–13. These two verses join the blessing of the sanctuary (almost certainly the one in Jerusalem) with God's presence as "the spring of living water" (cf. 2:13). That God is "the hope of Israel" has been used by Jeremiah before (17:13; see 14:8).

17:14–18. Here is another of Jeremiah's laments. Verse 14 draws a connection between healing and saving. Healing likely means the kind of restoration of emotional spirit and physical well-being that only God can grant. Since Jeremiah has been the object of scorn and ridicule, his acceptance by God is crucial to his survival. In 17:15 the prophet reports to God that he has been verbally abused by those who ridicule his prophecies. Their question points to the as-yet unfulfilled prophecies of disaster.

In poignant fashion the prophet reminds God that he has walked the path of discipleship. He has taken no joy in announcing a day of despair. It is almost as if waiting for the prophecies of disaster to be fulfilled has made Jeremiah feel separated from God, so he prays that God will be his "refuge" (17:17) when disaster falls. He also prays that God will deal strictly with his persecutors, so that they will know that in opposing Jeremiah they were opposing the word and prophet sent by God.

17:19–29. This is an autobiographical report in prose. It functions like a sermon on the fourth commandment of the Decalogue (Deut 5:12–15) to keep the Sabbath day holy. In his temple sermon, Jeremiah charged the people with several failures, including theft, murder, and perjury (Jer 7:9). These terms come from the Decalogue. The charge of violating the Sabbath is simply another example of his using normative covenant traditions in his critique of the people.

Jeremiah's mini sermon on the Sabbath, furthermore, has the familiar two-way formulation. This is entirely in keeping with the poetic texts that precede it. For example, the blessing or curse formulation in 17:5–8 is a brief exposition of the two-way paradigm. Here, keeping the Sabbath holy will result in receiving God's blessing, while failure to do so will bring destruction on Jerusalem.

Note that Jeremiah's specific accusation concerns carrying loads on the Sabbath, (i.e., working rather than refraining from labor). Resting from work helped make the Sabbath day holy. If God's people honor him by keeping the Sabbath, then not only Jerusalem but the various regions of Judah will be inhabited, and right worship will be offered to the Lord. This is the one place in the chapter that suggests a role for repentance and renewed obedience to God's law.

Application. Recovering the doctrine of the corporate nature of sin and its universal effects on individuals is a necessary condition for the proclamation that God has spoken decisively to the world in Jesus Christ. In the modern West, among the places perhaps to start a conversation is the prevalence of addictive behavior, racism, and random violence. All three of these phenomena in Western societies are symptomatic of larger issues of human existence, and they stand under the judgment of God's Word. Nevertheless, they defy easy explanation or cure. They are irrational, and they lead to more of the same in spirals of self-destruction.

JEREMIAH 18:1–19:15

Original Meaning. *18:1–17.* Readers receive an account of Jeremiah's visit to a potter's workshop and commentary on its significance. Verse 1 is clearly the work of Jeremiah's editor(s). What is reported, however, has an autobiographical element still preserved (the "I" of 18:3; the "me" of 18:5). For his contemporaries, Jeremiah's visit to the workshop and his announcement of God's word have the profile of a symbolic act, what might be termed a parable in action. Jeremiah's readers and hearers can use their imagination to envisage the workshop and the efforts of a potter to shape wet clay into a vessel ready to be fired and then used as a container.

God (the potter) has the sovereign right to make and remake the clay as he sees fit. Wet clay is malleable, which means it is capable of being formed in a variety of shapes. But it is also capable of collapsing its shape or of being ill-mixed and thus unsuitable for firing. Not just any wet clay will do, and not just any individual can shape a vessel properly. It takes a correct mixture of clay and the skills of a trained artisan to form a pot for successful firing.

The meaning of this illustration is clear. Just as the potter may form and reform the same clay until he is either satisfied or decides to dump the clay completely, so God can form and reform the house of Israel (18:6). This affirmation of God's sovereign right over the people he has formed is followed by the "two-way" formulation of God's dealings with any nation. If God announces judgment on a nation and that nation repents, then that judgment can be reversed or simply canceled. Correspondingly, if God has announced goodness for a kingdom and it acts faithlessly, then that good can also be reversed.

The two-way formulation implies that a wholehearted repentance on the part of Judah can avert the judgment that looms over them. Verse 12, however, puts a quote in the mouth of the people to the effect that they will follow their own stubborn heart.

God does not take "no" for an answer easily. The poetic

reply in 18:13–17 begins with an indignant question. An appalling thing has happened; God's people have forgotten him and worshiped other deities, worthless idols unable to help them. Verse 17 has a surprising metaphorical turn to it: In the coming day of judgment, God will show his "back" to the people "and not [his] face."

18:18–23. Jeremiah's opponents are again the issue. In 18:18 they intend to attack him verbally and pay no attention to anything he says. In 18:19–23, in another personal lament, Jeremiah prays for God's judgment on his enemies. Jeremiah prays, in essence, that his enemies may fall into the pit they have dug. Since they have committed an evil in attacking an innocent person, may the evil they intend fall back on them.

19:1–13. God now instructs Jeremiah to perform another symbolic act (a parable in action), also with a pottery jar. Presumably the actions described were carried out, though only the instructions and a brief report in 19:14–15 remain. God commands Jeremiah to buy an earthenware jar and to take a group of elders and priests to the Valley of Ben Hinnom where the Topheth, a place for human sacrificial rites, is located. Jeremiah must prophesy judgment on the kings of Judah and the inhabitants of Jerusalem. The failures of these addressees are listed as the worship of other gods, the spilling of innocent blood, and especially the worship of Baal through the burning of children in a sacrificial fire.

With the breaking of the jar, Jeremiah indicates the irrevocable judgment to come. Just as the smashed earthenware cannot be repaired, Judah cannot be reformed. For original hearers and readers there is likely added significance to the earthenware pot. The Topheth was not only the place of ceremonial slaughter; it likely also contained a section where earthenware jars with the charred remains of sacrificial victims were collected.

Jeremiah understands the Topheth as a place of defilement and its earthenware jars as symbolic of slaughter. Indeed, he gives the valley a devastating nickname—"The Valley of Slaughter" (19:6; cf. 7:32). Judgment will come on Jerusalem in such a way that there will be no other place to bury the dead except in the Topheth, the place of ritual slaughter and cultic defilement. One of the characteristics of Topheth is the crowded nature of the burial section, where pots full of bones and charred remains are stacked together.

19:14–15. Jeremiah leaves the Topheth and goes to the courtyard of the temple to proclaim that God will "bring on this city and all the villages around it every disaster I pronounced against them, because they were stiff-necked and would not listen to my words" (19:15). His presence in the temple courtyard is tantamount to bringing the defilement of the Topheth into the temple, as any reader familiar with the purity laws of the Old Testament would recognize (a cemetery or a corpse rendered a person ceremonially unclean). Furthermore, the reference to "stiff-necked" people catches up the failure of the people to recognize the possibility of repentance that was announced as possible in 18:7–11.

Application. In authentic discussions about God's purpose and goodness, there is an inherent reference to a future entrusted to God; it is a future not completely understood from a finite human perspective. One is called to trust in the work of the potter, to walk by faith and not by sight, and to accept God's judgment in the present in the hope that the Potter will reshape the future.

Certainly, one of the stupendous events of the twentieth century happened with the collapse of Soviet domination of Eastern Europe, beginning with the fall of the Berlin Wall in November 1989. The impact of this collapse is still being worked out. Each state has its own version of the impact as do the churches in the region. Can anyone say for sure where the collapse will lead? No Christian should doubt the role of God in this process; the contribution of the churches to the collapse is widely recognized. Here is a paradigm of the surprising providence of God being worked out. Was the collapse predicted in the Old Testament? Not precisely, but the God who reshapes history and speaks authoritatively is revealed in the Old Testament, and he is still at work.

JEREMIAH 20:1–18

Original Meaning. *20:1–6.* Pashhur represents the religious establishment, especially the priests who care for and officiate at the temple. In fact, he is described as the chief officer at the temple. This probably means among other things that he heads the security detail for the large complex, providing oversight for the Levitical personnel who keep the gates and who restrict access to and activities within the temple courts.

Pashhur is from a segment of the population who prove to be some of Jeremiah's most persistent persecutors. With the temple looming in the background, Jeremiah's treatment is portrayed as God's judgment on him, carried out by the priests who care for God's house. Upon his release, Jeremiah gives Pashhur a new name, "Terror on Every Side" (Heb. *magor missabib*; 20:3). The Hebrew expression occurs elsewhere in Jeremiah to describe the plight of Judah when the foe from the north comes against the state and its capital city.

Jeremiah announces in the name of the Lord that Pashhur has "prophesied lies" and that he will enter Babylon as a captive (20:6). Perhaps his actions against Jeremiah are a form of prophecy, not unlike Jeremiah's visit to the Valley of Hinnom and his coming to the temple complex to prophesy (19:14–15). Indeed, Jeremiah's prophetic witness in the temple may have prompted his arrest and thrashing. As a priest, however, Pashhur almost certainly took the opportunity to speak a word of judgment in public about Jeremiah and his actions. These would take the form of repudiating Jeremiah's words and actions and claiming divine judgment on him.

20:7–18. The prophet is persecuted because of "the word of the Lord" (20:8). His persecutors lie in wait to ambush him and ridicule him with his own phrase, "terror on every side" (20:10), as if to say that Jeremiah is a deluded madman who speaks incessantly about terror to come. In his frustration and bitterness Jeremiah accuses God of "deceiving" him (20:7), a strong term that can also refer to seduction. The prophet has reached his wits' end and is unable to articulate a sense that God will rescue him from this situation.

Verse 11 affirms that God is indeed strong to save. In context this means that the prophet's persecutors will fail. The next verse affirms that God is an infallible judge and will see to the judgment of the persecutors. Jeremiah's prayer in this respect takes on the form of setting his "cause" (20:12) before God.

The prophet also rues the day he was born (20:14–18; cf. 15:10), as he, like Job, suffers unjustly. It is difficult to know whether the lament/complaint of 20:7–18 should be read sequentially, as if the movement of the prayer/complaint is significant. If so, it suggests that Jeremiah goes back and forth in his confidence and on his resolve to carry out his prophetic work. That should surprise no one who takes seriously the humiliation suffered in the "Upper Gate" (20:2).

Application. There is much to learn from the frank expression of Jeremiah's human limitations. One may—with Christ's help—bear innocent suffering with a certain grace. But it is no failure of Jeremiah's that he feels crushed by the burdens of the prophetic office. What he gets finally is a taste of the insidious opposition to the word of God that cloaks itself in all manner of religiosity and patriotism. He experiences the sinking feeling that not only is all lost but that God seems involved in his pain. It will take the humiliation of Christ for the redemptive element of suffering to emerge, but in his own way Jeremiah suffers on our behalf. He demonstrates what it is like to feel the burdens of human failure and personal frustration as a part of his calling, and he does so to instruct us about the cost of discipleship and also for a testimony that God is faithful still—beyond our finite comprehension and in spite of our complaints.

JEREMIAH 21:1–10

Original Meaning. Zedekiah is king—the first reference to the last king of Judah since the superscription to the book of Jeremiah—and the date is circa 588 BC. With the Babylonian army surrounding Jerusalem, a royal official named Pashhur and a priest named Zephaniah are sent to Jeremiah for him to inquire of the Lord. The name Pashhur is the same as that of the priest in chapter 20, although they are two different people.

Pashhur and Zephaniah ask Jeremiah to inquire of the Lord and to intercede for the nation. This is something that King Zedekiah would seek from Jeremiah on more than one occasion (37:3; 38:14). The Lord's reply is full of the judgmental language seen in virtually every previous chapter. What is new (for those reading through Jeremiah) is a specific reference to Nebuchadnezzar, king of Babylon, and the specifics of the siege of Jerusalem. Babylon itself is mentioned specifically for the first time only in the previous chapter (20:4–6). Elsewhere the agent of judgment to come was merely described as the foe or enemy from the north.

According to the divine oracle, God will not war against the Babylonian army but against Judah for its faithlessness and wickedness. Yes, God is a valiant warrior, but the enemy at the moment is Judah, not Babylon! The fall of the city, therefore, is certain. God's resolve to judge the city is described in Hebrew as "the setting of his face" (NIV "determined to do), an idiom for single-minded determination (21:10).

Jeremiah mediates part of God's reply to the state officials in language reminiscent of Deuteronomy 30:11–20. Jeremiah tells the people that God is setting before them the way of life and death (Jer 21:8–9). Death is the fate of those who stay in the city; those who leave and are taken captive by the Babylonians will escape with their lives.

Ominously, there is no call for repentance in the text of the divine oracle. God is on the side of the Babylonians for the historical moment, and the best that can be done for the Judeans is to convince them to capitulate to the Babylonians and thereby save their lives. There is specific reference to the destruction of Jerusalem by fire.

Application. Christians may see in Jeremiah's hard words here an example of the "razor edge" of biblical theism. God fights against the powers of evil and corruption—and as with every fight, the results are not pretty. God will fight the powers of evil when they oppress his people, but God can also use the powers of evil in this world to judge his people. God is not indifferent to the sins of his people.

JEREMIAH 21:11–22:30

Original Meaning. *21:11–14.* These verses can be read as further commentary on Jeremiah's word to Zedekiah in 21:1–10. They are meant for any and all members of the house of David who live in the palace and assist in carrying out the affairs of the state.

The command in 21:12 to "administer justice every morning" and to "rescue from the hand of his oppressor the one . . . robbed" has a close parallel in Micah's critique preserved in Micah 2:1–2. Early morning was the time when people in towns and villages rose and met one another on their way to perform daily tasks. When they met at the gate of the city or village, they also worked out administrative-judicial affairs and witnessed agreements. Jeremiah's charge to the royal house, therefore, is to be a court of appeal for the oppressed "every morning" (Jer 21:12).

22:1–9. Readers should not overlook the verb "go down" (22:1). Since the palace of the king is located at one of the highest points of Jerusalem, about the only place from which Jeremiah can "go down" is from the temple mount. This incidental comment tells us much about one important place where Jeremiah receives his prompting from God. Readers learn from another incidental comment in 22:2 that the royal palace had gates. Since some matters of state and cult were carried out at the royal palace (likely located near the temple), the gates would be those entry points to a public courtyard or hall.

Monarchs and their servants should prevent the shedding of "innocent blood in this place" (22:3). This is a foreboding topic since "innocent blood" required atonement and other ceremonies to deal with its expiation; otherwise, responsibility for the shedding of innocent blood fell on the whole community. In essence, the two ways set before the royal house are the same as those set before the people.

22:10–12. Of the three kings addressed directly, the briefest prophecy concerns Shallum, that is, Jehoahaz, the son and immediate successor to Josiah. He was placed on the throne after the death of his father but was subsequently removed by the Egyptian pharaoh after a brief reign. Jeremiah calls for bitter weeping (mourning) on his behalf, although his personal evaluation of Jehoahaz is not clear. The fate of this king foreshadows that of the people. The call in Jeremiah 22:10 not to mourn the death of Josiah is intended only to call attention to the sad fate of Jehoahaz.

22:13–23. Jeremiah pronounces a judgmental "woe" (22:13) on Jehoiakim, the older brother of Jehoahaz, who succeeded his younger brother on the throne. Apparently, the people of the land (Judean property owners?) recognized Jehoiakim's unsuitability for rule when they initially bypassed him for Jehoahaz. They were loyal to the dynasty of David but did not want the eldest son to follow Josiah.

Verse 13 describes Jehoiakim's activities as "unrighteous" and as examples of "injustice." These terms, of course, are the negative counterparts to justice and righteousness (cf. 22:3). Jehoiakim's arrogant building project is described as "his palace" (22:13). Almost certainly this is not a primary residence since the royal palace in Jerusalem had been in existence as long as the temple.

By contrast with Jehoiakim, his father Josiah is described as one who lived the life of a king (he ate and drank) but who also did what was "right and just" (22:15), defending the cause of the poor and needy. Jeremiah describes this activity as an example of what it means to "know" (22:16) the Lord. Josiah is the only one of the monarchs from his day whom Jeremiah praises.

The fate of the arrogant and selfish king is that he will not be mourned at his death and will not receive a proper burial. Extant sources do not give details of Jehoiakim's burial or the precise circumstances of his death. The latter came apparently during the time of the Babylonians' siege of Jerusalem in 598/597 BC.

22:24–30. This address to Jehoiachin has several grammatical complexities. The gist of the message is that he too falls under the judgment of the historical hour. His personal failings are not listed, and it may be that the query in 22:28 recognizes the incongruence of his circumstances. More precisely he and his family will go into Babylonian exile, and the young king will be reckoned as childless—although he has descendants—since his sons will not sit on the throne of David and rule as kings in Judah.

Application. The harsh word to Jehoiakim also contains an affirmation of what it means to know God. In his case, the contrast with his father, Josiah, is telling. The test of knowing God is the commitment of the person to the things of God—justice and righteousness for God's people. To know God is to be committed to his revealed will in the places of responsibility (ministry) where one lives and works. Of course, to know God means also to be rightly and personally related to him.

JEREMIAH 23:1–40

Original Meaning. *23:1–4.* Punishment and crime are linked for the shepherds in this brief prose text. God will bring judgment on them because they have not cared for their flock. Verse 2 charges them more specifically with not caring for "my [i.e., God's] people." The scattered flock is identified as the exiled remnant of God's people, who will be brought back to their homeland (23:3, 7–8). This passage, therefore, probably originated after the first wave of exiles was taken away to Babylon in 597 BC.

23:5–6. This passage begins with a typical formula about the future: "The days are coming" (23:5). God will raise up for his scattered people a shepherd who will rule justly and wisely. He will be a king from David's line. His wonderful name, "The Lord Our Righteous Savior" (23:6), is a pun on the name Zedekiah (= Righteous is Yahweh), the last king of Judah (who reigned from 597–587/586 BC). For the generation of Jeremiah, the symbolic name of this "righteous Branch" (23:5) is probably a sarcastic judgment on Zedekiah; moreover, it points to God's resolve to restore his people and fulfill his promises to the Davidic line.

This prophecy, like the prose text that begins chapter 23, should be read in the context of the previous section (21:11–22:30) and its concern with the injustice and failures of the Davidic monarchs. The judgment to fall on the shepherds comes because they have failed to fulfill the duties of their office.

The name of the king represents significant claims about the work of God.

1. In his days Judah and Israel "will be saved" (23:6) and will dwell securely.
2. The righteousness indicated in his name is for the people, even though it is not fully their own.

23:7–8. Prophecy of a future change in the circumstances of the people continues in these two verses. Just as something new and wonderful will emerge from David's line, so a second exodus will occur, and the exiled people will return to their land.

23:9–10. Perhaps the first clause of 23:9 ("Concerning the prophets") is a heading for the materials that follow and not just for Jeremiah's anguished comments in 23:9–10. Jeremiah reacts to the dire straits of his people and the power of his prophetic opponents to mislead them. He mentions drought conditions as one element of his horror (cf. ch. 14). The magnitude of God's words of judgment have rendered the prophet like a drunken man. It is not clear whether this is metaphorical language to describe Jeremiah's strong emotional reaction or if he actually manifests physical symptoms.

23:11–12. God's first reply notes that the wickedness of prophet and priest is in "my temple" (literally, "my house"; 23:11). These verses confirm that the prophets and priests who serve there are also offering oracles of assurance that the nation will not fall.

23:13–14. Prophets of Samaria prophesied by Baal and led God's people astray (cf. 23:27). This historical comment interprets the fall of Israel and Samaria in 722/721 BC. Something equally heinous is then reported with respect to the prophets in Jerusalem: They are adulterers and living a lie. Verse 14 offers a familiar analogy to describe the folly of Samaria and Jerusalem; the two cities are compared to Sodom and Gomorrah.

23:15–24. The introductory formula of 23:15 is like that of 23:9. Concerning the prophets, it seems to introduce several oracles from the Lord. There are additional rhetorical formulae in 23:16, 23, and 24. The command "do not listen to . . . the prophets" (23:16) is addressed to the people. There will be no peace or security for a people who despise God.

The oracle about judgment on the prophets notes that the people will better understand this matter in "days to come" (23:20). It is the function of a book like Jeremiah, which was published in the aftermath of Judah's demise, to make clear that the people had trusted in lies.

God denies sending these prophets (23:18, 21). If they had been in God's council, then they would have proclaimed the evil deeds of the people and attempted to turn them from their acts and the consequences.

The rhetorical questions of 23:23–24 are also intended for the people's hearing. Whether near or far, the people and their deeds are known to God, who fills heaven and earth (with his presence).

23:25–40. These prose comments continue the criticism of Jerusalem's prophets. One of their modes of communicating is dream reports. Verse 28 makes a distinction between the faithful reporting of God's word and the reporting of a dream. The implication is that the reception of the word is a different form of experience, but it is not further defined. In effect, it is like the hammer that shatters rock.

Verses 33–40 begin with a play on one of the words for "message" (*massa'*), which can also be translated as "burden." Perhaps the link between the two meanings of the word comes from the concept of bearing or carrying something.

It is important to note that in all the criticism of the prophets, the expression "false prophet" is not used. Some of these prophets probably deserved the description, for they looked to Baal for their inspiration or simply lied about their reception of a message from Yahweh. Some, however, might not deserve such a description. Perhaps they had been of service in the cause of the Lord in times past, and they sincerely hoped that their message of peace and security had its origin with the Lord.

These judgments against the religious leaders of the people are related to other passages in Jeremiah. Various narratives and oracles make it clear that Jehoiakim and Zedekiah failed as shepherds of the nation. That some members of the priesthood were hostile to Jeremiah is clear from 20:1–6. Jeremiah will have a memorable encounter with a prophet named Hananiah in chapter 28, and he will be involved (via letters) in debate with Judean prophets in Babylon (29:21–32). His prayers of lament are derived, in part, from his experiences of ridicule and humiliation at the hand of these leaders.

Application. Jeremiah was a true prophet because the word he received from the Lord was vindicated in the events of history. Clearly, the timing of the fulfillment was a point of consternation for him. He spent years proclaiming a judgment that came only after much anguish on his part. That his word about the future eventually did occur is one of the tests for true prophecy (according to Deuteronomy). With the life of the people in crisis, Jeremiah announced that Judah had to change or judgment would come. Eventually he understood that any repentance would be too little and too late. Those prophets who disagreed with him were wrong historically and theologically. In essence, their denial of judgment was a denial of the

Lord at work redemptively through historical judgment. Their words diverted the people's attention from seeking the Lord to a false assurance that he would protect them.

Is this not like the turmoil over Jesus's public ministry, where he continually called people to a life of commitment and spiritual discernment in counting the cost of discipleship? Discipleship (i.e., following Christ) is also a form of leadership, and vice versa. Christ came not to be served but to serve (Mark 10:45). That is the point of Christology; it is the point for all shepherds in the church.

JEREMIAH 24:1–10

Original Meaning. Jeremiah's observations at the temple become a vehicle for God's address to the people. The setting is in Zedekiah's reign, sometime between 597 BC, when Nebuchadnezzar took Jehoiachin and a number of the leading citizens of Judah into exile in Babylon, and 587/586 BC, when the Babylonians besieged and destroyed Jerusalem. The date is probably close to 588 BC, the beginning of the second Babylonian siege of Jerusalem.

Jeremiah observes two baskets of figs left as offerings at the temple, one of which contains ripe figs and the other rotten figs. The Lord tells the prophet that the good figs are like the Judeans taken into exile, while the rotten figs represent Zedekiah and those who remain in Jerusalem and Judah. The Lord promises to do good to the exilic community, to bring them back from exile, and to give them a heart to know him. Concerning those remaining in Judah, however, the Lord promises judgment.

One finds in this autobiographic prophetic report a shorthand version of what the larger book of Jeremiah intends to accomplish. For those on whom the judgment of the exile has fallen, God announces that he intends to "build them up" and to "plant" (24:6) them again in the promised land. Return to the land is not all that God intends, although the return is a sign of something more fundamental—a wholehearted return to the Lord. Thus, there is also the promise of a heart prepared by God to know him as well as the reinstitution of the covenant relationship (24:7).

Application. God is just in judgment and yet one who justifies (accepts as righteous) those who trust him for their salvation. This is a paraphrase of Romans 3:26; it also captures the intent of Jeremiah 24. God brings judgment on those who spurn him and reject his covenant. But he also seeks to save that which is lost and to give a new heart to those whom he calls into fellowship. The divided fate of the two communities in Jeremiah's day illustrates God's use of the historical process for judgment and restoration.

JEREMIAH 25:1–38

Original Meaning. *25:1–14.* The material in 25:1–14 reports oracular material that God gives to Jeremiah. That it is also a summary statement is clear from 25:3—a reference to twenty-three years of preaching on the part of the prophet. Jeremiah's work is set in the context of God's ongoing prophetic witness among the people. The refusal of the people to heed Jeremiah's warnings and earlier calls for repentance (cf. 25:5) has now led to the brink of judgment. Babylon, and, more particularly, Nebuchadnezzar, are identified as a foe from the north. The judgment to come on Judah and Jerusalem is only part of what Nebuchadnezzar will do. Other nations will also come under his domination.

Verse 9 describes Nebuchadnezzar as God's "servant." This is a shocking term to use but fully consistent with Jeremiah's message. The prophet portrays the historical judgment to come on Judah as God's work against his sinful people. The king's servanthood does not make him morally superior or grant him saving knowledge of God. One may compare the language of "anointed" used to describe Cyrus (Isa 45:1–7).

In the judgments against Judah, a servitude to Babylon of "seventy years" is projected (Jer 25:11–12). The actual period was about sixty-six years, if one reckons from the first year of Nebuchadnezzar's kingship in 605 BC to the fall of Babylon in 539, or seventy years almost exactly if one reckons from the destruction of the temple in 586 BC to its rededication in 516 BC (cf. Ezra 6:15). More likely, seventy is a round number representing the fulfillment of an extended period. It should be contrasted with the short period predicted by Hananiah for Babylonian hegemony (Jer 28:3–4). That Nebuchadnezzar and Babylon are the Lord's servants in the historical process does not make them immune from his standards of justice, however. Babylon too will be judged for its iniquities (25:12–14).

25:15–38. This section vividly depicts the imagery of the nations drinking from the Lord's "cup" (25:15) of wrath. Such a cup, which presupposes the staggering of someone inebriated and out of control, is a metaphor for the turmoil to come among the nations when God's sword of judgment is unleashed.

A long listing of states and rulers comprises a summary for "all the kingdoms on the face of the earth" (25:26). All the nations are caught up in the description of the judgment to come. It is not just Jerusalem, "the city that bears [God's] Name" (25:29), who will bear judgment. God is depicted as cosmic judge, and the imagery employed suggests a type of sweeping judgment beyond the circumstances of the late seventh/early sixth centuries BC. The face of the earth is strewn about with the effects of destruction. Here is prophetic proclamation like that in Daniel and Zechariah, which depict cataclysmic change in apocalyptic form.

Application. The claims of chapter 25 play a significant role in assessing what is meant by God's historical providence.

1. The prophetic perspective on God's historical judgments is not so much a blueprint about the future as it is a revelation about God's purpose. Judgment in the historical process can be self-incurred, but its moral dimension is shaped by the Creator in surprising ways.
2. While God's purpose in judging and reforming his people takes shape in the historical process, God's providence was not limited to Israel, nor is it now limited to the church. Other nations, as part of God's universal purpose, are judged and shaped as well.
3. Judgment is not all that God intends for the future of nations (cf. Gen 12:3) as his near and far purposes are worked out.
4. The work of God is a process and not just an occasional event. Historical events are part of his proximate designs and are used in service of his eternal designs, which no one fully grasps. God's judgments are unsearchable (Rom 11:33); they stand, however, in the service of his undeserved mercy—the ultimate goal of his providence.

In light of these affirmations Christians cannot assume that the misfortune of every nation is God's judgment and that a period of relative peace is evidence of his favor. God's work through the historical process is more complicated than that. There is no time in world history when this confession lacks application. The larger pattern can only be glimpsed by faith, and that faith must allow for a transhistorical culmination that cannot be fully grasped at any one point in history.

JEREMIAH 26:1–24

Original Meaning. *26:1–6.* Jeremiah warns the people that if they fail to follow the instruction (26:4) of the Lord, they will bring calamity on themselves. This is a typical form of the act-consequence claim: Disobedience brings disaster. The temple will be destroyed in the coming judgment, just like the destruction of the worship center at Shiloh during the days of the judges and the prophet Samuel.

Jeremiah's words about the temple strike a chord with his audience. It is God's "house" (26:2), and the assumption of many in the audience is that God will protect it no matter what. Also, for some in the audience, to speak against the temple is tantamount to speaking against God himself. This is blasphemy. The historical fate of the temple is actually influenced by the actions of the people.

26:7–19. Opposition to the "temple sermon," with its prediction that the temple will be destroyed, is widespread and intense. Priests and prophets (cf. 26:16), as well as "the people" (26:8), propose the death sentence for what appears to them as both blasphemy and treason. The essentials of a public trial ensue when certain officials take their seat in the New Gate of the temple complex (26:10). Such a location lends gravity to the situation and the charges against the prophet. He will be judged in the context of the temple complex against which he himself has just announced the possibility of judgment (cf. also ch. 20).

Jeremiah defends himself as one in the line of prophets whom the Lord has sent to warn his people about the consequences of disobedience to his instruction (cf. 26:5). He recognizes that he is "in [their] hands" (26:14)—that is, he is on trial—but he warns them that if they execute him, they will incur the judgment of bringing "innocent blood on yourselves" (26:15). There are two implications of this claim.

1. The shedding of innocent blood will bring guilt on the assembly and the place.
2. Jeremiah is thereby reminding the people indirectly that as "innocent" (26:15) of their charges, he is one of the prophets sent by the Lord. To put it in a kind of syllogism: If Jeremiah speaks a word against the temple in the name of the Lord yet is innocent of blasphemy, then the word he speaks must come from the Lord.

This second point, at least, gains a hearing for Jeremiah among some of the people. He has spoken to them in the name of the Lord. He meets, therefore, at least one of Deuteronomy's criteria for judging prophecy (Deut 13). Some elders of the land add that Jeremiah is no different from Micah, who prophesied in Hezekiah's reign that Jerusalem would be destroyed (Jer 6:18 = Mic 3:12). Apparently, they agree that Micah was one of God's servants the prophets. King Hezekiah, they remind the court, did not execute Micah; instead, he feared the Lord, and the Lord relented concerning the announced judgment. The elders conclude that by the present course of action, the people are doing great harm to themselves. This is a tacit recognition of Jeremiah's claim.

In referring to the prophecy of Micah, the people engage in a type of exegesis or interpretation of their religious traditions. Just as Jeremiah drew a comparison between the Jerusalem of his day with the Shiloh of Samuel's day, so they draw a comparison of Jeremiah's message with that of Micah. The elders put the work of Micah and the response of Hezekiah together in a more explicit way than either 2 Kings or 2 Chronicles (the two narratives about Hezekiah's reign) or the book of Micah itself does. The people understand, however, that Hezekiah's reaction to the prophecy was genuine repentance and that God used the unconditional prophecy to move the king and people toward change.

26:20–24. A prophet named Uriah, however, was not given the reprieve accorded Jeremiah. King Jehoiakim's anger against prophets who announced the Lord's judgment on Judah led to the extradition of Uriah from Egypt (where he had fled) and his execution. The narrator notes incidentally that the body of Uriah was thrown in the burial place of the common people. This was intended as a further sign that Uriah was not a real prophet.

Jehoiakim's execution of Uriah thereby brings the judgment of "innocent blood" on himself and his administration. Jeremiah too might have been executed except that an important official, Ahikam son of Shaphan, stood on his side. With Ahikam one gets a glimpse of someone who sympathized with Jeremiah and his prophetic task. His brother later lends to Baruch, Jeremiah's scribe, his office overlooking the temple complex (36:10).

Application. Judgmental prophecy does not reach its final goal when (or even if) a predicted disaster occurs. Micah was a true prophet in that he brought about a change in Judah, although the judgment he announced did not come to pass. Judgmental prophecy is a sharp way of defining who God is, a God who takes his people seriously as covenant partners in his work of bringing justice and redemption to the world. Does God have standards? Yes! Is he committed to the righteousness and integrity of his people? Yes! While God may vindicate his righteousness through judgment of the wicked (and thereby instruct others), such judgment (enacted in history or simply announced) may also serve the larger ends of renewing his people. Both righteousness and renewal are goals of God according to the broader scriptural witness. Attaining these goals through refinement is a consistent pattern of God's dealings with his people.

JEREMIAH 27:1–22

Original Meaning. Jeremiah's message in chapter 27 is that God has given a limited historical sovereignty to Babylon and Nebuchadnezzar. To oppose Babylon at this time is to oppose God's will as Creator and Lord. In this style of presentation, Jeremiah shows himself to be a prophet to the nations (cf. 1:5).

In keeping with prophecies made elsewhere, the end of Babylonian supremacy is also acknowledged. Babylon's end is noted (27:7), as is God's intent to restore the temple vessels taken by Nebuchadnezzar and those of his people now in exile (27:22).

The majority of chapter 27 concerns the work of other prophets who oppose the message of Jeremiah (27:9, 14–18). Jeremiah's years of proclaiming an assault on Jerusalem have proved true, but the city itself has survived. Those who prophesied "peace" have been proved wrong, but the Judean state and its capital are still intact.

Verse 9 provides an intriguing list of mediators and specialists for determining the will of the gods. Five specialists are mentioned: prophets, diviners, interpreters of dreams, mediums, and sorcerers. In times of threat and calamity, such people have plenty of customers. The text does not make any distinction between those practitioners who have sought the Lord's will through their rituals and those who may have consulted another deity. All alike are rejected.

With all of the language of judgment in chapter 27, the concluding verses point to a time when God will bring back temple vessels from Babylon to Jerusalem (27:16–22). Babylon did not take them away because God was impotent—Nebuchadnezzar is God's servant, not vanquisher. The vessels will be returned when God is ready. This concluding comment makes for a transition to the account of Jeremiah's encounter with Hananiah in chapter 28. There too the concern is ostensibly about the temple vessels and related matters, but the deeper issue remains the same.

Application. A modern application of this message must be quick to deny that all peoples who languish under oppressive regimes or that all individuals who suffer emotional and physical exile are bound in these conditions by God's judgment. Scripture gives no blanket warrant for such a claim. Some people (including some Christians) find unpalatable any thought of oppression and exile as God's refining judgment. Scripture gives no warrant for that claim either. The issues with which Jeremiah 27 are concerned are those of God's timing and the larger design of his historical purposes in forming a people for himself. It is simply true that God's timing is often not *our* timing and God's ways are not our ways (Isa 55:8). What Jeremiah calls his contemporaries to believe is that their first impulse is wrong. They have yet to see the error of their ways, and until God has dealt with that, there will be no successful liberation from political oppression or anything else.

JEREMIAH 28:1–17

Original Meaning. *28:1–11.* Hananiah bears all the marks of a prophet of the Lord. His name means the "The LORD is [*or* has been] gracious." When he speaks, his words are prefaced by the announcement, "This is what the LORD Almighty, the God of Israel, says" (28:2). Hananiah prophesies that God will restore to Jerusalem the temple vessels taken by the Babylonians in 597 BC and the exiled Judean king. Hananiah represents one of the unnamed prophets, noted in chapter 27, who are leading the people astray.

Hananiah performs a prophetic symbolic act in breaking the wooden yoke that Jeremiah is wearing. Hananiah believes in the power of the Lord to overcome Babylonian rule and to restore the exiled king Jehoiachin, the other exiles deported in 597 BC, and even the temple vessels taken by the Babylonian army. Throughout the chapter Hananiah is described as "the prophet." Both the terminology and the form of his public address indicate that he is a Yahwistic prophet, perhaps even one who has served God faithfully on previous occasions. Now, however, the content of his oracle is wrong.

Hananiah makes his announcement in the courtyard of the temple complex (28:2–4). On several occasions Jeremiah publicly prophesied in the temple. Jeremiah's encounter with Hananiah in the temple symbolizes their differing viewpoints on what it means that God dwells in the midst of his people. Hananiah seems to think that God's presence means that God's defense of the house and the people is always near at hand.

Jeremiah's first reaction to the oracle of Hananiah ("Amen!" 28:6) seems to indicate that the prophecy impresses him. This reaction is in spite of the fact that Hananiah's proclamation goes against what he himself has prophesied. Jeremiah is open to hearing God speak through Hananiah. By way of first response, Jeremiah reminds Hananiah and their audience in the temple that prophets of the Lord have habitually announced disaster and judgment—the prophet who predicts peace will be vindicated only when that word comes to pass (28:8–9). A prophecy of disaster or judgment, however, is evaluated differently. It is intended to evoke consternation and provoke people to action.

28:12–17. When Hananiah breaks the yoke worn by Jeremiah, Jeremiah does not reply immediately. This is another indication of the seriousness with which he takes Hananiah's prophetic efforts. Subsequently the word of the Lord comes to him, and he confronts Hananiah with the message that Babylon rules with God's explicit assent and that Hananiah has made the people believe a "lie" (28:15). Indeed, Hananiah's words are a rebellion against the will of the Lord. In place of the wooden yoke broken by Hananiah, Jeremiah proclaims that God will now place the people in servitude to Babylon through an iron yoke. In a somber word, Jeremiah announces that Hananiah will die within the year (28:12–17). That death is interpreted as judgment on him and his word.

Application. An authentic prophet cannot overlook the barriers between what God has called his people to be and what they in their human fallibility actually represent. Wherever there is an automatic reliance on God's will to save without an acceptance of his refining judgments as a process of sanctification, there is the real possibility of misrepresenting God to any generation.

JEREMIAH 29:1–32

Original Meaning. *29:1–3.* Jeremiah writes a letter to the Judean community in Babylonian exile, that is, to those Judeans taken into exile with Jehoiachin in 597 BC. Several prophets and diviners among the Judean exiles have provoked the community with announcements of the imminent demise of Babylon and a return of the exiles to Judah (29:8–9, 15, 21–28). Some of the agitators are named (Ahab and Zedekiah, 29:21–22; Shemaiah, 29:24), although nothing else is preserved about them beside what is contained in this chapter. These figures show awareness that Jeremiah's prophecies are known in Babylon.

Chapter 29 contains the same charges against the exilic prophets as was made against Hananiah in chapter 28. They cause the people to trust in a lie (29:9, 21, 23, 31), and their words are, in effect, rebellion against the Lord (29:31–32). Jeremiah's struggle against prophets who prophesy falsely in the Lord's name extends even to the exilic community.

29:4–9. The first line of the letter contains a shocking truth, but it points to the good news to follow. God is the subject of the phrase "all those I carried into exile." Nebuchadnezzar was the historical agent who took the people into exile, but in 29:4 the theological point is made that it is actually the work of God himself. The affirmation is followed by the commands to settle down in exile. Exile is not the end of existence as God's people but the beginning of a new phase of relating to God. Babylon, in effect, is the authority of God over them for a prescribed time. More positively, the people are to seek the prosperity of Babylon because it will affect them as well. Most important, they are to pray for their captors.

29:10–14. These hopeful verses help prepare readers for the section that follows in the prophetic book, a section known to interpreters as the Book of Consolation. Jeremiah notes that the future of the people in exile rests on God's "good promise" (29:10; literally, God's "good word"). In 29:11 the gracious promise is described as plans God has for the people. A tangible element to the future consists in the restoration of the people to their homeland. The restoration, however, is predicated on their seeking God with their whole heart.

29:15–23. Certain prophets believe no more disaster will befall Judah and Jerusalem. Jeremiah describes God as making King Zedekiah and the people in Jerusalem like "poor figs that ... cannot be eaten" (29:17). This metaphor is the same one as given to Jeremiah in 24:1–10. Because the king in Jerusalem and his people refuse to acknowledge God's judgment and refuse to embrace his covenant stipulations, they will be given over to the disasters of the sword and plague. The last part of this section warns the exiles not to listen to these prophetic agitators.

29:24–32. A particular opponent of Jeremiah, Shemaiah the Nehelamite, is singled out for criticism and announced judgment.

Application. There are some surprising things to be learned from and experienced through prayer. Such is the rich testimony of Scripture and saints alike. As a general rule, communities and individuals who do not regularly pray indicate by this that they do not have an adequate theology. The command for Jeremiah not to pray is thus a special case and comes as a radical illustration of the spiritual deadness of the people. Fervent prayer means confidence in God and an openness to his surprising leading. Prayer is a form of applied theology. The issue here is not belief in God but communion with God through prayer. The devil and his assistants do not pray to God, but they believe in his existence.

Prayer is not for the benefit of God, although both praise and petition belong in a relationship with God. Prayer changes both the perceptions of those who pray and their actions. Through prayer one can look at opponents or problems as more than someone or something to be overcome. They can become a means of education and sanctification, the agents through whom one finds growth in relationship with God.

JEREMIAH 30:1–24

Original Meaning. *30:1–3.* Although the text does not provide a specific setting for these prophecies in Jeremiah's life, the command in 30:2 to write them in a scroll suggests that they are to stand as instruction and witness for the future. The primary claim about the future is that the affliction of "Jacob" (30:7, 10, 18) will be removed and the people will be restored to their land and to a better relationship with God.

These prophecies presuppose a unity to God's people that transcends their current political and geographical circumstances. Jeremiah announces a restoration of the covenant relationship between God and his people that assumes a unity for that people (30:22).

30:4–7. This portion of chapter 30 is a bit cryptic with respect to the future turmoil it presupposes. A rhetorical question in 30:6 suggests that the dismay on the part of human beings will not be permanent. The point is that Jacob will be saved from a time of trouble.

30:8–11. The introductory phrase "in that day" (30:8) is a rhetorical device used by prophets to speak of a decisive time in the future. Yokes and bonds will be removed from Jacob, and the people will no longer be enslaved by foreigners. The expression "David their king" in 30:9 likely means someone from David's line. Since no king from David's line ruled Jacob in the postexilic period, this hope finds its ultimate fulfillment in the New Testament proclamation that Jesus is David's greater Son.

The injunction "do not be afraid," addressed to Jacob as God's "servant" (30:10), reminds the reader of the exilic prophecies in the book of Isaiah. Jacob has received judgment, but his judgment has been disciplinary in form. A day of reckoning still awaits the nations.

30:12–17. In these verses humiliated Jerusalem is addressed. The description of her guilt and her helplessness remind the reader/hearer of the book of Lamentations. Judgmental language predominates in these verses, but its effects on Jerusalem are not without merciful limits. There is also announcement that Zion's enemies will be destroyed, and that the city will be restored.

30:18–22. The announcement that Zion will be restored continues in the proclamation that Jacob's fortunes will be reconstituted. There is also an allusion to future leadership that will spring up from among the people (30:21). The concluding verse reiterates the covenant formula (30:22; cf. 24:7).

30:23–24. This surprising section puts the future under the claim of God's righteous judgment and also in the context of divine intentions that cannot be fully grasped. The final verse (30:24) is cryptic. Only the future (literally, "in the latter days"; NIV "in days to come") will reveal the extent of God's purposes. Thus, the earliest recipients of these prophecies are informed that the full significance of these prophecies will only be realized at considerable distance from their time of origin.

Application. A glance at biblical prophecy confirms that God has been faithful to his promises, but his faithfulness comes in surprising ways. It is true that God announced through prophets both the exile of his people and their return. But the return did not usher in the final age. God also announced that a new David would come to lead the people, but not everyone could accept that Jesus was the fulfillment of this hope. In this regard, oftentimes it is at some distance that people of faith can see more clearly what God has done. Perhaps what is more important for people of faith today is to concentrate on the "constants" in the eschatological prophecy of the Bible rather than on a blueprint mentality that believes it can "figure out the future in advance."

What are some of those constants? One is certainly that God is the Judge of all people. In addition, God has called people into fellowship and has promised to be their God. These two things will not change.

JEREMIAH 31:1–40

Original Meaning. *31:1.* "That time" is a reference to a decisive time of divine activity and the resulting changes brought to fruition as a result. How far into the future is not specified by such references; the emphasis is on the *qualitative* changes between the present grim circumstances and the future God has promised.

31:2–6. God's people are addressed in familiar imagery. He reminds them that they can find his favor even in the desert.

The future rebuilding of "Virgin Israel" (31:4) indicates that God has loved them with an "everlasting love" and drawn them back to himself with "unfailing kindness" (*hesed*; 31:3). This latter term refers to commitments that spring from affection and loyalty rather than those prescribed by law.

Zion will play an important role in the future restoration. Those in Ephraim will call to one another with the request to "go up to Zion" (31:6). There they will come to the Lord their God. This is pilgrimage language.

31:7–9. The Lord proposes a song of praise for a saved remnant. Readers should take note of the term *Israel* in context. Verse 9 uses the term to refer specifically to the former Northern Kingdom by way of comparison with Ephraim, God's "firstborn" (31:9). Perhaps the remnant reference here has a particular focus on those exiled by the Assyrians in the eighth century.

31:10–14. The poetry of 31:11 links two terms to describe God's reacquisition of his people. The NIV translates *pdh*, the first verb, as "deliver." The term is used also for the ransom of a slave (Exod 21:8). The second verb is translated by the NIV as "redeem" (Jer 31:11). The word has its roots in family custom, where a relative could use his possessions and influence to extricate other family members from such difficulties as debts or other social obligations.

In its primary sense the passage refers to the new exodus, which God is about to accomplish by bringing his scattered people back to their homes. The language of joy and delight in 31:12–14 is every bit as extravagant as the thorough language of judgment used elsewhere in Jeremiah. "Mourning" will be turned into "gladness" (31:13).

31:15–20. The mourning of the promised land for the loss of "her" (31:15) children is described through the metaphor of Rachel weeping. Rachel died in childbirth with Benjamin and was buried between Bethel and Bethlehem (Gen 35:16–26). A monument was built to mark her tomb. Jeremiah's reference to weeping in Ramah (meaning "hill" in Hebrew) apparently refers to the place of this monument. Rachel's children are coming home. This means that there is a hope for Rachel's future.

Verses 18–20 in Jeremiah 31 can be taken as a separate oracle from 31:15–17. The speaker changes from Rachel to Ephraim. The sentiment, however, in these verses is similar. The Israelites who have sinned and been cast from their land are personified in Ephraim, who confesses his failures. God tenderly accepts his repentance, describing Ephraim as his "dear son" (31:20; cf. 31:9), a child for whom his heart yearns. God's parental mercy is paramount in these verses.

31:21–26. This section is combined of both poetry and prose. The poetry (31:21–22) calls for highway markers to be erected so that "Virgin Israel" (31:21) can find her way home. The text describes her return to her homeland as a new thing that God will create—"the woman will return to the man" (31:22). The phrase points to a surprising and compassionate act of God in making new life possible for those who were estranged in exile.

Restoration of the people is the theme of 31:23–25. While this theme is familiar in the immediate context, it is still important to note that God is the subject of the verbs "bring back," "refresh," and "satisfy" (31:23, 25). He is the chief actor in the drama of the return.

31:27–30. Not only will God pluck up and destroy Judah, but he will also build and plant Israel and Judah. The use of both names conveys totality (cf. 31:31). The form of their life together is not stated. Furthermore, the future will bring an end to the complaints that corporate judgment is unjust (31:29–30). Each person will indeed bear his or her own sins in God's judgment of the people.

31:31–34. This well-known passage, with its proclamation of a new covenant, is a summary of Jeremiah's message. It moves from the righteous judgment that has come on Israel and Judah because of their disobedience to the restoration of God's people in a new relationship with him. God's torah ("law," the verbal expression of his will) will become a constituent part of a person/people when God writes it on their hearts.

The objects of God's restoration are "the people of Israel and . . . the people of Judah" (31:31). As in the previous section (31:27), these terms denote inclusivity as referring to all of God's people. They do not disqualify any other peoples among the nations from being included, but such possibilities are not mentioned either. What is "new" (31:31) about the new covenant is not the covenant partner but the quality of the community created by God's amazing acts.

The imagery is the writing of God's instruction on the human heart rather than on the tablets of stone. Knowledge of God, therefore, is internalized. Furthermore, the ability of sin to disrupt the relationship is made obsolete by the astounding announcement that God will not remember sins and their effects on the relationship.

This famous "new covenant" passage proclaims that an ultimate restoration of the covenant relationship between God and his people includes the transformation of corporate existence. In essence, it is a summary of all that God will accomplish in the renewing of his covenant relationship with his people.

31:35–40. The fidelity of God to his people is cast by analogy with the fixed order of the cosmos. Just as the order of the cosmos is sure, so is God's commitment to his people. The final claim is for the rebuilding of Jerusalem, but it is not a simple rebuilding of the city that is envisioned. The city, like the people of the new covenant, is to be transformed and will never again be overthrown.

Application. Jeremiah 31 is the voice of an inspired spiritual ancestor who spoke to his contemporaries about the shape that God's action would take in their lives and that of their descendants (e.g., return from exile, a purified worship, knowledge of forgiveness). Perhaps in the present we can think of things in our lives that are signs of God at work, things whose shape and function portray the work of God. These things may be personal; they may concern the family; they may be part of the life of fellowship one enjoys among friends and in the activities of a congregation. Signs of redemption should point not only to what has already been accomplished in Christ but also to what still lies ahead. There is always a future tense to the life of believers.

JEREMIAH 32:1–44

Original Meaning. *32:1–15.* The historical setting of chapter 32 is clear. Babylon has besieged Jerusalem for a second time, and Jeremiah is confined in the city by a royal guard. Apparently, the Babylonians began the siege late in the year 588 BC.

Jeremiah's continual prophecies about the sovereignty of Babylon over Judah and Jerusalem have been perceived as seditious, and as a result he is imprisoned or confined on several occasions. His announcement to Zedekiah here (32:3–4) that Jerusalem and the king will be handed over to Babylon is essentially repeated in 34:2–3.

Jeremiah purchases some family property. A particularly significant element of what defined most families was its patrimony or its inheritance. This property, unlike perhaps other things the family possessed, was not to be sold to those outside of the clan (the kin of the family). Thus, when there were economic difficulties or other types of hardship, the property could be used as collateral and sold to members within the clan (or even tribe), but it was not to be alienated permanently from the family of possession.

According to Jeremiah 32:7 the prophet has the right of redemption to the property owned by Hanamel. His right comes by virtue of family ties. Needless to say, a time of siege is not the time to be buying property. Whatever the specific reason behind the request of Hanamel, such a request reflects a time of desperation as families seek whatever means they can to keep life and limb together.

Jeremiah's purchase of Hanamel's property becomes a vehicle, a symbolic act, intended to illustrate his message. At one of the darkest moments in Judah's history, when the Babylonian reduction of the country is in an advanced state and the successful siege of Jerusalem seems merely a matter of time, Jeremiah purchases the property because there will be a future restoration to their land after the pain of defeat and the trauma of exile (32:15).

Baruch assists Jeremiah in carrying out the purchase and the preparation of the necessary records. He is a scribe (36:32); that is, the preparation, reading, and preservation of documents are skills of his profession. Baruch will assist Jeremiah in the preparing of a scroll of prophecies in chapter 36. The preservation of the purchase documents is described in some detail. In time to come they will serve as verification of Jeremiah's prophecy that land and fields will again be bought.

32:16–25. In a prayer Jeremiah praises God as creator, as merciful and righteous judge in the historical process, and as the true God who chose Israel as his own. Also, he acknowledges that the Babylonian siege is God's work. This prayer ends abruptly with the statement that God has commanded Jeremiah to go and buy the field.

32:26–44. God speaks to Jeremiah after the prophet's prayer concludes. His communication is a summary of what Jeremiah has proclaimed for years, that a righteous judgment will befall Judah and Jerusalem and that it will proceed not from God's weakness over against the powerful Babylonian deities, but from his intention to discipline and purge his people. Considerable space is devoted to the articulation of God's anger at the failures of the people. Verse 37 describes God's response as "furious anger and great wrath."

In addition to the articulation of wrath, God reiterates the significance of Jeremiah's land purchase as a sign of the Lord's resolve to restore and bless his people. Both current calamity and future blessing are the work of God.

God's announced future holds forth the miraculous promises of an "everlasting covenant" (32:40), a changed heart for the people (32:39), and life again in the promised land (32:41). These prose promises are related to the poetic announcements in chapters 30–31, which also concern the people's future.

Application. Redemption always costs something. This is a truth that should never be ignored. Whether it is the purchase of property or a theory to explain the atonement, the whole concept of redemption rests in the dynamics of a gift on behalf of those unable to gain something for themselves. For redemption to work, it requires those who have to give on behalf of those who don't. It is usually easier to argue about the faults of those who don't have rather than to celebrate that God has provided the opportunity to give so that others might live. Evangelism and social ethics both work best when they follow the scriptural pattern of joyful giving without concern for an accounting of merits. It is amazing what can be "redeemed" by the simple giving of talents bestowed by the Lord.

JEREMIAH 33:1–26

Original Meaning. *33:1–3.* The emphasis in this chapter is on God speaking (33:2, 10, 12, 17, 19, 23), almost as if the divine commentary that concluded chapter 32 is picked up again, with continued emphasis on the future turning of Judah's fortune.

33:4–9. God reiterates his promise to redeem Judah and Jerusalem. The turning fortunes of the people are here described as God's "healing" them (33:6). Healing also includes forgiveness, along with such tangible signs of restoration as resettlement in the land of promise, rebuilding Jerusalem ("this city" in 33:9), and security while dwelling there. These promises reiterate those made in previous chapters. Other peoples will learn to fear God because of Judah's restoration. Here again the theme of Jeremiah as "prophet to the nations" (Jer 1:5) comes to the fore.

33:10–13. These verses continue to emphasize a joyful future for the people as a reversal of the judgment on and the misery suffered by Judah. Cities in Judah will again be inhabited. The temple will again have worship. Verse 11 contains a familiar refrain from the temple liturgy: "Give thanks to the LORD Almighty, for the LORD is good; his love [*hesed*] endures forever." This is the characteristic phrase of the temple singers appointed by David (1 Chr 16:41) and is known from the praises of the Psalter (Pss 106:1; 118:1, 29; 136; cf. 100:4–5). For someone who had been as critical about the temple as Jeremiah, such a text reminds us that his criticisms presuppose no enduring hostility to the temple, only toward its misuse and corruption.

33:14–18. There is more than one chronological moment to the "good promise" (33:14) that God provides. These verses are introduced by the prophetic formula for the future: "The days are coming" (33:14). Both Israel and Judah are included in the future transformation. In addition to the corporate restoration of the people, Jeremiah announces that "a righteous Branch . . . from David's line" (33:15) will arise and execute justice and righteousness (see also 23:5–6). This promise is messianic in that it depends on the promises made by God to David's family. Jerusalem will even receive a new symbolic name: "The LORD Our Righteous Savior" (33:16).

33:19–22. The work of Davidic rule and that of priestly ministry will not cease. These announcements indicate that God's promises (when finally realized in their completeness) will never end. God will undergird two fundamental institutions of the people in perpetuity. Someone from David's line will be head of the people, and descendants of Levi, the priestly tribe, will always be available to officiate in public worship.

There is an allusion to the promises made to Abraham. He was promised descendants like the stars of heaven and the sand on the seashore (Gen 15:5; 22:17); here God promises innumerable descendants to the Davidic line and the Levitical priests.

33:23–26. God has heard the despair and cynicism of his people. Those who conclude that God has simply rejected them are wrong. God has not broken his covenant with day and night (cf. 33:20), nor has he rejected his people. The use of covenant language in this context is appropriate. A covenant (*berit*) is a solemn promise often undergirded by an oath. God's covenant with day and night is not an agreement with those inanimate parties but the expression of his sovereign resolve to maintain a beneficent order. Because of his mercy, the people still have a future.

Application. Contemporary Christians, particularly in the West, may find this dynamic an odd one: Lose your freedom and find out more about God; be in despair and find yourself instructed about the power and mercy of God. God often finds an opportunity to reconstitute people's horizons about themselves when they are suddenly limited in their freedom. So it was for Judah, so it was for John on the isle of Patmos and the suffering churches of Asia Minor.

Charles Colson is a modern example of someone whose freedom was taken from him by the state because he had broken the law. While there, Colson dealt with more than the humiliation of imprisonment; he wrestled with his sinfulness before God and emerged from prison with Christian zeal. The lives of many prisoners and congregations have been dramatically changed because of his witness. God's promised future has the power to change the present circumstances of people as they yield themselves to the leading of the Holy Spirit.

God's promise that someone from David's line will reign over his people is made eternal in the resurrection of his Son (born of the house of David). He is the ultimate head of God's people. Truth and reconciliation can take lasting shape only if they are understood by people to be joined in Christ, the head of the church.

JEREMIAH 34:1–22

Original Meaning. *34:1–5.* The fate of Zedekiah and of the city and nation are bound together. The statements about the future should be understood as announcements contingent on the reactions of king and people to the Babylonian siege. Verses 2–3 voice a familiar word of judgment on the city and its king. Their present course of disaster will lead (as it were) inevitably to a tragic conclusion. Verses 4–5, likewise, should be understood as contingent on some response of Zedekiah, even at this late date. These prophecies indicate the possible mitigation of the king's threatening circumstances.

Later on, Zedekiah was captured while fleeing the besieged city. His last days were spent in darkness because the Babylonians blinded him (39:5–7). One should note the information provided in 34:21. It is a commentary (an update) on the word to Zedekiah in 34:4–5, perhaps anticipating the king's continuing recalcitrance and his sorry fate. Zedekiah's actions condemned him to the same fate as the rebellious city.

34:6–7. These verses seem to be an incidental comment regarding the timing of Jeremiah's communication to Zedekiah. As a result of archaeological work, however, they have become an interesting commentary on the formation of the book. According to 34:6–7, the two cities of Azekah and Lachish were still holding out against the Babylonian forces when Jeremiah made his prophecies to Zedekiah. During the 1930s an expedition excavated at the site of Lachish. Near the gate and near the interior fortress the excavation team found several ostraca (letters written on pottery shards), dating from the time of Jeremiah. One of the letters states that the signals from Azekah, located a few kilometers to the north of Lachish, could no longer be seen.

34:8–22. King Zedekiah had initiated a covenant with his subjects regarding their Judean slaves, that they were to be set free. The reason is not stated, but most likely the dire circumstances of the Babylonian siege lay behind the ceremony. After the release of the slaves, circumstances apparently improved enough so that the solemn oath of the covenant was broken, and the slaves were taken back by their owners. Apparently, there was a temporary lifting of the siege (cf. 37:7–8). This is the best interpretation of the comment in 34:21–22 that the Lord will "bring . . . back" the Babylonian army that "has withdrawn."

No context or background is given for the first acquisitions of the slaves, but their enslavement is primarily debt related. Debts and warfare were the two most common reasons for someone to become a slave in antiquity. In a caustic response to the events, God (through Jeremiah) alludes to the debt-slavery laws of Deuteronomy 15. In the indictment for breaking their word and re-enslaving the slaves, the people are also accused of breaking the covenant God made with them when he brought them out of Egypt.

The allusion to Deuteronomy 15 in Jeremiah 34:14–15 is important to understanding God's anger over the injustice done to the slaves, since the Pentateuchal legislation links the obligation of justice toward slaves with the content of the covenant stipulations given to their ancestors. Jeremiah underscores this same dynamic. The ancestors of the Judeans were slaves in Egypt, and God brought them out of the house of slavery. God has not gone back on his good word and work, so neither should the slave owners in Judah.

If the people can "proclaim freedom" for the slaves, only to take them back when it is convenient, then God will "proclaim freedom" (34:15) for Judah and Jerusalem. Readers will detect the sarcasm in this proclamation easily enough. God's freedom proclamation to Judah and Jerusalem is "freedom" (34:17) to fall to Babylon. In this announcement of judgment, the punishment to come fits the crime. There is a link between crime and punishment.

Verses 18–19 refer to the owners and officials who pass between the parts of the calf; this probably indicates a self-imprecation and promissory oath as part of the solemn covenant ceremony. The best parallel to the report comes in Genesis 15:7–21, where Abram prepares for a sacrificial ceremony by slaying the proper animals and dividing their carcasses. In such ceremonies, those who walked between the parts of the slain animals enacted symbolically their passing through death and dismemberment as a pledge to keep their word. "Walked between the pieces" (34:19) thus became a symbolic act to bind the word of promise as an imprecatory oath. Since the Judeans passed between the parts of the calf when making an oath to free the slaves but subsequently did not keep their word, they themselves will be like the sacrificial animals.

Application. One wonders what later historians will say of the tumultuous social changes that have swept through much of the Western world (and affected other parts of the globe as well) in the last half of the twentieth century. Surely the accelerated pace of change itself will be seen as one of the remarkable characteristics of the period. Perhaps future generations will be making the necessary adaptations to cope with the pace of societal changes. Change seems to dictate for many people that they keep their options open, that they try to remain flexible, and that they make no commitments unless an easy point of extrication is identified. Perhaps the Christians of the future will have the courage of conviction to point out that promises, divine and human, are the rock on which all relationships stand.

JEREMIAH 35:1–19

Original Meaning. *35:1–11.* Uncertainty remains over how best to describe the Rekabites. Some scholars have seen them as an anti-Canaanite faction and also as conservative representatives of a nomadic ideal from Israel's past. This is due mainly to their rejection of wine, agriculture, and houses (cf. 35:6–10), plus the account in 2 Kings 10 that links Jonadab, the founder of the Rekabites, with Jehu's revolt against the Omrides. Others have seen them more as an alternative community or commercial guild associated with the design and building of chariots.

Verse 3 raises an interesting question with respect to the formation of the Rekabite community. Jeremiah reports that he went to Jaazaniah, the head of the community, to offer them the opportunity to drink wine. That community is comprised of Jaazaniah's brothers and sons, "the whole family of the Rekabites" (35:3). One cannot tell from this description whether the community is literally comprised of Jaazaniah's biological extended family or whether the kinship terminology of brothers and sons serves to identify a close-knit community. Jonadab, the founder of the Rekabites, is described as the group's "forefather" in 35:8. Literally, the term can be translated as "father" (*'ab* in Hebrew).

Whatever the origin of the Rekabites, their constancy regarding their community's values becomes a prophetically appropriated sign against the lack of integrity in Judah and Jerusalem. According to their self-designation, Rekabites do not live in houses, plant crops, or drink wine. Instead, they live in tents (and apparently trade goods for grain and other agricultural products). Their presence in Jerusalem is the result of pressure put on the Judean countryside by the Babylonian army and their Aramean companions (35:11). Jerusalem is a place of refuge for them because of its stout walls. This indicates that otherwise the Rekabites would normally have lived in tents outside the city in obedience to the command of their founder, Jonadab.

The prophetic symbolism of the account is accentuated by the scene of wine cups set before the Rekabites in the chambers of Hanan's sons (35:4; their family was founded by Igdaliah, "the man of God" = prophet). Their reply—that they do not drink wine—is narrated for the effect such a scene will have on the larger community of Judah and Jerusalem.

35:12–19. God instructs Jeremiah to report the encounter with the Rekabites to the people of Judah and Jerusalem. The fact that Jeremiah has invited the Rekabites to meet him at a room near the temple (35:4) ensures that they are observed by other members of the community. The incident contrasts Rekabite obedience to their community standards with the faithlessness of Judeans to theirs. It is part of a history of disobedience, for Judah has consistently disobeyed the word of God's servants, the prophets (35:15). The prophetic communication, therefore, concludes that a call to repentance is neither timely nor warranted. God spoke (in the past), but Judah did not listen; he called, but they did not answer.

The final word of the chapter is addressed to the Rekabites. They are promised that they will always have someone to "serve" (35:19) the Lord; that is, they will never be forgotten by God, and their place with him is secure.

Application. Several things can be said about the nature of faithful witness on the basis of Jeremiah 35 (and the book of Jeremiah as a whole).

1. Faith in God is expressed by living in community with other believers. The community of faith (i.e., the church) helps give shape not only to what one believes but how one lives responsibly as a result of faith.
2. God has called people to lead public lives of obedience to his revealed will. Obedience is not just pleasing to God; it can be an effective witness to the larger culture in which believers find themselves.
3. The exercise of the Christian faith may entail giving up certain practices common to a culture for the sake of the gospel.

JEREMIAH 36:1–32

Original Meaning. *36:1–7.* Jehoiakim's fourth year (36:1) is 605 BC. In that year Nabopolassar, the ruler of Babylon, died; his young son, Nebuchadnezzar, ascended the Babylonian throne, and his forces defeated the Egyptians in battle at Carchemish. Since Jehoiakim had been placed on the throne in Judah by the Egyptians (2 Kgs 23:34–37), this defeat was potentially an ominous sign for him and the Judean leadership. Jeremiah 25:1 bears the same date as the heading to a chapter of judgmental sayings against Jerusalem and Judah.

Just why Jeremiah had been banned from preaching in the temple is a mystery (36:5). Since his words were often judgmental and divisive, a restriction on his preaching in the temple precincts could have come at almost any time in the reign of Jehoiakim. Possibly the temple sermon Jeremiah delivered at the beginning of Jehoiakim's reign (26:1; cf. ch. 7) led to his restriction from delivering oracles at that site. It should be recalled that Jeremiah narrowly escaped a lynch mob at that time. Ahikam, the son of Shaphan, stood on the prophet's side in that setting (26:24). In the narrative of chapter 36, other descendants of Shaphan are instrumental in Baruch's delivery of Jeremiah's words (36:10–12; cf. 29:3). The influential family of Shaphan appears sympathetic to Jeremiah, and its members may be part of the largely anonymous group who have preserved the words of the prophet.

Baruch is a scribe (36:26); that is, his profession is in recording and interpreting documents. In a way he is a disciple of Jeremiah. Since Jeremiah is restricted from preaching in the temple precincts, Baruch is commissioned with delivering the prophet's message in the temple. This comes, however, after Baruch has copied Jeremiah's oracles onto a scroll. He knows the material intimately and is able to represent the prophet in his absence.

Here readers encounter another theme of the chapter. The written scroll of Jeremiah's prophecies is an adequate substitute for the living voice of the prophet. Baruch's brother Seraiah also assisted Jeremiah in delivering prophecy to Babylon (51:59–64). Probably scribal activity was a family profession; both the father and grandfather of Baruch and Seraiah are named (51:59), as if the family and its work were well known in Judah.

Jeremiah hopes that the hard words he wants delivered to the people will be a catalyst for repentance and change (36:7). Ominously, the possibility of repentance is not mentioned in the summary statements of 36:27–31. One function of the narrative in chapter 36 is to confirm the obduracy of Judean leadership and even the collective will of the people.

36:8–19. In the ninth month of Jehoiakim's fifth year (i.e., December 604 BC), a solemn fast is declared, and many people in Judah stream to the temple to pray (36:9). This is a year or so later than the chronological notice in 36:1. The solemn fast becomes the occasion for Baruch to deliver the prophetic message of Jeremiah. At this time Nebuchadnezzar's army was on the Palestinian coast, and the Philistine city of Ashkelon was sacked by the Babylonians. The text does not say why the fast is called, so the link with the ominous arrival of the Babylonians is speculative, but some perceived threat prompts this assembly. Another possibility is the effects of a prolonged drought.

A close reading of the text shows that the words of the scroll delivered orally by Baruch are accorded the same prophetic authority as that of Jeremiah. Baruch is asked in an initial interrogation whether these are the words from the mouth of Jeremiah; he replies that they are (36:17–18). Pointedly, the narrator (Baruch?) gives no account of the people's reaction to Baruch's oral recital in 36:10. He seems to assume that the words are familiar and that the people have not responded as hoped, although the words of the scroll aimed for repentance (36:3). The only one described as hearing anything at the temple is Micaiah the son of Gemariah, the son of Shaphan, who "heard all the words of the LORD from the scroll" (36:11). This detail is not coincidental. The chain of authority runs backward from Baruch to Jeremiah to the Lord. The prophetic word rejected by the people is ultimately that of the Lord.

It is unlikely that the officials named in 36:10–14 are simply listed for verisimilitude. On the one hand, they represent Judean leadership. On the other, some of them represent people sympathetic to Jeremiah. Gemariah has taken a big risk in allowing Baruch to use his office as the location for preaching to the crowds in the temple courtyard (36:10). This suggests that he, like his sibling Ahikam (26:24), has heard something authentic in Jeremiah's preaching.

After hearing for themselves the contents of the prophetic scroll, the officials request that Baruch and Jeremiah go into hiding. In taking that advice, Baruch and Jeremiah may have preserved their lives until the turmoil around the oracles dies down a bit.

36:20–26. The callous rejection of Jeremiah's words by Jehoiakim is described in a manner intended to remind readers of his father, Josiah, and to contrast father and son. When Josiah heard the words of the Torah, he tore his garments as a sign that he recognized the authority of the prophetic scroll to judge him and his nation (2 Kgs 22). In contemptuous fashion, Jehoiakim cuts the scroll in pieces and does not rend his garments (Jer 36:23–24).

The use of a knife to cut the scroll probably indicates a scroll that contained more than one piece of tanned animal skin. Typically, sections of tanned animal skins were sewn together to make a continuous roll for written contents. The easiest way for Jehoiakim (or anyone else) to cut a scroll would be to slice along the join of two sections where thread held them together. If this is correct, this also indicates that Baruch has copied a number of different oracles for presentation to the temple crowds.

36:27–32. Jehoiakim and Judah's fate is sealed by their indifference and even hostility to the prophetic word. According to 26:20–23, Jehoiakim became upset with the preaching activity of Uriah and sent a delegation to Egypt to arrest him. Subsequently, Uriah was executed for his prophetic activity. Baruch's reading of Jeremiah's scroll is the second recorded time that the prophet's words have been given at the temple and incite consternation; the delegation to arrest Baruch and Jeremiah may not itself have been empowered to execute the two men, but had they been found, the arrest might have ended in execution. The narrator notes, almost in passing, that the Lord had hidden them.

One supposes that the Lord's command to compile another scroll comes while Jeremiah and Baruch are hiding from the royal officials searching for them. Along with the command comes a revelation to Jeremiah that judgment will come particularly on Jehoiakim and that it will be extended broadly to Judah and Jerusalem. No mention is made of any hope that they will repent. The second scroll is longer than the first. Its contents are not otherwise revealed except to say that the additions are similar to what was included in the first scroll.

Application. The account of the prophetic scroll in Jeremiah 36 illustrates the old English word "heedless." Neither people nor king were prepared to heed (i.e., hear and obey) the word of the Lord. Thus, at one level the account becomes a testimony to the consequences of heedlessness. But at another level, there were those who did heed the word of the Lord. They preserved the account for posterity, so that God's judging word from the past might be God's correcting and instructive word to future generations. It is the nature of God's word that it always accomplishes its purpose. This question is valid for all of us today: Who recognizes the judging, correcting, and restorative nature of God's word?

JEREMIAH 37:1–21

Original Meaning. *37:1–2.* According to 37:1, Zedekiah was placed on the throne in Judah by the Babylonians. These two verses are actually a summary statement of Zedekiah's eleven years of reign. Details of his kingship and of his relationship with Jeremiah are picked up in 37:3 and continue through the end of chapter 38.

37:3–10. An Egyptian army is moving toward Judah in a manner intended to threaten the Babylonian army. According to 37:4, Jeremiah was not confined or imprisoned during all of

Zedekiah's reign, but the rest of chapter 37 confirms that he was confined in a variety of circumstances.

Verses 6–10 report on a revelation given Jeremiah that he is to transmit to Zedekiah: Babylon will succeed in taking the city. The Egyptian army will not turn the tide of the Babylonian intent to take Judah and Jerusalem.

37:11–15. The appearance of the Egyptian army causes a temporary lifting of the Babylonian siege. According to the summary statement in 37:12, Jeremiah wants to go to the Benjamite tribal area in order to get his share of the property. The guards of the city are suspicious that the prophet wants to leave the city in order to desert to the Babylonians. He is beaten and placed in confinement.

37:16–21. Zedekiah appears to be a classic case of a divided mind under pressure. On the one hand, he desperately seeks guidance, including his requests that Jeremiah pray to God (37:3) and that Jeremiah mediate God's will to him (37:17). On the other hand, the word of the Lord causes him consternation and demands what his self-serving nature will not allow. Zedekiah mistreats the very prophet he approaches for help.

Jeremiah is confined to a house belonging to a scribe (37:15) and later to a place associated with a guardhouse (37:21). Neither place appears to be a prison in the modern sense of the word, although Jeremiah's personal circumstances are painful. He is beaten at the scribe's house, and his rations in the guardhouse quarters are minimal. In 37:18 Jeremiah inquires of the king in what way he has sinned against the king or the people that he should be treated in this manner. The implied point is that he has told the truth and that Zedekiah is persecuting him for it.

Application. It is important to remember how easy it is to assault the messenger rather than to listen carefully and to learn humbly from him or her. It is more convenient to reject an "unfriendly" assessment than it is to look in the mirror of God's Word.

Paradoxically, there is also hope in this disquieting account. Even in judging Zedekiah and the people, God is still at work to keep his promises. Zedekiah's family (i.e., that of David) will still be privileged to play a crucial role in God's economy. Moreover, what most Judeans think is an awful tragedy—the fall of the state and the resulting exile—is also the seedbed of new beginnings.

JEREMIAH 38:1–28A

Original Meaning. *38:1–6.* The men named in 38:1 are "officials" (38:4). These officials have much autonomy in dealing with Jeremiah, as Zedekiah concedes in 38:5. The officials are angry with Jeremiah because his words about Babylonian supremacy are "discouraging" (literally, "weaken the hands"; 38:4). This is not a common phrase in the Old Testament, but it occurs in a secular letter from the time of Jeremiah, where it describes the effect of bad news. The officials lower Jeremiah into a cistern that has mud but no water. This is vindictive treatment by his opponents. Indirectly this comment tells the reader about the desperate circumstances of the siege. An empty cistern indicates water scarcity. Jeremiah is trapped in the cistern and unable to move easily or to rest.

38:7–13. One of the palace officials, a eunuch from Ethiopia, courageously approaches Zedekiah to overturn the order consigning Jeremiah to a slow and painful death. He secures an agreement from the king (who is holding court in the gate of Benjamin) and goes with thirty men to pull the weakened prophet from the muddy cistern.

One gains an idea of how weak the prophet has become from the description of Ebed-Melek's manner of extricating him from the mire. The men provide some worn-out rags to place under Jeremiah's arms so that the rope harness will not injure him. Jeremiah is freed from his sentence of slow death, but he is still kept under confinement with Zedekiah's guards. The actions of Ebed-Melek later receive a commendation of God and the promise of personal deliverance when the Babylonians finally take the city (see 39:15–18).

38:14–28. The chapter concludes with the notice that Jeremiah remains in the court of the guard (cf. 37:20–21; 39:11–14) until the day that Jerusalem is captured. But Zedekiah is not through with the prophet. As in earlier cases (21:1; 37:3), the king seeks spiritual advice from him. Initially, Jeremiah seeks assurance that he will not be killed, and the king swears not to hand the prophet over to those who want to kill him.

Readers learn from the narrative that Zedekiah is as worried about his personal safety and future as he is about the city and the state. Jeremiah sets before the king the alternatives of surrendering and trusting the Lord for his safety or holding out and seeing the Babylonians victorious. The latter scenario includes the burning of the city (38:23).

Zedekiah asks Jeremiah not to reveal their conversation. This is another indication of the king's divided mind and his vacillation with respect to listening to the prophet. One gains the impression from all this that both Jeremiah and Zedekiah are the subject of rumor and conspiracy, and that Zedekiah has precious few people whom he can trust. The chapter concludes with the comment that Jeremiah remains in the courtyard of the guard until the Babylonians take the city. This last comment sets the stage for the narrative in chapter 39.

Application. Fear does strange things to people. Some people are frozen by fear, unable to make a decision because they cannot clearly see a resolution. Not to decide on a course of action may be prudent, just as staying a familiar course can be the better of options, but neither is satisfactory when God has called his people to accountability and to action. In the case of Zedekiah, not to act decisively and obediently to Jeremiah's prophetic word means simply keeping on with the old and tired policies of failure. In his case, not to decide is actually to make a fateful decision.

God's providence is so designed that people may inevitably face their fears and choose among difficult options. This is not necessarily bad news. The issue is first discernment and then trusting God, who sends such matters our way. The Gospel narratives provide us with portraits of a Jesus who spoke his word in season and stood by his claims. It is true that he prayed for the cup of suffering and shame to be taken away (Luke 22:39–44). Yet what remained paramount for Jesus (and remains so for us) is the discerning of God's will. And once his will is discerned, trust in God is a conviction about life and our place in it.

JEREMIAH 38:28B–39:18

Original Meaning. *38:28b–39:7.* The first line of this section introduces the account of Jerusalem's fall, but the narrative quickly shifts to a description of Zedekiah's fate. To put it succinctly, his fate is essentially the same as that of the city and people (39:4–7). He attempts to escape the consequences of Jerusalem's fall by fleeing to the Jordan Valley. He is caught by the Babylonian army with gruesome results.

39:8–10. These verses describe succinctly the actual burning of the city. Named in particular are the royal palace and houses of the people. The walls are also pulled down. Nothing is mentioned about the temple here.

Nebuzaradan, a high Babylonian official, organizes much of the surviving population into a group for exile. Some of the poorest people in Judah (probably those who do not own land) are left to tend the land. Thus, the former state of Judah is not totally depopulated, and the Babylonians will be able to extract tribute from those who remain to tend the land.

39:11–14. Nebuchadnezzar himself orders that Jeremiah be released from confinement. Reasons for his release are not cited, but Jeremiah's confinement serves no Babylonian purpose, and perhaps Nebuchadnezzar has heard secondhand that a Judean prophet proclaimed his supremacy. Moreover, the Babylonians turn him over to Gedaliah son of Ahikam, son of Shaphan. In the next chapter we learn that Nebuchadnezzar will appoint Gedaliah as governor of Judah. Here we see again the illustrious family of Shaphan, whose members had been supportive of Jeremiah. Gedaliah's fate also mirrors the Judean tragedy, even though his personal commitments are closer to those of Jeremiah than Zedekiah's.

39:15–18. The narrator provides a retrospective account of an oracle Jeremiah received about Ebed-Melek, the eunuch who saved his life during the darker moments of the siege. God has granted Ebed-Melek his life. Even though he is an official of the despised Zedekiah, he will not be handed over to the Babylonians.

Application. Is there such a thing as an *expected* tragedy? So often what makes an event or circumstance tragic is its unexpectedness. Certainly, readers of the Old Testament can point to the account of Jerusalem's fall and say that the city's fate was announced beforehand. A tragedy that is anticipated and yet comes to pass is, in some sense, doubly tragic, because if it is anticipated, there should be ways of mitigating its harshness.

In Judah's case, we may question why one would even call such an event a tragedy rather than simply a reflection of God's judgment. It is really both, and therein lies something for us to think about. Tragedy suggests that an event or process does not have to turn out that way. In theological terms it suggests that God may have preferred it otherwise (cf. Ezek 18:32), that he took no pleasure in the fall—indeed, that he sent a string of prophets to try and turn Judah from its self-destructive folly. Whether tragedy or judgment, the circumstances of Judah's fall were both allowed and then used by God in the history of his people.

Yet there can be a personal word from God that comes in the midst of tragedy or judgment. One sees it in the gift of life to Ebed-Melek. Such a word just comes. Is it expected? Hardly so, if one calls such a thing a word of grace. Grace happens, but it cannot be presumed upon. God is the God of new beginnings as well as the God of historical destiny. How judgment and new life work out in God's economy is what gives shape to the Christian life and confirms God as Lord of all circumstances.

JEREMIAH 40:1–41:18

Original Meaning. *40:1–6.* Nebuzaradan, a Babylonian official, addresses Jeremiah (39:9), stating that God has given Judah and Jerusalem into the hands of Babylon in order to judge them. This may sound strange to modern readers, but many people in antiquity affirmed the power of a local deity in its sphere of influence. There is no reason to suspect sarcasm or insincerity on the part of Nebuzaradan.

Jeremiah is also given a choice whether to go to Babylon or remain in the land with Gedaliah. From the point of view of personal security, it would likely be better for Jeremiah to accompany Nebuzaradan to Babylon, but he chooses to remain with the remnant in the land. In this choice the prophet signals a commitment to the land and to renewal, just like his symbolic purchase of property during the Babylonian siege of Jerusalem

(32:1–15). So, Jeremiah becomes a member of the remnant band associated with Gedaliah. He seems to know nothing about the plot against the governor. That Jeremiah is given provisions and a "present" by the Babylonians (40:5) is recognition on their part that the prophet predicted their success.

40:7–16. Remnants of Judeans begin to gather around Gedaliah at Mizpah, about five miles north of Jerusalem. Included in the group are Ishmael son of Nethaniah and Johanan son of Kareah, two people whose actions will affect decisively the fortunes of both the little province and the prophet Jeremiah. Johanan is a member of the Judean army but also seemingly well-connected to the remaining officials in Judah. Ishmael is related to the royal family of Judah (41:1). Johanan discovers that Baalis, king of the Ammonites (40:14), has concocted a plot with Ishmael to assassinate Gedaliah. Indeed, Johanan apprises Gedaliah of his knowledge, but Gedaliah does not believe the report.

Verses 10–11 remind us of the continuing impact of the Babylonian siege. When the Babylonian army first marched into the area, a number of Judeans had fled their homes to take up residence in surrounding territories. Now that the Babylonians have completed their siege and the main elements of the army returned to Babylon, many of these Judeans now return to see what remains of their former property. Upon doing so, they also find that additional property needs tending.

All in all, it is a precarious time for those who remain in the land. They can be called the "remnant of Judah" (40:15), and the tasks of bringing corporate life back to a more even keel are daunting. Gedaliah may well have been able to represent the interests of the remnant to the Babylonian provincial administration. Unfortunately, this will never be known because of his tragic and untimely demise.

41:1–3. Chapter 41 narrates quickly Ishmael's treacherous murder of Gedaliah. The massacre is both a strike against the Babylonians and an attempt by Ishmael to usurp power. In addition to Gedaliah, Ishmael murders "all the men of Judah" (41:3), the Judean men who work with Gedaliah in administrative affairs. Verses 10 and 16 report the survival of some persons from the town of Mizpah.

41:4–18. The day after the murder at Mizpah, a group of pilgrims from Shiloh, Shechem, and Samaria come south on the hill-country road to Jerusalem. They have cut their beards and torn their clothes as signs of ritual humiliation, and they intend to worship at the site of the temple in Jerusalem (41:4–8). Here is unintended commentary on the importance of the temple for people who lived outside the territory of Judah. The pilgrims from the north want to present grain offerings and incense at the temple in Jerusalem. Perhaps an altar has been erected and repositioned in the courtyard, or perhaps the ceremony envisioned by the pilgrims is for prayer and lamentation, and their gifts a symbolic gesture. The text does not say, and interpreters should be wary of speculation.

In yet another treacherous act, Ishmael gains their confidence and brings them to Mizpah, only to murder most of them and then to cast their bodies into the large cistern built by a former king. A few are spared who offer him provisions they have hidden in a field. Ishmael then gathers the townspeople and sets out to cross over the Jordan River to the Ammonites. Among his captives are daughters of the king. Most likely these are daughters of Zedekiah from marriages with women of prominent local families. Johanan and his soldiers attempt to intercept Ishmael. The two groups met near Gibeon, with the result that most of the captives taken by Ishmael are recovered by Johanan and his officers, but Ishmael and eight of his men escape.

The question faced by Johanan and his band is, "What now?" Their fear of Babylonian reprisal and the treachery of men like Ishmael lead them toward a decision to flee the region. Their choice of venue is Egypt, where already a sizable group of Judeans live.

Application. For North American readers, the depressing account of Gedaliah's murder and the continuing downward spiral in Judah may strike a responsive chord in their historical memory. Abraham Lincoln announced that a "house divided against itself cannot stand." He knew he was quoting a biblical text (cf. Mark 3:24–25), and he believed that God would judge the United States for its folly in the slave trade and its continuing bitter conflict over ways to resolve the matter.

After four years of civil war (1861–1865), with the southern states in tatters and the whole nation exhausted from the senseless bloodletting, Lincoln began to look for ways to rebuild the nation and to reconcile its various factions. Lincoln was not perfect (nor was Gedaliah!), but he represented the possibility of moving past the consequences of moral and spiritual failure. A twisted soul named John Wilkes Booth assassinated Lincoln before he could put his plans for reconciliation into effect.

What does one say to such a lesson? One should begin by affirming that the painful historical process came about as self-incurred failure. Its effects linger on. The issues are not just in the past. Christians, however, should go on further and, like Lincoln, confess the hand of God at work in judgment.

Are there not additional things that we as Christians can confess? One of them is that Lincoln (like Gedaliah and Jeremiah) is something of a tragic figure. In a mysterious way, he bore corporate failure in his person and suffered along with the nation—and not just in his death. The christological analogy is not complete: Lincoln (Gedaliah or Jeremiah) did not atone for the sins of others, but they did suffer as part of their calling.

Their tragedies raise interesting questions. If God uses their tragic circumstances to instruct his people and to evoke measures of repentance and sympathy, then they serve a larger purpose. Moreover, failure can be the prelude to and even the beginning of new directions. In the midst of a national humiliation, Gedaliah advises his contemporaries not to fear. Jeremiah chooses the more difficult road rather than setting off to Babylon. Do those who have tasted new life in the crucified and risen Lord have eyes to see and ears to hear what the Spirit is saying?

JEREMIAH 42:1–43:7

Original Meaning. *42:1–6.* Should the remnant associated with Johanan (and until recently with Gedaliah) flee to Egypt or not? They seek the counsel of God through Jeremiah and promise obedience to the prophetic word. There is an implied self-curse in 42:5, should the company of Judeans not heed the Lord's instruction. Jeremiah agrees to seek counsel from the Lord and to tell them everything the Lord reveals.

42:7–22. Jeremiah's reply to the request of Johanan takes two forms. After ten days he begins with the preface, "This is what the LORD . . . says" (42:9), where the gist of the message is that God will preserve the remnant of Judeans if they stay in the land. In language associated with Jeremiah's call, God promises to build and to plant them in the land and there to protect them from the wrath of Nebuchadnezzar (42:10–12). Should they choose to disregard his word and to flee to Egypt, judgment will come on them there.

This indication of judgment should be read in light of 42:5, where the people ask that God be a "true and faithful witness" against them if they disobey his revealed word. Jeremiah adds his personal word to the group (42:19–22), indicating that a choice for Egypt means that they are self-deceived and will not escape judgment.

43:1–7. Members of the group accuse Jeremiah of lying to them and of engaging in a conspiracy with Baruch, who wants the group to stay in the land. Why Baruch might be an agent of subterfuge is not clear from their accusation. Their reaction to Jeremiah's prophetic oracle is similar to that of Zedekiah. The latter specifically asked Jeremiah for a word from the Lord, but when he didn't like what Jeremiah provided, he simply refused to obey.

The end result is that Johanan leads the group to Tahpanhes in Egypt. Jeremiah and Baruch are taken with them, but not willingly. Tahpanhes (cf. 2:16) is located in the eastern section of the Nile Delta. It is one of the first communities that a traveler from Palestine would encounter when approaching the Nile Delta from the east. As 44:1 makes clear, it was one of several cities in Egypt with a Judean population.

Application. Christians should not understand obedience to God's revealed will as an irrelevant burden or needless constriction; obedience is the proper response needed to fulfill one's calling. In biblical terms obedience is virtually a synonym for the path of discipleship. It is certainly easy to complain that we don't always know God's will and to offer that as a reason why we don't do something. One should not make light of the intellectual difficulties associated with discerning God's will, but it is more frequently the case that the hindrance to discipleship comes from moral sloth and failure to trust than from inability to discern at least the basics of a course of action.

A former teacher once said that truth is only known through commitment. What he meant is that the intellectual approach to God or the dialogical form of inquiry can be helpful, but personal commitment to God (and being known by God) is where the truth of God's sovereignty and goodness is revealed. What a tragedy that Jeremiah's companions could commit themselves in advance to following God's will, only to reject it when it did not suit their predilections.

JEREMIAH 43:8–44:30

Original Meaning. *43:8–13.* At God's initiative, Jeremiah takes some large stones and buries them in the courtyard of a government building in Tahpanhes. He explains this act by saying that God will grant his "servant Nebuchadnezzar" (43:10) a seat over these stones when the Babylonian king spreads out his royal canopy. Jeremiah's prophetic depiction of Nebuchadnezzar's presence is an indication that Babylon will conquer Egypt. Moreover, judgment will come on those Judeans who think they have escaped the reach of the Babylonians by fleeing to Egypt. The prophet also predicts that the Babylonians will set fire to temples in the land of Egypt and break the obelisks in the city of the sun, that is, Heliopolis, located just northeast of modern Cairo.

44:1–14. The bitter exchange between prophet and people in chapter 44 underscores the deep cultural and religious fissures in the Judean community. These verses are Jeremiah's prophetic invective against Judean people in Egypt. They concentrate on Judean idolatry and syncretism, if not outright apostasy against their ancestral faith.

Verse 7 contains a rhetorical question: "Why bring such great disaster on yourselves?" The point is another one familiar to readers of the book. Acts have consequences; the idolatry and apostasy of Judeans in Egypt will have the same self-incurred consequences as did idolatry and apostasy in Judah. The prophet concludes with a statement that Judeans in Egypt seem not to have associated the fall of Judah and Jerusalem as judgment on their faithlessness to the Lord. As the following reply to the prophet makes clear, some have not made the connection.

44:15–19. The people's testy reply to the prophet's judgment speech reflects two significant assumptions about religious practice on the part of Judeans.

1. Religion has the primary function of securing the health and safety of a group.
2. The worship of the Queen of Heaven was stopped earlier in Judah (by Josiah?) and subsequently resumed. The fortunes of the people, so they claim, have turned out better with her than with the Lord (44:17). As a result, the Judeans in Egypt intend to maintain the worship of the Queen of Heaven as did their ancestors and their kings in Judah.

In particular, the Judean women reply that their worship of the Queen of Heaven was done with the acquiescence of their husbands (44:19). Although Jeremiah's previous comments have not singled out either Judean women or worship of the Queen of Heaven, their role in her cult takes center stage as the example of idolatry and apostasy.

44:20–30. Jeremiah's reply to the people's resolve to commit apostasy is that judgment will come on them for their act of faithlessness toward the Lord. He judges implicitly their claim that things are better with the Queen of Heaven than with the Lord.

Jeremiah recognizes that his give-and-take with the crowd has set out both their resolve to remain worshipers of the Queen of Heaven and God's resolve that his word of judgment will come to pass. He predicts, therefore, that Pharaoh Hophra, the current ruler of Egypt, will be given over to the hands of his enemies as a sign of God's mastery of affairs, even in Egypt. In 569 BC Hophra was killed by one of his officials in a military coup.

The prophet does identify a future for a Jewish remnant, a future in which the remnant will recognize whose word stands the test of time. Jeremiah predicts that it will be the word of the Lord that stands the test of time, not that of the Queen of Heaven and her worshipers.

Application. "The fear of the LORD is the beginning of knowledge" (Prov 1:7). The pathway to life begins by acknowledging that every road leads to death except the one charted by God. Jeremiah's contemporaries in Egypt simply could not face the fact that they had been (and remained) part of a failed political and religious enterprise. Tragically, they were willing to do almost anything to hear from God: kidnap Jeremiah and Baruch, worship the Queen of Heaven, and so on. What they refused to do is to acknowledge their failure and depend on the God of grace, who can make all things new.

JEREMIAH 45:1–5

Original Meaning. The prophecy concerning Baruch is out of place chronologically with the preceding chapters (chs. 37–44). Verse 1 provides a date in the fourth year of Jehoiakim (605 BC), which coincides with the command from the Lord in 36:1 for Jeremiah to prepare a scroll of his prophecies. The fallout over Baruch's reading from the scroll may have been an early occasion for public persecution of this scribe, who was Jeremiah's secretary and companion. According to 36:19, 26, Baruch was forced into hiding because of his reading of the scroll at the temple complex. After the fall of Jerusalem, the Judeans accused him of playing loose with the truth (43:3). Subsequently he and Jeremiah were taken to Egypt by a band of Judeans.

Why does this account come at the end of the description of the Egyptian sojourn of Jeremiah and Baruch? These words to and about Baruch owe their literary placement to their thematic and theological value as a divine confirmation that Baruch served God and would be enabled to perform his calling. Moreover, the placement of this prophecy as a conclusion to the narratives about life in Egypt serves to reinforce the claim that Baruch's presence in Egypt is not the result of God's disfavor. Thus, although neither prophet nor companion will escape the fate of the nation, God will vindicate them nevertheless.

Baruch's "woe" (45:3) is a counterpart to the laments of Jeremiah. There is a cost to serving the Lord in times such as these. The divine oracle to Baruch repeats the language of uprooting and tearing down used at Jeremiah's commission to the prophetic office (1:10). In the tragic affairs of Judah and Jerusalem, God has been at work to uproot and tear down. Baruch has no more "right" (to use modern Western language) than anyone else to expect that he will escape the consequences of corporate and historical judgment that have swept through the region.

In that light, all that can be said is that God calls Baruch to be faithful and that his personal safety resides with God. God promises him that his life has been granted to him "wherever" (45:5) he might go. Readers are given no additional information about where his service to Jeremiah and to God may take him. His life is a gift, and he has been called to use it well.

Application. Christians who feel isolated or depressed over their circumstances, who have been forced into unfamiliar territory, or who are caught up in destructive forces that overwhelm their lives are invited to measure their lives against a scriptural pattern including saints such as Abraham, Joseph, Moses, Jeremiah, and Baruch. Abraham made mistakes in Egypt. Joseph was unjustly imprisoned there. Moses committed murder there and struggled against Pharaoh and his minions to mobilize his people to leave. Jeremiah and Baruch were kidnapped and brought to Egypt.

None of these saints, however, lacked the attention of God, who remained faithful to them in times of upheaval. This did not cause their pain to go away. Their lives were gifts in service to the Lord in and through the difficulties. And through their difficulties God formed disciples. No wonder that the idiom for Baruch is that his life is a prize of war. It is certainly given to him in the midst of struggle.

In Baruch's case, he assisted in the formation of a book that now instructs us all. That is his greatest gift.

JEREMIAH 46–49

Original Meaning. *46:1.* There are two prophecies against Egypt: 46:2–12 and 46:14–26. Only the first one is dated. The fourth year of Jehoiakim was 605 BC, the year of the fateful battle at Carchemish (in northern Syria) between the forces of Pharaoh Necho and of Nebuchadnezzar (mentioned explicitly in 46:26). The Egyptians were routed, and Babylon began the process of claiming hegemony over the states in the eastern Mediterranean. Egyptian demise is predicted as part of the judgment in the historical process but not the end of the Egyptians themselves.

46:2–12. This oracle is directed to the army of Pharaoh Necho. In 609 BC Pharaoh's army had marched from Egypt toward Syria in order to join forces with the remnants of the Assyrian army and to oppose the emerging power of Babylon. At that time Josiah had attempted to head off the Egyptian army at Megiddo and was mortally wounded in the unsuccessful effort to thwart the Egyptian advance (2 Kgs 23:29–30; 2 Chr 35:20–24).

As noted above, the date of this oracle against the Egyptian army is the fourth year of Jehoiakim (605 BC). Jehoiakim was the Egyptian choice among Josiah's sons to follow his father in rule. The martial language of the oracle depicts elements of the Egyptian army preparing to fight and then fleeing in terror. Furthermore, the boastful pride of the Egyptians is described in imperialistic terms (46:8), only to be reversed by divine judgment on a day that "belongs to the Lord" (46:10). It is a day of vengeance to be directed against the Lord's foes, of which Egypt is one. In fact, the language of judgment on that decisive day is described in sacrificial terms.

Egypt is also described in familial terms as "Virgin Daughter" (46:11). She who seeks a balm in Gilead will find that there is no healing for her.

46:13–26. Verse 13 is a prose introduction to the prophecy that follows. Unlike the companion oracle in 46:2–12, this prophecy is undated. Nebuchadnezzar did not invade Egypt until 570 BC, late in his reign, but there were periodic encounters of various kinds between Egypt and Babylon throughout Jeremiah's lifetime. Essentially the prophecy announces that Babylon will work God's judgment on Egypt. At a basic interpretive level, such a claim is little different from those Jeremiah directed at Judah. In both instances Babylon and Nebuchadnezzar serve as the rod of historical judgment used by the Lord.

The disastrous event is a day in the future (46:21). For some in Egypt it will be defeat and exile. As in the previous oracle, Egypt is personified as a female ("Daughter Egypt," 46:24) who will be put to shame by a people from the north. Part of the judgment to come is directed at Amon, one of the Egyptian deities (46:25). Judgment, however, is not the end of Egypt as a nation; it will again be inhabited (46:26).

46:27–28. Following the oracles against Egypt is a prediction of the restoration of God's people. Those on whom God's judgment has fallen have been disciplined justly, but in his mercy, God will not make an end of them. Correspondingly, those whom God used to discipline his people (such as the Egyptians) will suffer the fate of those whose hubris, cruelty, and idolatry have kept them from acknowledging the work of God.

47:1–7. The Philistines lived in some of the cities on the coast of Palestine. They had been neighbors and often enemies of Judah since the days of the judges. They were immigrants to the area, having come from some of the Aegean islands and southwestern Turkey in the twelfth century BC.

Two Philistine cities are named here: Gaza and Ashkelon. The occasion for the oracle against the Philistines possibly comes with Nebuchadnezzar's preparations to attack Gaza (cf. 47:2). No extrabiblical records survive of a Babylonian attack on Gaza, but it is completely understandable that the Babylonians either fought against Gaza and subdued it or received the city's surrender. Gaza was a trading center and an important point of contact between Egypt, the states immediately to the north and east (e.g., Judah, Moab), and the Arab tribes from Sinai and the fringes of sedentary existence.

The assault in question could have been perpetrated by the Egyptians between 609 BC, when Necho moved from Egypt to north Syria, and 605 BC, when the Egyptians were defeated at Carchemish. A first reading of 47:1 refers explicitly to an attack by an unnamed Pharaoh. There are two problems with this interpretation, although neither are insurmountable.

1. The Greek version of this verse omits the reference to the Pharaoh.
2. There is no record of an Egyptian attack on Gaza or Ashkelon in the period 609 BC and later.

At the present state of knowledge, therefore, it is difficult to place this oracle in a specific historical context, but there are several plausible options because of frequent military actions in the region.

In form and vocabulary, the oracle against the Philistines is similar to the preceding oracles against Egypt. The Philistines will be defeated on some future day (47:4). People will mourn for Gaza and Ashkelon. God's historical judgment is personified through a poetic address to his sword (47:6).

48:1–25. The Moabites receive an extensive address in 48:1–47 that preserves a significant knowledge of geography. Over twenty different cities (settlements) are named in the poetic indictment of Judah's eastern neighbor. The Moabites and Israelites were distant relatives. Later, David's family was related to the Moabites through Ruth, his great-grandmother (Ruth 4:13–22). Solomon married a Moabite princess and built for her a temple to Chemosh, the chief Moabite deity, on the hill east of the temple mount in Jerusalem (1 Kgs 11:7).

The repetition of a concluding prophetic formula ("declares the LORD") in 48:25, 30, 35, 38, 43, 44, 47 suggests that more than one prophetic announcement has been collected in Jeremiah 48.

Apart from 48:1a and the last phrase of 48:25, this long section does not have introductory or concluding formulae to break up the sequence of verses. It is possible that 48:1b–25 is a single unit of speech, offering mourning language, prediction of judgment and exile, and sarcasm in poetry, all designed to humiliate Moab.

Verse 7 mentions Chemosh. One way to refer to Moab was to call them "the people of Chemosh" (Num 21:29). He, like his people, will suffer defeat and go into exile. In the future, Moab will be ashamed of Chemosh, just as Israel was ashamed when trusting Bethel (Jer 48:13). The name "Bethel" here likely refers to a deity rather than a place.

Some of the judgment language in this section is frightful. There are references to salt (48:9), an agent that ruins agricultural products, and to curses (48:10) on whoever is lax in doing the Lord's work of execution. As with Egypt and Judah, Jeremiah uses familial language for Moab. Her cities will be ruined, and she will wail a funeral lament. Even physical mutilation is mentioned. Moab's "horn" (48:25), a metaphor for strength, will be cut off and her arm broken.

48:26–47. These prophecies continue the depiction of Moab's humiliation and degradation. As with the previous oracle, the language is graphic. Moab will wallow in vomit (48:26), cries of dereliction will be heard (48:34, 38), fire will scorch the country (48:45), and the children of the nation will be taken into exile (48:46).

So moved is the prophet by the intensity of depicting Moab's downfall that he portrays himself in mourning (48:31–32). The historical agent of all this destruction is not named explicitly. Moab will be judged because "she defied the LORD" (48:42).

The last line of these intricate poetic prophecies is one of restoration (48:47). This is the same phrase God uses elsewhere in predicting the restoration of Israel.

49:1–6. The oracle against the Ammonites is much briefer than the one against Moab. According to Genesis 19:30–38, Ben-Ammi, the ancestor of the Ammonites, was the incestuous son of Lot. Ammon's chief deity was Milcom. Solomon married an Ammonite princess and built a temple for Milcom's worship on the hill east of the temple mount in Jerusalem (1 Kgs 11:7). Baalis, king of Ammon at the time of Jerusalem's fall, plotted with Ishmael to murder Gedaliah, the Judean governor appointed by the Babylonians (Jer 40–41).

Rabbah is the capital city of Ammon. Its remains form part of the impressive citadel at the heart of modern-day Amman, Jordan. The judgment to come on Ammon is depicted as defeat and exile. No biblical or Babylonian accounts exist to document an official defeat of Ammon (or Moab), but both states fell under the control of Babylon.

In 49:1 and 3 the NIV refers to "Molek" as having taken possession of Gad and then being sent into exile with his priests and officials. Elsewhere in Jeremiah, Molek is the name of the deity to whom child sacrifices are offered in Judah (32:35; cf. Lev 20:2–5; 2 Kgs 23:10). The NIV translators have rendered the Hebrew term *malkam* (literally, "their king") in 49:1, 3 as Molek based on the reference to Molekas the Ammonite deity in 1 Kings 11:7. This seemingly logical move, however, concerns a complicated matter over which considerable uncertainty remains.

As a name, Molek is a polemical hybrid because it combines the consonants of the word king (*m-l-k*) with the vowels from the word "shame." Molek and Milcom have the same consonants. In comparing the biblical references to Molek, it is not clear whether Milcom is the same deity as Molek. Jeremiah also refers to the deity of child sacrifice as Baal (19:5). In brief, the Hebrew term *malkam* in 49:1, 3 can be rendered "their king," "Milcom," or (by inference from 1 Kgs 11:7) "Molek."

As with Moab (with whom the Ammonites are sometimes linked), the Lord promises to restore the fortunes of Ammon.

49:7–22. Like Ammon and Moab, the Edomites are related to God's people—in their case, through Esau (Gen 36). Esau is mentioned explicitly in Jeremiah 49:8, 10 as a synonym for Edom. The bitterness reflected in the relationship between Jacob and Esau was reflected later in the relationship between Judah and Edom in the days of Jeremiah and into the postexilic period. According to the lamentation of Psalm 137:7, Edom gleefully celebrated the fall of Jerusalem. Unlike the prophecies to Moab and Ammon, Jeremiah makes no reference to Edom's restoration.

The polemic against Edom begins with a reference to wisdom. Those who lived east of Palestine were celebrated as wise. Jeremiah's polemic against the Edomites depicts its day of judgment as the loss or failure of its wisdom. The region of Dedan (49:8) is in the Arabian desert, but its inhabitants were linked with Edom through trade.

Bozrah (49:13, 22) is the capital city of Edom. Its ruins are located near the modern Jordanian village of Buseirah. Bozrah will drink the cup of wrath. Edom's strongholds on mountains and in cliffs will not save them from destruction. Verse 19 depicts God as a lion coming upon Edom. His plan is to destroy them, which will come on a day that strikes fear into the heart of a warrior.

49:23–27. Damascus is another object of prophetic judgment. Perhaps Damascus is named among the oracles because of the Aramean raids reported in 2 Kings 24:2. Damascus suffered devastating attacks from the Assyrians in the ninth and eighth centuries because it was a persistent ringleader in the region for anti-Assyrian activities. History repeated itself when Babylon took Damascus.

Hamath and Arpad, two cities in northern Syria, are named in this oracle as regional cities who will be dismayed by the bad news of judgment to fall on the area. Damascus is personified as a weak woman with pain like that which comes with labor. The reference to Ben-Hadad (Jer 49:27) comes in an "update" of Amos's prophecy (Amos 1:3–4) against Damascus. Hadad is a well-known Aramean deity, and the name Ben-Hadad designates a king as the adopted "son" (Hebrew *ben* means "son") of the deity. Several kings from Damascus had this name/title.

49:28–33. Kedar is a region of northern Arabia. Hazor is something of a mystery since no location with that name is known in northern Arabia. Kedar and Hazor most likely refer to Arab tribesmen who were attacked by the Babylonians in Nebuchadnezzar's sixth year (winter of 599 BC). The "people of the East" (49:28) are associated with Kedar. They live in tents, travel using camels, and keep sheep and goats. These peoples are known in other sources as Arabs.

49:34–39. The prophecy against Elam is dated early in the reign of Zedekiah. Just why Elam is singled out is a mystery. Elam will also be restored by God. As with other matters of grace, no merit or reason is cited for this announcement.

Application. Mysterious affirmations come at the end of the oracles against Egypt, Moab, Ammon, and Elam, which proclaim restoration after their judgment. The good news is that God's judgment is often in the service of a wider saving purpose. His church will be comprised of people from every nation. In heaven this joyful fact is part of a song sung by the redeemed (Rev 5). Should this not also be a song of the church on earth?

Attempts to discern meaning and purpose in the fate of nations is a most difficult task. Read any of the oracles against the nations in Jeremiah and one is reminded instantly that injustice and cruelty are constant historical companions, but so are the words of grace and future hope.

JEREMIAH 50:1–51:64

Original Meaning. *50:1–10.* The fall of Babylon is to be proclaimed among the nations. Perhaps this is because Babylon had subjugated a number of them, and there will be rejoicing in more than one corner of the former empire. Another reason perhaps is the public declaration of the Lord's sovereignty by announcing the fact in public and in advance.

As in the prophecies in the book of the covenant (chs. 30–31), remnants from Israel and Judah will seek the Lord and a way back to Zion. They are currently like lost sheep, but they will return to their true shepherd, "the hope of their ancestors" (50:7). The prophet urges them to flee out of Babylon (cf. 51:6). This is not contradictory to the advice given in 29:4–9, that the exiles should build houses in Babylon and pray for the welfare of the city. That same chapter indicated a coming time when God will restore his people. The defeat of Babylon will indicate that restoration is on the horizon.

50:11–17. Babylon's joy in pillaging Judah (God's "inheritance," 50:11) will be turned to great shame. Babylon is personified here as the mother of the Babylonian people. Portraying cities as female persons is common in the Old Testament, but this imagery will be taken up in the New Testament, where Babylon is portrayed as a great prostitute (Rev 17–18).

In poetic reversal pattern, Babylon will be besieged and defeated. Verse 15 is a somber cry: "Since this is the vengeance of the Lord, take vengeance on her; do to her as she has done to others." This proclamation is also an example of the "act and consequence" theology espoused by many biblical writers. What Babylon has set in motion will come around to her.

50:18–32. Imperialistic Babylon is compared to Assyria, the earlier conqueror of Israel and much of the Near East. As with Assyria, so with Babylon—God will judge the oppressor. Twice the language of judgment against Babylon uses the Hebrew verb *ḥrm* ("to devote to ritual destruction"). Vengeance on God's part is another motive for judgment (50:28; cf. 51:11).

50:33–46. God is strong, not just as judge of iniquity, but as the redeemer of his people. Verse 34 celebrates God as the one who vindicates his people's cause.

The overthrow of Babylon is compared to that of Sodom and Gomorrah. Again, the prophet uses the language of military attack and siege to describe the coming fall of Babylon. Verse 44 alludes to either a people or an individual who will do God's bidding and take Babylon. As Jeremiah 50:9; 51:27–28 indicate, God has summoned several groups against Babylon. These claims elaborate on the theme that a foe from the north will attack Babylon.

51:1–23. Chapter 51 continues the contrast between the coming deliverance of Judean exiles and the judgment to befall Babylon. Much of the imagery of judgment on Babylon and redemption for Israel is repeated from or similar to that in chapter 50. One of the poetic symbols Jeremiah uses is that of the "cup" (51:7), a vessel that indicates the future when its contents are consumed. In 51:7 Babylon itself is depicted as a cup from which Judah and the nations drank, but now it is ready to be smashed.

Verses 15–19 celebrate the creative power and wisdom of God. The sentiments expressed here are similar to those in chapter 10, where again the character of the true God is set in the context of the foolishness and idolatry of the nations. In contrast to human idol-makers, God is "the Maker of all things" (51:19).

51:24–58. These verses portray four of Babylon's neighbors as threats. The Medes are mentioned twice (51:11, 28). They were a people to the north and east of Babylon who were incorporated into the Persian state created by Cyrus the Great. Ararat, Minni, and the Ashkenaz (51:27–28) were also peoples from the north and northeast of Babylon. Along with the Medes and the Persians, they may reflect collectively the foe from the "north" (51:48) who will strike Babylon.

In 51:34–40 personified Jerusalem speaks, and the Lord replies that judgment will come on Babylon. In this context she (Jerusalem) speaks of the torment she has received from Babylon. Her first-person speech is similar to that found in the book of Lamentations.

The gods of Babylon are also judged in the fall of the city. Specifically mentioned is Bel (51:44). The imagery of judgment against Babylon alludes to the tower of Babylon (Babel) in Genesis 11:1–9. God will send destroyers against Babylon, even if the city reaches the sky (Jer 51:53).

51:59–64. The chapter concludes with a prose account of Seraiah, brother of Baruch, who traveled to Babylon in Zedekiah's fourth year (594/593 BC). Seraiah was from a family of scribes and was capable of writing and interpreting documents. While in Babylon he performed a symbolic act to depict the judgment that would ultimately befall Babylon. Just as the written scroll sank when Seraiah threw it into the river, so will Babylon sink and rise no more.

The last line of the chapter states that "the words of Jeremiah end here" (51:64). Readers do well to recall the way in which Jeremiah's work began. He was called to be a prophet to the nations. The literary arrangement of his words concludes with an extended prophecy against Babylon, the great imperial power of the day. But note how Jeremiah's words in collected form have lasted much longer than the great political and military foe of his day.

Application. In pondering the judgments of history, perhaps no region is more strife-ridden and more difficult to understand than the Middle East. While Israelis and Arabs debate and fight—which they seem to do at the same time—there is the ongoing exodus of Arab Christians from the region. Understandably, Christians in other parts of the world lament the fact that brothers and sisters from the land of the Messiah are fleeing in such numbers that if current projections continue, virtually all churches in Israel and Jordan will be museums in decades to come.

Yes, the fleeing of Arab Christians is a tragedy. It may also be one of the ways in which God saves his people from a more terrible historical fate looming on the horizon. Hindsight often improves judgment, even for the church. Christians may find much about judgment in Jeremiah 50–51, but it is the hidden work of God to which we should also be drawn.

In all these questions about the judgment of oppressing nations, the Christian church finds itself caught up in debates about morality and the just exercise of force. These debates are good when they remind Christians that God is not mocked and that no nation or ethnic group will have the final say on judgment day. They can mislead if they allow people to think that it is only the "other side" that is wrong and sinful in God's assessment.

No group comes out unscathed in the book of Jeremiah. There is plenty of folly and failure to go around, whether in Judah or in Babylon. God's promise to rescue his people comes not because they are morally perfect, but because of the grace of his promise to them. His standards of judgment are a stark reminder of how much grace is needed for the rescue of the saints in any generation.

JEREMIAH 52:1–34

Original Meaning. *52:1–11.* The date of the ninth day and fourth month (52:6) refers to the last year of Zedekiah's reign. The details of Zedekiah's capture should be compared with 39:1–7 and 2 Kings 25:1–7. Second Chronicles contains no narrative of Zedekiah's capture.

52:12–16. This brief description of the city's fall should be compared with 39:8 and 2 Kings 25:8–12. A reader only of Jeremiah 39 would not know that Nebuzaradan was the official in charge of burning the city and the temple. Indeed, 39:8 does not even mention the burning of the temple, as do the other two accounts.

52:17–23. These verses include a brief report of the looting of the temple (see also 2 Kgs 25:13–17). A comparison of the account here and that in 2 Kings is fascinating. Each begins with a report that the Babylonians broke the bronze pillars, and there are similar details preserved between them. Nevertheless, each account preserves some distinctive elements. The Jeremiah account, which is the longer of the two, has more details about the carved pomegranates and the bronze pillars.

52:24–27a. These verses closely parallel 2 Kings 25:18–21.

52:27b–30. These verses preserve references to two waves of exiles during the reign of Nebuchadnezzar. The first wave came during the reign of Jehoiachin (597 BC), and the second came in 582 BC.

52:31–34. This notice about Jehoiachin, which concludes Jeremiah, is paralleled in 2 Kings 25:27–30, which also concludes 2 Kings. It is far more than a simple report about a minor monarch being long exiled. The report undergirds a type of muted but stubborn faith. Even when the land of Judah and the city of Jerusalem lie in ruins, one from David's line still lives.

Application. It is possible for those who "wait on the LORD" to renew their strength (Isa 40:31). It is possible because God provides the strength we need in our times of need. It is possible because no matter how strong or resilient the enemy, the future belongs to God, who is faithful. How this happens is the mystery of grace. One cannot explain it by a formula; one can only point to the God of new beginnings as the faithful God and Lord of life and death.

Matthew's genealogy of Jesus runs through the line of Jehoiachin (Matt 1:11–12). What a story is packed into that simple genealogical list. Here is inspired commentary on sacred history. It is a reminder of how decades and centuries play a part in God's redemptive work, even when their twists and turns seem only confusing. Who would have thought that a king exiled for thirty-seven years meant much of anything other than years of frustration?

Jeremiah 52 is the final word about an influential epoch in sacred history. It is the final witness of the prophet Jeremiah's book. What we do with the witness is the way in which the ending of the book becomes an instructional piece in the unfolding drama of our lives. Jehoiachin died in captivity, yet he provided the means by which the Davidic family and the promises to it could continue. Jehoiachin's greater Son arrived in the fullness of time only to die at the hands of another imperial power. The story of which the book of Jeremiah is a part is still unfolding because Christ is alive and because he calls the current generation of God's people to discipleship and faithful living. So, comfort one another with these words.

LAMENTATIONS

INTRODUCTION TO LAMENTATIONS

The book of Lamentations consists of five chapters of Hebrew poetry, joined together by the common themes of sorrow over the destruction of Jerusalem in 586 BC and the humiliation of Judah's population. No author is named in the Hebrew version, and the book appears not in the prophetic section of the Hebrew Bible but in the last section, entitled the Writings. The earliest claim to human authorship comes in the Greek translation, where the first verse explicitly attributes the book to the weeping prophet Jeremiah.

Although it is unlikely that Jeremiah is the author of Lamentations, its association with him is one of several indications that the work fits into the broader context of the prophet's later life and times. The perspective of the voices in Lamentations is that of the Babylonian exile. At some point in the exile, Judeans began to lament corporately and publicly in order to remember Jerusalem, the capital city, the location of the temple, and the symbolic mother of the people.

BOOK OUTLINE

I. The Royal City of Jerusalem Mourns like a Widow (1:1–22)
II. Jerusalem Mourns the Day of the Lord's Anger That Fell on Her (2:1–22)
III. The Poet Speaks of Judgment and Mercy (3:1–66)
IV. Jerusalem Is Examined Before and After Destruction (4:1–22)
V. The Community Remembers and Asks God to Remember What Happened to Them (5:1–22)

LAMENTATIONS 1:1–22

Original Meaning. This chapter is an acrostic. Each verse begins with a word whose initial letter follows the twenty-two-letter sequence of the Hebrew alphabet. More than one voice speaks in chapter 1. The poet (the author's voice) begins, and it is complemented by that of personified Jerusalem. When the chapter is read as a unit, the "back and forth" of the two voices mutually reinforces the tragic dilemma of Jerusalem. The two voices are arranged as follows:

A. 1:1–9a are the voice of the poet.
B. A quotation is attributed to personified Jerusalem in 1:9b.
C. 1:10–11a are the voice of the poet.
D. An extended quotation is attributed to personified Jerusalem in 1:11b–16.
E. 1:17 is the voice of the poet.
F. An extended quotation is attributed to personified Jerusalem in 1:18–22.

Verse 1 indicates the theme of the chapter; it depicts the noble city of Jerusalem in the mourning position of a widow. The imagery for Jerusalem, personified and otherwise, runs throughout the chapter. She is a widow, once a noble woman and now a slave (1:1). The NIV rendering in 1:1, "she who was queen," translates the Hebrew noun *sarah*, which indicates nobility or royalty but does not necessarily refer to a queen. It is the word used for the name of Abraham's wife, Sarah.

In 1:2 *sarah* is forsaken by her "lovers." The term has a sexual overtone when used in a similar context by the prophets, where it refers either to other gods pursued illicitly or to stronger neighbors with whom Israel or Judah sought to ingratiate themselves. Because of her sinfulness, the Lord has judged her, and her children have gone into exile (1:5; cf. 1:16, 18).

The language of chapter 1 refers to the sinfulness of Judah and to a resulting sorrow and suffering. These things are related to one another; sinfulness has led to judgment and suffering. Their link is expressed succinctly in 1:5, "the Lord has brought her [i.e., Zion] grief because of her many sins" (cf. 1:8, 14, 18, 20, 22). The emphasis falls, however, on the grief, the suffering, and the pitiful nature of the city. She "weeps" (1:1–2, 16) and "groans" (1:8, 21–22), and is "in bitter anguish" (1:4) and "distress" (1:20–21). Nothing here points to the relief of the city's woes.

The voice of the poet depicts Jerusalem in the posture of "remembering" her days of affliction (1:7). This posture of remembering or bringing to mind again captures much of the reason for the book of Lamentations as a whole. What is depicted for Jerusalem is actually what the readers (or performers) do when reciting the poem.

In 1:22 Jerusalem asks that the evil done to her by her enemies be brought before God so that he can deal with them. An answer to this sentiment also lies largely outside the book. In texts like Obadiah and Isaiah 47 readers again may get an intertextual echo of Lamentations and the desire for vindication.

Application. In the summer of 1999 John F. Kennedy Jr. died in a tragic airplane crash. Subsequent investigation concluded that he had likely miscalculated his navigational skills for nighttime flight. He, his wife, and her sister were killed in the single plane crash. For American readers, JFK Jr. was close to royalty. With regard to his tragic death, one headline read: "The End of Camelot."

Just as some could now ask, "What will life be like without the ideals represented by JFK Jr.?," so God's ancient people asked, "What will life be like without Zion and Judah?" How difficult it is for God's people to see themselves in light of their failures. They first must know that to be God's people is a precious privilege, and then that it is possible for something to threaten that privilege so that they cannot take it for granted. The poetry of Lamentations is one of the most articulate voices for confession of sin and lament over failure. The poems themselves point first to the consequences of failure; as tragedy they loom larger than life and seemingly out of proportion to the failure. But most important, they are directed to the only One who can hear them fully and adequately respond.

LAMENTATIONS 2:1–22

Original Meaning. Careful examination of chapter 2 reveals several changes in the speaker's form of address. Verses 1–10 describe, in the third person, the suffering and anguish of the city through what God has done to them. God has covered the city with "the cloud of his anger" (2:1); he has "burned in Jacob like a flaming fire" (2:3; cf. 2:5); God has "given the walls of her palaces into the hands of the enemy" (2:7); and so on. Verses 9–10 describe Jerusalem in her pathetic state.

In 2:11 the poet uses the first-person "I" to describe his weeping and torment with respect to the awful condition of "my people." This is a most interesting verse, since the pattern from chapter 1 suggests that the first-person speech belongs to that of personified Jerusalem. Indeed, some commentators take it that way. However, the first person of 2:13 is that of the poet addressing Jerusalem, and it seems best overall to take 2:11 as also the voice of the poet. The alternation between description and first-person lament gives poignancy to the circumstances of Jerusalem's humiliation.

First-person references come also in 2:13 and 22. The former is the voice of the poet addressing Jerusalem, but 2:20–22 is perhaps better taken as the voice of Jerusalem. Verse 22 refers to those whom the speaker has cared for and raised—verbs associated with child-rearing. Since Jerusalem is frequently personified as a mother, it seems best to see her as the final speaker of chapter 2. In fact, 2:18–19 seem to address the wall(s) of Jerusalem with the urge to cry out. If correct—and 2:18 is textually difficult—this call to the wall(s) of Jerusalem is an example of metonymy, a literary device whereby something is represented or personified by a constituent part.

We may therefore set out the chapter's voices as follows:

A. 2:1–10 is the poet's description of Jerusalem's anguish and humiliation.

B. 2:11–13 is the poet's first-person response to Jerusalem's wretchedness.

C. 2:14–17 is again the poet's description of Jerusalem.

D. 2:18–19 is a call to Jerusalem's walls to cry out to God.

E. 2:20–22 is addressed to God by Jerusalem (perhaps more specifically her "walls"; cf. 2:18).

Both the city (2:13–19) and God (2:20–21) are addressed directly. These are second-person references ("you . . . your"). The effect overall of this chapter is to move beyond a surface description to give a more nuanced and personal portrait of those judged and bereaved and to ask God about the rightness of the devastation.

The great distinction of Zion's calling is reflected in 2:1. She is the "splendor" (Heb. *tiperet*) of Israel. This word can be used of an ornament or jewel. In Isaiah 60:7 God describes the temple as "my glorious temple" (*bet tiparti*). In Psalm 99:5 the ark of the covenant is described as God's "footstool," a term also used in Lamentations 2:1 in parallel with Israel's splendor. The city was "the perfection of beauty, the joy of the whole earth" (2:15; cf. Ps 48:2), until it came crashing down.

In Lamentations 2:3 the poet laments the fact that God has "cut off every horn of Israel." The term *horn* can be used as a metaphor for strength or honor, though it can also refer to the upraised corner or protrusions at the ends of a sacrificial altar (Exod 29:12; Lev 4:7; Ps 118:27). It was customary in Israel that those who "grasped the horns of the altar" had asylum and would not be slain (cf. 1 Kgs 1:49–53). Thus, the comment that God has cut off every horn in Israel can mean that God has destroyed the pride and nobility of the people and/or that God has removed any means of seeking asylum from the judgment fallen on Jerusalem and Judah.

God is so angry with Jerusalem that he is destroying "his" things that are within her. God has "laid waste his dwelling" and "destroyed his place of meeting" (Lam 2:6). Verse 7 elaborates on this matter: God has "rejected his altar and abandoned his sanctuary." The presence of the sacred temple in the midst of Jerusalem was no guarantee of God's benevolence or protection. The so-called "temple sermon" of Jeremiah made this view quite clear (Jer 7 and 26). Even parts of the city are personified to underscore the horror of what has befallen God's jewel. The walls of the city lament and weep over their destruction (2:8, 18).

Judgment is unsparing on those leaders who should have led the people in a different direction. The king is rejected and exiled (2:6, 9); the visionary task of the prophets failed them and their people (2:9, 14, 20). Priests are spurned, and now torah is gone (2:6, 9, 20).

God used the enemy to judge his people and his city. In remarkably pointed and anguished language, the poet asks God whether he has ever treated anyone else like this (2:20). It is as if God has become the enemy by using the enemy.

Application. The frankness of the language in Lamentations should persuade people that God is open to their real feelings and their honest reactions to tragedy. There is no "answer" in the immediacy of overwhelming tragedy, and one's prayers ought to reflect that. The great miracle of the gospel is that the One to whom despair and bitterness are directed is the One whose only Son suffered the travail of the cross. God, who strove against Jerusalem and Judah, also engaged the principalities and powers to gain an eternal victory for his people.

Yes! All things work together for good to those who love God and who are called according to his purpose (Rom 8:28). His purpose is to conform us to the image of his Son. That means quite a bit of chiseling and disciplining for us. Not everything is good, but things that happen work toward the good purpose of our incorporation into Christ.

LAMENTATIONS 3:1–66

Original Meaning. It is worth asking whether in chapter 3 we as readers are dealing with an individual voice in the fully modern sense of that term (i.e., an individual whose suffering and experience is provided in autobiographical form), or whether the "I" is the poet's voice in service to the larger community of readers and those who pray the Lamentations. The balance of probability favors the latter. The individual voice of chapter 3, which includes "we" and "our," speaks in order to provide a voice for the suffering members of his community. The first generations of readers would understand the formulaic language of chapter 3 to be paradigmatic of the poet's time and generation.

The "I" of chapter 3 is likely the poet of the book. He has seen the destruction of the city and its people, and the language of pain and suffering is filtered through both self-reference and shared experience ("we" and "our"). The language of individual travail is also reminiscent of Job, whose "speeches" are much like psalms of individual lament/complaint, especially in the description of his sufferings, in the recounting of the machinations of his "friends," and in his appeal to God for deliverance. Likewise, the affirmation of God's benevolent faithfulness is derived from the central confessions of the Old Testament.

The poet first sees God as the source of trouble, who has turned his rod and hand against the poet (3:1–3). God has besieged and walled him in (3:4–9), as if the fate of the city and the poet are the same. God is a lion or bear, or more menacingly, an archer taking aim at the poet (3:10–12).

In slightly different language the enemies of Zion have condemned and hunted the poet (3:46–54). They plot, insult, and mock him (3:58–63). He recapitulates in his person the suffering endured by the city and its inhabitants. Because his experience is shared by his contemporaries, it is relatively easy to follow the shift in the language from "I" to "we."

Memory plays an important role in a lament. Sometimes the poet asks God to remember and sometimes he himself remembers or recalls the previous deeds of the Lord. Such is the case in 3:19–24. Both suffering and redemption are part of the poet's experience, and he sets their memories side by side. God is the source not only of judgment but also of deliverance. Since he knows that God is strong to save, he says he has "hope" (3:21, 24). The resignation seen elsewhere in Lamentations is tempered by the realization that God, who has struck both Jerusalem and the poet, is the same One who can overturn the shame of public judgment and humiliation.

In 3:22 the "great love" of the Lord renders the Hebrew term *hesed*. While love is not a wrong translation, the term also carries the meaning of kindness and loyalty. Closely related to the term *hesed* is that of compassion(s)—*rahamim* in the Hebrew of 3:22. The best analogy is that of parental concern, for in the singular, *rehem* can mean womb. Finally, the poet confesses that God is great in faithfulness (3:23).

One can read the claims of Lamentations about judgment and mercy and see them as the outworking of this great self-definition of God. The corporate judgment that fell on Judah and Jerusalem is like the judgment that falls to the third and fourth generation, since what is likely meant by them is the claim of completeness. To judge the third and fourth generation is to deal with all involved. By contrast, to show mercy and forgiveness to thousands is to claim that mercy and forgiveness abound further than the third and fourth generation of complete retribution.

As with psalms of lament/complaint, the poet speaks of the "pit," which seeks to claim his life (3:53, 55). In the stanzas of 3:52–57, the poet prays like the beginning of Psalm 130: "Out of the depths I cry to you, LORD." The poet then reminds God that he has seen and heard what the enemies have done. His own life is like a judicial case (Lam 3:58), where God the judge should rule in his favor. The chapter, again like some of the psalms of lament/complaint, concludes with the plea of the poet for God to judge the enemies. In this the poet is also reminiscent of Jeremiah, who sought judgment on his tormenters (Jer 11:20; 15:15; 17:18; 18:19–23; 20:12).

As is sometimes also the case with psalms of lament/complaint, the poet is moved to speak about repentance (Lam 3:40–45). Significantly, the language is first-person plural: "Let us examine . . . let us return . . . let us lift" (3:40, 41). This indicates that the poet's experience is linked with that of his community. They become one before God. It also signifies the function or impact of Lamentations as a whole. The poems move readers to consider their lives in light of God's holiness and his cleansing judgment.

Application. *Quest for spirituality.* It is illuminating to set the language of Lamentations 3 in the context of the modern quest for spirituality. We must distinguish carefully between interest in a subject and the particular content or truthfulness of the subject material. Chapter 3 of Lamentations comes in the context of historical experience and inherited revelation. It has several marks of authentic spirituality.

1. He sees the tragedy of Jerusalem's fall as a revelation of the Lord, not as the entry of a new and foreign deity into his life or the stubborn arrival of an irrational mystery. Judgment is consistent with the character of God revealed in torah, prophecy, and the psalms.
2. He learns that prayer and confession directed toward God bring him into fellowship with God.
3. He finds that repentance is more than a concept, that it is a tangible way of relating to God. Repentance is not a magical elixir but a series of steps taken toward God in obedience to his will. For many people, failure to acknowledge the truth about God is less an intellectual matter and more a moral matter; and more particularly a matter of the will. That is why confession and repentance are integral to authentic spirituality.
4. He seeks God for deliverance and healing. He is able to see that his circumstances are the occasion for fresh prayers and newfound vows.
5. It probably never occurs to him that his spirituality can be a private matter. His confession that God is faithful also includes affirmation that "we" are not consumed. His call to repentance offers steps for "us" to return to the Lord.
6. For the poet, "waiting" on the Lord includes the practices of prayer and repentance and does not assume that waiting is merely marking time.

LAMENTATIONS 4:1–22

Original Meaning. One shocking effect of the Babylonian siege was the enormity of the changes that happened to families with children. Such dire circumstances give rise to a speculative thought concerning death. The poet suggests that those who died from the sword are better off than those who died from famine (4:9). It is not clear whether the poet really believes this is so or whether he states the comparison for its effectiveness in depicting the horror of Zion's fall.

The poet of Lamentations underscores the pain and despair of his generation rhetorically by noting how much longer and more painful it is to starve than to die by the sword. Perhaps we should interpret similarly the comment about the punishment on Zion as greater than that for Sodom (4:6). Sodom—it should be recalled—was wholly consumed in fire in a way that Zion was not.

The poet picks up a strand of teaching about Jerusalem's failure that is given elsewhere in the Old Testament, namely, that the leadership of the people shed "the blood of the righteous" (4:13, i.e., innocent blood). Whether this means by active persecution or by allowing injustice is not stated.

There is a reflection of the popular "theology of Zion" in 4:12, a belief that Jerusalem was sacrosanct and that God would not allow the city to fall. The poet of Lamentations notes (perhaps rhetorically) that foreign kings were surprised at Zion's fall, as if everyone knew of Zion's special status.

Lamentations 4:17 picks up on another theme given in prophetic accounts, namely, that help from another state would not save Zion. Jeremiah notes that the Babylonian siege was temporarily lifted because of an approaching Egyptian army (Jer 34:21–22; 37:5–11). Hopes for relief, however, quickly died when the siege was reinstated.

The poet speaks movingly of Zedekiah, Zion's reigning monarch at the time of the city's fall (Lam 4:20). He uses a striking phrase to describe his royal role—that Zedekiah was the very "life breath" (4:20) of the people. Comparison of this statement with the strong polemic of Jeremiah against Zedekiah is one reason why some scholars conclude that Jeremiah cannot be the author of Lamentations. However one decides that issue, 4:20 reflects poignant appreciation for the royal office ("the LORD's anointed"). The royal messiah (i.e., "anointed one") represented and gave life to the people. Metaphorically his "shadow" (4:20) provided security for the people like the shadow or wings of the Lord for the righteous (cf. Ruth 2:12; Ps 17:8; 91:1, 4).

Finally, Lamentations 4:21–22 refer to an end to Zion's punishment and the beginning of Edom's judgment from the Lord. Apparently, the assistance Edom gave the Babylonians in taking Zion was a particularly bitter pill for Judeans. After all, Judah and Edom were joined by blood. Nothing is said directly about an Edomite role in the fall of Jerusalem, but the vitriolic language of Psalm 137:7, Joel 3:19–21, and Obadiah 10–14 make it clear that Edom had committed treachery.

This oracle-like conclusion to chapter 4 has a strong ironic bite to it. Edom is actually called on to rejoice and be glad (in the present) because the cup is about to be passed, and they will be harshly judged in the future. Partaking of a celebratory cup—which turns on its drinker and leads to drunkenness and judgment—is a proverbial motif of judgment throughout the Old Testament. The content of the cup initially tastes good, but it contains the wrath of judgment soon to be dispensed.

The judgment that fell on Zion was severe, but it will have an end (4:22a). In succinct fashion the two parts of this affirmation show the major function of Lamentations. On the one hand, judgment has fallen, and the resulting tragedies are everywhere in evidence. On the other hand, a confession on the part of the people helps prepare the way for the new thing God will do in bringing an end to Jerusalem's bereavement and humiliation.

Application. The past, present, and future alike come under the judging, refining, and transforming work of God. We are called to moral and spiritual accountability. All of us have a past as well as a future in which we are held morally and spiritually accountable. There will be harsh and tragic words in the future for those who think that freedom and pleasure are the goals of human existence. By God's grace they can be gifts in due season, but that is a far different matter than the goal of radical autonomy. The latter is a false god and leads ultimately to catastrophe.

LAMENTATIONS 5:1–22

Original Meaning. The dominant voice in this chapter is first-person plural. The chapter—with its challenge for God to remember and its plea for God to restore—invites conversation between the people and God. A corporate call to God typically comes in the context of worship, and the topic of conversation here—the very possibility of an ongoing relationship between Judah and God—is best approached through prayer and confession.

The poet of Lamentations 5 offers a catalogue of characters whose lives have been shattered by the loss of Jerusalem. Corporately the joy is gone from the people's hearts (5:15). The voices of the text sound weary, resigned, and accusatory.

The last verse both raises a question and provides an implied answer. There is no doubt in the mind of the poet that God has rejected and judged his people. But has God irrevocably and utterly rejected them, and is his anger beyond measure and without appeasement? No final answer can come solely from the side of the people, for they are not capable of restoring themselves to God. An answer, nevertheless, is intimated, even though only God can bring it to pass. It is intimated in the confession of God's daily mercy (3:22–24), in the claim that Judah's exile will not be forever (4:22), and in the request for God to restore the people to himself (5:21).

Application. Of all the concentration camps established by the Nazis, Auschwitz seems to evoke the most horror. Each plaque says essentially the same thing, although each is inscribed in a different language. The English plaque reads: "Forever let this place be a cry of despair, a warning to humanity." No visitor can avoid the feeling of evil that pervades the place, even though the camp has not been used in over half a century.

The book of Lamentations preaches the cross in a historically based typological sense. In doing so, it unmasks the pretense and hypocrisy of humankind in any generation, pushing all who read its despairing poetry to reflect on the meaning and purpose of their own lives. Within the dominant despair of the book are indications that God has spoken a renewing and redeeming word. In the fullness of time that Word was enfleshed, crucified, and resurrected. Through his Word, God is not aloof toward despair, even despair of its own making, but has taken despair into and upon himself through the cross and resurrection of his Son, expending its death-dealing curse and bringing healing and immortality to light.

EZEKIEL

INTRODUCTION TO EZEKIEL

Who wrote the book that bears Ezekiel's name? In recent academic work, there has been something of a resurgence of support for a more conservative position regarding the relationship of the prophet and the book. The excellent commentaries by Daniel Block in the New International Commentary on the Old Testament series and by Moshe Greenberg in the Anchor Bible series acknowledge in principle the possibility that there may have been editorial additions and revisions made by the disciples of the prophet. Yet both commentaries assume that the present contents of the book of Ezekiel essentially come to us from the hand of the prophet himself. It is the firm conviction of this writer that they are fundamentally accurate in their assessment. When the text is allowed to speak for itself, it conveys a coherent and consistent worldview that addresses the situation of those exiled from Judah in the sixth century BC. There seems, therefore, little reason to assign significant portions of it to late redactors. It is simpler to accept the testimony of the book itself than to multiply unnecessarily complex theories of authorship.

Ultimately, however, the authority of the text does not lie in our ability to demonstrate that it comes to us directly from the mouth of the prophet. Though there may be supporting witnesses, for us to be convinced of its divine origin and authority over us requires a work of the Holy Spirit in our hearts. Only this internal illumination will enable us to recognize the book and receive it for what it really is: nothing less than the word of the Sovereign Lord.

BOOK OUTLINE

I. Ezekiel's Call and Commissioning (1:1–3:27)
   A. Preface: The Prophet's Social and Physical Location (1:1–3)
   B. The Vision of the Divine Throne-Chariot (1:4–28)
   C. The Prophet's Call (2:1–3:15)
   D. Commissioned as a Watchman (3:16–27)
II. Oracles of Doom (4:1–24:27)
   A. Prophecies against Jerusalem and Her Land (4:1–7:27)
   B. The Vision of the Temple (8:1–11:25)
   C. Further Oracles of Judgment (12:1–24:27)
III. Oracles against the Nations (25:1–32:32)
   A. Oracles against Ammon, Moab, Edom, and Philistia (25:1–17)
   B. Oracles against Tyre and Sidon, and Judgment for the Nations (26:1–28:26)
   C. An Oracle against Egypt and Her Ruler (29:1–32:32)
IV. Oracles of Good News (33:1–48:35)
   A. The Turning Point (33:1–33)
   B. Oracles of Restoration (34:1–37:28)
   C. The New Order Put to the Final Test (38:1–39:29)
   D. The Renewed Temple (40:1–48:35)

EZEKIEL 1:1–3

Original Meaning. The opening three verses of Ezekiel serve to locate the prophet's ministry in time and space. Verse 1 tells us that the prophet received his call on the fifth day of the fourth month in the thirtieth year, among the exiles beside the Kebar River. What is clear and underlined in the present form of the text is that the opening vision of the prophet Ezekiel is placed in the fifth year of Jehoiachin's exile, that is, 593 BC, while the prophet lived among the exiles of Babylonia. Historically and socially, therefore, Ezekiel's message was addressed to those in exile.

There in exile, Ezekiel was confronted by a dramatic spectacle: The heavens were opened and he saw "visions of God" (1:1). The prophet was taken behind the scenes, as it were, and given a different, divine perspective on the events unfolding around him. The phrase "visions of God" encompasses not only the opening vision of the divine throne-chariot but all of the visions that play such an important part in Ezekiel's message. God is dramatically at work even in the apparently hopeless situation of the exiles, a work that the prophet is invited to "show and tell" to those around him.

Application. How do we live with the reality of life in a world where victories are frequently hard to come by and right living does not always lead to success? The answer is to balance the biblical models of exodus and conquest with the equally biblical models of wilderness and exile. As exiles, we are not homeless and hopeless. We do have a home—it is just not here. Why do we love to read the Scriptures daily? Because they speak to us of home. Why do we live differently from those around us? Because we remember that we are soon going home (1 Pet 4:1–7). Why are we willing to suffer and even die for our faith?

Because we are sure of what we hope for and certain that to be with God, even through pain, is better by far than to be comfortable without him (Heb 11:1–2, 13–16).

EZEKIEL 1:4–28

Original Meaning. Two kinds of imagery dominate the opening vision of Ezekiel: images of motion and images of judgment. In contrast to Isaiah's static temple imagery, Ezekiel's vision is filled with movement. Whereas Isaiah saw the Lord seated in the temple, Ezekiel's vision opens with the Lord in the midst of a motion-filled "windstorm" (1:4) in the land of the exiles. Movement dominates Ezekiel's description of the approach of a mighty windstorm. The windstorm itself is in motion, while the living creatures it contains not only have legs but wings as well. Torches are moving back and forth between the creatures (1:13), while alongside the creatures are various wheels, with each "wheel intersecting a wheel" (1:16). All of these wheels move together and stop together under the control of "the spirit of the living creatures" (1:20). Everywhere the prophet looks, he sees bustling activity.

What is more, the activity has ominous import. Ezekiel's vision, however bizarre it may seem to us, draws on a number of traditional ancient Near Eastern elements. The imagery of the Lord riding on the storm, surrounded by fire and lightning, was a common way of describing the coming of the Divine Warrior. Frequently, the image of God as a warrior was adopted by the prophets to speak of the Lord's coming to deliver his people. In this instance, however, it is significant that the windstorm is coming "out of the north" (1:4), the traditional source of Judah's foes. The Divine Warrior is here approaching to wage war against his own people, not to deliver them.

The Lord's throne-chariot is supported by living creatures, which are instantly recognizable as cherubim from their role as throne-bearers (cf. Ps 18:10) and indeed are explicitly identified as such in Ezekiel 10:1. They have four faces each—that of a man, a lion (the highest wild animal), an ox (the highest domestic animal), and an eagle (the highest bird)—symbolizing the fact that they embody within themselves all of the highest attributes of living creation.

As well as being God's throne-bearers, the cherubim are the guardians of God's holiness, God's heavenly bodyguard. The threatening nature of their presence comes from their role as enforcers of divine judgment. Thus, when the man and the woman were thrown out of the garden of Eden, cherubim were appointed to bar the way back into God's presence, preventing any intrusion of the profane into the realm of God's holiness (Gen 3:24).

While the emphasis of Ezekiel 1 is almost exclusively on the gathering clouds that threaten rain, the mention of the rainbow (1:28) allows the possibility of a ray of hope even in the midst of the gloom. God's judgment must fall on his rebellious people, yet because of commitment to his covenant he will not wipe them out.

But where can one flee from this impending judgment of God? The message of the vision is that flight is useless. The throne-chariot can proceed as easily to any of the four points of the compass, without even having to turn, symbolizing God's omnipresence (1:12, 17). The wheels are covered with eyes, symbolizing the omniscience of God. In the face of such an awesome, ominous appearing of God, it is small wonder that Ezekiel fell on his face (1:28).

Application. God is living and active and constantly doing new things. Should the existing structures of the church grow moribund and useless, he can and does raise up for himself new organizations and denominations to achieve his purposes. The encouragement and challenge to our contemporary churches is that the living God will achieve his purposes—with or without us! Given that truth, Christians need to adopt a balance between progressivism and traditionalism. On the one hand, not everything that is new is of God. On the other hand, neither is everything new automatically suspect. Our understanding of the Scriptures and how they are to be applied to our present times is constantly growing as new challenges drive us back to reread old passages and reevaluate the traditions we have received.

EZEKIEL 2:1–3:15

Original Meaning. God comes to Ezekiel entirely unsought and reveals himself to the prophet to commission him for a task and to entrust to him a message. On the most basic level, the call, vision, and commissioning serve to authenticate Ezekiel's ministry, both to himself and to his audience. Ezekiel is being sent to the Israelites, who are a "rebellious nation" (2:3).

The essence of the people's transgression lies in their refusal to recognize God's sovereignty over them. In that attitude they have hardened themselves, externally and internally, becoming "obstinate" and "stubborn" (2:4). Even though the people will not listen to his words, yet "they will know that a prophet has been among them" (2:5). That is, when the predicted disasters befall Israel, they will recognize that God had previously warned them of what was about to happen.

Throughout the vision, Ezekiel is the very picture of compliant obedience, not because of some special measure of holiness intrinsic to Ezekiel but because of an infusion of divine Spirit (2:2). God not only hands the scroll to Ezekiel, but he also causes him to eat it (3:2). He is the One who will strengthen Ezekiel to make him as tough as his opponents. Without God's power, Ezekiel literally can do nothing.

This depiction of Ezekiel as the model of Spirit-infused submission suggests that there is more than one dimension to the Lord's characteristic address to Ezekiel as *ben-adam*, usually translated "son of man" (2:1, 3, etc.). This form of address sharply distinguishes Ezekiel from the Sovereign God. But this expression may perhaps also mark him out from all of his contemporaries. They are the "sons of Israel" (*beney yisrael*, 2:3, NIV "Israelites"), the true descendants of the one whose nature was to strive with God (Gen 32:28); Ezekiel, on the other hand, is literally designated "the son of Adam" (NIV "son of man").

Like the first Adam, Ezekiel faces a test of obedience that revolves around the idea of eating, though in his case he is to eat whatever the Lord commands him to (Ezek 2:8). In another reversal of the original sin, what Ezekiel is given to eat is anything but "good for food" (Gen 3:6); rather, it is a scroll covered on both sides with words of lament and woe (Ezek 2:10). But though its appearance is unattractive, to the obedient eater it tasted "as sweet as honey" (3:3).

Yet the vision ends on what appears at first sight to be a discordant note in 3:14–15. The prophet who has been called, empowered, and equipped is found sitting down, overwhelmed, filled with feelings of anger. These verses underline, however, the dual nature of the prophet's task. On the one hand, he remains under "the strong hand of the LORD" (3:14) and therefore begins to feel the feelings that the Lord has toward the people—feelings of wrath and anger. On the other hand, he sits among the exiles, living where they live, and thus sees the effects of God's wrath from the other side: the forthcoming overwhelming devastation of his people (3:15).

Application. Are those who today labor for many years in the difficult areas of the Middle East or Japan, while seeing only a handful of converts, operating in the wrong place? If the primary goal of missions is to see the world converted, then the answer to both questions is yes. But if the primary goal of missions is the same as the goal set before Ezekiel—faithfulness to the task to which one has been called, no matter what the consequences, so that God may be glorified—then the answer is different. In biblical perspective, reaching the world is only the secondary goal of missions, behind the primary goal of bringing glory to God through faithful obedience.

EZEKIEL 3:16–27

Original Meaning. The idea of the prophet as a "watchman" (3:17) is a familiar one in the Old Testament. In this case, the "enemy" of whom the people have to beware is none other than God himself!

Ezekiel has been shown the reality of judgment to come. To those who heed his warning of judgment, it will be a message of life; to those who refuse him, it will be a message of death. In either case, his responsibility is the same: to sound the warning note clearly. Otherwise, he too will share in the judgment.

Just as a watchman has to shout his message of danger to everyone in the city, so also Ezekiel must address his message of judgment to all, whether righteous or wicked, and whether they listen or fail to listen (cf. 2:7). Thus, 3:17–21 does not expand the scope of Ezekiel's ministry beyond what is already required of him in 2:7. What it does is set before him clearly the consequences of any failure to fulfill his responsibilities.

Those who respond faithfully to his proclamation will "live" (3:21), a term describing not merely physical life but rather the fullness of relationship with the Sovereign Lord that flows from obedience. Death, on the other hand, means estrangement from both God and the covenant community.

The wicked are not closed out from life by their present status; there is still time to turn and live. Similarly, the righteous must listen to the word of the prophet in order to live. In other words, what marks out those who "live" from those who "die" is the fact that they listen to the word of the Lord through the prophet and respond to it.

When he is placed on his feet by an infusion of the divine Spirit, Ezekiel is ordered to remain confined to his house and told that he will be mute (3:24–26). The nature of the prophet's isolation will be twofold: He is to be confined to his house and he will lose his power of free speech. The time for appeals for mercy is past; the appeals process is exhausted. The prophet's role, at least up until the fall of Jerusalem, is restricted to the delivery of the divine sentence of judgment (3:27).

Application. Not all are called to fulfill the distinctive kind of prophetic ministry to which Ezekiel was called; yet as Christians, we too have a calling from God. The spirit of God that inspired the prophets now indwells us; only instead of swallowing a scroll, as Ezekiel did, we imbibe a book, the Bible, through whose pages God continues to speak to his people and to the world. This is the message we have been given to communicate and to which we are confined. Though we may be creative in the way we communicate the message, we are not free to be creative in the content of the message that we are to deliver.

EZEKIEL 4:1–17

Original Meaning. The first of Ezekiel's sign-acts symbolizes the siege of the city of Jerusalem and the reason for it. Acting the part of the Lord, Ezekiel is to set up a large iron pan between himself and the city (4:3), symbolizing the cutting off of relationships between God and his people. There is now no channel by which the people can communicate with God, even if they wanted to do so. In the previous chapter, the prophet had been told that the appeals process had been exhausted. By his pantomime, Ezekiel is to make the invisible aggressor visible.

At this point the sign changes to a new sign-act, more complex in terms of interpretation. Not only were the rations small and unappetizing, but Ezekiel was also instructed (at first) to prepare them by baking them over human excrement, rendering him ceremonially unclean. This would be particularly abhorrent to a priest like Ezekiel. However, in response to Ezekiel's protest, the Lord permitted the prophet to substitute animal dung as the fuel.

For Ezekiel the "people of Israel" (4:5) is the whole covenant people of God, and their sins are centered in the Jerusalem temple, the heart of the Southern Kingdom. Their 390-year history of sin, pictured by the prophet's 390-day prostration on his left side, stretches back in time to around the construction of the first temple. Likewise, the "people of Judah" (4:6) appears here to be a designation for the community of the exiles in Ezekiel.

When we combine this approach with the dual significance of the phrase "bear their sin" (4:4), the following interpretation emerges: Ezekiel is to lie on his left side for 390 days, representing 390 years, bearing the guilt of the entire covenant community of Israel. The iniquity of the community is placed on him (4:4). During this period, the prophet symbolizes Israel's long history of accumulated sin, which culminates in the siege and fall of Jerusalem, concretely depicted by eating siege rations throughout the 390 days (4:9). Then during the period of forty days, he represents the punishment of the exile, which he depicts in terms of the symbolic figure of forty years. Just as Israel's ancestors in the desert were a lost generation, spending forty years in the desert for their sin (Num 14:34), so the exilic generation is condemned to a similar fate for the nation's long history of sin.

Ezekiel's diet during this period has a twofold aspect: small rations of poor quality, symbolizing the siege diet of the people of Jerusalem, and cooking in a ceremonially unclean way, symbolizing the unclean food for those in Jerusalem and in exile. Moreover, Ezekiel is instructed to cook in a ceremonially unclean way, symbolizing the defiled food that the Israelites will eat in exile (4:13). By this means, the twofold message of judgment is proclaimed on all Israel, both those who remain in Jerusalem and those who are in exile. Yet Ezekiel asserts that he has never consumed anything defiled, and the decree is promptly emended by the Lord to allow the prophet to maintain his ceremonial purity. Ezekiel thus stands as a picture of a righteous remnant.

Application. Well-executed drama has an affective function, touching emotions not easily reached by words while stimulating and holding interest. Yet we should not fail to see the differences between the prophetic sign-acts and contemporary dramas. The prophetic sign-acts were more than mere visual aids or attention-getting devices. They were delivered with divine authority and thus functioned as the divine word made visible and sure. In Ezekiel's case, the message took over the messenger in a life-dominating way.

EZEKIEL 5:1–17

Original Meaning. The image of relentless judgment that we saw in Ezekiel 4 reemerges at the beginning of chapter 5. Here Ezekiel is called upon to shave his head and his beard, a sign of humiliation (cf. 2 Sam 10:4). The instrument of this humiliation is described as both a "sharp sword" and a "barber's razor" (Ezek 5:1). The first term serves to link this image with what precedes and what follows, underlining the military nature of the coming disaster, while the latter term shows that what God calls Ezekiel to do is to act out in concrete form. The prophet's hair itself becomes the medium for the last sign-act, representing the different fates that will meet the inhabitants of Jerusalem (5:2–4).

The interpretation of these last two signs is given in 5:5–17. The language Ezekiel adopts in these verses is not his own creation but is largely borrowed from Leviticus 26, a chapter that lays out the blessings and curses attached to the covenant. They have committed idolatry and thus defiled the sanctuary (Ezek 5:9, 11). More generally, they have not followed the Lord's decrees or kept his laws (5:6; cf. Lev 26:14–15). As a result, the curses of Leviticus 26 will be operative in their midst.

This covenant context is important because it demonstrates that the judgment that will befall Jerusalem is neither arbitrary nor unfair. The judgments coming on that city are not random afflictions thought up on the spur of the moment, as if God has lost his temper; they are the execution of the curses on the covenant breakers. Indeed, Israel has not merely failed to live up to God's standards; they have not even lived up to the standards of the nations around them (Ezek 5:7). Instead of being a light to the nations, they have led the nations further into the darkness. The Lord will not show pity or spare his beloved but rebellious people (5:11).

Both Leviticus 26 and Ezekiel 5 hold out the hope that the Lord's anger will reach an end before Israel will. Yes, God's anger and wrath must be poured out on Israel so that they may know the Lord as a jealous God (5:13; cf. Exod 20:5), a God who will not share the devotion of his people with another. For now, they will be a ruin and reproach in the sight of the nations (Ezek 5:14). But God's anger will cease, and his wrath will subside once it has been fully vented (5:13), for the Lord is merciful and gracious as well as jealous (Exod 34:6, 14). To put it more precisely, God has covenanted himself to his people and has made a commitment he will not break, even though his people are unfaithful (Lev 26:44). The purpose of this present chastisement, therefore, is not to destroy them utterly and forever but in order that the Lord may once again amaze the nations by accomplishing a new exodus of his people.

Application. Even though God is faithful and loving, he is also just. He is a holy God, of purer eyes than to look upon evil. So how can he forgive the guilty and still be just? Ezekiel does not give us a very clear answer to that question. He leaves it open. He knows that it is true, for God has revealed it to him, but he doesn't know how it can be true. But we who live this side of Christmas have a much clearer understanding. How can God be just and still forgive the guilty? How can the fire pass over us and not completely burn us alive? It is only because it has already passed over Jesus and poured its heat out on him.

EZEKIEL 6:1–14

Original Meaning. Whereas before the prophet addressed the city of Jerusalem, the political and religious center of the land, now he is told to set his face against the mountains of all Israel. While the borders of Israel expanded and contracted at different times in Israel's history, the hill country was always Israel par excellence. It was the Lord's "home turf."

Yet it is precisely into that home turf that idolatry has penetrated. For the hill country is also the location of "high places" (*bamot*, 6:3). Prior to the building of the Jerusalem temple, the people were permitted to use the high places as locations for offering sacrifices to the Lord (1 Kgs 3:2). Once that structure was completed, however, the worship of Israel was to be centralized in Jerusalem (Deut 12). These local high places became the entry points for Canaanite religious ideas and images. Syncretism was at times officially encouraged, while at other times the authorities simply turned a blind eye to it.

It was not uncommon in the ancient world to defile altars by burning corpses on them, putting the profane in the place of the holy (1 Kgs 13:2; 2 Kgs 23:16). The places of idolatry will be rendered unfit, and the idolaters themselves will be put to death (cf. Deut 13:9). God will do what successive generations of kings failed to do and put an end to this abomination.

When God acts decisively in this way, the result will be that Israel "will know that I am the LORD" (Ezek 6:7). This so-called "recognition formula" stresses the fact that the knowledge of the Lord comes about as a direct result of God's actions in history. A remnant will survive the coming judgment who will look back from exile and recognize that the Lord is the God who acts in history.

The content of what the people will remember about the Lord is his grief at their adulterous actions, and the result flowing from that remembrance will be self-loathing at their evil ways (6:9). As much as their sin of idolatry delighted them in the past, now it will become an object of horror in their eyes.

However, in keeping with the focus on the dark side in these chapters, Ezekiel does not end his oracle on this happy thought. Instead, he returns to the theme of judgment on the house of Israel because of their abominations (6:11–14). The threefold judgment of sword, famine, and plague is once again unleashed on the land (6:11). When the people are slain around their idolatrous altars and the entire land from south to north is turned into a desolate waste, the knowledge of the Lord will be established.

This twofold ending to the two oracles seems to envisage two opposite possibilities: repentance and return to the Lord (6:8–10) or the total devastation of the land and the wiping out of the entire people (6:11–14). Both are indeed possible endings to Israel's story; in either event, the Lord's justice will be seen and known.

Application. The people who say, "It doesn't matter what you believe about God as long as you are sincere," are those to whom belief about God is inconsequential. But if, in fact, there is a God who designed the whole cosmic and human story with a purpose, so that the chief end of humanity is indeed to glorify this God and enjoy him forever, then what you believe becomes a matter of supreme and decisive importance.

EZEKIEL 7:1–27

Original Meaning. Many people think of the message of the prophets as, "Repent, the end is near." Ezekiel's message in this chapter, however, is: "It's too late to repent; the end has come." There is a twofold expansion in Ezekiel 7 regarding the scope of the judgment from that described in his previous messages.

1. It is once more expanded geographically. The prophet widens his scope of attention to include judgment on the whole "land of Israel" (7:2).
2. Ezekiel insists repeatedly that doom is not merely imminent but has actually arrived. Thus 7:7 announces: "The time has come, the day has arrived" (author's translation). The prophesied end is coming on the whole land of Israel (7:2), and it is coming now (7:3). Measure for measure, they will receive what they deserve for their abominations (7:3), without favoritism or pity, resulting in an understanding of the Lord's power and holiness.

The second oracle (7:5–9) picks up from the first oracle the theme of the personal nature of divine judgment on the people's sin. All of the first-person verbs from the first oracle expressing the outpouring of the Lord's wrath recur, along with a significantly modified version of the recognition formula, "Then you will know that it is I the LORD who strikes you" (7:9).

The third oracle (7:10–27) unfolds the theme of the comprehensiveness of judgment from the first oracle. It begins with a brief introduction (7:10–11), which draws out the organic connection between Judah's sin and her punishment. According to 7:10–11, Israel's "doom has burst forth, the rod has budded, arrogance has blossomed! Violence has arisen, a rod to punish wickedness." Alongside Israel's blossoming pride and violence, however, the rod of God's judgment has been growing, namely, Babylon (7:21).

Suitably to its theme of comprehensive judgment, the oracle is itself massive and wide-ranging, consisting of two parallel cycles of judgment scenes that move from the general to the particular. These may be broken down as follows:

A: the futility of commercial transactions (7:12–13)
  B: the announcement and arrival of war and devastation (7:14–16)
    C: universal ineffectiveness, terror, and mourning (7:17–18)
A′: the futility of gold and silver (7:19–20)
  B′: dispossession, looting, and desecration (7:21–24)
    C′: ineffectiveness, terror, and mourning by all classes (7:25–27)

When the threatened judgment falls, commercial transactions will lose their meaning; there will be no such thing as a good deal or a bad deal, whether for the buyer or the seller (7:12). Even gold and silver will be worthless, able neither to save their owners nor to satisfy them (7:19). Indeed, these precious metals will be worse than worthless; they will not simply be regarded as trash, because gold and silver furnished the materials for the people's idolatry (7:20).

The nature of the disaster is the focus of the next section in the cycle: Judah will be given over into the hand of her enemies, and all her possessions will be handed over as plunder (7:21). The Lord will turn away his face (7:22), allowing the wicked of the earth to pollute the land and even to desecrate "the place I treasure" (7:22). Since Israel failed to distinguish between true and false places of worship and did not destroy the high places, now God's judgment will be similarly nondiscriminatory, destroying not only the pagan sanctuaries but his own temple.

In the face of this disaster, no coherent policy will be formulated or implemented. All hands will hang passively by their sides. Paralyzing fear will result in loss of control of bodily functions (7:17). The people will put on a show of mourning by means of their clothes and their shaven heads (7:18), yet no mercy or forgiveness will be found there, as God already announced (7:4). The people will seek peace and not find it (7:25), whether they seek it through the channel of religious leadership or political leadership. There will be no effective guidance through the religious leadership, whether the prophet (from whom a vision might be sought), the priest (from whom torah, or instruction from the priestly law, might be sought), or the elders (from whom wisdom and counsel might be expected). Nor will there be effective leadership in the political realm.

Application. Why do we strive so hard to accumulate possessions that will not last and to gain influence and power that will not ultimately benefit us? The reason is that we have given ourselves over to our various idolatries and have forgotten our inescapable accountability to the one true God. Even believers will have to give an account for their actions, as the apostle Paul reminds us (2 Cor 5:10). We need to learn to see the end from the beginning, to envisage the future vividly here and now, and to let that vision dominate our lives.

EZEKIEL 8:1–9:11

Original Meaning. The vision opens with a date: the fifth day of the sixth month of the sixth year (of Jehoiachin's exile); in our reckoning, that would be September 18, 592 BC. Although the date formula serves to mark chapters 8–11 off from what precedes, the close connection with chapter 7 is maintained. Thus, it would not be inappropriate to say that Ezekiel 8–9 depicts in visionary form what Ezekiel 7 stated in oracular style.

The vision of Ezekiel 8–11 is intended for a specific audience, "the elders of Judah" (8:1), who have gathered at Ezekiel's house. As the vision opens, Ezekiel sees a glowing figure in human form, corresponding to what he had seen in 1:27. Once more he is transported by the agency of the Spirit and shown a vision; the context of the vision, however, is no longer the situation of the exiles but the defiled city of Jerusalem. The prophet is shown four scenes of increasing abomination, with the offense to God being greater as the scenes in which they take place move nearer to the center of the temple.

1. His tour begins with a vision of an idol (8:3) at the north gate of the city (8:3–6). The focus of the attention is the effect that this image has on the Lord. It "provokes [him] to jealousy" (8:3); God will not share Israel's worship with other gods, and he has proof of her infidelity.
2. However, abominable though this idolatry is, worse is yet to come. Next, Ezekiel is shown seventy elders of the house of Israel, leaders among the lay community, offering incense to idols in a secret chamber (8:7–13).

These non-Spirit-filled elders find justification for their conduct in the belief that the Lord does not see (8:12). One of their number is named as Jaazaniah, who is designated the son of Shaphan—and thus equally shockingly associated with a family that was prominent in the reforms of Josiah's days (2 Kgs 22:3–14).

In the light of what they saw as God's abandonment of them, they felt justified in pursuing other deities who might help out. Far from the Lord's having abandoned the land, it is they who have driven the Lord away (Ezek 8:6). Far from their incense-burning being an effective means of warding off dangers, it is one of the causes of God's impending judgment on them. Ironically, it is their vision that is clouded, not the Lord's.

3. Worse still is the sight of women weeping for Tammuz at the north gate of the temple itself (8:14–15). With each new scene we approach closer to the heart of Israel's worship. Weeping for Tammuz was a Babylonian ritual, marking the death and descent into the underworld of the god Dumuzi, whose mythological course of death and "resurrection" (or more accurately, "return") was thought to be parallel to the annual rhythm of nature.
4. The final and supreme act of idolatry takes place within the inner court of the temple itself, where Ezekiel sees twenty-five men turning their backs on the temple proper and prostrating themselves to the east in worship of the sun (8:16). This is the ultimate abomination: Instead of bowing down to worship the Lord and seeking his face, they turn their backs on God and worship the created order.

In four brief scenes, then, Ezekiel has been shown the comprehensive nature of the sins of Jerusalem. Their sin extends from outside the city gate to the inner courtyard of the temple itself. It involves both men and women, even the seventy elders, symbolic of the leadership of the whole people. It includes idolatry imported from all sorts of surrounding nations (Canaan, Egypt, and Babylon) and involving all kinds of gods (male and female human figures, animal figures, and stellar bodies). This is a unified, universalized religion, the ultimate multifaith worship service. From the Lord's perspective, however, the picture is one of abomination piled on abomination.

The Lord summons six "guards" (NIV: "those who are appointed to execute judgment") each of whom appears armed with a club (9:1). These figures are normally interpreted as angelic beings because of their superhuman role in the vision and the symbolic nature of their total number (seven). On the one hand, in the vision they are the angelic servants of the Most High, wreaking his judgments on the earth; on the other hand, those same judgments are carried out in history through human agency, so the six destroyers may equally aptly be seen to represent the Babylonian invaders. If this much is true, is it not also true that the seventh figure, the priestly writer, acts in some sense as Ezekiel's own alter ego? He obediently passes among the people prior to the judgment, distinguishing the righteous from the wicked, marking out those who sigh and over the detestable things done in Jerusalem (9:4).

Hard on his heels come the agents of destruction, who themselves take on the attitude of God toward the people (9:5). All those without the mark are to be slain—young and old, male and female (9:5–6). The categories listed demonstrate that even the defenseless, the frail, and the innocent are condemned to destruction.

The slaughter is to begin at the temple with the chief idolaters: the twenty-five elders who were worshiping the sun (9:6; cf. 8:16). The killing takes place within the temple itself (9:7). It is already so contaminated by their idolatry that God himself has no compunction about defiling it further.

In the midst of the carnage, Ezekiel is left alone (9:8) and he cries out. The Lord's answer to the prophet's question appears to be yes. He points to the depth of the abominations and sin of the house of Israel and Judah. They can expect no pity or compassion but just retribution for their actions, which is the final proof that he has indeed seen everything that has transpired.

Yet at this critical juncture, precisely when it appears that all hope is gone, suddenly the priestly figure with the writing kit reappears, saying, "I have done as you commanded" (9:11). His appearance also answers Ezekiel's question concerning the remnant, for he stands as mute testimony to the Lord's purpose to save those who sigh and mourn over the abominations of Jerusalem. We are not told how many he has marked—indeed, we are not even told that he has marked any—yet his presence acts to mitigate slightly the awful severity of the judgment, just as the rainbow of 1:28 tempers slightly the coming windstorm of God's wrath.

Application. We, too, face an abundance of idols all around us in our multicultural age. Frequently, people speak of ours as being an age of pluralism, as if that somehow makes our time distinct from the past. This is palpable nonsense, for at many times in the past, not least during the New Testament era and the time of the exile, God's people have found themselves placed in a melting pot of world religions. The options available in the "marketplace of religions" have often been just as diverse in previous centuries as they are at present. The hallmark of any pluralistic age is that idolatry comes in all shapes and sizes and encourages us to attend regularly the church or religious institution of our choice.

EZEKIEL 10:1–11:25

Original Meaning. Chapter 10 opens with a continuation of the judgment scene of Ezekiel 9. There we saw the city being overrun by divinely appointed executioners. Now, on top of that destruction of life, follows the destruction of property. The seventh angel returns to the fray. At the Lord's command, he takes burning coals from beneath the heavenly throne in order to burn the city to the ground (10:2). Ezekiel is here simply giving us a glimpse behind the scenes at the cosmic realities that underlie history.

After the priestly figure departs to carry out the Lord's bidding, there follows a renewed description of the divine chariot with its supernatural attendants. The divine chariot is drawn up on the south side of the temple (10:3), as far away as possible from the abominations on the northern side of the city. Then Ezekiel sees a cloud filling the inner court and the glory of God on the move once more. It departs slowly, haltingly, as if reluctant to leave. First it passes from the earthly cherubim in the Most Holy Place to the threshold of the temple (10:4), then from the threshold of the temple to the divine chariot over the (real) cherubim (10:18). From there the glory moves to the east gate of the temple courtyard (10:19), where there is a pause during which the prophet receives a further oracle and vision. Finally, the glory moves on to the Mount of Olives, east of Jerusalem, outside the city limits. The city itself is now effectively doomed, cut off from divine aid from its true protector, waiting for the ax to fall. The Lord has abandoned the city to the empty hope offered by the idols for which the people abandoned him.

Not everyone within the city of Jerusalem has the same perspective, however. At the entrance to the east gate, Ezekiel sees a group of men whose number (twenty-five, 11:1) and whose function (giving advice, 11:2) suggest them to be elders. Ezekiel is told that these leaders have been "plotting evil" (11:2). In opposition to the prophetic word of forthcoming judgment on Jerusalem, they have apparently been arrogantly asserting the security of their position. The exact meaning of the terse expression in 11:3a (literally, "not near building houses") has been much debated. The NIV, along with most translations and commentators, takes the Hebrew word for "near" in a temporal sense: "'Haven't our houses been recently rebuilt?'" However, a better sense is obtained if "near" is taken in a spatial sense. The phrase then becomes, "It is not for the one who is near to build houses," with an obvious reference to the letter that Jeremiah sent the exiles urging them to "build houses" (Jer 29:5).

This understanding seems to fit better with the second half of the statement: "This city is a pot, and we are the meat" (Ezek 11:3b). This may be interpreted as a statement of the relative value of those who remain in Jerusalem and the exiles (the best part, the "meat," is put in the cooking pot while the undesired portion, the offal, is thrown into the fire). A contrast is implied between those who remain in Jerusalem and the exiles, a contrast that favors the inhabitants of the city. They regard the de facto situation as an expression of God's favor on them and displeasure with those in exile (11:15). They think of themselves as the true remnant while those in exile are under God's judgment.

In the oracle that follows, the Lord rejects their claim. Because of the violent crimes committed by these leaders, by which they have filled the city with corpses, the city will provide no protection for them (11:7). The sword that they fear will come on them and they will fall by it (11:8, 10). The land will not be their possession; rather, the Lord will bring them out of the city to judge them at the very edge of the land, at the "borders of Israel" (11:10).

In this prophecy there is a challenge to the Jerusalemites' claim to possess the land. The language is carefully chosen to depict their fate as a kind of anti-exodus. The Lord will "drive [them] out of the city," just as he earlier brought Israel out of the land of Egypt (11:9; cf. Exod 6:6). The judgments that once fell on Egypt (Exod 6:6; 12:12) now fall on the inhabitants of Jerusalem (Ezek 11:10). Far from the land of Canaan being their "possession" (11:15; cf. Exod 6:8), the inhabitants of Jerusalem will die outside the land because of their failure to keep the Lord's decrees and laws. Ezekiel's response to this demonstration of the reality of God's judgment is to fall on his face and cry out the question: "Sovereign LORD! Will you completely destroy the remnant of Israel?" (Ezek 11:13; cf. 9:8). Up to a point, Ezekiel shares the presuppositions of the Jerusalemites. God's land and God's people are an indivisible unity.

The response to Ezekiel's cry (11:13) is a glorious declaration that the future of Israel lies among the exiles (11:15). Yes, they have been sent far away from the land of Israel, but even there they have not been cast out of the Lord's presence (11:16). By this we see that the Lord's movement is not simply a departure *from* Jerusalem, but also a departure *to* Babylon, to be a sanctuary for his true people there.

But the Lord's exile, like that of his true people, is only a temporary state of affairs. The counterpart of the anti-exodus of the Lord's nonpeople from Judah will be a new exodus of the Lord's true people from all the nations to which they have been scattered (11:17; cf. Exod 6:6); the land that Ezekiel cannot redeem for his redemption relatives (Ezek 11:15) will be redeemed for them by the Lord (cf. Exod 6:6). The detestable idols and vile images with which the former inhabitants filled the land (7:20; 8:3–17) will be removed by the new inhabitants (11:18).

The reason for this change in behavior is, quite literally, a change of heart. The Lord will create in his new people "an undivided heart" (11:19), in the sense of undivided loyalty to the Lord. In contrast to the present occupants of the land, who neither follow the Lord's decrees nor keep his laws (11:12), his new people will observe both decrees and laws (11:20). The result of such renewal will be nothing less than the fulfillment of the goal of the first exodus (11:20; cf. Exod 6:7). This is the first substantive indication in Ezekiel of a solid hope for the future for God's people in exile.

There is, however, no such promising hope for those who remain in the land: They remain committed to idolatry and abominations, for which the judgment they receive will be fully deserved (Ezek 11:21). Thus ends Ezekiel's temple vision: The glory departs from the temple and moves off onto the Mount of Olives, across from Jerusalem, as if waiting to see the judgment on the rebellious city completed, while the prophet is returned to his own people in exile.

Application. Most assume that things are as they appear and that we can easily identify those on whom God's favor rests. We may put our confidence in the traditions of the past, for example, and assume that forms hallowed by repeated usage must be pleasing to God in the present. God's presence is not so easily discerned. He does not always continue to bless forms and institutions that he has blessed in the past, nor is he always found in the large and apparently successful churches.

In the Bible, he is most often found with the poor and the weak, the despised and rejected, those whom the world regards as castoffs. So, when Jesus comes, he visits the temple, but his primary teaching and ministry takes place in the open air. He will eat with the scribes and the Pharisees when they invite him, but he is known rather as the friend of tax collectors and sinners (Matt 11:19). When he seeks twelve disciples, he goes not to the religious training schools but to the workplaces of ordinary men and women. The essence of his training program is not a rigorous course of book study, but three years of being in his presence.

EZEKIEL 12:1–20

Original Meaning. If Ezekiel cherished any hopes of seeing a revolutionary change in the thinking of the exiles as a result of his message, he is quickly disabused of his notions in chapter 12. They do not see what the Lord shows them, nor do they hear what the Lord says, not because they lack the physical organs of sight and hearing, but simply because they are rebellious (12:2). In the language of 11:19, they are still characterized by the heart of stone, a stubborn will that rejects obedience.

This saying of 12:2 underlies the sign-acts that follow it. This section is made up of a sign-act of exile (12:3–7), the interpretation of this sign-act (12:8–17), and a second sign-act of fear and trembling (12:18–20). The initial sign-act that the prophet performs depicts the action of going into exile. Ezekiel is first to put together an exile's pack. These preparations are to be made in the daytime, though the departure is delayed until evening. This delay serves both the practical purpose of allowing time for a crowd to gather to witness the sign-act and a symbolic purpose, representing God's delaying of judgment until the proper time, the gathering gloom of evening (12:4). All of this has symbolic meaning: The Jerusalemites and their prince will go into exile just as he has acted out (12:11).

The symbolic meaning of the otherwise rather enigmatic sign is expounded in 12:10–16. It concerns the fate of Zedekiah along with the house of Israel in Jerusalem (12:10). Many of the details of the sign-act are capable of more than one interpretation.

Some of these complexities may be due to reading the text in the light of its historical fulfillment recorded in 2 Kings 25:4–7; however, some are due to the prophet's penchant for complex, multivalent images, which involve plays on words and sounds. Though the imagery is complex, the essential message seems reasonably straightforward. Not only will there be a further exile, bringing out those still remaining in Jerusalem and Judah, but this anti-exodus will center on the person of the prince, Zedekiah.

All this will happen not because of the desire of Nebuchadnezzar for a little more *Lebensraum* ("room to live") but because the Lord has set a snare for Zedekiah and for the people he represents (Ezek 12:13). The Lord is the one who will bring Zedekiah to Babylonia and will scatter his forces to the winds, pursuing him with drawn sword (12:14). The Lord is the one who will disperse his followers among the nations (12:15–16). Their defeat and dispersal are evidence of the Lord's wrath in action, evidence aimed at curing the willful obtuseness of those remaining in Judah.

To this initial sign-act and interpretation, a further one is then added: Ezekiel is to eat and drink with trembling and shuddering, depicting the anxiety that the inhabitants of Jerusalem and Judah will feel (12:18–19). The land of Judah and all who remain in it are doomed.

Application. The word Ezekiel received took flesh in his actions—actions that were uncomfortable and costly (breaking through his own wall with his bare hands!), actions that were embarrassingly odd (pretending to go into exile, eating and drinking with violent trembling). Through his actions, along with the accompanying words, a message of judgment on their dearest hopes was imparted to his hearers.

How though does God's Word take flesh through us? Evangelicals have sometimes been accused of making the Word who became flesh back into words again. We can talk a good talk but don't always have the walk to match it. A world with ears tightly closed against the truth needs to see the reality of our faith written in changed lives.

EZEKIEL 12:21–13:23

Original Meaning

Confusion Over Prophecy (12:21–28). As he does on a number of other occasions, Ezekiel addresses these issues by presenting two current popular sayings or slogans.

1. The first "proverb" of the people asserts the ineffectiveness of the prophetic word in general (12:22). The people had grown so used to hearing visions proclaimed that never came about that some had come to the conclusion that all prophetic visions were nothing more than empty words. The Lord's response was to throw a slightly revised form of their saying back in their faces (12:23).

   Indeed, every vision would be fulfilled because of a twofold action on the Lord's part. In the first place, there would be no more false visions or flattering divination among the people of Israel (12:24). False prophecy would be silenced so that the people might no longer be led astray by it. In addition, however, true prophecy would be vindicated: The Lord will speak, and what he speaks will happen with no more delay (12:25). This is God's answer to the skeptics of Ezekiel's day.
2. Yet alongside these unbelievers was apparently a second party, the delayers. They simply hoped that this particular word of judgment would not take effect until a future generation (12:27). This second group also receives a "no more" answer from the Lord: There will be no more delay; the Lord will fulfill whatever he has spoken (12:28).

   In order for every prophetic word to be fulfilled, it was necessary that judgment should come to silence the self-proclaimed prophets. This idea, mentioned in passing in 12:24, is unfolded throughout chapter 13 in two halves that show considerable symmetry. Ezekiel first addresses the false prophets (13:1–16) and then the false prophetesses (13:17–23).

Address to the False Prophets of Israel (13:1–16). The foundational difference between Ezekiel and "the prophets of Israel" (13:2a) is the *origin* of their prophecy: The false prophets "prophesy out of their own imagination" (13:2b), whereas Ezekiel declares the vision that the Sovereign Lord has revealed to him (cf. 11:25). In 13:3 Ezekiel calls these people "foolish prophets." They confidently proclaim the divine origin of their words (13:2) while using the oracle formula, "The LORD declares" (13:6–7). They even hope to see what they have prophesied established (13:6), though in actuality they have no calling from Yahweh (13:7).

Ezekiel also criticizes the content—or rather, lack of content—of their messages. Their visions are false and their divinations a lie (13:6). What their message consists of is revealed in 13:10. Such false comfort has had catastrophic results. In speaking according to their own hopes rather than the word of the Lord, they have seduced God's people into a false security that will be devastatingly exposed on the coming day of judgment.

This criticism of the prophets is expressed in a series of pictures.

1. They have acted "like jackals among ruins" (13:4).
2. Intent on pursuing their own prey, these skulking scavengers have failed to take on the dangerous but necessary task of standing in the gaps to build up a solid protection for Israel on the day of the Lord (13:5).
3. The third picture Ezekiel uses to describe the "prophets of Israel" also involves a wall. In 13:10–16 the image is of a poorly constructed wall, which the prophets, rather than rebuilding properly, merely cover with "whitewash" (13:10), thus giving it a misleadingly solid appearance. Its true nature will be exposed, however, by the coming of the storm (13:12–15).

The concern of the passage is not so much the fate of those who trust in the whitewashed wall but that of the false prophets. The divine hand will be raised in judgment on them (13:9). To be excluded from "the council of my people" (13:9) was to be cut off from the true Israel. It is surely a fitting fate that those who have falsely claimed to be prophets, and thus to have access to the council of the Lord (Heb. *sod yhwh*), will ultimately be excluded even from the council of his people. They will not "enter the land of Israel" (13:9). When Israel returns from exile, the false prophets will not participate in that return.

Address to the False Prophetesses of Israel (13:17–23). Whereas the prophets of Israel were apparently prophesying in forms indistinguishable from those used by Ezekiel, the practices adopted by the women seem to have had magical overtones. Exactly what those practices are has been a matter for some debate because of the obscure terminology employed. It seems that the women were involved in tying magic bands of some kind (13:18), though whether the object being tied up was the medium herself, the inquirer, or an image of the victim is not clear.

Further, the prophetesses are charged with making *mispahot* for their heads (13:18). The term occurs only here and in 13:21, and the common translation "veils" is at best a tentative suggestion on the basis of the context; they may equally well have been amulets worn around the neck. Whatever the precise form of their actions, however, they are not those of a true prophet of the Lord.

The prophesying women are apparently concerned more with the future of individuals than the fate of the nation. They mediate life and death to "the righteous" and "the wicked" (13:22). The women are not criticized for dealing with the wrong questions but for giving the wrong answers (13:22). In other words, their magically-derived oracles are afflicting those who ought not to have been afflicted and comforting those who ought not to have been comforted.

In doing this, the prophesying women are motivated not by divine calling but by pursuit of personal profit in the form of small payments of barley and bread. The result of their activities is deadly, killing "those who should not have died" and sparing "those who should not live" (13:19). They are, in a graphic image, "ensnar[ing] people like birds" (13:20), that is, regarding both their clients and their communities as disposable objects to be exploited in whatever ways proved profitable. The women's destructive work in this area prevents the wicked from becoming aware of their true state, putting both their lives and the women's own lives in jeopardy (13:18).

The closing verses of the chapter (13:22–23), while still grammatically addressed to the women, pick up themes from the first section to round off the whole. The "prophets of Israel" (13:2) are a stumbling block to the reception of Ezekiel's message of national judgment by the people, while the "[women] who prophesy" (13:17) undermine his calling to proclaim life to the righteous and to warn the wicked to turn from their ways. To be opposed to the prophet God has sent is to be a false prophet, ensnaring the people rather than setting them free, causing distress to the righteous and false confidence to the wicked.

Application. Satan's strategy is to imitate God's means of self-revelation in order to confuse the message. We are therefore not automatically to believe those who claim to be speaking the word of God to us. As John instructs us, we are to test every spirit (1 John 4:1). The need to test those who claim to bring God's message to us did not come to an end in Ezekiel's day; it was true in New Testament times, and it is true today.

EZEKIEL 14:1–11

Original Meaning. The elders in exile are tainted with the same fundamental sin as those left behind in Judah: internal idolatry. Even while externally willing to go through the orthodox motions of inquiring of the Lord, their hearts belonged elsewhere. The phrase "wicked stumbling block" (14:3), which occurs six times in Ezekiel, is also invariably linked to idolatry. Because the hearts of the exilic elders are divided between the Lord and idols, the Lord will give the elders no answer to their inquiry except an answer of judgment (14:4).

The people in exile are equally implicated in this half-heartedness. Those who feel abandoned by God find that the pull of seeking out other gods increases, other gods whom they think can deliver the sense of security and significance they seek. The result is that all of the exiles have, in their hearts, deserted the Lord for their idols (14:5). Such people—whether native-born Israelite or proselyte (14:7) —should not expect to receive a word of divine guidance through the prophet. Instead, the Lord will answer them himself (14:7) by direct action rather than through a prophet. Do they want a word from the Lord? The Lord will demonstrate his attitude toward them. They will become a "byword" (14:8), a proverbial warning of the dangers of divided loyalties.

The judgment with which they are threatened (14:8) has often been interpreted as a form of excommunication; however, in view of the divine destruction threatened on a prophet in the following verse, the death penalty is more likely indicated here. A similar judgment would apply to any prophet who attempted to provide an oracle for them. Those who sought false gods rather than the true God would find what they sought—lies in place of the truth. Those who attempted to counteract God's will by speaking when he had not spoken would find that they were doing nothing other than God's will, confirming the guilty ones in their guilt.

Yet the goal of God's judgment on the exiles is not their total extermination, but rather their salvation. There is still room for God's people to repent and return to God (14:6). The result of God's purifying judgment will be a faithful and undefiled people, cleansed from their transgressions (14:11). The goal of the covenant—God's dwelling in the midst of his people—will certainly not be thwarted, not even by Israel's sin (14:11).

Application. What is "just good enough" when it comes to your commitment to God? The answer is that all of us who claim the name of Christ have divided hearts. Outwardly, our appearance may "fit": We go to church regularly and appear to be decent, religious people. Yet when it comes to the tough decisions in life, there are other standards operating than God's word, which demonstrates the existence in our hearts of other gods than the true God.

EZEKIEL 14:12–23

Original Meaning. This section of Ezekiel's prophecy focuses on the inevitability and justice of God's decision to destroy Jerusalem. Behind the implied universality, the actual reference is clearly to Israel, for the phrase "by being unfaithful" (14:13) refers elsewhere to a breach of a covenant relationship. This may be through marital infidelity (Num 5:12, 27), misappropriation of an object belonging by rights to the Lord, as in the case of Achan (Josh 7:1), or other action that violates the covenant between God and his people (e.g., Lev 26:40; Ezek 17:20). Such a breach of the covenant inevitably brings on the offending nation (i.e., Israel) the curses attached to the covenant in Leviticus 26.

These covenant curses are itemized individually in the form of four test cases (Ezek 14:13–14, 15–16, 17–18, 19–20). In each case, a different covenant curse is envisaged: famine, through cutting off the bread supply (Lev 26:26); wild beasts (Lev 26:22); a sword (Lev 26:25); and finally plague (Lev 26:25). The curses of Leviticus 26 will descend.

What is common to all four cases is the hypothetical presence in the land of three righteous men: Noah, Daniel, and Job. Each of these men was noted for righteous behavior in the midst of a corrupt generation. The point in each case is that even three such outstanding citizens would be unable to rescue their closest relatives out of the divinely decreed disaster for covenant violation (Ezek 14:14, 16, 18, 20); their righteousness would suffice merely to save themselves.

The repetition of the four cases in which the sentence and the outcome are the same while only the form of the judgment is different underlines the inevitability of Jerusalem's destruction (14:21). Her situation is worse on two counts than that of the hypothetical land of 14:12–20. Not only does she lack such righteous men as Noah, Daniel, and Job, but in addition she is faced with not one kind of judgment, but all four at once.

Unexpectedly, some will survive the catastrophe (14:22). The purpose of saving this remnant is not for their sake but to "console" (14:22) those already in exile by allowing them to see the extent of Jerusalem's depravity. When the exiles see the impious behavior of this unspiritual remnant, then they will know that the Lord has not acted without cause (14:23).

Application. The astonishing fact is not that God judged Jerusalem, but that God allows our contemporary society, with all its sins, flagrant and secret, to continue to exist. We should not regard that patience as inability to act, however. God's "slowness" is patience in order to allow time for all of his chosen people to repent.

EZEKIEL 15:1–8

Original Meaning. Ezekiel 15 is a brief parable, a pictorial story with a sting in the tail. Yet the message of chapter 15 only becomes plain when the interpretation is added to the parable. The prunings cut from the vine were familiar objects, and it is immediately apparent to all that they serve no useful purpose. Frequently among the ashes of the fire, half-burnt pieces of vine would be found, the ends burned away and the middle charred. Were such pieces thereby made more useful? The conclusion of 15:5 is inescapable.

He then proceeds to apply the metaphor, to press home a less acceptable proposition: Jerusalem is like that vine wood, and its fate is therefore (inevitably) going to be that of half-burnt vine branches, fit for nothing but to be thrown back onto the fire and consumed completely. As in 14:12–23, the unfaithfulness of the land to its covenant overlord in pursuing idols will result in its being made desolate.

Application. Fruitful branches are pruned just as fruitless ones are cast off (John 15:2, 6). Suffering is a part of every life, but for the Christian it is a fruitful part of life, bearing a harvest of righteousness (cf. Heb 12:11). As we suffer, we are further conformed to the likeness of Christ, the Suffering Servant. As we suffer, we are detached from our passionate absorption with ourselves and this present world and taught to refocus our attention on the glories that await us in the place where suffering will be no more. Outside the vine, the outlook is as bleak as that which Ezekiel prophesies for Jerusalem: Unbelievers are headed on a course toward certain destruction.

EZEKIEL 16:1–63

Original Meaning. Ezekiel 16 is an "in-your-face" condemnation of Jerusalem. With graphic imagination and violent force, Ezekiel strips away the popular fiction of "Jerusalem the Golden" and replaces it with the figure of "Jerusalem the Prostitute." Here we have an exposé of Jerusalem's true nature, with the prophet taking the part of prosecuting counsel in the divine courtroom.

The story starts out by depicting Jerusalem's dubious origins. In contrast to Israel, who in her creed traced her heritage back to "a wandering Aramean" (Deut 26:5) whose arrival in the land of Canaan was the result of God's action in fulfillment of his promise, the city of Jerusalem's roots in the land are entirely natural and pagan. Jerusalem's prominent position is based on the accidents of history, not the acts of God; even before David captured it and made it his capital city, it was an important (pagan) city in its own right.

The child Jerusalem was born to heartless parents, however, who revealed their own depravity by abandoning the newborn infant. Into that situation of helplessness and hopelessness, however, came God's intervention. Passing by this sorry spectacle, he spoke his life-giving word, causing her to live and thrive like a plant of the field. The word of the Lord was all it took to turn the field from a place of death (16:5) to a place of life (16:7). Subsequently, she grew up, reached sexual maturity (16:7), and attained an age appropriate for marriage (16:8). Historically, this period corresponds to the pre-Israelite period of Jerusalem's history, during which time she existed and prospered but was not yet directly included in his purposes.

At the end of this time, the Lord spread a corner of his robe over her, symbolically covering her nakedness (16:8). This was an act with quasi-legal status. The Lord then entered into a covenant relationship with Jerusalem. In the terms of the metaphor, he married her. Again, the historical reality lies buried beneath the surface in the establishing of the Davidic covenant, which entails not simply the election of David and his descendants (2 Sam 7) but also the election of Zion, David's city, as the city of the Great King (Ps 48:2).

The Lord's choice of Jerusalem was a true love match on his part (16:8–9), in a reversal of the circumstance of her birth (16:4). He provided her with a wardrobe fit for a queen (16:10). This is not merely elegant or royal clothing, however. She is clothed in materials that are elsewhere associated with the tabernacle, underlining her symbolic identity as the home of the temple.

In addition, the Lord lavished on her an extensive supply of fine jewelry (16:11–12). Finally, she was fed with the very best (16:13). On account of her natural beauty and of the splendor with which the Lord had endowed her, her fame spread far and wide (16:14).

But instead of remembering that it was the Lord who had endowed her with all these blessings, she trusted in her beauty and prostituted her reputation. The beautiful clothes were used to adorn the high places. The gold and silver were used to manufacture the idols themselves; the flour, oil, and honey, which had been given to her for food, were offered instead to her idols (16:16–19). Even her children, those whom she had borne to the Lord, were not safe; they were sacrificed to the idols she had made for herself (16:20–21). Again, this history of idolatry corresponds to the general trend of Israel's behavior according to the account of the book of Kings.

This depiction of Jerusalem's idolatry in terms of adultery has its roots in Hosea 2:4–14. Hosea's Israel was simply a foolishly promiscuous woman; Ezekiel's Jerusalem is a thoroughly depraved and degraded prostitute. Her behavior descends to ever deeper depths in Ezekiel 16:23–34. Indeed, Jerusalem did not even act like a normal prostitute, for Jerusalem has been so perverse in her lust that she pays everyone to join in her depravity (16:34).

But far more expensive in the eyes of the Old Testament prophets was the cost in religious terms. Behind every act of international diplomacy stood the gods of the nations as guarantors of compliance. International cooperation inevitably involved a measure of recognition of the existence and power of the gods of the nations, along with an implicit affirmation that trusting in the Lord alone was not effective.

For Jerusalem, the natural and inevitable consequence of an adulterous lifestyle was an adulteress's death (16:38). The punishment is in accord with the crime. The normal practice was for adulteresses first to be exposed naked in public (16:37; cf. Nah 3:5), followed by their stoning by the assembly (Deut 22:22; Ezek 16:40). Similarly, Jerusalem's places of idolatry would be torn down, her wealth and possessions stripped away, leaving her in the state in which she began, naked and bare (16:39; cf. 16:7). Only then, when full circle had been reached and the one initially chosen for life had been sentenced to death and executed, would the Lord's wrath finally be turned aside (16:42). Even then, it would be the silence not of mercy but of completion of the judicial sentence: All that she did had been returned on her head (16:43).

In 16:44 the imagery changes from the husband-wife relationship to mother and daughter. Whereas Jerusalem had previously been considered in relationship to her adoptive "family," she has proved herself to be a chip off the old block by despising her husband and children. She is like her mother, the Hittite, who was married to an Amorite (16:45).

In addition, Jerusalem has a family resemblance to her natural sisters, Samaria and Sodom, who are the primary focus of this section. Samaria, the former capital of the Northern Kingdom of Israel, is described as her older sister. Here, "older" (16:46) refers to her size rather than age. Sodom, the "younger" (or "littler"; 16:46) sister, is physically smaller. Jerusalem is surrounded by sinners and fits naturally into their company, delighting to go along with the crowd.

According to Ezekiel neither of these twin icons of sin could match Jerusalem's record. She did more detestable things than either of them, making them seem (comparatively) righteous (16:51). God judged Sodom because of her sin and if he judged Samaria because of her sin, how will Jerusalem escape from his wrath?

However, if the similarity between Jerusalem and her sisters serves to justify further God's action in completely destroying her (16:58), that is not the only focus of attention here. Rather, the purpose of this comparison with her sisters in crime is designed to evoke a sense of shame on Jerusalem's part (16:52). Just as in her pride Jerusalem once scorned Sodom for her sin, so now that Jerusalem's sin has been uncovered, the surrounding nations scorn her (16:57). Now, instead of looking down her nose at Sodom and Samaria as beyond redemption, she will herself only be redeemed alongside them (16:53). Paradoxically, it is in that redemption itself that shame will be experienced as the inhabitants of Jerusalem realize how much worse they have been than the bywords of iniquity, Sodom and Samaria.

Though they have despised God's oath and broken his

covenant and must therefore be judged (16:59), judgment is not God's last word. For though Jerusalem does not remember the days of her youth (16:22, 43), the Lord will remember the days of her youth and will therefore establish an everlasting covenant with her (16:60). In so doing, he will create in her the two qualities that are signally lacking in her at present, memory and shame (16:61). On the one hand, she will be profoundly aware of having broken the covenant, shattering it so completely that it can no longer stand as the basis of her self-identity vis-à-vis other nations (16:61). She will be aware of the depths of her sin and ashamed of it.

On the other hand, she can also look back to the days of her youth, the days when, in the imagery of Ezekiel 16:4–6, she was similarly naked and bare before the Lord. If he chose her once, not on the basis of anything in herself but simply his own sovereign will, can he not do so again?

Yet that is precisely what the Lord affirms. The nations will view Jerusalem as an object lesson of the wideness of God's mercy. On the day when the Lord "makes atonement" (Heb. *kipper*) for Jerusalem (16:63), she will remember and be ashamed; her tongue will be stilled and her pride humbled once and for all.

Application. How else do you explain the obscenity of the cross? An innocent man—the only truly innocent man who ever lived—is convicted in a rigged trial, abused by his guards until he can scarcely walk, yet forced to carry his own cross on a back that has been flayed raw. Nails are forced through the living flesh of his hands and feet, and he is jerked upright to hang until, too tired to lift himself one more time, he suffocates. What good God could permit such a death? What awful thing could be so bad that only such an atonement could pay for it?

The answer is *sin*. In the cross, we see sin revealed in its starkest, most abominable ugliness. There, if we sweep away for a second the prettification with which we sentimentalize that terrible moment, we see God's "R" rated answer to my sin. There is the "atonement" that God made (16:63), the ransom that he paid for his people (cf. Mark 10:45). The cost of our salvation was not silver and gold but the precious blood of the Lord Jesus Christ (1 Pet 1:18–19).

EZEKIEL 17:1–24

Original Meaning. Ezekiel continues to utilize metaphorical language, this time in a form that combines "riddle" (NIV, "allegory") and "parable" (17:2). A "riddle" is a statement that hides the truth it imparts, while a "parable" elucidates the truth that underlies it by putting it in a fresh light. In other words, this chapter functions both to conceal and reveal. Perhaps this section best fits into the genre of "fable," a story that communicates its concealed message by transposing the realities it describes into the world of plants and animals.

The political realities depicted in this fable are little more concealed from the original hearers than when in contemporary American political cartoons the Republican Party is depicted by an elephant and the Democrats by a donkey. So, there is a certain irony in Ezekiel saying to his audience: "Do you not know what these things mean?" (17:12). His hearers could probably have supplied for themselves the interpretation that follows. The first eagle is the king of Babylon, while the cedar sprig is Jehoiachin, whom Nebuchadnezzar carried off to Babylon, along with Ezekiel himself. The "seedlings of the land" (17:5) whom Nebuchadnezzar put in his place is clearly Zedekiah, Jehoiachin's uncle, whom Nebuchadnezzar installed in Jehoiachin's place. The second eagle is Egypt, from whom Zedekiah was seeking aid to break free from the Babylonian yoke.

The meaning of the parable is therefore self-evident: Zedekiah's foreign policy is worse than foolish; it is suicidal. His revolt cannot stand on the basis of seeking help from a (disinterested) lesser superpower against the dominant superpower in the contemporary ancient Near East. Will he thrive? No way!

But is the fable's meaning as clear as it appears at first sight? The fable is a riddle as well as a parable; it conceals a deeper truth as well as reveals an obvious lesson. For instance, Lebanon is not only the proverbial home of all cedars but also the name of one of Solomon's palaces (cf. 1 Kgs 7:2; Jer 22:23). So, the discerning reader is invited to consider who planted "the cedar in Lebanon" (Jer 22:23) in the first place. Who established the Davidic dynasty in Jerusalem (2 Sam 7:8–9)? Further back still, who was it who had brought them "to the land of Canaan" (Gen 12:1; 15:7), just as Nebuchadnezzar brought Jehoiachin "to the land of merchants" (Ezek 17:4)?

Moreover, the vine planted in conditions suitable for growth is a classic picture of the Lord's provision for Israel (Isa 5:1–7); indeed, the imagery of "no effort spared," which seems more than a little overdone with reference to Nebuchadnezzar, fits perfectly for the Lord's care. He is the one who, according to Psalm 80, brought a vine out of Egypt and cleared the ground in order to plant it in the promised land (Ps 80:8–11). Likewise, Ezekiel's address to Judah as "this rebellious people" (Ezek 17:11) describes the history of their relationship with the Lord much better than their history (to date) with Babylon.

Taken together, these hints supply a deeper significance to the breaking of Zedekiah's oath of loyalty to Nebuchadnezzar. There is a fundamental *analogy* between Zedekiah's rebellion against his covenant overlord, Nebuchadnezzar, and Israel's rebellion against her covenant overlord, God himself. If Zedekiah's abandoning of his (relatively) prosperous situation in favor of the Egyptian option is a suicidally foolish breach of the covenant relationship, what may we say about Israel's abandonment of the Lord and their history of rebellion against him?

Thus, at just the moment when it might seem that Ezekiel has unpacked the meaning of the fable, he launches into its *real* meaning with the word "therefore" (17:19). The political leadership in Judah has not only despised and broken Nebuchadnezzar's covenant; on a deeper level they have despised and broken the Lord's covenant (17:19). The result is that the coming judgment is not merely a harsh taste of *Realpolitik*, but the judgment of God on a rebellious house.

The deeper message of the fable thus paints the hopelessness of Zedekiah's revolt against Nebuchadnezzar in its blackest hues, pointing out that he was not just rebelling against the mighty Babylonians but against the sovereign Lord, the God who made heaven and earth. At the same time, however, the latter part of this chapter also reworks the fable in more positive terms (17:22–24). The Lord himself, no longer acting through intermediaries, will take a new shoot from the cedar and plant it on a high and lofty mountain (17:22). A new cedar will grow on the mountain heights of Israel into a lofty tree, which will provide in its branches shelter for birds of all kinds (17:23). In contrast to the vine, which even in ideal conditions rebelled and failed to fulfill its potential (17:8), the cedar will achieve the eagle's initial purpose. In that way, all the trees of the field (the nations) will be brought to an understanding of the Lord's sovereignty in history, seeing that the rise and fall of empires is entirely his doing (17:24).

The interpretation of this postscript to the earlier fable is a straightforward development from the deeper level of meaning of those verses. What does the future hold after the Lord's judgment on Judah? Is there any hope for the uprooted vine? The logical answer would be no, but Ezekiel affirms, against all logic, that the Lord will intervene to reverse the failures of the past. Just as Nebuchadnezzar once installed Zedekiah, so Yahweh will install his own vassal on Mount Zion. In contrast to the vine that rebelled and would soon wither (17:7–10), the cedar of Yahweh's planting will thrive and bear fruit (17:23).

Application. We suffer from the same rose-tinted myopia that Zedekiah did. On a societal level, we think the problem with our world is essentially political. We should work for political change and we should plan for the future. Yet we can be so busy doing the good things that we miss out on the one insight that is really necessary, the best thing—maintaining our personal and corporate spiritual life with God.

EZEKIEL 18:1–32

Original Meaning. This chapter continues the pattern of pictorial speech found in the preceding chapters, but this time the proverb comes from the mouth of the people, not delivered from the Lord. It is an erroneous proverb—or at least a proverb erroneously applied—and such has been its misuse that the Lord swears that all use of it will be eliminated from Israel (18:3).

The Lord's response to this proverb is a categorical denial of its applicability. Both father and son "belong" to the Lord; indeed, everyone belongs to him (18:4). The Lord is not only sovereign over all flesh, but he is also a just judge. There is no unfair attribution of punishment to the next generation for the sins of the fathers (18:4). To the temptation to question God's goodness, Ezekiel affirms the justice of God's ways. These specific temptations and their answers underlie the course of the disputation that follows.

The first part of that disputation is a case study covering three successive generations. The three generations described are a righteous man who is succeeded by a wicked son, who is in turn followed by a repentant, righteous son. The behavior of each is assessed against a checklist of righteous behaviors, a kind of miniature Ten Commandments.

The first man mentioned is orthodox in his religious practice (see 6:3–7). In addition, this righteous man does not oppress those in debt to him (18:7). There were a multitude of ways in which an unscrupulous lender could take advantage of the desperate. Far from robbing, however, this righteous man feeds and clothes the poor out of his own resources (18:7). To summarize, this person "follows my decrees and faithfully keeps my laws" (18:9a). What is the verdict on such a person? "That man is righteous; he will surely live" (18:9b).

On the other hand, suppose this man's son is the antithesis of all his father stands for. He does everything bad his father abhorred and fails to do any of the good things his father did. Point by point, Ezekiel checks off his sins. What is to be the verdict on such a person? "Will such a man live? He will not!" He will die, and his death will be no one's fault but his own (18:13).

But suppose this second man also has a son who swims against the tide. He is like his grandfather in doing what is good and right, not like his wicked father. He sees what his father does and deliberately follows a different course. According to Ezekiel, "he will surely live" (18:17).

At this point, Ezekiel envisages a hypothetical objection (18:19a). By providing this *reductio ad absurdum*, the complaint of Ezekiel's audience is undermined. In such a clear case, no one can dispute the justice of Ezekiel's assertion (18:19b–20). If this generation is experiencing the "death" of exile and if God deals justly with each generation, then the only possible conclusion is that they too must also be tarred with guilt before God.

Ezekiel's point is that the present generation is not guiltless. They themselves have shared in the sins of past generations. Therefore, although the judgment they are now undergoing is certainly in part a judgment on the result of the sins of previous generations, the present generation are not innocent bystanders but *guilty* bystanders. They too have shared in eating the sour grapes, so they cannot pass the buck for the unpleasant aftertaste onto others.

Since their death sentence is decreed, ought they not simply to eat, drink, and try to be merry in the time that remains to them? Ezekiel 18:21–32 addresses that question by propounding another pair of case studies. The first concerns a wicked person who turns from his sins and does what is right (18:21). Grace is possible for the one who repents; his transgressions will be remembered no more (18:22–23). By contrast, the righteous person who "repents" of his righteousness and abandons his service of God will not escape judgment. Thus, just as this generation is not guiltless but brings on its own head divine judgment, so also as long as it exists, this generation is not fixed on its present course. Change, real change, is always possible.

The essential point the prophet is making is introduced by the word "therefore" in 18:30. Judgment is coming! But even now it is not too late! Even wicked, condemned sinners can still leave their transgressions behind, repent, and acquire for themselves a new heart and new spirit (18:31). Even now death is not inevitable. They can still return to the God of all grace and live (18:32). Everything leads up to the passionate appeal to turn from death, to choose life and live (cf. Deut 30:15–20)!

Application. We have not begun to grasp the reason why we suffer if we have not first considered the suffering of Christ in our place. For it was on the cross that his suffering made it possible for my suffering to be for good, for God's glory in my redemption, for God's glory in my growth in grace. That doesn't make it any less suffering. It is indeed painful, frequently very painful, as we endure it. But it does mean that for Christians, suffering is not for our judgment but is the means of God's gracious work in our lives, by which we are increasingly conformed to the image of Jesus Christ.

Ezekiel's passion to convey that message of life for everyone who will repent fits the cost paid by Jesus to make it possible. The only appropriate response to the cross is to plead and exhort and pour out our lives to communicate the gospel of Jesus Christ. Like Ezekiel, we must confront men and women here and now with their desperate need to turn from their sins and to receive forgiveness and new life through Christ, and thus live forever with God and his people.

EZEKIEL 19:1–14

Original Meaning. Ezekiel moves from prose into poetry, adopting the form of a lament or dirge. Ezekiel's lament is made up of two distinct images: a lioness and her cubs, and a vine and its branches. Both were familiar images for the royal tribe of Judah. The first image is of a mother lioness who produces a number of cubs. Out of them, she chooses one to be the leader of the pack. He behaves in lionlike fashion, tearing the prey and even consuming people (19:3). As a result, he is hunted by the nations, captured, and carried off to Egypt (19:4). In his place, she appoints a second cub, who acts with even greater destructiveness (19:6–7). He too is hunted by the nations, captured, and carried into exile, this time to Babylon. The point is that the current rulers of Judah are simply the latest outcroppings of the rock of oppression and pride from which they were hewn.

In the second image, a vine is planted in a vineyard beside abundant waters. The perfect conditions provided for her lead to abundant growth and, in particular, many strong branches suitable for a ruler's scepter (19:11). Pride goes before a fall, and the lofty vine is uprooted, withered by the east wind and stripped of its fruit (19:12). Its strong branches are burned, and the vine is replanted in the desert, in a dry and thirsty land (19:13). Indeed, the destructive fire itself comes from one of the branches and consumes its fruit; the result is that no strong branch is left suitable for a ruler's scepter (19:14). The vine is Judah, planted by the Lord in perfect conditions. As a result, she produces many scions capable of ruling. But pride is her downfall.

Echoes of chapter 17 are evident throughout this second picture. Both describe a vine planted in conditions suitable for growth (17:5–6), then uprooted in wrath (17:9) and shriveled by the east wind (17:10). The tall tree is brought low (17:24). Though the focus is different, placed on divine action rather than human action, the conclusion for Zedekiah is the same: no escape.

Application. The assertion that God has a wonderful plan for our lives often rings hollow when measured up against the realities of day-to-day life. We make New Year's resolutions and plans to quit this bad habit and abandon that sin and start to do this good thing and generally overhaul our lives. We think, "Next year, I'll be a little better than this." Ezekiel's lament tells us that New Year's resolutions aren't enough, just as a new Davidic king wouldn't be enough. God will have to do something far more radical to save us. The good news is that in Jesus Christ, God has done precisely such a radical new work.

EZEKIEL 20:1–44

Original Meaning. It is now the summer of 591 BC. The elders have assembled before Ezekiel in order to "inquire of the LORD" (20:1). Now, as a life-stance, "inquiring of the LORD" or "seeking the LORD" would have been commendable. But seeking the Lord can never be simply one part of a broadly-based religious strategy. Seeking the Lord is, by definition, exclusive.

This is precisely where the elders fail the test. It is not *what they ask* that the Lord finds unacceptable but *who they are*.

Although the Lord will not answer them in terms of what they are seeking, he has a message for them to hear, addressed directly to their sin (20:4–5; cf. 14:4). Ezekiel is called to join God in judging the elders by confronting them with their sin (20:4).

The three generations Ezekiel chooses here for his case study are the generation who lived in Egypt at the time of the exodus (20:5–10), the desert generation (20:11–15), and their children (20:18–23). Each generation's history is presented as a six-stage cycle:

1. The Lord's self-revelation (20:5–6, 11, 18–19)
2. A challenge to exclusive devotion (20:7, 12, 19–20)
3. Israel's rebellion (20:8, 13, 21)
4. The threat of the Lord's wrath (20:8b, 13b, 21b)
5. Wrath limited/deferred for the sake of the divine name (20:9, 14, 22)
6. Act of limited judgment (20:10, 17, 23)

According to this schema, each new generation is confronted for itself with a fresh revelation of the Lord. To each comes the gracious self-announcement "I am the LORD" (20:5, 20, cf. 20:12). The basis for this self-revelation is not Israel's merit but divine election and a covenant oath sworn by God to bring them to the promised land (20:5). But this decisive act in Israel's history required a response on the part of Israel of exclusive devotion to the Lord.

But Israel's consistent response to this gracious self-revelation was rebellion. Three times that rebellion is detailed, not simply in general terms but specifically as the failure to keep themselves distinct (20:7, 12, 19–20). Three times the Lord threatened to pour out his wrath on them once and for all, destroying them utterly. Yet each time he held back his hand (cf. Num 14:15–16).

Nonetheless, in each case limited judgment does fall: First-generation Israel exits Egypt and finds itself not in a beautiful land flowing with milk and honey, but in the desert (Ezek 20:10). The next generation does not inherit the promised land either but are doomed to die in the desert (20:15). The third generation not only fails to inherit the promised land but will be scattered among the nations (20:23).

To this threefold cycle of gracious election, rebellion, and limited judgment, a coda is added in 20:27–29. Israel's present is exactly the same as Israel's past: vile images, child sacrifice, and idolatry (20:31). Such people need not expect any reply to their attempts to inquire of the Lord (20:31).

But what should they expect from the Lord? The answer given in 20:32–44 may surprise us, though it is already implicit in the account Ezekiel has given of Israel's history. God will act, not to destroy his people utterly but rather to fulfill his original purposes in election: to establish a purified people to worship him (20:40–41). He will do this through a new exodus, not because of any merit on Israel's part but for the sake of his own name (20:44).

This answer, as we have said, is already implicit in Ezekiel's rendering of history. There is an analogy to be drawn between the exodus/desert generation and his own. The present position of the exilic generation in the cycle of sin and judgment is that Israel's rebellion has led to a limited judgment on the Lord's part—specifically, the scattering among the nations, mentioned in 20:23. But as the three-generation cycle makes clear, *that can never be the end of the story!* God's people cannot be destroyed completely, not because they do not deserve it but because God has staked the reputation of his own name on the covenant promises made to them. His divine nature requires faithfulness to his promise, even in the face of unrelenting human sin (cf. Hos 11:8–11).

Therefore, there must necessarily be a new act of salvation on God's part, a new exodus. Israel cannot be abandoned (Ezek 20:32)! Whether that thought is one of desire or of despair is not really the issue; rather, the focus is on the impossibility of such a thing happening for God has staked his reputation on them (cf. 36:22–23).

Divine election cannot be revoked; the Lord will reign over them (20:33). The echoes of 1 Samuel 8 are not coincidental. There, too, the people had sought to become "such as all the other nations" by having a king (1 Sam 8:5), which is interpreted as a rejection of the Lord's reign over them (8:7). They are warned of the real consequences of their choice (8:11–18), yet ultimately their election is not revocable. They do not, indeed cannot, become like the nations around them: instead, even their rebellious wish for a monarchy is subsumed in the providence of God. The Lord himself gives them the kings of his own choosing, good and bad, to prepare the way for the coming of the King of kings.

Similarly, the message of God's kingship exercised in a new exodus is not necessarily good news. Yes, his reign comes with a mighty hand and outstretched arm, as in the first exodus. But in addition, his reign comes with outpoured wrath. Just as the unfaithful Israelites were brought up out of Egypt only to die in the desert, so too the regathered Israel will be purged in the "wilderness of the nations" (Ezek 20:35). There God will meet with his people "face to face," just as he met with Moses "face to face" in the tent of meeting (20:35; Exod 33:11).

But this face-to-face meeting will not be that of two friends, as it was with Moses, but rather a meeting of personal judgment. God will go to court against the rebels among his people, singling out the transgressors from the faithful just as a shepherd counts and separates his sheep by passing them one by one under his rod (Ezek 20:37).

The application to the present generation comes in 20:39. The choice is, in one sense, theirs to make. They may go and serve their idols if they wish, but they must remember this: that God's purpose in the election of Israel will stand (20:40).

This looks forward in seed form to the full description of the renewed Israel at worship on a high mountain in chapters 40–48. The positive result of the new exodus will be pure worship offered by a purified people, in whom the Lord's holiness is publicly displayed to the eyes of the nations. There the oath made in Egypt (20:5) will be fulfilled (20:42), and there the remnant who survived the desert judgment—not on merit but by grace—will appreciate the immensity of their own sin and the faithfulness of God to his covenant promises (20:44).

Application. Rebellion is never simply against an abstract conception of God, however, but against the personal God of grace. Satan always seeks to persuade us, as he did our first parents, that God is a harsh taskmaster who will exploit us and abuse us if we allow him, and that he seeks to deny us things that are good (Gen 3:1). The reality is exactly the opposite, for them and for us. God had made a perfect world for Adam and Eve to live in and placed them in the most perfect spot within it, a paradise. Their area of personal freedom was large; the restriction minuscule. Yet being deceived into reading that minuscule restriction as bondage, they gave in to temptation, only to discover too late what true bondage was.

So also in our day many seek meaning, significance, and purpose—but only on their own terms. Spirituality is a growth market. We are surrounded by a generation of seekers who assume that God can be found whenever and wherever they choose to seek him. For them, "seeking" is another word for "shopping." But, as the elders discovered, God is not a cosmic merchandiser for whom "the customer is always right." It is possible, indeed inevitable, that the determinedly open-minded seeker will not find an answer from Israel's God.

EZEKIEL 20:45–21:32

The passage begins with the command to Ezekiel to face toward the south of Israel and preach against it (20:46); fire is coming on the southern forest, which will consume every tree, "both green and dry" (20:47). It will be publicly recognized as the work of the Lord and will not be extinguished (20:48). But the people's response to this message is apparently total lack of comprehension (20:49).

The judgment is all-consuming in its *content*, both green tree and dry; in its *geographical scope* (from the south northwards); and in its *temporal scope* (it has been kindled and will not be extinguished). Yet the precise focus of the parable is not immediately clear: Who is the "southern forest" (20:47)? Without that critical piece of information, the parable remains an obscure riddle.

That information is supplied in the interpretation that follows. The three Hebrew terms for "south" in the parable (*teman*; *darom*; *negeb*) are matched by three objects of judgment: Jerusalem, the sanctuary, and the land of Israel (21:2). With that identification in place, other elements of the parable are put into sharper focus. Israel is the southland. The image of fire is linked with that of the sword of the Lord, which is coming to cut off both righteous (the green tree) and wicked (the dry tree), from the south to the north of the land. The sword has been drawn from its scabbard and will not return there.

To underline that fearful certainty, Ezekiel is instructed to perform a sign-act (21:6). When people ask him why he is sighing, he is to respond with a somewhat cryptic statement (21:7). What event has come that merits such a response? Ezekiel 7, where the final judgment was threatened in virtually identical language, is now a present reality.

The twin judgment images of cutting and burning are maintained in the twin actions of sharpening and burnishing (note the connection between polishing and lightning in 21:10, 15). Together, these actions serve to prepare the weapon for action. Israel will be surrounded, hemmed in on all sides with no place to run and no place to hide (21:14–16). The prophet's threatening gesture is merely a public display of the Lord's own determination to satisfy his wrath in his decimation of the people.

In 21:18–27 we are introduced to the human agency that executes the divine will, the sword of the king of Babylon. The prophet is instructed to perform another sign-act, this time marking out a three-way road junction with a signpost. Ezekiel is to act out the forces of the king of Babylon coming to this parting of the ways and deciding which route to follow.

Ezekiel pictures the king utilizing all the pagan means of decision-making (21:21). The irony is that this use of pagan means of discerning the will of the gods is here an accurate discernment of the will of the true God. The "lying divinations" that had found such favor with God's people (13:7) now become the very means through which judgment comes on them (21:23).

That punishment falls not only on the people but also upon Zedekiah. By introducing him by that title rather than by name, Ezekiel puts the focus of the judgment on the office, not the person. It is not simply that Zedekiah will be stripped of the insignia of royalty, the turban and the crown (21:26), but that in him the old order of things has reached a conclusion. A divine reordering of society is called for, in which the Lord will exalt the lowly and bring down the exalted (21:26; cf. 17:24).

Ezekiel has reshaped the traditional messianic oracle of Genesis 49:10 into a threatening oracle of judgment. Now the scepter will not depart from Judah until the coming of the judge . . . Nebuchadnezzar! Yet precisely this method of framing the judgment oracle reminds us of the Judge behind the judge, the Coming One behind the coming one. Heathen Nebuchadnezzar may be God's chosen instrument of judgment in Ezekiel 21, yet the dominant reality in both cases is the plan and purpose of God.

Judgment is not limited to Judah. The (pagan) oracle that directed Nebuchadnezzar toward Jerusalem is more a stay of execution for Ammon than a reprieve. They too, like Zedekiah, are among the profane wicked whose time of punishment has come (cf. 21:29 with 21:25). Therefore, they too will feel the cutting edge of the sword of God's judgment.

Babylon is neither above God nor independent of God in its furious power. Rather, it is merely his creation, a tool to be taken up and used for his purposes and then put down when its usefulness is over. What the Lord has lifted up, the Lord can also reduce once more to nothing. In that way it will become clear that it is the Lord who has raised her up and put her down, not any supposed power of her own gods.

Application. The destruction of Jerusalem in 586 BC was terribly comprehensive when God handed over judgment to the sword of Babylon. However, it was merely a sideshow when compared to the comprehensive judgment of the world that awaits the coming of the One to whom judgment belongs. God's wrath is aroused at the rebellious thoughts, deeds, and words of those whom he has created. When the Judge of all the earth comes to settle final accounts, the sword will fall on uncleansed sinners to their eternal doom.

The doctrine of eternal torment in hell is not popular these days. In fact, it probably never has been, even in the heyday of Puritan preaching. In the modern world, however, it is rarely the topic of sermons. Far more often, it is the subject of attempts to present the biblical teaching in a kinder, gentler light. Like the erstwhile inhabitants of Jerusalem, we are convinced that the Judge will choose the other road and we will be spared. We don't really believe that the Bible's teaching on eternal punishment should be taken literally, at least not with reference to ourselves. But it is precisely with reference to us that we should consider this doctrine.

EZEKIEL 22:1–31

Original Meaning. In this chapter, the prophet is called on to act as prosecuting counsel. The prophet begins by presenting his indictment in outline form (22:3–5): Jerusalem's sins involve both social sins—that is, sins against humanity—and cultic sins—that is, sins against God (e.g., the manufacture of idols, 22:3). These two broad classes of sins have resulted in two respective consequences: social sins lead to "guilt" (22:4), the forensic state of deserving punishment, while cultic sins lead to "defilement" (22:4), the ritual state of being unfit to appear in the presence of God. The combination of these in Jerusalem's case means that the end of her years have come (22:4). The result of that judgment will make Jerusalem into an "object of scorn" to the nations around her (22:4, 5), famous for her cultic and social sins, which have led to her downfall.

Verses 6–12 give the first catalogue of Jerusalem's crimes, showing how she has offended against God's law. The charges are directed against the "princes of Israel" (22:6), a phrase normally understood as designating the former kings of Judah. Thus, in view are not merely present sins but a continuing history of sin on the part of Judah's leadership.

The sins listed here are an accusation of having violated the laws of the Pentateuch, especially those of the so-called Holiness Code of Leviticus 18–20; 25. Though the charges themselves are largely drawn from the Holiness Code, the specific turn of phrase is in many places influenced by Deuteronomy, for instance, in the final concluding phrase: "You have forgotten me" (Ezek 22:12; cf. Deut 8:14, 19). The end result, then, is a comprehensive indictment of the former rulers of Judah on the basis of the law of Moses. The "holy nation" (Exod 19:6) has become thoroughly unholy.

Such a comprehensive catalogue of sins can have only one outcome. As Deuteronomy 8:19 makes clear: "If you ever forget the LORD your God . . . you will surely be destroyed." So, the next two sections (Ezek 22:13–16, 17–22) deal with the Lord's response to his people's sin under the twin images of *judgment by scattering* and *judgment by gathering*. The literary device of using two diametrically opposite images together underscores once again the comprehensive nature of Judah's doom.

Verse 13 acts as the link between the accusation and the threat of punishment, summarizing the accusation by putting together the last charge ("unjust gain") with the first ("blood you have shed," cf. 22:3). Because of these things the Lord will now act, dispersing Judah among the nations and scattering them through the countries. In this way, the Lord will bring an end to Judah's uncleanness (22:15).

Paradoxically, there appears also a judgment by gathering, as the house of Israel is gathered into Jerusalem to experience the destructive impact of the full outpouring of the Lord's wrath (22:18–22). This is paradoxical not merely because "gathering" is the logical opposite of "scattering," but also because the terminology of gathering is elsewhere normally used in a positive sense.

The image of judgment as the refiner's fire, purifying the dross to leave only the pure metal, appears several times in the Bible, but in Ezekiel 22, the refining process has a purely negative product, with nothing but unpurged molten dross produced. The purpose of this divine act of judgment, then, is not to purify his people but merely to pour out on rebellious sinners his fiery wrath.

This outpouring of God's wrath has not yet happened to Judah, notwithstanding the disasters of 605 and 597 BC. She remains "a land that has not been cleansed" (22:24). The concept of rain on the land as an element of judgment is present in the flood narrative (Gen 7:4, 11), and the expectation of a future destructive flood is reflected in Ezekiel 13:11 and 38:22. Because of this lack of cleansing in the past, the land remains full of oppression, detailed in the following verses, which will lead to a final pouring out of indignation on the people (22:31).

All of the leadership classes in Judah are charged and found guilty of wrongdoing. The "princes" have wreaked havoc through a series of social sins (22:25). In effect, they preenacted the societal devastation that the Babylonians would bring to full measure when they destroyed Jerusalem. The "officials," described as "wolves," have likewise misused their power for the purpose of "unjust gain" (22:27).

Even the "priests" did "violence to my law and profane[d] my holy things" (22:26). They have failed in their task of protecting Yahweh's holy things by not teaching the proper distinction between holy and unholy, clean and unclean. The unusual phrase "they shut their eyes to the keeping of my Sabbaths" (22:26) seems to indicate the priests' failure to prosecute those who transgressed the law. Meanwhile the "prophets" are condemned in terms similar to Ezekiel 13 as unreliable whitewashers, telling people what they wanted to hear in the Lord's name, when he had not sent them (22:28).

The "people of the land" (22:29), who in this context should be identified as a group of powerful men in Jerusalem with close ties to the Davidic house, have also been taking advantage of their position. They have been exploiting those unable to defend themselves (22:29).

After the conclusion of the second catalogue of sins, we again read of the Lord's twofold response. He first of all sought for "someone among them who would build up the wall and stand before me in the gap on behalf of the land" (22:30). In other words, he sought a true prophet—someone who would take on the difficult and dangerous task of interceding for the people, just as Moses did successfully after the incident of the golden calf (Ps 106:23). But this time no one was found to deflect God's wrath, and thus the all-consuming fiery anger of God will descend on Jerusalem (Ezek 22:31). As if to emphasize the connection to the destruction of Jerusalem depicted in chapters 9–11, the last, ominous words of the Lord are the same in both cases: "[I will bring] down on their own heads all they have done" (22:31; cf. 11:21).

Application. Modern people are unconvinced of the reality of their sin. Even those who still talk about sins have frequently lost the sense of the comprehensive nature of our sin. Preachers (and churches) tend to have a shortened list of actual sins that they preach against. Along with the loss of the sense of sin goes the loss of understanding of God's wrath. A knowledge of sin and the understanding of God's wrath go together. It should therefore be no surprise that in a society where sin is no longer believed in, the wrath of God is not understood.

EZEKIEL 23:1–49

Original Meaning. Two women are introduced in the opening verses as sisters, sharing a common mother (23:2). This is intended to denote not merely the historical fact of a shared heredity between the Northern and Southern Kingdoms but a deeper commonality: Though they are two in number, they are one in nature, living parallel lives. This essential identity is underlined by the names they are given. The similarity of their names draws our attention: Oholah and Oholibah go together like Tweedledum and Tweedledee.

These sisters have behaved alike from their youth. Already in Egypt they gave themselves over to prostitution (23:3). But in spite of that, the Lord married them, and they became the mothers of his children (23:4). Thus far, there is nothing controversial about Ezekiel's retelling of history. Israel's undistinguished past in terms of their faithfulness to the Lord was not particularly news to those familiar with the events recounted in Exodus and Numbers.

In the next verses, however, Ezekiel brings his hearers down to the present in a hurry with a brief sketch of the history of the older sister, Oholah (i.e., Samaria, the Northern Kingdom; 23:5–10). Not content with the Lord, she traded her attentions elsewhere. She lusted after the Assyrians. They all appeared to her as warriors (23:6).

It was also tantamount to a rejection of trust in the Lord in favor of Assyria's idols, with which Israel now defiled herself (23:7). It was a return to her former way of life in Egypt, from which the Lord had redeemed her (23:8). The Lord gave her over into the hand of her lovers, the Assyrians (23:9). The very things that attracted her to them rebounded against her. Their warrior power was exerted against her, and far from clothing her in similar manner to themselves, they stripped her naked and killed her (23:10).

But Oholah is not Ezekiel's real interest. The brief sketch of her history merely sets up a paradigm of sin and punishment to which the subsequent history of her southern sister can be compared (23:10). The question is, "Has her younger sister applied to herself the lessons to be drawn from the older sister's fate?"

As the chapter unfolds, it is evident that she has not. Oholibah is not merely like her sister; she is *worse* than her sister. Nor is this depravity the result of ignorance: Her sister "saw" and yet still became more depraved in her lust, committing more adulteries than her sister (23:11). She first sinned in exactly the same way with the Assyrians (23:12), and then added to her little black book the Babylonians (23:14). She was worse not merely in the number of her lovers (two as against one) but in the nature of their relationship. She was attracted to the Babylonians by a mere wall depiction; entranced by the vision of them she herself sent messengers to Babylon to get them (23:16). She was thus not merely willing to be seduced but was herself the active seductress.

Submission to these relationships is nothing less than spiritual adultery against their true covenant head, the Lord himself. Once again, the prophet seeks to challenge Judah's complacent sense of moral and spiritual superiority to her former northern neighbor.

Her adulterous liaisons did not satisfy Oholibah. Having been defiled by her lovers, she became disgusted with them and turned away from them (23:17). But in turning away from her adulterous lovers, she continued her prostitution openly so that the Lord turned away from her, just as he had earlier turned away from her sister (23:18).

Yet even this did not deter her from her course. She remembered the days of her youth in Egypt, not as the time when the Lord delivered her from bondage but as the time when they enjoyed pleasures no longer theirs. In her lust, she was not even limited by natural relationships; instead, she sought those whose sexual capacities were not merely superhuman but positively bestial (23:20).

The result of such thoroughgoing depravity is predictable (23:22). As with Oholah, the things that attracted Oholibah to her lovers are now used against her (23:24). This combination of divine and human judgment is further developed in the following verses (23:25). As Jerusalem's sins were worse than her sister's, so also will her punishment be. She will not only be stripped but also disfigured, and her children will not only be taken from her but will also fall by the sword and be consumed by fire (23:25). The goal of this judgment is a proper amnesia: forgetting the prostitution begun in Egypt (23:27). Her lovers have now become her enemies, who will strip her and plunder her (23:28–29). As she followed in the pattern of her elder sister, so now she will share her elder sister's fate and drink from the same bitter cup of sorrow, all the way down to its dregs (23:32–34). In her shame, she will tear out the bodily members that led her into sin in the first place, her breasts.

In the remaining verses (23:36–49), Ezekiel is once more cast into the role of prosecuting attorney as the point of the metaphor is driven home. Jerusalem is to be confronted with her adultery and bloodshed. Adultery has taken place at home and on the road, with domestic and foreign idols. At home, sanctuary and Sabbath have been defiled, and even their children have been sacrificed (23:38–39). Not content with such "homegrown" heresies, they have sent messengers far and wide to all comers (23:40). But in spite of their beauty preparations and makeup, their true nature is becoming clear to all: an aging, worn-out prostitute, desired not for her charms but for her availability and price (23:43).

Once more, the conclusion of the sisters' activities is clearly stated: An army will come, plundering them, stoning them, and putting them to the sword. Their children will be slaughtered, their homes burned (23:47). Thus, the Lord will bring to an end all such adultery. This time the object lesson will be heeded, and "all women" will be chastened and not do likewise (23:48). The chapter closes with the recognition formula: "Then you will know that I am the Sovereign LORD" (23:49).

Application. There is no message of hope in Ezekiel 23. The stone is rolled away to reveal the gaping mouth of the tomb, which is ready to swallow up defiled Jerusalem, just as it had earlier swallowed up defiled Samaria. But for those reading Ezekiel 23 from a New Testament perspective, the opened mouth of another tomb speaks a word of comfort even to those as defiled as Jerusalem. Because Christ has died in our place, and more than that has risen from the dead, there is now no condemnation for us who are in Christ Jesus! My death is swallowed up in his victory; my defilement is replaced by his purity, credited to my account. In the name of the Lord Jesus Christ, I too have been washed, I have been justified, and I am being sanctified. What is more, this is true in spite of the sins that I continue to commit daily. Although I am unfaithful to my commitment to God and continue to sin against him regularly in thought, word, and deed, the gospel continues to be good news for me, a sinner.

EZEKIEL 24:1–27

Original Meaning

The Day of Reckoning for Jerusalem (24:1–14). Following the Hebrew more literally, this is the day when Nebuchadnezzar "leaned on" (24:2; *samak*; NIV "laid siege") Jerusalem, a word with overtones of the sacrificial system. By Ezekiel's use of this terminology, Nebuchadnezzar is depicted as designating Jerusalem as the sacrificial lamb.

This sacrificial language leads into a parable. In the parable, Jerusalem is compared to a cooking pot in which abundant meat has been placed to be cooked (24:3). The sacrificial animal has been cut up and all of its pieces "gathered" (24:4; NIV "put") to be boiled, presumably as a fellowship offering.

The wood has been piled up under the pot and the pot has been brought to a nice simmer.

Thus far the expectations of the audience have been moved in a positive direction. But in a classic twist, typical of the genre of parable, what ought to be a tasty sacred meal is, in fact, a foul, profane mess (24:6). This filth that is inside her will not "come out" (24:6; NIV, "go away"), a phrase that has a double meaning. In terms of the imagery of the pot, the filth that will not come out reflects the frustration of a burned-on mess that cannot be removed. On the level of the metaphorical meaning, "come out" is precisely what Jerusalem's inhabitants hope to do at the end of the siege.

Their only exit from the pot will be for judgment (24:6). Lots will be cast over the pot, for all the meat is destined for the same end, reprobation (24:6). There will be no escape.

The blood Jerusalem has shed in her midst is left uncovered, poured out on a bare rock rather than on the ground (24:7). Covering the blood with earth (Lev 17:13) was required for the blood of all animals slaughtered for meat in Deuteronomy 12:16, 24. Blood left exposed would provoke the wrath of God, so their action was nothing less than a deliberate act of sacrilege.

The empty pot is now transformed into a kind of refiner's furnace in a final attempt to try to melt away the impurities (Ezek 24:11). But once again, all efforts to remove the defilement have proved ineffective. God's wrath must be satisfied on Jerusalem if she is ever to be clean again (24:13), and it is time for that definitive final action to begin. The time for words has ended; now it is time for deeds (24:14).

The Death of Ezekiel's Wife (24:15–27). The sword that is going to strike Jerusalem first strikes the prophet himself in the most painful and personal of his prophetic sign-acts. His own wife, the delight of his eyes, is suddenly taken from him (24:16). This is no random turn of fate but a sudden stroke directly from God. Yet Ezekiel is not permitted to mourn publicly in the traditional ways, by lamentation and tears, disheveled clothing, and special food (24:17). All he can do is "groan quietly" (24:17). Outwardly, he is to behave as if nothing has happened.

This strange behavior is to be a sign to the people of the significance of what is to come (24:24). The temple in Jerusalem was their pride and joy; it had become as precious to the Jerusalemites as the closest of relations (24:21). This building, the delight of their eyes, will be desecrated by God. Yet the people will not weep or wail or mourn publicly for the temple (24:22). The normal channels of community support will be gone in the face of such universal loss; only inward grief will be possible (24:23).

But on the very day when the blow falls on Ezekiel's compatriots, when the news of the fall of Jerusalem is confirmed by a fugitive, Ezekiel's lips will be opened, and he will be dumb no more (24:27). With the destruction of Jerusalem, his words of judgment for the city will come to an end; their time will be complete.

Here ends the first lesson, we might say—the lesson of inevitable and incredible judgment poured out on sinners. In the chapters that follow, it will be time for the prophet to speak words of judgment on the surrounding nations, Israel's enemies (chs. 25–32), and then, when the promise of the removal of dumbness is fulfilled (ch. 33), words of hope to God's chosen people (chs. 34–48).

Application. Just as the deepest night for Jerusalem is the beginning of the end of God's wrath on his people and the turning point to hope in Ezekiel's message, so also the death of Jesus Christ on the cross is the turning point in the history of redemption. The blackness of Good Friday causes the light of Easter Sunday to break out with fresh power for Christ's disciples. The taking away of their Lord, the delight of their eyes, to lay him in a tomb, paradoxically, is the means by which they may be enabled to enjoy him forever.

Since God did not spare his own Son, surely he has the right to ask us not to spare even the delight of our eyes, whatever that is. We should be willing to give it up freely for the sake of spreading the good news and for the sake of the glory of this great God. Nor is it enough merely to be willing; sometimes, God actually takes from us that which is most precious to us. In those moments, as we are enabled by his grace to say, "Not my will, but yours be done, Lord," we become living signs to the world around us of God's grace and glory. We become living demonstrations of the fact that we do not regard God as our accomplice, whose job is to ensure that we live comfortable and fulfilling lives. Rather, he is our Lord, who has bought us with a price and owns us and everything we have. Moreover, we do not mourn as the world mourns, for in the midst of our sadness and real sense of painful loss, we know the assurance that just as our Lord has risen, so also will all his people.

EZEKIEL 25:1–17

Original Meaning. With this chapter, we move into a new section of Ezekiel's prophecy: a series of oracles against the surrounding nations (chs. 25–32). In this oracle the Lord tells the prophet to set his face toward the Ammonites and prophesy against them (25:2). They exulted in noisy triumph when the sanctuary was desecrated, the land of Israel laid waste, and the people of Judah exiled (25:3). They saw it as proof positive that the triangular relationship between the nation of Israel, her land, and her deity was broken forever.

Because of that attitude, the Ammonites too would experience judgment (25:4). Their produce would be eaten by others and their people cut off, exterminated, and destroyed—a threefold fate to match their threefold rejoicing (25:4, 7). As a result of this judgment the Ammonites "will know that I am the LORD" (25:7). The nations will recognize the Lord's sovereignty when he acts to judge not only his own people but them as well. In so doing, he will demonstrate that he is the only one with power to judge or to deliver; in the face of the Lord's fury, their gods are impotent to save them.

The oracle against Moab (25:8–11) charges them with saying, "Look, Judah has become like all the other nations" (25:8). The irony is that there was not a little truth in that statement: Judah had indeed in large measure become like the nations. But it could never be true in the sense in which Moab had intended, so that this statement is nothing short of blasphemy on her lips. They are the ones who will be left unremembered on the stage of world history (25:10).

The Edomites (25:12–14) seem not merely to have gloated over the downfall of Judah but to have actively participated in it. Although they were, from a biblical perspective, close kin of the Israelites, they had no compassion on their brothers. The result will be God's execution of vengeance on them, using his own people to do so (25:14).

In 25:15–17 the Philistines are likewise charged with trying to settle old scores, seeking to work out their "ancient hostility" (25:15) toward Israel in the destruction of the chosen people. They too will experience the vengeance of God (25:17).

Application. God's judgment is real in history as well as beyond history, but it should never be contemplated lightly. We would do well to remember the words of Jesus that the measure we use in judging others will be the same one used on us (Luke 6:38). Rather, with reverent fear and trembling before the awful reality of the judgment of God, we should seek to persuade all people to flee the wrath to come (2 Cor 5:10–11).

EZEKIEL 26:1–27:36

Original Meaning. The oracle against Tyre is composed of three distinct but essentially parallel literary panels, each of which ends with the same concluding phrase about Tyre's going down to the realm of the dead (26:21; 27:36; 28:19). The purpose of this panel construction is to invite the reader to place the three oracles side by side and see essentially the same message presented in three different ways.

The First Panel (26:2–21). The charge against Tyre is similar to that raised against Judah's other neighbors: She rejoiced when Jerusalem fell, seeing in that event the opportunity for personal gain (26:2). A potential rival for her trading empire has been eliminated, opening up new avenues to prosperity.

Ezekiel is quick to point out the flaw in Tyre's thinking. The God who brought judgment on Jerusalem is also against Tyre and will judge her in an almost exactly corresponding manner. Does Tyre hope to become the new meeting place for the nations? The Lord will bring many nations against her (26:3). Did Tyre rejoice to see Jerusalem's doors shattered? Her walls will be destroyed and her towers torn down (26:4). Did Tyre expect to prosper? She will become plunder for the nations (26:5).

The assault of the nations on Tyre is described as being like the waves of a stormy sea (26:3), which is a peculiarly apt image for the city of Tyre. It was originally built on a coastal island about a mile long and half a mile wide, whose strength came from its position surrounded by water.

The general expression "many nations" (26:3) resolves into the specific figure of Nebuchadnezzar, king of Babylon (26:7). The assault and destruction of Tyre is described in great, if rather stereotypical, detail (26:8–12). But the end result is exactly the same: Tyre will be reduced to a bare rock, the haunt of local fishermen rather than of long-distance trading vessels (26:5, 14). Her former glory will never be regained (26:14).

The terrible fall of Tyre will have an impact on her maritime trading partners, the "coastlands," or "islands" (26:15). They will tremble and adopt the customs of mourning, with their rulers coming down from their thrones and setting aside their fine robes (26:16), taking up a lament for the fallen city. It will be as if the island city has sunk into the heart of the chaotic "ocean depths" (26:19), its inhabitants condemned to "the pit" (*bor*, 26:20), never to return again. The "deep" was an element of the primeval chaos that God transformed into cosmos in Genesis 1 (cf. Gen 1:2), while "the pit" was the shadowy underworld of the dead, the nightmare end of those abandoned by God. Though people seek for Tyre, she will have utterly vanished, sunk by God's torpedoes, never again to be found (Ezek 26:21).

The Second Panel (27:1–36). The second panel (27:1–36) proclaims essentially the same message as the first but in the form of a lament. Ezekiel describes in great detail the glory of Tyre under the metaphor of a majestic ship. She was a legend in her own mind, beautiful to the point of perfection (27:3). She was fitted out with prime timbers for her construction and fine cloth for her sails and awnings (27:5–7). Her crew had been recruited from the best manpower available (27:8–11b), bringing her beauty to perfection (27:11c). Could there ever have been a more perfect ship?

Her beauty was not merely cosmetic. The merchant ship Tyre is depicted as a highly efficient business machine, trading in all kinds of costly goods. The cargo list seems to be organized by geographic areas, starting with Mediterranean locations and those in Asia Minor (27:12–15) and moving on through Palestinian regions from south to north (27:16–17) to Syria (27:18–19), Arabia (27:20–22), and finally Mesopotamia (27:23–24). By covering all points of the compass and virtually every imaginable precious commodity, the picture is established of Tyre as the commercial crossroads of the world.

But the paean of praise for her beauty and commercial importance only heightens the tragedy of her downfall. Her apparent invincibility contains the seeds of her own downfall. She is "filled with heavy cargo" (27:25), a description that fits the city Tyre literally as well as the ship Tyre metaphorically. But when the stormy wind blows, the sea that provides the source of the mariner's wealth can easily become an enemy. An east wind (from Babylon) will start to blow, and the mighty vessel will flounder with the loss of all hands (27:26–27). The rapidity with which her demise can be described contrasts starkly with the lengthy description of her beauty. Her beauty and security count for nothing when the storm strikes.

As in the first panel, once again those who watch from the sidelines tremble, and a lament is raised for the doomed city. This time those who adopt the customary forms of mourning are the sailors and seafaring people in company with the kings of the coastlands and the merchants (27:28–36). Tyre's joy over the destruction of "the gate to the nations" (26:2) is seen to be thoroughly misplaced, for the one who judged Jerusalem will also judge Tyre, the marketplace of the "nations" (27:33, 36). The end result for Tyre is the same as the first panel: Tyre will "come to a horrible end and will be no more" (27:36).

Application. The true answer to seduction is to open people's eyes to the shallowness of the "beauty" on offer. In Revelation 17–18 Babylon is modeled after Ezekiel's description of Tyre. She sits on many waters (Rev 17:1), she is the ultimate trading nation (Rev 18:12–13), and when she falls the kings of the earth and the sailors mourn (Rev 18:9, 17). "Babylon" here is a cipher for Rome, and her trump card is wealth and luxury, in short, materialism. However beautiful and powerful Rome may appear, the book of Revelation reveals the truth that her beauty is only skin deep, and her power is merely temporary. Judgment is coming, which will uncover the true nature of all things and put them into proper perspective.

Today seduction lives in materialistic excess, drawing the world away from God and proclaiming her name more widely than the good news of Jesus Christ. Consumerism is making disciples in all nations through its seductive charms.

At the heart of seduction, however, is a lie: that what you see is what you get. And Satan, the eternal liar, is skilled at making us see things from their most attractive perspective. Like an artful angler, he hides the hook and shows us only the juicy worm. Not until too late does the fish discover the steel within. Satan's tackle box is well equipped with lures, but the truth in each of these cases is that we will indeed pay later for what we buy now.

How does God wean our hearts from the seductiveness of this world? The way for us to learn to resist the attractiveness of Satan's seduction is to learn to fix our eyes on the truth, on Jesus. If Jerusalem's beauty was spiritually discerned even during its prosperous days, then it was not surprising that many would be seduced away by the apparent beauty of its rival during her humiliation at the time of the exile. So also, there are many today who are unable to discern the beauty of Christ crucified. Their eyes are blinded to the truth. The world still seems to offer far more attractive alternatives than the Son of Man.

EZEKIEL 28:1–26

Original Meaning

The Third Panel (28:1–19). The third panel combines both straightforward prophecy and lament, this time directed at the ruler of Tyre, who in his person and fate acts as a kind of personification of the city. He is accused of overweening pride (28:2). He claims to exercise the divine authority that comes from sitting on the throne of the gods.

The evidence on which the king of Tyre rests his claim to the status of a divine being is twofold: his wisdom and his wealth. In the first place, he claims to be as wise as a god, wiser than the ancient hero Daniel (28:3). This enormous wisdom, in his estimation, is what has brought him his great wealth. That his treasuries are full of gold and silver is attributed to his skill in trading (28:4–5); thus, along with his wealth his pride has grown enormously (28:5).

The Sovereign Lord will quickly put the king of Tyre in his place. His vaunted wisdom and claimed divine status will not help him when the true God brings the nations against him (28:6–8). The most objective demonstration of his human status will be his helplessness in the hands of those who capture him as they put him to death (28:8–10). What kind of god is he if he can be so easily slain? Far from being a god, he will go down to "the pit," dying the death of the slain in the chaotic heart of the seas (28:8).

The king's destiny is underlined in the command to the prophet to raise a lament for the king of Tyre (28:12). A lament presupposes the death of the person concerned, thus emphasizing from the outset his humanity. Yet the lament (with perhaps more than a hint of sarcasm?) in its eulogy appears at the outset to take his claims of divinity seriously (28:12–13).

In keeping with his claims of semidivine status, the king of Tyre is described as having been present at the beginning of the world in Eden, the garden of God, adorned with every precious stone (28:13). He was even anointed as a "guardian cherub" (28:14), one of the heavenly beings described in Ezekiel 1 and

10 and known from the account in Genesis 3 as the guardians of the sacred garden. He had access to the center of the divine presence (28:14).

But his greatness and privilege as the protological man simply serves to underline the greatness of his fall from grace. The abundance of his trade brought with it not merely riches but also violence and pride; his "wisdom" became corrupt and led him into wickedness (28:16–17).

Far from being a god, who by a theophany might sanctify a piece of ground as a suitable site for a sanctuary, his very presence had the opposite effect, defiling sanctuaries. Cast down to the ground, he was made a public spectacle before the kings of the earth and consumed by fire from within (28:18).

The end result of this judgment is that the king of Tyre, like his city, will come to a horrible end and will be no more (26:19). When the great ship Tyre sinks, her captain will go down to the depths along with her.

Oracle against Sidon (28:20–23). After the three-panel depiction of Tyre's judgment comes a brief oracle against Tyre's neighbor, Sidon (28:20–23). She, like the other nations, will find that Judah's God is not to be trifled with. The Lord will gain glory for himself by executing judgments on Sidon—plague, bloodshed, and the sword on every side (28:22–23). Then indeed the nations will experience personally the Lord's holiness and power.

Address to the Lord's People (28:24–26). These words of hope form the central fulcrum for the oracles against the nations, showing that their purpose is to build hope in Ezekiel's immediate audience. The judgments on the nations that the prophet describes are ultimately for Israel's own good, so that when the full regathering of the nation takes place, she may dwell in safety, free from prickly neighbors (28:24).

Indeed, God will demonstrate his holiness—the distinctiveness of his being—not only by judging the nations but also by once again gathering his own people to the promised land (28:25). The people will once again be able to build houses and plant vineyards (28:26), long-term projects that speak of settled security. Then all nations will see that Israel is God's people and he is their God, which has been the goal of his covenant relationship with them from the outset. This point is underlined in the modified version of the recognition formula used. Instead of the usual "then they will know that I am the LORD" (e.g., 25:17), the oracle closes, "Then they will know that I am the LORD their God" (28:26). Paradise, which the king of Tyre claimed and lost, may still be regained by God's own people.

Application. The wisdom of the world may offer a God-like ability to succeed in everything we attempt while living lives free of pain and sickness. It offers a seductively attractive path to those who are suffering physically or otherwise lacking in some area of their lives. The wisdom of the world, however, is foolishness to God (1 Cor 1:20). For the Christian, wisdom consists neither in consulting the experts nor in seeking inner enlightenment, but in consulting God and in living according to his word.

EZEKIEL 29:1–30:19

Original Meaning

The First Oracle (29:1–16). Ezekiel 29 opens with a word of judgment against Pharaoh, who is addressed under the figure of a great sea monster. This sea monster was a well-known element of ancient Near Eastern mythology. In Ezekiel, the mythical picture blends with the geographically appropriate image of Pharaoh as a great crocodile, resting secure amid the Nile streams, to give a picture of the ruler of Egypt as a superhuman, supernatural force of destruction.

For all Pharaoh's boasts of divine power, he will be trapped with hooks like an ordinary crocodile (29:4). He will be brought out into the desert and there executed along with "all the fish of your streams" (29:5), that is, either the nations allied to him or the members of his armed forces.

The reason for this act of judgment becomes clear in 29:6–7. Egypt has been an unstable support to Judah. Egypt's sin was to appear to be a source of military support in Judah's struggle against Babylon, encouraging her to rebel against her overlords. Once the battle was joined, however, she stood at a distance, leaving Judah to her fate.

God's people should indeed have known better than to trust in Egypt, but Egypt too is not guiltless for soliciting their trust and then proving dangerously unstable (29:7). Egypt's arrogant claims to creator status are a contributory factor in Judah's sin (29:9). As a result, she too will be judged by God and turned into an utter devastation (29:10). The whole of Egypt will be uninhabited for forty years (29:11), which is not only the standard length of a generation in biblical terminology but is also the length of the Judean exile Ezekiel had prophesied in 4:6.

To underline the symmetry of Egypt's fate with those who trusted in her, her people will be scattered among the nations and dispersed among the peoples, just like Judah. Even more strikingly, they too will be gathered by the Lord from among the nations, brought back from captivity, and returned to the land from which they originated (29:14). But Egypt will not be fully restored (29:16).

The Second Oracle (29:17–21). The second oracle recognizes the relative fruitlessness of Nebuchadnezzar's campaign against Tyre, of which Ezekiel had spoken in chapters 26–28. Though the effort expended was great, the booty achieved at the end of the campaign was minimal (29:18). In compensation, since they were working for the Lord (29:20), the Lord will give Egypt's wealth as plunder for Nebuchadnezzar's army (29:19).

Chapter 29 then closes with a brief oracle that reminds us that Israel remains the central focus of the prophet's interest, even in the oracles against the foreign nations (29:21).

The Third Oracle (30:1–19). In this third oracle, the content of the prophecy of the first oracle (29:1–16) is essentially replayed in the form of a lament. The prophet is instructed to wail and mourn for the coming of the day of the Lord's judgment on Egypt (30:3–4). Egypt's allies now come into focus as distinct nations and will fall along with Egypt (30:5–6). The entire confederacy will be reduced to a shattered and burned ruin (30:6–9), made desolate at the hand of Nebuchadnezzar and his ruthless army (30:10–12). From Memphis, Tahpahnes, and Heliopolis in the north of Egypt to Thebes in the south, the cities of Egypt will be destroyed (30:13–19).

The summary statement in 30:19 evokes repeated themes of the Exodus narrative, where both judgments against Egypt (Exod 6:6; 7:4; 12:12; Num 33:4) and the knowledge of God (Exod 7:5; 14:4, 18) are prominent. As in the exodus, this act of judgment will strike at both the gods of Egypt and their earthly rulers (Ezek 30:13). In the imagery of the cosmic day of the Lord, the light will be turned to darkness and the proud strength of Egypt brought to an end (30:18). By this means, God will demonstrate conclusively his existence and power in front of a watching world.

Application. Like Israel before him, Jesus faced the alluring attractiveness of the ways of the world. Whereas Israel failed, Jesus endured faithfully. He did so because he was not deceived by Satan. He saw clearly that things are not always as they appear. Satan offers a solution for our felt needs, immediate relief for the blister points of life. However, our felt needs are not always our real needs. Sometimes what offers temporary relief causes long-term problems. Jesus rejected Satan's quick-fix solutions in favor of a life lived in obedience to God's call, a path that led all the way to the cross. Why did he do so? Because he saw the ultimate realities of life: that men and women would be eternally lost without a Savior, someone who lived the life of perfect obedience in their place and who died the death their sins deserved. Jesus followed the hard road.

EZEKIEL 30:20–32:32

Original Meaning

The Fourth Oracle (30:20–26). The fourth of the seven oracles against Egypt declares that God has already begun to act. The date formula in 30:20 places it shortly before the fall of Jerusalem; the oracle itself rules out the possibility of any relief coming from the Egyptian direction (30:21).

The defeat of Egypt is described in terms of a breaking of Pharaoh's arm (30:21). The "arm" in the Old Testament is a symbol of strength. The fundamental contrast in this oracle is between the broken arms of Pharaoh and the arms of Nebuchadnezzar that have been strengthened by the Lord (30:24–25). This bout is clearly not an equal contest. Ezekiel even anticipates potential objections that though Pharaoh's arm has been broken, it may be healed (30:21). On the contrary, it will be broken again, along with the sound arm that remains (30:22). Egypt's power will be comprehensively destroyed, a prediction ultimately fulfilled in the conquest of Egypt by Cambyses in 525 BC.

In the background of this struggle between two world powers, however, there is another actor. In this passage the arm of the Lord is not directly referred to, but the Lord's action is everywhere evident. He is the one who will break Pharaoh's arms and strengthen Nebuchadnezzar's (30:22, 25). It is the Lord's sword that Nebuchadnezzar will draw against Egypt (30:25). It is the Lord who will scatter the Egyptians among the nations (30:26). The clash of the superpowers is under his control.

The Fifth Oracle (31:1–18). The fifth oracle against Egypt compares Pharaoh to a massive tree that is felled because of its pride. He himself recognized no equal, and in what follows Ezekiel takes his claims of greatness seriously. He is like a mighty cedar (31:3) in Lebanon; there follows a graphic picture of a tree of supernatural proportions. The myth of a tree that constitutes the heart of ordered existence was part of the lore of the surrounding nations.

Here Ezekiel puts this mythical picture to use as a description of Egypt's greatness. Her roots were fed by the deep springs under the earth (31:4). As a result, she grew higher than all the other trees of the earth, providing shelter for all the birds of the air and the beasts of the field (31:5–6). In fact, her greatness surpassed earthly proportions; not even the trees of Eden itself could match Egypt's beauty.

Pride once again precedes a fall from grace. In all the vivid word pictures used by Ezekiel in the oracles against the foreign nations, the nature of the glorious object described contains within it the seeds of its own destruction. Here, Egypt is a great world tree, but it will be felled by the cosmic lumberjack.

It was the Lord who had raised Egypt to her elevated status (31:9), but she considered her attainments something of which to be proud (31:10). The Lord can just as easily cast her down (31:11). The agency of execution is human (31:11), but the instructions come from on high. The tree no longer provides shade and protection; instead, its fallen branches are merely a convenient resting place for them (31:13). Just as her height was unparalleled in her time, so it will never again be surpassed; for all the dominant nations that come after her will share her mortality, treading along with her the way to destruction, bound for the underworld (31:14).

The cosmic scale of the tree is matched by cosmic mourning at its fall and descent into Sheol, the home of the unworthy dead. The cosmic springs are shut up, while Lebanon, the home of the mighty cedar, is darkened (31:15). The heights and the depths, the sources of light and subterranean water, are thus both clothed in mourning, a state also affecting those in between.

The nations of the world trembled at the sound of the tree's fall, whose echoes reverberated even into the underworld. Those of its predecessors who had envied it (31:16) were gratified in its sharing of their demise, while those who had allied themselves to it went down with it to Sheol (31:17). There they joined those killed by the sword, whose unpeaceful end was thought in some way to carry over to their state beyond death. Ezekiel brings out the point of the word picture explicitly in 31:18. Though Egypt's splendor and majesty were unrivaled in all the powerful nations who went before, she too will share their fate in the underworld among those outside the peaceful community, among the uncircumcised and those slain by the sword.

The Sixth Oracle (32:1–16). The lion and crocodile are two mighty beasts who appear all-powerful (32:2). Indeed, both images were regularly appropriated by the pharaohs as positive self-descriptions. Yet in spite of their strength, both may be hunted and killed. Once more through human agency (32:3), the Lord will cast his net over Pharaoh, a method of hunting suitable to either crocodiles or lions. His corpse will be thrown to the ground to provide a home and food for the birds of the air and beasts of the field. At this point, the scale of Pharaoh's demise takes on semi-mythical proportions: His body is big enough to be spread on the mountains and fill the valleys, his blood enough to water the land and fill the ravines (32:5–6).

The images of cosmic darkness and universal mourning are invoked. In an echo of the penultimate exodus plague on Egypt, the plague of darkness (Exod 10:21–22), the heavens will be darkened, and sun, moon, and stars will fail to give light (Ezek 32:7). The peoples will be appalled, and their kings will shudder because of the scale of Egypt's devastation, fearing for their own lives (32:9–10).

In this final onslaught against Egypt, the king of Babylon will shatter her pride (32:11–12). All people and animals are cut off from the land (32:13). The demise of the great animal-human of 32:2 is underlined by the ceasing of his thrashing around, muddying the streams (32:13). Now the waters of Egypt will flow as clear and smooth as oil, untroubled by any disturbance (32:14). Egypt will once again recognize the sovereign power of the Lord when he acts to strike down all who live there, this time with no exceptions (32:15). The lament is prepared; all that waits is the execution of the divine decree (32:16).

The Seventh Oracle (32:17–32). The final oracle against Egypt and the final oracle in the sequence of oracles against the nations sums up everything that has gone before by means of a comprehensive tour of the underworld, which is to be Egypt's new home. Six nations are named as already there. Egypt is the climactic and completing seventh nation of the underworld.

Once again, the oracle draws out and expands an idea present in an earlier pronouncement (31:17–18), which spoke of Egypt's descent into the underworld and the company she would keep there. Here, however, the picture is presented in graphic detail. Egypt's future home will be among the unquiet dead and those who fell by the sword (32:21). Though all these other nations were once mighty and had administered a reign of terror while they lived, now they bear the reproach for their iniquity. A place of punishment (32:24) is prepared for all such, and Pharaoh certainly qualifies to join the club (32:28). For the time of the Lord's appointing, he too spread terror in the land of the living (32:32), but soon he will become merely a part of the terror that is the land of the dead. The Sovereign Lord has spoken (32:32).

Application. The declaration on US bank notes is unequivocal: "In God we trust." Unfortunately, it is a single-mindedness that few of us, even as Christians, live out in practice. The temptation to trust in the paper on which the slogan is written rather than in the God of whom the slogan speaks is real. Yet on what does our faith in that piece of paper rest? The paper can be burned up, lost, or stolen. Even if the paper is retained, its value can be devastated through runaway inflation to the point where the note itself is virtually worthless. Moreover, even if none of these things happen, US dollars are not the local currency beyond the grave. How foolish we are, then, to place our trust in money! Yet how many of us still believe unflinchingly in its power to bless us, and that possessing more of it will make our life more meaningful and desirable! The number of people who participate weekly in the various state and local lotteries demonstrates the power of that myth in our society.

Or consider the power of the myth of career. How many people have devoted their lives to finding a fulfilling and rewarding job? In the process, they may sacrifice precious relationships and outside interests on the altar of success, which they have defined as career progress. How many find, if they finally reach the top of the ladder, that they wish they had climbed a different one? Even if they are content with the ladder they have climbed and they receive the benediction of their idol, do its blessings last? Sooner or later, through retirement or death, the ladder is put away. The job is turned over to someone else. Where will they be then?

But perhaps these are altogether too obvious idols to deceive us. Perhaps we have instead sacrificed everything on the altar of family. What could be more noble than laying down our lives for the sake of our loved ones? Yet if our trust is in our family to provide meaning and value in our lives, then we too are headed for disappointment sooner or later. In the short term, we should remember that we are investing our love in fallen sinners. Even faithful Christians see their spouses commit adultery or their children rebel and run away, in spite of their best efforts. The pain and sorrow of such traumas are real and intense. But in the life of someone for whom family has become the controlling myth, they are more than intense; they are devastating. Life loses all its meaning, for meaning was determined by the sense of family.

Yet, tragic though it is, such a painful loss may be God's way of demonstrating the powerlessness of "family" to save. It is a broken reed, which wounds those who lean on it. Even those who do not experience that kind of disillusionment through broken family relationships must still face up to the reality of death. The ultimate dissolution of all earthly relationships is a fact that cannot be gainsaid. Relationships by blood or marriage may serve to gain us citizenship in earthly kingdoms, but they will avail us nothing when it comes to citizenship in the kingdom of heaven.

EZEKIEL 33:1–33

Original Meaning. After the judgment oracles of Ezekiel 1–24 and the oracles against the foreign nations in chapters 25–32, we finally get to the good news in chapters 34–48. Ezekiel 33 opens with the depiction of the prophet as "watchman" (33:2), just as did his oracles of destruction in chapter 3. In chapter 3 the image functioned as part of a private message to the prophet. In chapter 33 it is part of a public proclamation (33:2, 7), pressing in on the people their own responsibility for their fate and the real possibility, even now, of repentance and return.

The proclamation starts from the general statement of a commonly accepted fact, that when the Lord sent a judgment against a land, the watchman was responsible for the consequences only if he did not warn the people (33:2–6). From this general principle, Ezekiel moves to the specific case facing the people in 33:7–9: Clearly the Lord has sent judgment against his people, and no one who has read chapters 4–32 can doubt the prophet's faithfulness to proclaiming the judgment to come; he is free from any culpability in the death of the wicked.

But does this mean that there is now no hope for God's rebellious people? This seems to have been the thought among at least some of the exiles (33:10). Now that Jerusalem is on the brink of destruction and they are finally taking the possibility of judgment seriously, despair is a real danger.

Ezekiel's answer to that was that the living God takes no pleasure in the death of the wicked but rather seeks their repentance that they may live (33:11). Even now, it is not too late to turn and be saved. The fundamental covenant choice of life or death is still open to the people (33:11). The prophet illustrates the reality of that choice by appealing to two case studies. In the first case, someone "trusts in [past] righteousness" and does evil; he will surely die and not live (33:13). In the second, a wicked man turns from his sins and does what is right; he will surely live and not die (33:14–15). The prophet's point is that neither judgment nor salvation is an automatic process, but each works itself out through a life lived in accordance with the terms of the covenant (33:15) or in violation of it.

The problem that the people face is not that of God's justice (33:17). His path to life is continuously held open to rebels. The problem is with the people's lack of righteousness (33:17). They have consistently chosen the path to death over the path to life. That is what makes it bad news that God will judge each according to his own way (33:20)! Nonetheless, the point of the case studies is that there is a remedy for the bad news.

This is the context in which Ezekiel places the news of Jerusalem's destruction (33:21–22). This is the radical turning point in the fortunes of God's people and in Ezekiel's own life. His dumbness, with him since his commissioning as a prophet in 3:26–27, is now removed, just as the Lord promised in chapter 24. The possibility of a new beginning for God's people similarly exists. But which will they choose: life or death?

The prophet is not left long in suspense. The following two sections make it clear that the hearts of God's people have not been fundamentally changed even by this radical act of judgment. Both back home in Judah (33:23–29) and among the exiles (33:30–33), it is business as usual. Those who remain behind in Judah, inhabiting the ruins of God's judgment, see the situation as an opportunity for economic gain rather than personal and societal repentance. Claiming to be Abraham's children, they interpret God's covenant promise of the land to Abraham as an inalienable right, an unconditional covenant. If Abraham as one man was able to possess the land, how much more his many descendants still living in the land (33:24)?

The people are, in fact, corporately in a situation analogous to the first case study described by Ezekiel. The prophet describes their disobedience in the stereotypical terms (33:25–26). These covenant-breakers will continue to inherit the three classic curses of the covenant: the sword, wild animals, and plague (33:27; cf. Lev 26:22, 25). The land will continue to suffer God's judgment until it becomes a desolate wasteland (Ezek 33:28–29; cf. Lev 26:32–33).

Nor are matters any better among the exiles. The news of Jerusalem's fall appears to have given Ezekiel's message a certain popularity and topicality. He is now the subject of conversation in the cities and doorways (Ezek 33:30). To use a contemporary analogy, his fame is like that of a pop star, whose declarations on spiritual matters may arouse curiosity but are scarcely accorded authoritative status. People may have been humming along to his tune, but they are paying no attention to the true meaning of his lyrics.

Time, however, will prove the power of the word of the Lord through Ezekiel (33:33). In that day, just as all will know experientially the power of the Lord, so they will also be forced to recognize the authenticity of the Lord's prophet.

Application. For some, a major life crisis may cause them to attend church, but only as superficial hearers. Like Ezekiel's audience, they may find the form of the message interesting and stimulating, but they never feel its power in their hearts as a life-changing reality. Those of us who are preachers need to be careful that we do not foster such shallow attention. In our day, there is a focus on "seeker-sensitive" services that will present the gospel in a way that will be attractive to such people. The end task of the church, however, is not to assemble seekers but to make disciples.

EZEKIEL 34:1–31

Original Meaning. This chapter opens with an oracle against "the shepherds of Israel" (34:1–16). The title *shepherd* was a well-known ascription of both kings and gods in the ancient Near East. A similar notion of the relationship between the king and God was present in Israel. Thus, when the tribes came to David at Hebron to make him king over them, the basis of their action was the Lord's declaration concerning David (2 Sam 5:2).

In Ezekiel's oracle of judgment, however, the Lord is coming *against* his shepherds—the former kings of Judah—because they have failed to fulfill their role of shepherd properly. These shepherds have viewed their position as an opportunity for personal gain, ruling harshly and brutally, feeding only themselves, not the flock, and even slaughtering the choicest animals (Ezek 34:2–6). Because of the shepherds' sinful self-interest, judgment is coming on them (34:7–10). In the absence of a true shepherd, the flock has been scattered and plundered (34:8). But now the Lord will step in and remove the false shepherds from their office. Their shepherding will be brought to an end as the Lord acts to rescue his sheep (34:10). Now the Lord will himself search out the flock and take care of them, gathering them from all the places where they were scattered (34:12).

This metaphorical image of shepherd and sheep is made from a concrete promise of return from exile in 34:13. They can look forward to a return to the "mountains of Israel" (34:13), the heart of the promised land. There they will experience the full blessing of the Lord's shepherding (34:16).

This last thought leads into a further oracle of judgment (34:17–22) against the "rams and goats" (34:17) or the "fat sheep" (34:20). These are the broader class of leaders of the community, who had oppressed the weak. Even what they did not need for themselves they spoiled, thus denying it to others (34:18–19). They had abandoned the traditional responsibility of the upper class for the social well-being of the other classes. The Lord will intervene to execute judgment within his flock, judging between sheep and sheep (34:22). He will thus deal with both external and internal dangers to the peace and security of his flock.

As elsewhere in Ezekiel, we see in this chapter a double critique of the failures of the past: the divine response of punishing those responsible and the divine promise of intervention to reverse those failures. The intervention takes the form of setting up over them "one shepherd, my servant David," who will act as their "prince" (34:23–24). His relationship to them is not simply *primus inter pares* (first among equals) but shepherd to sheep, a relationship that involves authority as well as service.

Indeed, the change to be wrought in Israel's situation is not so much a change in the nature of the office as in the nature of the occupant. This good shepherd will be like the great king David, the king after God's own heart (1 Sam 13:14), the archetypal picture of a strong king ruling with justice and fairness.

This future ruler is nothing less than the fulfillment of the covenant with David. God promised David that he would raise up his offspring to succeed him and that he would establish his kingdom (2 Sam 7:12, 25). Solomon subsequently received the promise that, if he followed the pattern of his father David, his throne would be established forever. That dynastic oracle will be fulfilled with the raising up of a new David (Ezek 34:23), who would be the Lord's servant and his people's shepherd.

In addition, the Lord will make "a covenant of peace" with his flock (34:25). In place of the curses of the Sinai covenant (Lev 26:14–35), they will now experience the blessings of the covenant (Lev 26:4–13). The state of experiencing the blessings that flow from a harmonious relationship with God is what makes this distinctively a "covenant of peace." This covenant is thus not so much a *new* covenant as it is the experience of the blessings promised in the original covenant. They will be his sheep and he will be their God.

Application. What does it mean for a pastor to be a shepherd? It is a unique combination of afflicting the comfortable and comforting the afflicted. The bad shepherds of Ezekiel 34 were criticized because they ignored the fat sheep who were oppressing the other sheep, while they lived comfortably off the products of the flock. In contrast, the good shepherd will both confront the fat sheep and tenderly care for the weak sheep (34:16).

Most of us who are shepherds fall far short of this standard. Sometimes, we don't challenge those who are comfortable for fear of stirring up conflict—after all, the fat sheep are often big givers who underwrite the church's budget (and pay our salaries). Nor do we always comfort the weak sheep as we should. Taking care of the weak sheep is hard, painful, time-consuming work, and we have been told that there are more important things to do with our time. As a result, we gradually turn into managers of the flock, and as long as the flock is growing in numbers, no one around us complains. God is against such shepherds, however. He is the one to whom we are ultimately accountable, and what will it profit us if we grow a sizable megachurch yet neglect our calling to shepherd the sheep? We will stand under his condemnation.

EZEKIEL 35:1–36:15

Original Meaning. Ezekiel 35 comprises an oracle against the nation of Edom. This larger oracle against Edom is linked together with the oracle that follows it (36:1–15) as a pair of contrasting panels of darkness and light. The chapter opens with an address through the prophet against Mount Seir, the symbol of Edom (35:2). Edom, the nation to the southeast of Judah, had apparently taken advantage of the power vacuum left by the destruction of Jerusalem to move into Judean territory and take it over. The Lord declared that judgment would come on Mount Seir (35:3), exactly the same fate he had earlier brought on the mountains of Israel (6:14).

The reason for God's judgment is given in 35:5: Because of the "ancient hostility" between the two nations, the Edomites gave the Israelites over to the sword in their time of judgment. This hostility reached all the way back to the time of their progenitors, Jacob and Esau (also known as Edom), as recorded in Genesis 27–28. When Judah was under God's wrath and Jerusalem was judged, Edom saw an opportunity to reclaim the stolen birthright by helping the Babylonians. To match their perpetual enmity toward Israel, now they will become "desolate forever" (35:9).

The source of Edom's perpetual enmity toward God's people becomes clear in 35:10. This ambition will be thwarted by the Lord's intervention (35:11–12). Just as they rejoiced at Israel's downfall, many nations will rejoice at theirs (35:15). Then indeed they will know that the Lord stands behind the assignment of the land of Canaan to Israel as a lasting inheritance (Num 34:2); his present abandonment of the land is not permanent.

Though the vassal Israel has been temporarily removed, the land of Canaan remains the rightful property of the Lord. The living God will not be mocked or trifled with (35:13). Edom's foolish boasting will ultimately be seen as the empty words of the godless, who think to overthrow God's kingdom.

If Ezekiel 35 gives the dark side of the future, 36:1–15 gives the bright side—the return of God's people to the land of promise. Edom will be brought down to the depths; Israel will return to possess the land that is now in the hands of many nations (36:2–3).

Edom's fate is therefore representative of all who oppose God's plan; all who seek to benefit from Israel's misfortune will meet the same end at the hands of Israel's jealous God (36:5). Whereas in the past God's jealousy and wrath were poured out on the mountains of Israel so that they became the object of scorn for the nations, that scorn will be returned on the head of the nations (36:7). Israel has once again become "my people" (36:8). The mountains of Israel will burst forth with a primeval fruitfulness as the Lord turns his face toward them in blessing (36:9). People and animals will multiply and be fruitful for the Israelites (36:11), an echo of the creation mandate in Genesis 1:28. This re-creation will not merely be a return to the former status quo but will be something even better than their original state (36:11). The mountains of Israel, Israel's heartland, would once again be a place of prosperity and blessing, experiencing the positive fruits of divine election; no longer would it be a barren and undesirable place under God's curse because of the people's unfaithfulness to their covenant overlord.

Application. God has determined from all eternity to save a people for himself, and that purpose must stand in spite of all that the forces of the evil one can throw against it. God did not choose Jacob because he was better than Esau or Israel because she was better than Edom. He chose them simply because of his own good pleasure and purpose. In spite of Israel's sin and rebellion against God, the honor of his name required him to act to preserve for himself a people. Astonishingly, the way in which he has chosen to do so is by engrafting the gentiles into a new nonethnic entity, the true Israel of God (Rom 11:17, 26; Gal 6:16). We were engrafted into the vine not because we chose him but because he chose us to bear lasting fruit for him (John 15:16). All is of grace, even our fruitfulness, so that no one can boast in the presence of God.

EZEKIEL 36:16–38

Original Meaning. The prophet begins by pointing out the motivation for God's wrath in the past. The people, while they lived in their own land, polluted it by their actions (36:17). As a result, they could not remain in God's presence, and he could not remain in their midst. Communication with the living God through the various Old Testament means of grace was impossible as long as one was in a state of impurity as a result of contact with death.

What Israel had done while they lived in their land was to turn it into a permanent place of death, making it a place unfit for divine habitation by the living God (36:18). God had no choice but to bring on them the curses of the covenant they had broken, in wrath scattering them among the nations, just as he had threatened when they first entered the land (Deut 29:22–28).

This action, however, created a new problem for God. He had established a relationship between himself, his people, and the land. Yet now the nations could see that the Lord's people were absent from his land (Ezek 36:21). That three-way relationship had been broken. The conclusion drawn by the surrounding nations would be natural: The Lord's power was insufficient to bring about that which he promised. Thus, as long as Israel was scattered among the nations, they continually profaned the divine name (36:20) *simply by being in exile instead of in the land of promise*, all of which brings Ezekiel to the reasons for God's future mercy.

It is not because God shrinks from dealing out judgment that he stays his hand from crushing Israel comprehensively and finally. However, the Israelites of Ezekiel's day were not completely destroyed. Why not? Because though he has no compassion on them, God will nonetheless have concern for his name, which he had inextricably linked to Israel by entering covenant with them. Because of that sovereign, irrevocable act, mercy not only may but must be shown to Israel. The honor of God's name will be vindicated by a show of power among the nations when he brings Israel back to her land (36:21–23). The Lord will act, not for Israel's sake, but for the sake of his own name. The root of God's action in restoring his people is grounded not in his love (which might suggest something lovable about the object of his affections) but in a demonstration of his holiness.

But this act through which God's power is demonstrated involves a total change in their nature. His people must be redeemed not merely outwardly but inwardly, truly. Israel will indeed be gathered and returned from the nations to their own land (36:24). Then she will be sprinkled with clean water, symbolizing her cleansing from all her past impurities and idolatries, the things that had made the land unclean (36:25).

This outward act of initiation is then followed by a deeper, internal change, whereby Israel's heart and spirit will be made new. Unresponsive, unyielding stone will be replaced by warm, living, responsive flesh (36:26). The spirit of God, which brings life and power, will indwell them and create in them both the will and the ability to follow God's decrees and laws (36:27). Then, finally, they will be fit to live in God's land and be his people, and he in turn will not be ashamed to be called their God (36:28).

Then the Israelites will experience the blessings of the covenant, the fruitfulness of the land, rather than the covenant curse of famine that had made them a reproach among the nations (36:30). Such a salvation will not bring about pride in the renewed nation but rather a profound sense of shame, for they will realize it is a free gift of sovereign grace.

In addition to the act of self-glorification that results in the restored people being returned to the land, God will also restore the land to a better-than-original state. It will become "like the garden of Eden," the ultimate symbol of fertility and fruitfulness (36:35). The garden land will be filled with restored cities; the places that once were torn down and desolate will be inhabited and fortified (36:35). In place of the one original *adam* and his wife, the new garden land will be filled with "flocks" (36:38) of *adam*, that is, numerous "people" (36:37–38) who will fill the cities to overflowing. The chief blessing, however, will be that God will permit himself to be sought by them to act on their behalf (36:37).

Application. The motivation for seeking change is frequently the perception that one's life is in some way *dysfunctional*. Such individuals feel they are not living life to the full, but instead are engaging in lifestyle choices that result in a diminished quality of life. If only they could solve their behavioral problem or find and fix its underlying psychological root, their life will surely be fuller and more meaningful. Then they will be "cured."

In contrast to this human predicament, Ezekiel has presented the Lord's diagnosis of Israel's situation. The work of God in believers is a two-stage process, just as it is depicted in Ezekiel 36. First there is an initial work of *purification*, which corresponds to the outward sprinkling of water on the restored Israel (36:25). Then there is an ongoing work of internal *renovation*, which Ezekiel describes under the figure of receiving the new heart and new spirit through the internal work of the divine Spirit (36:26–27). These two stages are both necessary to being a Christian, and this passage may well be the one that lies behind Jesus's statement to Nicodemus in John 3:5.

EZEKIEL 37:1–14

Original Meaning. From an oracle depicting flourishing garden-cities filled with vibrantly alive people (36:33–38), the prophet is confronted with a scene of total death. The valley is filled not merely with slain corpses but with skeletal remains, and dry skeletal remains at that. The Lord's question to the prophet, "Son of man, can these bones live?" (37:3a), seems redundant. It seems as if God's people have been utterly destroyed for their sin. The covenant curses have been executed and the corpses of the slain left unburied. No life remains in the bones. End of story.

Recognizing the sovereign power of God, however, the prophet is unwilling to give a negative answer. Rather, he turns the question back to God (37:3b). God certainly has the power to bring the dry bones back to life; the question remains as to whether it is his will to do so. That question is swiftly answered in the affirmative: God wills that the dry bones shall indeed live.

The means by which regeneration is brought about is through an infusion of the Spirit (Heb. *ruah*) in response to the prophetic word. Thus, Ezekiel is told to prophesy to the bones and require them to listen to the word of the Lord; in response, the Lord will make breath (*ruah*) enter them and bring them back to life, not as ghostly skeletons but as living flesh (37:5–6).

The prophet obediently speaks the word and sees the power of God instantly unleashed. While he is prophesying, the bones come together—but still without life; there was no breath (*ruah*) in them. It seems as if the bones are too dry even for God. But almost before the thought has been framed, it is answered by a second command to prophesy. This time Ezekiel is to prophesy to the wind (*ruah*). Like the creation of the first *adam* in Genesis 2, so the re-creation of this mighty army is a two-stage process of forming and filling.

Ezekiel personally experienced a similar infusion of the Spirit at the outset of his ministry. Twice, confronted with the awesome majesty of God, he was reduced to prostration (1:28; 3:23); each time the Spirit entered him, raising him to his feet (2:2; 3:24). This is exactly what happens to the dry bones after they have been re-formed into bodies (37:10).

The oracle that follows the vision (37:11–14) merely serves to make explicit what the vision has already recounted. The dry bones are the whole house of Israel, helpless and hopeless, cut off from God's life-giving presence (37:11). Without contradicting this self-perception that their present situation is hopeless—indeed, reinforcing the accurateness of the idea—the Lord still affirms that there is nonetheless hope for the future. The promises of a new spirit and a return to the land made in Ezekiel 36:27–36 will indeed be fulfilled. Ezekiel's visions will come about, and the people will be restored to their land and revitalized through the internal work of God's spirit.

Application. Just as the dry bones in Ezekiel did not remain dead, so also Christ did not remain in the tomb! He burst forth with resurrection power, raised from the dead by God! Just as surely, if we have been truly buried with him in baptism, receiving the reality as well as the sign, we also are made alive in Christ. Our sins are forgiven; the hold of the law over us is broken, nailed to the cross (Col 2:14). We are not dry bones any longer, but living, breathing, Spirit-infused children of God (Rom 8:16). What Ezekiel saw in visionary form has now become a reality!

EZEKIEL 37:15–28

Original Meaning. This passage contains a sign-act and a related oracle concerning the future reunification of God's people. The sign-act involves the prophet's taking two sticks, each of which he is to inscribe with a name (37:16). Strictly speaking, the two rivals for first place among Jacob's sons are Judah and Joseph; hence the proper designation of the sticks as "Belonging to Judah . . . belonging to Joseph" (37:16). Historically, however, the rivalry had become essentially a struggle between (the tribes of) Judah and Ephraim. Ezekiel is then instructed to join the sticks together in his hand so that they become one stick (37:17).

The writing on the sticks makes the symbolism of the act entirely transparent. Clearly, the reunification of Northern and Southern Kingdoms is anticipated. Because the action itself is so transparent, the expected question from the audience (37:18) is a question about the deeper significance of the sign. The Lord's reply, therefore, merely reiterates the sign without further explication, while adding the emphasis that "I" will accomplish all this, a divine act of reuniting his people.

Just as the division was caused by a failure in the area of servant leadership, so also the reunion will be affected by the Lord's providing a single servant-leader, "my servant David" (37:24). Just as the division resulted in the setting up of separate sanctuaries, so also the reunion will result in a return to a single, divinely approved sanctuary in their midst (37:26). The reunion will be established on the basis of a fundamental new spiritual unity, affected by God in the hearts of his people. The Lord's hand is the place where the sticks are rejoined.

The nation will be purified and cleansed by God, thus allowing for a restoration of the covenant relationship between God and his people (37:23) and the blessings that flow from such a relationship (37:25). What is more, those blessings will be enduring (37:25). The covenant of peace will be "an everlasting covenant"; the sanctuary will be restored to their midst "forever" (37:26).

The permanent restoration of the sanctuary to Israel's midst will result in the nations' recognizing that the Lord has endowed his people with a new level of holiness (37:28). The significance of the temple's restoration as crowning blessing, then, is this: It is objective evidence of the successful completion of the Lord's purposes to make for himself a holy people, a purpose announced already in 36:27 as the expected result of the outpouring of the Lord's Spirit.

Once the new, united Israel has been settled in the land (37:14) and is at peace, then the nation's thoughts will naturally turn to temple building. Thus, the promise of the Lord's sanctuary in the midst of his settled people is a fitting capstone to the prophecies of restoration. Though her enemies will once more descend on her (chs. 38–39), it is so that they may be defeated by the Lord, who will then establish his final temple (chs. 40–48).

Application. Christ himself is our true temple because he accomplished in himself everything to which the tabernacle and temple of the Old Testament pointed. When the Word became flesh, he "made his dwelling [literally, tabernacled] among us" (John 1:14), manifesting God's glory in our midst, just as the Mosaic tabernacle was the place where God's glory was manifested in the desert (Exod 40:34). In him, God's glorious presence is experienced in the midst of his people. Moreover, to act against his person is to do nothing less than to assault God's temple. That is why, referring to his own body in John 2:19, Jesus said, "Destroy this temple, and I will raise it again in three days."

Because Jesus is our temple, he himself is what unites his people together in worship. When Jesus met with the woman of Samaria, he prophesied an end to the divisions between Jews and Samaritans founded on their separate temples (John 4:21–24). This marks a radical change in the old order of things, which anticipated the nations' coming to worship God at Mount Zion. With the coming of Christ, the old division between Jew and Samaritan in worship is broken down, not by Samaritans coming to the temple in Jerusalem but by Jew and Samaritan alike being incorporated into Christ himself, as the final temple.

Likewise, Christ has broken down the old wall between Jews and gentiles through his death on the cross, building both together into a new, holy temple to the Lord (Eph 2:14–22). There is but one temple of God in this age, the church, the body of Jesus Christ, in which Jews, Samaritans, and gentiles are all brought together as one. As Galatians 3:28 puts it: "There is neither Jew nor Gentile, neither slave nor free, nor is there male and female, for you are all one in Christ Jesus."

EZEKIEL 38:1–39:29

Original Meaning

The Defeat of Gog (38:1–23). The oracle opens with a summons to Gog and his allies to arm themselves and to prepare an assault against God's people dwelling peacefully on the mountains of Israel (38:2–9). The biblical Gog is no mere historical figure but rather a fear-inducing figure of cosmic proportions; and to make matters worse, he is not alone. He is the commander-in-chief of a coalition of forces gathered from the ends of the earth (38:5–6). It is no coincidence that together these make up a total of seven nations, and it is significant that they are gathered from the uttermost parts of the world known to the prophet.

Ezekiel foresees the nations streaming toward God's holy land in the latter days to take up their weapons in the "mother of all battles" against the Sovereign Lord and his people. But even such an act of rebellion is itself instigated by God. Though Gog and his allies are far from unwilling participants in the coming conflict, the controlling force in all this is the Lord, who directs them by (38:4).

Once the unholy alliance has been prepared by God, he will summon them against his restored people at a time of his own choosing. Israel is depicted in terms borrowed from Ezekiel 34–37: They now live in safety (38:8), a peaceful, unsuspecting, and undefended people (38:11), grown rich in livestock and goods (38:12). They are dwelling "at the center of the land [earth]" (38:12), a description that is theological rather than geographical. This position at the center of God's favor, which Jerusalem had forfeited through her sin, has now been restored to the land.

This description of the state of God's people underlines the motives of the evil alliance. Israel is at rest, trusting in the Lord. Yet trust in the Lord does not eliminate the possibility of conflict. The ungodly will cast greedy eyes in Israel's direction, encouraged by the traders from east and west (38:13), and will advance against them like an overshadowing cloud (38:9, 16).

But in spite of all his planning and preparation, Gog has fundamentally misread the match-up. It is not a matter, as he supposes, of his vast and well-equipped army ranged against a defenseless nation (38:14–16). Rather, by tangling with Israel Gog is taking on Israel's God. Indeed, the only reason for Gog's being permitted to come is so that the Lord may demonstrate his greatness and his holiness in defeating this monstrous alliance (38:16).

Therefore, the judgment of God falls on Gog in 38:17–22. The judgments that earlier fell on his people now fall on their enemies. God's hot anger, zeal, and fiery wrath are all emotions of which Israel has felt the weight in the earlier chapters of Ezekiel. Now these same feelings are turned against Gog (38:18–19). The Divine Warrior will let loose a mighty earthquake, which will cause all creatures to tremble in his presence (38:19–20). The sword, plague, bloodshed, torrential rain, hail, burning sulfur—judgments, most of which were experienced first by Israel—are now experienced by her enemies (38:21–22). Now God will reveal his power and holiness to the nations not by the destruction of his unholy people but by the protection of his restored people (38:23).

The Disposal of Gog (39:1–29). Ezekiel begins in chapter 39 by announcing the slaughter of Gog (39:1–8). His seemingly invincible power will be broken and his body left exposed for the birds of the air and the beasts of the field (39:4). The fire of God's wrath will be poured out on his homeland and the homelands of his allies (39:6). The destruction they had planned to wreak on a people living "in safety" will return on their own heads (39:6; cf. 38:8).

Unlike past times when, because of his people's sins, the Lord had allowed his name to be profaned by bringing on them the catastrophe of exile (36:22–23), this time the Lord will act to prevent such profanation by defending his people against all assault. This too will demonstrate the holiness of his name by showing that his power to save is as mighty as his power to judge (39:7). The future salvation is as secure as the past catastrophic judgment (39:8; cf. 21:7).

Once God has decisively dealt with Gog as a threat, then for the first time Israel is called to act. She plays no part in winning the victory; she merely carries out the mopping-up operation of spoiling the corpses and disposing of the remains (39:9–16). The Israelites collect six kinds of weapons, which for seven years serve them for fuel (39:9). Ironically, these flammable materials seem to have been the only things not harmed by the descent of God's fiery wrath! Those who came to plunder are now plundered (39:10).

In addition to plundering the fallen, however, Israel will also be active in purifying the land by burying the corpses. The whole house of Israel will be engaged in this burial process (39:12). After that, there will be a further period in which two squads of professional morticians will pass through the land (39:15) until the whole of Gog's army is safely laid to rest.

The dramatic, though not the chronological, climax comes in 39:17–20. Here the birds and the beasts are invited to come to join in a kind of gruesome "messianic banquet." But on this occasion, instead of animals being slain to feed the appetites of the human guests from north and south and east and west, here the humans have been slain to feed the animals from all around.

The lesson Israel is to draw from these chapters is explicitly laid out for them in 39:21–29. The Lord is sovereign in history, a sovereignty that is displayed before the nations in two separate movements.

1. In the first, God demonstrated his sovereignty by sending his own people into exile because of their sin and unfaithfulness (39:23). He hid his face from them, and as a result they became easy prey for all their enemies.
2. But in the days to come a new period in Israel's history is beginning. God's people will return from exile; he will have compassion on them. They will take responsibility for their past actions when they are restored to their land and dwell in safety. Then they will know that it is the Lord their God who sent them into exile and the Lord their God who returns them from exile (39:28). The tragic events of 586 BC will never repeat themselves, for the covenant-keeping God will pour out his Spirit on his people as he once poured out his wrath on them, and he will never again hide his face from them (39:29).

Application. Christians naturally, and rightly, respond to the general atmosphere of end-of-the-world anxieties by turning from the world's stories to God's stories. At times like this, many turn to the apocalyptic literature of the Scriptures, such as Ezekiel 38–39 or the books of Daniel and Revelation, seeking an infallible word from the Lord. But what do you do with these stories? Many contemporary Christians treat these passages as checklists on the road to Armageddon, providing a countdown on the road to the end of the world. However, as we have shown above, this is not how the passage was intended to be read. Rather, it is a dramatic statement of the central truth that no matter what the forces of evil may throw at God's people, in the final analysis God's purpose and victory stand secure.

Do you see how comforting this truth is for all of us? Christians have, historically, suffered a great deal for their faith. From the time of Nero, when Christians were dipped in pitch and set alight to illumine the emperor's pleasure gardens, down to the present day, when believers continue to be tortured and killed for their faith in Sudan and elsewhere, the spiritual forces of opposition are real. Often those forces are institutional rather than individual, an organized and orchestrated attempt to destroy the church. For those enduring such times of persecution, Ezekiel 38–39 provides a powerful message of hope.

God is going to win. This may seem a simple, even simplistic, point, but it is central to the thrust of the Gog narrative. No matter how big the opposition, how well organized they are, how powerful their weaponry, or how paltry the resources of God's people, ultimately the plans of God's enemies will come to nothing. As in Psalm 2, the nations may conspire together and the kings of the earth take a stand against God, but all their posturing causes mirth rather than worry in the heart of the Most High. Ultimately, no matter what Satan throws against the church, the full number of the elect from the north and south and east and west will be brought in and will sit down together at God's table to share in the heavenly feast.

EZEKIEL 40:1–42:20

Original Meaning. Whereas the opening vision of the heavenly King on his throne had been dated from the exile of the earthly king, Jehoiachin, this vision of the heavenly city is dated from the destruction of the earthly city, Jerusalem. Fourteen years have passed since that momentous, earth-shattering event, twenty-five since the beginning of the exile. In these dates, especially the fact that the vision took place on the tenth of the first month, a reference to the Jubilee year is generally seen (Lev 25:8–13).

It was on this very day that Ezekiel saw his "visions of God," whereby he was taken up to a high mountain in the land of Israel (Ezek 40:2). This journey is equivalent to Moses's ascent up Mount Sinai to receive the law of God; indeed, Ezekiel is the only person in the Old Testament apart from Moses who imparts God's legislation to the people. Moses also received on the mountaintop a detailed design for building the tabernacle and establishing its worship; Ezekiel is likewise shown a heavenly sanctuary and instructed about the requirements for its worship. As with another mountaintop experience of Moses (Deut 32:48–52), Ezekiel surveys the promised land that has been prepared for God's people, though he himself will never enter it. But the "very high mountain" (Ezek 40:2) also represents Mount Zion, the mountain of the temple, concerning which Isaiah had prophesied (Isa 2:2–3).

There on the mountaintop Ezekiel is met by an angelic figure who will be his tour guide around the temple; in chapter 8 he received a similar tour of the defiled Jerusalem temple and all its abominations. That vision culminated in the departure of "the glory of the Lord" from the temple (10:18), just as the vision in chapters 40–42 culminates in the return of that glory to the new temple (43:1–5). The focus of the temple vision, then, is the reversal of the divine abandonment of God's people that had culminated in the destruction of Jerusalem.

The angel is equipped with a linen cord and a measuring rod to enable him to measure the various parts of the temple (40:3). Ezekiel is instructed to look and hear, to pay attention to all that he is shown so that he can tell the house of Israel what he sees (40:4). In other words, the purpose of his vision is instructional (see 43:10–12).

It is highly significant that the first thing the prophet sees on his tour is a wall surrounding the whole temple area (40:5). Walls mark territory as "inside" or "outside" and to regulate access to the "inside" space. This wall is some ten feet, six inches tall and ten feet, six inches thick, providing a solid dividing line between the "holy" and the "profane," the area outside. A wall depends on its height and thickness for its effectiveness in keeping people out, so these dimensions take on a particular importance.

What gates this wall possesses! The three sides that permit access (there is no entry on the west side) are dominated by massive fortress-style gatehouses, almost forty-five feet wide and ninety feet deep (40:13, 15). The defensive nature of these gates is underlined by the fact that they have a portico or vestibule not on the outside, where one would expect it (and where it is on the inner gatehouses), but on the inside.

The gatehouses are further specified as having no fewer than six rooms for guards, three on each side. To add to the sense of inaccessibility, there is a flight of seven steps to be climbed before the worshiper even reaches the gate (40:6, 22, 26). There is no doubt as to the initial impression that Ezekiel's temple is intended to have: It is a mighty fortress that clearly separates the sacred from the profane.

The area of the outer court is of little interest to the prophet or his angelic guide. It is passed over with a brief reference to a paved area all around the court, with thirty rooms opening off from it (40:17–19). The single key measurement in the outer court is its breadth, roughly 175 feet from the outer gateway to the inner gateway (40:19). This substantial dimension is intended to provide a substantial buffer zone around the holy things in the inner courtyard.

The inner courtyard itself is strongly separated off from the outer courtyard. It is defended by gates identical to those of the outer court, though with the portico on the outside rather than the inside (40:28–37). It is further elevated, probably by about eight feet, with the gates being approached by a flight of eight steps (40:31, 34, 37).

At this point, the prophet's progress inward is briefly halted, while his attention is drawn to the purpose of some of the spaces in the inner courtyard. There are rooms beside the portico of each of the gates for washing the sacrifices (40:38), while the porticoes themselves were used for slaughtering the sacrifices (40:39–43). The precise details concerning the function of these rooms underline the fact already that the primary function of this temple is as a place of offering sacrifice. In the exilic and postexilic situation, the need for a sacrifice to atone for the people's sins and enable them to stand in God's presence became a dominant theme. In contrast, key descriptions of Solomon's temple highlight its importance not only as the location for sacrifice but also as the center for prayer (1 Kgs 8:28–54; Isa 56:7).

In addition to these rooms, the prophet also sees two rooms for the Zadokite priests, who have overall responsibility for the temple and altar (Ezek 40:44–46). These Zadokites are further defined as "the only Levites who may draw near to the Lord to minister before him" (40:46). Thus, the function of both sets of spaces specifically identified within the inner court serves the overall thrust of the vision: separating off access to a restricted space, which is reserved for the priests, so that proper sacrifices may be offered. Both ideas of holiness and sacrifice are present in the summary statement of 40:47.

1. The inner courtyard is a perfect square, one hundred cubits in each direction, for the square is the shape of the holy.

2. At its geometric center is the altar, the only piece of furniture noted in the courtyard, which is the place of sacrifice.

Having briefly described the outer and inner courts, Ezekiel is led on to the central feature of the new temple complex, the temple structure itself (40:48; 41:26). Its importance is marked in three ways.

1. It is located at the protected center at the heart of the complex, with walls and zones of controlled access all around it.
2. The temple building is conspicuous in its elevation, as the highest point of an edifice that is itself on top of the high mountain.
3. Its key significance is reflected in the extent and nature of the description accorded to the building. It is the space of the temple complex that is described in most detail and with the most precise measurements.

The temple building is a tripartite structure, comprising portico, outer sanctuary, and inner sanctuary, whose architecture focuses attention on the inner sanctuary, that is, "the Most Holy Place" (41:4). This is the only square space within the temple building itself, and it is reached by passing through three openings of increasing narrowness. The door from the inner court into the portico is fourteen cubits (almost twenty-five feet) wide; the door from there into the outer sanctuary is ten cubits (seventeen feet) wide, while the door into the inner sanctuary is a mere six cubits (ten feet) wide. This design feature underlines the sanctity of the Most Holy Place, a sanctity so great that Ezekiel himself is not permitted to enter it (41:3–5).

All around the temple building are no fewer than ninety rooms on three levels (41:5–11), while behind the temple to the west there was a restricted area of twenty cubits breadth and a "building" of unspecified purpose (41:10, 12). The rationale for this building may simply have been to protect the rear approach to the temple building; from now on no one would approach God "from behind," as it were.

Returning to the description of the temple building itself, it is described as completely paneled with wood and decorated with images of palm trees and cherubim (41:17–18). This makes it more ornamented than the gates of the courtyards, which were simply adorned by palm trees (40:16). Ezekiel's decoration scheme is simpler than that of the first temple, and the focus on the cherubim recalls the ominous presence of these enforcers of divine judgment in Ezekiel's opening vision.

The only piece of furniture mentioned within the temple building is an "altar" of wood in the outer sanctuary, which is designated "the table that is before the Lord" (41:22). This is presumably the table on which the "bread of the Presence" was laid out before the Lord (1 Kgs 7:48). It is mentioned here because it will later be referred to as one of the places at which the Zadokite priests have the privilege of ministering (Ezek 44:16), a situation that is the necessary corollary of its location in the outer sanctuary, where only they had access.

Having described the temple building, Ezekiel is now headed outward once more in his description of the complex. His attention is first drawn to a series of rooms for the priests, located north and south of the unnamed building behind the temple. The details of the construction of these rooms are not entirely clear, but they are built on three levels, and it appears that the priests could enter at the top from the inner court (42:12) and emerge from the bottom into the outer court (42:9). This serves to underline the status of the rooms as boundary areas for activities that, if not properly contained, might violate the gradation of holiness. These, therefore, are the rooms where the sacrifices and sacred offerings were to be consumed (42:13).

Eating these offerings was both a privilege and a responsibility. It was a *privilege* in that it was a means of providing for the physical needs of the priests, who as Levites had no land of their own to farm (44:28–30). But it was also a *responsibility*, since the consumption of the sin offerings was the required way of disposing of the low-grade contaminated material produced by the purification process. The carcass of the animal was regarded as having absorbed impurities during the sacrificial ritual, which were then dealt with by being ingested by the priest.

In addition to eating the sacred offerings here, the priests were also required to leave the sacred clothes in which they had ministered in these rooms (42:14), so that they might not bring that which was holy into dangerous contact with the profane. Both of these restrictions represent a significant raising of the differential between priest and nonpriest when they are compared with the perspective of the book of Leviticus.

Having completed his tour of the inner court, Ezekiel was brought back out to survey the temple from the outside. Its overall dimensions are square, five hundred cubits by five hundred cubits (42:16–20). It might seem only natural that a sacred building would adopt the most sacred shape, but once more the stakes have been raised from the arrangements of the Mosaic and Solomonic eras. In the tabernacle, for example, only the Most Holy Place is square; the other external spaces are increasingly non square. In Ezekiel's temple, however, the entire structure bears an increased level of sanctity that is expressed in its overall shape.

The final note on the layout of the temple brings us back to where we started, to the wall (42:20). This inclusion highlights the wall and its function: It serves "to separate the holy from the common" (42:20). Never again will the profane intrude on the realm of the holy as it did in the past. In the future, the lines will be clearly drawn. The walls must be clearly established, with a place for everyone and everyone in his or her place, so that the Lord can return to his place at the center of his people.

Application. Ezekiel's visionary temple addresses the believer who lives in a world in which God seems absent. His answer is to lift the veil and show us the black-and-white realities of the world as it really is, the heavenly order of things. In this world there is a place for everything, and everything (and everyone) is in its place. In Ezekiel's vision, society has been reordered and transformed. But most significantly, it is a world where God is once more in his place, for the entire description of Ezekiel 40–42 leads up to the climactic reentry of the glory to the temple in chapter 43.

There are no walls that keep us out of God's presence, not because we are more holy in ourselves than Ezekiel and his hearers but because we have been credited with the perfect righteousness of Christ in place of our filthy rags. His once-for-all sacrifice has affected the transition that turned us from aliens and strangers, without God and without hope in the world (Eph 2:12), to insiders who are able to "approach . . . with confidence" (Heb 4:16). Should we not therefore rejoice at the greatness of the salvation accomplished for us and strive to be pure, even as our Lord Jesus was pure?

But we should also remember that one wall still remains and that many are still outsiders to God's grace. Some live beyond the sound of gospel proclamation. Others have heard the gospel proclaimed over and over again, yet have repeatedly rejected it. Nothing and no one impure can ever enter God's heavenly holy city. Even the most moral person, if he or she does not believe in Christ, is outside the wall; left to themselves, such people must perish utterly. Our calling as priests of the new temple is to teach these people the one way to holiness through trusting in Christ, seeking to draw them into the new world we have been given, where paradise once more stands open to God's people and the tree of life is freely accessible to all.

EZEKIEL 43:1–27

Original Meaning. The return of the glory of the Lord to the new temple is the high point of chapters 43–46. This return, which reverses the abandonment of the temple and its destruction described in equally visionary form in chapters 8–11, is the fulfillment of the central promise of restoration: the Lord dwelling in the midst of his people forever (37:26–28).

The glory returns to the temple through the east gate, from the same direction in which it had earlier left (10:18–19). Whereas its departure was slow and halting, its return is rapid and direct. On its return, the glory of God not only fills the temple (1 Kgs 8:10–11), it even causes the land itself to shine (Ezek 43:2). As with the other visions, the prophet's response to the revelation of God's glory is to fall on his face (43:3b).

The overwhelmed prophet is once again picked up by the Spirit and dropped in the inner court, in order for him to hear the word of the Lord (43:5). That word is an assertion of the Lord's kingship and of his "liv[ing] among the Israelites forever" (43:7). What is new is not the Lord's claim to kingship or the area over which he makes that claim; it is the assertion that his kingship will be exercised there *forever*.

In the past, the house of Israel and their kings had defiled the Lord's name by their prostitution and by setting up memorial stelae to their monarchs within the temple grounds (43:7–8). There is no room for these stelae in honor of the human king in the place dedicated to the worship of the divine King. Because the former kings defiled the Lord's name by their detestable practices, their position in the future kingdom will be further removed from the center. This is a necessary precondition for the Lord's perpetual dwelling in the midst of his people (43:9).

Ezekiel is being shown these things so that he can relay them to his own generation. They must consider the design and "be ashamed of their [former] sins" (43:10). What specifically about the temple design is to move them to shame? The temple vision is a pedagogical tool that speaks by its shape and size, and particularly by its permission or denial of access ("exits and entrances," 43:11). These regulations all serve a single overriding purpose: that the whole area all around the temple may be most holy. In order for God to continue to live in their midst forever, regard for his holiness must govern not simply access to the Most Holy Place but the entire temple mount (43:12).

Ezekiel's attention is now drawn once more to the altar in the inner court, the central piece of furniture mentioned in the earlier tour. The importance of this altar to Ezekiel's plan is evident not merely from its detailed description, but also from its place at the geometric center of the temple complex. The contrast is made clearer by the fact that in the tabernacle the altar was the least sacred of the cultic articles, located in the outer court; its geometric center pointed rather to the ark. Once more this represents an overall raising of the standards of holiness compared to the old ways, assigning the altar an equal sanctity to the furnishings of the Most Holy Place.

The dimensions of the altar are eighteen cubits by eighteen cubits (thirty-one feet, six inches square) at the lowest level and fourteen cubits by fourteen cubits (twenty-four feet, six inches square) at the highest (43:13–17). At each corner of the top level there are projections, or "horns," to which blood is applied during some aspects of the ritual (43:20). The whole edifice stands nine cubits (about fifteen feet) high and is approached by a flight of steps from the east. This is a reversal of the normal ancient Near Eastern practice whereby the priest faces east when offering sacrifices. In Ezekiel's temple the priest faces west, toward the Most Holy Place, thus avoiding any suggestion of a repetition of the sun worship of 8:16, the crowning abomination of the earlier temple vision.

Having described the new altar, Ezekiel is then given instructions for the eight-day purification process that fits the altar for sacred use (43:19–27). He himself is assigned a key role in this consecration process, just as Moses had instituted the cult given on Mount Sinai. On the first day he is to offer an unblemished bull as a purification offering, while on days two through eight he is to offer a male goat as a purification offering and a bull and a ram as burnt offerings.

The body of the purification sacrifice is then disposed of by burning it outside the sanctuary. The burnt offerings are also to be offered with salt (43:24). Salt was the preservative par excellence in the ancient Near East and seems to have featured prominently in covenant ceremonies. Although it is elsewhere only specifically required in the regulations for the cereal offering (Lev 2:13), it may well have formed part of all of the offerings made by fire.

The purpose of this ritual with the repeated presentation of purification offerings is to "purify the altar and make atonement [*kipper*] for it," so that the holy space can be used for the regular ministry of offering sacrifices (43:20). The concept of making atonement (or expiation) expresses the idea of ritually wiping away the impurities and sins that adhere to a person or object. Israel's past sins have penetrated even to this heavenly sanctuary and must be cleansed before the work of the cult can be restarted. Without a spiritual spring cleaning of the altar, none of the offerings made on it will be acceptable to God. Once Ezekiel has completed his inaugural ministry, assisted by the Zadokite priests (43:19), the priests will be able to carry out their task of offering burnt offerings and fellowship offerings on the altar, the ongoing means of assuring God's blessing on his people. They will once more be acceptable to God (43:27).

Application. When Christ comes into our lives, he does so in only one role: as King. One of the problems that existed in Judah was a confusion over who was really sovereign, a confusion that demonstrated itself in the proliferation of memorial stelae glorifying earthly kings in a building intended to glorify the heavenly King. That may seem an alien problem to us until we start to examine our own hearts and ask how much of our lives are lived to our own glory and how much to God's glory. Who is really sovereign in your decision-making? Who calls the shots in how you spend your money and your time? Who is Lord in how you arrange your priorities? Who occupies the center of your thoughts? All of a sudden, the questions strike closer to home. Although we may confess with our mouths that our bodies are temples of the Holy Spirit, all too often our lives tell a different story.

EZEKIEL 44:1–31

Original Meaning. This section begins with an absolute prohibition of access: the outer east gate is closed and will forever remain closed (44:1–2). Because the Lord entered through it on his return to the Most Holy Place, it has acquired a special sanctity and may not be used by anyone else. However, the space within the gate may be used by the prince for his sacral meals before the Lord (44:3). In this way, both the privilege and restriction of the prince's position is emphasized. The royal figure has a limited, though still honorable, position.

That the concern of this section is with access—or, to use the language of the passage, "exits and entrances" (43:11)—is further underlined by the brief recapitulation in 44:4–5. The continued presence of God is contingent on the proper control of access to these areas.

It was a failure to control access in the past that leads to the condemnation of the house of Israel in 44:6. The sin of the past lay in bringing "foreigners uncircumcised in heart and flesh into my sanctuary" (44:7). This probably refers to the well-attested practice of employing foreign guards in the temple (2 Kgs 11:14–19). The people failed in "carrying out [their] duty in regard to my holy things" (Ezek 44:8); instead, they assigned that charge to others. This sin will be repeated no more; uncircumcised foreigners will have no right of access into the sanctuary (44:9). Verse 10 continues the thought of what precedes by identifying the legitimate temple guards, the Levites. The flow of the main train of thought is as follows: The foreigners will not enter the sanctuary (44:9), but the Levites will (44:10); they will be in my sanctuary serving as armed guards at the gates of the house (44:11).

Once again, the walls of separation have been raised in Ezekiel's temple in comparison to the preexilic situation. The sin of the Levites, whatever its precise form, has consequences in terms of restriction on access and service. The greater sin of the people has even greater consequences. The purpose of these regulations is to induce shame in the hearers as they consider their detestable practices (44:13).

In contrast to the Levites and the people, whose access is restricted because of their sin, the Zadokite priests receive the privilege of sole access to the inner court and the offering of all sacrifices at the altar and the service at the table inside the sanctuary itself (44:15–16). This privilege is explained as being due to their faithful service in the time of Israel's apostasy (44:15). This is not because the narrator in Ezekiel 44 is unaware of the criticisms aimed at the priesthood in 22:26. In fact, it is precisely these sins that he insists will be done away with in the future, when the priests observe God's law and keep his Sabbaths holy (44:24).

Because the Zadokite priests penetrate closer to the Most Holy Place than any others, they face additional restrictions on their behavior (44:17–27). They must wear linen rather than woolen clothing when they minister so that they do not defile the inner court with their sweat (44:17–18). Sweat may have been undesirable because it was regarded as belonging to the general category of bodily emissions that rendered one unclean (Deut 23:9–14). Moreover, they are to distinguish between the "sacred" clothes they wear for ministry and the "other [profane] clothes" (Ezek 44:19) they wear for the rest of life.

In Israelite law, holiness was not dangerous by itself. It was dangerous only to one who was contaminated with impurity or who acted in contravention of its laws. Therefore the priest, who daily handled the holy things, had to take special care with regard to his ritual cleanliness and actions. Of particular danger was the contamination associated with contact with the realm of death, either through contact with a corpse (44:25) or through the ritual mourning practices of shaving or loosing the hair of the head (44:20). The possibility of potentially fatal errors induced by the consumption of alcoholic beverages is also taken into account (44:21).

The need for pure priestly stock, which flows from restricting access to the descendants of the seed of Zadok, is present in the restriction of priestly marriage to unmarried Israelite women or to the widows of priests (44:22). That provision assured that no offspring conceived by a former husband of a different tribe would be accidentally assumed to be of priestly stock. In all these ways, the priests are to be living models of what they teach—that there is a difference between holy and profane, between clean and unclean (44:23).

Since the priests belong to the Lord, they are to have the Lord as their inheritance alone (44:28). Unlike the other tribes, they are to be allotted no territory of their own in the new promised land. Instead, they are to be provided for through the sacrificial system. They are to eat the grain offering, the sin and guilt offerings, and all the things vowed to the Lord that cannot be redeemed, along with all "the firstfruits" and the "special gifts" (44:30). Birds or animals found dead or torn by wild animals are not to be eaten, however (44:31).

Throughout this chapter, the concern over the holiness of those having access to the central regions of the sanctuary is evident. Those who enter the inner parts of the sanctuary to minister in God's service must have a past history of faithfulness and must continue to walk in the ways of the holy, lest they be destroyed in an instant by the holy God whom they serve.

Application. The privilege of close access to God is a reward we do not have to wait for eternity to begin to experience. We get to sample the firstfruits of the pie ahead of time. Even now, we can approach the throne of God with boldness, presenting our praises and our petitions, basking in the glory of his love. But if we expect to experience the full blessing of communion with God, our behavior must reflect his holiness. For the Zadokites, access to God's presence meant heavy restrictions on their lifestyle. There were things they could not touch, places they could not go to, food they could not eat, and clothes they could not wear if they were to minister in the presence of the all-holy God. So too for us, if we expect to experience the blessing of God's presence with us, then our lifestyle will be (from the world's perspective) restricted.

EZEKIEL 45:1–46:24

Original Meaning. The primary focus of the division of the land for the prophet here is not safeguarding human equality and land rights, but rather asserting divine sovereignty and safeguarding the divine presence in their midst. Hence, Ezekiel's first concern in introducing the concept of a new division of the land is to insist that the people are to "present to the LORD" as an offering the central portion of the land as a "sacred district" (45:1).

The primary purpose of this sacred district is to provide a zone of graded holiness outside the temple, exactly analogous to that inside the temple. The entire temple complex is, from the perspective of the land, a "Most Holy Place" (45:3). The area immediately around the sanctuary is therefore reserved for the priests, in which they are to build their homes (45:3–4). The strip parallel to the priestly portion and to its north is reserved for the Levites and their cities (45:5), while the half-size strip to its south is for the city (45:6). To the east and west of the 25,000 cubit sacred square, the remainder of the sacred strip is to be allocated to the prince as his inheritance.

The same principles of graded access that applied within the temple complex have thus been extrapolated to the land itself, resulting in an entirely temple-oriented geography. This is evident not simply from the central position of the temple within the land and the restricted access allowed to different groups and individuals, but even from the east-west alignment of the strips into which the land has been divided.

At the center of this Holy Land is the temple, not the city or the king. The old Zion theology, which found its focus in the twin pillars of the election of Jerusalem and David, is now refocused on the central assertion of Yahweh's kingship and rule in the temple.

Even the future kings of the land, now addressed as "my princes," are subject to the Lord's oversight (45:8). These princes in Ezekiel have no active part to play in distributing the land. The divine king has already allocated it (45:8). Examples of abuse in Israel's past are too numerous to require documentation.

The primary focus of the prince's duties is temple-centered, as with virtually everything else in Ezekiel 40–48. Thus, the prince is responsible to ensure that accurate weights and measures are used in gathering up the offerings and gifts of the people (45:10–12). All are required to participate in the sacred offerings provided by the prince (45:13–16), and it is foreseen that this might be viewed as a possible means for the prince to enrich himself at the cost of the people by using disproportionate measures.

But although the people provide the materials for the regular offerings (45:15–16), it is the prince's responsibility from his own resources to provide the offerings for the special occasions (45:17). In both the regular and the special offerings, the prince has a central role as the representative of the people in worship (45:17). This is a great privilege, especially given the central significance of purification and atonement in chapters 40–48.

Mention of the sacrifices on these special occasions in the ritual calendar leads into a discussion of the ritual calendar itself. Like the vision of the temple itself, Ezekiel's calendar appears to be a stripped-down, focused edition of what had previously been in force. There is no mention of the Feast of Weeks, the third annual festival, and the remaining two festivals (Passover and Tabernacles) have become virtually symmetrical festivals of purification (45:18–25). Of the two, the Feast of Passover retains more of its distinctive features (45:19–21). Yet its original character as a festival of the Lord's deliverance from Egypt is now subordinated to a concern for purifying the sanctuary.

The Passover feast proper is now preceded by a dual ceremony of cleansing the temple on the first and seventh days of the first month (45:18–20). During the seven days of the feast, the prince is to provide seven bulls and seven rams daily as a burnt offering, along with the daily purification offering of a male goat (45:23). This represents a substantial increase from the sacrifices demanded for the Passover in the Mosaic legislation of Numbers 28.

If the Passover feast is still named and recognizable, the festival in the seventh month, which takes place at the time of the Feast of Tabernacles, has lost all its original distinctiveness. It lacks any name or description, except for the fact that the prince is to provide the same offerings for it as at the Passover (45:25). There is apparently no comparable purification ceremony before it, nor is any ceremony recorded that might correspond to the Day of Atonement ceremony associated with this festival in Leviticus 16. The primary annual ritual purification of the central sanctuary now takes place at the beginning of the year. But Ezekiel's special interest in purification remains clear in the prominent place given to the sin offerings in the list of 45:25. Both festivals thereby come to share the same interest in atonement for sin.

The prince is also required to provide the offerings for the Sabbath and New Moon festivals (46:1–8). He has the unique privilege as a layman of approaching the threshold of the inner east gate and prostrating himself there before the Lord (46:2). "The people of the land," however, are only permitted to approach the entrance of the gate (46:3). In Ezekiel's program, the laity are being kept at a "safe" distance from the holy things.

At the annual festivals, God's people are required to present themselves and prostrate themselves before the Lord (46:9). The community at large is assigned no other tasks in the cult. Even their annual processions through the temple are in the "profane" north-south or south-north direction (46:9), at right angles to the "holy" east-west orientation of priestly ministrations at the altar of burnt offering (43:17). Though the people are clearly expected to offer sacrifices of their own (cf. 46:24), these are relegated to footnote status, barely perceptible in the peripheral vision of the prophet.

The representative nature of the prince as chief worshiper is clear from the fact that he enters in the midst of the people and goes out with them (46:10). But his privileged position is clear also from his access to the east gate of the inner court, which is opened for him whenever he wishes to offer a freewill sacrifice (46:12).

The section on the sacrifices closes with the requirements for the daily sacrifice, which is now limited to a single morning sacrifice of a year-old lamb, with its associated grain offering (46:13–14). The former practice of offering also an evening sacrifice, attested in Numbers 28:4 and 1 Kings 18:29, 36, goes unmentioned.

After his discussion of the sacrifices, Ezekiel returns to his previous topic, the inheritance of the prince (46:16–18; cf. 45:7–8). The purpose of this regulation is straightforward: In an economy where the king typically rewarded loyal service by gifts of land, there would have been a perpetual temptation for the king to acquire ever more land with which to reward his followers. Not so in the new Israel, which will be reconstituted as a nation of free peasants with an inalienable claim to their own land.

That this powerful assertion against land stealing brackets the sacrificial regulations emphasizes the fact that the driving force behind the division of the land is not egalitarianism but divine sovereignty: The land is the Lord's and he divides it. The prince is thereby continually reminded that he is a vassal of the great king and must behave as such.

The entire section of 44:1–46:24 is rounded off by a return to the beginning. The heavenly messenger, inactive since 44:4, returns to guide the prophet out of the inner court via the sacred rooms where the priests cook and eat the sacred offerings that are not permitted to leave the sanctity of the inner court (46:19–20). Together they arrive back at the outer court, where the prophet is shown "the kitchens" at its four extremities, where the Levites are to cook the sacrifices of the people (46:21–24). The tour of the temple is thus neatly completed, having gone from the outside to the center (40:5–41:4) and back out again twice.

Application. True worship should preserve the law-gospel dynamic, which lies at the heart of the best historic liturgies. In other words, in order to appreciate the good news of the gospel we need to confront ourselves again with the reality of God's perfect law, which condemns our own sin and points us to Jesus as our sinless substitute. Without a deep appreciation of our sinfulness and impurity, real worship is not a possibility.

In that worship, all God's people now have a central part to play. Here is where our privilege far exceeds that envisaged by Ezekiel. Whereas the ordinary people in his vision were to be kept at a distance from God's presence because of their past sins and a concern to protect his holiness, now, covered in the blood of Christ, we may draw near to the Most Holy Place itself (Heb 10:19). We need no human priests to interpose between us and the holy God, to conduct our worship on our behalf, for we have a great priest, Jesus, who has perfectly met our needs (Heb 10:21).

In light of that incredible privilege, let us indeed count it a great blessing to draw near to God in worship and adoration. Let us hold unswervingly to the hope we profess, and let us stir one another on to love and good deeds and lives of purified holiness, until the approaching day comes when Christ our King will return and we will be exiles no more (Heb 10:22–25).

EZEKIEL 47:1–12

Original Meaning. Ezekiel's tour of the temple is now complete. His vision at this point turns outward to the rest of the land and the influence that the thorough restoration of the temple as the place of God's dwelling will have on it. That influence is nothing short of a total transformation from death to life, a transformation expressed in the visionary form of a life-giving river that flows out from the temple.

The source of the living water is the temple itself (47:1). This was the site of the "Sea" in Solomon's temple, a massive bronze pool whose practical purpose was to provide the water required for cleansing (1 Kgs 7:23, 39). The Sea now becomes the source of a life-giving river that flows out from the temple. The archetype of this river is the earth-fructifying stream that flows out in four branches from the prototypical sanctuary of Eden (Gen 2:10–14).

The river flowing from Ezekiel's temple follows the sacred route eastward from the inner court, out through the (closed!) east gate of the outer court (47:2). Because Ezekiel cannot follow it through there, he is brought round by the north gate and sees it trickling out of the south side of the gate. The stream that starts out so pitifully small miraculously becomes progressively larger the further he journeys along it. At first, it is a trickle; after 1,000 cubits (1,500 feet), it is ankle-deep (47:3); after another 1,000 cubits, it is knee-deep (47:4), then waist-deep (47:4), and finally an uncrossable torrent (47:5). The guiding angel asks him to pause here and ponder its significance (47:6).

This river is also a transforming force wherever it flows. It brings fertility to the ground surrounding it, indicated by the presence of a great many trees on both sides of the river (47:7). The river transforms the Dead Sea, healing its waters—that is, turning its salty water into drinkable, life-supporting water (47:8). This Edenic river will induce paradise-like levels of fertility, teeming with all kinds of swarming creatures (47:9), like the waters of Genesis 1:20 (Ezek 47:10 cf. Gen 1:21). To sum up the pictorial message in straightforward speech: "Where the river flows everything will live" (Ezek 47:9).

Nor is this abundant fertility merely fertility in the abstract. The abundant fish will support an equally abundant number of fishermen. Even while the waters of the Dead Sea will be healed, its one existing use, as the source of valuable salt deposits, will not be eliminated (47:11).

The numerous trees of 47:7 are now more closely defined as "fruit trees" (literally, "food trees," 47:12). They will not suffer from any lack of moisture. Indeed, they will be so full of life that they will bear new fruit every month to feed the population, and their leaves will be for healing (47:12). All of this will be brought about because they are fed from the source of life-giving fruitfulness, the stream that flows from the temple.

Application. In a postmodern society, where fewer and fewer people feel any sense of guilt over their lifestyle, it is important that we recognize there is another way of presenting the gospel. In this approach, similar to that which Jesus used with the Samaritan woman, the focus is on bondage or emptiness, not guilt, as humanity's basic problem. One's basic need then becomes liberation (freedom from the slavery and futility of sin), and the gospel is the means whereby we enter the freedom to be what we were created to be—God-centered worshipers. This is Paul's approach to the gospel in Galatians: You were in bondage to a futile, empty lifestyle, but Christ came to set you free.

EZEKIEL 47:13–48:35

Original Meaning. The passage opens with the description of the boundaries of the new promised land (47:13–20). The area circumscribed is broadly similar to the original area allotted to Moses in Numbers 34:1–12. This is a larger area of territory than was ever controlled by Israel, even at the height of the Davidic empire; however, of greater significance than its absolute size is the fact that it is the same land that God promised to Moses. In receiving this land, the people receive the fulfillment of the covenant promise.

Strikingly absent from the land to be divided is the territory in the Transjordan. This land, historically the home of Reuben, Gad, and half of the tribe of Manasseh, is no longer considered part of the promised land, for the simple reason that it was not part of the original promise.

Equally radical is the distribution of the land itself (47:21–23). It is to be distributed "according to the tribes of Israel" (47:21), which represents a return to the premonarchic state of affairs. In place of the preexilic historic reality of two divided kingdoms, the reunited people receive the land as twelve tribes. Yet it is a return to the beginning that takes into account the intervening history, for the twelve tribes are now united under a single "prince" (48:21).

Further, there is to be an inheritance in the land not merely for the native-born Israelite and his children, but also for the resident alien (Heb. *ger*; 47:22–23) and his children. If he and his household were circumcised, he could partake of the Passover meal (Exod 12:48), and he could present sacrifices to the Lord just like a native-born Israelite (Lev 22:18). The status of these proselytes is confirmed by Ezekiel through the allocation to them also of a hereditary portion in the renewed land. Given the significance of the land in Ezekiel 40–48, this is high privilege indeed.

In chapter 48 the prophet moves on to the division of the land itself among the tribes. Each of the twelve tribes is assigned an equal portion (47:14), running in a strip from east to west. This is a way of orientating the entire land along the sacred east-west axis of the temple.

This contrasts dramatically with the division of the land in Joshua 14–21, whose roots are in historical rather than theological geography, where the boundaries between the different tribes are clearly defined. However, it corresponds exactly with the trend within the temple complex itself to define precisely the areas within the most holy zone. Holy space is important, so it must be completely defined.

The arrangement of the tribes within the land is not a random process. The number twelve is maintained, even though the tribe of Levi has no portion of its own, by treating the two half-tribes descended from Joseph (Ephraim and Manasseh) as tribes in their own right, as in the original division of the land (47:13). The four tribes most distant from the sacred zone, and therefore in the position of least honor, are Dan, Asher, Naphtali, and Gad, the sons of Jacob's concubines, Zilpah and Bilhah (48:1–3, 27–28). The eight sons of Jacob's wives, Rachel and Leah, take the four strips immediately to the north and the four to the south of the sacred zone (48:4–7, 23–26). Of these, Benjamin and Judah, historically located immediately to the north and south of Jerusalem, are immediately north and south of the sacred zone (48:7, 23).

It should also be noted that the site of the temple itself seems to have migrated north in Ezekiel's vision. Given that the tribal strips are equal (47:14) and that there are seven to the north of the sacred reservation and five to the south, the site of the temple ought in strict geographical terms to be located somewhere close to Shiloh, thirty miles north of its old location. The shift in theological geography may also have been driven by a simple desire to locate the temple closer to the center of the land, in the midst of the people, while still (in deference to history) slightly south of center.

The sacred portion is certainly the spiritual center of the land (48:8–22). The sacred strip is twenty-five thousand cubits (almost eight miles) wide and extends across the breadth of the land (48:8). At its heart is a twenty-five-thousand-cubit square, which is itself comprised of three east-west strips, two of ten thousand cubits breadth and one of five thousand cubits.

The first of these ten-thousand-cubit strips is assigned to the Zadokite priests (48:10–11). It is "a sacred portion within the sacred portion of the land" (author's translation, 48:12), a kind of Holy of Holies for the land. The second ten-thousand-cubit strip, which most commentators locate to the north of the priestly portion, is allocated to the Levites (48:13–14).

The remaining five-thousand-cubit strip along the southern edge of the sacred portion is the location of "the city" (48:15–19). The city functions as a visible symbol and focus of the unity of the tribes, inhabited and maintained by workers from all of the tribes (48:19).

Flanking the square sacred portion on both sides and occupying the remainder of the sacred strip is the land belonging to the prince (48:21–22). This is land of an intermediate level of holiness. It is part of the sacred strip but not part of the central square. In this context it serves to indicate the prince's status: He ranks above the ordinary lay members of the tribes of Israel, yet below the priests and Levites. The entire land is assigned to God's people on the basis of a graded hierarchy, in exactly the same way (and with the same gradations) as was the temple itself.

The closing verses of the book (48:30–35) bring us back to contemplate the city and some of the major themes of the vision of chapters 40–48. The prophet notes the exits of the city. Like the temple, the city is a precisely measured square. With its twelve gates, named for the twelve tribes of Israel, the city functions as a visible focus of the unity of the restored people.

Yet the city is not an end in itself: It faces north, toward the temple, the center of the renewed land. For that reason, the north wall and north gates are described first and assigned to the favored tribes of Reuben, Judah, and Levi, the three most significant tribes descended from Leah. The other three tribes descended from Leah (Simeon, Issachar, and Zebulun) are assigned the southern gates. The gates to the east are the tribes descended from Rachel (Joseph and Benjamin) and one from her servant Bilhah (Dan), while the least-favored west gates are assigned to Gad, Asher, and Naphtali, descendants of the concubines, Bilhah and Zilpah (48:34).

Finally, the city is given a new name, reflecting the focus of the entire temple vision: "THE LORD IS THERE" (48:35). The language of God's dual presence is necessary in order to communicate both God's transcendence and his immanence.

Both of these themes have been developed in Ezekiel 40–48: The high walls of the temple underline God's transcendent presence in the midst of God's people but separate from them, while the river of life speaks of God's immanent presence for blessing in the midst of his people. Similarly, God's transcendence is emphasized in the separation of the temple from the city, while at the same time his immanence is asserted by the sacred shape given to the city and its new name, "THE LORD IS THERE" (48:35).

Temple and city are where Ezekiel 40–48 started out (40:2), and they are where the vision ends. Both are transformed versions of the defiled and destroyed earthly institutions. In place of the earthly temple, contaminated by the sins of the people and abandoned by the presence of God (chs. 8–11), Ezekiel has seen an undefiled temple, refilled by God's glory (chs. 40–43). In place of an adulterous city named Jerusalem, which is put to death on account of her sins, Ezekiel has seen a holy city named "THE LORD IS THERE" (48:35), the habitat of the twelve renewed tribes of Israel. In place of a devastated land, Ezekiel has seen a land of peace and prosperity, watered by the river of life. In short, Ezekiel's entire temple vision is the unfolding of his earlier prophecy (37:26–27)

Application. We are to live lives completely centered on the new covenant temple, Jesus himself (Heb 12:22–28). Such lives revolve around the powerful worship of the awe-inspiring God, the living presence in our hearts of Jesus Christ our King, and the life-giving activity of his Spirit in our lives. So nourished, we are empowered to take the gospel out to all the nations of the earth. The inheritance that is ours in Christ is offered not simply to the twelve historic tribes of Israel, nor even to those who are resident aliens in their midst, but to all to whom the word of God comes. As Peter put it on the day of Pentecost: "The promise is for you and for your children and for all who are far off—for all whom the Lord our God will call" (Acts 2:39).

Thus, the nations will be brought in from the north and south and east and west and will sit down to feast with one another in the heavenly city, and the Lord of hosts and the Lamb will be there in their midst. Then indeed the heavenly city, the new Jerusalem, will fittingly bear the name that Ezekiel ascribed to it, "THE LORD IS THERE" (48:35).

DANIEL

INTRODUCTION TO DANIEL

The book of Daniel sets Daniel in the sixth century BC, where major figures from the time period play an important role in the book, such as Nebuchadnezzar, Belshazzar, Cyrus, and Jehoiakim. Concerns regarding dating, however, persist since the historical narrative of the first six chapters of the book are otherwise surrounded by issues of historical accuracy. At the same time, the second six chapters of the book, which include prophetic material, are uncannily accurate and precise through the second century BC, at least up to a definite point.

The conundrum is that interpreters find themselves on two sides of the debate. On the one hand, there are those who believe it is necessary to stick to a sixth-century composition. Others feel that the text drives them to a second-century date, and if they believe that the Bible is the word of God, they must then struggle with the theological issue of a book that, at least on the surface, attempts to deceive its audience into thinking it is prophesying future events when in reality it is casting the past into a future tense.

These are difficult issues that will divide faithful interpreters for years. We must resist the temptation to turn this issue into a simple litmus test. I interpret the book from the conclusion that the prophecies come from the sixth century BC. I find the problems amenable to hypothetical solutions and the theological issues of a late date difficult to surmount. In short, while the present commentary still finds a sixth-century date defensible, it refuses to discount all those who interpret from a second-century date.

BOOK OUTLINE

I. Daniel and the Three Friends in Nebuchadnezzar's Court (1:1–21)
II. The God of Wisdom Reveals Nebuchadnezzar's Dream to Daniel (2:1–49)
III. God Saves the Three Friends from the Fiery Furnace (3:1–30)
IV. Nebuchadnezzar's Pride Takes a Fall (4:1–37)
V. The Writing on the Wall (5:1–31)
VI. Daniel in the Lions' Den (6:1–28)
VII. The Vision of the Four Beasts (7:1–28)
VIII. The Ram and the Goat (8:1–27)
IX. Daniel's Prayer of Repentance (9:1–27)
X. The Vision of a Heavenly Messenger (10:1–11:1)
XI. The Scope and End of History (11:2–12:13)

DANIEL 1:1–21

Original Meaning

Jehoiakim Delivered into Nebuchadnezzar's Hand (1:1–2). In 605 BC Nebuchadnezzar was the head of the army in Syria. He defeated the Egyptians at Carchemish, a victory that opened the rest of Syria and Palestine to the Babylonian forces. Nebuchadnezzar cowed Jerusalem and took away some of the temple vessels and, as we will find out in the next section, a few of the noble youth. To the human eye, it appeared that Nebuchadnezzar had power; Judah did not.

Training for Service (1:3–7). Nebuchadnezzar was trying to control Judah without actually taking it over. His purpose with Daniel and the others was to train them in Babylonian ways for political and propaganda purposes. These members of the elite classes would become enamored with Babylonian ways and customs and either return to positions of influence at home or stay in Babylon in important positions, perhaps even serving as quasi-hostages. The elite of subdued nations were pressed into service in the interest of Babylonian Empire building.

In 1:6–7 we learn that the names of Daniel and the others were changed. In the ancient Near East, the name, which often contained the name of the one's deity, was integrally connected with a person's identity. Thus, the Babylonians began the process of reeducation by giving their captives new names.

Avoiding Defilement (1:8–16). Daniel and his three friends are in a process of education and preparation for service. Their minds as well as their bodies are being fed by the Babylonian court. If they prosper, then to whom should they attribute their development and success? The Babylonians. However, by refusing to eat the food of the king, they know it is not the king who is responsible. Only God could have done it.

Success Given to Daniel and His Friends (1:17–20). The description of Daniel here and his actions later remind us of Joseph, who played a similar role in the court of the Egyptian pharaoh. God blessed him as well with the ability to interpret dreams in a style that even this pagan monarch could recognize. God can utilize even the forms of pagan wisdom for his purposes.

The Extent of Daniel's Ministry (1:21). Daniel 10:1 locates the concluding vision in the third year of Cyrus. There are various ways to harmonize 1:21 and 10:1, but we should not miss the intention of the verse to identify Daniel as the prophet of the exile. This message provides both encouragement and hope to those alienated from their land with the message that success without compromise was possible even in the midst of captivity.

Application. It is striking how the contemporary church finds itself in a situation similar to Daniel's. We too live in a strange land. The god of modern culture is not the God of the Bible but is ultimately the self. This strange god demands worship that creates values different than those of Christianity. Indeed, many Christians have a sense of oppression and even hostility as they live their lives in the public square. Daniel imparts the liberating yet frightening news that there are multiple ways to be a believer in an unbelieving world. Much depends on the person and his or her specific cultural situation.

DANIEL 2:1–49

Original Meaning

The King and His Advisors (2:1–13). Nebuchadnezzar had a dream that disturbed him greatly, so he called his professionals—not psychologists, of course, but the ancient equivalents. These people were the political consultants, trend spotters, and religious gurus of the day. Babylonian religion encouraged looking for portents of the future in dreams and the fantastic occurrences of everyday life.

The biblical text does not clearly state why Nebuchadnezzar refuses to describe the contents of the dream to his interpreters. His reaction to the diviners' request to supply them with the content of the dream indicates that Nebuchadnezzar is testing their integrity.

In their exasperation, the diviners utter the statement that sets up the main lesson of the chapter: "No one can reveal it to the king except the gods, and they do not live among humans" (2:11). With that, the king orders all the "wise men" in Babylonia, present in the court or not, put to death.

God's Revealing of the Mystery to Daniel (2:14–23). Arioch informs Daniel on the situation that brings him to his doorstep. Daniel hears of the king's dream, the interpreters' inability to discern its contents, and their impotence in interpretation. After winning some time, he returned to his house, where he meets with his three friends. He knows that they have only one recourse: prayer. The Babylonian sages were only half right. While no human being could ever tell the king the contents and interpretation of his dream, God can, and, in contrast to the beliefs of the Babylonians (2:11), there is a God who lives among people: Daniel's God.

In his prayer, Daniel highlights two aspects of God's character that play a pivotal role in this chapter and indeed throughout the book.

1. God is powerful. Babylon and Nebuchadnezzar presume to have control over Israel and Daniel, but the prophet recognizes the truth of the matter. Nebuchadnezzar himself is a king because God is the one who "deposes kings and raises up others" (2:21).
2. God is wise. Indeed, Daniel understands that his wisdom is derivative from God's. The "wisdom and tact" (Dan 2:14) that we earlier saw him display toward Ashpenaz and then Arioch might be confused with the common sense available to any sensitive human being, but the ability to describe someone else's dream can only come from a divine source. He is the one who "reveals deep and hidden things" (2:22).

The Dream and Its Interpretation (2:24–45). Arioch brings Daniel into the presence of Nebuchadnezzar. The king gets right to the point: "Are you able to tell me what I saw in my dream and interpret it?" (2:26).

Daniel responds in a way that puts the focus where it belongs, not on himself but directly on God. Daniel bears witness to the God who speaks the life-granting answer; he is the "God in heaven who reveals mysteries" (2:28). He then proceeds with a description of the content of the king's vision.

The dream is of a huge statue. Besides its size, the statue is striking by virtue of its composition. Its head is gold; its chest and arms silver, while its belly and thighs are bronze and its legs iron. The feet are themselves composite, made of both iron and clay.

The statue is not the only character in the vision. Daniel next describes a rock made "not by human hands" (2:34). The rock smashes into the feet of the statue. After this, the rock becomes a huge mountain, filling the whole world.

In 2:36 Daniel moves from dream report to dream interpretation, and we begin on solid interpretive ground. Speaking to Nebuchadnezzar, Daniel says, "You are that head of gold" (2:38). Nebuchadnezzar must have rejoiced at this news. After all, in the scheme of "things to come" he was at the top, represented by the most precious of all metals.

After Nebuchadnezzar, Daniel interprets the remaining metals as symbolic of nations rather than individual kings. The identity of the following kingdoms has been much debated over the centuries, particularly in the past hundred years. Historically, two main approaches have dominated: the Greek view and the Roman view.

In the light of interpretive confusion, we must entertain

seriously the idea that, though it starts in the concrete present, it is a wrong strategy to proceed through history and associate the different stages of the statue with particular empires. The vision intends to communicate something more general but also more grand: God is sovereign; he is in control despite present conditions.

Not allowing ourselves to be distracted by the above debate, we notice some crucial theological principles in the dream. We see, for instance, while human beings operate on the idea that we get better and stronger with time, God's vision undercuts our understanding, informing us that the opposite is true. A statue that starts out in grandeur and beauty ends in weakness.

The other important principle in this dream-vision is seen when this statue is contrasted with the object of its demise, the rock. The statue is an object made with human hands and ingenuity. The rock, however, is explicitly said not to be the result of human intention or energy. In the interpretation, Daniel identifies the rock as God's kingdom (2:44–45). The rock obliterates these human kingdoms. God's kingdom will expand and take over the world, just as the rock becomes a huge mountain.

The King's Response (2:46–49). The concluding scene gives us a powerful picture that reinforces the theme of our book: The most powerful pagan in the world lies prostrate before an exiled Jew. Chills of excitement and the flames of hope will rise in the hearts of those who identify with Daniel and his God.

Application. Biblical wisdom is more than a knowledge of facts; it is a more like a skill (a "knowing how" rather than a "knowing that") based on our relationship with Jesus Christ. Wisdom is a divinely-given ability to have insight as to the best way to live life. What does this mean in practical terms? It means we live life in a troubled and confusing world in relationship with Christ. We gain our wisdom in conversation with him. And how do we converse with Christ? Through prayer and reading his word. Through prayer we enhance our relationship with him through praise, and we draw on his wisdom through sharing our problems and confusion. We then listen to his answer as he speaks to us through the Bible.

DANIEL 3:1–30

Original Meaning

Nebuchadnezzar's Image of Gold (3:1–7). Daniel does not inform us whether the image was a god or the king himself. Whether deity or the divinized king, the command was to worship and bow down to this statue. Such a command was impossible for a faithful follower of the true God to obey, and that is the point of the text.

The gold of this statue links the story with Nebuchadnezzar's recently described dream in which he was the head of gold. The size of the image is startling. Nebuchadnezzar not only built the statue; he demanded a public demonstration of adoration. For this purpose, he issued a call to attend its dedication. With this rather imposing list of officials, we encounter a lengthy list that is repeated a number of times in the chapter. These lists appear ponderous to us, but their literary effect is to heighten the tension and the feeling of danger toward the three friends, who will soon be singled out of the group. The second lengthy list of musical instruments heightens the tension, focusing on the moment of obedience or disobedience.

The Accusation against the Three Friends (3:8–12). We should note that this is an accusation by *some* astrologers against *some* Jews. It is not a class action against a whole people. These men appear to be motivated out of professional jealousy. They beat them out for best honors in their school (ch. 1), and now they are rapidly rising in the ranks of the government—and they are foreigners to boot! Close attention to the words of the astrologers reveals their strategy. In a phrase, they appeal to his sense of vanity.

The Confrontation with Nebuchadnezzar (3:13–18). Nebuchadnezzar's insecurity is apparent in his treatment of the wisdom teachers in chapter 2, as well as in his happiness after learning that he was the head of gold. The premise of this chapter is the enforced worship of Nebuchadnezzar's golden statue, which, whether idol or royal statue, is a way of compelling a display of loyalty. The report of disloyalty among the three friends causes an explosion of anger on his part. He immediately has them brought into his presence for a personal loyalty test. The tension reaches fever pitch when Nebuchadnezzar orders a personal ceremony for the three, instructing the band to strike up the introit, at the end of which they are to worship the image.

The three friends begin by acknowledging God's ability to save them, but then they envision the possibility that God may choose not to do so. In other words, they answer Nebuchadnezzar in light of the possibility that they will be burned to ashes in the blazing furnace. Whichever is the case, they say, they will not worship the golden image. No matter what the result, deliverance or death, they will not give into the evil powers of the world. They will stay faithful to God.

The Miraculous Deliverance (3:19–27). The three friends' speech, courageous in our ears, exasperates the king. He grows even more furious. He orders the furnace, apparently burning in the background of the scene, to be superheated, reflecting perhaps the heat of his own anger. Is there a "god" (3:15) who can rescue them from the hands of such a powerful ruler?

Nebuchadnezzar himself gives us the answer: "I see four

men walking around in the fire, unbound and unharmed, and the fourth looks like a son of the gods" (3:25). The king quickly gets the message and orders the three out, and then Nebuchadnezzar and all the others, including the accusers, witness the extent of the miracle of deliverance. It was as if they were not even in the fire (3:27). In this way, God is showing Nebuchadnezzar who is in charge.

Nebuchadnezzar Worships God (3:28–30). As in chapter 2, Nebuchadnezzar is moved from anger to praise toward God and his followers. In his concluding speech in the present chapter, he again mentions the mysterious fourth person. Was this God himself, as "a son of the gods" (3:25) might lead us to believe, or an angel?

In one sense, it does not make any difference. Even if the fourth figure was an angel, it was *God's* angel; God is still the redeemer. Even Nebuchadnezzar recognizes this. He further acknowledges that the three have been right to obey this God rather than a king like him.

The king then issues a command that, while not instituting worship of the true God, will not allow anyone in his kingdom to show such a powerful deity any disrespect. Furthermore, Shadrach, Meshach, and Abednego get a further promotion, thus completely thwarting the intentions of their accusers.

Application. At first it is difficult for us as Christians living at the turn of the millennium to identify with the challenge facing the Jewish people on the plain of Dura. But the issue transcends the worship of a particular statue and concerns instead the constant threat to dilute the worship of the true God by elevating anything or anyone else to a comparable place of importance in our life. We are constantly, even as Christians, in a struggle with this temptation.

Our addictions can make pleasure an idol, so that all our efforts and thoughts are directed toward where we will get our next high, whether through alcohol, drugs, sex, or some other cheap thrill. We might seek power in order to control our world or simply to have the resources of revenge toward those who have hurt us in some way. We may make relationships, or one particular relationship, an idol. We may be gearing our life and decisions not around what we understand to be God's will but rather the will of a spouse, a child, or a friend. The list is vast, which is why the danger is so real. The seduction is subtle, which is why we can slip so easily into idol worship.

DANIEL 4:1–37

Original Meaning

Nebuchadnezzar's Decree to Praise the Lord (4:1–3). The last two chapters concluded with Nebuchadnezzar's praise of the Lord, but Daniel 4 departs from the pattern and begins (as well as ends) with Nebuchadnezzar's praise. The content of his praise is somewhat general, but it highlights God's sovereignty and the wonderful nature of his interaction with the world. The following story is the specification of the events behind the general praise.

The Dream Report and the Search for an Interpreter (4:4–18). A dream intrudes into the king's peaceful mind, tormenting him with doubt and fear. His first impulse is to call his professional wise men into his presence. On a psychological level, the modern reader might ask why he waited to call Daniel, considering his earlier success. The text does not give us the king's motives, but the delay does differentiate Daniel from those who used traditional dream interpretation techniques and emphasizes his superiority, who is wise only because of the gift Yahweh has given him.

That Nebuchadnezzar still really hasn't gotten it is indicated by the parenthetical comment at the end of 4:8. He refers to Daniel by his Babylonian name, which connects him to the king's native god. Moreover, he speaks of Daniel as the one in whom the "spirit of the holy gods" dwells (4:8). Being a polytheist, Nebuchadnezzar has the intellectual framework to subsume Yahweh into his already existing theology.

The king then relates the contents of his dream. Its main feature is a huge tree in the middle of the land. This use of the tree as an image of the life-giving nature of the king has previously been used in biblical tradition (cf. Ezek 17:1–10; 31:3–14). The story also connects with the ancient Near East. There is little about a sacred or cosmic tree in the literature of Mesopotamia, but the tree occurs as a major motif in the iconography. The implications for Daniel 4 are clear: Nebuchadnezzar's dream shows that he identifies himself with the cosmic tree; he is the keeper of the cosmos, the true image of God, the perfect man.

After the description of the tree, the king narrates the plot. It begins with the appearance of a "messenger" (an Aramaic word better translated "watchman" or "watcher," cf. NIV footnote, 4:13). No doubt a supernatural being is meant. The watcher barks orders for the dismantling of the cosmic tree. The dream ends with the watcher's proclamation concerning the motive behind this desolation. It is clearly expressed in 4:17.

The Dream Interpretation (4:19–27). The dynamic between Daniel and the king is a remarkable one, considering that this is the king who destroyed Jerusalem, but God's prophet shows concern for the well-being of the king, not vindictiveness. After receiving encouragement from the king, Daniel reveals the referent of the tree symbol. It is Nebuchadnezzar himself. Since Nebuchadnezzar is the tree, he is also the subject of the coming judgment. As the tree will be desolated, so he will be desolated. As the subject of the dream will be reduced to an animal-like state, so Nebuchadnezzar will be reduced from his humanity and become beast-like.

This is the message of judgment that confronts Nebuchadnezzar, but it is a conditional message. Daniel's advice is to avoid sin and be kind. In other words, he should not fall prey to the temptation to think himself a god. In spite of his greatness, he must retain his humility.

The Fulfillment of the Dream (4:28–33). The narrative does not let Daniel's hope live long. Verse 28 reports in a summarizing fashion, "All this happened to King Nebuchadnezzar." We learn from 4:29 that a period of twelve months passed before the crucial moment. We are perhaps to understand that the dream and its interpretation frightened Nebuchadnezzar into a temporary compliance. Or perhaps he pretty much continued his sinful (4:27) course, but God waited until this moment of monumental pride to exercise his judgment. We cannot be sure.

As we learn from ancient texts and the results of archaeology, the Babylon of Nebuchadnezzar was grand indeed. Nebuchadnezzar had much to do with the greatness of Babylon. From biblical and ancient Near Eastern records contemporary with his reign, we know he had great wealth and was an accomplished builder. He gave the orders and paid the bills. However, his power and accomplishments led to a pride that blinded him from broader realities.

While God gave him time after his first warning, no time elapses ("the words were on his lips," 4:31) before a heavenly voice decrees his doom. From being the most powerful man in the world, he is reduced to roaming the steppe like an animal.

Healing and Concluding Doxology (4:34–37). We get little insight into Nebuchadnezzar's mental processes. But we are told that the divine prescription works. At the appointed time (the end of the "seven times," cf. 4:25) Nebuchadnezzar "raised [his] eyes toward heaven, and [his] sanity was restored" (4:34). The action of looking toward heaven is obviously meant as an acknowledgment of God's ultimate superiority. Nebuchadnezzar now understands his place in the scheme of things. Thus, Nebuchadnezzar is restored to sanity and to his relative grandeur as great king of Babylon. The lesson is learned and the moral of the story is the last word (4:37).

Application. God humbles the proud. It began in the garden of Eden. Another story is the account of the Tower of Babel in Genesis 11. Again, pride led to rebellion, even an assault on heaven itself. The humble faithful can find comfort in these accounts of the reversal of pride into shame. Apart from Old Testament anticipation, the New Testament makes it even more clear that God is in control. He has won a victory over an enemy even more powerful than Nebuchadnezzar, over a kingdom even more deadly and oppressive than the Babylonian Empire. He has defeated Satan and death itself.

DANIEL 5:1–31

Original Meaning

The Profanation of the Holy Vessels (5:1–4). The Persians are knocking at the door of the Babylonian Empire. Belshazzar must have known that an attack would come sooner or later. It was in this context that the banquet described in our chapter took place. Was it to rally and encourage the leaders? To give them a diversion in the face of the onslaught? To feast today for tomorrow we die? Perhaps a bit of all three, but we are safe to assume that tension permeated the air in the Babylonian capital at this time.

Wine flowed abundantly at the banquet. The text does not emphasize the drinking to provide a moral lesson on the dangers of thinking under the influence of alcohol. No, the focus shifts to the holy goblets that Nebuchadnezzar had removed from the temple. These precious temple vessels are about to be profaned by being pressed into common use. Belshazzar's impiety portends dire consequences.

We cannot be certain what was going on in Belshazzar's mind at this time. He surely had a propaganda purpose in mind. But what? He may have been making claims to power by comparing himself to his "father" (5:2) Nebuchadnezzar. Perhaps in the midst of the present crisis Belshazzar is claiming more power than Nebuchadnezzar, a boast vain enough in itself. In the final analysis, it does not matter what was going on in Belshazzar's mind; his very act is like spitting in the eye of God.

Belshazzar is not only committing blasphemy, but he also combines it with idolatry. Here is where his profanation surpasses that of Nebuchadnezzar. He uses God's holy goblets to toast the lifeless idols of his own religion. Those objects made out of precious metals are not objects of worship, but Belshazzar's perverted religion puts their material cousins at the heart of his confidence and hope for the future.

The Enigmatic Writing on the Wall (5:5–12). A hand suddenly appears without explanation. The faithful reader of the past and present has no doubt who is behind the writing, though to be sure, Belshazzar has no clue. As a polytheist, he could have seen the hand as controlled by any of a number of different divinities. Immediately, however, he suspects that the enigmatic writing has a message that intends calamity toward him.

Belshazzar cannot make heads or tails of the writing, so he calls for the wise men. By now the reader of the book of Daniel cannot help but picture these men as incompetent fools, and they don't disappoint our expectations. The wise men are baffled by the inscription. This means at the very least that they cannot interpret the significance of the inscription. It may also imply that it was written in some kind of code, because it has been written in Aramaic, the common language of the day. Their inability cannot be the result of a simple inability to read the script if it were written out in a normal manner. The text ultimately does not let us know.

At this point, the queen whisks onto the stage without detailed introduction or explanation, again leading to speculation. Who is the queen? Whoever she is, she has the solution to Belshazzar's problem: "Call for Daniel" (5:12).

Daniel's Interpretation of the Inscription (5:13–28). The king first identifies him as one of the captives: "Are you Daniel, one of the exiles my father the king brought from Judah?" (5:13). Such an address intends to remind Daniel of his place before Belshazzar. Belshazzar is king; Daniel is his captive.

Belshazzar then launches off a series of honorifics that cite Daniel's abilities and character, but a close reading of the speech shows that the king himself does not endorse the reports. Twice he begins his words with "I have heard," once when speaking of Daniel's endowment with the divine spirit, insight, intelligence, and wisdom (5:14), and again when saying that Daniel is one who can give interpretations and solve difficult problems (5:16).

Daniel has not missed the slight. Daniel begins by refusing the gift. He will interpret the writing on the wall free of charge. Perhaps having read the inscription already, Daniel knows that the reward means nothing. The king has nothing really to give.

But before actually giving the interpretation, Daniel delivers a stinging rebuke to the king. He uses Nebuchadnezzar, Belshazzar's predecessor and by far superior, to redress the upstart, who is not only probably young and really the second in command to his father Nabonidus but is also on the brink of disaster. Nebuchadnezzar was great, but when God confronted him, he ultimately acknowledged his subservience. Belshazzar did not learn the lesson.

For the first time, then, we as readers hear the words: "MENE, MENE, TEKEL, PARSIN" (5:25). As presented in the text, these are three different nouns, the first repeated for emphasis. As nouns, they are units of money and may be translated: "Mina, mina, shekel, and a half." Daniel's interpretation takes these nouns and interprets them as verbal forms, passive participles to be exact. The three verbal roots in order may be translated "numbered," "weighed," and "divided."

That Belshazzar has ruled at all—indeed, that Babylon has achieved ascendancy as the major power of the world—has been at God's sovereign determination, but it was a temporary period now at an end. Belshazzar and the Babylonians have not measured up, and so now another power will come to the throne, one dominated by Persia, which includes the Medes. No further explanation is needed from Daniel; the message is clear, and it spells doom.

Reward and Punishment (5:29–31). God's judgment is double-edged. As he punishes his enemies, so he frees and rewards his people. Here, two individuals represent the dual fates of the godly and the ungodly.

1. Belshazzar bestows the purple garments, the gold chain, and high political status on godly Daniel. Earlier he had treated the possibility of reward with disdain, but now he accepts them without recorded objection. While the text does not give us a window to Daniel's motivation, the scene shows us that the godly ultimately receive their reward even from hostile and reluctant oppressors.
2. The chapter ends by narrating the consequences of Belshazzar's ungodly acts. Thus, we witness the reward granted to insolence, idolatry, and blasphemy.

Application. Is there a contrast between an Old Testament God of judgment and condemnation and a New Testament God of grace and mercy? By no means! The New Testament teaches that God, in Jesus, judges evil and condemns the wicked (John 8:26; 12:31). God is still judge in the New Testament (2 Tim 4:8).

But there is also clear and strong teaching that God's followers are not in a position to judge others. Perhaps the most well-known teaching in this regard is found in Matthew 7:1–2. Paul echoes this understanding as he also emphasizes God's role as judge in Romans 2:1–4. God judges, indeed, but we cannot know with certainty when suffering and death is God's judgment and when it is not. Therefore, we must keep our mouths shut. We must never point to a person who suffers and say, "Behold God's judgment!"

DANIEL 6:1–28

Original Meaning

The Plot against Daniel (6:1–9). By now, we are not surprised that Daniel distinguishes himself from all the other authorities whom Darius has placed in important positions throughout his kingdom. The king's intention to promote him above everyone else is apparently leaked to the others, who for obviously selfish reasons want to block his swift rise. Unfortunately for them, Daniel's behavior conforms to his spotless reputation. They know that Daniel's religion is the fundamental guiding principle of his life. He would betray the king before he would betray his religion. Thus, they lay their trap to trip him up.

Their approach to the king is a masterpiece of political

deception to achieve their illicit ends. These "administrators and satraps" (6:6) are clearly lying to the king, since they claim that the proposal they are presenting has been unanimously approved by all of his subordinates. Of course, Daniel, the king's favorite, does not even know about it.

The proposal appeals to the vanity of the king, especially if the king is feeling any insecurity about his popularity or power. Perhaps this explains his ready acceptance of such a bizarre suggestion. Daniel will find himself in an impossible situation from a human point of view, for the decree may not be repealed according to the custom of the Persians and Medes.

The Trap and Reluctant Punishment (6:10–18). We move from the court to Daniel's home where he hears of the king's decree. His response is simple: He goes upstairs and prays with the windows open toward Jerusalem. The impression the narrative intends to impart is Daniel's unflinching obedience. He does not question, doubt, or worry; he acts.

Why does Daniel bow toward Jerusalem? Essentially, his act is motivated by 1 Kings 8:35–36. The context of these verses is Solomon's prayer of dedication of the temple in Jerusalem. Of course, at the time of Daniel's prayer the temple was in ruins. God had abandoned his earthly home (Ezek 9–11) because of the presumption of the people (Jer 7) and had allowed the Babylonians to tear down the temple (book of Lamentations). Nonetheless, Judeans in exile, such as Daniel, turned regularly to the city with longing in their hearts and hope for the future.

The mention of the "three times a day" (Dan 6:10) indicates that Daniel's prayer on this occasion is not stirred on by the decree; it is part of his regular habit. He is neither flaunting nor hiding his religious practice. After all, he is praying in an upper room and with the windows open. He is not on public display, but neither is he hiding from determined spies.

And determined spies there were. The conspirators present news of Daniel's actions craftily. They know where the king's sympathies lie, so before they accuse Daniel, they remind the king of his earlier decision and its binding character. They then confront the king with the news that indicts Daniel. The king reacts with extreme dismay. However, he is trapped by his own unchangeable words and must carry out the punishment.

As decreed, Daniel is thrown into the lions' den. The king's concern for Daniel continues through the night. He cannot eat or sleep. As he discovers the next morning to his surprise, his evening has been much more difficult than Daniel's!

Daniel's Rescue and the Accusers' Demise (6:19–24). The coming dawn finds Darius rushing to the lions' den in order to discover the fate of Daniel. Darius must have had at least a glimmer of hope that Daniel would survive the night. After all, he had commended Daniel into the hands of the prophet's God and called out to him the moment he reached the den.

Perhaps it is best to consider the lions' den a trial by ordeal rather than an execution per se. An individual was subjected to an ordeal when he was suspected of a crime, but there was some uncertainty as to his guilt. Daniel's survival attests to his innocence.

But perhaps the lions weren't hungry that night. Or perhaps someone sympathetic to Daniel, say Darius, had had the lions fed to the full or even drugged beforehand. Any such doubts are dispelled in the following verses when Daniel's accusers and their families are thrown into the den. The viciousness and hunger of the lions are vividly displayed by the fact they were attacked and killed before "they reached the floor of the den" (6:24). The accusers set a trap for Daniel, but in the end, they were caught in their own trap—and not only the accusers themselves but also their families.

Darius's Decree (6:25–28). The plot of Daniel 6 was set in motion by Darius's issuing a decree that prayers could only be directed toward himself either as a divine figure or, as is more likely, the only mediator with the divine realm. The chapter ends with a second decree, this time promoting Daniel's God throughout his vast empire.

Darius proclaims the God of Daniel "the living God" (6:26). This indicates that he not only exists but is active in the world. Certainly, the prophet's rescue shows that in a dramatic fashion. God and his kingdom will never end, and he rescues his people in astounding ways. Specifically, his rescue of Daniel from the lions' den demonstrates that "he rescues and he saves" (6:27).

After Darius's speech, the chapter, which brings to a close the court narrative part of the book, concludes with the narrative statement that "Daniel prospered during the reign of Darius and the reign of Cyrus the Persian" (6:28). Indeed he did. He prospered throughout his entire lifetime in the court.

Application. At times, Western Christians misapply the example of Daniel. A prime example is the complaint about the lack of prayer in our public schools. Our present law prohibits a teacher from offering a prayer in our state-run schools. This bothers some Christians, who believe that Daniel 6 provides the motivation for objection. A similar kind of argument is presented in the analogous cases of Christmas displays on government property or the hanging of the Ten Commandments in a judge's courtroom.

But are these situations really analogous to Daniel 6? I suggest they are not. Daniel was not prohibited from praying in a certain location like the court; he was forbidden to pray to God at all, even in private!

The confusion in the United States and probably other Western democracies arises because some Christians insist that their country is the modern equivalent of Israel. However, it cannot be urged too strongly that there are and can be no modern equivalents of Israel. There is no such thing as a "Christian nation," except in the sense of a nation where most of the inhabitants happen to be Christian at that particular historical moment.

DANIEL 7:1–28

Original Meaning. We change genres from the first half of the book to the second. Apocalyptic replaces court narrative, demanding that we change reading strategy. Apocalyptic is a metaphor-rich genre. Metaphors and similes teach by analogy. They throw light on difficult concepts and things by relating them to something we know from common experience. As such, images speak truly and accurately, but not precisely. Caution and reserve are virtues in the interpretation of apocalyptic literature.

Horror by the Sea (7:1–8). Daniel's vision comes about by means of a dream, and with this note we get an indication of another difference between the closely related genres of prophecy and apocalyptic: they share many similarities, most notably that both at times concern the future. Apocalyptic is slightly different in terms of the mode of revelation. The prophet is God's spokesperson; he brings God's word to the people. A different dynamic is at work in apocalyptic literature. God speaks to Daniel through a dream or through a mediator (e.g., Dan 12:5–13). He is not commissioned to speak to the people but rather to write it down.

Daniel's report of the vision begins on the coast of the sea, where the winds are whipping the waves into a frenzy. Deep in the psyche of the people of the ancient Near East the sea was more than a dangerous place. It was a threatening force that was ranged against the beneficial forces of creation. The description of the sea at the beginning of Daniel's vision evokes horror and an anticipation of evil.

Out of the chaotic sea arises four great beasts, one after the other. They are symbols of forces ranged against God and his creation order. These beasts are bizarre; they are mutants, perversions of what God intended by his creation. As such, they evoke not only horror in the original reader, but also revulsion.

The beasts come out of the chaotic sea one after the other. The first is described as "like a lion, and it had the wings of an eagle." (7:4). As with the statue in chapter 2, we begin in the present. There the head of gold was explicitly identified as Nebuchadnezzar (i.e., the Babylonian Empire). Here, in the waning years of that same empire, the most natural interpretation of the symbolism is that it stands for Babylonia.

The second beast rises out of the sea, the bear. For whatever reason this beast is not a hybrid, but it still is a ferocious animal of prey. It is with this second beast that the classic debate begins. Is the bear Medo-Persia or Media? We find ourselves on slippery ground when it comes to specific and concrete historical identifications of the imagery of the four beasts. It is my argument that this is an intentional effect of the imagery of the vision. The purpose is not so much writing history in advance as making a theological statement about the conflict between human evil and God.

The intentional ambiguity continues with the third beast. As we look for the point of the imagery, we are drawn immediately to the characteristic of speed. Leopards are fast cats, and with the addition of wings, we are to imagine blazing speed. Is the significance of this imagery the blazing speed of the Persian army, or does it point to Alexander's blitzkrieg through the Near East and the four generals who divided his vast empire after his early death?

The fourth kingdom is the most enigmatic of all. It appears to be only vaguely animal-like. The metallic composition of its weapons (teeth and claws) highlights its destructive power and ruthlessness. There is little concrete description here by which we may argue for a specific identification, so the classic approaches to this text have recourse to simple historical sequence. If one has already identified the first three as Babylon, Media, and Persia, then the fourth must be Greek. If, on the other hand, one has combined Media and Persia and identified the third as Greece, then the fourth kingdom must be Roman.

Heavenly Power (7:9–14). Verse 9 is an abrupt transition from the scene by the sea to a courtroom. The two main characters are described in human-like terms. In essence, we have gone up the chain of being. Evil human kingdoms were described as horrifying hybrid animals; the divine realm is imaged as human beings.

The first figure is called the "Ancient of Days" (7:9). He is God, specifically in his role as judge. As such, he is imaged as an old and presumably wise human judge sitting in his courtroom. The second figure, "one like a son of man" (7:13), is more startling in this Old Testament context. He is riding the cloud chariot, which is the prerogative of God alone.

Cloud imagery associated with the Lord's appearance is as old as the exodus and the pillar of cloud by day and the fire by night (Exod 13:21). During the climactic theophany on Sinai, the mountain was covered by a cloud (19:16). In the tabernacle, God appeared in the cloud that was present in the Most Holy Place (Lev 16:2). We learn of the vehicular cloud in the Psalms and Prophets (Pss 68:4, 104:3–4; Isa 19:1, Nah 1:3). Like the sea image, the motif of God riding clouds also has an ancient Near Eastern background.

Daniel 7:1–14 presents the reader with two image clusters. On the one hand, we have four beasts and horns, which represent depraved human kingdoms; on the other hand, we see two human figures, the Ancient of Days and one like a son of man, who image the divine realm.

Divine Victory (7:15–28). Much energy has been exerted as to the identity of the fourth beast and the associated horns. A strong case can be made that the fourth beast is Greece and the ten horns are the kings that followed Alexander, with the climactic horn being associated with Antiochus IV Epiphanes.

Critics, however, have pointed out that although Antiochus himself died, his death could hardly be said to be followed by the incoming of God's kingdom. For this reason, other scholars have argued that the fourth kingdom must be Rome and the ten horns should be identified as ten kingdoms that arise from that political entity, to be followed by a climactic rebel to be identified as the antichrist in the New Testament.

It remains to comment on the enigmatic phrase "a time, times and half a time" (7:25). This expression is often taken to mean "one year, two years, and half a year," that is, three and a half years. Questions must be raised about attempts to make this symbolic number so specific. It is better to understand this reference to be as vague as it sounds on first reading. The rebellion of the little horn will get off to a fast start and seem like it is going to last forever but then is suddenly cut off.

Application. Daniel 7 paints a horrifying picture of human evil. Many Christians around the world know and experience the harsh rule of regimes that hate Christianity. These brothers and sisters have no trouble recognizing the beast-like nature of the world in which they live. Christians who are fortunate enough not to live in a literal battle zone understand that life is a struggle, sometimes just annoying but at least occasionally a battle of nearly epic proportions. The picture of the beasts in Daniel 7 is consistent with the lesson we learn throughout the Bible—every man and woman at heart is a self-seeking rebel against God.

DANIEL 8:1–27

Original Meaning

The Vision of a Ram and a Goat (8:1–14). The description of the success and travail of the ram and the goat are simply a prelude to the focus of the passage, which centers on a small horn that grows out of one of the four. Already, we know that the symbol of the horn points to a king or a kingdom. This small horn takes on large proportions as it grows to the south, to the east, and toward the "Beautiful Land" (8:9), Israel.

It grows until it attains the "host of the heavens" (8:10) and enters into a conflict with this heavenly army. Strikingly, the text reports that the small horn achieves some measure of success against its rivals in the sky. Then, climactically, the horn challenges "the commander of in chief of the LORD" (8:11). Significantly, its incursion against the commander is described as harm done to the formal worship of Israel.

Verse 12 is difficult and its interpretation uncertain. In a word, it is clear that God's side will take some blows during the struggle "because of rebellion" (8:12). Is this the rebellion of the little horn or of God's people? Within this chapter little evidence exists for the latter view. God's people suffer at the hands of a power that rebels against God and seeks to take his place. The astounding fact is that this little horn succeeds at least for a while and that the "truth" (8:12) was thrown to the ground.

How long will the sanctuary and its ritual be disrupted? While the one celestial being directs his question to the other, it is notable that the answer is addressed not to the celestial being but rather to Daniel (8:14): "It will take 2,300 evenings and mornings; then the sanctuary will be reconsecrated."

The Interpretation of the Vision (8:15–27). The vision has come to an end and Daniel struggles to understand. Suddenly, a humanlike figure appears before him. The first figure is Gabriel (meaning "God's hero"), a leading angel in God's heavenly army. The source of the voice is not named, but we are surely to believe that it is the voice of God himself, who commands this powerful angelic being to reveal to Daniel the meaning of the vision that he has been watching.

The first words from Gabriel announce the interpretation of the vision under a general heading: It "concerns the time of the end" (8:17). This general introduction might at first lead us to believe that the vision concerns the end of history, but the clear interpretation of the context of the vision's climax places it squarely in the middle of the second century BC.

Unlike chapter 7, where the animals are said to be "four kings" (7:17), here they are identified with particular and well-known political entities. The ram with the two horns represents the "kings of Media and Persia" (8:20). In the vision itself, one horn grew larger than the other, which is surely a reference to the fact that the Persian part of this empire soon swallowed the Median part and assumed dominance.

The goat with the single horn that speedily devastated the ram is Greece, the single horn being its first king—Alexander the Great. He achieved an unprecedented domination from Italy to India in unbelievable time; but he died suddenly at age 33 in 323 BC, leaving behind two young sons, Alexander and Herakles. These boys were ultimately murdered, and the world was carved up between Alexander's powerful generals, the Diadochi. The Diadochi are the "four prominent horns" (8:8; cf. 8:22).

The vision then skips over about two centuries of history. For now the focus goes immediately to one particular horn. Scholars almost universally agree that the horn that grew out of one of the four is the second century BC Seleucid ruler, Antiochus IV Epiphanes. We know much about this king from intertestamental writings like the Maccabees.

Antiochus IV ordered the cessation of temple sacrifice in 167 BC and profaned the temple by introducing a holy object sacred to the god Zeus, to which he sacrificed a pig, abhorrent to Jewish religion. This holy object has been suggested to be a meteorite that became a cult object that the Jews referred to as "an abomination that causes desolation" (9:27).

Such actions against the formal worship of God's people were far more than an affront against the people; it was an attack against heaven itself. Antiochus indeed took a stand against the "Prince of princes" (8:25), that is, against God. But such arrogance can only lead to one conclusion: utter defeat. The ultimate power behind the Maccabean freedom fighters was God himself, who gave them the victory and allowed them to restore the temple.

Finally, the angelic interpreter reaffirms the time frame of the suffering and its end: "The vision of the evenings and mornings that has been given you is true, but seal up the vision, for it concerns the distant future" (8:26). Interestingly, even in historical retrospect we cannot be dogmatic about the meaning of the 2,300 evenings and mornings (8:14).

The number is given not so much so that those who read Daniel's sixth-century prognostications in the second century could compute when the suffering would stop as much as to assure them that God had things under control. This number is typical of chronological numbers throughout the book of Daniel. They may not be used for date settings or for establishing apocalyptic calendars. Moreover, if we cannot be certain of numbers used in prophecies that have already been fulfilled, how likely can we figure out the numbers that point to times in the far distant future?

Application. The church is constantly bombarded with claims that someone has finally figured out the difficult apocalyptic numbers and has determined that we are living in the period of the end. Every generation has seen the signs of the time. This is why we are tempted, particularly when we have not listened to Jesus's clear teaching about not knowing the precise time, to think that our time is that special time.

The misuse of these apocalyptic dates is an attempt to wrest control from God and place it firmly in our own sinful grasp, but the result is disruption in the church and in our lives. Such vain speculation leads, as in the case of the people I mentioned above in the Application for chapter 7, to a complete disregard for present realities. God calls us to live in the present while waiting with hope for the future.

DANIEL 9:1–27

Original Meaning

Preparation for Prayer (9:1–4a). Darius's first year as king of Babylon would have coincided with the first year of Cyrus as the great king of the Persian Empire—also the year, therefore, that witnessed the decree to allow some Judeans to return to their homeland. Daniel's prayer seems to have taken place in anticipation of this decree. His witness to the fall of Babylon (539 BC) may have caused him to turn to the Scriptures with new eyes.

Though verse numbers are not given, Daniel certainly had passages like Jeremiah 25:11–12; 29:10 in mind. In essence these passages teach that the king of Babylon will dominate the ancient Near East (including Judah) for seventy years, after which time Babylon itself will come to an end. In the first year of Darius, Babylon has come to an end as a world power, being replaced by Persia. Daniel recognizes this as the time when the exile may come to an end.

Note that seventy years, counting backward from 539 BC, is 609 BC. What happened in 609 BC? As far as Judah and the exile is concerned—nothing. The first incursion we know about is the one mentioned in Daniel 1:1–2, dated to around 605 BC. The interpretation of this number becomes even more complex when we examine two later biblical books (2 Chr 36:20–22; Zech 1:12).

When we compare these passages and reflect on the number itself, we reach the conclusion that the number is not literal, nor even referring to one specific period of time. This should not concern us; it is the predominant way in which numbers are used in apocalyptic literature. The recognition of this fact should also prepare us for the even more extravagant use of numbers later in the chapter.

Invocation and Confession (9:4b–10). The prayer paints a powerful picture of the Lord, especially in contrast to his people. Daniel acknowledges him as "great and awesome" (9:4b) as well as faithful to the covenant. However, Daniel confesses that God's people have not obeyed his commands but have rebelled against him instead.

The prophets were sent, according to Daniel, to all strata of society—from kings to common people. None of them, however, responded. They are in exile because they have rebelled against the covenant God made with them through Moses.

God's Punishment (9:11–14). In the next section of his prayer, Daniel draws a direct connection between the sin of the people and their present suffering. Between the law of Moses and the Prophets, God's people had no excuse. They knew what the consequences of their actions would be, but somehow they rationalized it. They wrongly reasoned that if God's residence was the temple, there would be no way that an enemy could defeat their city. What they did not consider was the possibility that God would abandon his temple (Ezek 9–11). The destruction of Jerusalem and the exile of Judah were not acts of an arbitrary God, but rather the consequences of the sinful attitudes and actions of God's people, about which they were repeatedly warned.

Appeal for Mercy (9:15–19). Here the prophet calls on God as the one who delivered his people out of Egypt. The exodus was a pivotal event in the life of God's people. It defined them as a nation. In essence, the return from the exile would be a sort of second exodus.

Though the plea for God's mercy follows the confession and could not proceed without it, it is wrong to think that the confession is the basis of God's restoration. Daniel knows that the people are still sinful and if there is any hope for them, it is in God's righteousness and not their own (9:16, 18). Daniel's appeal is ultimately based not on the people's plight but on the reputation of God himself.

The Prophecy of the Seventy Weeks (9:20–27). Daniel has prayed for forgiveness and restoration, and Gabriel now communicates the heavenly answer by reinterpreting the seventy years as seventy "sevens" (9:24). During this period six actions will be completed:

1. the finishing of transgression,
2. the end of sin,
3. the atonement of the wicked,
4. the bringing in of everlasting righteousness,
5. the sealing up of vision and prophecy, and
6. the anointing of the most holy (9:24).

While the first three actions describe the eradication of the negative, the next three are more positive in focus. These six actions take place during the entire period of seventy "sevens." They describe the eradication of evil and the establishment of righteousness. In the present, Daniel and his companions know an imperfect world, but in the future things will be wonderful.

Far from concluding his speech, Gabriel continues. We are already used to this enigmatic way of referring to future time periods, so we are not surprised at the questions that arise from these numbers. Why exactly is the first seven "sevens" separated from the next sixty-two (9:25–26)? Apparently, we are to think of that shorter period as having a kind of integrity of its own.

The actions of the seventieth week are the work of a destructive force. The unspecified "he" (9:27) confirms a covenant for one "seven," presumably the seventieth, but in the middle of it he cuts off sacrifice and offering. While it may be possible to construe the latter in some way as positive, the erection of "an abomination that causes desolation" (9:27) clearly is not. The period of the prophecy ends with the end of this disruptive person.

Application. Daniel turned to the writings of Jeremiah to hear the voice of God. God then spoke to him further through the agency of Gabriel, an angel. Where do we go to hear God speak today? The opening verses of the book of Hebrews (1:1–4) points us in the right direction. Jesus is God's fullest revelation of himself to us. He is God in human form. Where do we meet God in Jesus today? Most directly in the Bible.

DANIEL 10:1–11:1

Original Meaning

A Heavenly Vision (10:1–9). Daniel then describes for us, the readers, what he was doing at the time of the reception of the vision. For three weeks up to that moment, he has been in mourning. From the later words of the supernatural being we understand that this period of mourning was accompanied by prayer for understanding (10:12). He denies himself to gain a special hearing from the Lord. Daniel was in a state of prayerful turmoil.

Then, on the twenty-fourth day of the first month, Daniel receives a vision of a heavenly being that terrifies him. He has a human appearance, dressed like a priest in linen and wearing a belt of gold. His physical description looks more like a statue than an actual human being. His voice booms "like the sound of a multitude" (10:6b). Those around Daniel do not see the vision, but somehow they sense some great power because they immediately flee the scene and hide.

A Conversation with a Supernatural Being (10:10–11:1). The present section opens with supernatural ministrations (see also 10:16, 18). Daniel is a highly desired, precious man, coveted by God. With these words, Daniel receives courage enough to stand, though he is still trembling.

As the supernatural figure continues to speak with Daniel in 10:12, he again encourages the waning prophet. The supernatural speaker almost casually mentions the "prince of the Persian kingdom" (10:13), but questions immediately rise in our minds. Who is this "prince" who can resist a heavenly being? These verses give us a hint at the cosmic battle that parallels the earthly struggles of God's people. The "prince of the Persian kingdom" is a supernatural being who fights on behalf of that human kingdom.

The picture that emerges from Daniel 10:12–14 is that of a heavenly conflict. The speaker, who is an unnamed angelic power (if not God himself) and Michael fight on God's side. On the other side stands "the prince of the Persian kingdom" (10:13), who himself is powerful, but we are to understand that he is evil as well.

After describing the conflict that led to the delayed answer to Daniel's prayer, the heavenly messenger announces the substance of his message (10:14). Some believe that the language here suggests that the vision will at some point address the time just before the end of history as we know it.

Again, Daniel is overwhelmed by the vision and bows to the ground, unable to speak. Again, a supernatural being ministers to him by touching his lips so he can speak. Though this being is referred to with a phrase similar to that found in 7:13 ("one like a son of man"), we should not be too quick to identify the two, since the phrase could be used of any human-like appearance of God or angels. Thanks to the supernatural ministrations, the prophet announces that he is ready to receive the vision.

We have already pointed out that chapters 10–12 are a unit. In 10:20–11:1, the figure, probably an angel, gives a general overview of what is to come before outlining the details (the bulk of ch. 11). He is going to tell Daniel "what is written in the Book of Truth" (10:21). The fact that God has scripted history and that the rescue of his people is the punch line is cause for great optimism and celebration.

Application. In Daniel 10 the veil is pulled back slightly, and we see the divine realities behind human conflict. We are to fight, just as Israel was to fight. But also like Israel, we need to recognize that we will have victory only as we allow God to use us. We are not to be passive; we are to stand firm. But our strength to do this comes only as we put on the armor of God. Our ultimate enemy is Satan and his demonic powers. We should not underestimate our enemy's strength. To do so will lead to the temptation to fight our battles in our own strength, and our own strength will lead to our quick and easy defeat. When we realize that we have no power to ourselves to fight the battles of life, we are driven to Jesus, our Divine Warrior.

DANIEL 11:2–12:13

Original Meaning

Persia and Greece (11:2–4). It may seem odd that the angel begins by asserting that what he says is true. Would Daniel have expected anything else? Of course not, but the statement reminds us that we are to imagine Daniel in the sixth century hearing detailed events that cover the next few centuries. The specific events are so well documented that we will not footnote the connections we make between the prophecies and the actual events. Such may be found in any reputable history of the period.

We are not certain who the fourth king is, the one who "will be far richer than all the others" (11:2). To be frank, we cannot be sure how to construe the mind of the author at this stage. We know with certainty the identity of the "mighty king" of 11:3—none other than Alexander, whom we call "the Great." But as soon as he came on the scene, he disappeared from it. Power passed into the hands of Alexander's four leading generals. In the north, the rulers eventually became known as the Seleucid dynasty, and in the south, the Ptolemies ruled. The story of the third and second centuries BC is an account of how Judah passed back and forth between the Ptolemies and the Seleucids.

Struggles between the Kings of the North and the Kings of the South (11:5–20). The king of the south was Ptolemy I. The king of the north was Seleucus I. When Ptolemy and Seleucus defeated Antigonus in Gaza in 312 BC, the struggles between the various Diadochi were resolved. It was at this time that Syria-Palestine was assigned to Seleucus. However, his long-standing ally Ptolemy moved against his holdings and occupied Palestine. Seleucus and his successors never gave up claim to this area, however, so there was tension between the two.

In 11:7 we have an allusion to the fact that Ptolemy III came to the throne in 246 BC and waged war against Seleucus II, who had inherited the northern throne. In the process of the successful campaign, Ptolemy III stole the images of the gods and returned them to Egypt. However, his success was not long-lived for Seleucus II attacked the south and, though he did not take Egypt, recovered his land. The battles continued.

The sons of Seleucus II, alluded to in 11:10, are Seleucus III, who ruled from 227–223 BC, and one of the most famous of all the Seleucid rulers, Antiochus III the Great, who had a long reign from 223–187 BC. The story of Antiochus III the Great's reign continues through 11:19. The significance given to his reign likely has much to do with the fact that it was through his agency that Palestine finally shifted from Ptolomaic control to Seleucid control, thus setting the scene for the horrors of his son's reign.

Antiochus never tired of ambition, and in accordance with the prophecy of 11:18 started annexing parts of Asia Minor as well as some Greek islands. His son Seleucus IV Philopator (187–175 BC) succeeded him. Seleucus IV died under mysterious circumstances just as his younger brother was returning to his homeland. That younger brother's name was Antiochus IV, who got the nickname Epiphanes. The attention of the text turns now to this highly significant figure.

The Climactic King of the North (11:21–35). Antiochus received the news of his brother's death while in Athens. Antiochus rushed home to come to the aid of another nephew, who was also named Antiochus. He reached Antioch and ruled for the next five years as coregent with young Antiochus. In 170 BC the latter died, and Antiochus IV ruled alone.

For our purposes, it is only important to point out that Antiochus took increasingly aggressive steps against what God's faithful people would call proper worship. Most distressing was his stopping the daily sacrifice on the altar and placing in the temple an idolatrous object, probably a meteorite representing Baal Shamem (the Syrian version of Zeus). This object is called "the abomination that causes desolation" in the book of Daniel.

The people of God were split into two parties (11:32): those who supported Antiochus and his program of Hellenization of Judea and those who did not. Jason had earlier been removed from the high priesthood and replaced by a person named Menelaus, who was not even a member of the right family to be a priest. While Antiochus was waging his second Egyptian campaign, Jason, the deposed high priest, heard a rumor that Antiochus had been killed and so he moved against Menelaus. However, Antiochus, upset about the frustrations of his plans in Egypt, was far from dead. Thus, upon his return he had many massacred and sold as slaves.

The King Who Will Do as He Pleases (11:36–45). The issue is: Who is in mind in 11:36–45? Further complicating the issue is the question of whose "mind" are we referring to, the human author or the divine author? It is our understanding of the nature of revelation that the human author did not fully understand the implications of what he was speaking about. In other words, it is conceivable that Daniel thought he was still describing the climactic king of the north, but the divine intention may have been much broader.

There are several signals for a broader intention.

1. The language takes on bigger-than-life terms, language that lifts us above mundane, earthly activity.
2. We have the language of the "time of the end" (11:40), which, of course, was not achieved at the time of Antiochus Epiphanes, as horrible as his reign was.
3. Finally, we know that 11:40–45 simply do not work when applied to the life and death of Antiochus Epiphanes.

My own opinion is that Daniel is speaking from the sixth century and is looking into the future. It is from this perspective that I will interpret the verses. Biblical prophecy was often presented as one event, but as we witness its fulfillment, we see that it was really more complex than that.

The pride of this king will be enormous. He will exalt himself not only above every other human being but above the gods themselves. Interestingly, he is castigated not only for rejecting the true God, but also for disdain showed toward his own ancestral religion, perhaps mentioned because it reinforces the idea that he is a man of incredible pride.

Verse 40 begins with the phrase "at the time of the end," begging the question "the end of what?" At this stage of biblical revelation, we are getting some of the earliest glimpses of final things. The New Testament will provide much more on the final judgment. We should be extremely cautious in our treatment of these truths. Indeed, all I feel safe asserting is the following: Verses 40–45 look forward to a violent end to history. The next section goes on to talk about the other side of the coin, the great eschatological reward for those who are on God's side in the conflict.

The Salvation of God's People (12:1–4). The chapter division obscures the fact that 12:1–4 is integrally connected with what preceded at the end of chapter 11. Just as the ideal king of the Psalms was grounded in the Davidic reality but anticipated the messianic glory, so the wicked king of the end of Daniel is grounded in the Antiochene reality but anticipated the horror of the antichrist. Thus, when chapter 12 begins "at that time," we find ourselves again in that flux between earthly and heavenly reality. We deal with the definitive end of Antiochus's persecution of God's people as well as their final struggle.

We have been introduced to Michael already (see 10:13, 21) as God's warring angel. Verse 1 has military and judicial overtones. Distress is no sooner announced than the fact of deliverance is introduced. This deliverance is spelled out in more detail in 12:2. Of course, we must not develop a whole doctrine of the afterlife from this one verse, but we can confidently affirm that it celebrates the vindication that will come, both in the reward for the righteous and in the punishment for the wicked. The righteous will shine "like the brightness of the heavens" (12:3).

The best understanding of the "many will go here and there to increase knowledge" (12:4) is a negative one (cf. Amos 8:12), that is, people will scurry about desperately trying to find knowledge in their own power but will fail in their attempt.

Final Words (12:5–13). Daniel again finds himself in the position of overhearing a conversation between celestial beings. One of the angels on the bank addresses a climactic question to the other one, obviously the superior, hovering over the water (12:6). This question, though delivered by the angel, would be of dire interest to Daniel and his spiritual heirs.

Before answering, the hovering figure dressed in linen garments makes an unprecedented gesture (12:7): He lifts both hands toward heaven and swears "by him who lives forever" (12:7). The double-handed gesture, at least as far as we can tell, is a statement of emphasis and certainly evokes a solemn atmosphere around what is to follow.

This figure then delivers an enigmatic answer that reminds us of the answer given in 7:25 (12:7). But Daniel, like us, wants more information. Thus, he asks in 12:8, "My lord, what will the outcome of all this be?" The reply comes, not harshly but clearly, that now is not the time. The celestial being again emphasizes closed nature of the revelation (they are "rolled up" and "sealed"; 12:9).

Nonetheless, the being does expand his earlier comments on the period to follow (12:10). We are, I believe, to take them as words that describe the period from Daniel's time to the end. The wicked will continue to be wicked and not understand, while those who are wise will understand.

But the enigmas continue in 12:11–12. Two more time periods are specified. Both are impossible to pinpoint with real events or to correlate with each other. God alone knows—and that seems to be the point. God knows that there is an end that he has determined, but we cannot figure it out because we are not supposed to. Leave it to God, the angel says to Daniel, and through him he speaks to us. This is a fitting conclusion for Daniel and for the book. You may suffer now, but God has given you a glimpse of the coming glory.

Application. That God is sovereign is true in spite of the fact that when we open the morning's newspaper or listen to the news on the TV or the radio, we may have a different idea. Besides sports scores and weather, we hear the accounts of the latest scandals, wars, and local murders and other crimes. It is easy to be melodramatic and say that the streets of our cities are a war zone, but without resorting to hyperbole it is still obvious that social and moral chaos is evident all over the world. It is tempting to believe that when we step out into that world every morning, we are prey to incredible risk. Who knows whether, when we step out of our homes (or even before) in the morning, our time is up and we will find ourselves the victim of crime, disease, or accident?

The good news is that God is no less in control today than he was in antiquity. To hear some modern Christian leaders talk, we might not believe this is the case. With a note of panic in their voice, they tell us that things have gotten out of control in the seat of our government. If we do not act immediately (often by sending in a check), our whole society will be turned over to the devil!

I am not prepared to defend the moral quality of our government, nor do I want to argue to "let go and let God." God does expect us to work for righteousness' sake. What I object to is the shrill note, the panicky mood, the sense of loss of control. God *is* in control.

HOSEA

INTRODUCTION TO HOSEA

The book of Hosea says nothing about the prophet's early life, where he was born, what his occupation was before he was called to be a prophet, or his age when he became a prophet. It is impossible to trace the prophet's life history in any kind of clarity. The story simply looks forward to and then records the marriage and the birth of three children. These events highlight the love of Hosea and God for undeserving partners. The chapters do not provide a detailed biography of the prophet's troubled family life but draw out comparative theological lessons from his experience with Gomer and God's experience with Israel.

BOOK OUTLINE

I. Unfaithfulness in the Family of God (1:1–3:5)
   A. Hosea's and God's Broken Family (1:1–2:1)
   B. Confronting Unfaithful Wives (2:2–23)
   C. Restoration of Broken Families (3:1–5)
II. God's Lawsuit for No Knowledge of God (4:1–6:6)
   A. The Priests Do Not Know God (4:1–19)
   B. Judgment of War (5:1–14)
   C. Possibilities of Restoration for the Seeker (5:15–6:6)
III. God's Lawsuit for Lack of Steadfast Devotion to God (6:7–11:11)
   A. Israel's Unfaithfulness to the Covenant (6:7–7:16)
   B. Destruction, Captivity, and an End to Israel (8:1–9:17)
   C. Sin is the Reason for Israel's Fall (10:1–15)
   D. God's Love Provides Hope for Restoration (11:1–11)
IV. God's Lawsuit for Deceitfulness (11:12–14:9)
   A. Charges of Deceit (11:12–13:3)
   B. Punishment of Destruction (13:4–16)
   C. Restoration for the Repentant (14:1–9)

HOSEA 1:1–2:1

Original Meaning

God's and Hosea's Symbolic Marriage (1:1–3). The brief historical superscription places these events in the prosperous days of King Jeroboam II of Israel (1:1). God instructed Hosea to marry an "promiscuous woman" (1:2). In accepting God's plan for his life, Hosea submitted his wishes to God's will. He set himself up to feel and know a little bit about the bitterness of God's pain, as well as the depth of his love for undeserving people.

God's and Hosea's Symbolic Children (1:4–9). If Gomer represents the nation and its evil culture, the children represent the individual Israelites who later witness against their mother (2:2, 4). The first child was Hosea's, and God named him Jezreel. This child was to remind Hosea's audience of what had happened in the Valley of Jezreel, where king Jehu poured out the blood of innocent lives in order to solidify his political power (2 Kgs 9–10). This implies that a violent situation at the beginning of Jehu's reign will parallel a violent situation that will end the dynasty of Jehu.

The second child (Hos 1:6–7) was a girl named "Lo-Ruhamah." This child's name reveals that God will end his tender feelings of deep affection (like a mother's deep affection for the fruit of her womb) that are foundational to his covenant relationship with his people. They will no longer be rescued when they are in trouble, for God's compassionate mercy will no longer be extended to them.

God gives the third child the name "Lo-Ammi . . . not my people" (1:8–9). Now it is official; the covenant connection is broken. Israel's unfaithful adultery will lead to the dissolution of the covenant relationship. They will no longer be the children of God; their identity will change because they have committed themselves to another lover.

God's and Hosea's New Children (1:10–2:1). This section ends with a great paradoxical surprise and a reversal of the meaning of the children's names. The change is jarring and breathtakingly quick. At one moment God rejects his people, and in the next he accepts them back as his covenant partners. These promises should cause them to remember that the covenant relationship promises two possible destinies for Israel (curses and blessings), to realize that their harlotry will result in their judgment, and to understand that God's plans to bless his faithful people will happen after a period of judgment. His sermon may have encouraged some to recommit themselves in faith to God's future plans.

Application. Just as he was with the rebellious people of Israel and Gomer, God is not pleased with believers today who do not maintain a loyal covenant commitment to him. He still looks at sin as prostitution—a serious and disgusting breach of a love relationship. The theology of Hosea 1 is not limited to the negative implications of sin in a person's life, however. Because of God's grace, people can be assured that his eternal plans and promises will be accomplished.

HOSEA 2:2–23

Original Meaning

The Rejection of Adulterous Ways (2:2–5). The Lord instructs the children to "rebuke" (literally, "accuse, contend with"; 2:2a) their mother, but it is really God who is doing all the talking. The basis for God's claim is the "adulterous look" and "unfaithfulness" between his wife's breasts (2:2b). The reference to breasts suggests the sexual nature of the nation's unfaithfulness. God is trying to persuade Israel, his people, to remove the pagan culture of Canaan and its sexual fertility cult temples that dot the landscape.

This call for change is accompanied by a threat that God will bring shame on the nation and dry up the land so that there is no fertility (2:3). Since Baal was the god of rain and fertility, this would be a clear sign of his powerlessness and the extreme consequences of unfaithful prostitution with other gods.

The sins of the nation are present in the "children of adultery" (2:4) as well as in the "mother" (2:5). In fact, this unfaithfulness was a purposely planned pursuit of other lovers. Like a bold strutting prostitute hunting down customers, the people of Israel quickly invited and pursued the Baal fertility religion that promised to bring more fertility for their crops of grain, grapes, and oil (2:5).

God's Redemptive Plans for His Unfaithful People (2:6–15). Verse 6 begins a series of three "therefore" clauses (see also 2:9, 14) that describe what God plans to do to win back his unfaithful people. He will symbolically hedge his wife. This is for her own good and for the good of their relationship (cf. 3:3). It will protect her from straying off and returning to love other gods. God will frustrate Israel's pursuit of Baal by discrediting the idol's power (2:7). It will appear as if Baal is not listening or has no power.

The second "therefore" (2:9) reemphasizes how God will transform the people's thinking by reversing what he usually does. He will not allow the land to be fertile. God will strip her naked by stripping the land of any agricultural produce.

The third "therefore" (2:14) describes a dramatic new step in God's tactics to win back his wife, Israel. Using sexual terminology, God will "allure" (2:14) Israel back to himself. He will speak the tender love language that the people understand, for he deeply cares for this wife who rejected him. The resulting reversal of God's attitude toward his wife, Israel, and Israel's rejoicing (2:15) indicate that this meeting in the desert will bring about a renewal of the covenantal relationship of love between God and Israel.

The New Covenantal Relationship (2:16–23). The second half of this oracle is structured around three "in that day" promises, which refer to events at some unknown time in the future (2:16, 18, 21). This period will begin with the reaffirmation of Israel's covenant commitment to God (like repeating wedding vows), in which she will cease to confuse God with Baal. God will be "my husband," not "my master" (Heb. *baal*; also possible to translate "my Baal/my lord"); thus, they will no longer confuse the significant difference between God and Baal (2:16).

The second thing God will do "in that day" will be to reestablish a covenant relationship with his people and with nature (2:18–20). God's new covenant will remove the fear of death and war (cf. Isa 2:4; Mic 4:3) because peace and security will exist among all peoples.

The final "in that day" promises (Hos 2:21–23) describe the effects of this new relationship on life in this world. Once God's people know and love him (2:15, 20), he can respond to their love by restoring the natural bounty and beauty of the created universe. Thus, God in his magnificent power, not Baal, will reinvigorate the heavens above so that the sky will function as it was originally designed and give rain to the ground (2:21). But the sowing of God will not be limited to just planting crops; he will also "plant" his people in their promised land (2:23). God's beautiful plan for this world will be accomplished through his grace in spite of the present rebelliousness and unfaithfulness of his people.

Application. In an individualistic materialistic culture such as Western society today, we are constantly being tempted to depend on human abilities rather than on God. Moreover, it is easy to get sucked into the business worldview that places no reliance on God and substitutes for it an undue dependence on a job, the stock market, personal savings, or Social Security. Like Hosea, we must challenge our audiences to evaluate what their trust is based on. Do people actually see God as the final source of all economic blessing (Deut 8:17–18)? Or is prosperity just the result of fortunately being at the right place at the right time, of smart farming procedures with the latest chemicals and fertilizers, of great investment advice, or of having the right genes to produce a high IQ? A central theme of Hosea 2 is that God is the only source who can meet people's needs. Any attempt to replace his proper role is seen as a prostitution of loyalties.

HOSEA 3:1–5

Original Meaning. Hosea's love is demonstrated by his action of buying his wife. Some compare the price to the price of a slave, but we have no idea what a female slave cost in the time of Hosea. It is better to suppose that Hosea is simply paying off Gomer's debts. Gomer is now free to live with him for the foreseeable future (3:3).

This restoration is parallel to the restoration between God and Israel (3:4–5). Just as Hosea cut Gomer off from the men who led her into adultery, so God will remove the factors that have caused Israel to destroy her relationship with him. Then, "in the last days" (3:5), the covenant relationship between God and Israel will be restored. Both Hosea and God will love their wives and give them the blessings of their renewed covenant.

Application. *Showing love.* No one should ever question the availability of God's love. The question, rather, is this: Will people respond to God's love? Scripture assures us that God loves everyone in the whole world and does not want any to perish (2 Peter 3:9). Paul also reassures the church at Rome that nothing can separate them from God's love (Rom 8:38–39).

HOSEA 4:1–19

Original Meaning

God Has a Covenant Lawsuit against His People (4:1–3). This breakdown of covenant relationship results in the cursing of Israel's land, just as the covenant predicted. The sign of this curse is the disappearance of vegetation, animals, birds, and even the fish. Hosea does not say whether this will happen through a drought, a military invasion, or a combination of these factors. What is important is that morality has an effect on the economic and political status of the nation. God has inserted into the fabric of covenantal theology a reciprocal relationship between loving or obeying God and blessing the land, and between unfaithfulness and cursing the land. Hosea warns that all who live on the land will feel the consequences of their sins.

Accusations against the Priests (4:4–10). In 4:4a some interpreters suggest that a person in Hosea's audience objects to his bold attempt to present this case against Israel in 4:1–3. It is better (following NIV) to see all of this verse as Hosea's report of what God has said. The prophet is encouraging the people to listen to what God has to say and not dispute his charges. The evidence will show that the priests, the spiritual leaders of the community, are guilty.

The prophets (4:5) and even the mothers and children of the priests will suffer under God's punishment. This comes about because the priests have destroyed the people by failing to instruct the people concerning God's divine revelation in the Torah. How can they ever know God's character or ways if the priest never explains the "Bible" of that day? If the truth were told, the priests actually enjoy sinning and relish their evil lifestyle (4:8). The priests have even gotten involved with the drinking and prostitution going on at these temples.

Accusations of Worthless Worship (4:11–14). The second charge explains how ignoring God's revelation is affecting the worship celebrations of the people. What is going on at the temples is astonishing: prostitution, drunkenness, idol worship, divination, and all the perversions that go with them. These practices lead people astray into unfaithful acts against God (4:12). Without proper teaching from Israel's priests, the population of Israel is filled with the "spirit of prostitution" (4:12) and blindly led away into a sensuous and selfish worldview that promotes debauchery rather than godliness.

This paragraph ends with God's decision not to cast the primary blame on the young women who are involved or who submit themselves to this sexual cultic activity at the Baal temples (4:14). Instead, God will punish the men (probably older) who set up, promote, and probably demand this perverse sexual activity.

Israel Is Hopeless (4:15–19). God warns the Israelites not to influence the people of Judah with this unfaithful behavior of prostitution. The people think God and Baal are the same divine being. Because of these confusions, it is almost impossible for the stubborn people of Israel to change (4:16).

When people are this hardened, about all one can do is to leave them alone (4:17b) and let them wallow in their shameful ways (4:18b). They will wake up soon and realize the shamefulness of what they are doing. They have given themselves over to such a depraved way of thinking that there is not much Hosea or God can do.

Application. The blame for Israel's spiritual decline is put at the feet of her spiritual leaders. It is always dangerous to oversimplify the complexities of life, but the failure of spiritual leadership is one of the top reasons why people in the church fail to acknowledge God and to be faithful and true to him.

HOSEA 5:1–14

Original Meaning

Leaders Are Accountable for Israel's Promiscuity (5:1–7). Hosea begins the verdict by calling the priests and political leaders to hear what the judge will say about their leadership. The verdict in 5:1 ("judgment") comes for several reasons. The first is related to failures at Mizpah, Tabor, and probably Shittim. Hunting images suggest an atmosphere of deception and violence as individuals or groups try to control the political scene. Another reason for judgment is the religious prostitution the priests have encouraged (5:3). A third problem that Hosea raises is the nation's "arrogance" (5:5). The people selfishly refuse to admit anything is wrong. A final stumbling block to recovery is God's abandonment of the people (5:6). Although some may bring a sacrifice to a temple to worship, God will not be there.

Warnings about the Impending War (5:8–11). With God's verdict legitimated (5:1–7), a terrorizing announcement of war is proclaimed by trumpet blasts around the countryside. This warning of Israel is interrupted by a condemnation of Judah because she has moved certain boundary stones that mark the border between Judah and Israel (5:10a). He reveals that God will pour out his wrath on Judah for their sins and destroy their land like a flood.

Fearful Images of God (5:12–14). Hosea ends this section with several astonishing metaphors of God's future dealings with Israel and Judah. God, their loving covenant partner, will be like "pus" (author's translation; NIV "moth") in an open wound and a "rot" to these people (5:12). These daring comparisons suggest that Israel and Judah will be like an injured soldier whose wounds are festering with terrible infection. The second image pictures God as a destructive lion (5:14). He will tear his prey to pieces and carry off what remains, and no one will be able to stop him.

Application. When God is excluded from the solution process, he may actually exacerbate the problem rather than heal the situation. In fact, what people sometimes interpret as an earthly problem among humans may actually be a divine fight in which God himself is against us. The ultimate resolution to this kind of problem is to reject sin, seek God, and humbly plead for restoration.

HOSEA 5:15–6:6

Original Meaning

Seek to Know God (5:15–6:3). In the past God's people ignored his revelation and confused him with Baal, but in the future they will earnestly "seek my face" (5:15). The confession of 6:1–3 is the prophet's intercessory confession. He hopes his audience will accept this confession as their own decision to seek God. Hosea is confident God will respond quickly to the people's turning to God—in two to three days (6:2). Hosea motivates any doubters with the promise of the reliability of God (6:3).

God's Frustration with Israel's Seeking of God (6:4–6). God's response to Hosea's invitation begins with a lament of disappointment. God's dissatisfaction with the devotion of his people is based on the fleeting nature of their covenant love for him (6:4b). Like dew, it disappears as quickly as a vapor. They need to know God by having a living relationship with him. Their worship at their temples does not satisfy the Lord because he wants them to love him, fear him, worship only him, serve him, and obey him (Deut 10:12). Going through the religious motions will not cut it with God.

Application. Revival is not an optional course of action for a church. It needs to be a vital part of every church calendar and a prayer concern of every believer. Revival is about living for God and glorifying his name. It encourages people to be restored from a cold, deadened condition to a living state of joy and peace. Spiritual leaders in the church need to encourage people to return to God, to look to him for restoration, and to desire to live in his marvelous presence. If a spiritual leader rejects the path of revival, the church will die.

HOSEA 6:7–7:16

Original Meaning

The Sins of the Priests (6:7–10). The priests' violent action of shedding blood in some kind of ambush (6:9) on the road to Shechem is characterized as a betrayal that violates the agreement between God and Israel. A second sin that implicates the spiritual leadership of the priests is the cultic prostitution that fills the land. God sees this "horrible thing" (6:10). It is not hidden from his sight, and he will not overlook it.

Restoration Is Impossible Because of Sin (6:11–7:2). Just as Israel's sins will be exposed when God comes to heal his people (7:1), so Judah's judgment will be necessary when God comes to restore his people to their covenant relationship (6:11). The focus is on the sinfulness of the people, which necessitates judgment. In 7:1b–2 Hosea lists some of the sins that God will expose. Most surprising is the utter callousness of the people toward these sinful acts.

Political Corruption in Government (7:3–7). At first the people referred to here appear to be friends of the royal court (the king and his princes) because they delight the king by joining him in all kinds of evil deeds. Hosea describes these rulers as "adulterers" (7:4), a word that refers to someone who is unfaithful to another person. Like a hot oven these people burn in their passion for political power. Instead of protecting the king, they are in on the plot.

Political Dependence on Alliances (7:8–12). Instead of depending on God to protect them and guide their political decisions, the new kings consolidate their power by forming alliances with other nations (7:8). These alliances are hurting the nation because they require payment of heavy tribute and encourage cultural and religious compromises to keep the peace with the Assyrians. This syncretistic trend drains the nation of its financial resources, its independence, and its moral strength (7:9). The surprising thing is that the people do not see how this creeping compromising is gradually undermining their identity. These are selfish acts of pride and self-determination that are not based on God's direction (7:10). Like a foolish dove, Israel's foreign policy flips and flops back and forth without consistency or any lasting commitment (7:11). God responds (7:12) by capturing these senseless birds in his net.

God Laments Israel's Coming Destruction (7:13–16). The reactions of God's people to his great deeds of power and grace are lamentable. They have rebelled against his authority, strayed from his instruction, and lied about their love and loyalty to him (7:13). They do not cry out to God from a heart of love, but when they worship and bring their sacrifices to the temple, they worship other gods, using pagan methods (7:14). All their deception will catch up with them, and then their former allies will laugh and "ridicule" them (7:16). Israel will get what it deserves from God and receive no sympathy from its former political partners.

Application. God still hates sin, and the result of sin is still death. Evangelists must faithfully persuade their secular friends and neighbors that after death there will be a court of justice, where all people must give an account of their deeds (Rom 14:10–12). The great hope for redemption from the penalty for sin has been provided through the death of Jesus Christ.

HOSEA 8:1–9:17

Original Meaning

The Destruction of Gods and Government (8:1–14). The theme of destruction in 8:1–3 is implicit in Hosea's charge to sound the trumpet to warn the people about an approaching military threat. The people have broken their covenant relationship with God by rebelling against his instructions in the torah (8:1b). These covenant stipulations were supposed to guide the people so that they would know the meaning of loving God with all their hearts. The rebellion against these instructions (the "good" thing mentioned in 8:3) is thus a willful rejection of the authority of God and a repudiation of the unique relationship that has set them apart from all the other nations of the world.

Verses 4–6 describe Israel's rebellion against God in the area of politics and worship. Hosea reminds his audience that they have removed one king and appointed another without asking God for direction or identifying his chosen leader (see 2 Kgs 15). The people have also made idols of gold and silver, particularly the golden calves at Dan and Bethel (Hos 8:5–6; see 1 Kgs 12). God's "anger burns against them" (Hos 8:5) because these bull images were quickly confused with the Canaanite god Baal, thus syncretizing perverse pagan ideas with the pure revelation of God revealed in the Torah. Therefore, God rejects this calf and will have it cut to pieces (8:4b, 6b).

In 8:7–10 Hosea laments because Israel's sowing of friendly alliances with other nations will result in reaping the whirlwind of destruction. This has happened because the nation willingly went to sell herself like a prostitute (8:9–10) through her alliance with the Assyrians.

Verses 11–14 draw a logical connection between God's condemnation of Israel for giving unacceptable sacrifices and her rejection of God's instructions in the Torah. The people's "sacrifices" (8:13) on the many pagan altars around the nation have brought greater sinning instead of expiation of sin and divine pleasure (8:11). Therefore, in the near future God will demonstrate his power and destroy these proud cities and the homes in them.

Captivity Will Bring an End to Israel's Festivals (9:1–9). Hosea argues that the people should not be conducting their feasts like the pagans in other nations (9:1). Apparently, this festival changed over the years into a pagan celebration by adding activities common in Baal festivals, such as sacred prostitution at their threshing floors. In response, God will reverse their false theology and remove the fertility of the land, thus proving that Baalism does not work (9:2); he will also reverse the people's security by exiling them from God's holy land and putting them in some other countries (Egypt and Assyria). In these pagan countries the Israelites will be unable to give to God their Levitical sacrifices (Lev 1–5; 23:13; Num 15:1–10), so it will be impossible to please him.

In a final summary statement Hosea declares that the days of final reckoning and divine vengeance are close at hand (9:7). This statement draws a strong reaction from Hosea's audience. Since they do not see their own action as sinful, Hosea is branded a radical reactionary. But Hosea sees himself differently. He speaks for God, for God is with him, and his Spirit inspires him with the words he speaks. He is God's "watchman" (9:8), who warns the people of approaching danger to help them avoid destruction.

Bereavement for Israel's Sins (9:10–17). The story of Israel starts with positive images of God's joy and excitement when he first entered into a covenant relationship with them. This experience compares to finding sweet, juicy grapes in a hot and dry desert, or to enjoying the first fruit from a fig tree. But this joy was abruptly turned into something shameful when the people worshiped an idol at Baal Peor (9:10b; see Num 25:1–5). In these sins the people set themselves apart to an idol instead of God—presumably a reference to the vile sexual rituals that some Israelites participated in at Baal Peor (Num 25:6–8).

God's curse on the nation for these detestable acts is described in 9:11–13. These warnings remind us of the covenant curses that predict the people will be bereaved and not have any children (Deut 28:18, 41). Hosea interrupts this dire prediction of slaughter with a brief prayer in 9:14. Hosea is not pleading for mercy or trying to keep back God's wrath. He is sorrowfully agreeing with God's earlier statements: God should remove the fertility of the nation and curse their offspring (see Deut 28:4, 11).

The final subparagraph (Hos 9:15–17) recalls Israel's sins at Gilgal. Hosea does not mention a specific sin at this city near the banks of the Jordan River, but there was a pagan temple there, and at this place Israel's first king was inaugurated (1 Sam 11:15). God hated the present political system that sprang from this initial event and the worship practices that spread from Gilgal to infect the whole nation. As a result, he will drive them out of his land; he will love them no longer because there is no one to lead the people back to God.

Once again Hosea interrupts this prediction of judgment with a prayer (9:17) that agrees with God's conclusion. God should reject them as they have rejected God. This truly is a depressing ending—without hope, without divine love, and without a prophet to intercede.

Application. If people do not please God with their worship and political leaders do not allow God to guide their decisions, how can God bless them with prosperity and children? Eventually these nations will end up like Israel. God will hate them because of their sinful deeds, no longer love them because of their rebellious leaders (9:15), and reject them because they have rejected him. If people do not put pleasing God as a priority, God will not be pleased with them.

HOSEA 10:1–15

Original Meaning

Idols and Altars Will Be Destroyed (10:1–8). Israel is like a destroyed vine because she has selfishly used its fruit for herself. God will hold the people accountable, take away their abundance, and demolish the altars and sacred pillars (10:2). One should not confuse God with an idol or give an idol credit for God's rich blessings.

One way of understanding the quotation in 10:3 is that the people reject God as their divine king and sovereign ruler. They do not fear or call on him for help because they do not think he can do anything to change their situation. Instead of humbly confessing their failure to fear God, the people have made false promises and oaths to God and are unfaithful to their covenant with him (10:4).

Verse 5 describes the people's deep commitment to the golden calf at Bethel. The people will be ashamed and disgraced because the true colors of their ugly wooden idol will finally be known. They have been fools to trust it. When the captive people finally see the impotence of Baal and the uselessness of faith in this idol, they will want to die (10:8b).

A Devastating War Because of Wickedness (10:9–15). Hosea is removing any false hopes his audience may have. They will be chastened through military defeat by a much stronger army (the Assyrians) and put in bonds to go into captivity for two sins (10:10). Perhaps Hosea is referring to the two calves at Dan and Bethel, to the two times the people sinned at Gibeah, or to idol worship and trust in their army; these, however, are only educated guesses from the context.

Hosea quickly changes metaphors in 10:11 to draw on his audience's understanding of agriculture. He compares Israel to a good heifer, who was well trained and a hard worker at threshing time. God was impressed with this animal and wanted to make it his own (symbolic of his having a covenant relationship with the people). So, he put his willing heifer to work plowing for him—an analogy that suggests God's election of his people to do his service. Unfortunately, Israel instead planted unrighteous seeds, and they will now reap a harvest of evil (10:13), just what they deserve.

Because of Israel's trust in their army, God will destroy their military establishment and the fortifications that are designed to protect the army from attackers (10:14). The historical battle when Shalman devastated Beth Arbel is unrecorded elsewhere in history, though the heartless brutality and gross inhumanity of this battle will be replayed when God brings an enemy on the most evil city of Bethel, where its pagan temple with the golden calf dwells (10:15). God will use this enemy to completely destroy them.

Application. What kind of deceptions or misunderstandings are present in churches today? The most serious reified self-deceptions are theological. This happens when people give absolute divine authority and status to humanly created perceptions that do not fully represent what God has said or what he desires. To reify one cultural means of expressing praise to God into a universal, unchangeable norm is an erroneous approach to understanding the spirit of true worship.

HOSEA 11:1–11

Original Meaning

God's Love for His Rebellious Son (11:1–4). God demonstrated this love supremely in his deliverance of a great multitude from Egypt. This experience established the father-son relationship and gave the Israelites a unique identity as "my son" (11:1). Verse 2 emphasizes how quickly the nation fell into apostasy. But like a loving parent, God did not immediately give up on his son. The metaphors in 11:4 of cords, ropes, and yoke suggest aspects of control. But by defining these as "cords of human kindness, with ties of love" (11:4), one gets a picture of gentle leading rather than forced labor. The final line in 11:4 describes God's tender care.

No Repentance Leads to Punishment (11:5–7). One would expect that a people receiving this kind of love and care would naturally follow God. Instead, Israel will end up losing their land and going back in bondage (11:5). The Israelites refuse to repent (11:5b) and turn back to the worship of God alone; instead, they stubbornly and consistently turn away from following him (11:7a). Eventually his patience will run out and his rebellious children must be judged. Although they may cry out for mercy, like a child about to receive a spanking, God's judgment will fall on Israel.

God's Lamenting Compassion for Israel (11:8–9). God is not a cold computer or a philosophical abstract concept. He has an intimate relationship of commitment that involves him with his people's lives in more than a legal or contractual way. The husband-wife or father-son relationships help humans understand in an oblique way the personal caring involvement that a holy, mysterious God has with his people. In compassion God declares that he cannot totally give up on his people; he cannot totally annihilate Israel as he did Zeboiim and Admah.

God's Restoration Promise (11:10–11). At some point in the future God will act like a lion and roar, calling his people to follow him and to return from the land of their captivity. At that time, they will come back to their land in a new exodus and dwell in their own homes. God's love will accomplish his plan; human sinfulness will not triumph over his compassion. This is his promise.

Application. If evangelism is a sign that believers have God's love in them and its transformational power compels them to tell others, one must wonder why there is such a small amount of the love of God exhibited in the life of so many church members (in evangelism). Is it fair to say that a person who does not evangelize has never experienced the glories of God's love?

HOSEA 11:12–13:3

Original Meaning

God's Charge of Deceit (11:12–12:2). Israel is trying to find help from gods who cannot fulfill her desires. By going after something that is illusive and without substance, she shows her stupidity and the uselessness of her quest. Because of these deceptive actions, God is bringing another charge in his lawsuit (12:2; cf. 4:1).

Warning to Israel Not to Be like Deceptive Jacob (12:3–6). Hosea begins his case by going back in history to the story of Jacob, the founder of the nation of Israel. Hosea tries to persuade his audience to "return to your God" (12:6) as Jacob finally did, to have steadfast covenantal love for God, to follow the just practices outlined in the covenant stipulations in the Torah, and to earnestly wait for God in difficult times.

Forgetfulness by Israel's Merchants about God's Gifts to Them (12:7–10). Those in the upper class boast about their illegally gained wealth (12:8). Now God is going to bring an anti-exodus event and return them to the desert existence. Their wealth will not protect them from God's conclusion that they are guilty.

Israel's Choice of Deception Instead of God (12:11–14). Apparently, the wickedness of Gilead was infamous (see 6:8) and Gilgal was a well-known place where people worshiped other gods (see 4:15; 9:15). As punishment Gilead will be reduced to a "worthless" thing (12:11). The stones on the altars at Gilgal will look like unorganized piles of rocks on a plowed field rather than a sacred altar for worship.

Through Jacob's own efforts he managed to survive Esau's hatred and worked for a wife, but the nation of Israel was freed from working as slaves by God's grace through Moses. The implication is that Hosea's audience should not follow the patterns of Jacob (self-effort and deception) but should allow God to care for them and bring them freedom through another prophet (Hosea).

Israel's Deceptive Worship (13:1–3). The contrasts between Israel's past (13:1), present (13:2), and future (13:3) continue to provide additional evidence of the nation's guilt and deception. The positive past depicts a time when Israel was a powerful nation. Although Israel had many things going for her at the time of Jeroboam II, the people turned away from God. This led to the death of the nation rather than to fertility and life as Baalism promised. The consequence (13:3) of this deceptive idolatry is stated in another verdict: Israel will disappear!

Application. One way church members can ensure a proper relationship with God and avoid his condemnation is never to forget what God has done for them. Values and beliefs are cemented in the minds of people by repeatedly reemphasizing them. Transformation comes when people's hearts are so touched by the past work of Christ that they are willing to take up their cross and follow him (Matt 16:24).

HOSEA 13:4–16

Original Meaning

God's Past Caring Will Turn to Tearing (13:4–8). God's care is defined (13:4–6a) by who he is and by the relationships he has established through his great acts in salvation history. He is the covenant-making God, who cared enough to deliver his people from Egyptian slavery. A second demonstration of God's care was his provision for the nation while they were traveling for forty years in the hot and dry desert of Sinai (13:5). If God had not cared, they would not have survived. The third stage in God's relationship with his people was his abundant blessing of them in the promised land (13:6a). This brief historical background sets the stage for the verdict of the lawsuit in the rest of this chapter. God will now turn against his people and tear them apart (13:7–8).

Since Israel Rejects God's Leadership, God Rejects Israel's Leaders (13:9–11). There is no mystery about God's plan, no hidden agenda that the people cannot figure out. They know what God desires, but they reject him. Verses 10–11 seem almost as a taunting explanation of where the nation went wrong. They trusted in human leaders instead of God.

Israel Will Die, But Death Will Not Overpower God's Plan (13:12–16). The final part of the verdict that began in 13:7 emphasizes the nation's death, using the analogy of abnormal childbirth, drought, and violent death in military conflicts (13:13, 15, 16b). In the middle of this announcement of judgment comes a caveat similar to 6:4 and 11:8–9. God is overcome with love and refuses to totally destroy his people. Hosea 13:14 seems to be a bold refusal on God's part to completely reject his people. This taunt of death is based on his redemptive power to overcome the curse of death (13:14a).

The final clause in 13:14, "I will have no compassion," abruptly returns to the theme of judgment on Israel. How can God say they will die (13:12–13), then they will not die (13:14a-b), and then he will have no compassion on them and they will die (13:14c–16)? Hosea is not deceiving the people in 13:14 by telling them that God will not judge them. No, God will bring death on the nation soon, but death will not have final victory over God or his plans. In the midst of or after this judgment, he will ransom some from the power of death. That eschatological group will again be called the people of God.

Application. Through his provision of salvation and forgiveness of sins, the sting of death is removed and eternal life with God is possible. This is just one more example of God's care. In light of God's past, present, and future care for us, how should we act today? Can we forget what God has done and proudly act as if we can take care of things ourselves?

HOSEA 14:1–9

Original Meaning

A Call to Repentance (14:1–3). This simple but profound prayer asks for forgiveness, then openly and honestly admits the failures that broke fellowship with God. The first step in renewing any relationship is a humble admission of one's mistakes.

God's Promise of Restoration (14:4–8). Hosea clearly reveals how God will respond when people turn to him and worship only him: He will heal their sinful waywardness (14:4). People need a miraculous act of God's healing grace to enable them to respond to his gifts of restoration. This love is a free expression of divine commitment and deep emotional care for undeserving people.

The fruitfulness of the nation is compared to a bountiful grain field, a blossoming grapevine, and the famous wine from Lebanon (14:7). These are all pictures of God's rich blessing. God will lovingly give his returning people the covenant blessings he promised long ago. The nation will serve God, and he will bless them.

Exhortation to Choose Wisely (14:9). If you want to be considered an upright or "righteous" person in God's eyes, you must follow what he has said. If, however, you reject what God has said or refuse to apply his word, you will "stumble" and be ruined. You cannot be wise and continue to refuse to submit to God's will.

Application. Preaching repentance is necessary since there is no other way to begin a relationship with God. Repentance is not just a negative theme of rejecting or "turning from"; it also has a positive theme of "turning toward." If the abundance, joy, and hope of Hosea's presentation of repentance are contrasted with the hopelessness of the status quo, suddenly repentance becomes a positive change that has appeal. If God calls people to repent and follow him, then repentance must be preached today. It is his way of entering a relationship with people.

JOEL

INTRODUCTION TO JOEL

The prophecies of Joel are directed toward Judah and Jerusalem. An unidentified army threatens Judah (2:1–11), while other peoples are explicitly identified in 3:4–8, raising the prophecies onto the world stage. There is no direct evidence from the book itself to determine its historical setting conclusively, though circumstantial evidence has been mined for assistance.

BOOK OUTLINE

I. Heading and Warnings to Judah (1:1–20)
II. Invasion of a Locust Army (2:1–11)
III. Turn Back to Me! (2:12–17)
IV. Yahweh Responds (2:18–32)
V. Judah's Enemies Judged (3:1–12)
VI. The Day of the Lord for Nations and God's People (3:13–21)

JOEL 1:1–20

Original Meaning

Heading (1:1). Joel's prophecies are headed by two elements in addition to his name. First is the designation "the word of the LORD." The Hebrew term lying behind "the LORD" is *yhwh*, the personal name of Israel's God. Joel's father is Pethuel. His name means "a youth of/belonging to El," which reflects his parents' understanding of the divine source of offspring.

Warnings to Judah (1:2–14). *To the people (1:2–4).* The message starts with rhetorical questions, which draw the audience into the message from the beginning, seeking a response rather than asking for actual information. Verse 3 moves from two generations past (self and ancestors), who have not seen such a thing, to four generations yet to come (self, children, their children, and future generations), who are to be told of it. Verse 4 finally reveals the subject of the message, the elusive "it": the devastation resulting from swarms of locusts. Their arrival always means devastation and despair.

Sound the alarm (1:5–14). The second audience must lament for the wine that is newly pressed at this time of devastation. Not only are Israel's sustaining sources of nutrients, her grain foods and drink such as wine, devoured, the latter also serves to lessen the hardships of daily life.

In 1:10 the grounds for the deprivation and mourning are established: Three staples of life—grain, wine, and oil—fail from earth and field. Devastation comes to the cultivated field as it does to its grain, the source of flour for daily. Food and drink, which make the heart glad, by their absence now remove that gladness.

Lament (1:15–20). The cry begins in 1:15 with an interjection of woe, "alas," and concerns the proximity of "the day of the LORD" (1:15), a statement familiar from other prophecies. Some anticipate the day as positive. Joel quickly corrects their misconception. His own people realize that judgment curses face them right before their very own eyes.

Both "food" and "joy and gladness" (1:16) are denied to the temple. With an exclamation of wonder, the writer notes in 1:18 that the domesticated animals, important for Israelite household and cultic economy, also feel the negative effects.

Finally (1:19–20), the writer turns to Yahweh himself, to whom he now calls. The destruction now takes a different slant, comparing voracious locusts with all-consuming fire and flame. This may be yet another metaphor for the all-consuming locust swarms, or an indication that all of nature works together at one time against these poor folks, hitting them either simultaneously or sequentially with locust, drought, and fire. The latter is a natural consequence of the death and desiccation caused by the former, leaving tinder-dry remains, vulnerable to the first spark.

Application. While it does no good to provide pious platitudes of hope to those heading for destruction unless they alter their path, it is also unhelpful to present unmitigated woe to those defeated and beaten down. Great prophets like Joel, Jonah, and Jesus read the times and spoke elements of God's truth relevant to those times. Does our message today need to look beyond self-actualization and the abundant life, which are indeed provided by God, to the message that our lifestyle as Christians in many areas puts our relationship with God in question? When do we mix warning with weal?

JOEL 2:1–11

Original Meaning

A Warning Concerning the Day (2:1–2a). A new section commences with the speaker turning from addressing Yahweh to Yahweh addressing the people (2:1). The section begins with an urgent series of commands. The place where the alarm is raised is called "Zion" and "my holy hill" (2:1). The reason for this alarm is again "the day of the LORD" (2:1).

Expansion on the Nature of the Day (2:2b–11). Joel now expands on the nature of this day. It is like a "mighty army" (2:2b). The encroacher pursues a scorched-earth policy. Previously there was land "like the garden of Eden" (2:3), a place of beauty, fruitful and luxuriant. After the marauders' passing, it is as lifeless as a desert.

Verses 4–5 provide different comparisons of the locust horde. Like runners in their lanes, each soldier moves straight ahead, "through" (2:8) rather than around obstacles. Verse 9 describes the actual progression of events for the marauding forces: ranging around the city, attacking the walls, and climbing up to and into the house windows. In 2:10–11, the elements of the universe are in turmoil. Even the heavenly bodies—the sun, moon, and stars—lose their light as God removes his favor from his wayward people.

The mounting litany reaches its climax in 2:11. The focus moves from humans (attacker and attacked) to the earth and heavens, and now specifically to Yahweh, Israel's own covenant God. The locust swarm is not just some freak of nature, a random storm that, though devastating, is entirely natural. It is rather a force brought and controlled by God himself. The "day of the LORD" (2:11) is not just approaching; it is already here, and it is overwhelmingly unbearable.

Application. While this passage describes a bleak and chilling picture, it is bracketed by rays of hope—acknowledgment that God hears and that he can turn back to them in grace if they respond to him in an appropriate way. Though the darkness is rising, it will be overcome by the light. In reality, that light has already dawned (e.g., Isa 9:2; Matt 4:16).

JOEL 2:12–17

Original Meaning. When Yahweh next speaks, it is not in warnings of judgment but in tones of grace. The appropriate response to the devastation brought by God is repentance (2:12). It must be total, accompanied not only by the traditional outward signs of grief, but also with a true, inner reflection of sorrow ("with all your heart," 2:12).

Repentance is to be based on who God is, not on anything of the one who repents. The whole section expresses characteristics of God, not only a judge but also someone who wishes to temper his judgment, if the correct response is forthcoming. It is theologically vital to note the hesitancy, however, "Who knows?" (2:14). God is by no means obligated to show compassion and forgiveness.

After establishing that there is reason to hope for God's gracious restoration, the people are called to assemble for "sacred" (2:15) purposes. The priests request that God's own be spared from becoming an international "byword" (2:17) or word of contempt. In the case of Israel, their claim to be God's people and inheritance would become a lie if they were destroyed.

Rather than thinking that the disaster that befell them is only a fluke of nature, the people realize that it is from God. While God is instigator, he also desires to restore the relationship and actually commands his people to approach him for restoration. All society has suffered; now all must turn to the Lord for aid. Their attention is now directed away from the calamities of the past and toward the possibility of restoration through God's response in the future to their previous laments.

Application. In an experience of personal crisis, there seems to be much more practical assurance of hope in knowing that I am in the hands of a God who loves me and cares for every aspect of my life than in knowing that I have to do with a God who is emotionless and dispassionate

JOEL 2:18–32

Original Meaning

Yahweh's First Response (2:18–20). Verse 18 is a literary pivot in the book. Up to now, the problem has been presented and the response of the people has been called for. Now God's response unfolds. The locust army will be driven away from the land.

People, Rejoice! (2:21–24). The verbs in 2:21–22 revert to imperative-like forms in a call to praise, not directed only to people who suffered but also to inanimate creation and dumb beasts, who are also directly affected. Those previously summoned to fear, weep, and pray in Zion now join the rest of creation in celebration. The basis of their rejoicing is God himself and secondarily his actions on their behalf.

The final stage of restoration follows (2:24). After the locusts are expelled and the trees start to bear because the rains have returned, other crops are prepared for consumption and storing away. The locusts previously destroyed all of these, but God makes them good in abundance.

Yahweh's Second Response (2:25–27). This is a theological pivot point of the book, the truth that provides the nation with the psychological boost they need to overcome their extreme distress: Yahweh exists, Yahweh is present with them, and Yahweh, and no natural phenomenon of force, has divine power over them.

Yahweh's Third Response (2:28–32). The recipients of the outpouring are clear from the text: "all people" (literally, "flesh"; 2:28). Moses's prayer that all might be prophets (Num 11:29) is fulfilled at this time. This all happens "in those days" (cf. Joel 2:29b; 3:1). Sometimes this phrase describes events both predicted from the viewpoint of the writer but then fulfilled within the period of the Old Testament. Sometimes, however, there are elements that are not ever fulfilled in this way, such as the predicted restoration of both Judah and Israel and a turning by all nations to Israel and Jerusalem as the only source for help and guidance from God, neither of which have happened up to this day. There can be, therefore, an eschatological implication with this phrase, referring to a much later Pentecost (Acts 2:1–21) and beyond (Rev 8:7).

Displays in the astral ("the heavens") and terrestrial ("the earth") spheres accompany the Spirit's outpouring (2:30). All of these phenomena are harbingers of the "day of the LORD," which this time is not described by its proximity but by its character; it is "great" (2:31). Relief is not automatic, however, but must be requested. Calling on God's name (2:32) means invoking him, praying for his help, and even expressing allegiance and belonging to him. Unfortunately, there are casualties, since those making the request of God are "among the survivors" (2:32), a synonym of those delivered earlier in the verse. This implies that there are also some who have perished.

Application. God's jealousy is to shower his people with all good blessings, wanting to raise them to the heights rather than keeping them low and impoverished. He desires all of their allegiance and love to be directed toward him, since it is finite and should not be squandered on another deity. His infinite blessing, however, is completely available to those who so worship him.

JOEL 3:1–12

Original Meaning. Still looking to the future, God directs his attention away from his own people, as he has been doing, to speak judgment and restoration on the nations. The entire passage is bracketed as a unit by mention of judgment in the Valley of Jehoshaphat. God's people have been subject to great loss through natural phenomena as well as at the hand of her neighbors. Now those nations in general will suffer at the hand of God.

Wrongs Committed (3:1–8). The nature of the evil of these nations is scattering God's people "among the nations" (3:2). They misuse both male and female children as the means of barter, treating them like foreign chattel slaves by selling them. They give or sell them in exchange for the means of debauchery, prostitutes, or wine. Verses 5–6 detail some of the wrongs for which the nations are to be repaid. The slave traders receive the same treatment they inflicted on Judah: They too will be sold.

You Nations! (3:9–12). Verse 11 shows an impatient prophet who is almost saying, "Enough talk, God. Get moving!" Yahweh's directions resume in 3:12. He repeats his call for the arousal and ascent of the surrounding nations to the same valley to which he promised they would be gathered in 3:2. Over this entire procedure, Yahweh sits as a mighty, enthroned king or judge.

Application. In 1999, the CIA estimated that between 45,000 and 50,000 women and children are trafficked into the United States each year. Most of these women and children are used within the sex industry, for prostitution and/or pornography. Christians also make use of both of these, especially through internet viewing or pornography. There are members of our churches who are supporting this slave trade through their participation, and it must be addressed. Each of us needs to come to a position on this and many other vital ethical issues, since theology cannot stay just in our heads but must also live through out hearts in our hands.

JOEL 3:13–21

Original Meaning

The Valley of Decision (3:13–17). God commands an unidentified group to set its hands to attack, using a harvest metaphor. God promised agricultural abundance for his people (2:24), and now this is applied metaphorically to the wickedness of the nations. For this cause, they are cut down like grain.

The valley, previously fully identified as that of Jehoshaphat, is now identified twice as that of "decision" (3:14). Once again, the approaching "day of the LORD" (3:14) is mentioned, this time as it affects the nations rather than God's people. Nations experience the same upset of earth and heavens as Judah suffered, with the exact clauses of 2:10 repeated in 3:15.

In marked contrast to the turmoil facing the nations, Yahweh stands firm on behalf of his people. The tabernacle and temple are called holy places, and this sanctity, deriving from the presence of God within them, extends to the entire city when what is unclean is removed. The foreigners are to be kept away permanently, for they will "never again . . . invade her" (3:17).

In That Day (3:18–21). The new wine, previously cut off from drinkers' lips, is now restored in abundance. The "hills will flow with milk" (3:18). Not only milk, but also an even more valuable commodity—water will flow. Not only will there be sufficient water for her needs, but its "fountain" (3:18) is a source of fresh water for others. The nations, in contrast, receive no blessing but rather the devastation that once was Judah's.

God's own people were previously called to repentance,

and this is the promise that forgiveness is granted. The entire prophecy comes to a close with these two positive sentiments to God's people: I will forgive you, and I am with you. Though locusts, droughts, enemies, and devastation come, from natural causes or from their own guilt, Yahweh is there.

Application. Church is not an end in itself; rather, it is a means to a greater end, developing an intimate relationship with God. The aim of the church should not be to get people to know about God, but rather to get to know God. While God is one party in the relationship, and he knows and loves those who are in relationship with him, we must spend time, not only in our talking to him in prayer, but also in our listening to him, in reading Scripture, and in being in his presence. The church needs to return to a realization that we very much need to know God.

AMOS

INTRODUCTION TO AMOS

The book of Amos never states the purpose for writing down the prophecies Amos spoke in Israel; in fact, the book never clearly states who actually did write down the oracles. Although some critical scholars question whether Amos wrote the sermons contained in the book, I do not believe the evidence supports the view that there was a long editorial history for its composition. Amos's ministry covers less than two years (1:1), somewhere between 765–760 BC, and his sermons are given at two key cities: Samaria, the capital and center of Israelite government, and Bethel, a center of Israelite religion.

BOOK OUTLINE

I. Introduction (1:1–2)
II. A War Oracle against the Nations (1:3–2:16)
  A. Oracles against the Foreign Nations (1:3–2:3)
  B. Oracles against Judah and Israel (2:4–16)
III. The Verification of God's Judgment on Israel (3:1–6:14)
  A. The Relationship between Cause and Effect and the Confirmation of Israel's Punishment (3:1–4:3)
  B. Israel's Worship Is Not Acceptable (4:4–13)
  C. A Lament over Israel, the Dead Nation (5:1–17)
  D. Woe Oracle Concerning False Hopes (5:18–27)
  E. Woe Oracle Concerning False Security (6:1–14)
IV. Visions and Exhortations of the End (7:1–9:15)
  A. Compassion in Visions of Judgment (7:1–6)
  B. Visions of Destruction Cause Conflict (7:7–17)
  C. Wailing at the End, Not Forgiveness (8:1–14)
  D. No Sinner Can Escape from God's Hand (9:1–10)
  E. The Restoration after God's Judgment (9:11–15)

AMOS 1:1–2

Original Meaning

The Superscription (1:1). Amos is largely unknown except for the sermons in the book of Amos. The text says nothing about his family of origin or whether he has a wife and children. He comes from Tekoa, a small rural Judean (not Israelite) village about ten miles south of Jerusalem.

The Theme (1:2). The poetic part of the introduction announces God's roaring revelation from Zion in what appears to be a hymnic description of a theophany. This hymn emphasizes God's roaring voice, his thunderous appeal from Zion (i.e., the temple in Jerusalem where he resides).

Application. Many of the great men and women of God in our time started out much like Amos. They were common people who had no special status and limited potential in the eyes of their friends and family. Yet God chose them to demonstrate his power through their weakness (1 Cor 1:27).

AMOS 1:3–2:3

Original Meaning

Oracle against Syria (1:3–5). As the audience listens to Amos begin his prophecy, they hear a word about the past atrocities of a Syrian military battle and that nation's future punishment. The rebellious act of the Syrians that Amos mentions is undated, but it probably happened years earlier. The punishment Amos announces involves the destruction of the king's house and military fortresses that have given him security and protection from reprisal.

Oracle against Philistia (1:6–8). The Philistine rebellious acts against God's authority involve capturing whole communities. Since both foreign and Israelite law allowed for taking prisoners of war (Deut 20:10–11; 2 Chr 28:8), the crime cannot refer to a military action in war. Instead, this is a wholesale kidnapping of peaceful people for the purpose of turning a profit. Philistia's punishment is similar to Syria's.

Oracle against Phoenicia (1:9–10). The oracle in 1:9–10 follows the same initial pattern as the two previous messages: God has spoken; Tyre, the leading city of Phoenicia, has rebelled many times; and God will act in wrath against them. The punishment statement is brief. God will go into action against the people of Tyre, bring down the thick walls of the city, and cause its strongly fortified palace-fortresses to go up in flames.

Oracle against Edom (1:11–12). Edom's rebellious acts involve chasing his brother with a sword, having no compassion, and exhibiting a continuous attitude of rage that flames out in an uncontrollable manner. Scripture describes years of animosity between these two brothers. The punishment clauses are brief and devastating announcements of God's intention to end the terror that Edom has unleashed on its neighbors.

Oracle against Ammon (1:13–15). The fourth and fifth oracles against the two tribes that descended from Lot return to the formal structure of the first two messages. God's judgment on Ammon involves the destruction of their capital, Rabbah (modern Amman, Jordan), and the military fortresses in it.

Oracle against Moab (2:1–3). The last foreign nation mentioned is Moab, the sister nation of Ammon. Their willful rebellious act has been to burn the bones of the king of Edom, but the Moabites have gone one step further by using the king's remains as lime, possibly to plaster the walls of a house. God's judgment of Moab is similar to what will happen to Ammon.

Application. If one is looking for situations to apply the principle that God holds every nation accountable for its acts of inhumanity against people, one can look for atrocities in peaceful foreign nations that have a poor record on human rights, discover how military personnel treat innocent civilians in war time, or move away from the national focus to examine the way individual people use their power to abuse others.

AMOS 2:4–16

Original Meaning

Oracle against Judah (2:4–5). The willful sin of Judah is not described as an oppressive act against some foreign nation but a direct refusal to follow God's stipulations and instructions in the torah. Many Judean people have turned to follow lies, which leads them astray from God. Because of this direct refusal to accept what God has said, God will treat Judah just like every other nation.

Oracle against Israel (2:6–16). The first accusations in 2:6 involve the unnecessary foreclosure on small loans by money lenders. The accusations in 2:7 emphasize the physical abuse of the helpless and weak. The third rebellious act in 2:7 is the sexual abuse of a servant woman by both a father and son. The law provided some protection for female slaves because they were so vulnerable to mistreatment by their masters. The final accusations of oppression in 2:8 chronicle additional ways the powerful exploit the destitute.

In 2:9–12 Amos now changes his approach to describing Israel's rebelliousness. He emphasizes what God did for Israel in the past by rescuing them when they were oppressed by stronger nations. One would expect Israel to be thankful to God and obey his covenant stipulations because of his grace. One would also assume that the Israelites would understand from their past history that God consistently fights against oppressors and on behalf of the oppressed.

Some Israelites in Amos's audience apparently oppose the Nazirites and prophets. In 2:12 the prophet reports that these Israelites coerce people who have taken a Nazirite vow into drinking wine and thus force them to break their vows of abstinence. This is in direct conflict with what God required and is a blatant attempt to substitute their own cultural rules for God's expectations.

The punishment statement in 2:13–16 against Israel does not begin like the judgments on the kings and the fortified cities of the foreign nations. Instead, it focuses on the utter annihilation of Israel's army. Israel's strong military force will collapse and run, and none will escape death. This will be an awesome demonstration of God's power! As Amos's audience in Samaria hears these words, they must have been astonished and petrified. How can such a thing happen? Will God actually do this? What will happen to them if such a disaster does take place?

Application. In a sense, Amos is living in a post-covenant moral era for most Israelites and a pre-covenant era for the pagan population in and around Israel. If one looks at the cultures around the world today, one could suggest that some countries (especially Western) appear to be in a post-Christian era. The church should be less concerned about its loss of status in influencing the general values of society and concentrate more on getting its own house in order.

AMOS 3:1–4:3

Original Meaning

A Chosen, Covenantal Status Does Not Guarantee Blessing (3:1–2). The people were led out of Egypt to be God's people, not a people who followed their own whims and worshiped Baal. If the Israelites forget what God did for them and do not live as his people, the curses of the covenant are inevitable (Deut 27–28).

There Is a Reason for Everything (3:3–8). Each question in 3:3–5 expects the answer no. In 3:6–8 Amos lists the cause before the result. Only a stupid person ignores a watchman's signal. Most Israelites would agree that cities are destroyed by divine action. But if this is true, God is also the one who has the power to cause the destruction of Samaria.

The flow of this long series of questions is broken in 3:7. God does not just destroy cities or nations on a whim. The implications are too obvious to miss. Why has Amos given this news about God's plan to destroy Israel? God has revealed them to the prophet because he intends to act in the near future, and he desires to have one of his servants warn those he will judge. The final verse (3:8) encourages the listener to be aware of the cause (God's roar) and to accomplish the intended results (fear God).

An Enemy Will Destroy the Places of Violence (3:9–12). The Israelites are full of "unrest" and "oppression" (3:9), which characterize the lifestyle of the rich and famous. God will bring an unnamed enemy nation to oppress the royal and noble inhabitants of Samaria, and they will receive the same treatment they have given to others.

God Will Destroy Their Places of Security (3:13–15). To drive home God's main point, Amos describes the removal of two of Israel's sources of security: the altars where they worship and their strongly fortified mansions. The altars of Bethel include those in the king's state temple (7:13), where the golden calf was located (see 1 Kgs 12:28–32). God will also remove the royal court and the wealthy's social status, financial security, and physical protection (Amos 3:15) when he tears down their homes.

God Will Exile the Oppressors (4:1–3). A few have understood the "cows of Bashan" (4:1) as a symbol of the leaders of Samaria or a reference to the Baal fertility cult, but most conclude that this imagery is a cutting reference to the rich women in Samaria. These pampered, self-indulgent, and bossy ladies maintain their lifestyle by exploiting the poor. Verses 2–3 are God's irrevocable oath of judgment against these women. Amos communicates in the most powerful way possible the unalterable will of God.

Application. Are possessions and wealth evils that God hates, or can people have possessions if they do not let them become a source of security? Those without abundance must be content, and those with abundance must be content and generous with what they have (Phil 4:12; 1 Tim 6:17–18).

AMOS 4:4–13

Original Meaning

A Sarcastic Call to Worship (4:4–5). In other worship contexts the priests call God's people to the sacred assemblies. Amos follows this traditional pattern by mimicking a call to worship, but he twists it in dramatic ways by changing the vocabulary. He does not just encourage people to go to the temples in Bethel and Gilgal; in 4:4a he sarcastically exhorts them to multiply their rebellious acts of worship. This paradoxical statement reveals that their sacrifices do not bring forgiveness of sin but add to the people's sinfulness before God.

Amos's second encouragement (4:4b) mocks the people's overemphasis on the repeated bringing of sacrifices (every morning) and tithes (every three days, not every "three years" as in the NIV). The prophet wants his audience to ask themselves whether God is primarily impressed with the number of religious acts his people do, or is it something else?

The third exhortation involves offering up or burning a thank offering of leavened bread (4:5). The Levitical regulations did allow for thank offerings of leavened bread (Lev 7:13), but there is no instruction to burn this bread. Thus, the problem Amos is pinpointing here relates to the pious person's bragging about his or her thank and freewill gifts. Their worship has little to do with glorifying God; they are far more concerned about honoring themselves.

No One Turns to God, Even After Chastening (4:6–11). This paragraph is divided into five short sections by the concluding phrase, "'yet you have not returned to me,' declares the LORD" (4:6, 8, 9, 10, 11). By the repetition of this phrase, Amos hammers home the central message that the Israelites do not have a proper relationship with God. The paragraph is also unified by the recitation of five different curses God has already brought on the nation (no food, no rain, no crops, no life, and his overthrowing of them). These are the covenant curses God said he would bring on the nation if they disobeyed him (see Lev 26; Deut 27–28).

God Will Meet Israel with Judgment (4:12–13). The sermon comes to a climax with a final warning that the people of Israel must "prepare to meet . . . God" (4:12). They can no longer avoid God because he is coming to meet them. In an almost oath-like formula (cf. 1 Kgs 2:23) the Lord declares what he will do to them. His patience has ended, and he will no longer chasten them with additional curses in hopes of bringing them into a dynamic covenant relationship.

The hymnic fragment in 4:13 describes this God as the creator of the earth, the one who reveals his thoughts—whose judgment can turn day into night and whose name is "the LORD God Almighty." This doxology may have quoted a popular hymn that the people regularly sang but never thought much about. Indeed, it is a fearful thing to fall into the hands of an angry God.

Application. We no longer offer burnt offerings or thank offerings with leavened bread in churches today, but we do have a variety of symbolic rituals that represent spiritual truths. Our prayers, songs, liturgies, and repeated acts can become just as dead as the meaningless offerings that some offered in Israel.

AMOS 5:1–17

Original Meaning

Lamenting the Death of the Nation (5:1–3, 16–17). This funeral song begins and ends by emphasizing the horror of the death of the nation of Israel. This once vibrant virgin now lies totally helpless without hope of revival. She has been deserted by friends, family, and God. The bitterness of the prophet's grief is evident, and the finality of Israel's destruction is clear.

Verse 3 points out why the nation has no hope: Its army has been decimated (90 percent of the troops have been killed), exactly as Amos predicted in 2:13–16. Everyone will mourn because death will touch every family. Amos has told them that this death will come about when God "pass[es] through your midst" (5:17), a phrase borrowed from the exodus and Passover events (Exod 11:4; 12:12). What a reversal of fortunes! God has turned the great Exodus themes into death threats.

A Call to Seek God and Live (5:4–6, 14–15). Next to these devastating lamentations is what appears to be a prophetic call of hope. I have difficulty in seeing this as a real offer of hope for the whole nation. It seems more likely that it functions rhetorically in two ways:

1. as a partial explanation for why God is judging the wicked—they are not seeking God but wasting their time at various temples; and
2. as an encouragement to a small "remnant" of seekers (5:15) to respond positively to God and not get fooled by all the religious activity at Israel's temples.

Accusations of No Justice (5:7, 10–13). In the midst of this wailing lament song is a series of accusations that seem to function as another reason for God's plan to destroy the nation of Israel. Perhaps some are wondering why God would want to destroy his people. The straightforward answer goes back to the way these people treat others. Some in Israel have perverted the central religious and social ideals of righteousness and justice. Their moral values are not governed by relationships of justice in the courts, honesty, fairness, equality (5:10, 12), and respect for the norms of the covenant.

Hymn to Yahweh (5:8–9). Amos reminds his audience that he is not talking about a weak power or a pantheistic personification of nature. In this muted polemic against the pagan astral gods, Yahweh is seen as the one who created the magnificent spectacle of nature that people see every night in the heavens—the constellations of Pleiades and Orion (5:8; see also Job 9:9; 38:31; Isa 40:26). The prophet is using positive traditions to support his view of God; he may even be quoting from a well-known hymn that the people sing in their temple worship services.

Application. Amos, Job, and the psalmists allow us to face our deepest fears and sorrows simply because they voice their grief. They do not face this pain alone but bring it to God, who can do something about it. Underlying the sorrow is a faith that believes God is trustworthy and understanding; he is a resource who can change the lament orientation into assurance and praise.

AMOS 5:18–27

Original Meaning

The Day of the Lord Will Bring No Hope (5:18–20). Amos describes his audience as people longing for or yearning for the coming day of the Lord (5:18). When Amos laments over those who want this day to come, many of his listeners probably wonder what is wrong with this crazy prophet. Why would anyone not look forward to the time when God will bless his people and defeat their enemies? Amos's answer to his rhetorical "why" question in 5:18b reveals that Israel will suffer God's judgment with the ungodly because they are a sinful people, just like the foreign nations.

God Rejects the People's Ritualistic Worship (5:21–24). Amos reintroduces his critique of the nation's sacrifices and singing with powerful persuasive clauses that claim God's vehement opposition to what is happening at Israel's temples. Verse 24 exhorts the people to pay close attention to the implications of what it means to worship God. If you worship him, you must walk in his ways. If worship does not further the development of spiritual character, it may just be empty emotions.

False Worship Will Bring Exile (5:25–27). This message ends with a concluding statement of punishment that outlines the consequences of improper worship of God. There is no doubt about what will happen, who will do this, or where the people will go. God will exile the Israelites into some nation far away, into an unknown land beyond Damascus. Later records in 2 Kings 17:23–24 verify that God did send these people into Assyria about forty years after Amos's prophecy (721 BC).

Application. Although many churches are struggling with people's preferences for different styles of worship format (seeker, contemporary, or traditional), a much deeper and more serious issue is the lifestyle people follow after the worship service is over. True and acceptable worship is not so much about issues of the style adopted by a particular congregation, but the extent to which the worshiper's life is transformed by being in the presence of a holy God.

AMOS 6:1–14

Original Meaning

Lament, for Complacency and Affluence Will Bring Destruction (6:1–7). The first part of this woe oracle laments the nation's false sense of security (6:1–3). Amos sorrowfully remembers that the people in Zion, the capital of Judah, as well as the people in Samaria, the capital of Israel, have a deceptive feeling of well-being and security (6:1). The people in Samaria are no better than those in surrounding cities (6:2). Because of Israel's misperception of its political situation, there is a real possibility that they may be defeated (6:3).

The second half of the woe (6:4–7) laments the people's careless ease and security derived from their wealth. With their money and power, they have everything they want. They are happy, so they ignore and deny the true status of their sick and dying nation. Amos ends his sorrowful lament with a dire warning of exile for the upper class. He ironically announces that these people—the citizens of the "foremost" nation in the Near East (6:1)—will be the "first" to go into captivity (6:7).

God's Oath of Destruction for Pride (6:8–14). This paragraph contains two parts: 6:8–11 is God's oath and a description of the effects this oath will have on the nation, while 6:12–14 describes the absurdity of Israel's military pride. The oath expresses God's deep feelings of abhorrence for Israel's trust in her strong, fortified cities (6:8, 11). In 6:9–10 Amos illustrates what will happen to the people who live in these fortresses. Since they are all dead, it will not do any good to call on God to save someone. In a similar context David ceased praying for his son once he knew the boy was dead (2 Sam 12:16–23).

The final subsection (Amos 6:12–14) abruptly begins with a series of absurd questions. By using these ridiculous rhetorical questions, Amos makes it easier for them to see the absurdity of their own action of turning righteousness into something vile, bitter, or poisonous. This type of injustice is as absurd as riding a horse over a rocky field; it makes no sense.

Application. Amos saw how riches and wealth cause the upper-class people to base their security in having the best money could buy. Does this mean that believers today must buy old pine furniture instead of new oak pieces, or that a wedding party for your daughter should serve only crackers and cheese plus a wedding cake? No one would want to suggest that it is wrong to have money, or that money always corrupts, or that people do not need money. Money is not the problem; we are.

AMOS 7:1–6

Original Meaning

The Vision of Locusts (7:1–3). The timing of this plague is critical, for the locusts are being formed after the king's share of the crop has been harvested. This suggests that the royal needs have been met but that the average peasant farmer will be in serious trouble. The prophet prays for compassion, like Moses at the golden calf (Exod 34:6). Since there is no sign of any repentance by Israel, Amos is asking for an act of pure grace that was undeserved.

God's relenting (Heb. *niham*) on his plans in 7:3 is an anthropomorphic way of explaining his personal interaction with the prophet and his people. Compassion for the people is not inconsistent with God's character; rather, it reveals the depth of his patience and his openness to hearing the prayers of righteous intercessors (Jas 5:13–18).

The Vision of the Fire (7:4–6). The second vision has a structure parallel to the first vision. Whatever the source of the fire, Amos intercedes with a prayer for God to stop the fire before it destroys the land of Israel. God stops the fire. More time is provided for the Israelites to respond.

Application. Does the church still realize that God takes no pleasure in the punishment of the wicked (Ezek 18:23) and that he desires that no one should perish but that all will come to a knowledge of the truth (2 Peter 3:9)? Is the problem more related to the fact that they have not taken the time to get personally involved with unbelievers? It would not surprise me if we will be asked one day: Who were the sinners you prayed for?

AMOS 7:7–17

Original Meaning

Vision of the Plumb Line (7:7–9). Just as a builder tests the straightness of a wall with a plumb line, God exposes the true state of his people's moral character and covenant faithfulness with his plumb line. God has decided to spare "my people Israel" no longer (7:8). God's patience has been exhausted; his punishment will not be delayed. The final part of the vision (7:9) explains God will destroy both the religious places of false worship and the dynasty of the king of Israel.

Conflict over God's Words (7:10–17). Amaziah's strong accusations (7:10–13) that Amos's words are a "conspiracy" (7:10) suggest an organized plot to overthrow the government. This would be considered rebellion, sedition, or subversion by those in authority. Amaziah communicates his concern over Amos's words to King Jeroboam II. His quotation of Amos (7:11) is not exact. Amaziah seems to reinvent Amos as a dangerous dissident who might stir up support from the poor people of the land or political rivals of the king.

This is not just an argument about where Amos can speak; this is a spiritual battle about accepting the message of the Lord or rejecting it. This conflict demonstrates Amaziah's guilt before God and his unworthiness to be the spiritual priestly leader of the nation of Israel. Such action justifies God's judgment on Amaziah and shows the bankruptcy of the religious beliefs and practices promulgated at the temple at Bethel.

Application. There are times when people must take a strong stand against those who reject true doctrine and who oppose what God is trying to accomplish. Each person should be aware that such confrontations (like confronting an alcoholic parent) may be difficult emotional experiences, but people should not let fear prevent them from taking responsibility to oppose the spiritual forces of evil in this world. This may not reduce persecution or conflict, but it will establish the truthfulness and authority of what God has said. It is the foundation of our faith, and it is worth fighting for.

AMOS 8:1–14

Original Meaning

Vision of the Ripe Summer Fruit (8:1–3). This is a dramatic picturing of future events that reemphasizes the finality of God's decision to destroy "my people Israel" (8:2). What a tragedy! Not only will the king and temple be destroyed (7:9), but God's own special covenant people will cease to exist in the near future. All one can do is gasp in horror at the enormity of the slaughter, turn one's eyes away from the mutilated carnage and bloated bodies, and flee from the unbearable stench of death and rotting flesh. The Bethel temple will not protect the worshipers, for God will bring mass destruction.

The End Will Bring Wailing but No Word from God (8:4–14). Amos focuses on the acts of the oppressors in 8:4 and their motives and methods in 8:5–6. Those who need help and cannot make it on their own receive no compassion or assistance but are taken advantage of. Those with the economic ability to help refuse to assist them; in fact, they purposely exacerbate the problems by manipulating things to their own advantage.

God is angry over this greed and these injustices, so he swears an oath that he "will never forget" (8:7). By this oath God binds himself to a specific, unalterable course of action. He will not change or pass over this brutality against the poor for any reason.

Amos describes how the land will tremble and mourn. In addition, there will be unusual signs of God's power over the heavens. Amos is not predicting the final end of the world as Isaiah 24 does; rather, he is predicting the approaching day of the Lord for Israel when the religious, political, and social status quo will end (fulfilled in 722 BC, when the Assyrians captured Samaria). The final paragraph (8:11–14) warns the people that on that final day there will be no word of help or comfort from God or from any of the pagan gods they worship.

In the midst of this death and mourning, the Israelites will remember that the Creator is all-powerful, and they will look to him for help in their deep distress. But when they go to a temple or inquire of a prophet for a word of hope from God, there will be nothing. Like a desperate and confused traveler who does not know where to find water, these confused people will be unable to find any message from God. The final verses (8:13–14) deepen the hopelessness of "that day" by noting that the strongest members of society will grow faint and end up resorting to other gods.

Application. Part of any discussion on business ethics must deal with attitudes and motivations people have toward their business activities. Believers need to be motivated by basic convictions of honesty and truthfulness, the challenge of fulfilling their God-given purpose in life, accepting responsibility for their choices, and honoring God in what they do.

AMOS 9:1–10

Original Meaning

The Vision: No One Can Escape (9:1–4). The vision in 9:1–4 removes all hope and security; no exceptions are noted until we get to 9:8. To convince the audience of the impossibility of any hope of survival, a series of five conditional clauses is presented (9:2–4). Each gives a possible way one might try to escape from God's mighty hand of judgment, but each is a useless waste of effort because there are no limits to the power of God's eyes or hands.

The Hymn: God Has All Power over the Heavens and the Earth (9:5–6). Amos uses this hymn of praise to God, which probably celebrates God's power over Israel's enemies, to support his claim that this omnipotent God will judge Israel. There is no way to avoid him or escape his wrath.

The Dispute: Does Israel Have a Special Protected Status? (9:7–10). The final paragraph refutes an implied or real objection by the audience. They question Amos's conclusion that Israel will actually be destroyed by God. They argue instead that "disaster will not overtake . . . us" (9:10), basing their confidence in God on what he has done in the past and the promises he made to their forefathers. How can God now reject his own people?

Amos does not dispute any facts of history but raises questions about how the Israelites have theologically interpreted these events. They have reified these ideas into absolute guarantees (focusing only on God's promises in his covenant relationship), thus disconnecting the nation's future from their daily covenantal relationship with him. But the covenant conditions state that if God's people do not follow him or maintain their covenant relationship with him, he will not automatically bless them. Past election (3:1–2) and past acts of divine grace (2:9–10) do not rule out the possibility of future punishment.

Application. People who have grown up in the church may think that they have the right to God's protection and blessing because of their past experience with God. No one should falsely think that all God requires is for us to be baptized or to join the church, though some do believe this because the truth of Scripture has not been adequately explained. Strong Bible teaching is necessary to ground people firmly so that they are not led astray with deceptions.

AMOS 9:11–15

Original Meaning

The Coming Day Will Bring the Restoration of the Davidic Kingdom (9:11–12). The coming day of hope is set somewhere in the unknown future. Verses 11–12 do not explain how this Davidic rule will be restored or clarify details about the ruler; it merely states that God himself will bring it about. The consequences of this Davidic revival will impact other nations so that they may gain inclusion into this future kingdom (9:12).

The Coming Day Will Bring the Restoration of the Land (9:13–15). Once the political status of the new kingdom is explained, Amos focuses on God's transformation of the fertility of the land. The abundance of the crops will be beyond everyone's imagination and exceed human ability to collect them. The grapes that are harvested around August and September will be so numerous that they will still not be finished at planting time in November. This salvation oracle ends with an unending covenantal promise of God's eternal granting of the land to his people (9:15). They will no longer be sojourners but landed citizens, deeply rooted in the place God has given them.

Application. The final words of Amos offer hope to the faithful remnant who will suffer with the wicked when God brings destruction on the nation of Israel. It also challenges unbelievers with the choices they can make: Reject God and suffer his curse or turn to God and accept this offer of hope. Everyone needs to have some hope in his or her life. Hope is not based on an eschatological chart or eliminated by difficult circumstances. God is the one who offers hope to those who will believe in him. Therefore, he must be at the center of all eschatological teaching.

OBADIAH

INTRODUCTION TO OBADIAH

The short prophecy of Obadiah, just twenty-one verses, finds Judah facing a difficult situation: Her next-door neighbor, Edom, whose inhabitants are related to the Judeans by blood, not only stood by when the Babylonian world power moved against Judah, she actively collaborated in that aggression. What Judah needs to be reminded of is that neither geographical nor military advantage is the sole deciding factor of international relations, especially when these involve the very people of God. While Obadiah's message is a promise of hope to Judah, the message primarily presents itself as a threat to Edom and to all others who mistreat God's people.

BOOK OUTLINE

I. Superscription and Yahweh's First Message (1–4)
II. Yahweh's Second Message: Pillage and Perfidy (5–7)
III. Yahweh's Third Message (8–18)
IV. Home Again (19–21)

OBADIAH 1–4

Original Meaning. Edom vaunts herself because of the strategic advantage she enjoys over her neighbors. Unfortunately for Edom, her survey does not include a glance heavenward, where the greatest threat to arrogance lies. It is not a human army who brings Edom down but the warrior God.

Application. There is a fine line between self-confidence, self-reliance, and pride. Pride, an inordinate opinion of one's own importance or superiority, characterizes our age, at least in Western culture. "I did it my way," says a popular song of not too long ago, and unfortunately the same attitude invades the church.

OBADIAH 5–7

Original Meaning. Edom in its punishment is completely denuded. Rather than criminals or ancient enemies plaguing Edom, it is her former friends and allies who turn against her. Rather than receiving the support expected from friends, Edom finds them to be enemies. The Edomites are forcefully expelled from their dwellings and driven to the periphery of their land.

Application. Most people today depend on things other than agriculture for their livelihood, but the threat of financial and medical loss is a good comparison. While dependence on the state for assistance may be helpful for some, the church should also provide care, much like the people of Israel in the Old Testament, who dispersed God's covenant bounty equitably through such things as leaving part of the crops for the poor (e.g., Lev 19:9–10; Deut 24:19–21), or the church in the New Testament, through distribution of wealth (e.g., Acts 2:44–45).

OBADIAH 8–9

Original Meaning. Yahweh promises that he will not only deprive Edom of tactical geographical advantage and strength derived from either wealth or allies, but he will also deny them two other means of national support, the wise and the strong. The "wise men" (8) are important figures in the court, providing sage intellectual insight or good sense as well as practical skill. Trained soldiers are called upon to act with valor, but those of Edom are terrified.

Application. The fact that neither today's society nor the church seems to be bothered about the loss of both moral vision and the ability to accomplish good in leading society is a concern. Where are today's leaders who will base decisions on integrity rather than on either pragmatism or politics?

OBADIAH 10–15

Original Meaning. Edom will receive back on her own head what she had done to her own "brother" (10, 12). This is not just an outrage against an enemy, or even a neighbor; this is against one's own blood! The most despicable acts are those in verse 14, where Edom physically lays hands on defeated and fleeing neighbors. Edom aids the exile of a defeated people by turning over the defeated survivors. Those to whom she commits them are not mentioned, lest they also share the blame, which is here left wholly on Edom. Edom will receive as she has given. As she exploited Judah's days of calamity (11–14), so a day will cause her distress.

Application. There needs to be education within the church as to what constitutes violence and abuse, what its results are, and what the logical consequences of it should be. Often the behavior is not recognized as being hurtful, so discussion and teaching need to start addressing the issue. The state has taken some initial strides in this area, and it is a shame if the church should be lagging behind.

OBADIAH 16–18

Original Meaning. Attention now turns from Edom, the oppressor of God's people, to the people of Judah themselves. God's holy city will be restored, and so will his people. Edom will suffer what Judah has suffered at her hand. Unlike Judah, which has survivors, even if Edom betrays them, Edom herself has none.

Application. While the US constitution calls for a system of checks and balances between the branches of government, the church needs to be ready and willing to bring a theological perspective to bear on what is constitutionally a secular enterprise. Both foreign and domestic policy need to be scrutinized biblically, and decision-makers need to be held accountable to standards derived from concepts of equity and justice rather than just national economic well-being.

OBADIAH 19–21

Original Meaning. What is of primary importance for the passage is not the starting point but the destination of the returnees. They come back to the ancestral holdings of Israel. Freedom from oppression is won for beleaguered Israel, and one of the oppressors, Edom, is herself subjugated. While Israel is yet in exile, her King promises that he is on his way back to his throne.

Application. Both the Old and New Testaments affirm that "the earth is the LORD's" (Ps 24:1; 1 Cor 12:26), all things and everyone included, and humanity has been mandated to look after it, supporting the helpless, widow, orphan, and alien. If they do not, Yahweh himself will be their support. As Yahweh takes the part of his exiled people in the book of Obadiah, will he not do the same for his dispossessed creatures today?

JONAH

INTRODUCTION TO JONAH

The book of Jonah contains only fifty-eight verses, but those few verses include a storm at sea, the conversion of sailors, a miraculous rescue, a song of praise, the repentance of Israel's archenemy, and an intensely honest dialogue between Yahweh and Israel's most reluctant prophet. The book reveals the nature of Yahweh's relationship to the gentile sailors, to Israel's enemy Nineveh, to nonhuman creation (the wind, a fish, vine, worm, and cattle), as well as to his messenger Jonah. The book is, in many ways, a microcosm of God's relationship to his whole creation in history.

The prophet Jonah, son of Amittai, is mentioned just twice in the Old Testament (2 Kgs 14:25; Jonah 1:1). The dating of the final form of the composition is widely disputed and includes a vast array of suggestions, ranging between the eighth and fourth centuries BC.

BOOK OUTLINE

I. Death and Life (1:1–17)
II. Jonah Gives Thanks for Yahweh's Great Fish (2:1–10)
III. Preaching, Repentance, and Compassion (3:1–10)
IV. The Creator's Love and Jonah's Anger (4:1–11)

JONAH 1:1–17

Original Meaning

A Reluctant Prophet and Yahweh (1:1–3). These three verses are full of detailed action, drawing us into the story. The word of Yahweh comes to Jonah in 1:1 (and will come to him a second time in 3:1). Yahweh tells him to preach against the wicked city of Nineveh, but Jonah runs in the opposite direction, heading for Tarshish. He goes down to Joppa, finds a ship, pays the fare, goes aboard, and sets sail. The detail gives readers the sense of being on board with him when Yahweh's great windstorm hits and threatens to break the ship apart.

The name "Jonah" means "dove." In Genesis 8:10–11 the dove Noah sent out from the ark returned with the branch of an olive tree—an enduring symbol of peace and compassion. The "dove" (Jonah) of peace will be Yahweh's agent. Jonah, however, chooses to flee in the opposite direction (1:3).

The Sailors and the Reluctant Prophet in Yahweh's Storm (1:4–12). Verse 4 turns our attention to the sailors and captain of the storm-bound ship and their situation in relation to Yahweh and Jonah. They are afraid because of the storm and cry out to their gods, and they then proceed to throw their cargo overboard (a radical action for freight haulers). The captain wakes Jonah to enlist him to pray, and the men cast lots and discover Jonah's sin.

Jonah is passive in 1:5–7. Exhausted from his struggle and decision to flee, he sleeps. He has temporarily escaped the pressure of God's word, but by fleeing he has also turned from the possibility of calling on his God. The irony of Jonah's decision is that he will die in either case. If he says nothing, the storm will kill them all. If he confesses, he knows he alone will die. God has reduced his decision to the question, "Will your life/death save the lives of others, or will it be an ordinary death at sea in a storm with pagan sailors?"

Jonah does not seem to be capable of simple repentance. He could have sought forgiveness during the storm (as the Ninevites do later) and committed himself to go to Nineveh. Yet Jonah does have compassion on the innocent sailors and does not want *them* to die. He will accept death for them, not in obedience to God but, nonetheless, in their place.

The Sailors and Yahweh (1:13–16). The sailors make vows to Yahweh. Vows were a public expression of the intent to continue in faithful worship. The actions of sacrifice and vows are precisely the actions of worship later declared by Jonah for *his* deliverance (2:9). The change in the sailors' relationship to Yahweh, evident in 1:16, is later paralleled in the Ninevites' repentance in chapter 3. Even in Jonah's disobedience, Yahweh has made him effective in his calling as a prophet, bringing people to faith in Yahweh.

God's Fish (1:17). Jonah's rescue from drowning via a "great fish" is an unbelievable development, at which even an ancient reader might have stopped and made an assessment concerning whether this was a legend or a miraculous account. Yet the safety of Jonah is assumed in the narrative. He does not die within the fish but somehow survives.

Application. We should not run from God, but we do. Even our piety, as in Jonah's righteous indignation with God's mercy, can cause us to run. Until we admit we are on the run, we are lost. But when, with Jonah, we admit our true situation (1:10), we have real hope.

Without mission, Christianity has no commission. In spite of this, many congregations struggle to support missionaries and evangelism. At the beginning of the twenty-first century more than 144 million persons in 815 ethnic people groups have virtually no access to the gospel message. Yet, the most affluent churches in the world often dedicate only small parts of their budget to mission projects outside of their locality.

JONAH 2:1–10

Original Meaning. Jonah 2 is Jonah's psalm of thanks from within the belly of the fish. The song primarily recounts Jonah's distress in the water and gives thanks for his rescue. It begins with a summary of his cry for help (2:2) and continues with four more stanzas describing Jonah's sinking in the water before he is swallowed by the fish (2:3–6). In the refrain (2:7–9) Jonah summarizes his cry for rescue and declares Yahweh as the true source of salvation. Then, the narrator tells us, Yahweh talked to the fish, and "it vomited Jonah onto dry land" (2:10).

The amazing context of this poetic prayer is Jonah's gratitude *while inside* the fish. He fully expected to die in the water. His thanksgiving within the belly of a fish is a proclamation of joy, with the realization that God has delivered him in spite of his running. Though he is not yet on dry land, his faith reaches a new dimension of understanding. He seems to have no doubt that, as he was delivered from drowning, he will also eventually be delivered safely to the shore.

Application. Jonah's song of thanksgiving demonstrates the power of praise and thanksgiving in any circumstance for the one who turns to Yahweh (2:4, 7). It is far more than a poetic interlude in the narrative. Although Jonah's song is not full of repentance, it is enough in this situation that he turns toward Yahweh in worship. Jonah, like all believers called by Yahweh, must be reborn by God's grace.

JONAH 3:1–10

Original Meaning. Jonah's preaching, the Ninevites' repentance, and Yahweh's compassion comprise the primary action of chapter 3. This chapter is neatly summarized in 3:4–5: Jonah threatens that the Ninevites "will be overthrown," and they "believed God." In response, God sees how they have turned from evil and has compassion. This chapter provides a convincing demonstration of God's argument with Jonah concerning what ought to be done with violent enemies: They should have an opportunity to hear from Yahweh, turn from their violent ways, and be forgiven.

Chapter 3 begins with Jonah's obedience in proclaiming Yahweh's message (3:1–4). This time Jonah does immediately go to the "very large city" (3:3) and begins proclaiming the "overthrowing" (3:4) of the city within forty days. On the first day of the three-day job, the Ninevites believe (3:3–5a), and the rest of the chapter continues with the Ninevites' dramatic public repentance of evil and violence (3:5–9).

When the king hears, he issues a proclamation of fasting and sackcloth, even for the animals (3:6–8). He says in humility, "Who knows? God may yet relent . . . so that we will not perish" (3:9). The chapter concludes with Yahweh's compassion and forgiveness (3:10). This is a great miracle. Even Israel's worst enemies—the most unlikely people—believe, repent, and receive God's compassion and forgiveness.

Application. Assyria was a long way from Jerusalem (about 500 miles). It dominated the ancient east for about 270 years, including a harsh domination of Israel and Judah. Yet, the Old Testament records God's concern for this distant and wicked people. This surprising fact has led interpreters to consider the Creator's "mission to the world" as a key theme of Jonah. The Creator seeks reconciliation with the whole creation.

JONAH 4:1–11

Original Meaning. Jonah 4 again focuses on the prophet's relationship with God as they dialogue about Jonah's anger over the ways of Yahweh. God argues his preference for compassion, even in horrible circumstances. God has compassion for what he has made, no matter how ignorant, abusive, or violent the culture. Jonah is angry about God's compassion, and God gives Jonah an object lesson in the form of a vine. He attempts to convince Jonah (and the reader) that the basic response of compassion for living things is more important than strict justice. God's primary argument is creational: "If you are moved to pity over the destruction of a vine you did not create, shouldn't I have pity over the destruction of people and animals I did create?" (4:10–11 paraphrased). God loves all his creation, for he is "gracious and compassionate" (4:2).

Application. We can make many significant applications of Jonah 4.

1. God's love for the whole creation is placed in front of the reader in the final question of the book ("Should I not have concern . . . ?"; 4:11). A city distant from Israel, filled with ignorant people (and all its cattle), is placed before us as a primary object of God's concern and love. The answer to God's question is left open for us, but the answer God seeks from Jonah and from us is clearly, "Yes." God's intention is for all to know his love, insider and outsider alike. We are called to affirm his intention

and to participate in the communication of his concern and love.

2. Another significant application is our common human experience of protection and exposure in relation to God. So many of our actions to protect or shield ourselves from life are vain attempts to ward off catastrophe or trouble. Only God can save. Seeking protection apart from God leads to false security because life is fragile and unpredictable. Jonah constantly searches for shelter, and each shelter (ship, fish, hut, plant) fails him in the end, even when provided by God. Jonah even seeks shelter inside his narrow worldview and narrow theology, both of which God deconstructs for him.

MICAH

INTRODUCTION TO MICAH

Micah writes little about his own personal life, his occupation before becoming a prophet, or his family of origin. Evidence from the sermons in his book suggests a ministry that stretched from about 725 BC to 690 BC. His role as a preacher is to speak God's words with courage and to emphasize the theme of God's justice (3:8). Micah's theology works itself out into a practical appeal for people in Judah to recognize what God will do to those who reject him. This possibility causes him to lament at the thought of such a disaster (1:8–16). If God's people do not rid themselves of their deceptive theology and if their leaders do not rule justly, there will be no hope. Micah's theology is principled by God's character and applied to bring about change. The leaders in the days of Ahaz and Manasseh reject God's ways, but Hezekiah transforms his theology and God answers his prayers (Isa 37:14–20). Indeed, acting on the basis of good theology changes everything.

BOOK OUTLINE

- I. God Is Coming in Power to Establish Justice (1:1–2:13)
  - A. God Is Coming to Destroy His People (1:1–16)
  - B. The Reason Why Judah Is God's Enemy; God Will Gather a Remnant (2:1–13)
- II. Just Leadership Will Come to Zion (3:1–5:15)
  - A. Evil Leaders Will Be Removed (3:1–12)
  - B. God Will Establish Justice in Zion (4:1–8)
  - C. Jerusalem Will Be Afflicted and Delivered (4:9–5:9)
  - D. God's Removal of All False Hopes (5:10–15)
- III. Coming to God in Justice, Covenant Loyalty, and Hope (6:1–7:20)
  - A. A Covenant Lawsuit for Not Coming to God Properly (6:1–16)
  - B. Trusting in God for Hope in a Time of Despair (7:1–20)

MICAH 1:1–7

Original Meaning

The Superscription (1:1). The prophetic book of Micah begins in the usual manner: announcement of the divine source of the words that follow, the identification of the prophet who receives these words, the time periods when the prophet preaches, and a brief comment about the subject of the prophecies.

God Will Come to Judge the Earth (1:2–4). Micah begins by describing the Lord's appearance in a theophany. This evokes not only a sense of awe and fear but also a sense of joy in his Hebrew listeners. The awe and fear arise because the power and glory of the majesty of God are seen coming to earth. The joy arises because of the Hebrew expectation that God is coming to defend his people and defeat their enemies as he did in earlier appearances.

God Will Judge Israel and Judah (1:5–7). In 1:5–7 Micah explains why God is coming in power to judge. God accuses the northern nation of Israel of insurrection or rebellion against himself, an idea that the people in Micah's Jerusalem audience readily support. God predicts the total destruction of the northern nation of Israel. The stones of her city walls and houses will be removed down to their foundations (1:6), and her idols will be destroyed (1:7).

Application. People need to realize that no power can stand in the presence of a holy God when judgment is determined. If mountains melt like wax before his power, we should all consider what we will say when we meet him and have to take responsibility for our deeds. The only hope for us as sinners is to turn from the sin that enrages God and rest in the power of his grace, which brings forgiveness.

MICAH 1:8–16

Original Meaning

Announcement of a Lament (1:8–9). Micah is following the ancient Near Eastern cultural pattern that expressed profound grief and sorrow over the approaching death and destruction of a nation. This symbolic action is also meant as a sign-act of things to come in the future; that is, Micah is behaving as the people will behave when this terrible disaster finally reaches Judah.

Lament on Six Cities in Judah (1:10–12). These towns seem to be chosen because puns can be made with their names. The puns are like saying: Watertown will be covered with water, Washington will be washed away, and Waterloo will meet its waterloo. In each case a disaster will happen, and the town will suffer an evil end related to the meaning of its name. The God of Judah is sending it on them.

Lament on Five Cities in Judah (1:13–16). The second stanza of the lament continues the puns of the first stanza. Town after town will be affected, from the smaller villages to the major fortresses like Lachish. The friends he grew up with and his parents and relatives who live in these towns will have to face this terrible day of disaster. This makes the coming attack personal for Micah. His family will have to suffer as well.

Application. Unfortunately, there is little talk in the church today about lamenting the lost of this world, who will suffer the punishment of eternal death, and far too little talk of ending war. Moses, Amos, Micah, Jeremiah, Jesus, and Paul found grieving a fitting way of communicating to the people in their audiences their deep sorrow for those who will die (many without a relationship with God).

MICAH 2:1–13

Original Meaning

The Powerful Covet and Steal Property (2:1–5). The timing of the evil deeds described in 2:1–2 is not when one usually expects crimes to happen. Most thieves work at night when no one can see them; ironically, these powerful thieves brazenly operate in broad daylight by using legal and illegal means to take what they want from others.

The messenger formula in 2:3, "the LORD says," and the direct first-person address by God ("I am planning") emphasize the authority and sureness of what will happen. Micah then sings a brief sarcastic lament (2:4b), which will be sung by an unidentified lamenter. Today one might mockingly say: "Isn't it too bad! It is so unfortunate, what these rich people had to go through. What they coveted and stole is now being coveted and taken from them."

The Powerful Reject God's Word (2:6–11). Micah's prophetic words do not please his audience. Consequently, they dispute his theological perspective, and they even try to get him to stop prophesying. Of course, the reason why they do not approve of Micah's messages is his condemnation of them as the enemy whom God will judge. Therefore, Micah weighs in with additional evidence to support his claim that these military and political leaders are oppressing God's people (2:8–10) and deserve his judgment. These leaders are not interested in what God has said through Micah, but they are interested in hearing a windy discussion concerning what is the best wine produced in the land last year.

God Will Gather a Remnant (2:12–13). The larger section of Micah 1:1–2:13 is completed with a salvation oracle that provides the possibility of hope for a future gathering of a remnant after the judgment of the nation. Verse 13 focuses on God as the sovereign King who will bring about this great event, not on how this breaking out will actually be accomplished. God's people do not need all the details spelled out; they act in faith, trusting that God will do what he has promised.

Application. The character of God has not changed, and his actions on behalf of his people will continue into the future. These facts bring assurance and hope to God's people everywhere and cause them to trust him as they struggle through trials. Although no one can predict what God will do in any specific situation (not even Micah does this), Scripture contains promises (Ezek 36–39; Dan 7–8) that assure people today that God knows what will happen and that he will ultimately have victory over all forces of evil.

MICAH 3:1–12

Original Meaning

The Removal of Judah's Unjust Leaders (3:1–4). This message is given to the political and civic leaders. God's dissatisfaction with the justice being carried out in Judah is evident in 3:2–3. Micah's analogy apparently refers to the leaders' unjust stripping of people of everything they have and treating them like animals. The government and civic institutions, created to protect justice, use strong-arm pressure and outright violence to get what they want.

The Removal of Judah's Prophetic Leaders (3:5–8). This second paragraph focuses on the unprincipled prophets who "lead my people astray" (3:5). Their downfall is that they love money and treat those more favorably who happen to slip a little extra cash in their hands (3:5). Micah's filling by the Spirit is the opposite of the false prophets' abandonment by God.

The Removal of Judah's Political, Civic, and Spiritual Leaders (3:9–12). Jeremiah 26:17–19 remembers how Hezekiah and the people of Judah heard this divine message from Micah. When the king and all Judah realized what would happen, they feared the Lord and entreated his favor so that this disaster would not fall on them. Because they turned to God, God graciously decided not to destroy Judah at this time.

This demonstrates the true persuasive power of Micah's message and how God's spirit is able to use these words to pierce the hearts of unjust and deceptive people. This response by Hezekiah (see Isa 36–37) changes the course of history for

Judah, but it happens only because Micah is willing to declare the sins of Judah.

Application. If leaders cannot be trusted to do the right and just thing, how can one respect their decisions and follow them? Too often a leader's selfish goals and desires are given higher value than justice (3:5, 11). Money corrupts, and the pressure for big donations can tempt leaders to do things in secret that are not above board. Although it may seem contradictory and surprising to some in leadership, many citizens and church members wonder if their leaders (political and religious) are not far more interested in their salary packages and benefits than in issues of justice. God sees when any leaders treat others unjustly and will hold each of them accountable for acts of injustice and selfish attitudes toward money.

MICAH 4:1–8

Original Meaning

God's Transformation of Zion and All Nations (4:1–5). The prophecy in 4:1–5 provides Micah and his audience with a vision of what God will ultimately do in Zion. Micah 4:1b–2 picture throngs of endless people streaming to Jerusalem from many nations to hear the words of God, to be taught his ways, and to understand the "law" (Heb. *torah*, 4:2) from God himself. Every individual will have plenty to eat, be free of anxiety, and have a peaceful sense of security (4:4). Verse 5 is a response of faith and commitment by some of the godly people listening to Micah.

God's Transformation of the Weak into the Strong (4:6–8). In 4:6–8 Micah assures his listeners that God has not forgotten any of them. God's promise that "the former dominion will be restored to you" (4:8) further emphasizes this return to Judah's ideal state. These promises give hope for the future to a people who have little to look forward to.

Application. Since God has a future plan to establish his kingdom, all believers should commit themselves to walk in God's ways and trust in his leadership, for he is the only basis for hope (4:5). Although this seems basic and taken for granted by many, if this principle were actually practiced by every believer, every church committee, and every leader, the church would be transformed with the removal of petty politics and anemic faith.

MICAH 4:9–5:9

Original Meaning

Zion Will Be Attacked and Later Delivered (4:9–5:4). Micah sees three steps in the near future that will cause the people to writhe in agony: They will leave the city of Jerusalem (a reference to its conquest), then camp in the open field for a period of time (a reference to their journey into exile), and finally end up in Babylon (4:10a). Ending this oracle with the good news of hope should have caused Micah's audience to look realistically at their present danger, to cry out to God for help, and to put their present problems in the larger framework of God's ultimate plan for his people.

The second paragraph (4:11–13) has an announcement of many nations gathering against Jerusalem. To emphasize the foolishness of this haughty people, Micah contrasts the attacker's ideas with God's thoughts (4:11–13). Sometime later God miraculously destroyed 185,000 Assyrian troops. The third paragraph (5:1–4) is speaking to the militarized populace in Jerusalem, encouraging them to prepare to defend their city because of the approaching siege in 701 BC.

The positive message of hope in 5:2–4 reminds the people about their tradition of the messianic promise of the eternal reign of David's Son. Verse 3 briefly interrupts the flow of thought with the clarification that this ruler will not come immediately and prevent the present disaster the nation is facing. After this brief clarification Micah begins to describe the reign of this new messianic ruler in 5:4. His kingdom will be a universal rule, including all the nations of the earth. Their temporal setback is part of God's plan and will not prevent him from establishing his rule over the earth in the future.

The Conquest of Zion's Enemies (5:5–9). The expressions in 5:5–6 seem to betray a significant contrast between what Micah has said about what God will do through the Messiah and what the audience is confidently saying about what "we" will do through "our" military strength. Verses 7–9 offer corrective ideas to persuade his listeners not to count on what "we" can do (5:5–6) in "our" strength, for humans can do little to determine the future; people cannot even control the dew. All they can do is trust the sovereign plan of God and wait for him to act. The divine initiative will accomplish all he has promised in its appropriate time.

This oracle ends with a statement of victory over Judah's foes (5:9). Micah now cries out to God for help. Micah is putting his total confidence in God. Some of those who hear this prayer, Micah hopes, will follow his example and commit their lives to his care and protection.

Application. Those with a high view of God, who recognize that God is the sovereign King of this world, will be more likely to bring their problems to him. If, however, you live around self-reliant and independent people who proudly struggle through problems with a stiff upper lip, then calling on God for help may not be an immediate response to troubled times.

Looking at this idea from the positive side, one can exhort people not to follow the mistakes of the past but to seek God's help in times of crisis.

MICAH 5:10–15

Original Meaning

False Political and Military Hopes Will Be Purged (5:10–11). In 5:10–11 Micah is reacting against the nationalistic fervor of war that optimistically imagines that military might is the key to the success of a nation. The nation needs to put its confidence in the name of God rather than in horses and chariots. Although massive buildings and huge walls appear to provide hope to the nation, God's removal of them will leave the people with nothing to depend on but God.

False Religious Hopes Will Be Purged (5:12–14). Isaiah 2:6 and 8:19 describe some of the witchcraft and sorcery that gradually infiltrated into Judah (during Uzziah's and Ahaz's reigns). The final purging of the land will remove this stumbling. Part of the false religious hope in Judah was tied to the people's dependence on idols of foreign gods. By purging the nation of these idols, God will help the people focus on their true source of hope.

The Purging of Those Who Do Not Obey God (5:15). The Hebrew word translated "vengeance" does not mean spiteful, vindictive revenge. This refers to the just execution of divine control over the affairs of the world. In the process of exercising this full control, some who have ignored God's ways and not obeyed him will reap their just reward.

Application. Few would argue that idols and graven images do not present a false hope to the worshiper, and most would concede that the flimflam con artists in the religious world provide no real hope to those who are deluded by a lot of fast talk. Equally serious are the deceptive false hopes that are more realistic imitations of the truth, especially the hope offered by cults that make some use of the Bible.

MICAH 6:1–16

Original Meaning

God Brings a Covenant Lawsuit against Judah (6:1–8). *The initiation of God's lawsuit (6:1–2).* God exhorts his prophet to arise as a plaintiff in the court and plead the case. The mountains (personified) know about the people's immorality and false worship of other gods. Verse 2 reveals that God has serious accusations of covenant unfaithfulness to bring against them.

A defense of God's action (6:3–5). God appears to be searching his own heart to determine if there was some evidence of unfaithfulness on his part or some unreasonable burden he has put on his covenant partner. God defends his past behavior by reciting his great acts of grace on behalf of his people. An obvious implication of this evidence is that the fault does not lie with God.

A defense of Israel's action (6:6–7). The questions in 6:6–7 are rhetorical statements in which the people try to defend themselves by explaining how faithful they have been to God. But they focus on excessive giving, as if God is primarily interested in the size or cost of the gifts. Were they just a means of bribing God by giving him an enormous quantity of gifts? No, they were much different. They were an outward sign of the inner attitude of a person's broken and contrite heart.

What God requires (6:8). Micah is not attempting to reveal some new standard of conduct or give an expanded or secret list of requirements previously unknown. God has already communicated he wants three basic things. Micah's delineation of God's requirements is noteworthy insofar as it includes no negative statements about what is forbidden to the Israelites. It presents the key to a full life within the covenant.

Accusations and Verdict (6:9–16). *Accusations of covenant disloyalty (6:9–12).* God now raises specific examples demonstrating that the people in Jerusalem have failed to live up to their covenant agreement. There has been no justice for others, no deep desire or commitment to maintain their loyalty to covenant principles, and no attempt to walk circumspectly with God.

Verdict of punishment (6:13–16). Because of Israel's infidelity, the only possible verdict for this lawsuit is: guilty as charged. By giving this terrible conclusion, Micah is hoping to convince his audience of the seriousness of their sins. God will abandon the inhabitants of the city of Jerusalem and allow them to be ruined and annihilated by their enemies, and the nations will scornfully mock them. This is God's verdict if there is no immediate turning from their evil ways.

Application. One way church members today can ensure a proper relationship to God and avoid his condemnation is never to forget what he has done for them. This is why Paul encourages the church at Corinth to celebrate the Lord's Supper, basing it on the memory of what Jesus did at his last Passover and on the cross.

MICAH 7:1–20

Original Meaning

Micah Laments Judah's Decadent Social Situation (7:1–6). At the end of Micah's life, when he hoped to look back with satisfaction on what the Lord has accomplished through him, he sadly finds that there is official opposition from the political and religious leaders and a decline in public morality. Micah continues to weep over this decadent social situation (7:3). He compares the best and most upright of these oppressors to "briers" and "thorns" (7:4).

Having wept over the problems in Judah, Micah gives a brief prophetic prayer of confidence. After this confident statement of divine retribution, Micah returns to lament how the present social upheaval has destroyed the normal peaceful and trusting relationship within the family and neighborhood (7:5–6).

Confession of Trust in God (7:7–10). Verse 7 becomes a key focal point for repositioning the prophet's mental perspective on God's sovereign control of life. Micah's concentration on God rather than his problems enables him to see a ray of hope for the future. He will wait, trusting that his saving God will act.

Knowing that God is a holy God and Judah is sinful, Micah immediately expresses confidence that God will deliver them from their fallen state (7:8), forgive them of their sins (7:9), and shame those who have mocked God (7:10). Micah accepts the inevitability of the nation's judgment as a result of its sins, but in faith he believes that the nation will rise once again in the future (7:8).

Oracle of Salvation for Judah (7:11–13). These promises confirm that the expectations of the prophet (7:8–10) are not just pie in the sky or ungrounded imaginations of a false prophet. The audience should be persuaded to believe Micah's message of hope because it fits what God has already promised to do. God has not forgotten them; he is not impotent, and his purposes have not changed. Those who mock will be defeated and trampled into the dust when God annihilates the evil inhabitants of the earth.

Intercession for God to Act (7:14). Being reminded of God's glorious plan for his people, Micah requests that God, as divine Shepherd-King of his people, take charge of his own flock by graciously ruling over them with his scepter.

Oracle of Salvation (7:15–17). The yearning for the ancient situation in Micah's intercessory prayer (7:14) may be the impetus for God's response that recalls his marvelous deeds in the ancient past at the time of the exodus from Egypt. When God miraculously intervenes on behalf of his people, the nations that oppress them will see his power and be ashamed of their own puny strength (7:16). The nations will be powerless, devoid of ability to stand against God; thus, they will fearfully bow in submission before the God of the universe (7:16–17).

Hymn of Praise to God (7:18–20). Micah's time of prayer ends with words of praise to God. The process of lamenting naturally brings a person from bitter complaints at the beginning, through petitions for help, to statements of trust and confidence, so that at the end one can refocus on the character and power of God in words of praise. This hymn is made up of two parts: a celebration of God and what he has done (7:18) and praise for what God will do (7:19–20).

When he makes an oath to establish an eternal covenant relationship with a people, he does not back out halfway along the road. When God swore an oath to Abraham, he did not speak lightly without considering the cost and commitment of his promises. His eternal plan to use the seed of Abraham to bless all the nations of the earth and to make of them a great nation is the only plan he has. For Micah and his audience, that plan may have seemed like a lost cause in the days of Manasseh, but through God's love and forgiveness he will miraculously accomplish his will on earth. Micah's bold hymn of faith in God's victory over sin gives real hope for the future.

Application. For Micah, the depression of hopelessness turned not only to the possibility of hope but to the confidence that victory over sin is sure. Like Micah, we can gain some semblance of hope by focusing not on the terrible plight of our world but on God, his past promises, and his ability to deal with the source of hopelessness—sin itself.

NAHUM

INTRODUCTION TO NAHUM

The book of Nahum darkly promises Judah's release from the oppression and cruelty of Nineveh. Nahum's prophecy celebrates the fall of the sadistic empire and is a word of judgment against it. The book of Jonah is similar in its prophecy of doom to the Assyrian Empire (Jonah 3:4; Nah 1:1–2), and both books end with questions from God, one of hope and one of despair (Jonah 4:11; Nah 3:19). Both books also deal with God's reputation as a just judge *and* a forgiving God (as revealed in the golden calf incident in Exod 34:5–6). Nahum focuses on judgment for the wicked, and Jonah focuses on grace to the repentant. Nahum ends without repentance, and history records Nineveh's fall to Babylon in 612 BC.

BOOK OUTLINE

I. The Lord's Wrath against Cruelty (1:1–15)
II. The Destruction of the Destroyers (2:1–13)
III. An End to Nineveh's Endless Cruelty (3:1–19)

NAHUM 1:1–15

Original Meaning. Nahum 1:1 provides the reader with brief introductory information. The "prophecy" (Heb. *massa*, literally, "something lifted up, burden") refers to Nahum's message, or oracle, lifted before the people. Oracles were often "against the nations" that threatened Judah (Isa 13:1; 15:1; 17:1; 19:1; 21:1; 23:1; NIV "prophecy"). The written document (the book of Nahum) communicates the oracle that Nahum received as a "vision."

The theme of chapter 1 is Yahweh's wrath against cruelty. A longer section (1:1–10) and a shorter section (1:11–15) are its basic rhetorical parts. The longer part describes the strength of Yahweh's opposition to the Ninevite kingdom and serves as the introduction to the book. Three subtitles present its subject matter. "Vengeance" (1:1–3a) describes Yahweh's anger against those "guilty" of violence. The "way" of the Creator (1:3b–6) describes Yahweh's powerful use of the creation to accomplish his purposes (in Nineveh's case, the Babylonian army is an element of the creation). The "good" and the "trouble" (1:7–10) declares that Yahweh is a good "refuge" for those who trust in him but an "overwhelming flood" for those who plot against him.

The shorter rhetorical section (1:11–15) ends with a word concerning the reversal of Judah's situation ("I will break their yoke from your neck," 1:13a). Nineveh's reversal will be from plotting "evil" (1:11) to the "grave" (1:14).

Application. Two common responses to Yahweh's avenging are present in the opening verses of Nahum. Those who have suffered violence may find that God's vengeance brings them comfort. God's goodness in the midst of catastrophic events may strike a sympathetic chord. Others may be horrified at God's wrath and the violence of his judgments. Life experience deeply influences how these verses are heard and interpreted.

NAHUM 2:1–13

Original Meaning. Nahum 2 vividly describes the destruction of the destroyers. It begins with the final battle inside Nineveh (2:1–10), as Nahum paints a word picture of the coming war. Nineveh's impressive preparations for battle are described in colorful detail, followed by its unexpected fall (2:6). The chapter concludes with a short mock lament over the end of the torturous "lions' den" (a term for Nineveh's walled city, a haven for its violent military "lions" and their human spoil, 2:11–12). It ends with Yahweh's direct quotation, "I am against you"; he will destroy her "chariots . . . young lions . . . prey . . . [and] messengers" (2:13).

Application. In certain times in the life of the church, images of warfare were used in thinking about the advance of the gospel. The gospel of Mark in particular presents Jesus's confrontations with the spiritual enemy in his healing ministry. Paul describes how warfare against enemies is to be engaged in by heaping fiery coals of kindness on their heads (Rom 12:14–21). The early church took hope in this verse as a promise of the resurrection of the martyrs in the last day — that they would experience victory over the enemies of death and the opponent of life, Satan.

NAHUM 3:1–19

Original Meaning. The main theme of Nahum 3 is the end of Nineveh's endless cruelty. The graphic description of its coming woe is presented in three parts.

1. A section on Nineveh's cruelty and exposure (3:1–7) has many similarities to chapter 2. They are like panels on a wall with similar content, matching in some ways but arranged differently. It begins with a vivid description of Nineveh's bloody war-making (3:1–3; cf. 2:3–6) and with a strong sorceress metaphor for its deep offenses (3:4; cf. 2:11–12). It continues with "the LORD Almighty's" second declaration, "I am against you" (3:5), and with a description of Nineveh's coming exposure (3:5–6; cf. 2:13). Human response to the judgment follows (3:7; cf. the lion's den metaphor in 2:7–10).
2. A unit on Nineveh's vulnerability (3:8–13) compares Nineveh to the stronger cities of Egypt that have already fallen (3:8–11). Two metaphors taunt Nineveh's warmongers, comparing their fortresses to ripe fig trees and their troops to peace-loving women (3:12–13).
3. The final section on Nineveh's corruption and the joy of the surrounding nations over its fall (3:14–19) mocks Nineveh's futile battle preparations and corrupt leadership. With the final metaphor of locusts (grasshoppers), Nahum indicates that Nineveh's fall will be completed through its self-serving leaders who will plunder what they can and flee (3:14–17). The last word concerning the end of Nineveh's cruelty (3:18–19) is to the king of Assyria, who will be abandoned by all his people and fearful allies. Everyone will celebrate, for who had not been overwhelmed by his oppressive actions?

Application. A natural response to the most uncomfortable parts of Nahum is to create distance between the book and our present situation. The descriptions of the abusive exposure of the harlot in 3:5 and the killing of infants in 3:10 are especially disturbing. Avoiding these passages of Scripture is the most obvious way to apply our contemporary discomfort. This avoidance sometimes rests on the claim that Christ's command to love our enemies has made some texts insignificant for the Christian (Joshua and Nahum are usually at the top of the list). Yet something may be learned from this part of God's word. At the other end of the spectrum, the book may be applied as an excuse for *human* violence against evil. This involves putting humanity in the place of God, something that is commonly called sin.

Between these two extremes, Christians have used a wide range of strategies for understanding Nahum. Many have the effect of pushing the violence into a neat interpretive corner. These rationales avoid the possibility that God will afflict us and those who are dear to us. God's violence against the woman and against the infants is a warning that catastrophic violence may also come into our communities and require a response from the faithful. Those who have taken Nahum's word to heart may be prepared to speak and to act in accordance with the gospel. On that occasion Christians will have the opportunity to stand with the suffering and earn the credibility of a witness to God's power both to kill and make alive. The alternative is to distance oneself ideologically from the suffering (even one's own) and to lose credibility and even one's faith in a good God.

HABAKKUK

INTRODUCTION TO HABAKKUK

The book of Habakkuk is a dialogue between Habakkuk and Yahweh during a vision Habakkuk receives from Yahweh. It begins with Habakkuk's complaint against local corruption and leads to a prophecy that spans ninety years, as he is drawn into a progressively more difficult understanding of faith. It begins with the persistent question, "Why . . . ?" (1:3, 13) and ends with a sung prayer ("In wrath remember mercy," 3:2) and a confession of faith ("Though the fig tree does not bud . . . yet I will rejoice in the LORD," 3:17–18).

The prophet Habakkuk was probably an official temple musician-prophet (1 Chr 25:1). He was a contemporary of Nahum, Zephaniah, and Jeremiah and prophesied the fall of Judah to Babylon in the year of the Babylonians' victory over the Egyptians at Carchemish in northern Syria (605 BC).

BOOK OUTLINE

I. Habakkuk's Dialogue with Yahweh (1:1–17)
II. Yahweh's Revelation (2:1–20)
III. A Song to Yahweh (3:1–19)

HABAKKUK 1:1–17

Original Meaning. The entire book of Habakkuk is an oracle given as a dialogue between Habakkuk and Yahweh. Chapter 1 records the prophet's first set of questions ("LORD . . . why do you tolerate wrongdoing?" 1:2–3), Yahweh's first response ("Look . . . I am raising up the Babylonians," 1:5–6), and the second set of questions ("LORD . . . why then do you tolerate the treacherous?" 1:12–17). Habakkuk's second set of questions rephrases, intensifies, and expands the original question in light of the new information given in Yahweh's response. The key question of the chapter (and book) is asked in both sets: "Why do you tolerate wrongdoing?" (1:3b), and "You cannot tolerate wrongdoing. Why then do you tolerate the treacherous?" (1:13b).

Application. Habakkuk is a difficult book, especially in the modern context. Why does God give us a book with the death of Habakkuk's community as the basic plot? We are increasingly aware that such horrors are a current reality for many in the world. For anyone who has experienced or may experience the loss of a good way of life, cultural displacement, or abrupt change in cultural security, the message of Habakkuk is both relevant and timely. It does not sugarcoat reality. Within just a few years of the conversation, Jerusalem was completely destroyed.

God's message is fundamentally that soon the internal corruption that Habakkuk dislikes will give way to a much worse external enemy. Habakkuk's response gives us an opportunity to see how a believer may deal faithfully with news of impending death and destruction. Habakkuk responds like a person who has just heard that someone he loves has a cancer that will certainly kill him or her. The prophet's way of life and his life itself will soon come to an abrupt and painful end. We do not know whether Habakkuk survived the exile (as Jeremiah did).

HABAKKUK 2:1–20

Original Meaning. Habakkuk 2 gives Yahweh's revelation of the fall and the "woes" of Babylon. In 2:2 he tells the prophet to take notes (literally, "write a vision"; NIV "write down the revelation") on the future. It is a revelation within a revelation. The prophet waits on the city wall to see what answer Yahweh will give regarding his question about the wicked (2:1). God tells him to write down and publish two ways in the world: puffed-up desire and faith (2:4–6a). The way of puffed-up desire leads to five "woes" from the mouths of the Babylonians' captives (2:6b–20).

The revelation addresses the prophet's questions from chapter 1: "Why . . . do you tolerate the treacherous?" (1:13b), and "Why are you silent while the wicked swallow up those more righteous than themselves?" (1:13b). The question about God's toleration is addressed succinctly in 2:4b. This half verse may be the best known part of the book: "The righteous person will live by his faithfulness." The second question has a much more lengthy answer (2:6–20). Together these responses form Yahweh's plain truth for dealing with the situation and the persistence of wickedness in the world.

Several important points of God's reputation are at stake in Habakkuk's questions and in the answers given in chapter 2. As noted in 1:12–13, God is everlasting, holy, solid as a rock, and too pure to look on evil, and he cannot tolerate wrong. Three issues emerge.

1. How can the faithful believe if Jerusalem falls?
2. How can God's reputation stand in the world if the Babylonians (and the wicked in general) prosper?

3. How does Yahweh's reputation stand up to Babylon's idolatry? The first issue is addressed in 2:4b. The second is answered in the prophecy of Babylon's end (and the implied restoration of the people in the land; 2:7–8, 10b, 16). The third is answered between the lines in 2:11 (as creation itself will cry out against the Babylonians), in 2:14 (where the earth will be filled with the knowledge of God's glory), and in 2:20 (as the entire world is commanded to be silent before Yahweh in his temple).

Application. Habakkuk 2 provides practical help for times when our foundations are shaken. When we receive bad news that someone we love will soon die, that peace and security are quickly moving toward war and destruction, or that our religious leadership is falling from grace through corruption—our personal world can be shaken to the core. In Habakkuk 2, through his complaint, the prophet is seeking a word of good news from Yahweh. He waits and is told to make the message plain in writing, so that everyone in need can understand it. Yahweh gives him words (five woes) to speak against the source of their suffering (2:6–19) and reminds them to participate in worship (2:20). God gives the woes (or taunts) as a bit of wisdom, to teach the foolishness of the way of power. Power used to create unjust wealth will also be used to undo that wealth.

In the Christian tradition, Babylon and its fall have come to represent the sting of death and its defeat in the resurrection. We may, like the prophets, be racked in pain and fear, but the message on the wall is announced to all the people. Death and its oppression have been defeated. Scripture gives us the freedom to grieve with the faithful prophets when we experience severe loss, but it sends us up onto the heights to look for the word of victory from the Lord.

Yahweh's message through Habakkuk does not promise a quick and false solution to their suffering. He wants them to understand the reality of their future. He does not lie about the pain that must be endured (2:3). The plain truth is that God is with them in their suffering and dying and will deliver them in time. This message can be trusted; the righteous will live by faith in it.

HABAKKUK 3:1–19

Original Meaning. Habakkuk 3 is a song to Yahweh about his power and way in the world. Some have argued that Habakkuk 3 was added to the oracle rather than being a part of the original oracle. True, it is different in form and content from the rest of the book. Like a psalm it has a title that sets it apart. Nevertheless, it is integral to the book. The concluding verses (3:16–19) enclose the song into the whole revelation. They refer back to Yahweh's revelation of the rise of the Babylonians and their demise (ch. 2). The song functions as a response to the revelation within the book. It continues Habakkuk's dialogue with Yahweh concerning the success of violent people. It is an integral conclusion of the entire oracle, received in a vision by Habakkuk and announced in 1:1. The words of the prophet, even those spoken *to God* in chapter 3, are a gift *from God*. This circle of inspiration is a legacy of biblical prophecy in general.

As Habakkuk's song comes to its conclusion, the form and content change. In musical terms this is called a "bridge," which introduces a new musical theme and sometimes a change in key or tempo. The lyrics, as in Habakkuk's song, often offer a counterpoint to the previous theme of the song. The counterpoint cannot be more powerful than it is in Habakkuk's song. In 3:2–15 he sang of the visible power of Yahweh. Now, in 3:16–19, he will sing of his joy, even when the simplest sign of Yahweh's favor (food on the table) is absent.

Even though Habakkuk believes that Babylon will eventually fall (ch. 2), he knows it will be a horrible wait and goes on to describe the experience of oppression and poverty that will settle on the conquered. These are the conditions the prophet expects and anticipates overcoming in patience. He will not be a victim. He will be a survivor. Habakkuk rejoices despite the lack of goods and protection. He shows he is prepared to live by faith in unseen promises, even in suffering. Habakkuk's faith has found its sure footing *as faith*. He does not hope or believe in what he sees but in what he has heard as promises from Yahweh. His feet are established on the path by Yahweh, even on the difficult and rocky heights.

Application. This chapter demonstrates the necessary process of struggling with our previously held conceptions of God as well as growing into God's revelation of his way in the world. Through the centuries, people of faith have used 3:16–19 more often than 3:1–15. The last four verses represent a more seasoned, deepened, and stalwart faith than the earlier verses. They are the necessary maturing of a lasting faith, free of illusions.

Nevertheless, 3:1–15 is not just an immature stage or process that must be left behind. Their strength is given by Yahweh in Habakkuk's vision as a necessary memory of God's power. The verses are a necessary confession of the historic deeds of God and the awe inspired by his majesty in acts of ongoing creation.

ZEPHANIAH

INTRODUCTION TO ZEPHANIAH

Zephaniah prophesied during Josiah's reign (630s BC), perhaps setting the stage for the king's religious reform. The book of Zephaniah is one of judgment against Judah and its capital city, Jerusalem (chs. 1 and 3). In the midst of this judgment comes God's call for a faithful remnant who will be sheltered when Jerusalem and its enemies are destroyed. God's promise of joy returning to Jerusalem concludes the book.

BOOK OUTLINE

I. The Dark Day of Yahweh against Judah (1:1–18)
II. Yahweh against the Nations, and a Remnant Sheltered (2:1–15)
III. Jerusalem's Judgment and Jerusalem's Joy (3:1–20)

ZEPHANIAH 1:1–18

Original Meaning. The prophecy of the dark "day of the Lord" was spoken against Yahweh's own beloved people. Chapter 1 begins and ends without compromise. God says, "I will sweep away everything" (1:2, 3), and the prophet concludes, "He will make a sudden end of all who live in the land [NIV earth]" (1:18). The offenses that demand this harsh judgment are listed as indictments against the people of Judah. Corrupt worship is at the top of the list, including syncretism—the worship of Yahweh alongside the worship of many other created things (1:4–6). The wealthy leaders of corrupt worship themselves will become the consecrated sacrifice on the day of Yahweh (1:7–9). Believers who trust in commerce and wealth are also indicted, as the complacency of Jerusalem's better neighborhoods is noted and described (1:10–13). Finally, the prophet describes a great "day of darkness" (1:15) and graphic death in Jerusalem.

In Scripture the jealousy of Yahweh is not simply an emotion but a comprehensive concept, focused on the Creator/creation and Deliverer/delivered relationships. The two main biblical settings for understanding God's jealousy are the first part of the Ten Commandments (Exod 20:1–7) and the golden calf incident (read Exod 32:7–8 with 34:5–9, 14). God's jealousy is easily misunderstood. God is "jealous" not because he is lacking in himself (a common human form of jealousy), but in the positive sense of being zealous for his precious creation that is in danger of corruption and death. When the human creation turns away from the source of its life (Creator/Deliverer), it is on a path toward death. God's "jealousy" is a prejudice *toward life* for his created and delivered people.

God's jealous consuming the "whole earth" (Zeph 1:18) is for the expressed purpose of establishing a remnant of the faithful—in a sense to rescue or preserve the faithful from the corruption of all life. God's "jealousy" for a future remnant to live in the freedom, innocence, and justice of the world he intended required a cataclysmic act against his own people. The only hope for their rescue as a faithful people was in the suffering of exile and captivity (Isa 37:32). It is this same "jealousy" or "zeal" that leads to the announcement of a coming King.

Application. God sounds angry in Zephaniah 1:1–18. It is perhaps the most graphic description of his anger in the Bible. The intensity of language, its magnitude, and its detailed descriptions of Jerusalem's demise demonstrate that God is more than angry; he is enraged. The intensity of that anger is a measure of how much he cares about the human subject. In Zephaniah we encounter God's ultimate concern for us.

What makes God this angry? The source of that anger is the same today. It is the response of One who has cared, loved, and invested deeply in people who have prospered under his care but have turned away. This warped view of reality and the sources of our successes may be reformed through repentance and by returning to the biblical view of wealth. Many of the commands of Sinai concern wealth, and many of Jesus's teachings address its use. Jesus vociferously reminds the religious people of his day not to neglect the tithe and to practice justice, mercy, and faithfulness.

ZEPHANIAH 2:1–15

Original Meaning. The theme of chapter 2 is the cleansing of other nations from the land so that it may be possessed in the future by the humble remnant of Judah. The chapter begins with the possibility that a remnant that seeks Yahweh will survive (2:1–3) and goes on to declare that survivors will live again in the land (2:6–7, 9b, 11; see also 3:9–10, 12–13). The prophet calls on the humble and obedient to seek Yahweh in hope of protection on the day of the Lord's wrath.

This clearing and cleansing of the land is described in the remainder of the chapter (2:4–15). The violent "day of the

LORD" (2:7; a judgment against Judah in ch. 1) is against the others living in that land in chapter 2. Gaza and the Philistine cities (2:4–7) will be completely destroyed. Moab and Ammon (across the Jordan) will be plundered and possessed for their pride and taunts (2:8–11). Ethiopia (Cush) and Assyria will be turned into wild lands (2:12–15).

This clearing of the nations from the land prepares it for a new beginning. In the midst of the emptied land, we see a future with the survivors in the pastures and meadows (2:6–7). In the north will be domestic herds, wild animals, and birds (2:14). The land, its animals, and a humble remnant will be renewed by God. The hope of this chapter is whispered in the possibility of surviving the day of the Lord, but also in the vision of a new beginning. For most people, however, the day of the Lord will mean an end to life in the land, a reality the Babylonians later accomplished.

Verses 10–11 may be the most revealing expression of both Yahweh's complaint and desire for the nations. After reading 2:10 in this prophecy of doom, the listener would expect to hear another description of physical devastation and death (as in 1:9). Instead, Zephaniah speaks this amazing revelation: In place of pride, Yahweh will be "awesome to them," and "distant nations" will bow down in worship before the Lord (2:11). Yahweh's desire is not simply to eradicate arrogance but to replace it with true worship in every land.

Application. God's opposition to arrogance is clear. Biblical humility is not, however, simply a life of personal religious devotion. The purpose of humility is societal justice and service toward those in need. Humility is relational and brings saving help, such as Moses helping his community to resolve their disputes by administering justice (Exod 18:13–18). The great hymn of Christ's humility calls us to have a similar attitude, looking to serve the needs of others (Phil 2:3–8). Christ did not cling to his equality with God but became a servant in human form. He humbled himself, obediently submitting to death on a cross for our sake. His humility was not abstract but led to the salvation of those in need. He even allowed himself to be deprived of justice in order to help us (Act 8:33). He calls us to walk with him in the miraculous "rest" of this kind of humility (Matt 11:29).

ZEPHANIAH 3:1–20

Original Meaning. In 3:1 the focus abruptly shifts from the nations back to Jerusalem, summarizing and expanding the themes of destruction and survival. This chapter begins with Jerusalem's judgment (3:1–8) and ends with her joy (3:9–20). The central verses (3:8–9) form a bridge, 3:8 speaking judgment and 3:9 announcing joy's beginning.

The judgment of Jerusalem is divided into two parts.

1. The city's sins of arrogance and corruption are described (3:1–5), sins that are against both God and people. The sins continue, although Yahweh has been faithful.
2. Yahweh describes the futile warnings he has given (3:6–8), but Jerusalem will not accept correction; "therefore . . . the whole world will be consumed" (3:8).

The joy of Jerusalem (3:9–20) may also be read in two parts.

1. In 3:9–13 God makes promises for the remnant. He will establish those who trust in his name in purity, humility, and safety.
2. The last verses (3:14–20) describe part of the day of joy in Jerusalem. They will sing in security because Yahweh will be near to them. Speaking directly ("I . . . you"; 3:18–20), Yahweh makes seven direct promises to those who trust in his name.

This chapter contains many changes in voice. The subject of the verb shifts between "the LORD" and "I" (God speaking in the first person). The object of the verb also abruptly shifts. Verses 1–10 are words of judgment spoken to the entire city of Jerusalem in the third person ("them"). Verses 11–20 are a word of hope spoken to the remnant ("you"). This combination of the "I" and the "you" makes the last half of the last chapter of Zephaniah powerfully personal for the community of faith.

Verse 20 fills out the last four of the seven promises. "'At that time I will gather you; at that time I will bring you home. I will give you honor and praise among all the peoples of the earth when I restore your fortunes before your very eyes,' says the LORD." For an exiled people, no set of promises carries more hope (see Ps 137). To be gathered home, to have what was lost restored, and to be honored by other peoples of the earth are the normalcy and health for which every culture longs. For believers in Zephaniah's Jerusalem, hearing the promise before any of this is lost will expand their view to the greater good God desires for them. Their culture will pass first through the great Babylonian crucible of purification. Then the people will understand that their previous cultural successes have come only through God, who gives all good things.

Application. The world experiences God's judgment against sin daily, especially sins of human arrogance against God and his good creation. The violence of war maims children. Human pollution destroys soil and drinking water. Famine emaciates. Children suffer the sins of parents' uncommitted dalliances. Greed is eventually judged through calcified corruption that handcuffs economies and traps the populace in cycles of uncertainty and poverty. National corruption and the lies of government propaganda are judged through a populace's frustration, radicalization, or acts of terror. God's judgment of corruption in the world's societies is reported as news every day.

These judgments are not the final judgment, but they are, nonetheless, real judgments in Zephaniah's tradition.

We are under judgment when see the negative effects on children exposed too early to violence and greed through the media in our homes. We recognize judgment when deep anxiety disrupts sanguine lives for no apparent reason. We are judged when substance abuse takes its vengeance on dear relationships. Judgment reigns through the self-destructive tendencies of laziness and overwork, failure to worship and pious self-righteousness, habitual self-deprecation and smug satisfaction, and the hidden powers of sensuality and the pride of asceticism.

Our arrogance is not limited to personal and social realms. We are under God's judgment for contaminating air and thereby threatening public health, the fouling and mismanagement of soil and its threat to agriculture, and the pollution and waste of clean water. Individuals reap what businesses and nations sow in every aspect of God's creation.

Judgment denied is like alcoholism denied. Admitting our true situation and complicity with our inherited condition is the beginning of our only hope. Ignoring it doesn't make it go away but guarantees that it will kill again. Many societies since Zephaniah's oracle have suffered Jerusalem's fate. Some people in ancient Judah understood his warning and turned to Yahweh. They heard and saw the judgment before it arrived. As a result, they also heard and saw the hope that God offered.

HAGGAI

INTRODUCTION TO HAGGAI

The prophets Haggai and Zechariah complement each other (see Introduction to Zechariah below). Both prophets announce an imminent restoration inaugurated by the return of God, dependent on repentance of the people. For Haggai, repentance can be shown in the rebuilding of the temple. The prophet's message is summarized with Yahweh's message to the people in 1:8: "Build my house, so that I may take pleasure in it and be honored." For both Haggai and Zechariah, the ultimate goal is the return of the presence and blessing of God to his people in order to transform the cosmos.

BOOK OUTLINE

I. Exhortation to Rebuild the Temple (1:1–15)
II. Encouragement for Restoring the Former Glory (2:1–9)
III. Prophetic Message on the Day the Foundation Was Laid (2:10–23)

HAGGAI 1:1–11

Original Meaning. Haggai's message comes at a significant time not only in the history of the Persian Empire, but also in the yearly and monthly rhythm of the Jewish people. At the center of the prophetic message is the call for the people to action, followed by two responses by Yahweh (1:8). On each side is the dialogue, and, although in this dialogue one does not hear the voice of the people, God's speeches anticipate and voice the people's thoughts and hearts. This is seen in 1:2–7 when God says: "These people say . . ." (1:2) and in 1:9–11 when the Lord declares: "Why?" (1:9). In both dialogues there is a connection between two basic issues: the house of the Lord and the poverty of the people. At first the connection is made subtly through the use of the interrogative, "Is it a time for you yourselves . . ." (1:4), and the reflective verbal expression, "Give careful thought to your ways . . ." (1:5). But as we move into 1:9–11, the connection is made directly and abrasively: "Why? . . . Because . . ."(1:9). God makes this clear in 1:11.

There is much in this initial prophetic encounter that addresses the predicament of the people. They are experiencing curses at the hand of Yahweh, who is displeased with their lack of attention to rebuilding the temple. The prophet is calling them to action and warning that inaction will mean further curses. However, this human action is linked to God's purposes and activity. The ultimate purpose of this project is the pleasure and glory of God. Ultimately, they are not to do it for relief from curse but for the pleasure and glory of God.

Application. This passage, read in light of the New Testament's redefinition of the temple as the Christian community, challenges us to release our resources for God's kingdom work beyond the physical structures of a building and to reconsider funds invested in such structures. Haggai also moves us to see our world from God's perspective, to make his priorities our priorities and see the consequences of not sharing these priorities. It places, then, at its center not the human predicament (that is only a means to an end) but rather divine desire, a desire defined as God's pleasure and glorification.

HAGGAI 1:12–15

Original Meaning. Verses 12–15 describe the people's response to Haggai's message in 1:1–11, which is given both from the divine and human perspective. At the center is the core promise: "I am with you" (1:13). This response represents a massive step of faith. Nearly two decades prior to this, an earlier group of Jews under their governor Sheshbazzar had responded to the invitation of Cyrus and began to work on the same temple site, yet with little success (see Ezra 1; 5:15–16). Now amidst threats from those in adjoining Persian provinces (see 3:3; 4:1–5; 5:1–6:15), a different generation begins the temple project anew. The message of God's promised presence is essential to bolster the faith of these underdogs.

Application. Haggai 1:12–15 reminds us that God graciously grants us the resources to fulfill his priorities, making it clear that even the human response is a work of the Almighty God as he stirs his people to action and then promises his presence to sustain the work. This does not preclude human involvement; rather, it assumes it. However, in the new covenant, God accompanies the call with his empowerment (see Jer 31:31–34). He provides the spiritual resources, especially through the Spirit, to fulfill his mandate within our generation. The resources are provided by the sovereign God as we respond to his call.

HAGGAI 2:1–9

Original Meaning. Ezra 3:1–6 suggests that by the first day of the seventh month, the sacrificial and festal system had been reinstituted on the rebuilt altar on the temple site. Haggai 2:1–9 places this oracle on day twenty-one of this seventh month, which was the busiest month in the Israelite festal calendar. By day twenty-one of this month (2:1), the lack of progress on the project coupled with the enormity of the task yet to come may have been accentuated by the frustration of celebrating a festal event in the unsightly ruins. In sum, Haggai calls a disgruntled and discouraged community to work with renewed strength and without paralyzing fear.

Application. It is easy to become trapped into evaluating the present experience of the church with past paradigms of spirituality rather than remaining open to the ways in which God is impacting the present generation in culturally relevant ways. It is possible to focus so intently on the experiences of past giants of the faith that one begins to live vicariously through these stories and examples and squelches one's own immediate experience with God. Such reflection on the past is not entirely illegitimate. There is something good in this longing to experience afresh the glory of the past. However, when such reflection on the past leads to inaction, we need to hear the message of Haggai 2:1–9.

HAGGAI 2:10–23

Original Meaning. The book of Haggai records the date of the prophet's prophecies in order to provide a historical backdrop for the reading of the text. To this point the dates have been linked to the feasts of the Jews—not surprising from a prophet whose name means "feast" and whose message is focused on the temple, the destination, and physical context of the feasts. Although at first sight this third pericope does not seem to follow this pattern, a closer look will reveal that it is connected to a significant celebration related to the temple rebuilding.

The date coincides with the third month anniversary of the beginning of the rebuilding project and, more importantly, with "the day when the foundation of the LORD's temple was laid" (2:18). On this day, Haggai addresses not only the people as a whole on the topic of blessing (2:15–19), but the priestly caste on the topic of purity (2:10–14) and Zerubbabel on the topic of royal power (2:20–23). Thus, this passage preserves the trend established in previous pericopes. Haggai's message is once again linked to a ritual celebration, but this time with a ceremony connected with the rebuilding of the temple. This is an important signal to the Persian authorities as well as to the Jewish people that substantial progress has been made on the temple structure.

Haggai 2:10–23 functions as a positive encouragement for the people, affirming their decision to move forward in the rebuilding project and to lay the foundation of the temple. This encouragement is offered by comparing the dismal past with the promised future, linking blessing to the obedient response of the people. This future blessing is ultimately linked to the reestablishment of the royal house represented by Zerubbabel, who becomes a symbol of hope for the community of God.

Application. As human beings our acts of sacrifice and worship are defiled by the touch of our fallen hands. Only through Jesus, the one who transforms our fallenness through his death and resurrection, can our sacrifices be acceptable before God. Those who are redeemed by Jesus can now walk in obedience by the Holy Spirit. However, even this new covenant community can become trapped in the meaningless practice of sacrifice without obedience. It is easy within the church today to bring our sacrifice, whether our verbal worship, our material contributions, or our gifts and abilities, and yet be walking in disobedience either because of a heart that is disengaged from the God of covenant or because of a pattern of life contrary to God's standards.

There is a climactic and triumphant tone to this final prophetic message in Haggai. Although the temple structure is far from completion, Haggai sees implications for the project far beyond the mere reversal of the dire human situation of the Jews in 520 BC. Haggai sees it as the first step in the establishment of God's rule on earth.

The coming of Christ means that we can live with far more hope than those who lived in Haggai's time. Jesus has come, fulfilling the prophetic hope of the Old Testament. This grants to us far more closure and certainty than those who longed for the coming messianic age. We continue to live, though, in faith as Haggai's audience of old, awaiting the ultimate shaking of the cosmos, the overthrow of all earthly power through the arrival of the Divine Warrior in the last days (Rev 19).

ZECHARIAH

INTRODUCTION TO ZECHARIAH

The prophets Haggai and Zechariah complement each other (see Introduction to Haggai above). Both announce an imminent restoration inaugurated by the return of God, dependent on repentance of the people. For Zechariah, repentance is demonstrated in the people's purity in their covenant relationship to Yahweh. The prophet's message is encapsulated in Yahweh's plea in 1:3, "Return to me . . . and I will return to you." For both Zechariah and Haggai, the ultimate goal is the return of the presence and blessing of God to his people in order to transform the cosmos.

BOOK OUTLINE

I. Sermon and Narrative: God's Call and Promise to Return (1:1–6)
II. Vision of Horses, Oracles of Comfort (1:7–17)
III. Vision of the Horns and Plowmen (1:18–21)
IV. Vision and Oracle: Jerusalem's Walls and God's Presence (2:1–5)
V. Oracle of Return of People and God (2:6–13)
VI. Vision, Sign-Act and Oracle: Joshua, the Shemah, and Blessing (3:1–10)
VII. Vision and Oracle: The Lampstand, the Olive Trees, and Prophecy (4:1–14)
VIII. Vision and Oracle: The Flying Scroll and God's Judgment (5:1–4)
IX. Vision of the Flying Ephah (5:5–11)
X. Vision of the Four Chariots (6:1–8)
XI. Sign-Act of the Two Crowns (6:9–15)
XII. Sermon, Narrative, and Oracles: From Fasts to Feasts (7:1–8:23)
XIII. Return of God, King, and People (9:1–17)
XIV. The Restoration of the Tribes (10:1–12)
XV. The Crisis and Cleansing of Leadership (11:1–17)
XVI. Future Victory and Cleansing of God's People (12:1–13:6)
XVII. The Shepherd Struck, the Flock Scattered (13:7–9)
XVIII. Future Victory and Submission of the Nations (14:1–21)

ZECHARIAH 1:1–6

Original Meaning. Penitential prayer arises from the agenda for renewal presented in the blessings and curses of the Torah and Solomon's prayer of dedication for the temple. In penitential prayers, one finds that the former generation, who did not listen to the prophets are attacked, and the present generation responds by confessing their culpability while affirming Yahweh's justice. By the time of Ezra and Nehemiah the penitential prayer tradition is clearly associated with the priests. Zechariah, arising out of the priestly context as a prophetic voice, is a good candidate to set the agenda for true repentance to accompany such liturgical acts of penitence.

An initial read through 1:2–6 may cause some confusion. In the short space of five verses, one finds multiple layers of quoted material: God speaks to Zechariah, telling him to declare to the present generation a message that includes a quotation of former prophets who were relaying a message from God to a former generation. Although difficult at points to follow, the passage reflects a rhetorical trend in later prophecy in which Yahweh is emphasized as the source of the prophetic speech, even if that is at the expense of literary flow.

Zechariah 1:6b is a report of the reaction of the people to Zechariah's initial message and picks up the narrative thread that begins in 1:1. Zechariah 1:2 sets the context for the prophetic message with a look to the past, expressing God's anger toward the former generation. This is explained in more detail in 1:4–6a and is a negative example for Zechariah's contemporaries to avoid. Verse 3, "return," then looks to the future, identifying the goal of this prophetic message, which has both a human ("repented," 1:6b) and divine (1:7–2:13; "return," 1:16) element, using the same verb (*shub*) for both.

Application. Biblical repentance is a matter of turning *to* as well as turning *from*, an abandonment into the arms of a God passionate for relationship. Biblical repentance is not just focused on behavioral patterns, but more importantly and more fundamentally on relational patterns: someone to love, not just some way to act. By reorienting our perspective on sin and repentance, we do not reduce but enhance the call to purity and holiness. Set in this covenantal context we are encouraged to live faithfully before God in all areas of life, not just in areas prescribed in our limited list of vices and virtues.

ZECHARIAH 1:7–17

Original Meaning. In the overall scheme of Zechariah 1–8, 1:7 is the doorway into the visionary world of the prophet.

This series of visions in 1:7–6:15 is often referred to as the "night visions." This first vision comes "during the night" (1:8). What we find in this first vision is a scene drawn from a military context. A group returning from a worldwide reconnaissance mission is reporting back to the commanding officer in a secret location. Such a military scene reminds the readers that the Lord is in control of their history, even if it is not always evident in the experience of those under foreign hegemony.

The report of the reconnaissance mission appears at first to be positive, for the angels have found "the whole world at rest and in peace" (1:11). This, however, is hardly comforting to the angel of the Lord, who appears to be looking for evidence of an upheaval that will usher in a new day for God's people. He takes on the intermediary role of the prophet and cries out to Yahweh: "How long?" (1:12). The allusion to "seventy years" (1:12) clearly refers to the exile, the purpose of which was to discipline God's people.

Even before we hear God's message, we are prepared for a positive response, for he speaks "kind and comforting words" (1:13) to the angel. The Lord expresses his message in highly emotive terms. His promise flows out of his character and is secured by his intense loyalty to his people. The zeal of God for his people is linked with the anger of God toward the nations (1:15).

After describing the present situation, the prophetic message makes a transition to the announcement of salvation with the word "therefore" (1:16). Yahweh promises to "return to Jerusalem with mercy" (1:16). Not only will God rebuild his house and his city, but he will also make them prosperous as he comforts and chooses them.

Application. The visionary scene accentuates the sovereignty of God over the affairs of the world. The reconnaissance mission symbolizes his omniscient awareness of the situation of his people. Similarly, the question "How long?" asked by the angel of the Lord in 1:12 expresses the assumption that God is superintending the experience of his people. Faith in God's sovereignty is essential to the walk of faithfulness as we await the return of Christ. The words of the apostles in Acts powerfully express such faith for us as Christians. Fresh from persecution they "raised their voices together in prayer to God" and began with the simple cry: "Sovereign Lord" (Acts 4:23–30). May that also be our cry as the people of God.

ZECHARIAH 1:18–21

Original Meaning. With the proclamation of Yahweh still ringing in their ears, one that offered hope to Israel and warning to her enemies, the reader now enters a second visionary scene. In this second vision, Zechariah sees four horns and what are often identified as four craftsmen. The angel tells Zechariah that these horns are those that have "scattered Judah, Israel and Jerusalem" (1:19). The horn is a common image for the military might of a nation.

The devastation of the exilic experience for both nations is summed up in 1:21 in the Hebrew idiom "no one could raise their head." In the negative form it is used for loss of freedom, and in the positive for regaining of independence. In this second vision Zechariah sees a scene that offers hope to his community. The nations that have scattered Israel will be driven back to their places, powerless to abuse the Jewish community any longer. This second vision, then, offers a revelation of what must precede this rebuilding project: the smashing of the power of the nations. Zechariah is also shown God's passion for his people, expressed in his punishment of Babylon.

Application. The ultimate symbol of this principle is the incarnation. Christ came in a helpless state and conquered through the helplessness of the cross. This is not only the basis for our vulnerable walk of faith, but it is an example to those who take up their cross and follow him. The weak things of the world conquer, not because of their weakness but because of the necessity for faith. Helplessness forces the believer to trust in the only One who can rescue them from their predicament.

ZECHARIAH 2:1–5

Original Meaning. This encounter with an individual holding surveying equipment in his hand fits the historical context in which the prophet Zechariah was living. The people had returned to the land and were in the midst of a major building project as they restored the temple in Jerusalem. The vision of Zechariah 2:1–5 unpacks the promises of the initial vision in 1:8–17, in particular, the promise that God will return (1:16), rebuild the temple and city (1:16), and restore prosperity (1:17). This continues the tone of comfort that began in 1:13 in response to the initial penitence of the people (1:1–6).

Application. Transformed vision and faithful living are possible only for the community that experiences God's personal presence in their midst. The glorious message of the New Testament is that God has graced us with his presence through his Holy Spirit, who enlivens his faithful community. Yet our churches and lives are often bereft of manifestations of his presence. As communities of faith, we are often unaware of God's absence in our midst and need to cry to him to pour out his Spirit. Without that presence, the challenges of this vision, to which we now turn, will never be realized.

ZECHARIAH 2:6–13

Original Meaning. The oracle in 2:6–13 builds on the previous visions and calls the people to respond to God's initial work and promise by returning to his land and city, where he promises his presence. Verse 11 introduces a surprise into the oracle by declaring that foreigners will enter the community of the Lord on the day when God's presence returns to Israel. That the expression "many nations" (2:11) does not refer to the exilic community living among the nations but to the nations themselves is clear from other prophetic contexts that use this verb and imagery. The universal vision will be realized through the particular reinstatement of Judah and Jerusalem as God's special possession. God's return to his land, city, and temple has implications for all humanity.

Application. This oracle balances the call to God's community to escape "the corruption in the world caused by evil desires" (2 Peter 1:4), but also to embrace God's redemptive plan for the world. Zechariah reminds us of God's passion for the nations, a passion that informed his purposes for his people from the outset of redemptive history and climaxed in the revelation of his Son Jesus Christ and the community he established. Of course, this impact on the nations is possible only for the community that has been redeemed from the bondage of sin and cultivates God's presence in its midst through worship.

ZECHARIAH 3:1–10

Original Meaning. The Lord shows Zechariah a scene that features Joshua, a priest representing the priesthood. Joshua is the focus of a meeting of the heavenly council in which the Lord is surrounded by his angelic messengers. On the right side of Joshua stands "Satan" (3:1), who brings an accusation and seeks a guilty verdict. Rather than deny the accusations, the Lord rebukes the accuser and declares his intention to change the deplorable condition of the high priest because of his election of Jerusalem. The removal of sin in one day alludes to the high priest's role as representative of Israel who, through the rites of the Day of Atonement, made atonement for the sins of the people and for their defilement of the sanctuary.

In summary, Zechariah 3 uses Joshua's investiture as high priest for two purposes.

1. It is an opportunity to speak to Joshua as high priest, assuring him of God's blessing and calling him to faithfulness in his duties.
2. It is also an opportunity to speak to Joshua as representative of his priestly line, which is a sign-act of something far greater—a new era in redemptive history that will culminate in the coming of a royal Davidic ruler. Key to this new era is the removal of guilt from the land and prosperity for its inhabitants.

Application. It is the sovereign choice and gracious provision of God in Zechariah 3 that ultimately undermine the arguments of the accuser. This can be applied to our ultimate spiritual adversary to whom is often attributed two great lies. Before we fall into sin, he whispers in our ear that such a sin is of no great consequence—only afterward to turn on us and remind us that the same sin has made us eternally unworthy for God's kingdom. Zechariah 3 reminds us of God's sovereign election and free grace, assuring revelation from God that silences both accuser and accusation.

ZECHARIAH 4:1–14

Original Meaning. The vision of the lampstand and olive trees emphasizes the role of the prophet in the restoration of the early Persian period. The lampstand, signifying the role of the temple as the location from which God's presence and sovereignty emanate throughout the earth, is fueled by oil supplied by the prophets.

Zerubbabel's involvement in rebuilding the temple is well attested in the Old Testament. These oracles are messages of encouragement and hope for Zerubbabel and the activity he commences. The details of these two oracles bolster the relationship between vision and oracle in Zechariah 4. In both, the royal and prophetic offices are intertwined. The power of the Spirit well associated with the prophetic office and linked to the empowerment of the royal office is promised to Zerubbabel, who undertakes the temple building project in the first oracle. The promise of the prophet confronts the skepticism against Zerubbabel in the second oracle. Surely the "oil" of prophecy fueled the building project, bringing God's presence on earth.

Application. Zechariah 4 calls the church back to the empowerment of God's spirit for its life and mission. The Spirit's empowerment provides us with the courage to overcome the incredible challenges that stand in our way. For Zerubbabel the challenge was represented by the pile of rubble that stood before his community as they commenced the rebuilding project. God's word through Zechariah came at the right time and reminded Zerubbabel of his need for the Spirit's empowerment to accomplish this task. So also today, as communities of faith we face formidable tasks that remind us of our desperate need for God's empowerment.

ZECHARIAH 5:1–4

Original Meaning. The scroll in 5:1 has several unusual features. The first peculiarity (suspended above the earth) grants the scroll the ability to fulfill its purpose of judgment with swiftness while providing access to a large territory. The second oddity (double-sided) links the scroll to the foundational covenant document delivered to Moses on Mount Sinai. The significance of the third irregularity (large size) most likely signifies a scroll that displays a section of the law and is commensurate with the size of transgression and territory. This vision raises the profile of the law as the guide to life in covenant relationship.

Application. This message has enduring significance for the Christian community as we seek to embody individually and corporately the values of this ancient law. With the confidence that Christians now live in the new era of the Spirit, we must be a community transfixed by the law of Christ, which is being written on our hearts.

ZECHARIAH 5:5–11

Original Meaning. Whereas the vision in 5:1–4 confronted covenant infidelity in human relationships, the second vision confronts covenant infidelity in the people's relationship with God. Yahweh is a jealous God who will not tolerate any rival.

The prophet is commanded to observe a new scene: a measuring "basket" (5:6) exiting the sanctuary. The angel identifies this container as "the iniquity of the people throughout the land" (5:6). The contents of the basket is a goddess or her idol, representing the idolatrous worship of the people. The "one" woman in the basket is clearly distinguished from the "two women" who elevate the measuring basket "between earth and heaven" (5:9).

Zechariah asks the obvious question: "Where are they taking the basket?" (5:10). The angel replies that the destination is "the land of Shinar" (5:11; lit., NIV "Babylonia"). It was in Shinar that the infamous episode of the Tower of Babel was set, a story that expresses the aspiration of humanity to invade God's heavenly abode and overthrow his rule. The resting place of the measuring basket with its dangerous contents is a temple built specially for it. Because it contains an idol, we can assume that this new structure will function as a shrine for the worship of the goddess contained therein.

Application. Gone are the days when the worship section of our services was considered the "preliminaries"—that is, those elements that preceded the main event, the sermon. To be a worship leader today demands a high level of theological and spiritual training. Worship teams desperately need to be mentored in their study and experience of God so that they may help lead others into relationship with God.

ZECHARIAH 6:1–8

Original Meaning. The prophet encounters a scene at the entrance to the divine council. Exiting it are the four winds of heaven, God's agents for judgment, depicted as four chariots each drawn by different colored horses. These powerful beasts are ready for war, pawing the ground, straining to go forth, yet awaiting their master's permission. When they are finally released, the Lord turns to the prophet and highlights the actions of the two chariots headed north. They bring judgment on "the land of the north" (6:8), venting God's wrath on the nation who exiled his people. This vision depicts in broad terms God's punishment of Babylon. God's comforting words have become reality as he unleashes his might on the helpless Babylonians.

Application. Zechariah 6:1–8 declared to believers living in the early Persian period that God had fulfilled his commitment to break the oppression of Babylon. But this message continued to speak throughout the history of redemption as God consistently rescued his people. This redemption came to a climax in the work of God in Christ, who is represented as both the community longing for release from exile and the God waging divine war on their behalf.

ZECHARIAH 6:9–15

Original Meaning. In this sign-act the prophet is told to take silver and gold from Jews who have recently returned from Babylon and to bring them to another returnee who is in charge of the growing temple treasure. Zechariah is to oversee the manufacture of two crowns from these metals, one of which is to be placed on the head of the high priest Joshua, who then receives a special message from God. This message concerns a figure who will fulfill Jeremiah's promise of a Davidic descendant ("Branch," Jer 23:5–6; Zech 6:12) and rebuild the temple. The priest will have a major role to play when this individual arrives, and they will work together. The building of the temple will not commence until others have joined them ("those who are far away," 6:15). The prophet exhorts them to await the fulfillment of his prophecy.

Application. What is the ultimate purpose of the church? I am convinced that the main purpose of the redeemed people of God is to participate in the restoration of God's rule in this world. Christ came proclaiming this rule of God ("kingdom of God"; e.g., Matt 12:28; 19:24) and inaugurated it through his death, resurrection, and ascension. As the church proclaims the gospel, it is fulfilling this purpose by announcing the kingdom. As the church worships the Lord, it attests to this rule on earth.

As the church serves its community, it extends the kingdom. As the church equips the saints by teaching them obedience to Christ, it is expanding the rule of God qualitatively deeper into the life of a community of faith.

ZECHARIAH 7:1–14

Original Meaning. Zechariah 7:1 sets this prophetic passage in the wider context of ancient Near Eastern history and, in particular, the redemptive history of Israel. The scene opens with some people from Bethel approaching the officials at the temple in Jerusalem for a decision on a liturgical matter. Zechariah offers not only the message of the earlier prophets but also a history lesson in the consequences of ignoring or rejecting God's message (cf. 1:1–6). In doing this, the prophet is not on a tangent unrelated to the original question of the delegation. This review of Israel's story began with his question: "Are these not the words . . ." (7:7), which were related directly to his concern over the fasting practices during the past seventy years. Zechariah is doing something more here than merely reciting the story of Israel and laying the foundation for his challenge to his own generation. He is using the very liturgy from the days of fasting in order to drive home his point about the people's lack of repentance.

Application. It is instructive that the revelation of Jesus Christ and his grace was preceded by the prophetic call to repentance through John the Baptist. God was serious about a covenant relationship with his people, a relationship based on extending his grace to a sinful people. But such grace required the sincere repentance of his people. This principle is reflected in the hope of Zechariah 7–8 and needs to inform our own experience with God today.

God demands fidelity in relationship and calls us to repentance as he extends grace to us through Christ's death and resurrection. As people are invited to respond to God in faith, they should also reflect deeply over the condition of their hearts and lives, renouncing their past life of sin even as they embrace the Spirit's enabling new life in Christ. In a rush to get people to pray a prayer of faith to God, Christians often present a truncated view of conversion, that is, one that involves a turning to God but not a turning from sin.

ZECHARIAH 8:1–13

Original Meaning

God's Salvation of the Remnant—Oracles (8:1–8). *Oracle 1 (8:2).* After having just encountered 7:4–14 with its description of God's discipline of the former generation, we expect an oracle of judgment directed at Judah. The surprise, however, is that Zechariah speaks of Israel's deliverance. The wrath is directed toward the nations who abused Israel.

Oracle 2 (8:3). Yahweh promises to return and dwell in Jerusalem. Zechariah's vocabulary of God's return to Jerusalem is closely linked to Exodus 25:8, which uses the same Hebrew phrase to describe God's dwelling in the tabernacle.

Oracle 3 (8:4–5). The prophet uses two images that represent life at its two extremes (children and the aged), the periods of greatest vulnerability. These images reveal life far above the subsistence level many have known since the judgment of 587 BC, a life with abundance of provisions and protection from harm.

Oracle 4 (8:6). Yahweh's passionate zeal results in his return to dwell in Jerusalem, transforming it into a city with the qualities of his character and with a renewed life of prosperity and peace.

Oracle 5 (8:7–8). Having identified the ultimate picture of a renewed Jerusalem, Zechariah now proclaims the means by which this miraculous God will fill his city. He will rescue his people from their exile and return them to Jerusalem.

God's Salvation of the Remnant—Sermon (8:9–13). Here we return to the style familiar from the book of Haggai with its regular use of the phrase "let your hands be strong" (8:9, 13) and "do not be afraid" (8:13), and an emphasis on rebuilding the temple and agro-economic woe and weal. The message here is designed to encourage those involved in the rebuilding project.

Verse 11 represents a turning point typical in prophetic speeches. God's new stance toward the community will be expressed through renewed blessing of the land (8:12). The final verse repeats themes of blessing and cursing and represents the main reason why this prophetic sermon was chosen for this particular place in Zechariah 7–8. Zechariah contrasts their experience among the nations as an object of curse with their experience in the coming era in which they will become a conduit for God's blessing to the nations.

Application. Zechariah 8:1 locates Yahweh's intention in moving from discipline to deliverance in his passionate zeal for his people. This reminds us that although this passage emphasizes human response, God is the one who must enact salvation for his people. He does not do so begrudgingly, but rather fervently desires to save and know his people. This revelation of God's heart is the greatest source of hope for every generation.

ZECHARIAH 8:14–23

Original Meaning

God's New Determination (8:14–15). Zechariah plays on the term "determined" (Heb. *zamam*) to signal a new era of redemptive history. The use of this term emphasizes "divine intentionality" and interestingly is only used elsewhere in the Hebrew Bible in reference to Yahweh's intention to enact discipline. Now instead of disaster, they will experience good.

God's Ethical Demand (8:16–17). The comforting words in 8:13, "do not be afraid," bring closure to this oracle of salvation, a regular feature of prophetic speech. The prophet, however, is not finished, for now he identifies the part the people must play in order to experience this turn in redemptive history. Verses 16–17 offer a list of admonitions to follow and prohibitions to avoid.

Transformation of Fasts to Feasts (8:18–19). The purpose of the intervening section has been to shape the fasting liturgy and to call the people to fasting, which will indeed accomplish the purpose for which it was designed: an expression of repentance from infidelity and a commitment to obey God's covenant demands. The previous imperatives in 8:16–17 have shown that this new era will not be inaugurated unless the people obey the ethical demands urged by the earlier prophets.

Impact on the Nations—Entreating Yahweh (8:20–23). Following 8:19 we find two additional oracles that expand the scope of the discussion. The first oracle (8:20–22) reflects a strong tradition in the prophetic movement in which the nations are drawn to Jerusalem to seek Yahweh. The second oracle (8:23) highlights the role of the Jewish community returning from exile. Their obedience will usher in the new era in which Jerusalem will fulfill its original purpose as the place of God's manifest presence on earth, from which his rule will extend over the cosmos and to which all nations will bend their knee either in glad adoration or broken submission.

Application. Zechariah looks to the future with hope. He envisions a day of restoration when a penitent people rejoice in the presence of their God. This reminds us that fasting is not an end in itself but has covenant relationship as its goal. Churches should take opportunities to enjoy fellowship meals together during their yearly rhythm of life as a congregation. These meals can become opportunities to share God's goodness with one another in word and deed. Celebrations on Easter Sunday or Christmas are important to the life of our faith communities.

ZECHARIAH 9:1–17

Original Meaning

God Returns in Triumph (9:1–8). Considering that the focus is on "all the tribes of Israel" (9:1), it is appropriate that traditional enemies of both the northern (Syria, Phoenicia) and southern tribes (Philistia) are mentioned. The vision of the sack and burning of Tyre sends shock waves down the coast of the Levant in 9:5–8. To the south along the great coastal highway lie the city-states traditionally associated with the Philistines, who realize that they are next in the path of this Divine Warrior. They know that if invincible Tyre is no match for this warrior, they have little hope. In 9:8 the Divine Warrior reaches his destination at the temple in Jerusalem. There God promises that there would never be a return to the conditions of the exile again.

The King Receives His Kingdom (9:9–10). The presence of a human king in Jerusalem/Zion is an essential component in God's rule over the nations of the earth (Ps 2). The Lord installed a human king on Zion and through him exercised his rule on earth. This king who arrives is not portrayed as a triumphant figure fresh from military success but as an individual faithful to the covenant and reliant on God for salvation. Such a figure enters the city not on a stately horse or glorious chariot, symbols of military prowess and success, but rather on a lowly donkey.

In line with the use of the donkey for the royal procession, the Lord declares his intention to remove all military equipment from his people. The "chariot," "warhorse," and "battle bow" (9:10a) are all essential for advanced warfare in the ancient Near East, but they will be unnecessary for this king who relies on the Divine Warrior for his victory and rule. Peace will be proclaimed to the "nations" (9:10b).

The People Return to the Kingdom (9:11–17). Having secured the promised land, the time has come for the return of a people. The basis of this promised liberation is the "blood of my covenant with you" (9:11). On the basis of this ancient covenant agreement, God promises salvation for his exiled people. God announces that the return to the city of these prisoners will be accompanied by incredible blessing. These freed prisoners will become weapons in God's hands for fighting battles. God as Divine Warrior is the archer who bends his bow (Judah) and places his arrows (Ephraim) against the string, an image of unity in the hands of God.

With 9:14 the prophecy switches from the first-person address of the Lord to third-person description of a battle involving the Lord and his people. The focus at the outset is on the military action of the Divine Warrior. But there is also a minor role for God's people in this battle. Protected by God, the people gain victory, not with the sophisticated weapons that have been removed from the kingdom but with the lowly sling, an allusion to David's victory over Goliath.

Application. Zechariah 9 calls us to recognize God's sovereign plan and power, to return to a theme that has often been ignored in the message of a church searching for "relevance." God is in control, and his past record and future promise reveal that he has no patience for the material splendor and military prowess of the nations.

God's sovereign plan, however, should not be construed in an exclusively negative manner. Zechariah 9 echoes the end of Zechariah 8, namely, that God envisions a community that transcends Israel's borders and ethnicity. The same is true for Christians today. In our pursuit of truth, justice, and redemption, we can villainize enemies of the faith to the point that we revel in their damnation. As Christ associated with those considered far less than holy, so also we need to reach out in love. We cannot lose sight of God's desire to bring blessing through us to all people.

ZECHARIAH 10:1–12

Original Meaning

Transforming Judah (10:1–5). With the picturesque scene of Jewish youth enjoying the plenteous fruit of the land still vividly in the reader's mind (9:17), 10:1 calls the community to trust God for this abundant harvest by asking him for the rain necessary for crops to flourish. The temptation to serve other gods was especially strong in matters related to agricultural activity. This connection between rain and idolatry is made explicit in 10:2.

The image of the shepherd and his flock is common in the literature of the ancient Near East in descriptions of the relationship between a king and his people. Shepherd imagery appears at regular intervals throughout Zechariah 9–14 as a description of both divine and human leadership. God's desire is to shepherd his flock, but they have abandoned his leadership. God thus addresses the human shepherds who have led the community astray (10:3).

Verse 5 confirms that the previous verse refers to a group of leaders rather than just one because "*they* will be like *warriors in battle*" (emphasis added). The identity of this new leadership caste from Judah is not specified. From our preceding discussion it most likely involves royal leadership, which has led many to see here a reference to a future messianic figure. Israel does not gain victory because of superior military tactics or weaponry but rather because of the Lord's overpowering presence.

Restoring Joseph (10:6–12). The "tribes of Joseph" (10:6) refers to those tribes from the Northern Kingdom who were taken into exile when Samaria, their capital, fell to the Assyrians in the late eighth century BC. God here promises to "save" this community and "restore" them to their former state (10:6). This promise links God's answer to an assumed cry from the exilic community: "I will answer them" (10:6). In 10:9 we are told that "in distant lands they will remember me." This kind of remembering is more than just a cerebral exercise since it involves the religious affections of the community.

God's restorative action is based on a double foundation: his compassion and his covenant. God's redemption will entail a reversal of their present condition. This defeated, depressed, and decimated people will become skilled warriors who are giddy with joy alongside a new generation.

Verse 12 brings closure to this section on the salvation of the northern tribes. Using the same verb with which he introduced the section in 10:6 ("strengthen"), now in 10:12 God promises the same benefits that the house of Judah enjoyed: to be strengthened by God. This strength will enable them to walk in his name. The restored community will regain control over their land.

Application. As we face challenges and decisions in life, the one to whom we turn for wisdom and direction and the way in which we process that enlightenment are indicators of whom we ultimately trust. Whether those challenges are uncertain conditions of agricultural enterprise as the community in Zechariah 10 or fluctuating fortunes of financial markets and unpredictable changes in one's physical condition, we must trust God's perspective on these issues, seek counsel from mature Christians, and reflect deeply on God's word.

ZECHARIAH 11:1–17

Original Meaning

Announcing Judgment (11:1–3). Verses 1–3 share many points of connection. These similarities should not veil the fact that each verse uses a unique image. Verse 1 mixes metaphors by envisioning a fiery conflagration of great cedars that are presently protected within the gates of a city called Lebanon. Verse 2 then picks up on the cedar of Lebanon but changes the imagery from fire to cutting as the cedars are fallen, ruined, and cut down. The addressee in 11:3 is uncertain as the imagery shifts to the destruction of rich pastures and lush thickets in northern Israel used by shepherds and inhabited by lions.

Prophetic Sign-Act of Shepherd and Sheep (11:4–16). In 11:4–16 three sign-acts can be discerned, each introduced by an exhortation (11:4, 13, 15). This exhortation places the prophet in the role of shepherd. The flock is one "marked for slaughter" (11:4), that is, a flock destined for complete destruction. The positive intention of this shepherd is confirmed by the fact that he takes two staffs, called "Favor" and "Union" (11:7), suggesting the two shepherding implements that guided and protected the sheep.

Verse 8 signals the beginning of trouble for God's appointed shepherd. He must rid the flock of the uncaring shepherds of

11:5. The removal of these shepherds appears to cause tension between the flock and the shepherd. This mutual rejection has serious repercussions.

The notice of the shepherd's departure is followed by two symbolic gestures linked to the staffs. Before reporting the breaking of the second staff in 11:14, the prophet reports his request for payment of wages. The "them" of 11:12 most likely refers to the "nations" of 11:10, who are the buyers of 11:5. Having terminated his contract with these nations, the shepherd now requests his wages, but he gives them the option of refusal.

Having received his wages, the prophet quickly reports a second sign-act (11:13). God instructs the shepherd to throw the payment to the "potter," who, according to the execution of this sign-act, is in "the house of the LORD" (11:13). The tone here is one of strong rejection of payment, highlighting the broken relationship with the nations. With this payment, the first symbolic gesture is completed, signaling an end to the covenant with the nations. In a second symbolic gesture, the shepherd breaks the staff called "Union" (11:14), an action that represents the shattering of the brotherhood between Judah and Israel.

Verse 15 introduces the final sign-act, where the Lord instructs the prophet to "take the equipment of a foolish shepherd." The folly of this shepherd is detailed in the explanation that follows in 11:16. In stark contrast to the good shepherd, who protected the vulnerable in the flock, the foolish shepherd will not only neglect these members of the flock but also turn on the remaining sheep and devour all edible meat.

Judgment on a Leader (11:17). In 11:17 the prophet pronounces judgment on shepherds who are compared with the inadequate shepherds of Ezekiel's day. By alluding to Jeremiah, the prophet announces that the idolatrous shepherds of his day will be judged by the sword in the same way that the idolatrous Babylonians with their false prophets were judged at the beginning of the Persian period.

Application. Zechariah 11 addresses serious leadership issues and is useful for addressing similar concerns in God's community today. One of the priorities of church leadership, whether clergy or laity, must be honest examination of motivations. The leader who invites honest examination displays strength, not weakness, and secures long-term vitality in ministry.

ZECHARIAH 12:1–13:6

Original Meaning

Introducing the God of the Oracle (12:1). The first two divine actions in 12:1 refer to God's creation of the cosmos, while the third action alludes to God's formation of the spirit of humanity. By using these snippets of praise the prophet establishes Yahweh's right to proclaim the message and his ability to act against or for the recipients.

Victory for Jerusalem and Judah against the Nations (12:2–8). The protagonists here are mainly Jerusalem and Judah, with some mention of the house of David. Throughout this initial section the author uses a variety of images to describe the triumph of Jerusalem and Judah. Taken together these four images emphasize God's victory over the surrounding nations through Jerusalem and Judah.

Grace and Supplication for Repentance and Cleansing in Victorious Jerusalem (12:9–13:1). In 12:10–14 the prophet reveals that accompanying salvation from external forces will be an internal renewal of the nation as God transforms their affections to seek him in repentance. God's pouring out his Spirit is a declaration of him placing his unique and manifest presence upon his people. The remainder of 12:10–14 describes the impact of God's spirit on the community. The people mourn over the fact that they had "pierced" (12:10) someone. Some see here an allusion to the suffering servant of Isaiah 53, a representative (often messianic) figure.

In the final phase, God will provide cleansing for the behavior of this people. The term "fountain" (13:1) here speaks of a spring that brings forth fresh water. The community that has slain their God has received the "spirit of grace and supplication" (12:10) in order to mourn their actions and be ritually cleansed, a symbol of God's acceptance.

Judgment on Idolatry and False Prophecy (13:2–6). This slaying of God has still not been defined. We know that this metaphorical slaying has brought defilement, but what is the nature of this slaying? Zechariah 13:2–6 brings clarity to this question, showing that the people have rejected their God by turning to idolatry. In Zechariah 13:2 impurity is clearly defined as idolatry and divination. Not only idols, but also their religious attendants, the prophets, will be removed from the land. The people will be so transformed by God that parents will enact the torah's judgment against their own child.

Verse 6 brings this section on false prophecy to a close. What should not be missed in all this is that these various aspects of renewal are inaugurated through the initiative of God. Although there are serious issues in view, human ability is not the way ahead. Rather, Yahweh brings victory and salvation for Israel, pours out the spirit of grace and supplication, provides a fountain of cleansing, and finally removes idolatry and false prophecy from the land.

Application. Within Christian traditions guilt is often used to motivate penitential response. But 12:10 declares that it is the Spirit "of grace and supplication" that stimulates such response. This means that it is an operation of God within the heart of his community, which in New Testament perspective means the work of the Holy Spirit within the life of believers. We do not conjure up this response to God; rather, it is his work. This is an important truth for the preacher as well as hearer of the gospel, both of whom must rely on God for this divine work.

ZECHARIAH 13:7–9

Original Meaning. This short section begins with an appeal to the "sword" (13:7). The sword is a regular metaphor in prophetic literature, an image of death and judgment. The phrase "awake . . . against" (13:7) is used for wielding a weapon in battle as well as for raising up an army against a nation. This shepherd is doomed, for the awaking is only the first of two imperatives directed to this sword. The second is devastating for the shepherd—the sword is instructed to "strike" (13:7).

Because the image of the sword is connected with God's judgment, this shepherd is apparently someone who is struck as a result of some offense. This is not surprising in light of the many negative depictions of shepherds elsewhere in Zechariah 9–14. However, precise identification of this shepherd is difficult to attain.

Because of the loss of the shepherd, the flock will be scattered, the expected result of a flock without leadership. This scattering leaves the "little ones" (13:7) vulnerable to attack. The attack comes from God, who turns his hand against them. This indicates that God will discipline the flock in order to purify them.

The process of purification is described in 13:8–9 as the community is divided into thirds: a third struck with the sword (representing those who fall by the sword outside the city) and a third scattered to the wind (representing those exiled). The final third survives but then undergoes further discipline.

The second half of Zechariah 13:9 reveals the result of this refining process. The covenant relationship between God and his people will be restored. Having been refined by God, they will now seek him, and to this people God promises to respond. He will declare them "my people" while they affirm that he is "our God" (13:9).

Application. A key theme throughout biblical theology is that of the remnant, namely, that from sinful humanity God forms a holy community. The gospel challenges the Western church's penchant for the health and wealth gospel. In the New Testament account, when people devote their lives to Christ, they are greeted with suffering more often than with success. We should not be surprised, then, at suffering but rather embrace it as part of God's purification of his remnant community (Rom 8:18–39; 1 Pet 4:17).

ZECHARIAH 14:1–21

Original Meaning

Judgment on Jerusalem (14:1–2). The phrase "a day of the Lord is coming" (14:1) emphasizes the doom about to strike the city. The description of the day does not announce victory for Israel. Thus, Zechariah 14:1 is an apt foreshadowing of the traumatic events described in 14:2.

These events are traced to the action of Yahweh. No reason is offered for the fact of this action, but one must assume that it is linked to the misdeeds of the people in the city. The incidents described are typical in the capture of a city. In the end half the inhabitants of the city are taken off into exile while a remnant is left behind in the city.

Appearance of Yahweh (14:3–5). While 14:1–2 envision disaster for Jerusalem and its inhabitants, 14:3 signals a reversal of fortunes for the city as the Lord marches out against the same nations that he previously sent against Jerusalem. He enters the fray as one who "fights on a day of battle" (14:3), but creation's violent response reveals that he is no ordinary adversary.

God's descent on the Mount of Olives wreaks havoc in the natural order. His appearance causes an earthquake, splitting in two the line of hills running north-south along the eastern edge of Jerusalem and creating a great east-west chasm. This newly created valley will be an escape route for those who have remained behind in Jerusalem. The valley will serve another purpose, providing a path for the triumphal return of Yahweh to his seat of rule. The "holy ones" (14:5) are the remnant that has fled from danger and now return under the protection of their Almighty God.

Transforming the Cosmos, Assuming His Rule (14:6–11). The vocabulary of 14:7 is reminiscent of the account of creation in Genesis 1. The congealing of the heavenly lights will return the cosmos to the conditions of the first day of the creation account, a day known only to the God who created the world. This image of a future era with perpetual light is a regular feature of apocalyptic literature.

The transformation of the cosmos continues in 14:8 as Jerusalem becomes a perpetual source of water for the entire land, supplying the seas to the east and west. This verse envisions a flow of water from within Jerusalem that will exceed the needs of the city, running throughout the land and emptying into the Dead Sea and the Mediterranean Sea.

God's right to rule the earth is intimately linked to his subjugation of the cosmos and nations. As conquering Divine

Warrior, he takes his legitimate place as king of the earth. Verse 10 envisions further transformation of the cosmos. Jerusalem will tower over the land, depicting the establishment of God's universal rule over the earth and of Jerusalem as the center, to which all nations stream. According to 14:11, this elevated and spacious city will be filled with inhabitants who will enjoy security.

Defeating the Nations (14:12–15). God strikes his opponents with an unprecedented plague. Their bodies will disintegrate on the spot: flesh, eyes, and tongues. This plague will generate overwhelming panic among the armies of these nations. The defeat of the armies is confirmed by the collection of plunder, including gold, silver, and clothing. The animals will not join this collection, for they will suffer the same plague as the soldiers.

Worshiping Yahweh (14:16–21). The defeat of these nations who attacked Jerusalem results in an annual pilgrimage of all these nations to Jerusalem. They will come to worship Yahweh as king, affirming the sovereignty already declared in Zechariah 14:9. The participation of the nations in the festal celebration is not the only surprising feature of the final section of Zechariah 14. There is a significant shift in perspective on ritual holiness in 14:20–21. In this new Jerusalem, that which was unclean will be made clean.

This new ritual condition of Jerusalem and Judah in which everything is consecrated for worship will eliminate the need for merchants in the temple precincts. The term "Canaanite" in 14:21 can denote the merchant class that bought and sold goods. This verse indicates, then, that there will be no more room for such merchants, who may have abused worshipers through exorbitant prices, or there will be no more need for them because of the availability of sacred utensils or the expansion of the types of offerings acceptable to Yahweh.

This final oracle brings not only Zechariah 9–14 but also the entire book of Zechariah to a climactic end. Its cosmic vision of the institution of the kingship involves the appearance of the Divine Warrior, whose very presence shakes the cosmos and, as a result, stirs the submission of both creation and culture to his mighty rule from his place of manifest presence, the temple in Jerusalem. God's people will be cleansed, and the nations will bend their knee before this mighty king and express their allegiance through annual worship of this Lord of the universe at the place of his holy presence.

Application. Zechariah 14 was written to a community with little reason for hope. But this chapter was written to raise their vision beyond their present circumstances, that they might see the world from God's eternal perspective and live accordingly. As Christians we need to hear this message of triumphant hope, not so that we can vindictively anticipate the demise of our enemies, but that we may be encouraged to live by faith in the present age, confident in our transforming message. As the Persian period community longed for God's arrival, so also we long for the arrival of Christ, who has come and will come again. Zechariah 14 grants us hope that our lives are not lived in vain, that God will someday transform the cosmic and political structures of our world.

MALACHI

INTRODUCTION TO MALACHI

Malachi is the last of the twelve Minor Prophets, closing the collection of the Prophets and, in the Protestant canon, the entire Old Testament. In the Jewish canon the books of the Writings follow Malachi. The location of the book of Malachi as the last of the Prophets strongly suggests a postexilic date. The book itself is unique in the Old Testament because of its form—a dispute or diatribe between God and those of his people who have become apathetic or even antagonistic to him. The prophet dialogues with both people and priests, showing particular concern for their unfaithfulness. The prophecy closes with a look forward to the day of the Lord, a time of judgment for those who misbehave.

BOOK OUTLINE

I. Heading and First Dispute (1:1–5)
II. Second Dispute: To You, Priests (1:6–2:9)
III. Third Dispute: We Are Unfaithful (2:10–16)
IV. Fourth Dispute: Coming Messenger (2:17–3:5)
V. Fifth Dispute: God Spurned (3:6–12)
VI. Sixth Dispute: God's Mercy (3:13–4:6)

MALACHI 1:1–5

Original Meaning. Verses 1–5 recall the strained relationship between Jacob, Israel's forefather, and his brother, Esau. What irony that the first statement God makes, and which they dispute, is that he loves them (1:2).

An emphatic contrast opens 1:3. This statement pair (love–hate) concerns election rather than emotions (cf. 2:16): Jacob (and his line) is chosen by God while Esau (and his line) is peripheral to the story of God's continued activity in the Bible. God's "hate" (1:3) for Esau is expressed in geographic terms. It is proud in its secure location. Rather than a place of refuge, it will be a "wasteland" (1:3), ruined by warfare.

In 1:5 Yahweh makes another declaration to Judah (see 1:2). Malachi emphasizes that it is Judah's own eyes that will see God's love. Judah, who questions God's love, will experience it through his greatness wherever in their land they might live. They are loved, even if they do not respond in kind.

Application. God maintains covenant love with his chosen people even though they regularly "un-chose" him, "hating" him by entering into a covenant relationship with others. This kind of covenantal, committed love must serve as a model to the church, since we are to love each other as God, in the person of Jesus his Son, loves us.

MALACHI 1:6–14

Original Meaning. God expected sacrifices and offerings to be taken from his good gifts and returned to him. They represented one's love, loyalty, honor, and, at times, sorrow for sin and wrongdoing (see Lev 1–7). Instead of respect, God receives "contempt" (1:6); he is despised and treated lightly, not even worthy of notice.

The priests know that what they are doing is "wrong" (1:8). Yahweh suggests that the priests should just try this presumption on him! Yahweh desires that the entire temple complex be closed. God is calling for the doors to close to protect the priests themselves from doing further unacceptable acts. Any such offerings are "useless" (1:10), having no effect.

In 1:11 God's name is not localized among his people but extends "among the nations." In 1:12 many of the terms and concepts of 1:6–11 are presented again with some variation. In emphatic contrast with the rest of the world who worship God correctly, the author returns to the priests who do not do so. In 1:13, inner contempt is exemplified and continued by outward actions: bringing unacceptable animal sacrifices instead.

The final verse of this section closes in response to the rhetorical question regarding lordship in 1:6. Yahweh is in fact the only true "Lord" (1:14) and should be treated as such. Also, his reverence, which is questioned there, is proclaimed here.

Application. We offer God our second best, thinking what we are able to do is good enough. Try offering that to a boss (cf. "the governor," 1:8), suggesting that he or she pay for forty hours of work a week, when we really only work thirty. That is not good enough for him, so why should we think it is good enough for God? Should we expect him to accept our second-best offerings? "Good enough" seldom is.

MALACHI 2:1–9

Original Meaning. Yahweh strongly warns the priests. The result of the noncompliance is a destructive curse (2:2), a clear and public display of their disgrace and inability to carry out the sacrificial functions of their office. Now no longer able to perform their functions, which require ritual purity, the priests are expelled from the camp, as is the unclean offal.

Verse 4 is equivalent of the admonition to obedience mentioned here and in 2:1. From the human perspective of the priests, the admonition/covenant involves cultic purity and ritual ministry, while from the perspective of Yahweh Almighty, it involves the blessings enumerated in the next verse. The priests, as beneficiaries of the covenant relationship, are again reminded in 2:5 that while the covenant is with Levi, it originates with God alone ("*my* covenant").

Truth characterized the speech of the priestly ancestor, Levi. His very lifestyle exemplifies covenantal peace and integrity or uprightness. As a result of this positive lifestyle, "many" (2:6, 8) completely change their own negative lifestyle. The ideal established by Levi is that his descendants, the priests, should live what they speak (2:7). The priests are in stark contrast to this ideal, however. They are humiliated "before all the people" (2:9). Those in whose presence the humiliation occurs are most likely the same as the "many" of 2:6 and 8.

Application. We teach by our words, but we also teach by our lives. This is at heart the message of the definition of "integrity," an unbroken wholeness where, in the matter under discussion, there is no gap at all between words and deeds. This must characterize the life of the Israelite priest as well as that of each Christian as a member of a kingdom of priests (Exod 19:6; Rev 1:6).

MALACHI 2:10–16

Original Meaning. In 2:11–12 Judah is held up as an example of polluting perfidy. These wrongdoers attempt to cover their continuing sin by surface religiosity, that is, by bringing offerings. The use of three terms of emotional distress ("tears," "weep," "wail"; 2:13) denotes extreme agitation. All three arise from a break in the relationship between Israel and her covenant God, which is supposed to be maintained by ritual purity. As long as Yahweh no longer acknowledges the efficacy of ritual, the relationship is severed. The passage ends with a human picture of breach of relationship (in marriage) that exemplifies the breach in divine-human relationship.

Application. One area in which the church should hang its head in shame is its acknowledgement of, and approach to, domestic violence and abuse among its members. On what I feel to be an incorrect reading of Malachi 2:16, women are sent back into this abuse, "encouraged" by the misunderstanding of another passage about wives submitting to their husband (Eph 5:22). How should we address this problem in the light of both Malachi and Paul? We must remember that Malachi addresses only the husband, the wife having no opportunity to initiate divorce in Israelite society. A valid reading is to see domestic violence in itself as being a divorce; if the man has done this, he has de facto broken the covenant relationship, initiating a divorce in a hateful way.

MALACHI 2:17–3:5

Original Meaning. Israel now impugns God's personal character. The disturbing claim is that this evil is in fact "good" (2:17) in God's estimation. In the second statement, the people ask God about a characteristic they perceive as lacking, namely, his "justice" (2:17). But in 3:1 Yahweh strongly rebuts this notion, indicating his action is imminent. The people are facing "the day of his coming" (3:2), referred to in other prophecies as the eschatological "day of the LORD" (4:5; cf. "day" in 4:1, 3). He comes first as a "refiner's fire" (3:2). The prophets use this process metaphorically to signify eliminating sinful behavior through the hot fire of God's judgment and wrath. Yahweh serves as a witness to "testify" (3:5) against an array of evildoers. To summarize, Yahweh claims that the wrongdoers exhibit a lack respect for him.

Application. Too many Christians today live as if they have a spiritual form of what is now called "dissociative identity disorder," previously known as "split personality disorder." They take Jesus's words in Matt 22:21 ("Give back to Caesar what is Caesar's, and to God what is God's") completely out of context by saying that life is bifurcated; part of what I do is religious, and the rest is secular, and never the twain shall meet. A healing from our "dissociative identity disorder" is much needed. We need to open our eyes, or possibly a better metaphor, we need to tear down our church walls, thus eliminating this artificial and unbiblical separation and acknowledging that this is all God's world.

MALACHI 3:6–12

Original Meaning. Yahweh states that he has not changed. Since her covenant God is steadfast, in spite of her own fickleness, Israel is "not destroyed" (3:6), though that is her due. Justifiable grounds for God's turning his back on his covenant promises include Israel's dereliction of her covenant duty (3:7). Hope is not lost, however, since God makes an offer to his people: Mutual restoration is possible if only they return to him.

Not learning from their previous attempts, the people again enter into dispute with God. Their question regards the means of their return ("How?"; 3:7). This could be an honest act of repentance. More likely in the context of their previous responses and of God's following rebuttal, however, this is a sarcastic protest of innocence.

God asserts that they are robbers. The results of repeatedly robbing God are severe: They are "cursed" (3:9). This apparently refers to the gamut of socioeconomic hardships that the postexilic Hebrew community is facing.

In 3:10 the prophet provides a remedy for Israelite wrongdoings: Present the tithe. The destination for the tithes is the facility associated with the temple that kept the supplies of the priests and Levites. The purpose of bringing the tithes is food or provisions for the house of God.

God promises to open the heavenly floodgates. Rather than a drought of withheld rain, blessing waters pours out. God then promises to address the blights hindering the land's fruitfulness. Judah will become a "delightful land" (3:12). Where previously God was not delighted with useless sacrifices brought by unrepentant disputants, now that the correct covenant relationship is restored, delight and acceptance are restored as well.

Application. There is also a wider issue beyond this particular passage. God's promises do not change, but neither do their recipients. God pledges blessings, but they are conditional. The recipients of God's blessings are those who obey the LORD. Act as a child of God and you will be treated as one.

MALACHI 3:13–4:6

Original Meaning. For the last time, Malachi's hearers dispute a divine claim. Israel has no authority to overturn her God, but she acts as if she does, actively speaking against his demands and desires. They are impugning the worth of following and serving God.

Verse 16 shows the more acceptable response of others in the prophet's audience. This group is made up of God fearers, those showing appropriate awe and reverence for God and his ways. Yahweh himself attentively hears this discussion and responds by memorializing those who fear him. This "scroll of remembrance" (3:16) is kept for God's use, like the Persian record kept for royal consultation. God continues to declare his actions, sparing the people in his pity, compassion, and grace from the punishment that is their due as covenant breakers.

The coming day in which God acts now receives greater definition. A characteristic of this day is indicated by how it comes: "burn[ing]" (4:1). God's fiery judgment is so fierce that nothing remains. Judgment is not the final word for all of Judah, however, but only for the wicked. Others revere God's name. Such reverence is lacking among the Israelite wrongdoers, but since all such evildoers are to be destroyed, the remaining faithful are blessed.

The "sun of righteousness" (4:2) has been understood as referring to God himself, a divine title with messianic overtones. But "sun of righteousness" could also be an objective genitive, where the righteousness is produced or caused by the sun, suggesting that God brings about the righteousness, where the passage's structure seems to contrast the wickedness done by some in Israel with the righteousness. Whatever interpretation is adopted, the sun is a fitting evidence of a new day that dawns.

In 4:4 the audience is commanded to "remember" and act upon the Mosaic law, just as God himself remembers his covenant with Israel and acts according to it. In the biblical notion of remembering, cognition is not sufficient; it also requires faithful obedience.

Before that day arrives, another event deriving from God himself will precede it. He is about to send a messenger in the person of Elijah. Elijah's mysterious disappearance, with no mention of his death (2 Kgs 2:11–12), leaves open the possibility of his reappearing and continuing his prophetic ministry. In Malachi, this ministry becomes associated eschatologically with the coming day of Yahweh. Elijah's ministry will be one of restoration and repentance, something God desires.

Application. Christian communion is a reminder of the great sacrificial work of Christ on the cross, and in eating, we make a covenant commitment to God, sacrificially offering ourselves. Remembering also has eschatological ramifications. It directs us first of all to the initial, close relationship between God and humanity as established in creation. This directs one's attention to the coming day when creation will be restored, with humanity restored to a new heaven and earth, a new and eschatological Eden when human-divine relationship will be restored, not by human effort but by divine sacrifice.

MATTHEW

INTRODUCTION TO MATTHEW

The Gospel according to Matthew was the most widely used Gospel in the formative years of the church. It has retained its appeal throughout the centuries and exerted a powerful influence on the church. One of the main reasons why this Gospel is so important is because of its verification that Jesus was the long-awaited Messiah of Israel, who had brought salvation not just to the Jews but to all nations.

Against the backdrop of a world increasingly hostile to Christianity, the author solidifies his church's identity as the true people of God, who transcend ethnic, economic, and religious barriers to find oneness in their adherence to Jesus Messiah. His Gospel becomes a manual on discipleship, as Jew and gentile are made disciples of Jesus Messiah and learn to obey all that he commanded his original disciples.

Little is known of Matthew Levi except for the widely attested tradition that he is the author of the Gospel that now bears his name. As a tax collector he would have been trained in secular scribal techniques, and as a Galilean Jewish Christian he would have been able to interpret the life of Jesus from the perspective of the Old Testament expectations.

No precise date for the writing of Matthew is known, although Jesus's prophecy of the overthrow of Jerusalem (24:1–28) has been used to indicate that the Gospel may have been written after AD 70. However, such a conclusion is necessary only if one denies Jesus the ability to predict the future. Matthew tells us that as of the time he was writing, the "field of blood" in Jerusalem continued to be called by that name (27:8), showing his continual connection with conditions in Palestine and hinting that this is prior to the devastation in Jerusalem in AD 70.

Matthew's popularity is explained at least in part because of the following distinctives that are found throughout this Gospel.

Christology. The church has consistently drawn on this Gospel as the foundational clarification of the identity of Jesus Christ, who is the Son of God, the king of Israel, and the Lord of the church. Matthew focuses on Jesus's identity as the incarnate Son of God.

Salvation-historical particularism and universalism. The terms *particularism* and *universalism* indicate that Matthew's Gospel places striking emphasis on both the fulfillment of the promises of salvation to a particular people, Israel, and the fulfillment of the universal promise of salvation to all the peoples of the earth. The church, made up of every nationality, has cherished this Gospel because Matthew aims to record the continuation of the history of salvation to all nations.

The bridge between Old and New Testaments. Matthew's Gospel has been a pivotal book throughout church history to help the church understand the relationship between Old and New Testaments. Matthew demonstrates repeatedly that Old Testament hopes, prophecies, and promises have now been fulfilled in the person and ministry of Jesus. The early church likely placed Matthew first in the New Testament canon precisely because of its value as a bridge between the Testaments.

A "great commission" for evangelism and mission. This first Gospel has held special status in the missionary and evangelistic outreach of the church because of the prominent placement of the Great Commission, which climactically concludes the story of Jesus's ministry (28:18–20). This Great Commission has been at the heart of evangelistic and missionary endeavor throughout the history of the church.

The new community of faith. Facing the threat of gathering Roman persecution within a pagan world, Matthew addresses a church that is representative of the emerging community of faith. The church has consistently found in Matthew a call to a new community that transcends ethnic and religious barriers to find oneness in its adherence to Jesus Messiah. The church has continually been challenged by Matthew's message that former barriers to discipleship have now been abolished.

The disciples, crowds, and Jewish leaders. These three groups provide a background for Matthew's story of Jesus. The "Jewish leaders" are the antagonists, the one's responsible for Jesus's crucifixion. The "crowds" are a basically neutral group; they are the object of Jesus's ministry of preaching, teaching, and healing, but as a group they do not exercise faith in him. The "disciples" are Jesus's true followers, true believers.

The role of Peter. Matthew emphasizes Peter's leadership role but also shows how Peter is an imperfect leader in process of development, as Jesus prepares him for the early days of the church ahead.

The structure of narrative and discourse. Matthew has collected the most complete compilation of Jesus's teachings, exhortations, prophecies, and parables found anywhere in Scripture.

BOOK OUTLINE

I. The Arrival in History of Jesus Messiah (1:1–2:23)
II. John the Baptist Prepares for the Appearance of the Messianic Kingdom (3:1–17)
III. Jesus Messiah Begins to Advance the Messianic Kingdom (4:1–25)
IV. First Discourse—The Sermon on the Mount—Kingdom-Life Proclamation (5:1–7:29)
V. The Authoritative Power of Messiah: Kingdom Power Demonstrated (8:1–9:38)
VI. Second Discourse—Mission Mandate—Authoritative Mission of Messiah's Messengers (10:1–42)
VII. Opposition to the Messiah Emerges (11:1–12:50)
VIII. Third Discourse—Parabolic Disclosure—Mysteries of the Messianic Kingdom (13:1–52)
IX. The Identity and Suffering of the Messiah Revealed (13:53–17:27)
X. The Community of the Messiah Revealed (18:1–20:34)
XI. The Messiah Asserts His Authority over Jerusalem (21:1–23:39)
XII. Fifth Discourse—Olivet Discourse—The Delay, Return, and Judgment of Messiah (24:1–25:46)
XIII. The Crucified Messiah (26:1–27:66)
XIV. The Resurrection and Commission of the Messiah (28:1–20)

MATTHEW 1:1–17

Original Meaning

Jesus Messiah Brings a New Beginning for Humanity (1:1). The Greek word that the NIV renders "genealogy" in 1:1 is *genesis*. Just as Genesis gave the story of one beginning, so the Gospel of Matthew gives the story of a new beginning—the arrival of Jesus the Messiah and the kingdom of God. In tracing the ancestry not only to David but also to Abraham, Matthew holds a light of hope to the entire world. The covenant God made with Abraham established Israel as a chosen people, but it was also a promise that his line would be a blessing to all the nations.

Jesus Messiah's Genealogy (1:2–17). *From Abraham to King David (1:2–6a).* "Abraham was the father of Isaac." This expression emphasizes the human descent of each generation, which paves the way for a dramatic change of construction in 1:16, where Matthew points to the divine origin of Jesus. David is not simply the son of Jesse but is "King David" (v. 6), an explicit emphasis on royalty in the genealogy of Jesus.

From King David to the Babylonian exile (1:6b–11). Matthew traces Jesus's genealogy through David's son Solomon. The striking characteristic of this section is the alternating series of godly and wicked kings that ruled Israel. God worked through them to bring about his salvation.

From the Babylonian exile to Jesus Messiah (1:12–16). After the return of Israel from the exile, the Davidic line continues through Jeconiah.

The culmination of Matthew's genealogy in Jesus Messiah (1:16–17). Matthew writes, ". . . and Jacob the father of Joseph, the husband of Mary, and Mary was the mother of Jesus who is called the Messiah" (v. 16). The English obscures two important points that Matthew makes about Jesus in the Greek text.

1. The feminine gender of the relative emphasizes that Mary is the biological parent, preparing the reader for the virgin birth by shifting attention from Joseph to Mary.
2. The expression "was the mother of" translates the verb *gennaō* in a passive voice, which many grammarians call a "divine passive," where God is the assumed agent of the action.

Application. *The apologetic value.* Jewish readers would immediately recognize the significance of Matthew's opening verses for establishing Jesus's claim to the Davidic throne and clarifying his messianic identity. This Gospel can speak directly to the needs of our Jewish friends and neighbors, offering them a clear understanding of how Jesus can indeed fulfill their hopes and dreams.

Roots. As he traces Jesus's lineage back to Abraham, he clarifies that the covenantal promise includes all humanity. Matthew shows us that we have another set of roots—roots of faith. Once a person becomes a Christian, he or she is immediately adopted into a family of faith that has a long and well-documented genealogy.

History. Christians are historians, with the theological foundation of their faith firmly embedded in the facts of history. All of us as Christians are called to solidify our faith in a careful and credible understanding of the earthly ministry of our Lord Jesus Messiah. This is one of the primary purposes for our study of Matthew's Gospel.

MATTHEW 1:18–25

Original Meaning

The Angelic Announcement of the Conception of Jesus Messiah (1:18–21). The marriage customs of Jewish culture at that time usually included two basic stages of the relationship, the betrothal and the wedding:

1. The betrothal stage involved the choosing of a spouse. In a formal prenuptial agreement before witnesses, the young man and woman entered into the official state of betrothal. This was a legally binding contract and could only be broken by a formal process of divorce. Sexual unfaithfulness with another person during this stage was considered adultery, the penalty for which was death by stoning, although by New Testament times stoning was rare.
2. In a formal ceremony about a year after the betrothal, the marriage proper took place.

By the time of the narrative in Matthew, Mary is approximately four months pregnant. Without knowing of the supernatural origin of the conception, Joseph naturally thinks that Mary has committed adultery. Into this dilemma comes the stunning appearance of the angel of the Lord, who announces in a dream to Joseph the miraculous conception of the child (v. 20).

The angelic appearance in a dream provides the guidance Joseph needs. The angel dramatically announces to Joseph that the conception of the child is from the Holy Spirit. Here at the beginning of the New Testament age, the Holy Spirit plays a crucial role. Jesus Messiah is God incarnate, whose miraculous conception and origin are only explained through the work of God the Holy Spirit.

The name *Jesus* was popular in Judaism of the first century, given to sons as a symbolic hope for Yahweh's anticipated sending of salvation. A widely held expression of this hope was the expectation of a messiah who would save Israel from Roman oppression and purify his people. But the angel draws on a less popular, although perhaps more important theme: salvation from sin. Matthew points his readers to the central purpose of Jesus's earthly life and ministry: he himself "will save his people from their sins" by giving his life as a ransom for many (v. 21).

The Prophesied Immanuel (1:22–23). The narrative continues with the reader being informed that the events of Jesus's miraculous conception fulfill a prophecy from the Lord through the prophet Isaiah. Here, Matthew declares that the events surrounding the conception of Jesus directly fulfills the prophet Isaiah's sublime prophecy made during the dark days of national threat under the reign of Ahaz, king of Judah. Isaiah declared that God would maintain the promise that a descendent of David would sit on his throne forever (2 Sam 7:11–17). In order to confirm this, Isaiah prophesied that the Lord would give to Ahaz a sign: a virgin would give birth.

God was giving a sign that had historical significance and fulfillment in the days of Ahaz. Isaiah prophesied that a woman who was a virgin at the time of Ahaz (734 BC) would bear a son named Immanuel. The woman would marry, conceive a child, and, when he was born, give him the name Immanuel, perhaps as a symbolic hope of God's presence in the dark times of national difficulty.

Matthew looks back to the Old Testament and declares that the birth of the child Jesus, who would save his people from their sins, ultimately fulfills the prophecy of Isaiah 7:14. The sign given to Ahaz and the house of Judah was God's miraculous prediction of military salvation, but it was also a prediction of a future messianic figure who would provide spiritual salvation from sin, a future messianic deliverer named Immanuel, truly God with us.

Joseph's Immediate Obedience (1:24–25). When Joseph awakes from his sleep, he is obedient to the angel's directive and carries out the second phase of the marital process by engaging in the formal wedding ceremony. Matthew emphasizes Joseph's remarkable character. Not only is Mary seen as a godly woman, but Joseph takes the lead in carrying out the angel's instructions.

Application. *The picture of Jesus.* Two things especially stand out in this passage.

1. Matthew records in straightforward fashion the most incredible miracle of history, the conception and birth of Jesus to a virgin mother through the Holy Spirit.
2. Jesus the Messiah came to be Savior for the sins of his people. In these two emphases is a unique story of a unique person with a unique conception and a unique message and ministry.

The virgin birth. Jesus's virgin birth has profound significance for our Christian faith and life.

1. To begin with, the virgin birth points to the divine nature of Jesus. His conception, ministry, and resurrection are nothing short of declarations of his divine nature, which impels us to regard his claims upon our lives as second to none.
2. The account of the virgin birth speaks of one person in whom is united full deity and full humanity. This supremely points to how the sacrifice of this human on the cross could atone for the sins of humanity. Jesus is enabled to carry the sins of the world to the cross only because his divine nature is infinitely capable to sustain his humanity.
3. The virgin birth signals Jesus's true humanity without inherited sin. The sinlessness of Jesus throughout his life is centered in the fact that his divine nature is so powerful in its determination to do good that it cannot be overcome by any temptation to his human nature. Thus, he is enabled to be the unique, human, sinless sacrifice for our sin.

4. The virgin birth of Jesus denotes the beginning stage of the redemption of humanity that had been created in the image of God but had been distorted by the effects of sin. Since the outworking of the image of God is seen most fully in Jesus, the Christian life means to pattern ourselves after him.

Learning from Joseph. Joseph is an important person in Matthew 1, as are the angel of the Lord, the Holy Spirit, and Mary. Matthew gives special attention to Joseph. We may see from this that Matthew has given awareness to Joseph to accentuate aspects of his role that have significance for our own lives.

1. In the first place, Joseph is an example for us in the way he establishes his priorities. As a young man still in the passions of his youth, Joseph provides us an example of a godly young man who attempts to establish the values of God's will for his life.
2. Joseph's obedience to the law is not legalistic. Matthew demonstrates to us in Joseph's balanced example that the people of Israel at that time did not wholesale adopt a rigid legalism of dos and don'ts.

The role of the Holy Spirit. The explicit nature of the role of the Holy Spirit in this passage enables us to begin to see the unfolding revelation of God throughout Scripture. This activity of the Spirit is more explicit in the expansion of the church in the book of Acts and in the teaching of later New Testament authors, but we begin to see it come into play with the conception and birth of Jesus Messiah.

What a privilege and responsibility we now have to live at this stage of history. In their obedience to the work of the Spirit, young Joseph and Mary give us a precursor of how godly relationships can be pure and characterized by serving one another. Today, that is the real basis on which we can pursue a godly marriage and family and, indeed, see the transformation of any of our relationships, both within and outside the church, through the transforming work of God's Spirit.

MATTHEW 2:1–12

Original Meaning

The Magi's Journey to Jerusalem (2:1–2). The events Matthew is about to narrate take place "during the time of King Herod" (v. 1). He most likely died in March, 4 BC. Since Herod is still alive when the magi arrive in Jerusalem as much as two years after Jesus was born, the dating of Jesus's birth is placed by most scholars somewhere between 6 and 4 BC.

The universal significance of the birth of the child Jesus is heralded immediately because magi from the east arrive in Jerusalem seeking to worship the one born "king of the Jews" (vv. 1–2). The term "magi" (*magos*, "magician") originally referred to a priestly caste in ancient Persia. There were significant Jewish centers of learning in Babylon at the time of the magi. Gentile religious leaders in the east were regularly exposed to Hebrew Scriptures, prophecy, and teachers.

Through the Jewish community in their homeland, the magi would have become familiar with Balaam's prophecy, "A star will come out of Jacob; a scepter will rise out of Israel" (Num 24:17). In many quarters within Judaism this prophecy was understood to point to a messianic deliverer.

Herod's Cunning Duplicity (2:3–8). Not only is Herod disturbed at the arrival of the magi, but so also is "all Jerusalem with him" (v. 3). The word "Jerusalem" represents the religious and political leadership of Israel. The leadership may be disturbed along with Herod because they know the consequences they might suffer if he were to fly into a rage at the perceived threat of the arriving forces with the magi. But more likely their reaction gives a clue to the spiritual health of Israel's leadership. They have aligned themselves politically with Herod, and if his power base is threatened, so is theirs.

The central leadership of the Jews was lodged in the "chief priests" and the "teachers of the law" (*grammateus*, v. 4). The chief priests were members of the Sanhedrin, joining the high priest in giving oversight to the temple activities, treasury, and priestly orders. The term *grammateus* came to signify the official interpreters of the Old Testament.

The Magi Worship the Child (2:9–12). The purpose of the magi's pilgrimage to see the child is accomplished as they "bowed down and worshiped him" (v. 11). The word used to describe the magi's "worship" is one normally reserved for the veneration of deity. It is doubtful that at this time these quasi-pagan religious figures understand Jesus's divine nature. Yet despite their blend of pagan religious background with Jewish influence, their worship is probably far more than even they understand.

"Gold" (v. 11) is the most-often mentioned valued metal in Scripture; as in modern times, it was prized throughout the ancient world as a medium of exchange as well as for making jewelry, ornaments, and dining instruments for royalty. "Frankincense" was used for secular purposes as a perfume, but in Israel it was used ceremonially as part of a recipe for the only incense permitted on the altar (Exod 30:9, 34–38). The Jews did not practice full embalming of corpses, but a dead body was prepared for burial by washing, dressing it in special garments, and packing it with fragrant "myrrh" and other spices to stifle the smell of a body as it decayed.

Dreams were commonly understood in the ancient world to be a means of divine communication to humans. Joseph is the primary recipient of dreams. In most of these an angel is specifically mentioned as the one who engages Joseph.

Therefore, it seems plausible that the angel appears also in this dream to the magi, warning them of Herod's duplicity. If so, the warning in a dream is consistent with the view that the star guiding them was an angel, who now directs them back to their homeland.

Application. *God's love—and ours.* The very act of sacrificial giving defines what it means to love each other. The magi in Matthew's story may have been impelled by that kind of love in their worship and gift-giving at the arrival of the king of the Jews. Our sacrificial worship and love of Jesus will produce true, sacrificial love for one another.

Personal response to Jesus. We rightfully focus on the magi, but we certainly must focus on the sacrificial love of God, of which the apostle Paul tells us, "God demonstrates his own love for us in this: While we were still sinners, Christ died for us" (Rom 5:8).

The purpose of the magi's visit was to worship the one born "king of the Jews." If these gentile magi have recognized Jesus as Israel's king, then the Jews should certainly acknowledge him as the Messiah. But will they? As Matthew turns to the response of the Jewish leadership to the magi's astounding announcement, he tragically records only duplicity and treachery.

At this most fundamental level, Matthew teaches us that Jesus's arrival in history to initiate the salvation of his people from their sins surely requires that we give ourselves to him. When we do so, his life becomes the pattern for our own lives. The apostle Paul strikes that note when he declares, "Husbands, love your wives, just as Christ loved the church and gave himself up for her" (Eph 5:25).

MATTHEW 2:13–23

Original Meaning

The Family's Escape to Egypt (2:13–15). Once the magi escaped safely, the angel of the Lord again appears in a dream to warn Joseph about Herod's scheme to murder the child. The angel makes explicit what has been implicit in the narrative to this point—Herod's paranoiac grasp of the throne drives him to attempt to kill the infant king of the Jews. The angel instructs Joseph how he is to care for the child and mother, and Joseph is again immediately obedient, escaping to Egypt by night with the child and his mother.

Matthew points to the flight and later return from Egypt as a fulfillment of Scripture. This allows us to see that Matthew has a multifaceted perspective on the way that Jesus fulfills the Old Testament Scriptures.

1. In some cases, "fulfill" indicates the way in which the events of Jesus's earthly life and ministry bring to actualization predictive prophecy.
2. In other cases, "fulfill" can indicate the way in which Jesus brings to its intended full meaning the entire Old Testament Scripture.
3. In still other cases, Matthew's use of "fulfill" can indicate the way in which Jesus's earthly life and ministry corresponded analogically or typologically (some say recapitulated or repeated) to certain aspects of the national history of Israel. This is apparently what Matthew has in view when he cites the prophet Hosea at 2:15 (Hos 11:1). Jesus actualizes the promise to the nation Israel of redemption that was initiated with the Exodus and Passover.

The Massacre of Bethlehem's Boys (2:16–18). No other historical records exist of this incident, which is not surprising, since Bethlehem was a somewhat small, rural town at this time. The number of infant boys massacred was a huge loss for Bethlehem, but it was not an incident to stand out significantly when seen in the light of other horrific events in Herod's infamous career.

Matthew's use of the Jeremiah narrative is a case of analogical correspondence. The events of Jesus's earthly life correspond analogically to an earlier attempt by a foreign power to wipe out God's chosen people. But the advent of Jesus's life also marks the arrival of the comfort promised to the Jews sent into exile.

Herod's Death (2:19a). Not long after ordering the grisly murder of the infant boys at Bethlehem, Herod died at the age of sixty-nine at his palace in Jericho in March, 4 BC. After remaking his will at least seven times, Herod had finally settled on dividing the kingdom between three of his remaining sons, Archelaus, Herod Antipas, and Herod Philip. Herod Antipas is the most prominent of Herod's sons in the New Testament because he ruled the region of Jesus's primary ministry. His chief infamy comes from his execution of John the Baptist and from his interview of Jesus prior to his crucifixion.

The Family's Return to Nazareth (2:19b–23). When Herod the Great dies, the angel appears once again to Joseph in a dream. The angel instructs Joseph to bring the child and mother back to Israel, because the threat from Herod is over. The family probably stayed in Egypt no more than a year. When they discover that Herod's son Archelaus is ruling over the region of Judea in his father's place, Joseph is warned in another dream not to return to Bethlehem. Therefore, the family takes a detour to Nazareth in the region of Galilee, a region governed by Herod Antipas.

Nazareth was originally settled by people from the line of David, who gave the settlement a consciously messianic name, connecting the establishment of the town with the hope of the coming *nētser* ("Branch") of Isaiah 11:1. Matthew also uses "Nazarene" as a slang or idiomatic expression for an individual from a remote, despised area. This Messiah did not come with fanfare or glory but was born in relative obscurity in Bethlehem.

Matthew intends for his readers to see a double meaning in the expression of Jesus as a "Nazarene." Used by his followers, it denoted faith in him as the messianic deliverer (Acts 2:22; 3:6; 10:38), but used by his enemies, it was a title of scorn to deny his messianic identity (Matt 26:71; Mark 14:67).

Matthew says nothing about Jesus's early years in Nazareth. Education was valued highly in Israel even among the poor, so most young children received the rudiments of schooling, including reading and writing. Jesus's education would have also included learning the skills of his father—carpentry. Jesus grew up in a multicultural environment in which a number of languages were spoken by the common people—Aramaic, some form of vernacular and literary Hebrew, and some Latin, which was spoken especially by Roman military personnel.

Application. *He will be called a Nazarene.* The name "Nazarene" was for Jesus a title of honor as he became for Israel the long-awaited redemptive messianic Branch. But it also was a title of scorn as he became for Israel the despised suffering Servant.

We are called "Christians." As the name "Nazarene" was for Jesus, so the name "Christian" is a badge of honor, but it is also a badge of scorn and a designation for persecution. For many in the world today, wearing the name Christian is similar to what it was like for the early church. In places like Indonesia, buildings are burned just because they are known to be Christian houses of worship. In communist China, people are placed in jail simply because they possess and distribute Christian literature. And in the face of worldwide radical Islamic terrorism, persecution for being a Christian has come even closer to home.

Our walk with Jesus in this world will involve some kind of suffering for his name. Jesus suffered when doing the right and good thing. Persecution marked the fate of the church from its earliest days, yet it did not dim their passion for following Jesus, no matter what the cost.

Joseph, the adoptive father. A unique thrust of Matthew's Gospel is the way that Jesus's earthly father, Joseph, stands out. In chapter 1 we see his love for his wife displayed as he first desires to protect her from disgrace. And in chapter 2 we see his love for his wife and son displayed as he goes against all the forces of the political and religious establishment to obey God and protect his family.

In this way, Joseph continues to be a powerful example to all of us as parents, because our children also are truly not our own. They are a gift to us from God, their true Father. That, I believe, is one of the most powerful lessons to be learned from infant dedication services or whatever your church tradition may call them. Young parents must start out their parental privilege by giving their own little baby back to the Father. This is what Joseph teaches us as an obedient father of an adoptive son. For all of us, whether biological or adoptive, parenting means to obey our child's true Father.

MATTHEW 3:1–17

Original Meaning

John the Baptist Prepares the Way (3:1–6). *John's message (3:1–3).* As similar as John's message is to the Old Testament prophets, there is a distinctly new sound to it. He calls the people to repent because "the kingdom of heaven has come near." John is the one foretold by Isaiah who would be privileged to prepare the way for the Lord's arrival and kingdom (3:3; cf. Isa 40:3).

John's appearance (3:4). Like his message, John's appearance stirred up recollections of the prophecies of Elijah's return. John the Baptist's garment of camel's hair probably visualized the repentance to which he called the people. John's diet of locusts and honey from wild bees supplied him with a crude but fairly balanced diet. His diet and clothing embody in his lifestyle the message of repentance he preaches.

John's baptism (3:5–6). John's baptism was both similar to, yet distinct from, other forms of baptism in Israel at the time. Accompanying as it did repentance and confession of sin, it was symbolic of purification. But in contrast to forms of baptism such as those at Qumran and by the Pharisees—both of which were highly structured and had regular, repeated washings—John's was a one-time baptism. His baptism called for a personal commitment to God's new activity within Israel. It became the backdrop of Jesus's and his disciples' practice and of the early church's baptism.

The Impact of the Kingdom of Heaven (3:7–12). *Warning to the religious leaders of Israel (3:7–10).* The Pharisees were a lay fellowship or brotherhood connected with local synagogues and thus were popular with the common people. Their most-pronounced characteristic was their adherence to oral tradition, which they obeyed rigorously in order to make the written law relevant to daily life. The Sadducees, by contrast, were a small group with aristocratic and priestly influence who derived their authority from the activities of the temple. They held the majority membership on the Sanhedrin but were removed from the common people by economic and political status and their support of Rome's rule over them.

Despite the fact that the Pharisees and Sadducees normally opposed one another, they are united in coming to where

John is baptizing. John sees through their hypocrisy and has harsh words for them. John is not attempting to subvert the Pharisees and Sadducees, the official leadership of Judaism, by publicly ridiculing them. Rather, he is calling them to their proper responsibility as examples for the nation. Of all people, they should be the ones who honestly and openly prepare their hearts for the coming of the Messiah. They have had the privilege of studying Scripture more carefully. They should have been the first to prepare themselves to receive kingdom life. Instead, they will receive judgment.

The coming of Messiah (3:11–12). Here we get to the core of John's ministry. He points ahead and beyond himself to another person. Although there is continuity between their messages and ministry, John especially emphasizes the contrast between himself and the Coming One.

1. John realizes that he is not worthy even to carry the sandals of this messianic deliverer. He is not lacking an adequate self-image. He knows himself and knows clearly the identity of the One to come. John is the herald; the Coming One is the messianic deliverer.
2. John accentuates further the contrast between himself and the Coming One by differentiating their baptisms: John's baptism was only preparatory. The Coming One will baptize the repentant—those who are prepared to receive him—with the blessing of the Holy Spirit. But the unrepentant he will baptize with the judgment of eternal fire.

By the use of a second metaphor, John declares that the time of this baptism is near. At the end of a harvest season, the farmer took a large pitchfork and tossed the wheat into the air, where the wind blew the lighter chaff away. The wheat was then stored in the granary for later grinding into flour to make bread, but the chaff was raked into piles and burned.

John Baptizes Jesus Messiah (3:13–17). What does Jesus mean that in his baptism he and John will "fulfill all righteousness" (v. 15)? Most likely Jesus means this in a salvation-historical sense. Jesus now will bring to fulfillment the ministry John began. He fulfills the hope of righteousness as the Davidic king and righteous Servant. But more important, he is also Immanuel, "God with us" (1:23), and Jesus, the one who will "save his people from their sins" (1:21). He identifies with John's salvation-historical ministry, but he does so from the water, identifying with the very people he has come to save. Hence, Jesus will now receive the anointing of the Spirit and the confirmation of the Father to accomplish his mission, further indications of the reason for his baptism.

Out of that unassuming scene comes a dramatic enactment of God to present Jesus for his messianic mission, as he experiences a threefold revelation:

1. As Jesus comes up from the water, "heaven was opened" (v. 16). This "divine passive" hints that God himself is opening the communication gates of heaven to reveal something momentous.
2. Jesus then "saw the Spirit of God descending like a dove and alighting on him" (v. 16). The Spirit does not take the form of a dove but rather some visible manifestation, indicating the real descent of the Spirit on Jesus. Jesus's anointing by the Spirit is both the coronation of Israel's Messiah and the commissioning of God's righteous Servant for the work he will now carry out in the power and presence of the Spirit. The one who is to baptize with the Spirit, who will be guided and empowered by the Spirit, who will inaugurate the messianic age of salvation through the Spirit, is now anointed by the Spirit for his public messianic ministry.
3. In the declaration of the Father, Jesus is heralded as the Servant who is enabled by the Spirit's anointing to bring justice to the nations. Through the anointing by the Spirit, the Father formally inaugurates Jesus into his public ministry as the unique Son, who is the triumphant messianic king (Ps 2), yet the humble Servant (Isa 42). He will accomplish his Father's will in coming to his people Israel, yet he brings hope to the nations.

Application. We can see from the incidents surrounding John the Baptist's announcement of the kingdom, along with Jesus's baptism and anointing as the Messiah of the kingdom, several important implications.

A warning of judgment, but also an invitation to life and change. We don't like to offend. But John does warn us, as will Jesus later, of the coming judgment for those who reject the message of the arriving kingdom of God. We can create a warped view of God and the gospel by overemphasizing the judgment to come, but we just as surely distort people's view if we minimize the reality of judgment.

But John isn't just holding out death. He is inviting those who respond to his message to experience life, to escape from the wrath to come, and to await the baptism of the Holy Spirit that the Coming One will bring. No message of judgment should ever be given without the accompanying message of promised life for those who respond.

The snare of spiritual pedigree. Religious pedigree does not guarantee participation in the kingdom of heaven. Participation in the kingdom of God is a *heart* matter. Repentance means first and foremost to have one's heart rightly directed toward God, which will then be evidenced by the fruit of one's life.

Humility. We must take God's calling on our lives with deadly seriousness, but we must not get caught up with appearances. John not only had a large following but also demonstrated authority as he rebuked the religious leaders for their hypocrisy. Yet he did not get carried away with his own importance.

The one who can make us most uncomfortable here is, of course, Jesus. He laid aside both the glory and the independent exercise of his deity to live a life like you and me. That is why he is the very real, very tangible example of what our lives are being transformed into.

MATTHEW 4:1–11

Original Meaning

The Setting of the Temptations (4:1–2). Matthew gives key insights in these first two verses.

1. The Spirit came on him at his baptism and now leads him to the desert. That same Spirit will give power to Jesus in order to withstand Satan's temptations.
2. Satan intends to get Jesus to go contrary to the Father's will, but in the middle of those circumstances the Father uses Satan's evil intention to a good purpose of strengthening Jesus for his messianic role.

First Temptation: Turn Stones into Bread (4:3–4). "If you are the Son of God . . ." This key phrase reflects the tempter's overall intent to manipulate. Satan does not doubt Jesus's identity as the Son of God, nor is he trying to get Jesus to doubt it; rather, he is trying to get Jesus to misuse his prerogatives as the Son of God.

Jesus has it within his powers to perform such a miracle, but for Jesus to have turned the stones into bread would lead Jesus outside the Father's will for the Son's incarnational experience. Temptations are one of the enemy's ways of trying to get a person to go contrary to God's specific will. Yet what is the Father's will for the Son?

Second Temptation: Jump Off the Temple (4:5–7). By intentionally putting himself in harm's way, Jesus would be inappropriately testing his Father's love, trying to manipulate him to send a rescuing force of angels. Such a spectacular display would gain Jesus a messianic following, but not by the Father's pathway—obediently proclaiming the gospel of the kingdom and suffering whatever consequences may come.

Third Temptation: Worship Satan (4:8–10). Jesus has laid aside his own glory to gather the nations into the kingdom of God. But before he sits on his royal throne, he must hang on the cross. So the devil offers a shortcut. Satan tries to sidetrack him from that mission by getting him to take a shortcut to gain the kingdom that will someday be his via the hard way of the cross.

"Away from me, Satan!" In this response Jesus exerts his rightful authority over Satan by issuing his first command and quotes for the third time the book of Deuteronomy. As powerful as Satan may be, and as frail as Jesus must be because of the extended fasting and the intensity of the temptations, Jesus vanquishes him with a word.

Outcome of the Temptations (4:11). Matthew adds a comforting, if not touching, comment: "and angels came and attended him." That is, angels attend to Jesus's physical needs after his long period of fasting. But more important, this comment indicates the cosmic significance of the scene that has just played out. The Son has begun the invasion of Satan's domain. All of heaven knows the significance, and the angels serve the Son, who now advances the kingdom.

Application. A temptation is not usually something inherently evil but rather consists of a good thing used for wrong purposes. Therefore, one of the most important considerations when addressing temptation is to understand the proper purpose for anything we face. Said in another way, what does God want for us in a situation? Being tempted is not a sin. Succumbing to the temptation is when it becomes sin.

Jesus's example for Christian leadership. A variety of temptations confront Christian leaders when they engage in ministry. We think immediately of moral or ethical temptations because most of us have cringed as we heard the media expose sinful behavior by Christian leaders. To be relevant, popular, and powerful are not bad per se, but a desire for them can corrupt ministry. Looking at Jesus's pattern, we will find a better example for our own leadership.

Jesus's example for daily temptations and spiritual warfare. Jesus's temptations are important examples for our personal daily victory over temptations and the spiritual warfare we encounter in our own experience. We can summarize Jesus's example like this: *Resist the devil in the power of the Spirit through the guidance of the word to accomplish the will of God.*

1. *Resist the devil.* When temptation arrives, the beginning of the victory comes in saying "No!" We have been called to put on the full armor of God and take our stand against the devil's schemes.
2. *In the power of the Spirit of God.* As we claim the same power that Jesus drew upon through the Spirit, we are able to resist the devil, who *will* flee from us (Jas 4:7).
3. *Through the guidance of the word of God.* The Bible has been given to show us the truth. Satan twists the context of Scripture for the purposes of temptation, but in his temptations Jesus exemplifies for us the right use of Scripture.
4. *To accomplish the will of God the Father.* When temptation comes, we should ask regarding any contemplated action, "Is this what God wants for me? Can I do this and truly love God and delight in him?"

MATTHEW 4:12–25

Original Meaning

Jesus Messiah Begins His Galilean Ministry (4:12–17). Returning to Galilee, Jesus goes first to his hometown of Nazareth but then makes Capernaum his base of operations. Jesus's arrival in Zebulun and Naphtali in Galilee provides a fertile place of ministry and fulfills another Old Testament prophecy. The inhabitants are called "the people living in darkness" (v. 16), a description of Jews who awaited deliverance while living among the hopelessness of the gentiles. Here, these Jews are the first to see the great light of God's deliverance in Jesus. The message that begins to unfold is of messianic grace, for it comes first to those least expecting it.

The phrase "from that time on Jesus began . . ." (v. 17) marks a significant turning point in Matthew's narrative. This phrase indicates that the preparations for Jesus's messianic ministry are complete. The prophesied miraculous birth and infancy of Messiah have been established.

Matthew's summary of Jesus's message is the same as that of John the Baptist: "repent, for the kingdom of heaven has come near" (v. 17; cf. 3:2). When people hear Jesus announce that the kingdom of heaven is near, they expect Jesus to inaugurate the kind of kingdom consistent with their hopes.

Jesus will indeed fulfill the prophetic hope. But he will bring this hope to complete fulfillment only when he returns as the Son of Man in glory (cf. 24:29–31). This dual phenomenon is the "already-not yet" nature of the kingdom. Jesus has *already* inaugurated the kingdom, but it has *not yet* reached its final form. The kingdom is now present with the arrival of the messianic king, and its arrival will confront a variety of expectations among those who experience its impact. But some of what others expected to occur immediately—especially full judgment and restoration—awaits final fulfillment.

Jesus Messiah Calls Fishers of Men (4:18–22). The kingdom of God advances in a unique way as Jesus walks along the shore of the sea of Galilee. Jesus sees two men, Simon Peter and Andrew, his brother, "casting a net" into the sea (v. 18). Jesus approaches these men and calls out, "Come, follow me . . . and I will send you out to fish for people" (v. 19). Surprisingly, in the middle of their workday, they immediately leave their nets and follow him.

Next, Jesus sees two other brothers, James and John, the sons of Zebedee, who are mending their fishing nets for the next commercial excursion on the lake. Caring for this equipment took up much of a morning after a night of fishing. But as with Peter and Andrew, Jesus interrupts their busy activities and calls them. They also leave everything behind to follow Jesus, including their boat and their father. By obeying Jesus's call, they are relinquishing commitment to the family business, their assets, and their livelihood, surely having an impact on varied family relationships, responsibilities, and obligations.

Discipleship to Jesus was going to be different from what many might have anticipated. It was not going to be simply an apprenticeship program. Discipleship was a life that began in relationship with the master and moved into all areas of their experience. This is the beginning of kingdom life.

Jesus Messiah Displays the Gospel of the Kingdom (4:23–25). The threefold profile of Jesus's ministry is highlighted by three participles and their objects:

1. "Teaching" is often related to explanation of truth to those already familiar with the content: Jesus will *teach* the disciples in the Sermon on the Mount.
2. "Proclaiming" or preaching is generally related to the pronouncement of truth to those unfamiliar with the content. The gospel of the kingdom will be *proclaimed* to the world as a witness to the gentiles.
3. This good news is not only taught and proclaimed, but it is also demonstrated through Jesus's *healing* every disease and sickness among the people. Both proclamation and miracle announce that Israel's hoped-for kingdom promise is at hand.

Those coming to Jesus are still primarily Jews, but they come from everywhere. Jesus is generating a tremendous stir in Israel with his message of the arrival of the kingdom, which has been validated by such widespread healings.

Application. Three points emerge from the inauguration of Jesus's ministry to Israel.

The light that dispels darkness brings life. The darkness of our own world is real even when we, or those around us, don't notice it. To be away from Jesus is to be in darkness. We can't let the superficial appearances of people mask the real needs that even they might not recognize. To reach them most effectively we must take as our calling the joy of living in the light of Jesus and continually allowing our lives to shine into theirs with the true kingdom life.

Jesus's call today. Whatever our profession, discipleship means that we place as the priority of our lives joining with Jesus in reaching our daily world with the good news of life in the kingdom of heaven. Our lives find fullest meaning as we follow Jesus's call to join him in advancing the kingdom of heaven.

A life-transforming message of the kingdom of God. We can be so intent on building our ministries that we don't go to where people are hurting. Instead, we just take care of our own. As Jesus's disciples, we all have the incredible privilege, and obligation, to carry the message of the gospel of the kingdom to those who live in the darkness all around us.

MATTHEW 5:1–2

Original Meaning. Matthew specifies three primary groups of people around Jesus in his earthly ministry. The *disciples* are those who have made a commitment to Jesus as the Messiah. The *religious leaders* are Jesus's opponents for much of his ministry, represented especially by the Pharisees. The *crowd* is basically neutral, a curious group of people who are astounded by his teaching and ministry but who have not yet made a commitment to him. Jesus's objective was to make disciples from among the crowd.

Application. *Matthew's discourses develop a full-orbed description of our discipleship to Jesus.* From the biblical point of view, all Christians are disciples, so the teaching in the Sermon on the Mount is not for a few more-committed believers. Matthew is a manual on discipleship, and throughout most of church history this Gospel has been used to provide the content of instruction for full-orbed Christian living.

MATTHEW 5:3–16

Original Meaning

The Beatitudes of the Kingdom of Heaven (5:3–12). *1. Blessed are the poor in spirit . . . (5:3).* The "poor" are those who have encountered unfortunate circumstances from an economic point of view, and also persons who are spiritually and emotionally in need of God's help. This also includes those who recognize that they can produce no spiritual or religious self-help before God. These are the "poor" to whom Jesus has come to announce "good news" and who will experience their most complete personal fulfillment as they draw on the resources of the kingdom of heaven to guide their lives.

2. Blessed are those who mourn . . . (5:4). Those who have reached the bottom of the barrel, whether it is spiritual or emotional or financial, or those who see the bankruptcy of those around them, will mourn. Mourning characterizes life in the "already-not yet" presence of the kingdom. We mourn oppression, persecution, personal sin, and social evil because we mourn the things that God mourns. But as we mourn, we become instruments of the good news of the kingdom as we share with others the comfort of God with which we ourselves have been comforted.

3. Blessed are the meek . . . (5:5). This shifts the focus to interpersonal attributes, people who do not assert themselves over others in order to advance their own causes. This does not imply weakness, however, for this same term is applied to Jesus. He will be strong enough to face the most torturous death possible as he endured the cross. Ultimately "they will inherit" points to the reign of Christ on this earth, but even now Jesus's disciples have entered into their spiritual inheritance.

4. Blessed are those who hunger and thirst for righteousness . . . (5:6). Persons who hunger and thirst will perish if they are not filled. For those who deeply long for God's multifaceted righteousness, divine satisfaction will come in a final sense in God's future reign. It will be experienced in the present by those who respond to Jesus's invitation to kingdom life and enter into a relationship with him as he fills their deepest personal hunger and thirst for righteousness.

5. Blessed are the merciful . . . (5:7). In God's great mercy he does not give humans what they deserve; rather, he gives to them what they do not deserve. The true disciple has experienced God's merciful forgiveness toward an undeserving sinner, which in turn should produce such overwhelming gratitude and deep understanding of forgiveness that he or she will in turn demonstrate that same mercy toward other undeserving sinners.

6. Blessed are the pure in heart . . . (5:8). Jesus declares here that a pure heart is what produces external purity, not vice versa. The pure in heart are those who have given undivided loyalty to God and his ways. Those who have set their heart on God and not simply religious ritualism are invited to enter into a fellowship with him in which they will experience the unthinkable—they will see God in Jesus.

7. Blessed are the peacemakers . . . (5:9). The theme of peace permeates the biblical record. It indicates completeness and wholeness in every area of life, including one's relationship with God, neighbors, and nations, and the true peacemakers are those who wait and work for God, who makes whole the divisions created by humans. Those who respond to Jesus's ministry are heirs of the kingdom and reflect the character of their heavenly Father as they carry Jesus's mission of peacemaking to the world.

8a. Blessed are those who are persecuted because of righteousness . . . (5:10). Persecution can take the form of physical or verbal abuse, or both, but it especially points to the way that the religious leaders hounded the populace and excluded from their fellowship any who did not meet up to their standards. Jesus gives hope to the people who have stood up and contended for God's form of righteousness against the self-righteousness of the religious leaders. Although they have been persecuted for it, Jesus says that the kingdom of God belongs to them, not the religious leaders, and all they need to do now is to respond to his invitation to join the kingdom.

8b. Blessed are you when people insult you . . . (5:11–12). In this instruction Jesus prepares his disciples for the time when persecution will indeed come to them. It may not look like it from a religious, economic, or social perspective, but the kingdom is theirs nonetheless—and in this they will truly rejoice.

Salt and Light (5:13–16). *You are the salt of the earth (5:13).* Since salt had a varied use in the ancient world, Jesus is using it in a broad, inclusive sense to refer to a vital necessity for everyday life. Jesus indicates with this metaphor that his disciples themselves ("*you* are the salt") are necessary for the welfare of the world.

"But if the salt loses its saltiness . . ." Imposter disciples, who simply attempt to put on the flavoring of the kingdom life, will be revealed. Their salt is only an external flavoring, not a real personal change. This imposter cannot be made salty again because he or she never had that kingdom life in the first place.

The light of the world (5:14–16). Jesus's disciples possess kingdom life, which produces good deeds from a changed life. Bearing the light of the gospel in both message and life will bring people to know that the kingdom of heaven is truly in the world, and they will glorify their heavenly Father.

Application. *The applicability of the Beatitudes.* The individual characteristics of the Beatitudes are not self-produced. The Beatitudes are neither a means of entering nor of advancing in the kingdom. They are expressions of Spirit-produced kingdom life, revealing to the entire world that a transformation of creation is beginning in Jesus's disciples. That is why we are blessed.

The applicability of the sayings on salt and light. We must declare the saving message of the gospel. People can't change until they have heard the message. But the old adage is true that actions speak louder than words. We must show by our lives that we are different. In so living, we will be revealed as sons and daughters of God, the true salt of the earth and the glowing light of the world.

MATTHEW 5:17–20

Original Meaning. *Fulfilling the law (5:17).* Jesus makes clear at the beginning of his teaching ministry that the arrival of the kingdom does not do away with God's prior revelation through the Law and the Prophets. The idea of fulfillment is more than his obedience (i.e., keeping the law), although that is included. Jesus has come to actualize the Scripture and take his disciples to a deeper understanding of its intended meaning—and this in distinction from many Jewish leaders, who have misunderstood and misapplied Scripture's intent.

The lasting validity of the Old Testament (5:18). While some elements of Scripture will be accomplished in Jesus's ministry, the Old Testament remains a valid principle. For example, the teaching of death and the shedding of blood to atone for sin has been "fulfilled" or "accomplished" once for all in Christ's atonement on the cross. Thus, this commandment from the Old Testament is no longer legally binding as a practice. Nevertheless, the Old Testament principle of penalty and payment for sin remains valid and needs to be taught and understood as God's will.

Jesus's view of the inspiration of Scripture extends to the actual words, even letters and parts of letters. This is in accord with a verbal plenary view of inspiration—that is, the very words, and all of the words, of Scripture are inspired. Scripture does not simply contain the word of God; the words of Scripture are the very word of God.

Doing and teaching the commandments (5:19). A disciple's status in the kingdom of heaven accords with whether one trifles with the revealed will of God or obeys and teaches it as truly the word of God. "Least" and "great" are ways to acknowledge in this present life those who have been faithful in word and deed to the revealed will of God as it is taught by Jesus.

"Inside-out" righteousness (5:20). This may have been Jesus's most shocking statement—a tacit disclosure of the central principle of life in the kingdom of heaven; namely, that kingdom righteousness operates from the inside-out, not from the outside-in. The arrival of the kingdom of heaven produces spiritual transformation in the disciple's heart, which will ultimately produce transformation in the disciple's external ethical life. In the antitheses to follow, Jesus contrasts his internal, spiritual interpretation with the external, legalistic interpretation of the Pharisees, which dead-ends in an external, superficial self-righteousness.

Application. *The Christian's relation to the law.* The law is a revelation of God's perfect righteousness. We trifle with God's will if we set aside some aspects of his word. It was given to point out humanity's sinfulness and lead humanity to Christ. Jesus is objecting to misinterpretations of the law, not the law itself. A tendency existed in Pharisaic Judaism to make their interpretations as binding as the law itself. Jesus rejected their practices, not the law itself.

Jesus fulfilled the law and proved to be the perfect God-man, who is therefore able to become the means of our justification or right standing with God. Therefore, we are not under the law as a means of gaining salvation. At the same time, Jesus is the interpreter of the law, showing what is binding principle and what is temporary symbolic ritual. Jesus demonstrates that the entire Old Testament hangs on love for God and neighbor.

Inside-out transformation. As the disciple continues to respond obediently to the word of God taught and preached by Jesus and energized by the Spirit, the newly transformed heart directs the transformation of the person from the inside to the outside. The indwelling Spirit directs the renewing of the mind, the disciplining of the body, and the purifying of social relations so that the disciple says yes to God with his or her entire person. The disciple bears the fruit of the Spirit in a life given to God that is being transformed to be like Jesus.

MATTHEW 5:21–48

Original Meaning

Murder . . . Nurturing Relationships (5:21–26). Although Hebrew possesses seven words for killing, the verb used in Exodus 20:13 makes "murder" (*ratsah*) a more accurate rendering than "kill." The fact that men and women have been created in the image of God lies behind this prohibition. This penalty was already in force before the Mosaic law in the decrees to Noah.

Jesus's declarative statement, "but I tell you" (v. 22), introduces three ways that a person's life is removed besides the physical act of murder. In each case, punishment is due.

1. Jesus gets at the source of murder, which is anger.
2. Calling another disciple "Raca," a transliteration of an Aramaic term implying "empty-headed."
3. Saying "you fool [*mōre*]" to a disciple. *Mōre* is most likely a case form of the Greek word *mōros* (the origin of the English word *moron*), indicating a person who consistently acts like an idiot. To treat a person with such contempt was to strip away his personal identity and wrongly make the person into something he or she was not.

The expression "fire of hell" is *geenna* (v. 22), from which we get the English transliteration *Gehenna*. It is a transliteration of the Aramaic form of the Hebrew *ge bene-hinnom* ("valley of the sons of Hinnom"), a valley west and southwest of Jerusalem. Here Ahaz and Manasseh sacrificed their sons to Molech, which caused Josiah to defile the place (2 Kgs 23:10). Later the valley was used to burn refuse from Jerusalem, so the constant burning made the valley an appropriate reference to fires of punishment. Jewish apocalyptic writers began to call the Valley of Hinnom the entrance to hell, later hell itself (4 Ezra 7.36). By the time of Jesus, the term was used to indicate the state of final punishment (cf. Matt 18:9).

Fulfilling the law's command not to murder is not accomplished simply by avoiding legal homicide. Jesus reveals that the intent of the law is to nurture relationships. Anything we do that strips away the personal distinctiveness of a brother or sister is sin, and it is our responsibility to become reconciled.

Adultery . . . Marital Oneness (5:27–30). Adultery was considered one of the most serious offenses because it broke the relationship that reflected the relationship between God and his people. Adultery was often used to describe the way in which the people of Israel went after gods. It is not enough for spouses only to maintain physical purity. The purity of marriage includes exclusive devotion to one another in every aspect of their lives.

Jesus uses hyperbole (deliberate exaggeration) for the sake of emphasizing the seriousness of single-hearted devotion. Jesus is not advocating physical self-mutilation, but through dramatic figures of speech he indicates the kind of rigorous self-discipline that committed disciples must display.

Divorce . . . Marriage Sanctity Inviolate (5:31–32). Since divorce was a widespread phenomenon in the ancient world, God instituted a regulation through Moses that was designed to do three things:

1. protect the sanctity of marriage from "indecency" defiling the marital relationship;
2. protect the woman from a husband who might simply send her away without any cause; and
3. document her status as a legitimately divorced woman so that she was not thought to be a harlot or a runaway adulteress.

Jesus goes back to the original intention both for God's institution of marriage and for the Mosaic regulation. God intended marriage to be a permanent union of a man and woman in a "one flesh" relationship (see Gen 2:24). God hates divorce, because it tears apart what should be considered a permanent union (cf. Mal 2:16). Therefore, Jesus states categorically that divorce creates adultery, the despicable nature of which he has just declared, because an illicit divorce turns the woman into an adulteress when she remarries.

However, as did Moses, Jesus allows for an exception—namely, when a person has committed *porneia*. *Porneia* includes any sinful sexual activity that intentionally divides the marital relationship. Jesus states unequivocally the sacredness of the marital relationship but allows divorce in this case to protect the nonoffending partner, as well as to protect the institution of marriage from becoming a vulgar sham.

Oaths . . . Transparent Honesty (5:33–37). Jesus goes to the heart of the law's intent regarding oaths when he says that his disciples are not to swear "at all" (v. 34). Jesus's disciples should be people of such integrity of character and truthfulness of heart that whatever they say is absolutely believable and dependable. A person of integrity is one who in daily conversation is so truthful, dependable, genuine, guileless, and reliable that his or her words are believed without an oath.

Eye for an Eye . . . Servanthood (5:38–42). The common person was at the mercy of the Romans everywhere—on the street, in the court, in the presence of the military occupying forces, and in the everyday world of financial need. Within this oppressive atmosphere, Jesus points to the motivation of the individual disciple who has been taken advantage of and wronged. Jesus's disciples are not to think first about retribution. Even when they are being abused, they must think of ways to advance the kingdom of heaven and its influence on this earth. Jesus himself lived out this radical principle and became a vivid example for his followers. He loved so much that he gave himself for sinners.

Love and Hatred . . . Unconditional Commitment (5:43–47). Jesus takes the competing attitudes of love for neighbor and hate for enemy and brings them together in a way that goes contrary to what was occurring in many quarters in Israel but that actually preserves the love that God has for all humans. All of God's creatures are his own, and he loves them and desires that all will come to repentance. Jesus's disciples are to look at people in this world as God does and to love them enough to reach out to them with the message of reconciliation, even to "pray for those who persecute" them as Jesus's disciples (v. 44). When Jesus states that "you may be children of your Father in heaven" (v. 45), he is not giving the means by which one becomes a child of God but indicates that love makes explicit the relationship between God the Father and Jesus's disciples.

Conclusion: The Pursuit of Perfection (5:48). The new birth for entrance into the kingdom of heaven enables the transformation of Christ's disciples into his own image. Since Jesus is both the perfection of the image of God in humans as a full human being and the perfect image of the invisible God as the divine Son of God, he is the ultimate example for his disciples to follow as they hear the command, "Be perfect, as your heavenly Father is perfect." That statement implies a realistically ideal goal that Jesus's disciples are to pursue with restful dissatisfaction in this life until their final perfection in eternity.

Application. *Treating people with dignity (5:21–26).* We are not to do anything that demeans a person's dignity. That is why we should be so careful with our words and actions. We can never take back a word uttered, and a hurt inflicted often leaves lasting scars.

Jesus's teaching is sometimes used to advocate opposition to capital punishment. But the prohibition of the Old Testament that Jesus continues to uphold is against murder, not killing per se. Moreover, Jesus is addressing personal activity, not governmental responsibility.

Purity in marriage (5:27–30). In the listings of qualifications for leadership in the church, Paul emphasizes the health of leaders' marriages (1 Tim 3:2, 12; Titus 1:6). There is perhaps no more powerful testimony to the reality of the presence of the kingdom of heaven than leaders who have an unreserved commitment to their spouses, which means to pursue an unqualified purity in all relationships.

Faithfulness in marriage (5:31–32). Respecting the purity of marriage also allows Jesus's disciples to understand God's original design for marriage and to be unreservedly committed to its permanence and sanctity. We should also be careful not to read into Jesus's statement what he did not imply. He did not declare the exception of *porneia* to require divorce. Reconciliation and forgiveness are always the goal. Jesus also did not state that remarriage in the case of a legitimate divorce is invalid. Further, he did not state that illegitimate divorce and even illegitimate remarriage are unpardonable sins. While there are always consequences for going contrary to Jesus's intentions for us, we must be careful not to create oppressive burdens that cancel out God's grace and restoration.

Keeping our word (5:33–37). Truthfulness is one of the basic necessities in the daily activities of life. When each person's word is honest, we are liberated to trust each other freely. When a person's word or handshake on a matter cannot be trusted, we must bring in all kinds of legal safeguards, which complicate daily life. Jesus is not suggesting that all oaths are wrong. He himself testified under oath in his trial before the Sanhedrin. In a court of law, a person is operating under the jurisdiction of governing authorities who are trying to establish human norms. To submit to taking an oath is complying with those norms and, by extension, is submitting to God.

Securely serving one another (5:38–42). Jesus is not countering the Old Testament law of retribution. Jesus does not deny justice in any way; as he goes to the cross, he will be the ultimate payment for the penalty of sin. What Jesus counteracts is the way that the law of retaliation was used to excuse *personal* retribution.

The fifth antithesis emphasizes the goal of servanthood in Jesus's disciples. This means not to think first about our own harm but about the other's good. We are to give to the person what is needed for his or her good. Our ultimate example is Jesus himself.

Loving as God loves (5:43–47). What does it really mean to love someone? Love may be defined as *an unconditional commitment to an imperfect person in which I give myself to bring the relationship to God's intended purpose.* Whatever it is that God has designed for my various relationships, I give myself to them unconditionally. That varies from the love commitments that I have for my wife or children or students or next-door neighbors. It will look differently as I give myself to people I don't like or who don't like me. But what I am asking in each is, "What does God want for this relationship, and how can I best give myself to bring it about?" It's with this kind of guidance that we can give ourselves wisely and maturely, even to our enemies.

Be perfect (5:48). In its simplicity this may be one of the purest statements of spiritual formation in all of Scripture. But we may become uneasy before its magnitude. Instead of being uneasy before Jesus's magnificent summons, we can practice a balance of what we may call "restful dissatisfaction." We rest content with what Christ has done in our lives and with the growth that has occurred, yet at the same time we balance that contentment with the desire to move on. Jesus's disciples experience the powerfully life-changing presence of the kingdom of heaven in such a way that becoming more like the Son produces the very perfection of God the Father. That is what we should hear in Jesus's summons to be perfect as our heavenly Father is perfect.

MATTHEW 6:1–18

Original Meaning

Acts of Righteousness (6:1). If Jesus's disciples fall into the attention-seeking display of public piety, "you will have no reward from your Father in heaven." The term for "reward" is *misthos*, which can indicate payment of "wages" (20:8) or, as here, the recompense of a person's good deeds with a good prize. Those who perform them out of the fullness of a heart transformed by God's righteousness will be rewarded with inner growth in kingdom righteousness in this life and final perfection in the afterlife.

Giving to the Needy (6:2–4). The term translated "hypocrite" was originally used for actors on a Greek stage who put on various masks to play different roles. Jesus here censures the religious leaders for a particular form of hypocrisy: performing external acts of righteousness that mask, even from themselves, their own inner corruption. The tragic irony is that they will "receive in full" the reward of public acclaim for their pious activities, but they will receive no reward from God.

Jesus's disciples are to go to the opposite extreme and keep their acts of piety secret. God will reward Jesus's disciples with inner righteousness in this life and complete perfection in the afterlife. Human acclaim for giving to the needy cannot be compared to the value of being recognized by God for secret giving.

Praying (6:5–15). *The pretentious prayer of hypocrites (6:5–6).* Prayer can be perverted from a true act of piety into an act of hypocrisy when the external act masks an inner corrupt motive. In contrast, Jesus directs his disciples, when they pray, to go to their inner "room." The focus is on the intimacy of communion with God in one's heart, which is at the center of all prayer, whether it happens to be given publicly or privately.

The repetitious prayer of pagans (6:7–8). Though God already knows, we should not hesitate to ask. Long, continued prayer is not improper, because Jesus himself prayed through whole nights. He also commended in a parable the perseverance of the widow in prayer and repeated the same request in his prayer to the Father in the garden of Gethsemane. Prayer is much about changing *us*, our character, our will, and our values, even while we seek for God's response.

The model prayer for disciples: "The Lord's Prayer" (6:9–13). The way Jesus uses "*my* Father" to address his heavenly Father is exceptional because Jesus is the unique Son (e.g., Matt 7:21; 12:50). But by calling his disciples to share in the kingdom of heaven, they now have entered into a relationship with his Father as well. God is "*our* Father" (6:9), expressing the relationship we have with one another as disciples and with Jesus as our brother, and the corporate intimacy we have with the same Father.

God's name (6:9). The purpose of hallowing the name (the name signifies the person) is that God might be sanctified or set apart as holy among all peoples and in all actions. Jesus's disciples will honor God's name in their prayers, but especially as they submit to his power and authority when they present themselves to baptism in the *name* of the Father, Son, and Holy Spirit (28:19).

God's kingdom (6:10). This petition is reflected in a prayer expressed in the early church's appeal, "Come, O Lord!" (*marana tha*), the oldest Christian prayer of which we have record (1 Cor 16:22). Jesus's earliest disciples had invoked the name of their covenant God as "Lord" in synagogue worship, but in 1 Cor 16:22 Paul applies the same divine title to Jesus the Messiah, who has inaugurated the kingdom of heaven and who will bring its final manifestation. Here in Matthew 6:10, "your kingdom" refers to God the Father's kingdom.

God's will (6:10). God reigns in heaven absolutely, which means that all of heaven experiences his perfect will. Jesus prays that earth will experience that same rule of God. Jesus's own utmost act of obedience in his earthly ministry was to submit to will of God the Father. Jesus's disciples are the present living testimony to the world that God's will can be experienced today.

Sustenance (6:11). In the same way that manna was only given one day at a time, disciples are to rely on daily provision for life from God, helping them to develop a continuing, conscious dependence on him. We are to rely on God for all physical sustenance but to be concerned for only one day at a time.

Sins (6:12). Sin creates an obligation or debt to God that we cannot possibly repay. Jesus's disciples are not simply to relish their own state of forgiveness; they are also to forgive others. This does not teach that humans must forgive others before they can receive forgiveness themselves; rather, forgiveness of others is *proof* that the disciple's sins are forgiven and that he or she possesses salvation.

Spiritual battle (6:13). This petition indicates that the disciples should pray either for relief from testing or for their testing not to become an occasion for temptation.

Satan's influence is behind every attempt to turn a testing into a temptation to evil, so Jesus teaches his disciples that they must rely on God for moral triumph and spiritual victory in all of the spiritual battles of life.

Forgiveness and prayer (6:14–15). Salvation does not rest on human merits but only on the grace and mercy of God. Once disciples have received forgiveness and salvation, they are to forgive with the same forgiveness with which they have been forgiven. This is the evidence that they are indeed forgiven.

Fasting (6:16–18). Jesus assumes his disciples will fast because he says simply, "When you fast" (v. 16). Jesus does not prohibit his disciples from fasting, but neither does he make it a required practice. Jesus's disciples are to celebrate life while fasting. Other people do not need to know of their religious discipline. Fasting is to be done in the secrecy of the heart, with only God the Father as audience. The reward for fasting is the same as the reward for other acts of righteousness—continued development of inner righteousness in this life and the final perfection of righteousness in the age to come.

Application. *Congruency of inner life and external practice.* Throughout church history the practice of the full panoply of spiritual disciplines has been a key to spiritual growth. These disciplines are viewed from different perspectives. However we might view them, the important point is to remember that the righteousness of the kingdom of heaven is an inside-out process, which Jesus intentionally orients to counteract the hypocritical practice of operating only on the surface.

Personal transformation begins in the inner person through the work of the Spirit of God, which produces change on the outside as we discipline ourselves to be more Christlike. We must develop an inside-out mentality so that Spirit-produced growth of the inner person is in harmony with outward obedience.

Eliminating elitism. One of Jesus's purposes in the Sermon on the Mount, and particularly in addressing the practice of acts of righteousness in this section, is to eliminate an elitist conception of discipleship. The practice of the disciplines is a normal outgrowth of discipleship to Jesus.

Practicing disciplines in secrecy. Jesus further emphasizes that one key solution to religious hypocrisy is to be sure that an act of righteousness is carried out "in secret" (vv. 4, 6, 18), which means essentially that the deed be performed in the privacy of one's heart.

Giving to the needy in secret (6:2–4). Inner motivation drives outward actions, so Jesus's disciples are to give to the needy from the secrecy of their heart. Years ago, before giving a prayer for the offering in the little church where I was pastor, I used to tell the people that if they were grudging that morning in their giving (2 Cor 9:5), or if they were tempted to give to be noticed by the pastoral staff or the leadership, or even their own family, they should put their wallet or purse away. God doesn't need their money given with bad motives. The elders of the church gasped almost visibly. But then I went on to say that even if they had mixed motives in giving, God could change their hearts in a moment. So if they were ready, we could pray and ask God to purify their motives. The elders were much happier! It is within our responsibility to check our motives, to ask the Spirit of God to purify our motives, and then to move on, knowing that he will continue to cause us to grow in this area if we really desire it.

Praying in secret (6:5–15). We've all been conscious at times of being in a prayer group when it seemed as though the one praying is addressing us more than God. Or our grand prayers were really aimed at impressing the audience more than reaching God. The motivation of private prayer is the intimacy of communion with God in our heart, which is at the center of all prayer, whether it happens to be given publicly or privately.

Fasting in secret (6:16–18). Of the sixteen or so references to fasting in the New Testament, roughly half speak of corporate fasts, including those that seem to indicate that it was the regular practice of the early church. Corporate fasting encouraged the church to express sorrow for sin, seek community forgiveness, concentrate on the work of God, and seek his guidance. But even corporate fasting needs to be conducted in the privacy of the heart, with no self-adulation of the church taking pride in its serious rigor. Fasting has lost much appeal in the modern church. This is a sad misreading of Jesus's teaching. He does not condemn fasting, not even corporate fasting, but only fasting with the motive of receiving acclaim from other people.

MATTHEW 6:19–34

Original Meaning

Choose Your Master: God or Wealth (6:19–24). *Two treasures of the heart (6:19–21).* The accumulation of wealth for its own sake is deceptive, because one can find in material treasure a false sense of security or an inaccurate assessment of one's spirituality. But those things that some people value are subject to the destructive effects of life in a fallen world. Moth, rust, and thieves represent those forces that cause earthly treasures to diminish in value and finally be destroyed.

The contrast of "treasures on earth" with "treasures in heaven" implies a contrast of values. Whatever the disciple has placed as his or her highest value is a gauge of the condition of the heart. The righteous value must be God himself. This will set a trajectory for healthy discipleship, including one's priorities, motives, righteous deeds, ambitions, security, personal self-worth, and relationships.

Two eyes of the heart (6:22–23). Since the heart is the true repository of treasure, Jesus now indicates that when the eye focuses on something of value, it becomes the conduit that fills the heart with what has been focused upon. If the eye is good, it is the conduit that allows the heart to be filled with the light of God's treasure. If a disciple's eyes are fixed on earthly treasure as his or her value, personal significance, and earthly security, then the heart will likewise be full of darkness. When we focus on something evil, the eye becomes the conduit by which evil fills the inner person.

Two masters of the heart: God and money (6:24). The term for "serve" is *douleuō*, indicating the work of a slave, not an employee. One might be able to work for two employers, but a slave is sole property of one master, which implies an exclusive owner who demands exclusive service. The biblical notion of "hate" and "love" understands them to be patterns of life, not simple emotional reactions. This prepares for Jesus's radical summons of unconditional commitment to him, to the point that one must hate, or completely reject, anything that hinders attachment to him, and love him, or give oneself completely to him.

Choose Your Provider: God or Worry (6:25–34). *The principle about worry (6:25).* The principle about worry is expressed in the imperative, "Do not worry [*merimnaō*] about your life." Sometimes *merimnaō* expresses an appropriate feeling of intense concern and care for something, such as the Lord's work (1 Cor 7:32) or someone's welfare (Phil 2:20). In this case we can render this word in English as "concern." Concern is appropriate when it is directed toward right things, kept within bounds, and causes us to do our proper duty. However, *merimnaō* is inappropriate or wrong when it is misdirected, is in wrong proportion, or indicates a lack of trust in God. It is this latter sense that Jesus addresses here.

The example of life and food (6:26–27). The first reason Jesus gives as to why his disciples should not worry is the Father's care for his creatures. Birds expend energy in doing what is natural, yet it is actually God who feeds and clothes them. The point is that when Jesus's disciples are responsible to carry out the proper ways of life as ordained by God, God is faithful to carry out his end of the order.

The example of clothing (6:28–30). This expression draws to mind God's provision in nature for flowers growing wild. If God's sustaining care extends to such a transitory part of his creation, "will he not much more clothe you—you of little faith?" "Little faith" (*oligopistos*) is a favorite expression of Jesus, found mainly in this Gospel. It is only directed to Jesus's disciples, indicating not *absence* of faith but *deficiency* of faith.

The Father's interest in all things (6:31–32). Here, the emphasis is on those who operate outside of God's values. Those with faith in God's provision will not worry and will reject the pursuits and values of unbelievers.

The proper priority (6:33). The use of the imperative "seek" does not mean to look for something not present, for Jesus has already announced the arrival of the kingdom. In this context it means that his disciples are to make the kingdom of heaven the center of their continual, daily priorities.

Eliminating worry (6:34). All the worry in the world today can do nothing about the cares and problems of tomorrow. As disciples learn to let God care for them today, including their "daily bread" (v. 11), they will become increasingly secure in his care for them tomorrow, regardless of whatever evil may come. Jesus's disciples don't know what tomorrow will bring, but the Father does. It takes a great deal of worry from us when we live that way daily.

Application. *The idol of materialism.* The pursuit of material wealth is a feeble attempt to fill the dark void that can only be filled by a good eye fixed on Jesus as our sole master and provider. Money, wealth, and possessions have at least three primary purposes in Scripture:

1. to give appropriate care for one's own family and prevent them from becoming a burden to others (1 Thess 4:11–12; 2 Thess 3:6–15; 1 Tim 5:8);
2. to help those who are in need, especially the family of faith (Prov 19:17; Acts 11:27–30; Rom 15:25–27; 2 Cor 8:1–15; Gal 6:7–10; Eph 4:28; 1 Tim 5:3–7); and
3. to encourage and support God's work in spreading the gospel of the kingdom both at home and around the world (1 Cor 9:3–14; Phil 4:14–19; 1 Tim 5:17–18).

If we put Jesus at the center of our lives to serve and love him with all that we are and have, we will use appropriately all the blessings of life and avoid the modern idolatry of materialism.

The idolatry of worry. We probably do not think of worry as a form of idolatry, but it is when we allow it to take our eyes off of Jesus. We substitute despair, hopelessness, or fear in place of God and turn to our own efforts at trying to control our environment. This can be a harsh world, and worry about the outcome can consume us. A way of reversing the trend toward anxiety is to look around at what we have and what God has done and then say, "Thank you." He is our master and provider, the one who has given us kingdom life, kingdom priorities, and kingdom values, by which we can truly say, "Thank you."

MATTHEW 7:1–12

Original Meaning

Judging Others Inappropriately (7:1–5). The warning about judging is the reverse of the positive blessing Jesus advocated in the fifth beatitude: "blessed are the merciful . . ." (5:7).

The warning also recapitulates the point of the fifth petition of the Lord's Prayer: "forgive us our debts . . ." (6:12). True disciples, who have been impacted by the mercy of God in the arrival of the kingdom of heaven, will exhibit mercy toward one another, not judgment. The responsibility that disciples have to help each other remove the "speck" (v. 3) of sin from each other's lives must come from a humble and self-examined life that has first removed the plank of self-righteous judgment.

Evaluating Others Appropriately (7:6). Jesus next addresses a problem at the opposite extreme of judging hypocritically: naive acceptance. To modern readers the mention of "dogs" conjures up images of well-groomed household pets, but in the ancient world dogs lived in squalor, running the streets and scavenging for food (Ps 59:14–15). The reference here includes all those who are hostile to Jesus's disciples. The gospel of the kingdom must not be defiled by those who are unreceptive to, or have rejected, Jesus's invitation.

Although pork was a highly prized food among many people in the ancient Mediterranean world, it was rejected by Jews, probably because pigs, like dogs, were scavenging animals. "Pearls" symbolize the value of the message of the kingdom of heaven. Something so valuable should not be given to those who have no appreciation for such precious truths; their nature is demonstrated by their rejection of that message.

God's Guidance in Relationship to Others (7:7–12). *Ask, seek, and knock (7:7–8).* Jesus is indicating a rising scale of intensity in one's prayers and points to the persistent manner of life lived before the Father. "Ask" indicates coming to God with humility and consciousness of need, as a child fittingly comes to her father. "Seek" links one's prayer with responsible activity in pursuing God's will, as when a person prays for a job and at the same time checks out leads. "Knock" includes perseverance in one's asking and seeking, as when the disciple perseveres in praying for his unbelieving family's salvation and speaks and lives the gospel throughout his lifetime. Jesus's disciples are to ask the Father continually as a manner of life, to be constantly responsible in pursuing God's will, and to maintain an unremitting determination in expecting the Father to answer.

Bread . . . stone . . . fish . . . snake (7:9–11). Jesus clarifies the open-ended teaching on the certainty of the answer to the disciples' prayers by demonstrating that the Father will answer with what he knows is good for his children. If a responsible father will supply his children precisely with what they need on a daily basis, the heavenly Father, who is absolutely trustworthy, will always give to the disciples what they really need.

The Golden Rule (7:12). This moral maxim of the Golden Rule occurs in various forms in other traditions, stated both positively and negatively. Jesus's teaching on prayer and the Golden Rule brings to light two significant points about stability in one's discipleship. First, stability will come as his disciples learn how to depend on their heavenly Father. To love God is to trust him to take care of us. Second, stability will also come through a healthy commitment to live for the benefit of others. When appropriate trust in another's care is linked with trust in the Father's care, Jesus's disciples never have to think about their own needs being met; those needs are met in the loving community of disciples who emulate the Father's commitment to care for us.

Application. *Balance.* The kind of balance advocated here means to take two seemingly opposite truths and live with them both at the same time, even though we may not be able to understand completely how they fit together. It is a process that includes the following points.

1. Think sensibly. Don't be carried away by emotional reactions. Such reaction to apparent contradictions may cause us to become immobilized or carried away to an extreme.
2. Be honestly open to both truths, regardless of past experience or background.
3. Hold those seemingly opposing truths at the same time. If they are both biblical, they will both have value in the decision-making process and ultimately will reveal themselves as complementary, not contradictory.
4. Apply both sides of the issue to life at the same time. Since Scripture is a guide to life, both principles may be more easily lived out than fully comprehended.

In this section we come across a number of issues that require us to balance two truths. Rightly approached, proportional living is a fulfilling way of thinking and exploring all of life, because it leads us into the fullest realization of truth. But it is also the most demanding, because we are always thinking and weighing our actions and thoughts. We must recognize that we are always in process. But the pursuit of the goal to understand and apply all of God's truth is what will enable us to keep balanced.

MATTHEW 7:13–29

Original Meaning

Narrow and Broad Gates and Roads (7:13–14). The broad gate and road is inviting, offering plenty of room for those who would follow the cultural and pious norm of the religious leaders. One can enter and travel comfortably and unmolested on this roomy road. However, the comfort is deceiving, because it ends in "destruction" (*apōleia*), a common word for eternal punishment. The narrow gate and road is much more restrictive, because it is limited to Jesus and his manner of discipleship.

Those traveling this narrow road will experience difficulty, especially because the challenge of Jesus's way of discipleship will prompt oppression, even persecution, from those of the majority way. Jesus himself is the narrow gate through which people pass as they respond to his invitation to the kingdom of heaven. The way of discipleship then stretches throughout one's years on earth, ultimately leading to life eternal.

True and False Prophets (7:15–20). False prophets first seem to be genuine members of God's flock by their talk and association with the group, but their intentions are evil, like a wolf who ravages a flock for its own gratification. Jesus admonishes his disciples to be "fruit inspectors" of those passing themselves off as prophets. False prophets will produce bad fruit, which includes leading the people away from God to follow false gods or speaking prophecies that are not fulfilled. Bad trees are good for nothing except to be used for firewood, a striking metaphor of the judgment to come for false prophets.

True and False Disciples (7:21–23). Not only will false prophets enter the community, but some within the community itself will be false disciples. These false disciples claim prophetic status and point to their charismatic activity as a sign of their discipleship: "Did we not prophesy in your name, and in your name drive out demons and perform many miracles?" (v. 22). Exorcism and performance of miracles regularly accompany the gospel proclamation of Jesus and the Twelve; such activities confirm the authenticity of the message. False disciples are able to gain power "in Jesus's name," but their activities are meaningless for their own eternal destiny. They do not come to Jesus as the true gate to the kingdom and so do not engage in these activities according to the Father's will.

The ultimate revelation of the authenticity of one's life will come at the time of judgment. So Jesus evokes an eschatological scene of eternal judgment and banishes them from him. This is a stark, straightforward rejection of a person who does not have a true relationship with Jesus as his disciple. For Jesus to place himself as the one who has authority to determine who enters the kingdom and who is banished to eternal punishment is to accrue to himself the highest christological claim. Here Jesus claims the divine prerogative to know the inner recesses of a person's heart.

Wise and Foolish Builders (7:24–27). The audience of the Sermon on the Mount would readily understand the surface meaning intended in the parable, because they would know how foolish a person was who would choose the easy way and did not build on bedrock. But would they see beyond the parable to Jesus's point? Would they reject the present secure but shallow shifting sands of the religious leadership of the scribes and Pharisees and choose instead Jesus's words as the foundation for their lives? The religious establishment was advocating a form of surface righteousness that masked an unstable foundation of religious hypocrisy. Eventually its instability would be revealed as not having the answers to the deepest needs of the people.

The wise person shows that he or she has carefully viewed the shifting sands of life's teachings and understands that Jesus is the only secure truth of life. The wise person thinks ahead to when there will be storms and sacrifices and builds his or her life on the rock of Jesus's words. The choice is no less stark in our own day. Wise men and women build their lives on Jesus, regardless of the cultural or religious weather.

The Reaction of the Crowds (7:28–29). Matthew's conclusion is ironic. Amazement at Jesus's teachings does not indicate acceptance. The term "amazed" is the passive form of *ekplēssō*, which in Matthew is not a description of faith. It indicates a variety of emotional responses but not a commitment to Jesus's messianic ministry. Amazement is not the same as a commitment of faith. Only when a person accepts Jesus's invitation and enters the kingdom of heaven does he or she become a disciple.

Application. *Narrow and wide gates and roads (7:13–14).* A perpetual problem of those who consider Jesus's invitation to the kingdom is that it is not the popular way. We cannot always discover God's will by appealing to the majority, because our ways are not always God's ways. When we are motivated by a desire to please people, we will find that it might not at all please God.

Jesus's invitation to the kingdom is that it is not the easy way. The words "wide" and "broad" not only clue us to the numbers of those who will take the highway to hell, but they also imply an easy way, without the troubles and oppression and rigor of discipleship to Jesus. Jesus calls would-be disciples to carefully consider the alternative of life in the kingdom of heaven, as narrow and as difficult as it may be, with the popular road that leads to destruction.

An additional problem that can surface from Jesus's challenge of the gates and roads is that if we don't get the order right, we may think Jesus is implying a system of works. But by looking closely at Jesus's saying, we have seen that the gate comes first. Jesus offers by grace the invitation to salvation and a life of walking with him.

Good and bad fruit (7:15–20). Two important implications draw our attention. First, real transformation is the test of the reality of the impact of the kingdom of heaven in a person's life. The virtuous life of the kingdom of heaven that Jesus taught in the Sermon on the Mount cannot be produced by a person who has not experienced the kingdom's transforming power.

Second, we are called to examine the fruit of those who profess a message from God, for they may be impostors. Jesus's warning of false prophetic voices is as relevant today as it has been throughout church history. A multitude of false messengers hype a promise of life, but it will only take them and their followers into the fires of hell.

Hearers and doers of the Father's will (7:21–23). In this third warning, Jesus addresses those who make profession of faith in him, who even perform miraculous deeds in his name, but who are really not his own. It is no different today. It is discouraging to see how many are attracted to preachers who assert the authenticity of their message by dramatic exhibitions of "spiritual" power. The final proof of any ministry is whether it promotes obedience to the Father's will.

Wise and foolish builders (7:24–27). Jesus's fourth warning compares the wisdom of finding one's righteousness in Jesus's proclamation of the kingdom of heaven with the foolishness of pursuing the self-righteousness of the religious establishment. The solid rock that has provided true stability, security, and hope throughout church history is none other than Jesus, and him alone, and the life of kingdom righteousness that he has announced in the Sermon on the Mount.

MATTHEW 8:1–9:8

Original Meaning

Healing the Marginalized (8:1–17). In three brief scenes, Matthew demonstrates how Jesus's messianic ministry breaks down purity, ethnic, and gender barriers so that all may respond to his invitation to the kingdom of heaven.

Cleansing the leper: purity boundaries (8:1–4). As he reaches out to touch the leper, Jesus does not violate the Old Testament purity laws, for instead of becoming unclean himself he cleanses the leper with his healing hand and spiritual purity. By commanding the leper to perform the prescribed ritual of presenting himself to the priest, Jesus fulfills the law required of lepers for reentry into society (Lev 14:1–32).

Jesus's desire for silence is a theme that characterizes Jesus's historical mission. Although miracles will attest the authenticity of his gospel message about the arrival of the kingdom of heaven, Jesus does not want crowds clamoring for the miracles alone. He will guide his disciples and the crowds to understand that his primary mission is to bring forgiveness of sins, which brings true cleansing.

Healing the centurion's servant: ethnic boundaries (8:5–13). Returning again to Capernaum, Jesus encounters a centurion, a Roman military officer. The *centuria*, a group of a hundred soldiers, was the smallest unit of the Roman legion. The centurion of Capernaum must have been an able and responsible official who maintained good relations with the Jewish populace.

This Roman centurion displays a remarkable sensitivity for Jewish traditions by considering himself unworthy to receive the Jewish teacher into his gentile home. Entering the home of a gentile rendered a Jew ceremonially unclean. But the centurion goes beyond the Jewish aversion to gentile homes in his recognition of Jesus's personal superiority as the one who can heal his servant. This centurion pays homage to an even greater authority in Jesus, whose word alone, like God's word, can heal.

The centurion understands that in Jesus is the hoped-for deliverer, whom Israel as a nation should have recognized. Hence, Jesus's statement both singles out the centurion for exemplary faith and censures Israel for its lack of faith. The Old Testament had anticipated the inclusion of all the peoples of the earth in the eschatological banquet. The covenant made with Abraham to be a blessing to all the nations of the earth, which has been fulfilled with the arrival of Jesus, is now made public in the pronouncement to the centurion.

At the same time that Jesus assures the inclusion of gentiles, he dramatically foresees the exclusion of those who seem to have an assured place. Israel's claim to the kingdom will leave outside any who have not repented, unless they follow the path of faith in Jesus that the centurion has exemplified. This declaration must have shocked Jesus's listeners, but it is consistent with the Old Testament prophets, who consistently called Israel back to God. Those who do not turn to him in faith as the messianic deliverer will receive just punishment, whether Jew or gentile. The gentile mission has not yet been declared, but Jesus's reply to the centurion indicates that the door to the kingdom is open to whoever believes.

Healing Peter's mother-in-law: gender boundaries (8:14–15). Jesus has crossed purity and ethnic boundaries, and in this third healing miracle he breaches a gender boundary to heal a woman, another person often marginalized in some circles of Judaism. Matthew's expression "lying in bed with a fever" indicates that Peter's mother-in-law is in the throes of a severe illness, perhaps malaria, because fever was considered a disease, not a symptom.

Jesus heals the woman with a touch. "And she got up and began to wait on [*diakoneō*] him." Matthew's use of *diakoneō* has significance beyond simple meal preparation. The woman's actions indicate instantaneous gratitude for being healed, a strikingly significant motivation for all discipleship to Jesus.

Exorcising and healing many (8:16–17). Matthew once again emphasizes that Jesus's life and ministry is the fulfillment of the Old Testament, specifying that his healing ministry fulfills the prophecy of Isaiah 53:4: "Surely he took up our pain and bore our suffering." The Servant bears the sicknesses of others through his own suffering and death. Matthew draws on this prophecy to link Jesus's healing ministry with the substitutionary theme. Jesus does not himself become ill but takes and removes illness by his healing power. All sickness and death is ultimately rooted in the entrance of sin to human existence, so Jesus's entire ministry in his inauguration of the kingdom of heaven begins to reverse the cycle of suffering and death.

Expected Discipleship Disappointed (8:18–22). *A would-be disciple's professional expectations (8:18–20).* The teacher of the law has in mind the kind of master-disciple relationship in which a potential disciple examines various masters and then enlists himself with the most popular or the best-equipped one. Jesus's noticeably stern reply checks this enthusiastic recruit, because Jesus's form of discipleship is a different sort from what the scribe has experienced in his prior training. The expression "no place to lay his head" does not indicate a homeless philosopher but rather that his ministry will not result in an institutional establishment with comfortable benefits, and this will also be the lot of those who follow him.

The expression "Son of Man" did not have popular associations attached to it, such as were attached to titles like "Messiah," "Son of David," or even "Son of God." With a general threefold progression, Jesus uses the expression to clarify who he is and what his ministry is. First, the Son of Man is the humble Servant who has come to forgive the sins of common sinners in his earthly ministry (8:20; 9:6; 11:19; 12:8, 32, 40). Second, the Son of Man is the suffering Servant, whose atoning death and resurrection will redeem his people (16:13, 27–28; 17:9, 12, 22; 20:18, 28; 26:2, 24, 45). Finally, the Son of Man is the glorious king and judge who will return to bring the kingdom of heaven to earth (10:23; 13:37, 41; 19:28; 24:27, 30, 37, 39, 44; 25:31; 26:64).

A would-be disciple's cultural expectations (8:21–22). Now "another disciple" comes forward. Jesus tests this disciple's commitment. The disciple asks, "Lord, first let me go and bury my father." Jesus's response is surprising, if not shocking: "Follow me, and let the dead bury their own dead." Jesus is elevating his call to "follow me" above all other allegiances. Anything that gets in the way of unqualified commitment to him must be set aside.

Overpowering Satan's Strongholds (8:23–9:8). *Calming a storm: authority over nature (8:23–27).* Traversing the Sea of Galilee by night was a common experience for fishermen, who used trammel nets throughout the night. This must have been a powerful storm for these disciples to be afraid. They cry out, but their appeal to him isn't quite enough, because Jesus chides them. The disciples have faith, but it is not functioning properly. Jesus calls them to understand more clearly who he is and then act on it. True faith will enable them to trust in God's care even when the circumstances do not look promising.

Jesus is able to command even the forces of nature in the same way that in the Old Testament God rebuked the sea, a demonstration of his sovereign control over all of nature. The reaction of the disciples says much about whom they are beginning to understand Jesus to be. The term for "amazed" is *thaumazō* and does not indicate a clear understanding of Jesus's identity (v. 27). Perhaps Matthew signals this deficiency by calling them here simply "the men" instead of the usual "his disciples."

Exorcising the demoniacs: authority over the spirit world (8:28–34). Jesus is now in the predominantly gentile region of the Decapolis, which explains why pigs are being raised, an animal unclean to Jews. As Jesus arrives in the region of the Gadarenes, "two demon-possessed men coming from the tombs met him" (v. 28). Mark and Luke single out the spokesman and describe him in more detail, citing his name as "Legion"—a figurative expression for the number of demons possessing the men. A Roman army legion had six thousand men.

The demons immediately recognize Jesus's true identity as the "Son of God" (v. 29a). From the demons, the use of the title trumpets their recognition that another stronghold of Satan, the sphere of the spirit world, is being invaded and overpowered. These demons apparently know quite well an appointed "time" when the forces of Satan will be judged (v. 29b). In Jesus's ministry that "time" has already begun with his ministry of exorcism.

The request of the demons to enter the pigs has a sinister purpose. Demons are elsewhere known to cause injury and pain to God's creatures, and they do whatever they can to stimulate opposition to Jesus and his invasion of Satan's stronghold. The destruction of the pigs leads the gentiles of the region to ask Jesus to leave. This response is a sad commentary on the perversion of their values, for one would think they would rejoice at a victory over Satan's demons. The darkness of the scene implies that the legion of demons go from the drowned swine looking for others to inhabit, an ominous thought for these people who have rejected Jesus. Jesus does not destroy the demons but rather allows evil to run its course in this world until that final day when all will be rectified.

Healing the paralytic: authority over sin (9:1–8). The connection between sin and sickness was suggested earlier, but now Jesus states explicitly that they are related. The entrance of sin to the world brought corruption and death, and the only way of reversing this worldwide phenomenon is to have the sin problem corrected. While individual sin is usually not the direct cause of a person's sickness, at the heart of humanity's problem is sin. Once sin is forgiven and redemption has occurred, all sickness and death will ultimately be abolished.

The teachers of the law rightly understand that Jesus is making a profound equation of himself with God as he offers forgiveness of sin, but they have evil thoughts against him.

They assume Jesus is wrong and label him with the charge of blasphemy. Later the Sanhedrin (which includes teachers of the law) likewise charge Jesus with blasphemy and condemn him to death because he tells the truth of who he actually is, thus presenting a threat to the establishment.

Jesus's rhetorical question assumes, of course, that it is easier to say your sins are forgiven, because there is no way of confirming whether or not it has happened. It is obviously much more difficult to declare a person healed, because it can be immediately confirmed by the person's ability to walk. Then Jesus, using the title "Son of Man" (v. 6), reveals another aspect of his identity by declaring that he has authority to forgive sins. As the teachers of the law have already ascertained, this is tantamount to an explicit claim to be divine. The evidence of Jesus's authority is demonstrated as the man gets up and goes home.

Application. *Facing fears.* One thing every wise person learns early on when adapting to the ocean is that it deserves a healthy respect and an appropriate fear of its awesomeness. The Sea of Galilee is a microcosm of the ocean, where the disciples of Jesus also face the full force of nature's wrath. For these veteran fishermen to express their fear and plea for help to a *carpenter* indicates that they know he can do what they cannot do for themselves. But what do they think he will do? After all, when he calms the storm they ask, "What kind of man is this?" (8:27). They have faith, because they place as much confidence in Jesus as they think he can accomplish. But it is "little faith" (8:26), because it is deficient to the task at hand. A more complete knowledge of who he really is and what he is able to accomplish would allow them to trust him fully and without fear.

Facing sin's fears. Having the right perspective on our eternal destiny enables us to have a different perspective on daily challenges. With our sins forgiven, we know that our own mortality will eventually lead to a secure eternity. When we experience suffering in this life, we can rest secure in the knowledge that the Savior who suffered death on the cross for the forgiveness of our sins not only awaits us in our eternal resting place but also travels with us as we endure the travails of this life. The authority of Jesus over all of life's challenges enables us, with an eternal perspective, to trust him fully wherever he may call us to follow him.

MATTHEW 9:9–38

Original Meaning

Unexpected Discipleship Revealed (9:9–17). *Matthew called (9:9).* The form of discipleship that Jesus institutes is unexpected and shocking, because he breaks down barriers between social classes, overturns religious conceptions of well-being, and abolishes slavish adherence to religious cultural traditions. It begins with the calling of a local tax collector, Matthew.

Matthew's tax booth probably stood at some place where the Via Maris passed close by the lakeshore on the outskirts of Capernaum. The expected tax revenue was a heavy toll to extract from the people of Galilee, who already had a hard life. So Matthew is likely not well respected in the region. In fact, the population probably considers him a traitor, selling out his own people to Roman occupation and rule.

Then Jesus shows up. Likely, this is the culmination of a prior relationship, similar to the call of the two sets of brothers—Peter and Andrew, and James and John. The wording of Matthew's call is somewhat different from that used of the four, but it carries the same connotation, and the wording used to describe his response is identical.

For Jesus, Matthew is a notorious convert. For Matthew, discipleship has an immediate cost, for collecting taxes not only filled the coffers of the governor but also meant a lucrative income for the tax collector. A fisherman could always go back to fishing, but it is less likely that a tax collector could return to the booth. But our author doesn't expand on what that sacrifice entails, perhaps a subtle indication of the identity of the humble Matthew as author of this first Gospel.

As a tax collector he would have been trained in secular scribal techniques, and as a Galilean Jewish Christian he would have been able to interpret the life of Jesus from the perspective of Old Testament expectations. Eusebius said that Matthew first preached to "Hebrews" and then to "others," including places such as Persia, Parthia, and Syria. The traditions are mixed regarding Matthew's death, with some saying that he died a martyr's death and others that he died a natural death.

Tax collectors and sinners (9:10–13). Matthew immediately follows Jesus and arranges a banquet for him and his other disciples at his own home (cf. Luke 5:29–30). Since tax collectors were generally better off financially and yet despised by the local populace because of their extortion practices, Matthew's calling and response are completely out of the ordinary and require nothing short of a miraculous turnaround in his life. To the banquet are invited "many tax collectors and 'sinners,'" most likely Matthew's closest companions up to this point.

The term "sinner" (*hamartōlos*) is often used by the Pharisees to point to an identifiable segment of the people opposed to God's will as reflected in their understanding of obedience to the law and their interpretations. To the Pharisees, a sinner is a person who has violated the law according to their interpretations. But to Jesus, a sinner is any person who remains opposed to God's will. The Pharisees consider themselves to be righteously healthy before God because they define righteousness by their observance of the law—their "sacrifice." But they are blind to their real sinfulness before God.

Jesus reaches out to blatant sinners and social outcasts, and he even takes one of them and calls him to be an apostle, one of the foundational leaders of the church to come. The Pharisees are so engrossed with their religious self-righteousness that they cannot see their own hardhearted sinfulness. Jesus's merciful outreach demonstrates for us our own calling: to seek out those who are sinfully sick and invite them to experience healing by coming into fellowship with and discipleship to Jesus.

Discipleship and religious traditions (9:14–17). Jesus's banquet with tax collectors and sinners is offensive to the Pharisees, but it is also offensive to the disciples of Jesus's forerunner, John the Baptist. These people gathered around John as the prophet who would usher in the messianic age.

Jesus's response is an important guideline for a proper perspective on spiritual growth and traditional practices. Spiritual growth is not automatically assured through ritual observance of certain spiritual disciplines. Traditions are what humans have designed to apply biblical principles to everyday life, but they are not commands from God. They can be helpful if practiced appropriately, but they can be stifling if they become more important than scriptural revelation itself. First, if a person puts an unshrunk new patch on an old, washed, shrunk garment, the new patch will shrink when washed and will tear away from the old cloth, leaving a larger hole. Jesus has not come just to patch up the old religious traditions; rather, he offers a new garment.

Second, wineskins were made from tanned and sometimes skinned animal hides. Over time they stretched to their limit and eventually became brittle. New wine that is still fermenting expands and will cause old skins to burst if new wine is poured into them. The new wine and old skins will both be lost. New wine requires new wineskins. In other words, Jesus has not come to fill the old Jewish system of traditions with new life.

Unexpected Miracles Demonstrate Extraordinary Compassion (9:18–34). *The dead have life (9:18–26).* One of the leaders of the Jewish community comes forward with a pressing need. Matthew's reference to him as a "synagogue leader" (*archōn*) denotes either a community leader or the head of a synagogue board. Perhaps in a smaller community this man functions as both a community and a synagogue leader. By kneeling before Jesus, he indicates the extreme honor he gives to him, because kneeling is the appropriate position one takes before a king or superior. The ruler has the same confident trust in Jesus's ability to heal as did the leper, the centurion, and the paralytic and his friends, but his trust is profound enough to believe that Jesus can raise his daughter from the dead.

Jesus's emergency trip to the man's home is interrupted briefly by another dire need. This condition is all the more difficult because this woman would be considered ritually unclean and excluded from normal social and religious relations, since others making contact with her would also become unclean. She has suffered with her condition for twelve years and has sought help from all known medical care. Nothing has brought healing, so she approaches Jesus and touches "the edge [*kraspedon*] of his cloak" (v. 20). The term *kraspedon* is rendered "tassel" in 23:5, which may be the meaning here as well. On the four corners of a garment worn by men were "tassels" attached with a blue cord, conforming to Numbers 15:37–42 and Deuteronomy 22:12. These tassels reminded the wearer to obey God's commands and to be holy to God.

Jesus's expression, "Take heart, daughter," again underscores his compassion, while his declaration "your faith has healed you" points to the source of healing (v. 22). Faith itself does not heal; God does. The woman has faith in Jesus's ability to heal her, which has brought her into this precarious public arena to seek out his healing. Her faith brings her to the place where God can heal her. By making her healing public with his announcement, Jesus removes the public stigma of her physical condition and thus facilitates her reentry into normal social and religious life.

Matthew may indicate that an even more profound event has transpired in this woman's life because both Jesus's statement ("has healed)" and Matthew's narrative ("was healed") use the verb *sōzō*, which often means "to save" (v. 22). It may well be that her act of faith in coming to Jesus for healing is also the moment in which she exercises faith in Jesus as the one who can save her from her sins.

Jesus then continues on to the man's home, where he encounters a typical Jewish mourning scene (v. 23). In the family of a prominent person like the ruler, many professional mourners would have joined the family and friends in expressing their grief. Jesus, however, indicates that the death of the little girl is merely "sleep," at which the mourners laugh (v. 24). So he clears the house of the skeptics. With the same compassionate touch that healed Peter's mother-in-law, Jesus takes the girl by the hand and brings her out of her sleep of death. This scene confirms for all believers that death is merely a state of sleep of one's body while awaiting the final resurrection.

The blind receive sight (9:27–31). Blindness was one of the grimmest maladies in the ancient world and was considered to be only a little less serious than being dead. The messianic age promised to bring healing to the blind (Isa 29:18; 35:5; 42:7), which Jesus told John the Baptist was one of the signs that he indeed was the expected Coming One. Jesus's healing of the blind is one of his most frequent miracles. These men have connected Jesus with the prophecies concerning the Son of David who would heal blindness, and they ask for that gift of messianic mercy.

The demand for secrecy is a regular aspect of Jesus's ministry and may be a reason why he waits to heal them until they are indoors. He carefully avoids stirring up in the crowds a misunderstanding of his messianic identity. Although miracles will attest the authenticity of his gospel message about the arrival of the kingdom of heaven, Jesus does not want crowds to clamor for the miracles alone or to think of him simply as a messianic wonder-worker; he is the Savior, who has come to bring salvation from sin.

The mute have a voice (9:32–34). The final miracle in this collection of miracle stories involves both healing and exorcism. "While they were going out, a man who was demon-possessed and could not talk was brought to Jesus." Demon possession takes a variety of external forms. In the case of the two demoniacs in the area of the Gadarenes, the manifestation produced violent behavior that threatened people (8:28). Here the phenomenon in some way prohibits the man from speaking (cf. 12:22). The exorcism of the demon and the concurrent healing of muteness is a powerful demonstration that the kingdom of heaven has finally arrived.

Without eyes of faith, the Pharisees cannot see beyond their parochial experience that God is doing something unique in Israel in the word and work of Jesus. So they gather their opposition to Jesus, both protecting their religious domain and thinking they are protecting the people from Jesus. This is an ominous tone, which tragically sets a trajectory for the cross that will inevitably come.

The Messiah at Work Enlists Workers (9:35–38). The crowds continue to be the object of Jesus's ministry, and the motivating force is his compassion. The verb "have compassion" is *splanchnizomai* ("to be moved in the inward parts"), which usually indicates deep feelings in the heart and affections. Elsewhere this word describes Jesus's motivation to heal and feed the crowd and heal the blind (e.g., 14:14; 15:32).

The metaphor of sheep and shepherd was well-known in Israel's history. The job of the shepherd is to ensure that the sheep are led peacefully beside still waters and that they lack for nothing, but these leaders are harassing the helpless crowds. They are suffering under the oppression of the occupying Roman forces, plus they have all of the daily concerns, heartbreaks, and difficulties of life beating down on them.

In the preceding miracle stories, Jesus has healed the diseased and sick, raised the dead, calmed the stormy sea, and exorcised demons. Those needs are hugely important, but woven throughout the scenes is Jesus's recognition of an underlying destitution that is far worse. In a word, the problem is sin. Jesus is the promised suffering servant of Isaiah 53, who will take on himself not only the infirmities of his people but also their sins. The deeper illness of the paralytic and the spiritual sickness of tax collectors and Pharisees alike is their sin. Jesus sees deeply into the need of the crowds and has been bringing healing to both body and soul.

The "harvest" is the crowds within Israel who have such tremendous needs, as the following mission discourse makes clear. Even as Jesus's mission is to bring the gospel of the kingdom to the needy, he wants his disciples to join him, because "the harvest is plentiful but the workers are few" (v. 37). Jesus will send out the Twelve on a special mission within Israel, but as long as there are needy crowds, he calls disciples throughout the ages to become harvest workers. The harvest mission includes the immediate assignment of the Twelve to take the gospel message only to Israel, but also the long-range mission of the disciples throughout the world until the Son of Man returns.

Application. *Evil is real.* We observe scenes of evil on a daily basis. Whether it is going through suffering with loved ones who are experiencing disease and death, watching the tragedy of an unwitting young idealist entrapped by a religious cult, or observing the incredible cruelty of city gangs, evil is real in this world. But into these overwhelming scenes of evil, Jesus's messianic mission comes to offer hope. He healed the sick, exorcised demons, and confronted religious hypocrisy in the first century, and he brings the same salvation to our sin-sick world. Today that includes sinners like you, me, and the raucous neighbor down the block. He has come with mercy and grace to save us from our own helpless state.

Opposition will come. As Jesus came with his plan of deliverance, he almost immediately encountered opposition. We too will face opposition if we are doing God's work in God's way. We will not be popular with the current secular culture and will often encounter opposition if we speak the truth about sin or give a biblical evaluation of current trends in film or culture or social media. We should expect opposition, but the heartbreak will often be the hardest when it comes from those who are close to us and who we dearly love and respect. For example, it may arise when one of your own family members objects to your decision to follow Christ or go into ministry.

Jesus is compassionate. For Jesus, the message of the kingdom's saving power was primarily a ministry of spiritual healing. But this is not license for the church to neglect the role of ministering to the whole person. We should do all we can to alleviate suffering. A proper sense of balance comes from keeping an eternal perspective on our compassion. Our responsibility for being salt and light among the evil of this world will not result in the eradication of evil. Regardless of how much healing of physical, emotional, or psychological problems we provide, each individual will someday have an eternal reckoning. Our compassion for the world is insincere unless we keep this eternal perspective.

MATTHEW 10:1–42

Original Meaning

Commissioning the Twelve for Mission (10:1–4). *Twelve disciples (10:1).* In the gathering of the twelve disciples, we find the hint that Jesus is indeed the messianic king of Israel who has come to unite the people of God in all ages. The same authority that characterized Jesus's ministry in chapters 8–9 is now given to the Twelve. Like Jesus, this authority enables them to drive out evil spirits and to heal every kind of disease and sickness (10:1; cf. 4:23; 9:35). All that the Twelve will accomplish is based on their having received Jesus's authority.

Twelve apostles (10:2–4). "Apostle" has narrow and wide meanings in the New Testament. The narrow sense, as here, is the usual meaning, signifying the special authoritative representatives chosen by Jesus to play a foundational role in the establishment of the church. Paul normally used the term to refer to the Twelve, but he includes himself among them as a special apostle to the gentiles. The wide sense of "apostle" derives from the verb *apostellō*, "to send," and therefore can mean merely "messenger" (John 13:16), refer to Jesus as our "apostle" whom we confess (Heb 3:1), or designate an individual such as Barnabas, Titus, or Epaphroditus within the group of missionaries larger than the Twelve and Paul.

Instructions for the Short-Term Mission to Israel (10:5–15). *The prohibition (10:5–6).* The key to the prohibition is found here. Jesus's attention to Israel underscores God's faithfulness to his covenant promises, the continuity of his purposes, and his plan for Israel. Jesus is dispelling any doubt as to whether he truly is the Messiah who fulfills the promises given to Israel and God's program of salvation history. But there is also a warning here. The eschatological ingathering is beginning. This is Israel's opportunity, and from here on it will be fully responsible for its own decision.

Message and miracles (10:7–8a). The message of the disciples is the same as that of both John the Baptist and Jesus. They also go with the same authority as Jesus. The power of the Twelve is clearly an extension of Jesus's own power and is to be exercised in the same manner.

Equipment for the mission (10:8b–10). The disciples are not to accept payment from those to whom they minister, which would otherwise make it a mercenary venture. The Twelve are not to spend time procuring extra supplies as though they are going to be out in foreign lands for an extended period of time. There are two reasons for this prohibition. First, this is a relatively quick preaching tour through the Galilean countryside. To procure extensive supplies is unnecessary. Second, Jesus insists that "the worker is worth his keep" (v. 10). It is the responsibility of those to whom they minister to support their mission. Although they may not charge for their ministry, the Twelve are to accept the hospitality extended to them from those to whom they minister.

Worthy of the mission (10:11–14). The word "worthy" (*axios*; translated as "deserving" in v. 13) does not point to a person who has a high moral or religious stature but indicates someone who responds positively to the message proclaimed by the disciples. If the household does not receive God's message and messengers, then the missionaries are to shake the dust off of their feet when they leave. For the missionaries it is an acted parable of judgment on those rejecting the message.

Judgment for rejecting the mission (10:15). The preaching of the gospel becomes for Israel a threat as well as a promise. Increased light of God's revelation makes for increased responsibility, and those who have been exposed to Jesus's ministry and the witness of the disciples have greater responsibility for that privilege. The whole scene exudes urgency because the time of Jesus's earthly ministry is short, and both the blessings of the kingdom and the punishment of judgment are awaiting a decision from Israel.

Instructions for the Long-Term Mission to the World (10:16–23). *Sheep among wolves (10:16a).* In the first part of the commissioning, Jesus gave instructions to the disciples about their short-term mission to Israel during his earthly ministry. Now he is giving them instructions about their long-term mission throughout the world after that ministry. Matthew makes no reference to the Twelve either actually going out or returning from their mission. In this way, the commission is sufficiently open-ended to include both instructions for an immediate mission to Israel and the ongoing mission to the nations until the end of the age. The historical setting of Jesus's sending of the Twelve to the people of Israel has provided an occasion for him to lay down instruction for Christian missions to all nations.

Wise serpents, harmless doves (10:16b). Jesus warns his disciples that wariness, yet innocence, will be necessary in the future mission. The serpent was the emblem of wisdom, shrewdness, and intellectual keenness, while the dove represented simple innocence. Without innocence the keenness of the snake is crafty, a devious menace; without keenness the innocence of the dove is naive, helpless gullibility.

Flogging in the Jewish synagogue (10:17). The synagogue was not only the place of assembly for worship but also an assembly of justice, where discipline was exercised. Note that it is not "our" or "your" synagogues. The synagogue belongs to those opposed to Jesus's disciples.

A witness to gentiles (10:18–20). The disciples' future mission will bring them "before governors and kings as witnesses to them and to the Gentiles." At the time of their trials, they will witness to these ruling figures of the truthfulness of the gospel message brought by Jesus. The Spirit is the creative, empowering, guiding force in Jesus's own life. Through this same Spirit his disciples will find their own empowering and guidance to give their witness.

The disciples' opposition and endurance (10:21–23). Moses had warned the people that even if one's own brother or sister or wife or closest friend tries to beguile a person into idolatry, this person was to be stoned (Deut 13:6–11). In the future, some may think that the disciples are leading the people into idolatry with their call to worship Jesus; as a result, the mission-disciples will be delivered over to persecution and death. This will be a tragic misperception of Jesus's identity and message.

Along with family betrayal because of their commitment to Jesus's exclusivity, his disciples will feel the wrath and hatred of "everyone . . . because of me" (v. 22; cf. 24:9). An element of hyperbole may be included, but this statement indicates an unavoidable consequence that comes from attachment to Jesus and his message. Jesus's disciples will have the privilege of carrying his name, but it also brings suffering, because the hatred directed against him will naturally fall upon his followers.

Those who endure until the end of the age, when the Son of Man comes, or to the end of their lives will be saved. His *promise* is that the one who remains committed to his name to the end will not be consumed by the persecution but will experience the full blessing and peace of the kingdom and of salvation. The *reminder* is that the test of a disciple's real commitment to Jesus is whether he or she remains steadfast to the end despite hardship and persecution. Jesus through his Spirit will provide the resources to withstand whatever difficulties may come; in fact, Jesus himself will be with them to the end of the age to see them through (28:19–20).

What does "before the Son of Man comes" mean in this context (v. 23)? Some suggest that Jesus is promising the disciples that they will witness the final coming of the Son of Man while they are on their first Palestinian mission, or at his resurrection, or at Pentecost, or at the destruction of Jerusalem in AD 70. Others contend that this promise is to be associated with the coming of the Son of Man at the end of the age.

The latter seems to fit the larger context here. There will be a continuing mission to Israel alongside the mission to the gentiles until Christ returns. Despite Israel's hard-heartedness, God will remain faithful to his covenant promises to her. This is a powerful apologetic to the Jews both in Jesus's ministry and to those within hearing of Matthew's Gospel. God has not abandoned his covenantal promises. It is also a challenging yet sober call to the mission-disciples to endure to the end with the message of the gospel to all peoples —both Jew and gentile.

Characteristics of Missionary Disciples (10:24–42). *Disciples and the Master in mission (10:24–25).* His disciples have received his authority, so they go out with his message and power. The harsh treatment that he is now beginning to receive from the religious leaders will be their lot as well in the ongoing mission. The Pharisees had accused Jesus of casting out demons by the "prince of demons" (9:34). The accusation that Jesus has formed an alliance with Satan to carry out his work will naturally be lodged against his disciples as well.

Fearless followers (10:26–31). Jesus then gives three reasons why his followers should not be afraid. First, the truth about his ministry will become known. Eventually the subversive opposition to his ministry conducted in the hidden counsel of the religious leaders will be revealed as false. Second, their eternal destiny is secure. If the disciples persevere, they will be rewarded, but if they are disloyal to the truth of the gospel message, they will face ultimate condemnation. Finally, the "sparrow" is proverbially the smallest of creatures, and the "penny" (*assarion*) is one of the smallest and least in value of the Roman coins (v. 29). If the heavenly Father gives constant sovereign supervision to such insignificant creatures, surely he will do so for mission-disciples whose every detail, even to the number of hairs on their head, he knows.

Acknowledging Jesus's supremacy in public (10:32–33). The test of a disciple's commitment to Jesus and his mission will come when opposition arises. The easiest way to avoid persecution is to deny that one is Jesus's disciple. But the true disciple will publicly acknowledge or confess Jesus as her master and God, the Son of the heavenly Father. But the disciple who attempts to avoid persecution by public denial of Jesus reveals that he is not a true disciple and has not publicly confessed Jesus as his master and God. Such denial results in eternal rejection by the Father.

Allegiance to Jesus's supremacy at home (10:34–39). The "sword" in 10:34 is a metaphorical sword, as proven by Jesus's rebuke of those who took up an actual sword to defend him in the garden of Gethsemane (26:51–52). The sword can be a metaphor of God's judgment or, as here, a metaphor of separation between those who believe and those who don't, even if it is in one's family. Jesus's disciples can expect division to occur in their family as members try to prevent them from furthering Jesus's mission.

Furthermore, discipleship to Jesus means that he has unqualified supremacy over the disciples' lives. Jesus indicates his form of discipleship calls for giving him ultimate supremacy beyond parents or children, something not even the most esteemed rabbi would demand. This is an implicit declaration of his deity, because only God deserves a higher place of honor than one's father and mother. Jesus's statement here is in line with the call to give priority to Jesus as God above all else, even one's dearest loved ones. To take up one's cross is a metaphor that means to take up God's will for one's life, in the same way that the cross was the Father's will for the Son's life. Taking up God's will for one's life will result in gaining true life as Jesus's disciple.

Reward for receiving Jesus's mission-disciples (10:40–42). Mission-disciples go in the authority and with the message of Jesus himself, so to receive them is to receive Jesus. This includes a "prophet," a "righteous person," and a "little one." The "prophets" and the "righteous" refer to Christian prophets and righteous persons. To receive either means to receive Jesus's gospel of the kingdom and live under its authority and so receive life's greatest reward—kingdom salvation and kingdom life.

Application. Television news anchor Tom Brokaw wrote a best-selling, gripping tribute to what he calls *The Greatest Generation*. When we read the story of Jesus's mission of the Twelve, we can also think of them as the greatest generation of the church. They were called out of the hardship of occupation by the Roman Empire, but they went on to fight a battle, not with swords and chariots but with the good news of the arrival of the kingdom of heaven and a message of transformation. They went on to lay the foundation of the church, and according to tradition most of them suffered martyrdom for the name of the Lord Jesus.

Scripture likewise speaks of our own discipleship using the language of warfare, although it is not a war against flesh and blood (e.g., Eph 6:10–20; cf. 1 Tim 1:18). Christians are everyday people who have been called to advance the kingdom of God in an alien and hostile world. We are the church, the body of Jesus Christ, some of whose service results in external and public honor while others carry out their service in the humility of obscurity. But each individual is vitally necessary to the proper functioning of the church in this world.

Mission-driven discipleship. Every disciple is a missionary. Some of us tend to avoid passages like this mission discourse by saying, "Well, how does this relate to me? Those were the twelve apostles. I'm not like them!" But while it does have special significance for the Twelve in their historical ministry, it has immediate relevance for disciples in every era.

Every disciple is a missionary, but not every missionary goes overseas. While all of us may not become full-time missionaries, it is clear that all disciples are called to join in mission in some fashion. And whether we are more directly involved in mission or conduct more of a support role, the rewards are the same. The specifics of how one engages in mission should be tailored to one's giftedness and abilities, but a disciple of Jesus will see that carrying the message of salvation to the world is a vital part of our discipleship.

Support of worldwide mission is the responsibility of all disciples. We are to support missionaries "in a manner worthy of God" (3 John 6). God gives generously to us, his disciples, so we should likewise give generously to mission-disciples involved in full-time mission.

Transformational discipleship. Discipleship refers to the process of how Christians are equipped and transformed for this life and battle, to be light in a dark world to those still held in the clutches of the prince of the power of the air. Those first twelve disciples/apostles are a great deal more like us than we usually imagine. The Twelve are not to be idealized. We can look at each of them and find that they are not much different from us. Try identifying realistically with even one of the Twelve, with their individual strengths yet also with their foibles and failings.

The persecution and suffering of discipleship. Persecution is closer than we think. Believers who stand for the name of Jesus as we enter the third millennium are increasingly facing persecution similar to that experienced in the first centuries of the church's existence.

The increasing secularization of Western culture does not bode well for us. Christians are discouraged from denouncing practices condemned in Scripture, such as obscenity, pornography, and homosexuality. In the name of "freedom of religion" many of the normal practices of faith once enjoyed have been stripped away. The agenda of much public policy seems more like freedom *from* religion, and the consequences for those who decry this secularist public policy will grow increasingly harsh.

Jesus suffered when doing the right and good thing, and persecution marked the fate of the church from its earliest days. Yet it did not dim passion for following Jesus, no matter what the cost. For the Christian, suffering is not something to be avoided at all costs. Suffering, when it comes, can be a means of furthering our union with Christ, who promises to be united with us in our deepest hour of need.

Guarding our hearts in the real world. One of the central cautions of Jesus in this mission discourse is that as we live out our lives with him in the world, our hearts become vulnerable to hurt, temptation, and spiritual attacks. Guarding our hearts in this world is a difficult yet necessary balance as we, mission-disciples, carry the message of the gospel of the kingdom to a world that is dying eternally without its message of grace and salvation. We probably shouldn't fancy ourselves as part of a "greatest generation," but we are to know that we are called to unwavering commitment to bring the gospel of the kingdom to our generation and to those who follow. That is the clarion call of Jesus's mission discourse to every generation of the church.

MATTHEW 11:1–30

Original Meaning

John the Baptist Questions Jesus (11:1–6). *Transition (11:1).* The conclusion to the mission discourse, "After Jesus had finished," serves as a transition to the next section of narrative.

John questions Jesus through his disciples (11:2–3). John sends some of his disciples to Jesus. Along with John they were becoming increasingly alarmed as to the future of the messianic program. John's question seems out of character with his earlier bold and courageous declaration of Jesus as the Coming One. It is natural for John to experience perplexity as he languishes in prison, much as had earlier prophets when their human experience did not fully correspond with God's message through them. John rightly expected the Messiah to be a judging figure, so events are not unfolding as he anticipated. The divine judgment and time of messianic blessing do not seem to have arrived as he projected. Jesus is not carrying out judgment; rather, he seems to be concentrating on healing and helping. John needs to have his understanding of the messianic program reconfirmed.

Jesus responds to John's questions (11:4–6). Jesus reiterates to John's disciples that the way his ministry has unfolded is in line with the prophetic promises. Thus Jesus confirms for John that the blessings of the messianic age have arrived with his ministry. But Jesus likewise mildly rebukes John and his disciples by calling them to see the bigger picture in his ministry. John and his disciples must use eyes of faith to recognize both blessing and judgment. Jesus has brought the blessing of healing and good news to the poor and oppressed, yet those who reject his ministry and message face certain judgment, which even now is pronounced by Jesus.

Jesus's Tribute to John the Baptist (11:7–19). *John is more than a prophet (11:7–10).* Through three rhetorical questions Jesus gives the crowds contrasting options about John, which will force them to acknowledge his true identity and mission.

1. Was John a "reed swayed by the wind?" (v. 7). The metaphor suggests weakness and vacillation with every changing wind of opportunity or challenge. John, by contrast, languishes in prison because of the strength of his resolve to confront every challenge and speak the truth.
2. Was John "a man dressed in fine clothes?" (v. 8). The expected answer is, "Of course not!" John consistently lived an ascetic lifestyle in keeping with his call for repentance. John's question about Jesus did not come from materialistic opportunism.
3. John was like the Old Testament prophets because he was God's spokesperson who called the nation to repentance and declared God's program of salvation. But John was more than any prophet of the Old Testament because he was the one about whom a prophecy had been given—the prophet who would announce the arrival of the Messiah and the inbreaking of the kingdom of heaven.

John's greatness and the greatness of the messianic kingdom (11:11). Jesus continues to defend John by pointing to the greatness of his ministry, yet he gives a surprising twist by pointing to the greatness of those in the kingdom of heaven. John is the greatest of those born during the Old Testament era because of his crucial role in preparing the way for the Messiah and his kingdom. His mission was great because of the greatness of the one he introduced. But those in the kingdom are greater because of their privilege to have actually entered it.

Violence and the kingdom of heaven (11:12). This saying of Jesus has been widely debated, with the difficulty arising primarily because the verb *biazō* (NIV "subjected to violence") and the noun *biastēs* (NIV "violent people") can be taken in either a positive or a negative way.

Since the verb *biazō* and the noun *biastēs* are related, Matthew intends them to reflect a parallel expression by Jesus, meaning that both clauses should be interpreted more naturally with the same force. Thus, in the light of the negative circumstances of John the Baptist and the rising opposition to his own ministry, Jesus points to the ongoing opposition that the kingdom of heaven has encountered since the days of John the Baptist. The saying foreshadows the gathering opposition to Jesus, which will come to a climax in his arrest, trial, and execution by the Jewish high priest, Caiaphas, and the Roman governor, Pontius Pilate.

John and Elijah (11:13–15). Jesus's tribute to John peaks with a powerful testimony to the role John has played. John is the culmination of a long history of prophecy that looked forward to the arrival of the messianic kingdom. That prophetic hope has been realized in John's preparation for Jesus's inauguration of the kingdom of heaven.

Malachi prophesied that Elijah would prepare the way for Messiah (Mal 3:1; 4:5). John fulfilled Malachi's prophecy in that at his conception he was designated as the one who would minister in the "spirit and power of Elijah" (Luke 1:17). For those who receive John's ministry, he is the fulfillment of Malachi's prophecy. This call to recognize John as the fulfillment of Malachi's prophecy is even more dramatic when we recall that Elijah would prepare for the coming of the Lord himself in the great and terrible day of the Lord. Jesus equates his ministry as Messiah with God's own arrival, another awe-inspiring revelation of his divine identity.

The discontented generation (11:16–19). This is not a blanket condemnation of Israel, because Jesus's own disciples are

Jews and large crowds of Jews still follow him around, but it points sadly to the fact that only a small minority of the current generation will enter the narrow gate to the kingdom by accepting John's and Jesus's invitation.

When children invite other children to join them in playing games, childish children insist on having their own way. The current generation is like such children, who continually want to set the agenda of games. Likewise, this generation rejects the invitation to the kingdom of heaven because John and Jesus don't play the game that they want.

Wisdom (*sophia*) was often personified in Judaism as a woman giving her children practical guidance in everyday affairs. The personification exemplified the way in which those who are guided by God's practical approach to life make right decisions. The saying here appears to be proverbial. God's wisdom will be "proved right" (or "vindicated") by her actions in the ministries and lifestyles of John and Jesus (v. 19). If this generation had taken John the Baptist and Jesus for who they said they were, the knowledge of them as forerunner and Messiah would have been proved right by their actions, as seemingly opposite as were their lifestyles.

Judgment and Invitation (11:20–30). *The privileged unrepentant cities (11:20–24).* Jesus turns up the heat by denouncing the cities who have rejected his gospel message. The privilege of witnessing Jesus's miraculous ministry should have moved them to repent and accept the invitation to the kingdom of heaven. Repentance was the appropriate response to Jesus's miracles, which validated his message of the kingdom.

A prayer of praise to the Father (11:25–26). The things that are both hidden and revealed are presumably the activities of the good news of the presence of the kingdom of heaven that required humble eyes of faith to see God's hand in them. The "wise and learned" are not academic specialists but those who stubbornly refuse to repent and learn from Jesus the true way to God. The contrast is between those whose pride and self-sufficiency have caused them to reject Jesus's message and those whose humility and recognition of their own neediness allow them to be open to God's unqualified care through Jesus's announcement of the arrival of the kingdom. It is the Father's will that all receive his care in the same way, as humble and repentant children.

The unique relationship between Father and Son (11:27). Jesus follows his brief prayer with an astonishing statement of his relationship to the Father. Jesus has a profound divine self-consciousness. He was validated at the baptism as the Son (3:17), tested as the Son of God (4:3), worshiped as the Son of God (14:33), confessed as the Son of the living God (16:16), validated at the transfiguration as the Son (17:5), alludes to himself as the Son in the parables of the landowner and wedding banquet (21:33–46; 22:1–14), refers to himself as the Son of the Father (24:36), emphasized as Son of God strongly in the trial and crucifixion (cf. 26:39, 63; 27:43, 54), and associated with the Father and Holy Spirit in the baptism of new disciples (28:18–20). The Son theme is one of the high points of Matthew's Christology as well as Synoptic Christology generally.

In both his incarnate and eternal state as Son, Jesus and the Father enjoy a direct, intuitive, and immediate knowledge that is grounded in their divine relationship as Father and Son. Jesus's sonship involves more than a unique filial consciousness; it involves an exclusive essential relationship between Father and Son. In his incarnate state, Jesus received from the Father the exclusive authority to reveal the Father, which does not imply the Son's inferiority to the Father but the process of revelation. Humans can know the Father only through the sovereign will of the Son's revelation. God's program of salvation history derives from the unique, divine relationship of Father and Son.

An invitation to the weary and burdened (11:28–30). With an invitation found only in Matthew's Gospel, Jesus, who alone reveals the Father and the divine plan of redemption, calls out, "Come to me," a tender call to intimacy with him for all those who are weary and burdened. "Weary" evokes the image of persons exhausted from their work or journey, while "burdened" indicates persons weighted down with heavy loads.

Jesus's invitation is in stark contrast to the religious burden of Pharisaism or the militaristic burden of foreign oppressors. His yoke—a metaphor for discipleship to him—promises rest from the weariness and burden of religious regulation and human oppression because it is none other than commitment to him. His disciples learn directly from him. As the messianic inaugurator of the kingdom of heaven, Jesus offers rest in himself for their souls through his authoritative understanding of God's truth.

The yoke of discipleship brings rest because Jesus has come gently, preaching and teaching the good news of the arrival of the kingdom of heaven, and in humble human form he has brought healing to sin-sick humanity. This is the true eschatological rest for which Israel has long hoped. Jesus's teaching is the true fulfillment of the law, and those who come to him will enter into a discipleship that produces rest for the soul (cf. Jer 6:16).

While discipleship to Jesus brings relief from the burden of Pharisaic regulations, it is not lawlessness. In fact, in Jesus's interpretation of the law the challenge of following him may be seen as even more demanding than the Pharisees, because he calls his disciples to fulfill the law from the obedience of the heart, not simply through external obedience. Yet his Spirit provides the strength to carry the load.

However, in the quest to learn from Jesus how to live God's truth, it is critical to remember that Jesus's disciples can also turn his yoke into an unbearable burden unless we consciously recognize that discipleship to Jesus is not essentially a religious obligation. Rather, ours is an intimate relationship with the one who calls, "Come to me" and "learn from me." As complicated as life may become, discipleship is at heart simply walking with Jesus in the real world and having him teach us moment by moment how to live life his way.

Application. *Rest.* Of the many different types of people who gather together in Christian worship each week, one group deserves special attention: those who come to the Lord with a questioning heart in need of rest. It may be a person who suffers at work under an uncaring boss; it may be a person in a marriage with an uncaring or cheating spouse; it may be a faithful parent with a spiritually wayward child; or it may be a young person who has lost a friend in a tragic death. Oftentimes these kinds of people will come into a worship setting to question—sometimes respectfully, other times not—the Lord's control of life. They are seeking some kind of resolution in their heart to a big question in their lives for which they have no answer and for which they may even doubt that God has an answer. What they need is rest, the rest that only Jesus can ultimately give. It is the wise disciple who recognizes just how many people come to church with this need for the Lord's rest and in pastorally wise, loving, and sensitive ways seek to lead people to Jesus and the spiritual rest only he can provide for the anxious and weary soul.

MATTHEW 12:1–50

Original Meaning

Confrontations with the Pharisees over the Sabbath (12:1–14). *The Pharisees' accusations against Jesus's disciples (12:1–2).* While it is doubtful that Pharisees regularly patrolled the fields watching for people violating the Sabbath, with the mounting opposition to Jesus's ministry they are now likely looking for opportunities to accuse him and his disciples of crimes against the law. The disciples could have been guilty of several rabbinic rules as they plucked grain heads, separated the chaff from the grain, and ground the grain in their hands to prepare it to eat. But not everyone shared the Pharisees' view of the Sabbath, which heightens our awareness of the tension that is growing between Jesus and the Pharisees.

Jesus defends his disciples (12:3–7). Jesus's reply puts the Pharisees on the defensive because he uses the Old Testament itself, on which they prided themselves as experts, to combat their accusations against his disciples. Instead of rebuking his disciples, Jesus cites two Old Testament examples that render ineffective the Pharisees' charge. He then goes on to give a third response that clarifies his use of these examples. He is not entering into their rabbinic debate but, as in the Sermon on the Mount, will show how his authoritative arrival and teaching has fulfilled the law.

First, Ahimelech understood that as God's anointed, David was serving God and was thus entitled to the bread at his time of need. Ahimelech served God's purposes by feeding the fleeing David. The intent of the law is to serve God's people, not for God's people to serve the law. The next two responses clarify this point.

Second, priests regularly violated the Sabbath when they performed their duties on the Sabbath, yet they were considered guiltless. Jesus emphasizes that if the guardians of the temple were allowed to violate the Sabbath for the greater good of conducting the priestly rituals, how much more should Jesus and his disciples be considered guiltless when doing the work of God given to them. After all, he is someone greater than the temple.

Jesus's third response takes the argument one step further by quoting a second time from Hosea 6:6 (v. 7; cf. 9:13). If they had not just read the prophet but had understood him, they would have known that in their adjudication of the Sabbath they should have extended mercy, not demanded more sacrifice. Jesus attacks the very core of the Pharisaic tendency to add burdens to the daily lives of people by their accumulation of oral traditions.

Lord of the Sabbath (12:8). Jesus concludes the argument with another remarkable clarification of his identity and authority. Jesus has revealed himself to Israel as their long-anticipated Messiah. The messianic Son of Man has the authority to give the true interpretation of the law, including the role of the Sabbath (cf. 5:17–48).

In other words, Jesus does not challenge the Sabbath law itself but the prevailing interpretation of it. Jesus answers the charge against his disciples by showing from the Old Testament itself that the Sabbath is not fulfilled by the scrupulous observance of the Pharisees but in living out the intent and motive of the Sabbath, which was designed to bring rest. As the Lord of the Sabbath, Jesus gives the true interpretation of its intent, bringing rest under his easy yoke and light burden of discipleship (cf. 11:28–30).

Healing on the Sabbath (12:9–13). The identity of Jesus's accusers is not stated, but presumably they are the Pharisees of the preceding controversy, who plot Jesus's demise at the end of this confrontation. The man with the withered hand has likely had the condition for some time, and his life certainly is not in danger, so he could wait until the next day. According to the Pharisees, he is not a proper candidate for healing.

Jesus counters with a question of his own. "If any of you has a sheep and it falls into a pit on the Sabbath, will you not take hold of it and lift it out?" (v. 11). The question is not simply rhetorical. There was active debate in Judaism at the time on just such a point. Jesus contends that the higher principle is not simply abstaining from activity on the Sabbath but doing good on the Sabbath.

The miracle confirms Jesus's authority to make these pronouncements about the Sabbath, once more validating his claim to be the messianic Son of Man. Without uttering a command of healing or even touching the withered limb, Jesus heals the man's hand completely.

Plot of the Pharisees (12:14). The seriousness of these issues is now revealed, for in reaction to Jesus's actions and pronouncement about the Sabbath, the Pharisees understand clearly that Jesus's claim to messianic authority to interpret the law is, in their eyes, a heretical claim worthy of death. They are now convinced that Jesus is not God's agent.

God's Spirit-Anointed Servant (12:15–21). Once again in response to a threat, Jesus withdraws. He is not trying to escape opposition but to keep it at bay until the time for his predicted betrayal, arrest, and death. He is still in full public view, because "a large crowd followed him, and he healed all who were ill" (v. 15).

Matthew uses his typical fulfillment formula to introduce the longest Old Testament quotation in his Gospel, which identifies Jesus with the messianic servant of Isaiah 42:1–4. In this fulfillment quotation, Matthew gives one of the clearest declarations of Jesus's intent as Messiah: He is the gentle, Spirit-endowed, suffering servant, who advances a mission of justice to the nations. The "justice" Jesus brings to the "nations" combines the sense of grace and judgment that has characterized the theme of inward righteousness that accompanies the arrival of the kingdom of heaven (v. 18). The servant will pronounce the arrival of the kingdom that is an invitation to kingdom life, but it is also a sentence of judgment on the rulers of this world.

The suffering servant's advance of justice will not break those who are abused, nor will it smother those who are nearly out of resources; rather, he will provide the ultimate victory for those who respond to the invitation to enter the kingdom. The strong and the mighty are often victorious in this life because they advance their own causes by abusing others and withholding care from the needy. But even as Isaiah knew that evil would not have the ultimate victory, so Matthew points to Jesus and declares that victory is at hand for those who seek God's justice.

Confrontations with the Pharisees over the Source of Jesus's Miraculous Power (12:22–37). *The Pharisees accuse Jesus of demonism (12:22–24).* The people are astonished at Jesus's healing of this blind and mute demoniac, so they exclaim, "Could this be the Son of David?" (v. 23). It is perhaps stretching the crowds' understanding to comprehend that this gentle healing person is indeed the Son of David who will shepherd his people and usher in the kingdom of God.

In contrast to the reaction of the crowds, the Pharisees accuse Jesus of drawing on the power of "Beelzebul" (or better, "Beelzeboul," the ruler of the demons) to cast out the demon from the blind and mute man (v. 24). This is a most serious charge, because practicing magic under the influence of Satan was a capital offense, punishable by stoning.

Jesus's defense (12:25–29). Jesus first defends his ministry of exorcism with two short parables, then he follows it with two scathing denunciations of the Pharisees. First, Jesus shows the illogical nature of their thinking. If Satan wants to maintain rulership of this world, he would not work against himself by exorcising a demon that had control of a person. Second, Jesus alludes to his role of inaugurating the kingdom as entering a well-guarded house (the household of Satan and his demonic cronies) and plundering the possessions of the owner. Before Jesus can release through exorcism those held captive, he must "tie up" or bind Satan (v. 29). Jesus declares here that Satan's powers are now limited because of the arrival of the kingdom of God.

Jesus's offense (12:30–37). Jesus now goes on the offensive and declares two scathing denunciations.

1. There is no middle ground with Jesus. He is either Messiah, or he isn't. The Old Testament regarded deliberate, defiant sin against God and his ordinances to be blasphemy, the guilt of which remained. Rejection of Jesus's ministry as validated by the Spirit is defiant, deliberate sin. As long as the Pharisees continue to reject that evidence, they cannot enter the kingdom and receive forgiveness.

   This also goes along with the role of the Spirit in convicting individuals of sin, righteousness, and judgment (John 16:8). As long as one rejects the Spirit, one can never find forgiveness for sins. Apparently Jesus knows the state of these Pharisees' hearts and knows that they have now reached a place where they have hardened their hearts nearly beyond the point of no return.

   This passage has caused many unknowing believers anguish, thinking that somehow they have committed this sin through a verbal assault on the Holy Spirit, resulting in eternal condemnation. This sin can be committed today only by unbelievers who reject the ministry of the Holy Spirit leading them to salvation. Ultimately, once a person has either hardened his or her heart to an irretrievable point in this life or has died without repenting, the chance for forgiveness has passed.

2. Jesus's second offensive strike forces the Pharisees to recognize that their charges against him come from their own evil nature. The Pharisees attempt to hide their own wicked blasphemy by calling Jesus a blasphemer. But their slander is actually blasphemy of the Spirit of God. Since they refuse to repent, they will be held accountable for every word at the judgment.

Confrontations with the Pharisees over Their Demand for a Sign (12:38–42). The problem with a sign is that it can be interpreted in different ways. The Pharisees here ask Jesus to perform some kind of on-demand spectacular display of power that will irrefutably convince them that his power is from God, not from Satan. However, although their request appears innocent enough, they are not asking in good faith. They are asking for a sign that they can use against him. Jesus recognizes their evil motive, so he refuses to fall into their trap of giving them further ammunition for their charges against him. Because of their evil intention, the only other sign that Jesus will give to them is a sign of God's coming judgment on them, as Jonah was to the people of Nineveh.

The culpability of the Pharisees and teachers of the law for not repenting at the arrival of Jesus extends to the entire generation who followed their misguided lead. They have had the greatest privilege, but the ones who will point a figure of condemnation are those who had far less privilege—the pagans of Nineveh—who repented when God's messenger, Jonah, arrived.

A second figure of condemnation against the Pharisees is another pagan—"the Queen of the South" (v. 42), that is, the queen of Sheba (1 Kgs 10:1–29). She too allowed God's revelation to penetrate to her pagan heart.

Jesus's arrival with the kingdom of God has exceeded all that Israel has witnessed in her history. But tragically, and ironically, the gentiles see what the Pharisees and that fateful generation do not.

This Wicked Generation and the Return of the Evil Spirit (12:43–45). After the scene of judgment for rejecting Jesus Messiah's inauguration of the kingdom of heaven, Jesus gives a parabolic revelation of the warfare within that adulterous generation. Jesus begins with a general statement of how demons operate. The verb "comes out" implies that the demon has come out through an exorcism (v. 43a). The "rest" implies that although a demon can exist in a disembodied state, its evil purpose is best performed in an embodied state (v. 43b). The demon seeks re-ownership of a person's entire immaterial and material self. Demons tend to be persistent in wanting to maintain ownership of a person. The number seven is linked in Scripture with completion, fulfillment, and perfection. Here it may point to the completeness of demon-possession once the demon returns.

The evil generation that Jesus addresses has experienced his powerful ministry, especially through his exorcisms. That has been a good thing for Israel. But Israel has not repented and turned to the kingdom of heaven. Therefore, that generation is more susceptible to the power of the evil one than ever before.

Without kingdom transformation, a "cleaned-up" person is more vulnerable to the renewed and persistent attack of the demonic world to take back ownership. He can easily be repossessed by the demon and seven more wicked cronies and will be in far worse shape, completely dominated by the entourage of wickedness. But if this person does receive Jesus and the kingdom, Satan will flee from the presence of God in this disciple's life.

Jesus's Disciples Are His True Family (12:46–50). Matthew 12:9–45 did not include any reference to the disciples. This is a clue that the topics discussed there were about entrance into the kingdom, not instruction about life within it. Now, however, as Jesus continues to address the crowd (v. 46), his mother and brothers stood outside, wanting to speak to him. Jesus has focused on proclaiming the gospel of the kingdom to all with an open-ended invitation. That invitation continues, but he now begins to require accountability of those to whom the invitation has been extended.

Mary and Jesus's brothers arrive at the place where Jesus is speaking in order to escort him back to Nazareth. But Jesus will not be deterred from his messianic mission, even if it means disruption of biological loyalties. Jesus has already accentuated to his disciples the inevitable separation that will occur between family members because of a commitment to him (10:34–36). He has not come to abolish the family, but Jesus is here demonstrating the preeminence of commitment to him and the kingdom of heaven, which places people in a new spiritual family.

Jesus specifies the central feature that creates and characterizes this spiritual family. A person's genealogical relationship to Israel does not guarantee a place in the kingdom of heaven, nor does a person's family relationship. Each individual must respond to the will of the Father and obey Jesus's call to the kingdom and become his disciple. Jesus is the ultimate example of the will of the Father revealed and obeyed, so to follow his example in discipleship and become like him will enable his disciples to do the Father's will on a daily basis.

Application. *Obedience to the Father's will.* There are several points of application for us as modern readers of this account, but obedience to the Father's will stands at the center. Rightly applying the Old Testament by imitating Jesus's example, encountering persecution while engaging in spiritual warfare, and developing community discipleship are all themes of this chapter. And all hinge on rightly obeying the Father's will as it is now revealed by Jesus Messiah.

Evaluating the opposition that will come. The opposition that we encounter will be of a variety of different types. In the increasingly secular society of the twenty-first century, we will encounter opposition to our faith from popular culture. As with Jesus, we may encounter opposition from our own family if they do not understand the way in which we want to serve God. On a more drastic level, Christians can expect opposition when we proclaim the message of the gospel.

Emulating Jesus's response to opposition: tips for wounded disciples. Within Jesus's prediction of the inevitability of opposition, we also should look for his example in dealing with it. Matthew develops his narrative in such a way that as one looks at the life of Jesus, one not only learns what it is for Jesus to be Messiah but also what it is to be his disciple by emulating the life he lived. Jesus was hurt deeply in all ways possible, as those he came to rescue rejected him, as his own forerunner questioned him, as his family members attempted to deter him, and ultimately how his own people, including the crowds and the religious leaders, sought ways to have him arrested and executed. But Jesus did not allow his own massive hurt to dislodge him from his mission.

Every person who reads these words, every person to whom we minister, has been hurt. Not as deeply as we see in Jesus, but we have all been hurt by seemingly well-intentioned people who, in their own misguided sincerity, have attacked us, called into question our motives, or perhaps even slandered us. How should we respond? How do we maintain our commitment to the Father's will while loving those who oppose us and have hurt us?

We have all encountered opposition. We've all been hurt. The opposition Jesus encountered and the hurt he experienced in his earthly life is beyond comprehension. But for those of us who may be his wounded disciples, his example is necessary to guide us in our response to opposition and to those who have hurt us. His example is the most profound display of love imaginable, of giving himself to bring others to God's intended purpose for their lives.

MATTHEW 13:1–52

Original Meaning

The Setting for the Parabolic Discourse (13:1–3a). Jesus next leaves the house to go sit "by the lake," that is, the Sea of Galilee (v. 1). The crowds come in great numbers to hear him. Such large crowds only heighten the animosity of the Pharisees, who up to now have been popular with the people and see their influence continuing to shift to Jesus.

The Parable of the Sower and Soils (13:3b–9). *(1) Seed on paths (13:4).* Seed was sown "broadcast" style by scattering it in all directions while walking up and down the field. It was common for seeds to be scattered accidentally on the hard paths that surrounded the fields. Birds would swoop down and eat those seeds.

(2) Seed on rocky places (13:5–6). Conditions for farming in many areas of Israel were not favorable. In many places the terrain was uneven and rocky, with only thin layers of soil covering the rock. Seed that landed on this shallow soil would begin to germinate more quickly than seed sown in deep soil, but it couldn't put down deep roots and would soon wither and die in the hot sun.

(3) Seed among thorns (13:7). The plants battled for nutrients from the soil, and the wild thorny plants were well adapted to rob whatever they needed from the soil. As the thorny plants grew up with other plants, they choked out the less hardy agricultural plants.

(4) Seed on good soil (13:8). As the seeds germinated and matured, they kept on yielding a range of a hundred, sixty, or thirty times what was sown. The straight meaning of the parable is that only seed sown on good earth yielded a crop. The seed sown on good soil yielded to the maximum what it was created to produce, with varying amounts that reflected individual potential.

Spiritual ears (13:9). The parable is not for just anyone to hear but rather is for those with spiritual ears who have the ability to hear the spiritual message embedded in the parable.

Jesus's Purpose for Speaking in Parables (13:10–17). The distinction between the disciples and crowd is crucial in order to understand Jesus's purpose for speaking in parables. He uses the parables to cause the listener to make a decision about the kingdom of God.

The secrets of the kingdom of heaven (13:11). The reason why Jesus speaks to the crowd in parables is because God has given "the secrets of the kingdom of heaven" to the disciples, not to the crowd, to know. Jesus's message from the beginning has declared that the kingdom of heaven has arrived, but it hasn't always been apparent to those observing. Jesus gives to his disciples an understanding of that kingdom as it is now, and will be, operating in the world. The kingdom is present, but not yet in its fully manifested power.

The mysteries are not that God will establish his kingdom, which was a well-known prophetic hope within Israel, but that it has arrived in a form different from what was anticipated. The initial understanding of the secrets of the kingdom of heaven that the disciples now have, as given by God through Jesus, will be enlarged upon, so that they will have full understanding. But whatever understanding the crowd has, even that will be taken away. In other words, not only do the parables *not* reveal truth to the crowd; they even take away what the crowd already has.

Sovereignty and responsibility (13:12–13). The crowd must make a decision, and the parables force the issue. God knows those who will harden their heart against Jesus's message, so the parables are used to sovereignly harden the person's heart to the point where eventually he or she will be unable to respond (v. 15). God also knows those who will respond to the message of the gospel, so the parables elicit a positive response to come to Jesus, become his disciple, and ask for explanation (cf. v. 10). Thus, both sayings balance God's divine sovereignty with each individual human's responsibility.

Hard-hearted crowds (13:14–15). Jesus quotes Isaiah 6:9–10 to indicate that even as Israel had a long background of unbelief and rejection of God's prior prophets, so the crowd is now hardened against him. The crowd mirrors the people of Israel to whom the prophet Isaiah ministered. God does not force anyone to accept the message of the kingdom, so the crowd's response to the parables is dictated by the nature of their heart. If a person in the crowd has no spiritual ears, his or her heart will be increasingly hardened and will turn away from Jesus and the healing that comes with the kingdom of heaven.

Blessed disciples (13:16–17). The significance of the catchphrase that concluded the parable of the soils is now revealed. Jesus's parables are designed to test the spiritual "ears" or life of his audience. The spiritually alive disciples will seek further understanding from Jesus, causing their life and understanding to be enhanced. All that the prophets and righteous people of the Old Testament had longed to see, Jesus's disciples are privileged to take part in.

Therefore, we can say generally that with the parables Jesus accomplishes two important feats. First, the parables test the heart of the listener. They act as a spiritual examination, prompting a response from the listener that will indicate whether the person's heart is open to Jesus's message or is hardened. Second, the parables give instruction to those who are responsive. They teach Jesus's disciples about the nature of the kingdom of heaven, clarifying its secrets or mysteries, which thus shows how the kingdom operates in this world in a very different way from that expected by the religious leaders and the crowds.

Interpretation of the Parable of the Sower and Soils (13:18–23). *Hard hearts (13:19).* Jesus indicates that it is the Son of Man who sows the good seed. All of Jesus's seeds are good, so the emphasis falls on the type of soil, whether it is good or bad. Some in the crowd have hardened their hearts against Jesus's message. That hardness of heart prevents the seed of the gospel from taking root, and they cannot understand its truth. It makes them vulnerable to Satan, the "evil one," who "snatches away what was sown in their heart." In other words, the preaching of the gospel of the kingdom did not impact this type of person.

Shallow hearts (13:20–21). This type of heart exhibits a superficial reception of the gospel, but it does not take root. This is like those of the crowd who have not made a personal commitment to be Jesus's disciple. The seed of the gospel message was not able to penetrate to produce the change of regeneration in the person's heart.

Thorny hearts (13:22). This type of heart receives the gospel but has competition from the world. The message of the gospel is not able to transform the person into a true disciple because of his or her competing priorities. The combined priorities of worry and wealth choke out the life of the message of the kingdom of heaven, so that it is unable to bear fruit.

Receptive hearts (13:23). This represents a true believing disciple. Only those whose hearts have been receptive to the work of Jesus's message will produce the fruit of kingdom life, the evidence that they are truly children of the kingdom. Seed sown on good soil will yield to the maximum what it has been created to produce, with varying amounts that reflect individual potential.

Further Parables Told to the Crowds (13:24–35). *The parable of the wheat and the weeds (13:24–30).* Like the parable of the sower and soils, Jesus begins with a man sowing seed. Now, however, the seed is described as good seed and is contrasted with an enemy of the farmer, who attempts to disrupt the growth of good wheat by sowing among it *zizanion*, a kind of weed. Jesus sounds an eschatological note with this parable that resounds throughout the rest of the discourse. The kingdom of heaven has indeed come into this world, but its advance does not mean that the enemy will be completely vanquished during this age. That awaits the final judgment, which is surprisingly delayed. Jesus will later explain the meaning of the parable to his disciples at their request.

The parable of the mustard seed (13:31–32). The mustard seed was the smallest seed known in Galilee at that time. The proverbial smallness of the mustard seed as a metaphor that describes the kingdom of God would have shocked the crowd. Israel always believed that when God's kingdom was established on the earth, it would be great; they were not prepared for an insignificant beginning. But through this parable Jesus declares that the kingdom is already present, although only as a tiny manifestation. The image of a large tree with birds alighting on its branches recalls several Old Testament references to a great kingdom (cf. Ezek 17:22–24; 31:2–18; Dan 4:9–27).

The parable of the yeast (13:33). Jesus reverses the common evil connotation associated with yeast for the purpose of once again prompting the crowd to try to understand the presence of the kingdom. Scripture uses leaven almost exclusively as a negative metaphor, probably because fermentation implied disintegration and corruption. But Jesus uses yeast to symbolize the positive, hidden permeation of the kingdom of heaven in this world. Jesus's arrival did not bring the expected immediate, external, dramatic change. So his parable teaches the crowd that they must not let the present, inconspicuous form of the kingdom fool them from understanding what will be its final result. The kingdom of heaven is indeed active, although it is not at that time fully observable, because it begins with an inner transformation of the heart.

Parables that reveal hidden things (13:34–35). The crowd has had the opportunity to hear Jesus's proclamation of the gospel of the kingdom. Now they must respond. The parables are one of the means by which he tests the hearts of those in the crowd, prompting them either to be with him or against him. Their day of opportunity is nearly over. They cannot stay in the middle ground forever.

Explanations and Parables Told to the Disciples (13:36–50). *Interpretation of the parable of the wheat and weeds (13:36–43).* The explanation of the parable of the wheat and weeds is unique for the way in which Jesus identifies the main elements of the story, leading to an eschatological conclusion. Each of these elements is helpful for interpreting other parables. Several elements are not identified, which reminds us that not every element has significance in the metaphor. Jesus gives additional explanation of the events that will transpire at the end of the age and concludes his explanation of this parable with the familiar refrain to yield to the will of the Father as it is being proclaimed by Jesus—anyone who is willing to hear should listen and understand.

The parable of the hidden treasure (13:44). The kingdom of heaven is like a treasure that lies unnoticed because of its hidden nature. However, Jesus stresses that the man is not searching for the treasure. He happens upon it and instantly recognizes its value. By selling all that he has to purchase the field, he is gaining something far more valuable than any of his possessions and far more valuable than the field itself. The emphasis is on the supreme worth of the treasure that is unseen by others; it is worth far more than any sacrifice one might make to acquire it.

The parable of the costly pearl (13:45–46). As with the parable of the treasure, this one stresses the incomparable quality of the kingdom of God. But a contrast between the two primary figures illustrates that instead of simply stumbling across a hidden treasure, a diligent search by one well qualified to know its value will ultimately lead to the kingdom. The point is not on buying one's way into the kingdom but on recognizing its supreme value. The religious leaders of Jesus's day were certainly those whose expertise qualified them to understand the magnitude of the kingdom of God that Jesus announced, but they were blinded by their hypocrisy and their desire for a pious reputation and honor from people. Jesus's disciples are to understand that there is nothing more valuable in all of the world than possession of the kingdom of God.

The parable of the dragnet (13:47–50). Jesus uses this parable to describe the end-of-the-age judgment when the good will be separated from the bad, similar to the way that the parable of the wheat and weeds depicted an end-of-age separation. When Jesus comes in power, he will consummate the establishment of his kingdom on the earth. The statement of judgment of the wicked at verse 50 reiterates verbatim the words of 13:42. The final arrival of the kingdom of heaven will then extend its net throughout the world.

The Parable of the Householder's Treasure (13:51–52). Since Jesus is speaking to disciples here about the consequence of their understanding (cf. "therefore," v. 52), he now likens them to teachers of the law, who are in turn likened to owners of a house (*oikodespotēs*). An *oikodespotēs* is used in Jesus's parables to refer to God, Jesus, or Jesus's disciples and is sometimes pictured as distributing his wealth, whether as wages for his workers or as a rental property for farmers. Jesus extends the metaphor here to indicate that the householder brings from his treasure box both new and old things. He does not do so simply to ogle his wealth but to dispense it for the benefit of others.

The contrast is thus drawn between the teachers of the law within the Judaism of his day and the disciples of Jesus. The Torah-trained teachers of the law studied under great rabbis and passed on their traditions and interpretations. But all those who have become disciples of the kingdom of heaven have Jesus alone as their teacher, and they will in turn faithfully pass on to others what Jesus has taught them. In the same way that Jesus has developed them, they are to make disciples of all the nations and teach these new disciples all that they have been taught by Jesus.

Application. *Hidden but powerful.* Jesus clarifies with his parables that the kingdom of heaven has secrets associated with it. It is hidden but powerful in its spiritual transformational working. It is small in its beginning, but it will bring the reality of salvation from sin to all those who dare to come to it with eyes of faith and an open heart. God's judgment of the evil one and his followers is certain and will come with power, but it may not always appear that way during the present age. Jesus's return in glorious power to liberate this sin-sick world is a concrete promise that energizes us and gives us purpose for our own lives. These are the truths of the parables that reveal the secrets of the kingdom of heaven and that have provided guidance and hope and revelation of God's powerful, yet hidden operation during this age.

The transforming power of the kingdom of heaven—the parable of the sower and soils (13:1–9, 18–23). Just as Jesus had varied responses to his message, so will we. Faithfulness in sowing the gospel message is paramount, not the numbers that respond. The results are ultimately in the hands of God as well as in the choice of the individual. Our responsibility is to sow the seed, as did Jesus, to trust God, and to understand that inevitably there will be mixed responses. Nothing is comparable to the gospel message itself. It alone has potential power to produce life in dead soil. There are many stories of missionaries who labor for years in a foreign country before seeing even one conversion. Contentment comes through obedience and trusting God with the results.

Ultimately, it is the ongoing production of fruit that differentiates those who have truly responded to the kingdom from those who have not. The person who receives the gospel of the kingdom into his or her heart will experience the transformation of kingdom life, the very life that Jesus described in the Sermon on the Mount. So we should not just hope for transformation but should expect it as a result of the life-giving power of the gospel of the kingdom as energized by the Spirit of God. The responsibility for the production of fruit lies in the life-giving operation of the Spirit-empowered gospel, but that does not eliminate the disciple's own responsibility. We must be careful to supply proper nutrients and care for our well-being by continually being watered with the word of God and enfolded in a protective community of other believers. We likewise must be careful not to allow the weeds of this world to choke us, as the next parable points out.

The looming judgment of the kingdom of heaven—the parables of the wheat and weeds (13:24–30, 36–43) and the dragnet (13:47–50). Although the kingdom of heaven has been inaugurated in this world through the sowing of the gospel and many have become Jesus's disciples, the arrival of the kingdom has not vanquished the enemy or prevented the survival of evil people in this world. There will be a mixed nature in the world, which will continue in a form that seems counterintuitive to contemporary notions of God's reigning kingdom.

While the parables speak of the coexistence of the sons of the evil one and the sons of the kingdom in this world, there is secondary application to the church. The parable of the wheat and weeds allows us to be aware of the plans of the enemy—that Satan will attempt to infiltrate the church. We must be aware of how to be on guard, which should encourage us to pray against the plans of Satan. The true nature of those who are gathered in will not always be readily apparent, as Judas Iscariot sadly exemplifies. Only at the judgment will the full implication be known.

The surprising appearance of the kingdom of heaven—the parables of the mustard seed and yeast (13:31–32, 33). These parables should caution us about the popularity of our faith. In centuries past these parables were understood as referring to the church as the manifestation of the kingdom. The church has experienced remarkable growth at various periods of time in the world's history, but often at the expense of contamination from the world. The parables of the mustard seed and yeast caution us against expecting the popularity of the kingdom of heaven during this age. It will remain inconspicuous and hidden except to eyes of faith, awaiting its final manifestation. As citizens of the kingdom, we are the salt of the earth and the light of the world (5:13–16), and we seek to bring people into a loving community within the church, but our popularity is never to be the final gauge of the real influence of the kingdom.

The incalculable value of the kingdom of heaven—the parables of the hidden treasure (13:44) and costly pearl (13:45–46). Salvation and the righteousness of the kingdom is a greater treasure than all that the world has to offer, and it is the source of greatest joy. Unfortunately, it is all too easy to lose sight of this value and so lose the joy.

MATTHEW 13:53–14:36

Original Meaning

Jesus Rejected at Nazareth (13:53–58). At the beginning of his ministry, the townspeople were incensed by his inclusion of gentiles in God's plan of salvation, but now they are incredulous at the reports of the wisdom and miracles that he has demonstrated throughout Galilee. Since they know his human roots, the townspeople conclude that since Jesus had no other training than that of a carpenter, he cannot be a proper source of wisdom, nor can he lay claim to supernatural powers.

Jesus aligns himself with the Old Testament prophets who revealed God's will for the nation. Those messengers had consistently been rejected by the people of Israel. Jesus is likewise rejected. Because of the hardness of their hearts, they are not open to Jesus's ministry. While Jesus could apparently heal people elsewhere whose faith was not a significant factor in the miracle, hard-heartedness and rejection prevent the ministry of the Spirit's healing, even as it prevents the forgiveness of sin.

John the Baptist Beheaded by Herod Antipas (14:1–12). Herod Antipas's capital city, Tiberias, was only eight and a half miles down the coast of the Sea of Galilee from Capernaum, the base of Jesus's ministry. Somehow Jesus's widespread popularity among the masses of people throughout Israel, Perea, and the Decapolis reaches the ears of Herod. Herod's guilty fear for having executed John combines with a confused notion of resurrection, probably based in part on Pharisaic beliefs along with semi-pagan superstitious ideas of returning spirits.

On Herod's birthday a great celebration was held in his honor at the palace at Machaerus, where John was imprisoned. On this fateful occasion, Herodias's daughter performs a dance for Antipas. The girl is probably only twelve to fourteen years old, but in this degraded, deceptive setting she dances what is likely a highly sensual dance.

Herodias steps in immediately to orchestrate the elimination of another threat to her husband's reign. Herod Antipas knows that John is a prophet, popular with the people, and does not want to execute him. But he does not want to lose face in front of his guests.

Compassionate Healer and Supplier (14:13–21). *Beginning withdrawal from Galilee (14:13–14).* Matthew's narrative comment strikes a melancholy note. The implication may be that Jesus hears about the death of John and withdraws for a period of personal contemplation and mourning. But since John was most likely executed some months prior to this, others suggest that Jesus's withdrawal is connected to Herod Antipas's reaction to Jesus's ministry.

Twice in this narrative Jesus goes off alone, which he often did at a momentous time in his ministry. A key to his ministry was the way he listened to and then obeyed his Father's will, which often took place through the discipline of solitude. With his impending withdrawal from Galilee in order to make the final destined trip to Jerusalem and the cross, Jesus seeks the fellowship, solace, and guidance of his Father. However, his popularity with the people has not diminished. Word spreads that he is on the move, and many from the surrounding towns follow him on foot along the shore. When he lands, a large crowd is there to meet him. Even though the crowd is a fickle lot, Jesus has compassion for them. They have carried the sick to him from out of the towns, so Jesus heals them.

Feeding the five thousand (14:15–21). After the day of travel and healing, Jesus's disciples approach him with a logistical problem. The remote region offers no food for the people to eat. Such a large crowd might have presented problems to any surrounding villages, since abundant staples were not usually on hand. Thus, Jesus turns the problem back to the disciples and tells them to give the crowd something to eat, showing them the importance of compassion for the needs of people.

Apparently the disciples have no more food of their own either, but they scrounge around and come up with five loaves of bread and two fish. The season is spring, when the grass is lush and the streams are running full, so Jesus directs the crowd to sit down on the grass. He takes the loaves and the fish and looks up to heaven, a typical posture for prayer. He gives thanks or offers a blessing and breaks the loaves. Jesus does not bless the bread but blesses God for what will be the miraculous supply of bread.

He gives the disciples the miraculously multiplied bread, and they in turn pass among the crowd and give the pieces to the people. Matthew narrates almost casually that the crowd eats until they are satisfied, and "the disciples picked up twelve basketfuls of broken pieces that were left over" (v. 20). The number twelve is obviously significant for both the twelve tribes of Israel and the twelve disciples/apostles, but the significance here is uncertain. Gathering up the leftovers demonstrates that they should not neglect what God has already provided.

The crowd apparently thinks that Jesus will now restore the throne to Israel. They cannot get their eyes off their physical needs long enough to hear Jesus's message. So Jesus leaves to focus on those who will accept his offer of salvation. But the miracle also has a lesson for the disciples. They see the size of the need and the smallness of the human resources available. They must learn to see as Jesus sees.

The Son of God Is Worshiped (14:22–36). *Jesus walks on the water (14:22–27).* After the crowd and disciples leave, Jesus is finally alone. On a mountainside he spends concentrated time in prayer with his heavenly Father throughout the evening and into the night. At this significant turning point in his ministry, Jesus is readying himself for the journey into gentile regions, with the cross in Jerusalem looming on ahead.

While Jesus is alone on the mountain in prayer, the disciples are having a difficult time trying to cross the Sea of Galilee. They battle the storm for over nine hours—from before sundown until "shortly before dawn" (v. 25; literally "the fourth watch," i.e., 3:00 to 6:00 a.m.). In the previous incident of stilling the storm, Jesus was with the disciples, although he was sleeping in the stern of the boat. Now he comes walking to them on the sea.

The disciples are afraid when they see Jesus walking on the water, thinking that he is a "ghost" (*phantasma*). In Greek literature this word is used for dream appearances or spirit appearances, but in the Old Testament it means a deception. The disciples may be thinking that some evil spirit is attempting to deceive them. Jesus gives them immediate assurance that he is no deceptive evil spirit but truly their master: The expression "It is I" (v. 27; literally "I am") may allude to the voice of Yahweh from the burning bush (Exod 3:1–6). Throughout this section Jesus continues to reveal his true nature to the disciples, and this powerful statement accords with his miraculous calming of the storm.

Peter walks on the water (14:28–32). Amazingly, as Peter hears the voice of Jesus, he shouts back above the storm, "Lord, if it's you, tell me to come to you on the water" (v. 28). The expression "Lord" (*kyrios*) was used elsewhere to address Jesus with a title of respect or as a false declaration of faith, but here it means far more. Jesus is walking on the water in the middle of a furious storm, something that elevates him above any other figure that Peter has ever known. But likewise, if Jesus truly is the Lord and not an apparition, there is no need for fear. Peter's focused faith in Jesus's true identity enables him to overcome his fear, call out to him, and recognize that Jesus can enable Peter also to come to him on the water.

In reply to Peter's request, Jesus authoritatively says, "Come" (v. 29). Peter obeys by getting down out of the boat and miraculously walks on the water toward Jesus. We are not told how far or for how long he walks on the sea, but suddenly reality hits. He loses his focused faith in Jesus's divine identity and begins to sink beneath the seas. But then most importantly, Peter cries out, "Lord, save me!" (v. 30). The same Lord who could walk on the water himself and then enable Peter to walk on the water is more than able to save Peter from sinking.

Jesus immediately catches Peter by the hand to rescue him and says, "You of little faith, why did you doubt?" (v. 31). "Little faith" (*oligopistos*) is not the same as the "no faith" of the hard-hearted townspeople of Nazareth. A person with no faith would not recognize Jesus and call out to him. Peter has faith; it is just not functioning properly. Peter's faith enables him to recognize Jesus's true identity and to request to come out to him on the water, but it is like a burst of emotional energy. Jesus thus directs Peter to understand more clearly who he is and then act on it. Faith is not like a commodity of which Peter needs more. Rather, faith is consistent trust in Jesus to accomplish what Peter is called to do.

Jesus is worshiped as the Son of God (14:33). Worship is an action in Scripture reserved for God. One may prostrate oneself before other esteemed personages as a symbol of respect, but in the context of such works of divine significance, the disciples are gripped with the reality that Jesus is much, much more; he is the Son of God, and so they worship him.

They are understanding more clearly that Jesus is uniquely related to God the Father. Connected with the confession, their worship of Jesus is similar to the spontaneous reaction of people in the Old Testament to divine disclosures. Baffled as they must be as to who Jesus really is, they give homage to him in a way that is only rightly accorded to God.

The Son of God heals at Gennesaret (14:34–36). The region of Gennesaret did not figure prominently in Jesus's ministry as recorded in the Gospels. When the people recognize who he is, they spread the word throughout the surrounding country, and the response to him is remarkable. They bring their sick to him, believing that if they only touch the edge of his cloak, they will be healed. As on the occasion of the woman with the hemorrhage, "all who touched it were healed." This is a remarkable display of faith, in stark contrast to the Pharisees and teachers of the law.

Application. The wide range of reactions to Jesus's gospel of the kingdom that are found in this narrative hinge on one common element: an exercise of faith in Jesus's identity and message. The faith of people today ranges from the same extremes, with similar results. These narratives offer helpful growth in our own faith in Jesus's identity and message.

Offensiveness of the message and messenger. People don't like to forget others' pasts. If a person is not particularly striking or gifted at one point in life, then family, friends, and neighbors often won't let them grow into something more significant. This is an issue that almost every church has wrestled with at some point or another. Those of the older generation ought to keep wisely in mind that the upcoming generation is often a threat to their own identity. But does the older generation allow the younger the opportunity to earn their respect by giving them a chance to prove their giftedness and calling from God? Or are they rejected out of hand simply because they are too familiar with them?

We should also consider the ramifications for anyone bearing God's message. The viciousness of an attack on the messenger is especially unleashed when our message gets in the way of another's ambition. To call into question a colleague's motivation, to point out a lie, or to reveal a cover-up of an unethical business practice threatens one's power track to success, and you may find yourself facing not only anger but also bodily or emotional danger. But such is sometimes the responsibility of disciples, who are to be salt and light in a dark world.

Two caveats. We need to at this point interject two caveats about these lessons from Jesus's and John's experiences of rejection. First, we must learn to live with the consequences if we attempt to minister to people who are too familiar with us. We cannot demand respect; we have to earn it. Second, we must recognize that sometimes the *inappropriate* offensiveness of the messenger causes a rejection of the message. There are Christians out there who are jerks. They have poor social skills and poor manners. They treat people, both Christian and non-Christian, with disrespect. They run roughshod over others in the name of their own crusade. Some Christians are so legalistically narrow-minded that no one is right about anything except them. Jesus and John embodied a powerfully truthful message that called the nation into accountability, but they did so with appropriate, not inappropriate, personal offensiveness.

Eliciting discipleship and leadership through faith and worship. Leadership under Jesus demands effective faith in his divine power. We all face many circumstances for which we are unprepared. The difficulties we face change from day to day. But the one constancy we have in this life is Jesus. As we go through life focused on an intimate walk with Jesus through each and every circumstance, we learn how to apply his consistency to our situations. We may never be in such a position as

Peter was, but we can learn from him. When the Lord called him, whether to get out of the boat or later to become a leader in the early church, Jesus was always there to see him through.

The events of this narrative also teach us that discipleship and leadership under Jesus demand humble worship of his divine identity. A balanced, rounded understanding of Jesus needs to incorporate all aspects of his character and nature. A faulty vision of Jesus will cause us to reject him or to base our lives on only a partial understanding of what he has come to accomplish in our lives. But a clear and accurate vision of Jesus will cause us to worship him, which means ultimately to give our lives completely to him as our God.

MATTHEW 15:1–39

Original Meaning

The Traditions of the Jewish Elders (15:1–9). *The charge against Jesus's disciples (15:1–2).* The earlier charge of the Pharisees against Jesus's disciples was that they defiled the Sabbath. Now the Pharisees and teachers of the law from Jerusalem lodge a charge against the disciples that "they don't wash their hands before they eat" (v. 2). Bodily cleanliness was highly valued in the ancient world. The hands were a particular concern for cleanliness, as something unclean could be transmitted to oneself and others, so the priests were required to wash their hands and feet prior to offering their service. The Pharisees adapted the concern for hygienic cleanliness to ceremonial purity and applied it to common Israelites.

Jesus's countercharge (15:3–9). Jesus counters the Pharisees' charge against his disciples. In his question he goes to the heart of the problem, which is the relationship of the developing oral law to the written law. The tradition of the elders was not simply a preferred way of living, but it became equal in authority to the written law. Jesus makes it clear to them that the Old Testament came from God, while their traditions are simply the pronouncements of human elders.

Jesus drives home the point that their tradition has caused them to violate the law, so that they "nullify the word of God" in their zeal to practice a human tradition (v. 6). The Pharisees and teachers of the law perform religious rituals externally, but their primary motivation has not been to commit their entire inner person to God. Therefore, not only does their human tradition and teaching nullify God's word, but their worship is empty of any real meaning. This is a disturbingly sweeping indictment by Jesus of Israel's leading religious establishment.

Purity and Impurity from the Heart (15:10–20). *A warning to the crowd (15:10–11).* Since the Pharisees and teachers of the law are so influential among the common people, Jesus turns to the crowd to warn them of falling into the same trap. Those in the crowd who are unreceptive will turn away from this saying to follow the Pharisees and teachers of the law, while those who are receptive will respond by becoming his disciples and seeking further understanding through his teaching.

Jesus states categorically that spiritual impurity is not contracted through eating foods that are not ceremonially cleansed. He thereby renounces publicly the Pharisees' tradition that required ritual cleansing before eating. He is not speaking of hygienic cleanliness but of spiritual purity. Ceremonial cleansing is not the key element in producing godliness. A hypocritical show of devotion to God can mask a heart that is more intent on gaining a religious reputation than it is on seeking to do God's will as revealed in the Old Testament.

In challenging Jesus about conformity to the tradition of the elders, the Pharisees reveal that their inner life is unclean. They have not repented in the light of the arrival of the kingdom of heaven and received the righteousness that is Spirit-produced. They continue to rely on their own practice of external righteousness, which does not allow them entrance to the kingdom. They have not only deceived themselves but have misled the people with their traditions, so Jesus gives due warning to the crowd.

A warning from the disciples (15:12–14). The disciples are probably worried not only about Jesus finding himself at odds with these religious leaders but also with those who are influenced by them. And they are also probably worried about their own reputation. They rightly understand that Jesus has elevated himself as a critic of their entire religious tradition, which will undercut their influence with the people.

Jesus replies to the disciples' warning with two parables. First, he likens the fate of the Pharisees to that of a plant. Reminiscent of the parable of the weeds and the wheat, this saying declares that the Pharisees have not been planted by the Father (v. 13). Jesus also likens the Pharisees to blind guides (v. 14). Not only does the hypocrisy of the Pharisees blind them to their own inner impurity, but in their blindness they lead the people astray because they cannot see the truth of God's will in the Old Testament.

A question from Peter (15:15–16). Peter asks for the interpretation of the parables. Understanding Jesus's parables and teaching is a key element of discipleship, because true disciples have spiritual ears to hear and spiritual eyes to see the truth of Jesus's teaching, something the crowd does not have. But Jesus rebukes the disciples here for not being as spiritually perceptive as they should. As elsewhere, the real key to understanding is Jesus's teaching, so he goes on to give an explanation of the parable.

Jesus's explanation of the role of the heart in spiritual purity (15:17–20). In his explanation, Jesus outlines to the disciples the central role that the heart plays in spiritual purity. Traditions of the elders have nothing to do with true spiritual cleanness, because they only focus on the external physical activities. They do not make a person unclean before God. God's judgment concerns behavior that originates in the heart of a person. The spiritual heart is evil, and it must first be cleansed, which will then produce lives that exemplify righteous purity in word, thought, motivation, deed, and relationships.

This is an explicit statement about the heart that was implied in Jesus's teaching in the Sermon on the Mount. Jesus came to fulfill the Old Testament revelation about God's will for his people and to bring about the righteousness of the kingdom of heaven in those who respond to his message. That righteousness is an inside-out transformation that begins with the heart and works throughout the process of the disciple's life to produce external righteousness while pursuing the perfection of the Father.

Healer and Provider for Gentiles (15:21–39). *Jesus withdraws to gentile regions (15:21).* Jesus now explicitly withdraws to gentile territory, to the infamous cities of Tyre and Sidon. The Jews of Galilee have been privileged to hear and see Jesus's message and miracles that authenticated his announcement of the arrival of the kingdom of heaven, but their lack of repentance condemns them, so Jesus withdraws. He and his disciples proceed to gentile regions before heading to Judea and the final destination, Jerusalem.

A gentile woman acknowledges Jesus as the Son of David (15:22–28). His first encounter in this gentile region is with a Canaanite woman. This woman, a "Canaanite" (i.e., a pagan non-Jew) demonstrates familiarity with Jewish messianic tradition by calling Jesus "Son of David," and she pleads for his merciful, miraculous ministry of exorcism for her suffering daughter (v. 22).

Jesus does not reply to the woman's cry for help, which the disciples apparently take as his way of rebuffing the woman's request. But this woman's great need to have her daughter exorcised drives her to be persistent, which is a sign that she knows that Jesus certainly can come to her aid. Jesus still maintains his commitment to his mission to Israel. The "children's bread" emphasizes the care that God promises to provide for his covenant children (v. 26). As a metaphor, "dogs" is a humiliating label for those apart from, or enemies of, Israel's covenant community. Jesus used the metaphor similarly in the Sermon on the Mount to indicate that the holy message of the gospel of the kingdom must not be defiled by those who are unreceptive to, or have rejected, Jesus's invitation.

This perceptive woman, who has already confessed Jesus as the messianic Son of David, now presses Jesus by calling on the extended blessings promised to the gentiles. Although Israel receives the primary blessings of the covenant, gentiles also were to be recipients of blessing through them. The woman draws on that promise to seek the aid of Jesus Messiah.

She understands the program of God to go to Israel first, but she persists. In a sense, Jesus is testing her. Will she see through the salvation-historical distinction between Israel and the gentiles and recognize that God ultimately desires to bring healing to all people? She passes with flying colors because she acknowledges that as the Messiah of Israel, Jesus is the master of all, and he will care for the needs of all, whether Jews ("children") or gentiles ("dogs"). Her response is called by Jesus an exercise of "great faith," which is rewarded by having her daughter healed that very hour (v. 28).

Many gentiles glorify the God of Israel (15:29–31). Gentiles increasingly become the focus of Jesus's ministry now that the religious leadership is working to turn the people away from him. As Israel rejects the kingdom, gentiles frequently come into view as recipients of his message and healing. Like the crowd in Israel, they are amazed when they see his miraculous ministry, and they "praised the God of Israel" (v. 31). But like Israel's crowd, it is not enough to be amazed. They must believe in him as the Messiah of Israel and become his disciples.

Feeding the four thousand (15:32–38). This is the second time that Jesus feeds a crowd of thousands miraculously after spending time healing those brought to him, although this time he is in the gentile region of the Decapolis. Jesus addresses the disciples with the needs of the crowd, challenging them to recall the earlier miraculous supply of the five thousand. But the disciples still have not fully grasped the magnitude of Jesus's identity, because they question where they will find supplies to feed such a massive group. Once again Jesus will teach them with a miraculous illustration.

In this feeding the number of small bread cakes is seven, and there are seven baskets left over. If the number of twelve baskets left over in the feeding of the five thousand is symbolic of Israel, as most suppose, then the number seven here, which is normally symbolic of perfection or completion, may symbolize the completion or fullness of God's meeting the needs of all peoples, now including gentiles.

A brief return to Jewish territory (15:39). Magadan (perhaps a variant spelling for Magdala) is generally identified with Migdal Nunya ("Tower of Fish") of Talmudic times, about three miles north of Tiberias on the Gennesaret plain. The name suggests that this town was the center of Galilee's fish-processing industry, making it one of the most important fishing centers on the Sea of Galilee and the administrative seat of the surrounding region. Archaeologists uncovered in Magdala, in the ruins of a first-century AD home, a decorative mosaic depicting a boat with a mast for sailing and oars for rowing.

Application. *The ultimate authority of the word of God.* Jesus's confrontations with the religious leaders of his day, especially the political rationalism of the Sadducees and the religious authoritarianism of the Pharisees, give us the right guidance to understanding God's will in our own day. The word of God as revealed in Scripture must be understood as the sole authority that contains all that is necessary for salvation and the spiritual life. That word must be elevated above any human tradition. It is in God's word that we have the clearest understanding of God's will for our daily lives and the life of our communities of faith. Teachers, preachers, and doctrinal formulations are helpful guides to individuals and churches, but Scripture must continually be upheld as the final authority.

Transformation from the heart. Jesus's condemnation of the Pharisees for elevating human traditions over the word of God brought to the light a precipitating problem—the evil of one's heart cannot be cleansed by religious activity. Spiritual hearts become hardened in two primary ways. First, hearts harden from the inside when we say no to what God wants from us. Put simply, our hearts harden when we sin. Yet second, our hearts also harden against the outside when we try to protect ourselves from being hurt. Every person reading these words has been hurt by other people, and we often try to protect ourselves from being hurt again by hardening our heart against those who might bring pain into our lives. This kind of hardening of the heart can result in fearfulness, arrogance, or bitterness as means of protecting ourselves.

The only cure for spiritual heart disease is through the penetrating, transforming work of the kingdom of God in a person's life. As we allow Jesus to unleash the power of the Spirit in our hearts, we will experience an inward transformation that will begin to influence our thoughts, our actions, our emotions, and our relationships.

Great faith and ungrateful privilege. Privilege demands accountability, and faith in Jesus's identity and mission brings the touch of the kingdom's blessing. This blessing is not that of wealth—quite possibly the woman already had that—or even that of health, for the mother herself receives nothing, and her little daughter will eventually die physically. Rather, like the centurion, this gentile woman of great faith is a foretaste of the promise of the eschatological feast of salvation that all those from every point of the compass will enjoy who respond to Jesus's summons to the kingdom (8:10–12). This wonderful story of the persistent mother warns and instructs us that Jesus always responds to those who have the courage to come to him with their desperate need, because true privilege comes through openness to him in faith.

MATTHEW 16:1–28

Original Meaning

Jesus Gives No More Signs of His Identity and Mission (16:1–4). The Pharisees and Sadducees want a sign from God, most likely one that will be displayed in the skies. Mariners are notorious for developing maxims that predict the patterns of weather, which they must heed daily, if not hourly, in order to conduct safe passage on the seas. Jesus uses a similar maxim drawn from his cultural milieu to contrast the religious leaders' familiarity with natural phenomena in the "sky" (*ouranos*) with the supernatural phenomena from "heaven" (*ouranos*) that they request, but about which they are so spiritually blind that they cannot recognize it. Because the Jewish religious leaders are not seeking in good faith, the only validating sign Jesus will give them of his messianic authority will be his resurrection, which will be like the appearance of Jonah to the Ninevites. The actions of the pagan people of Nineveh who repented at Jonah's preaching forms the judgment on all who do not repent at Jesus's announcement of the arrival of the kingdom of God.

Spiritual Leaven of the Pharisees and Sadducees (16:5–12). The prior use of yeast in the parable of the mystery of the kingdom of heaven should have prepared the disciples to understand that he was using it metaphorically again, but they are so preoccupied with their physical needs that they overlook the direction of Jesus's spiritual teaching. But Jesus patiently leads these fumbling disciples into the meaning that he intends them to understand. Their openness to his teaching about the yeast of the Pharisees and Sadducees leads to their understanding the threat that these religious leaders are to Jesus and his mission.

Who Is the Son of Man? (16:13–14). At the time that Jesus and his disciples traveled there, Caesarea Philippi was an important Greco-Roman city, whose population was primarily pagan Syrian and Greek. This region, long a bastion of pagan worship to Baal, then to the Greek god Pan, and then to Caesar, becomes the site where Jesus calls for a decision about his own identity. At this pivotal time, having basically concluded his Galilean mission, he attempts to elicit from his disciples not only what the people have gleaned but also what his disciples have come to understand about him. Thus, Jesus asks, "Who do people say the Son of Man is?" The disciples' response is striking. Each response indicates a prophet, in line with one of the popular messianic expectations held in Israel.

Peter's Confession of Jesus's Identity (16:15–16). Peter steps forward once again as a leader and spokesperson for the others. Prior to this, the expression "Messiah" has occurred only in Matthew's narrative; now it is used for the first time by a person to address Jesus directly. "Messiah," or "Christ," is a title, the translation of the Greek term *Christos*, which is a translation of the Hebrew term for "anointed" (*mashiah*). Peter further expresses Jesus's identity as "the Son of the living God," an expression that has special significance in the area of Caesarea Philippi with its plethora of ancient Baal, Pan, and Caesar worship. Jesus is the Son of the God who is living, not like those mythical, superstitious figures etched in stone. Even more significantly, this expression bears witness to a relationship that has characterized Jesus and God throughout the Gospel of Matthew.

Peter's confession is not the first recognition of Jesus as Messiah, but it is the fullest to this point. But Peter confesses more than he really understands about Jesus's identity, and he does not yet fully understand Jesus's mission, because he will soon attempt to deter Jesus from his redemptive objective. But his understanding is certainly increasing, as is that of the rest of the Twelve, as they pay attention to God's revelation of who Jesus is and what he has come to accomplish.

Jesus's Pronouncements about Peter (16:17–20). Once Peter makes his grand confession about Jesus, Jesus in turn makes a grand pronouncement about Peter. Jesus's pronouncement is not a conferral of unique, individual supremacy. Peter is given a special recognition for all he is and is to be, but he is never placed above or apart from the disciples. Peter is crucial for his role in the foundation of the church, but he is not the only part of the foundation.

As Jesus looks down the long corridor of history, he gives an absolute promise that his church will endure to the end of the age. Hades, or Sheol, is the realm of the dead, and the word "gates," which are essential to the security and might of a city, indicates power. So the expression "gates of Hades" referred to the realm and power of death (v. 18). Jesus thus promises that death will not overpower the church, his own family of faith.

Peter's mission is to give people access to the kingdom, and this mission involves especially his preaching of the gospel. Peter, the representative disciple who gives the first personal declaration of the Messiah's identity, is the one in the book of Acts who opens the door of the kingdom to the Jews on Pentecost, to the Samaritans, and finally to the gentiles. Once Peter used the keys to open the door to the kingdom of God, he passes from the scene. The door to the kingdom now stands open throughout the ages, so the keys are no longer needed.

Peter is the one who is given authority to declare the terms under which God grants entrance to, and exclusion from, the kingdom. Peter's authority is tied directly to his confession. Through the revelation of the Father and the personal confession of Jesus as the Messiah, the Son of the living God, Peter receives a blessing and becomes the foundation of the church. His confession is a condensation of the gospel, and through Peter's preaching of the gospel and the preaching of others who follow him, sins are forgiven and entrance is gained to the kingdom.

Jesus warns against his public identification as the Messiah (16:20). Peter's confession has released Jesus's identity as the Messiah/Christ, but it is still subject to misunderstanding by the crowds and even by his own disciples, as even Peter will soon display. So Jesus warns his disciples not to disclose further to the crowds that he is the Messiah.

Jesus Messiah Predicts His Suffering and Resurrection (16:21–23). *The suffering and risen Messiah (16:21).* This is the first of four times in which Jesus predicts his arrest and crucifixion, but as much as he tries to get his disciples to understand the necessity of that mission, they continually misapprehend its significance. By claiming the necessity of suffering death at the hands of the religious leadership of Jerusalem, Jesus begins to reveal the ultimate destiny and purpose for his life's ministry.

Peter's presumption (16:22–23). With audacious presumption Peter steps forward, likely once again as spokesman for the rest of the shocked disciples, to try to save his master from the announced fate of suffering. Although this may appear to reflect appropriate concern, Jesus understands the source of Peter's admonition. Satan tried to tempt Jesus away from carrying out the Father's will at the start of his earthly ministry (4:1–11). Now he uses a different strategy by trying to hinder Jesus's mission through Peter, one of Jesus's own disciples, the same one who has just been privy to a revelation from God the Father.

Peter here sets his mind on human ways, not on God's. He may have gotten carried away with his own significance in understanding Jesus's identity and mission, which made him vulnerable to Satan's temptation. He undoubtedly thinks he is protecting Jesus. Jesus will now show Peter that God's way is the way of the cross, for him and for all disciples.

The Cost of Discipleship (16:24–28). *Taking up one's cross (16:24).* Jesus's path of suffering and death on the cross is the ultimate example of obedience to the Father's will. Indeed, the cross symbolizes the central purpose for Jesus's life. The cross is, for Jesus and those who follow him in discipleship, a metaphor of the Father's will for a disciple's life.

The reasons for taking up one's cross (16:25–28). Verses 25–28 give three related reasons for the necessity of taking up the cross of discipleship.

1. *Saving and losing one's soul (16:25).* The person who tries to hang on to his own will and reject what God desires for him ultimately loses eternally all that he is attempting to protect in this life. The new life of the kingdom of

God is discovered only by giving over to Jesus one's old life and finding new life in following him.

2. *The value of a kingdom soul (16:26).* All of the physical riches, pleasures, and powers of this world will do no one any ultimate good if one forfeits his or her spiritual existence. The acquisition of all the world has to offer cannot match the blessed riches of finding true life through obeying God's will in following Jesus's summons to the kingdom of God.
3. *The reward of gaining kingdom life for one's soul (16:27–28).* It is urgently necessary to take up one's cross in discipleship, because the coming of the Son of Man will bring an abrupt accounting as to whether each person has taken up God's will by responding to Jesus's call to kingdom life. Whether at the end of one's life or at the unexpected time of the return of the Son of Man in glory, all must give account for the choices they have made.

What does Jesus mean by saying that the Son of Man "is going to come" in his Father's glory (v. 27)? Jesus gives a specific application to the Twelve standing there with him. The phrase "truly I tell you" typically introduces an important declaration. Here it signals a concluding clarification of the reward that will be given to those who have followed Jesus's form of discipleship by taking up God's will as symbolized in the cross. Some of the Twelve standing with Jesus in Caesarea Philippi will remain alive until they see the Son of Man coming in his kingdom. Jesus's saying in this context points to the urgency of his disciples' taking up their cross. As they will see, Jesus will be transfigured in kingdom glory in just a few days. They must not themselves delay to take up their cross and adopt God's will for their lives, because in some sense, every day brings with it the possibility of impending reward or judgment.

Application. *Consistency.* In Matthew 16 we can see at least three areas where we must develop consistency in our daily walk with Jesus, regardless of our circumstances: consistency in our spiritual perception and reception, consistency in our motivation to know Jesus on his terms rather than ours, and consistency in our willingness to live with the cross.

Consistency in spiritual perception and reception. The perceptiveness of our hearts is different from the perceptiveness of our intellect or mind. A heart open to spiritual cues will hear God's voice, whereas a heart hardened against God cannot hear or see him. Openness to God as his disciples is related to spiritual perception.

This reinforces the importance of placing ourselves in proximity to where we can learn, such as in a church setting or an individual or group Bible study. But mere proximity doesn't guarantee adequate reception. Our receptivity to God's leading and teaching must balance appropriate personal responsibility with adequate reliance on God's provision.

Consistency in knowing Jesus on his terms, not ours. To conduct ourselves appropriately as Jesus's disciples is to understand that we can do nothing of eternal value apart from clearly knowing his will and experiencing his enablement. We can each display a rocklike consistency in our lives if we know who we are as created and gifted and called by God (and no more!), and if we then commit ourselves to maximizing all God wants to do through us as his uniquely gifted vessels. To do so is to be motivated to know Jesus on his own terms, not ours, and to take his calling on our life with deadly seriousness—but not take ourselves too seriously in the process.

Consistency in living with the cross as both invitation and instruction. Another way of learning consistency in our discipleship to Jesus is illustrated by the metaphor of the cross. It not only is the cruel instrument of Jesus's death and the symbol of the purpose for his incarnation, but it is also emblematic for following him in our own lives. Consistency in our discipleship involves a continual willingness to live with the cross, because taking up our cross to follow Jesus involves both the initiation of the Christian life as well as the ongoing standard of discipleship.

We should not emphasize examining ourselves so heavily that we dissolve the confidence that we should have when we believe on Jesus as the true Son of God for eternal life (cf. 1 John 5:13–15). But persons who have truly denied themselves and have taken up the cross will stand out in this world as they follow Jesus and live his kingdom values in transformed lives.

MATTHEW 17:1–27

Original Meaning

The Transfiguration of Jesus (17:1–8). *A high mountain (17:1).* This mountain is not identified. Mount Tabor has been favored by much of church tradition. It is only six miles from Nazareth and twelve miles from the Sea of Galilee, but few today contend for this as the site, primarily because we now know that it was occupied by a Roman garrison during Jesus's time. Most scholars favor Mount Hermon. Its primary peak is snow-capped for much of the year, with a series of two other peaks rising at less altitude. If this is the location, Jesus and the disciples probably do not ascend to the top but go to a secluded spot.

Jesus is transfigured (17:2). Jesus experiences a physical transformation visible to the disciples. It is a reminder of Jesus's preincarnate, divine glory and a preview of his coming exaltation. That glory designates the royal presence, for in his person the kingdom of God is with his people.

Moses and Elijah appear (17:3). Both Moses and Elijah had visions of the glory of God on a mountain—Moses on Mount Sinai and Elijah on Mount Horeb. Both of them had unique endings—Elijah was taken directly to heaven, while Moses, whose grave was never found, is said by rabbinic tradition also to have been taken directly to heaven. Both are mentioned together in Malachi 4:4–6 in the giving of the law through God's servant Moses and the sending of the prophet Elijah before the coming day of the Lord. Their appearance on the mountain with Jesus indicates the greatness of Jesus, who transcends them both as the one who will be declared the Son of God.

Peter's response (17:4). It is difficult to understand Peter's comment and suggestion. Perhaps the best that can be made of Peter's suggestion is that he, in trying to make sense of this overwhelming transfiguration of Jesus and the appearance of these great figures, wishes to make some sort of memorial fitting to their stature. As the next verses indicate, however, Peter does not grasp fully the stature of Jesus, for he is not just another Old Testament figure like Moses and Elijah. Jesus is superior in every way, and his transfiguration confirms the eschatological inauguration of the kingdom of God.

The Father's declaration (17:5). A "bright cloud" appears, reminiscent of the way that God appeared at different times in the Old Testament. The voice of God the Father from the cloud gives the same public endorsement of Jesus that was given at his baptism, indicating that Jesus is both Son and suffering servant. An experience of the awesome reality of God's presence commonly produced fear in the people of the Old Testament. But Jesus tenderly touches his frightened disciples and tells them not to fear. This gives them reassuring confirmation that he is the same master that they have known, even though they have just experienced a stunning revelation of his divine nature.

When the disciples look up, they see no one except Jesus. Their focus is now exclusively on Jesus, the way Moses and Elijah would have desired, for their ultimate significance was in preparing the way for Messiah, the Son of God, and his redemptive mission. The disciples have received the most explicit revelation of Jesus's identity, but they still do not comprehend fully what they have experienced.

John the Baptist and the Coming of Elijah (17:9–13). *The need for silence (17:9).* The disciples may tell others of the stupendous events of the transfiguration only after he has been raised from the dead. Otherwise, the disciples and the crowd may think that Jesus's transfiguration and meeting with Moses and Elijah indicates that the time has come to effect national and military liberation, thus misunderstanding his mission. Jesus's message must be understood to focus on forgiveness of sins through his suffering on the cross.

Elijah and John the Baptist (17:10–12). Jesus's disciples do not understand how Malachi's prophecy of Elijah as the forerunner can be fulfilled in Jesus if he truly is the Messiah. Jesus is there with them, and Elijah has only now appeared on the mountain. He has not preceded Jesus, so how can Jesus be the fulfillment of Malachi's prophecy?

Jesus clarifies Malachi's prophecy in the light of John the Baptist's ministry, his own arrival, and the response of the people of Israel to both John's and Jesus's announcement of the kingdom of God. John's ministry was a partial fulfillment of Malachi's prophecy. John was the fulfillment of the arrival of the anticipated Elijah, but neither John's nor Jesus's ministry was accepted fully. Instead, John was executed, as will be Jesus. Thus, the complete fulfillment of Malachi's promise of restoration and judgment cannot now be accomplished. Another Elijah-type figure will have to come in the future, again preparing the way, but then for the final consummation of the day of the Lord prophesied in Malachi, preparing the way for the returning Son of Man who will at that time restore all things and bring God's wrath on the unrepentant.

The disciples understand (17:13). Jesus's clarification of the role that the prophesied Elijah figure will play jogs the disciples' memory. Matthew emphasizes how Jesus and his teaching bring enlightenment in the path of discipleship.

The Healing and Exorcism of an Epileptic Boy (17:14–20). *The epileptic boy not healed by Jesus's disciples (17:14–16).* The boy's father approaches Jesus with great reverence. The man respects Jesus as an esteemed and pious master by calling him "Lord" (v. 15), but he goes beyond that to anticipate that Jesus can extend mercy to heal his son. The father had such confidence in Jesus's ability to heal that he assumes that his disciples have this ability as well. But his confidence has been dashed.

The generation's "no faith" (17:17–18). "Unbelieving" (*apistos*) indicates that the current generation has not as a whole placed their faith in Jesus as the anticipated Messiah; "perverse" (*diestrammenos*) indicates that they have become distorted in their evaluation of Jesus, likely a result of their own willfulness in rejecting Jesus's demand for repentance as well as the influence of the religious leaders on them.

Jesus reveals a conscious understanding not only of the contrast between the glory of his transfiguration and the realities of this world, but of his heavenly origin with his Father. Jesus will only return to his heavenly glory after going through this world of demonic activity, faithlessness, and eventually the cross. Demonstrating that he has ultimate authority over the satanic source of this illness, Jesus rebukes the demon, it comes out of the boy, and he is immediately healed.

The disciples' "little faith" (17:19–20). The disciples do have faith in Jesus and his mission, but here it is not functioning properly; it is "little faith," or defective faith. Apparently in the present incident the disciples were either relying on their own abilities to do the exorcism, or else they were doing something that God had not called them to do; perhaps they were trying to put on a show for their own acclaim.

The accomplishments of "effective faith" (17:20). By using the contrast to the mustard seed, he declares that even the smallest amount of faith can accomplish tremendous feats. The disciples themselves would declare that they have a larger amount of faith than that of the size of a mustard seed. Jesus is getting them to look at the real nature of faith. It is not the *amount* of faith that is in question but rather its *focus*.

Faith is confidence that we can do what God calls us to do—it is taking God at his word. Therefore, the disciples should not place confidence in what they have but have confidence that if God calls them to do something, they can do it in his strength.

The Second Passion Prediction (17:22–23). This second prediction adds an ominous element: Jesus will not just be arrested by the religious leaders—he will be betrayed. Along with an increased understanding of the tragedy ahead, the knowledge that a duplicitous, evil betrayal lies behind it causes the disciples to be "filled with grief." Little do they know they will experience even greater grief upon discovering that the traitorous betrayer is one of their own and that they themselves will abandon Jesus at his moment of greatest human need.

Paying the Temple Tax (17:24–27). These collectors of the temple tax represent the Jewish religious establishment in Jerusalem overseeing the temple. The grammatical structure of the question indicates that these temple-tax agents are attempting to elicit an affirmative response: "He does pay the tax, doesn't he?" These representatives from the temple establishment may have been attempting, with duplicity, to confirm charges of Jesus's disloyalty to the temple.

Peter knows of Jesus's loyalty to the law (5:17–19), so he answers in the affirmative. He is correct on one level, but once Jesus gets him alone in the house, he gives Peter a more profound insight to the issue. He asks: "From whom do the kings of the earth collect duty and taxes—from their own children or from others?" (v. 25). Peter's reply is expected. Rulers do not collect taxes from their own children but from their subjects. This completes the analogy, as Jesus concludes. The temple is his Father's own house, so since Jesus is the Son of God his Father, he is exempt from the temple tax. And Jesus's disciples, now part of the Father's family, are likewise exempt. This is a profound christological statement, indicating not only Jesus's relationship by analogy to his Father, the ultimate king, but also the way in which he is the fulfillment of the law.

Jesus, and by extension his disciples, are not under obligation to pay the tax. But so as not to offend the conscience of those Jews who have not yet experienced liberation through Jesus and his end to the temple, they will both pay the tax. To make a striking impression on his disciples that they will long remember, Jesus instructs Peter to throw out a fishing line, where he will find the coin for paying the tax.

Application. Matthew presents three primary scenes—from the mountain of transfiguration to the village of faulty faith to the sea of the miraculously supplied coin—to demonstrate the centrality of Jesus Messiah in God's program of salvation history and to persuade his followers to give him ultimate centrality in their worldview.

Obedience means to listen to Jesus. As rational, reasoning humans, we can go a long way toward understanding this world in which we live, but the revelation of God through Jesus is the final and ultimate word. Thus, we must learn to submit ourselves to the authority of Jesus, which means to evaluate our lives in the light of his revelation, being obedient to what he calls us to be and to do. Once we hear his words, we cannot pick and choose which ones we like. Hardship may accompany being one of his disciples, but if we want to find true life, we must embrace that to which he calls us.

Faith means to stay focused on Jesus. Jesus pointed to the *effectiveness* of faith. The smallest faith can accomplish the greatest deeds, such as moving a mountain, if it is properly focused. It is not the amount of our faith that works miracles. It is the focus of our faith on Jesus who will work miracles through us according to his will. Jesus's point is that anyone with any amount of faith can do the most unthinkable things, if that is what God has called us to do. Therefore, we should not place confidence in what we have; rather, we should be confident that if God calls us to do something, we can do it in his strength, even the most absurdly impossible-sounding things from the world's point of view.

Freedom means the ability not to demand our rights, but to do the right thing. We often think of freedom as simply the ability to do what we want to do. There is truth in that concept. But there is another sense of freedom that comes from the biblical understanding of the effect of sin on humanity. Humanity is under the curse of sin, which chains us to self-centeredness and rebellion against what God wants us to do. But when we come to know the truth from Jesus about our sinfulness and receive his atoning sacrifice, we are set free from our bondage to sin. That freedom enables us to do the right thing, which we were not able to do before. Therefore, true freedom does not mean the unrestricted ability to do whatever we want but the ability to sacrifice ourselves for the good of others. The kingdom life must characterize the church, and our walk of discipleship in this world is not so much about asserting our rights as it is the freedom to benefit and serve others.

MATTHEW 18:1–35

Original Meaning

The Greatness of Humility (18:1–4). Jesus's disciples have all sacrificed significantly by following him around the countryside these last two to three years, and they want to attain to the highest level of commitment to Jesus's kingdom agenda. But as the following interaction indicates, the disciples have a different type of greatness in mind from what Jesus meant. One of Jesus's primary goals in chapter 18 is to revise their understanding of "greatness" to the way God thinks about it.

Jesus begins this process with a visual aid by calling a little child and having him stand among them. The humility of a child consists of the inability to advance his or her own cause apart from the help and resources of a parent. Yet Jesus celebrates the humility that comes from the child's weakness, defenselessness, and vulnerability. Those who wish to enter the kingdom must turn away from their own power and self-seeking, and in childlike humility call on God's mercy to allow them to enter the kingdom of heaven.

Shelter for the Humble (18:5–9). *Care for humble disciples (18:5).* The "child" is the true disciple who has humbly received God's enabling mercy to enter the kingdom and who is now serving God. Receiving a little child in the name of Christ means accepting and believing the witness of a Christian disciple.

Warning about taking advantage of humble disciples (18:6–7). The phrase "cause . . . to stumble" does not indicate a single isolated indiscretion. Rather, drawing on the metaphorical nature of the verb *skandalizō* ("cause to stumble"), it points to a person who has been led astray into sin and fallen badly in his or her walk with God. To practice a lifestyle that regularly leads Jesus's humble disciples to sin indicates that one is headed for eternal damnation, so it would be better to cut one's life off quickly than to risk staying on that trajectory.

Warning about allowing one's own passions to lead oneself into sin (18:8–9). Jesus is not advocating physical self-mutilation, but through dramatic figures of speech he indicates the rigorous self-discipline needed for committed disciples. A person who consistently yields to sin is worthy of eternal condemnation since such sin reveals that he or she is not a disciple of Jesus. The fires of the eternal hell of Gehenna await those who receive God's judgment.

Angelic Protection of the Little Ones (18:10). Angels are well-known to be active in the affairs of humans, but in a strikingly personal way Jesus refers to "their" angels. Whether or not Jesus's statement implies guardian angels who watch over individual believers on an ongoing basis, it does confirm that the heavenly Father uses angels to care for childlike disciples. Jesus's statement that they "always see the face of my Father" indicates that the disciples' angels have constant access to and communication with God.

The Divine Search for Lost Sheep (18:12–14). Jesus uses a parable concerning safe and wayward sheep to make his point. The metaphor naturally becomes associated with Jesus, as he here seems to imply, as a central part of his mission both to Israel and to all of humanity. The joy of finding the lost sheep does not mean that it has more value than the others. Rather, the shepherd's joy demonstrates the depth of his concern, care, and love for all his sheep. The depth of that love is often only experienced when faced with the possibility of loss.

Disciplining Wayward Disciples (18:15–17). Jesus enunciates four steps for dealing with a sinning member of the discipleship community, which has as its intended goal the restoration of the sinning brother or sister to a state of purity and the reestablishment of the fellowship of the body.

1. *Personal confrontation.* Such an encounter must be undertaken with privacy so that if it is resolved, no undue attention will be given to the tragedy of sin committed by a member of the community. The ultimate objective of the encounter is not punishment but restoration—winning over a brother or sister so that he or she can be restored to the faithful path of discipleship.
2. *Witnesses to the confrontation.* If the first step does not result in repentance, one or two other members of the community should go back to witness the confrontation and the sinning brother or sister's refusal to repent. They will be able to help arbitrate, or in the case of stubborn rebellion, become witnesses of nonrepentance.
3. *Involvement of the church.* The third step, in the case of nonrepentance, is to bring the complaint before the church. The way in which this was carried out in the small house churches of the early church may be quite different than today. Such a sin would become immediately evident to the community. This may work most effectively when the church leaders are made aware of the situation and are brought into the process of attempted restoration rather than just making a public announcement.
4. *Treat as an unbeliever.* The fourth step of discipline is to treat the sinning brother or sister who refuses to repent like a pagan (*ethnikos*, literally "gentile") or tax collector, the common titles for those who are

consciously rebellious against God and his people. This is best carried out when the church considers the sinning individual not to be a believer. Confessing disciples who live with unconfessed sin indicate by their lives that they are not truly members of Jesus's spiritual family and are not to be allowed to enjoy its fellowship. They should be treated as unbelievers, with the same compassion and urgency needed to encourage them to repent; they are not to receive the same openness to the inner fellowship of the community that is reserved for fellow disciples.

Consensus on Community Discipline and Life (18:18–20). *Consensus in discipline (18:18).* In this context, the community of disciples, the church, is given authority to declare the terms under which God forgives or refuses to forgive the sin of wayward disciples. In other words, the disciples as a whole have a responsibility for declaring the terms under which sins are forgiven or how a person is to be excluded from the fellowship of the local church. The church is the instrument of God, who alone can grant forgiveness of sin or consign a person to judgment. Jesus's statement assures the church that God in heaven confirms its judgment on a sinning brother.

Consensus in praying for God's will in the community (18:19). The correspondence sought in the community of disciples between earth and heaven also promises to guide the church's attempt generally to carry out the will of the heavenly Father on earth.

Consensus in experiencing Jesus's presence within the community (18:20). Jesus himself assumes the place of the divine presence among his disciples, guaranteeing that when his followers reach a consensus as they ask in prayer for guidance in matters of discipline, his Father in heaven will guide them as they carry it out. A special emphasis of Matthew is that Jesus, who is Immanuel ("God with us," 1:23), endows his people with his abiding presence even until the end of the age (28:20). Jesus's risen presence within his community brings radical transformation, with the result that they steadfastly carry out the Father's will in imitation of Jesus's own unswerving commitment to his Father's will.

Forgiveness in the Community toward Sinning Disciples (18:21–35). *Repeated forgiveness (18:21–22).* The teaching within the Judaism of Jesus's day was that three times was enough to show a forgiving spirit. Peter's question appears to be following in that line, wondering how many times he should forgive a person who repeatedly sins against him. His offer to forgive the person seven times, more than double the above-mentioned statement, is magnanimous, reflecting a desire for completeness that the number seven usually evokes.

Jesus's astonishing response is that Peter must forgive not the magnanimous number of seven but countless times. In essence, Jesus seems to be saying that the number doesn't matter. Peter and the rest of the disciples are to continue to forgive without keeping count. The reason for such an unheard of thought is given in the parable that immediately follows—Peter should go on forgiving because the reality of his own forgiveness is demonstrated in the way in which God forgives others.

The parable of the unforgiving and unmerciful servant (18:23–35). Jesus tells Peter and the other disciples what forgiveness is like for those who have encountered the kingdom. That kingdom is like a king who wanted to settle accounts with his servants.

The expression "settle accounts" rings an ominous note of judgment by setting the stage for an accounting of what is owed the king (v. 23). Altogether, the man owes at least two and a half billion dollars. As extreme as those figures are, comparisons are difficult to appreciate since such a sum in first-century Judea or Galilee would be far more disproportionate to the same sum in modern times. Some estimate that the amount is the equivalent of hundreds of billions of dollars.

Since the man is unable to pay such an astronomical figure, he and his family are to be sold to repay the debt, implying that the king will sell them into slavery, a practice common in the ancient world. The servant of the king makes a ridiculous petition, suggesting that with just a bit of patience he can repay the debt. But his overwhelming plight evokes pity from the king and prompts him to give to the servant what he does not deserve: he cancels the debt and releases him. This first scene is a powerful display of the forgiveness that God, who alone is king, displays toward those who have offended him.

But the one who has been forgiven so much does not respond with the same pity, but rather the opposite. The second servant pleads with almost the identical actions and words as the first servant. But instead of reacting with the same compassion and grace, the first servant delivers physical punishment by choking him and, instead of selling him into slavery, throws him into the debtor's prison, an even more severe punishment than that threatened him by the king and which made repaying the debt impossible.

The mercy and benevolence of the master toward the first servant should have so impacted his life and values that he would shower mercy and benevolence on others. Instead, his wicked nature has only taken selfish advantage of the master. Now he will receive the punishment that he deserved in the first place. He is handed over to the "jailers to be tortured" (v. 34). Since it would be impossible for the servant to repay the vast amounts owed, the scene concludes with the grim certainty that he will experience that punishment forever, a harsh metaphorical allusion to an eternal destiny of judgment.

A person who has truly experienced the mercy and grace

of God by responding to the presence of his kingdom will be transformed into Jesus's disciple, which, in a most fundamental way, means experiencing a transformed heart that produces a changed life that gives the same mercy and grace to others that one has received from God. Such a transformation will be evident in the words and actions of a disciple's life. A person who has not truly experienced God's grace and mercy will not experience his forgiveness. He will, like the first servant, accept the personal benefits, but it will be only superficial. It will not penetrate a hard and wicked heart to produce transformation. Such a person will thus experience eternal condemnation. Jesus's disciples must be forgiving to others, for through God's grace and mercy they have experienced his forgiveness.

Application. *Community.* We pride ourselves on our ability to take care of ourselves, to get along without needing anyone. But that's not the way that we were created to be. Community is an important element of God's creation. Despite the devastating effects of sin, community is a stabilizing force that God has established to perpetuate his creation. As the crown of God's creation, humans are designed as the exemplary apex of community.

However, sin disrupts community, because individual humans prioritize their own good over that of the community. But with the arrival of the kingdom of heaven, with its radicalizing of life for those who respond to its invitation, community is now reenvisioned. Three destructive issues are noted: competition, independence, and retribution. Likewise, three qualities to overcome these destructive elements are also noted: humility, accountability, and mercy. This kind of church community will function faithfully as a witness to the presence of Jesus in this age.

Humility reverses competition. The humility Jesus proposes is one in which we place ourselves in an unqualified state of vulnerability to God. That happens in this passage in two primary ways, as humility both creates and advances community.

Instead of aggressively pursuing our own status and life goals by our efforts, we receive life as a gift of the kingdom of heaven. As we enter into that life, we find our own personal worth as disciples of Jesus. As we humbly experience God's grace in being established as Jesus's disciples as we enter the kingdom, community is created.

Humility also advances community. Instead of competing with others to be personally the greatest, our unique individual relationships to Jesus allow us to serve one another for everyone's ultimate good and for the good of God's kingdom in this world. Comparison is a cancer in our relationships that robs the uniqueness of the other person as we elevate ourselves over them. Jesus emphasizes that as we enter the kingdom of heaven as little children, we are likewise to protect others who have humbly entered it (18:5–9).

Accountability overcomes independence. The fierce independence that many desire in the modern world is another evidence of a subtle sinfulness. What overcomes that independence is a proper sense of accountability—others need us. Once we gain God's heart for his children, which prompts him to provide ministering angels for their every need, our own eyes are opened to the needs of those for whom he has given us responsibility, and an accountability relationship is established that creates God's kind of community.

The parable of the lost sheep carries over to the spiritual well-being of all disciples in the community. When we love individuals and desire to treat them with the respect their kinship in the kingdom entitles them, we care much about the direction of their lives. We must never get too preoccupied with our own advancement in Christian service and maturity that we forget that we are here to help other disciples on the path, including those who backslide. We must give ourselves to the prayer, pursuit, and restoration of those gone astray.

Discipline is not usually a popular topic. But it is important for us to try to work through the process practically. The discipline of brothers and sisters is not a pleasant task, but as we follow Scripture's teaching, it will help contribute to a community of disciples that is a faithful witness to the presence of the risen Lord Jesus in our midst. And it is important always to keep in mind that the goal is not discipline itself, or even punishment. The intended goal of all discipline is restoration of the sinning brother or sister to a state of purity and the reestablishment of the fellowship of peace within the body.

Mercy annuls alienation. The key to forgiveness is to stop focusing on what others have done *to* us and focus instead on what Jesus has done *for* us. An unspiritual community is one that does not live in relationship to the reality of the cross and resurrection of Jesus. Rather, it lives according to the prevailing cultural paradigm of values. We may try to gather around like interests, or geographical location, or even political ideologies. But the kind of community that Jesus advances is based on having received mercy and forgiveness, which in turn will impel us to demonstrate mercy and forgiveness.

True reconciliation is not simply a tolerant attitude toward one another in the same living space. It is a real, personal, loving connection between individuals that Jesus desires, and without a heart attitude of forgiveness, this type of connection is not even possible.

Another important facet to consider is that often our forgiveness of others points people toward God's forgiveness of them. Forgiveness not only sustains the intimacy of the community, but it is a powerful device that allows people to make changes in their own lives and to move on toward deeper intimacy with God.

MATTHEW 19:1–30

Original Meaning

Journeying through Judea to Jerusalem (19:1–2). Following his teaching concerning forgiveness, Matthew records events that reveal what life is to be like in his community of disciples.

Sanctity of Marriage in the Community (19:3–12). *The question of divorce (19:3–9).* A hotbed of discussion surrounded the interpretations of Moses's divorce regulation (Deut 24:1). The more conservative school of Shammai held to the letter of the Mosaic law and said that the word "indecent" means "unchastity." The more liberal school of Hillel interpreted "indecent" to mean that "he may divorce her even if she spoiled a dish for him."

Jesus goes back to the beginning of creation to demonstrate God's intention for the institution of marriage (Gen 2:24). God designed his human creatures as male and female, with marriage a permanent bond of a man and woman into one new union that is consecrated by physical intercourse. God hates divorce, because it tears apart what should be considered a permanent union (cf. Mal 2:16). So Jesus avoids the Pharisaic argument and demands that humans should go back to God's intention and understand that marriage is part of God's original design. Divorce separates what God brought together.

But the Pharisees point to the Mosaic law that allowed a husband to give to his wife a certificate of divorce. Since sinful abuse of a marriage partner was a harsh reality in the ancient world, Moses instituted a regulation designed to do three things:

1. protect the sanctity of marriage from something "indecent" defiling the relationship;
2. protect the woman from a husband who might simply send her away without any cause; and
3. document her status as a legitimately divorced woman, so that she would not be thought a harlot or a runaway adulteress.

Jesus counters by once again going to God's original intention with marriage. Somewhere in each relationship that experiences divorce, something has gone wrong that shouldn't have. So Moses gave God's prescription for dealing with sin. Jesus emphasizes that divorce should never be understood to be a morally neutral option. It always evidences the presence of sin, the hardness of heart. The Pharisees are focused on the wrong issue. They are not looking at God's original intention but at Moses's prescription.

Jesus allows for an exception to protect the nonoffending partner and to protect the institution of marriage from being an indecent sham. Such an occasion occurs when a person has committed *porneia*. Since "adultery" is already specified by another word (*moicheuō*; 5:27–28; 19:9), *porneia* must be something less specific than sexual infidelity, but, following the Mosaic intention, more than a frivolous excuse. The semantic range of *porneia* includes whatever intentionally divides the marital relationship, possibly including, but not limited to, related sexual sins such as incest, homosexuality, prostitution, molestation, or indecent exposure .Jesus does not require divorce but allows it to occur to protect the person violated.

The question of singleness in the community (19:10–12). Jesus does not contradict his earlier confirmation that the right order of God's creation is for men and women to marry and remain so permanently, but neither is he going to adopt the disciple's cynical attitude toward a life of singleness. Singleness is an appropriate alternative for those for whom it has been given as their lot in life, whether they are a literal (either born or man-made) or figurative eunuch. But nowhere in Scripture is celibacy seen as a higher form of spirituality than being married.

The Kingdom Community Belongs to Children (19:13–15). The disciples probably do not want the children brought to Jesus because they had an insignificant societal status and are interrupting what they consider to be more important matters of proclaiming the kingdom of heaven. Jesus once again turns prevailing societal values on their head to show that childlikeness is not only a prerequisite for entrance to the kingdom but is also a necessary lifetime characteristic for Jesus's disciples. As weak, defenseless, vulnerable children, they must continue to maintain dependence on their heavenly Father for the purpose, power, and significance of their life of discipleship.

The Tragedy of the Rich Young Man (19:16–22). This young man seems to believe that there is something deficient in obeying the law to gain eternal life. Jesus gets the young man to focus on God alone as the only one who is good, to whom he must come to gain eternal life (v. 17). Jesus is not denying he is good or that he is equal with God, but he is trying to get the rich young man to see that only in understanding God as good can he discover that good deeds beyond the law do not obtain eternal life. Jesus takes the young man back to obeying the law as an expression of faith in the truly good God. This is not to *earn* life eternal but is to humbly obey the law in childlike faith in God's goodness.

In verse 18 the young man responds to Jesus's directive to obey the commandments by asking, "Which ones?" Jesus replies by giving a representative listing of the law, including five of the commandments in the second part of the Decalogue and the second of the two greatest commandments. With unblinking confidence, the young man declares that he has kept them all. And he does not mean only those commandments cited by Jesus, for he understands these commandments as representative of the entire law. His obedience to the law is complete.

But obedience to the law still does not satisfy this young man. He senses that he still lacks something: "What do I still lack?" (v. 20). Jesus could have challenged him further to find where some lack of obedience might be found and corrected, but the issue is not one of external performance. Instead, Jesus takes the young man to the inner place where his values are formed (his heart) and challenges him to see what his most cherished value actually is—in essence, the ruling god of his life.

His wealth has become his means to personal identity, power, purpose, and meaning in life. It has, in a real sense, become his god. Thus, Jesus calls him to exchange the god of wealth for following him as the one true God. He will continue to lack until he becomes like a child—powerless, defenseless, and needing his Father's influence.

The response of the young man comprises one of the truly heartbreaking verses in Scripture. The young man knows that Jesus has correctly pinpointed what is lacking in his life. He knows what issues are at stake. His many possessions have captivated his heart, and he cannot exchange this god for Jesus. So he goes away with great distress, knowing deep in his heart that his decision has eternal consequences. He knew all along what he was lacking for eternal life, and when he is offered it by Jesus, he rejects the invitation to life.

The Gracious Reward for Those Who Follow Jesus (19:23–30). *The difficulty of rich people entering the kingdom of heaven (19:23–26).* The disciples are shocked at Jesus's statement about the difficulty of wealthy people entering the kingdom of God, because wealth was often equated with the blessing of divine favor. Jesus knows that riches can keep people's eyes off of God. But he also knows God's operation in the lives of people and says that even if it is impossible with humankind, if a rich person truly trusts God, God will make it possible. All we need to do is to acknowledge what rules our lives and exchange that treasure for the treasure of Jesus as one's God.

Reward for following Jesus (19:27–30). Peter gets Jesus's point, but not fully. He rightly understands that the focus is not solely on the rich person but on all people, because it provides a pattern for everyone. He and the others have left all to follow Jesus. But Peter should have left it there. He has already entered the kingdom of heaven and found salvation. Instead, he focuses on rewards.

Jesus ends by showing that serving him and the kingdom of heaven for the primary purpose of receiving rewards and gaining personal prominence is the least noble of motivations for a disciple. Those who serve for the purpose of gaining rewards will be last, but those who serve for the motivation of obeying Jesus's summons will be first.

Application. *Community.* The life of Jesus becomes the life force of the church as we witness to the reality of the kingdom of heaven. Our witness comes through both our declaration of the gospel message and our example of living out the gospel message as a family of faith characterized by humility, purity, accountability, discipline, reconciliation, restoration, and forgiveness. Two primary areas call for our attention: the sanctity of marriage and the "god" of one's life.

The sanctity of marriage. The same God who established marriage gives the courage and strength to complete that marriage. Those who receive the love of God in a personal relationship with Jesus Christ have an inexhaustible store of love for each other by which they can commit themselves to what God wants to do through them to serve each other. Thus, marriage is a mystical union and a source of grace to all who enter it under the blessing of God, and it remains a bond of peace with Christ at the center. This is what marriage can be, if we beautify and enrich it by our tender care, our attention to the little things, and our patience and sacrifice to each other.

A bride and groom are committing themselves for life, for the long haul. Many today do not make that kind of vow. Their vow is conditional, whether they say so or not. A marriage that is centered in Christ vows from the first to remain together no matter what comes between them.

Divorce is an exception. So if divorce is not to be considered an option, why does Jesus allow it? Jesus allows divorce as an exception because some destructive sin has entered into the relationship and destroyed the union God established. Divorce is permitted to protect the nonoffending spouse. By allowing divorce as an exception, Jesus is condemning the hardness of heart that leads to sinful behavior and is indirectly proposing a renovation of the heart, as seen through his kingdom program, which will affect these areas of life. Allowing divorce and presenting the certificate to protect the rights of the injured party prevents further damage in a fallen world.

Adultery and desertion. In the case of *porneia*, which we understand to be basically equivalent to adultery but includes anything that intentionally divides the marital relationship, divorce and, by extension, remarriage are permitted. The apostle Paul included another exception: desertion by an unbelieving partner. Together, Jesus's and Paul's teachings address the two main components of the marriage covenant—interpersonal intimacy culminating in sexual relations and personal allegiance or loyalty.

Those within a marriage that is experiencing either of these exceptions should not see divorce as mandatory; they should seek all avenues to have the sinning partner repent and attempt to restore the marriage to a healthy state. This is not easy because of the hurt that has been experienced, with the resulting absence of trust. But the reality of kingdom life that Jesus brings is the divine source of healing and recovery that brings the Spirit's regenerative powers into all relationships within the community.

The sanctity of singleness. Those who have chosen to remain single need us as their community of brothers and sisters. Jesus declares that celibacy is an acceptable lifestyle for those for whom it is given by God. Unfortunately, many of our churches endorse marriage as a sign of maturity, and those who are married tend to get the more "responsible" ministry opportunities in the church. Single people are sometimes seen as those who have not yet "settled down." We should reevaluate the way we view and value single people within our ministries—after all, both the Lord Jesus as well as the apostle Paul were single.

Reconciliation and restoration. Divorce is not the unpardonable sin, but we tend to go to extremes with those who have unbiblically divorced and remarried. We either relegate them to an outcast status with permanent stigma, or else we glibly act as though it never happened. The themes of repentance, forgiveness, restoration, and reconciliation that marked Jesus's community instructions in chapter 18 must guide our thinking in all of these situations.

The "god" of a person's life. Even Christians can misplace their allegiance, so each person must be honest with themselves to know what is the treasure of their heart. In order to claim Jesus as Savior, each person must exchange the god of his or her life to have Jesus as God. The cost varies from person to person according to the god of each person's life, but it must be faced. So what rules our lives? What must be dethroned as that which is keeping us from experiencing freedom and fullness of life?

Salvation is not earned. It is received by faith through God's grace. But at the same time salvation is costly. It cost Jesus his life, and it costs us our lives as well. Being a disciple of Jesus is for those who have counted the cost and want real life, eternal life, received from a Savior who came to earth to seek and to save us and who lovingly and persistently transforms us into his image. These are tough words if we fear and resist him. But they are words of hope, promise, peace, and joy if we are tired of ruling our lives ourselves.

MATTHEW 20:1–34

Original Meaning

The Parable of the Vineyard Workers: Gratitude and Service in the Kingdom Community (20:1–16). Jesus pictures harvest time, when a landowner hired seasonal workers to help with his harvest. He went early to the marketplace, where laborers gathered. The agreed-upon sum of a denarius was expected because a denarius was a day's wage for a laborer. The landowner needed more laborers for his abundant harvest, so he went back to the marketplace and found people, expecting most likely to receive a proportionate reduction from the day's regular denarius. The abundance of the harvest was such that the landowner went again at the sixth hour (12:00 noon) and the ninth hour (3:00 p.m.). Needing still more laborers, the landowner went back to the town marketplace and found workers who would have expected only one-twelfth of the amount of those who worked for the denarius.

At the end of the day, a shocking development unfolds. The laborers who were hired last are paid the full denarius, the wages expected for a full day's work. This built up the expectations that those who worked longer would receive a proportional increase in their wages. But no! Those who worked the entire long, hot day received the same wage as those who only worked an hour, which unsurprisingly causes the first laborers to protest that the others didn't deserve equal treatment.

With a measure of gentleness but with the intent to straighten out this attitude, the landowner addressed one of the first hired laborers as "friend" (v. 13). The expression "are you envious" (v. 15) can be rendered literally, "Is your eye evil," indicating that the laborer could not be thankful because he was blinded by his self-centered envy. If a disciple's eyes are fixed on earthly, material treasure as his or her value, personal significance, and earthly security, then the darkness of that evil value is the state of that person's heart. When we focus on something evil, the eye becomes the conduit by which the evil fills the inner person.

So this parable is a lesson on gratitude and motivation in service. The parable is not about salvation or gaining eternal life, because salvation is not earned by works. Nor is the parable about rewards for service, because God will reward believers differently according to their service. Rather, this is a profound parable about what should be the disciple's motivation for service. We should serve out of gratitude, for it is only through the intervention of Jesus that any disciple receives anything. We should be concerned only to rejoice when others are called to the kingdom without serving as long or as hard as we have.

The Third Passion Prediction (20:17–19). With the fateful event in Jerusalem only weeks away, Jesus takes the Twelve aside to give them another prediction of his impending betrayal. This is the third of four predictions of his arrest and crucifixion, but the drama is heightened by the first reference to Jerusalem, the first mention of the religious leaders' condemnation of Jesus to death, and the first mention of the gentiles who will carry out the execution.

The Example of Jesus for Community Sacrifice, Suffering, and Service (20:20–28). The mother of Zebedee's sons comes up to Jesus with her sons and, "kneeling down, asked a favor of him" (v. 20). This woman has been a faithful follower of

Jesus. Later identified as Salome, she is among the women who attends Jesus at the cross and witnesses the empty tomb. She is likely the sister of Mary, Jesus's mother, and so she is Jesus's aunt, and her sons, James and John, are his cousins on his mother's side.

As she kneels before Jesus, Salome shows her deference to Jesus as her messianic master, but she also comes apparently to exercise her earthly kinship advantage with Jesus. The mother's request for a favor is forthright. She is not pushing her sons into something that they do not want, but together they are demonstrating their commitment to support Jesus in what lies ahead. The mother desires for her sons to have the highest positions of importance when Jesus inaugurates his future kingdom.

Jesus addresses the brothers directly. They (and their mother) have only a faint idea of what lies yet ahead. The "cup" (v. 22) throughout Scripture refers figuratively to one's divinely appointed destiny, whether it was one of blessing and salvation or of wrath and disaster. Jesus is referring to his forthcoming cup of suffering on the cross, to which he has just given his third prediction.

The brothers' response, "We can" (v. 22), indicates that they misunderstand Jesus to be challenging them to see if they are willing to endure the difficulties that lie ahead in the battle to establish the eschatological kingdom. The disciples will reaffirm their commitment to Jesus and his destiny in the Upper Room, but they have little knowledge of what lies ahead. Their bravado is commendable for its commitment to Jesus and their willingness to face difficulties for the reward of future glory, but they don't really know themselves or the future.

Jesus looks down the corridor of time to when the brothers will suffer for the kingdom of heaven. James became an early martyr of the church (Acts 12:1–2), and John experienced persecution and exile, although apparently not martyrdom (Rev 1:9). They will share in Jesus's cup of blessing, but they must submit to the Father's will for their future, just as Jesus is doing. Jesus has come to fulfill the task assigned by the Father, which is not the path of glory but of servanthood. The disciples will see that there is no less requirement of submission for them as well.

The other disciples are probably indignant, not so much because of the immodesty of the request of James and John, but because of the attempt to use their mother's family relationship to Jesus as an unfair advantage to get what they themselves want. Jesus gathers all the disciples together to overturn their strictly human ambitions by making a contrast between the world's conception of greatness and that in the kingdom of heaven.

Jesus's disciples have the ambition to be greatest and to be first, so Jesus gives them the means by which they can do so according to the values of the kingdom of God. They must arrange their lives with the goal of giving themselves for the benefit of others. The ultimate example for the disciples is Jesus's own life. Jesus has willingly set aside that prerogative for a higher purpose—namely, to serve by giving his life as a ransom for many.

Merciful Healing of Two Blind Men in Jericho En Route to Jerusalem (20:29–34). This city was not the ancient city of Old Testament fame, which was still inhabited. The new Jericho refers to the developments surrounding a huge palace complex first built by the Hasmoneans on a three-acre site about a mile south of the ancient city mound, which was greatly expanded by Herod the Great. Matthew records this healing as Jesus is leaving Jericho, while Luke writes that Jesus is drawing near to Jericho (Luke 18:35). This can be most easily reconciled in the light of the phenomenon of two Jerichos still being inhabited, with Jesus leaving the old site and entering the new Jericho on his way to Jerusalem.

A similar scene earlier in the Galilean ministry indicates that this type of encounter was relatively frequent as Jesus passed through new areas. His remarkable reputation preceded him. The blind men understand Jesus to be the "Son of David"—a messianic title—so they ask for the gift of messianic mercy to heal their blindness (v. 30). Although he has experienced increasing rejection from his own people and will face ultimate betrayal and rejection when he enters Jerusalem, Jesus continues to have compassion on those in great need, so he touches their eyes and heals them. Thereupon they follow Jesus.

The contrast in this incident is on the crowds who try to silence the two blind men. Yet the two men are the ones to whom Jesus directs his ministry; the crowds remain only spectators. Those without natural ability to follow Jesus are able through his healing touch to follow him.

Application. Unless we watch our motives, we can do the right things for the wrong reasons and fall into hypocrisy. As we look at this concluding section that deals with the community of Jesus's disciples, we must evaluate our own actions in the light of two primary motivations for service—gratitude and servanthood. The more we focus on the example of Jesus in his earthly ministry, who came not to be served but to serve, the more we will be able to purify why we do what we do.

The attitude of gratitude. Gratitude is the response of the believing person to the goodness of God's grace in creation and redemption, making gratitude the authentic hallmark of the disciple of Jesus. We know there is nothing we have that we have not first received. And out of that knowledge comes the wellspring of gratitude that affects what we are, what we do and say, and how we conduct our lives. Gratitude impels our worship, motivates our service, and inspires our continual thankfulness.

The profound significance of gratitude is that it impacts not just the one toward whom we should be grateful but all other relationships as well. Those who give to the needy, pray, and fast in the secrecy of the heart will be rewarded. But rewards are mentioned as the by-product of a life that is free from self-advancement.

What we do in giving ourselves in service of the kingdom of heaven flows from a grateful heart. God created the original man and woman to serve as stewards of his creation. Tragically, with the entrance of sin came the distortion of this stewardship, so that men and women became self-centered, with the desire to take instead of give, to dominate instead of serve, and to hate instead of love. But when God's love impelled him to give his Son, a fundamental change occurred in those who humble themselves to receive his gift. That transformation reverses the impulse from taking to giving, from self-centeredness to other-centeredness. Because of the impact of God's love in our lives, we can now love (1 John 4:19). And because of the transforming impact of God's gift of grace in our lives, we can now give ourselves to serve others.

That is what lies behind the concept of the Christian life as being able to be generous and to give all day and every day as a pattern of life. The giving of ourselves—including our careers, our relationships, our talents, our resources, and our time—flows from a transformation of our lives produced by God's giving to us. The motivation for devoting ourselves to service comes simply from a grateful heart.

The ambition to serve. Think of your own career, your involvement in community activities, or even your own church. The way of the world is getting ahead by being more aggressive, more powerful, more intimidating, more demanding than the other person. In our passage, James and John incurred the anger of the other apostles when they approached Jesus and asked for prominent positions in his kingdom. They were ready and willing to endure whatever hardship was necessary, whatever sacrifice was required, as long as they could get positions of prominence in Jesus's kingdom.

Sacrifice is a concept that is readily understood when we think of it in terms of our own benefit. "No pain, no gain" is an old adage. It communicates a well-known and appreciated value—we must sacrifice present pleasure for personal future gain. That may mean the pain of physical exercise for the gain of a healthy heart, or the pain of sacrificing to save enough to gain that long-anticipated vacation. Jesus does not overturn that principle completely, but he does reverse the focus: "My pain, *others'* gain."

But this does not mean that all ambition is bad. Ambition is bad when it is greedy, when it hurts and uses people, when it exalts us over others, when it is prideful. But the right kind of ambition involves hitching our aspirations to selfless servanthood. James's and John's strength was a weakness because it was greedy and selfish. But when ambition is selflessly directed toward service, God can use it in powerful ways. John's ambitious drive guided and nurtured the early church in Jerusalem. James's zeal resulted in his being the first apostle to suffer martyrdom, which became a turning point in the courage of the church. Disciples of Jesus are to be just as goal-oriented as anyone in the world, but our ambition must be linked to selfless servanthood—giving our lives as a source of blessing to those for whom we have responsibility.

MATTHEW 21:1–46

Original Meaning

The Climactic Entry into Jerusalem: Jesus's Authority as Messiah (21:1–11). *Preparations for the entry (21:1–7).* Near Bethany is the town of Bethphage, which Matthew tells us is the place from which Jesus directs his entrance to Jerusalem. Jesus sends two disciples into Bethphage, where they are to obtain the donkey and colt for Jesus's entry into Jerusalem. They are to untie them and bring them to Jesus, and if anyone questions their actions they are to say, "The Lord needs them" (v. 3). The term "Lord" (*kyrios*) can designate one's earthly master or one's deity. It is difficult to say what either the disciples or anyone else would have understood *kyrios* to mean in this context, but Jesus plainly intends it to refer to himself as the one who sovereignly superintends these events. At this climactic time of his earthly ministry, Jesus reveals himself with increasing clarity.

Jesus intentionally declares his identity to the nation. Jesus's descent from the Mount of Olives into Jerusalem evokes images of Zechariah's prophecy of the Lord's fighting against the nations with his feet on the Mount of Olives and liberating Jerusalem (Zech 14:3–21). Further excitement is stimulated by Jesus's riding on a colt, fulfilling Zechariah's prophecy of the messianic king who comes to liberate his people (Zech 9:9–13). The acclaim of the crowds comes from their own expectations of what they want Jesus to be. But for Jesus it is a self-disclosure to Israel, which will seal the fate of his people but will also be a testimony to his disciples once they reflect on these events with eyes of faith after his crucifixion and resurrection.

The fulfillment phrase, "this took place to fulfill what was spoken through the prophet" (v. 4), is most likely Matthew's comment that Jesus's entrance into Jerusalem on a colt fulfills the prophecy of Zechariah 9:9. The time has now come for Jesus to declare openly that he is the righteous Davidic Messiah. He comes as the righteous one who offers salvation, not as a conquering military leader. He comes with reconciliation, as did rulers who sometimes rode a donkey in times of peace. Through this event, Jesus delineates that he is not coming to bring military conquest.

The disciples place their outer cloaks on both animals, but Jesus sits on the cloaks placed on the foal. There is no mistaking that he proceeds into Jerusalem as the anticipated king, the messianic Son of David. But his entry is triumphant in a paradoxical sense because his victory will come by way of death on a cross.

Jesus's climactic entry to Jerusalem (21:8–11). The events for which Jesus has prepared the disciples now begin to unfold. As he descends from the Mount of Olives to enter the city, "a very large crowd" gathers to acknowledge his arrival in Jerusalem (v. 8). Palms symbolized Jewish nationalism and victory, such as when Judas Maccabeus and his followers recovered Jerusalem and the temple desecrated by Antiochus (2 Macc 10:7; cf. 1 Macc 13:51). Many coins at the time of Jesus contain palms, expressive of nationalism generally, both Jewish and Roman.

This large crowd is a mixed sort. Within the crowd are also those who are not Jesus's disciples but who are part of the typical crowds that followed Jesus throughout his ministry. They follow with their own particular expectations, here thinking perhaps that Jesus has come to liberate Jerusalem and the people of Israel from Roman oppression. Others are there most likely out of curiosity and are caught up in the excitement.

The crowds shout out "Hosanna," which is the transliteration of the Hebrew expression that means, "O save" (v. 9). As the advancing crowd enters the city, "the whole city was stirred and asked, 'Who is this?'" (v. 10). The expression "the whole city" indicates that the religious establishment is once again paranoid of this person whom they believe may attempt to usurp their power, and they want an explanation of who Jesus intends to present himself to be.

The crowd's answer generally is, "This is Jesus, the prophet from Nazareth in Galilee" (v. 11). That answer indicates the mixed nature of those attending Jesus's entrance. Some in the crowd call him a prophet, which many in his ministry saw him to be. Others who have called out "Hosanna" seem to expect Jesus to bring liberation, as had the kings of ancient Israel and the Maccabees of more recent times.

But Jesus has undertaken a different kind of "triumphal entry" from what many among the crowd expected. Jesus will triumph over the enemy of sin, bringing salvation to his people through his righteous sacrifice on the cross that looms ahead. Although the crowd gives great acclaim, Jesus knows why they are really welcoming him. He knows their nationalistic ambitions and fickleness; thus, Luke in his Gospel tells us that Jesus weeps over the city (Luke 19:42–44).

The Temple Actions: Jesus's Pronouncement on the Temple Establishment (21:12–17). Matthew condenses some of the narrative of Jesus's activities during Holy Week, which is the case with his narrative here of the chronology of the temple activities. A comparison of the other Gospels indicates a fuller sequence of events. After his climactic entry to Jerusalem, Jesus goes to the temple precinct area and surveys the activities being conducted (Mark 11:11). Later that day (i.e., Sunday afternoon), he returns to Bethany with the Twelve (Mark 11:11), where they spend the night. Early on Monday morning Jesus and the disciples return to Jerusalem, but on the way he symbolically curses the fig tree (Mark 11:12–14). After entering the city, Jesus proceeds to the temple. At this point Matthew picks up the narrative.

Jesus's action in the temple (21:12). Jesus immediately begins to drive out all who are both buying and selling and overturns the tables of the moneychangers and the benches of those selling doves. Both the moneychangers and those buying and selling are making this simply a commercial operation, and the temptation for abuse is real, since surplus tax was consigned to the temple fund. Doves were the sacrifice made by the poor (who could not afford animal sacrifices) as well as by those making a variety of types of personal offerings. Temple commerce was at times notorious for exploiting the disadvantaged.

A den of robbers (21:13). The religious leaders are treating the temple as robbers do their dens—a place of refuge for both accumulating illicitly gained wealth and for plotting future illegal activities (Jer 7:11). The term "robber" (*lēstēs*) often designates an insurrectionist. This may be a subtle use of the term to indicate that the temple authorities are making it a nationalistic stronghold, or more subtly, a place where they are insurrectionists against God's intended plan for the temple.

Jesus's action here has often been called a "cleansing" of the temple. While corrupt practices are certainly being rebuked, Jesus goes beyond cleansing to intentionally enact a symbolic act of judgment against the religious leadership of Israel. This is also a dramatic statement on Jesus's authority over the purposes of the sacrificial practices at the temple, which will be fulfilled with his impending crucifixion, as is so dramatically announced by God in the tearing of the veil or curtain at his death (Matt 27:51).

Healings and praise (21:14–16). Jesus's actions in the temple in pronouncing judgment and healing the blind and lame should have caused the religious authorities to acknowledge his authority as the Messiah, the Son of David, whom the children innocently and unknowingly identify. Instead, they become "indignant" at Jesus's challenge to their authority (v. 15). The word "indignant" (*aganakteō*) is the same term used of the ten disciples' reaction to the sons of Zebedee and their mother's attempt to use kinship privileges to obtain places of privilege in Jesus's kingdom (20:24). The religious leaders recognize Jesus as a threat to their positions of religious prominence.

Return to Bethany (21:17). After the dramatic events of this Monday of Holy Week, Jesus leaves the religious leaders, most likely with their fury beginning to boil. He will return to the city and the temple the next day to engage them in extended debate, but for now he returns to Bethany. Jerusalem was packed with pilgrims during the Passover season, and many found shelter outside the city. Most likely Jesus stays at the home of Lazarus, whom he raised from the dead, and of his sisters, Mary and Martha.

Cursing the Fig Tree: Jesus's Judgment of the Nation (21:18–22). The appearance of leaves on a fig tree in this region was a promise of the sweet early fig. But the tree is unproductive, with no figs at all. This becomes an appropriate object for Jesus to use to indicate Israel's spiritual condition, providing a striking lesson for the disciples. Just as the fig tree's fruitfulness was a sign of its health, so fruitfulness was a sign of Israel's faithfulness to God's covenantal standards. Now that Israel, especially represented by its religious leadership, has perverted the temple practices and has not repented at the appearance of Jesus Messiah proclaiming the arrival of the kingdom of heaven, Israel is being judged by God.

The disciples are amazed that the fig tree can wither so quickly, simply at the word of Jesus, but he tells them that they also can do such a thing, and even more. Jesus's cursing the fig tree is not a fit of temper but a symbolic act, demonstrating that God's creatures must produce that for which they were created—to carry out God's will, which means entering into a discipleship relationship with him and then demonstrating fruit from that relationship in a life of faith empowered by prayer.

Using the handy object of the Mount of Olives or perhaps even the Temple Mount across the Kidron Valley, Jesus says that one with faith can throw the mountain into the sea. Then, similar to an earlier saying (see 17:20–21), Jesus declares, "If you believe, you will receive whatever you ask for in prayer" (v. 22). The point here is not the disciples' amount of faith to do great things but rather their trust in accomplishing God's will in God's power. If God directs them to move a mountain, God will supply the power for it to be accomplished. They simply must be obedient and say yes to his will.

Controversies in the Temple Court over Jesus's Authority (21:23–27). Since Jesus had the previous day symbolically judged the religious leaders publicly, shaming them before the crowds over whom they exercised religious authority, they respond by asking, "By what authority are you doing these things?" (v. 23). Instead of cowering before their challenge, Jesus engages the religious leaders in a series of rabbinic-type debates that follow a typical pattern: a hostile question, followed by a counter-question, admission, and final rejoinder.

Jesus's question is whether they think John the Baptist had divine or merely human authority to carry out his ministry of calling all Israel to repentance in the light of the soon-coming arrival of the Messiah. Jesus lays a logical trap. They cannot alienate the people by saying that John's highly popular prophetic ministry was not from God, but neither can they endorse the very prophet who had condemned them for not repenting. The implication that Jesus demands them to admit is that John's authority as a true prophet was derived from God, and John had pointed to Jesus as the Messiah. If they respond that John's authority came from God, that would validate Jesus's authority to say and do what he wishes, even in the temple, which would be a clear answer to their question. If these religious leaders will not endorse the prophet from God who pointed to Jesus, they surely will not endorse him as the Messiah, whose most recent actions have demonstrated that he has come to judge their leadership in Israel.

These religious leaders recognize the dilemma Jesus has put them in, so they refuse to answer. That refusal shows their dishonesty, and they must accept their culpability. Therefore, Jesus feels no obligation to answer their question about his authority, since he has forced them to accept their own responsibility for how they have responded to him. They are spiritually dishonest by not acknowledging the truth they know and have hardened their hearts against God's revelation. This draws dangerously close to the unforgivable sin that the Pharisees were precariously close to committing earlier in Matthew's Gospel.

Parables of Condemnation Directed toward the Religious Leadership of Israel (21:28–46). *The parable of the two sons: the religious leadership did not heed John the Baptist (21:28–32).* The first parable is about two sons who were asked to work in their father's vineyard. This parable presses Jesus's point that the religious leaders have not rightly recognized John the Baptist's divinely endowed prophetic ministry. This parable and the next bring to mind the religious leaders, who have been called to serve God by serving the nation of Israel. In the parable, one son initially refuses to go, but then does go. The other initially agrees to go, but then refuses.

The son that originally refused but then obeyed is like those in Israel who were disobedient to the law, such as the tax collectors and prostitutes. But when John arrived with the message of true righteousness through the announcement of the arrival of the kingdom of God, they obeyed God's call through John and were repentant. By contrast, the religious leaders are like the son who agreed but did nothing. They were externally obedient to the law, but when God sent his messenger, John the Baptist, they did not obey God's message through him.

The parable of the wicked tenants: God takes away the kingdom from Israel (21:33–46). Jesus continues the vineyard metaphor of the previous parable. Clearly alluding to Isaiah 5:1–7, he intensifies his rebuke of the religious leadership by pronouncing God's judgment: the kingdom will be taken away from Israel and given to another people.

Many absentee landowners were notorious for their harsh treatment of their tenants. Here the scene is reversed, and the landowner's servants are abused when they come to collect a portion of the harvest. The treatment of these servants calls to mind the same fate that befell God's prophets throughout Old Testament history.

Finally, the landowner sends his own son to make a collection. This is an unmistakable allusion to God the Father's sending of his Son, Jesus, which is further evidence of Jesus's self-consciousness of his identity as God's unique Son. Through this parable Jesus is making a public assertion of his divine sonship to the religious leadership and the crowds.

The story turns unthinkably ugly when the tenants say, "'This is the heir. Come, let's kill him and take his inheritance.' So they took him and threw him out of the vineyard and killed him" (v. 38). The religious leaders have not acknowledged Jesus publicly as God's Son, nor have they publicly condemned Jesus out of fear of the crowds. But Jesus foretells what they will do to him.

Yet the Jewish leaders cannot get away with their duplicity. Jesus concludes the parable by foretelling their demise. He places their self-condemnation in their own mouth by asking these religious leaders what the vineyard owner will do to those wicked tenants when he comes. They reply with the only just thing that should be done. This is fitting self-condemnation, which Jesus makes explicit as he foretells their judgment and rejection.

Jesus climaxes his indictment of the religious leadership with a stinging pronouncement: "therefore I tell you that the kingdom of God will be taken away from you and given to a people who will produce its fruit" (v. 43). The privileged role of the religious leaders in caring for God's "vineyard" is now being taken away. But this is also a hint that Israel's privileged role in the establishment of God's kingdom will be taken away and given to another people. "People" is the singular *ethnos* (v. 43), which prepares for the time when the church, a nation of gathered people, will include both Jew and gentile in the outworking of God's kingdom in the present age.

The two parts of the stone imagery in verse 44 are somewhat enigmatic, but the emphasis on judgment is clear. The first half speaks of the personal culpability of individuals who stumble or fall into sin by not rightly recognizing the identity of Jesus. This probably draws on the imagery of Isaiah 8:13–15.

The second half of verse 44 emphasizes the absolute judgment that will fall on those who stumble over Jesus, probably drawing on the well-known stone imagery in Daniel 2:34–35, 44–45. Jesus returns to the stone motif to issue a warning to Israel and her leadership. Not only will the privileged position and role in the outworking of the kingdom of God be taken away, but judgment also will come on those rejecting the Son. Those who stumble over the stone and try to destroy it, such as the religious leaders, will be destroyed. At the end Jesus will come as judge and fall on those who have rejected him.

Application. *Walking with Jesus through Holy Week.* The magnitude of the Holy Week events for the future of humanity must be understood correctly. We must understand what Jesus intended in Holy Week so that our own expectations and dreams are kept in line with his. Perhaps to help with this we might begin the practice of "walking" with Jesus through Holy Week. Try to visualize what Jesus was doing every day of that week, starting from the celebration with his disciples on the Saturday evening prior to Palm Sunday, all the way to the resurrection on Easter Sunday. Try to imagine what Jesus was doing at each hour of each day—was he enjoying the last fellowship with his disciples, or was he alone preparing for the experience of the cross? Perhaps try to put yourself in his place to feel what he was feeling. Was it poignant joy when Mary anointed his feet, or painful rejection as Peter and the other disciples denied him? What was he feeling as Judas betrayed him?

We might also attempt to imagine his incredible suffering as he endured the horrors of his crucifixion and separation from God, yet we may also try to imagine the incredible joy as he experienced the resurrection with his victory over sin accomplished. As we walk with Jesus through these various events, we can have an incredibly wide range of experiences, from feelings of tenderness and intimacy with him, to anger at what others did to him, to utter amazement over the profound experience of our Lord on the cross and out of the empty tomb in resurrection.

The impact of Holy Week on our lives. We can be drawn into a more intimate relationship with Jesus after having walked with him through all of the events of this week. We will have entered into the fellowship that he experienced with his closest followers that fateful week—the adrenaline rush of the entry into Jerusalem and the clearing of the temple, the tenderness of the final moments of silent Wednesday and the Upper Room supper, the heartbreak of seeing them turn away from him in his hour of greatest need and then even deny him. We will have followed Jesus into the garden where, in utter anguish, he prays for a different path but then resolutely accepts the Father's will of going to the cross. We will have drawn as close as we dare to witness his physical pain of scourging and crucifixion and have tried as feebly as we can to comprehend the abandonment he experiences from God. And we will have, as Paul says, experienced being raised with him from the dead as we reconsider and reclaim our own salvation experience. Walking with Jesus during Holy Week is a practice worthy of our consideration.

MATTHEW 22:1–46

Original Meaning

The Parable of the Wedding Banquet: Responses to the Invitation to the Kingdom (22:1–14). *Rejections of the invitations to the wedding (22:1–7).* The parable takes its first surprising turn because some have apparently overlooked the initial invitation to the wedding. Although one might overlook a first invitation, the refusal of a direct invitation from the king would be unthinkable—a dangerous affront to the monarch. Yet the king's graciousness wins the day, and he reissues the invitation, now elaborating on the bounty of the celebration.

Some of the invitees still reject the king's invitation—with trivial excuses. The rest actually abuse and kill the king's messengers. This is an unbelievable insult to the king, who severely punishes his insubordinate subjects with death and fire. This kind of punishment was used only in case of the most serious treason and revolt against a king.

An open invitation to the wedding (22:8–10). Instead of the privileged few being invited to the wedding, the undeserving and unworthy receive an invitation. This continues a theme that Jesus has emphasized throughout his ministry. It is not the externally righteous or healthy but sinners and the sick who are invited to the kingdom of heaven. Only those who recognize their personal helplessness cast aside their self-reliance and self-worthiness to accept the grace of God. The wedding hall is filled with these undeserving guests who respond to the gracious invitation.

Inappropriate garments for the wedding (22:11–13). The third part of the parable focuses on one of the guests who has gained entrance to the wedding but does not have the appropriate wedding garment. The implication is that the guest has proper clothing available but has declined to wear it. The man is bound and cast into the outer place of weeping and gnashing of teeth, language that commonly refers to eternal judgment. This once again points to the accountability of everyone's response to Jesus's invitation to the kingdom of heaven. Any who insult God's gracious offer of the kingdom of heaven by presuming on it without honoring the Son will receive due judgment.

Many invited, few chosen (22:14). Israel and her leadership had been known as the "chosen," but even this privilege is lost through unresponsiveness to Jesus's invitation to the kingdom of heaven. Therefore, while there is an open invitation to the kingdom, from the divine perspective it is only God's sovereign choice that effects salvation. From a human perspective it is only those who respond to the call appropriately that are part of the banquet. Only an appropriate response reveals God's divine election.

Four Debates with the Religious Leaders concerning Jesus's Authority and Identity (22:15–46). *Paying taxes to Caesar: disciples of the Pharisees and the Herodians (22:15–22).* These disciples are most likely those in training to become full initiates to the brotherhood of the Pharisees and have been immersed in the Pharisaic commitment to the oral law and rigorous practice of their traditions. The Herodians were supporters of the Herodian family and dynasty. They most likely are a loosely organized group with a vested economic and political interest in advancing the Herods' influence in Israel. Although the Herodians and the Pharisees would be at odds on many political and religious issues, here they combine to combat the common threat to their respective power bases.

Calling Jesus "teacher" (v. 16) is an attempt to ingratiate themselves with him by using a title of respect, the equivalent of the Hebrew title "rabbi." They are shamelessly hypocritical in their attempt to disarm Jesus with their flattery. This address, however, is far truer than they realize and is the opposite of their own hypocrisy and that of the religious leaders whom Jesus has condemned throughout his ministry. If these disciples of the Pharisees and Herodians really mean these words, they will become Jesus's disciples.

These visitors to Jesus try to ambush him with a seemingly innocent question. This question reveals a volatile issue in Israel. The people were seething at the exhausting taxation. Some estimate that a Jewish family paid approximately 50 percent of its annual income to these various taxes. If Jesus answers that it is indeed right to pay taxes to Caesar, it will put him in disfavor with the burdened people, who will think that he has capitulated and is now in league with Roman oppression. If Jesus answers that it is not right to pay taxes to Caesar, it can be used against him with the Roman authorities to support their case that he is an insurrectionist. The Pharisees know that either answer will jeopardize Jesus's mission—exactly their intent.

But Jesus reverses the confrontation by taking the offensive. He asks for a coin used for paying the tax, the denarius, which they produce. Replying to their statement that Caesar's portrait and inscription are on the denarius, Jesus avows, "Give back to Caesar what is Caesar's, and to God what is God's" (v. 21). Jesus is not merely attempting to wiggle out of a sticky, logical riddle by offering another. Rather, behind his answer is a profound statement of his role, as well as the way those in the kingdom of God will operate in this world. He has not come as a military or political threat to the established rulers of this world. His kingdom is revolutionary, but until he returns in glory the kingdom will operate within the existing political order. Jesus again is not establishing a political kingdom to oppose Caesar.

We are to pattern our lives in such a way that we show we are God's stewards of all he has created, and we are to use what is his in the way he has designed it to be used. This implies that even what belongs to Caesar is only his in a secondary way. Allegiance to God takes precedence over allegiance to Caesar, especially when Caesar attempts to usurp allegiance to God's will.

Jesus's profound logic undoes the attempt of his enemies to entrap him with their contrived conundrum. They go away, probably back to those who sent them. They are surely chagrined at their failure to trap Jesus, because the Pharisees have sent them after carefully preparing the ambush.

Marriage at the resurrection: Sadducees (22:23–33). Like the Pharisees, the Sadducees try to create a theological trap to demonstrate that Jesus holds to doctrines that are biblically unsubstantiated. They assume their question will stump Jesus theologically. The case they bring could possibly have happened, but they have more malicious intentions. They hope to disclose that Jesus is not qualified as a theological leader and has no right or authority to challenge their authority. Since they do not believe in the resurrection, their question reveals a hypocritical attempt to confound Jesus and others who do believe in the resurrection.

Once again Jesus turns the logic back on his questioners. He starts with their underlying foundational failure. They should recognize that the rest of the Old Testament is also Scripture, where the doctrine of resurrection is clear. He also chides them for denying the reality of the resurrection, for what lies behind any thought of resurrection is the power of God to do so.

Jesus then turns to the specific issue that they have raised. Jesus draws a parallel to angels in order to note that resurrected humans will not continue the practice of marriage. Jesus does not suggest that humans become angels; rather, in the same way that angelic beings do not marry or procreate, the resurrected state ends the practice of marriage and ushers in entirely new relationships between resurrected humans.

Jesus develops a further clinching argument from the Sadducees' authoritative base, the Pentateuch. Drawing on the present tense in Exodus 3:6, Jesus states that the logical implication is that even though the patriarchs have died physically, they still exist as seen by the fact that God continues in a relationship with them as their God, which cannot be sustained with those who no longer exist. If they are still alive even though physically dead, and if the rest of Scripture points to the reality of resurrection, the Sadducees should believe God's power to raise the patriarchs to enjoy his continued purposes for humanity in the kingdom of God.

The crowds express amazement at Jesus's profundity in responding to the Sadducees, but this is not the same as faith. The crowds will soon be swayed by the religious leaders to ask for Jesus's death. Astonishment is not faith; faith comes from conviction, not emotion.

The greatest commandment: A legal expert of the Pharisees (22:34–40). This encounter is initiated by an "expert in the law" (*nomikos*), who approaches Jesus to "test" him (*peirazō*, v. 35). A regular debate went on among rabbis to determine the weighty and light commandments. This legal expert is probably well aware of this discussion.

Jesus's reply is not unexpected. He quotes Deuteronomy 6:5. Jesus continues by quoting from Leviticus 19:18. Jesus is not simply advocating an emotional attachment or an abstract love. In the same way that individuals are called to care for themselves responsibly and attune their lives to carry out God's will in their lives, they are to give themselves to others to care for them responsibly and help them attune their lives to carry out God's will.

These are the greatest commandments because they go to the essence of the way God has created humans to live: giving oneself to God and to others to fulfill his purposes for us as the crown of his creation in displaying in our lives the glory of God's kingdom on earth. Jesus's inauguration of the kingdom enables this to be a concrete reality for his disciples.

The son of David: Pharisees (22:41–46). Jesus goes on the offensive as he poses a question to the Pharisees. Jesus goes to the heart of the issue, challenging their ability to rightly interpret one of the most important messianic texts in the Old Testament. So he prods them: "What do you think about the Messiah? Whose son is he?" (v. 42).

This must have seemed like a simple question to the Pharisees, who answer with, "The son of David." This is the automatic reply, based on common knowledge that the prophesied Messiah (*ho Christos*, "the anointed one") was from the line of David. This is confirmed by common practice, with the recurring declarations of Jesus's messianic identity as "Son of David."

But Jesus presses them further to plumb the depths of their understanding of the true identity of the Messiah from the Old Testament prophecies. The point that Jesus is making is taken from Psalm 110:1, which he quotes—the most quoted Old Testament passage in the New Testament. Familial respect would not expect an older person, such as David, to refer to his offspring as "lord"; rather, the offspring, "son," should refer to David, his "father," as "lord."

In other words, Jesus uses their own Scriptures to point out the obvious implication of these combined points, which the Pharisees cannot avoid. "If then David calls him 'Lord,' how can he be his son?" (v. 45). David says that the coming Messiah is one who is not just his special human descendant but is his "Lord."

The Messiah is more than what the Pharisees have understood the son of David to be. He is more than a human descendant of David. Since the Pharisees do not adequately understand the Old Testament prophecies regarding the Messiah, they cannot possibly understand Jesus's identity. They do not understand the depth of the personal identity of the Messiah in relationship to Yahweh, so they cannot understand the relationship of Jesus to Yahweh.

Matthew narrates the combined reaction to Jesus's final spar with the religious leaders in the temple. Their silence and reticence to question Jesus further is not only the conclusion to the preceding pericope but also the conclusion to the series of controversies that stretch back to 21:23. Jesus has given increasing clarification of his identity everywhere in these controversies. They have not been able to entrap him. Instead, he has revealed clearly his identity and his authority.

Application. *The invitation to insiders to come inside.* The striking, almost frightening, point of the parable of the wedding celebration (22:1–14) is that the ones who are condemned the most severely are insiders. The parable should cause us to take stock of our true membership within the kingdom. The church does contain people who are not true members of the kingdom. There are children of solid church members who are "insiders" but who have not truly responded to the invitation of the gospel.

Let's be careful not to fall into the Pharisaic legalism that counts fruit in others. The reality of the mixed nature of those who are insiders allows us to be comforted as realists about life until Jesus's return. It *will* be a mixed bag of the good wheat and bad weeds until Jesus comes. As we learn to examine ourselves and to help others learn to examine themselves, we can back off and leave the judging to God.

Advice for making a difference in this world. Jesus's response to the religious leaders about paying taxes to Caesar stands as one of the most important principles for Christians living in this world until the Lord returns. Both Caesar and the kingdom of God have rights in their respective areas as ordained by God, but the way of fulfilling our obligations to earthly authorities is by first fulfilling our obligations to God.

The danger for religious leaders is a tendency to go to extremes. On the one side they either withdraw completely from Caesar, like the Essenes in the Qumran community, or withdraw socially, like the Pharisees. On the other side they may capitulate by joining league with Caesar, like the Sadducees and Herodians, or they may take matters into the own hands and fight against Caesar, like the Zealots. As we look around at the various groups within the larger world of Christendom today, we find similar kinds of extremes. Some separatist Christians withdraw to their own world, like the Amish, or stay socially separated, like some fundamentalist groups. Others go to the other extreme and embrace politics as their primary agenda, while others use violence to advance their cause. Jesus's words should help us stay balanced. Christians must never forget that our first allegiance is to the kingdom of God.

Letting God be God. The important example for us is set by Jesus's censure of the Sadducees. We must commit ourselves to knowing the full teaching of Scripture, not just those selections or books that we find comfortable or compatible with our own worldview. The Bible will make us uncomfortable with our sin. It will also point out that it is incompatible with our secularist cultural baggage and philosophies. As much of a fan of John Lennon that I was, I had to evaluate his secularist philosophies in light of the Bible—and they were incompatible.

Furthermore, we must commit ourselves to know the power of God, which can change lives, make a difference in this world, break the chains of addictions, and enable marriages to last and flourish. The power of God is available for every Christian, every day, every hour.

Love as God's overarching will for disciples. Christians who are also college students regularly discuss God's will for their lives—what he wants them to study, what job or ministry they should pursue, where they should live, whom they should marry. All of these are important issues. Finding God's will for our lives is a heavily debated topic among such young people. They might consider Augustine's oft-quoted dictum, "Love [God], and do as you will." That is the kind of love about which Jesus spoke to the Pharisaic lawyer. And that is the kind of love that, when practiced in giving ourselves to God so that we can love our neighbor, opens up the freedom of living in obedience to his will.

Jesus under fire. If you are to live a life of integrity before God, it is imperative that your beliefs be true and that your questions have intellectually satisfying answers. Jesus provided those for the first century, and he does so for us today. Without him, we are spiritually bankrupt and hopeless. The kind of Messiah envisioned by the Pharisees or by modern reinventions cannot offer eternal salvation or the power to live life as we know we should.

These truths lie at the center of Christian claims. If Jesus is truly the one whom he declares himself to be, we have a unique message to proclaim. Jesus is unlike any figure ever to walk the earth, for he is not simply a messenger but the Son of God. The religious leaders' silence is outspoken testimony that the straightforward implication of the text cannot be avoided. The Messiah has a special relationship to Yahweh, which Jesus claims for himself. Their silence is also outspoken testimony of their own hypocritical avoidance of the implications for themselves. They should acknowledge Jesus as their own Lord and Messiah. Yet ultimately none of us, Christian or non-Christian, can ignore that Jesus demands nothing less from all of us than to be accepted, served, and worshiped as our Lord.

MATTHEW 23:1–39

Original Meaning

Warning the Crowds and the Disciples (23:1–12). *Warnings about demanding legalistic performance (23:1–4).* This "seat" (v. 2) was often viewed as a figurative expression, referring to the authority of Moses. However, recent archaeological evidence points to a literal chair. Jesus's statement confirms the use of the "seat of Moses" as a place from which experts in the law teach. Jesus recognizes their official capacity when exercised in the proper manner. Any and all accurate interpretation of Scripture is to be obeyed. Jesus does not condemn the pursuit of righteousness itself; rather, he points to specific issues in which the Pharisees preach one value but do not practice it themselves. This is a form of hypocrisy. The hypocrisy that Jesus condemned in the Sermon on the Mount was that the Pharisees were doing right things for the wrong reasons. Both forms of hypocrisy are included below in Jesus's criticism.

Throughout his ministry, one of Jesus's core censures of these religious leaders has been that they burden the people. Heavy "loads" put on people's shoulders denote the rabbinic oral tradition that was a distinctive feature of the Pharisaic branch of ancient Judaism. It was intended to make the Old Testament relevant to life situations where it seemed irrelevant, such as the complex sacrificial system in contexts removed from the temple, both in time and in locale.

The oral tradition was also a means of protecting Torah itself. Since the oral law was considered to be of divine origin, its massive obligations became far more burdensome than Scripture, and with the passing of years and the addition of more and more prescriptions, the rabbis could not lessen the burden without overthrowing the whole system. This is the inherent conflict with Jesus and the Pharisaic system, because they were so committed to their system that they missed the movement of God among them in the person of Jesus.

Warnings about pretentious public displays of piety (23:5–7). The expression "for people to see" here focuses on two related practices: wearing of religious garments and positioning for religious prominence. Phylacteries are small leather cubical cases containing passages of Scripture written on parchment. They were worn as an attempt to obey literally the admonition of Deuteronomy 11:18. The tassels reminded the people to obey God's commandment and to be holy to God (Num 15:40). Jesus chides these religious leaders for extending the tassels as a display of their piety, which is another way that they try to gain the admiration of the people.

Sought-after religious positions of honor come in for a second criticism. Seating at special dinner occasions was bestowed on guests according to their rank or status. Seating in the synagogue varied from location to location, with some synagogues having stone benches along one, two, three, or four of the walls, with removable benches or mats brought in for the majority of the congregation. There is ample evidence that the elders and other synagogue leaders had places of prominence.

Honorific public recognition to trumpet one's religious position in the community is especially odious. The rabbi was generally a master of the Torah, and the title usually refers to the head of a rabbinical school. The school was a holy community, and the people regarded the members as a whole with great deference. These academic institutions were distinguished from the synagogue, with the academy a place to promote Torah study and the synagogue a place to promote prayer.

Warnings about exploiting titles (23:8–10). With Jesus a new form of discipleship emerges. A disciple of Jesus will always and forever be only a disciple, because Jesus alone is Teacher. Nor are Jesus's disciples to abuse the term *father*. The use of the term *father* as a title of honor, respect, and authority had deep roots in ancient Judaism. The expression "father of the synagogue" was used in rabbinic times of an individual holding a place of honor and leadership within the synagogue affairs generally.

Matthew uses a word found only here in the New Testament to describe the third title that Jesus's disciples are to avoid—*kathēgētēs* ("instructor"). The term *kathēgētēs* occurs in Greek literature to designate especially a private tutor, which may point to the individual authority an instructor has over a student. Jesus's disciples are not to seek out personal authority as an instructor over other disciples, because as the Messiah, Jesus alone is Instructor.

A new type of leadership (23:11–12). Jesus's disciples must place servant leadership as the highest priority. The ideal servant lived to care for, protect, and make better the lives of those over him or her. Jesus warns his own disciples about trying to thwart this new servant-leader paradigm. If they follow the world's thirst for power and prestige, they will be humbled. Jesus's disciples who exalt themselves will be humbled and lose their place of leadership. But those who live out the humble role of servant will be exalted as true sons and daughters of the kingdom. This does not indicate exaltation over each other but the equal exaltation that all disciples of Jesus enjoy as those who are brothers and sisters of one another, with Jesus as master and his Father as their own.

Woes to the Teachers of the Law and the Pharisees (23:13–36). *First woe: the shut door (23:13 [14]).* Jesus condemns these leaders for hypocrisy. The term "hypocrite" (*hypokritēs*) was originally used for a play actor. He condemns them for the type of hypocrisy in which they deceive the people through their fallacious leadership. Not only have they rejected the offer to enter the kingdom themselves, but their teachings and opposition to Jesus's ministry influence the people to reject that invitation as well. This is a terrible abuse of their responsibility. Jesus condemns them for their hypocrisy—that is, attempting to bring the people into a righteous relationship with God while at the same time not being in a genuine relationship themselves.

Second woe: entrapped converts (23:15). Perhaps the primary point of Jesus's invective is best understood by recognizing that the Pharisees, not all of Judaism, are the primary targets here. The Pharisees were ardent advocates of their own sectarian understanding of Judaism, contending that their way was the primary avenue of living a life of true devotion. Therefore, Jesus does not condemn proselytizing per se but criticizes the way that the Pharisees, zealous to win people to their own brand of Judaism, place them under their particularly burdensome code of conduct in the oral law. The expression "twice as much" may be literary hyperbole, or it may point to the zeal of a recent convert who, knowing no other way, is more easily indoctrinated to the way of error and is far less likely to escape.

Third woe: binding oaths (23:16–22). Jesus now intentionally addresses the teachers of the law and the Pharisees by the characteristic that has so led themselves and others astray. Their clever casuistry has blinded them to the truth, which in turn causes them to lead others away from the truth. Included in Jesus's criticism may be an inconsistent hypocrisy in the religious leaders' teaching when they declare some oaths binding and others not, and also in their behavior, when they themselves are inconsistent when they take oaths.

Fourth woe: neglecting the weighty matters of the law (23:23–24). Jesus does not tell the Pharisees and teachers of the law to neglect the tithe, but their scrupulous attention to ceremonial detail consumes so much of their time and attention that they have no time to plan how they will daily exercise the more important matters. The law declared that many winged creatures were unclean, which the rabbis applied by straining wine to keep out small insects that made wine unclean. While attending to the minutiae of legal matters, they overlook the largest animal in their land, the camel, which was also ceremonially unclean. This may be the clearest example of the kind of hypocrisy that demonstrates inconsistency in their personal behavior.

Fifth woe: clean outside, filthy inside (23:25–26). The heart is the source of all thoughts, motives, and actions. The greed and self-indulgence of the Pharisees and teachers of the law, especially their lust for public religious acclaim, are inner motivations that impact external behavior. A root of hypocrisy is pride, the desire to have others see one as better than one actually is. This deceptive and pretentious attitude fuels a drive for power and prestige by those in a position to take advantage of those who are vulnerable. Moreover, hypocrisy has caused the Pharisees to miss the more important internal, moral issues that are foundational to the operation of the kingdom—justice, mercy, and faithfulness. Jesus accuses them of being clean on the outside but dirty on the inside; if the inside is clean, the outside will follow.

Sixth woe: whitewashed tombs (23:27–28). The teachers of the law and the Pharisees were like these ossuaries—on the outside they were deceptively ornate, but inside there is nothing but impure death. Jesus makes his point plain. These religious leaders give the appearance of having avoided unrighteousness by their attention to their many legal requirements, but inwardly they are unrighteous, for they have not attended to the transformation of the heart that can come by responding to Jesus.

Seventh woe: descendants of murderers of the prophets (23:29–32). Like the preceding woe, this is a blatant contrast between the religious leaders' fastidious outward observance of cleanliness and the wickedness of their inward motives. They build beautiful monuments to the prophets, but Jesus declares that they are motivationally descendants of those who killed them. They deny that they would have killed the ancient prophets, but as they secretly prepare to have Jesus executed they demonstrate their wicked, spiritually corrupt lineage to the ancient murderers.

Final invective: murderers of the righteous (23:33–36). "Snakes" as used here with "brood of vipers" are synonyms to heap up the culpability of these religious leaders (v. 33). Jesus gives a blood-curdling prediction: "Therefore I am sending you prophets . . ." (v. 34). This prophetic statement points ahead to the Christian era, when Israel will still be a focus of Jesus's gracious invitation through his messengers, but they will continue to reject that message.

Along with the prophecy that the religious leaders will murder his messengers, Jesus includes a prophecy of the judgment that will come on them for their murderous activities. The first righteous person in human history to be killed was Abel, slain by his brother Cain in an act of unrighteous jealousy. The last murder recorded in the Old Testament in the canonical order of the Hebrew Bible (Law, Prophets, Writings) is Zechariah, a son of the high priest, murdered in the courtyard of the temple.

Lament over Jerusalem (23:37–39). Jesus continues to desire the gathering of his people. But he will not force himself on anyone; they must determine their own fate—"and you were not willing" (v. 37). Jesus is especially burdened in light of Israel's coming judgment. He predicts the destruction of Israel's "house" (v. 38), an expression for the temple in the Old Testament. This is possibly its meaning here as well, although it may point more widely to judgment on Jerusalem's leadership. Jewish authority will be lost with the destruction of the temple in AD 70. This is the theme to which Jesus turns next.

Jesus concludes his address to the people of Israel with a dramatic prophecy. This is the last time that Jesus addresses the crowds, who have had their opportunity to repent. The christological implications of Jesus's quotation of Psalm 118:26 in verse 39 are profound. The same words were cited earlier in 21:9 at Jesus's entrance to Jerusalem, shouted by those identifying him as the messianic Son of David. Now as Jesus cites the same passage, he identifies himself with God's Messiah, Israel's Savior, the "Coming One," who will once again return to his people after a time of great judgment, when they will have no other choice but to acknowledge him as Lord, either in great joy or in great sorrow.

Application. One of the most humbling aspects of reading the Gospels is recognizing that many of the criticisms that Jesus lodges against the Pharisees can also be lodged against us. This is especially true of Christian leaders. We have seen how Jesus pointed out many troublesome, indeed sinful, characteristics: pride, public showmanship, one-upmanship, bull-headedness, politicizing of one's position, and, of course, hypocrisy.

Matthew's Gospel is the source from which leaders can derive insight into the errors of the Pharisees as well as help in establishing more consistent leadership qualities.

Live by example God's message of grace (23:1–4). The gospel of the kingdom is grace, not practicing works to gain God's favor. We must demonstrate grace toward those to whom we minister and love and accept them regardless of their performance.

Earn respect and honor, don't demand them (23:5–7). We must earn respect by the daily, long-term development of our personal godliness, not in artificial and ostentatious displays of piety but in developing our prayer life, controlling our temper, and maintaining an appropriate demeanor when in front of people. It is a temptation to hide behind titles and positions and pretentiously posture as a leader, but your people need to see plain old you—a regular person like them, who is also in process of growing into the image of Christ. Don't demand respect and honor by manipulation.

Wear titles lightly that point to God (23:8–10). Don't use your titles or degrees or education to manipulate people into following you. Use it to bless them so that they can be drawn into an even more intimate relationship with Jesus. Wear your titles lightly by allowing them to make you wiser, more understanding, and more effective as a servant of Christ.

Serve God's people to empower them to advance the kingdom of God (23:11–12). For those that have been placed in positions of prominence, such as a teacher, minister, or executive, the goal of each position is to advance the kingdom; the means is to give yourself to all so that they can best accomplish God's calling on their lives.

Be a signpost to the doorway to the kingdom (23:13). The fifth principle for leaders is that in all that we say and do, we are to be a signpost to the doorway to the kingdom. We are to provide a personal example of the teaching concerning the reality of life lived in the power of the presence of Jesus through the indwelling Spirit of God.

Make converts to the kingdom, not to yourself (23:15). We must take God's calling on our lives seriously, for people's responses to the gospel we proclaim have eternal consequences. But we are not to take ourselves too seriously in the process. If we overstep our bounds, God will use others. Be absolutely sure to maintain a grip on the truth by sticking as close to Scripture as possible. We must passionately pursue converts to life in the kingdom of God, not to ourselves.

Maintain personal accountability (23:16–22). It is important for leaders to maintain personal accountability by weaning ourselves from artificially imposed ways of remaining accountable to God. The most straightforward approach is the transparency of a life lived in the intimacy of a relationship with Jesus.

Major on the majors of the kingdom (23:23–24). Like the first warning, it is easy to get caught up in minor issues that lead to legalistic demands and expectations. To understand what the really important concerns are—doctrinally, ecclesiastically, relationally—is to give our time and energies to what will really count for eternity.

Pursue pure motives for leadership in ministry from the inside out (23:25–26). It's easy to put on a show. Run a glitzy worship service, and people are convinced that they have really worshiped. But leaders can be tempted to draw attention to themselves instead of to God. This illustrates the importance of team ministries that are honest and transparent, where others call us out on our self-indulgent motives and help us promote pure motives.

Develop personal identity as a leader from the inside out (23:27–28). As we open ourselves up to be known by God, we embark on one of the most important aspects of our growth as leaders: to know ourselves as God knows us. Opening up to God enables him to help us understand ourselves more accurately. Find out who you are. What makes you tick the way you do? What are your problems? Our continuing transformation will occur as we know ourselves as God knows us. Let your self-worth grow out of who you are in Christ, not what you do for him.

Carefully choose the traditions you will represent (23:29–32). Jesus's leaders must carefully choose the traditions we represent. There are many voices out there, but our calling is to listen to the voice of God and those who represent him.

Listen to God's other messengers, because leadership has stricter condemnation (23:33–36). We as leaders must listen to God's message through his other messengers and be careful when we see ourselves stifling every voice with which we disagree. Jesus rebukes the religious leaders because they are muffling God's righteous voice so that their own can be heard. God will avenge those who have lived righteously and have been abused by powerful leaders. There are other people out there who speak for God; we are not the only ones. We must examine those voices, but we will be wiser, more balanced, and better equipped when we learn from others and join with them in advancing the kingdom of God.

MATTHEW 24:1–35

Original Meaning

The Setting of the Olivet Discourse (24:1–3). The road from Jerusalem to Bethany traverses the Mount of Olives, giving a spectacular view of the temple behind and below them. In response to exclamations over the beauty and magnificence of the temple, Jesus paints a dark picture of its future. This must have startled the disciples, because Jerusalem was the holy city, and the rebuilt temple was the pride of the nation. Now Jesus is prophesying its destruction (which did occur in AD 70).

Jesus sits on the Mount of Olives, perhaps pondering his prophetic forecast, when his disciples approach him to ask his private understanding of the incredible events to which he has just alluded. Jesus's reply initiates an extended discourse forecasting the events that will stretch on down the course of history. The content of the discourse is in response to the disciples' questions. The disciples ask two questions (v. 3):

1. "When will this happen?"
2. "What will be the sign of your coming and of the end of the age?"

The way in which the disciples ask both questions may indicate that to them, the destruction of the temple and the parousia are not separated, which clues us to Jesus's reply.

In this discourse we have historical and eschatological references, with Jesus prophesying both the fall of Jerusalem and his own parousia. We may see, then, three basic parts to Jesus's discourse.

1. Part one describes events, generally chronological, prior to the coming of Jesus (24:4–31).
2. Part two gives lessons on watching, waiting, and being prepared for the coming of Jesus (24:36–25:30).
3. Part three concludes the discourse with a warning of judgment and a promise of reward at the time of his coming (25:31–46).

The Beginning of Birth Pains (24:4–14). *Sufferings throughout the world (24:4–8).* Many events may deceive the disciples into thinking that the end of the age has arrived. Instead, all of these events are general characteristics of this present age of "birth pains" (v. 8). Jesus explicitly outlines a number of conditions that must not be seen as indicators of the end of the age.

False messiahs (24:4–5). Prophetic figures and messianic deliverers had long attempted to incite revolution against occupying forces. Throughout the ages, many have attempted to claim messianic identity. Jesus's disciples must not be deceived.

Wars and calamities (24:6–7). Jesus next warns that wars and rumors of wars will occur repeatedly throughout this age, with nations and kingdoms rising against each other. But Jesus emphasizes that these cataclysmic activities will be a regular part of the suffering of this life until the return of Jesus begins the redemption of all creation.

Birth pains (24:8). The imagery points to an expected time of suffering that will characterize the period prior to the messianic age. Although the inauguration of the kingdom of heaven brings redemption to its citizens, the whole world continues to experience birth pains as it awaits final redemption, as do even believers who have the firstfruits of the Spirit.

We may think that the imagery of birth pains contradicts Jesus's statement that the time of his coming is unknown (24:36), since such pains presage the imminent birth of a baby. But the baby does not come on the first pang, but once the pains begin, all know that the inexorable process has commenced. We do not know if the baby will come on the fifth, the fifteenth, the fiftieth, or the five hundredth. Throughout the labor we must remain on guard.

Sufferings of Jesus's disciples (24:9–13). Persecution (24:9–11). The disciples will be handed over to *thlipsis* ("persecution," "distress," or "tribulation"). Jesus's disciples will feel the wrath and alienation from humanity for following him and proclaiming his message. The phrase "because of me" (v. 9) is literally "because of my name" and is an important christological expression that harks back to the Old Testament significance of God's name as the representation of his person as being the sole focus of Israel's worship and allegiance. Jesus's disciples will have the privilege of carrying his name, but it also brings with it suffering, because the antagonism and hatred that is directed toward him will naturally fall on his followers.

Betrayal (24:10). It is not easy to endure persecution, and those who only hold on to Jesus because of their own comfort will find it easier to turn away from him and avoid the suffering. They not only will seek their own escape from suffering, but they will become enemies of Jesus and turn against his followers, their former fellow disciples. They will betray them to the persecutors, and the love that had characterized the relationship between them will be turned to hate as they utterly reject Jesus. This apostasy is the evidence that they never were true disciples.

Deception (24:11). Not only will false messiahs try to deceive the world (v. 5), false prophets will surface within the community to try to deceive Jesus's disciples.

Wickedness and lovelessness (24:12). All of the preceding phenomena are described as the increase of wickedness, which points to the spiritual death of those who fall away and those who have attempted to deceive the community. The chief characteristic of spiritual death is that it causes love to grow cold. This is a somber picture of the community of disciples being impacted by apostasy.

Standing firm (24:13). Active resistance may be included in standing firm, but much more in view is the enduring fortitude of the disciples under any circumstance, including the most hateful persecution. "Saved" does not speak of rescue from physical death, because many true disciples have experienced martyrdom. His promise is that the one who remains committed to his name until the end will not be consumed by the persecution but will experience the full blessing and peace of the kingdom's salvation with his arrival. Jesus likewise reminds them that a disciple's real commitment to him is demonstrated in whether he or she remains steadfast.

Preaching the gospel to all nations (24:14). Although the increase of events in 24:9–13 indicates that the parousia is near, the only explicit condition to be met is the proclamation of the gospel to all the nations. After that proclamation has occurred, the end will come. During Jesus's earthly ministry, the disciples' mission was restricted to Israel. The future mission shifts to all the nations, which will fulfill the Abrahamic covenant, though it will include a continued outreach to Israel. This future mission will be inaugurated with the risen Jesus's "Great Commission" (28:19–20), but it is prophesied both here and earlier in the missionary discourse in Matthew 10.

Description of "Great Tribulation" (24:15–28). *The abomination that causes desolation (24:15).* Jesus quotes Daniel directly to clarify that the fulfillment of the "abomination that causes desolation" is yet future (Dan 9:27; cf. also 8:13; 11:31; 12:11). Both Matthew and Mark include the phrase "let the reader understand" (cf. Mark 13:14). This is an aside intended to get the reader of Daniel to see that in Jesus's words, one will find the real fulfillment of the prophecy. With the onset of the abomination that causes desolation as spoken of by Daniel, the period of "great distress" begins (Matt 24:21). This desolating sacrilege is the predominant event of this period of tribulation, which corresponds to Daniel's period of "seven," during which in the middle of the "seven" a ruler will set up "an abomination that causes desolation" (Dan 9:27). When we look at Daniel (esp. 9:25–27) and the events of Revelation (see the number of days of 1,260 in Rev 12:6, which equals three and a half years), this marks the second half of the seven years of tribulation, the time of "great distress [tribulation]." Apparently the first three and a half years was a time of relative peace and quiet.

As discussed in the introduction to this discourse, Jesus's prophecy is an answer to both of the disciples' questions. He predicts the destruction of Jerusalem and the temple in AD 70, but he looks beyond to a future time when another abomination that causes desolation will arise in Jerusalem to lead astray God's people and bring destruction on all who resist him.

Flight of believers (24:16–20). In a series of five warnings taken from everyday life in Israel, Jesus accentuates the immediacy of danger that will accompany the fulfillment of the arrival of the abomination that causes desolation.

1. When the abomination occurs, those who have heeded the prophecies of Jesus will know that immediate and utter destruction is coming on Jerusalem and many will die, so they are to flee with great haste.
2. The impending destruction means that there will be no time to gather provisions in the home. The flat rooftops on many homes in Israel were a place to find a cool breeze in the evening and were considered part of the living quarters.
3. The outer coat was an essential garment for traveling, often used as a blanket when sleeping outdoors, and only those in the greatest hurry would think of leaving it behind.
4. The danger of travel in this perilous time is greatest for those most at risk, especially pregnant mothers and their infants.
5. Flight in winter, when roads are washed out and rivers are swollen, presents even more difficulty for those fleeing the horrors of approaching ruin.

In prayer the disciples must cling to God's presence and ever-ready help, even though they may have to disrupt even the most devoutly held religious traditions, such as the Jewish Sabbath.

"Great distress" (24:21). While the time of the siege and destruction of Jerusalem were horrible, Matthew's description here indicates a time of tribulation that did not occur during the fall of Jerusalem. The horrors that fell on the Jewish people and on the entire world with the two world wars of the twentieth century are a somber warning that the devastation that comes from humanity's unleashed depravity will yet be unequaled. The vision Jesus paints must yet be ahead.

The days cut short (24:22). If the wickedness of humanity and the wrath of God were allowed to run unchecked, there would be no end to the terror, and no one would survive. This is a promise that the time of tribulation will not last indefinitely, because God is in control. In the time of future great tribulation, when Israel will once again be used by God for witness to bring in a multitude of believers from all the nations who worship God and the Lamb, the expression "the elect" includes all who believe on Christ during this period.

Warnings about false messiahs (24:23–28). The desert had messianic overtones for diverse groups within Israel, who associated it with God's forthcoming deliverance. Messianic pretenders often gathered their followers in the desert prior to their public appearance. The Messiah will not come in a secretive manner only to his exclusive group of followers. Rather, the Son of Man will come in a spectacular manner, like lightning that is visible to all.

The warnings about secret workings of false messiahs and the declaration of his own spectacular appearance prompts Jesus to give a puzzling saying: "Wherever there is a carcass, there the vultures will gather" (v. 28). This proverb may indicate the sphere of operation from which people can see high-circling vultures converging on the carcass of a dead animal; so will be the visibility of the return of the Son of Man when he comes to bring judgment on the deadness of this corrupt world. This view seems to make most sense in the context of Jesus's allusion to his lightning-like appearance, but it is awkward in that it seems to make Jesus parallel to a vulture. But such incongruities often characterize Jesus's proverbial sayings and parables for effect.

Description of the Coming of the Son of Man (24:29–31). The Son of Man will come after that time of tribulation. Here "distress" (*thlipsis*) in verse 29 connects with verse 21 to point to a specific period of great tribulation. The adverbial expression "immediately after" (v. 29) emphasizes that the celestial signs and the coming of Jesus will occur after the time of "great distress" just described in verses 15–28. Once again, the mixture of prophecy referring to both the fall of Jerusalem and the end of the age should be acknowledged. Although the judgment that will be brought on Israel in AD 70 with the fall of Jerusalem does seem to be in Jesus's mind, the primary emphasis rests on the end of the age when he will come as the Son of Man in great universal power.

Heavenly disturbances (24:29). Jesus uses typical apocalyptic imagery as he alludes here to passages such as Isaiah 13:10 and 34:4 to describe his coming with a mixture of literal and figurative language. Such language may point to both physical phenomena and political and spiritual disruptions. The darkness at Jesus's crucifixion was an indication that he had conquered the forces of evil on the cross, and the darkness during his second coming is an indication that he will now exert his rule over all forces, especially those of the demonic prince of the powers of the air.

Heavenly appearances (24:30–31). As in his first coming, when Jesus's ministry and resurrection were sufficient signs that he was indeed the Messiah, the Son of God, so his second coming will be the sign to "all the peoples [*phylai*] of the earth," who will then mourn. The term *phylai* can be rendered either "peoples" (NIV) or "tribes" (NASB). Matthew regularly uses *ethnē* to refer to the nations (e.g., 24:9; 28:19), and the only other time he uses *phylai* it refers specifically to the twelve tribes of Israel (19:28); thus, here it should be rendered as "tribes," calling to mind the twelve tribes of Israel.

This language would hold special meaning to a Jewish audience, since the prophecy of Zechariah 12:10 speaks of the people of Israel mourning when they look on the one whom they have pierced. This is a kind of mourning that produces repentance, or else it stems from recognition of their coming judgment. In the light of the place that Paul gives to Israel's future repentance and conversion (Rom 9–11; cf. Matt 23:39), repentance is more likely in view.

Jesus continues the description of his coming. This picture coincides with the sovereign Son of Man accompanying the angels of heaven, who "will gather his elect from the four winds, from one end of the heavens to the other" (v. 31). The "elect" is another reference to all believers, both Jew and gentile, who have come to believe in him during this time of great tribulation.

The Lesson of the Fig Tree (24:32–35). Jesus uses the fig tree as a parabolic lesson taught from nature to the disciples. It teaches a principle of nearness concerning the abomination that causes desolation of the temple and the return of the Son of Man. Jesus stated earlier that the general distressful events of this age must not be interpreted to mean that the Lord is near (24:1–8). However, as the end grows closer, subtle increases of difficulty begin to mark the end. The budding tree can be overlooked; it is not spectacular and can even be unnoticed until too late. The point is that people must stay alert and must be forewarned by certain signs at the very end.

The identity of "this generation" has vexed interpreters (v. 34). Perhaps it is best to see a twofold reference, as Jesus has done throughout the discourse. In other words, the saying is a word of warning, both for those of the generation of Jesus as well as for those in the future who have not yet repented, that the arrival of the Son of Man will bring judgment. But the saying is also a word of encouragement to his followers that tribulation will not go on forever, as it may appear to those who are suffering in it. Summer is near.

In the final words of this section, Jesus gives a profound word of assurance to all those looking down the corridors of history and seeing the incredible events he has just described. Throughout history will come birth pains and tribulation that may seem as though history itself is out of control. But Jesus's rock-solid prophesying of his return to establish his kingdom on the earth provides the assurance needed by his disciples to maintain hope and determination.

Application. *Prophecy today.* All of us need to move from speculation to implication in our study of prophecy, because the Bible does not record prophecy of end-time activity simply for curiosity's sake. The study in this commentary of Jesus's life and teaching understands that the offer and establishment of the kingdom of God is an "already-not yet" proposition—it is present and fully operative in the lives of those who respond, but it yet awaits a final manifestation, when Jesus Messiah will reign on the earth and Israel will experience the realization of her covenantal promises. This premillennial outlook on Jesus's eschatological discourse leads to important implications.

Godly living in the present. The study of the future should spur us to godly living in the present. Jesus's signal statement, "See, I have told you ahead of time" (24:25), stands in the middle of his prophecy of future events. He prophesies future events so that we will discipline ourselves to maintain and expand personal kingdom-righteousness in our daily lives regardless of the circumstances. He does not tell us these things so that we will be obsessed with dates, events, and speculation about the minute details of his prophecy, but to encourage us to godly living.

Conviction about the future. A second implication is that our study of prophecy should produce conviction about what is going to happen in the future. We should admit we may be wrong on certain points, which will help us avoid a narrow dogmatism; but when we have done our homework and settled on what we believe to be the Bible's teaching, we should develop conviction, for appropriate conviction affects our character and our attitudes. Even though we must guard against excess and obsession with this kind of study, we will have no peace or security without a proper understanding of revelation concerning the future.

Warning of difficult times ahead. There is also an important warning in Jesus's prophecy of difficult times ahead. Jesus spent much of his time in the discourses preparing the disciples in advance for the harsh realities of life during this present age. Jesus's prophetic words, as well as much of prophecy generally, are an encouragement for believers amid persecution, not a handbook for future prediction or simply a hope of escape from an imperfect world. Jesus gives us this information so that we can endure and live appropriately until his return.

Warning of impending judgment. Yet there is another kind of warning in Jesus's eschatological forecast—impending judgment. Not only is prophecy an encouragement to godly living; it is a stimulus to repentance. An appropriate preaching, teaching, and evangelism from prophetic passages must include warnings of judgment, or else the full message has been ignored. This calls for wisdom in our presentations, compassion in our approach, and urgency in our message.

Missions and evangelism. The conviction of Jesus's return, therefore, should fuel a vigorous involvement in missions, evangelism, and church planting. When we are gripped with the fact that the souls of men and women are at stake, we will move our study of prophecy beyond academic debate or idle curiosity. No matter how bad things may get within public opinion or the political arena, no matter how much government may legislate against the Christian faith, or no matter how much persecution is mounted against it, the gospel cannot be stopped until the end, when Jesus returns in glory and power.

MATTHEW 24:36–25:46

Original Meaning

The "Time" of Jesus's Coming (24:36–41). *The day and hour of coming is unknown (24:36).* The theological doctrine of Christ's *kenosis* (meaning "emptying"; cf. Phil 2:7) generally contends that in Jesus's incarnation he voluntarily limited the use of his divine attributes so that he could experience the full human life. While he did not in any sense give up his deity, Jesus voluntarily limited the use of those divine characteristics so that he could experience human life in its entirety. It was only at the will of his Father that he could use his divine attributes, if it was the Father's will for him to do so. He acted primarily in his humanity and was empowered by the Spirit. In his human consciousness, Jesus restricted himself to normal human knowledge while retaining omniscience in his divine nature.

Analogy of the days of Noah (24:37–39). The people in the days of Noah did not heed the warnings of judgment that were given to them. By contrast, Noah and his family went about with preparations for the coming flood even though they saw no specific signs of its coming and did not know when it would arrive (see Gen 6). Jesus's return will catch unaware all who do not heed whatever warnings are given and who are spiritually unprepared.

Some will be taken, some left (24:40–41). The "taking" and "leaving" are intriguing. These expressions may indicate that one is taken away to judgment (like those swept away by the flood in Noah's day) and the other is left to enjoy the blessing of salvation at the arrival of the Son of Man (as Noah and his family were saved by God's warning), although the verb for "taken" in verses 40–41 is different from the verb for "took them all away" in verse 39. Or vice versa, one is taken away to safety to enjoy the blessing of the arrival of the Son of Man (like Noah and his family in the ark), while the other is left to experience the wrath of the Son of Man (like those who died with the arrival of the flood). The point is that the Son of Man gathers his people at his return to enjoy the full manifestation of the kingdom of God, while the rest experience his judgment.

The Parable of the Homeowner and the Thief (24:42–44). This is the only time that the expression "your Lord" occurs in Matthew's Gospel and accentuates that Jesus, as the coming

Son of Man, is the disciples' Lord. Jesus draws a comparison between his coming and the unexpectedness of a thief's activity, calling his disciples to recognize and know the lesson he is teaching. This parable stresses that vigilance is necessary if a thief should appear.

The responsibility for the safety of each home lay upon the "owner of the house" (v. 43) since the modern conception of a police force was nonexistent. The parable here stresses the alertness necessary to thwart a burglar who might attempt to dig through a roof that was covered with reeds and a layer of clay or tiles. Like many parables, one particular aspect of the parable is used as a comparison—here, unexpectedness. Other aspects of the parable have no comparisons, such as the fact that Jesus is not a thief who has intent to steal. Alert watchfulness is important, but perhaps more important is preparedness.

The Parable of Two Kinds of Servants (24:45–51). *Faithful servant (24:45–47).* The servant (*doulos*) placed in a position of responsibility to oversee and care for other servants in the master's household was often called a "steward" (*oikonomos*). This man is the chief servant, head over the master's household affairs and staff and expected to care for the master's personal affairs. The test of his responsibility occurs when the master is absent; will he faithfully carry out his tasks? If he has done so, when the master returns he will be given more responsibility.

Unfaithful servant (24:48–51). The long absence of his master allows the servant to abuse his authority, mistreat his fellow servants, and consort drunkenly with bad acquaintances—activities that are characteristic of idolaters, pagans, unbelievers, and those who have turned away from the faith. When the master does return, the slave is caught unaware. As a result, he is cut in pieces. His place with hypocrites deserves treatment that is proverbial for the eternal condemnation of hell. The wicked servant is a false, professing disciple.

This parable is not talking about rewards or punishment for believers, nor is it advocating cutting off believers who have fallen away. It is a contrast between true and false believers and addresses the consequences of those who show by their lives that they are deserving of hell.

What prompts the servant's wickedness is his noticing that his master has been away a long time. The way one thinks about the Lord's return will eventually influence what one says and how one acts. Perhaps the servant thinks that the master will never return or that he can get away with his wickedness before he is caught. This may be a subtle hint here that Jesus's return will be delayed, which will act as a test to the heart of each person.

The Parable of the Ten Virgins (25:1–13). This parable specifically teaches readiness in the light of the unknown time of the coming of the Son of Man. The ten virgins are bridesmaids who are not yet married. A groom left his parents' home with a contingent of friends to go to the home of his bride, where nuptial ceremonies were carried out. After this, the entire wedding party formed a processional to a wedding banquet, normally at the home of the bridegroom. The lamp (*lampas*) was a larger dome-shaped container with rags soaked in the oil to light the way while a person was walking outside.

After the long wait, the cry rings out in the middle of the night. The wise virgins awake and trim their lamps to get the brightest light possible for the procession, but the parable takes a surprising turn when the foolish virgins say to the wise, "Give us some of your oil; our lamps are going out." The wise virgins cannot comply because their own lamps will go out if they share, so they tell the foolish virgins to find their own at a local shop. While the foolish virgins are off to find oil, the procession with the bridegroom finally arrives. The reason for referring to the virgins as "wise" in all the prior references is now revealed: they are "ready" to go with the bridegroom to the wedding banquet (v. 10b). The foolish virgins are not, which Jesus accentuates by stating, "and the door was shut" (v. 10c).

The foolish virgins finally arrive, but the bridegroom calls out to them as they stand in the darkness of the night, a stark, straightforward statement of rejection of a person who does not have a true relationship with Jesus. As in the preceding parable, this is another distinction between two types of people—those who are truly disciples of Jesus and those who are not. Disciples of Jesus will be ready for the arrival of the Son of Man. The previous parable (24:50–51) and the following parable (25:29–30) both speak of hell as the destiny for those who do not "watch" correctly by being properly prepared with salvation to accompany the Son of Man when he arrives.

The Parable of the Talents (25:14–30). *Talents (25:14–18).* Wealthy landowners often entrusted their property and affairs to trustworthy servants (*doulos*) when they went away on business or for personal dealings. In terms of today's value, the landowner disperses perhaps approximately two million dollars to the three servants.

Faithful servants (25:19–23). The sums dispersed by the homeowner apparently symbolize personal giftedness or abilities, but only generally: "each according to his ability" (v. 15). After a long interval, the master returns and settles accounts with them. The identical statement of praise to both servants indicates that the point of the parable is not on the total amount earned but on faithful responsibility in living up to one's potential and giftedness. The reward of earnings bestowed may differ, but both servants received the identical joy in the presence of their master.

Wicked servant (25:24–27). The wickedness of the third slave primarily stems from his attitude about his master, which in turn has led to laziness and bad stewardship. The servant's misperception of the master has produced alienation, mistrust, fear, and then personal sloth. Had he truly loved his master, he would not have attempted to place the blame on him but would have operated out of love. The blame in the servant is because he was not industrious enough to seek to earn his master interest on the talent.

Abundance and punishment (25:28–30). The punishment is not simply taking away the talent from the wicked slave, now called "worthless." The master instructs that he should be thrown "outside, into the darkness, where there will be weeping and gnashing of teeth" (v. 30). As in the other parables, the contrast is between those whose eternal destiny is salvation in the presence of the long-expected Son of Man and eternal damnation.

Judgment at the End (25:31–46). *Sheep separated from goats (25:31–33).* The scene switches now to the glorious coming of the Son of Man. He is accompanied in his glory with all the angels, and he sits on his throne of glory. Before him all of the nations will be gathered (v. 32). The debated expression "the nations" is most likely intended to mean both Jews and gentiles who throughout this age are the combined object of the Great Commission (28:19–20). The nations as entities are not judged but rather the people within them: "He will separate the people one from another as a shepherd separates the sheep from the goats" (v. 32).

The shepherd metaphor softens the judgment image but does not diminish the foreboding consequences of separating the sheep from the goats. There seems to be no significant reason why Jesus contrasts sheep with goats, except for the symbolism that will be attached to both in a surprising manner.

The reward of the sheep (25:34–40). The king represents the Son of Man sitting on the throne, bringing to mind Daniel 7:13–14, where "one like a son of man" receives the kingdom from the Ancient of Days. The king addresses the sheep on his right as "blessed by my Father" (Matt 25:34). The blessing consists of their inheritance, which is the kingdom they now receive, not because they have earned it through their own efforts but because it is a gift of their relationship with the Father and the Son. God's assured purpose is carried out as the blessing of the inheritance of the kingdom for the sheep is realized.

The transitional "for" in verse 35 introduces the explanation why the sheep receive the inheritance: kingdom inheritance is the reward for caring for Jesus's physical needs. The sheep cared for Jesus when he was in need with hunger, thirst, being a stranger, naked, sick, and imprisoned. The surprise of the "righteous" sheep comes from their taking his words literally, because they can recall no time when they have done this to the king (v. 37). Such surprise indicates that these were not intentional meritorious acts to gain access to the kingdom. Rather, these acts of mercy function as evidence that the sheep belong to the kingdom, just as the preceding parables pointed out external behavioral evidence of a person who has truly received the gift of salvation and the resulting transformation by the Spirit.

Jesus responds, "Truly I tell you, whatever you did for one of the least of these brothers and sisters of mine, you did for me" (v. 40). Following on the surprise of the righteous, this statement of Jesus is a central principle of the passage—in caring for the needs of "the least" of these brothers and sisters of Jesus, they have served Jesus.

Jesus affirms that believers are to care for one another, but especially the least and insignificant among them. This does not absolve a general mercy that Christians must demonstrate toward all in need. We should also reiterate that these good deeds are not the works by which one enters the kingdom; they are rather the substantiation of the kind of kingdom life that has been produced through the transformation of the heart of his disciples through regeneration.

The punishment of the goats (25:41–45). The goats are just as surprised as the sheep, but they are surprised like those in the preceding parables. Here, sins of omission are also worthy of eternal damnation, because they are evidence that a person has not been made righteous by association with Jesus and the kingdom of God. Righteous acts spring from a heart sanctified by the Spirit of God, while persistently unrighteous acts, even of omission, indicate a heart lacking in the Spirit's work of transformation.

Eternal punishment and eternal life (25:46). The important point throughout this scene is clear: judgment will come. This judgment scene provides a dramatic conclusion to the entire discourse and a sequential culmination to the preceding parables. As has been the emphasis throughout the Olivet Discourse, and ultimately throughout this Gospel, there are only two types of people. Those who have not followed Jesus are actually against him and will endure separation from him in their eternal punishment. Jesus's disciples are with him and will enjoy with him life that is eternal. This should produce the greatest joy in Jesus's disciples, as they consider their eternal destiny. But the fate of the wicked should also weigh heavily upon them, provoking the same kind of anguish that the apostle Paul experienced as he considered the eternal fate of his fellow Jews who had rejected Jesus (Rom 9:1–3; 10:1–2).

Application. Faithful discipleship to Jesus while awaiting his return is demonstrated in those who *watch by being prepared.*

The three following parables demonstrate how: we must be *responsible* (the two kinds of servants; 24:45–51), *ready* (ten virgins; 25:1–13), and *productive* (the talents; 25:14–30). The concluding scene of the judgment of the sheep and the goats (25:31–46) brings a climactic conclusion by announcing that watching and waiting throughout one's life, and throughout history, requires us to be *accountable* to our discipleship.

Prepared (24:43–44). Our entire worldview must be kingdom oriented, as Jesus has been emphasizing throughout his ministry. Our hope lies in God's fully established kingdom on earth, not in the kingdoms we create. We wait with all of creation for its full liberation, but our waiting and watching means that we are prepared by responding to the invitation to the kingdom on earth now and by experiencing the beginning of regeneration as our own souls are washed and renewed by the Holy Spirit. As we nurture the blessed hope of Jesus's return daily, the grace of God teaches us to say no to ungodliness and worldly passions. When this is our daily, even hourly, focus, we watch and wait for Jesus's return, fully equipped to meet him with peace and confidence.

Responsible (24:45–51). The parable of the two kinds of servants continues that theme by teaching that a person truly demonstrates that he or she is prepared with kingdom life by *responsible* behavior. Whether we are with other believers or not, whether we think that we will be caught or not, a pure heart is intent on producing responsible behavior. It is our responsibility to make known the gospel by all that we are and say. When we live with the blessed hope of Jesus's soon return, we are motivated to live up to our responsibilities. This means we are ethically responsible for daily purity in the light of the expectation of Jesus's coming. Someone has said well, "Live each day so that you will neither be afraid of tomorrow nor ashamed of yesterday."

Ready (25:1–13). The parable of the ten virgins continues the theme of watchful preparation—namely, being prepared for the Lord's coming by our *readiness* to meet him at any moment. We are ready when our relationships with God and others are what they should be. We are ready when at any moment of our day we are not ashamed to have the Lord meet us. We are ready when past grievances have been acquitted. A suitable attitude of readiness in the church and in our own lives allows our anticipation of eternal things to make more insignificant some of our petty concerns and more manageable some of our bigger concerns.

Productive (25:14–30). The parable of the talents also demonstrates that disciples are prepared for the Lord's coming by their intentional *productivity*. It is vitally important to have a correct biblical perception of God's character, his activities, and his goals for us. This is the important role of solid Bible teaching and preaching, for our view of God determines our behavior. The parable reveals that the wickedness of the servant impelled him to pervert the image of his master, which then provided him with an excuse for his personal irresponsibility. The parable teaches us that a truthful understanding of God will bring about the productive investment of our lives.

Accountable (25:31–46). The scene of the judgment of the sheep and goats brings these parables and the discourse to a dramatic conclusion with the pronouncement that we will all be accountable for what we do in this life while awaiting the return of the king. Humble ministry to the lowliest demonstrates Jesus's own humility in leaving the glories of heaven to bring salvation's story to the weak and the downtrodden, the tax collector and sinner, the sick and dying. We cannot serve these solely out of a motivation of religious obligation, for then we do so out of our own prideful strength. We serve because we have been served, we love because we have been loved, we lift up because we have been lifted up—and we never forget it.

Life is fragile and fleeting. This is the message of Jesus's exhortation as he concludes the Olivet Discourse. We must be ready to meet him as our master and Lord, whether at the end of life or at the end of this age. Yet we are all called to account for what we have done with our lives. *Live as though Jesus is coming back today; plan as though he is not coming back for a hundred years.*

MATTHEW 26:1–46

Original Meaning

Jesus's Prediction and the Plot of the Religious Leaders (26:1–5). *The Passover (26:1–2).* The Passover feast was celebrated annually to commemorate Israel's escape from Egypt. This is now the fourth and last time that Jesus predicts his arrest and crucifixion. Although this prediction is briefer than the others, Jesus connects his death with the celebration of Passover.

The religious leaders plot Jesus's arrest and execution (26:3–4). The chief priests, controlled by the high priest and the wealthy aristocracy of Jerusalem, were dominated by Sadducean influence. They are among the most eager in Jerusalem to get rid of the threat to their influence in the temple posed by Jesus and his messianic following, so they plot to arrest and kill him. As the conspiracy against Jesus proceeds in Matthew's narrative, the close cooperation between Caiaphas and the Roman government will be important in accounting for the way in which Jesus is so readily condemned and crucified.

For the first time in Matthew the high priest is identified as "Caiaphas," who is son-in-law of the previous high priest, Annas (who still wielded much influence). Because the Roman governor appointed and deposed the high priest, the office was essentially a political one, and apparently Caiaphas knew how to manipulate it well. Because of this, the reputation of the office was ruined. The Qumran community was especially critical of the high-priestly leadership, whom they called the "wicked priest."

The plot to arrest Jesus (26:5). The chief priests and elders cannot arrest Jesus openly because of his popularity with the people. They saw the tumultuous welcome Jesus received from the crowds just two days prior at his triumphal entry into Jerusalem. At this time of Passover, with thousands of pilgrims jamming Jerusalem and with nationalistic fervor running high as they celebrate the way that God liberated their ancestors from bondage in Egypt, the people have been stirred by the rumors that Jesus is their expected Messiah. The religious leaders will bide their time until the most propitious, secretive moment to arrest Jesus.

Jesus Anointed at Bethany (26:6–13). Matthew recounts the story of Jesus's anointing thematically, placing it in the context of the conspiracy to arrest Jesus. Placed in this context, the woman's act of homage stands out conspicuously against the duplicity of Judas and the plotting of the high priest, Caiaphas.

Mary anoints Jesus (26:6–7). On Saturday evening, just after the end of the Sabbath at sunset, Jesus and the disciples attend a dinner at the home of "Simon the Leper" in Bethany. Since Simon is hosting a meal in his own home, he has probably been healed of leprosy by Jesus, for lepers were required to live away from the common population. During the dinner, a woman (identified in John 12:3 as Mary) approaches Jesus carrying an alabaster jar of very expensive perfume. The perfume is pure nard, an oil extracted from the root of the nard plant grown in India. This is an expensive perfume oil used for a solemn and special act of devotion. By breaking the flask, Mary shows that she is not just pouring a few drops to enhance the aroma of the feast but is performing the highest act of consecration to Jesus, even anointing his feet.

The disciples' objections (26:8–9). The perfume costs at least three hundred denarii, equivalent to about a year's wages for the average worker in the time of Jesus. John's Gospel informs us that Judas Iscariot is the one who expresses the feelings of some of the apostles, especially his own, that the perfume could have been sold for money and given to the poor (John 12:4–5). But John likewise exposes Judas's real motives (12:6), since he regularly pilfered money from the moneybox. The other disciples do not know of Judas's thievery, but they also think that this is a waste of precious funding. Poverty was a pervasive problem in Jerusalem and throughout Israel.

An act of memorial (26:10–13). Jesus is not relieving the disciples of caring for the poor. Jesus here emphasizes that the woman is performing an act of homage to him that can only be done at this time while he is with them. There are special circumstances that affect the disciples' practices while Jesus is still with them.

Jesus goes on to show the even more profound significance of Mary's deed. Whatever her actual motivation, Jesus tells his disciples that what she has performed is an act of homage far more significant than even she knows. She unknowingly has begun the preparations for his burial, which will come sooner than any of them conceives possible. She is memorializing his death for all generations to come. In the proclamation of the gospel, the true story behind this story will be told that she is performing an act of worship to her Lord in setting him above all other values.

Judas Arranges the Betrayal (26:14–16). Judas leaves Bethany and travels the two miles to Jerusalem, where he meets privately with the chief priests to ask what they are willing to pay him to betray Jesus. Matthew is the only Gospel that specifies the agreed-upon amount of thirty pieces of silver. This amount is not only the price of a slave accidentally gored to death by an ox but is also apparently a way of indicating a paltry amount. Once Judas receives the amount, he probably returns to Bethany to join Jesus and the other disciples and to watch for an opportunity to hand Jesus over to the temple authorities.

As Judas enters this plot, his spiritual nature is revealed; he is not a true believer. Many reasons have been suggested as to why Judas does this, but most likely he is disappointed in the spiritual nature of Jesus's messiahship and decides to recoup what losses he has suffered in following Jesus for three years. Whatever the reasons, Judas's betrayal stands as history's most infamous act of treachery.

The Passover and the Lord's Supper (26:17–30). *Issues of chronology.* There have been several attempted explanations of the differences between the Synoptics and the Gospel of John, but the two most promising are as follows.

1. One view suggests that Jesus and the disciples celebrated the Passover according to a solar calendar known from a work called Jubilees and possibly used by the Qumran community. In this view, the Synoptic Gospels follow the method of the Galileans and the Pharisees, by whose reckoning the day was measured from sunrise to sunrise. Jesus and his disciples had their paschal lamb slaughtered in the late afternoon of Thursday, Nisan 14, and ate the Passover with unleavened bread later that evening. John's Gospel, however, follows the method of the Judeans, especially the Sadducees, in reckoning the day from sunset to sunset. These Jews had the paschal lamb slaughtered in the late afternoon of Friday, Nisan 14, and ate the Passover with the unleavened bread that night, which by then had become Nisan 15. Thus, Jesus

had already eaten the Passover meal when his enemies, who had not yet celebrated the Passover, arrested him.

2. Another view is perhaps stronger. This view suggests that the passages in John that seem to contradict the Synoptics all point to a use of the expression "Passover" for the weeklong series of events, not just the Passover meal itself. In other words, Jesus and his disciples ate the Passover meal on Thursday, the beginning of Nisan 15 and the weeklong feast, at the same time as the rest of those assembled in Jerusalem.

Preparations for the Passover (26:17–19). Knowing that Jesus has come to Jerusalem to participate with them in the Passover meal, his disciples ask where they should prepare for the celebration. Finding a man carrying a water jar would not be difficult, since women normally lugged water. Either Jesus has made prearrangements for the room with friends in Jerusalem in order to avoid the Jewish authorities, or else these were divine arrangements.

The betrayer revealed (26:20–25). During the Passover, Jesus reveals the betrayer. Jesus has anticipated the betrayal and even warned the disciples on their journey to Jerusalem, but his prediction of the treacherous act at the meal apparently comes as a surprise to all. Hence, they "were very sad" or distressed (v. 22). They do not expect a betrayal to come out of their tight-knit group that has experienced so much together for the last three years.

Jesus prolongs their dismay as he states, "The one who has dipped his hand into the bowl with me will betray me" (v. 23). Each of those around the room have dipped their bread into bowls that served the group, so this implies no more than one of those at the meal at that time will betray him, but no one knows who.

Even with the treachery, the betrayal does not thwart God's plans, for the Scriptures have prophesied the coming of a slain Messiah. This points again to the profound interplay of God's sovereign control over all human activity with each one's personal responsibility and culpability for one's own decisions. Judas has sealed his own destiny by his personal choice, and he is now personally accountable.

Matthew accentuates the contrast between the larger group around the table, who address Jesus as "Lord," and Judas, who addresses Jesus as "rabbi." Significantly, Judas is never recorded to have addressed Jesus as "Lord." This is perhaps a clue to the fact that Jesus knew all along those who did not truly believe in him as their Lord and who would betray him.

Judas, the one who will betray him, says, "Surely you don't mean me, Rabbi?" (v. 25). The tone of his reply is disingenuous, deceptively sincere, expecting a negative reply from Jesus. Judas has been carrying out his arrangements for the betrayal in secret, with no thought of anyone knowing about it. But Jesus's knowledge is divinely revealed: "You have said so." The NIV rendering of this phrase accurately reflects the literal Greek expression: "You yourself have said." Judas's own question has indicted him. Although Matthew does not record Judas's response or his exit, he most likely leaves at this point to make final arrangements for the betrayal. His deception is known, but he is satanically driven to accomplish his treachery.

The institution of the Lord's Supper (26:26–30). With the traitor gone, Jesus continues the Passover with the rest of the Twelve. He dramatically brings the symbolic significance of this meal to its intended fulfillment as he institutes what becomes known as "the Lord's Supper."

The bread (26:26). The Haggadah of Passover was the set form in which the exodus story was told on the first two nights of Passover as part of the ritual Seder (literally "order"). Central to the meal were three foods—unleavened bread, bitter herbs, and the Passover offering (a lamb in temple days)—along with the four (traditional) cups of wine. Jesus uses the bread as a stunning illustration, saying: "Take and eat; this is my body."

Jesus's twofold injunction with the explanation demonstrates that his body will be the fulfillment of the ceremonies surrounding the Passover lamb, as he becomes the sacrificial atonement for the "passing over" of the sins of the people. It is significant that Jesus uses bread, not the paschal lamb, to initiate the commemoration. Because of his death, the killing of a lamb will no longer be necessary. The later theological debates about the meaning of "body" and its relation to the presence of Jesus in the bread would not have even entered the minds of those hearing Jesus's words. They are having difficulty enough understanding the symbolism. But once the events of the cross transpire, they will, like Paul, recognize that the bread and the cup are profound memorials of the single most important event in history.

The cup (26:27–28). Continuing the symbolism, Jesus takes a cup, gives thanks, and asks all of them to join in drinking from it. Of the four cups of wine consumed at a Passover celebration, this is most likely the third cup. This third cup was often called the cup of redemption, corresponding to God's third promise in Exodus 6:6, "*I will redeem you* with an outstretched arm and with mighty acts of judgment." The death of the Passover lamb and the smearing of its blood opened the way for the redemption of God's people from Egypt, but the shedding of Jesus's blood, which this cup foreshadows, opens the way for the redemption of all humanity to enter into a new covenant relationship with God.

The poignant promise (26:29). Jesus gives a surprising twist to the occasion as he states, "I tell you, I will not drink of this fruit of the vine from now on until that day when I drink it new with you in my Father's kingdom." Jesus's words hold out a poignant promise (that his sacrificial death will bring forgiveness of sins) and a sad indication (that he will have to go away), but also an assurance (that he will return). When he comes again and brings the final establishment of the kingdom on earth, he will bring to fulfillment the time of peace and redemption for which his disciples are waiting and the consolation for which the people of Israel await.

Prediction of the Falling Away and Denial (26:31–35). After they sing together, Jesus goes with the Twelve to the Mount of Olives. They are most likely on their way back to Bethany, where they have spent each evening during Holy Week. Earlier Jesus predicted that one of the Twelve would betray him; now he implies that all of them will lack courage. The expression "fall away on account of me" (v. 31) indicates that there will come that night an extreme test of their loyalty to him as their master. They will not cease being his disciples, but they will fail the test of courage to stand up for him.

Their failure was also prophesied by Zechariah, as Jesus demonstrates: "I will strike the shepherd, and the sheep of the flock will be scattered" (Zech 13:7). This quotation demonstrates that even when God's actions are carried out by others, they are a result of his sovereign activity.

With his usual bravado, Peter does not listen to Jesus's warning and heed its caution, and his false bravado leads the rest of the disciples to join him. Jesus warns Peter that he will fail even more than the others. The crowing of the rooster is proverbial for the arrival of the day. Thus, the denial will take place before dawn.

The difference between Judas and Peter (and the rest of the disciples) is demonstrated by their behavior *after* their failures. Judas is satanically driven to accomplish his treachery because he never was a true believer. Peter and the other disciples falter, but their repentance later brings them back to Jesus for restoration.

Gethsemane: Jesus's Agonizing Prayers (26:36–46). *Gethsemane (26:36).* On their way out of Jerusalem, Jesus and his disciples stop at a place called Gethsemane, which John calls a "garden" (John 18:1, 26). At least four current sites have been suggested as the actual identity, but two primary ones claim scholars' attention. The first site now houses the Church of All Nations, which is adjacent to an olive grove about fifty-five yards square, with olive trees perhaps more than a thousand years old. The second, more likely site is located a few hundred feet north of the traditional garden.

Watching and praying (26:37–38). Once at Gethsemane, Jesus asks the inner group of three disciples (Peter, James, and John) to stay awake with him while he prays. Jesus does not ask them to pray but to watch. As he grievously anticipates his looming death, his overwhelming sorrow reveals a heart broken almost to the point of death itself, because he knows that he will experience his Father's forsakenness. This reveals the depth of Jesus's need for human relationship, which he feels is necessary to sustain him in his time of greatest need. It may be difficult to grasp that the Son of God had such needs, but to do so gives us a more adequate understanding of his incarnation.

Jesus's first prayer (26:39). Matthew reveals one of the most profound insights into the intimacy between Father and Son. With harmless urgency and trustfulness, Jesus lays his life into his Father's hands as he calls out with tender intimacy, "My Father." He started his earthly ministry by being tempted by the devil in the desert; now, at the moment when he is ready to accomplish his life's mission, the temptation is intensified to its maximum. This is the devil's last-ditch effort to attempt to convince Jesus that the cross is unnecessary. But Jesus has demonstrated a complete confidence in his Father's sovereign power and perfect will throughout his life, so at this moment of greatest temptation, he turns to his Father for guidance.

It is not death itself that evokes this plea from Jesus, but the kind of death. Although dreading the prospect of pain and death on the cross, the prospect of separation from the Father is a greater horror and a greater sorrow. But doing the will of the Father is Jesus's only motivation because he knows that millions of men and women, both before and after his triumph over sin at the cross, will be reconciled to the Father through his death.

The disciples' first failure (26:40–41). After intensely wrestling in prayer, Jesus returns to find the trio of disciples sleeping. Jesus called them to watch with him so that they could support his prayer to the Father. They have failed that charge, but he calls them to continue, yet now they must also pray about their own temptation. Jesus draws a contrast between their human spirit (not Holy Spirit) and its aspirations and their human nature that is impacted by sin, specifically here their physical humanness. Jesus is not creating a proverbial expression to excuse human weakness but is giving an example of how obedience to God's will is accomplished. Spiritual disciplines of watching and praying enable the spiritual heart to direct all aspects of a person's human nature so that the entire person is obedient to God.

The second and third prayers and failures (26:42–44). Now there is the conscious recognition that it is not possible for the cup to be taken away and that Jesus must drink its wrathful onslaught. He consciously submits to that destiny. This is probably what the writer of Hebrews understood when he wrote that Jesus "learned obedience from what he suffered" (Heb 5:8).

But the disciples have not yet learned this obedience, because again Jesus goes back to find the trio sleeping. They have not learned the discipline of spirit over flesh. As he goes away to pray again a third time, Jesus prays the same thing. Although there may be some development in Jesus's understanding of the nature of the temptation and the Father's will for him, Matthew allows us to see that even from the start, there is no deficiency in Jesus's prayer. He continues only to seek the Father's will.

The betrayer arrives (26:45–46). The divine clock ticks inexorably on; the time for Jesus to accomplish his mission of salvation through the cross has arrived. Jesus has perhaps watched the troop of temple police being led by Judas cross the Kidron Valley coming to the garden with torches. Instead of fleeing, he calls his disciples to meet this challenge head-on.

Application. *God is in control.* Perhaps the most important lesson that we can learn from this section of Matthew's passion narrative is that God is in control. When we rest in God's known will, we will find our peace. God is ultimately in control of all events around us. Human power structures, no matter how powerful they look, are not powerful enough to thwart God's intention to fulfill his ultimate desires and ends.

How to experience this in our day-to-day activities is one of the chief growing points of our discipleship to Jesus. You may have been laid off work. Your church board and pastor may be experiencing a deepening rift. Your youngest child may have been diagnosed with autism. You may have an erratic neighbor who threatens to sue you over water rights to his farm. You may have an ongoing struggle with your spouse. You may have sustained an injury that wipes out your chances of getting that potential scholarship to college. All of these can be a threat to the stability of your life. But the lesson from each of the passion-narrative scenes is that God is there to walk us through anything, if we will only turn to him.

The Lord's Supper as life's schematic. The institution of the Lord's Supper gives us a crucial experience of God's will for us, individually and corporately. It is not simply a religious exercise but a schematic for our lives. We will do ourselves much good to explore continually the many dimensions of the Lord's Supper, of which there are at least six.

1. *Backward.* The Lord's Supper points backward to Jesus's historical accomplishment of salvation as a finished act. As a memorial to his sacrifice, the Lord's Supper is a powerful reminder of the historical bedrock of our faith in his finished work of the cross.
2. *Forward.* The Lord's Supper looks forward to the time when we will enjoy the consummation of the kingdom of God and enjoy fellowship with Jesus in drinking the cup anew together with him. We also look forward with sober recognition that he will come again to reward those who long for his appearance and judge those who eat unworthily.
3. *Inward.* The celebration of communion is also an important time of self-examination, as Paul reminds us. Communion times can be important occasions of looking inwardly at one's heart and holding oneself personally accountable before God.
4. *Upward.* The Lord's Supper also looks upward as we remember that Jesus's death on the cross and burial in the tomb is not the end of the story. His resurrection is the foundation of our faith that we too have been raised with him, so that we set our minds on things above.
5. *Around.* Communion is also a time to emphasize the corporate nature of the Lord's Supper. Jesus's disciples need each other to help them stay faithful, and times of communion are powerful opportunities to renew our service to each other in the body.
6. *Outward.* The corporate nature of communion also points to the outward dimension of the Lord's Supper. The world is dying without the message of the good news that Jesus has provided salvation from sins through his death on the cross. As we renew our common commitment to that message, we are renewed individually to walk with that risen Savior in a world that waits to hear our personal testimony.

Jesus, the Prince of Peace. Christians live in the anticipation of the establishment of the kingdom, when Jesus will return to bring worldwide peace. But Christians also live in the reality of the new-covenant peace that Jesus brought through his work of the cross. The new covenant brings personal peace through the forgiveness of sin. The new covenant enables Jesus's disciples to be instruments of peace in this world through their message and their lives, and it enables them to have personal inward peace regardless of the circumstances of this world.

Jesus found peace in the garden of Gethsemane as he rested in obedience to his Father's will—and that despite knowing that his worst battles were yet to come. We likewise will find our life's greatest peace as we rest obediently in God's will for us individually and corporately.

MATTHEW 26:47–27:26

Original Meaning

Jesus Is Arrested (26:47–56). *Judas and the armed temple troop (26:47).* The most heavily armed of those coming with Judas would be a contingent of Roman soldiers assigned by Pilate for temple security, who were authorized to carry swords (*machairai*), the short, double-edged weapon used in hand-to-hand combat. Levitical temple police and personal security guards of the chief priests and Sanhedrin carrying clubs also probably make up another large detachment in the arresting crowd; they represent the highest authority of the Jewish people and are endorsed by the Roman governor's own forces.

Judas's kiss of death (26:48–49). This was the customary way of greeting a venerable rabbi and would have seemed to the other disciples as a greeting of peace rather than shameless hypocrisy. From this event onward, Judas is forever known in biblical and historical infamy for his betrayal of Jesus.

An insider betrayal (26:50). Jesus's response can be rendered as a question (RSV: "Why are you here?"), but the NIV appropriately renders it as a command continuing the theme of divine inevitability that permeates the passion narrative ("Do what you came for").

A disciple's armed resistance (26:51–54). Simon Peter tries to defend Jesus by taking the sword he is carrying and striking the high priest's servant. But he only grazes him, cutting off his ear. But Jesus tells Peter to put away his sword. Peter's use of force is not guided by kingdom priorities but by the human desire to retaliate.

Circumstances may indicate that Jesus's mission is thwarted, but events are not out of control. Jesus has come to carry out God's plan of redemption as prophesied. Jesus does not point to a particular prophetic passage here but to the Scriptures as a whole that indicate the purpose of his earthly ministry, which "must" (*dei*) lead him to the cross (v. 54). As was the point in the prayers at Gethsemane, obedience to the Father's will for his life is Jesus's ultimate desire, not pursuing his own will.

Jesus is no rebel (26:55–56a). Jesus mocks the contingent that has come out so heavily armed to arrest him, for he has been within their reach in the temple precincts teaching throughout the week. The question in the NIV, "Am I leading a rebellion . . . ?" shows that Jesus has no intention of being a militaristic insurrectionist. Their clever manipulations cannot thwart God's purposes. Jesus declares to these representatives of the religious authorities that God has ordained their deception long ago. In "the writings of the prophets," God's spokespersons predicted their wickedness. The evil deeds of the religious establishment will accomplish God's plan, but it will be to their ultimate personal and national demise.

The disciples abandon Jesus (26:56b). Jesus predicted the disciples' cowardice, which they rebuffed with false bravado, but Jesus's prophetic word comes to pass. Once again at Jesus's greatest time of personal need for human support, his closest followers desert him. He faces the cross alone.

The Jewish Trial of Jesus (26:57–68). Scholars have long noted the irregularities of the Jewish legal proceedings against Jesus according to later Mishnaic procedures. The anomalies of this trial do not invalidate the historicity of the Gospel records; rather, they point to the devious expediency by which the trial is conducted. Matthew highlights the fraudulence of Jesus's arrest and trial by pointing out that the teachers of the law and the elders have already assembled with the high priest. They are waiting to make a quick pronouncement of doom. None of the Gospel writers gives a full account of the judicial process leading to Jesus's death, but the overall pattern that emerges is that the Jewish authorities first try Jesus and convict him of blasphemy. Then they take him to Pilate and change the accusation to treason.

The house of Caiaphas (26:57–58). After his arrest in Gethsemane, Jesus apparently is taken to the home of the high priest, Caiaphas, which is a palatial mansion, so that Jesus's double appearance in a short period of time in the early morning hours is entirely within reason. Peter demonstrates a personal courage that compels him to follow Jesus and the arresting delegation to the courtyard of the high priest, where he sits down incognito among the guards. Peter is able to watch as Jesus is shuffled from hearing to hearing.

False witnesses (26:59–60). For the first time Matthew notes that "the whole Sanhedrin" is assembled to try Jesus, which means that the necessary constituents are in place. When a capital case was involved, the sages required that twenty-three members must make up a quorum. Instead of presuming innocence until proven guilty, the Sanhedrin tries to find false witnesses who will testify against Jesus that he has violated the law. The entire proceedings are a sham, for the Jewish leaders are manipulating the events to get Jesus out of the way as quickly as possible.

Destroying and rebuilding the temple (26:61–63a). Finally, out of the pack of false witnesses are two who testify that Jesus made the declaration, "I am able to destroy the temple of God and rebuild it in three days" (v. 61). Matthew does not explain why this charge catches the attention of the high priest when the others have not, but he considers this a serious charge against Jesus, for he stands up and confronts Jesus. The high priest apparently views Jesus as exalting himself over the temple of God.

Jesus is silent (26:63a). Throughout this long night Jesus has spoken of the divine inevitability of these events. The Scriptures have prophesied them, and the Father's will superintends them. The theme of silence is noted at various times during the trials, fulfilling Isaiah 53:7 and placing the responsibility for his death back on his accusers.

Are you the Messiah? (26:63b). "Messiah" and "Son of God" are basically equivalent expressions in this context, emphasizing that the expected Messiah is both the Son of David and the Son of God (16:16; cf. 2 Sam 7:14; Pss 2:7; 89:26–27). The high priest is not thinking of Messiah in a Trinitarian sense that we know today to be true of Jesus. Rather, Caiaphas draws on the Jewish conception of Messiah as the Davidic king, God's anointed, who will rule his people forever.

Jesus as the divine messianic Son of Man (26:64). Jesus affirms that he is the Messiah, but it allows him to go beyond Caiaphas's inadequate conception to give a further clarification of the kind of Messiah he is and in what way he is the Son of God. Jesus avoided those kinds of titles in his ministry because of the way that they could be misunderstood. Jesus declares that he is not just a human messianic deliverer; he is the divine Son of Man foretold in Daniel 7:13–14 and the object of the psalmist's reference to the divine figure who sits at the right hand of God (Ps 110:1–2), cited earlier in his debates with the Pharisees. He is the Messiah, the Son of God, but in an exalted way that they cannot possibly conceive. Jesus is making himself to be equal with God.

The charge of blasphemy (26:65–68). From the standpoint of the Jewish law, Jesus deserves death because he has made himself to be divine. From the standpoint of Roman law, however, blasphemy is not a crime deserving of death. Therefore, they will have to manipulate the charges and focus on Jesus as a common messianic pretender who is dangerous to Rome as an insurrectionist and is gathering around himself men whom he will lead in an uprising against the military government.

With what they perceive to be the height of blasphemy, the Sanhedrin officials spit in his face, strike him with their fists, and mock him. Spitting on him shows disdain for his claim to divine status, striking him shows how powerless he is, and slapping and mocking him for not knowing who has hit him attempts to demonstrate that he has no prophetic gift to know the future.

Peter's Denials of Jesus (26:69–75). *First denial—a servant girl (26:69–70).* Peter has courageously stayed through the early morning hours in that hostile environment. But when his own personal safety is threatened by public exposure of his affiliation with Jesus, Peter's courage deserts him. He does not deny her charge but evades it by denying to all within hearing range that he does not know what the girl is talking about. Obviously, he misses the chance to declare his allegiance to Jesus.

Second denial—another girl (26:71–72). This second girl's confrontation escalates from the first, and Peter's denial also escalates. The oath is not vulgar swearing but the invocation of something sacred to affirm the truthfulness of one's statement. Peter is sinking deeper into personal denial as he denies his allegiance to Jesus.

Third denial—those standing there (26:73–75). This third and final confrontation escalates the threat to Peter, so he intensifies his own denial by calling down curses on himself and swearing, which are most likely a doubling up of emphatic invocations of God's wrath on himself if he is lying. The more likely to others that Peter is lying, the more emphatic become his attempts to dupe the crowd with his deceptive sincerity—a well-known tactic of flagrant liars. His third and final denial takes the same form as the second: "I don't know the man!" (v. 74).

The brutal poignancy of Peter's self-revelation is starkly stated: "and he went outside and wept bitterly" (v. 75). The bitter weeping is recognition of his betrayal of Jesus; he has thrown away all that has given him a new identity as Jesus's disciple. But the weeping is perhaps also the first sign of his repentance.

Jesus Condemned by the Sanhedrin and Delivered to Pilate (27:1–2). Since the Jewish religious leaders at this time did not have the liberty under Roman law to perform capital punishment, they bind Jesus and take him to Pilate. Pilate was the Roman prefect and governor of Judea under Emperor Tiberius. When Pilate first became governor, he attempted to impose Roman superiority throughout Israel. He hung images of the emperor throughout Jerusalem and had coins bearing pagan religious symbols minted. But he was exposed to increasing criticism from the Jews for such acts, which may have encouraged the religious leaders to capitalize on Pilate's vulnerability, leading them to align themselves with him in his attempt to maintain peace. Their demand for a legal death sentence on Jesus, a falsely accused rival to Caesar, would not have been an unwelcome way of putting down a popular uprising.

Judas's Remorse and Suicide (27:3–10). *Judas' remorse (27:3–4).* Matthew shows the magnitude of Judas's remorse but appears careful not to suggest that the betrayer repents of the sin. Judas confesses that he sinned by betraying innocent blood; had he truly repented of his pattern of rebellion, he would have been impelled to seek forgiveness of his sin from God. Instead, he turns to the chief priests and the elders, who are just as guilty of Jesus's death.

Judas's suicide (27:5). The traditional reconciliation of the accounts of Judas's death by hanging in 27:3–10 and by falling headlong in Acts 1:18–19 is that the priests used the money of Judas to acquire the field, whereupon Judas hanged himself out of remorse (either in this field or elsewhere). Part of the structure on which he was hanging (perhaps the branch of a tree) broke, resulting in his falling headlong on some obstacle (perhaps rocks) and his insides spilling out.

The religious leaders purchase the potter's field (27:6–10). After Judas leaves, the chief priests are fixated on scrupulous adherence to religious custom but hard-hearted about their unscrupulous complicity in the betrayal of Jesus to death. The irony is that they are careful not to defile the temple treasury with blood money, but they are the very ones who earlier schemed to provide the money that shed the blood of an innocent man. Drawing on a combination of Jeremiah and Zechariah (Zech 11:12–13; cf. Jer 19:1–13; 32:6–9), Matthew demonstrates that the events surrounding Jesus's fateful journey to the cross are not the random tragedies of history but prophesied actions in which God superintends the redemption of humanity.

The Roman Trial of Jesus (27:11–26). *Jesus before Pilate (27:11–14).* The significance of the change of legal venues is evident in Pilate's first question posed to Jesus. This is similar to the question asked by Caiaphas, though Caiaphas had a different emphasis. This new charge focuses on treason and insurrection, that Jesus claims to be a rival king to Caesar. Jesus replies in the same indirect manner. His answer affirms the question but places the responsibility back on Pilate to discern properly what the question implies.

Pilate has certainly heard of Jesus prior to this encounter, but he is not prepared for the sovereign silence that Jesus maintains in the middle of these threatening circumstances. Jesus recognizes the trial is a sham, so he does not grace the charade with a reply. His refusal to speak may bring to mind among Matthew's readers the servant of Isaiah 53:7.

The crowd, Barabbas, and Jesus (27:15–18). Pilate's position as prefect gave him the authority to acquit a prisoner, whether or not already convicted and condemned. In an ingenious way of attempting to enfold the people to his favor, he apparently initiated a custom in earlier years in which he released a prisoner at Passover whom the crowd favored.

Matthew calls the prisoner Barabbas "well-known" (v. 16), evidently for his reputation as a freedom fighter esteemed by the people. Social unrest was common, instigated in part by these guerillas. The two criminals between whom Jesus was crucified are also called by this same term. These bandits were popular with the common people because they preyed on the wealthy establishment of Israel and created havoc for the Roman government.

Pilate knows that the high priest and Sanhedrin have not indicted Jesus because they care about the potential threat to Roman rule. Rather, they are envious of Jesus and his popularity with the people, and they want him out of the way. Moreover, his authoritative ministry threatens their entire way of life. Jesus's threat to their religious establishment has come to a climax, so now they know that they must get rid of him. Pilate is wise to their maneuverings, and he thinks that he has found a way to ingratiate the crowds to himself while subtly putting the Sanhedrin back in their place.

The dream of Pilate's wife (27:19). Matthew alone records the incident of Pilate's wife attempting to dissuade him because of her dream. Dreams have figured prominently in Matthew, so perhaps this dream is a supernatural one used by God to make clear to Pilate that Jesus is innocent of any crime. Nevertheless, the Romans often took dreams as omens. Since there is no indication that Pilate's wife is either a God-fearer or a disciple of Jesus, this dream may be a natural, though profound, premonition. In any case, whether supernatural or natural, her plea to her husband is an exoneration of Jesus for Matthew's readers. But Pilate does not heed his wife's warning.

The chief priests and elders persuade the crowd (27:20). Throughout Jesus's ministry, the "crowd" (*ochlos*) has been the object of his offer of salvation and discipleship, but all along it was an either-or matter. But now the religious leaders attempt to persuade the crowd to join them and go against Jesus. They are simply that—a crowd. They have shouted with amazement and enthusiasm at his teaching, miracles, and triumphal entry to Jerusalem. But when something better is offered, they give up their shallow allegiance.

The crowd turns ugly (27:21–23). Pilate understands that Jesus is not the dangerous hero whom the religious leaders are trying to portray. But he also understands that Jesus has claimed the title "Christ" as one who offers spiritual hope. That seems harmless enough to Pilate, so he tries to get the crowd to recall that many of them, even recently, have pinned their hopes on Jesus. But the crowd is unifying into a mob, and they "all" answer, "Crucify him!" (v. 22). This is the first time that this verb is used in the passion narrative, though it will recur six more times as the climactic events move inevitably forward. The crowd is well aware that the alternative fate for the one not chosen to be released will be death on a cross.

Pilate's charade (27:24). There is abundant background from Jewish as well as Hellenistic sources for the practice of washing one's hands as a way of showing public innocence. This is a virtual admission that Pilate has not found anything in Jesus deserving of the death penalty. But his duplicity cannot force the full responsibility of Jesus's death on the crowd or the religious leaders, for he still could have, and should have, released Jesus for lack of any evidence of insurrection and treason.

Israel's responsibility for Jesus's blood (27:25). Matthew now switches to a different word, "people" (*laos*), in the expression "all the people answered." In doing so, he emphasizes that the crowd and the religious leaders have had their opportunity. Now they must bear responsibility for not repenting and for asking for Jesus's death. *Laos* is the word that Matthew normally uses to designate Israel as a nation (e.g., 1:21; 2:6; 4:16; 15:8). Used here, the implications are ominous. The Jewish leaders and the crowds claim responsibility for Jesus's death as they declare boldly, "His blood is on us and on our children!"

In his first public sermon at Pentecost, the apostle Peter indicts the religious leaders, the Jewish crowds, and the Romans for Jesus's death. But to those who acknowledge their guilt, he also extends an offer of forgiveness of sins and salvation. Thousands of Jewish people, including many priests, received that offer in the first days after Pentecost (see Acts 2). In their ignorance they called down responsibility on their children, but this does not in any way excuse any form of anti-Semitism, then or now. Everyone is responsible for his or her own actions, but God's forgiveness awaits any who repent.

Jesus is flogged and sent for crucifixion (27:26). Roman flogging was different from Jewish flogging. The word Matthew uses for flogging (*mastigoō*, 23:34) in the Jewish synagogue is different from the word used here (*phragelloō*). This is a horrific method of torture. Whereas flogging in the Jewish synagogue was limited to forty lashes, no such restrictions limited Roman flogging. A condemned man (women were not flogged) was tied to a post and beaten with the cruel *flagellum*, a leather strap interwoven with pieces of bone and metal that cut through the skin, leaving it hanging in sheds. The repeated flaying often exposed the bones and intestines, and in many cases it was fatal. Flogging weakened the accused before crucifixion. With the Sabbath approaching, the Romans flog Jesus nearly to death so he will not be left on the cross after sundown.

Application. *Caiaphas—religious conviction forced by a leader.* Religious leaders today have responsibility to understand God's message and with it to shepherd God's people for him. Their certainty about biblical truths must be their unwavering passion, but there is always the temptation to believe that their convictions equal the truth itself.

Pilate—political conviction compromised by a leader. It is impossible to get into Pilate's head to understand all that he experienced and all the options that he considered, but it is obvious that he operated out of a political frame of reference. By contrast, Jesus's resolve to maintain the "good confession" (1 Tim 6:13) was expressed with silent witness to what his entire life had expressed. He did not resort to double-dealing or compromise to accomplish his life's ambitions. His silence before Pilate is deafening testimony to his unwavering commitment to God's calling.

They may not be many, and they may not come often, but there are hills that are worth fighting and dying for, even when they may come in the relative obscurity of our own little worlds. We may be far from centers of power and acclaim, but the responsibilities allotted to us have untold consequences. When the opportunity presents itself, each of us must contend for what we know to be right and for those for whom we are responsible, regardless of whether we think that the outcome will ever be known by others.

People—responsibility claimed does not deserve discrimination. Those who reject Jesus, whether Jew or gentile, will bear consequences. Today each individual Jew must consider the claims of Jesus and the message that the apostles bring. Only days after the crucifixion, thousands of Jews do repent at Peter's preaching about the Jesus whom they put to death (Acts 2:23, 37–41), and even many of the priests will become believers (Acts 6:7). The responsibility of Christians today is to love the Jewish people as God does, to recognize the special place they enjoy in God's plan for the ages, and to share the gospel with them as we would any other people. No one can support racial bigotry toward Jews by appealing to Matthew's record.

Peter—personal defeat requires intentional restoration. J. Glyn Owen followed Dr. Martyn Lloyd-Jones as the minister of Westminster Chapel in London, England. Over the course of several years, he preached a series of messages about Peter. The special concentration of the series of messages, which was later transcribed into book form, was on the transformation of Simon into Peter—from an eagerly rambunctious fisherman into the rock-solid foundational character of the church. The encouraging nature of this transformation is that it has much to offer us as an example for our own. Peter learned his lesson and stands as a powerful example of one who denied his Lord, but he was courageous enough to allow Jesus to restore him so that in turn he could help to restore others.

MATTHEW 27:27–66

Original Meaning

The Soldiers Flog and Mock Jesus (27:27–31). Typical of the treatment given to those about to be crucified, the soldiers strip Jesus of his own clothing and put on him a scarlet robe. Roman soldiers in Jerusalem at the time were known to play a cruel game with condemned prisoners, especially revolutionary brigands. The charges against Jesus make him fair game for this torturous pastime. The soldiers dress him up and mock him as the "king of the Jews" (v. 29).

The Journey to Golgotha (27:32–34). Criminals condemned to die were customarily required to carry to the scene of crucifixion the heavy wooden crosspiece (*patibulum*) on which they were to be nailed. The *patibulum* usually weighed thirty to forty pounds and was strapped across the shoulders. The scourging and loss of blood had so weakened Jesus that he could hardly walk and carry the *patibulum* because of the tremendous injury to his skin, muscles, and internal organs.

Simon of Cyrene (27:32). Cyrene was a town in North Africa that had a large Jewish population. Simon is likely a Jew who has made a pilgrimage to Jerusalem for the Passover. Tradition tells us that this incident of carrying Jesus's cross so impacted Simon that he became a Christian, perhaps through Peter's preaching on Pentecost.

Golgotha (27:33). The soldiers escorting Jesus and Simon arrive at the crucifixion site, which Matthew says is called "Golgotha." The name is a transliteration of the Aramaic word for "skull," which Matthew clarifies by providing a Greek translation, "which means the place of the skull." The common designation "Calvary" comes from the Latin word for skull, *calvaria*.

Wine and gall (27:34). Feigning that they are offering Jesus a cup of refreshment, the wine has instead been mixed with "gall," a bitter herb that may even be poisonous. When Jesus tastes the bitter drink, he knows it is not for refreshment but is only another way of torturing him. The bitterness will only intensify his parched thirst, so he refuses.

Jesus Is Crucified (27:35–38). *The guards cast lots and keep watch (27:35–37).* In the first of a series of allusions to Psalm 22, Matthew quotes nearly verbatim the Greek version of Psalm 22:18. Yet his readers know that as the soldiers divide up his clothing by casting lots, this fulfills Scripture. Here the lot is a form of gambling by the Roman guards as they divide up whatever is left of Jesus's clothes, which is probably not much. By so doing they take away his final external dignity and protection from the flies and elements that torture his beaten body.

As a deterrent to any Jews thinking of continuing his sedition or causing any other kind of uprising against Rome, the soldiers place a placard above Jesus's head. Perhaps Jesus wore this placard strung around his neck as he walked to Golgotha. Ironically, however, this is a statement of truth about Jesus. He *is* the king of the Jews, who has been rejected and framed by the very people he came to redeem.

The two robbers (27:38). The two sons of Zebedee had requested the privilege of being seated at Jesus's right- and left-hand side in his kingdom; with bitter irony, Matthew records that two rebel criminals form Jesus's right- and left-hand attendants on a cross, not a throne.

The Mocking of Messiah (27:39–44). *The people (27:39–40).* "Those who pass by" may include people randomly entering or leaving the city, but also those who have witnessed the trials. The expression "hurled insults" is literally "blasphemed," indicating that they deride Jesus for his blasphemous claims and for the bogus assertion that he would destroy the temple and build it in three days. This derision mocks Jesus's claim at supernatural power. If he has such powers, he should be able to save himself. Matthew's readers will hear in these taunts from the passersby another allusion to Psalm 22 (Ps 22:6–7).

The religious leaders (27:41–43). The religious leaders who comprise the Sanhedrin join in the mocking. How can Jesus save others and not himself? Matthew again alludes to Psalm 22 as the religious leaders mock Jesus's supposed trust in God (Ps 22:8). If he really is the Son of God, God would not allow him to die on a cross. Although they taunt him to save himself, Jesus must pursue his life's mission to the very end, because there the Son of God will truly save humanity.

The robbers (27:44). The two between whom Jesus is crucified join in the mockery by heaping insults on Jesus.

The Death of Jesus Messiah (27:45–50). *The darkness (27:45).* Darkness here displays a limitation on the power of Satan, God's displeasure on humanity for crucifying his Son, and God's judgment on the sins of the world.

Eloi, Eloi, lama sabachthani? (27:46). The connection between the darkness and Jesus's cry is close—the darkness is a symbol of its agonizing content. Once again the crucifixion scene recalls the lament of King David in Psalm 22:1. Matthew gives us a singular focus on Jesus's feelings of being abandoned on the cross. He must be separated from the Father in order to bear the sin of his people. He bears the divine retribution and punishment for sin, as the Father's cup of wrath is poured out on him in divine judgment.

Not only does Jesus bear the load of humanity's sin, but he becomes sin on our behalf. He became cursed by God for us. Jesus was not separated in his essence or substance from the Father as the second person of the Trinity. Rather, Jesus's divinely sustained humanity consciously experienced the full penalty of death for the sins of humanity. This lays the foundation for the theological doctrine of the atonement, in which Jesus's sacrifice on the cross is one of "penal substitution" or "vicarious atonement"—Jesus suffers our punishment for our sin.

But even in the depth of Jesus's abandonment to his atoning sacrifice, he still knows that this experience is not one of despair—he still calls his Father "my God, my God." The relational separation while bearing the sins of humanity cannot separate him entirely from God, because his consummate trust in the Father expects that he will not be abandoned forever and because the oneness of their ontology is indissoluble.

The bystanders think of Elijah (27:47–49). Jesus's call to God in Aramaic (*eli eli*; v. 46) sounds similar to the Hebrew name for Elijah (*eliyyah*), so the bystanders misunderstand him to be attempting to summon the prophet. At the sound of his cry, someone in the crowd runs to get a sponge, which he fills with *oxos*, a sour wine used by common people and soldiers as a daily drink with meals. Perhaps one of the bystanders is offering an act of kindness and mercy to Jesus. Or perhaps this person is continuing the earlier mockery; nothing indicates that the mockery of the crowds has ceased.

Jesus gives up his spirit (27:50). Jesus cries out again in a loud voice. Neither Matthew nor Mark gives the content of Jesus's final cry, but the implication is that this is one final agonizing experience of separation from the Father as he bears humanity's sin-punishment. Then "he gave up his spirit." Matthew shows that to the very end Jesus maintains volitional control over his destiny. He approaches his death willingly. The redemption that Jesus came to achieve was accomplished once for all.

Testimonies to Jesus's Death (27:51–54). *Testimony from the temple (27:51).* The curtain was an elaborately woven fabric of seventy-two twisted plaits of twenty-four threads each, and the veil was sixty feet high and thirty feet wide. Since only the priestly aristocracy would have known about the tearing of the veil, when only a few weeks later a number of priests became believers (Acts 6:7), they would have informed the Christian community of this event. The tearing of the temple curtain testifies that Jesus's sacrifice on the cross has fulfilled the hopes expressed in Israel's years of temple sacrifice. Jesus is the great high priest, whose sacrifice is the permanent satisfaction of God's wrath on humanity's sin (Heb 4:14–5:10). Jesus is the permanently accessible new temple in whom all who turn to him are reconciled to the Father.

Testimony from the dead (27:51b–53). Matthew's unique record of these events emphasizes the victory over death that Jesus's sacrifice on the cross accomplishes. Those who are raised are described literally as those "who had fallen asleep" (v. 52; NIV "had died"), a common New Testament idiom for a person who has died but whose eternal destiny is secure. As with the preceding miraculous testimonies, the supernatural raising of the bodies of these holy ones and their appearances in Jerusalem is striking testimony to Jesus's accomplished work on the cross and thereafter his resurrection.

The miraculously opened tombs at the time of Jesus's death are a prolepsis of the resurrection of Jesus, and the bodies of the holy people follow in a mere three days. Their appearance to people in Jerusalem is a witness to the efficaciousness of Jesus's work on the cross and the declaration of his victory over death in his, and their, resurrection. Matthew does not answer all the questions we would like answered about these miraculous events, but in narrating them he presents a unified testimony to the supernatural confirmation of Jesus's identity and mission.

Testimony from gentiles (27:54). The centurion has probably been in attendance since Jesus's Roman trial and subsequent flogging and mocking by the soldiers. He has probably witnessed many crucifixions, but the cataclysmic events of the earthquake and opened tombs, plus the manner of Jesus's death, combine to evoke the statement, "Surely he was the Son of God!"

The centurion is gaining insight into Jesus's true identity. The charge of blasphemy from the Sanhedrin was in part lodged against Jesus's claim to be the Son of God, to which Jesus responded with an affirmative. The centurion is certain to know the various charges against Jesus, because the military chain of command necessitates that he know about potential uprisings to rescue the convicted Jesus. As he watches the events unfold, he and his men are overwhelmed by the realization that the identification is truthful. Jesus is innocent of the contrived charges, which then leads to the logical conclusion that he is truly who he claimed to be—*the* Son of God, who sustains a divine relationship to the Ancient of Days as the Son of Man.

The centurion's evocation is in dramatic distinction from the religious leaders and the bystanders at the cross, who mocked Jesus for his claim to be the Son of God. It is a striking picture for Matthew's readers. The cataclysmic events recorded here testify to Jesus's true identity, and the centurion and his men make a step of faith to acknowledge the truth of that testimony.

The Women Followers of Jesus (27:55–56). Matthew now narrates a peaceful, yet melancholy scene of the women who have faithfully watched these events unfold. The expressions used to describe these women concur with the evidence elsewhere that they are Jesus's disciples. As the women followed Jesus, they cared for his needs, called him Lord, and worshiped him after the resurrection. These descriptions not only designate the women to be disciples but also describe them as *exemplary* disciples of Jesus. They are displaying a commitment to Jesus that the Twelve themselves should have displayed.

One of the most important perspectives on the women is that God used them as witnesses not only to the central redemptive act of history, Jesus's death on the cross and the sealing of the tomb, but also as witnesses to his resurrection from the dead. Since the women are present for Jesus's death and his burial by Joseph of Arimathea, they can verify that Jesus is truly dead, not just unconscious. God is bestowing a special honor on them. They are exemplars of true discipleship to Jesus, and because of their faithfulness and courage, they are given the special honor of being witnesses to these profound events.

The Burial of Jesus Messiah (27:57–61). *Joseph of Arimathea (27:57).* Matthew now narrates the remarkable arrival of a man named Joseph who claims the body of the crucified Messiah. Joseph is a member of the Sanhedrin, who appears as an exemplary Jew anticipating the arrival of the kingdom of God. He is an example of a person who apparently did not follow Jesus around in his earthly ministry but who was still considered his disciple, even while continuing to serve within the religious establishment of Israel.

Joseph requests Jesus's body from Pilate (27:58). Joseph's high standing within the Jewish community allows him access to Pilate, to whom he goes to request the body of Jesus so that he can give it a proper burial. Pilate releases Jesus's body to him immediately. Pilate attempted futilely to wash his hands of responsibility for Jesus's execution and perhaps sees in Joseph's request an opportunity to relieve himself of any responsibility for Jesus's burial. Joseph's action in initiating the burial of Jesus is both an act of obedience to Jewish law and an act of devotion to his lord.

Joseph prepares Jesus's body for burial (27:59). John's Gospel fills in some other details, such as another secret disciple, Nicodemus, unveiling himself at this critical moment to aid Joseph (John 19:39–40). The Jews did not practice cremation or full embalming of corpses, but the body was prepared for burial by washing it, dressing it in special garments, and packing it in the linen cloth with fragrant spices. Along with stifling the smell of the body decaying, myrrh and other aromatics represented the preservation of the body, which to the Jewish mind was the prerequisite of resurrection. Joseph of Arimathea and Nicodemus perform acts even more significant than they themselves understand.

Joseph's new tomb is Jesus's burial place (27:60). After the body is wrapped in the linen cloth, Joseph places it in his own new tomb cut out of the rock. After Jesus's body is laid in the tomb, Joseph rolls a large stone in front of the entrance. He and Nicodemus return to the city. Although part of the preparation for burial has been accomplished at this point, because the Sabbath is approaching they cannot work with the dead and thus must return after the Sabbath to complete the preparations.

The women's sad vigil (27:61). Matthew tells us that at least two of the women who witnessed Jesus's crucifixion sit opposite the tomb and witness the sad and lonely ceremony. These faithful women still stay with Jesus even in death. It is even possible that these women (and perhaps others) who have followed Jesus from Galilee and who have been close to Jesus and his family worked together with Joseph and Nicodemus to prepare Jesus's body for burial.

The Guard at the Tomb (27:62–66). *Wanting to keep a dead man dead (27:62–63).* On at least one occasion Jesus specifically predicted to the Pharisees that he would rise in three days. They have not forgotten. What they understood by Jesus's declaration is unknown, but they assume Jesus's followers will come to their senses and gain courage to continue the movement by perpetuating Jesus's deception. The Jewish religious leaders sense that things may get out of control, so they enlist Pilate's aid in keeping the tomb secure.

A deceptive attempt to prevent deception (27:64). The religious leaders allege that Jesus's first deception was his claim to be the Messiah, and his second deception is his claim that he will be raised from the dead. If this kind of rumor gets spread, they know it will be far more difficult to squelch the stories about Jesus's claims. But Matthew makes it clear that the real deceivers are the religious leaders, who actually deceive themselves.

Pilate orders a guard placed at the tomb (27:65–66). Pilate orders a guard to be placed. After a family placed the body of one of its members in a burial recess in the tomb, a stone was placed over the entrance and was often sealed with clay. However, the "seal" here seems to be more of an official security device, so it was more likely an apparatus such as a cord attached to both the stone that blocked the entrance and to the rock face of the tomb, with wax imprinted with the Roman seal anchoring both ends so that any tampering could be detected. The military contingent standing guard acts as the final security seal. While the religious leaders and Pilate have gone to extreme lengths to prevent a hoax about Jesus's resurrection, they provide another witness to the factuality of the empty tomb and the resurrection of Jesus, to their own judgment.

Application. *The outrageous cross commands our contemplation.* We must not minimize the outrageousness of the cross, because it is there that the God-man suffered a death that was unique. The Son of God bore the load of sin for humanity and experienced ultimate separation from God, while retaining in his consciousness a painful intimacy with his Father.

As we ponder the cross, the New Testament tells us that we will find in its shadow an example for our own lives—not in some kind of mindless self-abasement but in a lifelong conforming of our lives to the example of Jesus, who saw in the cross his life's mission of giving his life so that others could live. This is sometimes called *cruciformity*—that is, the salvation experience of dying and rising with Christ that embarks us on a lifelong process of being conformed to his image in a life expressed in faith, love, power, and hope. The cross commands our continual contemplation as we open ourselves to God's transforming and conforming power.

The empty cross creates our peace. To meditate on an empty cross should bring us the greatest expectation of our own destiny. In so doing it will become one of our most important messages to the world around us. Western culture idolizes the young, the beautiful, the strong. At times that same idolization creeps into the church. But if we wisely face our own mortality and appropriately emphasize our eternal destiny, we will give much more prominent place to the elderly saints among us who have so much knowledge, experience, and wisdom to pass on to the succeeding generations. Part of that is how to die well. Jesus's empty cross is a call to each of us to expand our vision of this life and courageously face life, and death, with the peace that passes understanding.

The wondrous cross demands our all. A contemplation of the wondrous cross of Jesus should cause us to take serious pause and ask *Why?* Why would Jesus do this for me? It should leave us with a sense of gratitude as we determine it is simply a result of his love for us. But it should also leave us with a sense in which we are bound up with him in such a way that when God sees us, he sees Jesus and the sacrifice he made for us, allowing us to be justified in his sight; we no longer need to take the penalty for our own sins. As a result, we are now free to live for him, to become who we were intended to be before sin had its devastating effect upon the world.

Consider the little-known figures around the cross. Their diversity is remarkable, but the confession of their lips and life is uniformly exemplary for us. We may not ever accomplish great feats in the eyes of the world, but when we are gripped by the profound truths that Jesus accomplished on the cross, we too will be energized by the Spirit of God to be men and women whose service to our master is a courageous witness that the gospel of the kingdom has triumphed. Jesus's amazing, divine, sacrificial love for us demands our soul, our life, our all, whether we are hotel housekeepers or hotel owners, school children or school teachers, ex-cons or police officers. That is the only proper response of a life that surveys the wondrous cross.

MATTHEW 28:1–20

Original Meaning

The Women Disciples of Jesus Discover an Empty Tomb (28:1–4). *After the Sabbath, at dawn (28:1).* Most of the same women who courageously witnessed Jesus's gruesome crucifixion and burial plan to visit the tomb in order to assist the family in finalizing the body for burial. The women go to the place where Jesus was laid prior to the Sabbath. Matthew focuses only on Mary Magdalene and this other Mary.

An earthquake, an angel, and a rolling stone (28:2–4). The conjunction "for" (*gar*) that begins the phrase "for an angel of the Lord came down from heaven" (v. 2) suggests that the earthquake accompanies the appearance of the angel or is the means used by the angel to roll the stone away, or perhaps the angel's moving the stone causes the earthquake. The brilliance of the angel of the Lord is often associated with descriptions of lightning, as is Jesus's own return. The white clothing symbolizes brilliant purity.

When the guards see the angel, they are so afraid that they shake and become "like dead men" (v. 4). These guards are battle-hardened veterans, used to facing fearful situations. But nothing has prepared them for this encounter. After the angel speaks to the women, the guards hurriedly go into the city to report to the chief priests.

The Angel Announces the Resurrection of Jesus (28:5–6). *The angel calms the women (28:5).* For the first time the angel speaks to the women: "do not be afraid, for I know that you are looking for Jesus, who was crucified." The perfect participial phrase "who was crucified" is used substantivally in apposition to Jesus. We can render this as "Jesus, the crucified one." The perfect tense generally indicates an ongoing result as a result of the completion of past action. Here and elsewhere in the New Testament, Jesus remains the crucified one.

The angel announces Jesus's resurrection (28:6). Jesus has indeed been raised from the dead. The agent of the passive voice "was raised" is not expressed, but this is a clear use of the divine passive, where agency is left unexpressed since it is obvious from the context that God the Father is the one who raised Jesus from the dead. He has made the final affirmation and declaration of the Son's identity and ministry by raising him. To complete the verification of the resurrection, the angel invites the women to enter the tomb to see the place where Jesus was laid just a few short days earlier. Jesus was not just raised spiritually but was resurrected physically; his body was no longer in the tomb.

The Angel's Instructions to the Women Disciples (28:7). *Women witnesses.* One of the most important perspectives on the women here is that God uses them as witnesses not only to the central redemptive act of history, Jesus's death on the cross, but also to his resurrection. They are designated by both the angel and Jesus to carry their witness to the other disciples as the first to testify to the reality of the resurrection.

Galilee. Galilee was the central location of his earthly ministry. Now Galilee continues as a central place of his ascended ministry.

The Risen Jesus Appears to the Women Disciples (28:8–10). *The women run to tell the disciples (28:8).* The women heed the urgent directive from the angel to go quickly to tell the disciples of Jesus's resurrection. They came to the tomb expecting to find death, but now everything is turned upside down, and even their wildest dreams pale beside the astonishing message that Jesus has been raised. Their future now includes the risen Jesus, the long-anticipated and now fully realized Messiah of Israel and Savior of the world.

The risen Jesus appears to the women, who worship him (28:9). As the women go, the risen Jesus meets them to confirm the reality of their hopes. He "suddenly" appears and gives an ordinary greeting, one they must have heard him utter on many occasions but now prompts them to fall at his feet to "worship" him. The presence of the risen Jesus turns their fear into worship. By mentioning that they "clasped his feet," Matthew subtly emphasizes that this is no mere spiritual vision but a physical resurrection.

Many scholars consider God's choice of these women as the first witnesses of Jesus's resurrection to be one of the bedrock truths of the resurrection narratives and the historicity of the resurrection itself. It is unlikely that any Jew would have created such a story as fiction. First, there was disagreement among some of the rabbis as to the acceptability of a woman giving testimony in a court of law. Some rabbis did not accept women as valid witnesses, for they were said to be liars by nature. However, this seems to be a minority opinion, for a number of others did allow women to give testimony. But because of that disagreement, it would seem unlikely that a Jew would fictionalize a woman's testimony in the case of Jesus's resurrection.

Second, the cowardly picture painted of the men hiding away in Jerusalem while the women boldly carry out their responsibilities to prepare Jesus's body for burial would certainly offend the sensibilities of Jewish readers and doubtless would not have been recorded unless it were true.

Finally, the listing of the names of the women weighs against being fiction, because these women were known in early Christian fellowship and would not have easily been associated with a false account.

They will see Jesus in Galilee (28:10). Jesus's intention in directing these women to call for his brothers to meet him in Galilee marks an important salvation-historical turning point. Since they are the first witnesses to the resurrection, this suggests that they should be regarded as equal in value to men and be restored as coworkers with men in the community of faith, a role they had been assigned from creation. The return to Galilee harks back to the region of "Galilee of the Gentiles" (cf. 4:15–16), thus preparing the way for Jesus's commission to make disciples of all nations. The historical precedence of going to Israel has been fulfilled. Now the family of faith includes all who are Jesus's disciples, from every gender, every ethnicity, and every religion.

The Conspiracy to Deny the Truth of Jesus's Resurrection (28:11–15). Matthew is the only Gospel writer who recounts these incidents, which has led some to doubt their historicity because of their obvious apologetic nature. However, if no rumor had ever been circulating, it is difficult to imagine why Christians would make up such a story and put this idea into other people's minds. And if the tomb were not empty, the religious leaders would have pointed to the evidence of a body. Rather, Matthew is writing for a Jewish-Christian audience who have presumably heard about the charges circulating among the Jews that Jesus's body was stolen by his disciples, while the audiences of the other evangelists may not have been aware of such charges. Therefore, rather than being a late legend created by the Christian community, in this story Matthew addresses a situation that is of uniquely pressing concern to his readers.

The guards report to the chief priests (28:11). While some of the guard apparently stay at the tomb since they have not been officially relieved of guard duty, others go into the city to report to the chief priests. Their report presumably includes what transpired up to the point when they fainted away—the earthquake, the stone being rolled back, the appearance of the brilliance of the angel, and the empty tomb. They apparently did not see the risen Jesus, only the results of his resurrection. But they know that they have failed their orders to secure the burial scene, because the tomb is empty.

The chief priests conspire with the elders (28:12). As soon as the chief priests hear the guards' report, they gather together with the elders for an immediate attempt at damage control. If Jesus were known to be raised, as he predicted, it would be a validation of his messianic claims, and the people will turn to him—which thousands do at Pentecost and thereafter. Even as the chief priests and the elders bribed Judas to betray Jesus, so now they bribe the guards to concoct a story. One might wonder how these deliberations became known to the Christian community until we recall that some of Jesus's own followers, such as Nicodemus and Joseph of Arimathea, were privy to the highest echelons of the Jerusalem religious elite.

The concocted story (28:13). Why do the religious leaders concoct such a dubious story? And why do the guards agree to be implicated for negligence of duty? As noted above, the religious leaders are desperate and want to hide what really happened. The guards are likewise in a predicament. If they accept the plan of the Jewish religious leaders, they are putting themselves in jeopardy with their Roman superiors for falling asleep. But at the same time, they are already in jeopardy because they have allowed the security of the tomb to be breached. They cannot deny the tomb is empty, and who would believe them about some angelic being? Additionally, they failed to put up a fight. Either way, therefore, they face possible execution for dereliction of duty. Thus, with the backing of the Jewish leaders, they at least have a chance to escape punishment, and the religious leaders see in their proposal a crafty way of accounting for the empty tomb.

The Jewish leaders' ruse (28:14–15). It would do Pilate no good to have rumors circulating that Jesus has been raised from the dead, so the Jewish leaders are confident that they can maintain a collaboration with Pilate to hide the truth of the empty tomb and at the same time cast the disciples in a negative light for trying to perpetuate a deception of Jesus's resurrection.

Matthew writes upwards of thirty years after these events, and yet he states, "And this story has been widely circulated among the Jews to this very day" (v. 15). This Matthean aside indicates an active attempt by the Jewish leaders to counteract the increasingly widespread declaration that Jesus was raised from the dead in vindication of his claim to be Messiah. The truth is often harder for a person to believe than a lie, and many then, and even now, fall for this conspiracy to avoid the radical truth of Jesus's resurrection.

Jesus's Great Commission (28:16–20). *The risen Jesus appears to his disciples in Galilee (28:16–17).* For the first time in

Matthew's narrative, the disciples encounter the risen Jesus, and appropriately their response is to worship him. All along Jesus has been leading them to understand his true identity as the Son of God, a fact in his earthly ministry that was difficult for them to comprehend. But now that he has been raised, which is the declaration that he is indeed God's Son, they are prepared to give him the homage that is due him.

But then Matthew strikes a jarring, although remarkably believable, note when he comments further that "some doubted" (v. 17). Since Matthew mentions only the eleven disciples, is he saying that some of them doubted? How many are "some"? The eleven disciples, who have received at least two or three appearances from the risen Jesus in Jerusalem prior to this appearance (according to the other Gospels), are prepared to worship him. Perhaps other disciples with them from Judea and Galilee, who have not yet seen the risen Jesus, are those here who doubt. It is difficult to grasp how those who doubt Jesus here could be those very eleven who have witnessed the dramatic removal of Thomas's doubt (see John 20:24–28), but this is likely the most straightforward reading of the text.

The risen Jesus gives his Great Commission to the disciples (28:18–20). As Matthew comes to the final three verses of his Gospel, he encapsulates the primary thrust of the whole book. In this famous Great Commission, Jesus declares that his disciples are to make more of what he has made of them. In that sense, the commission encapsulates Jesus's purpose for coming to earth, and its placement at the conclusion of this Gospel indicates Matthew's overall purpose for writing. Jesus has come to inaugurate the kingdom of God on earth by bringing men and women into a saving relationship with himself, which heretofore is called "discipleship to Jesus."

Jesus comes close to them and addresses them in order to bring strength and calm. He was and is and always will be their master, whose presence and words are what bring meaning and guidance to their daily lives. His first words are an essential foundation for the disciples' personal security, but also for the commission to follow. The all-inclusiveness of the Great Commission for the present age is indicated by the repetition of the adjective *pas* ("all"): "all authority," "all nations," "all things" (NIV "everything"), "all the days" (NIV "always").

The Great Commission contains one primary, central command, the imperative "make disciples," with three subordinate participles: "go," "baptizing," and "teaching." The imperative explains the central thrust of the commission, while the participles describe aspects of the process. These subordinate participles take on imperatival force because of the imperative main verb and so characterize the ongoing mandatory process of discipleship to Jesus.

Jesus's Great Commission implies more than securing salvation as his disciple. Implied in the imperative "make disciples" is both the call to and the process of becoming a disciple. Jesus spent a great deal of time guiding and instructing the disciples in their growth. He now sends them out to do the same.

Jesus demonstrates his messianic authority to call people of all the nations to be his disciples. This is the third time in Matthew's Gospel that he uses the verb *mathēteuō*. In the first two uses, *mathēteuō* has a passive flavor: "has become a disciple" (13:52; 27:57). Here the verb takes on a distinctively transitive sense, "make a disciple," in which the focus is on calling individuals to absolute commitment to the person of Jesus as one's sole master and lord.

Being a disciple of Jesus was primarily not an academic endeavor like the Pharisees, nor even commitment to a great prophet like John the Baptist. A disciple of Jesus comes to him and him alone for eternal life and will always be only a disciple of Jesus. The object of making disciples is "all the nations" (v. 19). People of every nation are to receive the opportunity to become Jesus's disciples. Jesus's ministry in Israel was the beginning point of a universal offer of salvation to all the peoples of the earth.

The first participle that modifies the command to make disciples is "go." Because Jesus now exercises universal authority, the entire earth is to be their mission field. To obey Jesus's commission may require some to leave their homeland and go to other parts of the world, but the imperatival nature of the entire commission requires all believers to be involved in it. The completion of the commission is not simply evangelism. Rather, it means calling unbelievers to be converted and to embark on the process of being transformed into the image of Jesus in lifelong discipleship.

The participle "baptizing" describes the activity by which a new disciple identifies with Jesus and his community, and the participle "teaching" introduces the activities by which the new disciple grows in discipleship. With the initiation of the new covenant through Jesus's death and resurrection and the arrival of the Spirit, Jesus's form of baptism is unique. It is the symbol of conversion, indicating a union and new identity with Jesus Messiah who has died and been raised to new life. In the act of baptism, the new disciple identifies with Jesus and his community of faith and gives public declaration that she or he has become a lifelong adherent to Jesus.

Baptism in the "name" (v. 19; note the singular) of the Father, Son, and Holy Spirit associates the three as personal distinctions, an early indication of the Trinitarian Godhead and an overt proclamation of Jesus's deity. This is the clearest Trinitarian language in the Gospels and is often accused of being a later theological formula inserted by Matthew, because it is purported to be too theologically developed to have been used by Jesus at this stage. However, this is not the earliest such Trinitarian expression in the New Testament (cf. 1 Cor

12:4–6; 2 Cor 13:14; Gal 4:4–7), and even in Jesus's earlier ministry and teaching we catch beginning hints of the plurality of the nature of the Godhead.

We have noted regularly how difficult it was for Jesus's followers to move from strict theological monotheism to recognize the plurality of the Godhead in the person of Jesus in relation to his heavenly Father. Now in his risen state, however, the cognitive dissonance is so profound that the shock has enabled a more complete paradigm shift to occur. The risen Jesus is at the heart of the Christian life and the tangible picture of the living God. He is not so much giving a formula as he is emphasizing a theological truth symbolized with baptism. Baptism is a ceremony of entry into the family of God, the family of the new covenant, so what one does in the name of Jesus one does in the name of the Father, Son, and Holy Spirit.

The final participial phrase in Jesus's Great Commission, "teaching," indicates the process by which disciples of Jesus are continually transformed through discipleship and the discipling process. *Discipleship* is the process by which a disciple is transformed, while *discipling* is the involvement of one disciple helping another to grow in his or her discipleship.

The pronoun "them" indicates that everyone who has become a disciple of Jesus is to be involved in the process of discipleship. All of his disciples—women and men, gentile and Jew, poor or rich—must be taught to obey everything he has commanded. The activity of discipleship is involved with "teaching." The emphasis is not simply on acquiring knowledge; the distinguishing feature is always that disciples are to obey or conform their lives to the teaching. All disciples, new and mature, are to be taught to "obey everything that I [Jesus] have commanded [*entellomai*]" (v. 20), so that they increasingly become like him. Jesus is not pointing to particular commands but rather to the full explication in his life and ministry for disciples. All that Jesus communicated by word of mouth is included in his commands, whether they are teachings, proverbs, blessings, parables, or prophecies.

But we should go even further to suggest that all of Jesus's *life* is included in *entellomai*. This verb unifies Jesus's words and deeds and therefore recalls the entire Gospel of Matthew. Jesus's life, whether in word or in deed, fulfills God's will in the Old Testament, and as his disciples teach other disciples to obey his commands, their lives will reflect the transforming will of God in their own every word and deed.

What Jesus did in making disciples of his first followers, succeeding generations of the church will do in the making of new disciples of Jesus. In other words, in the Great Commission it would be inappropriate for Jesus to state, "teaching them to obey everything I *taught* you." He did more than teach. He gave a new authoritative basis for life as a disciple in this age.

Jesus's entrance into history is encapsulated in the name Immanuel, "God with us" (1:23), and his abiding presence with his disciples is evident in his concluding assurance, "I am with you always" (28:20). A true Israelite would proclaim only God to be eternal and omnipresent, so here Matthew records a concluding claim by Jesus to his deity. Thus, Jesus concludes the commission with the crucial element of discipleship: the presence of the Lord. Both those who obey the commission and those who respond are comforted by the awareness that the risen Jesus will continue to fashion all his disciples.

This wonderful promise of Jesus's continual presence invites us as readers into the story. This should not evoke fear or a guilty conscience; rather, it should spur all his disciples on to proclaim the good news of the presence of the kingdom of God in our lives. We are the ongoing chapter of this story, walking receptacles of the presence of the risen Jesus and living demonstrations of the power of the kingdom of God. May we be faithful and obedient disciples of Jesus as we walk in closest intimacy with him and proclaim this good news that he is with us to the very end of the age.

Application. Although brief, Matthew's account of Jesus's resurrection and postresurrection appearance to the disciples in Galilee yields some immensely significant points for us to ponder.

Resurrection perspective on life. As we learn to view life through the empty tomb, it puts everything else into perspective. Our career takes on an eternal perspective, so that we can put our priorities of time and finances and success in line with God's will for our lives. Likewise, our marriage becomes a shared life with a fellow disciple of Jesus as we support each other to fulfill God's calling for us individually and as a couple. Similarly, whether it is the illness of our parents, the death of our child, or our own sudden battle with cancer, the empty tomb puts all our sorrow into perspective when we know that because Jesus lives, we can face tomorrow and plan for an eternity.

Resurrection power for life. Think of the power of an eight-cylinder truck or an immense construction crane. Think of the power that is behind lighting a city the size of New York. Think of the massive power of a hydrogen bomb that can eliminate a city that size. We have much power as humans to do good, and much to do evil. But with all that power, we do not have the power to raise someone from the dead. It took the power of the Godhead to raise Jesus, and that is but a portion of his power that he exercises.

Now that the risen Jesus indwells each of his disciples, that is the kind of power available to us to live the kind of discipleship to which he calls us. When we live with a resurrection perspective, we must focus our lives so that we can tap into resurrection power. We will then have the power to accomplish anything to which Jesus calls us—controlling our temper, overcoming addictions, remaining faithful to our commitments, maintaining patience with a parent demonstrating increasing dementia. Whatever in life comes our way, discipleship to the risen Jesus includes the power to accomplish it.

Maintaining a resurrection perspective on life has the same potential to light *our* lives on fire with resurrection power. If we grant the benefits and inherent power in the resurrection, what have we to lose? Death no longer has its sting; it can no longer keep us down, as it was unable to keep Jesus down. This gives us great boldness as we go about taking the message of the gospel to the world and committing our lives to Jesus's kingdom program.

Resurrection persuasion against lies. The resurrection of Jesus will always have its dissenters. People still use the stolen-body hypothesis to try to discredit the Christian faith, and we cannot become slack in our defense of the gospel and endorsement of the Christian worldview in a culture that brings Jesus's resurrection into question. As we saw earlier, much of the hardness of heart of the religious leaders had to do with their preconceived notions of what it is to be in right relationship with God. Today, the preconceived notions that prevent individuals from accepting the reality of Jesus's death and resurrection include a naturalistic worldview, which insists these types of miraculous occurrences are impossible; hence, there must be some sort of naturalistic explanation. The reasons may be different, but individuals will always find reasons to reject God's revelation to us, and our approaches must adjust to address these objections.

Resurrection purpose for life. The conclusion of any book, letter, or treatise usually contains an explicit statement or summary of the author's purpose for writing. Matthew is no exception. Matthew points to Jesus as the supreme Lord and Teacher and emphasizes that his life and teaching produced obedience to and understanding of the truth of God's revelation in his disciples. That same obedience and understanding will continue to be the hallmark of disciples, and his Gospel is readily usable for this purpose.

For much of church history the Gospel of Matthew was used as one of the primary catechetical tools for teaching disciples how to obey all that Jesus commanded. With its alternating sections of narrative and discourse, it gives one of the most complete pictures of Jesus's actions and words. In other words, Matthew has collected the entire life ministry of Jesus so that it can be passed on to succeeding generations of the church. Since discipleship is basically equivalent to the teaching on spiritual formation that we find in Scripture, Matthew has provided us an invaluable tool for our growth as disciples of the Lord Jesus.

The final saying of Jesus in this Gospel is what gives us the greatest assurance that we can carry out his purpose in our lives, because he promises unconditionally, "Surely I am with you always, to the very end of the age" (28:20). Our discipleship to the risen Jesus continues to be our greatest source of comfort, power, and security. As Matthew has demonstrated over and over, the arrival of Jesus began the greatest revolution that history has ever known. It begins in the heart, where Jesus enters and begins the transformation. But then it extends to every area of our lives, so that our entire lives are impacted by the power of the kingdom of heaven. As we conclude our study of this magnificent Gospel, may our prayer be that our lives will be transformed by our Lord's abiding presence with us.

MARK

INTRODUCTION TO MARK

Authorship. The earliest testimony connects Mark's name to the Gospel. It comes from Papias, bishop of Hierapolis in Asia Minor, who noted Mark's relationship to the apostle Peter. Although some modern scholars question whether Papias knew what he was talking about, the early attribution of this Gospel to Mark is credible. Why would the church want to credit someone who was not one of the Twelve for writing this work if it were not so?

To think that just anyone could write a Gospel that early Christians would accept as authoritative stretches credibility. Matthew and Luke testify to Mark's authority since they allowed themselves to be guided by him when they wrote their own Gospels. Matthew confers even greater prominence to Peter in his Gospel, which reveals the authority he invests in this apostle. It is not unreasonable to assume that Mark's Gospel, therefore, reflects the teaching of the apostle Peter, just as Papias reported.

Setting. Mark should be read as a pastoral response to stressful times. The church faced major crises in the 60s. Christians had to cope with the death of eyewitnesses, which created the need to conserve and stabilize the traditions about Jesus. Mark also composed his Gospel to encourage Christians facing increasingly trying conditions and to remind them of the foundation of their faith. Mark does not complain about the inhumane suffering that Christians undergo but shows that persecution should lead to confession—the confession by Christians that leads to the confession of others.

BOOK OUTLINE

I. Prologue (1:1–13)
II. Jesus's Ministry in Galilee (1:14–9:50)
III. On the Way to Jerusalem (10:1–52)
IV. Confrontation and Death in Jerusalem (11:1–15:47)
V. Resurrection (16:1–8)

MARK 1:1–13

Original Meaning

The Structure of the Prologue. The prologue briefly lets the readers in on what are otherwise secrets that will remain hidden in various degrees to all of the characters in the drama that follows. The point of these opening scenes is to let the reader know from the start who Jesus is and to stress that he comes to fulfill divine promises and his divine commission. Because we who read know who Jesus is, our failure to follow and obey makes us more culpable than the characters in the story.

The Title for the Entire Gospel (1:1). The first verse of Mark's Gospel functions as the title to the entire work. It contains three key terms that are vital for understanding what this work is about: the gospel (NIV "good news"), Christ (NIV "Messiah"), and Son of God. The first term, "gospel," refers to what is preached about God or about Jesus as the Christ, the Son of God. It refers to the whole story about Jesus—the words, deeds, death, and resurrection of Jesus and what it all means as God's act to save humanity.

Second, this work is about Jesus "Christ" or Jesus "the Messiah." For Jewish readers, expectations varied, but "Messiah" was often a title of the coming deliverer anointed by God who would carry out specific tasks related to the liberation of Israel. But Mark in his Gospel will fill the word in with his own distinctive understanding, and one must read carefully to see how Mark wants his readers to understand what it truly means for Jesus to be the Christ.

Finally, the title tells us that Mark's Gospel is about the "Son of God." The phrase does not appear in all early copies of Mark. Jesus as God's Son, however, is an important theme in Mark. The title emerges at pivotal junctures in the story: the baptism (1:11), the transfiguration (9:7), and the crucifixion (15:39). Jittery demons shout out this title (3:11; 5:7), and it appears on the lips of an outraged high priest (14:61). For Mark, being the Messiah and the Son of God are one and the same thing.

The Promise of Scripture Fulfilled and the Ministry of John the Baptizer (1:2–8). *The promise of Scripture fulfilled (1:2–3).* By quoting these verses, Mark certifies that the Torah (Exodus), the Major Prophets (Isaiah), and the Minor Prophets (Malachi) confirm what he is about to tell.

The ministry of John the Baptizer (1:4–8). Mark has little interest in John except as the forerunner of Jesus. In Mark, he is simply John the Baptizer, who comes preaching and whose baptizing has to do with the forgiveness of sins. John apparently demands that all come for his baptism. To call all Israel to baptism implies that in some way all Israel is defiled. Mark tells us that, for whatever reason, they come to John in droves to get this cleansing in the desert.

John's clothing and diet suggest two things. First, to go out to someone like this in the desert requires a break with the institutions and culture of Jerusalem. The way that is prepared will not be a comfortable path; it will require forgoing pleasures long taken for granted. Second, this description of John is reminiscent of Elijah. The crowds presumably believed that he was Elijah reappearing for his second career, to prepare for the imminent coming of God.

Mark is primarily interested in John's announcement that one who is more powerful than he is coming, who will baptize with the Spirit.

Jesus's Baptism (1:9–11). *Jesus of Nazareth baptized by John (1:9).* Unlike the urban sophisticates who come from Jerusalem, Jesus comes from a town that did not even rate a mention in the Old Testament. He does not come with some special aura or halo.

The ripping of the heavens (1:10a). Mark does not use the word "open" (*anoigō*), as some translations render it. Instead, he describes that the heavens are "torn" (*schizō*), as one might imagine a bolt of lightning tearing through its domain. It is a significant difference. What is opened may be closed; what is ripped cannot easily return to its former state. When Jesus comes out of the water, Mark tells us, all heaven breaks loose.

The descent of the Spirit (1:10b). The same Spirit that once hovered over the primeval waters in the beginning of time now descends on Jesus. The beginning of the gospel is then also the beginning of a new creation. This time, however, the Spirit hovers over a human being, not over a formless void, which suggests that God intends to transform humanity.

The declaration of the voice from heaven (1:11). The announcement conveys several things to a reader attuned to the Old Testament. First, in the Old Testament, God is delighted in Israel when Israel is obedient. What the Scriptures ascribe to Israel, Mark transfers to Jesus. Second, some suggest that this phrase may be an allusion to another biblical "beloved son"—Isaac, whom Abraham offered up (Gen 22:2). Finally, Mark's language recalls Psalm 2:7 and Isaiah 42:1. One can interpret the voice at Jesus's baptism as God's announcement that Jesus has been chosen to rule over his people and that he assumes royal power as king.

Testing in the Desert (1:12–13). The Spirit's descent on Jesus drives him deeper into the desolate desert and into the clutches of Satan and the wild beasts for forty days, a biblical round number. The beasts are malevolent and are the natural confederates of evil powers. The desert represents the uncultivated place of the curse, paradise lost, and the realm of Satan. Now Satan must contend with a new Adam, who has the power of heaven at his side and angels as his cornermen.

Application. Mark shows no interest in listing Jesus's human credentials, because those things might cause the reader to miss the divine dimension of who Jesus is. Jesus's status does not derive from his family pedigree but from God. The narrator gives us access to this divine dimension in the prologue so that we know in advance the answers to the questions raised by a variety of baffled characters in the story.

The opening section of Mark is frequently used as an Advent text in lectionaries. Most Christians consequently associate it with preparing the way for a babe in a manger and assume that it has something to do with getting ready for the coming of the Christ by catching the Christmas spirit. It is questionable, however, whether this text calls for us to do anything to prepare the way for the Christ. Jesus is the one who must be out in front, blazing the trail and leading. Disciples are those who follow in his way.

The problem is that the way that Jesus prepares for us is not the one we want to travel. It is arduous and paved with suffering, but it is one that we must journey to get home. In following the way that Jesus has prepared, disciples will encounter many enemies, just as Jesus did. God's activity has been hidden from human beings, and even when it is revealed through Jesus, many will be unable to see. Those who do see will take comfort when they pass through the desert. They will know that Jesus has already been there and knows the way. All they have to do is follow.

MARK 1:14–15

Original Meaning. *John's arrest (1:14a).* John's arrest sets the stage for the proclamation of the gospel. Herod Antipas may have thought he was getting his prophetic nemesis out of the way, but in reality it is all part of preparing the way for the coming of the kingdom of God.

Jesus's message (1:14b–15). Jesus returns triumphantly from the combat in the desert to Galilee and joyously announces the good news of God. The coming of the kingdom of God is the central theme in the Gospel. Jesus announces that the time of waiting for God's intervention is over, which means that all that God had said and done in history is reaching its denouement. When God steps onto the stage of human history, it always comes as a surprise and as a scandal to those whose field of vision is limited to merely finite human possibilities and whose time is measured only by the tenure of transient human kings. In the midst of the present moment, one can easily forget that God bestrides time and history and works by a different clock.

The dominion of God has come near—so near that Mark believes people can touch it in Jesus. The future created by God is no longer a flickering hope light years away; it has become available in the present. The divine rule blazed abroad by Jesus, therefore, requires immediate human decision and commitment: repentance, submission to God's reign, and trust that the incredible promises of Scripture are finding their fulfillment.

Application. *The proclamation of victory.* Jesus's clash with Satan in the desert clearly did not end in a tie, because the preaching of the good news of God that immediately follows is the proclamation of victory. The victory peals throughout Jesus's ministry in many ways in commands and announcements. Christians are not to be defeatist but confident in their proclamation that the victory has already been won.

The announcement of victory. Jesus is confident that God has prepared the end of the age of this world. The kingdom of God has come near and is about to foreclose on the bankrupt kingdoms of this world. Christians need to give evidence of the victories that are being won.

Response by those who hear. The preaching of repentance encounters at least four obstacles today. First, people tend to wince when they hear talk of repentance because that cry has so often been used to harangue others. Jesus's call to repent is not a caustic reprimand but an invitation to switch allegiances. Second, another problem in preaching repentance to our generation is created by the human penchant to become infuriated at anyone who would dare to tell us we need to change. This pride first reared its ugly head with Adam. Adam tried to blame both Eve and God for his sin. Eve tried to shift blame to the serpent. The problem is that when we lose any sense of sin and responsibility, we also lose any burning desire for pardon. If we do not admit that we have a problem, then we do not get down on our knees and come to God for the solution. Third, our contemporary culture has a shallow view of *sin*. Many have no sense that they have rebelled against God. Some even argue that there is no such thing as sin, and they are perplexed and dismayed by how so many Christians in history have been tormented by their sin. Finally, our contemporary culture has a shallow view of *repentance*. Many have washed, deodorized, and perfumed their spiritual lives through a variety of religious rituals and believe that they have done their duty before God while countless unconfessed sins lurk within.

The call "to believe the good news" indicates that repentance is not an end in itself but the first step of faith. Where faith is absent in the characters in the story, it must be because repentance is absent. Only those who have turned their lives toward God will be able to see and believe what is not self-evident to others, because the evidence is not compelling but veiled and paradoxical.

MARK 1:16–45

Original Meaning

Jesus's Call to Discipleship (1:16–20). Jesus abruptly appears by the Sea of Galilee and without warning calls unsuspecting fishermen to be disciples. The disciples are called to be agents who will bring a compelling message to others that will change their lives beyond recognition. Jesus's call has the same effect on them. The call so overpowers these disciples that their lives will never be the same again.

Teaching with Authority (1:21–28). The next scene, depicting Jesus teaching in a synagogue, concludes with a stunned crowd extolling him as one who teaches with authority and with the news of his feats rocketing through the Galilean countryside. The crowds detect that one is in their midst who speaks for God and not simply about God, as the scribes do. Jesus confronts demons with destruction and Judaism with a new teaching. Consequently, both demons and the religious authorities will be threatened by him.

An outburst from a man with an unclean spirit interrupts Jesus's teaching. Most would take steps to remove the troublemaker from a place of worship, but Jesus moves to deliver the troubled man. Only demons and angels fathom the mysteries of the unseen world at this point in the narrative. They recognize that Jesus is not just another exorcist, but the one God has anointed to break the rule of Satan.

The unclean spirit's noisy recognition of Jesus may be viewed as a panicked defensive stratagem or as a reverent acknowledgment of his power. Jesus tells the spirit to shut up. One might think that Jesus would appreciate the free advertising before the synagogue crowd. The unclean spirit is right, but Jesus does not want testimony that is demonic. The demon's recognition of Jesus also can only mislead others. Jesus's healing miracles do not simply remedy human physical maladies; they represent a war against demonic forces.

Healing Fever (1:29–31). In this incident, Jesus goes to Peter's mother-in-law and raises her up by seizing her hand, and the fever forsakes her. A literal rendering, "the fever forsook her," suggests, as do the other two references to fever in the New Testament, that the cause of the fever was supernatural (either induced by demons or as a divine chastisement). What is significant is Jesus's miraculous ability to extinguish a heavenly fire—something that only God or God's agent could do.

Summary of Healing and Jesus's Affirmation of His Ministry (1:32–39). The Sabbath ends in the evening, and the next scene pictures the whole city pounding at the doors. The next morning finds Jesus venturing out to "a solitary place" to pray (v. 35). The desire for secluded prayer makes it plain that Jesus is not a sorcerer working by magic independent of God's help. His authority, strength, and power come from God alone.

Jesus meets temptation again in this lonely place when Simon and those who are with him "hunt him down" (*katadiōkō*; NIV "went to look for him," v. 36). They are looking for him in Capernaum because of the miracles, not because of his words. Jesus is not interested in the fleeting adulation of crowds and refuses to go back to Capernaum because he is to go to preach to all Israel. The good news cannot be static. Throughout the Gospel, Jesus keeps his bags packed, traveling hither and yon. He will not be distracted from his divine purpose, even by success, and will not remain as a localized guru or healer.

Healing the Leper (1:40–42). A leper comes to him and begs him on his knees, "If you are willing, you can make me clean." At verse 41 the updated NIV (2011) has replaced "is indignant" for the earlier NIV (1984) reading, "filled with compassion." If Jesus's first response is anger, he is not annoyed at the man for breaching the ritual barriers that bar him from any contact with others. He may be expressing the anger of God toward the ravages of the disease. His compassion for the man is expressed in his touch, probably the first time another "clean" human has touched this social outcast in a long time. He also commands him to "be clean" (v. 41). At Jesus's word, the leprosy leaves the man immediately. Jesus just as immediately sends him away.

The Commands to Keep Silent (1:43–45; cf. 1:25, 34). Mark 1 records the first of Jesus's frequent commands to demons and to those whom he healed to keep silent. The command makes clear that as a miracle worker Jesus wants to remain hidden; Jesus has no interest in taking on the role of a celebrity healer. Jesus does not trust a faith based on spectacles, and he knows that the clamor of the moment will not last. He also knows that God's power is not revealed solely through miracles. It becomes clearest in the crucifixion, but those who want only miracles can see nothing.

Jesus also prefers to keep the news of his miracles quiet so that it will give him more time to put off his inevitable destruction by the powers that be and to sow the word. Whenever someone disobeys this command, the next scene begins by mentioning the crush of the crowds. The hubbub restricts Jesus's free movement, as he is harried by the increasing numbers of supplicants and autograph hounds. Ironically, Jesus's attempts to cloak himself in secrecy only serve to magnify his reputation.

Further, as far as Mark is concerned, the command to secrecy makes it clear that any charges of insurrection made against Jesus are false. Consequently, Rome has no reason to fear him as king of the Jews, intent on fomenting an uprising of the people.

Finally, the failure to hush those who are healed reveals that the news of his power to heal is not something that can be kept hidden. One cannot keep silent, and the good news will spread to the ends of the earth.

Application. *Discipleship.* The call and the instant response of these fishermen reveal something of what discipleship to Jesus entails and should shatter our comfortable world of middle-class discipleship. Few would make the radical commitment these first disciples made, and most would hope that Jesus might offer a less rigorous category of auxiliary discipleship, which would promise the same rewards while allowing one to continue the pursuit of money and success.

Jesus's authority and ours. To evaluate religious leaders today, we must judge them by the standard of Jesus. Do they share his aversion to publicity and acclaim? Do they want to receive credit for all that happens? Are they primarily interested in a power grab, in building empires for themselves, and in serving their own needs? Do they truly speak in the name of the Lord from sincere motives? Are they accessible to those in need, not just the wealthy and influential but those from the margins of society?

Healing and our ministry. If Jesus is the model for the church's ministry, we see that he never condemns the afflicted. He never tells people that they are sinners or that they are possessed by unclean spirits. We see, instead, one who is confident in the power of God, who touches the unclean and restores the banished to his community and the sick to a meaningful role of service.

If one does believe that God wills our physical and spiritual wholeness and that God's power remains available to us and can intervene directly in our lives, then one must allow for Christian healing today. Christians and Christian communities can be instruments of that power and love. It does not necessarily follow that because many persons today have not witnessed New Testament quality miracles, they therefore are no longer possible. We do not understand the vast world of microorganisms, let alone how God works in our world. It is best, therefore, not to place limits on God regarding healing.

MARK 2:1–12

Original Meaning

Healing and Forgiveness (2:1–9). The impenetrable thicket of people surrounding the house Jesus is speaking in presents a roadblock for friends of a paralytic man, who want to bring him to Jesus so that he can also be healed. The crowd is only one of the obstacles that needs to be overcome for the paralyzed man to be healed. As the story progresses, the reader learns of two other impediments: the suspicious skepticism of the teachers of the law and the potential hesitancy of the man to act on Jesus's command.

Digging through a roof and dropping their friend before Jesus is a silent but dramatic plea for healing, and Jesus recognizes that only a tenacious faith would have led these men to go to so much trouble. The merciful granting of their request comes when Jesus announces to the paralytic, "Your sins are forgiven" (v. 5). Mark does not report the reaction of the friends or the man to these words, only the silent misgivings of the teachers of the law, whose "sitting" contrasts with the active demonstration of faith of the men on the roof. They are asking themselves, "What possible redemptive authority can this man have?" To presume to forgive sins is an arrogant affront to the majesty of God, which appropriately can be labeled blasphemy.

Proof that Jesus speaks for God comes in his response to these teachers' unexpressed censure. He knows in his spirit that they question thus in their hearts. He skirts the issue of blasphemy with a riddling question of his own, in effect saying, "Which is easier, to make a theological pronouncement about the forgiveness of sins or to provide empirical proof that the man's sins have indeed been forgiven by virtue of his ability to get up and walk away?"

The Son of Man (2:10–12). To show the teachers of the law that his pronouncement of forgiveness is not just idle theological prattle, Jesus commands the paralytic to get up and walk so they may know that the Son of Man has authority to forgive sins on earth. The word confirms that their alarm is not misplaced. Jesus does presume to forgive sins on the basis of grace—something that a priest in the temple could not do, that even the law could not do. How is it that Jesus can usurp the prerogatives of God and proclaim forgiveness of sins, willy-nilly? How is he able to speak for God in such startling and untraditional ways? Can sin be dismissed so effortlessly? No! The crucifixion will clarify this matter.

The final obstacle to the man's healing is his own skepticism. This final obstacle to healing is overcome when the man displays the same faith as his friends by obeying Jesus's command and goes out before all, his mat tucked under his arm. Presumably the crowds now make way, and the roof is raised once more in an explosion of glory to God. Their praise confirms that what Jesus has done is no great impiety but reason to glorify God.

Jesus's climactic announcement refers to himself as "the Son of Man" (v. 10). No consensus exists about what this title, if it can be considered a title, was intended to conjure up in the minds of Jews in the first century. It is clear, however, that in Mark it most adequately expresses who Jesus is. Although the term Son of Man is undefined, we do learn what he does. He has authority to forgive sins. He is Lord of the Sabbath. He will be betrayed, suffer ignominy and death, and be raised on the third day. He comes not to be served but to give his life as a ransom for many. He will be seated at the right hand of power, return on the clouds, and gather his elect.

Application. Many today are skeptical of miraculous healing that does not use medical means. Our regard for the miracles of modern science often makes the church and the clergy seem superfluous. Many physicians, therefore, do not want the clergy interfering in the sickroom, especially worrying patients about the issues of sin, until the medical fight is over.

The healings of Jesus reveal that God is for healing and therefore can work through medicine and surgery as much as faith and prayer, but faith and prayer may not be neglected. As mind and spirit can effect the onset of a disease, they can also effect healing. Healing involves far more than the physical dimension; it involves mental, social, and spiritual dimensions as well. Faith, prayer, and a deep sense of the forgiveness of sins are therefore not simply religious placebos but are essential elements of discipleship to Jesus, the Son of Man. He has come to inaugurate the kingdom of God and make his people whole—if not in the present age, then certainly in the resurrection and the age to come.

MARK 2:13–3:6

Original Meaning

The Call of Levi the Tax Collector and Dinner in His House (2:13–17). Jesus returns to the lake. As he passes along the shore, he once again singles out a person and challenges him to follow him. This time it is a tax official, Levi son of Alphaeus, busy with his duties at the tax office, just as the fishermen had been with their nets. Levi is no tax baron but one who is stationed at an intersection of trade routes to collect tolls, tariffs, imposts, and customs, probably for Herod Antipas. Tax officials were hardly choice candidates for discipleship since most Jews in Jesus's day would dismiss them as those who craved money more than respectability or righteousness.

Levi responds to Jesus's call as promptly as the fishermen did and gets up and follows Jesus, but his obedience marks an even more radical break with his past. The other disciples can always go back to fishing, but not so a toll collector who abandons his post. The next scene finds Levi along with many other toll collectors and sinners who follow Jesus and eat at "his house" (literal translation, 2:15; against NIV's "Levi's house"). The "house" in Mark is connected to Jesus. On this reading, Levi follows Jesus and sits at table in *Jesus's* house, at the place where he is staying. Jesus then serves as the host of a ragtag assemblage of social pariahs.

In other words, Jesus does more than preach repentance to

sinners; he befriends them. This display of open acceptance of sinners appalls the Pharisees. Their dismay precipitates Jesus's comment about the sick needing a physician. No physician waits for the ill to recover fully before consulting with them. As their physician, Jesus offers the remedy that vanquishes the illness of these so-called sinners.

One should not picture Jesus as simply partying with notorious sinners. For one, they may have been labeled "sinners" by pietist groups such as the Pharisees out of disdain for their refusal to heed their guidance on proper holiness. For another, to follow Jesus in the full sense of the word requires repentance and obedience. His goal in reaching out to the sick is to bring about healing and transformation in their lives, not to gather them together for a fun time. Instead of sorting people into classifications, holy and unholy, clean and unclean, righteous and sinner, Jesus gathers them under the wings of God's grace and love.

The Question of Fasting (2:18–22). The query about fasting prompts three parabolic answers. The first response assumes that the kingdom of God, which has drawn near in Jesus's preaching and merciful activity, is not a funeral wake but a wedding party. The second and third responses draw on metaphors from everyday life to illustrate the significance of Jesus's ministry. He has not come to patch up an old system that does not match the revolutionary rule of God. The old, exemplified by the condemnation and exclusion of sinners in the previous controversy and the practice of fasting in this debate, cannot contain the new. Both will be ruined if they are combined.

Two Sabbath Controversies (2:23–3:6). This section concludes with two Sabbath controversies. The first (2:23–28) is provoked when the Pharisees, who seem to function here as a kind of religious police, spot the disciples plucking grain as they saunter through a field. Jesus's response recalls a Davidic precedent, when David took it upon himself to violate the law by eating the bread of the Presence (1 Sam 21:6). David was not just a hungry man, however. He was to become the king of Israel, the ancestor of the Messiah, and a type of the Messiah-King. His personal authority legitimated his actions. If the strict regulations regarding the bread of the Presence could be set aside for David, who was fleeing for his life, how much more can holy regulations be set aside for Jesus (and his companions), whom Mark presents as David's Lord (Mark 1:2–3; 12:35–37) and who is in a situation of far greater urgency in proclaiming the coming of the kingdom of God?

The second part of the argument moves in a different direction, with the premise that God created the idea of the Sabbath for the well-being of humans, not the other way around. The priority of human need always outweighs the need for humans to conform to ritual formalities. Jesus argues that it does not transgress God's will for hungry people to have something to eat on the Sabbath, even if it infringes on the Pharisees' narrow interpretation of what is permitted.

The third part of the argument consists of the climactic announcement that the Son of Man is Lord of the Sabbath. This statement boldly affirms that, as Lord, the Son of Man is the one who decrees what is lawful and unlawful, permissible and impermissible, and any customs ordained by the Pharisees or their traditions are thereby rendered null and void.

The second controversy over the Sabbath (3:1–6) augments the humanitarian purpose of the law by revealing how easily rules can get in the way of restoring people to health. It also exposes the true nature of Jesus's opponents. It begins with the notice that they are "looking for a reason to accuse Jesus," treacherously inspecting his every move (v. 2). They do not question his power to heal—that is presumed by now; they want to see if he will heal on the Sabbath and violate their interpretation of the law. A Sabbath violation, just like blasphemy, was worthy of death. The segment ends with the Pharisees joining forces with the Herodians to plot his death. Of what is he guilty? Bringing healing on the Sabbath! This reveals more about the opponents than it does about Jesus or what is permissible on the Sabbath.

With his defiant question in 3:4, Jesus frames the issue around doing good or doing evil, saving life or destroying it. The question contains its own answer: doing good is not to be limited to certain days. Even on the Sabbath one must make the right choice. Suffering may be alleviated at any time, and to refrain from doing good is to abet evil and to pick death over life.

The sharp reaction to what Jesus does in this incident is completely unwarranted. Healing by speaking is not a breach of the Sabbath. Jesus only violates the Pharisees' finespun interpretation of the law—an interpretation that fosters death because these self-appointed guardians of the Sabbath would insist that the man return the next day if he wants healing, so as to avoid any hint of desecrating the sacred day. These critics are so blindly cynical that they are incensed when Jesus does good and saves a life on a holy day, but they have no qualms about doing harm and plotting death on that very same day with the secular powers that be.

Application. *Reaching out to sinners.* Other religions are the result of a human search for God; the Christian faith presents itself as God's search for humans—even those the world deems the most unworthy. Many Christians today do not recognize that they harbor the very same attitude as these first-century Pharisees. We sing "amazing grace . . . that saved a wretch like me," but we have in mind only our kind of wretches. It is too amazing for us that the same grace is extended to save those whom we believe truly deserve punishment.

It is one thing to go to them to witness to them; it is quite another to treat them as if they were in some way respectable and acceptable, persons whom God loves as much as the righteous (healthy) who need no repentance. It creates religious confusion so that one cannot distinguish the righteous from the unrighteous. It scares those who are convinced that society will crumble if these barriers are not maintained. Yet this is precisely what Jesus did, and by so doing he makes it clear that one cannot win people with whom one is not willing to eat. The religiosity of the Pharisees is therefore something we must guard against.

Joy versus gloom. Jesus's ministry is associated more with table fellowship, even feeding huge crowds in the desert, than with ascetic fasting. The question about fasting forces us to question the purposes of our religious rites and observances. Fasting is only meaningful when it arises from concerns so deep that food does not matter, not when it is dictated by some rule book. All spiritual exertion that aims only at setting ourselves apart from and above others is to be rejected.

Keeping the Lord's Day. Christians are also not to be conformed to the world around them, and observing a day of worship and rest is one way they distinguish themselves from others and give witness to their faith. Instead of heeding the calls to bow down to the gods of materialism or to play with their pile of recreational toys, Christians set aside time to worship their God and celebrate their faith.

The observance of days and seasons is not to be the sole element that distinguishes Christians from others. What Jesus affirms is that the Sabbath is for doing good. Jesus never criticizes the law that requires the Sabbath to be treated as holy. He simply affirms that the Sabbath can become an occasion to do good rather than simply a time to refrain from work. The criterion is mercy, not ritual. The question then is not whether something is or is not allowed, but whether or not what we do helps or hinders those who are in need. To do evil is always prohibited, regardless of the day of the week. To do good is always required, regardless of the day of the week. Christians should be distinguished by their doing good.

MARK 3:7–35

Original Meaning

Summary of Jesus's Ministry (3:7–12). Jesus may withdraw to elude the conspirators, but he cannot escape his immense popularity. This exuberant crush of people stands in stark contrast to the grim verdict of the teachers of the law from Jerusalem and also explains why they are so worried about Jesus. His surging popularity threatens to undermine their leverage with the crowds.

The unclean spirits continue to know him immediately, fall before him in surrender, and blurt out his identity. The translation, "he gave them strict orders" (v. 12), is too mild. Jesus is not merely putting them under a gag order. The verb *epitimaō* is frequently translated "rebuke," but even this does not adequately capture its meaning. He also "rebukes" the wind and sea to "be still" (4:39), and the muzzling of the demons, like the quelling of the storm, is a sign that Jesus has overmastered them. He therefore both expels and silences the demons with a word.

Creating the Twelve (3:13–19). The huge multitude is thinned as Jesus invites "those he wanted" to come with him (v. 13). This call creates a distinction between those who follow after him desperately seeking healing, those who are only caught up in the spectacle of these strange events, and those who are summoned to follow after him as disciples with a particular task. Jesus "appointed twelve" out of this group who came to him (v. 14). The Twelve have symbolic significance, pointing to the restoration of the twelve tribes of Israel, and Jesus stands over them as leader. Implicit in the choice of the Twelve is a renunciation of the powers that be in Jerusalem.

The mission of the Twelve is twofold. Mark stresses the disciples' task of being "with [Jesus]" (v. 14). What does that mean? Most importantly, it denotes the Twelve as the witnesses to his ministry, who have learned from him and are qualified to pass on and authenticate the traditions about him. The Twelve will have to learn that there is a difference between hanging around with Jesus and truly being with him. The latter means that they must follow wherever he leads and share the toil of the ministry, the harassment of the crowds, and the same bitter draught of suffering.

The Twelve are also created because God requires human cooperation to touch, enlighten, and heal others. Their second task is to fulfill the commission of extending Jesus's work by preaching and casting out demons. Their companionship with him is to lead to service that benefits others. They are not merely on the receiving end of this outbreak of power but are to become channels by which it touches others.

The Reaction of Jesus's Family and the Pharisees (3:20–35). Mark reports two other groups besides the awestruck crowds who have heard of Jesus's deeds and who come to him, but they come with quite different designs. Jesus's family intrudes to round him up, not to rally around him. The scribal authorities from Jerusalem come with the ignoble intention of defaming Jesus and sabotaging his movement. Both groups receive a stunning reproof.

This segment is the first example of the Markan technique of bracketing (intercalation or "sandwiching"), where the narration begins with one story but is interrupted by another before it is concluded. This technique allows the two separate stories to make a similar point. Both Jesus's closest relations and the theological specialists from Jerusalem offer mistaken speculation about Jesus.

Jesus's mother and his brothers are not making a friendly visit but want to "take charge of him" (v. 21). Jesus's response to the visit from his family would have been a shock because it runs counter to the received wisdom of the age. In the Old Testament, "life" is used almost interchangeably with "family." One's family was one's life, and to reject family or to be cast out of the family was to lose one's life.

But Jesus affirms that life under God is not defined by relationships in a biological family, which was primarily geared for the preservation of the family line, its wealth, and its honor. One's ultimate devotion is owed to God, who is head of a new divine family, and becoming a member of this family is open to all persons regardless of race, class, or gender. The only requirement is that they share Jesus's commitment to God; however, becoming a member of this new family has its costs. Devotion to him is likely to bring abuse and persecution.

The scene shifts to irate teachers of the law from Jerusalem. Those in power in the holy city must have thought that the rumors regarding this popular teacher, preacher, and healer warranted sending deputies to investigate and to debunk any aura of holiness surrounding Jesus's ministry. He comes from outside the system, which can only create alarm and resentment for those inside, and these critics do not plot in hushed secrecy but go publicly on the attack.

On the one hand, people frequently attribute to Satan what they fear or do not understand. The teachers of the law may have concluded that one who flouts hallowed traditions and who does not kowtow to their authority could only be an undercover agent for Satan. On the other hand, they may be venomously attempting to undermine Jesus by branding him as the devil's spawn. The latter seems to be the case since Jesus warns them against blaspheming the Spirit.

Jesus speaks to them in parables, which draw out the absurdity of their accusation and open the way to the truth. If their accusation is correct, the demonic empire is either crumbling from a conflict between warring factions engaged in some takeover plot, or Satan is irrationally trying to do himself in. If Jesus does not work by Satan's power, however, another explanation is at hand: a stronger one has bound the strong man and is pillaging his house. With the advent of the kingdom of God, the battle is being waged not just against the petty tyrants and their domains but against the very kingdom of Satan itself, which has enslaved all humanity.

This encounter with the teachers of the law from Jerusalem marks a shift in Jesus's approach to his religious antagonists. Although he withdraws, from now on he will give no quarter to his opponents whenever they confront him. For their part, the Pharisees have become allies with the secular Herodians in hatching plots against Jesus. Their hardened hearts also cause them to align with Satan. Jesus will no longer attempt to coax these leaders to faith.

Application. *Blasphemy against the Spirit.* The church does not openly revile the Spirit as these bitter opponents of Jesus did, but her blasphemy against the Spirit may take more subtle forms. Vicious criticism of others in religious circles stems from a variety of motives: sincere distress over something radically new, genuine alarm over what is perceived to be heresy, a desire to reassure that we belong to the good guys by branding others as the bad guys, or a craven dread of losing power. One must pray for the discernment of the Spirit so that our pride, self-interest, and inflexibility do not cloud our judgment of what the Spirit is doing.

Authority over evil. The church is not to sit on the sidelines, watching the world go by and doing nothing more than offering people a different religious option for salvation. The church has the task of standing up and confronting evil in the arena of life. Jesus sends his disciples out to tackle evil that is larger than personal evil and to deliver people from whatever enslaves them. The temptation is for us to retreat from the world or to overlook the evil in our midst. We have been sent by Christ into the midst of an evil world to confront evil head-on with the power of God.

Jesus and the family. Jesus's statement about the family has enormous repercussions for the way we live out our family commitments and the way we should minister to families. Jesus's definition of family embraces those outside one's kith and kin as brother and sister. His understanding counters the ruinous tribalism and the ethnic strife that rears its ugly head in our cities and in nations around the world.

On the other hand, Jesus's definition of the family may create problems for many individuals instead of providing answers. The commitment to do the will of God may force some to make a wrenching choice between their biological family and God. While some may be forced to disengage themselves from close family relationships that would strangle their commitment to God, we as Christians still need special people in our lives, a family of folks who support us, who are committed to us and we to them. We were not created to live alone, but to live in families.

Jesus's words about the family can therefore become good news for everyone. If the church takes seriously Jesus's ideal of what the family is, one of its tasks is to create and nurture families that make a place for all those who want a relationship with God as Father and with one another. This requires more than sharing a pew on Sunday morning and a fellowship doughnut afterward. Instead, we are to allow these persons to become our parents, our children, our siblings. The church is to take those who know the hurt of the world and bring them into the healing of community acceptance.

MARK 4:1–20

Original Meaning

The Parable of the Sower (4:1–9). The parable portrays a sower who sows with abandon—casting seed upon a pathway, rocks, and thorns as well as on good ground. He is cultivating marginal ground and laboring against formidable odds, so the rate of failure is not surprising nor is the report of an average to good yield from the seed in good soil. Given the nature of the land, the average farmer meets with frustration and failure, but in the end he does receive a reward for his labors—a harvest where the seed has prospered in good soil and borne fruit. Jesus implies in the parable that he fully expects to meet with failure and success, but he fastens more attention on the reasons for the failure than the reasons for success.

Just as the field has different yields, the parable yields a number of points. The following ideas may legitimately be gleaned from the parable.

1. It makes all the difference in the world who tells this parable and what one's stance is toward that person for how one understands this parable. The astounding implication, which only a few will see, is that Jesus comes as the end-time sower of God. The metaphor of sowing takes on the greatest significance in that it implies that Jesus comes to renew Israel, and how one responds to his teaching decides whether one will be included or excluded.
2. The sower sows liberally even in unfruitful ground in hope of a harvest. Just as God sends rain on the just and the unjust, Jesus sows his word on good and bad soil. The parable therefore depicts a prodigal sower who excludes no one on principle.
3. The parable affirms that the farmer will have a harvest from good soil. The farmer does not go out to waste seed but to gain a harvest. One can be assured the harvest will come from the response of the good soil.
4. The parable reveals that the kingdom of God's appearance in the ministry of Jesus does not come in one dramatic fell swoop, which instantly upends the old age. Evil does not vanish straightaway with the coming of the Christ, and people do not universally respond.
5. The parable makes clear that fruit bearing is an essential mark of the kingdom of God. The text mentions fruit bearing before the growth.

The Explanation for Teaching in Parables (4:10–12). *The mystery of the kingdom (4:10–11).* The term "secret" (or "mystery," *mystērion*) refers to a heavenly truth that is concealed from human understanding but is made known by God. Mark does not tell us specifically what the nature of this mystery of the kingdom is. Those who possess the secret of the kingdom will eventually be able to see what others cannot: the kingdom of God is advancing not just through miracles but also through suffering and persecution. Only in its final stage will it be publicly manifest for all to see.

Because Jesus characterizes the parables as mystery, everyone needs his interpretation to understand them. The parables are not the only things that are opaque and require special insight; rather, everything, including the miracles, require interpretation.

The phrase "in parables" in 4:11 takes on a different meaning from its use in 4:2. It now means bewildering puzzles. Revelation becomes riddles and stumpers to the hardened, shallow, and indifferent mind, and the end result is puzzlement. These persons do not suffer from a thick skull but a hardened heart. Disciples are not quicker than others, nor are they able to unravel mysteries for themselves. The mystery is something that is "given" to them. The understanding comes by grace as Jesus's interpretation unlocks the mystery for them.

The quotation from Isaiah 6:9–10 (4:12). God tells Isaiah the prophet to preach despite warning him in advance that it will only harden the hearts of the hearers until God carries out the punishment. That command brims over with irony and scorn. God calls a faithful prophet to preach to faithless people. Jesus's explanation for the parables has the same ironic tenor and can be translated, "So that they may indeed see but not perceive, and may indeed hear but not understand, because the last thing they want is to turn and have their sins forgiven."

Insiders and outsiders. Disciples are no different from anyone in needing explanations for the parables, but they are different from outsiders in that they choose to come to Jesus for explanations. Being an insider, however, does not mean that one knows everything. Insiders are elite only in the sense that they have knowledge that will save their lives. But insiders can be baffled and deceived and must watch how they listen. So-called insiders can become outsiders; otherwise there would be no reason to caution them to pay heed to how they listen so that they can discern what lies hidden beneath the surface.

The Interpretation of the Parable of the Sower (4:13–20). The context in Mark assumes that there can be no understanding without interpretation, and Jesus provides one for those who ask. Jesus's preaching reveals the good earth as well as the bad. One knows something is good earth simply because it bears fruit. In contrast to the bad soil, good soil hears rightly.

As the seed fails in three different ways in the bad soils, it succeeds in three different ways in good soil; but the parable and interpretation do not expand on the reasons for this varying success.

Application. We can apply the parable to our role as sowers of God's word. First, the sower in the parable does not prejudge soil. He casts the seeds with abandon and does not decide in advance whether the soil has potential or not, whether it is a waste of time or not. There is no concern to hit target groups only. There is no fear of sowing outside the boundaries.

Second, the explanation for the parable indicates that success comes from God. Jesus affirms that insight into the mystery of the kingdom is something given by God. As sowers, we can take no credit for any success that comes from our sowing, nor need we beat ourselves down for any failure.

Finally, sowers are not called to be successful but to be faithful. As sowers, we are to aim for success—a harvest. But the peril is that we may become so consumed with the outward signs of success that we get converts with no deep root system that will support them over the long haul.

We can also apply the parable to our own responsibility to receive the word as good soil. Soil is unable to change its character, but humans can. Sometimes we can be like the hardened soil on the path. Nothing sinks in. Sometimes we are in danger of becoming like the shallow-rooted soil. Any hint of persecution or tribulation shrivels any faith we might have. Another danger is that of materialism, which cramps faith. The glut of how-to books flooding the market, which promise to teach the buyers how to relax their way to success, to be energetic and beautiful, to win big money, unlimited power, and control over others reveals that we live in a narcissistic age.

The parable identifies what makes bad soil bad. But the parable does not identify what makes good soil good so that it produces a good yield. What is a thirtyfolder, a sixtyfolder, a hundredfolder? Jesus tells us the reasons for the failures but not the precise modes of success. The parable does not tell us how to become good earth—only to be careful how we hear. One can only know this after reading the whole of the Gospel of Mark and learning from the example of Jesus.

MARK 4:21–34

Original Meaning

The Parable of the Lamp (4:21–23). God's means of making the kingdom manifest through hiding it may mystify those who prefer that God do things in ways that match human methods and expectations. The parable of the lamp affirms that God's purpose is not to shroud the light in darkness but to make it manifest to all.

The Parable of the Measure (4:24–25). The parable of the measure refers to the ways people respond to the light. Those who hear well will get more explanation of God's purposes and will have a superabundance of understanding. The one who snubs it has everything to lose; the one who risks faith in what now lies hidden has everything to gain.

The Parable of the Seed Cast on the Earth (4:26–29). That the farmer has no idea how it grows implies that he is not the cause of the growth and is ignorant of the process. The seed holds within itself the secret of its growth, and the earth is said to produce "all by itself" (*automatē*, v. 28). This sequence also assumes that whatever has transpired under the ground will become visible.

In deciding the meaning of the parable, one should allow the context in Mark to be a key factor. This parable is linked closely to the parable of the mustard seed, and like the preceding parables of the lamp and measure, they help interpret one another. Both parables address the deceptive insignificance of the coming of the kingdom before its final manifestation. God's purposes will be fulfilled in God's way, and God entrusts the secrets of those purposes only to those who are willing to trust him despite unpromising appearances. Can one believe that the kingdom of God advances through ignominy, through defeat, through crucifixion? Can one believe that Jesus of Nazareth, who was hanged on a tree, is indeed the judge of the living and the dead?

The Parable of the Mustard Seed (4:30–32). One could dismiss the microscopic seed as something inconsequential, but it has a power within itself to evolve into something that one cannot ignore and that eventually attracts the birds of heaven. The same thing, Jesus implies, is true of the kingdom of God. The kingdom of God is already present in the work of Jesus but remains concealed and modest. Many would never guess that this inconspicuous presence manifests God's power and dominion that will reach out to all the nations.

Conclusion (4:33–34). The description of the word of God in Hebrews 4:12 applies also to the parables; they discern the thoughts and intentions of the hearts of the listeners. To understand them requires more than intellectual comprehension; it requires submitting to the word in one's heart. Jesus uses parables to plumb the spiritual perception of the audience, because he knows that a Messiah who dies can only be perceived through a rare spiritual discernment.

Application. These parables should instill confidence that overcomes despair. When we cannot see what transpires under the ground as the seed winters in the earth, we can become discouraged. Observers can easily write off this movement, particularly in our hurried, pragmatic age that wants immediate gratification and results. The slightest failure may drive us to a sense of hopelessness. The parables assure us that when we sow God's seed, it will accomplish its purpose. We may not be the ones who harvest the bounty, but it is not our harvest (1 Cor 3:6–9). It belongs to God.

These parables make the case that the seed's success does not depend on our feeble efforts. Despite the assurance of the harvest—and no mention is made of its size—we are still left with a mystery of how it comes about. Success does not depend on the one who preaches, but on God. The parable allows us to stop concentrating on what we need to accomplish or have accomplished and to reflect on what God is accomplishing. It encourages us to trust the seed to do what seeds do in the soil.

The parables encourage patient faith. In an age of instantaneous communication and a time when children may ask their parents, "Why do microwave ovens take so long?", waiting can be intolerable. We are always in a hurry. The parables do not promise instantaneous growth. God gives the growth, and it follows an appointed order that cannot be hurried or bypassed.

MARK 4:35–41

Original Meaning

The Storm at Sea (4:35–41). The unit opens with Jesus urging his disciples to set sail for the other side of the lake. Obedience to this command requires leaving the crowd and joining Jesus in the boat. The disciples take him with them in the boat because the fishermen in the group are presumably the expert mariners. Ironically, they are the ones terrified by the unexpected storm, while Jesus, the carpenter, sleeps serenely. One can imagine that at the close of a hard, full day, preaching to hardened hearts, Jesus is physically exhausted. Those attuned to Scripture, however, catch a deeper significance behind his peaceful repose. Jesus's sleep amid a raging storm churning the sea around him and filling the boat with water is a sign of his trust in God and contrasts with the terror of the disciples.

The disciples, however, do not interpret his untroubled sleep as evidence of his trust in God, which will also ensure their welfare. They regard it as a token of his indifference to their safety in their hour of danger. They awaken Jesus with an indignant wail of complaint, as if he were in some way responsible for their plight.

Jesus's rest is another token of his divine sovereignty that the disciples do not yet recognize, and the formidable power of the tempest is promptly overcome when he arises and speaks. He answers their anxious cries by rebuking the wind with a word. If the disciples only understood that they had set to sea with one who has such power, they would confess that all their fears were groundless. The disciples' faith must continue to grow and become tempered as hardened steel by life's hard circumstances.

After calming the sea, Jesus rebukes the disciples for their hysteria. Faith is clearly not something that is inborn; it can ebb and flow, depending on circumstances, and is most likely to fizzle in situations of danger. Despite the disciples' fear and lack of faith, Jesus muzzles the storm and preserves their lives. What can he do when people show faith?

The fear of the disciples, however, does not alleviate after the storm quiets down. Instead, their fear intensifies as it shifts to the person with them in the boat, who has just shown his divine control over the sea. The disciples' awe before the numinous is appropriate, but they still have only the vaguest inkling of who this man is in their midst, who wields such power.

Application. We can easily claim to be courageous when everything is calm. We can have faith in God's deliverance when we do not sense any urgent need to be delivered. When we come under extreme pressure, however, the courage and assurance that Jesus cares for his own, let alone preserves them from ultimate danger, can fade fast. Reading Mark helps one learn to trust in a Savior who does not deliver us from storms but through the storms. The Christian faith is not a refuge from the uncertainties and insecurities of the world. Some may be too cowardly to get into the boat in the first place. Others may wish they never had embarked and want to retreat to the safety of the shore. But then they meet raging demons (5:2). There are no safe places in life, and one can only find security with Jesus and a serenity that this world does not know and cannot give. Christians know that Jesus has done battle with the strong man and won. He has beaten down the savage storms, and one has no reason to fear anything from nature or the supernatural, from life or death (see Rom 8:31–39).

MARK 5:1–20

Original Meaning

The Encounter with a Demon-Possessed Man (5:1–5). Wherever Jesus goes, his holy presence triggers an immediate reaction from the unholy. These demons do not cower in fear but cause the man to rush at Jesus. No one had the strength to "subdue" him. The Greek word used here (*damazō*) is used for taming a wild animal and is better translated, "no one was able to tame him." People treat him like a wild animal, and he acts like one. He is banished as an outcast from society and must dwell with those whose sleep will not be disturbed by his shrieks echoing through the night as he lacerates his body with stones. Malignant spirits always deface humanity and destroy life.

The Encounter with Unclean Spirits (5:6–13). These demons are feisty. In their desperate attempt to resist any exorcism, they are momentarily successful in creating a standoff. The evasive tactics consist of the demonized man prostrating himself before Jesus. Whether this action is counterfeit worship or conniving submission, the evil spirits employ subterfuge to persuade Jesus to leave them alone. They invoke the name of God to keep the Son of God off their back—to protect themselves.

Jesus seems to parry these diversionary tactics by asking for the demon's name. The evil spirits evade the question, however, by giving a number instead of a name: "My name is Legion" (5:9), the number in a Roman regiment (consisting of six thousand foot soldiers and 120 horsemen). The evil spirits request to be sent into an enormously large herd of pigs feeding on the hillside. Jesus seems all too gracious in granting the request, but it leads to the surprise ending. The very thing they want to avert happens. From a Jewish perspective, the scene is a joke: unclean spirits and unclean animals are both wiped out in one fell swoop, and a human being is cleansed.

The Encounter with the Townspeople (5:14–17). These townspeople do not seem to care that Jesus has such power; they just want him gone. Instead of giving him the key to the city, they give him a cold shoulder. The demons had begged Jesus to let them stay in the region; the townspeople now beg Jesus to leave. This benighted community becomes another example of the outsiders who see but do not see, who hear what happens but who do not hear.

Jesus's Instructions to the Restored Man (5:18–20). Jesus sends him to his own house so that he can be restored to his family. Jesus also reverses his usual demand of silence by telling the man to spread the news of how God has shown mercy to him. Jesus may grant the community's wishes for him to leave, but he leaves this disturbing evidence of his presence. The upshot is that the preaching of the gospel about Jesus expands into the Decapolis. The splash created by the testimony of the man is more effective in divulging who Jesus is than the splash created by the demons in the pigs.

Application. We may see a mirror of ourselves in this disturbed man—beaten down by others, divided against ourselves, a civil war raging within, living among the gloomy tombs of life, and feeling all alone. If we can recognize ourselves in this tortured man, we can also see that deliverance is not something that someone else needs—derelicts and foaming lunatics. The power of the gospel is also for us. We are just as battered, though we may do a better job of hiding it behind our coherent words, our well-kept homes, and our smart attire.

The problem is that those who need deliverance the most are those who sometimes offer the greatest resistance. Many counselors have experienced this resistance in their clients. Persons come for therapy, saying that they want to change, and then fight for all they're worth against changing themselves. Some people find security in the demons they know and are afraid to be delivered from them. One can derive comfort from Jesus's persistence in this account. He will not be put off by evasive tactics and does not give up the fight to deliver this one from his personal demons.

This incident also has to do with a community that resists supernatural power. They are callously indifferent to the restoration of a man. It is one thing to encounter the impersonal forces of evil in nature run amok in an individual; it is quite another to encounter them in a whole community. Whole societies and institutions can be caught in the grips of evil and never recognize it. The solution is a power that comes from without, but some may be too afraid to let that power loose in their own lives, let alone to unleash it on society.

MARK 5:21–43

Original Meaning. After Jesus returns from across the lake, an official of a synagogue falls before Jesus's feet and desperately begs him to come to his home to lay hands on his daughter that she might be healed and live. Jesus agrees, but the rush to the girl's side is interrupted by an anonymous woman. She is so desperate to be healed from her hemorrhaging that she sneaks up to touch Jesus's garments in hopes that it will restore her to health.

This woman suffers physically, living every day with the signs of her decaying mortality as the blood essential for life drains from her body. She suffers socially and psychologically, knowing that she is a contaminant. Her plight is compounded because she has become impoverished after wasting her living on the fruitless cure of physicians.

When she touches Jesus, immediately her fountain of blood stops. But just as immediately Jesus knows that power has gone forth from him, and he mystifies the disciples by asking who in the throng pushing around him has touched him. Jesus forces her to step out on faith and be identified. When she does, he blesses her and announces that her faith has made her well. Faith, then—not any magical properties in Jesus's clothing—accomplishes her healing and saving.

Meanwhile, the distraught father has been left to cool his heels. One can only guess what he must be thinking about this delay. He too must publicly demonstrate his trust in Jesus as the worst possible news comes. He had shown faith in coming to Jesus in the first place, and now he must continue. Both the woman and Jairus reveal that faith is something that trusts amid hopelessness.

Jairus obeys because he leads Jesus to his house, but his faith is again challenged by the grievous chorus of those already assembled to mourn the little girl's death. They do not have the faith of the woman and would undermine the faith of the father. Their skepticism puts them outside. There will be no miracles for the scornful throng.

In private, with only the parents and Peter, James, and John, Jesus grasps the little girl's hand to raise her up. Jesus does not utter some mysterious mumbo jumbo but an ordinary phrase. The offer of food shows that the child is really alive and not a disembodied spirit. The command to secrecy reveals that Jesus is not interested in turning jeers into cheers.

Application. The healings in these two scenes show that one appropriates Jesus's power through faith. An act of faith can make a person well. Faith opens the door to the power of God. Faith transfers divine power to those who are utterly powerless. Faith can be imperfect; it can be bold; it can be halting; it can be brave; it can be laced with fear and trepidation. What counts for it to be effective is for it to be directed rightly to Jesus and God.

Faith shows persistence in overcoming any obstacles. Faith goes forward in the face of mocking laughter and refuses to give in to fear and scorn. Faith is embodied in action. Faith is something that can be seen, like the men digging through a roof to bring their friend to Jesus. It kneels, begs, and reaches out to touch. It does not wait to see if the waters will divide and then step out. It steps out, trusting God to do what is needed. Faith is impelled by desperation that Jesus is sufficient to meet whatever need one has. Faith is able to hold on in the face of death, knowing that God has conquered death in the resurrection of Christ.

MARK 6:1–6A

Original Meaning. The reader learns more about Jesus's background from the incidental question, "Isn't this the carpenter? Isn't this Mary's son and the brother of James, Joseph, Judas and Simon?" (v. 3). These details are not crucial to the gospel about Jesus, but they stir our curiosity.

A "carpenter" (*tektōn*, v. 3) could work with wood, metal, or stone. In Jesus's context, it probably denoted a woodworking handyman. Jesus must have been technically skilled and physically strong. The people of Nazareth identify Jesus as "Mary's son" (v. 3). Normally a man is identified as the son of his father. Some suggest they refer to him in this way because his father is no longer alive and thus are expressing their familiarity with his mother, who resides there. The references to his brothers and sisters emphasize that he is simply "a local boy." They think they have Jesus pegged. This one is just Mary's boy, who used to be one of us. The upshot of their analysis of Jesus's origins is that they are scandalized by him.

Mark concludes this incident with a notice that Jesus can do no miracles in Nazareth except heal a few people and that he marvels over their unbelief. The negative reaction to Jesus in Nazareth makes them little different from the land where the pigs and pagans dwell, and one can better appreciate the difficulty faced by the one who is known formerly as the Gerasene demoniac and must give witness in his hometown.

Application. When we judge others by appearances, we may be dead wrong. If Jesus were issued identity papers, his profession would list him as a carpenter, not Messiah. He is blue collar. Those who evaluate Jesus by outward appearances will miss the truth about him. They are also likely to misjudge his commissioned messengers.

Mark tells us that his disciples accompanied him to Nazareth. Being with Jesus provides opportunities for learning. They can learn from this indifferent response to Jesus's teaching and miracles that rejection will come sometimes when and where it is least expected. Rejection is not the end of the world, however. Failure is common to the experience of anyone who sows the seeds of the gospel. Christian missionaries perhaps can take comfort from this episode from Jesus's life when they too meet with skepticism.

This passage can also apply to the contemporary phenomenon where persons raised as Christians search for the answers to life's questions by turning to other religions. One can only wonder why many Christians turn to something other than the faith of their youth for help in their lives or for meaning. Does familiarity with the stories about Jesus breed contempt? We must guard against the attitude that beset the synagogue of Nazareth: "I already know him from the Bible stories of my youth. What can he teach me now?"

MARK 6:6B–30

Original Meaning

The Mission of the Disciples (6:6b–13). Jesus launched his public ministry by calling Israel to repentance; now he expands that mission by sending the Twelve to their unbelieving countrymen to preach repentance, to cast out demons, and to anoint the sick. When Jesus gives them their marching orders, we might expect him to give detailed advice on what to do when they encounter unclean spirits, for example; but instead he instructs them on what not to pack for the trip.

Jesus instructs the Twelve to accept the first accommodations offered to them and not to move if they chance to find something better. This demonstration of commitment is a testimony of their devotion to their mission and not to themselves. It also reduces the chance that they will create jealousy by moving to better quarters, which will interfere with their mission.

The mission of the Twelve communicates in dramatic and harrowing fashion the seriousness of the need for Israel to repent now. Mark tells us the disciples obey Jesus's commission. They preach repentance, cast out demons, and anoint the sick with oil. But Mark tells us nothing more about the results of their mission, whether it is successful or not. Why? The best answer is that Mark sees it as preparatory for the later mission of the disciples after Jesus's death and resurrection. It introduces them to the requirement of total self-sacrifice in commitment to their mission. It also acquaints them with the reality of rejection. It therefore prepares them for Jesus's teaching about his destiny, which will follow.

The Death of John the Baptizer (6:14–29). The question raised by Jesus's disciples, "Who is this?" (4:41), is now rousing the interest of the political gentry, as Herod's court is abuzz with the news of him. One of the things that must have troubled someone like "King Herod" (6:14) is that Jesus and his disciples were proclaiming the kingdom of God. It boils down to the simple message: God is king, and Herod (and anybody else) is not.

The account of John's imprisonment and execution underscores the great impiety of Herod. First, John reproaches him publicly for marrying Herodias, his niece, who is already the wife of his half brother. His new marriage ignited religious protests at home because it was classified as incestuous. Ironically, Herod's young stepdaughter captivates him with her presumably erotic dancing, which also hints of incestuous lust.

Herodias understandably holds a grudge against someone who has called for her removal from the seat of power. Either Herodias seizes the moment to sacrifice her daughter's dignity by sending her in to dance to win Herod's favor or takes advantage of an opportunity to do away with her prophetic nemesis when her daughter comes to consult with her. The grisly detail of John's head brought to Herod on a platter caps off a banquet already polluted by excess. John dies according to the caprice of an evil woman and the weakness of her impotent and debauched husband.

The Return of the "Apostles" (6:30). In 6:30 the Twelve are called "apostles" for the first and only time in this Gospel. The title has in view their function as those sent out rather than some permanent office or status. They have fulfilled the particular commission Jesus gave them to do and now report to him. The mission of the apostles therefore brackets the account of the death of John. As we have seen before, recognizing this sandwich technique is crucial for unfolding Mark's theological purpose. The insertion does more than provide an interlude between the sending out and return of the disciples; it interprets the flanking halves. It foreshadows the suffering that comes to God's messengers. What happens to John will happen to Jesus in his mission and to the disciples in theirs.

John's death foreshadows the suffering of the Son of Man, but the sending out of the Twelve and their return "sandwiches" the account of his death. John's beheading, therefore, casts the shadow of death over the disciples' mission. The bracketing suggests that what happened to John the Baptizer presages what will also happen to any who preach the same message of repentance in a hostile world.

The world is filled with villainous people in high and low places, who will try to rub out the messengers of God and their disturbing message. But it will not work. When the princes of this world have done their stamping, God is not through. The world will not easily be rid of prophets like John because of the God who raises the dead and enables disciples to remain faithful. The kingdom advances despite the murderous evil in the world.

Application. While we must always trust God to supply all our needs, Jesus's charge dispatching his disciples on their mission without preparations or provisions hardly applies today. From a close reading of the text, we can draw the following principles about their mission that apply today. First, the disciples' mission is an extension of Christ's work in the world. They go as the voice and action of Christ. Jesus will not do it all. He sends out disciples to help make ministry happen.

Second, they are to be so dedicated to the task of their mission that personal comforts become inconsequential. When Jesus sends out his disciples, he expects them to concentrate more on getting the message out than getting the finest accommodations. He does not promise a successful career or protection from sickness, ordeals, or tyrants. We do not always get to choose where we will go. It may be next door; it may be to death's door. Answering the call to serve others is risky business, but ignoring it or scorning it is even riskier.

Third, the disciples' mission is not just a matter of preaching the good news but of bringing into effect in people's lives the good news of healing and deliverance. They do not offer people something new to believe in but something that tangibly changes their lives.

Finally, we should note the hint of triumph in the midst of suffering. The powers of evil seem to deal a dismal defeat with the arrest and death of John, but John's beheading does not silence God's message. Twelve messengers take his place, who, like Jesus, go about preaching, healing, and exorcising demons.

MARK 6:31–44

Original Meaning. A swarm of excited fans continue to besiege Jesus, making it impossible for him and his disciples even to take time to eat. This relentless pursuit of Jesus is further proof of his immense, superstar popularity. Jesus does not show any irritation with the crowds for chasing him down. Instead, he has compassion on them because they are "like a sheep without a shepherd" (v. 34). His first response to their need is to teach them.

Mark refrains from giving a full account of Jesus's teaching to the crowd, as is his tendency throughout the Gospel, but he describes instead a miraculous feeding of the crowd in the desert. The disciples stress that they are in a deserted place, and they ask incredulously how they can possibly feed such a number. The feeding in the desert evokes several biblical themes.

First, it recalls God's miraculous provision of food in several stories of the Old Testament. The disciples begin with hardly anything and end up with enough to satisfy five thousand. Jesus's banquet for the rabble of Galilee also foreshadows the messianic banquet and contrasts with the drunken debauchery of Herod's feast for the high officials, captains, and the leading men of Galilee. Jesus brings life-giving bread with an abundance of leftovers. His disciples feed and serve others.

Second, the feeding specifically recalls the exodus of the Israelites from Egypt and their being fed in the desert. Jesus quickly organizes the shepherdless throng and makes them sit in groups in rectangular sections, which makes it easier to feed them in an orderly fashion. More suggestively, it reflects the encampment of Israel. Jesus is able to provide the people in the desert what Moses could not. Moses had to contend with disgruntled people teetering on the edge of starvation. Those gathered around Jesus are all satisfied.

Third, Psalm 23 reverberates in the account of the feeding of the five thousand. Jesus has compassion on the people because they were like sheep without a shepherd, and his actions reflect the first line of the psalm, "The LORD is my shepherd." The barren desert has suddenly become green as the shepherd finds good pasture for his flock beside the waters of the sea. Most importantly, however, Jesus restores their soul and guides them in right paths by teaching them.

A fourth biblical echo comes from the Elijah/Elisha cycle. Elijah provided miraculously for the widow of Zarephath and mediated divine power by raising her son from the dead. Elisha fed the guild of a hundred prophets with twenty barley loaves; Jesus feeds five thousand people with five loaves. If we are meant to recall the works of these prophets of old, we see that in Jesus one greater than Elijah and Elisha is here.

Finally, the feeding account is a foretoken of the Last Supper in Mark. The action of taking bread, giving thanks, breaking it, and giving it to the disciples matches his action at the Last Supper. While this gesture is not out of the ordinary, the reader familiar with Jesus's action on his last night could not help but make the connection. The abundance of food left over after feeding five thousand means that there is more to go around and much more where it came from. Those who come to hear the teaching of Jesus and to share in the broken bread will receive the same abundant blessing.

Application. The image of Jesus as the good shepherd of the flock is prominent in this feeding episode. To say that the people were like sheep without a shepherd seriously challenged Israel's religious leadership. It was not that they did not have enough priests to go around. The problem was that the religious leaders were not doing what they were meant to do. What Jesus saw were spiritually and physically hungry people, wrapped up in all sorts of religious red tape. They were spiritually starved as well as materially impoverished, and nobody seemed to care. He would see the same things today. Jesus recognizes both needs and moves to correct them.

This incident also reveals that Jesus recognizes his disciples' need for rest. One cannot serve others twenty-four hours a day. The need can be overwhelming, and we are tempted to send the suffering and needy away empty-handed.

Disciples of Jesus need to do more than lament the crowd's hunger and the lack of food while sending them away with nothing. We have not done our duty if all we have done is point out the problems in society and lament them. The church cannot neglect either spiritual or physical hunger. In this account, the disciples are stymied when they think that the task is impossible or the cost too great. Only when they have faith to tap into the divine provision do they accomplish the job and provide everyone with enough. Disciples are always servants of others—called to feed the sheep and not just themselves. The lesson from this account is clear: they will always have enough to feed the church. The passage confirms that compassion combined with God's bounty and power can meet both the spiritual and physical needs of people.

MARK 6:45–56

Original Meaning. Separated from their master, the disciples undergo an ordeal, fighting against the waves. A storm does not endanger their lives as earlier, but they find themselves stuck in the middle of the lake, fighting against the wind after hours of strenuous rowing. Just as Jesus did not first feed the hungry multitudes but taught them, so he does not first rescue the disciples from their predicament but tries to teach them something by passing by them. Their eyes and ears are not up to it, however; they see only a phantasm, a ghost. The waves and the wind have not thrown them into a panic, but the sight of Jesus passing by on the water does. When Jesus comes strolling across the waters, he shares in the unlimited power of the Creator.

Mark's explanation that Jesus "wanted to pass by them" (6:48, literal translation) has caused confusion. This account is not about a rescue of the disciples on the sea. They are frustrated but not in peril. Since walking on the sea is something no ordinary mortal can do, Jesus's desire to pass by the disciples is not related to some mundane purpose. The verb *parerchomai* ("to pass by"), when connected to a divinity, refers to an epiphany.

Jesus displays his divine power further when he gets into the boat. His mere presence causes the wind to cease howling and enables the disciples to continue their journey. It does not calm their apprehension, however. Mark offers a surprising explanation for the disciples' terror and amazement: "for they had not understood about the loaves; their hearts were hardened" (v. 52). The two incidents are somehow connected. What is it that they do not understand about the loaves? What does it have to do with walking on the water? They do not recognize that the blessing pronounced at the meal applies also to Jesus. The disciples are drawing closer to Jesus's opponents than to Jesus in their life stance. The difference between them and the opponents is significant, however. The disciples may be confused and blind, but they are not hostile to Jesus.

Jesus sends the disciples off to Bethsaida, but they land in Gennesaret. Perhaps Mark wants the reader to see some significance in their going off course. They are unable to go to Bethsaida, just as they have been unable to understand about the loaves, and do not reach this destination until later (8:22). Meanwhile, the activities of Jesus comprise a second series of mighty works, intended to help the disciples to see. Jesus never gives up on the disciples despite their failures, but takes them through the whole process again so that they may understand. He does not require disciples to grasp things immediately. He veils his self-disclosure, and full understanding will not come until after his death and resurrection.

Application. Jesus's retreat from the throngs and his disciples shows that all humans need solitude, rest, and prayer (1:35; 6:31). In such moments we can meet ourselves face to face and hear God speaking most clearly. We can look at this passage from the perspective of the disciples, who face adversity, feel separated from Jesus, and are distressed in the rowing. Many people may feel that way as they serve in the church. They keep rowing but seem to make no progress. Discouragement sets in when one always seems headed into a gale. They feel cast adrift and may ask why they ever left the shore in the first place; they long to go back.

Jesus does not rescue his disciples out of the sea but enables them to continue the voyage. Often Christ may pass by our lives in ways that we fail to see and that might frighten us. How do we see him while we struggle in the dim hours of the night in this present age, besieged by windy opposition? It may only become clear in retrospect, as it did for those first disciples. We realize that in that horrible hour we were in the very presence of God and that Christ revealed his glory to us. We were too blind, too petrified to see it. One should then be alert that in the times of discouragement and greatest fears Christ is passing by, showing his love and power and leading us across troubled waters.

MARK 7:1–23

Original Meaning

Confrontation Over the Tradition of the Elders (7:1–13). The conflict in Mark 7 revolves around the issue of defilement. The Levitical system regarded uncleanness as something transferable to persons, vessels, clothes, and even houses by touch, lying, or sitting. Layers of impurity could be removed by ablutions. To disregard such concerns means that Jesus redefines what it is that inhibits fellowship with God.

Jesus's counterattack cites an extreme example to show how the tradition of the elders sanctions the subversion of God's will. God commands children to honor their parents, and in Jewish tradition that requires providing them with physical necessities. In the case example, the Pharisees would allow a son to duck that responsibility by informing his parents that what support they might expect from him is "Corban" (v. 11), dedicated to God, and therefore it cannot be touched to help them.

From Jesus's point of view, the command to honor parents soars above the command to honor vows. The Pharisees' tradition turned the law on its head by insisting that the sanctity of the vow superseded the parents' right to support.

Jesus assumes that such a vow, whether made spitefully or not, is automatically invalid because it violates God's command to honor parents. One cannot elude God's commands by resorting to shrewd legal loopholes. Jesus exposes these sticklers for the law as more interested in legal niceties than the requirement of love, more devoted to unwritten traditions than the written law, and more concerned with property than care of one's parents.

A Public and Private Explanation of Purity (7:14–23). Jesus now goes much further by explicitly rejecting the proposition that contact with anything profane defiles a person. Jesus does not differ with the Pharisees only over details such as washing hands; he rejects their whole approach to God's law. They are concerned about surface impurity and piety; Jesus is concerned about internal impurity that one cannot wash away by washing the hands. They do not understand that true holiness that imitates God and opens one up to God is something internal.

Jesus illustrates his point by reminding them of what happens to food when it is consumed. The only defilement that the disciples need worry about has to do with the heart, not the hands, with evil thoughts that leak out from within a person, not food that ends up in the latrine. The list of vices that come from the heart deals with behavior that harms others. One needs more than a little water poured over cupped hands to cleanse this impurity.

Application. Many engage in heated religious arguments over what they regard to be life and death issues that to the outside world and to the average Christian are much ado about nothing. The root issue has to do with what one considers proper or pure (which becomes one's sacred tradition) and improper or impure. It results in a church devoted to turning the Christian faith into an unassailable fortress by building impregnable walls to keep the pure in and the impure out. The concern for purity directly affects evangelism. This closed system, more often than not, shuts one off from fellow human beings and from real fellowship with God.

Jesus is like those who want to run the church for those who do not yet attend. How do we include them into the family rather than exclude them? His teaching had a direct impact on Christian missionary practice when Paul advised the Corinthians to eat whatever was set before them. We can imagine how we would respond if guests turned up their noses at the food we offered them because it somehow did not meet their religious standards. What if their rejection of our food also implied that we were somehow impure, somehow untouchable? It would hardly dispose us to hear their message. In applying this passage, we should ask ourselves, "Are there subtle and not so subtle ways in which we communicate to others that they are 'dirty' and unfit for contact with us? How does it hinder our ability to evangelize them?"

Hypocrites may fool themselves that they have done all that God requires by doing this or that with the greatest of care. They play by the rules but allow them to run roughshod over others. How many times do Christians ignore the vices in the list and concentrate on minor pieties? They wind up with a religion that affects only the hands but that never touches the heart. The church needs reminding again and again that it can be correct in outward form and theology but not have the spirit of Christ. Goodness comes from inner purity, a life transformed within, rather than from the pure observance of rules and doctrine.

MARK 7:24–30

Original Meaning. Jesus travels to the region of Tyre. When word leaks out that he is in the vicinity, a woman whose daughter is a victim of an unclean spirit immediately begins to hunt for him to ask his help. We see a token of her faith in seeking him out and her resourceful determination when she detects his whereabouts.

She is a gentile pagan, which introduces a new wrinkle in the story. Gentiles were impure simply because they were gentiles. The humble request of this gentile woman, therefore, creates dramatic tension. Will Jesus be as gracious to this lady from Tyre as he was to the unclean outcasts within Israel?

The resulting dialogue between Jesus and his gentile petitioner offers many surprises. First, Jesus is not the affable fellow we imagine him always to be. He dismisses her appeal out of hand with a sharp insult. The word "first" (v. 27) implies that gentiles have some ray of hope, but for the time being this woman must wait patiently for her turn. Jesus comes as the Messiah of Israel, and she has no right as a gentile to jump the queue to receive benefits from him.

The second surprise unfolds in the woman's unwillingness to be put off by this less-than-genial response to her request. This clever woman recognizes, without any prompting, that "the children" in the parable represent Israel and "the dogs" represent the gentiles (v. 27). She understands and accepts the riddle's implications: Israel has precedence over gentiles, and the time for gentiles has not yet come.

But the implied insult does not embitter her. Instead, she becomes the first person in the narrative to engage Jesus in a constructive exchange about his mission. She does not selfishly worry that others have an advantage over her, and her cheerful acknowledgment of Israel's preeminence leads to another surprise. She refuses to accept his dismissal and will not take no for an answer. She is not asking for a catered, full-course meal, just a little crumb of Jesus's power for a little dog.

The woman's response reveals that she comprehends more about the bread that Jesus offers than even his disciples do. They have witnessed the feeding of the five thousand and will witness the feeding of four thousand, but they still do not understand the bread that Jesus offers. This woman, who did not partake in either feeding, begs to receive only the bread crumbs falling from the diners' laps. She knows that she cannot insist on God's mercy and does not take offense when Jesus tells her so. She will gladly accept the rank of household dog if it means getting fed.

Jesus relents and grants her request. The little dog is now accepted as a little girl. Her witty comeback expresses sincere humility. She concedes the differences between children and dogs. She accepts Jewish priority—the bread rightly belongs to the children, Israel. This willingness to humble oneself is a key requirement for discipleship and something the disciples of Jesus have difficulty learning. They have trouble receiving the kingdom as "little children"; she has no qualms about receiving the kingdom as a little dog. When Jesus says that the demon has left her daughter, she does not insist that he go home with her to make doubly sure. She goes in faith as she came in faith.

Mark 7 opened with the Pharisees' rebuking Jesus's disciples for eating with unwashed hands—these seemingly impious disciples were too unclean to eat at a Pharisee's table. It concludes with bread crumbs now being offered to dogs, who are at the bottom rung of the ladder when it comes to being clean or unclean. The reader should grasp the implication that God will heal gentiles, no matter how unclean or how far away from God they may seem. Those who exercise humble faith will receive bread.

Application. One can use this passage in an oblique assault on prejudice by substituting a contemporary object of bias for the Syrophoenician woman. The listener may be outraged that Jesus would speak to someone in such a tone and would consider withholding the help she so desperately wants. Then the listener may realize that this sympathetic figure belongs to a group that excites hatred or disdain. It may allow the listener to see the prejudice in a new light. The passage may allow one to recognize that all humans share the same desperation when demonic powers and sickness batter us about. All yearn for help—high and low, rich and poor, urban and rural, Jew and gentile. Jesus turns no one away who comes with humble faith.

The woman shows the greatest humility when she begs for a few crumbs from the bread sent to the Jews. She does not become caustic or bitter about the privilege of others. She accepts that she is unacceptable. Jesus's ministry reveals that God has not sent him to reward the deserving but to serve the needy, whoever they are and wherever they may be found. God helps those who confess that they are needy and deserve nothing. Pride stiffens the knees so that they will not bow down, and it muzzles our voice so that we do not call out in humble supplication.

MARK 7:31–37

Original Meaning. The mention of Tyre, Sidon, and the Decapolis emphasizes that Jesus passes into gentile territory. Just as the Jewish crowds in Galilee brought their sick to Jesus, so a gentile crowd brings a deaf and speechless man to him and begs him to place his hand on him. Jesus ushers the man away from the crowd. He shuns self-promotion and has no interest in turning his ministry into a three-ring circus.

In healing this deaf man, Jesus uses a sequence of actions, not just a spoken word. The vivid account creates an atmosphere of mystery and drama. He begins by putting his fingers in the man's ears, symbolic of opening them. Next, he spits and touches his tongue, symbolic of loosening his tongue. Then he looks up to heaven, the source of his power, and sighs deeply, a gesture of prayer. Mark gives us Jesus's healing words, "Ephphatha," which he translates, "Be opened!" so that the reader will not mistake it for some hocus-pocus incantation (v. 34). Immediately, the man's ears are opened, and his tongue is loosened.

Jesus can command storms, demons, and illnesses, but his orders for people to keep silent fall on deaf ears. The failures to obey his command for silence reveal that what Jesus does is so sensational that it is hopeless to try to hush it up. But the command to keep silent also underscores for the reader what needs special attention. While onlookers may jabber excitedly about what Jesus has done, the magnitude of what it signifies escapes them. They do not have all the pieces of the puzzle to see a completed picture.

The chorus of Jesus's admirers nevertheless proclaims the truth even if they do not fully understand it. When one interprets Jesus's miracles from the contours of the biblical landscape, one sees again that Jesus does what only God can do. The Lord had responded to Moses's excuses, for example, with these words: "Who gave human beings their mouths? Who makes them deaf or mute? Who gives them sight or makes them blind? Is it not I, the LORD?" (Exod 4:11). Jesus's actions here show that he has that same divine power.

Application. Spiritual deafness in the Scriptures often applied to the people of God. Today God's people still do not always open their ears to God. Christians need to hear more clearly and to remedy their slurred speech. Mark's narrative shows that Jesus seeks to cure his disciples' blindness and deafness by taking them away from the pressing crowds and teaching them. Modern Christians may need to have times when they retreat and allow the miracle of Jesus's power to penetrate plugged-up ears so that they may hear God's word afresh and speak it to others more clearly.

Spiritual deafness is also the condition of the world. How does one break through to tell the gospel? Mark's account—which describes Jesus looking up to heaven, groaning, and shouting out in Aramaic—emphasizes the difficulty of the miracle. Perhaps the church needs to act out the message of good news for those who cannot understand in a language that is universally understood—deeds of loving-kindness. The church needs to love as Christ loved, to touch those who need assurance, and to pray visibly for healing.

MARK 8:1–26

Original Meaning

The Feeding of Four Thousand (8:1–10). Note how this feeding occurs immediately after Mark has recorded how Jesus crossed purity boundaries and social barriers. The context suggests that Jesus is now offering a predominantly gentile crowd the same opportunity to be fed by his teaching and by his miraculous power that he offered to the Jewish crowd. We may think that it is only fair that gentiles get a share in Christ's benefits, but from Mark's Jewish perspective the inclusion of gentiles is a token of the end-time reign of God. The miracle signifies that Jesus is the redeemer of the world, offering redemption to more than just the people of Israel.

The present account brings into bold relief the arrested development of the disciples. They were in on the first miracle feeding of five thousand in a deserted place, but this does not stop them from asking Jesus, "But where in this remote place can anyone get enough bread to feed them?" (v. 4). The answer to their question is obvious: from Jesus. Again, Jesus patiently has the disciples go through their inventory of provisions. They do not yet realize that even with their scanty supplies, they have in Jesus enough to feed the entire world.

Seeking a Sign (8:11–12). Why does Jesus oppose giving the Pharisees a sign from heaven? Some incorrectly argue that Jesus resolutely refuses to give any signs in Mark's Gospel. The reason Jesus balks at giving a sign here revolves around two issues: the meaning of the expression "a sign from heaven," and the defiant disposition of these opponents.

First, the Pharisees specifically ask for a sign "from heaven." Ironically, this request comes after the miraculous feeding, a miracle that pointed to the blessing, not the destruction, of gentiles. Jesus refuses to give the Pharisees a sign from heaven because God has sent him to give his life on the cross for all humanity, not to smash the enemies of Israel or to give the nation political mastery of the world. He will not give in to pressure to take a course of action different from God's purposes.

Second, the Pharisees have already received plenty of proof in Mark 1–2 of the source of Jesus's power, and they come now only as detractors who wish to tempt him. Those who claim to know God and to teach God's law to others do not recognize the signs that God has already displayed through Jesus because they are spiritually blind.

The Disciples' Incomprehension (8:13–21). This last scene in the boat opens with an awkwardly phrased notice that the disciples forgot to bring loaves, "except for one loaf they had with them in the boat" (v. 14). Why the contradiction between no loaves and one loaf? Mark wants the reader to recognize Jesus as that one loaf who can multiply one into an abundance of loaves to feed thousands.

The Pharisees are insisting that Jesus provide a sign conforming to their own goals and aspirations before they will commit themselves to believe. Jesus thus warns the disciples not to fall victim to this same insidious unbelief. Their worry about where their next meal is coming from makes them deaf to the warning about not hearing and blind to the warning against blindness. Mundane concerns distract them too much, and they do not catch the subtle connection.

Jesus believes that the feedings in the desert are the key events that should explain everything for the disciples. The meaning of the event clearly escapes them, but Jesus implies that it should point them on the way to recognizing Jesus as the Messiah, who works by the power of God. They are mired in their own little world with its petty alarms and cannot see God's reign breaking into their midst.

Healing a Blind Man (8:22–26). Since the man does not recover his sight immediately, the reader gets the impression that his blindness is stubborn and hard to cure. The miracle shows Jesus's power to heal even the most difficult cases. The Markan context, which portrays Jesus's struggle to get his disciples to see anything, gives this unusual two-stage healing added significance. The blind man's healing occurs between two examples of the disciples' blindness. This physical healing of blindness serves as a paradigm for the spiritual healing of the disciples' sight, which also comes gradually and with difficulty.

Application. These incidents depict opponents and disciples as blind to what God is working through Jesus. The blindness stems from many causes. Jesus has a vision of what the kingdom of God looks like. The disciples see nothing, no matter how hard they strain their eyes. Everything looks to them like a barren landscape. They may remain in the dark, but Jesus calls them to trust his vision.

Belief can exist and not affect one's conduct. One can believe statistical evidence that flying in an airplane is far safer than traveling the highways in a car, but fear of flying may prevent one from ever booking a trip on a plane. Trust, on the other hand, results in certain actions. Both belief and trust intertwine.

MARK 8:27–9:1

Original Meaning. The rapid pace of the Gospel slows down to a deliberate march in this large unit. Jesus is no longer simply on the go, moving from town to town and back and forth across the lake. He now leads his disciples "on the way" (v. 27). The journey now replaces the boat as the classroom for the disciples' lessons.

Jesus As the Messiah (8:27–33). The first course of instruction takes place in the unlikely location of Caesarea Philippi, which lay on the border between the Holy Land and gentile territory and was famed for its cultic associations with the nature god, Pan. Jesus teaches his disciples by asking them probing questions. The first one is: "Who do people say I am?" (v. 27). The disciples report his favorable ratings in the polls. The man in the street holds a good opinion of Jesus.

These people have not hit on the truth, however. Jesus is more than just another in a long line of messengers God has dispatched to the people. Thus, Jesus probes further. Peter moves to the head of the class by giving the answer that makes sense of all that they have witnessed: "You are the Messiah" (v. 29). His confession occurs in the very center of the Gospel. This passage serves as a hinge between the first half of the Gospel, where Jesus's power is so prominent, and the second half, where his weakness becomes predominant.

This confession represents a significant leap of faith, given the current expectations associated with the Messiah. The reader knows that Peter's answer is correct from the title of the Gospel (1:1). It seems a major breakthrough. Peter has finally caught on, and the reader might expect that the disciples have finally begun to shake off their persistent stupor. The secret will soon be out. But Jesus does not confirm Peter's confession or praise him for his insight. Instead, he rebukes him to tell no one because his understanding of what "Messiah" means is wrong and needs correction.

After rebuking Peter, Jesus explains that it is necessary for the Son of Man to suffer; and this announcement plunges them back into an uncomprehending daze. Jesus undermines Peter's newfound faith to lead him to a higher level of faith.

Jesus does not explain his mission to his disciples simply to predict future events but to verify for his disciples that what is about to happen fulfills God's plan. The disciples can understand it only after the fact because this plan runs counter to everything they were conditioned to expect. Lofty visions of majesty fill up their eyes, and the noise of cheering crowds plugs up their hearing so that Jesus's teaching about suffering and death flies in one ear and out the other.

Peter displays astonishing nerve by trying to set Jesus straight on what is and what is not necessary. His counter-rebuke reveals his ignorance about the nature of Jesus's messiahship and his deep offense at Jesus's teaching. Preconceived notions about the Messiah blur his vision, and he only appraises things from a human perspective. He has begun to understand that Jesus's great manifestation of power means that he must be the Messiah, but he does not have any understanding of how Jesus's passion ties into his identity.

Peter, therefore, shows himself at cross-purposes with Jesus, and along with the other disciples, he wants to impose his own private agenda on how Jesus will live out his vocation as Messiah and how they will benefit as his followers. He looks for a human reign, while Jesus tries to prepare them for the reign of God. He thinks in human terms, while Jesus seeks the divine will. This conflict leads the reader to wonder how he and the other disciples can ever overcome the scandal of the cross and see a transformed vision of God's power. It also reveals that the quest to uncover Jesus's identity does not end with the confession that he is the Christ. The disciples cannot know who Jesus really is without accepting the necessity of his suffering and death, and they cannot be his disciples unless they accept that fate for themselves.

Jesus's second touch to heal this blindness begins with a second "rebuke" (v. 33). He turns around, looks at the disciples, and calls Peter "Satan." That Jesus looks at the disciples when he rebukes Peter may suggest that he is not alone in his opinion about Jesus's suffering, just more daring in voicing it. On the other hand, the other disciples may have been following properly behind their master, while Peter had moved out in front of Jesus or alongside him. Whichever is the case, Jesus chides him publicly for trying to block the way.

The Demands of Discipleship (8:34–9:1). *Three demands (8:34).* First, Jesus insists that if the disciples want to follow him, they must deny themselves. Those who deny themselves have learned to say, "Not my will but thine be done." Second, Jesus demands that his disciples take up a cross. This vivid imagery must have sounded strange before Jesus's crucifixion and resurrection but would have communicated danger and sacrifice. Third, Jesus tells his disciples to follow the way he has chosen, not the way they would choose for themselves. Jesus does not want a convoy of followers who marvel at his deeds but fail to follow his example.

The rationale (8:35–37). Jesus appeals to the basic human desire to secure one's life as the rationale for making such a sacrifice. Humans seek to guarantee their lives but usually choose ways destined to fail. If we give up our lives for his sake and the gospel, we will be given the only life that counts, life from God.

A solemn warning (8:38). Jesus next warns his disciples about the judgment, when each one will have to give an account before the Judge. Jesus uses the threat of judgment to induce his followers to be faithful. Giving one's life in service to God may mean losing a few years on earth, but the result will be spending eternity with the glorified Son of Man.

A confident promise (9:1). Jesus concludes this first lesson on discipleship requirements with a solemn promise that some of them will not taste death before they see the kingdom of God coming in power. The best option assumes that the promise in 9:1 is somehow fulfilled within the story and in the events that take place after the resurrection. The visible manifestation of God's mighty rule does not appear in a form that people will expect. It comes as a hidden mystery. The cross and resurrection transform the meaning of power and glory and the way God will establish his reign on earth.

One therefore may no longer think of power and glory in the ways that humans usually think. Many imprisoned under the powers will see nothing of what God is doing in the world and will be judged. Others will see in the darkness at noon, the splitting of the temple veil, the empty tomb, and the reunion with the risen Lord the kingdom of God coming in power.

Application. Modern scholars tend to make Jesus over into their own image and, in the process, eliminate any eternal claim he might exert on their lives. Some present him as a revolutionary who gathered a band of desperadoes to bring about a social liberation of the oppressed peasants. Others present him as an itinerant, nonviolent teacher spouting pithy maxims; still others as a charismatic healer trying to reform Judaism. These speculations, all dressed in the garb of academic expertise, are no closer to the truth than the best guesses of Jesus's contemporaries, but the media will often seize on these opinions. We cannot put him into nonreligious categories that allow us to evade the claim that God makes on our lives. He is the Messiah whom God sent to suffer and save his people through his death and resurrection.

The temptation for Jesus to meet the expectations of his little band of followers must have been enormous lest they desert him in disappointment. But Jesus pledges to do only God's will, even if he must die all alone. His commitment serves as the model for present-day ministers who face the same kind of pressures to conform to the expectations of what others think a minister ought to be and do.

Many church members treat their ministers as coolies whom they have hired to take them to the top of a spiritual Pike's Peak. They act like stockholders who have retained a CEO to shape up the bottom line. Expectations are diverse. Some expect the minister to bring instant success to the church so that people overflow into the aisles. It is often a lonely business when one must leave the pack and head off in a direction demanded by God. To preach Christ crucified and to live it means that one will court rejection and ridicule.

We face the temptation to seek worldly security rather than risk our lives for Christ. Those whose sole aim is material well-being lose the one life that is worth living; those who sacrifice for others gain it. Many devote themselves to gaining the security that this world provides, but there is a difference between feeling secure and being secure. Trying to ensure one's advancement in this life leads only to the irreparable loss of something far more valuable to oneself. Many people today, if they do a little serious soul-searching, will find themselves coming up empty-handed. They have sold their souls for what will prove to be utterly worthless. Those who give their lives to Christ get self-fulfillment by not seeking self-fulfillment.

MARK 9:2–13

Original Meaning

The Transfiguration (9:2–8). Mark has made no attempt to fix times or dates for the reader in his narrative, but the transfiguration account begins with a chronological note. This specific logging of the time recalls Moses' six-day preparation before God appeared to him on the mountain (Exod 24:15–16). The transfiguration has other parallels with Moses's ascent and descent of Mount Sinai. These echoes suggest that a Moses typology undergirds Mark's shaping of the transfiguration. What happened to Moses on Sinai sheds light on the meaning of Jesus's transfiguration. Since Jewish traditions interpreted Moses's ascent of Sinai as an enthronement, the parallels with the transfiguration cast Jesus as a king.

The chronological note also expressly connects the transfiguration to the previous incident. Peter confesses Jesus to be the Messiah, and Jesus divulges his future suffering, warns of the coming judgment, and promises that some present will see the kingdom coming in power before they die. The transfiguration occurs on the seventh day after this incident and connects Jesus's announcement of suffering with the foretaste of his promised resurrection glory that occurs at the end of the passion week. The transfiguration, therefore, serves to confirm that the suffering Jesus will endure is not incompatible with his glory.

A third theme relates to the presence of Elijah and Moses conversing with Jesus. Since Mark reports nothing of the conversation, the significant element is their appearance with Jesus. Their presence with Jesus on the high mountain rouses Jewish hopes about the final redemption of Israel and suggests that the time has been fulfilled. The kingdom of God has drawn near.

A fourth theme emerges in Peter's unthinking response to these sights. Whatever Peter has in mind, his remarks are ill-advised. He continues to see and react to things from a human perspective, and fear continues to cloud his mind. If the offer to build three shelters suggests some desire to venerate the trio, he mistakenly puts Jesus on a par with Elijah and Moses and fails to recognize his true rank. Elijah and Moses, great as they were, do not share God's glory with Jesus.

Jesus has spoken plainly of his suffering and death; now God speaks plainly about the Son. Peter and the rest of the disciples must keep quiet and bend their minds around what Jesus says about his suffering. Announcements that God's reign advances through the death of the Messiah surround the transfiguration. Jesus's appearance, bathed in divine glory, attended by the great saints of old, and heralded by the voice of God, may take away the sting of these announcements about suffering by offering assurance of ultimate vindication, but it does not remove the necessity of travail for him and for all those who follow him.

The Question about Elijah (9:9–13). As they descend, Jesus commands the three disciples to keep silent about what they saw and heard until the Son of Man should rise from the dead. Mark reports that the disciples hold fast to the word but are confused about the reference to the resurrection from the dead. The disciples are stumped because Jesus's teaching that he must suffer has not yet sunk in, which explains why Jesus orders them to keep quiet. Their bewilderment reveals that Jesus must continue to drill into their heads that God's plan entails that the Son of Man must suffer and die.

It may appear that Jesus agrees with the scribal doctrine about Elijah's coming (v. 12), but he gives it a twist by announcing that Elijah has already come. Clearly he has John the Baptizer in mind. Jesus's statement means that, contrary to received opinion, Elijah's return does not herald the approach of messianic happy days. Eschatological expectations have been fulfilled in totally unanticipated ways. Elijah does come first and has already come, but they did to him whatever they wished. The disciples, however, still question if Jesus has got it right. How can the Messiah be rejected and suffer? Jesus answers that their expectations are all wrong. Elijah goes before the Messiah in the way of suffering and death.

Application. Most readers would prefer to be with the disciples basking in the glory on the mountaintop than to trudge along with them as they struggle and fail to help an epileptic boy and end up surrounded by hissing opponents and a disgruntled crowd. We spend most of our lives, however, down below in the valley, where the shadow of death hovers over us. Earthly life cannot be all heavenly visions. Sometimes the memory fades, and one may doubt if it was real. Was it all a mirage or hallucination? The words of our Lord remain constant, however. One must continue to listen to Jesus, whose words are able to sustain us when tingling visionary moments have grown dim.

Many in the church today suffer from a form of Bible amnesia. They remember only the parts that promise wealth, happiness, and glory and forget, or fail to listen to, the calls for self-sacrifice, suffering, and bearing one's cross. They want to skip Suffering 101 and move on to advanced placement in Glory 909. The Gospel of Mark emphasizes that the Messiah must shoulder a cross, embrace humility, and renounce brute force, and his disciples must do the same if they bear Christ's name.

MARK 9:14–29

Original Meaning. When Jesus appears from the mountain, the crowds respond with fearful amazement and run to greet him. Is it his sudden arrival, his air of authority, or something about his countenance—some residual effects from the transfiguration that stirs their astonishment? Mark does not tell us. He focuses instead on the spectacle of the disciples' glaring failure.

"How long?" (v. 19) does not convey a wish to be rid of inept disciples but refers to how little time he has left to soften their hard-heartedness and to acquaint them more fully with the power that can expel evil. Time is short. Will they ever catch on? Faced with his disciples' failure and the crowd's unbelief, Jesus does not throw up his hands in disgust but immediately takes action to rectify the situation.

At the heart of this exorcism is the struggle for faith, not the struggle with a demon. Jesus's probing questions reveal the problem's severity and prompt the father's cry for compassion. Seeing his son's renewed torment on top of the disciples' miserable failure can only pierce the father's heart even more and drain away his faith that Jesus can do any better than his disciples. He has not lost all hope, however. His plea reveals that he does not doubt that Jesus would like to do something if he could, but he is uncertain whether Jesus can prevail in such a pernicious case. The implied skepticism of his plea, "If you can" (v. 22), meets with a sharp comeback from Jesus. His capability is not at issue: "Everything is possible for one who believes" (v. 23). This affirmation does not mean that faith can accomplish anything but that those who have faith will not limit God.

Whom does Jesus have in mind when he singles out "one who believes"? Does he refer to the miracle worker's faith or the faith of those who seek miracles? The answer is both. Unlike the disciples, Jesus as a miracle worker possesses unlimited power because of his potent faith. He therefore chides the father for putting limits on what he can do to help him. But petitioners also need to possess faith in him, and aggressive faith has been a characteristic of all those who beseech him for healing in the Gospel.

The faith of both the miracle worker and the petitioner leads to success. The father belongs to the unbelieving generation, but we see him straining to have this faith. Unlike the people at Nazareth, who refuse to believe, the father's unbelief is repentant. He pleads for help just as he is, a doubter.

The third scene presents Jesus doing battle with the spirit as he commands it to leave the boy and never to enter him again. Jesus's presence throws demons into fawning submission or into a fury, and this one defiantly flails his young victim about in one last gasp of malice. Jesus seizes his hand as he did Jairus's dead daughter and raises him up. One should not miss that Mark uses resurrection language in verse 27: "he raised him" (*ēgeiren*; NIV "he lifted him to his feet"), and "he was raised" (*anestē*; NIV "he stood up"). Jesus drives the evil spirit out and gives the boy new life.

In the final scene, the disciples want to review their failure in the privacy of the house. Jesus's response, "This kind can come out only by prayer," implies that they failed because they had not prayed. The disciples were too busy arguing among themselves and with the opponents to pray. Since Jesus did not offer up a prayer to exorcise the unclean spirit, the prayer that he has in mind is not some magical invocation but a close and enduring relationship with God.

Application. The cause of the disciples' power failure becomes clear in the final scene: they had deficient faith and insufficient prayer. Their prayers were mute. A life of prayer goes hand in hand with effective ministry. It makes one receptive to the action of God. One cannot get ready for the moment by quickly uttering a special prayer; one has to be ready through a prayerful life when the moment comes.

The disciples must have felt quite empty and useless when they failed to make any headway with the demon controlling the young lad. They came to Jesus wanting to learn how to fill themselves so that they would not bungle things in the future and look so absurd. What Jesus teaches them applies to us. They need to learn from their emptiness and their failures that all healing comes from God, and they must depend entirely upon God.

The most severe challenge to faith comes when loved ones suffer or die, particularly when they are very young. When hopes are raised only to be dashed, one finds it hard to dare hope again for God's benevolent intervention. The father in Mark 9 has almost reached the point where he has given up all hope when Jesus encourages him to have faith. Faith unleashes a new power in one's life, but several cautions need to be raised.

First, people too glibly say to others, "Just have faith," and mouth platitudes about the great power of faith. Living out one's faith is never easy, and it grows harder when tragedies buffet one's life. This father tethers what little faith he has to Christ and asks for help just as he is. Jesus does not expect him to summon up a mighty faith before anything can be done but only to trust that God can act decisively through him.

Second, Dwight L. Moody said there were three kinds of faith. There is struggling faith, like a man in deep water desperately swimming; clinging faith, like a man hanging to the side of a boat; and resting faith, like a man safely within the boat and able to reach out and help others get in. The Gospel of Mark intends to lead the reader to a resting faith, but it reveals that it can only come by divine aid.

Third, faith requires humble trust. The father comes to Jesus hesitantly, not with a bold swagger, and humbly stammers his plea. Jesus is not put off by the humble honesty of one who says, "I believe, but I am not certain of it." He grants what is asked.

Next, faith comes as a gift and is sustained by the power of Jesus, the same power that can cast out the evil that held the boy captive. God offers help for faith as well as healing.

Finally, faith and prayer make a powerful combination. Faith is not just an inner comfort; it changes human reality.

MARK 9:30–50

Original Meaning

The Second Prediction of Jesus's Suffering and Resurrection (9:30–37). Jesus needs privacy to continue teaching his small band of disciples about the suffering and death that God requires of him and about what he requires of them. They do not comprehend what he is talking about, but they are afraid to ask him what it means. Either they are wary of being rebuked if they say anything, as Peter was earlier, or they prefer to live in a state of denial. They may not have wanted to understand the unpleasant reality staring Jesus in the face. The disciples should worry who it is who might betray him, but instead they spar with one another about who ranks the highest.

When they arrived in Capernaum, Jesus exposes their spat and their misunderstanding by asking them what they were discussing on the way. The picture Mark presents has tragic-comic dimensions. Jesus walks ahead in silence on his way to his sacrificial death, while his straggling disciples push and shove, trying to establish the order of the procession behind him.

The dispute opens the door for Jesus's teaching on selfless service. He presents them with a paradox: the one who wants to be first must become last of all and servant of all. To reinforce the lesson, Jesus places a little child in their midst. The point of comparison is the insignificance of the child on the honor scale. The child had no power, no status, and few rights. Jesus requires his "great" disciples to show humble service for the humble. Jesus follows this up with another paradox: when his followers serve those without any status, they receive Jesus, and the one who sent him.

The Unfamiliar Exorcist (9:38–41). John proudly announces to Jesus that they saw someone casting out demons in his name and they obstructed him. Their reason for intervening? "Because he was not one of us" (v. 38). The complaint drips with irony. The disciples only recently bungled an exorcism, yet they do not hesitate to obstruct someone who is successful but who is not a member of their team.

Jesus's explanation for condoning the exorcist's success in Mark's account is practical, not theological. He argues that they cannot use his name to do mighty works and speak ill of him later. Jesus then opens the doors wide to include on his side all those who are not against him. He knows that both he and his disciples are locked in a life-and-death struggle against evil, and he is prepared to accept any ally willing to join the fight.

Warning about Causing Others to Stumble (9:42–48). Jesus promised a reward to outsiders who show his disciples a bare minimum of goodwill (9:41), but he threatens his disciples with dire judgment if they cause a little one who believes in him to slip. He uses hyperbole to make the point. A string of maxims warns disciples that they need to be more worried about the evil within them than about outsiders. Again, Jesus uses hyperbole. Jesus did not intend for followers to take this advice literally. Maiming sometimes was substituted for capital punishment and was considered more merciful than executing a death sentence. Jesus applies this principle to the disciples' spiritual life. It is better now to take every precaution and to cut off everything in their lives that leads them to sin than to be punished later in fiery Gehenna.

Salt (9:49–50). Jesus concludes his teaching in this section with two enigmatic sayings about salt. The first, "Everyone will be salted with fire," appears only in Mark. An early interpretation of this saying appears in a textual variant: "for every sacrifice will be salted with salt." Salt was used for purification, and the one who substituted this gloss associated fire with persecution. If they endure to the end, the suffering they undergo will not destroy but purify them for God.

The second salt saying divides into two halves. If salt fails to salt food, it is not salt and is worthless. The same applies to disciples. If they do not manifest the distinctive characteristics Jesus requires, they are not real disciples and are worthless to him. The second half is in synonymous parallelism. To have salt among yourselves means to share salt, a reference to having meals together in the context of fellowship and peace. These concluding sayings present peaceful fellowship as the model for disciples' relations.

Application. Jesus has consistently avoided self-acclamation, but his disciples are all too ready to exalt themselves over others. In seeking leaders for the church, committees and bishops usually consult their references, which are often written by peers or superiors. It might be wise to consult those who have worked under their leadership, such as the secretaries and janitors. One can discover the true spirit of an individual by learning how they treated those under their authority. If people know that is how they will be evaluated, they may treat these persons differently. Jesus seems to imply that God looks for these things in evaluating us.

Jesus uses the child as a symbol of the little ones who are little esteemed, who are needy, who are socially invisible and easily ignored, who can be hurt and dominated without anyone knowing or protesting. But these little ones are not insignificant in the eyes of their Lord. As there is no insignificant family member, so there is no insignificant member in a church. These are the ones to whom Jesus ministered and through whom God works.

One can use the text about the unfamiliar exorcist as a helpful corrective for any community that would presume that God can act only through them. The Christian world is becoming increasingly divided. So-called liberals afraid of so-called evangelicals denigrate them, and vice versa. Each regards the other with deep suspicion and as a lesser caste of Christian. We must guard against the attitude of superiority that says, "You are different from me, and I despise you for being different." You can uncover this spirit by asking yourself and members of your church how they feel about the other churches in the area. Would they pray that another church in the neighborhood might have success in its ministry even if it would siphon off members from their own church? Would they pray for that success if it were of another denomination?

In the battle against evil, we must recognize that whatever particular group we belong to is not the only group of Christians in the world. We can then learn from others who worship the same Christ as Lord and Savior but who may use different language and emphasize different parts of Scripture from what we do. Perhaps when we lay aside our labels, we will recognize that together we are all Christ's servants and will then find ways to cooperate rather than to compete in serving him. Without compromising our convictions, we can have fellowship (have salt) with one another. We may not think the same thoughts, but we will have the same mind in Christ Jesus (Phil 2:1–4). Our unity will be a sign of what God's power can do to drive out the evil and chaos infecting our world.

MARK 10:1–16

Original Meaning

The Question about Divorce (10:1–12). The specific question the Pharisees ask Jesus is about divorce, though they are really interested in something more than Jesus's legal opinion on this issue. Jesus typically fends off his opponents by going on the counterattack. When the Pharisees ask whether divorce is lawful, he asks them, "What did Moses command you?" (v. 3). This rejoinder exposes a fatal flaw in the Pharisees' whole approach to the law. They come at the law asking, "What does it allow me to do?" or, to put it more bluntly, "What can I get away with?" This preoccupation with legal subtleties ultimately neglects God's will, which is primarily concerned with love for neighbor. Jesus's question uncovers their sinful hearts hidden behind the mask of legal rectitude.

The Pharisees respond to Jesus's counterquestion by citing the Mosaic regulations covering the divorce process: Moses permitted divorce, provided the husband gives his wife a certificate of divorce. The instruction in Deuteronomy 24:1–4 does not outline the grounds for divorce, nor does it endorse it. Jesus's line of reasoning becomes clear. If the Mosaic legislation on this issue had its roots in men's hardness of heart—willful defiance against God—then it cannot reflect God's will. Divorce is sin in God's eyes because it originates in human hardness of heart.

The Pharisees need to discover what God commands, not what Moses has permitted. Jesus addresses marriage from the perspective of God's intention at the beginning of creation. One does not find God's true intentions for marriage in Deuteronomy 24:1–4 but earlier, in Genesis 1–2, which is also a "book of Moses."

As has been his custom, Jesus gives his disciples additional instruction when they privately ask him for an explanation. Not only does he maintain that divorce is wrong, but he declares that remarriage after divorce is even more wrong and labels it adultery. Deuteronomy 24:3–4 forbids a husband from remarrying his divorced wife, who has since remarried and been divorced again, and labels it an abomination. Jesus brands remarriage to anyone after a divorce as adultery. Divorce stems from hardness of heart, and it can lead to more hardness of heart.

Blessing the Children (10:13–16). Others have brought the paralyzed and the blind to Jesus; now parents bring children for Jesus to touch. The disciples act like truculent bouncers. These aspiring leaders want to be the gatekeepers, who determine not only who can use Jesus's name (9:38) but also who can have admission to his presence. He must indignantly intercede on behalf of the children and inform his disciples that the kingdom of God belongs to such as these.

In the ancient world, children had no status. The little ones are easily pushed aside because they are weak, but God works most powerfully in weakness. When one is appropriately little, like a child, or poor in spirit, one is more open to receiving the reign of God. Children are also more open to receiving gifts than adults. Adults want to earn what they get, as the next scene with the rich man reveals.

Application. Despite the changes in our culture, the church needs to take a stand against the rising tide of easy divorce in our society. Christians are not to be conformed to this world—and this includes its indifference toward the marriage vow. But one has to steer between the Scylla of being too lenient on the sin of divorce and the Charybdis of being too harsh. On the one hand, one must be careful to proclaim God's intention for marriage to be a permanent covenant relationship. The church needs to infuse in its youth a deep sense of the sanctity of the marriage commitment to counterbalance all the messages they receive from our culture.

On the other hand, one must also be sensitive not to beat people over the head with the Bible when they are already bruised and broken. While the church should proclaim God's will for marriage and announce God's judgment on sin, we must also proclaim God's forgiveness of sin and acceptance of sinners. The church must direct sinners to God's offer of forgiveness and provide a place for them to experience God's healing. Divorce recovery groups may provide an excellent opportunity to minister to people when they need help the most.

What should the church do with its members who divorce? Is there Christian life after divorce and remarriage? Should churches allow divorced persons to serve in any capacity? Should they be allowed to attend seminary? Should they be ordained? How is one to be faithful to Scripture and also gracious and not legalistic? All these questions become important in applying Scripture to real-life situations.

MARK 10:17–31

Original Meaning. This faithful Jew who believed in the life to come must have been taken aback by Jesus's initial response. This brusque response gets to the core issue raised by this encounter. The man's salutation assumes that one can find goodness in human resources and accomplishments. As the scene develops, God's demands turn out to be far more costly than he bargained for, and Jesus's teaching reveals another paradox: goodness and salvation do not come from our own valiant efforts but only as a gift from God.

After turning aside the greeting, Jesus directs the inquirer to the Ten Commandments, which he already knows. Either the man is disappointed to learn nothing new from Jesus or pleased that his hunch about his good prospects in the age to come has been confirmed by a religious specialist. His response is then either a defensive reaction or a triumphant exclamation.

Jesus does not sneer at his claims to have obeyed the law. He believes what he says about his obedience; but because he loves him, he directly challenges him. The command to sell all sounds quite unreasonable to us, but most in the ancient world would have heard it as radical but sound advice for those who were seriously devout.

Jesus insists, however, that the wisest investments accrue interest in the treasuries of heaven. In this man's case, it means giving all that he has to support the poor. His unhappy departure reveals that he does not want to enter life under Jesus's guidance. He goes off, presumably in search of a second, more accommodating, opinion. Jesus will not renegotiate the terms, however. One can imagine the disciples standing with mouths agape as they observe this exchange. Jesus lets a good man slip away, whose deep pockets could help advance the kingdom cause—or at least their meager treasury. Jesus astounds them further by observing that the rich will have a hard time entering the kingdom of God.

The disciples' reaction to Jesus's bombshell about the rich matches many people's reactions: shock and consternation. Even those who know in their heads that money does not buy happiness or heaven still wish in their hearts that they had more. Consequently, Jesus repeats himself to drive home the point.

Jesus resorts to colorful hyperbole to reinforce the point that those who are ruled by money cannot be ruled by God. The rich will find entering the kingdom of God (coming under God's rule) more difficult than trying to squeeze a camel through the eye of a needle. Shocked by this statement and assuming that the prospects of entering the kingdom of God are hopeless for those who usually get whatever they want in this life, the disciples ask, "Who then can be saved?" (v. 26).

Jesus corrects the implicit assumption in the rich man's initial question. He assumed that one could attain eternal life by doing something. Since he wanted something he could do, Jesus obliged him: sell all that you have and give it to the poor. The disciples are to learn from this encounter that God requires something more than reverence for Jesus as a good teacher and earnest attempts to obey God's commands. To enter the kingdom of God one must submit to God's rule so that God reigns over every aspect of life.

Disciples must be prepared to give up everything. Peter quickly reminds Jesus that they have done exactly that. Jesus promises that their sacrifice will not be for naught. At this point, many walk away from Jesus, which lays bare the decision of the Twelve and other followers to stick by his side. These others fall away because they are not yet ready to accept the hundredfold persecution that comes with following Christ and with bearing a cross. The first will become last in the end, and the last will become first. The disciples need to learn how to make themselves last.

Application. The values of our materialistic culture seep in and can undermine that spirit proper to a follower of Jesus. We need to confront the materialism of our culture that has infiltrated the church. Jesus said that the rich man in this story lacked one thing, though he did not specify what it was. In applying this passage to our contemporary situation, we can imagine that he lacked the very things that we ourselves may lack. First, this man lacked for nothing. He had too much to give up. Money brings people many things (honor, respect, admiration, power, beauty, sex), which is why it is so alluring. Wealth cannot make one holy or purchase eternal life, and it does not offer any deep happiness, even when people get more than their fair share.

The second thing this man lacked was trust. God requires something more than simply reverence for Jesus and zealous attempts at obedience. God requires radical trust. Like so many today, this rich man wanted to serve God on his own terms. To have life, one must trust God and give up the quest to create one's own security.

Third, this man lacked compassion for others. Possessions set humans against other humans and against God. A recent survey has revealed that a low but significant percentage of Americans would still buy clothing even if they knew it had been produced by slave labor in a sweatshop. The cheaper cost would override any compassion or justice. Many cannot envision life without things they cherish. They are in danger of losing the only life that counts.

MARK 10:32–45

Original Meaning. The disciples and Jesus are marching to Zion. Jesus goes there as the Messiah, who invites all Israel to come under God's mysterious dominion, not just those living in Galilee. Jesus constructs the way of the Lord, while the disciples, still worried about the order of procession behind him, trail behind. Mark tells us that they are amazed and afraid.

As Jesus draws nearer to his ordeal, the disciples do not draw nearer to understanding. Each time he speaks to them about his suffering, his words go in one ear and out the other. Immediately after his announcement, James and John come sidling up to him with a special request. The earlier dispute about status and rank among the disciples was silenced but not buried.

These two are no different from Peter as they misinterpret what it means for Jesus to be the Messiah and assume that when he ushers in the new age, they as his friends will receive special privileges. Either Jesus's words about his suffering whistle right by them or they must hope that his travail will only be a temporary setback, quickly reversed.

Jesus responds to their ill-timed and selfish request with grace: "You don't know what you are asking" (v. 38). He informs them that the Father has not placed him in charge of the seating arrangements in the kingdom. He then asks whether they think they can drink the cup that he drinks and be baptized with the baptism with which he is baptized. The cup is a metaphor for suffering (Isa 51:17, 22), and baptism is a metaphor for being plunged into calamity (see Pss 42:7; 69:1). He will not be sprinkled with a bit of suffering but be submerged in it. He asks them if they are willing to share his fate and be doused with the waters of hardship and trial. James and John are as self-confident in their own abilities as the rich man was.

The other disciples are not livid because James and John have been so insensitive to make such a request just after Jesus has shared about his coming suffering and death. Rather, they are angry because James and John beat them to the punch and may now have an edge over them for the power slots. Jealousy creates turmoil in the ranks. The disciples would rather bear a grudge than a cross.

Jesus tries to channel their desire to be great into humble service: be great servants of others. The disciples have taken pagan rulers as their models, whereas they need to take Jesus as their model. The way of Jesus is self-giving service. They are not to be on the receiving end but on the giving end of service.

Jesus has told his disciples that he must die, but this is the only passage in Mark that tells us why he must die. The term "ransom" (*lytron*, v. 45) was used for compensation for personal injury or a crime, for purchasing the freedom of an enslaved relative, and for the price paid as an equivalent for the sacrifice of the firstborn. The concept of ransom, therefore, is connected to the idea of cost, substitution, and atonement.

Jesus thus provides the answer to the question that he asked his disciples earlier, "What can anyone give in exchange for their soul?" (8:37). The psalmist asserts that no ransom avails for one's life (Ps 49:7–9). That is true if we think we can pay the ransom ourselves. But this text affirms that Jesus pays a price for others that they cannot pay themselves.

Application. Despite all the warnings in Scripture, pagan values continue to seep into the church and govern its actions. Many ministers still dream of the big church, of the presidency of an institution or of a denomination, or of being acclaimed in national magazines as a mover and a shaker. All too frequently, these people achieve their dreams because of their single-minded purpose to attain them at all costs, regardless of how much suffering they cause others along the way and how much they cause the work of Christ to suffer. The church has had to endure power struggles that make it look no different from the pagan corporate world.

But the church cannot thrive if its leaders are competing with one another for positions of power. Looking at James and John is like looking in the mirror. We can see our own selfishness, and Mark hopes that we can see how foolish we look.

MARK 10:46–52

Original Meaning. Anticipating the generosity of pilgrims headed toward the Holy City, a blind man reduced to beggary sits by the roadside. Such a man in the ancient world was totally dependent on others for charity and for guidance and protection. He was one of society's expendables.

That is exactly how the crowd treats him, for they offer him no help. When he cries out to Jesus as the Son of David, they chide him for making a nuisance of himself. The blind man will not be put off by reproaches from the crowd and yells more desperately. Jesus has reached the last stage of his journey to Jerusalem. Despite the shadow of the cross looming ever larger across his path, he can still hear the cries of others in distress.

The crowds tell Bartimaeus to keep quiet. Jesus, however, stops and says, "Call him" (v. 49)—further evidence that he came to serve, not to be acclaimed. He springs up to come to Jesus, who then asks him, "What do you want me to do for you?" (v. 51).

This question may seem an odd one to ask a blind man, but Jesus forces him to reflect on what he truly wants from him. His answer demonstrates enough faith to transform him from a blind man begging along the way to a person who sees and follows Jesus on the way. He believes that Jesus is able to fulfill Isaiah 35:5 and give sight to the blind.

This miracle takes on symbolic significance as it caps the discipleship theme in this section. Jesus has told others he has healed to go and that their faith has saved them. Bartimaeus, however, does not choose to go off his own way. With his eyes now open, he decides to follow Jesus as every disciple is called to do. Like the first disciples Jesus called, he abandons his former way of life and leaves everything. The cloak he leaves behind is not much perhaps, but it is his sole worldly possession. The cloak would have been placed before him to collect alms by day and would have been his source of warmth by night. He will have no encumbrances in following Jesus. Leaving just a garment may seem easier that selling all that one has, but that is why Jesus indicated how hard it was for those having possessions to enter the kingdom.

Application. Many resonate with this blind man's encounter with Jesus. It matches the healing grace they have received in their own lives. They know what it is like to sit figuratively in the dust, a beggar for grace, calling out desperately for help and shouting all the louder when others would drown out their cries or try to silence them. They know what it is like to learn that Jesus cares—enough to hear the cry above the din of the crowd, to stop, and to extend the call that gladdens the heart.

If we treat this healing as a paradigm for the contemporary restoration of sight, we see several motifs. Healing does not always come easily for those whom Jesus heals. Before Bartimaeus receives healing from Jesus, he must overcome the crowd's determination to throttle his cries for help. He persists in calling out Jesus's name until he hears Jesus call out his own name.

If healing requires persistence, one must be intentional in coming to Jesus for relief. Bartimaeus does not simply want to meet the famous prophet from Nazareth in some misty-eyed emotionalism. He cries out specifically to Jesus because he believes that he will have mercy on him and can give him his sight.

"What do you want me to do for you?" is the most important question God ever asks us, and the one to which we most frequently give the wrong answer. We ask for all the wrong things in life. One can think of many examples, but Mark provides two notable ones. Herod asks his dancing stepdaughter essentially the same question, "Ask me for anything you want" (6:22). Her answer: "The head of John the Baptist" (6:24). Pilate asks the crowd a similar question (15:9, 12). Their answer: "Barabbas" and "Crucify him!" (15:11, 13). Our answer to this question will reveal whether we want death or life, whether we want to be healed from our blindness or selfishly want to use God to do our bidding and fulfill our own desires.

The aphorism, "He who hesitates is lost," applies in this situation. Bartimaeus cannot hesitate: "Maybe I will wait until Jesus passes this way again in a less crowded, less hectic time." Those who are healed in Mark act decisively and throw pride and caution to the wind to seize the one chance they get when Jesus passes by. Otherwise, the opportunity for healing will be lost.

After being healed, Bartimaeus moves into action. One cannot sit on the sidelines as a spectator while others lay their lives on the line. When people are healed from a debilitating disease, they usually want to make things right in their life. When one receives sight, one must follow the way behind Jesus.

MARK 11:1–11

Original Meaning. Jesus orchestrates a grand entrance that departs significantly from his previous patterns of movement in the Gospel of Mark. He has walked everywhere else in his ministry except for the times he crossed the lake in a boat. The animal he chooses has never been ridden, which makes it suitable for a sacred purpose and worthy of a king. Jesus enters Jerusalem as Israel's Messiah (cf. Zech 9:9). This also deviates from previous attempts to avoid calling attention to himself. What occurs now is a complete reversal: Jesus encourages public rejoicing by his provocative entrance.

The excitement generated by Jesus's arrival ends with somewhat of an anticlimax when he enters the temple, only to look around and leave. Mark raises the readers' expectations that something grand will happen, but nothing does. He tells us that "it was already late" (v. 11). Late for what? Did time run out on Jesus before he could do anything; or is time running out for the temple? This colorless ending to Jesus's dramatic entry into Jerusalem depicts more than meets the eye. Jesus enters the temple to inspect it, and the next day's events reveal that he comes not to restore it but to pronounce God's judgment on it.

Application. The crowd shouts, "Hosanna! Save us!" thinking that Jesus has come to save them from their political enemies. What we need most is for him to save us from ourselves. Human nature and aspirations change little over the years, and this incident reveals that we still need saving. We must be saved from a petty nationalism that divides the world into tiny enclaves set over against one another. We must be saved from a mercurial faith that abandons Jesus at the first sign of trouble. Jesus does not welcome cheers from throngs who will not pray with him in dark Gethsemane or go with him to an even darker Golgotha. We must be saved from foolish expectations of glory so that we can see God's power truly effected on the cross. God does not win by sending armies into bloody battles but by sending his Son to the cross. As a king who gives his life for others, Jesus reigns with a kind of power that earthly kings cannot match.

MARK 11:12–33

Original Meaning. The fig-tree incident sandwiches the temple incident. Interpreting either in isolation from the other leads one in the wrong direction. We will first look at Jesus's actions in the temple and then show how the cursing of the fig tree helps explain what it means. It is common to refer to this event as the temple cleansing. The cursing of the fig tree brings that interpretation into question.

The Temple Action (11:15–19). Many suggestions have been offered to explain Jesus's actions in the temple. A key question to ask is why Jesus would attempt to reform or purify something that he predicts, without any great anguish, will soon be destroyed (13:2)? The best answer is that he does not intend to reform the temple. Jesus has been acclaimed as a prophet. Prophets do not simply make announcements; they also engage in prophetic actions to communicate. Jesus appears in the temple as a charismatic prophet and graphically acts out God's rejection of the temple cult and its coming destruction. While actions may speak louder than words, they are not always as clear.

The interpretation that Jesus gives to his action is crucial for understanding what he intended. This teaching transforms a simple display of protest into an announcement of divine judgment (see 12:9). The disciples and the readers of Mark's Gospel also have the added advantage for understanding this incident because they see the cursing of the fig tree.

The passage cited from Isaiah 56:7 in verse 17 means that God did not plan for the temple to become a national shrine for Israel. Isaiah 56:1–8 contains God' promise of blessing for all who might think they are excluded from God's salvation: the foreigner, the eunuch, and the outcasts of Israel. Most assumed that Isaiah 56 spoke of some distant future, but Jesus expects it to be fulfilled in his day.

In Jesus's day the temple had become a nationalistic symbol that served only to divide Israel from the nations. If it were to become what God intended, "a house of prayer for all nations," walls would have to crumble. Indeed, walls will soon collapse, and barriers will be breached. When Jesus dies, the temple veil is split from top to bottom, and a gentile confesses that he is the Son of God.

By quoting from Jeremiah 7 (also in v. 17), Jesus reminds the people that something holy can be perverted. He claims that the same abuses that sullied the temple cult in the time of Jeremiah taint it now. The temple, God's house, has been made into "a den of robbers." One needs to read the context of Jeremiah 7:1–15 to understand the allusion. The reference to the "den of robbers" has nothing to do with the trade in the temple. Instead, it denounces the false security that the sacrificial cult breeds.

In other words, the robbers are not swindlers but bandits, and they do not do their robbing in their den. The den is the place where robbers retreat after having committed their crimes. It is their hideout, a place of security and refuge. Calling the temple a robbers' den is therefore not a cry of outrage against any dishonest business practices in the temple. Jesus indirectly attacks them for allowing the temple to degenerate into a safe hiding place where people think that they find forgiveness and fellowship with God no matter how they act on the outside. The sanctuary, supposedly sanctified by God, has become a sanctuary for bandits who think that they are protected from God's judgment.

The Cursing of the Fig Tree (11:12–14, 20–25). The fig-tree incident brackets the temple action and interprets it. It reveals more clearly that Jesus does not intend to cleanse the temple. Instead, his actions visually announce its disqualification. The fig tree that has not borne fruit is cursed, not reformed or cleansed.

Why curse a fig tree for not bearing figs out of season? Jesus surely knows it is not fig season. This detail is a clue for the reader to look beyond the surface meaning and to see its symbolic meaning. This action is not about a particular unfruitful fig tree; it has to do with the temple. The word "season" (*kairos*, v. 13) is not the botanical term for the growing season, but the religious term found in 1:14–15 denoting the time of the kingdom of God. Moreover, the tenants do not produce the fruits of the vineyard "at harvest time" (12:2; literally "in season"). The barren fig tree represents the barrenness of temple Judaism that is unprepared to accept Jesus's messianic reign.

As the fig tree's time is barren (cf. Luke 13:6–9), so is the temple's. Time can run out for fruitless trees and prayerless temples. The locus of salvation now shifts from the temple to Jesus and his death and resurrection. Faith in him will become the way to God, not the sacrifice of animals in the temple. Thus, when Jesus dies, the curtain of the temple is torn from top to bottom.

When Jesus and his disciples pass by the tree on the next day, the fig tree is "withered from the roots" (v. 20). For a fig tree in full leaf to shrivel so completely within a day is a miracle, and it conveys that the temple's condemnation is not a temporary measure. It is everlasting. This event also contrasts the sterility of temple Judaism with the authority and power of Jesus. Jesus is said to "answer" the tree (NIV "he said," v. 14). What he answers is the tree's false advertising with leaves that hide its fruitlessness. The tree gives the impression that it might have something to eat, just as the temple gives the impression that it is a place dedicated to the service of God. The temple profits only the priestly hierarchy; it profits nothing for God.

Jesus does not say "mountains" but specifies "this mountain" (v. 23). In the Markan context he is most likely referring to the temple mount, Mount Zion. Despite the widespread belief that God's earthly address was the holy of holies, the temple, Jerusalem, the Holy Land, the temple would no longer be the focal point of God's presence among the people. The holy place is wherever disciples preach Jesus's gospel and wherever his people, Jews and gentiles, gather.

Jesus assures his disciples that the effectiveness of prayer has nothing to with the temple or its sacrifices. When he dies on the cross, access to God is not closed off but opened up for all. His death creates a new house of prayer, a temple not made with hands, which will be without barriers or limitations.

Jesus concludes his explanation with the promise, "And when you stand praying, if you hold anything against anyone, forgive them, so that your Father in heaven may forgive you your sins" (v. 25). Relationship with God is based simply on faith and forgiveness. If one can unleash God's power by faith and find forgiveness through prayer and a forgiving spirit, the temple cultus has been bypassed, and a house of prayer that has become a den of brigands has no more use than a dead fig tree. God's power will become available to those, including gentiles, who have faith that it can be unleashed apart from the temple. The temple with its priesthood, sacrifices, and taxes is no longer the place of God's presence, where one meets God and where sins are forgiven. By the time Mark writes, the temple is either besieged or already destroyed. He wants to convey to his readers that broken altars do not prejudice atonement with God.

The Reaction of the High Priests (11:18, 27–33). The chief priests (former high priests and priests with permanent duties in the temple), the teachers of the law (learned legal experts), and the elders (laymen drawn from the wealthy aristocracy) are the very ones Jesus predicted would conspire to kill him. They challenge Jesus to present his credentials.

They ask by what authority Jesus could assail the cultic system, and he refers back to the ministry of John the Baptizer. John came preaching a baptism of repentance for the forgiveness of sins that bypassed the temple cult. It was free; no sacrifice was required except that of a repentant heart. No money exchanged hands. Jesus implicitly aligns himself with the ministry of John, and if John's ministry was from heaven, then the temple has become passé.

The authorities attempt to sidestep the challenge, but the damage is done. These corrupt leaders do not want to lose credibility with the crowds or alienate them because that may disrupt their scheme to do away with Jesus. Mark's comment that "they feared the people" (v. 32) reveals that their authority derives from humans because they do not fear heaven. These leaders only dread losing face before the crowds and will ultimately lose their souls. They may evade Jesus's question, but they cannot evade God's judgment. Their logic reveals something about Jesus as well as themselves. Their answer reveals that they have no understanding of God's working and consequently no authority.

Application. *Jesus and the temple.* This incident in Mark 11 should cause us to examine the theological and political ramifications of Jesus's actions and words.

First, attacking religious corruption is no less dangerous than attacking political corruption. People are easily hoodwinked by a show of piety. If one attacked a similar sacred cow today, one could meet with the same results.

Second, Jesus's attack made clear that God's requirements are not ritual but ethical. Cultic sacrifice is meaningless because everything is a matter of the heart: faith, prayer, and forgiveness of others.

Third, by denouncing the temple, Jesus also denounces the system of domination it represented. The temple had become the center of power for the nobility who dominated, controlled, indoctrinated, and exploited others who ranked lower on the social scale. The temple preserved the status quo by extending privileges to the few and by resisting the transforming power of the kingdom of God in society. Jesus did not simply help individual poor people; he went to the very source of much of the injustice in society in his day—the temple and its priestly hierarchy.

Next, the temple system fostered xenophobia and ethnocentrism. The strain between Jew and gentile, male and female, would never be settled as long as the temple stood with its series of holy barriers, each saying to a different group, "No entry!" If any can say of a church fellowship, "It is easier for a camel to go through the eye of a needle than for some people to be accepted there," it needs to be condemned.

Finally, Jesus attacks the merchandising of religion that obstructed the access of others to God. No ministry can legitimately take advantage of the presence of God to make a profit or to give the impression that they are hawking a religious commodity.

The power of prayer. People regarded the temple as the place of prayer. Jesus expected it to be a house of prayer for all nations, though he went on to predict its destruction. In his explanation of the fig tree's withering, Jesus envisioned a future without a temple. But its demise would not bring an end to effective prayer. What does prayer look like in his community?

First, the community needs to pray receptively. Prayer is not imposing our will on God but opening up our lives to God's will. Second, people are to pray confidently. This text does not invite one to attempt magical miracles. When Christians pray in Jesus's name, they may be confident of God's response, but what they ask must be compatible with his teaching, life, and death. There are some things that Christians should not ask and some things that God will not give. Next, the new community is to pray expectantly and without discouragement. Our prayers should not only focus on our own small worlds and our immediate futures but should fix our attention on the long term and the large scale. Finally, the community is to pray with a forgiving spirit. We cannot make peace with God if we bear animosity for others.

MARK 12:1–12

Original Meaning. Jesus's allegory of the wicked tenants continues his response to the leaders' challenge of his authority and brings matters to a head. The story is an allegory of God's troubled relationship with Israel that is nearing its climax. Jesus's original audience, however, would not have made this connection immediately. As the allegory unfolds, they become aware that their initial assumptions are false and must be revised. The sending of the servants and their callous rejection turn the tide. The word "servant" is a frequent designation in the Old Testament for the prophets whom God sent to the people. The servants' treatment in the allegory surely called to mind the ill-treatment of the prophets. The abuse of the servants in the allegory becomes progressively worse. Popular wisdom in the time of Jesus believed that prophets inevitably were rejected and suffered a martyr's fate.

The allegory reaches its denouement after the servants fail to collect the fruit. The owner has one more card up his sleeve. He will send the son "last of all" (v. 6). He is identified as a "son, whom he loved" (an idiom for an "only son"), which recalls the voice from heaven identifying Jesus as "my Son, whom I love" (1:11; 9:7). The son's mission is the same as that of the servants before him.

The tenants recognize the son as the heir and wickedly want

his inheritance for themselves. After they assassinate the son, they throw his body outside and leave him unburied. To refuse to bury a corpse was an incredible offense in the ancient world.

The owner suddenly changes from one who is seemingly impotent to one who can exact revenge. He is now the Lord of the vineyard, who will destroy the tenants who killed his servants and son. But the Lord is not through. He will give the vineyard to others. Although the true heir is rejected and killed, the inheritance still belongs to him and his community. Jesus terminates the confrontation with a citation from Psalm 118:22–23, the psalm that the crowd chanted when Jesus entered the city. The block of stone that the builders discarded becomes either the cornerstone or the capstone of a new structure. The image implies a new temple. Mark's readers will understand that Jesus is the stone of stumbling that the psalmist talked about.

The final part of the quotation, "The Lord has done this, and it is marvelous in our eyes" (12:11), attributes Jesus's condemnation of the temple to God's work. The tenants' destruction, the giving of the vineyard to others, and the transformation of a rejected stone into the capstone are marvelous to the ones who have eyes to see God's plan. The impotent animal sacrifices in a fruitless, racist, chauvinistic, stone structure will end. The Son whom these leaders will put to death will be raised by God and will become the locus of salvation. Mark does not present Jesus despised and rejected by the people of Israel but by the leaders of the people.

This allegory has christological significance. It reflects Jesus's full consciousness of his sonship in relation to the Lord of the vineyard and his full awareness of his impending death at the hands of the authorities. Those who question the authenticity of the allegory tend to question both possibilities.

Application. The parable particularly applies to the church today. Israel was chosen by God to fulfill God's gracious purposes for the whole world. God equipped them specially for the task, but the leaders mistook that assignment as special privilege and wanted to be accountable only to themselves, not to God. If one asks what fruit God requires from us today, the answer comes from what immediately precedes and follows the parable: God requires that our place of worship be a house of prayer for all nations. God also requires our community to be a forgiving one. We are to render to God what belongs to God. We are also to love God with all our heart, soul, mind, and strength, and our neighbors as ourselves. In other words, God expects the vineyard, God's people, to be an accepting, prayerful, forgiving, devoted, and loving fellowship built around his Son, the one stone that binds everything together. When it becomes something other than this, it courts God's judgment.

MARK 12:13–17

Original Meaning. The chief priests, teachers of the law, and elders send Pharisees and the Herodians to ensnare Jesus in a carefully laid trap. These interrogators bait the trap by asking a yes or no question about an explosive issue, taxes. The question asked of Jesus is loaded because it raises the issue of fidelity to the God of Israel. Can one pay taxes to Caesar and still give allegiance to the God of Israel? Are people traitors to God for supporting Caesar's hegemony over the land?

Jesus knows his questioners' hypocrisy, adroitly evades their ambush, and sets a trap of his own. By asking for a coin, which he does not possess, he throws them off guard. The opponents produce the coin, and Jesus asks them to identify whose image it bears. Jesus can now answer their question. Caesar's coins belong to him. Since they have no qualms about doing business with Caesar's money, they had better pay Caesar's taxes. And since they are able to produce the coin, Jesus also exposes that they have no qualms about bringing an image of Caesar and an emblem of his worldly power and his pretension to deity into God's temple. He makes them look foolish and impious.

Jesus does more than balance this statement when he tells them to render to God what is God's. God is Caesar's lord. One may owe Caesar what bears his image and name—money. One owes God what bears God's image and name. Exactly what we owe God becomes clear in Jesus's answer to a certain teacher of the law: we owe God love from all our heart, soul, mind, and strength (vv. 30, 33).

Application. Jesus's response to his opponents in this section serves as a model for his followers. He speaks God's truth with such utter conviction that people listen. We as Christians may hold citizenship in heaven, but that does not exempt us from being exemplary citizens on earth. Jesus does not call us to disengage from the world, nor does he confer us with special status that allows us to escape its obligations. Christians may be free from the Mosaic law, but we are not free from civil law designed to promote order.

An unhealthy union between church and state has been the undoing of both churches and governments throughout history. One must always be cautious about politicizing the church, for that inevitably means that the church becomes involved in power struggles that will detract from its mission, even if its members are fighting for a good cause. The church can become identified solely with political agendas and not the proclamation of the gospel, which transcends society and government. The church must deter politicians from girding their policies and programs with divine authority or branding their opponents as inherently evil or sinful. The church must be far enough removed from the political machine to allow it to speak prophetically.

MARK 12:18–27

Original Meaning. What little we know about the Sadducees derives almost entirely from their bitter opponents, who preserved memories of conflicts with them. Their conservatism led them to reject any theological innovations they regarded as derived from something other than the Pentateuch. The belief in the resurrection fell into that category since the books of Moses never mention it. The Sadducees bait Jesus with a teasing conundrum based on the law of levirate marriage, which prescribed what should happen when a man died with no heirs.

Jesus follows his pattern of dealing with hostile questioners by going on the attack. The Sadducees are deceived because they are ignorant of Scripture and underestimate the power of God. Jesus first corrects the Sadducees on their view of the resurrection. The resurrected are transfigured into a new dimension of life that we have never experienced. Jesus then corrects the Sadducees' biblical ignorance by reminding them of the "bush" passage in the Torah that identifies God as the God of Abraham, Isaac, and Jacob (Exod 3:6). Would God claim to be the God of ghostly shadows or of those who no longer exist? The living God would hardly identify himself as the God of corpses. Jesus's parting shot, "You are badly mistaken" (v. 27), affirms that some truths are not open to debate.

Application. The media gives its fantasy version of what happens in death through popular movies. Those images have an enormous subliminal affect on both Christians and non-Christians. The church must give its answer. It needs to proclaim its message clearly to a confused world that is much deceived, as the Sadducees were. We should avoid attempts to describe what heavenly life is like. Instead, we should highlight the necessity of a close relationship to the heavenly Father, who keeps his promises.

How can we comprehend anything except in earthly images? It would be like trying to explain to persons who lived all their lives isolated on Arctic tundra what a tropical beach is like. Only with difficulty could one describe palm trees, a sandy beach, colorful birds, fish, shells, and coral to someone who has no conception of such things. It would be easier to describe the landscape by telling them what was not there: no snow, polar bears, ice floes, freezing winds. The Sadducees pictured the resurrection in terms of what they were familiar with in earthly life, and it naturally made no sense. Jesus only tells them what is not there: no marriage or giving in marriage.

MARK 12:28–44

Original Meaning

The Greatest Commandment (12:28–34). In this passage, this teacher is not asking which laws need to be obeyed and which can safely be ignored. He is asking, "What is the fundamental premise of the law on which all the individual commands depend?" Jesus gives an orthodox reply from the daily confession of Israel known as the Shema.

Love is our inner commitment to God that is expressed in all our conduct and relationships. Those who do not show love to others can hardly claim to love God. The statement that no other command is greater than these two can mean that the other commands simply spell out different ways in which to apply these two primary ones. Or it may be more radical: these are the only two commands that matter.

The teacher of the law affirms that Jesus has answered his question well. He had assumed a superior position from which he passed judgment on Jesus's teaching. Jesus puts things in proper perspective as the final arbiter of the interpretation of the law and, what is more important, as the one who knows who is near or far from the kingdom of God. Can this teacher of the law take the next step and accept Jesus as the Son of David and David's Lord?

Jesus's Question about David's Son (12:35–37). Jesus cites Psalm 110:1 to point out a conundrum. If the Messiah is the Son of David, why does David address him "by the Holy Spirit" as "Lord" (v. 36)? It is hardly customary for fathers to address their sons in this way. One expects quite the reverse. How then can the Messiah be David's Son?

Mark frequently challenges his readers to understand more of Jesus's full identity by posing questions. This tantalizer serves to correct the crowd's exultation over "the coming kingdom of our father David" (11:10). Jesus does not wield the political and military authority of David, yet he is greater than the great king of Israel. The kingdom that he brings is greater than that of "our father David"; it is the kingdom of the Father.

The Denunciation of the Teachers of the Law (12:38–40). After commending a particular teacher of the law and citing the Jewish theological leaders' opinion about the Son of David, Jesus proceeds to denounce them as a class. First, he chastens them for their desire to wear distinguished dress—they like to parade about in long robes. Jesus also condemns the longing of these teachers of the law for human adulation. Jesus accuses the teachers of the law of devouring widows' houses. Finally, Jesus castigates the prayers of these teachers of the law. Prayers supposedly addressed to God are spoken to win accolades from human eavesdroppers. They do not recognize how despicable their insincerity is and fool themselves into believing that human admiration for their piety accords with God's admiration for it.

The Widow's Offering (12:41–44). The resounding of the trumpet, when the rich toss in their silver, dwarfs the tinkling of the widow's two coins. But her sacrificial devotion eclipses their perfunctory donations. The rich give from their abundance, but they do not sacrifice their abundance. This poor widow gives all that she has to live on, which is next to nothing. Her unassuming piety sharply contrasts with the conspicuous impiety of the scribes in the preceding denunciation. She shows radical trust in God to provide for her and gives what is surplus for this day to God.

Application. Our love for God is a response to God's love for us. Those who try to straddle the fence by allotting God only token love while maintaining a bosom friendship with the world are doomed to be frustrated in this world and doomed in the world to come. With God, it is all or nothing. Love cannot be tithed like money. Few can honestly sing, "All to Jesus I Surrender," but God requires nothing less.

We must love God with all our heart. In the Bible, the heart is the command center of the body, where decisions are made and plans are formed. It is the center of our inner being, which controls our feelings, emotions, desires, and passions. The heart is where religious commitment takes root.

We must love God with all our soul. God gave breath to the soul of humans. The soul is the source of vitality in life. It is the motivating power that brings strength of will. Together with the heart, the soul determines conduct. When we are commanded to love God with all our soul, it refers to the power of our lives.

We must love God with all our mind. The mind is the faculty of perception and reflection that directs our opinions and judgments. Our love for God requires more than an emotional response or a swirl of activity in God's name. We must love God with our intelligence.

We must love God with all our strength. "Strength" refers to one's physical capacities, including one's possessions. The widow provides the best example of this love.

We must also love our neighbors as ourselves. This command assumes a healthy egoism and encourages an enlightened self-interest. We want others to deal with us according to their highest ideals rather than according to our merits.

MARK 13:1–37

Original Meaning

Introduction (13:1–4). As Jesus departs the temple, the disciples are overawed by its magnificence. Anyone who has seen reconstructed models of the temple or read descriptions of it can understand why. Just as marvels of engineering prowess in our towns or cities kindle pride in us, so this imposing structure glistening in the sun inspired the disciples' awe. The temple also gave the Jews a sense of security because it was the place where God lived. How could God ever abandon this beautiful house or allow it to be destroyed?

Jesus reproaches them for their reverence and wonder. What has been implicit in Jesus's actions in the temple now becomes explicit. He openly prophecies its complete destruction. When he earlier predicted his death and resurrection, the disciples never asked when it would happen; but talk of the temple's destruction sends off alarm bells in their heads. Peter, James, John, and now Andrew want to know exactly when this will occur and what is the sign so that they can prepare themselves for the catastrophe and perhaps escape its terrors.

Warnings about the Destruction of the Temple (13:5–23). *Warning about deceivers who feed false hopes (13:5–6).* Jesus warns that they must "watch," though this command does not mean simply to "be on your guard." The disciples will need uncommon spiritual acumen to be able to withstand the deceivers and to weather the storms of persecution. They will need to keep their wits so that they will not be led astray amid crises and cries of confusion.

The deceivers lay claim to divine authority that rightfully belongs only to Jesus. These messianic pretenders easily dupe their followers with dramatic gestures and daring declarations. The disciples must steel themselves to see through these impostors and not be caught up in the excited delusions of the crowd.

Warning about wars and earthquakes that feed false fears (13:7–8). Jesus also warns about international commotions and natural disasters. Jesus identifies these things as the "beginning of birth pains"—a time of suffering. When the world is collapsing around them, Jesus-followers may impatiently yearn for deliverance from their present distress. They must prepare themselves for the long haul, however. Yet by comparing the travail in history to the birth process, where the pain gets worse just before delivery, Jesus conveys that things are not hopeless. The end is certain, and the torment will result in God's deliverance of the elect.

Warning about persecutions that can break resolve (13:9–13). The disasters described in 13:5–8 overwhelm everyone in the path of the armies or situated on geological fault lines. The persecutions sketched in 13:9–13, however, specifically target Christians because they are Christians. They will be singled out for persecution because they faithfully follow their Lord.

When these things happen, astute disciples will realize they are suffering precisely what their Lord has prophesied. They also suffer what he himself endured. He hopes that his disciples will understand that, through their suffering, the kingdom of God silently advances as they proclaim the gospel amid trial and tribulation.

Amid this bleak landscape of wars, starvation, atrocities, earthquakes, persecutions, and treachery, the one bright light is God's intention to get the word of the gospel out to all. It is necessary for the gospel to be preached first to the whole world. This prophecy that the gospel will be preached to the whole world also assures the reader that the pre-Easter cowardice of the disciples will somehow be transformed into bravery. It makes clear that the empty tomb is not the end of the gospel, only the beginning.

Warning about the war in Judea (13:14–20). The warning in these verses applies specifically to the first and second generation of Jesus's disciples, who will witness the war in Judea that will result in the destruction of the temple. The cue to take flight comes when they see the "abomination that causes desolation" (v. 14), which refers to what is detestable and rejected by God and causes horror and destruction among humankind. The term derives from Daniel 11:31. Since Jesus specifically mentions Judea and uses a phrase from Daniel referring to an enemy's desecration of the sanctuary, he is predicting some horrifying event in the temple. Therefore it applies to a time when the temple was still standing.

The allusion remains inside information that the original audience of the Gospel understood, but we are left only with guesses. It may refer to some specific first-century phenomenon related to the war against Rome when it made sense to flee Jerusalem. It would be useless to flee to some mountain redoubt at the end of the ages. Whatever that abomination was, Mark intended the audience to understand it as a fulfillment of Daniel's prophecy and another sign of the beginning of the birth pains.

When this event occurs, there will be no time for the refugees to retrieve precious possessions or even such essentials as cloaks. Those who are slowed in their flight by the need to care for children will be particularly vulnerable. If it occurs in the cold of winter, escape without provisions over flooded rivers and dangerous mountain passes will be precarious.

The temple no longer symbolizes God's abiding favor and protection, since God will allow it to be desecrated and destroyed. Any reverence of the temple and its cherished heritage or belief that its sanctity still ensures God's blessing is more than simply mistaken devotion to a lost cause. To reverence the temple means to disavow trust in Jesus and his commands. His followers should not allow themselves to become entangled in the fate of the doomed nation and its temple.

Warning about deceivers (13:21–23). This unit about the war in Judea concludes as it began—with a warning about deceivers. False prophets will arise who will exploit catastrophes for their own ends and add to the miseries of the people. Both deceivers and the deceived will perish.

However compelling the signs and portents and however persuasive their interpretations, disciples must ever keep on their toes to resist their lures. They must guard against religious leaders who appeal to false hopes and want to exalt themselves and expand their influence. They must not allow the yearning for God to deliver them to cause them to embrace mirages, fantasies, and errors. Jesus urges them to hold fast to the certainty that God's Messiah has already come and is hidden in heaven, not on earth. He will not come to save the temple from its fate.

The Coming of the Son of Man (13:24–27). The hope of Jesus's coming enables disciples to endure any affliction, but Jesus gives no precise timetable about how long it will take for the end to come after the temple's destruction. Two things are clear: the end of the temple must happen before the end of time, but it does not denote the end. Jesus is silent about what might lie between the two events. He simply says, "But in those days, following that distress . . ." (v. 24).

How long following that distress? The ambiguity is deliberate, and Jesus does not intend for us to try to unravel it. Otherwise, he would have given more definite clues. He expects his disciples to be ready for anything anytime. Busying oneself with calculations about dates is thus a fruitless exercise that can only distract from the mission that God has called the church to do—to preach the gospel.

One knows that the end is certain, and the cosmic tumult will make it obvious to all. There will be no secret appearances so that people need to search here and there. Only in the parousia will the veil that cloaks the Son of Man in mystery be completely lifted for all to see. The clouds of his coming unveil his glory as the one who shares in the majesty and power of God, who also comes in clouds.

The images of the sun darkening, the moon not giving its light, the stars falling, and the powers in the heaven shaking are woven together from the Old Testament (Isa 13:10; Joel 2:10). Jesus's coming means salvation for the elect as angels are sent out to gather them. The elect are those who have faithfully responded to the gospel. The gospel begins with the one who is faithful to the very end and is raised up by God; it will close with the gathering of the many elect who remain faithful to the end.

Final Warnings to Watch (13:28–37). *The lesson from the fig tree (13:28–31).* Many questions surround these verses, and even more answers have been proposed. Yet it appears that the simplest explanation is to take the fig-tree parable and the statement that all these things will come upon this generation as a reference to the woes preceding the destruction of the temple (13:5–23). It sums up Jesus's warning in this unit. One can see the evidence of the coming destruction of Jerusalem as surely as one can tell that a budding fig tree means summer is near. Jesus's predictions about the temple's destruction will come true. Those things that humans believe are the center of the universe will disappear from the face of the earth. Only Jesus's words abide.

The unknown time of the end (13:32). Just as it is not in Jesus's power to grant to anyone to sit at his right hand or left, so Jesus must be obedient to the sovereign will of God, who determines the time. No apocalyptic calculations beforehand can violate that sovereignty. The end comes without any warning. No one will have time for last-second preparations.

The parable of the doorkeeper (13:33–37). This parable applies to the coming of the Son of Man. Its key element is that the servants have no advance warning when the master of the house will return. The doorkeeper must keep alert throughout the watches of the night. Jesus's warnings affirm that only those who are valiant under fire and vigilant during the delay will be vindicated in the end. We are to work faithfully because our Lord will return; we are to work with assurance because it is the Lord who returns.

Application. Christians today want Jesus to give them a crib sheet to help them identify precisely when the end will come. Despite Jesus's disclaimer in 13:32, some today claim to have decoded the mystery and to speak for God. Obviously, they think they comprehend more than Jesus and can arrange all events on a timetable.

Although history is riddled with vain predictions about the timing of the end, such speculation continues. Without any embarrassment, people revise their calculations for the dates of the rapture and Christ's merciful return again and again. Some compile a "Rapture Index," toting up all the earthquakes, wars, and other disasters to gauge the probabilities that the time will be soon. Christians are bombarded with paperback-book prophets, both secular and religious, who have produced libraries of books that forecast an era of war, nuclear holocaust, famine, ecological disaster, economic ruin, and pestilence just around the corner.

The most important thing that Christians have been called to do is to preach the gospel to all the nations (13:10). When the Son of Man comes, he will not quiz people to see whose predictions on the date were accurate. He will want to know what we were doing. Were we proclaiming the gospel to all the nations? Were we enduring suffering faithfully? Were we fulfilling the assigned tasks? Those who have been asleep on the job or buried in the task of trying to map out the times rather than carrying out the mission will be more than just embarrassed; they will be judged. That is why Jesus warns his disciples to be on their guard (13:9).

MARK 14:1–11

Original Meaning. During the Passover festival, an estimated eighty-five to three-hundred thousand pilgrims flocked to the city of Jerusalem, which had a population estimated at sixty to one-hundred twenty thousand. The atmosphere may have been much like a state fair. Passover commemorated the liberation of the nation from Egypt, when God sent a plague that claimed the lives of the Egyptians' firstborn sons. The Israelites were spared by dabbing their doorways with the blood of a slaughtered lamb. Many in Jesus's day saw this first deliverance as the model for their final liberation. It was a particularly nervous time for the high priests and their police force since the chance for an outbreak of riots increased dramatically during this time.

The Jewish leaders begin to make good on their determination to do away with a dangerous rabble-rouser, who menaces the temple and their priestly class. Because of his popularity, they plot to arrest him by stealth and to kill him.

The next scene finds Jesus dining at the home of Simon the leper. Mark gives no details about who this Simon is or how Jesus happens to be in his house. He is only interested in what happens when an anonymous woman breaks into the company of men and pours precious perfume over Jesus's head. She breaks a costly jar containing pure nard, and the even more costly perfume streams out.

What is going on in this woman's mind as she pours out the precious contents of the jar on Jesus's head? In the Old Testament, kings were anointed in private, and it sometimes signaled a revolt. Maybe she hopes it is time for God to intervene in the affairs of Israel with this king. We may not know what this woman was thinking, but Mark does tell us exactly what is going on in the minds of the bystanders who witness this scene. They complain about the waste of something so expensive. But Jesus cherishes this woman's devotion and defends her.

The anointing reveals that Jesus has prophetic knowledge both of his death and of his ultimate triumph. Good news pierces through the tragedy. Jesus announces that this woman's devotion will be remembered wherever the gospel is preached in the whole world.

Application. The malicious scheming against Jesus surrounding the act of sacrificial love reveals that people did not come pouring out of the saloons and peep shows to kill Jesus. It was the religious politicos and one of Jesus's intimates who did him in. The church tends to look for threats from without and to ignore the threats from within. Those who hold the reins of power may honestly believe that what they are doing is in the best interests of God's cause on earth. They may convince themselves that the end justifies the means. They may never see that self-interest motivates their words and actions and that it leads them into their greatest guilt.

Jesus's commendation of this anonymous woman also reveals that one can never be fully aware of one's own significance or role in God's kingdom. The woman had no idea of the worldwide significance of her action, nor did the high priests, Judas, or Pontius Pilate. Albert Einstein said, "It is a tragic mistake for those in power to think that they are in control." It is also a mistake for us to think that our sacrificial devotion is wasteful or insignificant. Who knows how God will use it?

Caring for the Poor. Jesus says that what this woman did was good because she was anointing him for his burial. Since Jesus has died and risen again, how today do we best show our love and devotion to Christ when we have a lavish gift to give? Perhaps we help to build elaborate church buildings? Such gifts are likely better directed to supporting missions or giving to alleviate the needs of the poor. As we relate to the poor, we relate to our Savior.

Judas's Betrayal. Modern readers usually want to know more why Judas betrayed Jesus than why the woman was so generous. Mark offers no motive at all for the betrayal. Luke tells us that Satan entered Judas. According to Matthew, greed was the chief motive. In John's Gospel, Judas is identified as a thief concerned about money and as one in league with Satan.

Attempts to find the reason or reasons to explain why Judas did what he did are diversions that prevent us from looking at our own potential betrayal. If we convince ourselves that Judas acted for this or that reason, we can also convince ourselves that we would not succumb to such perfidy. If no specific reason can be given except greed or Satan, then we all are susceptible. We too can betray Jesus for all the temptations in life that may snare us.

MARK 14:12–31

Original Meaning

Preparations for the Passover Meal (14:12–16). Mark notes that the disciples are anxious to make preparations for the Passover meal. Jesus gives the disciples directions that may reflect some secret arrangement on his part with coded signs. Finding the room is so similar to finding the donkey in 11:1–6, however, that the scene may be intended to show that Jesus knows everything in advance and has total control of the situation. The emphasis falls on the conclusion: "The disciples . . . found things just as Jesus had told them" (v. 16).

The Last Supper (14:17–25). The scene begins with Jesus's grave announcement that one of the Twelve will betray him. All the disciples ask him one by one, "Surely you don't mean me?" Jesus reassures no one but gives only an ambiguous response: "It is one of the Twelve . . . one who dips bread into the bowl with me" (v. 20). This statement adds no new information but reiterates that the betrayer has infiltrated their midst and is eating with him.

When Jesus breaks the bread and distributes it to the disciples, it means that what has happened to this bread will happen to him. The broken bread given to the disciples also symbolizes that his passion will benefit them and is an acted-out parable of his offering up his life for the many. What is significant is that Jesus uses an article of food so simple and so universal that the disciples can never again recline at a meal, take bread, bless it, and break it without thinking of the last night that they were together with their Lord.

After the blessing of the cup, Jesus gives it to them. Mark reports that after they have all drunk from the cup, Jesus announces, "This is my blood of the covenant, which is poured out for many" (v. 24). Years of taking communion have so conditioned us that we hardly blink an eye over this statement. Think of what that might have meant to a Jew in the first century. You have drunk from the cup, and the host says, "This is my blood."

What do Jesus's statements, "This is my body," and, "This is my blood," imply? First, when Jesus makes his statements, he is saying that his death is a new sacrifice offered to God. No more sacrificial victims need be killed, only bread broken and shared, wine poured out and shared. Second, Mark makes it clear that they all drank from the one cup. Drinking the cup of someone meant entering into a communion of relationship with that person, to the point that one shared that person's destiny, good or ill. They also had to follow in the way of their Lord and accept his destiny of suffering for themselves. Finally, blood sealed or inaugurated a covenant. Jesus's sacrificial death is also a covenant-making event. It marks a new act of redemption and begins a new relationship between God and the people—one that supersedes the old.

Gloom predominates the Last Supper in Mark. But whenever Jesus speaks of his death, he combines it with a positive note of his vindication. A glimmer of joy emerges when Jesus speaks of drinking the fruit of the vine anew in the kingdom of God. The supper that begins on such a sad note ends on a note of joy. In the face of death, duplicity, and desertion, Jesus exudes confidence that ultimately he will be vindicated by God's reign.

To the Mount of Olives (14:26–31). Jesus has worked hard all through Mark's narrative and now at the end has little to show for it. Even his small band will be thrown into confusion and scatter in all directions. The citation from Zechariah 13:7 at verse 27 reveals, however, that what happens is all in God's control.

Jesus again gives them a cheering promise, "After I have risen, I will go ahead of you into Galilee" (v. 28). For the fifth time in the Gospel, Jesus predicts his resurrection. The future of Jesus's movement depends entirely on God's direct intervention, not on the disciples' individual bravery. Jesus will "go ahead of" them, which implies that he will resume his shepherding role, leading them and calling them together.

Peter insists that he will prove himself more trustworthy than the rest, who, he implies, probably will fall away. This competitive egotism, "Even if all fall away, I will not" (v. 29), will never go willingly to a cross. Consequently, Peter's failure at the crucial moment will be immortalized.

Application. The Passover was not intended to be a gratifying memento of God's past deliverance of Israel. The celebration was meant to place each generation in touch with that event and make it a present reality. In the same way, the Lord's Supper is not a memorial of something past and gone but reminds us of what the Lord has done for us and makes his death and his presence a living reality.

The Lord's Supper works for good. It reminds us who we are, what our story is, what our values are, and who claims us as his own. In the Lord's Supper, the gospel confronts all five of our physical senses. We see, hear, taste, smell, and touch what it meant for Christ to die for us. It also binds the past, present, and future together. We look back to Jesus's Last Supper and experience the beginning of the new covenant with God (see Jer 31:31–34). We experience Jesus's death for us, and the power of our sins being forgiven in the present. We look forward to the future celebration in God's kingdom when all will acknowledge Jesus as Lord. When Jesus distributes the wine to his disciples, he solemnly assures them that he will be vindicated by God and will drink it anew in the kingdom of God.

The presence of Christ's saving power in the Eucharist manifests itself when we recognize our common union with one another. Churches should compare their ecclesiastical tradition regarding the Lord's Supper critically with the New Testament witness. Perhaps they will discover that they need to develop ways to convey the presence of Christ's saving power in new and different ways. Perhaps this can be communicated best if we return to the practice of the New Testament in observing the Lord's Supper at a shared meal. We can celebrate our fellowship with the Lord and with one another.

MARK 14:32–52

Original Meaning

The Gethsemane of Jesus (14:32–36). Although Jesus wants the support and prayer of Peter, James, and John, he knows that even these three disciples will be of no help to him now and goes off a little farther alone. Mark uses a word to suggest the greatest possible degree of horror and suffering (*ekthambeō*) in 14:33. He boldly allows us to see Jesus suffering psychological anguish before his physical suffering. Jesus is in the grip of a shuddering horror as he faces the dreadful prospect before him. Jesus's prayer of lament follows a well-known pattern of lament found in the Psalms.

Jesus here expresses his intimacy with his Father as well as his confidence in his nearness and loving care. His prayer does not try to run counter to the Father's purpose but explores the limits of the purpose without trying to burst its bounds. Might there be another way? Might he escape the horrifying cup?

The cup may represent God's wrathful judgment, the awful consequences of God's judgment on sinful humanity. On the other hand, the cup may simply refer to Jesus's death and the suffering he must endure. Jesus uses the cup and baptism as symbols of his redemptive death. Jesus prays to be delivered from death; instead, he will be delivered through death and glorified by the resurrection.

In Gethsemane, Jesus meets the dreadful silence of heaven. Jesus overcomes the silence, fights off the human temptation to do as he wills, and through prayer acquiesces to God's will. He will not try to evade the cup either by slipping away in the dark or by resorting to violence. He will accept the nails of the cross as he accepted the stones of the desert.

The Gethsemane of the Disciples (14:37–42). One can interpret Jesus's checking on the disciples both positively and negatively. On the one hand, Jesus returns to them as the Good Shepherd, who, confronted with the threat of the destruction of the flock, returns repeatedly to look after it. On the other hand, Mark underscores the failure of the disciples at this most crucial point.

Jesus's prayer in Gethsemane ends when he senses that the hour has come. Jesus knows that he will not be delivered from the cup but will be delivered into the hands of sinners. He has freely accepted God's will for himself and through prayer has steeled himself for what lies ahead. By contrast, the disciples have squandered the opportunity for prayer by sleeping. Consequently, they will fold under pressure.

Jesus's Arrest (14:43–50). A grim realism stamps Mark's account of Jesus's arrest. A misguided rabble, deputized by the temple officials, invades Gethsemane with swords and clubs. Ironically, Jesus castigated the temple for being a robber's den instead of a house of prayer for all nations. Now temple goons arrest him in the middle of his prayer, as if he is a robber.

The sad performance of Jesus's disciples in this crucial moment dominates this scene. Judas gives Jesus no sign that their fellowship has been broken. He wants everything to appear normal up to the last second, when guards rush to capture him. He turns him over to a certain death with a warm gesture of love and the customary greeting of respect, turning a sign of intimacy and goodwill into a sign of infamy and death. Mark does not record any response from Jesus. Judas vanishes from the story, though not from memory as the one guilty of vile treachery.

Despite the well-laid plans to avoid any ruckus, "one of those standing near" drew his sword and struck (v. 47). Whether by accident or intentionally, the high priest's servant has his ear cut off. Jesus condemns the violent demeanor of the arresting party and then announces that the Scriptures are being fulfilled.

The disciples have awakened sufficiently by this time to make their shameless getaway. They all forsake him and flee (v. 50), but not before the announcement about the fulfillment of the Scriptures. Jesus's arrest sets in motion a whole range of Scriptures that will be fulfilled. This explains why the one who has exhibited so much power throughout the Gospel willingly submits to this mob. The Son of Man is handed over in accordance with God's will as attested by Scripture.

The Young Man's Flight (14:51–52). Mark alone includes the account of a young man, identified only as one who was following Jesus, being grabbed by the arresting party and wriggling free from their grasp. He runs away into the darkness naked. The disciples' panicked flight sharply contrasts with the quiet dignity of Jesus, who has kept watch and is ready. Jesus now will become increasingly alone and must face the horror of his death without any human support. The craven fear of this young man who is seized and stripped and escapes into the darkness compares badly with the courage of Jesus, who is seized and stripped and does not escape but is crucified.

Application. Mark's readers need not shy from crying to God to be spared from their own cross that they must bear, but they can learn from Jesus to accept God's plan through prayer. We can learn to handle pain and suffering from Jesus. Jesus was on such intimate terms with God that he did not shy away from vociferously laying bare his thoughts—like a hurting child crying to a loving parent. His prayer shows that we can express our feelings honestly to God.

Jesus models what he means when he tells his disciples to "watch" in 13:37. Watching is not what we might first think it is. Jesus does not tell them to watch for the end of all things. The disciples expected cosmic upheaval that would come with plenty of warning, with sirens blaring, swords flashing, and angels descending. They did not recognize that we fight against demonic powers and not just the powers of flesh and blood. The trouble is that we never know when the crisis will come. Spiritual drowsiness is dangerous and will prove the Christian's undoing.

First, spiritual drowsiness is to stop praying. We often do not pray because we are unaware that we are in the midst of trial. Second, spiritual drowsiness is to be unable to recognize the onset of trial or to accept it as God's will. The disciples heard only what they wanted to hear and tuned out Jesus's teaching on the necessity of suffering and the requirement of taking up a cross. They are totally unprepared for the pop quiz. Third, spiritual drowsiness is to presume that the Spirit is willing without being mindful of the weakness of the flesh. One must be ever mindful how close we are to falling. The good news, however, is that failure in times of crisis is not permanent. Finally, spiritual drowsiness is to assume that we have arrived. The sudden arrival of the hour of trial can be a cruel reminder how mistaken false confidence in past spiritual achievements is.

MARK 14:53–72

Original Meaning

The Hearing before the Sanhedrin (14:53–65). Mark's trial scene pins the primary responsibility and initiative for Jesus's death on the high priest and his Sanhedrin. Nocturnal trials were abnormal and were later forbidden under rabbinic law. A hearing in the middle of the night suggests the kangaroo justice of a lynch mob dressed in hooded sheets, but it also shows that these leaders are under time constraints.

Apparently, it is not enough to arrest and flog Jesus, which was in their power; the ruling priests want him dead and disgraced before the crowds. They presume his guilt because he is a threat. The hearing will serve to convince anyone with misgivings that he is worthy of death and will fix the charge they will present to the Roman governor.

Mark has told us that the high priests, teachers of the law, and elders "were looking for evidence against Jesus" (v. 55) that will put a noose around his neck. The law allowed the condemnation of an accused person only on the evidence of two or more witnesses who agreed. Mark relates that many volunteer testimony against Jesus, and he fastens on one particular charge.

Jesus has indeed made menacing noises against this man-made temple with his daring protest against the money changers and dove sellers. He also predicted privately to his disciples that the vast temple complex would be destroyed. Since what the witnesses say about Jesus's stance toward the temple seems close to the truth and since this charge resurfaces when passersby taunt him with it while he hangs from the cross (15:29), how is their testimony false?

Most likely Mark emphasizes that the testimony of the witnesses is false primarily because of the second element in the charge. His first readers may have held out hopes that Jesus as the Messiah would build another temple. Since Scripture mentions that David's offspring would build a house for God's name, some probably assumed that Jesus would do that (2 Sam 7:13). Mark therefore makes it clear that Jesus never claimed he would build another earthly temple, and thus no one should expect any kind of earthly temple.

Like the suffering servant of Isaiah 53 and the righteous person in the Psalms, Jesus remains silent before his false accusers. The high priest takes charge and asks Jesus directly, "Are you the Messiah, the Son of the Blessed One?" (v. 61). He piously avoids God's name with a circumlocution while using underhanded means to get rid of an enemy.

Jesus publicly accepts that he is the Messiah, with his reply: "I am" (v. 62). Jesus here affirms his identity before the high priest and his council and continues with, "And you will see the Son of Man sitting at the right hand of the Mighty One and coming on the clouds of heaven."

The drama heightens as the high priest labels his response as blasphemy and tears his garment to underscore his judgment. This gesture was an ancient way of expressing distress, mourning, or outrage and is a fitting response to perceived blasphemy, but it also may be a grandstanding display to get others to see things his way. To the high priest, the evidence is conclusive: Jesus has incriminated himself, and the council unanimously condemns him. They judge him to be worthy of death.

What is blasphemous about Jesus's answer in verse 62? The high priest's reaction follows Jesus's complete statement that they will see the Son of Man sitting at the right hand of God. Jesus claims to be more than the Messiah, the Son of the Blessed One. He understands his sonship to be on a higher plane than that implied in Psalm 2:7 and 2 Samuel 7:14 for the Davidic king. His affirmation far surpasses any current conception about the Messiah because he implies that he has divine authority, and they will one day see it.

The two charges that emerge from this hearing are religious in nature and have to do with the temple and the Messiah. They will resurface as two taunts at the cross. Two events occur at Jesus's death that parallel these taunts. The temple curtain is torn from top to bottom, and a Roman centurion confesses, "Surely this man was the Son of God" (15:38–39).

The hearing before the Sanhedrin, which has made a mockery of justice, concludes with callous mockery of Jesus. Certain people spit on Jesus as a sign of repudiation, slap him around, cover his face, and taunt him to prophesy. The reader can see the irony of all this. Jesus's prophecies have been fulfilled or are being fulfilled at this very moment.

All of these prophecies are being fulfilled, but Jesus has just uttered another prophecy in this scene that is of a greater magnitude: They will see the Son of Man sitting on the right hand of the Mighty One, coming with the clouds of heaven. Having seen Jesus's prophecies fulfilled to the letter, the reader knows that this prophecy is neither blasphemous nor ridiculous and can trust that it also will be fulfilled. Jesus will be vindicated in his resurrection and will judge his oppressors. The blindfolded Jesus is therefore the only one who sees, while his tormentors are blinded by their hatred.

Peter's Denial (14:66–72). If Mark were simply interested in giving a factual report about what Peter did during the trial of Jesus, he leaves us with many loose ends, and Peter drops out of the narrative the same way that he drops out of Acts, with many questions left up in the air.

Mark is not interested, however, in solely reporting what happened to Peter. Peter's trial in the courtyard is a parody of his Lord's. While Jesus is under fire inside, Peter warms himself by the fire outside (see vv. 53–54). As Jesus confesses under immense pressure and hostility that seals his fate, Peter capitulates under the gentlest of pressure and lies to save himself.

In his third denial, Peter invokes a curse. The verb "call down curses" has no object in the Greek text (v. 71). It may be that he calls down curses on himself, as the NIV translates it. He denies Jesus under oath and curses himself if he is lying. Or he may have pronounced a curse on Jesus. In my opinion, Mark implies that Peter commits this blasphemy. This would make Peter's fall all the more dreadful and his restoration all the more remarkable.

Application. Jesus was killed by self-serving religious leaders in control of the temple who were intent on preserving their power. They were embedded in a prosperous and mighty institution, and institutions can forget their original purpose and become concerned only with self-preservation. Even institutions dedicated to God can become taken over by evil and can try to thwart God's will rather than serving as an agent of God's will. Jesus confronted a corrupt institution and threatened its existence. What happened next should not surprise us. Confront those that exist today and see what happens.

Many Christians today in the West do not face the fierce persecution that engulfed the first Christians. Few are forced to choose between Christ and imprisonment or execution. Consequently, our denials of Christ may take more subtle forms, such as timid silence. We may not want to be identified as Christians. We do not speak out against those who sarcastically dismiss Christianity as a fantasy. We try to blend into the crowd of our Lord's enemies because we do not want to be jeered by others or to rock any boats.

The Christian faith calls for us to stand out from others. When the Hall of Fame baseball player Mickey Mantle was on the verge of death after years of abusing his body with alcohol, his many friends gathered around his hospital bed to say their farewells. One former teammate who came to his bedside was Bobby Richardson. As a Christian he had not joined the wild partying of his mates and had become a minister after his retirement from the game. Mickey Mantle used to make fun of him as "the milk drinker," but as his life ebbed away, he most wanted to talk with Bobby Richardson. The testimony of Bobby's life amid the jeers had made its impact.

One can also take solace from the account of Peter's denials. Peter was the most prominent of Jesus's disciples, yet he was still a sinner in need of God's mercy. He thought he would die for Jesus, but he needed Jesus to die for him. Mark is the Gospel of the second chance. There were probably members in Mark's church who already had betrayed and denied their Lord. If Peter could be restored after denying his Lord and even cursing him, then there was hope for others who might be guilty of the same or worse. Peter's tears of remorse mark the beginning of that restoration.

MARK 15:1–20

Original Meaning

The Charge against Jesus (15:1–5). A Roman governor would not have put a native Jew on trial for his life simply because he had violated Jewish religious regulations. Thus, the high priests reformulate the charge against Jesus in a way that the Roman governor will understand and have to take seriously. If Jesus claims to be a king, he is guilty of a crime against the sovereign power of Rome. Sending him to Pilate in tethers also insinuates that he is a threat to public order.

Much to Pilate's consternation, Jesus chooses to answer the charge enigmatically and then to remain silent. Jesus's answer is less direct, "You say so," or "Whatever you say." Jesus refuses to defend himself and implicate his fellow Jews in a gentile's court. His silence before such charges evokes Pilate's amazement. The governor may want to release Jesus, but he cannot release someone who refuses to deny such a serious charge. Jesus leaves it to God to provide the answer to the charges and to the evil massed against him. Even after God acts, many will be blind to truth.

Barabbas (15:6–15a). Pilate is perplexed that the crowd cries for the release of the murderous Barabbas instead of the harmless Jesus. Mark offers no reason why they choose Barabbas and call for the crucifixion of Jesus except that the high priests have stirred them up. Crowds, of course, can be easily manipulated. The crowd that these leaders so feared has now become their willing pawn, and things turn ugly.

Barabbas had been arrested for committing murder in an insurrection. Barabbas may have been a right-wing extremist, fighting to deliver Israel from the pollution of Roman rule, or he may have simply been a bandit. Social banditry plagued many parts of the empire. The rich man's terrorist, however, is frequently the poor man's Robin Hood. The impoverished common people, from whose ranks the bandits came, looked to them as heroic figures who justly exacted vengeance against their oppressors. Barabbas may have been a hero in the eyes of the crowd, which explains their choice. The crowd's choice is ironic. Barabbas, a brigand guilty of murder, will go free because Jesus has taken his place on the cross intended for him. Pilate is indifferent to his responsibility to carry out justice.

The Scourging and Mockery of Jesus (15:15b–20). Prisoners to be flogged were bound to a pillar or post and given strokes with a flagellum. This lash consisted of leather thongs plaited with pieces of bone, lead, or bronze. It was fittingly called a scorpion. There were no prescribed number of lashes, and sometimes the scourging itself was fatal. The balls (sometimes having hooks) would cause deep contusions as the flesh was literally ripped into bloody ribbons. Significant blood loss could also occur, critically weakening the victim.

Mark reports that the whole company of soldiers (around six hundred in a cohort) joins in the mockery of Jesus in the courtyard of Pilate's praetorium. They deck him out in royal purple and twist together a crown of thorns. The crown may also have been simply a clump of thorns heaped together.

The soldiers' mock homage climaxes the masquerade. They hail him as "king of the Jews" and bow down before him (vv. 18–19). Their ridicule probably expresses as much contempt for the Jews as it does for Jesus. Officially the Jews had had no king after the death of Herod the Great. The mockery implies that this pitiful, weak figure is the kind of king they deserve.

The recognition of Jesus in Mark's passion narrative is almost complete. A woman had lovingly anointed him in the home of a leper, but he announced that it was for his burial. The high priest asked if he was the Messiah, the Son of the Blessed One, and he responded with a yes. Pilate called him the king of the Jews, and the soldiers mockingly saluted him as a king. While on earth, Jesus was a different type of king, as ruffians anointed him with spit, crowned him with thorns, and prepared to enthrone him on a cross. At this point, everyone has abandoned Jesus, and now only God can deliver him.

Application. People with no moral compass and no moral backbone often cave in to satisfy the crowd. Many today are like Pilate. They prefer Jesus to the envious, malicious high priests and the violent Barabbas, but that is as far as it goes. They see no harm in him, but they see nothing else, and therefore they see no reason to risk anything for him.

The choice of Barabbas represents our basic instinct to protect our interests, with violence if necessary. If the vote came today, then, Barabbas would likely win again, hands down. We are more comfortable with the violent machismo of the knight-errant than with the passive suffering of a seemingly powerless savior who submits to beatings and mockery.

In other words, we have learned little since the day the crowd hailed Barabbas and called for Jesus to be crucified. Barabbas's way only doles out more violence in a never-ending cycle. Jesus's way soaks up the injustice, evil, and oppression like the venom of a sting and unleashes a far more powerful force of love and forgiveness.

Jesus took the place of a condemned man. He did not volunteer to die specifically for Barabbas, but he was chosen by God to die for all sinful humanity. He accepted the bitter cup of judgment and took the place of a murderous Barabbas and all guilty humans. He is silent, answering nothing, taking nothing—except the lashes from their scourges. We can learn of him how to endure suffering with peace and grace, trusting in God to deliver us.

MARK 15:21–47

Original Meaning

To Golgotha (15:21–27). Mark does not tell why Jesus does not carry his own cross, but it is easy to guess. He is either too weak or too slow from the severe lashing, and the soldiers must conscript an innocent onlooker to carry the crossbar. Mark identifies Simon as from Cyrene in North Africa and as the father of Rufus and Alexander. Most likely his name is remembered because he later became a Christian. Mark mentions the names of his two sons (who do not figure in the plot) because they were known to the first readers of this Gospel.

The procession ends at a place called Golgotha, which Mark interprets for his Greek-speaking readers as "the place of the skull" (v. 22). Mark does not describe the details of Jesus's crucifixion. Nearly everyone in the ancient world knew what crucifixion was like, and it served no purpose to sketch its horrors. The details Mark does isolate have theological significance.

Wine mixed with myrrh had a narcotic property. This act may have been a compassionate attempt to somewhat relieve the pain. It is unlikely, however, that the executioners are now showing Jesus charity after mocking and scourging him. They may only have wanted to give their exhausted victim a spurt of energy so that he would last longer and suffer more. Jesus rejects the offer. He had made a vow of abstinence at the Last Supper not to drink from the fruit of the vine until he would drink it anew in the kingdom of God. He has been destined to drink the cup of God, not of men, and he wishes to remain fully conscious to the bitter end as he accepts his suffering. Jesus is not going to sleep on the cross as the disciples slept in Gethsemane.

It was customary for executioners to share out the minor personal belongings of the person being executed. This detail would not have been mentioned by Mark if it had not been recognized that the division of garments also appears in Psalm 22:18. The linkage helps the reader see that this moment of absolute humiliation for Jesus is fully consonant with God's will.

The Derision (15:29–33). The victim of crucifixion customarily became the butt of contemptuous abuse. For some perverse reason, certain people relish witnessing the agony of others and enjoy adding to it. Individuals from all walks of life heap insults on Jesus, from the low criminals who are crucified with him to the high priests gathered to gloat over their triumph. The scene drips with irony as these scoffers spout their derision from their own blind point of view and unknowingly proclaim the truth about Jesus.

The passersby "hurled insults at him" (v. 29). Mark may use this verb (*blasphēmeō*) to mean simply "to deride," but he may also intend an ironic contrast with the blasphemy charge leveled by the high priest against Jesus at the conclusion of his initial interrogation. The reader must decide who is the real blasphemer—Jesus or the spectators.

The scoffing aimed Jesus's way recalls the charges raised before the high priest and his council. They taunt him as the one who would destroy the colossal temple and rebuild it in three days. Seeing this feeble and exhausted figure strung up on a cross naturally makes such a boast seem laughable. Their mockery, however, testifies to a truth beyond their range of vision. Jesus's death does destroy the temple made with hands and builds a new one not made with hands.

The chief priests and the teachers of the law join the fray next. They scoff that he saved others but cannot save himself. The reference to saving others recalls the verb used in Jesus's healings (*sōzō*). This impotent object of scorn was without form or comeliness and looked absurd as a savior. They could hardly see how God could be with someone so abandoned and tormented on a cross. By their reasoning, if he were a savior, he ought to be able to save himself.

Their jeers underscore Mark's point. He saved others—the disciples in the midst of a sea storm, the woman with a hemorrhage—and he truly cannot save himself. Were he to save himself, he could not save others from something more deadly than storms or illnesses.

Because they cannot see, they next demand a miracle. They want him to come down from the cross so that they can see and believe. They claim that some miraculous display of power or a miraculous escape will finally convince them, but they are only taunting his helplessness. A miraculous rescue would have proven only that he was a superman, not the Messiah, the Son of God. Those who want tangible proof of the divine presence will never see anything.

Jesus said that darkness would announce the great day of the Lord. The Pharisees earlier demanded a sign from heaven, and Jesus refused. Belatedly, the leaders do receive a sign from heaven, but it is not the kind they want or that they can read.

Jesus's Cry from the Cross (15:34–37). Jesus's ghastly cry, "My God, my God, why have you forsaken me?" which are the last words he speaks in this Gospel, continue to perplex Christians. It has summoned many explanations, and interpreters are divided whether to consider only the words written (which come from Psalm 22:1) or to weigh them against the entire psalm, a lament that ends with a triumphant hope of vindication. Jesus's death establishes the sovereignty of God, who sends his beloved Son to give his life as a ransom for many (Mark 10:45).

The scoffers either misunderstand Jesus's final prayer or deliberately distort his words as a final jest. They think he is calling for Elijah, presumably to rescue him from the cross. Someone in the crowd runs to fill a sponge with sharp wine. Others stop this man and mockingly wait for a miraculous deliverance from Elijah, who was himself taken up in a chariot of fire. Their jeer, "Let's see if Elijah comes to take him down" (v. 36), turns his cry of desperation into a heartless joke; but the joke is filled with irony. After all, the reader knows that Elijah has already come, and Elijah (i.e., John the Baptizer) has already been put to death and will not return to rescue Jesus.

With this last taunt, Jesus lets out a great voice and "breathed his last" (*ekpneō*), a euphemism for death (v. 37). The loud cry is unusual since crucified victims normally died of exhaustion and lack of breath.

The Tearing of the Temple Veil and the Centurion's Confession (15:38–39). This closing scene of Jesus's life parallels the opening scene of his baptism (1:9–11).

1. In Jesus's baptism, John appears in the garb of Elijah. In the crucifixion, bystanders think that Jesus is calling for Elijah to rescue him.
2. Both incidents also record the rending of a holy place (the verb "torn" [*schizō*] appears only in these two scenes in Mark). When Jesus ascended from the waters at his baptism, he saw the heavens, which Isaiah likens to a curtain (Isa 40:22), "torn open" (Mark 1:10). The temple veil was also likened to the heavens, embroidered with blue and fine linens and typifying it.
3. The divine presence descends on Jesus like a dove at his baptism and a voice sounds forth from heaven announcing, "You are my Son, whom I love" (1:11). The centurion echoes that voice from heaven: "Surely this man was the Son of God" (15:39).
4. While the tearing of the fabric of the heavens at the baptism scene was a private revelation for Jesus—only "he saw" (1:10)—the crucifixion is a public revelation for all to see. For the first time human beings can fully see what God intends to reveal.

The confession from the leader of the death squad comes as a surprise. The confession marks the beginning of the fulfillment of Psalm 22:27, "All the families of the nations will bow down before him." With Jesus's death, the reader begins to see a new temple, which will be "a house of prayer for all nations" (Mark 11:17), becoming a reality.

The Burial (15:40–47). A somber group of grieving women who have followed Jesus from Galilee look on at the execution of Jesus from a distance and witness his burial. Unlike the disciples, they have not vanished from the scene, but they are not close by to give testimony to their love and support. Standing at a distance may show delicacy; they do not gaze at his nakedness at close hand. Their stance, however, parallels that of Peter, who followed Jesus "at a distance" so that he might disguise his discipleship (14:54). They witness his death but do not confess as the centurion does.

Joseph of Arimathea takes the initiative in securing Jesus's body for burial. To ask for the body of someone executed for high treason could be looked upon as sympathizing and could earn one the same fate. But as a member of the council who condemned Jesus to death, Joseph is above suspicion. Pilate's only concern is to ascertain that Jesus is already dead. The centurion who confessed Jesus as the Son of God affirms that Jesus is really dead. Jesus's quick death amazes Pilate as much as his silence before his accusers. That Pilate readily grants the body to Joseph either confirms that he did not seriously consider Jesus guilty of treason or suggests that he willingly accedes to Jewish sensibilities.

Mark has been tolling the watches as they tick by during the passion and the hours during the crucifixion. The passion began in the evening when Jesus came with his disciples for his Last Supper; it now ends in the evening with his burial. Joseph (presumably with the help of servants) wraps Jesus's body up in a newly bought linen cloth and buries him in a tomb carved in rock.

Application. The cross is the point at which the blind rage of humanity against God is unleashed with a horrible intensity and is shown for what it is. The Gospel story depicts many of the sins that put Jesus on this cross: pride, envy, jealousy, betrayal, cruelty, greed, indifference, cowardice, and murder. We need only add our own many sins to complete the list. The old spiritual, "Were you there when they crucified my Lord?" must be answered, "Yes." We were not there as loyal supporters to sing hymns, however. Human beings still need saving from evil's power. The cross reveals at least six profound truths.

First, the cross reveals the truth about humankind but also

about God's incredible power. God's power absorbs the toxin of human sin and hatred and turns it into salvation for all who put their trust in a God who loves this much and who works in this way. The gospel is the only thing that makes sense of a world so ugly and so beautiful.

Second, the cross reveals God's incredible love. We truly see who God is when we see the Son of God crying out from the cross and then raised in glory, and when we hear the offer of forgiveness of sins ring out ever more loudly.

Next, the cross reveals that things are never what they seem in our world. It seems as if God is absent. But God remains in control and accomplishes God's purposes, planned from creation.

Fourth, the cross reveals that God's love and power can win those one might never have dreamed would respond. The actions of the centurion who put Jesus to death and of Joseph, the respected and wealthy council member who condemned Jesus to death, mean that one can never write off an enemy.

Fifth, the cross also reveals the pain of the human situation. The Son of God took on our humanity and absorbed all the bitter suffering and anguish of the world. We cannot obscure the hurtful side of life. It might be helpful in giving pastoral care to those suffering from enormous grief to teach them about biblical lamentation that cries out boldly to God. We do not cry out from the depths simply to cry out. We cry out because God is the only one who can deliver us and can answer the question "Why?"

Finally, the cross reveals a new way of life. Those who taunted Jesus assumed that anyone with power would use it to extricate himself from a personal life-threatening situation. The disciples heeded the call to save themselves when they fled into the night. Peter heeded it when he denied Jesus three times. The high priest heeded it when he moved quickly to eliminate this threatening prophetic figure. Pilate heeded it when he refused to take a stand for justice. Jesus lives out his teaching. The one who tries to save his life will lose it. The one who gives up his or her life will gain it and will give life to others.

MARK 16:1–8

Original Meaning. The women followers of Jesus rise to unexpected prominence at the very end of the story. Their emergence as the key witnesses oddly attests to the truth of what Mark reports since it is highly unlikely that the church would have invented a small group of women to furnish evidence for such events.

The Report of Jesus's Resurrection (16:1–7). The women come to the tomb wondering how the stone can be moved; they leave wondering how the stone could have been moved. The tomb is open so that the women can enter and see that Jesus is not there. But the tomb is not empty. Looking into the tomb, the women find a young man clothed in a white robe. He is an angelic figure, who gives a typical angelic reassurance, "Don't be alarmed" (v. 6). Mark's Gospel began with God's messenger announcing what God was about to do; it closes with God's messenger announcing what God has done.

The women must go to the disciples, who must in turn go to Galilee. This command is the first time that Jesus's followers are told to tell something about him. The crucifixion and the resurrection, therefore, mark a turning point. There is no need for silence or secrets now.

The resurrection revokes death and destruction, and it also revokes sin. A special nod to Peter hints at his full restoration despite his extraordinary breach of faith. Jesus does not give up on his disciples, no matter how great their failure or how many their faults.

The announcement that "he is going ahead of you" (v. 7) is as important as the word that "he is not here" (v. 6). The verb used here (*proagō*) does not simply mean that Jesus has gone on ahead of his disciples. As the risen Lord, he will regather them into the fold. Just as the earthly Jesus led his frightened disciples to Jerusalem by going before them, so the risen Jesus goes ahead of them still, leading the church.

The command to go to Galilee does make one thing clear: Jerusalem is not the center of God's movement. The disciples' future lies elsewhere. Jerusalem has become the city of the fruitless and doomed temple, the stronghold of hostility to the gospel, and the place of Jesus's savage execution. In the Gospel, Galilee has been the place of calling, faith, compassion, healing power, and authority. By going back to Galilee where Jesus will be, the disciples go back to the promising birth of their call to discipleship. There they can regroup and begin again the journey of discipleship.

The Conclusion to the Gospel and the Women's Fear (16:8). In the earliest and most reliable manuscripts, Mark's Gospel ends with verse 8. Such an abrupt ending has perplexed readers for centuries. The abrupt ending both surprises and creates suspense. Mark may have felt no need to relate resurrection appearances to readers who had heard them so often. The ending goads the reader to react. We must assume that the disciples reunite with Jesus, otherwise this Gospel would never have been written. We must now become participants because we are forced to fill in the unnarrated events from the clues Mark has offered thus far. When presented with this ending, we must ask, "What happened? What will happen?"

This conclusion about Mark's ending raises questions about the women's departure from the tomb and the nature of their fear. One might expect them to run quickly from the tomb with fear and great joy and tell his disciples, but Mark reports that they dash away in incoherent silence. Are their flight and silence to be attributed to faintheartedness and disobedience or to urgency and awe? Is one to understand their silence as only temporary incapacity because of the breathtaking nature of the news or as another sad example of abject failure by Jesus's followers?

Some contend that the women's silence depicts the effects of a frightening encounter with divine power. The women's fear may be interpreted as awe that befalls one who stands before God's presence and action—an explanation that makes Mark's conclusion less grim. Jesus's resurrection from the dead is so astounding that one cannot grasp it all, and the women need time to collect their thoughts.

But this is not the only possible interpretation. People respond with fear throughout Mark. The disciples were awestruck when confronted with Jesus's overwhelming power to calm the sea. A woman feared when her plague was healed by simply touching his garments. The disciples were filled with fear when they saw Jesus walk on the sea. Humans have been deaf and silent to God's glory throughout the story. Why should we not expect this same reaction when these women meet with the most powerful divine act of all, Jesus's resurrection from the dead?

It is not a closed-minded disbelief that muzzles their voices; that would drain the power of the gospel. Rather, the cause is pure and simple fear. Fear surfaces among Jesus's followers both before the cross and after the resurrection. The resurrection does not mean that all now is set right and that everyone will live happily ever after. The flesh is still weak. Many will suffer the same fear as the women and will try to take cover in silence. Disciples need to learn to lose their lives to save them, which means losing their fear.

Application. Mark's ending teaches us that Christians after the resurrection must still live with ambiguity. We want the Gospel to conclude on a note of victory and good cheer, but that was not Mark's situation. The ache of death is not so easily assuaged. Mark writes for those who never will experience Jesus's physical presence. Followers will still experience confusion. Only at the end of time, when the Son of Man is manifest in all his glory, will all ambiguity be eliminated.

Like the first auditors of this Gospel, we have only the reports from the eyewitnesses to confirm the resurrection, no scientific proof. How will we know for sure that what they say is true? Will we be willing to stake our lives on that truth? Will we demand something more from God before we will make a commitment? Mark's ending shows that the historical question, "Was it real?" ignores the more crucial question, "Is it real?" Something other than a pious dropping by the tomb once every Easter and looking in to see that it is empty is required to spark faith.

The ending of this Gospel means that the last scene in which Jesus speaks is from the cross. In Mark one sees most vividly the power of God working in the crucifixion. The ending therefore means that one cannot proclaim the glories of the resurrection to the neglect of the suffering of the cross. The confession, "Surely this man was the Son of God!" (15:39), comes when Jesus dies on the cross, not at the empty tomb.

The ending touches on the problem that fallible humans must live with failure. The way of discipleship is not a triumphant procession through the world, like a hot knife cutting through butter. It is a way pocked by personal failure after personal failure. It may seem that the Gospel ends on a pessimistic note because Mark does not report that the women successfully fulfill their commission. Mark's story, however, is not about the disciples' foolishness and failure. The gospel is about the power of God, which overcomes human dysfunction and disaster. We know that Jesus's resurrection was proclaimed and is being proclaimed throughout the world, just as Jesus said it would. This means that God's will and Jesus's promise have been fulfilled despite human disobedience.

Mark's ending, therefore, reveals that with God our failure is not fatal. But we cannot jump for joy and give one another high fives as members of winning sports teams do. We consistently fail. We must humbly and consistently turn to God for help and can give only God the glory when failure turns into victory by divine power.

The fulfillment of this promise to go to Galilee suggests to us that Jesus's other promises will come true as well.

- John prophesied that the one coming after him would baptize with the Holy Spirit (1:8). Mark does not narrate the fulfillment of this prophecy, but the auditors know it has come true because they have experienced this baptism for themselves.
- Jesus promised Peter and Andrew that he would make them fishers of men (1:17).
- He promised his disciples that some would not taste death before they saw the kingdom of God come with power (9:1).
- He promised Peter that those who have made sacrifices to follow him will receive a hundredfold more and in the age to come, eternal life (10:29–30).
- He promised James and John that they would be baptized with his baptism and would drink his cup (10:39).
- He promised that before the end comes, the gospel will be preached to all the nations (13:10).
- He promised that the woman's extravagant anointing of him for his burial will be remembered wherever the gospel is preached in the whole world (14:9).

- He assured his disciples that he will drink from the fruit of the vine anew in the kingdom of God (14:25).
- He promised the high priest and his council that they would see the Son of Man sitting at the right hand of the Mighty One and coming on the clouds of heaven (14:62).

Because Jesus's foreknowledge of what was to come has been proven, we can trust that what he says will come true despite human muddling and satanic opposition, not only in the lives of his first disciples but also in the lives of persons today.

The last word, therefore, ultimately belongs to God, who will accomplish all things. This truth puts in a new light the disciples' failures in this Gospel to understand, to exorcise demons, to stand with Jesus during the fiery test, and to herald the resurrection. Failure does not mean the end of discipleship or the defeat of God's purposes. The words of Jesus will not fail, and his promise will overcome the disciples' bungling and dereliction of duty.

Discipleship is established by Jesus's call and can only be sustained by God's mercy and power alone. We can take comfort from this fact when we also fail in our commission, as we inevitably will. Everything depends on God, not us. When we do succeed, we can therefore only give credit to God.

This ending fits the title of Mark's Gospel: "The beginning of the good news about Jesus the Messiah, the Son of God" (1:1). The burial of Jesus and the news of his resurrection bring the narrative to a close, but the resurrection is not the end of the story, only the beginning. How does one end such a story?

We cannot allow the resurrection account to become a faded if cherished memory that is to be placed in a photo album and taken out once a year and admired. The ending forces us to enter the story. We are the next chapter. What would we have done if we were those first women let in on the tremendous news? The question then becomes not what will the women do—how long will they keep silent?—but what will we do now that we have been let in on the news? Will we flee in fear and become silent? Will the story die with us? Will we obediently follow Jesus to Galilee or try to hunker down in our safe cocoons?

The Gospel of Mark leaves us with unfinished business to preach the gospel to the ends of the earth. The ending (which is not an ending) becomes a new phase of an unfolding story as the baton passes on to us to join in the race and spread the news. Mark's stunning ending raises the question, Who will tell the story? His Gospel is the account of the beginning of the gospel; will we now join in its continuation?

Peter asks, "Who is going to harm you if you are eager to do good?" (1 Pet 3:13). The answer in the first century was, "Plenty." Enemies were everywhere, and their threats naturally elicited fear and inhibited witness. The kinds of people who killed Jesus are still out there, ready to kill his followers. No one enjoys being hated or hunted down. It is safer to remain silent, to treasure all these things in our hearts (Luke 2:51) rather than to bare our hearts to others. One might understand why those facing the persecution might be reticent to speak, but what excuse do those have who enjoy all the comforts of life and the freedom of worship?

LUKE

INTRODUCTION TO LUKE

We are accustomed to highlighting the diversity of people in our world. Ours is a multicultural and multidimensional world in the way it sees things. The Gospel of Luke explains how God can take those many ethnic backgrounds and dimensions and mold them into a new, special community. In Jesus, though we have different roots, we can come to oneness. The more we closely examine first-century people, the more we see that they are just like us. Their problems and attitudes concerning sin, money, anxiety, hope, community, rejection, vengeance, pride, humility, and God's direction mirror questions we face. The Gospel of Luke gives insight into how Jesus addressed such topics, and he makes clear how we can come to know God.

Neither Luke nor Acts gives the name of its author. We must therefore examine evidence in these books and church tradition to determine authorship. Given the options available, the tie to Luke is impressive evidence of the memory of the church about the third Gospel's author. What we know about Luke suggests that he was not Jewish, though it is possible that he was a Semite, perhaps a Syrian from Antioch rather than a Greek (Col 4:10–11). His knowledge of the Old Testament and his discussion of God-fearers may suggest he had some previous connection to Judaism and may even have been a God-fearer. The connection of Luke to medicine comes from Colossians 4:14.

Many date this book after AD 70, usually in the mid-eighties, based on the fact that the texts on the judgment of the nation are so specific about Jerusalem's destruction. A more likely date is sometime in the sixties. The last event in Acts is dated AD 62; since Luke appears to be closely related to Acts, the release of the two volumes would have been fairly close to each other. This date is suggested because Paul's death is not noted in Acts, and time must be allowed for the other sources, which included either Mark or Matthew, to circulate.

BOOK OUTLINE

I. The Infancy Narrative (1:1–2:52)
II. Preparation for Ministry (3:1–4:13)
III. The Galilean Ministry (4:14–9:50)
IV. The Journey to Jerusalem (9:51–19:44)
V. Jerusalem: The Innocent Slain and Vindicated (19:45–24:53)

LUKE 1:1–4

Original Meaning. Part of the certainty one gains from Luke's account comes from these roots. The fact that this material has been "handed down" (v. 2) highlights its being part of a stream of tradition, something the Jews knew how to handle with care. In the same way as the previous accounts came from eyewitnesses who were servants of the word, so Luke's account has been constructed with care. He wants to join this tradition of rendering the Jesus story, adding new material and eventually providing a sequel, the book of Acts.

Luke tells us four things in verse 3 about his work before he tells us why he writes.

1. He has "investigated" the story. That is, he has taken a long and careful look at what he is about to tell us.
2. He went back to "the beginning." This is why he starts his story with John the Baptist, the forerunner, who points to Jesus.
3. Luke was thorough, having studied "everything." This is undoubtedly why there is so much fresh material in his account. About 30 percent of this Gospel is not found elsewhere, including several of Jesus's parables.
4. Luke worked "carefully," taking great care to develop his orderly account in a way that told the story clearly. Luke wants to reassure Theophilus, in order that he "may know the certainty of the things [he has] been taught" (v. 4).

Application. The three points of application from the preface are linked to the two strands of contact we already noted.

1. Luke tells us of God's acts in history *through Jesus*. This main character is not a Savior made up in the image of a person's imagination. After all, who on his or her own would create a Savior who makes us all responsible for our sin and then chooses to pay the penalty for that sin by offering himself? The unusual nature of the story is a testimony to its authenticity. Its reality is the basis for the assurance Luke wishes to give his readers.
2. God wants us to sense that we fit into his community. He wants us to see that the Jesus story is not only about him, but about us—God reaching out with both power and humility to lift us up and bring us into his presence. God takes people who are "outside" his care and makes them "insiders," involved and related to the God of the universe.

3. We can trust the Gospel as we read it. Luke, as a solid ancient historian, records the real Jesus for us and reveals the heart of God in doing so. He worked under God's direction, carefully passing on a tradition from those who saw what they preached (v. 2). We can read Luke with full confidence that God is introducing us to Jesus. God reveals himself in the word so that we may know our real need and story.

LUKE 1:5–25

Original Meaning. Luke begins his story by placing it in an established historical setting—the reign of Herod the Great (37–4 BC). Herod had done much building up of the nation. When the angel appears to Zechariah, we are near the end of his reign.

In his goodness, God picks an important moment in the career of Zechariah to make his divine move. As a priest he served at the temple for two one-week periods a year. A priest only officiated at the sacrifice once in his life, having been selected by lot. The angel appears as Zechariah places the incense on the altar. How appropriate to pick a moment of worship and a time when people recognized their need for cleansing from sin!

The initial encounter produces terror in Zechariah, though that is not uncommon when one senses that God or an agent of his is present. After comforting Zechariah, the angel announces why he has come. His name, Gabriel (v. 19; cf. Dan 8:15–16; 9:21), probably means "God is my hero," though Luke makes nothing of the name.

Luke continues to use language and imagery drawn from the Old Testament as he tells the story of Zechariah and John the Baptist. The birth of this child is similar to other births to formerly barren wives or other announcements of the birth of a special child. Telling the story in this manner indicates that God has renewed his work among his people.

John has a special place in that plan. This prophet will live an ascetic lifestyle, like the special people of God who took vows to show their devotion to God. He may drink no strong drink. This is likely not a Nazirite vow, however, since there is no mention of not cutting his hair.

Going before the Lord describes John as a prophet of the period of restoration of the promise. His preparation for the Lord refers to God's powerful coming through his agent, Jesus. God is the subject because Jesus has not even been mentioned yet. "To turn hearts" and "make ready a people" (v. 17) reflects John's call for repentance as he turns the nation's attention back to God and to righteousness.

The third element in this passage is the personal story of Zechariah and Elizabeth. Sometimes righteous people do have disappointments in life. Zechariah and Elizabeth had prayed about their difficult situation. Then one day the angel announces the coming of a child. This promised child answers two prayers at the same time: for a child in the house of Zechariah, and for God to work redemption in the nation.

But Zechariah and Elizabeth represent two different kinds of righteous people. Zechariah raises doubts about the angel's message, for the prospective parents are now beyond normal childbearing age (v. 18). Sometimes even good people have doubts about God's promise. The angel tells Zechariah in effect, "Just be quiet for a while and watch God work."

Elizabeth is the picture of the righteous saint who takes her burden to God and rejoices when that burden is lifted. Elizabeth does not react as a victim who has been bitter at God for her lack of a child. In fact, she seems to have accepted this fate and served God faithfully anyway. Thus, when the burden is removed, she rejoices as the object of God's personal concern.

Application. The application of this text in terms of God's plan is basic. It will be a refrain through the entire Gospel. Are we prepared for God, and do we respond to his work through the one he sent to lead us to him? John will point the way. Do we take the path of sensing our need for God and of responding to the one who offers forgiveness to us? Are we humble before God, taking the path he calls us to, or do we opt to go our own way?

John's greatness is not found in his choice of lifestyle but in the fact that in understanding his calling, he pursues it fully and carries out God's will faithfully. As a servant of God, John became a catalyst who encouraged others to live before God in a way that honored him. Not everyone responded to John, so success need not be measured by numbers. John's mission to be a source of stimulating others to find God is something we all can seek to follow.

We can also apply the lessons that Zechariah and Elizabeth teach us. We must not presume upon God by either always seeing struggles in life as evidence of the presence of sin or by calling on God to bless us with everything we desire. Elizabeth teaches us to take our sense of grief over our disappointments to God, and to be sure to take our rejoicing to him as well.

Finally, God is gracious in seemingly mysterious ways. Sometimes we are deprived of something because God has better things awaiting us down the road. When we wait patiently on the Lord, he often gives us more than we imagined possible. Zechariah and Elizabeth wanted a child; what they got was a prophet. God's ways are set to his clock, and they are often filled with things that cause us to wonder as we rejoice at his surprises.

LUKE 1:26–38

Original Meaning. The announcement in Nazareth shows that Mary came from humble, agrarian roots. Galilee was not a respected region. It was hardly the expected locale for one sent from God. Gabriel, the same angel who spoke to Zechariah, brings the divine message. Luke identifies Mary as a virgin, engaged to Joseph; that is, she was pledged to him sometime in the previous year. A Jewish betrothal involved two steps: the formal engagement including a contract and exchange of a bridal price, and then about a year later, a wedding.

Mary is "highly favored" (v. 28), receiving God's grace on the basis of his sovereign action. One can always rejoice when God chooses to show his presence through his grace. Thus the Lord is with her (v. 28). Her initial fear is calmed when the angel explains the reason for his presence. She has "found favor" (v. 30)—a second indication that she is the object of God's grace.

She is honored by God not because of her own merit or because of anything she has done, but simply because she is the chosen vessel for this demonstration of God's grace. Mary's response reveals her character. This was no simple matter. She is being asked to bear a child as a virgin without being married. In standing up for God and his power, she will probably become the object of much doubt and ridicule.

Again, Luke has not only explained how the plan of God is advanced by telling the details of the birth announcement, but he also has revealed the character of those surrounding the birth of these two great men of God. All the figures involved are examples of spirituality as they respond to what God is doing among them. Woven throughout the cosmic story are human stories. The narrative wants the reader to sense both levels of the story.

Application. God shows his greatness by working with anyone on the street who is willing to be used by him. Spiritual greatness is not a matter of social class, monetary clout, or degrees but is a function of the heart. God can do great things through those who entrust the journey with him to his care. That means when God leads, the believer must simply reply, "May it be according to your will."

This passage suggests four other important lessons:

1. the certainty that God will perform his promise, since nothing is impossible with him;
2. Mary's example as one chosen to serve God, a prime example of someone willing to be used by God for his purposes;
3. the significance of the virgin birth of our Savior; and
4. the importance of sexual faithfulness throughout our lives.

LUKE 1:39–56

Original Meaning. The remark about the Spirit's filling Elizabeth is crucial, for it indicates that her remarks and emotions are directed by God. The humility reflected here by John's mother in feeling honored just to be in the presence of the child is expressed more fully by her son in John 3:30: "He must become greater; I must become less." The sense of privilege and favor at being used by God finds fresh expression here. Elizabeth knows God does not owe her such a central role, yet she is amazed at God's involvement with her.

Alongside her amazement is the lesson of Mary's blessing. We should not miss the significance of the testimony about these children that comes through this grateful mother-to-be. Three points are central:

1. Mary's child is especially blessed, being at the center of God's fresh activity;
2. there is amazement in being any part of these astounding events; and
3. joy and blessing come to those who believe that God does what he says.

Mary's hymn, a thanksgiving psalm, comes in two parts. That it is a praise psalm is indicated by "my soul glorifies the Lord and my spirit rejoices in God my Savior" (vv. 46–47), similar to Hannah's praise to God (1 Sam 2:1). Luke 1:46–49 gives Mary's personal praise for her specific situation, while the rest of the hymn praises God's activity in more general terms. A shift of tenses from present (vv. 46b–47) to past (v. 48a) to future (v. 48b) shows the broadening scope of her basis for praise. The idea that all generations will praise her (v. 48b) leads to the idea of how God treats other God-fearers (vv. 49–53). This mention of "those who fear [God]" (v. 50) may especially open up this psalm to Luke's audience, which likely included former gentile God-fearers. Though Israel is clearly in view in the psalm (vv. 54–55), the implication of the general praise in verse 50 opens up the possibility that others outside the nation may also be blessed.

Mary will be honored "from now on" by all generations (v. 48), not because she is special but because she is the model and representative of what it is to experience God's grace and mercy. Luke loves to note how events tied to God's activity change everything "from now on" (5:10; 12:52; 22:18, 69; Acts 18:6).

Mary's feelings are clear. God owes her nothing, while she has received everything from him. But her story illustrates how God treats others, so she goes on to indicate that her story could be repeated a thousand times over. God's "mercy" extends to those who fear him (v. 50). This mercy is his loyal love, what the Old Testament calls God's *hesed*.

These texts should not be read merely as a sociological

commitment by God to the poor. The lead line into the general refrain makes it clear that "those who fear [God]" are the blessed. The poor are the "pious poor," or those whom the Old Testament often calls the *anawim*. They recognize their need and are thus less reluctant to turn to God. Mary expresses hope for Israel's vindication before her enemies. God will deliver this and more through Jesus. Those who turn to God can expect him to show his love and justice on their behalf in a time he deems appropriate. God does so because he "remembers" his promises (Luke 1:54).

Application. Luke aims at the heart with these texts. Believers must take God at his word and be amazed at his involvement with the details of their lives. God owes us nothing; we who have trusted Christ owe him everything. As the child leaped in Elizabeth's womb, so should our hearts leap in our chests when we consider the many blessings of God that we experience. God does what he says, and he has said much on behalf of the believer. The key is to expect a reversal of fortune and a deliverance in the future. Whatever our lot in this sinful and fallen world now, those who fear God can expect vindication.

Those who know God and his grace can well echo Mary's song. We do not have the honor of giving birth to the Savior of the world, but we do have the blessing of becoming one of his children. The promises God makes to his humble and poor children, revealed by Mary in her hymn of praise, are promises in which we share. No deed is more powerful or heroic than rescuing humanity from sin. No act is more gracious than God's extension of mercy through his powerful, faithful, compassionate hand.

There is no doubt that God expects the church to show compassion to the poor, because they are in a unique position to appreciate that they must be dependent on God. On the other hand, this text is not a political manifesto that simply says the poor are right and so one can fight and even take up weapons for them. This text has often been used as the basis of a theology of liberation because of the passage's strong support for the poor. Such theologies have even defended taking up arms on behalf of the poor. But the vindication God supplies does not come through the barrel of a gun but through a heart turned to God.

Finally, let us note what causes Mary to be grateful. In an age where we expect so much as a matter of personal or human rights, we develop an attitude that much is owed us. How we can give or serve is not high on our priority list. We even risk treating God more as if he were a friend or neighbor to be joked with or negotiated with rather than as the Almighty Creator. Mary understands the difference and recognizes the honor given her to have God actively involved in her life. The sense of privilege, lacking any hint of merit, spills over into a waterfall of praise and gratitude—praise that is refreshing for its passion and sense of wonder.

LUKE 1:57–80

Original Meaning. Amid great joy and the recognition that God has been merciful to this priestly family, the time has come for the circumcision and naming of the child. Events like this are filled with custom. Perhaps given Zechariah's recent debilitating condition, the crowd expects the child to be named Zechariah Junior. But Elizabeth gives her son the name "John," sending shock waves of surprise through the crowd. The neighbors are so convinced an error had been made, since the name has no family precedent, that they ask the father through sign language. On a wood tablet probably covered with wax, Zechariah writes the name the angel had given him for the child.

Immediately his tongue is freed, and he speaks in praise to God. The long silence has allowed him to reflect on what God called for him to do, and he is now prepared to do it. Zechariah has learned that even righteous men have something to learn from God.

With his lips freed to speak, Zechariah now praises God for what he is doing. Whereas Mary's hymn spoke in personal and general terms, this hymn of praise anticipates and overviews the careers of the two children whom divine destiny has brought together. Luke introduces it as a response to the Spirit's filling of Zechariah. As is often the case in Luke, the Spirit leads to bold testimony and praise.

The psalm's main theme appears in verses 68–70, while its elaboration is the remainder of the psalm. The Lord God of Israel has once again acted on behalf of his people by visiting them and redeeming them. The appeal to David's house makes it clear that God is doing what the prophets promised long ago. Zechariah anticipates messianic redemption and thanks God for it.

So what does Zechariah look forward to? What Zechariah desires most is to be rescued from his enemies so that he can serve God his whole life without fear and in righteousness and holiness (vv. 74–75). Here is the pious person's creed: "I want to serve you with my whole life, O Lord; enable me to do so and vindicate me in my pursuit."

Zechariah speaks as a righteous Jew here. He longs for the nation's vindication, possibly from Rome and the forces that direct her. In Luke's story, however, the scope of the hymn's hope may even be broader. He will show how the promised one from David's lineage has power that extends beyond the political forces that sit over Israel. God has "raised up" this significant figure onto the world's stage. The Son of David will become a servant himself. He will take on the cosmic forces that oppress humanity and bring pain and suffering into the world.

Zechariah indicates that his own son will be a prophet for

the Most High God, preparing a people for this coming visit of the Lord by telling them about "salvation through the forgiveness of their sins" (vv. 76–77). The message about salvation and the forgiveness of sins, which John preaches, will be like the commission Jesus gives to the church in 24:44–47, except that at that later commission events will have filled in details that are only vague here.

God will not only work through John. He will send "the rising sun" (v. 78; literally "the morning star"), a likely allusion to Numbers 24:17 and Isaiah 11:1–10. The Son, who serves as a bright morning light, comes from heaven and shines on those in darkness and death, guiding them into the path of peace. Significantly Zechariah puts himself among those in darkness. As a spiritual man, he knows that the only way to walk righteously is to follow the path God sets. Zechariah knows that the Messiah is coming. He will be powerful, but more than that, he will be light.

Application. Besides the overview and description of the careers of John and Jesus that serve as the foundation for this text's teaching, several key attitudes are central to the application of this text. The lesson that pious Zechariah learns is important, especially to those who have a rich spiritual heritage. He is a man of lifelong faith who still needed to grow. It is all too easy to view one's spiritual life as something that can be mastered rather than something to be maintained.

Though our God is awesome and powerful, he uses that power in surprising ways. He sends a king who leads initially not with a sword but with his word. He rescues not through a bloody war but with a new way. He leads not just with might but with light—his teaching and life. When we think of a promised king, we think of a palace and knights, the king's army arrayed to defend his people. Jesus's kingship does not seclude itself in a palace, nor does he have a round table. This king walked among his people and lived as they did. He was baptized by the one pointing the way to him, because life is not a function of power, as the world tends to think, but is a reflection of character and light.

How do we define life? Is it in power and in the ability to take control, or is it in following the one who is in control? The text leaves no doubt that we should follow the one who is the source of light. The only road to righteousness and peace, even for a righteous man like Zechariah, is to be prepared to see the light and follow it. The text raises the question and answers it with notes of praise. See the morning star, Jesus, and follow the light in the way of peace. What precisely that pathway involves is the rest of this Gospel's story, for which this hymn serves as a guiding introduction. In a real sense, the application of this text is found in the entirety of this Gospel's message.

LUKE 2:1–21

Original Meaning. Jesus's birthplace is determined in part by the need to fill out a census—probably a means to register for paying taxes. The journeying of everyone "to their own town to register" (v. 3) appears to be a sensitive decision by the Romans that allowed the Jews to follow their own custom of going to one's ancestral home. So Joseph and Mary go to Bethlehem, a place identified as "the town of David" (v. 4), because of Joseph's lineage in the family.

Though modern renditions dramatize a search for a room, the text tells the story with exceptional brevity. Such inns would have been either the second story of a house that housed animals below or a one-story building with a stable next to it. Since no such locale has a vacancy, the couple finds shelter where they can. Jesus therefore enters the world in as mundane a way as possible.

The testimony to Jesus's birth from the angelic host to shepherds is significant in scope. Heaven meets and greets the average person through the angelic announcement to these pastoral figures. Jesus's birth is more than a family affair. The announcement indicates that God desires to speak to every person about the coming of Jesus, since all humanity is impacted by his coming.

The titles the angel uses for the newborn child are significant (v. 11). "Savior" (*sōtēr*) reflects the call of Jesus to deliver his people, as Mary's and Zechariah's hymns had declared. This term is rich in Old Testament roots, especially as a figure for divine deliverance. "Messiah" (Hebrew for "anointed one") is a rare term in the Old Testament. Psalm 2:2 is the main technical regal use. What about "Lord"? Of the three titles, this one is left unexplained in this context. One could well argue that the rest of this Gospel and the book of Acts serve to explain the nature of Jesus's authority and lordship, as well as the extent of the exercise of his power in overcoming sin and the forces of evil.

The angelic revelation of a sign implies that the angel wanted the shepherds to go and see the child for themselves. They will recognize the child when they see a newborn baby in the town of David "wrapped in cloths and lying in a manger" (v. 12). This is the third sign in the infancy material (1:19–20, 36).

As if the announcement were not enough, the heavenly choir strikes up in praise to God, giving him honor for what is taking place. Glory should be given to God in the most exalted of ways, while on earth one should see that this child means peace for those "on whom his favor rests" (v. 14). The picture of being a person of God's favor was a Jewish way of saying that someone was numbered among God's chosen people. This remark makes it clear that salvation and its fullness are not automatic for everyone. Only those who respond to God's grace and follow the path lit by the rising sun will experience the peace into which that path leads.

The shepherds find the child in the manger, just as the angel has said. They respond with obedience and cannot contain themselves from testifying to what God has done in making Jesus's presence evident to them. Luke's reader is supposed to identify with their response to God's first revelation of this birth to the human race.

As is often the case when God's work is reported, those who hear their testimony are amazed, while Mary simply ponders it all. The event closes with the shepherds returning to their flocks and giving glory and praise to God, for things were just as he said. God will perform his word. This is the final note that Jesus's birth should bring.

Application. The birth of Jesus is a lesson in God's faithfulness, but it also reveals God's heart and character. For God identifies with the human race, and this birth reflects such identification. The most humble birth for the most exalted figure ever born shows that the key values of life are found in the life itself, not in the accouterments that come with life.

The birth of Jesus also shows that greatness is not a function of the size of one's bank account or one's social résumé. Status does not make the person, for God recognizes the quality of the inner person. God shows his greatness by walking with us as we are where we are, not in elitist isolation and insulation, which is often the way the powerful live in the world. We learn to see things the way God does if we do not pay attention to addresses, clothes, bank accounts, or résumés, but consider who honors God (Jas 2:1–5).

What the angels announced to the shepherds that night is announced on behalf of all humanity. Their journey to see these things should be every person's journey to see what God is up to in Jesus. When people see that everything happened according to what God had told the shepherds, they and we should sense that God does what he says. Their sense of amazement should be matched by our own. The best way we show our amazement is with the response of a grateful, faithful walk that is marked with praise.

The variety of reactions to the birth of Jesus noted here should not surprise us. People respond to him differently. Some are amazed but do not engage him at any deeper level. Others offer praise, while some ponder what Jesus's significance will be. There is no doubt that in this passage Mary and the shepherds are the central exemplary characters, reflecting the testimony and obedience that should characterize God's people.

Our rejoicing starts with Jesus in the story of his birth, but it does not stop there. He is involved in our lives even now. By the Spirit his presence continues to express itself in us. As believers we belong to a great train of witnesses spanning the ages, who have lifted their voices and offered their souls in gratitude for what this birth meant. One day in heaven, face to face with men and women of every generation and nation, we will offer thanks before him. There is nothing wrong with getting in a little practice now.

LUKE 2:22–40

Original Meaning. Jesus was born to parents who kept the laws of Judaism. The journey of Jesus's parents to the temple combines three separate ceremonies as recorded in God's law: the purification of a woman forty days after the birth of a child, the presentation of the firstborn to God, and the dedication of the firstborn into the Lord's service. Though this dedication to service is like many others that took place in Israel for centuries, this one is unique because of the call of this child.

The rite of purification involved the offering of a burnt sacrifice and sin offering. The mention of turtledoves indicates that Joseph and Mary utilized the offering of the poor, though middle classes also made such sacrifices. All these sacrifices indicate how seriously Judaism took approaching God in worship and how prepared a heart and soul one should have as they address God.

As Joseph and Mary proceed, they meet a pious old man, Simeon, either in the court of the gentiles or the court of women (since Mary is present). Whereas the shepherds symbolized the average person on the street, Simeon represents the testimony of a wise elder who has walked with God. Part of his wisdom is seen in that he is looking for the hope of the nation, the consummation of God's promises. Those in touch with God's heart often wait expectantly for the completion of God's promises. This revered saint is led to see what the arrival of this child means.

The locale of Simeon's prophecy, the temple, is significant for Jewish readers, for this prophet is testifying to Jesus amid the nation's most sacred locale. Simeon begins by saying that God can take him now, for he has fulfilled his call of seeing the child who is the Christ. Once again, Luke has emphasized how God has performed his word.

This child is the salvation of God and represents the public display of God's concern for people. Jesus is light, a theme already noted in 1:78–79. Simeon's remarks recall Isaiah 60:1–3, where the light of salvation comes with revelation and glory as the result. Jesus serves two constituencies with his salvation, Israel and the gentiles, but each in a slightly different way. He is a "revelation" to gentiles (v. 32a), for they will be brought into blessing through his coming. Jesus is "glory" to Israel (v. 32b), for through him they will perform their service of ministry to the world. When the promises of God come, they come through the promised one of Israel.

As the parents marvel at the note of praise, the more somber notes of promise are revealed. Jesus will split the nation in two. Some will see him as someone to be opposed. But his ministry reveals where the thoughts of one's heart are. As the salvation of God and the expression of God's will, the reaction to him reveals one's reaction to God. The opposition he produces will be a source of pain to Mary. The mother's pain will emerge from the intense rejection the child will experience and from his priorities in ministry.

The second prophetic witness in this section of Luke is Anna. She is merely introduced and her career summarized. In all likelihood, she is over a hundred years old, having served God faithfully with worship, prayer, and fasting for years. While her words are not recorded in Luke, her testimony makes everyone aware that God is doing something special in this child. Those who are faithful to God will hear her report and share in her praise.

Application. A clear theological point dominates the application. To see Jesus is to see God's salvation. To see Jesus is to see God's light and revelation. To see Jesus is to see God and his way revealed. Jesus is no longer visibly around so that we can look him in the face, but he is in the world in his body, the church, the people into whom he pours himself in order to express his fullness. This means that in a real sense we become little incarnations of Jesus.

Simeon's sense of identification with doing God's will and then surrendering to the timing of his own death shows just how committed he is to God's timing. Furthermore, having seen Jesus and knowing him, Simeon is at peace. Everything else in his life pales in comparison. Simeon knows that he can be content with his life, since he has had the honor of witnessing God's salvation. This attitude is important because it puts the other events and traumas of life into perspective. If this can be how Simeon feels, knowing that death is approaching, how should we feel when many of us have much of life still ahead of us?

Why do resolutions for the most part deal with external matters? Is the soul so unimportant? If exercise is valuable for physical well-being, should we starve our inner being? If contentment is based on externals that slowly wither away, will we not set ourselves up for disappointment if we focus on such goals? Simeon suggests a better way. To know God is best. Simeon can be content even as he faces death, knowing that he has been carrying out the Lord's call. His goal is knowing God, with whom he will have a relationship forever. Contentment means knowing the source of life who can help us see even beyond our death.

LUKE 2:41–52

Original Meaning. The annual trip for the Passover was one of the highlights of the Jewish year, one of three annual festivals that were celebrated in the capital. On this particular occasion, Jesus remains behind in Jerusalem. Only after a day's travel do his parents discover he is not with the group, for they do not find him with relatives. They undoubtedly assumed Jesus was somewhere in the throng, though the text itself does not explain how he could go unmissed for a day. They discover Jesus among the teachers in the temple, listening to them, asking questions, and giving reply. Even at this young age Jesus has amazing knowledge of the things of God. In fact, those listening to him are astonished at his understanding.

A frustrated mother asks her budding adolescent how he could have behaved this way, leaving his parents with a major anxiety attack (*odynaō*, v. 48). Jesus's reply is just as direct: "I must be about the . . . of my Father" (literal translation). Jesus's point is that his career must be about instruction in the way of God, for the temple was not only a place of worship but was also a place of teaching. Jesus has a call to instruct the nation. Though he is twelve now, a day is coming when this will be his priority. All Mary can do is ponder such events in her heart, something Luke's reader is also to do.

Application. In a real sense the reader is in a similar dilemma as the one Jesus's parents faced. Who is Jesus, and is his authority such that even the most basic human relationships, like the parent-child relationship, are transcended? As with many texts in this Gospel, the basic question is: What do you think of Jesus's authority? Will you respond or reject his claims? Our relationship to God is determined by this response, since this unique one is so closely related to him.

There is another key implication here. The world tells us to treat Jesus as one great religious figure among many in history. Luke does not give us that option. Rather, as the unique Son, Jesus has exclusive rights to reveal the way of God, and one either accepts or rejects that revelation.

In moving from Jesus to us, the text also raises the issue of another common tension among God's people—namely, the hard decisions that have to be made in prioritizing God, family, and ministry. The pangs of Jesus's priorities are what Mary and Joseph felt here. It is not unlike the pain some parents feel when children choose to serve God on the mission field or opt to go into ministry instead of into a "real profession." Sometimes the pain is a helpful reminder that our top priority is to serve God. Sometimes parents may need to let go of their children, because the children are faithfully serving God. Yet those busily engaged in ministry also need to check whether their ministry has taken precedence over caring for their family. There must be a balance here.

One final application emerges from Jesus's stop at the temple. Sometimes we think adolescents are beyond useful spiritual reflection, having entered a twilight zone from which they hopefully will emerge in their twenties. Our children should be encouraged to develop spiritually, whether through their involvement in church or in discussion of topics that matter with their parents and others. Jesus could sit with the rabbis; maybe our children can as well, if we will be sensitive to the potential they have and relate to them at a level to which they can respond.

LUKE 3:1–22

Original Meaning. Luke portrays John's ministry as a call to repentance. His ministry in the Jordan River region is designed to get people ready for the arrival of God's salvation by having hearts open to respond to the coming Messiah. That is why in citing Isaiah, Luke mentions the leveling of obstacles in the way of God's arrival. If the creation bows to God's coming, certainly human hearts should as well.

The rite of baptism is unprecedented. Judaism knew of repeated baptisms for temporary cleansing, but this was a call to prepare for the arrival of salvation, a one-time baptism in honor of the arrival of the eschatological era of salvation.

Though the Greek word for "repentance" (*metanoia*, v. 8) means "a change of mind," the concept of repentance has Old Testament roots in the idea of turning to God. To be prepared for God's salvation, one's heart must be open to his message. John is a sentry keeping watch over God's plan and blowing a trumpet to announce preparation for the Messiah's arrival. When it comes, all humanity will see the salvation of God.

The possibility of salvation also implies the approach of judgment. Thus, opportunity will become tragedy if one does not respond. John warns the people as he prepares them by mentioning the ax lying at the root of the tree. Relying on ancestry and heritage will not commend one before God. Salvation is not by family inheritance but by faith, by turning in trust to the living God.

Again, as John proclaims the approaching salvation, the good news has a flip side—the threat of judgment for failing to respond to God. In effect, John is asking if they understand what his baptism is really about and what is at stake. So he issues an ethical call in common Old Testament style. The people are to produce fruit worthy of repentance. If one turns to God, one's life should look different. Awareness of our accountability to God should make us more sensitive to how we treat others. For John the horizontal, ethical dimension of life is fed by our sensitivity to our vertical relationship with God.

John's audience may have assumed that because they were Jews, having Abraham as their father, they were guaranteed salvation as part of the elect family of God. John warns that such a heritage means nothing to an individual who does not personally turn to God. God is able to make his children out of objects of creation, such as stones.

The crowd understands the message and asks what they can do to avoid the wrath to come. The repetition of the word "do" or "produce" (*poieō*; vv. 8, 10, 12, 14) shows the link between John's remarks and the crowd's response. The crowd knows that the important issue is not getting baptized but responding to God with a certain kind of heart and life.

John tells the crowd to be generous, giving a tunic to one who needs it and food to those who lack it. The hated tax collectors also respond. John tells them to collect only what is required. Finally, the soldiers, who kept the peace and wielded great power, are told not to use that force to extort money or accuse people falsely, but to be content with their wages. The word for "to extort" (*diaseiō*, v. 14) is particularly descriptive, since it means "to shake violently."

John preaches personal preparation, but he also points to Jesus (vv. 15–17). When the issue is raised whether John might be the Messiah, he denies the speculation and explains how they may know that the Christ has come. There is in fact so much difference between the two that John feels he is not worthy to do the most menial of tasks that a slave might do, to untie the thong of the coming stronger one's sandal.

Baptism with Spirit and fire represents a presence and a purging that divides. That presence and purging are in view is made clear by verse 17, where the "winnowing fork" is said to be ready to clear the threshing floor. The harvesting image refers to a wooden fork that lifted beaten grain in the air, so that the wind could drive away the light chaff and the grain fall to the floor to be gathered. The Spirit's baptism will gather some, while others will be left to the wind.

John's message reaches the upper echelon of society, and no one escapes his penetrating call to repent. He takes Herod to task for his marriage to Herodias, both of whom left marriages to marry each other. Herod responds to this with the typical reaction of a hardened sinner—by striking back and locking John in prison. Given the choice of repenting or denying sin, the ruler tries to remove the source of accountability. Luke moves up the account of this jailing, so that when he turns to Jesus, he can tell the story of that ministry uninterrupted.

As we turn to consider Jesus's baptism, few moments are as important as when heaven speaks (in this event and in the transfiguration). This event has three significant points.

1. When Jesus submits to this washing, he is declaring that John's message is true and that people must get prepared to receive salvation.
2. Jesus is praying when the Spirit descends like a dove on him. Luke loves to mention how Jesus bathes his life in prayer.

3. This is probably a private experience of Jesus. The voice speaks directly to him; Luke does not record any reaction or response from the crowd, as in other cases when such events occur.

More important is the anointing that takes place. The Spirit descends like a dove on Jesus. The symbolism of the dove is difficult to ascertain. The Spirit is associated with the presence of God in his creative work and in the presence of his grace. The most important feature of the text is the endorsement itself: God identifies Jesus as his Son as he anoints him for ministry. This event confirms the call of Jesus and names his function.

The remark about "my Son, whom I love; with you I am well pleased" (v. 22) weaves together three Old Testament allusions.

1. Jesus is identified in Psalm 2:7 as the messianic Son.
2. The next allusion comes from Isaiah 42:1, a servant passage.
3. Whether a third allusion appears in "whom I love" is debated. A likely option is to see an allusion to Isaiah 41:8, where the ideas of a chosen servant and a beloved person line up. The stress here is on the chosen nature of the Son's position and on his special relationship to God.

This event coronates Jesus's ministry, not by making him what he was not before but by recognizing that now the beloved Son will launch out into actively exercising the authority he possesses.

Application. The preacher must bear good news as well as news that exposes sin. Some preachers in the past tended to emphasize sin so much that one wondered where grace might be found. Today our problem might be the opposite. A preacher of God's message must be balanced in delivering both messages. Forgiveness cannot occur except where one realizes responsibility for sin and repents of it.

When we are forgiven after turning to God, such forgiveness should yield a transformed life as a response to the grace of God. John assumes that repentance will bear fruit. In other words, a transformed life transforms our ways of relating to others. People are not to be ignored, used, or abused. God honors those who honor others. As the Father has shown his goodwill to us, so we should show it to others.

John's faithfulness leads to a final observation. Sometimes doing God's will is not popular; it may involve personal risk. John speaks up and has to suffer the consequences of his public stand. He describes what sin is and calls people to account before God for it, but he also shows the way out of its sinister grip. The church today needs to do the same.

The primary application of this text comes in its Christology. When one comes to Jesus, one is not approaching one truth among many. Religion is not like a line in a cafeteria, where one has a choice of what meal to eat. The message of Jesus is unique. The road to the Father comes through him. Nor is religious faith in the world like a vast interstate highway system where many roads lead to God. Jesus is available to all humanity, so the offer he makes is not an exclusive one. But in order to know the Father, one must know the Son. That message may cut against the grain of our current cultural pluralism, but it does reflect that Jesus is unique: "You are my Son, whom I love; with you I am well pleased." With a divine endorsement like that, we must listen to him.

LUKE 3:23–38

Original Meaning. Ancestry can be revealing. In the case of Jesus, this is especially so. Several features stand out about Luke's genealogy in comparison to Matthew 1:1–17. Luke places it between Jesus's baptism as Son and the temptations that test him. Luke is answering the question: Is Jesus qualified to be God's promised Son? Luke's list goes from the present to the past. Luke goes all the way back to Adam. With this touch, Luke indicates that Jesus's story is humanity's story. There are also some differences in the listing, the explanation for which is not entirely certain. There is no way to establish the superiority of one of these options over the other, except to note that a reconciliation between the lists is possible in a variety of ways.

The overall intention of Luke's list is clear. He wants to show Jesus's connection to David, to Abraham, and to Adam. The connection to David establishes his rights as regal heir; Jesus can be king of Israel. The connection to Abraham links Jesus to the national promise and hope. The connection to Adam allows Luke to argue that Jesus represents all humanity. So, in Jesus, God has carefully designed affairs so that as the Son, Jesus can realize both the hope of the Old Testament and the hope of creation.

As Luke introduces his genealogy, he gives the age of Jesus at the start of his ministry as being about thirty (v. 23). He also notes that Jesus was "thought" to be the son of Joseph, reaffirming his earlier assertions about the miraculous birth through Mary. Despite this qualification, legal paternity was still the source of ancient ancestry, so it is likely the line is Joseph's. It is this distinction that makes Luke's line a "legal" line.

Application. In this list is a variety of humanity. Some of the people are well-known Old Testament people who made a great mark; others are known to us only in this listing. Jesus represents both the well-known and the unknown of the world.

Churches mirror this truth. Some who function in the Christian community receive much public attention; others are barely known. Yet God knows them all and honors all faithfulness, no matter how much public acclaim such faithfulness receives when it is done. One of the great examples of such truth is to hear the testimony of great believers, only to realize that God got their attention through a grandparent, relative, or friend the world never knew. God's work often takes mysterious twists and turns.

Finally, Jesus's roots go back to Adam, the figure through whom all of us are connected to one another. In a day when ethnic diversity and hatred are raised to almost religious levels, we do well to reflect that even in our diversity humanity is one. Jesus came to reconcile us to each other (Eph 2:11–22), and he is in a unique position to accomplish that goal. God's plan of salvation indicates that he did not want to be a tribal god of only one people or of only one region. He came for everyone.

LUKE 4:1–13

Original Meaning. Before beginning his ministry, Jesus faces off with Satan after being led by the Spirit into the desert. Luke makes such leading clear by noting that Jesus was "led by the Spirit into the wilderness" (v. 1). What occurs here, therefore, takes place under God's direction. Jesus's testing takes place in an environment opposite to the one Adam faced. The cosmic confrontation of Jesus with Satan recalls that earlier encounter, which had such dire consequences for humanity. Another major biblical event surfacing in this passage is the exodus, for Jesus uses the book of Deuteronomy to reply to each satanic temptation.

Jesus's successful encounter with the devil reveals how thoroughly dedicated he is to God's will and call. Jesus will take only the road God asks him to follow. He will not take any shortcuts. He knows that a successful walk with God only goes where the Father leads.

The first temptation questions God's provision and care. Satan's premise is that Jesus's sonship must mean that God does not want him to starve in the desert, so the mighty Son should simply turn stone into bread and meet his basic needs under his own power. But Jesus understands that the request is not a challenge to be strong, but to be independent. Jesus's reply comes from Deuteronomy 8:3b, arguing that life is run by more than food. To follow God is to live.

The second temptation is an invitation to worship Satan and abandon loyalty to the Father, a direct challenge to the first commandment. The proposal is of an alliance between the Son and Satan. Jesus can leave behind the rejection and suffering for quick access to power. Though Satan possesses great authority, he really cannot grant this wish. Jesus opts to receive from the Father what is the Father's to give. Therefore, Jesus replies with Deuteronomy 6:13. Only one being is worthy of worship—the Lord God. True service means remaining allied to God.

The third temptation involves a vision-like experience. Jesus is taken to the temple in Jerusalem—probably on the royal porch on the temple's southeast corner, which looms over a cliff and the Kidron Valley some four hundred and fifty feet below. To cast oneself down from such a height and survive would take divine intervention. Satan adds to his enticement by quoting Scripture himself, citing Psalm 91:11–12, a text that promises God's protection for his own. As spiritual as this sounds, Jesus recognizes the remark as a presumptuous test of God's care. So Jesus replies with Deuteronomy 6:16, a text that rebuked Israel for testing God. Jesus will not test God or characterize his ministry with a flashy display engaged in for selfish purposes.

Application. The first application emerging from this event is about temptation itself. Tests in life are not bad; in fact, they can be divinely sent (Jas 1:2–4). The main issue is my response to a test. Do I respond in a way that looks to God to guide me through it? Do I trust him, or do I put him to the test? If I am to grow spiritually, I can expect trial. If I am to grow spiritually, I need to look to God in the midst of it.

Such trust can extend to provision. The pursuit of material goals can become a driving force in our lives. But where does God's word and leading stand? Will Satan succeed in testing us to take bread that God is not asking us to eat, while we ignore the most basic meal of all, his will? Sometimes God provides marvelously in the midst of a sacrifice made for his will. Seeking to have less materially may mean having much more.

Another way we show lack of trust is to grab for power that is not ours or to take power in a way it is not intended to be received. The implications of such a power grab extend into how we exercise authority in the home, how we conduct our businesses, and how we relate to others. The best authority is one exercised not under threat but because of earned respect. The most genuine authority is not that which is seized, but that which is received from the God who honors faithfulness.

A final way we tend to show a lack of trust in God is to try to force him to act on our behalf. This type of spiritual wagering does not involve leaping from tall buildings, but in walking into events where we say in effect, "If you care for me, God, then this situation will turn out this way." This kind of testing is an attempt to control God, not follow his leading. We are setting ourselves up for disappointment, since it may be in our best interest for events to go in a different direction than we desire.

LUKE 4:14–30

Original Meaning. Luke 4:14–15 introduces and summarizes the general character of Jesus's ministry during its early Galilean stage. As with his temptations, Jesus is under the guidance of the Spirit. Luke loves to note how Jesus is responsive to God's leading. As he ministers, his fame spreads. In the ancient world, these reports went by word of mouth. What catches people's interest is his teaching, so much so that they "praise" him (v. 15). This word (*doxazō*) is normally reserved for praise to God.

When Jesus preaches in the synagogue in Nazareth, the people are impressed with him, though not necessarily persuaded. This account of Jesus's teaching ministry should be paired with Luke 4:31–44, which highlights his ministry of miracles. Jesus combines word and event. This event becomes a snapshot of what Jesus's entire Galilean ministry will be like: people will be amazed at his teaching and claims, but they will not flock to him.

To appreciate what happens here, one must understand the synagogue service order. The congregation recites the *Shema*, the confession recorded in Deuteronomy 6:4–9. Then they share in prayer. Then comes a reading from the Torah followed by a reading of the Prophets. Then follows an exposition that usually ties the readings together, and the service closes with a benediction.

Presumably Jesus speaks during the exposition section of this service. He not only cites Isaiah 61:1–2 but mixes into it an allusion to Isaiah 58:6. The mixture may represent a summary of a larger reading or set of remarks. Since Jesus speaks of himself as fulfilling this text, he is the one to whom the text applies. Insofar as the text speaks explicitly of being anointed by the Spirit, this anointing looks back to the bestowal of the Spirit on Jesus at his baptism by John.

Jesus makes three points here: (1) he is anointed by the Spirit to perform a specific ministry; (2) he is a prophetic figure who declares the arrival of the new era; and (3) he will actually bring about the release that he proclaims. The combination means that Jesus functions as both prophet and Messiah. This combination is important, because the following verses compare Jesus to the prophets Elijah and Elisha, but his anointing recalls his messianic function.

Jesus concludes his remarks by telling his audience that they are seeing the fulfillment of these words of Isaiah. Isaiah 61 was associated with the decisive end-time salvation of God, which Jesus has begun to introduce. That program is going to come in phases, as will be made clear in the rest of Luke, but here Jesus notes that the fulfillment has started. The crowd reacts with marvel and are overwhelmed by the content of his message. Despite their amazement, they are skeptical.

The townsfolk want him to show his stuff. Jesus notes how a prophet is without honor in his own land. Jesus then singles out the period of Elijah and Elisha, one of the lowest, most apostate periods of the nation's history. He reminds the people that during that time, the prophets did no work in the nation but they did heal a couple of gentiles! Jesus is warning his audience that their reaction recalls some of the lowest years in Israel's past. A choice surrounds Jesus, and to choose wrongly is to lose opportunity for blessing.

Jesus's remark angers the crowd, and they want to remove him and cast him over the cliff—possibly an allusion to their perception that he is a false prophet worthy of complete rejection. Instead, Jesus walks away. The opportunity for blessing has become a moment when paradise is lost.

Application. It is important to appreciate how central good teaching is to ministry. In an era when feelings and interpersonal relationships are high on the agenda, it is wise to reflect on why Jesus spent so much time instructing people. One of the fundamental biblical assumptions is that human cultures distort reality. Our minds need reshaping and renewing, so that our feelings and reactions will be more like what God desires. It takes careful cultural discernment to know how to respond to the subtleties our culture feeds us.

It is not merely a matter of teaching doctrine and facts but also of relating that teaching to life and putting flesh and blood on it. We speak to hearts, not just minds. But there must be content to send to the heart, or else we are ministering with nothing more than what a person can get in the lifestyles section of the bookstore or what they can receive from their neighborhood counselors.

The major application emerging from the scene where Jesus preaches in the synagogue involves the nature of his mission. The church's call is but an extension of Jesus's mission. The fulfillment he proclaims is part of the fulfillment that the church proclaims. Values reflected in this mission should be reflected in the church's outreach. For example, the church should engage in its preaching and evangelistic task with an understanding that the gospel message is more suited to those who are poor and already live in a dependent context. Independent, well-to-do people often have a false sense of security about life, as if it is really within their control.

Expressing concern for people can become a powerful tool in evangelism. Jesus communicated this sense of redemption to notorious sinners and those who stood in dire need. His relating to people's pain had much to do with it. The people not only heard his message of repentance, forgiveness, release, and fulfillment of promise, but they also saw his compassion and care.

Another major application of this passage centers on the nature of salvation. The one metaphor that dominates Jesus's declaration of fulfillment here is *release*. The picture of Jubilee, which foresees a total release from all enemies and debt, wonderfully describes the essence of salvation. The books are wiped clean; all legal obligations are removed through the grace Jesus provides.

According to this passage, the church must care about the oppressed. Yet Jesus focuses less on how to change societal structures and more on how to change the individual.

Structures cannot change until the people who operate them are changed. Part of the liberty of the gospel is coming to the Father with the recognition that he supplies what we really need to release us from perspectives in life that chain us down and cause us to mistreat others. This is why in other texts where Jesus describes his mission, he makes it clear that he focuses on calling sinners to repentance and on finding the lost (5:31–32; 19:10). The way to start fixing what is wrong in the world is to start with fixing ourselves. Only then will we have the eyes to see how we contribute to the problems that sometimes make the world a painful place of broken relationships.

The church has a difficult task. On the one hand, to discuss redemption and release we must mention sin. On the other hand, the offer of the gospel is ultimately positive, so that the goal is not a message of doom but of hope. Granted there is a choice at stake, but the offer is made to anyone who will enter. God has an open door for any heart that is open.

LUKE 4:31–44

Original Meaning. Luke introduces here two of his five examples of Jesus's performing miracles on the Sabbath. He has declared the fulfillment of God's promise at a synagogue in Nazareth on the Sabbath. Now he shows the presence of such fulfillment. As important as miracles are as events in the life of Jesus, they also serve as visual indications of deeper realities. All Jesus's miracles in some way reflect a visual representation of some significant spiritual reality—often the depth of the cosmic struggle associated with his ministry. Since his work represents the powerful arrival of the force of righteousness into God's world, is it any wonder that Jesus must go in hand-to-hand combat with the forces of evil? In a real sense, the miracles pull back a veil on the cosmic forces at work within creation.

The major feature of the initial summary of Jesus's ministry in verses 31–32 is the recognition of the authority inherent in his teaching. Most rabbinic arguments took on an anthological approach to teaching, where each rabbi's opinion on a matter was set out in a kind of listing and where truth was often a matter of establishing a precedent for an idea. Jesus does *not* teach this way. He declares God's will directly, even keeping his direct use of Scripture to a few limited situations. The crowds recognize his distinct approach to teaching and are astonished by it.

The first miracle of this Gospel is an exorcism. The major opponent in Jesus's ministry consists of the spiritual forces of evil. Demons are noted twenty-three times in this Gospel, with fourteen of those references occurring between here and 9:50 in the Galilean ministry section. Judaism believed that in the messianic times demonic power would be crushed. Jesus has already met with Satan; now he is facing off against Satan's cohorts.

Luke distinguishes demon possession from physical illness, as does the rest of the New Testament—though on occasion the concepts overlap. A distinguishing feature of demon possession is erratic behavior or severe physical distortion.

Jesus's presence makes the demon nervous, and it cries out through the man, asking him what he is planning to do. Jesus rebukes the evil spirit, and immediately the man is restored. He also silences it. Apparently Jesus wants nothing to do with demonic confession of him in public. Even the demon's attempt to harm the man by throwing him to the ground fails to have results. The destructive tendencies of evil are overcome by the authority that Jesus possesses to deliver humanity from the clutches of the demons.

The next healing is less dramatic but just as significant. Jesus encounters Peter's mother-in-law at Peter's home, sick with a high fever. Jesus acts against another distinct threat to life. As he has just done with the demon, so now with disease. He rebukes the illness, and the woman is restored to life and begins serving them. This remark not only testifies to her recovery; it also reflects her gratitude.

Word spreads quickly, and Jesus finds himself dealing with people who come to him with all kinds of maladies. Healings continue without interruption. There is no unevenness in his ministry. His authority flows constantly. In addition, demons are exorcized regularly. They confess Jesus to be the Son of God, meaning that they recognize him as the Christ. The Anointed One is showing the evidence of his unique calling. As he has done earlier, he silences any attempts at demonic confession.

Jesus on occasion withdraws for a private time of prayer, but the people look for him. Those in Capernaum want him to stay, but Jesus's mission is not provincially limited. Jesus has been called to preach the kingdom of God elsewhere, so he must go where he is sent. This means that Jesus must preach in other synagogues throughout the land.

Application. Many missionary organizations and churches in recent history have organized benevolent ministries and hospitals as expressions of the type of compassionate service Jesus performs here. Such a connection is justified. What the healings and exorcisms show is God's power and concern for humanity. The church should show no less compassion today. When we deal with the ravages of disease or show concern to those who are hurting, we are reflecting the kind of love God has for people who live in a fallen world.

Another application emerges in the area of counseling. We can minister to people's souls by helping them wrestle with the presence of sin and the fall in their lives through a biblically centered counseling approach that seeks to understand who people are and why they are hurting. This is not to argue that mental health and exorcism are the same, for they are not. But it is to suggest that the type of compassion that engaged in exorcism is similar to the type of compassion needed for one to minister to a hurting soul afflicted by a mental disturbance.

What is needed is good counseling—counseling that integrates the truth of Scripture about the character of sin and fallenness in our world and environment with the study and analysis of the symptoms and causes of our struggles. To ignore either aspect, so that personal responsibility for our condition is avoided or a person is always made to feel the blame, is a mistake.

In Jesus's ministry we see the exercise of whatever resources he had to aid those who were afflicted by the forces that attack humanity and debilitate it. Though the form of such ministry today might differ, the compassion that motivates such service does not.

LUKE 5:1–32

Original Meaning

The Call of the First Disciples (5:1–11). Sometimes service for Jesus starts out rather innocently. Just ask Peter. The entire episode is both surprising and revealing. The crowds are pressing around. To avoid the crush, Jesus decides to get on Simon's boat and pushes out from the shore a little so that he can address the crowds. After teaching, Jesus tells Peter to head out and go fishing. Conditions were certainly not right for fishing, as Peter notes. Nevertheless, at Jesus's word Peter agrees to cast the nets. This indicates potential in Peter, for he responds to Jesus's leading.

The effort is successful, almost too much so. The boat overflows with fish and begins to sink. Peter calls out to James and John for help. The nets are breaking, and fish are spilling out everywhere. In the rush, something profound dawns on Peter. What has taken place is no accident; only an agent of God could have produced such a catch in the middle of the day.

In words full of respect and awe, he asks Jesus to depart. The premise behind this remark is that a man of God surely would want to have nothing to do with an everyday sinner. What Peter does not realize is that admitting one's inability and sin is the best prerequisite for service, since then one can depend on God. Peter's confession becomes his résumé for service. Humility is the elevator to spiritual greatness.

Thereupon Jesus notes that Peter will start catching people. He issues a call to Peter to enter into the process of gathering people and rescuing them from the danger of a fallen world. Unlike fish, which are caught to be flayed and devoured, Peter will catch people and bring them into life.

The miraculous catch indicates how miracles are pictures or metaphors of spiritual realities. The miraculous catch of fish produces the metaphorical call to catch people. Jesus's prophetic leading and insight powerfully illustrate his call, indicating graphically the mission Peter has before him.

The disciples respond to Jesus's call by leaving all and following him. That was the last time they spent the day just as fishermen. Jesus changes people's priorities. A call to ministry transcends their previous vocation.

Two Healing Miracles (5:12–26). After this initial call, Luke relates two miracles that present further details about Jesus's authority and compassion. Luke introduces the first healing by mentioning that Jesus is venturing to other parts of Galilee, as he said he must do. A man full of leprosy approaches him. Having this disease led to social isolation. Jesus's ministry to a leper therefore reveals his attention to the outcasts of society, demonstrating that such people can have access to God's blessing.

The man approaches Jesus with humility, bowing before him. His request raises the question of Jesus's willingness to heal, not his capability. In fact, the leper assumes Jesus can do it. Jesus responds to the leper's request by declaring his willingness and announcing that he is cleansed. The picture of redemption should not be missed. Those who turn to Jesus for cleansing receive it from him because he willingly gives it.

Jesus tells the man to go to the priest and not say anything to anyone. According to the Mosaic law, this testimony before the priest will take a week. The ritual pictured the cleansing and removal of sin, so even the follow-up program for the leper reinforces the message of what Jesus has done. The fact that the testimony is for the priests is not surprising, given their need to understand what Jesus represents.

Luke bridges the two miracle stories and the hectic pace Jesus is leading by noting that he stops for prayer. In the quietness that comes privately after a rapid rush of events comes the solace and gaining of perspective that keeps Jesus close to God. Luke regularly notes such commitments to prayer.

The next healing is that of a paralytic man. Pharisees and teachers of the law (better known as scribes) have joined the crowd. The Pharisees were one of four religious parties in Judaism (Sadducees, Zealots, and Essenes are the others). They were a non-priestly, lay separatist movement that developed many traditions and oral rulings to establish how the Mosaic law should be applied in their generation. These leaders are now watching Jesus.

As Jesus is teaching, a group of men try to bring a paralyzed man to him for healing, but the crowd is too large. Therefore, they go on the roof. Working their way through the tiles, they lower the man before Jesus. Getting a hole in the roof would have involved working through a muddy layer above the roof beams.

Jesus sees "their faith" (v. 20), a remark that is easy to move past. Faith in this text must mean the visible expression of faith, not a mere attitude, since Jesus sees it in the actions of the men.

As a result, Jesus acts, giving the man much more than he was seeking. He declares his sins to be forgiven.

A chain reaction follows. The Pharisees and scribes begin to think about the theological implications of what Jesus just said. They know that only God forgives sin, so to claim to do what God does is blasphemy, a slander against God.

Jesus asks the Pharisees to ponder a question that is really a dilemma. Is it easier to declare sins are forgiven or to tell a paralytic to get up and walk? Logic tells us that it is easier to say one's sins are forgiven, since that cannot be seen; but in fact that is more difficult, since one must have the authority to do that. Then Jesus links the two issues together. He acts so that the audience can know the Son of Man has authority to forgive sins. He tells the man to walk. He enables the hard thing—having the paralyzed man get up and walk—in order to show the even harder thing—the power to forgive sin.

This event reveals one further picture. The ability of the paralyzed man to resume his walk of life is a picture of what Jesus does when he saves. His message is a liberating one.

The Calling of Levi (5:27–32). Sometime after the healing of the paralytic, Jesus goes out and spots a tax collector at his toll booth, whose job is to collect the surcharge as people travel from city to city. Jesus initiates the entire encounter, asking him to become a disciple. Just as sinners can enter into an intimate relationship with God, so can tax collectors. In other words, *anyone* who responds to Jesus can receive a blessing. Levi responds to the invitation, leaving his vocation and financial security behind to follow Jesus.

Levi then throws Jesus "a great banquet," a feast (v. 29). Invited to the table are Levi's circle of notorious friends, "tax collectors and others," whom the Pharisees call "sinners" in verse 30. The associations Jesus makes cause other religious figures to raise questions. In ancient culture, to sit at table with someone communicated acceptance. The Pharisees avoided sinners to avoid the suggestion that they endorsed the sinner. The two perspectives cannot be more opposite.

Jesus then gives the theological and missiological rationale for his actions. Jesus notes that a healthy person does not seek a physician; it is the sick who need one. So Jesus's mission is not to call the healthy but the sick "to repentance" (v. 32). In other words, Jesus's call goes out to those who realize they need help. Jesus calls on those who are not well to get better by coming into the grace God offers them. If they desire to know God, the Lord will not reject them but will begin the process that will make them well.

Application. Peter understood that there is no greater call than to cast nets for Jesus and minister to those who find their way into the saving net of the gospel. When he first encountered God's power, he thought Jesus must leave, because the teacher was amid sinners. Jesus taught Peter that sinners who turn to God are the people God can use the most. So Peter simply followed Jesus.

The most significant lesson from the cleansing of the leper story is that even outsiders can experience God's healing grace. The church is called by this example to reach out to those on the fringes of society. The leper's healing pictures Jesus making someone clean from sin. This text warns us not to take any sin lightly, for it makes us unclean. God took sin so seriously that he gave his own Son to purify us from its stain.

Jesus's sojourn for prayer is an important note at this point in his ministry. He teaches us how important it is to commune with God, especially when we tend to ignore him because things are so busy. Sometimes the best thing we can do amid the rush of life is to slow down and listen to God. We err seriously if we argue that we do not have time, for what we need under pressure is God's presence and calming involvement in our lives.

The healing of the paralytic reveals that faith expresses itself in diligent trust. That is what the paralytic's friends show and what Jesus commends. This faith is active, going to great lengths to seek Jesus's presence. Such faith catches Jesus's eye and touches God's heart.

Note Levi's response in both following Jesus and hosting a banquet for him. Here is a sinner whose life takes a total turn because of Jesus and who cannot wait to share Jesus with the friends of his former circle. Frequently for a new Christian, evangelism is strongest in the first two years after conversion. Then the change of one's circle of friends cuts off further opportunity. Perhaps we isolate ourselves as the pious Pharisees did.

Jesus's initiative is also revealing. He seeks sinners, keeping his eye out for them, and makes reaching out to them a priority. For evangelism to be effective, the unsaved must be reached, since they are not looking to come into the church! The attitude of the Pharisees, in contrast, is censured in this text. They are so concerned with appearance that people are crushed or ignored in the process. Purity at the expense of serving people is not purity; it is isolationism—and sin.

LUKE 5:33–6:5

Original Meaning. Fasting in Judaism was a major rite of piety. Highly regarded as an act of worship, it took place at major events, like the Day of Atonement. Fasts usually involved penitence, mourning, or a plea for deliverance. Pharisees fasted twice a week. In the Judaism of Jesus's time, fasting was regarded as a virtue. The failure of Jesus's disciples to fast could be read as reflecting a lack of respect for God, a severe absence of piety.

Jesus not only explains why he does not fast but also explains the deep significance of the refusal. The picture he uses is a wedding—a symbol often used to describe God's relationship with his people. Since the groom is now present and the wedding is taking place, there is no need to mourn or seek deliverance. But in the future, the groom will be taken from them; then fasting will be appropriate. Here is the first hint of Jesus's approaching suffering. It is no accident that Jesus makes this point as the opposition is rising. When the groom is gone, then God's people will long for the completion of redemption. Then fasting will be appropriate again.

A new era with new perspectives has arrived. The time Jesus brings is like a new piece of cloth. One does not take such cloth and sew it onto an old garment. One cannot mix what Jesus brings with the old ways without creating a destructive mix. Jesus's era is also like wineskins. The old wineskin cannot expand with the fermentation. Its age and brittle quality causes it to rip, and the wine is lost. Jesus is more than a reformer of Judaism; he has come to refashion it into something fresh. Those who like old wine do not try the new, for their minds are already made up: "The old is good." So Jesus expects many not to respond to his new way. They are comfortable with life and piety as it is. Jesus's remark is both a description and a warning. Jesus knows that some do not want change.

Luke moves immediately into the next event, the plucking of grain on the Sabbath (6:1–5). Jewish tradition specified what one could and could not do on the Sabbath. The Mishnah (an ancient Jewish rule book) contained a list of thirty-nine prohibited activities. According to that list, the disciples are guilty of reaping, threshing, winnowing, and preparing food.

Some Pharisees just happen to be keeping an eye on Jesus's disciples. The text does not tell us why, but the fact that they know what the disciples are doing shows how carefully the disciples are being watched. They ask them, "Why are you doing what is unlawful on the Sabbath?" (v. 2). The question is specific, since it uses the legal term *exestin*, which refers to what is legally allowed.

Jesus defends the actions of his colleagues by citing Scripture. Jesus knows the Pharisees have read 1 Samuel 21:1–7 and 22:8–9, but he argues they have misunderstood it. So his reply begins with an implied rebuke. In that passage, David gathers showbread from the tabernacle so that he and his men can eat it—a clear violation of the law. Since David was not disciplined by the high priest at the time, the Old Testament suggests that what he did was appropriate. Jesus's reply has the Pharisees in a dilemma. In effect, if they condemn him on this issue, they criticize David as well.

But Jesus is not done. He adds a note about his authority, arguing that the Son of Man is Lord of the Sabbath. The fact that Jesus is Son of Man means that he has the right to regulate what takes place on the Sabbath. This remark underlines his unique position. His actions are not the issue; his authority is. The question for all to ponder becomes: "Does Jesus reveal God's way and have authority over it, or does he not?"

Application. The Christian is "between eras." We share in the benefits that Jesus brings, yet we still await his full redemption. Jesus no longer tells us to fast regularly on fixed days set by the law, but acts of worship in anticipation of his future coming and our full redemption are commendable. The bridegroom has been taken from us, and we long for his return. Not only can we celebrate this reality through fasting, but it is recalled whenever we share in the Lord's table—an affirmation not only of our relationship to Jesus but also of our belonging to the same confession with one another (1 Cor 11:23–26). All of this makes us aware that though we share in the initial benefits of the new era, we have not experienced all God has for us, and life on this earth is but a preliminary stage in what God is doing.

The passage also warns against syncretism between the Christian faith and any other religion. If syncretism were possible, one would think that Judaism would be the best candidate. Judaism was older, worshiped the same God, shared the same hope in the Messiah, and prayed for the same deliverance. Jesus makes it clear that although he is the fulfillment of promise, the new way he brings is not to be mixed with the old. If the Christian faith cannot be mixed with Judaism, its closest cousin, then certainly it cannot be mixed with anything else available in the world's cafeteria of religions. To do so will destroy both.

We also learn how people resist change, even change directed by God. Christians can fall into such ruts of ritual contentment today as well, assuming the way they worship is the way everyone must worship. Music styles or certain church practices are elevated to the level of necessity, rather than seen as means to an end.

While some resist because they are hostile to what Jesus is doing, others resist because they are content with life as it is. We should be sensitive to the difference as we seek to share Jesus. It is hard to convince a person who is content that he or she is not; these are often the hardest people to reach.

In the end, the correctness of what Jesus does with his disciples rests on his claims. Does he have authority as the Son of Man, so that his analysis of the Old Testament and the present situation are authoritative over the law? If so, who then is Jesus? This is the fundamental question in this text. The Pharisees do not believe Jesus has the authority to say what he is teaching. Today people still challenge Jesus's authority. But if he is the Son of Man, he must be heard, for he reveals the way to God.

LUKE 6:6–16

Original Meaning. While teaching in a synagogue, Jesus sees a person in need, a man with a shriveled right hand, and takes the initiative to heal him. The scribes and Pharisees watch Jesus. The Greek word for "watched" (*paratēreō*, v. 7) means "to spy on" or "to watch out of the corner of one's eye." They want to level a charge against Jesus. This attitude is emerging out of what is becoming a growing opposition.

Jesus raises a fundamental question, "Which is lawful on the Sabbath: to do good or to do evil, to save life or destroy it?" (v. 9). The question has an ironic edge, because Jesus is looking at the Sabbath from a relational angle. In fact, the way he pursues the question almost suggests that a failure to act here would be to do evil.

The action becomes a test. Will God vindicate Jesus and reveal the answer to Jesus's question? Jesus asks the man to stretch out his hand, and the man is able to respond, indicating that healing has occurred. But rather than rejoicing at his restoration, the leadership becomes angry at Jesus's success. The word for their anger (*anoia*) in verse 11 is a strong term (NIV "furious"), describing irrational anger, even pathological rage. A turning point has come. Refusing to accept the evidence Jesus has laid before them, they reveal hardness of heart and cast their vote against Jesus.

Rising opposition means that Jesus must organize his followers. His selection of the twelve is preparation for the missions to come, as well as an anticipation of his future departure through death. He spends the entire previous night in prayer. Thus, his selection is set in a context of communion with God. This is the only place in the New Testament where an all-night vigil is noted. Jesus selects twelve men. The number is designed to suggest a parallel to Israel. Only Luke calls the group "apostles" as he lists their names (v. 13). That title indicates their role as commissioned representatives of Jesus on behalf of the kingdom message.

Application. This passage demonstrates the priority that showing mercy has in the mind of God. He is compassionate and wants us to help others whenever possible. Even a day of rest, like the Sabbath, is no reason to opt out of doing good. Jesus goes out of his way to show his opponents that this is how God desires others to be treated. He dedicated himself to serving others, especially others in need. He acted at the first opportunity. Our rapid response should match his as well.

The major emphasis in the passage is the rising opposition to Jesus and its cold, irrational nature. Jesus met such opposition by simply continuing to minister with love to those who needed compassion. Here we see his heart in contrast to a heart that does not respond to the moral call of God to serve at all times. Even if facing strong opposition, those who walk with Jesus are called to a ministry of service and love.

When we turn to the selection of the twelve disciples, Jesus consciously selected a diverse group of people, presumably to keep his ministry team balanced. Their central bond was Jesus. The new community he builds today is just as varied, and our differences should not prevent a unity from forming among this nucleus, as Jesus bonds us together.

The inclusion of a Judas in the group also has its lesson. Not everyone remains a team player, and defection can come from the innermost ranks. Close association with Jesus does not necessarily reveal the real condition of the heart. Unfaithfulness and denial eventually show themselves, but for a significant period of time it is hard to tell where Judas really is.

A final question emerges from this selection. How do we choose our leadership? What criteria do we use? Does character count for much? Jesus was looking for a few good men and chose them in the hopes of building their character to the point where they could lead the church he left behind.

That goal makes another key point about leadership. The best leader is one who so prepares his community for the future that when he departs, he is barely missed, since solid leadership is left behind. If the Twelve as a group are measured by this standard of leadership, then Jesus's choice for successors was a strategic one, since this group came to shake and shape the world.

LUKE 6:17–49

Original Meaning. Jesus ministers here to three groups: the apostles, "a large crowd of his disciples," and "a great number of people" (v. 17). The people gather for two reasons: to listen to Jesus's teaching and to be healed by him. Teaching and compassionate service combine to touch the people. Jesus's message of God's kindness is supported by his actions. The healings involve both sicknesses and exorcisms. The power that proceeds from Jesus indicates the authority with which he works.

Call of Blessings and Woes (6:17–26). The first part declares God's grace of blessing to those who identify with him. In contrast, the woes, unique to Luke's Gospel, show God's displeasure on those who oppose the blessing Jesus gives and who persecute his disciples as a result.

The "poor" are discussed first (v. 20). The poor are the pious poor, who are blessed because they have a position in the kingdom of God, the delivering rule of his presence. These poor are the special objects of Jesus's ministry, as Luke repeatedly mentions. Such people understand that they must depend on God, because life is beyond their control.

Those that hunger now are promised satisfaction in the

future. Hunger is a result of religious persecution and harsh treatment by people of power who take advantage of others. The blessing they will receive transcends any lack they have now.

Those who are poor and hungry are also sad because of the strain of life, but there will come a time when they will laugh with joy. God sees their tears, and their tears will become smiles. Disappointment and pain will turn into joy. Those who weep have paid the price of painful rejection for lining up with God.

The last unit is the key remark of the blessing sequence because it shows the religious dimensions of those who are blessed (v. 22). These remarks clearly presuppose a life that has faced religious persecution, and the four descriptions depict an escalating negative reaction to their association with Jesus. A choice for Jesus meant the loss of family fellowship, dismissal from the synagogue, and removal from social contact. The call to "rejoice" is the one command among the blessings (v. 23); everything else is promise. God's grace will help them overcome their suffering for their faith.

The "rich" are singled out because they often take advantage of the poor (v. 24). The remark is, of course, a generalization, since some rich do respond to the gospel. But the warning is serious, for wealth can create a sense of independence that results in distance from God and callousness toward others.

The next woe is against those "who are well fed now" (v. 25). In a classic case of reversal, they will be hungry on the day of judgment. Those who ignore God and place their hopes solely on the good life here have little comfort for the future.

The final woe reveals the spiritual depravity of these people (v. 26). They are spoken well of by others, just like the false prophets of old. They have settled for an approach to life that does not challenge them to live any differently. They wrongly see themselves as unaccountable to God.

Call to Love and Mercy (6:27–38). Jesus turns to address the disciple's ethical character and call. Fundamental to ethics is love—not a love like the world's, but a unique love that endures. Love evidences mercy, just like the Father, so that the result is a hesitation to judge and a readiness to forgive.

Four exhortations in verses 27 and 28 make the key point. The special objects of love are one's enemies. The love Jesus commands is not an abstract love tucked away in the person's inner recesses, but a love that demonstrates itself in concrete action. The exhortations expect action, not just a private expression to God. In the context of rejection, Jesus calls for extraordinary trust in God. Disciples should reflect such love constantly.

Lest there be any doubt that Jesus calls his followers to active, visible love for their enemies, four illustrations guarantee that this is his focus. Turning the cheek pictures a person slapped on the cheek in rejection (v. 29a). Numerous examples of this kind of use of violence appear in Acts. Yet the early church consistently turned the other cheek by continuing to share the gospel with those who rejected them. They never fought back in kind, but attempted to overcome evil with good.

The second illustration continues the picture of being vulnerable. Those who take the outer garment should also be allowed to have the undershirt (v. 29b). Jesus's point here is not to stand on a street corner and allow oneself to be robbed, but that ministry in the context of rejection, which includes economic isolation, requires being vulnerable again and again.

The disciple should also be compassionate and generous and should thus give to the needy (v. 30a). The giving of alms to the poor was an important part of Jewish piety. Such compassion represents a fundamental expression of love.

The final illustration involves retribution for wrong done (v. 30b). Jesus does not want a disciple to seek to get back what has been taken from him. It is better to be defrauded than to bring reproach on Jesus's name. Those who strike against the disciples should be treated differently by the disciples.

All of these exhortations assume that the disciple understands that God is watching over him or her. Any vindication should be left in his hands. The greatest vindication of all is to transform the enemy into a friend of God through the example of love. The essence of love is a sensitivity to the needs of others, deferring to how they prefer to be treated. Such love takes great sensitivity and a spirit that desires to hear what others have to say. It is another way of showing respect for others.

Jesus drives home the point with a series of questions. The fundamental point is that if we love only those who are kind to us, that takes no special effort. Even sinners love that way. The call of the disciple is to a greater love, a distinct love, a love that is unique in the world.

Jesus then restates the exhortation: love your enemies, do good, lend while expecting nothing back, and expect a reward from the God who lives in heaven. Such love is rewarded because it marks out the presence of the children of God, who reflect the character of God. In other words, the standard of the disciple's behavior is the merciful character of God. To be his child is not only to be brought into a relationship where God has forgiven us but is the beginning of a process of reflecting God's gracious, merciful, and forgiving character to the world.

In imitation of God the disciple should also be slow to judge (v. 37). Love for one's enemy does not fix a view of him in stone. Moreover, the measure we use toward others is the measure God will use toward us. In the ancient marketplace, a seller placed grain in a container then shook the container to get the grain to level out so that he could put more grain in the measure. That is how God measures for the generous and those who give. This abundant measure God pours into the "lap" or fold of one's ancient garment (v. 38). God honors a compassionate spirit.

Call to Righteousness, Fruit, and Wise Building (6:39–49). Jesus begins the final unit with a warning that calls disciples to pay attention to which teachers they follow. Blindness is a common figure for spiritual blindness; thus, Jesus is warning here about religious leadership. One should follow the right teacher and not apply too much authority to one's self. In the context of this discourse, only one such teacher exists—Jesus.

Jesus continues to attack a critical spirit, like that of the Pharisees, by mentioning the quickness with which we are hypocritically aware of a little fault in someone else but ignore the log in our own eye. The way to deal with it is by paying attention to our own faults first and dealing fully with them before turning our attention to the treatment of the little faults of others.

How can one know the character of a person? Jesus says to check the fruit. Jesus highlights speech here. The tongue is a litmus test of the soul, and the product of one's life is a litmus test of the heart. Each one should examine one's own self in this regard, not others.

Finally, Jesus returns to the issue of his authority. Any disciple who respects Jesus should do what he says. How can one call him "Lord" and not do what he says? To hear Jesus and do what he says is like building a home with a solid foundation. Such a home can stand up against the floods of life. Even when the surging waters beat against the house, it stands, because it is well built. It is therefore foolish to build a house without a foundation. Likewise, it is foolish not to listen to Jesus.

Application. *Call to Blessings and Woes.* The blessings and woes possess two central points. First, God is aware of what we are going through, and he promises to vindicate the faithful. To love in a way that is unlike the world risks being misunderstood. Only those who rest in God's care and have assurance of his blessing can endure that hard path. Acceptance comes from the Father, whom we seek to imitate. As a result, acceptance from others matters less.

Second, the blessings and woes also reflect God's values. Whom does he honor? He responds to the poor, the hungry, those who mourn, and those who are rejected. In the Western world, such questions also cry out for consideration in some of our troubled urban centers. God cares for people such as these—not only to save their souls but to bring them into a community that evidences God's care for them in terms of life's basic needs.

It is appropriate to ask: Why does God single out the poor and suffering and issue such stark warnings to the wealthy? Surely God is affirming the dignity of people whom the world treats as trash. If God cares for such as these, should his church not do the same?

This suggests that the church be more involved than it is in ministries that reflect this priority. Such an emphasis does not represent an acceptance of a social gospel, since the social gospel is devoid of the redemptive message that is so central to God's saving work. What it does represent is the recognition that God seeks to redeem the total person and to create a community interested in all dimensions of life for those who are saved.

Call to Love and Mercy. To exemplify love in a hostile world is difficult. It takes a supernatural perspective and a change of thinking. We often have a hard time showing that love in the way we communicate with those who possess different values from our own. We must hold to our convictions while communicating a sensitive, loving concern. The world may misunderstand us, but that does not allow us to be insensitive or to harbor misunderstanding toward them.

Love, doing good, blessing, and praying for those who are our enemies also assumes another reality—namely, that we are in relational contact with the outside world. The ability to be struck on the cheek means we are in striking distance and have risked making the effort to have contact. The fortress mentality that sometimes invades the church is a form of retreat, as well as a denial of what Jesus calls for from disciples in this sermon. To love in a way that does not reflect some personal payback is to offer the world a different kind of love that is not based on what the self receives but on what we can give. It is to love in a way different from sinners.

Sadly, we often do not love in this way even within the community of God, much less show it to our enemies. By failing to love, we fail to reveal the loving and merciful character of God. Perhaps one reason evangelism fails is because people cannot see the grace of God evidenced in our relationships to one another in the church.

The connection between God's blessing and our ability to love should not be missed. Because of his blessing to us and our appreciation for him, we are able to love others. Because he gave, we can give. Because we know the joy of receiving from him, we are motivated to give to others. The actions Jesus calls for in his sermon apply to others what he has already applied to us. The deeper our understanding and appreciation of what God has done, the better prepared we will be to reflect his character to others.

Call to Righteousness, Fruit, and Wise Building. Many who teach about character are committed to developing character in a self-focused way, in a way that is effective in getting what we want or in a way that takes the easiest path possible. Trying to build ethical character while staying self-focused is the essence of blindness. We should choose our models carefully, following those who themselves are clear about following our Lord. Only one teacher is worthy of being followed—Jesus himself.

If there is to be accountability, it must start with us. Those who do the best job of restoring others in their walk are those who can restore themselves. That means being able to receive rebuke and honestly going before the Lord so that our beam may be removed.

The mouth is a litmus test of who we are spiritually. If we evaluated the character and tone of our daily speech, would it register like acid on litmus paper or yield the sweet presence of a person secure in God's care?

The issue of our loyalty as disciples comes down to responding to Jesus in terms of what we do. The disciple who learns to see and act in the world as Jesus calls the disciple to do is able to face the floods—that is, the disappointments and injuries that life often brings. Jesus's sermon's final word to the disciple is, in effect: "Apply yourself to apply my teaching; it is wisdom that stands up when things get tough."

Three final points need to be made about the sermon's imagery of trees and fruit.

1. Jesus's remarks here are not designed to examine individual moments in life but the pattern of a lifelong walk with God. The overapplication of a text like this with reference to a particular sin can do great damage, particularly to someone who sensitively reacts to his or her spiritual failure.
2. The text indicates that although fruit may not be a certain indicator, it can be a suggestive one. There are significant pastoral lessons about how to proceed with the "difficult" cases here. Some believers do turn away from God for a time. Such cases need to be challenged, but we must be careful not to ignore what Jesus warns in this sermon about judging as we seek to address someone in such a condition.
3. Scripture does seem clear that regenerated people do bear fruit. Total absence of fruit, particularly love, does raise the question about the presence of regeneration and faith. We are not saying that works save. Salvation is by grace through faith, but that grace bestows a changed heart that accepts God as Father and responds, at least to some degree, to his presence. If the seed of new faith is present, it will sprout.

LUKE 7:1–17

Original Meaning. The centurion, who as a military man would be among the wealthy in the society, has come to appreciate what Jesus has been doing. Though we do not know his national background, we do know he is not Jewish. This centurion has a slave near death. He sends a delegation of Jewish elders to ask Jesus to heal this man. The emissaries not only bring the man's request, but they also lobby for him, arguing that he is worthy of aid. The question raised here is significant at two levels: Will Jesus minister to someone from outside of Israel, and will he minister to a wealthy man?

Jesus turns to go to the man's house when a second delegation arrives. They report the response of the centurion in the first person, indicating that they are speaking for him. He understands Jesus's authority and knows that if he just issues the order, the healing will occur. These remarks amaze Jesus, insofar as a gentile has such faith. What impresses him is both the centurion's humility and his understanding of Jesus's power. One can argue that the essence of faith is humility: the recognition of the uniqueness of God's power and our unworthiness before it, while trusting in God's care.

From the raising of a widow's only son in 7:11–17 emerge two basic questions about Jesus: What kind of understanding does the Israelite public have of him, and why do they think of him this way? In that culture a widow without children was alone and in need of protection. Jesus stops the procession just outside the city and touches the burial plank. That touch renders him unclean, but it also expresses his compassionate concern. Jesus simply tells the corpse to arise, a cruel remark unless he has the power to bring it to pass. The dead man—or better, formerly dead man—sits up. Jesus has restored the previously broken relationship between mother and son with renewed life.

The crowd concludes that Jesus is "a great prophet" (v. 16). Luke will show that granting Jesus prophetic status is not enough. The crowd also realizes that God is visiting the people, for these kinds of miracles are not everyday affairs. The ancients often recognized that unusual events signaled God was in their midst. The crowd here sees a connection between God and Jesus.

Application. The first point of application regarding the centurion is that he, even as an outsider, had developed a good reputation with people from other backgrounds. The Jews, in turn, were responsive to him, indicating how mutual respect is one means of overcoming cultural and ethnic barriers. Luke is pointing out here that Jews and gentiles can respect one another if each side makes the necessary effort, especially when each group is open to God's way.

In our country, as we become more diverse, Christians will need to develop cultural sensitivity if we hope to share the gospel in all possible contexts. The Bible communicates a respect for "God-fearers" like Cornelius (Acts 10) and this centurion. With such openness we can build new bridges for the gospel where we might have formerly isolated ourselves through fear or ignorance.

Another application is that a position of power and wealth

can be used in ways that do not use people but serve them. Here is a man of wealth who used his resources and power to the benefit of those around him. Here is a man of wealth who seemed open to the worship of God. The Jews argued that the centurion was worthy of Jesus's attention. Part of the reason was his exemplary generosity and openness toward the people of God to whom Jesus came to minister. Should we who know him be any different?

The central lesson of the centurion story is the nature of the man's faith. He believed Jesus could heal by a simple sovereign word even at a physical distance. And he knew that Jesus cared enough to do so. Such faith and humility in approaching God's power are what amaze Jesus. This passage calls us to possess a similar faith.

In the story of the resuscitation of the widow's son we see the powerful reversal of death. Jesus deals here with the most fundamental obstacle we will ever face. Thus this miracle testifies to a central aspect of Christian hope. Its touching image reminds us that renewal and reunion are not an impossible dream. God promises to restore to life those who know his touch. In Jesus God takes the initiative to accomplish this renewal.

Death is not the end for those who know Christ. It involves a transfer into a level of life not known on this earth. While this miracle reminds us of our frailty and mortality, it also shouts out to us about God's power to raise and transform. No wonder the crowd who saw this miracle was filled with awe. We should be also, as we contemplate his creative power and compassion.

LUKE 7:18–35

Original Meaning. John's question emerges because his disciples report to him what Jesus is doing. The word of his miracles gives encouragement that Jesus is a significant figure, but something still does not fit right. Where is the powerful sovereign judge John predicted? He does not wonder whether Jesus has been sent from God; he simply wants confirmation that his ministry is the promised ministry of deliverance. Even the best of God's servants need reassurance from time to time. The reference to "the one who is to come" (v. 19) recalls John's own words in 3:15–16. So John is asking if Jesus is the Messiah.

Jesus's reply is not direct, but it does call for an inference. Before recording the reply, Luke interjects a reminder about the scope of Jesus's ministry; it has involved healings, exorcisms, and even sight given to the blind. Jesus's ministry graced many with restoration. The envoys are simply to report what they have seen, using a collage of Old Testament phrases from Isaiah, all of which refer to the coming period of decisive deliverance. Jesus's ministry signals fulfillment of these prophecies. The reply closes with a beatitude that calls for faith. Blessing belongs to the person who is not offended by Jesus.

Jesus then raises the question about John for the crowd. People did not go to see John because of the scenery at the Jordan River or for a fashion statement! They came for another reason: to see a prophet. In fact, John was more than a prophet. At the time of his birth, he was the greatest man yet born, since he represented the end of an era and pointed to the dawn of a new era of realization in God's plan. God was pointing the way in this forerunner, a witness to the approaching realization of promise.

Yet John's greatness is nothing compared to those who participate in the new era's blessings and benefits. Jesus's remark in verse 28 is one of the greatest affirmations of the believer's status in Scripture. To belong to the kingdom is a great privilege. John is the bridge between the two eras, but those who follow where the Baptist points come into a closer, more intimate relationship to God that transcends even the best the old age offered. That is how great Jesus's work is in this new era.

Jesus warns the current generation of religious leaders about their response to John. He does so through a parable, as he often does when discussing the kingdom or God's plan. He compares them to an ancient game of children at play. One can call this comparison "the parable of the brats." They are the children who are seated and refuse to play, complaining that John and Jesus do not dance to their tune. Whether they play a light tune on the flute or a funeral dirge, these two men do not follow the Jewish leadership's desires. They charge John with being demonic and Jesus with gluttony and questionable friendships. Jesus's open effort to reach sinners represents a repudiation of the leadership's more separatist approach.

Those who respond, wisdom's children, are contrasted with those who do not. The divine attempt to reach out to sinners means that they should not be ignored but pursued. The rebuke through the parable is another way to say that the leadership is hard-hearted in its rejection of God's way.

Application. Often we feel that the prophets of old had all the advantages. We think how great it would have been to be with Moses, Isaiah, or John the Baptist. How wonderful to see God "really" work. But this passage indicates that anyone who truly knows Jesus has greater blessings. Just think, we have the Spirit of God within us and within our communities. We possess a forgiveness that is complete because of Jesus's finished work on the cross. They are greater than the more temporary, individualized bestowals of the old era. God has given the church all the gifts we need to be effective in ministry, provided everyone does his or her part.

Jesus's ministry is one of substance, not mere claims. Claims are a dime a dozen, but in-depth ministry speaks volumes. Jesus simply let John deduce who he was on the basis of his works. They indicate that Jesus is the Messiah promised in the Old

Testament. Our ministries should have similar substance that points the way to their origin.

The value of John's struggle should not be missed. Here is a man of God needing reassurance that Jesus is truly the one he anticipated. We sometimes think that the great people of God never doubted. In doing so, we deny that they were normal human beings. Scripture is honest and open about such struggles and doubts, just as the Christian community today should be.

The response to tax collectors and sinners also suggests that we can anticipate being surprised at who might respond to the gospel. In fact, some of those we might least expect will respond. This is why we can never anticipate who God might bring to himself through us. We must be ready to share the gospel with anyone, even with those who at first may seem impossible cases.

We also learn something here about those who reject Jesus. The parable of the brats indicates how superficially pious people sometimes want God to approach them on their own terms. They want God to respond to their music rather than follow God's tune. The blessing of being greater than a prophet comes only from following his call to enter into God's grace and to dance to the music of the divine musician.

LUKE 7:36–8:3

Original Meaning. Jesus is asked to dinner and accepts the invitation. Even though the Pharisees oppose him, he accepts the opportunity to visit with some of them. As was common in the ancient world, the guests recline on cushions beside the table. Since Jesus is a public figure, the door to this meal likely remains open, so that interested people can enter, sit on the edge of the room, and hear the discussion. The rebuke in verse 39 is not because the woman has come to the meal, but because she did not stay on the sidelines.

The woman says nothing in this narrative, but her actions produce a wide range of discussion. Her sin is not identified. Perhaps she is a prostitute or has engaged in some other promiscuity to gain her reputation. But she boldly enters into the room and anoints Jesus's feet with a jar of expensive perfume. That act reflects great sacrifice, for such perfume was very costly. If she used nard, for example, the cost would be about three hundred denarii a pound, an average person's annual wage. Such perfume, like myrrh, was used for burial or to purify priests. Moved by the moment, she weeps as she anoints Jesus and kisses his feet. The action reflects her humility.

But the action is shocking to Jesus's host. Taken aback, the Pharisee begins to think to himself that Jesus must not be a prophet to allow such a woman to come into contact with him. The leader clearly doubts Jesus's prophetic credentials. Ironically, Jesus reads his mind and tells a parable that explains his actions.

The parable pictures two debtors: a two-month's debt versus a twenty-month debt for a basic wage earner. The debt collector discovers that neither of them can pay. Yet unlike most collectors, who would turn up the heat, he forgives each debt. Now, Jesus asks, who would love the collector more? Simon gives an astute reply: the one who has been forgiven more. Here is the heart of Jesus's relational ethic. Unlike the Pharisee, who can only dwell on the sinner's past record, Jesus prefers to see the potential that love and forgiveness possess for changing a person's heart. So he points out how the woman cared for him in a way his host has not.

But there is a reason for her love—her many sins now stand forgiven. The one who is forgiven little, on the other hand, loves little. To understand Jesus's point, the parable and his remarks must be put together. According to the parable, the basis of love is a previously extended forgiveness that produces a response of love. So Jesus indicates that the woman's actions reflect her experience of forgiveness from him. The Lord's declaration to her of forgiveness of sins serves to confirm what the parable has already indicated. There also is an implied warning from Jesus to the Pharisee: "Your love may not be great, because you have not appreciated the depth of forgiveness God has made available to you. Instead, you judge this woman in order to gain a good feeling about yourself." Jesus challenges such a way of looking at sin.

Jesus's words of forgiveness are also significant. Earlier the Pharisee raised the question whether Jesus is a prophet. But here he is forgiving sins, an act limited to God, as the Pharisees well know. They know that Jesus is appropriating to himself the ultimate level of authority. But that does not stop Jesus, who turns to the woman amid the objections and tells her to go in peace because her faith has saved her.

This final comment is significant, since up to this point the issue has been the presence of love. Jesus's remark reveals a crucial theological sequence: first an offer of forgiveness from God, then the faith that saves. Such faith evidences itself in the acts of love that she has performed for Jesus. Such is the fundamental cycle of relationship that exists between God and a believer.

In 8:1–3, unique to Luke's Gospel, the evangelist notes the work of three women of faith. As Jesus ministers, he draws followers who come from a wide variety of backgrounds. Mary Magdalene serves after having seven demons exorcised by Jesus. Joanna, as the wife of Herod's steward Cuza, gives evidence that Jesus's message has reached even into the palace. When these and other women come to faith, they immediately give of their resources to enable Jesus's ministry to continue. This note is important, since the passage makes clear that those contributing to Jesus's ministry span both gender diversity and the social scale. The pattern of grace received and ministry pursued emerges in the exemplary response of these women. Their ministry comes at two levels: personal involvement and the contribution of resources. Both levels of involvement are important to effective ministry.

Application. In our era, there is much debate about "user-friendly" churches that openly seek outsiders. Important questions surface, such as whether the church should minister primarily to God's people and whether truth will have to be watered down when outsiders are let in. We must look at Jesus's own teaching style and consider how he carried out his mission. He used illustrations from commerce and agriculture, plugging into the very activities of life that all people, including unbelievers, experienced.

This is not to say that the church should not seek to minister to the people of God or that teaching deep theological truth is not a part of the church's call. But we should not be harsh on those who feel called to target those who have not yet come to faith. The church needs more workers in the fields.

The sinful woman illustrates some basic truths about faith. In terms of faith, she demonstrates an ability to overcome barriers, such as the popular perceptions about her. As a woman, even to contemplate publicly drawing near to Jesus was a risk, because women did not do such things in that culture. The fact that she was a sinner only heightened the risk, since a religious figure like Jesus might reject her. Yet her gratitude and humility were so great that drawing near to Jesus was all she cared about. She counted the cost and reckoned that Jesus would respond to her humble approach toward him. Her faith was honored. One wonders how many of us today would be so bold as to come forward and identify with Jesus in the face of known public rejection of our approaching him.

Regarding the Pharisee's response, how many believing communities are guilty of thinking about sinners and relating to them as the Pharisee did? It is so easy to wall people off subtly from God and give the impression they are beyond God's reach, rather than sincerely trying to bring them into the sphere of God's forgiveness. Jesus is the one who calls the heart to change. We as believers serve and point to him. Any righteousness we possess comes because he has worked in our lives. We have not earned it but received it because of his grace. We are all in the position of the woman at Jesus's feet. We must never forget that truth, so we can show to others the way to his feet.

Luke 8:1–3 highlights three women for special mention who ministered with their resources. In dealing with ministry and resources, we can look at ministry as simply a matter of throwing money at a need. But ministry without heart, even well-financed ministry, is not ministry in God's eyes. The opposite error is to argue that resources do not matter and are best left undiscussed. Money is an important aspect of ministerial stewardship for the believer. All of us should be generous, and if the Old Testament is any guide, those who minister in the temple should be well provided for, so they can concentrate on the task of ministry. One of the reasons Jesus and the Twelve were so effective in their ministry was because disciples like these women stood totally behind their ministries.

LUKE 8:4–21

Original Meaning. As Jesus gathers disciples and gains opposition, the question about how people respond to his message surfaces. As the parable explains, just because Jesus is God's chosen agent does not mean people respond to him automatically. Diversity of response exists, though not because of a variation in his teaching. It is all a matter of the soil, the heart of the hearer.

The imagery draws on standard Palestinian farming practices. Sowing took place from late October to early December. The sower carried a bag of grain, usually slung over his shoulder. He tossed the seed in rows. Jesus specifies four different types of soil on which the seed falls. The seed on the road not only has no chance to become embedded in the ground and draw nutrients from the soil, but it is also trampled upon. The rocky soil, at least in Palestine, is hard to spot, since in the hill country, much topsoil is set thinly over a limestone rock base. Weeds are also plentiful, with some able to grow up to six feet in height. The parable also speaks of a hundredfold yield in a culture that expected a seven to tenfold yield.

Jesus tells the parable without explanation and then calls on his audience to hear what is said in it. The disciples then ask Jesus why he speaks in parables without comments. His answer reveals a twofold role. First, the disciples have the benefit of parabolic instruction because they are receiving the revelation of the mysteries of the kingdom. The concept of mystery (*mystērion*) describes making a divine revelation clear. The disciples receive parables as a revelatory gift of God's grace. Second, to outsiders, the presence of parables is a form of judgment, a revelation concealed that prevents understanding.

The major topic of Jesus's parables is the kingdom of God. The kingdom refers to the manifestation of God's promised rule. In Jesus's ministry, this era has arrived, though in the New Testament it arrives in phases. Jesus prepares for its coming through his ministry and by his work on the cross, which enables the new-covenant promise of forgiveness of sins to be put into place and allows the disciples to begin preaching its offer to all. The sign of the coming of the kingdom is the arrival of the Spirit. But there is more to the kingdom than spiritual blessing, for Jesus will someday exercise authority over the entire earth in the future manifestation of the kingdom.

His preaching has to do with this promised kingdom program, since as Messiah he was and is the king of the kingdom. The parables deal with life in the kingdom both now and in the era to come.

Thus, Jesus explains to his disciples that the seed is the word of God, that is, the revelatory message about the kingdom that goes out into the world as Jesus, the sower, tosses the seed. The focus of the parable is on the soils, not the seed, since the seed gets four different reactions.

Fruit is never a matter of an overnight exercise. It takes nurturing. Thus, Jesus's teaching does not look at the reaction to God's word in a single moment but over a period of time, which may be why the planting analogy is used. Jesus's point deals with how response to the word is a product of a process. Only one soil meets the goal for which the seed was planted, the fourth soil.

This observation raises a question of interpretation that unfortunately often becomes the main focus of this parable: Which soil represents "saved" people? Clearly those represented by the first soil are not saved, while the fourth are clearly among the redeemed. The debate stems from the second and third soils, especially since Luke notes that those pictured by the second soil have faith, at least for a time. I contend that the parable is deliberately ambiguous here. Though the text's portrait is not explicit on this question since it is treating another issue, the literary thrust of the image of the second soil questions its healthy status. The same can be said for the third, where faith is not mentioned.

Verses 16–18 calls people to respond to the light because of the dire consequences of not doing so. Jesus notes that one does not light a lamp to hide it but to make its light available by placing it on a lampstand. The function of light is to make visible that which was previously hidden in darkness. So it will be with Jesus's message. Everything that is hidden will be made known, and all secrets will be brought to light. One must therefore listen with care since we will all be held accountable. There is much at stake, for whoever has, in terms of responding to revelation, will get more. On the other hand, those who do not have because they refuse to respond will lose what they seemed to have, ending up with nothing.

Verses 19–21 also highlights the importance of responding to God's word. Jesus's family wants to see him, but the crowds make it difficult for them to get to him. When Jesus is told they are seeking him, he replies with a proverbial-style remark that indicates where his family can be found. Jesus's family consists of those who hear the word of God and do it.

Application. Many things can get in the way of responding to Jesus. Some people never seem interested. Others are initially drawn to God's word, but as the difficulty of being a Christian in a world that often does not understand devotion to Christ becomes clear, their interest wanes and they drop out of sight. Still others flirt with a Christian walk, but life is either too tempting or too demanding for them to respond in a way that draws them to Jesus. The difference seems to be the condition of the heart. A healthy heart clings to God's word; it beats fast for him and responds to him. A damaged heart has trouble seeing him over the distraction and attraction of other things. To respond to God is not a matter of spiritual cruise control. It takes conscious effort to focus on God and his ways so that we become consistently fruitful.

Fruitfulness takes patience. As we labor to sow the seed of the kingdom, we must remember that different responses are inevitable. We must also be clear to discuss the many pitfalls to fruitfulness. Whether riches, fame, success, desire to be accepted, the pursuit of pleasure or comfort, or fear of letting God have control, the road to fruitfulness is littered with massive potholes that can swallow up any progress toward spiritual vibrancy.

It is easy as adults to think we are only accountable to ourselves, but Jesus warns that such a view is a delusion. All of us are accountable to God, especially for how we respond to his revelation. He has put that revelation on a lampstand, where it is visible. Thus we all need to pay attention to what his truth reveals about where we are and what we are doing.

There is another implication from this section. If Jesus teaches light and we are his representatives today, then we are called both to teach and to reflect light. Some churches, in hopes of not offending their audiences, have stopped discussing sin as a topic. If a pastor is not preaching biblically about what life looks like when one is pursuing righteousness, then we as church members are not being prepared to walk a life of light. To grow, our ways need exposure to the light so that we can better reflect who God wants us to be. The goal of God's shining light is to make us light, so we can shine for him.

LUKE 8:22–25

Original Meaning. The Sea of Galilee is located some seven hundred feet below sea level and has hills surrounding it. The eastern side has a particularly steep set of hills. It is not unusual for a cold wind to shoot through the gaps and collide with warm air over the lake in a weather pattern that any meteorologist would recognize as dangerous.

As Jesus rests, such a weather cycle occurs. Before the disciples have time to react, a whirlwind emerges, and they find themselves at risk in the boat. Waves sweep over the edge and threaten to capsize them. Sensing the danger, the disciples cry out to Jesus of their impending doom. Can he do anything? Jesus turns and rebukes the wind, and immediately there is calm. Then he asks them a crucial question, "Where is your faith?" (v. 25). Do they not trust God to see them and care for their best interest? The dialogue stops here so that the event can be an object of reflection.

Luke goes on to record the disciples' reactions of fear and amazement. They ask a central question: "Who is this? He commands even the winds and the water, and they obey him" (v. 25). The question is crucial because the Old Testament makes it clear who has authority over nature: God does. Although other biblical stories have major figures imploring God or describe God's people experiencing protection from the presence of severe weather, Jesus works directly here. Luke purposefully wants the question of Jesus's identity and uniqueness to be kept before his reader. The disciples are beginning to appreciate just how unique he is.

Application. This passage is a call for a deeper, trusting faith, even amid circumstances beyond our control. There is no telling how often some of the disciples, as former fishermen, had been on the lake in the midst of a storm. Yet it was clear that they were powerless to deal with such forces. Though their faith was weak, they did the right thing in turning to Jesus for help. Only their cry that they were perishing was in error. Had they understood God's care, they would have realized that divine care never takes a break, even when it leads into rough waters. Jesus's call for faith is also a call to reassurance that God is aware of whatever storms we are going through and is watching over us.

The second question in the text deals with further reflection on the identity of Jesus. Those in our world who wish to relegate Jesus to the status of sage or teacher fail to reckon with texts such as this one. The disciples, as they lived with Jesus and saw him work, came to understand that they were not following an ordinary rabbi. Luke has the disciples ask here, "Who is this?" and the rest of his Gospel shows the answer to this question. That answer is a central issue of life: he is the unique Son of God. Here is a Savior with the power to deliver and bring life out of death.

LUKE 8:26–39

Original Meaning. The detailed description of the demoniac shows the destructive power of the demons, for the man has totally withdrawn from society, living unclothed in tombs. We are told how he has been seized many times and bound with ropes, chains, or both. But he shattered them and could not be restrained. In the Roman world, *legion* referred to a company of thousands of soldiers. In other words, Jesus is engaging in a major battle here. He is outnumbered, but not overmatched.

The demons ask to be sent into a herd of pigs rather than into the abyss. This request has produced much speculation, none of which is answered by the text. What the incident involving the pigs does indicate is the real impact of demonic presence and influence—namely, the destruction of life.

Word spreads fast as those tending the pigs flee into the city and country to report what has happened. When many people go out to the area, they see the new character who now inhabits the formerly possessed man. He is seated calmly at the feet of Jesus, restored, clothed, and of sound mind. Jesus has rescued him from life among the tombs and brought him into the real world again. The scene is a picture of new life.

The local people do not care for Jesus's work, however. Luke does not tell us exactly why they ask him to leave other than their fear, but Mark 5:16 makes it clear that Jesus has had a negative economic impact on the region. They do not want to lose more livestock. Their fear has turned into rejection and a desire to have nothing more to do with the presence of divine authority.

The healed man wants to join Jesus's traveling group of disciples, but Jesus has another calling in mind. Someone must be left behind to share what God has done in the area. That is the man's task. He does that and more, preaching and proclaiming what Jesus has done for him. Those whose lives are most radically transformed often end up being the strongest witnesses for Jesus.

Application. Our world plays with spiritual forces rather than taking them seriously. Attraction to the devil and the demonic has recently taken on an avant-garde air. One senses that those who engage in this practice are having fun and trying to be cute. It is a way of expressing rebellion. But there is a serious side to this reality. The exorcism in Luke 8 is but one picture of the dangerous character of such activity. Encounter with demons is not a neutral undertaking.

One must be careful not to overreact, however. Some people see a demon behind every bush, while our culture, being enlightened, often makes the opposite error of dismissing such talk as reflecting a primitive worldview. Both approaches are a victory for the dark side. One never fights against what one does not believe is there. On the other hand, to be preoccupied with the demonic can produce a type of fixation that does not reflect spiritual balance and can deflect taking spiritual accountability. "The devil made me do it" can turn sinners into victims who have no control over whom they decide to ally themselves to. Jesus's power over such forces should deliver us from any tendency to attribute too much to demonic power (Eph 1:15–23).

A significant human quality appears in this text. The people who ask Jesus to leave their region recognize his power, but they are afraid to be too close to him. Many fear divine accountability, preferring to be left on their own and to fend for themselves. Perhaps the biggest tragedy of all is to see God at work and pretend nothing has really happened.

The delivered man gives us a final point of application. This newly healed and transformed man did not need to raise support to find his mission field; he simply needed to start sharing—which, in fact, he did. He could not tell the story of God's work in his life without discussing Jesus.

LUKE 8:40–56

Original Meaning. Jesus finds himself in the midst of a crowd, which has been expectantly waiting for him. Among them stands a synagogue ruler, Jairus—a man in charge of arranging the service and the progress of worship. As Jesus approaches, the leader falls before Jesus and asks him to come to his house where his only daughter, a twelve-year-old, is near death. Jesus starts heading for his house, but along the way another person also needs Jesus. A woman, who has suffered from a flow of blood for twelve years, wants Jesus to heal her. This condition renders her constantly ceremonially unclean, isolating her from Jewish religious life. Getting herself into position, she touches him as he walks by, and immediately she is healed. This is not an act of magic. She simply believes that Jesus possesses great power.

Jesus stops to find out what has just happened. He turns to the vast throng of the pressing crowd and asks, "Who touched me?" He is conscious of the fact that power has proceeded from him. The touch he asks about is not just a physical touch but a touch that pleaded for help and found it. The silent faith of the woman needs exposure.

With great fear, she comes forward, revealing the reasonableness of Jesus's seemingly strange question. She falls before him and relates her story. Jesus commends her, noting that her faith has saved her. There is nothing in Jesus's treatment of her that indicates rebuke. What the woman needs is reassurance and confidence that her actions need not remain secretive. Given the opportunity, she summons up her courage and gives her testimony to her now enhanced faith.

One can only imagine the desperate frustration Jairus feels as this delay, orchestrated by Jesus's question, proceeds. Then things get worse. Someone from Jairus's house appears to tell him it is too late, and that Jesus need not be troubled. His daughter has just passed away. I suspect with this announcement that pain, disappointment, and anger flooded Jairus's soul. But Jesus relates words of comfort to the synagogue ruler, telling him not to fear but to believe. Whereas the woman's faith needed bolstering because it was shy, Jairus's faith needs to be calmed, persistent, and trusting.

When Jesus gets to the house, he allows only the family, Peter, John, and James to enter the room where the corpse is lying. Outside, the mourners have gathered. They are only called after it is clear that death has taken place. Amid community sorrow, Jesus calls on them to stop, for the girl "is not dead but asleep" (v. 52). The agent of God will move to reveal the extent of his power over forces that reveal the mortality of humanity.

The crowd laughs. Surely no one can resuscitate someone from the dead. We often regard the ancients as gullible, but the reaction here shows they can be as empirically based as most moderns. Once inside, Jesus grasps the girl's hand and tells her to get up. The girl sits up, her spirit revived within her. Someone immediately gives her food. Her parents are amazed. The call to faith that Jesus made to Jairus has now received its answer.

The account closes with Jesus's instruction to say nothing about what had happened. To broadcast this healing far and wide will turn him into a wonder-worker, with all the public attention focused on that ministry. Jesus wants the attention elsewhere, on his central teaching, and will have nothing to do with the promotion of actions that place the emphasis in the wrong place. The miracles point to more fundamental realities. Jesus wants to major on the major issues.

Application. It is often the case that what we think God ought to do right now God chooses to act on later, while what we would put off he chooses to handle right away. In a sense the juxtaposition of these two miracles is an exercise in time management, where everything is turned upside down. The critical life-and-death situation must wait for a healing and testimony that could have been done under less urgent circumstances. Part of the faith that Jairus is called to exercise not only needed to believe that God could deal with his recently deceased daughter, but also had to rest in the trauma that the seeming delay had created. Ultimately, trusting in God's care means accepting his timing for events.

The testimony of the previously timid woman is also instructive. It can be frightening to speak up for the Lord sometimes, but this woman found the strength by God's grace to overcome her fears and to tell the story of what Jesus had done for her. A timid faith can become a testifying faith.

The most fundamental lesson in this passage is the combination of characteristics tied to faith. Faith should seize the initiative to act in dependence on God and speak about him, yet sometimes it must be patient. In one sense faith is full speed ahead, while in another it is waiting on the Lord. Our lives require a vibrant faith applied to the affairs of life, but it also requires a patient waiting on the Lord, for the Father does know best.

LUKE 9:1–9

Original Meaning. Jesus intends to get the message of the arrival of kingdom hope spread across the nation of Israel. To accomplish this, he commissions the Twelve to minister for him in the towns and villages of the nation. He sends them out with the same authority that he has exercised, including the power to heal and to exorcise. They are to preach the kingdom and heal the sick. This combination reflects Jesus's ministry of word and deed, linking the proclamation of hope for the promised arrival of God's rule with the demonstration of compassion. The disciples leave on this mission, preaching the good news and healing.

A linkage in this passage should not be missed. In verse 2 the disciples are to "proclaim the kingdom of God," while in verse 6 they are "proclaiming the good news." In other words, the gospel announces the arrival of blessing through Jesus in conjunction with the kingdom of God. The deeds of healing make evident the rule of God. God has the power to deliver humanity from forces hostile to us. In these acts, God's power and concern have been put on public display.

Verses 7–9 continue to ask a basic question in this Gospel, "Who is Jesus?" This time it surfaces in Herod's court. Jesus's healing activity and challenge to walk with God remind many of the prophets of old. But the offer of the kingdom means that more is being offered by his ministry.

Application. Evangelism requires engagement. What is needed are more engagement-oriented ministries, where the church "travels light" and engages the community with service, not just words. Such outreach-intensive ministries are the hardest to produce and sustain because they require a great deal of labor to make them effective. Nonetheless, such ministries have the potential of speaking the gospel more clearly than words alone do. Acts of care reinforce the claim that God cares, putting flesh and blood on the claim.

Herod appears interested in Jesus only as a matter of curiosity. He longs to see him, but only because he has heard so much about him. This is not the best way to approach Jesus. His ministry is not a matter of popular, sociological inquiry, as if he were a figure in *People* magazine. Rather, one should take seriously the claim that he has been sent from God as the Messiah and that he shows us the way to God (9:18–20). Herod pictures a figure who almost tragically trivializes Jesus and his ministry.

LUKE 9:10–17

Original Meaning. This miracle of provision obviously indicates how Jesus meets needs. But there is a second key to the miracle, in that this provision comes through the disciples. The disciples have returned from their mission and report to Jesus on all they have done. That this report is the setting for the miracle is no accident. Luke is indicating the importance Jesus gives to the concept that he will minister through his servants. They will do great things through his enabling power.

The disciples, who always keep the practical questions in front of them, begin to wonder where and how they will feed the crowd of five thousand men. Jesus surprises his disciples by telling them to provide the food. The food accountants in the group take inventory: five loaves and two fish. It is impossible to feed five thousand with this small amount. Procuring sufficient provision for this crowd will be a logistical nightmare, even for twelve men. Surely Jesus should reconsider!

He does. He tells them to group the crowd into units of fifty. Then taking the five loaves and two fish, he invokes the blessing of God. He breaks the bread and hands the food to the disciples to distribute. Through their connection to Jesus, the disciples provide enough food for all present, with twelve baskets left over. No details of how the multiplication of loaves and fish takes place are given. Rather, Luke stresses the provision itself. Jesus has a ministry that can meet our most fundamental needs. Moreover, the disciples can do all things necessary for ministry through the Christ who enables them. In a sense Jesus is preparing to pass the torch of ministry to them. So lessons are present, both for those who receive the provision and those through whom Jesus provides it.

Application. There is no one way to reach people. The ministry of provision takes many forms. But one dynamic is a constant: to be effective, the one who leads in setting out the provision must be Jesus. Whether one ministers through visiting someone in the hospital, providing meals for a family whose members are unable to provide for themselves, or simply being available to listen to someone's emotional trauma, those who seek to provide what Jesus offers bring a picture of God's compassion to those they serve.

There is another note in this event. The simple scene of reclining together in fellowship paints a picture of the community that Jesus seeks to provide. As the food was distributed and the meal provided, there was a sense that Jesus had ministered to all of them, since there was more than enough food provided for all those present. This setting is a statement against privatized religion, where my only concern is what God is doing with me. Jesus teaches us to minister to the multitudes and gather them together as a community.

Jesus later instituted the Lord's Supper to make the same point. The meal of fellowship we enjoy at Jesus's feet means we are all seated at the same table. We should minister with the awareness that the table is his and the food he has provided is his. We all partake of one loaf and one cup, and in that meal we make a joint proclamation of our allegiance to Jesus.

LUKE 9:18–22

Original Meaning. The disciples have been with him and know that he is not a mere teacher of God's word or one of many agents of God; he is the promised deliverer sent by God. The crowd believes that Jesus is a prophet of some kind or the reappearance of John the Baptist. In contrast, Peter confesses Jesus as the Messiah, though this category is short of a full confession of deity. More time with Jesus and more reflection on the significance of his resurrection will produce that deeper understanding of Jesus and his messianic function.

Peter's confession can lead to misunderstanding about what is ahead for Jesus, so Jesus immediately moves to correct that possibility. The disciples anticipate a direct route to glory. He predicts the suffering of the Son of Man in rejection, death, and resurrection. A combination of Old Testament teachings clearly make these associations, including the imagery of the suffering servant in Isaiah 53 and the idea of the suffering of the righteous in the Psalms. Both these themes teach that suffering precedes glory. It is this surprising route to glory that has caused Jesus to call for silence about the earlier confessions of him as Messiah, for the Messiah was seen as a triumphant figure who did not suffer at all. The disciples must have God's true plan explained to them before they can share it with others.

Despite the need for more instruction, Peter's confession is a crucial turning point. In recognizing Jesus as the promised Messiah of God, he sees that Jesus is unique. Such a building block is fundamental to understanding God's plan of redemption and its accomplishment through Jesus. To be a Christian is to understand this unique role of Jesus. There is no one else like him in the plan of God. He is the only foundation that can be laid to build the house of God.

Application. Many contemporary portraits of Jesus fall short of understanding who Jesus is. Some attempt to accept him as a religious teacher, a member of the religious Hall of Fame, but do not see him as unique. This approach to Jesus is popular in our culture since it is a tolerant stance that does not foist his uniqueness on anyone. Our culture's attempt to relativize one of Jesus's fundamental claims is not consistent with regarding him as the great teacher. How can one respect Jesus's religious greatness as a teacher and then reject or relativize his most fundamental claim to be the unique Son of God? One cannot have it both ways. Either Jesus was unique in fulfilling the promise of God, or else his claims were a distortion of truth—hardly a standard for a religious teacher of note.

This passage also makes clear that blessing often requires great cost and pain, and one must be prepared to face the same sort of reaction Jesus faced. Some parts of the world have an inherently better understanding of this part of the walk with Christ than what exists in the West. One of the advantages of being at a seminary with students from around the world is hearing the differing conditions believers must live in as they confess Jesus. It is not unusual to hear about those who lost promotions or jobs or were forced to work on Sunday simply because people found out they were believers. Some faced prison for their beliefs. In some contexts, confessing Jesus literally meant suffering. For those of us who live in a society where sharing Jesus is not outlawed, such testimonies should encourage us to be bold.

LUKE 9:23–27

Original Meaning. Luke 9:23 has an interesting sequence of tenses. All three verbs are imperatives, but the call to "deny [one]self" and "take up [one's] cross" are in Greek aorist tenses, while the call to "follow [Jesus]" is in the present. This means that discipleship involves the fundamental commitment of self-denial and bearing one's cross, while the call to follow Jesus is constant, growing out of those base commitments. Discipleship therefore requires a basic shift of orientation as we align ourselves with God's will through a humble renunciation of our own agenda. To deny ourselves in the context of cross-bearing means that the world may "kill" us for walking outside its paths, but we are ready to do so because God has called us to walk a different way. Verse 24 summarizes the point nicely. If you try to save your life by preserving yourself from the opposition of the world and/or by accommodating yourself to the world, what results is loss of real life.

Jesus's rhetorical question in verse 25 drives the point home. "To gain the whole world" means that all the provision, power, and property the world can provide is available to us. To Jesus, it makes no sense to live this way, for it makes one a loser at real life. Jesus faced a choice between walking on the path God called him to take or accepting the kingdoms of the world by bowing before Satan. Jesus knew, of course, that the choice was not a real one, for Satan could not give him what God could. Thus, Jesus calls on disciples here to follow the example he has already established. To gain the world at the expense of one's soul is a bad investment and a losing proposition.

What will such sacrifice gain? Jesus uses a negative picture to answer the question. Those ashamed or afraid to confess the Son of Man (i.e., Jesus) will face his rejection when he returns with all of heaven's glory. They will get what they have chosen: separation from him. On the other hand, by implication, those who ally themselves to Jesus will experience the kingdom of God.

Jesus concludes his remarks with a note that some present with him will not taste death until they experience the kingdom of God. This remark appears to have two points of reference. First, some of the Twelve will journey with Jesus to the mountain and experience the transfiguration, where they will receive a glimpse or preview of Jesus's coming glory. They will "see" the kingdom of God to come. Second, the reference may well anticipate also the type of blessing that descends on the church at Pentecost, since there the power of the risen Jesus manifests itself in the distribution of the Spirit. Thus, Jesus notes that with the hard road of discipleship comes association with the rich blessing of being a part of God's kingdom.

Application. Denying oneself means different things in different contexts. To a parent, it means not just seeking one's own desires but serving the child in their best interests in terms of the investment of time and energy. To a spouse, it means not just asking what can be done for you but considering how one can be of help to your partner. To a neighbor, it means considering how one can be of service and show concern in the affairs of life. To a colleague at work, it may mean not seeing how you can advance the responsibilities you have to undertake but how you can be of service to them. Most importantly to God, it means seeking his will and spending time before him so that he can lead and guide you in the way you should go. Discipleship means being a learner, a follower. It means that our attention is turned to how we can follow Jesus, not how we can make him follow us.

This means that we are seeking his kingdom, not our own. Materialism and the pursuit of power, independence, and security are probably the biggest obstacles to spiritual advancement. Everything in our culture from commercials to our education pushes us in the direction of advancing our standard of living for more comfort. Bearing a cross may mean leaving behind dreams created for us long ago by a citizenship we have now left behind.

Finally, Jesus saved us for discipleship. There is more to salvation than heaven. He saved us to change us, to make us different in the world than we were before we came to know him. So discipleship is a full-time job, not a weekend hobby. As a lifestyle and commitment, it never takes a holiday. That is why Jesus says we should bear our cross daily.

LUKE 9:28–36

Original Meaning. Jesus opts to go to a mountain to pray and takes Peter, John, and James with him. The mountain's not being named suggests the exact locale is not significant, though Jesus's being in northern Palestine indicates that his central ministry takes place outside of Jerusalem, outside the beaten path.

During his time of prayer, Jesus is transformed into a glorious figure with a brilliance like lightning. His glory recalls the description of Moses on the mountain in Exodus 34:29–34. Jesus is not alone, as he is joined by Moses and Elijah. These two Old Testament witnesses highlight that Jesus represents the realization of Old Testament hope, since the two figures also span both the early and late periods of Old Testament history. Moses and Elijah are discussing Jesus's "departure" (Gk. *exodos*, v. 31). Luke is the only Gospel to note this topic of conversation. The "exodus" alludes to the journey Jesus is taking, with its turning point being his death in Jerusalem.

The disciples are napping but wake up to find the discussion in process. Peter, in his excitement, asks Jesus if three booths should be built—an allusion to the Feast of Tabernacles, which looked forward to the arrival of the end times through recalling God's provision for the nation in the desert. Peter correctly understands that Moses and Elijah represent hope and fulfillment, but he wants three booths in a way that ranks the three figures equally. Luke signals that Peter speaks with ignorance, for he does not know what he is saying.

The presence of the cloud recalls the presence of God in the exodus. The disciples are filled with fear, but need only listen as the voice commends his Son, the chosen one, who must be heard. The description "whom I have chosen" (v. 35b) elaborates on the "whom I love" of the baptism scene at 3:22. The addition of "listen to him" (v. 35c) marks out the disciples' responsibility. They must pay attention to what Jesus is saying, for they have much to learn.

After the endorsement only Jesus is left. The event is so startling that the disciples say nothing about it for some time. They are best silent until they understand it. Some events need reflection before there can be adequate commentary.

Application. In our pluralistic culture, we long for spiritual examples, and like Peter we want as many booths to be built in a row as possible. Our culture desires to assemble a religious hall of honor from as many religious traditions as possible, all in honor of our commitment to religious toleration. But Jesus does not ask for a booth alongside the others. The heavenly voice notes that he transcends all cultures and is called to minister to all humanity as God's chosen servant. Any devaluation of Jesus distorts who he is.

He is not the equal of Moses, Mohammed, or Joseph Smith. These current popular perceptions of Jesus are a major distortion of who he is. He is the glorified and chosen one of God, who one day will manifest himself with all the glory that the mountain scene revealed.

A new heart leads us to sit at Jesus's feet, ready to learn and listen. What is in view here is not the pedantic memorization of religious facts or the ability to indicate where something is in Scripture, but a reflective interaction with Scripture and one's walk with God. This dynamic between God's word and life enables us to interact wisely with the culture and with the people who God brings into our lives.

LUKE 9:37–50

Original Meaning. The disciples still have much to learn from Jesus. Nothing makes this more evident than the failure of nine disciples to heal a demon-possessed boy while Peter, James, and John are on the mountain with a transfigured Jesus, hearing God's voice. Their impotence in working by their own means surfaces vividly here. This is also the first of a series of passages where the disciples need serious correction. As the voice in the cloud said, disciples must listen to Jesus.

Jesus encounters a man who has an only child in desperate straits. He is possessed by an evil spirit that causes convulsions and leaves him bruised. Jesus's reply to the man's request for healing indicates that something is wrong, for he describes the current generation as "unbelieving and perverse" (v. 41). The spirit suddenly casts the boy down, and Jesus issues a command for it to come out. The rebuke works. Not only does the demon depart, but the boy is left unharmed. Jesus's protection is total.

Amid the crowd's marveling, Jesus makes a second prediction of his coming passion, reiterating the coming betrayal of the Son of Man. They do not understand how betrayal can happen to a figure whom they have just confessed as Messiah. The text is vague on who has "hidden" the truth from them (v. 45). Is it God in the context of his plan of salvation? Or is Satan at work? In God's sovereignty, whatever is needed for them to hurdle this lack of understanding is not yet in place, though by the end of the Gospel the blinders will be removed. God certainly is most active in that removal, as the Emmaus scene in 24:13–35 shows.

Two brief incidents close Luke's report on the Galilean ministry. In the first, the disciples are haggling over who has the greatest position in the disciples' Hall of Fame. Jesus knows of their petty dispute, so he takes a child and points out to them the value of receiving such a child (who is culturally viewed as powerless and irrelevant). There are no unimportant people. Second, neither is ministry a copyrighted monopoly. Jesus wants all to serve and encourages all to do so. All who serve the Lord faithfully deserve our support.

Application. Sin is a powerful force in our lives. Satan is a strong adversary, and the opponents of righteousness in the world are formidable. But Jesus is against righteous wimps who think Satan and evil are unbeatable Goliaths. With all the resources available in Christ, there is no reason for sin to prevail, for our humanness to lead to failure, or for demonic forces to remain in control. When we fail spiritually, it is because we have not used what God has made available. To fail to draw on such resources is spiritual neglect, like trying to use a bicycle to go across the country when a jet plane is available.

One of the times we struggle in our Christian walk is when God takes us on a journey using a path marked "unknown." We may feel unprepared and untrained, but God is saying, "Just trust me for the direction I am taking you." He takes us to our destination and wants us to trust him that walking with him does not always mean we understand him. He has his reasons, though it may be that the only result we discover is that we know him better.

By highlighting the value of a child, Jesus raises everyone's stature. If the lowly are to be welcomed in Jesus's name, all are to be welcomed. We are all important to our Lord. If he died for our sin, then he has elevated the potential stature of every person who serves him, since forgiveness and full restoration are grounded in faith in him. To welcome a child is to welcome Jesus, which in turn is to welcome the God who sent them both. When the least is the greatest, all are great and the search for greatness becomes unnecessary.

Finally, a disease that plagues ministry is the belief that we are indispensable, that only we can perform it. But ministry is not a franchise with an exclusive license. The disciples must learn that in order to blanket the world, many laborers are needed, and Jesus enlists many into the ranks of ministry. Jesus wants his disciples to appreciate the right that others have to minister. No one performs in the church as a lone ranger. The one who is not against us is for us; and we need all the allies we can get.

LUKE 9:51–62

Original Meaning. This section opens with the remark that Jesus sets his face to go to Jerusalem. The journey is not a straight-line trip, however, for in 10:38–42 Jesus is in Bethany near Jerusalem, in the south, while later he is traveling between Samaria and Galilee, in the north. Luke describes a journey of destiny, which has as its destination Israel's capital. So Jerusalem is a city of fate and destiny, where God's plan and the rejection of the prophet are realized. Luke highlights these themes through the journey motif in a way the other Gospels do not.

The journey starts with Jesus's expanding his ministry into Samaritan territory. To Jews, this ethnic group was comprised of traitors and considered a collection of half-breeds. The Samaritans intermarried with the pagan nations and were thus seen as unfaithful to the nation of Israel. The fact that Jesus reaches out to them indicates his desire to broaden his ministry. But he meets rejection there.

The disciples are not pleased with the lack of response in Samaria and ask Jesus if fiery judgment should be called down from heaven. Surely to reject the coming of God deserves instant eradication and vengeance. But Jesus rebukes them.

In a series of three encounters, Jesus shows the high priority he places on discipleship. The central term in this section is "follow." The first exchange begins with a confident statement by a man that he will follow Jesus wherever he goes (v. 57). This remark requires reflection, so Jesus warns the man precisely what that will require. It requires viewing this journey with total dedication, especially since the Son of Man will not have a home (v. 58). Rejection will be a given, and finding a home may be difficult. Jesus is preparing his prospective follower for those times that lie ahead.

In the second case, a prospective follower wishes to bury his father before joining the group (v. 59). But taking care of funeral rites for a family member is a lower priority. Instead, this man must go and proclaim the gospel (v. 60). More important than caring for the dead is preaching the offer of life. Disciples must move forward to share that need, not memorialize what is past.

A similar request surfaces in the third encounter (vv. 61–62). Again Jesus issues what on the surface seems a harsh warning: those who look back are not fit for the kingdom. The picture of looking back while plowing is apt, since in Palestine the terrain is rugged. To look back while plowing was asking to make mistakes in preparing the field. The task required a focused eye on what lay ahead. So discipleship demands attention to the rough road before us. To look back risks being knocked off course.

Application. The disciples respond to the Samaritans with natural instinct, in effect saying, "Let's wipe those foolish people off of the face of the earth." When I think of this text and Jesus's rebuke, I consider how angry many Christians appear at the world as they address it. It is not unusual today to see an angry Christian face on television, expressing some form of condemnation on our society at large. Truth, justice, and the divine way are lifted up as a banner, and those who walk differently are left to hear only words of judgment. Some have even resorted to brute force or violence to try and stop sin. Is that our only option?

There will come a time when judgment is called for, when God's righteous anger will be shown to hard hearts, but in the current era the call of the church is to love and continue to intercede for those who reject the gospel. That does not mean that confrontation is excluded, but there is a way to confront that also holds out the invitation that forgiveness is obtainable with a change of heart. As with Saul, the keeper of the cloaks at Stephen's execution, a little forgiveness may sow a seed that the Lord can reap.

What kind of servant does Jesus desire? What type of service does he expect? Several analogies surface. In the military, as the soldier trains for service, he or she is often required to leave home for a long time. Whether in boot camp or on call somewhere in the world, there is no time to stop and bury the dead or have contact with the family. Like a commitment to serve one's nation, discipleship is a call to serve God. Personal agendas end up suspended in the face of national realities. Jesus says the call of discipleship is like that.

Discipleship has an urgency to it that should have first place. And once we go, we should not look back. God does not issue his call for a season but for a lifetime. Service for the kingdom begins at the moment we receive Jesus and continues until the Father calls us home. What does this look like? In detail, it is different for each person. Some are called to serve where they grew up; others are called to journey thousands of miles away. Some live in hardship and lose their life for the faith, like Peter who died for his faith, while others live a long life, like John who apparently died of old age. What is the same for all is the call that discipleship should have priority over everything else.

LUKE 10:1–24

Original Meaning. Jesus sends out another mission, this time involving seventy-two. Jesus sends them out in pairs. What they do is only a start, since they are to pray for more workers for the harvest. The fact that these workers emerge as a result of intercession stresses that God is the sovereign source of such blessing. He is Lord of the harvest, he leads the mission, and he is responsible for "sending out" workers into the field (v. 3). Missions is not a matter of marketing but of the Lord's directing his people to share faithfully the grace they have experienced.

Such ministry is not easy, for the workers are "like lambs among wolves" (v. 3). There is danger and hostile rejection on all sides. Despite the danger, the disciples must go forth to perform their calling. Such danger requires the workers to travel light. They must not be concerned with the normal affairs of life as other people are; ministry is their priority. They are also to rest in the knowledge that God will provide for them. Their main responsibility is to heal the sick and declare the arrival of God's kingdom. The mention of God's kingdom is central, because these disciples reflect the approach of the new era Jesus brings. God's ruling power in deliverance is coming.

To announce the kingdom is not to say that everything associated with Jesus's authority is now manifest, for he also taught that there are things he will do when he returns. But the rule of God through Jesus has begun. The power to deliver from Satan's power has started to work itself out in history and among humanity. The deeds of ministry support that claim by showing that evil forces and the presence of death cannot resist Jesus's authority.

If the disciples are rejected, then they must shake the dust from their feet and move on. This act declares a separation between God and the rejecting city, exposing their accountability to him for their decision. To reject such a gracious invitation is dangerous. Even Tyre and Sidon, two gentile cities with reputations for evil, will come out better in the judgment than the Galilean cities of Chorazin, Bethsaida, and Capernaum. The risk of rejection is eternal.

What is not often appreciated is the unbreakable link Jesus places between himself and his messengers. They are commissioned in such a way that they represent him. For people to hear them is to hear Jesus; for people to reject them is to reject Jesus.

The mission is a success, since the disciples return filled with excitement at the power they possess. In Jesus's name, even demons have submitted to them! Such power was exciting to contemplate. Yet such power is not the true ground for their rejoicing. That is, the submission of evil spirits to them is nothing compared to the fact that they are registered among the saved in heaven. Here is the real cause for joy. In fact, it is cause for continuous joy. True and eternal life with the everlasting God is the essence of blessing.

To underscore the point Jesus intercedes with a note of praise to God. God's sovereignty sends such blessings to "little children" rather than to the wise and learned (v. 21). Those of simple faith, not those who rest in their own wisdom, have come to see the blessing of God. He honors those who in simplicity rely on him.

But there is another fundamental link that holds the chain together. There is a chain of revelation that extends from God through the Son to those who respond and bear the Son's message. That is why this mission was so important and why knowing him is so crucial.

There is a blessing of divine approval in sharing in the task of the Son. So Jesus concludes with a beatitude for those who see what the seventy-two have seen. King and prophets longed to experience what they are experiencing, but they did not get this special honor. As great as the eras of Moses, David, and Isaiah were, they are nothing compared to those who have seen the Messiah.

Application. Mission must still be built through dependence on God. Such dependence starts with prayer and ends with a sense of joy in being a part of such a grand, long-standing mission. Through prayer, wise effort, and the strength to face rejection, each generation looks to God's direction to supply workers to the tasks of evangelism and mission. As rich as the history of the faith is, what is preached is what makes the task so precious. The call to share in God's blessing is the greatest vocation one can possess. Every believing community needs to highlight and teach its people to join in the task. Some will go great distances; others will share with friends and neighbors. But all are called to do something. Jesus did not leave the ministry only to the Twelve. Neither today are pastors or missionaries the only ones called to share God's blessings with others.

There should be no doubt that eternal life and death are the issue when it comes to Jesus. Our era has made it easy to pass off religious opinion as if we were choosing flavors at an ice-cream store. God is not so cold as to allow such important matters to be left to human whim. In offering his Son, he has put the true life to death, so that men and women can experience life. Strange as it may seem, the world often accuses God of narrowness for opening the way so wide through his Son. What seems as a narrow way in Jesus is in fact a door that opens up to a vast field of blessing.

The gospel, so simple in this basic element of turning to God for forgiveness in Christ, is often too hard for many to comprehend, much less accept. Yet it is this very simplicity that caused Jesus to compare those who see and embrace it to little children. The ways of God are not to be figured out when it comes to the gospel. For what Jesus offers are things that prophets and kings longed to experience. Those who know Jesus reside in a palace whose walls will never become a museum.

LUKE 10:25–37

Original Meaning. The incident begins innocently enough. Knowing that the Old Testament alludes to the eternal inheritance one can possess, an expert in Jewish tradition asks Jesus what he must do to inherit eternal life. What must he do to share in the resurrection of the righteous? When future blessing comes, how can he know he will receive it?

Jesus responds with a question of his own. He turns to the law, asking the lawyer what he sees it saying. The scribe replies with a part of the *Shema* from Deuteronomy 6:5, that portion of the law that a Jew recited daily and that calls on the nation to love God fully. He also cites the portion of Leviticus 19:18 that calls for the love of one's neighbor. This combination was known as the "great commandment."

Jesus commends the answer by noting that if the lawyer meets these demands, he will live. Love for God that comes to a person responding as a child to God means that the call of God will be heard. So Jesus rightly says, "Do this and you will live" (v. 28).

Luke tell us that the lawyer wants "to justify himself." So he asks Jesus, "Who is my neighbor?" (v. 29). Does the lawyer seek to limit the scope so as to be able to say he has fulfilled the command? The lawyer's question is really an attempt to create a distinction, arguing that some people are neighbors and others are not, and that one's responsibility is only to love God's people. The suggestion that some people are "non-neighbors" is what Jesus responds to in his story.

Jesus picks a Samaritan as the highlight of the story because such a person is a non-neighbor in the lawyer's eyes. A Samaritan, as a "half-breed" and renegade, would be the last person from whom one could expect compassion. Another cultural detail is important. Jesus picks the treacherous road from Jericho to Jerusalem as the site of the incident. This seventeen-mile journey was well known for its danger. So this man is stripped of his clothing, beaten, and robbed. He is left for dead, cast off at the side of the road.

Two opportunities for aid appear next. But both the priest and the Levite, pious though they may be, pass by on the other side of the road to avoid serving this man in desperate need. Why do they pass by? Perhaps they fear being rendered unclean from touching what looks like a dead corpse, though the oral law allowed for exceptions involving priests where no family was present. But the text makes no mention of any motive, and it is best not to speculate.

Next comes a Samaritan. This is surprising, since one might expect a Jewish layperson to appear here, not this half-breed. But the Samaritan has pity on the wounded traveler. Jesus details in a series of verbs just how active this man is in ministering to his newly discovered needy neighbor: he goes to him, bandages him, pours oil and wine on his wounds, puts him on his donkey, carries him to the inn, and takes care of him, even to the point of leaving enough money behind to make sure the man has two weeks' lodging to recover. In addition, he tells the innkeeper to keep a running tab, so that when he returns he can pay for any cost overruns. Here is a ministry that underwrites the victim's recovery from start to finish.

Jesus then asks a simple question: "Which of the three ... was a neighbor to the man?" (v. 36). The scribe cannot bring himself to identify the man by his race. Jesus tells the man to "go and do likewise" (v. 37). The point is obvious. The lawyer wants to know if he can be a neighbor to a select, elite few. Jesus tells him through the Samaritan's example. Rather than worrying if someone else is a neighbor, Jesus's call is to be a neighbor to those who have need.

Application. One often hears that the task of dealing with pain in the world is so vast that we do not know where to begin or how we can even hope to make a dent in what needs to be done. Such thinking can become an excuse for inaction. If I cannot know where to begin, I will not even start to help, because if I do, I will be overwhelmed. A better attitude is to pitch in where one feels a sense and ability to help.

LUKE 10:38–42

Original Meaning. This short passage is unique to Luke, and its story can be considered from two angles. One involves the perspective of Martha. Martha is performing a worthy task, but she is consumed with what others are doing. Jesus does not criticize her for what she is doing but for being concerned about others' activities.

From the standpoint of Mary emerges the example of someone willing to sit at Jesus's feet and fellowship with him as his disciple. There is something tranquil in what Mary does. Often in the hustle and bustle of life, we need to pause for a moment of reflection before the Lord. Discipleship sometimes requires that tasks be suspended while fellowship is maintained.

Application. Mary's sitting at the feet of Jesus portrays a person willing to learn from him, while Martha's busyness pictures someone serving him. Disciples need to do both. In other words, discipleship is a balanced combination of two things: service and reflection. Mary shows the importance of reflecting on what Jesus teaches. Today that translates into time in Scripture and in the church's instructing of disciples about their role in the world. It may involve moments of silence before God in prayer, listening for his voice. It is a great temptation to serve at the expense of being fed spiritually. That is what Jesus's remark to Martha means. Some activities can wait. There is a time to work and a time to listen.

LUKE 11:1–13

Original Meaning. The prayer opens with an address of the "Father" (v. 2). Disciples are called to childlike trust, not to a shallow, childish intimacy. Though God is a unique and great figure, he is not unapproachable. Jesus's stress on God's proximity and the access believers have with him for his provision and care make his view of God deeply personal in emphasis.

Access that develops close relationship need not destroy respect. So the first address to the Father is the statement that his name be "hallowed" (v. 2), that is, kept holy. God is unique and set apart in character. Whatever awe we give to anyone in a prominent position on earth is nothing compared with the respect owed to God. Thus the opening remark sets a proper tone for our spirit as we begin.

Next is the request for his kingdom to come. We pray that God's just rule be totally manifest on the earth. The people of God know that one day God will reveal himself in power and rule in glory. This request longs for that hope. Life is lived more effectively when one appreciates where history is headed. In the context of eternity, our temporal requests make more sense.

The third remark contains a request for God to provide food for each succeeding day. The expectation and recognition is that God is our provider, down to the food that sustains us each day. If the earth did not provide food, where would our nourishment and sustenance come from? The disciple acknowledges God's care at this basic level.

The disciple also seeks forgiveness of sin but does so recognizing that he or she must give in return what is asked for. Thus, not only is the request made that our sins be forgiven, but that we are ready to forgive others who are indebted to us. It is wrong to ask from God what we are not willing to give to others.

The final request is for spiritual protection. Why should we ask God not to "lead us … into temptation" (v. 4)? The request reflects a depth of spiritual sensitivity, since it understands just how prone to sin we are if we do not seek God's face.

Jesus has told us what to pray, but how should we come to the throne of grace? We should pray with a spirit of dependence and humility, looking for God's gracious provision. Jesus therefore goes on to present a parable that emphasizes that God is approachable, gracious, generous, and ready to hear our requests.

To understand this parable, we must appreciate certain aspects of first-century cultural expectation. Food was not as readily available as it is today. Bread was baked each day to meet daily needs. A visitor was to be welcomed and cared for, regardless of the hour of his arrival. Here, then, we have a dilemma: a late evening guest, but no food. What would the host do?

Jesus poses the dilemma and then asks, "Which of you would have the nerve to go wake up his friend in the middle of the night to ask for bread?" The request for three loaves would meet the need, provided his neighbor still had some leftovers from the day. The answer shows the tension. He replies that he cannot be bothered, since the children are in bed and he is unwilling to risk rousing them!

Jesus then comes to his main point. The neighbor does respond, not because he is a friend but because the petitioner has "shameless audacity" (*anaideia*, v. 8). This Greek term combines two qualities: boldness and shamelessness. This man has nerve to make such a request. In recognition of his boldness, the neighbor honors the request.

Then Jesus gives another illustration. If a child asks for a basic meal—fish or eggs—will the father give him something dangerous instead, like a snake or scorpion? The Father delights in giving the basic spiritual provisions that the disciple needs to negotiate his or her way through life. If one needs strength or insight from God, he will provide it if we but ask.

The dependence expressed in this disciples' prayer should also lead them to trust God fully. We can seek a neighbor's aid in moments of need, or a child might seek help from a parent. Surely the most intimate of relationships, our need for God, works in the context of similar care, where we can rest in the knowledge that he cares for us and hears us.

Application. God is not a cosmic grouch. He loves and cares for us, desiring what is best for us. He shows the extent of his commitment to us in the sacrifice of Jesus. Nothing can separate us from a close connection with him but ourselves and our failure to accept the care, provision, and access that come from his hands. A relationship takes more than words claiming his presence; it must be nurtured through time and effort. That is why prayer is so crucial to the Christian walk.

The pursuit of spiritual discipline is receiving renewed attention today. This is only right. Our world is so hectic that often all we think we have time for is a quick "check in" with the Father above. In fact, however, the more hectic the pace, the more we need him. The application is simple: make time to seek his face.

God is not a buddy. He is both Father and Lord. The petitioner who recognizes his uniqueness appreciates the privilege of entering his presence. He sits enthroned in the heavens above. Thus, humility is fundamental to the ways of discipleship.

God desires prayer that is bold, even shameless, in its approach to him. The reason we can be bold emerges in the more subtle argument of the parable. If a human responds affirmatively to the earthly request of his neighbor, surely a gracious God will respond to our requests about basic spiritual needs. We are to come to the Father, knowing that his arms are open for us. We can be bold because he cares. We can seek his face because he is there, waiting to hear and embrace our spiritual needs.

LUKE 11:14–23

Original Meaning. To understand the significance of Jesus's miraculous work, especially his exorcisms, one must understand 11:14–23. The issue here is Jesus's authority. When he exorcises a demon that is the source of a man's mute condition, the discussion begins about the unusual character of Jesus's ministry. Two approaches emerge. Some assign his work to Beelzebub. This name, probably originally referring to a pagan god, was applied to Satan, designating him as "lord of the flies." Others prefer to sit on the fence and wait for something more from Jesus. Apparently some type of visible sign involving activity in the heavens is in view.

Jesus knows the speculation about him and addresses it. He rejects the connection to Satan on a simple premise. If Satan's goal is to destroy and Jesus is reversing the effects of destruction by healing, then how can one tie Jesus's work to the archdemon? That would mean a house divided and a kingdom ready to fall. Satan's kingdom cannot stand if Jesus is driving out the demons by this power.

Jesus adds one more point to his assessment—namely, that others are also driving out demons. The meaning of this point is disputed. Is Jesus pointing to all Jewish exorcists here, asking how they manage to do their work? This meaning seems unlikely. More likely, the allusion is to Jesus's disciples, who are also Jewish but who do their work through Jesus's commission. His point is that there is more than one figure in the movement that shows this authority. Divine endorsement extends to those he has commissioned.

Jesus outlines two possibilities for explaining what is taking place. Either he works by satanic power or through divine connection. There is no third option, no neutral ground. His use of the phrase "the finger of God" (v. 20)—which occurs in the biblical account of the Exodus (Exod 8:19), another great moment of divine activity—shows that God is directly involved in history through Jesus with the powerful touch of his grace.

The point about God's kingdom coming is also significant. Jesus claims that his miracles are audiovisuals of the presence of God's victorious rule. Jesus's work is a divine painting etched by the finger of God and pointing to the one through whom the forces in heaven manifest themselves on earth. He is exhibiting his authority over Satan, establishing the earth as a place where righteousness can and does triumph over destruction. Redemption comes through him. All that remains is for people to choose for him.

Jesus then summarizes his main point with a parable. A strong man occupies a house and guards his possessions. When a stronger one comes, the armor of the original man is stripped away, and the spoils are divided among the victors. Jesus claims his miracle portrays such a victory. He has superior strength over Satan. That also implies that Jesus does not work with Satan but against him. There are only two sides, and the choice of allies in this cosmic battle is crucial.

Application. This text has significant applications concerning the nature of the kingdom of God and the meaning of Jesus's victory. Christ's rule is designed to establish the presence of righteousness on the earth through the formation of a people who reflect his character before others. Though his kingdom will be powerfully visible one day when he returns, Jesus has gathered around himself a community of redeemed people who demonstrate the transformation and real life that his victory purchased. This new community is to be a people who evidence reconciliation. Early glimpses of what this new type of community is like appear in Acts as believers shared with each other, even to the extent of raising money to meet needs across racial and geographical lines.

The power Jesus gives includes the enablement to live as reconciled people in a community that displays love and reconciliation in the context of renewed relationship. The victory Jesus describes clears the road of any claim that obstacles exist that cannot be overcome in the church community. If failure occurs, it is not because enablement has not been provided but because we fail to make use of the victory Jesus provides.

The potential exists to live righteously as we walk with and respond to God's Spirit. The Spirit does not come and go, though our tendency to draw from him can waver if we fail to draw on his resources. To share in the kingdom is to share in the benefits that give us new life, not just in heaven but now.

Such theological background means that the fundamental application of this text is to reaffirm and pursue our identity with the stronger one who overran Satan. To decide that Jesus has been sent from God is to decide that "in him is life" (cf. John 1:4). If his coming means the finger of God has come with evidence of his guiding rule, then our call is to follow where he points.

LUKE 11:24–36

Original Meaning. The first remark is about spiritual response (vv. 24–26). If God's grace frees someone from the presence of evil temporarily, or at least offers to do so, and then a refusal to respond comes, a dangerous situation emerges. The "house" is left clean (v. 24), and the door remains open for those forces to return more determined than ever to live there. The end result is then worse than the first. Revelation missed becomes one step closer to being left in evil hands. Refusing to respond to God's grace is not a matter of being neutral but of remaining in destructive hands.

Next comes a short exchange that concludes with a beatitude (vv. 27–28). It was not unusual to honor a mother in that culture by the accomplishments of her sons. But Jesus transforms the remark into another opportunity to declare where real blessing in life resides—in those who hear and obey God's word.

Jesus then turns to history as he issues a warning about the endless pursuit of signs (vv. 29–32). Jesus makes it clear that such a continual quest, especially in light of what has already been done, is sinful. Someone greater than both Jonah and Solomon stands before them, and his teaching offers what they longed to see. In other words, Jesus's miracles and signs point to the more important issue—his teaching. In fact, this queen and the men of Nineveh will stand at the judgment to testify against this generation for what they are missing in Jesus. Their testimony will condemn them. The remark is a warning. To refuse Jesus is to face rejection in judgment and the condemnation of previous generations who understand the unique opportunity that Jesus's preaching provides.

Finally, Jesus uses the image of light to make his point more strongly (vv. 33–34). Light not only has to be lit; it has to be received by the eye. The eye is a lamp in the sense that it is a doorkeeper. What the eye lets into the mind makes up the person. Of course, what is let in reflects where our heart is. Jesus, therefore, calls for people to be full of light. They are to respond to the light of God's word by receiving it. To take in light is to shine from the inside.

Application. The application of Jesus's claim to reveal light and of his call to be careful how we respond to God's presence and revelation is to take seriously the claim that he offers light. In our society, responsibility for truth has been abandoned to the black hole of shifting public perception. The church may never again function in a world where objective truth is seen as a given. The life raft to get to the human heart lost in this sea of relativity is not merely to refight the battle for objective truth but simply to affirm the immense responsibility of living in a universe where one is responsible for one's choices. Our choices come at great risk.

The challenge of the church of our age is to have people see that there is no escape from responsibility for reflecting over ultimate questions. In the future, God will ascertain the fate of every person's decision. The church's role is to set forth its message in the public square and make clear what is at stake.

There is another crucial application here. No religious discussion is a private affair. One's decision made about religion is privately made and considered, but the consequences are decidedly public, since character and morals are often the product of our religious choices. Our culture's commitment to relegate religious discussion to the sidelines of life represents one of the great abdications of intellectual and spiritual well-being in the history of humanity. To pursue every other avenue of life with diligence and energy while ignoring the soul is to produce people whose lives may be full of activity but whose souls are empty shells, houses waiting to be filled with something. Hollow people often live shallow lives. If any discussion should fill the public square, it is that of religion. The possibility of the existence of light means that discussion about where it can be found should proceed with vigor for everyone.

LUKE 11:37–54

Original Meaning. The setting of this section is a meal. The catalyst is Jesus's failure to wash his hands in preparation for eating. Jesus knows what his host is thinking, so he addresses all of the Pharisees about the question. He begins with a rebuke.

The general complaint is that the Pharisees clean the outside of the cup and dish, but inside there is the filth of extortion and greed. Did not God create both the inside and the outside? God is concerned with both spheres. In fact, the inside is especially of concern to him. This figure means that a person should give energy to the care of the heart, like a person who might perform the venerated act of offering alms to the poor. That is, one should be sensitive both to God and to others. Alms was an honorable religious act, so this attention to the inner life is honorable as well. In doing so, the inner life will be clean.

Jesus then treats tithing, even of the smallest herbs, as the Old Testament calls for, while ignoring justice and love. They should be sensitive both to tithing and to their character.

There also is the issue of pride. They love the front seats in the synagogue and the special greetings they receive on the road. Jesus describes them as being like an unmarked grave over which people walk without knowing, conductors of spiritual uncleanness, because they do not model real spirituality.

Someone at the table comes to the Pharisees' defense. A scribe notes that if Jesus insists on condemning the Pharisees, he must include the scribes also. So Jesus issues more rebukes, this time with the scribes in view. The first rebuke is about showing lack of compassion to others as the burdens of the rules are pursued. They call on others to bear the weight of tradition on their back, but they do nothing to help them carry the load. In effect, Jesus calls on them to be more considerate and compassionate.

The condemnation becomes even stronger when a historical tie to the past is made with a twist. They are like their ancestors, who not only built the tombs but helped to put the prophets there by denying their message! They killed the prophets, and the scribes honor the tombs they created.

In the strongest remark of all, Jesus condemns the scribes for being the exact opposite of what they think. They believe they possess the key to knowledge. But in fact they are an obstacle to truth. There can be no greater rebuke for teachers of religion.

These woes are a devastating condemnation of pride and self-assurance in the pursuit of piety. The reaction is immediate. The scribes and Pharisees begin to "lie in wait" for Jesus, or, as the NIV says, "besiege him" (v. 53). The woes Jesus pronounces do not lead to repentance but to hardness of heart.

Application. Legalism can manifest itself in various ways. Frequently legalists refuse to speak directly to those whose behavior bothers them. The Pharisees disagree here about what Jesus is doing, but they discuss it only privately, in their own inner circle.

Legalists major in minors and ignore the major relational requirements God asks of his followers. Jesus is not decrying tithing or watching out for one's spiritual walk. What he does condemn is a pretense of being so self-focused on spiritual matters that one ignores the condition of the heart and fails to notice those who are truly hurting.

The close association of pride with legalism is no accident. Pride tends to turn us into bad listeners and causes us to slip into a legalistic, arrogant, judgmental mind-set, which is death to genuine spirituality.

A legalist is often quick to criticize but slow to help. In making sure others know their spiritual responsibilities, they often are the last in line to encourage others in the pursuit of those goals. The absence of relational commitment is a symptom of a deeper problem. If there was one thing Jesus's ministry shows us, it is a commitment to people.

In contrast to the characteristics of legalism, Jesus is a model of how to pursue righteousness. He encourages those who feel out of touch with God so that they can know him. Though he points out sin, he also points the way to righteousness, simply noting the consequences of a failure to respond. In our battle with our culture, which often thinks little of spiritual discipline, honesty, integrity, and justice, the church can learn from Jesus's model of forthright but gentle persuasion.

Finally, Jesus's pronouncement of woes means that everyone, including those who claim an association with God, are accountable for their choices. Our culture loves to claim the right to choose. One must also embrace the responsibility that comes with the choice. So choose wisely.

LUKE 12:1–12

Original Meaning. Jesus turns his attention to the disciples in 12:1–12, as they deal with the huge crowds pressing around them. Their press raises an issue that becomes a temptation to the disciples: hypocrisy. An effort to maintain popularity easily leads to hypocrisy. Jesus calls them to be on guard against "the yeast of the Pharisees." Yeast refers to their teaching and its hypocrisy, which can permeate in a community like the substance people put in bread.

To enhance the warning, Jesus emphasizes that everything will be disclosed before God when our lives are evaluated. Nothing will be concealed. On that coming day, disciples will have their stewardship of God's gifts and opportunities examined, and they will be rewarded accordingly, though forgiveness and eternal life come only through drawing on the forgiveness Christ provides. Those who do not know the Lord will have their actions condemned.

Jesus discusses the issue of whom to fear because the world's rejection for identifying with him is a real prospect—so real that some may back off from coming to him. But to fear the multitude and to turn away from God is to make the wrong choice. In fearing God, we have nothing to fear from anyone else, for we are worth more than the sparrows.

This message about fearing God is reinforced in remarks about Jesus as the Son of Man (vv. 8–9). This juxtaposition of fearing God with the Son of Man again shows the close connection between Christ's ministry and God's call. Virtually every passage in this Jerusalem journey section highlights the importance and consequences of choosing to believe in Jesus.

Verse 10 is one of the most enigmatic in Luke. The sin of denying the Son of Man can be forgiven, but to the person who blasphemes the Spirit there will be no forgiveness. Speaking a word against the Son of Man refers to a specific act of rejection, while rejecting the testimony of the Spirit refers to a permanent rejection of that message of salvation. This decision about the testimony the Spirit gives is the key issue for Jesus.

This connection is reinforced in verses 11–12. There is nothing to fear in persecution because the Holy Spirit will teach his people what to say before the synagogues, rulers, and authorities. Their message will be his message. If they reject them, they reject Jesus, but he will serve as the source of strength and wisdom for his people. Thus, by fearing God, disciples have nothing to fear from people.

Application. As Christians we often must face people who do not understand us, who reject the principles we live for, or who may even be hostile to our beliefs about God. Sometimes in having the opportunity to share him we must risk the possibility of being rejected. Our values may cause us to do things or not do things that produce a negative response to us. All of this can come with the territory of identifying with Jesus.

In a sense, Jesus does not call for action here but for an attitude. To fear him means to respect his presence, to trust in his care, and not to worry about how others react to us. It means not going along with popular opinion, for the majority may not always be right. With this recognition, we can respond with inner strength and dependence to situations that emerge where our faith is challenged.

Another application relates to the serious nature of the choice of rejecting the testimony of the Spirit about Jesus. The unforgivable sin is rejecting what God has offered in the forgiveness present in Jesus. There can be no "it makes no difference" approach to Jesus's question. Our culture may say there are many routes to God, but Jesus does not provide that option.

The "no escape" conclusion of this passage indicates just how seriously Jesus took the prospect of final judgment. Texts like Revelation 20:10–15 and 22:15 suggest that the unrighteous continue to exist outside the presence of God. In what are surely the most tragic texts of the Bible, these passages teach that to reject God and to come into judgment is one of the most despairing experiences possible. For after the judgment, a person knows for certain that there is a God and that they have forever missed the chance to know him. That is why the teaching about judgment is so important, and that is why it is so crucial to share Jesus with those who need to know him.

LUKE 12:13–21

Original Meaning. Jesus is being treated like a rabbi here, since he is asked to become an arbiter on this family squabble—except that the request is not really to arbitrate but to be an advocate for the petitioner against his brother. He refuses to be drawn into choosing sides, preferring instead to raise a question about greed, which can cut through relationships, especially family relationships, like a knife.

The main issue in this parable is not wealth. Rather, it is one's attitude to obtaining wealth. The man in the story did not acquire his harvest immorally; he simply had a good year. His error comes in how he views what has become his. Five times in verses 17–19 he speaks of what "I" will do, as if he owns it all. He speaks about "my" crops, "my" barns, "my" surplus grain, and speaks to himself ("I'll say to myself . . ."). His goal is to ease back and withdraw from life. He will "eat, drink and be merry" (v. 19). He feels no concern or responsibility for anyone else. The essence of greed is keeping what resources God brings your way for yourself.

This is the ultimate "you can't take it with you" parable. Jesus calls the man a "fool" (v. 20), an Old Testament term that describes someone who either acts without God or acts without wisdom in a self-destructive way. His approach to his stumbling upon wealth is to become self-centered and therefore self-destructive.

Jesus concludes that this is how it will be for any who pile up treasures for themselves but are not rich toward God. Richness toward God means responding to life and blessing in a way that he desires, in a way that honors him—through service and compassion. The conclusion condemns greed as the attitude that piles up stuff simply for one's own use.

Application. This text calls for self-examination. How do I feel about what God has given to me? Is it mine? Am I a steward of what has come my way? Both the wise use of resources and the absence of greed are addressed here, since one attitude is the cause of the other.

A test of our hearts is in how we give. Are we generous or are we hoarders? This is a test that we have to engage in privately before the Lord. No one can tell someone else exactly how to answer such questions, for there is no magic percentage that is to be reached. The Old Testament standard of a tithe (10 percent) might be too low for what we are capable of doing.

LUKE 12:22–34

Original Meaning. Jesus begins with a call not to worry. The Greek present imperative used here implies that we should be constantly free of anxiety. The first example Jesus gives involves an unclean creature, ravens. This choice is significant, since ravens were among the lower rank of living creatures. God is aware of their needs. They do not plant or store grain, yet God feeds them. If he cares for them, how much more will he care for us!

From this illustration Jesus takes up some practical considerations about anxiety. What does worry contribute? Does it add any length to one's life? Anxiety, though perhaps a natural response to sensing events that are beyond our control, is one such profitless activity.

Examine beautiful flowers like the lilies. There is no labor in their existence; they simply do what they are created to do. Even the grass, which lives for a short period and then is cast into fire, is cared for and clothed by God. If God cares for them, he will care for human beings.

Worry casts doubt on God's care. So Jesus addresses them as people "of little faith" (v. 28). The essence of trust is to recognize that God will take care of what is in his hands. The Father knows what his disciples need. Jesus's shift to mentioning the Father adds an image of family and concern to his remarks. Every good father watches over his children.

Jesus calls for a single issue to be a disciple's major concern: God's kingdom. God will care for the rest. To "seek [God's] kingdom" means to live as his representatives (v. 31). We must represent him and reflect his righteousness in a world unconcerned about knowing God. That is the constant call of the disciple, as the Greek present imperative "seek" indicates.

There is nothing to fear in this task, since God desires to give this kingdom to his sheep. Sheep can be among the more skittish of creatures and tend to be frightened easily. Jesus casts God as a caring great shepherd who cares for his own and gives them what they need in order to do what he has called them to do.

If we do not need to worry about the provisions of life, then we can be generous with what God has given us. Such generosity God honors; he gives us "treasure in heaven" (v. 33). Such treasure involves God's commendation and reward for service that pleases him.

How we use our resources communicates our values. If we invest in earthly possessions, we show we care about things. If we invest and care for people, we radiate our love for others. God's kingdom is about people.

A life attached to possessions becomes a stumbling block, because it leads to high anxiety. Jesus indicates that one way in which disciples can be different in their testimony is to reflect that people and needs have priority over possessions and ownership. The ethics of an absence of anxiety is also an ethics that is aimed at relating to people through generosity, because we are confident of God's care.

Application. We all want to feel secure. Yet we are fooling ourselves if we think we are in control of our lives. Doctor's offices and hospitals are filled with people who are emotional wrecks because they have abruptly come to realize that they are not in control.

The first step in wisdom is to know better. We can attempt to create a safe environment for our lives. We can try to create a world where we control others. We can seek the accolades of peers to give ourselves worth. We can withdraw so that we are safe in our own little world. Each of these attempts is really an evasion of the need to seek identity in the one source who can give it, the tender care of God.

A major obstacle to pursuing God's call is to think that we need to get security in other areas of our lives before we can be freed up to serve as he wishes. In the process we short-circuit what God calls us to do and get distracted with personal security issues. The spiritual life as Jesus sees it is not a life of comfort but of risk, exposure, weakness, and vulnerability. The call of God will never take us to a place where the grace of God cannot sustain us.

Are we really called to sell all our possessions? Jesus's point is that we must give up viewing what we call ours, as if it were a private possession to be hoarded. "My resources are not mine, but yours. Show me how to use them for your glory, O God." That is the prayer of a disciple who seeks to apply what Jesus teaches here. Beyond the prayer are the moments of truth, when we take our resources and give them up or put them to use so that others can benefit from their use.

LUKE 12:35–48

Original Meaning. Disciples should prepare for the Lord's return by living in a way that honors him when he comes to assess our walk with him. An ancient way of calling for that preparation was to "gird up your loins" (NIV "be dressed ready for service," v. 35). The Greek perfect imperative implies a constant state of readiness, a readiness that once taken up is to remain in place. They must be on the constant watch, even during the darkness of the night. Disciples should be like servants not knowing exactly when the master will come home from a wedding. They should be ready to open the door when he arrives.

As always, Jesus's images carry a twist. Here the twist is that the master, on finding the house well cared for, turns around and serves the servants. In other words, blessing awaits those whom the master finds ready and waiting at his return, even if he comes at a time when others might not be ready.

Jesus then uses the picture of the thief to illustrate his point. The reality of the return in the face of the uncertainty of its timing demands vigilance. Accountability to the Lord is a major New Testament theme. Grace does not end accountability. Rather, the goal of grace is to create a people who are faithful and zealous in their service for God. God cares what we do with his gifts, and at Christ's return he will honor those who are faithful and discipline those who are not.

Peter understands the drift of Jesus's remarks and asks if the Lord is only speaking to the leaders like the Twelve or to everyone. Jesus tells of a servant who is responsible for giving the other servants their allowance of food while the master is away on business. When he returns, blessing comes to that servant who does his job well; he will be promoted to serve in a higher capacity.

What if the servant decides that the master will be gone for a long time? Instead of caring for the servants, he does the opposite. What will the master do when he returns unexpectedly? He will punish that servant.

To understand how serious this possibility is, we must look at verses 46–48 and compare the three punishments. The servant who is outright disobedient, doing the opposite of what is commanded, will be dismembered, and the Lord will assign him a place with unbelievers. Someone who knows what his master wants and who simply fails to obey that command will receive many blows. The picture here is of a disciplinary judgment. But for the servant who fails to obey because he does not know what he must obey, he will be beaten with a few blows. Jesus pictures an accountability here that varies depending on what one does and what one knows.

Jesus closes by saying that to whom much is given much is demanded, and those entrusted with much will be asked much. In the Western church, where resources of instruction and communication are readily available, most of us have access to much, making us responsible for much.

Application. One major application is to live in such a way as to honor the Lord and be ready for his return, which can come at any moment. When that happens, our Lord will assess how we have walked with him, especially in the community of faith. The issue most in view as a basis of his evaluation is how we serve others in the community. Do we build up or destroy the people of God?

Often when believers beat one another up, as is alluded to in this parable, it is over disputes about what we believe. Most of us are aware of vehement disagreements on topics such as the Lord's return, the permanence of spiritual gifts, lordship salvation versus an emphasis on grace, modes of baptism, Calvinism versus Arminianism, and so on.

The central truths of the faith are things about which we must have firm convictions. These truths can be hard to identify amid the many areas of theology and interpretation. If we may hazard a guess at the key themes, they are the authority of all

Scripture, the Trinity, the deity and humanity of Christ, the unique work of Christ, the need for faith in Jesus to save from sin, the effective presence of the Spirit as the transforming agent of God in the believer's life, the blessings of grace for the believer, the importance of the church as God's community, the practice of baptism and the Lord's Supper, the reality of the Lord's return, the reality of judgment and eternal punishment for those who do not know God, the centrality of prayer and worship for the health of the believer, the importance of ethical integrity, and the call to evangelism. These are themes we must hold to as central.

We will be held accountable to the Lord at his return. This concept is frightening only if we have something to fear because we are unfaithful. With his return comes the hope of casting off our sinful humanity for a glorified and purified existence forever with God. These texts exhort us to live like what we shall become. If we live righteously, we will have nothing to fear when the Lord returns.

Not everything in this passage warns of judgment. Is there a more amazing promise in Scripture than that the Master will serve the faithful at the table? Thus, at the heart of the Lord's return is a reminder of where our relationship with God should take us—namely, to make us more like him. In all the speculation about when and how he might come, we should perhaps pay more attention to who we will be when he comes.

LUKE 12:49–13:9

Original Meaning. Jesus's "I have come" statements, like this one in verse 49, are designed to summarize his ministry. The image of fire can refer to judgment or to the Spirit. Jesus's message reveals the judging and purging work that his ministry represents: to provide the way for people to make decisions about where they stand and to offer them the opportunity to be healed. But before he can exercise such judgment and authority, he must undergo his own baptism, so he is limited in what he can do until then. "Baptism" is a reference to his approaching death (v. 50).

Jesus knows that he forces choices, so he does not bring peace "but division" (v. 51). Families will be divided as some opt for him and others choose against him. The choices are real, and people will go different ways. No one should be surprised that in forcing choices, division of opinion will emerge.

But there is guidance for the decision. Jesus calls on the crowd to reflect on their skills of discernment. They can read and anticipate the weather just by looking around. Yet they are unable to discern the nature of current events that surround Jesus. In calling them "hypocrites" (v. 56), Jesus is trying to shock them into reflection, as if to say: "How can you miss all that is going on around you in my ministry?" Their poor judgment leaves them at great risk.

The magistrate is like a sheriff in charge of a debtor's prison. In Luke's context of warning, the remark makes sense as a reference to a debt before God. Jesus is urging us to settle our accounts with God, or else the prospect of judgment remains. The central idea is not that one can get out of hell but that one will be held accountable for every sin one commits.

Luke next turns his attention to issues related to the nation of Israel and its citizens (13:1–9). In the discussion of the two tragedies in verses 1–5, the question emerges whether a worse level of sin causes a person to suffer a special judgment, either in being the victim in a series of events or in being the victim of a natural catastrophe. Jesus responds by changing the import of the question, making it a question about the possibility of eternal punishment.

Jesus deflects the question about the degree of sin because it distracts from the real question, the presence of sin, no matter what its form. Often we compare sinners so that we may excuse ourselves as not being as bad as others. Jesus wants no such escape from responsibility here. So he centers his thoughts on the most visible question. That is why he cites no specifics about sin in this passage.

The call to repent is a fundamental theme in Luke. Jesus has in mind that change of direction that comes from a change of orientation after hearing God's messenger. With repentance comes a change of mind that effects a change of direction, since one's orientation of life is directed in faith to God.

The closing parable discusses the nation, using a variation on a standard figure about Israel—a vineyard or a tree garden (vv. 6–9). The image describes the unfruitful state of the nation of Israel and indicates that the time for the nation to respond is limited. The parable also pictures God's patience. He will give the nation a short time yet before exercising judgment. But the shortness of the time also highlights the importance of making a decision quickly before it is too late. The judgment came on Israel in AD 70, but as Paul indicates in Romans 11:12, 14, 26–27, it will not be a permanent judgment, because God is gracious and will bring the broken branches back into the plant.

Application. This text calls each reader to consider where he or she stands before God. The Jesus of popular culture does not force such choices, but we may not manipulate the biblical Jesus into our own image. The Gospels are clear that many reacted against him because he challenged them in a threatening way with his prophetic call.

Another application of this passage is that it is important to clear the books with God. It is a wise thing to assess one's debt correctly and have it paid it off before the case is closed. To remove accountability to God for sin is to remove one of the realities that make grace so powerful. In trying to exalt God's love by ignoring sin, we remove the most powerful evidence of its presence.

Repentance is not an emotion or a mere mental assent to a proposition. It is a reorientation to a new life. To repent is not merely to regret things we have done or to apologize for them or to recognize a wrong has been committed. To repent is to agree that a change of direction is required, and then to respond accordingly.

God is patient, but there does come a time when it is too late to repent. Often in sharing the gospel we give ourselves a sense that there is much time for people to decide. In a sense that can be true, for God is patient and does delay his judgment. But in a sense it can lull us to sleep. As we share Jesus, we can get complacent. Although ultimately the Spirit causes people to respond to Jesus, if we take a laid-back attitude we will not be as sensitive to opportunities to share as we could be. Note how the caretaker kept trying to fertilize the fig tree. We also should try to keep feeding those who need to hear the gospel with the seed of truth.

LUKE 13:10–17

Original Meaning. Jesus is in a synagogue. Among the people is a woman who has suffered for eighteen years from the presence of a spirit that caused her to be weak and bent over. The mention of the length of her suffering underscores the seriousness of her condition. In this culture, being a woman and suffering from such a malady makes her an outsider on two counts. Jesus notices her, lays hands on her, and she straightens up immediately. Luke loves to note instant healing. This would have been cause for immediate rejoicing except for one fact: it was the Sabbath.

The synagogue leader argues that Jesus has violated laws of working on the Sabbath. It is crucial to see what his work consists of in order to appreciate the complaint. Jewish tradition was particular about Sabbath labor. The rules are specific, though it is not clear precisely which rule Jesus has violated. All he has done is to address the woman and touch her.

Jesus responds sternly, addressing those who agree with the synagogue ruler as "hypocrites" (v. 15). He cites an example of their own practice by raising a question that in Greek expects a positive reply. Do they not lead their donkey or ox to water on the Sabbath? If people show so much compassion to animals on the Sabbath, how much more compassion should a human receive!

Jesus drives the point home. Should not this woman, bound by Satan for eighteen years, be set free on the Sabbath? What more appropriate day for this to happen to a daughter of Abraham, a daughter of promise? What more appropriate day to defeat Satan and release people from his bonds than the day of rest when God is to be contemplated? Here is a day to remember God and celebrate the goodness of his healing grace. The connection of this language to the remarks of 4:16–30 is obvious. Jesus is exercising his ministry of deliverance and release. He is Lord of the Sabbath. Yet Jesus's approach to the issue is the exact opposite of the Jewish leadership's view.

The reaction is instantaneous. The leadership stands humiliated, while the crowd is delighted with what Jesus has done. In the cosmic battle over the woman, a ministry of compassion has emerged. Those who wish to apply the rules improperly stand rebuked. Legalism stands condemned.

Application. The image of salvation as release from Satan's clutches is the major positive picture in this text. Jesus has come to free us from the prison of Satan's grip. He can damage both physically and emotionally, causing us to depend on substances or behaviors that are compulsive and destructive. Whether the challenge is being "bent over" and "brought low" by alcohol, drugs, sex, or some other debilitating situation, Jesus's deliverance is designed to free us up to relate to him in a way that enables us to shed the limitations Satan sometimes chains us with.

The picture of physical deliverance here serves notice that deliverance is possible through Jesus. The establishing of a relationship with God and the access to the power of God's presence in his Spirit empower us with resources to renew our lives. Any time is appropriate for such a move toward restoration. It is what Jesus's ministry—and the church's ministry today—are all about.

Finally, we must be careful not to let our pursuit of religious practices according to our preferred custom outweigh our responsibility to be compassionate. We must not allow the tyranny of comfort in practice or even the tyranny of keeping to some type of predetermined schedule prevent us from being sensitive to others around us.

LUKE 13:18–35

Original Meaning. Jesus now turns to a brief discussion of the kingdom he brings (vv. 18–21). His remarks are important in light of the Jewish expectation that the kingdom would come all at once and with great power. The parable of the mustard seed and the yeast make fundamentally the same point—that the kingdom starts out small but will eventually cover the whole earth. What the Jews expected to come all at once will grow gradually into greatness.

Jesus tells these parables to call for trust. He is building the kingdom, and people should trust God that it will come, even though the movement starts out looking so insignificant. God's plan is advancing; his kingdom will come. Nothing will stop its coming in fullness.

The parable in verses 22–30, though filled with conceptual parallels elsewhere in the Gospels, is unique to Luke. It serves as a warning to Israel. Since the kingdom is coming, people should respond now, before the door closes. Many of those originally invited, descendants of those to whom the original promise came, will miss the blessing if they do not respond. There is nothing more tragic than being close to God's blessing and then missing out.

Someone asks Jesus if only a few are going to be saved. Perhaps he senses that Jesus's rebukes of Israel mean that salvation will not be as automatic or as based on genealogy as some had thought. Jesus's reply makes it clear that this man's suspicion is correct.

The verb "make every effort" (*agōnizomai*, v. 24) speaks of laboring to get in. This implies that there is a specific route by which to enter; that is why Jesus mentions a *narrow* door and sets forth what it is. For individuals, the door shuts at death—if not before, because of the hardness of one's heart.

The banquet image looks at the time after Jesus returns, when those who trust in him are gathered to share in the celebration of salvation. There are no ex post facto opportunities. Entry comes through the means Jesus provides or not at all. External contact with Jesus counts for nothing; what he desires is an inward response from the heart that issues forth in repentance and faith in him.

The end result for those outside is "weeping" and "gnashing of teeth," a sense of pain and frustration at having missed the moment (v. 28). Though their birth made them excellent candidates, they did not respond and have missed the blessing. The effect of Jesus's remarks has altered the theoretical nature of the original question to a practical level. The question, "Will the saved be few?" has become, "Will the saved be you?"

In verses 31–35 Jesus warns the nation by mentioning the city that represents her, Jerusalem. Verse 31 opens with the Pharisees warning Jesus that Herod is seeking to kill him. While their statement looks like one of concern, it is really expedient. They have been consistently portrayed as doubting and challenging Jesus, so to have them now looking out for his welfare is totally out of character.

Jesus replies by stating that he will complete his mission. Nothing will stop him. So they are to tell the one who wants to destroy Jesus that he will continue to exorcise demons, heal people, and then complete his task. He must go this way, since a prophet cannot perish outside of Jerusalem. Death is not to be avoided but is in fact the pivot point in his ministry. Jesus's presentation of himself as a prophet underscores his function as the revealer of God's will. Just as God at the transfiguration told the disciples to "listen to [Jesus]" (9:35), here Jesus asserts his prophetic mission to Israel. In rejecting him they are rejecting the call of God through him.

Then comes Jesus's lament (vv. 34–35). Jesus's pain comes from realizing the privilege of Jerusalem's position as representative of the nation in contrast to the history of her response in killing and stoning the prophets. Jesus speaks in the first person for God, as is typical of a prophet, and explains how he has longed to care for and protect Jerusalem as a hen cares for her chicks. Is there a more tender image than this? However, the chicks did not want to stay in the nest, an allusion perhaps to the nations' lack of desire to be gathered again before him in the protective care of his salvation.

One of the tragedies of rejecting God's will is that people get what they ask for, including the dire consequences. The nation and its citizens face abandonment to their own weak devices. Until Jesus garners acceptance, the nation is at risk. They must recognize Jesus as the figure the Baptist announced and the one whom God has been attesting to through his works. The word "until" (v. 35) suggests that though this judgment is serious, it is not forever. If the nation of Israel turns, God will again take them under his wings.

Application. The program of God's kingdom gives us hope. It offers rest to those who share in it. Describing the kingdom this way should result in a greater trust of God's direction. What he presents is a community that offers protection until its task is done. When the time comes, God will reveal the commitment he has to the fullness of the kingdom's promise and to its people as he exercises his authority over all the earth through the extension of its presence in the age to come. Those who know Jesus are a part of its history, heritage, and growth.

In the meantime, the kingdom is present in a more hidden form today. It does not manifest the fullness of power that it will possess one day, nor is its call to any one nation, party, or human institution. Rather, the kingdom is found wherever God's people are found. To manifest the kingdom's presence is not to build buildings or pass laws but to honor God with a life that is full of the transforming work of his Spirit.

Verses 22–30 issue a warning. People should be sure they have responded to the one who brings in the kingdom. It is easy to think we automatically qualify—by birth, by cultural connection, or by church membership. But to Jesus, a relationship with God requires personal appropriation on the path Jesus has set (John 1:12).

This principle is fundamental in a culture that argues that there are many ways to God, as if the road to heaven is a complex interstate highway system that offers dozens of routes and interchanges. Jesus uses a more focused image, the narrow and soon-to-be-shut door.

Though in our hearts we may want God to take in everyone, that is not what Scripture teaches. He wants people to consciously enter into relationship with him, aware of their sins and shortcomings, their need for God, and the salvation Jesus has achieved for them.

According to verses 31–35, nothing will block God's plan from taking place. Efforts to try to thwart the presence of the truth abound. They range from cries that the Christian faith is outdated to attempts to bully and threaten Christians in Third World countries, where persecution is overt and martyrdom is a real possibility. Yet whatever happens through the social and political processes of the nations, God's ways will not be thwarted.

Finally, Christ's compassion should be noted. His heart is to show mercy to all. Israel's error is painful, and Jesus suffers as he issues his warning. Judgment is not relished, but its reality must still be declared. Here is a heart that is worthy of emulation as we stand amid a hostile world.

LUKE 14:1–24

Original Meaning

A Healing (14:1–6). As Jesus enters the house for the meal, a man suffering from dropsy is there, a condition of retaining bodily fluids. Many see the condition as a result of God's judgment. So Jesus takes the initiative and asks the Pharisees and scribes if it is lawful to heal such a person on the Sabbath. They remain silent. Jesus then takes the man's hand, heals him, and sends him on his way. Luke is trying to show that, even after all these demonstrations of power and compassion, the leaders do not get the message. Despite numerous opportunities, the leadership fails to see what God is doing.

A Discourse on Humility (14:7–14). This passage highlights the importance of genuine humility. Jesus pictures a gathering where many prominent people are invited, such as a wedding feast or some other special feast, and he discusses the fundamental question about how to approach being honored. In the background are the issues of God's relationship to us and of the nature of our standing before him. According to Jesus, you should not seek a seat of honor, for a more distinguished person may arrive who gets your seat. Then the host will ask you to move, and you will have to move to the least important seat. The mention of shame is important because, in that ancient culture, honor and shame were key issues of a person's identity, worth, and character.

If you are a wise person, Jesus says, you will take the least important place, so that when the host comes and sees you in a seat that is not worthy, he will beckon you up to a better place. Then, instead of shame, glory (*doxa*; NIV "honor")—that is, approval and commendation—will result (v. 10). Such honor God will also give in the age to come. God will exalt those who humble themselves. On the other hand, those who exalt themselves will be humbled by God.

Jesus expands the call in verses 12–14 as he calls us to serve those who cannot repay our kindness. Jesus's point is that loving and hosting those who love you and are your friends is not inherently morally commendable. One expects that to be the case. Rather, we should invite "the poor, the crippled, the lame, the blind" (v. 13). The best hospitality is that which is given, not exchanged. Then divine commendation will come. True righteousness does not look for a payback but is offered free of charge, graciously, just as God in Christ has forgiven us free of charge.

A Closing Parable (14:15–24). This final portion of the meal scene serves as a summary of all that Jesus has warned the nation about in these last few chapters. A remark from one of the guests about the blessedness of those who sit at the banquet table in the kingdom leads Jesus to tell another parable. The remark probably is designed to remove some of the tension Jesus's remarks and actions have created. Jesus challenges some of the assumptions in that remark.

Jesus tells the story of a man who is planning a great banquet at his home. This is a major affair, which includes an initial invitation and an ancient form of RSVP. When the time for the party comes, the owner sends out servants to announce the beginning of the meal. To opt out of the meal at this point is rude.

At this moment the story gets interesting. Three of the invitees, who have previously accepted, opt out of coming. Each has what he considers a good excuse. One wants to check out a recently bought field, a post-purchase inspection that will seal the deal. The second excuse involves the purchase of five oxen. The third excuse is a commitment to a recent marriage—the Old Testament sometimes allowed newlyweds to beg off certain vital responsibilities. Since the banquet probably includes just the men, this third invitee opts out because his new bride cannot attend.

Rather than waste what has been prepared, the party will go on as scheduled. So the servant goes out and invites the poor, maimed, blind, and lame. With the first round of secondary invitations, the room begins to fill with people, but there is still room for more. So the host sends his servant out to the edges of the city. There he must urge others to come to the banquet. These folks will not know the host, even second-hand, so they will need encouragement to come. The master intends to have a fully attended party.

Here is the crux of the parable. The original invitees represent Israel. Although the nation as the originally invited is not responding, the time for the arrival of the kingdom has come, and the initial celebration of its blessings will go ahead. Others previously thought excluded from the celebration will get invitations. These people represent the spread of God's blessing beyond the bounds of the needy of Israel. Israel, though first in line, is missing her present chance to sit at the table. The first have indeed become last.

Application. The Pharisees were not ready for any surprises. They wanted to define the limits of God's work. We sometimes risk missing what God is doing because we think we know how he will act. Those who wish to see God at work must be careful not to dictate to him. He acts as he wills, and he has revealed aspects of his will to us, but that does not mean that he cannot sovereignly choose to manifest his grace in new ways not yet revealed to us. God will accomplish his plan, but we can be sure that it may come in surprising ways.

That verses 7–14 offer a call to humility is obvious. But actually developing a humble spirit and living in light of it is difficult. Do we ignore "unimportant" people? Do we seek attention? Do we act sensitively only to those who can repay us with kindness or status?

A good litmus test of a community is to see how many activities it engages in that are outwardly directed as opposed to being self-serving. Selfishness can surface not just individually but corporately. It can be instructive to examine programs in the church or in the budget and ask how many activities are used on our own interest versus how many represent genuine giving. Our personal use of time and resources can be assessed similarly.

We must be careful not to presume that God will eventually bless us, either because he is not judging us right now or because we can repent at the last minute. Scripture warns that the longer we refuse the offer, the more likely we will have a hardness of heart that becomes callous to any word from God. There are many excuses people give for not responding to the gospel.

God is not caught by surprise when some reject him. The celebration of blessing goes on without the original invitees, and by God's grace others are invited to the table. The important question is not when we are invited to the table, but that we come when invited.

LUKE 14:25–35

Original Meaning. Jesus's attention turns here to his followers, asking them to assess what discipleship requires. He makes these remarks to the multitude, unlike earlier remarks, where only disciples were present. He has no desire to hide his requirements from those who want to follow him, as if he wants to get our decision first and then tell us the rest of the story. Jesus makes it clear to everyone just how much following him requires.

Jesus gets right to the point. If anyone wants to follow him, he must hate father, mother, wife, children, brothers, sisters, and even his or her own life. The meaning of "hate" carries a comparative force here. The idea is that in comparison to Jesus, if we are forced to choose, the winner in that choice must be Jesus. In a first-century context, those who loved family more would not even consider Jesus. Those who loved their own lives more also would not consider Jesus, since trusting him might eventually mean martyrdom. People should understand the cost.

To get his point across clearly, Jesus uses two illustrations. One is of a man who builds a watchtower over his land or over a city (vv. 28–30). Such an undertaking is expensive, and it is best to estimate the cost before starting to build. How sad to start construction and not have the money to finish. In other words, moving toward successful discipleship takes reflection; it is not an automatic exercise. There is no positive testimony in a walk with God that is abandoned because the cost has not been properly assessed. Rather, it is tragic.

The second parable pictures a king assessing his strength in preparation for war (vv. 31–32). If he realizes he cannot win, he will send a delegation and negotiate peace. Similarly, says Jesus, those who want to be his disciples must make such an assessment (v. 33). A person must negotiate peace with God. He or she can go one's own way, with the result being taking a stand against God. One can take a wiser approach by suing for terms of peace on the Lord's gracious terms. This second option means giving the Lord his due and then following him. No one can know at the start of the walk everything involved, but one can enter the journey with an understanding that God has access to all that we are.

In this part of the ancient world, salt could maintain its potency for up to fifteen years. Whether used as a type of seasoning or as a catalyst for a fire, it was only useful when it was salty. If it ceased to function as salt, it was thrown away. The remark notes that God can dispense with disciples who do not complete their call. This means that discipline can come from God. That is why he calls us to hear what he says. Discipleship takes dedication and focus, and God is concerned how his disciples walk. Different eras involve different walks, since not everyone is called to suffer as many Christians did in the early centuries. But those differences do not alter the need to walk as faithful disciples. Jesus wants everyone on the journey to bring to it an understanding of what it requires and to resolve to stay on the path every step of the way.

Application. The fundamental question about discipleship is to consider its relationship to faith. Jesus calls us into a relationship, not just to a decision. As a learner, a disciple enters into relationship with Jesus and embarks on a lifetime journey of learning. Grace brings a relationship with God as a gift, but included is the journey of walking by God's grace.

Another application of this text requires serious self-reflection. Do I yield to the Lord in every area of my life—my possessions, my family, even my own life? Do I really trust him to care for me? Or do I have to help him along by seizing control or by being careful that I avoid some of the tension that inevitably comes into the process when one takes a position of representing Jesus to a needy world?

Sometimes a decision for Jesus means refusing to offer support to a family member for a decision that may be immoral in God's eyes. Taking that stand may be painful but necessary. It may mean refusing to endorse a relationship before God that has been conducted in a way that dishonors him. It may mean discussing destructive behavior at the risk of never speaking to that person again. It may be perceived as loving God over family or friends, when ironically it means loving both!

The choices of discipleship are not always easy. To follow Jesus and share his cross may mean that neighbors and friends do not always understand why we do what we do. Sometimes they will not support us and may even do things that hurt. Our understanding of what counting the cost means is only theoretical until we are put in such circumstances. But those who have contemplated counting the cost will be ready when the moment comes. They must rely on God and turn to him for wisdom if and when a time comes to choose God over family, self, or possessions. Those who wish to follow Jesus should give attention to who has priority, even when they are just considering starting the journey with him.

LUKE 15:1–10

Original Meaning. In a series of three parables in Luke 15, Jesus defends his involvement with the lost. (The third is related in the next unit, in vv. 11–32.) God is committed to finding the lost, as this chapter explains. Jesus deals with the contrast between this divine attitude and the temptation among many believers to ignore the lost. Jesus once again chooses the scribes and Pharisees as the foil for his comparison. They cannot believe that he is spending so much time receiving sinners and eating with them. Such table fellowship represents an absence of the separation they think righteousness demands. Jesus argues, however, that the call of God demands time be spent seeking the lost.

Anyone who has ever searched for something lost knows how maddening it is to look for it and not find it. That frustration underlies this text. Jesus's first story fits the agrarian and pastoral setting of Palestine (vv. 1–7). A shepherd counting a hundred sheep comes up one short. The flock belongs to an owner of modest means (the average flock ran anywhere from twenty to two hundred head). It is possible that the owner and the shepherd are the same person since there is no watchman to help him.

The shepherd goes to look for the lost animal. We are not told if he leaves the rest of his flock with neighbors, though that is likely in the natural understanding of the situation, for he would hardly put the ninety-nine at risk for one sheep. On the other hand, sometimes parables are intentionally surprising, and the twist may be a part of the drama. If so, then Jesus is saying that finding the one is so important that he is willing to take such a risk. The hunt is successful when he finds the lost animal, not shred to bits by some wild animal but alive and well. The shepherd rejoices at finding his valuable sheep.

The note of joy fits the cultural context, since such animals had commercial value. But Jesus's point is not a self-serving one about recovery of lost property but is a comparison of the effort the shepherd makes to recover the lost sheep with his own effort at evangelism. The model of God's care should be our model in relating to the lost. The recovery of the lost sheep leads to shared joy. The shepherd calls his friends and neighbors to celebrate the recovery of his animal. Here is a picture of God's heart and joy at the turning of one sinner back to him. Jesus searches for sinners because heaven rejoices at their recovery.

The second image is similar (vv. 8–10). This time a woman hunts for a lost coin. The "silver coin" that is in view here is equal to a denarius or a day's wage for an average worker (v. 8). It is a modest sum. Her search takes time and effort. When she does find it, she is as excited as the shepherd was. She also calls her neighbors to celebrate with her. Again, this is a picture of heaven's joy at a sinner's repentance.

These two parables are among the simplest stories of Jesus, communicating both truth and emotion. God wants servants who understand his heart to restore sinners. In both cases, the search takes work. In both cases what is searched for seems, on the surface, to be a modest object. In fact, the search becomes a priority. Yet in both cases, the recovery of what was lost leads to rejoicing with others. This imagery underscores God's desire for disciples to share the goal of winning the lost back to him. Note that the focus is on the joy at the recovery of a sinner, not on the fact that Jesus is the only one to do it. The listener is brought into the story as the shepherd. Jesus is training other disciples after him to do as he has been doing.

Application. This passage says much about the heart of God in engaging those who are not interested in him. He cares enough for them to go looking for them, even when they have consciously stayed away. We should be like raiders in search of great treasure, only the treasure we seek are the lost souls of vulnerable sheep. The search is not always easy, but the joy at the end makes the effort worth the cost.

Believers should be engaging the lost in meaningful relationships. Often in the church, however, we see the opposite. We withdraw from the multitudes for fear of compromising our testimony. Evangelism requires time and energy, like the shepherd's and woman's search, in order to reclaim the lost. Some searches even take years, but our Lord calls us to get out among people and build the relationships that allow us to draw others to God. In our fast-moving and busy culture, developing such relationships can be hard. The best opportunities come from work, school contacts, and neighbors. In each case opportunities exist that can lead to deeper relationships.

LUKE 15:11–32

Original Meaning. This parable is often called "The Prodigal Son," but it is really about different reactions to the prodigal. The key reaction is that of the father, who is excited to receive his son back. Thus a better name for the parable is "The Forgiving Father." A subtheme is the reaction of the older brother, so that one can subtitle the parable with the addendum: "and the Begrudging Brother."

The parable is almost allegorical, since each member in the story contributes significantly to its meaning. The father pictures God the Father in heaven. The prodigal pictures the sinner who repents. The older son pictures the attitude of the Pharisees in not desiring sinners to turn to God. Jesus is defending his right to associate with sinners for the sake of the gospel. In fact, the gospel is for sinners, and his mission fits his message.

The parable begins when a younger son asks for his portion of his father's estate. As the younger son, he would have received one third. The father in the parable grants the request. This detail pictures a father who is letting a sinner make his own decisions and go his own way.

The son squanders his fortune in a distant land. Throwing away his inheritance, he lives and plays hard. But a famine when his money runs out presents a predicament. He needs to eat. This pictures the dire circumstances that sin produces.

So the son acts prudently and gets a job feeding pigs. This detail is significant, since in Judaism a pig was an unclean animal. This job is thus a dishonorable one. And he is still hungry, longing to eat what the pigs have for a meal. With no one to help him, he is living a tragedy.

Then he recognizes things have to change. He decides that he will be better off as a slave of his father than working on the edge of the earth alone. He comes "to his senses" (v. 17). How foolish to starve when his father's slaves live better than he does. So he resolves to confess to his father and ask for status as a slave. He has sinned against heaven and his father, and he knows he should admit it. Here Jesus pictures the humility of one who comes and places his spiritual welfare in God's hands, asking nothing but his grace. He will rest in the father's mercy.

The son heads home. But the father does not wait for him to walk up to the house. This part of the story is a cultural surprise. Normally a father waits to be addressed by the son and to receive some indication of respect before responding. But God's compassion is exceptional.

The son is not deterred. He begins to confess, but he does not even get through his response before the father makes it clear that full restoration awaits him. The son is received back into the family with full honor and privileges, as if nothing has happened. He gets the best robe, a family ring, and sandals, and there is a big celebration. The feast declares that the lost son has been found. Here is God's joy at a sinner returning to him.

The older brother, unaware of what has occurred, returns from a hard day's work and hears music. He asks a servant what is going on and hears about his brother's return and the celebration. He is angry and refuses to go in. He wants nothing to do with his lost and wayward brother, even though he has returned. To drive the point home, the older brother notes that "this son of yours" (v. 30; note: not "my brother"!) has squandered property and lived with prostitutes.

The father responds without defensiveness, noting that the older son already has access to what is the father's. Given that the older son represents the Pharisees, this detail suggests that the full rights of sonship are the older son's as well, if he asks for them. But the celebration for the sibling ("this brother of yours"!; v. 32) is necessary, since he is back from the dead. A sinner found is a cause to celebrate.

The story ends here. The parable pictures reversal: the son who was out of the house is now very much in, while the older son sits on the outside. The story also concludes with a point to ponder in that we are not told how the older son responds to the father.

Application. The attitude of the Father is at the center of the parable. We can be assured that God approaches sinners who turn to him with open arms. Even more, God goes on the active search for sinners, taking the initiative with them, for he sent the Son of Man "to seek and to save the lost" (19:10). He rejoices to bring us into his family, and he celebrates our turning to him.

Those with especially sensitive consciences about whether they are saved should be careful not to doubt God and his gracious desire to welcome us. Faith is trusting in the presence and care of God, that he is the rewarder of those who seek him. This is the central issue of the parable. Do we believe that God embraces those who turn to him? This text calls us to see that he does and then to rest in the encouragement that such love and grace generates.

Another major application of this text involves how people respond to the lost. The parable justifies Jesus's involvement with sinners and urges us to rejoice when we see someone come into the Christian community. Jesus wants a community filled with people who can forgive and restore those who turn to God. He is displeased with any who are disgruntled and sit sulking on the outside.

LUKE 16:1–13

Original Meaning. The account begins with a rich man who has a manager in charge of administering his affairs. He apparently serves as a bill collector. Some bring charges against him that he has wasted the master's resources. The master apparently believes the charges and orders the manager to account for his stewardship in a type of audit. With the audit will come the loss of his position.

Facing a future on the streets, the fired manager contemplates his options. He does not want to work as a daily laborer, for he is not strong enough. The alternative, begging, is not particularly attractive either. Contemplating his options, he develops a plan whose goal is simply to ingratiate himself to his master's debtors so that they will help him. He is a prudent planner. Having lost the protection of his former master, he looks for help elsewhere.

The manager takes inventory, one at a time. In each case, he lowers the creditor's bill. The first bill involves a hundred baths of olive oil (about nine hundred gallons). By eliminating the manager's commission, the debt is reduced by half. The second example concerns a thousand bushels of wheat, representing the yield of about a hundred acres and costing 2,500–3,000 denarii, anywhere from just over eight to nine and a half years' wage. This bill is reduced to eight hundred bushels. Again, the manager sacrifices his commission.

Jesus is ready to make the point. He notes that the master commends "the dishonest manager" (v. 8). He has prepared the soil for his future care by what he has done. Such foresight is worthy of commendation. The manager has acted in light of what the future may bring, and he is ready for it now.

In this first of several applications, Jesus notes that people in the world give more thought to their physical well-being than the righteous do to their spiritual well-being. Wealth of this world should be used generously to gain friends, so that when the resources are gone, that disciple will be welcomed into eternal dwellings. When the end comes and no more money is available, the one who has seen into the future and acted prudently will have handled the resources and stewardship God has given wisely.

In addition, those who can be trusted with little can also be trusted with much, just as those who are dishonest with little will be dishonest in much. Who can entrust people with significant things of real value if they cannot handle worldly wealth? Jesus drives for a character in his disciples that reflects God's integrity, generosity, and grace.

The decisive point is then made. A person in this world is faced with a fundamental choice of allegiance. No servant can serve two masters. If the resources we receive are a stewardship from God to be used in service to him and to others, then to serve God is to give our resources to meet the needs of those around us. Someday God will evaluate our use of resources, whether we have handled them in a way that anticipates his desires and values; if we have, his commendation will follow.

Application. Luke highlights the role of money throughout his Gospel. This parable, especially the applications at the end, argues that the use of resources is a litmus test of spiritual stewardship. This is a dangerous area to discuss. On the one hand, the church has to be careful in handling money (and in asking for it) so that it does not succumb to the seductive power of money to distort our values. In addition, the church must be careful not to talk about money so much that what it preaches on this issue seems as if it is the topic that determines spiritual success.

It might seem odd to highlight an application that starts with how the church appeals for money, since the exhortation of the passage is an appeal to individuals. But how can individuals learn to use resources and give wisely if the church is guilty of exploitation in how it obtains what God makes available?

We should support ministries that help people care for themselves, but too many people see giving to those who suffer in our society as evidence of a commitment to some distorted social agenda. Yet centuries ago, pious Christians were the ones committed to a witness reflective of biblical values, leading efforts to meet the needs of widows, orphans, and the other poor who needed evidence that God cared about them.

How conscious are we that what we own is not really owned by us but has been loaned from the Lord, who wishes to see how faithfully we handle his resources to serve those in need? Jesus will soon reinforce such questions in 16:19–31, where he raises the question of how a poor, needy man, Lazarus, was treated by a rich man.

God's call to be generous means that one will be on watch for valid ministries and needs. Some of that giving may be directed to local churches and ministries. But just giving to the local church may narrow our vision too much. We should also contribute to the work of agencies by laboring in areas of need, whether it be feeding the poor, working with agencies that promote education in areas where family support for education is not present, or dealing with unwed mothers in need, or the elderly.

LUKE 16:14–18

Original Meaning. The Pharisees' scoffing indicates that they do not understand the values that Jesus insists are reflective of his kingdom. Their love for money has put them out of touch with his message. Jesus can hardly use a stronger word than what the NIV translates as "detestable" (v. 15). On the continuum that measure values, God and the Pharisees are on opposite ends.

God's plan divides into two periods: Law and Prophets, and kingdom. The boundary line is John the Baptist's ministry. The call of Jesus is the beginning of the realization of promise. Now the kingdom is being proclaimed.

The last part of verse 16 is disputed. The NIV suggests acceptance of the gospel that is more widespread than Scripture portrays. The word "is forcing" (*biazetai*) can be read differently, however, since the form is a middle-passive voice. We prefer to read a passive here and translate it: "Everyone is urged insistently to enter in." With this reading, the emphasis is on the preached word, which is what Jesus gives here.

Jesus closes with a note about divorce to illustrate that the ethical call of the kingdom is rooted in an integrity that matches the integrity of the period of the Law and the Prophets. If anyone makes a commitment before God in marriage and then divorces, this represents adultery, not only because it is an act of unfaithfulness but also because it is a violation of the original vow made before God. To break that commitment and remarry is to commit adultery.

Application. The basic application to this small unit is to respond with obedience to the kingdom demand for ethical integrity, whether it be in how we deal with our resources or how we approach our marriages. To honor God means to be faithful to him in all areas of life.

The message of the kingdom is a message about the beginning of fulfillment. Believers are urged to encourage others to enter into its blessings. That is why others are urged insistently to enter in, not in a sense of coercion but with a pleading that says, "Be reconciled to God" (cf. 2 Cor 5:20).

The Christian community should be a place where transformation and growth are evident. God has brought us into relationship with him in order to renew us as his image bearers. The essence of the community is that its dynamic will change us so that we become more like Christ. We must think through how to keep this fundamental dynamic of the Christian life vibrant and not shaped by the values of our fallen world.

LUKE 16:19–31

Original Meaning. An important feature often discussed about this passage is whether it is truly a parable. The story does differ from other parables in not being about a repeatable everyday situation but rather a specific story. In this sense it is like the parable of the good Samaritan. Still, the account does not recount a historical interchange between a specific rich man and a specific Lazarus, but rather depicts it. The details of the discussion in the afterlife, including the rich man's ability to engage Abraham in discussion, are apocalyptic-like features in the account that show its rhetorical, parabolic, and symbolic character. Yet realities about accountability before God are portrayed.

The first portion of the account contrasts the condition of the rich man with that of Lazarus. The man is very wealthy. He lives in a home with a gate, and he wears clothes made with purple dye, one of the touches of luxury in that era. He dresses in fine linen, a description of the quality of his undergarments. In contrast, Lazarus, a man with nothing, lies at his gate. He is begging, full of sores, longing to get the crumbs from the rich man's table, and having his sores licked by the wild dogs on the streets. This licking is significant since it makes Lazarus ceremonially unclean. His situation is as tragic as the rich man's is sumptuous.

But death is the great equalizer, and here it even reverses fortunes, because after death the one thing that counts is the human heart. Possessions and status symbols are left behind. What God considers is not written down with numbers and dollar signs. Lazarus is in; the rich man is out. The standards of the afterlife are different from those of the appearances of this world.

The rich man looks up and sees Abraham and Lazarus together. Several points are worth noting here. First, the heat of torment may well depict the intense agony of what it means to be confined to the underworld, knowing that God exists and knowing that one is not in heaven. Second, the rich man knows who Lazarus is. During the time on earth, he knew the poor man was out there, had needs, and even knew his name. Finally, the rich man's view of Lazarus has not changed since his death. He still views him as beneath him, as someone who might be sent to give him relief. This reveals the lack of heart in the rich man.

Abraham must give the reply for eternity. In effect, Abraham notes that there was a time when the rich man could have done for Lazarus what he is asking that Lazarus do for him now, but he refused to give Lazarus aid. What he measured in the past is being measured to him, only with one crucial difference: the current setup is permanent.

Understanding that all is lost for him, he intercedes for his five brothers, whose attitude is similar to his own. He pleads for Abraham to send Lazarus to warn them. Abraham's reply here is crucial to understanding what was said both to the rich man earlier and to Luke's readers. If one wants to understand what God asks of his people in terms of caring for others, one need only read the Old Testament. God's word has made clear what he desires. Our devotion to him is seen in our care for others.

There is irony in this reply. What Abraham refuses for the brothers is accomplished for the readers of the parable by warnings issued for them. We hear a person in torment warn us to respond with compassion to those around us. In this parable, the grave speaks so that we might hear.

The rich man persists. He insists with Abraham that if one were sent from the dead to warn them, they will repent. Something spectacular and supernatural will change people's minds. Those reading the parable in the Gospel, knowing the story of Jesus, are aware of how true this remark is. Jesus's resurrection convinced only some that God was working through him. The parable closes with a dark and tragic note about how humanity often misses the opportunities God makes available to them.

Application. The parable is designed to have us reflect on how we respond to people like Lazarus. Though illustrated negatively, the parable is about defining compassion. A compassionate heart sees need and moves to help. If we find it difficult to help someone in need, then this parable exposes the hard quality in our heart that God desires to soften.

Implications of a text like this touch on lifestyle choices we make and the way we use resources. But it is important to appreciate that aid to those in need is not limited to simply throwing money at people, even though in the short term that may be necessary. Expressions of compassion in contexts of need are not merely a matter of money but of true compassion. The positive example in Scripture of giving more than mere resources is the example of the good Samaritan, who fully involved himself with the man who fell among the thieves. This text challenges each one of us to ask: "What am I doing?"

The parable also portrays the stubborn nature of sin. Apparently not even the resurrection is a good enough witness for some. Therefore, we need not be surprised when some do not respond to God's call. The failure to see what God is doing applies not just to failing to see his revelation but failing to see the evidence he leaves behind that points to his revelation.

Finally, one can point to the parable's underscoring of the sufficiency of all of Scripture. If we are to see what God desires from us, Scripture is the place to find it. Scripture must not just be read but must be put into practice. Through it we see the heart of God for us and for others in need.

LUKE 17:1–10

Original Meaning. The warning (vv. 1–3a) treats the topic of causing someone to sin. Jesus says the fate of the culprit is worse than if a huge millstone were placed around his neck and he were cast into the sea. In sum, death would be a better fate than to face God's judgment for his crime. That is how seriously Jesus takes causing others to sin.

But though the warning about sin is serious, equally important is the need to forgive (vv. 3b–4). Sin is to be rebuked, which reveals the community's commitment to righteousness. Yet the sinner's repentance should produce the church's forgiveness. Disciples pursue spirituality in dependence on one another other for support. Following Christ is not a private pursuit but a shared family responsibility. This family is to be a supportive environment where forgiveness is central.

The possibility of forgiveness raises the question of how often forgiveness should follow repentance. Jesus answers that seven times a day is required—a figurative way of saying that as often as repentance occurs, forgiveness should be given. Accountability for keeping relationships working comes from those involved in the events. Often in such situations, the participants refuse to interact with each other, but Jesus argues that maturity handles such matters directly.

Another key characteristic of discipleship is having faith (vv. 5–6). The issue for Jesus is not the amount of faith but its presence. The disciples ask for their faith to be increased, but Jesus replies that all that is needed is faith the size of a mustard seed.

A final image in the passage is a short parable about service (vv. 7–10). No thanks is offered to the slave since he is simply doing what is commanded. The service of Jesus's servants works in precisely the same way. Our attitude should be that we have only done our duty. Obedience is not a matter of merit (though God does honor it), but of duty.

Application. The church today is prone to pay too little attention to details of doctrinal teachings in God's revelation, a response that puts the community at risk. Some practical errors emerge because theological errors stand behind them. These admonitions suggest that truth and integrity belong together. God cares about character as well as truth. Both need to be pursued with diligence and tender, loving care.

A major applicational test of this balance is whether a community is recognized simply for being a watchdog about sin or has a reputation for compassion that seeks quickly and unconditionally to restore a sinner, even again and again ("seven times in a day"!). Sin must be acknowledged and dealt with. But once confessed, the blood of Jesus is sufficient cleansing to prohibit any additional requirements being added on top.

This passage also requires us to reflect on why communities are so slow to forgive. It is too easy to want to make people pay in full for their failures rather than to create an environment where restoration is possible. We must consider how to make our communities sensitive to sin, but not closed to grace.

When one thinks of the issue of trust, the applications are

numerous. Do I trust God that he desires what is best for my spiritual welfare? Do I trust God to fight for me when I uphold his honor? Can I trust God to reverse a severely damaged relationship? The spheres in which true faith can exercise itself in uprooting trees and planting them in the sea are endless.

Of course, the remarks about uprooting trees and planting them in the sea are figurative for doing amazing things. Jesus does not call for a magic amount of faith, just its presence. When we lean on him, his strength can carry a long way and will accomplish amazing things.

The major application of this text with respect to service is to avoid getting in a bargaining position with God. In fact, we should not have a reward mentality at all. Service, obedience, and duty are not rights we negotiate with God to exercise. They are the natural outgrowth of appreciating his act of grace in saving us, so we might bring honor to him.

LUKE 17:11–19

Original Meaning. Luke begins this miracle story by drawing our attention again to Jesus's journey. Jesus is now moving east to west along the boundary between Samaria and Galilee (v. 11). In other words, Luke's journey section is not a straight-line journey, but a journey of fate.

The miracle contains a double level of cultural tension, since the main figure is both a leper and a Samaritan. Lepers were culturally isolated, and Samaritans were detested by Jews for their religious defection and for being racial half-breeds. As Jesus enters a village, he is approached by ten lepers. The fact that they draw near to him says much, since lepers were expected to isolate themselves from people.

The lepers ask for mercy. This is a cry for compassion, a request that comes frequently to Jesus. Jesus immediately removes any doubt about his desire to show compassion. He tells them to go show themselves to the priest, as the law commands. One does not go to the priest until he or she has been healed, so Jesus's telling them to go indicates healing will occur. If they believe Jesus, they will obey. As the lepers turn, they are healed. This event pictures God's grace.

One of the men breaks from the group. Full of praise for God, he falls at Jesus's feet and offers thanksgiving for his cleansing. Luke notes that the man is a Samaritan. He commends the example of gratitude in the Samaritan, and he also shows that response to him is possible from those outside the people of Israel, the chosen people of God. In some cases, those most sensitive to the gospel come from those outside the community of faith.

Jesus then issues a final encouraging commendation. He tells the man that his "faith has made [him] well" (v. 19). Jesus is probably saying that although ten have experienced the blessing of healing, only one has faith and has turned to establish ties with Jesus that indicate the presence of salvation. Faith and salvation again merge.

Application. Praise is important because it reestablishes our relationship with God on its proper terms. Allowing time for *personal* thanksgiving is also important. Much of the evangelical tradition highlights the quiet time. Such time is important not only because we learn about God in Scripture, but we grow in a personal and deeper relationship with him as we converse with him in prayer—praising him for who he is, thanking him for his gifts of grace, and asking him for the things we need.

The reaction of the nine in not returning thanks to Jesus shows how often we tend to take God's gracious actions for granted. When the blessings of life are seen as a result of God's grace, it makes us into gentler, more grateful people. Such an attitude prevents us from assessing life in terms of what we are owed, an attitude that can sow seeds of anger and bitterness.

As with many texts, a fundamental picture of salvation is present here. The Samaritan showed how he personally appropriated the blessing Jesus had given him. In return, the Lord gifted him even more—the declaration that faith had made him well. Luke calls for us to follow in the Samaritan's footsteps.

The fact that the Samaritan is the example warns us against unduly limiting our ministry and whom God might bless through it. Sometimes faith shows up in surprising cross-cultural places. Our ministries may have a natural audience, but in such ministries we must communicate values and attitudes that make it clear that the gospel is for all who trust in Jesus.

LUKE 17:20–18:8

Original Meaning. It is possible that the Pharisees not only ask when the kingdom will come, but what signs will accompany its arrival. Jewish expectation held that the kingdom would come as a part of the ultimate day of the Lord and that cosmic signs would accompany its arrival. Jesus begins his reply by noting that the kingdom does not come with signs to be observed. The kingdom of God is present among them in the person of Jesus.

Luke 17:21 is one of the key verses in the New Testament about the kingdom. It is best to take verse 21 as teaching that the initial manifestation of the kingdom has come with Jesus's ministry. The Pharisees do not need to look for the kingdom's coming in the sky, because it is already here in him.

Jesus indicates that the expected day of the Son of Man's coming in power is a day they will long for but will not see. That is, the powerful display of that day is still coming. One crucial event must precede all of this. That central event is the suffering of the Son of Man. Suffering precedes glory for Jesus. Rejection must come before glorious rule can follow.

Jesus compares the nature of the messianic judgment to two great periods of judgment against humanity. Just as they did then, people will engage in the affairs of life with little attention to God. Both comparisons picture the absolute finality of God's judgment. The days of the Son of Man will be like those ancient days of judgment. The idea that there is a second chance on the judgment day is a myth as far as the Bible is concerned. If the world is not careful, they will not be prepared for the judgment when it comes, being too tied to the things of earth to hear the voice of God.

Such misplaced allegiance is why Jesus says that the person who seeks to save their life will lose it, while those willing to lose their lives will save them. Deciding to honor God may mean some suffering now, but it means eternal glory to come. For Christ's followers this is the crucial point of the passage—we must be faithful until he comes.

Jesus's words that "one will be taken and the other left" involve the separation of the righteous from the unrighteous (vv. 34–35). The disciples' question "Where?" (v. 37) asks about the locale of such judgment. Jesus deflects the question by pointing to the mood and reality of what he is saying: the day of the Son of Man will be a day of judgment. When he is done, only vultures will remain for those left in judgment.

Luke 18:1–8 contains a parable and an application that portrays the importance of prayer for God's vindication of the saints. If they minister in a world that will not accept them, how should they handle the injustice of that rejection? The answer comes in a call to pray persistently without losing heart. It is important to maintain faith in the light of patiently awaiting his return.

What makes this parable so effective are its two characters, with whom it is easy to identify. The widow who needs help is persistent, a quality Jesus makes exemplary in the story. Jesus's argument goes that if a judge, who is no respecter of persons, hears the cry of the widow, how much more will a compassionate God hear the cries of his people.

The Lord asks us to reflect on the judge's reaction to the persistent requests of the woman, which in turn picture the prayers of the people of God. God will vindicate his people who constantly cry out to him. God will judge those who persecute the righteous. He will not delay, but will vindicate them with "justice, and quickly" (v. 8a).

The remark about quick justice has received much attention, since total vindication has not yet come. It can be understood in two ways.

1. Luke desires to emphasize that the return can come at any moment, without specifying when that is. Vindication is the next thing on the divine calendar, and once it comes, in light of the eternity that follows, it will be a quick exercise of justice.
2. The vindication comes in part in the protection that God offers to his own. Even though they suffer, they do not perish, and that is a sign of their vindication. God longs to vindicate his people, and he will do so. In the meantime, he protects us.

One final thought remains. When total vindication comes, will the Son of Man "find faith on the earth?" (v. 8b). In other words, will the delay, which is to some degree assumed in the parable, affect the faith of some, since Jesus calls us not to give up? No answer is given to this question.

Application. The initial phase of the kingdom of God calls us to be worthy citizens. We are servants of the Lord, who represent him on earth; we must not define our lives through earthly or cultural attachments.

To experience the divine favor that comes from sharing in the kingdom promises, Jesus tells the Pharisees they must deal with him. It is no different today. In the face of great debate whether Jesus is the only way, the Lord's stress is that the road to blessing and participation in God's presence goes through him. To follow him is to be different.

No area of theology breeds more speculative attention than the end times. Some ministries devote their full attention to such concerns. On the other end are those who view such speculation as a waste of time and energy. Both approaches are overreactions. The only way for us to make sense of life today is to appreciate where the future is going. Scripture outlines that future, not with detailed dates but with a general outline of what is to come. That outline is designed not to have us prepare charts but to prepare our hearts.

Jesus talks about the end in grim terms and gruesome detail to make clear how serious an issue judgment is for God. Judgment means accountability. In a society that tends to view adults as accountable only to themselves and their own consciences, it is a critical reminder that God does hold us responsible for our actions. This text urges every person to choose wisely when it comes to the things of God. There is too much at stake to make an erroneous choice.

Furthermore, every moment until the Lord returns is an opportunity to be God's instrument in changing the destiny of someone who does not yet know him. God is delaying the day of judgment, being patient and allowing time for others to come to him. Thus, the moments that remain should motivate the church to be the vessel through which others come to see and enjoy the grace of God.

The major application of the parable in Luke 18:1–8 is to keep our eyes focused on the hope that is yet to come. The parable also reveals something significant about prayer. Many prayer meetings we attend take on a predictable character. What is often missing in such meetings are the types of concerns reflected in this parable's call for persistent prayer. The prayer most like the one called for here in Scripture appears in Acts 4:23–31, where the church asked for enablement to perform what God had called them to do, even in the face of fierce persecution. They desired vindication, that God would show his presence powerfully through their ministry. We should do no less.

LUKE 18:9–17

Original Meaning. This parable is really the parable of the two prayers. In those prayers appear two kinds of hearts, whose contrast is not only seen in the way they make their requests but also in the way they approach God. The text is explicit about its audience: those "who were confident of their own righteousness and looked down on everyone else" (v. 9). It is easy to compare ourselves to people who do not measure up to us, at least in our own eyes!

The Pharisee is grateful that he is not like other people. He honors God by fasting and by tithing. But this prayer is actually a distortion of the praise psalm, because when the Pharisee is done, his prayer in effect is, "I thank you, God, that I am so great!" In fact, one gets the impression that God should be honored that this "faithful" Pharisee is on his team.

In contrast, the tax collector does not stand up but approaches God with a sense of distance. He does not look up to heaven, a sign of contrition, but beats his breast, fully aware that he approaches God as a sinner. He comes to God desiring only to improve his relationship to God.

Jesus's comment closes the passage. He endorses the tax collector's humility. The one justified before God, the one whose prayer is heard, is not that of the religious man with all of his works. The prayer that God hears is the cry for mercy. Jesus explains why. Those who exalt themselves will be humbled, while the humbled will be lifted up. Bravado and appearance mean nothing. Résumé and social status mean nothing. Self-reliance means nothing. What counts is a heart that appreciates what God can give.

When Jesus is ministering, many seek to have him touch their little children. The disciples try to stop the parents from coming. Jesus takes the opposite attitude. He invites the children to come to him because they are important people. One must trust God with the simple faith and humility of a dependent child. Entrance into the kingdom is a matter of humility that recognizes a need for God. What is commended in children is their inherent dependence, for they bring nothing but themselves to the feet of Jesus.

Application. In our assertive society, pride often gets the accolades, despite what it does to relationships and character. Pride means that the task is more important than the people. The objective becomes the obstacle to human relationships. Jesus condemned pride because it is so insidiously destructive.

Humility is harder to discuss because it does not discuss itself. It simply gets out there and serves, often with sacrifice. It does not claim rights; it tries to do what is right. It does not brag about integrity; it displays it. Sometimes it is easy to miss what does not point to itself. But God sees the humble heart and lifts it up in honor. That is Jesus's challenge.

Many pious folk are proud of their achievements and often identify themselves by talking down to others who "do" less. A parable like this applies to them. Insofar as they feel they can learn little from others, something is wrong.

The tax collector may also be someone who is faithful to his or her spouse, fulfills responsibilities, and yet knows when he or she fails to live in a God-honoring way that the best thing to do is seek forgiveness from a gracious God. They do not wear a badge on their shirt that says "religious." They just try to be faithful to God.

We should look at a child hanging on its mother's arm and ask, "Do I turn to my Father in heaven like that?" We are to place our hands in his and walk by his side, letting him direct our steps. Such humility, trust, and dependence calls on us to seek the face of our heavenly Father and stay close to him as we walk with him.

We should also note the precious nature and importance of children. Children are often most open to God and less impacted by a fallen world that wants to draw them away from God. If Jesus can take them into his arms, so can and should we.

LUKE 18:18–30

Original Meaning. Contrasts echo throughout this text. The rich man stands in contrast to the disciples in verses 28–30. Interestingly, we know this man as the rich *young* ruler, but Luke does not relate his age. Luke is more interested in the man's attitude than suggesting any kind of immaturity, since the attitude is destructive no matter how old a person is. This rich man also stands in contrast to the blind man who seeks Jesus's healing in 18:35–43. That man, though blind, sees clearly, while the rich man, though possessing eyes, has his vision clouded by his possessions.

The ruler addresses Jesus as "Good teacher," perhaps in an attempt to gain a good hearing (v. 18). But Jesus puts the ruler on notice at the start that he will not be won over with a flattering greeting, warning the man that only God is good. When Jesus exhorts the ruler to go in a difficult direction with his wealth, the teaching is not accepted as good but is rejected with a change of countenance.

The issue of goodness raises the question of honoring God. Loving God first from the heart means not being drawn away into various expressions of idolatry that the world offers. One of the key dangers of wealth is that possessions come first and people slip down the list. Adultery, murder, stealing, and lying should not be a part of a believer's walk, while honoring parents should be. Jesus calls for character that is not self-serving and does not take advantage of others.

The ruler replies that he has been obedient to these commands since his youth. Jesus replies by adding an additional test to see if the man will serve God. Jesus calls on the man to sell everything he has and give to the poor; by doing so he will receive treasure in heaven. After that, he must follow Jesus and join him in walking with God.

The combination is crucial to understanding the nature of Jesus's reply. Will this man prefer what earth can give him or what heaven offers? This is not a test of works but a probing of his heart, an examination of his fundamental allegiance. In sum, Jesus wants to know if his faith is in the things of the earth or in the way of God.

The man reacts with sadness. He is wealthy and would have to give up much. Jesus implies that the personal identity of a rich person is so bound up with the things of this earth that it is all but impossible for him to turn everything over to God's care. The remark about the eye of the needle is sharp. If a camel going through the eye of a needle is impossible, where does that leave the rich for whom entry into the kingdom is even harder?

Jesus's remarks to the rich man have traumatized the disciples. The rich were often seen as the blessed. Have they done what Jesus is asking the ruler to do? Jesus's reply basically responds affirmatively to Peter. Anyone who leaves home, wife, children, or the family for the sake of the kingdom of God will receive much more family in this life, the family of God, and eternal life in the age to come.

The passage ends with the same topic that began it: "eternal life" (v. 30). We must ally ourselves in relationship to Jesus and rest all our welfare on his care. We call this faith. Trusting Jesus with our welfare is to enter a new family and to receive the gift of life. Jesus is saying to Peter that he has that gift. God has made possible what would have otherwise been impossible.

Application. This passage challenges us to ask where our fundamental anchors of identity lie. Possessions can be one such anchor. They can shade our sight from what is ultimately important and chain our hearts to the wrong point of identity. What is really frightening is how easy it is for all of us to choose earth over heaven. We do not, of course, have to be perfect to be saved, but God's people must recognize just how important trust in him is. Through hearts focused on the Lord, we receive eternal life and come to know him more fully.

The text also suggests we should carefully consider how to use the resources God gives us. In a world where a few people, relatively speaking, hold the majority of the world's resources, application of this passage is not easy. Needs exist everywhere. The rich who have turned to God should act concretely by performing deeds of ministry and service to those who have genuine needs.

Perhaps the most fundamental application is one that Peter later develops—that Jesus's followers are as "foreigners and exiles" on this earth (1 Pet 2:11). Our resources cease to be ours; they become tools of heaven in order to serve Christ. Only when we have a sense of detachment from the things of earth can we give our all to God.

Another encouraging feature of this text is that such detachment is possible. Peter asked if they had done it, and Jesus assured them that they had. In the end, they gain far more than anything they give up.

Finally, the text makes it clear that we gain an entire new family when we come to Jesus. This truth is particularly important in context where many come from fragmented families. The church becomes a place where new brothers and sisters provide encouragement, emotional support, and other forms of sustenance. We note this especially whenever a local church rallies to a family's needs amid a crisis. Through such support, taking the difficult road of discipleship becomes a little easier.

LUKE 18:31–43

Original Meaning. Verses 31–34 of this unit present the sixth direct allusion to Jesus's death in this Gospel. The disciples cannot comprehend how Jesus's death will accomplish God's will. The coming events will clarify their understanding.

Jesus announces that they are heading to Jerusalem to fulfill all that the prophets have written. This note of fulfillment emphasizes that the events about to occur are part of a divine design that must happen. Nothing catches Jesus off guard. Jerusalem has been identified as the city of destiny for some time already in this Gospel.

Jesus will be given over to the gentiles. In the events to come, the opponents will mock, insult, spit on, flog, and then kill him. On the third day, he will rise again. After suffering will be glory and vindication.

The disciples do not understand this. Jesus's life fulfills Jewish prophecy, yet it is full of surprises as to how that fulfillment comes. How is it possible for the promised Messiah to die? All of these events are initially incomprehensible, even to those who follow Jesus. The approaching death of one honored as the Son of Man is but one of the many surprises we now take for granted in the church. It is often difficult to appreciate just how surprising the road Jesus takes was for the original disciples. But God's subsequent actions will make clear what is currently hidden to them.

Ironically, while many struggle to see who Jesus is, a blind man has full clarity of vision. As Jesus travels near Jericho, a blind man is begging by the road and hears the commotion. He asks what is going on. They tell him that "Jesus of Nazareth" is passing by (v. 37); the blind man has apparently heard about Jesus and knows that he is not merely an inhabitant of the town of Nazareth. Everything in his response to Jesus shows that he has heard something about this man and believes he can change his life. In calling Jesus the "Son of David" (v. 38), the blind man recognizes that Jesus is the promised Messiah of God. The blind man wants Jesus to exercise the power he has heard about on his behalf.

The popular perception is that this blind man is too insignificant for Jesus to pay any attention to. He should be quiet and leave the teacher alone. But the rebukes solidify the blind man's resolve, and he cries out even louder for mercy. The crowd is wrong. Jesus is concerned about people like the blind man. God looks on the heart, not a person's social status. Jesus asks the man what he wants, probably to elicit his desire publicly and to draw out his faith. The blind man replies he wants to see again. Jesus then grants his request and notes that his faith has delivered him.

This exchange symbolizes much more than the ability to see again. The blind man trusts that, by asking the Son of David to provide what his power can deliver, he will be restored. Jesus then not only opens his eyes but also affirms that the blind man can walk on the road with his eyes on God. His faith has brought deliverance and sight. Those who approach God in confidence that he can make them see are given spiritual sight.

Application. Jesus is part of an organized plan to send the promise of hope and salvation to humanity. What Jesus did was not part of a second or backup plan of God because plan A failed. God had predicted that his servant would be despised and rejected by his own people and would die. Scripture also promises that the one who was put to death will return to exercise his authority over the earth. Those remaining parts are just as certain to be realized as was the first part of the plan. Thus, God is moving the events of history to realization in their proper time.

The disciples' failure to see God's ways challenges us to ask ourselves whether we miss God's direction in our lives because we do not want to see those parts of his call that ask us to take the hard road. Such questions are answered in the silent moments of private reflection or through interaction with those who know us well. Are we hesitant to step out in faith because we cannot guarantee the results? The road God wants us to travel is not always the most comfortable one.

The switch from begging at the side of the road to journeying along with Jesus pictures the change of direction and status Jesus brings to life. No matter how low our social position has been, when we come to Jesus we are elevated to the highest possible station in life, the position for which we were created—a relationship with God.

A church that is open to involvement in a multiethnic environment can develop a depth of sensitivity that one-dimensional churches lack. Sometimes we think ministry can only go from the haves to the have-nots. This passage reminds us that sometimes those who lack see better than those who have. We must not be too quick to make judgments about what a person can offer to the body of Christ because of what he or she appears to lack.

Of course, the recognition of Jesus as Son of David is the basis of everything pictured in this passage. Luke never stops making the person of Jesus the issue of this Gospel. This passage asks the questions in visual terms: Do you see who Jesus is, or are you blind? Blindness becomes sight when one turns to him.

LUKE 19:1–10

Original Meaning. Zacchaeus is a wealthy man, though many consider his wealth ill-gotten. As Jesus moves through Jericho, Zacchaeus longs to see the famous teacher, but his short stature and the crowd prevent him from doing so. But he is resourceful, so he runs ahead and climbs a sycamore tree, a tree with a short trunk and wide, lateral branches. Jesus breaks the ice by noticing Zacchaeus in the tree. He stops and tells him to come down out of the tree, because he "must" (*dei*) stay at his house today (v. 5). Jesus's stay with the tax collector is a necessity because it pictures what his ministry is all about—to lead to God those whom others have given up on, to call those who need to repent.

Zacchaeus welcomes Jesus gladly. One who has simply sought to get a glimpse of the teacher now gets to meet him face to face. His development of intimacy with Jesus underscores how one who approaches God on the Lord's terms gets more than they may have expected.

The reaction to Jesus's choice for a host does not meet with popular approval. Zacchaeus is indeed a sinner, as his own remarks will show, but he is not beyond the reach of God or his call. Jesus does not write off those who remain open to God. He does not worry about the impression on his testimony this association makes, because his priority is to associate closely enough with the lost that they may come to know the grace of God.

Zacchaeus expresses his appreciation of Jesus's acceptance of him by declaring his intent to be a different man. Because of his new relationship with God, he will do two things: half of his possessions will now go to the poor, and those he has wronged will receive restitution at four times the amount taken. Both actions stand out in light of cultural expectations. In Zacchaeus's changed heart, love for God expresses itself in love for others.

Giving away half of one's possessions serves as a rhetorical way of stating that one should see their possessions as under the stewardship of God. The resources we possess are the Lord's, and he guides us in how we are to use them. Such giving as Zacchaeus intends is not required by God's law, but it does reflects a heart given over to God.

Jesus endorses the response fully, noting that this very day "salvation has come to [Zacchaeus's] house" (v. 9). This statement testifies to a heart changed by the presence of God. The Lord has been reclaiming a formerly lost child. He has taken the initiative to point to Zacchaeus as a man who can know God's acceptance, and the tax collector has embraced the opportunity.

Application. One of the errors the pious can make is to separate themselves from the world in such a way that they lose contact with sinners. Usually two factors feed such isolation: a healthy desire not to succumb to standards of living that destroy moral integrity, and a subtle but deadly feeling of superiority so that we feel we are inherently better than others. This second element in the equation can squeeze out our ability to empathize with the sinner's plight. It forgets that our blessing is the result of God's gracious work, not our inherent character.

To want to live a moral life is part of God's call for believers. Along with that is the desire to keep one's distance from morally suspect practices. This principle is a good one. However, it risks being applied so thoroughly that one ceases to associate with unbelievers for fear of what comes with the relationship.

Those of us who did not grow up in the church often are brought to the Lord by friendships. A Christian roommate who modeled Christ in the midst of my desire to enjoy my freshman year at college was primarily responsible for leading me to the Lord. We must not give up on those whose hearts God may draw through our life and witness.

Another key application in this passage comes in the portrait of faith. Faith transforms people. A transformed faith responds to wronging others differently than our natural instincts do. One of the most painful things we can do in a relationship is to commit a wrong and then pretend it never happened or did not do any damage. Such blindness builds up resentment and eats away at the relationship. Admitting wrong, asking for forgiveness, and trying to make restitution are like a spring shower that can open up the possibility of a fresh start.

The Christian faith is the ultimate "recovery" movement because what is recovered is the fundamental relationship with God that allows recovery in other areas to take place. Some of the most moving services in the church are those where sinners tell how God recovered them from lostness and brought them back into his fold. As they exposed their sin before God, he brought them back into relationship with him and with others.

We do too little of sharing our testimony in our communities as an act that can bind us together. A church made up of "perfect" people who cannot confess sin does not give evidence of the gospel's transforming power. We are new creations in Christ, but in him we are under continual renewal. The moment we forget our continual need for renewal, we slip into the self-delusion of being spiritually independent. Nothing is more devastating for the Christian walk than forgiven sinners who think they can live like saints on automatic pilot. Independence is not the essence of faith; humility and dependence are.

LUKE 19:11–27

Original Meaning. This is the last parable in Luke's record of Jesus's final journey to Jerusalem. Luke is clear about why Jesus tells the parable. Jesus must inform his disciples that the full expression of kingdom authority will not come until his return, and he must explain what he expects of them in the interim.

A man of noble birth goes to a far country "to have himself appointed king and then to return" (v. 12). The Greek expression literally refers to his "receiving a kingdom"—a remark that pictures Jesus's reception of the kingdom after the vindication of his upcoming resurrection and ascension. While gone, the nobleman's interests need to be administered. So he calls ten servants and gives each of them a mina. The servants represent anyone following Jesus.

In addition to servants are subjects who hate the ruler and do not want him as king. They send a delegation to those making the selection to inform them of their complaint. This pictures the rejection of Jesus by Israel.

Returning home, the newly appointed king requests an accounting by his servants. Have they used the resources in a way that benefited him? The story is kept compact by relating the situation of only three servants. The main exchange takes place between the master and the third servant. The third servant has no sense of loyalty to his master. Why should he honor him with his labor? This rhetorical detail about the servant's attitude is important because it shows that although he is associated with the master, there is nothing that indicates any trust of the master.

The master's reaction to the servant is strong and clear. This wicked servant will be condemned on his own testimony. The master's remarks in verse 22 are not his confession that he is a hard taskmaster but a condemnation of the third servant's failure to follow through on how he viewed the master. Verse 23 shows that the third servant's attitude should have led to a different response. He is measuring the servant by the servant's own standards, a measure he fails to live up to.

Jesus then makes the application. The one who has gets more, but the one who has nothing loses even what he has. Jesus applies a mathematical warning to the third slave. Nothing from nothing leaves nothing. The one who has no trust in God's goodness, even though he or she has a "connection" to God, has no relationship with God and ends up with nothing from him in the end. The third servant represents all those tied to the community who neither trust nor know the goodness of the master, Jesus. Mere association with the community counts for nothing; what counts is personal relationship to Jesus.

Jesus deals with one more group in the parable—the subjects who did not want the nobleman to be king. These enemies are slain. This represents the fate of those who reject Jesus outright. They are judged and excluded from blessing. This detail represents the irreversibility and severity of the final judgment.

Application. We are all accountable to God for how we conduct our journey through his world. One day he will render judgment. This concept is not popular in some circles today, but it is a biblical concept. God will require each person to render an account of their life, and he will vindicate those who are truly his.

As our culture grows more independent from God, many claim they are not his subjects, or they try to create God in their image and form him in the frame of their expectations. Yet we all are accountable to God. Our lives last a short span in this world, and they will be subject to examination by the God who is the source of all life and breath.

This parable also emphasizes that God has given kingship to Jesus. He undertook that rule when he rose to the side of the Father after his death. His kingship includes judgment. Scripture consistently presents the judgment of God through his Son Jesus as an inevitable stop in the journey of each life. This parable declares God's right to hold us accountable.

The third servant also represents a strong warning. Connection to a Christian community is not what makes a Christian, even if that person has stewardship responsibilities in that community. A Christian is a person who has a relationship of trust with Jesus. This parable calls on us to examine whether our perceived relationship to God is purely formal or real.

The parable suggests on the surface that the third servant lacks fruit in his life, but there is really a more basic complaint. He is condemned on the basis of his own words—that is, on the basis of his own heart attitude to God, for he sees the master as a hard and unjust taskmaster. Behind his lack of fruit is a lack of recognition of God's grace. Membership in a church is not a union card to heaven; knowing and embracing God's grace is.

A positive note in the story is the recognition that Jesus will reward the faithfulness of those who walk with him. The provision of additional responsibilities to the first and second servants shows that God sees and commends faithfulness. Jesus exhorts us here to apply ourselves fully to the task so that in the day of his assessment, our stewardship may be an occasion for rejoicing.

LUKE 19:28–44

Original Meaning. As Jesus approaches Jerusalem, he begins to direct events. Near Bethphage and Bethany at the Mount of Olives, some two miles east of Jerusalem, he tells his disciples to procure an animal for entry into the capital. The disciples must untie the animal, and if anyone asks what they are doing, they are simply to say that the Lord needs it. The cultural background for this response is the *angaria*, where a dignitary could procure use of property for personal reasons. This right extended to people like rabbis. So the request is not unusual.

The disciples do just as Jesus has instructed them, and everything happens as he said it would. In effect, Jesus is directing the sequence of events that leads to his death. The disciples throw their cloaks on the colt and put Jesus on it. As he proceeds, people spread their cloaks in front of him as well, much as a red carpet functions today. The description uses language from several Old Testament passages. While the background is regal, the ride on a humble animal denotes not a Messiah of raw power but of humility and service.

Luke stays focused on the person of Jesus. The disciples praise of God is also praise of Jesus. They proclaim the hope of Psalm 118:26, where blessing falls on the king who comes in the name of the Lord (Luke 19:38). The disciples, by echoing the words of the psalm, declare that Jesus is the sent king who comes with authority given by God. They are also filled with joy as they note the presence of peace and glory in heaven. For disciples, this is a great moment. For the crowds, as the parallels tell us, this is a time to join in.

Luke has left two sets of clues as to who Jesus is. One appeals to Old Testament background, while the other treats the events of Jesus's ministry (especially the miracles). Each explains the other. Jesus is the promised one who John the Baptist mentioned; he is also the one who comes in the name of the Lord, who Jesus predicted would be slain in Jerusalem.

But the vote is not unanimous. The Pharisees come and ask Jesus to reject the claim and rebuke his disciples. His reply makes clear how appropriate the remarks are: if the disciples do not speak, creation will. This remark contains an inherent rebuke, in that inanimate creation knows more about what is taking place than they do. The situation cannot be more tragic, as the tears of Jesus will soon show.

As Jesus approaches the city, we get a glimpse of his heart. He declares pending judgment for the nation. Rejection of the divinely selected king will cost it greatly. The prediction of national judgment shows just how seriously the decision about him should be taken.

Despite the fanfare, the entry is not a pleasant one for Jesus. He knows what lies ahead and that the pain he will suffer will not be limited to himself. The nation has made a frightful choice, with dire consequences for itself. A major opportunity has been missed. If they had known it, they could have experienced blessing. But now, something more dire lies ahead.

What Jesus predicts is the consequence for covenant unfaithfulness. The roots of his prediction go back to Deuteronomy 28–32, where God warned that such unfaithfulness would lead to his judgment through other nations. They are continuing to miss the moment of truth, and they are now responsible for their decision.

Jesus's reference to "the days will come" indicates a prophetic oracle (v. 43). Here it is an oracle of doom. When the enemy finally enters the city, everyone will be slaughtered and there will be total destruction. Jesus knows what he is talking about. The decision to reject Jesus is a fundamental violation of covenant trust.

Application. Jesus infuses his evangelism with a humility of service that is represented even in the way he enters Jerusalem as king. Like her Messiah, the church needs to be a community, not just of testimony and words, but of presence and service among those whom it seeks to reach. The touch of God's presence reveals his mercy. Proclaiming and revealing Jesus are more than a matter for the head.

The wedding of life to theology is important because God has revealed his attributes in a similar way. His character is not revealed in a set of philosophical propositions. It comes through what he is doing in people's lives. We proclaim him most truly when we wed our knowledge of him from Scripture to his direct involvement in our lives. This assumes, of course, that we live a life of faith attuned to seeing him and recognizing him.

We can expect a variety of reactions to Jesus. The church's message to a culture that does not believe that God speaks truth is to call that culture to consider the responsibility they undertake if they are wrong. It is a tragic, even permanent, mistake to misjudge what God has revealed.

The importance of making a wise decision about Jesus is a constant theme in this Gospel. Acceptance of him leads to great blessing, while rejection leads to great pain. A time will come when we will each have to own up to our decision. Making the right decision determines the character of that meeting.

LUKE 19:45–20:8

Original Meaning. Luke succinctly tells the story of the temple incident. Jesus drives out the merchants and quotes a composite Old Testament citation. The first part calls for justice and acknowledges the way to God is open to all, including foreigners and eunuchs, if they are faithful to God's law. The second part declares that God's people have made the temple "a den of robbers" (v. 46). With the support of the prophets behind him, Jesus condemns the desecration of the temple's holy function.

Jesus's action strengthens the resolve of the leadership to deal with him. He cannot be allowed to dictate how worship will be conducted at the temple and thus blatantly challenge priestly practices. But his popularity makes them hesitant. How can they do it when people are hanging on his every word? That is why they try to trip him up into saying something inappropriate.

Luke 20:1–8 returns to the central issue of the Gospel. Where does Jesus's authority come from? Such concerns motivate the priests and teachers of the law to probe Jesus as he teaches in the temple courts and shares the good news of the kingdom. Their question comes in two forms. By what authority does Jesus do these things, and who has given it to him?

Jesus responds with his own question. He asks them to assess John the Baptist's ministry. The question is brilliant because John's roots were as obscure as those of Jesus. The principle by which the leadership is judging Jesus—namely, he has no official priestly credentials—will also result in the rejection of John's ministry, but John has already been accepted by the people as a prophet. Jesus has put them in a corner.

The character of the leadership emerges in their deliberations among themselves. The issue they discuss is not the truth but appearances. The Jews decide to take a safe route and punt, claiming they do not know the answer to his question. The refusal to take a position leaves the door open for Jesus to refuse to commit himself, not because he does not wish to make a claim but because the answer is obvious and need not be debated. They refused to recognize John, and now they are maintaining their distance from Jesus. The time for debate is past. The leadership has made their decision, and they should own up to it. Their failure to do so is the narration's indictment on their action.

Application. Our culture may be right about certain expressions of the Christian faith when it accuses us of being too commercial. When money and prospering through the faith become more central than the worship of God, a distortion like that which occurred at the temple has taken place.

Neutral organizations like the Evangelical Council for Financial Accountability (ECFA) audit and verify the integrity of a ministry's financial practices. One should check to see if a ministry has such financial oversight and accountability before giving.

No doubt the leadership would have pled in their resistance to Jesus that they were merely trying to prevent someone from coming in and creating havoc at the temple. But failure to engage in serious self-examination led to further sin. Sins, like lies, tend to travel in packs and devour like wolves. Untreated, sin becomes a thoroughly destructive force.

Preaching the arrival of God's promise and clearing the temple are acts that either are sanctioned by God or are wrong. Jesus is not just a good man here. The kind of benign respect our culture pays him is not a possible category that the Bible leaves open. He does not allow fence-sitting. He should either be embraced as Savior and Lord or opposed.

The negative character lesson of the Jewish leaders' deliberations has been noted above. But do we do the same things? Do we hesitate to speak up for our association with Jesus in contexts where it might not be popular? Do we use evasive tactics to hide previous actions that we now know were wrong? Do we tell people in public debate we are searching for truth when our mind is already made up? Are we manipulative like the leaders here?

LUKE 20:9–19

Original Meaning. This significant parable summarizes the history of God's activity with Israel. Its placement here provides the answer for the questions of the origin of Jesus's authority. He is the only Son, sent from God. The picture in this parable is a common one. It was not unusual in Jesus's day, as in many parts of the world today, for land to be owned by one person and farmed by others. When a man plants a vineyard and rents it out to tenants, he expects to collect proceeds from the profit on the crops. Even if his absence is long, he expects the land to remain profitable.

In the parable, when harvest time comes the owner sends servants to collect the proceeds from the vineyard. Yet all the owner's efforts to collect his share are rebuffed with impunity. The owner decides to send "my son, whom I love" (v. 13). This expression may well be a way of describing him as an only son, since the tenants expect his death to lead to their being given the land. The owner assumes the tenants will treat his son with respect. But when they see the son arrive, they see an opportunity. How will killing the heir reap benefits for them? How twisted sinful thinking can be. Blindness can see strange things in the dark. The allusion here is to the Jewish leadership's approaching execution of Jesus, which is the parable's key point. Jesus knows exactly what they are about, even though it makes no logical sense.

Jesus asks the people how the owner will respond to the execution of the son. The owner will come, kill the tenants, and lease the land to others. The crowd gets the point about the shift in who gets to tend the vineyard and exclaims, "God forbid!" (v. 16). Surely Israel and her leadership could never be guilty of such reckless disobedience.

Jesus cites Scripture and a popular proverb to drive home his point. Psalm 118:22 teaches that the righteous one rejected by others is exalted by God as the key figure. Old Testament Jews would have thought of their king in these terms. The rejectors would have been the nations. Jesus turns the image upside down, noting that now the king is rejected by his own people. Everyone who falls on the stone is broken, and those on whom the stone falls are crushed. Either way it is a problem to oppose the precious stone whom God has exalted—his Son Jesus.

Opposition to Jesus grows more intense, for they know Jesus is challenging them, just as he did earlier at the temple. He accuses them of being in the exact opposite place of where they see themselves. They want to arrest him, but the people remain an obstacle. Jesus is still too popular with them. He will have to be discredited first. To this effort they turn their attention.

Application. Though this text seems harsh in portraying God's casting aside of Israel, it is important to look at how patient and long-suffering God was. He rejects people only after a long effort of trying to gain a response from them. Jesus wept as he entered Jerusalem because judgment is not what God desires to bring on anyone. Judgment comes only because we fail to respond to God's compassion and mercy.

The text again highlights the centrality of Jesus. He is the cornerstone, and to oppose him is to face rejection by God. God seeks honor from the community among whom he lives, as well as from those who refuse to give it. One day all will acknowledge him. It is better to do so willingly now than to be forced to acknowledge him later.

LUKE 20:20–26

Original Meaning. The Jewish leadership now tries to trip up Jesus on political grounds. The issue is the Roman poll tax. This unpopular tax represented one of the most decisive examples of Rome's sovereignty over Israel. The plot thickens by the way Luke describes the setting. The leadership is looking for anything Jesus might say to allow them to hand him over to the governor on a political charge. In Roman custody, Jesus could be subject to the death penalty for treason, thus sparing the leadership of any direct blame for his death. In addition, Rome would appreciate the Jews looking out for Rome's interests.

These infiltrators have a brilliant plan. They ask Jesus: "Is it right for us to pay taxes to Caesar or not?" (v. 22). If Jesus supports Rome, his allegiance to Israel will be questioned. If he sides with the Jews, then Rome can be called. Their initial praise of him as one who teaches "what is right" (v. 21) only highlights their hypocrisy.

The question is posed in either/or terms. But Jesus is aware of their craftiness, calls for a coin, and asks who is responsible for its inscription. The Jews were carrying such coins in their pockets, proof that they already lived under Rome's sovereignty and accepted it by participating in its commerce.

Jesus turns the question into a both/and. Government has the right to exist and function, but its presence does not destroy one's allegiance to God. Jesus is not a political revolutionary who rails against Rome, nor is he an ardent nationalist. No one can charge him with political subversion. He does not step into the trap set for him, and the leadership recognizes their effort has failed.

Application. How should the church view government? Does God desire a Christian nation? And what does that phrase even mean? If we mean that God desires the structures of society to relate to people in a way that honors God and humanity, then the answer is surely yes. But if we mean that God has a special contract of blessing with any given nation, the answer is no, since only Israel had a special relationship with God.

The church today risks looking for God's nation in the wrong place. That Christian nation is not in a political capital. That nation is the community Jesus has formed to be the world's light, a citizenship whose roots are in heaven and whose call is to reach out to people in every nation and tribe to be a part of this community. To render to God what is God's is to give to God faithful service on behalf of his kingdom amid the nations.

What does this imply about political activity? Christians have the right to be full citizens in any country, even the duty to do so. The church has the right to contend in the public marketplace for those values that make for a healthy community. But the church is not in the business of wielding secular power or the sword. God himself lets people refuse to be a part of his community and then holds them responsible for the choice.

The political motto of the church is to love God and one's neighbor. The application of that credo can take so many forms that it is limited only by the church's imagination and energy. The church has much work and reflection to do in this area. Our capital is found at the right hand of God.

Though we can seek it, the church's call is not to reform culture, because reformation cannot take place by changing structures alone; hearts must be changed. The church should be able to show the world what healthy relationships look like, how the needs of the poor can be met with compassion, what absence of racism looks like, how people can engage in business with integrity, how reconciliation takes place when people have failed one another, and so forth.

What does this perspective mean for our involvement in politics? The church as an alternative to the culture must stay above culture in its critique of how government or any other institution does business. Government exists to protect the people, administer law and order, collect taxes, and serve the common good as a principle of justice; the church exists to nurture hearts and souls.

These questions become more difficult when one gets specific. What about abortion? This is an issue of public morality. It is an inherently religious and philosophical discussion in a culture that does not know how to have such discussions. As we make the case, we will need to offer ourselves as good neighbors, willing to help on the follow-through of a choice to bear a child, especially in contexts where emotional and financial support is lacking.

What about prayer in school? Here is a delicate question. I am all for prayer and teaching the value of prayer to God, but how will we pray in a multicultural environment? We cannot argue, I believe, that we are a monoreligious community, for we are not. The best prayers in our multireligious contexts are those that allow the individual time for personal prayer. Otherwise, battles will ensue over who gets to write the prayers that the class prays. What is rendered unto God should be rendered sincerely, not by coercion.

LUKE 20:27–40

Original Meaning. The next new angle in challenging Jesus is a theological one. The protagonists are the Sadducees. They raise the issue of the resurrection, which finds them on the opposite side of the Pharisees, for the Sadducees did not believe in resurrection. The Sadducees had a standard question they liked to pose on the resurrection to try to show how ludicrous it was. The Sadducees do not really want an answer, for they are convinced that the dilemma shows the lack of logic concerning resurrection. They also assume that the afterlife is like this life.

Jesus notes that the afterlife is not like this life in that there will be no marriage in the age to come. As a more subtle point, Jesus implies that not everyone will be resurrected. He speaks of those "considered worthy of taking part" in that age (v. 35). Therefore, some risk being excluded from that era. This second point does not relate to the question, but it raises the issue of who gets to receive the resurrection to everlasting life.

To solidify his argument, Jesus notes how God said to Moses that the Lord is the God of Abraham, Isaac, and Jacob. God is the God of the living, not the dead. So if God *is* still God to the patriarchs when he speaks to Moses, who lived long after their deaths, they must be alive or present somehow with God.

In other words, Jesus's reply takes two forms. The Sadducean marriage dilemma misunderstands the afterlife since marriage does not occur there. Thus, the problem the Sadducees pose is a pseudo-problem. And Scripture does teach resurrection in the Torah in how it mentions the patriarchs. If God makes promises to them and the afterlife is known, then resurrection seems an appropriate deduction. This is a fundamental doctrine of hope.

The reaction to Jesus's answer is instant. Some, no doubt of the Pharisees, like his defense of resurrection. Jesus also silences his opponents so that they do not want to ask him any more questions. Jesus knows more about God's will and where he is going than his opponents. He may be outnumbered a few thousand to one, but he can be trusted to teach the way of God.

Application. That you only go around once in life is good theology. The Bible knows nothing of return visits in new forms of existence. The proper response to that reality is vastly different than the view of advertisers. Rather than grabbing for all the gusto one can, the uniqueness of our journey means that we should pay careful attention to our one chance to walk with God. We should live as we have been created to live. You only go around once in life, so grab for all of God's goodness you can get.

Regarding the resurrection, we do not just go to heaven when we are raised from the dead; we are transformed. Life after the resurrection takes place in a transformed community, where sin no longer exists. It is not just where we are going that makes the hope so great, but who we will be when we get there.

LUKE 20:41–44

Original Meaning. One favorite identification of the Messiah among the Jews was to mark him as "Son of David." Jesus wants to test that identification, not as wrong but as incomplete. He uses a rhetorical argument like that used by later rabbis, where two conflicting ideas are placed next to one another, not to deny either but to relate them to each other. At the center of the discussion is Psalm 110:1, the most popular Old Testament text used by Jesus and the early church.

This psalm is a regal promise psalm that articulates the hope of what Israel's ideal king will be. Jesus notes that David is the speaker of the promise. If David is the speaker of this psalm and addresses the regal, messianic figure as his "Lord," how can the title "Son of David" be the best title for Messiah? A father normally did not bow to a son. So the dilemma in the question is why David shows this figure such total respect and submits to him if this "Lord" is his son rather than his ancestor.

The text ends here with no answer. The question is posed for reflection. That is precisely how Luke uses it. The issue of Jesus's identity will be the central point of debate as he goes to the cross. What emerges from the image of being seated at God's right hand is that Jesus is both Lord and Christ.

Application. This text functions as yet another call for reflection and decision about Jesus. As one who is both Son of David and his Lord, he should be honored with an allegiance worthy of a king. His rule does not emerge through congressional committee, nor does he serve at the whim of humanity. His commission comes from a higher call and functions at a permanent plane.

In Jesus's position as Lord, we see how powerful our Savior is and what his position entitles him to do in the future. Our responsibility to him is greater than to any other being, and we stand before him not as peers but as servants. That is why Paul often begins his letters by describing himself as a servant of Christ Jesus. He knows who his Lord is and that he ought to respond faithfully to him.

LUKE 20:45–21:4

Original Meaning. Jesus warns of the pride of the teachers of the law, revealed in their long robes and the special greetings in the marketplace. Jesus also condemns their misuse of widows' funds. Apparently in managing widows' affairs, the teachers of the law took a large cut for themselves. Their pretentious long prayers for others in the face of such inconsideration made matters worse. They claim to lead the people and to be examples of God's will, but their callousness shows through.

Luke 21:1–4 shifts to a different type of response to God. In contrast to the Pharisees and the rich who shower gifts into the treasury, a poor widow comes with two copper coins. These coins were the smallest ones made—each worth 1/100 of a denarius (about five minutes of labor at minimum wage). The woman here is not looking for credit, but for how she can humbly serve God.

But God does not see things as we do. He does not count but weighs. Jesus calls this widow's gift the greatest gift of those that his disciples have been observing. What others give comes out of their excess, and they will hardly miss what they toss in for the temple. But this woman is giving out of her poverty. She gives what little she has, even though she needs it to live on.

Application. What is subtle about pride is that it develops at such unconscious levels in the mind that it is often unnoticed by the person who has it. But it does emerge in the way others are treated. Proud leaders manifest a condescending attitude toward others, which is reinforced by the way our culture honors them.

In order for giving like the widow to take place, we must

give consciously and with planning. What we give to God deserves priority. He should not receive our leftovers. As is all too common, the leftovers mysteriously shrink in size to take care of things that are not necessities. On the other hand, giving to God that is set aside from the first inevitably limits what we use for ourselves.

Another important point about giving surfaces here. No one is too poor to give. The issue is not the amount but participation. God loves cheerful givers—people who give as they are led by God. Believers should institute personal structured programs where they agree to up their giving until it reaches a level that they feel God has led them to. To those who do give and at great cost, this text reminds us that God sees what we are doing.

LUKE 21:5–38

Original Meaning. Jesus here treats many themes that connect to the Old Testament hope of the day of the Lord. While prophetic remarks dominate verses 7–24, apocalyptic elements appear in verses 25–28. What is the difference between these two? *Prophetic promise* frames itself in terms of everyday history where God works through agents already present, while *apocalyptic* speaks explicitly of God's breaking into history in a marvelous way. Though Jesus does not say so explicitly, the predicted events begin with persecution in the early church and end with the Lord's return, a time frame we now know represents centuries.

The discourse begins in verse 5 with an observation about the temple in Jerusalem. Jesus and his disciples have just been at the temple, watching the widow make her offering. Some of the disciples comment on the temple's beauty, especially its noble stones and the ornaments that made it such a unique edifice. Certainly a building so grand would have a long life. After all, it was decorated by gifts from many of the surrounding nations and was a building that had received notice around the Roman world.

Jesus notes immediately that the building will not be permanent. With these words he predicts the destruction of Jerusalem in AD 70, for the only way the temple can be leveled is if the city comes under severe attack. Jesus's remark is devastating, since the temple was the heart and soul of Israel's worship. How could God allow the sacred locale of worship to be reduced to rubble after so much effort had gone into restoring it?

Three points about Jesus's extended answer need attention. First, it is important to see how Luke lays out the chronology since his account is more specific than the other Synoptics. A careful look at verses 8–9, 11–12 shows that Jesus answers the question by working at points in the discourse backward in time, with the events of verses 12–19 looking to events that come before Jerusalem's fall in verses 20–28, but only after explaining what the period all the way to the end is like in verses 7–11. The two key phrases in the sequence are: "but the end will not come right away" (v. 9b) and "but before all this [i.e., the end]" (v. 12a). His answer begins with a warning not to be deceived (v. 8) and with an assurance that the end is not yet (v. 9). So verse 12 speaks of events that take place before the things he mentions in verses 8–11. At verse 20, the fall of Jerusalem is central. Then the thing that will happen at the very end of history begins in verse 24.

Second, the events tied to Jerusalem's fall mirror events that bring the Son of Man's return. In other words, the discourse discusses the character of an entire period from the time of Jesus's remarks through the destruction of Jerusalem and into the period of the Lord's return.

Finally, the presence of wars and rumors of wars should not startle them either. Great calamities, like those that engulfed Jerusalem in AD 66–70, should not take them by surprise.

But even before the claims of messianic pretenders and the cosmic chaos comes the persecution of God's people. This actually starts almost immediately after the crucifixion, and large portions of Acts can be read as initial fulfillments of this prophecy. One reason this discourse is so important for the disciples to hear is because Jesus wants them to understand that before the end arrives, believers will experience rough times.

Through these opportunities, the disciples will "bear testimony" to Jesus (v. 13). The theme of witness is a major one in Acts, beginning with Jesus's instruction and promise of the Holy Spirit in Acts 1:8. There is hardly a role more important for the disciple than that of witness. These disciples will have the chance to step up to the public microphone and testify to Christ.

Luke remains focused on what is going to happen soon as the gospel goes out to the Jewish community. Such opportunity for testimony requires resolve because of the uncertainty that results from being under such pressure. Jesus says he will give them the words to say, while in Luke 12 it was the Spirit. The difference indicates how closely together Jesus and the Spirit work. He is the one who sends the Spirit, who in turn enables his people to stand for him. Jesus will give them answers to silence their opponents.

Parents, brothers, relatives, and friends will be involved in the persecution. Some may even be martyred for their faith. Deciding for Jesus can be serious business.

Jesus goes on to give a word about ultimate protection (v. 18; cf. 12:1–5). Though death may come, not a hair on any believer's head will perish. When it comes to life that counts, eternal life, believers can know God will welcome them. To stand with Jesus is to have salvation.

At verse 21:20 Luke is interested primarily in the short-term destruction of the capital and only indirectly in the end-time event. Verses 20–22 review predictions already made in 19:43–44. Jerusalem will be surrounded by armies, so its desolation is near. The Jewish historian Josephus, a contemporary of Luke, tells us that a million Jews were killed and nearly a hundred thousand taken captive. Though some argue the numbers are high (Josephus is known to exaggerate at times), they do indicate how devastating this invasion was. The judgment was horrific; children were even cooked for food.

Jerusalem should be avoided at all costs during this time. Those in Judea should flee to the mountains, while those in the city should try to get out. No one should enter Jerusalem. The language of "desolation" is important. Matthew 24:15 and Mark 13:14 allude to the desecration of the temple. Luke appeals to the term as a general reference to judgment (Luke 21:20).

All these events take place "in fulfillment of all that has been written" (v. 22). There are no surprises in God's plan. Israel's being overrun and the temple's being destroyed do not indicate anything amiss in the plan.

Gentiles will have a role in the city until "the times of the Gentiles are fulfilled" (v. 24). This phrase, which marks out an era, suggests that a time will again come when Israel will be prominent in God's plan. This point is debated among Christians, since many hold that with Jesus's return come the new heavens and new earth. This position argues either that there is no thousand-year reign with Jesus's return (*amillennialism*) or that the church is the kingdom today and as such fulfills millennial promises (*postmillennialism*). But others argue that Jesus's return will begin a thousand-year earthly rule (*premillennialism*) and include a central role for Israel in that rule.

When "the times of the Gentiles are fulfilled" (v. 24), then God's promised plan will move toward completion, a plan Jesus launched in his earthly ministry. So at verse 25, Jesus addresses "the end" that begins with his return. Accompanying that return will be great cosmic signs, and for this reason one will not have to search to find it. The disturbances will be so great as to bring great distress and anguish. One need only picture the trauma that comes at a major catastrophe and multiply it many times to get a feel for what is described here.

At such a moment of insecurity, the Son of Man will appear riding on the clouds. The Son of Man's presence—that is, Jesus's return—will mean that vindication has come near. God's people present at that time can lift their heads, for their redemption is near. In place of the fear (vv. 25–26) comes hope.

As bad as the fall of Jerusalem is, it is not the end of the story. The Son of Man's return means that God's people will see victory. That is why the disciples should keep watch.

To drive home the point Jesus notes how one can tell the time of year by noting the condition of a fig tree. When it sprouts leaves, one knows summer is near. So also, Jesus says, when one sees these things happening, one knows that the kingdom is drawing near. So in effect the parable says to keep one's eyes open for what God is doing.

"This generation" appears to set a specific time frame for these events, all of which did not take place in the lifetime of the disciples (v. 32). It seems clear that whatever "generation" means, it did not refer to the generation of Jesus's time or that of Luke's readers. The view preferred here is that the "generation" that sees all these things refers to the generation present in verse 25. In other words, those who see the beginning of the end in the cosmic signs will see the arrival of the decisive era in the Son of Man's return. Once the events of the final act commence, they will take place rather quickly.

Jesus is so certain that what he is saying is true that he argues that creation will pass away, but not his words (v. 33). The discourse is designed to inform and encourage faithfulness. To do so, what he declares about vindication must take place. Jesus's disciples can count on that fact.

Jesus then continues to warn the disciples to be sure that the day does not take them unaware like a trap. When the Lord does come back, everyone will be faced with the reality of his return and his powerful presence. Some will be ready for it, while others will be surprised. Jesus calls his disciples to "be always on the watch" in looking for his return (v. 36). We must pray in order to escape what lies ahead, both short term in Jerusalem and long term in the end. The ultimate goal is to "stand before the Son of Man" (v. 36). All those who identify with the Son of Man will stand in that day.

Application. This passage tells us something about God, about Jesus, about Israel, and about ourselves (both unbelievers and believers). We will consider the applications for each one of these.

First, sometimes we get impatient with God's control and timing. Like the psalmists, we complain that God does not hear the cries of his people and that evil seems to be victorious. Jesus in this discourse asserts God does control the direction of history. He calls us to be patient and to use our time in presenting the gospel of God's grace to others.

Second, Jesus taught about the end, but he did not major in it. He longed to lead people into a healthy relationship to God in the here and now. We must constantly watch, but only in a way that serves God honorably so that Jesus's return is a reason to rejoice without shrinking back. We must live ethically in this world.

Third, the lesson for Israel is a call to reflection. Why did she lose her precious temple centuries ago? With love and tears, the church proclaims that she missed her time of visitation. In doing so, she became an example, to herself and to all, of the painful price of turning away from God's call. In her persecution of God's children, Israel paved the way for her own judgment.

Fourth, these sections cause us to ponder where we stand before God. God has provided through Jesus the means whereby we can gain forgiveness for any wrongs we have done. We cannot provide for our own salvation. The road of proclaiming one's own self-righteousness was the road the Jewish leadership had taken, and this text makes it plain where Israel ended up. The warning to us is to not make the same mistake.

Finally, what does this text say to believers? We must keep watch, stand fast, and trust God's timing with the reassurance that one day our deliverance will surely come. Events may be painful, for even our families may oppose us and hostilities may feel like they are going to overwhelm us. Yet even though we cannot see it, we can see Jesus, the author and defender of our faith, who promises that one day he will return for us in great power and glory. So, looking to him, we serve and wait with great expectations.

LUKE 22:1–6

Original Meaning. The events in 22:1–38 leading to Jesus's arrest provide his final opportunity to share with his disciples before his departure. This final meal functions much like his last will and testament. The time has come to face the cross. The disciples will need to conduct their faith walk in light of his departure. The moment of truth for all has come.

The Jewish leadership has been powerless to do anything about Jesus because of his popularity. All of that changes when Judas goes to the leadership to discuss how he might hand Jesus over to them. The chief priests' presence shows that the decision is being made at the highest levels. The guard is present because they will have to carry out the arrest.

It is hard to appreciate just how great a break this offer is for the Jewish leaders. Now they can figure out Jesus's private whereabouts, and they have in-house testimony against him. All that is needed is to find an appropriate time to arrest the teacher. It must be a time when crowds are not present. Judas will determine that time. Sinister forces are behind Jesus's death.

Application. We see vividly how Jesus was rejected and betrayed. The hypocrisy of celebrating the Passover and plotting Jesus's death adds to the pathos of it all. What is so tragic is that if we stop and analyze the role of sin in our own lives, we see the same types of behavior and choices. One sin often leads to more sin in the effort either to set it up or cover it up.

Another lesson in the pattern of rejection from the leadership and Judas is the tendency of sin to make someone else the sinner. Sin subtly tends to create a layer of insulation in a form of rationalization. Such a diabolical barrier is built when a man who is cheating on his wife maintains that her coldness forced him to look elsewhere for tender nurture or when children blame the other child's behavior for the right to strike back.

If Satan opposed Jesus here, he will also oppose the church. Defection from within is one of the most effective means he has to discredit the church. Faithfulness to God's will prevents Satan from getting such a foothold.

LUKE 22:7–20

Original Meaning. Jesus sends his disciples to prepare to celebrate the Passover at a house that is ready to host them. Peter and John must not only obtain a locale but also secure the lamb for the sacrifice and pick up the bitter herbs and unleavened bread that are part of the meal.

What is unusual about this instruction is the detail that comes with it. The details given may reflect that some type of prearrangement is in place, since Matthew 26:18 suggests that the host knows who this "Teacher" is. The disciples go and find things just as Jesus has told them.

Luke 22:14–20 occur during the fifth of seven meal scenes in Luke. Such intimate events are the context for much of Jesus's teaching, which can be characterized as "table talk." The meal is also known as the Last Supper, and it forms the basis of the Lord's Supper. The background of the meal is likely a Passover meal.

The hour comes for Jesus to recline at the table and share this final meal with his disciples. He notes how he has "eagerly desired" (a Semitic expression indicating great emotion) to celebrate this meal before he suffers (v. 15). The mention of approaching suffering adds pathos to what follows.

Jesus will not celebrate this meal again until "it finds fulfillment in the kingdom of God" (v. 16). Jesus has in mind here the fulfillment of the kingdom in the consummation. At that time a meal like the Passover will celebrate the completion of the promise. Jesus longs for that moment, but until then this is the last such celebration he will engage in.

This will be the last moment of sustained, shared fellowship with him for some time. But his death means far more than the end of his ministry. The bread Jesus takes is a part of the third course of the meal, eaten along with the lamb and bitter herbs. Jesus makes a fresh symbol out of the bread in light of his death. He takes it, gives thanks, breaks it, and passes it around the table. In that moment the Jewish meal becomes Christianized, a memorial act in memory and proclamation of Jesus's death. The bread symbolizes the broken body of Jesus offered on behalf of his community. It gives them a chance, as one body, to reaffirm what God has done for them. This meal is like a new start.

Thanksgiving to God for the bread is also thanksgiving for the offering that clears the way for a relationship to God. Exactly how Jesus's body is offered for them is not specified here. The Passover was a time when judgment came to the Egyptians in the death of their firstborn, but Israel's firstborn were "passed over" and spared the judgment because blood of a lamb was placed on the lintel of the door at their homes (see Exod 12:13). Jesus now becomes the symbol of such protection.

Jesus goes on to refer to the cup as "the new covenant in my blood" (v. 20). The reference to blood looks at Jesus's coming sacrifice as that which inaugurates the covenantal provision that the disciples will benefit from as a result of Jesus's death. Jesus's blood shed for them clears the way for the distribution of the blessings of this covenant and opens up a new era of God's blessing (see Jer 31:31–34).

In sum, the meal and its memorialization commemorate and declare Jesus's sacrificial death. To share in this meal in the future is to affirm the relationship established by what Jesus is about to do. The meal affirms an intimate oneness between Jesus and those who identify with his death.

Application. Jesus is dedicated to the way and will of God. Facing betrayal and death, he calmly leads his disciples into the celebration of God's goodness in salvation. Though he will soon go to the cross and experience rejection, he leads his disciples in worship and reminds them of their call to follow in his steps.

All of this is reassuring to those who read Luke's account. God's control even amid dire circumstances is important to recall as we face the painful circumstances of our own lives. Though our modern difficult circumstances may not involve martyrdom, there are moments where we or others face desperate circumstances.

Through prayer and supplication, Jesus lets his requests be made known to God, and God's peace serves to guard him. At the base of his assurance stands the God who is represented in the meal he is sharing with his disciples, a God who provides for the deliverance that really counts when all else seems awry.

This supper was never designed to be an element of worship tacked on at the end of the service. In the Lord's Supper, we acknowledge the presence of our Lord, his death, and his coming again. Sharing in the elements together, we affirm our oneness before him and our submission to him, and we recall how we came to receive such grace. The ultimate commemoration of the Lord's table is a righteous life. If new life comes through his death, new life is what should be manifested in response.

LUKE 22:21–38

Original Meaning. Jesus notes with the sharing of the meal that the hand of the betrayer is at the table. He is fully aware of what is taking place, and he goes to his death willingly. It is hard to imagine what Judas must have felt when Jesus reveals his awareness of the betrayal. As the disciples discuss who this person might be, the message that Jesus is soon going to his death is sinking in.

Ironically, as Jesus faces his death and Judas engages in betrayal, the disciples worry about their status before Jesus. The dispute is significant because it impacts the unity of the community. Jesus's reply is like his remarks in the other Gospels. Ruling in Jesus's dictionary means service, not power. Elitism and debate about status are out.

To drive the point home, Jesus offers an illustration. Who is greater in the eyes of the world—the one who is served at the table or the servant who delivers the meal? By noting the character of his own ministry, Jesus sets forth a contrast that is the new example. Better to be a servant than to be served.

Jesus is not uninterested in their status question. He just does not want them to compare themselves to each other. Their constancy is noted and rewarded. The eleven will receive what Judas misses.

God the Father has assigned Jesus a kingdom, so Jesus appoints his disciples to a role in it. This marking out of authority over the twelve tribes shows that Jesus is forming a new community from his disciples. Their authority is not only for this era, but for the one to come as well.

Jesus singles out Peter for special attention because Satan has zeroed in on this central disciple, asking to take him through the sieve. But Peter does not face this alone. At his side stands Jesus, who intercedes for him and for his faith. Jesus goes on to note that when Peter has "turned back," he will be called on to strengthen the people (v. 32). This implies there will be a temporary failure. In the restoration, the ultimate success of Jesus's intercession emerges.

Peter obviously comprehends by this time that death awaits Jesus, and he is confident Jesus need not face it alone. But Jesus knows Peter better than Peter does. He predicts that before the cock crows in the hours just before dawn, Peter will have denied Jesus three times.

Jesus must prepare them to face future realities. Earlier, when Jesus sent them out, God provided for them through people. But now it will be necessary to take a purse, a bag, and even a sword. They are now going to minister in a world that may well be hostile to them. The disciples must be prepared for what lies ahead and understand that ministry takes place in a context of opposition.

The disciples misunderstand his rhetorical remarks about defending themselves in the face of opposition. The sword inventory they really need is an inner one. Jesus thus makes a dismissive remark: "That's enough" (v. 38). This phrase closes the discussion.

Application. At Acts 20:29–30 Scripture warns about wolves who emerge from within the Christian community to ravage the church. We must be careful with this, of course. The last thing churches need are heresy hunters who take it upon themselves to sniff out the least suspicion of error. Yet the New Testament does issue warnings for people to remain faithful to God and to his word. Professions of faith and association with the church are not in and of themselves signs of true faith. Faith does, of course, save, and such faith continues to believe, as the saying "once saved, always saved" implies. God is, after all, thoroughly committed to those who genuinely trust him.

In the world, the leader gets all the perks and receives service. He wields power and authority with a recognition that his rank gives him the right to direct and coerce others into action. Jesus's approach to leadership is the exact opposite. Leadership is a responsibility and a trust to exercise one's skills and energies to serve those who are led.

Christian leadership is not the raw exercise of power but rather a sensitive display of compassion, care, and service. It is the sharing of spiritual resources and energy in a way that leads by example. God exalts those who humble themselves, even as they lead by serving.

The example of Peter warns us that we can easily turn our backs on Jesus when we are under pressure. The disappointment of Peter's denials needs to be balanced with the lessons of the rest of his life. Sometimes we can see complete restoration from a severe fall. The resources Peter had are the same ones we have today. Through the work of Christ and the power of the Spirit, transformation and restoration are possible.

Wars are never won when allies are divided. All our energy and resources should go into making sure we have the provisions necessary to carry out our mission. We can continue to talk about the most effective strategies, but to accomplish our call we must respect those we recognize are on our side and keep the real enemy in our sights. The disciples needed such unity when they launched the church through the Spirit's enabling in Acts. We need to regain such unity to continue her task effectively today.

In contrast to this tendency to fight in-house, Jesus urges preparation and a recognition that we as a community must provide for ourselves. This means the church cannot expect the world to come to its defense. Rather, we must stand together. The defense called for here manifested itself in Acts as the community looked out for, prayed for, and protected figures like Peter and Paul. Our opposition must not be a militant or violent one, a reaction Jesus specifically disapproves of in Luke 22:50–51. Yet it is a form of defensive engagement where the community stands up for its own, offering them protection or caring for them, even if they are called to send them along to a location where they may be at risk. We must work with one another and support one another as we seek to share the gospel in the world.

LUKE 22:39–46

Original Meaning. Jesus takes his customary evening trip to the Mount of Olives, and the disciples accompany him. Before he himself prays, he tells them to pray so as to not fall into temptation. One almost has the sense that he is exemplifying what he calls for from them. Prayer is important since it brings us into communion with God and allows us to draw on his presence with us. Jesus's command to "pray," written in a Greek present imperative, may suggest an ongoing commitment to pray as opposed to a single moment of prayer (v. 40).

Jesus kneels down and intercedes, asking if there might be some other way to accomplish what lies ahead. The request is couched in the fundamental commitment Jesus has to doing God's will. Jesus wants the cup of wrath to be passed from him, but only if there is another way. Jesus has bracketed his request on each end to a commitment to do God's will. The importance of the angelic appearance is that the strengthening from above shows heaven's willingness to stand beside Jesus as he faces his calling.

Here is a very human portrait of Jesus, facing his death with a range of emotions. Luke's portrait of Jesus does not hide behind his deity. He presents a Jesus who can identify with our weaknesses and traumas.

Finally, Jesus gets up and returns to his disciples, finding them "exhausted from sorrow" and asleep (v. 45). They have begun to understand that rejection for Jesus lies just ahead, and it has wiped them out emotionally. The only way they will be ready for what is ahead is if they prepare for it as he has. Faithfulness is grounded in being in touch with God.

Application. Jesus reminds us that prayer is important, even in the most frantic of times. And his prayer is not a matter of merely checking in; it is full of honesty, emotion, and pain. Jesus manifests honesty and humility in prayer. He sincerely desires that God will not make him go through what lies ahead and honestly shares that request, yet he is even more committed to being in God's will. Jesus can walk with God because he regularly seeks God.

The disciples are a stunning lesson in contrast, for they sleep rather than pray. This type of procrastination argues that time or fate itself will settle such matters. Maybe it reflects a view that prayer really accomplishes little. We as his disciples must not regard prayer time at our meetings and functions as a formal preamble but part of the work of ministry itself.

As committed to God as Jesus is, heaven is just as committed to him. The remark about angelic strength should reassure us that as we turn to him, he will strengthen us. Other texts are clear about how God provides "the way out" for us if, as we face temptation, we recognize our need for him (e.g., 1 Cor 10:13).

LUKE 22:47–53

Original Meaning. The betrayal comes as a crowd approaches and Judas comes forward to give Jesus a kiss. The text notes that Judas is one of the Twelve, thus underscoring how far his rejection has penetrated. The kiss, a sign of affection, has become a sign of defection.

The disciples recall Jesus's remarks about swords. One of them (Peter, according to John 18:10), strikes at the servant of the high priest, severing his right ear. Jesus puts a stop to the action. Then he picks up the severed ear and heals the servant. We do not know what effect this may have had on the temple guards, but it does not stop them from carrying out their duty. Everything about the arrest is told in a way that indicates how amazing it is that anyone seeks to arrest Jesus.

Jesus adds one more note. He questions the chief priests, the officers of the temple guard, and the elders whether they really needed to come as if to arrest someone "leading a rebellion" (v. 52). Jesus complains that they act as if he is a common criminal, whereas he has been with them daily in the temple, and they did not arrest him then. There is only one explanation for what is happening. Satan's attempt to stop Jesus is underway. Ironically, the cross will accomplish the exact opposite of what the darkness wishes. Though the Jewish leadership seems to be in control, God and his agent are really in control.

Application. Did Judas hope his act of betrayal would be covered up as the arrest took place? That sin tries to cover its tracks is not at all unusual. One can think of examples where people pilfer funds designated for the needy as they work for relief organizations. Such actions show how hard sin works to disguise itself.

In contrast stands Jesus. As his enemies arrest him and approach him as a dangerous criminal, he gives testimony by healing the high priest's servant. The irony and the picture are a cameo of the gospel. Jesus ministers to sinners in need. Luke is asking those reflecting on his Gospel to think through which side they identify with.

To reject Jesus and his claims is to side with those who arrest him, since their premise is that Jesus is not who he claims to be. Thus, as this passion account proceeds, the constant question is, "Which side represents God?" Luke asks the reader to ponder the question and respond not just with an intellectual choice but with a decision to embrace the forgiveness and blessing Jesus offers those who recognize him through faith.

There is a subtle strength in facing persecution as Jesus did, passively resting in the active defense of his God. The power of such a defense can be seen in our own time with those who have taken a similar approach to ethical issues in the public square. The church today has all the resources to be as bold for Jesus as the early church was.

LUKE 22:54–71

Original Meaning. After his arrest, Jesus is brought to the house of the high priest. Peter has trailed at some distance and ends up sitting down by a fire in the courtyard area of the location where Jesus is being held. One of the maidservants recognizes Peter as one of Jesus's followers and says so. But Peter denies that he even knows Jesus. The disciples have failed to pray in preparation for this moment, and Peter's confidence, so strong in the privacy and safety of a meal, has wilted.

Sometime later, someone else repeats the claim. Peter replies instantly. Peter's denial here is not only of knowing Jesus but also of having any association with his fellow disciples.

The last denial follows about an hour later. Peter's accent identifies him as a man from the northern region of Israel, and he responds. He claims they have the wrong person. The "rock man" (which is the meaning of Peter's name) has been crushed to pieces by the pressure.

With the third denial, the rooster crows, just as Jesus predicted. In an additional touch of drama, the Lord looks at Peter, an act that indicates he knows what Peter has just done. It is too much. Peter departs, weeping bitterly. He has experienced a major failure of nerve. The Lord's word, as always, has come true. He knew Peter better than Peter did.

Meanwhile the soldiers—in all likelihood, the temple guards who arrested Jesus—are having a grand time with Jesus, mocking him mercilessly. In their mocking, they identify him as a prophet, the most popular conception of Jesus. But the Jewish leadership needs a stronger charge than that Jesus is a troublesome prophet. Rome worried about would-be kings, not prophets.

At daybreak, the council meets with Jesus. The account of the trial has several irregularities. Listed below are a few of the procedures that are at variance with the rules in the Mishnah.

1. The proceedings did not take place at the temple.
2. Jesus is allowed no defense.
3. Jesus does not blaspheme in the technical sense of the term by using the divine name.
4. The verdict comes on the same day as the trial, when two days were required for capital crimes.
5. Jesus is being tried on a feast day, normally prohibited.
6. Contradictory testimony is supposed to exonerate the defendant.
7. The high priest is not supposed to issue the pronouncement of guilt.

Exceptions to some of these procedures might be allowed in certain situations, but the mass of them indicates just how quickly (and illegally?) the trial proceeds.

With chief priests and teachers of the law gathered together, Jesus is examined. Luke narrates only the central question:

"'If you are the Messiah,' they said, 'tell us'" (v. 67). He subtly raises the question whether they really want to have a fair trial here or if their minds are already made up. Jesus will go on to say, "From now on, the Son of Man will be seated at the right hand of the mighty God" (v. 69). He makes three claims here. First, he predicts that he will eventually be seated at God's right hand in heaven, an allusion to his approaching resurrection-ascension. Second, he claims to have authority from God, an authority he will exercise from this moment on. Finally, he has authority over them. This may be their trial, but he is the one who will ultimately judge. Jesus answers their question indirectly, but his reply is actually more than they may have anticipated.

Note how Luke is weaving titles together here: Messiah, Son of Man, and Son of God. Jesus replies to the Son of God question with, "You say that I am" (v. 70). The audience takes it positively. They have their man.

What the leadership has been unable to do—namely, to get convicting testimony against Jesus—the Lord brings against himself. In essence, Jesus is the witness the leadership sought and sends himself to the cross. Jesus, of course, spoke as he did because his claim is true.

Just what did Jesus say that was so condemning in Jewish eyes? The key remark appears to be his claim to be Son of God, not merely in a regal sense, but *as it is tied to the claim of being the Son of Man of Daniel 7:13–14*. Jesus in effect is claiming the right to go directly into God's presence and be seated with him in heaven. To Jewish ears this is highly offensive—worse than claiming the right to walk in and permanently reside in the holy of holies at the temple, since the temple represented God's presence in heaven. In a real sense, Jesus sends himself to the cross because he is faithful to his identity amid an audience that rejects his claims. So the Sanhedrin sends him on to trial before the Roman governor.

Application. Christianity is a historically grounded faith. Without a cross, the Christian faith is reduced to a mere form of moral suasion, of no more value than many other religious ethical systems or forms of psychology that seek to make us stronger people. Throughout this Gospel we have seen Jesus make himself the issue; reducing Christianity to moral teaching eliminates the unique person of the Christ from Christianity. Without him and what he accomplished in his death and resurrection, there is not much sense to the faith. Luke wants us to ponder whose side we are on.

Note the varied character of rejection in this passage. The soldiers take Jesus frivolously. We all have met people who have no time for religion and love to mock its existence. The leadership reveals another side of rejection. Though often giving the appearance of fairness, there is a sense in which the jury is stacked in its soul. A hard heart is a tough nut to crack. That is why evangelism in the end must be a supernatural undertaking. We do not always know how our testimony will strike those who are opposed to us. Sometimes the Spirit uses our lives and words to melt a hard heart.

The lesson of Peter is tragic. What is encouraging about Peter's story is that he learns from his failure. Only a few chapters down the road in Acts, we see this same man risking everything to tell about the forgiveness he has found in Jesus. If anyone appreciates what forgiveness and restoration mean, it is Peter.

In fact, the entire story of Peter underscores an important principle about the Christian walk. The goal of the church is not to shoot its wounded to death but to restore them. Though Peter's failure is great, his victory comes through his restoration, a restoration made possible because Jesus is ultimately about forgiveness.

Jesus prepares to bear his cross, something Peter has failed to do. Christ testifies boldly to his identity, even at the prospective cost of his life. In doing so, he becomes an example of a bold witness for the gospel. Several figures in Acts will take the same risk, and many of God's people since have done likewise, as the classic work *Foxe's Book of Martyrs* documents.

LUKE 23:1–12

Original Meaning. After the Jewish trial, the entourage heads for Pilate. No doubt the meeting is quickly arranged. The heart of the case is a threefold accusation: (1) Jesus subverts the nation; (2) he opposes payment of taxes to Caesar; and (3) he claims to be Christ, a king. For Pilate the most dangerous charges are the second and third, though the first charge may suggest Jesus is a source of public unrest. It may be the first charge is general, while the second two are more specific.

The first charge, subversion, naturally leads into the other two complaints. An internal religious dispute is of no interest to Pilate, so more concrete political charges are needed. Since Pilate is responsible to keep the peace and collect taxes, the taxation charges challenge his ability to do his job faithfully. This second charge is blatantly false, as readers of Luke recognize from 20:20–26.

The third charge is the one Pilate pursues. He simply asks, "Are you the king of the Jews?" (v. 3). Jesus responds with a mild affirmative. Jesus is saying yes, but not quite in the sense Pilate intends. It is not clear here what leads to Pilate's decision, but he concludes there is "no basis for a charge" against Jesus (v. 4). He has done nothing worthy of death. This should have been the end of the matter.

Yet the leadership continues to press Pilate, noting that Jesus has stirred up the people from Galilee to Judea. In effect they are saying, "It would be dereliction of your duty to let him go, Pilate!" On hearing mention of Galilee, Pilate thinks up a brilliant solution. He will send Jesus to Herod, since Herod has authority over that region. Now any decision Pilate makes will have Herod's consultation, and Pilate will be protected either way.

Herod is excited about meeting Jesus. He has heard about him and wants to see the Galilean perform miracles. But he is disappointed by Jesus's lack of response. The Jews "vehemently" press their case (v. 10); they are the catalysts in these events. The roles of Pilate and Herod are more passive, but they contribute enough to the situation that they share blame.

In the face of Jesus's silence, Herod and others react with more mocking. They dress Jesus in some type of regal clothing and make fun of the "king," who in their view possesses so little power. Then they send him back to Pilate. Pilate's plan works, for from that day he and Herod are friends.

Application. When we engage in sharing Jesus, we can expect a wide array of responses to him. Some will be decidedly hostile, while others will be more disinterested, just as in the trial scene. But both constitute rejection. Evangelism often requires patience. Our primary responsibility before the Lord is to continue to share him.

LUKE 23:13–25

Original Meaning. Gathered together are the chief priests, the rulers, and the people. A representation of the entire nation in her capital assembles to issue a judgment on Jesus. Though the authority for that verdict resides with Pilate, he negotiates Jesus's fate. Pilate makes his clearest statement yet on how he sees the matter. Pilate concludes that "he has done nothing to deserve death" (v. 15), the same verdict Herod reached. It sounds like Jesus's release is coming.

But Pilate knows he has a political hot potato. So he compromises by offering to flog Jesus and release him. This judgment receives a public reaction: "Away with this man! Release Barabbas to us!" (v. 18). The response must surely have caught him off guard, for Barabbas was incarcerated for leading an uprising and for murder. The leadership and people desire the release of a clearly more dangerous man than Jesus.

Pilate is not the first, nor the last, public official to keep his eye on opinion polls. Like a tennis match, the crowd smashes away Pilate's proposal. They insist on crucifixion. Only Jesus's death will satisfy them.

Crucifixion was designed to deter criminals. That is why the executions were public. Treason and evading due process were the normal grounds for such a death. The crowd wants Jesus not just to die, but to experience this most gruesome form of execution. He is counted among the worst of criminals.

Pilate insists that nothing worthy of death has been done, and he repeats his earlier verdict to chastise and release Jesus. This agitates the crowd even more, and the voices get louder. Pilate has moved from a private hearing to a near riot on a feast day when the city is full of people. He finally relents. Barabbas is released, while Jesus is surrendered to the will of the people. It is not justice that sends Jesus to the cross, but a mass of humanity.

Application. The passion is narrated for our reflection. As we read or hear it, the text calls for us to make decisions about the various reactions to Jesus. The leadership fabricated charges and rejected a solution that would spare an innocent life. Luke leads the reader to see that there was something criminal in Jesus's death, and it was not him.

The fickle people also represent something not quite right. Days before, some hailed Jesus as a king. Now, however, a murderer is better than him. In just a few days, everything has changed. The people reflect a shallowness of conviction and an ability to be swayed that warns against a superficial approach to these issues.

Pilate is a man who tests the wind more than assesses the truth of Jesus's claim. He does not stand up to his responsibility. The world often passes off major religious decisions as Pilate did. Religious issues need to be thought through, not simply reacted to, as if a Gallup poll can decide religious truth. How many other Pilates might there be in our world?

Barabbas's story is our story. Jesus freed us by his death, just as Barabbas was freed. One who saves a life is owed a life. The Christian walk is a statement of gratitude to the one who has taken our place. He did not complain as he bore the cross for the murderer and for us. Those who have been rescued from the penalty of sin understand that in Barabbas's freedom is a portrait of their escape from death through the gracious work of Jesus.

LUKE 23:26–49

Original Meaning. Jesus goes to his death after a long day and night of emotion. Without sleep and after a scourging, he needs help in bearing the cross. Simon from Cyrene is drafted to carry the cross. Jesus's going to the cross is not a private affair. It involves others because of what he is accomplishing there. As he goes to the cross, another person, just like us, shares in his journey there.

Behind Jesus is a host of people. The crowds that urged his execution have stayed on to see it carried out. With them is a group of women, wailing in mourning. Jesus urges them not to weep for him. Painful as his death will be, he knows that he will be taken care of, since his vindication in resurrection is only hours away. The real issue moves beyond what Jesus will suffer to what his death means for those who reject him.

Jesus then exercises a prophetic role on his road to the cross. Hard days lie ahead for the nation, in which "childless women" will be blessed (v. 29). Here is a reversal of the normal Jewish view that blessing comes from a fruitful womb. That is because the judgment to come on the nation will be harsh. People in Jerusalem will be crushed because of their failure to recognize what they are doing.

The locale of the crucifixion is a place called "the Skull" (v. 33). In Aramaic, the name is "Golgotha"; in Latin, *calvaria*, which is why we refer to this site as Calvary. The hill where executions take place protrudes out of the ground like a skull. Jesus's cross is situated between the two criminals. This is revealing, since in the debate between the criminals one of them will soon confess him and be saved. Jesus is the bridge by which the unrighteous can become the righteous.

As he awaits his death, Jesus turns again to the Father in prayer, asking that the actions of his enemies be forgiven. By praying for his enemies, Jesus has fulfilled an ethical standard he himself noted: to pray for one's enemies. Jesus evidences his love and compassion here and models his own instructions on discipleship.

The soldiers at the cross are simply biding their time until the execution is complete. They divide up his clothes among them by casting lots. This remark alludes to Psalm 22:18, which is a psalm about the suffering righteous and how they are treated. Another part of the psalm shows up in Jesus's cry from the cross about being forsaken by God. He is hanging on the cross as an innocent man, willingly dying for those who do not understand his death and who mock it.

This execution fits the pattern of public crucifixion known in the ancient world. The people "watch" what is taking place, and the leaders "sneer" (v. 35; both verbs appear in Ps 22:7). Their sarcasm shows just how much confidence and passion that Jesus's enemies have. They are comfortable with his execution. The ultimate irony, however, is that God will actually perform their request in Jesus's resurrection.

The soldiers add to the mocking. They offer a dry "wine vinegar" that was used among the poor (v. 36). Their taunt is for Jesus to save himself if he is the king, which shows that compassion is not their real motive. At this point Luke records the notice of the crime: "THIS IS THE KING OF THE JEWS" (v. 38). He consistently shows how it is Jesus as the Christ who goes to the cross.

The scene turns back to the criminals. One of them feels free to be a part of putting Jesus down. Like the leaders, he calls on Jesus to deliver himself if he is the Christ. In addition, he should save them too. But the other criminal speaks up and rebukes the first criminal. He stresses that their sentence is just, since they are getting what they deserve. In contrast, Jesus is innocent.

This criminal accepts the claim that Jesus is a king, and he wants to share in his coming rule and to be among the righteous in the judgment. Jesus's reply indicates that an answer to his request will come sooner than the criminal hopes. Even this very day, they will be together "in paradise," a word that refers to the place of the righteous (v. 43). Jesus is saving people even as he hangs on the cross.

At midday it becomes dark for three hours. Now even the heavens testify to the nature of the hour. In the Old Testament darkness often indicates judgment. God is signaling his presence. The sun is nowhere to be found. The real hour of darkness has come.

The curtain at the temple is torn in two. A time of judgment has come, and the temple is included in that judgment. Since the temple is the center of Judaism's religion, this is a significant judgment for the nation. The tearing of the curtain also suggests an opening of the way to God. The curtain shielded access to God. By ripping it open, restricted access no longer exists.

Jesus's final words come from Psalm 31:5. Jesus trusts the Lord to care for him. This psalm describes a righteous sufferer, just as Jesus is. What happens from this point on is up to God. He will have to give his testimony about Jesus by what he does in the next few days.

A centurion then has some insight into the event, which serves as the final commentary Luke supplies for the whole event. He declares that Jesus is surely "righteous" (v. 47). The centurion thus becomes a second witness to affirm Jesus's legal innocence as he is dying, and the fourth person in Luke 23 to do so.

The crowds also react. They depart, beating their breasts. The cosmic signs may have given them pause. Imagine slaying the Messiah of God and realizing that the mistake has been made when it is too late to reverse it! Such mourning may have prepared the way for the openness Peter meets with in his speech in Acts 2, since these events became well-known.

The disciples see things from a distance. Among them is a group of women who have been with Jesus from the start of his ministry in Galilee. The one thing this death has is numerous witnesses. Luke has noted many different groups who share in what has just taken place. He has also noted the variety of perspectives about the event. Which one is true? The closing words of the centurion leave no doubt.

Application. The New Testament uses many images to describe what the cross is and how we should see it. It is a ransom, a payment for the debt of sin. It is a substitution—Jesus offers himself in our place. It is a propitiation, satisfying the justice of God by dealing with sin. It represents Jesus's exaltation, and through it Satan is overthrown. It is the means by which the church is purchased. It is the sacrifice that ends all other sacrifices for sin.

The cross probably should not be so much discussed theologically as meditated over and pondered. I sometimes wonder if a Good Friday service should not allow for a long period of silence and prayer before the Lord, where each person can reflect quietly on just what the cross means to him or her. Silence is usually not popular in our culture. But the cross is an event that should be absorbed, not just described.

The cross is at its heart the offer of God's gracious forgiveness to those who embrace it. To embrace the cross means to renounce our own works as the basis of our salvation. Our relationship with God comes through trusting in Jesus and in his finished work. Our spiritual well-being rests solidly and securely in the hands of a caring heavenly Father.

For those who have made that decision, the cross reminds us where it all started. Our relationship with God is a response of gratitude for all he has done to bring us to himself. Grace calls us to live in a way that honors God by reflecting the new life he has provided for us. Reconciliation with God not only transforms our relationship with God, but also alters the way we relate to others. In a real sense, the ultimate application of the cross involves relating to others on a different basis, because we now operate in the world as forgiven people who know where and how they fit in creation. The cross becomes the ground of all Luke's passages on discipleship. Another way to say this is that at the center of God's plan stands Jesus, and at the center of Jesus's work stand the cross and resurrection.

One final application is important here. The cross is described through appeal to a variety of psalms that point to Jesus's suffering as a righteous and innocent person. He is an example of someone offering everything to show his love for his neighbor, even when the neighbor unjustly treats him. Jesus thus shows how the person who walks with God should reach out to the lost. The least we can do is to proclaim to everyone the forgiveness that Jesus died to provide.

LUKE 23:50–56

Original Meaning. Joseph of Arimathea does not think it appropriate that Jesus should be buried in a pauper's grave. He takes possession of the body, brings it down from the cross, and wraps it in linen—probably a fine cloth. Joseph places the body in a previously unused tomb, probably tunneled out of the side of a rock, having a small door-like entrance of perhaps a yard in height. Such tombs were present just north of the city. Jesus receives an honorable burial.

His action does not take place privately, for some women observe him as he lays Jesus in the tomb. The fact that these women are from Galilee indicates that they have been disciples for some time and know Jesus well. They will not make a mistake as to whether and where Joseph has taken Jesus.

As the women prepare for the Sabbath, they also prepare spices and perfumes, a custom common for Jews since they did not embalm. The spices and perfumes were placed on the body to reduce the stench and decomposition. These women fully intend to return to the tomb. They want to continue to honor the Lord. There is no indication they expect a resurrection that involves Jesus's body.

Application. One of the charges some make today is that the resurrection was an event created by the early church in order to allow Jesus's memory and teaching to continue. If that were the case, the authors of the Gospels have certainly found an unusual way to describe the preparation for it. Their testimony is that the resurrection caught the disciples by surprise. When Jesus died, they figured he had departed. Even though Jesus prophesied his resurrection, it did not sink in. If the resurrection were a fabrication, would its creators portray the disciples as being so much at a loss to understand what Jesus was predicting? It is more incredible to believe in a fabricated resurrection, for which some of Jesus's followers even died, than it is to take the possibility of resurrection seriously. The implications of this contrast lead directly to a decision for the resurrection and to Jesus's claims about who he is.

LUKE 24:1–12

Original Meaning. At the break of dawn on the day after the Sabbath, certain women journey to the tomb with their spices to anoint Jesus's body, fully expecting to find it in the tomb. The first hint that something unusual has taken place is that the stone is rolled away at the entrance of the tomb. The women enter the tomb only to find that "the body of the Lord" is missing (v. 3). Note that the predominant title for Jesus in this chapter is "Lord," the name that, through Jesus's resurrection, reveals his lordship and points to his exaltation and vindication by God.

At this point "two men" appear (v. 4). Their clothes gleam like lightning, suggesting that the term "men" is a euphemism for angels. They appear to function as two witnesses. The women know that they are in the presence of some type of supernatural beings, so they bow before them in respect.

The men speak to them by asking a simple question: "Why do you look for the living among the dead?" (v. 5). In other words, Jesus is alive. The tomb could not hold him. The verb "has risen" is passive and implies that God is responsible for Jesus's return to life (v. 6a). God has intervened, just as Jesus promised.

"Remember how he told you . . ." (v. 6b). This remark is both a call to remember and a rebuke. God often says things we fail to understand because we have trouble accepting them. But when God speaks, we must listen—not according to the categories we are used to but with hearts that recognize who is speaking the promise.

The angels' remark leads the women to recall Jesus's words. God's words are indeed coming to pass. If we want to find the fulfillment of God's promises, we must look to Jesus.

The women journey back to where the disciples and others are gathered and tell their story. Despite these numerous female witnesses, their story is not viewed as credible. Not only is it hard to accept, but culturally such a story from women would be viewed with suspicion. One of the main proofs that the resurrection story is credible is realization that the first-century church would never have created a story whose main first witnesses were women. Luke is clear just how skeptical the first audience is that hears about the resurrection. The first skeptics Jesus faces are his disciples.

But Peter knows better than to doubt the Lord's word. During his denials, he has learned that the Lord knows better than we perceive. So he runs to the tomb, bends down to glance in it, and sees the grave clothes present and the body absent. He leaves the tomb "wondering to himself what had happened" (v. 12). Using a word short of full faith, Luke adds to the drama by having Peter ponder what is going on. The first steps are here, while the full conviction comes in the following accounts.

Application. Perhaps we should be less surprised when people initially stumble over the resurrection. After all, the disciples hurdle it only after much persuasion. The Bible is real as it tells its story. The doubt of the disciples is set forth with crystal clarity. Their slowness to believe is not exemplary, but it is instructive. Resurrection is a doctrine that is hard to believe. For that reason, the Spirit needs to work in hearts as the gospel is shared.

According to the Christian hope, God gives everlasting life to his children in a world that he will remake and renew. If such a world is to come and if God keeps his promises, preparing for it is more important than any short-term issues we face today. Visionary thinking, so popular today, is designed to consider the long-term picture. There is nothing more visionary than thinking about our long-term relationship to God.

In sum, resurrection changes everything. Luke wants us to ponder the "so what" of Jesus's resurrection—that Jesus is alive and offers forgiveness, so that I can have a new relationship with God through him. For believers, resurrection is a reminder that new life is a gift from God that calls us to a life of gratitude. To those who do not know him, Scripture calls them to embrace what the resurrection means.

LUKE 24:13–35

Original Meaning. The encounter between Jesus and the two disciples on the road starts with another journey. Two men are traveling to Emmaus. These disciples apparently are heading home after a traumatic weekend.

They find themselves discussing what has taken place. Perhaps they are disputing the meaning of the empty tomb. Jesus approaches them as they talk, though they cannot tell it is him. Jesus's first post-resurrection appearance in Luke is both normal and mysterious at the same time. This description adds to the drama and the mystery of resurrection.

Jesus asks them about their discussion. One of the two, Cleopas, is amazed. Of course, Jesus knows exactly what has happened, since it happened to him! Nonetheless, Jesus asks, "What things?" The disciples answer immediately, "About Jesus of Nazareth," and note his prophetic work (v. 19). They note how the chief priests and rulers handed him over for death by crucifixion. The disciples themselves thought Jesus was more than a prophet and hoped he would be the one to redeem Israel. That was the hope they saw nailed to a cross in the capital city.

But there is more to tell. Three days later, some of the women among the disciples stunned the group. They went to the tomb only to find it empty. They also reported angels telling them that Jesus was alive. Other companions went to the tomb and found it empty, just as the women reported, but Jesus was nowhere to be seen. How ironic the report is, in light of Cleopas's audience! The two disciples are baffled by what has taken place. The last thing they expect is a resurrection.

Jesus then launches into a rebuke, whose rationale becomes clearer as events move on. For Luke's readers, this is a call to believe and not slip into the fog that these two disciples are currently in. They must believe all that the prophets have spoken, a brief way of referring to the messianic promises of the ancient Scriptures. These things "have to" be (v. 26), since they are part of God's effort to restore relationship with humanity. Jesus then begins to explain these promises to the two travelers, working from Moses through the Prophets.

As the three near their stop at the village, it appears as if Jesus will journey on. But the two men persuade him to stay with them, since the day is nearly over. As Jesus reclines at the table with them, he shares a meal. In a setting with a pastoral feel and a picture like that of the Last Supper, he takes the bread, gives thanks, breaks it, and gives it to them. Suddenly, their eyes are opened. They see that it is Jesus. But as soon as they recognize him, he is gone.

Cleopas and his friend acknowledge how amazing their walk and talk have been. Had not God been at work through Jesus's words to help them see what God was all about in the suffering and the glory of Jesus? Was it not the promise of God that they have just experienced? Now it all makes sense.

They return at once to Jerusalem. There the Eleven and the others are still gathered and quite excited. Before the two from Emmaus can get their story out, the report of the truth of the women's story fills the room. "It is true! The Lord has risen and has appeared to Simon [i.e., Peter]" (v. 34). The Emmaus disciples then tell what has just happened to them on the road and how Jesus revealed himself to them at the table. Despair becomes delight as the truth about Jesus's resurrection begins to sink in.

Application. The most basic application of this section, as with all of the resurrection accounts, is to reassure us that Jesus has arisen and is alive. Such reassurance should deepen our faith each time God's work for us is affirmed. First Corinthians 15 explains exactly how the resurrection achieves this hope by calling Jesus's resurrection the "firstfruits" (v. 20), with more resurrections (ours!) to come.

The declaration of Jesus at the right hand of God found its way into the oldest creeds of the church (e.g., the Apostles' Creed). This is not an abstract declaration. Central realities of the Christian life are bound up in this affirmation. Jesus's place at the right hand of God means that he possesses authority over all those forces that stand opposed to humanity, both in this age and in the age to come. Such authority stands behind his ability to give us new birth.

This aspect of resurrection hope is important, since we often feel that our sin or the devil is more powerful than we are. Yet in the context of Jesus's power obtained through his resurrection, we have access to the one who enables us to overcome whatever obstacles Satan places in our path. The letters of the New Testament, besides being commentary on the cross, are commentary on the resurrection, since everything that we have in Christ ultimately is only possible through the resurrection.

The resurrection and the word of God combine to illustrate the reality of the realization of God's promise. At the one end stands the word revealed and moving toward realization. As revelation of God, it is to be embraced and believed, something the disciples were slow to grasp. On the other end stands the resurrected Lord Jesus, exercising the many prerogatives the word attributes to him in fulfillment of God's promises. Some of those promises still remain to be fulfilled. When the Lord returns, he will finish what he has started. So the resurrection is a bridge into new life and the first step of glory that leads to the consummation of his promise.

LUKE 24:36–53

Original Meaning. The present passage is an extension of the previous passage, where the reporting of Jesus's various appearances continues. The momentum of his appearances is stacking up, as one meeting follows another in rapid succession. As the disciples are sharing reports, Jesus himself stands among them and gives a beatitude that sums up his ministry in triumph, "Peace be with you" (v. 36). It is a greeting of comfort. The group is frightened by his appearance, since they think Jesus is a spirit (v. 37; NIV "ghost").

Jesus asks the group why they are troubled and why they have doubts. Jesus's remarks suggest some are still doubting even after the appearances. So he invites them to look at and touch his hands and feet, where the evidence of his crucifixion remains. The resurrection body is both the same as and different from the physical body, retaining aspects of physicality while existing in a glorified condition. Jesus does everything he can to reassure his disciples that he is truly alive. To drive the point home even further, Jesus asks for something to eat.

Jesus then explains what has taken place. A crucified and resurrected Messiah is not an adjustment in God's plan; this road was in the design all along. In fact, everything written about Jesus must be fulfilled. The disciples are experiencing what Scripture promised and what the saints of old longed to see.

Jesus then instructs in the Scriptures. Note that the church has developed its understanding of the Old Testament from Jesus. His instruction regarding basic elements of divine promise is summarized by three verbs: "suffer," "rise," and "be preached" (vv. 46–47). All three of these stages are reflected in the Old Testament. The Christ, the Messiah, was to suffer and to be raised, and the disciples must now engage in preaching to the nations.

To repent is to change direction from allegiance to idols to serving the living and true God. This change of perspective embraces Jesus and produces the forgiveness he offers. This message of salvation extends to all the nations. They must preach to every tribe and nation—a fact we take for granted today but that was revolutionary at the time, since religions had a stronger ethnic character to them.

The disciples saw Jesus hang on the cross and have now seen him in his resurrection. Their calling is to share that what they know has taken place according to the Scriptures. Jesus will send them out, but not before he has equipped them. To this end he will send to them the Spirit from his Father. The allusion here is to Joel's promise of the Spirit in the end time (Joel 2:28–32) as part of the promise of the new covenant (Jer 31:31–34; Ezek 36:26–27). The Spirit is the one who enables us to witness and testify to Jesus effectively. As God's plan moves ahead, the disciples are a major part of its advance. But until the Spirit comes, they must remain in Jerusalem.

Luke's Gospel closes with Jesus's taking the disciples out to Bethany, lifting up his hands, blessing them, and departing into heaven. Jesus blesses the disciples as he departs to continue his work from God's side. What follows for them are worship and joy. They return to the temple, where Luke's story began with Zechariah, in order to praise God for all that has taken place. Luke never forgets that the heart of a believer's walk involves responding to God with joy.

Application. The commission in Luke 24 calls us as a community to take the gospel to all nations. But how can we do that effectively? We must offer that gospel message in terms that the particular culture can comprehend. Paul, for example, cited Greek poets or used terms of the Greek culture. As the church continues to take the gospel to the world, we must think through how to communicate its truth through pictures familiar to our audience.

We can speak of *repenting* when considering where we start from at conversion. We can speak of *turning* to describe the change of direction that comes from embracing God. We can speak of *faith* in Christ to highlight the object of our hope. We can speak of *receiving him* to emphasize the personal appropriation of faith that is more than mental assent. We can speak of *coming to him* to describe the act from Jesus's perspective. We can talk of *confessing him* as an expression of how faith verbalizes its presence. All these terms highlight the saving act of faith where people embrace Jesus with a trust that he will forgive them by his grace and bring them into relationship with himself.

Another issue raised by this text is Jesus's resurrection, because its presence proves that there is an afterlife. Death is not an end but a transition. The critical question is, a transition into what? Will a person enter into eternal life or into a second, more permanent death? The choice for life involves a choice for Jesus.

It is a privilege to be witnesses to Jesus. We often hear people say they are afraid to witness because they are not sure what to say theologically. They do not feel capable of debating with their lost friends, or they do not always want to. But we do not need to learn a list of theological terms or a ream of apologetics in order to be witnesses; we simply need to tell our story.

Lest we get too nervous about evangelism, let's remember that we do not share Jesus by ourselves. Jesus has provided his Spirit, who indwells us to help us make sense of our testimony. The disciples waited for the Spirit in order to be empowered and enabled to share with conviction. To see how effective the Spirit can be, we need only contrast the Peter of the three denials with the Peter of the speeches recorded in the book of Acts.

What other movement has been able to span the centuries and the variety of cultures that the Christian movement has touched? Where else can people of a wide variety of national backgrounds be woven together in a rich fellowship? Part of the gospel's power is surely seen in the success of the commission that was launched from the original apostles.

We have an opportunity to share in that march of faith throughout history. God is at work in it all, fulfilling what he promised centuries ago in the Old Testament. He is as present in our own sharing as he was in the commission Jesus issued to a small group of mostly Galilean followers in the first century. The march of faith moves one era at a time, one person at a time, one testimony at a time. Centuries ago, Luke wrote to reassure Theophilus that he belonged in that honored line of march (Luke 1:1–4). Fortunately for us, God made sure that Theophilus was not the only one to be reassured about his grace through Jesus.

JOHN

INTRODUCTION TO JOHN

The Fourth Gospel provides no explicit internal evidence concerning its author. The best solution is the traditional one: John son of Zebedee. This man was one of the Twelve and along with James and Peter formed an inner circle around Jesus. Patristic evidence seems to confirm this conclusion. Irenaeus, writing at about AD 200, says that the Beloved Disciple was John, the disciple of Jesus, and that John originated the Gospel at Ephesus.

Fixing a certain date for the publication of the Gospel is difficult because objective data is slim. The latest possible date is AD 125. Traditions about Jesus that John preserves most likely stem from the earliest apostolic period—perhaps AD 60–65. But the final edition of the Gospel may have been published later. John and/or his disciples may have edited the work, making additions and sharpening its message for later Christian faith. Tradition tells us that the place of writing was Ephesus, and no decisive reasons have been raised against it.

To a greater extent than the Synoptics, each section of the Fourth Gospel contributes to a central theme: the appearance of the Son of God in human history. John explores two facets of this appearing: its revelation and its redemption. Offending every modern sensibility, John writes that in Christ we behold the glory of God—even though he appeared in flesh. But the gift of Christ is not simply his revelation of the Father. John's second message concerns redemption. There is hope for us in the world. The message of history's invasion is also a message of sacrifice and redemption. Those who embrace this revelation, who identify with the light and have faith, will gain eternal life.

BOOK OUTLINE

If we scan the entire Gospel, we at once can see some natural divisions. Scholars have been quick to note these divisions and label them. Chapters 1–12 are called the "Book of Signs" since they record Jesus's numerous revelatory miracles. Chapters 13–21 (uniting the upper room and passion sections) are called the "Book of Glory," since on the cross Jesus is glorified.

The Book of Signs (1–12). *The Prologue (1:1–18)*

I. Jesus and the Baptist (1:19–51)
II. Jesus and the Jewish Institutions (2:1–4:54)
III. Jesus and Jewish Festivals (5:1–10:42)
IV. Foreshadowing Jesus's Death and Resurrection (11:1–12:50)

The Book of Glory (13–21). *The Passover Meal and Farewell Discourse (13:1–17:26)*

I. The Suffering and Death of Jesus (18:1–19:42)
II. The Resurrection (20:1–31)
III. Epilogue (21:1–25)

JOHN 1:1–18

Original Meaning. One reason why the Gospel of John was symbolized in the ancient church by the eagle is the lofty heights attained by its prologue. This prologue may well have been an ancient Christian hymn. We know of other hymns extant, especially in Paul's writing, and here too there is an artful flowing of language and theology. This prologue is also an overture to the story of the rest of the Gospel. More precisely, verses 11–12 reflect the layout or the emphasis of the Gospel's entire structure. The first half of the Gospel (chs. 1–12, the Book of Signs) describes the rejection of Jesus by Judaism. The second half of the book (chs. 13–21, the Book of Glory) describes the "flock of Jesus," those who have embraced his messiahship and followed him.

The First Strophe: The Logos and God (1:1–2). John begins by establishing the preeminence of the Word existing before the creation of the world. The initial allusion to Genesis 1 cannot be missed. This is a Gospel that will record the re-creation of men and women, the giving of life in darkness where there is no hope.

John begins by introducing Jesus as "the Word" (*logos*) and is building here on much contemporary Jewish thought, where the word of God took on personal creative attributes. John identifies this Word as Jesus Christ. As such John can attribute to him various divine functions, such as creation and giving of life.

But John goes further. He is ready to infer some personal identity between the Logos and God. "And the Word *was* God." John is making an absolute affirmation about the eternal existence of the Word. It did not come into being nor was there ever a time when "the Word was not." Whatever we can say about God, we can and must say about the Word.

Some have argued that because *theos* ("God") does not have an article, the better translation would be, "The word was divine," thereby limiting any absolute claim for the Logos. But this cannot be the case. Greek has another common word for divine (*theios*), and in other passages John omits the article but does not imply a change in meaning.

This is John's overture to Christology and the beginnings of his Trinitarian thought. We will be introduced to Jesus time and time again, and in each case we will be forced to picture Jesus with increasingly profound images. He is the greatest of all people; he is the Messiah of Jewish expectation; yet more—and this is John's unique message—he is the Son of God, the divine messenger from the Father.

The Second Strophe: The Logos and Creation (1:3–8). Once John has identified the Logos with God, he continues to mark the relation of this Logos to the world. As God's creative agent, he was responsible for the creation of the world. John's language here is careful and specific: the Logos was never created. *Nothing* came into being without him. John stresses not merely that who God is, the Logos is (the first strophe), but that what God does, the Logos does. Therefore, in the Gospel what Jesus does is divine activity.

The entry of the Logos into the world (his incarnation) is described as light shining in the darkness (v. 5). Even though John the Baptist's testimony was clear, still Jesus experiences rejection. The darkness is hostile. There is enmity.

John suggests that the darkness cannot defeat or overcome the Word. This theme gives us some hint of the struggle between light and darkness that will sound throughout the Gospel. The opposition to Jesus will be severe.

John emphasizes the true nature of the Baptist's ministry and shows how he came as a witness to Jesus; this theme is clear in the other "Baptist" sections of the Gospel. What does the writer say? John the Baptist was *not* the Messiah or the light. Instead, he came as a witness to tell the truth about what was happening in the world.

This is the first time we see the word group for "witness" (v. 8; Gk. *martyreō*, *martys*, *martyria*) in the Gospel. As if in a courtroom, evidence and witnesses will come forward to verify the truth of Jesus's case. John the Baptist is the first of these literary witnesses. Essential to John's mission is a denial of his own significance: "He himself was not the light" (v. 8). John's main role is simply to identify and glorify Jesus.

The Third Strophe: The Logos and Revelation (1:9–13). John the Baptist was bearing witness not to an abstraction or a hope, but to a reality. The "true light" was coming (v. 9). The virtue of this divine entry is in how it reaches all people, particularly those hostile to God. In John's vocabulary, the "world" (*kosmos*) is an important theological term, appearing seventy-eight times in this Gospel alone. For the most part, references to *kosmos* are decidedly negative. The world is not the created order of things; it is not the natural environment per se. It is the sphere of creation that lives in rebellion against God.

But if the world is hostile, how can the true light enlighten *everyone*? Does its arrival illumine every heart? Perhaps John is thinking of the accessibility of everyone to this one source of illumination. The light invades the darkness, shining on every person and exposing them for who they are.

Despite the presence of the Logos in the world, despite his creative work making the world and leaving the marks of general revelation, still the world failed to recognize him. Similar to the parable of the vineyard owner and his renters, the residents repudiated his visit. Therefore, John has made a startling claim. Even though the focus of revelation has been in Israel, the natural home for the truth of God, the Word has come for the entire world, not merely for the Jews.

John indicates, however, that the light has its followers; Jesus has his disciples. Even though his own people—adherents to Judaism—spurned his message, those who did receive him obtained power to become God's children. Verses 12–13 anticipate the story of Nicodemus, in which this rebirth is explored (see 3:1–21).

Those who follow the Word, who believe and obtain divine power, will share in divine birth. This is John's understanding of conversion: deliberate faith joined with divine transformation. In other words, there will be a powerful transformation of those who embrace this light, who align themselves with the light instead of the darkness, who cling to the Messiah instead of the world.

The Fourth Strophe: The Logos and Incarnation (1:14–18). Verse 14 is one of the most important verses in the Bible. The Word did not just appear to be human; *the Word became flesh*. This assertion stunned the Greek mind for whom the separation of the divine spirit and the mundane world ("flesh," *sarx*) was an axiom of belief. But the second phrase is equally stunning for the Jew. This Word "made his dwelling" (*skēnoō*) among us and revealed his "glory" (*doxa*, v. 14). This verb for dwelling is employed in the Greek Old Testament for the tabernacle of God. In other words, Christ is the locus of God's dwelling with Israel *as he had dwelt with them in the tabernacle in the desert*. Hence the glory of God, once restricted to the tabernacle, is now visible in Christ.

This experience of glory is concrete. The glory of God took up tangible form in the person of Christ. This glory was not merely a display of power. For John the deepest irony is how glory is to be found in the cross of Christ, again and again described as Jesus's *glorification*. His signs and miracles showed his glory, to be sure, but it is in the cross that the mysterious, unfathomable glory of God is to be found.

It is curious that the word *grace*, so common in the rest of the New Testament, is virtually unused by John and appears only here in the prologue (four times: vv. 14, 16 [twice], 17) and then disappears. John likely has in mind the generous work of

God in sending his Son, which results in our salvation. Grace is found in God's coming and working *despite* the hostility and rejection of the world. John emphasizes our experience and reception of this grace as its chief merit.

The more important word for John, however, is *truth*. Most simply it is the opposite of falsehood; but John sees truth as penetrating far deeper. Truth is the self-disclosure that alone comes from God; truth is not just what is right but what is divine—*and this is right*.

John the Baptist's cry as a witness to Jesus repeats his role as witness. Even though Jesus comes after John chronologically, this does not give John priority. These words pick up on the theme in all of the Baptist texts, where John's secondary status is underscored. Jesus does not have a relative superiority but an absolute superiority.

Throughout this Gospel, it is clear that the apostle John and his community are struggling with the counterclaims of the Jewish synagogue. John does not intend to show that the grace of Christ stands at odds with the revelation of Moses. The law likewise contains the grace of God and is an earlier display of it.

Verse 18 joins verse 1 as the closing frame of the prologue, offering a summary statement about the divine origin and exhaustive knowledge of the Son. Christ's revelation is unique for ontological reasons: it is his identity, his being, the essence of who he is that makes his words God's words. Indeed, Christ is fully God, who in his incarnation is revealing *himself* to the world.

Application. *Voices.* The world in which we live is looking for a diagnosis of its condition and its possibilities for renewal. There are countless voices providing messages that promise to alleviate the struggle of life or the questions that trouble us. These prophets of our day offer services that are deeply needed and useful, but their voices cannot replace the voice that John 1:1–18 introduces.

Three strands. The prologue provides a theological template, weaving together three strands of thinking that, when taken together, form the essential fabric of the Christian message.

Definitive Christology. Jesus is God-in-flesh. There never was a time when the Son did not exist.

This notion challenges a major shift in the way the modern world views reality. Western society had emptied modern life of the ability to see the world *theocentrically*. We must uncover today's *pagan cosmology*. The cosmos is not merely explained by cause and effect. God is the architect of history, who delights in making himself known and who enters our reality through word and miracle, showing his glory and power. Christ is God once more at work, disclosing himself to his creation.

Complete rejection. The great irony of Christian theology is that the very medicine that can cure the human condition is rejected. Christian theology affirms that humanity is in a state from which there is no freedom. John understands that we do not live in a nice world that God desires to make nicer. Humanity must be reborn.

Absolute transformation. The natural eye cannot see the glory of God since it is dimmed by sin. Instead, it is necessary for God to work, to self-disclose, to send his Son, who alone has exposed God's heart. When God takes this initiative, new possibilities are born. Divine power is released into the broken world and its broken lives so that new life is possible. Transformation is not an inspired human work; it is a divine work through and through.

JOHN 1:19–51

Original Meaning. The author's purpose in these verses is the nature of discipleship and what it means to meet, know, and follow Jesus. In each case, disciples are invited to have a personal contact with Jesus and to recognize who he truly is.

John the Baptist's Self-Denial (1:19–28). John's baptizing activity at the Jordan River attracted a great deal of attention, leading many people from Jerusalem and the surrounding regions of Judea to come out to him either to be baptized or to inquire about his work. One such delegation was sent by "the Jewish leaders" to interrogate the Baptist (v. 19). The term in John's Gospel generally represents the Jewish leadership in Jerusalem who are hostile to Jesus. It has a specialized usage stemming from John's own world, a world in which synagogue and church were struggling.

What we have here is an interrogation by emissaries from "official Judaism," from the temple and its interests. John the Baptist was an odd phenomenon and needed investigating. Three names are at stake, and together each of them probe John's intentions vis-à-vis Israel.

1. John first denies that he is "the Messiah" or "the Christ." "Christ" is a Greek translation of the Hebrew word for "Messiah." Throughout the late Old Testament period and especially in intertestamental Judaism, hope in a coming Messiah was widespread. It is no accident that in the days of Greek and Roman oppression, the term *Messiah* was filled with political connotations.
2. If John were not the Messiah, perhaps then he was Elijah. Jewish speculation proposed that he was mysteriously alive and would return at the end of time. John denies that he is Elijah who has returned.
3. "The Prophet" (v. 21) is likely a reference to Deuteronomy 18:15–19, where a prophet "like Moses" would return to Israel sometime in the future. John's answer is succinct: no.

Following this series of denials John now identifies who he is. He is "a voice" and quotes Isaiah 40:3 in order to identify his role in Jesus's mission (v. 23). He is a tool in God's hand, pointing to another on the horizon. John's message said that the dawn of the messianic era was at hand and virtually no waiting was needed.

Baptism was generally reserved for gentiles who had converted to Judaism. It was a total cleansing that marked a threshold crossed. John, however, was calling *Jews* to be baptized, and of course this prompted the question, "What is the new order that would change us as Jews?" The promise on the horizon is not a new religion but a person. John describes him as so great that by comparison, John will be less than a slave.

John the Baptist Bears Witness to Jesus (1:29–34). The episode on "the next day" is a continuation of John the Baptist's testimony to Jesus (v. 29). While previously John could only hint at the coming of Christ, now he identifies Christ plainly. Note how confidently the Baptist can speak of his knowledge of Jesus (v. 33). It was knowledge that had come to him through revelation—when the Spirit descended on Jesus (v. 32).

1. Jesus is identified as "the Lamb of God . . ." (v. 29). Here we see Jesus as a gift provided *by God* to take away sin. As a lamb he becomes a sacrificial animal whose death "takes away" a condition that is prohibited in the presence of God. Since this Gospel highlights the festivals of Judaism, and in particular the Passover, it is not unreasonable to see Passover imagery here as well.
2. John's second testimony on this day occurs in verses 32–33. Here his testimony is remarkable. The Spirit descended and *remained* on him. This is a permanent anointing; this is an anointing unlike anything witnessed before in Judaism; this is the messianic anointing. Moreover, this Jesus is not merely anointed himself with the Spirit at his baptism, but he will baptize others in the Holy Spirit as well. Indeed, John has witnessed the dawning of the messianic era.
3. The final testimony given by John the Baptist in this day appears in verse 34: "I have seen and I testify that this is God's Chosen One." "Chosen" likely comes from Isaiah 42:1, which emphasizes the Spirit-anointing of the Messiah and uses this title for him.

Peter and Andrew in Judea (1:35–42). In verse 37 we learn that two disciples hear John testify to Jesus. One is Andrew, Simon Peter's brother. But that leaves unanswered the identity of the other disciple in verse 37. It is no accident that this unnamed disciple may be our first hidden reference to the apostle John, likely the person behind the mysterious title "Beloved Disciple" used elsewhere in the Gospel.

The language of verses 38–39 is the explicit language of discipleship. This language is consciously designed to describe discipleship: to "follow" (*akoloutheō*), to "come and see," and to "stay, remain" (*menō*) each describe aspects of discipleship. As we explore the wider meaning of this discipleship, we will examine these words with some care.

We are told that these events occur "about four in the afternoon" (v. 39). This is not only one more indication that John is providing an eyewitness account, but it may refer to the fact that here Jesus has invited them to spend the *entire* day with him. This visit becomes a teaching session, in which Jesus discloses not only his messianic identity but likewise his mastery over these new followers.

In Jewish culture naming is a significant event. Names unveil something of the character of the person, and renaming indicates something of the authority of one person over another. Jesus is here asserting his authority over Peter and telling him that he is a different man, a man who is about to acquire the character of his true name, a name he has likely forgotten. It is striking that "rock" is not the image that comes through the portrait of Peter. Peter is impulsive and in the end will deny Jesus. But despite Peter's frailty, this name signals Jesus's vision for what Peter will become.

Philip and Nathanael in Galilee (1:43–51). The north shore of the Sea of Galilee hosted a number of fishing villages (Bethsaida means "house of fishing"), and Jesus based his Galilean ministry among them. They were important places because they resided on the main highway that brought traffic from the coastal hills of Judea to the northern regions of the country.

Philip and Nathanael were from Bethsaida. Philip appears only rarely in the Gospels. Nathanael is not listed among the apostles; this has led to speculation that perhaps he should be identified as Matthew or even Bartholomew. In all three Synoptic stories Bartholomew is listed with Philip. But we cannot be sure.

Jesus sees in Nathanael a good man, an honest man. And much to Nathanael's surprise, Jesus refers to seeing him "under the fig tree" at an earlier time (v. 48). Jesus has a capacity for knowing that which is more than humanly possible. At once Nathanael, who now has experienced Jesus for himself, addresses him with a litany of titles. It is such a man who recognizes the true identity of Jesus.

This chapter has one more surprise. Verse 51 introduces Jesus's first use of the "*amēn, amēn*" formula (obscured in the NIV's "very truly"). Literally Jesus says, "Truly [*amēn*], truly [*amēn*] I say to you . . ." Jesus describes angels ascending and descending on the Son of Man as the heavens open. This image springs from Jacob's life. In Genesis 28 when Jacob is en route from Beersheba to Haran, he stops in Bethel and sleeps. In Hebrew, Bethel means "house of God," and Jesus is indicating that this is precisely who he is in his own person.

Verse 51 also introduces us for the first time to the curious phrase "Son of Man." While "Son of Man" is likely a Hebrew self-ascription meaning "I," in Daniel 7:13–14 it appears as the title of a heavenly personage who is given ultimate authority by God. Jesus likely picks up this term and uses it extensively in order to avoid titles that were loaded with political ideas. With it he can forge his own identity that is sufficiently ambiguous and that conveys overtones of divinity and authority.

Application. *Love for God and knowledge about God.* John 1:19–51 is a theological model for what it means to follow Christ. As a model, it urges that personal piety ("loving God") must be wed to theological sophistication ("knowing God"). This twin emphasis on personal piety and theological sophistication is desperately needed in the church today. Pews are filled with men and women whose love for God is strong and yet whose understanding of the content of the faith is diminishing. They cannot explain it, and when intellectually challenged they struggle to defend it. Honed theological expertise is as valuable as personal spiritual experience. It is the anchor that will keep disciples committed with their minds as well as their hearts when the going gets tough.

JOHN 2:1–25

Original Meaning

The Cana Story (2:1–12). In the village culture of Palestine, weddings were important events, announced well in advance and recognized by the entire village. Following a public betrothal that was far more permanent than a modern engagement, the family announced the wedding date, and elaborate preparations were made for a ceremony that could last for as long as a week. Gift-giving was carefully considered, not as a simple gesture of goodwill but as a means of bringing honor on the couple and their families. This gives us an interesting insight into the concern of the servants when the feast suddenly runs out of wine. This is not merely an embarrassing situation; it is a dishonoring crisis for the host.

Mary's statement in verse 3 prompts Jesus to respond in an unexpected way. The English tone of this seems harsh, but it is simply formal. In some sense, Mary is presuming on her relationship with him as her son, yet Jesus must follow the course that has been determined for him by God. Jesus's orientation for activity is elsewhere. The important Greek word "hour" [*hōra*] in verse 4 is used throughout this Gospel to look forward to Jesus's important work on the cross. Mary's request for activity is thus given an ironic spin inasmuch as Jesus will not act merely on behalf of this wedding but for the entire world. His death on the cross will provide far more than wine.

The story gives us an important clue as to its meaning when we discover that six stone jars will now be the source of the new wine. The note that they are stone is a signal that they are for Jewish purification washings. The six jars hold considerable volume, each with a capacity for over twenty gallons.

The stewards are then told to take some of the water that is now wine and bring it to the head steward. The head steward makes a pronouncement with telling significance: in most banquets, the best wine is served first. Jesus is delivering something to the banquet quite unexpected. It is superior to anything the banquet has witnessed before. John's emphasis, therefore, is on the quality of this wine and its timing; things served before this wine are inferior.

John consistently refers to Jesus's mighty works as "signs" (*sēmeiōn*; v. 11). A miracle underscores power and is generally received with awe. A sign is revelatory, disclosing something from God, something hidden before. The signs are not merely acts of power and might, but they unveil that God is at work in Jesus and indeed is present in him. Since he radiates the presence of God, he appropriately shows forth God's glory.

The Temple Story (2:13–25). In the first section, Jesus worked a miracle on Jewish purification vessels. Now Jesus comes to Jerusalem for a major festival in the city. He enters the temple (a place of sacrificial purification) and likewise does a symbolic work, demonstrating that it also will experience replacement and fulfillment (just as the stone water vessels in Cana were filled with new wine).

The Synoptics place the temple cleansing at the end of the ministry of Jesus, while John introduces it at the beginning. I suggest that John has recorded his own version of one cleansing, and while it is a historical record he has moved it chronologically for theological reasons. Using uncompromised historical material, John is creating a theological portrait of Jesus's display of signs in the context of Judaism. Jesus is the fulfillment and replacement of Judaism's festivals and institutions. And the temple is high on his list as a place that soon (through his death) will no longer serve the purposes of God.

Passover was an annual festival celebrated each spring. Over the centuries Passover had become a pilgrimage festival in which Jewish families were expected to travel to Jerusalem and participate in sacrifice, a symbolic meal, and reflective study of Israel's deliverance from Egypt in the exodus. Since pilgrims would need approved animals for sacrifice, a considerable business grew in the city at this time of year. Jesus is attacking the financial machinery of the festival system, which certainly would put him at odds with Caiaphas and the temple leadership.

His disciples recall Psalm 69:9 (v. 17). Theologically this is John's way of indicating two things. First, Jesus is acting out of his relationship with the Father. As Messiah and God's Son, he is driven to defend and promote God's interests in the world. Second, John often uses the Old Testament at the major junctures of Jesus's life. He is working out the purposes of God—purposes he knows have already been outlined in Scripture.

When confronted with his actions, his critics demand that he show some sign to demonstrate his authority to cause such upheaval. Curiously, Jesus refers to his *own* destruction and resurrection. Jesus's audience misunderstands him and thinks he is referring (ironically) to the Jerusalem temple.

In Judaism of this period, many spiritual leaders expected that a new temple would be built and that the present temple in Jerusalem would be replaced. Even after the Roman destruction of the temple in AD 70, Jews continued to retain a hope in the coming of the Messiah, who would bring a newly built temple. But Jesus's deeper meaning referred to his body, which would serve the same function as the temple, even replacing it. Jesus is predicting his death and resurrection, which will create a new covenant with God and make the services of the Jerusalem temple obsolete.

John provides a telling wordplay in verse 24. The same Greek word translated "believe" in verse 23 appears in verse 24: even though some of these people *believed* in him . . . Jesus would not *believe* in them. Jesus understood about all of humanity and its capacity for deception and duplicity. John is making a sweeping theological affirmation. God alone knows the hearts of men and women—and now Jesus has this same capacity.

Application. *A wedding in Cana.* It is easy for us to spiritualize the work of Christ today and conclude that he is only in the business of saving souls and renewing lives. But is he really interested in the commonplace events of my life? Is he really interested in the simple conundrums of everyday living? The Cana story says yes. We can invite Christ into dilemmas that seem embarrassingly inconsequential—dilemmas that seem ridiculously practical—and ask him to help.

There is also an important theological message that this story is telling us. John is telling us something about Judaism and history. The arrival of the Messiah means that something unparalleled is happening in the world. Jesus's public display of glory here is a definitive event. The glory of God has suddenly become visible in human form. John has in mind the Shekinah glory that resided first in the tabernacle and then in the temple of Jerusalem. Jesus Christ is a man, and yet no mere man can bear this glory. Hence Jesus Christ is also divine, God's Son, who has united with humanity in perfect union.

If indeed God is at work in the world in unprecedented ways, then his appearance among us ultimately alters the value of all religious ritual expressions. Vessels of purification cannot be put to their former use. The Messiah has touched them and made them obsolete for purification. This is an idea that must be brought into my contemporary world. We have created a world of religious vessels no less traditional than the ones described in Cana. God has arrived, and Christ desires an immediacy, an intimacy with us that will not be impeded by ritual forms that no longer bring life.

Finally, the Cana story forces us to probe the relation of faith and miracle. The disciples saw the sign and believed in Jesus. Does this mean that experiencing the miraculous can be an avenue to faith? The chief problem with faith anchored to the miraculous is that miracles become an end in themselves. People begin to seek bread rather than the bread of life. Yet, having sounded this note of caution, we still need to note that Jesus worked wonders and through these displayed his glory. Miraculous signs may become a powerful means to discover or strengthen faith.

Disruptions in Jerusalem. Jesus came to the center of Jewish life, and he acted there in what was considered an outrageous way by those who witnessed it. It was a center where in that day politics, religion, and law were virtually inseparable. Our society has intentionally separated church and state, and their domains appear completely distinct. Yet it is not so simple. For one thing, secular society does indeed promote an innocuous sort of religion that is a brew of patriotism, self-sacrifice, tolerance, and openness. "Aren't churches supposed to promote good things like this?" argue the priests of that temple.

But we are also called to be participants in our society; to respect it, yes, but also to be a witness for God's interests. To be salt and light. To be a light on a hill that cannot be missed. We need to be agents for change that not only speak the gospel to our world but also who are angered by the things that anger God. Evangelical Christianity is not often outrageous. Yet Jesus went to Washington. He was outrageous.

JOHN 3:1–36

Original Meaning

Jesus and Nicodemus (3:1–21). The story of Nicodemus is another story in which Jesus continues to reverse the prominence of institutions in Judaism—to replace them, to show their incompleteness in light of his arrival, and to supplant their function with his own life and work. The notion in this and so many other discourses is that unless some deficit is met (generally faith or the Spirit), deeper penetration into the words of Jesus is impossible.

We know that Nicodemus was a member of the Jewish ruling council and that he was a Pharisee. We also know he was a rabbi, a teacher no doubt of some fame. When this rabbi comes to Jesus at night, it may simply refer to his desire for privacy stemming from fear. He might worry that the temple authorities, whom Jesus has just challenged, might see him as a collaborator.

But "night" (v. 2) is also likely a theological symbol (used frequently by John) that expresses Nicodemus's spiritual relation to the truth. Nicodemus is a man of the darkness, while Jesus is the light. John's subsequent commentary says this plainly: Jesus is light that has come into the world, but men and women prefer darkness (v. 19). In this case, however, Nicodemus has stepped into the light to make inquiries.

Nicodemus's first question shows admirable respect launched by one theologian to another. Two terms require definition. First, although the Old Testament does not use the phrase "kingdom of God" in full (v. 3), the notion of God's sovereign, kingly rule is implicit throughout Scripture. Judaism taught that this was to be a future kingdom and that all Jews who faithfully kept the law would be admitted to it freely. Second, however, Jesus asserts that there is a new prerequisite to see or enter this kingdom. "No one can see the kingdom of God unless they are born *again*" (v. 3). In order to enter the kingdom, in order to understand divine revelations such as this, one must have an experience that transports beyond the mere observation of "signs" (v. 2). The language Jesus uses would have seemed unusual to Nicodemus. Jesus is driving at something comprehensive, a complete renewal of the whole person.

Nicodemus's question shows that Nicodemus is outside the kingdom and that he cannot penetrate its deeper truths. Thus Jesus must explain more fully. Divine birth is now explained as birth "of water and the Spirit" (v. 5).

This critical phrase has given interpreters difficulty. A likely view is to see this as a reference to John the Baptist's baptism, which the Gospel has already introduced in the narrative. Nicodemus (by this reading) must submit to the baptism of repentance offered by the Baptist at the Jordan. Following this he can experience the Spirit and transformation.

Another option suggests that "water and Spirit" form a unified concept to express the eschatological renewal promised in the Old Testament. This figurative pair appears again and again in the Old Testament, and no doubt Ezekiel 36:25–27 is the most important eschatological image of all. Here Israel's heart will be transformed.

Jesus is here pointing to the dawning of a new eschatological era. John the Baptist has inaugurated this era, and submission to his message—his water baptism, which is the precursor for Christian baptism—is expected. Jesus now is one who baptizes "with the Holy Spirit" (John 1:33), who will complete the dawning of this time. But above all, Nicodemus must understand that this era will be an era when the Spirit of God moves among humanity. Jesus compares this with the "wind," another Greek wordplay, since *pneuma* can mean either "spirit" or "wind" (3:8). Its origin and movements are mysterious, and they cannot be contained by the human religious systems Jesus has already challenged.

Nicodemus's final question is rhetorical in the narrative. "How can this be?" likely disguises a thoroughgoing and lengthy inquiry by the rabbi, whose religious categories have now been upended (v. 9). He is baffled. He is disturbed. He is a man standing on the frontier, looking at a new country and wondering how such momentous events will unfold.

Jesus begins his answer with (literally), "Truly, truly I say to you" (v. 11), as if to underscore the importance of what he is about to say. The irony of his response is that he refers to Nicodemus as a rabbi, just as Nicodemus had referred to Jesus, but now we see that this teacher does not know the answers. Jesus is the only true rabbi who can explain the deeper mysteries of God.

But the problem is far deeper. It is not really a problem of knowledge. The signs and Scriptures are accessible here on earth, and if these cannot be understood and believed, it is not possible for profound heavenly things to be believed. People who stumble on the elemental teachings of Jesus cannot hope to grasp the deeper realities. Jesus is unique among all others to disclose these heavenly truths because he is the only one among humankind who has truly entered heaven's realms. Human teachers do not have access to this sort of revelation.

Jesus then refers to a story from Numbers 21, in which Moses built a serpent of bronze and elevated it among the Israelites so that whoever gazed on it would be healed from the snakes that bit them in the desert. In the same manner, Jesus says, he must be "lifted up" in order to become the source of eternal life for all who believe (John 3:14). The Greek *hypsoō* ("lift up") is an important Johannine verb to describe Jesus's "ascent" or "lifting up" to the cross (3:14; 8:28; 12:32, 34). John has in mind that the cross will not simply be a place of sacrifice and suffering but a place of departure and of return, when Jesus resumes his life with the Father. Jesus *ascends* to the cross. As we will see later in this Gospel, the cross will actually be a place of glorification.

The statement that God loves *the world* is surprising (v. 16). Judaism rarely (or never) spoke of God's loving the world outside of Israel. It is a uniquely Christian idea to say that God's love extends beyond the limits of race and nation. For John, *kosmos* is the realm *of humanity* arrayed in opposition to God. Thus Jesus enters this world in his incarnation, knowing that hostility will result and that sacrifice will be needed in order to redeem the world. The Son did not come to the world to save a select few; rather, he came to save *the world*, namely, the all-encompassing circle of men and women who inhabit this planet, people who embrace darkness habitually.

In this respect, the entry of the Son into the darkness of this world is an act of judgment (3:19; cf. 9:39) inasmuch as divine light has penetrated and unveiled the darkness for what it is. Yet Jesus has not come to condemn the world but to provide a way of escape for those shuttered in the darkness. Those who see this light and recognize the tragedy of their own situation have one responsibility—to believe.

Yet the affections of people in the world are corrupt, their desires are fallen, and they are not eager to be redeemed. Evil and darkness do not ignore the light; rather, they wage war against it, trying to bring it down. But despite these efforts, the darkness launches a battle that brings about its own defeat.

By contrast, those who love the coming of the light, who look on and trust the upraised, crucified Son, who believe in Jesus and "live by the truth" (v. 21) not only enjoy eternal life but come to the light and yearn for its truth. John is describing what happens when those in the world make a choice to believe—they are transformed into children of God. Such people live righteously because God is at work in them, not because they have a native desire to be godly.

Jesus and John the Baptist (3:22–36). Following his conversation with Nicodemus, Jesus and his followers move into the regions east of Jerusalem, where he conducts a ministry much like that of John the Baptist. This is an interesting note since it is our only record that Jesus had a baptizing ministry. But we must remain clear that at this point Jesus is conducting a baptism of repentance since the Spirit (a feature of *Christian* baptism) has not yet been given.

The dispute described in verses 25–26 is the root of the problem that the Baptist's subsequent speech in verses 27–30 will address. These verses indicate that the Baptist had followers who knew about the events surrounding Jesus's baptism, who knew John's testimony concerning him, and likely knew Jesus by name. They seem disgruntled, unhappy that Jesus is becoming a celebrated leader.

The Baptist's rejoinder corrects the rivalry. God has provided the successes and increases enjoyed by Jesus. Such growth should not be criticized. Above all, John affirms that he is not the Christ but his forerunner. Jesus is superior because of his heavenly origins. Truth is something that *descends*, not something that is discovered through human labor. It is foreign. It comes from outside and thus runs the risk of rejection.

The two Greek verbs at the center of verse 33 are in the aorist tense. This describes men and women who have made a firm decision once and for all. John's imagery is graphic. In antiquity wax seals were used to give authentication and ownership to letters and possessions. Hence, to embrace Jesus is to set a seal, to confirm, and to defend an entire constellation of beliefs central to Christian faith and God.

What is at stake here is the nature of Jesus and his authority. God's love for the Son is so complete that *nothing* is beyond the Son's reach. The Father has commissioned the Son to come to us. Above all, the Father has provided the Son with the Holy Spirit. Verse 34 does not refer to Jesus's giving the Spirit to us, but to God's giving the Spirit to his Son, underscoring the remarkable interconnectedness of Father and Son once more.

Jesus bears a divine nature and carries God's authority. Therefore, the gift of life and Spirit that the Son will distribute comes from the gift of life and Spirit that the Son already enjoys. It is a gift that will be distributed once the Son of God is glorified.

In verse 36b John then looks at salvation from the other point of view. Those who reject the Son will not see life; instead, God's wrath rests on them. This verse does not indicate that God is angry in light of their rejection. Rather, it means that the world of darkness and unbelief stands under the judgment of God, and those who refuse the light, who reject Jesus, remain in the darkness and thus continue to live under that divine judgment.

Application. *The conversion of Nicodemus.* The longer we are in the church, the more we are likely in need of conversion stories. To convey the decision that faced Nicodemus and the prospect for his renewal, we have to tell stories that describe what would have happened if Nicodemus had been "born again." Nicodemus was challenged to think about the frontier between what is above and what is below, between the darkness and the light. The drama of belief, of choosing to come to the light, is a drama that must remain before us so that as disciples we can understand where we stand and where an unbeliever must move in order to enter the light.

There is also a provocative, secondary message here, which has to do with cultural and intellectual bondage. There is a link between spiritual receptivity and the degree to which we are settled into a system of life and belief. The greater our comfort, the less our chances to receive a new word, a transforming word from God. This is probably the reason why as people age, the possibility of their conversion tends to decrease.

Our arena of comfort also has to do with the scope of our religious knowledge. Nicodemus was a man skilled in religious rhetoric. He knew Scripture and had no doubt built his own "systematic theology" that explained God, his world, and his relation to both. His problem was not a lack of knowledge; in fact, his great knowledge in some fashion may have anesthetized him from true spiritual conversion. Religious knowledge can become a shield, a defense with which we protect ourselves from the very God we claim to know. It is like visiting a Pentecostal worship service with a theologian or a sociologist.

They can always explain what is going on without reference to genuine divine power.

But is John 3 a message that only pertains to the non-Christian? To be sure, the invitation to believe in Jesus and to be born of water and Spirit is an invitation to Christian discipleship. But Nicodemus was a man steeped in religious tradition; he knew how to teach and defend it. I firmly believe that there are men and women in the church today who have not really heard the Nicodemus story. They have grown up in their tradition, they have taught and defended it, but it has become a tame and predictable thing. Jesus is talking about mystical experiences and spiritual power. One can harness this Spirit no more than one can harness the wind.

A final contemporary note has to do with the work of Christ and Christology. The imaginative picture used by many to express the work of Christ is that Jesus has died in order to placate an angry God, whereas the cross expresses the love of Christ for us and his work appeases God's threatening wrath. This makes God an opponent and an adversary while Jesus is our ally.

But this is not what John says in 3:16. "God so loved the world . . ." The work of Christ is *God* at work, *God* saving the world, *God* extending himself into the condition of our humanity and bringing about reconciliation. God himself is on our side. God himself is at work on our behalf. He did not send a messenger (Jesus) to do the dirty work. God himself came to the cross and suffered in order to bring his beloved creation back to himself.

John the Baptist and charismatic leadership. The impulse to follow a charismatic religious leader is with us today as much as it was with the first disciples in the first century. We have simply replaced those ancient names with contemporary names of spiritual heroism and theological insight. In some cases, these are nationally known names, men and women whose writing and speaking become the model against which a pastor's sermons and skills are compared.

The problem is not necessarily with their contributions but with their followers, who have a personal interest in elevating them to levels that the leaders would not accept for themselves. John the Baptist was doing exactly what God had gifted and called him to do; contemporary leaders are often doing the same. But their followers exploit the leader's stature as a means of leveraging their own power or position in the kingdom of God.

John 3:22–36 is all about the fragmentation that results in the kingdom of God when Jesus is made to compete with human vessels in this world. No one will admit that they are competing with Jesus. No one will say that they are impeding the kingdom's growth. Words like envy, jealousy, and rivalry are never admitted. But just as the Baptist's followers were interested in making him into an institution, so too the Christian church can become a human institution built on the foundation of human enterprise and personality.

JOHN 4:1–54

Original Meaning

Jesus and the Samaritan Woman (4:1–26). By Jesus's day, a smoldering tension existed between the regions of Judea and Samaria. Partly based on race and religion, it echoed many centuries of terrible political fights. Therefore, when we read that Jesus, in passing through the region, meets a "Samaritan woman" (v. 7), the story does not mean that she is a resident of the city of Samaria but that she is from the region of Samaria. She is a woman bearing the history, language, religion, and attitudes of people on the far margin of Judaism. A first-century reader would barely expect Jesus and the woman to acknowledge each other's presence, much less speak.

In John 4:6 the Greek word for "well" actually refers to a "spring" (Gk. *pēgē*), that is, a free-flowing water source or fountain (such as Jerusalem's Gihon Spring). Jesus arrives at the well and sits on the wall at its edge to relieve his fatigue. Throughout this Gospel, John emphasizes the divinity of Jesus in the strongest terms. But here he easily and comfortably shows an incidental human feature: Jesus is tired. John's Christology does not emphasize one dimension of Jesus at the expense of the other.

It is noon. In this culture, water collection was a responsibility of women. In a world that isolated women socially, the task was not entirely burdensome but became an opportunity for women to meet and talk. Historically, water-drawing took place either in the early morning or at dusk in order to avoid the Mediterranean heat. She draws water when other women are absent. Later, of course, we learn the reason for her isolation: she has doomed her reputation and broken the morals of her community. This makes Jesus's overture and conversation all the more remarkable. In this world men rarely speak to women in public. Single men *never* speak to or touch women at any time. Above all, a rabbi would observe these ideals scrupulously. The surprising thing is not that Jesus would ask her for help with a drink; rather, it is that he would ask her *anything.*

The conversation between Jesus and the woman is a delightful, dramatic play. Woven through are two questions, two challenges launched by Jesus in 4:10: Will this woman comprehend the gift of God and its giver? Will she ask for a drink? We are left in suspense, wondering if the woman will have the courage to ask Jesus to be her water source and will identify him accurately for who he is.

Jesus says something unexpected: he is able to provide "living water" (v. 10). "Living water" refers to water that flows as in a spring, river, or stream—that is, *moving* water. Living water was precious and was the only water that could be used in ritual washings to make pure unclean worshipers. Everyone knew that Shechem had no rivers or streams. How could a Jewish outsider, someone who barely knew the terrain, offer water that no one else had found?

But the woman stumbles on the metaphor and misunderstands. She is curious about the possibility of a nearby stream or spring, but Jesus wants her to look beyond, to the spiritual significance of what this water means. Living water is life nourished by God. God is the source of spiritual renewal, and other avenues simply must be rejected.

Jesus is talking about a new life that is available through the Spirit of God. Water has become a symbol of this new reality since the beginning of the book and later will be defined as the Holy Spirit. Christ himself is the source of precious living water, which can transform even this woman in her isolation.

But Jesus takes this promise a step further. It is not simply an experience that changes our state, but it is a dynamic experience that makes a life as living as the water itself. The water (or Spirit) will transform a life into a well that "wells up" (*hallomai*, v. 14). The woman in search of a well discovers that the Spirit could transform her life into a well that does not require reaching and dipping, but which roils and gurgles with water until it spills over its rim.

The woman has requested water, but she does not understand the gift, nor does she know the identity of the giver. No doubt Jesus's request that she summon her husband was a shock. Her response that she has no husband may have been true were she divorced or a widow. But Jesus reminds her that she has had five husbands, and her current lover is either a sixth husband or a man to whom she is not married.

She has sinned, and the reputation that has dogged her incessantly now has surfaced again. But Jesus is not simply judging her. She rightly sees that this uncovers his abilities as a messenger from God, and so she recoils, looking for a way to deflect the moral probing of this stranger.

The Samaritans understood the expectation of Deuteronomy 18:18, which said a great prophet would follow Moses. But this was to be the messianic figure of the final day. Therefore, in referring to Jesus as a prophet the woman unwittingly has opened the subject of messianism for Jesus.

In verse 20 the woman launches what she hopes will be her most potent salvo. She refers to the historic religious division between Jews and Samaritans. Both groups understood that God had commanded a place be set aside for worship, but they had serious disagreements about its location. King David decided to select Jerusalem, and after he acquired land and brought the tabernacle there, his son Solomon built God's temple.

The Samaritans rejected this tradition. In the Pentateuch, the first place where Abraham built an altar was at Shechem beneath Mount Gerizim. Given their historical commitments, it made sense that this mountain was deemed to be the place chosen by God. Even following the destruction of the Samaritan temple in the second century BC, priests continued to sacrifice and worship there. Jesus is therefore being invited to enter this historical-religious quagmire and give comment. But once again Jesus deflects her appeal to racial division and supplies a sharp commentary on worship.

Jesus comments on the inadequacy of Samaritan worship. Jesus is a Jew. The Messiah was to be a Jew. Therefore, Judaism is the trajectory of religious history through which God has been at work. Jesus indicates that the debate between Gerizim and Jerusalem is only marginally important anyway since both places will soon be obsolete. A cataclysmic change will occur *in worship* when Jesus goes to the cross, offering himself as sacrifice. Finally, Jesus defines carefully what is coming and what is even now dawning on earth. Worship in "spirit and truth" (NIV 1984; NIV 2011: "in the Spirit and in truth") is the key phrase that controls what Jesus means and is no doubt tied to Jesus's affirmation that "God is spirit" (v. 24). Jesus is describing something of the dynamic and life-giving character of God.

Worship in spirit is dynamically animated by God's Holy Spirit. But it is more. This is worship empowered by God but also informed by the revelation of God and provided to humans by the one who is the truth, Jesus Christ. This is worship not tied to holy places but impacted by a holy person, who through his cross will inaugurate the era in which the Holy Spirit will change everything.

The woman's final statement to Jesus again tries to deflect his clarification. The Samaritans did believe in the coming of the Messiah and understood that this person would explain everything to them. But the woman implies that both she and Jesus will have to wait. To this woman, Jesus does not qualify to be this Messiah, but such spiritual explanations are on the horizon for them. But unwittingly, she has used the very words that best describe Jesus. With simple dignity, Jesus accepts the titles for himself. The woman has rightly identified Jesus.

The Greek phrase of 4:26 (literally "I am—who speaks to you") holds a term that is peculiar to the Fourth Gospel and will recur with some frequency: "I am" (*egō eimi*). The phrase is emphatic and unusual. As we will see later, it is not always just a term of self-identification that bears a predicate. It is also the divine name of God uttered on Mount Sinai to Moses. Throughout John we will see Jesus's absolute use of this phrase without a predicate to disclose more of his divine identity.

The Food of Jesus (4:27–42). Jesus's disciples, who had left to get food, now return and express normal amazement that he is talking with a woman, much less a Samaritan. Of course, they are likely thinking about the prohibitions lived in tradition and written in law that forbade a man to talk casually with a woman. But they may also have been intrigued that Jesus would engage a woman *theologically*. The rabbis taught that theological education, that is, instruction in the law, was for men alone.

Much has been made of the woman leaving her jar behind (v. 28) in order to report to her neighbors. Her zeal to share her discovery made her leave behind anything that would hinder her. One sign of discipleship is the testimony given to others—words that eagerly spill out because of the preciousness of discovery. Potential converts need only to come and have their own experience with him.

In the woman's absence, the disciples urge Jesus to eat. Jesus's claim to possess food baffles them since their assignment was to acquire food. Did someone (the woman?) give him food? Their misunderstanding enables Jesus to press their thinking to another level. Obeying the Father is Jesus's more deeply satisfying task.

In verse 35 Jesus reminds his disciples of a farming proverb in order to point them to their present obedience. Jesus is thinking about the span of time between planting and harvest when the grain is growing but not mature, when the fields are full but not ready for cutting. The farmer relaxes and enjoys the promise of plenty. But Jesus abruptly changes the image. The fields are *now* ready for gathering! Jesus is in the world, God has invaded the field with seed, and it is bearing fruit already.

Sometimes those who do the preparatory work are not the same as those who harvest. But what does Jesus mean by "others [who] have done the hard work" (v. 38)? This is possibly John the Baptist or Jesus himself. Either way it is an important theological statement since it defines Christian mission in terms of what has gone on before, what God has been doing in advance of our efforts.

In verse 39 the Samaritans reenter the scene, and the harvest is at hand. Their faith is based on the woman's testimony, which underscores the value of human witness to the work of God. Evangelism is a cooperative effort, in which the preparatory work of God joins with our witness to what he has done and is doing in the world.

The narrative's final statement is an important summary of the fruit of the woman's labor. The Samaritans evidence what every believer must have—a faith that is not secondary or dependent on someone else. *Rather, they have come and seen and experienced Christ for themselves.* This personal experiential feature is a constant concern for John.

Jesus Returns to Cana (4:43–54). This small story brings us full circle from where Jesus began his public ministry—namely, in Cana. In fact, the story provides a closing "frame" to the section of the Gospel that outlines Jesus and four institutions of Judaism (purification, temple, rabbi, a well). Each Cana miracle is even numbered for our convenience.

John is writing with genuine irony in verse 45 when he talks about the Galileans' welcome. As the next section in Galilee makes clear, they do not understand him; in fact, they readily misrepresent his aims, and some of his disciples even fall away. As a Jew, Jesus is commenting on his home culture, Judaism, which cannot provide one of its own prophets with honor.

When Jesus visits Cana, he is approached by a man from Capernaum whose son is desperately ill and about to die. He was an important man since he likely worked for Herod Antipas in Galilee. The man asks Jesus persistently if he will come down to Capernaum to heal his son. Jesus heals the boy at a distance instead of traveling to Capernaum. Later, as the man returns home, his servants meet him with news of the healing that occurred precisely when Jesus uttered his words of healing.

Even though the official and his family believe in Jesus, the critical sentence in the story is verse 48: "'Unless you people see signs and wonders,' Jesus told him, 'you will never believe.'" The attitude of the Galileans is the issue here. In this case, the Galileans miss the *revelatory sign* Jesus has given and press him to do something spectacular so that they can believe. Jesus's point is sharp: they simply want miracles, but they do not want to see what God is really doing among them.

Application. *Jesus and the world.* Where is Samaria today? I am not referring to the geographical location of hills a few miles north of Jerusalem. I am thinking about Samaria as a metaphor that represents a major political and cultural boundary that stands between the church and a needy people. We must think about those social, economic, and political boundaries that circumscribe the church's activity, and we must cross them.

Not every evangelical is comfortable with Jesus's evangelistic strategy here. It is not until Jesus utters a word of prophecy that suddenly the woman's eyes are opened in a new way. *Jesus exhibits the power of the Spirit at work for her and thereby models the power of the Spirit that may someday be within her.*

Jesus affirms that our abilities will imitate his (14:12), explaining that the endowment of the Spirit given to the disciples following his glorification will equip them in a way similar to his. But what does this mean for evangelism? Is a convincing testimony simply about a coherent presentation of belief or a persuasive presentation of the facts? It must be more. Those outside the kingdom deserve to see signs; they deserve to see the Holy Spirit in us before they will step closer to faith themselves.

I believe that John is also telling us something about the incapacity of this woman—or any other person, for that matter

—to grasp the things of God by themselves. We live in darkness. God's effort in the incarnation is an attempt to penetrate this darkness in his Son, Jesus Christ. Moreover, the Holy Spirit is his effort to penetrate our hearts so that we can believe and understand.

Jesus, tradition, and "place." Both Jews and Samaritans had their sacred mountains. Mount Gerizim and Mount Zion (Jerusalem) both held a sacred history that anchored the religious identities of their people. Religious mountains can have as much to do with the truth as a well in Shechem has to do with the living water offered by God. Jesus is not interested in identities any more than he is interested in credentials. The questions remain the same: Have you discovered living water? And do you know who supplies it?

Tradition is not the evil some evangelicals would think, however. Tradition can give needed perspective and depth, which today many seek and value. However, religious tradition can become a badge that is more important than our faith itself.

Jesus, miracles, and faith. Miraculous signs do not automatically lead to faith, nor do they vanquish the darkness that haunts us. John 4:43–54 opens a question that it does not entirely answer—namely, what are the advantages and disadvantages of a faith based on miraculous signs? For John, a sign is a divine revelation that leads to an enlightened faith in God. But most who live in this world can only experience the surface apprehension of power. For each of us burdened by human frailty, God must help.

This is not to say that miraculous signs have no place in the ministry of the church. They do. But John 4:43–54 suggests to us that they have a limited scope and usefulness. The human capacity to seek after God and to identify him and worship him is entirely broken. It was as true in Galilee as it is today.

JOHN 5:1–47

Original Meaning. John 5 is a trial—perhaps it is "the trial" of Jesus played out for us. This episode serves a literary role for John that exceeds its particular setting in Jesus's historic life, showing us the kind of accusation and rejection Jesus experienced, his defense, and above all the genuine spiritual jeopardy his opponents are in.

The Crime (5:1–15). The story opens with Jesus coming to Jerusalem during a feast (which is the Sabbath, v. 9) and arriving at a gate in the city's northeast wall called the Sheep Gate. It is interesting that this northeast section of the walled city has continued to sponsor a sheep market one day per week just outside St. Stephen's Gate. The NIV refers to the name of a pool there called in Aramaic "Bethesda" (v. 2). Today this pool, complete with five porches, is located adjacent to the Church of St. Anne inside Jerusalem's Old City.

We learn in the story that many people viewed the pool as a healing sanctuary. The people understood that occasionally an angel would descend and stir the water of the pool, and the first one to touch the water would be healed. The man Jesus meets had been ill for thirty-eight years. This area was likely a regular place for him to spend the day. Here he could beg from people coming to the pool and take his chances at being healed.

Jesus takes the initiative with the man (as he generally does in the Gospel) with words whose meaning likely goes beyond the mere miracle at hand: "Do you want to get well?" (v. 6). The man then appeals to his dilemma: as a paraplegic, he cannot outrace the others getting into the pool for healing. Jesus ignores both the superstition surrounding the pool and the man's complaint: "Get up! Pick up your mat and walk" (v. 8). The healing is immediate. The man simply obeys and is healed.

The importance of the story comes to us in verse 9b. It is the Sabbath when Jesus heals the man, and immediately the story takes an abrupt and unsettling turn. A self-appointed enforcer of Sabbath law upbraids the man.

The man does not know Jesus. He simply points to his own healing, and no doubt with joy that matched his inquisitors' zeal, he says that a man with the authority to heal told him to do this. For the first time in the Gospel, Jesus's opponents show themselves in all their hostility. Their question shifts rapidly from the error of the healed man to the identity of the healer who has incited this breach of law.

When Jesus meets the former paraplegic in the temple, there is an important exchange. We can surmise that the man has gone to the temple to offer praise to God for his healing or perhaps to confirm his healing with priests. When Jesus sees him, he says two things. "See, you are [literally have become] well" is no doubt a recognition that his cure was not short-lived, as many supposed cures were (v. 14a). But then Jesus remarks, "Stop sinning or something worse may happen to you" (v. 14b).

Is Jesus making some link between sin and physical ills? The man's sin and his condition are linked. Scripture indicates that some tragedies may be the result of specific sins, and this may be why Jesus has chosen the man for healing. But those with an infirmity have not *necessarily* sinned, and those who sin do not necessarily endure suffering as a consequence. Luke 13:1–5 and John 9:3 provide Jesus's correction of that sort of thinking. Suffering is *not* an index of a person's sin. But having said that, specific suffering may still come from specific sins.

The Decision to Prosecute (5:16–18). We dare not miss the pivotal importance of these three verses. The Jewish leadership has located two crimes that are major offenses deserving the death penalty. If we keep John's fascinating trial motif in mind, these verses contain the legal complaint that the Jewish authorities held against Jesus.

The Greek of verse 16 says that the persecution is tied to Jesus's habit of doing such things on the Sabbath. Jesus was viewed as indifferent to divine Sabbath law as mediated through Jewish tradition, and observers to such violations were obligated to punish the offender.

The second charge against Jesus has to do with blasphemy. Jesus's defense of his Sabbath activity is given in verse 17 (literally): "My Father is still working, and I also am working." If God (who made the Sabbath) can continue to work positively while commanding rest, and if Jesus's works are the works of God, then Jesus's works on the Sabbath are defensible. Jesus is assuming divine prerogatives (v. 19).

If the defense is true, a breathtaking claim is being set before Judaism. If it is false, a serious crime has been committed. Jesus is claiming equality with God. As God's divine agent, Jesus has the right and the ability to do what God does. Therefore John interprets the persecution and eventual death of Jesus as leading from Jesus's divine claims about himself.

Jesus Goes to Trial (5:19–47). *Jesus and God (5:19–30).* The central motif in the discourse is the relation of a father and a son as it would be viewed in this culture through the trade or skill the son was learning. His activity is never independent or self-initiated but always dependent, deriving its purpose from his Father's will. The Son does not simply draw inspiration from the Father but imitates him tirelessly and successfully. What makes this possible? John provides three answers.

The most important affirmation is that the Father loves the Son. The Greek present tense suggests an ongoing, continuous affection here, which leads to complete disclosure of the deeper mysteries of the Father. Jesus is unique inasmuch as he has seen and heard things no one else has.

This love spills into two tasks entrusted to the Son that belong exclusively to the Father. Jesus is sovereign over life and judgment. That God alone has power over life and can raise people from death is no surprise. That Jesus can do it too sets him apart. Since Jesus is in this world, since he is the one through whom light and life are mediated, he becomes the catalyst of divine judgment. Those who love darkness find themselves under judgment already. Whoever believes in the Son has life already.

This makes Jesus God's premier agent in the world. In antiquity, being an "agent" referred to a role in which authority and power were delegated to do a task. The agent's words were binding both on his audience and on the king who sent him. Therefore the agent had to be completely trustworthy. This is the imagery Jesus has in mind. As verse 23 makes explicit, whoever wishes to honor the Father must likewise honor the Son who represents him. And whoever dishonors the Son offends the Father whose presence stands behind him.

Now that the groundwork has been laid, Jesus expands and interprets what life and judgment really mean. To hear the words of Jesus (i.e., to accept his entire presence and message) is to believe God (who sent him). God's word and Jesus's word are one and the same, and so to embrace one is to embrace the other.

The key in these verses is to see that Jesus is expanding his divine claim. His authority over the Sabbath leads now to authority over eternal life. Because of *who* he is, Jesus can do what God does.

Witnesses for Jesus's case (5:31–40). Verse 31 is crucial in Jesus's trial. In Old Testament law, more than one witness was needed in order to condemn someone. Jesus's claims are extraordinary. But if he is the only one making them, they will carry little weight with his audience. But if the claims are corroborated, they stand.

Jesus therefore identifies five witnesses whose words and deeds buttress his claims.

1. The first witness is God. God's word and power are within Jesus, he has been sent by the Father, and these data point to the truth of who he is.
2. The next witness is John the Baptist. John preceded Jesus, identified him, worked with him, and directed his followers to become Jesus's disciples.
3. Jesus points to his own works, which demand some explanation. These point not merely to Jesus's identity but to the Father, who alone can enable such things.
4. Jesus adds the Scriptures to his list of witnesses. First-century Judaism was zealous in its study of the Scriptures. Yet, Jesus says, his contemporaries do not see the central message about Jesus and how he fulfills the Scripture.
5. The final witness is contained in the next element of Jesus's defense. It is Moses, who is represented in Scripture, but his words about the Messiah are unequivocal (Deut 18:15). Moses is the patron saint of Judaism. But, Jesus remarks, even Moses's words have gone ignored.

Jesus prosecutes his opponents (5:41–47). A remarkable and unexpected feature of the discourse is the way in which Jesus finishes by attacking his opponents. Jesus turns the tables and moves from defense to prosecution. The final impact of his defense in verses 31–40 leaves the impression that Jesus's hearers bear some responsibility for what God has done. If they cannot see the Father's work in their midst, something must be profoundly wrong. Their disbelief is deliberate and the diagnosis severe: they do not have the love of God in their hearts. They love the religious life, but they have forgotten how to love God.

Jesus's final reference to Moses in verses 45–47 points not only to Moses's role as a witness (cf. above), but also to his role as judge. Judaism took great pride in Moses. But if Moses is possessed and not obeyed, the very words of Moses will come back to judge. To possess the Bible and to know the Scriptures but to not know God is to be in the most precarious place of all.

Application. *Ministry to the suffering.* Among the many at Bethesda looking for healing that day, Jesus does not reach out to those who are spiritually on the margin but socially "safe." Instead, he reaches out to someone whose suffering and isolation are beyond measure. What implications does this have for where the church goes today? What social risks does John 5 insist that we take?

Spiritual heroism. Jesus models something that we, bearing the name and Spirit of Jesus, ought to consider. Are there areas of contemporary life that need to be violated in the name of God so that God's person and justice can be seen by everyone?

The identity of Jesus. Jesus Christ makes *ultimate* claims for himself in the Gospels. To make an absolute claim about Jesus is to invite precisely the thing that John 5 describes: persecution. A strong witness to Jesus *necessarily* offends. This is as true today as it has ever been. We live in a world of pluralism and tolerance that exerts enormous pressure on us to refine away the distinctives of our faith that might offend.

John 5 poses a terrible question for us: Are we willing to be labeled as blasphemers to the religious canons of our day when our hour comes? Are our churches equipped to do this? Are we ready to be judged and expelled, to experience social shame and public damning *in the name of religion* because we are holding on to an absolute faith in Jesus, the Son of God?

Spiritual sickness. The final matter that must attend us concerns the spiritual sickness of Jesus's opponents. Jesus's inquisitors represent the religious establishment for whom the vigorous preservation of religious tradition counts more highly than the spontaneity and openness of faith. These people know their Scriptures and use them to defend all the wrong things.

On a national level we have seen evangelicals unsheathe their religious swords over arcane doctrinal matters. On local levels many of us have likely seen older church members viciously lash out because "the contemporary service" isn't to their liking or they perceive that their power and influence are diminishing. We have also perhaps seen younger church members unlovingly lash out at the older members because they are "stuck in their old ways" and don't have "true faith." All of it, John 5 suggests, is empty religion, religion that seeks its own glory. In the end, it is religion that would condemn and crucify Jesus as a *religious* duty.

JOHN 6:1–71

Original Meaning

The Feeding of the Five Thousand (6:1–15). We need to pause and underscore some of the motifs that were well-known in the Passover story. Among Moses's many miracles in Egypt, two stand out as particularly remarkable:

1. his departure through the sea (Exod 14), and
2. his miraculous feeding of the people with manna for forty years in the desert.

In John 6, Jesus appears at Passover, repeating many of these themes. The people are a multitude not unlike those in the desert; Jesus feeds them with heavenly bread; and following the feeding, when the disciples are on the sea, Jesus comes to them walking on water.

These parallels offer some intriguing conclusions. This Passover story of Jesus makes direct connections with prominent Old Testament motifs that tumble over one another in rapid succession. They provide a growing impression that in some fashion the hero of Passover, Moses, has now been superseded by Jesus, who not only provides "bread from heaven" (6:32) but is himself "the bread of life" (6:35).

This feeding miracle must have had widespread fame and was locked into the collective memory of early Christianity as a key event in Jesus's life. John provides insights no other Gospel possesses. Jesus not only wants to provide food, but he wishes to test the developing faith of Philip. Philip's response indicates that he does not yet grasp Jesus's miraculous ability.

But Andrew, Peter's brother, locates a young boy carrying five barley loaves and two salted fish. Only John mentions that the bread is barley, which is a signal of the poverty of this crowd. These details are important because in 2 Kings 4:42–44 is another Old Testament miracle, where Elisha feeds a hundred men with twenty barley loaves and is assisted by a young servant. As with the twelve baskets left after Jesus's miracle, Elisha had baskets of food left over.

What is happening here? These images and motifs from the Old Testament suggest that Jesus is fulfilling and re-creating images from Israel's sacred past. John's point is to underscore that Jesus is the provider of food, the source of life for these people (as thus far we have seen him be the source of rebirth, living water, and healing).

The crowd interprets Jesus's miracle as messianic. *He has just re-created the miracle of Moses!* For many, Moses had become the image of the ideal Messiah, unifying images of king and prophet. Most disturbing is what happens next. "Jesus, knowing that they intended to come and make him king *by force*, withdrew again to a mountain by himself" (v. 15, emphasis added). This reflects a crass misunderstanding by the crowd. The crowd wants to *force* Jesus to define his mission and work politically, to become a king who will rival the Herodians or the Romans. Jesus wants no part of such a kingship. Thus he must flee and must push his disciples out to sea in order to preserve himself and his work from the political ambitions of the crowd.

Jesus Walks on the Water (6:16–24). While Jesus leaves for the mountains of upper Galilee (near Mount Meron?), the disciples set sail, heading for the lake's northeast shore. East/west winds are common on this sea, and fishermen watched for them carefully. Their fear of the rough water, however, was surpassed by their terror at seeing Jesus walking to them on the water. Again, we have another motif that reminds us of the moment when Moses led Israel through the water. Psalm 77 describes this moment in Israel's life and explains that it was in fact God who led them.

When Jesus arrives at the boat, he identifies himself with a term that was sure to evoke further images of the exodus story: "It is I" (*egō eimi*, v. 20). The verb "to be" (*eimi*) possesses no predicate here and thus reflects God's divine name given to Moses on Mount Sinai (Exod 3:14). Even Jesus's call not to fear echoes Moses's fearful response on the mountain when he learned God's name and saw the burning bush (Exod 3:6). Jesus approaches, and even though he is now providing an awesome and overwhelming presentation of his power, the disciples need not fear.

While the Gospel of Mark says that Jesus stilled the storm when he entered the boat, John 6:21 almost implies that the disciples barely were able to get him into the boat when they reached their destination. Many interpreters suspect that here we have yet another miracle, as Jesus leads his disciples to their port. Again, Jesus is fulfilling the role of God—feeding, protecting, rescuing, and guiding his followers despite the natural calamities that surround them.

Questions surface the next day when the crowd discovers that although Jesus did not accompany the men on the boat, he nevertheless arrived with them at their destination. More boats arrive at the site of the feeding, and when Jesus is not found the people, charged with excitement, travel to Capernaum to see if he can be located. Their arrival in the village of Capernaum introduces Jesus's major "bread of life" discourse (6:25–58), in which he defines carefully his relation to the miracle and its deeper meaning.

Bread from Heaven (6:25–34). As Jesus teaches in the synagogue, he desires to lift his hearers above a material understanding of his miracle. He argues that their efforts should be focused not on the loaves and fish but on the greater food that lasts forever. But the synagogue audience offers a challenge. If it is true that in the days of Moses the treasury of manna was opened, and if it is true that Jesus is making some messianic claim, then what sort of sign can Jesus give to validate his word? Is he claiming that he has re-created the messianic miracle of Moses?

Jesus's interpretation of the manna follows rabbinic lines perfectly. First, the true source of the manna was not Moses but God. If God is truly the source of true heavenly bread and if Jesus has been sent by God, the shocking turn in verse 33 should come as no surprise. The bread of God is a person who gives life to the world. With a stroke of genius, Jesus has done precisely what he has done throughout the Gospel: he exploits some feature of Jewish belief and ritual and reinterprets it to refer to himself.

"I Am the Bread of Life" (6:35–50). Jesus here presses the logic of his case to the next level. Jesus is "living bread," as once before he offered "living water." This famous saying ("I am the bread of life") heads the list of what we call the "I-am sayings" in John (v. 35). In each of these sayings, Jesus is taking a motif from Judaism and reinterpreting it for himself. He now supplies that which Judaism sought in its activities and stories.

With remarkable candor, Jesus announces his disappointment with the crowd. The crowd is either twisting Jesus's mission or demanding more evidence, but they are unwilling to come to Jesus and confess their hunger and thirst. Jesus says that their first step must be belief, but they refuse to take it. Such belief is not a leap into the darkness, for they have had the opportunity to see. Hence their decision is a willful refusal to act on what God has set before them.

Throughout verses 37–40, Jesus speaks confidently about the success of his work and the fulfillment of his mission. The determinism of these verses is sometimes softened by verse 37b: "Whoever comes to me I will never drive away." The idea is about Jesus's keeping people whom the Father has given into his care. Jesus will not lose a single one of those who have come to him.

The sayings that began at verse 35 serve the larger program of the "bread of life" discourse because they place in abstract what Jesus has been saying parabolically all along. God is the supplier of divine bread, and whoever eats of it will live forever. The identity of this "bread of life" is actually Jesus, just as the object of faith now should be Jesus.

But this is the great turning point that the synagogue audience cannot bear. It is one thing to say that we should have faith in God and be fed by him, but it is quite another for Jesus to say that he is the source of that meal, the object of believing vision. The "grumbling" described in 6:41, 43 (and 61) is reminiscent of the "grumbling" or "murmuring" of the Israelites against Moses in the desert (e.g., Exod 15:24; 16:2, 7–8), and it completes yet one more Passover theme. But this time there is a Johannine literary twist. The crowd misunderstands Jesus just as people and crowds have misunderstood him in most of the discourses since chapter 2.

After Jesus's firm exhortation to stop grumbling, it is interesting that he does not defend himself against their complaint but instead returns to the problem of their spiritual receptivity. The idea of Jesus's divine origin and descent is impossible for the crowd unless God in some fashion illumines them. God must move the inner heart of a person before he or she can see the things of God. And this takes place on God's initiative.

The Flesh and Blood of the Son of Man (6:51–58). The first two thoughts of verse 51 repeat what we have already seen: Jesus is the living bread that came down, referring to his incarnation, and one must eat this bread, referring to the decisive moment when one believes. But it is in the third sentence of the verse where Jesus makes a pivotal statement, "This bread is my flesh, which I will give for the life of the world." When Jesus refers to his "flesh" (*sarx*), we are at once reminded of 1:14, where *sarx* was used to describe the comprehensive life of the Son.

But *sarx* is a surprising, even graphic word that runs deeper than 1:14, and it will become the unifying thread of this portion of the discourse. *Jesus is flesh offered in sacrifice.* The gift of Jesus is nothing other than a sacrifice, a blood sacrifice, a temple sacrifice, that will benefit the world.

If Jesus's audience was amazed that he miraculously fed the multitudes, they were startled when he described himself as the heavenly bread from God. Now they are aghast as he makes the next step. Earthly bread—heavenly bread—Jesus as bread —Jesus as bread to eat—Jesus as sacrifice. It is all too much. Of course, Jesus is not proposing religious cannibalism. Earthly symbols must be converted into spiritual truths. How, then, are we to understand this life-giving meal? What deeper spiritual truth needs to be uncovered?

Jesus's answer in verses 53–58 has proven difficult for almost every commentator. The only Judeo-Christian setting where such words make good sense is the Christian Eucharist. It is significant that John does *not* record the words of institution later in Jesus's upper-room discourse. When we look at his language here, it echoes Luke's language at the supper: "This is my body given for you" (Luke 22:19).

Certainly, as Jesus speaks these words, their graphic and shocking character stuns the audience. Regardless of their theological meaning, they are graphic, compelling, and confusing. This eating and drinking gives eternal life and forms the basis of the interior, intimate experience one may have with Christ.

Some Disciples Fall Away (6:59–71). If Jesus's revelation that he himself was bread made the crowds grumble, this new revelation offends Jesus's own disciples. This difficult teaching sifts Jesus's followers: some of them fall away and refuse to follow him any longer, while one other disciple likely finds in this a catalyst for his own personal rebellion and betrayal.

These are the deeper things of Jesus, and only with divine help can anyone comprehend them. Therefore, Jesus points to yet one more feature of this coming hour. If his death brings offense, what of his ascension? If the first idea of death was scandalous, this further idea will be even harder. Not only will he die, but he will return to heaven. It is through this complete work of Christ that life can be given to the world.

There is an important gift, however, a vital endowment, that will be a part of this life-giving work. The "flesh" that is of no avail in verse 63 recalls the literal flesh of verse 53. Jesus clarifies that taking his words literally is not the point. If eucharistic symbolism is at work, it is not a mechanical sacramentalism that Jesus has in mind, for the life-giving gift is the Holy Spirit.

With some of his following now collapsing, Jesus turns to the Twelve to inquire if they wish to depart as well. This is clearly a turning point for Jesus. The mystery of his person and work has now been laid out in full. For Peter this difficult exchange provides an opportunity to give a courageous confession: "Lord, to whom shall we go? You have the words of eternal life. We have come to believe and know that you are the Holy One of God" (vv. 68–69).

Jesus recognizes the confession not simply as a tribute to Peter's courage but also as evidence of God's supernatural movement in his life. These deeper things cannot be embraced by just anyone, but only by those whom God has enabled.

Application. *The pursuit of bread.* The needs of the crowd in Galilee were obvious. In some way they represent the needs of humanity from the beginning of time. We need the things necessary for survival ("Give us today our *daily bread*," those famous words from the Sermon on the Mount at Matt 6:11). And if those needs go unmet, if hunger goes ignored, then the pursuit of any higher virtue (religious or otherwise) collapses. This is why Jesus rightly ensures that the crowd is fed. It is ethically responsible to care for the body before nurturing the soul.

If bread is what we need to survive in order to feel well and wholesome, the pursuit of bread becomes complicated when people determine that their needs include things unnecessary for true life. Living in a consumer society fueled by sophisticated advertising and relative affluence, we have been given the means and the motivation to pursue countless forms of bread. Christians are not exempt from the seductions of the material culture around us. We define the "bread" we need with lives of remarkable indulgence.

The religious pursuit of bread. Even among those people who embrace an utterly pagan worldview, deep spiritual instincts lead them to explore everything from meditation to philosophy.

When the human instinct for religion is unleashed, it rarely reaches its true goal. Americans are as religious as ever, and now they are seeking religious bread wherever they can find it.

There is another way we can look at the crowd's attempt to "take Jesus by force" (v. 15). They come to kidnap him, to promote him as a hero, to make him a *religious figure* in their own image and to serve their own agenda. But evangelicals have taken "Jesus by force" as well. We identify social platforms, national security interests, and moral crusades, and we baptize them in the name of Jesus. Many of us have difficulty being critical of these agendas since for the most part we agree with them. When Jesus is taken by force to serve as a pawn in our religiously sanctioned political program, we are no different than the crowds in Galilee.

Being fed by God. All Christian traditions, Protestant as well as Catholic, provide forms and traditions that are designed to feed us, to nurture us. Being fed by God is so simple that in a world congested with busyness, it has become hard to understand. Like the pursuit of joy, the more we run after it with strategies and plans, the more it seems to flee. It is not gained by ministry accomplishments, righteous efforts, or the intellectual mastery of the Bible. Being fed by God requires a conversion of thinking, a discovery that God is eager to give life and renewal to anyone who can listen in simplicity and piety.

Does this mean that religious forms should be discarded? This sort of response finds no sympathy from John. The apostle provides a critique of sacramental worship that has lost any connection with the life-giving Lord present in the church through the Spirit. I believe he would have us use the sacraments correctly so that they become true vehicles of encounter and not fossilized instruments of religiosity.

Rebellion. Hearts that are religiously inclined can become angry when the formulas change, when things don't show up as predicted, when conventions become upset. It is a religious rebellion that in some fashion disguises itself as piety, as light—but in the end is darkness nonetheless. Christ may have things to say that we cannot accept. I must forever keep in mind that Judas Iscariot's traitorous act is born when Jesus reveals the deeper things about himself. With Peter, we must always be willing to relinquish our position, to hold our assumptions loosely, and to say in faith, "Lord, to whom shall we go? You have the words of eternal life" (v. 68).

JOHN 7:1–52

Original Meaning. The literary outline followed by John in chapters 5–10 is organized around the festivals of Judaism. Chapter 5 centers on the weekly feast of Sabbath, while chapter 6 is organized around Passover. Jesus appears at these festivals, exploits some feature of their imagery, and launches major discourses in which he identifies himself and his mission through their historic themes.

Jesus's visit to Jerusalem now at the Feast of Tabernacles (John 7–9) follows this same pattern. It is almost impossible to interpret John 7 without some acquaintance with the Jewish Feast of Tabernacles and how it was celebrated in Jerusalem in the first century. It was an old festival of agriculture from the ancient Near East that adopted the Israelite story of redemption. To this were added Jewish intertestamental motifs of water and light, and even these the rabbis interpreted spiritually. Tabernacles then blended a variety of images from agriculture (harvest), climate (sun and rain), and theological history (Israel's desert wandering). Jesus makes these motifs serve his purposes as he stands in the feast and makes his identity known.

The Beginning of the Festival (7:1–13). Jesus has been avoiding Judea because he knows the depth of hostility waiting for him there. It is not inappropriate to hear cynicism in the encouragement of Jesus's brothers for him to attend the autumn festival. They may be reminding him of his religious obligation (despite the danger) or even pushing him to place his messianic identity into full public view. Either way, they do not believe in him (v. 5) and do not see in the Jerusalem visit a fruitful disclosure of the truth about him.

When Jesus says that he will not "go up" to the festival, he explains that he cannot because it is not yet his time (v. 8). Jesus's brothers take his words at face value. They see things from an earthly perspective and assume that Jesus is simply going to avoid the feast. Jesus intends no deception and attends the feast on his own, keeping his identity as quiet as possible in order to avoid those who would like to harm him.

Jesus's arrival brings controversy and division. The crowd is "whispering"—*gongysmos* (v. 12), a word that reminds us of 6:41 and the desert grumbling (Exod 17:3; Num 11:1). In their search for Jesus, some from the crowd describe him as "good" while others describe him as a deceiver, a fraud (John 7:12). But overshadowing all is the fear of the common person for the Jewish leaders (not "the Jews" in general), who have decided to kill him.

The Middle of the Festival (7:14–36). At the midpoint of the feast, Jesus enters the temple courts for the first time and teaches publicly. Questions are launched by Jesus's listeners that permit him to describe his identity and mission more completely. But the questions disclose how little his audience really understands. Three scenes are anchored to three questions with three ironic answers.

Scene One (7:14–24). Educational standards for rabbis were well established in the first century. Jesus possessed no such credentials. The Jewish leaders, in effect, wish to see these, and Jesus complies by saying that his diplomas are divine. God has taught and commissioned him; God has given him the things he teaches. Moreover, Jesus explains that if their lives are in harmony with God, they will recognize the character and source of his teaching.

The Jewish notion of authority was specialized. Authority was passed down and conferred from rabbi to rabbi through ordination. Jesus's problem is that he is not ordained. What is the source of his authority? Jesus's answer is clear: his authority stems directly from God. Unlike a rabbi, Jesus is authorized to speak much like a prophet because he bears the words of God, not religious tradition.

It is clear from verse 19 that the Sabbath debate of chapter 5 still dominates Jesus's relation with these authorities. Jesus here returns to his line of argument expressed then: those who do not keep the law of Moses in its entirety should be reluctant about judging others. On more than one occasion the New Testament reports that some people were so intent on their hostility toward Jesus that they made plans to kill him. In these months before Passover, Jesus has to be cautious, protecting himself from those who want to assassinate him. "You are demon-possessed" likely carries no theological weight and can simply be translated, "You're crazy!" (v. 20).

Jesus now expands his line of reasoning. If a boy can be *partially* healed on the Sabbath in this context, why should not a man be *completely* healed on the Sabbath? Jesus sees himself not simply liberalizing the law but fulfilling what the law was meant to do—to bring renewal and redemption to God's people.

Scene Two (7:25–31). Once again the ironic misunderstanding of the crowd is displayed by their statement in verse 27: "We know where this man is from; when the Messiah comes, no one will know where he is from." The crowd is examining Jesus on an earthly level and thinks that since they can trace Jesus's human origins, he is disqualified from messianic status.

Jesus leaves the confusion unchallenged but goes on to make his claim more astounding. He has come from God, whom he knows with unparalleled intimacy. This is paramount to a divine claim that breaks with all the canons of Judaism. Jesus is claiming to know God and be something of a personal liaison or confidant—a Son!—who now has authority in Jerusalem not by virtue of his education alone (scene one) but also by virtue of his origins (scene two). It is Jesus's ontological status with the Father that empowers not simply what he does but who he is.

The episode with the crowd comes to a dramatic climax with a division within their ranks. It is a division we see throughout the Gospel, where some express openness to Jesus while others either deny him or attempt to inflict harm. Some in the crowd try to arrest him for making divine claims, but their efforts are frustrated. Jesus is sovereign over his life and will choose when his time has come.

Scene Three (7:32–36). The first two scenes raised ironic earthly questions about Jesus's schooling and Jesus's background, both of which found an unexpected answer: heaven. In scene three the audience shifts to the chief priests and Pharisees, who enlist police from the temple to arrest Jesus. No doubt it leads Jesus to think about his death at their hands.

Jesus will view his as a departure, a "going away" that will put him beyond the world's reach since he will have returned to heaven. As in the previous scenes, this statement inspires earthly misunderstanding. The Jewish leadership speculate that Jesus is simply leaving Israel. But Jesus is talking about where they *cannot* go—heaven.

The Last Day of the Festival (7:37–52). Each day of the feast witnessed a water ceremony in which a procession of priests descended to the south border of the city to the Gihon Spring. Judaism saw this water ceremony on multiple levels. On the one hand, it was a plea to God for rain since the autumn is a time of threatened drought in Israel. On the other hand, it was a source of rich symbolism. In the desert, God brought water from a rock, and here water was flowing from the sacrificial rock altar of the temple. Ezekiel and Zechariah had visions of rivers flowing from the temple in a miraculous display of God's blessing (Ezek 47; Zech 14:8). In a drought-stricken land, it was a spectacular vision of water, life-giving water flowing from God's life-giving temple.

On this final day of celebration, Jesus steps into public view and makes his most stunning pronouncement of the feast. This announcement parallels symbolically what Jesus did in John 6 at Passover. Just as earthly bread led to memories of heavenly bread (manna), which concluded with Jesus offering himself as the bread of life (John 6:35), so now Jesus is doing the same. Needed rainfall and water ceremonies lead to memories of miraculous desert water, water given from heaven, which concludes with Jesus's offering himself as the source of the water of life.

The punctuation of 7:37–38 has inspired numerous debates among scholars. The NIV punctuates the verses to make *the believer* the one in whom the living water is flowing. A second Western or christological punctuation views Christ as the source of the living water. The second christological view is compelling for a number of reasons. Not only is it grammatically defensible, but theologically it fits the literary setting of both John 6 and 7, wherein Jesus supplies the spiritual gifts promised in the festival.

Another difficulty in this passage is the Scripture citation in verse 38. Most scholars believe we have a composite quotation describing visions of the coming blessings of the messianic age.

John also has in mind the desert water image of the rock struck by Moses at Meribah to feed the Israelites and their flocks (Num 20:2–13).

At the Feast of Tabernacles, then, Jesus is saying he is not only the new temple and source of living water but also the eschatological rock that, when struck, will yield life-giving water. Is it any surprise that when Jesus is struck on the cross with a spear, his "belly" (literal translation of *koilia* in John 7:38) yields blood *and water* (19:34)?

John's theological comment in verse 39 is likewise critically important. He explains that Jesus was referring to the Holy Spirit in this pronouncement. This gift of the Spirit is not available during Jesus's earthly ministry. It must await his "glorification" in order to be distributed. As we watch the passion story unfold, we will do well to observe how the Spirit becomes a signal feature of Jesus's departure from the world and return to the Father.

We next meet Jews who hold that the Messiah will fulfill prophecy, descend from David, and be born in Bethlehem. The crowd only knows that Jesus is from Galilee, and if the prophetic fulfillment is important Jesus is disqualified. But this is misunderstanding at work once again. Jesus was born in Bethlehem. Thus, once more knowledge about Jesus is just out of reach of those trying to grasp it.

The complete frustration of the Sanhedrin becomes clear. Even the temple police are impressed with Jesus. Nicodemus speaks up, urging caution and fair play. The Sanhedrin's objection that Jesus cannot be a prophet since he has come from Galilee is outlandish and unfounded. The prophets Jonah and Nahum came from this very place.

Application. *Questions Christians should ask.* John 7 provides another scenario about religious debate. Can Christians become religious debaters? Can they ever oppose a new thing God may be doing? Are they not also today genuinely affected by the sinful impulses that permeated the audiences in John 7? John understands that even those who claim to believe in Jesus sometimes choose to reject his word and deny him his way. As we interpret this passage and bring it to our generation, we have to wrestle with the sobering truth of this possibility and its implications.

Standing with Jesus. The most obvious application of John 7 has to do with the reactions of the world to the revelation of Jesus Christ. It is naive for Christians to think that the "good news" of the gospel is going to enjoy a warm reception when it is given in the world. It is naive to think that if people simply understand the truth correctly, if they have the message of Christ fully explained, or if they meet a "true" Christian, they will be converted. It is presumptuous to think that the world is an eager, receptive vessel waiting to be filled by the presence of God. *The world is in rebellion.* It is skilled at asking religious questions and feigning spiritual interest, but such inquiries are nothing more than disguised, sophisticated rebellion.

When the gospel is preached in the world, Jesus goes on trial. Every hearer must choose which voice he or she will embrace, which side he or she will choose, for there is no middle ground. We really do not know what voice is ours until there is risk involved in speaking up. As soon as the opponents of Jesus express their will—and John 7 is filled with hints of conflict and violence—the crowd must decide if their faith is stronger than their fear.

Standing against Jesus. It is not simply the world in all of its pagan self-indulgence that settles in as Jesus's great opponent. Just as there is a worldly opposition to Jesus, there is likewise a religious opposition to Jesus. What does this opposition mean? Does the religious reflex that came alive in the temple—a reflex that builds and preserves religion, that weighs obedience to its statutes, that finds quibbling ways to dissect fidelity to its mission—ever arise in the church?

Jesus is offering a spiritual mysticism and encounter with God that *always* makes the custodians of traditional religion nervous. This can be especially true in those tightly drawn circles of conservative theology that seem impenetrable. To propose new freedom, new spontaneity, new thought—that is, to step outside the canons of traditional religious behavior or thinking—is to experience what Jesus experienced at the Feast of Tabernacles.

JOHN 7:53–8:11

Original Meaning. This story is absent from all of the major Greek manuscripts that bear the strongest, earliest witness to John's original form. The whole range of Greek patristic literature virtually ignores it, while it seems to have a strong currency only in the West. The story also seems artificial to the narrative of John 7 and 8. Without the story, the Tabernacles narrative flows smoothly from 7:1 to 8:59. Scholars also point to numerous words and grammatical forms that are not Johannine. In other words, this story was likely an independent account that circulated freely for some time and was only later attached to John.

While scholars are reasonably convinced that this story does not belong originally to the Fourth Gospel, many are confident that it is an ancient narrative that stems from the same pool of stories that contributed to the Synoptic Gospels. This is a typical Synoptic "conflict" story in which Jesus is placed on the horns of a dilemma. He chooses to stand against the representatives of the law in favor of the needs of the woman. Jesus refuses to get embroiled in the legalism of sinners who want to judge sin.

The Woman Caught in Adultery (7:53–8:11). This story has numerous arresting details that richly repay careful study and provide excellent insight into the thought and ministry of Jesus. The setting of the story must have been typical of Jesus's ministry in Jerusalem, particularly during his final visits there. On this particular day, the group with Jesus is joined by Pharisees and teachers of the law.

The religious leaders are making a legal claim: they possess strong testimony from two witnesses who saw the couple in a sexual context. The two witnesses had to see these things at the same time and place so that their testimonies would be identical. Such evidence virtually required the witnesses to set a trap. The law also expected that if a person witnessed another about to commit a sin, compassion required them to speak up. These witnesses stand silently, neglecting their moral obligation to give guidance to the woman. They want to catch her and use her.

We must ask if the woman is married or betrothed to another man. A woman who is sexually unfaithful to her fiancé was to be stoned to death along with her lover. Unfaithful wives were likewise, but the law did not indicate the method of death. In the present passage, the woman therefore must be engaged. But if so, where is her lover? If they were caught in the act, he was caught too. The accusers have permitted him to get away clean.

These witnesses bring the woman to Jesus before a crowd and heap public shame on her. They could have kept her to one side and brought her case to Jesus privately. But their approach to the problem indicates that they wish to trap Jesus, and her personal life is incidental. They have no interest in a trial. They are thinking about a public lynching, and they want Jesus to make a judgment.

It is impossible to know what Jesus wrote in the dust. For some interpreters, Jesus was simply drawing to give himself added time. If his writing seemed to stall things, 8:7 indicates that these men persist to force the question of judgment on him before the crowd. Jesus responds with his often-quoted statement, "Let any one of you who is without sin be the first to throw a stone at her." This does not mean that this woman's accusers must be sinless or morally perfect in order to bring charges against the woman. In such a case, accusations would be impossible at any time. This is simply a direct reference to Deuteronomy 13:9 or 17:7, which says that those who witness a crime and bring home a successful accusation must be the first to stone the victim.

But then the accusers must engage in self-examination. The world of antiquity was little different from our own when it came to sexual sins. Women who transgressed social mores could find themselves in legal jeopardy much more quickly than their partners. Jesus may thus be cutting through the double standard in order to force the men to reflect on their own hypocrisy.

Jesus resumes his writing, and the religious leaders begin departing one by one. John uses an imperfect verb here to build a picture of one teacher departing, who is then followed by a succession of people eventually walking away, so that the accusers arrayed against the woman crumble bit by bit. No doubt they are stunned, and perhaps the audience is embarrassed. But in the end, Jesus and the woman are left alone.

Because Jesus must have been sitting and the woman standing, he now straightens up (v. 10) and speaks to her for the first time. His questions do not imply that the woman is innocent since in verse 11 he warns her to cease a sinful life that has been her habit. He simply points to the absence of accusers. They have disappeared. Her response shows considerable respect for Jesus. Jesus's final words again do not imply innocence, but they do reflect his sovereignty to forgive sin. The story's crisp ending captures the seriousness with which Jesus views sin and judgment—even the sin of those who accuse the woman—and his gracious, forgiving outlook on those who are caught in its grip.

Application. *The woman.* Christ's forgiveness in each of our lives diminishes as we lose touch with the depth of our own sinfulness. When we no longer see ourselves in the drama of the woman, when we feel we are free from accusation and judgment, we lose sight of God's grace. This drama of Jesus and the woman gains power when I become that woman and reflect on the seriousness of my own jeopardy. Through this new vision, I gain a new glimpse of Jesus's love and mercy.

The judgment. There are other subsidiary issues that the drama raises, and we would do well to think about them today. Despite the woman's sin and the requirements of the law, Jesus does not permit the accusers to carry out the punishment. Jesus did not punish the woman. There is no punishment, no penance, no restitution. Should not the woman do public service at an orphanage for a couple of years in Jerusalem?

We are not suggesting that our story teaches us to free all convicted criminals. But it does raise questions about the purpose of capital punishment. We have had the opportunity to meet a number of former convicts who are now growing Christians. One meeting with them and suddenly we will carry the burden of new questions that did not trouble us before. If Jesus can forgive, transform, and set free in the temple, what happens if he does it in our prisons? Will we join him or those religious leaders who prefer to see one woman dead?

The accusers. The deeper motive among these men is to trap Jesus. Their strategy includes trapping the woman. Perhaps entrapment characterizes a good portion of their religious effort. They are religious police. People with religious obsessions like this rarely see themselves this way. Evangelicals who take godly righteousness seriously rarely see themselves this way either. Are we religious police? Does our healthy commitment to righteousness ever lapse into an obsessive preoccupation with the details of people's personal lives?

Sex and sin. Sin is sin, and sexual sin is sin. Yet as we look at the contemporary church, it is fascinating to observe how we do not share the same impassive reaction of Jesus. Is our reflex to judge and expel or to forgive and heal? We are not compromising the seriousness of sexual sin when we raise this question. Neither was Jesus. But Jesus had different reflexes.

Women, sex, and sin. Societies have a higher tolerance for male misconduct than female misconduct. "He's all boy" is a convenient label for a child who challenges the rules and tears his jeans. "He's out sowing his wild oats" is another convenient label for boys when they are much older. If it is true that gender plays a role in our perception of wrongdoing, what does it mean for women when they are unmasked in their sin? When men accuse them? Is there a different level of severity? Different levels of tolerance? Are the social ramifications different? Are signals sent and labels made that mark the woman permanently? These are troubling questions that require soul-searching honesty if we are to get to the heart of them. No doubt the place to begin is to ask *a woman* what it means when she *alone* is dragged before the religious authorities. Many of us men might hear some surprising answers.

JOHN 8:12–59

Original Meaning

"I Am the Light of the World!" (8:12–20). This is Jesus's second "I am" saying that is followed by a predicate: "I am the light of the world" (v. 12). Tabernacles occurred in the late autumn and celebrated the harvest of tree and vine. The autumn equinox (where night and day are of equal length) provided the context for a light ceremony that was popular in Jerusalem and orchestrated during Tabernacles. Tabernacles witnesses the converging of multiple motifs—harvest, drought, the coming winter darkness, Israel's desert wandering, and eschatological vision all merge in the temple ceremonies.

Four large stands each held four golden bowls; these were placed in the heavily used court of women. These sixteen golden bowls (reached by ladders) were filled with oil. When they were lit at night, all Jerusalem was illumined. Choirs of Levites would sing during the lighting, while people danced in the streets, carrying torches and singing hymns. Imagine the scene! In the very court where the lighting ceremony takes place, Jesus stands beneath sixteen lit bowls of oil and says that he is not only the true light of Jerusalem, but of the whole world!

Jesus's use here—and the entire scene we have just built—is thoroughly Jewish. Jesus is referring to the countless times that God's saving work in the world is described as "light." John 1:5 reflects this tradition. Since in John's Gospel Jesus is the realization or incarnation of God's own presence in the world, it is unsurprising that "light" is used to describe the work of Christ sixteen times.

Jesus's self-reference as light guiding people through darkness (as the pillar of light guided the Israelites in the desert) is quickly challenged. The Pharisees' argument echoes what occurred during Jesus's last visit to Jerusalem in chapter 5, when he referred to the legal qualifications of judicial witnesses. Unfortunately, his opponents have forgotten that in the earlier Jerusalem debate, Jesus showed that there were ample witnesses verifying his claim. Now Jesus must repeat again that his Father is a second witness (8:18).

But something important has now been added. Jesus would hardly say that whenever he speaks alone his words are invalid, as if they must be weighed by the double-witness judicial rule. Jesus's judgment is true, and his words are true, not because of their inherent persuasiveness but because of their *origins*. This is the new and unexpected authority behind Jesus's testimony.

Jesus comes from the Father. He does not speak on his own authority but is echoing what the Father has told him to say. The root problem with Jesus's opponents, then, is that they do not know the Father. They are incapable of having true spiritual discernment because they do not know the source of all spirituality, God himself. Without a deep knowledge of God and his love, it is impossible to recognize his Son.

"I Am Going Away!" (8:21–30). The question of Jesus's origins remains at the center of the discussion. Jesus will depart eventually to return to where he came from. The crowd concludes that Jesus must be going to his death—a departure they would prefer to avoid for themselves. Jesus will indeed die, and this departure will be a return to his Father in heaven.

Jesus's answer in verses 23–29 provides a critical insight into his identity and his incomprehensibility before his listeners. It also explains the urgency of humanity's condition. Once Jesus departs, once the opportunity to hear him and believe in him is gone, the world is lost. But the crowd misses the point altogether. Jesus is not simply a prophet with divine things to communicate, but he bears divinity in himself. He is not a man with religious insight (from below, from the world), but God's Son (from above, from heaven). This prompts his audience to ask its most important question. Not: "What do you mean?" But: "Who are you?" (v. 25).

The supreme moment of revelation is when Jesus is "lifted up" (v. 28), which is not merely the cross but the series of events that lead to his glorification: betrayal, trial, crucifixion, resurrection, and ascension. Through these events, the world will see *not* that Jesus is simply telling the truth but that he is the bearer of God's divine name ("I am"; see Exod 3:14). "When you have lifted up the Son of Man, then you will know that I am" (v. 28). Again, verse 28 leaves off the predicate, making Jesus's audience wonder and marvel at the amazing claims he is making.

In the Synoptic Gospels there are three instances when Jesus specifically predicts his coming death in Jerusalem. The Fourth Gospel parallels this with three statements about the "lifting up of the Son of Man"; in each we see John emphasize how it is God's sovereign will that determines his Son's fate (see also 3:14; 12:32–34). Jesus's remarkable sense of the Father's presence, even as he describes the cross that awaits him, is linked to his perfect obedience to God's will.

The faith of some of the Jews in his audience provides an interesting counterpoint to what we learned in 8:20. In the first section (8:12–20) the discussion concludes with speculation about Jesus's capture. Now we have a description of some who believe. These two reactions parallel what we observed elsewhere in the Gospel where Jesus's audience divides: some completely oppose him, while others are receptive and welcoming.

Spiritual Ancestry (8:31–59). In the first round of debate (vv. 31–41), Jesus challenges a widely held assumption in Judaism. From the earliest chapters of the Old Testament, the people of Israel understood the importance of their election. They would be a blessing not only to God but to other nations. However, the sense of obligation and responsibility that this inspired was eventually replaced with feelings of privilege and protection.

With its history of slavery and bondage, freedom was a precious treasure among the Jews. Yet, Jesus claims, it is not religious heritage that brings true freedom, but truth (v. 32). "The truth will set you free." But to be set free means that there is a bondage from which you need to be freed. The captivity, of course, to which Jesus points is a bondage to sin. Jesus is urging that the more devastating bondage is not to any political power but to spiritual and moral depravity. The Jews consider themselves to be free (sons of Abraham), but in actuality, Jesus insists, they are slaves (of sin).

Thus, because they are slaves, their residence in God's family may be in jeopardy. Lineage from Abraham is a matter of faith, and any claim to blood heritage that brings spiritual privilege always stands in question. The "son" who is secure and permanent is likely Jesus himself. If the son in such a large household sets a slave free, he will be free indeed (v. 36). Imagine, then, if the Son of God sets a slave free. The freedom enjoyed would be indescribable.

Jesus acknowledges that his audience bears the bloodline of Abraham, but because of their desire to kill him and their refusal to accept his word, they betray that their lives are not guided by the Father, whose voice Jesus obeys. True Jewishness is inward, not physical and outward. Jesus implies that their activity points to another spiritual father.

As the argument unfolds, Jesus's opponents see clearly where he is leading. Without Abraham, they cannot belong to God's people. "We are not illegitimate children" is now a defense and an attack (v. 41). "We" is emphatic and implies comparison: *we* are not illegitimate (but *you* certainly are). Some scholars argue for a hint here of speculation about Jesus's extraordinary origins and its irony. By claiming to have God as Father, Jesus cannot have a human father, which is precisely the argument from the Synoptic nativity stories. Yet illegitimacy was a slur used by Jews against the Samaritans (and vice versa), and this will come up in verse 48 for Jesus.

If Jesus will not permit them Abraham, certainly (they think) he cannot forbid them an appeal to God. But even this is rejected. Since Jesus himself has come from God the Father, then if their parentage stemmed from God the Father, they would love the things of Jesus. But, in fact, they do not. They do not "belong to God" (v. 47) and are therefore working against his purposes. It is not as if Jesus's opponents disagree with him; the problem is more essential. Given who they are, they cannot recognize the truth, the Father, or anyone sent from the Father speaking the truth. The problem is not intellectual, but spiritual.

The climax of these implications is finally given in verse 44. His opponents' desire to kill Jesus unmasks the true nature of their spiritual ancestry: Satan. The murder the devil promoted "from the beginning" refers either to Cain and Abel or to the fact that it was through Satan's work that death came into the world, making him the architect of death. This is contrasted with Jesus, the architect of truth and life.

The opponents of Jesus now turn back accusations on him (v. 48). If it is true that his opponents are children of the devil, then he must be a Samaritan and demon possessed. This is a radical dishonoring. By Jesus's day, the enmity between Jews and Samaritans was intense. This slur likely had become a curse, much like *heretic* or *unbeliever*, so Jesus does not even take the time to refute it. The charge of demon-possession is far more serious. Rather than seeing God's work in Jesus, his opponents now point to Satan.

Jesus has made numerous absolute claims. He comes from the Father and bears the truth; their inability to see this truth betrays their separation from the Father and his purposes. Is this self-promotion? Jesus cannot deny the essential relationship he has with the Father. The Son glorifies the Father, and likewise the Father glorifies the Son. If his opponents cannot understand the truth about Jesus, they cannot understand this either.

Next Jesus makes a claim about life and death (vv. 51–58).

That Jesus can promise life eternal to those who obey him sets him apart from every spiritual luminary in Judaism, Abraham included. The force of verse 53 is literally, "What are you making of yourself here?" It is antagonistic and aggressive. But Jesus's defense is that he is *not* glorifying himself; instead, he is faithfully witnessing to his relationship with the Father. Jesus is simply living in fidelity to his word, and because God is the author and sustainer of life, all who know him will share in that life.

If Judaism could make an appeal to their ancestry in Abraham, Jesus now makes a parallel appeal (v. 56). No rabbi would object to Jesus's claim that Abraham would see the messianic era. But Jesus does not say this. Instead, he says: "Your father Abraham rejoiced at the thought of seeing *my day*; he saw it and was glad" (emphasis added). But how can Jesus and Abraham know each other since Jesus is not even fifty years old?

The climax of the entire chapter arrives at verse 58. This is an absolute claim to preexistence anchored in the absolute "I am" (*egō eimi*) echoing the Greek translation of God's divine name given in Exodus 3:14. To exist before the birth of Abraham—and yet to stand here today—is the boldest claim Jesus has yet made. It recalls the affirmation of the prologue that the Word existed even at the beginning of time. His existence has been continuous since his life is completely drawn from God's eternal life.

That Jesus's audience interpreted his words as a divine claim is seen in their reaction. They are furious because they believe they have heard blasphemy, for which stoning is the legal response. Jesus slips away, not as a result of his own ingenuity, but because God has appointed an hour when his death will be necessary. There is a divine plan, and no action of a mob will interrupt it.

Application. *The custodians of tradition.* The deepest paradox of John 8 is that Jesus suffers *religious* persecution. Jesus steps into a religiously devout environment and immediately splits his audience. Those who follow him become passionate believers. Those who stand opposed, who defend their traditions with zeal, suddenly become zealous opponents, enemies of God's work in the world. This passage warns the custodians of tradition that their defense of these spiritual habits and rituals may well be their undoing.

Karl Barth in his 1919 commentary on Romans wrote about such people. Their lives are like those who are headed on a long journey and along the way find a sign pointing them westward. The signpost is there to convey them to their destination, but instead they stop and create a life for themselves under its painted words. They build a civilization there, celebrating the signpost and telling stories of how they arrived at the marker. Rituals evolve and songs are written. Books are published and liturgies follow. A few travel on and return, confirming that the sign does indeed lead to the place promised. But the second and third generations have built a life around the signpost and have forgotten the meaning of the journey. Their lore is built on stories of past travel, not on stories of arriving or on the prophetic call to get on with the journey themselves.

Jesus in our century. It is a troubling question, but we must face it. If Jesus stepped into our century, if he walked into our evangelical churches, if he picked up a religious symbol and challenged the symbol's original meaning, would we cheer or would we fight? Suddenly we might find ourselves defending *Christendom* instead of the Christian faith. This reflex that cannot see God in the prophetic voice of Jesus, that rebels and fights and attacks, is the work of Satan. It is Satan's work among *religious* people. It is a work that appeared within Judaism and that appears just as often within the Christian church. It is the work of darkness that is commonplace to the human heart. Above all, it is a voice that makes a human voice preeminent to the voice of God.

John 8:12–59 is a severe call to Judaism that it must repent. But it is a call for us too, who have taken up the mantle worn by the temple leadership of Jerusalem.

JOHN 9:1–41

Original Meaning. In the present chapter, a man who lives in "darkness" is miraculously given "light." Through the story of this man's healing, we see another parable beginning to unfold. Physical healing becomes a symbol of spiritual healing, while physical blindness is replaced with spiritual blindness. At the end of the story a splendid reversal appears: the man who once lived in darkness now has light (in both eye and heart), while those arrayed against him have sound eyes but nevertheless live in spiritual darkness.

The Healing of the Blind Man (9:1–7). Blindness was a problem in antiquity, far more common than we would think. Eye disease had few cures, and unsanitary conditions increased risks considerably. The man whom Jesus meets at the Feast of Tabernacles has been blind from birth. This leads his disciples to ask about the origin of his suffering. They assume there must be a connection between sin and suffering, so they probe who is responsible, the man or his parents. Jesus rejects this entire line of questioning. However, the NIV and most English translations invite gross confusion with Jesus's answer (v. 3). It hardly takes a careful reader to see the theological implications following this line of thought: God brought suffering to this man so that he might glorify himself in his healing. While a sound theology cannot doubt God's sovereignty to do as he pleases, thoughtful Christians may see this as a cruel fate in which God inflicts pain on people simply to glorify himself.

However, the "purpose clause" of verse 3b ("so that the works of God . . .") can just as well be applied to verse 4, and no doubt it should. We may translate it as follows: "'Neither this man nor his parents sinned,' said Jesus. 'But so that the work of God might be displayed in his life, we must do the work of him who sent me while it is still day.'"

The purpose clause now explains that Jesus must work *so that* God's work may be displayed in this man's life. God had not made the man blind in order to show his glory; rather, God has sent Jesus to do works of healing in order to show his glory. The theological nuance of the two translations cannot be more different.

In antiquity, spittle was thought to have medicinal power. Thus, Jesus's action is not unusual. Jesus then tells the man to go and wash in the Pool of Siloam. This is an important detail for two reasons. It was the source of water in Tabernacles. If Jesus is the source of the Feast of Tabernacles water (7:37–39), this man has now experienced such water in a profound way. The name of the pool bears symbolic importance for Jesus. More than twenty times in this Gospel, Jesus is described as the one who has been "sent" by God. In other words, the blind man is being told to go wash in the place called "sent" (9:7), by the one who was "sent" by God. Jesus, then, is the source of his healing, not the pool.

Interrogation (9:8–34). The dramatic healing of this man must have made a significant stir among his immediate friends and family. The community's investigation of this man's experience is given to us in abbreviated form in the following verses. We can imagine hours of debating and discussing as the community tries to verify not only the identity of the man *as blind* but the identity of the healer, Jesus.

The neighbors (9:8–13). John provides a cycle of four scenes where questions are launched concerning the man and his healing. In the first scene (vv. 8–13), the neighbors interrogate the man and in disbelief work to verify that he is indeed the man they knew as blind. They do not reject the miracle, but they look to the Pharisees, the established theological leaders in the synagogue, for counsel.

The Pharisees (9:14–17). The Pharisees question the man about the healing, but their chief worry is about a violation of the Sabbath.

The man's parents (9:18–23). The Pharisees turn next to the man's parents in order to confirm that indeed a miracle has occurred. The leaders are incredulous, but the parents fear them because they know of a conspiracy that will expel anyone from the synagogue who stands with Jesus. They deflect the Pharisees' questions and direct them back to their son.

The formerly blind man (again) (9:24–29). The leaders turn to the man for a second time. While he can hardly make a comment about Jesus's sinfulness, he cannot deny the miracle. In exasperation, he presses the Pharisees boldly, and the tension of the story mounts. The miracle demands an explanation, and its sheer magnitude points to only one source: God. But if this is the case, since God does not listen to sinners—and God has listened to Jesus—Jesus cannot be a sinner. Here we have the sharpest division between the man (who supports Jesus) and the leaders (who do not).

As the story progresses, Jesus is more closely revealed by name: he is "Jesus" (v. 11), then he is called a "prophet" (v. 17), then "the Messiah" (v. 22), and finally he is declared to be "from God" (v. 33). It is easy to see the christological progression of each name as the story develops. While the Pharisees repudiate Jesus and his role, the discussion drives home his true identity.

Ironically, the entire episode of interrogation ends with an accusation hurled at the man from the leaders (v. 34). This is telling, since it echoes the verses that began the chapter. In the former instance, sin supposedly brought physical blindness; in the latter, his sin supposedly brought spiritual blindness (or religious ignorance). They are wrong on both counts. Nevertheless, the interrogation ends with the healed man expelled from the synagogue.

Spiritual Blindness (9:35–41). Jesus meets with the blind man privately to unveil the true depth of what he experienced. His confession of faith ("Lord, I believe," v. 38) and his worship indicate that he no longer lives in darkness in any sense. This is an open embrace of Jesus—a commitment to him as the Messiah of Israel. The blind man thus becomes a model of every believer who embraces Jesus's lordship and suffers persecution as a result.

The Pharisees, by contrast, have come forward to judge both the man and Jesus. But in the end, Jesus judges them. The light/darkness motif that surrounds the Feast of Tabernacles creates a delightful double meaning. Jesus's opponents are physically sighted, but in reality they are spiritually blind. The blind man has had both conditions reversed.

But the most serious condition these opponents possess (v. 41) is their insistence that they are innocent, that they understand fully the theological point Jesus is making, and that they reject it. Because they *claim* that they can see, their guilt is underscored since they are self-affirming in their religious position against Jesus.

Application. *The blind man: a model of belief and conversion.* This man's life should be depicted as a hopeless tragedy. He sat at the roadside and begged. No employment, no prospects for marriage, no social honor. He was at the bottom of the social ladder. His future was bleak, and he knew it. This hopelessness and darkness provide us with a potent image because John describes men and women without Christ to be in a crisis no less desperate. Jesus refers to those who "walk in darkness," and this is precisely the condition of the blind. Jesus lifts this image above the commonplace in order to make it a spiritual metaphor for the condition of the world that he has come to remedy.

Healing was important to Jesus's work, and likewise it should be important in the church's work today. We do not want to spiritualize this story utterly, making the spiritual renewal of the blind man the only important thing; Jesus also recognized that making the blind man whole was a gesture of his love for the man. Unfortunately, many of us are predisposed not to believe in healing such as this.

God is glorified when ministry happens in this manner. This is ministry that invites God to act in a powerful, dramatic manner to utterly transform. Sometimes evangelicals are prone to view ministry through the lens of a twenty-first-century scholasticism.

The model of this man's conversion, however, is not simply about desperation and healing. He is courageous. He valiantly holds fast to what he cannot deny. His intellectual courage is matched by his personal fearlessness as he suffers persecution for his courage. This drama is also a part of John's conversion model. To embrace faith in Jesus Christ will come with consequences: social isolation, punishment, perhaps martyrdom.

It is significant that John's story moves quickly away from the sheer fact of Jesus's miracle-working capacity to the identity of the one who heals. The man's faith is not in the miracle-working ability of Jesus. This is only the springboard. His faith quickly connects with the true identity of who Jesus is.

The temple leadership: a model of spiritual intransigence. Perhaps the most troubling questions to surface in this passage have to do with the profile of Jesus's opponents. They stand against Jesus from an informed theological standpoint. If they rejected Jesus out of ignorance, it would be a different matter. But they reject Jesus out of knowledge, and so their "guilt remains."

John opens a question that he does not answer. Is it possible to "be blind" and yet not be guilty of sin because of genuine spiritual ignorance? This would be a person who is in the darkness, who cannot recognize God's work in Christ and who thus rejects Jesus—but the rejection is based on ignorance. John would almost certainly affirm that anyone who is in the darkness is in spiritual jeopardy, regardless of his or her intellectual, religious position.

John's real interest is to examine the position of a person who has a knowing, willful religious rejection of Jesus. In the church there has always been (and continues to be today) those from within our own ranks who reject Jesus knowingly. They know the rudiments of the orthodox faith, they know our theological traditions, they may have experienced the life of a Christian, but they say no. This is called *heresy* or *apostasy*, and we need to be able to name it when it appears. Hell will have more than its share of thoughtful theologians.

JOHN 10:1–42

Original Meaning

The Good Shepherd (10:1–18). Jesus is stepping into a venerable Old Testament tradition when he describes himself as the good shepherd of Israel. In the Old Testament, God is the shepherd of Israel. Moreover, shepherding became a helpful image explaining the spiritual and practical leadership among God's people. Moses and David, for example, were shepherds. Impious kings in Israel were commonly understood to be false or bad shepherds.

The occasion for this discourse, John reminds us, is the Festival of Hanukkah (v. 22). This is the only reference to this minor, intertestamental festival in the Bible. Since the conquest of Alexander the Great in 332 BC, Jewish resistance to Hellenization met opposition not only from Greeks but also from Jews who had compromised their commitment to Jewish culture and their faith. In the 160s BC the Maccabean War erupted, pitting conservative Jewish fighters against Greeks and Hellenized Jews. Hanukkah thus became a season that asked hard questions about failed leadership and false shepherds.

Jesus assumes his audience understands the scene he is constructing. In the desert at night sheep were often herded into walled enclosures. Not only can sheep identify rightful shepherds by their access through the main gate, but they also recognize the voice of their shepherd. Just as Arab shepherds today can separate personal sheep from larger flocks by using peculiar calls, so Jesus knows his own sheep, they can recognize his voice, and he leads them (v. 4).

It is not surprising that Jesus's audience does not understand the figurative saying. They understand the nature of shepherding, but they fail to grasp the spiritual point he is making. The Middle East delights in the dark saying that must be unpacked, and every good teacher must know how to use the proverb and the symbolic story. In John the theme is consistently Jesus's identity; stories unveil who he is. But in each case, the problem is not necessarily intellectual. The problem is often an unwillingness to respond to the challenge of the saying.

Jesus's explanation turns the story creatively. The first image of the parable that Jesus does not interpret concerns his entry into the sheepfold. The watchman permits him entry, making him God's shepherd. He is the rightful leader who goes through the gate. He has authority to lead the sheep (while others do not).

In his interpretation Jesus shifts some of the images. He becomes *the gate*. He alone is the sentry, the one through whom access to the sheep can be found. He stands in the gate, and any who enter without his permission (who sneak into the flock) are not to be trusted. This implies some endorsement of those who enter into leadership in Christ's name. But it also implies a warning, for there are illegitimate shepherds whose entry he prohibits. Who are these "thieves and robbers" who have come before Jesus (v. 8)? The most likely target of Jesus's criticism is the Pharisees.

Jesus is the gate for the sheep; only those sheep who find him will enter the sheepfold and find safety. They alone will know his leadership and exit to find safe, lush pasture. The image here is a flock of sheep in a threatening desert. Food and water are scarce. Predators are everywhere, and they know the sheep are vulnerable. Jesus's image is that of well-fed sheep whose shepherd knows how to lead them to pasture and water daily, and who at night gives them safe rest in the sturdy walls of the sheepfold.

At the final level of his interpretation, Jesus claims that he is the "good shepherd" (v. 11). It is important not to overly sentimentalize the image given here. This is not a portrait of a kindly man holding cuddly lambs. "Good" (*kalos*) can just as well be translated "noble." The shepherd's job was severe, tiring, and hazardous. The hired hand is distinguished by his lack of commitment to the sheep. When danger comes, he flees and the flock is attacked. His own self-interest refers directly to the leaders of Israel graphically chastised during the Hanukkah festival. The good shepherd, by contrast, "owns the sheep" (see v. 12), which speaks to his unique, passionate commitment to them.

The most important feature of Jesus's role as shepherd is that he lays down his life for the sheep. He cares for them so much that he is willing to come between his flock and danger. He is *willing to die* for them. To die "for" (Gk. *hyper*) the sheep is significant (v. 11). Throughout the Fourth Gospel, *hyper* is used almost exclusively in a sacrificial context, generally describing Jesus's sacrificial death on behalf of others. Therefore, Jesus is pointing to the depth of his love for the flock of God and his commitment to die for them in obedience to God's will.

Perhaps the most startling feature of Jesus's interpretation is his description of the intimacy of the sheep and their shepherd. We have already learned that the sheep "know" the shepherd's voice (v. 4), but now we learn that this knowledge is mutual and exhaustive. Moreover, the model for this intimacy is the mutual knowledge shared between the Son and the Father; as he and the Father share profound love, so too Jesus and his flock share this quality of love. This explains the willingness of Jesus to die for his sheep. Jesus is willing to die because of his profound commitment to the ones he loves.

Jesus further says there are "other sheep" that do not come from this sheepfold (v. 16). If they come from a different fold, they come from outside of Judaism, which no doubt refers to gentiles. They too will recognize Jesus's voice and follow him, so that there will be one flock and one shepherd. This is Jesus's vision for the unity of the church: Jewish believers and gentile believers living together under Christ's leadership. For the first time, Jesus is anticipating in detail the wider scope of his ministry to reach the world.

Jesus next probes the deeper meaning of the Father's love for him. The fundamental element in this relationship is Jesus's dependence on and obedience to God's will. This is expressed utterly in his willingness to die on the cross. We must avoid the idea that in giving his life, the Son wins the Father's love. The Father has loved the Son from the "creation of the world" (17:24). Jesus's voluntary death therefore is a hallmark of his union with the Father's will and an expression of the love they share together.

This is underscored at the beginning of verse 18. Jesus is not a victim of human conspiracies. He was not a martyr whose life was ended as a tragedy. He obediently participates in the plan of God. The early Christians who interpreted Jesus's death reinforced this view.

The final aspect of Jesus's uniqueness as the good shepherd is the authority he bears not only to die but to retake his life in resurrection (vv. 17b–18). The resurrection, therefore, is not an afterthought wherein God rescues his Son from an unexpected tragedy. As the tomb could not contain God, so too Jesus, in his union with the Father, possessed the authority and power to vanquish the death he had embraced on Good Friday. He takes his life up again.

But even in this act he is not working independently, as if he submits to God's plan of sacrifice but recovers through his own power of resurrection. Jesus's authoritative, powerful activity, from Good Friday to Easter Sunday, operates in harmony with God, who has authorized and directed it.

The Reaction of the Crowd (10:19–21). John's chief interest here is in the opposite reactions now forming. Some believe that Jesus is "demon-possessed and raving mad" (v. 20). The reaction is antagonistic. Still others in the audience are impressed with Jesus. This part of the crowd fails to identify Jesus accurately or exhibit belief. Nevertheless, they are open to new possibilities and unwilling to judge Jesus outright.

The Controversy Intensifies (10:22–42). This final section is a critical revelation for the Fourth Gospel. This is Jesus's final public disclosure of himself to his people. It will be an ultimate disclosure of his complete identity. The account ends with his returning to where it all began—the Jordan River, where John had baptized him.

The crowd is looking for an unambiguous statement about Jesus's identity. "How long will you keep us in suspense?" (v. 24) can also be translated, "How long will you annoy us?" Are these people seeking clarity or are they antagonistic? What they want is an open, clear statement from Jesus about his messiahship, and no doubt they are poised to judge him if his answer is not to their liking.

Given the explosive, highly politicized views of the Messiah in this period, it is not surprising that Jesus has used restraint so far. Now his audience wants a plain statement. Yet we have already learned that even if Jesus were to speak plainly, only his "sheep" would recognize his voice (v. 26). Ironically, his shepherd sermon was just such a disclosure, but they have not "heard" it.

The root problem is unbelief. The character of Jesus's life and his works or miracles wrought by God's power indicate his true identity. But the true problem, which is a deep theological issue, is that only those who are Jesus's sheep can understand these things. The "other sheep" cannot understand his voice, he does not know them, and they do not follow. This does not excuse them; it simply says that nothing in Jesus's life is happening outside of the sovereign plan of God.

Not only is this faith a gift, but so are eternal life and security. This shepherd will die for his sheep, but those outside the fold will remain in jeopardy. Jesus's assignment has been to gather up "all those the Father gives" him (6:37–40). Therefore, his skill as the good shepherd secures them from all predators and thieves (10:29).

The astounding affirmation given in verse 30 serves as a high point in the chapter. Earlier Jesus spoke about his working in cooperation with the Father and in accordance with the Father's will. The sheep here belong both to the Father and the Son and enjoy fellowship with both simultaneously. "One" in Greek is neuter and does not refer to "one person." Therefore, Jesus is affirming a unity of purpose and will. The protection of the sheep results from the joint work of Father and Son.

This formulation of oneness is stronger than what we see elsewhere, and the response of the crowd in verses 31, 33 suggests that they hear something different too. This is not a man who is saying he has joined his efforts with God; this is a man who is saying something dangerous, something more, something blasphemous.

Such statements by Jesus demand a response. In chapter 8 Jesus's summary disclosure of his relationship to Abraham ended in an attempt to stone him. The same thing happens here. The perceived problem is not Jesus's miracles but his words. While charges have been given against Jesus's illegal work on the Sabbath, here the problem is blasphemy. His opponents believe he is claiming to be God. This statement is likely John's typical use of irony, where the antagonist affirms the very truth about Jesus.

Jesus's defense in verses 34–39 is carefully nuanced and takes advantage of the symbolic motifs present at the Hanukkah festival. He defends himself by citing Psalm 82:6. If the word "god" can be applied to those other than God himself in the Scriptures, why are Jesus's words blasphemy?

Moreover, Jesus is the one whom God "sanctified" (*hagiazō*; NIV "set apart") and sent into the world (v. 36). The NIV obscures 10:36a with a paraphrase. The Greek verb *hagiazō* means to consecrate or make something holy. This points to the meaning of Hanukkah itself. Judas Maccabeus had reclaimed the temple after he conquered his Greek oppressors. In 1 Maccabees 4:48 we read, "They also rebuilt the sanctuary and the interior of the temple, and consecrated [*hagiazō*] the courts." Jesus, then, is the object of Hanukkah's interest. He is the "sanctified place," the "holy place," the "temple" of God celebrated in this season. Not only is his title "Son of God" justified by Psalm 82, but his identity as the locus of God's presence, as the divine courier from heaven, gives him an incomparable status.

Jesus's departure from Judea (vv. 40–42) is as much a theological statement as it is geographical. He is moving away from the area of conflict in Jerusalem and returning across the eastern deserts near the Jordan River, where John the Baptist had worked. As such it forms a literary bookend that matches the John the Baptist stories at the start of the Gospel. Jesus has come full circle. He has concluded his public ministry among his people, and now it is time for him to "stay" (v. 40b) there until his hour does come. In a few months he will appear in Jerusalem at Passover to be glorified as God has planned.

For the last time, John the Baptist's role is affirmed. Echoing the words of 3:22–30, his ministry is placed in perspective. He was a trustworthy and reliable witness to the truth about Jesus. Jesus alone has provided divine signs that point to the hand of the Father in his life, but John provided a voice, a voice in the desert, calling men and women to faith.

Ironically, the evangelist adds, "And in that place many believed in Jesus" (v. 42). Jesus finds faith not among the ranks of the religious in the holy city of Jerusalem. Rather, he finds it when he moves to the desert and works among those who must travel at some hardship to find him. "Many people came to him" in the desert by the Jordan and believed in him (v. 41), recognizing that this was God's hand behind Jesus's works and God's voice within his words. But the leaders of Jerusalem will not see him again until they are given an opportunity to crucify him.

Application. *The desert.* The desert in Israel is tremendously important in order to understand the Bible. During the bulk of the year, the desert is inhospitable to life. Water is scarce, food is rare, and dangers are everywhere. Competent shepherds must have skills and tools, or else their sheep will become prey either to the elements or to wild animals in this region. When the flock is attacked, a "good" shepherd will never throw a lamb to the attacking animals in order to save the flock. He tries to find a sheep pen and then stands between the flock and danger.

This is precisely the image that we need to construct for our audience. The desert is a desperate place. Our shepherd is skilled and courageous. If we remain under his leadership, if we recognize his voice, we will find safety and flourish. To make this come alive, we need to recognize the perilous environment of our lives, our need of guidance, and the requisite skill that can tell the right voices from the wrong voices.

It takes little convincing to show that the environment of the world is as treacherous as a Judean desert. The environment of the world is hostile at every turn. We do live in a modern desert. Amid this moral chaos, in this threatening desert, whose voice, which shepherd, do we follow?

Testing. Every communicator of biblical truth needs to sound the alarm and point their audience to their need of a true shepherd who can genuinely lead them from the desert. John has given us a direct and simple solution. Jesus is the true shepherd, and he is the only one who can endorse others who will lead the sheep. The final test of a shepherd's credentials is his or her fidelity to the leadership of Jesus.

Ancillary issues. That Jesus has "other sheep" not of "this fold" means in its historic setting that Jesus has sheep among those on the margins of Jewish society (most likely, the gentiles) that must be included in his flock. When the body of Christ—or the flock of Jesus—embraces these "other sheep," remarkable things happen. As modern interpreters, we need to wrestle with the identity of these sheep for the churches in which we live. Who lives on the margins of our world? This is also a warning to those sheep whose control of the fold has made it homogenous and exclusive. The vision here is for a unity that breaks the bonds of racial, economic, and cultural divisions, that sees a person's identity in Christ first, while all other markers fall away.

The second ancillary question concerns the divine sovereignty alluded to throughout the chapter. Thinking Christians will pick up on this immediately. "If God's will is sovereign, then there are no autonomous human decisions." We have to strike a balance that pays appropriate respect to both of these themes. God continues to work in powerful ways, but his work always invites our participation, and even demands our participation. In John 10 Jesus's sheep are those whom God has given into his hand, and they are also sheep who have decided to believe.

Finally, the nuanced ending of the chapter is troubling. The suggestion here is that once Jesus has completed his direct revelation within Judaism, he is ready to remove himself and remain outside Judea until the coming festival of Passover, when he is killed. Perhaps the application of this theme points to the limited opportunities we possess to hear the gospel. Practically, the messenger from God who speaks the gospel to me today may not be here tomorrow. Consequently, "today" must be the "day of salvation."

JOHN 11:1–57

Original Meaning. John 11 and 12 stand together as marking a new and significant step in the life and work of Jesus. These two chapters are about both death and life. The Lazarus story is a story about one man who Jesus rescues from the grave; but it is also a parabolic story, telling us far more about Jesus, his power, and his upcoming experience in the grave.

The Death of Lazarus (11:1–16). Bethany was a village just east of Jerusalem over the Mount of Olives, about one and a half miles away. When he was in Jerusalem, Jesus used Bethany as his base. This is why the Gospels contain multiple stories related to the village and why Jesus likely lived here during the final week of his life.

Here in this small Judean community lives a family extremely dear to Jesus; Mary, Martha, and Lazarus may have become something like an extended family for Jesus. No indication is given that they live together, and we should not assume it. It would be most natural for them all to be married. That Jesus loves this family is affirmed again and again.

It is interesting that the women know how to find Jesus. Does this suggest that they have been keeping up with his movements? Or is there a network of supporters the sisters tap? Although they do not request Jesus to come, it is implied, since he is well-known as a healer and later both women express regret that if Jesus had only come on time, Lazarus would not have died. No doubt they are in a dilemma. They know about the hostility of the Jerusalem's leadership toward Jesus and conclude that for Jesus to visit would mean considerable risk.

When Jesus hears the report about Lazarus's illness, his response parallels his comments about the man born blind. The final result of this tragedy is that God will be glorified, not that death will win the victory. The tragedy is not by God's design, but God will use it for an opportunity to glorify his Son.

John reports that Jesus does not respond immediately and come to Bethany. He waits two days. Note that Jesus's delay is not the cause of Lazarus's death. When Jesus arrives in Bethany, Lazarus has been dead for four days. It likely took the messengers one day to find Jesus, Jesus continues to work where he is two days, and then he takes one more day to travel to Bethany. This means that Lazarus likely died right after the departure of the messengers. When they meet Jesus, Lazarus is already buried.

Nevertheless, we should assume that in the narrative Jesus has divine knowledge of what is happening in Bethany. If Jesus has this knowledge and if he knows the moment of Lazarus's death, his delay serves not to promote the death but to heighten the significance of his own miraculous work. His aim is to reveal the glory of God's work in him and thereby to promote the faith of his followers.

The decision finally to go up to Judea must have been frightening to Jesus's disciples. Throughout the story we have learned of the growing tensions surrounding Jesus's contact with the religious leadership. During the previous autumn celebration at the Feast of Tabernacles, the authorities tried to arrest him, and rumor was out that they wanted to kill him. At one point a crowd tried to stone Jesus. A few months later at Hanukkah they tried to arrest him, and again there was the threat of stoning. The threat is not simply to Jesus but to his disciples as well, so that Thomas speaks up, "Let us also go, that we may die with him" (v. 16).

We should probably see these words as another case of Johannine irony. Thomas likely does not understand the profound truth he utters. This parallels the role of Caiaphas later in the chapter, when the high priest says that Jesus's death will be expedient for the nation (vv. 49–50). Indeed, it will be—but not as Caiaphas imagines it. So too being a disciple will pose dangers, even martyrdom, for anyone who follows Jesus.

Jesus Comes to Bethany (11:17–37). When Jesus finally arrives in Bethany, Lazarus has been dead for four days. This note is significant. There was a well-known Jewish belief that the soul of a dead person remained in the vicinity of the body for three days, but once decomposition set in, the soul departed. John wants us to know clearly that Lazarus is truly dead and that the miracle of Jesus cannot be construed as a resuscitation.

Lazarus's death was not a private period of mourning for his family. Life in New Testament Palestine was lived publicly, and community ties were strong. Formal mourning lasted for seven days, and it commenced immediately on the day of burial, which took place on the same day as death. We can assume that Lazarus was buried in a rock-cut tomb of the type that has been discovered throughout the hills of Judea. After a year or so, the body was removed, and the bones were placed in a limestone burial box (an ossuary). The tomb was closed (and reopened for further burials) with a wheel-shaped "rolling stone" fitted to cover the entrance in a stone channel.

Therefore, when Jesus arrives on the outskirts of Bethany, the tomb is closed, and there is tremendous commotion surrounding Martha and Mary. The extent and passion of mourning reflects the honor and esteem of Lazarus in the village. Friends and family from far off came to join the scene. By referring to Jerusalem, the text increases our sense of Jesus's jeopardy when he arrives. His presence in Bethany just over the Mount of Olives would certainly become known to his enemies in Jerusalem.

The story follows the two sisters as each makes contact with Jesus. First Martha, then Mary, talk with Jesus; this is followed by the miracle itself. The sorrowful complaints of both women (vv. 21, 32) are virtually the same.

Martha meets Jesus before he enters the village (v. 30), and her words in verse 21 are an affirmation of faith in Jesus's healing ability. Despite what she says in verse 22, she likely does not expect Jesus to raise Lazarus from death since in verse 39 she objects when Jesus wants to roll open the tomb. Instead, she is expressing faith, not wanting to imply any criticism of Jesus since he was not in Bethany to rescue her brother. Martha's words can be paraphrased: "If you had been here, you could have healed Lazarus. Nevertheless, I still believe in you, that God works through you mightily."

But Jesus pushes Martha to a second, deeper level of discussion (vv. 23–27). Martha misses the more immediate application Jesus has in mind. His correction leads to one of the most famous and significant "I am" sayings in John's Gospel. Jesus does not say that he can provide resurrection and life. That in itself would be astounding. Jesus says that *he is* resurrection and life (v. 25).

In other words, eternal life and rescue from the finality of death are not merely gifts obtained by appeal to God; they are aspects of what it means to live a life in association with Jesus. If Jesus is life, then those who believe in him will enjoy the confidence and power over death known by him. This does not mean that Jesus's followers will not die a physical death (v. 25b), but that life will be theirs beyond the grave; they will not suffer death in eternity. Moreover, they will have a life now and do not have to await the end of human time and history in order to enjoy the benefits of Jesus's power.

Jesus's question to Martha, "Do you believe this?" (v. 26) is asking if her faith can embrace a belief in Jesus's lordship over death itself. If it is true that in Jesus the power of resurrection life is present in Bethany, the logical implication is that this may lead to something for Lazarus. Lazarus's resurrection becomes a proof of Jesus's statement.

She says yes, when undoubtedly the implications of this yes are beyond her comprehension. She is trusting in Jesus's power as a personal commitment, but she is also ready to make a cognitive commitment to who Jesus must be. If he has this sort of authority, he must also be the "the Messiah, the Son of God" (v. 27).

Mary then enters the scene while Jesus is still outside the village and inaccessible to the crowd. It is a deeply touching scene, since Jesus knows that his ministry here is not simply to Lazarus but to both of these women whom he has known. Mary (like her sister) explains in dismay their sorrow over Jesus's absence while Lazarus was alive, and then is overcome with grief. The NIV's "weeping" leaves the impression of quiet tears of sadness, but the Greek tells a different story. The verb *klaiō* describes loud wailing and crying, which is echoed by the people standing around Mary (v. 33a).

When Jesus sees and hears their wailing, he is moved powerfully. But the NIV's "deeply moved" may not be the best reading of the Greek verb *embrimaomai* (v. 33b). For humans it describes outrage, fury, or anger. This is seen in the explanation John attaches: Jesus was not only outraged but "troubled."

Why is he outraged in the deepest level of his being? He is certainly not angry at Martha, Mary, or their mourners. Rather, he is overcome by the futility of this sorrowful scene in light of the reality of the resurrection. Jesus is angry at death itself and the devastation it brings.

Jesus's tears are not for Lazarus. He knows what good surprises are in store for his good friend. Jesus's tears should be connected to the anger he is feeling so deeply. The public chaos surrounding him, the loud wailing and crying, and the scene of a cemetery and its reminders of death—all the result of sin and death—together produce outrage in the Son of God as he works to reverse such damage.

Lazarus Is Raised to Life (11:38–44). As Jesus steps to the tomb itself, he is "once more deeply moved" (v. 38). The verb used here is the same one as in verse 33 (*embrimaomai*), which suggests he is outraged at what he sees. The Lord of life is now directly confronting his opponent, death, symbolized in the cave-tomb before him.

Martha's response in verse 39 is critical for John's report of the scene. She warns that since Lazarus has been dead four days, decomposition has set in and there will be an odor. All of this serves to remind us that Lazarus is truly dead and that the miracle of Jesus is not simply one of resuscitating his friend. He must be "awakened" *from death*.

When the stone is rolled back, Jesus prays. This prayer is interesting on several counts. First, it implies that Jesus had prayed *already* for Lazarus and that he is now coming to this great miracle fully prepared for what will take place. This is not a last-minute request. Second, Jesus prays publicly, and he does so "looking up" (v. 41). This was a common posture for Jewish prayer. Audible prayers were more common in Jesus's world than private prayers. Jesus is certainly not praying to impress the audience of mourners. But his followers could use prayers to learn things about the life and thought of their Lord. Thus, Jesus is aware that his prayer is also for the benefit of these bystanders (v. 42). Finally, Jesus addresses God as "Father" (not "our" father) and shows his personal intimacy with him. He also demonstrates that his work is done in concert with God's will, for he never acts autonomously.

The dramatic high point of the story is reached in verse 43 when Jesus calls to Lazarus to come out. This is not a whisper or a firm request. It is a shout of raw authority. When Lazarus emerges from the tomb, he is bound in grave wrappings, which were strips of fabric wound around his limbs and filled with burial spices. Jewish burials likewise tied the jaw closed and covered the face with a linen cloth.

Lazarus's coming from the grave must have been an amazing spectacle witnessed by a growing crowd of people, many of whom carry news of this miracle back to Jerusalem. Lazarus stands before Jesus wrapped tightly. Jesus is no doubt talking to him (what does he say?), and the crowd undoubtedly shrinks back in awe. Jewish superstitions took great interest in cemeteries (as do most cultures), and strict ritual laws of purification (clean/unclean) were attached to dead bodies. Should anyone come near the man? Martha? Mary? Jesus loved Lazarus, and it is not hard to imagine him being the first to embrace his friend. Jesus remains in command and orders that someone unbind him.

The Sanhedrin Plots to Kill Jesus (11:45–57). Most of the miracles and discourses in the Book of Signs (John 1–12) led to a sharp division in the audience. The same occurs here. Many of the Jews in Bethany who witnessed the events of that day "believed in him" (v. 45). John's sharp contrast with "some of them," who go directly to the Pharisees, suggests that these do not believe (v. 46).

The Sanhedrin deliberations are noteworthy. There is genuine fear that the populace will accept Jesus as the Messiah. This is not simply religious rivalry but a paralyzing concern that if a messianic claimant is embraced by the city, the Roman armies will suppress it. The Romans had shown their intolerance to this sort of messianism in the past (viewing it as a political challenge), and Jerusalem's leadership know the seriousness of the threat now.

John summarizes the view of the reigning high priest, Caiaphas. This man ruled the Sanhedrin from AD 18 to 36 and took personal responsibility for the political stability of the country. For Caiaphas, then, political expediency is the key: if there must be a sacrifice, better to lose one man than the entire nation. Therefore, the high council begins planning how they can kill Jesus.

These voices say more than even they expected. John knows this and tips us off to look beneath the surface. Indeed, both of the comments from the Sanhedrin bear some truth. The Romans will eventually come and bring their judgment on the city and its temple. But Caiaphas is also right in a way he cannot perceive. Jesus will die for the salvation of the nation. An unwitting prophecy here points to the cross since the salvation Judaism needs has less to do with Rome than it does with Jerusalem's spiritual jeopardy.

John knows that the death of Christ will perform a work that is far more profound than anyone imagines. It is not simply for the city of Jerusalem but for the "scattered children of God" (v. 52). To a Jew, such a phrase would describe Jews living in the diaspora (or the dispersion) of gentile countries around the Mediterranean. But here John is no doubt referring to gentiles, who likewise need to come into the family of God.

Jesus cannot risk being a public figure in the same manner any longer. He knows the hour of his glorification and will not permit anyone or anything to interrupt his mission. With characteristic geographical precision, John says that Jesus moves to the village of Ephraim (v. 54). Here Jesus is safe from the Sanhedrin, but he is also close enough to attend the upcoming Passover in Jerusalem.

Residents of Jerusalem no doubt spread the story of Lazarus, and the city is buzzing with talk about the intentions of the religious authorities. An open announcement of arrest is circulating for Jesus. If he is seen, he will be captured. There will be a showdown.

But from Jesus's point of view, his public ministry among his own people is completed. No longer will he provide any miraculous signs for them. No longer will we hear of new audiences of Jews believing in him. Jesus is finished. He now will spend concentrated private time with those families (e.g., Martha, Mary, Lazarus), friends, and followers who know him, trust him, and believe in him. Jesus will indeed return to the public square once more during the Passover feast following his triumphal entry, but only to give an impassioned plea for belief (12:44). No longer will he provide public signs that evoke belief. The next time after this he appears in public, he will be a prisoner.

Application. Every age struggles with the finality of the grave and the incomprehensibility of death. In some respects, we also live in an age that does its best to deny death. Today this process has been sanitized, taken over by professional hospitals, hospices, and morticians. All of this is cultural, springing from the heartfelt wish to make death pleasant. But it masks a profound anxiety that even the prettiest funeral service cannot disguise. Perhaps this is why in the work of the church, funeral services become such potent opportunities for ministry. Here the raw vulnerability of our lives stands naked, and we are confronted by a personal fate we would rather not look at directly.

Sign and explanation. There were many standing among the mourners of Bethany that day who were friends with Lazarus, who knew he was dead, and who participated in his burial. But when he stepped from the grave, they refused to believe in Jesus. This is amazing. Signs alone cannot provoke faith.

This understanding of the limited success of the miracle is at the root of John's link between sign and explanation (or miracle and discourse). A sheer experience of the power of God is insufficient to persuade the human heart. Therefore, in the activity of the church, words must accompany deeds. It is foolhardy to think that if God supplies us with a compelling miracle, our spiritual communities will be energized. Signs from God must have a spiritually true context to be understood correctly, to be grounded as they should.

The power and confidence of Jesus. Lazarus eventually died (again!). But imagine for a moment Lazarus's thoughts as he laid on his second deathbed some years after the death and resurrection of Jesus. Normal feelings of worry and fear were there in the corners of his soul, no doubt. But he had confidence. He knew that Jesus had a relationship with death like no other. Jesus was "resurrection and life," and so he was not going to the grave alone.

Jesus's death and resurrection. John is taking the long view of Jesus's work when he describes the events that surround Lazarus's new life. Jesus proves he has power over death; but more, we also learn that Jesus's death will play a role in the work that he still has to do. That Jesus must die is said explicitly in the chambers of the Sanhedrin. Moreover, we learn that Jesus is the one man who must die *for the people.* We also know that Jesus is "the resurrection and the life." Therefore, in order to vanquish death for himself and in order to bring the benefits of his work to the world, he too will demonstrate his power by his own resurrection from the tomb.

The raising of Lazarus thus provides us with theological foreshadowing. It points us elsewhere, reminding us that Jesus's work is greater even than this. Jesus is not demonstrating that death has a limited grip over humanity. It does not. But *his own death and resurrection* affect the reality of death permanently for those who believe in him.

Our graveside experience. While the chief thrust of chapter 11 is theological, the dramatic setting of the story also invites reflection. In some Christian circles, Jesus's power over the grave is embraced with such conviction that there is no permission to mourn the tragedy of death. To grieve is to show a lack of faith; funerals are to be celebrations of eternal life and victory. To a degree this is true, but it denies a basic human need to express the sorrow and dismay that comes with loss. Jesus did not impede this family's grieving; instead by joining with them, he gives generous permission.

Moreover, Jesus is expressing a truth that is sometimes missed. Resurrection describes an aspect of life that we can experience *now.* Martha says that Lazarus will be raised in the future. But Jesus says that Lazarus is going to be raised *now.*

This means that there is a real power available in the present experience of Christ that is unknown to the Jewish framework of Martha and Mary. The power of God resident in our lives today is the same power that will enable us to live for eternity.

Two minor notes. John 11 has two minor notes with some genuine practical importance. First, Jesus must die not only for the nation (of Israel) but "to bring [the scattered children of God] together and make them one" (v. 52). As modern Christians we need to wrestle with our worldviews, inquiring who are those "scattered people" for whom Christ died. Second, it is noteworthy that Jesus treats Martha and Mary with such respect. Jesus dignifies these women as full participants among his followers. If he is their rabbi, they are his disciples (not unlike the other men who followed him).

JOHN 12:1–50

Original Meaning. John has now finished recording the events of Jesus's public ministry. John 12 is the final chapter of the Book of Signs (John 1–12), in which the evangelist records three events in the days just prior to Passover. We have in this final page of the Book of Signs a variety of themes rolling over one another: excited popularity, imminent death, promised glorification, rejection, and unbelief.

Mary Anoints Jesus in Bethany (12:1–11). The account of Jesus's anointing in Bethany is recorded in Matthew and Mark (Matt 26:6–16; Mark 14:3–9) as well as here in John. Most likely Mark and John are recording the same story. Parallels are extensive, and the major differences really only work to supplement one another.

It is difficult to be precise concerning the location of the meal. Is it Martha's home? Mary's? Do they live together? At any rate, it is an important meal attended by many who want to honor Jesus publicly and remember the great event of Lazarus's life.

It goes without saying that Mary's dramatic gesture is astonishing. While Judas objects, Jesus finds in it a pleasing expression of devotion. Nard was a rare and precious spice imported from northern India. Note that Mary's gift is called "pure" nard (v. 3), meaning it had no additives. A pound of the spice would have been huge and lavish. Its value of three hundred denarii represents one year's wage for a day laborer. Mary has purchased the very best. The average Jewish family would not be able to do such a thing.

Mary anoints Jesus generously, not simply on his feet but also his head, which no doubt runs down and perfumes his garments. The quantity is so great that the entire house is filled with its fragrance, which underscores the extravagance of the gift. John emphasizes Jesus's feet to show the sheer act of humble devotion on Mary's part and to provide a contrast with the foot washing of the next chapter. That she uses her hair to dry his feet is peculiar. Women did not let down their hair in public, and the only one who saw a woman's hair was her husband. Mary is acting with abandon, extravagant abandon, hoping that the close circle of friends will understand.

That Judas objects comes as no surprise. The legitimacy of Judas's complaint is tarnished by his own reputation. As treasurer of the group he would steal money from their holdings. But John reminds us that Judas is also the one who will betray Jesus.

Jesus's defense of Mary (vv. 7–8) is difficult to translate. The NIV gives a paraphrase that extends the Greek but likely gives the best sense. The idea is no doubt that she had kept this perfume for some later use, but now (unknowingly) has kept it for Jesus's embalming. Like Caiaphas in 11:50–51, her deed (like his words) bears a meaning far beyond what is intended. Jesus has now been prepared for burial (figuratively) as he heads toward the day of his death and glorification.

Jesus's final words in verse 8 place in tension pure personal adoration and social responsibility. This is not to deny our responsibility to the poor, but it alerts us to the wonder of who Mary and Martha are hosting that day.

Many people begin to arrive in Bethany. Not only is Jesus in Judea, but they can see Lazarus too. Lazarus has become a source of new faith in Jesus. The Sanhedrin determines that Lazarus must likewise die.

Jesus's Triumphal Entry into Jerusalem (12:12–19). John's abbreviated account focuses on the crowds, who have come to Jerusalem to celebrate the feast of Passover. It is important to keep in mind the significance of these crowds. Many scholars believe that the regular population of Jerusalem in this period was about fifty thousand and that during Passover it grew to perhaps between one hundred and one hundred twenty thousand. The social dynamic of this change was immense. The city could not contain the population, and as a result thousands of people lived on the hillsides surrounding the city. The crowds brought tension to the leadership of the city, who knew that any social disruption that began at a festival could explode violently.

The branches from date palms were abundant in Israel and had become a symbol of Jewish nationalism. When the temple was rededicated during the Maccabean era, palms were used in the celebration. Thus this act of celebration is by no means neutral. It symbolizes Israel's national hopes, now focused on Jesus, being hailed as he enters the city.

The cry of "Hosanna!" (v. 13a) is an Aramaic phrase meaning "save us now!" The following words quote from Psalm 118:26 and announce a blessing on the pilgrim arriving in Jerusalem (v. 13b). But what comes next ("blessed is the king of Israel!") is not in the psalm and departs considerably from its intent (v. 13c). Suddenly we gain the impression that the crowds are greeting a national liberator.

"Triumphal entries" were common in the ancient world. A conquering hero or king would return to his city, bringing the spoils of his battles and stories of conquest. This scene is awash in Jewish political fervor. After Jesus fed the five thousand, the crowd attempted to take him "by force" and "make him king" (6:15). Jesus was misunderstood then; now he is misunderstood again.

Jesus's use of a young donkey is an attempt to calm the zeal of the crowd, which John interprets for us with a quote from the Old Testament. The triumphant king is not a man of chariots and war horses, swords and bows (Zech 9:10), but one who will bring peace to all nations. His gift is a gift of life, not conquest. Hence, Jesus is forcing a messianic reinterpretation of his purposes for the crowd, which is caught up in a frenzied passion for Jesus's kingship.

Not only do the crowds fail to understand the true nature of Jesus's kingship, but the disciples likewise misunderstand "all this" (v. 16). It was not until Jesus was glorified—when they saw the nature of Jesus's person and work and were filled with God's Spirit—that they understood the true picture of what was happening.

At this point we are also reminded that the Pharisees have begun to despair at Jesus's popularity (v. 19). When the Pharisees say "the world" has gone after him, the deeper irony is that these words point to the fulfillment of Jesus's primary mission. It is no accident that the next episode records characters from that larger Mediterranean world—namely, some Greeks who are eager to see Jesus.

The Hour Has Come (12:20–36). The word "Greeks" (Gk. *Hellēnes*, v. 20) was a label for anyone not Jewish. They are likely "God-fearers," gentiles who admire the Jewish faith and respect its traditions. The lands surrounding Israel were filled with Greek-speaking peoples who knew and admired these grand festivals. Such gentiles were invited to the feasts but were permitted to go no further than the court of the gentiles within the temple precincts.

They approach Philip, probably because he has a Hellenistic name and comes from a Greek region (Bethsaida, 1:44). But for John it is their theological symbolism that is important. These God-fearers represent the "scattered children of God" of 11:52. They are the "other sheep" of 10:16. They want to "see" Jesus (12:21). On one level it refers to an opportunity to talk with Jesus and ask questions. However, the verbs of seeing often mean far more. They are invitations to belief; these are foreigners who now stand ready to join the flock of Christ.

Curiously, the arrival of these God-fearers triggers "the hour" we have been hearing about throughout the Gospel (v. 23). Many times we have listened to Jesus say that the hour has not yet arrived. Something has changed; the Greeks signal the closing of a chapter for Jesus. His ministry in Judaism is finished, and he now belongs to the wider world.

Jesus then offers an extended discourse that gives insight into the meaning of this hour. Just as a seed must "die" in order to give life (v. 24), likewise Jesus must die in order to give life to the world. This same law applies to disciples. To relinquish one's hold on life—to give it up—is the key to participation in the kingdom.

But we should note that the results of this sacrifice are different for Jesus and for the disciples. Jesus's sacrifice brings about life for others, but his disciples must practice this discipline so that they can procure life for themselves. Following Jesus involves self-sacrifice (v. 26a)—an echo of similar Synoptic sayings about bearing one's cross. The chief difference in the Johannine version, however, is a promise: ". . . and where I am, my servant also will be." This promise points to a unity of purpose between Jesus and his servants. It also points to a guarantee that such servants will be with Jesus in heaven.

Jesus's turmoil (*tarassō*, v. 27; NIV "troubled") recalls his agitation and anger when he stood before Lazarus's tomb and will come up again when Judas betrays him. This turmoil should not be minimized. Thus, he wonders what he should say. The words in verse 27b can be read either as a question or as a statement. If a question, it implies that this is something Jesus does not really pray ("What shall I say? 'Father, save me from this hour'? No!"). But if it is a genuine prayer (which is likely), it can be read as a statement in the following manner: "What should I say? [pause] Father, save me from this hour—but no! It was for this very reason that I came to this hour."

Here we are listening to Jesus's genuine anguish and the strength of his obedience as he conforms his life to his Father's will. In this sense, the prayer is similar to Jesus's words in Gethsemane, which are followed with a word of obedience. The prayer that concludes Jesus's spiritual wrestling unveils his final commitment: "Father, glorify your name!" (v. 28).

Jesus's prayer is a conversation with God, who now responds audibly. God affirms that he has *already* glorified himself in his Son; here we no doubt should think of the incarnation and the work of Jesus. But he says he will glorify it again; this will be the final act of glory, the cross. Some think the voice is only thunder. Others assign it to an angel. This voice, Jesus says, is for those listening, not for him. God is continuing to supply the world with evidence of himself.

The glorification of Christ brings catastrophic change to everything right now. The "now" of verse 31 must be underscored and taken seriously. The cross of Christ inaugurates judgment. It unmasks those aligned with Satan and opposed to

God, who will crucify the Son. The cross also identifies those who are children of the light, who believe and are saved. As he is lifted up from the earth in crucifixion, he is visible to all. Like light shining in darkness with all of its radiance, so now every hidden darkness will be exposed.

Jesus's view seems incomprehensible. What sort of Son of Man or Messiah is this who finds glory in death? Jesus denies them an answer (vv. 35–36a), refusing to enter into speculation about the theological role of the Messiah in popular thought. Instead, he appeals to them to believe. The crowd must make a choice and *make it quickly* before the light disappears. To reinforce this urgency and to model what he means, Jesus disappears, intentionally hiding himself from them. The public revelation of Jesus is now complete.

The Dilemma of Unbelief (12:37–41). Jesus's public work is completed; his signs have been displayed in the world; his discourses have been delivered. *And yet, the signs have been rejected.* The theological message of verses 37–41 is anchored to Isaiah's experience. God called Isaiah to speak to Israel but forewarned him that his words would find no acceptance. People would hear, but fail to understand; they would see, but fail to comprehend. Therefore, Isaiah did not fail but rather fulfilled God's purposes. Likewise, Jesus did not fail in his ministry but was continuing the prophetic experience of Isaiah; he was simply filling up or completing what Isaiah described in his own time. The Jews should therefore hear John's words and see them as an exhortation to repent of their disbelief and turn to the messenger who can save them.

In fact, it is doubtful if biblical writers like Isaiah or John were thinking about a philosophical causality as some would argue for it today. In John's Gospel, God's sovereignty and human responsibility are held together consistently. Jesus calls for people to believe, and we learn that many do indeed make this choice. Throughout his Gospel, John never compromises the demand Jesus makes for decision and faith.

However, John is describing what we might call a "judicial" hardening that settles on a people who are already guilty. When revelation comes, we must believe. But if we refuse to believe, the light disappears (12:35–36), and when God's light departs from the world, the darkness (which is the default state of the world) closes over unbelieving hearts.

It is also important to see that rejection is hopeful in the plan of God. In John's understanding, the hardness of Israel is purposeful: through Christ's rejection, salvation will be won for Israel at the cross and the glory of God revealed. Unbelieving Jews will crucify him. Moreover, through their refusal the gospel goes out to the rest of the world.

The link with Isaiah is further reinforced in verse 41. This brings us back to Isaiah's vision in Isaiah 6:1–4, where the prophet saw the Lord "high and exalted" and surrounded by "his glory." Isaiah had seen the Messiah, and the glory witnessed there glimpsed something of the glory Jesus will presently reveal in his "hour" (John 12:23).

Jesus's Final Plea for Belief (12:42–50). The struggle for belief in the world has now entered its final stage. John introduces us to leaders in Judaism, such as Nicodemus, who are keenly interested in Jesus and some of whom have decided to believe in him. But they refuse to make this faith public, so that many of their colleagues do not even know about them. John is harshly critical of them, and the stinging rebuke is given in verse 43.

The Book of Signs closes with Jesus's making a final plea for belief, probably in the precincts of the temple. For John this is no doubt a final theological summary, comprising the main motifs that have been publicly revealed in the ministry of Jesus. But we also have a warning. Jesus's word will remain as a deposit of revelation by which human lives may be judged. Moreover, discipleship is not just a matter of knowing Jesus's word; it is also a matter of "keeping" and doing what Jesus has (v. 47).

The seriousness of Jesus's revelation is reinforced in the end when he returns to his first subject: the Father (v. 50). Without doubt, the presence of the Father in the life and work of Jesus is the theme John does not want us to miss. The greatest error of all is for someone to see this light and reject it, thinking it has no connection with God. When the world makes a decision about Jesus, it is really making a decision about God.

Application. *Mary's extravagant gift of nard.* The extravagance of the gift is a problem. It is breathtaking. Surely she could have poured half the bottle and sold the rest. Maybe she could have instead sold the entire bottle and used the money to honor the work of Jesus in some way (an endowed scholarship or trust somewhere?). Judas's complaint would likely be echoed by many church elders today.

For some Christians this has resulted in a spirituality that has promoted personal austerity and commitment to the poor as the highest virtues. Is it possible to cherish and honor Jesus today in the world in ways that seem extravagant? When an impoverished African community pools its resources in order to build a church on a scale that is "extravagant" by local standards, is this "nard" that has been wasted? Western visitors will look at the poverty surrounding the church and see such expense as misdirected. But the poor may see it otherwise.

Of course, there can be abuses, and that is where the debate begins. When extravagance is pursued at the expense of the ministry to the poor, there is a problem. And there may be an extravagance that discerning Christians may consider completely out of bounds. Nevertheless, Mary's gift may be something we may worthily imitate today—with caution and with discernment, of course, but nevertheless it is there.

Celebrating Jesus in Jerusalem. The crowd in Jerusalem assumed that Jesus and his movement would serve their cause. Their vision for society and Jesus's presence could together make changes they dearly desired. Jesus's failure to satisfy those visions (religious, political, and social) leads to a cry for crucifixion one week later.

In what manner do we likewise use Jesus to fuel our own visions for social and political change? Evangelicals have agendas for social change, which they wed to their religious convictions. To be "biblical" is to affirm a platform of political commitments, and to question them is to place in jeopardy one's theological orthodoxy. Jesus wants our praise and celebration. But too often we only see him through the issues of the day, issues about which we are confident he stands with us.

The arrival of the Greeks. In order to understand what is at stake here, we must have some comprehension of Israel's passionate commitment to racial purity. The world was divided into harsh categories: clean and unclean. And keeping oneself "clean" was a religious pursuit of the highest order.

The entry of Samaritans, God-fearers, or gentiles, therefore, into the early church was not just a matter of racial diversity and tolerance. To argue that Cornelius is indeed a child of God was one of Peter's most dramatic moments (see Acts 10:1–11:18). Today we may live in an era that talks openly about racial diversity, but not far beneath the surface racial divisions flourish. These divisions are central to the fallen human experience. Any Christian who fails to welcome a "Greek" does not understand the radical nature of Jesus's community.

Belief and unbelief. John is not saying that God has forced into unbelief men and women who otherwise would have believed. It is wrong to conclude John supports an extreme determinism in which God assigns otherwise neutral people to faith and others to unbelief. John's comment here is that people who refuse to believe will experience judgment.

The significance of this is twofold. First, it underscores the urgency of coming to faith. Those who refuse the light will find it extinguished and the darkness closing over them. Next, it assures us that when we are confronted with hardened unbelief, it does not mean that God has lost control.

The implication of this section is sobering. As Jesus hid from his audiences in Jerusalem, likewise God's judgment can fall in the present on an era and a people who have utterly rejected him.

JOHN 13:1–38

Original Meaning. The Book of Glory (John 13–21) shifts our attention. The focus of the first half of John is on *the signs* of Jesus, evidences of his identity borne by miraculous works. The focus of the second half of John is on *the hour.* Jesus now must say farewell to his followers and begin his return to the Father through his arrest, crucifixion, resurrection, and ascension. In 13:1 Jesus recognizes that "his hour" has come to depart out of the world, and he focuses his attention on "his own," whom he has loved.

The problem of the meal in John 13. Many readers readily assume that this is Jesus's Passover meal described in the Synoptic Gospels. However, there is a puzzle here that every interpreter must study. Many commentators believe that John is at odds with the Synoptic chronology. But as I hope to suggest, this is not an impossible problem.

The main problem in John's Gospel is that the author says Jesus was crucified on the "day of Preparation"—presumably when the Passover lambs were being killed (John 19:14, 31). Therefore, if Friday was Nisan 14 (the day of Preparation), then the meal of Jesus Thursday evening was also Nisan 14 and could *not* have been his Passover meal.

It is clear that John understands this meal to be the same meal as the Synoptic meal. The reference to Judas Iscariot solidly links the two. But what do we do with the passages that imply Jesus was crucified on the "day of Preparation?" The argument that, according to John, Jesus was crucified on Nisan 14 (the day of Preparation) is anchored to five texts that imply that the Passover had not yet happened when Jesus is crucified. We will look at these verses later in the commentary, but for now we note that they do not necessarily imply that the meal in John 13 was before Passover.

If this line of reasoning is correct, John's chronology fits the Synoptic outline perfectly. Thursday evening began Nisan 15, when Jesus hosted a Passover meal; on Friday afternoon Jesus was crucified "on the day of [Sabbath] Preparation of Passover Week." I recognize that this explanation is perhaps a bit complex. But it is important. In critical discussions of the historical reliability of John's Gospel, the problem of chronology and the Johannine passion narrative always come up for examination.

Jesus Washes His Disciples' Feet (13:1–17). It may seem odd that although John records Jesus's final meal before his arrest, he does not record the well-known details of the Lord's Supper as we have them in the Synoptic Gospels and Paul (1 Cor 11:23–26). This is certainly not because John felt the meal was irrelevant. John wants to supplement (or interpret) the well-known tradition with new things that will give a more complete theology of the sacrament not seen elsewhere.

In the Synoptic setting, two important motifs appear. First, Jesus uses the imagery of the meal to point to his death (body broken, blood poured out). Next, Luke tells us that there was a dispute about greatness that night, and Jesus responds by telling the disciples about true servanthood. In John 13, these two themes appear in sequence.

If we are correct that John views the meal as a Passover meal, 13:1 likely hints that the footwashing was an event that took place just prior to the celebration of the dinner. As the meal is being served, Jesus interrupts the ceremonies in order to demonstrate the depth of his love for his followers.

Jesus's decision to wash his disciples' feet is anchored in his assurance of his relationship with God. He knows both his origins and his destiny and thus understands the authority he has been given. This gives him the courage to do something his followers never expected. The task of footwashing was so menial that Jewish slaves were exempt, and the job kept for gentiles. When done by a wife (for her husband), a child (for his/her parents), or a pupil (for his teacher), it was always an act of extreme devotion. In no way do we find those with a higher status washing the feet of those beneath them. When Jesus takes off "his outer clothing" and wraps a towel around himself (v. 4), he is adopting the posture of a slave.

Peter reflects how shocking the deed must have seemed. The depth of his devotion to Jesus defines the strength of his objection. But Jesus is not simply giving them a lesson in humble service; he is doing something that symbolizes his greater act of sacrifice on the cross. Only after "the hour" when Jesus is resurrected will any of this make sense. But Peter continues to object in the most strenuous way, and Jesus's rebuke is carefully worded. "If *I* do not wash you . . ." means that the question is not simply one of washing, but a question of *who* does the washing. Peter must participate in the work of Jesus (vv. 8–9). He lacks a cleansing that only Jesus can supply.

If Peter is not washed, he cannot have any "part" (Gk. *meros*) in Jesus (v. 8). Jesus is talking about eternal life and union with him. If so, then the footwashing is symbolic of something more than a gesture of fellowship. It is only the death of Jesus (and its acceptance by the believer) that brings eternal life.

Peter's zeal to gain this inheritance is one more example of Johannine misunderstanding. Peter concludes that if footwashing gains an inheritance with Jesus, what would a thoroughgoing washing gain? Jesus's initial reference to bathing points to his own work. This is the bathing that makes one clean all over. The plain sense of Jesus's words seems clear and almost proverbial: if you have been cleansed already, you don't need to wash further. The cleansing work of Jesus—footwashing, symbolizing spiritual cleansing on the cross—is complete in itself and therefore Peter does not need to pursue more.

The curious return to the subject of Judas in verses 10b–11 indicates that Jesus's work of footwashing has not changed Judas's heart. The fact alone that Jesus washed Judas's feet is stunning and is a testimony to Jesus's patience and love for his followers (even the man who betrays him). Judas is now a man in the grip of the darkness.

As with so many of Jesus's powerful acts, here too he provides a discourse explaining what he has just done. But while the subject of the footwashing in verses 2–11 pertained to Jesus's salvific work on their behalf, his teaching now points to how they might imitate his deeds. These themes are different, though related. Jesus's sacrifice will be the supreme token of his overwhelming love for the world. In his farewell discourse, Jesus now wants his followers to exemplify that same love to one another.

Jesus's proverb in verse 16 echoes well-known words from the Synoptic Gospels. His prefacing words, "Very truly" conceal the literal phrase "truly, truly" (Gk. *amēn, amēn*). Jesus is reinforcing the importance of this often-repeated truth. Servants should not consider themselves to be greater than their masters; if this is so, what is applicable to the master (sacrifice) is likewise applicable to the servant.

Jesus Predicts His Betrayal (13:18–30). For the third time, the subject of Judas's betrayal enters the story. Jesus's interpretation returns again to thoughts of him (vv. 18–19). This builds the impression that the betrayal of this man weighs heavily on him. Jesus makes clear that his choice of Judas was no mistake. The blessing pronounced in verse 17 is not directed to Judas, whose intentions Jesus knows perfectly. "I know those I have chosen" in verse 18 should not be read to say that Jesus chose the eleven and Judas has been rejected from the beginning.

Jesus knows each of these men now with him in the room. There have been no surprises after so many years together in ministry. Jesus wants *each* of them. Jesus's citation of Psalm 41:9 underscores the personal affront that this betrayal meant. To "eat bread" is a cultural symbol that refers to personal intimacy, and to expose the bottom of the foot is another symbol of personal contempt. Jesus possesses divine wisdom into these events and yet experiences bewildering dismay as they unfold.

Jesus returns to his subject of the servant and the master in verse 20. As servants are obligated to reflect the work of their masters in every respect, so too such servants enjoy the respect and the authority that comes from working in their master's name. Both verse 16 and verse 20 are proverbs (preceded by "very truly"; literal translation: "truly, truly"), and both echo well-known sayings in the Synoptic Gospels.

This is the third and final time we read that Jesus is "troubled" (v. 21, *tarassō*; cf. its use at Lazarus's tomb, 11:33, and at the prospect of the cross, 12:27). His words predicting his betrayal in 13:21 were firmly fixed in the Gospel tradition. In all four Gospels the Twelve immediately begin questioning the identity of the betrayer. But since the Fourth Gospel is preserving the eyewitness testimony of the Beloved Disciple, it is not surprising that John records a story unlike any other.

Since the disciples are eating a Passover meal, it is necessary for them to recline. The Beloved Disciple enjoys a place of honor, seated on Jesus's right. This explains why he can easily lean back and place his head near Jesus's chest and speak to him privately, asking Jesus to divulge the name of the betrayer. Peter is not as near and so must call to the Beloved Disciple. Judas likewise has a place of honor near Jesus because Jesus is able to dip some bread into a common dish and serve the morsel to him.

Meals were eaten with flat, baked bread, and a broken portion of this bread was then dipped into common bowls on the table. Jesus says that the betrayer is the one to whom he provides some dipped bread, and then he promptly serves Judas. The disciples could have taken it as a simple honoring gesture for Judas. If so, it is particularly ironic since this gesture of respect is the last thing Jesus can do for Judas, and it compares with Judas's last gesture of betrayal in the garden.

At this point, Satan controls Judas's fate, and Jesus dispatches him to pursue the course he has set for himself. Even though the disciples seem unaware of what is happening, the story implies that John understood everything. He had been given the key to the morsel, and he sees the consequences of the gift.

The departure of Judas is at "night" (v. 30). Night represents the antithesis of Jesus, who is the light. It is the darkness of unbelief and opposition, where people stumble and find themselves in a fruitless search for life. It is the setting of Nicodemus, a man who must choose to leave the darkness and be reborn to join Jesus (3:2; 19:39). Therefore, Judas represents a person described in 3:19.

Jesus Begins His "Farewell" (13:31–38). The departure of Judas into the night marks a solemn divide in the plot of this Gospel. Jesus is now left with "his own," to give them his final instructions. The arrival of the Greeks in 12:20 signaled that the "hour" was near at hand. Now in 13:31 it has arrived.

Numerous academic studies have compared Jesus's farewell discourse with those of dying teachers and leaders in antiquity. Jacob's last words in Genesis 49 are typical of this form, as is Moses's farewell in Deuteronomy 31–34. Jewish testaments imagine the dying (or departing) person surrounded by his most intimate friends and family. Standard literary elements generally appear. For instance, they always show a concern for the comfort and encouragement of those left behind. Often there is an exhortation to obey the law, and a deposit of writings is left behind. In some cases, the departing person passes his "spirit" to his followers or successor. Moses and Elijah do this respectively for Joshua and Elisha.

In the farewell of Jesus many of these elements appear. He encourages his disciples and comforts them. He also urges them to be obedient, and from John's perspective the "literary deposit" Jesus leaves behind is the Fourth Gospel itself. Moreover, Jesus promises that his Spirit will indwell and empower his followers following his death. In other words, we have in John 13–17 all of the elements of a Jewish farewell.

With the departure of Judas Iscariot, Jesus speaks directly of his glorification. Throughout Jesus's life of perfect obedience, God has been honored. God's power has also been made visible through the many signs of Jesus's ministry. Now the hour of glorification has dawned; even in washing his disciples' feet, Jesus has revealed something more of God's glory. Jesus's glory thus occurs when God's glory radiates through him.

The supreme place where this divine radiance will be visible will be on the cross. This future glorification, then, is not some distant event at the end of time or in heaven. It is the series of events that will unfold at the end of this momentous week: Jesus's death, resurrection, and ascension.

John 13:33 is a crucial thought for the farewell discourse. It is balanced by the words of assurance that are threaded through the balance of the discourse for his intimate friends. He is departing so that he can prepare for their arrival. His desire is not to abandon them or to orphan them, but to enjoy their fellowship in perpetuity. Jesus possesses life that goes beyond the grave, and those who believe in him will possess the same life with him. Therefore, Peter will shortly be assured that soon after Jesus's departure he "will follow" his master to where he is (v. 36).

That the disciples are to love one another is nothing new. That they are to love each other with the sort of love modeled by Jesus is something dramatic. Disciples are to reflect the sort of love known to Jesus—a love expressed through committed obedience. "As I have loved you" (v. 34) points to Jesus's most immediate act of love (the footwashing) and means that to truly love another, they must pursue a life of servanthood and sacrifice.

But the word "new" (*kainos*) may mean something more (v. 34). This "new command" may be a signal that Jesus is talking about life in a new era, a messianic era. In that era, love must characterize his followers—a love patterned on the generous, loving act of God that saves his people.

Peter is eager to be with Jesus even if it costs him his life, and his words echo the language of the good shepherd. Jesus goes on to prophesy that Peter's nerve will fail at the last moment. His good intentions to lay down his life, uttered so bravely, will not hold when confronted with genuine danger. Peter's eventual death ("but you will follow later," v. 36) will come up again in 21:18–19. Peter will have an opportunity to show his faithfulness in death and so "glorify God" (21:19); this is reinforced when Jesus returns from the grave.

Application. *Jesus and footwashing.* Jesus's act was powerful not because of the footwashing itself but because of the role he was assuming by doing it. To serve *as Jesus served* requires humility. It requires sacrifice. It means taking up the lesser role for the benefit of someone else. Jesus's love and service for us transforms and empowers us. Without such knowledge, we *cannot* wash another person's feet as Jesus would have us.

Judas Iscariot's betrayal. Judas is a more disturbing figure than Pilate or Caiaphas or any of the Jewish leaders. He saw the light and understood it, but he chose the darkness anyway. We too, then, are in danger—in danger of misunderstanding Jesus and of being seduced by our own dreams and visions for life. In doing this work, we betray Jesus. The "betrayer" is someone who "hands over" Christ to his enemies and who (unwittingly or not) serves the forces of darkness rather than the light.

The love command. The command to love was one of John's foremost concerns. The problem with this verse is that it may be impossible to order someone to love. Unless one has a profound experience of being loved, it is virtually impossible to express profound love for another.

Nothing so astonishes a fractured world as a community in which radical, faithful, genuine love is shared among its members. There are many places you can go to find communities of shared interest. There are many places you can go to find people just like yourself, who live for sports or music or gardening or politics. But it is the mandate of the church to become a community of love, a circle of Christ's followers who invest in one another because Christ has invested in them, who exhibit love not based on the mutuality and attractiveness of its members but on the model of Christ, who washed the feet of everyone (including Judas).

JOHN 14:1–31

Original Meaning

Jesus's Departure from this World (14:1–11). On three previous occasions we learned of Jesus's deeply troubled feelings (11:33; 12:27; 13:21; Gk. *tarassō*). Here in 14:1 the disciples must face the same feelings. Jesus is charging his disciples to hold fast in light of the upcoming crisis.

In his departure he will be working on their behalf, preparing a place for them. God's "house" (*oikia*) is a place with many "rooms" (*monai*; v. 2). This latter word is related to the common Johannine verb *menō*, to "remain" or "abide." He is promising that death will not interrupt intimacy enjoyed with him.

To have a place in heaven reserved for us is one thing; confidence in getting there is quite another. But Jesus promises that he "will come back" (v. 3). When will this "coming" occur? The best view takes verses 2–3 as a plain promise of the second coming. As the chapter develops, Jesus points to other returns he will make, but these are separate from what he affirms here.

While Jesus affirms that they know where he is going, Thomas speaks up and presses for more clarification. Jesus's answer in verse 6 is the premier expression of the theology of this entire Gospel. Access to the Father's presence in heaven will only be through Jesus and no other. He is the only one who can lead his followers back to the places he will prepare.

This is the case because Jesus is the "truth," the authoritative representative and revealer of God. He discloses God exhaustively unlike anyone else can because he has seen God. Those who follow Jesus, who come to the Father through his "way," will be the ones who gain eternal "life."

Jesus has disclosed more than anyone expected. Instead of simply defining his destination, Jesus takes the next inevitable step: only the Father can lead us to himself—*and the Father is genuinely present in Jesus.* This is an echo of the prologue (1:1–2), which explained the ultimate union (and differentiation) of the Son and the Father. If his followers know Jesus, they will know the Father as well. This is not a rebuke but a promise. Since they have known him, there is more to come, and they will discover the Father who is present in him. Moreover, they have seen the Father *already.*

Philip does not understand that *no one* has seen God (1:18a). It is beyond human capacity. But in Christ Philip has before him the full embodiment of God as it *can* be seen by humanity. This is one of the high points of John's Christology. Jesus is not simply a religious teacher or guide, nor is he simply the means to some other destination. He is also the end, the goal. He is the one in whom God can be found.

Such a claim requires justification, and Jesus supplies it. At its most basic level, Jesus is God's envoy. Jesus (as God's agent) is authorized both to work for and to speak for his sender. But "agency" barely touches the surface of Jesus's thought. Jesus and the Father enjoy a reciprocity of life: the Father is in him and he is in the Father. This is not merely a functional unity, as if Jesus's life could be summed up by his obedience. This is an exhaustive, substantial unity—an ontological unity—that at last explains statements hinted in the public ministry: "I and the Father are one" (10:30; cf. 10:38).

The First Promise of the Spirit (14:12–17). Once Jesus departs, two promises will be realized in the community of faith: great works will accompany those who believe, and prayer will be answered. Note that the promise of verse 12 does not simply point to miracles. What Jesus has been doing includes deeds of humility, service, and love as well as miraculous signs. Jesus's followers will do works that are "greater" even than these.

What is "greater" is that these works will be done by regular people in whom the power of Christ has taken up residence following his glorification. This is why the departure of Jesus is crucial, for only through that can the Holy Spirit become a reality to all who follow him. The coming of the Spirit after Christ's glorification will inaugurate an eschatological reality not known in the world.

One hallmark of the intimacy shared between Jesus and his disciples will be their ability to hear one another's voice. This theme that Jesus will do what his disciples ask (in prayer) is frequent both in the farewell discourse and in the Johannine letters. Such prayer is given in Jesus's "name" and directed to Jesus (v. 13).

However, John can just as easily refer to this prayer as directed to the Father; no doubt we should not make too much of this difference since every prayer must come in "Jesus's name." This promise of answered prayer is really a continuation of what is given in verse 13. Such answered prayer is another "great work" that Jesus will accomplish among them.

Next, as Jesus anticipates his departure he describes the Spirit that is coming. The Spirit's gift in these verses is controlled by verse 15a, "if you love me." The gift, then, is an outgrowth of the loving relationship between Jesus and his disciples, not an entitlement earned by the disciple.

Jesus uses an unusual term in verse 16 for the Spirit. The NIV's "advocate" translates the Greek *paraklētos*. It occurs in secular Greek literature for an advocate in a court of law, who comes alongside a person to speak in his or her defense and provide counsel. It is interesting that Jesus calls the Spirit *another* Paraclete. Jesus is a Paraclete, who is now sending a second Paraclete. This means that the ongoing work of the Spirit will be a continuation of the work of Jesus during the disciples' lifetime.

Jesus has been on trial, and like an advocate he has produced evidence and witnesses for the truth about God. The Paraclete, then, will pick up where Jesus leaves off. It is no surprise that he is also called "the Spirit of truth" (v. 17). He communicates the truth about God, which is the essence of God's work in Christ. Moreover, we know that Jesus is "the truth" (v. 6), and inasmuch as the Spirit duplicates and sustains Jesus's work, he will continue to defend the truth of Jesus.

In John's Gospel, the "world" (*kosmos*) refers to the human environment that is in rebellion against God and in need of salvation (v. 17). Jesus recognizes that such people cannot perceive or penetrate the deeper things of God, such as the mystery of the Holy Spirit. The disciples, however, can know the Spirit of truth because he (i.e., Jesus) has been with them all along—and will be in them in the future (i.e., in the Spirit).

Jesus's Return to His Disciples (14:18–24). Jesus has already reassured his followers that he will return to rescue his disciples from this world. In the meantime, they will be empowered by the Spirit to sustain his mighty work in the world. Moreover, the Spirit will not be merely an ambiguous force coming upon them, but in a genuine way he will sustain what they have loved about Jesus thus far. The Spirit-Paraclete will be "another" Paraclete (v. 16), another presence who will re-create the person of Jesus within them.

"I will come to you" (v. 18b) means that Jesus will not leave them desolate. But does this refer to the coming of the Spirit (vv. 16–17)? Subtle clues suggest that this is Jesus's coming after his resurrection on Easter. The time frame is specific ("before long," v. 19), and the disciples are to look for "that day" (v. 20). While from the world's perspective Jesus will disappear from view (in his death), in his resurrection he will return to them and validate that the power of the Father has been with him all along.

But the coming of Jesus on Easter will mean more than a mere return of Jesus to life. His aim is to establish the sort of intimacy and unity he has promised throughout the discourse. The oneness he enjoys with the Father parallels the oneness the disciples will enjoy with him. *Thus the Easter return will be the bridge that will inaugurate the spiritual union Jesus wants with them.* The call to obedience (v. 21) is a clue that Jesus is speaking of a union that will include the coming of the Spirit. Out of love for his disciples, Jesus will "show" himself to them (v. 21), which will result in a profound spiritual union beyond the world's comprehension.

Again (for the third time) Jesus talks about obedience as a key to what is planned: those who love Jesus show it by their fidelity to his word. But those who fail to invest faith in Jesus—who do not love him and refuse to obey him—are not connected either to Jesus or the Father and so cannot share in this divine union.

The delicate play on words in chapter 14 should not be missed. In 14:2 we learned that Jesus will depart in order to make heavenly "rooms" (*monai*) for his followers. But when he returns at Easter, he and the Father will reside within them, making a "home" (*monē*) within them (v. 23). That is, the places of dwelling promised in 14:2 will be realized as places of "indwelling."

The Second Promise of the Spirit (14:25–31). The rudimentary Trinitarian implications of verses 25–26 are inescapable: the Father will send the Spirit in the name of Jesus. Therefore, this spiritual revelation promised by Jesus is in fact the effort of God himself (in every dimension) working for our benefit.

Jesus then emphasizes the conserving and teaching roles of the Spirit. During the earthly ministry of Jesus, understanding was difficult. But now, Jesus promises, the Spirit-Paraclete will recall the things Jesus has done and said and fix them in the minds of his followers.

It was the resurrection—and its gift of the Spirit—that

provided the meaning of Jesus's works. The inspiration of the Spirit, therefore, does not bring forward new revelations about Jesus but simply gives correct meanings and applications for what he did in history. Just as Jesus's primary work was revealing the Father, so now the work of the Spirit-Paraclete is revealing the "Jesus of history" to his followers.

The discourse of chapter 14 closes with words of reassurance similar to those offered at the beginning. "Peace" in verse 27 refers to the Hebrew greeting *shalom* and for Jesus refers to the aim of his work on earth: to restore the equilibrium and richness of humanity's relationship with God. Nothing in the world can offer such a gift.

Jesus mentions again that his disciples are troubled (v. 27). Jesus points to himself. Their love for him should lead to celebration because he is returning to where he began, to the Father. To receive the Father's gifts is blessed; to return to live with the giver is beyond comprehension.

Few verses have caused more controversy than verse 28b. This verse has been used to deny the divinity of Christ. Taken in isolation, this may appear to be the meaning of the verse, but if so this verse jars the overwhelmingly divine portrait we have of Jesus in this Gospel. Making Jesus a lesser divinity or a lesser God would offend the solid Jewish monotheism of the Gospel. Making Jesus merely a human being loses the plain sense of his origin and unity with the Father in places such as the prologue, where incarnational Christology seems clear.

Classic exegesis has taken one of two paths out of this interpretive forest. Some interpreters have sought to make this "lesser" status refer to Jesus's humanity limited in the incarnation. Others have pointed to eternal distinctions between the Father and Son that do not compromise the Son's divinity. But these views owe more to later theological Trinitarian debates than the Gospel itself. Arguments about ontology are likely far from John's mind. The Father's greatness springs from his role as the origin and sender of Jesus, just as a ray of light might refer to the sun from which it came.

The word picture Jesus often uses to describe his life is the agent sent on a mission. Within this agent/sender relationship, the originator of the mission has greater authority. As courier of God's message, Jesus is acknowledging the relationship, the source, of what has brought that message to life.

Not only should the disciples take comfort and rejoice because Jesus is returning to his origin, but they should realize that the events unfolding in Jerusalem for him are not controlled by Satan. In fact, his specific description of these matters should prove to encourage their faith because when they occur, the disciples will recall his words and see his predictions fulfilled. Moreover, Jesus's obedience to God's plan should be seen as an example of his love for the Father. Following the discourse Jesus says, "Come now; let us leave" (v. 31b).

Application. *The departure of Jesus.* Possessing an anticipation for heaven builds in us an eternal vantage point. We live in a world that continually offers us temporal securities and comforts, a world that keeps our eyes on the near horizon of the present, that denies the limitations of our own mortality. Jesus offers a positive incentive. Our true home, our complete security, has already been built for us by him in heaven. Once we embrace the significance of this notion, our attitudes toward this world completely change.

Jesus and the Father. In a world of religious pluralism, anyone making an exclusive truth claim will find opponents who will object not necessarily to the religious system offered, but to the *exclusivity* of any such claim. But this is precisely the truth claim we have in Christ. The theological idea that anchors this belief is that God *himself* was in Christ. It is centered on our claim that God was fully present in Christ to reconcile the world to himself. Jesus's way is true because *in him* we find God drawing us to himself.

Jesus is coming. Threaded throughout the discourse, Jesus says, in effect, "I will come again," in three different contexts.

1. *The second coming.* My experience among young people in their twenties is that they hold a sense of historical despair: war, overpopulation, environmental crises, infectious disease, and moral decline are some of the items they will check off quickly. Oddly, when asked to describe their hope in this apparent mess, the "blessed hope" of the second coming rarely comes to view. Jesus's promise is that he will come, that he will return to save his church and rescue his followers. This teaching needs to be revitalized in the church today.
2. *The empty tomb.* Jesus's resurrection is not merely a display of his divine power over death, but it is motivated by his interest in coming to his followers and aiding them. While the resurrection is a step in Jesus's glorification and return to the Father, it also provides an opportunity for him to meet with his disciples, encourage them, and equip them. Disciples today need to have a confident grasp of the meaning of this return. In virtually every sermon in the book of Acts, Jesus's return from the grave lies at the center.
3. *The Holy Spirit.* John 14 urges us to see the Spirit as intimately tied to Jesus. The unity of Jesus and the Spirit means that we should not talk about receiving Jesus without incorporating some notion of receiving the Spirit. To have this Spirit is to have the catalogue of gifts listed in this chapter. Powerful works (v. 12), effective prayer (v. 13), and the peace of God (v. 27) all deserve careful application today. But this does not mean that the work of the modern minister will exceed the work of Jesus. This is not Jesus's point. It is the distribution of his powers to the wider world that facilitates a remarkable outpouring of mighty works.

JOHN 15:1–16:4A

Original Meaning

The Vine and the Branches (15:1–17). What prompts Jesus to use this image? If Jesus left the upper room in 14:30, he may have stopped at the temple to teach and to pray. At the entrance of the holy place (west of the altar), steps led to a linen curtain. Above the curtain (beneath the roof line) grew a gigantic grapevine of pure gold, representing Israel. Wealthy citizens could bring gifts to add to the vine (gold tendrils, grapes, or leaves), and these would be added by metal workers to the ever-growing vine. Josephus claims that some of the grape clusters were the "height of a man."

The vine and the vineyard were old and sacred images in Judaism (as in most Mediterranean societies). The vine represented the covenant people of God. In his final "I am" saying in this Gospel, Jesus declares that *he* is the true vine (15:1). That is, in this ancient imagery he has taken the place of Israel as God's true planting. The new concept is that God's vineyard holds *one vine*, and Israel must inquire if it is attached to him. No longer is Israel automatically seen as a vine growing in God's vineyard. Men and women are now branches growing from one stock.

The picture of attachment to Jesus as a branch is attached to a vine is an apt description of the interior spiritual life Jesus has described since chapter 14. Here, however, the key word is "remaining" or "abiding" (*menō*), which is used throughout the discourse. Discipleship is not just a matter of acknowledging who Jesus is; it is having Jesus spiritually connected to our inner lives.

That connection also means being "pruned." The Greek word for trimming or pruning in verse 2 (*kathairō*) is closely related to the adjective in 15:3, "You are already clean [*katharos*]." Those who remain in the vine are being readied for more fruit-bearing by the word Jesus is giving them.

To fail to "remain" in Christ, to fail to find life in the vine (i.e., Jesus), risks separation from the vineyard and consequent destruction. There is only one evidence if a branch is truly alive: Does it produce clusters of grapes? Note carefully, however, what the metaphor is not saying. Fruit-bearing is not a test; that is, a branch does not have to demonstrate a level of productivity to be safe from destruction. Rather, fruit-bearing is a byproduct. Fruitfulness will be the inevitable outcome of an interior spiritual life with Jesus.

Jesus concludes the metaphor in verses 7–11 by drawing out some of the implications that come from "remaining" in him. Verse 7 compares remaining in Jesus and remaining in his word. No doubt this recalls the commands to obedience, in which keeping Jesus's word is how we demonstrate love for him. Those whose lives are so in harmony with Jesus will find their prayers controlled by his word, and such prayers will be answered and bring added glory to God. The disciple steps into a relationship of love with both Jesus and the Father, out of which a transformed life, a fruit-bearing life, will flow.

Jesus desires "that *my joy* may be in you" (v. 11, emphasis added). It is likewise a gift of the Spirit, a gift of Jesus dwelling within, that makes this joy supernatural and substantial. Jesus's joy has come through his reliance on God and his obedience to his Father's will. We inherit the capacity given through the Spirit to enjoy God in the same manner.

Having described the life-giving vine, Jesus moves on to describe life among the branches. This is the second time that Jesus has commanded his followers to love one another. Such love for one another is a fulfillment of God's love for us and in us, and to refuse to love leads John to describe such people as "liars"—people who show that they have neither seen nor experienced God's love (1 John 4:20). Such love is an outgrowth of a life that has witnessed the dramatic quality of God's love when his Son died on behalf of those he loves. Such love requires that we also love God with our entire heart, soul, and strength.

Jesus then calls his disciples "friends" to distinguish them from servants, who do not know the deeper thoughts of their masters (vv. 14–15). This title is unusual and speaks of the highest relationship possible between God and a human being. Jesus chooses us as friends, which gives us tremendous security that his affection for us will not disappear.

Where true friendship exists, true disclosure (or revelation) accompanies it. Disciples possess the word of Jesus, and they will receive ongoing revelations of Jesus. Disciples thus know God's heart. When they therefore pray, their desires and God's will harmonize, making them participants in God's efforts in the world.

Conflict with the World (15:18–25). Jesus explains the hatred of the world as a continuation of the hatred he personally witnessed throughout his public ministry. Because the disciples are now separated from the world by virtue of their faith in Jesus, they qualify for similar treatment. Christians have passed from death to life and so should not expect the world's affections.

Jesus repeats the proverb about servants and masters—not to compromise his disciples' status as friends, but to teach that they now share his status as persons no longer welcome in this fallen world. This anticipation of conflict recalls the role of the prophets in the Old Testament. As bearers of God's word, they expected harsh treatment when their announcements were unpopular.

Jesus discusses the guilt of the world by explaining that it is accountable before the revelation of God. Jesus's ministry provided both words and works that pointed to God. Now that they have seen and heard him, their guilt is immovable.

The Third Promise of the Spirit (5:26–16:4a). As we learned earlier, *paraklētos* should be taken as "advocate," since it is a judicial title describing someone aiding a legal argument. The Spirit-Paraclete will not only live in the disciples, enabling them to recall the words of Jesus; now he will become a witness, supporting their trial. The disciples are witnesses, and they will be empowered as they deliver that message to the world.

The disciples will be forced to witness about Jesus as they are confronted. But the words they utter will be "the truth" because they are speaking about the work of God in Christ through the power of the Holy Spirit (v. 26). The truth (in the power of the Spirit of truth) is not a compelling spiritual experience in the first instance; it is the capacity to point faithfully to what is known about Jesus's historic ministry from its onset.

Jesus has taught them "all this" so that they will not "fall away" (Gk. *skandalizō*, 16:1). This word refers to someone who stumbles, such as when a person trips because of darkness. The greatest thing, therefore, that the disciples have to fear is that they will renounce their faith or commit apostasy.

Throughout his ministry, Jesus was candid about the social consequences that came with discipleship. Suffering and even martyrdom may be theirs. In John's own Gospel the story of the blind man (John 9) serves as a paradigm of what is to come.

But Jesus's point is that to know in advance is to be equipped (16:4a). To step into suffering and recognize that it follows the pattern of Jesus's life and fulfills his word may strengthen men and women for whom faith comes at a severe cost. Verse 16:4a does not refer to "when their time comes" (NIV) but "when *their hour* comes." Throughout John, "the hour" refers to Jesus's death and glorification, but now it is the disciples' "hour" that will test their devotion to their faith.

Application. *Spiritual attachment.* The Christian faith is not simply about believing the right things (though this is important). Nor is it simply a matter of living a Christlike life (though this is important too). Christian experience must necessarily have a mystical, spiritual, nonquantifiable dimension. To be a disciple means having the Father, Son, and Holy Spirit living in us (14:23–26). What are the outcomes of this sort of life? The fruit Jesus expects from the branches is first and foremost love. As Jesus enjoyed the Father's love and reflected it to his followers, so now his love should fill their lives. Fruit then becomes a sign of spiritual life and vitality; fruit is not an evidence by which we demonstrate that we belong in the vineyard.

Can branches be broken off? The viticulture of the Middle East teaches us that every good farmer knows how to read the health of his vines. Living branches are trimmed; dead branches are removed insofar as they do not have the life of the vine coursing through them. The principle is simple: Jesus (the vine) is the source of life; to fail to have him is to fail to have life. To refuse to "remain in Jesus" is to refuse the gift of life he offers. He provides this analogy to talk about his essential, life-giving work, not to discuss the history of individual branches.

Spiritual attachment and the Eucharist. Early Christian readers who knew the institution of the Lord's Supper would recall how the contents of the cup are described as "the fruit of the vine" (Matt 26:29; Mark 14:25; Luke 22:18). Further, the saying of the vine is given on the very night in which Jesus provides the Lord's Supper. In this paragraph he even refers to his sacrificial death. Surely (many suggest) there must be eucharistic overtones here.

Christians who do not come from a liturgical background will at once object to this reading of John 15. Many of us are eager to see spiritual realities in the chapter, but less so to see them as linked to ritual observances or sacraments. I would urge that learning to see spiritual reality within liturgical ritual is a gift. Those who possess it hold something precious.

Our incarnational Christology insists that God's work in Christ took seriously the natural, material world in which we live. God used the form of this world, the full humanity of our lives, in order to accomplish his work. God is still using the concrete things of this world to attach himself to us.

Conflict with the world. John's Gospel has preserved some of Jesus's strongest teachings about the world and its ill will. It would not be far wrong to see that the worldview John offers is "world rejecting." Such teaching needs to be balanced against other teachings in the New Testament that express God's love for the world and the readiness of the world to be evangelized. But this teaching also needs to be placed in reserve for times when the world's hostility is acute and when suffering, including martyrdom, may come to us. The world always has the potential to turn on the church and see it as an impediment to some social, political, or ideological program.

The vineyard and the land. John 15 is the Fourth Gospel's most profound theological relocation of Israel's holy space. Jesus is here revising Israel's theological assumptions about territory and religion. He is changing the place of rootedness for the people of God. Jesus here says God's vineyard has one vine, he is that vine, and attachment to God comes through attachment to him. It is no longer a matter of possessing the vineyard; it is now a matter of knowing the one true vine. *In a word, Jesus spiritualizes the land.* He replaces the image of the vine and the promise of the land held so sacred in Judaism.

The practical implications of this are profound. Deep within the New Testament is an announcement of a radical reversal. Just as Jesus is a replacement for the religious functions of the temple, so too Jesus replaces the religious inheritance of the land. Jesus is the locus of God's habitation. He is the sole link to the vineyard, and to promote a vineyard without him, to promote a territorial salvation, is to miss entirely the thrust of his message about the land.

JOHN 16:4B–33

Original Meaning

The Fourth Promise of the Spirit (16:4b–11). Jesus's candor about the coming sufferings stems from his awareness that he will not be with his disciples to absorb the hostility that is coming their way. In past times he has been with them, but in the future, while he will be within them in the Spirit, they will have to bear the brunt of persecution. As in the earlier chapters, Jesus's departure brought dismay, so now Jesus returns to the subject of his going away.

Jesus's statement in verse 5 has perplexed many since in 13:36 and 14:5 this is precisely what Peter and Thomas ask. His interest here is that in light of his disclosures about persecution, no one is pressing him about his departure. This question thus must be linked to 16:6. Sorrow has so swamped the disciples' lives that they have forgotten that Jesus's death is not the end of everything; it is rather the beginning. The point is the goal of his glorification—namely, the Father's presence.

If he does not go away, if he is not glorified, then the Spirit cannot come. In some fashion, then, it is mutually exclusive to have both this Spirit and Jesus on earth. The Spirit is a gift that must await the trigger of Jesus's departure.

In verses 8–11 Jesus gives another description of what the Spirit will do in this difficult relationship with the world. Precisely how we are to understand the work of the Spirit in these verses has been difficult. One important issue involves the Greek verb *elenchō*, translated "prove the world to be in the wrong" (v. 8). In the New Testament, *elenchō* has to do with exposing sin and its guilt.

In John the judicial context sharpens it further: this is exposure leading to conviction and judgment. The fundamental idea is that the world has already conducted its trial of Jesus and found him guilty and deserving of death. But in fact, Jesus is innocent, and the world stands accused of error and sin. Its guilt will be exposed. It cannot deny that the verdict has been given any more than a criminal can miss the judgment passed on the final day of their trial. Since the world cannot receive the Spirit, this operation will be effected through the work of the church, which has the Spirit and which provides a bold testimony to the truth.

The three clauses given in verses 9–11 each offer important descriptions of the errors of the world and the bases of its conviction. The first error is the refusal to believe. The second error thinks that through Jesus's death his *unrighteousness* will be demonstrated for all to see. But God plans to make the cross a place of glorification in which Jesus's innocence and righteousness are proclaimed. The third error concerns judgment. Jesus has not been judged by his trial; rather, the world has been judged. Jesus identifies the source of this error to be the "prince of this world" (no doubt Satan, v. 11). As the hour of glorification approaches, Jesus realizes that it is the world's "hour" as well (cf. 12:31). This Jesus who has been rejected and who now sits enthroned has become the world's chief judge.

The Fifth Promise of the Spirit (16:12–15). While the work of the Spirit in 14:26 stressed "remembering" the historic words of Jesus uttered in his ministry, 16:12–15 suggests that the Spirit will provide supplementary revelations that the disciples have not yet heard. Jesus speaks of a future time when new things will be disclosed. The historical Jesus and his ministry stand alongside the ongoing living Jesus-in-Spirit, who is continuously experienced in the church.

The revelation of Jesus will continue in the community, and the Spirit-Paraclete will be the authoritative channel through which he is heard. Yet these revelations may not depart from what Jesus uttered in his historic ministry. Historic revelation must always be the measure by which new revelations are tested.

Verse 13b likely refers to a genuine prophetic gift that will disclose the future—a gift like that exercised in the book of Revelation and described in 1 Corinthians 12:29–30. The Spirit's "making known" (v. 14) is not of Jesus's previous historic teachings nor is it confined to the eyewitnesses of the apostolic era, whose prophetic work will close with the canon.

Jesus's Return, the Disciples' Joy (16:16–22). The departure of Jesus and its distress for the disciples has been a constant theme in the upper room. Jesus does not let them ignore the reality of his departure, and in verse 16 he brings it up again. Seven times in this chapter Jesus refers to "a little while" (*mikron*), which prompts the central question of the section: "What does he mean by saying, 'In a little while . . .'?" (v. 17). The confusion of the disciples is understandable.

This is not intentional ambiguity on Jesus's part. Rather, he is simply referring to his return in resurrection. He is departing from the world in his glorification, and the world will no longer have access to him. When he returns in resurrection, it will be his followers' final opportunity to see him as he has always been.

Prayer and Understanding (16:23–33). This joy at seeing Jesus will not only result in a renewed relationship with him, but it will have two notable effects: the joy of understanding and the joy of efficacious prayer. The confusion described in 16:16–18 will no longer be theirs. At last, they will understand. The momentous event of the resurrection will at once dispel their apprehensions.

Of course, these faithful men had on many occasions asked God for things in prayer. But the new theological order stipulates that they ask *in Jesus's name*, which is something new, something that belongs to the new spiritual era inaugurated by Jesus's work. Jesus is their shepherd, their patron who will take care of their needs. The intimacy that will result from his indwelling them and their obedience to his word assures their success.

Jesus had taught "figuratively" (v. 25), but the Greek word used here (*paroimia*) does not simply mean illustrative speech or the use of metaphor and parable; rather, it is speech that is obscure and enigmatic. For the Middle Easterner, this is the dark saying, which typically possesses prophecy or wisdom.

The "hour" (v. 25; NIV "time") is the hour of glorification, that departure of Jesus out of this world when he returns to the Father and sends to his disciples the Holy Spirit. There is a new circle of fellowship possible, which now includes not simply Jesus and the disciple but Jesus, the disciple, *and the Father*.

One might call verse 28 a summary of John's doctrine of Christ. His origins are divine, and he comes from God; he was sent on a mission to the world; he will return to the Father after completing his work. This is the essence of the Christian faith, distilled to its most essential form. It shows the paradox of the incarnational service of the Son.

The disciples immediately celebrate and feel confident that in Jesus they have gained access to unsurpassed wisdom. But this is one more example of tragic misunderstanding, such as we have seen in every other discourse. This final discourse must also end on the same note. The time of complete understanding is coming with the hour of glorification—when the Spirit is given to them as a powerful and unique endowment. They do not believe with the rigor or insight that they think. At the "hour," in fact, they will be scattered in their fear. If they had understood, if they had believed fully, they would have the strength to cross this obstacle, but they do not.

While his disciples will desert him, Jesus says that nevertheless he will not be alone because the Father will never leave him. This verse does not contradict Jesus's cry of desolation on the cross. In John, Jesus is comparing the faithfulness of God through the hour of glorification and contrasting it with the faithlessness of his disciples.

Verse 33 records Jesus's final words to his disciples before his arrest. Last words are always precious. Jesus supplies comfort and reassurance. His exhortation was for their benefit since the days to come will be difficult for each of them. The solution is "courage" (*tharseō*, 16:33b; NIV "take heart!"). Despite the circumstances, the victory of Jesus ("I have overcome the world") outweighs the jeopardy of the present crisis.

Application. *The conviction of the world.* One mission of the church is to be the *one voice* that holds an honest assessment of the world, that speaks of the way it twists the meaning of sin, righteousness, and judgment, and that describes boldly its absence of justice and compassion and its failure to promote true virtue in the fear of God. This is the courageous testimony that the Spirit seeks to engage and empower.

If the church talks about the Holy Spirit only in terms of the emotional healing it may bring or the praise and worship it may generate, the church has missed part of the Spirit's work. Charismatic gifts, healings, and signs and wonders are only part of the Spirit's mission. The Spirit is also engaged in the prosecution of the world.

The Spirit and revelation. In the first instance the work of the Spirit brings a Spirit-directed illumination as we interpret the Bible. This is God's word, which God's Spirit opens for us. But Jesus says that the Spirit will unveil things they have *not* heard. Such an understanding, of course, has led to countless abuses over the centuries, as self-appointed teachers and new-age prophets have laid claim to the Spirit's authority as they unveiled new, unbiblical teachings. These abuses have made modern exegetes understandably cautious about such ongoing revelation, and some of them claim that we are doing nothing more than pressing modern issues of church life on John's ancient text. But this is not the case.

The best evidence for the view that John's followers understood the Spirit to have ongoing revelatory power can be seen in the abuses John had to combat in his first letter (1 John). Since many false prophets have gone out into the world, John's followers need to start testing the spirits to see if they belong to God. John does not disqualify the spiritual endowment in his argument with these teachers; he calls for the testing of the gift.

Therefore, as we look at the work of the Spirit today, we see that not only does the Spirit recall, authenticate, and enliven the teaching of Jesus for each generation, but *also* the Spirit works creatively in the church, bringing a new prophetic word. This word never contradicts the historic word of Jesus and never deflects glory away from Jesus, but it may faithfully bring the church to see its message and mission in a new way. To restrict the Spirit's voice to the work of historic recitation—that is, to the application of the biblical text—is to restrict the Spirit's effort to speak to contemporary issues. The Spirit both equips those who guide the church into the deeper meaning of Scripture (teachers) and those who have a contemporary word, a dynamic word for the church in its world today (prophets).

Resurrection and resolution. Running through John 16 is Jesus's repeated assurance that "in a little while" his disciples will see him again. As I argued above, this "seeing" points to the resurrection. But what about us today? This is perhaps where an application of John 16 requires that we understand clearly that Jesus participates in four episodes of self-revelation.

1. There was Jesus's earthly ministry, which was filled with ambiguity for his followers.
2. His resurrection provided the confirmation and clarity they yearned to experience.
3. Jesus promised the Spirit, who would serve as his personal, indwelling presence during his absence.
4. We await his glorious second coming, when we once more will *see* him again.

Our experience (episode 3) is similar to that of the disciples (episode 1) inasmuch as we struggle to understand and yearn for perfect clarity. But we have one sterling advantage: we possess the Spirit, who gives us insight and understanding inaccessible even to the apostles. Jesus's resurrection was the disciples' ultimate confirming experience, and while we can only point back to it (as a confirmation of their authority), we must point *forward* to Christ's return. *That is, the second coming serves the church much the same way that the resurrection served the apostles.*

"In the world you will have trouble." It is curious that Jesus here speaks of peace and trouble in the same breath. This forces us to carefully define what this peace really is. One sort of peace means the absence of all enemies; the other is freedom from anxiety while struggling with enemies. It is essential that we keep in mind that peace and trouble do not negate one another. The peace of Jesus is a condition that takes the uncertainties and struggles of this world seriously, but like a seagull riding the surface of a turbulent sea, is able to climb swells and drop into valleys without worry.

If Jesus is more than a human, if he is indeed the Son of God who overcame the world not simply for his own sake but for our sake as well—for all of humanity, if his victory in his life can become a victory that we enjoy—a victory extended to us when we embrace him in faith, then his triumph can become our triumph. This is the great departure of the Christian faith from every other religious faith. It does not simply set out an ideal or a moral code; it offers a means of achieving it. It is the offer of God to live in his followers and achieve in them the victory demonstrated in his Son Jesus Christ. And in that indwelling, an indescribable peace will be ours despite the fury and foment of the world around us.

JOHN 17:1–26

Original Meaning

Jesus Prays for Himself (17:1–8). This section of the prayer finds Jesus talking to his Father about his efforts on earth to glorify him and to be obedient to his will. Now, with the work of the incarnation complete (which assumes Jesus's descent from heavenly glory), Jesus anticipates his ascent, his resumption of the glory he had before creation.

Addressing God as "Father" was Jesus's habit, and in this prayer it occurs six times. Such intimate language for God was a hallmark of Jesus's spirituality. Jesus says that the "hour" (Gk. *hōra*) has come (v. 1), which points to the hour of glorification we have anticipated throughout the Gospel. For Jesus the cross is not a place of shame, but a place of honor. His oneness with the Father means that as he is glorified, so too is the Father glorified. This unique connection with the Father finds further explanation inasmuch as Jesus also possesses a divine authority over all humanity so that he may distribute to them eternal life.

Eternal life comes through knowing God (v. 3). The Hebrew notion of knowing encompasses experience and intimacy, and for Christians this means obedience to and love for God. Moreover, such knowledge *must include* a commitment to Jesus Christ, God's Son.

The first accomplishment of the incarnation was Jesus's display of God's glory for the world. Now Jesus says that he has accomplished this task God has given him to do. But does Jesus say that he is *finished* at this point in his life? It is best to see this finished work as including the hour of glorification in which Jesus is now engaged. This work includes his death, resurrection, and return to the Father, as much as it includes his revelation of the Father to the world.

What then is Jesus's summary of the work he finished in his ministry? Jesus has revealed God's "name" (v. 6, NIV "you"). It is no accident that throughout the Gospel, Jesus not only refers to his work as empowered by God's name but also that people should believe in "his name." Jesus bears the name of God. Thus, in revealing himself he has disclosed the personhood (the name) of God to the entire world.

But this revelation has not been distributed without purpose. While it has been offered to the entire world, only those who have faith have truly understood what was happening in this divine revelation. They know that Jesus has come from God and his words are divine. Jesus's disciples can be described as followers who belonged to God—a remnant, whom God delivered to Jesus. Of course, this at once sets in place a theological tension that we must examine (see below). How are we to interpret this divine sovereignty and human response?

Jesus Prays for His Disciples (17:9–19). The thought of this leads Jesus to pray for them specifically. They are precious because they belong to the Father and are now Jesus's responsibility. The failure to read these verses in the wider context of John's theology has led many to misrepresent them. God loves the world and entered the world in his Son for the sake of the world, to save it. Now Jesus's work in the world is near completion, and he is praying exclusively for his immediate followers who will be left behind as he departs. Like a shepherd about to lay down his life for his sheep, he prays for his flock whom he has led and who now must persevere in the wilderness.

Note the similarity between Jesus's prayer in 17:10 and that in 17:1. The pattern of glorification is now complete: God is glorified through his Son, and the Son is glorified through his disciples. Therefore, those features of Jesus's life that brought glory to God may likewise be the characteristics of discipleship that bring glory to Jesus. When a disciple's life bears fruit, God himself is glorified directly. Jesus is describing a pattern of divine life, of indwelling and mysticism, in which God and Jesus share an interiority that leads to this sharing of glory; he also anticipates that disciples will enjoy a similar unity with God and one another.

Jesus's first petition for his followers is that they remain united. Remarkably he desires that his disciples enjoy an intimacy and oneness that are analogous to the intimacy and oneness he shares with the Father. The reason for Jesus's concern is that his service, providing leadership and unity, will end with his departure.

His disciples, however, remain in the world. This is the environment not just of unbelief and cynicism but of abject hostility. The mission of the church, the task of Jesus's followers, is to challenge this world, to draw out those who love the truth and bring them into the flock.

Jesus's next point concerns his disciples' sustenance and strength in the world. Their assignment is dangerous, and so he prays for their equipment and protection. Jesus has given them his word, and the Spirit will recall it and keep it secure. This word, this divine revelation, will become essential equipment in their testimony and survival in the world.

Jesus also prays for their protection. He recognizes the power of evil, for he lost one of his disciples to Satan, and he understands that representing God in this world is an invitation to genuine battle. His disciples must contend with these powers since they remain in this world. God's "name" will be a refuge (v. 11).

Jesus's next concern has to do with holiness. They live in the world, and yet Jesus can say that they are not "of the world" (vv. 14, 16). This points not to their location geographically but to their position spiritually.

Jesus prays that his disciples might be "sanctified" (*hagiazō*) in the truth (v. 17). This Greek word refers to something made holy, but the means to achieving this holiness is through separation. To be holy, then, is not in the first instance a description of perfection (though this is included). It refers to a life that is so aligned with God that it reflects God's passions completely.

Jesus likewise was set apart for a divine mission. Sanctification is always for mission since it is God's activity in the world, bringing it truth, light, and salvation. Thus, the disciples have a mission similar to that of Jesus. They too should see their purposes for living as not their own, but as shaped by the mission God has for them.

Perhaps verse 19 is one of the key verses in the prayer. When Jesus says that he *sanctifies* himself (*hagiazō*), to what does this refer? Jesus is recommitting himself to the mission assigned by the Father. This priestly mission of service involves his sacrifice. Through his death on the cross, the disciples will experience something never known before. His death will enable them to experience a new holiness, an identification, a deep attachment with God.

Jesus Prays for All Believers (17:20–26). Jesus is aware that those who stand with him will also depart to be with him in his glory. This will leave those whom they disciple, the church, to represent the kingdom in the world. Therefore, Jesus next turns to pray for these followers whom he has not yet met, men and women who will follow the apostles, indeed the church today, which carries the mission set down by Jesus during his final week.

He first prays that they will have a unity like that of his first disciples. This unity must be visibly based on love so that when the world sees them, it will know immediately that they represent Jesus. This love is an outgrowth of the union Christians will enjoy with Jesus himself, a union modeled on the oneness of the Father and the Son, a union born when the Father and the Son indwell the believers when they are given new birth.

Jesus was the bearer of God's glory, and now the church bears that glory. The thought is of the glory of God passing to Jesus's followers, indwelling them. The confidence of the church's mission rests here: if it lives in the Spirit (and thereby in the Father and Son), if it reflects God's glory and love, if it shows a unity in its ranks born by a shared knowledge of God, then its testimony will astonish the world. Jesus prays that someday his followers will see the true glory, the true love, that has existed in heaven since the beginning of time.

This anticipated glory, however, finds its counterpoint in the prayer's last sentences. Jesus addresses God as "righteous Father" (v. 25), reminding us that it is God's righteousness that has led to his upright judgment of the world. The problem is not the world's access to the knowledge of God but that the world refused to acknowledge that God had sent Jesus.

Yet all those who accept the Son, who embrace him and the Father, will experience the ineffable love known only between Father and Son. These are the last words Jesus prays before his arrest: "that I myself may be in them" (v. 26). His last desire is to love his followers and indwell them, to fill them with the glory and joy he has known, so that their knowledge of God will be unsurpassed and overwhelming.

Application. We should see ourselves as the subjects of this prayer. Jesus is *our* Lord and shepherd as much as he was the shepherd of this small circle of men. Therefore, when he prays he invites us to listen, to hear the quality of the love and honor shared between himself and God. He invites us to listen as he prays for believers. We are the church, the body of believers built on the apostles' word.

A sensitive, spiritual reading of chapter 17 may even convert its many third-person sentences into second-person ones in order to get the full force of Jesus's passion for us. When we do this, suddenly the prayer takes on a remarkable force.

Jesus and spirituality. The Gospels point not only to Jesus's mighty works and profound words but also to his personal relationship with God. Within the personhood of God is a social dynamic, a desire for community, a yearning for fellowship. This means that, as we are invited into life with the Father, as the Father and the Son indwell us through Holy Spirit, spirituality is not a static experience. The Christian life is a conversation, a dynamic relationship in which, as a result of our new birth, the fellowship and relationship begin.

Jesus's interests. Jesus not only is preparing a place for us but is eager for us to join him there, to see his glory, to witness the tremendous love the Father has for him (and us). In Christ God has embraced us, expressing his genuine affection for us. He has brought the glory of God into the human sphere. Jesus did not come to change God's mind; instead, he came to express God's mind. If God so loved the world, Jesus loved us also.

What is striking in the prayer is that Jesus draws us not only into a divine union of life and conversation, but he invites us into participation with the glory of God. This is the *essence* of Jesus's vision for the church. The church is a community that invites people to touch the glory of God, to be changed by it, and to bear it to the world.

Jesus and the church. How does the church bear fruit that glorifies God? We suggest four basic roles that the church serves: transcendence, fellowship, teaching, and mission.

1. *Transcendence.* People are often looking for the reality of God. Of the world's 700 million evangelical Christians, fully 350 million are charismatic. And two-thirds of all Pentecostal Christians are found in Africa, Asia, and Latin America, where Christianity is growing at a fantastic rate. Jesus prays that his followers will know just this sort of reality. Jesus prays that they will *experience* the indwelling of God brought about through the work of the Holy Spirit.
2. *Teaching.* But religious quests must be anchored in the truth. The first thing such knowledge teaches is that any experience that departs from loyalty to Jesus Christ is mistaken. The Spirit of God never contradicts what has been given to us by Jesus Christ in history.
3. *Fellowship.* Not only are people looking for transcendent spiritual experience and sound instruction, but they are also looking for community. People feel alienated, lonely, and disconnected from place and kinship. Jesus prays that the church will be a genuine community of strong unity. Without a heroic love similar to Jesus's love, unity is impossible.
4. *Mission.* The church possesses a mission, a cause, just as Jesus had a mission in the world. The unity of the church and the quality of its life and experiences lead not only to the glory of God but to a powerful testimony to the world. When Christians are one with Christ and one with one another, the growth of the church is virtually inevitable.

JOHN 18:1–19:16A

Original Meaning

Jesus's Arrest (18:1–11). Jesus leads his disciples out of the city to a garden that he frequented. We should not think of a decorative garden like those built for pleasure in Europe or North America. This is an olive grove, which grew along the west shoulder of the Mount of Olives.

The appearance of a Roman "detachment" (*speira*) is likely a detachment large enough to warrant bringing along their commander and to be equipped with weapons (v. 3). During festival seasons the Romans were aware of the explosive atmosphere in the city, and reinforcements routinely came to Jerusalem. At the beginning, then, we have a signal of Roman interest in Jesus and a hint that Pilate may already be participating. The presence of chief priests and Pharisees recalls their appearances elsewhere in the Gospel. The entire world—both Jew and gentile—has come against Jesus. Responsibility for what happens next rests with all of them.

Jesus's foreknowledge gives him the ability to see the arrest before it unfolds. He steps forward and asks the first question, "Who is it you want?" (v. 4). They answer: "Jesus of Nazareth" (v. 5). Jesus then uses the "I am" formula we have seen elsewhere in the Gospel, which no doubt recalls God's divine name (v. 6).

Jesus's words provoke a response that even those who hear it likely do not understand. This is the biblical response of holy fear before the Lord. This is a theophany in which God has been revealed before mortals and the only response is to fall prostrate.

Jesus not only steps forward (thus taking charge of his own arrest), but he protects his followers from capture and so fulfills what he said in 17:12. Of those whom God has given to him, he has lost not one. This recalls the image we have of Jesus the shepherd laying down his life for his sheep and not letting them become victims left to the wolves.

Peter's sword is a *machaira,* a short sword or a long knife (probably worn with everyday garments), and Peter's clumsy use of it shows something of the chaos of the scene. We know nothing more of the priest's slave except that both John and Luke tell us that he loses his right ear. Luke closes the scene with Jesus's healing of the man's ear.

Jesus, Peter, and Annas (18:12–27). Under full armed arrest, Jesus is brought to meet Annas. Annas is well-known even though he appears second to Caiaphas in the New Testament. Five of Annas's sons became high priests as well as his son-in-law Caiaphas. Thus Annas enjoyed great power and was the patriarch of an influential priestly family, well-known for its wealth, power, and greed.

That Jesus is sent first to Annas is plausible if he is the de facto power behind Caiaphas. This meeting may have been arranged in advance if Caiaphas is seeking to broaden his base of support vis-à-vis Rome. Verses 19–24 represent the gist of Annas's questioning.

Each of the four Gospels record Peter's denials of Jesus during his interrogation by the Jewish authorities. Peter is accompanied by "another disciple," who remains unnamed (v. 15). This is curious since John has been careful to name people in his Gospel. Is this the Beloved Disciple, who figures elsewhere in the Gospel and is commonly identified with John son of Zebedee? The view that this is the Beloved Disciple has a great deal to commend it. Throughout the gospel, the Beloved Disciple frequently appears alongside Peter. His presence at the arrest shows his profound loyalty to Jesus so characteristic throughout the Gospel.

Peter feels his vulnerability because the small courtyard also hosts officers and other servants. Some of them may even remember that he attacked Malchus. So at the gate, to gain entry, Peter refuses to acknowledge his discipleship. Since it was now night and springtime, the bystanders in Annas's courtyard, including Peter and the Beloved Disciple, stand around a charcoal fire, warming themselves against the cold.

John next shifts the scene to what is transpiring inside. The words recorded here no doubt represent the barest summary of Jesus's meeting with Annas, who probes two things: Jesus's teachings and his disciples. To what extent is he a genuine threat? Does he have a strong following? Is he promoting some sort of conspiracy? A secret conspiracy? To what extent does he threaten their interests? Jesus's sharp answer—pointing out that Annas should be talking to witnesses—unmasks the priest's attempt to make Jesus incriminate himself. Twice Jesus demands that Annas produce witnesses and evidence; in other words, Jesus is demanding a trial, which the guards interpret as insolence. Thus, one of them strikes him (v. 22).

Note that Jesus here simply points to the truth (v. 23). There are no witnesses accusing him. Nothing he has said can be construed as incriminating. Annas is at an impasse. If Jesus is going to be prosecuted, if his case is to be carried successfully to Pilate, it will be necessary to have the explicit support of the Sanhedrin, Jerusalem's high judicial council.

A major meeting of the Sanhedrin takes place under the direction of Caiaphas that evening. While Jesus is with Caiaphas, John reports Peter's ongoing failings as a witness in the courtyard. A relative of Malchus, the man whom Peter attacked, speaks up. When Peter denies Jesus the third time, a cock crows, recalling Jesus's prediction of Peter's great failure. By weaving Peter's denials among the various interrogations of Jesus, John makes a theological point. Peter's triple denial will return in John's story, for in 21:15–17 Peter meets with Jesus in Galilee and is invited three times to affirm his love for him.

Jesus before Pilate (Episode 1) (18:28–40). Even though the Sanhedrin was Israel's highest judicial court, it did not have the power of capital punishment. Therefore, if it were to prosecute Jesus with a capital offense, it had to enlist the involvement of the Roman governor. The Sanhedrin possessed only one ongoing exception in this regard: any who violated the sanctity of the temple could be killed even if that person was a Roman citizen.

Pontius Pilate was the fifth Roman governor of the province of Judea, ruling from AD 26 to 36. Jewish and Hellenistic sources tell us a great deal about Pilate, most of which is extremely critical. He was a brutal ruler whose atrocities against the Jews were legendary. As a member of Rome's lower nobility, he was always aware of his vulnerabilities and so controlled Judea harshly, with an eye on the pleasure of his masters in Rome.

Early in the morning, the Jewish leadership brought Jesus to his residence (v. 28). Two historical notes are important. First, they do not enter Pilate's quarters because they did not want to become ritually unclean. This Jewish concern makes Pilate move in and out of the building throughout the story. Second, what meal do they wish to eat in verse 28 and so remain clean? They were concerned not with the Passover meal the night before, but with the many meals and celebrations that week in the Passover season, which continued until Nisan 21.

The irony of the scene is that here the leaders, concerned about their religious purity, now plot Jesus's death and claim that *he* is an evildoer. Such a charge would be meaningless to Pilate, who viewed this no doubt as an inter-Jewish squabble. But they urge that this is a capital case and so they *require* his involvement.

Where the crime might threaten the interests of the empire or where the execution of the accused was involved, the governor was held personally responsible. Thus Pilate's first question to Jesus, "Are you the king of the Jews?" is loaded with political meaning (v. 33). Is Jesus involved in political sedition? Is he one more Jewish terrorist-revolutionary with a head full of messianic notions and a band of well-armed followers?

Jesus does not answer directly but probes the source of Pilate's question. What sort of king does Pilate mean? Is this *his* question—and if so, what does he mean by it? Pilate is already being forced to make a judgment, to evaluate Jesus. But Pilate recoils, asking incredulously if Jesus thinks he would have any interest in matters related to Jewish theological squabbles. Nevertheless, if kingship is at issue, Pilate must uncover what sort of kingship it is.

Unlike the Synoptics, however, Jesus provides a definition of his kingship. The true test of his kingdom can be seen in the behavior of his disciples. They will not engage in combat or struggle against Rome's rule. He is no threat to Rome. The one instance of violence when Peter struck Malchus was promptly rebuked by Jesus.

A good paraphrase of verse 37a might be: "So you're telling me that you are indeed some kind of king?" Having said what his kingdom is *not*, Jesus can now say what it is—a kingdom of truth. His mission began in heaven and so he possesses a divine charge: he has come to unveil the truth to the world. "Truth" is a *theological* term. Truth is what we see when we see God. Jesus is thus the truth (cf. 14:6).

Jesus's revelation that he is working for the truth serves as an invitation for Pilate to join him. For Pilate to condemn Jesus is for him to condemn the truth. Jesus has thus reversed positions with Pilate. Now Pilate has been challenged (will he side with truth or falsehood?), and now he carries the burden of response. But his cynical question, "What is truth?" reveals his true position—that he cannot recognize the things of God and will avoid the light (v. 38).

When Pilate returns to the Sanhedrin emissaries, he announces Jesus's innocence. Having given this verdict (which is repeated two more times, 19:4, 6), the deeper question for Pilate is whether he will act on the truth he *has* seen. He does not see a man here who threatens Rome; Jesus does not qualify as a terrorist. Pilate therefore appeals to a tradition of Passover amnesty. John says that it was a valued Jewish custom, thus placing the outcome of the amnesty entirely in the Sanhedrin's hands.

The deepest irony of all comes in verses 39–40 when Pilate refers to Jesus as "the king of the Jews." It is difficult to interpret his motive. By bringing up the amnesty it is clear that he wants to have Jesus released. By using this title, he is endorsing it as something that is meaningless to Rome. But John and his readers can see it as a true identification of who Jesus is. This is one more example of Johannine dramas happening at multiple levels.

But irony often shocks, and the scene closes with the crowd calling instead for the release of Barabbas (v. 40). A man who *is* a genuine threat to Rome, a man with proven capability to challenge the military occupation of Israel, a man with demonstrated tendencies toward violence, is poised to go free. Jesus, by contrast, a man in whom there is no danger and whose followers will not fight, remains in custody.

Jesus before Pilate (Episode 2) (19:1–16a). Roman law recognized three types of flogging: *fustigatio*, *flagellatio*, and *verberatio*, each representing ascending levels of severity, although it is uncertain if the Gospel's original readers would have understood these differences. The lowest form (*fustigatio*) was reserved for troublemakers who simply needed to be punished and warned. In the present scene, Pilate chooses to employ *fustigatio*, not only to teach Jesus to be more prudent in the future but to satisfy the crowds who are demanding his death.

Since the task of flogging generally belonged to soldiers, the same soldiers also begin to mock Jesus and hurt him. The mock crown may have been a woven circular crown of twigs and thorns, pressed down to inflict pain. It may have been made of the thorny date palm, whose thorns can exceed twelve inches. These are woven together with some of the thorns sticking straight up around the entire crown. This made him look like a god-king with "radiating" beams coming from his head. The robe is likely a soldier's robe thrown on him, completing the picture of mock royalty. With this costume, they jeer and strike Jesus.

When Pilate escorts Jesus outside, his clear intention is to display Jesus in cruel submission, bearing the marks of his punishment, and thereby to obtain his release. Rather than pitying Jesus, the leaders are calling for his crucifixion, and in disgust Pilate calls back to them. Pilate is trying to avoid responsibility for the death of an innocent man.

The Jewish leaders had earlier played their political card, telling Pilate that Jesus was a king. Now they have a religious accusation: if Pilate truly discharges his duties in the province, he will uphold local law (when it is irrelevant to imperial interests) and thereby keep the peace.

Pilate is unnerved. John says that he is more afraid *than before*, which gives us an insight into his previous state of mind during the morning. There is something about this inquiry he does not like. While Pilate may not possess spiritual insight, he undoubtedly is highly superstitious, and the idea that in some fashion gods could appear in the world was not uncommon.

When Pilate escorts Jesus back into his praetorium (v. 9), his first question is terse. The question follows naturally from his worries in verse 8. This is not a question about Jesus's birthplace; it lies deeper. But Jesus supplies no answer, knowing that to fit himself into Pilate's religious schema would be useless.

Jesus and Pilate talk past each other, responding to ideas on utterly different planes. Of course Pilate has the power to crucify Jesus, but Jesus's retort explains the nature of *true* power. The real power above both Caesar and Pilate is God, and so Pilate has no grounds for boasting. Pilate is *powerless* before God's plan in this hour.

The verb in verse 12a is imperfect, meaning ongoing action ("Pilate *kept trying* to free Jesus"), but it is fruitless. Suddenly something dramatic happens. The Jewish leaders know they have one more weapon, one more bit of leverage on this governor that will make him pliable, like putty in their hands. "If you let this man go, you are no friend of Caesar" (v. 12b).

From this point, things proceed swiftly (vv. 13–16). Pilate returns to the porch outside with Jesus, where he occupies the governor's judgment seat and prepares to render a decision. Pilate is now positioned to speak with the voice of his office.

The closing scene is filled with Pilate's sarcasm. "Here is your king" (v 14b) echoes "here is the man" (v. 5), and Pilate now offers to crucify this royal Jewish monarch. The audience of chief priests supplies an acid tone to the conclusion and lays the groundwork for their own blasphemy. "We have no king but Caesar" (v. 15) is a direct contradiction of the injunction of the Bible that God alone is Israel's king. By rejecting Jesus, they have rejected God himself, as Jesus predicted.

When Jesus is handed over for crucifixion (v. 16a), he is placed in the custody of the Roman garrison that ordinarily handled such matters. While Jesus had been given a remedial flogging by Pilate's men, now the soldiers inflict the *verberatio*. He is bleeding profusely, his clothes are soaked in blood, his thorn-laced crown now digs deeply and painfully into his head, and he is nearly in shock. Jesus carries the cross himself for a good while (v. 17a), but according to the Synoptics his condition becomes so severe that he cannot carry it all the way to the site. A man named Simon, a visitor from North African Cyrene (in present-day Libya), must carry it for him. Visitors watching on the Via Dolorosa ("the way of suffering") would have seen a stunning spectacle and a roadway running with blood.

Application. *The betrayal of leadership.* This is a story about collusion, about secret agreements with some fraudulent purpose, about conniving and conspiring. This is a story about the betrayal of leadership, how Judaism's high priests abandoned all pretense of devotion to God and decided instead to conspire with the military arm of Rome.

How often do the Pilates of our world pursue a course of pragmatism and expediency, protecting their own self-interest, using the rhetoric of righteousness, feigning an interest in truth—but when backed into a corner, when pressed to make a decision with social consequences, they crumble? "What is truth?" is the question you ask when truth is the last thing you want to hear. In the end, Pilate is of the "world" and so represents a system that is filled with darkness.

But the most disturbing profile in this climax to the Gospel belongs to Annas and Caiaphas, figures who almost merge in the narrative. This is a story of religious corruption, of spiritual leaders who slaughter the sheep and ruin the flock. In their secret conspiracy to eliminate one man, a man who could upset their carefully built equilibrium, they sacrifice their souls. In the end, they are in the world as much as Pilate is; yet disturbingly they do not show any of Pilate's reserve or regret. *Caiaphas is a parable as much as he is a man.* He is a Christian in Washington cutting deals with political action groups. He is a theologian revising his teachings for the modern world in order to make the church palatable for the world.

Jesus the king. John's passion story is like a symphony, which seems to pursue one theme: the sorrow of Jesus's departure, his rejection by many, the dismay of the disciples, the betrayal of Judas, the denials of Peter, Jesus's imminent death—each of these are a part of the "hour" that beats its way through virtually every chapter of the Gospel.

But then there is a counterpoint, a secondary theme that works its way to the surface and makes itself known confidently but unobtrusively, a theme that could be missed if you were not watching for it. This scene, this hour does not belong to Pilate or Caiaphas, *it belongs to Jesus*. Jesus is in control of the situation.

A simple exercise brings the counterpoint to light. Take a pencil and circle every reference to "king" (or kingdom, kingship) in the story and watch what happens. Jesus is Israel's king, despite what his enemies are doing to him; Jesus is the *true* king, despite their refusal to recognize him. John's theological message is that despite the darkness of the hour, this is in fact *the hour of glory*. The passion story of John is indeed a story of tragedy, but it is not Jesus's tragedy; it is a human tragedy as we witness the futile and tragic efforts of people blinded by darkness, unable to see the true king in their midst.

JOHN 19:16B–42

Original Meaning

Jesus Is Led to Golgotha (19:16b–24). When Jesus is led away from the praetorium, he is bleeding profusely and nearly in shock. Nevertheless it was the tradition that under Roman guard, the victim had to bear his own cross to the site of death. The crossbeam (Latin *patibulum*) was placed over the neck, like a yoke, while the person's arms were pulled back and hooked around it.

John keeps the story to a bare minimum. The route of Jesus's walk (traditionally Jerusalem's Via Dolorosa) would have taken him from the praetorium of Pilate to a location outside the city walls, where people passing by would see the spectacle and some would even speak to Jesus or jeer. Public executions were designed to shock and warn the populace, but no doubt John sees another meaning here: Jesus is being lifted up so that now Israel can see its king.

The victim was laid on the ground with his arms stretched across the beam. After he was either nailed or tied, he was hoisted up and mounted on the vertical post. Romans nailed the ankles together, forcing the feet to lay sideways on top of one another. The key is to remember that nailing was not the means of death on the cross. Many factors, such as hemorrhaging, asphyxia, and shock, played a role.

Each of the Gospels say that Jesus was crucified with "bandits" (Gk. *lēstēs*). This word is best translated "terrorist" and increases the irony of Jesus's wrongful execution. Jesus is being aligned with terrorists, while another terrorist has gone free. Each of the Gospels also refer to Jesus's position between them. This may refer to a place of prominence or it may echo Psalm 22:16.

It was customary for the Romans to provide a public, written notice of the criminal's name and activity, and this was paraded before him. John is the only writer who notes that it came by Pilate's order, and it may be that this is Pilate's revenge on the Jewish high council.

It comes as no surprise that the chief priests understand that the sign implies a kind of sarcastic endorsement by Rome of Jesus's royal identity, and they do not like it. Pilate for the first time in the story stands up to them. He refuses to publish a lie. Thus the scene ends, and Jesus's kingship stands secure.

Roman guards take Jesus's "clothes" and divide it into four parts (v. 23). These four "shares" have led to speculation as to what Jesus possessed. No doubt they include a head covering, a belt, possibly sandals, an outer cloak, and an undergarment or tunic. The soldiers gamble for the undergarment, which John sees as a fulfillment of Psalm 22:18. Josephus describes the high priests' tunic as "seamless." Josephus's description seems to refer to a long outer robe decorated with gold thread and fringes. It is difficult to know if this is what John has in mind; if so, this may be an allusion to Jesus's priestly work on the cross.

Jesus's Final Deeds and Death (19:25–37). John records a number of people at the foot of the cross. These include his mother; his aunt ("his mother's sister"); Mary, the "wife of Clopas"; Mary [from the village of] Magdala; and the Beloved Disciple (vv. 25–26). The Beloved Disciple is being called here to take Mary into his family, and he does this obediently.

Jesus's second statement on the cross is a cry of thirst, which John alone records. Jesus speaks in order to fulfill Psalm 69:21, "They . . . gave me vinegar for my thirst." In response, the soldiers provide him with a drink (Gk. *oxos*), diluted wine drunk by soldiers and peasants. We must not confuse this drink with the offer of wine mixed with drugs extended to him earlier. Jesus refused this earlier narcotic. The detail of hyssop is important here since the plant was used at the Passover to brush lamb's blood on the lintels and doorposts of Israelite homes.

What Jesus knows about the finality of his work (v. 28) he now utters aloud (v. 30a). This confirms the sense we have seen throughout the passion story that here Jesus is accomplishing what he intends. He is *not* a victim but a servant doing God's bidding. This is *not* a cry of desolation ("at last it is over!") but an announcement of triumph ("it is accomplished").

At this moment John says that Jesus bows his head and "handed over the spirit" (NIV "gave up his spirit," v. 30). John uses an unusual verb here, which does not mean "give up." The Greek *paradidōmi* means to "hand over," and nowhere in Greek literature is *paradidōmi to pneuma* used as a reference to death. The expression may well be John's characteristic double meaning at work, giving the subtle, general impression that the gift of the Spirit is active at the time of the cross. This coheres with what we learned earlier, that the Spirit is a fruit of Jesus's death. Thus he bows his head, looking directly at those ideal disciples at the foot of the cross—and we recognize them as the recipients of his gift.

Symbolism may equally be at work in verse 28 in the images of water and thirst that run through these verses. A cry of thirst is remarkable from the one in whom rivers of living water run. *The source of living water now thirsts!* Elsewhere the language of "thirst" refers to his work as one who can satisfy all thirst. As his life escapes, as the Spirit is released, as this living water is poured out, Jesus is keenly aware of this emptying, which is felt sharply in his thirst.

John reminds us that it is the "day of Preparation" (v. 31), which most naturally refers to Sabbath preparation, not preparation for the Passover. The Jews wish to remove the bodies from the crosses because of the onset of dusk and the beginning of the Sabbath. We can assume that the same group of Jews who asked for a change to the title on the cross (v. 21) now wish to remove the three men from their crosses.

The squad of soldiers breaks the legs of the two men next to Jesus, but when they come to Jesus—and here John makes the point with absolute clarity—they do not break his legs since he is already dead. If they are confident of this, however, it seems odd that one of them takes a lance to test him further. But one does, and when Jesus's side is pierced, blood and water flow from the wound (v. 34).

Exegetes and physicians have explored this phenomenon of blood and water at length, and we can only provide the barest summary of their work. Few today hold the view that Jesus's heart "bursts," despite the homiletic possibilities this offers. Two solid theories are available.

P. Barbet once argued that the spear may have penetrated Jesus's heart, so that the blood from his heart as well as fluid from the pericardial sac were released simultaneously. Today many physician-interpreters favor this view. Yet the surgeon A. F. Sava objected to this theory since Barbet took his evidence from cadavers twenty-four hours old. His own experiments with four- to six-hour cadavers did not produce the same results. However, among victims of traumatic accidents (especially with chest injuries), massive fluids build up between the body lining and the lung, in some instances providing as much as two liters of fluid.

John's primary intention is to let his readers know that Jesus is most certainly dead. Theologically this is important for a couple of reasons. John is working to affirm the full humanity of Jesus, whose life was dependent on his flesh. Moreover, already in John's time false teachers were doubting the true incarnation of Christ, and it is likely that in 1 John 5:6–9 he may even be alluding to this event.

But just as with the many other events on this day, John no doubt sees symbolism that goes beyond the surface meaning of piercing. John may be making the point that the crucified Jesus qualifies as a Passover victim. He notes, for instance, that Jesus's legs are not broken, likely because it was illegal for any Passover sacrifice to have broken bones (Exod 12:46). The lamb must be a perfect sacrifice.

But there are more theological allusions to Passover. One of the responsibilities of the temple during Passover sacrifices was to verify that the lamb was not *already* dead as it was brought forward for sacrifice. The blood must flow, the Talmud later argued, *as water (or fluid)*. The image of Jesus on the cross evokes major Passover symbolism. His was a *living* sacrifice, a genuine life that had been taken.

As we discovered in John 7, the Feast of Tabernacles in the late autumn had as part of its celebrations a water festival, in which Israel remembered the miracle of water conducted by Moses when he struck the rock at Meribah. This struck rock became a vital part of the Jewish story. It was a rock that gave water and life, becoming a model for the eternal flowing that would spring from Jerusalem. When the rabbis were asked what this eternal water really represented, their answer was simple: it referred to the Holy Spirit. John 19:34 is then a symbolic fulfillment of 7:38, which Jesus gave *at the Feast of Tabernacles*.

We saw above how Exodus 12:46 helped interpret the failure to break Jesus's legs, and so John here paraphrases the verse (19:36). But John also reflects on Zechariah 12:10, where the prophet describes how Israel will look on the prophet (or God? or the Messiah?) and lament Israel's harmful lack of faith (John 19:37). As John stands at the foot of the cross—an eyewitness to Jesus's remarkable work—he contemplates the symbolism of Israel now gazing at the very messenger, God's Son, sent to redeem the world.

Jesus's Burial (19:38–42). Joseph is one of Jesus's disciples and comes secretly because he fears the Sanhedrin leadership (v. 38). This may be explained by his disagreement with the Sanhedrin's prosecution of Jesus (Luke 23:51). John's description of him, however, may be critical, given what he says in John 12:42–43 about secret followers of Jesus among these authorities, who out of fear refused to give a public witness. Nicodemus, another member of the Sanhedrin, joins Joseph. Joseph and Nicodemus redeem their images since in this final deed they make a public gesture that holds risk. Joseph risks ceremonial uncleanness from touching a dead body, not to mention challenges to his political and religious career. To place Jesus in a tomb of prestige implies some endorsement, some honor to this man the council has deemed a criminal.

Together these men bury Jesus in a garden tomb near the site of crucifixion "in accordance with Jewish burial customs" (v. 40). In the first century, bodies were prepared for burial by wrapping them tightly with cloth and spices. The powdered spice would either be fitted among the cloth wrappings or packed beneath the body. Coins were often placed on the eyes and a napkin covered the face. Nicodemus brings a considerable number of burial spices (v. 39), reminiscent of the excessive wine in Cana that marked Jesus's first public appearance (2:1–10).

First-century Jews carved cave tombs in the limestone hills surrounding Jerusalem's walls. The type of tomb described in the Gospels for Jesus was typically characterized by the following elements:

1. *A rolling stone.* The door of the tomb was a heavy, wheel-shaped stone placed in a shallow trough and held upright by a short wall on either side of the tomb opening. Rolling stones could be opened again for ongoing use but required great strength.
2. *A burial chamber.* Upon entering the tomb, one entered a square preparation room, encircled by a stone bench running along the room's perimeter. Here the body was laid and prepared for burial.
3. *Burial niches.* The prepared body was then slipped into a small, six-foot tunnel (height about twenty-four inches) that was carved in the wall until it decomposed.
4. *Bone boxes (or ossuaries).* After decomposition, the bones would be gathered into a decorated limestone "bone box" and kept on the tomb floor. These tombs were costly and generally contained numerous niches and ossuaries.

Application. The cross of Christ is *the great sign* we have awaited throughout the entire course of this Gospel. In his death, Jesus provides the gift that every other sign promised. The bread of Galilee pointed to heavenly bread, consumed when Jesus gave his flesh for the life of the world. The water of Samaria or Tabernacles is truly the Holy Spirit, which must look toward the hour for distribution. The new temple will only discover its true meaning when Christ has died and been raised to life. Lazarus's story is not that one man in a village is now alive, but that *the man* is present who reigns over death and life. The cross is therefore the great sign, the reality from which every other sign becomes like a shadow.

Jesus the king. We discovered in 18:1–19:16a that Jesus is Israel's king *incognito*. John constructs his story to make the regal glory of Jesus the central motif of his passion story. The title over the cross makes the imagery obvious. John notes that Jesus's title is written for all of the major languages of the Mediterranean: Greek, Latin, and Aramaic. This king is not a provincial ruler but a supreme monarch, whose authority now sweeps up those people speaking foreign tongues. Jesus is a *global* king, and in God's eye the cross included countless more languages than these three: Russian, Swahili, Swedish, Bemba, Arabic, Spanish, Mandarin, Hindi; 19:20 suggests that there is no limit.

But if Jesus is a king, he deserves a king's burial. It is no accident, then, that when we read about Jesus's tomb, similar themes prevail. His was no pauper's grave. *At great expense* a wealthy man provided a tomb, no doubt among other wealthy family tombs on the fringes of Jerusalem. *At great expense*, a religious leader brought a tremendous amount of burial spice to Jesus's grave. Jesus is buried in splendor, in beauty, in an unused tomb, as if it had been carved for him alone. Jesus is King!

The cross and sacrifice. At the beginning of the Gospel, we were introduced to Jesus by John the Baptist. "Look, the Lamb of God, who takes away the sin of the world!" (1:29). When we come to the passion story, John carefully reminds us that it occurred in the season of Passover, when Judaism celebrated its departure from Egypt through the spilled blood of a lamb. The imagery of Jesus as a Passover sacrifice is unmistakable. Jesus's legs were not broken because no lamb could come to the temple as a sacrifice with broken bones. Jesus's wound offered evidence sought by every priest that indeed he was a qualified lamb, an acceptable sacrifice, able to meet the stringent demands of the festival.

When Jesus bears his wooden cross at Passover—as a lamb whose limbs cannot be broken—Jewish readers may at once have recalled Isaac, the precious son of Abraham, whose story was repeated and cherished at this time of year. Genesis 22:2, 12, 16 describe Isaac as "the only son," a word translated in the LXX as the "beloved" (*agapētos*) son.

It was commonplace among the earliest Christians to look at Jesus as a sacrificial lamb, even a Passover lamb, slain for their benefit. We too at once should reflect on the benefits of his death for our lives. Re-creating this story for people today requires that we must both dramatically relive the Passover story and Jesus's participation in it, as well as generate modern stories that help us reexperience the meaning of costly sacrifice.

The cross and the Spirit. In Jesus's farewell discourse, the coming of the Spirit is dependent on the departure of Jesus. The promised Spirit will be Jesus's alter-ego, resuming the role of Jesus after his departure. The Spirit becomes an aspect of the life of Christ in John's Gospel, given as a gift when his life expires. Thus we see the irony of the source of living water experiencing thirst. Thus we see symbols at work on the cross that at the moment of death, when Jesus expires, the Spirit becomes free. In John's thought, Jesus Christ is like a precious vial of perfume, filled with the fragrant Spirit of God. It is a gift he offers throughout his life but cannot genuinely extend until "the hour" when the vial is broken, when the crystal is shattered and the fragrance of its contents fills the world.

The spiritual implications for this are significant. This means that the gift of Christ is not merely a gift of salvation, if by salvation we mean freedom from condemnation and the promise of eternal life. John affirms this and more. He understands that the gift of Christ has to do with transformation and renewal. Jesus offers *life*, not mere freedom from eternal judgment. Jesus offers *himself*, and the vehicle of this gift is the Spirit, by which he and the Father will indwell the believer.

Jesus as victor. Jesus is *not* a victim in this story. Why is this important? God has succeeded in accomplishing everything he designed to do in the life of his Son. In Jesus Christ, God himself was at work, demonstrating his love for us, revealing his will for our lives, and bringing about a reconciliation that needs no supplement. *Jesus's victory is the basis of our security.*

The tomb and the cross. This tomb is the resting place for the great King, the culmination of his work on the cross, the terminus of his journey through the hands of Caiaphas and Pilate. The resurrection for John is not a solution to a problem (Jesus's death and burial), but another step along the way, as Jesus moves from earth to heaven. Therefore, the tomb story offers little in the way of apologetic material for Easter but points us to motifs developed on Golgotha. It too, like the cross, is a place of glory and victory.

Joseph and Nicodemus. It has been the view of a variety of scholars that Joseph of Arimathea and Nicodemus are not merely historical figures but symbols. Joseph and Nicodemus are drawn out from their ambivalent positions at tremendous risk and publicly acknowledge Jesus's honor, pointing to the importance of the public visibility of faith among true disciples. John is setting before us a sterling example of two men who used their considerable resources to glorify Jesus—and in doing so, chose to become genuine followers of Christ.

JOHN 20:1–31

Original Meaning

Mary and the Empty Tomb (20:1–18). The name "Mary Magdalene" refers to Mary who came from the Galilean village of Magdala (v. 1). She appears in John for the first time at the cross and enjoys this lengthy and important episode on Easter Sunday. Jesus had expelled numerous demons from her and, along with other women, she followed Jesus to Jerusalem to care for his needs.

On Friday Jesus was left on the burial preparation bench in the receiving room of the tomb chamber. No doubt the women thought they could return following the Sabbath, roll back the stone, and complete the burial. Mary's discovery that the tomb door has been rolled to one side suggested immediately to her that someone has entered the tomb. Perhaps someone came that night—or was in the tomb at that moment. It is not hard to suppose that Mary examines the tomb's interior, sees that Jesus is gone, and flees to find some of the others.

Mary's report to Peter and "the other disciple" conveys something of her dismay and fear (v. 2). The reference to "they" ("*they* have taken the Lord") likely refers to the temple authorities. Mary's use of the plural for herself suggests that she is not alone but accompanied by other women. A woman would rarely venture out alone outside the city walls in the dark under such circumstances.

Peter and the Beloved Disciple immediately sprint to the tomb to see what has happened. The Beloved Disciple arrives first, and when he sees everything alongside Peter, he "believes" (v. 8). Oddly the story is silent about the faith of Peter.

John's description of the clothes includes some unexpected details. The scene is not chaotic or confused. Rather, something purposeful has transpired here. If someone had simply stolen Jesus's body, surely the clothes would be missing, or at least strewn about the floor. But here is a scene in which the body is missing but the clothes appear undisturbed. Jesus's body has simply left them behind.

The Beloved Disciple has penetrated the deeper meaning of this empty tomb despite the fact that he does not yet grasp the larger *biblical and theological context* in which these things are taking place (v. 9). Following the revelation of Jesus's person, the disciples' minds nevertheless need to be opened for them to grasp the larger picture of what this resurrection means. Hence the Beloved Disciple believes that Jesus is now alive—but as yet he does not know the scriptural and theological undergirding that have made this resurrection inevitable.

John notes how Mary alone experiences the first and most profound moment with the resurrected Jesus. Angels do not solve the riddle of Jesus's disappearance but suggest that sorrow is not what the present moment requires. She hears someone approach from behind and suddenly meets a man, whom she concludes must be the caretaker of the garden surrounding the tomb. He repeats the angels' words but deflects the question to a more profound level: "Who is it you are looking for?" (v. 15). Her conclusion indicates that she has not heard the man standing before her. Her mind remains on the problem of the tomb. Jesus's question points her in another direction. The reality of meeting him is more important than the riddle of the tomb.

When Jesus utters Mary's name, at once she recognizes him, and in her joy she uses the familiar Hebrew title "Rabboni" (which John translates for us as "Teacher," v. 16). Jesus tells Mary not to hold him because he has not yet ascended to the Father but then directs her to go and tell his disciples that he is presently ascending to the Father. This means that the final step of "the hour" is advancing. Jesus must honor one more promise mentioned throughout his farewell discourse. He will distribute to them the Holy Spirit as his parting gift.

Mary is thinking that the resurrection of Jesus is Jesus's resumption of normal relations with his disciples. In telling her not to hold on, Jesus is saying that his permanent "return" and presence must come in another form. Jesus's correction is a spiritual redirection away from Jesus's physical presence, a preparation for the Spirit that is about to be given.

The coming of the Spirit is still future (v. 22), and this will be the momentous gift that will return Jesus to them permanently. Therefore, the story with Mary can be seen as an *interpretive vehicle* to stress the transition now underway in Jesus's life and in his relationship with each of his disciples. Mary is then charged to ready Jesus's disciples for his coming—namely, his coming both in body (in the upper room) but more profoundly in the Holy Spirit.

Mary becomes a courier of news for the second time. She alone is the bearer of the report not only that the tomb was empty but also that the resurrected Jesus has come and that she has "seen" him (v. 18), thus fulfilling Jesus's promise in 16:19–22: "In a little while you will see me no more, and then after a little while *you will see me*."

Jesus and the Upper Room (20:19–23). It is the evening of this Easter Sunday, and the doors are shut. Fear has gripped their hearts, and they no doubt conclude that the tragic fate of Jesus may soon be theirs. The temple authorities will find them and arrest them too. But instead Jesus "comes" to them and stands in their midst (v. 19). No doubt this appearance is miraculous since John has just told us that the doors were shut tight. But we can hardly speculate how he has materialized among them.

His words, "Peace be with you," are far more than a greeting (v. 19). At a profoundly personal level, Jesus is summing up the essence of his work and presence in the world. Peace is the gift of his kingdom. Jesus promised that this peace would be his gift to them; now he has delivered it. The disciples' response to his appearance is likewise a fulfillment of what was promised. Once they see Jesus in this room, the disciples are filled with joy.

Jesus was God's special representative (or agent) in the world, so now also his disciples become Jesus's agents, working in the world and witnessing to the reality of God and the truth of Jesus's words. One feature of Jesus's commission is his empowering. God not only sent his Son but also empowered him with the Spirit.

To be commissioned as God's agent means being empowered as Jesus was empowered—obtaining the Spirit, just as Jesus was anointed and as Jesus promised. Thus verse 22 becomes the climax to the entire Gospel. The Spirit is now given to the disciples in a provocative and personal way. Jesus breathes (on them) and says, "Receive the Holy Spirit." The hour of glorification has reached its climax. Jesus is departing, and he places the Spirit that is within him in their lives.

We see this gift of the Spirit as a genuine transforming experience on Easter Sunday. The time in which the resurrected Jesus lived among his followers was no doubt a period of remarkable spiritual experiences. To be with him and to understand him, to see him as he truly was, required a gift of God's Spirit. It all began the moment Jesus returned on Easter. That they would be empowered again, in a different way, on Pentecost does not eliminate the possibility that they were filled earlier.

Christians who bear Christ's Spirit, who continue his efforts in the world, sustain his saving and judging work through their proclamation. Pointing to what God has disclosed in Christ, unveiling divine light in darkness, the prospect of judgment and salvation is suddenly placed before every man and woman. Christians do not distribute forgiveness on a whim (or retain the sins of any). As Jesus's life was a divine response of the Father's prompting (14:31), similarly Christians can do nothing except what Jesus-in-Spirit prompts them to do. Their life likewise must be a response to what Jesus is prompting through his Spirit in the world.

Thomas and Jesus (20:24–29). The following account carefully duplicates what transpired on Easter Sunday. Jesus has heard Thomas's challenge. The evidence he demands is now provided. Jesus's exhortation has a fine rhythm in Greek: "Do not become unbelieving [*apistos*] but believing [*pistos*]" (v. 27, literal translation). Thomas is being challenged to change, to become like the others who, upon seeing Jesus, embrace him with faith. His response is a confession of heartfelt belief in Jesus.

These words supply the closing frame of the Gospel, matching the high and lofty descriptions of Christ the Word in 1:1–18. As the Gospel comes to its close, no more explicit identification of Jesus can be imagined. But the climax of the passage comes in 20:29. Jesus does not disparage the faith of Thomas but simply goes on to utter a blessing on those who believe but have *not seen*. Jesus has in mind people (such as us) who are now reading this Gospel and have not had Thomas's opportunity to touch Jesus's wounds.

Conclusion (20:30–31). John acknowledges that Jesus provided many other signs with his disciples and that the collection offered here in his Gospel is a mere selection. This means that John is aware of a rich source of traditions about Jesus and that he, as an editor, has had to make a careful selection to suit his own literary needs. In 20:31 John discloses his purpose for writing the Gospel. Belief leads to life, and this life is a gift given through the power of Jesus Christ, God's Son.

Application. *The truth of the resurrection.* The reason that debates about the historicity of Jesus finally focus on his resurrection is that this one event, this one claim to history, becomes the most objectionable. Easter claims that divine events, such as the stupendous event of Jesus's emerging alive from the tomb, happen in history. Easter claims that such events should not only be catalogued and studied as genuine events in history but that they can be viewed as a reliable basis for belief. We believe in a *God who acts in history*, and those activities must be taken as serious disclosures of his revelation to humankind.

The Thomas episode is a dramatic gift for modern cynics. We are invited—no, we are challenged—to believe like Thomas. Yet John understands perfectly well that we do not have the same opportunities. This is why in the story of John 20 the Beloved Disciple becomes one of the most important figures. He looks into the tomb, sees the evidence, and believes. While not seeing the resurrected Jesus, he sees what has been left behind; he sees the remnants of divine activity in history in stone and fabric and decides to believe.

This is our situation today. John has provided us with the best evidence he can muster to persuade us that belief is not only a reasonable choice but a necessary decision if we are going to follow Jesus. Jesus is not an *idea* whose ongoing validity finds a home in our ideas or our ethics. Jesus is a person—he is God incarnate in human history—and in coming into history, he has left marks that we can see and measure and trust.

The centrality of the Spirit. Discipleship is defined not only by belief in Jesus but by the indwelling of the Son through the Spirit. Some theological traditions separate Jesus and the Spirit, urging that to accept Christ as Savior is one matter and receiving the Holy Spirit is a second, necessary experience. But this is an unacceptable division in John. To receive Christ is to obtain the Spirit; to be filled by the Holy Spirit is to experience the living presence of Jesus Christ within. Christian transformation is Christ at work within us, bringing about his glory in our Spirit-led renewal.

Other theological traditions, particularly in the evangelical community, create yet another theological problem by making the Spirit disappear into Christology. For these Christians, the chief evidence of the Spirit is found in conversion and sanctification. Little is said about the more mysterious and mystical work of the Spirit. John's own church was certainly "pneumatic" (or what we today might call charismatic). The evidence of his letters (and his emphasis on the Spirit in his Gospel) makes this evident. But those outside this world of experience often fail to see its importance.

The necessity of faith. It is striking that John never uses the noun "faith" (*pistis*) in his Gospel. Yet the verb "to believe" (*pisteuō*) appears almost a hundred times. John's interest is to underscore the act of believing (as opposed to the content of faith). Faith, then, is more a matter of relationship than of creed. On occasion it means accepting that a message given is true and trustworthy (2:22), but for the most part faith springs from confidence in the works Jesus has done (2:11; 10:38) and results in a desire to invest all hope in him. Faith is personal and transforming since it is dependent on a person who has demonstrated himself powerful and trustworthy. It is the decision whereby a person gains eternal life and the power to become a child of God (1:12; 3:16) and so marks himself or herself as a member of Jesus's community.

JOHN 21:1–25

Original Meaning

The Fishing Miracle (21:1–14). Peter decides to return to his long-neglected work of fishing. At sunrise they are finishing up when an unknown voice from shore instructs them to try the opposite side of the boat. "Throw your net on the right side of the boat and you will find some," Jesus called out (v. 6). To toss a cast net at random into the sea was virtually futile. Only a school captured by a trammel net could be picked up in this manner. But the stranger may have seen a large school of fish from the shore, and Peter quickly spins the net over his head and lets it sail, like a parachute, dropping onto the sea as he watches the sinkers take it down.

In these shallow waters, the miraculous catch cannot be mistaken. Pinned to the net are over one hundred fish (later counted at 153), and its weight is more than the boat can take. Immediately the Beloved Disciple recognizes Jesus on the shore and conveys the news to Peter. When he hears that Jesus is on the shore, he tucks or wraps his smock into his belt to give him a tight fit and leaps into the water.

In Judaism, an abundant catch was a sign of God's favor and blessing; this is precisely what Jesus has done. He blesses them further by greeting them with a fire and roasting fish together with fresh bread. While they are eating, John says that the men know it is Jesus but are also afraid to ask. He is the same Jesus, but the events of Easter have also made him unmistakably different. Jesus's offer of bread and fish precisely parallels what he did at the miraculous feeding in 6:11, and this no doubt serves as a signal that removes any uncertainties.

The Restoration of Peter (21:15–17). Jesus's three queries in verses 15–17 are perhaps the most celebrated exchange of questions and answers in the entire Bible. Three times Jesus asks Peter if he loves him, and three times Peter affirms his love. In each case he is commissioned to tend Jesus's flock. There are nuances of language here, however, that are often identified in the passage, and it may be helpful to outline the exchange in Greek.

[15] Jesus: Do you love [*agapaō*] me? Peter: I love [*phileō*] you.
[16] Jesus: Do you love [*agapaō*] me? Peter: I love [*phileō*] you.
[17] Jesus: Do you love [*phileō*] me? Peter: I love [*phileō*] you.

Interpreters have to make a decision. Do these two words for love convey some hidden difference of meaning? Some commentators have argued that *phileō* represents an inferior form of love and that Jesus is challenging Peter to elevate his level of commitment. One of the problems with this view is that if the conversation took place in Aramaic, such variation in Greek would not have been present—although this explanation fails to recognize that John is using Greek to represent the nuances of the exchange and his choice of words remains important.

This has led many exegetes to see the variation between *agapaō* and *phileō* as insignificant and to understand these two words as synonyms. The focus of Peter's conversation with Jesus has to do with his commission to tend the flock of Christ, not the quality of his love for him. Peter is thus upset (v. 17) not because Jesus has changed the verb for love but because Jesus has asked him the same question for the third time. Attempts to find deeper meaning in the connections among these words should be viewed with utmost caution.

The Death of Peter and the Beloved Disciple (21:18–23). We should no doubt read these verses together with 13:36–38. Peter *will* lay down his life for Jesus (13:37). He will be crucified also and will glorify God in the same manner as his Lord—but this must await a time in the future. "Follow me" in 21:19 now takes on a poignant and provocative new meaning. Peter will follow Jesus to the cross.

Interest now shifts to the Beloved Disciple in verses 20–23.

Throughout the Gospel this disciple is an exemplar of faithfulness and commitment. We are reminded, for instance, that it was he who spoke to Jesus about betrayal at their last meal. He was faithful, standing with Jesus at the cross, and later he was the first to express faith at the empty tomb. Here at the shore, Peter is charged to "follow" Jesus (v. 19), but we learn that John, the disciple whom Jesus loved, is "following" already (v. 20). Again, he is a model who on one level may be following nearby as Jesus talks privately with Peter, but who (on another level) is found to be the ideal follower whom Peter should emulate.

It is not Peter's privilege to know how or when John will die—or if, for that matter, John will remain alive until Jesus comes back in his powerful return. Again, Jesus tells the apostle to *follow*, and this time the form is emphatic. To paraphrase: "Peter, this matter is not your concern; it is mine. *You* have one duty: follow me."

Verse 23 corrects what must have been an unusual misinterpretation of Jesus's words that had circulated for some time in the church. No doubt among John's followers many believed that their beloved leader would not die but would remain until Christ returned. Disciples in the Johannine church could thus keep their hope in the second coming alive and then increase their anticipation as John grew in age. As Peter should not speculate about John, so too should John's followers abandon any eschatology linked to the apostle's fate.

Validating John's Testimony (21:24–25). John's disciples next explicitly affirm the veracity of their leader's work. When they write, "*We know* that his testimony is true" (emphases added), at once we are alerted to their presence in the narrative. Here we have a third party standing between John's reliable testimony and ourselves as readers. With devotion and humility, they now pen the Gospel's closing frame.

The Gospel's closing verse may well stem from the hand of John himself (following the quick editorial insertion of v. 24). John reminds us that there is far more to Jesus's life than what is recorded in his Gospel. This suggests again the possibility that John knew of other stories (Synoptic stories?) that he did not record (cf. 20:30). At best we can say that the Fourth Gospel is a partial rendering—but also a sufficient rendering—of a story whose scope surpasses any one effort.

With playful and delightful hyperbole, John says that even all the books of the world could not contain Jesus's story. John ends his Gospel with humility. The story is larger than anything he can imagine. His effort, while glorious for us to read, pales in comparison to the glory of the person whom his story describes.

Application. *Peter and Jesus.* Peter could have spent the balance of his life working for the kingdom and promoting faith in Jesus. He could have become one of the most zealous apostles, intolerant of those who might compromise, inflexible with any who didn't take discipleship with utmost seriousness. All of this energy would look excellent on the surface, but it would have been mere compensation—perhaps even overcompensation—for the failings of his earlier life. This sort of Christianity (so familiar to ardent conservatives) is destructive.

On the other hand, Peter could have become a man filled with despair. Seeing his own weakness so directly, knowing that Jesus had seen it and now even his fellow apostles knew about it, how could he still enjoy anyone's respect? Yes, Peter could have continued in ministry, having packed away the burden of his sin in some of the deepest recesses of his heart. But it would have eroded his soul. Self-criticism, depression, and a spiritual pessimism (disguised as a "theology of the cross") would have characterized his work.

Jesus wanted none of this. His first plan was a gift of such good humor that we can just imagine him smiling as he contemplated his friends hauling in a net full of fish. When Peter learned that it was Jesus who had done this—the fishing miracle-worker Jesus—it is no accident that he ran to the shore. He ran to the only one who could heal his memories, who could rewrite the terrible pictures and sounds of his recent past—the courtyard, the charcoal fire, the servant girl. The miracle demonstrated that despite Peter's failings, Jesus was still on his side, cooking a good meal for friends, having fun filling nets with fish.

Peter and John. Two strong men; one Christian movement. Yet John possessed intuitive skills that permitted him to grasp aspects of Christ's personhood in a way that may have eluded others. The leadership of the body of Christ demands a diversity of gifts, and John possessed his own unique set. For this we can be thankful. Christ's flock has need of many shepherds, and (thankfully) each will bring to the community a variety of gifts.

Peter and the church. Peter's restoration to Christ makes possible his service to the church. Peter—and each of us—is called to embrace the body of Christ, to love it, to tend it, and to protect it. The chief images of John 21 (fish and sheep) both speak to us about the work of the church. We must gather up those to whom Christ directs us and nurture those who live in his flock. This is labor, divinely directed labor, which must be inspired by our devotion to Christ.

Yet note that Jesus participates in these efforts too. We misuse the story of the great catch of fish if we use it to illustrate the work Christ has for us to do. We often view the story as Jesus's exhortation for Peter to give his fishing "one more try." Jesus is not calling for renewed skill or renewed energy, but for faith. He has challenged Peter to do what may appear ridiculous or fanciful. But in doing it, Peter discovers unmistakably that the fruit of his labor is a gift from God.

But how does Jesus continue to participate in the labor of the church? How does he assist his shepherds in their work? This answer is found in the sustained emphasis on the Holy Spirit in John's Gospel. The Spirit is not merely an ambiguous spiritual influence but is rather the Spirit of Jesus himself living in his followers. The work of the church, therefore, is not religious energy fueled by our sense of commission; it is a call to work, wed to a divine empowering; it is ministering knowing that Christ himself (through the Spirit) is ministering in and through our efforts.

Good shepherds are not people whose ministries promote ego and personal glory, who disguise their own ambitions in pursuits of "excellence" in so-called great churches and institutions. These are not people whose competitiveness harms other shepherds, who always look over their shoulder to see if someone else will enjoy a parallel glory. These are men and women who simply hear Jesus's words, "Follow me," and obey, thinking about their own discipleship more than that of others. The result is a rich life that glorifies God in humility as it bears witness to Jesus.

This profile no doubt describes the life of John. He has written his Gospel and supplied us with his testimony. His three letters also show that he was a man who loved the church and defended it with all his might. John's disciples knew that he was the "Beloved Disciple" because Jesus held a special affection for him. But this title also has another meaning (have we not seen countless double meanings in this Gospel?). This amazing title also describes one church's love for its own shepherd. John was *likewise* beloved among those he led, and this Gospel, this beloved Gospel now concluded by his devoted disciples, stands as a memorial of John's witness and work for the church.

ACTS

INTRODUCTION TO ACTS

The external evidence available for the authorship of Acts, gleaned from the writings of the church in the first few centuries, is unanimous that the author was Luke. When we look for internal evidence (found in Scripture itself), we note that Acts is linked closely with the third Gospel, which indicates common authorship. Both are addressed to the same person, Theophilus (Luke 1:3; Acts 1:1). Acts begins by summarizing the contents of a "former book" (1:1), whose contents correspond with the Gospel of Luke.

Luke writes in good literary Greek, which has led to the conclusion that he must have been well educated. He was probably a gentile, though this claim has been challenged. While there is no unanimity about where he came from, a strong early tradition connects him with Antioch of Pisidia. Paul refers to him as "our dear friend Luke, the doctor" (Col 4:14) and shows Luke as faithfully sticking with him at a time when most other Christians had shunned him—that is, during his second imprisonment in Rome (2 Tim 4:11).

Scholars have placed the date of writing of Acts from early to mid-60s of the first century to much later in the century (some estimates go as far as the late second century). The most evident point used in support of an earlier date is the fact that the book ends so abruptly with events that should be dated in the early 60s.

BOOK OUTLINE

I. Prologue and Preparation for Pentecost (1:1–26)
II. Witness in Jerusalem (2:1–8:4)
III. Witness in Judea and Samaria and the Beginnings of Gentile Evangelism (8:5–11:18)
IV. Witness to the Ends of the Earth (11:19–28:31)

ACTS 1:1–8

Original Meaning

The Former Book (1:1–2a). The opening section of Acts contains a prologue along with a historical introduction. The author begins by referring to his "former book," gives the name of the recipient (Theophilus), and summarizes the contents of the earlier book (the Gospel of Luke). Theophilus means "friend of God" or "loved by God." "Most excellent" could suggest that a high government official is being addressed, but that is not a necessary inference. In those days, it was common for books to be dedicated to distinguished persons.

Teaching and Instructions before the Ascension (1:2b–8). In the forty days before Jesus's ascension, his primary ministry related to the truth of the gospel (vv. 2b–3). The verb for instructing (*entellomai*) has the idea of commanding or giving orders. These instructions were given "through the Holy Spirit" (v. 2), which introduces a key theme of Acts: all Christian ministry depends on the activity of the Spirit in the minister and in the ones ministered to.

Luke then reports that Jesus's appearances were proof of his resurrection (v. 3a). The objective reality of the resurrection was the ultimate proof of the amazing claims that the apostles were to make about Jesus (17:31). The fact that the apostles were witnesses to this resurrection was a key to their preaching. So right at the start of his book, Luke presents the resurrection as an event attested by "many convincing proofs" (1:3a).

Jesus "spoke about the kingdom of God" (v. 3b), which refers to the reign or rule of God and was a key to his teaching. According to the Gospels, the kingdom of God came with the events of the life, death, and resurrection of Jesus, and it finds its consummation in the return of Christ as judge and king.

Verses 4–5 present the crucial promise of the gift of baptism with the Holy Spirit. The word *baptizō* basically means to dip or immerse. But it can take different meanings that must be determined by considering the context in which the word appears. Describing what happened when this promise was fulfilled, Luke writes that the disciples "were filled with the Holy Spirit" (2:4). The words "power" and "filled" in these verses suggest that the baptism with the Holy Spirit involves an experience of God's fullness.

It must have saddened the heart of Jesus to hear his disciples ask about the time of restoring the kingdom to Israel (v. 6). He had taught them about the kingdom of God, but they talk about the kingdom of Israel. Jesus's answer about not knowing times and dates set by the Father (v. 7) is consistent with what he said elsewhere on the topic of the timing of the last things.

Verse 8 begins with "but" (*alla*), suggesting that Jesus is presenting an alternative aspiration for the disciples. Their primary concern should not be the political power that will come with the restoration of Israel's kingdom. It should be the spiritual power that will come through the baptism with the

Holy Spirit, which will enable them to be witnesses "to the ends of the earth" (v. 8).

In a sense the disciples were already witnesses, for they had seen the risen Lord; that was the key to their witness (v. 22). But they also needed "power" to be effective witnesses, power that would come from the Holy Spirit (v. 8). The way the Holy Spirit makes witnesses and empowers witness must cover the entire witnessing process, and this is well illustrated in Acts.

Application. We find it difficult to integrate the subjective and the objective aspects of our faith today. The early church, therefore, challenges us here. We have churches that are "strong on the Bible" but which show little vitality because they suffer from a dead orthodoxy. Segments of the evangelical movement were for many years weak on the experiential aspects of the faith, especially when it came to evangelism—until the charismatic movement burst onto the scene.

The integration we are talking about comes from grappling with many areas of life at the same time, and that is difficult in our specialized world. We prefer to have our specialist scholars and specialist spiritual writers. As long as we permit such fragmentation of truth, we are going to have an anemic church that does not know the depth of what it means to know God out of a foundation of objective reality and an experience of deep spirituality. From Acts 1, then, we can infer that the ideal Christian teaching is done by Spirit-empowered individuals whose teaching is grounded on the objective facts of the gospel and should result in evangelism and witness.

Someone once said that 95 percent of what happens in many evangelical churches could be done without the Holy Spirit. Many people will come to these churches attracted by the comprehensive program the church offers. People want a weekly religious dose, and, in our entertainment-oriented culture, a church that provides an entertaining program that will attract people, just like a good concert or sporting event will attract people. But Christian ministry is ministry in the Spirit. Without the Spirit's power, our excellent programs are ultimately futile.

ACTS 1:9–26

Original Meaning

The Ascension (1:9–11). Jesus's ascension takes place after his giving the Great Commission for the last time (v. 9). In the early church the ascension was associated with Christ's exaltation to God's right hand (see Eph 1:20–21; Phil 2:9; Heb 1:3; 2:9).

The upward gaze of the disciples is interrupted by the appearance of two men (v. 10), whose white clothes suggest that they are angels (see Matt 28:2–3; John 20:12). There is a mild rebuke implied in their question (v. 11a). The angels specifically give Jesus's post-ascension abode as "heaven" (v. 11b). The promise that he "will come back in the same [exalted] way" (v. 11c) would have helped make some sense out of Jesus's repeated statements to the disciples about his second coming.

Waiting Prayerfully (1:12–14). The apostles' return from the Mount of Olives to Jerusalem was a Sabbath day's walk (v. 12), a little less than three-fourths of a mile. Since this happened forty days after Easter, it was a Thursday, not a Sabbath day.

Luke's list of who had gathered in the upper room (v. 13b) includes the eleven apostles—the same list as given in Luke 6:14–16, but without Judas. The order, however, has been changed; this list begins with the three prominent apostles who alone appear later in Acts—Peter, John, and James. Women are also mentioned, in keeping with Luke's practice of giving a prominent place to women in his writings. Faithful women were with Jesus during his ministry to minister to his needs (Luke 8:2–3); they were also prominently featured on the days of his death (23:27–31, 49, 55–56) and resurrection (24:1–10). Thus, it is not surprising to find them here as well (Acts 1:14).

Mary, Jesus's mother, is also mentioned here—her only appearance in Acts (v. 14). Luke had presented her as a model of trust and obedience in his Gospel (Luke 1:38). Jesus appeared to James, his brother, after his resurrection (1 Cor 15:7). The unbelief of the brothers, which was still there as late as six months before this death (John 7:5), is now gone.

Luke-Acts abounds with references to prayer (mentioned thirty-one times in Acts and appears in twenty of its chapters). Thus, it is unsurprising to find that, as the followers of Jesus wait for the promised baptism of the Spirit, they "all joined together constantly in prayer" (Acts 1:14). The word translated "together" (*homothymadon*) literally means "with one mind or passion" and is a favorite word of Luke.

Choosing Judas's Successor (1:15–26). To find a replacement for Judas, Peter addresses a group of "believers [literally brothers] ... numbering about a hundred and twenty" (v. 15). With his concern for accuracy in reporting, Luke likes to qualify his numerical data with a cautious "about," especially if a round number follows (2:41; 4:4; 10:3; 19:7). As this may not be the exact number present, the number one hundred and twenty is probably not significant, and Luke may simply be saying that the room was full.

Peter views Judas's act of betrayal as a fulfillment of Scripture (v. 16). That, however, does not take away from the pain of what happened, for, as Peter says, "he was one of our number and shared in our ministry" (v. 17). Peter's view of the divine authorship of the Old Testament Scriptures is evidenced in his words (v. 16).

Luke's digression about how Judas died (vv. 18–19) uses the word "wickedness," which shows that, while the betrayal was predicted in Scripture, it was a serious act of treachery. This eliminates the views of those who try to "rehabilitate" Judas by showing that his motives for betraying Christ were honorable.

Peter's predictions in verse 20 are from Psalms 69 and 109. The early Christians saw David, the righteous sufferer, and his enemies as types of Christ and *his* enemies (the antitypes). Differences between David and Jesus and between David's enemies and Judas in these psalms can be explained by the fact that the antitype is always greater than the type.

The theme of God's sovereign will at work in the suffering and death of Christ is one that occurs several times in the apostles' preaching, especially to Jews. When the disciples faced the first outlawing of evangelism, they again reflected on the sovereignty of God as it was manifested in the most terrible event in history: the death of Christ (Acts 4:25–28). This perspective helps us believe that God will turn the evil done to us into good (cf. Gen 50:20). It would have helped take away the bitterness that the disciples must have had over the betrayal of Jesus by one who had been so close to them.

Peter felt that it was "necessary" to find a replacement for Judas (v. 21). The same verb (*dei*) is used here as in verse 16, which presented the necessity of Judas's betrayal. Thus, the early church followed Jesus's practice of having exactly twelve apostles.

Note that the first period of the church's growth was in Israel and that in the Gospels the apostles had a special role in relation to Israel (Luke 9:1–6; 22:28–30). The qualifications required for the replacement had to do with the role of the apostles as witnesses (Acts 1:21–22). Witnessing to the resurrection was a crucial, never to be repeated role of a select group of men in the early Christian church.

The church cast lots since they felt a need for direct divine guidance on the final choice between two equally qualified people. But the use of lots comes only after prayer for God's guidance. That prayer shows what we should be looking for most in a leader: "Lord, you know everyone's heart. Show us which of these two you have chosen" (v. 24). The believers had found two people with suitable external qualifications, but those would be useless if the person's heart was not right. Only God knows the hearts of people unerringly, so they ask his help. Like most of the other apostles, the new apostle Matthias does not appear again in Acts. Later tradition presents him as a missionary to the Ethiopians.

Application. Just as Pentecost came after constant prayer by the disciples, the history of the church demonstrates that revival also comes only after persistent prayer. Revival is something that God sends sovereignly, and therefore we cannot predict when it will come. But, there is a statement, attributed to Matthew Henry, that when God wants to do something special in the world, he first gets his people to start praying.

The prayer that took place in Jerusalem was persistent or prevailing prayer. This can happen today as well. The Lord sometimes gives a burden to someone, which he or she shares with others. They pray about this over an extended period of time, and with time they find that the Lord has wonderfully answered their prayers. It is a simple principle, but one that we must be regularly reminded of, given our natural tendency to drift toward prayerlessness.

ACTS 2:1–13

Original Meaning. The fulfillment of Christ's promise of the Holy Spirit appropriately takes place during a Jewish harvest festival, Pentecost (v. 1). It was one of the three Jewish pilgrimage festivals (Exod 23:14–17). It is appropriate that the event that was going to propel the gospel to the ends of the earth took place at a time when people from the ends of the earth were in Jerusalem.

The wind and fire that accompanied the gift of the Spirit (vv. 2–3) are common biblical symbols for the activity of the Spirit (Ezek 37:1–14; cf. John 3:7–8). Wind was a symbol of regeneration. In the prediction of baptism with the Holy Spirit by John the Baptist, the wind (by implication) blows the chaff away (Luke 3:16–17). This is a symbol of judgment. Similarly, fire in this same prediction, which burns up the chaff, is a symbol of judgment. In other words, like the coming of the gospel message (2 Cor 2:15–16), the coming of the Spirit means life to some and judgment to others (as we will see with Ananias and Sapphira, Acts 5:3, 9).

The tongues of fire "rest on each of them" (v. 3). This does not negate the importance of the corporate relationship with God, as Paul's letters amply demonstrate. But from now on, the corporate arises out of a personal relationship with God through the Holy Spirit. This is in keeping with the prediction through Jeremiah that in the new covenant the law will be written on the hearts (Jer 31:31–34).

Two things happened to the disciples after the Spirit came: they "were filled with the Holy Spirit" and "began to speak in other tongues" (v. 4). The "tongues" are different from those described in 1 Corinthians 12–14 because, unlike there, "God-fearing Jews" from the diaspora were able to understand what was being said (Acts 2:5, 11). The gift of tongues generally seems to have been used for praising God (see 1 Cor 14). But this particular manifestation of the Spirit, in languages understood by the people, was most appropriate here since those who heard it were eager to listen to the preaching of the gospel.

The sign fit in with the Spirit's role in enabling the church's worldwide witness (Acts 1:8).

Those who heard the praise of God in their own languages were devout Jews (v. 5). Large numbers of pilgrims came to Jerusalem for the Feast of Pentecost. In amazement the people point out that those who are speaking are "Galileans" (v. 7a). God had broken earthly stereotypes of greatness and chosen people not held in high esteem in society in order to lead in a historic event (cf. 1 Cor 1:26–31).

Verses 12–13 give the two reactions of those who heard the faithful proclamation of God's word by the apostles. Some were touched and wanted to know more (v. 12). Others rejected the message and ridiculed what was said (v. 13). It is surprising that, in the face of such a spectacular miracle, some should mock what they saw. But as we will see below, this is in keeping with the theology of rejection that is clearly present in Scripture.

Application. To many, the Christian faith is restricted to entering the kingdom through a rational acceptance of the truth of the gospel, followed by their labor to live according to the Bible. This is indeed an important ingredient to the Christian faith. But Pentecost tells us that there is something more. The greatest contribution of the Pentecostal movement (and the Wesleyan Holiness movement that preceded it) is that it gave back to the church the importance of a subjective experience of Christ through the Holy Spirit in one's personal life and in corporate worship. At Pentecost, when the disciples were filled with the Spirit, they began "declaring the wonders of God" (v. 11). When we sense, through experience, that "God's love has been poured out into our hearts through the Holy Spirit, who has been given to us" (Rom 5:5), our hearts are filled with joy, and this joy expresses itself in praise.

While quality can be an expression of spirituality, it can never be a substitute for it. All Christians should give due attention to having quality in worship. But more importantly they must ensure that the Holy Spirit has ample opportunity to fill the service with the sense of God's presence and to lead the people to a deep experience of God. I fear that sometimes what we aim at is to entertain people through our quality. This can be an effective means of attracting people in our entertainment-oriented society, but it should never so consume our efforts that it becomes a substitute for seeking God's fullness in worship, as reflected in the Pentecostal experience in Acts.

ACTS 2:14–41

Original Meaning

Explaining the Phenomena (2:14–21). Peter launches his message by connecting with his audience through something they can relate to: the mockers' statement that they are drunk (v. 15). Then he points to the real reason for the surprising phenomena they have witnessed: the fulfillment of a prophecy by Joel (Joel 2:28–32).

The expression "last days" in this prophecy includes two distinct periods; the start of the second one is separated from the start of the first by a long time. But in a way typical of the prophetic perspective, these two events are juxtaposed side by side by the prophet Joel. What the people are witnessing is the beginning of the last days, when people of all types and ages will prophecy (vv. 17b–18). At the end of the last days will be cosmic disturbances (vv. 19–20; cf. Rev 6:12–14; 8:5, 7; 20:9), which will herald "the great and glorious day of the Lord" (v. 20b)—the day of judgment at the end of the world. For believers, this will not be a time to dread, for "everyone who calls on the name of the Lord will be saved" (v. 21).

The Miracles and Death of Christ (2:22–23). Peter begins with a reference to the miracles of Christ as evidence that he was accredited by God (v. 22). Next, Peter presents the death of Christ as having been caused by the audience, but also as being "by God's deliberate plan and foreknowledge" (v. 23). This is also a common theme in the evangelistic preaching of Acts (2:23; 3:18; 8:32–35; 13:27, 29).

This affirmation was the Christian response to the fact that a crucified Messiah was a stumbling block to the Jews (see 1 Cor 1:23). The first Christians must have thought hard about how to respond to this stumbling block in their evangelism with the Jews, and they came up with this strategy of presenting it as a triumph that God had planned from the beginning.

The Resurrection (2:24–32). The Bible often refers to the resurrection as an act of God ("God raised him," v. 24a), which is in keeping with the fact that it was God's accreditation of the person and work of Christ. The next statement, "It was impossible for death to keep its hold on him" (v. 24b), clearly shows that Peter is using the resurrection as a validation of Jesus's life and ministry.

In verses 25–28 Peter quotes Psalm 16:8–11, where David anticipates a resurrection. Then he goes on to argue that, since David did not rise from the dead, this passage must be referring to David's great Son, Jesus (vv. 29–31). Peter clinches his argument for the resurrection with his claim: "We are all witnesses of it" (v. 32).

The Exaltation (2:33–35). Peter next states that Jesus has been exalted to the right hand of the Father and connects the event of Pentecost with this exaltation. Jesus received the Holy Spirit from the Father and has poured out what they have just seen and heard (v. 33). While we often speak of the ascension of Christ, the scriptural term *exaltation* may be a more appropriate word since it implies the significance of the event. In the New Testament, the resurrection and exaltation of Christ are held in close association with each other, almost as if they constituted a single event.

As with the resurrection, Peter provides evidence for the exaltation of Christ. First, he appeals to their experience of the Holy Spirit (v. 33). Next, he quotes from another Davidic psalm (Ps 110) and, as before (vv. 29–31), claims that what David said there cannot apply to him (vv. 34–35). This quotation also gives us a clue as to what Christ is doing now in his exalted state: he is seated at the right hand of God and bringing to pass the complete defeat of his enemies.

Lord and Messiah (2:36). Peter's next statement represents the second major feature of the apostolic proclamation: a theological evaluation of the person of Jesus. The words with which he begins his major affirmation, "Therefore let all Israel be assured of this," are appropriate considering the convincing way he has argued his case up to now. His conclusion is clear: "God has made this Jesus, whom you crucified, both Lord and Messiah."

Peter claims first that Jesus is "Lord." In this speech, *kyrios* is used for Jesus in ways that were used for God in the Greek Old Testament (see vv. 20–21); moreover, Jesus as Lord has taken on divine functions, such as pouring out the Spirit (v. 33) and being the object of faith (v. 21). The title "Messiah" points to the hope of Israel for a deliverer. While the title "Lord" emphasizes the sovereign kingship of Jesus, the title "Messiah" emphasizes the salvation he brings.

A Summons to Repent and Receive Forgiveness (2:37–40). The third feature of the apostolic preaching is a summons to respond to the message. It comes as a result of the inquiry of the audience (v. 37). Peter gives two stipulations and promises two blessings. They must repent and be baptized, and they will receive the forgiveness of sin and experience the Holy Spirit. As Lord, Jesus demands repentance and baptism, which is an outward expression of allegiance to him. As Savior, he offers the unmerited gift of forgiveness. There is no separation of the lordship of Christ from his role as Savior here.

In this story, as in every story of conversion, the grace of God fills us with wonder. In his message, Peter has reminded these people that they put Jesus to death. Now this same Jesus offers them salvation. Peter is showing them how they can appropriate Christ's plea on the cross for their forgiveness.

The Response to the Message (2:41). The amazing response of three thousand baptisms illustrates Jesus's promise that with his going away and the Spirit's coming, the disciples will do even greater works than he did (John 14:12).

Application. Finding people's questions and making the connection between them and the gospel is an art we must develop. It helps to study and meditate over the issues people face and to pray about them, yearning to see them come into line with God's thinking. An even more important key is our personal ministry, which enables us to interact with people and thus informs our minds about how best to reach them. Failure may be an important aid here. We ask, "Why couldn't I get through to him or her?" Such questioning teaches us a lot about how to minister to people. We can then extend to our public ministries what we have learned through personal ministry.

ACTS 2:42–47

Original Meaning

Follow-Through Care of the Converts (2:42). There was immediate, regular, follow-through care of the first converts in the early church. The verbal expression "they were devoting themselves to" (literal translation) covers four activities. "Devoting" (*proskartereō*) is the same word as is used in connection with the persistent devotion of the disciples to prayer in 1:14.

1. The first feature is "the apostles' teaching." From the Gospels and Acts we can say that it likely included explanations of the nature of salvation, the person and work of Christ, the commands of Christ and other features of the Christian life, and the message of the kingdom.
2. The word *koinōnia*, which Luke uses for "fellowship," is a favorite word of Paul's, though this is the only time it appears in Luke's writings. Its basic idea is sharing, but it is used also to denote intimacy and fellowship in general. The nineteen occurrences of *koinōnia* in the New Testament suggest that the church used this word for the unique sharing that Christians have with God and with other Christians.
3. "The breaking of bread" was probably part of the ordinary fellowship meals as described in 1 Corinthians 11. As Paul's traveling companion, Luke would have been aware of this practice in the churches of celebrating the Lord's Supper and having fellowship meals together. It would have been confusing to his readers if he mentioned the breaking of bread without meaning the Lord's Supper.
4. The final feature in verse 42 literally reads, "and to the prayers" (see NRSV). The phrase could refer to prayer during the set times of the Jerusalem temple, which the disciples attended (3:1; cf. 2:46; 22:17). But there were also times when they prayed on their own (1:24; 4:24; 12:12).

The great contribution of Jesus to the Christian understanding of prayer was his intimacy with God, whom he called

"Father" (Mark 14:36). He taught his disciples also to share this intimacy, and even the gentile Christians used the characteristic Aramaic word that he used, "*Abba*," when addressing God (Rom 8:15; Gal 4:6).

The Community Life of the Church (2:43–47). The description of follow-through care of the new converts gives way to a description of the community life of the whole church. First we are told about the "awe" that everyone was filled with and about the ministry of miracles performed by the apostles (v. 43). These people could sense that God was at work.

Property was sold according to need. Thus, we do not have here a case of enforced sharing, as in communism. Nor was it a once-for-all disposal of all private property in the church. The important point is that the fellowship touched the pocketbook too.

Next we are told that the early believers went to the temple (v. 46a), just as Jesus did. They tried to remain within the Jewish fold; that attitude to Judaism prevailed among Christians in Judea throughout the New Testament era (see 21:26).

According to what we argued above, the breaking of bread mentioned in 2:46 included both the Lord's Supper and fellowship meals. Eating together "with glad . . . hearts" can be an important expression of fellowship in any culture, and in the early church it had an important place (v. 46b). The believers also had "sincere" hearts when they met. The word translated "sincere" can mean single-minded devotion, the absence of pretense, or simplicity and generosity.

When God's people come together and enjoy fellowship, "praising God" is the natural result (v. 47a). True fellowship focuses on God and helps people to remember the good things he has done, which, in turn, causes praise.

In the meantime, the church grew numerically. Luke never writes that these new conversions took place primarily through the preaching of the apostles. Personal witness through word and life added to the impact of the miraculous signs and the public preaching and resulted in a comprehensive evangelistic outreach.

But it was "the Lord" who "added to their number" (v. 47). Ultimately, God is the evangelist. God does use our efforts and our techniques, but we must ensure that we are in the place where he can use us and that our techniques are acceptable to him.

Application. Experience in evangelistic ministry shows that during the first few days after a commitment has been made to Christ, Satan will do all he can to ensnare new believers into his traps. They will face doubts regarding what has happened to them and be tempted to sin, sometimes even succumbing to it. This will make them fear that they do not have the strength to make it spiritually. Then they will face persecution and ridicule. They will become discouraged over the behavior of other Christians, and sometimes even become discouraged with God since he does not seem to answer their prayers. They may get entangled in the cares and attractions of the world and may trip and fall. These and a host of other factors will challenge the commitment they have made. Thus, like newborn babies, new believers need special care during the first few days of their spiritual life.

Usually, however, those involved in organizing a big evangelistic campaign are so drained of energy at the end of it that they need some rest, and the follow-through process gets delayed. This can be disastrous to the lives of babes in Christ. For this reason, it is important that plans for "neonatal care" be made before the birth of the babies and that this process of follow-through care occurs immediately after the evangelistic program. John Wesley considered this so important that he is reported to have said, "I determined not to strike in one place where I could not follow the blow." The organized system he developed to conserve the fruit is considered one of the secrets of the long-term effectiveness of the Wesleyan revival.

ACTS 3:1–26

Original Meaning

The Lame Man Healed (3:1–10). The story begins during one of the daily visits (2:46) that Christians made to the temple (3:1). This visit was about three in the afternoon, one of the Jewish times of prayer (the other two being nine in the morning and noon). As was common at entrances to places of worship, a man crippled from birth was begging at the temple gate called Beautiful (v. 2).

Following his plea for money, "Peter looked straight at him, as did John" (v. 4). The addition of John's name in verse 4, where it is almost an afterthought, may indicate that, though Peter was the prominent member of the team, John had an important role. Luke seems to alternate between the mention of both Peter and John and of Peter alone in this chapter. Peter's memorable words to the beggar (v. 6) indicate that they were in touch with the power of Jesus.

Peter's Speech (3:11–26). The exuberant response of the healed cripple gives prominence to the miracle, and that in turn becomes a launching pad for Peter's speech. Many features typical of evangelistic speeches to Jews in Acts appear here. A new feature is Peter's serious effort to deflect glory from himself and John. He asks why the people are staring at them (v. 12). Peter then refers to "the God of Abraham, Isaac and Jacob" (v. 13a)—a description relevant to his Jewish audience. The miracle is presented as glorifying the one they "handed . . . over to be killed" and "disowned" (vv. 13b–14).

Peter makes significant christological statements in this speech. As at Pentecost, the "name" of Jesus receives emphasis; Acts 3–4 have eight references to it. The speech begins and ends with the expression of Jesus as God's "servant" (vv. 13, 26). This directs us back to the messianic servant of Yahweh in Isaiah 42–53.

The death of Christ is again given as a fulfillment of prophecy (v. 18), and again God is said to have raised up Jesus, with the apostles being witnesses of it (v. 15). Jesus is the one appointed or designated as their Messiah (v. 20; cf. 2:36). This reminds us of Romans 1:4. The resurrection was something like an ordination of Christ, when he was confirmed on earth for who he really is.

Peter refers to the fulfillment of Old Testament promises when he says that times of refreshment will come as a result of their repentance (v. 19). This was part of the Jewish hope. But Peter clarifies that this will come only when God sends the Messiah following their repentance and cleansing (v. 20). This anticipates the second coming of Christ. Thus, while the messianic age has dawned, it has not yet been consummated. In the present age, "heaven must receive him" (v. 21a; cf. 2:33–35), but only until the time of the final restoration promised by the prophets (3:21b). The noun used here (*apokatastasis*, "restoration") is from the same root as the verb in the disciples' question about God's restoring the kingdom to Israel (*apokathistanō*, 1:6).

Jesus extends that restoration from Israel to all things, but it will happen at the end of time when God will be "all in all" (1 Cor 15:28). We can assume that these are all parts of Jesus's teaching about the kingdom and that they were included in Paul's teaching about the kingdom (Acts 19:8; 20:24; 28:31). Thus, we find two points of eschatology in this evangelistic sermon. On the positive side is the promise of the restoration of all things (3:19–21); on the negative side is the threat that those who do not listen to Jesus will be completely cut off (v. 23).

The use of the second-person plural "you" here is significant. At the start of his speech Peter clearly places responsibility for the death of Christ on his audience (vv. 13–14). In the middle of his speech, he gets conciliatory by saying that he knows they "acted in ignorance" (v. 17). He ends his speech on a positive note, reminding them that they are "heirs of the prophets and of the covenant" (v. 25) and that God's servant was sent first to bless them via repentance (v. 26). Just prior to that, however, he issues a strong warning about those who do not listen being cut off (v. 23). This warning is in the third person because it becomes real only if they reject the message. This message, then, is not an abstract and detached discourse on the Christian gospel. It is an urgent plea that pulsates with the need for personal response.

Peter cites many blessings to the audience. He reminds them of the promise of universal blessedness made to Abraham (v. 25). As Isaiah promised before (Isa 43:25), their sins will "be wiped out" (Acts 3:19). One of the blessings of Christ's resurrection is that people will be turned from their wicked ways (v. 26). This is in keeping with the many promises of the Old Testament regarding the new covenant, where God himself will give people the ability to keep the law (Jer 31:31–34; Ezek 11:19; 36:26–27). Repentance and forgiveness will also result in "times of refreshing" (Acts 3:19). We have already seen the blessings to come in connection with Christ's consummating history (v. 21).

Application. The value of team ministry today cannot be overstressed. Recently we have seen clergy with prominent ministries fall into serious sin. Many have noted that they did not have any group to which they were accountable. The pitfalls of a traveling ministry are well-known. Traveling ministers often stay in hotels, which cater to the sexual gratification of traveling businessmen. After a tiring day of ministry, when we are emotionally and spiritually drained and have no strength for serious activity like studying or writing, it is easy to watch something unclean on TV in the privacy of the hotel room. No one knows about it. But several such incidents can leave us seriously polluted and vulnerable to more serious sin.

Some prominent ministers never travel alone, though not all of us can afford this luxury. Even then, it would be good for us to ensure that we have the backing of a team. If traveling, perhaps you might send out a prayer letter to a few prayer warriors before your trip so that they will pray for you at every stage of your journey. Request prayer for personal purity. On your return, report to your colleagues on how you fared, especially in your TV watching.

Ideally we should be staying in homes, which will help us identify with the people among whom we are ministering. This was how it was done in the early church (see discussion on 9:43). In Bible times the inns were likewise morally and hygienically unclean. I have also found it personally helpful to ask for a roommate who will effectively be my teammate when I am doing high-pressure ministry, such as Bible expositions at a large conference.

ACTS 4:1–22

Original Meaning

Peter and John Arrested (4:1–4). The word for "people" (*laos*) appears five times in a generally positive light just before and after Peter's temple speech. As in the case of Jesus (Luke 19:47–48; 20:19; 21:38; 22:2), the popularity of the church with the people prevented the authorities from taking action against it. But soon, as with Jesus, the tide changed, so that by the time of Stephen's death the people also seem to have turned against the church.

Peter is seized by the priests (possibly the chief priests, who were all Sadducees), the captain of the temple guard (a powerful person who commanded the temple police force), and the Sadducees. They were particularly disturbed about the message of the resurrection (v. 2). To say that Christ rose would buttress the Pharisees' teaching regarding the resurrection, which the Sadducees rejected. They are deeply concerned, for "many who heard the message believed; so the number of men who believed grew to about five thousand" (v. 4). This growth is phenomenal, considering that women and children are not included in this accounting.

Before the Sanhedrin (4:5–12). The next day Peter and John are brought before the Sanhedrin (v. 7). Annas, who was actually the senior ex-high priest, and his son-in-law Caiaphas, the reigning high priest, had participated in the trial of Jesus some weeks before, but their hopes of getting rid of Jesus were short-lived. In a typical question that authorities ask when their position is threatened, they demand to know the source of the apostles' "power" and "name" (i.e., authority, v. 7).

Though the disciples are technically on the defensive, they switch to an attacking position in their response to the Sanhedrin's question (v. 10). Then Peter cites Psalm 118:22, which became a favorite text in the early church (v. 11). Then comes a proclamation of the absolute uniqueness of Christ as the only means of salvation (v. 12). Peter is referring here to a broader meaning than simple deliverance from sickness. He is talking about a change of status from being rebels to being accepted among God's people.

Warned and Discharged (4:13–22). The members of the Sanhedrin are "astonished" at the courage of Peter and John, for they are "unschooled, ordinary men" (v. 13a). Though Peter and John are professionally unqualified, they are boldly conducting their own defense with great eloquence before this august assembly. The Sanhedrin already knows that these men have been with Jesus. But this performance reminds them afresh how they have been influenced by Jesus, who also "taught . . . as one who had authority" (Mark 1:22). The apostles have a boldness that comes from confidence about their message and empowerment by the Spirit.

After ordering Peter and John to leave the Sanhedrin, the Jewish leaders discuss the dilemma they are in (v. 16; cf. v. 21). The only thing they can do is to command Peter and John "not to speak or teach at all in the name of Jesus" (v. 18). The two apostles reply that they must obey God (vv. 19–20).

Loyalty to God and the nature of the message combine to give compelling reasons to disobey the command of the Sanhedrin. Such is the dilemma of the Sanhedrin that even so bold a proclamation of defiance cannot bring about a punishment. All they can do is to threaten the apostles further and release them (v. 21).

Application. In the Bible numbers are important because they represent people for whom Christ died. This approach to numbers stands in contrast with the triumphalist approach. Yet if we are concerned primarily about *numbers*, we may be tempted to use wrong means to win people. We may lower our standards by watering down the gospel, not doing proper follow-through care, or not insisting on holiness. We may add unbiblical features to our gospel or indulge in sheep-stealing, evangelistic bribery, or manipulation. Living in such an environment, we may be tempted to accept such means as acceptable to make our churches grow numerically.

But when we use such methods, we can easily end up with fat but unhealthy churches. This is a danger in the megachurches of today. Some churches wisely have a policy of dividing and starting a daughter church the moment they get to a certain size, in order to maintain the family atmosphere that is essential to Christian fellowship. Effective megachurches must have numerous small groups, which are the real local churches where true Christian fellowship and accountability are practiced.

ACTS 4:23–31

Original Meaning

Praying Together (4:23–24a). The immediate response is to pray (v. 24). Though only one prayer is given, Luke says, "They raised their voices together." It was a common practice in biblical times to express assent by saying "amen." Deuteronomy 27:15–26 gives a recitation of the Levites, which elicited twelve "amens"—one after each affirmation. Quietly saying something like "amen" or "yes, Lord" helps a person to concentrate better and participate more fully in the prayer of someone else.

The word translated "together" is one of Luke's favorite words, *homothymadon*. The word indicates a unity among the Christians as they prayed.

Affirming God's Sovereignty (4:24b–28). The content of the prayer shows the wisdom of the translation "sovereign Lord" (v. 24b). When this title is put together with the Christians' affirmation that God is Creator, we see that his sovereignty over creation is being proclaimed. The implication is that the one who created the world is more powerful than those whom he created. Therefore, nothing can thwart his plans.

The prayer goes on to assert how God's sovereignty has been revealed in history. First comes a quotation from Psalm 2:1–2 about the power of those who are opposed to God (vv. 25–26). Verse 26 continues with the theme of opposition to God by presenting the general principle that throughout history, the powers of this world have stood against the cause of God and of Christ. Verse 27 cites the death of Christ as a specific application of this principle.

Verses 24–26 are saturated with Scripture. This is typical of many spontaneous prayers in the Bible. Scripture had been stored in the minds and hearts of biblical people, ready to be harnessed in times of need.

Two Requests (4:29–30). After the extended reflection on God's sovereignty, these believers give only one passing reference to their problem (v. 29)! The request they make is not for wisdom, protection, or favor with the authorities. All these are appropriate petitions, of course. But this prayer is for the ability to be obedient to Christ's command to them to preach the gospel.

The second request of the disciples is that God will show his power (v. 30). It is significant that the only two requests in this prayer have to do with evangelism, which has just been outlawed! These people have a consuming passion for evangelism, and the only practical things that come to mind in this time of crisis are related to fulfilling the evangelistic task.

God's Response to the Prayer (4:31). In the Old Testament the shaking of a place (v. 31) was a sign for a theophany—that is, a manifestation of God in a visible form (Exod 19:18; Isa 6:4). It was God's way of indicating that he was present there and would answer the prayer. Next, "they were all filled with the Holy Spirit." This is not a fresh baptism but a fresh filling. This is another instance in Acts where filling does not describe the characteristic of a person, but a special anointing. As in most of these cases, the result of the filling is proclamation. Thus, it is not surprising to find verse 31 ending with the announcement that the believers "spoke the word of God boldly."

Application. When we are under attack, it is easy to get discouraged and to lose our boldness and compromise by not being totally obedient to our call. It is also easy to act rashly, creating unnecessary problems to the cause of the gospel. The strength of community helps overcome these temptations.

It is therefore important that workers under threat or facing opposition be undergirded by companions in Christ. When we share our situation with our support group, we can unburden ourselves to them. How sharing clears the air! It helps us to look at problems rationally. When we keep it to ourselves, we can become so overwhelmed by the emotional influences of the situation that we cannot think straight about the problems.

When we are together with our support group, we can spend time praying together. The significance of partnership in a crisis is not only the strength that we give each other; being together also causes us to motivate each other to seek God, who is the source of our strength.

ACTS 4:32–35

Original Meaning. For a second time Luke describes the quality of the radical sharing that the first Christian community practiced (see 2:44–45). This time he describes it in greater detail. The fact that he mentions this issue twice suggests we should regard it with some importance.

Luke first presents what was at the heart of the practice of sharing—a deep unity (v. 32a). In the Gospels the disciples often quarreled among each other and had to be corrected by Jesus (Luke 9:46–47; 22:24–27), but in Acts the Twelve are a unified group (2:14; 5:29; 6:2–4), and this unity now spreads to the entire church. This is often the case that when the leaders are united; it helps the members to be united too.

"One in heart and mind" (*kardia kai psychē mia*) describes a comprehensive unity (v. 32). What joined them was not simply a common affiliation to the church. There was a spiritual unity and a unity of passionate commitment to a mission. Therefore, right in the middle of this description of unity we find the witness of the apostles (v. 33). Community life is never an end in itself; a vibrant community is a community in mission.

Included in this unity was the sharing of possessions among the believers. They did not consider their possessions as their own (v. 32b). This sharing extended to material possessions. As a result, "there were no needy persons among them" (v. 34a). But for that to happen, some costly sacrifices had to be made by some believers who sold their lands and houses (vv. 34b–35).

This practice of selling land and giving it to the church has been called Christian communism. But it is different to communism in two ways. First, it was an entirely voluntary renunciation of wealth. Unlike communism and the Qumran community of the first century, the sharing of property was not legislated. Second, private ownership continued in the church. Acts 12:12 mentions the house of Mary the mother of John Mark. Earlier we were told that people met in each other's homes for meals (2:46). Thus, what is mentioned here is not a renunciation of all private property by everyone in the church.

There are five verbs in the imperfect tense in 4:34–35. The imperfect describes continuous action in the past. In other words, this selling of land is something that took place regularly. The NIV rendering ("from time to time") attempts to express this idea (v. 34). In other words, whenever there was a need, those who owned land asked themselves whether the Lord wanted them to sell this land. Some did and then gave the proceeds to the leaders to distribute wherever there was a need.

These were probably not easy decisions to make. But some did make them, and the result was the elimination of poverty in the church.

Application. While being one in heart and mind is considered the usual model for Christian community life, it is not easy to maintain in today's individualistic society. We do not like having anyone pry into our personal lives, which would be necessary if the model shown in Acts were to be followed. For this reason, many have lowered their standards and settled for a functional unity that comes more from secular management studies than from God's word. People agree to work according to a plan, even though they may not be "one in heart and mind" with it. But can we jettison this biblical model so easily? Given the fact that there are so many commands to this model of unity, we should not be satisfied by lowering our standards.

This is an area where the church needs to be countercultural. In a society where people deny the community orientation that is part of human nature in order to protect their privacy, close Christian community life may be one of the most important prophetic messages we can give the world. No one can deny one's essential humanity without sooner or later feeling a void inside. The church must present itself as the group that can adequately fill this thirst for community in the heart of the human being.

ACTS 4:36–5:11

Original Meaning

The Generosity of Barnabas (4:36–37). After describing the spirit of sharing in the church (4:32–35), Luke gives good and bad examples of this sharing. Joseph, a man from Cyprus, was given the nickname Barnabas, translated in the NIV as "son of encouragement" (v. 36). The exact meaning of Barnabas, however, is not easy to arrive at. It seems to mean "son of prophecy" (*bar* means "son of" and *nabi* means "prophet"). The NIV translates the Greek word *paraklēsis* as "encouragement," a word that can mean encouragement but also consolation or exhortation. Perhaps we should translate Luke's definition as "son of exhortation."

Being a Levite from Cyprus, Barnabas was from the large groups of Hellenistic Jews who migrated back to Jerusalem. He must have been from a wealthy background, for the mother of his cousin Mark had a house large enough to accommodate a prayer meeting for "many people" (12:12).

The Deception of Ananias and Sapphira (5:1–11). The bad example of sharing is that of Ananias and Sapphira, who sold their property but kept back some of the money for themselves (5:1–2). "Kept back" (*nosphizō*) literally means pilfer, embezzle. The LXX uses this word for Achan (Josh 7:1). Wrong use of our possessions is a serious sin in God's sight.

Five important truths emerge from Peter's words to Ananias in 5:3. First, Satan had so filled and controlled Ananias's heart that he was carried away in his actions. Second, Satan's activity does not remove culpability from Ananias. Verse 3 attributes the act to Satan's infilling, but verse 4 places responsibility for his action squarely on Ananias. Third, the most serious thing Ananias did was to lie to the Holy Spirit, not keep back part of the money. Later Peter said that he could have done whatever he wanted with his money (v. 4). Fourth, when we lie to the church, we lie to the Holy Spirit. Saul/Paul finds out later that when he persecuted the church, he was persecuting Jesus (9:4). Later he expresses the treasured teaching that the church is the body of Christ (1 Cor 12:27; Eph 4:12; 5:23). Finally, since giving everything was not mandatory (v. 4), the particular desire that Satan had filled Ananias and Sapphira with was the desire for recognition by the church. They lied to win the same sort of esteem that Barnabas had won in the church.

Ananias first and then Sapphira fell down dead following Peter's forthright condemnation (vv. 5, 10). One can imagine how surprised the bystanders must have been as they saw Peter, probably not a rich man, rebuking the rich giver of a large contribution. But whoever the person and however big the gift, sin is sin, and it has to be dealt with decisively.

The result of the death of Ananias is that "great fear seized all who heard what had happened" (v. 5b). Luke repeats this affirmation at the end of the story (v. 11). In other words, the fear resulting from judgment is a key aspect of the story. This was a fear of displeasing God that comes from a knowledge of his holiness and the consequences of sin.

Application. If a survey were taken about all the possessions-related preaching from evangelical pulpits today, we may find more teaching on the promise of wealth than on the dangers of wealth. That goes against the entire tenor of the New Testament. Certainly, the Old Testament contains teachings about the promise of wealth. The biblical attitude is for the righteous to regard their wealth as a blessing from God, provided, among other reasons, for their enjoyment (1 Tim 6:17).

Yet both the Old and New Testaments contain numerous warnings about the dangers of wealth and advice on how to use wealth responsibly and charitably. That should be the primary emphasis in Christian teaching about wealth.

One of the best ways to avoid the pitfalls relating to possessions is to have people to whom we can be accountable about our use of money. It is wise for us to share with our accountability partners even significant personal gifts we have received. They can be a check to us that will help us avoid the snares of materialism and deception that are always looming near to us.

Most of the recent funds-related scandals in the church could have been avoided if those involved had been completely open to a responsible person about their income and use of funds.

ACTS 5:12–42

Original Meaning

Continuing Power (5:12–16). The fear that came on the people as a result of the deaths of Ananias and Sapphira (v. 11) did not reduce the evangelistic effectiveness of the apostles. They continued to minister in the miraculous (v. 12) and to reap an evangelistic harvest (v. 14). Their ministry in the miraculous intensified (vv. 15–16). The sick stayed out on the streets just to have Peter's shadow fall on them, and people were coming from neighboring towns as well. This is the nearest we have in the Bible to a modern-day healing campaign. Luke may be suggesting that the intensifying of signs and wonders indicated God's approval of the painful act of purifying the church in 5:1–11.

The emphasis on miracles, however, did not result in a situation where the gospel was cheapened and large numbers came into the church only for miracles. The church did not lower its standards in order to win the lost.

The Apostles Arrested, Tried, and Beaten (5:17–40). It is unsurprising that, with such spectacular ministry by the apostles, the Jewish leaders "were filled with jealousy" (v. 17). The success of the apostles upset the peace that reigned in the community as these leaders lost their power and control over the people. They had to respond with a corresponding show of power. As often happens, they used political power to attack the church rather than spiritual power (v. 18). Yet their plans are foiled through an angelic rescue (v. 19).

Angels appear often in Acts, giving directions (8:26; 10:3) or words of encouragement (27:23), delivering God's people from prison (5:19; 12:7–11), and judging the wicked (12:23). Here the angel not only delivers the apostles from prison but also encourages them in fulfilling their call by giving a fresh commission (v. 20).

In instances of threat and danger in Acts, the key word from God concerns boldness in witness (4:29–31; 18:9–11; 23:11). Three times in this passage the evangelistic ministry of the apostles is described with the verb "teach" (*didaskō*, vv. 21, 25, 28). There must have been a major emphasis on the content—the truth—of the gospel. Truth is communicated through what the Bible describes as preaching and teaching.

In the meantime, the meeting of "the full assembly of the elders of Israel" (i.e., the Sanhedrin) is ready to begin, but the prisoners are missing (vv. 21–23). The puzzled officials are then informed that they "are standing in the temple courts teaching the people" (vv. 24–25). The captain of the temple guard himself goes to rearrest them. It is ironic that those who probably had wanted to stone the apostles for blasphemy are now afraid that they themselves will be stoned by the people. Consequently, "they did not use force" (v. 26b). This time all the apostles are brought before the Sanhedrin to be questioned by the high priest (v. 27). They are accused of disobeying the orders to stop teaching and of making the Jewish hierarchy "guilty of this man's blood" (v. 28). It is possible that they said this because they were fearing a popular uprising.

"Peter and the other apostles" (v. 29) reply to the Sanhedrin. The Christian community is solidly unified. Peter's opening statement about obeying "God rather than human beings" (v. 29) is reminiscent of his closing statement during his previous trial (4:19–20); he is willing to die rather than disobey his Lord. Later he will say that the Holy Spirit is "given to those who obey him" (5:32). His obedience gives him a credibility that qualifies him later on to write to the church about obedience (see 1 Pet 1:2, 14, 22; 3:1, 6; 4:17).

The response given to the Sanhedrin is recorded in summary form here. Once again the apostles do not give what would be expected of a defense at a trial. Rather, they witness to the facts of the gospel (vv. 30–32). The apostolic proclamation is even more clearly explained here than in Acts 4.

- As always, Peter gives an introduction arising from the particular situation (v. 29). The apostles are responding to the question of the high priest about their defiance of his order not to teach in the name of Jesus (v. 28).
- Next the facts of Christ are presented, beginning with, "The God of our ancestors raised Jesus from the dead" (v. 30a). The words "from the dead" have been added by the NIV translators, though this may not be the intended meaning. The expression "the God of our ancestors" reminds the hearers of the great acts of God in Israel's history. Peter may be proclaiming that God has raised up Jesus as the Messiah, just as he had raised up other deliverers throughout Israel's history.
- Then comes a reference to Jesus's death: "Whom you killed by hanging him on a cross" (v. 30b; cf. 10:39). The idea of hanging on a cross probably alludes to Deuteronomy 21:23, which pronounces a curse for one who hangs on a tree. The early Christians applied this text to the death of Jesus. By the time Peter wrote his first letter he had developed the theological significance of the tree more fully (1 Pet 2:24). Paul developed this theme further (Gal 3:13; cf. Acts 13:29). Before Jewish audiences (for whom the cross is a scandal), the apostles typically did not hide Jesus's death but presented it as a triumph of God planned long ago.
- If 5:30a does not refer to the resurrection, then the resurrection is not mentioned in Luke's summary of this

speech. It is, however, implied in Peter's next statement about Jesus's exaltation (v. 31). How important the exaltation was to early Christian preaching (2:33–35; 3:20–21; 4:11), and how strange is our comparative neglect of this theme in our preaching!

- Next comes the offer of salvation. As a result of Jesus's exaltation, not only forgiveness but also repentance is given by Christ (v. 31b). Repentance is triggered through the hearing of the gospel, which brings the conviction of sin. But this act is not done by our own efforts; the grace to repent is given by Christ (v. 31b). Though Calvinists and Arminians may differ over the possibility of resisting the saving grace of God, they will agree, if they seek to be biblical, that the ability to respond to grace is a gift from God.
- Peter then buttresses his points about Christ by claiming, "We are witnesses of these things" (v. 32a). This is unique to the apostles. But as we noted in our study of the sermon in Acts 2, we, too, can have the same confidence of the apostles if the facts recorded in the New Testament about Christ and his resurrection are historically true. We believe that there is sufficient evidence for that claim.
- Finally, Peter insists that the Holy Spirit is also a witness and that he has been given to those who are obedient (v. 32b). In other words, the Spirit's witness is made through believers.

The fury and wish for capital punishment of the Sanhedrin (v. 33) is tempered by the comments of Gamaliel (vv. 34–40). He was the greatest teacher of his era and was considered the embodiment of Pharisaism. The apostles' miracles and escape from prison presumably made him suspect that God might indeed be blessing this new movement. He therefore advocates caution and restraint. He is confident that God will sovereignly show in history whether this movement is of him or not. Gamaliel feared that by opposing it, they may be opposing God himself (vv. 38–39). This advice persuades the Sanhedrin to drop their intentions of capital punishment, but it does not prevent a sound flogging of the apostles (v. 40).

After the Beating (5:41–42). Incredibly, the apostles rejoice over their flogging, because "they had been counted worthy of suffering disgrace for the Name" (v. 41). This is an oxymoron: the disgrace was an indicator of their worth, so they felt honored by the dishonor! We see here a new dimension in the exposition on suffering, a major subtheme of Acts: to suffer for Christ is an honor that causes joy.

Our passage closes with the report of the incessant witness of the church (v. 42). Since this report of incessant evangelistic activity comes immediately after the report of the beating that the apostles received, it seems as if Luke wants to point out that, far from reducing evangelism, the beating resulted in increased evangelistic intensity.

Application. Some have argued that presenting unpleasant truths of the gospel to an unbeliever can be deferred until the follow-through process; we must win a hearing first and only present these truths later. There is some truth in this, for even the evangelists in Acts started their proclamation with some common ground that the people generally agreed with—some point of contact. But before we ask people to accept the gospel, they need to know those aspects of the essential gospel that may be unpleasant to them. Otherwise they may feel cheated that they were not shown the fine print before they entered into a covenant with God. The holiness of God and his hatred of sin are important aspects of the gospel, and they cannot be eliminated from the basic message. As our passage shows, the Jerusalem church exhibited both the awesome holiness of God—which provoked fear among outsiders—and the power of God, which made the gospel attractive to outsiders.

The results of preaching the gospel without the holiness of God in recent times have been tragic. We see people who claim to have had a born-again experience but who continue in the sins of their past life. For example, reports of a prominent publisher of pornography publicly claiming to be born again did not give up producing pornography. We cannot, of course, automatically blame the church for this. But the fact that people living such flagrant lives of public sin can even claim to be born again may indicate that something is wrong in the understanding of being born again that the church is projecting to the world.

The most common objection to the Christian faith among the Buddhists in Sri Lanka is that we have a cheap religion. Christians, they say, can live any life of impurity and then receive forgiveness and happily go back to their impure life. That some famous preachers have done just that and that our newspapers have given those stories wide coverage have not helped.

The reason why evangelicals have been slow to battle exploitation and prejudice can in part be traced to a neglect of the holiness of God and its implications in our evangelistic preaching. We ask people to come to Christ to receive forgiveness of sins, but we do not ask them to repent of social sins such as prejudice against race, class, caste, and gender. Nor do we ask them to repent of sins of injustice, such as exploiting employees. We do not like to talk about personal sins like lying and greed. As a result, people accept a Christianity that is neutral on such matters. They enter into the fellowship of the church and become identified as Christians, even though they continue to do things that bring disrepute to the name of Christ. We are seeing this in countries torn by ethnic or religious strife, where many supposedly devout Christians express attitudes toward those of the other side that are decidedly contrary to the teachings of Jesus Christ.

Clearly in Acts the emphasis on God's holiness and its implications did not hinder the evangelistic effectiveness of the early church. Billy Graham stated at one point that when he started preaching about the lordship of Christ, many felt that less people would respond to the appeal to commit their lives to Christ. But he did not find that to be so. If anything, there was an increase in the proportion of people who responded to the invitation.

On the matter of God's power, when groups lose the experience of that power, they have only their identification with the people as a means of attracting them to Christ. As a result, they lower their standards and do not insist on holiness, claiming that this is necessary if they are to attract people. But the ministry of Jesus and of the early church show that we do not have to become sinners to attract sinners. Jesus paid the price of such identification, for he was accused of being a sinner himself because he moved so closely among them. But he never lowered his principles.

Today we are seeing a strange phenomenon in the church: people are expressing the power of God in their ministries through healing and other manifestations of miraculous gifts while living ungodly lives. How can this be? A tentative answer is to conclude that ministry gifts can become part of our personality and can express themselves for some time even after we have strayed personally from God. In an analogous manner, we have seen this with the gift of preaching, where gifted people who fell into serious sin still showed their giftedness for a time after their fall. But they cannot go on with this deception for long. Soon the fruit of a spiritually dry experience will become evident in their preaching.

ACTS 6:1–7

Original Meaning

The Problem (6:1). Jewish society had a system to help needy widows. Probably the isolation that resulted when these people became Christians made these sources less accessible to them. Grecian widows were particularly needy, as they were not native Judeans and did not have relatives to care for them. Many older couples came to die in Jerusalem so that they could be buried there.

Almost certainly the Grecian widows were not deliberately discriminated against. The cause of the problem was the increase in the number of disciples (v. 1a). In an active and expanding movement it is possible for less prominent people not to be noticed. But that is still wrong.

Problems among different ethnic and cultural groups have been common in the church. This contributed to the complaining that took place in the church. The word translated "complained" (*gongysmos*) is an unpleasant word, used in the LXX for the murmuring of the Jews against Moses in the desert (Exod 16:7). The church was now in danger of splitting. The problem might aggravate if it was not handled sensitively.

The Solution (6:2–6). The apostles did not focus attention on the complaining attitude toward the leadership. Nor did they talk about the priority of the spiritual and the relative unimportance of earthly food, as some may have done. There was a genuine problem, and the best way to quell doubts about prejudice was to solve the problem first. Thus, the apostles made an administrative decision. Thereby they not only averted a serious crisis of disunity, but also led the church to take a significant leap forward in terms of organizational structure. Though Luke does not use the word *deacon* here to describe the Seven, this decision laid the foundation for the diaconal order, which, while taking different forms in the history of the church, has rendered great service in mediating Christ's love to needy people.

The procedure adopted in choosing the Seven is instructive. The complaint came from the Grecians, "so the Twelve gathered all the disciples together" (v. 2). The entire group was given the task of choosing seven officials (v. 3). The apostles insisted that their own main task was to concentrate on "the ministry of the word of God" (v. 2; v. 4 adds "prayer"). Therefore, seven people had to be chosen to oversee the work of distributing food (vv. 2–3).

The apostles laid down qualifications for these men: they are to be known to be "full of the Spirit and wisdom" (v. 3a). We do not know how these seven were selected. Once the choice was made, the apostles said, "We will turn this responsibility over to them" (v. 3b).

"This proposal pleased the whole group" (v. 5), and they chose seven men, all of whom have Greek names. This does not necessarily mean that they were all Hellenists. Yet we know for sure that Nicolas was a Hellenist, since he was a "convert to Judaism"; Stephen was one too, for his ministry was in a Hellenistic synagogue (6:9).

The disciples then "presented these men to the apostles, who prayed and laid their hands on them" (v. 6). There we see the beginnings of church leaders laying hands on believers and commissioning them for specific tasks. The church has, over time, developed various orders of worship for such functions and given them names, such as commissioning, ordination, and induction services.

The Outcome (6:7). Luke is eager to show that this administrative change did not reduce the evangelistic fervor of the church.

So he adds another of his reports of evangelistic effectiveness (v. 7). The book of Acts is like a long hymn interspersed with refrains like this, which report on the spread of the church. Luke wants us to catch the spirit of this consuming passion for evangelism.

Application. Some leaders try to sweep problems like those faced in Acts 6 under the rug because they do not want to face the humiliation that comes if such problems surface. Others attempt to force a unity through exercises of worship or external affirmations of unity, like picnics and hugs. Others are overcome by hurt in that, despite their good intentions and hard work, people attribute bad motives to them. Still others may feel offended by the attitude of the grumblers and focus on that attitude without solving the root of the problem. Such delays in dealing with problems usually aggravate situations and open the door for mighty explosions, which result in major church splits.

Christ's teaching on unity problems is clear (Matt 5:23–24). Regardless of whether we think this brother or sister is justified to be angry with us and whether he or she has been honorable in their actions or not, we must go to him or her immediately. So urgent is the issue that we should hold back at the altar a gift we have come to give.

The church in many countries finds itself in places of ethnic turmoil, where its members are from both ethnic groups in the conflict. Often Christians do not talk about their problems with people of the other race; they keep their prejudices and complaints to themselves and discuss them only with people of their own group. Perhaps they are polite when they meet those of the other group, but there is an undercurrent of anger, which occasionally surfaces. When we act in this way, we cease to be a healing community in our lands. Christians must constantly be on the alert to the danger of unchristian prejudices reappearing in the church and deal with them decisively when they arise. We know that God is bigger than the problem and that what unites us is deeper than what divides us. Therefore, we must have the courage to face up to the problem squarely.

ACTS 6:8–7:53

Original Meaning

The Man Stephen (6:8–10). Stephen must have been an outstanding person because Luke mentions six features of his character and ministry in 6:5–10. First, he was "a man full of faith" (v. 5). This was a key requirement for one who blazed new trails for the gospel. Many opposed him. Probably even people within the church would have preferred for him to take a more cautious approach. But Stephen saw certain implications in what the Bible taught and what Christ did, and he was willing to risk all for the truth of those implications.

Second, he was "full . . . of the Holy Spirit" (v. 5). This need not have been mentioned since all of the Seven had to be filled with the Spirit (v. 3). Possibly there were some, like Stephen and Barnabas (11:24), who so exhibited the power of the Spirit that when people observed them they were struck by this fact, and it is thus given special mention. Acts 6:8a confirms this by saying Stephen was "a man full of God's . . . power." This feature manifested itself as he "performed great wonders and signs among the people" (v. 8b).

Third, he was "a man full of God's grace" (v. 8). Since this phrase comes just before the external manifestation of God's power, we can assume that it refers to the way God was manifested internally. Stephen had let God's grace impact him so much that it had made him a gracious person. Stephen was able to act in a Christlike way under provocation.

Fourth, the opponents who debated Stephen were "members of the Synagogue of the Freedmen" (v. 9). They came from four places: Cyrene and Alexandria, cities in upper Africa, and Cilicia and Asia, provinces in Asia Minor. The most important town in Cilicia was Tarsus, Paul's hometown. Did Paul (Saul) worship in this synagogue? We cannot be sure, but we know that he was involved in Stephen's death. This was clearly a Hellenist synagogue and may be the one to which Stephen himself once belonged.

The last two features of Stephen's character relate to his preaching: "They could not stand up against the wisdom the Spirit gave him as he spoke" (v. 10). "Wisdom" (*sophia*) appears only four times in Acts (6:3, 10; 7:10, 22). It was an inspired wisdom in that the Spirit gave Stephen the words to speak, in keeping with the promise of Christ (Luke 21:15). Then finally we also see this wisdom in Stephen's speech in that it is saturated in Scripture and applies Scripture skillfully to the challenges arising from the gospel. Speaking out of the Jewish worldview, using Jewish Scripture, and inspired by the Spirit, Stephen speaks in a way that cuts to the heart of their thinking, and his opponents cannot answer him.

Stephen Charged (6:11–15). After failing to silence Stephen through debate, the Jews try to silence him through the law. They persuade certain people to make accusations against him (v. 11), which allows them to take him to the Sanhedrin (v. 12) with this charge: He "never stops speaking against this holy place and against the law" (v. 13). This is elaborated with a claim that he said that Jesus "will destroy this place and change the customs Moses handed down to us" (v. 14). The Sanhedrin observes that Stephen's "face was like the face of an angel" (v. 15).

Stephen's Speech (7:1–53). Stephen argues his points from Israel's history as recorded in the Jewish Scriptures, the Old Testament. He stresses three major themes.

The activity of God is not confined to the geographical land of Israel. God spoke to Abraham in Mesopotamia (vv. 2–3) and Haran (v. 4; NIV "Harran"). He blessed Joseph in Egypt (vv. 9–16). He spoke to Moses in the desert near Sinai during the incident of the burning bush (vv. 30–34). He performed wonders and signs in Egypt, the Red Sea, and the desert (v. 36), and he also gave his people the law at Mount Sinai (v. 38).

Worship acceptable to God is not confined to the Jerusalem temple. The burning bush was holy ground, and Moses had to remove his sandals there (v. 33). Moses encountered God in Mount Sinai and was given living words (v. 38). The tabernacle was a suitable place of worship for the people of Israel (vv. 44–46). The Jewish Scriptures testify that God does not dwell in houses made by human beings (vv. 48–50).

The Jews have constantly rejected God's representatives. Joseph was rejected by the patriarchs (v. 9). Moses was rejected when he tried to intervene in a quarrel between two Jews (vv. 26–29), and yet this Moses was sent as Israel's deliverer (v. 35). The message of Moses they rejected and instead erected a golden calf (vv. 39–43). Stephen climaxes his message in vigorous language by claiming that Israelite history is a history of rejection (vv. 51–53). It is possible that Stephen has to end his talk abruptly at this point because his audience has become so restive.

There is little about Jesus and a lot about Moses in this speech. This is understandable since the charge against Stephen is about his rejecting Moses's teachings (6:11, 14). Stephen points to one significant thing that Moses said to the Israelites about Jesus (7:37). The other two references to Jesus are both in verse 52.

Stephen's final words of accusation (vv. 51–53) may make us wonder what has happened to his angelic face. After all, when we think of an angel, we think of a sweet, gentle person who has no place for wrath and judgment. This idea, however, does not come from Scripture, for some of the angels in the Bible are agents of judgment. Stephen is like Christ here. Though Jesus radiated the love of God as no one else did, he also expressed God's wrath against hypocrisy and sham, especially in his denunciation of the Pharisees (Matt 23:13–23).

The ministry of Stephen helped blaze new trails for the gospel. He opened the door theologically for the world mission of the church. We do not know whether he himself realized this, but he freed the Christian faith from the temple and therefore from Judaism. A short time later the church concluded that one does not have to be Jewish first in order to be Christian. Though Stephen ended his life an apparent failure, though he did not live to see the fruit of his theologizing, God revealed later that his ministry had borne great fruit. The trail he blazed was later followed by Paul—the one who approved of his death (8:1) and kept the clothes of those who stoned him (7:58), but who later became the apostle to the gentiles. Stephen is also considered the precursor of the later Christian apologists, especially those who defended the faith against Judaism.

Application. The call to be winsome radicals, like Stephen, is an important challenge facing Christians today. If we are faithful to God, we are sure to face anger and opposition from within and outside the church. We will be treated unjustly, and many will attribute unworthy motives to what we do. Our true worth will not be recognized, and perhaps we too will end our lives as Stephen did—as apparent failures. How can we remain winsome under such circumstances?

To be sure, many radicals are anything but winsome. They are cynical and angry people, whose worthwhile messages may go unheeded because of their disagreeable disposition. Cynicism can reach epidemic proportions in the church as a reaction to the predominance of appearance (looking good) that leaves room for hypocrisy (appearance without substance) to thrive.

Stephen's life shows us how to maintain winsomeness in a hostile world. He was "a man full of God's grace" (6:8). Whatever people may do to us, however severe their sins against us may be, we must be able to affirm the supremacy of grace—that God's grace "superabounds" (literal translation of *hyperperisseuō* in Rom 5:20 and *hyperpleonazō* in 1 Tim 1:14) over all sins and situations. We must affirm the principle that God will work good through what we have experienced because we "love him" and "have been called according to his purpose" (Rom 8:28). We must be able to say, as Joseph said to his brothers who had treated him so badly, "You intended to harm me, but God intended it for good to accomplish what is now being done, the saving of many lives" (Gen 50:20). We will need to battle in the presence of God, as the psalmist did (Ps 73), until we know that he has comforted us and that the vision of superabounding grace has overcome our bitterness. Then, having tasted of the comforting grace of God, we will be able to minister this grace to others (2 Cor 1:3–7).

Stephen clearly achieved his winsomeness through his contact with God. Evidence of this intimate relationship abounds in Acts 6–7. His communion with God seemed to deepen as the viciousness of the opposition deepened. When he was brought to trial, so close was his tie with God that his face looked like that of an angel (6:15). When he is then described as being filled with the Spirit, he had a vision of Christ and began to say the same things that Jesus said at his death (7:56, 59–60).

The key to maintaining winsomeness under pressure is maintaining our relationship with God, as Stephen did. We must develop the discipline of seeking God and his beautiful face first (Ps 27:4) whenever we are attacked, so that we can always operate out of an experience of grace. Then grace will make us gracious, and we will become winsome and faithful witnesses for Christ. Millions of Christians, by not waging a war against bitterness, have missed out on the opportunities to radiate God's grace through winsomeness and charm.

With this winsomeness Stephen had the face of an angel and expressed God's wrath against sin. Sometimes we hear people say, "He's such a saint, he never gets angry." This is because we have come to value an understanding of tolerance that is far from the biblical lifestyle. True, in the past we may have seen uptight religious people who were unpleasant to be around because they were always ranting and raving against evil. Nothing pleasant came from their lips. We must surely avoid this extreme, but we must also avoid the opposite extreme.

Our failure at times to get angry over wrong may be a reflection of our fallenness rather than our godliness. We may sin against children and colleagues by not expressing anger concerning things in their lives that dishonor God. When we do not show anger with our children when they sin, we may be opening the door for serious insecurity in their lives. Unconsciously we may be sending them the message that their sinful actions are not serious enough to merit an appropriate response. That in turn communicates the idea that they are not significant enough to be taken seriously. Many such children grow up to be delinquents, and through their wrong deeds try to grab the attention they were deprived of in their childhood.

ACTS 7:54–8:4

Original Meaning

Stephen's Vision (7:54–56). With his accusation against the Jewish people (7:51–53), Stephen brings his speech to an (abrupt?) end. Predictably, the reaction is bitter (v. 54). Yet the next verse starts with one of the many glorious "buts" found in the Bible, signaling a change in the direction or tone of events. The Greek literally says of Stephen, "But being filled with the Holy Spirit . . ." (v. 55a). Stephen had been filled with the Holy Spirit throughout his Christian life, and this fullness did not leave him at his time of crisis.

Stephen's vision is filled with deep significance. At his time of shame and apparent defeat, he "saw the glory of God" (v. 55b). He also saw Jesus and exclaimed, "Look . . . I see heaven open and the Son of Man standing at the right hand of God" (v. 56). This is the only New Testament occurrence of the title "the Son of Man" outside the Gospels. Stephen's statement reminds us of a similar statement made by Jesus to the same court only a few months before. For that Jesus was adjudged guilty of blasphemy and worthy of death (Mark 14:61–64).

Now Stephen is, as it were, challenging that judgment by affirming that Jesus is indeed the glorious Christ and is now at the right hand of God. The Sanhedrin had no choice but to condemn Stephen also, unless they were willing to say they were wrong about their verdict on Jesus. This vision must have given Stephen courage.

Why is Jesus *standing* and not seated, as the other Scriptures declare (v. 55)? As Stephen is rejected by earthly courts, he finds Jesus acting as his advocate and testifying on his behalf. But Jesus is also the judge, whose judgment alone matters from the eternal perspective. Therefore, there is nothing to fear. Rejection by his own people, the Jews, would have been hard to bear, but acceptance by that greatest of Jews, great David's greater Son, more than compensates for the pain.

Stephen's Death (7:57–60). With dramatic crispness Luke describes how the angry audience acts in haste to put Stephen to death. When they add these words about the vision of Jesus to his damaging statements about the temple, they have no choice but to kill him for blasphemy—just as they had killed Jesus. Their covering of their ears (v. 57) must have been a characteristic response to blasphemy. Stephen is dragged out of the city for stoning (v. 58a; cf. Lev 24:14). Luke mentions Saul at this point (v. 58b), in keeping with his habit of introducing major characters of his book in a narrative before they come into prominence (cf. 4:36–37; 6:5).

Stephen's last words are surprisingly close to two of the last words of Jesus just before he died. He asks God to receive his spirit (v. 59; cf. Luke 23:46) and not to "hold this sin against" his killers (v. 60; cf. Luke 23:34). Only Luke mentions the two parallel statements of Christ. Presumably he wants his readers to note the similarity.

The Church Scattered (8:1–4). The death of Stephen gives a new impetus to the anti-Christian forces with which Saul is now prominently associated. A great persecution arose that day (v. 1).

Stephen was buried and mourned over by "godly men" (v. 2). The language used for mourning suggests loud and deep mourning. It is comforting to find that in a culture where an honorable burial was a much-valued feature, the first Christian martyr received such a burial.

Acts keeps unfolding its deep theology on the subtheme of suffering as the book proceeds. God is not dormant; he actually feels the pain that Saul inflicts (see 9:4). For the moment, Luke gives us a glimpse of the victory that God is going to win out of this seeming tragedy (8:4). Perhaps Luke is conscious of a new dispersion coming into being.

With the benefit of hindsight, Luke sees great significance in these events. In fact, when he describes the preaching of the gospel to gentiles for the first time outside Palestine, he says that the ones who did this were "those who had been scattered by the persecution that broke out when Stephen was killed"

(11:19). Luke deliberately associates Stephen and the persecution with this important development in the church.

Application. Stephen's experience of a special anointing with the Spirit's fullness amid suffering challenges many prevalent notions of that fullness. We usually relate that fullness to some ministry activity, such as preaching, healing, or prophesying, or to an ecstatic personal spiritual experience, such as speaking in tongues. While that is certainly valid, we must not forget that the Spirit's fullness is also given to prepare us for suffering, which is such an important part of the life of obedience. God is powerfully at work both when the sun shines brightly and when the dark clouds loom over us.

We must, therefore, develop a theology of the fullness of the Spirit in the darkness. Such a teaching is not easy to grasp in this sensual, hedonistic world, which is afraid of suffering and does so much to avoid it. Yet the Bible tells us to anticipate suffering rather than avoid it. If we have a theology of the fullness of the Spirit in the darkness, we will eagerly seek the blessings we know God will give us through the darkness.

The Spirit's fullness in the darkness is so important for our spiritual health that God permits us to go through dark times in order that he can fill us afresh. Many preachers will testify that some of their best experiences of the freedom of the Spirit in preaching came during times of deep pain in their lives. I have personally found that before a major assignment that I know will be a drain on me spiritually (such as speaking at a large conference), I often first encounter some major crises. I have now come to recognize these as God's gifts to draw me nearer to him. Struggling with such crisis increases my dependence on him, which is a key to opening me to an experience of God's fullness.

The vision of God's glory and Christ's exaltation must have done much to encourage Stephen. Rejection by one's own people is always incredibly hard to face. But when we realize that God is on the throne and that he is for us, we can find courage and even joy amid our pain.

In our pain we will wonder whether it is worth suffering for the gospel. At such times we ought to fix "our eyes on Jesus, the pioneer and perfecter of our faith. For the joy set before him he endured the cross, scorning its shame, and sat down at the right hand of the throne of God" (Heb 12:2). With such a vision we can run with perseverance the race that is set before us, refusing to give up when the going gets tough and divesting ourselves of unnecessary earthly weights that so easily entangle us (12:1).

ACTS 8:5–25

Original Meaning

Samaritans Receive the Spirit (8:5–17). Among the scattered witnesses from Jerusalem was Philip, who went to Samaria (v. 5); we are not told which city. The Samaritans were awaiting a future deliverer in keeping with the promise of Deuteronomy 18:15–19 about the coming of a prophet like Moses (cf. the Samaritan woman in John 4:25). Philip seems to have built on this hope when he preached the Messiah there.

Verse 6 establishes a direct link between the miracles and the fact that the Samaritans "all paid close attention to what [Philip] said." Signs served to enhance the preaching of the word as the more important element in evangelism.

Philip "proclaimed the good news" (v. 12). The two expressions "the kingdom of God" and "the name of Jesus" (or expressions similar to them) are used often in Acts as a summary of the gospel. "Great joy" resulted from Philip's ministry (v. 8), though we are not told the exact reason for the joy. Was it the result of conversion or of so many people being healed?

Luke then introduces Simon the sorcerer (vv. 9–11). He was amazed by what he saw in Philip's ministry, and he too "believed and was baptized" (v. 13). As the story proceeds, however, it becomes apparent that his belief was superficial.

Peter and John are sent from Jerusalem to check out what has happened in Samaria (v. 14). It is a situation where a second-generation leader is doing the work that Jesus and the apostles have been doing, and the role of the apostles shifts from initiation to verification. After their prayer, the Spirit descends on the Samaritans (v. 17). We are not told how Peter and John knew that the Holy Spirit had come on the Samaritans. There must have been some external manifestation, such as speaking in tongues, that gave unmistakable evidence.

Regardless of what biblical theology we derive about the reception of the Holy Spirit, this section contains another important truth: it is providential that through the ministry of leaders from the Jerusalem church the Samaritans received the Spirit. It helped maintain the unity of the early church.

Simon's Misplaced Religion (8:18–24). Simon is attracted by what happened through laying on of hands by the apostles. He is not interested in his own receiving the Spirit; what he wants was the ability to lay hands on people with similar results. His offer of money for this ability evokes a strong response from Peter (v. 20). Peter's point is that this is a gift that God gives sovereignly; humans cannot manipulate him into giving us what we desire. That is what happens in Simon's magic kingdom, not in God's righteous kingdom.

Peter tells Simon that he has "no part or share in this ministry" (v. 21). The word translated "ministry" is *logos* and thus may mean gospel (literally "word"). Peter views Simon as still being unregenerate. The important thing, says Peter, is to have one's heart right before God.

After calling Simon to repent, Peter explains his condition to him (v. 23). The word "bitterness" (literally "gall of bitterness") comes from Deuteronomy 29:18. Peter may be referring to the potential that Simon has of causing much damage to the church—which, according to later tradition, is what happened. If so, Peter's statement reflects his desire to rid the church of this evil influence.

Simon is a good example of misplaced religion. He believed and was baptized, but it was obviously an inadequate belief. He sought God's power without any apparent interest in developing a relationship with God.

The Apostles Evangelize in Samaria (8:25). The story ends with Peter and John "preaching the gospel in many Samaritan villages" on their return journey to Jerusalem (v. 25). The lead taken by the junior person, Philip, is followed by the senior leaders. It is heartening to see the same John, who had earlier asked Jesus whether to call down fire on some Samaritan villages (Luke 9:51–55), now preaching the gospel to them.

Application. The example of Peter and John in not only accepting but also learning from and following the lead given by Philip is a challenge to all leaders today. There is a lot of talk today about passing the baton to a new generation of leaders. Pioneer leaders are sometimes reluctant to do this. Actually, passing the baton is not something that happens when a leader comes close to retirement age. It is the result of an attitude that is cultivated early in one's leadership—the willingness to learn, especially from younger, creative people.

After giving new ideas and trailblazing efforts due consideration, those that are valid should not only be approved but also encouraged. Sometimes we as older leaders ignore or delay looking at new efforts. We may be busy with existing programs, we find the new effort too different from what we are used to, or we feel threatened by the drive of the young initiators. The result is that creative leaders lose their motivation, become angry rebels, or just leave.

True, we should not naively accept every new idea that comes along. Examining a new work, as Peter and John do in this story, is important. This ensures that errors are avoided and helps bring the benefit of mature wisdom to the young person's plan. Such analysis also can become a source of encouragement to the young person. If we simply hand over responsibility to younger leaders and do not offer our assistance, they may soon be discouraged, for they will face problems along the way that could have been eased by the input of mature people.

Many groups flounder after their first-generation leadership ages because they have not cultivated creative, younger leadership. They have depended so much on the pioneer leaders and their creative energies that they have not prepared for the next stage of the movement. Younger leaders should do their pioneering while benefiting from the wisdom and encouragement of the older leaders. In the early church the pioneer leaders regarded innovative advances from a new generation of leaders as important. Therefore, not only did they encourage them, but they also learned from them and followed the lead they gave.

ACTS 8:26–40

Original Meaning. The story of the conversion of the Ethiopian eunuch occupies about the same amount of space as the story of Philip's ministry in Samaria (8:5–25). There is no unanimity about where the evangelist was when the angel of the Lord asked him to go south to a desert road (southwest of Jerusalem, v. 26). Was he still in Samaria, which is north of Jerusalem and therefore far away from that road? Was he in Jerusalem? Or had he by now settled in Caesarea, where he went after this episode and where we find him many years later (21:8)? We cannot be sure. In this vividly written piece Luke is uninterested in specifics of geography. Rather, he wants to show how God directly led Philip to do something significant.

Philip immediately obeyed this somewhat strange command. And the God of surprises shocked him with the appearance of an Ethiopian. He is called a "eunuch" (*eunouchos*, v. 27), but there is disagreement among scholars as to whether he was literally a eunuch, for this word was used also for trusted workers of a royal court. If he was a eunuch, he may have been restricted from full participation in the worship of the Jerusalem temple, for Deuteronomy 23:1 prohibits castrated people from entering the assembly. Isaiah 56:4–5, however, promises an everlasting name within the walls of God's temple for faithful eunuchs. What we know for sure is that he was a high official—something like the finance minister—in Ethiopia.

"Ethiopia" (Cush in the Old Testament) corresponds to what is known as ancient Nubia. It encompassed parts of what is now southern Egypt and northern Sudan. In ancient literature the Ethiopians were considered as living in the ends of the earth. In other words, with the gospel going to the Samaritans and then to the Ethiopian, it was going to the last two geographical spheres of the Great Commission as given in Acts 1:8. Luke does not mention the religious background of the Ethiopian. He had come to the Jerusalem temple to worship and had a copy of Isaiah with him—not something easy to obtain in those days. This suggests that he may have been a God-fearer or a proselyte.

Only the most well-to-do had chariots in those days, but the Ethiopian was in one, reading from the prophet Isaiah (v. 28). Considering the high standing of this official, it would have required some boldness for Philip to obey the Spirit's command to go to the chariot (v. 29). Since people almost always read aloud in those days, Philip heard him reading—and reading one of the favorite messianic passages of the early church. Philip's question about whether the eunuch understood what he was reading got the response he needed to share the good news with him (vv. 30b–31).

The passage the eunuch was reading was from Isaiah 53:7–8 and talks of the unjust humiliation and sufferings of the Lord's servant (Acts 8:32–33). His question about the identity of this servant becomes a launching pad for Philip (vv. 34–35). The Ethiopian must have had with him the rest of Isaiah 53 also, where the substitutionary nature of Jesus's death is presented. Matthew and John specifically apply Isaiah 53 to Jesus's healing ministry, whereas Luke presents Isaiah 53 as being fulfilled in the sufferings of Jesus. In the church these passages became important messianic texts because Jesus had applied these texts to himself.

It is the Ethiopian who suggests baptism when they come to some water (v. 36). Philip may have discussed baptism with the Ethiopian, or he may have already known about it because it was the initiatory rite for gentiles who converted to Judaism. Philip takes another bold step in baptizing the eunuch (v. 38). Considering all the signs of divine leading he had received, Philip must have been convinced of the genuineness of this conversion, even though not long before he had baptized Simon, whose professed conversion turned out to be fake. Thus, just a few moments after the eunuch's decision for Christ, Philip baptizes him.

Philip is then taken away suddenly by the Spirit of the Lord. But the newfound joy of the Ethiopian cannot be dampened by his disappearance (v. 39). Philip next appears in Azotus, some twenty miles north of Gaza, and continues traveling north, preaching incessantly until he reaches Caesarea (v. 40). It is there that we find him again about twenty years later, now the father of four unmarried prophetesses (21:8–9). Luke, who probably visited him on this occasion, describes him as "Philip the evangelist" (21:8)—a most appropriate title for one who was so mightily used in evangelism.

Application. Because the primary work of those called to be evangelists is with people outside the church, Christians may not recognize their value and not give them the support they need. I know of many evangelists who spend far too much time trying to raise their support. It would be much better to have local churches commission evangelists to go where God leads them. The churches can then give them the backing and accountability they need. An interdenominational evangelist may find it more appropriate to work outside the confines of one local church. Such people should have a good group to back them. Evangelists especially need support because evangelism is a spiritually draining work and because Satan is active to trip them, seeing that they are directly invading his territory.

ACTS 9:1–31

Original Meaning

Saul's Vehemence (9:1–2). Saul's later friend and partner, Luke, uses strong language to express the vehemence with which Saul persecuted Christians (v. 1), but that is something Saul himself did in his own descriptions of his pre-Christian behavior (see 26:11; Gal 1:13). The root of this was his zeal (Phil 3:6), especially his zeal for the traditions of his fathers (Gal 1:14). The idea of a crucified Messiah was an impossibility according to Saul's thinking.

The Sadducees were, according to Josephus, more heartless in their judgments than the Pharisees, and it may not have been natural for a loyal Pharisee like Paul to go and request letters from the Sadducean high priest (Acts 9:2). This is an indication of the extremes he was willing to go in attempting to stamp out this menace.

Saul left for Damascus. Damascus was an old city with a long history of being controlled by different national powers. Tens of thousands of Jews lived there, and it had several synagogues (cf. Luke's "synagogues" in v. 2).

The Last Post-Resurrection Appearance (9:3–9). As Saul approaches Damascus, he hears a voice and sees a bright light. The light Saul sees (v. 3) must have been strong, for it is around noon when he encounters it (22:6; 26:13). It would have reminded him of the glory of God in the Old Testament. Saul must have realized that he was in the presence of the Lord God.

The voice from heaven asks a simple question (v. 4). While Saul was hitting the church, Jesus has actually been feeling the pain. Paul later expounds in depth about the church as the body of Christ (1 Cor 12; Eph 3–5).

Saul had been coming to Damascus "to arrest all who call on your name" (cf. Acts 9:14). In the Old Testament "calling on the name" is a standard description of prayer to God. He had heard Stephen call on the "Lord Jesus" as he was dying (7:59). All this was blasphemy to Saul, and it had to be stopped. Now as he is on his way to do just that, he is jolted into the realization that Jesus is indeed alive.

Saul was spiritually blinded by wrong convictions until a greater light caused him to become spiritually enlightened, though physically blinded. The evidence is suddenly now too overwhelming. He has to accept "the Way."

This passage records the last of the post-resurrection appearances of Jesus. Paul calls this a "vision" in 26:19, but it is more than a typical vision, for his companions also see the light (22:9) and hear the sound (9:7). In his list of post-resurrection appearances Paul says, "and last of all he appeared to me also, as to one abnormally born" (1 Cor 15:8). By placing it alongside the other post-resurrection appearances, Paul says that it was as objective an appearance as those recorded in the Gospels.

Paul later describes his having seen the risen Christ as part of his qualification for apostleship (1 Cor 9:1), along with his receiving a specific commission from Christ; both these elements are met through the Damascus experience.

In Damascus the blinded Saul follows the most intense type of fast, spending three days without eating or drinking (v. 9). People engaged in such fasts only if they were repenting or seeking God's face. Both are involved here (cf. v. 11, where Ananias is told Paul is praying).

Ananias's Ministry to Paul (9:10–19a). Ananias was a wise choice to help Saul (22:12). As with Peter and Cornelius (10:1–23), God's arrangements are confirmed by a double vision (9:10, 12). Visions occur often in Acts when God intervenes to direct the church into some new thing.

"Straight Street" (v. 11) is still identifiable today. Saul is described to Ananias as "a man from Tarsus" (v. 11), which Paul later describes as "no ordinary city" (21:39). Tarsus was the principal city of Cilicia, the most southeasterly part of Asia Minor (in present-day southern Turkey). It was a city of great culture.

Ananias's protest is understandable, considering all that Saul had done to the "holy people in Jerusalem" and had been planning to do in Damascus (vv. 13–14). But his willingness to obey immediately, after the Lord's explanation (vv. 15–16), is commendable. So is his magnanimous act of "placing his hands on Saul" and addressing him as "brother Saul" (v. 17). According to the Lord's description to Ananias of his plans for Saul, the latter will go to "the Gentiles," "their kings," and "the people of Israel" (v. 15).

Right at the start of his spiritual pilgrimage, Saul is informed that he will suffer for the name of Jesus (v. 16). Suffering is a basic aspect of following Christ. But before Paul experiences this cross, he will experience Christ's power: Ananias says that he has come so that Paul "may see again and be filled with the Holy Spirit" (v. 17). Though there is no record that he was filled with the Spirit, we have no reason to doubt that this happened.

Early Attempts at Ministry (9:19b–25). At once Saul launches out on a preaching ministry in the synagogues of Damascus (v. 20). Later he wrote that new converts should not be leaders in the church (1 Tim 3:6), but the fact that he preached did not mean he was a leader. Besides, unlike most new converts, Saul was already well versed in the Scriptures.

Verse 23 finds Saul in Damascus "after many days had gone by." His trip to Arabia and his return to Damascus (see Gal 1:17) must have occurred during this time—probably doing both meditating and preaching. He spent almost three years in Arabia. Arabia was ruled by the Nabateans at the time, and Damascus may have been either part of it or bordering it. Predictably, opposition arose, and the persecutor Saul becomes the persecuted—with the Jews conspiring to kill him (vv. 23–24). Saul had to make an unceremonious exit from Damascus in a basket (v. 25).

Finally to Jerusalem (9:26–30). In Galatians 1 Paul makes much of the fact that he did not go to Jerusalem until three years after his conversion. This fact was evidence that he had received his commission as an apostle directly from Christ, not from Christian leaders in the holy city. It must have been an emotionally stirring time for Saul as he returned to the city he loved, where he had grown up, and where he had been such an eminent success. He could assume his former associates would shun him. But how difficult it must have been for him to find that when he tried to join the disciples, "they were all afraid of him" (Acts 9:26).

Another of the great "buts" of Acts introduces God's solution to the problem, as Barnabas takes him, not just to the disciples, but to the apostles themselves (v. 27). Paul spent fifteen days with Peter (Gal 1:18). Saul would have been filled in on many of the details regarding the life and words of Christ.

Saul gets busy in Jerusalem, "speaking boldly" and debating for the Lord (Acts 9:28–29). But the Jews try to kill him, and he makes a hasty exit to Caesarea en route to his birthplace, Tarsus. He next appears in Acts several years later, still in Tarsus (11:25).

The Church Remains Healthy (9:31). This section ends with the report of a healthy church (v. 31). We note that, though there is no specific record in Acts of any ministry in Galilee, there was a church there. This is to be expected, considering how many followers Jesus had in Galilee. The church now enjoyed a time of relative calm, which is true of most evangelistic communities that face persecution: there are periods of respite from serious opposition. The numerical growth of the church continued, for there is never a respite from the work of evangelism.

Application. Our task as witnesses is to lead people to Jesus so that they will encounter him as their Savior and Lord. We may discuss religion, argue for the truth of it, and seek to persuade people about its relevance and power. But the end that we aim at is to introduce people to Jesus. This is why it is advisable to help those who are ready to accept the Christian way to pray a prayer of seeking salvation. We may have them repeat words after us. However we do it, our aim is to lead them in this encounter with Christ to talk personally to him.

We must never take it for granted that all to whom we minister have a personal relationship with God. My mother led me to such an encounter when I was a religious fourteen-year-old, who was already knowledgeable of the Scriptures and active in church. When I was in seminary, a fellow student who had been nurtured in an evangelical background testified in class that he had encountered Christ for the first time a few days before. The Emmanuel Methodist Church in Madras, India, was finding it difficult to maintain its property because it had a small congregation. They were preparing to sell some of the property when someone suggested to the pastor, an American missionary, to have some revival meetings in the church. He invited a Baptist preacher, very different to him in theology and outlook, to preach at these meetings. On the first night when that preacher invited those who wanted to be born again to come forward, the first one to go up was the pastor of the church! He met Christ personally, and his ministry was so transformed that the church became and still is, a few decades after his retirement, one of the great centers of Christian witness in India.

ACTS 9:32–43

Original Meaning. Peter's visit to "the Lord's people" (*hagioi*) around Palestine indicates that he had a pastoral role throughout the church (v. 32). We can imagine him teaching, encouraging, correcting, and counseling the believers and leaders on these visits. *Hagios* (literally "holy person"; one of Paul's, though not Luke's, favorite words for Christians) appears three times in chapter 9 (four times total in Acts: 9:13, 32, 41; 26:10). The New Testament always uses the word for a group rather than for an individual believer. It is not a designation given to a special class of people, so that the emphasis is not on saintly character, as it became in later centuries.

Among the many healings performed through Peter's ministry, Luke mentions two here—those of Aeneas and Tabitha. Aeneas was from Lydda (vv. 32–33), twenty-five miles northwest of Jerusalem, and Tabitha was from Joppa (v. 36), thirty-five miles northwest of Jerusalem. Joppa was the seaport of Jerusalem (modern Jaffa, a suburb of Tel-Aviv). Aeneas had been relatively inactive for eight years because he was a paralytic (v. 33), whereas Tabitha had been extremely active in the service of the needy (v. 36).

With both healings, Peter clearly places the emphasis on Christ as the healer. The first time he says, "Jesus Christ heals you" (v. 34); the second time, before speaking, "he got down on his knees and prayed" (v. 40). After Aeneas's healing we are told that "all those who lived in Lydda and Sharon saw him and turned to the Lord" (v. 35). After Tabitha's healing Luke says that "many people believed in the Lord" (v. 42). We do not know whether Aeneas was a Christian, but Tabitha certainly was; this fact indicates that miracles in the church were performed not only on unbelievers but also on believers.

Tabitha, who "was always doing good and helping the poor" (v. 36b), had died. Great haste was needed in bringing the message to the apostle Peter and in getting him to come to Joppa from Lydda (a distance of ten miles). A body was normally buried before sundown on the day of death. But Peter made this journey on foot right away to help the lady who had helped so many presumably insignificant people. Upon arrival, he was confronted by a moving scene of widows weeping and showing things that Tabitha had made for them (v. 39). Peter, who was there when Jesus had raised Jairus's daughter, followed some of his procedures here (v. 40; cf. Mark 5:40).

Peter stayed on in Joppa in the house of Simon the tanner (v. 43). It was a demeaning trade in Jewish eyes, for strictly speaking, tanners were ceremonially unclean since they handled dead animals. A tanner's shop had to be on the outskirts of town because of the bad odor that came from it; Simon's home was by the sea (see 10:6).

In this whole passage there is no record of any preaching, though it must have been done. The focus is on service. In the next chapter Luke will refer to Cornelius's acts of charity (10:2).

Application. There is considerable controversy in the church today about whether, when someone is sick, we should have special people like Peter pray over him or her. Obviously, this practice is endorsed in Scripture. Yet I have heard people say, "Why should you go to special people? Don't we all pray to the same God? Why not just go to the people in your own church?"

I believe that we should go first to our own local church (cf. Jas 5:14–15). If we choose to go to someone else, our church should know about it. It is unfortunate that some church leaders get angry when their members go outside for help, so that it has to be done secretly. This did not seem to have happened with the leaders in Joppa when Peter was called. The fact remains that although all church leaders should pray with their sick, some have gifts of healing and/or faith that enables them to pray in faith that results in healing and glory to God (1 Cor 12:9).

I have personally prayed with countless sick people over the years. Perhaps there have been some (unspectacular) healings along the way. But I have friends who are able to pray with a faith that I do not have. One of these friends is an illiterate person, whose only way to study personally the Scriptures is to meditate on what he has heard because he cannot read. But when he prays there is great faith, and God answers his prayers wonderfully. We have come to recognize that he has the gift of healing.

We should beware of what may be called "panic praying," where people go from place to place seeking special prayers.

That may be an expression of our lack of faith in the sovereign will of God. I know of people who cannot settle down to any abiding Christian service because they keep going from one prayer meeting to another, seeking prayer for their problems. There are times when we may find that the answer we hope for is not forthcoming. On such occasions we will need to adopt the attitude of Paul, who, after pleading three times for release from his thorn in the flesh, was told to depend on the sufficient grace of God that perfects strength in weakness. Instead of panicking, Paul gladly boasted about his weakness (2 Cor 12:9).

At such times we should affirm that the answer we want has not come because God has something better in store for us (Rom 8:28). God does not have to answer our prayers in the precise way as we ask. Sometimes he may have a better plan that will take us through what may look like a disaster. Though we cannot understand what we are going through, we can remain at peace, for we trust God and know that he will do what is best for us.

Perhaps a word should be said about the possibility of raising the dead today. There have been reports of this happening in different parts of the world today. I met a missionary working with a tribal group in India who told me that among this group in the past few years, there have been seven cases of bringing dead people back to life. When someone among them dies, the believers pray for about three-and-one-half hours after his or her death. After that, if the person has not come back to life, the elders give the signal to prepare the corpse for burial.

ACTS 10:1–33

Original Meaning

Scene One: Cornelius's Vision (10:1–8). Cornelius lived in Caesarea (v. 1), a seaport on the Mediterranean coast that was rebuilt by Herod the Great and named after Caesar Augustus. It was the center of the Roman administration of the province of Palestine and even had a temple dedicated to Caesar. The Jews hated Caesarea. The population there had more gentiles than Jews.

Cornelius was a centurion, which means that he was nominally in command of a hundred Roman soldiers. Centurions generally appear in a positive light in the New Testament (Matt 8:10). It was a centurion who said at the cross, "Surely he was the Son of God!" (Matt 27:54).

Cornelius "and all his family were devout and God-fearing" (v. 2). There is some debate today about the meaning of the designation "God-fearer." It is usually held that God-fearers were those who attended the synagogue and honored Jewish laws and customs but had not been incorporated into the Jewish community through circumcision. But the view that "devout" and "God-fearing" may not have been strict technical terms is becoming more accepted now.

Cornelius had a vision at about three in the afternoon (v. 3). This was one of the three traditional Jewish times of prayer, and Cornelius later tells Peter that he was praying at the time (v. 30). Here we have another occurrence in Acts of direction through a vision and through the action of an angel. Luke uses a strong word (*emphobos*) to describe Cornelius's reaction of fear (v. 4). Often in biblical instances of human contact with the spirit world, godly people responded with fear, and God gave them words of reassurance.

The angel tells Cornelius to summon Peter from Joppa (vv. 5–6). His message says nothing about what will happen as a result of his coming. The mention of Peter's staying in the house of Simon the tanner may have come as a surprise to Cornelius, as this was not a highly esteemed trade. Despite the lack of details, Cornelius obeys immediately (vv. 7–8).

Scene Two: Peter's Vision (10:9–16). Peter, the one to whom the keys of the kingdom were given (Matt 16:19), is again chosen to open another important door for the gospel—as he did with the Jews on the day of Pentecost and with the Samaritans a short while later. We find him in Joppa, where he will disregard his prejudices, obey God by traveling to Caesarea, and open the door for gentiles to respond to the gospel—the very thing that Jonah resisted in the same city (Jonah 1:3). He goes to the roof of the house he is staying at around noon to pray (v. 9, not one of the prescribed Jewish times for prayer).

Peter receives a vision, given at a time when he was hungry (v. 10). The entire animal world is symbolized, and clean and unclean animals are included. Peter receives a command to kill and eat (v. 13), which would be unacceptable for him as a Jew, as some of the animals were not kosher. His answer (v. 14) contains a contradiction: he makes a categorical refusal to obey one whom he calls "Lord" (*kyrios*).

The answer Peter receives clearly brings God into the picture (v. 15). The adjective and verb translated "impure" (*koinos*, *koinoō*, literally "common") appear five times in Acts 10–11. Later, Peter's disciple Mark, after reporting on the discourse of Jesus on clean and unclean objects (Mark 7:5–23), would make an editorial comment stating, "In saying this, Jesus declared all foods 'clean'" (Mark 7:19b). Perhaps this vision recorded here in Acts 10 helped Peter understand the implications of that earlier discourse of Jesus. The impact of the vision on Peter is heightened in the present passage by its repetition two more times (v. 16). Peter will soon realize that he may not consider any group of people common or unclean either (v. 28).

Scene Three: Peter Meets the Messengers (10:17–23a). Cornelius's messengers stop at Simon's gate (v. 17), and the Holy Spirit instructs Peter to go with the men (vv. 19–20). While we are told that the Spirit spoke to Peter, we must note that Peter was in a fit state to receive a communication from God. Luke says he was "wondering about the meaning of the vision" (v. 17) and "thinking about the vision" (v. 19). While God led Peter clearly, he was earnestly seeking to find God's will. Peter's bold step of inviting "the men into the house to be his guests" (v. 23a) introduces an important emphasis in this passage, that of hospitality.

Scene Four: Peter and Cornelius Meet (10:23b–33). In keeping with the regular practice in the early church, Peter takes some brothers rather than go on this assignment alone (v. 23b). Cornelius seems to have been certain about the time Peter would come (four days after he saw the vision, v. 30), for Peter finds "a large gathering of people" at the house (v. 27). Cornelius shows great humility for a centurion (v. 25). But Peter will have none of this, as such reverence is reserved only for God (v. 26). Such acts of reverence to respected people were not unusual in those days. But Peter will not risk anything that might suggest that he is accepting the type of respect that is due to God alone.

Peter's discovery, as he explains to his audience, is the pivotal message of this whole passage (v. 28). A big shift has taken place in Peter's thinking, for he now realizes that no longer are the typical Jewish distinctions among people significant. They have been rendered void once and for all. In this episode Jew and gentile have come together. Rarely does an evangelist find as receptive an audience as Peter found here (v. 33). The stage is set to move to the next scene: the proclamation of the gospel.

Application. That Peter needed a drastic message from God to get rid of his prejudices about distinctions among people suggests that even mature Christian leaders may occasionally need a major paradigm shift in order to come into line with God's thinking. Peter's initial response to the command in the vision (v. 14) is typical. But to such thinking comes God's message: "Do not call anything impure that God has made clean" (v. 15).

The particular person whom God asked Peter to meet was a top official of the army of occupation in the hated city of Caesarea. Often even Christians find such people difficult to accept. Prejudice is often one of the last things that is touched by the process of sanctification.

Often Christians have not wanted to break the barriers of caste, class, and race because it is inconvenient to do so. Sometimes believers do not bring up these issues, fearing that doing so will affect the evangelistic effectiveness of the church. At other times it seems advantageous to treat those different from them as inferior. Some Christians thought that it would spell national economic ruin to accept slaves as equals in the British Empire and then in North America. Even today, some think it will bring shame to them if their children marry outside race, class, or caste. Once some Christian parents in Sri Lanka were upset when a youth ministry took their children to minister in what they considered outcast villages. The evangelical church in particular has a bad record in the areas of prejudice and condoning race, caste, and class distinctions. Muslims are now exploiting this by proclaiming the brotherhood of Islam as an alternative to the prejudice of Christians. And Islam is growing with converts from Christianity among peoples who were once treated as inferior by other Christians.

It is beyond the scope of this section to detail how we can remedy this problem in the church. I will only list a few essential things we must do if we are to rid the church of this terrible malady of prejudice. First, we must help people understand the nature of Christian identity, which does not depend on human distinctions. When people realize that they are accepted as significant and useful to the kingdom, not because of any merit of their own but only because of the mercy of God, they also realize that they cannot look down on anyone.

Second, we must teach and preach the biblical truths that combat prejudice regularly in our churches. Many so-called Bible-believing churches do not do this. This allows Christians to imbibe sinful attitudes from their environment without being told such attitudes are wrong.

Third, we must listen to the heart of those on the other side of an issue that divides people. Because this can be a painful exercise, Christians often keep feelings to themselves that deeply affect them.

Next, we must confront prejudice when it appears in church and society and condemn it with holy zeal, as Paul did when Peter gave in to prejudice in Antioch (Gal 2:11–13). This can be difficult, for vested interests are often touched in such situations. It also can earn us the reputation of being traitors to our own people.

Finally, we must stand up for and pay the price of helping people of the "other" group. This, too, can be costly in terms of reputation and convenience. But it helps heal wounds within people who have been hurt.

ACTS 10:34–11:18

Original Meaning

Scene Five: Peter's Speech (10:34–43). Verse 34 begins with words that literally mean, "And opening his mouth ..." This phrase is sometimes used to introduce a weighty utterance (cf. 8:35; Matt 5:2) and is appropriate here since Peter will announce the great discovery that he has made. Peter's first phrase implies his surprise at realizing that "God does not show favoritism but accepts from every nation the one who fears him and does what is right" (vv. 34–35). Jesus had already implied that he was bringing salvation to the gentiles (John 10:16;

12:32). But it took a special revelation before the full implications of these truths would be understood and practiced.

Peter introduces his message as containing "good news of peace through Jesus Christ" (v. 36). Peace was the content of God's basic promise to the Jews in the Old Testament. But by describing Jesus as "Lord of all," Peter extends this blessing to gentiles also.

Peter's speech here is the only evangelistic message in Acts where a summary of the ministry of Jesus is given (vv. 37–39a). In verse 38 Peter clearly attempts to show his audience that Jesus's ministry was accredited by God. These words remind one of Isaiah 61:1, which Luke cites Jesus as quoting when he began his ministry (Luke 4:14–22). As in Luke's Gospel (Luke 4:18–19), the good deeds and miracles of Jesus are associated with his anointing by the Holy Spirit.

After pointing out that the apostles were witnesses to what happened in the ministry of Christ (v. 39a), Peter presents the death and resurrection of Jesus (vv. 39b–40). That death is described in typical fashion. Peter implicates the opponents of Christ and implies the curse of hanging on a tree (v. 39).

A unique feature of Peter's sermon is the point that Jesus even ate and drank with the apostles after his resurrection (v. 41). Luke's Gospel is the only one that records this fact (Luke 24:41–43). As in the speeches in Acts 2–3, Peter uses arguments to demonstrate the validity of the Christian gospel. The New Testament evangelists were both heralds of the good news and apologists.

Next Peter speaks of the commission the apostles received to proclaim Christ (v. 42). *Preaching* shows that evangelism is a confident proclamation of important news; *testifying* points to the solemnity of the task—it is a matter of judgment and salvation—and to the fact that this is something that we have experienced and know to be true. Peter presents Jesus "as judge of the living and the dead" (v. 42). Judgment is an essential part of the evangelistic message.

In verse 43 Peter gives the scriptural authentication of the person and work of Christ. This statement implies that Peter's audience will receive the forgiveness of sins if they respond by believing in Jesus.

Scene Six: Gentiles Receive the Holy Spirit (10:44–48). Nowhere else in Acts does the Spirit come before baptism. It was accompanied by "speaking in tongues and praising God" (v. 46). Despite all the leading that God had given up to this point, Jewish believers are astonished that these gentiles have received the Holy Spirit (v. 45). With such unmistakable evidence that these gentiles have indeed been converted, Peter does not hesitate to baptize them immediately (vv. 47–48). This points to the role that experience plays in discerning God's ways. As we will see, it is not the only criterion for deciding what is true, but it is one contributing factor in the decision-making process.

With his scruples about table fellowship with gentiles overcome, Peter seems to have accepted Cornelius's invitation for him to stay a few days (v. 48). This gives time for the news of what Peter has done to travel to Jerusalem before he arrives there. The consternation of the Christians there must have been immense because not only had their leader baptized gentiles, but he was also having continuous table fellowship with them.

Scene Seven: The Jewish Christians Approve (11:1–18). A revolutionary thing had happened in the life of the church, and the news about it spread through the church in Judea (v. 1). When Peter arrived in Jerusalem, "those of the circumcision" (literally) criticized him (v. 2). Luke is probably referring to the group within the church who required circumcision of all gentile believers. The only objection mentioned is that they "went into the house of uncircumcised men and ate with them" (v. 3). It shows how important the issue of table fellowship was to Jews.

In response to the criticism, Peter explained everything (v. 4). Luke's report is an extended summary of chapter 10. We will not go into Peter's speech here except to point out two elements. First, the apostle stressed that he had with him "six brothers" (v. 12), who could confirm everything that he was telling the leaders in Jerusalem. Second, as Peter concluded his report, he commented that the Holy Spirit came on Cornelius and company "as [he] began to speak" (v. 15). This suggests that he was unable to complete his talk. He clarified that the Holy Spirit came on them "as he had come on us at the beginning" (v. 15)—that is, as at Pentecost. In verse 16 Peter recalled Jesus's promise of the baptism with the Holy Spirit. Just as this promise had been fulfilled among Jews at Pentecost, now it was being fulfilled among gentiles. This was indeed a gentile Pentecost!

With so much evidence of God's work, Peter dared not resist as he had done when he was told to eat unclean flesh in Joppa (v. 17). The evidence was too great for further objections. The church then praised God and affirmed a new principle about God's dealings with the gentiles (v. 18).

For the moment the circumcision party is silenced. They will emerge again in chapter 15 when they see what large numbers of gentiles have come into the church. Not everyone has undergone the permanent change of conviction that Peter has. They join in the praise now, but as they see the wider implications of this step, they will rise up again in protest.

Application. All who bring pioneering-type changes in the church—for that matter in any sphere of life—usually face criticism.

- When styles of music we are unfamiliar with are presented in church, many protest, saying it is irreverent, without really trying hard to understand why the changes have been made.
- William Booth, founder of the Salvation Army, broke new ground for the church by going out to the poor, the alcoholics, and others considered undesirables in society. But respected and devout leaders of the church criticized him. Even the great evangelical politician the Earl of Shaftesbury, who was himself a champion of the rights of the poor, once announced that after much study he was convinced that the Salvation Army was clearly the antichrist. Someone else even added that in his own studies, he learned that the "number" of William Booth's name added up to 666!
- When missionaries like E. Stanley Jones in India expressed solidarity with the Indian struggle for independence from Britain, evangelicals accused them of liberalism.
- Many immediately branded the Pentecostal revival as demonic because it did not square with their understanding of the place of some gifts of the Spirit in this dispensation.

Peter's actions show how important it is to take pains to get body approval for the directions in which we are moving. Yet we often try to sidestep this difficult process. Many evangelicals who try out previously untried applications of biblical social concern are accused of espousing a social gospel and turning theologically liberal. Unfortunately, some end up theologically liberal because it is the liberals who welcome their new ideas. This is partly because they do not try hard to contend for their viewpoint with other evangelical leaders. It seems easier and more efficient to fulfill their vision alone or through a group that is more sympathetic to it. Prolonged fellowship with "liberals" and alienation from evangelicals, however, can easily lead us to jettison our evangelical convictions.

Making a serious effort to convince the church of a new position takes hard work and sometimes comes only after a long and tiring struggle. Modern-day pragmatism, which does not have much place for commitment to long-lasting relationships, does not have patience for such a long struggle. They feel their agenda does not allow such a "waste of time." Thus, they simply leave the group and join a new one.

ACTS 11:19–30

Original Meaning

Gentiles Converted in Antioch (11:19–21). Those who went to Phoenicia, Cyprus, and Antioch shared the message with Jews only, but some from Cyprus and Cyrene shared the gospel in Antioch with Greeks as well (v. 20). While Luke tells us where these daring spirits who took the lead in this great step forward in the life of the church hailed from, we do not know their names—possibly because there were no famous leaders among them, and no one stood out as prominent.

Antioch in north Syria by the Orontes River was the largest of sixteen cities in the eastern Mediterranean bearing that name. They were so named because many kings of the Seleucid dynasty (who ruled the eastern part of Alexander the Great's empire after his death) bore the name Antiochus. With an estimated population of about three hundred thousand, Antioch in Syria was the third largest city in the Roman Empire, surpassed in population only by Rome and Alexandria. It was also the seat of administration of the Roman province of Syria. A large Jewish population lived there, estimates of which range from twenty-two to sixty-five thousand.

Antioch had lax morals, especially owing to cult prostitution at a shrine in Daphne, five miles south of the city. Because it was an international commercial center, it was a cosmopolitan city. People were accustomed to innovations there. It remained an important center of Christianity for many centuries. It is now a part of Turkey and is called Antakya, with a relatively small population of about forty thousand.

Encouragement from Barnabas (11:22–26). The problem with unknown people doing significant things is that they lack credentials for others to accept the validity of what they are doing. Therefore, a known and respected person was sent by the Jerusalem church to check out what was happening (v. 22). They made a wise choice in Barnabas, for he had distinguished himself as an encourager (4:36) and was known for his godliness (11:24). Moreover, he was a Jew from Cyprus, like some of those who had preached to gentiles in Antioch. He would have a broader perspective than those who had never been abroad. It may be that he volunteered his services for this assignment.

Barnabas's first response to seeing the evidence of God's grace in Antioch shows why he was given the name "Son of Encouragement" (v. 23; see again 4:36). The word "encouraged" (*parakaleō*) should take the meaning "exhorted" here. What Barnabas urged was not just perseverance along the Christian way. The discipline required for perseverance comes from a clinging love relationship with the Christ who loved them and gave himself for them.

The NIV unfortunately does not translate the first word of verse 24, *hoti*, meaning "because." That word connects Barnabas's ministry of encouragement (v. 23) to his Christian character (v. 24). Paul ranks goodness above righteousness in Romans 5:7. It is a quality that inspires loyalty and commitment. It can mean generosity (Matt 20:15), a quality that comes to the fore here with Barnabas's unhesitating acceptance of this new work. Sometimes it refers to good as opposed to bad, as in good fruit versus bad fruit in Matthew 7:17. In the parable of the sower in Luke, the good soil is said to refer to "those with a noble and good heart" (Luke 8:15). To sum up, when Luke uses "good" to describe Barnabas, he is describing someone with true Christian character, a man of integrity and wholesomeness.

While Barnabas is the only one described as "a good man" in Acts (11:24), others, like the Seven (including Stephen), are likewise described as "full of the Holy Spirit" (cf. 6:3, 5). Barnabas was also "full of . . . faith" (11:24), which probably means faith in God.

Next follows a typical Lukan statement, that "a large crowd was added to the Lord" (v. 24b; literal translation). The coming of the encourager/consolidator did not result in a reduction in evangelistic zeal and effectiveness. Soon, however, Barnabas realized that he needed help to adequately pastor this flock. Thus, he went in search of Saul and brought him back to help in a teaching ministry that went on for a whole year (vv. 25–26). The trip to Tarsus was about a hundred miles—a major undertaking. About ten years must have elapsed since Saul had left Jerusalem and gone to Tarsus (9:30). He himself says that he was in Syria and Cilicia (whose principal city was Tarsus) during this time (Gal 1:21). There is every reason to believe, especially considering his comments in Galatians 1, that he was evangelizing during this time.

Another reason why Antioch has a special place in the history of Christianity is that here "the disciples were called Christians first" (Acts 11:26), a name that has prevailed. This was probably a name given by the Antiochene population; Christians used it of themselves beginning only in the second century. In New Testament times, they preferred to use words like "disciples," "saints," and "brothers and sisters." In the New Testament only non-Christians (like Agrippa, 26:28, and the persecutors of Christians, 1 Pet 4:16) use the term. The gentiles must have heard the believers speak so often of Christ that they supplied a suffix to the word "Christ"—thus, "Christians" (meaning "the Christ people"). The Jews would not have given them this name, since "Christ" is the Greek word for the title "Messiah," and the Jews did not accept Jesus as the Messiah.

A Gift to Jerusalem (11:27–30). The message brought by the group from Jerusalem involved the use of prophecy, a gift that has a fairly prominent place in Acts and Paul's letters. Prophecies took the form of understandable messages in the speaker's ordinary language (unlike tongues) given under the direct inspiration of God—that is, by the revelation of the Spirit. Often, as here, prophecy involved prediction of future events. Paul considered it to have high value (1 Cor 12:28; 14:5, 24–25; Eph 4:11), even something to be desired (1 Cor 14:1, 39), for prophecies contained messages from God that edified Christians (1 Cor 14:3). Agabus used this gift twice to predict future events (Acts 11:27–28; 21:10–11).

Luke's comment that the famine "happened during the reign of Claudius" (11:28), who reigned in AD 41–54, helps us place this visit of Paul and Barnabas at around AD 46, during which time, according to Josephus, there was a severe famine in Judea. Scholars debate whether this visit of Paul to Jerusalem harmonizes with the one referred to in Galatians 2:1–10 as Paul's second post-conversion visit to Jerusalem "fourteen years later." The problem is that the first visit should be dated around AD 35; if the second visit was fourteen years later, it would be around AD 49, which would identify it with the Council of Jerusalem. We can harmonize the AD 46 date with the Galatians account only if we take the fourteen years Paul refers to as being fourteen years after his conversion (dated ca. AD 33). He says he "went in response to a revelation" (Gal 2:2), which would then be the prophecy of Agabus.

That this young church gave a gift to the mother church in Jerusalem shows how the missionary spirit had caught on so soon in a church that would be the mother church of gentile missions (vv. 29–30). What a quick reversal of missionary roles! The mother church in Jerusalem sends the gospel, and the daughter church in Antioch sends money to the mother church.

Application. The fact that non-prominent Christians did such significant work for Christ reminds us that the famous are not necessarily the most significant or most important people in the church. The famous have gifts that put them into the limelight—and that is not wrong. But neither is it necessarily great. Some of the most significant work for the kingdom has been done by unknown witnesses who are obedient to Christ right where they are and where they do not attract much attention. Today we associate significance and greatness with newsworthiness. Much effort is made to make an event look newsworthy, and thus it has to be associated with names—such as the names of those who write best-selling books or head a big organization. These names attract the people in the media.

Some people write books simply to become newsworthy. Some even pay others to do most of the writing for books that will go under their name! All this is unnecessary, for our task is to be faithful to what God calls us to do. If that does not put our name forward on earth, that should not bother us, for our aim in life is not to get our name in the papers but to hear our Lord say, "Well done." It is the prospect of this reward that thrills true Christians.

ACTS 12:1–24

Original Meaning

Herod, James, and Peter (12:1–19). This time the source of persecution is King Herod (Agrippa I), who makes James the first of the apostles to be martyred (vv. 1–2). When he realized that the Jews were pleased with the killing of James, he also had Peter imprisoned (v. 3a). This incident indicates how much the relationship between Jews and Christians in Judea had deteriorated from the earlier situation (2:47). We do not know whether the general public was in favor of the earlier persecutions. But this time, as the use of the general term *Jews* suggests, approval for James's death was widespread.

There is much irony in this section. According to Luke, the imprisonment of Peter took place during the Passover (v. 3b). At the time when the Jews were celebrating the deliverance of their nation through God's intervention, a herald of God's climactic act of deliverance was taken into custody to please the Jews. While they should have been celebrating a great salvation, they were hoping to inflict a great punishment on the representative of the Savior (v. 11).

To the gloomy picture of Peter in prison Luke adds the hopeful note of the church earnestly in prayer for him (v. 5). The word translated "earnestly" (*ektenōs*) literally means "stretched out" and could thus mean continuous, in which case it carries a similar idea as it does in 1:14, which gave us the idea of prevailing prayer. But the idea of continuous or repeated prayer is already carried by the use of the imperfect tense for the verb "praying." Luke's use of *ektenōs* here, therefore, seems more like his use of this word in Luke 22:44, where it refers to Jesus's earnest prayer in the garden (cf. Acts 26:7). This idea of earnestness (see NIV) comes from the idea of hands *stretched out* to God in fervent supplication. It gives the impression of wholehearted, urgent pleading to God. While Peter was fast asleep in prison in the middle of the night (the angel had to wake him, v. 7), the church was engaged in vigilant prayer for him.

The second instance of irony is the unbelief of Peter and the praying church that their prayers had been answered (vv. 9–11, 15). And this came after God had similarly released Peter from imprisonment on an earlier occasion—that time also through an angel at night (5:19–20). In fact, when the servant girl Rhoda was overjoyed over the answer to the prayers of the believers, they pronounced her out of her mind (12:14–15).

The statement "it must be his angel" (v. 15) reflects the Jewish belief in protecting and guiding angels. Thus the believers thought that Rhoda mistook Peter's guardian angel for Peter. The irony continues as Peter went on knocking while the believers argued among themselves (v. 16a). While the big iron gate of the prison opened with no effort to let Peter out (v. 10), he was unable to get past the gate of his own friend's home.

Peter wanted James to be informed about what had happened, which suggests that he had already become an important leader in the church (cf. also Gal 2:1–10). Because James was known to hold strongly to Jewish ways, he would not be in as much danger from the Jews as Peter was.

A third instance of irony is Herod's response to Peter's escape, which deflated his ego. He restored his image by having the guards executed (v. 19a). This extreme reaction is typical of people who seek popularity but are unexpectedly humiliated. Luke then says that Herod went to Caesarea (v. 19b). He begins verse 19b with the word "and" (*kai*), which means it is part of the same sentence about the executions of the guards. This suggests Herod may have left Jerusalem because of frustration over Peter's escape.

Herod's Death (12:20–24). Herod's deflated ego received a big boost at his conference with the desperate delegates from Tyre and Sidon, who, deprived of their food supply, resort to flattery to win him over (vv. 20–22). The account of this incident by Josephus supplements the partial account given here. There is irony here, too, for the man who was glorious on the outside was rotting of worms on the inside.

Immediately after the report of Herod's death, Luke gives a report of the growth of the church he had brutally tried to suppress. The customary summary of growth in verse 24 ends the description in Acts of the Christian mission to the Jewish world. The section closes on a positive note. The early popularity of the church has given way to hostility, but that does not hinder the forward march of the gospel. From the next chapter to the end of Acts, the focus will be on Paul and his missionary activity.

Application. In times of trouble, God's sovereignty can be expressed by rescue or no rescue. In the violence that engulfed Sri Lanka in the late twentieth century we saw five types of situations that Christians encountered that can be applied to difficulties in general.

1. Some experienced wonderful deliverances that could be explained only as miraculous interventions from God. There were stories of bombs missing houses or not going off, of mobs suddenly turning away and avoiding the houses of God's servants. These certainly remind us that God can and does save his children in times of crises if it is his will.
2. Others have gone through great crisis and earthly loss but remained so radiant with the love of Christ that they were powerful testimonies of God's sustaining grace. In a terrible riot in 1983, the home of Dr. Arul Anketell, who directed Hospital Christian Fellowship in Sri Lanka at the time, was burned. When I met him for

the first time after the event, he ministered the peace of Christ to me rather than vice versa. He was a wonderful testimony of the sufficiency of God's grace.

3. The faith of certain people was shattered by the problems they faced. Not only did they question why God allowed the tragedy and became engulfed in a cloud of gloom—both of which are natural—they also never recovered from the gloom. In bitterness of spirit, they turned their back on God.
4. Other people compromised their principles in order to avoid pain. For example, some Christians left the country by illegal means or by telling lies to visa officers at embassies.
5. Finally, some who had not cared for the things of God, owing to their relentless pursuit of earthly success, were jolted into realizing the unreliability of earthly treasures as a means of security. They turned to God for security and succor and found him to be the answer to the aching void in their hearts.

Whatever experiences God's providence permits us to go through, our primary commitment should be to obedience. All the threats from the authorities did not cause the early church to pull back on its commitment to proclaiming the gospel. Peter saw wonderful deliverance through the intervention of God, while James faced death for Christ. But the early Christians persevered in obedience, knowing that if God is sovereign he would use their obedience to win a great victory for the kingdom.

ACTS 12:25–13:12

Original Meaning

A Missionary Team Is Sent Out (12:25–13:3). When Saul and Barnabas returned to Antioch from Jerusalem, Barnabas's cousin (see Col 4:10) John Mark was with them. We cannot be sure whether Luke is suggesting in Acts 13:1 that the same people were both teachers and prophets or whether these gifts resided in different people. Certainly Paul exercised both teaching and prophetic ministries, as we will see below.

Barnabas is mentioned first, possibly because he was the leader of the group. He was a Jew from the Jerusalem church but was originally from Cyprus (4:36), an island west of Palestine. Simeon is a Jewish name, but he is called Niger, meaning black. Attempts to identify him with Simon of Cyrene have not been convincing.

Lucius was from Cyrene, which was in North Africa (present-day Libya). Some have suggested that this is Luke, but that is unlikely. Manaen is a Jewish name. The NIV translates *syntrophos* as "had been brought up with" Herod the tetrarch (13:1), but it means foster brother or close friend from childhood. How strange that Herod should end up beheading John the Baptist and being involved in the trial of Christ, while Manaen became a leader of the church. Saul, an educated Jew originally from Tarsus, is mentioned last.

The Holy Spirit sent a message to this church, probably through one of the prophets there, which propelled it into a new era of missionary involvement. It happened "while they were worshiping the Lord and fasting" (13:2). "They" refers either to the prophets and teachers or to the whole church; the latter is more likely. The word translated "worshiping" (*leitourgeō*) literally means "ministering." Twice Paul uses these words for help given to him (Phil 2:25, 30). The noun appears in this sense in Luke 1:23, referring to Zechariah's service in the temple. The word for service seems to have fitted into the Christian understanding of worship and prayer.

The church's prayer was accompanied by fasting, both when the church received the message and when they sent off the missionary team (Acts 13:2–3). When Paul and Barnabas visited the churches they had established on the way back from this first missionary journey, they "appointed elders for them in each church and, with prayer and fasting, committed them to the Lord" (14:23).

The sending-off ceremony with the laying on of hands was more a commissioning to a specific task than an ordaining to ministry. It is not surprising that at the end of the mission, Paul and Barnabas returned to the church in Antioch and gave a report of what happened (14:26–27). There must have been much more work to be done in Antioch. But God asked the church to release their key leaders for missions. To their credit the church did so, with no apparent hesitation. That is how important missions and obedience to the Spirit were.

Ministry in Cyprus (13:4–12). Verse 4 reminds us that the Holy Spirit is the one who ultimately sends his servants out. The first place of ministry for the missionaries was the area Barnabas came from, the island of Cyprus, southwest of Antioch, to which they sailed from Seleucia, the port city of Antioch. They began their ministry in the northeastern city of Salamis, preaching first in a synagogue in keeping with the principle of going to the Jews first (cf. Rom 1:16). But they soon took a new step, directly approaching a gentile official who sent for them (v. 7).

Luke inserts a note that "John was with them as their helper" (v. 5b). As a resident of Jerusalem, Mark may have had an eyewitness knowledge of events in the gospel story, especially relating to the passion narrative, of which Paul would have availed himself.

The team next went to the provincial capital, Paphos, on the opposite (southwestern) side of the island. In Paphos, Saul and Barnabas encountered a sorcerer, Bar-Jesus or Elymas, just as Philip and Peter did in Samaria. Like Simon in Samaria, Elymas faced a stern rebuke from the evangelist because of his adverse influence on the proconsul of Cyprus, Sergius Paulus (vv. 6–11). Elymas presumably opposed Paul and Barnabas because their ministry jeopardized his standing with the proconsul. Such opposition to the gospel for selfish reasons is common in Acts.

At this stage we are told that Saul "was also called Paul" (v. 9), and from now on this is the name used in Acts (except when he relates the story of his conversion [22:7, 13; 26:14]). As a Jew he would have proudly borne the name of Israel's first king, Saul, who like him was from the tribe of Benjamin (Phil 3:5). Roman citizens had three names: a praenomen, a nomen, and a cognomen. The apostle's first two are not mentioned in the New Testament. Paul (*Paulos*, meaning "little") was his cognomen, and inscriptions show that often the cognomen of Jews sounded like their Jewish name, as is the case here. As Paul entered the gentile phase of his ministry, he would have gone by his Roman name. Thus, the view that this name change resulted from his conversion is wrong.

Paul has severe words for Elymas (vv. 9–11). Luke is careful to say that he was "filled with the Holy Spirit" when he uttered them (v. 9), indicating that this was not an error on Paul's part. It is an example of the use of the prophetic gift through which the apostle communicated a direct and specific word of judgment from God. Verse 12 attributes the belief of Sergius Paulus both to his seeing the miracle and being amazed at the teaching of the Lord. As we will see below, these factors present two key elements of effective evangelistic ministry.

Application. The Spirit directed Barnabas and Saul to be set apart for reaching the lost. As we noted above, these were the top leaders of the church, and the young church in Antioch presumably had many needs. But when God calls, we must release even those we consider the most important and valued persons. That's how important missions is. One does not have to be brilliant (humanly speaking) to be a missionary. One has to be called, and God often calls "ordinary," unspectacular people to do special things for him (1 Cor 1:26). But sometimes he sends the most talented. When brilliant people respond to the missionary call, we may say, "What a waste! Their audience will be uneducated, backward people. Why should the most brilliant go to them?" But throughout history God has called some of the brightest people in their generation to the mission field.

Is this happening today too? I can think of many sharp people, young and old, who are on the mission field today. But I also see a hindrance to this happening. The church has been influenced by worldly standards of success, and going to the unreached is low on this status scale. The pastor of a church of 2,500 people may be considered a powerful person. If that person was called to go to the lost, he may at first have only two people in his church—himself and his colleague. For this reason, many opt for the big church instead of answering God's call to missions.

Paul also encountered these wrong values in the church. Toward the end of his life he wrote that no one was with him in his trial because they all had deserted him (2 Tim 4:16). Perhaps there was no status in associating with Paul. He himself often spoke of how he was, humanly speaking, abased. But today he is a hero and one of the most admired people in the history of the world. Heroes are often admired only from a distance, not when they are doing their great work. In their own time they are often regarded as fools or failures. Their heroism made them give up earthly glory, with the result that earthly people did not admire them.

May we not be reluctant to challenge all—the brilliant and the ordinary—to consider missions. And when such are called, may we release them wholeheartedly for this work. May we place missions high up in our list of priorities.

ACTS 13:13–52

Original Meaning

Preaching in Pisidian Antioch (13:13–41). Verse 13 records two interesting changes in the missionary team.

1. Paul seems to have taken the prominent role. Prior to this Barnabas was always mentioned first. Now Barnabas is not even mentioned but is included as one of Paul's "companions." Hereafter, except in the description of the proceedings of the Jerusalem Council (15:12) and the letter it sent to the churches (15:25), the order is always "Paul and Barnabas." This seems to be Luke's way of saying that Paul has taken over the leadership slot or at least the place of prominence.
2. John Mark leaves to return home to Jerusalem. Paul later describes this departure as a desertion (15:38), but we are not told why he leaves.

From Perga, Paul and Barnabas travel inland and northward to the higher altitudes, and they minister in cities of south Galatia. Antioch of Pisidia was an important civil and military center of the Romans (v. 14), which lay about 3,600 feet above sea level. In Galatians 4:13 Paul says that "it was because of an illness that [he] first preached the gospel" in this area.

As was their custom, Paul and Barnabas go to the local synagogue on the Sabbath, and they are invited to speak (vv. 14–15). We note that Paul addresses both Jews and God-fearers twice, using different designations each time (vv. 16, 26), and that the message is tailored to suit an audience with a background of knowledge about the Old Testament. While he covers some of the same ground in his historical survey of Israel's history as Stephen, his aim is different. Stephen wanted to demonstrate that the old era with the temple and the law of Moses had given way to the new. Paul's aim is rather to show how God's activity in history climaxed in the coming of Jesus. Thus he talks of how God worked with Israel in Egypt (v. 17a), in the exodus (v. 17b), in the desert wanderings (v. 18), in the conquest of Canaan (v. 19), in the period of the judges (v. 20b), and during the time of Israel's first two kings, Saul and David (vv. 21–22). From there Paul jumps straight to Jesus the Savior, who came as one of David's descendants (v. 23). The implication here is that Jesus fulfills Jewish aspirations.

From that point on, Paul argues for the validity of his claim in verse 23 that Jesus is indeed the promised "Savior." John the Baptist had anticipated his coming (vv. 24–25). Paul's hearers possibly knew more about John than about Jesus. After proclaiming that this message of salvation has been sent to them (v. 26), Paul proceeds to expound on the death of Christ with the characteristic apologetic presented to the Jews in Acts: he was innocent, and his death fulfilled Old Testament prophecy (vv. 27–29). Then, as in Peter's Pentecost sermon, Paul gives an extended exposition of how the resurrection was witnessed by credible people and was in keeping with what the Old Testament said (vv. 30–37).

Following the exposition of the Christ event is an offer of forgiveness (v. 38) and justification (v. 39). Verse 39 contains ideas that are typical of Paul's letters: belief, justification, and the inability to be justified by the law of Moses. Paul concludes his message with a quotation from Habakkuk (Hab 1:5)—a warning of judgment to those who reject God's offer of salvation (Acts 13:41).

The themes of the displacement of people and God's choice are keys to Paul's sermon. He speaks of the displacement of the nations and the choice of Israel (v. 19); the displacement of Saul and the choice of David (v. 22); the fact that "all the people of Israel" had to go through the sign of conversion to Judaism, baptism, if they were to avoid displacement (v. 24); the displacement of John by Jesus (v. 25); and the displacement of the Jews and the choice of Jesus (vv. 40–41; cf. vv. 46–48). Paul expresses God's plan of salvation for the world through the progress of history. Beginning with his salvation at the exodus, he shows how God systematically kept unfolding his purposes until it reached its climax in the Christ event.

The Aftermath of Paul's Sermon (13:42–52). Paul and Barnabas are invited to speak the next Sabbath as well (v. 42). In the meantime, "many of the Jews and devout converts to Judaism" follow them (v. 43). We can assume that Paul and Barnabas gave themselves to personal ministry with these contacts during the week. The last expression may not mean that they were converted; rather, they had become open to the grace of God working in their hearts, and they were now being urged to continue along that path.

The Jews probably did not expect to see nearly the whole city there on that day (v. 44). Their jealousy is aroused, and they oppose Paul's next message with abusive talk (v. 45). Paul and Barnabas respond to this by stating what became a feature of their ministry and of Paul's theology: they preach to the Jews first, but if their response is unworthy of eternal life, they go to the gentiles (v. 46). Paul backs that step from the Scriptures (v. 47). While he no doubt spoke with confidence on this occasion, this recurring phenomenon of Jewish rejection of the gospel hurt him deeply and inflamed his desire to yearn and pray for their salvation (Rom 9:1–3; 10:1).

In Romans 9–11 Paul uses his great theological skill for a profound exploration of the implications of and reasons for this rejection. In fact, a part of Romans 9–11 is in some ways an exposition of Acts 13:47. The receptivity of the gentiles was remarkable, considering the fact that the imperial cult (public worship of the emperor) was strong in Antioch. There was a temple of Augustus in the center as the city's most prominent building, and this cult dominated the city's daily life and annual calendar.

The gentiles receive Paul's word with gladness (v. 48a). After considerable emphasis on the human response to the gospel, both positive and negative, Luke redresses the balance by emphasizing God's foundational role in salvation (v. 48b).

The severity of the opposition to the gospel is such that the team has to leave town (vv. 49–50). Despite these problems the new believers are "filled with joy and with the Holy Spirit" (v. 52). As Paul and Barnabas leave the area, they express their verdict on the Jews by shaking the dust off their feet (v. 51).

Application. There are three key factors in today's world that impede making the content of the gospel central to the evangelistic process. First, the dominant philosophy of our age, pluralism, has given the idea of truth a severe bashing. Pluralism denies the importance of objective truth. In such an environment, apologetics is regarded as inappropriate and even presumptuous. The pluralist says that truth is subjective—something we learn from our experience. There is therefore no absolute truth that comes from objective revelation. Instead of apologetics they propose dialogue—by which they mean an exchange of beliefs and experiences that will result in each one enriching the other.

Second, we live in a technological era that concentrates so much on action and information that there is little time to think about ideas and truth. When people want refreshment, they go to something that will keep them active (like outdoor recreation) or that will numb their senses (like television or social media). Preachers have an abundance of computer programs available that have done a lot of the thinking they would usually have done. While these have a place, nothing can replace meditation and hard thinking about truth. It is from such lingering with truth that effective apologetics and proclamation emerge. We should use the marvels of technology to make us efficient in doing things and gathering information so that we will have more time to think well.

Third, many Christian groups are oriented to experience. While this is not wrong and is, in fact, desirable, it must never dethrone truth. Sometimes experiences like healing or being slain in the Spirit can become so prominent that people do not associate the gospel with intelligent and demonstrable arguments. Many are not willing to work hard at studying the background of the audience and tailoring the message of what Christ has done for our salvation in order to be relevant, as Paul did. People fast and pray in order to receive the power of God—and that is vital for evangelism. But so is the power of being equipped with God's word, which requires preparation time. For this power we must both pray and study.

In other words, we must exhibit the power of God's Spirit *both* in experience *and* in the world of thought. In this way we will have a balanced gospel that can withstand the dry spells that will surely come, when God's hand seems withdrawn from us. Christians are not immune to such experiences. Those whose faith is founded on the truth will persevere, knowing that nothing can take away the truthfulness of the gospel. They will have the joy that the Christian disciples in Pisidian Antioch had despite the problems they faced (v. 52). But those whose faith is founded on experience will flounder when they encounter times of darkness. One would hope that at these times such people will stumble on the more secure and unchanging realities of the Christian faith.

It is not wrong, then, to attract people to Christ by presenting them an attractive program that ministers to their felt needs. But that is not enough. We must get people to understand the glory of the truth of the gospel—something deeper and more lasting than experience. Then they will have joy in the gospel, a joy that can withstand the mysterious and difficult times of darkness in life.

In order to communicate this vision, we must know in our own lives the joy of truth. We must take time to feed our minds with the truth and to meditate on it so that it will glow within us. As a result, those to whom we minister will, by observing us, also acquire a respect and appreciation for the truth. They will catch our enthusiasm over it. We also will find ourselves refreshed and fed. This will help us remain fresh amid the debilitating challenges of ministry.

ACTS 14:1–28

Original Meaning

Ministry in Iconium (14:1–7). Iconium (modern Konya) was and still is an important junction along which the east-west road from Syria to Ephesus. It was about ninety miles southeast of Pisidian Antioch, and Paul and Barnabas continued on the Via Sebaste that brought them to Antioch. Lystra was less than twenty miles southwest of Iconium. The sixty-three miles from Lystra to Derbe was on an unpaved track.

Paul and Barnabas followed their usual practice of going first to the local synagogue (v. 1). Many Jews and gentiles believed, which resulted in opposition from the Jews who did not believe (v. 2; cf. 13:50; 14:19; 17:5–9). But Paul and Barnabas persevered with the ministry of the word and of miracles (14:3); the latter were a confirmation from God of the message preached. The confirmatory role of miracles is implied in the believers' request to God in 4:30 to send miracles to their ministry and is illustrated in the conversion of Sergius Paulus after Elymas was struck blind (13:12), but here it is explicitly stated. The gospel caused the city to be divided (14:4), and a plot against Paul and Barnabas forced them to flee to Lystra and Derbe (v. 6).

Ministry in Lystra and Derbe (14:8–21a). The healing of the cripple with which the account of the ministry in Lystra begins probably took place sometime after Paul and Barnabas had arrived in Lystra, for it is clear that by the time Paul was stoned, there were already believers in the city who went to his aid (v. 20). The report of the miracle has remarkable similarities to the healing at the temple gate (3:2–10). Both the subjects were born lame. Paul looked directly at the cripple, just as Peter and John did (14:9; cf. 3:4). Both men jumped up after being healed (14:10; cf. 3:8). Both are said to have had the faith to be healed (14:9; cf. 3:16). In both cases the preachers had to divert the attention from themselves to God (14:15; cf. 3:12).

The frenzied response of the Lystrans may be traced to an ancient legend retold by Ovid (43 BC–AD 17) in his *Metamorphosis*. Zeus and Hermes once visited the Phrygian hill country disguised as ordinary men. They were turned away from a thousand homes where they sought lodging, but they were finally taken in by an elderly couple into their humble home. The gods turned that house into a temple and destroyed all the houses that had rejected them.

Paul and Barnabas could not understand what was being said by the people since they were shouting "in the Lycaonian language" (v. 11). This accounts for their delayed response to plans to offer sacrifices to them. When they found this out, their response was swift and typically Jewish (v. 14).

Paul uses the situation to launch into a witness to the gospel, stating that he and Barnabas are presenting a much more sublime message than can be obtained from "these worthless things" (v. 15, i.e., either idols or the sacrifices being prepared). This is the first speech in Acts presented to an audience that has not been influenced by a Jewish synagogue and its beliefs.

Thus, Paul has to start at the beginning with information that those influenced by biblical religion already knew. His approach is clearly to distinguish the Lord God from the pagan gods by pointing out that he is Creator of everything that there is (v. 15), whose influence as sustainer of creation is felt throughout the whole world (vv. 16–17). He is also the living God, who calls us to turn to him in repentance (v. 15).

But once again we find Jews opposing the ministry of Paul and Barnabas. This time they have traveled from Antioch, 110 miles away, and Iconium, 20 miles away, indicating the urgency with which they were ready to stamp out this work.

Yet at this dark hour, there is support from the new believers of Lystra, who "gathered around" Paul and "went back into the city" with him (v. 20). What a source of comfort this must have been to him. He and Barnabas leave the next day for Derbe. The Lord blesses their efforts with "a large number of disciples" (v. 21), and there is no mention of opposition here.

Return Visits to Churches and Antioch (14:21b–28). Their return journey took Paul and Barnabas through the three towns they had just ministered at: Lystra, Iconium, and Antioch (v. 21b). They had been expelled from one of them (13:50) and had fled from the other two (14:6, 20). But this time they engaged in a new role in follow-through care of the converts rather than in pioneering evangelism. Four important truths are given about this ministry of follow-through care.

1. They strengthened the disciples (v. 22a).
2. They encouraged or exhorted (*parakaleō*) them to remain in the faith (v. 22b).
3. They warned them about approaching hardship in a statement that implies that hardship is a necessary requirement along the path to the kingdom. It literally reads, "Through many tribulations it is necessary [*dei*] for us to enter the kingdom of God" (v. 22c). The word "many" (*pollōn*) expresses a variety of different tribulations. This idea of variety in suffering is more clearly expressed in James 1:2, which uses the word *poikilois* ("many kinds") with reference to trials. Paul implies that Christians will not sail through trouble with consummate ease. Rather, they will struggle with difficult hardships of various kinds.
4. Paul and Barnabas helped the new churches get organized by setting up a leadership team (v. 23). The leaders are called "elders" (*presbyteroi*), a word that occurs sixty-six times in the New Testament. It was used originally for the Jewish leaders, and it occurs with this meaning in Acts (see 4:5, 8, 23; 6:12; etc.). Without explanation the word is suddenly used for the elders of the Jerusalem church in 11:30. The next use within a Christian context is the present passage, after which it appears in Acts eight more times to refer to the elders of the church and three more times to refer to the Jewish elders. The elders appointed by Paul and Barnabas are committed to the Lord, and once more the commissioning of leaders is accompanied by prayer and fasting (14:23b; cf. 1:24–25; 6:6; 10:9–16; 13:2–3).

The journey of Paul and Barnabas back to Antioch takes them through Perga, from where they had started their journey up to the mountains of southern Galatia. We do not know whether they had preached there on their earlier visit, but they definitely did so on this return visit (14:25a). From there they went to Attalia and finally sailed back "home" to Antioch, having completed the task they were commissioned to do (v. 26). The church must have been thrilled to hear the report of their mission (v. 27) and happy that "they stayed there a long time with the disciples" (v. 28). The Greek word for "disciple" (*mathētēs*, literally "learner") has now become a favorite term to refer to Christians, appearing four times in this chapter (vv. 20, 21, 22, 28) and twenty-eight times in Acts (it appears over 250 times in the Gospels).

Application. In the exhortation that forms an important part in the follow-through and strengthening of believers, the need to prepare them to suffer in order to enter the kingdom is an essential ingredient (v. 22b). Paul's letters suggest that he and Barnabas exhorted these Galatian converts. They urged them to resist Satan and false doctrine, to put away the old lifestyle and put on the new lifestyle, to pray and give thanks always, to give primacy to love in all they do, and to have a biblical attitude to possessions. In order that Christians receive such exhortation early on, we should teach those parts of Scripture that lend themselves to these elements (e.g., the Ten Commandments; the Sermon on the Mount; the practical sections of Paul's letters, such as Rom 12–15; Gal 4–6; Eph 4–6; the book of James).

Today some people shy away from exhortation, perhaps because of the influence of our pluralistic culture, which is skeptical of any dogmatic approach; because of the entertainment orientation that dominates much Christian proclamation today; or because of the loss of credibility of preachers through moral failures. Yet many sections of the Bible that teach believers are comprised of exhortation. Surely, then, Christian leaders should be exhorting Christians today.

Perhaps one way we can win back the credibility that will enable us to exhort freely is by becoming examples of sacrificial living. When Paul talked to these Galatians about suffering, his message was credible since they had seen how he suffered for the gospel. Paul occasionally appealed to his sufferings when he wrote something difficult to accept (cf. Gal 6:17). In Ephesians 4:1 he said, "As a prisoner for the Lord, then, I urge you to live a life worthy of the calling you have received." Being a prisoner gave him credibility to exhort people. Similarly, today, when our hearers know that we are truly committed people who have paid a significant price because of our loyalty to Christ, they often take note of what we say.

ACTS 15:1–35

Original Meaning

Paul and Barnabas Go to Jerusalem (15:1–4). The events are sparked off by "certain people [who] came down from Judea to Antioch" (v. 1). Verse 24 makes clear that they went "without [the] authorization" of the church leaders in Jerusalem. They must have significantly troubled the minds of the Christians in Antioch because they insinuated that the apostles and elders agreed with what they were saying. If Paul preached circumcision, there would be no scandal to the Christian faith. But since he preached that salvation occurs through no work of our own and only through the merits of the death of Christ, such a message was scandalous to the average Jew. The teachers from Judea were trying to remove this scandal. The church realized that something serious was happening.

Settling the Issue of Salvation and the Gentiles (15:5–19). The joy at Paul and Barnabas's report was broken by objections regarding the circumcision issue (v. 5). Therefore, "the apostles and elders met to consider this question" (v. 6). We cannot be sure whether the whole church was present at this meeting (cf. vv. 12, 22). If so, the deliberation and decision rested with the leaders. The theological controversy was not swept under the rug and allowed to simmer; it was brought into the open and fearlessly discussed.

After the discussion, Peter spoke up (v. 7). If this council met after the humiliating confrontation in Antioch where Peter was publicly rebuked by the younger Paul (Gal 2:11–21), as we think it did, it is indeed creditable that Peter should be the first to get up and speak on behalf of Paul's side in the controversy.

Peter's main point was that the opening of the door of salvation took place through God's initiative. He referred to the conversion of Cornelius and his friends and pointed out that this whole event had been of God's choosing (v. 7). "God, who knows the heart," confirmed that they had been truly saved "by giving the Holy Spirit to them, just as he did to" Peter and his company (v. 8).

Peter then explicitly stated the great truth that Paul later expounded in Ephesians 2:14–22, that God broke all barriers separating Jews and gentiles. With surprising candor Peter admits that the Mosaic law was "a yoke" (v. 10). Insisting that gentiles keep the law is to "try to test God" (v. 10), a serious issue. With this speech Peter bows out of the book of Acts.

The next to speak are Barnabas and Paul (v. 12). In Luke's writings signs and wonders have an authenticating function. James then makes his entrance (v. 13). He is not introduced here or in 12:17, which records his first appearance in Acts, probably because he was a well-known figure in the early church. From what he says and the way he says it, it becomes evident that he has become the leader of the church in Jerusalem. While not all scholars agree, this James is probably the brother of Jesus.

James's first statement (v. 14) is loaded with significance. James makes a revolutionary statement: "God first intervened to choose a people for his name from the Gentiles." In the Old Testament (LXX) the "nations" or "Gentiles" (*ethnē*) stand in contrast to the "people" (*laos*), which usually refers to the people of Israel. Deuteronomy 14:2 says, for example, "You are a people [LXX *laos*] holy to the LORD your God. Out of all the peoples [LXX *ethnē*, nations] on the face of the earth, the LORD has chosen you to be his treasured possession." In other words, the Israelites have been called out from the nations to be a people for the Lord God. James says the opposite: from *within* the nations God has taken a people for himself. James concludes that the church "should not make it difficult for the Gentiles who are turning to God" (v. 19)—perhaps referring to not requiring them to go through the painful (esp. for adults) step of circumcision.

Fellowship between Jewish and Gentile Christians (15:20–35). Once the issue of the requirements for salvation has been settled, James brings up an important issue that impacts fellowship between Jewish and gentile Christians. To many Jews, maintaining their purity was an extremely important aspect of their survival and identity, especially when they were under foreign rule and had dispersed far and wide into gentile territory. Thus, the issue of table fellowship with gentiles and the consumption of non-kosher food was a serious issue. But in the early church, eating together was also an important element of community life (2:46). If there was going to be openhearted fellowship between Jewish and gentile Christians, there would have to be some sensitivity to Jewish scruples by the gentiles. Thus, James proposes three prohibitions relating to food (15:20).

The prohibition of sexual immorality (*porneia*) seems to belong to a different category from the rest, and it appears out of place in this list. Surely it goes without saying that sexual immorality is prohibited for Christians. I think that there was so much immorality in some of these places, like Antioch (which was notorious for its immorality), that the churches were also affected by the immorality surrounding them. Therefore, a special warning was necessary.

The Jerusalem leaders decide to send some of their own people as a delegation bearing a letter from the council (v. 22).

The letter to the churches takes on a conciliatory tone. The trouble caused by certain Christians from Jerusalem is condemned in uncompromising language (v. 24). Barnabas and Paul are described in endearing and complimentary terms (vv. 25–26). The words describing the final position of the council are prefaced by words that show how unity had won the day (v. 28).

This letter emphasizes the unity and unanimity of the church in this decision. Verses 30–35 describe a situation where joy and encouragement have replaced the uncertainty of a few days before. The hard work of the past days had indeed been worth the effort. The church had taken another important step in fulfilling the Great Commission.

Application. When false teachers came to Antioch, what they said could not be easily dismissed since they had come from the mother church in Judea. In the same way today, teachers from reputed seminaries can come and cause great damage in the church by false teaching. This type of thing has happened in this century to many churches in the Third World, when liberal teaching came from the mother churches in the West, either through missionaries or through the seminaries where Third World ministers studied. It has caused havoc in older churches, resulting in spiritual death.

Just as the Judaizers sought to remove the scandal of the gospel, throughout the history of the church people have tried to remove the unpleasant aspects of the Christian faith. In the aftermath of the scientific revolution, many tried to divest it of its miraculous element, since it did not harmonize with the so-called scientific worldview. Today, when pluralism and religious tolerance hold sway, people have tried to divest it of its claim to uniqueness and its doctrine of eternal punishment.

In situations closer to what happened in Acts, some teachers have avoided the unpleasant doctrine of Christ's breaking human barriers and encouraged instead the growth of segregated churches or refused to speak up against racism. The message of integration in Christ is one of the most revolutionary features of Christianity in this world torn by strife. Those who proclaim it get into trouble with extremists. Consequently, many choose to play safe and ignore it, and Christians end up with racist attitudes. If there is no exposure to the Christian view on this issue, people will tend to go with the crowd in their racist thinking.

ACTS 15:36–16:10

Original Meaning

The Team Breaks Up (15:36–41). In discussing the idea of revisiting the churches with Barnabas, Paul disagrees with the suggestion that they take Barnabas's cousin Mark (Col 4:10) along, "because he had deserted them in Pamphylia" (Acts 15:37–38). Though the word Luke uses in verse 39 for the resulting conflict is a strong one (*paroxysmos*, NIV "sharp disagreement"), it does not give us a hint about who was right and who was wrong. That the team should have broken up because of this conflict is sad. It is encouraging to find out that later Paul and Barnabas seem to have become colleagues again (1 Cor 9:6; Col 4:10) and that Paul had not only come to appreciate Mark but also to depend on him so much that he asked for him to come to him toward the end of his life (2 Tim 4:11; cf. Col 4:10; Phlm 24).

The sovereignty of God as he works out his purposes even through human weakness is revealed as two separate teams now set out, and the area of the first missionary journey is divided between Paul and Barnabas. The latter goes to his native Cyprus with Mark (Acts 15:39), while Paul takes Silas and travels via Syria and Cicilia to South Galatia (15:40–16:1).

Silas was a leader in the church of Jerusalem (15:22) and a prophet who "said much to encourage and strengthen the believers" in Antioch (15:32). This must mean he was an enthusiastic backer of Paul's program of gentile evangelism. He was also a Roman citizen like Paul (see 16:37)—an asset in an itinerant ministry in the Roman Empire. Silas is probably an abbreviation of the Latin Silvanus, by which he is called in the letters. He is named as coauthor of the two Thessalonian letters.

Paul and Silas are commissioned and sent off by the church in Antioch (v. 40), just as the earlier team had been sent off (13:3). There the commissioning had included fasting, prayer, and the laying on of hands. The same may have been done here too. There is no mention of a similar send-off for Barnabas and Mark, but this may be because from now on Luke focuses on Paul's ministry. All true ministry stems from God's grace, but grace is often mediated through the prayers, concern, accountability, and provisions of other Christians. The laying on of hands itself was intended to signify the mediating of God's blessing. The church released Paul and Silas to the grace of God, but they would have pledged to do their part in continuing to mediate this grace.

The Macedonian Call (16:1–10). Acts 15:41 and 16:5 indicate that the first leg of this journey by Paul and Silas was essentially one of "strengthening the churches." One aspect of this ministry was that "they delivered the decisions" of the Jerusalem Council "for the people to obey" (16:4).

In Lystra, a well-spoken-of young man of mixed parentage, Timothy, becomes the newest member of the team (vv. 1–3). Paul's circumcising of him has received much discussion. It is alleged that the Paul of the letters, who spoke so strongly against circumcision, could not have done this, and therefore that the Paul of Acts may not be the authentic Paul of history. But we must remember that the Paul of Acts also considered the circumcision issue so important that he made the long trip to Jerusalem to battle the Jewish agitators. His battle was against insisting that circumcision was a condition for the full inclusion of the gentiles among the people of God. Here the issue was qualifications for ministry. No church today asks for a theological degree as a necessary condition for membership, but many require this for entrance into the ministry. Timothy needed to win the esteem of the Jewish Christians, and being circumcised would have given him openings in evangelizing Jews.

The providence of God is obvious in this section, hindering Paul from doing what he wanted in order to be led to the place where God wanted him to go (vv. 6–10). After ministering in Phrygia and Galatia he wanted to go southwest to the province of Asia, probably to minister in Ephesus, the important capital of Asia, but "the Holy Spirit" prevented him (v. 6). Then he traveled west to the border of Mysia and tried to go north to Bithynia, but again the Spirit—this time called "the Spirit of Jesus"—"would not allow them" (v. 7). Paul had ministered in the east, he cannot go north or south, so he can only go further west and comes to the seaport of Troas (v. 8). There he has the vision with a call from Macedonia (v. 9) and concludes that "God had called [him] to preach" there (v. 10). After this period of uncertainty about God's will, when the will is confirmed Paul and his team get ready "at once" to go to Macedonia (v. 10), and with that to a new horizon in the expansion of the Christian faith.

In verse 10 we have the first of the "we" passages of Acts, suggesting to some that Troas may be where Paul first met Luke or at least where they first began to travel together. Some have suggested that he joined the team in his capacity as a doctor (cf. Col 4:14), which is possible, considering Paul's frequent ill health. Luke got to know Paul intimately through being with him. He was the only one with Paul shortly before his execution in Rome (2 Tim 4:11). But Luke also gives other leaders, like Peter and James, their due place in Acts. Traveling with Silas would certainly have helped Luke get the perspective of the Jerusalem church.

Application. While it is true that this passage does not give us an excuse to quarrel, it does give us comfort if we have disagreements that do not end in amicable resolutions. It also gives hope, for just as Paul and Barnabas got together after the heat of the conflict had died down, so can we. Therefore, we must be sure that during the heat of a conflict we do not do or say things that complicate a final resolution. All too often when people are hurt and disappointed, they make public statements that are difficult to live down. Perhaps they write strongly accusatory letters that cannot be erased once written.

Because God is greater than the problem, we can always live with the hope of resolution. That hope will enable us to look beyond the hurt to the day when we will rejoice in a relationship restored. And that, in turn, should cause us to temper our actions and reactions. Therefore, it is always best to get the help of others who are less emotionally involved in the conflict to guide us. Because they are detached from the situation, they may be able to see things more clearly and advise us to act more wisely.

ACTS 16:11–40

Original Meaning

Lydia's Household Converted in Philippi (16:11–15). Verse 11 gives a detailed log of the journey. We find specific descriptions of the time taken and the places passed through; this is understandable since the author himself participated in this trip. Samothrace was a common stopover for ships. Philippi was about ten miles inland, so they landed at Neapolis. From Neapolis Paul and company used the Egnatian Way, a famous Roman road running east-west with Neapolis as its eastern terminus. Some cobbled sections of this road are still visible.

The region of Macedonia was separate from Greece at this time; now it is mostly part of Greece, with a portion in the former Yugoslavia and Bulgaria. Two famous Macedonian kings, Philip II (356–336 BC) and his son Alexander (334–323 BC), had led a united Greco-Macedonian empire. Macedonia became a Roman province in 146 BC. Philippi was a Roman colony, which means its constitution was patterned after that of Rome.

On the Sabbath Paul and his friends went to the river outside the city gate, expecting to find "a place of prayer" (v. 13). Though "place of prayer" was used in those days for synagogues, this must have been simply a place where people met to worship God. Being by a river facilitated any ceremonial washing rituals. One of the first converts in Philippi was Lydia, a seller of purple cloth from Thyatira, a city renowned for purple dye. It belonged to the ancient kingdom of Lydia (part of Asia in the first century).

The interplay between the divine and human parts in evangelism is well expressed in verse 14. Paul and his companions went to the people and shared the message, but God was the ultimate evangelist. After her whole household (possibly including her employees) was baptized, she asked them to stay at her home. Verse 15b suggests that it took some persuading for Paul and company to decide to go there. This may have been because she was a woman, possibly a single woman. Were the team members reluctant to go there because it was a gentile home? We cannot be sure, but it is unlikely that Paul would have had such hesitancy. Luke's interest in hosts is seen with the mention of hospitality in the homes of Lydia and the jailer (v. 34).

A Slave Girl Is Healed (16:16–24). The story of the slave girl who was delivered from an evil spirit has similarities with episodes involving evil spirits in Jesus's life. The spirits seem to have had supernatural powers that enabled them to recognize the divine source of the ministries of Jesus and of Paul's team (v. 17; cf. Luke 4:34, 41; 8:28). Today also soothsayers predict the future for gain; some are fakes while others do it through supernatural powers. This girl seems to have belonged to the latter category. Though what she proclaimed affirmed Paul's ministry, he is "annoyed" by it (*diaponeomai*, Acts 16:18). Why Paul delayed responding for a few days remains a mystery. But when he did attend to it, the power of God overcame the demonic hold over the girl's life.

This miracle, which caused a significant loss of income for her owners, brought about opposition to the gospel (cf. 19:23–28). Their official reason for opposition was that Paul and Silas were "advocating customs unlawful for us Romans to accept or practice" (16:21)—which the authorities had to take as a serious complaint. Clearly an attempt was made to alienate the missionaries and cause the magistrates to side with "us Romans." Little did they know that the missionaries were Romans too (v. 37).

The treatment Paul and Silas received should not have been given to Roman citizens. They were "dragged . . . into the marketplace to face the authorities" (v. 19), "stripped" (v. 22), "severely flogged," and "thrown into prison" (v. 23) "without a trial" (v. 37). They were sent to the maximum security "inner cell" of the prison, and their feet were fastened in the stocks (v. 24).

A Jailer's Household Is Converted (16:25–34). Despite the humiliation and pain they had experienced through being stripped, flogged, and imprisoned, Paul and Silas were "praying and singing hymns" around midnight (v. 25). Songs in the night of suffering have been a common response to suffering by the faithful throughout the ages. "The other prisoners were listening to them" (v. 25b), and it is interesting that they did not escape when their chains became loose after the earthquake (vv. 26–28). The jailer's near suicide over the possibility that prisoners had escaped (v. 27) is understandable when we remember that Peter's escape from prison resulted in the execution of the guards (12:19) and that the soldiers planned to kill the prisoners after the shipwreck en route to Rome rather than letting them escape (27:42).

In an amazing turn of events, the jailer rushed toward Paul and Silas, fell down trembling before them, and blurted out, "Sirs, what must I do to be saved?" (16:30). He presumably knew that, as the girl had said, they proclaimed "the way to be saved" (v. 17). Most people ignore such messages when they first hear of them. But significant events can make them open to the message—such as a miracle, an act of kindness, or (as here) the events of the evening. He wanted to know what he had to "do" to be saved (v. 30), but actually there was nothing that he needed to do, for everything had already been done for him by Christ. All that was required was to believe (v. 31). Those who say that Paul in his letters is different from the Paul of Acts must reckon with this statement, which is in accord with his letters.

The first part of verse 31, "Believe in the Lord Jesus, and you will be saved," presents the condition for salvation. Paul follows the offer of salvation by explaining the way of salvation (v. 32). This accords with what Paul tells the Romans, "Consequently, faith comes from hearing the message, and the message is heard through the word about Christ" (Rom 10:17).

When Paul extends the offer of salvation to the jailer's household, is he saying that his faith will convert his entire household (Acts 16:31b)? We should infer that Paul is offering salvation to everyone in his household on the same terms as he is offering to the jailer. We should not infer that his personal faith will save his whole family. As both the jailer and his household listened to the word of God, we must assume that they all believed before they were baptized.

As is often the case in Acts, baptism follows immediately after conversion, and here the whole household is baptized. Were infants included in this baptism? We are not told, and thus this passage cannot be used as giving conclusive evidence for infant baptism. The midnight hospitality in the jailer's home includes the compassionate washing of wounds and the serving of a meal, and it is spiced with joy over salvation (vv. 33–34).

Paul and Silas Released (16:35–40). The magistrates must have felt that the punishment meted out to Paul and Silas was sufficient, considering the trivial nature of their offense. Thus, they sent word to the jailer to release them (v. 35). Yet the missionaries insisted on a public apology, which would ultimately influence the public standing of the mission and the church there. Paul's claim to Roman citizenship proved to be a turning point again in Jerusalem (22:25–29).

Paul and Silas made a final visit to Lydia's home to encourage the believers before leaving. According to verse 40, "they [note the *third-person* plural] left" Philippi. Presumably, therefore, Luke stayed on in Philippi and joined Paul again after his return visit to Philippi, at which time the first-person plural reappears (20:6).

Application. Four principles of reaching the unreached are relevant today from this passage. First, we must always be looking for bridgeheads in order to penetrate a community with the gospel. Often the best way is to find some point of contact with someone in the community we wish to reach. Such a point of contact is usually established through a common interest. The interest may be related to a felt need that we know Christ can answer (e.g., sickness, insecurity, fear, marital problems). It can also be commonly held religious convictions, which is what Paul looked for when he made contact in a new community by attending a synagogue or a place of prayer. In Athens it was the philosophical bent of the Athenians (17:21–22). We have found that the love of sports, music, drama and adventure, and the need for extra tuition beyond what students receive in school can be effective means of making contact with unreached youth in Sri Lanka.

Second, the interplay between human initiative and divine quickening identifies our responsibility and reminds us that God is the one who ultimately gives the results. This dual perspective helps us avoid not only being lethargic about witness but also feeling ourselves under a bondage of having to produce evangelistic results. Our call is to be faithful in going out and in using the best methods we know; God will look after the results.

Third, the principle that conversion often takes place through whole groups coming to Christ needs some explanation. These have been called people movements. One of the pioneers in this method of evangelism was an American missionary to India, J. Waskom Pickett (1890–1981), who studied what he called "mass movements" in India. Pickett's studies had a great influence on Donald McGavran, the father of the church-growth movement. People movements are not instances of "group conversion." Rather, each person exercises saving faith, but this is done in consultation with and along with others in the group. In whatever culture one ministers, when working with non-Christians it is always helpful to consider the wider contacts of the persons we reach.

Finally, as with Paul and Silas, we should do all we can to protect the freedom to practice and propagate faith in Jesus Christ wherever we are. If an unconstitutional law hinders the practice of our faith, they should do all they can to stop this. But while an organized "sit-in" like Paul's may be acceptable, violent measures, such as those sometimes used outside abortion clinics, are never acceptable.

ACTS 17:1–15

Original Meaning

Ministry in Thessalonica (17:1–10a). Thessalonica was the capital of the whole province of Macedonia and its largest and most prosperous city. "As was his custom, Paul went into the synagogue" and spoke there on three Sabbaths (v. 2). He must have stayed there much longer than three weeks, for he later writes that he worked day and night in Thessalonica so as not to burden the people there (1 Thess 2:9; 2 Thess 3:8), and that while in that city he also received aid from the church in Philippi (Phil 4:16). The result of the ministry of Paul and Silas was the conversion of several Jews and God-fearers (Acts 17:4). Paul's comment in 1 Thessalonians 1:9 indicates also that many of those converted were pagans.

Seeing that their influence over various people had diminished, the Jews were jealous, and they resorted to ignoble means to fight the missionaries (v. 5a). It was not the last time that religious people used the very people they were supposed to be transforming into good people to do their dirty work. Because Paul and Silas had probably been taken to a safe place, their host, Jason, and some brothers were taken to the city officials (vv. 5b–6a).

Portraying the evangelists as "men who have caused trouble all over the world" (v. 6b) is severe. But it is true that turmoil often results when the gospel challenges people to change their lives, and usually such turmoil originates with those who reject this challenge. The charge against Paul and Silas was that they had defied Caesar, "saying that there is another king," Jesus (v. 7b).

There had been trouble in Rome in connection with the Jews for some time. The events in Thessalonica may have occurred in the spring of AD 50, shortly after Claudius expelled Jews from Rome (in AD 49) following riots associated with Jews and Christians. The authorities would not have wanted a repetition of such problems, and the Jewish opponents would have exploited that fact. Jason was released after posting bond, probably assuring the politarchs that he and the "other believers" (v. 6) would not cause any more problems and would see to it that Paul and Silas left the city. This is the presumed background behind Paul's statement that he, Silas, and Timothy were torn away from the Thessalonians and that Satan stopped them from returning (1 Thess 2:17–18).

Ministry in Berea (17:10b–15). Paul proceeded south from Thessalonica rather than following the Egnatian Way, which continued west toward Rome. His next stop is Berea (present-day Verria). Berea was not as important a city as Philippi and Thessalonica, but it was a Greek-speaking town unlike the western towns that belonged to the section known as "free Macedonia." The three Christian communities he founded on this trip were in a position to take the gospel westward (see 1 Thess 1:8).

In keeping with their usual practice, the team started off at the synagogue (v. 10b) and made the pleasant discovery that "the Berean Jews were of more noble character than those in Thessalonica" (v. 11a). Luke gives two reasons for this commendation (v. 11b). They expressed an attitude of humble receptivity that lies at the heart of faith.

Luke records that among the converts in Berea were many Jews and "also a number of prominent Greek women and many Greek men" (v. 12). One of the converts, Sopater, accompanied Paul on his last journey to Jerusalem (20:4). Both in Thessalonica and Berea prominent women were among those converted (17:4, 12). It seems that in Athens also prominent people were converted (17:34).

But Paul had to make a sudden and rushed exit from Berea as well. Jews from Thessalonica arrived and roused the crowds in Berea, just as they had done in Thessalonica. Paul was sent with a group from Berea to the coast and traveled to Athens. The first few weeks in the life of a new church are most important, and the new believers need to be provided for. Therefore, Silas and Timothy stayed on in Berea with instructions to join Paul as soon as possible (vv. 14–15).

Note Paul had to flee from all three Macedonian cities in which he ministered. This must have been difficult for him to take, but he left behind three stable churches.

Application. The key words for Paul's evangelistic preaching apply today. Paul expounded the death and resurrection of Christ even though it was a stumbling block to the Jews. In our eagerness to be relevant and sensitive to people's needs, we may be tempted to ignore the cross. Since many people have lost the sense of a holy God, they may not be aware of the seriousness of sin. Thus, as we seek to present Christ as the answer to their problems, we may feel tempted to concentrate on their felt needs rather than the needs they should be addressing. A good way to solve this problem is to start by showing the relevance of the gospel to felt needs and to deal with the questions people are asking. Once we have won their attention through this bridgehead, we can move to the questions they should be asking—how to be saved from sin in order to be right with a holy God—which Christ answered on the cross.

In other words, in the preliminary process of proclamation, healing and discussions on contemporary problems are helpful. But we must always look for a way to bring up the message of Christ and his death and resurrection. It seems to me that while the contemporary church is developing effective models to meet people's felt needs, it is not looking seriously enough for effective ways of communicating the message of the cross and empty tomb.

The philosophical idea of dialectic in classical Greek (reaching an idea through dialogue) might represent a closer model to current evangelistic proclamation than the biblical idea. It fits in with the pluralistic philosophy that has swept through much of our society. Pluralists are calling for apologetics to be replaced by dialogue. But the dialogue they speak about is a meeting of minds where no one wants to cause another to change religions. Rather, each one seeks to enrich the other.

Receiving feedback as to what our hearers are thinking through questions, observations, or objections is a necessary part of evangelism, especially when witnessing to non-Christians. It enables us to find out how they have understood what we have communicated. After giving an evangelistic message on John 3:16 at a Youth for Christ meeting, I spoke to a Buddhist youth who had been in the audience. He told me that his religion says the same thing as I had said, whereas I thought this message showed clearly the difference between the Christian faith and Buddhism. He had filtered my Christian terminology through the Buddhist way of thinking in his mind and emerged with a Buddhist message from my talk!

Commitment to proclamation does not preclude listening to others. When people describe their views, we must give them full attention. Sometimes, in a witnessing situation, we may listen more than talk, for we should not rudely interrupt someone else's description of his or her views. We are servants, and it should not bother us if they dominate a conversation. Of course, love for this person will cause us to look for every opportunity to share the liberating news of Jesus Christ with them. Part of our listening may involve reading what non-Christian writers have to say about their religion, rather than only reading apologetic material written by Christians.

I want to add here that there is another type of dialogue that often takes place between Christians and those of other faiths that should not be classed under evangelism but nevertheless may be a valid activity. We may have discussions where people of different religions participate and share each other's views. When I was in my late teens and early twenties, I did this regularly with a group of students in our neighborhood. We met in a Muslim home on Saturday nights. The majority of those who met were Muslims; there was also an atheist (a disciple of Bertrand Russell) and a somewhat nominal Christian. We discussed many things, including politics, sports, world affairs, philosophy, and religion. I always went there as a witness of Christ and often talked about my faith. I yearned for the salvation of these people, and they knew that. Our meetings were not strictly evangelistic events, yet what I learned from them has been important in my own pilgrimage.

ACTS 17:16–34

Original Meaning

Ministry in Athens (17:16–21). When Paul saw these exquisite works of pagan art, he was "greatly distressed" (v. 16). As in 16:18, Luke uses a strong, though different, word (*paroxynomai*) for Paul's reaction to seeing the city so full of idols.

Though Paul was in a rage when he saw the idols, he acted with restraint and respect in his outward behavior among the idolaters (v. 17). "Reasoned" here probably involved proclamation but left room for discussion at the end. The "marketplace" he spoke at was the *agora*, the main public place in the city, adorned with public buildings and colonnades. It was the economic, political, and cultural heart of the city. An ancient description of Socrates has him in the marketplace when it was most crowded, where he conversed with whomever he met. When Paul evangelized this city of Socrates, he used the method of Socrates.

From the time of Chrysostom (ca. AD 347–407), interpreters have suggested that some Athenians thought Paul was proclaiming two gods: Jesus and Anastasis (*anastasis* means "resurrection"; v. 18b). This is typical of how people with a different worldview misunderstand us as we proclaim the gospel. The accusation against Paul (v. 18) reminds us of a similar charge against Socrates, which resulted in his being taken to the Areopagus and condemned to death.

The Areopagus was the main administrative body and the chief court of Athens. We are not sure whether Paul was taken (v. 19) into this council for a proper trial or just to the location of the hill after which the council was named. These Athenians seem to have been curious philosophically (v. 21), and thus they were willing to give the "strange ideas" of Paul an official hearing (vv. 19–20).

The Areopagus Speech and Its Results (17:22–34). Paul's speech before the Areopagus remains a model of sensitive but forthright confrontation of an intellectual audience with the claims of the gospel. "Very religious" in Paul's opening statement (v. 22) is general enough that can mean several things depending on the context. Most likely, it was a simple observation, opening the way for Paul's comment about the altar to the unknown god (v. 23a). Ancient literature contains references to altars to unknown gods. Paul is highlighting an acknowledged need of the Athenians, and he presents the God whom he proclaims as the answer to that need (v. 23b).

Paul introduces his God and offers a critique of the Athenian gods, which took the form of idolatry (vv. 24–29). His basic statement is that God is the creator of everything in the world and that he is Lord of heaven and earth (v. 24). His comments about God are calculated to not only show the futility of idolatry but also to demonstrate that God is the supreme Lord of creation and therefore worthy of our allegiance.

Against idolatry Paul insists that God does not live in temples (v. 24) and does not need our insignificant offerings, for he himself is the provider of everything (v. 25). The apostle continues by focusing both on God's sovereignty over the affairs of the human race (v. 26) and on his creation in human beings of an innate thirst to find him, an incurable religiosity (v. 27). Since God is the immanent sustainer of creation, everyone's life depends on him (v. 28).

All these points lead to the conclusion (note the "therefore" in v. 29) that idolatry is unnecessary and lend weight to Paul's call to repentance that follows (v. 30). If this God is indeed the supreme Lord of creation, the wisest thing to do is to turn to him. This turning to God is not an optional extra that merely adds a new dimension to one's life. It is a command that goes out to all people everywhere. But the wisdom of such a step becomes all the more evident when we realize that this God is someday going to judge the world (v. 31).

Along the way Paul has answered another question that would have arisen in the mind of a philosophically oriented person. If there is a God who is supreme, why does he allow people to live in such open defiance of him without punishing them? His answer has three aspects: (1) God overlooked their ignorance in the past, but (2) now he "commands all people everywhere to repent" (v. 30), and (3) a judgment day is coming (v. 31a). In other words, God will not tolerate sin forever, for he is indeed just. The wicked who openly defy God may prosper for a time, but one day they will have to pay for their sin if they do not repent.

Paul has made some astounding claims—especially that the representative of this supreme God through whom he will accomplish his work is a man called Jesus. How does Paul know that these things are true? What proof does he have of these claims? Paul answers that this supreme God "has given proof of this to everyone by raising [Jesus] from the dead" (v. 31b).

This basic feature of the Christian message brings the growing sense of unease within some in Paul's audience to a head, and they begin to sneer at him (v. 32). Others, however, want to hear more, and the gathering ends on that note (vv. 32b–33). Luke rounds off the story with a report about some of the results of Paul's ministry in Athens (v. 34). A member of the Areopagus, Dionysius, is among those converted, as is a woman named Damaris, who must have been converted through Paul's earlier ministry in Athens (women were traditionally not invited to meetings of the Areopagus).

Paul's strategy of reasoning for the gospel with the Athenians is instructive. His message does not contain direct quotations or appeals to the Old Testament as did his talks to Jews and God-fearers. Such appeals would have meant nothing to hearers who did not accept the authority of the Scriptures. But despite that, the message was thoroughly scriptural. Interestingly, Paul quoted from writers whom the Athenians looked up to (v. 28). Of the two statements in verse 28 there is a question whether the first is actually a quotation, but the second certainly is. Paul would not, of course, have agreed with the philosophical system out of which the statement arose, but he did agree with this individual statement and thus used it to buttress his argument.

It is helpful to know that Paul did not create his arguments in this speech *ex nihilo*. As a scholar schooled in the highest educational structures that Judaism could offer, Paul had access to this Jewish wisdom of the ages. He made use of that when developing the case for the Christian faith to present to the pagan mind.

Application. If we are to maintain our fervor for biblical mission while we engage other religions in study and encounter, we should have three disciplines that we regularly practice in our lives.

First, we must live under the Scriptures. The biblical attitude to life is so different to the world's attitudes that we can easily get drawn into the world's way of thinking unless we are regularly impacted by the Scriptures. A healthy trust in the authority and sufficiency of Scripture along with comprehensive regular input from all the segments of Scripture into our lives will enable us to remain scriptural in our attitudes.

Second, we need the discipline of community. When we live under the yoke of spiritual accountability within a community, we find ourselves challenged by others if we try something new. While such challenges may be difficult to endure, it is healthy for our spiritual stability. Our friends can confront us if we veer away from the path of biblical faith.

Finally, we must live under the discipline of witness. There are few things that energize the soul and enable us to maintain our passion for the gospel as much as an evangelistic lifestyle. When we get close to people, see their lives, and yearn for their salvation, we realize afresh how vital the gospel is for their salvation and we experience afresh the power of energizing for witness by the Spirit (1:8). Such cutting-edge living is an effective safeguard against compromise.

ACTS 18:1–22

Original Meaning

Paul in Corinth (18:1). Corinth was a prosperous city, having the feel of an economic boomtown. It was the center for the worship of Aphrodite, the Greek goddess of love, and had a temple with a thousand sacred prostitutes. From the fifth century BC on, the verb "to Corinthianize" meant to be sexually immoral.

Paul reports that he came to Corinth "in weakness with great fear and trembling" (1 Cor 2:3). This is understandable considering the pain he had endured in his last few stops. Despite the divine call to Macedonia, he had been driven out of all three Macedonian cities in which he ministered. He was worried about the situation in Thessalonica and eagerly awaited the arrival of Silas and Timothy from there (1 Thess 2:17–3:5). Paul may not have anticipated encountering much receptivity to his message in Corinth because of its prosperity and reputation for immorality.

Evangelizing Corinth (18:2–11). In Corinth, Paul was blessed with the acquaintance of Aquila and Priscilla, who had recently been expelled from Rome along with other Jews (v. 2). Like Paul, they were tentmakers, and they soon became business partners (v. 3).

Paul worked on tents during the week and had a more public ministry in the synagogue every Sabbath (v. 4). In every new city Paul visited, he looked for a bridgehead from which he could launch his ministry. Here it was his trade and his contacts in the synagogue.

While Paul was doing this work, his colleagues Silas and Timothy arrived from Macedonia with great news of how the church there was thriving under persecution (v. 5a; see 1 Thess 3:6–10). They probably brought gifts from Macedonia for support of his work (2 Cor 11:8–9; Phil 4:15–16), and as a result he was able to devote "himself exclusively to preaching" (Acts 18:5b).

Verse 6 describes Paul's response when the Jews "became abusive" (*blasphēmeō*): "He shook out his clothes in protest" of their blasphemous attitude and as an expression of his exemption from further responsibility for them. He then explicitly stated this exemption with the words, "Your blood be on your own heads! I am innocent of it," and announced his intention to focus his efforts on the gentiles.

Leaving the synagogue, Paul went to the home of Titius Justus (v. 7), which became the center of the young church in Corinth and was probably where its first house church met. Romans 16:23 refers to Gaius, who provided hospitality for the whole church in Corinth, but Gaius may be another name of Titius. If Gaius provided hospitality to the whole church, he must have had a big house, which meant he was wealthy.

In addition to the open door provided by Titius, the conversion of "Crispus, the synagogue leader" (v. 8), must have done much to encourage Paul in his disappointment over his rejection by his kinsmen, the Jews. The biggest encouragement came from a vision Paul had in which the Lord promised to protect him and told him that he had "many people [*laos*] in this city" (vv. 9–10). The use of *laos* for the prospective Corinthian believers is the usual designation for Israel as the people of God in the Greek Old Testament.

Gallio's Crucial Verdict (18:12–17). Luke does not describe Paul's relatively long ministry in Corinth in much detail. His emphasis is on the response to the Christian faith of the proconsul Gallio, who was a well-known figure in the Roman Empire. His proconsulship of Achaia is attested in an inscription found in Delphi dated around AD 52 and in the writings of his famous brother, the Stoic philosopher Seneca. His positive response toward the Christian faith was a key building block in the church's case for a positive legal standing in the Roman Empire.

The Jews brought Paul to Gallio, charging him with "persuading the people to worship God in ways contrary to the law" (v. 13). The reason behind making this charge was to show that the Christian faith was not truly Jewish and therefore could not be included with Judaism or claim protection under Roman law. Gallio did not even give time for Paul to speak. Rather, he said that what Paul was doing was not a crime for him to judge; it was instead a matter of Jewish law, and he was not going to tackle issues pertaining to their theology (vv. 14–15). The ejection of the Jews from the court (v. 16) resulted in the ruler of the synagogue being beaten by the people. Unfortunately, Gallio did not stop the beating (v. 17).

Itinerating En Route to Antioch (18:18–22). Thanks to Gallio's favorable ruling, Paul was able to stay on in Corinth after he had been brought to trial. But after some time he set off for Antioch, taking Aquila and Priscilla with him (vv. 18–19a). Paul went into the synagogue in Ephesus, reasoned with the Jews (v. 19b), and won an invitation to spend more time with them. He declined it with the promise that he would return if it was God's will (vv. 20–21).

Paul left Aquila and Priscilla behind in Ephesus and set off for Caesarea, where he "greeted the church and then went down to Antioch" (v. 22). One would not go "down" to an inland city from a coastal city. This has led scholars to assume that the church he greeted was the church in Jerusalem, from which we could then speak of Paul traveling "down" to Antioch. This ended Paul's second missionary journey.

Luke adds a note about Paul's having his hair cut in connection with a vow he had taken before leaving Cenchreae, the eastern port of Corinth (v. 18). Hair was cut (usually shaven) after completion of a vow. It would probably be taken to Jerusalem and offered to God. Many have felt that Paul took this vow when he was in a discouraged state at the start of his ministry in Corinth, or perhaps in connection with the vision he received with the promise of God's blessing. If so, cutting his hair was an act of thanksgiving for protection while in Corinth.

Application. As we think of the challenge of evangelizing the Corinths of today, we might be compelled to conclude that the whole world has become a Corinth. The rampant disregard for moral standards is no longer confined to a few cities. It is brought right into homes through television and our phones. The church is inevitably affected by it. Just as some Corinthian Christians succumbed to the temptations surrounding them, contemporary Christians also give in to the loose moral lifestyles portrayed in the media. Sadly, it seems that far too many have been doing this, so much so that in certain Western countries the percentage of Christians involved in extramarital sexual activity is not different from the percentage in the rest of society. Even Christian ministers and evangelists succumb to immorality. There is equal cause for concern in the Third World church.

ACTS 18:23–19:7

Original Meaning

Paul's Third Journey Begins (18:23). Paul's third missionary journey began from Antioch with visits to Galatia and Phrygia, regions that he had previously evangelized. He had done this type of strengthening ministry before (14:21–22; 15:41; cf. 9:32).

The Completion of Apollos (18:24–28). Though Pergamum was the capital of Asia, Ephesus was the real seat of provincial administration. Ephesus was the center of the worship of the Greek goddess Artemis (Roman Diana), the goddess of fertility. It boasted a magnificent temple to Artemis, which was considered one of the seven wonders of the ancient world.

A learned Old Testament scholar, Apollos, receives an important place in this narrative because he played a significant role in the growth of the early church. We are not told from where Apollos first heard about Jesus. It may be that disciples of John who accepted Christ as the Messiah had gone there and taught him, for we are told that "he knew only the baptism of John" (v. 25). He not only had a good knowledge of the word, but he also knew how to communicate it accurately—that is, he had developed skills in Bible teaching. And when he taught, he did so with enthusiasm and fervency.

Into this situation Priscilla and Aquila entered (v. 26). Luke has changed the order of their names from his first mention of them (18:2), giving the wife's name first (see also vv. 18–19). Priscilla may have been the more prominent of the two.

We are not told whether Apollos lodged in Priscilla and Aquila's home, but this act of inviting Apollos into their home is typical of the open-home attitude that this couple had. Apollos was willing to learn from his hosts when they took him home to complete his education in the faith. We will see that this is a characteristic of a true student of God's word.

We are not told whether Apollos was rebaptized, as were the Ephesian disciples whom Paul brought to a more complete knowledge of the truth (19:5). Apollos was probably a true believer in Christ with a deficient knowledge.

The Completion of Twelve Ephesians (19:1–7). Paul had wanted to come to Ephesus for major ministry for quite some time, but he had to wait for God's time (16:6; 18:21), which had now come. It was an important place because from here he could reach the entire province of Asia (19:10). There were believers in Ephesus when he arrived (18:27).

Paul also found some people who are called "disciples" but who were seriously deficient in their beliefs, even though they are said to have "believed" (19:1–2). What is significant is that Paul specifically asked them whether they received the Holy Spirit when they believed (v. 2). This suggests that people can really know when they receive the Holy Spirit.

The problem was that they had only received John's baptism (v. 3). Unlike Apollos, they had not progressed much beyond John's teaching. Hence they needed to be told about believing in Jesus, which led to baptism in his name (vv. 4–5). This suggests that they were not true believers until then.

Verses 5–6 suggest that it was after they were baptized that "Paul placed his hands on them," resulting in the Spirit's coming on them accompanied by tongues and prophecy. Luke then notes that there were "about twelve men in all" (v. 7).

Application. Unlike what happened with Priscilla, Aquila, and Apollos, we have encountered situations of potential learning today that have gone sour. Often this is because the teachers have not been wise in the way they confronted a leader whose knowledge was defective. Unfortunately, some people are so uncomfortable with personal encounter that they prefer to resort to public denouncing or to writing letters or, worse still, writing articles, rather than talking privately with the person concerned. The result is much hurt and usually little teaching that gets through.

Yet leaders will not learn unless they are teachable. The teachable attitude we described above should be true of anyone who truly understands the nature of Scripture. On the one hand, its vastness makes us realize that our knowledge will always be limited. On the other hand, its glory makes us eager to learn whatever new thing we can. These two factors combine with the attitude of childlike faith, which is basic to the Christian life, and prepare us for a lifetime of learning. The teacher-learner distinction subsides as a result of the eagerness to learn more of God's truth. The teacher enters into every teaching situation humbled by the realization that God's truth is so vast that there is more to learn and that some of this learning may come from unexpected sources, such as students or simple, unlearned Christians.

ACTS 19:8–41

Original Meaning

The Evangelization of Asia (19:8–10). As in other cities, Paul uses the synagogue as his bridgehead for evangelism. Ephesus was somewhat different from other cities he went to, for a few believers and semi-believers were already there. He established contact with them and even ministered to them at the start of his stay (19:1–7). Yet Paul was not content with a smattering of believers in Ephesus. He wanted everyone to hear the gospel, and in his remarkable stay of at least twenty-seven months, he succeeded in bringing the gospel to the entire population of the province of Asia (v. 10).

Luke uses some familiar words to describe Paul's evangelism. In the synagogue he "spoke boldly" (v. 8; *parrēsiazomai*, which appears six times in Acts, each time to describe the ministry of Paul). In general, this word describes his ministry among Jews. Preaching the gospel to Jews who were so close to and yet so far from the gospel required much boldness because of their animosity to it.

Though the message of the kingdom of God does not appear as much in Acts as in the Gospels, it is mentioned seven times in Acts—to describe the preaching of Jesus (1:3), of Philip (8:12), and of Paul (14:22; 19:8; 20:25; 28:23, 31). Peter also echoed this message in his Pentecost speech, though he did not use the expression "kingdom of God." The sequence we have seen elsewhere is repeated here in Acts 19, for the Jews rejected the gospel (v. 9b). But here there was a slight difference in that Paul spoke at the synagogue for as long as three months, and only "some" (not most) of the Jews "became obstinate" (v. 9a).

Paul then moved to "the lecture hall of Tyrannus" and held "discussions [*dialegomai* again] daily" (v. 9b). Tyrannus was either the lecturer who taught there or the owner of the hall, who rented it out to Paul. According to the Western textual witness, Paul had the use of the hall from 11 a.m. to 4 p.m. During those hours, public activity came to a standstill in cities in this region and people took an afternoon nap. Paul's hearers must have been motivated to come for discussions at this time. The apostle himself probably gave mornings and evenings to tentmaking (see 20:34) and came to the lecture hall to teach the people in the intervening time.

The result of this two-year stint was that "all the Jews and Greeks who lived in the province of Asia heard the word of the Lord" (v. 10). This was in part achieved through people who came to the big city of Ephesus from other places in the province, heard the gospel, and took it back to their hometowns. It also took place through colleagues of Paul, who brought the gospel to the other towns in Asia. Epaphras, for example, took the gospel to Colossae, Laodicea, and Hierapolis and founded the churches there (cf. Col 1:7–8; 2:1; 4:12–13). Presumably the seven churches of Asia addressed in Revelation 2–3 were founded at this time.

Extraordinary Miracles (19:11–22). After Luke's summary of the ministry in Ephesus, he records a few incidents or pictures that help us understand the unique experiences Paul had there. Verses 11–12 summarize the apostle's ministry in the miraculous. The apologist who marshaled arguments for the gospel was also the healer. The expression "extraordinary miracles" indicates that something unusual happened in Ephesus.

Some background information on Ephesus will help us understand Paul's ministry. This city had a reputation as a center for the learning and practice of magical arts. In addition to Paul's evangelistic ministry (vv. 8–10), he also had a ministry that can be classed as a power encounter, where Christ's power over the forces that bound the people was clearly demonstrated.

Many of the actions that took place in Ephesus are related to this need to demonstrate the power of God over these forces. "Handkerchiefs and aprons . . . touched him [and] were taken to the sick" (v. 12). We cannot be sure whether Paul deliberately adopted this strategy or whether, as with the healing that took place through a woman's touching the edge of Christ's cloak (Luke 8:44), others took these objects representing Paul to the sick.

In a culture where people were steeped in the use of such items, it is understandable that they would use them in connection with healing in the name of Jesus. Luke, however, is eager to stress that God was the one who "did extraordinary miracles through Paul" (v. 11), not Paul himself or the aprons. As a result, the people's "illnesses were cured and the evil spirits left them" (v. 12). It is not surprising that the casting out of demons, which is more prominent in the Gospels than in Acts, gains prominence in a place under the grip of occult practices.

The next picture Luke gives us is of "seven sons of Sceva, a Jewish chief priest" (v. 14). They were among the "Jews who went around driving out evil spirits [and who] tried to invoke the name of the Lord Jesus over those who were demon-possessed" (v. 13). The evil spirit in the person being exorcised by the sons of Sceva attacked these exorcists, leaving them naked and bleeding (v. 16).

Luke goes on to paint the picture of a people seized with fear and holding the name of Jesus in high honor (v. 17). This came as a direct result of the demonstration of God's power and, as we will see, was an important aspect of effective evangelism among those under the grip of occult power. Related to this was the open confession of evil deeds, culminating in a grand scroll-burning session (vv. 18–19). "Openly confessed" (v. 18) probably refers to these people's revealing the content of their spells.

The scrolls burned were valued at fifty thousand drachmas, which was equivalent to about fifty thousand days' wages of an average worker—a great value. The scrolls burned must have been documents containing spells and formulae for which Ephesus was famous.

Verses 21–22 summarize Paul's plans for moving on from Ephesus. The apostle made his plans for leaving with joy, seeing that a strong church had been established there. He wanted to go to Jerusalem and from there to Rome. But he decided first to go to Macedonia and Achaia and complete the work on the contribution to the church in Jerusalem. His plan was to bring the gift there personally (see Rom 15:25–28; 1 Cor 16:1–11; 2 Cor 8–9). He sent two helpers ahead of him to Macedonia and planned to join them shortly.

The Riot Subdued (19:23–41). Luke has one more picture to give us from Paul's lengthy ministry in Ephesus. He seems to have omitted the battle with what Paul calls "wild beasts" (1 Cor 15:32) as well as the hardships that caused him to despair "of life itself" (2 Cor 1:8–10). The riot—especially its conclusion in the acquittal of the Christians—fits in with a theme that Luke considered important: opposition to the gospel. Luke consistently stresses the real reasons behind such opposition, especially because opposition was usually for reasons other than the content of the gospel.

Here in Ephesus (as elsewhere, see 5:17; 13:45; 17:5) the root of the opposition was jealousy. As in Philippi (16:19), it had primarily an economic reason, though it was couched in religious and patriotic terms when presented in public. The temple of Artemis was a key to the economic stability of Ephesus, for foreigners traveled there to worship and deposited money in the temple. This had become more significant in the time of Paul since the city was beginning to lose its significance as a center for international trade.

Demetrius must have been the president of the guild of silversmiths. The silversmiths made "silver shrines of Artemis" (v. 24). In his speech to his colleagues, Demetrius is frank about the way Paul's preaching had hit them economically (vv. 24–26). But it would hit the honor of the goddess (v. 27). That was the line they would take in their public agitation (v. 28).

The silversmiths succeeded in getting the whole city into an uproar and seized two of Paul's colleagues (v. 29). The apostle wanted very much to take the place of his colleagues, but the wisdom of the believers and Paul's influential friends prevailed, and he remained in hiding (vv. 30–31). The word translated "officials of the province" is *Asiarchai* ("Asiarchs," v. 31). While there is some uncertainty about the exact duties of these high government officials, their presence in Ephesus during the first four centuries has been clearly attested. Paul had wealthy and powerful friends at Ephesus.

Luke's terminology and description of the proceedings has remarkable parallels with the evidence that is emerging about the social structure of Asia, especially of Ephesus, in the mid-first century. The people gathered in the great theater of Ephesus, where meetings of the assembly were held (vv. 30–31). This was an unofficial or informal assembly, which Luke calls the *ekklēsia* (vv. 32, 41) and distinguishes from "legal assembly" (*tē ennomō ekklēsia*), which had its regular official meetings (see v. 39). The Jews seem to have become nervous about trouble coming to them, so they wanted to distance themselves from Paul by thrusting a certain Alexander to the forefront. But he had no chance to speak, for a mob mentality has taken over. The result is a two-hour-long shouting session (vv. 33–34).

At this stage the city clerk took over (v. 35). He appealed to the heritage of the city, which believed that the image of the goddess Artemis had fallen down from heaven (v. 35) and was thus of divine workmanship. His point was that the security of having such facts should cause them not to panic and do something rash (v. 36). Besides, there were legal ways to handle such issues (v. 38).

The concerns of the clerk about a bad report going to the Romans have been reflected by another writer, Dio of Prusa, who wrote about fifty years later. City assemblies were on their way out at that time because Rome wanted to eliminate these democratic elements. The clerk must have been fearing these trends when he cautioned his people about the Roman reaction to this commotion (v. 40).

Luke saw this event as another victory for the cause of the gospel. In his estimation, the existing legal system, if properly administered, could be relied upon to give the Christians a fair trial (cf. also the decision of the proconsul Gallio in Corinth in 18:12–17).

Application. We hear many voices today downplaying the value of truth-centered evangelism. Such people, including many who class themselves as evangelicals, claim we live in an age when people no longer think in categories that value truth. In its place, they advocate a needs-based evangelism, which shows Jesus as the answer to felt needs. Sensitivity to needs was certainly a key to Paul's evangelistic strategy (cf. Paul's ministry in Ephesus and elsewhere). But basic to his gospel presentation was the primacy of its truth. This will always be so, for the Christian faith claims to have God's complete revelation to humanity. Those who downplay the truthfulness and content of the gospel have sadly betrayed its heart and have given in to syncretism.

ACTS 20:1–38

Original Meaning

Encouraging the Churches in Macedonia and Greece (20:1–6). After encouraging the Ephesians, Paul leaves for Macedonia (v. 1). He travels through the area speaking many words of encouragement; eventually he reaches Greece (v. 2). Luke strangely omits the fact that from Ephesus Paul first went to Troas and restlessly waited for Titus to come with news of the situation in Corinth. Because the latter did not arrive there, Paul "had no peace of mind"; as a result, he went to Macedonia, where he received good news of the situation in Corinth (2 Cor 2:12–14; 7:6–7).

Encouragement is a key theme of Acts 20. The verb *parakaleō* ("to encourage") appears three times (vv. 1, 2, 12), and verses 18–35 give a sample of the content of the encouragement Paul gave. The wording of verse 2 suggests that he spent a substantial time in Macedonia, unlike his first visit where he had to leave three Macedonian cities in a hurry. Some scholars suggest that he stayed one to two years in this area. During this time, he wrote 2 Corinthians. He may have done some pioneer evangelism—for example, in Illyricum, the province northwest of Macedonia (see Rom 15:18–19). By now Paul had established churches in a good portion of the Greek world. His next plan was to reach the Latin world, possibly using Rome as his base of operations.

Paul may have wanted to go to Jerusalem in time for Passover. He was about to sail from Corinth on a ship bound for Syria, which possibly carried Jewish pilgrims on their way to Jerusalem for this feast. But he found out about a plot against him, possibly by some of the people traveling on this ship (Acts 20:3). As a result, he decided to take the long route on foot through Macedonia, traveling north instead of east. He spent Passover in Philippi (v. 6), a city that had had such a small Jewish population that it did not even have a synagogue. According to his revised plan, he hoped to be in Jerusalem in time for the next feast, Pentecost (v. 16).

An important task during these days was to raise a substantial gift for the poor in the church in Jerusalem. There is only one allusion to this collection in Acts (24:17), but it was a topic Paul often brought up in his letters (Rom 15:25–32; 1 Cor 16:1–4; 2 Cor 8–9). Just as prominent representatives of the diaspora Jewish communities took their annual temple tax to Jerusalem, Paul was planning to take this contribution of the churches as a tangible expression of the solidarity of the gentile Christians with the church from which the gospel first radiated. The long list of traveling companions mentioned in Acts 20:4 probably represented the churches that had made contributions. Almost all of Paul's gentile churches are mentioned. Corinth is not mentioned, but that may be either because Paul represented Corinth or because of strained relations between him and the Corinthian church. Philippi is also not mentioned, but Luke, who has now joined the group, probably represents Philippi. The "we" section that came to a stop after the first visit to Philippi (16:16) starts again here (20:6). From Philippi Paul and Luke sailed to Troas (v. 6), where there is a church that had probably not been started by Paul.

A Midnight Miracle in Troas (20:7–12). At Troas the Christians meet "on the first day of the week . . . to break bread" (v. 7). Here is the first clear reference in Scripture to the believers meeting for worship on the first day of the week. We are not sure whether Sunday worship had already become a regular practice in the church or whether this meeting's being on a Sunday was coincidental.

Luke adds an observation about "many lamps in the upstairs room" (v. 8), possibly to clear his hero Paul of responsibility for Eutychus's falling asleep. Doctor Luke must have been satisfied that Eutychus was indeed dead, unlike in Lystra, where Paul's opponents thought Paul was dead but were mistaken (14:19). Paul's comment, "Don't be alarmed . . . he's alive!" (v. 10b), refers to the young man's state after he was healed.

This occurrence has similarities with the two resuscitations performed through Elijah and Elisha in the Old Testament (1 Kgs 17:17–24; 2 Kgs 4:32–37). Paul "threw himself on the young man and put his arms around him" (v. 10a). The embrace was an extension of the more common practice of laying hands on a person during the act of healing. After breaking bread, Paul talked until daylight and left (v. 11), with the Christians greatly encouraged (*parakaleō* again).

Traveling on to Miletus (20:13–16). Paul's companions took a ship bound for Assos, but Paul left a little later and journeyed on foot (v. 13b). Was this so that he could avoid choppy weather? Did he want to stay a little longer to ensure that young Eutychus was well? Or did he just want to be alone? Or did he keep changing his plans because he was carrying a lot of money for the Christians in Jerusalem and did not want others (apart from his close colleagues) to know where he would be at a particular time? Whatever the reason, the twenty-mile walk alone would have done him some good. From Assos Paul headed for Miletus by ship (vv. 14–15). These two ports were on the western coast of the mainland of Asia Minor. Between them were the island ports of Mitylene, Kios, and Samos. Paul avoided going to Ephesus (v. 16), possibly to save time since he was subject to the schedule of the ship or possibly because it would have been dangerous for him to go there.

Encouraging the Ephesian Elders (20:17–38). Though Paul avoided Ephesus, he sent for the elders of that church to come to Miletus (about thirty miles by land), possibly while the ship was loading and unloading its cargo. His talk to this group follows the form of farewell speeches familiar at that time. The language of this speech is more like Paul's than Luke's.

This is the only record we have of a speech that Paul gave to believers, and its contents are remarkably similar to his letters (also addressed to believers). This is a strong point against those who allege that Acts cannot be historically reliable because of alleged differences between the Paul of Acts and of the letters. Paul's talk has three main themes.

1. He defends his behavior, presenting it as an example to the Ephesian elders (vv. 18–27, 33–35).
2. He presents a charge along with a warning (vv. 28–31).
3. Finally, he commits them to God (v. 32).

Paul's example (20:18–27). The first and most prominent theme of the speech is Paul's example—an element typical of farewell addresses. He says he was an example in four things.

1. *He identified with the people.* He lived among them (v. 18), serving God with humility and tears (v. 19) and going from house to house (v. 20). This enabled him to know what they needed to hear, so that he was able to preach everything that was helpful to them (v. 20a). He obviously had what might be called an openhearted approach to ministry. This is why he could spend a whole night chatting with the believers in Troas (vv. 9–10), and this is why he shed so many tears among the Ephesians (vv. 19, 31).
2. *Paul was a teacher.* He taught the Ephesians everything that was helpful to them, and he did so publicly and from house to house (v. 20). His teaching was relevant to their needs.
3. *Paul was a witness to the gospel.* Paul uses the word *diamartyromai*, translated "declared" at verse 21 (cf. 18:5). This word conveys the idea that evangelism is a serious responsibility, as it calls people to repentance and faith. Later Paul says that the preaching was comprehensive in that he did not hesitate "to proclaim to [them] the whole will of God" (v. 27). Because of that he was able to declare that he was innocent of their blood (v. 26). Verses 21, 26–27 remind us of the call to be a sentinel, with a responsibility to warn people adequately as described in Ezekiel 3:16–21; 33:1–9.
4. Paul's commitment to evangelism is closely tied in with the fourth area where he was an example: *Paul suffered because of obedience.* In verses 22–23 he attributes two actions to the Holy Spirit: a compulsion that is now driving him to Jerusalem, and a regular warning that he will suffer if he goes to Jerusalem. Verse 24 explains how these two seemingly contradictory messages can be reconciled: the goal of life is not to preserve our lives but to be faithful to our calling to testify to the gospel. If such faithfulness involves suffering and imprisonment, then such experiences should be taken on willingly.

After presenting what the Holy Spirit has communicated to him, Paul presents a personal conviction that he will not see them again (v. 25). That, in turn, prompts his declaration that he is "innocent of the blood of any of you" because he has warned them of God's truth (vv. 26–27).

A charge and a warning (20:28–31). Paul is aware of the danger of things going wrong in Ephesus. He therefore both charges them and sternly warns them. The charge consists of three points.

1. Most important, the elders must keep watch over themselves (v. 28).
2. They must watch over the flock as overseers (v. 28). The word translated "overseer" (*episkopos*) has often been rendered "bishop." As elsewhere in Scripture it is a synonym for "elder" (see v. 17). Whereas "elder" focuses on the maturity of the individual, "overseer" focuses on the function, which is to take care of the people. In this verse, this task takes the form of keeping watch over God's people. Believers are to be especially on guard for "savage wolves," who will come even from within the church and distort the truth (vv. 29–30). When Paul was there, he had warned people about this danger day and night with tears (v. 31).
3. The elders must shepherd the flock (see also 1 Pet 5:2–3), which is so valuable that it was bought by Christ's own blood. The reference to Christ's act of purchasing the church with his own blood reminds us that just as the good shepherd gave his life for the sheep (cf. John 10:11), we too must give our lives for the sheep.

Committing the people to God and his word (20:32). Paul finally commits the elders "to God and to the word of his grace." The message they received will enable them to stay close to God. Today we have this message in the Scriptures. Though Paul may not have intended both Old and New Testament here, we can legitimately extend it to the entire Bible, for unlike the time of the first apostles when their message carried final authority, today we have the word of God in which that message is contained.

Paul's example (again) (20:33–35). Paul concludes his speech by once more presenting the challenge of his own life as an example for the elders to follow. When he was with them, he showed sincere commitment. He did not covet what others had (v. 33). Rather, he worked hard with his own hands to provide for the needs of the team (v. 34), and in the process he demonstrated one of the Christian aims for earning money: helping those who are in need (see also Eph 4:28). There is a ring of credibility to Paul's appeals for money for the poor because he himself led the way by being generous in his own giving.

The farewell (20:36–38). The grief expressed at Paul's departure gives us an indication of how much he was loved. He had paid the price of opening his life to these people. They, in turn, reciprocated by opening their lives to him. They now accompany him to the ship, and he proceeds on his journey to Jerusalem—just like his Lord, who also "resolutely set out for Jerusalem" (Luke 9:51), knowing that death awaited him there.

Application. It is well-known that church leaders today find it difficult to motivate others to suffer for the cause of Christ. In fact, they often find it difficult to motivate Christians even to take on inconvenience for the sake of Christ. The three principles about suffering gleaned from this passage can help us here.

First, the greatness of the cause of Christ should fire us with an ambition to take on suffering as a natural response (v. 24). Have we presented the glory of this cause in our proclamation? Or has our proclamation been so this-worldly, so related to our little human desires, that people have lost sight of the glory of the gospel cause? In focusing so much on felt needs, have we neglected the grand theme of the kingdom of God, which is a cause worth dying for? This passage challenges us to rethink our proclamation so that our people will be fired up by the greatness of the cause of Christ.

How important it is to recover this biblical sense of the glory of suffering for a great cause. Perhaps because people have become obsessed with lesser causes today, those who suffer for the gospel are viewed as failures and are pitied in the church rather than admired. Fatigue, unpopularity, inconvenience, or loss of prestige on earth, taken on because of obedience, are regarded as signs of weakness and folly rather than strength and wisdom. This is particularly a problem in richer countries, where economic and technological advancement have made it possible for people to have many conveniences. Convenience itself has become a major goal in life. Even Christians today avoid inconvenience for the gospel and resent it when they are inconvenienced.

This pattern has posed a major problem to churches in poorer countries. They send some of their most capable people to richer countries for education, and these people return expecting convenience. They have become soft and do not want to suffer; when they do, they resent it. Not only do they end up having ineffective ministries, but they also drag the church down to their low level of commitment. We should work hard at trying to restore a sense of the glory of suffering in the church.

Second, leaders can motivate others to suffer for the gospel by themselves being examples of suffering. It is no secret that commitment breeds commitment. When a leader is willing to die for a cause, those who follow are also fired by their enthusiasm. A leader's willingness to die impresses others of the urgency of the task they are involved in, thrills them with its significance, and motivates them to commitment. Our Youth for Christ ministry in Sri Lanka works primarily through volunteers. One of the things we have found is that if the leader works hard at personal cost to himself or herself, that leader usually can recruit and keep committed volunteers. If the leader does not work hard, volunteers often get demotivated and are unwilling to pay a price.

Finally, to this discussion we must add the third priority of leadership gleaned from verse 28: Leaders are good shepherds who die for their sheep. Not only do we die for the cause, we also die for the people we lead. This principle is often violated by Christian leaders today. A gifted pastor leaves a struggling church that needs him badly when he receives an invitation to go to a vibrant church that pays a much higher salary. A professor leaves the struggling seminary of her small denomination that is desperately short of teachers, to go to a famous school that offers her a bigger salary for teaching less hours, along with a generous package that gives time for writing. A Sunday school teacher rejects the request of a distraught student to go home with him to help resolve a crisis with his parents because the time is getting late. These people are not willing to die for their flock. Such lack of commitment begets a selfish Christianity.

One of the keys to solving the commitment crisis in the church is for a few people to be willing to die for their flock. When a leader is willing to die for those whom he or she leads, they in turn become willing to die for the movement or church they are part of. We need to raise up a generation of radical Christians willing to pay the necessary price for us to shake this world with the revolutionary message of Christ. Most leaders are not willing to die for others because no one has been willing to die for them. They have not had a model to follow. But we do have the model of Jesus and Paul. If we start using that model, we may breed a new generation of leaders who are ready and willing to die for others in service and help multiply generations of committed Christians.

ACTS 21:1–36

Original Meaning

In Tyre and Caesarea (21:1–16). As Paul and his friends sail eastward, they stop first at the main port on the island of Rhodes and then at Patara on the mainland (v. 1). There they board a larger ship that travels on the high seas. After sighting Cyprus along the way, they arrive in Tyre, a city in Phoenicia (v. 3). The unloading and loading process takes a week, but they have made good time. Thus Paul's plans to get to Jerusalem before Pentecost (20:16) remain intact. The traveling group makes contact with the church in Tyre (21:4).

"Through the Spirit" (i.e., probably through the operation of a prophetic gift) the Christians in Tyre "urged Paul not to go on to Jerusalem" (v. 4b). How do we reconcile this with Paul's statement that his trip to Jerusalem was "compelled by the Spirit" (20:22)? The Spirit could not possibly have given two contradictory messages in such quick succession. Perhaps the solution lies in the fact that Paul himself placed the Spirit's prediction about impending persecution alongside the compulsion of the Spirit to go to Jerusalem. What the Christians in Tyre received from the Spirit was a prophecy that Paul would have trouble in Jerusalem. Out of that they may have inferred that the Spirit was prompting Paul not to go to Jerusalem. This explains why "through the Spirit they urged Paul not to go on to Jerusalem" (v. 4b).

In Ptolemais, a few miles south of Tyre, Paul and his company stay only one day, but again they greet believers there (v. 7). Next they come to Caesarea, where they stay in the house of Philip—one of the Seven (see 6:5), who is called "the evangelist" here (21:8). We saw his giftedness as both a public evangelist through his ministry in Samaria and as a personal evangelist with the Ethiopian (Acts 8). Luke notes that Philip had "four unmarried daughters who prophesied" (21:9).

In the early church, prophesy was one of the most cherished gifts (1 Cor 14:5, 39), but in that culture unmarried women normally did not have high standing. This may be Luke's way of pointing out that low-status people were included in positions of prominence in the church.

In Caesarea, the prophet Agabus, who had predicted the famine in Judea that prompted a collection from the church in Antioch (11:28–30), predicts that Paul will be bound and handed over to the Jews (21:10–11). He uses the form of an acted prophecy—a familiar method used by Old Testament prophets. The people plead with Paul not to go to Jerusalem, though Agabus apparently does not do this (v. 12). For the first time, it seems, Paul's traveling companions (cf. Luke's "we") also join in the plea. The people weep as they try to persuade Paul (v. 13a; see 20:37). Paul's answer that they are breaking his heart shows how hard all this is on him (v. 13a). But he explains his stand: he is not only willing to be bound but also to die for the cause (v. 13b). Finally the people give up, resigning themselves to "the Lord's will" (v. 14).

The journey from Caesarea to Jerusalem was sixty-four miles, so the company stops over somewhere along the way—we are not sure where—at the home of Mnason (v. 16). Like Barnabas, he is from Cyprus and one of the early disciples. He too may have provided Luke with valuable information about the early days of the church.

Paul Meets the Jerusalem Christians (21:17–26). Paul is warmly received by the believers on his arrival in Jerusalem (v. 17). The next day he and his company meet James and the elders (v. 18). His report of what God has done elicits praise to God, though there is no mention of the gift Paul brought (vv. 19–20a; but cf. 24:17). The "we" sections stop here and start again only with the journey to Rome (27:1), at which point Luke again shares common experiences with Paul. In the intervening events Luke is probably a bystander.

The sensitive nature of what the believers tell Paul is evidenced by the tone in which they introduce their point (vv. 20b, 22b). For the sake of the many Christians who are zealous for the Jewish law, they think it a good idea for him to dispel misrepresentations about his stand on the law by showing a willingness to submit to the law publicly. He can do this by paying for the expenses of four fellow Christians who have taken a vow. In order to do this, he must purify himself along with these people (vv. 24, 26). Lest Paul misunderstand their position, they affirm that they are in agreement with the position of the Jerusalem Council regarding requirements of gentile Christians (v. 25).

Is Paul being inconsistent here? We must remember that Paul himself took a vow a few years before (18:18), so we know that he was convinced about the value of vows for Christians. But what about his opposition to "the works of the law" in his letters (e.g., Rom 3:28; Gal 2:16)? This was opposition to the belief that such works were necessary for salvation. He himself was not opposed to the Mosaic law per se. We must not forget what Paul wrote in 1 Corinthians 9:20. His actions in Jerusalem are consistent with the approach expressed in this verse.

Paul Is Arrested (21:27–36). As Paul was coming to the end of his responsibilities regarding the vows, some Jews from Asia saw him in the temple. They had earlier seen Paul in the city with Trophimus (v. 29), a gentile companion from Asia (20:4), and they assumed that he was also in the temple. Had this been true, it would have desecrated the temple, for gentiles could only go up to the outer court of the temple (the court of the gentiles). They incited the Jewish people to attack Paul (vv. 27–28).

The rioters began beating Paul to death. The timely intervention of the Roman commander and some of his soldiers prevented this from happening (vv. 31–32). Paul was arrested so that he could be given a proper trial (v. 33), but because of the turmoil of the crowd he had to be carried by the soldiers (v. 35). The crowd kept shouting, "Get rid of him!" (v. 36). Luke must surely have felt the significance of the fact that some twenty-seven years earlier, another crowd had shouted, "Away with this man!" at a spot nearby (Luke 23:18).

Application. How can we apply the principle evident in Luke's writings that women and other people marginalized in society have a prominent place in God's kingdom? We ought to follow Luke in demonstrating to such people that they are truly important to God and to the church. Our application of Scripture should be relevant to all segments of God's people. We must show how biblical principles apply to men and women, to the rich and the poor, and to adults, youth, and children. In our illustrations, we should be representative in our use of examples. For us in poorer nations, where much of our literature comes from the richer nations, we should look diligently for examples from our part of the world. In multiethnic societies, we should look for examples from the different ethnic groups.

We should also avoid examples that entrench people in their prejudices. Things have become a bit sensitive recently because of an overemphasis on political correctness, and inclusive language has been used even for God. While we deplore such excesses, that should not prevent us from using language that does not eliminate one group of people (e.g., women). What was legitimate a generation ago may mean something different today, as meanings attributed to words change over time.

Having said this, we must also remember that the New Testament letters say some things about the roles of men and women that grate against the way many people are thinking today. We should be careful about radically reinterpreting these passages to mean something Paul did not mean. Insofar as our cultural backgrounds can cause us to be blind to certain facets of scriptural truth, we should always be willing to submit traditional interpretations to fresh study. But we have no mandate to reject a passage or to reinterpret it so that it ends up saying something clearly not intended by the author. This is a difficult issue, as the plethora of books with conflicting conclusions from authors, all of whom are firmly committed to the authority of Scripture, shows. But whatever our views, there should be no doubt in the minds of all biblical Christians about the equality, importance, and significance of those whom society considers unequal, unimportant, or insignificant.

ACTS 21:37–23:11

Original Meaning

Paul Speaks to the Mob (21:37–22:21). The commander originally thought that Paul was an Egyptian who had tried to lead some people in revolt against Rome (vv. 37–38). This Egyptian took a large number of people to the Mount of Olives, promising them God's intervention, but the revolt was aborted by Governor Felix with the loss of much life but the escape of the Egyptian. The commander expressed surprise at Paul's ability to speak Greek, but the response he received to his query about Paul's citizenship in Tarsus (v. 39) did not impress the commander as much as the fact he found out later—that Paul was a Roman citizen (22:26–29).

Luke's mention of the language Paul used to speak to the Jewish crowd is probably a loose expression for Aramaic (21:40). The fact that Paul spoke fluent Aramaic caused the people to become "very quiet" (22:2). Any who may have thought he was a diaspora collaborator with the gentiles would probably have realized that they were wrong.

Paul began his address respectfully, calling his audience "brothers and fathers" (22:1), just as Stephen had addressed a similar audience (7:2). Paul's first point demonstrated his excellent Jewish credentials (22:3): "I studied under Gamaliel and was thoroughly trained in the law of our ancestors"; that is, he had a thorough training as a Pharisee under the most revered teacher of the era. The description of his activity as a persecutor of Christians (vv. 4–5) opened the way for him to describe his conversion.

Paul's report of his conversion here is similar to that in Acts 9, but there are some interesting points that complement the earlier account. The present one focuses on his call rather than his conversion. He defends his work with the gentiles and shows that he is still a good Jew. This account has a greater emphasis on light than Acts 9: Paul specifies that it was around noon when he saw the light, which would make it a very strong light indeed (22:6). The first account reports that the men with Paul heard the sound but did not see anyone (9:7). Here Paul says that his companions saw the light but did not understand the voice speaking to him (22:9).

Paul does not mention Ananias's dialogue with the Lord, where he was commanded to go to Paul (9:10–16), but he adds a new point, important to his audience, about Ananias's being "a devout observer of the law and highly respected by all the Jews living" in Damascus (22:12). Also new is the word from God communicated by Ananias that Paul was to be a "witness to all people" and that he must be baptized (vv. 14–16). We know from Paul's talk with Herod Agrippa that God also gave this commission directly to Paul (26:17). But here it was important for Paul to tell his audience that a respected Jew had shared the vision of his future ministry with him. In keeping with the emphasis on light and the response to it, Ananias said that Paul was chosen "to know [God's] will and to see the Righteous One and to hear words from his mouth" (22:14). He was to witness to what he has "seen and heard" (v. 15).

Another new point in this account is Paul's description of a vision he had while praying in the temple some later time, where God told him to leave Jerusalem (vv. 17–21). Paul had expressed to God his personal desire to stay in Jerusalem and witness to the Jews, considering his unique background. There is probably a hint that the Jews listening to Paul now should have accepted the validity of his message but would not because of the stubbornness of their hearts.

Luke's earlier description of the circumstances surrounding Paul's departure from Jerusalem is from a different perspective. The brothers had heard about a plot against Paul and escorted him to Caesarea, from where he was sent off to Tarsus (9:29–30).

Paul Uses His Roman Citizenship (22:22–29). Paul's statement in verse 21 that the Lord had decided to send him to the gentiles served as a trigger for another outburst from the Jewish crowd. They shouted for his death, threw off their cloaks, and flung dust into the air (vv. 22–23). The latter two actions expressed both their frustration and their horror at blasphemy, possibly through their connecting the word "Gentiles" with Paul's alleged desecration of the temple. The crowd was too unruly for anything constructive to take place, so the commander had him taken into the barracks in order to give him third-degree treatment—questioning through torture with hope of getting at the bottom of the wrong that Paul had committed about which the Jews were so angry (v. 24).

The planned flogging was probably the Roman scourging with a whip that had thongs weighted with rough pieces of bone or metal. It could cause great harm and even leave people crippled for life. As Paul was about to be flogged, he told the centurion that he was a Roman citizen. Though Roman citizens who had been convicted of some crime could have scourging decreed as a punishment, they were exempt from it as a method of inquiry before trial. The commander was therefore saved from breaking the law any further, for he was wrong to even order the flogging. Thus, his alarm (v. 29) was understandable. He talked of the bribe that he had had to pay to acquire Roman citizenship (v. 28), while Paul said he had inherited his citizenship through birth.

Paul before the Sanhedrin (22:30–23:11). The commander still had to get to the bottom of the case. As it obviously concerned a religious issue, he decided to order the Sanhedrin to look into the matter (v. 30). When Luke says that Paul was "released" (v. 30), he probably meant that he was released from confinement to appear before the Sanhedrin.

Paul's first statement to the Sanhedrin proclaimed that he had fulfilled his "duty to God in all good conscience" (23:1). This is consistent with what he says elsewhere (24:16; Phil 3:6). He was not talking about fulfilling requirements for salvation through a life of obedience. He clearly argued that no one can do that (Rom 2–3). Rather, by Jewish standards of measuring faithfulness relative to conscience, he had lived a blameless and exemplary life.

The high priest Ananias orders that Paul be struck on the mouth for this statement (Acts 23:2). Paul responds with a typically human reaction to this slap. He calls the high priest a hypocrite and says that God will strike him too, for he had violated the law in commanding this (v. 3). It was a miscarriage of justice to strike a person before being convicted, and in this case he had not even been properly charged.

When Paul was told that he had spoken these strong words to the high priest, he made a godly retraction of his typically human reaction (v. 5). Why did he not recognize the high priest? Paul had visited Jerusalem only sporadically during the previous twenty years, and Ananias had become high priest in AD 48, about ten years before these incidents. So Paul would not have recognized him.

As Paul's first line of reasoning was not going to work,

he adopted a new line. The issue at stake here was the resurrection of the dead, which the Pharisees accepted but the Sadducees rejected. Was this simply a crafty ploy used by Paul to divide the group? Certainly there is wisdom, possibly even shrewdness, here. But he was also using a strategy that pointed to the heart of the Christian gospel, which was indeed a fulfillment of Pharisaism, so much so that a real Pharisee should actually become a Christian. He even calls himself a Pharisee here (v. 6).

Paul agreed with the Pharisees that the Jews' national hope depended on a future resurrection. Here he is saying that the first stage of this resurrection has been fulfilled with the resurrection of Jesus. Later Paul will also clearly present the connection between the resurrection of Christ and the hope of the Jews in his speech to Agrippa (26:8, 23). He had already made the connection in his earlier letter to the Corinthians (1 Cor 15:16–28).

Paul's statement results in total confusion in the Sanhedrin, some siding with Paul and others against him. Some even consider the possibility that an angel or a spirit revealed Paul's message to him (v. 9). The commander has to intervene and take Paul away from the scene. The next night the Lord stands near Paul and encourages him by telling him that he is going to testify in Rome (v. 11). Amid all of the confusion of these days, the apostle receives assurance that God is working out his purposes and that one of Paul's great dreams is going to be fulfilled—he will go to Rome.

Application. On several occasions God had to curb Paul's personal ambitions with his guidance. When he wanted to go to Asia, his efforts were thwarted until it was God's time (16:6–10; 19:1). Acts 22:17–21 reflects God's curbing of Paul's ambition to be the witness par excellence to the Jews. The apostle honestly thought that his background would give him such credibility that he would be a powerful witness to his people. But this was not going to be so, and God knew it. Thus, God directed him to leave Jerusalem.

This does not mean that ambition is wrong. Paul also had a great ambition to go to Rome (Rom 1:10–15; 15:22–32), and the Lord fed that ambition in a vision (Acts 23:11). It is good to dream great dreams, but we must place all these dreams at the altar of God and bow to his sovereignty, believing that he knows what is best for us. And we should also be conscious of the fact that when it comes to our ambitions, it is easy for fleshly desire to cloud godly and holy ambition. Since it is difficult for us to distinguish between these two, we must look to God to send obstacles along the way that alert us to dangers.

We should note also that the other Christians in Jerusalem had a part to play in Paul's leaving Jerusalem (see 9:29–30). In other words, the Christian community can be agents of God's warning regarding our ambitions. We usually resent these blocks that come our way and seemingly hinder us from achieving our goals. But we need to discipline ourselves to accept the perspectives of other believers as gifts sent by God, who in his sovereignty knows what is best.

Recently we have heard many sad stories of capable Christian leaders whose uncontrolled ambitions led them to break Christian principles and to end up with shameful failure. Many such people have testified later that their ambition led to their downfall and that they did not have frank advisors who could have helped them avoid the pitfalls. This is why the Bible advises us to seek advice regarding our plans (Prov 11:14; 15:22; 20:18).

This does not mean that we should give up our visions whenever hindrances develop. Paul's plans to go to Asia Minor and Rome were often hindered, but he finally got to both places. Believers also tried to stop Paul from going to Jerusalem at this time, but he strongly felt the Spirit was directing him to go. A key ingredient of faithfulness is a willingness to persevere amid discouragements. Most, if not all, people who have achieved great things for God have done so by persevering through circumstances that would have caused others to give up.

Often our visions are fulfilled by others, and our role may be to motivate them. We can then back this work with our prayers, rejoice when we see it happening, and help wherever we can. Long after Paul's vision of the Lord in the temple, for example, he agreed that Peter had the call to go to the Jews, while his own call was to go to the gentiles (Gal 2:7–8). Yet Paul never lost his burden for the Jews (Rom 9:1–4), and he kept praying for their conversion (10:1). Wherever he went, he started by witnessing to them. Although God took him away from ministry in Jerusalem, when he heard about a need there he took immediate steps to do something about it. This was what had brought him to Jerusalem on this visit—to bring gifts from the gentile churches for the Jewish Christians.

ACTS 23:12–24:27

Original Meaning

Paul Moved to Caesarea (23:12–35). As Paul sat in prison, some Jews devised a plot that began the long process that would send him from Palestine to Rome (v. 12). The intensity of the resolve of these men is evidenced by their decision to have a total fast until they have killed Paul.

At this stage Paul's nephew enters the story with his tip-off to Paul (v. 16). He was able to get in touch with Paul and even with the centurion because Paul was an unconvicted Roman citizen and had to be treated with due respect. When Paul said that he lost all the things that he could claim from a human standpoint because of the gospel (Phil 3:4–8), this must have included his family. His father, probably a wealthy person, likely disowned him. But something of family affection must have remained for his sister's son to take the risk of spilling out the plot of this murderous group.

The centurion took immediate action on hearing about the plot and made arrangements to transfer Paul to Caesarea, where the governor of Judea usually resided (he went to Jerusalem only at important times, such as during festivals). An unusually large military contingent accompanied Paul, possibly because of the threat of a revolt in Jerusalem and also because of the group that was waiting to kill Paul (vv. 23–24). Once they were a safe distance from Jerusalem in Antipatris (about thirty-five miles away) and the danger to Paul's life was diminished, a portion of the group returned to Jerusalem (v. 32).

The centurion sent a letter along to the governor, describing the circumstances of Paul's arrest and trial in Jerusalem. The account embellished the story about Paul with an untruth about the commander's rescuing him upon discovering he was a Roman citizen (v. 27). The commander specifically mentions that "there was no charge against him that deserved death or imprisonment" (v. 29); rather, Paul was being sent to Caesarea for protection (v. 30). Luke's stress on Paul's blamelessness before the Roman law is a major theme of this entire passage.

Felix had became procurator of Judea in AD 52, which means that he had been governor for about five years when Paul was brought to him. Felix came from a somewhat lowly background but rose to a high position because of his brother Pallas, who was for a number of years the head of the imperial civil service. The governor successively married three women of royal birth. His current wife was his third, Drusilla, the daughter of Herod Agrippa I. There were many insurgent uprisings during Felix's term of office, which he ruthlessly put down. After reading the letter Felix ascertained that Paul was from Cilicia and decided to hear his case (vv. 34–35).

The Trial before Felix (24:1–23). The seriousness with which the Jewish leaders took this case is apparent in that the high priest himself made the sixty-five-mile journey to Caesarea along with the elders and the lawyer Tertullus (24:1). The speeches of Tertullus and Paul (as well as Paul's speech before Agrippa in ch. 26) follow the form of forensic speeches of the time.

Tertullus begins with a typical *exordium* (introduction). He expresses the gratitude of the Jews for the peace that they have enjoyed under him. This was not really true, for there had been many insurrections that had been brutally stamped out by Felix.

Tertullus then brings several charges against Paul. His causing riots may refer to the trouble he supposedly caused in Asia. Paul is also charged with being a ringleader of the Nazarene sect, and he tried to desecrate the temple (vv. 5b–6). The term *Nazarene* probably derives from the fact that Jesus grew up in Nazareth (Matt 2:23) and was used of Jesus in the Gospels (Matt 2:23; Mark 14:67; 16:6). This is the only time it is used of the church. Tertullus asserts that an examination of Paul will show that the charges they bring are true (v. 8).

Paul's *exordium* also points to the competence of Felix to judge the case, but he is less lavish than Tertullus with his compliments (v. 10). Each statement recorded by Luke in this summary makes a telling point that convinces Felix of Paul's innocence (cf. vv. 22–27). Felix can verify when Paul arrived in Jerusalem (v. 11). His accusers did not find him doing anything anywhere in Jerusalem that might suggest he was causing trouble (v. 12); they have no proof of any of their charges (v. 13). Paul does admit that he is a member of the Way, but he goes on to show that this sect has similar beliefs to the Jews (vv. 14–15); this is a sect just like the Pharisees and Sadducees. Next Paul asserts his blamelessness (v. 16). No one can point a finger at him regarding his personal life—a powerful state indeed for an ambassador of Christ to be in.

Paul then gets specific about his visit to Jerusalem, giving the clearest reference in Acts to the gifts for the poor he brought with him. He also mentions bringing "offerings" (v. 17), a statement that has been variously interpreted. This may be referring to the gifts for the poor, to offerings he presented at the temple possibly in connection with a vow, or to what he did in the temple in connection with the Nazirites, who had taken a vow.

Then Paul denies the specific charges against him. He was ceremonially clean when he was found in the temple, there was no crowd with him, and he was not involved in any disturbance (v. 18). If the charge about his causing trouble all over the world (v. 5) refers to the trouble in Ephesus, then the people from Asia should be there to press charges (v. 19). One by one he has refuted all the charges against him.

But Paul has one more point to make: he was tried by the Sanhedrin, but they also found no suitable charge to bring against him (v. 20). In his full talk, the apostle may have mentioned the confusion in the Sanhedrin during his trial. He certainly implies this when he says that he had to shout a statement about the resurrection (v. 21), which divided the Sanhedrin. He admits to one possible point against him—a doctrinal issue that really was not within Felix's jurisdiction.

Felix should have released Paul, but he was reluctant to displease the Jews (see v. 27). So he delayed making a decision until the commander came (v. 22). But he gave Paul relative freedom (v. 23). Felix's delaying tactics went on for two whole years, at which time he was removed from his job (v. 27). Luke leaves us with no doubt that this Roman governor thought Paul was innocent of any crime against the state.

Felix and the Gospel (24:24-27). The conversations Paul had with Felix and his wife give us a good description of how many top officials respond to the gospel. Included in Paul's discussions about the gospel (v. 24) was discourse about "righteousness, self-control and the judgment to come" (v. 25a). These discussions made Felix afraid, which expressed itself in a couldn't-care-less attitude ("When I find it convenient, I will send for you"—v. 25b). We also see how mixed his motives were, for he was looking for a bribe (v. 26) and did not want to displease the Jews, even if that meant being unjust to Paul (v. 27). He probably thought that one who was a Roman citizen and who had just brought a substantial gift for the poor must have had access to substantial wealth.

Application. The early Christians not only outthought their opponents, but they also outlived them. In the writings of the early Christian apologists, the behavior of the Christians was a key aspect used in defense of Christianity. The force of blameless lives has been powerful in defending the faith against attacks from outside in every age.

The challenge to the church today to be blameless before the world has become acute, considering the great moral crisis facing the world today. In the West, there has been a general rejection of the Christian worldview that formed its moral basis for centuries. Many of its structures were based on moral absolutes. For example, much of American society operates on the principle of trust. With the current rejection of moral absolutes in postmodern Western society, one wonders how it can survive without deteriorating into serious confusion.

One can imagine that sooner or later many millions in the West are going to look for an alternative to this confusion. When they realize the ravages of sexual indiscipline and seek a purer sexual morality, will they see Christians as people who not only remain pure but have a wholesome enjoyment that is much more refreshing than the extreme asceticism that many opt for? When they realize the ravages of living without integrity, will they see Christians as people who live with a clear conscience before God and humankind?

Although many, tired of the materialism and moral indiscipline of Western society, are turning to Eastern spirituality for answers, they will soon realize that this resource is equally bankrupt. There is no ethical system within Hinduism that enables people to live holy lives. While Buddhism has a strong ethical system to strive for, Buddhists are finding that they do not have the spiritual resources to overcome the onslaught of modern immorality to which they are being exposed in the media. Most countries in the so-called Third World are unable to make progress because of rampant corruption. There is a growing disenchantment with existing structures since people have not been able to shake off the corruption destroying the fabric of many nations.

We do have a dynamic from the creator of human nature that alone can satisfy this homesickness for morality in the human soul. But how have we fared? The church seems to have become a reflection of the maladies of society rather than a witness to these maladies. We have been so enslaved by pragmatism that morality has been subsumed in our quest for results. Earlier we spoke of the valuable place that signs and wonders have as a means of attracting people to Christ. But it is easy to be so enamored by such displays of power that we neglect the priority of holiness over power.

Many churches that emphasize the miraculous today are weak in their teaching and reflections on Christian morality. As a result, people who are testifying to miraculous answers to prayer are underpaying their workers, are guilty of racial prejudice, or lie to make a sale. Evangelists who minister in the miraculous can get so enamored by their power that they give little attention to pursuing holiness. They find refuge in their ministries and thus ignore the voice of conscience that tells them that all is not well in their lives.

This neglect of moral instruction is seen in other branches of the evangelical movement too. Some churches are afraid to confront members who are living privately in sin. In keeping with the thinking of society around us, they do not want to pry into the private lives of others. Preachers are afraid to speak forthrightly against sins condemned in Scripture, fearing that they will be branded as bigoted and will lose members as a result.

I am thankful that prayer has seen a resurgence in many evangelical churches. There is much talk about the place of prayer and fasting in mission. Warfare prayer for breaking down strongholds and the place of prayer in evangelism are receiving fresh emphasis today. But there is little emphasis on praying for personal holiness, on fasting and praying for the revival of holy living in the church. If we examine the New Testament letters that teach about living the Christian life, we will find much more teaching on holy living than on warfare. While we do not discount the value of instruction on warfare and rejoice over its return to the life of the church, we must keep a scriptural balance.

Paul spoke of striving to keep his "conscience clear before God and man" (24:16). The pursuit of holiness is an exercise that must be carried out with utmost diligence. If we exaggerate in the pulpit, we must correct it in the pulpit, even though it may be humiliating. If we fail at home in front of our children, we must apologize in their presence. We must strongly refuse any temptation to pay a bribe or tell a lie to get something done. We must follow the laws of the land even if they may seem silly.

The church, then, must rediscover the priority of holiness and look for the ways prescribed in the Scriptures to release the dynamic of the Holy Spirit, who enables Christians to live holy lives. This is why the Christian faith is so unique. The religions of the world teach us to be good, but Jesus Christ and the Spirit give us the power to become good.

ACTS 25:1–26:32

Original Meaning

Paul Appeals to Caesar (25:1–12). Governor Festus made his first visit to Jerusalem three days after arriving in the province. He met with the Jewish leaders, who were quick to bring up the issue of Paul (vv. 1–2). Even two years after Paul's arrest their urgency over this case and their plans to kill him had not diminished. The first favor they requested of Festus was to have Paul brought to Jerusalem, with the intent that they might kill him on the way (v. 3). Festus apparently preferred to conduct most of his business from Caesarea, particularly in cases that could be drawn out. So he asked the Jews to come to Caesarea with him and promised to take up the case on his return (vv. 4–6).

As in the trial before Felix, the Jews made serious charges against Paul, which they could not prove (v. 7). Again Paul proclaimed his blamelessness before the Jewish law, the temple, and Caesar (v. 8; see 23:1; 24:16). He should have been released at this stage. But Festus bowed to Jewish pressure and, wishing to grant them a favor, asked Paul whether he would be willing to go to Jerusalem for trial. Luke uses the word "favor" three times in the space of ten verses (24:27; 25:3, 9), showing that the chances of a fair trial for Paul were bleak.

Since the process of justice had been stalled for two years, Paul now realized that there was no hope of his getting a fair trial in Judea. Instead, his life was in great danger. The famous Roman justice system that had served him well under Gallio (18:17) could not operate for his good here because of the influence of powerful locals. Paul must have felt that this problem would not be as serious in Rome. Besides, the Lord had told him that he would testify in Rome (23:11). Thus, he decided to appeal to Caesar (25:11)—a privilege granted to Roman citizens. Felix must have been relieved by Paul's appeal to Caesar, for he could now wash his hands of the case. It was clearly beyond his abilities to judge, considering his unfamiliarity with Jewish customs and beliefs. He conferred with his council and declared the appeal valid (v. 12).

Festus Consults King Agrippa (25:13–22). Festus was happy to use a visit from Herod Agrippa II and his sister Bernice to consult on the puzzling case of Paul (vv. 13–14). Agrippa II was the son of Agrippa I (the grandson of Herod the Great and the "King Herod" mentioned in Acts 12). He was in his early thirties. Rumors were rife about an incestuous relationship between Agrippa and Bernice, both of whom did not live exemplary private lives. Agrippa held the vestments of the Jewish high priest and had the right to appoint him. Paul acknowledged that Agrippa was "acquainted with all the Jewish customs and controversies" (26:3).

Festus explained the events up to that point (25:14–21). It was a straightforward explanation, and it is interesting to note that he saw the resurrection of Jesus as a pivotal point in this case (vv. 19–20). When Agrippa expressed a desire to hear Paul, arrangements were made for a meeting to be held the next day (v. 22).

Paul's Speech before Agrippa (25:23–26:23). The appearance of Agrippa and Bernice with great pomp to hear Paul speak at a gathering that included "high ranking military officers and the prominent men of the city" (v. 23) reminds us of the prediction God made to Ananias that Paul would appear before the kings of the gentiles (9:15). Though Agrippa cannot himself be called a gentile, the territory he ruled included many gentiles. Luke's expression "with great pomp" may suggest the transitory character and vanity of all the outward show.

Festus's recounting of the events surrounding Paul shows that he was not impressed by the mob approach of the Jews ("shouting that he ought not to live any longer" [v. 24]) and expresses his conviction that Paul was innocent (v. 25). His immediate dilemma was that he did not have any specific charges against Paul to present to Caesar when he sent him to Rome (vv. 25–26).

Paul's speech once again follows the standard pattern of defense speeches of the first century. It starts with the *exordium* (introductory address to the king [26:2–3]), proceeds to the *narratio* (the narration of events [vv. 4–18]), and ends with the *argumentio* (the proof of his case [vv. 19–23]). Paul acknowledges the acquaintance of the young king with "Jewish customs and controversies," thus implying his suitability to hear his "defense" (vv. 2–3). Technically this was not a legal defense, but the word is used in a general sense here.

The *narratio* gives Paul's testimony. This is his fullest testimony in Acts because it discusses his pre-Christian activity, his conversion, and his calling, which drives his mission. Nothing is said about the role played by the devout Jew Ananias, who had an important role in the testimony given before the Jerusalem crowd (cf. 22:12–16). After saying that the Jews know his past well, Paul affirms his strict background as a Pharisee (26:4–5). Then he says that it is because of the hope of the Jewish people that he is on trial (vv. 6–7) and immediately affirms that his audience should not consider it incredible that God raises the dead (v. 8). The hope of Israel and the resurrection of Christ are intimately bound together, as we will see later.

Paul insists that he once had the same attitude toward "the name of Jesus of Nazareth" as his opponents now do (vv. 9–11).

He vividly describes the vehemence with which he opposed the gospel and persecuted Christians; he was an official representative of the chief priests and their main prosecutor (v. 10a). His statement that he cast his vote against those who were put to death (v. 10b) has led some to conclude that he was a member of the Sanhedrin, where such a vote may have been taken. But he was too young to be a member of the Sanhedrin at that time (see 7:58). Rather, it signifies that Paul was one of the major leaders in the campaign against the faith and that he was actively involved in prosecuting Christians. He "went from one synagogue to another" (26:11), by which Paul shows to Agrippa that at that time the believers were still participating in the life of the Jewish synagogues.

Verses 12–18 give the third account in Acts of Paul's conversion and divine call. Here he recounts that Jesus spoke to him in Aramaic, suggesting that this was Christ's first language. Also to Christ's words are added the comment, "It is hard for you to kick against the goads" (v. 14). This proverb has been used to buttress the idea that Paul was a troubled person, fighting his conscience prior to his conversion. In our study of Acts 9, we discounted this view on the grounds that the autobiographical statements of Paul leave no room for such psychological unrest in the apostle.

Also unique to this narrative of Paul's conversion was his commission by Jesus himself (26:16–18). The account in Acts 22 mentioned two commissions—one by Ananias (22:14–16) and a later one by Jesus (22:21). Here Paul mentions a direct commission from Jesus right on the Damascus road, where he was appointed as a servant and a witness of Christ (26:16). Like the other apostles, then, Paul was to be a witness to the resurrection. Paul claimed apostleship based on this commission.

Two factors qualified a person to be an apostle in the early church with the uniqueness that the twelve apostles had: seeing the risen Lord (1 Cor 9:1; 15:8; see Acts 1:22) and being personally commissioned by him (cf. Rom 1:1; 1 Cor 1:1; Gal 1:1; 2:7). Both these things happened to Paul on the Damascus road. Paul cites one more feature as qualifying him for apostleship: his effectiveness in ministry (1 Cor 9:2; 2 Cor 12:12; Gal 2:8–9). This feature is also presented in the speech to Agrippa (Acts 26:19–23). A key to understanding his ministry is that he was obedient to a vision from heaven (v. 19).

Festus and Agrippa Respond to Paul's Speech (26:24–32). Paul's speech is too much for the practical Roman official, Festus, who knows little about the intricacies of Jewish theology. He recognizes that Paul is a learned man, but he cries out that his learning has driven him insane (v. 24). Paul responds by affirming that what he is saying is both true and reasonable (v. 25). Had Paul been addressing Festus primarily, he would have presumably presented his words in a way that Festus would have understood. But here he is speaking to Agrippa, and Paul knows that the king understands what he is talking about (v. 26a). He is positive that Agrippa already knows many of the facts about the Way because these things were "not done in a corner" (v. 26b).

Paul zeros in at this stage with a direct challenge to Agrippa: "King Agrippa, do you believe the prophets? I know you do" (v. 27). This challenge is for Agrippa to compare what the prophets foretold with what happened in Christ. The king is in a dilemma. As an expert on the Jewish Scriptures, he knows what Paul is speaking about. But he cannot afford to make connections between what he knows and what Paul is saying because then he will have to make a decision about the Way. He therefore brushes off the challenge with an evasive comment that means something like, "In short you are trying to persuade me to act the Christian" (v. 28). Agrippa has not come to this gathering with a view to making such a serious commitment. He simply wants to help Festus out by giving him advice about this case. He may also have looked forward to meeting one of the top leaders of this growing sect. Paul's response shows that he desires all to come to Christ—including rulers (v. 29; cf. 1 Tim 2:1–4).

As the gathering is adjourned, the general sense of everyone there is that Paul has done nothing to deserve punishment (vv. 31–32). Agrippa specifically states, "This man could have been set free if he had not appealed to Caesar." It was easy for the consultant Agrippa to say this after Paul made his appeal. Before that, for two whole years, Paul was kept in prison because the leaders did not have the moral courage to release him even though they knew he was innocent.

Application. While the resurrection is the cornerstone of the Christian faith (both proof of the message of Jesus and the onset of Israel's eschatological blessings), many within the church do not know how to proclaim that message. The victory of the resurrection is one that must be emphasized because, in our pragmatic world, we find it difficult to visualize how an event like this can affect our daily lives.

Through the stress given to the cross in evangelical preaching in this century, we have come to understand at least some of the deep meaning of the cross. But we may not have come to a corresponding understanding of the resurrection and its significance. Yet this is a key message for today's church because, with all our pragmatism and focus on how to live the Christian life, Christians seem to lack the theological and spiritual muscle needed to overcome the onslaught of the world upon the church. The answer to the moral and ethical poverty of today's church is not only more instruction to people on how to live. It is a good dose of theological truth that will enable them to understand the meaning of Christ's victory won through his work. Believers will then realize that in Christ and in the resurrection power he provides they have the spiritual and theological power to withstand the onslaughts that come from the world, the flesh, and the devil. There is a great need for Christians to rediscover the meaning of the resurrection and its implications for their lives today.

ACTS 27:1–28:15

Original Meaning

The Journey Begins (27:1–12). Luke returns to the first-person plural ("we/us"; v. 1) after leaving off with his arrival in Jerusalem (21:18). He may have been in Caesarea during the two intervening years and collected valuable information for his two-volume work (see Luke 1:3). Others in the traveling party included the centurion, Julius, his soldiers, other prisoners, and "Aristarchus, a Macedonian from Thessalonica" (Acts 27:2). The latter had been traveling with Paul for some time (19:21; 20:4); he is described as Paul's "fellow prisoner" in Colossians 4:10 and "fellow worker" in Philemon 24. These two letters were probably written from Rome in the early sixties.

In tracing this journey, it is helpful to have a map open. In the Phoenician city of Sidon (about seventy miles north of Caesarea), the centurion, in the first of his many acts of kindness to Paul, permitted him to visit "his friends"—probably members of the Christian community there (Acts 27:3; see 11:19). The western winds that blow during the summer months caused the ship to go east and north of Cyprus (traveling off the coast of Cilicia and Pamphylia). Luke must have made note of this fact since this was opposite to the route they used when coming to Tyre two years earlier (21:3).

The ship arrived in Myra in Lycia, and the passengers boarded an Alexandrian ship there (27:6)—probably one of the large Alexandrian grain ships that headed west from there. A strong northwest wind probably caused them to make "slow headway" (v. 7) and even to travel southwest, along the southern coast of Crete, rather than due west (v. 8).

With difficulty the ship arrived in Fair Havens, which, despite its name, was not a suitable place to face the rigors of winter. The group had already been delayed, for it was "after the Day of Atonement" (Yom Kippur, v. 9), which fell around October 5 that year. Paul felt it was not safe to venture out to find a better place for the winter (v. 10). This advice may have been given informally at a consultation with the owner/master of the ship, its pilot, and the centurion. We do not know whether this advice was given through direct divine guidance or through Paul's human wisdom. We know that on one point he was not accurate, for he predicted the loss of life if they ventured out, and that did not happen.

Paul was a seasoned traveler, who had already been shipwrecked three times and had spent a night and a day in the open sea (2 Cor 11:25). But he was overruled by the majority, who decided to go a short distance further west to the better harbor at Phoenix (v. 12). They needed to travel four miles west and about thirty-four miles west-northwest across a bay.

The Storm (27:13–26). A "gentle south wind" seemed to be ideal for the journey to Phoenix, so the crew weighed anchor (v. 13). Unfortunately, Paul's ship had to confront a northeaster with all its force. They eventually decided that they could not fight it, so they gave in and let it carry them along in the opposite direction, away from the island (vv. 14–15). The little island of Cauda gave them a temporary reprieve from the gale (v. 16), and they were able to take some emergency measures necessary under these conditions. The lifeboat that may have been towed behind the ship was hauled in (v. 17a), and the crew passed ropes under the ship.

As they were being driven along, a new fear confronted them—the dreaded shallows off the shore of Cyrene in North Africa called "Syrtis" (v. 17b). The crew "lowered the equipment or instrument" (literal translation, v. 17c), an action that has been given numerous explanations, as Luke is not specific about this instrument. This may be because Luke did not know what the instrument was or had forgotten its technical name. It was probably a floating anchor.

The next step the sailors took was to throw their cargo overboard (v. 18) and then the ship's tackle or spare gear (v. 19). By doing this they hoped to decrease the danger of the ship if it offered too much resistance to the storm. The sun or stars did not appear "for many days" (v. 20a), which meant that they could not now determine which direction they should go. They finally came to the stage of giving up hope of being saved (v. 20b).

As a result of this storm, most of the people on board would have become seasick and not have eaten for several days. In this hopeless situation, Paul came with a word of encouragement, having himself been encouraged by God through a vision. When he said that they should have taken his advice (v. 21), he was not making an "I told you so" statement but trying to win their attention. Twice he asked them to keep up their courage (vv. 22, 25), basing that appeal on his vision. God had a job for him in Rome, and because of that everyone would be saved (v. 24). After expressing his faith in God, he predicted the ship would run aground on an island (vv. 25–26). From this point on, Paul seems to have assumed a leadership role on the ship.

The Shipwreck (27:27–44). Luke mentions "still being driven across the Adriatic Sea" (v. 27), that is, the central Mediterranean. They wisely decided to drop anchor and wait until it was day so that the ship would not dash onto the rocks of these unknown seas (v. 29).

Paul asserted his leadership again when the sailors tried to escape from the ship and ensured that they would stay on for the crucial time when the people had to go to shore (vv. 30–32). His leadership is again seen when he urged the people to eat (vv. 33–34). They needed energy for the final challenge and would not be strong on empty stomachs. They found courage to eat when they saw Paul eating after giving thanks to God (vv. 35–36).

The crew saw a bay, which was probably what is now known as St. Paul's Bay in Malta, but they did not recognize the land. They decided to sail toward land and run the ship aground near the shore, but it struck a sandbar further out and became stuck (vv. 39–41a). The waves were too strong for the battered ship, and it broke to pieces (v. 41b). The soldiers would have faced severe punishment if the prisoners escaped, so they planned to kill them; but they were saved because the centurion wanted to save Paul's life (vv. 42–43a). Again, therefore, people's lives were saved because of Paul's presence on the ship. As Paul had predicted, "everyone reached land safely" (v. 44).

Ministering in Malta (28:1–10). The proposed forty-mile trip from Fair Havens to Phoenix ended two weeks later on the island of Malta, which was scarcely a day's voyage from the great port of Syracuse in Sicily. But the people had to wait three months in Malta because it was winter. The word "islanders" (v. 2) is *barbaroi* (literally "barbarians"), which was how those who did not speak Greek were referred to in those days. The islanders showed the shipwrecked travelers "unusual kindness." And Paul, despite his exhaustion from the preceding events, joined in setting up a fire, which was probably needed because of the cool autumn temperature (vv. 2–3).

The viper that stuck to Paul has caused problems for scholars. While present-day Malta has vipers that stick onto their victims, they are not poisonous. This may be the species referred to here. But if so, the islanders would not have expected Paul to swell up or fall down dead (v. 6). Perhaps there was a species of poisonous viper in first-century Malta, which has since been exterminated by the islanders. The reaction that Paul was probably a murderer (v. 4) is typical of superstitious people who see others going through misfortune—they assume that they are paying for their wrong deeds. When nothing happened to Paul, their superstition led them to change their verdict, saying that he was a god (v. 6).

As was typical, Paul had a healing ministry in the town following the healing of the chief official's father (vv. 8–9). The prayer and the placing of hands on him is similar to other healing miracles. The hospitality of the people was truly generous, for they even supplied the travelers' needs when they left three months later (v. 10).

Rome at Last (28:11–15). The ship that took Paul and company to Italy was also an Alexandrian ship, with a figurehead of the twin gods, Castor and Pollux. If they left three months after the shipwreck, that would have been around February 8, rather early in the shipping season. They first stopped at Syracuse in Sicily and then at Rhegium at the toe of the Italian mainland. They finally reached Puteoli, the port of Neapolis (modern Naples), where they disembarked (vv. 12–13). It is interesting that Paul was allowed to accept the invitation to spend a week with the Christians in Puteoli.

During this week, news of Paul's arrival in Italy reached the church in Rome, presumably through someone who went to Rome from Puteoli. Some believers decided to meet Paul on the way (v. 15). Some Christians met him at the famous Forum of Appia, forty-three miles from Rome, others at the Three Taverns (a settlement that had grown around an isolated inn by that name), thirty-three miles from Rome. "At the sight of these people Paul thanked God and was encouraged" (v. 15).

It was almost two and a half difficult years after the divine assurance given to Paul in Jerusalem that he would go to Rome. He finally met Christians in Rome, people whom he had longed with much eagerness to see. Luke's mention of arrival in Rome in verse 14 rather than in verse 16 has been variously explained.

Application. This passage is unique to the exposition of God's sovereignty amid hardship in Acts because here the hardship comes not from the sinfulness of people but from the forces of nature and the folly of humans. Paul and his team would have avoided the storm if the ship's officers had heeded his words of wisdom. This passage provides a needed check to prevent overapplication of the story of Christ's stilling the storm (see Luke 8:22–25). Indeed, Christ can still every storm, but he does not immunize Christians from problems that others in the world also face. Sometimes he miraculously delivers his people from such situations, while at other times he gives them the courage to endure natural and other disasters. We thank him for performing miracles but also for his sufficient grace that provides endurance amid storms.

Some Christians will testify how God has saved them from investing in a venture that went bankrupt, while others ponder the mysterious providence that permitted them to invest in the same venture after making all the necessary inquiries about it and praying about the decision to invest. One Christian will testify how a traffic jam caused him to miss an ill-fated flight, while the godly mother of three little children will face an uncertain future because her husband died on that flight. We should never say that the one who was saved was godlier than the one who was not. In fact, perhaps the one who suffered had a stronger faith, so that God felt that he or she was able to go through this circumstance. We must never glibly pronounce that a calamity faced by a believer is a judgment from God. This may be so, but most often it is not, and by making such a pronouncement we may unnecessarily intensify the suffering of the righteous (cf. what Job's friends did to him).

What use is it to refer to God's sovereignty in view of the Christian who was not spared the experience of disaster? Though Christ can still the storm, we can have the courage to face it when he does not, for we know that through the crisis God's sovereignty will work out something good (Rom 8:28). We live under God's promises, and these promises brace us to face such challenges.

ACTS 28:16–31

Original Meaning

A Rented Home in Rome (28:16). Once Paul arrived in Rome he was "allowed to live by himself," which means he must have rented a house (see v. 30). He had a soldier to guard him, and Paul was probably chained to him by the wrist. This soldier would be relieved every four hours or so. As a result, Paul and the gospel became a talking point among the members of the palace guard (cf. Phil 1:13). The environment was not ideal, but it was adequate for Paul to have a bold and unhindered witness in Rome for two years (Acts 28:30–31).

Paul and the Jews in Rome (28:17–28). Luke does not refer anymore to Paul's relations with the Roman Christians. Instead, he concludes his book by describing Paul's attempts at witnessing to the Jewish community and by giving a summary of his other evangelistic activity. These have been key themes in Acts. Paul first called the Jewish leaders to meet him (v. 17), which was the correct protocol in communities that had a strong sense of solidarity. He explained to them the circumstances of his coming to Rome, climaxing with the statement, "It is because of the hope of Israel that I am bound with this chain" (v. 20b).

The leaders replied that they had not received any letters from Judea concerning Paul (v. 21). This is surprising, considering the urgency with which the Judean leaders hounded Paul while he was there. Also surprising is the fact that the Jewish leaders said that they did not know much about the Christian faith despite the presence of a Christian community in Rome (v. 22).

The first point can be explained in two different ways. Perhaps a letter or representative had been sent but was delayed because of the complexities of winter travel. Equally plausible is that the leaders in Judea did not think that they had much of a chance of success in Rome after failing in Judea, where the Roman leaders were eager to do them favors (24:27; 25:3, 9). They may have preferred to let the case go by default, especially since Roman law was severe on unsuccessful prosecutors.

We see a familiar sequence in Acts 28:23–28. The Jews showed an interest in the Way, and a meeting was arranged (v. 23a). Paul tried to convince them about Jesus "from the Law of Moses and from the Prophets" (v. 23b). The familiar word *peithō* ("persuade, convince") appears twice in these verses (vv. 23–24). Some are convinced, "but others would not believe" (v. 24). Those who rejected the message had stubborn hearts that did not want to believe. The result of that meeting was unpleasant for Paul (v. 25). There isn't much new here. Luke underscores the tragedy of Jewish rejection of the gospel. What is new is Paul's use of a familiar text (Isa 6:9–10) about hardened hearts to explain Jewish resistance to the gospel (vv. 26–27).

Bold Preaching and Teaching (28:30–31). Acts does not conclude on the note of Jewish rejection of the gospel. Rather, Luke's conclusion presents a more glorious reality: the gentiles hear the gospel, and Paul has two years of bold witness about "the kingdom of God and . . . the Lord Jesus Christ" (v. 31). At the start of Acts, Luke gave his key verse (1:8), which predicted that through the Holy Spirit the gospel would be proclaimed "to the ends of the earth." The book ends with that prediction being fulfilled.

Paul had more freedom than a typical prisoner because he was able to live in his own rented house and welcome all who came to see him (v. 30). Paul probably wrote his Prison Letters—Philippians, Ephesians, Colossians, and Philemon—at this time, though scholars are not unanimous about this.

Why does the book of Acts end so abruptly? Is it because Acts was written shortly after the two years mentioned in this conclusion? There is a strong case for this, and many scholars date the book of Acts to the early to mid-sixties. We cannot be sure of what Paul did after the events described in Acts. Tradition affirms that he was released from this imprisonment, had more evangelistic campaigns, and probably visited friends in Macedonia and Asia. Did he go to Spain during this time, as he had wished to (Rom 15:24, 28)? We cannot be sure.

Paul was probably arrested again and wrote the Pastoral Letters during his second imprisonment in Rome. The last of these, 2 Timothy, speaks of his impending death. He was martyred sometime between AD 64 and 67.

Application. The description of Paul's evangelism in Acts 28:30–31 shows us various factors that go into making an effective evangelistic process that are as relevant today as they were in the first century.

People under God's sovereignty have confidence to evangelize. Acts affirms the sovereignty of God in the various situations Christians faced: in the first persecution of believers, which resulted in a prayer that reflected on sovereignty (4:24–30); in the scattering of believers that became the scattering of the seed of the gospel as refugees were transformed into missionaries (8:1, 4); in the mysterious way in which Paul was brought to Rome (chs. 27–28). Evangelism thrives under the shadow of sovereignty. We know that God is marching on with his agenda, even through what humans consider tragedies, and we may join in the stream of God's sovereignty by being active in his agenda. To one who lives under sovereignty, success is obedience to God. That is, even though Paul was bound to a chain in Rome, he was a success.

With his confidence in God's sovereignty, Paul carried on with his ministry as if nothing had happened on the Mediterranean Sea! In Rome he probably continued his tentmaking, wrote his four great Prison Letters, and carried on his openhearted ministry as he welcomed all who came to him (28:30). The palace guards ended up talking about Christ, and the other Christians were "confident in the Lord and dare[d] all the more to proclaim the gospel without fear" (Phil 1:13–14). Thus Paul affirmed: "What has happened to me has actually served to advance the gospel" (Phil 1:12).

The depth and effectiveness of Paul's ministry was greatly enhanced by this mingling of deprivation, sovereignty, and obedience. This has been so throughout the history of the church. It is well-known that suffering is often the context out of which great creativity emerges. When you add to that the operation of the sovereign God, who can turn tragedies into triumphs, you realize that deprivation is not something to fear but an occasion for God to express his glory.

Though we belong to the triumphant kingdom of the Lord of the universe, we may sometimes feel as if we are living under circumstances of defeat. The witness of Acts should encourage us to see obedience to God as the ultimate success and triumph in life. Some churches in the West that were once powerful in national life are gradually losing their power and political clout. I see Christians bemoaning this fact and responding sometimes aggressively against this loss of earthly power. Perhaps they should not be worried, for great spiritual power is often unleashed from environments of great deprivation. Paul's imprisonment shows us that the greatest activities of life can be successfully carried out in such situations.

The message is about the kingdom of God and Jesus Christ. Luke summarizes the message preached as being about "the kingdom of God and . . . the Lord Jesus Christ" (Acts 28:31). This too has much to tell us today. The kingdom of God has been a neglected topic among evangelicals in this century. Preaching about the kingdom of God presents the greater purpose of God than just what God can do for an individual. It affirms that God is working out his purposes through the vicissitudes of history and that his plan will finally be accomplished, with his kingdom ruling the world. We ask people to join in this great march forward with the Lord of the universe. In this world, where people are wracked by fear, this is liberating news.

If the truth of the kingdom were added to our evangelistic preaching, our evangelism would yield much stronger Christians. In today's evangelism we tend to focus on how Jesus meets our personal needs. This topic is, of course, appropriate. But sooner or later Christians are going to find that God does not meet some needs they consider to be urgent. At such times they may be tempted to stray from Christ and seek help elsewhere. But if the grand picture of the kingdom is firmly rooted in their minds, they will never forsake the Lord of the universe for a smaller, less powerful deity or force.

Also necessary to evangelistic preaching is a focus on Jesus. Again, we do not only tell what he can do for us in connection with our present needs. We also describe who he is and what he has done and is doing in the world. We must emphasize the Jesus who is preached in Acts. Such a portrayal of Christ will leave believers feeling secure, confident, and complete.

The method is to be open to people and to preach and to teach. We noted how Paul opened his home and welcomed all who came to him (v. 30). If we are to truly identify with those whom we are trying to reach, we must open our lives to them as Paul did.

In such situations, Paul preached and taught (v. 31). Preaching refers to a proclamation of the message that appeals primarily to the will of the individual. In teaching, the emphasis is more on challenging the mind. Often in Acts evangelism is described as teaching (5:21, 25, 28). Especially when evangelizing people who do not have a Christian worldview, teaching is important in order for them to understand what Christians are saying and thus to make an intelligent and informed decision. However impressed they may be by our oratory in preaching, they will interpret our message by sending its words through the grid of their own worldview. They may make a decision for Christ in response to our passionate invitation, but they may not have truly understood the gospel.

Since many people in the West today have rejected the Christian faith, their worldview is not Christian. Therefore, witnesses in the post-Christian West face the same challenge that we in so-called non-Christian countries do. A key to effective evangelism in both these environments is teaching people what Christians believe and being sensitive to their reactions. Teaching does not have to be boring! I have heard people say of some Christian communicators that they are teachers, not preachers. But what they really meant was that they were boring speakers. Teachers must use a wide variety of means to attract and keep the attention of the audience.

The priority of evangelism. Luke's decision to close his book with a report of ongoing evangelism reminds us that evangelism is the passion that ignites our activity. God has acted decisively in Christ to save humanity. Herein lies the ultimate answer to the problems of the human race. If we love this world as God does, we will want to tell it of this liberating good news. This work will consume our passion until the day we die.

ROMANS

INTRODUCTION TO ROMANS

Romans claims to be written by Paul the apostle (1:1)—or, we might more accurately say, composed by Paul, who uses Tertius as his amanuensis, or scribe, to "write down" what Paul dictates to him (see 16:22). The apostle has finished an important stage of his missionary work (15:19). Now Paul is ready for a fresh challenge, to plant churches in Spain (15:23–24, 28). But before he goes there, he intends to return to Jerusalem to hand over to the church there the money he has been collecting from the gentile churches (15:25–27). Then on his way from Jerusalem to Spain, Paul plans to stop off in Rome (15:23–24, 29).

Paul writes Romans while in Corinth during the third missionary journey (Acts 20:2–3). This is probably in AD 57, give or take a year. What is most significant for our understanding of Romans is the sense Paul gives us of having reached an important transition point in his missionary career. He has been preaching the gospel for almost twenty-five years; he has planted thriving churches over much of the northeastern Mediterranean part of the Roman Empire; he has hammered out his theology on the anvil of pastoral problems and debates with opposing factions. He thus writes Romans during a lull in his ministry, at a time when he can reflect on what he has come to believe and what it may mean for the church.

The church at Rome was made up of both Jews and gentiles, with gentiles having recently become the majority group. Paul's letter seems to reflect just this balance. A few scholars have tried to minimize one side of this evidence or the other, arguing that the letter is addressed only to Jewish Christians or only to gentile Christians. But such conclusions can only be achieved by suppressing one side of the evidence or the other. With the large majority of modern scholars, therefore, we conclude that Paul's audience in Romans includes both gentile and Jewish Christians, with gentile Christians in the majority.

BOOK OUTLINE

I. The Letter Opening (1:1–17)
II. The Heart of the Gospel: Justification by Faith (1:18–4:25)
III. The Assurance Provided by the Gospel: The Hope of Salvation (5:1–8:39)
IV. The Defense of the Gospel: The Problem of Israel (9:1–11:36)
V. The Transforming Power of the Gospel: Christian Conduct (12:1–15:13)
VI. The Letter Closing (15:14–16:27)

ROMANS 1:1–7

Original Meaning

Paul (1:1). Paul introduces himself to the Roman Christians by identifying his master, his office, and his purpose.

1. While clearly revealing Paul's sense of subservience to his Lord, the word "servant" also was applied especially to outstanding figures in Israel's history, such as Moses and David.
2. He is "called to be an apostle," one of those whom Jesus himself had appointed to represent him and to provide the foundation for his church (see Eph 2:20).
3. "Set apart for the gospel of God" probably refers to the time when God called him on the Damascus Road (Acts 9:1–19). The "gospel" is the central, unifying motif of Romans, and Paul signals its importance by referring to it three other times in the introduction to the letter (vv. 9, 15, 16).

Paul and the Gospel (1:2–4). Paul now elaborates his brief introduction, describing the gospel in verses 2–4 and his apostolic calling in verses 5–6. Throughout the letter he is at pains to demonstrate that the good news about Jesus Christ is rooted firmly in the soil of the Old Testament. The "prophets" (v. 2) to which he refers are not just the famous writing prophets, but Old Testament authors generally.

Verses 3–4 describe the content of the gospel: Jesus Christ himself. The verb translated "appointed" in verse 4 does not mean that the resurrection made clear what Jesus already was; rather, it qualified him to attain an entirely new status. However, this does not mean that Jesus *became* Son of God at the time of his resurrection. But Jesus's resurrection, concluding and validating the messianic work of redemption, gave him new power to dispense salvation to all those who would believe in him (see esp. v. 16).

Paul's Apostolic Ministry (1:5–6). In verses 5–6, Paul elaborates briefly on his apostolic status. He has received this "grace" for two purposes. First, from the time of his conversion (see Acts 9:15), the Lord made clear that Paul's primary mission was to bring gentiles to faith in Jesus. What marks God's people is no longer deeds done in obedience to the law but an obedience that stems from, accompanies, and displays faith. Second, the Christians in Rome, Paul asserts in verse 6, are included among those gentiles. One of Paul's concerns in this long prescript is to establish his right to address a group of Christians he has never met before. Thus he makes it clear that the Romans belong to the sphere of ministry God has assigned him.

The Roman Christians (1:7). Paul finally gets around to identifying the recipients of the letter. They are all the Christians in Rome, "loved by God and called to be his holy people." Both descriptions reflect Old Testament language about Israel. "Grace" (*charis*) comes from a verb (*chairein*) that often appears in Greek letters as a greeting (cf., e.g., Jas 1:1). "Peace," by contrast, reflects the Semitic world, for behind it lies *shalom*, the Old Testament word for the well-being of the righteous.

Application. Being an apostle is an act of God's grace. As Paul makes clear elsewhere (e.g., 1 Cor 12 and Eph 4), so are all ministries. Serving God and his people in specific ways is a product of God's unmerited favor toward us. When we serve the Lord and the church, we do what we have no right to do on our own: speak in God's name, reach out with his love, and lead his people. Only because God both calls us to minister and gives us the grace to do it can we accomplish anything worthwhile.

ROMANS 1:8–15

Original Meaning

Thanksgiving and Prayer (1:8–12). Paul's thanksgiving is expressed to "my God" and is mediated "through Jesus Christ" (v. 8). Christ has created the access to God that enables Paul to approach him in thanksgiving. The reason for Paul's thanks is the wide reputation the Roman Christians have gained for their faith. In verses 9–10 Paul reinforces the sense of commitment to the Roman Christians hinted at in verse 8 by emphasizing his constant prayers for them.

Paul's own spirit has been caught up in God's Spirit, and he now serves the gospel in and by means of that transformed spirit. Paul "constantly" (v. 9) brings them regularly before the Lord. One specific focus of Paul's prayer in relationship to the Romans is that he may be able finally to come to Rome to minister (v. 10b). Specifically (v. 11), he wants to go to Rome so that he may "impart" some "spiritual gift." Paul may have in mind an insight or ability given by the Spirit that he hopes to share to strengthen the faith of the Roman Christians. But Paul immediately qualifies this purpose. It is not, Paul hastily adds (v. 12), that the spiritual benefit will flow all one direction, from Paul to the Romans.

Paul's Plans (1:13–15). Paul wants them to understand that his failure to visit Rome was not because of lack of will but because of lack of opportunity. Paul had often planned to visit them but was prevented from doing so. It was probably the pressing needs of the ministry in the eastern Mediterranean. But Paul is still intent on getting to Rome, where he wants to enjoy a time of mutual edification in the gospel.

Paul's desire to preach in Rome is motivated not by a concern to expand his personal territory but by his deep sense of obligation to preach the gospel to all kinds of people (vv. 13, 14). "Greek and non-Greek" is Paul's way of referring to all of gentile humanity (v. 14a). The relationship between this first pair of terms and the second ("the wise and the foolish," v. 14b) is not clear, but it probably refers again to gentiles only. This, then, explains why Paul is so eager to "preach the gospel also to you who are in Rome" (v. 15). Paul has been given a commission from the Lord to be the apostle to the gentiles, and it is this divine mandate, not any personal benefit or emotional satisfaction or marketing strategy, that impels Paul to travel ever farther afield.

Application. Paul's zeal for preaching the gospel should serve as a model for us. As this passage reveals, he was motivated to evangelize and plant churches because he was a man under obligation. Few of us will have such clear direction about a call to ministry or about the direction our ministry should take. But the imperative to evangelize is an obligation, Paul suggests, that all believers share.

ROMANS 1:16–17

Original Meaning. These two verses belong to the introduction to the letter. But these verses are also closely related to the body of the letter that follows, as Paul introduces the theme he will develop in the following chapters. For this theme, we need to look at the word that heads these two verses: *gospel.* Picking up the key word "gospel" that has been a basic motif in the introductory verses (see 1:1, 2, 9, 15), Paul now briefly explains why he is so committed to spreading the good news and how that message is able to transform people.

Why is he not ashamed? Because he knows the gospel he preaches is the divinely appointed means to bring salvation to the world. "Salvation" (*sōtēria*) and the verb "to save" (*sōzō*) are important words in Romans. We sometimes use this language to describe conversion only, but Paul more often uses it to refer to final deliverance from sin and evil that will come to the believer at death or the parousia (see esp. 5:9–10; 13:11).

Announcing what will become a key theme in this letter, Paul insists that the salvation available in the gospel is for *all* who believe. In a significant advance on the Old Testament, which focused on Israel, the gospel is universally available. But also typical of Romans is the qualification Paul immediately adds: this gospel of salvation is "first to the Jew." In some sense, he will affirm, Jews still have a kind of priority in the plan of salvation. The juxtaposition of these two statements—"*everyone* who believes" and "*first* to the Jew"—drives the theological dynamic of Romans.

Why does the gospel transmit salvation to those who believe? Paul explains this in verse 17. The Greek is simply *dikaiosynē theou*, literally, "righteousness of God." Paul uses the phrase only nine times in his letters (see also 3:5, 21, 22, 25, 26; 10:3 [2x]; 2 Cor 5:21). Since eight of them come in Romans, clearly the phrase is significant for the argument of this letter. Each occurrence must be examined in its own context, but most agree that the references here, in 3:21–22, and in 10:3 have the same meaning and are key to the letter. Three interpretations are popular.

1. "God's righteousness"—an attribute of God. "Righteousness" can refer to God's faithfulness.
2. "Righteousness *from* God"—a status given to people by God. When God justifies the sinner, God gives that person a new legal standing before him—his or her "righteousness."
3. "Righteousness *done by* God"—an action of "putting in the right" being done by God. This view, held by a growing number of scholars, gives a dynamic sense to "righteousness." It is God's intervention to set right what has gone wrong with his creation.

The context does not point clearly in one direction. The verb "reveal," which has a dynamic sense (come into being, manifest; see 1:18) favors the third view. But the fact that this righteousness, as Paul goes on to say, is based on faith favors the second view. Perhaps the most important consideration, however, is the use of the language "righteousness of God" in the Old Testament. Here we find that key prophetic texts use this phrase to denote God's eschatological saving activity. We think, then, that Paul announces the arrival in history of this saving activity of God. But in the context of his larger teaching, and qualified as it is here by human faith, this saving activity takes a specific form: the act by which God puts people who believe in right relationship with himself.

A central motif in Romans, and in Paul's gospel in general, is the insistence that one can experience this righteousness of God *only* through faith. Paul emphasizes this point in two ways. First, he repeats the word "faith": (literally) "from [*ek*] faith into [*eis*] faith," which is probably correctly interpreted in the NIV as an emphatic construction, "faith from first to last." Second, Paul cites Habakkuk 2:4 for the connection between the righteous person, faith, and life. Is he emphasizing that righteous people should live by faith? Or is he asserting that it is only the person who is righteous by faith who will attain life? The syntax can go either way, but we think that the argument of the letter, in which Paul again and again asserts that a person is righteous (or justified) only by faith, favors this second reading.

Application. We, in ourselves, are *never* worthy, not even the best of us. The gospel is precisely "good news" (the literal meaning of the Gk. word *euangelion*) because it announces that God accepts us anyway; all that we have to do is receive his offer in faith—to be sure, a faith that must, by its very nature, always be accompanied by obedience (cf. Rom 1:5). Justification reminds us that our standing with God is by grace and that thankfulness should be the hallmark in all our dealings with him.

ROMANS 1:18–32

Original Meaning

God's Wrath against Sin and Its Basis (1:18–20). God's reaction to sin is not the anger of an emotional person; it is the necessary reaction of a holy God to sin. The Old Testament regularly speaks of God's inflicting wrath on people, both in the course of history and especially at the end of history. Paul is probably referring broadly to the sentence of condemnation that all people stand under—a sentence that God sometimes inflicts in the events of history but will carry out with finality at the end of history.

Especially important for Paul is his insistence that God's wrath falls on people who "suppress the truth" (v. 18). One can only suppress something of which one has knowledge. As a result, Paul goes on in verses 19–20 to show that this word is entirely appropriate to use in describing people's relationship to God's truth. Human beings do have knowledge about God. He has revealed it to them (v. 19b), manifesting some of his divine qualities in the world he has created (v. 20). Moreover, these qualities "have been clearly seen" by people (v. 20).

Peoples' Suppression of Truth and Its Consequences (1:21–31). This section is dominated by a thrice-repeated sequence:

"they . . . exchanged" (vv. 22–23)—"Therefore God gave them over . . ." (v. 24)
"they exchanged" (v. 25)—"Because of this, God gave them over . . ." (v. 26)
"their women exchanged . . . in the same way the men also" (vv. 26b–27)—"God gave them over . . ." (v. 28b)

In each case, human beings put their own god or sin in place of the truth God has revealed to them. God reacts by handing them over to the consequences of the choice they have made.

Just who the people are who make these exchanges is never clearly stated; throughout Paul uses the general "they."

While the story of humankind's original fall into sin has undoubtedly colored Paul's description, he has in view human beings generally, prone to turn away from God because of the original fall into sin. What he says, in other words, is typical of human beings who have been given some evidence of God's truth in the natural world around them.

The first "exchange" (1:21–24) focuses explicitly on idolatry. People "knew" God (v. 21a), but they refused to acknowledge him. "Their thinking became futile" (v. 21b), they prided themselves on their own wisdom (v. 22), and they traded the "glory of the immortal God" for their own self-made images (v. 23). Paul echoes language used in the Old Testament to describe Israel's fall into idolatry when the people fashioned a golden calf to worship (see Exod 32).

As a punishment for this idolatry, God "gave them over" (v. 24). God reacts to the human decision to turn from him by consigning people to the consequences of their actions. As Paul will show, this involves an ever-increasing cycle of sin, but he highlights sexual sins.

The second "exchange sequence" (1:25–26) reiterates the connection between idolatry and sexual sin established in verse 24. The end of verse 26 is then transitional, as Paul both unpacks this sexual sin in terms of homosexuality and introduces the third "exchange sequence" as well (vv. 26b–28). The focus on homosexual acts reflects Jewish tradition, which often saw in homosexuality particularly striking evidence of the gentiles' idolatry and depravity. At the end of this section, Paul indicates the consequences of the indulgence in homosexual acts (in this case, among men in particular), that they "received in themselves the due penalty for their error" (v. 27b).

At the end of verse 28, Paul finally introduces the "handing over" that corresponds to the "exchanged" of verse 26b. He has muddied their close relationship in his desire in verse 28 to emphasize the correspondence between sin and result. The relationship is intolerably awkward in English, but it would go something like this: because people did not "approve" (*edokimasan*; NIV "think it worthwhile") of God's knowledge, he handed them over to "unapproved" (*adokimon*; NIV "depraved") minds (v. 28). Sin affects not only our affections (idolatry) and our senses (sex) but our very thinking.

Another result is not surprising either: people end up doing "what ought not to be done" (v. 28b). In verses 29–31, Paul provides several illustrations of this sinful conduct. Similar lists of sins—usually called "vice lists"—appear elsewhere in the New Testament (Matt 15:19; Gal 5:19–21; Col 3:5; 1 Tim 1:9–10; 1 Pet 2:1; 4:3) and imitate a widespread secular form.

Concluding Indictment (1:32). At the end of this section, Paul reiterates its key themes. First, human beings are in a position to understand God's truth. Second, sinners deserve death. Death (*thanatos*) is spiritual death, the condemnation or wrath of God under which all human beings stand as a result of sin. Finally, Paul suggests it is worse for a person to "approve" those who practice sins than to do them oneself (v. 32). Paul would be the last to minimize the seriousness of actual sin. But he apparently wants to castigate especially those people who, while not themselves perhaps tempted by a particular sin, lead others into it by their approval of it.

Application. Not only has God left clear evidence of himself in the world he has made, but this evidence is actually perceived by people: "God has made it plain to them" (v. 19). The reality of natural revelation and its universal availability has consequences for one of the most often-asked questions about God's justice: What about the fate of those who have "never heard"? This is a question I myself asked when people were witnessing to me in my college days. It has no easy answer. But one thing we can say on the basis of Romans 1: all people *have* heard. God has revealed certain truths about himself in the world, and all people have access to that truth. Every person is guilty of rejecting that knowledge of God universally available.

Paul does not deny that these truths may help lead people to search for true knowledge of God or to illustrate that knowledge. An important passage here is Acts 17:22–34, where Paul uses natural revelation as a stepping-stone to the presentation of the gospel to intellectuals in Athens. Natural revelation has a real, but limited, purpose. The beauty and intricacy of the world can help people understand that there must be a Creator; that religious traditions can reinforce notions of sin, judgment, and atonement; and that history can point to a providential ordering of events. Such things can stimulate in people a search for the true God. But Paul emphasizes how limited such knowledge is. Apart from God's grace, it does not lead people to worship the true God. Without further revelation about Christ and his work on the cross, disclosed in the gospel, it cannot bring salvation.

ROMANS 2:1–11

Original Meaning

Self-Righteous Jews Are as Guilty as the Gentiles (2:1–5). How can Paul claim that Jews are doing "the same things" as the gentiles (2:1)? Probably he means the same kinds of things. Jews in the first century were not idolaters, nor was homosexuality common among them. But they did commit many of the sins Paul lists in 1:29–31. Perhaps he even thinks of their preoccupation with the law as a kind of idolatry. In any case, their judging of other people rebounds directly onto them. For since they are doing the same things as these other people, they condemn themselves at the same time. No one can escape this judgment. Moreover, God's judgment is "based on truth" (*alētheia*; v. 2). It is just and impartial, based on the facts. And relying on "the riches of [God's] kindness, forbearance and patience" to avoid judgment will not work (vv. 3–4). These words together connote God's grace and willingness to forgive. We must remember that the Jews' assumption of superiority over gentiles was not a matter of ego or personal boasting. Out of all the nations of the earth, God had chosen Israel as his people. Surely, Jews may well have reasoned, as God's chosen people, they are immune from judgment.

It is this assumption Paul attacks here. God's kindness, Paul says, was intended to lead "you to repentance" (v. 4). Instead, apparently the Jews were regarding it as a carte blanche to sin with impunity. As a result, concludes the apostle, the Jews are "storing up wrath" against themselves, a wrath that will be inflicted on the day of God's coming righteous judgment (v. 5).

God Judges Every Human Being Impartially on the Same Basis (2:6–11). This important paragraph supports a point that is implicit but vital to Paul's indictment of self-righteous Jews in 2:1–5: God assesses Jews and gentiles on the same basis. In effect, Paul argues, there is a level playing field when it comes to God's ultimate verdict. In verse 6 Paul quotes from the Old Testament to show that "works" (NIV "what they have done") will be the basis for God's judgment. Key to Paul's argument is the word "each person"—including both Jews and gentiles.

Paul makes a similar point in verse 11 by insisting that God "does not show favoritism." The word for "favoritism" was apparently coined by Christians to translate a Hebrew expression that vividly conveys the sense of partiality: treating someone on the basis of outward appearance. God, Paul claims, does not do this.

Paul's apparent application of the partiality principle to Jews in terms of their covenant privileges and the judgment is a new and radical concept. He seems to be denying the covenant itself and, implicitly, God's own revelation in the Old Testament. Already, therefore, we see emerging the question of the continuity between the Old Testament and the gospel that becomes so central to the argument of Romans.

Paul spells out the implications of God's impartial judgment based on works, for two opposite kinds of people. On the one hand (v. 7), God will "give eternal life" to those "who by their persistence in a good work are seeking glory and honor and immortality" (literal translation). On the other hand (v. 8) are "those who are self-seeking and who reject the truth and follow evil." Such people earn for themselves "wrath and anger." Just in case we missed the point, Paul goes over the same ground again in verses 9 and 10.

Application. We, too, can show contempt for God's kindness toward us by using it as an "open sesame" for sin. We grow cavalier toward our sin because we think God will simply overlook it out of his love for us in Christ. But sin is a serious matter, whether we are in Christ or not. To be sure, Scripture teaches that the believer is eternally secure in Christ, and this security puts the Christian in a different position than the Jew under the old covenant. But the Scripture also teaches that a lack of concern about sin is incompatible with true faith. Thus Paul's warning in this text about presuming on God's grace carries a warning for the Christian as well as for the Jew.

ROMANS 2:12–16

Original Meaning. Paul has argued in 2:6–11 that Jews are in the same situation as gentiles when it comes to God's judgment. But what Paul seems blithely to ignore is that Jews are hardly in the same situation as gentiles. They have many privileges and blessings from God that the gentiles do not have. Preeminent among these, especially in the eyes of first-century Jews, was the law. Paul intends to show here that the Jews' possession of the law does not give to them a decisive advantage over the gentiles (v. 12).

"Law" (Gk. *nomos*) refers to the law of Moses. It was to Israel alone that this law was given, and they were made responsible for it. Therefore, when Jews sin, they sin "under" it or in its sphere (Gk. *en*, v. 12b). Gentiles, by contrast, sin "apart from" that law (Gk. *anomos*, v. 12a). But why can the law not protect the Jews from God's wrath? Paul explains in verse 13. The teaching was not new with Paul; the rabbis made the same point.

Verse 13 again raises the question of whether Paul teaches that people can be put right with God by what they do. But as in 2:8 and 10, Paul is simply asserting the standard of God's assessment. No person ever actually meets the standard of obeying the law required for right standing with God.

Verses 14–15 are a self-contained unit that describe the gentiles' relationship to "law." Paul is noting that gentiles do, in a certain sense, have access to law. To be sure, they do not have *the* law—that is, the law of Moses, the Torah. But their frequent conformity to many of the requirements of that law shows that they have a knowledge of God's basic moral requirements—God's "law" in an extended sense. The gentiles' innate knowledge of God's law leads them often to do what is right. When this happens, their consciences, along with their thoughts, "defend" them, convincing them that they are doing what God requires (v. 15). But they will not always obey, and when they do not, the conscience has the opposite effect: it "accuses" them (v. 15). All gentiles sometimes do the law and sometimes do not, and their consciences therefore both accuse and defend them.

Paul's reference to God's judgment in Christ in verse 16 is not easy to integrate into his argument. The NIV takes verses 14–15 as a parenthesis. But it is better to take verse 16 with the final verbs in verse 15. The constant self-criticism of the gentiles finds its ultimate meaning in the judgment of God at the end of history. That judgment, Paul affirms, takes place "through Jesus Christ," whom God has appointed as the arbiter (v. 16). This christologically oriented judgment is fully in accord with the gospel Paul preaches.

Application. As was true of natural revelation in chapter 1, natural law is the subject of a lot of debate in our day. Our pluralistic environment raises pointedly the question of the basis for those fundamental moral norms by which a society governs itself. "Positive" law—that is, specific law enacted by a lawgiver or lawmaker—must have a universal basis if it is to be universally applicable or avoid being arbitrary. Under the impetus of such issues, the tendency increasingly is to base positive law on the notion of "the common good." But that idea is slippery and open to being imposed on the minority by the majority. The idea of natural law that Paul endorses here helps us to establish a foundation for universal moral norms and therefore for positive law, which will not be undermined by the whims of society or the convenience of the majority.

ROMANS 2:17–29

Original Meaning

The Law (2:17–24). In a series of "if" clauses, Paul begins by enumerating many of the privileges enjoyed by the Jews (vv. 17–20). All the privileges Paul lists are legitimate, and almost every one has explicit Old Testament warrant. The problem is not that the Jews are illegitimately boasting in what is not really theirs. The problem, rather, is that they are not living up to their claim.

The end of verse 20 reveals again Paul's preoccupation with the law in this section. His enumeration of general Jewish blessings ended with the words "because you are instructed by the law" (v. 18); now he states "because you have in the law the embodiment of knowledge and truth." In natural revelation, the gentiles have knowledge of God and are therefore "without excuse" when they sin (1:20). Jews have knowledge of God in the special revelation of God's law so that they, likewise, "have no excuse" (2:1) when they sin.

Paul breaks off his conditional sentence at the end of 2:20 (the break is marked in the NIV with a dash). He does this so that he can get the maximum rhetorical effect from the charge that he now levels against the Jews. Only two points in these fairly obvious charges need comment.

First, what Paul means by accusing the Jews of robbing temples (v. 22) is unclear. The obvious interpretation, of course, is that the Jews are guilty of robbing pagan temples. We have some evidence that Jews at this time were relaxing the Old Testament strictures against using precious metals melted down from idols. The action of robbing temples must be the opposite of the Jews' abhorrence of idols.

Second, note the summarizing character of verse 23. The NIV takes this verse as a question, but it may be an assertion, giving even more weight to it. Here is the essence of the matter for Paul. By failing to demonstrate in day-to-day living the qualities of the law they profess to love, they not only fail to be the light that God wants them to be but they actually harm the reputation of God. Paul highlights this point in verse 24 with his quotation of Isaiah 52:5.

Circumcision (2:25–29). Next to the law, circumcision was the most important distinguishing mark of Jewishness. It is natural, then, for Paul to discuss it along with the law (2:17–24) in his continuing attempt to erode the Jews' confidence in their inherited religious advantages.

Paul does not deny that "circumcision has value" (v. 25a) But its value is contingent on obedience: only Jews who "observe the law" will profit from it. What does Paul mean by observing the law? Circumcision has no value to rescue Jews from God's wrath because their obedience to the law never reaches the level required for salvation. Verse 25b simply states the negative corollary of this point: failing to obey the law can annul the value of circumcision.

Verse 26 draws a natural inference from verse 25: if doing the law, not circumcision, is what saves, then gentiles who, though uncircumcised, obey the law can be saved. Having put before the Jew with whom he is debating the figure of a gentile who has done the law and has therefore joined the people of God (v. 26), Paul brings the imagery home by talking about this gentile standing in judgment over the disobedient Jew.

Verses 28–29 are a kind of appendix to this argument. Paul has made clear that real Jewishness can never be determined by physical birth, by cuts on our skin, or by devotion to a particular book. To be a real Jew is an inward matter. It is marked by the "circumcision of the heart" (v. 29), a circumcision that comes in the context of the Spirit, not the "written code."

Application. Christians do not hate or despise Jewish people even if we are convinced that their religion does not provide for their salvation. Nor do we hate Arabs because we don't think that Islam saves, or Indians because we question the validity of Hinduism (or Buddhism), or secularists because we do not think materialism is the final answer to life.

But we need also to admit that anti-Semitism lurks right around the corner—particularly when we are dealing with texts such as Romans 2. We must draw the conclusion that Paul himself draws from his discussion: that the Jewish people cannot be saved in their own religion and need to hear and respond to the gospel. We should never compromise on this. At the same time, we also need to avoid any hint of triumphalism when we make these points. Indeed, if we are faithful to Paul, we will acknowledge that, from a natural standpoint, Jews start in a position of advantage to us (3:1). But rescue from our plight, coming solely as a matter of God's grace, is nothing we can take any credit for.

ROMANS 3:1–8

Original Meaning. If we have followed Paul's argument when he asks in 3:1, "What advantage, then, is there in being a Jew, or what value is there in circumcision?," we are ready to answer "none." But Paul surprises us (v. 2a).

Paul's "first" is not followed by a "second" (3:2b). It is likely that Paul intends to give a longer list, but he gets sidetracked by his concern to clarify the limitations on the Jews' privilege of possessing God's word.

Paul seems to be grappling here with the common Jewish belief that God's righteousness, his covenant faithfulness, gave the Jews virtual immunity from judgment. In response, Paul affirms that the marvelous blessing of knowing God's word (v. 2) is a double-edged sword. For God's word promises blessing for obedience, but it also warns about the curse that will fall on disobedience. God remains faithful (v. 3) and righteous (v. 5) in all his dealings. But Jews must understand that the ultimate standard of righteousness is his own holy character, and that holy character requires him to respond to sin with wrath (v. 6).

But the Jewish objector is still not satisfied, arguing it is unfair for God to condemn Jews for acts that enhance his glory (v. 7). Paul responds with a counterquestion intended to show the absurdity of such an objection (v. 8): Should we then take the view that any act is justified so long as it brings good in the end?

Verse 8 is Paul's own counterquestion, designed to show the absurdity of the objection in verse 7. If the objector is right, and if God should not condemn Jews when they sin because their sin enhances God's glory, then the general inference would be that sin is justified as long as it eventually brings good. In an ironic twist, Paul adds a parenthesis, noting that some people (probably Jews) have accused Paul of teaching this very thing! Therefore, Paul concludes, the "condemnation" of people who argue this way "is just" (v. 8). Jews cannot excuse their sin just because God uses it for good in his salvation-historical scheme.

Application. The Jewish tendency to think that the covenant made them secure from all threat of divine judgment has parallels in the Christian church. Even genuine Christians can err in this matter. Believers should not so presume on their "security" that they fail to make every effort to bring their lives into obedience to Christ. It is precisely for this reason that many contemporary theologians and preachers prefer the slogan "perseverance of the saints" to "eternal security." For the former contains the reminder that the saints need to persevere if they expect to attain glory. We believe that God gives every aid needed for us to persevere. But we must also recognize that our commitment and dedication to the cause is also required.

ROMANS 3:9–20

Original Meaning. The question-and-answer format of verse 9 resembles the style of verses 1–8, and the question is probably sparked by these verses. The question is whether there is any basic difference between Jew and gentile. In chapter 2 as a whole he has criticized the Jews to such an extent that some may conclude they are worse off than the gentiles.

The "not at all!" makes clear that the distinction Paul denies here has to do with the specific issue of rescue from God's wrath (v. 9b). The exact phraseology is important: people do not just commit sin, but they are "under the power of sin" (v. 9c).

Paul then moves to a series of Old Testament quotations that substantiate the universality of sin. Paul quotes mainly from Psalms and Isaiah. In verses 13–14, Paul focuses on sins of speech. Verses 15–17 then enumerate sins of violence against others. Verse 18, finally, returns to where Paul began: the basic human disregard for God.

In verse 19 Paul announces the conclusion to be drawn from this series of quotations. Those "under the law" are Jews, accountable by God for the law of Moses he has imposed on them. The conclusion Paul draws from this is interesting: "every" mouth is "silenced"; the "whole world" is accountable to God. But how can Old Testament verses that, Paul says, apply to the Jews bring all of humanity under conviction? By proving from the Old Testament that Jews are condemned, Paul feels it legitimate to extend that verdict to all people.

Paul is aware that Jews may well want to appeal to their relationship to God's law as a reason why they are exempt from the verdict. Paul meets this objection by claiming that the law is powerless to change the Jews' basic standing before God (v. 20).

Paul concludes by telling us what the law *does* accomplish: through it "we become conscious of our sin" (v. 20). "Become conscious" in the NIV translates the Greek noun *epignōsis*, "knowledge." But since "knowledge" in the Bible often refers to intimate acquaintance or understanding, the NIV rendering is on target here. By setting before people a detailed record of God's will, the law makes people vividly aware of how short of God's requirements they fall. It therefore brings awareness of sinfulness.

Application. People, by nature, are addicted to sin. They are imprisoned under it, unable to free themselves by anything they can do. Knowing this, then, God has sent to us not a teacher or a politician but a liberator—one who has the power to set us free from our sins. Teaching, of course, is a very good thing—at least it had better be, because I do it all the time! But we must understand that it can never be, by itself, the ultimate solution to any one person's problems or to the problems of the world.

ROMANS 3:21–26

Original Meaning

The Righteousness of God by Faith (3:21–22a). Paul beautifully captures in just a few words the continuity and discontinuity in God's plan of salvation. The discontinuity? God reveals his righteousness in Christ "apart from" the law of Moses. The Mosaic covenant simply cannot contain the "new wine" of the gospel. The continuity? The entire Old Testament ("the Law and the Prophets") testifies to this new work of God in Christ. The cross has been God's intention from the beginning to reveal his saving righteousness by sending his Son as a sacrifice for us.

At the beginning of verse 22, Paul reiterates this righteousness available only "through faith." Paul continues to be especially concerned to show that God's work in Christ is for everyone. His righteousness is "activated" *only* for those who believe, but it is also for *all* those who believe.

The Backdrop of Universal Sinfulness (3:22b–23). Why does God's righteousness need to be available for "all who believe"? Because "all have sinned." All are under sin's power, and all "fall short of the glory of God." God's glory (*doxa*) in the Bible is, first of all, his own awesome presence. But the Bible teaches that God's people are destined to share in that glory; thus *doxa* also describes the eternal destiny of believers. What the first Adam lost, the last Adam, Christ, will restore.

Justified through Redeeming Grace (3:24). The verb "justify" (*dikaioō*) brings us back to the initial topic of God's righteousness (*dikaiosynē*). We are justified by means of God's grace and on the basis of his redemptive work in Jesus Christ. "Grace" (*charis*) is a key theological idea in Paul. He uses the word to stress that all God does on our behalf is done freely and without compulsion. "Redemption" (*apolytrōsis*) has the basic sense of "to liberate by paying a price."

Christ's Sacrifice Vindicates God's Justice (3:25–26). Especially debated is the meaning of the word translated in NIV as "sacrifice of atonement" (*hilastērion*). In its only other use in the New Testament (Heb 9:5) and in twenty-one of its twenty-seven occurrences in the LXX, *hilastērion* refers to the "atonement cover" of the ark where sacrificial blood was sprinkled. This atonement cover is prominent in Leviticus 16, where the Day of Atonement ritual is described. The atonement cover, therefore, came to represent for the Jews the place where, or the means by which, God took care of his people's sin problem. The meaning, then, is broad, encompassing the acts of both expiation and propitiation.

In verses 25b–26a, Paul indicates why God had to redeem people by the costly giving of his own Son: it was "to demonstrate his [God's] righteousness." "Righteousness" translates *dikaiosynē*, which Paul has used in verses 21–22 to refer to God's saving righteousness, the process by which he puts people right before him.

In the Old Testament period, people who sinned should have suffered spiritual death, because they did not yet have an adequate sacrifice to atone for their sins. But in his mercy God passed over their sins. In giving himself as a "sacrifice of atonement," Christ paid the price for the sins of all people—both before his time (v. 25b) and after (v. 26a).

Consequently, Paul summarizes, we can see how God can be "just and the one who justifies those who have faith in Jesus" (v. 26b). He accepts as righteous before him sinful people who have faith, and he accepts sinners as righteous without violating his own just character because Christ has fully satisfied God's demand that all who commit sin must die. By faith in Christ, we are joined to him. He becomes our representative, and his death is accredited to us.

Application. A basic theme of Romans, coming to expression again and again in the letter, is the need for Christians to understand who they are. Paul will say much more on this subject in chapters 5–8. Yet he lays the foundation here by reminding us of the great turning point in world history: the revelation of God's righteousness in Christ, inaugurating a new age in which a restored relationship with the God of the universe is available for all. The "but now" transition from the old life to the new is something I have personally experienced. That helps me appreciate all the more how secure I now feel—secure because I am a child of God, experiencing daily his fatherly care. If you are reading these words, take some time to remember who you were and contemplate who you now are in Christ.

ROMANS 3:27–31

Original Meaning. Paul reverts in verse 27 to the question-and-answer format so popular in the diatribe. This suggests that he is again engaged in dialogue with someone about the significance of the gospel. As elsewhere in Romans, Jewish boasting in "works of the law" is representative of human boasting in accomplishments (vv. 27–28). Verse 28 is a famous statement of the doctrine of justification by faith. In denying that even the best human works can justify us (e.g., Jewish obedience to God's holy law), Paul is, in effect, denying that anything a human being does will ever justify one before God.

Verses 29–30 bring to the surface again one of the central subthemes of the letter: the equality between Jew and gentile before God. If, as Jews proudly confess, there is only one God, then this God must be equally God of gentiles as well as Jews. Rightly understood, this demolishes any ultimate difference between Jew and gentile before the Lord. Thus, Paul concludes, God will justify both on the same basis: through faith.

Paul's pastoral sensitivity reveals itself again in verse 31. The Mosaic law may not play a role in justification, but Paul does not want his readers to conclude that it plays no role at all in God's plan of salvation. Paul affirms the valid demand that God makes of people in the law. But one of the things Christ does is to fulfill the law on our behalf. We who are in Christ are therefore accounted as having fulfilled the law and been set free from its penalties for disobedience. It is, paradoxically, this very freedom from the law's condemnation that puts us into a relationship in which true obedience, motivated and directed by the Spirit, can come about.

Application. When we obey the Lord by avoiding a sin we were tempted to commit or by doing an act of kindness, it is entirely appropriate for us to have a sense of contentment and even of self-satisfaction. However, the moment we think that our good works exert a claim on God, we have moved from legitimate contentment to illegitimate boasting. All our works, however good they may be—and all our works in this life are inevitably stained by sin—are the product of God's grace, as his Spirit moves in us.

ROMANS 4:1–8

Original Meaning. As he does so often in Romans, Paul uses a question to introduce the next stage of his argument. The question he asks in 4:1 about what Abraham "discovered in this matter" relates to the argument of 3:27–31. One of Paul's purposes in Romans is to demonstrate that the gospel is in continuity with the Old Testament. Proving that the story of Abraham fits into Paul's conception of salvation history is an important step toward this goal.

Having introduced Abraham in 4:1, Paul now moves directly to the attack: "If, in fact, Abraham was justified by works [as, apparently, at least some Jews believed], he had something to boast about [and our argument in 3:27–31 that boasting is excluded falls to the ground]." Paul immediately responds to this line of argument: "but not before God" (4:2). The logic of Paul's argument, as 4:3–8 reveals, is to reject the possibility of justification by works at all. Thus, his response probably means something like "from God's perspective, Abraham has no right at all to boast because he was not, and could not be, justified by works."

Paul grounds this response in Scripture (4:3). Genesis 15:6 is a foundational Old Testament verse for Paul's characteristic emphasis on justification by faith (see also Gal 3:6). Paul probably reads Genesis 15:6 as a summary of Abraham's response to God's promise to him generally.

But what does "crediting" Abraham's faith "as righteousness" mean (Rom 4:3)? The Hebrew construction in this verse (awkwardly taken over in the Greek) suggests "crediting" Abraham's faith as righteousness means "to account to him a righteousness that does not inherently belong to him." When Abraham believed God, God granted him the status of "righteous"; he considered him "right" before God.

Paul himself is concerned to unpack the significance of this crediting of Abraham's faith for righteousness. Thus, in verses 4–5 he explains the nature of this crediting and in verses 6–8 furnishes further scriptural support for the idea. Note, then, how Paul returns to the language of "crediting" both at the end of verse 5, in verse 6, and again in the quotation in verse 8 (the word translated "count" represents the same Greek word [*logizomai*] translated "credited").

The logic of verses 4–5 is not easy to understand at first sight because Paul does not express the major premise of his argument. The fact that God always relates to his creatures by grace, freely and without compulsion, is a theological axiom in Paul. That is, this is a fundamental perspective on God that he never argues but assumes as self-evident. If God were to justify people on the basis of their works, this axiom would be violated: God would be giving people something they had earned. In the context of this argument, then, Paul's description of the Christian as one who "does not work" (v. 5) is referring to the fact that Christians do not base their relationship to God on their actions.

Paul then quotes Psalm 32:1–2a in verses 7–8. In these verses, David joins his testimony to that of Moses, revealing that it is people "to whom God credits righteousness apart from works" that are truly blessed (v. 6). Here we find the heart of the good news: God accepts us, through our faith, just as we are. In his grace he covers our sins, not counting them against us.

Application. If God justifies us while we are wicked, why should we bother trying to lead holy lives? God has already accepted us, right? This objection is an old one, as Romans 6 reveals. Paul's teaching about God's justifying the wicked cannot be seen in isolation. Paul insists that God does more than justify us when we become Christians. He also regenerates us, sanctifies us, and causes his Spirit to indwell us. These acts of God change us from within. But becoming a Christian is first and foremost a change in our status before God. Sentenced to eternal death because of sin, God intervenes in a sheer act of grace and declares us innocent before him.

ROMANS 4:9–12

Original Meaning. The "blessedness" Paul mentions in 4:9 refers to acceptance before God. Is this acceptance, Paul asks, available only to Jews—as most Jews believed? Or is it also available to the "uncircumcised," that is, gentiles (v. 9)? In verse 10, Paul finds an answer to that question by noting the chronological relationship between God's pronouncement of Abraham's righteousness (Gen 15:6) and the institution of circumcision (Gen 17). The righteousness, Paul points out, came first—according to one rabbinic tradition, twenty-nine years before the circumcision.

But simple chronology is not a conclusive point. Paul goes on in verse 11 to explain circumcision, in Abraham's case, was not the basis or even the condition for his righteous status before God. The rite simply put a seal on what was already true.

In verses 11b–12 Paul draws out the significance of what he has said in verse 11a. Gentiles who have faith can claim Abraham as their father. They believe as he did, and they receive, as he did, righteousness as a gift from God. As we will see in 4:16–17, there is another strand of teaching about Abraham in Genesis, a strand that emphasizes his role as the "father of many nations."

Abraham is also "the father of the circumcised who not only are circumcised but who also walk in the footsteps of the faith that our father Abraham had before he was circumcised" (v. 12). As the NIV translates, Paul makes Abraham also the father of Jewish Christians—people who are circumcised *and who also* believe as Abraham did.

Application. The inclusion of gentiles into God's people becomes the leading edge of a broader principle: the removal of all outward distinctions in the face of God's grace and the universal offer of the gospel. The implications for the church are far-reaching. The church is called to be a genuinely countercultural institution, in which the usual barriers to association—race, national background, economic status, and so on—have no relevance at all.

ROMANS 4:13–22

Original Meaning

Faith, Not Law, Secures the Promise (4:13–15). Genesis repeatedly mentions the fact that Abraham will be a blessing to all the world, but the focus tends to be on his biological descendants and the land God promised them. Jewish interpreters highlighted this ethnic element in the promise. Thus Paul's focus here on "the world" may have a polemical intent, carrying on his insistence that Abraham is the father of all who believe (vv. 11–12).

The introduction of "law" (v. 13a) also has a polemical purpose. As we have noted, many of Paul's Jewish contemporaries taught that Abraham's stature and role had much to do with his obedience to the law of Moses. Paul wants to make clear that the promise did not come because people obeyed the law, but "through the righteousness that comes by faith" (v. 13b).

Verses 14–15 explain why Abraham and those who came after him could never have inherited God's promised blessings through the law. People who try to base their hope of blessing on doing what the Mosaic law demanded eviscerate the very meaning of "faith" and "promise." How can the blessing truly be, from God's side, a matter of his sheer promise and, from the human side, a matter of faith if people can earn it through their obedience to the law? However, Paul is more likely making a simpler point: if the fulfillment of the promise depends on obedience to the law, it will never happen, for people can never obey the law adequately.

In the first part of verse 15, Paul substantiates the point he made in verse 14: the law "brings wrath." This assertion is startling when we remember that Jews typically viewed the Mosaic law as one of the greatest blessings they possessed. How can Paul claim that the law has produced wrath? The end of verse 15 implicitly provides the answer: "Where there is no law there is no transgression." Anytime we fall short of conformity to God's image, we sin; but only when we directly violate a commandment God has given us do we commit a transgression. For this reason, then, transgression is also a more serious form of sin, meriting greater judgment.

Because Faith Secures the Promise, Both Jew and Gentile Can Benefit from It (4:16–17). Verses 16–17 focus on the promised blessing guaranteed to *all* Abraham's "offspring." "Offspring" translates the Greek *sperma* (literally seed), a word important in both the Genesis promise passages and in Paul. At the end of 4:16, Paul specifies the two groups that make up this spiritual seed of Abraham: "those who are of the law" and "those who are of the faith of Abraham." His concern is to show that the promise to Abraham is valid for all believers. Almost certainly, then, he is referring to Jewish Christians and gentile Christians.

The end of verse 17 almost certainly alludes to the miracle by which God brought life out of the "dead" womb of Sarah (v. 19). But what Paul means by describing God as the one who "calls into being things that were not" is not so clear. Paul is describing from another angle the miracle that God wrought in bringing children to Abraham and Sarah. Even before they had children, God spoke of the "many nations" that would come from them as if they already existed.

The Character of Abraham's Faith (4:18–22). From a human standpoint, there was no hope that Abraham and Sarah would ever have children. He was a hundred years old, and Sarah's womb was "dead" (v. 19). Abraham did not ignore these facts. But they did not cause Abraham's faith to weaken. Why not? Because his faith was also "in hope"—the hope that springs from God's word of promise (v. 18b). Therefore, Paul concludes, Abraham did not "waver through unbelief regarding the promise of God" (v. 20a). He had his momentary doubts, it is true, but they were momentary and always overcome by his faith in the God who had promised. By doing so, Abraham glorified God, because he took him at his word (vv. 20b–21). This is why, Paul concludes, "it [faith] was credited to him as righteousness" (v. 22).

Application. In our achievement-oriented world, giving faith its necessary central place in our lives is not always easy to do. We are tempted to ground our relationship to God in what we do. God accepts us not because of what we do but because we have humbled ourselves before him and have received from him the gift of salvation. Doing God's will is a necessary result of faith, but it must never be put in its place as the mainstay of our relationship to God.

ROMANS 4:23–25

Original Meaning. As Paul draws his exposition to an end, he makes explicit what has been implicit throughout, that it has direct application to Christians. Paul often describes God as the one who raised Jesus from the dead, but he rarely makes God the object of our belief. He does so here to make Christian faith as similar to Abraham's faith as possible. In verse 25, Paul adds a description of this Jesus whom God raised from the dead.

Application. Abraham believed in the God *who had made certain promises*. His faith, as Paul makes clear, was oriented not just vaguely to "God," but to the specific promises God had made to him. In other words, Abraham believed in God and in what God had revealed about himself and about his plan. Those who argue that people in our day believe in God the same way Abraham did miss the vital point that "God" must be given content.

But we can go further. God reveals more and more of himself as his plan of salvation unfolds. Each of those further revelations becomes part of the "content" of God. One cannot claim to believe in the God of the Bible without including that content. In our day, God has definitively revealed himself in Jesus Christ. Were Abraham alive today, he could not be saved apart from faith in God as revealed in Christ. Thus, we must also conclude that only people who believe in this particular God as revealed in Christ have hope for salvation.

ROMANS 5:1–11

Original Meaning

Being Justified Means We Have Peace and Hope (5:1–4). Paul established justification by faith in chapters 1–4. Now he will elaborate the results of the new status God has given us in Christ. "Peace" is a rich biblical word. The Old Testament and Jewish conception of peace, *shalom*, is the objective state of harmony with God that believers who have been justified enjoy.

Another wonderful result of our justification is "access by faith into this grace in which we now stand" (v. 2). Grace here does not, as in earlier verses, refer to the freedom with which God acts toward his creatures. Rather, it is a state in which the believer lives. God's free giving to us does not stop when we become Christians.

The third result of our new justified state is that "we boast" (v. 2). The verb for "boast" (*kauchaomai*) suggests both the idea of taking confidence in and of rejoicing in. Paul introduces what becomes the theme of this paragraph: the hope we have as Christians to share in God's glory. But Paul quickly adds, "we also glory [*kauchaomai* again] in our sufferings" (v. 3). Yes, he says in effect, I know Christians will continue to suffer. But life's difficulties do not contradict what I have been saying about the wonderful blessings of being a Christian; in fact, God actually uses them to bring us even greater blessing.

The key is the way we respond to the difficult trials that come our way. What we must do is to recognize that God uses them to build into our lives "perseverance" (*hypomonē*), which, in turn, leads to "character" (*dokimē*, v. 4). Then we can truly rejoice in the midst of suffering, knowing that God is at work even in these evil things to bring us blessing. Paradoxically, Paul claims at the end of verse 4 that suffering can actually lead to "hope." Just as resistance to a muscle strengthens it, so challenges to our hope can strengthen it.

We Hope Because God Loves Us in Christ (5:5–8). Paul introduces the certainty that believers will indeed receive what they hope for. How can we be sure? In verses 5b–10, Paul gives two basic reasons: God's love for us in Christ (vv. 5b–8) and God's work for us in Christ (vv. 9–10). It is the Spirit, dwelling in the heart of believers, who communicates God's love to us.

Alongside this subjective evidence of God's love, we also have objective proof of that love in the cross of Christ (v. 6).

To make sure we do not miss this point, Paul reinforces it in verse 7 with an analogy. A difference between "a good man" and "a righteous man" seems to be the key to the interpretation. A "righteous" person is one we might respect, but a "good" person is one we might love. The awesome quality of God's love for us is seen in that Christ died for us while we were "still sinners"—hating God, in rebellion against him (v. 8).

We Hope Because God Has Acted for Us in Christ (5:9–11). Verses 9–10 remind us what God has already done for us through the death of Christ: he "justified" us (v. 9) and "reconciled" us to him (v. 10). "How much more," then, Paul reasons, can we be sure that God will complete his work by saving us from his wrath in the last day (vv. 9, 10).

Two specific points in these verses require comment. First, Paul interchanges "justify" and "reconcile" in his argument, two ways of describing what happens when God first accepts us. He declares us innocent and absolves us from punishment for our sins ("justify"), and he removes the hostility that existed between us and him because of that sin ("reconcile"). The former is a judicial idea, the latter a relational one. Second, Paul claims that being "saved" (the verb is *sōzō*) comes *after* we are justified and reconciled. We often use the word "save" to refer to our initial acceptance with the Lord. Paul does use the word this way, but he more often uses it to depict the believer's final deliverance from death and the wrath of God in the last day. Being justified and reconciled to God is the critical step on the way to salvation; if these are in place, eventual salvation is certain.

Application. The word Paul uses for "sufferings" in verse 3 is the plural of *thlipsis* (tribulations or sufferings). He sometimes uses this word to refer to persecution in the narrow sense—that is, difficulties experienced because of one's witness for Christ (e.g., 1 Thess 1:6). But I am not sure that we can confine the reference to persecution. In a certain sense, everything that a Christian suffers is on behalf of Christ. All suffering betrays the presence of the enemy and attacks our relationship with Christ. Furthermore, the end of chapter 8 and the beginning of chapter 5 are closely related. This means that the suffering Paul mentions in 5:3 is likely related to the trials he lists in 8:35. More than persecution per se is included.

ROMANS 5:12–21

Original Meaning

Adam, Sin, and Universal Death (5:12). Adam's fall introduced sin into the world, and death came as a result of sin. What is this death? Paul seems to think of death as both physical and spiritual: separation from the body and estrangement from God. Both are the result of sin. That a physical element is present in death is evident from verses 13–14. But verses 18–19, where Paul replaces the death of verse 12 with "condemnation" and being "made sinners," shows that his focus is on spiritual death. The sin Adam introduced into the world spelled spiritual disaster for the human race.

The second two clauses of verse 12 emphasize the universal extent of this nexus of sin and death. Death, Paul affirms, affects all people because all people have "sinned." In verses 18–19, where Paul repeats and completes the comparison we have in this verse, he suggests a close relationship between Adam's sin and the condemnation that all people stand under. Sin and the spiritual death that results from sin are universal.

Sin and Death Even Apart from the Law (5:13–14). Already in verse 12, Paul has begun to lose control of his syntax as he lapses into a series of run-on clauses. At the end of the verse, he abandons it altogether. Apparently, he is convinced that something he has said in this verse requires elaboration before he can move on to finish the comparison that is at the heart of this paragraph. As a result, as he has done throughout chapters 1–4, he brings the Mosaic law into the picture.

Paul is *reinforcing* his teaching about the universality of death. Many Jews believed that there could be no sin or death apart from the law. Paul affirms that, indeed, sin existed before the Mosaic law was given and that people were condemned for their sin. The presence of positive law turns sin into transgression (*parabasis*, v. 14). Sin may not be charged to one's individual account (v. 13b) apart from law. But sin is still sin and brings God's condemnation and wrath.

The Contrast between Adam and Christ (5:15–17). At the end of verse 14, Paul expresses the premise on which the whole argument of verses 12–21 is built: Adam was a "pattern [or type, *typos*] of the one to come," that is, of Christ. But before he pursues the similarity between these two as a result of this relationship, the apostle notes some of the differences. These differences boil down to one great fact: in Christ God deals with people on the basis of grace.

The word "grace" and the related word "gift" occur seven times in verses 15–17. What happened as a result of Adam's sin is entirely a matter of just desserts. "Death" (vv. 15, 17), "judgment," and "condemnation" (v. 16) inevitably and justly follow sin. But what has happened as a result of Christ is quite different. In place of condemnation, Christ brings "justification" (v. 16). Condemnation came as a result of "one man's sin," but justification "followed many trespasses" (v. 16). We see in this circumstance, Paul concludes, evidence of the overwhelming grace of God.

The power of God's grace operating through the work of

Christ means there is a "how much more" in the quality of what Christ accomplishes in comparison with what Adam has done (v. 17). Christ more than cancels the effects of Adam's sin—he enables those who have received the "abundant provision of grace" and "the gift of righteousness" not just to experience life but to "reign in life" (v. 17).

The Comparison between Adam and Christ (5:18–19). In verses 18–19 Paul returns to the idea of verse 12 and completes it. Verses 18–19 are similar in structure. Each features Adam in the first ("just as") clause and Christ in the second ("so also") clause. Each contrasts what Adam did with what Christ did. Adam committed a "trespass" (v. 18); he disobeyed (v. 19). Christ, by contrast, committed "one righteous act" (v. 18); he obeyed (v. 19). Where Adam turned away from God and violated his commandment, Christ turned toward God and continually did the will of his Father. The singular "righteous act" suggests Paul is thinking of a single manifestation of Christ's obedience to his Father—probably in submitting to the Father's will to die on a Roman cross.

Finally, and most important, each verse also contrasts the results of Adam's sin with the results of Christ's obedience. Because of Adam's sin, "the many" were appointed to or inaugurated into a state of sinfulness; and because of Christ's obedience, "the many" were appointed to a status of righteousness (i.e., they were justified).

The Conclusion: Grace Reigns! (5:20–21). Paul, of course, believes firmly in the enduring value of the Old Testament. But he is equally convinced that God intended the Mosaic law to have a *negative* role in salvation history: it was added "so that the trespass might increase" (v. 20). The law did not bring relief from the Adamic condition of sin and death; instead, it made it worse. Paul believes that the Mosaic law, by making people accountable to a specific and detailed series of commandments, brings greater judgment on those sins.

But God's grace has more than compensated. Under the law, sins were charged against us (v. 13), and so "sin reigned in death" (v. 21). In the dominion of death introduced by Adam, sin holds sway over us. But "through righteousness," that is, as a result of being justified, "grace" reigns (v. 21). If we are confident that sin has brought death and untold devastation into the world, we can be even more confident that the grace of God that justifies us will also save us from his wrath in the judgment.

Application. While Romans 5:12–21 does not have original sin as its focus, it still remains the most important text in the Bible on this vexing theological doctrine. Basic to the Christian worldview is a view of humanity as inherently bent away from God, with all the tragedy that comes from this sinful condition. Indeed, the Christian faith offers at this point a succinct and convincing explanation for the human misery and hatred we see in the world around us. Original sin may not make sense to many people; they may find it irrational or even unjust. But what better explanation for the extent and persistence of crimes against humanity?

ROMANS 6:1–14

Original Meaning

United with Christ in Death and Resurrection (6:1–5). Paul says that we "died to sin" (v. 2). What does he mean by this? It creates an obvious point of contact with the death of Christ, an important step in Paul's argument (vv. 3–4). It is a powerful image of a decisive shift in state. When someone becomes a Christian, Paul implies, their change of state in relationship to sin is as dramatic as a change from life to death.

In verses 3–5, Paul shows how the transfer from the state of sin to new life in Christ has taken place. In baptism, we are joined to Christ and to his death and resurrection. Christ's own death was a death "to sin," and his resurrection meant living "to God" (v. 10). Therefore, those who participate in Christ's death and resurrection also have died to sin and now live to God.

Paul here refers to water baptism as the point in time at which people become joined with Christ. When we were baptized "into" Christ (i.e., so as to be joined with him), we were baptized "into his death" (v. 3). Verse 4 then elaborates that "we were buried with him through baptism into death." Paul uses the verb "buried" because he is thinking of the way the Christian is identified with Christ in all of the major events of his redemptive work (cf. 1 Cor 15:3–4). We who believe have participated with Christ in each of these events. Baptism brought us into union with Christ and the powerful events of his redemptive work. The effects of these events are therefore at work in us. That means we now have the ability to "live a new life" (Rom 6:4b).

Verse 5 states what Paul has implied in verse 4: believers not only participate in Christ's death (so that we have died to sin), but also in his resurrection (so that we can live a new life). Paul uses a future tense to describe our participation in the resurrection (v. 5). The future is a genuine temporal future: while we do indeed now enjoy new life, our being raised with Christ awaits his parousia or second coming (cf. Phil 3:20–21).

The Results of Dying with Christ (6:6–7). In verse 6, Paul replaces the "we" of verses 3–5 with "the old self" (Gk. *anthrōpos*) and death by crucifixion. Paul refers to crucifixion to emphasize our participation in Jesus's death itself (cf. Gal 2:20). The phrase "the old self" is likely Paul's way of referring to what we were in Adam. Paul is especially concerned that we understand what follows from this action. The result is that the "body ruled by sin might be done away with" (v. 6). Our identification with Christ means we are no longer dominated by sin.

The Results of Being Raised with Christ (6:8–10). In verse 8, Paul shows that living with Christ automatically follows dying with him. In verse 9 Paul explains just what Christ's own resurrection means: he now lives in a state in which death is no longer possible and has no power over him. He has conquered death, and, Paul implies, we who belong to him also have the assurance of conquering death.

Why would Christ, the sinless one, have to "die to sin" (v. 10)? As a result of his real identification with human beings, he was subject to the power of sin. He was therefore tempted as we are (cf. Heb 2:14–17). In this sense, he, too, needed to die to sin's power.

Putting Our New Status into Action (6:11–14). The general structure of 6:1–14 reflects a common pattern in Paul: what God has done for us is the basis and stimulus for what we need to do for God. The indicative mode, in which Paul tells us of the wonderful redemptive events, leads to the imperative, telling us how we are to respond to those events. But verse 11 suggests an intermediate step: coming to grips with the truth of what Paul has been teaching. Only by constantly looking at ourselves as people who really have died to sin and been made alive in Christ will we be able to live out the new status God has given us. In verses 12–13, Paul moves into the realm of action.

Paul claims in verse 14 that sin is no longer our master—in effect, sin does not reign. Yet this does not prevent him from commanding us not to let sin reign. The victory over sin that God has won for us in Christ is a victory that must be appropriated. Verse 13 makes the same point in a different way. Paul brings before us a picture of all our varied capacities and abilities, which we are to withdraw from the use of our old master, sin, and place at the disposal of our new master, God.

Just in case we become overbalanced toward the imperative side, Paul concludes with one more reminder of the indicative: "Sin shall no longer be your master" (v. 14). Paul emphasizes that our freedom from sin's power is a continuing state we can look forward to enjoying forever. Why is this? "Because you are not under the law, but under grace" (v. 14).

Because we stand under the new covenant, the law of the old covenant no longer has direct control over us. The contrast between "law" and "grace" is a salvation-historical contrast: the Mosaic law dominates the old regime from which we have been set free in Christ; grace dominates the new regime inaugurated by Jesus.

Application. Baptism is an important part of the conversion experience. To use biblical imagery, it sets a seal on that experience. Thus, baptism in water should probably be administered to a person as shortly after that person's coming to faith in Christ as possible. Acts 8 is instructive in this regard. After bringing the Ethiopian court official to faith, Philip does not enroll him in a series of baptismal classes; he baptizes him, out in the middle of the desert, right on the spot (Acts 8:36–38).

When one asks Paul what a person must do to be a Christian, his answer is clear: believe in the Lord Jesus. It is always dangerous to put words into the mouth of a scriptural author, but I think if Paul had ever been asked about an "unbaptized believer," he would have responded: "Well, yes, such a person is saved; but why in the world isn't she baptized?"

ROMANS 6:15–23

Original Meaning. The questions that open the two main sections in Romans 6 reveal the common theme Paul pursues: "Shall we go on sinning so that grace may increase?" (v. 1); "Shall we sin because we are not under the law but under grace?" (v. 15). As the former question is sparked by what Paul said in 5:20 about the power of grace, so the question in 6:15 is stimulated by what he has just said at the end of verse 14. Proclaiming that believers have been transferred from the regime of the Mosaic law to the regime of grace may lead some Christians to think that sin does not matter.

Paul heightens the seriousness of the issue at the end of verse 16 by making it clear that we are ultimately confronted with a choice of only two masters to serve: sin and obedience. Paul wants to hammer home the importance of obedience, so he uses this word in a positive sense to denote the Christian moral demand. Serving sin leads to death, but serving obedience "leads to righteousness." Paul is obviously using *dikaio-* language in a different nuance here from what he did in chapters 1–4. Righteousness has a moral sense: conduct pleasing to God.

From what Paul has said so far, we may assume that we stand in a state of neutrality with respect to the choice of serving "sin" or "obedience." Paul reminds us that this is certainly not the case. "Thanks . . . to God," believers have left slavery to sin (vv. 16–17).

Verse 18 goes on to summarize the indicative of the believer's transfer from one realm to another: from "sin" to "righteousness." The necessary moral implications of conversion to Christ are again made clear: we have been made "slaves" of that moral conduct God expects of his people.

Verse 19a is something of an aside, as Paul explains why he is using the imagery of slavery: "because of your human limitations." "Human limitation" translates *sarx* (literally flesh), the word Paul customarily uses to describe the human condition apart from God. What he suggests, therefore, is that the limitations of our human understanding make it necessary for him to use imprecise, but still appropriate analogies.

Verse 19b is the center of this paragraph. A reminder of the new situation God has put us in comes just before it (vv. 17–18), and a further reminder of that same status comes immediately after it (vv. 20–23). But, as in 6:1–14, Paul does not want us to think that the indicative of God's act undermines or cancels the need for the imperative or our response. Using the same verb as he did in 6:13, Paul again appeals to us to "offer" (*paristēmi*) all our capacities and abilities (v. 19).

"Holiness" (*hagiasmos*) denotes either the *state* of holiness or the *process* of sanctification. In either case, Paul sees our commitment to righteousness as resulting in Godlikeness. Paul suggests that our commitment to serve righteousness should be just as strong as our previous commitment to impurity and wickedness. Our pursuit of righteousness and holiness should be just as dedicated.

The transfer from the realm of sin and death to the realm of righteousness and life (vv. 20–23) is the ground for the command in verse 19. Non-Christians often pride themselves on being free. Paul notes that non-Christians do, indeed, have a freedom—the freedom not to be able to lead righteous lives. Genuine autonomy is not an option. If one is not serving God, then, whether knowingly or not, one is serving sin. To bring to our minds even more forcibly the negative side of our pre-Christian past, Paul reminds us of the shame we feel for what we used to do (v. 21). Verse 23 not only explains the contrasting outcomes of death and life but also brings the chapter to a fitting conclusion.

Application. In Romans 6 Paul regularly intersperses his indicatives with imperatives that make us responsible for winning the battle against sin. Yet one thing is clear in Paul: the imperative grows out of the indicative. God takes the initiative. In grace, he acts to help his people, and he asks them to respond. Christians are called to "become what they are."

At the same time, God's acts on our behalf are not finished. He has more things to give us and to accomplish in us. This means that we can also speak of "becoming what we will be." What God will one day make us should be a spur to getting as close to that ideal as possible.

ROMANS 7:1–6

Original Meaning. The negative effect of the Mosaic law has been a recurring motif in Romans. In 7:1–6 Paul directly addresses the negative effects of the Mosaic law and its relationship to believers. Arising directly from the "not under the law, but under grace" contrast of 6:14–15, these verses assert that Christians have been set free from the binding authority of the Mosaic law.

This section begins with a general principle: "The law [*nomos*] has authority over someone only as long as that person lives" (7:1). *Nomos* refers to the Mosaic law throughout this context. This does not mean, however, that Paul addresses only Jewish Christians. Many of the gentile Christians in Rome had probably been sympathetic to Judaism without becoming converts. They would have known the Mosaic law as well as Jewish Christians.

Verses 2–3 are an illustration of the point of verse 1 with some application to verse 4. Paul simply wants to show that a death can indeed bring freedom from the law; at the same time, he hints that such freedom can also lead to a new relationship.

In verse 4, the heart of the paragraph, Paul draws an inference from verses 1–3: believers have suffered a death in relationship to the law, a death that frees them from the law and enables them to enter into a new relationship. Believers have not only been released from bondage to sin, but they have also been released from bondage to the Mosaic law. This release was accomplished through "the body of Christ"—probably a reference to Jesus's death on the cross (v. 4).

What lies in the background of Paul's teaching is his salvation-historical conception. The era of the law has come to an end with the redemptive work of Christ. Last in verse 4, but by no means least, is the purpose for which we are freed from the law and joined to Christ: so that we can "bear fruit for God." Practical works of service should flow from our new relationship.

In verses 5–6 Paul elaborates the salvation-historical background he has assumed in verse 4. "Realm of the flesh" is the way the NIV translates Paul's use of the word *sarx* in a negative, ethical sense. The apostle uses *sarx* in these contexts to denote human existence apart from God. To be "in the flesh," then, is to make decisions and behave without any regard for God or for the spiritual realm.

The results of this kind of life are obvious: "sinful passions" and "death" (v. 5). But, as Paul has insisted again and again in the letter, the law of Moses did not bring relief from the matrix of sin and death; instead, it made it worse. Those sinful passions, Paul claims, were "aroused by the law" (v. 5). As he will explain in verses 7–12, God's law arouses sin by stimulating rebellion. Thus, we can see why a person must be released from that law (v. 4) if he or she is to serve God.

This is precisely the situation in the new regime: We have died "to what once bound us" (v. 6). "Written code" translates *gramma* (literally letter). *Gramma* refers to the Mosaic law in contrast to the Holy Spirit. The context shows that it must refer to the same thing that *nomos* refers to. Paul shifts to *gramma* because it more clearly connotes the "outward" nature of the Mosaic law.

Application. We cannot restrict Paul's claim that believers have been released from the law to a certain function of the law or to certain parts of the law. The believer has been set free from the commanding authority of the Mosaic law—period. What this means in practice is that no part of the Mosaic law stands any longer as a direct and unmediated guide to Christian living. Like a person who is free from the laws of the state of Indiana because she has moved to Illinois, so Christians are free from the law of the old covenant because we now belong to the new covenant.

Does our freedom from the Mosaic law include even the Ten Commandments? Yes and no. Yes in the sense that those commandments as part of the Mosaic law no longer stand over us. But no in the sense that the teaching of nine of the ten commandments is explicitly taken up by New Testament authors and made part of the "law of Christ." (The one commandment that is not taken over is, of course, the Sabbath command.) What all this means in practice, then, is that we should look to the New Testament for those commandments that express God's moral will for us as new-covenant Christians. Its teachings, properly interpreted, are to be obeyed. But this does not mean that we should no longer read the Mosaic law. It remains God's word, given, as all Scripture, for our enlightenment (2 Tim 3:16).

Moreover, although the new-covenant believer does not stand directly under Old Testament law, that law itself serves an important function in helping us understand our obligations. New Testament teachings are informed by the Old Testament law. For instance, the New Testament prohibits *porneia*—unlawful sexual conduct. But what is included in such illegitimate sexual conduct? The New Testament writers never spell it out because the scope of this conduct has already been clearly defined in the Old Testament law. Thus, we continue to read the Old Testament law as a guide to our interpretation of New Testament law.

ROMANS 7:7–12

Original Meaning. Paul anticipates a key objection to his presentation of the gospel. For he seems to imply in verses like 5:20 and 7:5 that the law is an evil thing. But if this were really his view, he would forfeit any claim that the gospel is the fulfillment of the Old Testament. As some of the later gnostics did, the Old Testament would be severed from the New and the God of Israel from the God of Jesus Christ; the gospel would replace, not fulfill, the Old Testament. Thus, Paul resolutely denies any such idea, restating the point positively in verse 12.

Paul claims he came to "know" sin through the law and uses the tenth commandment to illustrate (v. 7). The Mosaic law helped him come to understand clearly the extent and seriousness of his sin. Paul gives an abbreviated citation of the tenth commandment (Exod 20:17; Deut 5:21) as a fit summary of the Mosaic law as a whole.

In the first sentence in verse 8, Paul takes the argument one step further. Not only did he come to understand sin through the law, but he also was led into greater sinning through that same law. He probably has in mind the power of a definite prohibition to stimulate in sinful people a rebellious reaction. Told not to do something, we desire all the more to do it. Note how Paul continues to picture sin as a power.

Paul is describing the experience that he and all Jews have gone through as part of the people of Israel. Jews in Paul's day had a lively sense of their involvement with the great acts in the history of Israel. It would be natural for Paul to merge his own experience relative to sin and the law with the experience of his people Israel. As he has made clear throughout Romans, the coming of the commandment (= the giving of the law of Moses) meant for Israel not "life" but "death" (v. 10). Their sin was exposed and magnified, and greater wrath came on them (4:15; 5:20).

Verse 11 reiterates the same point about sin, using the law as a bridgehead that Paul made already in verse 8a; the two then act as a kind of frame around the narrative of verses 8b–10. With the "so then" of verse 12, Paul comes back to his main point. Sin has indeed used the law to bring death to Israel. But the law is innocent; it provides the "opportunity" only (v. 11). Thus, it can be concluded that the law is not sin (v. 7); it is "holy, righteous and good" (v. 12).

Application. Most people have their own code of morality they try to live up to. Sometimes that code, via God's grace in natural law, reflects his own standards; sometimes it is far from divine law. But whatever the law may be, this text suggests, the sinful condition of all people renders it impossible to obey. We always fall short of the law, and the law therefore reveals the power of sin, our own helplessness, and the need for someone to liberate us from our miserable state.

ROMANS 7:13–25

Original Meaning

A Summary and Transition (7:13). This verse summarizes what Paul has taught in 7:7–12, so that we can consider it the conclusion to the previous paragraph. He again notes that God's law has been the occasion that enables us to see sin for what it really is. In other words, the law becomes an instrument that sin uses to bring death. The form of the verse, however, similar to 7:7 with its question and emphatic response, suggests that it introduces what follows. This verse, therefore, is transitional, gathering up the argument so far and launching the new focus: the problem with "me."

The Divided "I" (7:14–20). In verse 14, Paul characterizes the two chief actors in the drama that follows. The law of Moses, as Paul has made clear in verse 12, is "spiritual"—that is, it has a divine origin (v. 14a). But "I am unspiritual, sold as a slave to sin" (v. 14b). "Unspiritual" translates *sarkinos*, which means "composed of flesh." Paul can use this word to describe "carnal" Christians (1 Cor 3:1–3), so it does not necessarily mean that the "I" is unregenerate. But the following description seems to tilt the scales in this direction. Paul has used "under sin" to describe the condition of all people apart from Christ (Rom 3:9).

In verses 15–20, Paul graphically portrays the struggle he finds within himself to follow through on his conviction that "the law is spiritual" (v. 14a). This tension reveals two truths.

1. The fact that he wills what is good shows that he acknowledges the goodness of the law (v. 16).
2. But he finds that he cannot do the law (v. 17).

Paul is not disclaiming responsibility for his actions. Rather, he is trying to explain his actions by revealing the force within himself that leads him to act as he does. That force is "sin" (v. 17).

The beginning of verse 18 continues this analysis of "indwelling" sin. Two very different interpretations of this verse exist, each lining up with one of the major views of the identity of the "I" in these verses. Those who think the "I" is regenerate usually insist that Paul, the Christian, has a sinful nature that disposes him to sin. Those who think the "I" is unregenerate usually take the "that is" clause as a definition: Paul, the Jew under the law, is still in a condition in which sinful passions are aroused by the law (see 7:5). We incline toward this second interpretation because it better fits the way Paul uses *sarx* in this context. But the other is certainly possible.

In verses 18b–20, Paul once more rehearses the struggle between willing and doing that reveals his sinful condition and makes it impossible for him to obey the law.

The Conclusion: The Law of God versus the "Law of Sin" (7:21–25). Paul draws the conclusion from the struggle between his will and his act by using the word "law" (*nomos*). This word occurs seven times in these verses. Throughout the chapter thus far he has used *nomos* in his usual sense to denote the body of legislation given by God through Moses to the people of Israel. But several occurrences of the word in these verses do not fit this sense: "this law" (v. 21), "another law" (v. 23), and "the law of sin" (v. 25).

Most interpreters agree that *nomos* in verse 21 means "principle" or "rule." Here is a principle Paul derives from his struggle: "Although I want to do good, evil is right there with me." He goes on to explain this struggle in verses 22–23. Paul continues to emphasize the two sides of people: willing versus doing (vv. 15–20), "inner being" versus "in me" (vv. 22–23), "mind" versus "flesh" (NIV "sinful nature," v. 25).

In verse 23, Paul contrasts God's law with another law, "the law of sin." For just as God in his law makes a claim on our lives, so sin exerts its own claim on us. These two claims battle for our allegiance. The upshot, Paul says, is that we are "prisoners of the law of sin." God's law simply does not have the power to deliver us from the power of sin.

In verse 24 Paul finally reacts to the situation he has described. Paul has consistently used "death" in chapter 7 to refer to the state of spiritual frustration and condemnation. So the rescue he hopes for is probably deliverance from the sin-dominated body, spiritually dead because of sin (see 6:6).

In verse 25a Paul gives thanks for the rescue, provided through "Jesus Christ our Lord." Having expressed the desire for rescue from the frustration of not being able to do God's law that he felt as a Jew under the law, Paul the Christian cannot refrain from interjecting a thanksgiving for the source of the deliverance he has experienced. In other words, he sums up the struggle he has been describing throughout verses 14–25 in verse 25b.

Application. With Paul, we should break out in thanksgiving to God when we recognize the state from which he has rescued us. All of us who read Romans 7 as Christians can identify, to some degree, with the struggle and frustration Paul depicts here. Looking back at that time is good for us, for it moves us all the more to praise God for his rescue of us in Jesus Christ.

ROMANS 8:1–13

Original Meaning

New Life through the Spirit's Liberating Work (8:1–4). Because we are justified by faith in conjunction with our union with Christ, we escape the sentence of spiritual death that our sins have justly earned. Transferred into the new regime of life, we no longer fear that our sins will ever condemn us.

In verse 2 Paul explains why we need no longer worry about condemnation. "The law of sin and death" could, considering the argument of Romans 7, refer to the Mosaic law, used by sin to bring death. But Paul has used a similar expression in 7:23 to refer to the authority or power of sin. This is probably what he means here as well. The Spirit exerts a liberating power through the work of Christ that takes us out of the realm of sin and the spiritual death to which sin inevitably leads.

As verse 2 grounds verse 1 ("because"), so verses 3–4 ground verse 2 ("for"). The liberating work of the Spirit takes place "through Christ Jesus." Paul now elaborates. The Mosaic law was powerless to rescue human beings from the authority of sin and death. Its demands could not be met because the people to whom the law was given were in the realm of "flesh" (v. 3). But God in Christ has intervened to do what the law could not.

God won the victory over sin in the very realm where it seemed to rule unchallenged: in the "flesh." In claiming that Christ came "in the likeness of sinful flesh" to offer himself as a sacrifice for our sins (v. 3), Paul carefully balances Jesus's full humanity with his sinlessness. Calling that flesh "sinful" might suggest that Christ took on *fallen* human nature. If so, he would not have been qualified to be our sinless redeemer. So Paul clarifies by adding the important word "likeness." In other words, Christ did not, like every other person since Adam, succumb to the tyranny of the flesh.

The purpose of this work of God in Christ is spelled out in verse 4. Paul does not claim that the "righteous *requirements* of the law" are fulfilled in us; he says that "the righteous *requirement* of the law" was fulfilled in us. The singular word, along with the passive form of "fully met," suggests a different idea: God in Christ has fulfilled the entirety of the law's demand on our behalf. The people in whom the law is fulfilled are those who live in the realm of the Spirit.

Life in the Spirit versus Death in the Flesh (8:5–8). In verses 5–8, then, Paul presents a series of contrasts between flesh and Spirit. His overall intention is clear: to show that *sarx* brings death while the Spirit brings life (v. 6). Paul leads up to this key claim by tracing people's manner of life to their underlying way of thinking. The lifestyle of the flesh flows from a mind oriented to the flesh, whereas the lifestyle of the Spirit comes from a mind oriented to the Spirit.

Assurance of Future, Resurrection Life (8:9–11). Paul signals a shift in direction by turning directly to his readers. Christians have been taken out of the realm dominated by "flesh" and placed in the realm dominated by God's Holy Spirit. It is clear, then, that the "in flesh"/"in Spirit" language is metaphorical—a way of indicating that people are dominated by one or the other of these forces.

In whom does the Spirit live? In every person who is genuinely a Christian. Not to have the Spirit of Christ is not to belong to Christ at all. Every Christian really is "in the Spirit"—under his domination and control. We may not always reflect that domination (see vv. 12–13), but it is a fundamental fact of our Christian existence and the basis for a life of confidence and obedience to the Lord.

Paul goes on to comment about a situation in which the Spirit's dominance might not be so obvious: the believer's continued existence in a physical body that is doomed to die and is still all too susceptible to the influence of sin. Our bodies may be doomed to die, but the Spirit, the Spirit of life, the Spirit of the God who raised our Lord Jesus from the dead, dwells within us and guarantees that our bodies will not end in the grave. God, through the Spirit, will give life to those bodies again.

Our Obligation (8:12–13). God's gift of new life through his Spirit carries with it an obligation. That obligation is not to "the flesh," that power of the old regime from which we have been delivered. It is to the Spirit, the power of the new regime.

Paul breaks off his sentence at the end of verse 12 to emphasize the importance of our obligation in verse 13. We will ultimately inherit the new eternal life that God has promised us only if we actively use the Spirit. Continuing to live "according to the flesh" means that we will suffer spiritual death. The tension between the indicative of what God gives us and the imperative of what we must do comes to a head here.

Application. Having the mind-set of the Spirit is the crucial middle step between existence in the sphere of the Spirit (v. 9) and living according to the Spirit (v. 4b). Cultivating a Spirit-led, Spirit-filled disposition of heart and mind is necessary if we are to live in a way that pleases God.

If we are serious about progressing in the Christian life, we must seek every day to feed our minds with spiritual food. Too easily our "quiet times" can degenerate into routine exercises in which the mind is hardly involved. We read Scripture, but we don't really seek to engage it by asking what it means or how it applies to us. We pray, but we follow the same pattern every day. Our daily times with the Lord can be one way in which we develop the mind-set of the Spirit, but only if the mind is really involved.

ROMANS 8:14–17

Original Meaning. The recognition that we are God's own children is yet another basis for our assurance that, indeed, "there is now no condemnation for those who are in Christ Jesus" (8:1). In popular speech, Christians often use language such as "led by the Spirit" (v. 14) to refer to guidance: "I was led by the Spirit to witness to her." But as in Galatians 5:18, where the same construction occurs, "being led by the Spirit" in Romans 8:14 means "having the basic orientation of your life determined by the Spirit." The phrase is a way of summing up the various descriptions of the life of the Spirit in 8:4–9.

In verses 15–16, Paul pauses in his argument to elaborate the link between the Spirit and being God's children. Verse 15 centers on a contrast between two different spirits. Paul is using a rhetorical device to explain the nature of the Spirit we have received. He is saying, in effect, that the Spirit of God we have received is not a spirit of fear but the Spirit who makes us God's children.

The legal act of adoption was not practiced by the Jews, so almost certainly Paul uses the image of the Greco-Roman practice whereby a man could formally confer on a child all the legal rights of a birth child. This, Paul suggests, is what God's Spirit confers on every believer—the rights and privileges of God's own children.

Naturally, then, we are moved to cry out in a spontaneous outburst, "*Abba*, Father!" (v. 15). The Spirit enables us to experience the same kind of intimate relationship to the Father that Jesus did, who also called God "*Abba*" (Mark 14:36). Not only does the Spirit confer on us this status, but he also is the one who, testifying with our own spirits, gives us the inner certainty of knowing that we truly are God's dearly loved children.

Verse 17 resumes the main course of Paul's argument in this paragraph, which runs from "Spirit" to "children" to "heir." The transition is a natural one. The adopted child is guaranteed legally all the benefits of the natural child, including being the heir of his new father. But precisely because the adopted child is an heir, there is still something incomplete in his status. Though legally part of a new family, adopted children do not yet possess all the benefits of their new status. Thus, Paul reminds us, we Christians must still await the consummation of that new status.

Application. The feeling of being rejected is all too common in our world. Of course, no human relationship can ever provide ultimate security. But what our fellow humans can never supply, God does. Amid our disillusionment and doubt, he offers the most secure relationship imaginable: adoption into his own eternal family. Through our faith in Christ, the Son of God, we become his "brothers and sisters" (see Heb 2:10–13), children of God and coheirs with Christ of all that God has promised to those who love him. We belong to the ultimate in-group, those who are the dearly loved children of the God of the universe.

ROMANS 8:18–30

Original Meaning

Anticipation of Future Glory (8:18–25). As in chapter 5 (see 5:3–4), Paul does not try to hide the fact that believers suffer. But those sufferings aren't worth comparing to the glory that will be "revealed in us" (8:18). In verses 19–21 Paul accentuates the importance of this revelation of glory by tying the liberation of the whole of creation to it. Following the lead of the psalmists, Paul personifies the created world, using vivid poetic language to speak of its "frustration" (v. 20) and its eventual "liberation" (v. 21). God will one day set the created world free from the decay that mars everything after the fall of human beings into sin. The fate of creation is bound up with that of humanity. As it was through them that creation was marred, so it is through the glorified children of God that it will be restored again.

The pain experienced by a woman about to deliver a child serves as a vivid metaphor of suffering that has a joyous outcome. From a Christian perspective, suffering is but a momentary thing that eventuates in eternal joy (v. 18). Thus, Christians join creation in this kind of groaning (v. 23).

Once the Spirit, with his demand for holiness, enters our lives, we sense as never before just what God wants us to be. As a result, the Spirit increases our frustration at not meeting God's standard and our yearning to be what he wants us to be. What do we wait for? "The redemption of our bodies" (v. 23) refers to the rescue of the body from sin and death that will happen when it is raised from the dead (see vv. 10–11).

But how can Paul suggest that we yearn also for "our adoption to sonship" (v. 23)? Has he not said that we have already been adopted (v. 16)? Here we find a classic New Testament example of the "already-not yet" tension that pervades its teaching about the Christian life.

In light of this tension, therefore, it becomes clear that "hope" is an inevitable part of Christian living (v. 24). Nevertheless, Paul assures us, this hope is not of the normal human kind—"I hope I win the lottery." No, Christian hope is solidly founded in God himself. Thus, we can "wait for it with patience" or, perhaps better, "with endurance" (v. 25).

God's Provision for Our Time of Waiting (8:26–30). As hope sustains us in our time of suffering (vv. 24–25), so also the Spirit sustains us in our time of weakness. "Weakness," then, refers to the limitations of our human condition (v. 26a). Because of these limitations, "we do not know what we ought to pray for" (v. 26b). But the Spirit comes to our aid, interceding on our behalf with "groanings too deep for words" (v. 26c).

"Groaning" has been used metaphorically in the context (8:22). Moreover, the word translated "wordless groans" in NIV at verse 26 can mean either "unspoken" (not expressed at all) or "ineffable" (not expressed in *words*). Whichever it is, Paul's main point is clear enough: these groanings of the Spirit are perfectly in accord with God's will (v. 27). Thus God, who knows the heart, hears and answers those prayers. Our inability to pray as precisely as we would like is no hindrance to the working out of God's perfect will in our lives.

The famous promise of verse 28 is one of the great biblical descriptions of providence. God, through his Spirit, can cause "all things" to work for our good. For whom is this promise valid? All believers. Paul defines Christians from a human direction ("those who love [God]") and from the divine direction ("who have been called according to his purpose"). "Those who love" God is simply a way of describing God's people; it is not a qualification of the promise, as if Paul means that God only works good if believers love God enough.

The "purpose" of God mentioned in verse 28 is outlined in verses 29–30. God has instituted a series of actions that create, sustain, and bring his people to glory. The first action is the most controversial. The Greek verb "to foreknow" (*proginōskō*) generally means to know something ahead of time. In Scripture God's knowing often refers to his entering into relationship with someone. What Paul is saying, then, is that God's plan for us began in a decision to enter into relationship with us. This led, in turn, to his decision to "predestine" us. As the English verb suggests, this word (*proorizō*) simply means to direct a person to a particular goal. Paul spells out the goal: "To be conformed to the likeness of his Son" (v. 29). The last stage of Christian existence is to be "conformed" to Christ's own glorious body. God enters into relationship with us so that we may attain that goal.

Paul's reference to conformity to Christ as the goal of predestination interrupts his sequence of verbs. In verse 30 he continues the sequence, beginning where he left off, with predestination. "Calling" is not a general gospel invitation. It is God's effective summoning of us into relationship with himself through Christ (see 1:7). After setting us on the road to the goal of conformity to Christ, God in his grace and by his Spirit reaches out and brings us into his own people. He then "justifies" us, that is, declares us innocent before him (see chs. 1–4).

Finally, as the capstone to this series, he "glorifies" us (v. 30). This verb is in the same tense that often (though not always) refers to action in the past. Why Paul uses that tense here for a verb whose action is yet future is not clear. Probably the best explanation is that he is viewing matters from God's perspective. God has already made the decision to glorify all those whom he has justified.

This sequence of verbs is a famous debating ground over issues of soteriology—election, predestination, eternal security. But we must not lose sight of Paul's main point, namely, to assure believers that God has a plan he is unfolding, one that provides fully for our future glory. He wants us to come away from this text not with theological questions but with a renewed sense of assurance. The God who began a good work in us will indeed bring it to completion in the day of Christ Jesus (Phil 1:6).

Application. Christians in every generation have found inestimable comfort in the wonderful promise of Romans 8:28, and rightly so. This is surely one of the greatest promises of God to his people anywhere in the Bible. Essentially, it promises that nothing will touch our lives that is not under the control and direction of our loving heavenly Father. Everything we do and say, everything people do to us or say about us, every experience we will ever have—all are sovereignly used by God for our good. We will not always understand how the things we experience work to good, and we certainly will not always enjoy them. But we do know that nothing comes into our lives that God does not allow and use for his own beneficent purposes.

ROMANS 8:31–39

Original Meaning

The Work of God for Us in Christ (8:31–34). Paul here launches into a new direction with a question. "These things" (v. 31) refers to the many reasons for our confidence that Paul has rehearsed in chapters 5–8. All those reasons can be neatly summed up in one statement: God is "for us" (v. 31). Who, then, Paul rightly asks, can be "against us?" Of course, we know many people and things still oppose us. But Paul's point is that with God on our side, none of this opposition ultimately matters.

Verse 32 reinforces Paul's point. God's being "for us" is seen climactically in his giving of his beloved Son. If he has done that, we can be certain he will also give us "all things"—or, to put it in the terms of verse 31, nothing can ultimately oppose us.

"Bring [a] charge" (v. 33) is the first of several judicial terms. Again, Paul's point is not that nothing will ever try to prosecute us in the court of God's justice. But the prosecution will be unsuccessful, for God has chosen us to be his and has justified us already. Paul alludes at this point to Isaiah 50:8–9.

Verse 34 provides more evidence for the same point. No one can successfully condemn us because Christ has died for us and has been raised to life to be our intercessor before the Father. With such a defense attorney, it is no wonder the prosecution loses its case!

The Love of God for Us in Christ (8:35–39). The question at the beginning of verse 35 sets the tone for verses 35–39 by introducing Christ's love into the picture. Christ not only defends us but loves us and enters into relationship with us, and nothing will ever separate us from that love. To make sure we get the point, Paul specifies some threats at the end of verse 35. As a comparison with 2 Corinthians 11:26–27 and 12:10 reveals, Paul himself has gone through most of these. He has learned by experience that they cannot disrupt his relationship with Christ.

The quotation of Psalm 44:22 in verse 36 is a bit of a detour in the logic of Paul's argument. But the detour reveals two of his key concerns: to remind us that suffering is a natural and expected part of the Christian life, and to root the experiences of Christians in the experience of God's old-covenant people.

With verse 37, Paul returns to the main line of his teaching in verse 35. In all the varied difficulties of life, we are "more than conquerors." Paul concludes his celebration of God's love for us in Christ with his own personal testimony: "*I* am convinced . . ." (vv. 38–39). There is nothing in all the world—whether we are dead or alive, whether they are things we now face or things we will face in the future, whether they are above us or below us—that can separate us from the "love of God that is in Christ Jesus our Lord" (v. 39). As the chapter began with "no condemnation" (8:1), so it ends with the bookends of "no separation" (8:35, 39).

Application. Paul's emphatic assertion that no spiritual being can separate us from Christ is needed in the church today. We need to recognize and proclaim that God in Christ has won a victory over the "powers and authorities" (Col 2:15) and that they have no power to keep us from inheriting the salvation God has promised to all who love him. Nothing on earth can separate us from God's love for us in Christ, and neither can anything in heaven.

ROMANS 9:1–5

Original Meaning. For Paul there can be no good news in Christ unless what God has done in him is part of the one master plan that the Old Testament reveals to us. Ultimately, then, Romans 9–11 is not about Israel—it is about God. The theme of the section is found in 9:6: "It is not as though God's word had failed."

The first five verses of chapter 9 reveal that Paul was deeply concerned about the matters he writes about in these chapters. In verse 1, he goes out of his way to stress the sincerity of this concern. In fact, he has "great sorrow and unceasing anguish in [his] heart" (v. 2). What Paul says in verse 3 shows the problem is basic: Israel is not saved! In offering to become himself "cursed and cut off from Christ" for the sake of his fellow Jews (v. 3), Paul implies that Israel herself stands under this judgment.

As Israelites, Jews have been blessed. Paul's claim that the Jews enjoy "adoption" (*huiothesia*, v. 4) is striking in light of 8:16, 23, where he has applied that blessing to Christians. Probably he thinks of Israel's adoption as a national blessing that does not confer salvation on individual Jews.

Paul concludes in verse 5 with two final blessings enjoyed by Israel. The patriarchs are significant not so much in themselves but because God entered into a solemn covenant with them. The greatest blessing promised to Israel was the Messiah, that is, the Christ. From a strictly human point of view, the Messiah was to arise from the people of Israel. But from the divine point of view, he is more; indeed, he is God. This verse deserves to be numbered among those few in the New Testament that explicitly call Jesus "God."

Application. A strong revisionist movement today has challenged the traditional view of Israel's plight. To be sure, Israel has sinned. But her sin has not separated her from God. Rather, Israel's sin is the sin of selfishness—seeking to keep God's grace all to themselves.

Integral to this interpretation of Israel in Romans 9–11 is the assumption that the Jewish people are saved through their own "Torah covenant," while gentiles are saved through the "Christ covenant." This so-called "bi-covenantal" view arose toward the end of the 1800s but became especially popular in the last decades of the twentieth century and is still prevalent today.

Two factors external to the text have propelled the popularity of this alternative interpretation. The first is the Holocaust. By excluding Jews from salvation, Christians in effect deny the value of Judaism and open the door to persecution and anti-Semitism. Second is the pluralism of our age. Every religion, so we are taught, is but a different way to the same God. Judaism must be seen as valid as the Christian faith.

We will deal with these trends in light of the exegetical evidence elsewhere in chapters 9–11. But we want to get this broad concern out on the table as we begin working through these chapters. Our interpretation of Scripture is always affected by factors external to the text—from the specifics of our own personalities and backgrounds to the generalities of cultural movements and influences.

ROMANS 9:6–13

Original Meaning

The Thesis of Chapters 9–11: The Reliability of God (9:6a). In verse 6a we hear the thesis that Paul defends in these three chapters. To defend the gospel, Paul must defend God's faithfulness to his promises to Israel. For if God has gone back on his word to Israel, then a deep chasm between the Old and New Testament opens up, and the whole plan of salvation crashes.

The Thesis of 9:7–29: The "Israel" within Israel (9:6b). Verse 6b sets forth the thesis for verses 7–29. Paul differentiates two "Israels": what we might call a physical Israel, based on descent, and a spiritual Israel. What is the spiritual Israel Paul has in view? In Galatians 6:16, Paul refers to the entire church as "Israel." This, then, may be what Paul means here: not all Jews by birth belong to the "Israel of God," the church. All Jews belong to the larger Israel by birth, but only those Jews called by God belong to the true Israel.

God's Choice of Isaac over Ishmael (9:7–9). Jews belong to Abraham in different ways, Paul affirms. All who can claim him as their physical ancestor are his "children," but only those who have him as their spiritual father as well are his "offspring" (v. 7).

A quotation from Genesis 21:12 grounds this assertion. God determined that Abraham's offspring would be "called" (*kaleō*; NIV "reckoned"), a key word in Paul's argument. God spoke these words to Abraham when the latter expressed reluctance to banish his other son, Ishmael. Thus it is clear, Paul concludes in verse 8, that it is only the "children of the promise" who are "regarded as Abraham's offspring."

Paul wraps up this argument from the sons of Abraham with a final scriptural quotation (v. 9), a loose rendering of Genesis 18:10 or 18:14 (or perhaps both). The initiative, Paul makes clear again, is with God. Inheriting the promise is not based on birth alone; it depends on God's gracious intervention.

God's Choice of Jacob over Esau (9:10–13). This same point becomes even clearer in verses 10–13. To dispel any idea that physical descent plays a role in the promise, Paul brings us down one generation, to two children born to the same parents and at the same time. What makes Jacob and Esau different from Ishmael and Isaac is not only that they had the same mother as well as the same father but that they were conceived at the same time.

The syntax of verses 11–12 is quite muddled, but the NIV does the best job we can with it. The main clause comes only at the end of the long complex sentence: "She was told, 'The older will serve the younger'" (v. 12). This quotation (from Gen 25:23) neatly expresses Paul's key point, that God's choice reversed the natural order of birth.

God appointed Jacob over Esau to carry on the line of promise before the two boys had been born (Rom 9:11a). In this way, "God's purpose in election might stand" (v. 11b). Since God chose Jacob over Esau before they were born or had done anything, it is clear that Jacob's status was based not on works but on the God who calls.

Paul concludes his discussion of Jacob and Esau with yet another quotation: "Jacob I loved, but Esau I hated" (Mal 1:2–3). The Old Testament context is clearly covenantal, so that "love" means, in effect, "choose," while "hate" means "reject." Paul is thinking of Jacob and Esau here as individuals. He has specifically rehearsed their personal histories in verses 11–12, referring to their birth and their "works." It is difficult to think that Paul switches from this personal reference to a corporate one, without warning, in verse 13.

Application. However much we may want to claim that salvation is based on God's choice, we must also insist that the human decision to believe is also both real and critical. We are not puppets in God's hands, passively moving as he directs. We are responsible human beings, called by God to exercise faith in his Son. The evidence of Scripture compels us to maintain a fine balance at this point. The Bible teaches in passages such as Romans 9:6–13 that God is the one who ultimately determines, by his own free decision, who is to be saved. But it also teaches that every human being is called upon to respond to God's offer of salvation in faith.

ROMANS 9:14–23

Original Meaning

God Is Just Because He Acts for His Glory (9:14–18). Paul has taught that God chose Jacob and rejected Esau simply because it was his will to do so; nothing about them led God to act toward them as he did (9:10–13). The question, "Is God unjust?," is a natural one to ask in response to this teaching.

Determining right or wrong, what is just or unjust, demands a standard for measurement. That standard is ultimately nothing less than God's own character. God, therefore, acts justly when he acts in accordance with his own person and plan. This is precisely the point Paul makes in verses 15–18.

Paul first quotes Exodus 33:19 in verse 15, where God reveals to Moses a fundamental aspect of his character: he is free to bestow mercy on whomever he wishes. Receiving favor from God does not depend on anything a person can will or do, but only on God's own will to show mercy.

A second quotation reinforces the freedom of God to act as he wishes, but now from a negative side (v. 17). Paul now turns to Moses's antagonist, Pharaoh, and cites a word that God spoke to him (Exod 9:16). The essence of the message is that God brought Pharaoh onto the stage of history to accomplish his own purposes. By resisting God's determination to release his people from captivity, Pharaoh forced Moses to work a series of miracles to bring Israel out of Egypt. This display of God's power became known throughout that part of the world (cf. Josh 2:10). Verse 18 draws the conclusion not only from verse 17 but from verses 15–16 as well.

Many think Paul refers to the roles of Moses (and Israel) and Pharaoh (and Egypt) in salvation history. But again, we think that what he says here has direct relevance to the issue of personal salvation. It is God who determines who is to be saved and who is to be kept in a state of spiritual blindness.

God Is Free to Use His Creatures as He Wills (9:19–23). Paul's reassertion of God's sovereignty in salvation (v. 18) sparks another round of question and answer (the diatribe style again). Paul offers no logical explanation of how God's determinative will and human responsibility cohere. Rather than taking the defensive, Paul goes full speed ahead with yet further assertions of the freedom of God to do as he wants with his creatures.

What right, Paul asks, does this created being have to

question God's ways and complain about how God has made him (v. 20)? Paul uses the imagery of the potter with his clay to depict God's relationship to human beings. The analogy works well at the one vital point the apostle wants to make here: God's right to fashion from the clay the kinds of vessels he wants. The parallel with "objects of his wrath" and "objects of his mercy" (vv. 22–23) suggest he is thinking of God's freedom to choose some people to be saved and leave others in their spiritual deadness.

Paul concludes his excursus about God's freedom to bestow and withhold salvation as he chooses with a final complicated question. Verses 22–23 form a question that has no direct answer. The "what if" at the beginning suggests that Paul is saying, in effect: "What if God has acted in this way? Who will question God's authority?"

The word "choosing" (or "willing") at verse 22 has a causal rather than a concessive function. *Because* God wants publicly to display wrath and power, he has done so. By reserving the outward display of his wrath against sinners until the end of history, God is able to make his judgment all the more obvious. God has tolerated sinners not only so he can display his wrath and power all the more clearly; he has done so especially in order to "make the riches of his glory known to the objects of his mercy" (v. 23). The contrast between wrath and glory shows that Paul is writing about individuals destined for judgment on the one hand and individuals destined for glory on the other. Salvation is the issue.

Application. If the idea of God's unconditional election to salvation stirs controversy, imagine the level of reaction against the idea that God might also choose to send people to hell on the basis of his own sovereign decision. Yet we cannot avoid considering whether, indeed, Paul teaches this dark side of election, for three key texts in Romans 9:6–23 seem to suggest this idea (9:13, 18, 22–23). In each of these, Paul seems to suggest that God chooses people to be damned just as he chooses people to be saved. Hence theologians, particularly of a Calvinist persuasion, speak of "double predestination." Is the idea really taught in this passage? I cautiously conclude that it is. If God has unconditionally chosen some to be saved, the parallelism suggests that he also unconditionally destines others to wrath.

But before we conclude that the two acts are completely parallel, one other factor must be considered. Paul teaches that all people are involved in Adam's sin. God's decision to destine some people to wrath comes, we believe, *after* (in a logical sense) that sin. God's "hardening," then, does not cause spiritual insensitivity; it maintains people in the state of sin that they have already chosen. Perhaps we can turn what can seem to be a problem into a virtue by allowing Paul's presentation of the sovereignty of God in election and perdition to stimulate in us a new appreciation for the greatness and incomprehensible purposes of God.

ROMANS 9:24–29

Original Meaning. God's call is the sole basis for inclusion in the true people of God. Paul now takes a step further by taking this principle to its logical conclusion. Since God's grace is what matters, then he is free to call gentiles into his kingdom as well as Jews. The apostle makes this point in verse 24, the heading for the paragraph. He then grounds his assertion with quotations from Scripture. The structure of the paragraph is chiastic, the verses falling into an A B B′ A′ pattern:

A God calls (some) Jews (v. 24a)
  B God calls gentiles (v. 24b)
  B′ The Old Testament confirms God's call of gentiles (vv. 25–26)
A′ The Old Testament confirms God's call of (some) Jews (vv. 27–29)

Paul ends his series of quotations with another one from Isaiah (Isa 1:9, quoted in Rom 9:29). What probably drew his attention to Isaiah 1:9 is the word "descendants" (Gk. *sperma*), which is the key word at the beginning of this section (see 9:7–8). This word is much more positive, holding out hope to Israel because God is determined to preserve descendants for Israel—people who will inherit this promise to Abraham. The verse thus anticipates Paul's word of hope about Israel in chapter 11.

Application. Paul's reading of the Old Testament against a broad theological background says something to us about our own reading of the Scriptures. We should follow his lead in reading the Old Testament as a single integral story about God's plan of redemption that finds its fulfillment in Christ. Those of us who preach and teach need to take more seriously the importance of helping the people to whom we minister to see the big picture of the Bible's wonderful narrative of God's redemptive plan. All of us—preachers, teachers, and laypeople alike—need to learn the "old, old story" so well that we can revel in the marvelous interrelationship between all the parts of Scripture.

ROMANS 9:30–10:13

Original Meaning

Israel's False Pursuit (9:30–33). Gentiles had not been pursuing their own righteousness, ignorant as they were of God's promises, but when God offered it to them they responded in faith and so obtained it (v. 30). In contrast to the gentiles, however, is the situation of Israel. Paul claims that they were pursuing "the law as the way of righteousness" and that they failed to attain "it" (i.e., this "law," v. 31). Paul's formulation is probably an attempt to make two points at once: Israel pursued righteousness, but she did not obtain it because she elevated *nomos*, "the law," to the central position of concern. The people of Israel, therefore, focused narrowly on the works the law demanded and missed the larger demand of God to submit to him in faith. Thus they failed to obtain righteousness. Israel, myopically concentrating on the law and its demands, missed Christ, "the stone" that God placed in her path (v. 32).

Israel's Lack of Knowledge (10:1–4). Paul makes clear how deeply he feels about the failure of Israel to embrace the salvation God offers in Jesus (10:1). "Zeal" for the Lord finds its outstanding Old Testament example in Phinehas (Num 25). Jesus himself displayed zeal for the Lord when he cleared the temple (John 2:17). Paul regards the zeal of his fellow Israelites as a good thing. The problem, however, is that—like the pre-Christian Paul (Acts 22:3; Phil 3:6)—their zeal was not directed by knowledge. The Jews did not understand that God is now offering a right relationship with himself through faith in Jesus Christ, the culmination of salvation history.

Instead of submitting to God's righteousness, the Jews sought to "establish their own" (v. 3). Paul's ultimate criticism of Israel is not just salvation-historical—Jews failed to see that God was doing something new with the gentiles. It is also anthropological—Jews failed to seek a relationship with God in the right way. Both criticisms are found in this context. In failing to submit to God's righteousness, the Jews were guilty of missing the decisive turn in salvation history that had come with Christ, for God's righteousness in Paul is clearly bound up with Christ (see 1:17; 3:21–22). But in seeking to establish their own righteousness, they were also guilty of relying on their own works.

Verse 4 explains that Israel's pursuit of a righteousness based on the law completely misses the point that the era of the law has ended. Picture Israel as the runner, the law as the race, and Christ as the finish line. What Israel has failed to understand, Paul is saying, is that the finish line has been reached. As a result of Christ's coming and bringing the law to its culmination, righteousness is now available for everyone who believes. Faith, apart from ethnic origin or works, is the sole basis for experiencing this gift he offers to the world.

Righteousness for Everyone Who Believes (10:5–13). In verses 5–6 we find the third contrast between two kinds of righteousness. The "law as the way of righteousness" of 9:31 and "their own [righteousness]" of 10:3 is now described as "the righteousness that is by the law" in verse 10:5; while, as in 9:30, "the righteousness of God" (10:3) is defined as the "righteousness that is by faith" (v. 6). Paul then identifies each righteousness by means of the Old Testament.

The apostle cites Leviticus 18:5 in Romans 10:5 to describe legal righteousness: "The person who does these things will live by them." Paul is not suggesting here that Moses taught that one could be saved by doing the law. Rather, Paul's point is that any righteousness based on the law is, by definition, something one can get only by "doing." For "doing" is what the law is all about.

In contrast to this legal righteousness, then, is the "righteousness that is by faith" (v. 6). The general point he wants to make about the righteousness by faith is clear enough: through Christ's being brought down to earth (i.e., his incarnation, v. 6) and his being brought up from the dead (v. 7), God has made righteousness readily available (v. 8). All one needs to do to attain righteousness is to respond in faith to the gospel as it is preached.

Verses 9–10 draw conclusions from what Paul has said about "the righteousness that is by faith" in verses 6–8. Deuteronomy 30:14, which Paul cites in verse 8, refers to the "mouth" and the "heart." In verse 9 he elaborates each of these. The fulfillment of these two conditions brings salvation. Verse 10 elaborates further, only now in reverse order.

Verse 11 grounds verse 10 by showing from the Old Testament (Isa 28:16) that putting one's trust in Christ will bring vindication in the judgment. The quotation in verse 11 also anticipates what is to come. For it stresses that the faith that leads to vindication in the judgment is open to "anyone." Paul develops this in verse 12, returning to his central claim that the gospel opens the doors to salvation to all people on the same basis.

The verb "call on" (*epikaleō*, v. 13) is apparently the trigger that leads Paul to yet another Old Testament text that underscores the universality of God's offer in the gospel (Joel 2:32). The "LORD" in Joel is Yahweh, but Paul identifies this "Lord" with Jesus (see Rom 10:9, 12), the "stone" of Isaiah 28:16 (Rom 10:11). Verse 13, then, is important evidence that the early Christians identified Jesus with God.

Application. Offering the gospel to all nations and ethnic groups is the logical conclusion from the principle we see in these verses. The church of Christ in general has committed itself to this great and yet unfinished task. But we are easily deflected from that goal. Ironically, some theoreticians have put forth the "church growth" approach to missions. Quite pragmatic, this approach argues that the church should concentrate its resources on people groups who are receptive to the gospel. Decisions about where to send missionaries are not easy, but we cannot predict where God will call his people to minister. Nor should we direct or deflect that call on the basis of pragmatics.

ROMANS 10:14–21

Original Meaning. In verses 14–15a, Paul uses four rhetorical questions to outline the sequence if a person is to be "saved" (cf. v. 13). The steps are, in reverse order to what Paul cites: the sending of preachers, preaching, hearing the message about Christ, believing in Christ, and calling on "the name of the Lord" (v. 14). Paul sets up his indictment of Israel in verse 16 and following by first speaking generally about what is required for *any* person (see "everyone" in v. 13) to be saved. The quotation from Isaiah 52:7 at the end of verse 15 confirms that preaching the good news is needed if people are to hear and to be saved. It also suggests, however, that preachers have been sent.

Paul now turns to Israel. While Israel has heard the good news (v. 18), she has not believed (v. 16). After his condemnation of Israel in verse 16, Paul resumes the logical unfolding of the steps necessary for salvation in verse 17. He begins by restating the second step mentioned in verse 14: faith comes from hearing. The last part of verse 17, then, restates the third step in the salvation sequence (v. 14c): hearing, the kind that can lead to faith, can only happen when a definite salvific word from God is proclaimed (8–9).

In verse 18, Paul again demonstrates the freedom with which he treats the Old Testament, for Psalm 19 is about God's revelation of his character in nature. Yet Paul applies it to the preaching of the gospel. Also puzzling is Paul's apparent claim that the message has gone "into all the earth" and "to the ends of the world." We should probably view Paul's application of this verse as hyperbole. He simply uses the language given to him in the quotation to assert that the gospel had been proclaimed so widely that Jews have no excuse for not responding.

Having demonstrated that Israel has heard, Paul now wants to probe more deeply into the nature of this hearing. Was it superficial? Not at all. Moses, Paul suggests, was the "first" in a long line of prophets to suggest that God would eventually extend his grace beyond the confines of Israel (v. 19, quoting Deut 32:21). Isaiah is another prophet who predicted the inclusion of gentiles (v. 20, quoting Isa 65:1). Gentiles who were not seeking righteousness have found it (Rom 9:30); gentiles who did ask for God have found him (10:20). Paul quotes Isaiah 65:2 in verse 21 to make two points: God continues to extend his grace to Israel (he "holds out his hands" to them), and Israel continues to rebel (they are "disobedient and obstinate").

Application. The absolute need for people to hear the gospel preached if they are to be saved was one of the greatest forces impelling the modern missionary enterprise, begun in the early 1800s and flourishing yet today. Yet the tie between preaching the gospel and being saved is being severed in many churches and denominations. Succumbing to the flood of postmodern malaise and afraid of seeming intolerant, many churches have lost their missionary zeal. Reasons vary, of course. But some teach that other religions are also ways to God, so why bother sending missionaries if people can be saved within their own religion? Others teach that God reveals himself to all people in various ways, so that an oral or written presentation of the gospel is unnecessary.

But the text before us shows such viewpoints as the false teachings or easy generalizations they really are. Paul links salvation to belief, which he in turn ties to hearing the message about Christ. People must be "sent out" so that the message can be proclaimed to all people. Paul himself, of course, was among those whom God had sent out. In his own life of difficult travel, he illustrates the theology he teaches: people need to hear the gospel so that they can be saved.

ROMANS 11:1–10

Original Meaning

God's Faithfulness to Israel Seen in the Remnant (11:1–6). Paul has claimed that Israel stumbled over the rock of Christ (9:33), willfully turning away from God's righteousness in Christ (10:3). Does this mean, Paul asks, that Israel has now forfeited any claim on God's promises? Paul emphatically rejects any such conclusion and follows it up with a solemn assertion in 11:2a. As in 8:29, the verb "foreknow" (*proginōskō*) means "choose ahead of time." "Whom he foreknew" does not identify the "people" Paul is talking about; rather, it explains why God remains faithful to that people.

Paul, in other words, has all of (physical) Israel in view here, and he is reasserting the common Old Testament teaching that God chose Israel as his very own people. What the apostle does in chapter 11 is show what that corporate election of Israel as a whole means for the salvation of Jews in his own day and in the future.

The evidence Paul offers for God's faithfulness to that election of Israel in his own day is the existence of a "remnant" (vv. 5–6). But he leads up to that claim with two preliminary points. First, he begins with himself (v. 1b). Paul's reminder to his readers of his Jewish descent reminds us that he himself is both a Jew and a Christian—evidence that God has not abandoned his people. Second, in verses 2b–4 Paul quotes Elijah's lament about being left alone after the slaughter of the prophets (cf. 1 Kgs 19:10, 14) and the Lord's concluding reassurance to Elijah that he has preserved a remnant (1 Kgs 19:18). Like Elijah, Paul is confronted with the apparent downfall of Israel, but finds new hope in God's preservation of a remnant of true believers.

Paul now draws a conclusion: "So too, at the present time

there is a remnant chosen by grace" (v. 5). God's word affirms a continuing role for Israel in salvation history. But Israel cannot claim this role as a matter of right, for it is due solely to the working of God's grace. This polemical thrust becomes explicit in verse 6. "Grace" means that "works" have no role to play, and that God is entirely free to bestow his blessing on whomever he chooses.

Israel's Present Situation: A Summary (11:7–10). With the rhetorical question "What then?" Paul signals the conclusion he wants to draw from his discussion about the remnant. But his conclusion is also a fair summary of the situation of Israel in Paul's day as he developed it in chapters 9–10. Israel as a whole "sought" a right standing with God, but "did not obtain" it (11:7b). Paul then breaks the situation of Israel in general down into two specific entities. One is the remnant or the "elect" (v. 7c). Despite the rejection of Israel as a whole, many individual Jews have responded to the gospel. They are the Israel within Israel (9:6), the "remnant chosen by grace" (11:5). These Jews have obtained the right standing with God that Israel as a whole was seeking. The other, larger division of Jews consists of those who have not attained this right standing. They have been "hardened" (v. 7d).

The Old Testament quotations in verses 8–10 provide biblical support for the idea that it is God who hardens people. Paul, following Jewish precedent, quotes from every part of the Hebrew canon: the Law (Deut 29:4), the Prophets (Isa 29:10), and the Writings (Ps 69:22–23). In verses 9–10 Paul supports this idea by quoting from one of the famous imprecatory psalms. In Psalm 69, David laments the unjust persecution he is experiencing and asks God to bring disaster on his enemies. What David prayed that his persecutors would experience, God has brought on the majority of Jews in his own day.

Application. Some Jews made the mistake of assuming that God's election of Israel virtually guaranteed spiritual benefits to every member of the nation. Birth into that nation, circumcision (for males), and a reasonable faithfulness in observing the law were all that was needed to ensure one's salvation. Some segments of the church have much the same kind of attitude. People assume that they will go to heaven as long as they can claim such external credits as baptism, confirmation, church attendance, and acts of service.

ROMANS 11:11–24

Original Meaning

God's Purpose in Israel's Rejection (11:11–15). While Israel at present has not obtained the righteousness they were seeking, Israelites have not for that reason fallen into irretrievable spiritual ruin. Paul's purpose in verses 11–32 is to explain why that is not so. Their "transgression" (v. 11) of rejecting God's grace in Christ has led to salvation for the gentiles. Paul's own ministry as portrayed in the book of Acts reveals how this happened historically (see Acts 13:44–47; 14:1–3; 18:4–7; 19:8–10; 28:23–29).

But this pattern was more than a historical accident. As Paul makes clear in Acts by citing Scripture in support and now demonstrates in Romans by revealing God's purpose behind what has happened, Jewish rejection and gentile acceptance was God's plan for the salvation of all the world. In specific answer to his question in verse 11, Paul affirms that the salvation of gentiles has the purpose of making Israel "envious" (or "jealous").

In verse 12, Paul elaborates on the sequence introduced in verse 11. Paul spoke vaguely of Israel being made "envious" (v. 11); now he speaks of "their full inclusion." The Greek word for "full inclusion" is *plērōma*, and it may have either a quantitative or qualitative meaning. With the former, *plērōma* would refer to a great number of Jews; with the latter, to Israel's restoration to kingdom blessing. The latter is the more likely meaning, but the context also suggests that the blessing Israel is to experience comes by way of an increase in the number of Jews who are saved (see 11:25).

In verses 13–14, Paul interrupts his sketch of God's plan for salvation history in order to hint at the practical purpose for what he is saying. His ministry to gentiles does *not* mean that he is unconcerned about his own people. His ultimate purpose in bringing the gospel to gentiles is to arouse Israel to envy and so "save some of them" (v. 14).

Verse 15 returns to the main line of argument, as Paul reiterates one more time the salvation-historical sequence that dominates this passage. If God's rejection of Israel has brought "reconciliation to the world" (see 5:10–11), then "what will their acceptance be but life from the dead?" Far greater blessing than the offer of a new relationship with God for the gentiles will come when God "accepts" Israel once again.

But what will this blessing be? The phrase "from the dead" (*ek nekrōn*, v. 15) refers to the resurrection of the body in forty-six of its forty-seven occurrences in the New Testament. Underlying Paul's sketch of salvation history here is an apocalyptic worldview that focuses on the resurrection of the dead as the last and climactic stage in God's plan for history.

Thus, Paul suggests that the return of Israel to favor with God will occur at the climax of history when the dead are raised. This likely reference of "life from the dead" constitutes one important reason to think that Paul is describing a linear sequence of acts in salvation history that climax with the return of Christ in glory.

God's Purpose and Gentile Arrogance (11:16–24). In this paragraph, dominated by the olive-tree metaphor, Paul makes more explicit his concern to stifle gentile arrogance. Paul uses two metaphors to make his point, each of which uses the logic of "if the part, then the whole" to anchor Paul's confidence about a great future for Israel. The first one in verse 16a is drawn from Numbers 15:17–21. The salvation of the remnant shows that God still considers Israel "holy," with all the hope that this holiness implies.

In the second image, the "root" almost certainly represents the patriarchs (v. 16b). This being the case, it is likely that "firstfruits" of verse 16a also refers to the patriarchs. God's promise to the patriarchs has not been revoked; their descendants remain "holy." By this Paul does not mean that all their descendants will be saved. Rather, "holy" (*hagios*), as in the Old Testament and 1 Corinthians 7:14, means that the people continue to be "set apart" by God for special attention.

Paul then uses a conditional sentence (vv. 17–18a) that gets to the heart of his concern. The "if" clause rehearses the sequence of Jewish rejection and gentile salvation that we have seen so often in this passage. "Some of the branches" broken off (cf. "natural branches" in vv. 21, 24) are, of course, Jews, while the "wild olive shoot" refers to gentiles. Gentiles were not originally included in the people of God formed via God's promise to the patriarchs—they do not naturally belong to the olive tree. But now that they have been included, they have, Paul affirms in the "then" clause (v. 18a), no reason to boast over Jews. "Those other branches" (v. 18) refers to the branches cut off in verse 17, that is, to those Jews in Paul's day who have not responded to the gospel.

The context reveals that the gentiles were guilty of an arrogance toward Jews. Paul shows why such arrogance is wrong in verses 18b–23. He makes two basic points. First, gentile Christians receive the spiritual benefits they enjoy only through the Jews. Second, gentile Christians have not earned the right to be grafted into the olive tree. It was, rather, entirely a matter of "faith" (v. 20).

Jews forfeited their place because they failed to believe, while gentile Christians have been included because they believed the message (v. 20b). Faith, as Paul has shown earlier in Romans, gives a person no basis for pride, for it is a matter simply of accepting the gracious gift God offers (3:27; 4:3–5). The gentile Christians, therefore, need to replace their arrogance with fear (11:20b). For while God shows "kindness" to those who stand in faith, he shows "sternness" to those who fall (v. 22a). It is necessary to renew one's faith every day. Failure to do so means that one will be "cut off": removed from God's people and the salvation found only through that relationship (v. 22b).

After the warning to gentile Christians, Paul concludes the olive-tree imagery with a word of hope for the Jews. Just as gentile Christians run the risk of being cut off if they should stop believing, so Jews can be grafted back in if they turn from unbelief to faith (v. 23). For it is surely easier to graft natural branches back in than to do what God has already done, that is, graft in, "contrary to nature," wild olive shoots (v. 24).

Application. We must be cautious about finding more theology in an analogy than is justified. But this much is clear: there is only one olive tree. Ultimately, the olive-tree imagery shows that there is one people of God. Yet Paul's imagery makes clear that the turn of the ages did not bring into existence a new people of God. Rather, gentiles join the already existing people of God, "true Israel."

From this perspective, then, we see how wrong is the common idea that the church has replaced Israel. As a name for the New Testament community of faith, the church *is* "Israel." But that people include in its number both gentiles and Jews. Clearly, therefore, the church cannot replace believing Israel. But neither can it replace unbelieving Israel, for the two belong in different categories. Jewish unbelievers belong by birth to national Israel, and nothing can change that. But the church is a spiritual entity, made up of people from all nations, including Israel.

ROMANS 11:25–32

Original Meaning

"All Israel Will Be Saved" (11:25–27). Paul is hopeful that Israel will be grafted back into the olive tree again, *because* a mystery has been revealed to him. "Mystery" (Gk. *mystērion*) refers to a truth that has been "hidden" from God's people in the past but has now been disclosed in the gospel.

Paul has described Israel's "hardening" earlier (11:7; cf. 9:18). This hardening affects only part of Israel. Yet not only is the hardening partial, but it is also temporary. It lasts, Paul implies, only "until the full number of the Gentiles has come in" (v. 25). In other words, once that number is reached, Israel's hardening comes to an end.

The first clause of verse 26 is the storm center in the interpretation of Romans 9–11 and of the New Testament teaching about Israel in general. What does Paul mean by "all Israel"? We think "all Israel" refers to some Israelites as a representative whole. Note, for instance, 2 Samuel 16:22. The phrase almost always refers to Israelites living at a certain point in time rather than to Israelites in every generation of the nation's history.

If the reference is to a single generation of Israel, Paul can hardly mean anything but the Israel as it exists in the end times. This conclusion is borne out by 11:15, where, we argued, Paul connects Israel's "acceptance" by God to the resurrection of the dead. We conclude, then, that Paul here predicts the salvation of a significant number of Jews at the time of Christ's return in glory. The present remnant of Israel will be expanded to include a much larger number of Jews who will enter the eternal kingdom along with converted gentiles. Paul backs up his prediction of a significant turning to Christ for salvation among Jews in the last day by citing Isaiah 59:20–21 along with a phrase from Isaiah 27:9 in verses 26b–27.

The Wrap-Up (11:28–32). In verses 28–32, Paul both provides further evidence for his claim that "all Israel will be saved" (11:26a) and wraps up chapters 9–11 by reminding his readers once more of some of the basic points of his argument. Israel's failure to respond to the gospel has cut her off from God's salvation. From this standpoint, therefore, they are "enemies" of God (v. 28).

Nevertheless, the refusal of Israel to believe does not mean God has relegated Israel to the rubbish heap of history. How could he do so, since he has elected Israel (cf. 11:2), and "God's gifts and his call are irrevocable" (v. 29)?

Paul explains just how God will manifest his grace to Israel in verses 30–31. One last time we hear again the salvation-historical sequence that dominates the latter part of chapter 11. Verse 30 is clear enough as a summary of the sequence we have seen so often in the chapter: Jewish disobedience has resulted in the gentiles receiving God's mercy. Verse 31, then, describes the third step in the process, Jewish inclusion.

Paul's concern to put Jew and gentile on equal footing is reinforced by the solemn conclusion in verse 32. God has sentenced all people to condemnation. But his purpose is ultimately a positive one: he wants to "have mercy on them all." Interpreters of this verse err when they wrest it from its context and use it to prove universalism—namely, that all people will eventually be saved. The Greek allows and the context strongly suggests that Paul has a different purpose: to show that God has both shut up under sin and shown mercy to all kinds of people—especially, in this context, Jews and gentiles.

Application. Romans 11 does teach that a significant number of Jews will come to salvation in the last day, yet here we did not draw the inferences that many dispensationalists do. The conversion of these Jews will take place as they believe the gospel, not through some kind of "special way." Those Jews who are converted will, like any other believers, become integrated into the church—although perhaps a church on its way to heaven, if the conversion happens at the time of Jesus's parousia or second coming.

ROMANS 11:33–36

Original Meaning. In verse 33, we find three exclamations about God's wise plan. In verses 34–35, the apostle uses three rhetorical questions to remind us how far above are the thoughts and ways of God. Finally, verse 36 reminds us that God is ultimate in all things and that he is therefore deserving of our praise.

The three questions in verses 34–35 are obviously rhetorical and expect the answer, "no one." If the first two questions remind us how far we are from fully understanding God, the final question reminds us of God's grace, a great theme of these chapters. What God does in his plan of salvation he does not do because anyone has earned his favor or deserves his kindness, but solely out of his own great love for us.

The concept of God as source (*ek*), sustainer (*dia*), and goal (*eis*) of all things expresses well the biblical teaching of God's ultimacy: that he is far more important than his creation and must be therefore given the honor and glory due him. Paul therefore appropriately responds by ascribing glory to this wondrous and all-consuming God.

Application. Paul's reminder that God's thoughts are far beyond anything we could ever approximate and his plan more intricate and marvelous than we could even imagine certainly calls on each of us to exercise great humility in seeking to understand God and his word. On this side of glory, all our theologizing is uncertain and tentative. Humility, willingness to listen, and respect for others are the appropriate attitudes for us finite creatures as we seek to plumb the depths of God's character and truth.

ROMANS 12:1–2

Original Meaning. Romans 12:1–2 is one of the best-known passages in the Bible—and deservedly so, for we find here a succinct description of the essence of the believer's response to God's grace in the gospel of Jesus Christ. It functions as the heading for all the specifics Paul will unpack in the subsequent chapters. Our response is rooted in God's grace.

The command to "offer" ourselves to God reminds us of Romans 6, where Paul used this same verb (*paristēmi*) to express the basic response of believers to God's grace to us in Christ (see 6:13, 16, 19). Indeed, all of Romans 12:1–15:13 is an explication of this basic demand in chapter 6. As new-covenant Christians, we no longer offer animal sacrifices; we now offer ourselves as "living sacrifices."

This offering of ourselves to God constitutes, Paul concludes, our "true and proper worship." We give ourselves to God as his sacrifices when we understand his grace and its place in our lives. We offer ourselves not ignorantly, like animals brought to slaughter, but intelligently and willingly. This is the worship that pleases God.

Building on his "two-era" concept of salvation history, Paul demands that we "not conform" to "this age" (literal translation).

The NIV's rendition as "the pattern of this world" captures the general sense well enough. The old age to which we belonged in our pre-Christian past still exerts influence on us, enticing us to follow its pattern of sinful and ungodly behavior. Rather than "conforming" our conduct to that age, we must be "transformed" in our behavior (v. 2). The means by which we accomplish this transformation in conduct is the "renewing of your mind." A new orientation in our thinking leads to a new orientation in behavior.

Application. Modern airliners are guided by their onboard computers. Pilots are told where they are and where they are to go by those computers. But airports still have runway lights. Pilots check the accuracy of the computer by visually watching those lights. So also the Christian. We are guided by our minds, which are in the process of being renewed by God's Spirit so that they perfectly reflect God's will. But because that process will never be complete in this life, we still need the external guidance of God's commands as set forth in Scripture. Put the commands at the heart of ethics and we end up with a superficial and incomplete obedience. But exclude the commands and we end up with self-centered and erratic obedience.

ROMANS 12:3–8

Original Meaning. Paul underlines the importance of what he is about to say by reminding the Roman Christians of his own authority. The "grace" given Paul is his apostolic calling, a specific manifestation of God's grace (v. 3). Paul's exhortation plays on a Greek word (*phroneō*) that means to think, have a particular mind-set. We should regard ourselves, Paul is saying, with "renewed minds" (cf. 12:2) that deliver us from the self-centeredness typical of the non-Christian and enable us to look at ourselves objectively and realistically.

The standard of that measurement is "the faith God has distributed to each of you" (v. 3). Paul may mean the specific amount of faith that God has distributed to each person. He is then encouraging us to look at ourselves in light of the gifts we have and to evaluate ourselves accordingly. Another possibility is that the Christian faith in general is the standard of measurement. On this view, Paul is asking us to look carefully to the gospel faith and its requirements as we assess ourselves. The decision between these two options is not easy, but we incline slightly to the second alternative.

Paul backs up and illustrates his call by reminding us that the Christian community, while diverse, is at bottom a unity. The church, Paul says, is like our individual bodies (vv. 4–5). It has many different parts, each with its own function. But all the parts form "one body" (v. 5), and each part is needed if the body is to function as it should.

In verses 6–8 Paul develops this notion further by listing a number of gifts God has given the members of the body of Christ. Paul uses this word "gift" (*charisma*) elsewhere to denote a God-given ability to serve the community of Christ in a particular way. In verses 6–8, Paul not only cites gifts but also encourages those who possess them to be active in using them for the edification of the community.

Application. We all must participate in the local church to help others grow. Whatever gift or gifts we have been given, we are under obligation to our Lord to use them to serve his people. Other Christians need what each of us has to offer. As the human body is at a disadvantage without a foot, or an eye, or a kidney, so the local church is harmed when the full panoply of gifts are not being exercised within it.

ROMANS 12:9–21

Original Meaning

The Heading: Sincere Love (12:9a). The apostles follow Jesus almost to the letter in presenting love for other people as the central focus of their exhortations. But "love" can be a vague idea. The Greek for "sincere" is *anypokritos* (literally "not hypocritical"). The underlying word was often applied to the actor who played a part on the stage. Christians can avoid love that is mere play-acting if they put into practice the commands that follow.

The Many Facets of Sincere Love (12:9b–13). At the end of verse 9, Paul briefly unpacks the basic moral dimension of sincere love. Christian love is more than a feeling; it leads to a violent hatred of evil and a tenacious attachment to what is good.

Verse 10 features two commands that focus on the "one another" relationship among believers. The first exhortation uses two words from the *phil-* root generally applied to loving relations among family members. The second command exhorts believers to put other believers first as an expression of genuine love.

If the three exhortations in verse 11 all relate to zealous service, the three in verse 12 combine to encourage believers to stay the course in their fight with the world.

Paul concludes the first series of commands by returning to the theme of verse 10a. We exhibit the familial love of true brothers and sisters in Christ by sharing with other believers who are in need. While the NIV does not make this clear, the Greek calls on believers not just to show (perhaps grudgingly) hospitality to others, but to "pursue" (NIV "practice," v. 13) it.

Living in Harmony with Other People (12:14–16). Paul's commands in verse 14 remind us of Jesus's famous teaching from the Sermon on the Mount. These similarities suggest that Paul is quoting Jesus's teaching here. In fact, Paul shows more dependence on Jesus's teaching in this part of Romans than he does anywhere else in his letters. Verse 15 may continue the theme of verse 14, calling on believers to identify with unbelievers in both their joys and their sorrows.

The command to "live in harmony with one another" (v. 16a) summarizes the overall thrust of these verses with specific reference to the believing community. Perhaps the greatest obstacle to this unity of mind and spirit is pride.

Overcoming Evil with Good by Refusing to Retaliate (12:17–21). At the end of his brief outline of the shape of sincere love, Paul returns to a key ingredient of that love he mentioned in verse 14: responding to the persecution of unbelievers with kindness rather than with hatred.

But the followers of Jesus are to do more than avoid retaliation. They must also, positively, "do what is right in the eyes of everyone" (v. 17). Verse 18 qualifies the extent to which believers are to conform their behavior to the expectations of unbelievers. Christians must never seek approval with the world at the expense of God's moral demands.

With verse 19, Paul returns to the theme of non-retaliation: believers are not to seek revenge. One reason why they should not do so is that God himself is the one who avenges wrong. He follows up the prohibition of verse 19 about not taking revenge with a positive exhortation to do good to those who may be doing evil to us (v. 20). Paul urges us to show kindness to our enemies with the hope that they will become ashamed of their actions and seek the underlying reason why we can respond with such love.

Verse 21 wraps up this paragraph with an appropriate bottom line. Though redeemed and citizens of heaven, we believers still live in a world soaked in evil. We must battle constantly against the tendency to conform our behavior to this world (see 12:2). But more than the purely negative quality of resistance to evil is needed. God calls us to be active in using the grace of the gospel and the power of the Spirit to win victories over the evil of this world.

Application. Biblical love, as we are constantly reminded, is not an emotion. It is an attitude, a mind-set. This distinction is one that older writers, and a few contemporary ones, try to get at by using the word "charity" to describe what the Bible is talking about. We are commanded to love; it is therefore a choice we make, a matter of the will.

ROMANS 13:1–7

Original Meaning. The basic point of the paragraph is summed up in its opening words: "Let everyone be subject to the governing authorities" (v. 1). Two words in this command need special attention. First, "governing authorities," as the translation suggests, refers to any person who represents the power of the state. The second key word is "submit" (*hypotassō*). This word is broader in its scope than "obey." It calls on believers to recognize that they "stand under" government in the scheme that God has instituted for ruling the world.

With the "for" in the middle of verse 1, Paul introduces his first reason why believers should recognize government's authority over them. Throughout the Bible, God's providential rule over everything is specifically applied to the rise and fall of political leaders.

In verse 2, Paul draws the consequence from God's involvement in the appointment of all political authorities. When we rebel against what they tell us to do, we are rebelling against God himself, and judgment will result.

In verses 3–4 Paul specifies that one of the purposes of secular government is to act as "God's servant" in rewarding good and punishing evil. Political officials are servants *of God.* Unconsciously, they serve God's purposes in the world. They have the right, under God, to punish wrongdoers. As Paul puts it, the authorities do not "bear the sword for nothing" (v. 4). Since the state has a God-given responsibility to punish those who do evil, believers should do good. They will then be commended by the government.

With verse 5 Paul summarizes the argument of the paragraph thus far. Because we understand that God has appointed secular rulers, we must submit to them. "This" at the beginning of verse 6 probably points to this truth. Because we are aware of God's ordaining of governing authorities, we pay taxes. We must respect governmental authorities because they are God's "servants" (v. 6). The point is even stronger here, because the word for "servant" now is *leitourgos*, which is used in the LXX for people who served in the temple and in the New Testament of ministers of the Lord. Paul could not more strongly have shown that civic leaders are, in fact, serving God's own purposes.

Paul concludes (v. 7) on a practical note. God asks for more than a grudging outward recognition of the government's authority. Because they are ordained by God, believers are to respect and honor governing authorities, manifesting that submission in the paying of taxes.

Application. Implicit always in the idea of submission is the need to recognize that God is at the pinnacle of any hierarchy. While not always explicit, Paul assumes that one's ultimate submission must be to God and that no human being can ever stand as the ultimate authority for a believer. When they order us to do something incompatible with our allegiance to God, our higher authority, we must "obey God rather than human beings" (Acts 5:29).

ROMANS 13:8–10

Original Meaning. Paul cleverly plays on the notion of "debt" that he introduced in 13:7 to create a transition back into the topic of love. Believers are to pay their debts (cf. v. 7); they are not to be in debt to anyone (cf. v. 8). But, Paul acknowledges, one debt will never be discharged: the debt of love we owe to other people.

In verses 9–10, Paul explains just how it is that loving others fulfills the law. The love command, found in Leviticus 19:18, sums up all the other commandments. Paul cites as examples four of the most famous commandments from the Decalogue: the prohibitions against adultery, murder, stealing, and coveting. When we truly love "the other," we automatically do what the other commandments of the law require. As Paul puts it in verse 10, "love does no harm to a neighbor." Paul's use of "fulfillment" language in this paragraph (vv. 8, 10) suggests that he views the love command as the eschatological replacement for the various commandments of the Mosaic law (see Gal 5:13–15).

Application. Americans love debt. We borrow to buy houses, cars, technology, food, medicine, clothes, appliances, lottery tickets. College students take on staggering debts to finance their education. Churches borrow immense sums to erect buildings. What does Romans 13:8—"Let no debt remain outstanding"—say to our debt-ridden society?

A few interpreters, taking a more literal rendering of the Greek—"Owe nothing to anyone"—think that the Bible here prohibits any form of borrowing at all. Individual believers should not borrow money, nor should churches. We should wait to build the building, buy the house or car, purchase the sound system, and so on, until we have the cash to pay for it up front. But this is probably not what verse 8 means. The NIV rendering gets the sense of what Paul is saying. He is not prohibiting us from borrowing money but demanding we pay back what we owe. If I have entered into an agreement with a bank to pay them $1100 per month for thirty years to buy a house, I need to discharge my obligation by paying that money on time. So what the text calls on us to do is to be careful, prudent financial planners, not taking on any more debt that we are sure we can handle.

ROMANS 13:11–14

Original Meaning. Paul signals the summarizing nature of these verses with the transitional phrase "And do this." "This" (*touto*) probably includes all Paul has taught in 12:1–13:10. We should be motivated all the more to do all these things—think of ourselves in the right way, exercise our gifts for the good of the body, display sincere love, obey the government, love others—as we "understand the present time" (v. 11).

The day of Christ's return and of the glorification of the believer is getting closer all the time. Paul skillfully blends two important strands of tradition using the imagery of day and night. The day/night contrast was popular in general moral teaching in the ancient world as a way of distinguishing good behavior from evil behavior. Paul makes explicit these behavioral consequences in verses 12b–14.

Paul concludes with a final contrast. Picking up the imagery of verse 12b, Paul commands: "Clothe yourselves with the Lord Jesus Christ" (v. 14). We who are in Christ must envelop ourselves with him in such a way that he directs all our thinking and conduct. We must regularly make the decision to "put on" Christ. As the negative counterpart to putting on Christ, we are also not to consider how we might "gratify the desires of the flesh" (v. 14b). In commanding us not to "think about" gratifying the flesh, Paul is urging us not to allow our fallen human impulses to dominate our behavior.

Application. Some Christians think nothing of watching movies that contain explicit sex and raunchy humor. Yet exposure to the values propagated in such movies almost inevitably leads those who watch them to become tolerant of some of those same values. We need to ask not "*can* I do this?" (i.e., are Christians allowed to do this?), but "*should* I do this?" Does this activity glorify God and honor the Lord whom I represent? Will this activity tempt me to gratify the flesh and cave in to the ways of this fallen world?

ROMANS 14:1–12

Original Meaning

Stop Judging One Another (14:1–3). The Christian community at Rome was apparently divided into two groups, those who are "weak [in faith]" (cf. 14:1) and those who are "strong [in faith]" (cf. 15:1). While Paul wants both groups in the church to accept each other, he is clearly most concerned about the attitude of the strong. Thus, we should not be surprised that he opens his exhortation by implicitly appealing to the strong.

"Faith" refers not directly to one's belief generally but to one's convictions about what that faith allows him or her to do. What Paul wants the strong to do is not simply extend grudging tolerance to the weak, but to welcome them. They should not allow "disputable matters" to interfere with full fellowship (v. 1).

Verse 2 identifies one of these disputable matters: the eating of meat. In verse 3, Paul urges both groups to change their attitude toward the other. The strong should not "treat with contempt" the weak, but the weak must not "judge" (*krinō*) the strong believers. The word *krinō* means to pronounce doom, to deny someone one's right to salvation. God has accepted this strong believer. How can anyone reject from the fellowship one whom God has accepted? Here is the theological bottom line in Paul's critique of judgmentalism in the church.

Slaves of the Lord Jesus (14:4–9). In verses 4–9, Paul elaborates this fundamental principle. Paul singles out a specific person. "Who do you think you are?" is basically what Paul is asking this weak believer. In condemning the strong believer, the weak believer is, in effect, claiming to be that believer's master. But the Christian has only one "master": the Lord Jesus Christ (v. 4).

The Greek word for both "master" and "Lord" is the same: *kyrios*. This word is central to the argument of verses 4–9. "Stand" and "fall" in verse 4 may be paraphrased to mean "stand in favor with" and "fall out of favor with."

Paul then cites a second disputable matter that is creating tension between the strong and the weak: judging certain days to be "more sacred" (v. 5). Reference is probably to Jewish holy days, including various festivals and the Sabbath. In any case, Paul wants every believer to be firmly convinced in his or her own mind.

With verse 6 Paul resumes the theological basis for his rebuke of the judgmental Roman believers that he began in verse 4. Each, Paul argues, acts out of sincere regard for God and a desire to please him. That is why it is wrong for them to condemn one another.

No Christian acts (or should act) out of regard for himself or herself alone. We always have to take into account not just our own interests but the interests of the one who died for us and returned to life so that he might be our Lord (v. 9). In whatever state we find ourselves, therefore—whether in life or in death—Christ, our Lord, owns us and expects us to act in obedience to him. The Roman Christians are presuming to dictate to one another what their behavior should be—what they should eat or not eat, and what days to observe. But only the Lord has that right.

It Is God Who Judges (14:10–12). In parallel rhetorical questions, he effectively rebukes the weak believer for condemning (*krinō*; cf. v. 3b) the strong Christian and the strong Christian for looking down on (*exoutheneō*; cf. v. 3a) the weak believer. Both are engaged in an activity that is God's alone: "We will all stand before God's judgment seat" (v. 10). Paul is teaching that every believer is ultimately answerable to God, not to other believers, for their conduct in this life. In verse 11 Paul underscores the unique role God plays in the judgment by citing Isaiah 45:23.

Application. This text, along with the attitude toward the Sabbath command as a whole in the New Testament, suggests that observance of the Sabbath is no longer incumbent on believers. Christians are not required to rest on Sunday. Taking a job that requires one to work on Sunday, washing one's car on Sunday, playing basketball on Sunday—none is prohibited to us. Yet Christians also have the liberty to rest on Sunday if they choose and if they are able. I think that such a rest, while not mandated, is physically and spiritually wise.

One might think that consistency would demand that worship be put in the same category as rest: regular worship is required, but the day is optional. This may be right. But we should hesitate to assert this because of the explicit New Testament references to the "the first day of the week" (e.g., Mark 16:2; John 20:1) and to the "Lord's Day" (Rev 1:10). Sunday worship is not mandated in the New Testament, but it does seem to be a pattern because of the Lord's resurrection on this day.

ROMANS 14:13–23

Original Meaning

Don't Be a Stumbling Block (14:13–16). Paul plays on the Greek verb *krinō* as he moves from the first part of verse 13 to the second. In the opening exhortation, this verb means "pass judgment," but in the second part it means "decide, determine" (NIV "make up your mind"). Turning specifically to the strong, Paul warns them about putting "any stumbling block or obstacle" in the way of another believer (v. 13). Paul's point is clear: those who pride themselves on being strong should display their spiritual maturity by doing everything they can to avoid bringing spiritual downfall to a brother or sister.

In a deft rhetorical move, Paul tries to get the strong to listen to him by conceding that they are right on the basic issue (v. 14). In other words, Paul emphasizes that all food is kosher. He follows the lead of Jesus (Mark 7:19; cf. Acts 10:9–23, 28). But while the strong have the theory right, they must come to grips with the practice. People who have always believed that avoiding certain foods is necessary may not be convinced—at least emotionally and psychologically—that they can eat anything. For them certain foods are still "unclean" (v. 14).

Having explained how food can bring spiritual downfall to a person, Paul moves on in verse 15 to show that this is just what the strong are doing to the weak. Their eating food that weak believers feel convinced is unclean "distresses" (*lypeō*, to cause pain) them. More than that, it may even "destroy" (*apollymi*) them. In other words, the cavalier attitude of the strong may lead to the weak believer's damnation.

How? Paul does not explain, but there are two possibilities.

1. The peer pressure brought by the example of the strong believers may lead the weak believer to eat what he or she is still convinced is unclean. Paul suggests again in verse 23 that a person "is condemned" when he or she eats while harboring doubts about whether it is proper.
2. The strong believers' flaunting of their freedom to eat all food may so offend conservative Jewish Christians that they are driven from their faith altogether.

The Values of the Kingdom (14:17–18). Paul here reminds his readers that God's kingdom is not about eating and drinking. Paul typically uses "righteousness" language in Romans in a forensic sense to refer to our status before God, but Paul also uses this word to refer to ethical righteousness, that is, behavior pleasing to God. This meaning fits the present context better. "Peace" refers to the horizontal harmony that believers should manifest. When these blessings are present, "joy" results. All three of these characteristics are possible only where the Holy Spirit is at work.

Don't Cause Your Fellow Believer to Stumble (14:19–23). After the indicative interlude (vv. 17–18), Paul returns to the imperative. "Edification" translates a word that means "act of building" (v. 19), though it is usually used in the New Testament with a spiritual sense: the process of building up individual believers or the church in faith. The strong ought to be more concerned about the growth of the body as a whole rather than their own freedom and spiritual advancement.

In verse 20 Paul shifts from the positive to the negative: how foolish it would be to "destroy" (*katalyō*) the work of God over food. "Destroy," applied to the church, probably means "ruin"—disputes over food bring disunity, mutual distrust, and eventually the disintegration of a congregation. Paul then reiterates his conviction that all food is "clean" (v. 20b). Yet the strong Christian needs to recognize that it is wrong for him or her to eat food in such a way that spiritual harm comes to another believer.

Paul formalizes the point in a general principle in verse 21: believers should avoid doing anything that brings spiritual harm to another believer. But why does Paul include "drinking wine" here as an example of a practice to avoid (v. 21)? Most likely he introduces it because, along with eating meat and observing holy days, drinking wine is also an issue in the Roman church.

In verses 22–23 Paul draws conclusions from his teaching for both the strong (v. 22) and weak (v. 23) Christians. Paul urges the strong to keep their convictions about the matters in dispute to themselves. There is no need for them to broadcast their views or to be continually trying to convince fellow believers how right they are. The blessing at the end of verse 22 is the bottom line for strong believers. Paul wants those who, like him, have internalized the truth about the freedom Christians have in the new era to have clear consciences about the ways they use that freedom—out of love and concern for the edification of the community.

Yet, Paul reminds his readers again, there are those who are still unconvinced about freedom on these matters. Those believers, who still "doubt," should not eat (v. 23a). The weak believer who eats would not be eating "from faith"—that is, on the basis of a sincere conviction that eating meat is permissible (v. 23b). Such eating then is sin, since "everything that does not come from faith is sin" (v. 23c). Paul is again using "faith" (*pistis*) in the specific sense he gave the word at the beginning of the chapter (14:1–2): a conviction that one's faith allows one to engage in a certain activity.

Application. The need to limit the expression of our liberty out of love for God and fellow believers is the key principle in this chapter. Our culture insists on rights, and it is easy for Christians to bring that attitude into the church. But the spiritual health of the body is far more important than our rights. The freedom God has purchased for us through his Son is a precious gift, but it is a freedom to live as God wants, not as we want.

ROMANS 15:1–6

Original Meaning. Although Paul has indicated his agreement with the thinking of the strong group in Rome (14:14, 20), he here for the first time explicitly identifies with them, using the first-person plural to include himself within the scope of his exhortation. Paul is not asking them simply to put up with those who differ from them. The verb "bear" (*bastazō*) has the same force here that it does in Galatians 6:2, where Paul exhorts believers to "bear one another's burdens and so fulfill the law of Christ" (author's translation). The introduction of "neighbor" language suggests Paul is thinking of the love command that exhorts love for one's neighbor.

If Christ, powerful as he was, could give up his own right to life itself, these strong believers should certainly be able to give up their right to eat meat whenever they want or to drink wine or to ignore Jewish holy days. Why does Paul use Psalm 69:9 here in Romans 15:3 to illustrate Jesus's attitude? He is probably drawn to it because this psalm is used so often in the New Testament to describe Jesus's suffering. At a more specific level, he may also be thinking of the insults that the weak believers in Rome are heaping on the strong. Like Jesus, the strong in Rome should be willing to serve in love even those who are being nasty to them.

Verse 4 is parenthetical. Paul pauses to remind his audience that the Old Testament, while no longer a direct source of moral instruction (see 6:14, 15; 7:4–6), continues to play a central role in helping believers understand salvation history and their responsibilities as the new-covenant people of God. The ultimate goal of this instruction is "hope" (15:4). He may introduce the concept of hope as a subtle reminder to the strong at Rome—mainly gentile Christians—that they were once without hope in the world but have now been integrated into God's people by grace (cf. Eph 2:12). In order to preserve their hope, they must work for the health and unity of God's people, the basis for their hope.

In verse 5 he prays that God himself will grant to the community the ability "to think the same way" (literal translation). It is unlikely that Paul is praying here that all the Roman believers will come to the same opinion on the matters at issue. Rather, he is praying that they may possess a unity of purpose that transcends these differences. It is a unity and way of thinking founded on and modeled after Christ. But unity is simply one stage on the way to the church's final purpose: to "glorify" God (15:6). Only when believers cease to quarrel with one another and speak with one heart and one voice will they be able to glorify God as they should.

Application. When everyone seeks the good of the other and the church as a whole, disagreements can strengthen rather than weaken the community. Ultimately, the Scriptures call on each one of us to bring together two personality traits that do not always go together: tenacity in holding to the essentials of the faith and infinite patience and tolerance toward people who hold differing ideas on the nonessentials.

ROMANS 15:7–13

Original Meaning. To "accept" one another means not just to tolerate other believers but to welcome them as brothers and sisters in the body of Christ (v. 7). We are to welcome one another *because* Christ has welcomed each one of us. "In order to bring praise to God" may be the purpose of Christ's accepting people. But this phrase more likely depends on the ruling idea of the verse, namely, that we accept one another.

Paul draws attention to the significance of what he says next with the rhetorical opening "For I tell you" (v. 8). What he does in verses 8–9a is to summarize one of the key theological teachings of the letter: how the fulfillment of God's promises in the gospel brings blessing to both Jews and gentiles. It beautifully captures the fine balance Paul preserves in Romans between the priority of the Jew—Christ came as a "servant of the Jews"—and the full inclusion of the gentiles—Christ's ministry to the Jews fulfills God's promises and so enables gentiles also to "glorify God for his mercy" (v. 9). The weak (mainly, if not entirely, Jewish Christians) need to accept gentile Christians because God's ultimate purpose is to include them, and the strong (mainly gentile Christians) need to remember that the Jews have always been at the center of God's concerns and promises.

Paul supports what he says in verses 8–9a with a series of Old Testament quotations (vv. 9b–12). God intends for his mercy to Israel to spill over to the gentiles so that they can join together in praising his name. Paul cites each of the three sections of the Jewish Scriptures: the Torah (Deut 32:43 in v. 10), the Prophets (Isa 11:10 in v. 12), and the Writings (Ps 18:49 in v. 9b; Ps 117:1 in v. 11). Each quotation refers to the gentiles, and two of them (vv. 10, 12) make clear that their presence in the people of God depends on the Jews. Two of them also speak of praising God (vv. 9, 11).

Paul completes his exhortation to the weak and the strong with a final prayer-wish: an appeal to God to work among the Romans in such a way that the unity he urges on them becomes a reality (v. 13). Paul beautifully incorporates into this prayer some of the key ideas from the previous chapters. Only when Jew and gentile at Rome rejoice together in their *common* hope will they be able to praise God as he wants to be praised—with the united hearts and voices of a *community* of believers (see 15:5–6).

Application. We must keep things in balance. The heart of the gospel is the message of God's justifying work in Christ. The essential human problem is estrangement from God. Only when this estrangement is overcome and a person is reconciled to God by faith can we speak about God's good news having done its work. Our preaching and teaching must therefore confront people with sin and offer them redemption in Christ.

But God also wants to form people transformed by the gospel into communities that reflect the values of the gospel. Vertical reconciliation with God must lead to horizontal reconciliation with one another. Faithfulness to the gospel demands that any of us involved in ministry should seek to maintain a balance between the two perspectives.

ROMANS 15:14–33

Original Meaning

Paul's Ministry and Its Past Expression (15:14–21). With the prayer-wish of 15:13, we reach the end of the body of Romans. What remains makes up the closing. Paul is especially concerned to explain to the Romans why he has taken the liberty to write to them so "boldly" (v. 15) about the gospel. As he explains, he has been called to convert and strengthen gentiles so that he might present them as an acceptable offering to the Lord.

To be sure, Paul has written "quite boldly on some points."

But he did so not to impart new knowledge but to remind the Roman Christians of truth they already knew. Paul must mean by this that he has simply explicated gospel truth that they already know.

Paul's second excuse for writing so boldly is more important. It is introduced in the last phrase in verse 15—"because of the grace God gave me"—and elaborated in verses 17–21: God gave Paul the gracious ministry of bringing gentiles into obedience to God. Since the Roman church is mainly gentile in composition, it lies within the scope of the mandate God himself has given to Paul.

Paul's use of cultic language to describe this ministry is striking. Paul pictures himself as a priest, using the gospel as the means by which he offers his gentile converts as a sacrifice acceptable to God. But, like the animal sacrifices of the old economy, these new sacrifices also must be "sanctified by the Holy Spirit" if they are to be acceptable (v. 16).

Because God is the one who has given Paul this service, he can legitimately "glory" in it (v. 17). Glorying or boasting is appropriate when it is the product of God's own work (cf. 5:2, 3, 11). In verse 18 Paul pursues this idea further, explaining just how it is that his glorying is "in Christ Jesus" (v. 17). The goal of what Christ does through Paul is (literally) "the obedience of the gentiles," an important echo of the letter's opening (1:5). The means of Christ's work in Paul is both "word and deed" (literal translation; 15:18).

Verse 19 continues Paul's description of his ministry. "Signs and wonders" is standard biblical terminology for miraculous acts that accompany and give credence to God's word. The phrase is especially prominent in Old Testament descriptions of the exodus and in the book of Acts. Paul perhaps uses this expression to signal his importance in salvation history. God works miracles through him because he is God's "point man" to open up the gentile world to the gospel.

Paul has identified the agent of his apostolic ministry (Christ) and its purpose (leading gentiles to obey the Lord). In the second half of verse 19, he states the results of his ministry. More important than geography is Paul's sense of having completed a significant phase of the ministry God has given him. Paul has brought to the divinely ordained climax his commission to plant thriving, self-reproducing churches throughout the region he has described. He is now, therefore, in a position to move on. For, as he explains in verse 20, his ministry is to "preach the gospel where Christ was not known."

Paul's Immediate Travel Plans (15:22–29). Paul goes on to mention his next three destinations (in order of visit): Jerusalem (vv. 25–27), Rome (vv. 22–24, 28–29), and Spain (vv. 24, 28). His main concern is to explain why it has taken him so long to get to Rome (v. 22) and why, when he does get there, he does not plan to stay long (v. 28). He must fulfill his commission to bring the gospel where the name of Christ has not yet been heard, and Spain is a fertile field for pioneer church-planting. But a stop in Rome is necessary for the apostle to secure logistical support for this new outreach, so far from his original home base of Antioch.

The NIV makes verse 22 the concluding verse of the preceding paragraph. But it is better, following modern editions of the Greek text, to make it the first verse in the new paragraph. Because Paul has been "fully proclaiming" the gospel all the way from Jerusalem to Illyricum (vv. 18–19), therefore (Gk. *dio* in v. 22, untranslated in NIV) he has been hindered up to now from coming to Rome (cf. 1:13).

Now, however, things have changed. With his ministry in the east fulfilled, there is no longer a place for him in those regions. In other words, Paul has two reasons to come to Rome: a negative one (the hindrance of ministry in the east has been removed) and a positive one (he longs to see them). He will visit them and hopes to "enjoy [their] company," but he will not remain there long; he is "passing through" on his way to Spain (v. 24). Parts of Spain had been occupied by the Romans since about 200 BC. But the Romans had fully organized the area as a province only in Paul's lifetime.

The verb "assist" (*propempō*) that he uses in verse 24b has the regular New Testament connotation of missionary support. Paul hints, then, that he hopes to enlist the support of the Roman Christians for his new missionary effort in Spain. Spain is a long way from Antioch, his original sending church, and he knows he will need a new base of operations.

One obstacle, however, still remains in the way of Paul's trip to the western part of the empire: he is on his way to Jerusalem "in the service of the Lord's people there" (v. 25). "In the service" translates the Greek verb *diakoneō* (to serve, minister). The context reveals that Paul is referring to the specific ministry of "the collection" (2 Cor 8:4, 19, 20; 9:1, 12, 13). Paul initiated this enterprise on his third missionary journey, requesting contributions from the gentile churches he had planted to be sent to Jerusalem for the believers who were suffering from severe want (1 Cor 16:1–2; 2 Cor 8–9). The recipients of this collection are "the poor among the Lord's people in Jerusalem" (Rom 15:26).

In verse 27 we detect why the collection is so important to Paul. It is not just a charitable project; it is also designed to bring into closer fellowship gentile and Jewish believers. Gentile Christians derive whatever spiritual blessing they experience from the Jewish Messiah and the fulfillment of God's promises to Israel. The gentile Christians can partially repay this debt by sharing with the Jews their own material blessings.

By the time he gets to Rome the tension over the collection will be over. He will therefore be able to come to them "in the full measure of the blessing of Christ" (v. 29). Paul probably refers here to the mutual ministry of edification he anticipates when he comes to Rome (cf. 1:12).

Request for Prayer (15:30–33). Why does Paul denote ministry of prayer as a "struggle" (v. 30)? He invites the Roman Christians to participate with him, through their prayers, in his missionary work. Paul asks the Romans to pray for two things specifically (v. 31): that he will "be kept safe from the unbelievers in Judea" and that the saints in Jerusalem will accept the offering of the collection. Unbelieving Jews were especially hostile to Paul for his opening the doors of God's people to gentiles. But he is also concerned that Jewish Christians do not refuse the gift as being tainted by the "unclean" hands of gentiles.

Only when these requests have been answered will Paul be able to come to Rome "with joy" and be spiritually refreshed with them (v. 32). Paul concludes his request for the Romans' prayer with his own prayer for them: that "the God of peace," that is, the God who gives peace, may be with them (v. 33).

Application. Paul's call for prayer illustrates the biblical tension between God's determination of events and the situation-changing power of prayer. Paul undoubtedly sensed that God himself had inaugurated and was empowering this collection. Yet he still asks people to pray for it. To be sure, we have no evidence Paul saw the collection in terms of a divine prophecy, sure to succeed because God had said it would. But even if this were the case, evidence from other texts shows that he would still have asked prayer for it.

Our own enterprises come with no more (and usually considerably less) divine mandate than Paul's collection. We can fall into the error of assuming our own ministries or projects are so important for the cause of Christ that God, as it were, is bound to prosper them. We can fail to pray for them or to enlist others in prayer. No matter how hard we try to avoid it, the antisupernaturalism of our culture exerts a strong pull on us. Particularly at a time when the business world is becoming more and more a paradigm for ministry, it is easy for us in ministry to put our projects in the same category as a business enterprise and assume that the keys to success are the same: hard work, careful planning, effective execution. Prayer can get left out.

ROMANS 16:1–16

Original Meaning

Commendation of a Prominent Christian Worker (16:1–2). Phoebe is apparently going to be traveling to Rome, and so Paul commends to the church this "sister." But Phoebe is more than a sister; she is also a "servant [*diakonos*] of the church in Cenchrea." *Diakonos* can be applied to any Christian, called to serve God and his people. But the addition "of the church in Cenchreae" makes it more likely that Phoebe is probably a deacon, serving the church by ministering to the financial and material needs of the believers (see esp. 1 Tim 3:8–12; cf. also Phil 1:1). Paul gives a further hint of Phoebe's function in the church at the end of verse 2, where he calls her a *prostatis* "of many people, including me." Perhaps the best suggestion is to give *prostatis* the meaning it often has in secular Greek, "patron, benefactor." Phoebe was probably a wealthy businesswoman, who used her wealth to support the church and its missionaries (like Paul).

Greetings (16:3–16). Paul also conveys individual greetings to a whole host of people. Public recognition, as the letter was read aloud, of those Christians in Rome whom Paul already knew would help cement good relationships with the community.

Paul commends Priscilla and Aquila as "co-workers" (*synergos*, v. 3), a term he uses regularly to refer to people who minister with him in all kinds of ways. They have also "risked their lives" for Paul (v. 4). When this happened we do not know, although it may have been at the time of the riot in Ephesus (Acts 19). They must have been fairly wealthy, owning a house large enough for a group of believers to meet there regularly for worship (a "house church") (v. 5a).

Andronicus and Junias (v. 7) are the most debated names in the list.* Andronicus is clearly a male name. But who was *Iounias*? The Greek form can reflect a feminine name, Junia. Here we simply note that the case for a feminine name is strong. *Iounia* (the feminine) is a common Greek name; the contracted form of *Iounianos* (the masculine) is apparently unknown.

Andronicus and Junias, like Aquila and Priscilla (v. 3), were probably husband and wife. But how can Paul call them "apostles" (*apostolos*, v. 7) when they were clearly not among the Twelve? Some interpreters have suggested that we translate "esteemed *by* the apostles," but this is unlikely. More to the point is to remember that Paul uses *apostolos* in ways other than as a reference to the official, authoritative "twelve apostles." It can refer to a "messenger" (2 Cor 8:23; Phil 2:25) or a "commissioned missionary" (Acts 14:4, 14; 1 Cor 9:5–6; 15:7[?]; Gal 2:9). In this context, this latter meaning is the most likely.

Paul concludes his request for greetings with a catch-all request: "Greet one another with a holy kiss" (v. 16a). The kiss was a standard form of greeting in the ancient world generally and in Judaism in particular.

Paul ends this section by turning the tables and conveying

---

* Editor's note: The NIV 2011 reads "Junia" in a revision of the NIV 1984's "Junias."

greetings to the Roman Christians from "all the churches of Christ" (v. 16). This is clearly hyperbole; the reference is probably to those churches he has planted.

Application. Women were an important and public part of the Roman Christian community. Romans 16 suggests, and the rest of the New Testament confirms, that Paul recognizes women along with men, implying their equality in the community and their participation together in worship.

I cringe when I hear the modern debate put in terms of *women and ministry*—as if there is doubt about whether women can be *ministers*. Our unfortunate restriction of that term to a particular ministry (e.g., head pastor) blinds us to the New Testament insistence that every believer is a minister, that is, a servant of Christ and the church, with important contributions to make to the life of the body.

What, finally, of the contribution of Romans 16 to the continuing debate about restrictions on women in ministry? This text has become an important skirmish in the larger battle. On the one side are those who insist that the New Testament imposes no restrictions whatever on ministry for women. They frequently appeal to three points in Romans 16 to support their view.

Phoebe had an important ministry. But Paul does not call her a pastor or leader but a deacon and benefactor. Both ministries (the former more "official" than the latter) were vital to the health of the church, but neither involved teaching or having authority over a man.

Junia is not so easy to explain away. Many scholars insist that the name is Junias and that Paul is referring to a man. The lexical evidence, however, is decisively against this view. In this case the situation is complicated by the different meanings that Paul gives to the term *apostle* (Gk. *apostolos*). It is quite possible that Paul is using the word to describe these otherwise unknown early Christians in the sense of "commissioned missionary" rather than in the sense of "authoritative representative of Christ."

ROMANS 16:17–27

Original Meaning. Paul touches quickly on many different topics as he brings the letter to its conclusion, most of which are common in the endings of Paul's letters. But two are not: the warning about false teachers in verses 17–19 and the concluding doxology in verses 25–27. The former is certainly part of the text, and we will discuss just why Paul may have added it here.

The doxology, however, is textually uncertain. It is not found in a couple of manuscripts of Romans and is located elsewhere in other manuscripts. The vast majority of manuscripts, however, do include the doxology at the end of the letter, and the vocabulary is non-Pauline only if we think Paul did not write Ephesians. So the case for including these verses is strong.

Paul does not elsewhere launch into a warning about false teachers in the conclusion of a letter. Possibly he waits until now because the false teachers have not yet arrived on the scene, or because he only hears about the threat as he is finishing the letter.

Various theories about who these false teachers may have been and what heresy they are propagating have been suggested. But Paul does not give us enough information to make a decision. All we know is what he tells us here. As with most false teachers, they "cause divisions" (*dichostasias*), putting "obstacles" or stumbling blocks (*skandala*) in the way of believers (v. 17). They bring spiritual harm to believers by teaching doctrines contrary to the gospel. These people are not, then, serving Christ, "but their own appetites" (v. 18).

The false teachers are interested in their own pleasure and ease, not in helping people know God. These people mask their lack of truth by employing persuasive speaking methods. People who are "naive" or innocent (*akakōn*, v. 18) are susceptible to such an approach. Their very sincerity and desire to obey may make them easy prey for false teachers. So, in an ironic twist, Paul wants them to remain "innocent" (*akeraios*, v. 19) about evil.

In verses 21–23, Paul conveys greetings to the Romans from some of his own associates and from other believers where he is staying. Tertius (v. 22) identifies himself as the amanuensis of the letter—that is, the trained scribe who "wrote down" what Paul dictated. He is otherwise unknown to us.

Erastus (v. 23) may be the same Erastus referred to in Acts 19:21–22 (cf. 2 Tim 4:20). But an inscription has been discovered in Corinth that refers to an Erastus who was an *aedile* of the city. This title may be equivalent to Paul's use of *oikonomos* here in Romans 16:23 (NIV "director of public works"). Even if the two are not identical, Erastus may have first served as *oikonomos* before being promoted to *aedile*.

Paul appropriately concludes his letter with a doxology in praise of God. While Paul or others seek to establish believers in their faith, only God can ultimately do so. He works through the gospel, which Paul further defines as "the message I proclaim about Jesus Christ" (v. 25). This good news of redemption for all people in Christ is the climax of the plan of God, a "mystery hidden for long ages past" but now "revealed and made known" (vv. 25–26) for all to see. The fact and timing of the revelation of this mystery lay in God's plan; it was his "command" that put the gospel into effect (v. 26a).

God's purpose in doing so was that "all the Gentiles might come to the obedience that comes from faith" (v. 26b).

The Greek phrase is the same as we encountered in 1:5. As there, the phrase refers to the obedient lifestyle that must always be flowing from sincere faith in the Lord.

The concluding description of God (v. 27) reminds us especially that he has instituted a "wise" and wonderful plan for the redemption of his creation (cf. 11:33–36). Surely our response should echo Paul's, as we give glory to him through Jesus Christ!

Application. The wonderful doxology in 16:25–27 is an appropriate way to end a letter that so beautifully sets forth the truth of the gospel. All theology has its ultimate goal in the glory of God, and any true theology will always lead to this end. Theology, the "study of God," is not an intellectual pastime. Nor is it only for the good of the church. Its ultimate purpose is to enable God's people to glorify him more effectively and more passionately because they have learned more about him. We noted above how Paul weaves into this doxology so many of the motifs of the letter. It is as if he himself is led to burst out in spontaneous praise to God as he reflects on the marvelous truths he has taught in the letter. May our "bottom line" also be *sola dei gloria*—"to God alone be the glory."

1 CORINTHIANS

INTRODUCTION TO 1 CORINTHIANS

Paul planted the church in Corinth during his second missionary journey (Acts 18:1–17). One night the Lord spoke to Paul in a vision and encouraged him to stay in Corinth, because many would come to the Lord. So Paul remained a year and a half, substantially longer than he had in any of the other communities he had evangelized to date. We can date Paul's stay in Corinth fairly precisely, from AD 50–51.

First Corinthians was written approximately three years later, probably in the spring of AD 55. This makes 1 Corinthians the fourth letter Paul penned, after Galatians and 1 and 2 Thessalonians. But several important developments occurred between Paul's initial trip to Corinth and his writing of this letter.

To begin with, 1 Corinthians is not really the first letter Paul wrote to Corinth. First Corinthians 5:9 alludes to a previous letter that the Corinthians had misunderstood. We know nothing of its contents except that Paul must have told the church not to associate with immoral people. The Corinthians had taken him to be referring to non-Christians when in fact he had meant flagrantly immoral and unrepentant believers (vv. 10–11).

Second, Paul received an oral report from certain unnamed members of the household of a Corinthian woman named Chloe (1:11a). Paul learned of several distressing aspects of life in that congregation, most notably the divisions within their fellowship (vv. 11b–12). From his visitors, Paul presumably also learned of the problems of sexual immorality and litigation, which he addresses in chapters 5–6.

Third, Paul received a letter from some or all of the church asking questions about specific issues that were dividing the congregation. The way Paul introduces his references to this letter suggests that chapters 7–16 deal, in turn, with each of the issues it raised. This is why, for example, the NIV puts part of Paul's words in quotations at 7:1 and 8:1. Presumably he is quoting a Corinthian slogan and then proceeding to critique it.

BOOK OUTLINE

- I. Introduction: Greeting and Thanksgiving (1:1–9)
- II. Letter Body (1:10–16:4)
  - A. Paul Responds to Oral Reports about the Corinthian Church (1:10–6:20)
  - B. Paul Responds to the Letter from the Corinthians (7:1–16:4)
- III. Conclusion: Travel Plans and Final Greetings (16:5–24)

1 CORINTHIANS 1:1–9

Original Meaning. The conventional letter in the ancient Greco-Roman world began with a salutation, in which the writer identified himself and his recipients and gave a brief greeting. This letter is from Paul, the Pharisaic Jew converted to Christ (Acts 9:1–31), who became the apostle to the non-Jewish world (Acts 13–28). He identifies himself as "called" to be an "apostle" (1 Cor 1:1), not in the sense Luke uses that term for one of the twelve disciples of Jesus (Acts 1:21–26), but as one divinely sent out on a mission of church-planting. Paul will later identify apostleship as a spiritual gift (1 Cor 12:29). This calling was not of Paul's own choosing, as his Damascus Road experience makes plain, but was due entirely to "the will of God" (1:1). This letter is said also to come from "our brother" (v. 1), that is, fellow Christian, Sosthenes, possibly the synagogue ruler of Acts 18:17, if he was later converted.

The recipients of the letter are the Corinthian Christians. They probably comprise several house congregations, but Paul addresses them in verse 2 as a collective whole, "the church," or assembly of those God has saved. "Sanctified" in verse 2 does not mean "*made* holy," as often in Paul, but separated apart for God. It is virtually synonymous with the next phrase, "*called* to be his holy people." Paul is reminding the Corinthians of their overarching purpose in the Christian life. He then generalizes to include all Christians everywhere, though obviously not all would immediately read his letter for themselves. "Their Lord and ours" stresses the spiritual unity that all believers share in Jesus Christ (v. 2).

"Grace" (v. 3) reflects the conventional Greco-Roman form of greeting; "peace," the typical Jewish salutation. But each suggests theological overtones too. Grace is a free gift; peace is wholeness in every aspect of life. Paul Christianizes these conventional greetings by adding a reference to the origin of grace and peace—the one, true, living God revealed in Jesus Christ.

When Paul says he "always" thanks God (v. 4a), he means either "repeatedly," or "whenever I pray." His thankfulness for God's "grace" (v. 4b; from the same root as "gift") prepares the way for his references to spiritual gifts in verses 5–7. Paul is grateful that the Corinthian Christians have been "enriched" or made wealthy (v. 5), specifically with reference to the spiritual gifts of speaking and knowledge—most prominently words of knowledge and wisdom, prophecy, and tongues (12:8–10). This occurred as they responded to his preaching with faith and repentance and thus received the Spirit, who began to distribute his gifts among them. The truth of Paul's message was thus confirmed (1:6–7).

How can Paul be so thankful and positive about a church rife with divisions and abuses of these very gifts? Verses 8–9 supply the answer: God's character provides the guarantee. He will remain faithful to his promises ultimately to perfect his people, however immature they at times seem to be (vv. 8a, 9).

Application. Verses 8–9 have important implications for the "eternal security" debate. Those whom the Spirit has genuinely indwelt will experience transformation. Those who begin this process can rest assured that God will be faithful to complete it. Of course, such verses provide no assurance for professing believers who have never shown any evidence of the gifts of the Spirit. Eternal security is not a doctrine to be applied glibly to all who have claimed to be Christian, however superficial their commitment has seemed to be.

1 CORINTHIANS 1:10–17

Original Meaning. Verse 10 begins the actual body of the letter, which falls into two main parts—Paul's response to information about the Corinthians, which he has heard by word of mouth (1:10–6:20) and his reply to a letter the Corinthians sent him (7:1–16:4). In the first half, Paul refers to four problems he has heard about that are plaguing the Corinthian church—factions (1:10–4:21), incest (5:1–13), lawsuits (6:1–11), and sexual immorality more generally (6:12–20).

Paul deals with the first of the four problems at greatest length. First Corinthians 1:10–17 states the essential problem (rival factions) and Paul's essential solution (an appeal for unity). Paul's basic appeal for unity (v. 10) involves several key expressions. He exhorts the church in the "name" (power or authority) of Jesus that all of them "agree," literally meaning that they all "say the same thing." They must abolish "divisions," a political term for rival parties or factions. They should become "perfectly united," a verb probably better rendered "restored to unity."

Verses 11–12 then elaborate the nature of the Corinthian factions: people are quarreling because they are aligning themselves with different Christian leaders. In light of the dispute between Peter and Paul in Antioch (Gal 2:11–14), many have seen a theological debate here also between a more legalistic and a more law-free gospel. Apollos, we know from Acts 18:24–28, was a gifted orator. Perhaps those inclined to be impressed with lofty rhetoric and speculative wisdom rallied around him. But there is little evidence that Paul, Peter, and Apollos were themselves at odds with one another at this point. And the disparity between the haves and the have-nots at the Lord's Supper (1 Cor 11:17–34) suggests that a polarization along the lines of rich and poor may have been an even more fundamental factor in the divisions.

Paul's initial reply to these reports consists of three rhetorical questions all implying the answer "no" (v. 13). Christ is not divided, so how can his people be? Neither Paul nor any other human leader was crucified for the world's sins, so how can these Christians so exalt merely mortal authorities? Christian baptism was into the "name" (again implying power or authority) of Jesus (Acts 2:38), not into the names of Paul, Peter, or Apollos. Verses 14–16 then expand on this last observation as Paul tries to recall how many people he baptized in Corinth. The answer is few.

Here is perhaps another clue to the nature of the rivalries: these young Christians may have been idolizing the particular leaders who first brought them to the Lord. Baptism played a prominent role in the life of the early church as the outward ritual signifying repentance from sin and initiation into the Christian community. By saying Paul did not baptize many, he must mean that he delegated this responsibility to others. Verse 17a must thus be taken as referring to relative priorities. Paul's primary calling was to preach rather than to baptize.

Verse 17b introduces the thought that will form the main idea of 1:18–2:5. The focus of Christian proclamation must remain clearly centered on the message of the crucifixion rather than baptism or any other doctrine, however important in its own right it may be.

Application. The disunity of the church of Jesus Christ remains one of the greatest scandals that compromises its witness today. In John 17, Jesus prayed that his disciples might be united. In Ephesians 3, Paul expounds the unity of the church across the greatest sociological divisions of the ancient Mediterranean world—Jew versus gentile. The evangelistic potential of a united church extends to the most powerful anti-Christian forces in the universe (Eph 3:9–10). The only way this unity can have an impact on a non-Christian world is for it to be visible.

1 CORINTHIANS 1:18–2:5

Original Meaning. First Corinthians 1:18 provides the thesis sentence which sums up the point of the first paragraph of this section (vv. 18–25). Verse 19 supplies scriptural support for Paul's thesis. Verses 20–25 then begin to explain why the world so roundly rejects the cross-centered gospel and why the Corinthians should nevertheless believe it.

Paul's thesis affirms that there are only two kinds of people in the world—those in the process of perishing and those in the process of being saved (v. 18). Each will respond to the gospel message in diametrically opposite ways. Verse 19 quotes Isaiah 29:14 for support. Verse 20b makes it clear that Paul is not disparaging *Christian* wisdom, intelligence, scholarship, or philosophy.

Verse 21 explains how the state of affairs of verse 18 came about. People in their fallen, worldly wisdom rejected God, so God confirmed humanity in its rebellion with a plan of salvation that would seem foolish (cf. Rom 1:18–32). But in his omniscience, he had anticipated this all along, so that the whole plan itself was "in the wisdom of God."

Verse 22 then specifies two key ways that major ethnic groups of Paul's world found the Christian faith foolish. Many Jews looked for dramatic, miraculous confirmation of Jesus's claims, which he refused to give. Many Greeks considered speculative philosophies the highest human ideals, with their concomitant emphasis on rhetoric, esoterica, and elitism. For such people, the cross was a "stumbling block" (literally scandal) and foolishness (v. 23). But those whom the Spirit of God touches and convicts, from whatever ethnic background, will find in the cross both godly wisdom and power to transform their lives (v. 24).

First Corinthians 1:26–31 describes the status of most of the Corinthians in their society when they were first saved ("called," v. 26a). Although the majority of people in the church were not from the most destitute strata of society, they were outside the circle of the strong and mighty. Hence, Paul could term them "the foolish," "the weak," and "the lowly" (vv. 27–28), in direct opposition to the three attributes of verse 26.

Then Paul adds the perspective of the powerful on such people—they are "despised" and "things that are not" (v. 28). Yet these are the people God for the most part chose to be saved, to shame the wise and strong. In short, he removes any grounds for boasting in one's self-sufficiency (v. 29). And if the world deems people unfortunate who cannot boast about their own accomplishments, blessings in Christ far more than compensate. In him, believers receive true wisdom—the wisdom of the cross and all its benefits (v. 30). Christians can properly boast, not in their own achievements, but in the Lord (v. 31).

First Corinthians 2:1–5 rounds out this section by reminding the Corinthians of the content and style of Paul's own ministry when he was with them. Paul does not deny that he tried to present his message in as compelling a form as possible, merely that by the world's standards he was at best ordinary. Verse 2 cannot be taken absolutely as if the only doctrine Paul taught on was the crucifixion, but refers rather to its centrality in his preaching.

Verse 3 underlines Paul's sense of personal inadequacy and dovetails with the Lord's reassurance to him not to be afraid (Acts 18:9–10). The "wise and persuasive words" of verse 4 must again refer to worldly wisdom and persuasion, since they are contrasted with "the Spirit's power." Verse 5 restates the rationale for his strategy, complementing the contrast between 1:29 and 31.

In short, the Corinthians came to faith by focusing on the cross of Christ, which seemed so foolish to everyone else. They must now return to that focus rather than splitting the church by magnifying human leaders.

Application. Much Western Christianity has fallen to a "suburban captivity" that domesticates the gospel and loses the central focus of the Scriptures on the spiritually ***and physically*** poor and needy of this world. Healthy churches will combat this trend by expending significant portions of their budgets and personal attention on evangelism and social action, locally and globally, in balanced combinations. And 1:30 directs our attention to another pair of priorities that cannot be divorced—correct knowledge and correct behavior. Too many today, both inside and outside the church, more closely resemble the ancient Greek philosophers who drove a wedge between inward spirituality and outward morality.

1 CORINTHIANS 2:6–16

Original Meaning. While there is a foolishness to the gospel (1:18–25), there is also a wisdom that the Corinthians must understand in order to overcome their divisiveness. The content of that wisdom remains a profoundly cross-centered faith (1:23). First Corinthians 2:6–10a introduces the theme of this wisdom and its acceptance by believers and rejection by unbelievers (parallel to the contrasts of 1:18–25). Verses 10b–16 then elaborate those responses by contrasting those who have the Spirit with those who do not.

The "mature" of verse 6a are the opposite of "the rulers of this age" (v. 6b) just as Paul's "message of wisdom" (v. 6a) contrasts with the "wisdom of this age" (v. 6b). Because those who are not mature are unbelievers, the mature in this context must be all Christians, at least in principle, and not just some elite group of believers. But the irony is that the Corinthians are not living according to this reality but as if they were still unsaved and in the grip of the world's values.

The "rulers" refer at least to the religious and political authorities of the day, comparable to Caiaphas and Pilate, who crucified the Lord of glory (v. 8). But they may also refer to demonic powers behind the opposition to the gospel (cf. Eph 2:2). "Coming to nothing" at the end of verse 6 thus refers to the ultimate transience of this age and its powers.

"God's wisdom" (v. 7a) is literally "wisdom in a mystery." But the word "mystery" (*mystērion*) in the New Testament most commonly refers to components of the gospel once hidden but now revealed. The concept of a crucified Messiah was not clearly understood in Old Testament times and was still not grasped in Paul's day by those who rejected Jesus (v. 8). But this should not cause surprise; Isaiah himself had prophesied unexpected wonders surrounding God's coming salvation for his people (Isa 64:4, quoted and paraphrased in v. 9). And all along God had planned these wondrous events for the benefit of those who would respond positively (v. 7b). The Holy Spirit who brings people to Christ now reveals to them what once was unknown (v. 10a).

The contrast between those who possess the Spirit and those who do not (vv. 10b–16) begins with a syllogism—a three-part argument in which two premises, if true, logically entail a particular conclusion (vv. 10b–12).

1. The major premise observes that only a person's own spirit or mind knows that individual's thoughts unless he or she chooses to disclose them to someone else (v. 11a), an affirmation which is true for God as well as humanity (vv. 10b, 11b). "Search" (v. 10b) thus equals "knows a person's thoughts" (v. 11b).
2. The minor premise reiterates that Christians have God's Spirit living in them (v. 12a). "The spirit of the world" (v. 12a) refers to fallen, human nature and ideologies, not to anything more directly demonic.
3. The conclusion logically follows then that Christians can know God's thoughts, at least to the extent that his Spirit graciously reveals them (v. 12b).

Verses 13–16 reiterate the fundamental contrast of 1:18–2:5. "Human" wisdom (v. 13a) must thus refer to that which is *merely* human, that is, unregenerate. Verse 13b is notoriously difficult to translate but the NIV has probably captured it.

"The person without the Spirit" (v. 14) interprets the adjective *psychikos*, from the noun *psychē*, meaning "soul" or "life." Such a person "does not accept" Christian truths (v. 14a). This phrase makes it clear that the "understanding" described in verse 14b is not primarily cognitive but volitional.

Conversely, the "person with the Spirit" (v. 15a) refers to any Christian (cf. 12:13). "Makes judgments" comes from the same verb as "discerned" and helps to interpret it. Believers have the ability to bring God's perspective to bear on every aspect of life. Verse 15b must be interpreted in light of the entire context: Christians are not subject to any *merely* human evaluation—that is, one that does not take God's perspective into account. But Paul may also be anticipating his argument in 4:3–5 that even evaluation by fellow believers is provisional; the only judge who ultimately counts is God. Verse 16 rounds out the passage by quoting Isaiah 40:13 on the inscrutability of God's ways, but it echoes the thought of verses 7 and 10–12 that some of this mystery has now been removed in the messianic age, in which the Spirit brings Christ's thoughts to believers by living in them.

Application. In an age of specialization, we are bombarded by claims that the key to a happy, healthy Christian faith, individually or corporately, is to be found in some new technique of evangelism, practice of certain spiritual disciplines, strategy for church growth, self-help therapy, Sunday-school curriculum, form of music or style of worship, and on and on. When these so-called keys pit their agendas against the majority of believers' beliefs and practices and move away from the humbling, central focus on the cross of Christ, they have become elitist and potentially divisive and must be rejected.

So too the church has become increasingly populated by single-issue people, analogous to single-issue voters in the political arena. One person constantly clamors for apologetics to be taught as the cure for all the church's ills; another repeatedly insists that foreign missions must overshadow every other commitment. A third is captivated by the writings of a famous Christian celebrity and promotes them as if they never erred. A fourth harps on nothing but social activism.

This list could be extended indefinitely, but it illustrates how factions and ultimately heresies begin—when one aspect of God's agenda for humanity is so emphasized that other crucial, balancing aspects are ignored. That so many Christians today tolerate such imbalance is an indictment of the lack of effective, comprehensive, week-in and week-out teaching ministries of our local congregations, a lack that leaves believers feeling that they need seminars and specialists to teach them what they have become convinced they could not otherwise learn on their own.

1 CORINTHIANS 3:1–23

Original Meaning. Paul shifts from contrasting Christians (those with the Spirit) and non-Christians (those without the Spirit) to comparing two kinds of Christians—those who are being controlled by the Spirit and those who are not. The latter are described in 3:1–4 as factious. Their quarreling not only mocks the cross-centered gospel (1:18–2:5) but fails to recognize the fundamental equality of all believers when measured against the attributes and character of God.

"Worldly" in 3:1 is a slightly different Greek word than in verse 3, but both are pejorative. The KJV translates both as "carnal," that is, "fleshly" or dominated by one's sinful nature, in this context manifested by jealousy and quarreling. "Spiritual" must therefore mean not merely having the Spirit but having the Spirit *in charge*. Their squabbling is inexcusable. Their immaturity resembles that of adults acting like infants by still eating only baby food (v. 2). Or, to change the comparison, they are acting like unregenerate people (v. 3b) rather than those in whom the Spirit has come to reside. Verse 4 reminds us of the specific problem at hand and reiterates two of the slogans of 1:12.

Verses 5–9a clarify another problem with the Corinthians' divisiveness. Not only is their behavior diametrically opposed to a focus on Christ crucified, but it also ignores the fact that all Christian leaders are merely "servants" (v. 5) with relatively equal and insignificant roles to play compared to the role God plays in causing his church to grow.

Verse 5b confirms our suspicions from 1:13–17 that part of the factionalism involved allegiance to those individuals who had personally led different groups of the Corinthians to the Lord.

Verses 6–7 compare the church to a field and its leaders to workers in that field. Particularly in the first century, farmers were keenly aware that their own contribution to a successful harvest in any given year was rather minimal compared to the vagaries of nature, which were seen to be directly in the hand of God or the gods. Compared to God's role, humans' roles are nothing of consequence. All godly leaders have a common purpose (v. 8a), which is the growth of the church. The emphatic position of the word *theos* in all three of its occurrences in the Greek of verse 9 makes it clear that Paul is stressing *God* as the one to whom the "co-workers," "field," and "building" belong.

The end of verse 9 belongs with verses 10–15 as the start of a new paragraph. The NIV omits the Greek "you are" that prefaces "God's building." Just as Paul has described the church and its leaders with an agricultural metaphor in verses 6–9a, he now does so by turning to the world of construction (vv. 9b–17). Here again God's sovereign guidance comes to the fore. Paul likens himself to an expert "builder" (v. 10), literally a "wise master-craftsman" or "chief engineer." Paul deliberately chooses the word for "wise" to contrast his godly wisdom with the Corinthians' misguided claims to wisdom. The word for "builder" is the word from which the English "architect" derives, but in Greek it referred not so much to the one who drew up a blueprint as to the on-site supervisor. The foundation of any truly Christian edifice must, of course, be the cross-centered gospel of Jesus Christ (v. 11).

There remain, however, two quite different ways of building on that foundation. Gold, silver, and costly stones reflect valuable materials that do not easily burn. Wood, hay, and stubble cost less and are quickly consumed by fire (v. 12). In the ancient world, people would have built a temple out of the former and an ordinary home out of the latter. Verse 13 likens "the Day" (i.e., judgment day) to just such a fire. "It will be revealed" (v. 13b) probably refers to "the Day" and not to "the work." When Christ returns, all believers will have to appear before him (2 Cor 5:10).

"What has been built" (v. 14a) is not teaching salvation by works but is referring instead to Christ's assessment of the way Christians have lived their lives subsequent to salvation. The nature of believers' rewards remains unspecified here (v. 14b), but in 4:5 it will be described as "praise from God."

The "it" with which the NIV begins verse 15 is spelled out in the Greek as a person's "work." It may be that Paul has in mind also the loss of the reward—that is, diminished praise and increased shame as we stand before Christ's judgment seat and as we realize how much of our lives were spent in activity of no eternal value. Such believers are still saved, but by the skin of their teeth or, to use Paul's metaphor, like escaping from a burning house (v. 15b).

If the temple imagery is implicit in the metaphor of building with costly stones and metal (vv. 9b–15), Paul makes it explicit in verses 16–17. The church is not just any building; it is the most holy and valuable of edifices. Just as Jewish and pagan temples were believed to be the dwelling place of God (or the gods), so also the Christian fellowship is the special place of the Spirit's presence. That is why the threat of verse 17a is so harsh. Here Paul warns against any who would try to destroy the church.

Verses 18–23 close the chapter with Paul repeating his appeal to banish divisiveness. They must become foolish by the world's standards and embrace the godly wisdom that Paul has been expounding (vv. 18–19a). The futile end of those who fail to take this corrective action is again underlined by two Scriptures: Job 5:13 and Psalm 94:11, quoted in verses 19b–20. Verses 21–23 highlight a final reason for the futility of such attitudes: the Corinthians have everything they could legitimately need or want in Jesus.

Application. Campus Crusade for Christ (now Cru) has popularized the concepts of 1 Corinthians 2:6–3:4 with its well-known circle diagrams for the natural, carnal, and spiritual persons. The natural person does not have the cross of Christ anywhere in his or her life; ego is on that person's throne. The carnal Christian has the cross inside the circle of his or her life, but ego still remains on the throne. The spiritual Christian has the cross central and ego dethroned. These diagrams are both helpful and misleading. They correctly remind us that believers do not automatically have Christ in charge of every area of their lives. Christians are free to take back a certain measure of control and in essence do so every time they consciously sin. The diagrams also correctly capture the fundamental difference between Christian and non-Christian, though it is perhaps worth noting that ego is not always on the throne of an unbeliever's life. More noble, family-centered, or humanitarian concerns may be central, but the point remains that God is not.

1 CORINTHIANS 4:1–21

Original Meaning. With this chapter Paul brings the discussion full circle: having begun with the wrong way to treat the apostles (overly exalting them), he now elaborates the right ways to consider them. Verse 1 picks up one of the themes of 3:5–23 with two key terms to describe the nature of the apostles' servanthood. Instead of seeing Christian preachers as rival leaders, the Corinthians should recognize them as helpers and overseers. "Servant" (v. 1) referred to "an assistant to someone in an official position. "Those who have been given a trust" (v. 2) reflects the Greek noun *oikonomos* ("steward"), the highest ranking servant of a wealthy landowner, who was in charge of the entire estate in his master's absence. Together, both words compare Paul, Apollos, Peter, and their peers to servants answerable primarily to God but with authority over their charges.

The key task of a steward is faithfulness to his master, not yielding to every demand of his underlings (v. 2). Verse 3 must thus be kept in context. The Corinthians' view of Paul matters little *relative to* God's view of him. Even his own self-estimation pales against this divine assessment. "My conscience is clear" (v. 4) loosely translates "I am aware of nothing against myself."

All human judgments not only lack God's omniscient perspective but also remain premature. The "appointed time" is defined as when "the Lord comes," that is, judgment day (v. 5). Only then will all facts be known and all the thoughts and intentions of human hearts disclosed, enabling a wholly fair evaluation of a person's behavior.

Again Paul singles out himself and Apollos for special mention (cf. 3:5). For Paul, "what is written" usually refers to Scripture, our Old Testament. But there is no specific verse that states, "Do not go beyond what is written" (4:6), so probably he is referring more generally to the need to remain within biblical standards. Or Paul may be quoting a popular proverb of the day. In each case, however, the general sense would remain the same: observe proper behavior and put an end to rivalries. Verse 7 underlines this appeal with three rhetorical questions anticipating the answers, "no one," "nothing," and "no good reason." Together, the three questions remind the Corinthians that all their spiritual gifts and natural blessings came from God and therefore give them no grounds for boasting.

With verse 8 Paul shifts tone abruptly and unleashes a bitter invective, dripping with irony and sarcasm. Here is one of the key texts that discloses the prevailing "overrealized eschatology" (the idea that all of the blessings of the messianic age had already arrived) that afflicted the church at Corinth. If all the blessings of the messianic age had really come all at once, then Paul and his companions would have been experiencing the same freedom from imperfection that these Corinthians claimed.

Instead, verses 9–13 provide a poignant catalogue of the apostles' suffering. "It seems to me" alerts the reader to Paul's use of two metaphors throughout verse 9. First, he imagines himself and his companions as prisoners of war in a victory procession by the opposing army (cf. 2 Cor 2:14–15). Second, he envisions the frequent outcome of such capture—thrown to the gladiators or wild animals in the sporting arena, with death as the most common result. In verse 10, Paul returns to using irony to mock the way the Corinthians are viewing him as quite different from themselves. At one level, of course, his statements are true: by the world's standards, he is foolish, weak, and dishonored (recall 1:26). But spiritually, he is the exact opposite, and it is the church in Corinth that is ailing, impoverished, and inglorious.

Verses 11–12a provide a more straightforward list of Paul's hardships. Some of these result from hostility to the gospel, some from the arduous lifestyle of an itinerant minister in antiquity (cf. 2 Cor 11:23b–29). Verse 12a anticipates a criticism of Paul's ministry that chapter 9 will unpack. Verses 12b–13a give a remarkable model of how to respond in godly fashion to ungodly treatment and echo several sayings of Jesus from the Sermon on the Mount (cf. Matt 5:38–48 and esp. Luke 6:28).

Verse 13b introduces a measure of hyperbole. Ironically, the Corinthians' view of Paul too frequently matches that of the non-Christian world. "Scum" and "garbage" both refer to that which is removed by a process of cleaning. In short, whereas the Corinthians think that their relatively prosperous conditions reflect God's blessing, Paul points to his sufferings for the sake of the gospel as a more accurate measure of Christian faithfulness.

As abruptly as Paul's sarcasm began, it now equally abruptly gives way to tender tones (vv. 14–17). The right way for Corinth to view its apostles in general, and Paul in particular, is as special relatives. Their local leaders are only "guardians" (literally "pedagogues"—Greek slaves in charge of seeing that children got from home to school and back again safely), but Paul is their spiritual father (v. 15). This parental imagery unites all of verses 14–21 and accounts for Paul's concern and strong warnings.

Verse 16 introduces Paul's call to imitate him, just as a father in the ancient world regularly taught his sons a trade by modeling it as they studied under him as apprentices. Paul will repeat this call in 11:1 and qualify it. Because of his unique relationship to this congregation as their church planter and the one responsible for leading many of its members to the Lord, Paul has a unique responsibility and authority to oversee their spiritual growth. He would like to be personally present again to model correct Christian living, but he believes the Lord wants him to stay on in Ephesus a little while longer (16:8–9).

So he has sent Timothy as his personal surrogate (cf. 16:10–11), who will hopefully overcome his timidity and arrive soon. Timothy will thus remind the Corinthians, through his exemplary behavior, of the appropriate Christian walk, which Paul describes here as his "way of life" (4:17).

With verses 18–21, Paul closes this four-chapter section of his letter with a final warning. He is coming soon, Lord willing, even though some in Corinth are claiming that he is not (vv. 18–19a). He agrees with them that talk is cheap but disputes their claim that "his letters are weighty and forceful, but in person he is unimpressive and his speaking amounts to nothing" (2 Cor 10:10). If he speaks gently to them in person, it is out of love. But if necessary he will come with a rod, metaphorically speaking, just as faithful fathers in Paul's day made guarded use of corporal punishment as a disciplinary tool for their children.

What ultimately counts, however, is the presence of genuine spiritual power, as befits the presence of God's reign (vv. 19b–20). This kingly power must not be narrowly conceived. It consists of the edifying manifestation of spiritual gifts, of winning people to Christ and discipling them, of moral living, and of appropriate humble self-assessment, all in striking contrast to the regal roles the Corinthians thought they were playing (v. 8).

Application. It is difficult to maintain the delicate balance between not judging individuals and congregations at all, even in biblical ways, and judging every minute detail of their lives, often by secular criteria. So too we must walk the tightrope between never dealing with sin in our midst and becoming overly harsh or judgmental in constantly trying to purge it. Matthew 7:1 seems to have replaced John 3:16 as the most well-known Bible verse by non-Christians, and it is almost always taken out of context and misapplied.

In our radically individualistic, highly democratic society, "Let your conscience be your guide" sounds akin to biblical truth. First Corinthians 4:4 makes plain that it is not. The theological concepts of the "priesthood of all believers" and of "soul competency" have often been applied far more widely than their Reformation-era framers ever intended. The Bible does teach the ability of each individual to relate directly to God, to understand enough of Scripture to come to salvation, and to be valued in God's eyes as much any other human being. But these themes have increasingly been distorted to support idiosyncratic, personal interpretations of the Bible and to challenge the right of Christian institutions to uphold standards by exercising discipline and removing unrepentant offenders.

1 CORINTHIANS 5:1–13

Original Meaning. Chapters 5–6 may be seen as a loosely connected unit structured in an ABA pattern that discusses sexual sin (5:1–13), lawsuits (6:1–11), and sexual sin again (6:12–20). Common to all three of these sections is the manifestation of the libertine or hedonistic wing of the church that is flaunting its freedom in Christ.

A horrible state of affairs in the Corinthian church has captured Paul's attention. "Reported" in verse 1 is literally "heard." We do not know how widely the news had traveled, but it had at least reached Paul. "Sexual immorality" translates the Greek *porneia*, the most general of all terms for sexual sin. In this context, however, it is clear that the sin is a matter of incest.

"Father's wife" means that the woman is not the man's mother but his stepmother (v. 1). She may have been considerably younger than her husband and hence attractive to his son. Whether or not the son had legally married the woman is impossible to determine. This kind of incest was strictly forbidden in Jewish law (Lev 18:8). Despite the general moral laxity of the Greco-Roman world, this kind of incest remained one form of sexual sin that was relatively rare and widely condemned there also.

The church's reaction to this affair was as bad or worse than the affair itself. Instead of grieving over sin in their midst, they were actually smug over their newfound, "enlightened" tolerance as Christians (v. 2). Paul recoils in horror. They must rather remove this man from their midst ("fellowship"). That no mention is made of removing the woman suggests she was not a church member to begin with.

In verses 3–4, Paul asserts his authority to pronounce judgment on the situation and in so doing to reflect the power and authority of Christ Jesus himself. Although physically absent, his thoughts were ever with them, and by means of this letter they knew his intentions and desires. "In the name of the Lord Jesus" begins verse 4 in the Greek and could modify either "passed judgment" or "the one who did this" in verse 3. If the last of these is accepted, the problem in Corinth takes on even more horrifying proportions: the man has justified his sin by appealing to the authority of Jesus, presumably referring to his freedom in Christ. But the sentence is too convoluted in the Greek to know for sure.

Precisely what Paul commands the Corinthians to do in verse 5 remains hotly disputed. All agree that it *at least* involves excommunication. The dominant perspective in the early church, now being revived in a number of recent studies of this passage, seems preferable. The Greek reads literally, "so that his *flesh* may be destroyed." When Paul contrasts flesh and spirit, he usually does not refer to body versus soul but to the old versus new natures of a believer (or to the individual as oriented toward sin versus oriented toward God). In 1 Timothy 1:20, Paul describes how he handed two believers over to Satan to be taught not to blaspheme, so presumably they did not die. And a good case can be made for seeing the repentant sinner of

2 Corinthians 2:5–11; 7:8–13 as this same individual addressed in 1 Corinthians 5. In either event, Paul's purpose clearly remains remedial.

Verses 6–8 appeal to the Jews' practice of purifying their homes and their temple from all leavened bread prior to the Passover feast (Exod 12:15). Paul applies this imagery to the *moral* purity God requires of his new house/temple—the church. Citing in verse 6 what may have been a popular proverb (cf. Gal 5:9), he makes it clear that serious sin can infect the whole congregation. Thinking of Passover reminds him of Christ as our perfect sacrifice (v. 7). Jesus's atonement was not intended to free us *to* sin but to liberate us *from* sin. As he likes to do in many of his letters, Paul thus calls his audience to "become what they are"—to act according to the way God has already chosen to consider them in Christ. This means putting away all forms of evil and behaving in ways that genuinely conform to God's true standards (v. 8).

Verses 9–13 close this section by clarifying an apparent misunderstanding, or possibly even a deliberate misrepresentation, of Paul's previous letter. When Paul had told them not to associate with (literally "mix up together with") flagrantly immoral people (v. 9), he was referring to professing Christians, not avowed unbelievers. To drive home this point, Paul generalizes and lists several serious sins in addition to sexual immorality (vv. 10–11). Not only must the Corinthians remove from their fellowship people who repeatedly refuse to repent of their sins, they must not even associate with them in intimate social gatherings outside the church, such as table fellowship.

Verses 12–13 explain the logic of the commands of verses 9–11. The church's jurisdiction is restricted to its own membership. God will take care of unbelievers' sins; indeed, their fate will be bad enough that Christians ought not add to their agony but seek instead to lead them to Christ. So Paul concludes where he began, reminding the Corinthians to expel the incestuous offender.

Application. Ours is an age, tragically, in which even church leaders commit sexual sin or defraud their congregations, at times with virtual impunity. And if a period of discipline and restoration is established, they may refuse to agree to their church's terms. In still other cases, such a period of time seems woefully inadequate to demonstrate a genuine and lasting change of heart and behavior. Some Christian leaders even endorse a philosophy of restoring fallen leaders to ministry as soon as possible in the name of grace and forgiveness. But forgiveness and restoration to fellowship do not automatically carry with them the privilege of pastoring or leading a congregation. The criteria for overseers and deacons in 1 Timothy 3:1–13, including marital faithfulness and wholesome family life, are best understood as attributes that *currently* characterize one's life and *have done so over a long enough period of time* that they may be assumed to be enduring character traits.

The biggest problem, of course, with replicating the effect of biblical excommunication today lies with the element of ostracism originally involved. The few churches that do excommunicate the defiantly immoral usually watch those individuals go down the road or move to a new town, and join another church that pays little or no attention to the reasons they left their previous congregation. Churches even hire pastoral staff who have been let go from other ministries for unethical or illegal behavior without ever asking enough questions of the right people to find out that such behavior had occurred. Becoming a church or staff member should require that the church involved learn enough about an individual's past to determine if he or she is running away from problems left unaddressed. Sensitive but frank cooperation and networking between congregations becomes crucial if the original impact of "shunning" is to have any possibility of being reproduced in our transient world and having its intended remedial effect.

1 CORINTHIANS 6:1–11

Original Meaning. Paul turns to a second example of how the judicial process should work *within* the church rather than outside it. This section begins with Paul's disgust over what is going on. Some sort of complaint concerning property or business dealings seems to have been the problem. If this is what was going on at Corinth, then the disputants were among the minority of well-to-do believers in the congregation, since the vast majority of people didn't own land or homes in those days.

Verses 2–3 present parallel examples of the logic of arguing from the greater to the lesser. Drawing on Daniel 7:22, Paul reminds the Corinthians that they will help the Lord Jesus exercise judgment over the non-Christian world (both people and angels). Surely, therefore, they must be competent to handle earthly disputes in their own midst. "Trivial cases" (v. 2) does not mean that the Corinthian litigation did not involve serious offenses, merely that *all* human litigation is trivial when viewed in the light of judgment day.

Verse 5 contrasts with 4:14. Now Paul *is* prepared to shame the Corinthians. Their litigation incenses him even more than their factiousness because it so fundamentally compromises their witness before a watching world quick to ridicule and reject the church on such occasions. "Is it possible that there is nobody among you wise enough . . . ?" drips with irony, since the Corinthians had been claiming to be so wise (4:10). But Paul probably also believes quite seriously that among the godly (minority?) in the church there are some who bear the marks of true Christian wisdom (2:6) and perhaps also legal training, so that they might intervene constructively. "Believer" in 6:5 is literally "brother," as in verse 6.

Verses 7–8 proceed to the more radical of Paul's two points. "Have lawsuits" (v. 7) might better be rendered "get judgments" and is not limited to litigation in a secular context. Whether inside or outside the church, the attitude of demanding one's rights remains diametrically opposed to Christ's teaching (Matt 5:39–42) and example (1 Pet 2:23). If two Christians cannot resolve their disagreements short of both secular litigation and Christian arbitration, something is fundamentally amiss. Better to suffer wrong—God will one day vindicate all injustices—than to alienate a fellow believer by requiring redress.

The fraud and injustice that trigger lawsuits, and which can even be exacerbated by them, lead Paul naturally to think about those who are "wrongdoers" more generally (v. 9). So, as in 5:10–11, he warns against being sucked into the vortex of behavior that eventually calls into question one's very salvation.

Another vice list appears here, uniquely tailored to the most common and offensive of Corinthian perversions. The same items that Paul mentions in chapter 5 reappear, along with four new ones. "Thieves" (v. 10) cause no surprise in a list stimulated by the thought of lawsuits. "Adulterers" follow naturally after a reference to the "sexually immoral" in general (v. 9). So too do "men who have sex with men," better understood as referring to the more passive and more active partners, respectively, in any male homosexual act. By using nouns that become labels for individuals only after persistent sin in particular areas, Paul makes plain that temporary lapses do not cause an individual to forfeit salvation.

Paul concludes on a more hopeful note (v. 11). Such behavior characterized the pre-Christian lives of many of the Corinthians, but they have now generally abandoned such practices. Therefore, they ought to be able to give up suing each other also! To stress the new holiness of character God has imputed to them, and in which they are progressively but fitfully growing, Paul ends this section with a reminder that they have been "washed" (inwardly, but possibly thinking of the external rite of baptism as well), "sanctified" (made holy), and "justified" (declared righteous) (v. 11). The agency of Jesus and God's Spirit provides an important implicit Trinitarian reference to round out the paragraph.

Application. Under no conceivable circumstances can the Bible be made to defend the often-heard allegation that God created homosexuals that way. What genetic component may contribute to homosexual predispositions remains to be determined but, like inherent predispositions to alcoholism, violence, or various diseases, such a component, if demonstrated, would be an offshoot of the fall, not of creation. Equally crucially, genetic predispositions never exempt humans from biblical standards and accountability before God for moral or immoral behavior. Those predisposed to alcoholism may have to impose more severe restrictions on themselves, such as teetotaling, than others might. But that does not mean that drunkenness for them becomes morally acceptable. Those predisposed to homosexual practices may have to monitor themselves more carefully too, but that scarcely turns sin into a divinely ordained lifestyle.

1 CORINTHIANS 6:12–20

Original Meaning. Paul next turns to treat sexual immorality in general, but particularly manifested in prostitution, for which Corinth was infamous. With verse 12 Paul begins a pattern that will frequently recur throughout the rest of the letter—quoting a Corinthian slogan and thereby giving it a limited endorsement, but then at once substantially qualifying it. These Corinthian slogans (here the three sayings of verses 12–13 that the NIV encloses with quotation marks) all share four characteristics: (a) they are short, pithy, and proverbial; (b) they reflect the libertine wing of the church; (c) Paul himself could have conceivably uttered them in some specific context; and (d) apart from that context they were so misleading that abuse was almost inevitable.

Verse 12 quotes the first slogan twice (cf. also 10:23): "I have the right to do anything." Paul might have spoken this in the context of Christian freedom from the law. The slogan of verse 13 ("food for the stomach and the stomach for food") could reflect his more specific reference to freedom from the Jewish dietary laws. But apart from these contexts the slogans virtually invite people to sin, as the Corinthians apparently were doing. Hence Paul explains that Christians still must submit to moral principles—not because they obey all 613 commandments of the Mosaic law but because many things simply are not beneficial and not truly liberating.

The Corinthians were apparently inferring from the relatively accurate observation that food and stomach were made for each other that the body and sexual release were identically related. After all, both eating and having sex seem to be limited to this life. Not so, declares Paul! There may be no need for stomachs in resurrection bodies that do not need to eat, but there most certainly will be resurrection bodies! And sexual immorality affects one's entire body in a way that overeating cannot, as verse 18 will explain. Hence, that body is to be dedicated to the Lord in holiness and not to sexual impurity (vv. 13b–14).

Verses 15–17 form a syllogism (a three-part argument with two premises and a conclusion that necessarily follows):

1. The bodies of Christians are members of Christ himself.
2. Sexual intercourse unites two human beings (as taught already in Gen 2:24).
3. Sexual intercourse with a prostitute, therefore, unites the members of Christ with that prostitute.

Paul expresses his utter repugnance to associating something as impure as prostitution with Christ's perfect holiness. Prostitution also creates the grotesque connection of the one who represents ultimate commitment with the act that represents the most casual of sexual relationships. Worse still, this sex is for hire, epitomizing the abuse of human beings.

Paul understandably reacts to this monstrous mismatch with a strong present-tense command (suggesting ongoing action) to "flee" *porneia* (v. 18). This is the broadest term for sexual sin in the Greek language, embracing any form of intercourse between two individuals who are not united in heterosexual marriage (v. 18a). At first glance, however, his next reason for this command seems patently false (v. 18b). Surely gluttony and drunkenness, self-mutilation, and suicide also sin against one's own body. The solution to this problem lies with the term "body" (*sōma*), which can often carry the connotation of an individual in bodily, interpersonal communion.

Verses 19–20 reapply the temple imagery, with its connotations of holiness, to the bodies of individual believers. As in 3:16–17, Paul writes literally "your [pl.] body [sg.]" (v. 19). But given the context of verses 12–17 it is more likely that he is still talking about individual bodies here. Verse 20 alludes to Jesus's costly atonement, which should cause believers to want to glorify God out of gratitude for the salvation he has purchased for them.

Application. Drastically countercultural themes persist in these verses. Ever since the sexual revolution of the 1960s, large segments of our modern world have subscribed to the "if it feels good, do it" mentality. The Christian view of sex—abstinence except in heterosexual marriage—makes good sense in our world, completely apart from Paul's primary rationale. The AIDS epidemic has now infected the subculture of the heterosexually promiscuous, particularly prostitutes and their companions. Other sexually transmitted diseases remain widespread. The dangers of unwanted pregnancies and potential abortions only compound the problem. But the most central Christian reason for limiting sex to husbands and wives deals with the permanent commitment that should be implied by interpersonal relations this intimate. In countless ways, women and men defy God and confidently proclaim that they can have sex without that commitment and without any destructive side effects. Time and time again, they regret those choices. But this is not a sin we can test and then back off from; we must trust that God knows best. Once a person yields to temptation, in little or big ways, there are mental and emotional scars that may never entirely disappear, even though God's grace can bring substantial healing.

1 CORINTHIANS 7:1–16

Original Meaning. Here begins the second half of the body of this letter, as Paul turns to take up the issues about which the Corinthians had written to him. The Corinthians' concerns may have been phrased as questions or as challenges, but either way Paul recognizes substantial problems that need correcting. He must now address the opposite error from the problem of promiscuity. Here the ascetic wing of the church is advocating the virtue of celibacy.

The key to a correct understanding of this chapter is the recognition that 7:1 is Paul's reluctant and qualified endorsement of a Corinthian slogan or position, just as he did in 6:12 and 13. First Corinthians 7:1–16, 17–24, and 25–40 appear to form an ABA structure, with two sections of explicit response to the proponents of celibacy sandwiched around a discussion of analogous situations in life in which it is good for Christians to "remain" as they are. Applied to the issues of singleness and marriage, Paul's central point stresses that believers should not be in a hurry to change their marital status.

Paul uses a "yes, but" logic as his thesis for the entire chapter. Verse 2 offers Paul's qualification: sexual abstinence is, for the most part, inappropriate for wedded couples. Corinthian men unable to have sex with their wives would often look elsewhere.

Verses 3–7 unpack this first application of Paul's response to the pro-celibacy faction in Corinth. They advocated completely refraining from sex within marriage, but Paul can imagine only a very limited role for such abstinence. A husband and wife should have sex often enough so that neither is frustrated or tempted to cheat on the other.

"Fulfill his marital duty" (v. 3) reads literally "give back that which is owed." One's "body" (v. 4) probably carries the broader sense of an instrument of interpersonal communication, as in 6:18. Married persons no longer control their own bodies but must surrender authority over them to their spouses. "Do not deprive" (v. 5) should probably read "stop defrauding" (cf. KJV)—that is, cheating someone else out of what is properly his or hers. The only exception Paul will tolerate is if both partners agree that for a very limited time they will abstain from sex for the sake of some unusually concentrated period of communion with the Lord. But even this Paul says only by way of concession (v. 6); he never *insists* that married people abstain at all from sex with each other.

Verse 7 offers the first hint of what verse 8 will make explicit: Paul is currently single, and he likes it that way. He wishes all could share his enjoyment of singleness but realizes that only some have that gift, while others are gifted for marriage.

In verses 8–9 Paul turns from the currently married to the previously married. "Unmarried" is a masculine plural, just as "widows" is a feminine plural (v. 8). Given that verses 25–38 will address those who have never married, and given that the more explicit Greek word for "widower" was falling into disuse in the first century, we should probably understand the unmarried here to refer to men whose wives had died.

The ascetics would of course be telling widowers and widows never to remarry. Paul again affirms that this may be a good course of action but not if it leads to sexual immorality. "Cannot" (v. 9a) is absent from the Greek and somewhat misleading. The text actually reads, "If they *are* not controlling themselves, they should marry." "With passion" (v. 9b) is the NIV's attempt to interpret the Greek verb *puroomai* ("burn") and is probably correct.

Verses 8–9 also make it clear that Paul is single. If his words here are limited to widows and widowers, then perhaps his wife has also died. Rabbis were almost always married, and members of the Sanhedrin had to be married. It is likely that Paul was once married, but we simply cannot be sure.

In verses 10–16 Paul returns to address those who are married, but this time in light of a different proposal by the ascetics. The pro-celibacy faction encouraged people to get divorced if they could not live with a spouse without engaging in sex. At this point Paul's ability to side with this faction is drastically curtailed.

Paul's parenthesis, "not I, but the Lord" (v. 10), alludes to words of the earthly Jesus widely known in early Christian tradition (cf. Mark 10:11–12). Those already divorced must not remarry, in order to leave the door open for possible reconciliation with their estranged partners. The words translated "separate," "divorce," and "leave" throughout verses 10–16 are used interchangeably. Many spouses in antiquity left marriage without legal divorce proceedings, but the end result was the same. If there is any difference between the wife "separating" in verse 10 and the husband "divorcing" in verse 11, it may be that the man was legally entitled to divorce his wife, whereas the woman often had no recourse but to move out.

In verses 12–16, however, Paul addresses the members of mixed marriages. With all the new converts in Corinth, there were no doubt many couples in which only one of the two had become a Christian. Some believers seem to have feared that sexual relations with an unbeliever would defile them. Paul disagrees and insists that if the unbelieving partner is content to stay, the believer must not initiate divorce (vv. 12–13). Here he can cite no word of the earthly Jesus but relies directly on his own sense of how God is guiding or inspiring him (cf. vv. 25, 40). Verse 14 supplies the rationale for Paul's insistence on preserving the marriage: there are spin-off blessings for the non-Christian spouse and children that come from having even one member of the family follow the Lord. "Sanctified" and "holy" cannot here mean "saved," as verse 16 proves. Rather they refer to the impact of the believer on the rest of the family.

But the tension introduced by one partner in a marriage suddenly having a new allegiance to Christ at times proved intolerable to the non-Christian partner. If such a person chose to divorce (or simply leave) his or her spouse, the Christian partner was not compelled to try to prevent the separation (v. 15a). Often there would be nothing he or she could do anyway. "God has called us to live in peace" (v. 15b) offers another reason for Paul's permission to let the unbeliever depart. There is no guarantee that the non-Christian partner will ever be saved by staying, and the constant tension introduced by divergent loyalties may even exacerbate the unbeliever's alienation from both spouse and God (v. 16).

Application. Few Christians today advocate total abstinence from sex as an ideal for all believers. Our problems parallel those of the hedonistic wing of the Corinthian church far more than those of the ascetic wing. So any application of 1 Corinthians 7 must proceed with the caution that these changed circumstances dictate. Perhaps the closest analogies to this sexual asceticism remain in traditional Roman Catholic circles, which still insist on celibacy as a requirement for priests and various religious orders. Neither Paul nor any other biblical writer justifies this across-the-board requirement. Protestants, however, often continue to overreact against this extreme by inappropriately denigrating the single life. Some churches will not hire pastors if they are *not* married! Even single lay adults regularly testify to feeling like second-class citizens in the church. The recent boom in singles groups has helped to allay some of their loneliness, but it is questionable if these groups have succeeded in integrating singles into the larger world of married adults and families in the church.

1 CORINTHIANS 7:17–24

Original Meaning. Verses 17–24 form a preliminary summary of Paul's argument in chapter 7 thus far and apply it to two analogous situations. The main point can be paraphrased as, "Do not be in a hurry to change the external circumstances of your life simply because you have become a Christian."

Verses 18–19 illustrate this principle with the example of circumcision versus uncircumcision. Although it was one of the most fundamental ritual requirements of Judaism, circumcision is now a matter of moral indifference for Christians. "Keeping God's commandments" (v. 19) for Christians refers to the reinterpretations and applications of the Mosaic law for a new age, in light of the words and works of Jesus and the apostles.

Verses 21–23 give a second illustration of the theme "remain as you are." Here Paul contrasts the experiences of Roman slaves and freedmen. Neither state makes serving the Lord inherently easier than the other, and there are spiritual senses in which literal slaves are free in Christ and literal freedmen slaves to Christ. Yet Paul does add an exception here that he did not in the case of circumcision: "If you can gain your freedom, do so" (v. 21). Physical slavery is a form of oppression that displeases God, so when an opportunity for freedom arises, it should be seized.

Application. These verses directly challenge our contemporary individualism, which teaches people never to rest content with the status they have already attained but always to seek more money, power, influence, and control over their lives. The results include a highly transient, upwardly mobile population among the more affluent, who generally fail to notice that the numbers of poor and dispossessed often grow precisely as they climb their ladders and push others down.

The opposite danger is passivity. Verse 21a encourages us to try to improve our lot in this world, so long as we do not do it at others' expense or imagine that the key to happiness and a rewarding Christian life demands a change in our current status. Certainly we must avoid the tendency to suggest to new Christians that leaving a secular job for full-time Christian work is somehow *by definition* the desirable thing to do.

1 CORINTHIANS 7:25–40

Original Meaning. Verses 25–40 return to the topic of sex and marriage in response to the pro-celibacy faction in Corinth. Verses 26b and 27b repeat the theme of "remain as you are." Because these young people are single, like the widows and widowers of verses 8–9, Paul can be more enthusiastic about celibacy. But he quickly reminds them that his enthusiasm for abstinence does not carry over to the married (v. 27a) and, against those in Corinth teaching that sex and marriage were inherently sinful, he affirms that "if you do marry, you have not sinned" (v. 28a).

Verses 25–28 also introduce two new reasons for Paul's advice. The first deals with "the present crisis" (v. 26a), which is further explained in verses 29–31. There is no indication that Corinthian Christians were persecuted much, at least not more than most first-century Christians. So it is better to understand verses 29–31 as explaining verse 26a. Paul knows that after Christ's first coming, his second coming could take place very soon ("the time is short"—v. 29a). This does not mean that Paul had set any dates or necessarily expected the Lord to return within his lifetime.

All Christians should sense an urgency to serving the Lord, caused by the uncertainty of the time of the end, after which point it will no longer be possible to win any more people to Christ or to disciple them to maturity. Paul is well aware that the distractions of marriage may temper this urgency. So those who choose to wed must not become so preoccupied with their families that they can no longer effectively serve Christ (v. 29b). The same is true with other normal human activities—celebrations and wakes, commerce and shopping (vv. 30–31). All are legitimate endeavors, but all remain fleeting. The Christian should therefore be less involved in the affairs of this world than the non-Christian.

Verses 32–35 unpack Paul's second rationale for encouraging those who have never married to stay single. Even if Christ does not come back right away, attending to the concerns of spouse and children takes time away from ministering to the needs of others in both church and world (vv. 32–34). Yet once again Paul refuses to absolutize his preferences or endorse without qualification the stance of the pro-celibacy faction. Verse 35 supplies the most crucial clue in the whole chapter for determining when marriage is or is not appropriate. Whichever state enables one to "live in a right way in undivided devotion to the Lord" is preferable. Paul does not wish to "restrict" his audience (literally "throw a noose around" them), one way or the other.

Verses 36–38 focus on one specific kind of unmarried person. But as the NIV footnote demonstrates, the language is vague enough to be taken in two quite different ways. The early church almost without exception interpreted these verses to refer to a father considering whether or not to give his daughter's hand in marriage.

It is probably better to take the two people involved to refer to fiancé and fiancée. Engaged couples should not feel compelled to heed the pro-celibacy faction and refrain from marriage, but if they choose to do so, that is acceptable as well. Indeed, as in verses 7–8, 26, and 40, Paul reiterates his preference for the single life (v. 38), but he refuses to legislate it.

Verses 39–40 round out the chapter by reaffirming monogamy as a lifelong commitment. These verses also contain the only explicit reference to remarriage in this chapter. Christian widows and, by implication, widowers are free to remarry, so long as they marry fellow believers. As in verse 8, Paul reiterates his preference for the single life but will not absolutize it. "I think that I too have the Spirit of God" (v. 40b) does not reflect any doubt on Paul's part but represents a slightly sarcastic aside to the Corinthians, who felt that only they had attained true spiritual insight.

Application. Not many Western Christians give adequate consideration to the possibility of remaining unmarried for the sake of wholehearted devotion to the Lord's work. More need to do so. Examples such as the internationally influential

Anglican pastor, John Stott, or the widely heralded Southern Baptist missionary, Lottie Moon, have demonstrated how much one life can accomplish when freed from the demands of family. Many Christian preachers, from John Wesley to contemporary workaholics, would have been better off unmarried rather than going through the agony of watching their marriages fall apart after years of neglect. William Carey's marvelous missionary career remains somewhat tarnished because of the sacrifices he demanded of his wife, Dorothy, who eventually lost her mind. Some of this heartache could surely have been avoided if couples unprepared to count the cost simply had not married in the first place.

For all of us, single or married, if the end of the world truly could come in our lifetime, we should have an urgency about the Lord's work that contemporary Christians seldom reflect. And even if the Lord delays his coming, sudden death claims too many lives for any of us ever to assume complacently that we have a certain number of years or decades left to serve God more leisurely.

1 CORINTHIANS 8:1–13

Original Meaning. Paul now addresses the second issue raised by the Corinthians in their letter to him (see 7:1). Most meat sold in the town marketplace came from sacrificial animals that had been slaughtered at pagan temple ceremonies. Did these rituals somehow automatically taint the food? What about the various social events that often used the temple dining halls for their festivities? Could Christians participate and eat meat at these events?

Verse 1 introduces the issue. "Food" should be understood to refer to "meat," lest verse 13 be seen as narrowing the topic. Part of the meat of each sacrificial animal was burned on the temple altar, part was eaten in temple ceremonies, and part was sold in the Corinthian marketplace for consumption at home.

"We know that 'we all possess knowledge'" (v. 1a) probably represents another Corinthian slogan. This slogan more likely reflects the position of the "stronger" Corinthians, who probably overlapped with the more indulgent rather than the more ascetic wing of the church there. "Knowledge" translates *gnōsis* and must be interpreted as in chapters 1–4 to refer to prideful human religious speculation. As with the previous slogans, there is a sense in which Paul can agree but not without immediate qualification (vv. 1b–3). Love, not knowledge, must form the foundation of Christian behavior. True Christian knowledge is inseparable from *agapē* love, which can be produced only by God's prior choice to love us (v. 3).

Verses 4–6 provide the basis for Christian freedom to eat this sacrificial food—the idols to which the meat is dedicated have no objective spiritual existence. Steeped in his Jewish understanding of monotheism, Paul forthrightly declares that there is only one true God in the universe (v. 4). Paul goes on to acknowledge that not everyone believes as he does. Gnosticism believed in divine emanations (v. 5), but in reality none of these alleged gods or lords had anything to do with the creation, sustenance, or redemption of the world, as the God of Israel and the Father of the Lord Jesus did (v. 6).

Verses 7–13 unpack Paul's qualification of the exercise of Christian freedom: it may corrupt the weak consciences of certain fellow believers. Love must therefore limit freedom. Some of the Corinthian Christians could not eat idol meat, even in private homes and almost certainly not in temple dining halls, without recalling the past religious associations that the meat had for them. This would have been a special concern for some of the poorer members of the church, who probably would not have had regular access to eating meat except at temple rituals. For them, meat still had inherently religious connotations. Their "weak" conscience was not a poorly developed sense of morality or propriety but rather the overscrupulous restrictions they placed on believers' freedom in Christ (v. 7). Their inner thoughts unnecessarily accused them and led to feelings of guilt or defilement. Because they felt compelled to do that which did not proceed from faith, for them it *was* sinful (Rom 14:23).

Verse 8 continues Paul's qualification; the introductory "but" should probably be translated "and." Here is the first of three reasons Paul gives for voluntarily abstaining from idol meat in the presence of those unable to handle the practice. Precisely because it is a morally neutral issue, there is no inherent spiritual advantage in eating the meat or disadvantage in avoiding it. Therefore, concern for one's fellow Christian should take precedence. The "however" in verse 9 should again be taken as a mild continuative (e.g., "moreover"). Verses 9–12 combine to make the point that the Corinthians should not behave in ways that lead each other into sin.

Verse 10 is often understood to mean that while the "stronger" Corinthians could draw appropriate boundaries and eat meat from the marketplace without being tempted to go to the temple, the "weaker" Christians could not. Hence that which was morally neutral led the latter to go on to do that which was inherently sinful. Quite likely what the strong felt would build up the weak was actually daring them to do something destructive. Verse 11 thus spells out the second reason for voluntary abstinence. Flaunting one's freedom was actually damaging the spiritual lives of the weak.

Verse 12b gives the third reason for abstinence: to avoid sinning against Christ. When there is good reason to believe that exercising one's freedom in amoral areas will actually lead a fellow Christian into sin, restraint is always right. Paul models this principle by his own example and states it with an emphasis worthy of Mark 9:42.

Application. For most readers of this commentary, idol meat and its analogues in other world religions will not rank among their top one hundred moral dilemmas in life! Some contemporary analogies involve the overt religious associations that eating meat in idol's temples could at times have. Freemasonry, for example, has distinctively non-Christian religious rituals at its core, yet much superficial involvement with the organization can be maintained at a purely secular level, and the organization does good with many charitable and humanitarian activities. Christians, therefore, continue to disagree as to whether believers may be involved, and at what levels, with this kind of organization. Room must be left for that disagreement to continue, so long as Christians agree on the larger principles at stake.

Similar debate should be allowed to continue to surround participation by Protestants in the Eucharists of Roman Catholic and Eastern Orthodox congregations and vice-versa. In an age of ecumenism, not every church means what its predecessors have meant by Holy Communion. Each Christian must judge each context to see if he or she can partake in good conscience, in light of what that particular ceremony is believed to accomplish.

Where are the boundaries that differentiate Christian meditation, secular meditation, and Hindu or Buddhist (including transcendental) meditation? To what extent, if any, can one participate in a game like Dungeons & Dragons, which in at least some circles, but by no means all, can lead to the practice of witchcraft or the occult? The answers will vary from one context to another.

The most common contemporary applications of 1 Corinthians 8, however, usually do not involve activities that could lead to overtly anti-Christian beliefs or rituals. Rather they have to do with involvement in activities that can lead to excess and sin, but do not have to. These include drinking alcohol; wearing potentially suggestive forms of dress; listening to certain kinds of music; smoking or chewing tobacco; playing games that sometimes but not necessarily involve gambling; buying lottery tickets that support government, education, state parks, and the like; engaging in premarital physical contact of a variety of kinds; and so on.

1 CORINTHIANS 9:1–18

Original Meaning. Paul turns next to a second illustration of the principle that Christian freedom should be tempered by voluntary relinquishing of one's rights. But the illustration is scarcely arbitrary; it reflects one of the primary ways the Corinthians are challenging Paul. They have come to doubt his apostolic authority (9:2–3) precisely because he is not charging them for his ministry.

Verses 1–12a therefore present the case in some detail for Paul's right to charge for his services. Yet in keeping with his "yes, but" logic and in defense of his actual behavior, verses 12b–18 then explain why Paul has in fact renounced this right. Verses 19–27 generalize to the even broader principle that lies behind Paul's behavior on the issues in both 8:1–13 and 9:1–18.

The four questions of 9:1 are all interconnected. If the answer to any proves negative, then all Paul's claims are in jeopardy. But in fact Paul is free, he is an apostle, he has seen Jesus, and he has spiritually fathered the Corinthians. Thus verse 2 follows logically. No matter anyone else's opinion of Paul, for the Corinthians to question his apostolicity calls into question their own spiritual existence!

Verses 3–12a supply Paul's formal defense, via a barrage of further rhetorical questions. The answers to each of them are intended to be unambiguous. First, Paul reasserts his right to receive material provision for his ministry, by means of three questions in verses 4–6. Verse 5 implies that most of these other men were married and brought their wives along on their travels. The way Paul phrases the question of verse 5 makes one wonder if Paul had been married when he first began his itinerant ministry and if his wife had subsequently died. Verse 6 then gets to the heart of Paul's complaint.

In verses 7–12a, Paul begins accumulating a series of reasons why in fact he *does* have the right to request payment for his services. These continue into verses 13–14 as well. Verse 7 presents three analogies from the common practice of human experience in the areas of warfare, farming, and shepherding. Few in Paul's day would have disputed the logic of these examples.

Verses 8–11 argue from Deuteronomy 25:4, which verse 9 explicitly quotes. "Merely" is a correct interpolation in verse 8 and could easily be added in verse 9b as well ("Is it merely about oxen that God is concerned?"). Verse 10a should then read, "Surely he says this [also] for us." Paul is not claiming that this quotation from the Mosaic law never had anything to do with oxen, only that its application cannot be limited to animals. Verses 10–11 clarify, using imagery favored by Jesus in his parables of seed and sowing, that preaching the gospel is like planting a crop and making disciples like harvesting.

Verse 12a rounds out the formal part of Paul's defense with a third kind of argument. The Corinthians have already conceded the logic of everything Paul has said thus far with respect to their other leaders and itinerating Christian workers. It is the height of irony and injustice that they would refuse these same rights to the one who was most of all responsible for their spiritual rebirth.

Verse 12b begins as if Paul is ready to move to the "but" of his "yes, but" argument. Verses 13–14, however, continue by providing the final two arguments in defense of Paul's right to receive remuneration: the analogy of priests and Levites in the

Jewish temple (cf. Num 18:8–31) and the express words of Jesus during his lifetime (Luke 10:7b).

After the interruption of verses 13–14, Paul restates the theme of verse 12b ("I have not used any of these rights"—v. 15a) and goes on to explain why he has refused to charge for his ministry. Verse 15b clarifies that his defense has not been a subtle hint that he wishes to reverse his policy now. Verse 15c forms an emotional outburst in the Greek, literally, "For it would be better for me to die than—no one will empty me of my boast!" "Boast" here carries the sense of an appropriate pride in what the Lord has done despite Paul's weakness (cf. 1:31; 2 Cor 10:12–12:10).

But Paul cannot legitimately boast merely in his ministry of preaching (v. 16). God has placed an irresistible call on his life to preach (cf. Jer 20:9). Verse 17a ("if I preach voluntarily") is thus merely hypothetical; verse 17b ("if not voluntarily") expresses what in fact is true in Paul's case.

The rest of verse 18 answers this question.

Application. "Tentmaking" is making a healthy comeback, especially in missions circles, though it needs to be taken as a serious option by even larger numbers of Christian workers. There are no countries "closed" to the gospel, notwithstanding the frequent use of this expression to refer to nations with government bans on missionary visas. Rather, Christians prepared to employ their skills overseas in business, industry, or teaching English as a foreign language may regularly gain entry into those areas otherwise most hostile to professional Christianity.

Even at home in the Western world, bivocational ministry is increasingly needed. In many instances, small congregations of young Christians in working-class or impoverished neighborhoods should not be asked to try to support their ministers. Even when they are asked, they often cannot do so.

Tentmaking, nevertheless, has substantial weaknesses, not least of which is the amount of time available to devote to evangelism, discipleship, preaching, teaching, and so on. The paid professional minister is not likely to disappear from the horizon in the near future.

1 CORINTHIANS 9:19–27

Original Meaning. In verses 19–27, Paul makes plain the evangelistic principle underlying his attitude to both idol meat and money for ministry. Whatever he does, he wants to clear the ground of unnecessary obstacles that might hinder unbelievers from coming to Christ. Verses 19–23 enunciate this principle in terms of "all things to all people." Verses 24–27 describe the spiritual discipline involved in adapting oneself to diverse cultural and moral situations.

Paul understands that with the death of Christ the age of the law has come to an end (Gal 3:19–4:7). Scripture itself is still relevant for followers of Jesus (2 Tim 3:16) but only as it is interpreted in light of what Christ has done (Rom 10:4). Nevertheless, to Jews and others under the law, Paul at times acts as if he is still subject to all of the laws of Moses (cf. Acts 16:1–3; 21:20–26), so long as it is clear that his actions are not a proof of salvation or spiritual maturity in any way.

First Corinthians 9:22b–23 summarize the paragraph, repeating Paul's principle of flexibility one last time and noting an additional rationale for his behavior. As in verses 15–18, there is inherent blessing in fulfilling his commission and seeing the results—people saved from their sins.

Verses 24–27 have been taken as belonging more with 10:1–13 than with 9:19–23. But the theme of sharing in the gospel's blessings continues, and the analogies of strict discipline fit the single-minded passion Paul has articulated in verses 15–18. The Corinthians would have been familiar with all of these analogies from the regular athletic training and competition that surrounded the Isthmian games the city hosted every other year.

Verse 27 spells out the spiritual import of these two analogies. Verse 27a does not imply that Paul is promoting asceticism after all; rather he is now referring to the spiritual training and self-discipline that he exercises so that his ministry will not become futile. Verse 27b has been taken as Paul's concern that he might lose his salvation (a remarkable thought in view of Rom 8:31–38) or that "the prize" refers to some kind of rewards above and beyond eternal life itself (an idea for which there is no shred of contextual support). More probably, "disqualified" (*adokimos*) should be interpreted in light of the other reference to testing in the context of judgment day in 1 Corinthians (3:12–15). There Paul says God will "test" (*dokimasei*; v. 13) believers' works and give out corresponding praise or censure (see comments there). But neither one's salvation nor eternal status in heaven is at stake.

Application. Contextualization has become a buzzword among missiologists and missionaries. When a person tries to reach people of different cultures, the need for doing more than dumping a canned condensation of gospel truths becomes both apparent and acute. For many Western Christians living and working in relatively homogeneous secular settings, the most important lesson from verses 19–27 may relate to their choices of companions—who they spend significant time with, cultivating friendships and engaging in recreation or leisure-time pursuits. Many Christians barely know any non-Christians well enough to share their faith in less than superficial fashion. Many congregations insist on their members attending countless church functions, but the result is that faithful followers have no time left for a fallen world. Better to spend less time in church and more in the world, so long as that does not reflect a lack of commitment to Christ and mature Christian living.

1 CORINTHIANS 10:1–22

Original Meaning. In verse 1, Paul casts perhaps another subtle aspersion at the Corinthians' claims to "knowledge" by suggesting that they may in fact be "ignorant" after all. To correct this oversight, he reminds them of the behavior of their spiritual predecessors. The association of water with both cloud and sea prompts Paul to conceive of this deliverance as a kind of baptism "into Moses" (v. 2). Paul uses the preposition "into" to match the idea of baptism "into Christ" (Rom 6:3; Gal 3:27), a reminder of the fact that both "baptisms" initiated people into the fellowship of a body of believers.

The Israelites experienced further supernatural blessing when God gave them manna from heaven to eat (e.g., Exod 16:4, 35) and water from a cleft rock to drink (Exod 17:6; Num 20:11) on occasions in which they otherwise would have died from hunger and thirst. Paul recognizes Christ as the preexistent Son of God, active with God the Father in creation and redemption, and hence the agent of both physical and spiritual nourishment for his people in the desert (1 Cor 10:4b). Yet none of these miracles guaranteed that the children of Israel would reach the promised land (v. 5).

In verse 6 Paul exhorts the Corinthians to learn from this example. "To keep us from setting our hearts on evil things" reads literally "to keep us from lusting after evil." The four additional examples of verses 7–10 illustrate more specific forms of this improper lust. First, Paul cites Exodus 32:6, part of the story of the Israelites' idolatrous worship of the golden calf (v. 7). Second, he refers to the episode in Numbers 25:1–9, in which Israelite men engaged in immoral sexual activity with Moabite women (v. 8). Third, he alludes to Numbers 21:4–9, when the people complained against Moses and God (v. 9). Fourth, he recalls the characteristic grumblings and murmurings of the people, most notably in Numbers 16:41–50 (v. 10).

Verse 11 repeats the warning of verse 6, all the more crucial since Christians live in the climactic era of human history for which all previous ages were preparing. Verse 12 summarizes the significance of these warnings for the Corinthians—even those who think they stand securely should take care, like Paul in 9:27, lest they fall and be disqualified. Verses 1–12 are all balanced by the marvelous promise of verse 13.

Verses 14–22 then return explicitly to the topic of idol meat in Corinth, with which chapter 8 began. Although the food itself is morally neutral, Paul does make one absolute prohibition: eating it in the context of explicitly pagan worship services is always wrong. In such cases eating is idolatry (v. 14). Paul appeals to the Corinthian Christians to come to the same conclusion (v. 15).

To cement his position, Paul offers two further analogies, from the sacred meals of Christianity (vv. 16–17) and Judaism (v. 18). Partaking of the elements of the Lord's Supper—the bread and the wine—involves a "participation" (Gk. *koinonia*, "fellowship") with the risen Lord and an appropriation of the benefits of his shed blood and broken body. "Participation" in verses 15–16 includes both communion with fellow believers and partnership in Christ.

The application to religious temple feasts in Corinth follows naturally (vv. 19–22). Pagans too commune with the spiritual beings they worship, in ways that make it ghastly to think of Christians participating. In drawing this parallel, Paul anticipates an objection. He is not now contradicting his earlier claims that idols have no objective, spiritual existence (8:4). But he knows from the law that demons—fallen angels—are the true objects of pagan ritual, however unwittingly they may be worshiped (cf. Deut 32:17).

Application. First Corinthians 10:2 is one of the most crucial verses in Scripture to combat the persistent heresy of baptismal regeneration; that is, the view that baptism into a religious community is a requirement of or guarantees salvation. In evangelical circles, this view persists in certain branches of the Church of Christ and various independent Baptist groups. In mainline Roman Catholic, Episcopal, and Lutheran churches, official dogma usually maintains that subsequent confirmation is necessary to make one's baptism as an infant effective, but less precise language in such circles often equates "baptized" with "Christian."

Questions about the salvation of children too young to be confirmed often hinge on whether or not they have been baptized. And confirmation itself can at times become a meaningless ritual that adolescents are expected to go through to please their parents, but without genuinely experiencing saving faith. In Baptistic circles, some churches offer prebaptismal instruction classes for children in ways that put subtle pressure on them to go ahead with the rite whether or not they are ready to be serious about professions of faith. Even baby dedications have sometimes arisen as a kind of Baptist alternative to infant baptism to placate family members who think some kind of ceremony is what counts the most. Care must be exercised in each branch of the church to ensure that baptism or confirmation is undertaken voluntarily as a public affirmation of genuine, saving faith in Christ, which those undergoing the rite have sincerely professed.

The Lord's Supper has also come to be viewed as quasi-magical in numerous Christian traditions, so that members of liturgical churches often stress the need to partake frequently, especially as one is dying, to appropriate forgiveness for the most recent round of sins in one's life. This too needs serious reexamination in light of Scripture.

1 CORINTHIANS 10:23–11:1

Original Meaning. First Corinthians 10:23 restates 6:12 almost verbatim, except that here Paul substitutes "but not everything is *constructive*" at the end. Now he is thinking more of the corporate than of the individual effects of exercising freedom in Christ. Still, his "yes, but" approach to the Corinthian slogans remains unchanged. Verse 24 amplifies the qualification. Christians are free to serve others above self. Verses 25–30 apply Paul's principles to the two specific contexts of purchasing and consuming meat sold in the Corinthian marketplace (vv. 25–26) and eating it in a friend's home (vv. 27–30). In each instance, the likelihood was great that the meat would have been sacrificed to idols.

In the case of marketplace food, Paul's command is unqualified: feel free to buy it and eat it. Food and drink are part of God's good creation and have been given to his people to be enjoyed (vv. 25–26, quoting Ps 24:1). No food is unclean in itself (cf. Rom 14:14). In the case of a friend's home, even that of an unbeliever not likely to have any scruples about what is eaten, Paul is only slightly less enthusiastic. His general affirmation is equally sweeping—go if you like, eat, and don't ask any questions (v. 27). Only if someone else present makes an issue of the food having been sacrificed to idols should abstention even be considered (v. 28a). Presumably this person is a "weaker" fellow Christian (recall 8:7), since unbelievers would not likely have any scruples about eating idol meat. In this situation, one might decide to refrain so as not to risk leading the other person into sin or confusing his or her conscience (vv. 28b–29a).

Verses 28–29a should probably be punctuated as a parenthesis, as in the old RSV. Verses 29b–30 then resume Paul's primary line of thought. He defends his freedom to partake of food for which he is grateful to God and not to be paranoid about what the unspoken thoughts of others present might be.

First Corinthians 10:31–11:1 restates the twin principles of freedom and restraint one last time, now in the context of God's glory—that which conforms to his standards and priorities (v. 31). Paul tries to lead as few into sin as possible, both outside and inside the church, but his most basic underlying motive is the salvation of as many as possible (vv. 32–33; recall 9:19–23). And he has included this somewhat lengthy discussion of his actions and motives precisely so that the Corinthians might imitate him carefully, at least to the extent that he successfully models Christlike behavior (11:1).

Application. I would refer readers to the Application section of chapter 8 above. But a little more can be said here. Verses 25–26 contain implications for ecology and stewardship of the environment that go beyond the original issue of acceptable food to eat. As with biblical teaching on the subject more generally, Paul recognizes that the created world is categorically distinct from humanity, which alone was fashioned in God's image. So we have the right and the responsibility to use creation for good purposes (Gen 1:28). Mandating vegetarianism or elevating animal rights to the level of human rights blurs this distinction between humanity and the rest of creation, but the more common modern malady of a cavalier rape of the environment proves even more heinous in God's eyes.

More central to this section is Paul's preference for freedom over restraint when commending the gospel to unbelievers. Non-Christian stereotypes of conservative Christian faith consistently characterize us as dour, legalistic joy-killers. And at least part of this caricature is deserved. Evangelicals often do argue over where to draw the boundaries in morally gray areas.

Pleasant exceptions to this trend often occur in creative church youth groups and parachurch campus ministries that defy the stereotype, organize lots of fun activities, usually attract good crowds, bring many to genuine faith, and weather the criticisms of the "professional weaker brothers" in their communities. Unfortunately, there are not as many models of similar exuberance, creativity, and freedom among older adults either inside or outside the church. Service projects and target-group ministries may prove effective alternate approaches to reaching adults from a wide variety of walks of life. Our outreach can be even more effective if we adopt attitudes and lifestyles that are quicker to affirm the truth and goodness that appear in unbelievers' lives than to condemn their sins.

1 CORINTHIANS 11:2–16

Original Meaning. The next three topics Paul addresses all deal with behavior in worship. They include what men and women should or should not wear on their heads (11:2–16), proper conduct during the Lord's Supper (11:17–34), and the use and abuse of spiritual gifts (chs. 12–14).

In the case of head coverings, Paul continues his "yes, but" logic. Yes, he praises them for their faithfulness to his teaching—probably about freedom (11:2)—but they have carried things too far. Yes, it is true that men and women are equal in Christ before God, but that does not mean that all differences between the sexes may be blurred.

The events that lie behind verses 3–16 seem to proceed as follows. Because of their newfound freedom in Christ, women in the Corinthian church were praying and prophesying (v. 5a). Christian tradition from Pentecost on had approved of such practice (Acts 2:18), and it readily fit Paul's own emphasis on freedom. But these women were not merely speaking in worship but doing it in a way that unnecessarily flaunted social convention and the order of creation. So Paul has to encourage them to exercise restraint. As in chapters 8–10, knowledge must be tempered with love.

One of the keys to understanding 11:3–10 is to recognize Paul's play on the word "head." The main point of this paragraph is the claim that what one does or doesn't put on one's physical head either honors or dishonors one's spiritual head. Verse 3 establishes three such relationships of spiritual headship, but what the term for head (Gk. *kephalē*) means here is hotly debated. The word was not often used figuratively; when it was it seems that its two main meanings were either "source" or "authority." Paul appears to use both meanings elsewhere (e.g., Eph 1:22 more readily yields "authority"; Eph 4:15, "source"), so a decision will ultimately depend on the immediate context. But even here in 1 Corinthians 11 Paul sends mixed signals, supplying an argument from the origin of men and women in verses 8–9, 12 but speaking explicitly of authority (Gk. *exousia*) in verse 10. The other passage in which Paul calls a man "head" over a woman refers as well to wives' subordination to their husbands (Eph. 5:22–24), so "authority" seems somewhat more likely here too.

The order of the three parts of 11:3 also proves significant. Some commentators stress that the sequence does not set up a chain of command, as if Paul had written, "The head of the woman is man, the head of every man is Christ, and the head of Christ is God." On the other hand, since the problem in Corinth involved men and women (but not Christ) dishonoring their heads, it is natural that he should refer to the heads of the man and of the woman first. The rationale for placing Christ's relationship to God last is most likely to draw attention to it as an analogy for the relationship between men, women, and their heads (the same sequence in v. 12). Fortunately, the overall thrust of this passage remains clear even if one cannot agree on the precise meaning of "head."

Another disputed issue in verses 3–10 involves the translation of the words the NIV consistently renders as "man" (*anēr*) and "woman" (*gynē*). In every other place in Paul where they are paired, with the possible exception of 1 Timothy 2:8–15, they refer to husband and wife. It is much harder to understand how Paul could have claimed that every man is an authority over every woman and much easier to interpret the passage if husbands and wives are meant throughout (e.g., 1 Cor 11:5).

Verses 4–5a proceed with Paul's play on words. In each verse, the first use of "head" refers to the physical anatomy; the second to the spiritual authority or originator (depending on how one interprets *kephalē*). The reference to praying and prophesying shows that the context is public worship; the latter in particular required an audience to be effective!

"With his head covered" (v. 4) might refer to long hair rather than to some external covering like a veil or shawl. In verses 14–15 Paul is definitely talking about relative lengths of hair for men and women, so it is somewhat more natural to assume that he has been talking about hairstyles all along. Long hair on Greek men might well have led to suspicions of homosexual behavior. If an external covering is meant, then Paul is probably objecting to a practice that resembled that of Roman priests pulling their togas up over their heads while offering sacrifice.

Wives, however, should keep their heads covered (v. 5a). Again, the covering could refer to long hair. It could be that Paul wants them to keep it done up, as was the custom among married women, rather than loose and flowing—a sign in some circles of being unmarried or, worse still, of suspected adultery (among Jews) or pagan, prophetic frenzy (among Greeks).

In verses 5b–6, Paul remarks ironically that if women are going to send ambiguous signals about their sexuality or religious commitments through inappropriate hairstyles or lack of headdress, then they might as well go all the way and become bald (or discard all head coverings) and unequivocally send the wrong signals! Verses 7–10, however, state Paul's true preference—that the Corinthian husbands and their wives revert back to the culturally appropriate signs of marital fidelity and worship of the one true God.

Verses 8–9 ground the commands of verses 4–7 in a twofold argument from creation:

1. Adam was created first and then Eve (v. 8);
2. woman was created to be a helper suitable for man (Gen 2:18) and not the reverse (v. 9).

Verse 10 brings the first part of Paul's argument to a climax, but with a notoriously obscure statement. "For this reason" suggests that this sentence is giving a further rationale for women keeping their heads covered (either with lots of hair or with a shawl). Every other use of this three-word construction in the New Testament means "to have authority (or control) *over*." This suggests a translation more along the lines of "For this reason . . . a wife should exercise control over her head [i.e., keep the appropriate covering on it]."

"Because of the angels" proves equally perplexing (v. 10b). The suggestions that these are fallen angels who might be sexually seduced or human messengers or church leaders go against the consistent meaning of *angeloi* used without qualification elsewhere in the New Testament. It is better to see them as the angels who remain God's servants, watching over creation and protecting the worship of his people. They in particular would want to see services proceed with appropriate dignity and decorum.

Verses 11–12 introduce an important qualification into Paul's discussion. Beginning with a strong contrast (*plēn*, "nevertheless"), Paul reminds the Corinthians that as Christians, notwithstanding creation, husbands and wives (or perhaps men and women more generally) are fundamentally interdependent.

God is the origin of everything that belongs to redemption. He is therefore our ultimate and most important authority.

Verses 13–16 return to the specific problem of head coverings, this time explicitly referring to long hair on men and women, with three further arguments. After appealing to the Corinthians to conclude that what Paul is saying is true (v. 13a), he argues further from propriety (v. 13b), nature (vv. 14–15), and the widespread first-century custom (NIV "practice") of all believers (v. 16).

Verse 15b also supports the idea that hair length or style has been the issue throughout verses 2–16. "As a covering" might more literally be rendered "instead of a wrap-around garment." That is, rather than wearing the customary hair shawl as Greek women did, long hair, perhaps done up in a bun, will suffice for Christian women. On the other hand, if an external garment is in view in verses 3–10, then Paul will be drawing an analogy here. Just as "nature" teaches that women should wear long hair as a head covering, so it is appropriate for women to further cover their heads according to the established custom of the day. Verse 15 might be translated, "For long hair is given her so that she may wind it around her head."

Application. Clearly head coverings send virtually no sexual or religious messages in contemporary Western societies. Perhaps the only exception is in those few extremely conservative churches that still insist on women wearing hats, scarves, or hairnets. And the message these churches usually send to the culture at large is that they are hopelessly out of touch with modernity! For them it would be best to abandon the practice at once, so that they could better implement Paul's principle of being all things to all people in order to save as many as possible (9:19–23).

Whenever Christian faith enters a new culture, the hermeneutical principles at stake here will need to be discussed. Since the 1960s we have watched men's hair grow long and short again, and we have seen teens of both sexes fall in and out of love with punk styles. New generations will doubtless bring still different fashions and resurrect others tried in the past. To the extent that people's grooming or dress deliberately flaunts authority and social convention, such actions cannot be condoned by Christians, because it gives us an unnecessarily bad reputation among non-Christians. No doubt some of this occurred in the 60s and with punk. But wise Christians, like wise parents, will choose their battles carefully. We should not get overly upset by a person's outward appearance when there are more fundamental theological and ethical issues to be concerned about in our society.

1 CORINTHIANS 11:17–34

Original Meaning. For once Paul abandons his "yes, but" logic. Whatever the Corinthians may have claimed in their letter about faithfully celebrating the Lord's Supper (11:2, 22c), Paul has heard additional news that horrifies him (v. 18). Paul refers to "divisions" (Gk. *schismata*, as in 1:10). But here he is not thinking of the rival parties that possibly separate various congregations but of the gulf between the rich and poor within a given house church. The minority of well-to-do believers (1:26) would have had the leisure time and resources to arrive earlier and bring larger quantities and finer food than the rest of the congregation. Latecomers (the majority, who probably had to finish work before coming) would be seated separately in the adjacent atrium or courtyard. Those that could not afford to bring a full meal, or a very good one, did not have the opportunity to share with the rest in the way that Christian unity demanded. The result of the lack of consideration by the wealthy for the less well-to-do implies that they are not celebrating the *Lord's* Supper at all, merely "their *own* supper" (v. 21).

Instead of sharing in a kind of potluck and ensuring that all get plenty to eat and drink, some gorge themselves and get drunk at the expense of those who come later or have less. Jude 12 seems to reflect and address a similar problem, and it uses the popular early Christian term "love feasts" for these communal meals. They would have probably culminated in the Lord's Supper, based on Jesus's model from the final Passover festival he celebrated with his disciples (Matt 26:26–29; Mark 14:22–25; Luke 22:14–20). Paul doesn't object to the well-to-do enjoying a reasonable quantity or quality of food in the privacy of their own families (v. 22a). But in this church setting, their satiating themselves at the expense of the have-nots proves singularly inappropriate (vv. 22b).

The account of Jesus's Last Supper stands in striking contrast to the report of the Corinthians' behavior. Verses 23b–26 run closely parallel to the passages noted above in the Synoptic Gospels, especially to Luke's version (Luke 22:17–20). When Paul says he received this information from the Lord, he is referring to that which the Lord Jesus spoke while he was alive, words widely repeated and perhaps even memorized in the early Christian community. The focus of those reflections centers on Jesus's so-called "words of institution" about the significance of the bread and the wine (1 Cor 11:24–26). During the Passover, Jews ate unleavened bread to recall their hasty departure from Egypt when God rescued them from the hands of Pharaoh (Exod 12). The head of the household would open the meal in prayer and then distribute pieces of the bread broken from a common loaf (recall 1 Cor 10:17). This historical setting makes any literal rendering of "is" in Jesus's statement "this is my body" incoherent (11:24). No one sitting with Christ at table would have thought he was saying that the bread was somehow a literal extension of his flesh or spirit. Rather the bread *symbolized* or *represented* his coming bodily death, an atoning sacrifice for the sake of all who would accept the forgiveness of sins it made available. The last line of verse 24 (and v. 25) is probably best translated, "Do this as my memorial."

The cup that was drunk after supper would probably have been the third of four cups of wine consumed during the Passover meal, again with redemptive implications. This was the point in the ceremony at which the words "I will redeem you" from Exodus 6:6 were read. The reason Paul, like the Gospel writers, calls it the "cup" rather than using the word *wine* is because the expression would evoke Old Testament associations of suffering the "cup" of God's wrath (e.g., Ps 75:8; Isa 51:17). The message about the significance of Christ's death that this ceremony re-enacts should be proclaimed throughout church history. Only when the Lord returns (v. 26) will cross-centered Christianity become redundant, a fact that the Corinthians clearly had yet to learn.

In verses 27–34 Paul draws out the implications for the Corinthians of his appeal to tradition. Jesus's self-giving love for them makes their behavior (as described in verse 21) that much more shameful. "In an unworthy manner" in verse 27a translates the Greek adverb *anaxiōs* ("unworthily"). Paul does not use the adjective "unworthy," which would have referred to a person's character, but highlights instead the nature of their *actions*. "The body and blood of the Lord" in verse 27b again refer to Jesus's crucifixion and its significance. "Examine" (v. 28) means "test and find approved." If their behavior toward their fellow Christians is appropriate, then they qualify to participate themselves.

Verse 29 seems to reflect the same problem described in verse 27 (eating unworthily), which in turn looked back to verse 21 (overeating and overdrinking). Verse 30 unpacks what was involved in God's punishing the Corinthians for their profaning his holy table. "Sleep" was a common euphemism for death. The way to avoid such tragedy is to monitor one's own behavior (v. 31). Paul ends on a somewhat upbeat note by reminding his readers that God disciplines those he loves to protect them from further damaging themselves or others (v. 32). Verses 33–34 bring this chapter to a close by restating and summarizing Paul's solution to the Corinthians' unholy activity during the Lord's Supper.

Application. Debates still rage as to whether the Lord's Supper should be called an ordinance or a sacrament. The latter historically has suggested the unbiblical notion of a quasi-mechanical "means of grace." The former seems to limit the ritual to an act of obedience to Christ. Our culture is one of the few in the history of the world that has lost respect for the immense value of tradition, ritual, symbolism, and religious drama. Not surprisingly, evangelical liturgical churches thus prove very appealing to many who are more and more frustrated with this loss. Some evangelicals, unable to find such churches within their own traditions, have increasingly turned to Anglicanism, Catholicism, and even Greek Orthodoxy to recover those emphases. What we need are balances between liturgy and spontaneity in the Eucharist and in worship more generally. We also need balances between planned sameness to stress our link with the past and opportunities for creativity to keep services fresh and meaningful for different subcultures within our society.

1 CORINTHIANS 12:1–31A

Original Meaning. "Gifts of the Spirit" in verse 1 is either the neuter or masculine gender of the adjective *spiritual* and so could also be translated "spiritual things" or "spiritual people." In 14:1 it is definitely neuter, but "things" may include "people." The term probably reflects the prideful way the Corinthian leaders referred to themselves. So too Paul picks up on their claims to knowledge and with a tinge of irony fears that he actually needs to dispel their "ignorance" (recall 10:1).

Part of their problem is that they have not made a radical enough break from their pagan backgrounds. Some of them had doubtless spoken seemingly inspired utterances during various Greco-Roman religious rituals (v. 2). But in those settings, participants who had heard of Christ's claims might well have cursed him (v. 3a). Conversely, only Christians—those indwelt by the Spirit—can acknowledge Jesus as Lord (v. 3b). Here is the fundamental early Christian confession of faith, flying both in the face of pagan affirmations of some other deity and in the face of Jewish insistence that Yahweh alone merited the title.

Verses 4–6 continue with three closely parallel statements. Paul elucidates spiritual gifts from three different angles: they are bestowed freely by the Spirit's grace (v. 4), are intended to be used in a Christlike attitude of servanthood (v. 5), and are the result of God's powerful working in a person's life (v. 6). Verse 7 employs yet a fourth term, "manifestation," and stresses that all the Corinthian Christians have at least one such gift, which is to be used for mutual edification.

Verses 8–10 divide into three sections: wisdom and knowledge (v. 8); faith, healings, miracles, prophecy, and distinguishing spirits (vv. 9–10a); and tongues and their interpretations (v. 10b). All nine represent the more miraculous gifts. Paul repeatedly states that they all come from the same Spirit. And because it is the Holy Spirit, and not individual merit, who determines who gets what gifts (v. 11), they cannot be used to mark out anyone for special status within the church in Corinth.

A "message" (literally "word") of wisdom or knowledge (v. 8) reflects the ability to bring spiritual insight to bear in a timely, helpful fashion in a specific Christian context. If Paul intends any difference between the word of wisdom and the word of knowledge, it may be that wisdom is knowledge applied, particularly in moral contexts. "Faith" in verse 9 is not the trust in Christ that all persons must have in order to be saved, but a special measure of faith that God can work miracles. "Gifts of healing" refer to supernatural cures of physical maladies. The plurals suggest either that the gift may come and go for various occasions or, perhaps more likely, that there are different gifts for different kinds of illnesses. "Miraculous powers" (v. 10) include additional kinds of miracles, such as the apostles and other early Christians were enabled to perform, including, most notably, exorcisms.

New Testament prophecy builds on the background of prophetic activity in both the Old Testament and Greco-Roman religions, while differing in crucial ways from each. Both inside and outside of the canon, prophecy consistently included both "foretelling" (predicting future events) and, more predominantly, "forthtelling" (exhorting God's people, and occasionally his enemies, about his will for their present circumstances). It shares the common feature of a sense of declaring a message one believes one has received relatively directly from God (cf. 14:30). New Testament prophecy therefore included both conventional preaching, when the preacher had the sense of being gripped and convicted by the Spirit about his or her message, and more spontaneous, unpremeditated utterances. Prophecy is not on a par with Scripture, and their exercise of the gift, like that of all other spiritual gifts, is subject to error and misinterpretation (cf. esp. Acts 21:4 with vv. 11, 13–14).

"Distinguishing between spirits" (v. 10) probably refers to the God-given ability to discern if an apparently inspired speaker is ministering by the power of the Holy Spirit or by some counterfeit power. It cannot be the same as evaluating the contents of an alleged prophecy, since 14:29 assigns that responsibility either to other prophets or to the entire congregation.

"Speaking in different kinds of tongues" (v. 10) must not be confused with what happened to the disciples at Pentecost. There the audience understood what was being proclaimed without benefit of an interpreter (Acts 2:1–13); here an interpretation is required. It is best to understand the Corinthian experience as involving some kind of initially unintelligible verbal utterance. "Interpreting" tongues then refers to putting the otherwise unintelligible message into words that are understood by those present (v. 10).

In verses 12–26, Paul develops the extended metaphor of the church as the body of Christ. Verses 13–14 give a twofold rationale for permitting diversity within unity: those who are being saved come from all ethnic and socioeconomic brackets of the ancient world, and that is how a human body works. Spirit-baptism is not identical to water baptism but occurs at the moment of conversion. However, Paul probably associated the concepts closely together, inasmuch as water baptism in the early church regularly followed quickly on the heels of belief.

Verses 15–20 underline what is demonstrable with respect to a human body: all the parts serve an important function, regardless of any claims to the contrary. Without the diversity that comes from specialization of function, one no longer has an organism but merely one giant organ, unable to do anything.

Verses 21–26 continue the analogy but begin to apply it to the church. Where there is seemingly less value, power, or honor in the body, compensation occurs to preserve relative equality. In fact, the true value of a particular body part is often inversely proportional to its outward appearance. Paul's fundamental concern is that the gifts and/or people the Corinthians are demeaning should be affirmed, while those they are overly exalting should be put in more balanced perspective. Presumably he has in mind the more visible and dramatic gifts, but he may also be thinking of the more wealthy power brokers in the church.

Verses 27–31 complete this chapter with one final restatement of the body metaphor and another listing of sample gifts. But this time Paul's main point is that not one of the gifts is intended for all believers. The rhetorical questions in verses 29–30 all employ the Greek word *mē*, which demonstrates that the implied answer to each question is "no."

This list includes some of the same and some different gifts as in verses 8–10. "Apostles" (v. 28) in Paul's usage include not merely the Twelve but himself (1:1), other "brothers" (2 Cor 8:23; NIV "representatives"), Epaphroditus (Phil 2:25; NIV "messenger"), James, the Lord's brother (Gal 1:19), and Andronicus and Junia (Rom 16:7), the latter probably a woman's name. Clearly Paul is using the term in its root sense of those sent out on a mission, in this case a divinely commissioned one. Christians would later come to call such people missionaries or church planters. "Teachers" (v. 28) in the ancient world limited themselves largely to the communication of a fixed body of information to their students, often solely by rote memory work. To take "first," "second," and "third" in verse 28 as a ranking in significance would clearly violate the whole point of Paul's discussion thus far. So it is best to see in this enumeration a chronological priority (cf. Eph 2:20).

Application. In an age of increasing specialization in careers and knowledge more generally, it becomes all the more crucial for Christians to view spiritual gifts as broadly as possible. We ought to encourage believers to consider as spiritual gifts many kinds of abilities dedicated to the Lord's work. Surely music fits this category (cf. Eph 5:18–19), and probably trade skills do as well (cf. Exod 31:1–5). Doubtless many others could be added to the list. Specialization deserves its place within pastoral staffs, as the megachurches are increasingly recognizing. Instead of dividing up the labor merely into preaching, Christian education, youth, music, and evangelism, one may consider also administrative pastors, computer programmers, and even spiritual planning directors who help to identify individuals' gifts and mobilize them for service.

In all of this, however, we must beware of continuing to play down the significance of the behind-the-scenes people. Ours is an age that delights to exalt Christian celebrities, to demand that our pastors entertain, have charismatic personalities, and display more spiritual gifts than any one Bible character ever had! Little wonder that burnout from full-time ministry seems to be at an all-time high and that moral failure often results from the stress. We need to relearn the model of servant leadership (recall under 1 Cor 4) and to allow our leaders and ourselves to spend the majority of time doing those things at which we excel.

1 CORINTHIANS 12:31B–13:13

Original Meaning. More important than all the gifts is love (12:31b). First Corinthians 13:1–3 makes the point that without love the gifts are worthless. Verses 1–3 drive home the same truth repeatedly by using five of the spiritual gifts as illustrations of the identical principle: without love the most exemplary use of a particular gift profits a believer nothing.

In verse 2, Paul uses the example of gifts of spiritual insight and of a faith to work miracles. Here he may be echoing the tradition of Jesus's own words in Matthew 21:21, although the expression was proverbial for trusting God to perform great deeds. Verse 3 hammers home the point one more time with the most extreme example yet—seemingly total self-abandonment in exercising the gift of giving.

The NIV's translations of the various terms in verses 4–7 are generally quite good and self-explanatory. Taken together, verses 4–7 clearly portray love as selfless, seeking the good of the other first and foremost.

Verse 8 states the thesis of verses 8–13. Again Paul makes the point with sample gifts that were of particular importance in Corinth. Whereas faith, hope, and love endure, spiritual gifts prove less permanent. The NIV renders the same verb *katargeō* ("to destroy or abolish") four different ways in verses 8–11, but each of these captures an important nuance of the term.

Why will the gifts cease? It is because they are imperfect provisions for an imperfect world, rendered unnecessary when perfection comes (vv. 9–10). But to what does "completeness" refer (v. 10)? Nothing in Paul supports any consciousness of his writing near the end of an apostolic age or the close of a biblical canon. And the metaphors in verse 12 fit poorly with such interpretations. After the Bible was completed, Christians did not see God "face to face" (only "face to book"!) or know him to the degree that he knew them. When we recall that 1:7 pointed out the ongoing role of the gifts until the return of Christ, there can be only one possible interpretation of "completeness"—it is the life in the world to come after Jesus reappears on earth.

But love abides on into eternity. So too probably do faith and hope (v. 13a), if faith is taken as belief in Jesus and faithful service to him, and if hope refers to the expectant anticipation of the good things God has in the future for his people. Paul adds these other two virtues because the triad of faith, hope, and love is a favorite of his (cf. Eph 1:15–18; Col 1:4–5; 1 Thess 1:3; 5:8). But love remains the greatest (v. 13b) because it is the most foundational, essential, and central to Paul's understanding of the Christian ethic.

Application. The need for genuine, Christlike love remains as great today as ever. Yet one of our greatest problems is defining love. Popular culture—in literature, music, advertising, and the visual arts—uses the word to mean just about everything *except* what the Bible means by it. So even Christians are easily misled into thinking love is primarily a feeling, something you fall in or out of. We equate it with lust or sexual intercourse itself, speaking of one's "lover" (unless one is properly married, when the term actually *would* be appropriate) or of "making love." But in this chapter, as throughout Scripture, love is first of all an action, an unconditional commitment, a promise that is never broken.

In an age in which demanding one's rights is considered a virtue, we must read again and again that love "is not self-seeking" (v. 5). At the same time, when we understand love's limits, we will avoid codependency. The most loving thing to do for the repeatedly abusive, perennially alcoholic husband is not to cover up for him or to believe his empty promises of reform, but to insist that he seek professional help and to refuse to carry on with business as usual if he does not.

1 CORINTHIANS 14:1–25

Original Meaning. In chapter 14 Paul climaxes his discussion of spiritual gifts by encouraging the Corinthians to prefer prophecy to tongues. Verse 1 resumes the thread of 12:31, picking up the two themes of that verse (love and desiring the greater gifts) in reverse order. Paul now specifies one of those "greater" gifts, namely, prophecy. Verse 2 makes it reasonably certain that the misuse of tongues was one of the Corinthians' major problems in the exercise of their spiritual gifts during worship. Apparently they were manifesting glossolalia without interpretation. Verse 5b demonstrates that all of verses 2–5a must be understood as Paul's criticisms of tongues *when they are not interpreted*. When they *are* interpreted, they, like prophecy, contain a fundamentally instructional and exhortational component (vv. 3, 4b, 5b).

Unlike uninterpreted tongues, prophecy edifies the whole assembly, not just the individual speaker (vv. 3–4). Paul thus isolates two reasons why prophecy is greater: people, not just God, are addressed, and they can be more positively affected. Verse 5 does not contradict 12:30. Paul is not clandestinely commanding all the Corinthians to seek tongues, merely admitting that it would be nice if all could speak in them.

Verse 6 presents the thesis of the next paragraph (vv. 6–12), repeating the need for intelligibility. Verses 7–11 then give three illustrations of this principle. In order to be understood or appreciated, musical instruments must play a discernible melody (v. 7). Trumpet calls to battle must be clear enough for soldiers to distinguish "advance!" from "retreat!" (v. 8). And foreign languages remain unintelligible to those who have not learned them (vv. 9–11). Verse 12 concludes by repeating the point with which the first paragraph of this chapter ended (v. 5).

So what must a person do if God *has* given him or her the gift of tongues? Verses 13–19 address this question. The tongues speaker should pray for the ability to interpret his or her tongue. Verses 14–15 show that receiving the gift of interpretation benefits oneself first of all. Praying with one's spirit versus praying with one's mind (v. 15a) is probably equivalent to the distinction in verses 13–14 of speaking in tongues versus interpretation.

In verses 16–17, Paul turns to the effect on others present. Again, interpretation is crucial if the rest of the congregation is to be able to agree. "Amen" (v. 16) is a Hebrew interjection roughly equivalent to "this is most certainly true." "Inquirer" (v. 16) translates one Greek word that refers to someone who is not an expert or not initiated into a given sphere of activity. Even mature Christians play the role of the uninitiated when they hear uninterpreted tongues. They have no idea what the message means.

Verses 18–19 probably surprised Paul's original readers, who may even have been criticizing him for not using glossolalia. If Paul refrains almost entirely from its public exercise, these verses surely substantiate his extensive private use of tongues as a "prayer language."

Verse 20 forms the transition to the last paragraph of this first section of chapter 14. A preoccupation with tongues without concern for their effect on oneself and others is childish. There are ways Christians should be childlike (cf. Matt 10:16) but not in their use of spiritual gifts.

Verses 21–25 proceed further to justify Paul's appeal to prefer prophecy to tongues. Paul begins by citing parts of Isaiah 28:11–12 in verse 21, a passage in which God pronounces judgment against rebellious Israel at the hands of the foreign empire of Assyria. The verses that bracket this quotation in Isaiah use Hebrew syllables that resemble nonsense sounds. So Paul may have been inspired by that context to apply Isaiah's prophecy to the similar impression that glossolalia created.

To make any sense of verse 22, the sign to which Paul refers must again be a sign *of judgment*. Verse 23 thus explains verse 22a: tongues are a sign of judgment for unbelievers. Like the unbelieving Israelites, non-Christians in Corinth will remain lost in their sins because they will reject the gospel as the product of insane babblers.

Verses 24–25 go on to elucidate verse 22b. Prophecy is a sign of judgment for believers in the positive sense that it creates Christians by convicting unbelievers of their sins and bringing them to repentance (v. 25b echoes Isa 45:14). Verses 24–25 do not guarantee that all who hear prophecy rather than tongues will be saved. They simply stress that an intelligible proclamation of the gospel stands a far better chance of convicting unsaved people and regenerating their hearts.

Application. The value in both charismatic and noncharismatic circles of a clear proclamation of God's word over and above more unusual phenomena like tongues remains indisputable. In Paul's world, the more exotic phenomena at least reminded people of analogous practices in other religions so that they were not entirely foreign. In our modern day, however, many unbelievers seeing glossolalia for the first time will be all the more convinced that Christians are "out of their mind" (v. 23). Indeed, the excesses of the charismatic movement, especially through televangelism, are one of the major reasons all conservative Christian faith has been caricatured, stereotyped, and rejected as weird and out of touch with reality by many contemporary Westerners, especially in the media.

A much more positive use of tongues continues to appear in Christians discovering a private prayer language. Testimony after testimony describes how the Spirit intervened to liberate some frustrated individual from his or her fruitless quiet time, lifeless worship, or inconsistent walk with the Lord. Indeed, the winds of the charismatic movement seem to have blown freshest and most purely in the middle of dead, formal, traditional churches, where it has given to congregations such "radical" ideas, by no means distinctively charismatic, as singing choruses, using musical instruments besides piano or organ, clapping or raising hands, sharing praise items and prayer requests, and conversational prayer.

1 CORINTHIANS 14:26–40

Original Meaning. If intelligibility is a priority for the gathered community, how then should worship proceed? Verses 26–40 answer this question. Verse 26 insists that the Corinthians continue to worship in highly participatory and spontaneous fashion. This does not mean that every person present exercises all of the gifts, nor even that all exercise at least one in every service. But opportunity is made available for all whom the Spirit leads on any given occasion to contribute.

Once again Paul stresses the need for everything to be done so as to build up fellow believers. It is just possible that the shift in focus from evangelizing non-Christians in verses 22–25 to edifying believers in verse 26, together with the more informal and highly participatory model of verse 26, indicates that this is the pattern for the regular small home-fellowship gatherings, whereas the earlier verses reflect periodic larger, more public assemblies of multiple house churches.

Verses 27–32 again narrow the focus to the two key gifts of tongues and prophecy. In closely parallel fashion, verses 27–28 and 29–32 temper the spontaneity described in verse 26 by regulating the exercise of these two particular gifts.

The "others" of verse 29 are more naturally taken to refer to the rest of the congregation, not merely the other prophets. If "weigh carefully" meant exercising the gift of discernment (12:10), then there would be clearly no guarantee that those who had the gift of prophecy necessarily had the gift of discernment too. But even if, as we have suggested, exercising the gift of discernment is not what Paul means by carefully weighing prophecy, it is still unlikely that the prophets were the best persons to evaluate each other's messages.

Verse 30 parallels verse 27 in insisting that prophets, like tongues speakers, exercise their gifts in turn. Verse 31 parallels verse 5 in illustrating Paul's desire that all might exercise these gifts, without implying that all can or will. Verse 32 proves that Christian prophecy is not "ecstatic" in the technical sense of that term. In other words, believers in the process of exercising their spiritual gifts are never so out of control as to be unable to stop or regulate their behavior. Verse 33a concludes the unit of thought begun in verse 26 by giving the rationale for the regulations of tongues and prophecy just stipulated: orderliness and peace.

Verses 34–35 seem quite intrusive at this juncture. Why does Paul seemingly interrupt his discussion of these two spiritual gifts in order to silence women? Perhaps the best perspective is to take Paul's commands as prohibiting women from participating in the final church decisions about the legitimacy of any given prophecy. To begin with, "speak," in twenty of the twenty-one appearances of this verb in this chapter outside of verses 34–35, refers either directly or by analogy to one of four very particular kinds of speech: tongues, their interpretation, prophecy, or its evaluation. But the first three of these are spiritual gifts, distributed regardless of gender. An authoritative evaluation of prophecy, however, while requiring input from the whole congregation, would ultimately have been the responsibility of the church leadership (what Paul elsewhere calls elders or overseers), who, at least in the first century, seem to have been exclusively male. This interpretation also explains why these verses come where they do. The sequence of topics from verses 27–33 has been precisely: tongues, their interpretation, prophecy, and its evaluation, in that order. The obvious drawback of this approach is that it must infer a meaning for "speaking" that Paul never spells out. But that problem afflicts all of the views that take Paul's words as less than absolute at this point, and this view seems to have the least number of additional difficulties.

As in 11:2–16, the women whom Paul silences may be only wives. This would explain why they must not publicly challenge the church's prophecies but consult at home (v. 35). To do otherwise might be to challenge their husbands in church in ways that would contradict their God-ordained submission to them (v. 34). The "law" probably alludes to the order and purpose of creation in Genesis 2, as in 1 Corinthians 11:8–9 with respect to women's honoring their heads.

Verses 36–38 thus challenge the Corinthians not to reject Paul's counsel lightly. If every other Christian church practiced what Paul preached on this matter, who are they to be the sole exceptions (v. 36)? Those who contested Paul's teaching undoubtedly justified their rebellion by claiming the Spirit's direction (v. 37a). So Paul adds that if they are truly Spirit-led they will come to acknowledge his views as from the Lord (v. 37b). If they continue to go their own way, they demonstrate that they are out of touch with the Spirit, and the Lord will continue to ignore them and to accomplish his work without them (v. 38).

Finally, verses 39–40 bring all three chapters (12–14), but especially this last one, to a fitting conclusion, as they balance Paul's twin concerns for freedom and structure. Every gift has its place, but each must be used to build up the church in unity and love.

Application. Comparing 1 Corinthians 14:1–33a with contemporary Christian practice suggests two sweeping generalizations to which there are many exceptions. First, large segments of charismatic Christianity so dwell on alleged words of the Lord, under various labels, that are so trite, repetitive, and predictable in nature that one cannot help but suspect that most of them come from human manufacture. God is not in the business of using miraculous means consistently to call attention to the obvious or ordinary. Probably a few people in each of these circles experienced the genuine gift, others wanted or were encouraged to get on the bandwagon, and so they have imitated the genuine gifts in their own strength. Second, large segments of noncharismatic Christianity are so enslaved to traditional patterns of worship that the Spirit could not break through without substantial disruption. A considerable majority of the church members are convinced that their gifts don't count. Not surprisingly, they remain relatively uninvolved. Both groups typically re-create worship after the models of their immediate spiritual predecessors rather than genuinely seeking to overhaul their worship and bring it into conformity with 1 Corinthians 14.

We desperately need to allow one another the freedom to agree to disagree, to set up alternate models, and to encourage local fellowships to determine for themselves, according to their best understanding of Scripture. Verses 39–40 end with strikingly plain words that are nevertheless disobeyed by large sections of the contemporary church. Many noncharismatics flatly forbid tongues, while many charismatics seldom come close to worshiping decently and in order.

On the other hand, if a majority of Christians obeyed Paul's commands, most of the divisiveness of the charismatic phenomena could be prevented and Paul's dominant concern for the mutual strengthening of believers enhanced. In some circles, the best illustration of the balance Paul commands appears in the charismatic renewal movement within liturgical churches. But where they may achieve an exemplary combination of structure and freedom, other problems sometimes intrude, not least of which is the danger of authoritarian charismatic leaders compounding their heavy-handedness with the weight of an elaborate denominational hierarchy above them. A combination of true congregational governance, with a balance between spontaneity and structure in worship, would seem to reflect Paul's ideal. But such churches remain few and far between.

1 CORINTHIANS 15:1–34

Original Meaning. Chapter 15 falls into two main sections. Verses 1–34 present Paul's arguments for the certainty of the bodily resurrection, while verses 35–58 discuss the nature of resurrection bodies. Paul begins by "reminding" the Corinthians what they should have remembered (v. 1). With a twinge of irony, he actually says "I make known to you," using their favorite language about knowledge, as if they had never heard of this central doctrine before (v. 1). But this was what they believed when they first became Christians, and only by continuing to believe in a bodily resurrected Jesus can they demonstrate the reality of their faith and persevere until the end (v. 2).

In verses 3–7 Paul repeats the foundational tradition that he had first taught the Corinthians. "That Christ died" (v. 3) refutes those docetists who believed that Christ only seemed to be human (because they also believed that matter was inherently evil). That it was "for our sins" points to a vicarious atonement—paying the penalty we deserved to pay on our behalf. "According to the Scriptures" probably has in mind passages such as those in Isaiah 52–53 that speak of God's suffering servant. Jesus's burial (v. 4) again certifies that he really died and also points forward to the empty tomb and the reality of the resurrection. It is less clear which Scriptures point to the resurrection on the third day. Perhaps Paul meant only that the Scriptures testified to Christ's resurrection, with passages like Psalms 16:8–11 and 110:1–4 in view (cf. Acts 2:24–36).

Verses 5–7 proceed to supply a list of key witnesses to certify the truth of Jesus's resurrection. No other reference to an appearance to five hundred (v. 6) is found in Scripture, but that many of these people were still alive to be interviewed provided strong corroboration of Paul's claims. Neither is the appearance to James (v. 7, referring to the Lord's brother) described elsewhere, but it probably caused his conversion (contrast his attitude to Jesus in John 7:5).

After his ascension, which signaled the end of the resurrection appearances, no one expected to see Jesus in this way again. So Paul's "private viewing" here (v. 8; cf. Acts 9:1–31) came as a shock. "One abnormally born" (v. 8) translates the Greek word for "miscarriage." But of course a miscarriage is a premature birth; here Jesus's resurrection appearance to Paul was unusually late. Hence the NIV takes the point of the comparison to be something that was simply abnormal. But it may be that Paul had in mind that when Christ appeared to him, God's purposes for his life were so far unfulfilled.

In verses 9–11, Paul acknowledges his inferiority as an apostle because he had persecuted the first Christians (v. 9). But he turns this admission of weakness into an opportunity to magnify God's grace. And that grace did not lead to sloth but to greater effort and substantial accomplishment (v. 10). Yet lest his remarks be seen as prideful or competitive, he closes this paragraph by stressing that all the apostles agree on the message of the resurrection and that this belief is what initially led to the Corinthians' salvation as well (v. 11).

Verses 12–19 and 29–34 both argue for the absurdity of Christian belief and practice if the bodily resurrection is not true. In between, verses 20–28 gloriously reaffirm that it *is* true and point to some of the consequences of this grand doctrine. The main point of verses 12–19 is that if there is no coming bodily resurrection of all Christians, then Jesus himself was not bodily raised, and that makes the Christian faith futile.

But wonderfully none of this is true, Paul retorts. Christ *has* been raised bodily and has thus set into motion an inexorable chain of events that will culminate in the universal demonstration of the absolute sovereignty of God (vv. 20–28). Verses 20–22 describe how Christ's bodily resurrection guarantees the future bodily resurrection of all believers, just as the "firstfruits" of a harvest (v. 20) heralded a much larger crop to follow (cf. Lev 23:9–14). Paul points out the parallel between Adam's sin leading to the sinfulness of all humanity and Christ's resurrection leading to the resurrection of all his followers (vv. 21–22). Because Adam represented the entire human race that would descend from him, sin spread throughout the whole world. Because Christ, as fully human, represented the entire human race in bearing its sins, he is able to apply the benefits of his death and resurrection to all who will accept them. "All" in the statement "all die" (v. 22a) means "all who are related to Adam." "All" in the declaration "all will be made alive" (v. 22b) refers to "all who are related to Christ," as verse 23 makes clear ("those who belong to him").

But the general resurrection of believers at the time of Christ's return is just the beginning (v. 23). Verses 24–28 go on to explain what will subsequently occur. After some unspecified interval of time, "the end" or goal of human history will arrive (v. 24). By this time, Christ will have destroyed all opposition to his reign in the universe—both human and angelic (i.e., demonic, vv. 24–25). Finally, death itself will be destroyed, so that God's people will never again have anything to fear for all eternity (v. 26). But the last word is not Christ's but God's (vv. 27–28).

The "he" in verse 27a refers to God; the "his" to Christ, as verse 27b clarifies. As a representative of humanity and as the one doing what humans were supposed to have done but failed to do (i.e., exercise dominion over the cosmos, Gen 1:28), Jesus remains ultimately subordinate to God. Compare Psalm 8:5, in which humanity, including Jesus in his incarnation (Heb 2:9), was made "a little lower than the angels." Here Paul quotes Psalm 8:6 to stress Christ's corresponding conquests as well. Although God the Son is *essentially* equal to the Father, he remains *functionally* subordinate, just as his glorified humanity keeps him distinct from what he was prior to the incarnation.

In verses 29–34 Paul goes back to arguing the absurdity of denying the bodily resurrection. Here he uses three ad hominem and ad hoc arguments based on what he and the Corinthians were experiencing (note the references to "they" [NIV "those" and "people"] in v. 29, "us," "we," and "I" in vv. 30–32, and "you" as the implied subject of the commands in vv. 33–34).

The most puzzling of these is the first. Despite all sorts of ingenious alternatives that have been suggested, the plain meaning of verse 29 remains that of some sort of proxy baptism. Paul neither condemns nor condones such a practice but argues for its irrelevance if Christ is not raised. In other words, those who are baptizing people on behalf of the dead contradict their own theology that denies the resurrection.

In verses 30–32 Paul turns to a parallel pair of arguments from his own experience. Why should he continue to tolerate hostility from others and risk his life for the sake of the gospel if there is no hope of resurrection? Verse 32 is almost certainly not to be taken literally. Roman citizens were exempt from being thrown to animals in the gladiator's ring, and Paul would not have easily survived such an encounter. Paul may be alluding to some otherwise unknown personal attack or persecution that threatened his life (cf. 2 Cor 1:8–11).

Verse 32b reflects the flip side of the logic of verse 19. If this life is all there is, then people ought to live it up, as the Epicureans did. Paul cites their most famous slogan, as the prophet Isaiah and the author of Ecclesiastes had done centuries earlier (Isa 22:13; Eccl 2:24). But he immediately proceeds to reject such logic, since Christ has in fact been raised. Instead, he quotes another popular Greek proverb, this one first attributed to the fourth-century BC comic playwright Menander. Those who deny the resurrection make for "bad company" (v. 33), and their dualistic presuppositions ("matter doesn't matter") foster immoral behavior. Paul appeals to the Corinthians to reject this route (v. 34) by again chiding them for their lack of true knowledge and by trying to shame them into repentance (cf. 6:5).

Application. Denying the reality of the resurrection remains a central problem in contemporary culture. Atheism usually rejects the possibility of the existence of all supernatural powers, often claiming support in the "findings" of modern science. But with revolutions in modern physics associated with Einstein and Heisenberg, scientists who understand their discipline are often more reluctant to rule out God and the supernatural on scientific grounds than are students of the humanities and even of world religions! Historians usually recognize the absurdity of most of the proposed alternatives to the resurrection—the swoon theory, the stolen-body or wrong-tomb theories, mass hallucination, and so on, though that does not stop more popular writers from continuing to perpetuate such nonsense.

Christ's death and resurrection in space and time, as bona fide historical events, actually set the Christian faith apart from all its major rivals. Later Western religions that developed in part in reaction to Christianity do not claim deity or resurrections for their originators, merely prophetic status (e.g., Mohammed in Islam or Joseph Smith in Mormonism). Older Eastern religions do not even require the actual historical existence of their founders for their beliefs and practices to make sense. In some ways they are more akin to philosophies than to historical truth claims (e.g., Hinduism, Buddhism, Confucianism). But the Christian faith lives or dies with the claim of Christ's resurrection. To be sure, it is possible to believe in Jesus's resurrection and not become a Christian, but without the bodily resurrection the Christian faith crumbles. Finding the bones of Jesus would assuredly disprove our faith. But Christians must recognize the historical evidence that is on their side.

1 CORINTHIANS 15:35–58

Original Meaning. Verses 35–58 respond to the potential objection that verse 35 notes. "How are the dead raised?" was probably not so much a genuine question but a way of mocking the whole notion of bodily resurrection. Paul's reply again falls into three parts. Verses 36–44a provide analogies from the created world to describe the resurrection body.

The first analogy Paul uses to illustrate the resurrection body is that of seed and plant. By being buried in the ground, the seed seemingly dies, and it certainly decomposes. Yet on that very spot new life emerges, totally different in appearance from the seed, and yet somehow the mature plant remains the same living entity (vv. 36–38). In fact, the world is filled with different kinds of bodies (v. 39) that God has created. So why should it be thought incredible that he could create still one more kind—a resurrected human body? So too the heavenly bodies—sun, moon, and stars—differ in nature and brilliance (v. 41). And an even greater gap exists between the earthly bodies, which all have certain identifiable features in common, and the heavenly bodies, which also resemble each other in certain aspects (v. 40).

Verses 42–44a make clear where Paul is going with all of these analogies. There yet await for the Corinthians resurrection bodies that will be far more glorious than their present ones. Unlike their current bodies, these new ones will be fitted for eternity, never again to die or be limited by sin or impotence (vv. 42–43). Whereas humans in this world are animated by merely physical life, believers will one day be fully empowered by the Spirit (v. 44a).

Verses 44b–49 pick up on widespread ancient speculation in both Jewish and Greek circles that there were two primal human beings, an earthly one and a heavenly one. Paul agrees that there are two progenitors of humanity (v. 44b). But he makes Jesus the perfect "Adam" (using the Hebrew play on words in which Adam means "man") and stresses that he came *after* the first Adam (i.e., in Christ's incarnation), not before (vv. 46–47). So too believers who have shared in the finite, fallen likeness of the first Adam can look forward to sharing in the kind of perfect humanity Jesus embodied, but only after this life, when Jesus comes back again (vv. 48–49).

Verses 50–57 further unpack the need for bodily transformation. Frail, mortal humanity cannot survive in God's eternal and perfectly holy presence. Verse 51 supplies more information about the time at which this transformation will take place. The secret that Paul is revealing here is that believers' bodily resurrections will occur when Christ returns. Not all Christians will die first since some will be alive when he comes back. But all will undergo whatever transformation is necessary to give them their glorified bodies. This change will take place instantaneously, not gradually. The trumpet (v. 52a) was a stock metaphor in biblical literature to herald the end.

The climax of this series of events for believers is the destruction of death itself, as Isaiah had predicted (v. 54b, quoting Isa 25:8). Paul breaks out into a rhapsody at the thought of this marvelous prospect, quoting and slightly adapting Hosea 13:14 (v. 55). And, as in Romans 6–8, he recalls that sin is the primary culprit that has led to both physical and spiritual death, while the Mosaic law, apart from pointing people to Christ, serves only to promote sin, as it increases conscious rebellion against God's standards (v. 56; cf. Gal 3:19–24). But praise God that this deadly sequence has been interrupted by the victory over death that God has wrought through the death and resurrection of Jesus (v. 57)!

Appropriately, Paul returns from these lofty flights of theological reflection to the practical implications for the Corinthians (v. 58). Since Christ has been raised bodily, they too will one day be physically transformed. Therefore, they should remain unswervingly committed to orthodox theology and totally dedicated to the work of the gospel—the purity of living and the faithful exercise of their distinctive avenues of service. No matter what the cost in this life, they can count on the ultimate triumph of all God's people and all his purposes.

Application. The ultimate vanquishing of death with which 1 Corinthians 15 culminates surely speaks volumes to those who continue to live in fear of death today. It is not just Sartre who has raised the specter of suicide as the only serious question for humans to debate. Existential and ecological fears pervade much of the non-Christian world. Christians ought to fear less. They may grieve the loss of loved ones and have a certain anxiety related to the unknown factors surrounding their own death, but neither reaction ought to be "like the rest of mankind, who have no hope" (1 Thess 4:13). Funerals for Christians ought to be first of all celebrations of their "homegoing." While preserving a culturally appropriate solemnity, a spirit of joy and a message of hope should nevertheless pervade such ceremonies, which may even include a tasteful evangelistic address to unbelievers present. And the hope of resurrection should encourage those of us who remain alive to persevere in obedience over the long haul (v. 58).

1 CORINTHIANS 16:1–4

Original Meaning. Paul proceeds to the final topic of the body of his letter. The collection to which Paul refers here in verse 1 formed a major enterprise of his third missionary journey. Significant numbers of Jewish Christians in Jerusalem were impoverished (v. 3), and Paul spent substantial energy raising funds from various gentile churches to help meet their needs

(Acts 20:4). But in addition to alleviating physical suffering, Paul undoubtedly saw the collection as an opportunity to bring greater unity within the church across Jewish and gentile boundaries, to pay off a spiritual debt of sorts that the gentile congregations owed their mother church in Jerusalem (Rom 15:27), and to demonstrate the genuineness of gentile Christianity to skeptical Jewish Christians (cf. Acts 24:17). In addition, the offering would be a testimony to the unsaved world and to Christians everywhere of the faith and love of those who participated. More people might well be won to Christ, and others would grow in their faith and give an outpouring of thanks to God (2 Cor 9:12–15).

The Corinthians had themselves taken the initiative to contribute generously and had inspired other churches to imitate them, but now they were lagging behind in keeping their commitments. Sadly, Paul's brief words here did not adequately motivate them, because he has to return to the topic in much greater detail in 2 Corinthians 8–9. But Romans 15:26 demonstrates that ultimately the Corinthians came through.

"The Lord's people" in 1 Corinthians 16:1a translates the word for "saints" and refers to Christians in general—in this case in Jerusalem. Despite verse 1b, there is no reference to this collection in the letter to the Galatians, so we must assume that the instructions to which Paul refers here took place after that letter was written in ca. AD 49 (six years earlier). But Galatians 2:10 does include "remembering the poor" as an important principle that Paul, Peter, and James all agreed on when they met in Jerusalem to talk about Paul's ministry.

"The first day of every week" (v. 2a) refers to Sunday. It is natural, therefore, to take this verse as the first known reference to a weekly offering as part of Christian worship. Yet the language is more literally rendered "place by himself . . . treasuring," as if each person stored his or her contributions at home. Yet even if the Corinthians did not necessarily bring their monies to a weekly worship service, the fact that this storing was to take place on Sunday strongly suggests that the first day of the week, not the seventh (the Sabbath), had already come to be the most special day of the week for these Christians.

"In keeping with your income" (v. 2b) translates an expression that might better read, "to whatever extent one is prospered." Paul's instructions about representatives and letters of recommendation (v. 3) show his concern for financial integrity and accountability. Acts 20:4 reveals that these representatives came from numerous churches and territories in which Paul had ministered.

Application. A better understanding of the principles of stewardship and a more consistent application of them are both acutely needed in the contemporary Western church. The amount of money required annually to relieve the worst suffering of the two-thirds of the world that is desperately poor is far exceeded by the amount Americans spend each year on sports, leisure, recreation, surplus food and clothing, and so on. And a significant percentage of both that impoverished two-thirds of the world and the affluent West are Christian! Obviously, corrupt governments, civil warfare, supply blockades, and various other obstacles would still prevent the alleviation of all human misery, but far more significant progress could be made toward helping the poor than is currently being done. Governments may at times have more resources at their disposal, but they will not usually bring relief in the name of Christ or present the type of holistic antidote to both spiritual and physical maladies that churches and Christians can.

In short, Christians of the West need to be challenged to give. If they are not, many churches and Christian organizations will go out of business, as donor bases in this country are currently weighted most heavily in favor of senior citizens. Furthermore, they (and all Christians) must be taught to give to those individuals, organizations, and churches who themselves have their priorities straight, who maximize giving to support a reasonable but not excessive lifestyle for full-time Christian workers and a holistic mission to meet the physical and spiritual needs of hurting people worldwide.

1 CORINTHIANS 16:5–12

Original Meaning. The body of the letter has ended. Paul now concludes his letter with personal remarks (vv. 5–12) and closing greetings (vv. 13–24).

As frequently in his letters, Paul's personal remarks concern his current ministry itinerary (or about those of his representatives, when he was later imprisoned); these serve as a transition to his formal closing. His goal of coming to Corinth after revisiting Macedonia (v. 5) did eventually materialize (Acts 20:1–6), but not as quickly as he had first hoped. While here he anticipates leaving Ephesus shortly, the trip described in 2 Corinthians 7:5, which finds Paul at last en route to Corinth, must have taken place at least nine months later. If 1 Corinthians was written in the spring of AD 55, then Paul would have originally hoped to come during that same calendar year, whereas in fact he did not arrive for his prolonged stay until sometime in AD 56.

His initial desire to spend a full winter in Corinth (vv. 6a, 7a) may still have been fulfilled, however, even if delayed by a year. Paul's motivation was at least twofold. First, he wanted to have a significant period of time with the troubled Corinthians in hopes of substantially improving the situation in the church there. Second, he hoped to avoid having to travel during that season of the year in which the high seas were generally impassable and travel overland was much more arduous.

The verb translated "help . . . on my journey" (v. 6b) probably implies material assistance—food, money, and possibly even traveling companions for his trip. In all this planning he knows full well that he must leave the door open for the Lord to change his itinerary (v. 7b).

Verses 8–9 inform the readers of Paul's current location (Ephesus) and enable us to date the writing of this letter to the time of the events of Acts 19. There we see ample illustrations of the two principles of 1 Corinthians 16:9: "a great door for effective work" and "many who oppose me." The former included remarkable conversions and turning away from idols; the latter included occult opposition and town riots. The uprising instigated by Demetrius, however, has probably not yet occurred, since Paul seems to have left town shortly after that event (Acts 20:1), while here he envisions staying on for a while. "Pentecost" (1 Cor 16:8) was the annual Jewish harvest festival (the Feast of Weeks). On that day the Holy Spirit descended on 120 of Jesus's followers fifty days after his resurrection, to inaugurate the era of the new covenant (see Acts 2). Whether Christians had started to celebrate it as a festival is impossible to determine from this reference; it may simply be Paul's natural way to refer to that time in late spring.

Paul's concern in verse 10 over how Timothy will be received is certainly related to their conflict with Paul himself, and it is probably heightened by Timothy's youthfulness (1 Tim 4:12) and possibly even by his personality. "Send him on his way" (v. 11) employs the same verb as "help me on my journey" in verse 6. The unnamed "brothers" probably include Erastus (Acts 19:22), who served as the town clerk of Corinth (Rom 16:23), and they would have been known to the Corinthians.

Verse 12 appears to respond to the final question the Corinthians had raised in their letter to Paul (cf. 7:1). Not only does Paul again say "now about," but it is unlikely that he alone would have taken the initiative to urge Apollos to return to Corinth in light of the danger of inflaming the sectarian divisiveness there all the more. Apollos's reluctance to go could reflect his concern to wait for a more opportune time when things had settled down in Corinth. "He was quite unwilling" is more literally, "it was entirely not the will," leading some to suggest that we should think of God's will instead of Apollos's will. Presumably Paul would have thought the two coincided in this instance.

Application. The ministry of giving to itinerant Christian workers and providing hospitality for them when they are in our own communities can go a long way to rekindling some of the spirit of familial intimacy that Paul tried to instill in his churches. Giving to churches is good and should be generous, but it should often be supplemented by giving to individuals who have to raise their own support for ministry and by providing lodging and provision for visiting missionaries.

1 CORINTHIANS 16:13–24

Original Meaning. Paul begins his final greetings and sign-off with two verses of brief exhortation (vv. 13–14). Four parallel commands employ military metaphors to encourage resoluteness in the faith (v. 13). "Be courageous" should probably be rendered "be adults"—that is, "put away the immaturity that has led to so many of your problems and grow up in the Lord." Balancing these commands to be strong is the call to love in verse 14. As with Paul's discussion of spiritual gifts in chapters 12–14, all Christian activity must take place within the sphere of putting others above self.

In verses 15–18, Paul gives thanks for three Corinthian Christians who have come to him in Ephesus and encouraged him. "Devoted" in verse 15 is literally "appointed." "The Lord's people" are not the believers in Judea, as in verse 1, but refer primarily to the Corinthian Christians (and perhaps others) to whom these three men had ministered. Despite a vigorous debate on the meaning of "submit," its use in verse 16 most likely means to place oneself voluntarily under the authority of someone else. "Everyone who joins" (v. 16b) translates the Greek noun for coworkers. "Labors" differs from ordinary ministry in that it implies *hard* work. "Supplied what was lacking" (v. 17) refers first of all to the spiritual refreshment and encouragement that Stephanas and his companions gave Paul (v. 18a). These men not only renewed Paul's spirit but also encouraged the rest of the Corinthians. "Such men deserve recognition" (v. 18b) tones down the more forceful Greek imperative, "Recognize such people!"

Verses 19–20 convey greetings to the Corinthian church from four groups of fellow believers:

1. the various churches in Asia Minor, almost certainly including Colossae and Ephesus, and possibly some of the other seven churches established in the vicinity (cf. Rev 2–3);
2. Paul's good friends Aquila and Priscilla, coworkers with him in Corinth (Acts 18:2–3) and later partners with him in his ministry in Ephesus (18:18–19);
3. the specific house church that met in their home; and
4. Paul's other immediate companions in ministry.

The "holy kiss" (v. 20b) was probably borrowed from common ancient practice, both sacred and secular, Jewish and gentile. Customarily, men greeted other men and women other women by embracing each other and kissing one another on the cheek.

After verse 20, Paul stops dictating his letter to his amanuensis (the secretary writing down the letter)—was it Sosthenes (1:1)? Paul now picks up pen and papyrus himself to write the closing words in his own hand (v. 21), as was his custom (cf. Gal 6:11; 2 Thess 3:17). The one letter in which we definitely know the name of Paul's amanuensis is Romans, when that individual, Tertius, sent his own greetings at the end (Rom 16:22).

Both parts of verse 22 follow abruptly. They may reflect conventional liturgical utterances of the early church. Paul's curse utilizes the expression *anathema*, as in 12:3. "Come, Lord" is the more likely of two possible translations of the Aramaic *marana tha* (the other one being, "the Lord has come"). Together the two expressions reflect the profound seriousness with which the early church viewed faithfulness to Christ in view of his imminent return.

Verse 23 substitutes Paul's favorite word for "grace" (*charis*) for the more conventional Greek "good-bye" (*erroso*). And, as in his introductory greeting, Paul makes the Christian perspective of his farewell clear with a reference to the Lord Jesus. Verse 24 ends on an upbeat note with one final reminder of his love for these often exasperating Christians in Corinth. The "Amen" is missing from some of the oldest manuscripts and may well reflect a pious addition by an early scribe.

Application. Paul's cry of *marana tha* reminds us of how much our world, even our Christian world, lives in the present without longing for the age to come. We attempt to create paradise on earth rather than genuinely longing for Christ's return and the perfect new heavens and new earth that God has promised to create.

Fittingly, Paul closes with one final reminder of the centrality of "grace" and "love" (vv. 23–24). We continue to need both; indeed, we ought to crave them. If our generation has sometimes removed God from the concept of love, it has at least correctly captured the centrality of love for any viable human ethic. Love does "make the world go 'round," but the only truly life- and world-changing love that will last is that which is founded on a saving relationship with Jesus Christ.

2 CORINTHIANS

INTRODUCTION TO 2 CORINTHIANS

The letter we call "2 Corinthians" is actually at least the *fourth* letter Paul wrote to his church in Corinth: the previous letter mentioned in 1 Corinthians 5:9, canonical 1 Corinthians itself, the tearful, severe letter referred to in 2 Corinthians 2:3–4, and canonical 2 Corinthians. First Corinthians is a product of pastoral concern. Written in the spring of AD 54 or 55, approximately three years after Paul's founding visit, it provides the most detailed example of the way in which Paul applied his theological convictions to the practical problems of the church. In 1 Corinthians we see Paul the pastor, striving to fill in the cracks in the Corinthians' way of life. In 2 Corinthians we encounter Paul the apologist. Paul fights for his authority as an apostle not for his own sake, but because the gospel itself, and hence the very life of the Corinthians, are at stake (12:19). In it, Paul strengthens the repentant majority while at the same time seeking to win back the resistant minority. Moreover, behind the Corinthians stand Paul's opponents, whom he addresses indirectly throughout his letter as the immediate source of the current problem. Second Corinthians is undisputed as part of the Pauline corpus.

BOOK OUTLINE

- I. Letter Opening: The Identity of Paul and His Church (1:1–2)
- II. Prologue (1:3–11)
- III. Letter Body (1:12–13:10)
  - A. Paul's History with the Corinthians (1:12–2:11)
  - B. Paul's Apologetic for His Apostolic Ministry (2:12–7:1)
  - C. The Application of Paul's Apologetic to the Repentant (7:2–9:15)
  - D. The Application of Paul's Apologetic to the Rebellious (10:1–13:10)
- IV. Letter Closing: Exhortation and Benediction (13:11–14)

2 CORINTHIANS 1:1–2

Original Meaning. Letter openings in the first century followed the typical pattern, "(Sender) to (recipient): Greetings!" Paul customarily followed this form but expanded these standard elements to indicate his own authority for writing, the recipient's qualification(s) for receiving what is written, and his Christian perspective on what was desired for the readers. In 2 Corinthians, however, Paul foregoes a detailed elaboration in favor of a nearly standard salutation. His only expansions are the reminders that he is "an apostle of Christ Jesus by the will of God" and that the Corinthians are the "church of God," who exist "together with all his holy people throughout Achaia."

This unusual simplicity serves to emphasize that Paul *is* an "apostle" (Gk. *apostolos*) and owes his calling to the "will *of God*." Christ sends Paul in accordance with God's will. The simple declaration reminds Paul's readers of his divinely appointed role and authority among God's people, thereby opening the way for the defense of his apostolic ministry that will be the focus of so much of 2 Corinthians.

The designation "church" (*ekklēsia*) is one of two terms used in the LXX to define the local gathering of God's chosen people. Thus, just as Paul owed his life as an apostle to the will of God, so too the Corinthians owed their existence as Christians to the same mercy of God. Moreover, the Corinthians are part of a larger gathering of "all his holy people" scattered throughout the Roman province of Achaia.

At the point where Paul's hearers would have expected to hear "hello!" (*charein*), Paul wishes them "grace" (*charis*). Paul wishes his readers a continuing experience of God's merciful gifts, from forgiveness and justification to deliverance from the power of sin and eternal life. Paul can do so because Christ's death on the cross for those who deserve only God's wrath makes such grace possible.

Application. When preaching and teaching from Paul's letters, we too must not shrink back from their intrinsic and abiding authority, or from their ability to communicate persuasively to God's people. For this reason, the following commentary on 2 Corinthians takes as its working presupposition that Paul's intention is accessible and that it is relevant and authoritative for today. Because of our confidence in the authority and sufficiency of Scripture, we seek to move *from* the original meaning of the text *to* its application.

2 CORINTHIANS 1:3–11

Original Meaning

Paul's Prayer of Praise for the Comfort of God (1:3–7). The "comfort" in view here is not merely a subjective feeling of relief or psychological support. Rather, Paul is referring to his present state of peace because of his confidence in God's willingness and ability to deliver. In turn, Paul has the ability to comfort others no matter what comes their way. Likewise, the divine comfort Paul experiences also comes "through Christ" (v. 5), that is, through Christ's own experience of God's commitment and ability to deliver him, even from death.

Verse 6 applies the principle of "from comfort to comfort" to the Corinthians directly. The result is spelled out in verses 6b–7. Like Paul, they too can rely on God to comfort them. This ability to endure is Paul's "hope" for the Corinthians. Moreover, Paul's hope is certain *because* he knows their participation in his suffering, like his own in the sufferings of Christ, will never outdistance their common share in God's comfort (v. 7b).

Paul's "Sentence to Death" as the Pattern of His Suffering (1:8–11). Paul's argument in 1:3–7 raises the question of how his suffering and comfort actually produce this endurance among the Corinthians so that he can justifiably equate his experience with that of Christ's. He answers this question in verses 8–11 by revealing just how drastic the situation really was. Indeed, Paul's suffering was so severe that he saw no way out but death (cf. 1:9). But God's purpose was not to kill Paul. Instead, the apostle was brought to what he thought was the end of his life *in order that* he would in no way rely on himself, but only "on God, who raises the dead," an allusion to the resurrection of Christ (v. 9).

Just as God raised Christ from the dead, so too God delivered Paul (v. 10a). Thus, God's past deliverance of Paul establishes his confidence in the deliverance to come (v. 10b). This confidence for the future is the biblical notion of "hope," a hope that Paul will continue to maintain with the help of the Corinthians' prayers (vv. 10–11a). As a result of the many prayers being offered up on Paul's behalf, others will join in praising God for displaying his great mercy and comfort to his apostle (v. 11).

Application. Our praise of God should never be transformed into some sort of Christian mantra, nor should it be used to make things look better than they really are. We praise God in the midst of our adversity not because things are not as bad as they seem (they could be worse!), but because of who God is and of what he does in and through the reality in which we live.

2 CORINTHIANS 1:12–2:11

Original Meaning

The Content of Paul's Boast (1:12–14). Paul's point in verse 12 is that his outward behavior, rather than calling his ministry into question, actually confirms the grace of God's call in his life. To boast in one's honesty and sincerity, or in any other evidence of God's grace, is to boast or glory properly in what *God* has done in and through one's life, that is, to "boast in the Lord" (10:17). The content of one's boast, not the act of boasting as such, determines whether it is legitimate or not.

Paul's confidence that his actions reflect God's work in his life is supported by his willingness to write openly and clearly—that is, to "boast" about his recent change of plans (v. 12), which he proceeds to do in 1:15–2:4. Paul has confidence (i.e., "hope," 1:13) that when the Corinthians hear the rest of the story, they too will no longer doubt his credibility but will join him in boasting in what God has done in his life as their apostle.

In both cases, however, the proof of their respective legitimacy is to be found in the manner of their lives. For Paul this entails the way in which he behaved toward the Corinthians as their apostle; for the Corinthians it means the way in which they respond to Paul.

The Reason for Paul's First Change of Plans (1:15–22). Paul's opponents viewed his failure to carry through with his original plan as an indication that the Spirit was not at work in his ministry but rather that he made his decisions "in a worldly manner" (v. 17). He reminds the Corinthians that his first change in plans was being carried out in response to God's grace in his life (taking the "this" of v. 15 to refer back to vv. 12–14). Paul's change of plans was not the expression of a vacillating character but a display of God's faithfulness (v. 18). That such a change in plans did not reflect a lack of the Spirit is evident in Paul's purpose for the extra visit: that the *Corinthians*, not Paul, might "benefit twice" (v. 15).

Seen in this light, Paul's change of plans was not a duplicitous act of vacillation but a reflection of God's own faithfulness. Just as God has shown himself faithful by fulfilling his promises in Jesus Christ, so too Paul has acted in accordance with this same gospel as it was preached and confirmed to the Corinthians by several witnesses (v. 20a).

"Amen" is a transliterated form of a Hebrew word that means "to confirm" or "to establish." By his own change of plans toward the Corinthians, Paul "amens" God's demonstration in Christ of his divine faithfulness toward his people. The object of Paul's "amen" is "to the glory of God" (v. 20b). Again he reminds the Corinthians that the purpose of all things is to glorify God (cf. vv. 3, 11). The reason for giving God the credit is expressed in the images set forth in verses 21–22, which are best taken as referring to both Paul and the Corinthians.

God is the one who, like an ancient king, has "set his seal of ownership" on them and "put his Spirit in [their] hearts as a deposit, guaranteeing what is to come" (v. 22). Here Paul is referring to God's commitment to their consummation, sealed and certified by his having given them his Spirit as an *arrabōn* (NIV "deposit"). This is a technical, financial term referring to a first installment or down payment paid out as a pledge of faithfulness to a commitment.

The Reason for Paul's Second Change of Plans (1:23–2:4). In verse 23 Paul is testifying in the most earnest way possible that it was not his fear of rejection that kept him from returning to Corinth, but his wish to "spare" them the judgment of God. His decision not to come to Corinth a second time was an act of humble restraint in which he refused to exercise his authority toward them, even when it would have meant his own vindication.

So Paul canceled his return visit (2:1). Paul changed his plans not solely for the sake of the Corinthians, but for his own sake as well (v. 3). Paul had the confidence that his mercy toward the Corinthians would have its desired result: the Corinthians would repent and once again share Paul's joy in Christ (v. 3b). Paul's love for the Corinthians, expressed in the severe warnings and calls to repentance of his previous letter (v. 4), was the instrument God used to bring the majority of the Corinthians back to Paul.

The Application of Paul's Example to the Corinthians (2:5–11). Though Paul nowhere mentions the specifics of the offense itself, it must have involved some sort of slander against him and his apostolic relationship with the Corinthians. Most of the Corinthians had initially sided with this slanderer. Later, after the majority had repented as a result of his "tearful letter" (2:4; 7:8–13), they grieved with Paul because of the offender's influence over them. They consequently punished the offender (2:6), most likely by excluding him from the fellowship of the Christian community in accordance with the precedent set in 1 Corinthians 5:2, 5, 13.

The punishment had its intended, salutary impact. The offender had repented. In response, Paul calls the Corinthians to follow in his footsteps in showing mercy to the repentant. This is why Paul makes it clear that his confrontational letter was intended to "test" them to determine whether they would be "obedient in *everything*" (v. 9). By exercising such obedience, they will be following Paul's example in extending mercy to the Corinthians themselves. In turn, Paul's willingness to submit to the Corinthians' extending forgiveness to the offender is yet another expression of this same Christlike obedience (v. 10a).

As Paul concludes this section, his seriousness is striking. He ends by indicating that the ultimate purpose for his admonitions is to prevent Satan from using this situation against the church (v. 11a). Satan's "schemes" (v. 11b) revolve around destroying the mutual acceptance and forgiveness that is to characterize God's people, since they are the evidence of God's redeeming work in Christ and of the unity of the Spirit that it creates.

Application. In the face of the cultural pressures around us, we must resist the counterfeit "easy believism" that downsizes biblical faith into a decision of the will based on an intellectual assent to the truths of history. We must maintain Paul's understanding of *faith* as that dependence or trust in God in the *present*, because of his acts in the *past*, that leads inevitably to banking our *hope* on his promises for the *future* (cf. 1:20–22). Moreover, those who hope in God's promises *love* one another (2:4–11).

2 CORINTHIANS 2:12–3:3

Original Meaning

The Reason for Paul's Last Change of Plans (2:12–13). In anticipation of meeting Titus in order to receive word of how the Corinthians had responded to Paul's "tearful" letter (cf. 2:4), Paul moved back toward Macedonia by traveling up from Ephesus to Troas. Then, when Titus failed to show up, Paul's anxiety (literally Paul had "no rest in [his] spirit") over Titus and the Corinthians forced him to move on from Troas despite the open door for the gospel that he encountered there. The apostle was simply too concerned over Titus and the spiritual condition of the Corinthians to carry on his ministry. Certainly, then, Paul's opponents could point to this anxiety-ridden decision as apparently incontrovertible evidence that he lacked the power of the Spirit. How else could one explain the fact that Paul's anxiety drove him away from a clear opportunity to preach the gospel?

Just as Paul's concern for Titus and the Corinthians originally led him to Troas, so too his concern for them led him on to Macedonia (cf. 7:5–7). Nothing was more important to Paul than their welfare, not even an opportunity to expand his own ministry! By filling in the rest of Paul's recent itinerary, 2:12–13 bring us back to the central theme of Paul's letter: his suffering as an apostle.

"Led Unto Death" in the Ministry (2:14–16a). Paul's praise in verse 14 introduces the necessary and logical response to the suffering introduced in verses 12–13. Paul praises God for it as part and parcel of his apostolic life of suffering, through which God's power and presence are being revealed. In turning to praise God, Paul turns his attention to the main point of his defense against those who have called his ministry into question because of his suffering.

The content of Paul's thesis, first introduced in 1:3–11, is summarized in verse 14 in the two participles that follow his statement of thanks: "leading in triumph" (*thriambeuonti*;

NIV "leads us as captives in Christ's triumphal procession") and "making known" (*phanerounti*; NIV "to spread"). The triumphal procession was a lavish parade conducted in Rome to celebrate great victories in significant military campaigns. They demonstrated Rome's prowess as the victor not only by parading the spoils of war but also by leading in triumph the most important leaders and intimidating warriors of the enemy, now presented as conquered slaves.

This fact is so startling because Paul is not the one leading the triumphal procession; he is the one being led in it like a prisoner of war! The solution to understanding Paul's metaphor is to recognize fully what it meant to "be led in triumph." As the enemy of God's people, God had conquered Paul at his conversion call on the road to Damascus and was now leading him, as a "slave of Christ," to death in Christ, in order that Paul might display or reveal the majesty, power, and glory of God, his conqueror.

Far from calling his apostleship into question, Paul's point in verse 14 is that his suffering, here portrayed in terms of being led to death in the Roman triumphal procession, is the means through which God is revealing himself. This revelation of God's power and glory took place in two ways. Either God rescued Paul from adversity when it was too much to bear (cf. 1:8–11) or, having strengthened Paul's hope through such experiences of deliverance, enabled him to endure his adversity with thanksgiving to God (cf. 4:7–12; 6:3–10).

In 2:14b–16a, Paul continues to describe the nature and function of his ministry metaphorically, this time under the images of a "fragrance" and "aroma." It is probably best to read verses 14b–16a as a reference to Old Testament sacrifice. Taken in this way, Paul is practicing effective cross-cultural communication. First he introduces the familiar image of the Roman triumphal procession in order to portray the role his suffering plays as an apostle, and then he uses sacrificial imagery from the Scriptures in order to unpack its significance.

To encounter Paul in his suffering on behalf of his churches is to encounter a picture of the crucified Christ, who died for his people. For this reason, Paul supports his praise in verse 14 by pointing in verses 15–16b to the twofold impact that God's self-revelation in Christ brings about through Paul's suffering: those who are being saved welcome his suffering as an expression of the glory of God revealed in the crucified Christ, while those who are perishing reject Paul's suffering as foolishness, just as they reject the cross of Christ.

Paul's Sufficiency for the Ministry (2:16b–17). The magnitude of such a calling naturally leads to the rhetorical question of 2:16b: "And who is equal to [literally sufficient for] such a task?" In view of Paul's high calling, it is often suggested that the implied answer to this question is "no one." Yet Paul's implied answer to the question, "Who is sufficient for these things?" is better understood as, "I am!" In being "led to death" as the "aroma of Christ," Paul is confident that God *is* making himself known.

In verse 17, Paul supports his sufficiency for the ministry by comparing his practice of preaching the gospel free of charge to that of the "many" who accept, even demand, money for their ministry. Unlike them, Paul does not "peddle the word of God for profit." Paul is referring here to those opponents who have recently arrived in Corinth (i.e., the "false apostles" of 11:4, 13–15). Paul's choice of words in verse 17 indicates that his opponents' practice, like that of a retailer in the market, was suspicious (Gk. *kapēleuo* means to peddle for profit like a retailer). If anyone is trying to con the Corinthians, it cannot be Paul. His manner of life is a window to his sincere motives.

Paul's Letter of Recommendation for the Ministry (3:1–3). Beginning in 3:1–3, Paul vies for the validity of his apostleship based on the presence and power of the Spirit. If the means of Paul's apostolic ministry is his suffering, the Spirit is its content. By embodying the gospel, Paul mediates the Spirit.

In the ancient world, like today, the need for letters of recommendation indicated that someone lacked his own evidence to back up the claims being made. Letters of recommendation are a substitute source of credibility. But Paul's work as an apostle speaks for itself, especially his founding of the church in Corinth. That the Corinthians are "written" (literally "engraved," v. 2) on Paul's heart does not mean that he has warm feelings for them, but that he is committed to act on their behalf as their "father" in the faith. The very existence of the Corinthians as Christians testifies to the power of the Spirit in and through Paul's ministry. This is the point of verse 3.

Application. Paul's understanding of the nature of Christian ministry strikes a piercing blow against all attempts, whether in Paul's day or our own, to fashion ministries and messages around techniques and technology. As children of the entertainment age, our culturally conditioned reflex is to make creating right environments for hearing the gospel our priority, instead of relying first and foremost on the power of the Spirit to call people to repentance. Our tendency is to concentrate on working the angles instead of relying on Christ to work. Rather than viewing the pastor as a mediator of the Spirit in conjunction with the proclamation of the word, the minister becomes a professional whose job it is to manage the corporate life of the congregation and oversee the creation of meaningful worship events.

In response, our congregations often no longer view themselves as those whom God has called in Christ to seek and worship the Lord in the power of the Spirit. Nor does the church view herself through the lens of redemptive history as the people called to mediate God's glory to the ends of the earth. Instead, she becomes a conglomerate of consumers held together only by its common view that this or that particular church happens to be the institution in the area best designed to provide the services sought. Going to church is more like going to a supermarket than like getting together with family. As in Paul's day, so too today, the popular preachers are frequently those who give the people what they want, religiously speaking, thereby confirming them in their own self-understanding and self-reliance.

2 CORINTHIANS 3:4–6

Original Meaning

Paul's Confidence as a Minister (3:4–6a). When Paul says God "made us competent as ministers of a new covenant" (3:6a), he is referring to his Moses-like call on the road to Damascus as a legitimizing principle. Because he is an apostle (i.e., his office, cf. 1:1), he is a minister of the new covenant (i.e., his function). As a minister, he mediates the Spirit in establishing the church. Christ is the one who has made Paul's confidence possible, and God is the one before whose judgment Paul ministers (cf. 2:17).

Paul's Ministry of the New Covenant (3:6b). The content of Paul's activity as a minister is the "new covenant" (3:6a). As is well-known, the only explicit use of the expression "new covenant" in the Old Testament is found in Jeremiah 31:31–34. How we understand Paul's self-understanding as a minister of the new covenant will therefore primarily be informed by our understanding of the meaning of the new covenant itself as found in Jeremiah 31:31–34.

The Ministry of the Spirit, Not the Letter (3:6c). In the end, the character of Paul's ministry as an apostle, compared and contrasted to the ministry of Moses, becomes the key to understanding Paul's self-conception and defense. The heart of this comparison and contrast is the famous letter/Spirit contrast of 3:6.

The key to the meaning of the letter/Spirit contrast is its immediate context. In 3:3b, Paul had established a contrast between God's work in the past under the old covenant, in which he engraved his covenant document on stone tablets, and his present work under the new covenant, in which he engraves his "letter of Christ" on the "tablets of human hearts." Moreover, God's present work by means of the Spirit was seen to be the fulfillment of Ezekiel 11:19 and 36:26–27. Against this backdrop, Paul's concern is not with two distinct messages but with the two materials on which God wrote, corresponding to the two basic ages within the history of salvation. If anything is to be assumed as implicit in Paul's contrast in regard to the law, it is that those who have received the Spirit are now keeping the law, just as Ezekiel prophesied.

Paul is careful in verse 6 *not* to establish a contrast between the law itself and the Spirit. Nor is the Spirit to be read as a code-word for the gospel, so that the letter/Spirit contrast is transformed into a law/gospel contrast. The problem with the Sinai covenant was not with the law itself but, as Ezekiel and Jeremiah testify, with the people whose hearts remained hardened under it. The letter/Spirit contrast encapsulates this distinction between the role of the law within the Sinai covenant, in which it effects and pronounces judgment on Israel, and its new role within the new covenant in Christ, in which it is kept by the power of the Spirit.

Application. Paul's reminder that we are people of the new covenant drives home the absolute necessity of living in obedience to God's commands as the expression of our faith in his promises. The *indicatives* of what God has done, is doing, and will do for his people are therefore inextricably linked to the *imperatives* that flow from them. For example, God commands his people not to steal because he has committed himself to meet their needs. To steal is to disbelieve God's promise in this regard. To say, "All I need to be happy is Jesus and something my neighbor has" is to commit idolatry by failing to trust God's covenant commitment that he will be enough for us. Idolatry is looking to something or someone other than God as the source of our happiness and contentment for the future.

2 CORINTHIANS 3:7–18

Original Meaning

The Old Covenant Ministry of Death (3:7a–b). The issue at stake is the distinct consequences brought about by the respective "ministries" of Moses and Paul. Paul associates Moses's ministry, not the law as such, with "death," since it was Moses's mediation of the glory of God that brought the judgment of God on a rebellious people. This realization leads Paul to his final point concerning the glory of the ministry of death in verse 7.

The Glory of Moses's Ministry (3:7c). Paul's final statement in verse 7 is to describe the glory on Moses's face with the passive participle *katargoumenēn*, which is usually translated here and elsewhere throughout the passage as "transitory" (cf. vv. 11, 13). Paul is thus understood to be saying that Moses veiled himself to keep Israel from discovering that the glory was passing away in order to protect his own authority. The evidence, however, does not warrant such a translation and conclusion concerning Paul's argument. A study of *katargeō* throughout Paul's writings reveals its meaning is consistently eschatological and is best translated in accordance with its rare but unvaried use elsewhere in the ancient world, "to render (something) inoperative, ineffective, powerless," or "to nullify (something) in terms of its effects or impact."

Paul's result clause becomes, "so that the Israelites could not look steadily at the face of Moses because of its glory, *which was being rendered inoperative* (with special regard for the effects of such an action)." Because of Israel's hardened nature as manifested in her sin with the golden calf, Moses's mediation of the glory of God was a ministry of death. The very need itself for Moses's veil manifests Yahweh's judgment against his rebellious people. Moses's ministry was not only an act of divine mercy and grace but was also a ministry of judgment on a rebellious people.

The Glory of the Ministry of the Spirit (3:8). Paul argues that since the old-covenant ministry, which brought death, came in glory, as testified to by its having been veiled, "then how much more must the ministry of the Spirit exist in *glory*" (v. 8, literal translation), since it brings life (v. 6c). Paul is arguing for the very existence of glory in the ministry of the new covenant despite the absence of visible displays of God's presence, not its degree or kind. The basis of his argument is the consequence (i.e., life) brought about by the ministry of the Spirit in contrast to that of the ministry of the letter (i.e., death).

The Contrast between the Two Ministries (3:9–11). If God's presence is the instrument of condemnation, it is also surely the means of salvation. The presence of God's glory in the believer's life, evidenced by his or her new life in and through the Spirit (v. 8), is at the same time an expression of God's righteousness revealed in the death of Christ for the ungodly.

Literally translated, verse 10 reads: "For indeed that which has been glorified is not glorified in this respect because of the surpassing glory." The meaning of verse 10 can be paraphrased: "*Because* God's purpose and its results in the new covenant surpass what he has accomplished thus far in the old covenant, *therefore* that which formerly was the vehicle of revelation of God's glory is in this respect no longer the means through which God is revealing his glory." Once the new covenant arrives, with its primary purpose of granting new life in the Spirit, the old covenant, with its primary purpose of condemnation, is no longer the locus of God's glory in the world.

In verse 11 Paul brings this section of his argument to a close. The new covenant "lasts" since it reveals the righteousness of God that lasts forever. It is this abiding new covenant (v. 10) of the Spirit (v. 8), based on the righteousness of God (v. 9), that Paul was called to minister (vv. 4–6).

The Boldness of the New-Covenant Ministry (3:12–13). Paul's confident expectation is that through his own life and message as a minister of the new covenant (3:6) the glory of God is being mediated to God's people in the Spirit (v. 11). Because he has this "hope," Paul is therefore "very bold" (v. 12). Ultimately, this boldness arises from his assurance that his life and labors derive from God's grace in his life, that they are being carried out in God's presence, and that they will be vindicated before God's judgment.

Paul is not declaring that he is open and honest in contrast to Moses's conscious or unconscious deception. Rather, unlike Moses, he is free to preach the gospel in the knowledge that the present revelation of God's glory need not be veiled from those to whom he is sent, since its outcome (*telos*) is life, not death (cf. 3:6). Whereas Moses had to veil himself as an act of judgment toward a rebellious people, Paul need not "veil himself" before a people whose disposition toward God has been radically changed by the Spirit.

The Continuing Hardening of Israel (3:14–15). Decoded, Paul's symbolism is clear. Because Israel's hardened condition can only be rendered inoperative in terms of its impact "in Christ" (v. 14d), Israel's large-scale rejection of the gospel indicates that she remains in the same hardened condition that has characterized her history ever since the golden calf (vv. 14c, 15a). The very one whom they reject is the only one who can remove their blindness. Only "in Christ" can the Spirit remove the heart of stone (cf. 3:2–3, 8–9). This has consequences both for Israel's reading of the Scriptures and for her own spiritual state.

The Conversion of the Remnant (3:16–18). Having spoken to the issue of Israel's rejection of the gospel in 3:14–15, in verses 16–18 Paul returns to Moses's experience with the veil one last time. Now, however, he brings out its significance not for unbelieving Israel, but for those who have responded to Christ. For believers, as for Moses, the veil has been removed from their "dull" minds (3:14) as a result of having their heart of stone removed by the Spirit.

Paul is not identifying Christ and the Spirit. Rather, he is making it abundantly clear that Moses's experience of Yahweh in the tent of meeting is equivalent to the current experience of the Spirit in Paul's ministry. Paul's point is that those who are presently living under the new covenant in Christ are in direct continuity with the revelation of Yahweh begun at Sinai.

The "freedom" spoken of in verse 17b implies a freedom from the veil of hard-heartedness that is unable to enter into the presence of the Lord. Nevertheless, this *negative* reading as a "freedom *from*" is most likely not the major thrust of Paul's statement. In our present passage, this positive result is a freedom *for* an obedience to the law that flows from the power of the Spirit.

In Paul's words, transformation is taking place "with ever-increasing glory" (v. 18, literally "from glory unto glory"). To say that we are being transformed into his likeness "*from* glory" means that the believer's gradual growth in obedience pictured in verse 18 takes place in response to God's presence.

Application. Paul argued for his authority from the Scriptures, in contrast to his opponents, who relied on their personal power, mystical experiences, rhetorical prowess, and public reputations. So also we turn to the Scriptures because we are convinced that the authority of our gospel derives from the inerrancy, sufficiency, and power of the word of God.

2 CORINTHIANS 4:1–18

Original Meaning

Paul's Confident Boldness despite Rejection (4:1–6). Paul does not lose heart because *God* has commended him through the pouring out of the Spirit in fulfillment of the promises of the new covenant through Paul's life of suffering in Christ. The evidence of Paul's not losing heart is that he renounces the "secret and shameful ways" of his opponents (v. 2). Paul's preaching with sincerity has resulted from God's conversion-call in his life and from the knowledge that he stands before God, his judge. Because of his own clear conscience, he can boldly appeal to the conscience of others.

The problem is not with Paul but with those who spurn him. Those who fail to see God's glory in Paul's ministry do so because of their spiritual blindness. The cause for this hard-heartedness is given in verse 4: Satan's rule over the present evil age. People are not blinded because they choose to renounce the gospel; rather, they choose to renounce the gospel because they are blind. And they are not blind because they choose to be so, but because Satan has made them so.

The description Paul uses in verse 4 to depict the glory now being veiled from those who are perishing is one of the most important christological statements in the New Testament. The entire history of redemption is encapsulated in this statement. Adam was created in the glorious image of God but fell from it. God consequently barred Adam and Eve from his presence. Israel encountered the glory of God on Mount Sinai but fell from it. Moses consequently veiled his face. Christ did not fall but is the revelation of the glory of God to his people. Paul, as an apostle, encountered the glory of God in Christ on the road to Damascus and was converted. As a result, he mediates the glory of God in Christ, unveiled, in order to reverse the effects of the fall as manifested in Israel's history of hard-heartedness.

Paul's final argument that those who refuse his ministry are not revealing his insufficiency but their own blindness is given in verse 5. Paul does not preach himself as the foundation or object of faith. Jesus, the Messiah, is alone Lord, both over the church and over the world The gospel that he preaches is embodied in his own Christlike willingness to consider the needs of others more important than his own rights.

The "glory" of the "image/likeness of God" from Genesis 1:26 that is equated with Christ here in 2 Corinthians 4:4, 6 is the same glory of God's image/likeness that provides both the basis and goal of transformation. The "light" of the new creation used by God to transform his people is not the glory of God seen in the firmament, but "the light of the knowledge of God's glory displayed in the face *of Christ*" (v. 6b). It is this glory, spoken in God's word at creation and enfleshed in Jesus, that is proclaimed in the gospel and experienced in the church.

Paul's Confident Boldness in the Midst of Suffering (4:7–12). The power of the gospel is so great and its glory so profound that it must be carried in a "jar" (v. 7), lest people put their trust in Paul himself. Within its context, the "treasure" in view in verse 7 refers most directly back to "the knowledge" from verse 6. But the link between verse 6 and verse 4, where the glory of Christ is seen to be the content of the gospel, suggests that it can also refer to Paul's entire ministry as this is embodied in his life of suffering. The purpose clause in verse 7b seems to indicate that the point of contrast is God's power, so that the intention of the image is to highlight the weakness of Paul. Paul's weakness ensures that the power is from God and not from Paul (cf. 12:1–10).

The series of four adversative contrasts in verses 8–9 all modify verse 7 by illustrating *how* this divine power comes to expression in Paul's life. Despite Paul's being "hard pressed," nevertheless he is not "crushed"; he is "perplexed, but not in despair," and so on. Given Paul's weakness, his perseverance can be attributed only to God. Paul's suffering provides the platform for the display of God's power.

In verses 10–11 Paul then interprets the experiences of verses 8–9 in terms of the death *and* resurrection of Jesus in order to indicate the christological purpose of his suffering. The power of God revealed in Paul's suffering is, in fact, the same power revealed in the experience of Jesus. The categories of Jesus's death and resurrection are used to interpret Paul's experience of suffering and sustenance, thereby demonstrating that his life mediates the knowledge of God to the world embodied in Christ.

In verse 11 Paul again asserts that his sufferings are not merely coincidental but are part of the divine plan for the spread of the gospel. Paul himself is the living one who is given over to death by God. But this does not lead Paul to the conclusion that the "life" he mediates is his own—it remains the life of *Jesus* (v. 11b).

In verse 12 Paul draws the consequence of this purpose for the Corinthians: he is given over to death in the present so that God's resurrection power might be at work in their lives. Paul's life is not a second atonement, but a mediation of the death and life of Jesus. In his preaching and suffering, Paul stands between the glory of God and the life of his congregation as an instrument in God's hand to bring about new life among his people.

Paul's Confident Boldness in Light of the Experience of the Righteous (4:13–15). Since it is the Spirit who creates faith and conforms one to Christ's faithfulness in the midst of adversity, the "spirit" (v. 13) in view here is most likely the Holy Spirit as the source of faith, not the "spirit" as a reference to the "essence" or "nature" of faith. Like the psalmist, Paul's preaching not only takes place in the midst of adversity, but also leads to even more adversity itself (Ps 116:10b). Paul's proclamation of the gospel reveals God's glory in Christ and, in so doing, the grace of God is causing thanksgiving to overflow among many others.

Paul's Confident Boldness in Light of the Resurrection (4:16–18). The correspondence between 4:1 and 16 makes it clear that "outer" and "inner" do not refer to a dualistic body/soul dichotomy. Rather, they point to the moral transformation of Paul's life as a believer. The result of this renewal is that God will use these "light and momentary troubles" to achieve for Paul "an eternal glory that far outweighs them all" (v. 17). Instead of destroying Paul, his sufferings "outwardly" are the very instrument God uses to reveal the glory of his presence and power in Paul's life "inwardly" (v. 16).

This insight and assurance did not come naturally. Paul had to learn this profound truth (cf. 1:8–11), the process of which is itself an essential part of his inward renewal (4:16). Just as Paul has grown to trust God to sustain him under the weight of his afflictions, so too Paul has come to see that the weight of God's glory far surpasses that of his afflictions.

This is Paul's response to God's presence in his life. The power of God that sustains Paul in his weakness (4:7–12) causes him to remain confident in his proclamation (v. 13) and in his suffering for the sake of others (v. 16). All that God has done and is doing through the adversities of his life (vv. 1–15) leads him to focus on all that God will do (vv. 16–18), which in turn gives him confidence to endure the daily consequences of sin (vv. 1–15). This is the cycle of faith.

Application. When Christians suffer, they too, like Paul, can take courage from the fact that their lives will mediate to others the power of the resurrection, either through God's act of deliverance or, even more profoundly, through the testimony of their endurance and holiness. Even though the circumstantial suffering that was an essential part of Paul's call may be an occasional aspect of God's will for all believers, all of us can follow Paul's example of incurring the suffering that comes from considering the needs of others more important than our own.

2 CORINTHIANS 5:1–10

Original Meaning

Paul's Confident "Groaning" for the Future (5:1–5). The main point of 4:13–18 was that, in the midst of his adversities, Paul focuses on those things that are not presently seen (v. 18b), because these unseen things are what count, for they are eternal (v. 18d). Paul supports this conviction in 5:1: "*because* [Gk. *gar*; NIV "for"] we know that if the earthly tent we live in is destroyed [= life in the perishable, mortal body of this age of suffering, the temporary things now being seen from 4:18], we have a building from God, an eternal house in heaven, not built by human hands [= life in the glory of the imperishable resurrection body, the eternal, unseen things from 4:18]."

In 5:2, Paul's confidence in God's future provision (4:13–5:1) causes him, like all believers, to "groan" in the midst of his present suffering as he longs to inherit the glory that God has in store for him in Christ. Paul's point is that the groaning of anticipation that comes from this longing is itself evidence that God has promised believers more to come than the moaning of suffering and death. Being clothed with Christ is the theological foundation to being clothed with our eternal dwelling from God.

The positive groaning of verses 2–3 is matched by a negative one, expressed in verse 4. Paul's confident longing to inherit the eternal life of the age to come is supported by his desire to escape God's judgment. The purpose of Paul's desire to avoid being naked on judgment day is cited at the end of verse 4. The "life" in view here is the resurrection life of the age to come.

To end the first section of his argument, Paul makes explicit in verse 5 that the basis of his groaning, both positively and negatively, is God himself, since he is the one who has "fashioned us for this very purpose." God is the one who brought about Paul's longing for the resurrection, since he is the one who "has given the Spirit as a deposit, guaranteeing what is to come." Furthermore, this Spirit-wrought longing takes place amid the very adversities that fuel this same desire (cf. 1:22; Rom 8:23).

The Consequence of Paul's Confidence (5:6–10). Paul is reminding his readers that the source of a Christian's confidence is the recognition that to be "at home in the body" (v. 6, parallel to being in "the earthly tent," 5:1, 4) is not the end-all of life. Life in this world is not the believer's final reality.

Therefore Paul, like all believers, lives "by faith, not by sight" (v. 7). This is the first consequence of Paul's confidence. In the present, it is impossible to see the fullness of the resurrection glory still to come. Nevertheless, he trusts in God's promises as the ultimate reality and lives accordingly. He does not live as if his present suffering was the sum of life. Verses 8–9 restate verses 6–7.

The basis ("for," once again Gk. *gar*) for ambition to please the Lord is given in verse 10: Believers are aware that all people must appear before Christ as judge (cf. 1:14). The image of the "judgment seat" (*bēma*) in verse 10 comes from the practice of the Roman governors, who sat on such tribunal benches to render judgment in legal cases.

Application. We must stake out four important boundary markers of a distinctively Christian worldview:

- There is a universal judgment to come, not just for some people, but for all, including Christians.
- Christ alone is the one who judges.
- Only those who have experienced the mercy and power of God in Christ can have confidence as they anticipate this coming day of reckoning.
- The only basis of confidence on the day of judgment is the good deeds that constitute living by faith.

These points need to be driven home in a culture in which about two-thirds of adult Americans consider themselves to be Christian, even though a staggering number of all adults believe you can lead a full and satisfying life without spirituality of any kind.

2 CORINTHIANS 5:11–6:2

Original Meaning

Paul's Motivation for Ministry (5:11–15). Paul's commitment to persuade others of the truth of the gospel is grounded in his confidence that one day Christ will judge all people (5:10). Paul is referring to a strong desire to avoid the negative consequences of Christ's judgment. The apostle seeks to persuade others to join him in fearing the Lord so that they too will escape his wrath.

Though the fear of God motivates him, the goal of his persuasion is not to justify himself before God. In other words, Paul's persuasion is not an attempt in itself to win back the Corinthians. In the battle for the gospel that continued to be waged in Corinth, the issue remained whether the repentant could defend their faith in Paul's ministry against the attacks of those who "peddle the word of God" (2:17). Paul's concern here is to provide them with the ammunition needed to do so.

The word translated "out of our mind" (*existēmi*) in 5:13 is used negatively in Mark 3:21 to describe the reaction of Jesus's family to his messianic claims. But Paul's use of this verb in reference to God indicates a different sense here. To be "out of our mind" is best seen as a reference to Paul's own ecstatic experiences in private worship, most likely that of tongues and visions. Paul's point is that his love for others (here the Corinthians) causes him to consider their needs for persuasion more important than even his own spiritual, private communion with God.

Yet Paul's desire to persuade others necessitates his giving top priority when ministering to being "in [his] right mind" (v. 13), since people, not God, are the focus of his ministry. The basis and purpose for this radical reversal from self to others is given in verses 14–15. In short, Paul's life is now determined by the gospel as outlined in these two verses. Christ's love compels Paul for two reasons.

First, he is convinced that Christ's vicarious death is the true definition of what it means to be right-minded about life. Christ, moved by his love, considered the needs of others for reconciliation more important than his own glory and position with the Father. Second, Christ's death "for all" brings about the "death" of "all" for whom he died (cf. the "therefore" of v. 14c). Together with Christ's death as a model for his own behavior, this accomplished fact concerning the consequences of Christ's death "compels" Paul in his ministry (v. 14a).

To love like Christ, because of Christ's love, is to consider the spiritual growth of others more important than one's own status or security. To live *for* Christ is to live *like* Christ. What transforms the believer, therefore, is that the one who will judge (vv. 10–11) is also the Savior (vv. 14–15).

The Consequences of Paul's Ministry (5:16–6:2). Paul's statement in verse 16a most likely refers back to the practice of his opponents, who continue to criticize Paul's ministry because of its lack of worldly status and apparent lack of spiritual power. Paul understands this way of thinking since he himself "once regarded Christ in this way" (v. 16b). Paul disdained the cross as a radical contradiction to Jesus's messianic claims. In the same way, Paul's opponents disdain his suffering as Christ's ambassador.

Paul too preached that Jesus's suffering as the Messiah changed his people's lives. Against the backdrop of 2:14–4:18, the "new creation" of a people who live for Christ by living for others is the beginning of the restoration of God's people under the new covenant. This means that reconciliation with God through Christ (5:18–21) is the beginning of the eschatological redemption of the world, the inbreaking into this evil age of the new creation to come. For Paul, the new covenant, made possible by Christ's death, is the inauguration of the new creation.

One can legitimately argue that the personal transformation

brought about by the Spirit in 3:18 is the evidence that one is part of the new creation spoken of in 5:17. For Paul, the real evidence of the glory of the new creation is not spiritual ecstasy (5:13), but moral transformation. The magnitude of what Paul has just said leads him to declare in verse 18a that the origin of all this can be none other than God himself.

God is the source of reconciliation, while Paul is his instrument in bringing it to fruition. God's work of reconciling the world to himself *precedes* Paul's own reconciliation with God, just as Paul's being granted the ministry and message of reconciliation *precedes* his consequent call to others to be reconciled with God (vv. 18–20).

It quickly becomes clear, therefore, that the center of Paul's formulation of the gospel in verses 18–19 is the concept of reconciliation. The use of this metaphor to express the significance of God's saving activity is unique to Paul. Some have argued that his use of the term *reconciliation* (noun: *katallagē*; verb: *katallassō*) in verses 18–21 derives directly from its secular use during that period as a diplomatic and political term referring to the harmony established between enemies by peace treaties.

Others have more persuasively argued that the background to Paul's self-understanding in this passage is not derived primarily from the diplomatic language of his day. Rather, it comes from the prophetic perspective of Isaiah himself, from the Old Testament and Jewish understanding of atoning sacrifice, and from the contrast between Paul's ministry and the ministry of Moses. Paul's understanding of Jesus's death is significantly informed in this passage by Isaiah 52:13–53:12.

The Old Testament and Jewish understanding of atonement with God by means of a substitutionary sacrifice is the essential background for understanding *both* "reconciliation" in verses 18–20 *and* Christ's being made "to be sin" in verse 21. The explicit link between the Old Testament sacrificial system and the death of Christ is found in the fact that Jesus, as the suffering servant of Isaiah 52:13–53:12, bears the sins of God's people as their ransom. In his sacrificial death as the sinless Son of God, Jesus pays the penalty for our sin.

As a result of Christ's death, not only does Christ take on our sin, but we take on his righteousness. When God sees us in Christ, he sees the perfection of Christ having already been granted to us as a gift—even though our being made perfect in Christ is still to come at the consummation of the age, when we will see Christ face-to-face.

Application. As Paul's pleading with the Corinthians makes clear, it is never too late to return to God. Paul's call for reconciliation to a wayward people is God's means of rescuing his people from judgment. Paul's confidence is that those who have not accepted God's grace in vain will respond, repent, and return to the Lord. Moreover, what was true for Paul in his day is true in ours: now is the day of salvation.

2 CORINTHIANS 6:3–13

Original Meaning. The focus of Paul's commendation here in verses 3–10 is once again on his divinely enabled endurance amid adversity, which embodies both Christ's "death" (= Paul's suffering) and his "resurrection" (= Paul's endurance). At the same time, this endurance "commends" Paul as a servant *of God* (v. 4), who, like Isaiah, is a mediator of God's word to his people. In contrast, those who lack such a divine recommendation can only engage in *self*-commendation.

All of these phrases also support the conclusions and exhortation of verses 11–13 that Paul voices as the spiritual father of his "children" (v. 13), the Corinthians. As their father in the faith, Paul's pattern of living his life for the sake of the Corinthians points to the fact that he has conducted his ministry with open integrity and genuine affection.

Consequently, Paul puts the responsibility for the conflict at Corinth squarely at the feet of those Corinthians who are still in rebellion against him (v. 12). All Paul wants is a fair exchange, his love for theirs (v. 13a). If there has been any lack of openness, integrity, or family commitment, it has been on their part, not Paul's. Hence, they, not he, must "open" their "hearts" (v. 13b).

Application. Suffering is not a noble and purifying virtue. Rather, what distinguishes the suffering of the righteous from the suffering rampant in our fallen world is the transforming power of God's sustaining presence in their lives. Those whom God calls to suffer on behalf of others as an extension of Christ's love are not being called to masochism but to a mission.

2 CORINTHIANS 6:14–7:1

Original Meaning

Support Number One: The Identity of the Church (6:14b–16b). The necessity of separating from those opposing Paul is first grounded in a series of five rhetorical questions, all of which anticipate a negative answer (vv. 14b–16a). Taken together, they reinforce the basic incompatibility between righteousness, light, Christ, being a believer, and the temple of God on the one hand, and wickedness, darkness, Belial, being an unbeliever, and idols on the other. The fact that in verse 14 "righteousness" is contrasted with "wickedness" (literally "lawlessness") demonstrates once again that for Paul "righteousness" is a concept that includes both one's relationship with God in Christ (cf. v. 15a) *and* its outworking in a life of "light" (v. 14c) as a "believer" (v. 15b). Here "light" is not a mystical concept but a moral designation that refers to the new life of obedience to God, engendered by trusting in Christ and enabled by the power of the Spirit.

Paul's choice of the word used for "temple" in verse 16 (*naos*) highlights God's presence. The Corinthians are not to have anything to do with idolatry precisely because they are "the temple of the living God." The fact that this reference to the temple is the climax of Paul's string of contrasts highlights its significance. The most likely reason for this special emphasis is that Paul's last rhetorical question recalls the "new covenant" substructure of his apologetic as a whole, which began back in 2:14. Nowhere in the Old Testament is Israel ever identified with the temple.

Paul's point is clear. Whereas Israel as a people fell into idolatry and disobedience, the Messiah has brought the church back into the presence of God's glory and begun the process of transforming her into the image of God himself (3:16–18). The separation that is to characterize God's people under the new covenant is thus the positive counterpart to Israel's history of syncretism under the old.

Support Number Two: The History of Redemption (6:16c–18). Paul initiates a second line of support directly from the Scriptures. Verses 16c–18 do not function to support the fact that believers are the temple of God (v. 16b), but are introduced as a *single* citation, composed of six Old Testament passages, which, when read as a whole, support the command of 6:14 and its restatement in 7:1.

The first Old Testament reference is taken primarily from the promise of God's covenant presence in Leviticus 26:11–12. Paul here reflects his conviction that the original covenant promises and the prophetic expectation of their realization after the judgment of the exile are now beginning to be fulfilled in the Corinthian church!

In verses 17–18 Paul draws the scriptural conclusion that flows from a covenant relationship with God: three commands from Isaiah 52:11 and three ensuing promises from Ezekiel 20:34, 2 Samuel 7:14, and Isaiah 43:6. Since the Corinthians are already part of God's new-covenant people in fulfillment of the prophets' hopes (2 Cor 6:16c–e), they must separate from the unbelievers among them (v. 17a–c) in anticipation of God's final deliverance (v. 18). The promise of a continuing covenant relationship and final redemption (v. 18) is given only to those who keep the covenant stipulations (v. 17), which in this case entail demonstrating their covenant identity by separating from impurity (vv. 14–16). In other words, the kingdom is here, but it is not yet here in all its fullness. The emphasis falls on the responsibility of God's children to separate from those within the covenant who, in reality, do not belong and are therefore rendering it unclean.

The Command and Its Support Restated (7:1). In 7:1, Paul takes the strong language normally used in the polemic against pagan idolatry and applies it to his opponents. Paul's closing admonition here recalls his opening argumentation in 2:14–3:6. Within the polemical situation in which Paul finds himself, the specific application of his general command in 6:14, 17, and 7:1 is to flee anything that would keep one from being "reconciled to God" (5:20) and from accepting the grace of God "in vain" (6:1). *Positively*, this means having an "open heart" toward Paul (6:13; cf. 7:2–4); *negatively*, this means separating from those who reject him and his gospel (6:14; 7:1)—that is, closing one's heart to Paul's opponents with their "different gospel" (cf. 11:4).

Application. In order to determine the pockets of idolatry in our lives together as God's people, we must carefully evaluate the influence of our daily commitments, our social practices, and, most important, those values that we share in common with our culture. Most often, the idolatry we face is our culture's smothering covetousness, in which happiness is derived from more possessions and security comes from increasing our financial stability. As believers, we sanitize this covetousness by perverting God's power and presence into a means to some other end. Since all we need to be happy is Jesus *and* the Christian family, Jesus *and* material blessings, Jesus *and* a growing ministry, Jesus *and* my neighbor's spouse, Jesus *and* whatever it is we do not yet possess, we turn following Jesus into a means to these other ends. Such a perversion makes serving Jesus the means to satisfying our idolatry!

2 CORINTHIANS 7:2–16

Original Meaning

Paul's Command to the Repentant (7:2–3). In 7:2–16, Paul is speaking to those who have already proven themselves to be among God's people by their repentance. In making the transition from addressing the church as a whole in 6:11–7:1 to addressing those whom Paul knows to be believers within it, Paul is simply drawing out the implications of what it means for the believers in Corinth to be his true spiritual "children" (6:13). Making room for Paul will necessitate cleaning out those who are still in rebellion against him.

Paul supports his command with a threefold assertion. The Corinthians should make room for Paul because it should be clear by now that he has "wronged no one . . . corrupted no one . . . exploited no one" (v. 2b). These staccato-style statements sharply summarize his argument thus far in response to the criticisms being raised against him.

In verse 3, Paul assures the faithful that in giving this command he is not again condemning them, as he did earlier in his "tearful letter" (2:4). Paul's reversal of the normal order of "live" and "die" (note that the NIV reverses Paul's order!) most likely alludes to the death and resurrection of Christ as they are being played out in Paul's own suffering and endurance on behalf of the Corinthians.

Paul's Disposition Because of the Repentant: Comfort and Joy (7:4). In verse 4 Paul begins his extended argument in support of verse 3 by recounting his own disposition in response to the repentant in Corinth. Paul's boldness leads him to "great pride" (literally "much boasting") in the Corinthians since they are the evidence of the Spirit-endowed character of his ministry. The ability to boast in the Corinthians as a new creation leads Paul to be "greatly encouraged" (literally "filled with comfort"). The outworking of Paul's comfort is a life filled with joy in the midst of his afflictions.

Paul's Comfort and Joy Because of God (7:5–7). Paul returns to the story begun in 2:12–13 in order to show how God used his suffering as a means both to the Corinthians' salvation and to his own happiness. Paul's anxiety over Titus's delay in returning from Corinth had caused him to push on into Macedonia in hope of hearing about the church's response to his "tearful letter" (2:4). Paul's description in 7:5 of this same suffering expands on the lack of peace he experienced as he waited and searched for Titus.

God used Titus's arrival, and *even more so* the comfort Titus had received from the Corinthians because of their changed attitude toward Paul, to increase his joy more than ever (vv. 6–7). He experiences joy and comfort when others make progress in their faith.

Paul's comfort and joy are not merely the expressions of personal relief over his friend and his church, though they certainly are that. More important, they are expressions of God's presence and power, since Paul recognizes that God is the one behind the coming of Titus and the change among the Corinthians. Paul's joy in meeting Titus and in hearing about the Corinthians is a joy ultimately brought about by Paul's theology.

Paul's Comfort and Joy Because of the Corinthians (7:8–13a). In 7:8–13b, Paul recounts how his joy increased all the more when he received word from Titus that his ministry had, in fact, born fruit among the Corinthians. Paul initially regretted having sent its stark denunciation of their defiance, since he knew it would cause them sorrow (v. 8). His fears were unfounded. In response to his rebuke, the majority of the Corinthians had repented, as evidenced by their willingness to discipline the one who had led the charge against Paul.

Thus, despite the pain the letter caused, the sorrow it caused was not an end in itself but led to their repentance (v. 9). Paul is aware, however, that not all experiences of "feeling bad" lead to repentance. People feel guilty for all kinds of reasons. The reason the Corinthians' remorse led to repentance was because they "became sorrowful as God intended"—that is, they experienced the kind of genuine remorse that leads to a real change in one's way of life. "Godly sorrow" (v. 10) feels bad because it is missing out on God.

Paul's confidence that the Corinthians have indeed experienced a "godly sorrow" leading to repentance is not based on wishful thinking but on the sevenfold expression of their repentance outlined in verse 11. The consequence of their earnestness is that they have "proved [themselves] innocent in this matter" (v. 11c).

Paul knew that he had to confront the Corinthians for the sake of their own salvation. He did so by reminding them that they stood "before God"—that is, in his presence as judge (v. 12). Paul wrote it because he had reason to believe it would provide the stimulus needed to prove their genuineness *before God*, while at the same time exposing their true colors *to themselves* (vv. 12, 14). They have passed the test. As a result, he is encouraged in the midst of his afflictions (v. 13a).

Paul's Comfort and Joy Because of Titus (7:13b–15). In verse 13b Paul then emphasizes, as he did in verse 7, that his joy increases "even more" (NIV "especially") over Titus than over the Corinthians in and of themselves. Paul had put himself on the line for the sake of the Corinthians. He had risked embarrassment by declaring in advance that they would respond positively to his "tearful letter" (2:4) and to Titus's ministry, even though Titus himself had reservations about taking the letter to Corinth. Their reception of Titus as Paul's emissary "with fear and trembling" also increased Titus's affections for them (v. 15).

In Conclusion: Confidence and Joy (7:16). On the one hand, verse 16 restates verse 4. On the other hand, verse 16 provides the transition to chapters 8–9 by making clear that the reason for the emphasis on Titus throughout this passage is not due only to his role in judging Paul's confidence in the Corinthians, but also to his upcoming role in the collection for Jerusalem.

Application. All too often the church is emaciated when it comes to experiencing deep and lasting joy in the midst of adversity because we no longer gain our identity by living within the community of faith. What we love, and therefore what we get excited about, is no longer wrapped up with the progress of God's people. The basis of our contentment is not the growing Christlikeness of our church but the comfort level of our personal circumstances. Conversely, we are famished when it comes to feeling grief over sin because what we hate, and therefore what we feel remorse about, no longer revolves around the reality of who God is in our midst. What makes us sad is no longer the sting of our sin but the frustration of our failed dreams and the lack of freedom to get whatever we want.

Today we find it hard to believe that someone's own happiness could be so wrapped up in the welfare of others that to talk about *their* situation naturally leads to talking about one's *own* grief or gladness. Paul and Titus's own joy coalesced with the condition of the Corinthians. The focus of this text is on the joy that comes about because of another person's participation in salvation.

2 CORINTHIANS 8:1–15

Original Meaning

The Example of the Macedonians (8:1–7). Paul's introduction in 8:1 is not to inform the Corinthians but to draw out for them the implications of what the Macedonians have experienced. Only the grace of God can account for such generosity springing from the soil of their "extreme poverty" on the one hand, while *at the same time* issuing forth from their "overflowing joy" on the other (v. 2)! The Macedonians' generosity is also evidence that they passed the "test" (NIV 1984; NIV 2011: "trial") brought on by their afflictions (v. 2). The Macedonians' giving exceeded their ability, without being manipulated or coerced (v. 3). It was the result of their urgently pleading to be involved in the collection (v. 4).

The apostolic context of this passage is made explicit in verse 5, where Paul delineates the final reason the Macedonians gave so generously. The most important thing for Paul is not that the Macedonians gave their money to others, but that they gave their lives to God and to Paul as God's apostle. Indeed, since he is the apostle who brought the gospel to Macedonia, the two cannot be separated: to give themselves to the Lord means that the Corinthians gave themselves to Paul.

Encouraged by the Macedonians' response to God's *grace* in *their* lives (vv. 1–2), Paul sends Titus back to Corinth "to bring also to completion this act of *grace* on *your* part" (v. 6). Paul wants God to do for the Corinthians what he has done for the Macedonians. With their recent repentance has come the opportunity once again to give their money to Jerusalem and to give themselves to God and to their apostle. For as the experience of the Macedonians has testified, this is what happens when the grace of God takes root in the church.

The main point of the Macedonian example is made explicit in verse 7. Like the Macedonians, the Corinthians too "excel" or "overflow" in their experience of God's grace. Thus, just as the Macedonians responded by "welling up" (*perisseuō* in 8:2) in generosity, the Corinthians should overflow (*perisseuō*) in the "grace of giving."

The Example of Jesus (8:8–10). The point of verse 8 is not to deny that Paul is giving them a command, which he explicitly goes on to do in verse 11! Rather, Paul's point is that the need to complete the collection is not a direct command *from Christ*, but his own advice or opinion (v. 10) concerning the implications of God's grace in their lives. The point of verse 8, therefore, is the opposite of Philemon 8–9, where Paul refrains from commanding them "in Christ," even though he has every right as an apostle to do so. Here he exercises that right!

In turning his attention to Christ in verse 9, Paul wants to remind the Corinthians ("for you know") that Jesus himself is *the* example of how grace joyfully expresses itself in love. Spurred on by how the Macedonians have copied Christ, in verse 10 Paul extends to the Corinthians by implication the same call to participate in the collection. Paul's assumption is that his Spirit-led admonition will be received by those in whom the Spirit dwells.

Paul's Expectation for the Corinthians (8:11–15). Verse 11 makes it plain that there is an obligation to give, but no call to give beyond what one can afford. By comparing the Corinthians to the Macedonians, who were less well-off and yet gave *beyond* their means, Paul is not trying to manipulate the believers in Corinth to do likewise. Paul's emphasis in verse 11 on the priority of one's attitude over the amount given, as well as on the inextricable link between attitude and action, is grounded in verse 12. The example of the Macedonians illustrates that proportionate giving means that even the poor can make a great contribution.

The reason Paul stresses proportionate giving is because the purpose of the collection is not to relieve the saints in Jerusalem by impoverishing the Corinthians. Rather, the goal is to create an "equality" between them with reference to their basic necessities (v. 13), which is defined as a reciprocity in meeting each other's needs.

A key question concerning verse 14, therefore, is whether Paul envisions that one day the Jerusalem believers will reciprocate by meeting the financial needs of the Corinthians. Paul is probably referring to the gentiles' present contribution to Israel as an expression of their spiritual fellowship and identity and to Israel's ongoing spiritual contribution to the gentiles as part of the eschatological redemption of the world.

Paul's final support (v. 15) for this expectation is Israel's experience with the manna in the desert as summarized in Exodus 16:18. God's promise to provide for his people, as embodied in the manna and quail, has been reconfirmed in Christ and applied to the Corinthians as God's people of the second exodus.

Application. It is staggering that when it comes to giving, the church spends so little time and theological energy addressing our most cherished cultural values—namely, the materialistic accumulation of money and the idolatrous status and security that come through material possessions. When we do speak about giving, we are quick to adopt the motivational strategies and mores of our culture. The fact that Paul devotes so much of 2 Corinthians, his letter of restoration and apologetic for the truth, to the issue of the collection should be a sober reminder of the significance of this aspect of our Christian life. Nowhere is our materialism challenged more directly, and nowhere do we skirt the issues more often, than when it comes to expressing the genuine nature of our faith and the unity of the church through our giving.

2 CORINTHIANS 8:16–9:15

Original Meaning

The Necessity of Sending the Delegation (8:16–24). The evidence of Titus's eagerness was his willingness to accept Paul's assignment and the "enthusiasm" and "initiative" with which he took it up (v. 17). In the light of Paul's argument in 8:1–15, this zeal to complete the collection is a zeal for the good of the Corinthians themselves. *God* is the one who put the desire to help the Corinthians in Titus's heart. This is why Titus is commended, but God is praised.

Verses 18–21 concern the sending of the second brother, who remains unnamed. Though this "brother" is sent by Paul (v. 18), he is not Paul's personal envoy but a chosen delegate of the churches. The word translated "chosen" in verse 19 is a technical term for being elected by the raising of hands in the assembly. The churches commissioned this brother to travel to Jerusalem with Paul and the collection before it was decided to send him to Corinth too. The presence of this respected brother will help certify the integrity of the enterprise both before God and others (v. 21).

The third member of the delegation is introduced in verse 22. Paul's description of him as "*our* brother" suggests that he too, like Titus, has been appointed directly by Paul, not the churches, though his responsibility is not to represent Paul per se but the concerns of the congregations (cf. v. 23b). Like Titus, this man's zeal to serve the Corinthians had been fueled all the more by the renewed, Spirit-induced zeal of the repentant Corinthians themselves. Love begets love.

In verses 23–24 Paul describes Titus as Paul's own representative. The two brothers of verses 18–22 are designated "representatives," not of Paul but "of the churches." As such, they are "an honor to Christ." This means that to reject their work among the Corinthians is to reject the reality of Christ in his church and within her apostles. Paul concludes this section by calling the Corinthians to respond appropriately to the delegation's presence and purpose among them (v. 24). The delegation that has just been commended is, of course, the very one that has delivered the letter they are now reading (i.e., our 2 Corinthians) and are at work completing the collection. The Corinthians must therefore demonstrate the reality of their renewed love for Paul and his gospel by complying with the call to contribute.

The Necessity of Completing the Collection in Advance (9:1–5). Paul really has "no need" to write to the Corinthians about "this service to the Lord's people" (v. 1). Indeed, their earlier willingness had proved to be an example to the Macedonians (v. 2). Most likely, Paul employs the geographical designation of "Achaia" here to match his corresponding reference to the "Macedonians," especially since Corinth was the senatorial and provincial capital of Achaia.

Paul has sent the three brothers to ensure that his boast concerning the collection, which is the visible fruit of his ministry among them, will not be "emptied" (v. 3; NIV "prove hollow"). The genuine nature of the Corinthians' renewed repentance is at stake in completing the collection (cf. 8:8). A delegation of Macedonians will accompany Paul with the collection. He is well aware of the shame both he and they will incur if these Macedonians, to whom Paul has boasted about the church in Achaia, find the Corinthians unprepared (9:4b).

In verse 5, Paul is pointing to two opposite ways of giving: the kind of generosity that flows from experiencing God's blessing and from trusting in the sufficiency of God's grace, versus the kind of begrudging greediness and self-reliance that selfishly seeks to keep as much as possible for oneself.

The Theological Ground and Purpose of the Collection (9:6–15). Verses 6–15 therefore serves to support 9:5, the main point of 9:1–5, by expressing the collection's theological basis (God's abundant grace) and purpose (the praise of God's glory). Paul's argument begins in verse 6 with a proverbial statement. But Paul emphasizes the respective degrees of reward associated with sowing and reaping respectively. Since the manner of one's giving reflects the character of one's heart, there is a principle of divine retribution here.

The logical conclusion to be drawn from this maxim is Paul's counsel in verse 7. Paul's exhortation echoes Deuteronomy 15:10. Paul's use of Deuteronomy 15:10 is yet another indication that he understands the church, as the continuation of the faithful remnant within Israel, to be the eschatological people of God. What was given to Israel to do every seventh year is now, under the new covenant, to be the *daily* pattern of those in Christ.

Verses 8–9 continue to ground Paul's call to give by indicating why God approves only of those who give cheerfully (v. 7c). Giving to others is simply what trusting in God's promises looks like in a different dress. As a consequence of these promises, believers will always have "all that you need" (*autarkeia*; literally "contentment," v. 8). The quote in verse 9 from Psalm 112:9 is intended to provide scriptural support for Paul's affirmation in verse 8. Paul summarizes the point of verses 8–9 in verse 10 by alluding to two more passages from Scripture, Isaiah 55:10 and Hosea 10:12.

In the original text, 2 Corinthians 9:10–14 form one long, complex sentence. Verses 11–14 support verse 10 by detailing the way in which God will "enlarge" the Corinthians' "harvest": God will provide for the Corinthians "in every way" so that they can be generous to others (v. 11). These people in turn will give thanks and pray to God, for God is the one who makes all this possible. The Corinthians' own "harvest of righteousness" (v. 10) will increase as their lives are blessed through being instruments for the praise of God and as recipients of the love and prayers of those whose needs they meet.

In verse 14, Paul anticipates a deep bond being formed between those in whom God's "surpassing grace" has been poured out. This reference to God's grace at work in the Corinthians picks up the thread that Paul has woven throughout and repeats the point with which he began, thus cementing chapters 8 and 9 together. Paul is anticipating that the grace granted to the Corinthians will be no less than that given to the Macedonians, since God's grace is the basis of all giving.

It is fitting that in verse 15 Paul draws 8:16–9:15 to a close by returning to the thanksgiving with which he started. That the Corinthians' giving to others, which begins in God's grace, will also rebound to their own blessing from God in response to the praise and prayers of others is an amazing "gift" of grace worthy of praise.

Application. While giving must be done freely, it is not optional. The ministry of the gospel requires that this point be made strongly and consistently, especially in a culture drowning in materialism. Unfortunately, many pastors are afraid to mention giving too often, lest the congregation think that the church "just wants our money." Such fears are misplaced theologically and often reflect our cowardice in the face of the reigning idols of our day. To speak about our need to give is to emphasize that we are God's people through whom God glorifies himself. The Corinthians' participation in the collection was not "for the church," but evidence that they were the church. Indeed, to give to others is a manifestation of the righteousness of God, apart from which there is no salvation (9:9–11). The fact that believers often ask how much they should give reveals that they have not yet grasped Paul's perspective. Besides, our problem is usually not that we are in danger of harming ourselves by giving too much!

2 CORINTHIANS 10:1–18

Original Meaning

Paul's Warfare on Behalf of His Authority (10:1–6). Paul begins this final section of his letter by boldly asserting his authority because he is about to announce his third and final visit, which will bring God's judgment on those who at that time have not yet repented. Paul is being bold now so that he will not have to be "bold" when he arrives (v. 2).

As verse 1b itself indicates, his opponents had accused him of duplicity or cowardice because of the discrepancy between the powerful threats in his previous writing(s) and his apparent powerlessness or "timidity" when it came to carrying them out in person. According to his detractors, his being "bold" (v. 1) when absent was a coward's threat, while for the apostle his boldness was an expression of his confidence from Christ. So his goal was to show them that his boldness when absent was just as much an expression of the "gentleness of Christ" as his humility when present. But just as Christ's meekness must not be misinterpreted to mean that he winks at sin, so too Paul's restraint must not be seen as cowardice.

In verses 3–6, Paul plays off the accusation from verse 2 that he conducts himself "by the standards of this world" by developing a military metaphor to support his strategy of writing boldly from afar in anticipation of not having to act boldly when he arrives. Though Paul concedes that he "lives in the world," his battle plan is not worldly (v. 3) because his "weapons" (v. 4) are not worldly; by implication, they are expressions of the power of the Spirit.

In particular, Paul's weapons are the manifold proclamation of the truth of the gospel in the power of the Spirit. Their purpose is to "demolish strongholds" (v. 4), an allusion to the bulwarks erected by citizens to protect their city from invaders. The truth of the gospel will overcome anything or anyone standing in its way.

Verse 5 details the two ways in which Paul wages his war on behalf of the gospel. First, he demolishes the "arguments" and "pretensions" (literally the "heights" from which the defenders opposed the besieging army) that his opponents have raised against "the knowledge of God." Paul overcomes them by a clear presentation of the gospel and its implications, surrounded by an unabashed appeal to his own life as its verification. Second, once he has destroyed the enemy defenses, Paul takes every thought of the enemy "captive" by evaluating it in view of his own ministry of the cross and resurrection of Christ. Specifically, Paul argues for his conviction, and supports it evidentially, that as a true apostle of the crucified and risen Christ, he reveals the power of God in and through his weakness.

After demolishing the defenses of his enemies and taking

captive their counterattacks, Paul will punish those who remain in rebellion. But he will only do so once the repentant, by their obedience, have shown themselves to be on his side (v. 6). Paul wants to give them every opportunity to surrender to the gospel before he executes God's judgment.

The Purpose of Apostolic Authority (10:7–11). Concretely, this section issues a command to the Corinthians (v. 7a), which leads to a command concerning Paul (v. 7b), which in turn supports a command, albeit indirectly, to Paul's opponents (cf. v. 11). This reading of the passage is based on taking the verb in verse 7a to be an imperative, rather than an indicative statement (NIV "You are judging"). Paul is most likely not simply describing or questioning what the Corinthians *are* doing, but stating what he wishes they *would* do. Having begged them to avoid judgment in 10:1–6, he now calls them to do so by evaluating things as they readily appear to the Corinthians themselves rather than listening to Paul's opponents.

When Paul's life is compared to others in Corinth who claim to be Christ's (v. 7b), the transparent nature of his belonging to Christ becomes his support for the command of v. 7a. In making this comparison, Paul still has his apostleship in view. Nevertheless, interpreting verse 7b as a reference merely to his role as an apostle in comparison with other apostles is too narrow.

Since the Corinthians themselves are evidence of Paul's rightful standing in Christ (v. 7), he will not be ashamed before the judgment of God if he boasts exceedingly concerning his apostolic authority (v. 8a). Paul's boasting in chapters 10–13 is not the exercise of an uncontrolled ego but the expression of his love and calling.

In verses 9–11, Paul expresses the purpose for his boasting and warnings that are to come in the chapters ahead. He is aware that his opponents have accused him of trying in his previous letter(s) to frighten the Corinthians with empty threats from a safe distance (v. 9). He knows that the apparent contradiction between his "weighty and forceful" letters and his personal weakness and suffering has been used against him as proof that he lacks the power of the Spirit (v. 10). Nevertheless, he has made it clear throughout 2 Corinthians that his decision to support himself in Corinth, his ministry in the midst of his weakness and suffering, his change in travel plans, his "weighty letters," and his simple, "unimpressive" manner of presenting the gospel are all expressions of his apostolic commitment to the Corinthians.

Thus, Paul's opponents should be put on notice that he is more than prepared to carry out his threats of judgment when he arrives (v. 11). The contrast that began in 10:1–2 between Paul's presence and absence is concluded in verses 10–11.

The Basis of Apostolic Authority (10:12–18). Paul's burden in 10:12–18 is twofold:

1. to define the proper criterion for determining what is, in fact, a proper boast or claim to apostolic authority in Corinth, and
2. to demonstrate that his boast, not that of his opponents, actually meets this criterion.

Paul accomplishes these purposes by introducing a negative comparison between his opponents' practice of commendation (v. 12) and his own (vv. 13–18). To engage in comparisons was a common rhetorical practice in Paul's day. So his hesitancy does not come from the practice itself; he himself does so without qualification. Here, however, he refuses to participate with those who commend themselves because their *means* of comparison is faulty from the start: they measure themselves *by themselves* and compare themselves *with themselves*, thereby revealing that they are without understanding (v. 12).

From Paul's perspective, to support a claim to apostolic authority in Corinth by pointing to one's own abilities, spiritual power and experiences, and/or rhetorical prowess is to be without understanding; such factors are simply irrelevant to the question at hand. His opponents lack the commendation needed to establish their authority over the Corinthians. This particular commendation does not come by comparing oneself to others; it comes from the Lord.

In contrast to his opponents, who measure themselves by themselves, Paul asserts in verses 13–15 that he will not boast beyond "proper limits"—that is, beyond what God has apportioned for him (v. 13a). Paul's apostolic authority in Corinth is the simple fact that he founded the Corinthian church. That Paul was the one through whom the Corinthians received the Spirit (cf. 3:1–3) indicates clearly that he, not his opponents, is the one to whom God has delegated apostolic authority in Corinth.

Paul's boast is therefore based on his own divinely established "work" (10:15a). His opponents attempt to assert apostolic authority in Corinth, yet they have no relevant evidence to back up such a claim. Unlike Paul, they are "boasting of work done by others" (v. 15a).

By contrast, the Corinthians themselves are Paul's recommendation (see 3:2–3). His opponents wanted letters verifying their own spiritual power; Paul's spiritual power could be seen in the growing faith of the believers in Corinth.

Since the Lord is the one who determines the measure of one's ministry, the only true object and ground of boasting is the approval that comes from the Lord's commendation (10:17–18). His commendation of Paul's apostleship in Corinth was the fact that he had brought the great missionary to Corinth as the church's founding father in the faith. In the end, therefore, the ultimate foundation of Paul's apologetic is that the only genuine boast and basis of authority is boasting "in the Lord" (v. 17). For what matters is not the Corinthians' approval, but God's commendation (v. 18).

Application. As a continuation of Paul's own "warfare," this passage calls us to engage in apologetics and church discipline whenever the gospel is being denied or diluted. Paul's apologetic in his passage reminds us that genuine salvation is marked by perseverance in the truth. Today we must fight again for the recognition that a growing faith, not a past decision, is the sign of the presence and power of the Spirit.

2 CORINTHIANS 11:1–33

Original Meaning

The Necessity of Paul's Boast (11:1–21a). *The danger in Corinth (11:1–6).* In 11:1–4, Paul begins his justification for boasting like a fool by expressing his desire that the Corinthians "put up with" him (v. 1). Paul is not expressing jealousy over being rejected. Paul is fighting for the faithfulness of the Corinthians because of their current temptation to commit spiritual adultery. Paul's portrayal of the Corinthians as engaged to Christ in verse 2 recalls the Old Testament representation of Israel as betrothed to God. Like God's jealousy for Israel, Paul is jealous with a "*godly* jealousy" for the Corinthians (v. 2).

The reference to the fall reveals just how serious the danger facing the Corinthians really is. It is a warning that, in reality, his opponents are servants of Satan who are seeking to destroy the Corinthians' marriage with Christ in the same way that Satan spoiled Eve's relationship with God.

That his opponents preach another Jesus is clearly revealed in their refusal to take up their cross on behalf of the Corinthians (v. 4). Rather than following in the footsteps of the crucified and then risen Lord, they preach an exalted figure that they wrongly assert is reflected in their assertions of superiority and the demands that they lord over the Corinthians. Nevertheless, the Corinthians gladly "put up" with such mistreatment because the opponents' Jesus promises the power of the Spirit over all sickness and financial want to those who will accept their gospel (v. 4). To do so, however, is to go back on the true Jesus, gospel, and Spirit as first preached by Paul.

The "super-apostles" of 11:5 and 12:11 should not be equated with the false apostles of 11:4 or 11:13–15. Those who reject Paul are rejecting the one common, apostolic gospel. Paul is the one who represents the apostolic tradition. Paul's equality with the leading apostles means that even if he is an amateur in the art of professional rhetoric and public oratory, his knowledge of the gospel is not second rate. His knowledge is on a par with any of the apostles, just as he himself shares their apostolic authority in every way.

The necessity of Paul's boasting in his weakness (11:7–15). Paul returns to the theme of his self-support in verses 7–12 because his voluntary humiliation and suffering are at the heart of the debate among those still questioning his apostleship. From Plato through Paul's day, the Sophist philosophers and professional orators charged fees. Hence, Paul's refusal to solicit support from the Corinthians could be viewed as casting an aspersion on his teaching: he gives his gospel away because nobody will pay for it.

At the same time, Paul's self-support is an affront to the pride of the Corinthians, who most likely want to be viewed as Paul's benefactors or patrons, with him as their client. But as an apostle, Paul is *their* patron, representing *his* true patron, Christ. Far from calling his ministry into question, his preaching for free represents God's gift in Christ.

The two oath formulas of verses 10 and 11 undergird Paul's resolve to continue his boast of preaching the gospel for free in Achaia. No criticism can stop him from doing so (cf. v. 7), since his boast is an expression of the truth of Christ in his life. He can equate his commitment to preach for free with the truth of Christ because the humiliation and suffering that his practice of self-support entails derives from his love toward the Corinthians, as God himself can attest.

There is a second reason why Paul will not stop supporting himself in Corinth. Paul's preaching for free makes it impossible for his opponents to compare their missionary practice favorably with his own. In so doing, it removes their "ground" (v. 12). Indeed, that Paul willingly suffers like Christ for the sake of others calls into question the dictum of the health and wealth gospel that Christ has suffered so that his people need not do so. The opponents are actually afraid to compare themselves to Paul because of the clear testimony that his practice of self-support gives to the sincerity of his motives.

Thus, in verse 12 Paul goes on the offensive by turning his opponents' criticism on its head and exposing it for what it really is: an attempt to get Paul to compromise his convictions so that they will not look so bad by comparison. Paul maintains that his message and ministry are the true criteria of legitimacy by which the opponents are to be measured, not the other way around.

Paul must set himself up as the criterion for true apostleship because of the deceptive nature of his opponents, who are "masquerading as apostles of Christ" (v. 13). Paul is not surprised by this, since Satan too "masquerades as an angel of light" (v. 14). The point of designating Satan as a false angel of light is to highlight his counterfeit nature as a messenger of God.

The foolishness of boasting in one's strength (11:16–21a). Again, desperate situations demand desperate measures. But before he goes down this path, Paul hesitates yet again in verses 16–21a in order to make it clear just how inappropriate such boasting actually is. Nevertheless, Paul feels compelled to conform to such boasting for the sake of winning back the Corinthians, since they are gladly bearing with Paul's opponents, the real fools (vv. 18–19a).

In contrast to Paul's foolishness, in verse 19 those Corinthians who remain enamored with his opponents are pictured, ironically, as the "wise." Paul unmasks his irony in verses 20–21a. The progression of abuse the Corinthians have suffered from the false apostles details why they are not really wise but fools for accepting his opponents. The insulting "slap . . . in the face" received from his opponents most likely refers to their denigrating the Corinthians as second-class citizens in the kingdom (v. 20)—unless, of course, they side with the opponents, who pride themselves on their Hebrew and Israelite heritage (cf. 11:22).

Paul's Boast in His Weakness and the Boasting of a Fool (11:21b–33). *The boasting of a fool (11:21b–23b).* Paul's litany of boasts in 11:21–33 is arranged in an ascending order of emphasis. First, Paul marshals in increasing force his "foolish" claims to apostolic authority (v. 21b), climaxing with his boast in being a "servant of Christ" (v. 23). He then turns to his suffering, from his labors as an apostle to his being exposed to death, in which the generalized statements first given in verse 23c are unpacked in the details that follow.

In verses 22–23b Paul matches his opponents' foolish boast element for element. Paul too can boast in his ethnic identity as a Jew, in his religious identity as a member of God's chosen people, and in his identity as part of the remnant who have received the Spirit as the true descendants of Abraham. If heritage makes one an apostle, then Paul can claim the heritage of the most esteemed Jewish apostles.

In fact, if this is the way his opponents are prepared to argue, then Paul can claim to be "more" a servant of Christ than they are (v. 23). Nobody can top his well-known pedigree and his former life of zeal for the law and the Pharisaic traditions. But this way of arguing is madness. It denies the very basis of apostolic authority itself: the call of the risen Christ to take on the character of the crucified Christ.

The boasting of Christ's apostle (11:23c–33). Because of the absurd and sinful nature of such boasting in one's self, Paul abruptly cuts it short and turns to the suffering outlined in verses 23c–33 as the real proof and ground of his apostleship.

Paul's various arrests, imprisonments, and punishments referred to in verses 23c–26 were suffered as an apostle for the gospel. His more severe beatings refer both to the Jewish punishment of thirty-nine "lashes" and to the gentile punishment of being beaten with rods (v. 24). Five times Paul received synagogue punishment. It was the most severe beating Scripture allowed. Paul's receiving such punishment five times attests that the synagogue continued to be a strategic focus of his ministry.

Paul's ministry as the Jewish apostle to the gentiles also caused rifts within the Jewish and gentile social fabric as a whole. Hence, three times the Romans punished Paul for disturbing the peace by beating him with rods, a form of punishment usually reserved for noncitizens and slaves.

Of special note is the fact that within Paul's listing of his various dangers, "in danger from false believers" stands alone and unpaired at the foot of the list (v. 26). By calling special attention in this way to the danger posed by false brothers as the climax of all his dangers, Paul is subtly reminding the Corinthians of the serious peril they themselves are now facing by embracing his opponents.

Paul's catalog of affliction reaches its climax not with any of his specific sufferings but with a reference to the "daily . . . pressure of [his] concern for all the churches" (v. 28). This too is part of Paul's apostolic suffering, since the pressure he feels is brought about by his identification with the weak and by his indignation over those who lead others into sin (v. 29). Contrary to what his opponents maintain, Paul is "weak" not because of his own inadequacies but because of his willingness to identify with those to whom he has been sent with the gospel. The counterpart to Paul's weakness is his strong anger over the thought of someone falling away from Christ.

Paul's argument concludes with the principle stated in verse 30: if forced to boast, he will do so concerning his weaknesses. Of course, Paul's list in verses 23–29 has already made this point by way of illustration. But its surprising nature leads him to underscore the veracity of his declaration with yet another oath in verse 31.

To illustrate his boast one last time, Paul recalls his experience in Damascus after his conversion when he escaped. The most likely reason for Paul's adducing this experience at this point in his apology is that, as a result of his conversion-call on the road to Damascus, it was the initial and foundational example of his newly granted weakness as an apostle. As such, it stands in stark contrast to the strength in which he had originally left for Damascus to persecute the believers—the same foolish "strength" his opponents continue to boast in (v. 22).

Application. Paul's example drives us to ask why, when we advertise our church, we do not promote the death of Christ for sinners, boast in God in what we say and do, highlight our own weaknesses, and call attention to the voluntary suffering of our role models? Why do we seek instead to portray an image of ourselves as successful and "normal"? The reaffirmation of Paul's principle from 11:30 is just as essential today as it was in his own: "If I must boast, I will boast of the things that show my weakness." The goal of ministry is not attaining numerical growth, but fostering a growing experience of depending on Christ's grace and power, knowing that the one who gives the grace receives the glory, which is God's own purpose in all that he does as the Giver of all things.

2 CORINTHIANS 12:1–13

Original Meaning

Paul's Boast in His Weakness and the Boasting of a Fool (12:1–6). Paul begins 12:1 with a reference to his visions and revelations. However, since such boasting is foolish, he immediately qualifies it as useless; that is, "there is nothing to be gained" from it (cf. 11:23). This is the only reference to a "vision" or "visions" within Paul's writings, and only here and in the parallel reference in 12:7 do we find the plural "revelations."

This hesitancy to boast in his visions is also reflected in Paul's use of the third person to describe his own being caught up into heaven. He is trying to report his experience while at the same time not reporting it. He wants the Corinthians to evaluate him only on the basis of what they themselves can see and hear from him directly, not on the grounds of personal reports of private mystical experiences.

The experience Paul describes in verses 2–4 was a personal rapture into the "third heaven" (v. 2), which is equated with being "caught up to paradise." The parallel between the "third heaven" and "paradise" (v. 4) indicates that Paul's reference is to the highest spiritual realm, where one encounters the very presence of God.

Having "boasted" about his own visions and revelations in verses 1–4, albeit indirectly, Paul concludes in verse 5 that this is as close as he will get to declaring his spiritual pedigree, since there is nothing to be gained by such self-promotion based on private experiences. Accordingly, Paul restrains himself from such boasting so that no one will brag about him *beyond what can be evaluated objectively.*

Paul's Strength in His Weakness (12:7–10). In 12:7a, Paul states explicitly his concern that if he did share his private experiences, others would go beyond boasting in his apostolic work to glorifying him as an apostle; that is why he has restrained himself. Paul's restraint, however, was not the result of his own moral willpower. In verse 7b, he makes it clear that God kept him from such conceit by granting him "a thorn in [or against] his flesh," that is, "a messenger of Satan" sent to batter or torment him.

The exact nature of this "thorn" or satanic messenger has been a matter of much debate. Paul's "thorn in the flesh" and the parallel reference to his "weakness" in verse 9 are often taken to refer to personal sickness. The other options are to understand them as referring to his inner temptations (a view that no longer finds much support) or to his being persecuted by his opponents (a view first found among the church fathers, beginning in the fourth century AD). Those who favor this last view emphasize that it was not a thorn *in* the flesh, but a thorn *against* the flesh. They also advocate a parallel between the "messenger of Satan" in 12:7 and the "servants" of Satan in 11:15 and point to the use of the image of a "thorn" in the LXX of Numbers 33:55 and Ezekiel 28:24 to refer to the enemies of Israel.

Whatever its exact referent, Paul is not interested in the medical diagnosis of his weakness but in its theological origin (sent by Satan but given by God), in its cause (Paul's great revelations), and in its purpose (to afflict Paul in order to keep him from becoming conceited). In 12:7, Paul therefore turns his opponents' argument on its head. The more they call attention to the severity of Paul's weaknesses as a sick charismatic, the more they themselves point to the exalted nature of his revelations!

Paul's sufferings can never outstrip God's supply of grace (cf. 1:8–11). For this reason, he will "all the more gladly" boast in his weaknesses instead of his revelations, in order that the power of Christ may dwell on him (12:9b; cf. 1:9–10; 11:30; 12:5). *Thus, the revelation of Christ's power in Paul's weakness (v. 9b) and Paul's consequent contentment (v. 10a) form the high point of his argument in this passage and, in doing so, provide a summary of the theological substructure of 2 Corinthians as a whole.*

Paul's various weaknesses (listed in 11:23b–33 and now summarized in 12:10) are therefore his only legitimating boast as an apostle, since they are the means by which God makes known his glory in Christ among the Corinthians. For this reason, Paul boasts in the very things that cause others to slander him. His strength in verse 10b is not his personal strength, but the strength that derives from his divinely granted ability to endure adversity for the sake of the gospel. This then is Paul's strongest argument for the legitimacy of his apostleship: his weaknesses are the basis of Christ's power. For to boast in his weakness is, at the same time, to boast in what the Lord is doing by his grace and power.

The Superfluous Nature of Paul's Boast (12:11–13). The need to match his opponents in their boast should not have been necessary in the first place, since the Corinthians themselves should have recognized him as of equal standing with the eminent apostles of the church. Here too his positive comparison of himself to these "super-apostles" in support of his legitimacy indicates that the apostles in view in verse 11 are not his opponents, but the leading "pillar" apostles from Jerusalem.

That Paul has the pillar apostles in view is confirmed by his following disclaimer at the end of verse 11 that such equality is asserted "even though he is nothing." Many commentators think that in saying this, Paul is ironically parroting a taunt from his opponents, who have accused him of being of no account. However, if in verse 11 Paul is comparing himself to those who were apostles before him, then his disclaimer is intended to remind the Corinthians of what he had taught them previously in 1 Corinthians 15:8–9.

In 12:12, Paul supports his assertion of equality by affirming that in addition to his weaknesses, the "marks of a true apostle" (literally "the signs of the apostle") had also accompanied his ministry. God was the one who performed signs through Paul, thereby accrediting his apostolic ministry of the new covenant.

In addition to the signs of an apostle, Paul goes on to speak of *other* "signs, wonders and miracles" that accompanied these signs (v. 12). Paul's point is that the pouring out of the Spirit as the primary sign of apostleship was done among the Corinthians, the authenticity of which was further attested by other miraculous works.

Hence, Paul did not treat the Corinthians in any way as inferior to any other church, since he brought to them the same gospel that the apostles did. Likewise, this gospel was empowered by the same Spirit and validated by the same confirming miracles of the "second exodus" redemption in Christ. In a declaration steeped in irony, Paul acknowledges that the *only* way in which he treated the Corinthians as "inferior" to other churches was that he did not "burden" them financially, a "wrong" for which he now asks to be "forgiven" (v. 13b; cf. 2:17). In reality, however, the only one who has been wronged is Paul himself.

Application. Paul's boasting in his weakness challenges our very definition of spirituality. In view of Christ's own death and resurrection, we should not consider it a strange providence of God that, like Paul, our own greatest experiences of Christ's grace and power often (though not always) come through our experiences of suffering and difficulties. Indeed, Paul's testimony that Christ's "power is made perfect in weakness" (12:9) has been confirmed throughout the ages. In the end, Paul's boast in his weakness summons us to trust in the sufficiency of Christ today.

2 CORINTHIANS 12:14–13:14

Original Meaning

Paul's Final Appeal Regarding His Legitimacy as an Apostle (12:14–21). In announcing his impending visit, Paul emphasizes one last time his commitment to support himself in Corinth. This theme, above all, encapsulates his own claims as an apostle, while at the same time calling into question the counterclaims of his opponents. Unlike his opponents, he is not interested in benefiting financially from them. Instead, he "wants [literally seeks]" the Corinthians themselves (v. 14b).

In verses 14b–15a, Paul supports his affirmation that he is seeking the Corinthians' welfare, not his own, by returning to the imagery of parenthood to describe his relationship with the church. Because he is their spiritual father, Paul is responsible to give to his "children," not the other way around, even if this means pouring out his life on their behalf.

Thus, with yet another jab at his opponents, Paul uses a rhetorical question in verse 15b to draw the only conclusion that can possibly follow from this concrete evidence of his fatherly love toward the Corinthians. Paul's loving them "more" than his opponents by refusing to take their money should not cause the Corinthians to love him "less" than those who *demand* their money.

In verses 16–18, Paul presses home his point. Those Corinthians who are still rebelling against him must now make a final decision. Paul did not burden them by asking for their money (v. 16a). Titus's careful handling of the money and Paul's sending of the well-respected "brother" to Corinth also speak concretely against his opponents' accusation (vv. 17–18). Since Paul is the one who gave Titus and the brother their mandate, he can argue from their integrity to his own (v. 18).

In verse 19, Paul's rhetorical questions continue. Lest the believers in Corinth misunderstand his purposes, Paul wants it clear that his confidence in the integrity of his ministry means, in reality, that his apologetic is not a *self*-defense before them at all (v. 19a). Paul reaffirms that, as one "in Christ," he "has been speaking in the sight of *God*" (v. 19b), a reference to the fact that God is the judge of his proclamation, not the Corinthians (cf. 5:10). Thus, in defending himself, Paul has not been seeking the approval of the Corinthians but fighting to strengthen their faith (12:19c). Controlled by Christ's love and knowing the fear of God's impending judgment, Paul defends his ministry before God for the sake of the Corinthians (5:11, 13–15).

The basis of Paul's concern for the Corinthians' welfare, therefore, is his fear that the continuing rebellion of those who have not yet repented, as evidenced in their sinful lifestyles, will lead to their being condemned by God through Paul's hand (12:20–21). Apparently, the rebellion against Paul's authority, fueled by the arrival of his opponents, included an unwillingness to repent from the kind of sexual immorality that had been a problem in Corinth from the beginning.

This is what Paul means by the reference in verse 20 to his not finding the Corinthians as he wants them to be when he returns. At the same time, when Paul returns they will not find him as they want him to be either—that is, still willing to tolerate their sinful rebellion against the gospel. Those whom Paul does not find repentant when he comes this "third time"

(v. 14) will not find him willing to withdraw yet again in order to spare them.

Paul's Final Appeal for the Repentance of the Rebellious (13:1–10). Paul introduces the last major section of his letter with a final announcement of his impending third visit. In doing so, he refers to the legal requirements from Deuteronomy 19:15 for accepting evidence in a trial. Paul's promise to fulfill this legal mandate is his final scriptural word to the Corinthians. When he arrives, he will make his case against his opponents and those who follow them, which will be verified by multiple witnesses from within the congregation itself, and all those found guilty will be punished. This is, of course, a harsh declaration. For this reason, Paul warns them in advance, as he did on his second visit, that when he returns the period of patience will come to an end.

The theological foundation of Paul's warning, unfolded throughout chapters 10–13, is crystallized in 13:3–4. When he arrives, Paul will not spare the Corinthians. Believing that Christ was not "weak" but "powerful" among them, the Corinthians insisted that Christ's apostles should manifest such power as well (v. 3b). Paul turns the tables and uses their own emphasis against them. If they want to see the power of Christ, then it will come in judgment, even as the return of the risen Christ will mean the judgment of the world.

Paul could not agree more that the resurrected Christ is acting powerfully in the midst of the Corinthians. Christ "lives by God's power" (v. 4). At the same time, Paul will not concede that his suffering and endurance as an apostle are not just as much a revelation of Christ's resurrection power. In affirming Christ's resurrection power in verse 3, the apostle reintroduces the cross in verse 4 in order to remind the Corinthians that Christ too was "weak" for the sake of his people.

The parallels established between Christ and Paul in verse 4 show how Christ's power is made perfect in Paul's ministry (cf. 12:9). His primary purpose as an apostle is to mediate through his suffering in Christ the knowledge of God and the transforming power of the life-giving Spirit (2:14–3:18; 4:1–15). This is the way in which Paul usually mediates the power of Christ's resurrection. But toward those who reject the cross and power of Christ as embodied in his suffering and endurance, the resurrection power of Christ will be made known through his acts of judgment within the church.

In view of Paul's imminent return to bring God's judgment to Corinth, his commands in verse 5 again contain a severe warning. Like the prophets of the old covenant, Paul thus announces the coming judgment in advance in order to bring about the repentance of those who are truly God's people. The goal of the test is to make it clear that Christ is indeed in them.

The means by which the test is performed is Paul himself. Allegiance to him as their apostle is the criterion that determines whether Christ is present in their lives since Paul is confident that he himself has already passed the test (v. 6). To accept *Paul's* message of reconciliation is to accept *God's* message of reconciliation.

Paul's confidence in verse 6 and his corresponding prayer for the Corinthians in verse 7 are both buttressed by the conviction that the truth of the gospel will prevail over all contenders (v. 8). Not even Paul's inadequacies and infirmities can do anything against it. *Therefore*, Paul rejoices whenever he is "weak," but the Corinthians are "strong" (v. 9). The apostle is glad whenever, as an extension of the cross, he is being led into suffering on their behalf so that, as an expression of the resurrection, they are being consoled and encouraged in their faith.

This is why Paul prefers to be "weak" for their sake and why he prays for the restoration of those who have begun with Christ but have now been led astray by the false apostles (v. 9b). Paul takes no pleasure in having to judge the Corinthians. This is also why he is writing "these things" (v. 10)—a reference to the present letter, especially chapters 10–13. Paul's desire is that he will not be forced to exercise his authority harshly when he comes again to Corinth (13:10b).

Paul's Final Words of Exhortation and Benediction (13:11–14). Just as he did in his opening, Paul closes his letter by following the conventions common to ancient letter writing. Unlike other ancient letters, in which the closings were curt and only linked to the body of the letter in a general way, Paul expands the letter closing significantly, strategically employing it to echo specific themes from his letter. Paul closes his letter with additional commands (v. 11), greetings (v. 12), and two farewell benedictions, one for peace and one for grace (vv. 11, 13). In each case, his closing highlights a main theme of his letter.

We must be careful not to gloss over these commands, as if they were merely some closing remarks thrown in only to fulfill a rhetorical or literary purpose. From Paul's perspective, there is much at stake in issuing these exhortations. Moreover, the structure of his closing again reveals the structure of his theology. In particular, the movement from the admonitions of verse 11a–b to the benediction in verse 11c demonstrates that God's continuing presence among the Corinthians is inextricably linked to the purification and repentance of his people.

Paul's own greeting in verse 11 is matched by two final greetings in verses 12–13, both of which continue his emphasis on unity within the church by stressing its local and universal dimensions respectively. Paul first calls for a greeting of "one another with a holy kiss" (v. 12), a practice unique among believers that signified their mutual acceptance and oneness as a family. Next, Paul extends to the Corinthians a greeting from "all God's people" (v. 13), thereby emphasizing their oneness with the church at large.

Paul also adds "all" at the end of verse 14 to stress the inclusive unity of the church. This emphasis on love and fellowship recalls themes from chapters 1–9 not found in chapters 10–13. In so doing, Paul again subtly indicates his goal of incorporating those who are still in rebellion against him back into the church as a whole.

Paul's closing benediction signifies the blessing of the new covenant itself, in which the grace of Christ has made it possible to experience God's love, poured out in the Holy Spirit. It is not accidental, therefore, that Paul's letter climaxes with a reference to the fellowship brought about by the Spirit. The pouring out of the Spirit on God's people is *the* gift of the new covenant. So in closing, Paul prays as a minister of the new covenant that God will grant to all those in the church the unity of the Spirit that he has worked so hard to mediate. For after everything is said and done, and despite all her flaws and growing pains, the church remains the temple of the living God.

Application. The sober conclusion to 2 Corinthians does not derive from a religious moralism, but from the life-transforming reality of Christ that Paul himself had experienced. Paul's expectations for the Corinthians are expectations for God. His admonitions to them are expressions of his confidence in what God can do in the lives of sinners. There is hope for all who trust in Christ. Perseverance is not reserved for a Christian elite but is promised to *all* who belong to God.

GALATIANS

INTRODUCTION TO GALATIANS

The *origin* of Paul's letter to the Galatians is well-known: after Paul had evangelized the southern districts of Galatia successfully and established some churches during his first missionary journey, he returned to Jerusalem (cf. Acts 13–14). While there he caught wind of some Jewish-Christian teachers who infiltrated these Galatian churches with a polluted message that was, according to Paul, endangering the entire gospel.

Before Paul could get off on his second missionary journey (cf. Acts 15:36–18:23), and just before the Apostolic Council of Acts 15, Paul sent this urgent and emotional missive to Galatia with the prayer and hope that it would straighten out the Galatian churches. What happened to the Galatians and how they received Paul's emotional letter, we simply do not know. What we do know is that this letter, penned probably in the late 40s of the first century, has given both life-transforming instruction and heartfelt admonition to the church for nearly two millennia.

BOOK OUTLINE

I. Introduction (1:1–9)
II. Paul's Personal Vindication of His Message (1:10–2:21)
III. Paul's Theological Vindication of His Message (3:1–4:31)
IV. Paul's Practical Application of His Message (5:1–6:10)
V. Conclusion (6:11–18)

GALATIANS 1:1–9

Original Meaning. Paul's salutation has some interesting features that we need to examine, including the significance of the title "apostle" (v. 1) and the meaning of "the present evil age" (v. 4). To use the title "apostle" as the second word of the letter is to claim authority and to expect agreement on the part of the churches of Galatia. Paul, along with the testimony of the church, saw the role of the apostles to be a special one in history; he knew that they performed a crucial function in the period just after the resurrection of Christ. Paul, then, writes as an apostle—as one who has been called personally by Jesus Christ, who therefore represents Jesus Christ, and who has a crucial role in the history of the church. He expects the Galatians to listen; he knows that disagreement is heresy when it comes to the essentials of the gospel as made known through the apostles and prophets. Even Paul himself must submit to his own gospel (1:8, 10).

Paul's greeting is the typical early Christian mixing of the Greek and Jewish greetings ("grace and peace"). However, the grace and peace Paul invokes upon the Galatians is the grace and peace "from God our Father and the Lord Jesus Christ" (v. 3). In describing the origin of the greetings, Paul goes on to comment on Jesus, saying that Jesus Christ "gave himself for our sins to rescue us from the present evil age" (v. 4). Forgiveness of sins is important for Galatians, but they did not realize that this forgiveness was also sufficient to rescue them from "the present evil age." It was the present evil age that concerned Paul because he believed that those who consistently lived in Christ would not succumb to it.

Paul's introduction moves next to a description of the *occasion* for the letter (vv. 6–9). It has often been observed that this is the only surviving letter of Paul's that does not contain a thanksgiving for the church to whom he is writing. However, we should also observe that many hold this letter to be the first canonical letter Paul wrote and that, in light of this, it is hard to argue for a departure from his typical practice since that practice had not yet begun. It is just possible that Paul's practice of expressing thanksgiving in his letters developed later or that such a practice developed out of his harsh experience at Galatia.

The reason why Paul wrote this letter, and the reason we have it, is because the Galatians had changed positions on a crucial subject: the means of acceptance with God and the role Christ played in that acceptance. Paul is amazed that their change took place "so quickly" (v. 6). While Paul suggests this was a move to a "different gospel," he goes on in verse 7 to clarify this by saying that this is "really no gospel at all." The move of the Galatians was not one of those views of legitimate Christian differences; it was total and devastating. Gross perversions of the gospel are heresies. Paul's final words here are potent. He invokes a curse on anyone (including himself!) who distorts the gospel.

Application. If it is true that an apostle is a personal agent of Jesus Christ, and if it is true that an agent is a personal representative, then it follows that Paul's message is a message from Jesus Christ. Acknowledging this implies that every Christian must accept apostolic letters as authoritative, for their message is a message from Jesus Christ. Of course, this works out in various ways. For instance, we may be charmed by radical pluralism today with its attractive suggestion that all will eventually be saved. But if we accept the earliest definitions of an apostle, then we must also accept the message of Paul that states that additions to the gospel bring the wrath, not the acceptance, of God.

GALATIANS 1:10–12

Original Meaning. Galatians 1:10–2:21 is concerned with demonstrating the independence of Paul's gospel. The opponents of Paul were bent on demonstrating that Paul's gospel ultimately derived from Jerusalem and from the early Jewish apostles who operated out of Jerusalem. For earliest first-century Christianity, the crisis was whether Israel would have a privileged existence and status in the new movement. The issue then became Jewish distinctives as opposed to the heterogeneous and, often enough, non-Jewish life of the diaspora. Paul countered this by demonstrating that his gospel came from Jesus Christ and comprised all people.

Paul argues that his gospel is not in fact dependent on Jerusalem and its leaders. Instead, it is an independent expression. He does this first through a series of questions (v. 10), each of which implies that he is not seeking to please human beings but God. Paul's questions are important here. It is reasonable to argue that his questions contain their own answers. For Paul there is a radical difference between "trying to win the approval of human beings" and being a "servant of Christ" (v. 10). For him, to accept the mantle of being a servant of Christ was to eliminate once-and-for-all the desire to please people.

What is "the gospel I preached" (v. 11)? There are at least three dimensions to "Paul's" gospel. First, salvation is in Jesus Christ alone, in fulfillment of the revelation given through Moses in millennia past. Second, one becomes accepted by God solely by faith, apart from living in accordance with the law of Moses. Finally, this acceptance is open as much to gentiles as it is to Jews. While the first two have been the focus of theologians since the Reformation, the center of attention in Paul's day was the third. This view threatened the very existence of Judaism and created the social crisis behind the letter.

"I received it by revelation from Jesus Christ" (v. 12). Surely Paul is describing here his Damascus Road encounter with the risen Lord, in which experience he was both converted and received his call to evangelize the gentile world (cf. Acts 9:1–19). The term "revelation" describes something made known by God that would otherwise not be known or accessible. Revelation thus stands in glaring contrast to passing on sacred traditions. In fact, we must surely see here a criticism of the Jewish agitators, whose basis of knowledge was sacred tradition. Paul contends that while their gospel may represent some of the leaders in Jerusalem, his gospel is a direct revelation from Jesus Christ.

Application. Along with Paul, we need to examine ourselves to see if we are seeking to "win the approval of human beings" and succumbing to social and peer pressure (v. 10). Probably no feature of life is more difficult than to discern where our own line of approval is actually going. Is it going in the direction of God or is it being rerouted through the approval of human leaders, spouses, and friends? Are we doing what we think is right before God or are we trying to be diplomatic or political? This rerouting can be subtle indeed: from the glance of a spouse during a conversation to a letter to a Christian friend. When the conviction of our own faithfulness to truth and the apostolic gospel gives way to the desire of approval from another human being, we have joined the ranks of those whom Paul attacks.

GALATIANS 1:13–24

Original Meaning. Paul next provides his readers with a quick overview of his life, a mini-autobiography. But this life story is more than a family recollection of events in the past. As we have been arguing, the first section of Galatians is Paul's vindication of his gospel and its origins, validity, and authority.

The first argument in our section (vv. 13–17) concerns Paul's independence from human teaching. God's call came to Paul directly; he says that he did not "consult any human being" (v. 16). His pre-Christian history in no way prepared him to be an apostle. Paul's description of his past focuses on the sacred traditions that were passed on in Judaism, the very element Paul is arguing against in this chapter.

The second argument is the same in essence but concerns a different set of authorities. Paul next moves from human teaching to the churches of Judea (vv. 18–24). Paul learned something from Peter, but he spent only a few days with him—and, he adds, only "after three years" (v. 18). We must infer from the seriousness of Paul's tone here that the Jewish agitators were arguing that Paul's first visit to Jerusalem was one designed for his instruction in the rudiments of the gospel. Paul thus argues, in context, that his gospel came from Jesus Christ directly and that it was derived neither from human teaching nor from the Jerusalem-Judean churches.

Application. Paul's calling in life was *specific*. Paul had a clear sense of God's direction in his life. We have been taught that if we aim at nothing we will hit nothing. The same applies in Christian living. It is fundamentally important for Christians to discern their gifts and to use those gifts. When we sense the call of God on our lives, we need to stick to that calling and not let distractions prevent us from fulfilling God's will for us.

GALATIANS 2:1–10

Original Meaning. The first unit in this next section is concerned with *Paul's presentation of his message* (vv. 1–3). Barnabas accompanied Paul to Jerusalem because he was a significant and respected person with the Jerusalem churches. It is possible that Paul brought Titus, likely one of his early converts and a continual friend, as a test case. Since "those esteemed as leaders" of Jerusalem did not demand Titus's circumcision, it can be assumed that they did not think circumcision was necessary for salvation.

Paul's argument against the Jewish agitators from this incident has a further proof: when he was in Jerusalem he met "privately" with the leaders and "set before them the gospel" that he preached to the gentiles (v. 2). This gave Paul an even deeper argument: his gospel was both independent of, and confirmed by, Jerusalem.

The second unit is concerned with *the opposition to Paul's message* (vv. 4–5). Paul argues that the experience he and the Galatians were presently having with the Jewish agitators was identical to the one he had in Jerusalem. In light of Paul's comments in 1:6–9, we should not be surprised that Paul calls them "false believers" (2:4). Paul's response to the infiltrators (v. 5) is the theme of the entire letter.

The third unit is concerned with *the unity expressed by the Jerusalem pillars and Paul over Paul's message* (vv. 6–10). In chapter 1 Paul argued that the *source* of his gospel was independent of Jerusalem. In chapter 2, however, he argues that while his gospel was independent in source, it was also *endorsed* by the Jerusalem pillars. That endorsement, for Paul, was not necessary, but as long as it worked out that way he decides to use that endorsement as part of his case against his opponents.

Application. Fundamental to Christian unity is the recognition of different callings and movements in the church of Christ. We need to see how varied the church is and hear how vibrantly different it is in different parts of the world. It is not unwise for Christians to visit other churches in their local communities to find out what God is doing in various churches. True enough, sometimes we may be disappointed with what we see, but frequently we will be encouraged by finding the faith of others expressed in slightly (but just as valid) different ways.

GALATIANS 2:11–14

Original Meaning

The Confrontation (2:11). Paul here argues more than that Peter was simply wrong or inconsistent; Peter had actually perverted the gospel itself with his behavior. Paul publicly rebuked Peter for his hypocritical behavior because what he was doing was clearly contrary to life through Christ and in the Spirit.

The Explanation (2:12–13). Peter, in his life in the diaspora, had become accustomed to eating with gentiles. But when a party from Jerusalem arrived, he felt their displeasure (no doubt hearing about it from them). He "began to draw back and separate himself" from the gentiles. The table that had functioned wonderfully as a symbol of unity had become a table of separation once again for Peter.

The Charge (2:14). Paul charges Peter indirectly and directly in this verse. Indirectly, Paul says, Peter's behavior was essentially a failure to live in line with the truth of the gospel. Directly, Paul accuses Peter in the following words: "You are a Jew, yet you live like a Gentile and not like a Jew. How is it, then, that you force Gentiles to follow Jewish customs?" It was not wrong for Jewish missionaries to the gentiles to be Jews who lived like gentiles and not like Jews. But it became problematical when those same missionaries then "force[d] Gentiles to follow Jewish customs." This word "force" is the most important word in this verse, for it tips us off as to what Peter was doing.

So what was Peter doing? He had previously enjoyed unrestricted social fellowship with the gentiles. When the Jewish nationalists arrived, Peter began to *force gentile Christians to be circumcised (and to follow Jewish social laws), to reduce the threat of persecution he was beginning to feel from these ardent Jewish nationalists.* Peter, in effect, was destroying the gospel of Jesus Christ by demanding that the converts at Galatia become Jews.

Application. The adaptations and changes that Peter's new ministry involved were difficult for him. He needed to learn that there had to be considerable flex in his new life in Christ. What was hard to accept was that this new life needed to be consistent: consistent with God's Spirit (though perhaps not with the law of Moses). Consistency in Christian living is not conformity and uniformity. Consistency is measured by listening to God's word, to Christ, and to the Spirit of God. When we arrive in our Antiochs, in our new situations, we need to learn to live consistently within the freedom that God's Spirit provides. For some, this is scary; for all, it ought to be the adventure of living in faith.

GALATIANS 2:15–21

Original Meaning

The Fact of a Common Conversion Experience (2:15–16). To be a Jew "by birth" was a wonderful privilege because Israel had been given God's covenant and promises (Rom 3:1–2; 9:4–5; Eph 2:12). As privileged Jews, Peter and Paul came to the conviction to "know that a person is not justified by the works of the law, but by faith in Jesus Christ." In what follows we need to analyze three crucial terms for understanding this passage (and Galatians as a whole): *justification*, *works*, and *faith*.

Broadly speaking, *justification* is a metaphor of our acceptance with God that is drawn from the world of law and jurisprudence. The dilemma people find themselves in before God is that they are guilty because they have transgressed God's law and commandments. Their desire and only hope is that God, perceived in this metaphor as judge, will somehow forgive them, make things right, and eliminate their guilt. But since God as judge is purely objective and altogether morally righteous, and because he cannot simply overlook sin, humans find themselves in an awful predicament. But God surprisingly forgives; his agent in this forgiveness is Jesus Christ, who legally assumed our guilt and bore the curse of the law in his crucifixion (3:13). The result of Christ's work is that humans who trust in Christ and surrender themselves to him are declared fit before God.

What are the *works of the law*? Are they merit-seeking works done in order to gain favor with God? Paul probably does not have in mind a person's merit intentions (works done *in order to gain* favor with God) in this expression. Rather, as we read Galatians, we find that Paul must have in mind two ideas. First, he means behavior, or work, that conforms to the law of Moses as an expression of a confession that ultimate acceptance with God is to be found through a commitment to submit to the law of Moses. Second, he means behavior that separates Jews from gentiles—namely, the works of circumcision, table-food restrictions, and social regulations governing the behavior of Jews as they relate to gentiles.

Paul knew that implicit in conversion to Christ was a confession that a proper standing before God could not be had through a commitment to the law. Christ was the fulfillment of the law and went beyond it in his revelation (Rom 10:4; Gal 3:19–25). To do the law after Christ was to deny his sufficient work; it was to step back in salvation history to a period before Christ. For Paul, this was abominable and denied the very purpose of Christ's coming.

On the other hand, Paul is not against good works. For him, works has three primary ideas. First, there is the *principle of works* as the way one finds acceptance with God. This sense of works Paul opposed; the principle of works is never a means of acceptance with God. Second, there is the notion of *Mosaic works, or works of the law*, as found predominantly in Galatians, that describes the behavior of certain persons who were expressing their conviction that acceptance with God could only be had if one lived according to the law of Moses (e.g., 2:3, 11–14). *What* these people were doing was perverted by *why* they were doing it: to express their faith in Moses rather than in Christ alone. There was nothing wrong with living according to the law when it was done properly (Acts 16:3; 21:26). But when one obeyed the law to express one's confidence in it as a necessary step for ultimate acceptance by God, Paul took serious umbrage.

Third, there is the idea of *good works as a lifestyle* that is attractive, moral, and godly. We might say, for Galatians, that the "fruit of the Spirit" (Gal 5:22–23) is a description of "good works." This kind of works is the primary thrust of how Paul thinks Christians should live. Paul is not, or never was, against good works as an adequate description of a Christian's moral life and relations with others. Indeed, Paul says we will be judged by our works.

Now to our third expression. Justification comes to a person *by faith*, not by observing the law. We may define faith as *the initial and continual response of trust in, and obedience to, Christ by a person for the purpose of acceptance with God.* When Paul uses the term "faith," he is describing both the initial act of trust and the continuing disposition of trust and obedience. This is why faith in Christ and "works of the law" are opposites: one cannot opt for Christ's system *and* Moses's system at the same time because they are mutually exclusive options for salvation. One cannot live under both systems without destroying one or the other's integrity.

The Implications of a Common Conversion Experience (2:17–21). There are three implications of this common conversion. First, *the life of the Christian is not a "lawless" life in the sense of wicked antinomianism* (v. 17). Paul's emphasis here is that life in Christ is not life in sin. Rather, life in Christ, as he will elaborate in chapters 5–6, is life in the Spirit. Instead of promoting sin, Christ promotes purity, holiness, love, and morally attractive personalities. What was formerly found only in the law for the Jews (namely, God's will for his people) has now been fulfilled in God's great gift of the Holy Spirit.

Second, *in converting to Christ, the Christian, especially the Jewish Christian, forfeits the opportunity of ever returning to the law of Moses as the primary orientation governing all of life* (v. 18). Peter was rebuilding Judaism when he withdrew from open table fellowship, even though he had previously destroyed it when he turned away from Judaism to Christ. Peter became the "lawbreaker" when he returned to Judaism, for in going back he was adopting the law with its condemning force.

Third, *in converting to Christ, the Jewish Christian finds spiritual life through death, understood here as being crucified with Christ to the law so that the resurrected Christ might grant his new life to the believer* (vv. 19–21). The "Jewish ego," the privilege Jews thought they had—but had only until Christ—died to the law. The life that the Jew, Paul, now lives for God is the result of dying with Christ (v. 20). Yet also the life Paul now lives is a life of the indwelling Christ and the indwelling

Spirit. In opting for the Christ system, the Jewish believers were not setting aside God's grace. The accusation against them was that they were setting aside God's grace (understood as the law of Moses). Paul counters: "No, it is not we who are setting aside God's grace when we leave the law. Rather, you (who do not come with us) are missing the great grace of God in Christ."

Application. It is common today to hear that the only requirement for salvation is to "believe that Jesus Christ saves." This is true—if properly defined. However, the term *believe* has been frequently wrongly defined in this preaching, and the statement consequently becomes untrue. What is the misstep? Simply put, it is the reduction of the meaning of faith to "mere credence." That is, faith is defined as "believing that Jesus is Savior" and no more. Jesus is indeed Savior, but in order for him to become the Savior for a given person, that person must surrender himself or herself in trust and obedience for true faith to be expressed.

GALATIANS 3:1–5

Original Meaning

Paul's Personal Question (3:1). The term "foolish" captures Paul's point. The Galatian believers were illogical in committing themselves to the Pauline message of God's grace in Christ and then succumbing to the Jewish agitators' insistence on keeping the law of Moses. The intensity of their experience, their conversion experience, leads Paul to appeal to it first.

Paul's Questions about Experience (3:2–5). *The question about initiation (3:2).* Paul begins with their first experience, their initiation into Christian faith, their conversion. And he wants to know: How did they get the Spirit? By obeying Moses or by obeying the gospel of faith? The real issue here is *how the experience took place and what triggered it.*

The question about completion (3:3). To live in the "flesh" is to ignore the Spirit, and, in this context, Paul may be thinking partly in terms of circumcision.

The question about persecution (3:4). What Paul envisages is simple. After their conversion to Christ (according to the Pauline gospel), the Galatian converts experienced persecution at the hands of others (probably at the hands of Jews, and perhaps also the Jewish agitators; see 4:29). So, he asks, was this all in vain?

The question about miracles (3:5). Paul queries, what triggered God's power? By now the Galatians must be either hiding in shame or continuing the Jewish agitators' polemical responses by appealing to Scripture, which Paul goes on to rebut.

Application. Experience is an integral part of all of our lives. We can learn from this passage that arguments from experience can be a part of our theological argumentation. But we cannot think our appeals to experience are all that we need. Contextual reading of Paul's argument from experience shows that Paul did not stop here; he went on to arguments from Scripture and logic. And so should we. Our arguments from experience have no truth backing if they are nothing more than that.

GALATIANS 3:6–14

Original Meaning. Paul's point in verses 6–7 is that acceptance by God solely on the basis of faith is as old as Abraham. Paul's emphasis is that Abraham was pronounced as acceptable to God *before his circumcision*, making the implication clear: circumcision was not necessary for acceptance with God. For Paul, Abraham's descendants are those who simply believe; they are not those who believe and allow themselves to be circumcised.

In verses 8–9 Paul then argues the point that gentile acceptance by God on the same basis as Jews is also as old as Abraham. Having argued that Abraham was accepted by God because of his faith and that the true descendants of Abraham are believers, Paul argues that *gentiles* can be these true believers.

In verses 10–11, Paul argues that the law does not justify because its function is to curse. Those who opt for the law are cursed because they are choosing to omit the salvation that can come only through faith in Christ (now that he has come). In choosing for the law, they are left to find what they can for salvation in the law; but it can only condemn.

In verse 12, Paul then explains that the law operates under a different system; it is not a system governed by faith but a system governed by doing. Paul has established that the law does not bring acceptance with God—that, even as taught in the Bible (Hab 2:4), it comes instead by way of faith. Once again, however, Paul does not bring in merit seeking but *only that the law of Moses is not a faith system.* This is critical for our perception of Paul's logic.

Paul then in verses 13–14 argues that the curse of the law fell on Christ so others might escape. It was possibly particularly the Jewish Christians who raised the issue of what to do with the curse they incurred in living (especially previously) under the Mosaic law. The term "redeemed" here is drawn from the commercial world (v. 13). The essential ideas are that (1) people are by nature slaves to sin and under the curse of the law; (2) Christ paid the price of freedom by dying on the cross; and (3) those who trust in Christ's ransom price are set free from sin and the curse of the law.

How did Christ do this? Christ ransomed Jewish Christians from the curse of the law "by becoming a curse" (v. 13). What Christ did was to die the death of a transgressor. In so doing, he becomes the transgressor because Christ was publicly crucified. But because he was innocent and sinless, he can die on behalf of those who have sinned and so absorb their curse. And because he was divine, he could perfectly satisfy the justice of God (see Rom 3:21–26).

The redemption Christ accomplished freed Jewish Christians (Jews who believe) from the curse of the law and also made it possible for gentiles to be incorporated into Abraham's blessing (Gal 3:14). Furthermore, now the new people of God (both Jewish and gentile) can "receive the promise of the Spirit" (v. 14).

Application. A fundamental message in this passage is that gentiles are included into the people of God by faith and that their inclusion is permitted without having to nationalize (i.e., become Jews). By extension today, the gospel is for all, and therefore social barriers must be broken down by the gospel. We find that the principle that Paul is using is that God loves "all kinds of people" and works with "all kinds"; therefore, the church cannot construct barriers to prevent the inclusion of "some kinds." We must apply Paul's message to our world by seeing if our churches and the gospel we preach minister to all kinds who believe or only some kinds (usually our "own" kind). We must constantly explore the implications of this message for the church today and allow ourselves to be challenged by it if we are to remain faithful to Paul's gospel.

GALATIANS 3:15–18

Original Meaning. Essentially Paul's argument in verse 15 here is that the way a human covenant operates is certainly the same way as a divine covenant does. In verse 16 Paul realizes he must first prove that the Abrahamic covenant applies to the Christian era. He does this by means of a special form of interpretation, in which he sees in "seed" a corporate solidarity in Christ (v. 16). By stating that Christ is the "seed," Paul interprets Genesis 13:15 and 24:7 in a Christian manner and reveals that the Abrahamic covenant is the one that climaxes in Christ and those who believe in him.

In verse 17 Paul then applies the analogy of the law of covenants of inheritance. And his point is quite simple: the law of Moses was given 430 years (Exod 12:40–42) after the covenant was made with Abraham; therefore, since the covenant (made with Abraham, not Moses) is irrevocable, the law cannot change the arrangements God made with Abraham.

In verse 18 Paul then restates the argument. God did not demand of Abraham to obey the law. In fact, as Paul has shown, the law was not even around; it came 430 years later. This must mean that the way to inherit the blessing of Abraham is the way Abraham received it: by faith in God's promises.

Application. We read the Bible for personal blessing, personal guidance, and personal instruction, and we should. But sometimes our individual desires express a rank egocentric approach to life and Bible reading. While God uses our highly individual desires to teach us something, frequently our individual approaches lead us to find meanings that are not there and teachings that are simply not accurate. One of the goals of this commentary is to help us to learn to interpret the Bible more accurately, both in its original meaning and its application.

GALATIANS 3:19–25

Original Meaning

The Question about the Historical Purpose of the Law (3:19–20). The *question* Paul raises ("Why, then, was the law given at all?") is easy to understand. His *answer*, however, takes some unraveling. First, Paul answers the question by stating the *purpose of the law* (v. 19b). It was given in order to reveal certain kinds of behavior as sinful. Second, Paul's answer on the historical purpose of the law pertains to *the temporal limitations of the law* (v. 19c). The law was to govern God's people only until Messiah had come. Finally, Paul speaks about the *circumstances of the giving of the law* (vv. 19d–20) and infers that an arrangement between a person and God that has mediators is inferior to an arrangement that has no mediators, because the latter arrangement is directly from God.

The Question about the Historical Function of the Law (3:21–25). *A second question and its answer (3:21a–b).* Is the law working against the purposes of God in the Abrahamic promise (v. 21a)? Paul's answer is simple: "Absolutely not!" (v. 21b).

The reason for the answer (3:21c–25). Paul then talks about *the essential inability of the law to bring saving life* (v. 21c). In effect, Paul's argument is that the law is not intended to bring life; therefore, the Jewish agitators cannot be demanding the Galatians to follow the law of Moses *in order to be accepted by God*. The function of the *law* (v. 22a) was to reveal sin (cf. v. 19). The next three verses (vv. 23–25) then largely restate what has been said before about both the purpose of the law and its time limitations, but this time he uses other terms.

First, Paul speaks of *the time elements of the law* (v. 23). At verse 19 Paul had said that the law was to reveal sin until the Seed had come; now he says the same thing but uses different expressions for both elements. Second, he addresses *the effect of the law* (v. 24a). The law held those under it (probably Jews) as prisoners and locked them up (v. 23). The expression in verse 24a is a free translation of what literally translates, "the law has become our pedagogue [Gk. *paidagōgos*]." A "pedagogue" here describes a time of children being enslaved, and "until Christ" means that the law had a confining ministry until the era of Christ came.

Third, Paul turns to *the result of the law's effect* (v. 24b). All of Paul's argument assumes that the Jewish agitators agree that justification begins with faith in Christ; they also mistakenly assume that the "works of the law" perfect that faith. But now that Paul has shown that the law pertains to a limited time, he can say that justification is solely by faith because "works of the law" now pertain to a bygone era.

Finally, Paul draws it all together by speaking of *the suspension of the law* (v. 25). The law had a limited purpose, and this purpose was only for a limited time—until the Seed had come. Everything the law wanted to be when it was young (as revealed to Moses) is found now in Christ and in life in the Spirit. Thus, when a Christian lives in Christ and the Spirit, that Christian is not living contrary to the law but is living in transcendence of the law.

Application. One of the most significant implications of these verses is the conclusion that God's law (meaning the law of Moses) has been in some sense suspended for the Christian. How then do we work out moral problems today in light of this view of the law? Christians must begin with two assumptions. First, faith is the response God wants of us if we are to be accepted by him and that this faith works itself out in obedience. Second, life in the Spirit is our primary mode of operation as we seek to live obediently before God.

This has an important corollary: *Christians who are seeking God's will do not turn first of all to the law of Moses for direction.* Instead, they listen to God's Spirit and to the teachings of Jesus ("the law of Christ"; see 6:2); both of these teach them that they are to love God and love others. In following Christ and the Spirit, the Christian will actually do God's will.

GALATIANS 3:26–4:7

Original Meaning

The Thesis Stated: Sons of God and Heirs by Faith (3:26–29). *Statement of sonship (3:26).* The use of "children of God" is important for the Galatians' experience, for they learned to say "Abba" to God through conversion (4:6). Being a child of God is a special promise by God for the last days and describes that special relationship of intimacy that the people of God can have with God.

Restatement of sonship (3:27). As Paul restates his thesis, he makes several parallel comments. What is important for our analysis of verse 27 is to realize that Paul sees faith as being expressed originally in baptism and becoming "children" as the baptismal experience of being united with Christ and putting on Christ. Paul is probably thinking that, since Christ is the Son of God, being united with him and putting him on is what sonship is all about.

The explanation (3:28). To be "in Christ" is to be in spiritual fellowship with him through God's Spirit. Those who are "in Christ Jesus" are those who believe in him; those who believe in him come from all walks of life, from every nation, and from both sexes. Scholars have often observed that a Jewish blessing that was prayed daily by some Jews is reversed here: "Blessed be God that he did not make me a gentile; blessed be God that he did not make me ignorant [or a slave]; blessed be God that he did not make me a woman" (Tosefta Berakhot 7:18). This is possibly a first-century prayer. Paul is surely responding to such a demeaning classification of humans.

The implication (3:29). Since the Galatian believers are "in Christ" and since Christ is the Seed of Abraham (v. 19), then it follows that the Galatian believers are also Abraham's seed. And if they are Abraham's seed, then they also inherit Abraham's promise—a relationship with God that entails his blessing and goodness.

The Analogy and Its Application (4:1–7). *The analogy (4:1–2).* Here Paul provides an analogy to illustrate his point. A child who is destined to inherit an estate is no different than a slave as long as he is a child (until twenty to twenty-five years old), for he cannot inherit that estate until he becomes an adult. During this period he is subject to the "guardians and trustees," but only until the father's set time of inheritance.

First application: we were enslaved (4:3). Paul says that when they were "underage," his audience was enslaved under the "elemental spiritual forces" or "basic principles" of the world (Gk. *stoicheia*). What does this term mean? Paul uses this term again in verse 9, describing a return to either pagan life with its tribal/national religions (cf. v. 8) or to the Mosaic laws. It is best to see it as a reference to the Mosaic law in its negative and suspended features.

Second application: we were made sons (4:4–5). God sent his Son, and this Son lived under the law (though not under sin) so that he could absorb the curse of the law, exhaust the fumes of God's wrath, and redeem those under the law. Once the Son had done this, they could become sons of God (v. 5).

Third application: we are heirs (4:6–7). The Spirit of God enables the child of God to cry out "Abba." If the Galatian Christians are calling God "Abba," they are "children of God"; the ability to call God "Abba" is evidence of being a son of God. This means they are no longer "slaves." And since they are children, they have the inheritance.

Application. According to Paul, a child of God is one who learns to call God "Abba" because God has given his Spirit to his children. This was often the first term a Jewish child learned (along with *imma*, "mom" or "mommy"), and it can be translated "dad" or arguably even "daddy." Yet there is more to it than the language of a child. The father, the *abba*, in Judaism was also a commanding authority figure for the Jewish family, and children were taught never to disagree with and always to honor him. Thus, the term *abba* is not just the language of little children with their loving fathers playing games and talking together; rather, it is the term that Jews used for their relationship to their fathers that involved both relational intimacy and honorable respect.

GALATIANS 4:8–20

Original Meaning

The Problem (4:8–11). Paul here describes two religious dimensions of his audience's past. First, they did not know the God of Israel, the true God of the world. Second, the gods they did know were "by nature . . . not gods" (v. 8). Paul goes on to state that now that they are converted, they have *a good beginning*. That good beginning *has now become a bad situation*. Despite having received the knowledge of God, they have reverted back to their former ways. This bad situation leads to *Paul's fear*. Paul had worked hard on the Galatians' behalf. Any pastor knows the heartache and fear that come when a parishioner wavers, stumbles, and even falls away. His fear and frustration now give way to a plea.

The Plea (4:12–20). *Paul's example (4:12a).* Most likely Paul here means something like this: "Become like me by freeing yourself from the law of Moses, just as I abandoned the law of Moses as God's dominant revelation for his people" (cf. Gal. 2:15–21).

Paul's role in their defection (4:12b). "You did me no wrong." What does Paul mean here? He was a servant of God, not the center of God's work, yet he knew that to reject him was more importantly to reject God (cf. Matt 10:40–42).

Paul's reminder of their initial response (4:13–16). What was this illness? There have been many guesses but no consensus. More importantly, the illness did not bother the Galatians (vv. 14–16); they looked beyond it and saw in Paul's preaching the truth of God because his message was attended by the power of the Holy Spirit. Reminding the Galatians of their former commitment (and friendship) to him makes the present situation unbearable for Paul (vv. 15–16). This whole situation, Paul thinks, needs clarification, so Paul proceeds to explain it.

Paul's explanation of the situation (4:17–18). The term "zeal" is highly important for understanding the context. Were the Jewish agitators violent Zealots? Though "zealous to win you over" can mean nothing more than "working hard to proselytize you," in essence their "zeal" was Jewish nationalism.

To "alienate you" means "to enter you, through circumcision, into Israel." The Jewish agitators' goal, of course, was that the Galatians might be "zealous" for them: devoted so much to the Mosaic law that they would carry on their agenda of separating God's people from the gentile world by constructing the barriers that Jesus Christ had broken down.

Paul now pauses to interject a note about zeal: it is good to be zealous if one is zealous for God, as some of the saints of Israel had been. It is "for no good," however, if one's zeal is nationalistic and contrary to the promises of Abraham.

Paul's wish (4:19–20). Paul's description of the Galatians' situation leads him to think of his pastoral role to be one like giving birth to children. While he implies new birth here, he also implies that the opponents had caused what, in effect, might be considered an abortion. For them to grow, Paul senses that he would have to be there and "change my tone"—from this stern warning and harsh language to the gentleness of a love that would persuade them over to his side and "alienate them" from the Jewish agitators. Paul's letter, he implies, is a weak communication in comparison to his mighty presence.

Application. Paul's emotional response here is, without doubt, a critique of the "dry as dust" approach some advocate for teaching and preaching. Inasmuch as the gospel of Christ stirs our emotions, we should try to stir the emotions of those who hear it. Inasmuch as the message of sin pricks our consciences, so we should seek to convict others of sin. Inasmuch as the love of God is soothing and ennobling, so we should flood our people with a sense of their dignity because God loves them. The emotions attached to, and inherent in, a text ought to be there, and we ought to bring them out. Otherwise, we do not read the Bible aright. We dare not pretend that the Bible is a book for academics, designed only for intellectual stimulation and debate. The Bible is a book of reality, and part of reality is emotion.

GALATIANS 4:21–31

Original Meaning

The Sarah-Hagar Allegory and Its Implications (4:21–31). *The question (4:21).* Those who wish to be "under the law" (live according to the Mosaic law in such a way that Christ is eclipsed) need to learn to read the law in light of what God has done in Christ.

The biblical material (4:22–23). Paul alludes here to texts in Genesis 16, 21, and 25. Paul fastens his attention on (1) the two women, describing one as the "slave woman" and the other as the "free woman" (which fits his polemical agenda), and (2) the births of the two boys—one "according to the flesh" and one "as the result of a . . . promise."

The interpretation (4:24–27). These two women correspond to two covenants. Hagar is in the covenant established on Mount Sinai (the place of giving the law), and her children are all slaves. Jerusalem corresponds to this Mount Sinai, for since its inhabitants live under the law, its people are slaves. Such an association would have been shocking to the Jewish agitators and to all Jews.

Sarah is connected to Isaiah 54:1 by the word "barren." There we have promises of God that he would restore Zion. Thus, Isaiah is predicting the future Jerusalem. In fact, by associating that his readers are part of the true Jerusalem in the sense of fulfilling 54:1, Paul is saying that those who believe in Christ are living in the new era, the era of fulfillment. They are "more" numerous, meaning that God has blessed them more.

The application (4:28–31). Paul makes his application, arguing from experience. Just as Isaac was persecuted by Ishmael, so believers in Christ are persecuted by the "Moses plus Christ" Jewish agitators. As Sarah expelled Hagar and her son (Gen 21:10), so the Galatian believers ought to expel the Jewish agitators.

Application. Persecution is opposing a Christian for either obeying God or for declaring God's will and truth. While it is theoretically possible to follow Christ and not be persecuted, it is indeed rare. If we pursue Christ in the *realities of our world*, we will quickly discover that there are various types of persecution awaiting followers of Christ. The world is opposed to God because God is truth and reveals the world's rebellious orientation away from God. This means that the Christian cannot expect to find in the "world" an ally to the gospel. Only opposition can be expected. The fear of being disapproved and therefore talked about is something most Christians would simply like to avoid. The result, however, is that we fail to speak up and be faithful.

GALATIANS 5:1–12

Original Meaning

The Thesis: Free at Last (5:1). Following the Greek word order, we translate woodenly: "For freedom Christ set you free." There are only four words in Greek: (in order) "freedom," "you," "Christ," and "set free." The first and last, the two places of a Greek sentence where emphasis can be found, are concerned with freedom—one a noun and the other a verb. The verb is in the aorist tense, which tells us not when or how they were set free, but *that* they were set free. Paul's main focus here is with the *fact of their being free at last*.

For Paul, "freedom" is the very heart of the gospel: God sets us free through Christ and in the Spirit, so that we can love God and others. The *implication* of Christ setting us free is the negative side of the letter of Galatians: "Do not let yourselves be burdened again by a yoke of slavery" (v. 1b). Freedom must be retained, protected from contamination, and renewed at all times.

Application of the Thesis to Circumcision (5:2–12). *The assertion (5:2).* Simply being circumcised is not the issue. Rather, it is their *reason for circumcision* that provokes Paul. If the Galatians go ahead with circumcision *because of the influence of the Jewish agitators*, they will be confessing, in the act of submitting to the rite, that they think Christ is insufficient.

Paul spells out the ramifications: "Christ will be of no value." That is to say, Christ will not deliver them from the present evil age (1:4) or from the curse of the law (3:13), nor will they become children of Abraham's promise for those who believe (3:6–9, 19–25; 3:26–4:7).

The explanation (5:3–6). Paul now needs to back up a bit and explain what he means by "Christ will be of no value." He makes three points if they go to the law.

First, *they will be obligated to do the whole law* (v. 3). They become debtors to the whole law, and that means condemnation *because that is only what the law can do*. It is doubtful that Paul means to say that if they opted for the law, they had to do it all perfectly (and if they did it would bring them acceptance). What we find in Galatians is that opting for the law is a misunderstanding of what the law was supposed to do—a choice to live in an inferior era under an inferior system.

Second, *they will be separated from Christ and grace* (v. 4). They are choosing another way of becoming accepted by God, and the one they are choosing (the law of Moses) will not do the job. Verse 4 brings up a sensitive issue for many. Is Paul saying here that in being alienated from Christ and in falling "away from grace" these Galatians converts have lost their salvation? The overall teaching of the New Testament assumes that Christians will persevere; there are numerous utterances of the assurance that they can have of their final destiny. Yet there are enough "terrifying" passages to make one think apostasy is a real possibility and that in the case of apostasy one can forfeit one's salvation. Theologically, the *only sin that can sever a Christian's relationship to God through Christ is the sin of apostasy*.

Third, *they will miss what really counts: faith* (vv. 5–6). If the Galatian converts opt for the law of Moses and express that choice by personally undergoing circumcision, they will miss out on what really matters: the faith they previously exhibited (3:1–5). From first to last their experiences showed that everything good came as a result of faith, not from observing the law.

The application (5:7–12). Paul likens the Jewish agitators' activities to such unsportsmanlike activity: they were cutting in on the Galatians' progress toward their final goal and slowing them down. Paul evaluates this kind of activity (vv. 8–9), stating that it does not come from God and that just a little of it will cause large problems.

We then see Paul's confidence expressed pastorally (v. 10a). While Paul had confidence in his readers, when he pondered the problems from other angles, he lost that confidence. Thus, this statement is probably strategic in his entire letter: he becomes positive in order to help them make a good decision.

Without signal, Paul suddenly then responds to one of the criticisms the Jewish agitators have been making (v. 11). Paul's response includes his oft-made assumption: those who are persecuted are right (see above on 4:21–31). And, since he is being persecuted *by the Jews*, he must be right.

Finally, Paul sarcastically urges the Jewish agitators to go the whole way (v. 12). If they are going to get involved with this purifying act of circumcision, they ought to go the whole way, become eunuchs, and end the matter there! Classing the Jewish agitators with eunuchs is a way of discrediting and disparaging them.

Application. Christians have been set free so they can be healthy in their relationships to God, to others, and to themselves. And healthy self-discovery is one of many reasons God sets us free. Yet it is not for personal absorption and ego-staring. It is the freedom of God's Spirit, blowing with his gentle spirit into our psyches, that makes it possible to be healed before God and others. Paul's whole message in Galatians may be summarized as this call to freedom through Christ and the Spirit.

GALATIANS 5:13–26

Original Meaning

A Call to a Life of Freedom from the Flesh (5:13–15). A possible criticism of Paul's blanket endorsement of "freedom and Spirit ethics" is that it may lead to indulging the flesh, to anarchic behavior, and to life completely out of line with the law of Moses. But Paul insists that freedom should not be used "to indulge" (Gk. *aphormēn*) the flesh (v. 13). "Flesh" is unspiritual life. Flesh and law belong to an era that is now past; the new era is characterized by the Spirit and Christ.

The problem of the Galatians is typically human: egos enter into the debates between people, and before long the issue is who is going to win; it becomes *who* is right, not *what* is right. This was a major issue at Galatia. There were lots of internal fights, as a quick survey of 5:1–6:10 proves.

On the contrary, Paul says, their freedom in Christ is to be a platform for serving one another in love. In our passage, Paul says two things about love: the Galatians are to "serve one another" in love (v. 13), and the entire law of Moses is summed up in the commandment from Leviticus 19:18.

Paul's entire ethic can be handled in three simple expressions: the Galatians are to live in love (vv. 6, 13), or in the Spirit (v. 22), or under the law of Christ (6:2). These are all the same. This love of Paul is not passion. It is the love of God for us that changes us so we can serve one another in love.

A Call to a Life in the Spirit against the Flesh (5:16–18). Paul is dealing here with opposites. When a person lives in God's Spirit, he or she escapes the power of the flesh (v. 17a) and the power of the law (v. 18). This life of the Spirit is a battle—a battle over God's will; those who are engaged in it recognize that flesh and Spirit are opposites. When one lives in the flesh, one does not do what God's Spirit wants. The Christian life is a life of consistent surrender to the Spirit.

What Is the Fleshly Life? (5:19–21). Paul goes on to explain what he means by "life in the flesh" and "life in the Spirit," giving a list for each. The lists here of the works of the flesh and the fruit of the Spirit (see below) are not abstract listings, nor are they comprehensive. Rather, they are context specific. *In the context of church conflict, the observer will find the manifestation of the flesh in such things as factionalism and will find that the Spirit, when in control, will produce such things as love and patience.* In other words, we interpret these lists incorrectly if we take them out of context and pretend that they are complete listings of either the flesh or the Spirit. These are the kinds of things Paul wants to focus on because he is concerned with conflict. Had he written to the Ephesians, he would have had other items in both lists.

What Is Life in the Spirit? (5:22–26). Paul in 5:19 has described "flesh" under the term "works" (Gk. *erga*; NIV "acts"), while he sees the Spirit's work as "fruit" (v. 22). The former is plural while the latter is singular. The change of terms to "fruit" evokes a different image: from one of human responsibility to one of divine enablement. The image of fruit has a certain sense of passivity to it; it is the Spirit of God who produces such things, and they grow in the life of the Christian.

As if summarizing his whole point, Paul says that (1) those who have surrendered themselves to Jesus Christ "have crucified the flesh" and so should not be involved in the works of the flesh (v. 24); (2) those who have been given God's life by the Spirit and Christ should march according to the Spirit's orders (v. 25); and (3) those who live in the freedom of the Spirit should not be conceited and so fight with one another (v. 26). Once again, we end up with Paul's emphasis in this context, which is Galatian factionalism.

Application. Situations of conflict today are found between spouses, between parents and children, between denominations, and between various groups in local churches (to name a few). Conflict mediation teams will always remind us that when there is tension, the first order of business is *to clarify the issues*. This is what Paul does in the letter: he explains the problems that are confronting them, in both theological and social terms. Galatians can be seen as a letter that seeks to explain the options (albeit in a highly persuasive manner) and to clarify the issues that confronted the Galatians churches.

GALATIANS 6:1–10

Original Meaning

Spiritual People Should Bear One Another's Burdens (6:1–5). *The problem: restoring a sinful brother (6:1).* One problem that sometimes arises for those who live as a community of people who are striving to live in the Spirit is that someone falls into sin. In this situation, the community should take it upon itself to restore such a person, because this is one way a family expresses its love. Gentleness is crucial for restoration, and only the spiritual, those under the Spirit, should be involved. In so doing, however, those restoring must watch out (v. 1b). The temptation here is probably pride because of verses 3–4, which carry on Paul's point.

The principle: love one another (6:2). The "law of Christ" is nothing other than (1) submission to the teachings of Jesus that fulfill the law, and (2) life in the Spirit, which is essentially love and which itself fulfills the law of Moses. A specific example is to carry the burden of a brother or sister. Paul is here addressing those who are restoring, and so we must envision the restorer as a person who undertakes not only to point out problems and sins but also to carry the responsibility of helping the person become free of that entanglement.

The problem of pride (6:3–5). Pride is wrong (v. 3), and each restorer should check himself or herself (v. 4a) and not find personal status by comparison with others, especially with sinning brothers and sisters (v. 4b). In the final analysis, each person is responsible before God for what he or she has done (v. 5).

Spiritual People Should Support Teachers (6:6). Here we find that teachers worked full-time in their ministry so that they could study and teach effectively; they were apparently being disrespected in the Christian community to the degree that their students were not taking care of them. Such treatment was inconsistent with life in the Spirit because it was unloving and unkind (5:22–23).

Spiritual People Are Accountable to God (6:7–10). After the parenthesis of verse 6, Paul gives the strongest foundation that one can perceive: God is the judge, and people cannot sneer at him. A person's final standing before God will be determined by that person's relationship to Jesus Christ as revealed in his or her works. While it is absolutely true that our grounds of acceptance is the atoning sacrifice that Jesus Christ made on our behalf, our connection to that sacrifice is by way of a faith that works itself out in love and in the many good works of a person's life. Paul thus interweaves here in this passage two highly fundamental ideas for Christian ethics—mutual accountability and personal responsibility.

Application. Some will tell us that we do kind things to others because such actions are good and right and because others deserve it; this is called altruism. Christian ethics probably does have an element of altruism in it, but it is fundamentally wrong to think that the foundation of the Christian lifestyle is some supposed altruism. Instead, the foundation for Christian behavior is the grace of God that awakens us, the love of God that stirs us to action, and the holiness of God that stiffens our resolve to obey him. And behind each of these is the fact that God will be our judge, that we will give account to him for everything done in the body, and that God is completely just.

GALATIANS 6:11–18

Original Meaning

Paul's Signature (6:11). What does it mean that Paul used "large letters"? There are three options: (1) Paul had bad eyesight that left him with trouble in writing (based on reading 4:13–16 as a reference to an eye disease); (2) Paul learned to write well—unlikely since Paul was well-educated; and (3) Paul's "large letters" are an ancient style of our modern boldface or italics. This latter view has commended itself to a large number of scholars today.

Paul's Concluding Summary of the Situation (6:12–18). *The problems of the Jewish agitators (6:12–13).* While the leaders at Jerusalem did not "compel" Titus to be circumcised (2:3), the Jewish agitators were clearly trying to force the Galatians to accept circumcision to demonstrate their commitment to the law of Moses. Their motive was *fear* (6:12b)—a fear of persecution. These Jewish agitators were getting pressured themselves from the Jews and conservative Jewish-Christian parties in Jerusalem over the kind of life the converts of Paul were actually living. Paul saw in their succumbing to the pressure of the Jerusalem Jews a denial of the gospel, and that is the heart of his letter. This Jewish wing did not see what the cross of Christ did to nationalism and to the era of the law. They had come to their end in Christ, and now God's people were much larger than the Jewish nation. Their consistency was flawed (v. 13). Paul contends that those who pushed circumcision as the ultimate sign of commitment to the law did not even keep the law themselves.

Their goal in it all was to be able to return to Jerusalem and claim a prize, to claim that they had been successful and so gain the praise of the Jewish nationalists.

Paul's self-evaluation (6:14–17). Paul counters the approach of the Jewish agitators with his own. The agitators may glory in the flesh, he says, but he glories exclusively in the cross of Christ. Paul's entire goal was to glory in the cross of Christ, and so he would gladly accept persecution (v. 14).

Paul next declares his perspective on nationalism (vv. 15–16). Once again, neither belonging to the Jewish nation (being circumcised) nor being a gentile (not being circumcised) mattered: what mattered was that God had formed a new people, the church, and that this new people was an entirely "new creation."

As Paul had cursed those who preached a different gospel (the gospel of nationalism) at the beginning of his letter (1:6–9), so now he blesses with peace those who embrace his view. "Israel of God" refers to the church (6:16), whether to the church as a whole or to the whole church, including Jewish Christians.

Finally, Paul presents a case for being right: he is being persecuted. He claims that he bears on his body "the marks of Jesus" (v. 17). Paul uses this expression for the many scars on his body as evidence for his persecution for following Christ (see 2 Cor 6:4–6; 11:23–30). It is unlikely that the "marks of Jesus" on Paul have anything to do with the hundreds of cases of stigmatization that have occurred in the history of the church, most notably with Saint Francis of Assisi.

Paul's grace benediction (6:18). Having spent his entire letter spelling out the universalistic implications of faith in Christ, the ending of the Mosaic law in the death of Christ, and acceptance by God on the basis of surrendering to Christ, there is no wonder that we see here more in "grace" than a simple good-bye.

Application. Who are the primary targets of Galatians in our world today? The answer is not a specific group. It does no good just to point fingers at others, for the real problem is far more subtle than that. The target of Galatians today is *anyone who depreciates Jesus Christ as sufficient Savior and minimizes the power of the Holy Spirit as sufficient guide.* It is a disposition toward what God has done for us through Christ and in the Spirit. Whoever minimizes the sufficiency of Christ or discounts the power of the Spirit finds the finger of Paul pointing right at them. Galatians challenges each of us to let the Spirit have control of our lives—whoever we are and wherever we come from.

EPHESIANS

INTRODUCTION TO EPHESIANS

The witness of the early church for the influence of Ephesians as a letter from Paul is extensive. It was referred to early and often, from Clement of Rome (AD 95) onward. It is quoted by Ignatius and Polycarp and included both in Marcion's canon of Paul's letters (about AD 140) and in the Muratorian Fragment (usually dated about AD 180).

Moreover, Ephesians claims to be by Paul and has Pauline language and theology. Not until the nineteenth century was its authenticity as a Pauline letter questioned.

Whether Ephesians is from Paul or a disciple of his is of major importance for two reasons. First, if it is not by Paul, it cannot be used to reconstruct Paul's thought and that of the earliest church. Even if only subconsciously, all readers of the Bible carry in their heads a framework by which Scripture is understood. Assumptions about the occasion and time in which a document was written determine how it is understood. We do not read 1 Thessalonians the same way we read Philippians because of differing ideas about Paul the missionary in AD 50 and Paul the prisoner in AD 60. Do we include Ephesians in the attempt to understand Paul? Numerous books written on Paul's theology disregard Ephesians completely. If Ephesians is by Paul, the picture these works present is skewed.

Second, if Ephesians is not by Paul, it will likely be considered less important than Paul's other letters and will be used with less confidence. Those who date Ephesians to the latter part of the first century often see Ephesians as a movement toward "early catholicism" (usually a negative connotation). On this approach Ephesians is less focused on the Spirit, has less concern for the parousia, salvation by faith, and Christology, and has more concern with ecclesiology and order. True, Ephesians does show development, but it is not early catholicism.

Those who reject Pauline authorship often argue that no devaluing of Ephesians should result. In reality, however, most of these scholars do consider it less authoritative. So while decisions about authorship and purpose do not necessarily make Ephesians less authoritative, in practice Ephesians is given less attention and less voice. But Ephesians is "the real thing," and it deserves maximum attention and application.

BOOK OUTLINE

I. Salutation: Identification of Author, Recipients, and a Greeting (1:1–2)

II. The Body of the Letter (1:3–6:20)
   A. A Meditation on God's Gift of Salvation (1:3–3:21)
   B. Instructions to Live Worthy of God's Call (4:1–6:20)

III. The Closing of the Letter (6:21–24)

EPHESIANS 1:1–2

Original Meaning. Paul's identification of himself as an apostle appointed by God in verse 1 is his customary way of beginning his letters. The will of God is an important theme in Ephesians. Paul was an apostle because God wanted him to be. Paul's primary concern was to emphasize that just as he had been appointed by God to be an apostle, the Ephesians too had been separated to God. "Faithful" can refer either to someone who has proven *to be faithful* or to someone who is a believer, someone who *has faith*. The latter seems the better choice here.

The wording in verse 2 is paralleled exactly in seven other Pauline letters. "Grace and peace" are important themes throughout Ephesians. Both are key words that describe God's initial salvation, and both describe God's continuing work among his people.

Application. Paul used his culture's letter form to write specifically Christian letters, but his method raises a crucial question: How do culture and gospel relate? The primary ingredient for Christians in relating to culture surely is authenticity. We should not try to communicate Paul's experience of Christ; we must communicate our own. Our expression of the gospel in our culture must be a natural flow of the depth of our relationship with Christ, not the borrowing of mere words that we have labeled religious.

EPHESIANS 1:3–14

Original Meaning

God Blessed Us in Christ (1:3). The God who acted in Christ and chose Christians to live before him deserves praise. "Every spiritual blessing" has been granted to them in Christ. "Spiritual" refers to all that God's Spirit brings to enable life. As verses 13–14 show, the Spirit is the primary gift and the source of all the others.

The expression "in the heavenly realms" does not refer to a physical location but to a spiritual reality—God's world, in which believers have a share and which evil forces still seek to attack. It includes all of the believer's relation to God and the church's experience.

No simple definition of "in Christ" will do, and each occurrence must be analyzed individually and in context. But the most important use of "in Christ" has a "local" sense and points to incorporation into Christ or union with Christ. That is, Christ is the "place" where believers reside, the source in which they find God's salvation and blessings, and the framework in which they live and work.

Election (1:4–6a). This is one of the most important texts on election in the Bible. Election is not some strange, unnecessary doctrine but merely another way of speaking of God's grace and salvation. Words like "chose" and "predestined" (vv. 4, 5) underscore God's activity in setting apart a people for himself. Election results in a holy people.

The emphasis on adoption in verse 5 shows that the purpose of election is relational. God, for no other reason than that he is a loving God, chose to adopt people *into his family* through Jesus Christ. "Adoption" (v. 5) is family imagery used to explain the salvation experience, both present and future.

Usually when people speak of divine election, they think of the election of individuals and the benefit to them. Individuals are not elected and then put in Christ. They are in Christ and therefore elect. The ultimate aim of election is the glory of God, as the recurring phrase "to the praise of his glory" shows (1:6, 12, 14).

Inundated with Grace (1:6b–8a). "Grace" is the power that works salvation and is a summary word for the gospel. Elsewhere in Paul's letters, grace conveys a broad range of ideas. Grace does not refer just to the entrance to the Christian life but covers the whole of it. We are not only saved by grace but we also live by grace.

As election takes place in Christ, so is redemption found in Christ. The term "redemption" (v. 6) has its roots in the Old Testament idea of the covenant and in the language of the ancient marketplace; in both instances it involved the idea of purchasing or buying back some item or person that would otherwise be lost, taken prisoner, or destroyed.

The Revelation of God's Will (1:8b–1:12). Whereas the focus in 1:4–6a was on God's choice of people in Christ, Paul here shifts to the revelation of God's plan and how that plan centered on Christ. Words for God's will, purpose, and desire dominate verses 9 and 11. Paul emphasizes that God's work in Christ was not an afterthought or an incidental event in the universe. Rather, it is what God intended all along.

The gospel is first of all a revelation about God's purpose and work, and here his revealing activity is a cause for praise. The term "mystery" (v. 9) emphasizes the revelation theme further. Whereas in modern usage "mystery" refers to what is unknown, in Jewish and early Christian literature this word refers to the hidden divine plan now revealed by God.

The NIV understands verse 10 to refer to the end of time. Literally the text reads "the fullness of the times." While the primary intent in this text does concern the ultimate fulfillment of God's purpose at the end of time, Paul viewed that fulfillment as already having begun in Christ's life, death, and resurrection. Just as redemption is both present and future, the revelation of God's will points both to the present and to the future.

The Spirit (1:13–14). Seals were used in the ancient world in ways similar to today. Cargo was sealed before shipping or letters were sealed to guarantee the validity of the contents. The Spirit is called "the promised" Holy Spirit because of texts like Ezekiel 36:26–27 and Joel 2:28, which speak of an end-time outpouring of God's Spirit.

The Spirit is also a "deposit." The Greek word used here (*arrabōn*) indicates a down payment that guaranteed complete payment. The Spirit, in other words, is God's first installment on our salvation and the guarantee that the full future inheritance will be delivered.

Application. Awareness of the presence of God and of living in Christ are the keys to all of life. People sin because they forget God. How strange that we forget the "place" we live. If we know we live before God and in Christ, we know we live in a defining presence. Our lives become determined by the character of Christ and God. It becomes increasingly difficult to say, "I know I live in Christ, but I am going to do the opposite of what Christ expects." Christian ethics are grounded in our being in Christ. The alternative—rule-keeping—is always an inadequate foundation for Christian ethics, because it asks the individual to conform to an external norm. If one lives in Christ, however, Christ is that person's environment.

EPHESIANS 1:15–23

Original Meaning

Introduction to the Prayer (1:15–16). "For this reason" points back to the doxology, which affirms the foundational character of that passage. The way God has worked to accomplish salvation motivates both Paul's praise and his intercession. The intent of this prayer is that people will know in their own lives the benefits mentioned in the doxology.

Faith in Christ leads unavoidably to "love" for others whom God has set apart for himself in Christ. Note the trilogy of faith, love, and hope that appears here and in at least nine other New Testament passages.

Paul's Intercession (1:17–19a). The intent of Paul's prayer is clear: that people will receive revelation to know what they have in Christ. Paul focuses on what is accomplished for humans, but as 3:16 shows, he is thinking of the Holy Spirit as the one who performs this task. Paul prays that God's Spirit will continually give wisdom and revelation for life and understanding. In other words, the apostle prays the lights will go on inside people so that they know God and understand the benefit of the gospel.

As to the content of Paul's intercession, he wants his readers to know three realities about God. First, Christians should know that "the hope to which [God] has called" (v. 18a) them means that they should know the significance that God's call has for their future. Second, Paul points to the tremendous glory that is present when God inherits the people he has set apart for himself. "In his holy people" (v. 18b) means that the inheritance is found in, or consists of, these people. Finally, believers should know God's "incomparably great power" for people with faith (v. 19). Ephesians focuses on words for power more than any other New Testament letter. The focus on God's power here is on God's life-giving power as it is specifically available for believers.

The Exaltation of Christ (1:19b–23). In verse 20 the NIV, as most translations, reads "raised Christ from the dead." The Greek text actually uses the plural, "from the dead ones" (as do most passages in the New Testament referring to Christ's resurrection). The point is not that Christ was raised from a state of death, but that he was raised *out from* the dead ones. This is an important difference, for it suggests that his resurrection was not viewed as an isolated event but as an inauguration of the final resurrection.

"In the heavenly realms" here in verse 20 points to Christ's presence with God and to the larger reality of life with God. That Christ is exalted to the highest position possible shows the importance of his life, death, and resurrection. Further, his exaltation shows that a shift has taken place. Life's center of gravity is not earthly life; it is in the heavenly realm with Christ and God.

The imagery in verse 20 of Christ seated at the right hand of God and exalted over the powers is drawn from Psalm 110:1. Paul goes on in verse 22a to connect the subjection of the powers with Psalm 8:6b. These two Old Testament texts were also used to describe Christ's resurrection and exaltation in 1 Corinthians 15:25–28 and Hebrews 1:13–2:9.

In verse 21, the five categories of powers mentioned—"rule," "authority," "power," "dominion," and "name"—are a stacking of terms to emphasize that Christ's victory over them is total. No certain conclusions can be drawn about distinctions between these terms, and no hierarchy of them is in mind. The five terms almost certainly refer to spiritual beings, as the further development of the idea in 2:1–3 shows. Whatever powers exist—real or imaginary, human or nonhuman—they are *all* subject to Christ.

In verse 22 we have our first occurrence in Ephesians of the word "church" (*ekklēsia*), a subject that becomes one of the main emphases of the letter. No other letter is so specifically focused on the theology of the church as Ephesians, and no other letter expresses such a high regard for the church (see esp. 5:23–33). Whereas Paul's other letters normally use "church" to refer to an individual congregation, all occurrences in Ephesians are universal in scope.

When Paul uses "head" in Ephesians and Colossians, "body" always occurs in the same context (though "body" is used at times without mention of head). It expresses what we have already seen—that Christians live in Christ and take their identity from him. They are part of him.

"Fullness" (Gk. *plērōma*) in verse 23 can express a variety of nuances, but the primary idea seems to be "completeness." God's presence, his glory, later referred to as his Shekinah in rabbinic literature, filled the tabernacle and temple in the Old Testament, and the Spirit of God filled individuals. "Fullness," in other words, refers to God's making his presence and power felt. "Fullness" refers to Christ, and the phrase "which is his body" in 1:23a is a parenthetical comment about the church. Christ is the place where God's presence, power, and salvation are known, and the church draws from this fullness in him (cf. 4:15–16).

Application. The power Christians have is not intrinsic power, something they have in themselves, but a power that comes from God, defined by the resurrection of Jesus and his exaltation as Lord over every other power, both now and in the future. Because no other power can rival him and because in him the fullness of God lives, Christians do not have to look elsewhere to find what they need for life. What they need is in Christ. This power, however, is not power in the abstract; it is *relational power*—power that is known and experienced because of being bound to the one in whom power resides.

EPHESIANS 2:1–10

Original Meaning

The Former Way of Life in Sins (2:1–3). *Dead in transgressions and sins (2:1).* Paul viewed the former life before Christ as spiritual death, life without God, and a meaningless life hardly worth living.

Living in sins (2:2–3a). People live in one of two spheres or environments, either in Christ or in sin(s). The former way of life of these believers involved conformity with the present worldly age. Living in sins is also living in conformity with "the ruler of the kingdom of the air." The ruler has control of this godless domain, and instead of living in accord with God's domain, people choose an insidious tyrant instead of the good and loving God who created them.

Sinful nature and wrath (2:3b–c). The translation of *sarx* as "sinful nature" (NIV 1984; NIV 2011: "flesh") avoids misleading ideas that suggest humanity or the material world is negative. Paul uses *sarx* in various ways in his letters, often with negative ethical connotations as here.

The result is that all people are by nature "deserving of wrath" (literally "children of wrath"). Paul is not thinking of uncontrolled outbursts of angry passion on God's part nor of some impersonal wrath; rather, wrath points to God's constant displeasure and reaction against evil and sin.

This text speaks of the universality of sin, but it *does not reject the value of humanity.* Because of sins, humans are the living dead. They live in keeping with a world order that ignores God and in keeping with a dark tyrant who works to cause disobedience. In their enslavement they follow desires and distorted reasonings that leave God out of the picture, and therefore they are under God's wrath. Yet the main point of Ephesians—and especially of 2:1–10—is that *God will not stay out of the picture.*

God's Merciful Salvation in Christ and Its Purpose (2:4–7). *The mercy and love of God (2:4).* The picture was bleak, *but God* acted because of his love and mercy. Apart from God's mercy, no hope exists for humanity. The "love" of God is a major theme in Paul's understanding of salvation. God is not a detached onlooker in the salvation process or in an angry huff waiting to be appeased. Rather, he is the primary actor, the one who by his love deals with his own wrath and shows mercy to his people.

Raised with Christ from death to life (2:5–6). The two verbs in verse 6 ("raised us up with Christ and seated us with him") do not refer to future resurrection but to our being raised with Christ in the past, to being "co-resurrected" with Christ. Not only have Christians been raised with Christ, but they have also been seated with him in the heavenly realms. What is true of him (1:20) is true of us.

Note Paul's mention that believers are "saved" by grace (v. 5b). Salvation language points primarily to the idea of rescue from danger, but this is, of course, only one of several ways Paul speaks of God's redeeming activity. No single image—justification, salvation, redemption, reconciliation, freedom, or any other—is adequate by itself to explain the reality God has worked for his people.

Demonstration for the coming ages (2:7). The purpose of God's action in saving his people is to demonstrate in the coming ages how rich his grace is. In intervening for us, God shows his own character.

Further Explanation of Salvation by Grace (2:8–10). *Faith (2:8).* The term "faith" (*pistis*) cannot be limited to mental assent or to believing certain ideas. *Faith is relational*, describing reliance on a reliable God. Faith is a *covenant* word, expressing the commitment and trust that bind two parties together. People who believe do not merely assent to certain ideas but are bound to God and live in response to him.

What is the antecedent of "this" in the statement, "and this not from yourselves" (v. 8b)? The word most likely refers to the *whole process* of God's saving people by grace. Paul's point is that salvation is a gift from the trustworthy God, whom we believe.

Works and boasting (2:9). Boasting is a determinative part of Paul's theology. Much of his concern is to make sure that praise goes only to God. He seeks to destroy any conceivable ground for human beings boasting in themselves.

God's new creation and good works prepared beforehand (2:10). This new creation—like everything else in Ephesians—takes place "in Christ Jesus." The new creation is based in Christ's resurrection, the creation of life in the midst of death. This new creation is to be active and productive, like the Creator. Paul does not normally speak of "good works." When he does use "works" positively, he adds the adjective "good" to prevent misunderstanding. These works were prepared in advance for God's people to do, a statement that strikes a note of awe-inspiring sovereignty and provides assurance that God providentially guides believers' lives.

Application. We must distinguish the world that God created from the world that human beings subvert to their own purposes. The former leads to worship of God; the latter leads to the wrath of God. Once we have distinguished God's order from the old order, we are obligated to defiance, a defiance rooted in the confession "Jesus is Lord." If Jesus is Lord, sin and the old world order cannot be our geography, and Christians must say a constant "no" to the fallen world's attempts to define us.

EPHESIANS 2:11–22

Original Meaning

Distance From God until Made Near in Christ (2:11–13). *The former plight (2:11–12).* The labels "uncircumcised" and "the circumcision" were common *Jewish* ways of referring to gentiles and Jews respectively. Although the Jews were bad-mouthing the gentiles as the "uncircumcised," in Paul's mind Jews were no better off, for the circumcision in which they boasted was a mere human circumcision. Apart from Christ, they lived in the same dark and fallen realm as the gentiles, even with their circumcision. Verse 12 describes five elements in which the gentiles were deprived, disconnected, and distant.

God's solution to the human plight (2:13). In this text the blood of Christ brings people in Christ near to God. The formerly distant gentiles have been brought near to God in Christ. The implication of the sacrificial language is that Christ has died *for us*, which means both he died in our place and for our benefit.

Peace with God and His People through Christ (2:14–18). *Christ our peace (2:14a).* Christ is our peace, makes peace, and proclaims peace (see also vv. 15c–17). Paul seeks to connect Christ and peace as comprehensively as possible. He is the one who makes peace possible, who announces its availability, and in whom peace is enjoyed.

The destruction of the barrier that divides (2:14b–15a). The law is here viewed as an instrument of division, which it surely and intentionally was. Circumcision, Sabbath-keeping, and food laws were all primary indications of the distinctions between Jews and other people, leading to arrogance and name-calling. Paul does *not* abolish the law as the word of God or as a moral guide. What is abolished is the law as *a set of regulations that excludes gentiles.*

The unity of the new being (2:15b). Not only does Christ take the hostility *into himself* and destroy it, but also *in himself* he creates a new being. The new being is Christ himself, into which people are incorporated as his body. The two groups of people are made one. Divided humanity is reconciled in Christ and joined into a unified, worshiping community. In effect, Paul suggests that Christians are a "third race" beside Jews and gentiles; the two are one in Jesus Christ.

Reconciliation, Preaching Peace, and Access to the Father (2:16–18). God is always the one who does the reconciling. Even when people are hostile to God and God is angry, he loves and works to restore relations. The result of reconciliation through the cross of Christ is "access" to the Father (v. 18), the privilege of entering into God's presence.

The People of God as the Dwelling of God (2:19–22). *Gentiles Now Citizens of the People of God (2:19).* Because of the cross of Christ, Paul reiterates that gentiles are now full members of God's family, together with all believing Jews.

The new temple (2:20–22). The household of God is "built on the foundation of the apostles and prophets" (v. 20). "Prophets" almost certainly refers not to Old Testament but to New Testament prophets. This is demonstrated both by the order ("apostles and prophets") and by the reference in 3:4–5 to the mystery, which to other generations was not made known, but which now has been revealed to his "holy apostles and prophets."

Jesus Christ occupies a unique place in the foundation as the "chief cornerstone" (v. 20). Christ makes the whole building possible, including the rest of the foundation. The temple is a "holy" temple because God dwells there (v. 21); it is a temple set aside by and for God. The temple is holy, and the people who make up this temple are "the holy ones." *They* are set apart by and for God.

Application. Remembering is the way we name and process the past, the way we structure our minds to know how to live. Paul asks that we remember the life-determining change Christ has brought in us—that is, the radical movement from being dead in sins to life in Christ, from being excluded to being included—for this movement is still at work in our lives every day. Such remembering gives attention to the continuing change at work in us and will not allow us to become lax or guilty of pride. Remembering is therefore the key to loving and worshiping God. Balance is required, however. We do not remember the former life for its own sake or to wallow in its memory. It no longer determines us. We focus instead on Christ and the change he has brought and live in light of those realities.

EPHESIANS 3:1–13

Original Meaning

Paul the Prisoner (3:1). "For this reason" points back at least to 2:11–22, if not the whole of chapter 2. The gospel that gives life and includes the gentiles informs what Paul writes in what follows.

Where Paul was in prison is debated, but whatever decision is made does not affect the reading of this letter. The only reason why Paul was in prison was because he thought gentiles had the same access to God that Jews did.

Paul the Steward of Grace and Servant of the Gospel (3:2–7). *Paul's apostolic administration of God's grace and mystery (3:2–3).* Paul as apostle to the gentiles was responsible to administer God's grace to the gentiles. "Grace" and "mystery" are closely related. The word "mystery" (Gk. *mystērion*) refers to what is known only because God has revealed it, and specifically here it refers to the revelation that the gentiles are included in Christ as equals (see v. 6).

The new revelation (3:4–6). It is striking that wisdom, gospel, mystery, ages, revelation, and gentiles are brought together in several of these texts. In the New Testament the gospel is a gospel of revelation: God reveals himself as a saving God.

While the revelation extends to all Christians (1:9), the foundational revelation has come only to certain select individuals.

"Apostles" (v. 5) refers to the founding apostles who saw the risen Christ and were given insight about the significance of the gospel and the responsibility for handing it on. "Prophets" (v. 5), clearly New Testament prophets, does not refer generally to prophets in the early church but to those who had received revelation that helped frame how the gospel was to be understood and lived.

Revelation that enlists (3:7). The revelation that comes in the gospel is not only so that people will understand, but that they may be enlisted in the service of the one who has revealed it. Paul has been made a servant because of "the gift of God's grace." Through grace Paul became a servant and apostle of the gospel for the gentiles.

The Purpose and Significance of the Gospel (3:8–13). *To proclaim and to reveal (3:8–11).* Grace was given to Paul for three purposes: (1) to preach to the gentiles the riches of Christ (v. 8); (2) to make plain the administration of the mystery (v. 9); and (3) to make the wisdom of God known to the rulers and authorities in the heavenly realms (v. 10). These are not three separate purposes, for all three focus on revelation. Paul wanted everyone to know the secret hidden in God but now made known—namely, that the gentiles are accepted by God as equals with Jewish believers.

Verse 10 assigns a lofty and cosmic role to the church. The church's very existence and conduct are making known how great God's plan of salvation is—both to people and to the powers "in the heavenly realms." This gives an unparalleled importance to the church.

Privilege and perseverance (3:12–13). The text again returns to the privileges available in Christ. Because of access to the Father and confidence based in Christ's faithfulness, Paul asks his readers not to be discouraged about his sufferings for them. That he was in prison should not be discouraging. The discouraging thing would be that no one was willing to go to prison for the ministry to the gentiles.

Application. Surely the most important application of this text is in reproducing Paul's attitude toward the revelation that has come in Christ. If we do not value the gospel as revelation from God for us, it will not impact our lives. For us the one truly great value, the "pearl of great price" (Matt 13:46 KJV), ought to be God's revelation in Christ. We need a conviction that God truly has revealed himself in Christ.

EPHESIANS 3:14–21

Original Meaning

Father of All (3:14–15). Paul again emphasizes God as Father. No other description of God is used so frequently in the New Testament. No doubt this goes back to Jesus's teaching his disciples to address God as *Abba*, the Aramaic word for "father" used by both children and adults but considered by Jews to be too familiar to use without qualification in relation to God.

English translations cannot easily show the wordplay between "Father" (*patēr*) and "family" (*patria*). It is an attempt to be as inclusive as possible to emphasize the cosmic scope of God's reign and purposes. Paul saw the divisions among the human race as existing under the one God.

Prayer for Power to Know Christ and His Love (3:16–19). "Power" and "Spirit" (v. 16) are so commonly associated in both Testaments that they are virtually synonymous. The Spirit is the power of God at work in people. Paul prays for his readers that the Spirit will be so strong an influence at the controlling center of their being that their lives will show it.

Although the NIV begins verse 17 with "so that," the indwelling of Christ does not result from the Spirit's strengthening; it is the *manner in which* the Spirit strengthens. In other words, verse 17 explains verse 16.

The NIV's "established" (v. 17) hides the similarity of this text to two others. If translated more literally as "rooted and founded," we note its closeness to both 2:20–22 and to Colossians 2:6–7. God's love is the wellspring from which believers are nourished and the foundation on which they find stability.

How the four dimensions "wide," "long," "high," and "deep" (v. 18) should be understood is more problematic than the NIV suggests. The Greek text does not have "is the love of Christ," but merely ". . . grasp with all God's people what is the width, breadth, height, and depth." The goal is that they will comprehend Christ's love, as the continuation of the thought in verse 19 shows.

The first half of verse 19 is a good example of an oxymoron: Paul prays that they may know the love that is beyond knowing. This is language from someone who has been surprised and overwhelmed with Christ's love.

In experiencing Christ, Christians experience the fullness of God, his presence, and power. In experiencing that fullness, they themselves are made full by Christ. That is, they partake of God's own being and are made like him. This is an ongoing process.

The Doxology (3:20–21). This doxology sums up the intent of the first half of the letter. All Christ followers should praise God for his astounding work in Christ Jesus. Paul's point is not merely that God is able to do beyond what is expected. Rather, this power is already at work in Christ's people. God does not fit the limitations of human expectations. God's ways and thoughts are exceedingly beyond our ways and thoughts.

God is at work and eager to work in his people to achieve his purposes for salvation.

Application. The imagery of the text challenges our conceptions about faith. Rather than a small Jesus tucked away somewhere in our souls, the text assumes the presence of one who gives shape and strength at the core of our being, who takes up residence in and redefines us. If we are permeated with Christ, such cherished ideas as independence, self-determination, and self-fulfillment must be abandoned, at least as they are understood in our fallen society. Christ's indwelling means we are not our own.

EPHESIANS 4:1–16

Original Meaning

Live Worthy of Your Call Focused on Unity (4:1–3). Note that "calling" in verse 1 is used of every Christian, not of the professional ministry or an elite group. This one call is for all Christians to live in accord with what God has done in Christ.

The phrases in verses 2–3 are subordinate to the one main imperative—"live a life worthy of the calling you have received." Living worthy of the call requires eagerness "to keep the unity of the Spirit" (v. 3). The unity believers share in God's Spirit is based on that peacemaking act of Christ, which has created one new being and links Christians together.

Unity Is Motivated by Theological Oneness (4:4–6). Verses 4–6 are likely from a creed used in Paul's churches or one that Paul composed originally for this letter. The confession has a threefold triadic structure:

1. body, Spirit, hope;
2. Lord, faith, baptism,
3. one God and Father of all, who is over all, through all, and in all.

Seven items are preceded by the word "one," and in each case the oneness expresses both the uniqueness of the item and its foundational value for unity. All seven express the reality that there is only one gospel and that to believe that gospel is to enter into the unity it creates.

Each Person Has Received Grace to Build Up Christ's Body (4:7–16). *Grace for ministry to each believer and its scriptural support (4:7–8).* Like other passages on the body, Paul's concern for unity is balanced by an emphasis on diversity and the responsibility of each person. Once again "grace" has an unexpected meaning. It does not designate saving grace here, but grace for ministry. Paul could as easily have written, "To each of us *ministry* has been given." "As Christ apportioned it" (v. 7) is literally "according to the measure of the gift of Christ."

In his quotation of Psalm 68:18 in verse 8, Paul is interested primarily in the last line, "and gave gifts to his people." This provides scriptural verification that the ascended Christ gives gifts to his people. Paul understood the psalm to concern Christ's ascension, or he has at least adapted it to Christ's ascension.

Parenthetical comment on the ascension (4:9–10). Most likely, Paul here is referring to the incarnation: the one who descended in the incarnation is the same one who has ascended and is now exalted over all things—Jesus Christ the Lord.

People are given as gifts to serve and build up (4:11–16). This section is one long sentence in Greek, in which two subjects are treated: the ministry that takes place in the body and the maturity this ministry is to achieve. The gifts Christ gives to the church are *people* to promote serving and building up. This text teaches both about gifts and about institutional order.

Servants build toward unity and knowledge of Christ (4:11–13). This text does not set up a hierarchy of clergy and laity; rather, it speaks of people given to the church to assist its service and edification. The idea is not of gifts given to a special group, but of grace giving people to the church.

"Apostles" were specially authorized agents of God, responsible for explaining and disseminating God's good news. "Prophets" at times predicted future events, but usually they explained the relevance of the gospel and the will of God (see 1 Cor 14:3–40). The "evangelist" was a "gospeler," someone who focused on proclaiming the gospel and its relevance. "Pastors and teachers" (literally "teaching shepherds") obviously had teaching gifts and provided pastoral care. The figure of a shepherd leading and caring for sheep is a familiar Old Testament image applied to both God and human leaders.

Verse 12 is made up of three prepositional phrases, which, rendered literally, reads: "*toward* the equipping of God's people *unto* a work of service *unto* building up the body of Christ." The emphasis on each person receiving grace for ministry in 4:7 and the parallels in Romans 12:3–8 and 1 Corinthians 12:4–31 necessitate a focus on the involvement of all the people in the work of the church.

While the first part of verse 13 may have implications for the end-time, Paul's concern is that his readers will not be blown about theologically like little children *now, in the present*, not after the parousia. "Unity in the faith and in the knowledge of the Son" is not merely unity in the ideas that we believe, but a unity resulting from the experience of receiving the gospel and living with Christ.

A mature and growing faith, evidenced by truth and love (4:14–16). Again, Paul wants his readers to become mature *so that* they will not be carried away by erroneous teaching. Immaturity is described as being "tossed back and forth" and "blown here and there"—that is, being easily deceived.

With the transition to the description of maturity in verse 15, we encounter perhaps the most important ethical guideline in the New Testament, one that summarizes what Christian living is about: truth, love, and continual growth into Christ in everything. Speaking and living the truth of the gospel is set opposite the deceitful teachings that carry away the immature. Yet a broader concern for truth generally must be included. The truth of the gospel cannot be separated from truth generally, whether it is in explaining God's purposes or relating to other humans. We are to "grow" up into Christ in everything (v. 15). Living the truth in love is both the means of growth and the result of growth.

The idea of growth provides an easy transition back to the "body" imagery (v. 16). "Head" here in verse 15 as elsewhere points to the fact that he is Lord. Because he is Lord, he has the power and authority to provide what the body, the church, needs.

Application. This passage offers a blueprint for redesigning the work of the church and its leaders. To do so, Christians must break the monopoly the clergy has on the tasks of ministry. The body of Christ does not have two classes of members—clergy and laity—or two sets of expectations. Everyone has the same task of building up the body, even though responsibilities vary. Certainly some tasks are more appropriate to pastors and require at least some expertise, but even with those tasks pastors should include and train church members. Ministry is the only profession that retains nothing to itself, gives away all its knowledge for free, and invites those served to do the same work.

EPHESIANS 4:17–24

Original Meaning

The Old Life of Futility (4:17–19). The Greek word translated "I . . . insist on it" (v. 17) is literally "I testify" or "I declare." In contexts like this it has the connotation "urge" (cf. 1 Thess 2:12). Paul expresses his appeal to his readers with increasing strength as the letter progresses.

In verses 17b, Paul's primary concern is not with a list of specific sins, but with a distortion and disorientation of the mind. The word translated "futility" (*mataiotēs*) expresses meaninglessness, uselessness, worthlessness, or emptiness. Four elements in verse 18 trace the problem back to its source. Hardness of heart has prevented all loyalty to God. Hearts made insensitive to God have set off a chain reaction that turned out the light and led to meaninglessness.

If verse 18 traces the problem back to its origin, verse 19 shows its outcome. Insensitivity in one direction leads to "sensuality" in another. "Sensuality" (*aselgeia*), by implication, is the idol to which the gentiles have given themselves. The word translated "full of greed" (*pleonexia*) means literally "the desire to have more." Impure activity is rooted in greedy desire, the self-centered character of sin.

Learning the Messiah (4:20–24). *Knowing the Christ and Jesus (4:20–21).* Literally, verse 20 reads: "You did not learn the Christ this way." More is intended than mere learning facts about Christ. That is, the readers have firsthand knowledge of him and know how radically different his life is from that of the unbelieving gentiles. In verse 21, Paul goes on to emphasize they know better than to live the life he described in verses 17–19, for they know the truth that is in Jesus.

Old being–new being (4:22–24). This passage is evidence of Paul's frequent blending of the indicative and the imperative. His intent is to buttress his plea in verse 17 for a different lifestyle. Verses 22–24 show what the readers were taught, but the implication is that these words should also be put into practice.

Paul's main issue here is transformation—a change of identities. The language for "putting off" and "putting on" occurs in a variety of ethical contexts, including non-Christian sources. "Putting off" and "putting on" are another way of expressing the ideas of dying and rising with Christ, which also appear in discussions of baptism and ethics (cf. Rom 6:1–11; Col 2:11–3:4).

The old being fit the former way of living, and its ongoing corruption was fueled by "deceitful desires" (v. 22). Paul's thought is related to 2:3, which spoke of disobedience caused by following fleshly desires, although no mention is made here of the ruler of the air. The old being is the human self without God, deluded and deceived into a downward spiral by fleshly desires. The solution requires ongoing renewal and a new creation.

The language for the new being (v. 24) recalls Genesis 1:26–27 and the idea of humanity's creation in God's image. The image marred in Eden is being re-created in Christ. This new creation is viewed as a work that God has already accomplished and reflects the same ideas as Ephesians 2:10.

Application. If the fundamental problem of fallen humanity is distorted reasoning, we need a wholesale restructuring of the mind. Other texts in Ephesians have emphasized the role of the Holy Spirit in this process (1:17–18; 3:16–17), so no thought exists of a depraved mind repairing itself. The light of the gospel shows the channels along which new thinking must run, and the Spirit engages our spirit in reordering life. We must learn to think for ourselves along Christian lines.

EPHESIANS 4:25–5:2

Original Meaning

Lying and Anger (4:25–27). Given the focus on "truth" in 4:15, 21, and 24, it is unsurprising that truth-telling is the first of Paul's ethical injunctions here. In verse 25, the main imperative (literally "each speak truth with his neighbor") is a quotation from Zechariah 8:16. The motivation for telling the truth is that we are members of each other. "In your anger do not sin" in verse 26 is a quotation from Psalm 4:4. That the sun is not to go down on one's anger is a way of saying that anger must not endure but must be dealt with quickly. We must not give the devil room in our lives to operate (v. 27). Anger is one place of inroad for him, a Trojan horse for his attack.

To Harm or to Help? (4:28–29). While stealing may have been common among slaves, by no means should verse 28 be thought as addressed merely to them. Theft then, as now, was a common problem. The word "unwholesome" in verse 29 is used of spoiled fish or rotten fruit, but it is also used to describe stones that crumble. The metaphorical meaning connotes "foul" or "bad." Although obscene speech may be in mind (see 5:4), the concern for "building up" later in the verse suggests "destructive" language.

Christian Ethics in a Nutshell (4:30–5:2). *Do not grieve the Spirit (4:30).* Verse 30 marks the incongruity of grieving the one who is proof we belong to God and are destined for his future salvation. Why live contrary to him whose ownership seal we wear and in violation of our destiny? This verse stands in marked contrast with what is said of the devil in verse 27. No room is to be permitted for the devil, but through the Spirit, God is at work in us. The personal character of the Spirit is here simply assumed.

Goodwill, not ill will (4:31–32). The focus here is on the responsibility of believers to act. Such acts of believers, of course, are presumed to be aided by the work of the Holy Spirit. The contrast between verse 31 and 4:2–3, the description of a Christian's calling, is striking.

In contrast to the badness and malice of verse 31, verse 32 calls for goodness, which applied to humans is understood as being "kind" (the same root is used for God's kindness in 2:7). Paul also calls for compassion and forgiveness. Note again the focus on salvation taking place "in Christ" (cf. 2 Cor 5:19).

Be like God (5:1–2). The command to imitate God is breathtaking, but it is a thoroughly biblical idea and not unusual in Jewish or Greek thought. Elsewhere Paul urges readers to imitate him or to imitate him as he imitates Christ. The second half of 5:1 shows why the command to imitate God is legitimate: the readers are God's children, whom he loves.

The imitation of God and his love is changed in verse 2 to the imitation of Christ and his love. Love is the sphere in which the believer lives. The standard by which Christian love is shaped and energized is the self-giving love of Christ on the cross. Christ's death is presented here as an example for our lives, but his death is never merely an example. With it comes a theology of atonement grounded in the love of God and Christ.

Application. Christians are encouraged by this passage and others to keep short accounts with God. These accounts have to do primarily with how we have treated other people, so we need to keep short accounts both with God *and* other people. The habit of regular and frequent checks with God is necessary to determine whether we are grieving or pleasing the Spirit. To put it another way, if Jesus's self-giving sacrifice was a pleasing smell to God, do our lives provide such a pleasing smell, or is the smell rather foul?

EPHESIANS 5:3–14

Original Meaning

Avoid Shameful Sins (5:3–6). *Sexual sin and greed (5:3).* The shift from Christ's self-giving nature in 5:2 to the self-indulgence of verse 3 is striking. The three sins mentioned—"sexual immorality" (*porneia*), "impurity" (*akatharsia*), and "greed" (*pleonexia*)—were already mentioned at 4:19. *Porneia* is a broad word covering any sexual sin. It can refer to incest (1 Cor 5:1), promiscuity (1 Thess 4:3), sexual relations with a prostitute (1 Cor 6:13), or illicit sexual relations (John 8:41). *Pleonexia*, literally "the desire to have more," is further identified as "idolatry" in verse 5. These sins are totally contrary to what it means to be a Christian.

Sins of the tongue (5:4). The three words for sins of speech in this verse occur nowhere else in the New Testament, although cognates appear of the word translated "obscenity" (*aischrotēs*). The root expresses that which is shameful or disgraceful. "Foolish talk" (*mōrologia*) brings to mind the frequent condemnation of the fool in Old Testament wisdom literature. "Coarse joking" (*eutrapelia*) suggests something easily turned, a double *entendre*. What is fitting for God's people is rather "thanksgiving."

Motivation in the form of warnings (5:5–6). Paul reminds his readers that sexual sin and greed are not fitting for God's people and that those who commit such sins will not inherit the kingdom of Christ and of God. Not only are practitioners of such sins excluded from the kingdom, but a more dire fate awaits them in the form of God's wrath.

The Relation of Christians and the Disobedient (5:7–14). *Do not partner with such people (5:7).* If one is joined to Christ and shares in him, one cannot share in the lives of those practicing sexual sin and greed.

Live the light (5:8–10). The use of light and darkness themes in 1:18, 3:9, and 4:18 does not prepare the reader for the radical statement here. No text is as strong in its explanation of conversion. The underlying thought is based on Paul's "spheres of influence" theology. People take on the character of the sphere in which they live. When they are in him who is the light, they too *are* light.

Paul's ethic is always guided by "what pleases the Lord" (v. 10). The word translated "find out" (*dokimazō*) means "put to the test, examine, or discern," in the sense "determine the validity of." The Christian ethic is in large measure an ethic of discernment.

Let the light do its work (5:11–14). The separation Paul calls for is not so much a withdrawal as a confrontation. "Expose" (vv. 11, 13) often carries a nuance of correcting or convincing someone. Clearly Paul is not thinking of geographical separation and avoidance of contact, but of the refusal to participate in indecent actions. After all, contact with non-Christians is required if the light is to accomplish its purpose.

The last half of verse 14 is about Christ's transforming light. This is clearly traditional material, as "it is said" shows. These words are a confession or hymnic statement calling for people to wake up from their darkness and experience the transformation that the risen Christ brings. The wording may be drawn from passages on resurrection and light in Isaiah 26:19 and 60:1.

Application. Our society has a major problem handling sexuality. The problems of adultery, promiscuity, and the like are bad enough, but the extent of the problem is revealed even more by rape, incest, and sexual abuse. Conservative estimates are that one in six women will be raped and that one in ten children is a victim of incest. Our legitimate desires for love and intimacy have gone haywire, and the pride, power, and pleasure coalesced around sexuality have destroyed all sanity and control.

EPHESIANS 5:15–33

Original Meaning

Christians Living on Target (5:15–21). *Careful living (5:15–17).* The main statement in this section is verse 15a: "Be very careful, then, how you live"; the rest of verses 15b–21 provides description of what that entails. The call to live wisely is a call for moral discernment and a practical skill in making decisions.

In verse 16 the NIV's "making the most of every opportunity" is an interpretation of the phrase "redeeming the time." The expression is a metaphorical way to speak of using time well. A good translation would be, "Buy up every opportunity."

Life in the Spirit (5:18–21). Paul has been contrasting the unacceptable behavior of the unbelieving world with that of God's people. To write against drunkenness was a convenient way for him to call to mind the destructive and unacceptable lifestyle of so many in the culture around them. The contrast between drunkenness and worship or godly living has a long tradition.

The command to "be filled with the Spirit" (v. 18) is unexpected and unparalleled in the Bible. Possession of the Spirit is the mark of being a Christian. Paul's point is that the Holy Spirit is the controlling influence motivating and directing the lives of believers. Fullness expresses unity with the triune God and the completion that God's salvation brings. The call to be filled with the Spirit is a call to live in that unity and to enjoy the wholeness of life with God.

Of the five participles describing life in the Spirit, three have to do with singing (v. 19). This whole section is reminiscent of the initial doxology in 1:3–14. Singing is the natural expression of joy that God brings into a person's life. The presence of early Christian hymns gives some indication of the importance of songs in the early church. The purpose of singing is both praise to God and instruction of believers.

In addition to singing, life in the Spirit is characterized by giving thanks (v. 20). Thanksgiving is the believing acknowledgment of God and his purposes for good in Christ. Obviously such giving of thanks points to a lifestyle and not just to spoken words.

Christians are to give thanks to God always for everything "in the name of our Lord Jesus Christ" (v. 20). This text is christologically significant, for it is evidence of the worship of Jesus, of his being linked with God liturgically, and of the transfer to him of the title "Lord." The early church was aware that in encountering the risen Jesus, they were encountering God.

The last participle describing life in the Spirit is perhaps the most surprising. The Greek word *hypotassō* ("submit," v. 21) literally means "arrange under." It was used previously in Ephesians of everything being subjected under Christ's feet (1:22). Attempts to translate "submit" by "be supportive of," "be committed to," or "identify with" are unacceptable. It is important to note that this text does not ask some Christians to submit to other Christians. It asks *all* Christians to submit to *one another.* No privileged group is in view. Christians are called to live in mutual submission, and *without mutual submission they cannot fulfill their destiny.* Such submission is a strong and free act of the will based on real love of the other person (cf. 4:2).

The House Codes (5:22–33). *Instructions to wives (5:22–24, 33b).* We must begin by emphasizing that the instruction to wives to submit to their husbands is only the first example of the mutual submission required of all Christians. Christianity brought with it significant change for women, and apparently their freedom was a source of offense to non-Christians. In Galatians 3:28, for example, Paul wrote that distinctions like male and female no longer determined value.

What Paul meant by saying wives should "submit to [their] own husbands *as you do to the Lord*" is unclear (v. 22). The wife's relation to the Lord is the basis, motivation, and qualification of her submission to her husband. In verse 24 the words "in everything" indicate that all spheres of life are included in this submission, provided, of course, that it is in keeping with life lived "to the Lord."

Verse 23 is surely one of the most abused and debated texts in the New Testament. Its focus is *not* on the privilege and dominance of the husband, and Paul never intended to suggest that wives were servants, compelled to follow any and every desire of the husband. The text does not tell women to *obey* their husbands, nor does it give any license for husbands to attempt to force submission.

The debate has intensified in recent years over the meaning of *kephalē*, the Greek word for "head" (v. 23). The most important factor for determining the meaning is the *context* of Ephesians and Paul's other writings. The argument for "source" as the meaning of *kephalē* is not convincing. Paul is not arguing in verses 22–24 that the husband is the source of the wife as Christ is the source of the church. Scholars appear to have chosen this meaning only to avoid negative connotations for the discussion of male-female relations in modern times. Some connotation of authority appears to be included in Paul's metaphorical uses of *kephalē*.

Still, verse 23 does not focus on authority. The husband has a leadership role, though not in order to boss his wife or use his position as privilege. Just as Jesus redefined greatness as being a servant, Paul redefines being head as having responsibility to love, to give oneself, and to nurture.

Although Paul makes explicit the priority or responsibility of the husband, the text also assumes the oneness and equality of husband and wife in verses 28 and 31. Both headship and equality must be given their due. As elsewhere, the truth is in the tension of the text.

Instructions to husbands (5:25a, 28–29a, 31, 33a). Since wives are asked to submit, one might expect the text would ask husbands to *rule* in an appropriate way. It does not; instead, it asks husbands to *love* and give themselves with the same self-giving love that Christ had in giving himself for the church.

In the ancient world husbands had relatively few obligations beyond providing food and shelter. They were free to do as they pleased, whereas wives were obligated to do domestic chores and to do what their husbands required. Paul's words change the picture dramatically. Rather than being guided by self-interests, the husband is asked to place the well-being of his wife first and to give himself to caring for her.

Verse 28 applies the commandment to love one's neighbor as oneself (Lev 19:18) specifically to the husband. Paul here assumes a theology of the oneness of the husband and wife based on Genesis 2:24. Consequently, the idea of hating or neglecting one's wife is as strange as hating or neglecting oneself.

The words of verse 29 express a tenderness and nurturing expected from the husband so that the well-being and wholeness of the wife are assured. Christ's love motivated him to give himself for the good of the church. Husbands must follow the same pattern and love enough to give themselves for their wives.

The relation of Christ and the church (5:23b–24a, 25b–27, 29b–32). The marriage relation is seen as an analogy of Christ's love, his saving work, and his ongoing care for the church. Paul describes this relation as "a profound mystery" (v. 32). Paul uses this term to point to a *revelation* from God, something one would not know had not God revealed it. What Paul probably meant is this: "The revelation about Christ and the church is tremendous and profound."

Application. This text underscores both the love of Christ and the lordship of Christ. That *he* is head and the church submits to him ought to be a constant reminder that the church has no other agenda than that set and modeled by Christ. A greater sense that Christ leads the church, joined with mutual submission in finding his purposes, will move the church past many of its current problems.

EPHESIANS 6:1–9

Original Meaning

Instructions to Children and Parents (6:1–4). "Obey your parents in the Lord" (v. 1) means to obey as part of one's relation to the Lord. That children should obey their parents was a given in Paul's society, but for him it was "right" because of their relation to Christ.

In the ancient world, fathers had absolute control over the family and were sometimes harsh; that is why Paul includes the warning against provoking children to anger. "Bring them up" conveys the idea of nurture (v. 4). "Training and instruction of the Lord" most likely means that the instruction is subsumed under and determined by the Lord.

Instructions to Slaves and Masters (6:5–9). On the one hand, the directions given to slaves removes any suggestion that this new faith upset the cultural order; on the other hand, *these verses are still extremely subversive.* Slave owners may have been pleased with the service they would get, but in the process they lost control, for slaves now had a higher allegiance than to their owners. This section makes specific to slaves (and masters) what was asked of everyone in 5:10, 17, 21: pleasing the Lord, doing his will, and mutual submission. To apply mutual submission to slaves and slave owners was a startling redefinition of slavery.

In verse 5 we again meet the difficulty of understanding the word "fear" in the ancient world, but to this word is added "trembling" (NIV "respect and fear"). The combination expresses deference in a relationship, not actual quaking. The slave is not to play to a human audience. The primary motivation for this ethic is the final judgment. Paul assumes here that judgment is according to works, the consistent expectation of the whole Bible.

That masters are asked to treat their slaves "in the same way" is cryptic, but still shocking (v. 9). For them to follow this instruction, they would have to treat their slaves with respect and fear and with sincerity of heart as to Christ. That alone should have abolished slavery for Christians! A structural parallel exists between the knowledge slaves have about judgment (v. 8) and the knowledge owners have of a common Lord in heaven, who shows no favoritism (v. 9). Every thought of privilege evaporates before Christ.

Application. The very form of this text is an indictment of modern-day churches. As passages like this show, early Christian congregations were made up of a cross section of society, but the usual valuations of the society were rejected. In most of our churches today, the valuations of society are retained so that no real cross section comes together. We have churches for different socio-economic groups; we do not draw people to a common place where hierarchies and valuations are set aside and people know they stand on equal footing before God. As long as a church is a "group of our kind," it fails its mission. Application of the text requires creation of a place where grace is evident and all people come together as equals.

The application of the teaching on slaves and masters is obviously relevant for work relations, but it actually involves every relation and act. No relation is merely a relation; it is a context for relating to Christ. No job is merely work; it is a context for serving Christ.

EPHESIANS 6:10–20

Original Meaning. *Be strong and put on the full armor of God (vv. 10–11, 13).* Since Ephesians is about power for living in Christ, it comes as no surprise that the concluding exhortation has this emphasis. The passive form of the verb ("be strong") indicates that this empowering is something done to Christians, not something they do themselves; its present tense shows the empowering is continual.

"Put on the full armor of God" (vv. 11, 13) recalls the command in 4:24 to "put on the new self." Putting on the new self is in essence the same as putting on the armor of God. The "armor of God" can be understood as the armor that God provides, the armor that God himself wears, or even the armor that is God himself. In the end all the armor language is a way to talk about identification with God and his purposes.

The struggle with spiritual forces (v. 12). The word translated "struggle" refers primarily to wrestling, but it can be used more generally of a fight or battle. "Flesh and blood" is a Semitism for "human." What Paul means, therefore, is: "Our struggle is not with human beings, but with evil spiritual forces." This is the only place in the New Testament where the Christian life is described in this sort of language.

Of the four expressions used for spiritual forces in verse 12, only "rulers" and "authorities" appear in the earlier list of five terms for spiritual forces in 1:21. Precise identification of the various expressions is impossible because of the ambiguity and paucity of the terms.

The use of the term "spiritual" for evil forces is somewhat surprising. More surprising still is that the struggle takes place "in the heavenly realms." Since verse 12 explains standing "against the devil's schemes" of verse 11, Paul was surely not thinking about structures of evil such as government, law, or social conventions. Rather, he thought of personal spiritual beings seeking to disrupt life as God intended it.

The Armor of God (6:14–20). The armor described is that of a heavily armed Roman foot soldier, though Paul uses this analogy because of the influence of the Old Testament, the picture it presents, and its rhetorical effect. Speculation about the connection between specific virtues and specific parts of the armor is not helpful, especially when the breastplate and helmet are associated with different qualities in 1 Thessalonians 5:8.

The NIV uses "belt" (v. 14) to convey the idea of tying around the waist—the idea of girding in the ancient world, which is often associated with tying up long robes and designating readiness for action. For soldiers, reference is probably to a leather, apron-like covering tied around the waist to protect the lower abdomen.

The "breastplate of righteousness" is from Isaiah 59:17, which describes *God's* putting on armor to come in judgment. To put on the breastplate of righteousness means that Christians are to reflect the righteous character of God in their actions.

"Feet fitted with the readiness that comes from the gospel of peace" (v. 15) is adapted from Isaiah 52:7, which describes the messenger of good news. The paradox of armor given to those committed to a gospel of peace reminds the reader that the language is metaphorical.

With the shield, Paul has in mind the large shield Roman infantry used to protect their whole bodies. They were not merely defensive, for a line of soldiers with interlocked shields and weapons poised could push right through enemy ranks. To speak of faith is not to focus on human belief but on the faithfulness of God.

"The helmet of salvation" (v. 17a) is from Isaiah 59:17, describing God's own armor. God's salvation is the ultimate assurance of protection. From the treatment of salvation earlier in the letter, this salvation is both present and future.

The Spirit is the one who empowers the sword (v. 17b). Throughout Scripture, God's word is the instrument by which his power is shown. "Word of God" does not refer to the Bible but to the gospel message. The Greek word used here (*rhēma*) usually refers to a teaching or prophetic utterance or, more specifically, to the gospel.

"Pray[ing] in the Spirit" (v. 18) does not refer to speaking in tongues. Rather, it should be seen in connection with other passages on the Spirit in Ephesians, especially 3:16 and 5:18. The Spirit communicates God to us, and through him we receive all gifts and empowering from God. The instructions to pray and be alert are paralleled elsewhere in the New Testament. Prayer combined with perseverance is, in fact, the way to keep alert. Just as Paul started the letter by praying for his readers, he closes by asking them to pray for him (vv. 19–20).

Application. The command to "be strong in the Lord" presumes that God is eager and willing to provide strength and that any lack of strength results from our neglect. It assumes also that empowering is a choice we make about the relative importance of life with Christ. If you seek a religion to make you comfortable, the Christian faith is not it—despite all its focus on peace and benefit. A battle rages, and contrary to our deception we do not live on neutral turf. We either live for God or against him.

EPHESIANS 6:21–24

Original Meaning. *Tychicus, the letter carrier (6:21–22).* The description given for Tychicus is used of Paul's other close helpers. At the beginning of the letter, Paul described his readers as "the faithful in Christ Jesus" (1:1). Similarly, at the end of the letter Tychicus is described as a "faithful servant in the Lord," underlining the importance of both faithfulness and the idea of being in Christ.

The closing benediction (6:23–24). The benediction here is fuller and more liturgical than most, which is unsurprising, given the liturgical character of the whole letter. The NIV translation "and love with faith from God" is problematic. If the focus is on the love and *faithfulness* that come from God and Christ, the passage makes better sense. This option would be translated: "Peace to the brothers and sisters and love with faithfulness from God the Father and the Lord Jesus Christ."

A second translation difficulty comes at the end of verse 24. If translated literally the text reads: "Grace be with all those loving our Lord Jesus Christ in immortality." The problem is primarily understanding where "in immortality" should be connected. Several possibilities exist:

1. Connect the words to "love," as the NIV has done.
2. Connect them to "grace," as the NEB has done ("grace and immortality").
3. Connect them to "the Lord Jesus Christ," emphasizing that Christ already reigns in immortality.
4. See them merely as a general and cryptic way to refer to the eternal consequences of the gospel.

The third option seems the most likely, both grammatically and theologically.

Application. Perhaps the most important application of this section is the reminder that God and Christ are the substance of life. They are the willing sources of what we need to live, and all God expects from us is a loving response. God has provided all we need in Christ; therefore, we should live worthy of the gift.

PHILIPPIANS

INTRODUCTION TO PHILIPPIANS

Were Paul to visit a church in a twenty-first century Western democracy, he might wonder how his letter could be understood by people so different from him and from the Philippians. How can people who worship in cathedrals named after Saint Paul understand that God advanced the gospel through the apostle's imprisonment and the Philippians' persecution?

What does Philippians have to say to the modern church? Four theological themes seem to form the foundation on which Philippians was built. Each of these four themes presents a significant challenge to Western Christians.

First, and most important, Paul says that Christian unity is necessary for withstanding the onslaught of forces hostile to the gospel, for presenting a credible witness to the unbelieving world, and, above all, for being found blameless and pure on the day of Christ.

Second, Philippians has much to say to the church about the problem of suffering. Paul was suffering when he wrote Philippians. He was in prison awaiting a trial that could result in his condemnation and execution as a criminal. The Philippians were also suffering at the hands of hostile unbelievers in the society around them.

Third, the relationship between God's grace and human works is frequently an issue in Philippians. As paradoxical as it may seem, Paul affirms in Philippians that although God expects believers to make concrete efforts at obedience, at the final day we will not be acquitted on the basis of our obedience but on the basis of the righteousness that God gives to us.

Finally, and perhaps less obviously, Philippians says much about the church's relationship to the fallen world around it. The societal structures of the day were not friendly to the Philippian church, but Paul resisted the notion that the believer should retreat from the world. Our goal, like Paul's, should be to advance the gospel by engaging the culture, remembering the world belongs to God and that he loved it so much that he sought to reconcile it to himself through the death of his Son.

BOOK OUTLINE

I. Introduction (1:1–11)
II. The Significance of Paul's Circumstances (1:12–26)
III. The Challenge of the Philippians' Circumstances (1:27–4:9)
   A. Standing United (1:27–2:18)
   B. Two Examples of Christian Unity (2:19–30)
   C. A Warning against Theological Error (3:1–4:1)
   D. Concluding Admonitions (4:2–9)
IV. Conclusion (4:10–23)

PHILIPPIANS 1:1–11

Original Meaning

The Greeting (1:1–2). The opening words of first-century letters followed almost unfailingly the pattern "[Name] to [Name]: Greetings." Paul follows this pattern in verses 1–2 but expands it. Three changes are particularly important.

First, in verse 1 Paul includes a descriptive phrase: the recipients are "servants of Christ Jesus." Paul's word for "servants" (*douloi*) is the term commonly used in ancient times for slaves. Paul's readers would probably have understood the term to refer to people conscripted into the service of Christ.

Second, Paul modifies the standard letter opening by referring not merely to "all God's holy people" but to "the overseers and deacons." He wants the Philippians to know that the letter is addressed to them *all*, although he also wants to recognize the leaders of the church in a special way.

Third, Paul expands the typical "greetings!" (*charein*) into the term "grace" (*charis*) and by adding the Jewish salutation, "peace" (v. 2). By "grace" Paul means the grace in which believers now stand through the sacrifice of Christ on the cross. Similarly, the "peace" Paul commends to the Philippians is the blessing of reconciliation that has resulted from God's gracious work on their behalf.

Thanksgiving for the Philippians' Partnership (1:3–8). Paul follows the conventional pattern (vv. 3–11), but once again transforms it. In the first part (vv. 3–8) he reports to the Philippians his continual thanks to God for them and gives the reasons for his thankfulness. In the second part he tells the church he intercedes for them and describes the content of that intercession (vv. 9–11).

Intercession for the Philippians' Spiritual Growth (1:9–11). Paul's basic request is that they might express their love in ways that show both a knowledge of how to obey God's will generally, and, more specifically, of how to make moral decisions based on God's will.

If the above-mentioned characteristics mark the Philippians, they will "be able to discern what is best" and will "be pure and blameless for the day of Christ" (v. 10). Such devotion to the gospel will ensure that they bear "the fruit of righteousness that comes through Jesus Christ" (v. 11a). This fruit, he prays, will be evident in the Philippians' lives on the final day, and the result will be "the glory and praise of God" (v. 11b).

Application. How can we work for Christian unity? First, we must identify the barriers that divide people who claim to be Christians and ask whether they are legitimate. Some barriers are necessary. Some barriers, however, are illegitimate. If we are to be faithful to the spirit of Philippians 1:1–2, such barriers to Christian unity are intolerable. After identifying the barriers dividing us, we must be willing to follow the example of Paul's unselfishness in tearing them down.

Another aspect of sanctification is the principle of supporting other believers who are using their gifts for the advancement of the gospel. The modern church, like the Philippians in ancient times, should cultivate a type of support for other believers that is both sacrificial and consistent.

The church also needs to hear Paul's concern that the Philippians grow in love. Love for one another should include a determination to stand as sentinels over the commitment of one's fellow believers to the gospel, helping them not to be distracted from it by heresy and sin but to pursue single-mindedly "the prize for which God has called" believers heavenward (3:14).

Finally, this passage challenges the church to be as creative as Paul was in using the inherited traditions of his day in the service of the gospel. In our efforts to communicate the gospel creatively with the cultural tools available to us, it seems sensible to use tools that can convey the gospel message with as much power and fullness as possible.

PHILIPPIANS 1:12–18A

Original Meaning

The Gospel Progresses through Paul's Imprisonment (1:12–14). Paul begins the body of his letter with the statement that "what has happened to me has actually served to advance the gospel" (v. 12). Such an unusual statement demands an explanation.

He says that "it has become clear" that he is "in chains for Christ" (v. 13). The phrase "for Christ" is literally "in Christ" and probably carries the connotation of being in Christ's suffering. The purpose of Christ's suffering was the advancement of God's redemptive work. His own suffering has the same quality. The adjective "clear" (*phaneros*) probably means "known for what it really is." Paul has had the opportunity to explain the reasons for his imprisonment. Paul may be in chains, but the gospel has gone forward unfettered.

The Gospel Progresses through the Preaching of Paul's Rivals (1:15–18a). Paul's description balances the negative description of one group with a positive description of the other. The carefully balanced structure prepares the reader for Paul's remarkable conclusion: both preach Christ, and in this he rejoices.

Those whose preaching is motivated "out of goodwill" and "love" know that these circumstances are part of God's strategy for advancing the gospel (vv. 15b–16a). Those whose preaching is motivated "out of envy and rivalry" (v. 15a) seem to oppose the apostle for personal reasons and imagine that as they freely seek to persuade people to join their party, Paul himself looks on with envy from his imprisonment (v. 17).

Ultimately the stance of either group toward Paul does not matter, for "the important thing is that in every way, whether from false motives or true, Christ is preached," and this gives Paul joy (v. 18a).

Application. Whatever our own "chains" might be, we can look for ways in which the gospel might be advanced through them. Ridicule for our commitment to the gospel, a feeling of alienation from the wider society, or even lack of understanding from a church that has itself become too thoroughly accommodated to its culture are all ways in which forces beyond the believer's control can shackle the believer. In such situations our response should be a joyful attempt to discover ways of communicating the gospel in the midst of difficulty.

This passage teaches the modern church about the nature of joy. It is the settled peace that arises from making the gospel the focus of life. Paul was at peace with his circumstances because the advancement of the gospel was his primary goal in life. If we lack this kind of joy, then perhaps we should search our souls to be sure that our happiness is not more firmly connected to our comfort than to the gospel.

Specifically, this passage urges us to recognize that God can use people whose Christian commitment is self-serving and insincere. Our joy will remain intact if we remember that God is in control and that wherever Christ is preached, God can advance the gospel.

PHILIPPIANS 1:18B–26

Original Meaning

Christ Exalted through Life or Death (1:18b–20). All that has happened to him, Paul says, will result in his "deliverance" (v. 19, *sōtēria*). Even Paul's death, in other words, can result in his "deliverance," because the deliverance of which he speaks is unrelated to his physical release from the chains that bind him. It is instead his eschatological "salvation."

In what follows, Paul qualifies this statement in two ways. First, he claims that the events described in 1:12–18a "will turn out" for his salvation through the Philippians' prayers and through the supply of the Spirit of Jesus Christ (v. 19b). Those prayers are linked with God's furnishing of the Spirit to him, and together they provide the help he needs to face the Roman tribunal with courage.

Second, Paul qualifies his statement by saying that his salvation will occur according to his expectation that he will successfully endure the trials that lie ahead of him (v. 20). The noun translated as "eagerly expect" (*apokaradokia*) is unusually strong. The word refers to the intense expectation of something that is sure to happen. Paul sees the upcoming test in court as a divinely appointed opportunity to defend the gospel on his way to the final salvation he eagerly awaits.

In the contest that awaits him before that final vindication, he says, he will not "be ashamed," but Christ will "be exalted" in his body (v. 20). He will ultimately triumph over evil because his hope is in the Lord. God is still sovereign and will see him safely through to ultimate, eternal vindication.

Death a Gain, Life a Fruitful Labor (1:21–26). Whether he lives or dies, Paul says, he will be with Christ. To Paul, life means Christ (v. 21a). Death is gain, for it will mean the closest possible union with Christ. Such a perspective on the hardships of the present and on the possibilities of the future is possible for Paul only because Christ lives within him and gives him strength.

When Paul claims to "know" that he will remain in the flesh in verse 25, he does not shut out the possibility that he will be executed. Instead, Paul states his own difficult decision, based on his confidence that remaining in the body would be better for the Philippians, to choose life. The ultimate choice of life or death throughout the passage lies with God.

Although Paul's personal preference is unquestionably to depart and be with Christ, he is convinced that his acquittal and freedom to return to Philippi would result in "progress" for the Philippians in the faith (v. 25). Like Christ, Paul has put the interests of others ahead of his own interests, and the interests of the gospel above all.

Application. *The character of our intercessory prayers.* We tend to spend much of the time we devote to prayer asking God for things that will make our lives more pleasant. The first step in applying this passage to ourselves may simply be to ask God to give us a genuine love for other Christians and an understanding of their need for our prayers.

Our understanding of the Spirit's work. The church has historically taken a cautious attitude toward claims that the Spirit is at work in some new and powerful way. The reason for the caution is clear: anyone can claim to be possessed with the Spirit's power, and many have used this claim erroneously or deceptively for their own advancement.

Philippians 1:19 will not provide all of the guidelines we need to test the spirits, but it does provide two important ones. First, we should expect the Spirit to come upon Christians with surprising power. Second, we should pray for and expect the Spirit to come with unusual abundance on Christians who are undergoing suffering, particularly suffering for their faith.

Our attitudes toward life and death. Death is the worst possible event for those who believe that they have an inalienable right to "life, liberty, and the pursuit of happiness," and our way of coping with it seems to be to deny its existence. This can only cause us to clutch our material possessions more tightly for the security they can give and keep us from risking our lives in the service of God.

If we are to be as faithful as Paul expected the Philippians to be, we need to be aware of the needs of our suffering brothers and sisters, pray that God will supply them with an unusual abundance of the Spirit of Jesus Christ, and learn from their single-minded devotion to the gospel, in life and in death.

PHILIPPIANS 1:27–2:4

Original Meaning

Standing United against Opposition from Outside (1:27–30). The word "conduct yourselves" (*politeuesthe*, v. 27a) probably carries a deeper significance than is immediately apparent from most English translations. Paul is telling the Philippians to govern their lives according to the gospel rather than according to society's requirements for being a good citizen of Philippi. Although the temptation may be strong to compromise, their first consideration should be loyalty to the standards of God's commonwealth.

They should "stand firm" and "strive" for the gospel "in the one Spirit" and "as one" (v. 27c). The Philippians should be united in spirit (because they have all experienced the work of God's Spirit) and united in soul.

Turning their attention outward, Paul next says that the Philippians should not fear their opponents, and then gives two results that should encourage the Philippians. First, this very opposition is a "sign to them" (v. 28; cf. 1:10), probably a sign to any who are able to perceive it, that God will destroy those who persecute his people. Second, it is a sign of their salvation. It is a sign of the Philippian believers' salvation, on that day.

In the next phrase (v. 29), he explains their suffering for the faith is a gift. This startling statement probably has two characteristics of Christian suffering in view. First, suffering is a gift because, when successfully endured, it confirms the future salvation of the believer. Second, it is a gift because through it we become identified with Christ's suffering. Just as grace abounded in the suffering of Christ (Rom 5:20–21), so when believers suffer for him, grace abounds as well (cf. 2 Cor 4:7–12).

Standing United against Dissension from Within (2:1–4). The word "if" in 2:1 does not mean that the Philippians' possession of the qualities that Paul lists is hypothetical. Paul does not doubt that the Philippians have experienced the "encouragement" and "comfort" of Christ (v. 1). Paul's appeal is based both on his friendship with them and the blessings that belong to them because they belong to Christ.

Paul urges his readers to act on the relationship they have with one another because of what the Lord has done for them all. Paul describes this action as making his joy complete through cultivating a single mind. He then shows the Philippians how they can accomplish this unity of purpose with a list of brief clauses. Two clear interests emerge from this list: that the Philippians be united, and that they achieve this unity through promoting the interests of others rather than their own interests.

Application. Since earliest times the church of Jesus Christ has struggled with precisely what its relationship should be to the broader social order. Philippians 1:27–30 provides perspective for marginalized believers. The Christian way is to refuse retaliation and to live such exemplary lives that our persecutors not only become ashamed of their conduct but want to become believers themselves.

The same human tendency that urges us to retaliate against our detractors leads us to climb the ladder of selfish ambition at the expense of others. Against all of this Paul commands us "not [to look] to your own interests but each of you to the interests of the others" (2:4). The road to greatness among Christians is service to others.

PHILIPPIANS 2:5–11

Original Meaning. Paul begins in verse 5 by admonishing the Philippians to be unified, humble, and unselfish just as Christ Jesus was unselfish. In verses 6–8 Paul describes Christ's divine status as being in very "nature" God (v. 6a). Similarly, when Paul uses this same word in verse 7, he means that Jesus became a slave in his "very nature." Paul viewed divinity and servanthood as compatible, not contradictory, roles.

Christ's condescension was made possible by his own attitude toward equality with God: he did not consider it "something to be used to his own advantage" (v. 6b). He viewed his status not as a matter of privilege but as a matter of unselfish giving. This is the character of the biblical God.

In verses 7–8 Paul tells us that Christ "emptied" himself (Gk. *kenoō*; NIV "made himself nothing"). Christ did not literally empty himself of any divine attribute; instead, he metaphorically emptied himself by revealing the form of God in the form of a slave and in human likeness. The term "servant" represents the Greek word for "slave" (*doulos*, v. 7). The slave was deprived of the most basic human rights. In the same way, Christ refused to exploit the privilege of his deity and, giving up that right, became a slave.

The term "likeness" (v. 7c) does not indicate a difference between Christ and humanity but rather an essential identity. Christ Jesus became human in the *exact* sense, in every sense that makes one truly human.

In verses 6–7 Paul describes one way in which Christ expressed his deity. In verse 8 Paul describes a second way: Christ "humbled himself" by being found in appearance as a man and by suffering death by crucifixion. Christ went from the highest position imaginable to the lowest precisely because such selfless love was an expression of his deity.

In verses 9–11 God takes center stage, and Christ is the recipient of his action. Verse 9 begins with the two Greek words *dio kai* (NIV "therefore"), showing that God responded to Jesus's obedience in two ways: he "exalted" Jesus "to the highest place," and he "gave" to Jesus "the name that is above every name." The term "exalted" is a reference to God's exaltation of Jesus to a position of recognizable superiority over all creation.

Paul describes this exaltation more specifically when he says that God gave to Jesus "the name that is above every name." This can only mean that at Christ's exaltation the process began by which the equality with God that Jesus always possessed would be acknowledged by all creation.

The key lies in noticing that God takes the initiative. Jesus does not force God's hand, nor is the exaltation and granting of the name a payment for deeds performed. Instead, God initiated the exaltation of Jesus and freely "gave" (*echarisato*, v. 9) to him the most superior of names.

Paul next describes the result of this exaltation (vv. 10–11). It would be unwise to leave the impression that Paul's emphasis lay on Jesus's triumph over his enemies. Paul's concern lay not in Jesus's victory over those who opposed him but in Jesus's sovereignty over all creation. One day, Paul says, the universe will acknowledge what the small, persecuted community at Philippi confesses in its worship—"Jesus Christ is Lord" (v. 11).

Application. Paul advised the church at Philippi, and through them the church of today, to follow Christ's example. This means that the church and the believer must adopt an "incarnational" demeanor. Yet the strategies for dominance within the world have so thoroughly permeated the Western church that if the Word became flesh today, many churches might not even know of his existence, for he would be among the poor and disenfranchised.

In our mutual relations, Paul says that the hallmark of our lives should be giving rather than getting, serving rather than being served, obeying rather than dominance. In the hundreds of ways in which our lives touch others, we are to have the attitude of Christ Jesus. In matters as mundane as where we eat, what we do with our money, and how we act toward the members of our families, Paul tells us to imitate Christ.

Church members would do well to "pretend" to be Christ when they discuss divisive issues. This does not mean that such issues are unimportant or that a right answer does not exist. It only means that thoughtful and devout believers can disagree. Christians should be willing to listen respectfully and remain united in spirit. To do this takes the kind of humility Paul ascribes to Christ in this passage.

Our emphasis should rest on selfless service and obedience, in imitation of Christ. But how do we keep this emphasis central in our relationships? Paul reminds us of the final day on which we will have to give an account. For Paul, one of the most important reasons for speaking of the final day was to provide an incentive for ethical behavior in the present. All of us will one day stand before God, just as Jesus did at his exaltation. All of us should be found faithful on that day as he was found faithful.

PHILIPPIANS 2:12–18

Original Meaning

Keep Up the Good Work (2:12–13). Paul next begins to apply the example of Christ to the Philippian situation. He wants the Philippians to obey as Christ obeyed, and presumably this means to work for unity by avoiding the kind of selfish ambition that leads to dissension.

Paul frequently speaks of obedience in his letters and expresses concern that his congregations be obedient to the teaching he has left with them, whether he is present or absent. This does not mean that Paul expected his churches to obey his personal wishes; rather, he expected them to obey the gospel tradition he handed on to them.

One of the most important themes in Paul's theology is that human effort cannot even cooperate with God's grace to yield a right standing before God. What can Paul possibly mean, then, when he says that the Philippians should "work out [their] salvation with fear and trembling"? We must grasp the difference between Paul's use of the term *salvation* and his use of the term *justification*.

When Paul uses the term *justification*, he refers primarily to a status of innocence that God confers on the believer and to a condition of peace that God initiates. He frequently uses the verb *justify*, therefore, in the past tense (e.g., Rom 5:1). This justification comes entirely through God's grace and not through human effort.

The terms *salvation* and *save* have a different connotation in Paul. Most of his references to this salvation place it in the future, and he often connects salvation with the day of the Lord. Those who have been justified can be assured that they will be saved, but their salvation awaits the final day.

Paul perhaps recognized the danger, nevertheless, that someone would take his statement to mean that believers cooperate with God in the process of salvation, so in verse 13 Paul explains that salvation comes entirely at God's initiative and that God provides both the will and the ability to accomplish "his good purpose."

Redeem the Witness of Disobedient Israel (2:14–16a). Paul follows with a more specific command: the Philippian believers should, he says, stop complaining and arguing (v. 14), so that they may shine as beacons of light within the darkness of a world gone astray (vv. 15–16a), and so that they may join Paul on the final day in the presentation of an acceptable sacrifice to God (vv. 16b–18).

Paul begins this more specific exhortation with the command that the Philippians should do all things without "grumbling or arguing." The term "grumbling" (*gongysmos*) occurs frequently in the narratives of the Greek Bible that describe Israel's desert wanderings, where the Israelites "grumbled" against Moses (e.g., Exod 16:8). Paul believes that the Philippians stand in continuity with the ancient people of God and hopes that, unlike their spiritual ancestors, they will prove to be a beacon of light for the truth of the gospel.

Join Paul in Offering an Acceptable Sacrifice (2:16b–18). Paul begins with his hope that he will be able to present the Philippians' blamelessness and purity to God as his "boast" (v. 16b). If he is able to do this, his apostolic efforts will not have been in vain. Paul's language is indebted both to Greek and Hebrew cultural imagery of hard work, which, provided it is not frustrated along the way, ends in reward.

In verse 17a Paul describes himself as a "drink offering" that may be poured out. He probably has in mind the custom where drink offerings are made *in addition to* other offerings (cf. Num 15:1–10). Paul views the Philippians' continued obedience and steadfastness amid persecution as an offering equivalent to the offering of his own apostolic labors that may end in his death. Even if this happens, he will rejoice.

Application. The church's unity should be as clear as a beacon shining in the night. Sadly, the church too often fails to show the world concrete expressions of unity and so obscures an important witness to the gospel. What is the remedy? Paul's solution is to issue a warning. Those who place their own interest above the unity of the church, and thus the advancement of the gospel, should question whether they belong to God's people at all.

In addition to this strong medicine, Paul implies a remedy: "It is God," he says, "who works in you to will and to act in order to fulfill his good purpose" (v. 13). Any good that we as believers accomplish is the result of God's work in us. This is a deeply humbling truth, one that should give anyone pause who is bent on having his or her way.

PHILIPPIANS 2:19–30

Original Meaning

Why Not Timothy? (2:19–24). Timothy will not be coming right away. This news may have surprised and disappointed the Philippians, for Paul explains at length in the following verses why Timothy must stay with him until he knows the results of his trial. Timothy is an exceptional ally in times of trouble. Paul shows this by giving Timothy three commendations. First, Timothy understands what it means to be united in spirit with other believers (v. 20). Second, Timothy stands apart because he puts the interests of Jesus Christ above his own (v. 21). Finally, Timothy's mettle had been tested in the difficulty of apostolic service (v. 22). It is no wonder that Paul, in light of these qualities, feels that he can send Timothy only after he gains a clear view of the outcome of his imprisonment.

Why Epaphroditus? (2:25–30). Paul introduces Epaphroditus with a fanfare of complimentary language, leaving little doubt he returns with the apostle's blessing. As if this were not enough, Paul explains to his readers that the illness Epaphroditus suffered almost resulted in his death, and it happened because Epaphroditus was trying to carry out his commission faithfully (v. 30). For all these reasons, and despite their surprise at seeing Epaphroditus earlier than expected, the Philippians should "welcome him in the Lord with great joy" (v. 29).

Application. One of the most important ways in which an undivided commitment to the gospel can be expressed is in faithfulness despite hardship—a quality that is important because it produces assurance that we belong to God's people and will stand before him acquitted on the final day.

It is not a quality, however, that Western, and particularly American, culture presently reinforces. This is most clearly visible in the now well-known statistics on divorce in the United States. In such a climate, it is not likely that Christians will receive much encouragement from the broader culture to be faithful to their commitment to the gospel. The notion that someone might become a "slave" in the service of anything or risk one's health to fulfill a higher calling appears extraordinary, even abnormal. Yet it is precisely such people that Paul in this passage asks his Philippian readers, and us, to hold in high esteem.

PHILIPPIANS 3:1–11

Original Meaning

A Seam in the Letter's Argument (3:1). Paul hopes that the Philippians will maintain an attitude of joy and states why he issues the warnings that follow. His purpose is to keep the foundation of their faith free from the cracks he has seen develop in other churches.

Circumcision, False and True (3:2–4a). Paul calls his opponents "dogs" because, like dogs who intrude where they are not wanted, his opponents have invited themselves into Paul's churches (v. 2a). They are "mutilators of the flesh" because their confidence lies in circumcision (v. 2b). Paul says believers comprise the true "circumcision" (v. 3a).

The Old Testament recognizes that the physical rite should be symbolic of a "circumcision of the heart," and looked forward to a time when God would figuratively perform this operation (Deut 30:6; cf. Jer 31:31–34; Ezek 36:36–37). Paul's point here in verse 3 is that this time has arrived, and thus physical circumcision is irrelevant. Paul identifies true circumcision with the work of the Spirit within the worshiping community of both circumcised and uncircumcised believers.

We who are truly circumcised, Paul says, "boast in Christ Jesus" (v. 3b). Paul's word for "boast" (*kauchaomai*) is often used in his letters to indicate the ground of one's confidence. Paul's point is that the ground of the Christian's confidence is Christ rather than any human social privilege.

Paul follows this with the statement that believers do not put "confidence in the flesh" (v. 3c). In both the Old Testament and the philosophical literature from Paul's time, the term "flesh" (*sarx*) often signified human weakness and tendency to sin. Paul's point is that whereas Christians have placed their confidence in Christ, the Jewish opponents rest on a fallen human foundation that will inevitably collapse.

Paul's Fleshly Advantages (3:4b–6). In this paragraph, Paul compares the Jewish opponents' confidence in circumcision with his own advantages prior to his conversion. He was "blameless with respect to the righteousness that comes by the law" (v. 6, author's translation). This means that his parents had done everything for him that the law required Jews to do and that he had himself diligently observed the law.

Advantage Becomes Disadvantage (3:7–11). Like a bolt from the blue God apprehended Paul, and he saw his privileges and attainments for what they were—tainted with sin and unable to receive God's approval. They could now only be considered "loss for the sake of Christ" (v. 7).

Paul explores the ramifications of this great reversal in verses 8–11. He considers "everything" to be loss for the sake of "the surpassing greatness of the knowledge of Christ Jesus my Lord" (v. 8, author's translation). Paul does not mean that his Jewish upbringing, the law, and "everything" else were evil, but that his attitude toward them was evil. At his conversion, he had to accept the means for righteousness that God alone provided.

Paul next describes two results of this momentous decision. The first is that he might "gain Christ" (v. 8b). For Paul to gain Christ means that when Paul stands before God on the final day, he will not be found clinging to his own defective obedience but trusting in God's willingness to consider him acquitted because of Christ's death (v. 9).

Paul describes the second result of gaining Christ in verses 10–11. Just as Christ's death was the means through which God worked the miracle of the resurrection, so Paul's own suffering in faithfulness to his calling is the means through which God is bringing spiritual life to the congregations of believers he has been establishing.

The "somehow" that begins verse 11 sounds a startling note of uncertainty after the confident theme of reliance on God that runs through verses 7–9. Paul is certain that God will keep both him and his congregations faithful to their calling and conduct them safely through the final judgment, but he consistently refuses to presume upon God's mercy.

Application. How can the church prevent the abuses of boundary drawing that have sometimes plagued the church and hindered its witness? At least two principles should guide legitimate accusations of deviation from the truth of the gospel. First, the supposed false teaching should be a clear deviation from a principle that rests at the heart of the gospel or is clearly taught throughout Scripture. Second, those who draw theological boundaries, particularly if they are in power, must constantly examine their own motives.

Having protected ourselves from using the charge of heresy for selfish ends, however, it is important for every believer to know where the theological boundaries of the faith lie and to hold to them without compromise. For this purpose, every believer should be acquainted with the Apostles' and Nicene Creeds and be able to explain their contents.

The doctrine that salvation comes at God's initiative and through faith in Jesus is no less under attack today than in the time of Paul. Some groups effectively deny that faith in Christ alone is sufficient for salvation. A second, and more subtle, way in which inroads are often made into the doctrine of justification by faith alone is that believers do not allow the principle to inform their practice.

Philippians 3:1–11 also urges unbelievers to examine their own convictions. Paul plainly says that those who have rejected the gospel will be found on the final day with nothing to present to God but their own righteousness. Any righteousness that is not the righteousness that God himself provides, however, will be unable to withstand the time of judgment.

PHILIPPIANS 3:12–4:1

Original Meaning

Paul Forestalls a Misunderstanding (3:12–16). In verses 12–16 Paul affirms the incompleteness of his own journey, stating that, paradoxically, only those who understand their lack of perfection (*teteleiōmai*, v. 12) have reached spiritual maturity (*teleios*, v. 15).

In verses 12–14 Paul's language comes from the world of war and athletics and emphasizes the strenuous nature of his efforts. Together the two terms "press on" and "straining toward" connote a single-minded attempt to reach a particular goal. The goal Paul pursues probably remains all that he has described in verses 8–11. Paul vigorously pursues the knowledge of Christ because on the road to Damascus, Christ took hold of him. Had that event not taken place, Paul might still be busy "persecuting [*diōkō*] the church" (v. 6) instead of pressing on (*diōkō*) toward these goals.

Even more expressive of the difficulty of Paul's exertion to reach these goals is the athletic imagery in verses 12–14. Like a runner who knows that a backward glance will only slow his progress, Paul refuses to rest on his past successes but presses on toward that day when he will present the Philippians and his other congregations blameless to Christ.

What is this prize? The heavenly call is God's call to be part of the people, made up of both Jews and gentiles, who will stand justified before him on the final day because of their identification with Christ (vv. 8–11).

Paul's next statement (v. 15), at least in the Greek text, comes as a surprise. Having just denied that he has been "made perfect" (literal translation of *teteleiōmai*, v. 12; NIV "arrived at the . . . goal"), Paul now numbers himself among the "perfect" (literal translation of *teleioi*, v. 15; NIV "mature"). Why? When Paul applies this word to believers, it has the connotation not of perfection in the ultimate sense but of the maturity necessary to distinguish the wisdom of God from the wisdom of the world and to use spiritual gifts.

The Hellenistic world was full of notions of religious perfection and salvation, and it would have been easy to mix these notions with the gospel at Philippi. Thus, Paul offers the mild corrective in 3:15b: if some among the Philippian believers hold another position, God will reveal to them the truth.

Paul has only one request of them in the meantime (v. 16): the believers in Philippi should not turn back from the progress they have already made in living lives worthy of the gospel. God has begun a good work in the Philippians, but Paul does not want slight deviations from the truth to destroy their progress.

Paul Warns against Error (3:17–4:1). Paul next warns the Philippians against "enemies of the cross of Christ" (v. 18) whose "god is their stomach" and whose "glory is in their shame" (v. 19a). Such thinking can only result in eternal destruction and is the product of a mind focused on earthly things rather than on the things of God. "Earthly things" (v. 19b) are not the practical affairs of everyday life, but things that characterize worldly life in opposition to God.

Paul recommends two antidotes: he asks the Philippians to unite in their efforts to follow the example he and other mature Christians have provided for them (v. 17), and he admonishes them to remember that they are citizens of a heavenly commonwealth (v. 20).

To us it may at first seem brash that Paul would urge the Philippians to imitate him. Yet Paul's words are not an egocentric claim that everyone should act precisely as he acts. As Paul says elsewhere, his example is worthy of emulation only insofar as it in turn follows the example of Christ.

In addition to following Paul's example, the Philippians should remember that their "citizenship is in heaven" (v. 20). The term "citizenship" (*politeuma*) has political overtones. Paul encourages the Philippians to think of themselves as members of a commonwealth located in heaven. The fallen earthly realm is not the sum of their existence. The goal of their existence will instead be reached on the day when the Lord Jesus Christ returns.

Verse 21 echoes the description of 2:6–11. Just as Christ humbled himself (*etapeinōsen heauton*, 2:8) and was exalted as a result (2:9–11), so at that final day Christ will draw the lowly bodies (*to sōma tēs tapeinōseōs hēmōn*) of believers up into his glorious existence.

Application. Although Paul was certain that when God had started a good work he would complete it, he was unwilling to claim for himself in the present a victory that still lay in the future. The spiritual dangers of his apostolic labor were too vivid, the labor too strenuous to claim success. Instead, like an athlete, the apostle went into strict training and stretched toward his final goal, so that on the final day his running and labor would not be in vain.

Mature believers often realize how far they have to go before they finally lay hold of the ultimate victory, while the immature may claim victory too early. The biblical view is that if believers truly understand Christ's death and resurrection, they will then understand how much of sin's presence and power they had to be saved from and how far in this life they still have to go to be free of its effects, knowing that the final victory over sin won't take place until the day of resurrection.

PHILIPPIANS 4:2–9

Original Meaning

A Plea to Two Coworkers (4:2–3). Euodia and Syntyche must seek unity. Those who live within the sphere of Christ's lordship are equipped to overcome circumstances that would dishearten unbelievers and disrupt their friendships. Paul wants these two women to put this principle into practice in their relationship.

A Brief Set of Exhortations (4:4–9). The term "gentleness" (*epieikes*) in verse 5 was often used of an attitude of kindness where the expected response was retaliation. The words "be anxious" (*merimnaō*, v. 6) is often used in contexts where persecution is the issue. The term "guard" (*phroureō*, v. 7) likewise is frequently used to refer to the action of a military garrison.

All of this points to the context of persecution as the background for Paul's admonitions. The Philippians were suffering under opposition from their pagan neighbors, just as Paul and Silas had suffered when among them. They should remember that the Lord is near and replace their anxiety with thankful prayer about their suffering.

If the Philippians follow Paul's advice, he says, then "the peace of God, which transcends all understanding" will stand like a garrison over their hearts and minds (v. 7). The peace mentioned here transcends all understanding because God supplies an attitude in the face of adversity that does not fit the normal categories.

In verse 8, Paul tells the Philippians how they should *think*. In verse 9 Paul tells the Philippians how to *act*. The list of virtues that Paul asks the Philippians to "think about" is not a distinctively Christian list and could have been embraced by many right-thinking people in ancient times. This list, with its admonition to look for virtue in the wider world, reminds the Philippians that although society sometimes seems hostile and evil, it is still part of God's world and contains much good that the believer can affirm.

The four verbs Paul uses here in verse 9 all show that he is reminding his readers both of his personal conduct while with them and of the Christian tradition he passed on to them. The term "learned" (from *manthanō*) refers to learning from someone else's example. The term "received" (from *paralambanō*), on the other hand, refers to the reception of a particular body of teaching. The Philippians would have received this teaching by hearing Paul, and they would have learned from his example by seeing how he conducted himself.

Application. The history of the church has shown that when Christians act as a moral compass for society, they often act as a lightning rod as well. Christians are sometimes ostracized, and those who attempt to bring their Christian convictions into public-policy debates are told to leave. Paul's advice is for Christians in these circumstances to rejoice in the Lord and to make gentleness an obvious characteristic of their lives.

Christians today should not retreat from face-to-face encounters with the best unbelieving minds of the age but should engage them in the hope of learning truth, justice, and excellence from them and becoming more obedient followers of Christ. At the same time, Christians should strive for minds so steeped in Scripture and Christian tradition that they are able to approach the values of the unbelieving world with a critical eye and discern between what appears to be true but is, in subtle ways, false.

All of this is so important because the way we think determines how we act. Our thinking and our actions, then, are closely bound together. Indulging evil thoughts and tolerating sloppy thinking can have terrible consequences. Thus, if instead of loving my enemy I indulge the temptation to resent him, resentment turns to anger, anger to hatred, and the link between hatred and murder, as Jesus saw, is close (Matt 5:21–22).

PHILIPPIANS 4:10–23

Original Meaning

Thanks, Sort of (4:10–20). Verses 10–20 are basically an expression of thanks to the Philippians for a monetary gift they sent to him. Paul's expression of thanks is qualified, however, by two efforts to distance himself from the Philippians' gift. In verses 11–13 he claims that ultimately he did not need their gift, and in verse 17 he says that he did not seek it.

Why this concern? Paul was always circumspect about money matters. Charlatan philosophers were a frequent sight on street corners, and many were able to gather a following that was willing not only to hear and submit to them but to give them financial support. Paul was aware that misunderstanding could arise if he depended on the churches he established for his financial support.

Paul begins in verse 10 with an expression of joy that the Philippians have shown their concern for him. Perhaps because of their poverty, they had not been able to help Paul in this way recently. Thus, Paul rejoices "greatly" that the opportunity to show their concern for him has returned.

Despite this, Paul wants the Philippians to know that he has learned to be content in every circumstance. As long as Christ is being preached, Paul is joyful (1:18), and he does not want the Philippians to think that the physical comfort their gifts have made possible has increased his ability to cope with the difficulties at hand.

The apostle is also concerned that the Philippians not read his comments as ingratitude. Thus, he follows this qualification with a second expression of appreciation to the Philippians. In verse 17 the imagery is of a bank account that receives compounded interest.

In verse 18 the emphasis shifts again to gratitude. Paul at first continues the financial imagery and, perhaps with a touch of friendly humor, composes a "receipt," employing a technical term from the business world of Paul's day (*apechō*), which was often used to refer to the receipt of full payment for goods delivered or services rendered.

Paul says that God will meet all of the Philippians' needs (v. 19). If Paul's own understanding of "need" (vv. 11–13) is the key to understanding the term here, then surely Paul is promising that God will supply the Philippians with the greatest need of all—the ability to face all circumstances through the one who gives them strength (v. 13).

Paul ends his expression of gratitude to the Philippians for their partnership with a doxology that echoes the note of praise at the end of the letter's opening prayer (v. 20; cf. 1:11). Here, as there, this is more than a perfunctory expression of piety. It focuses the reader's attention on the primary goal both of Paul's apostolic vocation and of the Philippians' participation in it: God's glory.

Greetings and Grace (4:21–23). The way Paul phrases his personal greetings to the church is unique among his letters in its stress on each member of the congregation without distinction. Translated literally, the sentence says, "Greet every saint in Christ Jesus." He stresses the equal worth before God of each member of the congregation.

The greetings from Paul's associates are likewise general and all-encompassing in nature. They come not only from the brothers with Paul but from all of God's people in the area. Paul's only effort to make distinctions in the greeting comes in the last phrase of verse 22, where he singles out the members of Caesar's household for special attention. Perhaps Paul hopes to encourage them with the news that even some of the Roman emperor's staff have turned to the gospel.

Paul concludes the letter (v. 23) in much the same way as he began it (1:2), with a reference to "the grace of the Lord Jesus Christ." The same grace that transformed Paul from a persecutor of the church into its apostle will sustain the Philippians.

Application. For the unbelieving world, money takes on divine status. It is the god of this age, a god for which many people are willing to sacrifice their happiness, their children, their health, indeed their own lives. The workaholic father has now given way to the workaholic couple, who hardly know their children because they are too busy paying off expensive mortgages and car loans. This kind of zeal for income borders on the irrational, and we are hardly remiss in thinking of it as "religious."

The believer who possesses wealth should be wary of money's ability to gain the upper hand. Like the governing structures of the society in which we live, we must make use of it, but we should always do so with our eyes open, aware that it can subtly tempt us to do homage to it rather than to God.

How can Christians guard themselves from its deceptive tendency to take the place of God? Paul and the Philippians supply the antidote. The Philippians, by their very act of giving, have refused to let their wealth control them and have instead taken control of it. They have therefore taken away its power and refused to allow it sacred status. By giving their money, they demonstrated where their loyalties lay and strengthened their commitment to the God who would supply all that they ultimately needed through his riches in glory in Christ Jesus.

The most powerful antidote is to give generously from our wealth to those who have need, especially, as Paul would say, to those who are of the household of faith. In this way we provide equality among God's people and begin to view ourselves as the channel of God's blessing to others, rather than as the recipients of payment we have earned. This will in turn serve as a powerful reminder of a principle that runs like a thread throughout Philippians, and indeed through all of Paul's writings. It is perhaps best expressed in Romans 11:35–36:

> Who has ever given to God,
> that God should repay them?
> For from him and through him and for him are
> all things.
> To him be the glory forever! Amen.

COLOSSIANS

INTRODUCTION TO COLOSSIANS

In the last two centuries, many scholars have questioned whether Paul wrote Colossians. The cumulative evidence of differences in vocabulary, style, and theology from the undisputed letters by Paul have led many to this conclusion. But why would such a ruse have been undertaken? We should point out, however, that if Paul had nothing to do with the writing of Colossians, it must then be regarded as a deliberate forgery. The counterfeiter deliberately lifted names from Philemon to give verisimilitude to Colossians and to defraud readers into thinking that it was a genuine letter from Paul. In contrast to Philemon, which has simply a list of names, the Colossian author supplies further remarks for each name, summarizing their circumstances and work in the churches. Apparently the forger did not believe that the command not to lie to one another (3:9) applied in such a case. This problem is eliminated if Paul is the author of the letter. The close connection between Philemon and Colossians makes this the most reasonable conclusion.

The situation facing the Colossians is also similar to ours today. They faced opponents who challenged and belittled the sufficiency of Christ and their hope. Christians today live in a secular society that regularly scoffs at Christian faith. Many Christians in the West have become increasingly uncertain of their faith and consequently hold it uncertainly.

The letter to the Colossians argues that Christians must not only be solidly grounded in their faith but also be ethically above reproach. Discerning, confident, grateful, and ethical Christians lead lives worthy of the Lord, are pleasing to God, and will bear spiritual fruit in a spiritually blighted world. Paul intends in this letter to help form this kind of believer.

BOOK OUTLINE

- I. Salutation and Thanksgiving (1:1–23)
- II. Letter Body (1:24–2:23)
    - A. Paul's Commission, Message, and Struggle (1:24–2:5)
    - B. The Colossian Error (2:6–23)
- III. Ethical Admonitions (3:1–4:1)
    - A. The Things Above, and the Old and New Morality (3:1–17)
    - B. Commands about the Household (3:18–4:1)
- IV. Final Exhortations and Greetings (4:2–18)

COLOSSIANS 1:1–8

Original Meaning

The Salutation (1:1–2). Paul does not write as a privately interested party but as Christ's "apostle" who speaks with authority (v. 1). By identifying himself in this way, Paul is not trying to establish his badge of rank or to put his readers under his thumb. His authority is not increased by the use of the title apostle, just as it is not reduced when he omits it or substitutes "servant" (Phil 1:1) or "prisoner" (Phlm 1). Being an apostle is simply what he is.

Paul includes Timothy, "our brother," as a co-sender of the letter. According to Acts 16:1–2, Paul met this young man during his ministry in Derbe or Lystra. Although Timothy was not an apostle, Paul affirms him as one who carries on the same work and the same preaching task.

Paul greets the church as "holy" and "faithful" in Christ. Paul customarily identifies the recipients of his letters as "God's holy people," but he does not usually address them as "faithful." This expression most likely refers to their steadfastness under pressure. Their faith is not teetering on the brink of extinction, trapped in error, or at the mercy of those hawking false teachings. They are holding fast to the head (2:19), and Paul only warns them about others who do not. Their faith is not perfected, however, and Paul wants to buttress it further and revitalize their growth. In this greeting, he establishes their common commitments so that he can move on to instruct and warn them. His goal is to ensure that they remain securely established in their faith (1:23) and are growing in their knowledge (1:10).

To be in Christ means to be incorporated in him so that he encompasses the entire life of the believer. The recipients may be Colossians, but the only identity that matters to God is that they are Christians. That means that Christ determines everything in their lives. Paul will later make clear in the letter that Christ's death becomes their death, his burial their burial, his resurrection their resurrection, his victory their victory (2:6–23). Being in Christ gives Christians their true identity beyond their race, nationality, clan. Paul therefore calls the Colossians "brothers and sisters."

Paul confesses that both grace and peace come "from God our Father" (1:2). The thanksgiving that follows is based on all that God has done and will continue to do. The image of God as Father conveyed power, authority, and loving care.

The nearness and love of God as Father was something particularly esteemed by Christians, and Paul usually identifies God as the Father of Jesus Christ, as he does in 1:3.

Thanksgiving for the Colossians' Reception of the Gospel (1:3–8). Paul informs the Colossians that he regularly prays for the church and gives thanks for them in every prayer. He is thankful for their faithful acceptance of the gospel, which has spilled over into their love for others. If Paul is writing from Rome, news of their faithfulness has even reached the capitol of the Roman Empire. Their active love is a sign of a genuine faith based on a solid hope.

The faith that Paul commends in verse 5 is not faith in general but *faith in Christ Jesus*. It refers specifically to the belief that God raised Jesus from the dead and that he offers all believers, Jew and gentile, the same promise of life. It is a vibrant force that expresses itself in how believers live. Consequently, Paul commends them for faith proven by tangible demonstrations of love for God's people.

"Love" (v. 5) refers to the mutual love that Christians have for one another, a basic Christian virtue. Faith directed toward Jesus Christ is embodied in love for others. It is a supernatural, God-given love, because he refers to it a second time as "your love in the Spirit" in verse 8. Christians are not united solely by their mutual interest in personal salvation but are knit together in love.

A sure hope is the source of faith and love. What is interesting in this formulation is that hope is not grounded in faith, but the reverse—faith is grounded in hope. "Hope" (v. 5), therefore, does not here refer to a subjective attitude of expectation. Rather, it refers to the thing hoped for.

The second feature for which Paul gives thanks is the universal impact of the gospel as it sprouts up everywhere on earth, including Colossae. Paul notes how the gospel has swept across geographical and racial barriers. The truth of the gospel is also effective, "bearing fruit and growing" (v. 6).

The third cause for Paul's giving thanks is how Epaphras has laid a solid foundation for the Colossians in the true gospel (vv. 7–8). Paul did not believe that as an apostle he was the only one qualified to preach the gospel. He was commissioned by God to preach to the gentiles, but he could not be everywhere. He rapidly equipped his converts to spread the gospel in places where he could not go himself. Apparently Epaphras represented Paul in his home territory and may have founded all three churches in the Lycus valley: Colossae, Laodicea, and Hierapolis (4:13).

Application. The opening paragraph in Colossians speaks to our contemporary need to understand, uphold, and proclaim the Christian vision of the truth. Those who are able to detect counterfeit bills learn everything they can about a genuine bill; this same principle applies to distinguishing truth from falsehood. We must know what the truth looks and feels like before we can recognize what is false.

COLOSSIANS 1:9–14

Original Meaning

Intercession for the Colossians (1:9–14). Paul prays that God will fill the Colossians with the knowledge of God's will through spiritual wisdom and discernment of every sort. Yet Paul does not want his readers to gain knowledge purely for its own sake. Knowledge of God's will always has ethical implications, because it requires us to bring our daily conduct and thinking into line with it.

Paul affirms that God "has rescued" (v. 13) them from the harsh rule of the power of darkness. Like victorious kings who uproot whole populations and resettle them in other lands, God has wrested believers from the tyrannical rule of darkness and "brought [them] into the kingdom of the Son he loves" (literally "the Son of his love"). Changing lordships means changing kingdoms. Since these powers cannot obstruct our relationship with God, Christians need not fear them and must not pay them homage.

Paul caps off the mention of the beloved Son with the benefits he has bestowed on us—namely, "redemption, the forgiveness of sins" (v. 14). Forgiveness of sins is not simply a liberation from the past; it sets us free for the present and future. It opens the possibility of living a life worthy of the Lord. Paul says that the Colossians used to give their lives to sin, which brings only God's wrath, but now they give their lives to Christ, which brings joy and light.

Application. The thanksgiving sections in Paul's letters reveal how important prayer was for Paul. We are prone to pray only in emergencies—for those in need, in trouble, or in hard circumstances. Paul prayed continuously for his churches; he wrote them letters when trouble was brewing. We sometimes resort to prayer only when we feel under siege and then focus only on our problems. Yet Paul gave thanks in every situation, because he could always see God's resplendent grace at work throughout the world. He provides a model of intercessory prayer that we do not often emulate.

COLOSSIANS 1:15–23

Original Meaning

The Image of the Invisible God, the Firstborn Over All Creation (1:15–17). Paul could express his faith with majestic poetry. The poem of 1:15–20 begins by affirming that Christ is "the image of the invisible God." In Christ we see who God is—creator and redeemer; what God is like—a God of mercy and love; and what God does—one who sends his Son to rescue people from the dominion of darkness and brings about the reconciliation of all creation through his death on a cross.

Christ is also acclaimed as "the firstborn over all creation" (v. 15). We usually associate the term "firstborn" with birth, and it connotes to us the first child. In the Old Testament this title expresses status. God bestowed this title on Israel because of her divine election. The metaphor, therefore, distinguishes Christ from all created things as before them in time and as supreme.

The next statement explains why Christ is preeminent over all creation (vv. 16–17). Verse 16 contains a series of prepositional phrases: All things were created "in [*en*] him," "through [*dia*] him," and "for [or with respect to, *eis*] him." The imposing list of powers visible and invisible created by Christ accents his all-encompassing role in creation—all things in heaven and earth. We can see the tangible powers on earth, but we cannot see the invisible forces of heaven. They may be good or evil—that is, mediators of divine knowledge or malevolent foes in league with the power of darkness (1:13), or simply human patterns of authority. They, like all things, were created by Christ and for Christ.

The verb "hold together" (v. 17) can imply that they have their existence in him. Christ is more than the force that preserves the orderly arrangement of the cosmos; he is its rationale and its rhyme and reason. Even those who do not acknowledge Christ's reign and those who actively oppose him are entirely dependent on him.

The Head of the Church, the Firstborn from among the Dead (1:18–20). The poem's second strophe brings the cosmic Christ down to earth, where blood flows from a body strung up on a cross. The image of the invisible God entered the sphere of human experience in order to reconcile all things in heaven and on earth by means of his humiliating death. Christ establishes his lordship in house churches, prison cells, and families, as well as in the furthest reaches of the heavens.

The second strophe begins by proclaiming that Christ is "the head of the body, the church" (v. 18). It was not uncommon in Paul's time for philosophers to compare the cosmos to a body, but Paul applies it to the church, a historical entity. If Christ is the head of the church, it means that the destinies of creation and the church are bound together and that God's purposes for all creation gestate in the church's congregational life.

The focus is on Christ, however, not the church. Paul emphasizes the body's organic and dependent relation to Christ as head. The metaphor "head" designates him both as supreme over the church and as the source of the church's life. In the image of a living body, the head not only directs and governs the body but also gives it life and strength.

This second strophe includes declarations that explain why Christ is head of the church. The poem moves from creation to a new creation by identifying Christ as "the beginning and the firstborn from among the dead" (v. 18b). Christ's resurrection is the source of the new life for others. He is the first in a sequence that opens new possibilities for others who follow.

The goal of the resurrection is not merely to give individual believers the hope that they might also defeat death. God is not satisfied for Christ to be head only over a small band of devoted followers. The goal expressed in verse 18c is far grander: Christ is firstborn of the dead "so that in everything he might have the supremacy." Christ's death and resurrection were all part of the divine purpose to accomplish this end, and this mystery can now be seen by all. In the meantime, Christ exercises his worldwide rule in his church.

Verse 19 explains that Christ differs from other supposedly divine emanations in the world (such as angels). He is a full, not a partial, embodiment of God. God is pleased to dwell fully and permanently only in Christ. Christ supplants the temple, or any other house made with hands, and represents God in person (cf. 2:9).

God created all things through Christ; in the end, God will reconcile all things through Christ (1:20). Christ's majesty is rooted in God's love, shown in the earthly, historical reality of the cross. The grim reference to Christ's "blood" and "cross" brings us down from the lofty heights of preeminence and fullness to the squalid depths of human pain and suffering.

Paul uses "blood" to refer to the work of Christ's atoning sacrifice. The cross establishes a new relationship between God and humans, which overcomes the rupture created by sin—estrangement from God, estrangement from other humans, and estrangement from created things. That peace can only be found now in Christ's body.

Remaining Firm and Established in the Faith (1:21–23). Verses 21–23 conclude the opening thanksgiving section. The key words "faith," "hope," and "heard" (v. 23) are repeated from the opening verses (1:4–6). These verses also restate the theme in 1:12–14, that redemption comes in Christ. Thus this theme encases the poem in 1:15–20. These concluding words of the thanksgiving recall the believers' past ("once," v. 21), present ("now," v. 22), and future ("if," v. 23). They also declare the means of their redemption ("he has reconciled," v. 22), its effects ("holy," "without blemish," and "free from accusation," v. 22), and the extent of its impact ("to every creature under heaven," v. 23).

In concluding his thanksgiving, Paul expresses his deepest conviction that God's plan for the world, kept secret from the dawn of history until now, has at last been disclosed in Christ.

"[It] has been proclaimed to every creature under heaven" is an expression that echoes Old Testament language but which Paul does not intend literally. It means that the gospel is not obscure or some secret mystery. This verse also defines the scope of the church's mission field: the gospel is to go out to everyone everywhere.

Application. The poem found in this section shimmers in the exultant celebration of Christ's creative and redemptive work. It praises who he is, what he has done, and what he will do. It forms the basis of Paul's intercession and instruction in the letter, which is filled with exhortations to be thankful. Those who have lost an immediate sense of God's presence and glory tend to turn God into an object of study and the subject of theories instead of praise and adoration.

This poem professes that, in a way, Christ is the theological "theory of everything." He is the key who unlocks the meaning and purpose of the universe. But he is not a set of physics laws; he is a person who has shown his love for us by giving his life.

COLOSSIANS 1:24–2:5

Original Meaning

The Apostle's Suffering and Struggle (1:24). Complex exegetical questions immediately confront us in trying to interpret Paul's statement on his suffering in verse 24. A literal translation helps reveal the problems: "Now I rejoice in the sufferings on your behalf and I fill up what is lacking in the afflictions of Christ in my flesh in behalf of his body, which is the church." Several questions need answers. How can Paul connect his sufferings to the afflictions of Christ? How can these sufferings be understood as for the sake of the Colossians, a church he did not found and may not have visited? How does Paul dare to think that he can suffer in behalf of others as Christ did? More specific questions concern the meaning of various words and expressions: What does the verb "fill up" mean? What does the phrase "Christ's afflictions" mean? What is the "lack" in Christ's afflictions that his sufferings fill up?

Paul's thought reflects his sense of unity with Christ, something he stresses in the letter. Christians have been buried with Christ, raised together with him, and made alive together with him. As Christ's body, the church has a corporate personality. If Christians share in dying and rising with Christ, they also share in his sufferings and he with theirs. Christ, therefore, continues to suffer in his body, the church. This statement reflects Paul's deeply held conviction that he ministers as Christ's representative. Christ lives in him, and he serves in Christ's place as one who died with him and who lives for him. It is no great jump, then, for him to label the suffering he endures on Christ's behalf and as a member of Christ's body as "the afflictions of Christ."

But what is lacking in Christ's sufferings? Paul tells the Philippians that Epaphroditus risked his life "to make up what was lacking in your service to me" (Phil 2:30; literal translation). Paul is not complaining that they have failed to supply anything material. What is lacking is their personal presence with Paul, which Epaphroditus, as their representative, supplied. This same meaning applies in our text. What is lacking is Christ's bodily presence. Paul's physical suffering as a member of Christ's body represents Christ's continuing suffering for the world through his servants.

This explains how Paul connects his sufferings to the afflictions of Christ. He suffers as the representative of Christ, who is absent in body but present in spirit. He presents himself as an example of the indwelling mystery of Christ's cross working itself out in a human life, and he makes the astonishing claim that he is suffering for them as Christ would suffer were he present bodily.

How can these sufferings be understood as "for the sake of" the Colossians? Paul's suffering, unlike Christ's death on the cross, does not save them from their sins. Instead, it is connected to his gentile mission. Paul was in prison because he proclaimed the gospel, and that struggle on their behalf (2:1) has brought the benefits of the gospel to them.

Paul's Commission as Servant of the Church (1:25–2:1). Paul again identifies himself as a "servant" in verse 25. He was a steward commissioned to carry out an assignment for his master. Paul's mandate is "to present to you the word of God in its fullness" (v. 25; literally "unto you to fulfill the word of God"). The goal of Paul's preaching, teaching, and admonishing is to "present everyone fully mature in Christ" (v. 28).

Paul's purpose is to bring others to maturity in Christ so that they can fend off false teaching (2:2). It involves the heart as well as the head. Paul has in mind the full assurance that understanding brings. A greater grasp of God's saving purposes in and through Christ will enable his readers better to fend off false teaching (2:4). If they are firmly rooted in understanding the rich mystery of their faith, the Colossians cannot be deceived or deluded by arguments no matter how persuasive or plausible.

The Mystery Kept Hidden for Ages and Generations (2:2–5). Paul wants the Colossians to know "the mystery of God" (v. 2). In the New Testament, the "mystery" refers to a secret once hidden but that God has now revealed. In fact, God calls apostles to make it known to all who have ears to hear and eyes to see. Instead of guarding this secret from others, they proclaimed it to the entire world. God did not call Christians to control a monopoly on the truth but to share it with others.

The mystery revealed to Paul was that God intended to save

the gentiles *from the very beginning* (1:26–27). Christ "among the gentiles" (1:27) was not plan B after the gospel had been rejected by Jews. Rather, it was God's eternal purpose. Paul rejoices because God has chosen him to make this mystery known to gentiles everywhere. Even though it has cost him an enormous toll in suffering, Paul rejoices to be an active participant in God's astounding plan for creation.

Application. Few knew suffering better than Paul, who believed that all Christians must share in the suffering of their Lord. Christians can expect no better treatment than their Lord received. Suffering thus belongs to the Christian calling. Paul bore his suffering joyfully because he knew that he belonged to Christ. His suffering for the gospel confirmed that.

COLOSSIANS 2:6–15

Original Meaning

Loyalty to Christ the Lord (2:6–7). The opening statement of this section affirms that the Colossians have "received Christ Jesus as Lord" and distinguishes them from their opponents. In verse 7, Paul lists four characteristics of what it means "to live your lives in him" (v. 6), each expressed with a participle. The first participle ("rooted") appears in the perfect tense (expressing the continuing results of an action completed in the past); the next three ("built up," "strengthened," and "overflowing") are in the present tense.

The Flawed "Philosophy" (2:8). The warning in verse 8 provides the first direct clue in the letter that the Colossian church faces an outside danger. Paul describes the potential abductor as a "hollow and deceptive philosophy." Paul draws several contrasts between the gospel and this "philosophy."

The "philosophy . . . depends on human tradition." There is nothing inherently wrong with human tradition. Paul, however, discredits the philosophy as a tradition that derives from humans and contrasts it with divine revelation that the Colossians have received in Christ.

The term "elemental spiritual forces of this world" does not reflect some important feature of the opponents' teaching but derives from Paul's derisive appraisal of the "philosophy." It belongs to the domain of flesh, sin, and death, where demonic powers still wield their influence.

This term further likely refers to the quasi-demonic spirits to which humans have foolishly given their allegiance and awe. The contrast between "the elemental spirits of this world" and "Christ" in verse 8 probably signifies that Paul regards them as rivals to Christ. Paul contends that the philosophy he is warning against depends on these created, malignant powers, not on the beneficent creator.

Paul also characterizes this philosophy as devoid of truth. By contrast, the Colossians have received the word of God in its fullness (1:25), have the full riches of complete understanding in Christ (2:2; see 1:9), and have been given fullness in Christ (2:9–10).

The All-Sufficient Christ (2:9–12). To counter the attraction of the philosophy, Paul reiterates in verse 9 what he said about Christ in 1:19: he is "the fullness" of God. Paul distinguishes Christ from the hierarchy of intermediary and angelic beings who possess dashes of divine attributes. The *fullness* of the Godhead dwells in Christ.

Since Christ is the fullness of God and believers are in him, they have all the fullness humans can ever possess. The Colossians were in danger of being deceived. The opponents tried to disillusion them that the fullness they yearned for was unattainable either through Christ or through Christ alone. Paul counters that they have all the completeness they need in Christ and do not need to look anywhere else.

The "circumcision not performed by human hands" (v. 11) refers to something done by God as opposed to something done by human beings. It therefore stood over against the external rite for which Judaism was famous in the ancient world. The "circumcision of Christ" (author's literal translation; NIV "circumcision by Christ") is a vivid image for Christ's death. Paul interprets Christ's death as a vicarious circumcision for all believers.

What God Has Done (2:13–15). Paul portrays the Colossians' life before they were joined to Christ as a kind of nonexistence in the realm of the dead. Paul goes on to use a commercial image to describe this forgiveness: God nailed the incriminating list of unpaid debts to the cross. The IOU exacted a penalty for nonpayment—death. The note was not simply torn up and thrown away, however. The full penalty was exacted in Christ's death.

The final image in the clause is translated "triumphing over them" in the NIV (v. 15). The Greek verb *thriambeuō* can mean "to triumph over, to march in a triumphal procession, to make known, or to reveal." God has triumphed through Christ's death on the cross over every power and authority. The rulers put him to death without knowing that through his death he would conquer them decisively and escape their rule.

Application. Every generation of Christians faces new assaults on their faith. But these challenges are only a serious problem for those who are not thoroughly grounded and growing in their faith. Those who fill themselves only with themselves remain empty. Those who are filled by Christ do not feel any chronic dissatisfaction with life or sense of insecurity, and they long only to please God and to pour their lives out for others. They can even rejoice amid suffering and afflictions.

COLOSSIANS 2:16–23

Original Meaning

Let No One Condemn You (2:16–17). Paul here condemns those who use eating and drinking and the observance of feast days to pass judgment on others. Paul connects such rules to the mind of the flesh. Paul does not reject these practices outright as idolatry but insists they are only a shadow of what is to come. The shadow/reality contrast as used by Paul applies to promise and fulfillment. Since Paul would never describe pagan rituals as a shadow or outline of what was to come in Christ, the promise/fulfillment motif is more fitting as an evaluation of Judaism's teachings, based as they were on the Hebrew Scriptures (the Old Testament). Paul's conclusion is: Why play in the shadow world when you have experienced the real thing in Christ?

Let No Self-Important, Self-Appointed Umpires Arbitrarily Disqualify You (2:18–19). "Do not let anyone who delights in" renders the Greek participle *thelōn* ("wishing," "desiring"), and this translation assumes that Paul pictures the opponent as setting up "humility" as *his own goal.* The opponent then insists, "My way is superior to yours; it achieves goals you fall short of."

The participle *thelōn* can also modify the verb "disqualify": "Let no one willfully disqualify you." This reading has the advantage of preserving the parallelism with 2:16, where the matters the errorists use to condemn the Colossians are introduced by the preposition *en* ("with regard to"). The opponents declare the Colossians unfit because they fail to measure up on issues of humility, worship of angels, and visions. The errorists are puffed up and have the gall to gainsay the Christians' salvation.

The NIV has the errorists "delight[ing] in false humility." He may imply that it is a "false humility" particularly because it results in their becoming "puffed up." Another option is to interpret it as a reference to a specific form of humility—namely, fasting. Fasting may have been part of the preparations for the heavenly visions and revelations. Self-mortification, however, can become twisted into a perverse self-exaltation.

The phrase "worship of angels" could mean that Paul accuses the errorists of worshiping angels (objective genitive). Their so-called worship may only have involved propitiating them to ward off their evil effects or beseeching them for protection. Paul may only be disdainfully caricaturing the philosophy's ritual concerns and attention to New Moons as the worship of angels.

The next phrase in verse 18 is no less difficult to decipher: "Such a person also goes into great detail about what they have seen." Paul does not need to give the Colossians an objective description of the opponents' beliefs and practices and only wants to deflate their false boasts by subverting them with sarcasm. Their exaggerated visions are all smoke and mirrors, much ado about nothing. Their nervy conceit is all folly.

The root of the error is one's failure to hold fast to the head (v. 19). Paul may be underscoring the contrast between the Colossian Christians and their antagonists, who do not hold to Christ or observe his teaching. They hold to something other than Christ. Holding to anything other than Christ, the head (1:18; 2:10), will cause them to disintegrate and perish.

Why Allow a False Wisdom to Make the Rules? (2:20–23). Since Christians have been released from the rulers' and powers' slavery, why would they ever consider giving these powers new life by submitting to their irksome and irrelevant taboos? The opponents suffered from the law of unintended consequences. Their religious aim to serve God and to bridle the flesh only succeeded in serving the flesh and unleashing its power. From Paul's perspective it is all a sham, though it may impress gullible observers. The mystical experiences and devotional genuflections of the opponents accomplished nothing spiritual and were worth nothing.

Application. The Colossian opponents' attempts to squelch fleshly desires and establish their purity let loose a more deadly strain of sin—namely, pride. Many Christian groups want to draw the circle of acceptability ever tighter around themselves and reject others because of some failure to conform to their narrow vision of the truth. The problem is that we can worship the rules or our theological constructions more than we worship Christ. This process inevitably results in an ugly, smug arrogance and exacerbates the divisions between us rather than working to bring about reconciliation.

COLOSSIANS 3:1–17

Original Meaning

New Life with Christ (3:1–4). Being raised with Christ emphasizes the new status of believers, which requires a new way of life. It refers to the power source for living the new life. This transitional paragraph reaffirms the previous theological arguments and lays the foundation for the following ethical admonitions.

The new life gets under way with a new orientation as Christians set their hearts on (literally "seek") the things above. Since believers are in Christ, they already belong to the world above, where he is. Christians already have knowledge of that realm through their faith (2:12) and do not attain it by using other mediators. Since Christ is not one of the serving angels but reigns over all, all of our lives should be ruled by him. Every thought, aim, value, aspiration, and striving should come under his lordship.

Paul's second affirmation is that the believer's life is "hidden with Christ in God" (v. 3); it seals the previous warnings and also has ethical implications. A believer's life in the Christ who reigns over the whole cosmos has yet to become unmistakably evident to all observers; one's glorious appearance with Christ lies in the future (v. 4; cf. 1 John 3:2). A life hidden in the one who is seated at the right hand of God is completely secure. The new life of obedience does not depend on their own feeble moral resolve but comes from being united with Christ.

The Old Morality (3:5–9a). Paul attests that one is either dead in sin (2:13) or dead to sin (3:5). Believers, however, are still works in progress, which explains the need for the commands to "put to death . . . your earthly nature" (v. 5) and to "rid yourselves of all such things" (v. 8). A believer's members can be offered to sin as instruments of wickedness or to God as instruments of righteousness and holiness (cf. Rom 6:13).

Paul insists that Christians eradicate any persisting marks of the old pagan lifestyle—its values, customs, and practices. The vices are heavily weighted toward sexual sins. Paul considered sexual relationships outside of marriage to be sinful, and the term "sexual immorality" (v. 5) runs the gamut of forbidden sexual acts. The list is capped off by "greed, which is idolatry." Greed refers to the haughty and ruthless belief that everything, including other people, exists for one's own personal amusement and purposes.

Paul concludes this first list of vices by attesting that such behavior will incur God's holy wrath (v. 6). God demands that Christ's followers live worthily of him. If avowed Christians behave no differently from their surrounding culture, they betray their calling and defame the name of their God.

Paul next turns his sights on various manifestations of unrighteous anger, which destroy community. "Filthy language from your lips" (v. 8) does not simply refer to curse words. It has in mind the abusive language people use to hurt others. Lying is rooted in an attempt to gain advantage over others. It therefore is at odds with Christian love.

The New Humanity (3:9b–11). The image here of having stripped off old filthy rags and put on new clothes marks the transition from the list of vices to the list of virtues. The phrasing of verse 10 in Greek, "the new that is being renewed in knowledge" (literally), means that the new life does not come as the result of a successful, daily battle with temptation. Rather, the new life marks the starting point. Paul does not urge the Colossians to amend their lives for the better, to reform their ways, or to make minor modifications in the direction of their lives. One's whole nature must be first exchanged, not just revamped. Note here the allusion to Genesis 1:26–27 with its reference to the image of God. In Christ the image of God is being renewed in all believers.

Verse 11 proclaims that the new humanity re-created in Christ erases all the old sinful divisions that segregated humans from one another. The gospel breaks down man-made walls. It does not classify people by race, tribe, nationality, or class; nor does it calculate their worth from the various permutations of these divisions. Paul's conclusion is that being in Christ, not being from a certain race or class, is the only thing that matters.

The New Morality (3:12–14). Paul first addresses the Colossians as "God's chosen people, holy and dearly loved" (v. 12). The image of being "chosen" reminds them that their election comes at God's initiative, who has embraced them with the gift of unmerited favor. This image also takes over terms from Jewish self-identity. The language reminds the Colossians that they are full partners in the heritage of Israel, an Israel without racial and ethnic divisions. But being God's chosen people brings with it ethical responsibilities.

"Compassion" (v. 12) is all the more crucial when societies become consumed by the race to outdo others and become callous to the needs of the down-and-out. "Kindness" is gracious sensitivity toward others that is triggered by genuine care for their feelings and desires. "Humility" checks the incessant quest to attain honor and to rise in the pecking order. "Gentleness" betokens the willingness to make allowances for others. "Patience" refrains from exacting revenge or reprisals against enemies and is willing to endure wrongs.

The final virtue in the list is "love." The last phrase of verse 14 reads literally as "which is the bond of perfection" and may be interpreted to mean "the bond that is perfection." We cannot truly exhibit compassion, kindness, humility, gentleness, and patience without love.

Harmony and Thankfulness (3:15–17). The key word in each sentence of the last paragraph of this section has to do with Christ: "the peace of Christ" (v. 15), "the message of Christ" (v. 16), "the name of the Lord Jesus" (v. 17). In verse 16, Paul stresses that singing and gratitude should be the distinctive features that embrace all of a Christian's life. And the final admonition in this section in verse 17 prepares the reader for the next set of instructions in 3:18–4:1. Everything believers do should be done conscious of the Lord's calling, commands, promises, and sustenance.

Application. Sometimes it is those who walk most closely to God who are most acutely aware of how much they have fallen short of God's glory. They still see themselves as poor, wretched sinners. Others may see more of God's transforming presence in their lives than they do. Our assurance is that those who are in Christ are being transformed.

Paul asserts here that the old nature is not renewed or reformed; instead, it is put to death. This forceful image means that Christian renewal is not some new cosmetic that is painted over our sinful personalities. Paul does not tell us to put on new clothes over the old; the old must be stripped off and thrown away.

COLOSSIANS 3:18–4:1

Original Meaning

Wives and Husbands (3:18–19). The instruction that the wife submit to her husband fits the norm of what was regarded as becoming conduct for a wife in Paul's culture. Paul does not overtly dispute this cultural assumption. The change in women's status in our age and modern sensibilities lead many today to wish that he had. The command for wives to submit, however, was not inappropriate in his context. It reflects the legal state of affairs. The husband as the *paterfamilias* (the head of the household) was the only fully legal person in the family and had power over all property and almost absolute authority over every other member of the family.

The verb "submit" (*hypotassō*) does not convey some innate inferiority but is used for a modest, cooperative demeanor that puts others first. It was something expected of all Christians regardless of their rank or gender (cf. Eph 5:21). The command promotes a demeanor that was believed to help elicit kindness from the husband.

Some nuances may also help to mitigate the command's harshness to modern ears. In contrast to the commands to children and slaves, Paul does not tell wives to "obey" their husbands. The verb "submit," however, is in the middle voice and can imply a voluntary submission. It makes the wife's submission her willing choice, not some universal law that ordains masculine dominance.

Paul also qualifies this submission further with the phrase, "as is fitting in the Lord." Paul does not just say that it is culturally proper or correct but "fitting *in the Lord*." The Lord determines what is fitting or not. Some things may be culturally acceptable, but reflection on them "in the Lord" leads to the realization that they may be unfit for a Christian.

Husbands are presented with a much more demanding task. They are told to "love" their wives (v. 19). Paul is not writing to prop up the authority and rights of husbands. Instead, he reminds husbands of their obligations "in the Lord." In a Christian marriage, the husband knows himself to be dearly loved by God and is commanded to love his wife in the same way.

Children and Parents (3:20–21). Children were legally regarded as their fathers' property, and their status, theoretically, was little better than that of slaves. The command for children to obey their parents, therefore, fits a universal expectation. As a father, Paul expected obedience, but he believed that a father's discipline should be tempered by love, compassion, kindness, and patience.

Slaves and Masters (3:22–4:1). The command that slaves must obey their masters in everything is jarring to those who now consider the institution of slavery to be abhorrent. In the first century, however, it was an entrenched reality that the early Christians could neither change nor ignore. Paul does not sanctify slavery with these commands but subtly undermines its very premises while encouraging obedience as an expression of loyalty to the family group. The commands to masters and slaves attempt to minimize the most egregious evils of the system.

Application. *Marriage.* The instructions to wife and husband focus on how they are to live together responsibly, not on how they can get their needs fulfilled. Submission can only be done with a healthy sense of self. The love that Paul commands husbands to have always puts the welfare of the wife and her needs first.

Parental discipline. Youth associate their parents' kindness with their personhood; that is just a part of who they are. In a world that is becoming increasingly indifferent and uncivil, parents need to inculcate in their children the spirit of kindness and compassion by setting good examples, beginning with the way they discipline their children.

The workplace. Paul's counsel on slaves and masters has no application in our culture, which rightly considers slavery to be intolerable. The relationship between employees and employers in democratic societies is so completely different from that of master and slave in the first century that we must exercise extreme caution in making any correlations. We cannot make a one-to-one correspondence, where slaves equal employees and masters equal employers. We must look elsewhere in the New Testament for help on such things, but there are certain principles in these instructions that apply in any setting, including the workplace. The statement in 3:17, "And whatever you do, whether in word or deed, do it all in the name of the Lord Jesus," is the hermeneutical key for how this exhortation can be applied to our world.

COLOSSIANS 4:2–18

Original Meaning

Devoting Yourselves to Prayer (4:2–4). Devotion to prayer implies unrelenting persistence. "Being watchful" (v. 2) may be related to the unknown hour of the Lord's return and the world's end. But more likely Paul is warning them against spiritual lassitude so that they can fend off the temptations that can steal upon them. Vigilant prayer provides the spiritual fortitude to face down temptation.

Paul does not fear imprisonment, though the possibility of deliverance is important to him because it will open up unrestricted mission opportunities. Preaching the gospel does not always win friends and influence people. It can evoke enormous hostility and has led to his current imprisonment. Paul usually qualifies references to his chains with some comment on his commitment to the gospel. This subtly notifies his readers that proclaiming the mystery of Christ crucified is more likely to open the door to a prison cell for them instead of the door to financial and social success. Paul is bound more by his commission to preach the gospel than by his chains.

Being Wise in Reaching Outsiders (4:5–6). As a minority in a hostile environment, Christians were concerned about the impressions they made on their neighbors. They were not resentful that they were marginalized in their society. The Colossians share the responsibility of evangelizing unbelievers as much as the traveling missionaries. They must blend wisdom with a sense of reckless urgency that exhausts every opportunity to reach unbelievers.

Paul does not want the Colossians to be fearful, threatened, or isolated. Their words should always be gracious. "Seasoned with salt" was used to refer to witty, amusing, clever, humorous speech. Their saltiness will prevent them from being ignored as irrelevant bores. They need to have their answers ready for those who challenge or are curious about their faith. To do this they need to be well-grounded in their faith.

Introduction of the Bearers of the Letter: Tychicus and Onesimus (4:7–9). Paul's list of coworkers in his letters reveals several things about his ministry. Paul could not possibly do all that he did without the help and support of others, and he is not stingy in giving them credit and thanks. Paul inspired love and loyalty, and any picture of him as an embattled and embittered loner is mistaken. The early Christians relied much on a network of friends. Without supportive friends and partners throughout the world, Christians could never have succeeded in advancing the gospel across national barriers.

Tychicus, as the bearer of the letter, is the first coworker mentioned (v. 7). He appears in Acts 20:4, along with Trophimus, as a native of Asia. He receives the highest praise a Christian can receive: "a dear [literally beloved] brother, a faithful minister and fellow servant in the Lord." He comes to encourage the Colossians with news of Paul and his team.

Paul identifies Onesimus simply as a "faithful and dear brother" (v. 9; cf. Phlm 16) and as "one of you," without mentioning any ministerial role. He offers no explanation of how he had contact with him. We can only guess.

Greetings from Associates with Paul (4:10–14). Aristarchus, Paul's "fellow prisoner" (v. 10), could have rotated in voluntarily together perhaps with Epaphras (v. 12, called a "fellow prisoner" in the companion letter to Philemon [v. 23]), sharing Paul's quarters and hence his captivity, though they were not charged with any crime. Taking turns in sharing Paul's captivity would explain why Paul refers to them in this way.

Mark is identified as "the cousin of Barnabas" (v. 10). Barnabas was apparently a well-known figure in the early church, familiar to the Galatians (Gal 2:1, 9) and the Corinthians (1 Cor 9:6). This relationship presumably adds stature to Mark and makes it likely that he is the same John Mark we meet in Acts (Acts 12:12, 25; 15:37, 39). If so, then Onesimus is not the only one who has turned the corner (see Phlm 10–11). Mark is no longer a cause for dispute (Acts 15:36–41) but has become a source of comfort as a coworker.

Jesus, "who is called Justus" (v. 11), is mentioned along with Aristarchus and Mark as "the only Jews" (literally "of the circumcision") among his coworkers. Paul wants to remind them that some Jews, whom they know or know about, have been willing to throw aside their religious entitlements for the sake of the gospel in which there is no Jew nor Greek, circumcised or uncircumcised. They also serve with him in his mission among the gentiles.

Epaphras, like Onesimus, is identified as "one of you" (v. 12). If Epaphras founded the congregation, he did not forget it when he left but continued to pray for it, perhaps suffering from the same anxiety for the well-being of his church that plagued Paul. The verb "wrestling" (*agōnizomai*) may allude to Christ's struggle in prayer in Gethsemane, but Paul uses the word in 1:29 to refer simply to his missionary labor. Epaphras, like Paul, wants the Colossians to become less tenuous in their understanding of all that God has done in Christ so that they will not become easy targets for false teaching.

The greetings of Luke and Demas come last (v. 14), and Paul does not mention their specific mission tasks. Luke is identified only as "the doctor." Demas is mentioned only by name with no commendation, which may hint of his future desertion of Paul (2 Tim 4:10). He did not prove to be faithful in Christ.

Greetings to Other Christians in the Area (4:15–17). Paul also extends his greetings in this letter to the Christians in Laodicea and particularly to the church that meets in Nympha's house (v. 15). The reference to the church meeting "in her house" does not treat it as an unusual circumstance or anything worthy of special comment. She is probably either unmarried or widowed. Either status would give her more independence and flexibility in the ancient world as the head of her household than if she were married and under a husband's legal authority.

Paul concludes his greetings with a cryptic comment about Archippus's work: "Tell Archippus: 'See to it that you complete the ministry you have received in the Lord'" (v. 17). We can do no more than guess at the nature of Archippus's ministry, but it parallels what Paul says about himself in 1:25.

Final Greeting from Paul's Own Hand (4:18). Paul next signs his letter with a terse, final request for them to "remember my chains." The apostle customarily dictated his letters, but he takes the pen in hand for the final greeting. His brief benediction may hint at the difficulty of writing with manacles binding his wrists.

The call to remember his chains is not some forlorn plea for pity from a woebegone and disheartened apostle. It is better to regard this call as a note of encouragement for those who may also suffer persecution for their faith as well as another request for their prayer support. Following Paul's example requires more than a halfhearted commitment to the gospel. The letter itself becomes a means by which believers can see and experience God's grace even when things become difficult.

Application. *Guidelines for advancing the gospel.* A new technique to increase efficiency in automobile manufacturing is to have materials manufactured as needed. That tactic may work in industry, but it does not work in prayer. If we expect our prayer life to have any effect in our lives and in our world, it cannot be sporadic or haphazard. We cannot fall back on prayer only when we think we need it; we must "devote" ourselves to it, as 4:2 states.

Overcoming failures: Mark, Onesimus, and Demas. The stories of personal failures connected to these names present an opportunity for the pastor to explore the nature of failure with their congregations. Failure happens, but failure need not be final. God is the God of second chances.

1 THESSALONIANS

INTRODUCTION TO 1 THESSALONIANS

Near the middle of the first century AD, Paul wrote a pair of letters to a recently established congregation of Christians in the town of Thessalonica. The people to whom he addressed the two letters we now call 1 and 2 Thessalonians were for the most part new converts to the Christian faith, who had grown up in, and hence were thoroughly socialized in, a Greek cultural environment. One of Paul's major challenges was that of *resocialization*—helping these believers to learn, understand, and live by the very different social and ethical code of early Christianity. See Acts 17:1–14 for background to these letters.

BOOK OUTLINE

I. Prescript (1:1)
II. Remembrance and Encouragement with Respect to the Past (1:2–3:13)
   A. Opening Thanksgiving (1:2–10)
   B. Apostolic Attitudes toward the Thessalonians While Present (2:1–12)
   C. Second Thanksgiving (2:13–16)
   D. Apostolic Attitudes toward the Thessalonians While Absent (2:17–3:8)
   E. Third Thanksgiving (3:9–13)
III. Exhortation and Encouragement with Respect to the Future (4:1–5:22)
   A. General Introduction, Holiness, and Sexual Ethics (4:1–8)
   B. Mutual Love (4:9–12)
   C. Questions concerning the Parousia of Jesus (4:13–5:11)
   D. Congregational Conduct (5:12–22)
IV. Letter Closing (5:23–28)

1 THESSALONIANS 1:1

Original Meaning. With regard to the letter's structure, 1:1 forms a complete structural unit, the "prescript," and 1:2 begins a new section (the "thanksgiving"). Like any prescript, it identifies the senders and recipients and conveys an expression of goodwill. Of all the Pauline letter openings, this is the simplest and most like contemporary Hellenistic letter openings (typically "A to B, greetings"; cf. Acts 15:23, "The apostles and elders, your brothers, To the Gentile believers in Antioch, Syria and Cilicia: Greetings").

For reasons we can only guess at, 1 and 2 Thessalonians are the only letters in which Paul does not characterize himself or his colleagues in some way. The conjunction of the three names (which also occur in 2 Thess 1:1) and the frequent use of the first-person plural ("we") throughout the letter indicate that all three are cosenders of the letter.

In the Greek world, *ekklēsia* (in the New Testament routinely translated "church") could designate, among other things, a public assembly (Acts 19:32, 39) or a philosophical school—that is, a gathering or a movement. The local assembly of the Thessalonians is identified as "in God the Father and the Lord Jesus Christ." The close linkage of God and Jesus indicates their unity of purpose and action (cf. 2 Cor 5:18–21), without which and apart from which the Christian *ekklēsia* does not exist.

For Paul, God is the ultimate source of grace, which is the foundation and basis of all God's actions on behalf of his people. The phrase "grace and peace" calls to mind both the basis and the consequence of God's saving activity, which finds its focus in Jesus Christ.

Application. Team leadership, which can be instituted informally within the constraints of any number of different formal structures, offers important advantages. Accountability to other members of a leadership team works to reduce the chances of a leader falling into sin. Moreover, even in instances where there is significant moral failure of a leader, the presence of a team rather than a single individual in leadership reduces the odds that the failure will devastate the congregation.

1 THESSALONIANS 1:2–10

Original Meaning. The shift from "thanksgiving" to speaking directly to the recipients in 2:1 ("You know") clearly marks 1:2–10 as a distinct unit, which functions as the primary "thanksgiving" section of the letter. Thanksgiving, however, is not the only thing going on here. In the course of his prayer, Paul explains *why* he is thankful; thus on a second level the passage provides us with important details about the founding of the Thessalonian congregation. This thankful remembrance of the church's early history in turn, on yet a third level, serves to praise and confirm the Thessalonians and thus also to encourage and reinforce the behaviors Paul is praising. Clearly this is a complex and multifunctional prayer report.

In this opening thanksgiving, Paul characteristically touches on several themes that arise later in the letter. For example, in verse 3 "love" anticipates the discussion of *philadelphia* ("love for brother and sister") in 4:9–12, and "hope" anticipates the topic of eschatology in 4:13–5:11. In verse 5 "power" and "Holy Spirit" anticipate the advice about the Spirit and prophecy in 5:19–22. In verses 5–6 the reference to imitation of the founding missionaries prepares for 2:1–12 and 5:12–13. In verses 9–10, the comments on serving God while waiting for the Son anticipate the comments on holiness (4:3–8), vigilance (5:1–10), and mutual exhortation (5:11, 14–22).

This foreshadowing of later topics in the letter, however, should not obscure what Paul's primary focus is in this section: the Thessalonian believers themselves. In particular he focuses on their Spirit-empowered response to the gospel message that Paul and his colleagues shared with them. This focus comes out with clarity when we observe how quickly Paul's thanksgiving for the Thessalonians turns into a description of them.

Application. One way to apply this passage to our contemporary situation is to take the six observations about the Thessalonian congregation and turn them into a set of questions to ask about our churches (and, for that matter, ourselves).

- Are we a community rooted in God's grace, love, and election?
- Are we a community committed to Jesus Christ?
- Are we a community empowered by the Holy Spirit?
- Are we a community that bears witness to the gospel?
- Are we a community characterized by faith, hope, and love?
- Are we a community clearly differentiated from other religions?

1 THESSALONIANS 2:1–12

Original Meaning. In 2:1, the word *gar* ("for," omitted in NIV) opens this section; it marks the transition from the primary thanksgiving (1:2–10) to the body or central part of the letter (2:1–5:22). In this section, two points raised in chapter 1—the behavior of the apostles, which the Thessalonians imitated (1:5b–6), and the character of their visit to Thessalonica (1:9)—are developed in some detail. The repeated appeal to the Thessalonians' own knowledge of these two matters (2:1–2, 5, 9–11) serves both to minimize the distance between Paul and the Thessalonians and to reinforce the relationship between them—points characteristic of ancient "letters of friendship" (see discussion on 2:17–3:8 below).

There are several antithetical statements ("not *x* but *y*") in this section. These statements have led many to argue that Paul here is defending himself against charges or accusations of some sort. But antithetical statements are also frequently used (a) in nonpolemical situations, and (b) for describing moral examples. The heavy concentration of direct appeals in the last part of our passage (vv. 9–12), in which Paul reminds the Thessalonians of how he exhorted them to holy living, confirms that the primary function of this section is not defense or apologetics but exhortation. By reminding them of the behavior he and his companions modeled while in Thessalonica (behavior that stands in sharp contrast to that of religious charlatans or con artists), Paul implicitly encourages them to adopt and/or continue such behavior—in the face of hostility and persecution, if necessary (1:6; 2:14; 3:4), as did the missionaries (e.g., 2:1–2).

The repeated use of "for" (*gar*) in the passage (in Greek, at the beginning of verses 1, 3, 5, and 9) notwithstanding, there is no clear or obvious structure to 2:1–12, as the widely varying paragraphing in recent English translations indicates. With respect to content, in verses 1–4 the focus is on the missionaries' dependence on and responsibility to God; in both verses 5–8 and 9–12 the focus is on their behavior toward and care for the Thessalonians.

In contrast to charlatans and entertainers, who sought in some way either to fill their own pockets or to enhance their public renown, and despite having, as an apostle of Christ, certain "rights" that he could have insisted the Thessalonians recognize (cf. 1 Cor 9:3–18), Paul deliberately adopted a different strategy of ministry in Thessalonica. For the sake of the gospel, he avoided behavior that could call into question the integrity of the gospel. On the one hand, their speech was bold and forceful; on the other hand, their actions were characterized by gentleness and care and motivated by love.

To recapitulate, here in 1 Thessalonians 2:1–12 Paul focuses on the behavior and attitudes of the missionaries while they were in Thessalonica. Calling on both God and the Thessalonians as witnesses, he first emphasizes their reliance on and responsibility to God (vv. 1–4). He then describes the blameless and gentle, loving way they behaved toward and cared for the Thessalonians as they sought to encourage them to live lives worthy of God (vv. 5–12).

Application. *Goals and Priorities.* Most of us learn early on that life is a series of choices, some of which will irrevocably shape the course of the rest of our life. For some people making choices seems easy, while others are virtually paralyzed by the prospect of having to choose. The difference often (but not always, of course) is a matter of whether or not a person has a clear sense of goals and priorities.

Paul's example ought to prompt us to reflect on our own goals and priorities, especially the "big ones." What, for example, do I really want to do with my life? What *am* I doing with my life? What is it that I really value in life? Is serving Jesus and living faithfully in accordance with the gospel really the most important thing for me? Or am I really most committed to accumulating a big enough nest egg so that I can retire by a certain age, or some similar goal? Am I (perhaps without realizing it) trying to serve two masters at the same time? What do my activities say about my priorities? These are the kind of questions that Paul's example prompts us to ask.

Integrity. Integrity is not something that happens by accident. It involves the hard work of discerning what is right and of learning right from wrong, and then living out—consistently—what has been discerned. Paul's example reminds us of the fundamental importance of integrity on the part of all of us who have been entrusted by God with the gospel of Jesus Christ (cf. 2:4).

Love and commitment. Among the more subtle hazards faced by those engaged in ministry is a temptation (often unconscious) to meet personal needs by ministering to others, or to do things for people in order to win their approval or get them to like us. In giving of himself for the sake of others, Paul found happiness and satisfaction for himself. How different would our churches be if we focused more on meeting the needs of others and less on our own?

1 THESSALONIANS 2:13–16

Original Meaning. The presence in these verses of what appears to be a second "thanksgiving" section (see 1:2–10 for the first) has caused difficulty for attempts to understand the letter in purely epistolary terms (most letters have only one). But if one notices that this is actually the second of three places in the letter where Paul gives thanks, it becomes clear that "thanksgiving" is both a formal epistolary feature and a recurring theme throughout the first major part of the letter. In 1:2 Paul's thanks are ultimately rooted in God's choice of the Thessalonians (1:4); here in 2:13 he gives thanks for their acceptance of the message, and in 3:9 he will give thanks for their continuing steadfastness (3:8).

The passage serves a transitional role in the structure of the letter. In 2:12, Paul's focus shifted from the behavior of the missionaries (the primary subject of 2:1–12) to that of the Thessalonians. Now, still focusing on the Thessalonians, he picks up and develops further a point touched on in 1:6: the Thessalonians' acceptance of the gospel despite severe suffering (2:13–14). This reference to suffering in turn sets up what he will say in 2:17–20 (where his focus again shifts from the Thessalonians back to the missionaries). Verses 15–16 (whose harsh tone has led some to suggest that they are not part of the letter) have something of the character of a parenthetical editorial comment, prompted by the mention of "the Jews" (at the end of v. 14).

Throughout this section Paul's continuing goal of encouraging his readers is also evident, as he (1) reminds the Thessalonians of their praiseworthy past actions in order to encourage them to maintain that pattern of behavior in the present (v. 13), and (2) seeks to strengthen their sense of group identity and their resolve (vv. 14–16).

An immediate consequence of the Thessalonians' acceptance of the "word of God" (v. 13) was that they became the focus of hostility from their "own people" (v. 14, to be understood in a political or local rather than an ethnic sense). Acts 17:5–9 offers a clue as to why this happened: By their acceptance of "Lord Jesus," the Thessalonians implicitly rejected the claims to sovereignty of "Lord Caesar" and the civil religion of the imperial cult, and they thus were perceived as threats to the established social order and government.

Judgment is the subject of Paul's last statement in this section (v. 16). Whereas Jesus will rescue believers from that "wrath" (1:10), those who are opposed to God will be unable to escape it (cf. 5:3). It is perhaps best to interpret this last phrase along the lines of the idea expressed in John 3:18. That is, rejection of God's Messiah is in and of itself judgment, in that it means the rejection of the one through whom God has made salvation available to all.

Application. *Confronting the issue of Anti-Semitism.* Any allegedly Christian group that advocates anti-Semitism or other forms of racial discrimination forfeits any right to be called "Christian." Because the present passage can so easily be misunderstood and twisted to support anti-Semitic prejudices, it is important to stress that in this passage Paul is *not* anti-Semitic. There is a fundamental theological difference between Christianity and Judaism—the one acknowledges Jesus as Messiah, the other does not—and this *christologically based* opposition to Judaism as a religion is expressed throughout the New Testament. Scholars have labeled this "anti-Judaism." Regrettably, this theological difference has frequently given rise to racially based discrimination (or worse) against Jews—that is, anti-Semitism. It cannot be stressed too strongly that there is in the New Testament no basis whatsoever for anti-Semitism of any sort.

The dangers of using "insider" and/or hyperbolic language. The ease with which Paul has been misunderstood offers us an opportunity to reflect on the inherent dangers of using "insider" and/or hyperbolic language in inappropriate circumstances. What Paul wrote as an insider and shared with his close friends made sense and was understandable to them in that context. But as soon as readers lost sight of that original context, Paul's deliberately hyperbolic overstatements sounded different, and over the centuries they have been seriously misinterpreted. The fate suffered by Paul's words may serve as a warning to Christians today to pay careful attention both to what they say and how they say it, especially if what they say may be repeated or passed on in other contexts.

Response to persecutors. Paul will remind the Thessalonians that doing good, not retaliation, is the proper reaction to persecution (cf. Rom 12:20–21). This is an important point to reaffirm in an era when some Christians are becoming increasingly violent in their reaction to social pressures or in the way in which they approach social issues. Attempts to impose, create, or maintain by force a "Christian" society generally have led to unmitigated disaster. In Romans 5:8–10, Paul points out how, even when we were all his enemies, God's response was to demonstrate his love for us. Are believers in that God to act any differently toward their enemies?

1 THESSALONIANS 2:17–3:8

Original Meaning. This section falls into three clear subsections: Paul's report of his unsuccessful attempts to revisit Thessalonica (2:17–20), his sending of Timothy in his place to encourage the believers in the midst of persecution (3:1–5), and his reaction to the good news when Timothy returns (3:6–8, which spills over into 3:9, the third thanksgiving in the letter).

Apostolic Concern: Attempts to Revisit Thessalonica (2:17–20). The intensity of his feelings toward the Thessalonians is evident from his description of the repeated attempts he made to return to Thessalonica (vv. 17b–18a). But these attempts failed, he reports, not because of any lack of desire or effort on Paul's part but because "Satan blocked our way" (v. 18b). How Paul was blocked is not stated. In view of Acts 17:9, it is possible that there were legal barriers to his return.

In verses 19–20 Paul explains why (note the "for" with which v. 19 begins) he was longing so strongly to see them again: they represented both the fruit and the evidence of his God-given apostolic ministry. In v. 19 Paul takes for granted a belief he explicitly mentions in 1 Corinthians 3:8, 13–15; 4:5 (cf. Rom 14:12): at some point in the future, believers will be evaluated with respect to their stewardship of the ministry entrusted to them by God. The "crown" mentioned in our verse 19 is likely the laurel wreath, a symbol of victory.

Apostolic Action: Timothy Is Sent to Thessalonica (3:1–5). Timothy's task was to "strengthen" (or perhaps "firmly establish") and "encourage" the Thessalonian converts (v. 2). The urgency of Timothy's mission was generated by the "trials" that the Thessalonians were currently experiencing (v. 3). Whatever the precise nature of these events, they had the potential to "unsettle" the new believers to the point of causing them to abandon their recently adopted faith.

Apostolic Relief and Joy: Timothy Returns with Good News (3:6–8). Almost audible in 3:6 is the sense of relief that Paul felt when Timothy returned with the welcome news that the Thessalonians had indeed successfully resisted Satan's temptations. Moreover, Timothy also reported the Thessalonians had positive memories of Paul and his fellow missionaries and would welcome a return visit. Evidently they understood why Paul left so suddenly under such suspicious circumstances and did not hold it against him.

In verse 8b, the NIV ("since you are standing firm") hides what is really a conditional statement, "if you continue to stand firm" (NRSV). It functions both as an affirmation—it clearly acknowledges that they are currently "standing firm"—and as an implicit exhortation ("*if* you continue"). Finally, it is worth noting how 3:8 reveals the extent to which Paul bases his own sense of well-being on the continuing faithfulness of his converts.

Application. *Persecution.* I am a member of the "boomer" generation, who came of age during the turbulent 60s. I have witnessed firsthand the transformation of the United States from a society in which nearly all citizens, Christian or otherwise, embraced values and ethical norms based on the Judeo-Christian moral tradition, into a society in which traditional Christian ethical teachings and values are increasingly not only ignored, but explicitly rejected by a steadily growing (as well as influential and powerful) percentage of society. As American society continues this transition from a Christian to a post-Christian culture, those who seek to live in accordance with the gospel of Jesus Christ can expect to encounter the kind of trials or persecution experienced by Paul and the Thessalonians. What will we value more at that time: social acceptance and affirmation, or faithfulness to the gospel, whatever that may cost?

1 THESSALONIANS 3:9–13

Original Meaning. There is clearly a substantial connection between these verses and those that precede them. The single sentence in Greek comprising verses 9–10 is closely joined with 3:8 by the conjunction *gar*, and verses 11–13 form a benediction that draws to a close the entire first part of the letter (1:2–3:13).

Paul moves from thanksgiving in verse 9 to a twofold petition (v. 10): that he might be able (1) to visit the Thessalonians in person, and (2) to "supply what is lacking in [their] faith." In view of Timothy's enthusiastic report (cf. 3:6), "what is lacking" likely designates "things still needed" rather than some kind of spiritual or ethical defect. These needed things would include additional instruction on specific points of doctrine and conduct—things they lacked through no fault of their own, but because Paul had been forced to terminate his initial visit prematurely.

The content of verse 11 repeats the substance of the first part of verse 10. Verse 12 both affirms the accomplishments of the Thessalonians (as reported by Timothy, cf. 3:6) and implicitly encourages them to "increase and overflow" in "love," a word that encompasses for Paul the full extent of proper Christian behavior.

The punctuation of verse 13 as a separate sentence obscures the fact that this verse, rather than being an additional petition, indicates the goal or purpose of the petition in verse 12. That is, Paul prays that the Lord will cause the love of the Thessalonians to increase so that when they find themselves "in the presence of our God," they may be "blameless in holiness" (literal translation)—that is, fully acceptable to God (v. 13).

Application. *Paul prays with thanksgiving (3:9).* On one level, this is a matter of basic gratitude, of acknowledging God's graciousness toward us. But in giving thanks to God, we are also sharing (indirectly, at least) with others the reality of God's love and concern for us, and thus thanksgiving to God can become a form of testimony about God.

Paul prays that the Thessalonians might be strengthened through loving service to others (3:12–13a). This love is not merely a matter of emotion or feeling; in 1:3 Paul already gave thanks for the Thessalonians' "labor prompted by love." In short, how might the members of this relatively new church with deep needs of its own gain strength in the face of difficulties and challenges? Through serving others in love, Paul implies—which is advice that flies in the face of the narcissism and self-centeredness of much of contemporary culture.

Paul prays for the Thessalonians in light of the future (3:13b). In our contemporary culture, which is overwhelmingly oriented to immediate gratification and results, to pray that others might live in light of eternity rather than the present is no small thing—especially since praying in this way on behalf of others inevitably reminds us of our need to do the same.

Paul prays out of his own deep and sincere love for others (3:12b). If we do not pray for others out of a genuine love for them, why not? Is it because we secretly despise them, hold something against them, are resentful or bitter, or view them as some kind of a threat? Or are we simply too self-centered to care about them? Whatever the reason, it calls us to personal repentance. Serious prayer for others forces us to get serious with ourselves.

1 THESSALONIANS 4:1–8

Original Meaning

A General Introduction (4:1–2). Here Paul does three things. First, he reminds the Thessalonians of the instructions they had received from him during his time in Thessalonica. Second, he affirms and commends them for following those instructions. Finally, he exhorts them "to do this more and more."

Holiness (4:3–8). Paul next focuses on a single aspect of what his instructions entailed—namely, sexual morality. This topic would have been of particular significance for anyone recently converted from pagan culture, in view of the wide range of sexual mores and practices that existed in Greco-Roman society.

For Paul, sexual activity is not just an inconsequential private activity involving one or more consenting adults; on the contrary, it has an impact on both one's relationship with God and with other people. Therefore, it ought to be exercised in a way that is respectful of both. In short, sexual behavior ought to be altruistic (a matter of giving to) rather than self-serving (a matter of taking from).

In verses 6b–8, the seriousness with which Paul approaches this matter of sexual behavior is evident. Verse 6b ends the long sentence started in verse 3 by indicating *why* believers should not wrong or exploit one another: The Lord (i.e., Jesus) "will punish all those who commit such sins"—that is, sooner or later such sinners will be brought to judgment.

God does not merely define by his character the standard according to which his followers are to live, but he provides as well the power by which one can live. For Paul the presence of the Spirit was not simply God's gift as an option against sin, nor would he have understood the Spirit as present but ineffectively so. On the contrary, the dynamic that makes Paul's argument against sexual impurity possible is the experienced reality of the Spirit.

Application. While the following comments barely scratch the surface of the matter, they will indicate what a contemporary application of Paul's teaching might involve.

On a personal level. For those who are married, it means first of all faithfulness to one's spouse. It also means treating each other with respect. For those who are not married, it means obedience to the spirit, not just the letter, of the biblical teaching about the proper context for sex. There are those who interpret the injunction against intercourse outside of marriage as implying permission for just about anything else. This results in the odd circumstance of people who in a technical sense are virgins, yet who are in some respects more sexually experienced than some married couples.

On a congregational level. Secular culture is, for various pragmatic reasons, seriously reconsidering the value of the kind of sexual ethic traditionally proclaimed by the church. It is both ironic and tragic that at such a moment many denominations or segments of the church have lost their ability and authority to speak clearly on sexual matters. Paul's instructions to the Thessalonians offer a biblical antidote to our current confusion.

1 THESSALONIANS 4:9–12

Original Meaning. After signaling the beginning of this section with the phrase "now about" and announcing the topic (*philadelphia*, "love for one another"), Paul employs a figure of speech (*paraleipsis*) in which a speaker pretends to skip over a subject ("we do not need to write to you") that he does in fact discuss (v. 9). It offers Paul a diplomatic way simultaneously both to affirm the Thessalonians for what they are doing well (vv. 9–10a) and to encourage them to develop in areas that need further attention (vv. 10b–12).

Even as Paul affirms the Thessalonians for doing well with respect to *philadelphia* (v. 10a), he urges them "to do so more and more" (v. 10b). Verses 11–12 (which with v. 10b comprise a single sentence) spell out what Paul has in mind. Specifically, he wants them "to make it your ambition to lead a quiet life," "mind your own business," and "to work with your hands."

From its inception, the Christian community, willingly or unwillingly, had been visible in the public arena, with sometimes painful consequences for the new believers. Any member of the congregation who remained active in the public arena ran the risk of attracting continued negative public attention—that is, persecution—to the congregation as a whole. Paul is basically telling the Thessalonians to keep a low profile, to give attention to their own affairs, and to stay busy, and with the reasons that follow in verse 12: "So that your daily life may win the respect of outsiders and so that you will not be dependent on anybody."

Application. *Occupational choice.* Ours is a culture that largely measures an individual's worth not by the quality of one's character but by the quantity of one's wealth and possessions. Our culture defines success increasingly in material terms and places great emphasis on affluence as evidence of success. Thus lifestyle choices about the size and location of one's house, the vehicle one drives, the clothes one wears, the organizations one joins, or the places one visits all become ways of demonstrating one's affluence—concrete evidence of one's success (or lack thereof). Wealth is to be displayed ("If you've got it, flaunt it"), and excess and extravagance are widely celebrated. In view of this contemporary emphasis on material affluence, it is no surprise that people feel pressure to choose a job primarily for what it pays rather than for its social usefulness or value.

Yet if the church is to affirm and model choosing jobs in terms of service rather than salary, it will also have to affirm and model lifestyle choices that encourage people to live on lower levels of income. But here too the trends are disturbing. It is difficult not to draw a connection between the culture's emphasis on affluence and the stats that Christians who as their income rises could afford to give more in fact give less (as a percentage of income). It appears that many Christians, like their unbelieving neighbors, are making lifestyle choices based on affluence rather than *philadelphia*.

1 THESSALONIANS 4:13–18

Original Meaning

The Topic (4:13). In verse 13, Paul introduces the topic of Christian brothers or sisters who have died before the parousia of Jesus. Paul does not say that the Thessalonians should not grieve over them but that they should not grieve in the same way or to the same extent as those without hope. The hope that is characteristic of a believer must, Paul believes, affect the way one deals with death.

A Theological Affirmation (4:14). The resurrection of Jesus provides the foundation on which Paul bases his encouragement and the rest of this section. For Paul, so close is the connection between Jesus and those who believe in him that belief in his resurrection carries with it, as a necessary corollary, belief in the resurrection of his followers. Thus, Paul took it for granted that Christians should face death not with despair but with hope—a hope in what God will do, grounded in what he has already done.

Additional Information (4:15–17). In verses 15–17 Paul spells out the implications of all this for those who have already died. Those alive at the parousia are said to be "caught up" together with the risen dead "to meet the Lord" (v. 17). The word for "meeting," *apantēsis*, is used in the LXX for God's meetings with Abraham, with David, and with the Israelites at Sinai. In the New Testament *apantēsis* describes exactly this same kind of movement of a welcoming party going out to meet someone and escorting him back to the destination. The implication of Paul's use of this word here is that the resurrected dead and raptured living will together meet the descending Lord "in the air" (v. 17) and accompany him in glory and honor the rest of his way to earth.

Application (4:18). Having stated the topic ("those who sleep in death") in verse 13, Paul then shared the fundamental theological affirmation that God will bring with Jesus those who have died (v. 14). He then shared some additional information (vv. 15–17) and indicates how the Thessalonians should use this information: to encourage one another (v. 18).

Application. To believers who wonder about what happens or "where we go" when we die, Paul says: "We will be with the Lord forever" (4:17). Compared to the detailed answers available from other sources (e.g., the Muslim portrayal of paradise or those propounded by the New Age movement), this seems almost too basic, hardly sufficient to satisfy our intense curiosity. If Paul's answer about the future seems somewhat basic in comparison to other, contemporary answers, it nonetheless has something that the latter do not: a solid historical foundation. What God has already done historically in the resurrection of Jesus—rather than human speculation, unfounded optimism, or sheer wishful thinking—provides a solid foundation on which our genuine hope for the future rests.

More generally, the passage challenges us to confront our own mortality. It invites us to ask about the extent to which our thinking about and behavior regarding death is motivated by either fear or denial of it. It offers an opportunity to decide if we really believe, with Paul, that for believers "to die is gain" (Phil 1:21, 23). None of these questions are easy to deal with, because they force us to confront death. The good news is that we do not need to confront death only on the basis of our own resources, but we can lean on the God who has already conquered death in the resurrection of his Son, our Savior and Lord.

1 THESSALONIANS 5:1–11

Original Meaning

"Times and Dates" (5:1–2). The starting point in this passage is the issue of when the Lord will return. As to when the day will occur, Paul writes that the Thessalonians already know "very well" the only thing one needs to know about "when" it will occur: it "will come like a thief in the night."

"Peace and Safety" (5:3)?. At a time when all *appears* well, "destruction" will arrive with the suddenness of labor pains (a common biblical image for pain and agony, though here the emphasis is more on the suddenness with which they begin). Anyone who is not "with the Lord" will certainly *not* escape.

Alertness and Self-Control (5:4–8). Paul spells out two implications of the Thessalonians' status as children. Unlike the "others," who sleep in ignorance (and will thus be caught off guard), the Thessalonians are to be "awake and sober" (v. 6). The first word emphasizes the need for vigilance; the second conveys the idea of balance or discipline.

Salvation, Not Wrath (5:9–11). Paul has already stated a basis for his exhortations about vigilance and discipline; here in verse 9 he gives what amounts to an additional reason, one that states its theological basis. The Thessalonians' status as "children of the light" (v. 5) is grounded in God's activity on their behalf. That is, the Thessalonians can stay alert and be self-controlled in genuine hope because God himself has destined them "to receive salvation" (v. 9).

In verses 10–11 it becomes clear that Paul is linking 5:1–11 with 4:13–18 as well as 4:9–12. Given that Paul viewed Jesus's death and resurrection as two sides of a single coin, his mention of the former here cannot but bring to mind his mention of the latter. Paul's description in verse 10b of the purpose of Christ's death is phrased in words that obviously echo 4:15–17. In 5:11 Paul recalls what he said in 4:9–10 about *philadelphia*. Concerns about the fate of those who die before the parousia and questions about its timing do not, for Paul, override the need to practice *philadelphia*. On the contrary, they provide concrete occasions for its exercise, as believers comfort and encourage one another amid difficult circumstances, confident in the hope of a salvation grounded in the death and resurrection of the Lord Jesus.

Application. The proper preparation for the coming day of the Lord is service rather than speculation. Human beings are naturally curious, especially about the future. Add God to the mix, and it is easy to understand why speculation about the return of Jesus is so attractive and fascinating for so many people. In contrast to idle speculation, Paul exhorts believers instead to encourage and build one another up.

1 THESSALONIANS 5:12–22

Original Meaning

Congregational Responsibilities toward Leaders (5:12–13). Verses 12–13a comprise a single sentence in which Paul asks the congregation to "acknowledge" a specific group within the church. In short, Paul is calling for proper recognition and appreciation of "those who work hard among you, who care for you in the Lord and who admonish you."

Congregational Responsibilities toward Individuals (5:14–15). Paul here instructs the congregation first to "warn those who are idle." The verb clearly includes a note of disapproval. Paul's word here (*ataktos*) should probably be given its more fundamental sense of "undisciplined, irresponsible, disorderly."

They are also to "encourage [*paramytheomai*; see 2:12] the disheartened." The range of meaning of the uncommon word translated "disheartened" (*oligopsychous*) includes being worried, discouraged, fearful, inadequate, lacking in confidence, despondent, sad, and weak. "Help the weak" is similarly imprecise. The verb can be rendered "support, supply, help," or even "defend," while the "weakness" can involve moral temptation, spiritual shortcomings, physical weakness, or economic need.

The command to "be patient with everyone" should be

compared with Galatians 5:22 (patience as a fruit of the Spirit), 1 Corinthians 13:4 (a characteristic of love), as well as Exodus 34:6 (a quality of God). The relevance of this injunction to a community under pressure or stress (e.g., persecution and concern about deceased believers) is evident.

In verse 15 Paul appears to be quoting a saying that formed a part of his basic instructions to new converts. Verse 15a is a categorical prohibition against repaying evil for evil; verse 15b is an equally absolute command to "always" (the word order is emphatic) actively pursue or strive for "what is good."

Congregational Responsibilities toward God (5:16–18). In urging the Thessalonians to "rejoice always," "pray continually" and to "give thanks in all circumstances" (vv. 16–18a), Paul is giving instructions that he himself modeled. Thanks to God was to be given even if the circumstances involved the death of a believer because, even though death was an awful reality, it was not the last word or act. The last word or act belongs to God, and that last word is resurrection and eternal life. Thus for Paul, both rejoicing and giving thanks become forms of worship or praise of the God who sovereignly superintends all of life for the ultimate good of his people in Christ (Rom 8:28–30).

Congregational Responsibilities toward the Spirit (5:19–22). Paul next focuses on charismatic manifestations of the Spirit, specifically prophecy. Do not, he says, quench the Spirit by treating prophetic utterances with contempt. The proper solution to the problem of potential abuse is not to throw out the baby with the bathwater; it is instead to "test them" (v. 21a). Paul strikes a careful balance here. Prophecies are not to be accepted blindly just because someone claims to have the Spirit. The proper course is to "test" them, in the sense of examining or investigating something with regard to its trustworthiness or genuineness.

Once a prophecy has been tested, the next step is clear: hold on firmly to those that are good, and have nothing to do with those that are not (vv. 21b–22). Prophecies that pass the test are from the Holy Spirit and therefore ought not to be rejected or treated with contempt. On the other hand, any prophecy that fails the testing process is not from the Spirit and should therefore be rejected and avoided (the verb here, *apechō*, is the same as in 4:3, "avoid sexual immorality").

Application. *Congregational responsibilities toward leaders (5:12–13a).* Paul's instructions in 5:12–13a call on congregations today to do two things. First, they should recognize or acknowledge those who are actually doing the work of ministry. Second, the congregation should respect and hold its leaders in highest regard. This may be the greater failure of congregations today. We usually know who our leaders are, but far too often we do not respect or follow them.

Living in peace (5:13b). Paul's command to live in peace with one another is a hard saying for many people and congregations. The peace that the apostle has in mind is not merely the absence of conflict (hard enough to achieve for many of us!), but the presence of positive, healthy relationships.

Congregational responsibilities toward individuals (5:14–15). In nurturing those who are weak, in caring for those in distress, by encouraging those who are fearful, and, if necessary, disciplining those who require it, we can become ministers of the grace of the gospel, servants of God through whom he reaches out to those looking for him or in need of his presence.

Congregational responsibilities toward God (5:16–18). Just as reciting a formal written creed (such as the Nicene Creed or Apostles' Creed) is an intellectual statement of faith, so the actions of rejoicing, giving thanks, and praying are an experiential statement of faith. They are ways of expressing by our behavior what we believe with our heart, soul, and mind.

Congregational responsibilities toward the Spirit (5:19–22). There is a double responsibility in these verses: not to quench anything that is genuinely of the Spirit, and not to attribute anything false to the Spirit.

1 THESSALONIANS 5:23–28

Original Meaning

A Closing Prayer (5:23–24). The prayer in verse 23 essentially echoes the thought (and even some of the words) of the prayer in 3:13. Verse 24 takes the form of a solemn affirmation, in which Paul grounds his prayer and with which he probably hoped to reassure any who might still be concerned about their fate at the parousia of the Lord Jesus.

Closing Requests and Benediction (5:25–28). Even as Paul on more than one occasion in the letter prayed for the Thessalonians, so he in turn requests their prayers for him and his companions. Despite the difference in spiritual maturity between Paul, Silas, and Timothy, on the one hand, and the Thessalonians on the other, Paul implicitly acknowledges, by his request for prayer, their fundamental equality before God.

The probable explanation of the abrupt switch in verse 27 from the plural to the singular pronoun ("I") is that Paul took the pen from the scribe (Silas?) and wrote the last two sentences himself.

Application. *The importance of remembering what God has done.* Remembering what God has done in the past—not as dead history but as the living and ongoing narrative of a faithful and powerful God in his relationship with his people—provides the basis for life in the present and hope for the future. Our future as believers rests entirely on God as revealed through Jesus the Messiah.

2 THESSALONIANS

INTRODUCTION TO 2 THESSALONIANS

We know next to nothing about the specific circumstances that led to the writing of 2 Thessalonians. That it was sent by the same three people as 1 Thessalonians and reflects so closely the language and structure of this letter strongly suggests that it was written not long after the first letter, while Paul, Silas, and Timothy were still in Corinth.

BOOK OUTLINE

I. Prescript (1:1–2)
II. Thanksgiving and Encouragement in the Face of Persecution (1:3–12)
III. The Parousia of Jesus and the Man of Lawlessness (2:1–12)
IV. Transition (2:13–3:5)
V. The Problem of the Disorderly (3:6–15)
VI. Letter Closing (3:16–18)

2 THESSALONIANS 1:1–12

Original Meaning

The Prescript (1:1–2). The designation of God as "our" Father reflects Paul's understanding that believers come to be part of God's spiritual family when they place their faith in Jesus Christ.

The Thanksgiving (1:3–4). The Thessalonians' growth in faith and love was taking place under the most adverse conditions. The church's circumstances do not appear to have changed much since the time of Paul's writing 1 Thessalonians. But adverse external circumstances have not hindered the fellowship's growth in the critical areas of faith and love; if anything, they may have promoted it.

Consequently, Paul reports two more reasons why he gives thanks and "boasts" to other congregations about the Thessalonians. These are the "perseverance" and "faith" (primarily in the sense of "trust," but perhaps also a bit of the sense of "faithfulness") that they have demonstrated. In short, the Thessalonian brothers and sisters have become for Paul an exemplary model of enduring Christian commitment under difficult conditions.

Instruction and Encouragement (1:5–10). Paul interprets the fact that the Thessalonians are not only persevering and trusting amid persecution but are actually growing and increasing as a sign of God's blessing, not judgment. In other words, the growth, increase, perseverance, and faith demonstrated by the Thessalonians together give evidence that they are indeed part of God's people. They are, by God's power, in fact living such lives, and Paul helps them understand that the continuing persecution and afflictions they are experiencing are not evidence to the contrary, but in fact confirmatory evidence.

In verse 6 Paul picks up and develops the idea of God's righteous judgment. There are, he says, two sides to this judgment, one negative and one positive. The negative side is discussed further in verses 8–9. The troublers of God's people are part of a larger group identified as "those who do not know God"—that is, who "do not obey the gospel of our Lord Jesus" (v. 8).

The punishment that this group will experience is identified in verse 9. The words "and shut out" are not in the Greek, which reads "everlasting destruction from the presence of the Lord and from the glory of his power." This suggests that Paul is not talking about two things (destruction and separation) but only one thing. The second part of the sentence defines what he means by the first part: "everlasting destruction"—that is, separation from the Lord's presence and glory.

The positive side of God's judgment is explicated in verse 10. Believers will experience both the presence and the glory of the Lord himself (the very things the other group will not experience). This is because the Lord will "be glorified in his holy people." They will also "marvel," either in the sense of "admire" or (in view of the parallelism with the preceding phrase) perhaps "worship."

In the last part of verse 10, Paul applies his point directly to the Thessalonians. The group that will experience the Lord's presence, he assures them, "includes you." In the context of their present experience of affliction, the statement is both reassuring and comforting. At the same time, it is a veiled exhortation to keep on persevering, lest they find themselves in the other category.

All that Paul has been talking about will happen "when the Lord Jesus is revealed from heaven" (v. 7b). The phrase "is revealed" actually renders a noun, *apokalypsis* ("revelation"). Paul likely uses this word (rather than *parousia*) because of its nuance of present hiddenness. Even though Jesus currently is indeed Lord, not all of creation yet recognizes or acknowledges that fact—indeed, some actively persecute the Lord's people. But the day is surely coming when the lordship of Jesus will be revealed for all to see clearly, and with consequences that Paul outlines in verses 6–10 (i.e., either judgment or salvation).

A Prayer Report (1:11–12). His first petition (which resumes the idea of v. 5) is that "God may make you worthy of his calling." The verb here (*axioō*) is a simple form of the verb in verse 5 (*kataxioō*). There is considerable debate whether these two verbs mean "make worthy" or "consider worthy." The first option better fits the context, but the second option better fits with usage elsewhere.

The other petition is that God might "fulfill" or "bring to fruition"—the verb has the idea of finishing something already begun—"your every desire for goodness and your every deed prompted by faith." These two phrases are likely an instance of hendiadys, in which the second phrase explains the first.

All of this is due solely to "the grace of our God and the Lord Jesus Christ" (v. 12). The fact that grace is most often associated with the initial experience of salvation in the past should not cause us to overlook the fact that the present and the future of salvation are no less a matter of grace.

Application. A hard-to-miss characteristic of a modern consumer culture is choice. To walk into a supermarket or department store is to find oneself immediately surrounded by a mind-dazzling array of choices. But even as the range of choices has multiplied, the significance of those choices has decreased. But not all choices are trivial, and not all consequences of our choices can be avoided. Examples include choices about education, which person to marry, what career to pursue, whether to use drugs, whether to terminate a pregnancy, or whether to be faithful to a commitment. They are choices, in other words, that "make all the difference" in the fabric and shape of our lives, to borrow a phrase from one of Robert Frost's most famous poems, "The Road Not Taken."

Paul's description in 1:5–10 of God's future judgment focuses a spotlight on a particularly consequential and unavoidable choice: the decision whether to accept or reject "the gospel of our Lord Jesus" (1:8). When the time of judgment comes, those who believed the message and placed their trust in God will "be with the Lord forever" (1 Thess 4:17) in his presence. Those, however, who have rejected the gospel will find themselves "shut out" (2 Thess 1:9).

2 THESSALONIANS 2:1–12

Original Meaning

Has the "Day of the Lord" Already Arrived? (2:1–2). At least some in the congregation had come to the conclusion that the event that Paul in 1 Thessalonians 5:1–11 spoke of as yet future had already in some way begun. This conclusion was apparently based either on misinformation or on a misunderstanding of Paul's previous teaching on the subject.

Paul's Response: The Day Has Not Arrived (2:3–4). Paul emphatically denies both its attribution to him and its content. Any claim that the day of the Lord has arrived is false, he insists, because certain things that must happen first have not yet happened.

These things that must happen first include (1) the occurrence of "the rebellion" (v. 3), and (2) the revealing of "the man of lawlessness" (v. 3b). Paul takes it for granted (cf. v. 5) that his readers know what he means by "*the* rebellion [*apostasia*]" and says nothing further about it. The term could denote either political or religious rebellion; here the two ideas are likely combined, with the emphasis on the latter. Paul, like other New Testament writers, probably has in view a time of increasing wrongdoing and general opposition to God.

The leader of this rebellion is first of all a "man of lawlessness." That is, this person is characterized by *anomia*, a word that describes willful opposition to God as well as a sinful condition. Paul further characterizes this individual as one who not only "opposes" God but also "exalts himself over everything that is called God or is worshiped" (v. 4), a description that echoes Daniel 11:36–37.

The result of this arrogant and audacious self-exaltation is the attempt by this person to usurp the very power and position of the one true God. This occurs when "he sets himself up in God's temple," a symbolic action that involves nothing less than "proclaiming himself to be God." Moreover, like the Lord Jesus himself, this man of lawlessness will have his own "revealing" (2:3, 6, 8) or "coming" (Gk. *parousia*, 2:9), a devilish imitation of the real thing. This suggests that he is nothing less than a rival messiah or antichrist.

Additional Information about the "Man of Lawlessness" (2:5–12). One reason for uncertainty regarding 2:4 is that Paul takes for granted that the Thessalonians know what he is talking about. As verse 5 indicates, he had taught them about this matter previously. As a consequence, however, later readers are left in the dark regarding some aspects of what he writes. As a result, verses 6–8a are among the most difficult in the Pauline corpus.

The basic structure of what Paul says in these verses is clear enough: (1) "The secret power of lawlessness is already at work" (v. 7a), but (2) it is operating in a manner that is somehow restrained or held back. (3) At some future time, however, "the lawless one will be revealed" (v. 8) or have his own "coming" (i.e., *parousia*, v. 9), at which point (4) he will be overthrown and destroyed by the far greater power and splendor of the Lord's own *parousia*. In verse 7 Paul confirms that evil is currently at work in the world and is satanic in origin, but it is nonetheless in some way limited or hindered. What or who did Paul have in mind that he could refer to it in both impersonal and personal terms?

There is a general consensus that the restraining influence must be a force for good rather than evil. Once the restraining influence (whatever or whoever it is) "is taken out of the way" (v. 7), "then the lawless one will be revealed" (v. 8). That is, he will have his *parousia* (v. 9). The parallel with the coming of Jesus is obvious; this is nothing less than the "anti-parousia" of the antichrist, an evil parody of the true coming of the genuine Christ, the Lord Jesus.

Though the "coming" of the lawless one may be both grand (the terminology evokes the pageantry, pomp, and circumstance attending the arrival of the emperor) and cunningly deceptive, it will nonetheless be short-lived, for he is "the man doomed to destruction" (2:3b), "whom the Lord Jesus will overthrow with the breath of his mouth and destroy by the splendor of his coming" (v. 8b).

The counterfeit signs and wonders of the lawless one (v. 9) exercise their deceptive effect on "those who are perishing" (v. 10), a group clearly not part of the community of faith. They are perishing specifically "because they refused to love the truth and so be saved" (v. 10). As Paul puts it emphatically in verse 12b, when they could have "believed the truth," they instead "delighted in wickedness."

Verses 11–12a discuss the consequence (*not* the cause) of this choice: "For this reason God sends them a powerful delusion so that they will believe the lie and so that all will be condemned."

Application. *Keep the focus on Jesus.* The manner in which Paul emphasizes in 2:10–12 the importance of truth reinforces the importance of focusing on Jesus. Paul describes those perishing as those who refused to love or to believe "the truth." In this context, "the truth" is virtually a synonym for the gospel. And who is its focus? Jesus, of course. Moreover, Jesus himself is the truth (John 14:6; cf. Eph 4:21). In other words, to love or believe in the truth is to love or believe in Jesus. Since our response to the truth—that is, to Jesus—determines, as Paul here makes clear, our ultimate destiny, we have all the more reason to focus on Jesus, the true Christ, and not on his antagonist, the *anti*christ.

2 THESSALONIANS 2:13–3:5

Original Meaning

Thanksgiving to God (2:13–14). The "but" with which 2:13 opens contrasts the fate of those "who are perishing" (v. 10) with that of the Thessalonian believers. Paul's major goal is to reassure the Thessalonians regarding their fate (salvation), in contrast to that of those opposing and persecuting them. Regardless of the efforts of the coming "lawless one" to deceive them, their salvation is in God's hand.

Exhortation to "Stand Firm" (2:15). As usual, Paul's thanksgiving statements are multifunctional. The list of reasons why God ought to be thanked (vv. 13–14) quickly becomes the basis for further exhortation (v. 15). "So, then," he says, "stand firm," a command that stands as the positive counterpart of 2:2. Moreover, he wants the Thessalonians to "hold fast to the teachings." Pay attention, Paul says, to what he and his companions actually taught them, not what someone is claiming or alleging that they taught.

An Intercessory Prayer (2:16–17). Paul has two gifts in view in verse 16. The first is "eternal encouragement"—that is, encouragement that will outlast the afflictions of this age and the judgment to come, encouragement that sustains God's people until they fully experience eternal life. The second is "good hope," a contemporary secular idiom that Paul has Christianized by basing hope not on an individual's own behavior but on God's gracious love, thereby providing a solid basis for genuine optimism about the future.

Finally, it is worth noting that here talk about the future ends up serving the present. Paul's discussion of the future coming of the man of lawlessness ends with a prayer for encouragement in the present, based on what God has done ("loved . . . gave," v. 16) in the past.

A Request for Prayer (3:1–2). Having concluded his prayer for the Thessalonians, Paul proceeds in 3:1–2 to ask for their prayers on his behalf. Paul's first request is on behalf of the message (v. 1); the second one is for the messengers who proclaim it (v. 2): that Paul and his companions "may be delivered from wicked and evil people." The two adjectives (*atopos*, "wicked"; *ponēros*, "evil") are roughly synonymous and convey the idea of morally perverse people who maliciously obstruct the gospel.

Expressions of Confidence (3:3–4). Together verses 3–4 closely parallel the pattern of 2:13–15: reassurance of God's love and concern for the community (cf. 3:3 with 2:13–14) is followed by an exhortation to obedience and perseverance (cf. 3:4 with 2:15). Paul is preparing the way for the instructions he is about to give in 3:6–15.

Further Prayer (3:5). Finally, having slipped from prayer back into further exhortation, Paul prays that the Lord might "direct" the Thessalonians' attention to two important points. The first, "God's love," is assurance grounded in God.

The second, "Christ's perseverance," sets before them Christ as the example of what Paul has repeatedly been encouraging them to do—that is, to persevere.

Application. *Perseverance.* What keeps us going in the face of continuing struggles? Why do we persist? We persevere because, as Paul has made clear earlier in the letter, Jesus wins. The one who has been faithful in the past will prove to be faithful in the future, and this gives us courage and hope to remain faithful in the present.

2 THESSALONIANS 3:6–18

Original Meaning

The Apostolic Command and Example (3:6–10). From Paul's perspective it should not have been necessary to "command" the Thessalonians "to keep away from" any believer who is *ataktōs*, "idle and disruptive" (v. 6), because they themselves (v. 7) already knew what they ought to be doing about this problem. What Paul and his colleagues had taught during their initial visit (v. 10) they had also lived themselves; that is, they deliberately practiced what they preached. Paul asserts (repeating virtually word for word what he said in 1 Thess 2:9), "we worked night and day, laboring and toiling so that we would not be a burden" (2 Thess 3:8b).

Orders for the Disorderly (3:11–12). The apostolic example stands in sharp contrast to "some" among the Thessalonians who were "idle and disruptive" (v. 11) and thereby becoming burdens to the rest of the congregation. Paul spells out his solution to the problem in verses 12–15. Rather than wasting their time in pseudo-work or unproductive busyness and meddling (v. 11), they should engage in productive self-supporting activities, in accordance with the apostolic model.

Instructions for the Congregation (3:13–15). Even as Paul authoritatively commands the disorderly, he encourages the rest of the congregation to "never tire of doing what is good" (v. 13). Here we catch a glimpse of the negative impact the disorderly were having on the congregation. Those who were living responsibly, in accordance with the apostolic teaching, perhaps were being worn down by the burden of providing not only for themselves and any who legitimately deserved assistance, but also for those who refused to work.

The instructions in verses 14–15 have in view everything discussed since 3:6. Paul clearly hopes that the disorderly will comply voluntarily with his instructions. If this compliance, however, is not forthcoming, the congregation itself must take steps to enforce them. The verb for "associate" that Paul uses here in verse 14 is the same one that he later uses in 1 Corinthians 5:9, 11. It essentially calls upon the congregation to cease having contact with any such people and thus amounts to an early instance of what later came to be termed *excommunication*.

The goal of non-association is clearly spelled out: "in order that they may feel ashamed" (v. 14). In the Mediterranean culture of the day, shame was primarily a matter of concern for one's reputation. Paul expects that the one who is shamed (whose reputation, in other words, is at stake) will then respond with appropriate behavior—in this case, repentance and obedience to Paul's instructions.

In short, the disciplinary action is clearly meant to be redemptive for the individual. At the same time, however, note that it is also protective for the community. That is, if repentance does not occur, the congregation will nonetheless have been purged of a potentially corrupting influence.

The Letter Closing (3:16–18). The reference to "the Lord of peace" (in which "Lord" is almost certainly Jesus) is unique in the New Testament. The prayer is that the Lord Jesus, who is characterized by "peace," may grant to the Thessalonians "peace at all times and in every way" (v. 16).

The last part of the phrase indicates the breadth of Paul's concern. He has in view not simply an absence of conflict within the congregation. Peace, for Paul, also encompasses a state of well-being and wholeness characterized by reconciled relationships —with God, with each other in the congregation, and finally with those outside the community, to the extent possible.

It was not uncommon for a person dictating a letter to take the pen from the amanuensis (the secretary or scribe who actually wrote the letter) and write the last sentence or two in his (or her) own hand. Paul seems to have done this as a matter of habit (he refers to it as "the distinguishing mark in all my letters," v. 17). The closing benediction in verse 18 is virtually identical to 1 Thessalonians 5:28.

Application. *Work.* Even while Paul explicitly affirms that individuals who are able to work have a responsibility to do so, he takes for granted the responsibility of the congregation to meet the basic financial needs of its members. Both the affirmation and the assumption provide opportunities to reflect on the meaning, significance, and value of work.

Work is a fundamental characteristic of human life because work provides the means for sustaining life. Without work, there is no life. In the biblical tradition, there is an altruistic aspect to work. One works not just for self (i.e., to support oneself and one's family) but also for others (i.e., to support those unable to work).

Church discipline. One major problem encountered in applying the biblical texts today is defining what qualifies for discipline. As noted above, Paul does not list or define what qualifies for this last stage of discipline. We can observe, however, that it seems to be reserved for matters affecting the spiritual health or well-being of the congregation as a whole. In the absence of definitive guidance from Scripture, application requires careful prayer and consideration by a congregation and its leadership.

Paul's final word: The centrality of the Lord Jesus Christ. Our future rests entirely on the power and faithfulness of God as revealed through the Lord Jesus Messiah. That was a good place for the letter to begin; it is an even better place for it to end, as we persevere in faith (1:4) and await with eternal encouragement and good hope (2:16) the revelation from heaven of the Lord Jesus himself (1:7).

1 TIMOTHY

INTRODUCTION TO 1 TIMOTHY

The apostle Paul (1:1) probably wrote this letter after his release from his first Roman imprisonment (see Acts 28:16–31), perhaps on an otherwise unattested fourth missionary journey, about AD 62–64. He writes to his younger apostolic delegate Timothy, who is ministering in the city of Ephesus (1:3). The inhabitants of this important city of the Roman province of Asia worshiped many of the Greco-Roman gods and participated in the imperial cult. Ephesus was also a significant port on the Aegean Sea especially known for its temple of the goddess Artemis (the Roman Diana; see Acts 19:23–41). The purpose of the letter is to instruct Timothy how to lead the church there and to refute a false teaching that was threatening it.

BOOK OUTLINE

I. Salutation (1:1–2)
II. Timothy's Commission from Paul (1:3–20)
III. Demeanor in the Church That Will Further Its Outreach (2:1–15)
IV. The Importance of Respected Leadership in the Church (3:1–13)
V. Godliness (3:14–16)
VI. Further Specifics as to Timothy's Assignment (4:1–16)
VII. Social Relationships in the Church (5:1–6:2)
VIII. Strong Comments about False Teachers and Greed (6:3–10)
IX. Concluding Charge to Timothy (6:11–21)

1 TIMOTHY 1:1–2

Original Meaning

The Sender and His Authority (1:1a). Paul's identification of himself as "an apostle of Christ Jesus" is similar to the way he identifies himself in every other letter except Philippians and 1 and 2 Thessalonians. Here he attributes his ministry to God's "command." The strong word used here (*epitagē*) occurs also in Titus 1:3; 2:15.

Distinctive Elements about God and Jesus (1:1b). Paul calls God "our Savior." We are so used to thinking of Jesus as our Savior that the use of that term to describe God arrests our attention. Paul goes on to describe Christ Jesus as "our hope." Significantly, the words "God" and "Savior" reappear in connection with Jesus Christ in Titus 2:13.

The Recipient (1:2a). Timothy is Paul's "true son in the faith." The word for "true" (*gnēsios*) is different from the more common one (*alēthēs*), which means true as opposed to false. The present word means "genuine" as opposed to illegitimate or fake. The word could be used of a child born within a legitimate marriage, and the implication in the figurative statement here refers to the quality of Timothy's spiritual-kinship relationship to Paul.

Kind Wishes (1:2b). It was customary for letters in the first century to convey kind wishes for the continued well-being of the recipients. Paul uses some Christian terms for this purpose, but also uses common terminology with a Christian meaning. Here he expresses these thoughts with the words "grace, mercy and peace." In most of his letters, Paul indicates, as here, that these beneficial favors come "from God the Father and Christ Jesus our Lord."

Application. The biblical hope mentioned in this greeting often tends to be replaced by a subjective, fuzzy optimism about a future life. When we invite people to the Christian hope, we must do so with a clear explanation as to how the Christian message offers the only basis for sure hope. We must also proclaim this truth, as other truths, with biblical authority. This authority is an important theme in the so-called Pastoral Epistles (1 and 2 Timothy and Titus).

1 TIMOTHY 1:3–7

Original Meaning. Apparently Timothy was already at Ephesus when it becomes clear to Paul that conditions are critically unhealthy there because of false teaching by immoral persons. Paul therefore has to "urge" Timothy to "stay" there for a specific purpose: to command these false teachers to stop (v. 3).

The word translated "teach false doctrines" (*heterodidaskaleō*) in verse 3 reappears in 6:3. The word "or" at the beginning of 1:4 does not introduce something additional to the false teachings but identifies specific aspects of those teachings. It is unnecessary to identify the source or nature of the "myths" and "endless genealogies" (v. 4) precisely to realize their detrimental effect on Christian thought, which, in this context, is the important point.

That effect is to "promote controversial speculations" (v. 4), the latter word (*ekzētēsis*) being unique in the Greek New Testament. False teaching, spawning endless detrimental discussions, is the concern of this letter. It arises from disbelief in what God has revealed.

"Faith" (v. 4c)is a basic term in the Christian vocabulary, as is "love" (v. 5a). The "goal of this command," like the fulfillment of the law (Rom 13:8–10), is "love." The solidity of the love Paul speaks about in verse 5, in contrast to mere feeling, is established by the fact that it requires an integrity of character to exist: "a pure heart and a good conscience and a sincere faith" (v. 5b).

Paul pursues this matter of integrity further by stating in verse 6 that some people had "departed from these." The heretics turned *away* from Christian character *to* empty, "meaningless" talk, a striking contrast between steadfast doing or being and vacuous speaking. It is ironic that the same people whose speech is empty "want to be teachers" and that those who repudiate love, a pure heart, a good conscience, and sincere faith want to be teachers "of the law" (v. 7).

Application. *How to address error.* The message of the Pastoral Epistles for us today is not only how to identify a particular kind of heresy but is also (and perhaps even more important in some circumstances) the *way* such deviations are to be addressed. It will become increasingly clear in the study of the Pastorals that *how* the sound teacher should confront heresy shares the spotlight with *what* heresies to confront. A major application of the Pastoral Epistles today—and it can be argued that it is the distinguishing one in the corpus—is not simply maintaining correct doctrine, much less insisting on some form of church organization that we may discern in those letters, but the importance of *the integrity of doctrine and life*, both of its leaders and of its members.

1 TIMOTHY 1:8–11

Original Meaning. In a play on words, Paul says "the law" (*nomos*) must be used "properly" or legitimately (or "lawfully," *nomimōs*, v. 8). Paul speaks to this issue at length in more than one place, but reference may be most profitably made, besides the present passage, to Galatians 5:13–26. There the Mosaic law is summarized "in keeping this one command: 'Love your neighbor as yourself'" (v. 14). Here in 1 Timothy 1, Paul describes those whose actions are contrary to that law, not now in personal debauchery as in Galatians 5:19–21, but in opposition to God (1 Tim 1:9a) and in hostility to human beings (vv. 9b–10a). Such people love neither God nor neighbor. Verse 9 establishes a principle that the law has been made not for the righteous but for "lawbreakers and rebels." Those who resist doing what is right need to be confronted by a standard that clarifies what they are doing is wrong.

Verse 10 uses the rhetorical method of going from the particular to the general. After listing the sins that require judgment and correction by the law, Paul generalizes, "and whatever else is contrary to the sound doctrine." This is a vivid figurative expression, specially employed in the Pastoral Epistles to describe teaching that is not "sick" but wholesome and resistant to the disease of error. There is a further implication in the vocabulary of verses 10–11. The unsound, sick, and false doctrine has a formidable opponent, the "gospel concerning the glory of the blessed God" (v. 11). This gospel God entrusted to the apostle Paul (v. 11b).

Application. *On distinguishing truth from error.* Some Christians may be unprepared to discern the difference between truth and error because of insufficient biblical and doctrinal teaching found in many churches today. We need to put extra effort into seeing that new Christians especially are given the background that they lack as quickly as possible, so that they will be able to tell the difference between the gospel and heresy and thereby successfully resist the latter.

1 TIMOTHY 1:12–17

Original Meaning

God's Gracious Commission to Paul (1:12–14). Paul next proceeds to offer gratitude to "Christ Jesus our Lord," who gave him strength (v. 12). While the strength comes from Christ, faithfulness or being found "trustworthy" is required of Paul. This faithfulness is not a virtue that earns Paul a commission but rather is a requirement for God's "service" (*diakonia*, v. 12). Throughout the New Testament many different kinds of service are mentioned without confining service (or "ministry") to some special order or office. In Paul's case his service, as unique as his conversion, is to be the apostle to the gentiles.

Verses 13–14 form an interesting contrast to Paul's testimony in Philippians 3:4–6, where he portrays himself as formerly being proud of his accomplishments. There he cited his persecution of the church as evidence of his zeal. He did immediately follow those words with the demurral, "Whatever were gains to me I now consider loss for the sake of Christ" (v. 7), but that is mild compared to his strong self-condemnation here in 1 Timothy 1:13. It is striking that faith and love, which in verse 5 formed the goal of Paul's command to Timothy, reappear here in verse 14. Faith and love, like grace, are abundantly bestowed by God.

God's Mercy to Paul (1:15–16). This trustworthy saying contains the essence of the Christian message: "Christ Jesus came into the world to save sinners" (v. 15b). Two extremes are cited of those for whom Christ came. One is the group of sinners described in verses 9–10; the other is Paul himself, who, despite all his life under the Mosaic law, calls himself "the worst" of sinners.

It was not only as an act of kindness that God showed Paul mercy, true and wonderful as that was. Verse 16 explains that he was a showcase for God's "immense patience." Paul sees himself as a prototype of all hostile, sinful rebels against God, whom God tolerates while patiently waiting for their conversion. The result of this faith is "eternal life." We know from 6:12 that this life of the age to come is something that the readers could "take hold" of even now in their present situation.

Doxology (1:17). Verse 17 brings this moving testimony to a doxological climax. It is a doxology honoring God as (1) the "King," (2) beyond the limitation of time, (3) incapable of dying, (4) invisible, and (5) existing alone as God. All of the characteristics of God cited in this doxology accord with Old Testament descriptions. Honor and glory therefore belong to him alone.

Application. Paul appropriately concludes this section with a doxology. It is not trite to remind ourselves that our lives should be one continuous doxology, a life lived in praise of God.

1 TIMOTHY 1:18–20

Original Meaning. The interplay of vocabulary between the opening and closing verses of this chapter is striking. Paul calls Timothy "my son" in verses 2 and 18. In verse 3 he tells Timothy what to command (*parangellō*) the false teachers; in verse 18 Paul uses the noun form of the same verb (*parangelia*, translated "command"), but this time he commands Timothy himself. In verse 3 Paul mentions his prior urging of Timothy to stay at Ephesus; in verse 18 he mentions prior "prophecies" about Timothy. We do not know what the prophecies were, but 4:14 mentions a prophetic message as the agency of the gift Timothy received at the laying on of hands (see comments there below).

The word translated "which" in verse 19b, referring to what the heretics have rejected, looks back to "faith" and a "good conscience" in verse 19a; these were already mentioned in 1:5, just a handful of verses earlier. The heretics have suffered shipwreck with regard to their own personal faith.

"Hymenaeus" (v. 20) reappears in 2 Timothy 2:17. "Alexander" may be the same person who tried to speak during the uproar when Paul was at Ephesus (Acts 19:33). Acts mentions him as though he were known to the readers, which would have been the case if he were known in the Ephesian church.

Application. The message of this short section—and of 1 Timothy 1 as a whole—is that while truth is to be celebrated, error must be discerned and corrected. This is a difficult assignment for the contemporary Christian. As the Pastoral Epistles unfold, we will see the importance of patient, gentle wooing of false teachers back to truth as well as of sharp rebuke of those whose rebellion is destroying the church.

1 TIMOTHY 2:1–7

Original Meaning

Prayer for Rulers (2:1–4). Verse 1 begins with the inferential *oun*, "therefore" (NIV "then"), which connects this with what precedes. Paul has been establishing not only the need to oppose heresy but stating his own commission and passion for the gospel. In order for that gospel to gain the response it should, several things are necessary, as set forth in chapters 2 and 3.

Paul uses several words for prayer in verse 1, as he does elsewhere. While such a listing can be redundant, it is more likely that Paul is expressing the breadth of prayer in its various aspects, each of which is relevant here. The tight syntactical construction proceeds with the word "that" (middle of v. 2), which introduces the intended result of the prayers. Paul's goal and all-consuming passion is that the gospel might freely penetrate society, which will be forwarded most effectively in a peaceful context.

Paul emphasizes that Christians in general must be *fully* characterized by the twin virtues of godliness and holiness. The implication is that as the world sees the Christian character of believers, not only will the gospel go forward in an orderly, peaceful society, but also it will be recognized as genuine.

God is pleased with these prayers for "all people" (v. 1), because he is the God who wants "all people" to be saved (v. 4). "To be saved" and "to come to a knowledge of the truth" are not different but rather overlapping experiences. Salvation is the active work of God, who has compassion and strength to rescue. The truth is to be grasped, appropriated, and allowed to change behavior.

Basis for This Prayer (2:5–7). God's concern for people is comprehensive, and his being the "one God" (v. 5) is both exclusive and inclusive. It is *exclusive* in the sense that there is no other God, a truth implicit and explicit throughout Scripture. But *inclusively* he wants to be accepted as the God and Savior of all people.

This being the case, it is both logical and right that there is only one mediator (v. 5). Jesus Christ is prophet, priest, and king. Especially in his priestly role, being both divine and human and offering himself as the ultimate sacrifice for sin, he is the only true mediator. He gave himself as a "ransom"—that is, he released God's people from bondage (v. 6). The ransom was that he gave himself up in death. He did this "for" (*hyper*, i.e., "on behalf of") all people.

Application. *Our message to those without Christ.* When preaching the gospel, it is difficult today to keep from alienating people who have a contemporary aversion to any exclusive religious claims. As far as truth is concerned, we are convinced that Christ is the only way. But *how* we declare this in today's world can move people toward or away from the gospel. Without weakness or compromise we must declare the narrow way, but in doing so we must stress that there *is* a way, a wonderful way, a way for all people. It is important that we show the love of God in *providing* that way (John 3:16) and the grace of Christ in *becoming* that way through his sacrifice on the cross.

1 TIMOTHY 2:8–15

Original Meaning

Attitude and Behavior of Men in the Christian Church (2:8). The word translated "men" (pl. of *anēr*) usually means males, though there are examples in classical Greek rhetoric of its use to include women. Here, however, it clearly stands in contrast with "women" in verse 9. This policy is in accordance with public prayer in the Jewish synagogue, though women did pray in gatherings of Christians. "Everywhere" should caution us against any assumption that Paul's instructions in our passage apply only to the church at Ephesus. "Anger" and "disputing" are inconsistent with the life of holiness that God requires of those who pray publicly, but they are also counter to effective praying.

Attitude and Behavior of Women in the Christian Church (2:9–10). Paul insists that women's outward appearance should not be in conflict with their inner character. The description of the clothing, hairstyle, and jewelry suggests two reasons why they were thought improper. First, is the inordinate expense—the clothes are "expensive." Second is the traditional association of at least some of the clothing with immoral behavior. In sum, the believing women of the church in Ephesus are to avoid wearing what exudes wealth and what suggests immorality.

Special Instructions about Women Learning (2:11–15). The attitude of quietness in verses 11–12 can be understood as ruling out teaching and the attitude of submission as ruling out exercising authority. This would not have been surprising to either Jews or Greeks, since neither culture permitted women to teach. There is a considerable body of literature on the meaning of verse 12. Proper understanding of Paul's introductory words, "I do not permit," requires comment. Is this a prohibition? In English "I do not permit" does not sound as strong as "I forbid." However, permission and non-permission were strong expressions with which Jewish readers especially would have been familiar. Can it be paraphrased "I am not now permitting," with the implication that Paul may permit it in the future but does not at the present time for some temporary reason? That may be the case, though it seems more likely a normal use of the present indicative expressing a simple fact.

As to the meaning of "teach," given the use of the word and its cognates in the Pastoral Epistles, it probably refers to the authoritative communication of "the faith"—that is, the apostolic doctrine, with the witness to Jesus and his teachings at its core. To "assume authority" is not as clear in its meaning. The clause in verse 12 specifically limits its prohibition of a teaching and having authority to exercising these over a man (or, as some suggest, over a woman's own husband) and does not rule out, even in those circumstances, any other ministry for women.

The word "for" (*gar*) that introduces verses 13–14 can indicate either the grounds for the foregoing statement or provide an explanation for it. That is, the circumstances cited from Genesis can either *require* the restriction of women or *explain* it, in this case by an analogy.

Verse 15 has been the object of much study. The meaning of "saved" is debated. The word can mean to be rescued from some danger or disease. There is a prepositional phrase modifying "saved" ("through childbearing," or, literally "through the childbirth"). The phrase can mean:

1. saved "through the [ordeal of] childbearing" (in which case "salvation" reverts to its broader meaning of preservation or rescue);
2. saved "through the [means of] childbearing" (in which case it appears to clash with the doctrine of salvation by grace alone); or
3. saved "through [*both* through the ordeal of and by means of] bearing children."
4. A fourth possibility, however, takes special note of the fact that the genitive object of that preposition, *teknogonias*, has the article (i.e., "the childbirth"). This occurrence of the article makes it possible that a particular instance of childbirth is in mind, usually understood to be the birth of Christ.

Application. *The importance of consistency.* Paul's restriction on women's teaching made good sense in a world that refused to give women teachers a hearing. In the first century, Paul was willing to become all things to all people in order to save some (1 Cor 9:22). Would not the apostle think it inappropriate for us to forbid a female college president from teaching a Bible class composed of university students—men and women—when such a restriction could cause people to stumble and cause them to turn from the gospel? A different kind of question often being asked today is whether it is right for a church to be deprived of the spiritual gift of leadership God may have given a woman when she is limited to using that gift in the women's group.

These are real situations that raise legitimate questions. If, on the one hand, Paul's restrictions *were* intended to keep women from doing missionary teaching of men today, from leading a mixed Bible study, or from serving among a group of elders, those restrictions must not be ignored. If, on the other hand, Paul would have valued missionary principles such as not hindering people from the gospel as primary, and if he considered secondary such practices as head-coverings and restricting the teaching of a mixed group to males, we need to be consistent in that regard. No doubt thoughtful readers will see strong points on each side.

1 TIMOTHY 3:1–7

Original Meaning. Paul here in this next section takes another step to address the problem of the false teachers by ensuring that the Ephesian church has leaders who are morally qualified and above reproach. The word Paul uses in verse 1 for church leadership is *episkopē*. It is hard to translate; "overseership" might be the best literal rendering. It is noteworthy that Paul here defines being an overseer in terms of function ("a noble task"), not of status or office. Yet *episkopē* does describe a position of special responsibility and leadership.

In verses 2–7 Paul sets out some significant moral requirements for overseers. His first concern is that overseers be "above reproach" (v. 2). The phrase "able to teach" (representing one Greek word, *didaktikon*) refers to ability, not knowledge. The wording "not given to drunkenness" (v. 3) by implication allows moderate use of alcoholic beverages (cf. 5:23). A potential overseer must also not be a "lover of money." The manner of argumentation and the attitude toward money that characterize true or false teachers are such important topics that Paul will return to them in 6:3–10.

The next qualification, "he must manage his own family well" (v. 4), is not only more extended but also includes an explanation. The parallel between managing one's family and caring for the church requires careful attention. Paul stresses not authority but the caring side of leadership. Even at home the father should not discharge his duty just by giving orders. The children must not only "obey" their father; they must have proper "respect" for him. Once again the accent is on the elders' character.

The same observation can be made with regard to verse 6. The warning is not against doctrinal immaturity, serious as that would be, but against the danger of a character flaw, "conceit." Verse 7 underlines the importance, noted above, of "a good reputation with outsiders," in order to avoid "disgrace." But Paul also keeps in mind here the lurking danger of Satan. Paul is deeply conscious of his malevolent intentions.

Application. Church leaders for centuries have been preoccupied with determining which church order best represents biblical teaching and example. We must both find the broad features that New Testament churches had in common and recognize that variations do not necessarily compromise these features. First Corinthians 12, which stresses the charismatic work of God's Spirit in distributing gifts to the Lord's people, does not deal with, and therefore does not exclude, structure in church government. Also, when we look at passages that deal with this subject, we see leadership by elders. While this does not mean that there was no room for individual leadership, a plurality of elders and leaders seems to be assumed (see also Titus 1:5–9).

1 TIMOTHY 3:8–13

Original Meaning. Paul's concern with the demeanor and public reputation of church leaders continues with the deacons as "worthy of respect" (v. 8). Like the overseer (3:3), the deacon must exercise moderation in drinking and in regard to money. It may seem strange that there is a reference to doctrine ("the deep truths of the faith," v. 9) in connection with deacons, but not in the qualifications for overseers. The reason may be that this is taken for granted in elders but might not be thought of as important for deacons. Here the expanded phrase "mystery of the faith" (literal translation) expresses the broad body of essential truths.

Verse 11 interrupts the instructions about deacons with some directions concerning women. The word *gynē* can mean either "woman" or "wife," so it is impossible to tell whether these were the wives of the deacons or women who were serving as deacons. It seems strange that there are no similar instructions within the section on overseers. One would think that the character of their wives was at least as important as that of the wives of deacons. But if women were at that time serving as deacons but not as elders, and if those women were at first the wives of the deacons, the picture becomes clear.

Verse 12 about the deacons' family relationships corresponds to 3:2b, 4–5 about overseers, reinforcing the importance of marital fidelity and a strong family. "Excellent standing" reveals what a noble task serving as a deacon truly is (v. 13).

Application. *Servant leadership.* If we think of leadership as any ministry in which one person guides and develops the spirit of another, it can apply to even the most humble relationships. In the church, therefore, a person may be a servant leader either (1) by exercising leadership with a servant attitude, or (2) by serving in such a way as to lead by godly example. Either way, servanthood must characterize Christians, whether or not they serve publicly as leaders.

1 TIMOTHY 3:14–16

Original Meaning. Paul next provides here an explicit purpose for the writing of his letter to Timothy—namely, that Timothy "will know how people ought to conduct themselves in God's household," the church of the "living God" and the "pillar and foundation of the truth" (v. 15).

The introduction to Paul's great creedal statement in verse 16 begins with an affirmation, "Beyond all question." While this could apply to the reliability of the creed, grammatically it refers to the description "great" in the predicate nominative position. No one can disagree that the creed is indeed great, so that is what lies "beyond all question."

The word "mystery" (*mystērion*) describes God's revelation of his sovereign work throughout history. The function of the hymn in context is apparently to remind the Ephesian believers, through Timothy, about the foundation of the church that cannot be destroyed by false teachers. The doctrine of Christ is the unshakable foundation of the Christian faith. Since there will always be opponents of the gospel, this hymn is always necessary and foundational. While the structure of the creed is obviously less important than the content, to study it helps the reader to focus carefully on content and its points of emphasis. Among the possibilities include the two listed here.

Alternating Structure

Earthly	*Heavenly*
He appeared in a body. . . .	. . . . was vindicated by the Spirit,
Heavenly	*Earthly*
was seen by angels. . . .	. . . . was preached among the nations,
Earthly	*Heavenly*
was believed on in the world. . . .	. . . . was taken up in glory.

This scheme gives attention to the literary structure and is consistent within itself. Its bipolar structure causes the reader to focus on the two loci of the revelation of Christ.

Chiastic Structure

A. He appeared in a body,	Manifestation on earth
B. was vindicated by the Spirit,	Acceptance in spiritual realm
C. was seen by angels,	Comprehension by heavenly beings
C.′ was preached among the nations	Comprehension by human beings
B.′ was believed on in the world,	Acceptance in earthly realm
A.′ was taken up in glory.	Manifestation in heaven

Since chiasm (a literary structure that involves the repetition, in reverse order, of words, phrases, or, as here, ideas) was an acceptable structural scheme in ancient times to draw attention to the successive ideas and their relationships, it is legitimate to consider the possibility of one here. But one must be careful not to go beyond the intention of the author and force such a scheme on a text improperly.

Application. The message of the incredible christological hymn embedded in 3:16 is relevant for a multitude of contemporary concerns. Its very structure rests on verbs rather than nouns. It centers on the Christ who came to us and the response he has received and deserves to receive further from us. This proclamation and confession of Christ evokes a response from us. There is a sense of purpose and hope as Christ moves, so to speak, from his incarnation to his ascension. Those who feel misunderstood can identify with the Christ who needed vindication. Those who feel alone as Christians can be encouraged by the reminder of how widespread faith in Christ really is in our world. Those who are self-centered can be reminded by this Christocentric hymn where the center of our attention and affections belong. Those who need hope are reminded that Christ has taken his seat in glory at the right hand of God and begun to rule in exaltation and won't stop until God is all in all. Grounding this hope, our hope, is an objective christological foundation confessed in this ancient hymn.

1 TIMOTHY 4:1–5

Original Meaning. Paul next gives us a behind-the-scenes glimpse and reveals that the real perpetrators of heresy are not only the heretics but the evil spiritual forces that deceived and taught them (v. 1). The two false teachings cited in verse 3—"forbid[ding] people to marry" and "order[ing] them to abstain from certain foods"—are not easy to understand. The error seems to be a judgment against all marriage and against certain foods as being wrong in themselves. This conclusion is strongly countered by Paul's statement in verse 4 that "everything God created is good" (thereby alluding to Genesis 1).

To reject food is to negate God's creative work. To receive it and be thankful are to acknowledge that work and our dependence on God. Thanksgiving, prayer, and the word of God render the food legitimate to eat. While this does not mean that a formal act of blessing is necessary every time food is taken, it does suggest that an acknowledgment of its source and of the fact that "everything God created is good" is appropriate and desirable.

Application. *Facing the "last days."* Wherever we may be today within the total span of the church age and however far we may be into the "last days," most would agree that there seems to be intense activity now on the part of deceiving spirits. Scripture tells us that one of the gifts God gives his church is distinguishing between spirits (1 Cor 12:10). This gift is urgently needed today. But one does not need special gifting to study God's word and learn sound doctrine against which to test various claims. Churches that teach God's truth clearly, that emphasize major doctrines, that avoid a dogmatic attitude about things that matter less (the so-called *adiaphora*), and that stress love as the goal of God's commands are well able to deal with false teachings.

1 TIMOTHY 4:6–10

Original Meaning. The references to "the truth" (4:3) and "the word of God" (4:5) in the previous section lead Paul to remind Timothy of his training in the "truths of the faith" (v. 6), an important emphasis in the Pastoral Epistles. To "point these things out" (v. 6) is one way to express Timothy's assignment. "Command and teach" in verse 4:11 is a stronger way of putting it. By doing this he will be a "good minister of Christ Jesus" (v. 6). "Minister" (*diakonos*) is a word for anyone who serves God, as well as for the special group described in 3:8. This training in godliness is so important that it far surpasses physical training (4:8).

Two phrases in verse 10 require careful attention lest they be misunderstood: "Savior of all people" and "especially of those who believe." These words could be taken to mean that God ultimately saves everyone (an idea called *universalism*), though believers experience this in some special way. But this is not the case. Paul, Jesus, and Scripture in general make it clear that not all are saved, for some deliberately refuse to accept God's saving grace. In the present context "all" may mean "all kinds of," a possibility supported by the use of *anthrōpos*, which refers to humanity. The second phrase, "especially of those who believe," is not the best translation of the Greek words used here; more likely it means "in particular" or "I mean."

Application. *Spiritual formation.* In recent decades the term *spiritual formation* has been more common among evangelicals. There is a recognition that conscious attention should be given to such areas as spiritual growth, moral and ethical awareness, practical appropriation of Scripture, immersion in prayer and meditation, and involvement in the community of faith. What is still sometimes neglected is the development of *character*. Prayer, Bible reading, moments of spiritual insight, and even revival are all tremendously important. Isolated acts and events, however, do not necessarily develop character. Character is developed by bringing these spiritual disciplines to bear together on our lives, on our attitudes and decisions, and on our relationships and actions.

1 TIMOTHY 4:11–16

Original Meaning. Verses 11–16 contain a series of important imperatives that summarize and enlarge on the preceding sections. Paul tells Timothy, "Command and teach these things" (v. 11). The encouragement not to let people despise his youth (v. 12) raises the question of Timothy's age. If, as is probable, Timothy was in his thirties, words such as "young" and "youth" might give the contemporary reader the wrong impression, since we generally reserve these words for people in their teens and early twenties.

The word "life" (v. 12) translates *anastrophē*, which can describe one's conduct or behavior in a particular circumstance (Gal 1:13) or a way of life (Eph 4:22). Here it means the latter, in conjunction with the traits of character expressed in love, faith, and purity. This is a reprise of 1 Timothy 1:4–5.

"Until I come" (v. 13) serves both to support genuine Pauline authorship of the letter and to place Timothy's commission in context. His duties are not those of a pastor as we conceive of that ministry today. Timothy represented Paul in the doctrinal conflict at Ephesus as an apostolic delegate.

The call to perseverance in verse 16 is in accordance with Paul's words to others. In the context of the Pastoral Epistles, with their emphasis on the necessity of the Lord's servant leading a godly life under the scrutiny of others, this verse can best be interpreted by stating it negatively: "If you do not combine godliness with proper doctrine in your life, you will give the lie to your own claim to salvation and be a hindrance to others who seek to be saved."

Application. *The laying on of hands.* Most ordination rites today are intended to convey an ecclesiastical status and privilege not given to Timothy. Ordination should be reexamined as to its significance. It should be recognized that this is not the elevation of a privileged cleric to a superior exclusive class (as was the Old Testament priesthood), but the acceptance of one whom God has given to his church to work not above, but among, the people of God.

1 TIMOTHY 5:1–16

Original Meaning

Relationship in the Christian Family (5:1–2). Verses 1–2 provide a terse introduction to the next topic of the Christian family. The instructions are comprehensive, covering all four possible relationships: older men, younger men, older women, and younger women. The instructions are not directed to these groups, as they would be in the usual household instructions. Instead, they are directed to Timothy to guide him in *his* relationship to them.

The first of these is in the singular, "older man"; the others are plural. In this context it is clear that the Greek word *presbyteros* refers to age, not to a church elder. His attitude to the older men is not to be harsh even if they need correction. The verb used here for "rebuke" (*epiplēssō*) means to strike out at someone (in a figurative usage here, to strike verbally).

Caring for Widows (5:3–16). Care of widows was important in Jewish tradition. The Jewish concern for widows appears also in the New Testament (Jas 1:27). Acts 6:1–6 reveals the concern the early Jerusalem church had for widows, first those who were Hebrew-speaking and then those who spoke Greek. As for the Greco-Roman world outside of Judaism, a widow was to be cared for by her sons in her husband's home, or if that was not possible, she was to return to her parental home.

After instructing Timothy to honor those who are "really" widows (v. 3), Paul defines them first as those who are alone and have no family members to care for them. Moreover, they must trust in God in contrast to living for pleasure (vv. 5–6). Three further characteristics identify those who are to be put on "the list" (v. 9). To be placed on "the list" a widow must be over sixty (v. 9a), must have been faithful to her husband (v. 9b), and must have had a reputation for "good deeds" (v. 10). The next verses (vv. 11–15) explain why younger widows should not be on this list. The section concludes with a reprise on a family's care for its own widows, now focused on female family members (v. 16).

The contrast between younger and older widows in verses 11–15 is stronger than one might have expected. It is not merely that younger widows are likely to remarry and therefore not need financial help. They are to be refused rather than be enrolled, because their sensual desires may well come between them and Christ. The problem is not in young widows remarrying, since Paul counsels remarriage of young widows in verse 14. It is rather that they allow their impulses to alienate them from Christ.

Paul also counsels the young widows to "manage their homes" (v. 14). The word for "manage" is *oikodespoteō*, which is a remarkable term to use for the responsibility of the remarried young widow over her household. It indicates that this woman would have a strong management role in her new family.

Once more, and in conclusion (v. 16), Paul counsels family members to care for widows to prevent additional burden on the church. The person who should help is a believing woman. The end of the verse shows Paul's concern for truly needy widows.

Application. *Widows in Western society today.* First Timothy 5 refers to literal widows. There are, however, parallel situations in our contemporary world in which we can express the same blend of doctrine and life in helping those in need. Today there are many divorced people who are alone, hurting, feeling misunderstood, and perhaps having financial need. There are also children of divorces; recent studies have shown that divorce usually has an effect on children that continues even into their adult lives. They are not orphans, but they are children in need of love, which means understanding and care. There are also children who have been abused. They and abused women (with a few men as well) give opportunity for Christians to combine their faith with practice. Our churches should be centers of healing.

1 TIMOTHY 5:17–6:2

Original Meaning

Honoring Elders (5:17–20). The instructions in 3:1–7 concerning "overseers" certainly apply to elders, but since the usual Greek word for elder (*presbyteros*) does not occur there, this is the first unambiguous occurrence of substantial instructions concerning them. "Direct the affairs of the church well" (v. 17) is an enlargement on the Greek words for "rule well." The verb used here is *proistēmi*, the same one employed to refer to overseers and deacons managing their families (3:4, 12). The adverb "well" (*kalōs*) also appears both in that context (3:4, 12) and this one.

While the reference to the "respect" (3:4) that an overseer should have from his children is different from the "double honor" referred to here at 5:17, it is significant that evidence of an elder's dignity and recognition appears in both contexts. Commentators differ as to whether the phrase "double honor" means (a) respect, (b) remuneration, or (c) both; and whether, if it is (b), it means that they should receive literally twice as much remuneration as elders who do not rule well or who do not minister the word. In support of (a), honor was far more important in that society than in ours and would have been a deeply valued reward to the worthy elders. In support of (b), Paul elsewhere argues strongly for proper financial support for the Lord's servants (cf. 1 Cor 9:14). Finally, since the provision of needs would have been a practical expression of honor, the two possible meanings need not be mutually exclusive, and thus (c) is possible.

With verse 19 the passage takes a sharp turn from *honoring* to *accusing* elders, though the elders are still honored by the exercise of caution in making an accusation. The present tense of the word "sin" in verse 20 implies that the elder in question not only has been proved guilty of the sin charged but persists in it.

Further Instructions about Sin and Purity in the Church (5:21–25). The warning in verse 21 to avoid "partiality" and "favoritism" seems a matter of common sense and courtesy. However, since Timothy is working closely with the elders, his natural tendency might be reluctance to act strongly against a leader who has sinned. Paul initiates these instructions with the heavy artillery of a solemn warning just short of an oath, calling on "God and Christ Jesus and the elect angels" as witnesses (v. 21).

Paul's warning not to "share in the sins of others" and his exhortation to Timothy to keep himself "pure" imply the actuality or the possibility of sin in the original selection of the erring elder (v. 22). Clearly *neither* action—selecting or disciplining—should be done in such a hasty manner as to be undiscerning, careless, or slack as regards to sin.

Slaves and Masters (6:1–2). Paul next proceeds to discuss slaves and masters. Slaves are under a "yoke" (v. 1). While it was unnecessary to use that graphic word (since the term *slavery* itself conveys their miserable condition), "yoke" emphasizes that slaves have no rights of their own. Paul is not rubbing this in but rather setting the stage for his strong word that both in general (v. 1), and particularly when slaves have a Christian master (v. 2), they should give "respect" and not disrespect. Rather than taking advantage of Christian masters "because they are fellow believers," the slaves are to remember that their owners are also "believers" and beloved (NIV "dear to them").

Application. *Problems of defection among leaders.* The contemporary problem of moral defection among church leaders is real and serious. We note the following observations. First, the circumstances of moral defection are often complicated by the existence of heavy demands in contemporary ministry, of increasing tensions within the home, and of the high number of people entering ministry who come out of broken and abusive homes.

Second, when a pastor has not had stable, loving support and moral encouragement in early life, when he or she is tired, often occupied in counseling people with sexual problems, and when he or she is busy with frequent evening meetings that interfere with time at home with family and especially with spouse, temptations, especially of a sexual nature, can become strong.

Added to this are the burdens of spiritual warfare—the fact that a pastor is a likely target of the enemy of souls and of the realities of temptation described in James 1:13–15 that we all face. Understanding, compassion, and counseling are needed in such situations. Yet such understanding and counseling do not preclude definitive action on the part of the church if the leader goes astray, such as that which is described in this section of 1 Timothy.

1 TIMOTHY 6:3–10

Original Meaning

Description of the False Teacher (6:3–5). Verse 3 opens with a conditional clause, "if anyone teaches otherwise." Paul has already made it clear that there are indeed people who do this, and the conditional clause is a normal way of expressing an assumption. The false doctrine runs counter to "sound instruction" and "godly teaching" (v. 3). Both expressions are thematic in the Pastoral Epistles. The person who rejects "healthy" doctrine has an "unhealthy" or morbid obsession with "controversies and quarrels about words" (v. 4). The five results listed for these quarrels all have to do with disruptions in interpersonal relationships.

Contentment and True Godliness (6:6–10). In verse 6 Paul picks up the word "gain" from verse 5 and contradicts the utilitarian view of godliness criticized there. There *is* great gain in godliness, but only if it is combined "with contentment," the opposite of greed. The word "contentment" is *autarkeia*, a word used by the Stoics for the virtue of self-sufficiency. Paul used the related adjective in a Christian sense also in Philippians 4:11. The point he makes in verse 7 is expressed in an aphorism much like our "you can't take it with you." Verse 8 specifies the essentials necessary for contentment, "food and clothing." This embodies Jesus's strong teaching against greed and for trust in God for material needs in Luke 12:13–34.

The point of verses 9–10 is not that wealth is wrong but that desire for it is. The NIV properly avoids the article before the word "root" because Paul is not saying that the love of money is *the* root, but it is *a* root. The closing words of verse 10 show the interconnection between covetousness and departure from "the faith."

Application. *Keeping our checkbook in balance.* It would not hurt preachers—or any of us, for that matter—to draw up a series of pages with two columns, one labeled "need" and the other "want," and to list in the appropriate columns our homes with their market value, our cars, perhaps the number of clothes and shoes we have, and other items that need that kind of assessment, and then to set these lists before God in a time of prayer, determined to take the proper action as a result of our evaluation. One friend who had earned enough to live comfortably sincerely offered to God to downsize significantly and recalls the fear he then experienced as to what this might mean. Do we master our desire for material possessions, or do they master us?

1 TIMOTHY 6:11–21

Original Meaning

Honoring God by Fulfilling His Calling (6:11–16). Timothy is here commanded to distance himself from the people described in verses 3–10. Several imperatives follow in short order. "Flee [*pheugō*] from all this" in verse 11 refers to the evils mentioned in verses 3–10. Timothy is to pursue a series of virtues that will help him to maintain the character that Paul has been mandating throughout the letter.

The verb "fight" (v. 12) refers to an athletic contest, not military combat, and we also know that Timothy was to be kind and gentle as he was instructing unbelievers (2 Tim 2:24–25). Actually, the context of verse 12 is not a conflict against other people; it is the "good fight of the faith," which is Timothy's own "athletic contest" for personal mastery. In this connection Timothy is to "take hold" of eternal life. He has received this from God and is to appropriate it now.

Verse 13 contains another solemn charge by Paul, introduced by the word *parangellō*, "I charge." Paul's command has moral overtones. It was not only a *charge* to *do* something but a *mandate* to *be* something: "without spot or blame" (v. 14).

The doxology in verses 15–16 employs rich, lofty vocabulary to exalt God. It is introduced by a statement that includes the previous reference to the appearing of Christ. This statement emphasizes the sovereignty of God, who will bring about that appearing "in his own time." Another unique characteristic of God celebrated in this doxology is his immortality. This is the God who lives in light that cannot be approached.

Words to the Wealthy (6:17–19). The early Christian churches did not lack members of the upper, wealthier class. In whatever way they may have gained their wealth, possibly before they became believers, they now had it and needed instructions as to how to use it. Such people are to recognize that wealth is temporary, of "this present world" (v. 17), and will last only until the appearing of Christ just alluded to in the previous verses. Moreover, they should not be arrogant. They are not to "put their hope in wealth," because wealth is "so uncertain." Rather, the rich are to be "rich" in good deeds, to be generous, and to be willing to share with others who have less (v. 18). In this way they lay up treasure in heaven for themselves in the age to come and "take hold" of eternal life, which is "truly life" (v. 19).

Conclusion (6:20–21). Verse 20 begins a final personal word to Timothy. It is difficult to know what was "entrusted" to him. But immediately after telling Timothy to "guard" this, Paul writes about turning away from "what is falsely called knowledge." This command seems to be a summary of all the exhortations in this letter to follow and defend truth and oppose heresy. If so, probably what was "entrusted" and to be guarded carefully was the "sound teaching." Paul concludes the letter to Timothy with a prayer that God's "grace" would be with Timothy and his fellow believers in Ephesus (v. 21).

Application. *Doxology and worship.* The doxologies in the Pastoral Epistles are uplifting, directing our hearts to the God who is worthy of all worship and honor. We can miss a great opportunity, however, if we simply read these words in the course of our study or wait until the worship leader incorporates them into a Sunday morning service. They are there for our use at any time.

It is often said that our personal times of prayer should include worship. Such worship can be expressed, of course, in our own words—words inspired by the Spirit in the depths of our minds and hearts. It can also come through the words of hymns and devotional writings. This is not only a helpful way to expand our worshipful thoughts and vocabulary but also a means of joining in the voices of people from other Christian traditions as part of the great worshiping church worldwide. This has exciting possibilities. Personally, for example, I find it wonderfully stretching to offer an evening hymn when it is evening somewhere *else* in God's world, joining in with, and praying for, the believers in that time zone.

Best of all, however, is to worship God in his own words—through the Psalms, the songs of praise in Revelation, and other passages. The doxology found here in this final section of 1 Timothy, celebrating, along with 1:17, the immortal God, is a wonderful instrument of worship. It can also be a means of recalling the universal church and all those—believers on earth and in heaven, angels, and other beings—who for an eternity will worship God together.

2 TIMOTHY

INTRODUCTION TO 2 TIMOTHY

The apostle Paul (1:1) probably wrote this letter during a second Roman imprisonment (see Acts 28:16–31 for the first), perhaps after an otherwise unattested fourth missionary journey, about AD 64–65. He writes again to his younger apostolic delegate Timothy, who is ministering in the city of Ephesus. Paul senses that his execution is near (4:6–8), and so he writes a sort of fond farewell discourse to Timothy to encourage him to stand firm in the faith and fulfill his calling as his apostolic delegate and as a leader of the church. He bids him also come to Rome for a final visit (4:9). Paul further provides instruction concerning yet another false teaching and how Timothy should lead the church and refute it. Second Timothy is Paul's final extant letter.

BOOK OUTLINE

I. Salutation (1:1–2)
II. Personal Encouragement and Paul's Circumstances (1:3–18)
III. Exhortation (2:1–26)
IV. The Coming of Terrible Times (3:1–13)
V. The Power of Scripture (3:14–17)
VI. Paul's Final Charge to Timothy (4:1–8)
VII. Conclusion (4:9–22)

2 TIMOTHY 1:1–7

Original Meaning

Paul's Greeting (1:1–2). On Paul's apostleship (v. 1), see comments on 1 Timothy 1:1. His reference to the "will of God" stands alone in the Pastoral Epistles, though it is not unique among the Pauline letters. The reference to "Christ" in verse 1 is one of thirty-two in the Pastoral Epistles, almost always along with "Jesus." The prepositional phrase "in Christ Jesus" may be one of many uses by Paul where it conveys the idea of close relationship or union.

Remembering Timothy's Faith and Spiritual Giftedness (1:3–7). The word "serve" in verse 3 translates *latreuō*, which often refers to worship, especially with regard to the offering of worship in a cultic context. In the (Greek) Old Testament this word could refer to the worship offered to God in his temple.

What follows is a pattern of words about remembrance. Paul remembers Timothy in his prayers. He does so "constantly." He prays "night and day." Paul remembers Timothy's tears (v. 4). Paul then recalls Timothy's "sincere faith" (v. 5). It was clear to Paul when he met him that Timothy had an authentic Jewish faith, thanks to the piety of his mother, Eunice, and his grandmother, Lois.

The fourth remembrance is actually a reminder Paul gives Timothy to fan God's gift into flame (v. 6). Paul's words do not necessarily mean that Timothy's passion had abated, though the verb translated "fan into flame" can have the sense of rekindling a dying fire. The basis of Paul's exhortation ("for this reason") is Timothy's faith (v. 5), so we know that there is no lapse there.

The "Spirit" mentioned in verse 7 is the Holy Spirit himself, not the human spirit. It is something God gave and was probably part of the gift mentioned in verse 6. The gift seems to have been a measure or kind of power, love, and ability to control oneself that is beyond our normal capacities, which comes only from the Holy Spirit. He is not the kind of Spirit who brings fear or a "timid" spirit.

Application. *Today's Timothys.* The skills and professional knowledge needed for service to God today can be gained in many ways. What is less attainable is character and wisdom. What young Timothys today need especially is personal mentoring, but not merely mentoring in the sense of giving information and offering guidance. That is not what Christian discipling and mentoring are about. To mentor a Timothy means to be available, to spend time with him or her, to understand the differences, and to seek to facilitate rather than to control the use of that person's distinctive gifts. An athlete runs the race alone but does so after months or perhaps years of training and encouragement. And that may not be done just by a coach, but by others who are close to the athlete. Timothy had in Paul a person who was close to him, who listened and understood him, who recognized his individual giftedness, and who had confidence in him.

2 TIMOTHY 1:8–18

Original Meaning

No Cause for Shame (1:8–12). Verses 8–12 form one long sentence in Greek. It is introduced by the word "so" (or "therefore"), indicating that Timothy's ability to resist being ashamed lies in the gifts of power, love, and self-discipline (v. 7). In this context being ashamed stands in contrast to joining with Paul in suffering. This very suffering is "by the power of God" (v. 8). Verse 9 shows two ways in which God has expressed that power. One is by saving us; the other, by calling us.

The importance of the phrase "because of his own purpose and grace" (v. 9) can be realized more fully by noting Ephesians 1:3–14, where Paul makes it clear that God's grace is founded on his eternal purposes. That passage employs a remarkable series of words, phrases, and grammatical constructions that express the idea of God's purpose, wisdom, good pleasure, and plan, through which God's people are brought to salvation. The same concept is fortified in our verse 9 by the time reference, indicating that grace was actually given us "in Christ Jesus *before* the beginning of time" (v. 9b), but that "it has [only] *now* been revealed" (v. 10).

A couple of words in verse 10 are of special importance in the Pastoral Epistles. The word translated "revealed" (*phaneroō*) occurs in the important creedal statement in 1 Timothy 3:16 and in Titus 1:3 (cf. Titus 2:11, 13; 3:4). The word "Savior" (*sōtēr*) is also significant since, apart from 2 Peter, this noun is relatively infrequent in the New Testament (see 1 Tim 1:1; 2:3; 4:10; Titus 1:3, 4; 2:10, 13; 3:4, 6). In the New Testament, salvation—which is the work of God in the Old Testament—is now also the work of Christ.

The long Greek sentence that began in verse 8 continues with a participle in verse 10 ("destroyed" death), which is used adjectivally to describe the activity of Christ at his appearing. Christ made it possible for us to *have* eternal life through his resurrection, but the emphasis here is on that which "brought life and immortality *to light*" (v. 10). What accomplished that was the gospel.

Paul then speaks of his own ministry (v. 11) on behalf of the gospel. The three words "herald," "apostle," and "teacher" are not intended to be mutually exclusive in this context, but rather to express three distinctive ways in which Paul serves the gospel. The fact that "herald" appears first (rather than "apostle") suggests that Paul is not drawing attention to his status or authority but rather to the ways in which he forwards the cause of the gospel. The herald naturally comes first as the person who makes the announcement, who first brings the good news. The "teacher" explains God's truth with a view to edifying the church. The word "apostle" describes Paul's special commission, in the fulfillment of which he did both proclaim and teach, but which had other dimensions (such as representing the sender, the Lord Jesus Christ, and fulfilling his will wherever he went).

As Paul nears the end of his sentence, he gathers up in verse 12 what he has said about testifying to the gospel and declares that it is for this reason that he is "suffering as I am," probably meaning that suffering is also part of his commission, as it is Timothy's (cf. 3:12). Paul is doing his part in suffering for the sake of the gospel, committing his life and ministry to God as a deposit for the future day of reckoning. Timothy, for his part, must guard the teachings that God has entrusted to him, and God has given him the Holy Spirit to help him do this.

Keeping the Pattern of Sound Teaching (1:13–14). The emphasis given to "pattern" (being the first word in the Greek sentence), considered along with the key phrase "sound words" and with the instruction about guarding the deposit in verse 14, makes it unmistakably clear that Timothy is not at liberty to deviate from the apostolic teaching.

The Kindness of Onesiphorus (1:15–18). Verses 15–18 reveal some of Paul's personal feelings. The nature of the desertion of "everyone in the province of Asia" (v. 15) has been a matter of debate. Possibly prior to this writing some from Asia had been in Rome during Paul's imprisonment there and had not supported him. Phygelus and Hermogenes are not called heretics, as Hymenaeus and Philetus are (see 2:17), but probably are two stalwart associates whose defection hurt Paul the most. Onesiphorus stands in beautiful contrast to the others. Taking up the theme of Paul's imprisonment and the natural tendency of associates to be ashamed of him, Paul specifically says that Onesiphorus "was not ashamed of my chains" (v. 16).

Application. *Embarrassment as Christians today.* Because claims for the exclusiveness of the gospel run counter to today's doctrine of tolerance for all views, Christians do stand out for their witness to truth. But it is not only tolerance that is the problem, it is the common idea that *no* system, even one's own, can claim absolute truth. Most agree it is appropriate for a Christian to give a testimony as to how their personal faith has helped them in a given situation, but to go beyond that to make strong and universal truth claims relevant for everyone is frowned on. Those believers who do so can experience a kind of humiliation and shame.

2 TIMOTHY 2:1–13

Original Meaning

Forceful Words about Hardship (2:1–7). Following the emphatic "you," verse 1 continues with the word "then." This causes the reader to reflect on the exhortations and events referred to in chapter 1 and leads to the exhortation to "be strong."

Verse 2 may seem an unexpected intrusion into the flow of thought. But the need for what Paul teaches and commands to be passed on by Timothy (and Titus) pervades the Pastoral Epistles. In this case Paul does not refer to a direct command or written instruction but to his teaching as heard by Timothy and other "witnesses."

The three images in verses 3–6 appear elsewhere in Paul, but with different emphases. The military image here has to do not with warfare but with disciplined obedience; the athletic image deals less with success and more with conformity to the rules; the agricultural image stresses hard work.

Reasons for Enduring Hardship (2:8–13). Verse 8 moves from analogy to history. Whatever encouragement Timothy may receive from verses 1–7, it is the resurrection of Christ, the promised messianic descendent of David, that provides the strongest motivation. Paul refers in verse 9 to his own suffering in chains "like a criminal," but adds that "God's word is not chained."

Paul turns in verse 10 to his own willingness to endure anything necessary "for the sake of the elect." The words that follow, "that they too may obtain the salvation that is in Christ Jesus, with eternal glory," have elicited discussion. The whole concept of election stands to the side of the present passage because Paul's emphasis here is not on the matter of election, predestination, and the sovereignty of God, but on the need to *facilitate the salvation* of the elect. However one may address the matter of election, the conversion of a person involves the faithful ministry of the saving gospel.

The "trustworthy saying" (v. 11) is one of five in the Pastoral Epistles. The present saying in verses 11–13 is the only one that can be called poetic. Paul has already written strongly about spiritual identification with Christ in his death. Paul is not simply here thinking of something historical, though it is based on the historical death of Christ, and certainly not of something physical, for we have not actually been put to death. Rather, there is a personal identification with Christ in his death. If verse 11 deals with the kind of death and life referred to in Romans 6, the future tense "we will also live" refers to our present life in Christ (cf. Rom 6:8).

In verse 12, the endurance is, by its very nature, lifelong. The reigning is not something of a spiritual nature in this life but is eschatological. The word "disown" is a possible translation of the Greek *arneomai*, but since we tend to use it with regard to a parent disowning a son or daughter, it could give the wrong impression. The Greek word also means "to deny, refuse" or simply "to say no"; "repudiate" may be a proper translation here.

While Christ will repudiate the person who repudiates him, verse 13 tells us that if we are faithless, he remains faithful, for he cannot repudiate himself. Is it being faithful to his people, to his own righteousness, or to his judgments? Since all three are true and supported throughout Scripture, we do not lose any truth by leaving this question open here. What is most striking is that the saying of verses 11–13 concludes with a magnificent statement about Christ's character: he cannot repudiate himself!

Application. *Monitoring results in a mobile society.* Our occasional contacts with people are fleeting, such as with fellow passengers on an airline flight. Therefore, those who are hardworking farmers in the imagery of verse 6 may never know on this earth whether seeds they have planted have taken root and grown. Faithful Christians may not see the results or reap its rewards until heaven. We must depend all the more heavily on the promises of this passage as well as respond in faith to its commands.

2 TIMOTHY 2:14–26

Original Meaning

How to Deal with Destructive Teaching (2:14–19). The NIV "keep reminding" (v. 14) brings out the present tense of the verb. "Warn" is a participle, also in the present tense. This tense indicates that the task is not complete but requires constant attention. The contemporary reader of the completed New Testament is well aware that words are important and that precise wording is necessary for precise theology. But here Paul is warning "against quarreling about words." Paul does not enlarge here on what the controversy is about, but rather offers two clear reasons against allowing it: it is without value and does no good, and it ruins the listeners and therefore does evil.

This is the setting against which Paul writes the well-known words of verse 15. The words "do your best" represents the Greek verb *spoudazō*. The idea is doing something with diligence and perhaps with haste and urgency. It communicates the idea of zeal.

It may be asked why anyone would think that a workman might be ashamed. There is no suggestion that this workman might be ashamed of his product—that is, the gospel. Rather, the following clause indicates that it is the *way* the work is performed that might or might not give reason for shame ("who correctly handles the word of truth," v. 15b).

Verse 16 counsels against "godless chatter." This empty talk is devoid of religious value and consequently leads those who indulge in it to become "more and more ungodly." The sentence continues in verse 17 with a second reason for avoiding godless chatter. "Their" refers to the false teachers. "Teaching" is *logos*, with the use of that word standing in strong contrast to "the word [*logos*] of truth" in verse 15. "Will spread like gangrene" is a mixed metaphor.

Of the two false teachers named in verse 17, Hymenaeus was mentioned in 1 Timothy 1:20, while Philetus is mentioned only here. Their error is in saying "that the resurrection has already taken place" (v. 18). This refers to the future resurrection, which is like that of Jesus and not just a spiritual transformation. This is an error that seems to value Hellenistic ideas opposed to the biblical celebration of body and soul together, and it may draw on negative pre-gnostic ideas about the material world, including the human body.

Verse 19 responds to this troubling situation with the affirmation that "God's solid foundation stands firm." Paul merges several images next to convey the idea of that which (1) is absolutely firm, (2) is owned by God, and (3) stands despite the presence of destructive persons like Hymenaeus and Philetus. God does, after all, own the building.

The Imagery of Household Utensils (2:20–21). A large house, owned by a wealthy person, would have a variety of utensils. This is not simply a matter of better versus everyday tableware. It is rather that some utensils are used for purposes that have an overtone of dishonor, disgrace, or shame. Such a purpose might be for removing excrement, for example. This would be better understood by readers in cultures where, for example, the left hand is reserved for the dirty functions of living. It is this strong description that gives sense to verse 21 and its requirement to "cleanse" oneself from the latter group of utensils. This accomplishes the shift from the impersonal utensils of the image to the personal world of Timothy, who is to be an instrument "for special purposes," "holy [and] useful to the Master."

Personal Advice about Handling Controversy (2:22–26). Verse 22 presents two contrasting objectives: "the evil desires of youth," from which one should flee, and the pursuit of "righteousness, faith, love and peace." Verse 23 warns against arguments that produce quarrels, which must not characterize the Lord's servant (v. 24).

The positive attitudes in verse 24 are significant. The word for "kind" (found only here in the New Testament) carries the idea of gentleness and stands in contrast to a controversial spirit. Timothy must have this attitude "to everyone." The next word, *didaktikos* ("able to teach"), is one of the qualifications for overseership in 1 Timothy 3:2. The word translated "not resentful" appears only here in the New Testament and describes the way one handles evil opposition or pain.

Verse 25 describes the required active response: instruction with a view to the "repentance" of the opponents. Paul hopes that these opponents will "come to their senses" (v. 26), a phrase that translates a verb that can mean also "to become sober again." The key to the error and belligerent attitude of these heretics is their entrapment by the devil.

Application. *Fruitful dialogue.* Contemporary application of our passage should not be difficult if we share Paul's goals. It will always be more difficult to separate from those whose life and teachings are destructive if we know them personally than if they are merely names to us. Yet it should make us more concerned for them personally, and we can hope for an eventual turnaround if we do know them. In his house-church setting, Timothy must have had firsthand contact, perhaps weekly for a period of time, with the very people Paul warns him about.

2 TIMOTHY 3:1–9

Original Meaning

Terrible Times (3:1–5). The reasons why the last days are so terrible are cited in verses 2–9, introduced by the word *gar* ("for," omitted in NIV). The list in verses 2–5 calls to mind the vice catalogues found in Greco-Roman literature. The amazing thing is that these people, consumed by their own vices, have "a form of godliness" (v. 5a). This does not necessarily mean that they are in the church, but the fact that Paul counsels Timothy to "have nothing to do with such people" (v. 5b) may indicate that they are.

Victimization of Women and Others (3:6–9). Verses 6–9 continue the warning against the evil people so graphically described in verses 2–4. Since these evil hypocrites have a "form of godliness" (v. 5a), they are able to seduce some people into believing their heresies. Those described in verse 6 are women, specifically described as *gynaikaria*—a diminutive, demeaning form of the word for woman. It is important exegetically to understand this word as a particular class of women and not as a description of women in general, any more than the words in verses 2–4 describe men in general. These women may have been recent converts, possibly from lives of religious perversion or prostitution. Paul's main point in verses 6–7 is not to malign women but to show the treachery of the false teachers. These women are sadly "always learning but never able to come to a knowledge of the truth" (v. 7). The point is that they are susceptible to further encounters of this nature.

Verse 8 contains another description of the false teachers, this time by reference to "Jannes and Jambres," names Jewish tradition gave to the Egyptian magicians who tried to imitate the signs performed before Pharaoh by Moses and Aaron (Exod 7:11; 9:11). What they had in common with the false teachers at Ephesus was that they also stood against the truth, had "depraved minds," and were rejected "as far as the faith is concerned." These heretics "will not get very far" (v. 9). It would have been a great encouragement to Timothy to know that "their folly will be clear to everyone."

Application. *Social degeneration.* According to the Bible's descriptions of "the last days," the darkest hours of social degeneration may be yet ahead. Terrible as such things are, the common thread through all of this is selfishness. "People will be lovers of themselves," and the expressions of that—pride, ungratefulness, lack of love for others, ingratitude, and sensuous pleasure at the cost of other people—are descriptive of contemporary moral malaise.

2 TIMOTHY 3:10–17

Original Meaning

Paul's Sufferings (3:10–13). Paul's autobiographical notes here and elsewhere often serve several purposes. They may demonstrate the sovereign grace of God in his life, acknowledge that faithful service does bring suffering, and provides a model for others to emulate. The present passage accomplishes the second and third of those purposes. It opens with the emphatic "You, however" (v. 10), which calls Timothy as a witness to the difference between the false teachers just described and Paul's teaching and way of life.

Paul is not flattering himself but rather showing where his values are, values that are not optional or relative but of absolute importance in the life of the Lord's servant. Not only Paul's teaching, but also his character distinguishes him from the false teachers and the itinerant philosophers mentioned above. Paul has already alluded to his sufferings in the Pastoral Epistles, but those mentioned here refer to events in specific cities that took place prior to Paul's meeting with Timothy (v. 11). Persecution is not exceptional for those who want to live a life that is "godly" (v. 12).

Having moved from the sole figure of Paul to all those who want to live a godly life in Christ Jesus, we now face the contrasting figures of "evildoers and impostors" (v. 13). The tragedy of these impostors is compounded by the fact that they not only deceive but are themselves "deceived."

The Importance of Scripture (3:14–17). Verses 16–17 are the strongest statement in the Bible about itself. We understand that the word "Scripture" (*graphē*) includes the New Testament, since 2 Peter 3:16 cites the writings of Paul among the "Scriptures" (also *graphē*). The word translated "God-breathed" (*theopneustos*) in the NIV is more commonly translated "inspired," which is less awkward but also less accurate. The term *inspired* is much too broad in its common usage today to convey the force of the Greek *theopneustos*, which is formed from *theo* (the root form of the word "God") and *pneustos* (from a Greek root having to do with breathing). The inspiration of Scripture is foundational to its usefulness.

The first use of Scripture Paul lists is doctrinal. Its use for "rebuking" and "correcting" may not seem primary to the modern reader. However, given the major function of the Pastoral Epistles to address the problem of false teaching in Ephesus and Crete, these functions have obvious significance. The appearance of these two words here is probably due to their strength and appropriateness in the overall context of correction. There may be a sequence intended here: first, refuting the false teaching that Timothy was confronting, and second, straightening everything out. The final item in the sequence is providing an ongoing "training in righteousness." Structurally, "teaching" stands at the head of this series and the purpose of it all is expressed in verse 17, "for every good work."

Application. *The uniqueness of the Bible.* Unless the word of God is obeyed, preached, and taught as it should be, we are neither giving it due honor nor letting it do its job. Bible societies, Bible publishers, Bible translators and other missionaries who translate the Scriptures, Sunday school teachers who explain it, preachers who proclaim it—and everyone who studies it, lives it, teaches it, raises a family based on its teachings, witnesses from it, and prays to God and praises him from its message—all have a significant part in the obedient application of the "God-breathed" Scripture to the life of the church.

2 TIMOTHY 4:1–8

Original Meaning

The Charge to Timothy (4:1–5). Verse 1 begins Paul's final exhortation and appeal to Timothy. The seriousness of this charge is heightened by a reference to the fact that Christ "will judge the living and the dead" (v. 1). We gather from the various biblical texts about future judgment that this will be a complex event. Not only will there be a comprehensive judgment before the great white throne, resulting in eternal life or death (see Rev 20:11–15), but our lives as servants of the Lord will be evaluated before the judgment seat of Christ (2 Cor 5:9–10).

The contents of the charge are contained in verses 2–5. It opens with commands. The first ("preach the word," v. 2) echoes the repeated instructions to Timothy and Titus regarding the teaching and preaching of God's truth. The word must be preached because sound doctrine is going to be rejected.

People will "gather [teachers] around them," who suit the "desires" of the people (v. 3).

Timothy is to "be sober in all things" (v. 5a, literal translation). It is not enough to keep from losing his head; he must think clearly, fully aware of all that is going on. This means that he has to "endure hardship," an exhortation that recalls Paul's words about suffering in 2 Timothy 1:8, 12; 2:3. "Do the work of an evangelist" is a straightforward command, implying that Timothy might be so consumed with other needs and tasks that he is in danger of not pursuing the work he probably originally did with Paul on their travels together.

Paul's Reflections on His Life of Service (4:6–8). "Being poured out like a drink offering" (v. 6) likely alludes to the sacrifice of drink offerings in the Old Testament (Exod 29:40–41; Lev 23:13; Num 15:4–10; 28:7). "The good fight" probably has behind it an athletic rather than a military picture (v. 7). "I have finished the race," recalls Philippians 2:16. The phrase "to keep the faith" was a fixed expression in extrabiblical literature for those who remained faithful to God.

The idea of a "crown [or garland] of righteousness" in verse 8 is unique here. Paul knows he has already received righteousness and that this righteousness has been stored up for him in heaven. The Lord who awards this crown is "the righteous Judge." That fact both offers the assurance that God is right in bestowing that crown and gives a sobering context in view of the fact that God "will judge the living and the dead" (4:1). The word "appearing" in verse 8 is the significant *epiphaneia*, that future epiphany of our Lord Jesus Christ that provides motivation to live a godly life in the Pastoral Epistles (see 4:1; also 1 Tim 6:14; Titus 2:13).

Application. *Passing the baton.* Behind all these exhortations is the figure of the great apostle, ready now to commit the immense tasks he has been passing on to a younger man. This must have required a great deal of trust on his part. My wife, on reading this text and my comments on it, added this note: "How do you feel as a retired teacher? Can you turn it all over to the young?" That gave me reason to reflect, both as a retired seminary professor and as a retired pastor. Then, just before completing this section I had two phone calls. One was about a former student and his excellent teaching ministry overseas. The other was about another former student who is being sought as a pastor by several churches. How do I feel? I have cherished every God-given opportunity for personal ministry. Yet I cherish more the fact that this kind of ministry does not end with my retirement but continues in the hands of many competent Timothys. The same phenomenon is no doubt being experienced daily in countless ways in the global church.

2 TIMOTHY 4:9–22

Original Meaning. The reason given here for Timothy's coming is that Paul's companions have been leaving him. His distress will be compounded if Timothy is delayed by a long stopover because of the onset of winter. Demas made a choice for the present world. Titus has gone to Dalmatia, probably on a mission for Paul.

The statement in verse 11, "only Luke is with me," conveys some pathos. Some think it also offers a clue concerning the authorship of the Pastoral Epistles. Luke's presence would make it possible for him to function as a secretary writing at Paul's dictation.

"Get Mark" (v. 11b) implies that at some point after Paul's refusal to have Mark continue with him on his missionary journeys (Acts 15:37–40), a change took place in Mark or in Paul, or perhaps in both, that made it possible for Paul to trust Mark again as an associate in his ministry. Tychicus (v. 12) appears at several points as an important associate of Paul (Acts 20:4; Eph 6:21–22; Col 4:7–9). Paul may be sending this letter to Timothy by the hand of Tychicus. Another possibility is that Paul has already sent Tychicus on a mission that will end in Ephesus after this letter arrives.

It is impossible to tell whether "Alexander the metalworker" (v. 14) is the same person named in 1 Timothy 1:20. Paul does not offer any clear comment to distinguish the two from each other, although the word "metalworker" here could be understood as that kind of distinguishing comment.

What does Paul mean by "my first defense" in verse 16? If Paul was tried and acquitted after the end of Acts and is now for the second time imprisoned and awaiting the disposition of his case, this verse could naturally refer to that previous circumstance. On the other hand, "first defense" may refer to what was called in Roman law the *actio prima*, the first phase of his present trial. In this case we would have to understand verse 17 about the future proclamation of the gospel in another sense than Paul's going personally to further countries and gentile audiences.

Paul's final greetings and personal references in verses 19–21 are, in the best sense of the word, sentimental. Priscilla and Aquila have meant a great deal to Paul. The order of their names is significant. The best explanation seems to be that she gained more prominence as their ministry continued. For example, in Acts 18:26 Priscilla and Aquila (mentioned in that order) invited Apollos to their home and "explained to him the way of God more adequately." Any application of 1 Timothy 2:12 should take the Acts passage into account.

The reference to the "household of Onesiphorus" (v. 19b) may be a wonderful testimony to the entire household or, poignantly, a sympathetic word to his bereaved family if he had died. "Erastus" (v. 20) may be the same person mentioned in the same breath as Timothy in Acts 19:22. Paul's mention of Erastus without further description implies that Timothy knows him. "Trophimus" is also mentioned in Acts 20:4 in company with Timothy.

In verse 21 the verb *spoudazō* occurs (see again also v. 9), giving a note of urgency to Timothy's projected trip to see Paul "before winter" and the closure of the sea lanes. Paul then cites several otherwise unknown people: Eubulus, Pudens, Linus, and Claudia. Given the fact that many passages in Paul's writings referring to "brothers" clearly in their context include sisters, to add "sisters" in translation is legitimate (as is done in the NIV 2011).

Application. *Facing death.* To say farewell is also a good and thoughtful act on the part of the one facing death. Too many people have been unwilling to deal realistically with the prospect of death. They then lose the opportunity to say that last word of forgiveness or to ask for it. Paul was not courting death. Yet he was *ready* to die when it was God's time for him to do so, and that readiness speaks to us.

TITUS

INTRODUCTION TO TITUS

The apostle Paul (1:1) probably wrote this letter after his release from his first Roman imprisonment (see Acts 28:16–31), perhaps on an otherwise unattested fourth missionary journey, about AD 62–64. He writes to his younger delegate Titus, who is ministering on the island of Crete (Titus 1:5). For reasons lost to us, Paul had been ministering with Titus on Crete but left the island, leaving Titus behind to complete the work of establishing the church there. The fledgling church on Crete was in danger from a local Jewish false teaching (1:10–16), and the urgent need to combat it was to appoint godly and spiritually mature elders for every town where a church had been established (1:5–9). The purpose of the letter is to instruct Titus how to lead the church on Crete and to refute the false teaching that threatens it.

BOOK OUTLINE

I. Opening (1:1–4)
II. The Need for Elders in the Churches of Crete (1:5–16)
III. Ethical Teachings (2:1–15)
IV. The Importance of Doing Good (3:1–11)
V. Concluding Personal Remarks (3:12–15)

TITUS 1:1–16

Original Meaning. In the order of writing, Paul's letter to Titus almost certainly came close on the heels of 1 Timothy and well before 2 Timothy. Like Timothy in Ephesus, Titus was left by Paul on the island of Crete to organize the church and deal with a crisis situation of false teachers who had infiltrated the church.

An Expanded Introduction (1:1–4). It is natural to compare the opening lines of this letter with those of 1 and 2 Timothy. One difference appears at the very beginning. Paul identifies himself both as "a servant" (*doulos*, "slave") of God and as "an apostle" (Titus 1:1). The word *doulos* appears in Philippians 1:1, a letter he coauthored with Timothy. In all the other Pauline letters, except 1 and 2 Thessalonians (which were authored by Paul, Silas, and Timothy), Paul identifies himself simply as an apostle. Paul does not use *doulos* in a self-deprecating way. A slave was owned by another person to whom obedience was required. If slavery meant obligation, apostleship meant authority, but both meant responsibility.

The faith that Paul wants strengthened in the church at Crete is not some vague, subjective feeling but the faith of God's "elect," who stand in the tradition of the Old Testament people of God whom God had set apart for himself. The correspondence between "truth" and "godliness" probably means "truth that is appropriate to godliness" rather than "that leads to godliness" (NIV) or "truth that shows them how to live godly lives" (NLT). Genuine godliness requires a genuine foundation of truth. The false teachers lack both.

The same "hope" that enlivens Paul's correspondence with Timothy appears here (v. 2). It may seem strange that "faith" and "knowledge" rest on hope. However, this hope does not arise from the human heart, but has been "promised before the beginning of time" by "God, who does not lie."

The responsibilities of being faithful to a trust ("entrusted") and obedient to "the command of God" gives Paul not only responsibility but also authority (v. 3). He did not ask for this trust; it was given him by God's command. God has the right to decide how his saving message is to be announced.

The Need for Elders (1:5–9). There is some ambiguity in the words "put in order what was left unfinished" (v. 5). Put together, the words imply that there was some residual disorganization after Paul left, which could be remedied by what had not been done before: appointing responsible leadership. The Greek word in verse 5 for "appoint" is *kathistēmi*. The word for "elders" (*presbyteroi*) in Titus is apparently the same as the *episkopoi* in 1 Timothy 3 (see the use of *episkipos* in Titus 1:7 and comments below).

There is a difference between the latter part of verse 6 and 1 Timothy 3:4. In 1 Timothy the elder is to manage his family well and "see that his children obey him." Here the elder's children are to "believe," as well as not be open to the charge of being "wild and disobedient" (v. 6). This seems to make the parent responsible for a child's salvation. But the Greek word translated "believe" is an adjective (*pistos*), which can also mean "faithful" or "trustworthy." Thus, the meaning here may be broader than it seems at first. The children should not incur any accusation of being "wild" or "disobedient." Thus, the phrase in verse 6 describes outrageous behavioral activity that would bring public disrepute on the eldership and the church.

In verse 7, *episkopos* ("overseer") is used, suggesting that overseers and elders are identical. The overseer/elder is to be "blameless" (the same word as in v. 6) for a specific reason: he acts as God's steward. The series of qualifications that follows specifies behavioral patterns that cannot characterize an elder if he is to be considered blameless. The desirable characteristics cited in verse 8 describe the ideal character of all Christian men and women. Their function here is to portray a morally well-rounded person who will not disgrace the Lord and his church.

The Circumstances of the Church on the Island of Crete (1:10–16). This section introduces the people whose teachings must be opposed by doctrinally capable elders. Paul has the "circumcision group" particularly in mind (v. 10). The meaning here is not that people in the circumcision group cause more problems than others do, but that the rebellious people *are* the "circumcision group." There is an urgency about this. The false teachers at Crete are turning *whole families* upside down. Perhaps the "things they ought not to teach" include the kind of legalistic practices that, when followed by some members of a family, disrupt relationships. Further, these teachers on the island of Crete are not operating out of sincerity but "for the sake of dishonest gain" (v. 11b).

The quotation in verse 12 that begins "Cretans are always liars" has caused much discussion. The function of the quotation is to provide a reason for distrusting the false teachers and to point out that people in a society that promotes laziness and the satisfying of base desires easily foster the desire for "dishonest gain" in their false teachers.

At the beginning of verse 13 Paul inserts the second of two comments that form a bracket around the saying concerning the Cretans (the first being Paul's reference to the reputation of the saying's author as a "prophet"): "This saying is true." The next words may be translated "for this reason" or perhaps "on account of this"; the NIV's "therefore" lacks the punch of the Greek expression. "Rebuke" is a strong word.

Verse 14 states the two aspects of the teachings of the circumcision group that must be rejected. One is "Jewish myths." The presence of Jews throughout the ancient world provided a network through which those who promulgated nonbiblical deviant stories could circulate their errors. The other aspect of the heretics' teachings has to do with daily life: "the commands of those who reject the truth." Basic to both aspects of error is the rejection of the truth.

Paul's response in verse 15 to the commands of the circumcision group, which apparently have to do with ritual purity and food laws, is not theological but aphoristic. We might have expected a Galatians-like statement about freedom from the law. The assault on the false teachers reaches a climax in verse 16. The contrast is damning: those who claim they know God not only fail to match their actions to their words but by those actions actually deny him (cf. Rom 1:28–32).

Application. Strong discipline is sometimes required. Verses 10–16 require strong application. Although Paul's counsel, especially to Timothy, is to be gentle in correction, there are times when firm disciplinary action and public rebuke are called for, particularly those who are "rebellious" and deceivers (v. 10), "disrupting whole households" for "dishonest gain" (v. 11), "corrupted" (v. 15), denying God, "detestable," and "disobedient" (v. 16). It is hard to deal with such people if there is no strong, recognized leadership in the church.

This is a case where plural leadership is important. In one situation, in a small church blessed with a mature, wise congregation, there had seemed no need for elders. But when one member abused his wife and said (correctly) that no one had the authority to confront him, the church decided elders were needed. In time he threatened to kill one of the elders, and the church was at that point able to deal with him. The message of Titus 1:1–16 for today is that not merely leadership, but leadership vested with biblical authority is needed to handle any situation and any personal hostility that may arise.

TITUS 2:1–10

Original Meaning. "Teach" translates the Greek *laleō* (often translated as "speak," v. 1). The teaching must be consistent with the "sound doctrine" that Paul has been advocating throughout the Pastoral Epistles. The teaching here is not in itself doctrinal; it is practical instruction that is based on doctrine.

In the list of instructions that follows, the household image is once again invoked. It is more than an image because the Christian assembly *is* a household in its function. The older men in this household are not only to be venerated because of their age, as is common in many societies, but because of their character. The older women have a similar responsibility ("likewise" in v. 3), though the specific traits are different.

The word "urge" (v. 4) can imply a need to be reminded of something, in this case of the dimensions and implications of their original love for husbands and children, a love that can be diminished by circumstances or lack of response from others. The further content of the teaching of older women for younger women (v. 4) is an interesting complex of subjects, but not unexpected in a Christian household code in that society.

Paul goes on to tell Titus to instruct "the young men" (v. 6), but, after repeating (from v. 5) the injunction to be self-controlled, instead of issuing further instructions for them, the apostle tells Titus how *he* can be an example *to them*. "Doing what is good" (v. 7) reflects a repeated command in the Pastoral

Epistles (1 Tim 2:10; 5:10, 25; 6:18; 2 Tim 2:21; 3:17; Titus 1:8; 2:3, 14; 3:1, 8, 14). No one can understand the message of these letters without grasping this emphasis. The rest of the list emphasizes the kind of character Paul has urged throughout these letters.

The instructions to slaves (v. 9) are similar to those in Ephesians 6:5 and Colossians 3:22. In addition to being submissive in every area of the relationship, Paul urges integrity in word and deed. By showing that a slave can be "fully trusted," he or she will "make the teaching about God . . . attractive" (v. 10). Paul's instructions show Titus and Cretan Christians how character and good deeds can help win others to Christ.

Application. *Curves and angles.* If there is any passage in Paul's letter to Titus that needs to be applied today, it is this one. Christians must work hard to live so that they give no cause to unbelievers to "malign the word of God," have anything "bad to say about us," or find Christian doctrine unattractive. What may seem like straightforward advice that can easily be applied, however, turns out to have some curves and angles to negotiate. The preacher needs to call for obedience to ethical injunctions on the part of the congregation, but he or she also needs to have a more nuanced approach to those who do not share these values. Their meaning and legitimacy need to be established, and we must trust the Holy Spirit to convict the world of sin.

TITUS 2:11–15

Original Meaning. The fact of Christ's first and second comings underlies the instructions in 2:1–10. This basis is not only the *fact* of the two comings of Christ, but (1) the first appearing is an appearing of "the grace of God" (v. 11), which both brings salvation and teaches self-discipline, while (2) the second appearing constitutes a great hope, to be realized in the return of him who is not only the Savior, but actually "our great God" (v. 13).

The grace of God not only saves but it "teaches" (v. 12; perhaps better "trains"). The description that follows in verse 12 of what this training should accomplish demonstrates the meaning of the verb better than any single English word. There are two goals: a negative one, to renounce two specified undesirable habits of life; and a positive one, to adopt in their place three desirable habits. The negative goals are introduced by the words "to say 'No.'" What one should renounce or reject is "ungodliness" and "worldly passions." God's grace also trains us positively to embrace the Christian life in a way that is "self-controlled, upright [or just] and godly."

It is significant that Paul neither centers on the future consummation of our hope in the return of Christ to the neglect of our character and way of life here and now, nor centers on matters of conduct without setting these in the context of the Christian hope. In other words, before Paul addresses that "blessed hope" (v. 13), he mentions the virtues that grace teaches us to adopt and live out "in this present age" (v. 12).

Although the object of our waiting is twofold, "the blessed hope" and the glorious "appearing," it is a conceptual unity, with the two nouns joined in the Greek by one article. The NIV nicely expresses this by the use of a dash between them rather than with an "and."

"Who gave himself" in verse 14 points to the voluntary offering of Christ on the cross for us. Earlier, Paul noted that the training that grace gives us is in both a positive and a negative form. Here the same pairing is the result of our Lord's sacrifice: negatively, to "redeem us from all wickedness," and positively, "to purify for himself a people that are his very own, eager to do what is good."

Titus is to "teach" these things (v. 15). Two verbs follow: "encourage" and "rebuke." The word for authority here is *epitagē*, a specific command. Just as Paul functioned under the command of God, so Titus is to function under the apostolic command of Paul, though there is no indication that Titus had broad apostolic authority as Paul did.

Application. *Authority and its limits.* The application of verse 15 is complex and of immense importance. The principles must be derived carefully, with due regard for the differences between the unique commission of Titus as an apostolic delegate to a threatened congregation and the commission of those who care for churches today with a broader and less authoritative range of responsibilities. Yet this passage, like other passages in the Pastoral Epistles, teaches the importance of transmitting sound doctrine, and that doctrine carries divine authority. It is right for us to say, "Thus says the Lord" or, "The Bible says," making sure that we are properly teaching and applying Scripture so that God's people are equipped and "eager to do what is good."

TITUS 3:1–11

Original Meaning

True Conversion Should Make a Difference (3:1–8). Verse 1 opens with the word "remind," a gracious but insistent way in which Titus can reinforce teaching that the Cretans have already heard. The proper attitude toward the secular "rulers and authorities" is submission, obedience, and readiness "to do whatever is good." The fact that obedience is mentioned separately from submission indicates that not all submission requires obedience.

Verse 3 is joined to the preceding by the word *gar* ("for," untranslated in NIV). In other words, this section provides foundational or exemplary information pertinent to verses 1–2. The next word in verse 3 is *pote* ("once"; NIV "at one time"); it is paired with *hote* ("when") in verse 4. The next words, "we too," serve to identify the Christians' preconversion experience with that of those around them on Crete. The effect of all this is to keep the Christians humble (cf. v. 2), to offer hope to the present unbelievers, and to allow the use of strong words describing the unbelievers, since these characteristics had at one time been true of the converts.

Verse 4 provides the kind of gracious interruption found in Ephesians 2:4: "But God, being rich in mercies, because of his great love with which he loved us" (literal translation). In Ephesians 2 the great operative words are mercy, love, grace, and kindness. They reappear here in a different order: kindness, love, mercy, and grace.

Paul's emphasis is not only on the coming of Christ as Savior but also (1) on the merciful, gracious work of salvation and (2) on the fact that this was *God's* work, using once again the characteristic reference to God as Savior. The word translated as "kindness" in verse 4 conveys more than just goodness and includes the idea of benevolence.

The next two phrases in the Greek structure are prepositional phrases modifying the main verb of the sentence, "he saved" (v. 5). The first phrase expresses what we may call *false* grounds. The basis on which God saved us is not the good things we have done (literally "not out of works that we did in righteousness"). An emphatic "we" appears at the end of that phrase, stressing that it is not *our* doing (compare Eph 2:8–9). The second prepositional phrase stands in strong contrast to the first, introduced by the strong adversative conjunction *alla*; it indicates the *true* grounds on which God saves us: "his mercy."

The next word is the main verb, "saved," in the simple aorist tense, indicating the basic fact of that completed work. Paul then cites the means by which God has accomplished this. The use of the Greek genitive after the preposition *dia* ("through") is significant here and not entirely easy to understand. Illustrating this by grouping the English words together by hyphens, one can read it as "through-washing-of-regeneration and renewal-of-Holy-Spirit." In this reading, the washing is characterized by regeneration or perhaps produces it, and the renewal is accomplished *by* the Holy Spirit or perhaps comes *from* the Holy Spirit as a source.

These phrases can also, however, be understood as "through washing of regeneration-and-renewal of-the-Holy-Spirit." In this reading the regeneration and renewing are both functions of the washing. In either case it is difficult to separate the regeneration from the washing. The theological question is whether this teaches baptismal regeneration. We might say that the means of salvation are: the washing (represented by but not identical to baptism), the regeneration, and the renewing, while the agents of the renewing are the Holy Spirit and Jesus Christ our Savior, through whom the Spirit has been so generously poured out on us.

The purpose of this process includes one further circumstance that can be considered as further modifying "saved" (in sense although not grammatically) or else as modifying "we might become heirs" (v. 7)—namely, "having been justified by his grace." The overall point is clear: The purpose of God's mercy, grace, and kindness in our lives is "so that" we may be heirs of God, a concept closely linked to our having the "hope of eternal life."

The latter part of verse 8 sets out the importance of good works for those who have experienced God's grace. Paul makes the broad statement that such good works are excellent (cf. Titus 2:7, 14; 3:14) and profitable for everyone. Once again the apostle shows a concern for the world around him.

Final Words about Controversies (3:9–11). Controversies are "unprofitable and useless" (v. 9). After a couple of warnings, Titus is to have "nothing to do" with that person (v. 10). This does not mean that grace is never extended, for the person has already had a second chance (v. 10; cf. Matt 18:15–17). It has been established that this "divisive person" cannot be redeemed. He is not only "warped and sinful," but he has also condemned himself, so the responsibility is not on Titus (v. 11).

Application. *Dealing with the dark side.* Controversies and divisiveness that call for strong action on the part of Christian leaders require a rare blend of humility and authority, of love and uncompromising admonition. The stronger the reputation of a church and its leaders for expansive love, integrity, and civility in demeanor, the more effective will be their vigorous insistence on doctrinal purity.

TITUS 3:12–15

Original Meaning. Paul's final remarks in verses 12–15 include personal requests (vv. 12–13), a reprise of the latter part of 3:8 (which repeats the emphasis on doing good, v. 14), and finally greetings and a benediction (v. 15). The Pastoral Epistles are full of personal instructions, but the closing here allows for the kind of specific instructions contained in Ephesians 6:21–22 and Colossians 4:7–9.

Verse 14 picks up the latter part of verse 8, repeating the same words in the same order: "to devote themselves to doing what is good." This means believers are not only to provide for themselves in order to avoid being a burden to others but also that they should be productive in providing for others.

The closing greetings of verse 15 are warm and all-inclusive. The simple words "grace be with you all" conclude the letter—one final reminder of the saving grace of God our Savior.

Application. Many missionary letters and magazines today contain vivid pictures or descriptions of the people whom that particular mission or missionary is reaching for Christ. Christian agencies make pictorial appeals to provide Bibles for a certain tribe, to send missionaries to the remaining unreached people groups, and to support orphans. All this is good and can be facilitated by contemporary means of production and communication. Charitable organizations, such as those caring for children in deprived areas, must be sure to channel all the money possible from the donations received to those in need.

The conclusion to Titus also reminds us of the people right around us, people like Zenas and Apollos, who need encouragement along the way of missional endeavor. It serves as a reminder to us to be ready to practice hospitality and to invest in those who are doing gospel work, in order to ensure that their legitimate ministries continue without interruption due to lack of support.

PHILEMON

INTRODUCTION TO PHILEMON

Paul's letter to Philemon serves as a model of Christian compassion. In many ways, it parallels Jesus's parable of the prodigal son, which captures the gospel in a nutshell. The letter speaks of failure, the need for intercession, returning, forgiveness, and restoration. If we are genuine disciples of Christ, we will relate to our fellow believers with grace, forgiveness, and encouragement.

BOOK OUTLINE

- I. Salutation and Thanksgiving (1–7)
- II. Main Body (8–18)
  - A. The First Mention of Onesimus (8–12)
  - B. Paul's Unfulfilled Desire to Keep Onesimus with Him (13–14)
  - C. The Request to Receive Onesimus as a Brother (15–16)
  - D. The Request Backed by Paul's Pledge (17–18)
- III. Conclusion (19–25)

PHILEMON 1–7

Original Meaning

The Salutation (1–3). Paul begins his appeal to Philemon by identifying himself as a "prisoner of Christ Jesus" (v. 1), the only time this epithet appears in a salutation in Paul's letters. Paul not only addresses Philemon, Apphia, and Archippus but also "the church that meets in your home" (v. 2). This means that the letter is not an exclusively private note to Philemon; the whole church is included in the appeal.

Paul's Thanksgiving for Philemon (4–7). Philemon has an exemplary record for showing his love and helping fellow Christians, which gives Paul the confidence to ask him to show his love again for another believer. This particular saint, Onesimus, has done Philemon personal injury.

Paul moves in verse 6 from thanksgiving to an intercessory prayer. Paul prepares Philemon for his request. He intends to entrust the decision about Onesimus to Philemon's Christian moral insight.

Verse 7 gives the reason for Paul's thanksgiving and optimism. Philemon's past benevolence to fellow Christians shows him to be a man filled with Christian compassion, and his past generosity emboldens Paul to make an audacious request for Onesimus.

Application. Christians are not alone. When we are joined to Christ, we are joined to others. Recognizing how integrated we are with others who share the faith leads to greater understanding of its truth and to greater understanding of others. Our fellow Christians may be more toughminded in helping us put God's love to work in our lives.

PHILEMON 8–25

Original Meaning

The Return of Onesimus (8–12). Many have noted how reticent Paul is in this letter, only dropping hints here and there about what he wants his friend to do. Verse 9 explains why. He wants his friend to do what is right, but he will not command him, because he wants Philemon to draw his own conclusions and to make his own decision about what is fitting in Christ to do.

Forgiveness was not the norm in Philemon's world, but it is a fundamental requirement for Christians. Paul seeks to activate Philemon's Christian consciousness to make him aware of what is required for him to do in this situation. He expects Philemon, as a Christian who has been renewed in the image of his Creator, to show love and to forgive his grievance against Onesimus, just as the Lord forgave him his sins.

What is frequently overlooked is that Paul also expects Onesimus to act from love. Paul sends him home with a ringing endorsement, but he has no guarantee that Philemon will honor it. Onesimus must be willing to accept with grace whatever Philemon might decide in his case, which could include severe punishment or being sold to another master.

Paul pulls at Philemon's heartstrings by reminding him of his captivity for preaching the gospel (see v. 13) while appealing to an old man's privilege. The request for Onesimus may seem obvious and natural to those of us who live in societies that consider slavery to be a heinous sin against human decency. In Paul's culture, however, thoughts of abolitionist reform were unheard of, and a world without slavery was inconceivable.

Before making his actual appeal, Paul lets Philemon know that Onesimus has become a Christian. The father/son imagery used to relate this conversion conveys Paul's close relationship to Onesimus. Paul is careful to note that Onesimus had already been useful to him before he sent him back to Philemon. Paul intensifies his request by calling Onesimus his "very heart" (v. 12). Paul has already praised Philemon for "refresh[ing] the hearts of the Lord's people" (v. 7), referring to some benevolence that lifted their spirits, and he cannot imagine that Philemon will be callously indifferent to his own heart in the present situation.

Paul's Unfulfilled Desire to Keep Onesimus with Him (13–14). Paul expresses his personal preference, "I would have liked to keep him with me" (v. 13), but he puts aside his own wishes out of consideration for Philemon's rights and feelings. There are two reasons why Paul sends Onesimus home. Paul will do nothing without Philemon's specific consent (v. 14), nor will he try to make his ethical decisions for him. The other reason for sending Onesimus home is the premium Paul places on a face-to-face reconciliation between two believers, a slave and an owner. The apostle's personal wishes therefore must yield to this greater end.

The Request to Receive Onesimus as a Brother (15–16). Paul continues to speak with reserve and leads into his actual request with a "perhaps." The passive voice, "he was separated from you," is a euphemism for Onesimus's illegal flight. But the passive voice is also used in the New Testament to denote God's agency and further mitigates the seriousness of whatever Onesimus may have done by attributing it all to God's purposes.

Philemon has lost a slave for a brief time so that he can gain him back forever as a spiritual brother. Paul alludes to the new relationship between them. Philemon receives Onesimus back as a fellow Christian, and they will be together in eternity.

Paul speaks theologically of the transformed relationship between Onesimus and Philemon based on forgiveness and love. The phrase in verse 16, "both as a fellow man and as a brother in the Lord," translates an ambiguous Greek phrase that reads literally as "both in the flesh and in the Lord." Paul may only be asking that Onesimus be treated with love as a fellow Christian. In other words, Paul affirms that Onesimus, the man, is far more than a piece of property. He is Philemon's equal before the Lord.

Receiving him "no longer as a slave" (v. 16) is therefore a subtle but open invitation to free Onesimus. One can take it literally: "Since he has become a beloved brother, he should no longer be your slave." Paul, however, cannot bluntly ask this since it presents Philemon with a ticklish, practical dilemma.

The Request Backed by Paul's Pledge (17–18). Verse 17 is the letter's climax: "Welcome him as you would welcome me." Paul not only intercedes for Onesimus but identifies with him. Onesimus, the runaway slave, returns home as Paul's apostolic representative. Philemon's reception of Onesimus will represent his reception of Paul.

Paul is deliberately vague about how Onesimus has wronged Philemon, to avoid stirring up unpleasant memories and shifting attention away from the dramatic change in Onesimus. Whatever it is, Paul accepts the debt as his own. In effect he says, "I'll cover it from my own pocket" (v. 18). This pledge is astounding when one considers the historical context, and it emphasizes how committed Paul is to Onesimus. Few would be willing to take full responsibility for any debts that others may have incurred, let alone those of a slave, since most regarded slaves as morally irresponsible.

Conclusion (19–25). Since the letter is being read aloud to the church (v. 2), it is necessary for Paul to notify the listeners, who cannot see the change in handwriting, that he has taken the stylus to write out his promissory note (v. 19). This IOU is the same kind of bond that Paul refers to in Colossians 2:14.

With the phrase "not to mention that" (v. 19b), Paul uses a rhetorical gambit whereby one mentions what he will not mention. The apostle subtly reminds Philemon of the basis of their relationship and how he could even make such an unheard-of request. He suddenly converts Philemon from a creditor, whose debt will be paid in full, to a debtor, who cannot possibly repay the price of his life.

Verse 20 begins with an emphatic "Yes" (NIV "I do wish"). Friendship in the ancient world was a reciprocal relationship that continued when friends exchanged gifts, services, and benefits. Philemon's positive response will be a "benefit" to Paul that will "refresh" his "heart in Christ."

Paul's words in verse 21 exude confidence because he knows his man. Paul knows he will obey. The obedience is not to Paul but to the Lord, whom he has just referred to in verse 20, and to the command of love that undergirds the entire letter.

Paul makes one last request related to his hoped-for release from prison and his prospective visit. Paul has shrouded his supplication for Onesimus in a guarded indirectness. Now he makes a direct request: "Prepare a guest room for me" (v. 22). Paul's self-invitation would not have been a serious imposition in his culture.

Paul's arrival in Philemon's home would be a gracious answer to prayer. Paul again uses the divine passive "to be restored to you" (v. 22; see v. 15), which reveals that he would regard his release from prison as divine intervention.

Paul signs off with greetings from his fellow prisoner, Epaphras, and his fellow workers. The "you" in verse 23 is singular. Presumably, each of these people would vouch for Onesimus and concur with Paul's request on his behalf.

Application. *Facing moral dilemmas.* Sometimes social evils can overwhelm us. We may hear descriptions of an urgent need, the deplorable conditions, and a desperate plight and become immobilized because we suffer from compassion overload. We may also think to ourselves: How could we possibly do anything to alleviate so much suffering in so many places? Paul's letter to Philemon guides us to look at the person on our very doorstep. We may not be able to undo all the injustice in the world, but in our local neighborhood we can stand with those individuals who are oppressed victims who need a friend and a loving hand.

HEBREWS

INTRODUCTION TO HEBREWS

Few questions concerning the New Testament have fostered more curiosity and fewer firm answers than the query, "Who wrote the book of Hebrews?" This popular question has raised speculation since the second century, because Hebrews provides no personal introduction of the author to his audience. As with other matters of background, we are almost entirely dependent on evidence internal to the book. So, what does the work reveal of its author?

It is widely recognized that Hebrews begins like a sermon rather than a letter. At 13:22 the author himself calls the document a "word [or message] of exhortation," a designation used elsewhere to refer to a sermon. The author of Hebrews may be said to have been a gifted expositor, thoroughly versed in the Old Testament and trained in the homiletical skills of his day. Whoever he was, we owe him respect for his rhetorical craftsmanship, admiration for the depth of his theological reflection, and gratitude for this enduring word of exhortation.

BOOK OUTLINE

I. Introduction: God Has Spoken to Us in a Son (1:1–4)
II. The Son Superior to the Angels, with an Exhortation to Attend his Word of Salvation (1:5–2:4)
III. The Son Became Incarnate to Die, with Exhortations to Faithfulness (2:5–4:13)
IV. The Son Appointed as High Priest, with Exhortations to Mature in the Faith (4:14–7:28)
V. The Son a Superior Sacrifice, with Exhortations to Endure in Faith (8:1–12:29)
VI. Closing, Practical Exhortations (13:1–19)
VII. Benediction and Conclusion (13:20–25)

HEBREWS 1:1–4

Original Meaning

The Climax of Divine Communication (1:1–2a). The older revelation mentioned here was expansive but incomplete. By contrast, the revelation of these last days has come "to us," the receptors of the Christian message. The whole of the incarnation—Christ's person, words, and acts—should be understood as communicating God's ultimate word to his new-covenant people.

The Person, Work, and Status of the Son (1:2b–4). The author of Hebrews provides seven affirmations describing the Son's person, work, and current status.

1. "Whom he appointed heir of all things" affirms the present and anticipates the future rule of Christ (v. 2b).
2. "through whom he made the universe," affirms the Father as the source of the created order and the Son as the Father's agent in the creative process (v. 2c).
3. He is "the radiance of God's glory and the exact representation of his being" (v. 3a). These phrases highlight the divine nature of the Son. To see the Son is to view God's glory or manifest presence. The Son provides a true and trustworthy picture of the person of the Father.
4. The Son is also the one "sustaining all things by his powerful word" (v. 3b). As the world was created by the word of God through the Son, it is sustained by the Son's powerful word.
5. "Purification for sins" is the introduction's reference to Christ's sacrificial death on the cross (v. 3c). What the Son "had provided" was a forgiveness that would be permanent and lead God' people into the very presence of God.
6. At the heart of the introduction, the author centers on the Son's present status as the one who "sat down" at God's right hand (v. 3c). This allusion to Psalm 110:1 highlights Jesus's messiahship, vindication (through resurrection and exaltation), role as judge, lordship, and his intercession on behalf of believers.
7. The result of this exaltation is that the Son "became as much superior to the angels as the name he has inherited is superior to theirs" (v. 4). The Son has moved to a position of authority and governance above the status of the angels.

Application. The Scriptures were written to change, mold, and direct the lives of God's people. Yet grave danger lies in focusing on the "practical" teachings of Scripture to the neglect of the "theological." Theology and practice are both vitally important aspects of following Christ. Notice that in his introduction to the book, the author of Hebrews lays a robust theological foundation for his entire sermon. He uses sound doctrine as a precursor to praxis.

HEBREWS 1:5–14

Original Meaning

The Son's Unique Relationship to the Father (1:5). The author begins with a question: "For to which of the angels did God ever say . . . ?" Rather than a request for information, this query is rhetorical, a way of making an assertion. The writer is, in fact, proclaiming, "There is no angel to whom God has said . . . !" The two quotations in verse 5 continue a focus on the sonship of Jesus started in 1:2. Both Psalm 2:7 and 2 Samuel 7:14 had been adopted in earliest Christianity as pointing to the enthronement of Messiah.

The Inferior Position of the Angels (1:6–7). The term "firstborn" (*prototokos*) continues the idea of sonship established thus far in Hebrews. It had strong religious overtones in the consecration of the firstborn to Yahweh in the Old Testament. A firstborn son had a special place in the heart of his father, shared the father's authority, and inherited the lion's share of his property. It serves as a title for Christ, expressing his preeminence in the church and the cosmos, and is especially associated with the resurrection.

Verses 6–7 present the angels in two activities that imply their subordination to the Son. First, with the quote of Psalm 97:7, they are exhorted to "worship" the Son. In contexts accentuating God's power and majesty, angels worship him. It is therefore of no small significance that they here are said to worship the Son, an implicit acclamation of his deity. Second, Psalm 104:4 expresses their role as servants of God—a theme made more clear by the author's recapitulation of, and further comment on, this passage later at Hebrews 1:14.

The Eternality of the Son's Reign and Relationship to the Cosmos (1:8–12). The preacher's third pair of Old Testament texts returns full attention to the Son. These two passages focus on three overarching themes. First, they speak of the Son's authority. The Son sits on a "throne," has a "scepter," and has a "kingdom" (v. 8). Furthermore, he has been anointed "above [his] companions" as king (v. 9). He is also the one with the authority to lay "the foundations of the earth" and to mold "the heavens" with his "hands" (v. 10).

Second, the author's use of these texts draws attention to the Son's eternal nature. Messiah's kingdom is one that "will last for ever and ever" (v. 8). The Lord was there "in the beginning" (v. 10), and his "years will never end" (v. 12). By contrast, the created order changes, becoming old and perishable. Like old and worn clothing, the Son will fold it up at the end of the age (vv. 11–12), but he remains "the same" (v. 12).

Finally, in addition to the affirmation of the Son's deity implied in these creation statements, verse 8 has one of the most explicit references to Jesus as God found in the New Testament: "Your throne, O God, will last for ever and ever" (quoting Ps 45:6–7).

The Son's Position at the Right Hand in Contrast with the Position of the Angels (1:13–14). The author's string of Old Testament quotations comes to its zenith with his quote of Psalm 110:1: "Sit at my right hand until I make your enemies a footstool for your feet." The difference between the allusion to Psalm 110:1 found earlier at 1:3 and the direct quote of this text here at verse 13 is that the quotation here includes "until I make your enemies a footstool for your feet." The enthronement of the Son has a corresponding implication—defeat for the enemies of God and his Messiah.

Application. It is no exaggeration to suggest that Western culture in general and the church in particular are in the midst of an authority crisis. In this section, the author uses a chain of Old Testament quotations to a specific end. He focuses the listeners' attention on the preeminent position of Jesus in order to draw them to the preeminent authority of Jesus. Therefore, these verses speak volumes to an age grappling with issues of authority—to whom should we listen; whom can we trust; who has the right answers to our life questions?

HEBREWS 2:1–4

Original Meaning

A Caution against Drifting (2:1). The object of our attention is "what we have heard"—that is, the word spoken via the Son (1:2). The image of "drifting" could signify objects that slip away, such as a ring that slips off the finger or a ship drifting, missing a harbor it intended to enter because of strong currents or winds.

Motivation for Heeding This Admonition (2:2–3a). In verses 2–3a the author utilizes an argument "from lesser to greater" to motivate the congregation to action. Punishment received for rejecting what God spoke through angels under the old covenant constitutes the "lesser" situation in this case. The older covenant message delivered through angels was "binding"; to neglect that word brought about sure, severe punishment.

The preacher continues by presenting the "greater" situation in the form of a rhetorical question. God's punishment of the disobedient in the lesser situation provides a basis for the assumption that even more severe punishment will be forthcoming in the greater. The word rendered "ignore" in verse 3a means to neglect through apathy or not to care enough about something.

Those who care so little about the word of salvation that they neglect it will find no escape from the punishment they deserve.

The Message of Salvation (2:3b–4). Neither the author nor the recipients of Hebrews had directly heard Jesus preach the message of salvation; they were second-generation Christians, having received that word from "those who heard him." The word "confirm" carries the sense of firm assurance or guarantee. Thus, although the author and his hearers had not heard the message of salvation from the mouth of Jesus himself, it was something they could count on absolutely.

God has not simply spoken a word of confirmation but has acted in "signs, wonders and various miracles." The triple expression was used in early Christianity to speak of God's activity among his people accompanying the preaching of the gospel. The phenomena played a significant role in the apologetics of early Christian preachers.

Application. The author of Hebrews looks to the confirmation of the gospel by the first witnesses and by God himself as significant. Faith in the message is not a leap in the dark but a decision to commit oneself to God through Christ, based on the reliable testimony of the apostles. The apostolic tradition helps Christians stay true to the salvation preached by Jesus. To drift away from this message, to treat it carelessly, invites spiritual ruin. On the other hand, to pay close attention to the word of salvation provides stability in our trek as followers of Christ, for that word of deliverance constitutes a foundation stone in one's relationship to God.

HEBREWS 2:5–9

Original Meaning

Submission of All Things to Christ (2:5–8a). Judaism held to the belief that angels had been placed by God over the nations of the world. The basis for this belief went back to an interpretation of Deuteronomy 32:8, which referred to the boundaries of the nations as set according to the number of God's angels. The quote of Psalm 110:1 in Hebrews 1:13 gives rise to the statement here in Hebrews 2:5 that "it is not to angels that he has subjected the world to come, about which we are speaking." The author has in mind the part of Psalm 110 that reads, "until I make your enemies a footstool for your feet" (Ps 110:1). All the powers of the universe must submit to Christ—even those that do not do so willingly.

The statement about the incarnation in Psalm 8, as interpreted by our author in verse 7, reads, "You made him a little lower than the angels." The author is expressing the thought that Christ walked the earth as a human being for a brief time before being exalted back to heaven.

What We Do and Do Not See at Present (2:8b–9). Psalms 110:1 and 8:4–6 seem to contradict at a crucial point. Psalm 110:1 looks to the future, while Psalm 8:6 speaks of the subjugation as an accomplished fact. Given the potential puzzlement arising from the two passages, our author, in effect, answers the question, "Have all things been subjugated to the Son, or does his universal dominance lie in the future?" with "Both!" This tension between what is present reality but not yet seen expresses what may be referred to as the inaugurated rule of Christ.

To "see" Jesus (v. 9a) does not mean a physical perception, but rather a spiritual perception, recognizing both the witness of his earthly endurance and his present exalted position. The preacher specifies the means by which Jesus was crowned with glory and honor: "because he suffered death" (v. 9b).

Application. Why, at times, does God sometimes seem to refuse to respond to our desperate cries for help? The answer to our dilemma lies in our perception of reality and specifically the nature of the Christian faith. In the West especially, *feeling better has become more important than finding God.* To focus on our situations, our problems, our pains as primary (rather than the ultimate purposes of God) is to move away from an essential element of following Christ. We must follow Christ in the way of suffering. The problem of evil lies not in God's abilities, nor even in our perception of his will and timing, but in our perception of Jesus. As a pilot in a dense fog keeps on course by looking to the instruments, Jesus provides a reference point from which to assess the greater realities of any given situation. What we need is to "see Jesus" (2:8–9) in his incarnation and exaltation. The "in-between time" flanked by Christ's first and second comings is a time of tears, suffering, persecution, and death. But God's promise in Christ is ultimate salvation, healing, joy, and eternal life for God's people in the age of hope that looms on the horizon, dwarfing the pains of the present.

HEBREWS 2:10–18

Original Meaning

The Appropriateness of the Son's Suffering (2:10). In verse 10 the author proclaims that what God has done in the suffering of Jesus is in line with what we know of his character and purposes. God uses Jesus's death in "bringing" heirs with Christ to "glory," moving from earth to heaven. *Archēgos* (rendered "pioneer" by the NIV) might be translated better by "champion"—the divine hero common in the ancient Greek world—expressing a meaningful analogy that Jesus has come to our rescue.

Perfection in Hebrews has to do with fully completing a course, making it to the end of God's plan. That Jesus was made "perfect" through suffering, therefore, connotes his full obedience to his mission of death on the cross and, perhaps, the adequacy of that act for bringing the children of God to glory.

The Son's Solidarity with the "Sons" (2:11–13). The solidarity between the Son of God and the heirs of God results in a graciousness on the part of Christ: he is not ashamed to call us family. In verses 12–13 the author sets forth two texts, Psalm 22:22 and Isaiah 8:17b–18, as Old Testament support for Christ's solidarity with believers.

The Reasons for the Incarnation (2:14–16). The author next turns to address the necessity of the incarnation. It might help to work our way backward through the logic of his argument in verse 14. The goal of the incarnation was twofold. First, by becoming human the Son sought to "break the power of him who holds the power of death—that is, the devil." The devil was undone, and death's bite was rendered insipid by Christ's death, specifically his sacrifice for sin (cf. 1 Cor 15:56). Since death was the prescription for victory in this case, the only way the Son could accomplish the needed task was to die, and the only way to die was to become human. This is, for our author, the logic of the incarnation.

Second, in verse 15 the preacher considers the second happy outcome of the incarnation: a believer's fear of death no longer paralyzes and enslaves because Jesus has disabled death's master. As our champion, he has stormed the very gates of the enemy and laid hold of his stronghold, opening wide the doors of our captivity and pointing us to the path of freedom. The congregation, having been exposed to early Christian doctrine, would have understood that Jesus's sacrifice on the cross was not for angels but for those who inherit the promises of Abraham.

Conclusion (2:17–18). With the final two verses of this passage, the author sets up an effective transition to the great central section of Hebrews on Jesus's high priesthood. Through these concepts the preacher introduces an expansion on his reasons for the incarnation built around the high-priest motif, which he expounds in 4:14–10:25.

Application. What is missed both by those who deny the divinity of Jesus and those who reject his full humanity is that we as human beings needed a bridge between deity and humanity that could be built only by one who had experienced fully both sides of the gulf separating us from God. This is the biblical picture.

What is surprising is the form our champion took and the means of our liberation. The one of all power took the position of the powerless. The Lord of life drank deeply of death. The way he brought us up to God was by coming completely down to, and even below, our level, taking the form of a servant. Since we could not save ourselves, he did not save himself from the worst of human experiences. The limitless Lord of the universe took on limitations in order to free us from ours, and nowhere are our limitations more clearly recognized than in the face of death.

HEBREWS 3:1–19

Original Meaning

A Positive Example: Jesus's Faithfulness as a Son (3:1–6). The verbal form "share" in the NIV actually translates a plural noun meaning "partakers" or "sharers" (*metochoi*, v. 1). In the ancient world, this word sometimes meant a housemate or business associate. Here in verse 1 the term connotes an intimate relationship forged in a common spiritual reality.

The command to "fix your thoughts on Jesus" (v. 1) forms the core of the author's exhortation. "Fix your thoughts" renders the verb *katanoeō*, which can mean "consider, think about, notice, observe." The challenge seems to be to carefully consider the example of Jesus.

Hebrews 3:1 is the only place in the New Testament where Jesus is called an "apostle." This unusual designation for God's Son probably concerns his role as the one sent to proclaim God's name and message. Furthermore, we are to fix our thoughts on Jesus's being "faithful to the one who appointed him" (i.e., to God, v. 2). The focus of our attention, therefore, rests not only on the exalted Lord, but on the Incarnate One, who remained true to God's appointment amid adverse circumstances.

Jesus's faithfulness is comparable to that of Moses. They both were true to the calling they had received from God. That Moses was faithful over a "house" (v. 2) alludes specifically to Numbers 12:7 and means that his ministry involved establishment of and responsibility for a defined group of people in special relationship to God.

Whereas verse 2 draws a comparison between Jesus and Moses, verse 3 begins a treatment of the contrast between the two great figures—a contrast meant to highlight the superiority of Jesus's example. This proclamation of Jesus's superior worthiness expands in two directions. First, in verses 3–4 the author draws an analogy using architectural imagery, probably playing off the reference to "house" in verse 2. Second, in verses 5–6 he proclaim Jesus as worthy of more glory than Moses by comparing their respective earthly roles, executed in faithfulness to God the Father.

The author then shifts from the examples of Moses, and especially Jesus, to confronting the listeners with the question of their own faithfulness. The word rendered "hold firmly" (*katechō*) in verse 6 could be used by ancient authors to mean "hold to, keep, detain, contain, occupy, or possess." The word is used to speak of keeping a tight grip on the Christian faith, keeping it from slipping away. "Confidence" (*parēssia*, v. 6) connotes public boldness, the opposite of shrinking from an open stand with the community of faith. We may be considered part of the people of God *if* we hold fast to the Christian faith.

A Negative Example: The Faithless of the Desert (3:7–19). To change the direction of the discussion, the author employs Psalm 95:7c–11 as a catalyst. The phrase "as the Holy Spirit says" (v. 7) demonstrates the author's view that this admonition provides a direct, fresh, contemporary word to his listeners. The exhortation "do not harden your hearts" lies at the center of the first part (v. 8). The next portion ("as you did in the rebellion" and running through the end of verse 9) offers an example or illustration. The final segment confronts the hearers with the judgment experienced by that rebellious generation.

In verses 12–19 the author of Hebrews takes concepts from the psalm, weaving them into a potent commentary and exhortation. The hearers are to "encourage one another daily" (v. 13) so that none of them will experience a spiritual hardening brought on by sin's deceitfulness. If it was to be avoided, however, the recipients had to relate to one another in an atmosphere of encouragement.

Continuing with another sober word of warning, at 3:1 the author addresses the community as sharers "in the heavenly calling," but in verse 14 he places a condition on that designation. The condition placed on being companions of Christ has to do with holding "firmly to the very end." The word speaks of the dependability or firmness of a commitment expressed with assurance at the inception of each believer's relationship with the Lord. Thus, real Christian experience contains the quality of durability.

In verse 15 the preacher ends by quoting again the "exhortation" portion of the psalm (Ps 95:7b–8a). This section of the psalm serves as a summary for verses 12–14. The quotation in verse 15 also leads into the final segment of this unit.

In verses 16–19 the author follows a stylistic pattern of asking a question and then providing an answer. The questions at the beginning of each verse are taken directly from the quote of Psalm 95:7c–11. The answers provided, however, derive from other Old Testament passages that have to do with the desert wanderings (Num 14:1–38; Deut 9; Ps 106). The unit concludes with a summary statement in verse 19, explaining that at its core the wanderers' inability to enter God's rest stemmed from their unbelief, thus linking the concepts of unbelief and disobedience.

Application. Biblical theology provides a rich spectrum of truths about humanity and our relationship to God. From God's sovereignty to human responsibility, from grace to judgment, from the deity of Christ to his humanity, from conversion to salvation consummated (i.e., glorification), many doctrinal truths must be held in balance with related, equally important truths. To focus on parts of Scripture to the exclusion of other parts proves damaging to the church and individual Christians, and we often get things out of balance. This tendency suggests one reason why systematic, exegetical study of the Bible is so important. Through such study we confront the whole counsel of God and, hopefully, adjust our perspectives accordingly.

The qualifications in 3:6, 14 highlight areas in which many modern evangelicals have lost balance doctrinally and end up giving converts to the Christian faith false assurances in relation to salvation. The problem stems not from heresy per se, but from an emphasis on certain biblical teachings to the practical exclusion of others. Hebrews calls us to consider how we must adjust our thinking and practice.

We have no right to give assurance to those who have turned their backs on God—in fact, we should affirm their lack of assurance! We must never say, "I remember when you accepted Christ," or "You went through confirmation when you were twelve," using those experiences as a basis for giving them assurance of God's acceptance. We cannot look into a person's heart and see his or her spiritual condition. It would be better to say, "Since you have turned your back on God, the validity of your relationship with Christ has been called into question. You need to repent and examine yourself to see if you are in the faith." The author of Hebrews does challenge his hearers to remember their past confession of Christ (4:14; 10:23)—but as a basis for faithfulness rather than as a basis for assurance.

HEBREWS 4:1–13

Original Meaning

Transition: From the Problem of the Wanderers to the Promise of Rest "Today" (4:1–2). The author of Hebrews frequently uses the Greek word *oun* ("therefore") to introduce a given action that has been or should be undertaken. The word "since" interprets the participle *kataleipomenēs* as causal, that is, "because the promise . . . still stands." It would be better to understand the participle as temporal, communicating duration: "while the promise of entering his rest still stands." This clause anticipates a fuller argument in 4:6–10.

What gives rise to fear is the possibility that any of the community's number should appear to have fallen short. The author does not say unequivocally that any particular person has fallen short, but that appropriate caution is in order since that possibility exists. The perfect infinitive "to have fallen short" suggests that this spiritual state consists of one never truly having entered the rest of God.

This supposition finds further support in verse 2, which capitalizes on the negative example of the Old Testament fallen. The Israelite community physically may have heard words, but their hearing was "faith-less." The caution in verses 1–2 pertains to those of the community whose response to the gospel parallels the faith-vacant response of those who fell in the desert when offered entrance into the land of Canaan.

Identification of the "Rest" (4:3–5). What is this "rest" of which the preacher speaks, and which should be an object of concern for the community? The "rest" is something a believer enters (and thus experiences) now, but this rest in its fullness remains a promised destination for the future.

The Promise of Rest Still Stands (4:6–11). In verse 6 the preacher proclaims, "It still remains for some to enter that rest." That a rest "remains" for some means that the issue of rest was not closed with those disobedient ones to whom God had originally promised rest in the land.

An important clue to the specific Sabbath rest the author has in mind in verse 9 may be found in the book of Leviticus. It must be admitted, of course, that the author does not make an overt reference to Leviticus. However, the broader context in which he mentions the preaching of the gospel (4:1–2)—a message that included the forgiveness of sins—and the passage of our great high priest into the heavenly Most Holy Place (4:14), can be said to support such a tie. In this interpretation the Sabbath is a new-covenant Day of Atonement, in which God's people are cleansed from their sins.

In verse 11 the author follows with an exhortation and a rationale. Those of the author's community who have yet to combine faith with hearing the gospel must demonstrate their faith by active obedience rather than by passive repose.

Here, then, the reader confronts a paradox—the true, spiritual rest of God, in which one is cleansed from sin, may be entered not by cessation of effort but by its application. The hearers of Hebrews must not stop short of obedience to God's call. To stop short—that is, failing to combine hearing of the gospel with faith (i.e., trusting obedience, 4:1–2)—results in spiritual devastation.

Warning: Consider the Power of God's Word (4:12–13). Verses 12–13 evince masterful literary craftsmanship and have captivated the attention of Christians through the ages. The author describes God's word as "alive and active." It is not static and passive but dynamic, interactive, and transforming as it interfaces with the people of God. The sword imagery emphasizes that while God's word is a word of promise to those who would enter God's rest, it is also a discerning word of judgment. Verse 12 asserts that like a sword that cuts and thrusts, the word penetrates and divides, being able to reach into the depths of a person's inner life.

Lest one think carelessly about the extent of God's discernment, the author assures us through verse 13. The word translated "uncovered" (*gymnos*) calls to mind a complete inability to hide anything from God's gaze.

Application. Spiritual wandering and its resulting fatigue are not new problems. Jesus, the new Joshua, looks out on a desert-wandering humanity, and his solution is, "Come to *me*." Not, "Come to a set of teachings"; not, "Come to church"; not, "Come to your psychologist"; not, "Come to a vacation." No. Rather, he says, "Come to me." Jesus offers the ultimate source for true rest, for true rest is found only in a right relationship with God. The rest is *his* rest, for *his* people, found by obeying *his* word. In the wake of a culture leaving the fragmented, fragile, and fatigued in its wake, the church has the phenomenal opportunity of pointing people to the ultimate land of promise and spiritual well-being.

HEBREWS 4:14–16

Original Meaning

Hold Firmly to the Faith (4:14–15). The theme of Jesus's high priesthood occupies the author's attention from 4:14 to 10:25. For him, our high priest is "great" for a number of reasons that are explained in chapters 5–10. The present passage (4:14–16) focuses in part on the ministry of Jesus in which he entered the heavenly Most Holy Place to present his superior offering (cf. 8:2; 9:11, 23–24).

The author encourages his hearers with the words "let us hold firmly to the faith we profess" (v. 14). The author of Hebrews is calling the recipients of this sermon to remain committed to Jesus, holding to their public confession of him as the Son of God. Endurance in this commitment finds its basis in the follower's relationship to Christ as a heavenly high priest.

The author elaborates on Jesus's high priesthood in verse 15. We have a high priest who, because of his experience of temptation, can empathize with our weaknesses. In this passage, the word "empathize" does not necessitate a sharing of another's exact experience (cf. 10:34, where the hearers are said to have sympathized with prisoners, though not being prisoners themselves). Yet Christ, our high priest, does not stand aloof but cares for us in our human state of weakness.

Draw Near to God (4:16). The exhortation "let us approach" translates a present-tense form of the verb, indicating that drawing near to God constitutes an ongoing aspect of the Christian's relationship with God: "let us constantly approach." Under

Jesus's high priesthood, the people of God may enter the very presence of God on a continual basis and can do so with "confidence." Christians, therefore, should draw near to God with unabashed openness since God alone is the true source of mercy and grace.

Application. The fact of the matter is that we find it much more natural to drift or run away from God than to draw near to him. Thus, we leave the church or tune out the preacher, return to old, sinful patterns of life, or simply stop meeting with God for prayer and Bible study. In this fallen world the gravitational pull downward of the world, the flesh, and the devil at times makes a move toward God seem the most unnatural action in the world.

It is not natural to draw near to God; it is supernatural, and he has called us to himself away from the natural pulls and thoughts of the world. His invitation and promises still stand. Our part is to respond to his call and approach the throne. Our sympathetic high priest has experienced the temptation to bolt and run. He has been with us in our humanness and invites us to be with him at the throne of grace. Therefore, we may approach with unabashed boldness. Let us make that approach today, for we will surely find timely help for whatever we need.

HEBREWS 5:1–10

Original Meaning

Universal Principles of High Priesthood (5:1–4). When the author states "every high priest" (v. 1), he begins arguing for the superiority of Christ's high priesthood on the basis of commonly understood truths from the Old Testament. In essence he asserts: "This is how the office of high priest works according to the Scriptures." The high priest has a solidarity with people because he is taken "from among" them (v. 1). The author continues a theme treated in 2:10–18: the Son came down "among humanity" to accomplish something on our behalf.

Further, the high priest represents people "in matters related to God," especially in the offering of "gifts and sacrifices" (v. 1). By carrying out God's instructions, the high priest acts before God as a representative on behalf of the people, making atonement for their sins.

The next principle relates to another important aspect of the Day of Atonement: the high priest must offer a special sacrifice for himself before he can offer sacrifices on behalf of the people (vv. 2–3). Here the priest finds himself closed in by his own weakness, obligated to offer sacrifices for his own sins. It was for just this type of person—the person who, because of human moral weakness, has unintentionally wandered off the path of right living—that God designed the old covenant sin offerings.

Finally, the author of Hebrews next proclaims that the office of high priest is not one for which a person can enlist; God initiated the role, and any high priest must be called by God to be considered the authentic and authoritative representative for the people before God (v. 4).

The Appointment of Christ as High Priest (5:5–6). In verses 5–6 the author focuses on the glory bestowed by God the Father on the occasion of the Son's appointment to high priesthood, finding evidence for this honor in the Psalms. Once again the author draws on the rabbinic technique of "verbal analogy" to set up his argument, coupling Psalm 2:7 and 110:4 by virtue of their common elements. Both psalms contain a pronouncement by God in the second person ("You are . . ."). Consequently, the ancient exegete finds in these two passages a declaration made by God to Jesus.

The Path to Appointment (5:7–10). The phrase "during the days of Jesus's life on earth" makes an overt reference to Jesus's incarnation in general, but the rest of verses 7–8 hints at a specific event—Jesus's agonizing surrender to the Father's will in the garden of Gethsemane. While the outcome of Gethsemane may suggest that God did not "hear" that prayer in the sense of exempting Christ from the cross, God did "hear" it, affirming the righteousness of his Son's reverent submission through the resurrection.

When the author says in verses 8–9 that Christ "learned obedience" and was "made perfect," he is not suggesting that the Son had been disobedient and flawed. Rather, Jesus's call involved walking obediently all the way to the end of a path to which the Father had appointed him.

Verse 9 proclaims that the Son became "the source of eternal salvation." The affirmation links the perfection process closely to the cross, where our great high priest offered up himself as the sacrifice for sin. As a result of the Son's suffering, he has been appointed by God to fill the position of high priest according to "the order of Melchizedek" (v. 10).

Application. As an appropriate application of 5:1–10, we might begin by reflecting on our current motivations for engaging in Christ-following. Why are you doing what you are doing? Why am I? Is the fact that God has appointed Jesus to a position of honor in which we are called to obey him significant enough for us to serve as motivation for continuing in our commitment? Or are we more moved (as is evident by our actions and decisions) by the call of our world's system of values? Danger lies in embracing the world's value system, for she is a mother who often eats her young.

HEBREWS 5:11–6:3

Original Meaning

The Author Confronts the Hearers (5:11–14). Our preacher finds the hearers' condition especially egregious in light of their long-term involvement in the church ("by this time you ought to be teachers," v. 12). The content of the needed instruction is described as "elementary truths." The use of "milk" and "solid food" as metaphors for basic teachings were common in the ancient world. Spiritually they are acting like babies still suckling at a mother's breast, unconcerned with the rich, hearty foods of the adults' table.

The moral failure in the face of persecution must be understood as stemming from a lack of response to theological instruction (cf. 2:1–4). These milk drinkers have neither an understanding nor an inclination toward deeper matters of the faith by which one understands the importance and means of perseverance.

"The mature" (v. 14), on the other hand, are able to handle "solid food." In other words, they know how to make the right choices when confronted with critical decisions. The author's hope is that they will repent of their spiritual immaturity, grasp hold of the deeper matters of the faith, and ultimately endure in the face of persecution.

Moving on to Maturity (6:1–3). The author does not see these Christian principles as dispensable. Rather, the fundamental truths of the faith are presupposed in the continued trek toward maturity. "Cleansing rites" (or "baptisms," v. 2) may refer to the internal spiritual cleansing from sins found in the new covenant. The "laying on of hands" was with the coming of the Holy Spirit or anointing for ministry. "Resurrection of the dead" and "eternal judgment" provide theological cornerstones related to the end of the age. The author sums up the admonition by expressing his confidence in the hearers and his own submission to God's will.

Application. Life has a way of forcing us to deal with theology—that is, what we believe about God—sooner or later. The difficult experiences of life raise important questions about God and what he is up to. The New Testament pattern is to educate God's people in the tenets of the faith from the beginning of Christian experience, providing them with the basic theological nurturing they will need for the journey and maturing them through ongoing feeding on God's word. All who are Christ-followers need systematic teaching of biblical truth, both at the beginning of our spiritual formation and along the way as we grow to maturity.

HEBREWS 6:4–12

Original Meaning

A Harsh Word of Warning (6:4–8). The first three verses of this unit cohere around the central assertion, "It is impossible for those . . . to be brought back to repentance" (vv. 4, 6). These people have experienced "the heavenly gift" (v. 4). They "have tasted the goodness of the word of God" (v. 5). At the climax comes the clause "who have fallen away" (v. 6). The harshness of the descriptions that follow "fall away" demands that it be understood in terms of a serious sin—that of rejecting Christ. It is impossible for those who have done so "to be brought back to repentance."

The assertion must be considered in the broader context of Hebrews. True repentance can be experienced only in the shadow of Christ's sacrifice. Repentance in verses 4–6 is "impossible" because there is nowhere else to go for repentance once one has rejected Christ. The apostate in effect has turned his or her back on the only means available for forgiveness before God.

The language of crucifixion and public shaming in verse 6 is both potent and ironic. Instead of being blessed by accepting the forgiveness found in the crucified Christ, the ones who have fallen away identify with those who used the cross as an ultimate expression of rejection. Instead of being shamed in the eyes of the world by identification with the Son, the apostates stand with those before the cross who cast insults, disparaging Christ's claims as the true Messiah.

An Encouraging Word (6:9–12). Having become persuaded of their genuine commitment to Christ, the author communicates a personal conviction, based on his observations, that his readers are on a path that will end in the consummation of their salvation. What is the basis of the writer's confidence in these people? Their faith has been lived out. Verse 11, however, again bears witness to a basic, though often neglected, dynamic in this author's sermon—the uncertainty that surrounds any evaluation of another person's status before God apart from continued manifestations of God's grace. In other words, if the outward manifestations of genuineness cease, confidence evaporates. The author does not want his readers to lapse into laziness, but rather "to imitate those who through faith and patience inherit what has been promised" (v. 12).

Application. Anyone engaged in Christian ministry has certainly struggled with the pain and confusion of seeing those who have come into the church suddenly turn and walk away as if their professions of Christ were meaningless. How are we to respond? To those who have fallen away or are close to falling away we should offer strong warnings in line with Hebrews 6:4–8. For those who have come into the church, who have struggled to throw off spiritual mediocrity and maintain passion about Christian commitment, we should offer encouragement, pointing to God's approval of our diligence to remain faithful even amid dry and difficult times.

HEBREWS 6:13–20

Original Meaning

The Example of Abraham (6:13–15). For those oriented to the Jewish Scriptures, the author could have chosen no greater example of faithful perseverance than father Abraham. Especially apropos, the moment at which Abraham offered his cherished son, Isaac, at Moriah (Gen 22:1–18) forms the backdrop of the discussion here in these verses.

The Finality of Oaths (6:16–18). If truthfulness can be confirmed in human courts of law, it is even more assured when God himself swears an oath. God's oath shows the "unchanging nature of his purpose" in granting to the heirs their promised inheritance (v. 17). So the heirs need not worry that the terms of God's promised inheritance are going to change.

God intends that his heirs, "who have fled to take hold of the hope set before us," might find strong encouragement from his oath making (v. 18). We have turned from our former lives of sin and despair and to Christ for salvation, stability, and security. The foundation for our encouragement rests in the character of God, who cannot lie.

The Encouragement of a Firm Hope (6:19–20). Our hope, as an anchor for the soul, is both "firm" and "secure." Thus, our hope as an anchor offers both safety and a reliable basis for living. The security of our souls rests firmly in the eternal, high-priestly work of Christ, by which he has entered into God's presence on our behalf and made a way for us to follow.

Application. To this current age of despair Hebrews brings another perspective. God says that life is *more* than what can be seen immediately, and he offers us a wealth of spiritual resources to be found in relation to Jesus Christ. Those spiritual resources are accessed as we trust God's word and build our lives on it. His "oaths" help us to see beyond our limitations to his limitless power and provisions. Encouragement comes from knowing we play a part in a life both full of meaning and lasting. Thus, our current circumstances can never adequately define who we are or what we are about. This quality of hope produces hope. As Paul states, "May the God of hope fill you with all joy and peace as you trust in him, so that you may overflow with hope by the power of the Holy Spirit" (Rom 15:13). This age of angst asks, "Is there more?" The Christian conviction rings out: "Yes, and so we dare to hope."

HEBREWS 7:1–10

Original Meaning

An Exposition on Melchizedek (7:1–3). In verses 1–3 the writer to the Hebrews briefly expounds Genesis 14:17–20, demonstrating typological connections between Melchizedek and the Son of God. The writer capitalizes on Genesis 14's lack of any reference to Melchizedek's ancestry, birth, or death. His point is not that Melchizedek exists as some form of supernatural being. Rather, he focuses on the details of what the narrative does and does not say, anticipating a stark contrast between Melchizedek's priesthood and the Levitical priesthood, which he will develop later in the chapter.

The Greatness of Melchizedek (7:4–10). The author calls his hearers to grasp the greatness of Melchizedek, since Genesis has Abraham, the father of those who would become the Levites, giving a tithe to the priest Melchizedek, who obviously was not of the tribe of Levi (Heb 7:5–6). Thus the Levites, in a sense, paid a tenth to Melchizedek (vv. 9–10)! That father Abraham (and the Levites in his body) gave a tithe to this priest shows Abraham's deference to him and respect for his unique service on behalf of God Most High.

By virtue of his greater position, Melchizedek in turn blessed Abraham. Our author, based on his broader argument concerning the tithe and the eternality of Melchizedek's priesthood, parenthetically proclaims (rather than argues for) the superiority of Melchizedek in connection with the blessing offered by him. Melchizedek's superiority to the Levites primarily rests on his having received a tenth of the spoils from Abraham and the fact that Scripture gives no indication of his death.

Application. In Hebrews 7 the author is thinking critically and inviting us to think with him. His arguments are logical and well crafted, drawing us into analysis of the Old Testament material. We cannot deal with Hebrews 7 in terms of the heart alone. The head must come into play or one's reading of the text is awash. The author is leading us somewhere with his logic. We are moving once again toward a call to total commitment to Christ. Heart, mind, emotions, and strength all will be called upon shortly. Nevertheless, we must begin here, with rationales for why we must act a certain way. Here we, with the author of Hebrews, begin by loving God with our minds.

HEBREWS 7:11–28

Original Meaning

The Rules Have Changed (7:11–19). As a rhetorical question, verse 11 in reality makes a strong assertion. This assertion in the form of a question proclaims, "Since God's ultimate goal of establishing an eternal relationship between himself and people could not be attained through the Levitical priesthood, there was still a need for a priesthood to arrive that could bring that perfection."

Psalm 110:4 shows that a priest of a new order has come. In Hebrews 7:12, therefore, the author explains that a change to a Melchizedekan priesthood heralds a change in the law of genealogical descent. Jesus, the one appointed to high priesthood by God's oath of Psalm 110:4, does not meet the requirement of genealogical descent established under the Mosaic law (Heb 7:13–14). God has changed the rules for priesthood. In Jesus one understands clearly that this new high priest has been appointed not on the basis of ancestry, since he was from the tribe of Judah, but on the basis of his immortality, the author seizing on the term "forever" in Psalm 110:4 (Heb 7:16–17).

The argument continues in verses 18–19 by providing the reason for Jesus's having been appointed by God as a new type of priest. The old-covenant regulation concerning the priestly office could not and did not bring about God's ultimate relational aim for his people. Consequently, with the appointment of Jesus to priesthood, God introduces a "better hope" (v. 19).

The Power of a Divine Oath (7:20–22). The old-covenant priests became priests by genealogical descent—a completely different means of appointment than that seen in the case of the exalted Son. The writer to the Hebrews sees clearly that God, in Psalm 110:4, used an oath in his Son's case: "The Lord has sworn. . . ." Because of the unequivocal nature of God's oath, all danger of some change in the future has been wiped away. Thus, Jesus has become the "guarantor" of a better covenant (Heb 7:22).

The Permanent Priest (7:23–25). With verses 23–24 the author introduces yet another stark contrast between Jesus and the old-covenant priests. The mortality of its members may be seen as an inherent weakness in the old-covenant priesthood, and this weakness requires the genealogical aspect of priestly appointment under the old covenant. Since this weakness does not apply to Christ, neither does the genealogical requirement, and therefore his office will not be ceded to a subsequent generation.

Consequently, since Christ's priesthood lasts forever, there are no limitations on the mediation he offers between us and God. His priestly ministry brings a complete salvation in that it not only offers temporary deliverance from sin but perfects those who come to God through him for all time (cf. 10:1–3). In Jesus we have a priest who provides salvation for us perpetually and completely. Moreover, in his office of high priest, the Son makes continuous intercession on our behalf (7:25). The confession of the exalted Christ's intercession for his followers finds expression elsewhere in the New Testament.

A Summary and Transition (7:26–28). The descriptions here all emphasize the Son's sinless character in contrast to the sinfulness of the earthly priests. Unlike them he has no need to offer a sacrifice *for* himself but rather has offered the sacrifice *of* himself. Furthermore, whereas the ministry of the earthly high priest extended only to the tabernacle's Most Holy Place, Jesus's high-priestly ministry reaches into heaven. Unlike earthly priests, who must offer sacrifices day after day, this high priest's sacrifice has been made once for all time. The old priests were appointed by virtue of the law but were weak, but the Son was appointed by virtue of God's oath and has been "made perfect forever" (v. 28).

Application. In chapter 7 Hebrews proclaims the eternality of the Son's high priesthood. Thus, in the view of Hebrews, this order—this paradigm, if you will—by its very nature will not change. God's new-covenant way of relating to people, therefore, will never be altered. Thus, religions such as Islam and Mormonism amount to *contradictions* of Hebrews 7 rather than progressive revelations, since they suggest a different view of Christ than one finds in Hebrews and the rest of the New Testament. Consequently, Hebrews's view of reality, grounded in the eternal high priesthood of the Son of God, offers us lasting stability for life.

HEBREWS 8:1–13

Original Meaning

An Important Transition (8:1–2). These two verses make an effective transition because they point back to the writer's discourse on the Son's appointment, while at the same time anticipating the primary themes of the coming discourse on the heavenly high priest's superior service. The wording "in heaven" serves the author's purpose by mentioning a main motif of the following material: the location of the Son's ministry. This position makes it superior to the earthbound priesthood of the old covenant.

Introduction on Christ's Superior, High-Priestly Ministry (8:3–6). With verse 3, our author reiterates the thought expressed by 5:1. Here, however, he places emphasis on the required need of an offering. In 8:4–5 he continues his transition from the previous chapter by noting points of contrast between the Levitical priests and the exalted Son; yet the focus here rests on a differentiation between the two locales of their ministries—that is, the heavenly and earthly realms.

Since the old-covenant priests were limited in their effectiveness by their mortality (cf. 7:11–28), the old-covenant place of worship must be seen ultimately as an ineffectual copy of the heavenly reality. Consequently, "the ministry Jesus has received is . . . superior to theirs" (8:6), and this superiority of his ministry as mediator corresponds to the superiority of the new covenant over the old.

The Superiority of the New Covenant (8:7–13). The concept of the new covenant occurs elsewhere in the New Testament, but nowhere with such extensive explanation as in Hebrews. In the passage under consideration, the author focuses on the inadequacy of the old covenant, a concept presented as intrinsic to Jeremiah 31. The logic is simple: the announcement of a new covenant proves that something had gone wrong with the first. The first covenant came up short, missing the mark, perhaps by its inability to deliver the fullness of relationship God ultimately desired with humanity.

The quotation of Jeremiah 31:31–34 in Hebrews 8:8–12 has three parts. First, the Lord promises a time when he will make a new covenant with the people of God (v. 8). Second, following from the word "new," this promise is qualified negatively, in that this covenant would *not* be like the Sinai covenant. The reason for this change of arrangements is also given: those led out of Egypt did not remain faithful to God's covenant (v. 9). Finally, the details of the new covenant are described positively. The laws of God will be placed on the minds and hearts of God's people, the relationship between God and his followers will be firmly established (v. 10), and everyone within the covenant will know the Lord (v. 11), because God will forgive their sins (v. 12). The emphasis on relationship and the internal quality of the effect on God's people is unmistakable. The new covenant, in essence, establishes a relationship with God. In that relationship the laws of God are internalized, and the forgiveness of sins is foundational.

Application. It is possible to love others and treat them with dignity even if we disagree with them. Such respect does not mean we must set aside our own convictions or cease having conversations with others who are open to such conversations. On the contrary, we must share the gospel boldly to be true to the message of the New Testament. Yet respect does mean that we will conduct those conversations sensitively and with grace (cf. Col 4:5–6), listening as well as sharing our own perspectives.

Pluralism was as pervasive in the first century as it is in the present one. If those win the day who wish for a revision of Christianity as a nondogmatic religion, able to fit in with the plethora of religious systems offered modern humankind, then Christianity—that of the stripe proclaimed by Hebrews—will surely be lost. Thankfully, there are many who refuse to surrender that brand of the Christian faith and find in it their motivation for love, compassion, and respect for people of whatever religious conviction.

Many in broader culture try to redefine our religion for us in terms foreign to the new covenant described in Hebrews 8. But the Christian faith cannot be conceptualized as merely a social association, a set of rules that may be incorporated into a pluralistic, global scheme of morality, a psychological pathology of guilt or gratification, or a mystical experience similar to those of other religions. No, biblical Christianity as described in Hebrews 8 must be understood minimally as involving the forgiveness of sins, a transformation of the inner life in accordance with the laws of God, and an intimate relationship with the living God. Certainly more can be said of our faith, and the New Testament provides us with extensive development of these motifs. However, any definition of Christian faith that neglects these realities must be considered suspect.

HEBREWS 9:1–10

Original Meaning

Introduction to the Passage and a Description of the Tabernacle (9:1–5). In describing the old-covenant worship structure, the author spotlights the tabernacle of the book of Exodus rather than the temple of his own era, thus keeping with his characteristic practice of drawing his material from the Scriptures. The description found in verses 2–5 moves from the outer room of the worship tent to the inner. The lampstand was made of pure gold, having six flowered branches extending from its sides, three to a side. Seven lamps also were made to sit on the stand, and the stand was placed on the south side of the Holy Place. The table, made of acacia wood and overlaid with gold, held the bread of the presence. This piece of furniture was situated on the north side of the outer room.

The curtain separated the outer room of the sanctuary from the "Most Holy Place" (v. 3). Verses 4–5 then present us with two elements peripheral to the author's main point. First, the golden altar of incense was located in the inner room of the sanctuary with the ark of the covenant. The author of Hebrews clearly follows a tradition emphasizing the placement of the altar within the Most Holy Place. Second, the ark of the covenant, a chest made of acacia wood and overlaid with gold, was the most important element of the tabernacle, for above its cover, between the cherubim, God met with Moses. In all ancient literature, Hebrews alone says that in addition to the stone tablets, the jar of manna and Aaron's staff were placed in the chest. Hebrews may follow a strand of rabbinic tradition that presupposed that elements were later placed inside the ark, along with the tablets.

Regulations for Worship (9:6–10). Corresponding to his structural discussion, which relates in order the setup of the "first" and "second" rooms of the tabernacle (vv. 2, 3), the author next explains briefly the ministry performed in each part. He again begins with the outer or first room and shows this to be the domain of the priests, who entered this chamber for their service (changing the bread of the presence or the lighting of the lamps on the lampstand). The emphasis here, however, rests on the daily performance of their service rather than what that service entailed, and on the location of that ministry in the Holy Place.

In contrast to the daily ministry of the priests in the first room of the sanctuary, the high priest was the only ministrant to enter the Most Holy Place, doing so only once a year on the Day of Atonement. This important sacrifice involved the offering of a bull's blood for his own sins and the sins of his household, and the blood of a goat for the sins of the people. In both cases, the blood was sprinkled on the ark cover and in front of it. This atonement offering was for the cleansing of the Most Holy Place. Here for the first time the author mentions "blood" in a cultic context (v. 7).

The writer then turns to a lesson that the Holy Spirit wishes to teach through these old-covenant regulations: during the old-covenant era there existed no means of entrance into the presence of God. That way had not been disclosed "as long as the first tabernacle was still functioning" (v. 8). Up to this point in the chapter the phrase *prōtē skēnē* ("first tent") has been used with reference to the outer room the Holy Place. This should also be the interpretation in verse 8. The Holy Place portrays a barrier space separating the people of God from the presence of God.

Does the "illustration for the present time" (v. 9) refer to the entire old system of worship or to the front room of the tabernacle just mentioned at the end of verse 8? The latter interpretation offers a more consistent reading of the passage. The outer room of the tabernacle, therefore, illustrates the whole era managed by the older covenant. It was a time in which the general populace could not draw near to God because provision had yet to be made for their consciences to be cleansed.

The problem under the old covenant consisted of the sacrificial system's inability to resolve one's awareness of personal guilt. Thus, the outer room of the tabernacle illustrated the inner, spiritual condition of the people. More than external regulations that dealt with practices regarding food, drink, and certain washings would be required to make entrance to the presence of God possible.

Application. God does not leave us to make a way into his presence. He gives specific instructions, for he is holy and we are sinful. There can be no digging a tunnel underneath the walls of the Most Holy Place, no barging in to demand our right to see God, no philosophizing about the "social constructs of religious knowledge," and no musings on "pluralism in modern religious thought" that can win us entrance. This was God's idea; it's his tent, and he makes the rules. We must come in by the path of a high priest or not come in at all.

HEBREWS 9:11–28

Original Meaning

Introduction (9:11–12). The significance of the Messiah's appearance is that he comes as a high priest of "good things that are now already here" (v. 11). The Greek phraseology continues to build a stark contrast between the old- and new-covenant systems. The "good things" are all those blessings associated with the new covenant (8:6), blessings that have now been ushered in by Christ's establishment of that better agreement.

The writer has two prominent Old Testament images in mind as he walks us through this part of his argument: the high priest's Day of Atonement sacrifice, and the sacrifice made by Moses to inaugurate the Sinai covenant. Christ's death on the cross incorporates and fulfills the meaning of both. At present the author stays with his high-priest motif and proclaims that, as the earthly high priest passed through the outer to the inner room of the sanctuary, so Christ "went through the greater and more perfect tabernacle" (9:11). What he has in mind is simply Christ's passage into the very presence of God in heaven (8:1).

This high priest did not enter the presence of God "by means of the blood of goats and calves," but "by his own blood," shed in sacrifice (9:12). Christ's entrance with "his own blood" refers to his sacrificial death on the cross, which established his mediatorial relationship between us and the Father, after he obtained our "eternal redemption." The word "redemption" can also be translated "liberation" or "deliverance." The deliverance involves deliverance from sin's penalty and is eternal in nature, Christ having entered "once for all."

The Superior Blood of Christ (9:13–22). The old-covenant high priest offered the most important sacrifices of Israel's year on the Day of Atonement (Lev 16:1–25). As noted in our treatment of Hebrews 5:1–3, the high priest first offered a special sacrifice for himself and his household and then presented the sacrifice on behalf of the people. Having cast lots for the two goats taken from among the Israelites, he slaughtered one of the goats as a sin offering "for the people" (Lev 16:15) and brought forth the other goat alive from the tent. The high priest then laid hands on the head of the "scapegoat," confessing all the sins of the people before the Lord, and then he sent it away into the desert (Lev 16:20–21). God instructed Aaron to take the blood of both the bull and the sacrificed goat "behind the curtain" so that the blood of each might be sprinkled on the atonement cover (Lev 16:15). Our writer refers to these rituals in verse 13.

In addition to "the blood of goats and calves," the writer of Hebrews mentions a third sacrifice not associated with the Day of Atonement. In Numbers 19:1–21, God commanded the Israelites to bring Moses and Aaron a red heifer, perfect in body and never having been under a yoke. The heifer was taken outside the camp and slaughtered, its blood sprinkled seven times toward the front of the tent of meeting. Then the animal was burned and its ashes collected for later use. When needed for ceremonial cleansing, the ashes were mixed with water and the mixture was sprinkled on the unclean person. The tabernacle also had to be sprinkled when an Israelite had touched a dead body, thus defiling the worship center. These offerings fade in contrast to the offering made by Christ. Because of his perfection, his sacrifice of himself is able to "cleanse our consciences from acts that lead to death" (v. 14).

With verse 15 the discussion shifts from a treatment of Christ's sacrifice vis-à-vis the sacrifices offered within old-covenant worship to the inauguration of a covenant through sacrifice. Christ as mediator of the new covenant has stood between God and people and accomplished the bringing of the two parties together. The result for the new people of God is that they receive the eternal inheritance.

This mediatorial relationship was established by Christ's death, in which he served as a ransom to liberate people from sins. Christ has liberated us, establishing a means by which we might be forgiven for our transgressions. This constitutes a blessing of the new covenant, in which the sins of God's people are remembered "no more" (8:12).

Regarding verses 16–17, the interpretation of *diathēkē* as "will" is out of step with the immediate discussion. In context the author focuses on the old-covenant sacrifices (vv. 12–14) and the establishment of the old covenant through sacrifice (vv. 18–22). We interpret the word here instead as yet another reference to the "covenant," and verses 16–17 proclaim simply that someone (represented by the sacrificial victim) had to die in order for the covenant to be established.

This reading of verses 16–17 in terms of sacrifice squares perfectly with what follows in verses 18–22, which relate Moses's inauguration of the Sinai covenant with sacrificial blood. The first covenant was inaugurated with the shedding of blood. In verses 19–21 the details of this Old Testament event are summarized. This use of blood in cleansing the various aspects of tabernacle worship demonstrates the truth stated in verse 22.

The Heavenly Tabernacle (9:23–24). The law required that the various elements of the earthly tabernacle be purified with the blood from animal sacrifices. However, it may strike the reader as odd that it was necessary for the heavenly things to be purified at all. The need for purification of the tabernacle had to do with its association with a sinful people. This holy space was made fit for continued interaction between God and his people by sacrifices that addressed the problem of sin. Correspondingly, the heavenly tabernacle was made accessible to the new-covenant people of God by Christ's sacrificial death. The "heavenly things" are purified in conjunction with the purification of God's people. Rather than carrying out his high-priestly, Day of Atonement ministry in the earthly copy of the true tabernacle, Christ entered heaven to bring his sacrifice before God on our behalf (v. 24). That his appearance before God was "for us" marks his act as distinct from the earthly high priest, who also had to offer a sacrifice for himself (5:1–3; 7:27–28).

The Once-for-All Offering (9:25–28). If Christ's sacrifice of himself was an annual event, as was the Day of Atonement sacrifice under the first covenant, he would have had to suffer over and over again since the time of creation, but he has appeared "once for all" (v. 26) to do away with sin completely by sacrificing himself in death. His sacrifice, because of its superior quality, is able to reach back to the time of creation and forward to the time of the consummation of the ages, fully cleansing the people of God. Christ's sacrifice of himself will be followed by a second appearance in this earthly realm. Whereas the first coming was for the purpose of dealing with sin through his sacrificial death, the second coming will be to bring salvation—complete deliverance from this fallen, sinful world and its effects—to those who are anticipating his return (v. 28).

Application. With vast segments of the population, the Christian faith as popularly perceived has become a too-familiar, empty fixture of the culture. With the passage of time, images related to Christianity—such as the church building, the minister, and the cross (images that once represented significant referents)—have vaporized into faint echoes of their real counterparts: true bodies of believers, committed men and women of God, and a symbol of ultimate, atoning sacrifice. The concept of sacrifice, especially blood sacrifice, has been deemed such a primitive idea as to be completely irreconcilable to modern thinking.

We must retake this ground from the culture; we must take back our image of the cross and the sacrifice it represents. Why? Because the world must hear, and we ourselves must hear in a fresh way every day, that God loved us enough to experience voluntarily the death of his Son on our behalf. Christ volunteered to meet a need for us that we could not meet for ourselves. Therefore, we must not abandon the concept of the blood of Christ, for it lies at the heart of our redemption, even as we must also find fresh ways to interpret and communicate its significance for a modern audience scandalized by the "primitive sacrifice" concept.

HEBREWS 10:1–18

Original Meaning

The Limited Abilities of the Law (10:1–4). The author has already made the point that the old-covenant tabernacle was a "shadow." He now applies the same description to the law itself, specifically as it relates to the sacrificial system. What concerns the author most is the law's inability to "make perfect those who draw near to worship" God (v. 1). The perfection he has in mind does not involve a lack of flaws but rather a state of right relationship with God, in which the worshipers are once and for all cleansed from sin and delivered from a nagging sense of guilt.

The law's sacrificial system, rather than delivering worshipers from guilt, actually has the effect of reminding them of their sinfulness and thus their constant separation from God (v. 3). This is because the sacrifices of that system do not have the ability to remove sins (v. 4).

The Superior Sacrifice of Christ (10:5–10). Thankfully, Christ came into the world to set things right, and the author supports this assertion by quoting Psalm 40:6–8. The author takes the psalm quotation itself from the Greek translation of the Old Testament, as is his practice. This text has two primary components in which he shows special interest: God's dissatisfaction with the old-covenant sacrificial offerings, and the willing obedience of the speaker, whom our author understands to be Christ. Furthermore, in Hebrews 10:8 the writer explains that ritualistic sacrifice apart from a sincere commitment to God's will falls short of the divine intention for the sacrificial system.

In verse 9 the author explains that Christ's accomplishment of God's will has supplanted the use of animal sacrifices. The writer concludes by introducing the term "body" (v. 10), taken from the psalm text. It was by God's will, expressed in the sacrifice of the body of Jesus Christ once for all, that believers have been made holy.

Christ's Priestly Activity Contrasted with That of the Levitical Priests (10:11–14). The argument then turns again to the finality of Christ's sacrifice and sets forth several contrasts between the high-priestly service of Christ and that of the old-covenant priests. In verse 11 we find four elements that the author understands to characterize the older sacrificial service. In verses 12–14 the writer to the Hebrews demonstrates that, by contrast, Christ's sacrifice has the following characteristics:

1. it was offered "for all time" (v. 12);
2. it culminated in Christ sitting down at the right hand of God (v. 12);
3. it involved one sacrifice (vv. 12, 14); and
4. it accomplished perfection of those for whom the sacrifice was offered (v. 14).

In verse 12 the author, by allusion, reintroduces Psalm 110:1, to demonstrate the decisive, final nature of the Son's sacrifice. Psalm 110:1 proclaims that the exalted Christ has taken his seat of authority until his enemies are made a footstool for his feet; for Hebrews this truth demonstrates that the Son's sacrifice was completely satisfactory, never having to be repeated. In other words, the Son will remain seated until his second appearing (Heb 9:28), since no further sacrificial work needs to be accomplished. His task is finished until the final subjugation of his enemies is at hand.

In verse 14 our author expresses concisely the effect of Christ's work on new-covenant people. The word speaks of new-covenant people as having been made whole or complete. Christ has suited us for relationship with the Father. Our cleansing by the sacrifice of Christ (10:10) is the means by which we are made "perfect"—wholly adequate for a relationship with God (v. 14).

A Reflection on the Finality of Christ's Sacrifice in Light of the New Covenant (10:15–18). By the way the author introduces the quote of Psalm 40:6–8 at Hebrews 10:5, he clearly understands Christ as the speaker of that portion of Old Testament text. Here in verse 15, he introduces a Scripture passage once again by pointing to the Holy Spirit as its author. Psalm 110:1 indicates the finality of the Son's sacrifice (Heb 10:11–14). In a similar manner, the Spirit also proclaims the need for a new covenant and the decisive forgiveness of sins. In support of this last assertion, the author employs a loose rendering of two portions from Jeremiah 31:31–34. In verse 17 the writer to the Hebrews highlights the forgiveness of sins offered under that new covenant. That God "will remember no more" the sins of his people demonstrates that this covenant involves a superior sacrifice for sins by which those sins are dealt with fully. As the author points out in verse 18, this kind of forgiveness means that all future sacrifices for sin have been rendered obsolete.

Application. Most religions involve some form of human "doing" for God—sacrificing something to win favor with the Almighty. At the heart of the Christian faith stands the core truth that God has done something for us, through the sacrifice of his Son, that we could never do for ourselves. He has taken our sins out of the way, forgiven us completely, and relates to us, intimately and eternally. By that definitive sacrifice we, through the accomplishment of another, have been brought to the Father and brought into his family forever. This is the gospel.

HEBREWS 10:19–25

Original Meaning

Let Us Draw Near to God (10:19–22). The word "confidence" (*parrēsia*, v. 19), a rare word in Greek literature, has to do with free and open expression or conduct and, in an ancient Jewish context, relates especially to approaching God in prayer. Just as the old-covenant high priest was able to enter the earthly Most Holy Place by the blood of animals, the blood (i.e., death) of Jesus has won us confident entrance to the divine presence.

Our entrance, moreover, is "by a new and living way" (v. 20). The path is "new" in that it departs from the perennial, ritual requirements of the old covenant. Yet the word translated as "new" (*prosphatos*) can also carry the meaning "previously unavailable," which seems to fit the broader context nicely (9:8). Jesus has opened a path for us, a path unknown and inaccessible to people before the completion of his high-priestly work. Moreover, this way is "living" because we walk it in association with our resurrected Lord.

"The curtain" (v. 20), an allusion to the veil separating the outer and inner rooms of the tabernacle, ultimately points to a greater (i.e., heavenly) reality—the spiritual barrier through which one must pass in order to enter the presence of God. Closed to any but the high priest under the old-covenant system, this passage has now been opened to God's people by Christ's sacrifice. The author further draws an analogy between this curtain and the body of Christ. The best interpretations take the phrase "his body" to refer to Jesus's sacrificial death (v. 20).

Because of his person and work, our priest is "over the house of God" (v. 21), a reference reverberating from the writer's earlier discussion in 3:1–6, which sets forth a comparison of Moses and Christ as leaders of God's people. Christ's superior offering has established him as the one who by his work has brought into existence and has responsibility for a new people intimately related to God.

We must come "with a sincere heart" (v. 22), the word connoting the idea of being "real, genuine, loyal." "Full assurance [*plērophoria*] that faith brings" can also be translated "conviction" or "certainty of faith." The two concepts of "hearts sprinkled" and "bodies washed" allude to the ceremonies for the establishment of the covenant and the purification under that covenant for one who would approach God.

Commentators have been too quick to find in "having our bodies washed" (v. 22) a reference to Christian baptism; who can deny that the phrase *may* have been intended to draw such a connection? Yet the author gives no overt signals that he has the Christian rite in mind. What we do have in Hebrews are uses of the washing imagery in connection with the purification rites found in the Pentateuch (e.g., Heb 9:13). Thus, the writer continues his use of Old Testament imagery to communicate that the work of Christ has prepared believers to enter the presence of God.

Let Us Hold to Our Hope (10:23). In verse 23 the believer is challenged to hold onto the Christian hope, which the author so clearly has depicted as grounded in the person and work of Christ, without being moved by changing circumstances.

Let Us Encourage One Another (10:24–25). The final exhortation of this passage calls this community of Christ-followers to a life of mutual encouragement. Christians have a high calling to care for one another and stimulate one another spiritually and morally. The word translated "let us consider" (*katanoeō*) means to "notice, consider, pay attention to, look closely at." Believers are to rivet their attention on the need for conscious activities of encouragement among those in the Christian community. The need to be challenged to a love actively expressed is ever present in a Christian ethic and is a cornerstone of authentic Christian community.

The author explains the context for stimulation toward love and good works in verse 25, using contrasting expressions that mark out what the hearers must and must not do. What they must not do is stop meeting together on a regular basis. The author sees discontinuance of common fellowship and worship as fatal for perseverance in the faith. Encouragement cannot take place in isolation. Thus, what they must do is gather for mutual encouragement. Both consolation and encouragement to spiritual alertness are to be given in light of the great "Day" of Christ's coming. Believers must remind one another that we live from day to day in anticipation of that day at the end of the age.

Application. To come to God, to draw near to him, must be done with a sincere heart, one that has been sprinkled clean from a guilty conscience. This cleansing is only possible if one has a right understanding, a right belief in who Jesus is and in what he has accomplished on our behalf. Even for those who have new-covenant hearts, to persevere in this drawing near we must keep right thinking in place and yearning hearts engaged in the pursuit of God. It takes time to keep our lives focused on the right things. We are called to draw near to God on the basis of the completed work of Christ. Will we heed that call today, or will our hearts be yearning for other things? "Let us draw near to God with a sincere heart."

HEBREWS 10:26–39

Original Meaning

A Harsh Word of Warning (10:26–31). What the author has in mind here is a deliberate, sinful lifestyle of high-handed rebellion against the gospel. If a person keeps on sinning in this way after receiving a knowledge of the gospel's truth, no sacrifice for this kind of sin remains. Those whom the author has in mind demonstrate a continuity between the time before hearing the gospel and after, continuing a lifestyle of rejecting

God's word. In 10:1–18 the author has already made clear that the sacrifice offered by Christ has rendered all others obsolete. Where, then, can one go other than to Christ for an efficacious sacrifice? Once he and his provision have been rejected, there is nowhere else to turn.

What does remain is anything but pleasant. The expectation of certain judgment is said to be "fearful" (v. 27). Much more than a mere feeling, this expectation has to do with an awareness of an impending event—God's reckoning with the sinners' defiant rebellion against his grace.

In verses 28–29 the writer crafts an argument "from lesser to greater," much like that found in 2:1–4. He wishes to remind the hearers of the extreme penalty for rejection of God's revealed will under the old covenant. This, however, he presents as the *lesser* of two important situations, the greater situation being delineated in 10:29.

That greater situation, of course, is the rejection of the new-covenant high priest and his offering—see the words "how much more" at the beginning of verse 29. Those who have turned away from the work of grace accomplished in God's Son are faced with a more serious situation than the apostates of the old-covenant era.

The rebellion of those who have turned away from the gospel is depicted in terms of three actions graphically expressed. First, they have "trampled the Son of God underfoot" (v. 29a). Second, the rebels have "treated as an unholy thing the blood of the covenant" (v. 29b). Finally, those rejecting Christ and his sacrifice have "insulted the Spirit of grace" or caused him outrage (v. 29c). Those who turn away from the gospel and the Spirit's gentle promptings have committed a sin with eternal implications.

In verse 30 the author then reinforces his assertion concerning the seriousness of the situation by quoting two brief portions of the Song of Moses in Deuteronomy 32. This song, sung by Moses at the end of his life, eloquently delivered a warning to the people of Israel by depicting God's judgment toward a faithless people who had turned their backs on his covenant.

The author tersely concludes with "it is a dreadful thing to fall into the hands of the living God" (v. 31). There exists no means of escape for those who have rejected the grace of God in Christ (4:12–13).

Remember the Past (10:32–34). The believers had endured at least four forms of ill treatment. They had faced public ridicule and persecution. They had felt the pain of identification with those who were so treated. This solidarity extended from the public square to the prison cell, as the listeners "sympathized" or "suffered along" (*sympatheō*) with those incarcerated (v. 34). Finally, the believers "joyfully accepted the confiscation" of their property.

A key to the author's use of his hearers' past stance as a present example is the attitude of joy attendant in these circumstances. The hearers had joy amid their persecution because they knew that "better and lasting possessions" (v. 34) had been promised them by virtue of their identification with the Lord and his church.

Encouragement to Persevere (10:35–39). The author here continues to encourage the believers not to retreat, reminding them that such identification will be rewarded richly (v. 35). This reward, however, comes to those who accomplish God's will by persevering in their public confession (v. 36).

The quotation found in verses 37–38 brings together parts of two Old Testament texts (Isa 26:20–21 and Hab 2:3–4) and focuses on a contrast between the righteous who live by faith and the wicked. The Isaiah text carries with it strong overtones of the end of time, since it speaks both of resurrection and comprehensive judgment, and thus it has been adopted by our author to speak of Christ's second coming. The Habakkuk passage also lends itself for application to that eschatological event since it speaks of "the end."

The author of Hebrews applies these Old Testament texts to his hearers' situation. The concept of waiting for an impending time of reward and punishment fits the tension of their circumstances precisely. The author ends this section with a confident assertion that he and his community belong to those who have chosen the right path, for they walk the way of faith as "those who have faith and are saved" (v. 39b).

Application. Our past can also affect our present and future as we speak to ourselves from the past, as we remember those earlier days of our commitment to Christ. Perhaps there was a time when we as individuals stood in the face of severe trial. We should own and build memorials for the remembrance of those past times, using them for our own encouragement to endurance. If we as individuals have had no such experience, we can benefit from the example of our broader community of faith, looking to a time in the past at which they sacrificed greatly. Is there in the location where your church meets a place for people to remember the past boldness of your faith community, perhaps through photographs or written documents? Are there times during which your church celebrates those past stances publicly? How are you creating an organizational memory that can help people stand firm in their commitment to Christ in the present?

HEBREWS 11:1–40

Original Meaning

Overture (11:1–3). The writer of Hebrews begins his "hall of faith" with a two-part definition of faith. The first part includes the word *hypostasis*, translated by the NIV as "confidence" (v. 1a). We can translate this part of the verse as "now faith is the resolute confidence. . . ." The examples that follow demonstrate that faith entails a posture of firm confidence in the promises of God even though the believers had not yet received the fulfillment of those promises (cf. 11:39).

This interpretation stands in parallel with the second assertion about faith found in the second half of the verse: "and assurance about what we do not see" (v. 1b). Some realities are unseen because they belong to the spiritual realm, and some realities are unseen because they lie in the future, when that realm will break into the earthly sphere. In either case, the person of faith lives out of a strong conviction in God's greater realities.

Faith is what looks at the created order and has a firm and resolute confidence in the God to whom it bears witness, who, though unseen, has provided a foundation for such a confidence through his mighty acts (v. 3)

Movement 1: First Examples of Faith (11:4–12). The writer then follows, in sequence, great examples of faithfulness from Genesis, beginning with Abel and progressing to an initial discussion of Abraham's faith. In each example the emphasis lies both on an act accomplished by faith and the right spiritual posture of the exemplar.

By faith Abel presented God with a sacrifice superior to that of Cain (v. 4). Consequently, he was "commended" by God and still "speaks" today, even though he has been dead for a long time. His attitude and action were such that his example of faithfulness continues among people of faith. Hebrews emphasizes this vital link between internal attitudes and external actions.

The emphasis in the Enoch example (vv. 5–6) rests even more squarely on the importance of one's spiritual posture. This faithful believer, according to our author's interpretation of the Old Testament text, was taken out of this world by God without experiencing death (Gen 5:24). Why? Because Enoch was resolute in his commitment, thus bringing God pleasure.

The life of faith may be thus said to have at least three components (Heb 11:6). First, it involves a life of coming to God and seeking him earnestly. Second, this life of faith involves believing that God exists. Third, this life of faith involves confidence that God will reward those who exercise such faith.

Rounding off his account of exemplars prior to Abraham, the author introduces Noah (Gen 6:1–9:17), the first to act in faith based on a message from God. Noah acted on the divine warning in regard to a flood that was not yet seen. Accordingly, Noah built an ark to save his family and in this way condemned the world. His building of the ark both bore witness to the unseen God and his word and constituted a stark, prophetic rebuke to that godless generation.

The author next moves to an extensive treatment of the greatest example of faith in the Old Testament, Abraham the patriarch. Hebrews 11:8–12 focuses on two foundational events from the great exemplar's life as evidencing his faith. First, Abraham obediently followed God's call to move to a place with which he was unfamiliar (see Gen 12:1–9). Second, Abraham was enabled to become a father because he believed God (see Gen 18:10–15; 21:1–7). Faith, moving beyond the normal boundaries of possibility, works miracles.

The happy result, in accordance with the promise of God, is recorded in Hebrews 11:12: "And so from this one man, and he as good as dead, came descendants as numerous as the stars in the sky and as countless as the sand on the seashore." Out of nothing comes a multitude too numerous to count.

Interlude (11:13–16). The author here pauses in his person-by-person account of the faithful to tease out certain implications he wishes his hearers to recognize. The interlude is both didactic (the principles here are highly instructional for their current crisis) and rhetorical (the author, ever the skilled orator, interrupts his rapid-fire list to heighten his audience's attention). The focus continues on Abraham, his wife, and his son Isaac.

The author wishes to emphasize that the patriarchs' faith relationship to God was their preeminent commitment, not the obtaining of an earthly, secure place of residence. They died in a state of trust, never having seen their descendants' reception of the land. Thus, the true object of their deepest desire was God himself and God's city. Consequently, "God is not ashamed to be called their God" (v. 16).

The message to the original hearers must not be missed, for their circumstance must be seen as analogous to that of the patriarchs. Perhaps their current experience of persecution has highlighted the alien nature of their earthly existence. They cannot perceive the fulfillment of God's promises to them; all they can see is the difficulty of their present crisis. The writer's point is that this is normal for people of faith. The promises of God must be embraced even though their fulfillment lies in the future. Life must be lived in our challenging, terrestrial cities in light of a better, heavenly country that will be experienced in the future. God is not ashamed of identifying with those who live in this way.

Movement 2: More Examples of Faith (11:17–31). Verses 17–19 continue the author's exposition on Abraham, offering a third major event exemplifying this father's faith. Abraham, in a test by God, "offered Isaac as a sacrifice" (v. 17). This is the example par excellence of a magnanimous act of faith, born as it was of an excruciating decision placed before the patriarch by God. The crux of Abraham's crisis is the seeming contradiction between the promises of God, which were to be fulfilled through his heir, Isaac, and the command of God to sacrifice that heir. Thus Abraham was forced into a radical posture of trusting God. Our author's logical deduction is that "Abraham reasoned that God could even raise the dead" (v. 19)—the only way that both the promises and the command could be fulfilled.

The author of Hebrews moves rapid-fire through the next three generations in his example list, using his formulaic pattern cited above (vv. 20–22). Moses was specially venerated by Greek-speaking Jews of the first century as one who was unusually close to God. In certain expressions of Jewish tradition, he was considered to be the greatest person in history. Therefore, it is unsurprising that in his example list in verses 23–28 the writer gives sustained attention to Moses.

The author's treatment of Moses actually begins with the faith expressed by Moses's parents. Two points of the retelling are significant. First, the NIV translates Hebrews verse 23 with the phrase "no ordinary child." The writer, therefore, depicts the parents as having spiritual insight into his significance. Second, the author states that "they were not afraid of the king's edict," deducing this fact from their action of hiding the child. This lack of fear suggests a firm boldness in which they refused to shrink before the hostility of Pharaoh.

Moses himself also exhibited such boldness, and the writer to the Hebrews points out three events from the lawgiver's life that illustrate his faith. First, Moses chose to identify with God's people rather than with the godless (vv. 24–26). Second, by faith Moses left Egypt and persevered in the mission given him by God (v. 27). Finally, by faith Moses led the Israelites in the observance of the Passover ordinance (v. 28). The mention of "the application of blood" calls to mind the author's earlier references to Christ's sacrifice as paralleling the old-covenant sacrificial rituals (9:12–14, 18–22). Here, however, he specifically has in mind the smearing of blood on the Israelites' doorposts to avoid the death angel's work. This act was an act of faith since Moses led the Israelites in obedience to God's command with regard to an as-yet-unseen event.

The author rounds out his primary example list with three other events from the life of God's covenant people. According to the Old Testament narrative, this group of people in general was marked by timidity, complaining, and a *lack* of trust in God or his deliverance. However, when God told them to "move on" (Exod 14:15) they did so, and this constituted an act exemplifying faith. In obedience to another seemingly illogical command, the Israelites, under the command of Joshua, marched around the city of Jericho for seven days. Their obedience was rewarded with the walls falling down (Heb 11:30). Finally, Rahab, in accordance with God's will, helped the spies who had come to investigate the land (Josh 2:1–15). Her faith is expressed in her confession of Joshua 2:9 ("I know the LORD has given this land to you") and was rewarded with deliverance from death.

Crescendo and Conclusion (11:32–40). The author realizes that time constraints do not permit him to continue a detailed account of old-covenant men and women of faith. So, with the rhetorical "and what more shall I say?" he turns a corner (v. 32), finishing the section with a summary of Old Testament and perhaps intertestamental acts of faith.

The writer begins his summary with six figures spanning the era of the judges through the united monarchy, and to these adds the expansive "the prophets" (v. 32). The list of mighty deeds that follows would call to mind a whole host of those who lived faithfully before God in a hostile world. This is the intention of an example list—to provide a sample of people and events that point to a much larger body of data that can be brought to bear on a given subject—and the author brings his list to a crescendo with skill.

The passage then turns from the great performers of faith to their actions (vv. 33–38). They "through faith conquered kingdoms," especially calling to mind the period of the judges through the reign of King David (v. 33a). That they "administered justice" speaks of governmental administration and is an extension of their conquering (v. 33b). As God's servants they carried out his justice and righteousness to the people under their rule (e.g., 2 Sam 8:15; 1 Kgs 10:9).

These saints of old "gained what was promised" (v. 33c), an affirmation that can be interpreted as their reception of the promises themselves or as their reception of the *fulfillment* of those promises. From the context it would seem that the emphasis lies on God's giving them promises, some of which were not fulfilled in the receptor's lifetime (cf. v. 39). Nevertheless, the covenant promises to Abraham's children, such as the promised land and the promise of God's abiding presence with his people, are certainly in view. The author's twin points are that the promise-making God is faithful to his oaths, and that people of faith live in light of God's promises. With this confession the author echoes his earlier treatment of God's oaths in 6:13–20.

In the middle of verse 35 the writer shifts gears, from more positive outcomes encountered by faith to faith expressed in the face of great hardship. Although some "received back their dead," others expressed faith by embracing torture and death, refusing deliverance in light of a greater reward beyond the grave. The author has already stated that these uncomfortable circumstances had occurred among those in the community to which he is writing (10:32–34).

The author concludes his example list with a fitting epilogue (vv. 39–40), contrasting these great exemplars of faith, who were commended by God, with the new-covenant community. When the author notes that the great heroes of faith were "commended" by God, he means that God himself had born witness to their faithfulness (v. 39a). By living out faith in the unseen God, these men and women of history had established themselves as appropriate examples for the hearers, who were now being faced with choosing the path of faith or the alternative, the path of faithlessness.

The author's main point through his example list is that faith is the only right path for God's people. The heroes of faith demonstrate a resolute determination to live faithfully even though "none of them received what had been promised" (v. 39b). His point here is that they did not receive the eternal inheritance known through the new covenant established by Christ.

When the author says that "God had planned something better for us so that only together with us would they be made perfect" (v. 40), he means that historically these people of old did not experience the coming of Messiah and the new covenant. Their faith in God has been vindicated since God has broken into the world in the person of his Son, Jesus Christ. With us they now know the perfecting power of Christ's sacrifice and the eternal inheritance of the saints.

Application. How would you and I live today if we believed absolutely that God existed and loved us completely and had a destination for us that made all the world pale by just one square foot of its turf? How would we live if we believed that God cared about our every action and every concern and wished to reward us magnanimously for our faith? How would you and I live in the face of opposition if we believed in God, really believed as if our whole lives depended on him?

How would you live differently if you did not believe? Would there be much difference? This is a critical question.

If all I am and have and do differs little from my unbelieving neighbor, then I have embraced his world and his values and fool myself by saying I am living for another world and kingdom. My life must be radically different in what I embrace—the values of a heavenly kingdom. When I live by faith, I then will be one to whom God can bear witness and one who bears witness to God in such a way that others will be stimulated to faith. My life will portray that faith "works." Then I will be a hero in the best sense of the word, for I will live a life that helps others and honors God. Then I will be extraordinary, having chosen a narrow path.

HEBREWS 12:1–17

Original Meaning

Running the Race (12:1–2). The writer of Hebrews begins chapter 12 with the familiar race metaphor, presenting a forceful challenge for Christians to endure in a "marathon" commitment to Christ. Authors of classical literature used the image of a cloud to describe a large group of people, and our writer employs this metaphor with an added emphasis, pointing back to the multitude of persons listed or alluded to in chapter 11 as "such a great cloud."

However, the author intends more from this image than to conjure the faithful of the ages as passive spectators. Rather, they are witnesses in the sense that they bear witness to the Christian community of God's faithfulness and of the effectiveness of faith. The great cloud of the faithful through history offers the community motivation in its current struggle to stay the course of commitment.

The writer calls his hearers to "throw off everything that hinders and the sin that so easily entangles." The word could refer to a runner stripping of burdensome clothing or losing excess bodily fat. More specifically, we are to get rid of the entangling sin. The author does not seem to have a specific sin in mind, but rather understands any sin as hindering progress in the faith.

The main clause of verses 1–2a is translated with "let us run." The author has in view a marathon rather than a sprint, as seen in the phrase "with perseverance." The Greek verb *prokeimai*, translated here as "marked out," can also be translated "lie before, lie in view, be at hand"; the picture evoked in here is that of runners looking down the track at the course they must run. They know where they must go and now must bring their training and commitment to bear on the task of running the race successfully.

Yet, thankfully, the path is not all the believer sees. We are called to fix "our eyes on Jesus, the pioneer and perfecter of our faith" (v. 2). Jesus is the one who has run the path before us, and he offers the preeminent example of how the race is to be run. But he is more. That he is the "pioneer and perfecter of our faith" sets him apart from all the examples enumerated in Hebrews 11. Ultimately Jesus accomplished the perfection of our faith by his sacrificial death on the cross. In keeping with the race imagery, he has cleared the path of faith so that we may run it. The way is open, and although hurdles exist, the roadblocks have been removed.

That Jesus "scorned" the shame of the cross means that he treated it as insignificant or of little consequence. On the cross Jesus was treated as valueless, being mocked and ridiculed—in short, being scorned or shamed. He, however, turned the experience inside out, "scorning the scorn," or in the author's words here, "scorning the shame." The cross was insignificant compared to the joy set before our Lord. The end result of its shame was his exaltation to the right hand of God (Ps 110:1). Thus Christians are encouraged to look beyond their present difficulties to God's promised rewards.

The Discipline of Children (12:3–13). When the author says, "Consider him who endured . . . " (v. 3a), he restates the need to focus on Jesus as he endured the cross (v. 2), but here he gives the reason: "so that you will not grow weary and lose heart" (v. 3b). In this statement, the hearers' critical circumstance stands out clearly.

Consequently, a parallel exists between their situation and that of Jesus's cross. Because of this parallel, the persecuted community could draw strength from the positive outcome of Jesus's suffering. However, as verse 4 points out, those in this church, unlike Jesus, had yet to shed their blood in the struggle against sin. If Jesus endured through the pouring out of his life's blood, they could endure in the lesser persecution they were facing.

In verses 5–6 the author quotes from Proverbs 3:11–12. The emotional discouragement of his hearers prompts him to offer a gentle rebuke. The rationale for taking the Lord's discipline seriously and taking courage when facing his rebuke has to do with his motive of love. The Lord does not discipline arbitrarily, but rather does so as an expression of genuine relationship. This image is one of loving training given to amend actions and attitudes. Such training is only given to legitimate children.

The author begins his exposition of the proverb with the exhortation, "Endure hardship as discipline" (v. 7). They are to recognize in their current difficulties the Lord's hand lovingly training them in right character. The exposition that follows occurs in three movements. First, the original hearers of Hebrews could have interpreted the persecution they were facing as an indication of God's inattention. Yet the difficulties they face are actually a sign that they are true children of the Father. Discipline is a normal part of the parent-child relationship. Lack of discipline is a mark of illegitimacy (vv. 7–8).

Second, how then should one respond to the Lord's discipline? Human fathers are given respect in response to their discipline. God deserves even more reverence. Indeed, we should "submit" to him as "the Father of our spirits and live" (v. 9). We should bow our wills to the will of the Father, since his will is the path that leads to life.

The third movement occurs in verses 10–11 where the writer rounds out his exposition of the proverb by pointing out the benefits of divine discipline. The discipline of God, when received in the right manner, trains the Christian in right character, purifying the heart. The author admits that the experience of discipline is not pleasant but painful (v. 11a). However, the fruit of the discipline is worth the price of pain (v. 11b).

With verse 12 the author returns briefly to his earlier use of athletic imagery (vv. 1–2) and draws his material from Isaiah 35:3. The strengthening of the arms and knees is figurative of taking heart or hoping in the Lord; this message could not be more applicable to the original hearers, who were trudging along a path of persecution.

Verse 13 continues with a quote from Proverbs 4:26. The straight or level path is a common image in wisdom literature for God's way of right living, as is clear from Proverbs 4:25–27. In Hebrews 12:13 the author vies for his hearers to take courage in and choose the Lord's way of holiness so that their spiritual and emotional conditions might be strengthened.

The Importance of Choosing Holiness (12:14–17). The exhortations of verses 14–17 may seem somewhat disjointed from verses 1–13, but these verses continue with two themes that are central to the first thirteen verses: spiritual struggle and the need for holiness. Holiness has a profound impact on our relationships with other people. Holiness is indispensable for an authentic Christian life. The person who chooses to live an unholy life can be offered no assurance of "see[ing] the Lord" (v. 14b).

Verse 15 begins with a participle the NIV translates with "see to it." They are to see to it that no one "falls short of the grace of God," the state of rejecting the gospel and missing the forgiveness offered by virtue of Christ's sacrifice. The believers are further to see to it that "no bitter root grows up to cause trouble and defile many." Those among the original recipients who were jettisoning their confession of Christ were causing severe friction within the community, and relationships were breaking down.

The hearers are to see to it that no member of the church falls into the pattern of immoral Esau (vv. 16–17). Hebrews describes Esau in this way because of his misplaced values that led to his unwise decision to give up his inheritance. For something as valueless as a meal—simply a means of gaining immediate gratification for physical hunger pangs—he foolishly gave up his rights as the firstborn—that is, the double portion of his father's inheritance. Having given up his inheritance and being rejected from receiving the blessing, Esau, weeping, pleaded with his father to reverse the situation, but the patriarch could not. The author wishes to drive home the point that only tears and rejection await those who sell out the inheritance that God promises to his children.

Application. It goes without saying that all sins, including especially such sins as lust, greed, hatred, or pride, hamstring us in the contest and must be rejected over and over again if we are to run well and run long. For to run with perseverance means that we will grow in a pattern of obedience to God's word, day after day, year after year. It means that we will train ourselves to make the right choices, choosing the level path of righteousness. The premier sin to be jettisoned is the sin of abandoning Christian commitment altogether. We must strengthen our "feeble arms and week knees" if we are lagging in a rut of despair. This exercise is helped most by riveting "our eyes on Jesus," who has shown us what to scorn and what to hold as a cause of joy, and joy is set before us if we will persevere in the race to the end.

HEBREWS 12:18–29

Original Meaning

The Old-Covenant Mountain (12:18–21). Although the author of Hebrews never mentions Sinai by name, he clearly has that mountain in view in his poetic comments in these verses. He draws his depiction of the desert wanderers' encounter of God at Mount Sinai from the books of Exodus and Deuteronomy. The experience was terrifying.

These manifestations of God's presence at Sinai were visible, striking the eyes of the desert wanderers with awe. The manifestations of God's presence were auditory. The people did not see God's form but only heard the words. In response, they begged that God would speak to them no further. The people were aware of the boundaries God had placed between them and him and were terrified that the boundaries seemed to be dissolving under the weight of that terrible voice. In verse 21 our author concludes by noting that even the mediator of that covenant, Moses, was overwhelmed by the experience.

The New-Covenant Mountain (12:22–24). Thankfully, new-covenant believers have not come to Mount Sinai, a mountain of terror and separation from God. Rather, they have come to Mount Zion, the dwelling place of God. These images may be understood as creating a picture of the new-covenant assembly in the heavenly Jerusalem, and the contrast with the Sinai encounter could not be more pronounced. The author's picture of the gathered assembly at Mount Zion communicates exultation, warmth, openness, acceptance, and relationship, set off in bold relief against the dismal portrait of the Sinai assembly.

Mount Zion and the city of Jerusalem are so closely associated in the biblical literature that the two should be understood as conceptually synonymous, representing the dwelling place of God. Here, of course, as indicated by the adjective "heavenly" attached to "Jerusalem" (v. 22), the author has in mind the Zion and Jerusalem that are not of this creation. That God's true dwelling place, the place where he meets his new-covenant people, is in the heavenly realm forms a prominent aspect of the author's theological framework. This is the "heavenly" city of 11:16 and the "city that is to come" of 13:14. The multitude of angels in God's presence exults "in joyful assembly" (*panēgyris*), a sense of excitement, revelry, and well-being (12:22).

Those addressed by Hebrews also have come "to God, the Judge of all," and "to the spirits of the righteous made perfect" (v. 23). The author probably has in mind a strong note of the vindication of God's righteous people, a prominent theme in Scripture. In line with this motif of vindication, the new-covenant people have not come to Mount Zion for God to pass judgment on them, but for him to vindicate them before their wicked persecutors.

What does the author mean when he refers to the blood of Christ as speaking "a better word than the blood of Abel" (v. 24)? Abel's blood bore witness against Cain, indicating his guilt. Christ's blood, on the other hand, has won our forgiveness, "crying out" that people of the new covenant are no longer guilty, having been cleansed completely from sin.

A Final Warning (12:25–29). If those of the old covenant did not escape the wrath of God when they turned from his word, the judgment on those who reject the message of salvation received in the new-covenant era is even more certain. Their inheritance of an unshakable kingdom should inspire thanksgiving and reverent worship. On the other hand, those who, like Esau, reject such an inheritance, failing to be thankful and worship God appropriately, should be reminded that "God is a consuming fire" (Deut 4:24).

Application. Out of a desire to clearly reflect God's holiness, we can steer dangerously close to Sinai, not just as a necessary way station but as a permanent, spiritual destination, preaching a gospel of terror rather than a gospel of beauty. Do our sermons boom and flash with the darkness of Sinai more than they sing and gather people to the festiveness of Zion?

If we are not careful, grace can get lost amid our shouts. We can, in effect, be perceived as dragging people to the foot of Mount Sinai, attempting to hold their heads back and forcing them to face the storm, feel the white-hot flash of lightning, and tremble at the weighty voice of the fierce Almighty. Most unholy people still do not like Sinai and will respond, "I don't want to listen to that voice anymore!" In short, if we bear a message that lacks grace, they run the other way when they see us coming.

If our lives reflect the gloom of Sinai more than the glories of Zion, we do the kingdom poor publicity. This does not mean, of course, that we are always thrilled with the difficult situations in which we may find ourselves. But are we *characterized* by joy? That is a key question. If we are not, then the reality of Zion is not invading our lives. Perhaps we need a clearer view of that mountain and must hear again the song of the angels and the message of the sprinkled blood.

HEBREWS 13:1–25

Original Meaning

General Guidelines for Christian Living (13:1–6). *Love fellow Christians (13:1).* The concept of believers as united in a close spiritual family lays the foundation for practical exhortations to meet the needs of those in the family. Believers must live out love practically as an ever-present, foundational dynamic within the community.

Show hospitality (13:2). In the ancient world it was expensive to stay overnight at an inn, and such establishments usually had poor reputations. Thus, an aspect of Jewish and early Christian piety involved taking people in for an evening. In the Christian context, such admonitions to show hospitality have their foundation in the Old Testament and the teachings of Jesus.

Minister to those in prison and to those who are mistreated (13:3). Prisoners were not treated well in the first century, often having to depend on friends and family even for the most basic necessities of life. Christians could minister to fellow believers in prison, either by offering consolation and gifts or by praying for them.

Hold marriage as honorable and keep the sexual relationship pure (13:4). The institution of marriage was assaulted from two sides in the ancient world. For example, in some corners of Greco-Roman culture men were expected to take mistresses as their confidants and sexual partners. Others felt marriage stunted spiritual devotion and thus held asceticism as the ideal. As the verse develops, it is clear that the former, rather than the latter, error is in view. The "marriage bed" (*koitē*), used here as an idiom for the sexual relationship, is to be guarded or "kept pure." The defilement that the author has in mind is expressed in the explanatory "for God will judge the adulterer and all the sexually immoral." The former word, "adulterers" (*moichoi*), is more focused than the latter, referring specifically to those who betray their marriage vows. The latter, "the sexually immoral" (*pornoi*), refers to all those involved in sexual activity apart from the sanctity of the marriage relationship.

Be content with your financial status (13:5). The sins of sexual impurity and covetousness are linked in several New Testament passages, probably because their prohibitions are given side by side as the seventh and eighth of the Ten Commandments. Both the sexually immoral and those greedy for money pursue a myopic self-gratification that takes them outside the bounds of God's provision. Believers need not worry that their needs will go unmet. The Christian can profess with confidence, "The Lord is my helper; I will not be afraid. What can mere mortals do to me?" (v. 6). This response comes from Psalm 118:6–7 and asserts that the plans of the wicked will be thwarted by the provisions of God.

Guidelines on Church Leadership and Doctrine (13:7–19). In verse 7 the readers are exhorted to "remember your leaders." Used in a Christian context for a church office, the word finds expression in ancient Christian documents especially related to the city of Rome. The author exhorts his hearers to consider closely or scrutinize the fruit of their leaders' manner of living and imitate their faith. In other words, the leaders are placed in the same category of heroic examples as the paragons of biblical history listed in Hebrews 11.

Verse 8 sets forth a beautiful proclamation of Christ's immutability: "Jesus Christ is the same yesterday and today and forever." The theological perspective behind this concise christological formula has been developed well in the course of Hebrews. The author asserts the Son's role in creation (1:2, 10), certainly an aspect of "yesterday." Presently the Son sits in his exalted status as Lord of the universe, who intercedes for his people (1:3, 13; 7:26–28). The author has vigorously promulgated the perpetual nature of Christ's rule for all time into the eternal tomorrow (1:8a, 10–12).

With this christological statement the author reminds his audience that the same Christ who was so real to their community in the beginning, as they were ministered to by their former leaders, presently sits in his exalted state and will rule perpetually. Although their circumstances and perspectives change, Jesus Christ and his gospel do not.

It is important, therefore, that the congregation guard against "all kinds of strange teachings," to which some were being drawn (v. 9). These teachings evidently promised spiritual strengthening through ceremonial foods and apart from God's grace found in Christ. Some of the recipients of Hebrews are perhaps being drawn away from Christian fellowship and doctrine to theological expressions heralded within a community practicing Judaism. They are embracing aspects of Jewish community life and thought that are at odds with the gospel of grace through Jesus Christ. The author asserts that such ceremonial foods are not the true means of grace and spiritual strength. Although it is not clear exactly what he has in mind regarding the Christian's "altar" (v. 10), this much is certain: the participants of the new covenant draw spiritual sustenance and life from a source unavailable to those of the tabernacle, and that source is the sacrifice of Christ.

Leviticus 16:27 forms the backdrop of verses 11–14, which reiterates the author's interpretation of Christ as the Day of Atonement sacrifice (9:11–14, 24–28; 10:1–4). With verse 12 the author draws two parallels between Jesus's sacrifice and that of the Day of Atonement. First, "Jesus also suffered outside the city gate." Second, the purpose of Jesus's sacrifice was "to make the people holy." Jesus's high-priestly offering, however, was "through his own blood."

Having reasserted the superiority of Jesus's sacrifice and

thus the superiority of Christian doctrine, the author offers an application in verses 13–14: believers must reject the tempting security of Judaism and be resolute in their identification with Christ. The "camp" (v. 13) represents the religion of Judaism, grounded in the tabernacle rituals of the old covenant. For the listeners to turn their backs on Judaism will mean rejection and "disgrace," such as that experienced by Christ. Christians should hold to their confession of Christ in the face of opposition because his sacrifice means lasting holiness and his "city" is one that will endure (v. 14).

Although Christians should not participate in the Jewish cultic meals, they have their own appropriate "sacrifices" to offer (vv. 15–16). The writer details two spiritual sacrifices here. He exhorts the readers to "continually offer to God a sacrifice of praise" (v. 15). The "sacrifice" is the prayer of thanks. Yet also the Christ-follower is to offer a sacrifice of good deeds (v. 16). As the life of faith pleases God (11:6), so the sacrifices of praise and practical ministry give him pleasure.

With verse 17, the writer returns to the subject of the church's leadership, this time focusing clearly on current leaders. The members of the congregation have a responsibility to "obey" (NIV "have confidence in") these leaders and to "submit to their authority." The verb translated "obey" (*peithō*) as used by ancient authors had various nuances. It could mean to "conform one's actions," but it could also connote the idea of "being persuaded by" or "putting one's confidence in." The further injunction to "submit to their authority" (*hypeikō*) means the listeners are to have a readiness to comply and may suggest a strained relationship between the leadership and some members of the Christian community. These two commands involve yielding to and respecting the leaders as they give direction concerning right Christian doctrine.

Instead of working against them, the members of the congregation are to yield to their leaders so that their ministry may be carried out with "joy." The phrase "not a burden" can be translated as "not groaning." When members of the church fail to submit themselves to the leadership, the leaders end up working under an emotionally deflating burden that fills their lives with sighs and groaning.

The author rounds out his series of admonitions with a personal request in verses 18–19. The exhortation to pray is in the present tense and should be understood as durative: "keep on praying." He specifically asks them to pray that he "may be restored" to them, indicating that he was a member of this church, who, for whatever reason, had been prevented from rejoining them.

Benediction and Closing (13:20–25). In the ancient world, benedictions were important to an address, and in the Jewish context specifically a benediction was an aspect of worship. Thus, the author of Hebrews ends with a prayer containing the essential elements of his book. At the heart of his message is Christ's work of effecting the new covenant and God's work in believers to do his will.

The writer begins his closing in verse 22, urging the readers to bear with his "word of exhortation," a rather diffident request that is rhetorical in nature. The expression "word of exhortation" is probably a technical phrase referring to a sermon.

The "Timothy" of verse 23 is commonly assumed to be Paul's missionary companion. If so, his "release" indicates an incarceration not mentioned in Acts or elsewhere in the New Testament. The book closes with a formal greeting and a final blessing (vv. 24–25). His closing blessing states simply, "Grace be with you all."

Application. It is through the devoted living for God in common aspects of life that the truth of the gospel is proclaimed in a thousand varied voices and the kingdom is built. In the common practices of financial management, date nights, cleaning dirty faces and dirty bottoms, integrity at work, care for the burdened or oppressed, and hospitality God finds pleasure, for these are worthy sacrifices when presented on an altar made holy by the blood of Christ.

In areas such as marriage and money, the worlds of the spirit and the street meet. Such meeting places either become dance floors on which we move to the music of God's will or a stage of games on which we play at Christianity with dichotomized, hypocritical hearts. Everyday God wants us, and he wants us to want him in the nitty-gritty wonder, the plain and exalted dance of the everyday.

JAMES

INTRODUCTION TO JAMES

James wrote to a church beset by a number of problems. Giving shape to and electrifying these problems were the presence and popularity within the community of errant teaching. It allowed its followers to understand the church as one among many opportunities for social climbing and the exhibition of social snobbery. James combats this teaching. He points out that the rich will be humbled and the poor exalted, that the poor are God's elect, and that far from being a sign of divine displeasure, periods of adversity are used by God to purify and strengthen those whom he loves.

There is no good reason to suppose that James the brother of Jesus is not our author. Moreover, references to James in Paul (1 Cor 9:5; 15:7; Gal 1:15–2:12) and Acts (15:13–21) make clear that James the brother of Jesus held a prominent place in early Palestinian Christianity.

BOOK OUTLINE

- I. Address and Greeting (1:1)
- II. Building Christian Maturity (1:2–27)
    - A. Trials and Temptations (1:2–11)
    - B. The Evil Desire (1:12–18)
    - C. True Religion Is Compassion in Action (1:19–27)
- III. Building a Healthy Community (2:1–5:18)
    - A. A. The Effects of Sickness (2:1–26)
    - B. The Source of Sickness (3:1–18)
    - C. Symptoms and Antidote (4:1–5:18)
- IV. Conclusion: The Forgiveness of God (5:19–20)

JAMES 1:1

Original Meaning. James describes himself as the servant "of God and of the Lord Jesus Christ," a construction found only here in the New Testament. In part James may write it in this way to communicate that loyalty to Jesus Christ does not undermine loyalty to God; that, in fact, they are one and the same. He writes to "the twelve tribes scattered among the nations" (cf. 1 Pet 1:1). James addresses his letter to the scattered church comprised of both Jews and gentiles, but the native thought world of the letter is messianic Judaism.

Application. *Servanthood and authority.* James, like Paul in Philippians 2, issues a strong call for the basic character of the Christian life to be that of servanthood, after the model of Jesus himself. The witness of the Gospels is that Jesus was the Servant-Messiah. The model of servanthood is to be lived out especially by those in leadership in the church.

JAMES 1:2–11

Original Meaning

Trials (1:2–8). The "pure joy" James speaks of here is a complete, overflowing joy (v. 2). Although it seems strange, trials are to be occasions of such joy. Here "brothers and sisters" could be used of fellow Jews, but the overwhelming use in the New Testament is of fellow Christians in contradistinction to the world at large. Why should we rejoice in the face of trials? Trials have a purifying quality; they are the arena in which and the process through which something good develops. Trials can have this effect as a result of the means of "testing" (*dokimion*, v. 3). The root of this word means "approved character," so we can see the close link between the testing and its intended result.

The result of the testing of faith is "perseverance" or endurance (*hypomonē*)—a highly prized trait (v. 3). Yet *hypomonē* is a means to an end. We should not be satisfied with constancy, as important as this virtue is, but we should let it grow to its fullest, in order to become "mature and complete, not lacking anything" (v. 4). The "complete" person is one whose character is fully formed according to Christian standards; it is not "perfection" according to some standard common to popular culture.

While human beings are, at least in part, responsible for their moral development, wisdom comes only from God (v. 5). In the New Testament generally, wisdom is allied to understanding God's purposes and plan and indicates a determination to live accordingly. James goes on to say that God gives generously without hesitation. James conveys the notion that God's spontaneous generosity is unwavering, regardless of our previous record.

With the words "and not doubt" (v. 6a), honest intellectual doubts are not in view. After all, to doubt is human, as the Psalms attest. Yet amid this honest doubt as reflected in the Psalms, the psalmist is reminded of all that God has done for him in the past, and he gains the hope necessary to continue.

In verse 8 with the words "double-minded and unstable," James is speaking of someone who constantly changes allegiances and cultivates the appearance of faith, wrongly thinking mechanistic action to be the heart of faith. James calls us to be people of character whose faith manifests itself in action commensurate with what God has called us to be.

Poverty and Wealth (1:9–11). It is possible that the rich in James includes the wealthy of the Christian community whose pattern of life gave little or no evidence of Christian commitment, thereby disqualifying them from true membership. The humble should rejoice because their material poverty provides an arena for their faith to be tested and thus for endurance to grow, as well as because they will be eventually exalted, just as the prophets and Jesus had promised.

Application. *The wisdom of God.* With wisdom through prayer comes an appreciation for the timing of God. In trials we ask for wisdom in prayer, and trials push us to contemplate Scripture, to pray, and to seek God's face. In so doing we become more like God himself, as his love wells up within us more and more. This requires, and fosters, patience.

JAMES 1:12–18

Original Meaning

The Crown of Life (1:12). In calling Christians who endure "blessed" (*makarios*) in verse 12, James is saying that Christians *belong* to God. We are a part of his family and life. Like true children, we are to be like him. This idea includes intimacy with God and participation with him in accomplishing his purpose.

Temptations and Their Source (1:13–15). James knows the origin of temptation. It is not God, nor is it Satan and Satan alone. It is instead a personal desire born of self-interest that renders us susceptible to the evil inclination and therefore, at times, to the wiles of the evil one. We may wrongly seek to blame others, Satan, or even God, but ultimately we are morally responsible. According to him, we are "dragged away" and "enticed" by evil desire (v. 14).

The Father of Lights (1:16–18). In the phrase "the Father of the heavenly lights" (v. 17), James has combined two pairs of important theological ideas. The first is that God is the Father of the universe and that he has power over the heavenly luminaries as their creator (Gen 1:14–18; Ps 136:7; Jer 31:35); both concepts recall the creation account. The second pair is the notion of God as Father and of God as light.

James further describes God as one "who does not change like shifting shadows" (v. 17). God is light, and in him there is no shadow. God is also the creator of the heavenly luminaries, which do shift like shadows. As Father, God is ultimately reliable. He does not change, whether in the specific (he is always and will always be the one who gives good things) or the general (God is unchangeable and good).

God controls all of the things to which we wrongfully attribute power, whether we do so from ignorance or to avoid responsibility. God supervises and controls political forces, economic forces, Satan, fate, and the stars. Perhaps James is contrasting God as Father of the heavenly lights with the pretenders to his throne, the forces of the political order, which are mere shadows, unstable and unreliable.

The teaching of verses 12–18 might be summed up as follows. Since we were created by God with the full potential for truth and life, let us avail ourselves of it and do not foolishly squander it or trade it for the false lure. If we stand firm amid trial, if we do not capitulate to the evil desire to blame God and thus engage in sin, we will receive the crown of life in the age to come and its foretaste in the present. Let us remember that God is trustworthy and wholly good, and this will sustain us amid any difficulty.

Application. James calls us to learn spiritual discernment and to judge with right judgment, so that we will be able to see difficulties as opportunities for spiritual growth rather than suppose that in them is evidence that God does not care. To follow Jesus is to learn an attitude of mind and heart that is sensitive to the will and presence of God. God seeks and waits for our attention and for our hearts to be turned to him. The first step is the simple but profound one of opening the door to God in prayer, of asking God to be at work in our minds and hearts, and to change us into his image and likeness.

JAMES 1:19–27

Original Meaning

Receive the Word in Humility, Speak without Anger (1:19–21). The opening verb, "take note of this" (Gk. *iste*, v. 19), can by form be either indicative (a simple statement) or an imperative (a command). It is most likely a command, and it introduces the thoughts that follow: "Everyone should be quick to listen, slow to speak and slow to become angry."

James then turns his attention to two examples that illustrate his point: human anger and the righteous life that God desires. In verse 20 James seems to confirm our suspicion that in the background is to be found a concern with the character of Christian community, for he says that human anger does not produce the righteousness of God. James seems to have no particular type of anger in view, but puts before us the proposition that anger is deleterious to the righteousness God desires of us.

In verse 21 James opens with a brief catena of behaviors that should not characterize the life of a Christian. The first involves both restraint and renunciation: Christians should "get rid of" (NIV) or "strip off" certain behaviors (v. 21a). James instructs us to remove "moral filth" and "evil." These terms are among the strongest he has at his command and imply not only general moral evil, but also a premeditated, evil intent.

But turning from evil is not enough. James also places before us an alternative path: "Humbly accept the word planted in you, which can save you" (v. 21b). Humility is significant not only because the attitude is necessary in order to allow the word to flourish, but also because it is the essential attribute of the poor, those without resources who are dear to the heart of God.

God's word has the power to save us. We are to nurture it, for it is a motive force in the process of saving us. The result of this process is that we will achieve ultimate salvation.

Hearing without Doing Is Worthless (1:22–25). Living a life of holiness requires a life of action. James makes this point with the present imperative "do" (*ginesthe*, v. 22), which has the force of "continue to do." God's people must continue to grow in carrying out the commands laid on them by their hearing of God's word. This hearing is most naturally the public reading of the Scriptures in the context of worship. But hearing alone is insufficient. To hear and not to take action is to lie to oneself, to "deceive" ourselves. Having introduced the idea of eschatological judgment (v. 21b, the word is able to "save" us in ultimate salvation at the day of judgment), James's warning here takes on grave consequences.

In verses 23–24 James's point is that the image in the mirror, whether the product of a furtive glance or an adoring gaze, quickly dissipates; whatever impression forms in the mind and heart while looking in a mirror is temporary.

Verse 25 offers a positive example, but this verse is perhaps the thorniest theological problem in the entire book. For James "perfect law" and "word" are related. Like Jesus, James does not have in mind a new law, but rather the fuller expression or more perfect distillation of the Mosaic law. For the Christian this law is still the will of God, but a more refined apprehension of that will. The perfect law, the word implanted and allowed to take root, is ultimately the very teaching of Jesus.

Pure Religion (1:26–27). Two links connect this section to what has gone before. First, verse 26 highlights the sin of rash speech, the theme that opened the passage (v. 19). Second, here is provided an extension of the teaching of "not merely hearing but doing," in that worship is described as worthless without actions impelled by a godly character. In both this and the previous section, self-deception plays a significant role. The practice of "pure religion" is described here as the control of speech, acts of charity, and resisting temptation.

Application. *Intemperate speech.* While as children we may have chanted, "Sticks and stones may break my bones, but words will never hurt me," the ditty is actually an exercise in whistling in the dark. Words have great power to both wound and heal. Our speech has the power to encourage and nourish life or to snuff it out. Which shall we choose?

When is righteous anger justified? James cautions a slow and deliberate approach. When is righteous anger justified? Perhaps the best answer is to investigate biblical patterns, especially that of the prophets. The prophets certainly expressed righteous anger, as did our Lord Jesus. Yet James advocates slowness of speech. We easily become numb to injustice. Oppression of the powerless needs to be pointed out, and in whatever terms necessary. But not every situation is such a crisis. James would have us choose words that are, in fact, appropriate to the issue.

JAMES 2:1–13

Original Meaning

No Favoritism Based on Appearance (2:1–4). James gives a practical illustration of favoritism in the guise of a question (vv. 2–4). The situation posits the image of two guests at a church meeting. The first is obviously wealthy and not reticent to display that wealth. The second guest is adorned in the garb of the poor. The point is that it makes no sense to show favoritism to wealthy Christians just because of their wealth. After all, it is wealth and status that grants to non-Christians the ability to oppress the church. It makes no sense for Christians to show favoritism based solely on factors that on other occasions are used to exploit Christians.

James's question in verse 4 implies that the known and accepted norm within the Christian community was egalitarian. Such an ethic stands in stark contrast with the surrounding culture. The Old Testament affords no shortage of passages with a similar message.

The Wisdom of Experience Is against Favoritism (2:5–7). James links strong teaching and harsh words with the term *agapētoi* ("beloved"; NIV "dear," v. 5a). Ever the pastor, James conveys a stern message with the tones of gentle tenderness. James buttresses his case by employing an experiential argument. "Listen, my dear brothers and sisters: Has not God chosen those who are poor in the eyes of the world to be rich in faith and to inherit the kingdom he promised those who love him?" (v. 5).

The word James uses for "poor" (*ptōchos*) had by the late first century acquired the sense of the poor who put their trust in God and not in (the hope for) material wealth. For James the contrast is stronger than simply between materially rich and poor; it has to do with those who trust in God and with those whose trust in God is mixed with a trust in the standards of the world.

The phrase "to be rich in faith" indicates that these poor, unlike the rich, not only have "true riches" here in this life but also eschatological riches in that theirs is the kingdom. James lays out for us the proposition that it is not poverty alone that issues forth in this inheritance, but rather the faith that poverty germinates.

Despite the principles outlined by Jesus (and Paul), which James expects his readers to have known, the community has "dishonored" the poor (v. 6). This insult is rendered all the more unbelievable in that by favoring the rich, some in the church are favoring the very class of people who seek to harm the church, for it is the wealthy and powerful who drag Christians to court (v. 6) and slander the name of Christ (v. 7).

The wealthy, Christian and non-Christian alike, were presumably bringing suit against the poor within the church. James implies in verse 7 that whatever the charge, at least part of the reason had to do with the faith of the poor. Even if the charges were not in any sense motivated by the faith of the poor, one motivation would have to be the protection of the wealth and status of the rich, which is itself contrary to the gospel. James's point is that to curry favor with anyone simply because of their wealth is fundamentally to misunderstand the gospel and to do injury to the faith.

Scripture Is against Showing Favoritism (2:8–13). James refers to the specifically Christian understanding of the Old Testament law as "the royal law" (*nomos basilikos*, v. 8). The beauty of this law is that it takes seriously both law and mercy, both sin and grace. God does not excuse us from our sin, but he does forgive us. To excuse is to claim that the offending party is not, in fact, guilty of the offense or to deny the seriousness of the offense. To forgive grants full weight both to guilt and to its seriousness, but it nullifies the guilt.

James goes on to argue that showing favoritism is sin, and this behavior convicts one of breaking the royal law (v. 9). In verse 10 James again echoes Jesus's teachings when he says that to stumble at just one point of the law is to be guilty in all points. The point here is that the injunction to love the neighbor as yourself is total: Christians cannot pick and choose who is to be the neighbor or when they are to follow this law.

James links profession and action (see v. 12). His appeal to judgment is not foreign to the thought of the New Testament. Here is a strong reminder of the true center of the Christian life—the perfect law that is planted within us. For both Jesus and James, the law that is the fulcrum of judgment is the law of love for one's neighbor.

In verse 13 James continues to follow in the Jesus tradition by arguing that for those who do not show mercy, no mercy will be shown. A merciful attitude is one of the evidences that a person truly is alive in Christ. Few commentators argue that the judgment here is eschatological—that is, that one case of showing favoritism condemns the perpetrator to eternal damnation. This seems hardly the point. Rather, James is pointing to the danger of allowing this attitude to grow within both the individual and the church, because if its growth is not retarded and reversed, this attitude will result in a basic thrust of character and will come to dominate future decisions, which will, in fact, affect one's eschatological judgment. It is this total failure to live out the implications of the faith that James sees as evidence of no faith at all—faith without works is dead.

Application. *The peril of favoritism.* Our culture influences the evangelical church in the showing of favoritism, embracing certain expectations based on various markers. In America there are clearly defined roles and professions that, we think, deserve greater respect than others. Wealth is the clearest marker of social status in our culture. Compared to the first century, our age offers a variety of options for its display. James is not against wealth, but he is against the church becoming an arena for the display of wealth used to enhance status.

JAMES 2:14–26

Original Meaning

The Poor Christian Brother or Sister (2:14–17). The passage opens with rhetorical questions (v. 14). What good is faith without deeds? Can authentic faith find expression in a confession of right doctrine alone? Can authentic faith be expressed merely as sentiment that never reaches the point of action? Or is it by necessity a faith that goes beyond these to include practical action? The "faith" in view in the second question of verse 14 is workless faith, not faith per se. James is loathe even to dignify this position with the term "faith."

James then offers an illustration from the life of the church. He envisions a situation in which church members fail to display even the most basic forms of charity to one another. The example is stylized and so obvious that the point cannot be missed.

Having given a hypothetical example of crystal clarity, James surprises his readers with a response that seems unbelievable (v. 16). Who could respond to such a clear need in so deficient a manner, so obviously motivated by an empty heart! James goes on to say that faith without deeds is dead—fails to accomplish the aim of true faith. Without deeds faith is not really true faith—it is only a shadow, a shade, an impostor of true faith.

True Faith, Dead Faith (2:18–20). James next offers a rational argument in order to show that while there may be a type of "faith" that does not issue forth in deeds, such faith is dead; it has no saving power. True faith, he insists, always changes the heart and therefore results in acts of mercy and compassion. The view expressed at the end of verse 18—that there is a legitimate faith without deeds, and another faith with deeds—is consistently denied in James.

In verse 19 James then remarks that to believe in the one God is an excellent starting point, but such an intellectual conclusion is not true faith, for even the demons know this much. Religion that is worth something involves action that grows from the heart. While both James and his opponents believe that a faith with deeds exists and is a saving faith, James cannot agree with his opponents that there is a saving faith that exists without deeds.

In verse 20 the point is that "faith" without works is "faith" in name only. It cannot be saving faith, because it lacks the strength either to attain the proper end of faith (salvation) or the ability to understand that biblical faith is always tied to character and therefore to action. James even makes his point with a bit of wry humor in the form of a wordplay: faith without works (*ergōn*) does not work (*argē* = *a* + *ergos*).

The Example of Abraham (2:21–24). James next employs the example of Abraham to demonstrate the linkage between faith and deeds. This link is not new, he claims, but is in fact the desire of God from the beginning. "Was not our ancestor Abraham considered righteous for what he did when he offered his son Isaac on the altar?" (v. 21). It is possible that the opponent(s) of James had cited Genesis 15:6, which stated that God reckoned righteousness to Abraham because he believed. James, understanding the revered status of Abraham, wishes to point out that the faith of Abraham was not a sterile intellectual assent; rather, it was a faith that manifested itself in trusting actions that were often great risks, such as the near sacrifice of Isaac.

The Example of Rahab (2:25–26). James then uses the example of Rahab to further buttress his claim concerning the unity of faith and deeds. Although a woman of dubious reputation, her actions were evidence of faith. In Jewish tradition in the Babylonian Talmud, Rahab married Joshua and became the ancestor of Jeremiah and Ezekiel (b. Megillah 14b, 15a), and in Christian tradition she is included as among the ancestors of Jesus (Matt 1:5). She showed hospitality to the spies (just as Abraham did to the three strangers). This example is chosen because the church has refused to show hospitality to those whose outward appearance indicated that they had no ability to benefit the church. Yet both Abraham and Rahab showed hospitality to those whose outward appearance mirrored the poor in the church.

Application. In the hallowed halls of universities and colleges, in the sanctified confines of churches, issues such as community development, social action, and justice are studied and discussed. Yet Christian social reformers like John Perkins and his family have lived them out in the concrete, with their blood, sweat, tears, and joy. They offer to us a living monument to the potent caliber of hope for what can be—faith that results in action, a passion for the good of others, and compassion that flows from the very heart of God. James would have these virtues lodge in our hearts and minds, verities whose pursuit is worth the commitment of a lifetime.

JAMES 3:1–12

Original Meaning

Teachers and Pure Speech (3:1–2). Within the early church the position of teacher was one of high status. As noted earlier, the human desire for status was endemic to the Roman world, and some sought illegitimately to meet the need by joining the church and then seeking to become teachers. James provides a strong note of caution in view of the final judgment (v. 1). By nature of their position teachers have an inordinately great opportunity to influence others within the congregation—both for eternal benefit and harm.

In verse 2 James admits a very human truth—none of us is perfect; we all stumble frequently. Moreover, there is at least one sin that is common to everyone, the sin of the tongue. The notion of "perfect" must be that of completeness and maturity, just as in 1:4. This is completeness in Christian virtue, not sinless perfection.

The Tongue Can Control Us (3:3–5). In verses 3–4 James begins a series of illustrations from everyday life meant, in part, to bring home to his readers the power of the tongue either to corrode or to nurture. The first two analogies are not quite precise (the tongue does not control the body in the fashion that a bit controls a horse or a rudder a ship), but the meaning is plain enough.

In verse 5a James displays some of his literary skill, particularly alliteration: the tongue is a small (*mikron*) member (*melos*) but boasts of great things (*megala*). In verse 5b James turns to a new image, that of a fire set by a small spark. Here the image is clearly negative. Few disasters in the ancient world were more feared than fire, as the ancients possessed precious few resources to battle them. The point of the image is to emphasize the great destructive power of the tongue.

The Power of the Tongue (3:6–12). The statement that the tongue is a fire clearly echoes Old Testament imagery concerning the tongue and inopportune speech. But in choosing to use *kosmos* ("world"), James has left us with a term rich in various meanings. The linkage of this word with "evil" in verse 6 suggests that it here refers to the world and its forces opposed to God. James clearly believes that the false teachers are citizens of that world, or are at least under the influence of that world, even if they lack this self-awareness.

The tongue is often guilty of realizing its potential for evil and, in so doing, infects the rest of the body. This, in fact, is what James says at the end of verse 6, that the tongue can corrupt or stain the entire person (*sōma*, literally "body"). Here is another way of making the point that he has already registered: although small, the tongue controls the larger whole (3:2, 3, 4). The tongue can corrupt all of life, whether that of an individual or that of a community. In his phrase "is itself set on fire by hell" (v. 6b), James traces the root of evil, the mouthpiece of which are the teachers and the expressions of which are (particularly) favoritism and antinomianism.

In juxtaposition to the inability of human beings to control the tongue, James offers the idea that human beings can train, and have trained, members of the animal kingdom (v. 7). The inability of the human race to tame the tongue is evidence of the irrational nature of its orientation and effort. The image James uses here is of a barely and inadequately caged beast, which breaks forth with irrational destructive power (v. 8).

Having made the claim that the tongue is untrustworthy and duplicitous, James goes on in verse 9 to provide an example. The reference to "blessing" (NIV "praise") is of pointed significance, for it refers to and calls to mind God himself, as well as to the relationship between humans and God. The fact that the verb "curse" (*kataraomai*, v. 9) occurs in the present tense cements the interpretation that James has in mind a concrete and not hypothetical situation in the church. How can worshipers consciously mistreat their fellows and then expect to worship God in purity (v. 10)?

In verses 11–12, James continues to make the point that abusive speech is irrational. The triple image of the illogicality of expecting trees and vines to produce fruit not their own and of a salt spring to produce fresh water are all intended to round out the point he has made again and again.

Application. Several years ago, a group of friends was backpacking in northern California. On the morning of the last day, during a thunderstorm, they realized that a forest fire was not far away. As the day wore on, the air became increasingly thick with smoke. All day long they could hear and sometimes see the planes as they prepared to drop fire-arresting chemicals on the blaze. When they reached their car and turned on the radio, they learned that the fire had burned to the area where they had camped just the night before. After burning several hundred acres, the fire was arrested by a combination of the storm and the efforts of fire fighters. It had started as the result of one careless match. There is great potential stored up in the tongue, just as there is great potential in the position of teacher. Both must be exercised with the wisdom of God.

JAMES 3:13–18

Original Meaning. James begins this new section by offering an alternative vision of wisdom to that of his opponents—namely, that true wisdom is marked not by ambition and a desire for status, but rather by humility. Clearly the teachers whom James has opposed are in view. They have arrogated to themselves a position of authority as those qualified to instruct the Christian community, and in so doing have offered themselves as "wise" (v. 13a).

In verse 13b the phrase *en prautēti sophias* ("in the humility that comes from wisdom") is somewhat unwieldy, suggesting that its origin is Hebrew and not Greek. There are parallels in both the Old Testament and the New. Neither Moses (Num 12:1–3) nor Jesus (Matt 11:29) were interested in personal popularity or power, nor did they defend themselves, but in humility pointed others to God. In similar fashion the Christian in humility is to do good deeds to the glory of God. This is the spirit of true wisdom.

Verse 14 presents a contrasting picture: a bitter and selfish person. The term the NIV translates as "selfish ambition" is *eritheia*. Discord has come to the Christian community as a result of status-seeking, and some of these have usurped the spiritual offices of the church in order to teach and propagate this worldly philosophy.

Significantly, in verse 15 James does not call what his opponents espouse wisdom, preferring to refer to it in veiled fashion. Their "wisdom" is not from God, which can be had simply by asking (1:5). In saying this James makes a clear argument that the wisdom of these teachers is not neutral or trivial. He does this by arranging the sources of this "wisdom" in an escalating crescendo of perniciousness. The first is *epigeios*, or "earthbound" (NIV "earthly"). Here the image of the world, as elsewhere in James, plays a negative role. Next, this wisdom is *psychikos*, or "unspiritual." The term denoted beings possessing merely life, bereft of the touch of the Spirit of God. Finally, such "wisdom" is, worst of all, demonic in origin. This term, *daimoniōdēs*, is rare; it appears nowhere else in Scripture and is not to be found in Greek literature before James. Such teaching and its derivative behavior is instigated by demons and the fallen spiritual world.

In verse 16 James argues from the perspective of the practical. The wisdom of his opponents, rooted in "envy and selfish ambition," has done nothing to strengthen the body, but rather has served only to bring "disorder and every evil practice."

Their teaching has not added anything good to the church, but instead has caused the church to seriously question its direction, and even its heart and soul. Combined with this is all manner of evil practice.

In verse 17 James has arranged seven virtues to employ assonance, first with *e*, then with *a*: peace-loving (*eirēnikē*), considerate (*epieikēs*), submissive (*eupeithēs*), full of mercy (*mestē eleous*), good fruit (*karpōn agathōn*), impartial (*adiakritos*), and sincere (*anypokritos*). Such wisdom also creates a peace-making spirit (v. 18). This is of particular importance here, given the problem of discord in the church.

Application. Do not be fooled or cowed, James intones. False teaching, and the failure to recognize and resist it, is dangerous in the extreme. The poison begins innocently, in the fertile receptacle of our minds and hearts. It grows to dominate our actions. Finally, through our actions it spreads to infect the community around us. The most effective course to avoid this evil, James reminds us, is to walk firmly and with resolve in the path of heavenly wisdom and its fruits.

JAMES 4:1–10

Original Meaning

Prayers Offered in Anger and Desire (4:1–3). The church is beset by jealousy, selfish ambition, slander, anger, a willingness to depart from received teaching, and a host of other ills that follow the pattern of its culture. Certain teachers had won a following by offering a philosophy that encouraged the pursuit of status. Arrayed against these were believers loyal to the gospel who correctly understood the threat. The members of this group reacted variously to those following the teachers of false wisdom—some wanting peace at any price, others advocating a fight for the soul of the church.

Within the Christian community there is a wide variety of impulses. James says their disputes come from the "desires" within them (v. 1). In verses 2–3, James points out that the prayers his readers have offered are marked by their desire for "pleasures." The prayer was not answered positively because, in part, the prayer assumed a certain arrogance, the presumption that the one praying knew what was best. What is needed, of course, is patience and a willingness to be molded by God.

The Bane of Compromise (4:4–6). In verse 4 James adopts the mantle of elder and offers a rebuke as to errant children. By designating them "adulterous people," he recalls a frequent Old Testament rebuke and artfully holds out to his readers inclusion even as he wields the whip of chastisement. Many choose friendship with the world without realizing that it means enmity with God.

Verse 5 presents at least two problems of interpretation. First, what Scripture does James have in mind, for there is no Old Testament text to correspond to the quote? It is possible that James here summarizes the many Old Testament passages that speak of the jealousy of God. James's point is that God earnestly desires his spirit to reside in us. Second, what is the subject and what is the object of the verb "longs for" (*epipothei*)? The point is plainly that God desires with all of his heart for us to come home and to live with and in him. Instead, we follow the wisdom of the world, whether knowingly or unwittingly, and by following that errant path we can never achieve what we truly seek.

In verse 6 James holds out a lifeline to those who have apparently been ignorant of the gravity of their situation. God's grace, he says, is still available and abundant for them if they will humble themselves. Yet they are warned, for God's face is set against the proud.

Repentance and Forgiveness (4:7–10). Verse 7 opens a series of ten imperatives, or commands, built on the foundation laid in verse 6. These commands comprise James's recipe for humility before God. The idea of submission carries with it the full range intended by the term *repentance*, which is not only a change of direction but also a humble and contrite spirit. If this path is chosen, the response of God is forgiveness. James then expands these points.

The first component of submission to God is to "resist the devil" (v. 7b). The idea that the devil can be resisted is known in both Jewish and Christian thought. Within the theology of the New Testament the power of Satan was severely curtailed at the crucifixion and resurrection, and it is possible that James has this in mind. The correlate to "resist the devil" is "come near to God" (v. 8a).

To the admonition to cleanse themselves James adds obvious and perhaps even public acts of contrition (v. 9). In urging grief and a shift from laughter to mourning and joy to gloom, James reminds his readers that the false paths they thought would lead to true laughter and joy are dead ends and need to be abandoned.

Application. *Community.* James 4:1–10 offers a strong call to community, and especially community created by a spirit of humility and forgiveness. Certainly the congregation to which James wrote needed such direction. Our world is awash in facsimiles of true community. An avenue often attempted by evangelicals in America is that of reforming the state. Evangelicals must do more than work for structural change, for structures are weak and easily co-opted by Satan. The heart must change, for without these deeper values, the law is merely external. James implores us to draw near to God, not merely to adopt moral guidelines of which God would approve.

JAMES 4:11–17

Original Meaning

Pure Speech Does Not Condemn (4:11–12). The verb the NIV renders as "slander" is *katalaleō*, which means "to speak ill of," though it can also carry the more narrowly focused meaning of speaking falsely. James has in mind harsh criticism and condemnation. What is so keenly disturbing for James is the central place this command occupied in the ethical teaching of Jesus. To ignore this command is, in effect, to repudiate Christ and to render the self-description "Christian" a falsehood.

Here James is again in touch with a widely held tradition, that Christians should not judge others. According to James, when we judge others, we not only arrogate to ourselves what belongs to God alone, but we also invite and pronounce judgment on ourselves. This is not meant to exclude honest and healthy discussion among believers, but it is to make clear a strong warning that the line demarking proper from sinful discourse is easily crossed.

Do Not Boast, for Tomorrow Is Uncertain (4:13–17). Verse 13 contains a quotation; presumably James has heard that such statements have been on the lips of the merchants in the city. James is not arguing against the making of money or even against the desire to make money; rather, he is against the attitude of self-contained certainty, the same smug attitude that marked the teaching of the false teachers. Such certainty is revelatory of an attitude that does not take God seriously enough, a mind-set for which the making of money outstrips devotion to God in importance.

At this point it is proper to ask about these traders and merchants. We know of several New Testament Christians with wealth. Chloe, for example, a female leader in the church in Corinth, had enough money to send some of her people with a message to Paul (1 Cor 1:11). So the reference to travel and the considerable resources that such travel indicates do not necessarily preclude these traders from membership in the church.

The idea of the uncertainty of riches is universal, but Old Testament parallels are instructive. For James the real question is how to approach life when the outcome is uncertain. His answer is to trust in God's graciousness, not in human plans.

There is no clear biblical referent for the formula James records in verse 15, although the idea of the Lord's will pervades Scripture (e.g., Prov 19:21). This verse makes it clear that James is not against planning. Rather, James wants such planning to be given its proper priority, and none higher. God must be in control of such planning.

In verse 16, James sets limits on speech. He has already mentioned boasting. This boasting is the sin mentioned in verse 13: the merchants plan and carry on as if God were unimportant or did not even exist. Instead, they should have made their plans in prayer and in the anticipation that God may in fact change those plans.

In verse 17, James argues that sins of both commission and omission are grievous, especially when done knowingly. The making of plans as though the future is certain is itself a sin, because functionally it is a denial of God, either his importance or even his very existence. Then to boast about it is a further sin. James may perhaps be building on the saying of Jesus in Luke 12:47. Knowledge of right places us under a moral obligation to do right.

Application. *The folly of boasting in the uncertain.* When James counsels us that tomorrow is never certain, he is right. For Christians to rely on anything other than God is to lack integrity; it is to be double-minded. Jesus made decisions on the basis of principles rooted in Scripture and a sensitivity to the will of God. James would have us lead lives of similar fidelity—lives that integrate heart, mind, attitudes, and actions.

JAMES 5:1–6

Original Meaning

Condemning Introduction (5:1). James begins by condemning the unfeeling and selfish attitude of the wealthy landowners. These wealthy people must "weep and wail." The reason is not their wealth per se, but the fact that they have not sought to use their wealth to alleviate the sufferings of the poor.

A Catalogue of Futility (5:2–3). Having condemned the wealthy landowners for their indifference, James next points out that riches are worthless when it comes to eternal salvation. Just as it would be criminally ridiculous to hoard wealth when the parousia is imminent, so Christians who have heard Jesus's message and yet shortchange needy workers and hoard wealth are morally liable. The treasure awaiting them is not fine clothing or gold, but misery.

An Inventory of Selfishness (5:4–6). James then lists specific behaviors that have contributed to the hoarding of wealth. For one thing, they have not paid their hired laborers their due, thereby robbing their own neighbors of earned pay. Because God has already heard their cry, the voice of judgment against the wealthy has already begun to sound.

In verse 5 James turns his attention from the hardship imposed on others to the ease and sloth of the wealthy. The point of verse 5 recalls the parable of the rich man and Lazarus in Luke 16:19–31. In both the rich can expect nothing but torment in the next life.

The final accusation aimed at the landed class is their

plotting of the wrongful treatment and even murder of the innocent (v. 6). The death referred to here may be the result of starvation caused by the withholding of wages. They suffered and died, and the landed class was not even aware of their plight. This is perhaps an even more grievous offense than if the wealthy were watching this suffering with sickening glee.

Application. *The power and the peril of wealth.* What would James think of the way American evangelical churches and parishioners spend money? We are generally upper middle class, owning luxury cars, swimming pools, and the latest clothes. James warns us that our bent to ignore God and others while enjoying material goods and that our desire for money render us open to misery and judgment. The idea of judgment in the New Testament is enormously complex; it includes both chastening judgment, which has as its aim restoration (1 Cor 11:32), and separation from God and eternal destruction (John 3:19; Heb 10:27). It is unclear which James has in mind in our text, but neither is to be coveted. At the very least the "misery" he imagines is the realization that the wealth and the material goods in which we trusted have turned; they have proved untrustworthy, having rotted before our eyes.

JAMES 5:7–11

Original Meaning

The Call to Patience (5:7–8). Christians are enjoined to be patient until the Lord comes (v. 7). The use of *parousia* here signals the expected return of Jesus, and so "Lord," a term often used in James to refer to God (see, e.g., 5:4), here refers to Jesus. Some have argued that James is wholly without Christology. Here a statement of high Christology is present.

As a practical illustration of such patience, James refers to a farmer who waits patiently for harvest time and for the autumn and spring rains. In a similar manner the Christian and the Christian community must wait patiently for the coming of the Lord, for nothing can be done to speed the *parousia* on its way. Whether or not James envisioned an imminent return of Christ, perhaps the point here is that as Christians we are to live in community with one another as if the new day has already dawned.

Avoid Complaining (5:9). If we are correct in seeing that this section has as its primary audience the poor, then in verse 9 James has a warning for them as well: despite the abuse you have endured, do not grumble. Life does bring trials, of course, but no one is served by the cultivation of a spirit of complaining.

Biblical Examples of Patience (5:10–11). The prophets endured, patiently and hopefully waiting for the judgment and the mercy of God. Those who have gone into the presence of God with such a life of perseverance are truly "blessed." From the example of the prophets James turns to the specific example of Job (v. 11). As a result of his sufferings, he gained greater knowledge of God, which may indeed be God's purpose and the hope James has as the result of the sufferings that are the background to this passage.

Application. *Patience.* People in times of trouble naturally hope for release. But James uses the language of eschatology to prepare his readers for spiritual growth. Within the history of Christian spirituality, difficult circumstances are considered a normal and necessary part of the process of spiritual growth and bear certain results that prepare us for the age to come.

JAMES 5:12–18

Original Meaning

The Taking of Oaths (5:12). The point at issue in this verse is the taking of an oath—that is, invoking the name of God in order to buttress the truthfulness of what one has said. Here James is fully in line with the teaching of the Old Testament that false swearing and the giving of oaths is forbidden (e.g., Lev 19:12). James is likely drawing on a saying from Jesus here (see Matt 5:34–37). The problem is, of course, that sometimes people utter falsehoods knowingly, but at other times they are unable to accomplish what they intend. The prohibition recognizes this and serves to limit and to exclude these unintentional infelicities.

Prayer (5:13–18). While the most obvious feature of this section may seem to be healing—more specifically, the prayer over and anointing of the sick (v. 15)—the true theme of the passage is prayer (v. 16). The entire section is caught up by issues involving prayer, as prayer is mentioned in every verse. James here deals with the prayer of the individual (v. 13), the prayer of the elders (vv. 14–15), the prayers of friends and companions for one another (v. 16), and finally the prayer of the righteous prophet Elijah (vv. 17–18).

The first issue raised is that of suffering (v. 13a). In such times James advocates neither anger nor stoic resignation, for the former poisons the spirit and the latter dulls the mind. Instead, he advocates prayer. It is a response that allows us to be active and positive and keeps us in communion with God.

Then James discusses the case of those who are happy (v. 13b). The word he uses (*euthymeō*) refers to a deeply rooted happiness, a contentment of the heart. James wants his readers to remember that God desires and deserves our prayers and praise in both difficult and pleasant times.

The sick person is to be "prayed over" (v. 14b). It is obvious that the basis for this action is the firm belief that God is the source of healing. The chief issue is whether the verbs refer to eschatological and therefore spiritual healing, or to physical healing. While these verbs can be made to bear an eschatological nuance, the weight of the grammatical and lexical evidence is on the side of a physical understanding of the passage. After all, the person about whom this is written is still alive! James clearly teaches here that sickness caused by sin can be alleviated through public confession and prayer for healing.

James concludes with the thought that just as the prayer of the righteous Elijah resulted in the refreshing of the earth, so the prayer of the righteous believer can result in the refreshing and healing of a Christian afflicted by sickness caused by sin.

Application. *Prayer and joy in adversity.* We inhabit a social and cultural world in which a great premium is placed on the elimination of discomfort. In the face of this potent cultural norm, evangelicals need to go against the grain and appropriate a biblical understanding of adversity. God uses adversity in the interests of spiritual preparation. Prayer in adversity also urges us to renounce the materialism and the self-centeredness of the world. This has been a constant theme in James.

JAMES 5:19–20

Original Meaning. In this laconic conclusion James returns to the themes of sin and forgiveness. In so doing he reveals his pastoral heart. The passage is related to the previous section in that forgiveness follows confession.

The passage is short—in fact, a single sentence. But it should not be missed that in this one sentence James marshals no less than three significant theological ideas:

1. Christians have the opportunity and the responsibility to care for one another through the task of loving doctrinal and moral correction. The theme here is not evangelism but the care and maintenance of the Christian community.
2. The penalty for sin is death; James will not equivocate on this.
3. In this process, the agent of reconciliation "covers" a multitude of sins.

James ends his letter abruptly by reminding his readers that the wise person walks with God in wisdom. Sin is a problem both corporate and personal. It is subtle, tenacious, and dangerous; it should not be underestimated. Christians have a responsibility to their world and to one another.

Application. *Forgiveness and discipline.* The teaching of James throughout his letter often feels harsh and even rigid. Yet here, at the end of his letter, James provides a strong touch of grace. The note that has sounded softly through most of the letter here rings out loud and true. Forgiveness must be offered, but it must be balanced with faith that is active, faith that has captured mind and heart and body. James calls God's people to moral purity and to maintaining a heart of forgiveness. When we do so, we give evidence that we are true children of God, combining both faith and actions in the fashion that James has taught.

1 PETER

INTRODUCTION TO 1 PETER

The apostle Peter probably wrote this letter near the outset of Emperor Nero's persecution of the church—perhaps between AD 62–65. He wrote it to believers scattered throughout the Roman provinces of northwestern Asia Minor (modern Turkey, see 1:1). Peter's letter is an exhortation (5:12) to socially disenfranchised Christians to live steadfastly before God with faithfulness, holiness, and love. This steadfastness may lead to suffering, but a genuine understanding of persecution permits them to face it head-on and go forward faithfully. The foundation of their faithfulness even amid persecution is a clear understanding of their salvation that Peter paints so graphically in the letter.

BOOK OUTLINE

I. Salutation (1:1–2)
II. Exhortations Based on Salvation (1:3–2:10)
III. Exhortations Based on Social Groups (2:11–4:11)
IV. Exhortations Based on the Church (4:12–5:11)
V. Conclusion (5:12–14)

1 PETER 1:1–2

Original Meaning. Peter's salutation is one of the richest greetings to open a letter in the New Testament. It contains pastoral warmth and theological sweep. Peter's salutation contains both a penetrating description of the audience and a theological explanation of how they became Christians.

Peter as author of the letter was an "apostle of Jesus Christ." An apostle is one who was personally called by Jesus Christ to a special ministry of founding the church; the corollary of that calling is that an apostle represents, as an ambassador does a president, the one who sent him.

The geographical location of Peter's churches is not as important as the terms he uses to describe their social and spiritual status. To be "elect" means to receive God's grace; this benefit is the result of God's initiative, not ours. To be one of God's elect is a source of joy and comfort (for we know God's will cannot be thwarted) and of exhortation and demand (for we know God is working in us to enable us to do his will).

This group of churches was composed almost entirely of persons drawn from the slave classes and the disenfranchised. They were socially marginalized people, and their faith led to an association that had no social acceptance and therefore, at the very least, exacerbated their social conditions. They were not only castaways because of their social status but were also castaways because of their commitment to Jesus, to a life of holiness, and to a group of similarly disenfranchised people—the church.

As with other letters in the New Testament, the addressees are greeted in both a customary Greco-Roman way ("grace") and in a Jewish way ("peace"). Especially under the influence of early Christian and Jewish theology, these two terms exemplify not only friendliness to others but the rootedness of that friendliness in the gracious and peacemaking ways of God.

Application. There are numerous ways that these two verses might be readily applied today. One would be that, with the rising influence of Christian attempts at political activism in the Western world, particularly in the United States, the text offers two words of exhortation. First, this text urges us to act as Christians and in a Christian manner (especially in heated situations when divisive topics are being discussed), and second it urges us to understand that our individual and fundamental identity is as a child of God and part of God's chosen people, not as part of our social or political party.

1 PETER 1:3–12

Original Meaning

Praise Expressed (1:3–5). The sentence is simple in that it is a statement of praise to God, and the blessing is directed to the God *and* Father. This God and Father is blessed because he has given us new birth. This new birth is the result of his mercy, which grows into a living hope; that hope is defined as an inheritance. Put differently, Peter blesses God the Father because of his salvation and its manifold benefits.

Peter tells the readers that they have benefited from this new birth because of God's "mercy" (v. 3). Mercy is that pity God shows toward humans despite their sin and because of their total helplessness to right their wrongs; God permits them to be part of the special people of his favor (2:10). This great new birth sets off a chain reaction in his plan of redemption: his mercy stimulates their new birth, and their new birth stimulates a "living hope" (1:3).

The chain reaction continues. Not only does the new birth

stimulate a living hope, but that living hope is defined by "an inheritance that can never perish, spoil or fade" (v. 4). That inheritance is their completed salvation (1:3, 4, 5, 6–9) and eternal life in the kingdom of God. The only condition God sets for his people is that they must have faith (v. 5).

Digression on Joy and Love Despite Their Suffering (1:6–9). The problem facing these Christians in Asia Minor is that they are suffering "grief in all kinds of trials" (v. 6). They can be glad because they will survive this trial and find themselves in the glorious situation of salvation.

Since his readers will be found acceptable to God on the day when Jesus Christ is revealed, Peter turns in verses 8–9 to the present relationship of these Christians to Jesus. Their current response is that they love Christ in spite of not having seen him.

Digression on the Prophetic Search for Salvation (1:10–12). Peter contends that this salvation is the very salvation that the ancient prophets were seeking in all its details but never found. Peter's ultimate point is to demonstrate the privilege of enjoying salvation in his era, the privilege of living in the "AD" rather than the "BC" era.

Thus, Peter begins with the prophetic inquiry (v. 10). Their passion, whether they knew the exact longing of their hearts or not, was the grace that the Asian Christians found in Christ.

Verse 11 gives the topic of the prophets' inquiry. Peter writes that it was "the Spirit of Christ in them" that prompted their inquiry, and ultimately they were investigating "the sufferings of the Messiah and the glories that would follow." No matter how intense their search or profound their vision, Peter insists that these prophets, like John the Baptist after them, only served a preliminary role in the plan of God (v. 12). They were preparing the world and God's people for a later time—and that later time is now.

Application. Our world is so pluralistic that it has become anticultural to speak of *the necessity of salvation*. Furthermore, we have been easily led astray into following socially significant ministries rather than following the path of salvation as the road Christians should travel. The centrality of salvation, a cardinal doctrine of the Christian faith, is offensive to our culture. As a result, suffering often accompanies the preaching of salvation. Thus, the need to refocus our energies on the message of salvation stems in part from our fear of some form of cultural persecution.

The second problem staring Peter's message in the face today is the pervasive *lack or denial of a sense of any need for salvation* in contemporary society. To speak of such a need is to be old-fashioned, out of touch, and even offensive. At the root of this denial is a view that sees people as essentially good (though possibly hurting through some sickness or victimization) and not as sinners in the sight of God who need divine grace and re-creation. Accordingly, to speak to our society of the need for salvation in order to be acceptable to God is to speak a language that our culture simply does not hear or want to hear. While centuries have been crossed since Peter wrote this letter, this strangeness of the message of salvation remains similar. And as this strangeness led to suffering for the early Christians, so also it leads to suffering in our world.

1 PETER 1:13–25

Original Meaning

First Exhortation: Hope (1:13). Peter's first image is an ancient one that literally reads, "gird up the loins of your mind." This image is drawn from the ancient (and still modern for some in the Middle East) form of dress in which a man's long outer "shirt" draped down to his ankles, obviously preventing agile and quick motions and strenuous work. As a result, when such actions were needed, a man tucked his shirt into his belt and thus girded himself for action. Peter wants his churches to maintain a loose grip on this world and a tight grip on the world to come.

The second image is drawn from the all-too-realistic world of drunkenness; drunks have no control over themselves or their body. Peter's expression is metaphorical in that believers are to be totally in tune with God's plan in history, so much so that they set their hope on the future and live in light of that day.

Peter urges his readers to see history the way God has planned it. Though now they may suffer unjustly at the hands of evil people, someday Christ will return, and justice will be fully established. As a result, Christians are to live in light of that day of manifested grace.

Second Exhortation: Holiness (1:14–16). As Paul urged the Romans not to be conformed to this world (Rom 12:2), so Peter urges his readers not to be conformed to their former passions, which dominated their lives prior to their entrance into God's family. Since they are now children of obedience (v. 14a), they are to be holy, just as God is holy. We can assume that Peter has in mind here the similarity children are to have to their parents.

God is altogether holy. Because he had drawn Israel into a special relationship with himself, he expected his people to reflect his nature, including his holiness. The fundamental connection made here is twofold: Christians should be holy both because they have been converted (v. 14a) and because they are children of a God who is himself altogether holy (vv. 15–16). I can think of no section in the Bible that involves more interweaving of ethical exhortation and theological foundations for ethics than these three verses.

Third Exhortation: Fear of God (1:17–21). The flow of thought here again emphasizes the foundation of ethics. Peter says that if believers call as Father the one who judges indiscriminately, then they had better live in fear of this God, for he is altogether holy and will judge justly. Knowing that God is judge and that he judges with absolute fairness drives us to live in a healthy fear and awe of him. When his beautiful, holy love checks our thoughts and actions, we live in the light of his character, regardless of our social conditions.

To this fear of the judge Peter adds a second motive for a life of obedience: the nature of redemption (vv. 18–21). The former life of his addressees was an "empty way of life handed down to you from your ancestors" (v. 18). From this former life believers have been redeemed—that is, purchased with a price, the blood of Jesus Christ. As a result, we are now back in God's ownership as his servants, free from sin and death. Since we know we have been redeemed by the precious blood of Christ, we should be grateful to God for our new family and live in fear and holiness before him.

Fourth Exhortation: Love One Another (1:22–25). Peter's final exhortation is again rooted in the "before and after" of conversion. Their purification was by means of the sprinkling of Christ's blood, and they responded to God by obeying the truth of the gospel (1:2, 14). The result of obeying the truth was that they were ushered into the realm of love. Peter wants churches filled with people who love one another and where safe intimacy is the inevitable result of being made holy by God's grace.

Peter returns again to the foundation of their love: their regeneration (v. 23). Humans and humanly created things are like grass in that they will perish and vanish away. But the word of God, planted in Christians, is eternal and grows in those same Christians to give them an eternal existence.

Application. Ethics are either founded in ourselves (e.g., through reason, intuition, nature, moral instinct, conscience) or outside ourselves (e.g., through revelation, an established code of ethics, a governmental constitution). Christian orthodoxy teaches that *ethics flows from salvation* and that humans, by themselves, cannot discern the will of God. We know what is good from what is bad because God has told us.

Peter provides us with at least three foundations for determining whether an action is right or wrong. First, does it conform to the character of God? Second, is it the natural outcome of a life that has benefited from the salvation of God? Finally, will it stand up to God's scrutiny in that final day when he ushers us into his glorious presence?

1 PETER 2:1–10

Original Meaning

Fifth Exhortation: Desire the Word (2:1–3). "Pure spiritual milk" (v. 2) refers to the very things that nourish the Christian community in its growth: knowledge of God, prayer, instruction in the gospel, faithful obedience, and hearing God's preached word. This desire is accompanied by learning to "rid yourselves of" (v. 1) problems that arise in Christian assemblies when spiritual things are not desired.

If you, Peter says to his readers, learn to yearn for spiritual nourishment, you will "grow up in your salvation" (v. 2). Peter is concerned here about the church, regardless of its numerical strength, becoming desirous of spiritual nourishment and spiritual growth. If they yearn for spiritual nourishment, they will grow into that final salvation that is being protected for them by God as they continue in their faith.

All of this is founded on the fact "that you have tasted that the Lord is good" (v. 3). Because the Lord himself is spiritually satisfying, they are to focus their lives on spiritual nourishment and growth, for it is through this kind of development that they will attain their hope of salvation.

Sixth Exhortation: Build a Spiritual House (2:4–5). Peter exhorts believers to build a spiritual house. The churches in Asia Minor must see themselves as "living stones" (v. 5) connected to the "living Stone" (v. 4), and they must unify themselves so that they may become a spiritual house. That is, instead of being a simple group of social outcasts, they must find their identity and cohesion in their spiritual relationship to the living Stone. Jesus was rejected by human beings but chosen by God, just as his readers were being rejected by humans. This reflection about Christ is developed at 2:6–8.

Digression on Christ, the Rejected-Accepted Messiah (2:6–8). Peter's quotation is only one prophetic word drawn from the context in Isaiah ("stone"), but he assumes the entirety of the context in applying it. Peter sees in this word from Scripture a larger context that shows that the saying itself is to be understood in its former tragic sense: the Stone has been laid, but those who walk in Zion trip over it.

Peter then applies the text to the contemporary responses to Christ in Asia Minor and probably elsewhere. God's act of appointing Jesus as the living Stone has become both honor for believers and judgment for unbelievers; this was God's design, and everything happens according to his will.

Digression on the Church, the Acceptance Group (2:9–10). The four descriptors listed here do not describe individual Christians but the church as a whole. However, the function of the individual is a mirroring of the larger body, so that Christians individually do enjoy the privilege of access to God. The purpose of the church given here is to announce the good tidings of peace and joy that can be found in Christ. Peter also here in verse 10 appropriates the story of Hosea for the church, except that here "not a people" and "had not received mercy" describe their pagan past, while in Hosea these phrases describe God's judgment on Israel for their disobedience (see Hos 1:9–2:1, 2:23).

Application. One of Peter's major concerns in this letter can be broadly labeled "the relationship of the church to the state," though he did not think in those terms. Peter sees the primary business of the church to be concerned with itself, its own identity, and its own formation, not in terms of how it can either counter or enhance the state. The primary mission of the church is to grow as a spiritual community and to declare the virtues of God. Peter does not deny that Christians should be involved in society, nor does he insist (as nearly all sectarian movements do) that they must insulate themselves from the world's values by separating from the world. The entire sweep of the Bible teaches that Christians in non-Christian environments are not to be worried so much about changing their environments as they are to remain faithful in whatever kind of environment they find themselves.

1 PETER 2:11–12

Original Meaning

The Condition of the Believers (2:11a). The description of believers as "foreigners and exiles" here does not refer so much to their pilgrimage from this life to the next as to their particular social status as people without rights and without a permanent residence in the Roman Empire. These socially excluded Christians should provide no basis whatsoever for those above them and against them to persecute them or accuse them of improper behavior. Peter wants them to live an exemplary life to provide an attractive alternative to the pagan way of life. Such a life may even lead some to cast their lot with this Jewish Messiah, Jesus Christ.

The Exhortation to Good Behavior (2:11b). Peter then urges his readers to deny themselves the temporary pleasures of indulging in physical, sinful passions because those impulses prevent them from living a spiritual life. Abstaining from fleshly passions is the negative dimension of living a holy and obedient life.

The Purpose of Their Good Behavior (2:12). Peter situates this ethic of reputation in a specific *problem* (v. 12b): "though they accuse you of doing wrong." Peter urges his readers to live circumspectly and honorably when accusations are lodged against them and to refrain from insulting their unjust accusers.

Repeating himself, Peter offers once again the *alternative* (v. 12c): "that . . . they may see your good deeds." Yet this time he adds the *result*—namely, that the opponents will "glorify God on the day he visits us" (v. 12d). The issue here is what "on the day he visits us" means. Peter foresees judgment coming on the unbelieving world. He has the final day of judgment in view here, the day on which God will vindicate the good behavior of Christians and will drive the hostile accusers to see that they were wrong.

Application. We need to recognize that the forces working today to enculturate the mandates and truth of the gospel and to swallow holiness are *not as overtly physical as they were in Peter's day.* But the threat to the church is not to be minimized. In particular, we are dealing with the forces of modernization, privatization, and secularization. These forces war against our souls today, just as other forces warred against the souls of the Christians in Peter's day in Asia Minor. Why, for example, do so many Christians think that the essence of Christian living is to be disciplined and efficient? While such ideas are not absent in the Bible, they are hardly held up as core values. Do we not hold them up so high today because they reflect what we have found effective in our capitalistic society? Culture influences us more than we will ever know.

1 PETER 2:13–17

Original Meaning. If the early dating of 1 Peter is correct (early 60s), then the emperor to whom Peter is referring in verse 13 is none other than the rascal Nero. Such a setting has significant implications for the Christian attitude to the state, for it demonstrates that Christians are expected to be good citizens even in extreme situations.

The local governor mentioned in verse 14 has derived authority and often exercised it in a moral direction. Peter's concern is with the need for Christians to be good people so that the judicial arm of the governor is not raised over the churches. They must remember not only that their governor has authority to punish, but also that he can honor them for their good deeds.

A second part of Peter's discussion of the relationship to the state concerns the explanation for doing good (v. 15): they should submit to the various levels of governing authorities *because* in so doing their behavior will silence their accusing ignorance.

Next, Peter adds a condition for submitting to the authorities (v. 16). These socially excluded Christians are slaves of God, not Caesar. But they are not to use this freedom from human authorities as an excuse for living in chaos and insubordination.

Finally, Peter repeats his exhortation (v. 17). Peter details three specific manifestations of this proper respect. Their holy living, their abstinence from fleshly inspired passions, is to be manifested in respect for all people, whether that means the church, God, or the emperor. Such conduct is thus orderly and will prevent the gospel from disrepute and stave off some of the persecution that may be imminent.

Application. The Christian is to be obedient to the structures of society and to live within those structures, but such obedience at times may involve a justifiable civil disobedience to something unjust or idolatrous that remains within that governmental structure (cf. Acts 5:29). Christians at such times must speak out against the government. But this has to be done in ways that honor Christ and remain peaceful and nonviolent.

1 PETER 2:18–25

Original Meaning

The Exhortation (2:18). Peter here insists that Christian slaves should be obedient to all masters, regardless of their personal characteristics. The principles enunciated at 2:11–12 now become critical: the slaves are to be, like the social members of 2:13–17, obedient because it is God's will (cf. 2:19–20) and because through such obedience they will both witness to God's grace and provide him with a measuring stick for their opponents at the judgment.

Slavery is slavery, the ownership of another's body, whether it is ancient Rome, ancient Asia Minor, or the early American New World slavery. The Roman and Greek worlds anchored their entire economic system in this institution. In the Roman world, slavery was not usually a permanent condition of life. Rather, it was a temporary condition on the path toward freedom. In fact, it is entirely possible that one reason Peter urged Christian slaves to be submissive and obedient was that by living obediently, they could be set free.

The idea of slavery as the foundation of the Roman economy needs to be stressed, and this foundation may well lie at the heart of early Christian exhortations to remain submissive to masters. If Christians became known for opposing the institution, the Roman authorities would immediately, and perhaps even irreparably, damage the movement. Put differently, it was important to the survival of Christianity for its slaves to be good slaves. Since this was the case, one motive for Peter's exhortation would have been the desire for the fledgling church to survive as a movement.

The Motivation (2:19–20). What pleases God—if one is going to suffer—is suffering for doing good. If Roman slaves suffer in a submissive condition, then it is God's will for them to experience the suffering; if they suffer for insubordination, then they are acting outside of God's will for his people.

The Foundation (2:21–25). Peter proceeds to contend that suffering is the slaves' calling from God (v. 21) and, adding a new feature, suggests that the call to suffer is rooted in following Jesus. The suffering of Christ created a general pattern that believers were to follow. The reason his suffering is such a noteworthy example for Peter's teaching is because of the condition of perfection that Jesus achieved (vv. 22–23). That is, Jesus exemplified someone who suffered for doing good; he was perfect and yet suffered. Thus, Christian slaves should take this example as a paradigm for their lifestyle.

Application. The suffering of Christ is a paradigm of Christian existence. Churches today need to hear the message about the *cruciform nature of Christian existence*, especially since our litigant society is wasting far too much of its energy in defending personal rights. In such a society it is fundamental for Christians to sound forth a different message—that of Jesus Christ, who suffered injustice in order to testify to God's grace.

1 PETER 3:1–7

Original Meaning

Exhortation to Wives (3:1–6). *The Exhortation to Submit (3:1–2).* We must beware of the problem of hearing a passage today in a way that was never intended. To begin with, we must admit that great abuses have taken place and have led many to see in this passage some kind of moral subjugation of women by men.

What was it like for women in the ancient world? In Jewish perspective, while women were respected and protected in the laws, they were treated as inferior in most every way to men. Women in the Greco-Roman world, on the other hand, were in most cases better off. Roman society in particular allowed more property rights for women, permitted greater leverage for women in marriage and divorce situations, and encouraged more education for women.

Peter is urging the women of the Asia Minor churches to live a life that is respectable in society so that they will be able to maintain a good reputation for the gospel. That will mean that "submission" here probably does not refer to the same kind of restrictions in society that such a concept meant in Palestine. Furthermore, it makes Peter's injunction a more pragmatic one. That is, Peter wants wives to submit *because of the influence* (vv. 1b–2) they can exert on their non-Christian husbands. Peter's injunction to Christian wives is that they conduct their lives so as to win their husbands to the Christian faith.

Development of the Reason (3:3–4). Peter contrasts external beauty with internal beauty. Some have suggested that Peter's comments here actually prohibit Christian women of all ages from braiding their hair and wearing jewelry and fancy clothing, but the majority see a comparison of values: external appearance is relatively unimportant, but internal virtue is the prime pursuit of life. Peter urges them to regard their external appearance as a secondary matter to personal beauty and to dissociate themselves from the cultural trend of that day to adorn themselves so as to attract attention.

Examples of Good Behavior (3:5–6). Peter next legitimates his instructions to Christian wives about their good behavior by appealing to "the holy women of the past." What is noticeable here is that Peter extends the instruction to include women who had believing husbands, showing that his instructions to submit are not just some pragmatic expedient.

Exhortation to Husbands (3:7). Peter next addresses Christian husbands. The order for Christian husbands is one of being considerate—literally, of "living with one's wife knowledgeably." The verb *synoikeō* ("living together") was especially used for sexual relations between husband and wife, and that is no doubt the intended meaning here, though obviously not limited to that. The Christian man, Peter says, should be neither demanding nor selfish in his sexual and marital relations; he is instead to be considerate, sensitive, and serving.

The reason the Christian husband must be especially considerate in these relations is because his wife is "the weaker partner." This expression has given rise to two major interpretations: physical weakness and spiritual weakness. Inasmuch as the preponderance of evidence in the ancient world uses identical or similar language when describing a woman's physical condition, it is almost certain that Peter has in mind a wife's physical capacities.

Application. There are, in the United States alone, around sixty thousand reported cases of rape a year, not to mention many more that are left unreported. That there are between three to six million women per year who are victims of some form of physical violence in their homes staggers the imagination. Anger is the foundation of it all; angry men at home may be the biggest problem in our society, however they appear in the public square.

Against each of these acts of violence the words of Peter could be cited. Peter's advice is rooted in the notion that Christian husbands need to understand their wives. To be sure, wives need to understand their husbands as much as husbands need to understand their wives, but we are not talking here about what women need to understand. Husbands need to become lifelong, considerate learners of their wives because, just as husbands change over the years, so also do wives.

1 PETER 3:8–12

Original Meaning

Ethics for General Relations in the Church (3:8). While the previous three sections were addressed to specific kinds of people (slaves, wives, husbands), this exhortation is for "all of you." They must begin with harmony" in both mind and spirit. Harmony is, in part, a development of being "sympathetic." Christians are to love one another and any whom they encounter as good neighbors.

Ethics for Relations to a Hostile Society (3:9). Once again, Peter sees the Christian response to pressures from the outside world as one of passivity and grace, not aggressive retaliation. Why? Peter anchors their relationships to outsiders in their calling and promises them a "blessing." In line with his emphasis at 2:11–12, he imagines it will be a much better life for the churches if they are quiet, humble, and gentle, and if they refrain from retaliation and vindication.

Foundation for Ethics: God Is Watching Us (3:10–12). In Peter's principle that believers are to absorb some injustices for the sake of the gospel by not returning evil with evil, the apostle expresses a theological anchor that goes deep into the network of New Testament theology. The Christian is supposed to be motivated by a desire to receive a "blessing" from God (v. 9), a desire grounded in the fact that God is the final and ultimate judge. Christians have been called to inherit a blessing, which is God's reward for an obedient life.

The fundamental point Peter makes is that God is omniscient and omnipresent—he sees all, knows all, and is always present. People must not think that they can get by with evil behavior, for God is watching and evaluating; his eyes are on the righteous. Those who live righteously before God will, in the end, be vindicated by God on the great day of glory, but those who live sinfully and oppressively will receive condemnation from God Almighty on that same day of his glory.

Application. For Peter's day, as for ours, the church as a community was vital for survival, for sustaining one's faith amid threats and violence. We cannot identically compare our trials in the West to the ancient diaspora churches' experiences of persecution, but such an analogy can be made as long as we recognize its distance. If the early church was a community in which Christians found strength to carry on amid troubled times, then the church today ought to play the same role in our world, whatever the "trouble" might be. If our society is noted by an absence of moral values, then Christians need the family of believers to reinforce and strengthen their resolve to inculcate morals in their children and live a life of righteousness.

If our society is noted by pluralism and skepticism about knowing "truth," then Christians need the family of believers to confirm their grasp of the truth as taught in the Bible and to hold that truth high. If our society is noted by psychological battery with its increase in technology and its absence of treating workers as genuine humans in need of love, then Christians need the family of believers to be a society in which people are treated as those worthy of love and affection.

1 PETER 3:13–22

Original Meaning

The Pragmatic Issue and the Possible Problem (3:13–14). While it may be naive for someone to think that good behavior will *always* save the Christian from persecution, such naivete does not characterize Peter here. What we have, then, is a stance of hope that is baptized into a context of realism. But ultimately, Peter's assurances are grounded in his final hope: God will eventually (even if not now) establish complete justice.

While he believes generally in the rule that good behavior will alleviate suffering, he knows that not all opponents will be lenient. Peter's exhortation to his readers, when they do have to endure suffering, is not to fear the oppressors.

The Need for Preparation (3:15–17). Instead of fear, believers are to honor the Lord Christ by being ready to speak boldly about their "hope" (v. 15). This term is to be understood comprehensively, as all that drives the present history toward its destined future. Thus, this term includes concepts like salvation, inheritance, and final vindication (3:18–22). Christians are, in other words, expected to be prepared to speak at any moment about God's salvation.

Instead of brash defensiveness (which is frequently nothing more than an expression of insecurity), Christians ought to defend the Lord in a humble and respectful manner. Such a manner can lead both to conversions (3:1–2) and to leniency when persecution strikes (3:13). Moreover, if they live a good life before their opponents, they can have a "clear conscience" (v. 16). If God wills that they are to suffer, it is better that such takes place when the Christians are doing good rather than evil (v. 17).

A Digression on the Example of Jesus (3:18–22). Few passages have so many themes and different ideas intertwined as this section. It is no wonder that commentators have shaken their heads in despair! Yet the main point is not complex. Just as Jesus suffered as a righteous man and was vindicated, so too if the churches live righteously (as Peter has exhorted them to do), they will be vindicated and sit with Jesus in the presence of God. Such an understanding of this passage is a typical way of putting this section into focus with the previous verses (3:13–17).

It needs to be emphasized that we need to view this passage in light of its context and its overall theme of vindication. Jesus was righteous and suffered for the unrighteous; God vindicated him by exalting him to his right hand. The churches of Peter need to know that if they remain faithful, like Jesus they too will be vindicated. That is the hope that ought to sustain them as they endure suffering, the hope of which they are to be ready to speak, and the hope that Peter urges them to embrace.

Application. Where do Christians suffer injustice *because they are Christians*? Such people need to hear the message of Peter, the message of Christ's vindication and ours, and then to learn to live in light of that message so they can live beyond and through the persecution itself. Many of us know people who were fired because they were honest people trying to live out their faith in the workplace, or who suffered severe forms of ostracism because they sought to live Christian lives in the public sphere, or even people who simply felt "out of it" because they refused to run with the crowd. Such people readily discover the message of Peter applicable to their own lives and can find solace amid their trouble by reflecting thoughtfully on the ultimate vindication of God. They can learn to say, "Someday—" and so can learn to live in joy today despite their difficult situations.

1 PETER 4:1–6

Original Meaning. Peter here next provides an exhortation (v. 1a). To survive persecution in an obedient manner, Christians must have proper mental preparation (cf. 1:13): "arm yourselves also with the same attitude" that Christ had.

The first reason Peter gives is that it helps their obedience (vv. 1b–2). Christians ought to have the same mental approach as Jesus had "because whoever suffers in the body is done with sin" (v. 1b). In my judgment, the most likely interpretation of this difficult expression is that it refers to Christians who are suffering and that they learn not to sin by undergoing persecution. Thus, the theme of verse 2 follows naturally from our interpretation of verse 1b: "As a result, they do not live the rest of their earthly lives for evil human desires, but rather for the will of God."

Peter's second reason why the believers need to arm themselves with the same attitude as Christ's is given in verse 3. Just as good behavior will help get Christians out of tough situations, and just as suffering purges the Christian from sin, so also these same Christians have sinned more than enough for a lifetime, and it is time for them to get on with a life of obedience.

In verses 4–5 Peter explains that the very sins that once characterized the Christians' patterns of behavior have now been abandoned, partly because of the healing effects of suffering. But those behaviors continued among their old friends. These surprised former friends, who now abuse them verbally, are ultimately blasphemers. Accordingly, Peter informs the Christians of Asia Minor that "they will have to give account to him who is ready to judge the living and the dead" (v. 5).

Verse 6 has spirited a great discussion. Are the "dead" those to whom Christ preached after his crucifixion (3:19) the spiritually dead who are now alive, or the Christians of Peter's churches who have already died? The vast majority of commentators today argue that Peter is referring to Christians in Asia Minor who heard the gospel while alive but are now physically dead. Those who hear the gospel and respond, *even if they are killed for their faith*, will be vindicated ultimately before God.

Application. We know of a person who had to leave his "B.C. Group" (Before Christ Group) when he became a Christian because all they did together was drink to the point of drunkenness or take drugs until they were high. He missed them and longed for their conversion (and he shared the gospel with them frequently), but he knew he had to restrict his times with them because he was, due to his carnal nature, tempted to drink and do drugs. By the time he was "cured" of his desire for mind-altering substances, he had graduated from college and moved on to better things. His story is but one example of countless Christians who have experienced, as a result of their conversion, a complete change of social groups. Peter's churches had gone through that kind of change. They therefore provide an early example of what happens when people establish a lifestyle that follows Jesus.

1 PETER 4:7–11

Original Meaning

The Coming Day: The Foundation of Ethics (4:7a). Peter roots his ethical exhortations in 4:7b–11 in his perception of history and the judgment (v. 7a). Jewish prophets always envisioned the next big event on their "prophetic calendar" as the event that would usher in the last days—*and it never did.* Yet when the next event did not usher in the last days, no one thought the Jewish prophets were wrong. The reason they thought this way was not some kind of psychological denial but because the people of God recognized that a Jewish prophets' vision was telescoped and they could not see the entire chronology of God's plan. Thus, while Peter presented his ethical exhortations in light of a view that the end of history was imminent, his view is not mistaken. Rather, it was how Jewish prophecy worked.

Four Exhortations (4:7b–11). Peter's first exhortation here is that Christians keep themselves mentally and spiritually alert (cf. 1:13). Here the goal of such vigilance is so that they might pray effectively.

Next in verse 8, Peter exhorts his readers to "love each other deeply." Loving one another when things are tough is important "because love covers over a multitude of sins." The community that loves one another is able to forgive one another more rapidly when minor issues arise.

In verse 9 Peter offers his third exhortation—namely to be hospitable. Hospitality is a specific example of loving one another—this time by receiving others into our homes, making them feel welcome, meeting their needs, and providing for them a place of fellowship and acceptance.

Peter next offers his fourth and final exhortation that the believers exercise their gifts (vv. 10–11a). That the end is near prompts Peter to exhort believers to love one another beyond the idea of hospitality; they are to use their gifts "as faithful stewards of God's grace in its various forms" (v. 10). Whatever Christians are gifted to do, those gifts are to be exercised in such a way that they reflect their divine origin and purposes. That is, if God's Spirit prompts a person to speak to the congregation, that person ought to take the opportunity so seriously that the words spoken be considered with the utmost reverence.

In verse 11b Peter offers a doxology to conclude the section. It seems this doxology has Jesus Christ as its object. God glorifies himself through his Son, and the Son is at work in the prayer and loving ministries of the church.

Application. How frequently do we examine our lives in the light of eternity or of God's just judgment at the end of time? Once again, we find ourselves (most probably) in a situation where we have overreacted. The Christians of one or two generations ago, and beyond, were surely subject to far too many threats and sermons on hellfire. Our response has been one of embarrassment so that we have neglected the theme of judgment altogether. Yet that very theme is foundational to a Christian view of ethics—the foundation that God is the judge and that we are accountable to him for our behavior.

1 PETER 4:12–19

Original Meaning. Here in verse 12 Peter exhorts his readers to "not be surprised at the fiery ordeal" that has come their way. Presumably the early Christians were not generally surprised by opposition to the gospel, but the actual turn of events among

Peter's audience may have caught them off guard or shocked them. We are not told exactly what the "fiery ordeal" is. Instead of being shocked by these events and turning inward to wonder and doubt, Peter's readers are to "rejoice" (v. 13a). Peter sees the sufferings of ordinary believers as a special bond with their Lord. Being able to rejoice now amid suffering prepares one for being "overjoyed when his glory is revealed" (v. 13b).

Having lifted his readers spirits, Peter next in verses 14–16 reminds them of one important condition for enjoying that final, inexhaustible glory: they must remain faithful in doing good and not incur suffering because they deserve it.

The first comment speaks of being "insulted" (v. 14). Rather than taking these insults personally, Peter's readers must take these insults as an occasion to see that they are blessed. That is, they are blessed by God and are to glorify him because of the presence of his Spirit on them. This Spirit, especially when the saints are in stress, reveals the power, patience, and goodness of God to those who witness such events.

No matter what happens, however, Peter offers a warning: suffering for the name of Christ or for being a Christian is acceptable; suffering for doing bad things is unacceptable and deserving. Christians should live good lives, so that there may be no just cause of suffering (vv. 15–16).

Peter then gives in verses 17–19 the foundation for both exhortations: *they will someday have to answer to God for their behavior*. That God's judgment begins with the people of God is familiar to any reader of the Old Testament. This threat of judgment formed the basis for exhorting Christians to live faithfully.

We must understand that such persecution is *the beginning* of that judgment. In other words, the persecution these Christians are experiencing is the act of God whereby he purges his people to prepare them for his final display of salvation, insofar as he makes them fit for that judgment through suffering. In light of this statement, Peter then asks rhetorically: If the judgment is so severe that it deals a harsh blow for those associated with the family of God, then surely the pagans, who have no connection whatsoever with God's people or salvation, will be cut off entirely. Because of the severity of God's penetrating judgment, Peter exhorts these Christians to submit themselves to God by living a good life.

Application. Christians ought not to be surprised if they suffer shame and loss of status because of their faith. Even our suffering is one way God prepares us to be fit for his presence in the age to come. Whatever happens to us, Peter reminds us, we are not to ruin the cause of the gospel with filthy works of evil. Nothing is more damaging to the glory of God and the growth of the gospel than the sins of his people, especially those of well-known Christian leaders.

1 PETER 5:1–5

Original Meaning

The Address to Elders (5:1–4). In verse 1 Peter cites three traits that he and the elders of these churches share in common: they are all elders, they are all witnesses of Christ's sufferings, and they will all partake of the future glory.

Elders are responsible to shepherd "God's flock" (v. 2). Throughout the Bible the relationship of leaders to their charges was described metaphorically as a shepherd-like relationship. As shepherds cared for their flocks, so ought the leaders of Israel to care for Israelites. This is all rooted in the description of God as a shepherd to his people.

Peter exhorts his fellow shepherds to tend to the flock that God has appointed to them. What he has in mind is almost certainly the role that individual leaders played in a given house church—to tend to that house church as a group assigned to them by God. Without question, Peter ends any sense of possession by stating that it is "*God's* flock," not theirs.

Service in the church ought to be done with the proper motive—that is, with personal willingness and a sense of divine calling, not because of a sense of internal or external compulsion. Besides compulsion, greed is also an unworthy motivation for leading in God's house. The elders are not to serve in the churches in order to gain a profit. Instead, they are to do their ministry eagerly.

Finally, Peter urges the elders to lead by example, not by authoritative domination of their local churches (v. 3). Power is addictive. It leads to unworthy motives and pollutes decisions that are to be made under the guidance of the Spirit. Instead of seeking God's agenda, power-hungry church leaders pursue their own, doing what they can to increase their own reputation.

Peter incites them to the appropriate behavior by appealing to the promise they will receive for faithful discharge of their calling (v. 4). When Jesus returns as Savior and judge, he will give them a "crown of glory" for their faithfulness to him.

An Address to the Young and an Address to All (5:5). The exhortation here to the "younger" is to listen to the wisdom of the elders and live in accordance with their instruction—that is, they are "to submit." As stated in 2:13, the term *submission* should be understood as "living according to some constituted order"—here, the order established by the directives of the elders.

In 5:5b Peter then addresses the entire church. Whether leader or laity, whether old or young, Christians are to develop a deferential and humble attitude toward one another. Once again, Peter grounds his exhortations in the threatening judgment of God (see at 4:7, 17–19).

Application. Our text offers a list of three problems of motivation, and church leaders need to look over this list, examine their hearts, and ask themselves, "Why do I serve God in the church?" First, are you as a church leader motivated to serve in the church *because you have to or because you want to*? Second, are you, as a church leader, motivated to serve in the church *because of the money you can acquire or because of your enthusiasm for ministry*? Third, are you as a church leader motivated to serve in the church *because of your desire for power or because of the impact your life makes on others*?

1 PETER 5:6–14

Original Meaning

The Exhortation to Humility (5:6–7). As God's mighty hand was seen in the plagues of the exodus, so his mighty hand is now being seen in the persecution that the believers in Asia Minor are experiencing. By submitting to and waiting out God's deliverance, they can expect that same mighty hand to deliver them, just as the Lord delivered the children of Israel.

Peter grounds their submission to God in his loving care and protection. By turning over their fears and worries to God, they express their trust in him and rely on him to bring about vindication and justice.

The Exhortation to Vigilance (5:8–9). Christians resist Satan by refusing to succumb to his temptations to deny the Lord and to be faithless and fearful in the midst of suffering. Their encouragement comes from the worldwide family of God, for everywhere Christians are suffering.

The Doxology (5:10–11). Peter's letter ends on a note of prayer, which he begins with a theological reflection. The God they worship and serve is a God of grace. This theological reflection is then directed toward the specific calling God has given them: he made them his people so they could be with him eternally and praise him forever. This calling has in it a present condition, one that is not pleasant: suffering for a while. Finally, Peter's prayer is for their strength—strength to endure, to remain faithful, and to resist the temptations to the flesh.

Final Remarks (5:12–14). Peter concludes his letter in a manner similar to the endings of other letters: mentioning the amanuensis or deliverer of the letter (Silas), summarizing his intention (to exhort and testify), greeting them, and wishing them God's peace.

Our letters begin with greetings; Peter's ends with greetings. "She who is in Babylon, chosen together with you, sends you her greetings, and so does my son Mark" (v. 13). Because Babylon was a notorious place of sin, it became a figurative expression for any place known for its sinfulness. It surely describes Rome, and early Christian tradition confirms that Peter wrote from Rome.

Both Peter and Mark share their greetings. Peter then urges his readers to "greet one another with a kiss of love" (v. 14), the standard form of greeting in the ancient world and in many parts of the world today. Americans tend to shake hands, while other cultures hug one another or give one another a kiss. Peter's blessing then follows: "Peace to all of you who are in Christ."

Application. Our identity is not to be wrapped up in our social location, whether that be low (like Peter's churches) or high (like many churches today in the West), but in the fact that we are God's family and are related to him. As such, we are to serve one another with the gifts God has granted and live orderly and lovingly with one another. No matter how many adjustments we have to make as we read Peter's letter in our world, we are anchored to his world by the fact of the common salvation that transforms our behavior (1:3–2:10), we are challenged to live circumspectly in our society (2:11–3:12), and we are expected to live as the family of God ought to live (3:13–5:11). When we live like this, people will glorify him on the day he visits us (2:12).

2 PETER

INTRODUCTION TO 2 PETER

Many scholars find it difficult to believe that Peter, the Galilean fisherman, could have used some of the philosophical and religious terminology that we find in 2 Peter. But we should see this as evidence that Peter has adapted his message to his audience. By using "religious" language that his readers would have been familiar with, he contextualizes the gospel to meet their needs. The apostle Peter (1:1) likely wrote this letter somewhere just before AD 64–65 when reliable early tradition records Peter's death as a martyr at the time of Emperor Nero's persecution of Christians in Rome (note 1:13–14). In terms of his audience the best that can be surmised is that he writes to a predominantly gentile Christian audience probably living in Asia Minor, Macedonia, or Greece. He writes to combat a false teaching that saw in the free forgiveness of the gospel a golden opportunity to indulge selfish ambitions and desires (2:19).

BOOK OUTLINE

I. The Letter Opening (1:1–15)
II. The Body of the Letter (1:16–3:13)
   A. Christ Will Certainly Return, as Promised (1:16–21)
   B. Growth in Christ Requires That We Recognize and Resist False Christians (2:1–22)
   C. We Must Hold Fast to the Promise of Christ's Return (3:1–13)
III. The Letter Closing: Strive to Grow in Knowledge of Christ (3:14–18)

2 PETER 1:1–2

Original Meaning. In calling himself a "servant . . . of Jesus Christ," Peter here conveys his sense of humility in relationship to his Lord. Peter's right to speak authoritatively to these Christians is emphasized even more clearly in the second title, "apostle." This word (Gk. *apostolos*) can mean simply "messenger" and is so used occasionally in the New Testament. But the word more often has a technical sense, denoting those men chosen specially by the Lord to be his authoritative representatives.

Peter's description of his readers also anticipates some of the points he is going to make in the letter. These Christians, who are gentiles, have "received a faith as precious as ours." Gentile Christians are no second-class citizens in the kingdom of heaven.

"Grace" and "peace" appear frequently in these New Testament salutations. "Knowledge" is a key idea in the letter. Significantly, Peter both opens and closes the letter with a reference to the knowledge of God and or Christ. He refers to this knowledge again in 1:3 and 8 as the foundation for his readers' Christian experience.

2 PETER 1:3–11

Original Meaning

God's Provision (vv. 3–4). Spiritual maturity begins with God's provision (vv. 3–4). It is "his divine power" that has given to believers all that they need both for new spiritual life and for a "godly life" (v. 3a). Peter is referring to Christ's divine power. This power refers to his power to reclaim lost sinners, unleashed through his death and resurrection.

Godliness is prominent in this opening sermon of 2 Peter. The phrase "godly life" translates a Greek word that means literally "good worship" (*eusebeia*). It is a general word, and the biblical authors use it to summarize the behavior expected of Christians who have come to know the God of Scripture. Thus, Peter reminds us, God has made available to us all that we require to lead lives pleasing to him.

But God has made this power available in a specific way: "through our knowledge of him who called us" (v. 3b). As in verse 2, "knowledge" refers to an intimate and informed relationship that is the product of conversion to the gospel. Probably "him who called" is Jesus.

Peter adds that Christ calls us "by his own glory and goodness" (v. 3c). Christ lived a sinless life and went to the cross in obedience to the Father. It was through this "active" and "passive" obedience that he was qualified to offer himself as a sacrifice on our behalf.

The connection between verses 3 and 4 is not immediately clear. Peter's language here is elliptical: in saying "through these he has given us his very great and precious promises" (v. 4a), he really means that through these attributes, Christ has provided for the *fulfillment* of these promises. Christians now experience the fulfillment of those promises and thus have the remarkable privilege of enjoying intimacy with the God of this universe—or, as Peter puts it, "that . . . you may participate in the divine nature" (v. 4b).

"Divine nature" has a mystical or pantheistic ring to it. What Peter seems to mean is that believers come to share in some essential qualities that are characteristic of God himself. Peter must have in mind those divine qualities that enable believers to escape "the corruption in the world caused by evil desires" (v. 4c).

The Believer's Responsibility (vv. 5–9). Spiritual growth is a goal to which we need to give ourselves body and soul, every day of our lives. Verses 5b–7 describe, like the steps in a staircase, eight Christian virtues that must be added, one to the other, as we move upward in our pursuit of spiritual maturity. All of them are important, yet we doubt that Peter intends to say that we must pursue them in the precise order he gives them.

The way in which Peter begins his list of virtues might suggest that he thinks his readers at this point possess only faith and that they have to add all the others. But Peter goes on to show that this is not the case. In verse 8 he implies that they already "possess" these virtues. The issue is not one of having or not having them; the issue is one of growing in the degree to which the Christian exhibits them.

In verse 9 Peter touches for the first time on why, in his reader's own situation, this growth in knowledge of Christ is so important: spurious Christians, false teachers, were about. As Peter will make even more clear in 2:20–22, these fake Christians are people who at least claim to have had their sins forgiven by Christ but who are not now living as if that makes any difference to them.

The Importance of Godliness (vv. 10–11). Peter mentions two reasons why it is important for Christians to "confirm their calling and election" (v. 10a), one negative and one positive. Negatively, Christians are to respond in this way so that they "will never stumble" (v. 10b). This leads us to the positive reason: to bring "a rich welcome into the eternal kingdom of our Lord and Savior Jesus Christ" (v. 11). It is our effusive welcome into this eternal kingdom that should motivate us to move forward in the Christian life.

Application. Participating in the divine nature is a great and precious privilege. Through our union with Christ and the indwelling of the Holy Spirit, we share in something of God's own holy nature, separated from the corrupt world around us. And it is precisely "for this very reason" (v. 5) that we are called on to progress in holiness and godliness. But the very fact that Peter goes on to encourage us to make such progress shows that participating in the divine nature does not bring us into a state of sinlessness or even into a situation in which we can lay back and simply enjoy our new status. We must keep pressing forward by faith.

2 PETER 1:12–15

Original Meaning. The theme of reminding frames this passage, being found at its beginning (v. 12a) and again at its conclusion (v. 15b). Peter realizes that what he is saying to these Christians is not new. Not only have his readers heard already about the importance of pursuing godliness, but they have also been obedient to the exhortation. As Peter puts it, they "are firmly established in the truth" (v. 12b).

Peter wants especially to stress that the time available for him to continue his ministry of exhortation is limited. He knows he will soon be putting aside his earthly body. How does he know this? Because "our Lord Jesus Christ has made it clear to me" (v. 14). Peter refers to the prophecy about his death that we find at the end of John's Gospel. Jesus's words refer to Peter's death by crucifixion as a martyr. Faced with imminent death, then, Peter makes a last appeal to his readers. Yet he trusts that the force of this appeal will go on "after [his] departure" (v. 15).

Application. It takes the ministry of the Holy Spirit to bring to mind the truths of the gospel (John 14:26). But God's word, written and proclaimed, is the source of that reminder. And what Peter is indirectly suggesting here is that the repetition of the truths of the gospel, in both word and in acted "memorials" like the Lord's Supper, is a necessary component of a vital Christian experience.

2 PETER 1:16–21

Original Meaning

Peter's Eyewitness Testimony to the Parousia (vv. 16–18). Peter shifts from the first-person singular he used in verses 12–15 ("I will always remind you . . . I think it right . . . I will make every effort") to the first-person plural in verses 16–18. This "we" must refer to Peter and other apostles, since it was only they who were eyewitnesses of the transfiguration. Peter's point is that the fact of Christ's transfiguration, and thus also the belief that he will come again, rests on the testimony of several apostolic eyewitnesses.

Peter's reminder about the apostolic proclamation of the return of Christ may be the center of the verse grammatically, but the key point he wants to get across comes in the contrasting qualifications of this assertion: the apostles made known the return of Christ not in following "cleverly devised stories" but in being "eyewitnesses of his majesty." "Stories" translates the Greek word *mythos* (from which we get "myth"). This Greek word had a broad range of meaning, but the meaning most relevant to our verse is the sense "fictional account, fable."

Peter is not content simply to deny that the apostles' teaching about Christ's return was built on a myth, but he asserts positively that the teaching is the direct product of eyewitness testimony. It was on that occasion, as Peter puts it, that Christ "received honor and glory from God the Father" (v. 17a). Christ's exalted status is indicated in the transfiguration events especially by the accompanying signs and by the voice from heaven.

Peter was on the mountain to hear the voice, and thus it is reasonable to think that Peter is quoting the words from memory. The voice from heaven identifies Jesus as both Messiah and Suffering Servant.

In verse 18, he reminds his readers that he was an "earwitness": "We ourselves heard this voice." As the Gospel accounts make clear, the "we" here includes Peter, James, and John (see Mark 9:2 and parallels). Jesus selected these three from among the apostolic band so that they might be "with him on the sacred mountain."

Why does Peter allude to the transfiguration to confirm the truth of Jesus's return in glory? The transfiguration reveals Jesus as the glorious king, and Peter was there to see it. He therefore has utter confidence that Jesus will return as the glorious king and establish his kingdom in its final and ultimate form.

The Testimony of the Prophets to the Parousia (vv. 19–21). The reliability of revelation is the idea that links verses 16–18 and verses 19–21. Peter, James, and John can testify to the revelation of Christ's glory in the transfiguration. But also testifying to Christ's glorious appearance at the end of history are the prophets.

Confidence in the reliability of the prophetic word should lead to a firm adherence to its teaching. Consequently, Peter urges his readers to "pay attention to it, as to a light shining in a dark place" (v. 19b). The comparison of God's word to a light is common in Scripture. Peter wants his readers to pay attention to the prophetic word "until the day dawns and the morning star rises in your hearts" (v. 19c).

In verse 21 Peter reinforces what he has said about the origin of prophecy in verse 20. The belief that the prophets spoke for God is, of course, basic to the Scriptures. Peter is not denying that the prophecies were genuinely the words of the prophets themselves, men who consciously chose their words in accordance with their own vocabulary, style, and circumstances. What Peter does affirm, however, is that the words they chose to use were *also* the words that God wanted them to use to communicate the message he intended.

Application. *On the inspiration of Scripture.* For many, the Bible is "inspired" in only the loosest sense—as, for example, some might think Wordsworth was inspired as he wrote *The Prelude.* But among confessing Christians also we sometimes encounter those who insist that God must have accommodated himself to the human writers of Scripture. The result, they suggest, is that we still have errors in the Bible. Here, I would argue, we have an imbalance in which the divine author of Scripture is given too little place. God, by nature, does not lie; he cannot utter a falsehood. If, then, the words of Scripture are genuinely God's words, then the words of Scripture must be without error.

2 PETER 2:1–3

Original Meaning

A Profile of the False Teachers (vv. 1–3). Peter here gives a brief profile of the false teachers. First, they are *devious* in their manner. They are covering up the degree to which their teaching differs from the accepted apostolic teaching. Second, they are perpetrating a *serious error*: "even denying the sovereign Lord who bought them" (v. 1). The destiny of these false teachers is, like those who follow them, "destruction."

The popularity of these false teachers is great. "Many will follow their depraved conduct" (v. 2). Their impact on the Christian movement is disastrous. For by following this erroneous teaching, professing Christians bring "the way of truth into disrepute."

The false teachers are motivated by greed (v. 3a). Peter alludes to this motivation later in the chapter as well, comparing the false teachers to Balaam. The basis of their teaching is stories they have made up. It is the false teachers, not the apostles, who build their doctrine on the basis of "cleverly devised stories"—that is, on fabrications and forgeries.

Application. Peter's warnings about false teachers are, unfortunately, as appropriate today as they were in his time. Indeed, as we have seen, our Lord has warned us to expect such deviations from the faith. The church will always have to contend with both the outright opposition of those who reject Christ entirely as well as the more subtle threats of those who claim the name of Christian but twist and distort the Christian message. Indeed, precisely because they are more subtle, the latter threat is often the more dangerous one.

2 PETER 2:4–10A

Original Meaning

Examples of God's Judgment (vv. 4–8). A number of writers in the intertestamental period developed a story about angels who sinned and were punished by God at the time of the flood. Genesis 6:1–4 tells about "sons of God" who were attracted to the "daughters of men." It is likely here in verse 4 that Peter has this story in mind.

Peter's next warning example comes from the most famous judgment of God found in the Old Testament: the flood in Noah's day (v. 5). Peter uses similar wording to connect these first two examples: God "did not spare" the angels who sinned, and he "did not spare" the "ancient world" either.

With verse 6 we should not be surprised that Peter moves from the flood to Sodom and Gomorrah in order to illustrate God's judgment; the pairing of these two famous disasters was well established. Like the flood narrative, the story of Sodom and Gomorrah also has a positive side. God "rescued Lot, a righteous man" from the disaster, just as he rescued Noah and his family (v. 7).

The Application of the Examples (vv. 9–10a). What are the "trials" from which the "godly" will be rescued (v. 9)? Some commentators think that Peter is referring to the great trial of faith that will occur at the very end of history. Christians are no doubt already in the last days. Yet it is probably best to understand that Peter includes in the "trial" here all those challenges to faith that Christians experience in this world.

The first part of verse 10 is tied grammatically to verse 9, as Peter gives an example of those "unrighteous" who will be judged. But verse 10b, which is not tied grammatically to the first part, shifts the focus to a more extended description of these unrighteous people (see below).

Peter contents himself with two general characteristics of these unrighteous false teachers: They "follow the corrupt desire of the flesh," and they "despise authority." The NIV rendering of this first description is too mild. The reference is to sexual sin, probably including, in light of Peter's reference to Sodom and Gomorrah in verse 6, homosexuality. "Despising authority" is a general charge to the effect that the false teachers are self-willed and rebellious. Peter is not thinking of any specific authority; he is thinking of the principle of authority.

Application. Everywhere we look, we find people advocating ideas that the Bible clearly condemns yet claiming that they are the true way to find God, or "meaning in life," or spiritual fulfillment. What is the reaction of Christians to the increasing abandonment of Christian moral norms in the West? Many, to be sure, and to their credit, are responding vigorously, with a loving but firm restatement of the biblical perspective. But many of us are simply accepting what is happening without any undue fuss or concern. We are not "distressed" or "tormented" by what we see around us. Oh, we may be disturbed by these developments and deplore those who choose an unbiblical lifestyle. But few Christians experience the "torment of soul" that Lot felt as he faced the ungodliness of his society.

2 PETER 2:10B–16

Original Meaning

The False Teachers' Arrogance (vv. 10b–13a). What, exactly, are the false teachers doing? We begin with the word *blasphēmeō*. This "blasphemy" (v. 10b; NIV "heap abuse) may have taken a very basic form and involved a general denial of the existence of such beings. Or it is more likely that the false teachers were mocking the possibility that their sins might put them at the mercy of such evil spiritual beings. Though fallen, the evil angels still retain a rank higher than that of human beings. In their arrogance, the false teachers were in some way denying this fact.

Peter goes on to compare the false teachers to animals. In a word, they are "unspiritual." But if Peter is still referring to the false teachers' arrogance toward evil angels, then the point of comparison is between the animals' lack of rationality and the false teachers' sinful ignorance. Picking up a common ancient saying about animals, Peter reminds us that they are "born only to be caught and destroyed" (v. 12b).

We should make verse 13a the end of the sentence begun in verse 12. Being "paid back with harm for the harm they have done" provides a fitting addition to the prediction of the false teachers' ultimate destruction.

The False Teachers' Sensuality (vv. 13b–16). In Peter's day, as in ours, indulgence of sinful pleasure usually took place under cover of darkness. Practicing such hedonistic activities "in broad daylight" (v. 13b) is therefore a sign that the false teachers are completely shameless about their indulgence. The false teachers are further described as "blots and blemishes" (v. 13c). These are obviously general descriptions. The best way to define them is to recognize their opposites. With the words "reveling in their pleasures while they feast with you" (v. 13d), it is likely that Peter here rebukes the false teachers for indulging their own sinful pleasures even as they continue to join with other Christians in celebrating the atoning work of Christ at the church's fellowship meals.

"With eyes full of adultery, they never stop sinning" (v. 14a). Peter means with this that the false teachers are so addicted to sex that they look at every woman as a potential partner in their lust. "Seduce" (v. 14b) translates a Greek word that has its roots in the world of hunting and fishing; it suggests the bait used to lure a fish to the hook or an animal to the trap. They are also described as "experts in greed" (v. 14c). These false teachers, Peter implies, are so devoted and consistent in their greed that they must have worked very hard at it for a long time! The phrase "an accursed brood!" (v. 14d) conveys that Peter, overwhelmed by the enormity of the false teachers' sinfulness, once again interjects this reminder of their ultimate fate.

In verse 15 Peter next writes that the false teachers "have left the straight way and wandered off to follow the way of Balaam son of Bezer." Balaam's willingness to curse Israel for profit became a staple in Jewish stories about him. Moreover, the Jewish stories made Balaam responsible for Israel's rebellion against God in entering into sexual relationships with the women of Midian (see Num 25). Balaam had given himself to "madness" and so have the false teachers (v. 16).

Application. False teaching is often revealed in false living. "By their fruit you will recognize them," Jesus told his disciples as he warned them about false prophets (Matt 7:16). And so it always is: following bad doctrine leads to bad practices. The false teachers of Peter's day were propagating wrong ideas about Christ's return in glory and about judgment to come (cf. 2 Pet 1:16–21; 3:3–12). And Peter takes them to task for it. But he also paints this vivid picture of their sinful lifestyle in chapter 2 to show, from another angle, that these people cannot be trusted to represent the true Christian faith.

2 PETER 2:17–22

Original Meaning

Hollow and Deceptive Teaching (vv. 17–19). In the dry climate of the East, a spring of water is a marvelous blessing, giving—and sometimes even saving—life. Imagine the weary traveler's chagrin, then, when he or she finds the spring to be dry. So is the false teachers' message: it disappoints the spiritual pilgrim by promising spiritual vitality but not delivering it.

Yet the word "mist" (v. 17) can also denote the haze left after the condensation of a cloud into rain. But rather than producing life-giving rain, it could dissipate and, indeed, served as a harbinger of dry weather to come. The two metaphors, therefore, combine to characterize the message of the false teachers as hollow and therefore disillusioning. Peter adds at the end of the verse a quick sentence of judgment: "Blackest darkness is reserved for them" (v. 17b).

The false teachers' words, while superficially attractive, cannot produce the spiritual fulfillment that they promise. The false teachers also entice "by appealing to the lustful desires of the flesh" (v. 18b). The word "lustful" represents the Greek word *aselgeia*, denoting licentiousness, sensuality, and a pleasure-focused lifestyle of sexual promiscuity, gluttony, and drunkenness.

Yet the false teachers, Peter suggests, do not go after just anybody. Clever in picking their targets, they dangle their lure in front of "people who are just escaping from those who live in error" (v. 18c). It makes excellent sense to think that the heretics would go after new converts. In other words, Peter pictures these new converts as still in the process of distancing themselves from the values and lifestyle of the pagan society to which they recently belonged and in the midst of which they continue to live.

In verse 19 Peter continues to describe the false teachers' mode of operation. Another tactic to entice recent converts from their faith is to promise them freedom. This is about the only place in the chapter that Peter touches on the false teachers' doctrinal program. Peter has dwelt repeatedly on the false teachers' libertine lifestyle. And we have evidence from elsewhere in the New Testament of a tendency to abuse the free grace available in the gospel by turning it into a license to sin.

The Serious Plight of the False Teachers (vv. 20–22). Peter here continues his description of the false teachers. These false teachers gave every evidence of being Christians. Yet they run the risk of becoming "entangled" in the corruption of the world again and, indeed, of being "overcome" by it (v. 20a). So it is with people who embrace Christ but then abandon him for the world again: because they have knowingly and openly rejected the truth, their judgment will be worse than it would otherwise have been (v. 20b).

Peter has composed verses 20–22 almost entirely out of traditional material: a saying of Jesus in verse 20, a "better for them" warning in verse 21, and then, in verse 22, two extra-biblical proverbs. In fact, the NIV plural "proverbs" is a bit of a liberty. The Greek word is singular; Peter perhaps uses it because he views the two proverbs as functioning together to make the same point.

The meaning of the first proverb is clear enough: returning to the corruption of the world is like a dog returning to eat its own vomit (v. 22a) and like "a sow that is washed returns to her wallowing in the mud" (v. 22b). Having been washed clean by the blood of Christ, they are nevertheless anxious to return again to the filth of the world.

Application. *Consequences of turning away from the truth.* Peter implies in his warning a point that Scripture makes clear in many places: that the more we know of God when we reject his truth, the greater will be our punishment.

Sensitive believers and even unbelievers are often disturbed by this denial of the possibility of forgiveness. The very fact that someone is worried about having committed the unpardonable sin shows that he or she has not. Such concern and desire to believe suggests that the Holy Spirit, far from abandoning this person, is still at work in his or her life.

2 PETER 3:1–7

Original Meaning

Peter Urges His Readers to Remember the Truth (vv. 1–2). Peter mentions two specific sources for the teaching that he wants his readers to recall and put into action. First is "the words spoken in the past by the holy prophets." The second source Peter wants his readers to recall is "the command given by our Lord and Savior through your apostles." What is this command? Peter is describing the moral requirements that are placed on believers. Peter is thinking of the basic demand that believers conform to the image of Christ, becoming holy even as the God who called them is holy.

Peter Warns of Scoffers (vv. 3–4). Mockery is a general response to the truth of God. But the mockers or scoffers that Peter is particularly concerned about were not apparently mocking the faith generally. Indeed, they claimed to be following the faith (see, e.g., 2:18–22). Rather, they were scoffing at one particular teaching of the faith: the belief that Christ will return in glory at the end of history.

They based this rejection of the coming of Christ on a general belief in the unchanging nature of the world: "Ever since our ancestors died, everything goes on as it has since the beginning of creation." The false teachers were apparently scoffing at the idea of Christ's return at the end of history because they could not imagine the kind of change in the world and in the human situation that the church's teaching about the parousia assumed.

Peter Rebukes the Scoffers for Forgetting the Truth (vv. 5–7). Peter's general point in verse 5 is clear: God brought the universe into existence, and he did so by his own creative word and through the use of water. Therefore, the false teachers' assumption of an unchanging universe is without warrant. The very universe they are talking about has not always been here.

Through God's utterance the world of Noah's day was destroyed, and through "the same word" (v. 7) it will be destroyed again. This time, however, God will use fire rather than water to bring about the destruction. Thus, in response to the false teachers, who view the world as going on in the same way forever, Peter makes clear that God has destined it for a sudden and definite end.

Application. *God's role in history.* We must guard against the temptation to think we can precisely identify what God is doing in every event in history. But God has not stepped off the throne of the universe, nor has he stood aside to let events take their course. We need to recapture the biblical worldview, in which all of life is filled with the presence and activity of a personal, holy, and loving God, who is guiding history toward a definite end.

2 PETER 3:8–10

Original Meaning. One of the points on which Peter's audience needed reassurance was the issue of timing. Christians must realize that our perception of time is not the same as God's. What seems like long ages to us is a mere blip in time to him (v. 8).

Peter's second response has to do with God's purpose in delaying the return. Rather than being a sign of God's lack of concern (v. 9a), his delay in sending Christ in judgment is a sign of his deep concern for human beings (v. 9b). For in God's infinite patience, he is waiting for people to repent before it is too late.

With verse 10, Peter moves from argument to assertion. God may be delaying the parousia for his own beneficent purposes, but "the day of Lord will come like a thief." The time of Christ's coming cannot be calculated. Like a thief, he can appear at any time.

Application. Date-setters have arisen throughout the history of the church. Many sincere Christians have been led astray by these date-setters. We are called constantly to live in the light of the end of history, even if we can see no obvious signs of its end in the world around us. God can certainly use the world around us to wake us up and help us see the truth. But when all is said and done, we walk "by faith, not by sight." We must trust the promise of Christ's coming despite not knowing its timing.

2 PETER 3:11–13

Original Meaning. God did not build this world to last forever (v. 11a). That being the case, Peter asks, "What kind of people ought you to be?" (v. 11b). Peter makes the point clear enough by immediately answering his own question: "You ought to live holy and godly lives" (v. 11c). Having begun his exhortation to holy living with an eschatological reminder, Peter concludes it with another: "As you look forward to the day of God and speed its coming" (v. 12a). Peter has already claimed that the apparent delay in the parousia is because God wants everybody (or, as we argue, all God's people) to repent.

God has promised a "new heaven and a new earth" (v. 13). The important point here for Peter is not speculation about the exact nature of this "new heaven and earth," but that it will be "where righteousness dwells."

Application. Christians need to remember the ultimate purpose of biblical eschatology: to make us better Christians here and now. We must not study eschatology for its own sake or for the gratification of our curiosity. We must never forget, as Peter makes clear in verse 11, that biblical eschatology is to stimulate in believers a holy and godly lifestyle. In fact, we will find no passage in the New Testament on eschatology that does not have that kind of specific, practical focus.

2 PETER 3:14–18

Original Meaning

Concluding Eschatological Exhortation (vv. 14–15a). Peter next urges his readers to "make every effort to be found spotless, blameless and at peace with him." "To be found" has judicial overtones. It conjures up the scene of the court of law, where the judge "finds" defendants guilty or innocent. Motivated by the day of the Lord that is coming, believers should work hard to be found perfectly pure and blameless when God in Christ assesses our lives.

The command in verse 15 is parallel to the one at the end of verse 14. As Christians look forward to the end of history, they are to adopt an attitude toward the apparent delay in Christ's return that is exactly opposite to that of the false teachers. The latter considered the delay to be a sign of God's "slowness," concluding that judgment may never come. Christians, on the other hand, are to consider the delay as an opportunity to pursue salvation.

Appeal to Paul for Confirmation (vv. 15b–16). Calling Paul his "dear brother" would be perfectly natural for Peter and fits well with early Christian usage, for "brother" is often used to refer to coworkers in gospel ministry. Why does he refer to Paul as "our" beloved brother rather than "my" beloved brother? The "our" may refer to Christians generally or, perhaps more likely, to fellow apostles (see v. 2).

We cannot decide which of Paul's letters Peter may have in mind. Peter's language focuses more on the basis for what Paul wrote. What he wrote in his letters came not from his own study or imagination but from God himself, who gave Paul the wisdom to understand and apply the gospel in his generation.

The *implicit* point Peter is making emerges from his claim that the false teachers distort Paul's letters "as they do the other Scriptures." The word "other" (*loipos*) shows that Peter considers the letters of Paul to belong to the category of "Scripture." Peter therefore implies that the letters of Paul have a status equivalent to that of the canon of the Old Testament itself.

Concluding General Exhortation (vv. 17–18a). After his final warning, Peter issues a final positive exhortation: "Grow in the grace and knowledge of our Lord and Savior Jesus Christ." Here Peter summarizes his root concern—namely, that his readers, resisting the heresy of the false teachers, continue to grow spiritually, becoming more and more like the Christ whom they confess.

Doxology to Christ (v. 18b). Only here, in 2 Timothy 4:18, and in Revelation 1:5–6 do we find doxologies directed to Christ. The doxology here is unusual in at least one way. Peter uses a different expression—literally translated, "unto the day of eternity" (NIV "forever"). Christ's coming will inaugurate the eschatological age—a "day" that will last forever. We glorify Christ, looking to this day and earnestly waiting for it.

Application. The finality of our decisions in this life is assumed throughout the New Testament and, as we have seen, in 2 Peter 3 as well. Perhaps there are readers of this commentary who have not yet committed themselves in faith to Christ. For them, of course, the implications of this point are clear: now is the time to decide; death or the parousia may forever and at any time end all such opportunity. For those of us who do already know the Lord, the implications are also clear: now is the time to share the good news of Christ—with your neighbor, your coworker, your fellow team member—before it is too late.

1 JOHN

INTRODUCTION TO 1 JOHN

While Christian tradition has attributed these letters to John the apostle, the Johannine letters are anonymous, except that 2 and 3 John call their author "the elder" (2 John 1; 3 John 1). Unambiguous objective evidence for apostolic authorship is not at hand for the Gospel of John or the letters. But the absence of such evidence does not make such authorship implausible, and the burden of proof rests with those who want to dismantle the tradition. This commentary labels the author of the letters as "John," keeping in mind the limits of any historical investigation.

A date for all three letters sometime between 70 and 90 is not unreasonable. John wrote 1 John to correct doctrinal distortions (and their ethical implications) that arose within the Christian community (probably in Ephesus in Asia Minor) and that were causing a severe division among its members. Some had already seceded from the church.

BOOK OUTLINE

I. Prologue (1:1–4)
II. Part 1: God Is Light—And We Should Walk Accordingly (1:5–3:10)
III. Part 2: God Is Love—And We Should Walk Accordingly (3:11–5:12)
IV. Conclusion (5:13–21)

1 JOHN 1:1–4

Original Meaning

The Incarnate Word (1:1a). John's singular interest is not some abstract doctrine about Jesus or the importance of preaching about Jesus; rather, it is the reality of Jesus's personhood—his incarnation or his entry into history. To dispel any suggestion that this appearing in history was imagined or partial, John speaks graphically of the sensory confirmation (hearing/seeing/touching) that accompanied this revelation.

The Word of Life (1:1b–2). However, this is not simply a Word "about life," as if it were a message that explained the meaning of living. In other words, eternal life is not the by-product of some enlightenment or knowledge acquired mystically. Eternal life is historically anchored in what we may call *the scandal of particularity* unique to the Christian faith. The life of God has been channeled to us through a historical event, an event that John says has been verified by people who saw it.

The Word and Fellowship (1:3–4). Embracing this Word, experiencing this life, gaining this reference point—these are all prerequisites for Christian community. Christian fellowship is triangular: my life in fellowship with Christ, your life in fellowship with Christ, and my life in fellowship with yours. Christian community grows from a matured relationship with God in his Son, Jesus Christ. And no doubt where this relationship with Christ is absent, such community is an impossibility.

Application. There is no Christian faith if Jesus Christ is not at the center. True Christian community is hinged to true experiences of Jesus. Today the authenticity of our faith is likewise linked to the vitality of Jesus's life within us. If Jesus is a doctrine, our testimony will be hollow. If Jesus is a person, our testimony will be potent.

1 JOHN 1:5–7

Original Meaning

God Is Light (1:5). Since God is light, Jesus in bringing God to us has likewise brought light, divine light. Light unveils our spiritual identity—whether we abide in the Son—and it identifies those who live in darkness. Therefore, light also has a judging function, for it unveils.

Life in the Darkness (1:6). John's opponents were not just *in darkness*, they were living lives of darkness (conveyed by the present tense of *peripateō*, "to walk"). They were persistent, dogged, and tenacious in the habits they had chosen. They had not simply overlooked something about God; they were lying and self-deceiving in their conduct. Such conduct prefers to remain in darkness because living in the presence of God's light would expose its error.

Life in the Light (1:7). John is one of the few New Testament writers to draw the connection between our spiritual integrity and the quality of the communities we create. Walking in the light is the *only* way we can genuinely walk with each other.

Application. John is looking for a model of Christian life that is like a circle of light on a stage, perhaps a spotlight in a darkened theater. At once the darkness around it is most prominent. A boundary is evident. And yet the circle is created by God's penetrating light. It is a light that is pure, hard, revealing, and guiding. And those who walk in this light discover lives that are knit together by God's forgiveness and redemption. To walk in this light is ultimately humbling. But at the same time it is also healing, renewing, and invigorating.

1 JOHN 1:8–2:2

Original Meaning

Sin and Confession (1:8–9). John's opponents philosophically questioned the relevance of sin as something that can impede our relationship with God. John gives a stern warning that these people may not even be Christians at all! And their only recourse is confession. Confession is successful because of the character of God. His faithfulness to us has prompted him to make a way for our purification and thereby satisfy his demand for righteousness.

Sin and Jesus's Advocacy (1:10–2:1). Can someone claim that they have never committed any sins? Such a position impugns God's character, making him a liar (v. 10). But a second, equally severe, consequence follows. God's word "is not in" them either. "The word" may be a general reference to the Scriptures, or it may reference Jesus, who in John's writing is called "the Word."

Throughout these verses John has been telling us that sin is inherent to human life. Now he writes that he does not want us to sin. Which is it? When John talks about avoiding sin, he may be referring specifically to *the error of denying the reality of God's truth about sin*. John may also be worrying that some will take his teaching as a license to sin. God is eager to forgive our sins, but what is it that makes God's generosity accessible? Jesus Christ, in his ascended glory, represents us before the Father. Jesus's sinlessness and purity, his righteousness, gives him access to God's very presence.

Sin and Jesus's Sacrifice (2:2). The *basis* of Christ's case on our behalf, the power behind his advocacy, comes from his sacrifice on the cross. Jesus became a *hilasmos* ("atoning sacrifice") for our sins. A *hilasmos* was a sacrifice given to placate someone who was angry. In a religious setting, it was an angry God. By this interpretation God is the object of Jesus's sacrifice, making the sinner acceptable because God's disposition has changed. On the other hand, some have urged that the object is not God, but the sins themselves. The sinner is pleasing to God because the sins are wiped away. The two thoughts merge: sins are covered over *and* God's righteous anger is changed.

Jesus does not simply supply a *hilasmos*, he is one himself. Jesus is both *paraklētos* ("advocate," 2:1) and *hilasmos* on our behalf. He has supplied what was needed to effect our pardon. His righteousness made his sacrifice powerful (cf. Heb 7:26–28) so that it brings benefits not simply to a closed circle of Christian worshipers, but to the whole world. God's interest is not elitist, building a religious clique that excludes some (and this was no doubt one of the problems among John's followers). God's sacrificial work is comprehensive.

Application. The gnostics saw sin as unimportant because the moral arena of this world was unimportant. As we learn about many new religious movements today (Eastern mysticism, New Age, etc.), we note a similar phenomenon. Spirituality is being cultivated apart from the course of events in this world and is removed entirely from a rational, moral framework. John affirms that this world is important (hence his incarnational theology) and that the personal God who made it has moral expectations for all the humans who dwell therein. If either God is denied or if the standard is said not to apply to our world, accountability disappears.

1 JOHN 2:3–11

Original Meaning

Obedience and Spiritual Maturity (2:3–5). John's choice of words here is not accidental. He is concerned to stress obedience, but also to challenge those who boast in knowing. The Greek term *gnōsis* means "knowledge" and describes a religious disposition (hence, Gnosticism) that promoted enlightenment or mystical inspiration as the central feature of faith. "We know that *we have come to know* him" (v. 3) disguises a perfect-tense verb, which in Greek means not simply that knowledge is a one-time enlightenment but rather a past experience with ongoing present consequences. Knowledge for John reveals itself in the continuing reflex to obey God. The person who feigns intimacy with God and rejects obedience is a liar. On the other hand, the profile of true Christians is quite the opposite: they *keep* God's word (v. 5). To "obey [God's] word" expresses a zealous desire to adhere to God's will.

Obedience and the Life of Jesus (2:6–8). "To live in him" (v. 6) goes beyond merely imitating Christ in lifestyle or "living as Jesus lived." To know God truly is to abide in him deeply. The outgrowth of such knowing and indwelling is obedience. John holds up the earthly life of Jesus as a model to be imitated. *As earthly conduct is an essential part of faith, so too the earthly life of Jesus is an essential model for our lives.*

How is the command to love not new (v. 7)? On the one hand, it has been around since the Old Testament, and thus even Jesus appealed to it directly. And yet there is still something new in this (v. 8). The ancient command has taken on a new form since the coming of Christ. So once again John is providing a test for spiritual reality. In the first test, obedience was the natural outgrowth of an intimate life with God. Now we learn that the second test is a love that bears the quality of Christ's love.

Obedience and Love (2:9–11). The tests in this exhortation are cumulative: to know God and to abide in him mean to obey, and to obey is to exhibit Christlike love. But the ultimate test of such obedient love is whether we are able to love the unlovely. Thus John's severity is unrelenting: to hate a brother or sister in the church means one is "in the darkness" and has been blinded (v. 9); to love them means that one is living "in the light" (v. 10). Love becomes a genuine value only when it is tested, only when we must reach beyond ourselves and love someone we do not wish to love. This is the caliber of love John has in mind.

There is a curious phrase attached to verse 10. The NIV renders it, "Anyone who loves their brother or sister lives in the light, and *there is nothing in him to make him stumble.*" However, the Greek literally says, "stumbling [Gk. *skandalon*] is not in him/it." John may have in mind *Christian misbehavior* that may drive more people out of the church. Therefore, a better translation might be, "There is nothing in him to cause anyone to stumble." Naturally, such a warning would apply to the believer as well, but John has chiefly in mind indignant, persistent attitudes of anger that might widen the fissure already splitting the church.

Application. *Do we unwittingly neglect the call to obedience?* Many of us recoil at the mere word *obedience.* I often meet students who have grown up in conservative churches and families where obedience and righteousness were pounded home so often that today they have been pushed aside as vehicles of death and suffocation. This is a difficult paradox: personal righteousness and obedience *are* an essential component of our faith and yet do not form the basis of our salvation. It is no wonder that theologians continually debate the synthesis of these themes and ask if the "gospel according to Jesus" has long been neglected.

What if we disobey? Can the absence of obedience disqualify someone as a Christian? On the one hand, we dare not compromise the pivotal doctrine of grace. And yet there must be a call to discipleship that shows how such grace has transformed, and is transforming, the disciple. It must be a call that makes room for important, difficult passages, such as James 2:14–26. It must be a call that sobers, that makes us check our Christian resolve—all without sacrificing the loving character of God and the gospel of lavish grace.

The absolute command to love. The test of obedience to the command to love surfaces when we come to terms with those whom we have difficulty loving. And the first step in this direction is reconciliation. While John is eager to see love promoted, that does not mean that we are to be naive about those who hurt us. Even though we should be generously open and loving, we must also be shrewdly discerning and wise.

1 JOHN 2:12–17

Original Meaning

Words for John's Children (2:12, 14a). Two themes reassure John's followers of their place in God's household. First, their sins "have been forgiven" on account of Jesus's name (v. 12). Second, they "know the Father" (v. 14a). Freed from sin, they have been given a new consciousness of God's intimate fatherhood over them.

Words for Elders (2:13a, 14b). Like the children in 2:14a, fathers too have known God (vv. 13a; 14b). Everyone, mature and immature alike, shares this same privilege. But there is a difference, for fathers have known "him who is *from the beginning.*" This may refer to God exclusively—or it may refer to Jesus, whose preexistence is important to John. Those who are mature in the faith have a knowledge of God that is anchored securely in the things of the past. It is their seasoned wisdom that makes for steadfast faith in the present, difficult circumstances.

Words for Younger Christians (2:13b, 14c). If the elders of the community provide a steadfast anchor of faith, it is the youth who are here engaging the battle of living out that faith in the struggles of the world. Thus John affirms them by saying that they are strong and that God's word abides within them. That strength is there for a purpose: it has overcome the "evil one." In 3:8, 12 we learn that the spiritual life can be a war of spiritual forces, a conflict with the devil.

John does not, however, urge the young to defeat these forces. Rather, he says that they "have overcome" them already (perfect tense). Again and again the Christian life is being celebrated as an accomplished fact. Even though the world is under the control of Satan, those who have been born again, who know God, whose sins have been forgiven, are protected by Jesus Christ, who has conquered Satan through his cross and resurrection.

The Love of the World (2:15–17). John next turns to the principal exhortation of this section. Either we love the Father or we love the world. Affirmations for John's loyal followers now become warnings that they do not fall away into spiritual duplicity—parading spiritual things while the heart is possessed by the world.

When John uses the word "world" (Gk. *kosmos*, v. 15), he can mean either the created material universe, which is good, or the world of sin that stands in aggressive opposition to God. John says that we should "not love" this world. John has in mind that Christians are to avoid an infatuation with worldly godlessness, with the realm of darkness that brings base pleasures.

In verse 16 three things are mentioned that come "not from the Father but from the world":

1. *The desire of the flesh.* The Greek word *sarx* (literally "flesh") possesses various nuances. John has in mind any desire, any sinful interest, that draws us away from God or at least makes continuing fellowship with him impossible.
2. *The desire of the eyes.* The eye is often a metaphor for sinful passion that corrupts. Examples include Eve's looking at the forbidden tree or David's lustful looking at Bathsheba as she bathed.
3. *Boasting in one's lifestyle.* The third description moves from two forms of inappropriate interest and passion to an unholy pride in what one has. John has in mind an attitude of pretentious arrogance or subtle elitism that comes from one's view of wealth, rank, or stature in society. It is an overconfidence that makes us lose any notion that we are dependent on God.

These interests are wrongheaded. They do not spring from the Father and therefore will ultimately destroy a relationship with him. Christ has brought a completely new value system to history. And practically speaking, those who are utterly invested in the world and its passions will see it vanish. Only those whose passions rest in the Father will continue forever.

Application. Many of us fail to discuss the boundary between the church and the world. As a result, we fail to think of strategies to equip our people to manage a life lived in both spheres. John in this passage has provided strategies and given warnings to equip and strengthen the church for this situation.

Does assurance reduce vulnerability? The first threat to faith, the fissure in an otherwise rock-solid Christian life, comes when we doubt the validity or the certainty of our convictions. When someone comes along and suggests that *more complete knowledge* of God or *genuine certainty* of salvation is available elsewhere, I am forced to rethink the basis of my faith. If I am assured of our convictions and confident in the truth we embrace, such questions cannot make us vulnerable.

Senior believers are anchors of the faith. Those who understand the genesis of Christian belief, who recognize the importance of Jesus's life and work, and who know the Scriptures after long study are anchors of stability and wisdom. When such strength is set aside in favor of the exuberant zeal of youth, the church becomes vulnerable to those who would redirect it from its historic and biblical moorings.

Young believers can be exemplars of the faith. College students exhibit a zeal and abandon for God that can be found in few other places. They are eager to make new discoveries as they study. They listen for God's voice, and when they hear it, they are likely to leave their nets and follow Jesus. They are exemplars of faith. John knows that youth bring virtues that have been lost with the passing of years. When these virtues are absent, the church is vulnerable.

The theological problem of the world. We must be forthright that a *boundary* does exist between our lives in Christ and the life promoted in the world. Unfortunately, for many of us such preaching is difficult, if not embarrassing, because our lives are so utterly enmeshed with the world. And because we fail to warn believers in our churches about the character of the world, they become vulnerable to its influences.

1 JOHN 2:18–27

Original Meaning

The Problem: Dissolution and Controversy (2:18–19). In what sense is it "the last hour"? How can John be right since, to put it frankly, quite a few "hours" have passed since this letter was written and the end has still not come? John may be speaking theologically rather than chronologically. The early Christians understood that the first coming of Christ brought a change of eons, an unparalleled period in which the struggle with evil and the unveiling of God's power would intensify, though the exact knowledge of when the eschatological era was being culminated remained unknown. John is reminding his readers that the concentration of evil they are now experiencing fits perfectly the formula announced by Jesus and his apostles for the end of time.

But what has prompted John's interest in the end times? Verse 19 gives us our first explicit description of the secessionists, who once lived as a part of John's community but have now departed. Their departure is evidence, says John, that they were never a part of the church in the first place. Their falsehood has been unveiled.

The Protection: Anointing (2:20–21). When John speaks of the Christian's anointing, he likely has in mind their endowment with the Holy Spirit, a gift that is able to give all knowledge. John therefore tells his followers that they too have the Spirit; *they have an endowment of equal power* and must discern the truth spiritually—through the vehicle of the Spirit within them. The work of the Spirit must always submit to the revelation we have in Jesus Christ. If anyone comes along with a claim to have the Spirit and contradicts what we know of Jesus in history—that is, as recorded in the Gospels—his or her anointing is fraudulent.

The Heresy and Incarnational Christology (2:22–23). Just as the opponents of John have been explicitly identified, so now the false teaching they have been promoting is outlined for us. John's opponents struggled with the notion of incarnational Christology—namely, the notion that God could become human—fully flesh—when he sent his Son as the Christ. The Christian faith was agreeable everywhere with the exception of this one point. Greeks argued that God's divinity could not be compromised with the things of this earth. Spirit and flesh were utterly separate, and those who truly had the Spirit, who were initiated into secret wisdom and knowledge, realized the utter enmity between these two spheres. John's response is unequivocal. People who teach like this are "liars" (v. 22) and have nothing to do anymore with either the Son or the Father (vv. 23–24). In a word, they are no longer Christians.

Objective and Subjective Safeguards (2:24–27). John's antidote to this problem is twofold. He suggests two weapons that should always be available and ready in the Christian's arsenal. Objectively, John believes that right belief is rooted in our recitation of the historic facts about the faith. Subjectively, we need to hone our skills of spiritual discernment so that those who come bearing some spiritually compelling doctrine can be weighed by the Spirit of God within us.

Application. *Building an eschatological climate.* We can graph the church's life as an irregular line that moves between eras of comfort and eras of persecution. This cycle has repeated itself for centuries, and in some cases Christians have misunderstood their histories, urging an apocalyptic message that the end is at hand. John would have us build a climate in the church that heightens eschatological awareness so that when troubles overwhelm us, instead of confidently predicting the arrival of the end, we will say that we are in a period that hallmarks features of the end and that in this instance may actually carry us over the threshold that ends human history.

All of this serves one purpose: to equip Christians so that they are not discouraged when severe difficulties and turmoil erupt. *Eschatological readiness, in other words, has a pastoral function.* It interprets struggle and dispels the despair that accompanies it. It teaches us to watch for changes in history, to watch for "antichrists," and to be alert for times when history betrays elements of the end.

The problem of errant believers. John never tells us explicitly the history or the character of the people who have left the church. Were they faithful Christians once but had now moved into the darkness? While there may be a number of critical theological or spiritual issues that, if denied, place our lives in jeopardy, John's letter places significant emphasis on one issue: the doctrine of Jesus Christ. Whenever the exclusive place of Jesus Christ is jettisoned, when his lordship is lost, serious consequences follow.

Is division the ultimate pastoral catastrophe? When a congregation suffers a severe division in its fellowship and splits, pastors experience anxiety, shame, and loss. No matter what the explanation for the schism, most people on the outside will infer that there has been some pastoral deficiency, some failing in leadership, insofar as unity could not be maintained.

Unity is seriously valued by John. However, one awkward thought comes through these verses: *there comes a time when leadership must sacrifice unity for the sake of the truth.* Sometimes right belief is more important than cohesion and oneness. Unity is not the ultimate virtue in the Christian faith. John here is a co-conspirator in the splitting of his church because he has stood firm in the truth. Certainly he mourned for these people, but he did not ultimately regret his decision.

1 JOHN 2:28–3:10

Original Meaning

The Confidence of God's Children (2:28–29). Christ, John affirms, is going to arrive, and his appearing will at once dramatically set right the present circumstances and identify those who have been allied with him. John's warning about shame is not meant to threaten Christians, who are born of God. He is here addressing those who stand in opposition to Jesus, for whom his climactic coming will be a catastrophe of the first order. When we exhibit God's righteous character, we show that we are born of him, just as a child might show the features of his or her parents.

The Identity and Purity of God's Children (3:1–3). Again and again John repeats that *now* we are God's children. It is an established fact that God's love controls. In verse 2, John reflects on how this fact will have consequences in the future. If now we have a glimpse of what it means to have the presence of God within us, when Christ comes there will be yet more overwhelming experiences for us. He will appear, we will appear just like him, and then we will see him exactly as he is. In that day there will be an immediate and unmistakable unity between us and the Father.

Verse 3 contains the apostle's summary of his reasons for confidence in the Christian life. Fully knowing the Father's love, witnessing God's righteousness at work in us, experiencing the alienation of the world, and sharing a fresh confidence and joy at the prospect of Jesus's return—these things build renewed joy and assurance among Christians who may be struggling. John's pastoral purpose here is ethical. If we set our minds on the confident basis of God's promise, we will feel differently, and this will renew the character of our living.

God's Children and the Children of the Devil (3:4–10). John here does not only affirm the universality of sin once more but describes its inner character. *Sinners break the law.* The decision to sin or not to sin is really a decision to reflect the character of Christ or Satan. John is describing what it means to be a true child of God—or of the devil. Jesus came to destroy all sin. This means initially that his substitutionary sacrifice "took away" our sins and the punishment that accompanies them (v. 5). But John has more in mind. Jesus himself is pure—there is no sin in him—and if that is the case, his work also includes opposition to any sinfulness. In other words, Jesus's works include *both* removing the guilt of sin and defeating its presence altogether. Jesus is concerned with both justification *and* sanctification.

In order to make the point unmistakable, John goes on to say that no one who is truly in an intimate relation with Christ "keeps on sinning" (v. 6). The same thought is repeated in verses 9 and 10 with different nuances (see also 5:18). Those who are children of God keep themselves free from sin. In fact, verse 9 makes the statement boldly: Such people "cannot go on sinning" because they have "been born of God."

John's characteristically bold statements in these verses have led to numerous struggles for the average Christian. *Does this mean that perfect holiness is God's expectation for me?* John may well be emphasizing that ongoing, habitual sin should find no place in the believer's life. He is making a strong case for the holiness of the believer. In fact, those commentators in the Wesleyan or Holiness tradition point out that even within Judaism there was the expectation that in the era of the Messiah, surprising holiness would be commonplace (Ezek 36:27). Thus the New Testament writers (who viewed themselves living in that era) fully expect near sinlessness to accompany the Christian life.

This is a subject that will take some discernment in our application below. Its pastoral implications are immense, and we will have to ask how closely this teaching squares with the practical experience of the Christian life.

Application. *Assurance and rebirth.* We are instructed by John's teaching that *feeling* the power of rebirth is not the foremost measure of being reborn. For John it lies elsewhere. Our moral impulse to do right, to obey God's word, to live an ethical life, is the first by-product of divine rebirth. Admittedly, such ethical maturity lives in conjunction with a thoroughly informed orthodoxy (John would have it no other way). But it is Christian behavior, behavior that the world does not recognize and finds incomprehensible, that shows us that something divine has happened within us, that we have been reborn.

Assurance and adoption. It is astonishing how many believers, even after years in the church, need to learn (or relearn) about the unmerited love God has for us—how we are his children and he will never "unadopt" us. People weep over hearing such amazing news. Their tears have little to do with the character of the presentation; instead, they point to the *insecurity* they have learned in their church upbringing. "If I don't feel like God's child, maybe I'm not." "If I can't always act like God's child, perhaps I never was." We always need to keep circling back to the bedrock truth that God in Christ loves his people unconditionally and will never leave them.

Assurance and eschatology. Many Christians are filled with anxiety and fear at the thought of the second coming, and they wonder if *for them* it will be a day of joy. Many Christians teach that the day of Jesus's return will be a day of reckoning for everyone. John's purposes run along different lines. *Since* we bear Christ's image, when he appears we will be like him. The return of Jesus will disclose the truth about God's relationship with us, not evaluate whether that relationship is satisfactory.

1 JOHN 3:11–24

Original Meaning

The Tragic Example of Cain (3:11–15). The passions that fueled Cain's jealousy and hatred are fueling those opposed to the true Christians in John's churches. And this includes not simply non-Christians outside the church but also those who claim to be Christians—brothers and sisters—who reside within the fellowship.

John furthers his thoughts in verses 14–15. Those who exhibit love for Christ's family demonstrate that *already* they are enjoying the eternal life promised them. Verse 15 echoes the severe exhortation found in Jesus's Sermon on the Mount that our inner motives and attitudes weigh as seriously as our actions in God's moral economy (Matt 5:21–22). In other words, anyone who hates is willing to deny life to his or her opponent and in one sense already has committed murder.

The Superior Example of Jesus Christ (3:16–18). John uses the example of Jesus here in verse 16 for two reasons. First, Christ is a *model* for us to emulate. Christ as God's Son possessed more than we can ever imagine; yet he did not keep what he had selfishly but gave of himself voluntarily for others. Second, Jesus's death is also a *revelation* of God's work on our behalf: "Christ laid down his life for us" (v. 16). Jesus's death is not merely an ethical model; it is a genuine offering, a genuine giving of his life. Verse 18 serves as a sort of summary—and a plea. Love that fails to take the form of action on behalf of others is nothing more than religious rhetoric.

Shoring Up Christian Confidence (3:19–24). If we repunctuate verses 19–20, we can better clarify John's thought, particularly if we make the first clause clearly point to what comes before. Initially, therefore, John is making two points, which we can paraphrase in this manner:

> 19a: "In *this* [the love and obedience we exhibit, vv. 11–18] we will know that we are of the truth."
> 19b–20: "We will reassure our hearts in his presence whenever our hearts condemn us, because (1) God is greater than our hearts, and (2) God knows all things."

This paraphrase gives a clear strategy about what to think when moments of profound insecurity overtake us. Our assurance is anchored in God and God alone. If our conscience condemns, God overrides its verdict. This is possible for two reasons: God is mightier than our hearts, and he knows far more about us than we can ever imagine.

The astonishing statement in verses 21–22 echoes other similar forms of confidence found in passages such as John 14:13–14; 16:23–24. Here in our text John says that we must do "what pleases him"; this presupposes a quality of intimacy that is in touch with God's very heart. Therefore, prayer such as this springs from a fruitful and intimate relationship with God that has already matured.

The command of God to obey has two foci. We are to believe in God's Son, Jesus Christ, and to love one another. Therefore, John's description of the Christian life is at once theological *and* ethical. God has sent his Son, through whom we receive life, and in turn God has poured the life of his Son into us through his Holy Spirit. The virtues of the Christian life cannot be lived apart from a relationship with God, a relationship defined and sustained by Jesus Christ.

Application. *Is conflict justified?* Most of us are able to justify some sort of hostility when we perceive that our opponents are either incompetent or in the wrong. In Christian contexts, some of us have heard church leaders utter aloud words designed to destroy. In church committees, some of us have seen power brokers maneuver themselves over the lives and feelings of others without any hesitation. Of course, John's implication is that since these opponents fought us first, since they departed from the community, it proves that they do not have life in them (3:15). John then turns the thought on its head. *Their misbehavior, however, cannot ever become a justification for our misbehavior.* Fire must not be fought with fire.

High-fashion hatred. In what sense do we display attitudes that bring death to those around us? How often does polite civility disguise undisclosed feelings of antipathy and aversion? Usually such feelings can never be disguised completely, and in the end they destroy. Moreover, John draws a parallel between love and generosity in verse 17, but this time it is about apathy toward those in need. One measure of love is the degree to which people blessed with material wealth distribute that wealth within the community.

Sources of spiritual malaise. This entire section suggests that the church is to become a life-giving community. It should be a place where men, women, and children are healed, not hurt; where the rich take genuine responsibility for the poor and where lives flourish both spiritually and materially. Conflict, struggle, rejection, community fragmentation—all can lead to despair and doubt. When a community loses its solidarity, when its shared vision and life evaporates, personal faith begins to wane.

1 JOHN 4:1–6

Original Meaning

Dangerous Prophet-Teachers (4:1). We have seen suggestions throughout this letter that the schism that had John's community in its grip was being fueled by false teachers. House churches were isolated in cities throughout the Roman Empire. This phenomenon meant that churches could fall prey to unscrupulous itinerant prophets and teachers. Consequently, Christians had to be ready to assess the message they heard and the spirit that inspired it.

John's First Test: What They Say about Jesus (4:2–3). The first test centers entirely on one's view of Jesus Christ. Behind these words John is urging three things about our belief. First, the man Jesus of Nazareth is indeed the divine Word of God. Second, Jesus Christ was and is fully divine as well as fully human. Finally, Jesus is the sole source of eternal life since he alone reveals the Father to us and atones for our sins.

John's Second Test: What the World Thinks about Them (4:4–6). John's second test has to do with audiences. If false prophecies (such as those of the schismatics) originate with an ungodly spirit, these utterances will find a ready reception in the world (v. 5). On the other hand, it is the response of the church, the community of true believers, that can test the veracity of a word and whether it is from the Lord (v. 6). There is a harmony, a correspondence, between the Holy Spirit in the believer and the Holy Spirit in the prophet. When God's Spirit inspires a prophet, his people will discern God's truth.

Application. *The church is called to be the custodian of the truth.* It is not simply permissible but is incumbent on the church to weigh what is being taught within its ranks. But as soon as I say this, another question haunts me: *How do I cultivate a discerning spirit without becoming cynical?* John's interest in the importance of the gathered community—the church—is a signal reminder to us. The *church* is the custodian of the truth, and any impulse to critique, to analyze, or to judge must be worked out in the community of the church's leadership.

The centrality of Christology. What would happen to Christian theology if we neglected one of Christ's two dimensions? If he were not fully human, what would this mean for our confidence in his revelation of the Father? How would it affect his work on the cross or his return to the Father? If he were not fully divine, what would this mean for these same categories?

Where or who are these spirits today? John does not tell us about spiritual warfare as Paul does, but there is ample evidence to suggest that he led a "charismatic" or pneumatic community. The spiritual warfare described in Ephesians 6 was no doubt familiar to him. John wants us to be aware of and equipped for spiritual battle.

1 JOHN 4:7–5:4

Original Meaning

The Origin of Christian Love (4:7–10). The coming of Jesus Christ provides a compelling portrait of God's love for us. This theme—the compelling origin of divine love—weaves its way throughout this text (4:7–11, 16, 19). Christians who live out such love are exhibiting much more. They are also giving evidence that they *have been born* from God and *know* him (v. 7b; cf. 5:4). John goes on to point out that the reverse is also the case (4:8). Whoever does not love cannot possibly know God (also 4:20).

When verse 8 says "God is love" (cf. v. 16), John is saying that love is the essence of his being. John is carefully defining the character of who God is and what it means to live in relation to him. To genuinely contemplate the true identity of God is to become like him. A true apprehension of the personhood of God should lead us to change how we live and behave.

In verses 9–10 John carries his theological definition further with words strongly reminiscent of 3:16. The ultimate act of God's self-revelation is found in his activity in Jesus Christ. The NIV "showed" in verse 9 translates the Greek word *phaneroō* (literally "revealed"), a word that refers to the disclosure of things formerly hidden. Never before has God done such a thing in history! Christ is the unveiling of God's heart; he is God, displayed vulnerably before the world.

The Inspiration of Christian Love (4:11–16). Our obligation to love one another is a by-product of God's loving generosity toward us. Our love for others reflects the divine love already showered upon us. Moreover, John goes on to say that as we meet this obligation to love, we experience something unparalleled: God lives within us as his love is made complete through us. Those who obey God's commands live in him and *he lives in them.* God's own Spirit is powerfully alive within us as we obey (3:24) and love (4:13). Finally, John insists that through our proclamation—our testimony—the reality of God presses itself into our lives (vv. 14–16).

The Results of Christian Love (4:17–19). The most immediate result of this perfect love is assurance: we will have boldness or confidence on the day of judgment. Experiencing and expressing the love of God so powerfully and knowing unequivocally that God by his Spirit resides in our lives—all of this results in unbounded confidence as we approach the day when we meet God. Fear and love are mutually exclusive. To fear the character of God or to fear the final judgment paralyzes us. It destroys the perfection that love offers.

The Command to Love (4:20–5:4). This final exhortation does not rely on experience to fuel our love. For those whose lives require a stronger stimulus, John ushers a divine command: "Anyone who loves God must also love their brother and sister" (4:21). It is critical to keep 5:1–4 as a part of this discussion. John does not change his subject, but here gives it a different nuance. In 5:1a we learn that holding a true confession of faith is evidence of rebirth. Verse 1b adds a general principle: whoever loves the "one who gave birth" (NIV "father") loves his offspring. If you love God, you will love all his children. Therefore, using a family metaphor, John is broadening the ethical challenge. God has many children. To love him—or to love Jesus—demands that we love other children of God as well. The command mentioned in verse 2 is the command to love God's children, but this obligation springs from a profound affection for God in the first place. In verses 3b–4, John repeats what he said in verse 1. People who understand the true identity of Christ—those who love God and all his children, who obey his commands—these are people who have been born of God.

Application. *The grace of God and righteousness.* No one would deny a place for the law, for rules of conduct that place limits on behavior. But the deeper question is whether rules can inspire a life of devotion, love, service, and worship. Moreover, does a framework of law cultivate the sort of reflex to obey that inspires genuine spiritual maturity? In these verses, John is promoting a community that will exhibit spiritual maturity. Righteous Christian conduct is fueled by the realization that God has devoted himself to us so exhaustively that we can do nothing other than respond.

The risk of generous love. An immediate reaction among many Christians is the fear that without some disciplinary threat, without law, such generous love could be exploited. No doubt that is true. Paul's opponents in Galatia were saying the same thing. But it is striking that both John and Paul are willing to endure that risk.

The question of awe. To imagine God as completely loving runs another risk—namely, that of losing profound respect for him because we have made him too personal, too approachable. When we reclaim the awesomeness and power of God, giving him utmost respect, then his loving-kindness takes on new potency. This is the good news. The lion's paw is soft, yet powerful. Its growl is deep and loud, yet it utters our names with affection.

Christian victory and confidence. John raises a significant series of questions about spiritual confidence and certainty. The chief thrust of his message is to buttress the believer's understanding of God's love and to build a Christian ethic responsive to it. John is quick to charge his followers again and again with an exhortation to obey the command to love regardless of how they feel.

John's second suggestion makes many of us uncomfortable. It is mystical. The power to know God's love in reality, the power to love others as he loves us, the reassurance that gives us victory over our doubts—these things may come to us through an experience mediated in the Spirit. A vision perhaps? A Spirit-forged gift? An unexplainable resolve and peace? In any case, this gift is not intellectually obtained, nor is it the fruit of ethical behavior. It is ecstatic, mystical, otherworldly.

But are there other ways we might experience God's mystical love that John has not mentioned? One avenue is the body of Christ. When I am loved *supernaturally* by another Christian, when I am loved *supernaturally* by the body of Christ, I gain a fresh vision of God's love at work through them for me. When God's love feels distant (say, perhaps in our personal devotional time), the body's love can be tangible and real, and when I experience it my own ability to love is quickened. This also—this undramatic, less-than-fantastic, simple experience of love—is an amazing working of God's Spirit among us.

1 JOHN 5:5–12

Original Meaning

The Testimony of the Water and the Blood (5:5–6b). Some were teaching that the heavenly Christ descended on the man Jesus at baptism but departed before he was crucified. Hence, John says, Jesus came not only by baptismal water but also through the blood of the cross. It is Jesus's sacrificial death—not his incarnation alone—that gives life: not by water only, but by water *and blood.* Life and truth can only be found when a complete incarnation embraces a genuine death on the cross.

The Testimony of the Spirit (5:6c–8). Teachers claiming to bear the Spirit were pressing their views on the community. This was the spiritual terrain common to the Johannine churches. John is saying that Spirit-inspired teaching will not dislodge the historic events of salvation witnessed at the cross. This witness began with the apostle John (together with the other apostles) and has been nurtured within the community of believers.

The Testimony of the Father (5:9–12). John urges that since we accept human testimonies, we ought to accept a divine testimony all the more. It is God's divine authority that rests behind the testimony of the water and the blood. It is *God's* Spirit that is affirming truths about the gospel of Jesus Christ. The test of whether or not we accept God's testimony rests here: Do we embrace the truth about Jesus Christ? Since life comes to us through the death of the Son, to deny "the blood," to deny an incarnation that embraces the cross, to deny the salvific, substitutionary work of Jesus at the cross, puts our own salvation in jeopardy.

Application. *"The blood"—the cross—must remain central to all we are and preach.* The cross may not be demoted in *any* Christian soteriology. The mystery of what God is doing on our behalf is hidden there in all its particularity and severity. Christ is not simply one example of God's divine wisdom revealed to the world, a wisdom that can stand alongside other religious systems. Christ is *the* wisdom of God, and this wisdom is manifested in his salvific death within history at the cross.

The custodianship of the Spirit as preserver of the truth. In these verses John is reciting a traditional formula ("water and blood," v. 6) and encapsulating in them a symbol of orthodox conviction. This creedal recitation has become an anchor that should safeguard Christians from wrong belief. Throughout the letter John does the same thing, pointing believers to a recitation of what "was from the beginning" (1:1). Concrete foundations, therefore, not personal creativity and innovation, provide us with the substance and strength of our faith. This means that one avenue of the Spirit's work is the very human institutions that build and protect those foundations. This is undoubtedly one function of the church. The church, through its confessions and traditions, through its recitation of creeds and its defense of councils, lays a foundation from which secure things can be built.

No claim to spirituality is legitimate if it dismantles what God has said in Jesus Christ. Theological expression today must be tested against the bar of incarnational Christology.

The implications of this are enormous. It presses us to make hard judgments concerning theological diversity, it forces us to weigh the cost of affiliating the church with other religious movements, and it challenges us to wonder when we have emptied our creeds of Christ in environments that are inhospitable to him.

1 JOHN 5:13–21

Original Meaning

Prayer and Assurance (5:13–15). In the present section John wants to strengthen his followers' resolve and to reassure them of their place with God and the promises that accrue to those who hold fast to the faith. He wants them to know with full assurance that they have "eternal life" (v. 13). One of the results of this knowledge is confidence or boldness before God, particularly as we pray.

Jesus perhaps modeled this best. His will was always one with the Father, he always did the Father's works, and he always spoke what the Father wished him to say. John believes that through this oneness a profound intimacy will result, making prayer a genuine unity of wills. God does not simply hear us, but he understands and responds. Moreover, our requests are granted. No doubt the condition of verse 14 (abiding in God's will) applies not only to God's hearing but also to our receiving God's gifts. Union with God's will is a prerequisite for each.

Prayer and Sin (5:16–18). John has in mind a situation in which one believer sees another committing a sin. The chief difficulty in the verse is that John says this intercession should be done for "those whose *sin does not lead to death*" (v. 16). A helpful solution possibly comes from the Old Testament distinction between inadvertent sins and intentional sins. In the Old Testament, the temple sacrificial rituals only provided forgiveness for accidental or unconscious sins. When someone sinned intentionally and willfully, the sinner was either exiled or put to death.

Three Certainties (5:19–20). John concludes this section with three bold statements about Christian certainty. Verses 18, 19, and 20 each begin with the same statement, "We know" (cf. 3:2, 14), which gives the verses a rhythmic cadence. And in each case, the verses sound themes that have been dear to John's heart from the first chapter. The first addresses the ongoing righteousness of God's children, the second speaks of the fallenness of the world, and the third gives the hope that is in Christ as we live in this world. Sanctification, disintegration, and redemptive hope are John's final words to his readers.

John's earlier reference to sin (vv. 16–17) inspires a sweeping statement about Christians: they do "not continue to sin" (v. 18a). Why? Because all people who are genuine believers have been "born of God." Furthermore, Christ himself sustains and protects them from the evil one (v. 18b). Therefore, Christians do not engage in this sort of sustained, willful repudiation of God.

But we also know more (v. 19). The sustenance and protection of Jesus are essential because the world lies in the grip of Satan. John's imagery is striking. The world is not under siege by Satan; it hardly struggles against him at all. *The world rests in Satan's grip.*

Finally, John makes clear our hope. If the world is experiencing disintegration and there are many aligned with the forces of evil, what hope is there for us in the world? John's answer (v. 20) is that Jesus Christ has penetrated the world; he has worked as saboteur, undermining the systems of the world and reversing its possibilities. John describes the work of Christ as bringing knowledge (he "has given us understanding, so that we may know . . ."), but this should not be seen as a type of gnostic enlightenment—the very thing to which John is opposed! Christian knowledge is focused on genuine reality, things that happened in history. Thus, in verse 20 John does not say we merely know truth; rather, we know "him who is true [or real]."

John's final thought here is undoubtedly the most important. The NIV takes verse 20c as referring to Jesus Christ, and though interpreters differ, "he" can fully refer to the Son rather than the Father ("he is the true God and eternal life"). It is fitting that John's letter ends here. Throughout his writing he has promoted and defended the full divinity of Christ. To lose this one conviction is to miss not just Jesus but God himself.

Final Exhortation (5:21). Rather than closing the letter with a conventional greeting or blessing, John adds a final exhortation, using his now-familiar title "dear children." While Jesus keeps or sustains us (v. 18), we must be diligent and alert—never passive—when it comes to taking care of ourselves. John is urging his readers to watch out for anything that may become a substitute for God: religious shams, false religion, and even the error-filled words of those who claim to be true believers.

Application. *Christian confidence and doubt.* John emphasizes again and again the importance of Christians knowing with assurance essential facts about their relationship with God. We need to be bold about those things we know with certainty. We need to speak with conviction and assurance about God and his commitment to us. We need to say from lectern and pulpit, "God desires for us to be confident! God desires for us to be bold! God desires to purge doubt from our souls so that we can live enjoying the assurance of one who is eternally loved." When our assurance is truly anchored and secure, no conflict or disarray in the church can ever unsettle it.

Christian confidence and prayer. John has in mind a union, a mystical union, between our lives and the Spirit of God that will ultimately express itself in one voice. This is what the Johannine language for "in my name" is trying to depict. We become one with Jesus. Our will is then transformed freely to become his will. With God's stepping so deeply inside our lives, we have utter confidence that he knows the quietest thoughts of our hearts.

Sin that leads to death. John calls for serious involvement in the lives of people whose sins are not leading to death. These may be inadvertent sins or even minor sins. Either way, John calls for investment, active participation, and mutual ownership of the problem. What value is this? John says we must be alert to the lives of those living around us in the church. We must hold them up, pray for them, interrupt them, and confront them.

The "sin that leads" to death is possibly a reference to someone's ultimate turning away from God, a final repudiation of God (in apostasy), which leads to eternal death.

Confidence and the sustaining presence of Christ. Life in the church can be painful. And yet Jesus has not abandoned us. Pastors and mature Christian leaders can and will disappoint. But Jesus still remains committed and invested. Jesus is true even though all else fails. We are still children of God even though our spiritual family, the church, is oftentimes broken. And we can still discover the light and walk in it, even if those around us are succumbing to the darkness.

2 JOHN

INTRODUCTION TO 2 JOHN

For authorship and date of this short letter, see the introduction to 1 John above. Second John was probably written after 1 John to the same community in Ephesus and is an exhortation—a reminder—of things said before there in that first letter. By the time of the writing of 2 John, the rupture within the church reflected in 1 John seems complete (2 John 7). John writes the letter with two purposes in mind: to buttress his followers' commitment to the truth and to warn them about the severity of their opponents and the need to protect themselves.

BOOK OUTLINE

I. Personal Greetings (1–3)
II. Fidelity to the Truth: Commitment to Love the Family of God (4–6)
III. Protecting the Family of God: Specific Warnings (7–11)
IV. A Final Greeting (12–13)

2 JOHN 1–13

Original Meaning

Personal Greetings (1–3). Rather than give his name, the author simply calls himself "the elder" (Gk. *presbyteros*, v. 1a). On the one hand, he seems to know the church well—and is known by them. However, it is his *position* that is now important and the authority that comes with it. The elder (in our view, John) was an overseer of some sort, someone with pastoral oversight outside the congregation.

An ancient tradition has thought "lady chosen by God" (v. 1b) refers to a person. But this usage here is unlikely. The New Testament thinks of the church with feminine metaphors. Thus, we should view 2 John as a personal note written by John and sent to a particular congregation.

John's deep love for his church is expressed in his first sentence, "whom I love in the truth" (v. 1c), a community that has embraced Jesus Christ and experienced the indwelling power of the Holy Spirit. Thus, the threefold blessing of verse 3 is announced triumphantly as a promise, not a wish: "grace, mercy and peace . . . *will be* with us."

Fidelity to the Truth: Commitment to Love the Family of God (4–6). John's first message actually begins in verse 4, where he celebrates the continuing faithfulness and obedience of these Christians to the truth. "Truth" and "love" are the twin themes that echo throughout 1 John and here in verses 4 and 5 appear in summary form.

Couriers may have come to John reporting how faithful this remaining house church was. On the other hand, verse 4 may imply something different. John's rejoicing that "some of" the believers here remained faithful may suggest that *others have not*. John's call is for these believers to consolidate their besieged community and confirm the essence of their beliefs—in other words, to fortify themselves against those who are out to destroy them.

Protecting the Family of God: Specific Warnings (7–11). With stunning specificity, John moves in verse 7 from the truth and love that inspire celebration to the treachery and deception that are lurking just outside the church's doors. "Deceivers" (Gk. *planoi*, v. 7a) can also be translated "liars." Clearly these people have not only left the church and taken up residence in the world, but they have "gone out" into the world in order to spread their teachings (v. 7c). These false prophets have denied the complete incarnation of Christ and should now be seen as agents of the "antichrist" (v. 7d).

John says that orthodox confession affirms "Jesus Christ as coming in the flesh" (v. 7b). Why the present tense? This is likely not a reference to the second coming; rather, it is John's way of saying that Jesus Christ came *and still exists* in the flesh. In other words, through his incarnation Jesus swept up our humanity and carried it with him into eternity. To oppose this teaching is to be aligned with the antichrist.

Verses 8–9 form John's first firm word to his followers: he does not want them to lose all that they have gained so far. As evangelist and pastor, John has been a participant in the birth and maturation of the faith of the recipients of this letter. In other words, they are not the sole custodians of their church, free to do as they wish. John has been a builder among them, and his contributions and responsibility make him a justified critic of what is happening.

Verses 10–11 describe John's second firm word. The consequence of this false teaching is so serious that it demands a serious remedy: no hospitality should be extended to those people who bear such erroneous doctrine. An instruction like this is striking and peculiar in the New Testament, which generally encourages Christians to be generously hospitable.

These troubling verses should be viewed as "emergency regulations," tied directly to the crisis at hand.

A Final Greeting (12–13). John extends a greeting from his church and expresses his desire to make a personal visit rather than rely on "black ink and papyrus"—as the Greek puts it. We should note his confidence that his readers will receive him and heed his words. John's coming to these believers is aimed at renewing their fellowship so that both pastor and congregation will be joyful.

In verse 13 John's greeting from "the children of your sister" once again employs the metaphorical language we read in verse 1. Although this is the only place the phrase occurs in the New Testament, we can be reasonably sure that John is building on family imagery for the church (see on v. 1). Two "sisters" are talking with each other about conditions in the family, and their speech swings from expressions of love and intimacy to feelings of worry and concern.

Application. *Shutting the gates of the church.* John's teaching that Christians should show no hospitality to their opponents has met with severe criticism among some interpreters. Is there a place for "shutting the gate"? Despite what we hear in our popular culture, tolerance is not an ultimate virtue. Strong action is appropriate when individuals jeopardize the very integrity of the church. But John gives us little guidance concerning what matters would qualify as gate-shutting concerns. It is easy to be glib about this and refer to genuinely peripheral issues like the proper mode of baptism or tobacco. But matters become far more intense—and the questions more difficult—when we wonder about the legitimacy of other divisive issues. The answers here are often complex.

Using the doctrine of the church. John implies that Christians would do well to respect and learn from the consensus that has come to us from tradition, from the things passed down from the beginning. We ought to revive our creeds in which mature men and women of faith struggled to define orthodox Christian faith.

Guarding the message of the church. We will all at times experience a pressure to dilute the message of Christ that is no different from the pressure faced by the Johannine world. John's followers felt acute pressure from the sophisticated halls of Hellenistic *academe*—not to mention the popular voices of the marketplace—to reduce the person of Christ into someone less than he was. John calls his followers to stand firm, and he would have us do the same.

3 JOHN

INTRODUCTION TO 3 JOHN

For authorship and date of this short letter, see the introduction to 1 John above. Third John is a personal letter addressed to a dear friend and trusted believer named Gaius (v. 1). John wants to visit personally and address a situation that has arisen with a man named Diotrephes, but cannot at present (v. 14), so he writes to Gaius to encourage him to remain faithful to the truth until then.

BOOK OUTLINE

I. Personal Greetings (1–2)
II. Loving Christ's Emissaries (3–8)
III. Exhortations about Diotrephes (9–12)
IV. Closing (13–14)

3 JOHN 1–14

Original Meaning. Rather than outlining a number of theological doctrines, 3 John is a brief note dashed off to one heroic Christian (Gaius) who is standing firm while a community near him is struggling under the pressure of a single antagonist (Diotrephes). Rather than outline its themes, if we sketch the setting of the letter, its various parts fall into place.

Rebuilding the Scene. Imagine a house church located some distance from John's primary ministry. It is in the grips of the theological struggle. John himself once wrote to the church, but an influential man named Diotrephes rejected his letter. John then sent emissaries to the church, but Diotrephes forcefully stopped anyone who showed sympathy to the visitors or tried to speak with them. "Anyone who sides with these men from John," Diotrephes threatened, "gets thrown out with them" (cf. v. 10).

The missionaries found a courageous host, however, in a man named Gaius. He not only gave these emissaries from John rest and refreshment, but he sent them "on their way" (v. 6)—that is, gave them money—and they returned to John with their report about the rebellion of Diotrephes's church and about Gaius's faithfulness.

It is significant that John does not ask Gaius to intervene in the controversy by confronting Diotrephes himself. Christians are called to different roles, and Gaius has done enough if he stands firm for Jesus Christ and provides John and his couriers an entrée into the community.

John therefore writes this letter in anticipation of his upcoming visit. Verse 12 introduces the courier of the letter, a Christian named Demetrius. No doubt, John assumes, the hospitality and financial support shown to other Christian travelers will be extended to Demetrius, who is well known by the Johannine community and is a personal friend of John himself.

This strong affirmation of Demetrius surely anticipates what Diotrephes will say about him. Demetrius bears the authority of John himself, and since Diotrephes rejects John, he will likewise reject Demetrius. John's testimony should strengthen Gaius's confidence in Demetrius, but the problem will only be resolved when John confronts Diotrephes personally.

Reconstructing John's Struggle with Diotrephes. What was the nature of the problem with Diotrephes? Why was he so antagonistic to John? The tense of the Greek verb in verse 9 translated "will [not] welcome" is present. This construction means that John is not referring to a single event but to an enduring attitude. The verb itself can mean two things, both of which are at work here. Formally, it means "to receive or welcome" someone. Diotrephes was simply refusing to be hospitable to the missionaries. Yet second the verb also has a figurative meaning, carrying the idea "to accept or recognize" someone. Diotrephes was rejecting not merely his obligation to be hospitable but John himself as elder. This rejection of the missionaries was his way of refusing to acknowledge the authority of John, and this attitude was going to continue.

Scholars have offered much speculation regarding the nature of the tension in 3 John, and this letter has been made to serve theories of what was happening in the late apostolic period when leadership was shifting to a second generation. It is best to exclude grandiose schemes for this letter. Diotrephes was simply a powerful lay leader who had gained control and rejected John's authority. Possibly one way to undercut John's influence was to exploit the theological controversy that was circulating in the Johannine community. But there does not seem to be sufficient evidence to say that John viewed Diotrephes as a leading opponent in the secession.

Application. *John's first strategy.* John did not let go of this situation. John's first strategy for resolving this conflict is not to retreat but to remain in contact. This should be our strategy too. All too often our impulse when we must confront people of strong will and ambition is to retreat. The prospect of losing or of being shamed is so apparent that it seems better to wait and see what will happen, to stay on the sidelines, or to keep away from the perpetrators.

John's second strategy. Gaius becomes a point of reference that gives John pastoral objectivity in this remote congregation. Wounded pastors—John included—have trouble being objective. John needs Gaius. Without him, John can have no confidence that his approach in the situation is correct. Modern crises are no different than those of the first-century world. Pastoral objectivity that is anchored in the counsel of wise elders is always superior.

John's third strategy. The final, striking dimension of this letter is John's willingness to talk personally with Diotrephes. The temptation to avoid Diotrephes and fall silent must have occurred to John. It is one thing to write a letter or even send a messenger. But it is altogether another matter to go personally and confront your opponent. We can successfully rationalize conflict avoidance in countless ways. Powerlessness often masquerades as Christian piety and meekness, but it is neither of these.

JUDE

INTRODUCTION TO JUDE

While we can be rather sure that the letter of Jude was written by a brother of Jesus with that name, we can be sure of almost nothing else about this letter. Some date Jude by reference to its relationship to 2 Peter. To be sure, we cannot pin down the precise literary relationship between the two letters. But the degree of similarity between the two does suggest that they were dealing with similar false teaching and probably at about the same time. Second Peter was likely written toward the end of Peter's life, in the middle 60s. We should probably date Jude at about the same time.

BOOK OUTLINE

I. Introduction (1–2)
II. Occasion and Theme: Contending for the Faith (3–4)
III. Description and Condemnation of the False Teachers (5–16)
IV. Closing Appeal: Holding Fast to the Faith (17–23)
V. Concluding Doxology (24–25)

JUDE 1–2

Original Meaning. "Jude" is the brother of the Lord mentioned in Mark 6:3. "Servant" indicates Jude's subservience to the Lord. "James" must refer to the most famous James in the New Testament—the brother of Jesus, who attained a high position in the early Jerusalem church.

Jude identifies his readers as Christians. The key word in the description is "called" (*klētois*). This word reflects the New Testament conviction that being a Christian is a product of God's gracious reaching out to bring helpless sinners into a relationship with himself. Being "kept for Jesus Christ" means that God throughout this life exercises his power on behalf of Christians to preserve them spiritually intact until the coming of Jesus Christ in glory.

Application. Christians have many reasons to be anxious. But one thing we do not need to worry about is God's faithfulness in maintaining us in our faith. This is not to say, of course, that we have no part or responsibility in the matter. Jude makes clear that we do (v. 21). But we begin, as we always should in the Christian life, with God and his grace.

JUDE 3–4

Original Meaning. Jude explains the occasion and theme of this letter. The occasion is the intrusion of false teachers. To meet the needs of this occasion, Jude focuses on a single theme: maintaining the truth of the Christian faith as it has been handed down from Christ and the apostles (v. 3).

Clearly "faith" describes what Christians believe—such things as Jesus's atoning death and resurrection, the indwelling of the Holy Spirit, salvation by grace through faith, and (especially in Jude's situation) the holy lifestyle that flows from God's grace in Christ.

"Certain individuals" has a contemptuous ring. Rather than straightforwardly opposing the faith, these people pursue their agenda by stealth. Jude says four things about them. First, their "condemnation was written about long ago." Second, "they are ungodly." "Ungodly" (*asebēs*) is irreverence in an ethical sense. Jude clearly applies it in this way. Third, they pervert "the grace of our God into a license for immorality." Finally, they "deny Jesus Christ our only Sovereign and Lord." Exactly how were the false teachers denying Christ? Jude is thinking of a practical denial of Christ, of people behaving in a manner contrary to what Jesus the Lord demands of his people.

Application. What is Jude so passionate about? In a phrase, "the faith that was once for all entrusted to God's holy people." There is a set of beliefs, based in the teaching and work of Christ, developed and passed on by the apostles, that is nonnegotiable. To be Christian is to agree with these beliefs; to reject them is to cease to be Christian.

JUDE 5–10

Original Meaning

Three Old Testament Examples of Sin and Judgment (vv. 5–7). God's deliverance of his people seemed to be decisive and final, yet God still "destroyed" (v. 5b) them because of their lack of faith. Jude intends this as a warning to his readers: don't think, because God has decisively rescued you from your sins, that you can presume on his grace and mercy.

In Jude's day, a popular tradition about angels who sinned was associated with the enigmatic reference in Genesis 6:1–4 to "sons of God" who came down to earth and cohabited with "the daughters of men." These stories find their greatest elaboration in the intertestamental Jewish book 1 Enoch. These angels, says Jude, abandoned their "proper dwelling" by rebelling against God (v. 6). God therefore judged them.

Verse 7 introduces Sodom and Gomorrah. Jude not only mentions God's judgment but also tells us why God judged the cities: because they "gave themselves up to sexual immorality and perversion" (v. 7a). Jude concludes these sinful cities on the plain "serve as an example of those who suffer the punishment of eternal fire" (v. 7b).

Application of the Examples to the False Teachers (vv. 8–10). Jude lists three different sins the false teachers are committing. We give here a literal translation as a basis for our comments. They "dreaming, pollute flesh," "reject authority," and "blaspheme glories" (v. 8). The parallels between these three sins and those of the Old Testament sinners Jude has listed are generally clear.

Verse 9 is a contrast to the behavior of the false teachers. Perhaps the false teachers were disparaging the evil angels by presuming, apart from the power of the Lord, to dismiss their significance on their own behavior. Perhaps the experience of the Jewish exorcists in Acts 19:13–16 is something of a parallel. Jude's false teachers were probably not trying to exorcise demons on their own. But they may have been guilty in a general way of the mistake made by these Jewish exorcists: dismissing the power and influence of evil angels without the authority of Jesus to back it up.

With the "these" at the beginning of verse 10, Jude returns to his characterization of the false teachers. Jude is here describing the false teachers' sexual excesses. Rather than following the "reason" of God's word, they act at the level of pure instinct—like animals, with no moral compass or sense of right and wrong.

Application. *The issue of homosexuality.* Christians are reevaluating their understanding of homosexuality, and many today argue that we need to revise what is called the traditional view. Current secular theory about homosexuality is placing more and more emphasis on nature, rather than nurture, as the cause of homosexual behavior. Homosexuals, we are now being told, are genetically predisposed to this particular sin. But even if this is so, homosexual behavior is not unchangeable. Many people are predisposed, for all kinds of reasons, to certain sins, but this is no excuse in God's eyes. The important point is that the gospel offers people the power to turn from their sin, whatever their particular temptation.

JUDE 11–13

Original Meaning

Three Old Testament Examples (v. 11). Jude here compares the false teachers to three bad characters from the Old Testament. In what way does Jude think the false teachers "go the way of Cain"? He may be suggesting that as Cain murdered Abel, so the false teachers "murder" the souls of people (see Gen 4:1–16). Yet Jewish tradition also understood Cain to be the classic example of an ungodly skeptic and an instructor in wicked practices. It is hard to be sure exactly which nuance Jude has in mind here concerning Cain.

The second example from the Old Testament is Balaam, known especially for his greed, an emphasis Jude picks up also by claiming that the false teachers follow the way of Balaam out of a desire for "profit" or "gain." Balaam's story can be found in Numbers 22–24.

The third example is Korah, whose story is told in Numbers 16:1–35. He rebelled against Moses's leadership and in response God caused the earth to open up and swallow Korah and his followers in judgment. Such a similar fate is reserved for the false teachers if they do not turn and repent.

Application of the Examples to the False Teachers (vv. 12–13). Jude here provides six more brief descriptions of these false teachers. First, "these people are blemishes at your love feasts, eating with you without the slightest qualm" (v. 12a). Jude is suggesting that the false teachers, like a hidden reef that rips the bottom out of a boat, lie in wait to bring destruction upon the faithful. Second, they are "shepherds who feed only themselves" (v. 12b). The shepherd is the epitome of a person who selflessly watches out for others. But the false teachers were abandoning their natural responsibility to care for others, thinking only of themselves.

Third, "they are clouds without rain, blown along by the wind" (v. 12c). This is a natural metaphor for those who do not deliver what they promise. Fourth, they are "autumn trees, without fruit and uprooted—twice dead" (v. 12d). A tree that is still without fruit in the autumn has not fulfilled its purpose in being. Fifth, "they are wild waves of the sea, foaming up their shame" (v. 13a). Jude is thinking of the shameful deeds committed by the false teachers. Finally, they are "wandering stars, for whom the blackest darkness has been reserved forever" (v. 13b). Ancient people believed that the heavens should display order and regularity. They therefore had difficulty in accounting for the planets, which seemed to "wander" across the night sky in no discernible pattern.

JUDE 14–16

Original Meaning. Jude caps his denunciation of the false teachers with a prophecy. Jude takes this prophecy from 1 Enoch. This book was popular in Jude's day, and both he and Peter allude to it. It is not clear whether Jude intends to say in verse 14 that "Enoch prophesied about these men also [i.e., in addition to the wicked people of his own day]" or that "Enoch also [i.e., in addition to these other texts] prophesied about these men." But the NIV is probably correct to suggest the latter by simply omitting the "also" (Gk. *kai*). Like other New Testament writers, Jude assumes that the prophecies find their fulfillment in Christ and the church he founded. They can therefore apply the words of the prophets to their own circumstances.

In Jude's quotation of the prophecy, he goes out of his way to stress the "ungodly" character of these people. Indeed, the use of the word three times in one clause in verse 15 creates an almost awkward reading: "to convict all the *ungodly* of all the *ungodly* acts that they have done in an *ungodly* way" (literal translation). We certainly do not have to guess Jude's point!

But not only are these people judged for acting in an ungodly way; they have also sinned against God in speech. The transition from verses 14–15 to verse 16 is apparently this: Enoch prophesied about ungodly people who would be judged by the Lord. They are, Jude says, "grumblers and faultfinders." Who are they grumbling against and finding fault with? The biblical background of the term "grumbler" suggests that these false teachers are directing their complaints against God himself.

Jude's second description of the false teachers in verse 16 picks up the reference to their "ungodly acts" from the Enoch prophecy: "They follow their own evil desires." These evil desires probably encompass both the false teachers' sexual lust and greed. Jude's third accusation suggests the idea of arrogant speech about or even toward God.

Application. As believers, we should look forward to the day of Christ's coming with joy, for it brings our final deliverance from sin, temptation, and bodily weakness. But contemplation of that day should also lead to serious self-evaluation. For although we need not fear rejection and condemnation, we know our lives will be scrutinized as Christ asks what we have done with the precious blessings he has entrusted to us.

JUDE 17–23

Original Meaning. Jude here in this section tells the believers to do three things. First, they are to remember that the apostles themselves had predicted the kind of false teaching they are now experiencing (vv. 17–19). From a human standpoint, these false teachers have "secretly slipped in" (v. 4). But God knew all along that they were coming. Thus this reminder reassures Jude's readers that God knows what is happening in their midst. He is still in control.

Second, Jude's readers are to devote themselves to their own spiritual growth (vv. 20–21). They must not allow the false teachers to deflect them from their own development in the faith. Finally, Jude's readers are to reach out to those affected by the false teaching (vv. 22–23). Withdrawal into their own private spirituality is not enough; Jude's readers must do what they can to reclaim these people before it is too late.

Application. Jude wants us to be on our guard. We should not be surprised when we find people in our churches who teach or live lies. Being on our guard does not, of course, mean that we are to become critical and suspicious. But neither are we to be naive, assuming that because people have made a profession of faith, attend church regularly, or are even in a position of leadership, they must be above reproach.

JUDE 24–25

Original Meaning. Jude's doxology is a fitting conclusion to his letter. He has warned the church of a serious and threatening outbreak of false teaching. He has called believers not simply to batten down the hatches and ride out the storm but to reach out redemptively to those who are falling away. Believers can do that because their position with the Lord is secure: he has the power to preserve them intact until the day of judgment.

Application. We worry about our health, our money, our children, and our jobs. In sober moments we perhaps become anxious about death. God does not promise to take away these worries, but he does take away from us our greatest worry: where we will spend eternity. Do we reflect this confidence in the way we live? Do we truly value heaven enough so that our earthly worries, while sometimes pressing, fade in importance in light of our eternal destiny? To our God and Savior be glory for his salvation in and through Jesus Christ our Lord!

REVELATION

INTRODUCTION TO REVELATION

Although many details in Revelation (and in this commentary) are debatable, the basic thrust is not. The true and living God summons us from our preoccupation with the world to recognize what really matters and what does not. God first gave Revelation to a culture where people would hear and be struck by the full force of the book. It summons us to grapple with God's judgment on a world in rebellion against him.

If we take seriously what the book itself *claims*, then it was a book that must have made good sense to its first hearers, who in fact were "blessed" for obeying it (1:3). If today's newspapers are a necessary key to interpreting the book, then no generation until our own could have understood and obeyed the book (contrary 1:3). They could not have read the book as Scripture profitable for teaching and correction (cf. 2 Tim 3:16–17). If, however, the book was understandable for the first generation, subsequent generations can profit from the book simply by learning some history.

Early church fathers suggested that Revelation stems from the time of the evil emperor Domitian at the end of the first century, and that John returned from Patmos only after Domitian's death. Domitian so persecuted the church that their tradition explicitly viewed him as Emperor Nero's successor, who also persecuted the church, in the mid-60s. The church tradition that dates Revelation to the time of Domitian in the late first century is thus likely, around the mid-90s.

BOOK OUTLINE

I. Introduction (1:1–20)
II. Letters to the Seven Churches (2:1–3:22)
III. Visions of the Heavenly Temple (4:1–5:14)
IV. The Six Seals (6:1–7:17)
V. The Seventh Seal and the Trumpets (8:1–11:19)
VI. The Saints versus the Serpent (12:1–14:20)
VII. Bowls of Anger (15:1–16:21)
VIII. The Fate of Babylon (17:1–19:21)
IX. The Hope of the Saints (20:1–22:5)
X. Conclusion (22:6–21)

REVELATION 1:1–3

Original Meaning

The Revelation from Jesus Christ (1:1a). The title and subject of this book is "the revelation from Jesus Christ."

The Agents of Revelation (1:1b–2). *John and the angel.* That the author does not need to qualify which John he is may suggest that he is the most obvious John among the early Christians—namely, John the apostle, son of Zebedee, who had personally known Jesus in the flesh (cf. John 21:22).

John's testimony. John testifies "to everything he saw," which was "the word of God and the testimony of Jesus Christ" (v. 2). "Testify" is often courtroom language—appropriate for John and other early Christians, who would face law courts (cf. 1:9; John 16:2).

Those Who Read and Hear (1:3). That the book of Revelation was read in churches alongside Old Testament Scripture suggests that the early Christians began treating it as Scripture then or soon afterward. That one person would read the work ("blessed is the one who reads") and the whole congregation would hear it ("blessed are those who hear it") fits what we know of the time; even in urban areas, many people could not read much.

Application. Revelation announces that God is still in control and that he will conclude this stage of history the way he has promised. Precisely because he rules history, he can assure us of its outcome.

REVELATION 1:4–8

Original Meaning

Churches in Asia (1:4a). "Asia" was a designation for the Roman province of western Asia Minor (modern Turkey), where Christianity was flourishing by the end of the first century.

From God with Love (1:4b). "Grace" (*charis*) is related to the typical Greek greeting, "greetings" (*charein*), and "peace" translates the typical Jewish greeting, *shalom.* Early Christian letters invoked the Lord Jesus alongside God the Father, implying their belief in his deity.

Jesus the Deliverer (1:5–6). Each of Jesus's titles in verse 5 provides special encouragement to a suffering church. Jesus is the "faithful witness," who provided the ultimate witness of the Father (John 3:11) and stood faithful in his witness when on trial before Pilate (1 Tim 6:13). Jesus is also here the "firstborn from the dead" and expresses the fact that Jesus was the first person to rise from the dead (see also Col 1:18; Heb 1:6; cf. Rom 8:29). It was especially relevant for Christians who might soon face death for his name. As the firstborn, Jesus's resurrection was the guarantee that his dead followers would also be raised.

Jesus is also described as ruling over the "kings of the earth." The language alludes to Psalm 89:27. To believers suffering under agents of mighty Caesar, this title of Jesus would encourage them indeed!

In declaring that Jesus made us a "kingdom and priests," John reminds his audience that salvation is not just what God saves us from (our sins, v. 5), but what he saves us for—a destiny as his agents and worshipers (v. 6).

After John expresses his prayer for grace and peace from the triune God, he pauses to offer a doxology of praise to Jesus (v. 6). Whereas traditional Jewish texts praised God the Father, here the praise is apparently directed toward Jesus.

Concluding Promise and Affirmation (1:7–8). That Jesus would return in the clouds reflects Daniel 7:13; that those who pierced him would see him and mourn reflects Zechariah 12:10. Because the language of Matthew 24:30 reflects the same texts, it is likely that John here echoes an earlier saying of Jesus. No assurance could better encourage suffering believers than the knowledge that Jesus will come to set matters right. It is not altogether clear whether the "mourning" implies repentance or—more likely—fear, but the note of vindication is unambiguous.

Finally, John confirms once again that all history is in God's hands—the future as well as the present (v. 8); thus, his people need not fear as if something will happen to them apart from God's plan. The title "the Alpha and the Omega," like the one "who is, and who was, and who is to come," indicates God's eternality, that all of history from beginning to end is the same to him.

God not only is Lord over time, but he rules the entire universe: he is *pantokratōr*, "Almighty," a common title for God in this book (1:8; 4:8; 11:17; 15:3; 16:7, 14; 19:6, 15; 21:22). For Christians suffering under Caesar, the *autokratōr* or emperor, knowing that they served the "Almighty" must have provided strength.

Application. God saw our own generation and all the martyrs of history at the same time; the church of all ages is part of his plan, and we are part of a purpose that is bigger than us individually and that will not fail. He is the Almighty.

REVELATION 1:9–12

Original Meaning

Setting the Scene (1:9–10). "Suffering" and the "kingdom" are inseparable parts of our inheritance in Jesus. "Endurance" requires fortitude in view of God's promises (13:10; 14:12) during present tribulation.

John, in the context of speaking of suffering, declares that he was on the island of Patmos. Literally he was there "because of" God's word—as a punishment by the state for preaching and testifying about Jesus (cf. 6:9; 12:11). Though he probably experienced a more lenient form of banishment, his conditions would be harsh for someone of his age.

Because John was already in the Spirit when the vision began, perhaps "in the Spirit" begins here not with a visionary state, as in 4:2 and 21:10, but initially in worship that led to a visionary state. Such an interpretation helps explain John's mention of "the Lord's Day," likely used for corporate worship. Prophetically inspired worship characterized early Christianity (1 Cor 14:15, 26; Eph 5:18–19).

Among the Lampstands (1:11–12). John turns when he hears a voice "like a trumpet" (1:10). This expression presumably refers to the clarity of Jesus's voice, a voice that could therefore strike terror into the hearts of the unprepared.

Sometimes visionaries wrote by dictation as they saw their visions; this may be the case here (v. 11). Sometimes they wrote shortly after their vision, as in 10:4. John does not, however, need to wait until the completion of his visions.

What is most significant is that Jesus appears among the lampstands (1:12–13; 2:1), which represent the seven churches (1:20), probably suggesting Jesus's presence with his church (cf. John 20:19). The temple included a golden lampstand (Exod 25:31–35; 37:17–24; 2 Chr 4:7, 20), never extinguished by night or day.

Throughout the ancient Mediterranean world, this seven-branched lampstand, or menorah, stood as the most common symbol of Israel and Judaism. John encourages Jewish Christians excluded from their synagogues that it is not they but their opponents who are severed from their Jewish heritage (see comment on 2:9 below).

Application. One of Revelation's most important declarations is that Jesus appears among the lampstands (1:12; 2:1), which represent the seven churches (1:20). One need only skim the letters to these churches in chapters 2 and 3 to realize that five of them needed serious correction. Nevertheless, until a church has gone so far as to be withdrawn from its place (2:5), it remains the place where Christ's presence is found. When we see the flaws in churches, our tendency is sometimes to react with disdain, but we must never give up on the spiritual life that remains in the church, for the Lord of the churches, who offered his blood to redeem them, still loves them and walks among them (cf. 1:5; 3:4).

REVELATION 1:13–20

Original Meaning

John's Vision of the Son of Man (1:13–16). Revelation opens with Jesus as the revealer. The robe and girdle may recall the biblical high priest (Exod 28:4; Lev 8:7) and suggest that Jesus is his people's high priest. Jesus appears not only as king but as priest. The image weaves together imagery from sources in the book of Daniel. Two most important stem from the same passage: the reigning son of man (Dan 7:13–14) and the Ancient of Days (God), before whom the son of man appears (7:9).

Jesus's glory is *more* than that of an angel (Ezek 1:7; Dan 10:6). The voice like "the sound of rushing waters" (Rev 1:15) recalls the sound of God's own voice as many waters in Ezekiel 1:24 and 43:2. Jesus's title (Rev 1:13) recalls the figure who would reign as God's agent in Daniel 7:13–14; the hair like wool and comparison with white snow (Rev 1:14) allude to God himself, the "Ancient of Days" in the same Daniel passage (Dan 7:9–10).

Jesus's face also shines like the sun (Rev 1:16). The point of Jesus's fiery eyes, white hair, and bronze feet (vv. 14–15) is that he was radiating light or fire (v. 15)—like some visions of God in the Bible (Ezek 1:27; Dan 7:9–10). Other deities were portrayed as bearing swords, but this image in Revelation 1:16 is an allusion to Isaiah 11:4.

Jesus's Message (1:17–20). John responds to this revelation of Jesus's glory by falling down (v. 17; cf. Ezek 1:28; Dan 8:17), a standard response. When recipients respond in such a manner, the revealer often raises the recipient on his feet or declares, "Do not be afraid" (Dan 10:11–12; cf. Matt 17:7).

Most important, Jesus is "the First and the Last" (v. 17). This is exactly equivalent to "the Alpha and the Omega," a title appropriate only to God (1:8; 21:6), announcing Jesus's deity.

All the claims of verse 18 involve Jesus's triumph over death. Because of his victory over death, Jesus held the "keys of death and Hades." "Death and Hades" together represent death's power. Only the truly risen and Living One could release people from Hades, the realm of death.

When Jesus tells John to write (v. 19), he casts John in the typical role of a witness (1:2), one who must testify of what one has personally seen.

The "mystery" in verse 20 is not one which God wishes to keep secret (cf. 17:7). The stars in Jesus's hand represent the angels of the churches, and the lampstands among which he stands represent the churches. These indicate Jesus's intimate care for his people: he is among them (cf. 21:3), and their future lies in his hand (cf. John 10:28–29).

What are the angels of the seven churches? These angels most likely represent guardian angels of the congregations. Alternatively, one might view them as the heavenly representatives of congregational leaders, again functioning like guardian angels but of individuals (cf. Matt 18:10).

Application. Like Jesus's triumph over death (1:18), the fact that Jesus holds the churches in his hands (1:20) reassures us that in the end God's benevolent purposes will triumph.

REVELATION 2:1–7

Original Meaning

A Note on the Letters in General. The letters to the seven churches are "prophetic letters," a sort of writing that appeared earlier in the Bible (2 Chr 21:12–15; Jer 29). They resemble the biblical format of oracles concerning various peoples (Isa 13–23; Jer 46–51; Ezek 25–32), here applied more specifically to God's people dispersed in different cities.

Each letter is a prophetic word from Jesus through the Spirit (e.g., 2:7), who is inspiring John (1:10). Each letter follows a similar pattern, balancing praise and reproof:

- To the angel of the church in a given city, write:
- Jesus (depicted in glory, often in terms from 1:13–18) says:
- I know (in most instances offers some praise)
- But I have this against you (offers some reproof, where applicable)
- The one who has ears must pay attention to what the Spirit says
- Eschatological promise

Letter to Ephesus (2:1–7). The portrait of an evil world ruler demanding worship (13:12–15) would certainly be relevant to Christians in Ephesus. Ephesus honored Domitian at Olympic games just shortly before this book was written. Nor was the emperor cult the only prominent element of paganism there. Ephesus was known for the worship of Artemis (Acts 19:23–40) and the practice of magic (19:13–19). It also had a large Jewish community (19:8–9). All these elements would help make various features of the book of Revelation relevant to them.

Revelation 2:2 indicates that the church appears to have improved in discernment since Paul's day (2 Tim 1:15). That these teachers are self-styled apostles probably implies that they have arrived from outside Ephesus.

All that the Ephesian Christians are doing right is not sufficient to excuse their lack of love. Commentators today understand the phrase as love for one another (2:19). Those who once knew what was right should remember that they can repent and return (v. 5).

We can only guess the identity of the Nicolaitans (v. 6). The most reasonable guess is that they offer views similar to (but not identical with) those of "Balaam"—hence they condone immorality and the eating of food offered to idols (2:14–15), apparently common areas of assimilation among early Christians (cf. 1 Cor 6; 8–10).

For the church in Ephesus, "victory" (v. 7b) requires more than the vigilance of theological watchmen; it requires the internal unity of love. The reward of such overcoming is eating "from the tree of life" (v. 7c; see Gen 3:22; Rev 22:2).

Application. As a prophet and an apostle, John surely was not against prophets or apostles in general. Yet he demanded discernment in his day and would demand it no less in ours. If the Nicolaitans (2:6) supported the popular cultural values of sexual and religious compromise, they also serve as a warning to us to beware of modern purveyors of what people simply want to hear.

Yet despite important, notable exceptions, many of the churches most firmly committed to the truth of the gospel are also those churches that have drawn boundaries too tightly on secondary issues. In some of those cases, I have watched wounded Christians react against the rejection they experienced in their more traditional background in ways that discarded the proverbial baby with the bath water.

Even when we are dealing with clear cases of sin and error, does not Scripture call us to offer correction with love and grace (Luke 15:1–2; 2 Tim 2:24–26)? A church where love ceases can no longer function properly as a local expression of Christ's many-membered body.

REVELATION 2:8–11

Original Meaning. For three centuries, Smyrna had been one of the most important cities in Asia Minor; this as well as its location may have merited its place listing here among the churches. Smyrna was an important center of the imperial cult in Asia. Only Jews were exempt from worshiping the emperor. The recognition that Christians were a part of Judaism protected Christians from unnecessary persecution. Unfortunately, many synagogue leaders seem to have felt it necessary to make the Jewish Christians unwelcome in the synagogues. Many Asian Jewish leaders were probably nervous about being associated with prophetic, messianic movements like Christianity.

Such conflicts help explain "the slander of those who say they are Jews and are not" (v. 9). The synagogue of "Satan" also suggests involvement with "the devil," who would cast believers into prison (vv. 9–10). Many commentators thus recognize the likelihood that at least some members of the local Jewish community were collaborating with local officials to repress the Christian minority.

The passage envisions official persecution on the local level. Imprisonment (v. 10) was usually temporary detention until trial and then either official punishment or release. Believers must prepare for execution ("be faithful, even to the point of death," v. 10c); the Smyrnean Christians would thus understand what it meant to achieve victory while not loving their lives so much as to shrink from death (cf. 12:11).

The specific duration of the imprisonment ("ten days," v. 10b), like many others in Revelation, is probably a symbolic allusion to the Old Testament. Like Daniel and his colleagues (Dan 1:12–14), the believers in Smyrna would be "tested" for ten days. The very knowledge that imprisonment could include such torture demanded faithfulness.

Crowns (wreaths of olive, laurel, pine, or celery) were appropriate to victory in battle and more often in athletic competition; hence, they became a familiar symbolic image in Roman Asia. The term came to apply figuratively to any sort of honor or award. In this passage the "crown" (v. 10c) might also represent a subtle contrast with the city's claims to power: Smyrna's citadel was often compared with a crown, and nearly 20 percent of the inscriptions from earlier centuries contain the wreath emblem.

Whereas "victory" in Ephesus required restoration of love (2:4), in Smyrna it demanded withstanding persecution. But Revelation especially underlines the point in the image of the triumphant lion as a slain lamb in 5:5–6: we overcome not by returning hostility but by laying down our lives in the confidence that God will vindicate us.

Application. Of the seven churches, the only two that are unequivocally commended are the suffering churches in Smyrna and Philadelphia. Suffering has a way of reminding us of what in life really matters. It forces us to depend radically on God, and thus it purifies our obedience to God's will.

But it is important to know God's heart before we face suffering, so that we may understand our suffering in light of his love for us—in light of his sharing our suffering in the cross—rather than interpreting his heart toward us on the basis of our suffering.

If we have not prepared ourselves and our congregations to die for Christ's name if necessary, we have not completed our responsibility of preparing disciples (Mark 8:34–38). When we remain faithful in the face of rejection and persecution, Jesus promises us a reward far greater than the power and status our oppressors now enjoy.

REVELATION 2:12–17

Original Meaning. Pergamum was a famous city that had long prospered; it included between 120,000 and 200,000 inhabitants. The image of the "sword" in verse 12 may allude to the Roman government's right to execute capital punishment, in which case Jesus is reminding Christians that he holds the power of life and death (1:18). Such words would encourage the persecuted (2:13). Yet this letter focuses on false teachers in the church, so the "sword" may refer to the judgment of war, here with reference to the Lord Jesus, who will war against false teachers corrupting his church (vv. 15–16).

This church faced external as well as internal opposition. Although its general sense is clear enough, the precise referent of Satan's "throne" (v. 13) is disputed. Scholars think of the famous and huge throne-like altar of "Zeus the Savior," whose sculptures included serpents. As a center of the provincial imperial cult, Pergamum warranted Revelation's apt condemnation as Satan's throne.

Paganism in general or, more likely, the imperial cult in particular led to the martyrdom of Antipas mentioned in verse 13. As a "faithful witness" he is like his Lord (1:5; cf. 3:14). But despite Jesus's special sensitivity for a suffering church (2:8–11; 3:7–12), having suffered does not automatically validate everything we do or believe (2:14).

In addition to opposition from the outside, Pergamum is also experiencing internal problems. "Balaam" (v. 14) is undoubtedly not the prophet's own preferred name but a code name signifying that this prophet is a false one. Balaam acted out of greed for money (Num 22:16–19; Jude 11). He led Israel into sin, recognizing that this was the only way to destroy them (Num 31:16). The particular sins of Israel in connection with Balaam were sexual immorality and food offered to idols (Num 25:1–2), sins that remained temptations in later pagan society.

Scholars debate whether "sexual immorality" in our verse 14 refers to literal prostitution, such as the prostitution sometimes conducted in pagan temples, or to a spiritual adultery that leads astray from God. In view of the frequent use of the image in the Hebrew Bible (e.g., Jer 3:9; Hos 1:2) and especially in view of the "prostitute" later in this book (Rev 17:1), the spiritual sense seems more likely here. Balaam's promotion of food offered to idols means promotion of syncretism, in which God's people were lured into participating in the cults of other deities.

More to the point are the sorts of occasions where the meat was specifically doled out at pagan festivals or while participating in a guild banquet. One of the most difficult forms of this temptation may have been its challenge to the Christians' livelihood by denying their ability to participate in trade guilds. Trade guilds involved meals honoring a patron deity at their meetings, and in Thyatira trade guilds dominated city life.

For Christians in Pergamum, victory means to continue steadfast in the face of opposition (v. 13), but especially to stand against teachings of compromise with the world and to do their best to purge such teachings from their ranks (vv. 14–16).

To those who overcome, Jesus promises both the "hidden manna" and a "white stone with a new name written on it" (v. 17). The hidden manna probably alludes to a Jewish tradition that the manna deposited in the ark would be restored when the ark was restored in the end. This promised manna contrasts starkly with the idolatrous food for which Balaam's followers seem prepared to compromise their future reward (v. 14).

People used pebbles as admission tokens for public assemblies or festivities; the occasion here would be the celebration of heaven and the new manna of the messianic banquet (7:9; 19:9). Perhaps the most significant allusion is a reference to some ancient courtrooms, where jurors voted for acquittal with a white stone and for conviction with a black one. This pebble may also be white to symbolize eternal life or purity from sin. The "new name" alludes to Isaiah 56:5 and especially 62:2, which promises that God will give his people a new name, removing their shame (62:4); this fits the time of the new Jerusalem and new creation (65:15–19).

Application. The potential applications of this passage's warning against compromise are numerous; each pastor, Bible study leader, and individual guided by God's Spirit will recognize the most appropriate applications for his or her own particular settings.

REVELATION 2:18–29

Original Meaning. Economic pressures were inviting compromise on the part of Thyatira's Christians. The Asian churches may well hear in Jesus's biblical title "Son of God" (v. 18) a direct challenge to the imperial cult, where the emperor was honored with the same title. Apollo's link with Helios, the sun god, also could amplify the contrast implicit in Jesus's fiery features here. It may be more than coincidence that Jesus reminds hearers of his feet like bronze, specifically in a city where metalworking was a prominent industry.

Jesus knows that the Christians in Thyatira, in contrast to those in Ephesus, are doing his works more than they have before (2:5, 19), but one flaw in the congregation proves serious enough to offset this praise: unlike Ephesus, they are tolerating a false teacher of compromise (2:2, 20). Thyatira was known for its merchants, crafts, and their guilds. Those who participated in this aspect of public economic life would risk a substantial measure of their livelihood by refusing to join trade guilds. The guild meetings, however, included a common meal dedicated to the guild's patron deity.

A large number of commentators envision this situation as a primary contributor to "Jezebel's" appeal (v. 20). This Jezebel falsely claims to be a prophetess and to offer "deep secrets" (v. 24). Like Satan, she is a deceiver who misleads God's servants.

The biblical Jezebel was not a "prophetess," but sponsored 850 false prophets (1 Kgs 18:19); she also sought to take the lives of God's true prophets (v. 13). She is never accused of literal harlotry, but she sponsored spiritual harlotry by leading Israel away from its God (2 Kgs 9:22).

The Lord Jesus will not allow those leading his people astray to go unchallenged; he will strike "Jezebel" with sickness (v. 22). He will also kill her "children" (v. 23)—undoubtedly her disciples, perhaps members of house churches under her guidance. Killing with "death" reflects a familiar expression for the divine judgment of a plague or pestilence, sometimes associated with blasphemy (see Num 14:36–38).

Jesus promises those who overcome this threat of false teaching that they will share with him in his reign over the nations (v. 26), both during the "thousand years" (20:6) and eternally (22:5). They will share in Jesus's rule with an iron rod (2:27), a hope derived from the messianic promise of Psalm 2:9. Jesus shares his rule with his people, for God has delegated rule over the earth to humanity (Gen 1:26–28). Jesus will also give the morning star to those who overcome (Rev 2:28). Ancients emphasized the glory of the planet Venus, the "morning star," and could apply the image to magnificent rulers (Isa 14:12). In Revelation, Jesus is himself the morning star (Rev 22:16; cf. Num 24:17).

In other words, Jesus's promise to the church in Thyatira suggests that he will share not only victory in an abstract sense but himself as the morning star with his people (v. 28).

Application. The necessity of remaining faithful until the end (2:26) fits historic Calvinist and Arminian belief: the former argues that those who fall away were never ultimately converted, whereas the latter argues that they have lost their salvation—yet both concur that they will not be saved. Verses such as this one and countless others (Acts 14:22; 1 Cor 9:27; 2 Cor 13:5; Col 1:23; 1 Thess 3:5; 1 Tim 4:1; Heb 2:1–4; 4:1–2; 6:4–8; 10:19–31; 12:14–17; Jas 5:19–20) may prove uncomfortable to those who think that merely praying a prayer without truly persevering in Christian faith is adequate for salvation. The threats to perseverance vary among the churches today that are scattered across the earth—from persecution to lovelessness to compromise with paganism—but Scripture contains sufficient warning to summon the entire church worldwide to spiritual vigilance.

REVELATION 3:1–6

Original Meaning. Sardis had a significant and powerful Jewish community. In contrast to churches in Smyrna and Philadelphia, Jesus's followers seem to have coexisted peacefully with the synagogue community there, and therefore likely coexisted peacefully with the city establishment as a whole. Lacking the world's opposition, they may have grown comfortable in their relationship with the world.

Jesus's reproof of a church with a reputation of being alive yet is dead (v. 1) may have evoked a variety of local associations. Perhaps these Sardian Christians were identifying with the widely known ancient tradition of their city. Sardis maintained an ancient "reputation" (literally "name") as a great city from the time of its most famous ruler, Croesus. Whatever the specific basis for the imagery used here, however, its most important function is a deliberate contrast with the Lord himself, who was dead and is now alive (1:18; 2:8). The spiritual state of the believers in this city is hindering them from appropriating Jesus's own resurrection power.

Jesus's warning that he will come on them as a "thief" (v. 3), presumably unexpectedly as in the night, recalls Jesus's words about the end times (Matt 24:43). But this warning would also prove especially alarming to proud Sardians schooled from youth in the history of their city. Conquerors had never overtaken Sardis by conventional war but had twice conquered it unexpectedly because Sardians had failed to watch adequately.

That those who have not "soiled" their clothes will walk with Jesus "dressed in white" (v. 4) is significant. In the temples of Asia and elsewhere, worshipers dared not approach deities with soiled clothes; the normal apparel for approaching the gods in temples was white or linen. Jesus presumably promises here that his followers who have not polluted themselves with the paganism of their culture will participate in the new Jerusalem.

The promise that the overcomers in Sardis will not be blotted out "from the book of life" (v. 5) implies the obverse—namely, that much of the church in Sardis is close to spiritual death (v. 2) and will not see the kingdom. The image of "blotting out" stems from Exodus 32:32–33, which came to be applied to a heavenly book of life (Ps 69:28; Dan 12:1; Luke 10:20; Phil 4:3). The promise that Jesus will confess the faithful remnant before his Father echoes what he told his disciples (Matt 10:32).

Application. It is too easy for us to depend on past achievements instead of looking to God's call for us in the future (cf. Phil 3:12–14). We may recall the example of Gideon, who made a golden ephod to commemorate his victory yet failed to destroy this ephod even when his people began worshiping it (Judg 8:27). By lowering the standards, he set the stage for the return to Baal worship after his death and the disintegration of his spiritual legacy in Israel, and he effectively undercut the good he had achieved earlier in his life (v. 33). Gideon looked back to his past victory, but he should have made better plans for the future. We are warned by his poor example, and by Jesus's words here to those of the church of Sardis.

REVELATION 3:7–13

Original Meaning. In contrast to churches strong in their own sight (3:17), but like the Smyrnean Christians who acknowledged their poverty (2:9), the Philadelphian church has only a "little strength," but it has proved successful in standing in that strength (3:8).

Jesus is the one "who holds the key of David," with the authority to open and shut (v. 7). This means that Jesus is the one who controls entrance into the royal palace, a position of the highest authority in the kingdom (cf. Isa 22:15–25). As such Jesus determines who may enter his household and who may not.

As in Smyrna, believers in Philadelphia were like the Jewish Christians for whom John first wrote his Gospel, many of whom were likely expelled from their synagogues (John 9:34). Though these synagogues may have expelled Jewish Christians from their houses of worship, Jesus welcomes the believers into his own household. Jesus is the one who truly provides access to the new Jerusalem (Rev 21:12–14). This is the likeliest sense of opening and shutting the door here.

The biblical prophets had promised God's people that the gentiles would one day bow down to them (Isa 60:14). But here unbelieving Jews join unbelieving gentiles in bowing down before the faithful believers (Rev 3:9). They must recognize that God has chosen his people (Isa 49:7) and that he loves them. What marks them as Christ's people is that they have "kept" or guarded his word (Rev 3:10); he will thus guard them.

Verse 10 first introduces Revelation's typical contrast between those who live in heaven and those who live on the earth ("the inhabitants of the earth"). The earth-dwellers are normally the wicked who invite judgment (6:10), whereas the heaven-dwellers refer to the righteous (12:12). That the term *earth-dweller* does not normally include the suffering people of God on earth (though cf. 2:13) may suggest that though these people suffer temporarily on earth, their long-term home is heaven. The hour of testing is designed to test unbelievers; believers will be protected during it (see comment on 7:1–8 below).

Despite Jesus's praises for the Philadelphian Christians' perseverance to this point, however, "it's not over till it's over." They must continue to hold fast what they have (v. 11)—that is, to continue to keep the message that demands their perseverance (v. 10), lest their persecutors seize from them their crown (v. 11). Losing it means roughly the same as the warning to the preceding church: exclusion from the kingdom (3:5).

Those who do overcome, however, will not only be welcome in Jesus's household, God's temple, but they will constitute a part of it (v. 12). Thus, though expelled from Satan's "synagogue" (v. 9), they remain in God's temple. This image directly recalls Isaiah 56:5, in which foreigners and eunuchs will have a place and an eternal name within God's house, better than that of Israelites.

That Christ had established his people as one new temple made of both Jew and gentile was familiar imagery for Christians in Asia by this time (Eph 2:18–22; 1 Pet 2:5). Everyone would expect this new temple to include pillars (Ezek 40:9–41:3), just as the old one did (Exod 27:10–17), and personified pillars specifically functioned as an image of strength or blessing (Exod 24:4). That such pillars would bear the name of God, of the new Jerusalem, and Jesus's new name (Rev 3:12) merely confirms that they belong in the holy city.

The new Jerusalem "is coming down out of heaven" (v. 12); some take this as an iterative present, suggesting that the new Jerusalem always meets believers in the present as they submit to God's reign. More likely, however, the present tense merely vividly emphasizes the origin of this city as from above (21:2), which contrasts it with the merely human Jerusalem in which Israel's hopes were recently shattered (in AD 70 when the Roman army invaded Jerusalem and destroyed the temple), as well as with the synagogue community from which the Philadelphian Christians have been expelled (3:9).

Application. The Christians in Philadelphia have become broken by their exclusion from the synagogue, hence from their heritage. Faithfulness often means being excluded from circles that mean much to us—sometimes even from family. Those excluded today for their faith will wear the name that identifies them as citizens of the promised future world.

REVELATION 3:14–22

Original Meaning. Laodicea lay in Phrygia's Lycus Valley. Pagan worship, especially of Zeus but also of numerous other deities, flourished there. A significant Jewish community seems to have blended into Greek culture in many respects there.

By the third century, illustrations on some coins had mixed together Jewish and pagan versions of the flood stories.

Jesus pulls no punches when he addresses the Laodicean church (v. 14a). He is the "Amen" (v. 14b), a Hebrew term that suggests the assurance of all his promises. Likewise, he is "faithful and true" (v. 14c), a way of emphasizing again the certainty of his promises. Yet for the Laodicean Christians this was not exclusively good news. Jesus was also "the ruler" of the entire world (v. 14d)!

Laodicea boasted great resources (v. 17), but while the Laodicean Christians likely shared their Laodicean neighbors' pride over their self-sufficiency in many respects, they presumably also shared a common dislike for their water supply (vv. 15–16). The bad situation of Laodicea's water was well-known. Excavation of the city's terra-cotta pipes revealed thick lime deposits, which suggest heavy contamination in the water supply.

Laodicea lacked its own water supply, having no direct access to the cold water of the mountains or the hot water of the nearby springs in Hierapolis to the north. In contrast to its claims to self-sufficiency (v. 17), it had to pipe in its water. This water had grown lukewarm by the time of its arrival.

The point of lukewarm water is simply that it is disgusting, in contrast to the more directly useful "hot" and "cold" water (v. 15); all the churches would plainly understand this warning. Hot water (as long as it was not too hot) was useful for bathing. Cold water was useful for drinking, but Laodicea's water did not arrive in this state.

Jesus thus finds the church in Laodicea to be other than what he desires (cf. Isa 5:2–6). In today's English, he is telling the self-satisfied church in Laodicea: "You remind me of the water you always complain about. You make me want to puke." Earlier prophets also used images of rotten food to describe God's rejection of people who had grown disgusting to him (Jer 24), but Jesus contextualizes the image for Laodicea.

Jesus's challenge to the Laodicean Christians' self-sufficiency reminds us how readily we Christians absorb the attitudes of our culture without pausing for critical reflection on this behavior. Laodicea was known as a wealthy banking center. So arrogant was Laodicea about its wealth that when the emperor proposed to help rebuild Laodicea along with other Asian cities destroyed by an earthquake in AD 60, Laodicea refused the "federal disaster relief funds."

Laodiceans would doubt that they were "naked" (v. 17b); their city was famous for its production of textiles, especially cloth and carpets woven from black wool. Thus some commentators observe that Jesus's offer of "white clothes" (v. 18) probably provides a stark contrast with this black wool of Laodicea. They may also experience surprise that they need Jesus to supply them spiritual eye salve. Ancient sources report a first-century medical school located in Laodicea, ear ointment made there, a famous eye doctor practicing there, and eye salve made of Phrygian powder.

The Laodicean Christians, reflecting the values of their prosperous society, boast, "I am rich; I have acquired wealth and do not need a thing" (v. 17a). Jesus advises them to buy true wealth and garments from him (v. 18), which contrast starkly with the grandeur of the world.

Lest anyone misunderstand the tone and motivation of Jesus's rebuke, he makes clear that its purpose is love (v. 19). Indeed, not only does Jesus not reject them, but he wants to have dinner with them (v. 20), a familiar image for intimacy in antiquity. The personalized nature of the invitation suggests that not only the future messianic banquet (cf. 19:9) but a present foretaste of the intimacy is already available to those who respond to Jesus's call. Jesus is inviting the Laodicean Christians to realize how they have shut him out of their lives with their own self-sufficiency.

Jesus then provides a promise of sharing his reign to those who are "victorious" (v. 21). This is a familiar promise for the future in Revelation (2:26–27; 5:10; 20:6; 22:5). Although in the present believers already do share Christ's exaltation over the demonic powers (Eph 1:20–23; 2:6), the New Testament indicates that the fullness of the reign of God's people awaits Christ's return (Matt 5:5; Rom 5:17; 8:32; 2 Tim 2:12).

Application. Comparing the church in North America with churches in many other parts of the world, we should be concerned that the problems of Laodicea's church plague our own. We hear of massive suffering elsewhere and often find theological or sociological explanations for it to avoid the thought that we could experience the same hardships. Many of us are eager to export the profound learning of North American Christianity without humbly listening first to the lessons learned by other churches who have suffered far more than we have. We are materially wealthy and in danger of a spirit of self-sufficiency, which breeds a lukewarm disinterest in the things of the Lord Jesus Christ. We do not realize that we may be spiritually impoverished—"wretched, pitiful, poor, blind, and naked."

REVELATION 4:1–11

Original Meaning. John's throne vision in Revelation 4, like most of this book, resembles visions in the biblical prophets (esp. Isa 6:1–5; Ezek 1:4–28; Dan 7:9–14). Yet John frequently emphasizes the themes most dominant in a certain type of Jewish literature of his day, today known as *apocalyptic literature* (of which Revelation is the most well-known example). From an early period, Jewish apocalyptic texts focused on and developed particularly the throne visions of Ezekiel and Isaiah.

The "open" door in heaven (v. 1) signifies God's revelation. John does not have to force his way into heaven. Jewish tradition developed God's summons to Moses, eventually to the extent that many averred that it included an ascent to heaven.

If John's mode of entry into heaven (vv. 1–2) differs strikingly from the apocalyptic visions of his contemporaries, so does his vision of the heavenly court (vv. 3–11). Some apocalypses elaborate the character of God's throne in great detail to amplify his majesty; John presents his vision of God's throne without such adornment. The heavenly songs in Revelation provide the true picture of the events of the book: no matter what is experienced on earth, God is truly in charge of it all.

The "rainbow" (v. 3) recalls the radiance of God's throne in Ezekiel 1:28. "Jasper" was also crystal clear and brilliant, so John's audience will later recognize the new Jerusalem as the place of God's glorious dwelling (Rev 21:11, 18–20); in Ezekiel God's throne appeared like sapphire (Ezek 1:26; 10:1).

The twenty-four elders around the throne in our verse 4, like other worshipers in heaven, illustrate the appropriate response to God's glory: worship (vv. 10–11; 5:8–10, 14). Some regard them as angels, others as Old Testament saints. But most likely they represent all believers. The doubling of the twelve could represent the Old and New Testament peoples of God together. But given their function in worship they probably represent the twenty-four courses of priests in the Old Testament (see 1 Chr 24:4).

Because crowns were appropriate to victors in athletic competitions, the elders' crowns may signify that these are Christians who have persevered in faith to the end. But crowns were more often of gold when won in games sacred to a deity, and most often golden when worn by priests approaching a deity.

Elders were leaders of the people and stood as their representatives before God's glory at Sinai (Exod 24:9–10) as they would in the eschatological time (Isa 24:23). Thus these elders represent God's people as a whole, all of whom together are a "kingdom and priests" (Rev 1:6; 5:10).

The thunders around God's throne (v. 5) reveal his sovereignty. This would have been clear to Revelation's first readers; not only Jews (Ps 29:3) but other prominent Mediterranean religions portrayed deity associated with lightning and thunder. Most important, however, the thunder and lightning around the throne recall the revelation of God's majesty when he gave the law at Mount Sinai (Exod 19:16; 20:18).

The "sea" (v. 6) probably suggests to readers the great glory of the heavenly temple. John's most direct source is the bronze "sea" of Solomon's temple (1 Kgs 7:23–44), because heaven in Revelation appears like a temple. That the sea is of "glass, clear as crystal" reflects the sapphire that was "clear" in God's revelation to Israel at Sinai (Exod 24:10), but especially the heavenly expanse beneath God's throne in Ezekiel 1:22.

In view of descriptions of heavenly worship in Isaiah 6:1–4, Ezekiel 1:4–28, and Daniel 7:9–14, it is unsurprising that John's contemporaries believed that worship was a major feature of heavenly activity. The first Christians who heard John's descriptions of worship during their own worship services undoubtedly would have identified with the heavenly chorus.

Again, because Jewish descriptions of heaven nearly always started with what Scripture already said, it is not surprising that most emphasize the living creatures around the throne (Isa 6:2–3; Ezek 1:5–21). Like the portraits of most of his contemporaries, John's probably come directly from Ezekiel. That the creatures were "covered with eyes" (Rev 4:6; cf. Ezek 1:18) suggests that nothing on earth is hidden from them (Zech 4:10), with the implication, "How much less from God himself?"

These beings serve no other function than to extol the character of God (v. 8). John twice in the following breath reiterates that God is the sovereign one—the one who sits on the throne—and that he lives forever and ever (vv. 9–10). Falling on one's face was the gesture of honor, appropriately applied to worship of God. Revelation calls Christians to respectfully reserve true worship for God alone.

God alone should receive all glory and power, for he created all things (v. 11), a claim that again challenged the pretensions of Caesar in John's day. This text reminds us that all things were created for (or "by") God's will. The heavenly choirs of angels and redeemed people hail the true "Lord and God" (v. 11), who created and rules his universe.

Application. This passage in Revelation and others like it remind us that our primary job in heaven, like that of every other created being in heaven, is to worship God. In the present life, worship that focuses on God's worthiness—both his character and deeds—is our nearest foretaste of heaven, an experience in the down payment of the end-time Spirit. Worship also reminds us that, whatever else our calling or gifts now, all Christians become the same as God's worshipers; the eternal future leaves little place for gifts now valued, but our devotion to God will always rise (cf. 1 Cor 13:8–13).

REVELATION 5:1–14

Original Meaning. Jewish tradition often portrays scrolls or tablets in heaven containing God's moral decrees, people's destinies in life, or people's eternal destinies. Although the scroll in this text is never specifically identified, it may well represent the Lamb's book of life, hence the Lamb's legacy for his people (13:8). While some could suggest that the heavenly scroll is the prototype of this book of Revelation, reporting God's decrees for history (1:11; 22:7–10, 18–19), Revelation remains unsealed (22:10).

Most ancient people wrote on only one side of a scroll, generally the "front." The scroll in the present text clearly has a lot to say, as it has writing "on both sides." (v. 1). Then the scroll's user would roll the scroll up, tying it shut with a thread or, in legal documents meant to prevent tampering, several threads.

Legal documents normally closed by listing witnesses, usually about six in number. Such documents were normally sealed shut with hot wax over the threads that tied the scroll closed; then witnesses would press their personal seals (usually from signet rings) into the hot wax and attested that they were the witnesses. No one could open the scroll without breaking the hardened wax seals that held the threads in place, and no one could replace such seals without the witnesses' rings; hence no one could tamper with the legal document until it was time to publicly open it.

Like the scroll here, the scroll in Ezekiel 2:9–10 contains writing on both front and back, emphasizing the great quantity of suffering in judgment that the book records. Here, however, the judgments are not the contents of the book but the attesting witnesses in the seals (Rev 6:1–17). If this is the Lamb's book of life, God's judgments in history authenticate the promised inheritance of the people of God.

God holds the book in an open hand, and one of his angels issues the invitation (or challenge) to all creation: Who can open the book (v. 2)? Normally a scroll should be "loosed" (have its seals broken) only by those to whom it is addressed; moreover, these seals, on a book in the right hand of the living God, are too strong for ordinary mortals to break. After hailing God as worthy of all power (4:11), who can presume to be "worthy" (5:2) to have strength ("could," v. 3) to open it? Not yet recognizing that the Lamb is also worthy of all power (v. 12), John is traumatized with despair over the situation: the universe appears to lack a champion, and John weeps (v. 4).

But finally one of God's worshipers comforts John: the Lion from the tribe of Judah is the triumphant champion, and he has conquered (v. 5). The image of the "Lion of the tribe of Judah" comes from Genesis 49:9–10. The "Root of David" is the Messiah who comes from the truncated house of David, anointed by the Spirit and appointed to rule all the nations with peace (Isa 11:1–10).

But here the central paradox of Revelation and of Christian faith in general comes to the fore: Jesus conquered not by force but by death, not by violence but by martyrdom. The Lion is a Lamb! John turns, expecting to witness a powerful hero. Yet the Lamb, by contrast, provides an image of helplessness. Lambs were the most vulnerable of sheep, and sheep were among the weakest of creatures, typically contrasted with predators.

Most significantly for John, this is a *slaughtered* lamb, a sacrificed lamb. Plagues will fall on the disobedient world (Rev 6–16), but just as the blood of the Passover lamb delivered Israel from the climactic plague (Exod 12:23), so Jesus's blood will protect his people during God's judgments on humanity (Rev 7:3). Jesus's victory is like a new exodus (5:9–10; 15:3), and Jesus himself is the new Lamb.

Horns in prophetic literature sometimes represent power (Dan 7:7–24), but here the power is not human power but the seven spirits of God (Rev 5:6); this alludes to the ancient prophecy that the Jewish king must prevail not by human strength but by the power of the Spirit (Zech 4:6).

John identifies the horns here with seven eyes (Rev 5:6), which he probably understands as representing the Spirit in Zechariah's vision (Zech 3:9) as well as the seven lamps. But in Zechariah, the eyes belong to God himself; their application to Jesus the Lamb provides a clue to Jesus's true, exalted identity. Jesus's location by the throne (Rev 5:6) may also suggest a status that some texts reserve for divine Wisdom, but Jesus's status is higher even than divine Wisdom, for he ultimately sits in the midst of the throne, sharing the Father's supreme reign (7:17).

One of the many sorts of documents in the ancient world sealed by witnesses was a will. Once it was attested that the person who made the will was genuinely dead, the seals would be broken and the will opened, making public its contents. If this book is the Lamb's book of life, his legacy for his followers, it becomes theirs through his self-sacrifice.

John next states that Jesus went and "took" the scroll from God's hand (5:7); the verb's perfect tense may suggest that he not only receives the book but that he still holds it, and hence he reigns over the events of human history. The heavenly chorus offers not to God the Father but to Jesus the prayers of the saints (v. 8). A Lamb receives worship in God's heaven (v. 12), sharing with God himself as its object (v. 13).

Often worshipers in the time of the first temple offered God a "new song" (5:9; 14:3). Israel sang hymns to celebrate God's redemption of their people from Egypt in the Passover. But the perspective of the true heavenly chorus celebrates the redemption of God's people from among all nations by the blood of a new Passover Lamb (v. 9). Like ancient Israel (Exod 19:6), these people will also be a "kingdom and priests" (Rev 5:10). An audience immersed in the Old Testament would be most struck by the fact that this new act of redemption encompassed believers from all over the earth, "from every tribe and language and people and nation" (v. 9). Daniel announced the rule of the Son of Man over all these peoples (Dan 7:13–14), and John sees a literal fulfillment of this promise in Jesus Christ and the church.

That God has so many myriads (v. 11) to worship him reinforces the text's example for us that he is worthy of worship (cf. Dan 7:10). Not only all of heaven, but all of creation ultimately offers God glory (v. 13).

Application. That Jesus overcomes through dying challenges our ways of doing things. We like to gain political or social power and dictate God's terms from the top down. By contrast, Jesus shows us that the true victory comes in sacrifice and weakness, which force us to depend on God's vindication. Jesus's army of followers must imitate his example.

REVELATION 6:1–8

Original Meaning. John's depiction of judgment here reflects both literary artistry and immersion in Scripture. The list of four plagues resembles some from the Old Testament (Deut 32:24). The four riders appear to be angels of judgment. They most directly recall Zechariah 1:8, where many riders on four different colors of horses represent the Lord's patrol that report back to him about quiet on the earth (Zech 1:8–11).

The description of the rider on the white horse (v. 2) has occasioned various explanations, including an allusion to the antichrist figure Gog (Ezek 39:3). A more general allusion is possible; one might also reduce the significance of starting with the white horse by noting that such horses might be prized. Parthians were famous, like Scythians, for their horses. They were known as mounted warriors, and their cavalry were especially known for their formidable archery. Revelation uses this image merely to underscore the point of hostile invaders, not to predict a specifically Parthian invasion. The point is that Roman rule will someday collapse—not to yield to an eternal rule by Parthia, but ultimately to an eternal rule by God (Rev 11:15–19).

Bloodshed, the second rider, presents a grisly image (v. 4). Readers would likely catch an allusion to blood in the "red" horse. The "sword" represents the judgment of warfare and violent death.

Famine (the third horse) likewise constitutes a terrifying specter. The image of the balance (v. 5), normally used in the marketplace to weigh out the amount of food one could buy for one's money, suggests God's sovereignty over the food supply.

A denarius was roughly a day's wage in this period; a quart of wheat would feed a single worker for a day, but if he had a family to support he would buy instead three times as much barley, which was cheaper. One could eat, but the grain here costs at least five times and as much as fifteen times what it might in better times.

Why does the text mention the sparing of oil and wine (v. 6), less necessary to life than the grain? Some suggest that it indicates that the wealthy will still have the luxury items. Whether or not this proposal is accepted, this disparity probably points to inequities inherent in the Roman economy.

But the sparing of oil and wine also reveals God's mercy amid judgment. Ancient Mediterranean warfare included destroying the standing crops in the fields but not the vines and olive trees; destruction of vines and olive trees would produce a long-range devastation of the local economies (and so negate the entire point of conquering the land).

The coming of "Death" in verse 8 may sum up the result of the previous horsemen or may refer particularly to plague and pestilence (cf. 2:23). Death often appears personified in Jewish sources, typically as an angel subservient to God's design or sometimes as the equivalent of Satan, who also, however, cannot strike God's people apart from God's will.

Application. This passage underlines the recognition that God is sovereign over history. Terrible things may happen that seem beyond explanation, but on the larger scale God is using such forces to bring history to its climax. This text presents us not the God of deism promoted by Thomas Jefferson, Ben Franklin, and many other disciples of the Age of Reason; it declares the true and living God. The modern experiment to overcome the need for religion has failed. The modern world's values have proved inadequate to confront the threats our world experiences—continuing wars, weapons of massive destruction, and other plagues. Terror with teleology can only remind us of our mortality, our need to depend on someone greater than ourselves. Terror without teleology produces despair.

REVELATION 6:9–17

Original Meaning

The Fifth Seal (6:9–11). Earlier biblical prophets had predicted the witness of God's people to the nations (e.g., Isa 42:1), the conversion of the nations (Isa 19:19–25), and the suffering of God's people in the end time (Dan 7:21). The vision in Revelation 6:9–11, however, connects these three themes (as in Mark 13:9–10); the suffering witness of believers is a necessary prerequisite for the fullness of the gentiles to come in from among the nations, the event followed by the final turning of Jewish people to faith in Jesus (cf. Rom 11:25–27). All peoples must be evangelized before the end (Matt 24:14; 2 Pet 3:9–12; cf. Rev 7:9).

The position of these martyrs "under the altar" (6:9) undoubtedly recalls the place where priests poured the blood of their sacrifices (e.g., Lev 4:7). Jewish tradition recognized that the martyrs were with God and at peace and were sacrifices accepted by God. Here in Revelation the sacrifices are not vicarious per se, but the martyrs do share in Christ's sacrificial suffering; they are allies of the sacrificed Lamb of 5:6, 9 and will also share his exaltation (3:21; 20:4).

Although John tells us that they are told to wait, they receive divine assurance (6:11). God himself rewards them with white robes, and then he himself responds to their plea.

They should "wait" (literally "rest") until that time (cf. 14:13). "A little longer" is indeterminate by human time, measured only by God's standards (cf. 10:6), but nevertheless functions as an assurance that the time is finite.

The Sixth Seal (6:12–17). The sixth seal portrays the end of the cosmos as humanity knows it. Far from merely a repeatable judgment within history, like the four riders (6:1–8), this judgment includes the dissolution of the heavens (vv. 12–14) and the world finally recognizing that it stands under its Creator's wrath (vv. 16–17).

This graphic portrayal of destruction opens with an earthquake (v. 12), which is part of the movement of the mountains (v. 14) beneath which the wicked seek to flee (vv. 15–16). This earthquake seems to be no exaggeration: it is the climactic, eschatological earthquake that truly removes mountains (11:13). Because some of the cities whose churches are addressed in Revelation had been devastated by earthquakes only a few decades earlier, this image probably proved particularly graphic.

Discoloration or eclipsing of the sun or moon symbolized terrifying judgments both among Jews and pagans. The image here is worse than a mere eclipse (Isa 13:9–11). The rolling up of the heavens "like a scroll" (Rev 6:14) comes from "day of the Lord" imagery in Isaiah 34:4. For most of Revelation's audience, the picture likely evoked the mundane image of reading a scroll. But the mundane image here translates into one of terror for humanity!

The passage also indicates that it is ultimately loyalty to Jesus Christ, not social status, that determines one's fate. John lists the entire social order in 6:15, emphasizing that no marks of distinction will exempt anyone from judgment.

In verses 15–17 John recalls an image of inescapable judgment from Hosea 10:8 and Isaiah 2:19. Caves and mountain clefts were useful for hiding from human enemies. But such sites would prove utterly futile in obstructing the One who moved whole mountains in his wrath (Rev 6:14).

The flight of these people from God's wrath in the heavens may reflect the destruction of the heavens (vv. 12–14), but it also suggests some sort of image that reveals the coming of God and the Lamb in the sky (cf. Matt 24:30). Lambs were considered among the most docile creatures; hence "wrath of the Lamb" here is a striking and terrifying image (v. 16). Note that those who have not yet repented, who seek refuge from caves and mountains, do not cry out to God or the Lamb for mercy; it is now too late for that.

The final image of the sixth seal, in which the disobedient to God's will cry out, "Who can withstand [the day of wrath]?" (v. 17, adapting the language of Joel 2:11), prepares the reader for the answer that comes in the following vision: the servants of God can stand in that day (Rev 7:1–17). They can stand during the plagues within history (7:3), which in turn provides an assurance that God will be with them at the close of the age.

Application. As the martyrs cry for vindication in our passage, so do suffering believers today. That God grants the martyrs' request but that it does not come right away should encourage us to persevere. Many generations of American slaves cried to God for freedom (cf. also Exod 2:23–25) before the liberation from slavery came; many South Africans died fighting apartheid before it was finally abolished. God's time is not always our time, but even if we do not live to see the fulfillment of all our prayers, we can die in hope that God will bring about the things he has promised.

REVELATION 7:1–8

Original Meaning

Sealing the Tribes (7:1–3). The four winds correspond to the "four corners of the earth" (v. 1), a common phrase that simply means the four directions. Here they serve to show God's sovereignty over the furthest reaches of the earth, like Zechariah's four horsemen, who were the four spirits of heaven going patrolling in four directions (Zech 6:1–5). Here God prevents the winds from blowing in judgment (Rev 7:1; cf. 6:13) until he has provided protection for his servants (7:3).

The angel rising "from the east" (7:2) may recall God's glory returning to his house (Ezek 43:2) or the eastern orientation of the eschatological temple (46:1, 12; 47:1), or it may imply God's judgment from the east (Rev 16:12). But most likely the image points to the rising of the sun. His task is simply to pass on a message from God. God is sovereign over the sun (cf. 6:12; 7:16; 8:12; 9:2; 16:8; 21:23) as he is over the winds (7:1).

The angel's "seal" (v. 2) probably implies a signet ring, by which a king could authorize an agent to carry out an activity on his behalf. In this context, it may imply that the angel was one of God's agents of judgment who initially attested the plagues just mentioned (6:1–7). Scholars have proposed a variety of interpretations for the image of the sealing of the righteous here. Some cite the marking of soldiers or others on the hand, forehead, or neck; this could relate to the probable image of the 144,000 as God's army in 14:1–5. Because Christians are a kingdom and priests (1:6), John may have thought also of the engraving "like a seal" on the high priest's forehead (Exod 28:36–38), a fitting contrast to Babylon (Rev 17:5) or to servants of the beast (13:16). John envisions the mark as the name of God and the Lamb (14:1), the opposite of the name of the beast (13:17–18).

In any case, the seal does function to attest ownership (Isa 44:5), and its title contrasts with what is merely a "mark" (Rev 13:16–17). The most important source for the image is

Ezekiel 9, where God marks the righteous remnant to protect them from his judgments. As in the plagues of the exodus, to which many of Revelation's plagues allude, God draws a line of demarcation between his people and the world (Exod 8:22; 9:4; 11:7).

The Identity of the 144,000 (7:4–8). Who are the 144,000? The matter is open to question, but the form of the text may suggest a census to assess military preparation (Num 1:3; 26:2). This vision may thus represent an end-time army, prepared for a spiritual battle (cf. Rev 12:7–9).

Who constitutes this army? John is probably adapting a pattern of a Jewish end-time remnant to portray all believers. For John all believers have become part of the "kingdom and priests" (1:6), in contrast to those who falsely claim to be Jews (2:9; 3:9). Gentiles who believe in Jesus become part of the Jewish movement of faith in Jesus. The rest of Revelation leads us to expect that the numbers are probably symbolic. The numbers 12,000 and 144 elsewhere appear for the holy community (21:16–17); the new Jerusalem is laid out as a square and shaped as a cube (21:16). Thus, the 144,000 represent all those destined for the new Jerusalem.

Judah may be listed first (7:5–8) as the military leader and because the Lord Jesus descended from that tribe (cf. 5:5), with most of the others following birth order or pairing with the appropriate brothers. Scholars debate why the tribe of Dan in particular is chosen for omission. Perhaps if some tribe had to be omitted, one with more negative associations than others would be chosen first. The informed reader might think of Dan's association with a serpent (Gen 49:16–17; cf. Jer 8:16–17), which he or she might then link with the serpent of Eden (Gen 3:1–15), who represents the devil in Revelation 12:9. Others suggest that the omission was random; one tribe had to be omitted in order to include Levi, Manasseh, and Ephraim separately, yet end up with twelve.

It also seems simplest to read the upcoming second vision (7:9–17) as another interpretation of this first one (vv. 1–8), as second visions sometimes were interpretations of a first vision. John "hears" the number of God's servants (v. 4) but "sees" a countless multitude (7:9).

Application. Jesus Christ has not called us merely to stand our ground (Eph 6:11–14), but also to advance with our feet shod with the gospel (Eph 6:15). Christ has called us not to simply preach in our churches, waiting for the lost to come in or the fruits of past revivals to finish dying off; he has challenged us to take the news of our king outside the walls of our churches, to strike offensively as well as stand defensively. "Who wants to enroll in the king's army?" we proclaim. "Who is prepared to die in hope of eternal life?"

REVELATION 7:9–17

Original Meaning. If, as we argued above, the first vision portrays symbolically God's end-time spiritual army, then this second vision is a more literal interpretation of the first. All of us as God's people are his end-time army, and we vanquish our foes not by killing them but by martyrdom at their hands. In this, we are like our Lord.

That the multitude is countless in verse 9a probably echoes the promise to the patriarchs (Gen 13:16; 15:5; 32:12). But here the promised multitude is gathered from all nations; the hope of the gospel has touched all peoples. It is striking that Christians appear here as a group "no one could count." This vision would encourage John of the success of Christian witness.

"White robes" (v. 9b) are appropriate for worship but also may reflect their victors' attire and may well connect them with the martyrs of 6:11 and other overcomers of 3:4–5, 18. That they are washed in the Lamb's blood (7:14) may also suggest that they overcame by martyrdom, just as he did (12:11), though the focus of the image is sharing the effects of Christ's expiatory sacrifice on their behalf (cf. 1:5; 1 John 1:7).

"Palm branches" (v. 9b) most often reflect a military triumph, as with the Maccabean princes and probably with expectations during Jesus's triumphal entry in John (John 12:13). The end-time army John has heard about (Rev 7:1–8) actually hails the ultimate victor, Jesus, who has led them to triumph (v. 10), and all of heaven responds with further praises.

When the elder deliberately asks John a question that must provoke him to admit his need of the elder's answer (v. 13), he does not expect a knowledgeable answer. When the Lord asked Ezekiel a rhetorical question, the latter responded, "Sovereign LORD, you alone know" (Ezek 37:3; cf. Rev 7:14). Identifying the saints in white robes as those "who have come out of the great tribulation" (v. 14) undoubtedly refers to the superlative tribulation of Daniel 12:1, which Matthew (Matt 24:21) also calls a great tribulation.

If triumph in martyrdom sounds like an oxymoron, so does washing one's robes white in blood (Rev 7:14). But such vivid contrasts with human expectations prepare the hearer for the graphic picture of blessedness for those who have suffered this world's hostility. These people refused to deify the enthroned emperor; now they are before God's throne (v. 15). Now they are freed from suffering and sorrow, and all their needs are provided (vv. 16–17).

That this throng serves God day and night (v. 15) reminds us that God's people are a kingdom of priests, doing what priests and Levites did in the temple courts (1 Chr 9:33; Ps 134:1). God's spreading his tabernacle over his people (Rev 7:15) probably alludes to Isaiah 4:5–6, where God promised to restore his people Israel and cover them with his glory as a protective shelter.

Verses 16–17 especially recall Isaiah 49:10. In that passage God had already promised his people would no longer hunger or thirst, nor would heat or the sun beat down on them. Further, God as the one with compassion on his people would "lead them beside springs of water." God himself also promised to wipe away the tears of his people (Isa 25:8).

"The Lamb" in verse 17 clearly fulfills a role Isaiah had assigned to Yahweh; John is assuredly claiming deity for Jesus here. God's compassionately leading his people to water presents him as a shepherd (Ps 23:1–2; Isa 40:11), yet in Revelation the Lamb is the shepherd. Jesus is the shepherd precisely because he was the slaughtered Lamb, the one slain for his people (John 10:11; cf. Isa 53:7).

God promised an end to sorrow when he restored his people (Isa 35:10; 51:11), but here eschatological rest from pain for the righteous is available immediately upon death. Most notably a biblical promise to Israel becomes the hope of believers from all nations grafted into Israel's heritage of obedience to the true God (Rev 7:9).

Application. This text reminds us who the true hero is. Almost every hero in the Bible exhibits some flaws, whether major flaws like Samson and Jephthah or minor ones like Abraham and Samuel. The one exception is Jesus, the only true hero in the ultimate sense. That the martyr army holds palm branches to praise their conquering general reminds us of our dependence on Jesus and summons us to worship. The text reminds us most of all that our triumph rests on the finished work of Christ (7:14), and our future hope is in fellowship with him (7:15–17).

REVELATION 8:1–13

Original Meaning

The Seventh Seal (8:1). After six thunderous seals of judgment (6:1–17) and a dramatic interlude in 7:1–17, the reader may be pardoned for a sense of anticlimax when reaching the final seal and hearing—silence (v. 1). A specifically eschatological interpretation to the silence seems likely. In some ancient texts, silence characterizes respectful listening to another's speech. There is no speech mentioned here, but silence may similarly come from awe (Job 40:4). Texts also refer to the world's silence before God at the day of judgment (Zeph 1:7).

The Power of Prayer (8:2–6). The seven angels (v. 2) probably struck most of John's audience as the seven archangels of Jewish tradition (e.g., Tobit 12:15)—powerful angels authorized to act directly by God himself. The trumpets also mentioned in verse 2 likely recall those used in the temple for worship.

The altar of incense and censer are temple instruments implying impending judgment (vv. 3–5). The idea of a heavenly temple was an ancient one, probably even implied in the symbolism of the original tabernacle in the desert (cf. Heb 8:5).

Most importantly, however, the incense explicitly represents "the prayers of all God's people" offered before the heavenly temple (vv. 3–4), an idea those steeped in the Old Testament would easily understand (Ps 141:2). That judgment immediately follows this offering of prayers makes sense when we consider the prayers of the people of God offered so far: they have been crying out for vindication (Rev 6:10). They may wonder why the answer to their prayers has been delayed (6:10). Just as the full amount of proclamation and attendant suffering must be fulfilled (6:11), perhaps the prayers of God's people must also come to a particular level before the intervention takes place.

Thus, it is as fresh prayers for vindication are added to other prayers (8:3) that judgment is sent into motion. What takes place in heaven clearly affects what occurs on earth (v. 5), and though we cannot always see the processes, many judgments come in response to human prayers.

Punishment by Plagues (8:7–12). In verses 7–12, John reports the first four trumpets, a group set off to correspond numerically with the first four seals (6:1–8), to be followed by still more dramatic plagues (8:13). These plagues resemble those in the book of Exodus: God sent hail mixed with fire both in Egypt and in Revelation (Exod 9:23–24; Rev 8:7); he turned Egypt's water supply to blood (Exod 7:20–21; Rev 8:8–9); he sent the plague of darkness on Egypt (Exod 10:22; Rev 8:12). The righteous, however, are protected (7:1–8), just as Israel was (Exod 8:22; 9:26); in the end both are preserved by the blood of the paschal Lamb (Exod 12:13; Rev 5:5–6).

The blood and fire in the hail may portend the following plagues of bloody water (8:8) and the fiery stars or mountains falling into the seas (vv. 8–10). The transformation of water into blood (v. 8) recalls the first judgment on Egypt for refusing to release God's people from captivity (Exod 7:17). Although only one-third of the sea is affected here, allowing human life to continue on earth, the plague is severe.

The mountain's burning with fire (Rev 8:8) may recall Sinai and God's law (Exod 24:17), but it may also simply be another apocalyptic symbol of judgment. Heavenly stars (often symbolizing angels; cf. Rev 9:1; 12:4) can appear like burning mountains (1 Enoch 18:13; 21:3).

The third plague (Rev 8:10–11) resembles the turning of water into blood in verses 8–9 in that it also addresses the destruction of the water supply on which humanity depends. Thus it recalls the plagues but adds to them an allusion to the bitter, polluted waters of Marah, which God had purified (Exod 15:23); now pure water becomes poisoned.

The smiting of the celestial lights surely recalls the penultimate plague on Egypt (Exod 10:21–22), probably representing judgment against Egypt's highly esteemed sun god (Exod 12:12). Pagans also feared darkness over the land, which represented a catastrophic judgment. This sort of judgment (also Rev 9:2) foreshadows the ultimate smiting of sun and moon (6:12–13) and their absence in the new world (21:23).

The narrative sets the three remaining plagues off from the first four as particularly traumatic; they receive the title "woes" (8:13). John's Jewish-Christian audience would readily understand the harsh nature of these judgments.

The significance of "an eagle" in verse 13 declaring this message is more difficult. Perhaps it simply stands for a heavenly creature (4:7), but this leaves unexplained why an eagle is chosen here rather than another creature (cf. Mark 1:10). But while its message is judgment, this eagle is the messenger, not necessarily a symbol of its content (cf. Rev 19:17). Thus, symbolic interpretation is plausible, but uncertain. Yet Greeks viewed eagles as omens (whether of good or evil) from Zeus, and Romans, who sought to predict the future by the flight of birds, may especially see a symbol of a divine messenger here.

Application. God is sovereign, but in his sovereign plan he has chosen to make the prayers of his people part of the exercise of his will. These prayers have the power to shape the course of human history! One may compare Daniel, whose prayer becomes the battleground for angelic powers greater than the earthly rulers affected by them (Dan 10:13; 10:20–11:1). We often fail to see the effects of our seemingly insignificant lives. In Hannah's day, who would have thought that the future of Israel lay in her humble prayer rather than in the spiritual legacy of Israel's high priest, Eli (1 Sam 1:10–20)? Details for which we pray are sometimes answered "no," but in the big picture, the entire course of human history, God's plan is secure and is advanced in his sovereign will through the prayers of his people.

REVELATION 9:1–21

Original Meaning

Invasion, the Fifth Trumpet (9:1–11). In Revelation the abyss is a place of evil (11:7; 17:8) and a place where evil entities are imprisoned (20:1, 3; cf. Luke 8:31). That creatures from there oppose the evil forces of the empire (Rev 9:1–11) thus only emphasizes again God's sovereignty: he employs even evil agents to destroy other evil agents (cf. 17:17).

The fifth trumpet judgment may refer to a human invasion. "Locusts" (v. 3) undoubtedly appear because, in keeping with most of the other trumpet judgments, this one recalls a plague against Egypt (Exod 10:13–14). Locusts cloud the sky when they come (Joel 2:2, 10). Most hearers in urban Asia, no less than in the countryside, would have recognized that scorpions strike with their tails. Emphasizing God's sovereignty, Jewish people would recognize that God could use scorpions to execute his judgment (Rev 9:3, 10). Some existing creatures were considered composite, but such mixtures were more often considered frightening, sometimes supernatural. The centaurs of Greek myth mixed horses and humans; Babylonians portrayed mixtures of humans with scorpions or horses.

The specific description of these locusts, however, stems from the book of Joel (Joel 1:6; 2:4), where the locusts are described as an invading army (2:11, 20, 25), but an invading eschatological army also seems to be prefigured by the locusts (3:9–12). Clearly John does not envision normal locusts; locusts target the very sorts of vegetation that these locusts do not harm (Rev 9:4), but these locusts harm people. The human faces (v. 7) may indicate the composite design of an angelic creature (Ezek 1:10) but may also suggest that it is symbolic of a human army. That the locusts' wings sound like chariots (Rev 9:9) may also suggest a human army, though that too comes directly from Joel (Joel 2:5).

The "breastplates of iron" (Rev 9:9) may compare locusts' scaled bodies with the scales of eastern soldiers. "Crowns of gold" (v. 7) usually designate royalty or high office (cf. Exod 39:30; 1 Chr 20:2); hence they may suggest that each locust commands others, suggesting in turn an army far more vast than John can portray.

If Revelation has a particular army in view here, it is probably that of the Parthians (on the Parthians, see below). Some features that might recall the Parthians, such as the horses (Rev 9:7), simply stem from Joel (Joel 2:4; cf. Jer 51:27). But other details missing from Joel's locusts but present here may point to the Parthians, especially their long hair (Rev 9:8).

The "lions' teeth" (v. 8) reflect Joel's locusts (Joel 1:6), as does the appearance "like the thundering of many horses" (Rev 9:9; Joel 2:4) and the sound of "chariots rushing into battle" (Joel 2:5). By contrast, the case for a Parthian background in the sixth trumpet is much stronger.

The monstrosities from the abyss may represent angels of judgment. That God sets limits on their destructiveness, both in intensity (Rev 9:6) and duration (v. 10), may suggest his mercy and again underlines his sovereignty. Five months is approximately a normal locust's life span, and God does not choose to extend it. Scorpion stings usually bring terrible pain but not death to humans, although these are not purely literal scorpions. By preventing their death, God augments the pain of those who would rather be out of it (v. 6), so one can read this limitation as an increase in the judgment's intensity, which fits the context of fierce judgment.

Yet the purpose of such judgments is to turn people to repentance, so even this limitation may also serve to allow repentance (vv. 20–21). Five months of torment (v. 5) thus contrasts with eternal torment (14:10–11; 20:10). That the locusts harm only people without God's seal (9:4) reinforces the point: God specifically exempts his servants from this judgment, perhaps emphasized especially if this is a demonic army.

"Abaddon" (v. 11) was a subterranean place of the dead in the Old Testament (Job 31:12; NIV "Destruction"), which is regularly linked with death and the realm of the dead (Ps 88:11), equivalent to Hades, the sometimes-personified realm of the dead (Rev 6:8) over which God (20:13–14) and Christ (1:18) have ultimate control. But here the control is delegated temporarily to an evil angel, who appears to have been imprisoned with the other spirits of the pit.

"Apollyon" (9:11) is related to *apollymi*, the Greek verb meaning "to destroy" (cf. 17:8), but John may be adapting the title slightly to make his point. Thus, many suggest that this title is also intended to ridicule Apollo, the archer god, one of whose emblems was the locust. Domitian had sometimes portrayed himself as the god Apollo—which may imply the emperor himself will lead the demonic host in destroying Rome. Judgment will be horrifying, and those who do not embrace God's protection (v. 4) may as well prepare for such horrors.

A Parthian Invasion (9:12–21). The golden altar (v. 13) represents the incense altar (Exod 30:1–3), hence implying that this judgment represents a further response to the prayers of the saints (Rev 8:3–5). By reminding the audience that the final three trumpets are "woes" (cf. 8:13), 9:12 reinforces the dramatic nature of this sixth trumpet, equivalent to the sixth bowl of God's anger, that of Armageddon (16:12–16).

The mention of "the great river Euphrates" (9:14) leaves no doubt that Parthians are in view, for the Euphrates repeatedly appeared as the traditional boundary between Roman and Parthian territories. When Parthians crossed the Euphrates, it was to fight Romans.

Parthians were the archrivals of the Roman Empire, far more feared than the Germanic barbarians on the northern frontier. Though Rome claimed to subject the north, west, and south, they admitted that they could not defeat the Parthians to the east. Parthians were known for boldness in battle and could not be trusted; they were considered the appropriate enemies of Rome.

Evil angels were thought to be bound in various places, including subterranean chasms and bodies of deep water. The four angels bound in the Euphrates River (vv. 14–15) are thus likely evil angels whom God will use as agents of judgment by their stirring of the Parthians.

These angels have stings in tails (v. 19), as in the previous plague (v. 10). Parthian archers had perfected the art of riding forward while shooting backward. They often retreated up hills, and when the Romans followed, the mounted archers devastated them with a volley of arrows.

John heard their number, just as he had the godly army of the 144,000 (7:4); but as when he "saw" the 144,000 they turned out to be literally something different (7:9), perhaps this army will also turn out to be something other than mere Parthians (9:17). Smoke-belching fiery creatures (v. 17) may symbolize the ultimate form of God's judgments on humanity. In contrast to their predecessors (v. 5), these invaders kill (v. 18). That fire comes from their mouths indicates that like God's true prophets (11:5), this demonic army also exhibits supernatural power to execute judgment.

The specific images do transcend a mere army of Parthians from across the Euphrates. In contrast to iron breastplates (9:9), these warriors bore breastplates of (literally) "fire and brimstone" (v. 17). Although the NIV is probably partly right to render this description in terms of color, the literal rendering cannot be ignored here, for "fire, smoke and sulfur" also "[came] out of their mouths" (v. 17).

Then again, John explicitly says that what he saw was a "vision" (v. 17), which probably allows for considerable symbolic elements and enables us to hold that he is describing in horrific terms a literal human army. In either case, the images evoke terror.

The killing of one-third of the world's population (vv. 15, 18) is unparalleled catastrophe. Often in Revelation God's judgments strike only one-third (8:7–12; cf. 12:4) or even a tenth (11:13), indicating that he strikes a remnant rather than the majority, hoping that others will come to repentance (9:20–21).

The climax of the account comes in verses 20–21. God allows one-third of humanity to die and spares the remaining two-thirds to invite their repentance. Like Pharaoh, however, the world refuses to repent (Exod 7:22–23). They worship and probably seek help from false gods rather than the true God.

Jewish texts condemn those who worship gods of wood, stone, and precious metals (Isa 37:19; 44:19). Both early Christians and many Jews would have shared Revelation's view that pagans worshiped demons (Rev 9:20). That Revelation connects mistreatment of people made in God's image with rejection of God in idolatry (vv. 20–21) also should not surprise us.

Application. Revelation's main audience is Christians, and its main message at this point may therefore be twofold. First, Christians flirting with compromise with the world should think twice, because the entire fallen social order will be destroyed in God's judgments; Christ alone is an adequate security. Second, Christians suffering at the hand of the world should never envy the position of their persecutors. Their persecutors will suffer judgment. The invasions by other ungodly persons or spirits function as God's judgments on a wicked society and function as active vindication of his persecuted people.

Furthermore, John provides one perspective on troubles in the world that complements other biblical perspectives: God is not absent in times of the world's hardship but remains in control. Christians must also recognize another biblical perspective that summons us to work to heal the pain around us: the cross testifies that God loves a world hostile to him and even shared our pain to ultimately liberate us from it. Yet we also need Revelation's perspective, which addresses the stark division between God's martyrs and their persecutors. God does not merely wait until Christ's return to act in history on behalf of justice.

REVELATION 10:1–11

Original Meaning. In verse 1, John sees a magnificent angel. The rainbow on this angel's head probably functions like a brilliant crown (cf. 12:1; 14:14); the rainbow may represent the divine glory (4:3). Being "robed in a cloud" (cf. 11:12; 14:14–16) simply emphasizes his heavenly stature.

That this angel's feet are "like fiery pillars" (v. 1) may recall the ancient tradition in which the world was supported by pillars; that his feet straddle sea and land support this image of magnitude (v. 2). But appearing right after comparisons with the rainbow and the sun, his luminosity is probably emphasized more, alluding to the Jewish tradition of God's glory manifest to Israel as a pillar of fire in the desert, apparently extending to heaven (Exod 13:21–22; 14:24; Num 14:14; Neh 9:12, 19).

Scholars diverge widely in their views of the "little scroll" the angel holds (Rev 10:2). Because it becomes the content of John's prophecy (vv. 10–11), it seems likely that this scroll represents the substance of the book of Revelation (1:11; 22:7–10, 18–19). It is possible that this is the book whose seals are broken in 6:1–8:1 but whose contents constitute the entire message of Revelation—the book opened by the Lamb (5:1–9), which may in some sense include the book of life (3:5; 13:8; 17:8; 20:12, 15; 21:27).

The image of thunder is appropriate (10:3). The content of the seven thunders, however, is deliberately mysterious (v. 4). Some think John uses these thunders to explain why he has omitted one series of judgments revealed to him.

If the content of the seven thunders is related to the little book in the angel's hand, it may not be written in John's book (v. 4), yet it may be revealed in the prophesying of the one who ate the little book (vv. 8–11). Thus one can argue that the passage implies that God will reveal further details through John and through the two witnesses (11:3)—that is, through the testimony of God's people facing a hostile world. Such an interpretation does not violate the theology of the book. Although one dare not add to the book of Revelation itself (22:18), the book does not imply that God stopped speaking with the close of Revelation or even the close of the canon. Rather, anywhere that people testify about Christ, God will continue to be speaking (19:10). Appealing as this interpretation is, however, it seems more likely that the seven thunders will be revealed only at the time of the end, when God's "mystery" is finished (10:7).

Most likely the seven thunders remain mysterious in order to teach that the hidden things belong to God (Deut 29:29). Revelation, unlike Daniel, does not seal up most of its contents (Rev 22:10; cf. Dan. 12:9), but some things must remain sealed. God knows far more about the future than he tells us.

The angel lifts his hand to swear (Rev 10:5), hence emphasizing the certainty of his claim that the end will finally come. The specific description of the oath here recalls Daniel 12:7, where a revealing angel raises his hands toward heaven and swears by the one who lives forever that only three and a half years remain before the end. Here in Revelation, however, the tribulation period is already finished, and at the seventh angel's voice there remains no further interval before the end.

That "there will be no more delay" (Rev 10:6) means that no further interval of time remains before the end. John's point is probably that the prayers of the saints for final vindication await no further delay (6:9–11); judgment has come (11:18; 14:7).

The completion of "the mystery" (10:7) probably indicates that the seven thunders will no longer remain secret (v. 4); all will be revealed at the consummation. Although in Revelation anything symbolic may have been a "mystery" until explained (1:20; 17:5–7), the divine mystery here seems to involve God's kingdom (Dan 2:44, 47; Mark 4:11). God's purposes will be "accomplished," as promised to "his servants the prophets" (Rev 10:7).

At the command of a heavenly voice, John takes the small book from the angel's hand, similar to what Ezekiel did (Ezek 2:9). The voice from heaven, distinguished from that of the seventh angel, is probably that of Jesus. The angel instructs John to eat the book (Rev 10:9), just as God instructed Ezekiel (Ezek 2:8; 3:1); and as in Ezekiel, the book proves sweet as honey in his mouth (Rev 10:10; cf. Ezek 3:3). That it proves bitter in John's stomach (Rev 10:9–10) probably points to the message's content: sorrow and mourning. Eating the book symbolizes internalizing its contents, because the eater can then prophesy (v. 11; Ezek 3:1). But whereas Ezekiel was to deliver the message only to the house of Israel (Ezek 3:1), John will prophesy to "many peoples, nations, languages and kings" (Rev 10:11), like Jeremiah (Jer 1:10)—and the two witnesses (Rev 11:3).

Application. The thunders reveal that some matters are not yet ours to know. The hidden things belong to God alone. Until Jesus returns, we know in part only. This does not mean that we should not seek knowledge; it does mean that God has set boundaries to what is best for us to know, and we should acknowledge those boundaries. In other words, we should avoid undue speculation about matters on which we cannot be certain and should avoid speaking dogmatically about them. In contrast to this principle, some prophecy teachers fill in too many details on which the text does not comment. Prognosticators may satisfy our curiosity about the future, but the biblical expositor's job is to help us hear and obey the message of Scripture, not to add to it.

REVELATION 11:1–14

Original Meaning

The Temple (11:1–2). Some believe that verses 1–2 demands the rebuilding of the literal temple, but some factors incline us to favor a more symbolic reading of the passage. If the temple is symbolic, what does it mean? In early Christian literature, the temple regularly symbolizes Christians, both Jewish and gentile (1 Cor 3:16; Eph 2:18–22; 1 Pet 2:5). This is also what the temple symbolizes elsewhere in Revelation (Rev 3:12; 13:6).

Given the whole context of this passage, it is possible to adopt a more specifically Jewish-Christian reading. In this case, the *naos* ("temple") represents the church as the faithful remnant of Israel (including grafted-in gentile Christians). The trampling of the outer courts (11:2) then depicts the rule of the evil one who misleads the rest of the Jewish people, the end-time remnant who eventually understands and repents (vv. 8, 13). If we are correct, the use of the outer courts is profoundly ironic, for it was gentiles who were restricted to the outer court in the most recent temple that John's contemporaries remembered. But the exact meaning of the outer court remains open to debate.

What is the point of John's "measuring rod" (v. 1)? The most likely symbolic interpretation of the act of measuring here is a promise of preservation, as in the measuring of Jerusalem (Zech 2:1–2) or the temple (Ezek 40–42). No measurements are given here; this defers the mention of the measuring rod until Revelation 21:16, when John begins to measure the gloriously massive new Jerusalem, which is shaped like the Most Holy Place. The small, persecuted remnant oppressed during this age constitutes the glorious Holy City of the age to come.

The Identity of the Witnesses (11:3–6). Calling down fire (v. 5) recalls Elijah, who also was taken into heaven and who brought drought for three and a half years. Turning water into blood and sending other plagues recall especially Moses, who some Jewish traditions also claimed ascended.

While this passage does model the two witnesses after Moses and Elijah, it also deliberately modifies the connections. Thus, for example, fire comes from the witnesses' mouths (v. 5) rather than from heaven; this is figurative language for the power of God's word, as in Jeremiah's ministry (Jer 5:14).

Suggesting that the two witnesses are symbolic is not helpful unless we can determine what they symbolize. The most common view is that the two witnesses represent the prophetic witness of the church. Those who object to the witnesses being the church do so especially on grounds that the literal details, such as lying in the street for three days, do not fit the church; but few would insist, for example, that the women in Revelation 12 or 17 must represent literal individuals.

If the witnesses represent the church, one can view the 1,260 days as a symbolic number (11:3). In this case Revelation is borrowing Daniel's figure not to tell us the length of time but to inform us of the kind of time—that the era of the church is characterized by great suffering, as in Daniel's tribulation.

The dual nature of the witnesses provides a literary contrast with the two evil leaders in 13:11–12. This portrait reinforces John's contrast between the church and the world system; the latter holds power to kill God's witnesses, but the witnesses will triumph nevertheless. The two witnesses boldly challenge the evil rulers, who embody the spirit of the antichrist.

The History of the Two Witnesses (11:7–14). The "great city" (v. 8) may be Jerusalem in some sense here, but usually in this book it is explicitly Babylon (17:18). Unbelieving Jerusalem blends into the imperial world system of which it is a part, just as Jewish accusers of Christians to local officials have their synagogues linked with Satan in 2:9 and 3:9.

That the witnesses lie in the street indicates that they remain unburied, a fate normally reserved for the most vile of criminals. The enemies of God's servants exchange gifts after slaughtering them, yet many are ultimately converted (vv. 11–13). God's side will enjoy the final exultation (19:1–7).

The witnesses are protected for the duration of their ministry (11:5) but die at the end (v. 7). This may provide a way to show that God will preserve his church throughout the age for the sake of their witness, but that as the universal proclamation of the gospel is fulfilled, the world finally appears to crush the church through massive martyrdoms.

Thus the church will follow in the steps of its Lord: Christians will die but should look for the hope of the resurrection (v. 11). The "breath of life" (v. 11) alludes to God's care in Genesis 2:7 and contrasts with the false life imparted in Revelation 13:15. Like Jesus at the beginning of the era of hardship (cf. 12:5), these witnesses are caught up to heaven at its end (11:12), a sign of vindication and ultimate deliverance (12:5).

Given the world's persistent refusal to repent in the face of God's plagues, the repentance of the city in Revelation 11:11–13 is heartening. "And gave glory to the God of heaven" (v. 13) plainly involves worship (4:9; 19:7). This text may imply the eschatological conversion of the bulk of the Jewish people in Jerusalem who were not previously converted.

Application. *The two witnesses as symbols for today.* If the two witnesses are the church, they provide a direct model for us. Those who interpret them as two literal individuals can also recognize that they nevertheless provide role models for us, just as other men and women of God in Scripture do. We must therefore be Spirit-empowered witnesses to the world, ready to pay any cost and utterly dependent on God's power to accomplish his purposes.

REVELATION 11:15–19

Original Meaning. The closing verses of chapter 11 address the seventh trumpet. Although the final trumpet concludes the series of seven (v. 15), it also fits the occasion here; trumpets were normally blown at the accession of a king to his throne (1 Kgs 1:34–41; 2 Kgs 9:13; 11:14). The Bible had promised that the Davidic Messiah would reign forever (Isa 9:7); naturally Jewish people recognized that God would reign forever (Ps 10:16; 146:10). Daniel had emphasized the final triumph of God's kingdom over the successive world empires (Dan 2:44), a hope celebrated by many of John's contemporaries. Jewish people also emphasized that whereas the nations ruled now, God and his people would reign in the world to come. Here in Revelation 11:15, the kingdom "of our Lord and of his Messiah" probably recalls the language of Psalm 2:2, where the nations challenge them but will ultimately be crushed.

God's people often have praised him in response to his deliverance of his people (Rev 11:17–18; see, e.g., Exod 15:18). The wrath of the nations in Revelation 11:18 recalls the raging of the nations against God and his anointed king in Psalm 2:1–2, which in turn is met by God's wrath (v. 12). Here in our text their wrath is met by God's "wrath" on the day of judgment (Rev 11:18).

Jewish tradition also emphasized the rewards God would give his people at the time of the end (v. 18). Contrary to some Christian attempts to denigrate Jewish tradition, reward is no less a Christian concept, though the works it rewards are impossible apart from the grace experienced in Christ (Matt 5:11; 1 Cor 3:8; 2 John 8). Everyone, both righteous and wicked, receive their rewards at this time (Rev 11:18).

God's "servants the prophets" may be identified with "your people" and with "those who revere" God's name (v. 18). All believers are meant to be "prophets" in the general sense of Spirit-empowered witnesses for Christ (19:10), contrary to the arguments of some commentators. "Great and small" (11:18) is a common idiom meaning "everyone."

The reference to "those who destroy the earth" (v. 18) and so merit judgment is more difficult. It may refer to aggressors against God's people, invaders who seek to devastate the holy land (2 Kgs 18:25). That nothing in the context narrows the image specifically to the holy land, however, generalizes the image: the evil empire, like Babylon of old, devastates the whole earth. That those who harmed others will suffer an identical fate was a commonplace of biblical and broader ancient wisdom (e.g., Matt 26:52).

Revelation 11:19 is pivotal in that it introduces the following section (12:1–6), but we will discuss this verse here to avoid confusion. Jewish people generally believed that God had hidden the ark, but that it would be restored in the end-time. Thus, once the time for the final judgment has come (11:15–18), God unveils his heavenly temple, indicating the end (v. 19). Furthermore, regulations had previously prevented people on earth from viewing the ark when it was in the temple, for it remained shrouded in the Most Holy Place (Exod 40:21; Lev 16:2); the present revelation thus indicates an extraordinary change of affairs.

The picture of the ark suggests a variety of associations, especially involving the Sinai covenant, by which God demanded an accounting from a disobedient world. In the ancient Near East, a nation usually deposited a covenant with another people before the deity in the temple, thereby inviting the avenging curses mentioned in the covenant if it were broken. It may also be relevant that edicts were displayed in public places, such as temples. Further, just as the Israelites had taken the ark before them to war (1 Sam 4:3–9), so the Romans believed the numen of their state would go forth from its temple to war and return afterward. The meteorological phenomena here in Revelation 11:19 probably signify a new revelation from heaven comparable to the revelation of God's word at Mount Sinai (cf. 4:5; Exod 19:16).

Application. Those who face grief or any hardship in the world will find comfort in the message of these verses. They announce that this world ultimately belongs to God and that God will right all the wrongs of history in the day of judgment, shattering all opposition; they also invite worship as we contemplate God's coming intervention to rule. Moreover, they remind us that God will reward both small and great just as he will punish both great and small; God is no respecter of persons.

REVELATION 12:1–17

Original Meaning

The Mother (12:1). This woman is a mother, somehow the antecedent of the faithful bride of Christ, the new Jerusalem (21:2), and a contrast to the harlot, Babylon (17:5). The prophets portrayed righteous Israel as the mother of the restored future remnant of Israel (Isa 54:1; Mic 4:9–10), an image they mixed with that of Israel as a bride (Isa 62:5). The sun, moon, and twelve stars on the woman confirm this vision as symbolizing Israel or its faithful remnant (Gen 37:9).

Because the woman is Jesus's mother, many scholars naturally link her with Mary. Yet Revelation nowhere provides explicit teaching about Mary, and we cannot extrapolate from this passage about her without further comment in the text.

Labor Pains and the Dragon (12:2–4). As noted above, the prophets portrayed righteous Israel as the mother of the restored future remnant of Israel. In one passage God promises that suffering, pregnant Israel will truly bear new life in the time of the resurrection (Isa 26:17–19), the day of God's wrath in which he will slay the serpent (26:20–27:1).

For John, the dragon is especially the "ancient serpent" (Rev 12:9), the one in Genesis who led Adam and Eve to death by enticing them to disobey God (Gen 3:1–15). Jewish tradition sometimes identified the serpent with the devil or linked him with the devil in other ways.

The meaning of the stars also deserves comment. One can take their fall (Rev 12:4) as a description of cosmic catastrophe, but verse 4 probably implies more than that. In Jewish symbolism, stars could represent the righteous, as even in this context (v. 1; cf. Gen 26:4; Dan 12:3); hence this passage may be describing apostasy. But in Revelation the stars usually symbolize angels (Rev 1:20; 9:1). Jewish people recognized that Satan's revolt had long ago led to the fall of many angels (often associated with Gen 6:2), a view apparently supported in 1 Peter 3:19–22 and 2 Peter 2:4.

Yet John provides a Christocentric reapplication of this fall story: the greatest revolt of Satan and the ultimate goal of angelic apostasy was opposition to Jesus's mission on earth (Rev 12:4). But Satan and his angels failed, and precisely at Jesus's exaltation Satan's kingdom received its complete notice of defeat (vv. 7–9).

The Final Exodus (12:5–6). In the common myth of the time, the child born to the woman was a god or the emperor worshiped without controversy by the world system; John reinterprets the myth so that the child is the Lord Jesus. Jesus was "begotten" as king at his resurrection and enthronement (Ps 2:7). If read together with John's Gospel, Revelation may even depict Jesus's enthronement as beginning with the cross, where he was crowned "king of the Jews" (John 19:19–21); it was at the cross that Satan was "cast out" of heaven (John 12:31); it was by the cross that Jesus "prepared a place" for his followers (John 14:2–3; cf. Rev 12:6).

The "1,260 days" of verse 6 likely adapts Daniel's great tribulation (cf. Dan 12:11), three and a half years (Dan 7:25; 9:27; 12:7). Revelation seems to employ this figure to tell us about the kind of time rather than the length of time, emphasizing primarily that it is tribulation. Christians are already living in the final era, regardless of that era's length. John declares Satan's defeat in the past.

For several reasons, John's adaptation of his contemporaries' prophecy charts should not surprise us. First, Revelation rarely takes over Jewish symbols of the end without reapplying them in light of what Christians know about Jesus. Revelation is full of symbolic numbers. Second, the book of Daniel itself reapplies Jeremiah's seventy years prophecy to a much longer period (Dan 9:2, 24). Third, Jesus regarded Daniel's tribulation as at least partly literally fulfilled in the events of AD 66–70, when the temple was desecrated and destroyed. Finally, some of John's contemporaries had also symbolically reapplied Daniel's figure for the tribulation.

Revelation itself reads as if Jesus's exaltation is immediately followed by the tribulation (12:5–6). Satan's expulsion accompanies the arrival of "salvation" and God's "kingdom" (v. 10), and such language suits only two moments. One is Christ's return in glory (19:1), but this cannot be in view here, for that would hardly leave Satan even a "short" time (12:12). The other is Jesus's triumph through his death, resurrection, and enthronement (1:9; 2:27; 7:10), which therefore must be in view here. Believers will face tribulation in the world, but Jesus promises that his finished victory matters much more than such tribulation (John 16:33).

John uses the desert or "wilderness" in Revelation 12:6 symbolically to refer back to the first exodus, as in his Gospel (John 3:14; 6:31, 49), announcing a spiritual new exodus (1:23).

Celestial Combat (12:7–12). Revelation then shifts to a heavenly perspective on the events just described. Christ's triumph is envisioned in terms of a heavenly combat between God's and Satan's forces. Satan's fall here clearly refers to a past event (v. 9); "salvation" and God's "kingdom" (v. 10) are completed at Christ's return but were begun at his death, resurrection, and enthronement.

Michael and his forces cast down Satan's forces, because Michael and his allies represent the heavenly victory won by Christ on earth. God not only rules the world through events in the heavens but also fits these events to his acts on earth.

Ironically, Satan's loss of "place" (*topos*, v. 8) contrasts starkly with the "place" (*topos*) of refuge God provides his own people persecuted by Satan (vv. 6, 14). The Bible already declared that Satan functioned as an accuser (Zech 3:1), including directly before God's throne (Job 1:6; 2:1). Here, however, his accusations against the people of God have been silenced, for Christ's victory is sufficient to silence all objections of the once-heavenly prosecutor (Rev 12:10).

Satan's defeat in heaven does not mean an end to physical suffering on earth. God's people here continue to overcome the devil as they overcome the world—by faithfully testifying of Christ's victory even to the point of death (v. 11).

Satan accuses and oppresses Jesus's followers (vv. 10–12) and pursues the woman into the desert, just as Pharaoh pursued Israel in the exodus. The devil's "short" time (v. 12), like the "little while" between the cross and resurrection (John 16:16–19), is an interim period that involves both suspense and hardship—but whose outcome is predetermined.

The Dragon's Pursuit of the Woman (12:13–17). The woman fled to the desert for an extended period. The period (v. 14) refers to three and a half years, the period of great tribulation (Dan 7:25; 12:7). The exodus tradition spoke of God's bearing his people on eagle's wings (Exod 19:4), an image also applicable to the new exodus (Isa 40:31). The miraculous provision in the desert here echoes the manna God gave his people at the first exodus.

That "water like a river" comes from the serpent's mouth (Rev 12:15) may be a symbol for slander; Satan, who can no longer accuse God's people to God, accuses them to the world instead. In prophetic language, a "flood" could represent any sufferings (cf. Ps 32:6), including divine judgment (Isa 28:2), but also including unjust opposition (Ps 18:3–4). The earth, obeying God, helps the woman (Rev 12:16).

The dragon's rage against the woman carries forward his "fury" (v. 12) and that of his agents (11:18), but now at 12:17 he focuses his activity against her seed. The woman's "offspring" or "seed" here echoes the language of Genesis 3:15. These other offspring represent those who keep God's commandments—that is, true disciples of Jesus (Rev 3:10); they "hold fast their testimony about Jesus" (12:17).

Precisely how does the devil make war with the rest of the woman's seed? The answer is the theme of the following chapter, describing the world's repression.

Application. The image of conflict here reminds us that God's people must always be ready to confront the world's hostility; the contrast between the mother in chapter 12 and the prostitute in chapter 17 reminds us that the city of God and Babylon never coexist naturally in this world. Especially in view of the use of the image of labor pains in the Hebrew Bible, this image here further reminds us that God's purposes are often accomplished only through suffering (cf. John 16:21–22; Rom 8:22–23). The devil's hostility, probably expressed as slander, also warns us to expect false accusations, though we should do our best to prevent them.

REVELATION 13:1–10

Original Meaning

The Sea Beast (13:1–2). The beast in verses 1–10 recalls Daniel 7:3–8, where four beasts arise from the "sea" (Dan 7:2). The beast in Revelation differs from the fourth beast of Daniel, being a composite of different beasts. Composite descriptions can amplify the glory of a creature (Ezek 1:10), but here they amplify its hideousness. Thus, though John makes his allusion by way of Rome, the point goes beyond Rome.

The "ten horns" and "seven heads" (v. 1) connect this beast with its suprahuman mentor, another beast—namely, the dragon (v. 2). The "blasphemous name" (v. 1) probably evokes the arrogant boasts of Daniel 7:8, 20. Roman coins in the eastern Mediterranean announced that the emperor was "son of God" and "God."

Nero Strikes Again (13:3). Nero died June 9, AD 68, but even at the end of the first century many believed that he remained alive. Here in Revelation we read of a head that is wounded, then restored (v. 3)—an account that presumably points to the Roman ruler. Although the image of multiple heads on a beast may come from the four heads of one of the beasts in Daniel 7:6, a Roman tradition may also be of interest. Early Romans found a human head buried in the earth and understood it as a prophecy of Rome's future rule. What would retroactively clinch the allusion to Nero for informed members of John's audience is the riddle of Revelation 13:18 (or, if they failed to catch it, the riddle of 17:9–11).

None of this is to say that Revelation predicts a literal return of Nero from the dead. Rather, the final antichrist or the tradition of antichrist figures would be like Nero, just as John the Baptist was another Elijah (Matt 17:12–13; Luke 1:17).

After Nero's death, chaos ensued as rival candidates for emperor successively seized control of Rome; the peace of the empire had apparently died with Nero. But with the accession of Vespasian, Domitian's father, the empire regained a semblance of stability and power. The empire had, for all practical purposes, returned from the brink of death.

The Dragon, the Beast, and the Lamb (13:4–10). While the story of Nero's return provides a backdrop for the plot, the real plot action is a more deliberate picture of resurrection and its public consequences. The return from death is a parody on

Jesus; likewise, the ten-horned beast contrasts starkly with the seven-horned Lamb (5:6). The earth's first question, "Who is like the beast?" (13:4), parodies worship properly due God alone (Exod 15:11). But in contrast to imperial Rome, Jesus had defeated death and now ruled its domain (Rev 1:18).

Likewise, more horrifying than the image of a new Nero is the fact that those impressed by the "resurrection" recorded in 13:3 worship not only the emperor but the dragon who stands behind him.

The image of desecrating the temple was not unfamiliar to John's audience; Titus, the older brother of Emperor Domitian, had presided over the burning and desecration of the temple in Jerusalem in AD 70. But John means the heavenly temple, and he means it symbolically, as he explicitly notes (v. 6): God's people comprise God's tabernacle or temple, and whoever harms it will be judged.

That the beast "was given . . . authority" and "power" (vv. 5, 7), however, reminds John's audience that even the antichrist is a pawn in God's greater design on behalf of his people. In the end only God can authorize the devil or the beast to rule the nations (v. 7).

The unity of the beast's kingdom (vv. 7–8) reflects the understanding that God has permitted the world to stand together under a single evil empire to test his people. By contrast, God's people had their own multicultural unity (7:9–10), of which the world's was but a pale parody.

Nor is the beast's claim to rule the whole world to be taken completely at face value. Emperor Augustus had claimed to rule the entire inhabited world, having subdued even the Parthians, but in fact this was purely Roman propaganda to impress the empire's subjects. The beast "conquers" the saints (13:7), but their apparent defeat, like the cross, really spells their victory (12:11).

Jewish teachers often commented on the predestination of the righteous in God's book. Here, however, the book belongs to the Lamb (13:8). John's idea of predestination does not negate human responsibility. Anyone who proves able ought to respond to God's call immediately and find strength to persevere.

One can read verse 10 as a summary of the way that the people of God will be executed. But this passage probably claims that those not destined for eternal life (v. 8) are destined to die in various ways, a promise meant to encourage the faith of God's suffering people (v. 10).

Application. *How the devil works.* This passage reveals just how hideous evil is. Anthropological studies attest the pervasiveness of spirit-possession in various cultures, and the concrete existence of personal evil is one of the most empirically verifiable doctrines of the Christian faith. The frequent denial of the devil in the West is less rational than it pretends to be and plays into the devil's hands.

Yet what is truly horrific in this passage is that here, as in most of the Bible, the devil works not independently but through people. This passage testifies to the awfulness to which humans can descend in following the devil's ways (Eph 2:1–3)—the Neros, Hitlers, Stalins, Maos, and Pol Pots; the Arab and Western slave trade; the genocide in Rwanda; and so forth—these all testify to the reality of demonic power amplifying human sin and crushing its usual restraints.

At the same time, this passage offers hope to those who dare grasp it here: God is the one who gives the beast authority for forty-two months, and he does so to execute his purposes of judging the world by handing it over to its own evil ways. The promise of judgment is also given to encourage the saints (Rev 13:10); it reminds us that God is just, that there are some moral certainties and issues of justice in the world, and that God will vindicate justice in the end.

REVELATION 13:11–18

Original Meaning. That this second beast mentioned in verse 11 had two horns "like a lamb" reflects its imitation of the seven-horned Lamb of God (5:6), though the two horns may come from the ram of Daniel 8:3. But this "lamb" speaks like the dragon. Its message gives it away.

Not many years after Revelation was written, we have evidence of a legal tradition of executing Christians for refusing to worship the emperor's statue. John's audience would also think of Nebuchadnezzar's image, which was to be worshiped by all peoples.

Babylonian and Greco-Roman magic included rituals to seek to animate images; an entire branch of magic, called theurgy, specialized in animating statues so they could give oracles. The most important function of these signs in verse 13 is that they continued the parody on God and his agents (cf. 11:5).

The beast enforces a unity that cuts across all social lines (v. 16), though the attentive reader will remember that God's judgment also cuts across just such distinctions (6:15; 11:18). The use of a "mark" to enforce national or empire-wide unity already had a long history known to John's audience. Ptolemy IV Philopator, ruler of Egypt, required Jewish people in his realm to be enrolled in a census and to be branded with an ivy leaf (3 Macc. 2.28–29).

This mark stands in direct contrast to the seal of Revelation 7:3–4, which alludes to a "mark" on the righteous in Ezekiel 9:4–6. Whereas the symbolic mark of protection or judgment was normally on the forehead (Ezek 9:4), John adds here the "right hand" (Rev 13:16); branding soldiers on the hands was a sign of loyalty.

In John's day, one could not handle money without involvement in the imperial system. To withdraw from an economic system permeated with imperial worship—even to withdraw from trade guilds, whose meetings included meat offered to idols—was in many cities economic suicide.

But God would supply his people's needs, miraculously if need be (Rev 12:6, 14). Meanwhile, whereas many accept the mark to be able to engage in commerce (13:17), every following mention of the "mark" in Revelation implies the judgments its recipients merit (14:9–11; 16:2; 19:20; 20:4). Those with faith to believe God's warnings recognize that despite the world's perspective, the people of God are really better off in the long run.

What is the number of the beast's name (v. 17)? Ancients were adept at the use of symbolic numbers, of which Revelation includes several. The number 666 is a triangular number, with the root 36; 36 is also a triangular number with the root 8. Since the root of triangular numbers provide their significance, "8" may prepare the reader for the eighth ruler of 17:11, generally agreed to be a new Nero. Those interested in ancient numeric speculation would be familiar with 666. Most commentators find an allusion to Nero Caesar's name as written in Hebrew characters here.

Application. Because Satan's counterfeits imitate God's works, it is not surprising that false signs continue to lead many people astray today; some are fake, whereas others are demonic. One thinks, for example, of psychic healers and perhaps of some modern mind-science techniques. One Catholic scholar warns against false apparitions of Christ and Mary that exhibit signs yet teach what is false. Although God can do anything, it should also be noted that statues that are purported to weep or sweat are not a specifically Christian phenomenon. But missiologists comment on power encounters, noting that, as in the Bible (Exod 7:11–12; Acts 13:11), God's power is stronger than Satan's. The two witnesses prevailed with their signs until the appointed time of their martyrdom (Rev 11:7), and today's church should be able to demonstrate God's power more effectively than occult sources demonstrate theirs.

REVELATION 14:1–20

Original Meaning

The Army on Mount Zion (14:1–5). Perhaps most significant for our observation here is the location of the 144,000. They are with the Lamb on Mount Zion, God's dwelling, a place of Israel's hopes for salvation (Ps 53:6) and triumph (Obad 21). In Revelation, Zion is also the new Jerusalem, the holy city (Rev 3:12; 21:2–22:2), the antithesis of Babylon, whose demise is about to be introduced (14:8).

After John sees the 144,000 on Mount Zion, he hears a sound from heaven (v. 2). As his vision in 7:9–17 constitutes the interpretation of what he heard in 7:1–8, so here his hearing helps to interpret his vision of the 144,000. The "sound from heaven" is the song of 144,000 taken from the earth and now in heaven.

That the 144,000 are those "redeemed" (14:3) and "purchased" (v. 4) from the earth and from among humanity reminds us that they stand for all believers (5:9). That the Lamb bought them more than makes up for the fact that, a few verses earlier, they could neither buy nor sell (13:17). "Firstfruits" (14:4) is sacrificial language (Exod 23:19). These spiritual warriors are thus devoted to the Lamb.

God's people praise God for the victory of the Lamb, just as the Israelites praised God when he overthrew their enemies in the Red Sea (Exod 15:1–21). This "new song" is their unique experience shared by no one else in creation (Rev 14:3), just as believers have a new name known to no one else (2:17; 3:12).

Why are the 144,000 celibate? These 144,000 have refused to commit immorality with Babylon, the prostitute (cf. 18:3). The symbolism thus makes a strong point: Christians must be pure and faithful to Christ if they wish to be prepared for and engage in the Lamb's holy war.

That "no lie was found in their mouths" (14:5) contrasts God's faithful with the world's liars, who embrace the lies from the spirit of antichrist and whose fate is damnation (21:8). God's people speak the truth of the gospel and renounce idols regardless of the cost (6:9–11; 11:3; 12:11); this is part of what it means for them to be pure (14:4).

Four Heavenly Announcements (14:6–13). Because angels in Revelation often correspond to earthly realities, the angel's flight may correspond to the spread of the gospel through martyrs. Another sense of "gospel" (v. 6) is perhaps more likely here, however. In the prophetic tradition, "good news" is not just the announcement that God is restoring his people but also the announcement of judgment on their enemies (Nah 1:15); in context, this angel announces impending judgment (Rev 14:7).

The double "fallen" in the description of Babylon (v. 8) is emphatic and alludes to idolatrous Babylon's prophesied fall in Isaiah 21:9, perhaps viewed as fulfilled in Revelation 11:13; 16:19. Early Jews often used Babylon as a code name for Rome, as did early Christians (1 Pet 5:13). As Israel once experienced exile under the evil empire Babylon, now they are experiencing a new evil empire in Rome. Both Babylon and Rome destroyed the temple in Jerusalem.

Babylon is judged because she has made nations drink "the maddening wine of her adulteries" (Rev 14:8). This verse may introduce that cup of God's wine as anger *against* Babylon's "adulteries," which Babylon brought on all the nations with whom she committed such immoralities. Ancients normally diluted wine with two parts water to every part wine, except when they wished to get drunk. But God will administer this wine of his anger "full strength" (v. 10).

Those tormented will be able to look on the Lamb and the holy angels they despised (v. 10), now unable to evade the reality they once ignored. That the smoke of their torture rises "for ever and ever" (v. 11) must mean eternal torment rather than annihilation; this same phrase applies to God's and Christ's eternality (1:18; 4:10; 10:6; 11:15; 15:7), to the reign of the saints (22:5), and to the eternal suffering of the beast (20:10).

Finally, a heavenly voice promises peace for the martyr-witnesses of Jesus; the Spirit then confirms this with a prophetic assurance (14:13). Everyone is judged according to "works" (2:23; 20:12–13; 22:12), but the righteous can be satisfied in theirs (14:13). The key phrase is that these dead are "in the Lord" (v. 13).

The Harvests Have Come (14:14–20). In verses 14–20 the action shifts from heavenly announcements (vv. 6–13) to visions of symbolic actions. When Jesus appears in 19:12–13, his garments are spattered from treading out the winepress of human blood.

The primary exegetical problem in this text is whether to identify the grain harvest of the first vision with the grape vintage of the second harvest (a typical feature of Revelation is to have a second vision interpret the first), or to interpret them differently. This passage may be continuing the contrast between the fate of the righteous and the wicked found in 14:6–13; in the harvesting of the righteous the wicked are judged (cf. Matt 3:12; 13:40–42). Again, in Revelation a second vision often reinterprets the first (Rev 7:1–17). Yet it seems more likely on the whole that both visions involve judgment.

Whatever the point of the first vision, the meaning of the second vision is relatively plain. It portrays the wicked as gathered grapes now crushed into wine in God's winepress. God had already promised that he would go out and trample the blood of the wicked like wine in a winepress until his garments were stained with their blood (Isa 63:1–6); in Revelation Jesus assumes this divine role (Rev 19:13, 15).

The angel "who had charge of the fire" (14:18) keeps the fire of the incense altar (8:5). This image suggests that God again sends judgment in response to the cries of his oppressed people (6:9–11; 8:3–5).

The blood flows high "outside the city," vividly portraying a horrible end for Babylon (14:20). The image of blood flowing in terrible streams became standard in ancient descriptions of wars, both historical and fictitious. Sometimes the more extreme descriptions were merely figurative ways of expressing the horrific bloodshed (e.g., Ezek 32:5–6).

The "1,600 stadia" (v. 20) may be a rounded number with figurative significance; 1,600 is the square of the familiar biblical number forty. But while John rounds to a square number, its primary significance is to compound the grotesqueness of the image: none of the army will survive. Some commentators also suggest a contrast here: whereas the river of paradise flows from God's throne (22:2) to a significant height, the wicked will drown in a river of their own blood (14:20).

Application. The idea of eternal torment is so naturally revolting to most of us that modern readers have found a number of ways to circumvent it. Some teach annihilation, which seems to contradict a number of texts about eternal torment but which is not a pleasant alternative in itself. This view is not heretical, and it does not lessen the need for people to embrace Christ; but it is not likely correct.

Many today avoid trying to scare people into the kingdom. In a culture in revolt against authority and skeptical of threats, emphasizing God's loving invitation may be a more strategic approach. But John had no such scruples against scaring people, and as long as we speak the truth and are able to reason with people, there remain occasions when this approach is appropriate. A young atheist chose to consider the claims of Christ immediately rather than deferring the decision because the doctrine of hell made the stakes too high to ignore. Twenty-four years later, that former atheist remains a committed Christian—and wrote this commentary on Revelation.

REVELATION 15:1–8

Original Meaning. John makes it clear that what he sees is a symbolic portrayal of judgments (v. 1). Thus when he declares that these seven plagues are the "last plagues," completing God's anger, he probably does not imply that Revelation arranges all judgments in literal chronological sequence. Rather, "last" implies that these bowls begin John's final sequence of judgments. They are the last in terms of John's narrative.

The word used for the "bowls" of divine anger (*phialē*, v. 7; 16:1–17:1; 21:9) is also used for the bowls that contained the prayers of his people (5:8), suggesting a connection between the saints' intercession and their vindication through the world's judgments, as with the trumpet plagues (8:3–5). That the judgments in this passage issue from God's presence and follow worship by the conquering martyrs (15:2–4) probably implies that God has chosen to release his acts in history in response to the worship of his faithful people.

Those who have "been victorious over the beast" (v. 2) are God's people who overcame by way of the cross—that is, by being defeated on a purely earthly level by refusing to compromise with the agendas of the tyrannical beast (12:11; 13:7).

This is the same group already portrayed as God's conquering army in 14:1–5. The location of the overcomers is significant. The "sea of glass" (15:2) recalls the heavenly temple; perhaps the mixture "with fire" indicates that these believers have overcome the "lake of fire," although it has not yet been mentioned (19:20).

The song in 15:2–4 drives home the point. The harpists explicitly recall 14:2, and this passage spells out the "new song" of the 144,000 in 14:3; it declares how they have been victorious. Their song is the "song of Moses . . . and the song of the Lamb" (15:3), recalling the exodus both in terms of Moses's leading out of Egypt (cf. 11:8) and deliverance from God's plagues by the blood of the Passover lamb. The primary allusion is surely the song of the exodus in Exodus 15:1–18.

Israel sang this song, led by Moses and summarized antiphonally by Miriam (Exod 15:21) when God brought his people through the Red Sea and destroyed their enemies, the Egyptians. As God conquered Egypt in the sea, there figuratively slaying the primeval dragon (Ps 74:13–14; Isa 51:9), so here the 144,000 are the people of the new exodus, delivered and standing as conquerors on the sea of glass and fire.

The song in Revelation 15:3–4 praises God in language developed from Israel's ancient worship, especially Psalm 86:8–10. God's people address God as either "King of the ages" or "King of the nations" (Rev 15:3 NIV); both readings have significant support, and we cannot tell conclusively which is more likely the original reading. "King of the ages" means "eternal King." On the other hand, "King of the nations" also makes sense; God has triumphed over the nations as he triumphed over Egypt in the exodus, and now the nations will come to worship him (v. 4).

God's greatness and his "marvelous . . . deeds" (v. 3) recall Psalm 86:10, since verse 4 explicitly quotes Psalm 86:9. Yet the "great and marvelous . . . deeds" in Revelation's own context especially refer to the "great and marvelous" plagues of Revelation 15:1—that is, God's judgments. God is both "just and true" in his judgments (v. 3)—"just" or "righteous" in executing appropriate judgment (16:5–6), and "true" in his faithfulness to his people, whose blood he now vindicates (3:7, 14; 19:9, 11; 21:5; 22:6).

Yet whereas in the exodus God overthrew Egypt for oppressing Israel, here he welcomes those from all nations who have joined God's servants in resisting the world. The nations now come to God in worship (15:4), as in 21:24. Judgment brings representatives of all peoples to repentance.

As with the judgments of the seals (5:1–2) and the trumpets (8:2), the plagues from the bowls (16:1–17) are introduced with a scene in heaven (15:5–8), reminding us that earthly disasters are methodically arranged events determined by God's sovereign vindication of his people.

That this scene takes place in the heavenly temple is significant. The angels' linen clothing (v. 6) undoubtedly reminds the reader that these angels fulfill priestly acts in the heavenly temple (vv. 5–6; cf. Lev 16:4). The prerequisite for such service was righteousness (Rev 19:8). Priests in the heavenly temple respond to the earthly priests (1:6) of the oppressed earthly temple (11:1–2), whose prayers (6:9–11; 8:3–6) have invited the judgments about to begin.

That "smoke" filled the heavenly temple (15:8, note contrast with the smoke of the world's torment in 14:11) alludes to God's glory filling his house in some Old Testament theophanies (Isa 6:4; Ezek 10:3–4). God had filled the earthly tabernacle with his glory at its dedication and a time of celebration (Exod 40; cf. 1 Kgs 8); now he fills the temple with his glory in response to the worship of his martyred conquerors through history.

Application. For John, the songs of Moses and the Lamb were not two separate songs, as if Old Testament redemption and New Testament redemption were discontinuous and incompatible ideas. Jesus as the Lamb has provided the climactic act of redemption, akin to the paschal lamb of the first exodus, so the song of Moses is also the song of the Lamb.

REVELATION 16:1–21

Original Meaning

More Plagues (16:1–11). A voice here comes from "from the temple" (v. 1), the heavenly temple that has just been mentioned (15:5–8). The wicked have trampled the earthly temple (11:2), so judgment goes forth from the heavenly temple (11:19; 14:15, 17; 15:5–16:1; 16:17). The "seven bowls of God's wrath" (v. 1) represent urns in the temple, perhaps for libations of incense. The bowls are much like the trumpets.

Most of the bowls, like the trumpets, recall the plagues of the exodus: sores (v. 2), water into blood (vv. 3–4), and darkness (v. 10, and in this case its antithesis, v. 9). By recalling the plagues, this series of judgments also reminds believers that as God protected his own people in Goshen during the plagues (Exod 8:22; 9:26), so he will protect them from his judgments (Rev 7:1–8; 12:6, 16). The final two bowls represent the promised end-time battle and the completion of God's promises.

The water-into-blood plague is repeated for emphasis (16:3–4), to demonstrate the appropriateness of God's judgment (vv. 5–7). Jewish people believed God assigned various angels to superintend various features of nature (which Greeks attributed to gods or other spirits); here "the angel in charge of the waters," whose domain was turned to blood, praises God's justice (vv. 5–6).

The angel's and altar's praise provides the most striking feature of these judgments that adds to what the hearer already experienced in the trumpet judgments (vv. 5–7). The recitation of God's justice (or righteousness) and holiness (v. 5) develop the song of Moses and of the Lamb in 15:3–4, which also comments on God's judgments.

Our passage emphasizes the justness of his punishing the wicked (vv. 5–6). As God's enemies "have shed" (i.e., "poured out") blood (v. 6), so he "poured out" judgments (16:1–17), including blood (vv. 3–4); he avenges the world's repression of his servants, fulfilling his martyrs' anticipation (6:9–11; 14:20; 17:6; 18:24).

"The altar" confirms God's justice (16:7), undoubtedly because it harbors the prayers of the saints (6:9; 8:3, 5); hence it participates in the judgment (9:13; 14:18). It echoes the song in 15:3.

The plagues of scorching sun and darkness (16:8–10) recall the Old Testament plague of darkness, a judgment on Egypt's sun deity, Amon-Re; they may also recall other events of the exodus. That the darkness actually causes pain (v. 10) may reflect the darkness of Moses's day, which could be "felt" (Exod 10:21; cf. Ps 107:10). But instead of understanding God's justice and responding with repentance, the objects of his wrath here in Revelation grow harder against God and blaspheme him all the more (16:9, 11; cf. 9:20–21; 16:21).

Racing toward Judgment (16:12–21). The "great river Euphrates" (v. 12) recalls the terrifying image of 9:14, just as "prepare" recalls the same passage's emphasis that God will bring judgments at the appropriate hour. Although many rivers in the Near East occasionally dried up, the massive Euphrates was never known to do so under natural circumstances. This fact augments the terror of the image and is evidence of divine judgment (Isa 50:2; Hos 13:15; Nah 1:4).

The parting of the Jordan for Israel invited the conquest of Canaan (Josh 3:14–17; 4:23–5:1). People in the ancient Mediterranean remembered the Euphrates especially as the boundary between the Roman and Parthian Empires. Some people expected Nero to bring the kings of the East across the Euphrates to wreak his vengeance on Rome.

Revelation 16:13 may be suggesting the dragon, beast, and false prophet as a sort of a satanic trinity. That it speaks of frogs coming out of their mouths may recall another Egyptian plague (Exod 8:2–13), but like the plague of locusts (Exod 10:13–14; Rev 9:3) it is transformed into something different in Revelation's symbolism. Presumably there are three frogs because they issue from three mouths; because they issue from mouths, they probably represent propaganda (13:2, 5–6). These "demonic spirits" perform persuasive and miraculous "signs" (16:14), like the beast they serve (13:13–14).

The devil and his agents then gather the nations together in order to battle the true God, though in reality they were being gathered simply for God's great day—that is, for their destruction (16:14). The gathering of the wicked for their own destruction is a common end-time image (Joel 3:10–16; Zech 12:3–4; 14:2–3).

Such an announcement proves an appropriate point for John to remind his hearers that Jesus will come like a thief (Rev 16:15), as he stated earlier (3:3) and as most early Christians seem to have been warned (Matt 24:43; 2 Pet 3:10). Alluding back to this earlier warning (esp. harsh toward the sleeping church of Sardis), John insists that those found unprepared will be stripped instead of walking with Jesus in robes of white (cf. Rev 3:4–5, 17–18). The righteous must remain righteous without compromise, for terrible times are coming; but Jesus will come when the world does not expect him.

The meaning of "Armageddon" in 16:16—most likely Hebrew for "Mount Megiddo"—is obscure. Megiddo lay on a plain (2 Chr 35:22; Zech 12:11) rather than on a mountain, but apocalyptic geography allowed considerable symbolic flexibility. The Valley of Megiddo was the site of significant battles in history (Judg 5:19; 2 Kgs 23:29) and was strategically located for further ones. Although a valley would have worked well as an image of end-time judgment (Joel 3:12, 14), Megiddo may appear here as a mountain to symbolize its stature or as a contrast with Mount Zion (Rev 21:10), where the Messiah would do battle with the gathered nations (14:1).

The seventh bowl "poured out . . . into the air" in 16:17 refers to judgment either over the air (7:1) or over the entire world in the "air realm" (the lowest of the heavens in Greco-Roman thought). In either case it reminds the reader of God's continuing sovereignty over the cosmos. With this judgment, the judgments are "done" (16:17), as at the final trumpet (10:7) and the consummation of God's plan for history implied in the new creation (21:6).

The thunder, lightning, and earthquake in 16:18 suggest a revelation of God's glory as at Sinai (Exod 19:16), but the earthquake also signals the end of the age (Rev 6:12; 11:13). The "great city" in 16:19 is Babylon, called both "Babylon the Great" (14:8; 17:5; 18:2) and "the great city" (17:18; 18:10, 16, 18–21). Babylon likely stands as a symbol for Rome here. The city drinks the cup of God's wrath, a fitting image for one portrayed as sexually unfaithful (Num 5:23–24).

The moving of islands and mountains in 16:20, as in 6:14, is merely part of the image of dramatic, cosmic judgment (Isa 42:15; Nah 1:5–6), especially appropriate to the end time (Ezek 38:19–20; Mic 1:3–4; Zech 14:5).

As in Revelation 8:7, the "hail" mentioned in 16:21 recalls the plague against Egypt's crops (Exod 9:18–34), severe enough to kill those caught out in it (Exod 9:19). In contrast with the repentant of Jerusalem (Rev 11:13), Babylon's inhabitants become harder and curse God all the more when judged (16:21), having learned nothing from their unrepentance during earlier plagues (v. 11). The world dies in its sin, unwilling to repent.

Application. God sends judgments not only to vindicate his oppressed people but also to get the world's attention and offer them the opportunity for repentance. That many people do not repent when they face judgment is not too surprising. One survivor of a plane crash recounts that he always expected people who were dying to cry out to God for mercy in their final moments, but noted that he heard many respond with cursing, following the habits they had spent their lives developing. Whether God acts with justice or mercy, some refuse to believe. They are like the wicked who took Lot's admonitions about impending judgment as jesting (Gen 19:14), and when Lot tried to prevent homosexual rape, he was accused of being judgmental (v. 9). That the world dies unrepentant in the face of God's judgments (Rev 16:9, 11, 21) reveals their obduracy and the depth of human rebellion against God.

REVELATION 17:1–18

Original Meaning

The Mother of Prostitutes (17:1–5). An angel bids John to "come" so that he may "show" him the judgment of the prostitute (v. 1). He then carries him "away in the Spirit" (v. 3; cf. Ezek 8:3), just as an angel will later show him the bride, the prostitute's antithesis (Rev 21:9), and carries him "away in the Spirit" (v. 10). Here he sees a high-class prostitute who has intoxicated the nations with her immorality (17:2) but is herself drunk with the blood of the saints (v. 6). The image is calculated to put the evil empire's true hideousness in perspective. The heads, horns, and blasphemous names link the beast with the dragon and an earlier vision of the beast (v. 3; cf. 12:3; 13:1).

The Old Testament prophets often portrayed Israel as a woman, either God's faithful bride when pure or an adulteress when unfaithful to him (Ezek 16:20). Revelation contrasts two cities, Jerusalem and Babylon, as a bride and prostitute respectively (Rev 17:5; 21:2). In two Old Testament instances, the "prostitute" is not Israel, Judah, or Jerusalem, but an evil world empire: Nineveh or Tyre. Nineveh will seduce the nations with her prostitution and witchcraft (Nah 3:4); Tyre will play the prostitute (Isa 23:17), yet her wealth will ultimately be laid up for the righteous (v. 18).

In Revelation 17:4 the woman is described as if she is a queen. Some background for the image of the queen here may be found in Jezebel's pagan repression of God's prophets; she is condemned for "immorality" in Revelation 2:20–22. But Babylon sits as queen in Isaiah 47:5–7. Literal Babylon also lived by "many waters" (Jer 51:13), though most prosperous ancient cities (including Rome on the Tiber) had water; the "waters" (Rev 17:1) representing the nations here probably imply Rome's international power.

The "kings of the earth" who have "committed adultery" with the prostitute (v. 2) will suffer along with her. Some ancient writers used the term *kings* for any of the wealthy, but the expression was even more suitable for the client-rulers who ruled their people as local agents of Roman authority (cf. also 17:12, 16, 18). Thus Babylon is Rome here; its economic and political power made Rome a vehicle of propagating international idolatry and immorality.

That the woman sits "on a scarlet beast" with "seven heads and ten horns" (v. 3) identifies the beast with the seven-headed, ten-horned red dragon (12:3) as well as with Rome (13:1); this identification is something like calling Rome "Satan incarnate."

In more ways than one, Babylon is dressed to kill. Her clothing here in purple and scarlet (v. 4) indicates her wealth, and entirely purple garments were associated especially with high-class prostitutes. Her gold, precious stones, and pearls further contribute to this picture of wealth (cf. 18:12, 16), but also help underpin the impending contrast with the city of God, which was built of gold, had streets of gold and gates of pearls, and had precious stones on its foundations (21:18–21).

No scarlet or gold adornments will protect this sexually unfaithful figure from ultimate rejection and murder by her own lovers (17:16). The name written on her forehead contrasts with the name written on Jesus in Revelation 19:12–13 (cf. 13:16) As the "mother of prostitutes" (17:5), she is the prototype for prostitutes, the prostitute par excellence after whom the entire profession is modeled—a world in rebellion against God.

Seven Heads as Mountains and Kings (17:6–11). As Rome made others drunk with her immorality (v. 2), she also became drunk herself with the blood of God's people (v. 6). The image of drinking blood was a hideous one for Jews (Lev 17:14) but not unprecedented in deliberately terrifying oracles (Ezek 39:19). By John's day many believers had been martyred under Nero but probably not many under Domitian (Rev 2:13); yet in the centuries that follow, many more will die martyrs' deaths. John here is astonished, inviting the angelic response (17:6–7).

As the angel explains the mystery of the woman and the beast (vv. 7–18), only the purest semblance of subtlety remains; in several different ways, the beast is identified with Rome. First, the woman sits on seven mountains (v. 9); Rome was regularly portrayed in this manner. Second, the leader of Babylon is apparently the new Nero (vv. 8–11); although Nero was associated also with the Parthians, as a ruler in the series of the seven he will rule Rome. Third, this empire rules over the other kings of the earth (v. 18), who rules the nations gathered around the sea as a maritime power (v. 15). Finally, "Babylon" was a standard Jewish title for Rome by this period.

Revelation's symbolism is so transparent that non-Christian Romans would have immediately understood its import and regarded the document as subversive. But in addition to seeing Rome, many commentators also view the great prostitute as the evil world system that in principle continues beyond Rome's fall.

Many commentators do see an allusion to Nero in verses 8–11. The invitation to discern wisdom in verse 9 recalls the same formula in 13:18; while that does not necessarily imply a connection between the identities of the two mysterious kings, it draws attention to the connection between two passages that on other grounds seem to address the same revived ruler. The fact that the seven heads can represent both seven mountains and seven kings suggests that Revelation freely reapplies its imagery in polyvalent ways. Perhaps John even expects hearers to nod knowingly at his application of seven heads to the "seven hills" of Rome.

Who are the seven kings (17:10)? Daniel's beast had ten horns and another one that cast down three horns, which leaves seven (Dan 7:20, 24), but even if this is part of John's reason for numbering seven kings, Revelation probably wants seven of them anyway. It is not at all difficult to find a pattern of rulers that accommodates the revived Nero image that John seems to employ here. The king who "is" (Rev 17:10) must be Domitian; five kings back from Domitian easily includes Nero.

The "eighth king" mentioned in verse 11 is one of the rulers from the first seven who returns, undoubtedly the head earlier mentioned as wounded as if to death but recovered (13:3). This constitutes a parody of Jesus's resurrection—just as the phrase "[who] once was, now is not, and will come" (17:8) parodies the Lord "who is, and who was, and who is to come" (1:4, 8; cf. 4:8). The thought of Nero's return would be no less terrifying to the current Roman regime that had supplanted it than to the Christians, who had suffered under Nero's purges before.

Ten Horns (17:12–18). The "ten horns" as "ten kings" (v. 12) comes from Daniel 7:7, 20, 24, and in Revelation may simply refer to the continuing imperial system. Most likely they are viewed as Rome's client kingdoms; in the end, Rome's empire will collapse and turn on the one with whom they have committed prostitution. They have a common purpose with the beast (Rev 17:13; cf. Ps 83:5), but they will prove as unfaithful as the prostitute with whom they have had intercourse (Rev 17:16). They will reign with the beast briefly, "for one hour" (v. 12), to wage war against the Lamb (vv. 13–14); that their time is brief is emphasized by the repetition of "one hour" in the depiction of how instantly Babylon will be destroyed (18:10, 17, 19).

Whoever the kings are, they will inevitably fall after their "hour" (17:16). "King of kings" was the title of the Babylonian king long before (Ezek 26:7) and remained the title of the Parthian ruler in John's day. But the king here is not the Parthian ruler; it is Jesus, and the kingdoms of the world will soon be his (Rev 11:15). The Roman king thought himself ruler of all the other kings of the earth (17:18), but this role ultimately belongs to Jesus.

Jesus is the mighty conquering king, and his army is described as "called, chosen, and faithful" (v. 14). The first two terms designate the certainty of their victory, for the eternal outcome is already determined in God's sovereign foreknowledge. "Faithful" may involve their perseverance to the death (2:10, 13); it contrasts sharply with the disloyalty of the earthly kings (17:16).

The imperial system and the rulers of allied nations will eventually devastate Rome herself (v. 16); the world's allegiances are self-interested, hence temporary. Revelation will develop some of these images further: they will bring her to "ruin" (cf. 18:17); they will "eat her flesh" (cf. the carrion birds in 19:18); she will be burned (cf. 18:8). The prostitute's stripping may allude to the way one may disgrace oneself after having drunk too much (Lam 4:21). Stripping was also a standard ancient penalty for sexual unfaithfulness (Ezek 16:37–38; Hos 2:3). Burning was the normal fate of conquered cities (e.g., Josh 6:24; 8:28) and the promised fate of the final antichrist figure (Dan 7:10–11), but it was also the penalty for the most serious acts of promiscuity (Gen 38:24; Lev 20:14; 21:9). God had long before used betrayal by unfaithful lovers to punish Israel's unfaithfulness (Jer 4:30; Hos 2:7). Thus the diabolic system will meet a fitting end.

Perhaps the most striking statement about God's great rule is the fact that he is sovereign even in their evil, using it for his own long-range purposes (Rev 17:17). He can use evil powers to judge other evil people (e.g., Isa 10:5–15; Joel 2:11). To be sure, Rome ruled the kings of the earth (Rev 17:18). But in a far more important way, God ruled Rome and its enemies (v. 17). God remains the Lord of history, and his purposes will be accomplished.

Application. One may object that the American church is not responsible for the behavior of its culture, but when buying and television viewing habits of Christians differ little from that of our secular neighbors, can we deny responsibility for supporting an industry that glorifies violence and killing? Early Christians refused to go into theaters to be entertained by watching other people suffer. It is said that in the fourth century a monk named Telemachus visited Rome and was horrified by a gladiatorial fight in the Colosseum. Hurling himself between the gladiators, he sought to prevent either of them from being killed, until he was killed instead. As he lay still on the ground, one spectator got up in disgust, followed by others, until everyone had gone. This marked the end of gladiatorial contests in Rome's Colosseum. Unfortunately, what early Christians avoided in public, modern Christians invite into their living rooms.

REVELATION 18:1–24

Original Meaning

The Death of Babylon (18:1–8). "Fallen! Fallen is Babylon the Great" in verse 2 recapitulates 14:8, both of which recall the dirge over Babylon in Isaiah 21:9. The lament is especially joined by those who committed immorality with the prostitute (Rev 18:9–10) and the merchants whose prosperity likewise depended on it (18:11–19). By contrast, the dwellers in heaven rejoice (18:20; 19:1–3).

Mention that Babylon will become a dwelling place of unclean birds (18:2) is a creative way of announcing judgment. When cities were depopulated, no one could prevent animals from taking over. Thus Rome's population decreased from as much as a million in John's day to some 30,000 after its fall a few centuries later.

In Rome's propaganda, circulated by local elites (whose own rank depended on Rome's patronage), Rome brought good to many peoples; but in a scathing critique, the prophet here announces that Rome relates to other peoples only for her own personal gain. Three times the text zeroes in on Babylon's "luxury" (18:3, 7, 9). That the nations will mourn her destruction only reveals the extent to which they have been intoxicated and bewitched by her exploitive seduction (14:8; 17:2; 18:3, 23). But John's audience will not lose sight of God's sovereignty, for the language here echoes Jeremiah (Jer 51:7; cf. Zech 12:2), inviting mourning over Babylon (Jer 51:8) and the flight of God's people (Jer 51:6, 45; cf. Zech 2:7).

Those in Revelation 18:3 who mourn for Babylon include both "kings" and "merchants," Rome's political and mercantile allies; John focuses more on the latter group (vv. 11–19) than the former (vv. 9–10). His oracles against Babylon (18:1–19:8) are full of allusions to the Old Testament prophets, including not only prophecies against Babylon but also the oracle against Tyre in Ezekiel 26–28. Revelation borrows heavily from Old Testament images concerning Tyre because Tyre (also a prostitute, see Isa 23:15–17) was an economic power like Rome. Tyre, which many considered invincible despite Ezekiel's prophecy, ultimately met a terrible end at the hands of Alexander the Great in 332 BC.

Not all John's audience is persecuted by the beast at this point; some of them in Laodicea and Sardis, in fact, are prospering as part of the same system that elsewhere is killing God's people. The summons to "come out" in verse 4 may thus include withdrawal from the economic arenas that required compromise with emperor worship or other forms of idolatry.

Those who remain in Babylon will share Babylon's judgment, so Jeremiah had long ago prophesied to his people to flee (Jer 51:6), though he meant these words as a prophecy of future judgment rather than a present warning (29:7). This warning to flee comes in the same context as the mention that Babylon was an intoxicating cup for the nations and would be mourned (51:7–8). God urges his people to leave Babylon because they have a better city (Rev 21:2–3).

The judgment comes in 18:5 when Babylon's sins are piled as high as heaven; sometimes God delays judgment only to wait until the measure for judgment over several generations is full (cf. Gen 15:16). Such prophecies indicate that those who profit from the sins of their ancestors will also share the judgment due their ancestors, as well as that due their own sin. Those who destroy Babylon are repaying her double for her sins (Rev 18:6). Babylon will drink from its own cup (14:8–10).

The message of judgment against Babylon's arrogance in 18:7 reflects the language of an ancient oracle against Babylon. Babylon claimed to be an eternal "queen," living luxuriously and denying that she would be widowed or lose her children (cf. Isa 47:7–8). Thus plagues will come on her all "in one day" (Rev 18:8; cf. Isa 47:9); she will no longer deceive by her sorcery (Rev 18:23; cf. Isa 47:9).

The extent to which Rome glorified itself may be illustrated by the spread of the worship of the emperor and the goddess Roma, the personification of Rome. As a means of propaganda and social control, Rome expected worship of what it stood for. But a day is coming in which honor will be taken from the arrogant; punishment will come, because the Lord God who judges is "mighty" (Rev 18:8).

Die Hard: Crying Kings, Mourning Merchants (18:9–20). In this dystopian prophecy, the kings mourn the destruction of the evil empire (vv. 9–10); by contrast, the righteous remnant of all peoples will participate in the new Jerusalem, and their kings will bring their glory into it (21:24). The worldly rulers in the provinces have reason to lament here, for they profited personally from Roman rule (cf. 18:3), some rising to power and status because of the emperor's patronage.

"Kings of the earth" of verse 9 refer to Rome's client-kings (17:2, 18; 18:3), though the language is adapted to the Old Testament. The Messiah would rule the kings (Ps 89:27); they would gather against God's Son and be shattered (Ps 2:2; Rev 19:19); and they became wealthy through Tyre's trade (Ezek 27:33). Their cry of "Woe! Woe!" here in Revelation 18:10 is repeated by the merchants in verses 16 and 19.

The longest laments come from the merchants, who profited

from Rome's trade. Rome lived luxuriously on the basis of inequitable trade policies toward its provinces. In less than one year the usurper Vitellius wasted the equivalent of more than twenty million dollars, mainly on extravagant foods.

Rome's insatiable appetites and seductive wealth lured provincials with money to invest in what they could export to Rome rather than the needs of their people. Landowners in Asia Minor used so much land for export items like wine that Asia's cities had to import grain from Egypt; consequently, the landowners profited, but everyone else paid higher prices for basic food needs.

Rome's commercial interests also propagated its pagan religion (13:17). The merchant's lament that no one now buys their cargoes (18:11) is ironic retribution for those who worshiped the beast that they might buy and sell (13:17)! Many of the specific items of the list in 18:12–13 reveal Revelation's critique of luxury goods.

John concludes this list climactically with "human beings sold as slaves" (v. 13). Because this period did not produce sufficient wars to supply Rome slaves directly, Rome had to locate other sources to maintain its needs. Many poor people in the empire discarded babies they felt unable to raise. While many of these were eaten by birds and dogs, many were also rescued for slavery; Asia Minor exported a large number to Rome, probably through the port of Ephesus.

This is the longest extant list of products from the Roman period. John adapts Ezekiel's list of forty products in which Tyre traded (Ezek 27:2–24), but he updates it accurately for the trade realities of first-century Rome. Whereas Ezekiel's list is arranged geographically, John's is arranged topically, by type of cargo. John focuses mostly on expensive imports.

Revelation explicitly condemns Rome for profiting at the expense of the empire; the prostitute is decked with her imports (Rev 18:16; cf. 17:4). Although much of Revelation 18 condemns Rome's luxury itself, partly for its arrogance (v. 7), oppression is also in view (v. 24).

Those who mourn in verse 17 include those who work on ships, but this probably implies the sorrow of ship owners as well. The merchants were the "great" people of the earth (v. 23), which ranked them directly below kings in Revelation's scheme of worldly status (cf. 6:15). Because transport was cheaper by sea, Rome imported most of the goods listed in 18:12–13 through its port of Ostia. Shipwrecks could ruin ship owners, but some grew wealthy enough to own many ships, reducing the risk. With the fall of Rome, however, both ship owners and their employees would be out of business, little better off than the agrarian peasants Rome cruelly exploited with high taxes.

For a city that had burned less than half a century earlier (blamed by the first Nero on Christians in AD 64), the threat of such burning as verse 18 describes would be a vivid one. Casting dust on one's head (v. 19) was a traditional act of mourning.

Vengeance for the People of God (18:21–24). A "mighty angel" (v. 21) announces a message in verses 21–24, but the thought of the narrative continues from what precedes. Verses 20 and 24 bracket this paragraph with the theme of vengeance for the blood of God's people, a biblical theme that appears elsewhere (Deut 32:43; 2 Kgs 9:7; Ps 79:10; Joel 3:21).

In contrast to the earth dwellers' mourning, heaven rejoices over Babylon's fall (Rev 18:20). That God will pronounce sentence on Babylon on behalf of the martyred saints, apostles, and prophets suggests the continuing witness and suffering of these groups until the time of the end. Believers have been tried and executed in the world's courts, but it is the world that is really on trial.

God commanded Jeremiah to hurl a stone into the middle of the Euphrates to symbolize the permanent fall of Babylon (Jer 51:63–64). Here in our section this becomes a millstone into the sea (Rev 18:21), probably recalling Jesus's warning that those who cause any little ones to stumble will be killed in this manner (Mark 9:42); the words in each case refer to the huge millstone turned by a mule, not the kind a woman might use by hand. Such drowning was considered a terrible fate, and with such a heavy weight there would be no escape.

The angelic announcement shows that Babylon, oppressor of God's people, reaps what it has sown against them, mentioning also the stilling of mills, newlyweds, and lamps (Rev 18:22–23). By contrast, new Jerusalem will need no earthly lamp, illumined by the glory of God and the Lamb (21:23; 22:5), and that city herself will be a bride (19:7; 21:2, 9; 22:17). That the harpists will no longer be heard in Babylon (18:22) may contrast with the harpists heard in heaven (14:2). God's people struggled to use their harps in captivity (Ps 137:2–4), but the new temple city will prove a fitting place for harps (cf. 2 Chr 9:11; 20:28; 29:25).

The mention of "magic spell[s]" here in Revelation 18:23 is significant. Sorcery is linked with prostitution in the description of the biblical Jezebel (2 Kgs 9:22), a model for the prostitute in Revelation (2:20). More to the point, Babylon, who thought herself a queen and denied her impending widowhood (18:7), vainly thought to protect herself by sorceries (cf. Isa 47:9, 12). But if the prophecy against Babylon in Isaiah 47 supplies the concept, the oracle against Nineveh the prostitute supplies the language (Nah 3:4). Magic was a major practice in Asia Minor, especially Ephesus (Acts 19:13–19). But Revelation warns that anyone who practices it will be judged (Rev 21:8; 22:15; cf. 9:21).

But Babylon's greatest sin was "the blood of prophets and of God's holy people" (18:24), the witnesses of Jesus (11:3, 7; 17:6).

The addition of "all who have been slaughtered on the earth" (18:24) may refer to the prophets and saints, but it may also point beyond them to the broader critique of Rome's economic injustice (suggested in 18:5–19). Clearly in this context God is concerned about the crushing of Egypt's peasants, the brutality of slavery, and other methods by which Rome exploited most of the empire. John as a Jew likewise must have shared the pain of his people crushed by the Romans in AD 70, a bloody conquest the Romans widely commemorated on coins and by taxing all Jews throughout the empire. But given the parallel in language with verse 20, the climax of Rome's sin was its martyrdom of God's messengers.

Application. God warns his people to "come out" of Babylon (18:4). This is a call to holiness, but we must not misunderstand holiness. Holiness is not simply a matter of avoiding certain kinds of activities, as some traditional churches have emphasized; holiness is separation from the world to God. Thus one can express holiness by immersing oneself in God's word rather than in the world's values emphasized on social media; or by turning down a better-paying job because someone felt God wanted him or her to work in a different place, perhaps among the poor. Such holiness may cost us our place in Babylon and much more.

"Come out of her" also reminds us that we Christians may share in the judgments on our society, despite our forgiveness for individual sins. Nations and institutions as corporate entities can stand under judgment; we who participate in such institutions share in their responsibility before God unless we explicitly repudiate our complicity with them and declare their activities wrong. Most of all, the summons to "come out of her" reminds believers that we belong to a different city, whose true wealth is greater than Babylon's glory for which our neighbors strive.

REVELATION 19:1–21

Original Meaning

The Prostitute and the Bride (19:1–10). Most early Jewish readers, even those who used only Greek, would know that "Hallelujah!" (19:1, 3, 4, 6) meant "Praise Yahweh!" in a particularly emphatic form. Thus, the mourning over Babylon in 18:2 is purely a literary device; members of the audience that identify with the world and what it values may mourn (18:9, 11), but those who identify with heaven and what it values will rejoice (19:1, 3–5).

In a context of people hailing a conqueror, "salvation" (or "deliverance," v. 1) can refer to triumph (cf. 7:10; 12:10); the prostitute was stained with the blood of murdered believers (18:24), and God had exacted vengeance for them (19:2).

God's judgment does not simply stop Babylon's oppression; he avenges her incomprehensible injustices. Babylon, the city of the world system, is the new Sodom (11:8). The smoke of her death rises forever (19:3), suggesting eternal torment (14:11).

By judging the world system, God has begun to reign (19:6). Presumably among those who now join in triumphant praise are the martyrs, especially if the sound of "rushing waters" in our verse 6 recalls 14:2. All God's "servants"—that is, those who fear him—offer praise in verse 5; this group is also coextensive, at least in principle, with the martyrs mentioned in verse 2, because all true followers of Christ are potential martyrs. This group explicitly cuts across class lines, for like the world (6:15; 13:16; 19:18; 20:12), they include "both great and small" (19:5; cf. 11:18).

The "wedding supper" mentioned in 19:7–9 was a frequent figure for the coming messianic era. God had promised a splendid banquet, when he would destroy death and wipe away the tears and shame of his people (Isa 25:6–8). Some Jewish teachers even decided that Leviathan, the great many-headed serpent, would be slain (Isa 27:1) and served as the food at the messianic banquet. If this idea was pervasive when Revelation was written, it may be relevant that the marriage supper of the Lamb is contrasted with the great supper of God, in which birds feast on the carcasses of the wicked (Rev 19:17–18).

What does Revelation mean by the bride being "ready" (v. 7)? To make herself ready for the wedding a bride would bathe herself and adorn herself in special array. Here the special array is the "righteous acts of God's holy people," who comprise the bride (v. 8; cf. Isa 61:10). While white linen robes were appropriate for worship (Rev 4:4), they appear here also as appropriate for marriage.

The "fine linen" of God's people (19:8) contrasts with the fine linen of the prostitute (18:12, 16). High-class prostitutes were known for their elaborate garb, but God's faithful are dressed in wedding apparel beautiful to the groom. Presumably the prospective bride is also portrayed as believers in fine linen coming with Jesus in 19:14; by contrast, Jesus himself is clothed in a bloody robe (v. 13), for the task of just retribution will precede the wedding celebration.

That John begins to worship the messenger in verse 10 is unsurprising; his message is easily confused with God's (21:5–6). Yet the "fellow servant" here is not a fellow mortal but is an angel (cf. 22:8–9). Christians and angels have different functions, but both may proclaim God's message. The emphatic demand that God alone is to be worshiped challenges all forms of idolatry, including those offered the emperor in the name of loyalty to the state.

Most significantly, the angel declares that he is simply acting as God's agent (19:10b). The prophetic Spirit empowers those who speak the message about Christ; all believers are thus potential prophets, anointed with God's Spirit to speak his message in his place. The present activity of the Spirit in testifying about Jesus throughout Revelation would attest his identity as the true Lord. For those who too readily believed any prophecies without seeking to evaluate true from false and thus accepted messages from "Balaam" (2:14) and "Jezebel" (2:20), the reminder that true prophecy exalts Jesus (19:10) would be essential.

Holy War (19:11–21). If God's messenger in 19:10 is the wrong one to worship, verses 11–16 abruptly and immediately reveals the proper object of worship. As God's "Word" (v. 13), Jesus is "Faithful and True" (v. 11); earlier in Revelation "faithful" alluded to faithfulness in testifying to God's truth regardless of the cost (1:5; 2:10, 13). Moreover, Jesus "judges and wages war" (19:11). The former attribute belongs to God (6:10; 11:18; 18:8, 20; 19:2; 20:12) and to the Messiah, who will strike the wicked with his mouth (Isa 11:4; cf. Rev 19:15). The latter is the image of the end-time holy warrior, a final response to the worshipers of the beast (13:4). All along God has allowed the beast to make war with his people on earth (11:7; 12:17; 13:7); but when the right time comes, they will make war on the Lamb himself and be destroyed (17:14; 19:19; 20:8).

"The armies of heaven" with Jesus here at 19:14 execute no violence themselves; Jesus is the mighty warrior who strikes the wicked (vv. 11, 15, 21). Biblical prophets predicted God himself as the ultimate holy warrior (Isa 42:13; Hab 3:11–14; Zeph 3:17), cloaked for war (Isa 59:17), including the blood of the winepress as here (Isa 63:3); clearly Jesus assumes this divine role here.

John describes Jesus as riding on a white horse (Rev 19:11), as do his hosts (v. 14). Such horses were appropriate mounts for rulers, important officials, and conquerors entering Rome in triumph, but the idea of a "King of kings" (cf. v. 16) mounted on a white horse may be drawing on the image of the Parthian king. If Rome fears a Parthian invasion, how much more should it fear the true Lord from heaven.

Jesus's eyes "like a blazing fire" in verse 12a indicate divinity and fury, and his "many crowns" indicate that he is ruler over all the kings of the world. Moreover, Jesus has a hidden name (v. 12b). Perhaps this name is a secret only to the world, already accepted among God's people but revealed to all humanity at Jesus's coming—the "Word of God" (v. 13) or "King of kings and Lord of lords" (v. 16). His cloak "dipped in blood" in verse 13 draws from Isaiah 63, indicating that the world will finally realize at his coming that Jesus himself is God. The blood is from those slain from his winepress, the whole world, as in Isaiah 63:2. The army that overcame the beast by martyrdom (Rev 14:1–5) will now share Christ's final triumph (19:15).

Because the sword in verse 15 issues from Jesus's mouth, some interpreters apply it to an eschatological war of ideologies before Jesus's return; while such ideological conflict is likely, the allusion to Isaiah 11:4 and to Psalm 2:9 probably demands more than this in this passage (cf. 2 Thess 2:8), for it can also signify literal bloodshed (Isa 34:5; Jer 12:12; 47:6).

Jesus's title "KING OF KINGS AND LORD OF LORDS" in Revelation 19:16 may recall the title of the Parthian ruler, as noted above. Sometimes called merely the "great king," he was also called "king of kings." Ancient Judaism applied the title almost exclusively to God. Revelation applies the title consistently to Jesus (17:14; 19:16), the true ruler over the earth's other kings (1:5).

Whereas believers will partake of the promised messianic banquet (19:9), the wicked will be the banquet on which scavengers feed (v. 17). Their blood will flow as if from a winepress (v. 15), borrowing an earlier biblical image (Isa 63:2–3). The image of carrion birds feasting on the flesh of corpses killed in battle was a familiar one to ancient readers (1 Sam 17:44–46). Given common Greek views of one's image enduring in the realm of departed spirits, the only fate worse than death itself was death followed by lack of burial, in which one's remains are devoured by animals. Many of Revelation's original audience would recognize the clear and immediate source of the language of this passage: God invited beasts and birds to devour the flesh of the army that opposed him in Ezekiel 39:17–20.

John next describes God in Revelation 19:20 as hurling the leaders of Satan's army into "the fiery lake of burning sulfur." This burning sulfur may allude to the fate of Sodom (Gen 19:24), but the punishment in this lake of fire is eternal (Rev 14:10) and contrasts with the sea of glass in God's presence (4:6).

Application. This passage reminds us that the Spirit empowers us to speak for God. That the testimony about Jesus also implies prophetic empowerment by the Spirit has important implications for us today. Some Christians rank the anointing of other Christians based on their possession of particular spiritual gifts, but Christ gave all of us his Spirit to testify about him (Acts 1:8). Thus, every Christian who witnesses about Jesus experiences in some measure the empowerment of the Holy Spirit.

REVELATION 20:1–15

Original Meaning

The Thousand Years and First Resurrection (20:1–10). Interpreters of this chapter are divided into three broad schools of thought: *premillennialists*, who believe Jesus will return to establish a specific thousand-year kingdom; *amillennialists*, who generally believe that the thousand-year kingdom is symbolic for the present age; and *postmillennialists*, who believe that Christians help establish the thousand-year kingdom on earth prior to Jesus's return. Most evangelicals today are premillennialists or amillennialists.

As amillennial scholars note, it is difficult to interpret most of Revelation as a continuous chronological account; the seals, trumpets, and vials appear to be parallel in their inception and completion. Revelation emphasizes future eschatology, but it is not without some "realized eschatology" (implying blessings of the future available in the present). Further, many of the expressions about the end in chapter 20 plainly parallel previous descriptions of the end in Revelation. But these parallels may suggest merely that a later end repeats what was unfinished in a former one, if other factors warrant. Indeed, other factors do favor reading this thousand years as following the tribulation in the narrative plan of the book.

First, the binding of Satan during the thousand years hardly matches Satan's furious deceptive and murderous activity during the present era (12:12–13; 13:11–15; 20:2–3). Second, the saints have already been martyred, suggesting that the tribulation period precedes the millennium (20:4). Third, the resurrection of the righteous is parallel to and contrasted with the rest of the dead returning to life after the thousand years (vv. 4–6), suggesting a bodily rather than symbolic resurrection. Fourth, the beast and false prophet are already in the lake of fire before the millennium (v. 10); likewise, the devil cannot deceive "anymore" (v. 3), suggesting a suspension of his deceptive work that transpired from 12:9 on. Finally, in hindsight we recognize that the period between Jesus's first and second comings is longer than one thousand years, but in John's own day such a figure for the intermediate period must have seemed too long (1:3).

The idea of an intermediate, messianic kingdom appears frequently in early Jewish literature (see 4 Ezra 7:28–29; 1 Enoch 91:8–17). Although not dominant, some of these portraits of the end-time employ schemes that use thousand-year periods, sometimes with the seventh thousand years as a final Sabbath period. While John probably employs such background, to some degree he may also be interpreting the events according to their sequence in Ezekiel 36–48: resurrection and kingdom (Ezek 37); Gog from Magog (chs. 38–39); and the new temple and city (chs. 40–48). But the correspondence with Ezekiel is not exact or complete by itself; Ezekiel 37 lacks an explicit millennium, and Revelation 21–22 lacks a physical temple.

Premillennialists find in the typical intermediate period of apocalyptic literature confirmation that John likewise sees an intermediate period here; one can also argue for some delay of the final consummation in passages like Isaiah 24:22 and Daniel 7:12.

God delegates the "key" to the abyss to an angel here in Revelation 20:1. The idea of "binding" an evil angel (v. 2) appears regularly in Jewish texts. But Revelation draws on the more familiar use in apocalyptic texts, in which a spirit or evil angel is decisively bound until the day of judgment. In such texts, bound angels can also be thrown into the abyss. Once Satan is bound in the abyss, the angel "seals" it (v. 3), preventing any chance of his escape; Satan cannot act during that period as he does in the present.

The martyrs of verse 4 died "because of the word of God" and "because of their testimony for Jesus"; suffering for this cause is such a recurrent motif in Revelation (1:9; 6:9; 12:11) that it constitutes a virtual invitation to John's audience to participate in paying the price. Beheading believers who refused to worship the beast or his image recalls 13:15.

Recent chapters repeated the refrain of the blood of the righteous (16:6; 17:6; 18:24); Jesus's followers conquer the way he did, through death (3:21; cf. 5:5–6). But while the present world executes judgment against God's people, they will rule the future world (5:10)—both the "thousand years" (20:4, 6) and eternally (22:5). The righteous oppressed sought vindication (6:10); here it has finally come.

In contrast to the promise of the "first resurrection" is the "second death" (20:6); the resurrection to damnation is so horrible that its life is called "death" as opposed to the eternal life inherited by believers.

After the thousand years, Satan will be loosed to rouse Gog and Magog against the camp of the saints (vv. 8–9); in accordance with his nature, he gathers the nations for war again (16:16; 19:19). This army is numerically "like the sand on the seashore" (20:8), a common figure in the Hebrew Bible for saying a group of people are innumerable.

John draws this image from Ezekiel, but whereas in Ezekiel Gog is ruler of Magog, here Gog and Magog together merely symbolize all the nations, the nations "in the four corners of the earth" (v. 8).

Revelation may draw on the warning that God will cast fire on Magog in Ezekiel 39:6, and especially draws on the threat of 38:22—namely, that God will cast fire, hailstones, and burning sulfur on this army. This description portrays the fate of end-time Magog like Sodom. The point in Ezekiel is that God will be glorified through their destruction (38:16, 23) and will defend his people (vv. 14–16).

The holy city will be unwalled; otherwise, the inhabitants would spill out of the walls because there will be so many of them (Zech 2:4); thus God himself will be a "wall of fire" around her (Zech 2:5; cf. 9:8). But the language of a "camp" of the saints (Rev 20:9) probably alludes to Israel's experience in the exodus or as a unit of war. This reminds John's audience that even during the thousand years God's people must remain vigilant until their final victory, a reminder that invites even greater vigilance for believers in the present time.

Final Judgment (20:11–15). The scene of battle judgment gives way to the final judgment before God's throne. That there is "no place" for earth and sky (v. 11) reveals how dramatic is God's appearance as judge, and it paves the way for the new heavens and earth (21:1). The sight of God will banish creation; but in the new creation, his servants will see his face (22:4–5).

The "books" in 20:12 also contribute to this picture of dread for the wicked. The books here reflect those of Daniel 7:10. In Revelation 20:13–14, both "death and Hades" are judged. "Hades" is the realm of the dead, and those remaining in it are those not raised at the first resurrection (20:4–6), hence the damned. That the sea must give up its dead answers the concern of many people in antiquity, including some Jews contemplating the resurrection, concerning the fate of the unburied.

The stark picture of the banishment of the wicked to a place of fire is meant to grip the hearer's attention, but it would not surprise an early Jewish-Christian reader. Revelation prefers a graphic, oxymoronic picture of a "lake of fire" (vv. 14–15), over which God's people have come victorious. Although fire can communicate instant annihilation rather than eternal torment, earlier Christian tradition portrayed an unquenchable burning (Matt 3:12; Mark 9:43; Luke 3:17), and Revelation elsewhere speaks of eternal torment (14:10–11), implied also in this context for the lake of fire (20:10).

Application. The passage reveals that we may be outnumbered (20:8), but in the end God's purposes will triumph, and he will keep the church from being ultimately defeated by the world's evil oppressors. We can stand firm against evil even when the battle appears futile; victory belongs to the Lord.

The presumption of nations gathered against God is immediately revealed when he destroys them. Through much of history, God allows the suffering of his people; but this is a sign of his merciful restraint and sovereign purposes, not of his impotence. When he wills, he can slay his enemies in a moment.

Some skeptics have charged Christians with a hope that is merely "pie in the sky"—that is, with living for an uncertain hope while neglecting issues of pressing concern in the present life. Biblical hope, however, summons us to lives of holiness and love for neighbor in the present. The heavenly books in this passage remind us that the deeds we do in this life really do matter in an ultimate sense.

This passage, like most others in Revelation, provides preachers and teachers an adequate transition for what many evangelicals have called an "altar call." The knowledge of final judgment calls all to repentance in the present, for someday—when it is no longer possible to ignore God—it will be too late to repent.

REVELATION 21:1–22:5

Original Meaning

A New Creation (21:1–8). Two models of new creation—renewal and replacement—existed in early Judaism, but given such factors as the lack of any sea, Revelation seems to use at least the image of the latter. The lack of sea may have been extrapolated from the fact that Isaiah's promise mentioned only the new heavens and new earth, not any seas, but the absence of the sea probably also serves some other purpose. Within Revelation's own context, the drying of the sea may signify an end to any further need for mercantile trade (18:17); God will supply all the needs of his people (22:2). In the whole context of Revelation, the disappearance of the sea may well spell an end to the "many waters" of the followers of the beast (17:1, 15) that arose from the sea (13:1).

The new Jerusalem (21:2) had become a familiar Jewish expectation. That this city would descend from heaven is not surprising (Gal 4:26; Heb 11:16; 12:22). The point of its descent from heaven here is that the city comes from God, not by any human abilities.

Jewish people regularly called Jerusalem by the title "the Holy City," as here (Rev 21:2); God renews a holy city once defiled (11:2). Just as Babylon in Revelation represents the people of Rome and not simply its location, and just as "Jerusalem" in the Old Testament usually included the people and not simply the site, "new Jerusalem" (21:2) undoubtedly includes the people of God. This city is the "bride" (v. 2), just as we know the church is (2 Cor 11:2; Eph 5:23). Jerusalem's bridal adornment here is appropriate. Probably both Christ and the church play roles in "preparing" her for her marriage; 19:7 uses the active voice for the bride preparing herself, whereas 21:2 uses the passive voice.

The promise that God "will dwell" (*skēnoō*) with his people (v. 3) was a frequent Jewish hope that ultimately points back to a promise of God's covenant for Israel (Exod 25:8; 29:45–46; Lev 26:12; 1 Kgs 6:13; Ezek 37:27; Zech 2:10–11), including in the future temple (Ezek 43:7, 9). This promise is spelled out more clearly when the text reveals that new Jerusalem is a temple city (Rev 21:22) and is shaped like the Most Holy Place (v. 16). This will be the most explicit "tabernacling" of God with humanity since the incarnation, though deceased believers in heaven have already experienced it (7:15). This promise was expected for end-time Israel, but here all who "are victorious" receive it (21:7).

Emphasizing the presence of representatives from all nations fulfills the promise that many nations will become God's people and that he will live among them (Zech 2:11; cf. Isa 19:25).

John describes the new creation not to satisfy our curiosity about the future but to comfort us about the eventual change in the nature of this world. The passing of "the old order of things" (Rev 21:4), including suffering, directly echoes the new-creation promise of Isaiah 65:16–17; the deliverance from both tears and death echoes Isaiah 25:8. This passing of mourning is in stark contrast to the fate of the wicked (Rev 18:7–8). John is then again in 21:5 commanded to write because these words are "trustworthy and true" (cf. 19:9).

The announcement "It is done" in 21:6 suggests that God's purposes in history have come to their conclusion because he has created a people with whom he will live forever. By declaring that he is "the Alpha and the Omega" here, God reminds us that he is able to accomplish what he promises. By offering water from the spring of life, he recalls 7:17; this promise anticipates the fuller description offered in 22:1, 17. Offering this drink "without cost" (21:6; cf. 22:17) probably echoes Isaiah 55:1.

By itself suffering does not sufficiently qualify one for the kingdom; rather, one must overcome (Rev 21:7). In the context of Revelation, overcoming addresses such varied tests as compromise with the world's values (2:14, 20), dependence on our own strength (3:17), and persecution (2:10); but persecution is the test that Revelation particularly emphasizes for the end-time witnesses of Jesus (12:11; 13:7). Jewish texts often speak of inheriting the world to come, a common figure of speech among early Christians as well. Here in 21:7 the overcomers inherit "all this"—that is, the new and sorrowless world God has prepared for them.

The promise that God will be his people's God and they will be his people is the fundamental component of the ancient covenant formula (Gen 17:8; Exod 6:7; Lev 11:45; Num 15:41; Deut 29:13). The prophets rehearse the same covenant formula (Jer 7:23; Ezek 11:20; Zech 8:8). But our text slightly adapts it: God will be the overcomer's God, and the overcomer will be his own child (Rev 21:7). God had earlier declared Israel his children (Exod 4:22), but here in the end-time he publicly honors individual believers as his own children.

All these promises culminate, however, in a warning: those who fail to overcome, who prove disobedient, will experience the "second death" (Rev 21:8). The NIV's "they will be consigned" is more literally, "they will have their part [or share] in"; this is the language of inheritance, a deliberate contrast with the inheritance of the overcomers in verse 7. The "fiery lake" (v. 8) is the destination for all who will not inherit the new Jerusalem and the new creation of verses 1–6. "The second death" contrasts with the abolition of death in the new Jerusalem (v. 4). Those who begin as believers must overcome; apostates, like those who never professed Christ to begin with, will be lost.

Materials and Dimensions of the New Jerusalem (21:9–21). In verse 9 the angel invites John to see the bride, Jerusalem. Babylon was in the desert; Jerusalem descends from heaven. That John views the descent of the heavenly Jerusalem from a mountain may represent an ideal location for viewing this sight (Ezek 40:2; cf. Matt 4:8). But the mountain itself may point to the end-time Mount Zion (Rev 14:1; cf. Isa 2:2–3), thus contrasting with the seven hills on which Babylon sits (Rev 17:9).

John saw a glorious city in his vision (21:10–11). The older Jewish Christians among John's audience, who remembered the splendor of the temple destroyed in AD 70, would be touched by a description of new Jerusalem's glorious future.

That names were written on the gates and foundation stones (vv. 12–14) would not have struck ancient hearers as unusual; wealthy supporters who funded city building projects often had their names inscribed on them. Yet the benefactors named on the new Jerusalem were not wealthy supporters but those whose lives provided foundations for God's people. The presence of both the twelve tribes and the twelve apostles emphasizes the link and continuity between ancient Israel and Christ's church.

The gates represent the twelve tribes of Israel (cf. Ezek 48:31–34). Many Roman towns had three gates providing entrance on one side, but new Jerusalem provides such access on all sides, implying that it welcomes people from all directions.

In biblical tradition, twelve stones pointed to the twelve tribes (Josh 4:3–9); in the high priest's breastplate in Exodus 28:17–21 they are specifically inscribed with the names of the tribes. Here, however, the foundation stones refer to the twelve apostles of the Lamb, in keeping with the Christian image of the new temple's true foundations (Eph 2:20; Heb 11:10; 1 Pet 2:5).

The "measuring rod" mentioned in Revelation 21:15 is an important stage device that allows John to recognize the supernatural enormity of the city (v. 16). It recalls the measuring of Jerusalem (Zech 2:1–2) or the temple (Ezek 40–41) in the Hebrew Bible and reminds John's oppressed audience that the persecuted remnant whose measuring began in Revelation 11:1–2 is the prototype for the glorious future city. Ezekiel's new Jerusalem was 18,000 cubits all around; John's is nearly two thousand times larger. The symbolic numbers portray this city as the eternal dwelling of God's people.

The new Jerusalem is not merely square; it is cubic, despite the utter incongruity with all human imagination of a city 1,500 miles high. The cubic shape recalls the Most Holy Place (1 Kgs 6:20); not only will the entire city be like a temple, but it will be like the Most Holy Place. It is thus unsurprising that the city does not need a temple other than the Lord himself (Rev 21:22). Believers will experience God's presence in its full intensity, as never before.

The dimensions of the city are supernatural (vv. 15–16), contrasting starkly with the pretensions of the doomed "great city," Babylon (18:10, 16, 18–21). The purpose of the numbers is not literal so much as to emphasize the city's future glory and to suggest that, when history is complete, God's remnant through the ages will not prove as small as it now appears to persecuted churches of John's generation. The height is the most dramatic feature. What humanity could not accomplish in Babel—a city to the heavens (Gen 11:4)—God grants as an overwhelming gift.

Why does Jerusalem need a wall in the eternal era of peace? Certainly the purpose is not protection or to keep anyone out, since no one will ever close its gates (Rev 21:25). Ancient cities of substantial size always had walls, so one is needed in the description of the greatest of cities. Further, if there were no walls, there would be no description of the splendid gates! Without these gates, Revelation would miss an opportunity to reapply biblical symbolism in its specifically Christocentric way.

That the walls are of "jasper" (v. 18) means that they reflect God's glory (4:3), perhaps the most important feature of the city (21:19, 23); Isaiah had promised walls of precious stones (Isa 54:12). This jasper was "clear as crystal" (Rev 21:11), like the heavenly waters (4:6; 22:1), to allow the glory of God to shine through. That the city is of gold may reflect images from the original paradise (Gen 2:11–12) but more likely reflects the commonness of what is now regarded as wealth (cf. Rev 3:18), a stark contrast with the mere gold decorations of "wealthy" Babylon (17:4; 18:12, 16). That the gold is like glass suggests again God's glory (4:6; 15:2).

The "precious stone" of the foundations of the city (21:19–20) recall God's promise in Isaiah 54:11–12. John then lists the stones—derived from the priest's breastplate (Exod 28:17–20) and from Tyre's wealthy decorations (Ezek 28:13), omitting some of each to arrive at twelve but including nine stones that appear in both lists. Not only is this a priestly city (suggested by the allusion to the high priest's breastplate), but this city of economic sufficiency and justice contrasts sharply with Tyre, an economic exploiter. Jerusalem's true clothing puts to shame the ostentation of Babylon (Rev 17:4). The twelve gates of "pearls" here in 21:21 again contrasts sharply with the gaudy but inferior pearl decorations of Babylon (17:4; 18:12, 16).

Revelation's comment on the "great street" (21:21) is also significant. Those who remembered the first Jerusalem (destroyed probably over two decades earlier) might remember its major north-south and east-west streets (from ten to thirteen meters wide); but the vision of the new Jerusalem is far greater.

God's Presence and Glory in the New Paradise (21:22–22:5). The lack of a future temple in John's vision is not really a repudiation of Ezekiel's vision of a future temple in a new Jerusalem (Ezek 41–48); rather, the new city itself is wholly a temple, the dwelling place of God (Rev 21:3, 16, 22). God lives among his people, and they live in him—a present reality, taken to a deeper level in the age to come.

Not only will the city have no temple, but it will require neither sun nor moon (v. 23), which have been abolished; not only the city but the entire created order will walk in explicit dependence on God. The new Jerusalem is full of continual light.

Whereas some texts warn that God will destroy the nations (Isa 17:13–14), other texts indicate the nations will remain in the end time (Isa 2:4) and will serve God's people (Isa 45:14). Whereas some texts exclude gentiles from the future Jerusalem (Isa 52:1), in others they will bring their wealth into Jerusalem (Isa 45:14). This is the most positive vision of the future possible: whereas gentiles once trampled the temple city (Rev 11:2), now they honor it. The nations walk in the light of Jerusalem (21:24).

In Revelation the gifts that the nations bring are not simply wealth but "glory" (v. 24 [NIV "splendor"], 26); they offer their glory to God in light of God's greater glory (v. 23). They can enter the city, however, only because their names are in "the Lamb's book of life" (v. 27).

That the gates of the new Jerusalem are never closed (v. 25) suggests unlimited access. New Jerusalem welcomes all (22:17) and has no enemies to fear. But the promised joy of the new Jerusalem serves as a warning as well as a comfort, for not all will inhabit it (21:27).

"Then the angel showed me" (22:1) probably continues the vision of the new Jerusalem. It may be from a different perspective, but this paragraph continues elements of the previous description. In any case, 22:1–5 climaxes John's vision of a new creation.

That a "river" (22:1) flows from God's throne may reflect biblical images of water flowing from the future Zion (Ezek 47:1–12; Zech 14:8). This crystal river directly from God's throne replaces the earlier crystal sea (Rev 4:6). All strong cities must have their own water supply, and new Jerusalem has an eternal supply.

The river "of the water of life" (22:1) probably evokes the rivers of the first paradise (Gen 2:10), especially given the conjunction of this image with the "tree of life" (Rev 22:2). "Paradise" (2:7) literally meant "garden," and paradise-like images regularly included rivers and fruitful trees. Note that 2:7 also mentions the "tree of life." This could include the tree of life mentioned in the original paradise. Revelation's tree comes from the various fruit trees for healing on either side of the temple river in Ezekiel 47:12; unlike trees whose fruits were seasonal, these trees bear fruit every month.

Whereas shops often lined the main streets of ancient cities, Revelation presents a different kind of provision. To Ezekiel's "healing" Revelation adds, "of the nations" (Rev 22:2), emphasizing again that God's end-time community includes peoples from all nations grafted into his city (cf. 7:9).

The specific language of abolishing the curse (22:3) refers to Zechariah 14:11. But in this context about paradise, abolishing the curse also evokes a reversal of the fall (Gen 3:14, 17).

That his servants will "serve" him (22:3) may imply worship; this is a common Christian meaning of *latreuō*, the Greek word for "serve" used here; the other use of this word in Revelation also locates this worship in the heavenly temple (7:15).

The righteous "will see [God's] face" (22:4)—a statement that takes them beyond the vision granted to Moses, God's servant (Exod 33:20). God's children will live with him (Rev 21:3) and see his face and its glory (22:4–5). Such light obliterates the night (21:25; 22:5). The shining of God's face on people, used metaphorically, referred to his favor (Num 6:25), but when used as an end-time image connotes far more experientially than in the present world. The image of new Jerusalem's future glory is probably related to seeing God's face. When Moses saw God's glory, he reflected it (Exod 34:30).

Application. The time for adorning ourselves with "righteous acts" (Rev 19:8) is now. Even though Revelation emphasizes the new Jerusalem as a future city, it is being built in the present. If the character of Babylon is evident in the world around us, the glory of God's presence among us should be revealed at least in the way we live. In John's theology, God's glory is revealed in us through how we treat one another (John 13:34–35; 17:22–23; 1 John 4:12). In New Testament theology, though hope directs our attention toward the future, it also has implications for how we live in the present (Rom 12:12; Col 1:4–5; Titus 2:12–13; 1 John 3:3). The most faithful of John's audience (esp. in Smyrna and Philadelphia) would have seen themselves as a persecuted minority, but Revelation also summons them to see themselves as heirs of the future. If we see ourselves according to the destiny to which God has called us, we will act accordingly.

REVELATION 22:6–21

Original Meaning. The God of the prophets has spoken once again to "his servants the things that must soon take place," and "these words are trustworthy and true" (v. 6). Most of this verse repeats the announcement in 1:1 that God had sent his message by his angel, just as the promise of his coming and his blessing on the obedient in 22:7 echo 1:3, and "I, John" in 22:8 echoes the narrative introduction in 1:9. Because ancient writers often bracketed their writings or portions of their writings, these echoes are a way of letting the hearers know that the book is nearly at its end.

Those who heed this true prophecy will be rewarded, for Jesus is "coming soon" (22:7) to reward each according to one's deeds (v. 12). The promise of "coming soon" frames verses 7–12 and in a broader way verses 7–20, forming a recurrent theme of the closing section. Jesus's coming recalls 1:7 and the fuller description in 19:11–16; "soon" recalls 1:3; 2:16; 3:11. Now in 22:8, John mentions his own name for the first time since chapter 1 (1:1, 4, 9), and for the same reason: to provide eyewitness testimony, much as the beloved disciple does in the Gospel of John (John 19:35). That the prophetic angel refuses John's worship (Rev 22:8–9; cf. 19:10) reminds the reader that God and the Lamb alone are worthy of worship. Thus, by way of contrast, John once again underlines the deity of Christ emphasized elsewhere in the book.

God instructed Daniel to seal up his prophecy (Dan 12:4, 9), because the time of the end was a long time away (8:26). By contrast, Revelation must remain unsealed (22:10), for it addresses events that had already begun in that period. The time appears so near that each may as well continue in his or her current behavior (v. 11), receiving the reward that is due (v. 12). This passage probably also indicates that the end-time is at hand, because Daniel had spoken about the wicked continuing in their wickedness (Dan 12:10); the wicked will fulfill their negative role in God's plan in history.

In practice, however, God is not inviting anyone to continue in rebellion; rather, the language is ironic, serving the rhetorical function of challenging unrepentance, as often in the biblical prophets (Isa 29:9; Jer 44:25; Amos 4:4). God invites those who will to hear and those who choose rebellion to face the consequences of their rebellion (cf. Ezek 3:27). John would agree with his Jewish contemporaries, however, that once the end comes, the Lord will justly award each person according to what he or she has merited (Rev 22:12; cf. 20:12).

Where most of John's non-Christian Jewish contemporaries will find his words uncomfortable, however, is his claim that Jesus will be the judge on the final day (22:12), a role non-Christian Judaism reserved in its most exclusive sense for God. Those who catch the allusion to Isaiah will recognize even more plainly that Jesus claims to be divine here, for God promised to come with his reward ("his reward is with him") in Isaiah 40:10 and 62:11. Revelation reinforces this implication of Christ's deity in 22:13, where in three different ways the speaker is called first and last—hence God (Isa 41:4; 44:6; 48:12). By emphasizing that he is "the Beginning and the End" (Rev 22:13), Jesus also reminds the recipients of this book that he rules history.

The summons to "wash ... robes" (v. 14) sounds a strong note of warning especially to Sardians, the defilement of whose robes had already been declared to them (3:4). Such robes must be washed in Jesus's blood (7:14) to be ready for his imminent return (16:15), as noted in this context (22:12). Those who are prepared for Jesus's return, dependent on his blood, may partake of "the tree of life" (2:7; 22:2) and enter "through the gates into the city" (v. 14); the allusions back to the gates and the tree suggest that our verse 14, along with verse 15 (which alludes to 21:8, 27), summarizes what precedes.

But not everyone will be welcome to enter the city; future paradise for the faithful does not imply universalism. Just as the gates were open only for those in the Lamb's book of life in 21:25–27, so in 22:15 Jesus provides a partial list of those who will be excluded. Those who practice magic arts (9:21; 18:23), the sexually immoral (2:14, 20; 9:21; 14:8), and idolaters (13:14–15) all participate in the system of the beast; those who participate in the killing of Christians count as murderers (2:9–10; 13:15); those who love and live according to "falsehood" presumably include those deceived by the antichrist's system (3:9; 14:5; cf. John 8:44; 2 Thess 2:10; 1 John 2:22). "Dogs" may refer to a male homosexual prostitute (Deut 23:18), developing further the warning against sexual immorality.

Not only does John testify (Rev 22:8), but so does Jesus, who stands behind this entire revelation (v. 16). Jesus is not merely "the Offspring of David," but his "Root" (v. 16). Whereas the promised Messiah is a branch from David's family line (Isa 11:1)—and this could be in view here—given the whole context of Revelation's Christology this passage may present him as much more, as the very root from which David's line grew and on which it ultimately depends. As the "bright Morning Star" (Rev 22:16), Jesus compares his glory with a celestial body often worshiped by John's contemporaries, and also claims to be Messiah (Num 24:17).

"The Spirit" in Revelation 22:17 is probably the Spirit who inspires the prophets to speak. Perhaps the Spirit speaks through "the bride" here, presenting the bride as a prophetic community; or perhaps the Spirit speaks and is seconded by the bride. It is possible that with the word "Come" (v. 17), the Spirit and the bride are inviting the thirsty to drink, which is later echoed in a cry for Jesus to come (v. 20). But though Revelation is not addressed only to first-time readers, it seems noteworthy that one approaching the Spirit's and the bride's invitation will initially do so from the preceding context rather than the line that follows. Thus, it is more likely that in the word "Come," they are crying for Jesus to come, following his promise in 22:7, 12 and anticipating a final prayer of this nature in verse 20. This reality evokes the welcome of the thirsty to come and fits other early Christian teaching on the eagerness of the Spirit and God's people for Jesus's return.

This invitation to "the water of life" from God's throne (v. 17) probably indicates the present availability of the water as well as an invitation to drink in the future. One's "share in the tree of life and in the Holy City" (v. 19) refers to a future inheritance (21:7), but it is not incompatible with the present foretaste of the kingdom, like the concept of eternal life in John's Gospel (John 3:16).

The final of John's seven letters to the churches indicates that believers may dine with Jesus in the present (Rev 3:20) and so receive his spiritual adornment (21:2, 19), wealth (21:18), and healing (22:2) in the present era (3:18). If it is legitimate to read Revelation's description of the new Jerusalem together with John's Gospel, the fruit (22:2) may refer to the life of Jesus in believers (John 15:2), and the water of life flowing from the throne (Rev 22:1) may refer to the believer's present experience of the Spirit (John 4:14; 7:37–39; the term for "flowing" appears with the Spirit who "goes out" in John 15:26). We are promised future glory, but we can experience a foretaste of that glory in our present relationship with God.

Added to John's testimony in Revelation 22:8 and to that of Jesus in verse 16, plus that implied by the confident prayer of the Spirit and the bride (v. 17), are a solemn curse against anyone who tries to change the book (vv. 18–19) and another testimony by the faithful witness Jesus (v. 20). This is a standard sort of claim for a book or writing that claims to be inspired; it refers to the individual book of Revelation (though the *principle* applies to the rest of the Bible also, since its basis is the book's inspiration).

Revelation closes (immediately before its expected epistolary blessing in v. 21) with what was probably at that time the familiar prayer, "Come, Lord Jesus" (v. 20). Roughly the same prayer in Aramaic, "*Marana tha*" ("Come, O Lord"), appears in 1 Corinthians 16:22, which suggests that these words reflect the longing of even the earliest Aramaic-speaking churches, which already recognized Jesus as the coming, divine Lord.

Application. Not every Christian today feels comfortable praying, "Come, Lord Jesus" (Rev 22:20). Suffering Christians long for Jesus's return, but some people are more comfortable with the world and view the end of the present world order with anxiety. Sometimes we love things that are not wrong, but if we yearn for them more than we yearn for Jesus, those priorities are wrong. Any other longing we have will be but a shadow of our desire for the greatest and truest love available, the love to which the Lamb's shed blood stands as an eternal testimony.

SCRIPTURE INDEX

OLD TESTAMENT

Genesis

Leviticus

Numbers

Deuteronomy

Joshua

Judges

Ruth

2 Samuel

1 Kings

2 Kings

1 Chronicles

2 Chronicles

Ezra

Esther

Job

Psalms

Proverbs

Ecclesiastes

Song of Songs

Isaiah

Jeremiah

Lamentations

Malachi

NEW TESTAMENT

Matthew

Luke

John

Acts

Romans

1 Corinthians

2 Corinthians

Galatians

Ephesians

Philippians

Colossians

1 Thessalonians

2 Thessalonians

1 Timothy

2 Timothy

Titus

James

1 Peter

SUBJECT INDEX

A

C

D

H

J

M

N

O

P

S

T

U

X

Y

Z

Map 1: WORLD OF THE PATRIARCHS

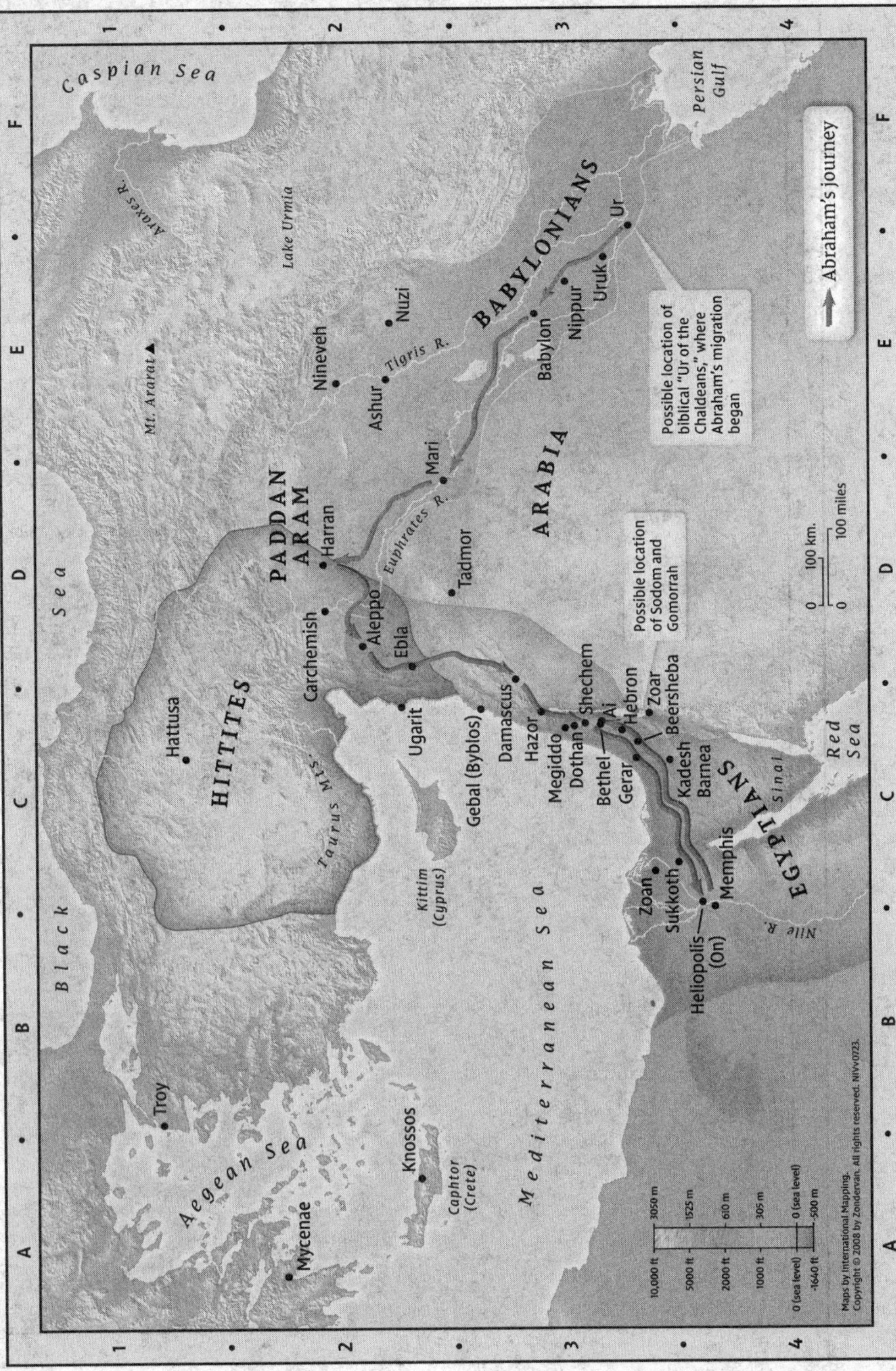

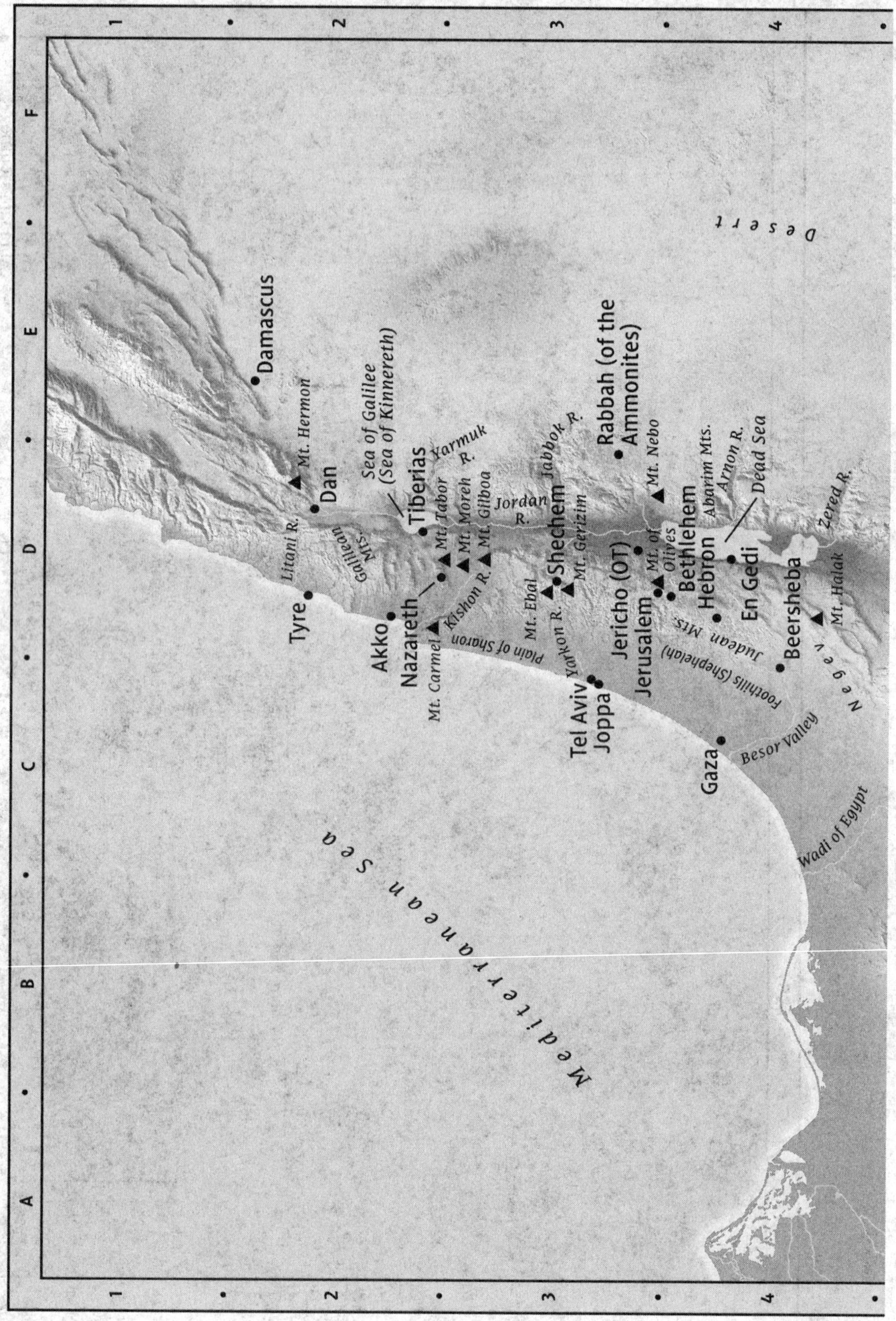

Damascus
Mt. Hermon
Dan
Litani R.
Tyre
Galilean Mts.
Sea of Galilee (Sea of Kinnereth)
Tiberias
Yarmuk R.
Akko
Nazareth
Mt. Carmel
Mt. Tabor
Mt. Moreh
Mt. Gilboa
Kishon R.
Plain of Sharon
Jordan R.
Jabbok R.
Mt. Ebal
Shechem
Mt. Gerizim
Yarkon R.
Tel Aviv
Joppa
Rabbah (of the Ammonites)
Jericho (OT)
Jerusalem
Mt. of Olives
Mt. Nebo
Bethlehem
Hebron
Abarim Mts.
Arnon R.
Dead Sea
En Gedi
Judean Mts.
Foothills (Shephelah)
Gaza
Besor Valley
Beersheba
Mt. Halak
Zered R.
Negev
Wadi of Egypt
Mediterranean Sea
Desert
A
B
C
D
E
F
1
2
3
4

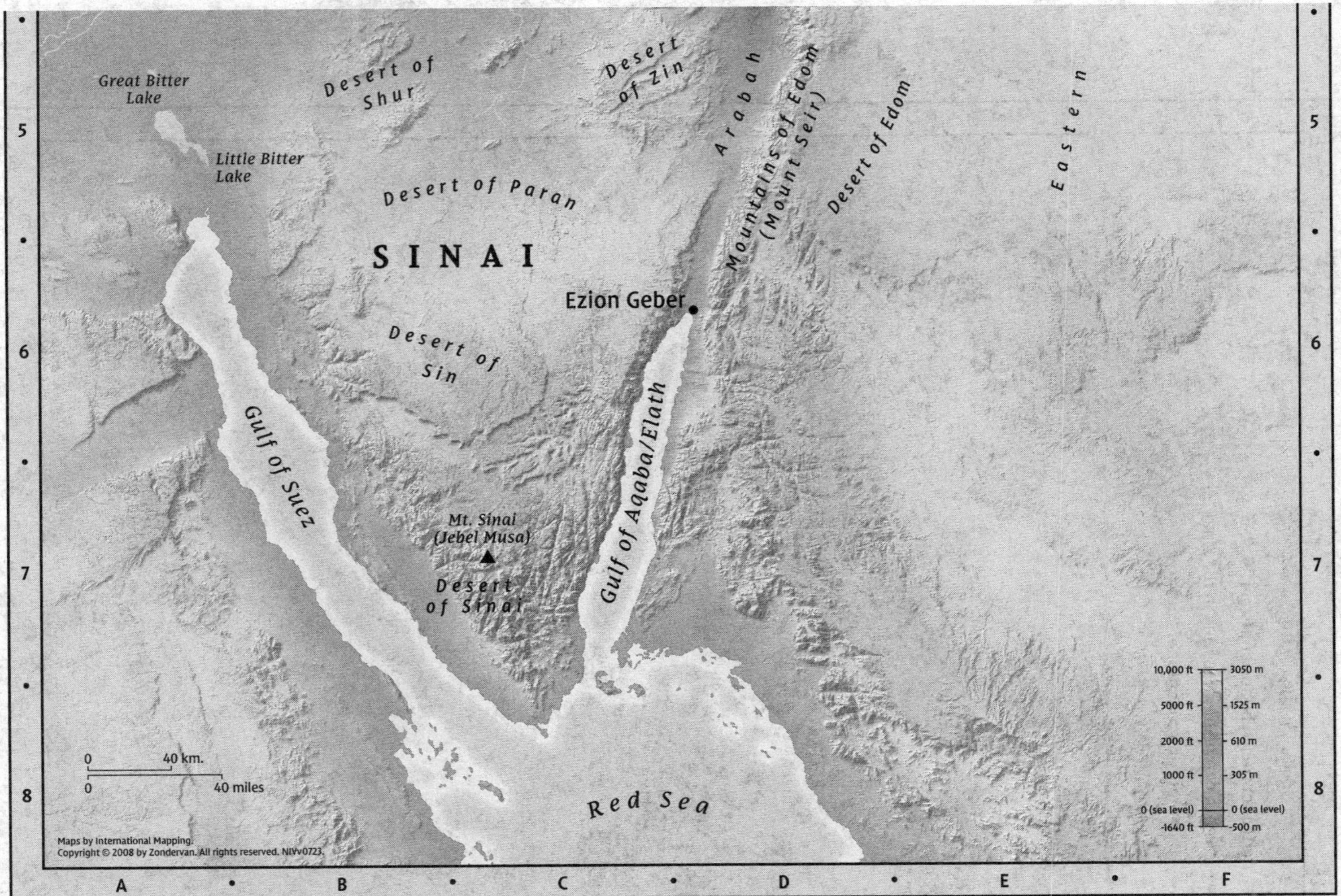

Great Bitter Lake
Little Bitter Lake
Desert of Shur
Desert of Zin
Desert of Paran
SINAI
Arabah
Mountains of Edom (Mount Seir)
Desert of Edom
Eastern
Ezion Geber
Desert of Sin
Gulf of Suez
Gulf of Aqaba/Elath
Mt. Sinai (Jebel Musa)
Desert of Sinai
Red Sea
0 40 km.
0 40 miles
10,000 ft 3050 m
5000 ft 1525 m
2000 ft 610 m
1000 ft 305 m
0 (sea level) 0 (sea level)
-1640 ft -500 m
A B C D E F
5 6 7 8

Map 3: EXODUS AND CONQUEST OF CANAAN

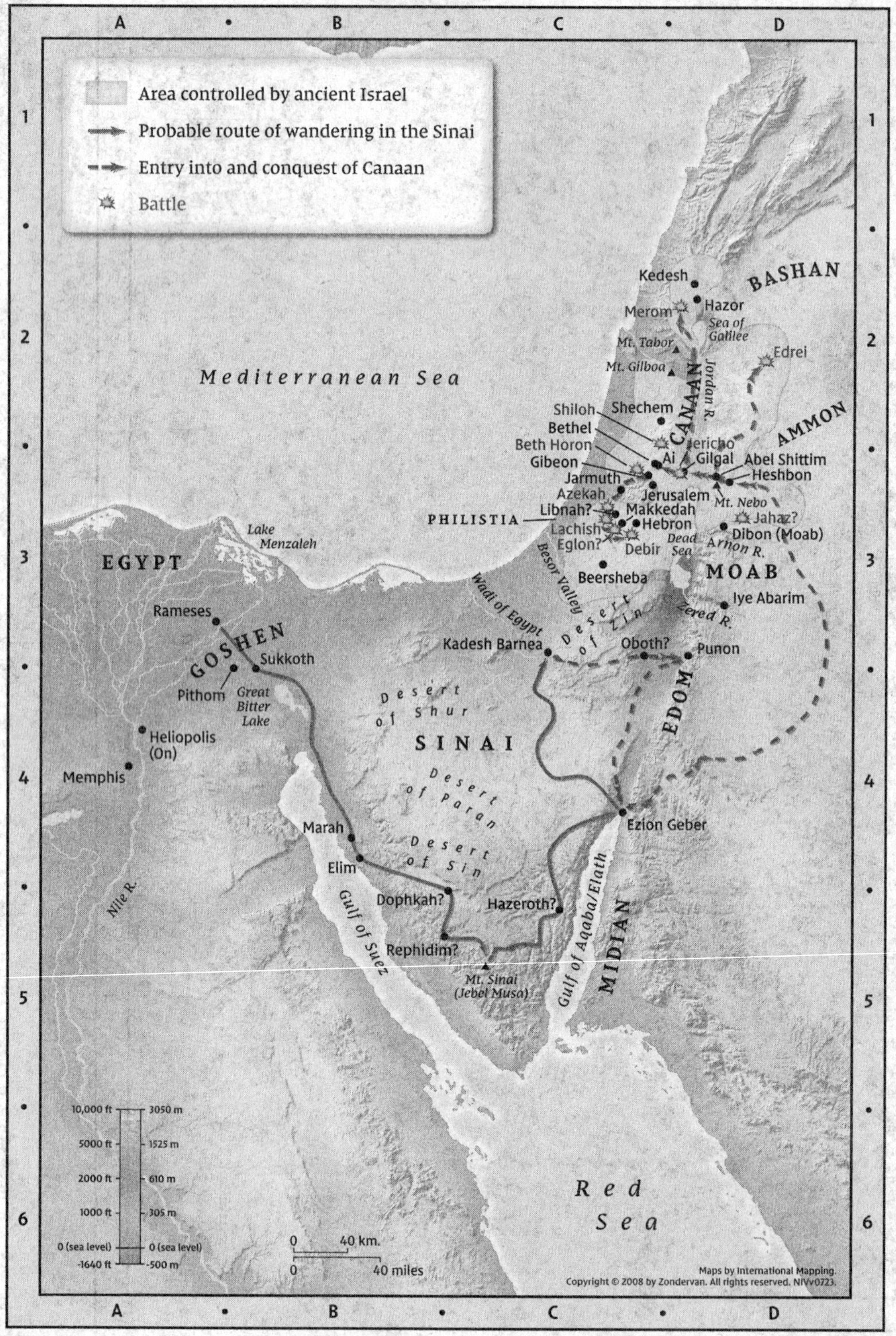

Map 4: LAND OF THE TWELVE TRIBES

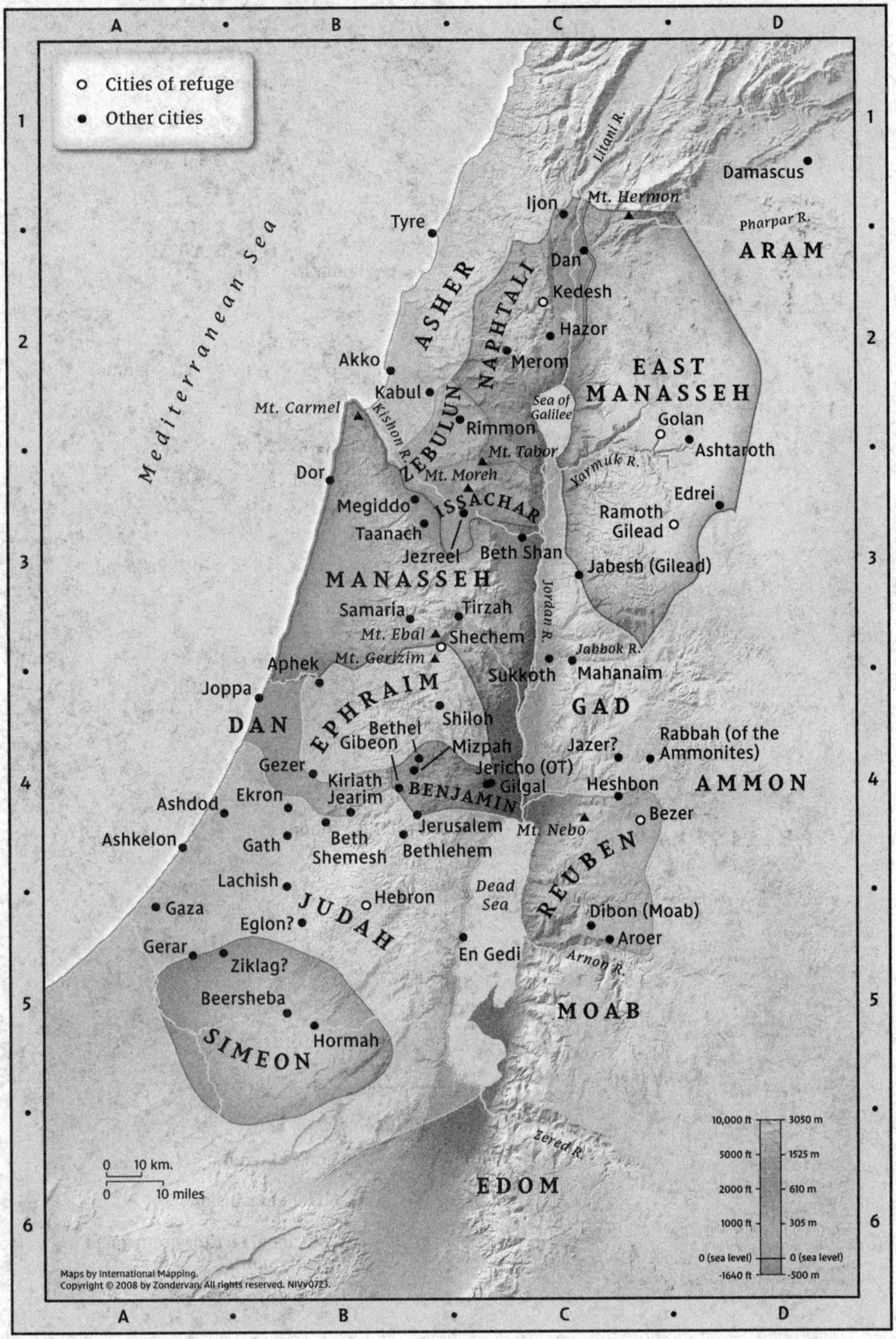

Map 5: KINGDOM OF DAVID AND SOLOMON

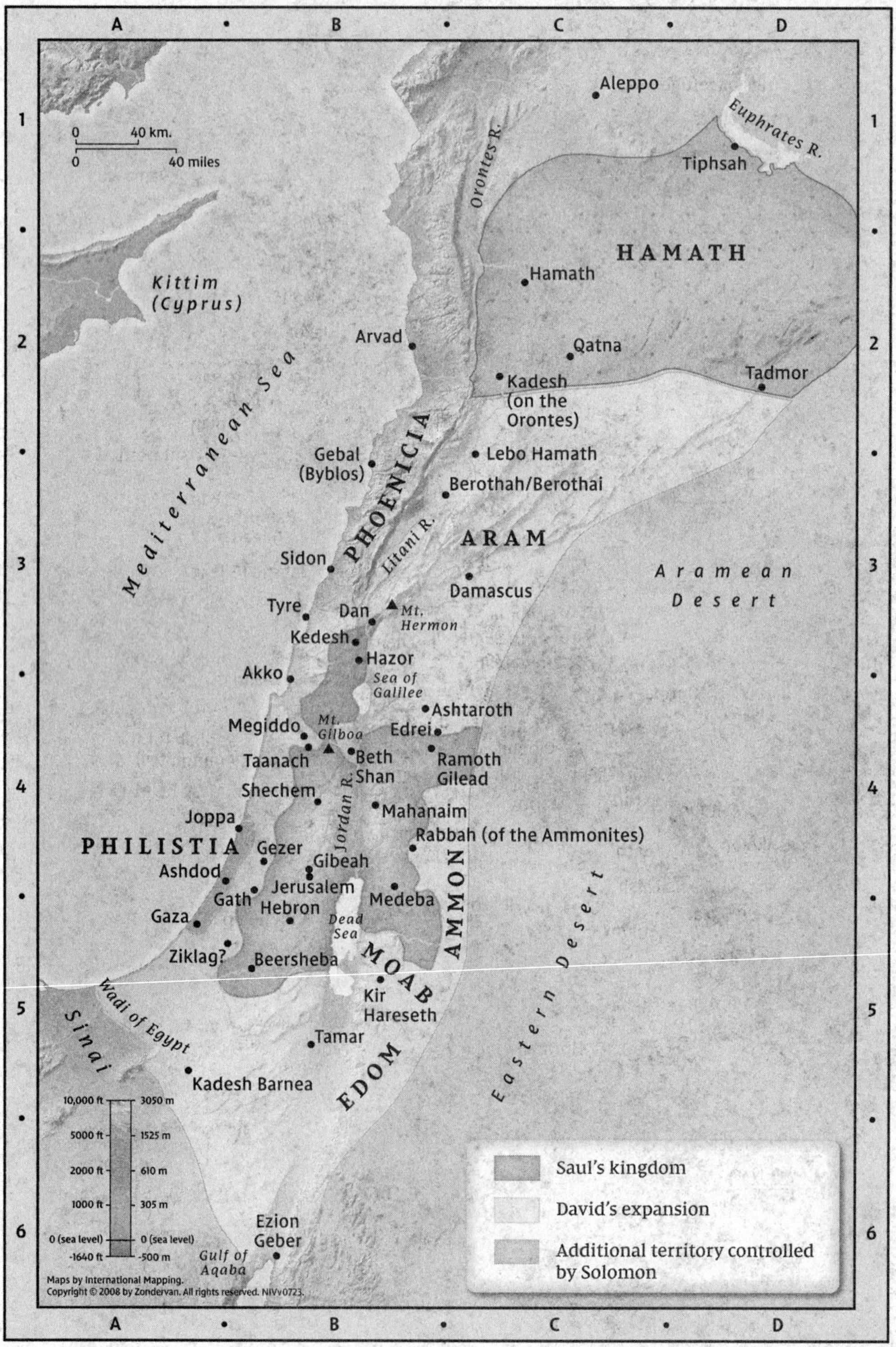

Maps by International Mapping.

Map 6: KINGDOMS OF ISRAEL AND JUDAH

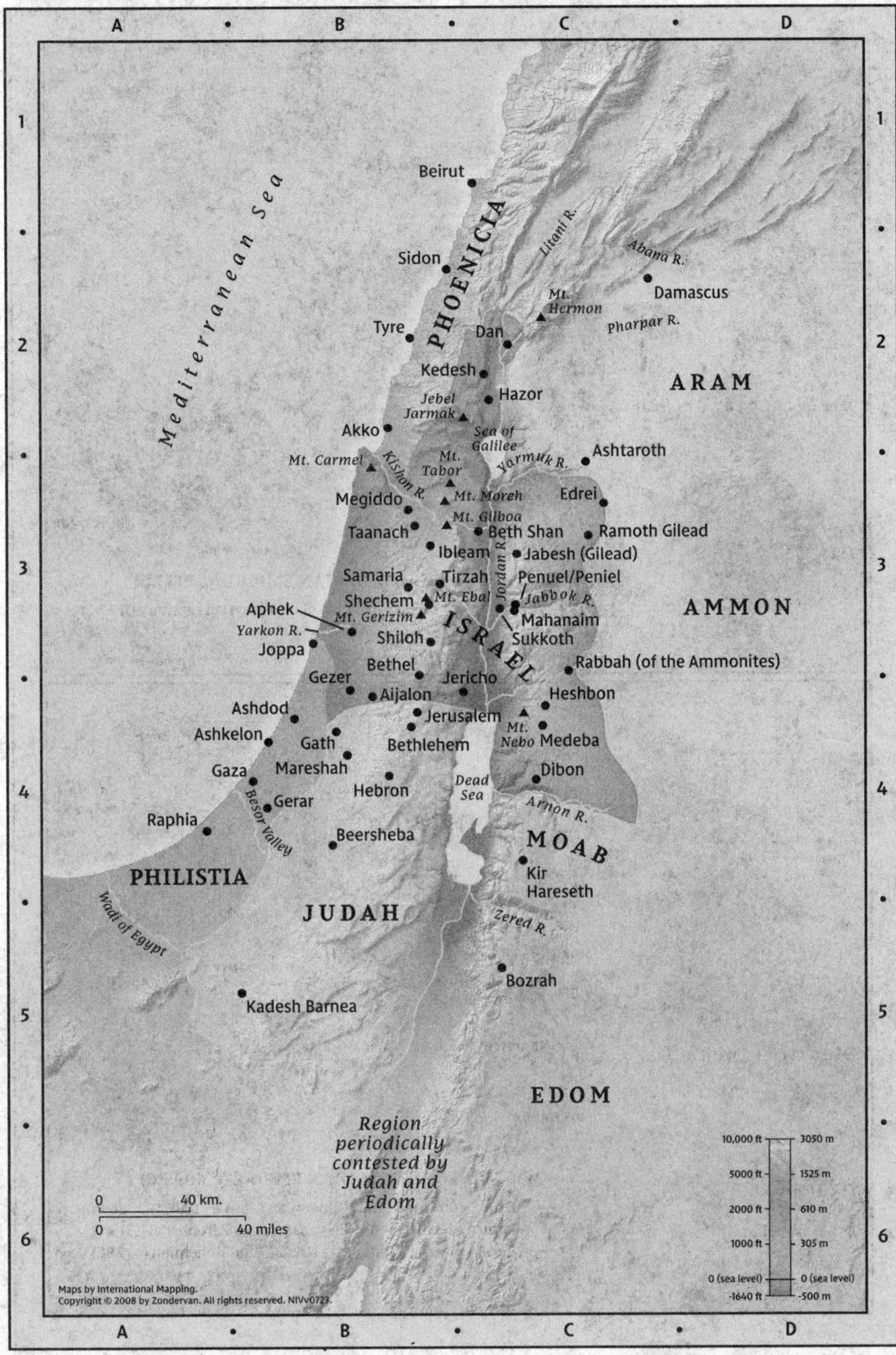

Map 7: ASSYRIAN AND BABYLONIAN EMPIRES

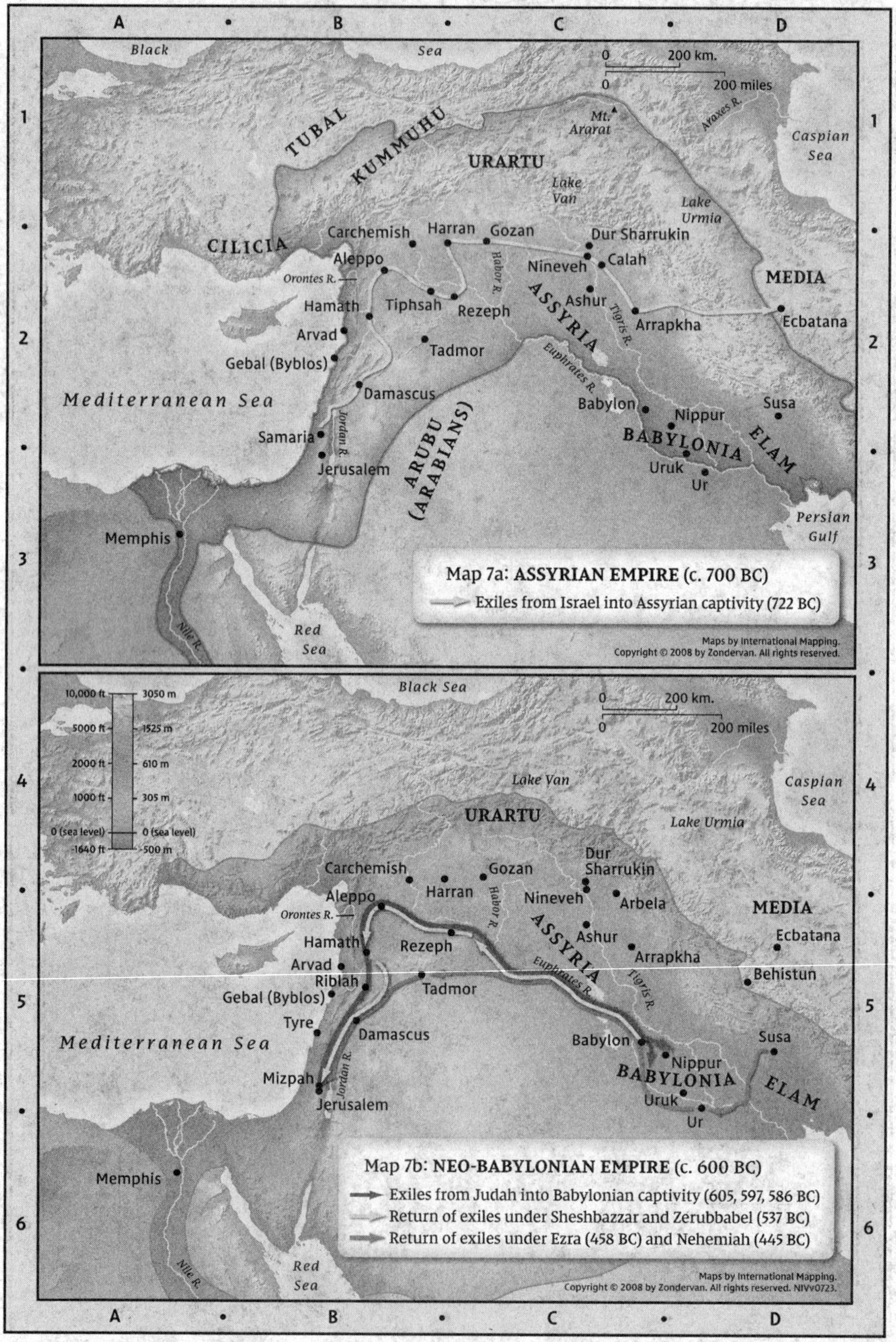

Map 7a: ASSYRIAN EMPIRE (c. 700 BC)
Exiles from Israel into Assyrian captivity (722 BC)

Map 7b: NEO-BABYLONIAN EMPIRE (c. 600 BC)
Exiles from Judah into Babylonian captivity (605, 597, 586 BC)
Return of exiles under Sheshbazzar and Zerubbabel (537 BC)
Return of exiles under Ezra (458 BC) and Nehemiah (445 BC)

Map 8: HOLY LAND IN THE TIME OF JESUS

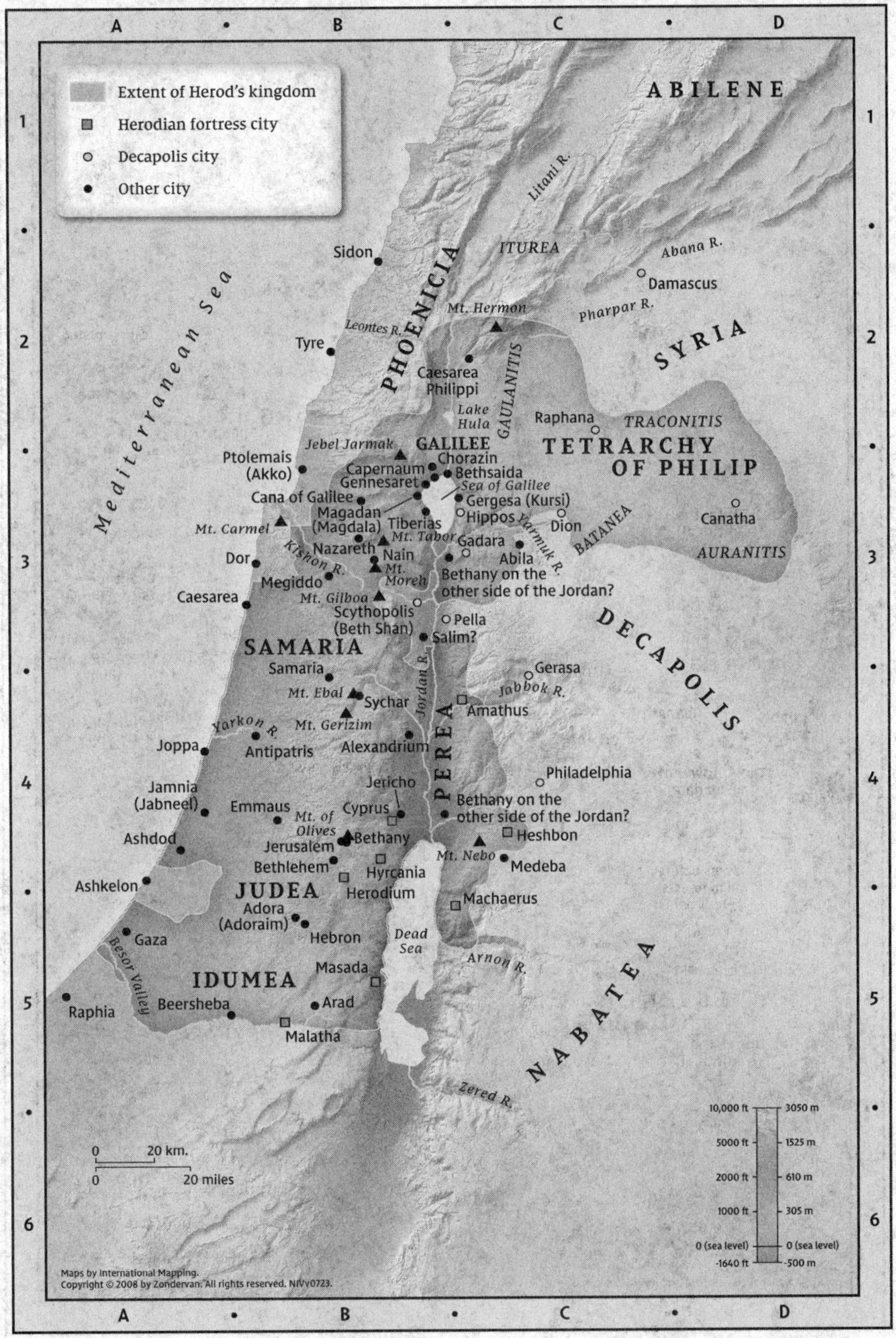

Maps by International Mapping.

Map 9: JERUSALEM IN THE TIME OF JESUS

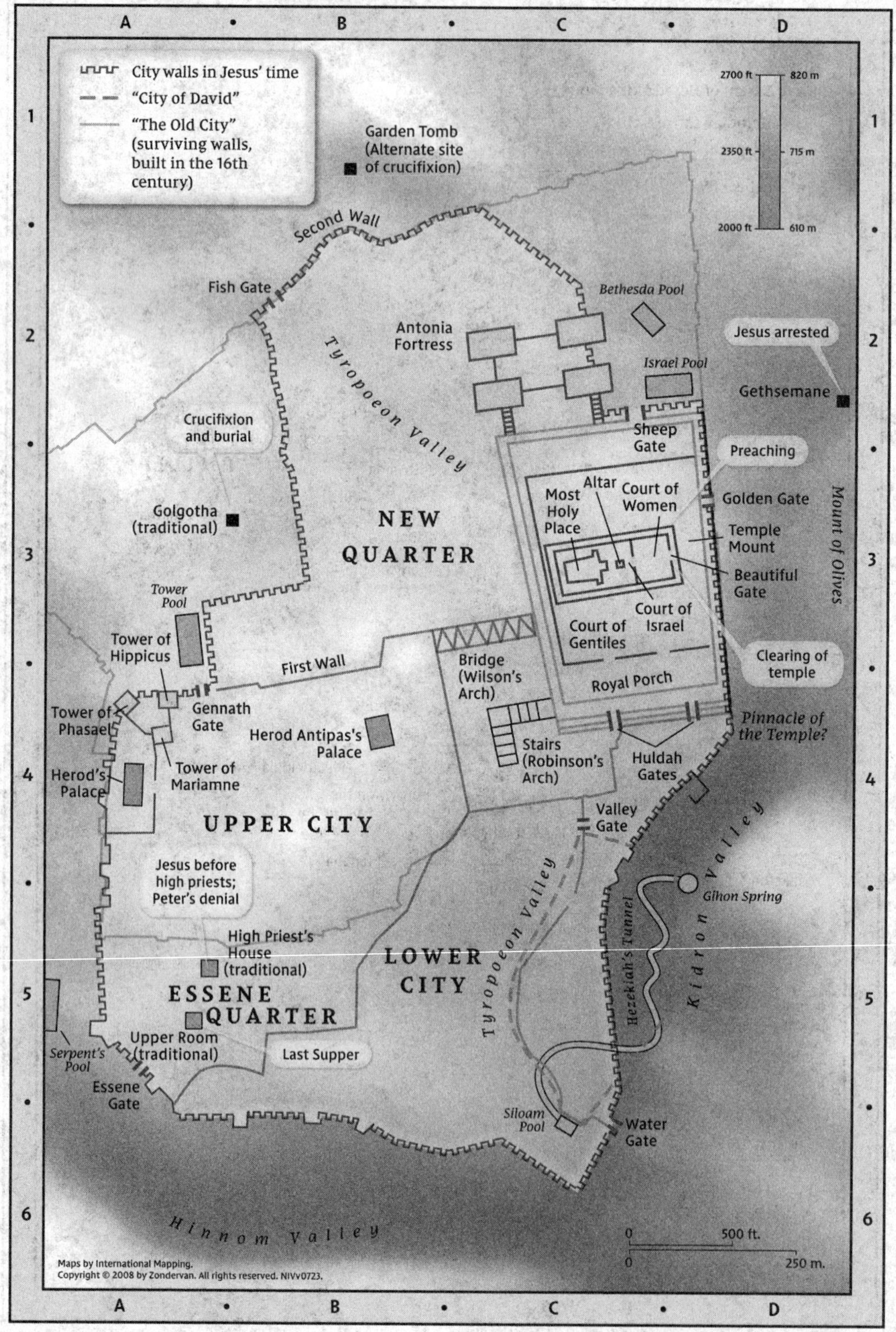

Map 10: ROMAN EMPIRE

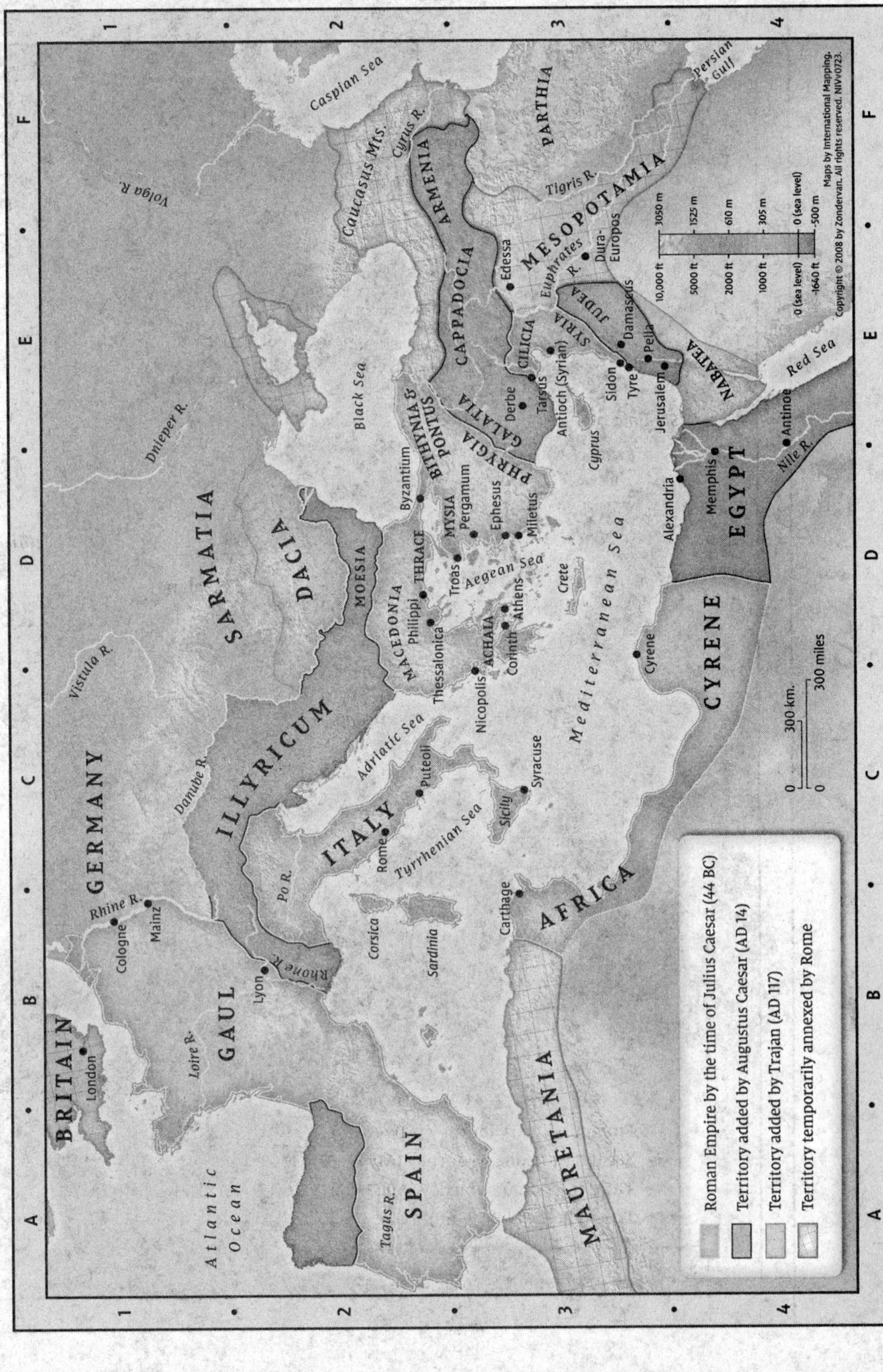

Map 11: PAUL'S MISSIONARY JOURNEYS

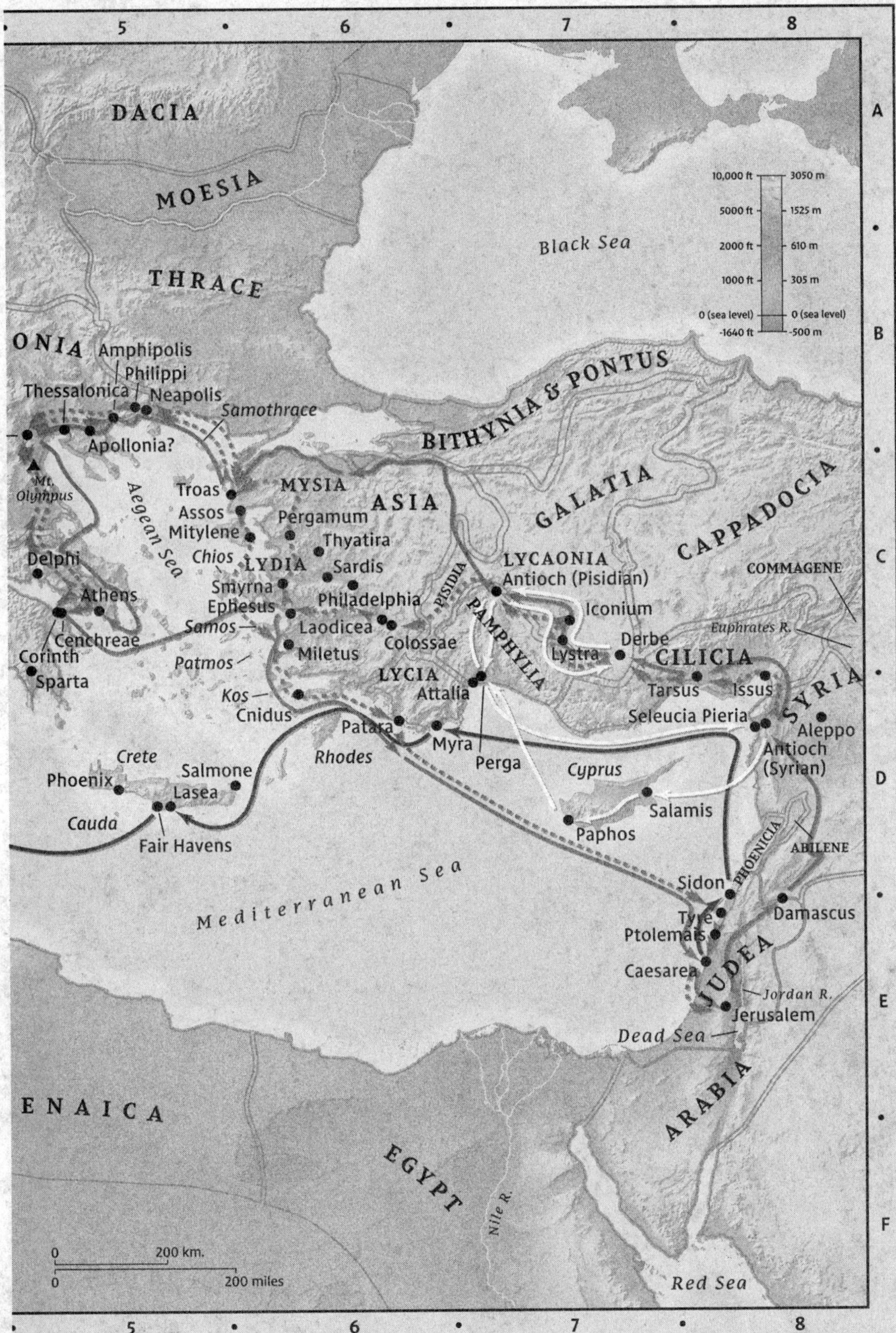

5
6
7
8
A
B
C
D
E
F
DACIA
MOESIA
THRACE
ONIA
Black Sea
10,000 ft
3050 m
5000 ft
1525 m
2000 ft
610 m
1000 ft
305 m
0 (sea level)
0 (sea level)
-1640 ft
-500 m
Amphipolis
Philippi
Thessalonica
Neapolis
Samothrace
Apollonia?
Mt. Olympus
Aegean Sea
Troas
Assos
Mitylene
Chios
Delphi
Athens
Corinth
Cenchreae
Sparta
MYSIA
ASIA
Pergamum
Thyatira
LYDIA
Sardis
Smyrna
Ephesus
Philadelphia
Samos
Laodicea
Colossae
Miletus
Patmos
Kos
Cnidus
LYCIA
Patara
Myra
Rhodes
Crete
Phoenix
Salmone
Lasea
Cauda
Fair Havens
BITHYNIA & PONTUS
GALATIA
CAPPADOCIA
PISIDIA
LYCAONIA
Antioch (Pisidian)
Iconium
PAMPHYLIA
Lystra
Derbe
Attalia
Perga
CILICIA
Tarsus
Issus
COMMAGENE
Euphrates R.
SYRIA
Seleucia Pieria
Aleppo
Antioch (Syrian)
Cyprus
Salamis
Paphos
PHOENICIA
ABILENE
Sidon
Tyre
Damascus
Ptolemais
Caesarea
JUDEA
Jordan R.
Jerusalem
Dead Sea
Mediterranean Sea
ENAICA
EGYPT
Nile R.
ARABIA
Red Sea
0
200 km.
0
200 miles